HOTEL GUIDE

GREAT BRITAIN AND IRELAND

1991

First published 1904

Published by RAC Publishing, RAC House, PO Box 100, South Croydon CR2 6XW

ISBN 0 86211 090 4

Typeset by BP Integraphics Ltd, Bath

Printed and bound by Redwood Press Ltd., Melksham, Wiltshire

Advertising Managers:
Kingslea Press Ltd, 137 Newhall St, Birmingham B3 1SF
Telephone: 021-236 8112

Cover picture: Middlethorpe Hall, York

Contents

The Royal Automobile Club

Patron
Her Majesty the Queen

President
H.R.H. Prince Michael of Kent

Vice Presidents
Sir Carl D. Aarvold, O.B.E., T.D.
His Grace the Duke of Richmond and Gordon, D.L.
The Rt. Hon. Lord Nugent of Guildford, P.C.
Sidney L. Lesser

Chairman
Jeffrey Rose

Vice Chairmen
J. A. Williams
B. K. McGivern
Sir John Rogers

General Secretary
M. J. Limb, F.I.M.I., F.I.B.M.

RAC MOTORING SERVICES

Chief Executive
A. R. W. Large, B.Sc., C.A., F.C.I.

The Automobile Club of Great Britain and Ireland was founded in 1897 as a Society of Encouragement for the motoring movement and the motor and allied industries in the British Empire, and the majority of the organisations in the Commonwealth are associated with it. In 1907, the title was changed to 'The Royal Automobile Club', following the granting of Royal patronage.

The Club House in Pall Mall was built by the RAC on the site of the old War Office and opened in February 1911.

In 1913, the RAC acquired Woodcote Park, Epsom – an estate of historical interest with an area of some 300 acres. The old Club House was destroyed by fire in 1934. A modern building in the same style was erected on the site and opened in 1936.

From the earliest days the RAC has done all it could to assist motorists, whether by representing their interests or by direct help from a fleet of patrolmen. Those motorists who were not interested in the Club's social activities, but did want help in emergencies, were enrolled as Associate Members of RAC Motoring Services Ltd. Starting in a modest way, this small offshoot of the Club has now grown to approaching 4,000,000 motorists who belong to the RAC but not to the full Club.

The RAC today through its Rescue, Recovery, At Home and Reflex Services is able to assist its Members wherever they may be, keeping up the traditions of the past. As a result of recent investment in manpower and resources, these services have never been better, reaching eight out of ten Members needing help within the hour.

As well as roadside services, the RAC offers a host of other services including car insurance, loans, ferry bookings, Eurocover, routes, motoring information, publications, technical and legal services.

Full details of RAC membership can be obtained from any RAC Office or ring Bristol 0272–232340.

Introduction

British hotels are accused of becoming too expensive. It is not just a case of prices going through the roof, it is more an impression of declining value for money, especially in terms of service. Harsh words these may be — but they are what we hear from people who stay in hotels — and those who do not! People who travel throughout Western Europe tell us they see this more keenly when they compare Britain with elsewhere.

But is this impression correct? On prices, we can certainly testify that they are rising faster in Britain than they are in Europe. This year, once again, many hotels in this guide are advising increases above the current high rate of inflation. These prices are also higher than the majority of equivalent European establishments in the RAC European Hotel Guide.

We talk to hoteliers, too, and they have strong arguments for their position. The high cost of land and building, the increases in rates and wage costs and a generally high rate of inflation are all put forward, and with good reason. In recent times, the very high cost of borrowing for investment has undeniably added to the hoteliers' woes.

In many hotels it is obvious to see that prices reflect substantial investment in new buildings, superior refurbishment of older properties or the addition of elaborate and extensive leisure facilities. But there are many who charge similar prices where there is no visible investment.

To many hotel guests the cost of staff argument would not appear to stand up to scrutiny. To most people the very idea of a hotel is that it offers service as well as a roof over your head. In many hotels the more obvious signs of that personal service are sadly fading away.

Too often there is no porter to carry your luggage or to show you to your room. A receptionist is often overworked to the point that a simple check in or check out can take 15 or more minutes. Self service breakfasts are fast becoming the norm — whether the guest prefers this or not. With that, too often, comes the heated tray of overcooked food in all its appetising splendour!

This lack of service might be acceptable in a budget-priced travel lodge or motel which advertises itself as such — but in a hotel? Indeed, we find many modestly priced hotels offering more service than some of their more expensive counterparts.

We know from our inspectors that there is much that is good about hotels in Britain, as evidenced by our extensive commendations announced in this guide. But, and it is a serious but, we believe hoteliers need to address the increasing criticism on the issues of high prices, poor value for money and declining personal service.

RAC Hotel Appointments

The RAC Appointment of hotels is made following an unannounced overnight stay by one of the Club's inspectors and a full inspection of the premises. Hotels are classified according to the following definitions which are intended to indicate the type of hotel rather than the degree of merit. The requirements of the lower classifications are included in the higher.

A change in the classification of an hotel from that held in previous years does not necessarily indicate a lowering of standards at the establishment.

This may well be the result of changes from time to time in the basic standards required by the RAC for the various classifications and which in turn reflects the requirements of guests.

★★★★★ Large luxury hotels offering the highest standard of accommodation, service and comfort.

★★★★ Large hotels with a full brigade of professional staff. Reception, porterage and room service at all hours. Telephones in all bedrooms. A high proportion of private bathrooms. Some bedrooms with private lounges; conference and/or banqueting facilities; or recreational facilities.

★★★ Small luxury hotels, or larger well-appointed hotels offering a high degree of comfort. Some room service. Telephones/intercoms in bedrooms. A good proportion of bedrooms with private bathrooms. Full meal facilities for residents and non-residents, including chance callers, on every day of the week.

★★ Formal reception arrangements and more employed senior staff. Greater provision for non-resident diners, including separate toilet arrangements. Lounge service available to residents.

★ Simple in furnishing, or menus, or service. May well be managed by the proprietor, with few employed senior staff. Usually only a small number of private bathrooms if any. Generally a more personal atmosphere than hotels with more stars.

Ap. Recommended hotels which do not conform to the minimum classification requirement in respect of porterage, reception facilities and choice of dishes; facilities for non-residents often limited.

Country House Hotels. Hotels, set in secluded rural surroundings which have many of the characteristics of a country house.

Small hotels, guest houses and similar establishments are also inspected by the RAC. Where standards are satisfactory they are included in the Guide as Listed hotels. Some of these small hotels provide excellent accommodation and facilities and are now designated Acclaimed or Highly Acclaimed. The Inn, whether in town or country is another type of establishment to come under scrutiny. Those which offer acceptable accommodation are included with the listed hotels, and the outstanding ones are awarded one to three tankards.

Unclassified hotels. Hotels under construction or undergoing major refurbishment are occasionally included in the Guide without classification. They obviously have not been inspected but are included for the convenience of readers, as they will be in operation during the currency of the Guide.

Symbols
(explained in three languages)

	English	Français	Deutsche
★	hotel classification	Classification de l'hôtel	Hotelklassifikation
[country-house symbol]	country-house hotel	Hôtel/manoir	Landhaushotel
[ribbon symbol]	Blue Ribbon	"Blue Ribbon"	Blaues Band
[C]	merit awards	Distinctions	Leistungsauszeichnungen
[telephone symbol]	telephone number	Numéro de téléphone	Telefonnummer
♿	facilities for the disabled	Aménagements pour handicapés	Einrichtungen für Behinderte
[bed symbol]	information about bedrooms	Renseignements sur les chambres	Informationen über Schlafzimmer
[hotel symbol]	facilities at hotel	Aménagements de l'hôtel	Einrichtungen im Hotel
[knife and fork symbol]	information about meals	Renseignements sur les repas	Informationen über Mahlzeiten
£	price information	Renseignements sur les tarifs	Preisinformationen
B&B	price of single room & breakfast	prix d'une chambre d'une personne + petit déjeuner	Preis für Einzelzimmer und Frühstück
HB	half-board	Demi-pension	Teilverpflegung
Bk	breakfast	Petit déjeuner	Frühstück
L	lunch	Déjeuner	Mittagessen
D	dinner	Dîner	Abendessen
fr	from	A partir de	von
WB	short breaks	Mini-vacances	Kurzurlaube
[V]	vouchers accepted	Tickets/Bons de réduction acceptés	Gutscheine werden angenommen
w/e	weekends	Week-ends	Wochenende
w/d	weekdays	Jours de semaine	Wochentage
cc	credit cards	Cartes de crédit	Kreditkarten
EC	early closing day	Jour hebdomadaire de fermeture anticipée	Tage mit frühem Geschäftsschuß
MD	market day	Jour de marché	Markttag
ns	no-smoking areas	Zones non fumeurs	Nichtraucher-Gebiete
NS	no smoking anywhere in hotel	Interdiction de fumer dans l'hôtel	Rauchverbot im ganzen Hotel
tcf	tea/coffee-making facilities	Equipement pour faire du thé/café dans les chambres	Tee-/Kaffee-Aufgußeinrichtungen
P	parking	Parking	Parken
G	garage	Garage	Garage
U	lock-up garage	Garage fermé	abschließbare Garage
CD	last dinner time	Dernière heure pour dîner	letzte Abendessenszeit
nr	no restaurant service	Pas de restaurant	keine Restaurantbedienung
[languages symbol]	languages spoken	Langue(s) parlée(s)	diese Sprache/n wird/werden gesprochen

Languages spoken

Fr French De German It Italian Es Spanish Po Portuguese Ja Japanese Du Dutch
Da Danish Sw Swedish No Norwegian Pl Polish Hu Hungarian Gr Greek Tu Turkish
Ar Arabic Hi Hindi Ur Urdu Ca Cantonese Ma Malaysian

How to use the Guide

A hotel entry in the Guide explained (the entry is fictitious)

★★ Grove House, Ridgeway MB5 2ZT (0569) 68681
Tx: 234466 Fax: (0569) 70134
Elegant Victorian mansion in 2 acres of well-tended gardens.
Swimming pool, tennis. Open Feb–Oct
10 bedrs, 8 en suite, (2 sh), 2 ba; annexe 5 bedrs, 5 en suite;
TV; tcf
lift, TV, dogs, ns, P 50, G 2, U 5, coach, child facs, con 20
LD 9.30, nr Mon–Wed lunch. Resid & Rest lic
£ B&B £20–£30, B&B (double) £30–£50; HB weekly £175–£275;
L £6, D £8·50; WB £82 (HB); [10% V w/d]
cc Access, Amex, B'card/Visa, CB, Diners; dep.

How to use the Guide

We have employed a minimum of symbols so that the Guide is easy to use. Each entry starts with the hotel's star classification (see p. 5), name, address, telephone, telex and fax numbers. Then follows, for Appointed hotels, a short description, sometimes accompanied by a picture.
The information about each hotel is in five sections:

bedroom information
10 bedrs: number of bedrooms
8 en suite: number with full en suite facilities (bath or shower)
(2 sh): number of rooms with shower cubicles (without WCs)
2 ba: number of general bathrooms
annexe: an RAC approved annexe
TV: available in at least some bedrooms
tcf: tea/coffee making facilities

facilities in the hotel
lift: to at least some floors
TV: available in a separate room or in the lounge
dogs: accepted at the manager's discretion. There may be limitations as to which areas of the hotel they are allowed in, or to size. To avoid disappointment, guests are advised to confirm the conditions under which dogs are accepted.
ns: no smoking areas available. Most hotels do not allow smoking in the dining room.
NS: no smoking anywhere in the hotel
P 50: number of parking places
G 1 (£1): number of garage places and overnight charge
U 2 (£3): number of single lock-ups and overnight charge
coach: coach parties accommodated
child facs: at least two of the following available: baby-watching service, baby listening service, cots, high chairs, special meals (baby foods), playroom, playground or playing area.
con 20: conference facilities and maximum number of delegates; see also Conference Hotels section.

meal information
LD 8: last time dinner orders taken.
nr: no restaurant service as shown; bar meals are often available instead
Licensing information: All hotels serve alcoholic liquor during permitted hours unless they are shown as unlicensed or are subject to any of the following limitations.
Club Licence. A licence granted to establishments at which it is necessary to become a member of a club in order to obtain alcoholic refreshment. To comply with the law, a period of 48 hours after joining should elapse before such club membership can take effect.
Restaurant or Table Licence (Rest lic). A licence whereby the sale of alcoholic liquor is restricted to customers taking meals.
Residential Licence (Resid lic). A licence whereby the sale of alcoholic liquor is restricted to residents at an hotel, guesthouse, etc., and their private bona fide friends entertained by them at the resident's expense.
Residential and Restaurant Licence. A combination of both of the above licences.
Temperance hotels (Temp.) do not allow the consumption of alcohol on the premises though
Unlicensed hotels (Unlic) may allow guests to consume their own drinks with their meals. Some may charge corkage if guests bring their own wine.

£ information on charges
B&B £20–£30: range of charges for one night bed and breakfast for one person
B&B (double) £30–£50: range of prices for one night bed and breakfast for two people in a double room
HB weekly £175–£250: cost of dinner, bed and breakfast for 7 nights for one person
Bk £5: price of full breakfast
L £8·50: price of table d'hote lunch
D £12: price of table d'hote dinner
WB £82 (HB): weekend or short break special offers available. Contact the hotel for details
[10% V w/d] 10% vouchers accepted on weekdays
w/e: at weekends

cc credit cards accepted
Access (includes Mastercharge and Eurocard)
Amex: American Express
B'card/Visa: Barclaycard and Visa cards
CB: Carte Blanche
Diners: Diners Club
dep.: deposit required on booking

The prices range from that for low season in standard rooms to that for superior rooms in high season.

Tariffs given in the Guide are forecasts by hoteliers of what they expect to charge in 1991. As the information is, of necessity, compiled well in advance of publication, varying conditions may have brought about increases in published charges. It is always wise to check with a hotel what the relevant charges are before booking.

All prices quoted should include VAT where applicable. They may or may not include a charge for service.

Shortened hotel entries. A number of hotels failed to provide detailed information for the 1991 season. In such cases only the classification, name, address and telephone number appear in the entry.

Maintenance of standards. All hotels listed in the Guide are inspected regularly. Nevertheless, we welcome reports from readers on the standards being maintained. We are also glad to have reports about hotels which are not appointed by the RAC; such reports may enable the RAC to extend the number of hotels appointed.

In cases of dissatisfaction or dispute, readers will find that discussion with the hotel management at the time of the problem/incident will normally allow the matter to be resolved promptly and amicably. The RAC will investigate any matter if this personal approach fails to produce satisfaction. Please submit details of any discussion or correspondence involved when reporting a problem to the RAC.

Cancellation of Reservations. Should it become necessary to cancel reserved accommodation, guests are advised to telephone at once to the hotel, followed by written confirmation.

If rooms which are reserved and not occupied cannot be re-let, the hotel proprietor may suffer loss and guests may be held legally responsible for part of the cost. This may also apply to table reservations in restaurants.

Arrival Times. Small hotels and inns may close for part of the afternoon. It is wise to inform them of your expected arrival time when booking, and courteous to telephone them if you are delayed.

Location of Hotels. All towns and villages in which there are RAC Appointed Hotels, Small Hotels, Guest Houses etc., are indicated on the maps in the atlas section by a purple circle. Having first located the town or village required, reference should then be made to the Guide where full particulars of the hotels, etc., will be found under the appropriate place name.

All the establishments named in the Guide are either "appointed", or "recommended" by the RAC. It should be noted, however, that the publication of an advertisement does not necessarily indicate, *except in the case of hotels*, that the advertiser has been granted RAC Appointment or Recommendation nor does it in itself confer the right to exhibit the RAC sign or to entry in the Guide.

While the RAC takes every care to ensure the accuracy of the particulars given in the Guide at the time of going to press, no liability can be accepted for any error or omission which may occur.

Information on towns

The RAC Hotel Guide is not a gazeteer and lists only those cities, towns and villages in which there are RAC Appointed Hotels, Small Hotels, Guest Houses and Inns. Every entry includes the appropriate map reference.

Mileages. The mileages shown are computed by the shortest practical routes, which are not necessarily those recommended by the RAC.

Group hotels

Hotels owned by the major hotel groups are identified as follows:

Commonwealth Holiday Inns of Canada	CHIC
De Vere Hotels	DeV
Embassy Hotels	Emb
Berni, Chef & Brewer	BCB
Greenall Whitley	GW
Hilton International	H. Int
Hilton National	HN
Holiday Inns	HI
Lansbury Hotels	Lns
Mount Charlotte Hotels	MtCh
Queen's Moat Houses	QMH
Scottish Highlands	SH
Stakis Hotels	Sk
Swallow Hotels	Sw
Thistle Hotels	ThH
Trusthouse Forte	THF
and	Cr/THF

Facilities for disabled visitors

Most hotels do their best to cater for disabled visitors. Some, in old or converted buildings, find it difficult to make the necessary alterations, whether because of a flight of steep stairs to the front door, or old, twisting passages, too narrow for a wheelchair to use comfortably.

Each year we ask our hotels if their accommodation is suitable for disabled visitors. Those hotels which are considered to have suitable facilities by their proprietors or managers are indicated in the guide by the usual symbol, ♿. Information on the specific facilities hotels provide can be found in '*On the Move*' the RAC's guide for disabled travellers.

Disabled visitors are recommended to **contact the hotel direct and to discuss with the manager whether the hotel can provide their particular requirements** and to let the hotel know what they will need in the way of extra service or facilities. Hotels are always glad to help, but are able to provide more if they are given advance notice.

RAC Hotels Department

To contact the RAC Hotels Department please write to:
RAC House
PO Box 100
Bartlett St
South Croydon
CR2 6XW
or telephone 081-686 0088

RAC Hotel Appointements

le RAC Hotel appointements est écrit à la suite d'un séjour imprévu d'une nuit par un des inspecteurs du club, et d'une inspection complète des lieux.

Les hotels sont classés selon les définitions suivantes. Celles-ci sont destinées à indiquer le type des hôtel plutôt que leur degré de mérite. Les exigeances des classifications les plus faibles sont comprises dans celles des meilleurs.

Une modification du classement d'un hôtel par rapport aux années précédentes ne signifie pas nécessairement une baisse de la qualité de l'établissement.

Elle peut aussi bien provenir du changement de temps en temps des normes exigées par le RAC pour les différentes classifications, reflétant les exigences des clients.

★★★★★ Grands hôtels de luxe offrant les plus hauts niveaux de confort, services et aménagements.

★★★★ Grands hôtels avec une équipe complète de professionels. Réception, concierge, service dans les chambres, possibles à toute heure. Téléphones dans toutes les chambres. Proportion élevée de salles de bain particulières. Quelques chambres avec salon privé; facilités de conférences et/ou de banquets; ou facilités de divertissement.

★★★ Petits hôtels de luxe ou grands hôtels bien équipés, offrant un haut degré de confort. Parfois service dans les chambres. Téléphone/interphone dans les chambres. Bonne proportion de chambres avec salles de bain particulières. Possibilité de repas complets midi et soir pour les pensionnaires et non pensionnaires, tous les jours de la semaine.

★★ Dispositions d'acceuil plus formelles, plus de personnel qualifié. Plus de facilités pour diner pour des personnes non pensionnaires, incluant des toilettes séparées. Possibilité de se faire servir des boissons, etc. . ., en dehors des heures de repas.

★ Simple au niveau de l'ameublement, des menus ou du service. Souvent dirigé par le propriétaire, avec peu de personnel qualifié. En general peu, sinon pas, de salle de bains particulières l'atmosphère est souvent plus personnelle que celle d'hotels mieux classés.

Ap. Hôtels recommandés, mais qui ne sont pas conformes aux exigences minimum des classifications concernant les portiers, les facilités de réception et le choix des menus.

Country House Hotel. Hôtels installés à la campagne, isolés, et bénéficiant d'un cadre particulièrement agréable (manoirs, relais, châteaux).

Petits hôtels, pensions de familles, et établissements similaires sont également inspectés par le RAC. Lorsques les normes sont satisfaites, ils sont inclus dans le guide en tant que "listed hotel" (hôtels recenses). Quelques-uns de ces petits hôtels offrent d'excellentes installations et facilités, et sont désormais designés par "Acclaimed" (approuvé) ou "Highly acclaimed" (Hautement approuvé). L'auberge, soit en ville, soit à la campagne est un autre type d'établissement examiné. Celles qui offrent des installations acceptables sont inclues dans les "listed hotels". Les meilleures sont classées, de une a trois chopes.

Hôtels non classés. Les hôtels en construction ou effectuant d'importants travaux de rénovation, sont à l'occasion inclus dans le guide sans classification. Ils n'ont évidemment pas été inspectés, mais sont inclus pour la commodité du lecteur, car ils seront ouverts pendant la période d'utilisation du guide.

Descriptions écourtées. Un certain nombre d'hôtels n'ont pas fourni d'informations pour la saison 1991. Dans ce cas seuls les classifications, noms, adresses et numéros de téléphone apparaissent.

Comment utiliser ce Guide

Nous avons utilisé un minimum de symboles afin que ce guide soit facile a utiliser.
Chaque entrée commence par la classification par étoile de l'hôtel, le nom, l'adresse, le numéro de téléphone, ainsi que les numéros de telex et de facs. Pour les "appointed hotels" (hotels classes) nous avons fait suivre une courte description, parfois accompagnée d'une photographie.

information concernant les chambres

10 bedrs: nombre de chambres
8 en suite: nombre de chambres avec salle de bain (douche ou baignoire)
(2 sh): nombre de chambres avec cabine de douche
2 ba: nombre de salles de bain communes
annexe: annexe approuvée par le RAC
TV: télévision disponible dans au moins quelques chambres
tcf: facilités pour obtenir du café ou du thé

facilités dans l'hotel

lift: ascenseur pour au moins quelques étages
TV: télévision disponible dans une pièce séparée ou dans le salon
dogs: chiens acceptés à la discrétion du gérant. Il peut y avoir des limitations de taille ou d'endroits autorisés. Pour éviter des déceptions, il est conseillé de demander confirmation des conditions auxquelles les chiens sont acceptés
ns: certaines parties de l'hôtel sont réservées aux non-fumeurs. La plupart des hôtels ne permettent pas de fumer dans la salle a manger
NS: interdiction de fumer dans tout l'hôtel
P 50: nombre de places de parking
G 1 (£1): nombre de places de garage et prix par nuit s'il y a lieu
U 2 (£3): nombre de garages particuliers et prix par nuit s'il y a lieu
coach: l'hôtel reçoit parfois des groupes en voyage organisé
child facs: au moins deux des services suivants sont disponibles: garde d'enfants ou simple surveillance, lits d'enfants, chaises hautes, menus speciaux, salle de jeux, cour de recréation ou aire de jeux
con 20: possibilité de conférences et nombre maximum de délégués

✕ information sur les repas

LD 8: heure limite de commande des repas, dans les hôtels classés.

nr: pas de service restaurant. Des repas au bar sont alors souvent disponibles.

Information sur les licences: Tous les hôtels servent de l'alcool aux heures légales, à moins qu'ils ne soient décrits comme sans licence (unlicenced) ou qu'ils ne soient sujets à une des limitations suivantes:

Club licence: Une licence est accordée à l'établissement, mais il est nécessaire de devenir membre d'un club pour obtenir des boissons alcoolisées. Pour respecter la loi une période de 48h doit s'écouler avant que celle-ci ne puisse prendre effet.

Restaurant or table licence (Rest lic): Licence par laquelle la vente d'alcool est strictement limitée aux clients prenant des repas.

Residential licence (Resid lic): Licence par laquelle la vente de boissons alcoolisées est limitée aux clients d'un hôtel, d'une pension de famille, etc. . . . et à leurs amis personnels, reçus aux frais du client séjournant a l'hotel.

Residential and restaurant licence: Combinaison des deux précédentes licences.

Temperance hotel (Temp): n'autorisent pas la consommation d'alcool sur les lieux, bien que les "unlic" (sans licence) puissent permettre aux clients de consommer leur propres boissons aux heures des repas. Quelques-uns peuvent faire payer un droit de débouchage si le client amène son propre vin.

£ information sur les prix

B&B £20–£30: étendue des prix par nuit et par personne, petit dejeuner compris.

B&B (double) £30–£50: étendue des prix par nuit pour deux personnes dans une chambre à deux lits (ou un lit à deux places)

HB weekly £175–£250: prix de la demi-pension par personne pour une semaine

Bk £5: prix d'un petit déjeuner complet

L £8·50: prix du déjeuner (table d'hôte)

D £12: prix du dinner (table d'hôte)

WB: offres spéciales pour le week-end ou pour quelques jours. Contacter l'hôtel pour avoir des détails supplementaires.

cc: cartes de crédit acceptées

Access: y compris Eurocard et Mastercard

Amex: American Express

B'card/Visa: cartes Barclays et Visa

CB: carte blanche

Diners: diners club

dep: caution exigée lors de la réservation

Les prix s'étendent de la chambre simple en basse saison à la chambre supérieure en pleine saison.

Les prix donnés dans le guide sont des prévisions faites par les hôteliers sur les prix qu'ils pensent offrir en 1991. Comme ces informations sont nécessairement traitées bien avant la publication, diverses conditions peuvent avoir mené à des prix supérieurs à ceux publiés. Il est toujours consieillé de vérifier avec l'hôtel les prix exacts avant de réserver.

Tous les prix cités comprennent la TVA là où elle est applicable. Ils peuvent ou non inclure le service.

RAC Hotels

Die Auswahl der Hotels durch den RAC erfolgt nach einer unangekündigten übernachtung durch einen der Inspektoren des Clubs und einer ausführlichen Inspektion der Anlage. Hotels sind nach folgenden Definitionen klassifiziert, die eingerückt sind, um den Hoteltyp zu bezeichnen und nicht den Leistungsgrad. Die Anforderungen, die an niedrigere Klassifikationen gestellt werden, sind in den höheren enthalten.

Eine Veränderung der Einstufung eines Hotels gegenüber früheren Jahren bedeutet nicht eine Verschlechterung des Standards in dem Etablissement.

Dies kann das Ergebnis von Änderungen der RAC-Anforderungen an Standardanforderungen innerhalb der Klassifikationen sein, die von Zeit zu Zeit vorgenommen werden und wiederum die Anforderungen der Gäste reflektieren.

★★★★★ Große luxuriöse Hotels von höchstem Standard für Zimmer, Service und Komfort.

★★★★ Große Hotels mit einem ganzen Stab ausgebildeten Personals. Rezeption, Gepäckträger und Zimmerservice stehen durchgängig zur Verfügung. Telefone in allen Zimmern. Eine große Anzahl privater Badezimmer. Einige Zimmer mit privatem Aufenthaltsraum; Konferenz- und/oder Banketteinrichtungen; oder Freizeiteinrichtungen.

★★★ Kleine luxuriöse Hotels oder größere, gut ausgestattete Hotels mit einem hohem Grad an Komfort. Beschränkter Zimmerservice. Telefon/Sprechanlage in den Zimmern. Eine Reihe von Zimmern mit privaten Badezimmern. Komplette Speiseeinrichtungen für Hotel- und andere Gäste einschließlich Laufkundschaft, sieben Tage in der Woche geöffnet.

★★ Formale Empfangsarrangements und mehrere höhere Angestellte. Einrichtungen für Gäste des Restaurants, die nicht im Hotel übernachten, darunter separate Toiletten. Aufenthaltsraumservice steht Hotelgästen zur Verfügung.

★ Einfach in der Ausstattung, der Menüauswahl und dem Service. Kann vom Besitzer persönlich geleitet sein, mit wenigen höheren Angestellten. In der Regel wenige oder keine privaten Badezimmer. Gewöhnlich mit persönlicherer Atmosphäre als die oben aufgeführten Sterne-Hotels.

Ap. Empfohlene Hotels, die nicht den minimalen Anforderungen bezüglich Gepäckdienst, Rezeptionseinrichtungen und Menüauswahl entsprechen; die Einrichtungen für Gäste, die nicht in dem Hotel übernachten, sind beschränkt.

Landhaushotels. Hotels in ländlicher Umgebung, die viele Charakteristika von Landhäusern aufwisen.

Kleine Hotels, Gasthäuser und ähnliche Etablissements werden auch vom RAC kontrolliert. Wenn der Standard zufriedenstellend ist, werden sie in den Führer unter Gelistete Hotels aufgenommen. Einige dieser kleinen Hotels verfügen über ausgezeichnete Unterkünfte und Einrichtungen und sind jetzt unter "Empfohlen" und "Sehr empfohlen" aufgeführt. Inns, ob sie sich in Städten oder auf dem Lande befinden, sind eine andere Kategorie, die der näheren Betrachtung unterzogen wurde. Inns, die akzeptable Unterkünfte bieten, sind bei den aufgenommenen Hotels aufgeführt, diejenigen, die herausragen, wurden mit einem bis drei Seideln ausgezeichnet.

Nichtklassifizierte Hotels. Hotels, die sich im Bau befinden oder bei denen größere Renovierungsarbeiten vorgenommen werden, sind in dem Führer in der Regel nicht klassifiziert, da sie noch nicht inspiziert werden konnten. Sie wurden aber dennoch für den Leser aufgenommen, da sie den Betrieb während der Gültigkeitsdauer des Führers aufnehmen werden.

Gekürzte Hotelbeschreibungen. Einige Hotels haben für die Saison 1991 noch keine detaillierte Beschreibung vorgelegt. In solchen Fällen sind nur Klassifikation, Name, Adresse und Telefonnummer in den Eintrag aufgenommen worden.

Benutzungshinweise

Zur einfacheren Benutzung des Führers wurde ein Minimum an Symbolen verwendet. Zu Beginn jedes Eintrags finden Sie die Klassifizierung des Hotels nach Sternen, den Namen, Adresse, Telefon-, Telex- und Telefaxnummer. Im Anschluß daran eine kurze Beschreibung der Ausgesuchten Hotels, einige davon mit Abbildung.

Die detaillierte Beschreibung der Hotels gliedert sich in fünf Abschnitte:

Zimmerinformation

10 bedrs: Anzahl der Zimmer
8 en suite: Anzahl der Zimmer mit Bad oder Dusche
(2 sh): Anzahl der Zimmer mit Duschkabinen (ohne WC)
2 ba: Anzahl der separaten Badezimmer
annexe: ein vom RAC abgenommenes Nebengebäude
TV: in mindestens einem Zimmer vorhanden
tcf: Einrichtungen zur Tee-/Kaffeezubereitung

Einrichtungen des Hotels

lift: Aufzug mindestens zu einigen Stockwerken
TV: steht in einem separaten Zimmer oder im Gemeinschaftsraum zur Verfügung
dogs: Genehmigung obliegt dem Leiter. Es kann Beschränkungen geben bezüglich der Bereiche des Hotels, in denen Hunde erlaubt sind, oder bezüglich der Größe. Um Enttäuschungen zu vermeiden, werden Gäste gebeten, sich über die Bedingungen zu informieren.
ns: Nichtraucherbereiche stehen zur Verfügung. In den meisten Hotels ist das Rauchen in den Speiseräumen nicht gestattet.
NS: Rauchen ist in keinem Hotelbereich gestattet
P 50: Anzahl der Parkplätze
G 1 (£1): Anzahl der Garageneinstellplätze und gegebenenfalls die Gebühr für eine Nacht
U 2 (£3): Anzahl der Einzelgaragen und gegebenenfalls die Gebühr für eine Nacht
coach: Busreisegesellschaften willkommen
child facs: mindestens zwei der folgenden Einrichtungen stehen zur Verfügung: Baby-Beaufsichtigung, Baby-Hördienst, Kinderbetten, hohe Stühle, spezielle Mahlzeiten (Babynahrung), Spielzimmer, Kinderspielplatz oder Spielbereich.
con 20: Konferenzeinrichtungen und maximale Teilnehmerzahl

Speiseinformation

LD 8: Entgegennahme der letzten Bestellung in Ausgesuchten Hotels.
nr: kein Restaurantservice; stattdessen werden oft Mahlzeiten in der Bar serviert.

Ausschankinformation: Alle Hotels servieren alkoholische Getränke während der erlaubten Ausschankzeiten, es sei denn, sie sind als solche ohne Konzession ausgewiesen oder unterliegen einer der folgenden Beschränkungen.
Clubkonzession. Eine Konzession, die an Etablissements vergeben wird, bei denen die Voraussetzung zum Ausschank alkoholischer Getränke die Mitgliedschaft im Club ist. Um den Gesetzen zu genügen, tritt die Mitgliedschaft im Club 48 Stunden nach Antragstellung in Kraft.
Restaurant-oder Tischkonzession (Rest lic). Eine Konzession, die den Verkauf alkoholischer Getränke auf Gäste beschränkt, die eine Mahlzeit zu sich nehmen.
Gastkonzession (Resid lic). Eine Konzession, die den Verkauf alkoholischer Getränke auf Gäste des Hotels, der Pension etc. beschränkt, und auf Freunde, die auf Kosten der Gäste bewirtet werden.
Gast-und Restaurantkonzession. Eine Kombination der oben aufgeführten Konzessionen.
In *Alkoholfreien Hotels* (Temp.) ist der Konsum alkoholischer Getränke nicht gestattet, Nichtkonzessionierte Hotels (Unlic) können allerdings ihren Gästen den Konsum mitgebrachter Getränke zu den Mahlzeiten gestatten. Einige erheben eine Korkengebühr, wenn Gäste ihren eigenen Wein mitbringen.

£ Kosteninformation

B&B £20–£30: Preis pro Person für eine übernachtung inklusive Frühstück
B&B (double) £30–£50: Preis für zwei Personen im Doppelzimmer für eine übernachtung inklusive Frühstück
HB weekly £175–£250: Preis pro Person für 7 übernachtungen, Abendessen und Frühstück
Bk £5: Preis für ein großes Frühstück
L £8·50: Preis für table d'hote Mittagessen
D £12: Preis für table d'hote Abendessen
WB: Sonderangebote für Kurz- oder Wochenendaufenthalte. Nähere Einzelheiten erfahren Sie direkt vom Hotel.

cc Kreditkarten werden akzeptiert

Access (einschließlich Mastercharge und Eurocard)
Amex: American Express
B'card/Visa: Barclay card und Visa cards
CB: Carte Blanche
Diners: Diners Club
dep.: Anzahlung bei Buchung erforderlich

Die Preise enthalten die Kosten für Standardzimmer in der Vor- und Nachsaison und für besser ausgestattete Zimmer in der Hauptsaison.

Die im Führer angegebenen Tarife sind von den Hoteliers für 1991 vorausberechnete Preise. Da diese Informationen notwendigerweise weit vor Veröffentlichung zusammengestellt wurden, können sich ändernde Bedingungen zu Erhöhungen der angegebenen Preise führen. Es wird geraten, die aktuellen Preise vor der Buchung bei dem Hotel zu erfragen.

Alle Preise enthalten MwST, falls zutreffend. Bedienung ist nicht immer enthalten.

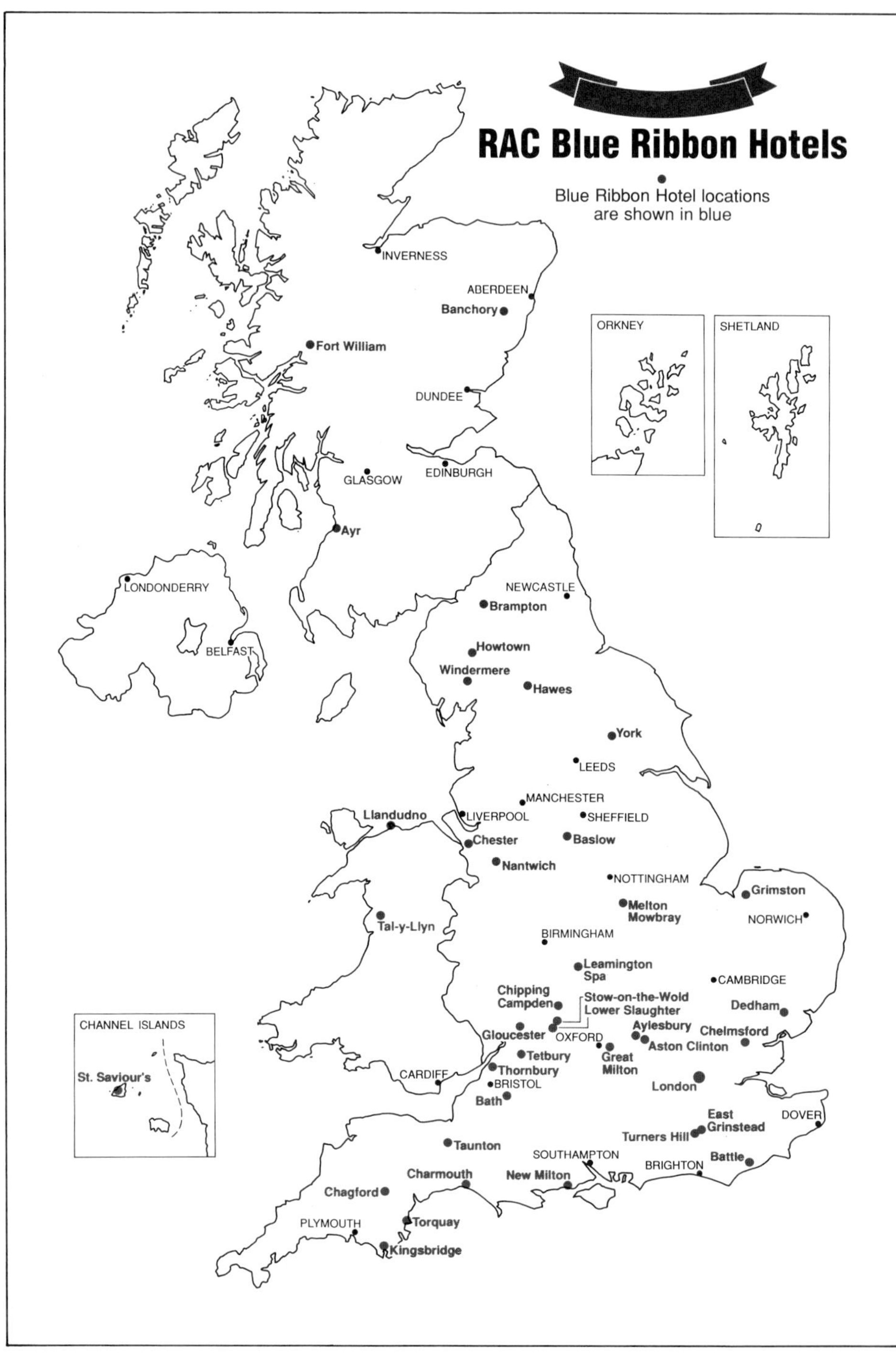

RAC Blue Ribbon Hotels
Blue Ribbon Hotel locations
are shown in blue
INVERNESS
ABERDEEN
Banchory
Fort William
DUNDEE
GLASGOW
EDINBURGH
Ayr
ORKNEY
SHETLAND
LONDONDERRY
BELFAST
NEWCASTLE
Brampton
Howtown
Windermere
Hawes
York
LEEDS
MANCHESTER
Llandudno
LIVERPOOL
SHEFFIELD
Chester
Baslow
Nantwich
NOTTINGHAM
Grimston
Melton
Mowbray
NORWICH
Tal-y-Llyn
BIRMINGHAM
Leamington
Spa
CAMBRIDGE
Chipping
Campden
Stow-on-the-Wold
Lower Slaughter
Dedham
Aylesbury
Chelmsford
Gloucester
OXFORD
Aston Clinton
Tetbury
Great
Milton
Thornbury
CARDIFF
BRISTOL
London
Bath
CHANNEL ISLANDS
St. Saviour's
East
Grinstead
DOVER
Turners Hill
Taunton
SOUTHAMPTON
Battle
BRIGHTON
Charmouth
New Milton
Chagford
Torquay
PLYMOUTH
Kingsbridge

RAC Hotel Awards

All hotels recommended by the RAC must reach the required standards for their classification. They must be well kept, comfortable, and offer good food and willing service to their guests.

Merit Awards

Some proprietors strive to offer their guests more than the standard; in some hotels it might be luxuries in the bedrooms, a greater degree of comfort in the public rooms, perhaps more space than one would expect; then there are those proprietors and managers, the born hoteliers, who look after their guests with concerned attention; and there are those hoteliers who are proud to offer food of a quality far beyond that which is required for their classification.

For each of these categories of excellence, there is an RAC Award: **C** for comfort, **H** for hospitality, **R** for restaurant quality. In this way we distinguish those hotels which in cold statistics can only be classified as, say, three star, but which offer guests more than other three-star hotels do.

Each year, awards are re-considered and must be earned afresh. If a hotel has changed hands, extra checks are made to ensure that the new owners are carrying on where the old ones left off. The **R** Award, in particular, is rarely awarded in a new owner's first year. We must be convinced that the restaurant regularly provides cuisine of an extra-high standard.

Blue Ribbon Award

The highest award the RAC gives is the Blue Ribbon. It indicates that the hotel is providing the highest standards of service, comfort and cuisine within its classification. The award is granted to hotels of one to four stars. Five star hotels are not eligible for Blue Ribbons because in order to become five-star hotels, they must prove to be outstanding in every department.

To be considered for a Blue Ribbon, an hotel must achieve Hospitality Comfort and Restaurant awards. In addition, it must offer that something extra, which is difficult to define but easy to recognise.

Blue Ribbons can be awarded to hotels of any size. Obviously a one-star Blue Ribbon hotel will not offer the same quality of comfort or standard of cuisine as, say, a three-star establishment, but it will be superior to its fellow hotels within its classification.

Blue Ribbon Hotels for 1990 are:

★★★	The Bell, Aston Clinton
★★★★	Hartwell House, Aylesbury
★★★	Cavendish, Baslow
★★★	Priory Hotel, Bath
★★★★	Netherfield Place, Battle
★★	Farlam Hall, Brampton
★★★	Gidleigh Park, Chagford
★★	White House, Charmouth
★★★★	Pontlands Park, Chelmsford
★★★★	Grosvenor Hotel, Chester
★★★	Charingworth Manor, Chipping Camden
★★★	Maison Talbooth, Dedham
★★★	Gravetye Manor, East Grinstead
★★★	Hatton Court, Gloucester
★★★	Le Manoir aux Quat' Saisons, Great Milton
★★★	Congham Hall, Grimston
★★	Simonstone Hall, Hawes
★★★	Sharrow Bay, Howtown
★★★	Buckland Tout Saints, Kingsbridge
★	Lansdowne Hotel, Leamington Spa
★★★★	Athenaeum Hotel, London
★★★★	Berkshire Hotel, London
★★★★	Browns Hotel, London
★★★★	Capital Hotel, London
★★★★	Dukes Hotel, London
★★★★	Goring Hotel, London
★★★★	Whites Hotel, London
★★★	Lower Slaughter Manor, Lower Slaughter
★★★★	Stapleford Park, Melton Mowbray
★★★	Rookery Hall, Nantwich
★★★★	Chewton Glen, New Milton
★★	Grapevine Hotel, Stow on the Wold
★★★★	Castle Hotel, Taunton
★★★	Close Hotel, Tetbury
★★★	Thornbury Castle, Thornbury
★	Fairmount House, Torquay
★★★★	Alexander House, Turners Hill
★★	Holbeck Ghyll, Windermere
★★★★	Middlethorpe Hall, York
SCOTLAND	
★★★★	Fairfield House, Ayr
★★★	Banchory Lodge, Banchory
★★★★	Inverlochy Castle, Fort William
WALES	
★★★	Bodysgallen Hall, Llandudno
★	Minfford Hotel, Tal-y-Lyn
CHANNEL ISLANDS	
★★★★	Longueville Manor, St Saviours

The Bell

The Bell, Aston Clinton

From a simply country inn, originally a coaching house on the old London – Aylesbury road, the Harris family have over the last 50 years created a gem of a small hotel. Discreet modernisation throughout has added the comfort required by today's guests to the atmosphere and charm of the original building. Carefully chosen furnishings set off antiques in the main rooms, luxury touches enhance the bedrooms, many set round the cobbled courtyard, and the garden is a riot of roses.

Hartwell House, Aylesbury

Hartwell House is an archetypal stately home, with a Jacobean *and* a Georgian facade, set in the appropriate landscaped parkland with a lake. The interior has notable plasterwork and panelling, which is well set-off by the fine paintings and antique furnishings, a Gothic hall and staircase with Jacobean carved figures, two exquisite dining rooms, lovely drawing rooms and some huge, elegant bedrooms. Truly a setting fit for a king – Hartwell House was for five years the home of the exiled King Louis XVIII.

The Cavendish

Cavendish, Baslow

Built in the 1780s as the coaching post between Buxton and Chesterfield, the Cavendish was restored in the 1970s under the personal guidance of the Duchess of Devonshire. Eric Marsh now runs this most English of hotels. There are log fires in the Georgian-style lounge and the Paxton restaurant is a lovely setting for the superb food. And from every room there are views over the Duke of Devonshire's Chatsworth estate whose exclusive fishing is available to guests.

Hartwell House

Priory, Bath

Two acres of lovely gardens surround this Victorian gothic house barely a mile from the centre of Bath. The country atmosphere extends into the hotel, which is delightfully furnished in Victorian style. The bedrooms offer every comfort, the service is excellent but unobtrusive, and the cuisine is of the highest quality.

The Priory

The Priory

Netherfield Place, Battle

A 1920s Georgian-style house, Netherfield Place stands in 30 acres of parkland, close to the ancient town of Battle. The spacious rooms, from the panelled dining room to the bedrooms with their delicate furnishings, have a restful quality, which will help you to relax. Fresh produce from the walled kitchen garden is a feature of the menus, which are complimented by a wine list of 300 bins.

Netherfield Place

Farlam Hall, Brampton

A creeper-clad, greystone house, peacefully set in 4 acres of mature gardens with a stream and lake, Farlam Hall makes a super setting for a holiday, lying as it does between the Lake District and Hadrian's Wall. The Quinion and Stevenson families are welcoming hosts and keep everything running smoothly.

Farlam Hall

Gidleigh Park

Gidleigh Park, Chagford

Gidleigh Park is a mock-Tudor country house set beside a rushing stream, deep in a wooded Devon valley below the stark grandeur of Coslon Hill on Dartmoor. Famed for its food and wine, Gidleigh Park has a typical English country house atmosphere, with big squashy sofas, log fires, chintzy bedrooms and fresh flowers everywhere.

The White House

White House, Charmouth

A pretty hotel in a pretty place, the White House in the centre of Charmouth has all the delicate charm of the best of Regency seaside architecture. Public rooms reflect this style in elegant decor and furnishings, while the tastefully decorated bedrooms offer all that the visitor requires. Concerned service from the resident proprietors and their helpful staff ensure that you are cared for as well as comfortable.

Pontlands Park, Chelmsford

From the moment the porter meets you, to take your luggage to reception, you know that you will be well looked after at this excellent hotel. A red-brick Victorian mansion, well-furnished and set in attractive grounds, Pontlands Park is run with flair by owner-manager Robert Bartella. The cuisine is as good as the service, the public rooms comfortable and the bedrooms charming, even the housekeeping is superlative!

Pontlands Park

Grosvenor Hotel, Chester

Right in the centre of historic Chester, the Grosvenor was built over a century ago, with the beams, gables and turrets dear to the Victorian heart. Inside, the sumptuous rooms have a Victorian feel to them too, with chandeliers, oil paintings and a superb central staircase.

The Grosvenor Hotel

Maison Talbooth

Maison Talbooth, Dedham

The vale of Dedham, immortalised by Constable, is still a haven of peace and tranquility. There, overlooking the river valley and the water meadows stretching away to the medieval church of Stratford St Mary, is Le Maison Talbooth, a quietly luxurious hotel in a Victorian country house, with sumptuous bedroom suites and an elegant lounge. Guests can dine at Le Talbooth restaurant or the spectacular Rotisserie at the sister Dedham Vale Hotel, both nearby.

Charingworth Manor

Charingworth Manor, Chipping Camden

The ancient manor of Charingworth lies in the beautiful Cotswold countryside. The manor house dates back to the early 14th century, and massive beams showing the original medieval decoration can still be seen. Furnished in a fitting country-house style with some fine antiques, Charingworth Manor is small enough to ensure that guests receive individual attention.

Gravetye Manor

Le Manoir aux Quat' Saisons

Gravetye Manor, East Grinstead

What can one say about this superb hotel, the doyenne of country house hotels? Others have followed the lead set by Peter Herbert, but Gravetye continues to hold its place amongst the best. A lovely Tudor manor house set in a famous garden – which is a place of pilgrimage for dedicated gardeners – furnished with fine antiques and equipped with every luxury. The ravishing cuisine and outstanding service complete a totally satisfying picture.

Hatton Court, Gloucester

A stone-built, 17th century manor house, 600 feet up in the Cotswold Hills, Hatton Court has superb views over the Severn Valley and Malvern Hills yet is only 3 miles from historic Gloucester. Extensively modernised, with additional bedrooms added in keeping with the main building, Hatton Court offers spacious rooms, well-chosen furnishings, a beautiful garden for summer visitors and log fires for winter ones. It is the management's proud boast that 'nothing is too much trouble' for the dedicated staff.

Le Manoir aux Quat' Saisons, Great Milton

In this exquisite manor house, Raymond Blanc has combined an English country-house hotel with a superb French restaurant. Elegantly furnished rooms help to create a relaxing atmosphere and the garden is a delight, while comfort is everywhere a priority. But the heart of this hotel is in the restaurant where M Blanc works his wizardry.

Hatton Court

Congham Hall, Grimston

There's a very personal touch to Congham Hall. Friendly owners have created an excellent hotel in this gracious Georgian country house. The well-proportioned rooms have attractive furnishings and the bedrooms are supplied with all those little extras from pot pourri to bathrobes, from books to fresh fruit, which make such a difference. The Foremosts pride themselves particularly on the cuisine at Congham Hall which is of the light and varied, modern mode.

Congham Hall

Simonstone Hall

Simonstone Hall, Hawes

Once owned by the Earls of Wharncliffe, this stone-built manor house is at one with the Yorkshire Dales landscape. There are incomparable views of Upper Wensleydale from the spacious drawing rooms, with their lovely panelling and ceilings. Up the stairs, with an heraldic stained glass window, are ten enchanting bedrooms, each one different. John and Sheila Jeffrys create a friendly informal atmosphere in which guests can relax and enjoy all that this outstanding countryside offers.

Sharrow Bay, Howtown

The Sharrow Bay is a very civilised and restful hotel, run in inimitable style by Francis Coulson and Bryan Slack. Standing on the shores of Ullswater, the views over the Lake to the fells beyond are a constant refreshment for the spirit. Exquisitely decorated and lovingly furnished rooms, superb food and wine, and wonderful service make this a very special hotel.

The Sharrow Bay

Buckland Tout Saints

Buckland Tout Saints, Kingsbridge

Buckland-Tout-Saints could be pictured in an architectural handbook as a perfect example of Queen Anne style. A red-brick country house set in a lovely garden, it is owned and personally managed by the Shepherd family, assisted by skilled, professional staff. Set in the lush countryside between Dartmoor and Salcombe, Buckland Tout Saints is a perfect base for a holiday, with its elegant public rooms and individually decorated bedrooms.

The Lansdowne

Lansdowne, Leamington Spa

A charming small hotel in adjoining Regency buildings close to the centre of Leamington Spa. Public rooms are welcoming and bedrooms have all been fitted with pretty furnishings and are as well equipped as those in much grander establishments. The Allens work hard to ensure that their guests are happy; Gillian's menus are short but offer something for all tastes, while David is here, there and everywhere.

Athenaeum, London W1

This busy hotel on Piccadilly is in contrast to most of our Blue Ribbon hotels in being a modern building, but none-the-less offers guests an equally agreeable stay. Amongst the best furnished hotels in London, the Athenaeum also prides itself on the quality of its service and the excellence of its cuisine.

The Athenaeum

The Berkshire

Berkshire, London W1

Just behind Oxford Street, the Berkshire is a most convenient place to stay, whether you are in London for business, on holiday or just for the shopping! Great care has been taken with the whole effect, with crystal chandeliers, specially lit pictures and plants adding the finishing touches and you may even find a harpist playing in the drawing room of this superbly run hotel.

Browns, London W1

Brown's is one of London's oldest established hotels. Opened by an ex-valet in the 1830s, it has offered 'the nobility and gentry' a home from home for the last 150 years but has not failed to move with the times and is thoroughly modern in most aspects. Only the service remains old-fashioned, being extensive, helpful and caring.

Browns

The Capital

Capital, London SW7

A small luxury town hotel conveniently placed in the heart of Knightsbridge, just round the corner from Harrods, the Capital with its elegant *fin de siècle* decoration is a restful retreat from the hurly burly of London. Tastefully fitted and decorated bedrooms offer every comfort required and the restaurant is excellent.

The Goring

Dukes

Dukes, London W1

A handsome Edwardian building, tucked away in a quiet cul-de-sac just off St James. Old gas street lamps lit by hand each evening, light your way through the entrance courtyard, and the opulent public rooms continue the theme of luxury Edwardian living. The suites and bedrooms are all individually decorated and boast marble bathrooms. Dukes restaurant has a well deserved reputation for good food and wine, while the service is of paramount importance – staff outnumber guests by two to one!

Goring, London SW1

Tucked away in a quiet backwater between Victoria Station and Buckingham Palace, the Goring is a very unusual London hotel. Privately owned and run, it has the quiet, relaxing atmosphere of a country house, unlike the bustle and excitement of some London hotels. Many of the rooms look out on to the charming garden and are furnished in a gentle traditional way that is as soothing as the excellent service.

Whites, London W2

An elegant hotel in an ornate Edwardian building overlooking Hyde Park and Kensington Gardens, Whites has great style, skilfully blending period ambience with modern amenities. The bedrooms have every luxury and the cuisine is well recommended.

Whites

Lower Slaughter Manor, Lower Slaughter

There has been a manor house here since before the Norman conquest, and the present building of Cotswold stone is listed as of architectural interest with some outstanding plasterwork ceilings. The restful atmosphere is enhanced by the tasteful antique furnishings and oil paintings and there are well-tended formal gardens with lawns and flower beds. But, overall, it is the warmth of the welcome and the genuine friendliness of everyone concerned which makes Lower Slaughter Manor so enjoyable.

Stapleford Park, Melton Mowbray

The Paytons' aim when they brought this one-time hunting lodge of the Earls of Harborough, was to restore it to its former grandeur. And they have succeeded! The house itself is an architectural delight and the park an eminently suitable setting for it. Inside, the public rooms have a stately grandeur, with leather sofas, panelling and oil paintings. The bedrooms have all been decorated by different personalities and designers; the result is quite charming and totally luxurious. The food and wine, too, is worthy of the house – not for nothing is this hotel owned by Bob Payton, *restaurateur extraordinaire*.

Rookery Hall, Nantwich

Standing proudly on a hill overlooking the Cheshire countryside, Rookery Hall is a Georgian mansion transformed into a Victorian château set in 28 acres of parkland. The beautifully proportioned rooms and fine details of ceilings and panelling make staying here an architectural experience as well as a pleasure. The excellent food and selected wines are all part of the success of this well-run hotel.

Lower Slaughter Manor

Rookery Hall

Stapleford Park

Chewton Glen

Chewton Glen, New Milton

Chewton Glen is a graceful country house in acres of glorious parkland on the edge of the New Forest. Privately owned, it is a hotel of rare charm, exquisitely furnished and with skilled and professional staff. Latest developments, to be opened at the end of 1990, include a superb new leisure centre with every facility that the most ardent sports enthusiast could want.

The Grapevine

Grapevine, Stow-on-the-Wold

There's a warm welcome from Sandra Elliott for guests at the Grapevine, close to the heart of this ancient town on the Fosse Way. There's a comfortable lounge, nicely furnished bar and charming, individually designed bedrooms, but the memorable feature of this hotel is the dining room, roofed by a spectacular 120 year old vine.

Castle Hotel, Taunton

Built partly around the ruins of the Norman castle, this lovely hotel offers guests a high degree of comfort. The public rooms are beautifully furnished and the bedrooms luxuriously equipped. Staff could not be more helpful and the food and wine in the elegantly refurbished restaurant are as notable as ever, with superb cooking of outstanding ingredients.

Castle Hotel

Close at Tetbury

Thornbury Castle

Thornbury Castle, Thornbury

A genuine castle, but Tudor, so the stone mullioned windows are large, the crenellations more decorative than functional and the chimney pots masterpieces of the bricklayers art. Inside, the furnishings point up the highly individual shapes of the rooms, with their high ceilings and lovely windows through which there are views over the Severn to Wales. All this and its own vineyard too!

Fairmount, Torquay

Above the lovely Cockington Valley, away from the bustle of the town, the Fairmount hotel has a delightful informal atmosphere; more like staying with friends than being in a hotel. You can sit in the suntrap gardens, relax in the cosy lounge, or join the other guests in the attractive conservatory bar, and at the end of the day there is a restful bedroom to welcome you.

The Fairmount

Close at Tetbury, Tetbury

Four centuries ago, a prosperous wool merchant built himself this house in the honey-coloured local stone. The 18th century roofed over the central courtyard with a superb domed ceiling and added two larger rooms, with Adam ceilings, on the garden-side. Today the Close at Tetbury is an elegant hotel with a surprisingly country feel for a town hotel – derived from the lovely gardens? the country house style furnishings? the freshest of fresh produce used in the meals? or all three together.

Alexander House

Alexander House, Turners Hill

Alexander House, a mellow, red-brick mansion, is an outstanding country house hotel. Public rooms are supremely elegant, whether panelled in bleached oak or hung with hand-painted silk panels of exotic birds. The elegant suites and bedrooms offer every luxury and the service is second to none.

Holbeck Ghyll

Holbeck Ghyll, Windermere

Holbeck Ghyll, a creeper-clad early 19th century building in Lakeland stone and slate, was once the country retreat of the Earl of Lonsdale. Now David and Patricia Nicholson have made it a charming small country house hotel, with carefully chosen furnishings, excellent food and wine, and attentive service, while the views across Windermere to the fells beyond are staggering.

Middlethorpe Hall, York

A grand and glorious William-and-Mary house set in parkland on the edge of York. The decorations, antiques and fine pictures have been carefully chosen as consistent with the period of the house and give an air of mellow comfort. The panelled dining room, a lovely backdrop to the imaginative food, looks out over the stately gardens and the individually decorated bedrooms have charming Edwardian-style bathrooms.

Middlethorpe Hall

Fairfield House, Ayr

A Victorian Glasgow merchant built this splendid house on the seafront at Ayr. Transformed by its refurbishment under the direction of Lady Henrietta Spencer-Churchill, it now offers incomparably luxurious bedrooms, spacious public rooms with distinctive decor, and service as good as anywhere. The cuisine, too, is excellent, and all the while the views out to sea entice the eye away.

Fairfield House

Banchory Lodge, Banchory

A gracious, Georgian house whose white walls and grey roofs stand out through the trees in the richly wooded grounds which are traversed by Banchory Lodge's main claim to fame – the River Dee. But you don't have to be a fisherman to enjoy staying here, anyone would revel in the good food, comfortable rooms, superb views and friendly caring service.

Banchory Lodge

Inverlochy Castle, Fort William

A Victorian 'castle' in the Scottish baronial style, Inverlochy is set in grand Highland scenery. Its 500 acre estate stretches down to the River Lochy with Ben Nevis towering on the other side, an incomparable view. As you enter the huge hall, you are enveloped in the atmosphere of a well-loved stately home, an impression enhanced by the lovely antique furniture, interesting paintings and carefully chosen ornaments throughout the hotel. The grandeur of the house is matched by the faultless service and the superb food and wine.

Inverlochy Castle

Bodysgallen Hall

WALES

Bodysgallen Hall, Llandudno

A skilfully and sympathetically restored 17th century house, furnished with antiques and a variety of pictures, Bodysgallen Hall is a superb hotel for a top level meeting; the conference rooms were converted from the 18th century stables! The restoration of the Hall extended to the beautiful gardens, which include a 17th century Knot garden. From its location just south of Llandudno, there are spectacular views of Snowdonia.

Minfford Hotel

Minfford Hotel, Tal-y-Lyn

The little Minfford is a coaching inn of charm and character, nestling beneath Cader Idris. There are magnificent views from the cosy lounge, the cheerful sun-room and the delightful cottagy bedrooms, and delicious food is served in the attractive beamed restaurant.

CHANNEL ISLANDS

Longueville Manor, St Saviours

Owned and run by the Lewis family, Longueville Manor dates in part from the 13th century. The magnificent oak-panelled dining room is the perfect setting for the excellent cuisine which is supplied in part by the hotel's own gardens; as are the flowers which add the finishing touches throughout the hotel. The spacious bedrooms are particularly charming with comfortable chairs for those who prefer to relax in the privacy of their own room rather than join their fellow guests in the convivial lounge and bar.

Longueville Manor

The Connaught – Five Star Hotel of the Year

The Connaught is a hotel like no other. New luxury hotels rise in a blaze of publicity, have a brief spell of fame and then settle down, as fashion and its followers move on to the latest sensation, but the Connaught continues on its way, utterly dependable in every facet of its excellence. By some magic, staff all know, and use, guests' names and are there to answer a request almost before you make it. The understated luxury of the furnishings and the quiet elegance of the decor are matched by the superlative food in classic British tradition. Tucked away in a quiet corner of Mayfair, the Connaught is a very special place. We are proud to award it our Five Star Hotel accolade for 1990.

'Credit to the Industry' Award

For nearly 30 years, the McMillan family have worked and worked to improve first the North West Castle Hotel in Stranraer and, since the early 80s, the Cally Palace in Gatehouse of Fleet, two popular hotels in the lovely south west of Scotland.

First, the McMillans made sure that the decor and furnishings were of a high standard, and that staff were offering guests real service. From this sound base, they have looked at the leisure opportunities at their hotels and have progressively added to and improved them. Both hotels have swimming pools, the North West Castle has a leisure centre while the McMillans are hoping to add a golf course at the Cally Palace soon. The North West Castle must be unique amongst hotels in having its own curling rink – both father and son McMillan have represented Scotland at this esoteric sport.

The dedication, care and imaginative flair displayed in these two excellent hotels make the McMillans worthy winners of our 'Credit to the Industry' Award for 1990.

Tankard Symbol for Inns

The inns of Britain have provided accommodation as well as refreshment for travellers for many centuries. They, too, have been urged forward to provide better facilities. Some now rival the best hotels in many ways, but remain inns because of the very style which is their charm.

The RAC introduced the Tankard symbol for inns to mark the achievements of those innkeepers who have not only upgraded the facilities of their establishment – for example at least three-quarters of the bedrooms of a three Tankard inn must be en suite and have a colour TV and a direct-dial telephone – but have also improved the quality of the service and of the cuisine.

Other inns, which offer comfortable accommodation but do not reach these high standards, will be found among the Listed hotels.

Listed Hotels and Guest Houses

Small hotels and guest houses have greatly improved the facilities and services that they offer guests. Some now provide facilities which in their own way may be as comfortable, even as luxurious, as those provided by star-rated hotels. The difference lies in the style of the hotel; listed ones are often much more informal and may only cater for residents and their guests.

Because they have a very different role to play in the tourist industry, we are publishing a new guide to Small Hotels, Guest Houses and Inns which will include full details of all these RAC listed establishments. Brief details of these are also included in this guide for the convenience of readers.

Merit Awards

There are three types of Merit Award:
H for Hospitality and Service
It is granted to those hotels where the quality of hospitality and service is superior to that expected in its classification
C for Comfort
Granted to those hotels where the overall comfort in bedrooms and in public rooms is superior to the general run of hotels in its classification.
R for Restaurant quality
Granted when the cuisine at a hotel is of a higher standard than is normally expected within its classification.

To help intending guests to choose hotels with above average qualities the **H C** and **R** symbols appear in the hotel's entry in the Guide. The Proprietor may also display the letters in brochures, letterheads and so on.

Hotels awarded all three Merit Awards

♣♣ ★★	Lovelady Shield	Alston
★★★	Alveston House	Alveston
★★★	Lansdown Grove	Bath
♣♣ ★★★	Beechfield House	Beanacre
★★★	Dragon House	Bilbrook
★★★	Crown	Blockley
★★★	Devonshire Arms	Bolton Abbey
★★★★	Norfolk Royale	Bournemouth
★★★	Langtry Manor	Bournemouth
♣♣ ★★★	Manor House	Castle Coombe
★★★	Castletown Golf-Links	Castletown – I.O.M.
♣♣ ★★★	Mill End	Chagford
★★★	Cotswold House	Chipping Camden
♣♣ ★★★	Ockenden Manor	Cuckfield
♣♣ ★★★	Dedham Vale	Dedham
★★★	International	Derby
★★★	Izaak Walton	Dovedale
★★★	Bell	Driffield
★★	Star & Eagle	Goudhurst
★★	Bishop's Table	Farnham
♣♣ ★★★	Hob Green	Harrogate
♣♣ ★★★	Hassop Hall	Hassop
★★★★	Royal Victoria	Hastings
♣♣ ★★★	Fairwater Head	Hawkchurch
♣♣ ★★★	Bel Alp	Haytor Vale
★★★	Black Swan	Helmsley
♣♣ ★★	Combe House	Holford
★★★	Mill House	Kingham
♣♣ ★★★	Lastingham Grange	Lastingham
★★★	Arundell Arms	Lifton
★★★★	Royal Lancaster	London
★★★★	Mountbatten	London
★★	Kersbrook	Lyme Regis
★★	Rising Sun	Lynmouth
★★★★	Fredrick's	Maidenhead
★★	Norfolk House	Maidenhead
★★★	Ivy House	Marlborough
★★	Remuera	Minehead
♣♣ ★★★	Monk Fryston Hall	Monk Fryston
★	Mill	Mungrisdale
♣♣ ★★★	Collaven Manor	Okehampton
★★★	Salterns	Poole
★★	Oaks	Porlock
♣♣ ★★★	Breamish House	Powburn
★★	Dean Court	Preston
♣♣ ★★★★	Quorn Country	Quorn
♣♣ ★★★★	Tylney Hall	Rotherwick
♣♣ ★★★	Rothley Court	Rothley
★	Rydal Lodge	Rydal
♣♣ ★★	Boscundle Manor	St Austell
★★★	Tides Reach	Salcombe
★★★	Charnwood	Sheffield
♣♣ ★★★	Daneswood House	Shipham
★★	Abbeydale	Sidmouth
★★★	Riviera	Sidmouth
★★★★	Victoria	Sidmouth
♣♣ ★★	Marsh Hall	South Molton
♣♣ ★★★	Whitechapel Manor	South Molton
★★	Hobbit	Sowerby Bridge
★★★	George	Stamford
★★★	Barton Cross	Stoke Canon
★★★	Swan	Streatley
♣♣ ★★★	Calcot Manor	Tetbury
★★★	Snooty Fox	Tetbury
♣♣ ★★★	Lords of the Manor	Upper Slaughter
★★	Lake Isle	Uppingham
★★	Downfield	Watchet
♣♣ ★★★★	Wood Hall	Wetherby
★★	White House	Williton
♣♣ ★★★★	Oakley Court	Windsor
♣♣ ★★	Westerclose	Withypool
★★★	Watersmeet	Woolacombe
★★	Royal Oak	Yattenden

SCOTLAND

★★★★	Craigendarroch	Ballater
♣♣ ★★★★	Invery Hosue	Banchory
★	Lubnaig	Callander
♣♣ ★★★	Dolphinton	Dolphinton
♣♣ ★★★	Montgreenan Mansion House	Irvine
♣♣ ★★★	Ardanaiseig	Kilchrenan
♣♣ ★★	Cringletie	Peebles
♣♣ ★★★	Murrayshall House	Scone
♣♣ ★★	Kilcamb Lodge	Strontian

WALES

★★★	St Tudno	Llandudno
♣♣ ★★★	Lake Hotel	Llangammarch Wells

CHANNEL ISLES
Jersey

★★★★	L'Horizon	St Brelades Bay

Two Merit Awards

♣♣ ★★★	The Elms	Abberley	H R
★★	Arrow Mill	Alcester	C R
★★	Grange	Alton	C R
★★★	Woodland Park	Altrincham	C R
★★	Borrans Park	Ambleside	C R
★★	Fisherbeck House	Ambleside	H C
♣♣ ★★	Kirkstone Foot	Ambleside	H C
★★★	Rothay Manor	Ambleside	H C
★★★	Moore Place	Apsley Guise	C R
♣♣ ★★★	Amberley Castle	Arundel	H C

Stars	Hotel	Town	Code
★★★	Tytherleigh Cott	Axminster	H R
★★	Cliff House	Barton on Sea	C R
🌲🌳 ★★	Overwater Hall	Bassenthwaite	C R
🌲🌳 ★★★	Woodlands Manor	Bedford	H C
★★★	Wild Boar Inn	Beeston	H C
★★	Riverdale Hall	Bellingham	H R
★★	White Lion	Bidford-on-Avon	H C
★★	Boltons	Bournemouth	H C
★★	Chinehead	Bournemouth	C R
★★	Chinehurst	Bournemouth	H C
★★★	Connaught	Bournemouth	H C
★★	Durley Chine	Bournemouth	H C
★★★	East Cliff Court	Bournemouth	H C
★★	Hinton Firs	Bournemouth	H C
★★	Finden Lodge	Bourton-on-the-Water	H C
★★	Parlors Hall	Bridgnorth	H C
★★	New Ravenstoke	Bridlington	H C
★★	Roundham House	Bridport	H C
★★★★	Brighton Metropole	Brighton	C R
★★★★	Lygon Arms	Broadway	H R
★★★	Carey's Manor	Brockenhurst	H C
★★★	String of Horses	Carlisle	H C
★★	Chester Court	Chester	H C
🌲🌳 ★★★★	Crabwall Manor	Chester	H C
★★★	Seymour House	Chipping Camden	H C
★★★	Waterford Lodge	Christchurch	H C
★★	Mynd House	Church Stretton	C R
★★★	Fleece	Cirencester	C R
★★★	Dunkenhalgh	Clayton le Moors	H R
★★★	Pines	Clayton le Woods	C R
★★	Old Bakehouse	Colyton	H R
★★	White Cottage	Colyton	H R
★★★	Rudloe Park	Corsham	H R
★★★	Brooklands Grange	Coventry	H C
★★★	Crooklands	Crooklands	H R
★★	Kittiwell House	Croyde	C R
★★	Crudwell Court	Crudwell	H C
★★★	Lord Daresbury	Daresbury	H C
★★	Tarr Steps	Dulverton	H C
★★	Exmoor House	Dunster	H C
★★★	Luttrell Arms	Dunster	H C
★★★	Duxford Lodge	Duxford	C R
★★	St George	Eccleshall	H C
★★★	Buckerell Lodge	Exeter	C R
🌲🌳 ★★★	Lord Haldon	Exeter	H C
★★	St Andrews	Exeter	H C
★★★	White Hart	Exeter	C R
🌲🌳 ★★★	Meudon Hotel	Falmouth	H C
🌲🌳 ★★★	Penmere Manor	Falmouth	H C
🌲🌳 ★★★	Throwley House	Faversham	H C
🌲🌳 ★★	Stock Hill House	Gillingham	H C
★★★	Crest	Gloucester	H C
★★	Oak Bank	Grasmere	H R
★★★	Swan	Grasmere	H R
★★★★	Wordsworth	Grasmere	H R
★★★	Ayton Hall	Great Ayton	H C
★★	Grizedale Lodge	Grizedale	H R
★★★	Holdsworth House	Halifax	H R
★★★	Lythe Hill	Haslemere	C R
🌲🌳 ★★★★	Down Hall	Hatfield Heath	H C
★★★	Alfoxton Park	Holford	C R
🌲🌳 ★★★	Deer Park	Honiton	H R
🌲🌳 ★★★	Foxdown Manor	Horns Cross	H R
★★	Grange Park	Hull	H R
🌲🌳 ★★★★	Hunstrete House	Hunstrete	H C
🌲🌳 ★★	Esseborne Manor	Hurstbourne Tarrant	H C
★★★	Rombalds	Ilkley	H R
★★★	Commodore	Instow	H R
★★	Grange	Keswick	H C
🌲🌳 ★★	Lyzzick Hall	Keswick	H C
★★★	Knights Hill Village	Kings Lynn	C R
★★★	Royal	Kirkby Lonsdale	H R
★★	Abbacourt	Leamington Spa	C R
★★	Tuscany	Leamington Spa	H C
★★★	Belmont	Leicester	C R
★★★	Royal Court	London SW1	H C
★★★	Royal Horseguards	London SW1	C R
★★★	Basil Street	London SW3	H R
★★★	Forum	London SW7	C R
★★★★	Britannia Inter-continental	London W1	C R
★★★★	Chesterfield	London W1	H C
★★	Delmere	London W2	H C
★★★	Bridge House	Longham	C R
★★★	Feathers	Ludlow	H C
★★	Dower House	Lyme Regis	H C
★★★	Lynton Cottage	Lynton	H R
★★★	Soar Mill Cove	Malborough	H R
🌲🌳 ★★★	Whatley Manor	Malmesbury	C R
★★★	Foley Arms	Malvern	H R
★★	Royal Malvern	Malvern	C R
🌲🌳 ★★★	Riber Hall	Matlock	H R
🌲🌳 ★	Old Rectory	Martinhoe	H C
★★	Conigre Farm	Melksham	H R
★★★	Manor	Meriden	H C
★★★	Manor House	Moreton in Marsh	H C
★★★★	Gosforth Park	Newcastle/Tyne	H C
★★★★	Nidd Hall	Nidd	H C
★★★	Springs	North Stoke	C R
★★	Windsor Lodge	Nottingham	H C
★★	Bark House	Oakford Bridge	H C
★★	Boultons	Oakham	H C
🌲🌳 ★★★	Penhaven	Parkham	C R
★★	White Swan	Pickering	H C
★★	Old Bakehouse	Piddletrenthide	H R
★★	Chequers	Pulborough	H C
★★	Saffron	Saffron Walden	H R
★★★★	Saunton Sands	Saunton	C R
★★	Seaview	Seaview, I.O.W.	H R
★★	Royal Oak	Sevenoaks	H C
★★★	Eastbury	Sherborne	H R
★★★★	Belmont	Sidmouth	C R
🌲🌳 ★★	Brownlands	Sidmouth	H C
★★★	Royal Glen	Sidmouth	H C
★★★	Westcliff	Sidmouth	C H
★★	Woodlands	Sidmouth	H C
🌲🌳 ★★★	Swynford Paddocks	Six Mile Bottom	C R
★★★	St Johns Swallow	Solihull	H C
🌲🌳 ★★	Glazebrook House	South Brent	H R
★★	Woodlands	Spalding	C R
★	Sea Trout Inn	Staverton	H R
🌲🌳 ★★★	Hanchurch Manor	Stoke on Trent	H C
🌲🌳 ★★★	Abingworth Hall	Storrington	H R
★★★	Windmill Park	Stratford on Avon	H C
🌲🌳 ★★★	Burleigh Court	Stroud	H C
★★★★	Belfry	Sutton Coldfield	H C
🌲🌳 ★★★★	New Hall	Sutton Coldfield	H R
★★★	Pines	Swanage	C R
★★★	Peartree	Swindon	H C
★★	School House	Swindon	C H
★★	Falcon	Taunton	H C
★★★	Temple Sowerby House	Temple Sowerby	H R
★★★	Spread Eagle	Thame	H R
★★	Sheppards	Thirsk	H R
★★★★	Thurlestone	Thurlestone	H C

★★★	Abbey Lawn	Torquay	H C
★★★	Corbyn Head	Torquay	H C
★★★	Livermead Cliff	Torquay	H R
★★★	Island	Tresco, I. of Scilly	H R
♣ ★★★★	Priory	Wareham	C R
♣ ★★★★	Bishopstrow House	Warminster	H C
★★	Bel Air	Wigan	H R
♣ ★★★	Lainston House	Winchester	H C
★★	Crag Brow Cottage	Windermere	C R
♣ ★★	Lindeth Fell	Windermere	C R
★★	Aurora Garden	Windsor	H C
★★★	Royal Oak	Winsford	C R
★★★	Grange	Winterbourne	H C
★★	Royal Oak	Withypool	C R
♣ ★★★	Seckford Hall	Woodbridge	C R
★★★	Bear	Woodstock	C R
★★★	Fownes	Worcester	H C
★★★	Grange	York	H C
★★	Heworth Court	York	H R
★★	Town House	York	H R

SCOTLAND

♣ ★★★	Raemoir	Banchory	H C
♣ ★★	Altamount House	Blairgowrie	H C
★★	Murray Park	Crieff	H R
★★★	Howard	Edinburgh	C R
★★★	Roxburghe	Edinburgh	H C
♣ ★★★	Kildrummy Castle	Kildrummy	H C
★★	Kilfinan	Kilfinan	H R
★★★	Inver Lodge	Lochinver	H C
★★	Haven	Plockton	H C
★★★	St Andrews Golf	St Andrews	H C
★★★	Creggans Inn	Strachur	H R
★★★	Holly Lodge	Strathpeffer	H R
★★★	Malin Court	Turnberry	H R

WALES

★★	Ty-Gwyn	Betws-y-Coed	H R
★★	Kilvert Country	Hay on Wye	H R
★★★	Empire	Llandudno	H C
♣ ★★★	Tre Ysagawen Hall	Llangefni	H C
★★	Tregenna	Merthyr Tydfil	H C
★★	Beaumont	Swansea	H C
★★	Windsor Lodge	Swansea	H R
♣ ★★	Maes-y-Nuadd	Talsarnau	H C
★★	Cross Lanes	Wrexham	C R

CHANNEL ISLANDS

Guernsey

★★★★	St Pierre Park	St Peter Port	H R
★★★	L'Atlantique	St Saviours	H R

Jersey

★★★	Château de la Valeuse	St Brelades Bay	H R
★★★	Little Grove	St Lawrence	H R
★★★	Lobster Pot	St Ouen	C R

One Merit Award

♣ ★★★★	Ettington Park	Alderminster	C
★★★	Fairlawns	Aldridge	R
★★★	Wateredge	Ambleside	H
★★	Riverside	Ambleside	C
♣ ★★★★	Eastwell Manor	Ashford	C
★★	Lord Crewe Arms	Bamburgh	H
★★★	Park	Barnstaple	H
★★★★	Royal Crescent	Bath	H
★★	Harrington's Hotel	Bath	H
★★	La Vieille Auberge	Battle	R
♣ ★★★	Beechfield House	Beanacre	C
★★	Knife & Cleaver	Bedford	R
★★	Blue Bell	Belford	C
♣ ★★	Bibury Court	Bibury	R
★★★	Durrant House	Bideford	C
★★	Riversford	Bideford	H
★★★	Royal George	Birdlip	C
★★	Riverhill	Birkenhead	R
★★★	Royal Angus Thistle	Birmingham	C
★★★	Millstone	Blackburn	C
★★	Olde School House	Bloxham	R
★	Old Ferry Inn	Bodinnick by Fowey	R
★★★	Burley Court	Bournemouth	H
★★★	Elstead	Bournemouth	C
★★★	Grosvenor	Bournemouth	H
★★	St George	Bournemouth	R
★★	Sun Court	Bournemouth	C
★★	Whitehall	Bournemouth	H
★★★	Post House	Bramhope	R
♣ ★★	Tarn End	Brampton	R
★★★	Berkeley Square	Bristol	C
★★★★	Balmer Lawn	Brockenhurst	C
★★★	New Park Manor	Brockenhurst	C
★★★	Bell Inn	Brook	C
♣ ★★★	Northcote Manor	Burrington	H
★★★	Riverside Inn	Burton on Trent	R
★★★	Angel	Bury St Edmunds	R
★★★	County	Canterbury	R
★★	The Bell	Charlbury	R
★★★	Charlecote	Charlecote	C
★★	Bedford Arms	Chenies	R
★★★	Hoole Hall	Chester	C
★★	Angel	Chippenham	R
★★★	Shaw Hill	Chorley	R
★★	Fishermans Haunt	Christchurch	H
★★	Corinium Court	Cirencester	H
★★★	Old Rectory	Claughton	R
♣ ★★	Court Barn	Clawton	R
★★★	Kingsway	Cleethorpes	R
★★	Redfern	Cleobury Mortimer	R
★★★	Woodlands	Cobham	C
★★	Coniston Sun	Coniston	H
★★★	Treglos	Constantine Bay	H
★★★★	Copthorne	Copthorne	R
★★	Methuen Arms	Corsham	C
★★★★	De Vere	Coventry	R
★★	Fleur de Lys	Cranborne	H
★★	Holcombe	Deddington	C
★★	Kedleston	Derby	R
★★★	Yalbury Cottage	Dorchester	R
★★★	George	Dorchester on Thames	R
★★★	White Hart	Dorchester on Thames	C
★★★	Palace	Douglas I.O.M.	R
★★	Downland	Eastbourne	R
♣ ★★	Eltermere	Elterwater	R
★★★	Royal Chace	Enfield	R
♣ ★★★	Evesham	Evesham	R
♣ ★★	Mill	Evesham	C
★★★	Imperial	Exeter	R
★★	Green Man	Fownhope	C
★★	Old Hall	Frodsham	C
★★★	Goodwood Park	Goodwood	R
★★★	Cliff Hotel	Gorleston on Sea	C

Rating	Hotel	Location	
♣♣ ★★	Graythwaite Manor	Grange over Sands	R
★★	Netherwood	Grange over Sands	H
★★★	Gold Rill	Grasmere	R
♣♣ ★★★	Manor at Newlands	Guildford	C
♣♣ ★★★★	West Lodge Park	Hadley Wood	R
★★	Harewood Arms	Harewood	C
★★★	Pheasant	Harome	R
★★	Gables	Harrogate	H
★★★	Grants	Harrogate	H
★★	Pier	Harwich	R
★	Flohr's	Henley on Thames	R
★★	Merton	Hereford	R
★★	County	Hexham	H
♣♣ ★★	Langley Castle	Hexham	R
★★	Lamb	Hindon	R
★★	Cottage	Hope Cove	R
♣♣ ★★★	Petersfield House	Horning	C
★★	Whitehaven	Hove	R
★★★	Bear	Hungerford	R
★★★	Old Bridge	Huntingdon	R
★★★	Ye Olde Bell	Hurley	R
★★★	Marlborough	Ipswich	R
★★	Garden House	Kendal	R
★★★	Gainsborough House	Kidderminster	H
★★	Tudor Rose	Kings Lynn	R
♣♣ ★★	Lee Manor	Lee Bay	H
★	Golden Lion	Leyburn	C
★★	Angel Croft	Lichfield	C
♣♣ ★★★	Milland Place	Liphook	C
★★★	Swiss Cottage	London NW3	C
★★★★	Royal Westminster	London SW1	C
★★★★	Lowndes Thistle	London SW1	C
★★★	Regency	London SW7	H
★★★★	Portman Inter-Continental	London W1	R
★★★★	Waldorf	London WC2	R
♣♣ ★★★★	Linden Hall	Longhorsley	C
♣♣ ★★★	Talland Bay	Looe	H
★★	Scale Hill	Loweswater	H
★	Central	Luton	C
★★★	Alexandra	Lyme Regis	H
★★	Bay	Lyme Regis	H
★★★	Devon	Lyme Regis	H
♣♣ ★★★	Passford House	Lymington	C
♣♣ ★★	Batch Farm Hotel	Lympsham	R
★	Rock House	Lynmouth	H
★	Chough's Nest	Lynton	H
★	Rockvale	Lynton	H
★	Seawood	Lynton	H
♣♣ ★★★★	Shrigley Hall	Macclesfield	R
★★	Pink House	Mealsgate	C
★★★	Three Ways	Mickleton	H
★★	Highfield	Middlesbrough	C
♣♣ ★★★	Fifehead Manor	Middle Wallop	R
★★★	Spread Eagle	Midhurst	C
♣♣ ★★	Milton Manor	Milton Abbas	C
★★	Beaconwood	Minehead	C
★	Kingsway	Minehead	H
★★★	Northfield	Minehead	H
★★	Windsor	Minehead	C
♣♣ ★★★★	Foley Lodge	Newbury	R
♣♣ ★★★	Millwaters	Newbury	C
★★★	County Thistle	Newcastle	C
★★	Queens	Newton Abbot	R
★★	Annesley	Norwich	R
★★★	Barnham Broom	Norwich	R
★★★	Smokies Park	Oldham	C
★★	Tree	Oxford	C
★	Oldway Links	Paignton	H
★★★	Redcliffe	Paignton	H
★★	Lindley	Parbold	C
★★★	Peterborough Moat House	Peterborough	R
★★★★	Swallow	Peterborough	C
★★	Naggs Head	Pickhill	R
♣♣ ★★★	Eldfordleigh	Plympton	C
★★★	Harbour Heights	Poole	C
★★★	Haven	Poole	C
★★	Quarterdeck	Poole	R
★★★	Anchor & Ship	Porlock Weir	R
★★★	Tickled Trout	Preston	R
★★	Arun Cosmopolitan	Pulborough	H
♣♣ ★★★	Nutfield Priory	Redhill	C
★★★★	Petersham	Richmond	R
♣♣ ★★★	Pengethley	Ross on Wye	H
★★★	Crest	Runcorn	H
★★★	St Michaels Manor	St Albans	H
★★★★	Carlyon Bay	St Austell	H
★★★	Slepe Hall	St Ives	R
★★★	Bolt Head	Salcombe	H
♣♣ ★★★	Wrea Head	Scalby	C
★★	Beach House	Seahouses	C
★★	Brickwall	Sedlescombe	R
★★★	Falcon Manor	Settle	H
★★	Little Court	Sidmouth	C
♣♣ ★★	Parrock Head Farm	Slaidburn	C
★★★	Thames Lodge	Staines	C
♣♣ ★★★★	Briggens House	Stanstead Abbotts	R
♣♣ ★★★	Gabriel Court	Stoke Gabriel	H
★★	Stow Lodge	Stow on the Wold	C
♣♣ ★★★	Billesley Manor	Stratford upon Avon	R
♣♣ ★★★★	Welcombe	Stratford upon Avon	R
♣♣ ★★★	Stonehouse Court	Stonehouse	C
★★★	Moor Hall	Sutton Coldfield	R
★★★★	Blunsdon House	Swindon	H
★★	Corner House	Taunton	R
✿✿✿	Hundred House	Telford	C
♣♣ ★★★	Madeley Court	Telford	H
★★	White Lion	Tenterden	C
★★	Swan	Thornthwaite	R
★★	Titchwell Manor	Titchwell	H
★★	Bute Court	Torquay	H
★★	Conway Court	Torquay	H
★★	Elmington	Torquay	H
★★	Gresham Court	Torquay	C
★★	Mount Nessing	Torquay	C
★★★	Orestone Manor	Torquay	H
★★★	Hilbury Court	Trowbridge	C
★★★	Brookdale House	Truro	H
★★★	Ye Olde Dog & Partridge	Tutbury	R
★★	Newcastle Arms	Tuxford	R
★★	Garden	Uppingham	H
★★	Wasdale Head Inn	Wasdale	R
♣♣ ★★★	Leeming House	Watermillock	R
♣♣ ★★★	Ramsbeck	Watermillock	R
★★★	Swan	Wells	R
★★	Crown	Wells-next-the-Sea	R
★★	Queenswood	Weston-super-Mare	H
♣♣ ★★★	Oatlands Park	Weybridge	C
★★★	Kilhey Court	Wigan	C
♣♣ ★★	Holbrook House	Wincanton	H
★★★★	Wessex	Winchester	R
♣♣ ★★	Bordriggs	Windermere	C
★★	Cedar Manor	Windermere	H

♣ ★★★	Langdale Chase	Windermere	H
♣ ★★	Lindeth Howe	Windermere	C
★★★	Wild Boar	Windermere	R
♣ ★★	Woody Bay	Woody Bay	H
★	Crossways	Woolacombe	H
★★	Devon Beach	Woolacombe	H
★★	Headlands	Woolacombe	H
★★	Waters Fall	Woolacombe	H
★★	Wroxham	Wroxham	R
★★	Imperial	Yarmouth Great	R

SCOTLAND

♣ ★★	Ledgowan	Achnasheen	H
♣ ★★★	Balcary Bay	Auchencairn	H
★★	Burns Monument	Ayr	R
♣ ★★★★	Kildonan	Barrhill	R
♣ ★★★	Auchrannie	Brodick, Isle of Arran	R
★★	Seafield	Campbeltown	R
♣ ★★	Cultoquey	Crieff	H
★	Gwydyr House	Crieff	H
★★★	Crinan	Crinan	R
★★★	Dundonell	Dundonell	C
♣ ★★★	Crutherland House	East Kilbride	R
★★	Harvesters	East Linton	C
★★	Ramnee	Forres	H
♣ ★★★	Kingsknowes	Galashiels	C
★★★	MacDonald Thistle	Giffnock	R
♣ ★★	Purves Hall	Greenlaw	H
★★	Kirklands	Hawick	C
★★★	Kingsmills	Inverness	C
★★	Ardvasar	Isle of Skye, Ardvasar	H
★	Isles	Isle of Skye, Portree	H
★★	Lagg	Kilmory	H
♣ ★★★	Ballathie House	Kinclaven	C
★★	Columba House	Kingussie	H
♣ ★★★	Gleddoch House	Langbank	R
♣ ★★★	Ladyburn	Maybole	R
★★	Burt's	Melrose	C
★★	Allt-Nan-Ros	Onich	R
★★★	Lodge on the Loch	Onich	H
♣ ★★★	Corsemalzie House	Port William	R
♣ ★★★	Rothes Glen	Rothes	C
★★★	Rufflets	St Andrews	R
★★	Scourie	Scourie	H
[symbol]	Hawes Inn	South Queensferry	R
★★	Letterfinlay House	Spean Bridge	H
♣ ★★	Port an Eilean	Strathtummel	C
★★★	Morange House	Tain	H
♣ ★★	Trigony House	Thornhill	R
♣ ★★★	Tweed Valley	Walkerburn	H

WALES

★★	Neigwl	Abersoch	H
♣ ★★★	Porth Tocyn	Abersoch	R
★★★	Menai Court	Bangor	R
★★	Telford	Bangor	H
★★	Park Hill	Betws-y-Coed	H
♣ ★★★	Coed-y-Mwstwr	Bridgend	C
★★★	St Pierre	Chepstow	C
★	Caerwylan	Criccieth	C
★	Henfaes	Criccieth	C
★★	Bryn Cregin Garden	Deganwy	C
★★	Padarn Lake	Llanberis	C
★★	Dunoon	Llandudno	C
★	Sunnymede	Llandudno	C
★★	Tan Lan	Llandudno	H
♣ ★★★	Bryn Howel	Llangollen	R
★★	Glansevern	Llangurig	R
♣ ★★★	Seiont Manor	Llanrug	C
★★	West House	Llantwit Major	C
★★	Tregenna	Merthyr Tydfil	C
♣ ★★★	Miskin Manor	Miskin	C
★★	Nanhoron Arms	Nefyn	C
★	Walton House	Penarth	R
★	Lorelei	Porthcawl	R
♣ ★★★	Egerton Grey	Porthkerry	C
★★★	Portmeirion	Portmeirion	C
★★	Radnorshire Arms	Presteigne	C
♣ ★★★	Fairyhill	Reynoldston	R
★★	Cambrian	Saundersfoot	C
★★	Atlantic	Tenby	H
★★	Fourtcroft	Tenby	H
★★	Hafod House	Trefriw	C
♣ ★★	Golfa Hotel	Welshpool	C

CHANNEL ISLES

Guernsey

★★	La Favorita	Fermain Bay	C
★★★	St Margarets Lodge	St Martins	C
★★★★	Old Government House	St Peter Port	H

Jersey

★★★★	St Brelade's Bay	St Brelade's	H
★★★	Shakespeare	St Clement	R
★★★	Apollo	St Hellier	C
★★	Laurels	St Helier	C

NORTHERN IRELAND

★★	Thornlea	Cushendall	H
★★★★	Culloden	Holywood	R

Discounts

Many hotels are prepared to offer readers of this Guide discounts on accommodation prices—which can be as much as £50 per visit at hotels offering 10% discounts, £25 per visit at others offering 5% discounts. These hotels are indicated by a [V] at the end of the price section of their entry. Use the vouchers on p. 703 to obtain your discount. Only one voucher can be used per visit.

Discounts are given on the appropriate full tariff for the room and the date. Vouchers will not be accepted for week-end breaks, rooms occupied by children at a reduced rate or against other tariffs already discounted. Hotels usually do not offer discounts over Bank Holidays, at Christmas and Easter or when there are local events in progress, for instance Gold Cup week at Cheltenham or major conferences in Harrogate.

Hotels may limit the day of the week or the time of year the vouchers can be used; this may be weekdays or weekends depending on whether the hotel is mainly a business one or mainly a holiday one. When you book, please inform the hotel that you intend to use an RAC discount voucher in part payment of your bill. Then if there is any confusion over when discounts are offered it can be sorted out easily.

Conference facilities at RAC Hotels

The tables on the following pages, and on pages 540–5, are designed to help those planning a conference to choose a hotel. The tables cover, first, the number of conference rooms and their capacities, plus the number of smaller, seminar, rooms; then the number of bedrooms at the hotel. The next columns indicate what conference facilities and equipment the hotel can offer. Most hotels can hire further items of equipment (videos, etc.) if required. Finally any sporting facilities *at the hotel itself* are listed.

Further details about each hotel plus the address and telephone number can be found in the main part of the guide.

ENGLAND Town	Hotel	No. of conf. rooms	Seating capacity of main room	Total seating of additional rooms	No. of smaller rooms	Maximum capacity of smaller rooms	No. of bedrooms	Exhibition hall space	Photocopying	Projection/Video	Closed circuit TV	Audio	Interpreting	Sporting facilities available at the Hotel	Use of fax
LONDON N4	★★Spring Park	3	50	100	1	7	58		✓	✓		✓		–	✓
LONDON NW1	★★★Harewood	2	60	35	2	–	93		✓	✓	✓	✓	✓	–	✓
	★★★Kennedy	5	100	190	10	10	360	✓	✓	✓		✓	✓	–	✓
	★★Ibis Euston	1	130	–	4	4	300	✓	✓					–	✓
LONDON NW3	★★★★Clive	5	250	–	5	10	96	✓	✓	✓		✓		–	✓
	★★★★Holiday Inn	2	400	90	6	20	303		✓	✓	✓	✓		[indoor pool] G	✓
	★★★Swiss Cottage	1	80	–	6	16	81		✓	✓		✓	✓		✓
LONDON SE3	★★Barden Lodge	1	22	–	1	6	39		✓	✓				–	✓
LONDON SE10	★★Ibis Greenwich	1	70	–	2	4	82	✓	✓					–	✓
LONDON SW1	★★★★★Hyatt Carlton Tower	2	150	26	1	16	224	✓	✓	✓		✓	✓	–	✓
	★★★★★Sheraton Park Tower	2	80	90	3	40	295	✓	✓	✓		✓		–	✓
	★★★★Chelsea	2	120	36	2	10	225	✓	✓	✓		✓	✓	–	✓
	★★★★Dukes	1	50	–	–	10	62		✓					–	✓
	★★★★Goring	1	40	–	4	30	90		✓	✓				–	✓
	★★★★Stakis St. Ermins	9	250	420	5	12	290	✓	✓	✓	✓	✓	✓	–	✓
	★★★Grosvenor	4	200	316	3	60	366	✓	✓	✓	✓	✓	✓	–	✓
	★★★Royal Court	1	40	–	4	10	102		✓	✓		✓		–	✓
LONDON SW3	★★★★Basil Street	1	50	–	2	25	92		✓	✓		✓		–	✓
	★★★★Capital	1	22	–	1	11	48		✓					–	✓
LONDON SW5	★★★★Swallow International	4	200	250	7	30	417	✓	✓	✓		✓		[indoor pool] G	✓
LONDON SW6	★★★Ramada Inn	1	1750	–	5	60	501	✓	✓	✓		✓		–	✓
LONDON SW7	★★★★Gloucester	3	400	–	2	45	550	✓	✓	✓	✓	✓	✓	–	✓
	★★★★Norfolk	3	70	26	5	12	96		✓	✓		✓		G	✓
	★★★Forum	1	400	–	5	–	911	✓	✓	✓	✓	✓	✓	–	✓
	★★★Regency	7	120	240	10	10	210	✓	✓	✓	✓	✓	✓	G	✓
	★★★Rembrant	2	220	80	4	35	200		✓	✓		✓		[indoor pool] G	✓
LONDON W1	★★★★★Ritz	1	50	–	2	30	130		✓	✓		✓	✓	–	✓
	★★★★Athenaeum	1	40	–	2	16	145	✓	✓	✓		✓	✓	–	✓
	★★★★Berkshire	2	50	70	2	20	147		✓	✓	✓	✓		–	✓
	★★★★Brittania Inter-continental	1	100	–	2	25	326	✓	✓	✓		✓		–	✓
	★★★★Chesterfield	3	100	40	3	20	110		✓	✓		✓	✓	–	✓
	★★★★Green Park	1	70	–	3	40	161		✓	✓		✓		–	✓
	★★★★Holiday Inn – Mayfair	4	70	25	5	6	186	✓	✓	✓	✓	✓	✓	–	✓
	★★★★London Marriott	1	375	–	2	40	223	✓	✓	✓	✓	✓	✓	–	✓
	★★★★Park Lane	10	300	300	15	20	320	✓	✓	✓	✓	✓	✓	–	✓
	★★★★Portman Inter-continental	3	360	–	3	40	272		✓	✓		✓	✓	[tennis]	✓
	★★★★Regent Crest	5	600	–	5	12	320	✓	✓	✓		✓		–	✓
	★★★★Washington	1	70	–	4	10	173		✓	✓		✓		–	✓
	★★★Clifton Ford	2	80	25	4	6	213	✓	✓	✓		✓	✓	–	✓
	★★★Londoner	3	90	20	–	6	144	✓	✓	✓	✓	✓		–	✓
	★★★Mostyn	3	150	150	5	10	122	✓	✓	✓	✓	✓		–	✓
	★★★Mount Royal	4	320	600	3	60	705	✓	✓	✓		✓		–	✓
LONDON W2	★★★★Hospitality Inn	1	40	–	6	8	175		✓	✓				–	✓
	★★★★London Embassy	1	78	–	–	6	193		✓	✓		✓		–	✓
	★★★★London Metropole	3	250	–	–	60	571		✓	✓		✓		–	✓
	★★★★Royal Lancaster	2	1400	85	1	–	418	✓	✓	✓		✓	✓	–	✓
	★★★★White's	1	20	–	1	18	54		✓	✓				–	✓
	★★★Park Court	6	120	–	4	30	398	✓	✓	✓				–	✓
LONDON W8	★★★★★Royal Garden	5	900	345	–	–	380	✓	✓	✓		✓	✓	–	✓
	★★★★London Tara	2	500	350	2	15	831	✓	✓	✓		✓		–	✓
LONDON WC1	★★★★Kenilworth	3	120	–	4	20	192	✓	✓	✓	✓	✓		–	✓
	★★★★Waverley House	1	25	–	1	12	110		✓	✓	✓	✓		–	✓
	★★★Bloomsbury Crest	1	600	–	6	20	284	✓	✓	✓	✓	✓	✓	–	✓
	★★★Bloomsbury Park	1	35	–	2	8	95		✓	✓				–	✓
	★★★Bonnington	2	120	–	6	40	215	✓	✓	✓	✓	✓	✓	–	
	★★★Kingsley	4	100	80	3	10	145	✓	✓	✓		✓		–	✓
	★★★London Ryan	2	50	40	4	8	211		✓	✓				–	✓
	★★★Royal Scot	5	180	250	2	10	351		✓	✓		✓		–	✓
LONDON WC2	★★★★Drury Lane Moat House	3	100	–	4	12	153	✓	✓					–	✓
	★★★★Mountbatten	2	75	35	–	–	127		✓	✓		✓		–	✓
LONDON AIRPORT HEATHROW	★★★★Holiday Inn Heathrow	8	100	–	14	8	380		✓	✓		✓		[indoor pool] [golf] G	✓
	★★★Berkeley Arms	3	100	–	2	4	56		✓	✓		✓		–	✓
	★★★Heathrow Park	3	700	300	11	60	306	✓	✓	✓		✓		–	✓
	★★Hotel Ibis Heathrow	1	1200	–	3	4	244	✓	✓					–	✓
	★★Stanwell Hall	2	25	14	1	10	18		✓	✓	✓	✓		–	
ABBERLEY	★★★Elms	3	50	40	1	12	25		✓	✓		✓		[tennis]	✓
ABBOTS SALFORD	★★★Salford Hall	5	50	32	4	14	34		✓	✓				[tennis]	✓

[indoor pool]=indoor swimming pool; [outdoor pool]=outdoor swimming pool; [golf]=golf; [tennis]=tennis; [squash]=squash; **G**=*gymnasium*

ENGLAND Town	Hotel	No. of conf. rooms	Seating capacity of main room	Total seating of additional rooms	No. of smaller rooms	Maximum capacity of smaller rooms	No. of bedrooms	Exhibition hall space	Photocopying	Projection/Video	Closed circuit TV	Audio	Interpreting	Sporting facilities available at the Hotel	Use of fax
ABINGDON	★★★Abingdon Lodge	7	130	70	3	15	63		✓	✓		✓		🎾	✓
	★★★Upper Reaches	2	60	12	3	–	26	✓	✓	✓				–	✓
	★★Crown & Thistle	2	60	30	–	–	21	✓	✓	✓				–	✓
ADLINGTON	★★Gladmar	1	45	–	1	12	20			✓		✓		–	✓
ALBRIGHTON	★★★★Albrighton Hall	8	260	60	4	50	38	✓	✓	✓		✓		⊟ ✱ G	✓
ALCESTER	★★Arrow Mill	2	60	40	2	10	18	✓	✓	✓		✓		–	✓
ALDEBURGH	★★★Brudenell	2	50	50	2	15	47		✓	✓				–	
ALDERMINSTER	★★★★Ettington Park	5	60	16	5	15	48	✓	✓					⊟ 🎾	✓
ALDRIDGE	★★★Fairlawns	4	70	70	2	30	36		✓	✓		✓		–	✓
ALFRISTON	★★★Star Inn	1	40	–	2	8	34		✓	✓		✓		–	✓
ALLENDALE	★★Bishopfield	1	20	40	3	10	12		✓					–	✓
ALNWICK	★★★White Swan	1	150	50	6	10	43	✓	✓	✓	✓	✓	✓	–	✓
ALSTON	★★Lovelady Shield Country House	1	10	–	1	–	12		✓					🎾	✓
	★★Lowbyer Manor	1	20	–	–	–	11							–	
ALTON	★★★Alton House	6	180	170	5	50	38	✓	✓	✓	✓	✓		⊟ ⊐ 🎾	✓
	★★★Swan	2	60	–	1	30	38		✓	✓		✓		–	✓
	★★Grange	2	45	25	3	6	34		✓	✓				–	✓
ALTRINGHAM	★★★Ashley	3	240	25	3	30	48		✓	✓		✓		–	✓
	★★★Bowdon	4	140	120	2	36	82	✓	✓	✓		✓		–	✓
	★★★Cresta Court	6	400	334	6	14	139	✓	✓	✓		✓		–	✓
	★★★Woodland Park	5	200	155	2	20	45	✓	✓	✓		✓	✓	–	✓
ALVESTON	★★★Alveston House	5	85	100	3	25	30	✓	✓	✓	✓	✓		–	✓
	★★★Post House	5	100	103	10	8	75	✓	✓	✓		✓	✓	⊐ ⛳	✓
AMBERLEY	★★Amberley Inn	1	16	–	–	–	14		✓	✓				–	✓
AMBLESIDE	★★★Waterhead	2	50	100	2	12	27		✓	✓					✓
	★★★Salutation	2	56	40	1	20	32		✓	✓				–	✓
AMERSHAM	★★Crown	1	25	–	–	–	25		✓					–	✓
AMPFIELD	★★★Potter Heron	2	100	50	1	10	60			✓				G	
ANDOVER	★★★Ashley Court	3	200	90	6	50	35	✓	✓	✓		✓		–	✓
	★★White Hart	1	60	–	–	–	20		✓	✓				–	
APPLEBY-IN-WESTMORLAND	★★★Tufton Arms	1	50	–	2	14	19		✓			✓		⊐ ⛳ ✱	✓
	★★★Appleby Manor Country House	1	28	24	3	12	30		✓	✓				⊟	✓
APPLETON-LE-MOORS	★★Dweldapilton Hall	1	40	–	1	12	12		✓					–	✓
APSLEY GUISE	★★★Moore Place	2	50	30	2	12	54		✓	✓	✓	✓		⛳	✓
ARUNDEL	★★★★Avisford Park	6	200	100	15	25	100		✓	✓	✓	✓		⊟ ⊐ ⛳ 🎾 ✱	✓
	★★★Norfolk Arms	3	100	20	1	8	34		✓	✓				–	✓
	★★Swan	1	40	–	1	20	13							–	
ASCOT	★★★★Berystede	8	125	–	8	25	91		✓	✓		✓		⊐	✓
	★★★★Royal Berkshire	8	75	25	150	8	82	✓	✓	✓				⊟ 🎾 ✱	✓
ASHBOURNE	★★★★Ashbourne Lodge	2	170	60	8	10	51	✓	✓	✓		✓		–	✓
	★★★Callow Hall	2	50	40	2	–	12		✓	✓				–	✓
ASHBURTON	★★★Holne Chace	1	40	30	3	12	12		✓	✓			✓	–	✓
	★★Dartmoor	2	70	30	2	10	32	✓	✓	✓				–	
	★★Tugela House	2	20	10	3	10	7		✓					–	✓
ASHFORD	★★★★Ashford International	2	400	300	8	25	200	✓	✓	✓		✓	✓	⊟ ⊐ G	✓
	★★★★Eastwell Manor	2	70	12	6	12	23		✓	✓	✓		✓	🎾	✓
	★★★Master Spearpoint	3	60	10	3	20/10	36	✓	✓					–	✓
	★★★Post House	5	120	60	–	8	60	✓	✓	✓	✓	✓			✓
ASHTON-UNDER-LYNE	★★★York House	2	30	20	2	20	34		✓	✓	✓	✓		–	✓
ASHURST	★★Busketts Lawn	2	100	20	2	12	14	✓	✓	✓	✓	✓		⊐	✓
ASKRIGG	★★Kings Arms	3	30	20	–	–	14	✓	✓	✓				G	✓
ASTHALL	Maytime	2	30	–	1	20	6							–	
ASTON CLINTON	★★★Bell Inn	2	200	20	–	–	21	✓	✓	✓	✓	✓		–	✓
ATHERSTONE	★Old Red Lion	2	40	40	–	–	22		✓	✓	✓	✓		–	✓
AXBRIDGE	★★★Webbington	12	1000	540	4	100	59							⊟ ⊐ 🎾 G	✓
AXMINSTER	★★Tytherleigh Cott	1	20	–	1	8	19		✓	✓				⊐ G	✓
AYLESBURY	★★★★Forte	3	80	–	6	8	94		✓	✓	✓	✓		⊟ G	✓
	★★★★Hartwell House	3	50	40	2	15	32		✓	✓	✓	✓		⊐	✓
BADMINTON	★★★Petty France	2	20	16	2	10	20		✓	✓				–	✓
BAGSHOT	★★★★Pennyhill Park	3	30	36	6	10	54		✓	✓		✓	✓	⊐ ⛳ 🎾	✓
BAKEWELL	★★★Rutland Arms	2	80	–	2	15	36	✓	✓	✓		✓	✓	–	
BAMBURGH	★★Victoria	2	50	20	–	–	23	✓		✓		✓		–	
	★Mizen Head	1	40	–	2	10	15							–	
BANBURY	★★★★Whately Hall	3	120	160	3	14	74	✓	✓	✓	✓	✓	✓	–	✓
	★★★Banbury Moat House	3	65	75	1	10	50		✓	✓				–	✓
	★★★Wroxton House	2	45	35	4	8	32		✓	✓		✓		–	✓
	★★Cromwell Lodge	2	25	10	–	–	32		✓	✓				–	✓

⊟=*indoor swimming pool;* ⊐=*outdoor swimming pool;* ⛳=*golf;* 🎾=*tennis;* ✱=*squash;* G=*gymnasium*

ENGLAND Town	Hotel	No. of conf. rooms	Seating capacity of main room	Total seating of additional rooms	No. of smaller rooms	Maximum capacity of smaller rooms	No. of bedrooms	Exhibition hall space	Photocopying	Projection/Video	Closed circuit TV	Audio	Interpreting	Sporting facilities available at the Hotel	Use of fax
BARNSLEY	★★★★Ardsley Moat House	8	300	200	5	8	75	✓	✓	✓	✓	✓		–	✓
	★★★Queen's	2	120	–	4	10	48	✓	✓	✓			✓	–	✓
BARNSTAPLE	★★★Barnstaple Motel	2	200	50	1	20	57	✓	✓	✓		✓		[indoor swimming pool] G	✓
	★★★Imperial	3	100	40	1	25	56		✓	✓	✓	✓		–	✓
	★★★Park	4	200	150	1	50	42	✓	✓	✓		✓		–	✓
BARROW IN FURNESS	★★★★Abbey House	4	100	30	2	20	27		✓	✓		✓		–	✓
BARTLE	★★★Bartle Hall	2	100	–	1	24	12	✓		✓				[outdoor swimming pool] [tennis]	
BASILDON	★★★Crest	12	300	300	9	20	110	✓	✓	✓	✓	✓		–	✓
BASINGSTOKE	★★★Crest	5	150	–	–	80	150		✓	✓		✓		–	✓
	★★★Hilton Lodge	12	150	70	6	10	144	✓	✓	✓	✓	✓		[indoor swimming pool] G	✓
	★★★Hilton National	8	160	70	3	8	135		✓	✓		✓		[indoor swimming pool] G	✓
	★★Red Lion	2	30	30	–	–	62		✓	✓		✓		–	✓
BASLOW	★★★Cavendish	1	20	–	1	–	23		✓	✓				–	✓
BASSENTHWAITE	★★★Castle Inn	3	200	110	2	40	36	✓	✓	✓		✓		[tennis] G	✓
BATH	★★★★Francis	2	80	60	–	–	94	✓	✓	✓				–	✓
	★★★★Hilton National	12	240	440	6	18	105							[indoor swimming pool] G	✓
	★★★★Royal Crescent	4	40	–	3	10	44	✓	✓	✓		✓	✓		✓
	★★★Lansdown Grove	4	100	140	2	10	45	✓	✓	✓		✓		–	✓
	★★★Pratt's	2	50	36	–	10	46		✓	✓				–	✓
	★★★The Priory	1	14	–	1	14	21		✓	✓		✓		[indoor swimming pool]	✓
	★★★Redcar	1	100	12	1	10	31		✓	✓		✓		–	✓
	★★Berni Royal	2	220	30	1	16	37	✓	✓	✓		✓		–	✓
	★★Compass	2	40	20	–	–	54		✓	✓				–	✓
BATLEY	★Alder House	3	80	16	3	40	22	✓	✓	✓		✓		–	✓
BATTLE	★★★Netherfield Place	2	24	12	–	–	14		✓	✓		✓		[tennis]	✓
	★★George	2	40	20	–	–	22	✓	✓	✓		✓	✓	–	✓
	★★La Viellie Auberge	1	14	–	–	–	7		✓	✓		✓		–	✓
BAWTRY	★★★Crown	7	130	300	4	12	57	✓	✓	✓				–	✓
BEACONSFIELD	★★★Bell House	6	450	400	8	8	136	✓	✓	✓		✓		[indoor swimming pool] [squash] G	✓
BEANACRE	★★★Beechfield House	1	24	–	2	8	24		✓	✓	✓	✓		[outdoor swimming pool] [tennis]	✓
BEBINGTON	★★Famous Olde Bridge Inn	2	100	35	–	–	16							–	
BEDFORD	★★★Barns	3	120	35	–	–	49		✓	✓		✓		G	✓
	★★★Woodlands Manor	2	60	20	2	8	29		✓	✓	✓	✓	✓	–	✓
	★★De Parys	1	60	–	3	30	29		✓	✓				–	✓
	★★Knife and Cleaver	–	–	–	2	12	9							–	✓
	★★Queens Head	1	12	–	–	–	12		✓	✓				–	✓
BEESTON	★★★Wild Boar	2	50	50	4	10	37	✓	✓	✓		✓		–	✓
BELFORD	★★★Waren House	1	25	–	–	–	9							[tennis]	
	★★Blue Bell	3	80	40	–	–	17		✓	✓		✓		–	✓
BELLINGHAM	★★Riverdale Hall	3	55	50	–	–	20	✓	✓	✓				[indoor swimming pool] [golf]	
BERKELEY	★★Berkeley Arms	3	100	50	2	30	10							–	
BERWICK-UPON-TWEED	★★★Turret House	1	250	–	2	10	13	✓	✓	✓				–	✓
	★★★Kings Arms	3	160	190	3	20	36	✓	✓	✓		✓		–	✓
BEVERLEY	★★★Beverley Arms	3	60	20	4	10	57	✓	✓	✓		✓		–	✓
	★★★Tickton Grange	2	40	16	–	–	16		✓	✓				–	✓
BEWDLEY	★★George	2	60	10	2	6	13	✓						–	
BEXHILL-ON-THE-SEA	★★★Granville	3	150	75	7	4	50	✓	✓	✓		✓		–	✓
BEXLEY	★★★Crest	4	70	115	5	6	106		✓	✓				–	✓
BIBURY	★★Bibury Court	2	20	20	3	10	18	✓	✓	✓		✓		[squash]	✓
BIDEFORD	★★★Portledge	5	–	81	3	32	35		✓	✓		✓		[outdoor swimming pool]	✓
	★★★Royal	3	150	20	2	15	30	✓	✓	✓		✓		–	✓
	★★Riversford	1	50	–	2	10	16	✓	✓	✓		✓		–	✓
	★★Yeoldon House	1	80	–	–	–	10	✓	✓	✓		✓	✓	–	✓
BILLESLEY	★★★Billesley Manor	4	80	60	3	15	41	✓	✓					[indoor swimming pool] [golf] [tennis]	✓
BINGLEY	★★★Bankfield	7	300	180	4	10	103	✓	✓	✓	✓	✓		–	✓
BIRDLIP	★★★Royal George	2	80	60	1	10	33		✓	✓		✓		–	✓
BIRKENHEAD	★★★Bowler Hat	1	120	–	2	12	29	✓	✓					–	
BIRMINGHAM	★★★★Albany	10	630	190	9	40	253	✓	✓	✓	✓	✓	✓	[indoor swimming pool] [squash]	✓
	★★★★Copthorne	1	200	–	8	12	212		✓			✓		[indoor swimming pool] G	✓
	★★★★Midland	7	200	200	4	65	111		✓	✓	✓	✓		–	✓
	Novotel	9	300	405	8	100	148		✓	✓	✓			G	✓
	★★★Post House	3	150	110	12	15	204	✓	✓	✓		✓		[indoor swimming pool] [outdoor swimming pool] G	✓
	★★New Cobden	3	120	75	6	10	250		✓	✓		✓		[indoor swimming pool] G	✓
	★★Norfolk	3	90	70	5	15	180		✓	✓		✓		–	✓
	★★Norwood	1	25	12	1	12	17		✓					–	✓
	★★Oriental Pearl	1	35	40	–	–	12		✓	✓			✓	–	✓
BIRMINGHAM AIRPORT	★★★★Birmingham Metropole	22	2000	–	6	50	807	✓	✓	✓	✓	✓		[squash]	✓
	★★★Excelsior	5	150	120	8	8	141							–	✓

[indoor swimming pool]=indoor swimming pool; [outdoor swimming pool]=outdoor swimming pool; [golf]=golf; [tennis]=tennis; [squash]=squash; G=gymnasium

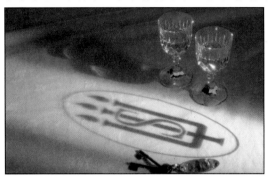

ENGLAND Town	Hotel	No. of conf. rooms	Seating capacity of main room	Total seating of additional rooms	No. of smaller rooms	Maximum capacity of smaller rooms	No. of bedrooms	Exhibition hall space	Photocopying	Projection/Video	Closed circuit TV	Audio	Interpreting	Sporting facilities available at the Hotel	Use of fax
BISHOP AUCKLAND	★★★Helme Park Hall	3	50	70	3	20	10			✓				–	
BISHOPSTEIGHNTON	★★Cockhaven Manor	1	100	–	2	50	12	✓	✓			✓		–	
BLACKBURN	★★★Mytton Fold Farm	3	300	60	1	10	27	✓	✓			✓		–	✓
BLACKPOOL	★★★★Imperial	10	600	500	6	30	183	✓	✓	✓	✓	✓	✓	▤ G	✓
	★★★★Pembroke	6	900	700	15	60	278	✓	✓			✓		▤	✓
	★★★Savoy	2	350	–	4	–	147	✓	✓	✓		✓		–	✓
	★★Carlton	2	130	60	2	30	57		✓	✓		✓		–	✓
	★★Claremont	3	250	250	–	20	143	✓	✓	✓		✓		–	✓
	★★Cliffs	6	350	400	8	20	165	✓	✓			✓		▤ ⛹ G	✓
	★★Gables Balmoral	4	100	75	4	20	70		✓	✓				–	✓
	★★Ruskin	2	200	200	4	30	80		✓	✓		✓		–	✓
	★★Sheraton	3	200	150	3	10	119	✓	✓	✓		✓		▤	
	★★Stretton	1	150	50	2	50	51	✓	✓	✓	✓	✓		–	✓
	★★Kimberley	2	130	25	3	20	54		✓		✓			–	
	★★Warwick	3	60	20	2	10	52		✓	✓		✓		▤	✓
BLAKENEY	★★★Blakeney	3	200	65	6	6	51	✓	✓	✓		✓		▤ G	✓
BLANCHLAND	★★Lord Crewe Arms	1	24	–	1	8	18		✓	✓				–	✓
BLANDFORD FORUM	★★★Crown	1	70	–	3	40	29		✓	✓		✓		–	✓
BLOCKLEY	★★★Crown Inn	2	20	10	2	5	21		✓	✓				–	✓
BLOXHAM	★★Olde School	5	72	120	2	22	39	✓	✓	✓	✓			–	✓
BOGNOR REGIS	★★★Royal Norfolk	2	65	25	4	8	51	✓	✓	✓				⊐ 🎾	✓
	★Black Mill House	1	45	–	2	15	26	✓	✓	✓		✓		–	✓
BOLNEY	★★★Hickstead Resort	6	200	150	2	20	49	✓	✓	✓			✓	▤ G	✓
BOLTON	★★★Crest	2	120	40	10	20	100	✓	✓	✓				–	
	★★★Egerton House	5	150	[illegible]	[illegible]	[illegible]	[illegible]	✓	✓	✓	✓	✓			✓
	★★★Last Drop Village	5	200	220	4	12	83	✓	✓	✓		✓		▤ ⛹ G	✓
	★★★Pack Horse	2	300	250	4	16	73	✓	✓	✓	✓	✓		–	✓
BOLTON ABBEY	★★★Devonshire Arms Country House	7	150	98	3	8	40	✓	✓	✓		✓	✓	◪	✓
BOROUGHBRIDGE	★★★Crown	4	150	76	–	–	42		✓	✓		✓		–	
BORROWDALE	★★★Borrowdale	3	45	30	3	8	34	✓	✓					–	✓
BOSHAM	★★Millstream	1	20	10	2	–	29		✓	✓				–	✓
BOSTON	★★★New England	1	45	–	–	–	15		✓					–	✓
BOTLEY	★★★★Botley	8	200	130	4	40	100	✓	✓	✓		✓		▤ ◪ 🎾 ⛹ G	✓
	★★★Botleigh Grange	4	120	155	4	8	43	✓	✓	✓		✓		–	✓
BOURNEMOUTH	Carlton	9	150	–	6	100	72		✓	✓		✓		⊐ G	✓
	★★★★★Royal Bath	7	500	250	7	30	131	✓	✓	✓	✓	✓	✓	▤ G	✓
	★★★★Bournemouth Highcliff	5	500	200	15	20	160	✓	✓	✓		✓	✓	⊐ 🎾	✓
	★★★★Norfolk Royale	4	80	15	4	15	95		✓	✓		✓	✓	▤	✓
	★★★★Palace Court	7	300	300	6	60	103	✓	✓	✓		✓		▤ G	✓
	★★★Anglo Swiss	7	160	200	5	20	70	✓	✓	✓		✓		⊐ G	✓
	★★★Belvedere	2	50	30	2	8	63		✓	✓				–	✓
	★★★Bournemouth Moat House	7	700	970	14	10	146	✓	✓	✓		✓		▤ G	✓
	★★★Chesterwood	2	150	200	3	30	52	✓	✓	✓		✓	✓	⊐	✓
	★★★Chine	2	120	155	7	10	97	✓	✓	✓	✓	✓	✓	▤ ⊐ G	✓
	★★★Cliffside	3	200	–	3	60	62		✓	✓		✓		⊐ G	✓
	★★★Connaught	2	300	150	7	30	60	✓	✓	✓	✓	✓		▤ ⊐ G	✓
	★★★Courtlands	2	45	45	2	10	60	✓	✓	✓	✓	✓		⊐	✓
	★★★Crest	6	100	80	4	8	102		✓	✓		✓		–	✓
	★★★Cumberland	4	100	100	102	12	102	✓	✓	✓	✓	✓		⊐	✓
	★★★Durley Hall	5	200	300	5	300	81	✓	✓	✓		✓		▤ ⊐ G	✓
	★★★Durlston Court	4	120	80	2	30	60	✓	✓	✓		✓		⊐ G	✓
	★★★East Anglia	4	150	–	2	20	73	✓	✓	✓		✓		▤ G	✓
	★★★Elstead	4	70	60	9	8	51		✓	✓		✓		–	✓
	★★★Embassy	5	150	235	2	40	72	✓	✓	✓	✓	✓		⊐	✓
	★★★Langtry Manor	2	60	50	4	20	27	✓	✓	✓		✓		–	✓
	★★★Marsham Court	5	200	100	7	24	86	✓	✓	✓	✓	✓		⊐	✓
	★★★Melford Hall	6	100	150	–	–	63	✓	✓	✓		✓		▤ G	✓
	★★★Miramar	2	75	90	2	10	39		✓	✓				–	✓
	★★★New Durley Dean	3	200	120	8	12	111		✓	✓				▤ G	✓
	★★★Pavilion	4	100	75	–	–	44	✓	✓	✓		✓		–	✓
	★★★Piccadilly	2	150	40	4	12	45	✓	✓	✓	✓	✓		–	✓
	★★★Queens	6	200	100	3	15	114	✓	✓	✓		✓		–	✓
	★★★Savoy	7	100	–	12	6	9		✓	✓		✓		⊐ 🎾 G	✓
	★★★Suncliff	4	150	30	5	8	95		✓	✓	✓	✓		▤ ⛹ G	✓
	★★★Trouville	6	60	240	12	15	80	✓	✓	✓	✓	✓		G	✓
	★★★Wessex	7	400	200	–	10	84	✓	✓	✓		✓		▤ ⊐ G	✓
	★★Cadogan	2	60	40	2	20	55	✓	✓	✓				–	✓
	★★Durley Chine	3	55	26	3	18	36		✓	✓				⊐	
	★★Durley Grange	1	50	–	2	6	50		✓	✓		✓		▤	✓
	★★Fircroft	2	80	60	2	30	49		✓			✓		▤ ⛹ G	

▤=indoor swimming pool; ⊐=outdoor swimming pool; ◪=golf; 🎾=tennis; ⛹=squash; **G**=*gymnasium*

ENGLAND Town	Hotel	No. of conf. rooms	Seating capacity of main room	Total seating of additional rooms	No. of smaller rooms	Maximum capacity of smaller rooms	No. of bedrooms	Exhibition hall space	Photocopying	Projection/Video	Closed circuit TV	Audio	Interpreting	Sporting facilities available at the Hotel	Use of fax
	★★Hinton Firs	3	20	25	1	10	52		✓	✓				[indoor pool] [outdoor pool]	✓
	★★Riviera	1	40	10	1	10	79		✓	✓		✓		[indoor pool] [outdoor pool]	✓
	★★Royal Exeter	3	200	65	–	–	36	✓	✓	✓		✓		–	✓
	★★Russell Court	2	60	30	1	30	62	✓	✓	✓		✓		–	✓
	★★St George	1	100	–	–	–	22		✓					–	
	★★Ullswater	4	35	40	–	–	42		✓					–	
	★★Winterbourne	2	80	40	3	12	41	✓	✓	✓		✓		[outdoor pool]	
	★★Winter Gardens	5	80	94	3	20	81	✓	✓	✓		✓		[indoor pool] [squash] G	✓
	★★Woodcroft	1	140	–	4	20	40		✓			✓		–	
BOURTON-ON-THE-WATER	★★★Old Manse	2	30	–	1	8	12		✓	✓				–	✓
BOVEY TRACEY	★★Coombe Cross	1	80	–	1	12	26			✓				–	
	★★Riverside Inn	2	280	25	2	40	10	✓	✓			✓		–	✓
BRACKNELL	★★★★Hilton National	12	200	–	5	10	167	✓	✓	✓				[indoor pool]	✓
BRADFORD	★★★★Stakis Norfolk Gardens	8	700	200	7	200	126	✓	✓	✓	✓	✓		–	✓
	★★★Victoria	3	230	130	2	30	59	✓	✓	✓				–	✓
BRADFORD-ON-AVON	★★★Leigh Park	3	120	75	4	6	21		✓	✓				[tennis]	✓
BRAINTREE	★★★White Hart	2	40	20	1	20	35		✓	✓				–	✓
BRAITHWAITE	★★★Middle Ruddings	1	25	–	1	16	12							–	
BRAMHOPE	★★★Post House	1	180	50	6	20	129	✓	✓	✓				[indoor pool] G	✓
BRAMPTON	★★Kirby Manor Country House	1	12	–	–	–	6							–	
	★★Tarn End	1	10	–	–	–	6							–	
BRENTWOOD	★★★Post House	3	100	200	10	8	117	✓	✓					[indoor pool] G	✓
BRERETON	★★Cedar Tree	3	200	15	2	15	28	✓				✓		[squash]	
BRIDGNORTH	★★Falcon	1	50	–	–	–	15							–	✓
	★★Old Vicarage	3	30	40	–	–	15			✓				–	✓
BRIDLINGTON	★★★Expanse	3	40	–	–	–	48		✓					–	✓
	★★★Monarch	2	40	20	2	20	40		✓	✓				–	✓
	★★New Revelstoke	2	150	20	2	15	29	✓		✓	✓	✓		–	✓
BRIDPORT	★★★Eypes Mouth	1	30	–	2	15	18		✓	✓				–	
	★★★Haddon House	2	40	25	1	25	13							–	
BRIGHOUSE	★★★★Forte	6	200	40	2	12	94	✓	✓	✓		✓		[indoor pool] G	✓
BRIGHTON	★★★★★Grand	5	300	430	7	12	163		✓					[indoor pool] G	✓
	★★★★★Hospitality Inn	1	300	–	6	80	204	✓	✓	✓		✓		[indoor pool] G	✓
	★★★★Brighton Metropole	11	1000	1000	15	60	328	✓	✓	✓		✓		[indoor pool] G	✓
	★★★Norfolk Resort	4	180	220	–	–	121	✓	✓	✓	✓	✓		[indoor pool]	✓
BRISTOL	★★★★Grand	7	600	–	2	50	178	✓	✓	✓		✓		–	✓
	★★★★Hilton	10	400	200	5	30	201	✓	✓	✓				[indoor pool] G	✓
	★★★★Holiday Inn	10	600	340	8	30	284	✓	✓	✓		✓		[indoor pool] G	✓
	★★★Avon Gorge	3	100	60	3	10	76	✓	✓	✓	✓	✓	✓	–	✓
	★★★Henbury Lodge	2	12	30	–	–	18		✓	✓				G	✓
	★★★Redwood Lodge	13	175	129	3	10	112	✓	✓	✓				[indoor pool] [outdoor pool] [tennis] [squash] G	✓
	★★★St Vincent Rocks	1	51	–	–	–	46		✓	✓				–	✓
	★★Parkside	2	200	200	3	30	30	✓	✓	✓		✓		–	✓
	★★Rodney	1	10	–	–	–	31							–	
	★★Seeley's	3	90	–	–	–	65		✓	✓	✓	✓		G	✓
BRIXHAM	★★★Quayside	1	20	–	–	–	30		✓					–	✓
BROADSTAIRS	★★Castlemere	1	30	–	2	28	37		✓	✓				–	
	★★Royal Albion	3	80	30	3	8	20	✓	✓	✓		✓	✓	–	✓
BROADWAY	★★★Dormy House	4	200	65	5	10	49		✓	✓	✓	✓		–	✓
BROCKENHURST	★★★★Balmer Lawn	7	90	230	5	20	58		✓	✓				[indoor pool] [outdoor pool] [tennis] [squash] G	✓
	★★★Carey's Manor	4	60	100	8	6	80	✓	✓	✓	✓	✓	✓	[indoor pool] G	✓
	★★★New Park Manor	4	30	20	2	8	26		✓	✓			✓	[outdoor pool] [tennis]	✓
	★★★Rhinefield House	5	150	–	3	10	34		✓	✓	✓	✓		[indoor pool] [outdoor pool] [tennis] G	✓
	★★★Forest Park	2	45	40		10	38		✓	✓				[outdoor pool] [tennis]	
BROMBOROUGH	★★★Cromwell	2	70	70	–	–	31		✓	✓		✓		G	✓
BROME	★★Brome Grange	1	150	30	2	12	22	✓	✓	✓		✓		–	✓
BROMLEY	★★★Bromley Court	13	150	260	8	60	122	✓	✓	✓	✓	✓		–	✓
BROMSGROVE	★★★Perry Hall	4	70	162	4	12	55		✓	✓				–	✓
BROMYARD	★★★Falcon	1	80	–	1	30	10	✓	✓	✓		✓		–	✓
BROOK	★★★Bell Inn	1	12	–	–	–	20		✓	✓		✓		[golf]	✓
BROXTON	★★★Frogg Manor	2	25	12	2	12	6			✓		✓		[indoor pool] [tennis]	
BUCKDEN	★★Lion	1	25	–	1	15	15		✓					–	✓
BUCKHURST HILL	★★★Roebuck	3	200	20	2	14	29	✓	✓	✓				–	✓
BUCKLOW HILL	★★★Swan	1	24	16	4	10	70		✓	✓				–	✓
BUDE	★★St Margaret's	2	30	10	2	10	10		✓	✓			✓	–	✓

[indoor pool]=*indoor swimming pool;* [outdoor pool]=*outdoor swimming pool;* [golf]=*golf;* [tennis]=*tennis;* [squash]=*squash;* **G**=*gymnasium*

ENGLAND Town	Hotel	No. of conf. rooms	Seating capacity of main room	Total seating of additional rooms	No. of smaller rooms	Maximum capacity of smaller rooms	No. of bedrooms	Exhibition hall space	Photocopying	Projection/Video	Closed circuit TV	Audio	Interpreting	Sporting facilities available at the Hotel	Use of fax
BUDE	★Edgcumbe	1	20	–	–	–	15							–	
BURFORD	★★The Golden Pheasant	1	15	–	–	–	12	✓	✓	✓				–	✓
BURGH HEATH	★★Heathside	2	190	70	6	8	73	✓	✓	✓		✓		[indoor pool] [outdoor pool] G	✓
BURLEY	★★★Burley Manor	2	80	–	–	–	30		✓	✓				[outdoor pool]	✓
	★★★Moorhill House	3	54	25	–	–	24							–	✓
BURNHAM	★★★Burnham Beeches	4	180		5	8	76		✓	✓	✓	✓		[golf] [tennis] G	✓
BURNHAM-ON-SEA	★★Dunstan House	1	60	–	1	20	7							–	
	★★Royal Clarence	2	100	20	–	–	17	✓	✓	✓				–	
BURNLEY	★★★Keirby	5	280	40	2	26	49		✓	✓		✓		G	✓
	★★★Oaks	3	120	58	7	14	58		✓	✓	✓	✓		[indoor pool] [squash] G	✓
BURNT YATES	★★Bay Horse Inn	1	20	–	2	10	16							–	
BURSCOUGH	★★★Beaufort	2	40	20	–	–	21		✓	✓				–	✓
BURSLEM	★★George	4	250	75	3	20	39	✓	✓	✓	✓	✓		G	✓
BURTON-ON-TRENT	★★★Newton Park	3	100	50	2	14	46	✓	✓	✓		✓		–	✓
	★★★Riverside	3	150	150	–	–	12	✓	✓	✓	✓	✓	✓		✓
	★★★Stanhope	3	200	60	2	60	28	✓	✓	✓		✓		G	✓
BURY	★★Bolholt	3	200	50	4	17	47	✓	✓	✓		✓	✓	[tennis] G	✓
	★Woolfield House	1	50	–	–	–	16							–	
BURY ST EDMONDS	★★★Angel	2	120	88	2	16	40		✓	✓	✓	✓	✓	–	✓
	★★★Butterfly	5	40	20	–	–	50		✓	✓				–	✓
BUTTERMERE	★★Bridge	1	30	1	1	20	22	✓						–	
BUXTON	★★★Buckingham	2	30	18	3	10	29		✓	✓				–	✓
	★★★Lee Wood	2	100	100	5	25	37		✓	✓				–	✓
	★★★Palace	7	400	300	–	–	122	✓	✓	✓		✓		[indoor pool] G	✓
	★★Portland	1	25	–	2	15	25		✓	✓		✓		–	✓
	★★Sandringham	2	60	30	–	–	35			✓				–	
CADNAM	★★★Bartley Lodge	4	80	75	2	20	19		✓					[outdoor pool] [tennis]	✓
CALNE	★★Lansdowne Strand	2	100	20	1	20	26	✓	✓	✓		✓		–	✓
CAMBERLEY	★★★Frimley Hall	3	70	70	1	12	66		✓	✓				–	✓
CAMBRIDGE	★★★★Cambridgeshire Moat House	8	200	165	7	8	100	✓	✓	✓		✓		[indoor pool] [golf] [tennis] [squash] G	✓
	★★★★Garden House	8	250	300	5	40	118	✓	✓	✓	✓	✓	✓	–	✓
	★★★★Post House	5	80	110	8	12	120		✓	✓				[indoor pool] G	✓
	★★★★University Arms	6	300	200	3	10	117	✓	✓	✓		✓		–	✓
	★★★Gonville	2	50	12	6	6	62		✓	✓		✓	✓	–	✓
	★★Arundel House	2	35	35	–	–	88		✓	✓				–	✓
CANTERBURY	★★★★County	3	180	140	3	40	73		✓	✓		✓		–	✓
	★★★Chaucer	2	80	40	1	20	45	✓	✓	✓		✓		–	✓
	★★★Falstaff	1	40	–	–	–	25			✓				–	
	★★★Slatters	2	100	40	2	4	31		✓	✓				–	✓
	★★Canterbury	3	20	–	15	27			✓	✓				–	✓
	★★Victoria	1	12	–	–	–	34		✓	✓				–	✓
CARLISLE	★★★Central	6	100	150	3	50	84	✓	✓	✓				–	✓
	★★★Crest	7	60	80	5	4	94	✓	✓	✓		✓		[indoor pool] G	✓
	★★★Cumbria Park	3	170	170	1	30	51		✓	✓		✓		–	✓
	★★★Hayton Castle	4	300	130	1	20	13	✓	✓	✓				–	✓
	★★★Swallow Hilltop	7	500	590	6	10	97	✓	✓	✓	✓	✓		[indoor pool] G	✓
	★★Carrow House	2	120	50	2	4	10	✓	✓	✓				–	✓
	★★Woodlands	1	15	–	–	–	15							–	✓
CARLTON COLVILLE	★★★Hedley House Park	2	100	50	1	20	16	✓	✓	✓		✓		–	✓
CARNFORTH	★★★Pine Lake Resort	3	100	150	45	10	68		✓	✓				[indoor pool] G	✓
	★★Royal Station	2	100	30	2	15	12	✓		✓				–	
CASTLE COMBE	★★★Manor House	5	60	66	4	4	36		✓	✓		✓		[outdoor pool] [tennis]	✓
CASTLE DONNINGTON	★★★Donnington Manor	4	90	150	3	20	37		✓	✓		✓		–	✓
CATTERICK BRIDGE	★★Bridge House	2	120	35	1	35	15	✓	✓	✓		✓		–	✓
CHAGFORD	★★★Gidleigh Park	1	18	–	–	–	16		✓					[tennis]	✓
	★★★Great Tree	1	25	–	1	8	12		✓					–	
CHARLBURY	★★Bell	2	55	12	1	12	14		✓	✓				–	✓
CHARLECOTE	★★★Charlecote Pheasant	6	140	30	6	6	60	✓	✓	✓		✓		[outdoor pool] [tennis] G	✓
CHARNOCK RICHARD	★★★Welcome Lodge	3	50	28	2	6	100		✓	✓				–	✓
CHATHAM	★★Crest	7	110	40	–	7	105		✓	✓		✓		[indoor pool] G	✓
CHELMSFORD	★★★★Pontlands Park	2	40	–	2	16	17		✓	✓		✓		[indoor pool] [outdoor pool]	✓
	★★★South Lodge Motel	2	40	30	3	4	41		✓	✓				–	✓
	★★Saracens Head	3	70	30	2	30	18		✓	✓		✓		–	✓
CHELTENHAM	★★★★Queens	4	200	150	2	20	77	✓	✓			✓		–	✓
	★★★Carlton	4	225	190	–	–	68	✓	✓	✓	✓	✓		–	✓

[indoor pool]=indoor swimming pool; [outdoor pool]=outdoor swimming pool; [golf]=golf; [tennis]=tennis; [squash]=squash; G=gymnasium

ENGLAND Town	Hotel	No. of conf. rooms	Seating capacity of main room	Total seating of additional rooms	No. of smaller rooms	Maximum capacity of smaller rooms	No. of bedrooms	Exhibition hall space	Photocopying	Projection/Video	Closed circuit TV	Audio	Interpreting	Sporting facilities available at the Hotel	Use of fax
	★★★White House	3	180	70	–	–	50	✓	✓	✓	✓	✓	✓	▣ G	✓
	★★George	2	40	40	–	–	40		✓	✓				–	✓
CHESTER	★★★★Chester Grosvenor	5	250	290	–	12	86	✓	✓	✓	✓	✓	✓		✓
	★★★★Chester International	3	500	250	13	12	152	✓	✓	✓		✓		G	✓
	★★★★Crabwall Manor	3	100	100	4	8	48		✓	✓	✓	✓	✓	–	✓
	★★★★Mollington Banastre	7	300	280	5	70	64	✓	✓	✓	✓	✓		▣ ⚔ G	✓
	★★★Abbots Well	3	200	100	3	12	127	✓	✓	✓		✓	✓	▣ G	✓
	★★★Blossoms	1	100	80	3	20	64	✓	✓	✓		✓	✓	–	✓
	★★★Hoole Hall	7	150	300	6	20	99	✓	✓	✓	✓	✓	✓	–	✓
	★★★Plantation	6	200	150	6	10	75	✓	✓	✓	✓	✓	✓	–	✓
	★★★Post House	3	100	100		10	107		✓	✓		✓		▣ G	✓
	★★★Rowton Hall	3	200	120	1	30	42							▣ G	
	★★Dene	1	20	–	–	–	49		✓		✓			–	✓
	★★Green Bough	2	15	12	–	–	16		✓	✓				–	✓
CHESTERFIELD	★★★Chesterfield	6	250	280	6	20	72		✓	✓	✓	✓		▣ G	✓
	★★★Ringwood	8	200	142	4	12	24	✓	✓	✓	✓	✓		–	✓
	★★Abbeydale	1	15	–	1	8	11			✓				–	
	★★Portland	3	60	15	–	–	27		✓	✓				–	✓
CHICHESTER	★★★Chichester Resort	7	350	100	5	8	76	✓	✓	✓	✓	✓	✓	▣	✓
	★★★Dolphin & Anchor	3	200	70	–	–	51		✓	✓	✓	✓		–	✓
CHIPPENHAM	★★Angel	3	76	65	–	–	44	✓	✓	✓	✓	✓		–	✓
CHIPPING CAMDEN	★★★Charingworth Manor	2	34	16	1	8	25		✓	✓				–	✓
	★★★Cotswold House	1	20	–	–	–	15		✓	✓	✓	✓		–	✓
CHIPPING NORTON	★★Crown & Cushion	3	190	30	5	20	29	✓	✓	✓		✓		▣ ⚔ G	✓
CHITTLEHAMHOLT	★★★Highbullen	1	20	–	–	–	35		✓	✓				▣ ⊃ ⊡ ♀ ⚔	✓
CHOLLERFORD	★★★George	3	35	30	–	–	50		✓	✓				▣	✓
CHORLEY	★★★Shawhill Golf & Country Club	3	–	–	2	16	22		✓	✓		✓		⊡	✓
	★★Hartwood Hall	4	120	90	–	–	22	✓	✓	✓		✓		–	✓
CHRISTCHURCH	★★★Waterford Lodge	1	16	6	–	–	20		✓	✓				–	✓
CHURCH STRETTON	★★★Long Mynd	6	80	50	5	12	52	✓	✓	✓	✓	✓	✓	⊃ G	✓
	★★Denehurst	2	150	40	–	–	15		✓			✓		▣ G	✓
	★★Mynd House	2	15	15	1	6	8		✓	✓				–	✓
CIRENCESTER	★★★Fleece	4	60	–	4	20	25	✓	✓	✓				–	✓
	★★★Kings Head	4	250	180	3	8	70		✓	✓		✓		–	✓
	★★★Stratton House	2	100	14	–	10	26		✓	✓				–	✓
CLAWTON	★★Court Barn Country House	1	35	–	1	15	8		✓	✓		✓		G	✓
CLAYTON-LE-MOORS	★★★Dunkenhalgh	8	350	200	6	50	67		✓	✓		✓		▣ G	✓
CLAYTON-LE-WOODS	★★★Pines	5	160	36	4	26	25	✓	✓	✓		✓		–	✓
CLEEVE HILL	★★★Rising Sun	3	60	20	–	–	25		✓	✓		✓		–	✓
CLEOBURY MORTIMER	★★Redfern	2	30	15	–	–	11	✓	✓	✓				–	✓
CLEVEDON	★★★Walton Park	3	150	230	2	40	36	✓	✓	✓					✓
CLIMPING	★★★Bailiffscourt	4	26	23	–	–	20		✓	✓		✓		▣ ♀	✓
COBHAM	★★★Hilton National	6	250	300	6	12	140		✓	✓		✓		▣ ♀ ⚔	✓
	★★★Woodlands Park	8	300	240	–	–	59	✓	✓	✓		✓		♀	✓
COCKERMOUTH	★★★Broughton Craggs	2	50	50	2	25	14		✓	✓				–	
	★★★Trout	1	55	–	–	–	22		✓	✓				–	✓
	★★Globe	1	80	–	2	15	80	✓	✓	✓		✓		–	✓
COGGLESHALL	★★★White Hart	1	40	–	1	10	18	✓	✓	✓	✓	✓		–	✓
COLCHESTER	★★★George	3	90	120	3	20	47		✓	✓				G	✓
	★★★Mill	3	80	60	3	6	55	✓	✓	✓				–	✓
COLERNE	★★★★Lucknam Park	1	26	–	3	10	39		✓	✓	✓	✓	✓	▣ ♀ G	✓
COLESHILL	★★★Coleshill	1	150	–	1	8	23	✓	✓	✓		✓		–	✓
	★★★Grimstock Country House	4	100	30	2	15	44	✓	✓	✓				–	✓
CONGLETON	★★Lion & Swan	2	180	30	4	20	21	✓	✓	✓	✓	✓	✓	–	✓
CONISTON	★★Yewdale	1	50	–	–	–	10							–	
COODEN BEACH	★★★Cooden Resort	4	100	–	4	20	42		✓	✓	✓	✓		▣ ⊃	✓
COPTHORNE	★★★★Copthorne	14	110	–	4	15	224	✓	✓	✓	✓	✓		⚔ G	✓
	★★★★Effingham Park	11	100	–	9	8	122	✓	✓	✓		✓		▣ ⊡ G	✓
CORBY	★★★Crest	2	400	100	4	30	70	✓	✓	✓		✓		–	✓
CORNHILL-ON-TWEED	★★★Tillmouth Park	1	38	–	1	6	12	✓	✓	✓				–	
CORSHAM	★★★Rudloe Park	2	100	20	2	15	17	✓						–	
	★★Methuen Arms	1	26	–	–	–	25	✓				✓		–	✓
COVENTRY	★★★★De Vere	4	500	524	8	40	190	✓	✓					–	✓
	★★★Ansty Hall	3	100	35	8	8	30		✓	✓				–	✓

▣=indoor swimming pool; ⊃=outdoor swimming pool; ⊡=golf; ♀=tennis; ⚔=squash; G=gymnasium

ENGLAND Town	Hotel	No. of conf. rooms	Seating capacity of main room	Total seating of additional rooms	No. of smaller rooms	Maximum capacity of smaller rooms	No. of bedrooms	Exhibition hall space	Photocopying	Projection/Video	Closed circuit TV	Audio	Interpreting	Sporting facilities available at the Hotel	Use of fax
	★★★Brandon Hall	8	100	215	6	30	60	✓	✓	✓				[golf] [squash]	✓
	★★★Crest	12	400	330	5	6	147	✓	✓	✓	✓	✓		[indoor pool] G	✓
	★★★Chace Crest	4	65	70	5	6	67							–	
	★★★Old Mill	2	30	20	–	–	20		✓	✓				–	✓
	★★★Post House	13	130	–	5	8	184		✓	✓	✓	✓	✓	–	✓
	★★Beechwood	1	14	–	–	–	24		✓					–	✓
CRANTOCK	★★Crantock Bay	2	80	–	3	20	36			✓	✓	✓		[indoor pool] [tennis] G	
CRATHORNE	★★★Crathorne Hall	8	160	–	6	30	39	✓	✓	✓		✓		–	✓
CRAWLEY	★★★Gatwick Manor	3	200	140	12	–	30	✓	✓	✓		✓		[golf]	✓
	★★★George	1	30	–	4	25	86		✓	✓		✓		–	✓
	★★★Goffs Park	2	120	75	3	16	65	✓	✓	✓		✓		–	✓
	★★★Holiday Inn	8	200	–	3	25	226	✓	✓	✓		✓		[indoor pool] G	✓
CREDITON	★★Coombe House	1	90	–	2	35	12	✓		✓		✓		[outdoor pool] [tennis]	
CREWE	★★★Embassy	7	100	240	7	30	53		✓	✓				–	✓
CRICK	★★★★Post House	2	223	223	2	12	96	✓	✓	✓		✓		[indoor pool] G	✓
CROOKLANDS	★★★Crooklands	2	100	40	1	5	30		✓	✓				–	✓
CROMER	★★Cliftonville	2	200	100	3	30	44	✓	✓	✓				–	✓
CROSBY	★★★Blundellsands	8	200	350	2	16	41		✓	✓		✓		–	✓
CROWBOROUGH	★★★Winston Manor	5	300	250	2	12	50	✓	✓		✓		✓	–	
CROWTHORNE	★★Waterloo	2	50	20	1	6	58		✓	✓	✓	✓		–	✓
CROYDON	★★★★Holiday Inn	6	300	210	9	10	214	✓	✓	✓		✓		[indoor pool] [squash] G	✓
	★★★★Selsdon Park	12	150	140	10	25	170		✓	✓	✓	✓		[indoor pool] [outdoor pool] [golf] [tennis] [squash] G	✓
	★★★Post House	5	200	100	85	6	85	✓	✓	✓		✓		–	✓
	★★Central	2	40	10	2	12	23	✓						–	✓
	★★Briarley	2	30	10	2	6	38		✓					–	✓
CRUDWELL	★★Mayfield House	1	16	10	–	–	20							–	✓
CUCKFIELD	★★★Ockenden Manor	1	25	–	–	–	22		✓	✓		✓		–	✓
	★★Hilton Park	1	30	–	–	–	13	✓						–	
DARESBURY	★★★Lord Daresbury	6	400	352	10	12	141	✓	✓	✓		✓		[indoor pool] [squash] G	✓
DARLINGTON	★★★★Blackwell Grange Moat House	9	300	90	7	10	99	✓	✓	✓	✓	✓	✓	[indoor pool] [golf] [tennis] G	✓
	★★★St George	5	200	130	4	50	59	✓	✓	✓		✓		[squash] G	✓
	★★Swallow Kings Head	5	250	96	–	–	60	✓	✓	✓		✓		–	✓
DARRINGTON	★★Darrington	1	70	–	1	14	28			✓		✓		–	
DARTMOUTH	★★★Royal Castle	2	60	–	2	20	25		✓	✓				–	✓
DARWEN	★★★Whitehall	2	50	20	1	20	18	✓	✓	✓	✓			[indoor pool]	✓
DATCHET	★★Manor	2	120	30	2	10	30		✓	✓		✓		–	✓
DAWLISH	★★★Langstone Cliff	6	400	200	6	20	64	✓	✓	✓		✓		[indoor pool] [outdoor pool] [tennis]	✓
DEDDINGTON	★★Holcombe	3	50	20	–	10	17		✓	✓	✓		✓	–	✓
DEDHAM	★★★Dedham Vale	1	16	–	–	–	6		✓	✓		✓		–	✓
DERBY	★★★Breadsall Priory	6	100	60	5	10	100	✓	✓	✓				[indoor pool] [golf] [tennis] [squash] G	✓
	★★★Crest	2	24	12	1	6	66		✓	✓		✓		–	✓
	★★★Gables	3	170	–	–	40	101		✓	✓		✓		–	✓
	★★★International	5	50	40	3	12	51		✓	✓	✓	✓		–	✓
	★★★Midland	6	150	200	4	50	60		✓	✓	✓	✓		–	✓
	★★★Pennine	6	–	–	–	8	94	✓	✓	✓	✓	✓		–	✓
	★★Clarendon	3	50	25	2	5	50		✓					–	✓
DEVIZES	★★Bear	3	120	35	1	12	24	✓	✓	✓				–	✓
DINNINGTON	★★★Dinnington Hall	2	60	10	2	10	10		✓	✓		✓		–	✓
DISLEY	★★★Moorside	8	300	90	4	15	96	✓	✓	✓	✓	✓		[golf]	✓
DONCASTER	★★★Danum Swallow	7	350	90	5	10	66		✓	✓				–	✓
	★★★Doncaster Moat House	8	400	90	–	10	70	✓	✓	✓		✓		–	✓
	★★★Mount Pleasant	2	60	20	1	12	36		✓	✓		✓		–	✓
DORCHESTER-ON-THAMES	★★★George	3	40	20	2	10	18	✓		✓	✓	✓		–	
DORCHESTER	★★★Kings Arms	2	80	30	2	10	33		✓	✓				–	✓
DORKING	★★★★Burford Bridge	7	300	60	–	6	48	✓	✓	✓		✓		[outdoor pool]	✓
	★★★White Horse	10	30	24	3	14	68		✓	✓				[outdoor pool]	✓
DOVEDALE	★★★Isaac Walton	3	40	25	2	12	34	✓	✓	✓		✓	✓	–	✓
	★★★Peveril of the Peak	3	65	12	4	12	47		✓	✓				[tennis]	✓
DOVER	★★★★Dover Moat House	2	80	80	5	10	79		✓	✓				[indoor pool]	✓
	★★★Crest	2	45	30	3	12	67		✓	✓				–	✓
	★★★White Cliffs	1	30	–	1	30	56		✓					–	✓
DOWNHAM MARKET	★★Castle	2	40	20	–	20	11		✓					–	✓
DRIFFIELD	★★★Bell-in-Driffield	6	300	250	3	40	14	✓		✓		✓		[indoor pool] [squash] G	
DRONFIELD	★★Manor	–	34	20	–	–	10								

[indoor pool]=*indoor swimming pool;* [outdoor pool]=*outdoor swimming pool;* [golf]=*golf;* [tennis]=*tennis;* [squash]=*squash;* **G**=*gymnasium*

ENGLAND Town	Hotel	No. of conf. rooms	Seating capacity of main room	Total seating of additional rooms	No. of smaller rooms	Maximum capacity of smaller rooms	No. of bedrooms	Exhibition hall space	Photocopying	Projection/Video	Closed circuit TV	Audio	Interpreting	Sporting facilities available at the Hotel	Use of fax
DUDLEY	★★★Ward Arms	5	100	20	4	25	48	✓	✓			✓		–	✓
	★★Station	4	200	60	3	40	38	✓	✓			✓		–	✓
DUNMOW GREAT	★★★Saracens Head	1	50	15	1	12	24		✓	✓				–	✓
DUNSTABLE	★★Highwayman	2	60	12	1	12	38							–	✓
DURHAM	★★★★Royal County	6	140	100	6	–	152		✓	✓		✓		indoor pool G	✓
	★★★Hallgarth Manor	3	350	30	1	30	23	✓	✓	✓		✓		–	✓
	★★★Three Tuns	3	400	60	2	15	48	✓	✓	✓		✓		–	✓
EAGLESCLIFFE	★★★Parkmore	3	80	100	3	15	55	✓	✓	✓		✓		indoor pool G	✓
EASTBOURNE	★★★★★Grand	6	400	800	20	20	161	✓	✓	✓	✓	✓	✓	indoor pool outdoor pool G	✓
	★★★★Cavendish	6	220	60	3	15	114	✓	✓	✓	✓	✓			✓
	★★★★Queens	7	300	540	7	20	108	✓	✓	✓		✓	✓	–	✓
	★★★Chatsworth	2	46	30	2	20	46		✓	✓				–	✓
	★★★Lansdowne	3	130	160	3	62	130	✓	✓	✓		✓		–	✓
	★★★Princes	1	60	36	–	–	46		✓	✓				–	✓
	★★★Wish Tower	3	80	40	3	25	67		✓	✓		✓		–	✓
	★★★York House	3	100	80	3	24	103		✓	✓		✓		indoor pool	✓
	★★Farrars	1	60	–	1	–	45	✓	✓	✓				–	✓
	★★Langham	2	60	40	2	25	87					✓		–	
ECCLESHALL	★★St George	1	18	–	–	–	10							–	✓
EDENHALL	★★★Edenhall	1	30	6	1	–	22		✓					–	
E. DEREHAM	★★★Phoenix	3	180	180	5	10	22	✓	✓	✓				–	
	★★Kings Head	1	40	–	–	–	15		✓					–	✓
E. HORSLEY	★★★Thatchers Resort	3	60	50	3	20	59		✓	✓				outdoor pool	✓
EASTLEIGH	★★★Crest	7	250	40	6	40	120	✓	✓	✓		✓		–	✓
EATHORPE	★★Eathorpe Park	3	100	50	2	50	12	✓	✓	✓				–	✓
EGGESFORD	★★Eggesford House	2	200	200	3	100	20	✓	✓					–	
EGHAM	★★★★Great Fosters	5	100	10	1	20	45	✓	✓	✓		✓		outdoor pool	✓
	★★★★Runnymede	26	400	216	26	18	125		✓	✓	✓	✓	✓	–	✓
EGREMONT	★★★Blackbeck Bridge Inn	1	40	–	–	1	22	✓	–	✓				–	
ELLESMERE	★★Woodhey	6	225	102	2	16	53	✓	✓	✓		✓		–	✓
ELSTREE	★★★Edwarebury	2	80	60	2	10	50			✓				tennis	
ELY	★★★Fenland Lodge	2	50	30	2	15	9			✓				–	✓
	★★★Lamb	2	100	40	6	15	32		✓	✓				–	✓
EMSWORTH	★★★Brookfield	3	50	30	2	30	41		✓	✓		✓		–	✓
ENFIELD	★★★Royal Chace	8	300	270	8	–	92	✓	✓	✓	✓	✓		outdoor pool	✓
	★★Holtwhites	1	20	–	1	20	30		✓					–	✓
EPPING	★★★Post House	1	100	20	7	10	82	✓	✓	✓				–	✓
ERMINGTON	★★Ermewood House	1	12	–	1	12	12	✓	✓					–	
EVESHAM	★★★Evesham	2	15	10	–	–	40		✓	✓	✓			indoor pool	✓
	★★★Northwick Arms	2	40	–	–	–	25			✓				–	✓
EXETER	★★★★Forte	6	80	18	4	12	110		✓	✓		✓		indoor pool G	✓
	★★★★Royal Clarence	3	120	90	2	90	56	✓	✓	✓		✓	✓	–	✓
	★★★Countess Wear Lodge	4	185	165	2	30	44	✓	✓	✓		✓		tennis	✓
	★★★Devon Motel	3	150	30	1	30	41		✓	✓		✓		–	✓
	★★★Exeter Court	1	160	20	1	20	63	✓	✓	✓		✓		golf tennis	✓
	★★★Gipsy Hill Country House	2	120	82	2	80	20		✓	✓				–	✓
	★★★Lord Haldon	5	140	195	4	20	20	✓	✓	✓		✓		–	✓
	★★★Rougemont	7	300	140	–	20	90	✓	✓	✓	✓	✓	✓	–	✓
	★★★St Olaves Court	2	30	12	2	12	17	✓	✓	✓		✓		–	✓
	★★★White Hart	3	70	20	2	50	62		✓	✓		✓		–	✓
EXMOUTH	★★★Imperial	2	50	12	1	–	57		✓	✓		✓		outdoor pool tennis	✓
	★★★Royal Beacon	3	100	60	2	15	30	✓	✓	✓	✓	✓		–	✓
	★★Barn	1	80	–	2	20	11	✓						outdoor pool tennis	
	★★Manor	3	100	110	4	10	42			✓				–	
	★Aliston	1	60	20	1	–	14							–	
FAIRFORD	★★★Hyperion House	2	50	10	1	10	30		✓	✓				–	✓
FALMOUTH	★★★Green Lawns	2	200	100	2	12	40	✓	✓	✓		✓	✓	indoor pool tennis squash G	✓
	★★★Penmere Manor	2	18	18	–	–	39		✓	✓				indoor pool outdoor pool	✓
	★★★Royal Duchy	2	100	10	1	10	50	✓	✓	✓		✓		indoor pool	✓
	★★★St Michaels of Falmouth	4	200	175	3	95	75	✓	✓	✓		✓		indoor pool tennis G	✓
FAREHAM	★★Maylings Manor	2	140	–	–	–	24		✓	✓		✓		–	✓
	★★Red Lion	3	120	40	1	15	44			✓				–	
FARNBOROUGH	★★★Queens	7	220	–	3	12	110	✓	✓	✓	✓	✓		indoor pool G	✓

indoor pool=indoor swimming pool; outdoor pool=outdoor swimming pool; golf=golf; tennis=tennis; squash=squash; G=gymnasium

ENGLAND Town	Hotel	No. of conf. rooms	Seating capacity of main room	Total seating of additional rooms	No. of smaller rooms	Maximum capacity of smaller rooms	No. of bedrooms	Exhibition hall space	Photocopying	Projection/Video	Closed circuit TV	Audio	Interpreting	Sporting facilities available at the Hotel	Use of fax
FARNHAM	★★★Bush	4	70	20	4	10	68		√	√				–	√
	★★★Frensham Pond	6	150	40	5	40	53		√	√		√		indoor pool, squash, G	√
	★★Bishops Table	2	20	15	1	10	18		√	√				–	√
	★★Trevena	2	45	15	3	15	20		√	√	√			outdoor pool, tennis	√
FAR SAWREY	★★Sawrey	1	35	–	2	10	17		√	√	√	√		–	
FAWKHAM GREEN	★★★Brands Hatch	7	150	108	4	10	29	√	√	√				indoor pool, [illegible], squash, [illegible]	
FELIXSTOWE	★★★★Orwell Moat House	5	200	50	5	12	58	√	√	√		√		–	√
	★★Marlborough	3	100	42	3	10	47	√	√	√				–	√
	★★Waverley	1	90	20	10	10	20		√	√		√		–	√
FERNDOWN	★★★★Dormy	12	250	245	6	20	129	√	√	√	√	√		–	√
	★★Welcome Lodge	3	100	20	2	20	28	√	√					–	
FINEDON	★★Tudor Gate	2	40	10	2	10	16		√					–	
FLEET	★★★Lismoyne	2	80	40	2	120	44		√			√	√	–	√
FLEETWOOD	★★★North Euston	2	100	80	2	30	60		√	√	√	√		G	√
FOLKESTONE	★★★Burlington	4	250	60	2	50	59	√	√			√		–	
	★★★Clifton	4	100	120	3	60	80	√	√	√				–	√
	★★★Garden House	3	80	35	–	–	42		√	√	√	√		–	√
FORDINGBRIDGE	★★Ashburn	2	150	30	2	8	22		√	√	√	√		–	
FOREST ROW	★★★Roebuck	3	100	50	2	12	28	√	√	√				–	√
	★★Brambletye	1	12	–	1	–	22	√	√	√		√		–	
	★★Chequers Inn	2	30	30	4	6	17		√	√				–	
FOWEY	★★★Fowey	1	25	–	–	–	30	√	√					–	√
FRADLEY	★★Fradley Arms	1	200	–	2	45	6	√	√	√	√	√		–	√
FRIMLEY GREEN	★★★Lakeside International	6	200	98	5	10	97		√					squash	√
FRODSHAM	★★Old Hall	1	30	6	1	–	21		√	√		√		outdoor pool	√
FROME	★★★Mendip Lodge	2	80	40	2	10	40		√	√				–	√
GAINSBOROUGH	★★Hickman Hill	1	50	10	1	10	8							–	
GARSTANG	★★★Crofters	3	220	36	2	2	19	√	√	√		√		–	
GATESHEAD	★★★Springfield	3	120	40	4	28	60	√	√	√		√		–	√
	★★★Swallow	5	350	190	4	12	103		√	√		√		indoor pool, G	√
GATWICK	★★★★Gatwick Hilton	25	450	275	18	6	552	√	√	√	√	√		indoor pool, G	√
GERRARDS CROSS	★★★Bull	4	200	200	4	20	95		√	√	√	√		–	√
	★★Ethorpe	2	26	16	1	–	29		√	√				–	√
GISBURN	★★★Stirk House	3	300	120	5	12	48	√	√	√		√		indoor pool, squash, G	√
GLOUCESTER	★★★Crest	10	100	130	5	–	123	√	√	√		√		indoor pool, G	√
	★★★Gloucester	5	180	100	3	10	107	√	√	√		√		indoor pool, golf, tennis, squash, G	√
	★★★Hatherley Manor	7	250	450	8	30	55	√	√	√		√		–	√
	★★★Hatton Court	6	60	108	3	28	46		√	√	√	√		outdoor pool	√
	★★New County	4	200	60	3	30	31	√	√	√				–	√
	★★Twigworth Lodge	1	20	–	2	–	30		√	√				indoor pool	√
GOODWOOD	★★★Goodwood Park	10	80	60	5	10	89	√	√	√				indoor pool, golf, tennis, squash, G	√
GOOLE	★★Clifton	2	40	10	2	10	10							–	√
GORLESTON-ON-SEA	★★Pier	2	100	30	1	30	20	√	√			√		–	√
GOUDHURST	★★Star & Eagle	–	25	–	–	–	11		√	√				–	
GRANGE-OVER-SANDS	★★Graythwaite Manor	1	25	–	1	12	22		√	√				tennis	
	★★Netherwood	3	150	50	2	50	33	√	√	√	√	√		–	
GRANTHAM	★★★Angel & Royal	3	25	25	2	6	30		√	√				–	√
	★★Kings	1	100	12	1	12	22		√	√		√		tennis	√
GRASMERE	★★★★Wordsworth	1	100	28	2	28	37	√	√	√		√		indoor pool, G	√
	★★★Prince of Wales	5	100	80	–	–	77	√	√	√				–	
	★★Red Lion	2	40	25	–	–	36		√	√				–	
	★★★Swan	1	46	6	1	8	36		√	√				–	√
	★★Moss Grove	2	10	10	2	10	14		√					–	√
	★★Rothay Garden	2	20	10	2	10	21		√	√				–	√
GRASSINGTON	★★★Wilson Arms	2	120	65	2	65	14		√	√		√		–	√
GRAVESEND	★★Tollgate	6	100	60	4	15	114	√	√	√	√	√		–	
GREAT AYTON	★★★Ayton Hall	1	250	20	2	20	9	√	√	√		√		–	√
GREAT MILTON	★★★Le Manoir aux Quat' Saisons	1	46	12	1	12	19		√	√				outdoor pool, tennis	√
GRETA BRIDGE	★★Morrit Arms	3	150	50	1	10	17	√	√	√	√	√		–	√
GRIMSBY	★★★★Humber Royal Crest	5	250	120	4	12	52		√	√		√		–	√
	★★★Crest	8	70	89	6	71	125	√	√	√		√		–	√
GRIMSTON	★★★Congham Hall Country House	1	12	–	–	–	14		√	√				outdoor pool, tennis	√
GRINDLEFORD	★★★Maynard Arms	2	50	20	1	20	13	√						–	√
GROBY	★★Brant	2	160	10	1	10	10		√	√		√		–	√
GUILDFORD	★★★★Forte	11	120	102	9	8	121	√	√	√	√	√		indoor pool, G	√

indoor pool=indoor swimming pool; outdoor pool=outdoor swimming pool; golf=golf; tennis=tennis; squash=squash; G=gymnasium

ENGLAND Town	Hotel	No. of conf. rooms	Seating capacity of main room	Total seating of additional rooms	No. of smaller rooms	Maximum capacity of smaller rooms	No. of bedrooms	Exhibition hall space	Photocopying	Projection/Video	Closed circuit TV	Audio	Interpreting	Sporting facilities available at the Hotel	Use of fax
GUISBOROUGH	★★Fox & Hounds	2	70	60	2	10	16							–	
HACKNESS	★★★Hackness Grange Country	1	26	26	2	38	26		✓	✓				[indoor pool] [tennis]	✓
HADLEY WOOD	★★★★West Lodge Park	4	40	36	2	32	50		✓	✓				–	✓
HALIFAX	★★★Holdsworth House	3	100	12	2	12	40		✓	✓		✓		–	✓
	★★★Imperial Crown	1	250	20	1	20	42	✓	✓	✓		✓		–	✓
	★★★Wool Merchant	1	60	–	6	10	25		✓	✓		✓	✓	–	
HALLAND	★★★Halland Forge	2	70	–	2	30	20		✓	✓				–	✓
HANDFORTH	★★★★Belfry	4	120	73	3	40	82	✓	✓	✓		✓		–	✓
HANLEY	★★★Stakis Grand	6	250	260	3	25	128	✓	✓	✓		✓		[indoor pool] G	✓
HARLOW	★★★Churchgate Manor	4	170	140	3	10	85		✓	✓	✓	✓		[indoor pool] G	✓
	★★★Green Man	2	60	–	1	12	55		✓	✓				–	✓
	★★★Harlow Moat House	15	150	196	10	16	120		✓	✓	✓	✓		–	✓
HARPENDEN	★★★★Harpenden Moat House	4	120	30	5	8	53		✓	✓	✓	✓		–	✓
	★★★Glen Eagle	4	80	20	2	12	50	✓	✓	✓				–	✓
HARROGATE	★★★★Crown	7	400	295	1	10	121	✓	✓	✓		✓		–	✓
	★★★★Majestic	8	450	995	6	30	156	✓	✓	✓		✓		[indoor pool] [tennis] [squash] G	✓
	★★★★Moat House International	7	400	190	9	25	214							–	
	★★★Grants	2	20	8	2	8	37		✓	✓				–	✓
	★★★Hospitality Inn	3	120	56	5	8	71	✓	✓	✓		✓		–	✓
	★★★Russell	3	16	5	2	6	34	✓	✓	✓		✓		–	✓
	★★★St George	4	150	90	3	90	93	✓	✓	✓	✓	✓		[indoor pool] G	✓
	★★Ascot House	2	80	15	1	15	24	✓	✓	✓		✓		[indoor pool] [outdoor pool]	✓
	★★Green Park	3	40	40	4	10	43	✓	✓	✓		✓		–	✓
HARROW	★★Harrow	3	150	45	8	12	100	✓	✓	✓	✓			–	✓
	★★Monksdene	3	100	12	3	12	90	✓	✓	✓				–	
HARTLEPOOL	★★★Grand	2	150	50	3	30	48	✓	✓	✓		✓		–	✓
HARWELL	★★★Kingswell	1	20	–	1	1	19		✓	✓				–	✓
HARWICH	★★Cliff	2	150	15	2	15	27	✓				✓		–	✓
	★★Tower	3	60	42	–	–	15		✓	✓				–	✓
HASLEMERE	★★★Lythe Hill	6	60	60	6	12	40	✓	✓	✓		✓		[tennis]	✓
HASSOP	★★★Hassop Hall	5	30	–	–	–	12		✓	✓				[tennis]	✓
HASTINGS	★★★★Royal Victoria	5	90	100	3	6	52	✓	✓					–	
	★★★Beauport Park	2	120	36	1	36	23	✓	✓	✓	✓	✓	✓	[outdoor pool] [golf] [tennis] [squash]	✓
	★★★Cinque Ports	7	300	80	4	10	40	✓	✓	✓		✓		[indoor pool]	✓
HATFIELD	★★★Comet	3	40	50	–	–	57		✓	✓				–	✓
HATFIELD HEATH	★★★★Down Hall Country House	22	320	320	22	15	103	✓	✓	✓		✓	✓	[indoor pool] [tennis]	✓
HATHERSAGE	★★★George	1	30	–	–	–	18		✓	✓				–	✓
	★★Hathersage Inn	1	12	–	1	12	15			✓				–	✓
HAVANT	★★★Bear	3	100	80	2	40	42			✓				–	
HAVERTHWAITE	★★Dicksons Arms	–	50	60	–	16	10		✓			✓		–	
HAWKHURST	★★Tudor Court	2	60	20	2	10	18		✓	✓		✓		[tennis]	✓
HAWKSHEAD	★★★Tarn Hows	5	40	12	3	12	22		✓	✓				[outdoor pool]	✓
HAWORTH	★★Old White Lion	1	100	–	1	40	14							–	
HAYDOCK	★★★★Haydock Thistle	14	250	120	10	20	139	✓	✓	✓		✓		[indoor pool] G	✓
	★★★★Post House	3	180	30	11	8	142	✓	✓	✓				[indoor pool] G	✓
HAYLING ISLAND	★★★★Post House	5	180	–	5	8	96		✓	✓		✓		[indoor pool] G	✓
	★★Newtown House	1	40	–	2	12	28		✓	✓		✓		[outdoor pool] [tennis] G	✓
HEADLAM	★★★Headlam Hall	2	20	20	2	10	19		✓	✓		✓		[indoor pool] [tennis] G	✓
HELMSLEY	★★★Black Swan	1	15	12	2	6	44		✓	✓	✓	✓		–	
	★★★Feversham Arms	–	–	–	1	24	18		✓	✓				[outdoor pool] [tennis]	✓
HELSTON	★★Gwealdues	2	120	25	1	15	12	✓	✓	✓				[outdoor pool]	✓
HEMEL HEMPSTEAD	★★★Post House	8	120	10	7	10	107	✓	✓	✓		✓		–	✓
HENLEY-ON-THAMES	★★Edwardian	1	80	10	2	10	22	✓	✓	✓	✓	✓		–	✓
HEREFORD	★★★Hereford Moat House	4	250	120	2	8	60	✓	✓	✓	✓	✓		–	✓
	★★Castle Pool	1	25	20	1	–	26		✓					–	✓
	★★Merton	1	60	10	1	10	19		✓					G	✓
	★★New Priory	3	15	45	2	25	8	✓		✓				–	
HERSTMONCEUX	★★Horse Shoe Inn	2	180	30	2	4	15	✓	✓	✓		✓		–	✓
HERTFORD	★★★White Horse	4	60	18	2	10	42		✓	✓	✓			–	✓
	★★Salisbury Arms	2	35	10	–	–	29		✓	✓				–	✓
HEXHAM	★★Beaumont	2	80	30	2	8	23	✓	✓	✓		✓		G	✓
	~~★★Langley Castle~~	1	120	–	–	–	8		✓					–	✓
	★★Royal	2	100	25	1	25	24	✓	✓	✓		✓	✓	–	
HIGH WYCOMBE	★★★Crest	7	100	156	4	8	110	✓	✓	✓		✓		–	✓

[indoor pool]=indoor swimming pool; [outdoor pool]=outdoor swimming pool; [golf]=golf; [tennis]=tennis; [squash]=squash; G=gymnasium

ENGLAND Town	Hotel	No. of conf. rooms	Seating capacity of main room	Total seating of additional rooms	No. of smaller rooms	Maximum capacity of smaller rooms	No. of bedrooms	Exhibition hall space	Photocopying	Projection/Video	Closed circuit TV	Audio	Interpreting	Sporting facilities available at the Hotel	Use of fax
HIMLEY	★★★Himley Country Club	2	50	30	2	10	76		✓	✓				–	
	★★Himley House	1	20	–	–	–	24		✓	✓				–	✓
HINTON CHARTERHOUSE	★★★Homewood Park	1	40	15	2	15	15		✓	✓				–	✓
HITCHIN	★★Firs	1	40	–	–	25	30	✓						–	✓
HOGS BACK	★★★Hogs Back	5	50	20	6	6	75	✓	✓	✓		✓		[indoor pool] G	✓
HOLLINGBOURNE	★★★Great Danes	11	600	–	6	42	126		✓					[indoor pool] [squash]	
HOLMES CHAPEL	★★Old Vicarage	2	30	10	1	6	22		✓	✓	✓			–	✓
HOPE COVE	★★Cottage	1	50	–	–	–	35							–	
HOPWOOD	★★★Westmead	3	300	50	–	–	60		✓	✓		✓		–	✓
HORLEY	★★★★Gatwick Penta	15	150	150	5	10	260		✓	✓		✓	✓	[indoor pool] [squash] G	✓
	★★★Gatwick Post House	1	120	8	6	8	216	✓	✓	✓				[indoor pool]	✓
HORNCHURCH	★★★Hilton National	8	250	30	6	8	137	✓	✓	✓	✓	✓		–	✓
HORNING	★★★Petersfield House	1	70	50	1	10	18		✓					–	✓
HORSHAM	★★Ye Olde Kings Head	1	50	–	–	–	43		✓	✓				–	
HORTON-CUM-STUDLEY	★★★Studley Priory	2	35	16	2	8	19		✓	✓	✓			[tennis]	
HORWICH	★★Swallowfield	1	20	–	1	–	31	✓	✓	✓				–	✓
HOUNSLOW	★★★Master Robert	4	135	50	2	10	100	✓	✓	✓	✓	✓		–	✓
HOVE	★★★★Dudley	2	150	160	6	20	80	✓	✓	✓		✓		–	✓
	★★★Alexandra	4	50	140	2	12	61		✓	✓				–	
	★★★St Catherine's Lodge	3	60	20	2	10	50		✓	✓	✓	✓	✓	–	✓
	★★Whitehaven	2	20	10	2	10	17		✓	✓		✓		–	✓
HOVINGHAM	★★★Worsley Arms	1	80	15	1	15	23		✓	✓		✓		[squash]	✓
HOW CHAPEL	★★How Chapel Grange	1	100	70	3	70	26							[outdoor pool] G	
HOWTOWN	★★★Sharrow Bay	1	12	–	–	–	12							–	✓
HUDDERSFIELD	★★★Briar Court	1	80	–	3	24	48	✓	✓	✓		✓		–	✓
	★★★George	4	120	80	2	12	60	✓	✓	✓				–	✓
	★★★Old Golf House	3	70	20	2	20	50		✓	✓	✓			[golf] G	
	★★★Penine Hilton National	14	400	100	8	8	118	✓	✓	✓		✓		[indoor pool] G	✓
	★★Huddersfield	3	50	20	3	12	37	✓	✓	✓		✓		–	✓
HULL	★★★★Marina Post House	32	120	75	10	10	99	✓	✓	✓		✓	✓	[indoor pool] G	✓
	★★★Grange Park	4	350	240	10	20	109	✓	✓	✓		✓	✓	[indoor pool] G	✓
	★★★Pearson Park	2	36	18	1	8	35	✓	✓	✓				–	
	★★★Royal	7	400	120	4	20	125		✓	✓		✓		[indoor pool] G	✓
	★★★Waterfront	2	100	40	–	–	30	✓	✓	✓		✓		–	✓
	★★★Willerby Manor	4	500	110	–	–	36	✓	✓	✓		✓		–	✓
	★★Maxims	2	100	40	1	20	14	✓	✓					–	✓
HUNGERFORD	★★★Bear	5	100	15	4	15	41	✓	✓	✓		✓	✓	–	✓
HUNSTANTON	★★★Le Strange Arms	5	150	90	5	20	40	✓	✓	✓		✓		–	
HUNSTRETE	★★★★Hunstrete House	2	40	24	2	24	24		✓	✓				[outdoor pool] [tennis]	✓
HUNTINGDON	★★★George	4	120	50	4	24	50	✓	✓	✓	✓	✓		–	✓
	★★★Old Bridge	5	50	38	2	6	26	✓	✓	✓		✓		–	✓
	★★Alconbury House	3	100	22	2	6	22	✓	✓					[squash]	✓
HURLEY	★★★Ye Olde Bell	5	140	–	4	91	25		✓	✓		✓		–	✓
	★★East Arms	2	100	80	2	36	11	✓	✓	✓	✓	✓		–	
HURSTBOURNE TARRANT	★★Esseborne Manor	1	12	12	1	–	12		✓	✓				[tennis]	✓
HURST GREEN	★★★Shireburn Arms	1	75	25	1	15	14	✓		✓				–	
HYTHE	★★★★Imperial	1	200	–	4	10	100	✓	✓	✓	✓	✓		[indoor pool] [golf] [tennis] [squash] G	✓
	★★★Stade Court	1	35	–	2	10	43		✓	✓	✓	✓		[indoor pool] [golf] [tennis] [squash] G	✓
ILFRACOMBE	★★★Trimstone Manor	2	70	10	2	12	17		✓	✓		✓		[tennis]	
	★★Arlington	1	70	–	1	40	29	✓	✓	✓				[outdoor pool]	✓
	★★Carlton	1	50	–	–	–	51			✓		✓		–	✓
	★★Tracy House	1	22	–	–	–	11		✓					–	
ILKLEY	★★★Rombalds	2	50	20	2	8	16	✓	✓	✓	✓	✓	✓	–	✓
INGATESTONE	★★★★Heybridge Moat House	5	500	100	2	30	22	✓	✓	✓		✓		–	✓
INSTOW	★★★Commodore	1	120	–	1	12	20	✓	✓					–	✓
IPSWICH	★★★★Hintlesham Hall	3	100	58	2	18	33	✓	✓	✓		✓		[tennis]	✓
	★★★Ipswich Moat	8	500	380	9	10	74	✓	✓	✓		✓		–	✓
	★★★Marlborough	2	24	12	3	4	22		✓					–	✓
	★★★Post House	2	100	60	6	10	118		✓	✓				[outdoor pool]	✓
	★★Great White Horse	3	150	40	2	40	57	✓	✓	✓	✓	✓		–	✓

[indoor pool]=indoor swimming pool; [outdoor pool]=outdoor swimming pool; [golf]=golf; [tennis]=tennis; [squash]=squash; G=gymnasium

ENGLAND Town	Hotel	No. of conf. rooms	Seating capacity of main room	Total seating of additional rooms	No. of smaller rooms	Maximum capacity of smaller rooms	No. of bedrooms	Exhibition hall space	Photocopying	Projection/Video	Closed circuit TV	Audio	Interpreting	Sporting facilities available at the Hotel	Use of fax
ISLE OF WIGHT															
BEMBRIDGE	★★Birdham	1	28	–	1	28	14							–	
FRESHWATER BAY	★★★Farringford	1	20	–	–	–	16							⊃ ▣ ⚲	
RYDE	★★★Ryde Castle	3	175	50	2	28	17	✓	✓	✓		✓		–	✓
SANDOWN	★★★Melville Hall	4	150	120	2	30	33	✓	✓	✓		✓		⊃	
SEAVIEW	★★Seaview	1	20	–	–	–	16							–	✓
SHANKLIN	★★Shanklin Manor	3	70	40	4	30	38	✓		✓		✓		▭ ⊃ ⚲ G	
TOTLAND BAY	★★★Country Garden	1	20	–	1	20	18							–	
VENTNOR	★★★Ventnor Towers	2	80	45	2	10	27		✓	✓		✓	✓	⊃ ▣ ⚲	✓
ISLEWORTH	Osterley	4	250	10	1	10	62	✓	✓	✓		✓		–	✓
KEGWORTH	★★★Yew Lodge	4	100	120	4	8	54	✓	✓	✓	✓	✓		–	✓
KENDAL	★★★Riverside	1	200	52	4	24	47		✓	✓		✓		–	✓
	★★★Woolpack	4	100	30	6	12	53	✓	✓	✓	✓	✓		–	✓
	★★★County	2	70	30	3	6	31	✓	✓	✓	✓	✓		–	✓
	★★Garden House	1	18	–	–	–	10	✓	✓	✓				–	✓
KENILWORTH	★★★★De Montfort	4	300	100	11	10	96	✓	✓	✓	✓	✓		–	✓
	★★★Chesford Grange	–	750	–	10	8	130	✓	✓			✓		–	✓
	★★★Clarendon House	2	120	16	2	16	31	✓	✓	✓		✓		–	✓
KESWICK	★★★★Stakis Lodore Swiss	1	80	–	4	8	70		✓	✓				▭ ⊃ ⚲ ⚔ G	✓
	★★★Derwentwater	1	70	30	2	15	83	✓	✓	✓				–	✓
	★★★Queens	1	20	–	–	–	36		✓	✓				–	✓
	★★Red House	3	30	50	2	12	22		✓	✓			✓	⊃	✓
	★★Lyzzick Hall	–	–	–	6	20	20							⊃	
KETTERING	★★George	1	52	25	2	10	52	✓	✓	✓	✓	✓	✓	–	✓
KEXBY	★★★Kexby Bridge	2	100	30	10	7	32	✓	✓	✓		✓		–	✓
KIDDERMINSTER	★★★Gainsborough House	3	250	155	3	25	46	✓	✓	✓		✓		–	✓
KINGHAM	★★★Mill House	2	30	20	3	–	21		✓	✓	✓	✓		–	✓
KINGSBRIDGE	★★★Buckland Tout Saints	2	20	14	–	–	12		✓					–	✓
KING'S LYNN	★★★Butterfly	1	55	80	4	20	50	✓	✓	✓				–	✓
	★★★Dukes Head	1	230	85	2	45	72	✓	✓	✓		✓		–	✓
	★★★Knights Hill	1	300	165	2	45	58	✓	✓	✓		✓		▭ ⚲ G	✓
	★★Globe	1	50	–	1	6	40		✓	✓		✓		–	✓
KINGSTON UPON THAMES	★★★Kingston Lodge	1	60	–	3	10	61		✓	✓				–	✓
KINGTON	★★Burton	2	150	30	–	–	15	✓					–	✓	
KINTBURY	★★★Elcot Park Resort	3	40	60	3	20	34		✓	✓		✓		–	✓
KIRBY LONSDALE	★★★Royal	2	60	50	1	10	19	✓	✓	✓		✓		–	✓
	★★Whoop Hall Inn	3	60	130	1	30	15	✓	✓					–	✓
KIRBY STEPHEN	★★King's Arms	3	40	120	2	–	10							–	
KNARESBOROUGH	★★★Dower House	2	70	20	3	10	32		✓					▭ G	✓
KNUTSFORD	★★★Cottons	6	200	360	2	20	86		✓	✓	✓	✓		▭ ⚲ G	✓
	★★★Royal George	3	80	60	6	6	31	✓	✓	✓	✓	✓	✓	–	✓
LANCASTER	★★★★Post House	5	120	120	6	8	117		✓	✓				▭ G	✓
	★★★Royal King's Arms	1	70	–	3	10	55		✓	✓		✓	✓	–	✓
LANGPORT	★★Langport Arms	3	180	70	2	40	8							–	
LARKFIELD	★★★Larkfield	3	80	65	–	–	52	✓	✓	✓				–	✓
LAUNCESTON	★★★Eagle House	1	170	–	2	20	10	✓	✓	✓		✓	✓	–	✓
	★★White Hart	1	250	–	2	40	27		✓	✓				–	✓
LAVENHAM	★★★★Swan	3	40	37	2	8	47	✓	✓	✓				–	✓
LEAMINGTON SPA	★★★Falstaff	5	60	65	3	10	65		✓	✓	✓	✓		–	✓
	★★★Manor House	4	100	60	4	15	53		✓	✓	✓	✓		–	✓
	★★★Regent	6	100	–	–	30	80		✓			✓		–	✓
	★★Abbacourt	1	30	–	1	20	26							–	
	★★Adams	2	14	14	–	–	11		✓					–	✓
	★★Angel	2	90	50	2	10	36	✓	✓	✓	✓			–	✓
LEDBURY	★★Royal Oak	1	140	–	2	50	10	✓	✓	✓		✓		–	✓
LEEDS	★★★★Hilton	9	400	–	8	20	210	✓	✓	✓		✓		–	✓
	★★★★Queens	13	700	800	5	10	188	✓	✓	✓		✓	✓	–	✓
	★★★Hilton National	14	250	100	10	25	144	✓	✓	✓	✓	✓		▭ G	✓
	★★★Merrion	1	80	–	3	6	120	✓	✓	✓		✓		–	✓
	★★★Parkway	2	250	100	6	5	103	✓	✓	✓		✓		▭ ⚲ G	✓
	★★Stakis Windmill	2	250	100	3	30	100	✓	✓					–	✓
	★★Golden Lion	3	100	140	–	–	89		✓	✓				–	✓
	★★Wellesley	2	200	50	5	–	54		✓	✓		✓		–	✓
LEEMING BAR	★★★Leeming Motel	2	90	30	4	8	40		✓	✓		✓		–	✓
	★★White Rose	1	40	–	1	15	18		✓					–	✓

▭=indoor swimming pool; ⊃=outdoor swimming pool; ▣=golf; ⚲=tennis; ⚔=squash; G=gymnasium

ENGLAND Town	Hotel	No. of conf. rooms	Seating capacity of main room	Total seating of additional rooms	No. of smaller rooms	Maximum capacity of smaller rooms	No. of bedrooms	Exhibition hall space	Photocopying	Projection/Video	Closed circuit TV	Audio	Interpreting	Sporting facilities available at the Hotel	Use of fax
LEICESTER	★★★★Grand	4	450	400	8	–	92	✓	✓	✓	✓	✓		–	✓
	★★★Belmont	4	120	65	3	10	68		✓	✓	✓	✓		–	✓
	★★★Forest Moat House	1	100	–	4	6	34		✓	✓				–	✓
	★★★Leicestershire Moat House	5	250	340	4	10	57	✓	✓	✓		✓		–	✓
	★★★Park International	7	400	555	5	80	209	✓	✓	✓	✓	✓		–	✓
	★★★Post House	4	120	120	5	12	172	✓	✓	✓		✓		–	✓
	★★★St James	1	[illegible]	[illegible]	[illegible]	[illegible]	[illegible]	✓	✓	✓		✓		G	✓
	★★★Stage	4	250	–	2	25	18	✓	✓	✓		✓		–	✓
	★★★★Holiday Inn	5	300	147	4	8	188	✓	✓	✓		✓		[indoor pool] G	✓
LEIGH	★★★Greyhound	1	60	–	–	–	48		✓	✓		✓		–	✓
LEIGH-ON-SEA	★Manor House	1	50	–	1	20	15	✓				✓		–	
LEIGHTON BUZZARD	★★★Swan	1	30	–	1	8	38		✓	✓				–	✓
LENHAM	★★Dog and Bear	1	60	–	3	6	21	✓	✓	✓		✓		–	✓
LEOMINSTER	★★Royal Oak	3	250	60	2	30	18	✓	✓	✓				–	
	★★Talbot	3	150	63	–	–	23	✓	✓			✓		–	
LEWES	★★★Shelleys	1	50	–	1	10	21	✓	✓	✓				–	✓
	★★White Hart	3	200	100	3	8	40		✓	✓				–	✓
LEYLAND	★★★Penguin	11	200	397	6	12	93	✓	✓	✓		✓		–	✓
LICHFIELD	★★★George	3	100	56	2	20	38	✓	✓	✓		✓		–	✓
	★★★Little Barrow	1	100	–	–	–	24			✓				–	✓
	★★Angel Croft	1	20	–	–	–	19		✓					–	✓
LIFTON	★★★Arundell Arms	3	60	42	2	–	29		✓	✓	✓			–	✓
LIMPLEY STOKE	★★Limpley Stoke	5	120	190	4	60	55	✓	✓	✓		✓		–	✓
LINCOLN	★★★★White Hart	4	90	120	3	15	50		✓	✓		✓	✓	–	✓
	★★★Eastgate Post House	4	70	25	1	6	71		✓	✓			✓	–	✓
	★★★Four Seasons	1	250	–	1	35	24	✓	✓	✓		✓	✓	–	✓
	★★★Moor Lodge	5	180	–	1	10	25	✓	✓	✓		✓		–	✓
	★★★Washingborough Hall	2	50	12	–	–	12		✓	✓				[outdoor pool]	
	★★Barbican	3	40	–	3	15	19	✓	✓					–	✓
	★★Hillcrest	1	20	–	–	–	17		✓	✓				–	✓
LISKEARD	★★Country Castle	2	40	12	–	–	11							[outdoor pool]	
LIVERPOOL	★★★★Atlantic Tower	7	110	190	7	8	226	✓	✓	✓	✓	✓		–	✓
	★★★★Liverpool Moat House	10	450	–	3	15	251	✓	✓	✓	✓	✓	✓	[indoor pool] G	✓
	★★★★St Georges	4	250	70	5	25	155	✓	✓	✓	✓	✓		–	✓
	★★★Cherry Tree	4	130	90	4	40	50		✓					–	✓
	★★★Crest	7	600	–	13	20	150	✓	✓	✓	✓	✓		–	✓
	★★★Park	2	100	60	2	25	60	✓	✓	✓	✓	✓		–	✓
	★★Grange	1	30	–	3	6	25	✓	✓					–	✓
	★★Green Park	1	80	–	1	12	23			✓		✓		–	
LIZARD	★★Housel Bay	–	–	–	1	20	23		✓					–	✓
LONGHAM	★★★Bridge House	1	100	–	2	15	37		✓			✓		–	✓
LONG MELFORD	★★★Bull	3	60	35	3	6	25		✓	✓				[indoor pool] G	✓
LOOE	★★★Talland Bay	1	50	–	2	8	24	✓	✓	✓				[outdoor pool]	✓
	★★★Hannafore Point	2	40	24	–	–	38	✓	✓	✓		✓		[indoor pool] [tennis] [squash] G	✓
LOSTWITHIEL	★★Restormel Lodge	2	80	40	1	14	34		✓	✓		✓		[outdoor pool]	✓
LOUGHBOROUGH	★★★Cedars	1	40	–	1	16	37		✓					[outdoor pool]	✓
	★★★Kings Head	2	120	50	2	20	78	✓	✓	✓				–	✓
	★★Great Central	2	80	30	–	–	18	✓	✓	✓	✓			–	✓
LOWER BEEDING	★★★★South Lodge	2	80	60	3	16	39		✓	✓				[tennis]	✓
LOWER DICKER	★★★Bishop Farm	2	120	40	–	12	46	✓	✓	✓				[outdoor pool] [tennis]	✓
LOWESTOFT	★★★Victoria	4	200	120	–	–	35	✓	✓	✓	✓	✓	✓	–	✓
LUDLOW	★★★Dinham Hall	2	24	10	2	10	12		✓	✓				G	✓
	★★★Feathers	2	100	60	5	40	40	✓	✓	✓				–	✓
	★★★Overton Grange	2	120	30	2	30	16	✓	✓	✓		✓		–	✓
LULWORTH	★Bishops Cottage	2	25	15	1	12	14							[outdoor pool]	
LUTON	★★★Chiltern	3	250	30	3	12	93	✓	✓	✓		✓		–	✓
	★★★Luton Crest	1	100	400	10	12	117		✓	✓				–	✓
	★★★Red Lion	1	50	–	1	20	39		✓	✓				–	✓
LUTTERWORTH	★★★Denbigh Arms	1	60	–	2	15	34	✓	✓	✓	✓	✓		–	✓
	★★★Greyhound Coaching Inn	2	64	20	1	10	29		✓	✓				–	✓
LYME REGIS	★★★Mariners	1	42	–	–	–	16		✓					–	✓
	★★Buena Vista	2	35	30	2	12	19	✓	✓					–	
	★★Orchard Country	2	25	20	–	–	12			✓			✓	–	
LYMINGTON	★★★Stanwell House	2	20	20	1	16	35	✓	✓	✓				–	✓
LYMM	★★★Lymm	2	120	–	3	30	69		✓	✓		✓		–	✓
LYMPSHAM	★★Batch Farm Country	1	70	–	2	20	8	✓		✓				–	
LYNDHURST	★★★Beaulieu	1	75	–	1	5	10		✓					–	✓
	★★★Crown	4	70	55	6	10	40		✓	✓	✓	✓		[squash] G	✓

[indoor pool]=indoor swimming pool; [outdoor pool]=outdoor swimming pool; [golf]=golf; [tennis]=tennis; [squash]=squash; G=gymnasium

ENGLAND Town	Hotel	No. of conf. rooms	Seating capacity of main room	Total seating of additional rooms	No. of smaller rooms	Maximum capacity of smaller rooms	No. of bedrooms	Exhibition hall space	Photocopying	Projection/Video	Closed circuit TV	Audio	Interpreting	Sporting facilities available at the Hotel	Use of fax
	★★★Forest Lodge	1	120	–	3	20	19		✓					outdoor pool	✓
	★★★Lyndhurst Park	2	150	120	3	20	59	✓	✓	✓		✓		tennis, outdoor pool	✓
LYNTON	★★★Lynton Cottage	1	20	–	–	–	17		✓	✓			✓	–	✓
	★★Crown	1	50	–	2	–	16	✓		✓		✓		–	
LYTHAM	★★★★Clifton Arms	3	300	250	2	20	41		✓	✓		✓		–	✓
	★★★Chadwick	2	70	70	6	25	70	✓	✓	✓		✓		indoor pool	✓
	★★★Dalmeny	6	200	200	15	15	99		✓	✓		✓		indoor pool, squash	✓
	★★Bedford	3	150	120	1	25	36	✓	✓	✓		✓		G	✓
	★★Glendower	6	100	90	7	70	60	✓	✓	✓		✓	✓	indoor pool	✓
	★Lindum	1	70	–	4	10	80		✓	✓		✓		–	✓
MACCLESFIELD	★★★★Shrigley Hall	5	200	125	4	25	58	✓	✓	✓		✓	✓	indoor pool, golf, squash, tennis, G	✓
	★★Park Villa	1	25	–	2	15	7		✓	✓		✓	✓	–	✓
MAIDENHEAD	★★★★Fredrick's	3	50	75	1	18	37		✓	✓	✓	✓		–	✓
	★★★★Holiday Inn	5	400	–	6	40	189	✓	✓	✓		✓		indoor pool, squash, G	✓
	★★★★Monkey Island	1	150	–	4	16	27		✓					–	✓
	★★★Taplow House	1	60	–	3	12	30		✓	✓		✓		–	✓
	★★Norfolk House	2	30	25	2	15	12		✓	✓	✓	✓	✓	outdoor pool	✓
	★★Thames	1	65	–	2	6	34		✓					–	✓
MAIDSTONE	★★★★Tudor Park	6	275	–	4	10	119	✓	✓	✓				indoor pool, golf, tennis, squash, G	✓
	★★★Wateringbury	2	80	50	–	–	28			✓				–	
	★★Grangemoor	2	150	45	1	22	36		✓	✓		✓		–	✓
MALMESBURY	★★★Old Bell	3	25	25	–	–	37	✓	✓	✓				–	✓
	★★★Whatley Manor	2	35	20	2	8	29		✓	✓		✓		outdoor pool, tennis	✓
MALVERN	★★★Abbey	6	350	250	4	16	106	✓	✓			✓		–	✓
	★★★Colwall Park	2	100	20	1	10	20		✓	✓				–	✓
	★★★Foley Arms	2	120	60	3	20	28		✓	✓				–	
	★★Mount Pleasant	4	90	50	3	30	15	✓	✓	✓		✓		–	✓
	★★Royal Malvern	1	12	–	–	–	14	✓	✓					–	✓
MANCHESTER	★★★★★Hotel Piccadilly	8	70	300	10	10	271	✓	✓	✓		✓		indoor pool, G	✓
	★★★★Copthorne	1	150	–	7	10	166	✓	✓	✓				indoor pool, G	✓
	★★★★Holiday Inn	9	600	947	7	6	303	✓	✓	✓	✓	✓	✓	indoor pool, squash, G	✓
	★★★★Sashas	8	700	–	–	–	223	✓	✓	✓	✓	✓	✓	indoor pool, G	✓
	★★★Post House	7	150	–	10	15	200	✓	✓	✓		✓		–	✓
	★★★Willow Bank	1	50	–	3	10	122		✓	✓				–	✓
	★★Royals	3	80	80	4	10	34		✓	✓		✓		–	✓
	★Baron	2	30	20	2	10	16	✓		✓				–	
MANCHESTER AIRPORT	★★★★Excelsior	4	220	65	6	6	300	✓	✓	✓		✓		–	✓
	★★★★Hilton International	4	200	150	9	8	223	✓	✓					indoor pool	✓
MANSFIELD	★★Pine Lodge	1	50	–	2	20	21		✓	✓	✓	✓		–	✓
MARAZION	★★Mount Haven	1	20	–	–	–	17		✓	✓				–	
MARGARETTING	★★★Ivy Hill	1	12	–	4	12	18		✓	✓				outdoor pool, tennis	✓
MARKET DRAYTON	★★★Goldstone Hall	2	80	26		60	20	✓	✓	✓					
	★★Corbet Arms	2	180	24	1	12	12	✓	✓					–	✓
MARKET HARBOROUGH	★★★Three Swans	2	75	45	2	8	37		✓	✓		✓		–	✓
MARLBOROUGH	★★★Castle and Ball	1	30	–	3	10	36		✓	✓				–	✓
MARLEY HILL	★★★Beamish Park	2	80	25	–	–	47		✓	✓	✓	✓		–	✓
MARLOW	★★★★Compleat Angler	3	125	55	1	12	46		✓	✓	✓	✓	✓	tennis	✓
MARKYATE	★★★Hertfordshire Moat House	7	200	400	16	8	95	✓	✓	✓	✓	✓		–	✓
MARYPORT	★★Ellenbank	1	300	–	1	15	26							–	
	★★Waverley	1	40	–	2	20	20		✓			✓		–	
MATLOCK	★★★Riber Hall	1	14	–	–	–	11		✓	✓				tennis	✓
MATLOCK BATH	★★★New Bath	1	150	–	5	30	55	✓	✓	✓	✓	✓		indoor pool, outdoor pool, golf, tennis	✓
	★★★Temple	3	80	120	2	8	14	✓	✓	✓				–	✓
MAWGAN PORTH	★★Tredragon	1	60	–	3	20	30		✓	✓				indoor pool, G	✓
MAWNAN SMITH	★★★Budock Vean	1	60	–	3	10	59		✓					indoor pool, golf, tennis	✓
MELKSHAM	★★Conigre Farm	1	40	–	1	20	9	✓						–	
	★★Kings Arms	2	30	20	1	10	14							–	✓
MELTON MOWBRAY	★★★★Stapleford Park	2	300	50	2	–	35	✓	✓	✓	✓	✓	✓	tennis	✓
	★★Sysonby Knoll	1	24	–	1	8	26							outdoor pool	✓
MERIDEN	★★★Manor	4	300	202	4	8	74	✓	✓			✓		outdoor pool	✓
MICKLETON	★★★Three Ways	3	75	95	3	12	40		✓					–	✓
MIDDLEHAM	★★Millers House	1	15	–	1	10	7							–	
MIDDLESBOROUGH	★★★★Hospitality Inn	5	400	–	–	10	180	✓	✓	✓		✓		G	✓
	★★Highfield	1	75	–	–	–	23		✓	✓				–	✓
MIDDLETON	★★Jersey Arms	1	20	–	2	6	16		✓	✓				–	✓
MIDDLE WALLOP	★★★Fifehead Manor	2	20	10	–	–	16		✓				✓	–	✓
MIDDLEHURST	★★★Spread Eagle	2	35	14	2	8	41		✓	✓	✓	✓		–	✓

indoor pool=indoor swimming pool; outdoor pool=outdoor swimming pool; golf=golf; tennis=tennis; squash=squash; G=gymnasium

ENGLAND Town	Hotel	No. of conf. rooms	Seating capacity of main room	Total seating of additional rooms	No. of smaller rooms	Maximum capacity of smaller rooms	No. of bedrooms	Exhibition hall space	Photocopying	Projection/Video	Closed circuit TV	Audio	Interpreting	Sporting facilities available at the Hotel	Use of fax
MIDSOMER NORTON	★★★Centurion	5	100	75	–	–	44	√	√	√		√		▤ ⛳ 🏃	√
MILDENHALL	★★★Riverside	1	60	–	–	–	20	√		√		√		–	√
	★★★Smoke House Inn	10	120	300	10	10	110	√	√	√	√	√	√	–	√
	★Bell	2	120	26	–	–	17	√	√	√				–	√
MILFORD ON SEA	★★★Westover	3	45	45	3	20	15	√	√	√		√		–	√
MILLAND	★★★Milland Place	1	18	–	1	14	18		√	√	√	√	√	–	√
MILTON COMMON	★★★Belfry	12	250	150			67	√	√	√	√	√	√	▤ G	√
MILTON KEYNES	★★★★Post House	3	150	–	12	8	163		√	√				▤ G	√
	★★★Broughton	1	50	–	2	10	30		√	√		√		–	√
	★★★Friendly	1	120	–	3	25	50		√	√		√		G	√
MINEHEAD	★★★Northfield	1	100	–	2	12	24	√	√	√				▤ G	
MINSTER-ON-SEA	★★Abbey	1	70	–	2	12	50	√	√	√		√		–	√
MORECAMBE	★★★Elms	4	200	120	3	50	40	√	√	√		√		–	√
	★★★Midland	2	150	40	1	–	46	√	√	√		√		–	√
	★★★Strathmore	1	250	–	5	80	51		√	√				–	√
	★★Clarendon	3	60	50	3	10	31					√		–	
	★Channings	1	40	–	2	20	20	√						–	
MORETON-IN-MARSH	★★★Manor House	1	60	–	1	12	38	√	√					▤ 🎾	√
	★★Redesdale	1	80	–	2	10	17	√	√	√		√		–	√
	★★White Hart Royal	1	70	–	2	15	18		√	√				–	
MOTTRAM ST. ANDREW	★★★Mottram Hall	1	220	–	5	10	95		√	√		√		▤ 🎾 🏃 G	√
MUCH BIRCH	★★★Pilgrim	1	45	–	1	10	20		√	√				–	√
MUDEFORD	★★★Avonmouth	2	25	15	1	6	41		√	√				⌓	√
MULLION	★★★Polurrian	2	100	60	2	10	40		√	√				▤ ⌓ 🎾 🏃 G	√
NANTWICH	★★★Alvaston	5	300	105	4	40	88	√	√	√	√	√	√	▤ 🎾 🏃 G	√
	★★★Rookery Hall	4	60	90	4	12	45		√	√	√	√	√	🎾	√
NEWARK ON-TRENT	★★Grange	1	20	–	–	–	9							–	√
NEWBURY	★★★★Foley Lodge	4	200	–	6	12	70	√	√					▤	√
	★★★★Regency Park	5	65	–	3	18	50	√	√	√	√	√		–	√
	★★★Chequers	1	70	–	3	12	56		√	√		√		–	√
	★★Enborne Grange	1	60	–	1	6	25		√	√				–	√
NEWBY BRIDGE	★★★Lakeside	1	100	–	4	30	79	√	√	√				–	√
	★★★Whitewater	1	70	–	3	6	35		√	√	√	√		▤ 🎾 🏃 G	√
NEWCASTLE UNDER-LYME	★★★Clayton Lodge	3	300	80	3	30	50	√	√	√		√		–	√
	★★★Post House	3	60	40	12	10	126	√	√	√				▤ G	√
	★★Borough Arms	2	90	35	–	–	45	√	√	√				–	√
	★Deansfield	1	30	–	1	15	11		√	√				–	
NEWCASTLE UPON TYNE	★★★★Holiday Inn	3	400	160	4	12	150	√	√	√	√	√		▤ G	√
	★★★★Swallow Gosforth Park	3	600	300	8	12	178	√	√	√	√	√		▤ 🎾 🏃 G	√
	★★★Airport Moat House	3	400	100	10	8	100	√	√	√		√	√	–	√
	★★★Crest	7	500	120	12	–	166	√	√	√	√	√		–	√
	★★★Hospitality Inn	2	120	–	4	60	89		√	√	√	√	√	–	√
	★★★Imperial Swallow	5	130	115	5	8	129	√	√	√				▤ G	√
	★★★Northumbria	1	70	–	–	–	70		√	√	√	√	√	–	√
	★★★Novotel	3	250	100	3	16	126	√			√	√		▤	√
	★★Cairn	2	50	40	–	–	51	√	√	√		√		–	√
NEWMARKET	★★★Newmarket Moat House	2	50	50	2	18	49		√	√	√	√		–	√
NEW MILTON	★★★★Chewton Glen	7	80	50	–	8	58	√	√	√	√	√	√	▤ ⌓ ⛳ 🎾 G	√
NEWPORT	★★Royal Victory	1	150	–	4	30	24	√	√	√		√		–	√
NEWPORT PAGNELL	★★★Coach House	2	220	60	7	6	49		√	√		√		G	√
	★★Swan Revived	2	80	40	2	16	40	√	√	√				–	√
NEWQUAY	★★★Barrowfield	2	100	–	2	50	81	√	√	√		√		▤ ⌓ G	√
	★★★Riviera	2	100	70	1	6	50	√	√	√		√		⌓ 🏃	
NEWTON ABBOT	★★★Passage House	1	150	–	2	16	39	√	√	√				▤ G	√
	★★Queen's	1	125	–	–	–	24	√						–	√
NEWTON FERRIERS	★★River Yealm	1	60	–	–	–	19	√						–	
NORMAN CROSS	★★★Crest	2	35	–	4	–	96		√	√	√	√		▤ G	√
NORTHALLERTON	★★Golden Lion	2	100	100	2	10	28		√	√		√		–	√
NORTHAMPTON	★★★★Swallow	1	220	–	11	14	122	√	√	√		√		▤ G	√
	★★★Grand	3	125	130	–	10	62	√	√	√	√	√		–	√
	★★★Heyford Manor	3	80	60	2	6	55		√	√	√	√		G	√
	★★★Northampton Moat House	5	600	400	9	50	140	√	√	√	√	√	√	–	√
	★★★Westone Moat House	3	150	150	4	15	66	√	√	√	√	√		G	√
	★★Queen Eleanor	2	80	20	–	–	20		√	√				–	√
NORTH STIFFORD	★★★Stifford Moat House	4	120	200	4	16	98		√	√		√		🎾	√

▤=indoor swimming pool; ⌓=outdoor swimming pool; ⛳=golf; 🎾=tennis; 🏃=squash; G=gymnasium

ENGLAND Town	Hotel	No. of conf. rooms	Seating capacity of main room	Total seating of additional rooms	No. of smaller rooms	Maximum capacity of smaller rooms	No. of bedrooms	Exhibition hall space	Photocopying	Projection/Video	Closed circuit TV	Audio	Interpreting	Sporting facilities available at the Hotel	Use of fax
NORTH WALSHAM	★★Felmingham Country House	1	15	–	–	–	18		✓	✓		✓		outdoor swimming pool, tennis, squash, gymnasium	✓
NORTH WALTHAM	★★★Wheatsheaf	1	80	–	1	10	28			✓				–	
NORTHWICH	★★★Nunsmere Hall	1	16	–	1	–	15		✓	✓				–	✓
	★★Blue Cap	1	150	–	–	–	12		✓	✓				–	✓
NORWICH	★★★Barnham Broom	3	250	–	4	16	52	✓	✓	✓		✓		indoor swimming pool, golf, tennis, squash, gymnasium	✓
	★★★Maid's Head	1	130	–	–	–	81		✓	✓		✓	✓	–	✓
	★★★Nelson	2	90	40	3	10	121		✓	✓		✓		–	✓
	★★★Norwich	2	300	80	3	50	100	✓	✓	✓		✓		–	✓
	★★★Post House	1	100	–	4	10	116		✓					indoor swimming pool, gymnasium	✓
	★★Lansdowne	3	120	69	4	6	45	✓	✓	✓				–	✓
	★★Oakland	1	140	–	3	–	39	✓	✓	✓		✓		–	✓
NOTTINGHAM	★★★★Albany	3	600	180	6	20	139	✓	✓	✓		✓		–	✓
	★★★★Nottingham Moat House	1	200	–	11	90	–		✓	✓		✓		–	
	★★★★Royal Moat House	14	500	–	–	20	201	✓	✓	✓		✓		squash, gymnasium	✓
	★★★★Victoria	10	200	–	6	20	166	✓	✓					–	✓
	★★★Bestwood Lodge	1	200	–	6	35	39	✓	✓	✓		✓		tennis	✓
	★★★Walton's	1	20	–	–	–	17							–	✓
OAKHAM	★★Boultons	2	100	50	–	–	25		✓	✓				–	✓
OLDHAM	★★★Avant	4	300	80	4	30	103	✓	✓	✓		✓		–	✓
	★★★Bower	2	200	80	2	20	65	✓	✓	✓		✓		–	✓
	★★★Smokies Park	4	400	150	10	10	47	✓	✓					gymnasium	✓
	★★High Point	1	30	–	–	–	18		✓	✓		✓		–	✓
OLD SODBURY	★★★Cross Hands	2	70	60	2	15	24	✓		✓	✓			–	✓
ONNERLEY	★★Wheatsheaf	1	24	–	–	–	5		✓	✓		✓		–	✓
OSSETT	★★★Post House	7	160	–	8	8	160	✓	✓	✓		✓		–	✓
OSWESTRY	★★★Wynnstay	3	200	–	3	40	26	✓	✓	✓		✓		–	✓
OTLEY	★★★Chevin	2	120	50	3	40	52		✓	✓		✓		tennis	✓
OTTERBURN	★★★Percy Arms	1	70	–	2	30	28		✓	✓		✓		–	✓
OTTERY ST. MARY	★★Tumbling Weir	1	120	–	–	–	13		✓	✓				–	✓
OUNDLE	★★★Talbot	4	80	100	2	15	39		✓	✓		✓		–	✓
OWER	★★★New Forest Heathlands	5	200	170	11	12	52		✓	✓	✓	✓	✓	–	✓
OXFORD	★★★★Randolph	4	30	–	4	6	109		✓	✓	✓	✓	✓	–	✓
	★★★Cotswold Lodge	3	100	–	9	8	50	✓	✓	✓	✓	✓		–	✓
	★★★Eastgate	1	15	–	7	6	43		✓	✓				–	✓
	★★★Linton Lodge	5	120	175	2	6	71	✓	✓	✓		✓		–	✓
	★★★Oxford Moat House	10	150	–	19	8	155		✓	✓	✓	✓		indoor swimming pool, squash, gymnasium	✓
	★★Royal Oxford	2	50	40	6	8	25		✓					–	✓
	★★Victoria	1	20	–	–	–	23							–	
	★★Westwood Country	1	50	–	2	24	27		✓	✓				gymnasium	✓
OXTED	★★Hoskins	2	35	20	1	10	11		✓	✓				–	✓
PADSTOW	★★★Metropole	1	40	–	1	15	44		✓	✓				outdoor swimming pool	✓
PAIGNTON	★★★Palace	1	45	–	2	12	52		✓	✓				outdoor swimming pool, tennis, squash, gymnasium	✓
	★★Sunhill	1	50	–	–	–	29			✓				–	✓
PANGBOURNE	★★★Copper Inn	2	60	16	1	10	22		✓	✓		✓		–	✓
	★★George	1	120	–	3	10	17	✓	✓	✓				–	✓
PARKGATE	★★★Ship	1	24	–	–	–	26		✓	✓				–	
	★★Parkgate	4	110	170	–	–	27		✓	✓		✓		–	✓
PATELEY BRIDGE	★★Harefield Hall	2	70	20	3	6	26			✓		✓		–	✓
PEASLAKE	★★Hurtwood Inn	3	30	20	2	6	18	✓	✓	✓		✓		–	
PENCRAIG	★★Pencraig Court	1	25	–	1	12	11							–	
PENRITH	★★★★North Lakes	4	200	175	7	12	85		✓	✓	✓	✓		indoor swimming pool, squash, gymnasium	✓
	★★★George	2	140	30	1	6	30			✓				–	✓
PETERBOROUGH	★★★★Swallow	3	300	–	11	30	163	✓	✓	✓	✓	✓		indoor swimming pool, gymnasium	✓
	★★★Butterfly	1	80	–	5	40	70		✓	✓				–	✓
	★★★Moat House	9	400	600	4	8	125	✓	✓			✓		indoor swimming pool, gymnasium	✓
PICKERING	★★Forest and Vale	2	120	60	3	40	17		✓					–	✓
PICKHILL	★★Nags Head	2	34	20	–	–	15		✓	✓		✓		–	✓
PLYMOUTH	★★★★Copthorne Plymouth	2	34	20	–	–	15		✓	✓		✓		–	✓
	★★★★Plymouth Moat House	6	425	340	10	20	213	✓	✓	✓		✓		indoor swimming pool, gymnasium	✓
	★★★Duke of Cornwall	6	300	–	2	20	70	✓	✓	✓		✓		–	✓
	★★★Mayflower Post House	1	80	–	4	12	106		✓	✓				indoor swimming pool	✓
	★★★Strathmore	1	90	–	1	16	54							–	✓
	★★Camelot	1	80	–	–	–	17		✓					–	✓
	★★Langdon Court	1	25	–	2	12	15	✓	✓	✓				–	✓
	★Imperial	1	30	–	–	–	22	✓	✓	✓				–	
PLYMOUTH PLYMPTON	★★Elfordleigh	2	100	30	1	6	18	✓	✓	✓	✓			indoor swimming pool, outdoor swimming pool, golf, tennis, squash, gymnasium	✓
POCKLINGTON	★★Feathers	1	20	–	2	–	12							–	

indoor swimming pool = indoor swimming pool; *outdoor swimming pool* = outdoor swimming pool; *golf* = golf; *tennis* = tennis; *squash* = squash; **G** = gymnasium

ENGLAND Town	Hotel	No. of conf. rooms	Seating capacity of main room	Total seating of additional rooms	No. of smaller rooms	Maximum capacity of smaller rooms	No. of bedrooms	Exhibition hall space	Photocopying	Projection/Video	Closed circuit TV	Audio	Interpreting	Sporting facilities available at the Hotel	Use of fax
POOLE	★★★★Hospitality Inn	1	60	–	2	6	68		✓					–	✓
	★★★Dolphin	1	60	–	1	20	66		✓					–	✓
	★★★Haven	5	150	–	13	10	96	✓	✓	✓		✓		▤ ⊇ ℛ G	✓
	★★★Salterns	1	50	–	3	25	16	✓	✓	✓		✓		ℛ	✓
	★★★Sandbanks	7	170	–	6	8	105	✓	✓	✓		✓		▤ G	✓
PORLOCK WEIR	★★★Anchor & Ship	1	40	–	3	10	46		✓		✓			–	✓
PORT ISAAC	★★Castle Rock	–	36	–	2	6	17	✓				✓		–	
PORTSCATHO	★★Roseland House	1	50	–	1	10	18							–	
PORTSMOUTH	★★★★Holiday Inn	4	300	290	4	15	170	✓	✓	✓	✓	✓		▤ ℛ G	✓
	★★★Hospitality Inn	2	250	60	3	50	115	✓	✓	✓		✓		–	✓
	★★Arcade	2	70	40	–	–	144		✓	✓				–	✓
	★★Keppel's Head	2	60	30	2	15	27		✓	✓				–	✓
PRESTBURY	★★★Bridge	2	50	28	2	8	23	✓	✓	✓	✓	✓		–	✓
PRESTON	★★★★Broughton Park	7	200	100	4	10	98	✓	✓	✓				▤ 🎾 ℛ G	✓
	★★★Barton Grange	4	300	–	5	10	66	✓	✓	✓		✓		▤	✓
	★★★Swallow Trafalgar	7	250	200	6	12	78	✓	✓	✓		✓		▤ ℛ G	✓
	★★★Tickled Trout	5	100	175	10	10	72	✓	✓	✓		✓		▤	✓
PRINCES RISBOROUGH	★★Rose and Crown	1	20	–	1	15	17		✓					–	✓
PRINCETHORPE	★★Woodhouse	1	60	–	2	12	17	✓	✓	✓		✓	✓	⊇ 🎾	✓
PULBOROUGH	★★Chequers	2	16	14	–	–	11		✓	✓		✓		–	✓
RAMSBOTTOM	★★★Old Hill	2	30	30	–	–	36		✓	✓	✓			▤ G	✓
RANGEWORTHY	★★Rangeworthy Court	1	15	–	–	–	–		✓	✓				⊇	✓
RAVENGLASS	★Pennington Arms	2	60	30	2	30	17							–	
RAVENSCAR	★★★Raven Hall	5	100	126	3	40	54		✓	✓				⊇ ⛳ 🎾	
READING	★★★★Ramada	8	220	8	8	59	196	✓	✓	✓				▤ G	✓
	★★★★Reading Moat House	7	80	205	9	6	96		✓					G	✓
	★★★Mill House	1	30	–	–	6	10		✓	✓				–	
	★★★Post House	3	120	35	10	10	143		✓	✓		✓		▤ G	✓
	★★★Rainbow Corner	1	40	–	–	–	22		✓					–	✓
	★★George	2	30	15	–	–	68		✓	✓				–	✓
REDBOURN	★★★Aubrey Park	3	75	60	10	12	119		✓	✓		✓		⊇	✓
REDCAR	★★★Royal York	3	300	200	2	50	51	✓	✓			✓		–	✓
REDDITCH	★★★South Crest	1	106	15	2	50	58		✓					–	✓
REDHILL	★★★Nutfield Priory	7	100	126	5	20	36		✓	✓				▤ ℛ G	✓
REDRUTH	★★★Penventon	5	250	130	5	30	55	✓	✓	✓	✓	✓	✓	▤ G	
	★★Aviary Court	1	25	–	–	–	6							–	
REIGATE	★★★Bridge House	2	40	30	–	–	40	✓	✓	✓		✓		–	✓
	★★★Reigate Manor	5	200	240	4	–	51	✓	✓					G	✓
RETFORD	★★★West Retford	4	120	105	–	8	63	✓	✓	✓	✓	✓		–	✓
RICHMOND	★★★★Petersham	2	80	20	2	32	56		✓	✓				–	✓
	★★★Richmond Hill	7	180	88	5	6	130	✓	✓					ℛ	✓
RIPON	★★★Ripon Spa	3	160	110	2	20	40		✓			✓		–	✓
	★★Unicorn	4	66	22	3	10	33		✓	✓		✓		–	
ROCHDALE	★★★Norton Grange	5	180	180	5	80	50							–	✓
ROCHESTER	★★★★Bridgewood Manor	7	200	200	24	10	100		✓	✓	✓	✓		▤ 🎾 G	✓
	★★Royal Victoria & Bull	2	100	60	1	60	28	✓	✓					–	✓
ROCHFORD	★★★Renouf	1	50	–	–	–	24		✓	✓		✓		–	✓
ROMALDKIRK	★★Rose & Crown	1	12	–	1	12	11		✓	✓				–	✓
ROMSEY	★★★White Horse	1	40	–	1	40	33							–	✓
ROSEDALE ABBEY	★★White Horse Farm	1	30	10	2	10	15		✓					–	
ROSS-ON-WYE	★★★Chase	4	260	71	3	71	40	✓	✓					–	✓
	★★★Pengethley Manor	2	60	115	3	72	22		✓	✓				⊇ ⛳	✓
	★★★Royal	3	85	76	3	14	40		✓	✓	✓			–	✓
	★★Orles Barn	–	12	40	1	10	9							⊇	
ROTHERHAM	★★★★Rotherham Moat House	5	250	270	3	8	83	✓	✓	✓		✓		G	✓
	★★Brentwood	4	50	66	2	36	47		✓	✓				–	✓
	★★Elton	1	10	16	2	8	31		✓	✓				–	✓
ROTHERWICK	★★★★Tylney Hall	9	100	58	9	8	91		✓	✓		✓		▤ ⊇ 🎾 G	✓
ROTHLEY	★★★★★Rothley Court	4	–	60	3	20	36		✓	✓				–	✓
ROWSLEY	★★★Peacock	–	–	–	1	16	20		✓					–	✓
RUNCORN	★★★Crest	9	450	79	5	80	134	✓	✓	✓		✓		▤ G	✓
RUSHYFORD	★★★Eden Arms Swallow	4	100	30	5	8	46	✓	✓	✓				▤ G	✓
RUSPER	★★★★Ghyll Manor	3	150	50	2	10	28	✓	✓	✓		✓	✓	⊇ 🎾	✓
RYE	★★★George	2	150	20	1	20	22		✓	✓				–	✓
	★★Flackley Ash	2	100	12	2	10	30		✓	✓		✓		▤ G	✓
ST. ALBANS	★★★St. Michaels Manor	2	18	10	2	10	26		✓	✓		✓		–	✓
	★★★Sopwell House	14	400	160	11	20	65	✓	✓	✓	✓	✓		–	✓

▤=indoor swimming pool; ⊇=outdoor swimming pool; ⛳=golf; 🎾=tennis; ℛ=squash; G=gymnasium

ENGLAND Town	Hotel	No. of conf. rooms	Seating capacity of main room	Total seating of additional rooms	No. of smaller rooms	Maximum capacity of smaller rooms	No. of bedrooms	Exhibition hall space	Photocopying	Projection/Video	Closed circuit TV	Audio	Interpreting	Sporting facilities available at the Hotel	Use of fax
ST. AUSTELL	★★★★Carlyon Bay	2	160	40	1	40	69	√	√	√		√		⊟ ⊃ ⊡ ϙ	√
	★★★Cliff Head	1	100	10	1	10	–				√	√		⊟ ⊃	√
	★★★Porth Avallen	2	100	14	2	14	24	√	√	√	√			–	√
ST. IVES (Cambs)	★★★Dolphin	1	100	10	1	10	22	√	√	√		√		–	√
	★★★Slepe Hall	2	220	50	2	220	16	√	√	√	√	√		–	√
ST. LEONARDS	★★★St. Leonards	3	175	165	1	25	33			√				G	
ST. MELLION	★★★St. Mellion Golf & Country Club	2	220	120	3	50	24	√	√	√		√		⊟ ⊡ ϙ Ѫ G	√
ST. NEOTS	★★Old Falcon	1	90	–	–	–	8	√		√				–	
SAFFRON WALDEN	★★Saffron	1	100	100	–	6	21	√	√			√		–	√
SALISBURY	★★★Red Lion	3	100	60	3	20	57	√	√	√				–	√
	★★★Rose & Crown	4	95	60	2	20	28	√	√	√		√		–	√
	★★County	2	100	15	1	12	31		√	√		√			√
	★White Horse	1	25	–	1	1	11	√	√					–	√
SALTBURN	★★★Grinkle Park	1	50	20	2	20	20	√	√	√				ϙ	√
SANDBACH	★★★Chimney House	2	100	100	4	20	50		√	√		√		G	√
	★★★Saxon Cross	3	80	40	3	6	52		√	√		√		–	√
	★★Old Hall	1	40	–	1	10	15			√	√	√		–	√
SANDIACRE	★★★Post House	2	75	20	10	10	107		√	√		√		–	√
SAUNTON	★★★★Saunton Sands	2	150	150	1	30	92	√	√	√		√		⊟ ϙ Ѫ	√
SAVERNAKE	★★Savernake Forest	7	60	–	3	–	16							–	
SCARBOROUGH	★★★★Holbeck Hall	2	175	20	2	20	31		√	√	√	√	√	–	√
	★★★★Royal	6	260	250	10	70	134	√	√	√		√		⊟ G	√
	★★★Wreahead Country	2	40	20	2	3	21		√	√		√		–	√
	★★★Esplanade	4	150	90	3	40	73	√	√	√		√		–	√
	★★★Palm Court	2	200	120	3	10	50		√	√		√		⊟	√
	★★Brooklands	4	120	100	2	30	61	√				√		–	
	★★Gridleys Crescent	–	25	–	1	25	20		√					–	√
	★★Red Lea	2	40	30	3	10	67		√	√				⊟ G	√
	★★Southlands	3	100	60	3	30	58	√	√	√		√		–	√
SCOLE	★★Scole Inn	1	36	–	1	10	23		√	√				–	√
SCOTCH CORNER	★★★Scotch Corner	10	350	155	3	10	90	√	√	√		√		–	√
SCUNTHORPE	★★★Royal Hotel	4	250	–	–	8	33		√	√				–	√
	★★★Wortley House Hotel	4	300	200	2	15	38	√	√	√	√	√		–	√
SELBY	★★Londesborough Arms	2	45	40	2	6	27		√	√		√		–	√
SEVENOAKS	★★Royal Oak	2	20	10	1	10	40		√					–	
SHAFTESBURY	★★★Grosvenor	2	150	80	–	10	41	√	√	√				–	√
	★★★Royal Chase	7	320	–	3	20	35	√	√	√	√	√	√	⊟ G	√
SHALDON	★★Ness House	2	12	14	2	–	12		√					–	√
SHAP	★★Shap Wells	4	200	330	2	30	90		√	√		√		ϙ	√
SHEDFIELD	★★★Meon Valley	9	120	60	6	10	84	√	√					⊟ ⊡ ϙ Ѫ G	√
SHEFFIELD	★★★★Grosvenor House	11	450	210	10	35	103	√	√	√	√	√		–	√
	★★★★Hallam Tower Post House	7	220	142	7	7	136	√	√	√	√	√	√	⊟ G	√
	★★★★Swallow	3	100	30	4	10	141	√	√	√				⊟ G	√
	★★★Beauchief	3	100	20	2	20	41	√	√	√			√	G	√
	★★★Charnwood	1	100	25	4	25	26	√	√	√	√	√	√	–	√
	★★★Rutland	10	70	–	5	25	90	√	√	√	√	√		–	√
	★★★Sheffield Moat House	5	500	160	3	20	95	√	√	√	√	√	√	⊃ G	√
	★★Andrews Park	2	30	20	2	20	13		√					–	√
	★★Roslyn Court	2	35	10	1	10	31							–	√
SHEPPERTON	★★★Shepperton Moat House	7	300	180	8	8	185	√	√					G	√
SHEPTON MALLET	★★★Charlton House	3	90	50	2	12	20	√	√	√				⊟ ϙ G	√
SHERBORNE	★★★Eastbury	3	80	55	1	20	15		√	√				–	√
	★★★Post House	2	100	200	10	12	60	√	√	√	√	√	√	–	√
SHIFNAL	★★★★Park House	4	200	80	4	20	54	√	√	√		√		⊟	√
SHIPHAM	★★Daneswood House	2	20	20	2	10	12		√	√				–	√
	★Penscot Farm House	2	30	30	–	3	18	√		√		√		–	
SHIRLEY	★★★Regency	7	150	170	3	60	112		√	√				⊟ G	√
SHRAWLEY	★★★Lenchford	2	80	12	2	12	16	√						⊃	√
SHREWSBURY	★★★Prince Rupert	3	90	45	3	5	65		√	√	√			–	√
	★★★Radbrook Hall	3	200	130	1	4	28		√	√		√		Ѫ G	√
	★★Shelton Hall	–	50	–	3	12	10							–	
	★★Shrewsbury	1	50	–	–	–	24	–	√	√		√		–	
SIBSON	★★Millers	2	40	24	2	15	40		√	√				–	√
SIDMOUTH	★★★★Belmont	2	50	20	1	20	54		√			√		⊟ ⊃ ϙ	√
	★★★★Victoria	2	100	25	1	25	63		√	√		√		⊟ ⊃ ϙ	√
	★★★Riviera	1	85	–	4	8	34	√	√	√				–	√

⊟=indoor swimming pool; ⊃=outdoor swimming pool; ⊡=golf; ϙ=tennis; Ѫ=squash; G=gymnasium

ENGLAND Town	Hotel	No. of conf. rooms	Seating capacity of main room	Total seating of additional rooms	No. of smaller rooms	Maximum capacity of smaller rooms	No. of bedrooms	Exhibition hall space	Photocopying	Projection/Video	Closed circuit TV	Audio	Interpreting	Sporting facilities available at the Hotel	Use of fax
SIDMOUTH (*contd.*)	★★★Westcliff	2	80	50	3	12	40	✓	✓	✓		✓		G	✓
	★★Littlecourt	2	35	50	1	20	21		✓					outdoor swimming pool	
	★★Royal York & Faulkner	3	50	100	2	30	68	✓	✓	✓				G	✓
SITTINGBOURNE	★★★Coniston	1	200	35	1	35	60	✓	✓	✓		✓		–	✓
SKEGNESS	★★Vine	2	75	25	–	–	20		✓					–	
SKELWITH	★★Skelwith Bridge	2	50	40	2	40	29		✓	✓	✓			–	✓
SLOUGH	★★★★Holiday Inn Slough	1	350	82	16	80	302	✓	✓	✓		✓		indoor swimming pool, tennis, G	✓
SOLIHULL	★★★Arden	6	130	390	6	67	76	✓	✓	✓	✓	✓		indoor swimming pool, G	✓
	★★★George	7	150	100	6	15	74	✓	✓	✓		✓		–	✓
	★★★St. Johns Swallow	7	800	330	3	20	206	✓	✓	✓		✓		indoor swimming pool, G	✓
SONNING-ON-THAMES	★★★Great House at Sonning	9	80	12	8	12	36		✓	✓				tennis	✓
SOUTHAM	★★★De La Bere	7	140	60	4	12	57	✓	✓	✓	✓	✓	✓	outdoor swimming pool, tennis, squash	✓
SOUTHAMPTON	★★★★Polygon	6	300	250	5	6	120	✓	✓	✓	✓	✓	✓	indoor swimming pool, G	✓
	★★★Dolphin	5	100	100	3	25	72		✓	✓	✓	✓	✓	indoor swimming pool, G	✓
	★★★Novotel	5	500	–	4	12	121	✓	✓	✓		✓	✓	indoor swimming pool, G	✓
	★★★Southampton Moat House	6	200	115	5	30	70	✓	✓	✓	✓	✓	✓	–	✓
	★★★Southampton Park	2	200	34	71	6	71	✓	✓	✓		✓		indoor swimming pool, G	✓
	★★Avenue	2	100	60	7	20	48	✓	✓	✓		✓		–	✓
	★★Elizabeth House	1	30	16	1	–	24							–	
	★★Hotel Ibis Southampton	4	80	60	2	60	93	✓	✓	✓	✓	✓		–	✓
	★★Star	4	100	65	5	10	45	✓	✓	✓				–	✓
SOUTHEND-ON-SEA	★★★Airport Moat House	5	300	100	2	25	65	✓	✓	✓	✓	✓		tennis, squash, G	✓
	★★Tower	2	40	30	3	35	32		✓	✓				–	✓
SOUTH MILFORD	★★★Post House	2	300	135	10	14	103	✓	✓	✓				indoor swimming pool, tennis	✓
SOUTH NORMANTON	★★★★Swallow	14	220	120	11	25	161	✓	✓	✓		✓		indoor swimming pool, G	✓
SOUTHPORT	★★★★Prince of Wales	9	450	560	–	4	15	✓	✓	✓		✓	✓	–	✓
	★★★Royal Clifton	4	300	350	5	40	107	✓	✓	✓	✓	✓	✓	indoor swimming pool, G	✓
	★★★Scarisbrick	3	180	50	14	25	66	✓	✓	✓		✓		–	✓
	★★New Bold	2	30	40	–	–	22		✓	✓	✓			–	✓
	★Talbot	1	60	–	1	10	24			✓		✓		–	
SOUTH SHIELDS	★★★Sea	4	120	80	4	10	33		✓	✓		✓		–	✓
SOUTH SHORE	★★★Normanton Park	2	60	20	3	12	16	✓	✓	✓		✓		outdoor swimming pool, golf	✓
SOUTHWELL	★★★Saracen's Head	1	150	–	1	8	27		✓	✓				–	✓
SOWERBY BRIDGE	★★Hobbit	2	60	16	1	8	23		✓					–	✓
SPALDING	★★Cley Hall	2	40	–	2	10	11	✓	✓	✓				–	✓
	★★Woodlands	2	60	34	2	14	17		✓	✓		✓		–	✓
STAFFORD	★★★Tillington Hall	4	200	120	6	8	90	✓	✓	✓		✓		indoor swimming pool, tennis, G	✓
	★★Garth	5	50	–	–	–	60		✓	✓		✓		–	✓
	★★Vine	1	8	–	–	–	27			✓	✓	✓		–	✓
STAINES	★★★Thames Lodge	1	55	–	3	8	44		✓	✓				–	✓
STALHAM	★★Kingfisher	1	100	–	1	10	16	✓	✓	✓		✓		–	✓
STAMFORD	★★★Garden House	2	50	20	–	–	20		✓	✓				–	✓
	★★★Lady Anne's	3	120	45	2	10	28	✓	✓	✓				–	
STANDISH	★★★Almond Brook	4	150	112	4	8	102	✓	✓	✓		✓	✓	indoor swimming pool, G	✓
STANSTEAD ABBOTTS	★★★★Briggens House	4	100	80	–	–	54		✓					outdoor swimming pool, golf, tennis	✓
STEEPLE ASTON	★★★Hopcrofts Holt	8	175	–	8	10	88	✓	✓	✓	✓	✓		–	✓
STEVENAGE	★★★Hertford Park	6	200	130	2	12	100	✓	✓	✓	✓	✓	✓	–	✓
	★★★Roebuck Inn	2	65	10	10	8	54		✓	✓				–	✓
	★★★Stevanage Moat House	1	200	–	2	16	60	✓	✓	✓		✓		–	✓
STOCKBRIDGE	★★★Grosvenor	1	70	–	–	–	25			✓				–	
STOKE CANON	★★★Barton Cross	1	12	–	2	8	6			✓				–	✓
STOKE FLEMING	★★★Stoke Lodge	1	100	–	2	35	24	✓	✓	✓				indoor swimming pool, tennis, G	
STOCKPORT	★★★Alma Lodge	5	250	125	4	6	58	✓	✓	✓	✓	✓	✓	–	✓
	★Acton Court	3	180	80	4	6	37	✓	✓	✓		✓		–	✓
STOCKTON-ON-TEES	★★★★Swallow	4	300	60	2	10	124	✓	✓	✓		✓		indoor swimming pool, G	✓
STOKE GABRIEL	★★★Gabriel Court	1	50	–	2	20	20							outdoor swimming pool	
STOKE-ON-TRENT	★★★Hanchurch Manor	2	14	8	–	–	12		✓	✓			✓	–	✓
STOKE	★★Crown	1	120	–	1	20	40	✓		✓				–	✓
STONE	★★★★Stone Manor	4	150	225	3	150	53	✓	✓	✓	✓	✓		outdoor swimming pool, tennis	✓
STONEHOUSE	★★★Stonehouse Court	4	150	70	–	–	37	✓	✓	✓				–	✓
STONE	★★★Stonehouse	4	250	270	–	–	50		✓	✓		✓		indoor swimming pool, tennis, G	✓
STONEY	★★Cock	1	30	–	–	–	28		✓	✓	✓			–	✓
STORRINGTON	★★★Abingworth Hall	1	40	–	2	10	21		✓	✓				outdoor swimming pool, tennis, golf	✓
	★★★Little Thakeham	1	15	–	1	6	9		✓					outdoor swimming pool, tennis	✓
STOURBRIDGE	★★Talbot	4	150	70	3	80	25	✓	✓	✓				–	✓
STOURPORT ON SEVERN	★★★Stourport Moat House	4	350	40	6	8	68		✓	✓				outdoor swimming pool, tennis, squash, G	✓

[indoor swimming pool symbol]=indoor swimming pool; [outdoor swimming pool symbol]=outdoor swimming pool; [golf symbol]=golf; [tennis symbol]=tennis; [squash symbol]=squash; G=gymnasium

ENGLAND Town	Hotel	No. of conf. rooms	Seating capacity of main room	Total seating of additional rooms	No. of smaller rooms	Maximum capacity of smaller rooms	No. of bedrooms	Exhibition hall space	Photocopying	Projection/Video	Closed circuit TV	Audio	Interpreting	Sporting facilities available at the Hotel	Use of fax
STOW-ON-THE-WOLD	★★★★Wych Hill House	2	40	88	4	12	31		√	√				–	
	★★★Unicorn	2	14	12	–	–	20		√	√				–	√
	★★Fosse Manor	1	40	–	2	10	20	√	√	√				–	√
STRATFORD-UPON-AVON	★★★★Moat House International	9	420	150	10	10	249	√	√	√	√	√		indoor pool G	√
	★★★★Shakespeare	6	100	60	4	15	70	√	√	√				–	√
	★★★★Welcombe Hotel & Golf Course	6	150	–	–	–	76		√	√	√	√	√	golf tennis	√
	★★★Alveston Manor	3	200	120	6	10	108	√	√	√	√	√	√		√
	★★★Falcon	9	200	180	4	20	73	√	√		√	√	√	–	√
	★★★Grosvenor	1	60	–	2	35	51		√	√				–	√
	★★★Swans Nest	4	150	50	3	6	60		√	√		√		–	√
	★★★White Swan	2	20	8	–	–	42		√					–	√
	★★Swan House	2	20	10	–	–	12		√	√	√	√		–	√
STREATLEY-ON-THAMES	★★★Swan Diplomat	6	100	100	3	10	46	√	√				√	indoor pool G	√
STREET	★★★Bear	2	100	15	2	30	15		√	√				–	
	★★★Wessex	2	250	35	–	10	50	√	√	√		√		–	√
STROUD	★★★Bear of Rodborough	3	60	50	2	16	47	√	√	√	√	√		–	√
	★★★Burleigh Court	1	20	–	1	–	17		√	√				outdoor pool	√
SUDBURY	★★★Mill	2	70	30	4	12	49	√	√	√		√		–	√
SUNDERLAND	★★Roker	1	400	–	–	–	45	√	√	√		√		–	√
SUTTON BENGER	★★★Bell House	1	40	8	2	8	14							–	√
SUTTON COLDFIELD	★★★★Belfry	19	300	677	14	–	219	√	√			√		indoor pool golf tennis squash G	√
	★★★★Penns Hall	3	400	150	11	30	114	√	√	√		√		indoor pool squash G	√
	★★★Moor Hall	7	320	100	5	60	75		√	√		√		indoor pool G	√
	★★★Sutton Court	0	00	30	0	10	61		√	√					√
	★★Berni Royal	3	200	130	–	–	22	√	√	√		√	√	–	√
SUTTON-ON-SEA	★★★Grange & Links	3	200	–	1	20	30			√		√		golf tennis	√
SWAFFHAM	★★George	3	150	8	–	–	28	√	√					–	√
SWANAGE	★★★Pines	2	100	–	4	20	51		√	√		√		–	√
SWINDON	★★★★Blunsdon House	8	300	315	7	10	89	√	√	√	√	√		indoor pool tennis squash G	√
	★★★Crest	3	80	62	3	6	94		√	√				–	√
	★★★Goddards	3	200	80	10	6	65	√	√	√				–	√
	★★★Pear Tree	3	60	12	2	6	18	√	√	√	√	√	√	–	√
	★★★Post House	2	100	80	8	8	104	√	√	√	√	√		indoor pool G	√
	★★★Wiltshire	2	200	90	2	12	93	√	√	√		√		–	√
	★★Ibis	1	140	–	4	30	120	√	√					–	√
	★★School House	1	10	–	–	–	10	√	√	√		√	√	–	
SYMONDS YAT	★★Paddocks	2	200	–	1	30	26	√	√			√		outdoor pool tennis	√
TAPLOW	★★★★★Cliveden	1	28	–	2	8	31		√	√		√		outdoor pool tennis squash	√
TAUNTON	★★★★Castle	5	90	–	3	12	35	√	√	√	√	√		–	√
	★★★County	4	400	200	3	20	66	√	√	√		√	√	–	√
	★★★Crest Hotel	6	230	30	4	6	101	√	√	√		√		G	√
	★★Corner House	2	40	15	1	12	30							–	
	★★Falcon	1	50	–	2	15	11		√	√		√		–	√
TAVISTOCK	★★★Bedford	2	70	45	–	–	31		√	√				–	√
TEBAY	★★★Tebay Mountain Lodge	1	12	–	–	–	30		√					–	√
TELFORD	★★★Buckatree Hall	1	100	–	2	35	37		√	√		√		–	√
	★★★Telford Golf & Country Club	4	240	220	2	10	59	√	√	√		√		indoor pool golf squash	√
	★★★Telford Moat House	12	500	430	6	35	148	√	√	√		√		indoor pool G	√
TEMPLE SOWERBY	★★★Temple Sowerby House	1	20	–	2	15	12		√	√				–	√
TEMPSFORD	★★Anchor	1	40	–	–	–	10		√	√				–	√
TENTERDEN	★★White Lion	1	55	–	2	8	15		√	√		√		–	√
TETBURY	★★★Calcot Manor	1	20	–	1	10	16		√	√				outdoor pool golf	√
	★★★Close	2	36	60	–	–	15		√	√				–	√
	★★★Snooty Fox	1	20	–	2	8	12		√	√		√		–	√
TEWKESBURY	★★★Bell	2	45	20	2	10	25	√	√					–	√
	★★★Royal Hop Pole Crest	1	12	–	4	–	29		√	√		√		–	√
	★★★Tewkesbury Hall	2	200	50	2	16	16	√	√					–	√
	★★★Tewkesbury Golf & Country Club	8	150	100	2	10	78	√	√	√				indoor pool golf tennis squash G	√
	★★Tudor House	4	40	60	2	6	19		√	√		√		–	√
THAME	★★★Spread Eagle	1	250	–	4	45	33	√	√	√	√	√		–	√
THAXTED	★★★Swan	1	30	–	1	5	21		√	√				–	√
THETFORD	★★★Bell	4	80	52	–	–	47		√	√		√		–	√
THIRSK	★★Golden Fleece	3	220	–	–	–	22		√	√				–	√
	★Old Red House	1	40	–	–	–	12							–	

indoor pool=indoor swimming pool; outdoor pool=outdoor swimming pool; golf=golf; tennis=tennis; squash=squash; **G**=*gymnasium*

ENGLAND Town	Hotel	No. of conf. rooms	Seating capacity of main room	Total seating of additional rooms	No. of smaller rooms	Maximum capacity of smaller rooms	No. of bedrooms	Exhibition hall space	Photocopying	Projection/Video	Closed circuit TV	Audio	Interpreting	Sporting facilities available at the Hotel	Use of fax
THORNABY	★★★Post House	7	120	100	5	10	135	✓	✓	✓		✓		–	✓
THORNBURY	★★★Thornbury Castle	1	24	–	–	–	18		✓				✓	–	✓
THORNE	★★Belmont	2	60	20	2	8	23		✓	✓	✓		✓	–	✓
THORNLEY	★★Crossways	3	150	200	–	12	23	✓	✓	✓	✓	✓		–	✓
THORNTHWAITE	★★Ladstock Country House	3	180	70	4	12	22	✓	✓	✓		✓		–	
THORNTON CLEVELEYS	★★Regal	1	60	–	3	15	41	✓	✓			✓		–	
THURLESTONE	★★★★Thurlestone	1	100	–	2	30	68	✓	✓	✓	✓	✓		[indoor pool] [outdoor pool] [golf] [tennis] [squash] G	✓
TITCHWELL	★★Titchwell Manor	2	20	20	–	–	16		✓					–	
TIVERTON	★★★Tiverton	4	250	140	2	60	75	✓	✓	✓		✓	✓	–	✓
TODMARDEN	★★★Scaitcliffe	3	200	50	4	15	13	✓	✓	✓	✓	✓		–	✓
TODWICK	★★★Red Lion	2	80	15	1	15	29		✓	✓				–	✓
TONBRIDGE	★★★Rose & Crown	3	100	30	–	30	50		✓	✓		✓		–	✓
TORMARTEN	★★Compass Inn	6	40	200	6	15	33	✓	✓	✓				–	✓
TORQUAY	★★★★★Imperial	6	400	200	12	12	167	✓	✓	✓		✓		[indoor pool] [outdoor pool] [tennis] [squash] G	✓
	★★★★Grand	6	300	300	6	30	112	✓	✓	✓	✓	✓	✓	[indoor pool] [outdoor pool] [tennis]	✓
	★★★★Palace	2	350	305	9	30	140	✓	✓	✓		✓		[indoor pool] [outdoor pool] [golf] [tennis] [squash]	✓
	★★★Abbey Lawn	4	120	110	–	15	65	✓	✓	✓		✓	✓	[outdoor pool] [tennis]	✓
	★★★Belgrave	3	150	60	2	20	68	✓	✓	✓	✓	✓		[outdoor pool]	✓
	★★★Corbyn Head	2	40	20	4	8	50		✓	✓	✓	✓		[outdoor pool]	✓
	★★★Livermead Cliff	3	80	75	6	6	64	✓	✓	✓		✓		[outdoor pool]	✓
	★★★Livermead House	4	80	130	2	20	62		✓	✓		✓		[outdoor pool] [tennis] [squash] G	✓
	★★★Orestone Manor	1	30	–	1	15	20		✓					[outdoor pool]	✓
	★★★Overmead	5	130	140	3	20	55	✓	✓	✓		✓		[outdoor pool] G	✓
	★★★Toorak	4	200	–	2	35	90	✓	✓	✓		✓		[indoor pool] [tennis] G	✓
	★★Bowden Close	1	30	–	2	10	20		✓					–	
	★★Burlington	2	100	25	–	–	55		✓	✓		✓		[indoor pool]	✓
	★★Conway Court	2	30	20	6	10	38	✓	✓	✓		✓		–	✓
	★★Sefton	2	100	50	3	10	47		✓					–	✓
TOTNES	★★Royal Seven Stars	2	60	16	–	–	18	✓	✓			✓		–	✓
TRICKETTS CROSS	★★Coach House	4	160	180	6	6	44	✓	✓	✓		✓		–	✓
TRIMSTONE	★★★Trimstone Manor	2	70	–	2	12	17							–	
TRING	★★★Rose & Crown	1	80	–	2	60	28		✓	✓		✓		–	✓
TROTTON	★★★Southdowns	1	120	–	4	20	22	✓	✓	✓		✓		[indoor pool] [tennis] G	✓
TRURO	★★Royal	1	50	–	2	12	34		✓	✓			✓	–	✓
TUNBRIDGE WELLS	★★★★Spa	6	300	200	6	150	76	✓	✓	✓	✓	✓		[indoor pool] [tennis] G	✓
	★★★Calverley	5	130	110	–	–	43	✓	✓	✓		✓		–	✓
	★★★Royal Wells	2	80	30	–	–	25		✓					–	✓
	★★Mt Edgcumbe House	2	28	12	–	–	6			✓		✓	–		
TUNBRIDGE WELLS	★★Russell	1	20	–	4	8	26							–	✓
TURVEY	★★Laws	1	75	–	1	15	11		✓	✓				–	
TUXFORD	★★Newcastle Arms	2	70	30	–	–	11		✓	✓		✓		–	✓
TWO BRIDGES	★★Two Bridges	2	40	40	4	15	23		✓					[golf]	✓
UPHOLLAND	★★Holland Hall	2	150	30	3	10	34		✓	✓		✓		–	✓
UPPER SLAUGHTER	★★★Lords of the Manor	2	24	24	2	10	29		✓	✓	✓	✓	✓	–	✓
UPPINGHAM	★★★Falcon	3	50	70	3	14	27	✓	✓	✓	✓	✓	✓	–	✓
	★★★Marquess of Exeter	1	50	–	1	10	17		✓	✓				–	✓
UPTON-UPON-SEVERN	★★★White Lion	1	12	–	1	–	10							–	
VERYAN	★★★Nare	1	50	–	2	12	39		✓					[outdoor pool] [tennis] G	✓
WADEBRIDGE	★★Molesworth Arms	1	80	–	1	15	14							–	
WAKEFIELD	★★★★Cedar Court	14	400	200	6	40	151	✓	✓	✓	✓	✓		–	✓
WALLINGFORD	★★★George	1	100	–	2	15	39		✓	✓	✓	✓		–	✓
	★★★Shillingford Bridge	3	40	12	–	–	37	✓	✓	✓				[outdoor pool] [squash]	✓
WALLSEND	★★★Newcastle Moat House	13	500	80	–	–	151	✓	✓	✓		✓		[indoor pool] G	✓
WALSALL	★★★Friendly	3	180	60	4	15	125		✓	✓		✓		[indoor pool] G	✓
	★★Abberley	1	45	–	1	8	29		✓	✓			✓	–	✓
	★★Bescot	1	30	–	3	20	13							–	✓
	★★Royal	4	240	120	9	50	32	✓	✓	✓		✓		–	✓
WALTHAM	★★★★Swallow	1	250	–	7	1	163	✓	✓	✓		✓		[indoor pool] G	✓
WALTON	★★★Waterton Park	3	100	110	2	90	31		✓	✓		✓		[indoor pool] [squash] G	✓
WANSFORD	★★★Haycock at Wansford	2	150	60	6	15	51	✓	✓	✓		✓		–	✓
WANTAGE	★★Bear	1	60	22	2	12	37	✓	✓	✓				–	
WAREHAM	★★★★Priory	1	20	–	2	10	19		✓					–	✓
	★★★Springfield Country	1	140	–	4	30	32	✓	✓	✓				[outdoor pool] [tennis]	✓

[indoor pool]=indoor swimming pool; [outdoor pool]=outdoor swimming pool; [golf]=golf; [tennis]=tennis; [squash]=squash; G=gymnasium

ENGLAND Town	Hotel	No. of conf. rooms	Seating capacity of main room	Total seating of additional rooms	No. of smaller rooms	Maximum capacity of smaller rooms	No. of bedrooms	Exhibition hall space	Photocopying	Projection/Video	Closed circuit TV	Audio	Interpreting	Sporting facilities available at the Hotel	Use of fax
WARMINSTER	★★★★Bishopstrow House	2	50	30	2	–	32		✓	✓				[indoor pool] [outdoor pool] [tennis]	✓
	★★Old Bell	1	100	–	1	25	24	✓	✓	✓				–	✓
WARRINGTON	★★★Fir Grove	3	200	110	3	8	40	✓	✓	✓		✓		–	✓
	★★Old Vicarage	1	60	–	3	20	26		✓	✓	✓	✓		–	✓
WARWICK	★★★★Hilton National	15	150	–	10	30	180	✓	✓	✓	✓	✓		[indoor pool] G	✓
	★★Lord Leycester	3	200	20	3	8	53		✓	✓		✓		–	
	★★Warwick Arms	3	95	65	–	–	35		✓					–	✓
WASHINGTON	★★★Washington Moat House	4	200	90	6	20	106	✓	✓	✓		✓		[indoor pool] [golf] [squash] G	✓
	★★★Post House	1	100	–	6	12	138	✓	✓	✓	✓	✓		–	✓
WATCHET	★★Downfield	1	20	–	1	15	8		✓					–	✓
WATERMILLOCK	★★★Leeming House	1	12	–	–	–	40		✓	✓				–	✓
	★★★Rampsbeck	2	60	20	–	–	19							–	
WATFORD	★★★Dean Park	5	200	135	4	4	90	✓	✓	✓		✓		–	✓
WEEDON	★★Globe	2	20	10	1	6	15		✓	✓				–	✓
	★★★Crossroads	4	50	100	3	12	48		✓	✓				[tennis]	✓
WELLINGBOROUGH	★★★Hind	3	100	130	4	6	34		✓	✓				–	✓
	★★Columbia	1	24	–	–	–	29		✓					–	✓
WELLS	★★★Swan	2	70	30	–	–	32		✓	✓	✓	✓		[squash]	✓
WELWYN	★★★Crest	4	100	60	–	6	58		✓	✓				–	✓
WEMBLEY	★★★★Hilton National	5	300	600	10	20	300	✓	✓	✓		✓		–	✓
WENTBRIDGE	★★★Wentbridge House	3	60	90	2	30	12		✓	✓		✓		–	✓
WEST BROMWICH	★★★West Bromwich Moat House	4	180	320	16	30	180	✓	✓	✓		✓		–	✓
WEST CHILTINGTON	★★★Roundabout	1	20	–	2	15	23	✓	✓	✓				–	✓
WESTERHAM	★★★Kings Arms	–	–	–	1	20	18		✓					–	✓
WESTGATE-ON-SEA	★★Ivyside	5	120	150	10	12	67	✓	✓	✓		✓		[indoor pool] [outdoor pool] [squash] G	✓
WESTHOUGHTON	★★★Mercury	2	150	150	1	50	21	✓	✓	✓		✓		–	✓
WESTONBIRT	★★★Hare and Hounds	4	40	70	2	12	30	✓	✓	✓				[tennis] [squash]	✓
WESTON-SUPER-MARE	★★★Commodore	1	120	–	2	30	20	✓	✓	✓		✓		–	✓
	★★★Grand Atlantic	3	230	125	–	–	76	✓	✓	✓		✓		[outdoor pool] [tennis]	✓
	★★Arosfa	4	100	–	2	12	47	✓	✓	✓	✓	✓		–	✓
	★★Beachlands	1	80	–	2	30	18			✓	✓	✓		–	
WESTON-UNDER-REDCASTLE	★★★Hawkstone Park	5	200	120	2	10	59		✓	✓		✓		[indoor pool] [outdoor pool] [golf] [tennis] G	✓
WETHERALL	★★★Crown	5	175	164	4	8	49		✓	✓	✓	✓		[indoor pool] [squash] G	✓
WETHERBY	★★★★Wood Hall	2	40	40	4	14	22		✓	✓		✓		–	✓
	★★★Penguin	11	160	150	5	6	72	✓	✓	✓	✓	✓		–	✓
WEYBRIDGE	★★★Oatlands Park	6	200	90	4	10	131	✓	✓					[tennis] [indoor pool]	✓
WEYMOUTH	★★Crown	3	120	70	1	15	79					✓		–	✓
	★★Hotel Rex	1	20	–	–	–	31		✓	✓				–	✓
	★★Prince Regent	3	200	100	3	20	50	✓	✓	✓		✓		–	✓
WHATTON	★★Haven	2	120	40	–	–	17			✓		✓		–	
WHICKHAM	★★★Gibside Arms	1	100	–	1	25	45	✓	✓	✓		✓		–	✓
WHITBY	★★Saxonville	1	120	–	1	10	24	✓						–	
WHITCHURCH (H&W)	★Crown	1	30	–	–	–	5	✓	✓	✓	✓	✓	✓	–	
WHITCHURCH(Salop)	★★★Doddington Lodge	1	65	–	1	30	10	✓		✓				–	
	★★Redbrook Hunting Lodge	1	70	–	1	15	13	✓	✓	✓		✓	✓	–	✓
	★★★Terrick Hall Country	1	40	–	1	10	22							[golf] [tennis] [squash]	
WHITEHAVEN	★★Chase	1	40	–	–	–	10							–	
WHITLEY BAY	★★Ambassador	1	15	–	–	–	28		✓	✓				–	✓
WHITLY BAY	★★Windsor	2	150	50	–	–	50	✓	✓	✓		✓	✓	–	✓
WHITWELL-ON-THE-HILL	★★★Whitwell Hall Country House	1	70	–	3	8	23		✓					[indoor pool] [tennis]	✓
WIDNES	★★★Hillcrest	4	120	20	3	12	57		✓	✓		✓		–	✓
WIGAN	★★★Kilhey Court	5	150	103	4	12	53	✓	✓	✓		✓		[indoor pool] [golf] G	✓
	★★Grand	2	125	40	2	12	38		✓	✓		✓		–	✓
WIGTON	★★Greenhill Lodge	1	80	–	3	20	7		✓					–	
WILMSLOW	★★★Wilmslow Moat House	6	300	120	6	8	125	✓	✓	✓		✓		[indoor pool] [squash] G	✓
WIMBORNE MINSTER	★★★Kings Head	2	40	54	1	14	27	✓	✓	✓				–	✓
WINCANTON	★★Holbrook House	1	15	–	1	12	20			✓				[outdoor pool] [tennis] [squash]	
WINCHESTER	★★★★Wessex	1	80	–	2	14	94	✓	✓	✓				–	✓
	★★★Lainston House	4	100	40	4	14	32	✓	✓	✓	✓	✓	✓	[golf] [tennis]	✓
	★★★Winchester Moat House	6	250	495	6	10	72	✓	✓	✓				[indoor pool]	✓
WINDERMERE	★★★★Bowness	3	120	100	3	14	82		✓	✓		✓		[outdoor pool]	✓
	★★★Beech Hill	2	90	70	4	24	46		✓	✓		✓		[indoor pool]	✓
	★★★Belmont Manor	2	100	–	3	12	13							–	
	★★★Belsfield	6	150	260	4	121	66	✓	✓	✓		✓		[indoor pool]	✓
	★★★Burn How	1	30	–	3	10	26		✓	✓				–	
	★★★Merewood Country House	3	50	42	3	10	20	✓	✓	✓	✓			–	✓

[indoor pool]=indoor swimming pool; [outdoor pool]=outdoor swimming pool; [golf]=golf; [tennis]=tennis; [squash]=squash; G*=gymnasium*

ENGLAND Town	Hotel	No. of conf. rooms	Seating capacity of main room	Total seating of additional rooms	No. of smaller rooms	Maximum capacity of smaller rooms	No. of bedrooms	Exhibition hall space	Photocopying	Projection/Video	Closed circuit TV	Audio	Interpreting	Sporting facilities available at the Hotel	Use of fax
WINDERMERE (*contd.*)	★★★Royal	2	60	28	4	12	29	✓	✓	✓		✓		–	✓
	★★★Wild Boar	1	40	–	1	10	36		✓	✓				–	✓
	★★★Windermere Hydro	4	250	180	4	15	96		✓	✓		✓		[golf]	✓
	★★Holbeck Ghyll	2	14	14	–	–	14		✓					–	
WINDSOR	★★★★Oakley Court	9	140	440	5	15								[golf]	✓
	★★★Castle	6	420	250	2	8	103	✓	✓	✓	✓	✓	✓	–	✓
	★★Ye Harte and Garter	2	180	50	2	6	50	✓	✓	✓		✓		–	✓
	★★Royal Adelaide	2	–	–	3	–	40		✓	✓				–	✓
WINTERBOURNE	★★★Grange Resort	5	130	46	3	17	52		✓	✓		✓		[indoor pool] G	✓
WISBECH	★★Queen's	1	70	–	4	12	18	✓	✓	✓		✓		–	✓
	★★White Lion	2	80	30	–	–	18	✓	✓	✓				–	
WITHAN	★★★Rivenhall Resort	6	200	75	5	15	54	✓	✓	✓		✓		[indoor pool] [squash] G	✓
WITNEY	★★Marlborough	1	70	–	1	15	23		✓	✓	✓	✓		–	
WOBURN	★★★★Bedford Arms	1	60	–	3	14	55	✓	✓	✓				–	✓
WOLVERHAMPTON	★★★Connaught	3	250	75	3	25	61	✓	✓	✓		✓		–	✓
	★★★Goldthorn	1	120	–	4	26	93	✓	✓	✓		✓		–	✓
	★★★Park Hall	9	400	120	9	10	57	✓	✓	✓				–	✓
	★★★Patshull Park	5	120	120	4	10	48	✓	✓	✓		✓		[indoor pool] [golf] G	✓
	★★Fox	1	75	–	–	–	33	✓						–	✓
WOODBRIDGE	★★★Seckford Hall	2	100	40	2	12	34	✓	✓	✓		✓		[indoor pool] G	✓
WOODFORD GREEN	★★★Woodford Moat House	3	150	48	3	6	99		✓	✓		✓		–	✓
WOODHALL SPA	★★★Golf	4	150	100	3	50	51		✓	✓		✓		–	✓
	★★★Petwood	4	160	155	–	–	46	✓	✓	✓		✓		[indoor pool] [golf] [tennis] G	✓
WOODSTOCK	★★★Bear	3	70	46	1	12	45		✓	✓				–	✓
WOOLACOMBE	★★★Watersmeet	1	30	–	–	–	25		✓					[outdoor pool] [tennis]	✓
	★★★Woolacombe Bay	4	200	130	2	40	59	✓	✓	✓	✓	✓		[outdoor pool] [golf] [tennis] [squash] G	✓
WOOLER	★★Tankerville Arms	2	50	25	2	15	15	✓						–	
WORCESTER	★★★Giffard	5	140	55	–	–	103		✓	✓		✓		–	✓
	★★★Star	2	100	45	1	35	46		✓	✓	✓	✓		–	✓
WORKINGTON	★★★Washington Central	2	200	50	1	20	40	✓	✓			✓		–	✓
	★★★Westland	3	400	750	2	75	110	✓	✓	✓		✓	✓	[golf]	✓
WORKSOP	★★★Charnwood	2	65	50	2	8	20		✓	✓				–	✓
WORTHING	★★★Burlington	2	75	50	2	50	26	✓	✓					–	
	★★★Chatsworth	10	120	200	10	8	105		✓	✓	✓	✓		–	✓
	★★★Kingsway	1	30	–	2	10	28	✓	✓			✓		–	✓
	★★Cavendish	2	36	12	–	–	17			✓	✓			–	
	★★Windsor House	1	120	–	2	30	33	✓	✓	✓		✓		–	✓
WROTHAM HEATH	★★★★Post House	4	60	120	10	8	120		✓	✓		✓		[indoor pool] G	✓
WYMONDHAM	★★Abbey	4	40	20	3	8	26		✓	✓		✓		–	✓
	★★Sinclair	1	30	–	1	10	20		✓					–	
YARMOUTH, GREAT	★★★Embassy	1	50	12	2	12	24		✓	✓				–	✓
	★★★Carlton	2	150	90	2	25	95	✓	✓	✓		✓		–	✓
	★★Imperial	2	140	60	4	40	41	✓	✓	✓		✓		–	✓
	★★Palm Court	2	120	120	7	30	77	✓	✓	✓		✓		[indoor pool] G	✓
	★★Star	2	140	60	4	10	40		✓					–	✓
YELVERTON	★★★Moorland Links	3	80	30	–	6	30	✓	✓	✓		✓		–	
YEOVIL	★★★Four Acres	1	80	–	2	25	24	✓	✓	✓				–	✓
	★★Three Choughs	1	45	–	–	–	35		✓	✓				–	✓
YORK	★★★★Crest	5	180	65	–	2	30	✓	✓	✓		✓		–	✓
	★★★★Middlethorpe	1	63	–	1	10	30	✓	✓	✓	✓	✓		–	✓
	★★★★Viking	12	300	200	7	10	188							G	✓
	★★★Ambassador	3	70	120	1	40	19		✓	✓		✓		–	✓
	★★★Dean Court	1	16	–	–	–	41		✓					–	✓
	★★★Hudson's	3	60	80	–	–	28		✓	✓		✓		–	
	★★★Penguin Abbey Park	4	100	70	3	30	85		✓	✓				–	✓
	★★★Swallow Chase	1	180	–	4	40	112	✓	✓	✓		✓	✓	[indoor pool] G	✓
	★★★Post House	2	100	70	8	12	147	✓	✓	✓		✓		–	✓
	★★★York Pavilion	1	30	–	2	20	21		✓	✓				–	✓
	★★Abbots Mews	1	50	–	2	10	48	✓	✓	✓	✓			–	✓
	★★Ashcroft	1	60	50	2	20	15	✓	✓	✓				–	✓
	★★Elmbank	1	80	–	3	30	48		✓	✓	✓	✓		–	✓
	★★Heworth Court	1	14	–	2	12	25	✓	✓	✓				–	✓
	★★Knavesmire Manor	1	24	–	1	12	22		✓	✓				[indoor pool] G	✓
	★★Town House	1	25	–	–	–	23		✓					–	✓
	★★Savages	1	30	–	–	–	18		✓					G	

Conference hotels in Scotland, Wales, Isle of Man, Channel Islands & N. Ireland are listed between Scotland and Wales.

[indoor pool]=*indoor swimming pool;* [outdoor pool]=*outdoor swimming pool;* [golf]=*golf;* [tennis]=*tennis;* [squash]=*squash;* **G**=*gymnasium*

LONDON

Pop Greater London 7,211,910.
Inner London (former admin county) 3,200,484.
RAC Pall Mall Clubhouse, *Pall Mall, SW1Y 5HS* ☎071-930 2345
Street Maps. See pp. 82–99. *Cross references to these London street maps are given at the end of entries of RAC Appointed hotels as appropriate.*
ⓘ Victoria Sta Forecourt, SW1 ☎071-730 3488

E1
★★★★ **Tower Thistle,** St Katharine's Way, E1 9LD ☎071-481 2575 Tx: 885934 Fax: 071-488 4106

Striking, large, modern hotel on riverside by picturesque St. Katharine Dock. (MtCh)
🛏 808 bedrs, 808 en suite; TV; tcf
🏠 lift, ns; P 136 (charge), G 116 (charge); child facs; con 250
✕ LD 12 midnight
£ room £99, double room £112, Bk £8·95, L £18·75, D £24·50; WB
cc Access, Amex, B'card/Visa, CB, Diners. (*London street map 8B1*)

E18
Grove Hill, 38 Grove Hill, South Woodford, E18 2JG ☎081-989 3344. *Hotel.*
£ B&B £23–£32

EC1
★★★ **New Barbican,** Central St, EC1V 8DS ☎071-251 1565 Tx: 25181
Custom built 5 and 6 storey buildings forming modern hotel in the heart of the City.

N4
★★ **Spring Park,** 400 Seven Sisters Rd, N4 2LX ☎081-800 6030 Tx: 265218 Fax: 081-802 5652

Discount vouchers
RAC discount vouchers are on p. 34. Hotels with a [V] shown at the end of the price information will accept them in part payment for accommodation bills on the full, standard rate, not against bargain breaks or any other special offers. Please note the limitations shown in the entry: w/e for weekends, w/d for weekdays, and which months they are accepted.

Large 4-storey Edwardian villa with modern extension conveniently set near Manor House tube station.
🛏 39 bedrs, 33 en suite, 2 ba; TV; tcf
🏠 dogs; P 50, U 2, coach; child facs; con 50
✕ LD 10·30, nr all Sun & Sat lunch.
£ B&B £45–£55, B&B (double) £55–£63; L £9·50, D £9·50
cc Access, Amex, B'card/Visa, CB, Diners
(*See advertisement on p. 66*)

★ **Royal Park,** 352 Seven Sisters Road, Finsbury Pk, N4 2PQ ☎081-800 0528 Fax: 081-802 5185
Three former residences joined to form a conveniently placed hotel. ✻ Fr
🛏 17 beds, 1 sh, 6 ba; annexe 16 bedrs, 9 en suite, 2 ba; TV; tcf
🏠 P 30, coach
✕ LD 9·
£ B&B £25–£30; B&B (double) £35–£40. [5%V].

Redland, 418 Seven Sisters Rd, N4 2LX ☎081-800 1826 Tx: 265218 Fax: 081-802 7080. *Hotel.*
£ B&B £30

N8
Aber, 89 Crouch Hill, N8 9EG ☎081-340 2847. *Hotel.*
£ B&B £16–£18.
Highgate Lodge, 9 Waverley Rd, Crouch End, N8 9QS ☎081-340 5601

N10
Raglan Hall, 8–12 Queens Av, Muswell Hill, N10 3NR ☎081-883 9836 Fax: 081-883 5002. *Hotel.*

En suite rooms
En suite rooms may be bath or shower rooms. If you have a preference, remember to state it when booking a room.

NW1
★★★ **Harewood,** Harewood Row, Marylebone, NW1 6SE ☎071-262 2707 Tx: 297225 Fax 071-262 2975

Purpose-built 6-storey modern hotel opposite Marylebone Station. ✻ De, Es, Du
🛏 93 bedrs, 93 en suite; TV; tcf
🏠 lift; coach; child facs; con 60
✕ LD 10; nr Sat & Sun lunch
£ B&B £75–£80, B&B (double) £108–£114·50; L £12·50, D £12·50
cc Access, Amex, B'card/Visa, Diners

★★★ **Kennedy,** Cardington St, NW1 2LP ☎071-387 4400 Tx: 28250 Fax: 071-387 5122

Large modern purpose-built hotel near Euston station. ✻ Fr, De, Es, Da (MtCh)
🛏 360 bedrs, 360 en suite; TV; tcf
🏠 lift, dogs, ns; G (£10), coach; child facs; con 100
✕ LD 10.30
£ B&B £80·75–£93·25 (w/e £36·50), B&B (double) £106·50–£116·50; L £11·50, D £11·50; [10% V]
cc Access, Amex, B'card/Visa, Diners.

★★★ **White House,** Regents Park, NW1 3UP ☎071-387 1200 Tx: 24111 Fax: 071-388 0091 ♿
Large, white, almost star-shaped building, originally a block of flats, close to Regent's Park. Sauna, gymnasium.
🛏 567 bedrs, 567 en suite; TV
🏠 lift, ns; P 6, coach; child facs; con 100

★★ **Ibis Euston,** 3 Cardington St, NW1 2LW ☎071-388 7777 Tx: 22115 Fax: 071-388 0001 ♿
Modern 4-storey purpose-built hotel close to Euston Station. ✻ Fr, It
🛏 300 bedrs, 300 en suite; TV
🏠 lift, dogs; coach; child facs; con 130

London N4

London NW3

London NW3

✕ LD 10.30
£ B&B £53, B&B £59; L £8·50, D £8·50
cc Access, Amex, B'card/Visa, Diners.

NW2
Clearview House, 161 Fordwych Rd, Cricklewood, NW2 3NG ☎081-452 9773. *Guest House.* ⚒ Fr, It
£ B&B £12
Garth, 72 Hendon Way, Cricklewood, NW2 2NL ☎081-455 4742

NW3
★★★★ Clive Hotel at Hampstead, Primrose Hill Rd, Hampstead, NW3 3NA ☎071-586 2233 Tx: 22759 Fax: 071-586 1659

A modern hotel in a quiet leafy residential location close to Regents Park. ⚒ Fr, De, Es, Du (HN)
🛏 96 bedrs, 96 en suite; TV; tcf
🏠 lift, dogs, P 1[illegible], coach, child facs, con 300
✕ LD 9.45
£ B&B £78–£105; B&B (double) £93–£105; D £12·95; WB £38. [10% V Dec–Aug]
cc Access, Amex, B'card/Visa, Diners.

★★★★ Holiday Inn Swiss Cottage, King Henry's Rd, NW3 3ST ☎071-722 7711 Tx: 267396 Fax: 071-586 5822 ♿
Large 7-storey modern luxury hotel. Indoor swimming pool, sauna, solarium, gymnasium. Fr, De, It, Es, Ar, Eg (CHIC)
🛏 303 bedrs, 303 en suite; TV; tcf
🏠 lift, dogs, ns; P 120, child facs; con 400
✕ LD 10.30. Resid & Rest lic
£ room £120–£140 (w/e £47·50); double room £150–£175; Bk £7·25, L £15; D £16. [5% V w/e]
cc Access, Amex, B'card/Visa, CB, Diners.

★★★ Post House, Haverstock Hill, Hampstead, NW3 4RB ☎071-794 8121 Tx: 262494 Fax: 071-435 5586
Modern hotel on Haverstock Hill and close to Underground station. (THF)
🛏 140 bedrs, 140 en suite; TV; tcf
🏠 lift, dogs, ns; P 70, coach; child facs; con 30
(*See advertisement on p. 66*)

Complaints

If you are dissatisfied with the facilities or service offered by a hotel, please take the matter up with the Manager WHILE YOU ARE AT THE HOTEL. In this way, any problems can usually be solved promptly and amicably.

The RAC will investigate matters if a personal approach has failed to resolve the problem. Please submit details of any discussion or correspondence when reporting the problem to the RAC.

★★★ C Swiss Cottage, 4 Adamson Rd, NW3 3HP ☎071-722 2281 Tx: 297232 Fax: 071-483 4588

Victorian building in residential area. Furnished with fine antiques. ⚒ Fr, De, It, Es
🛏 64 bedrs, 58 en suite, 3 ba; TV
🏠 lift; P 5; child facs; con 80
✕ LD 9.30
£ B&B £45–£86, B&B (double) £70–£120; L £12·50, D £12·50; WB £250; [10% V Oct–Apr]
cc Access, Amex, B'card/Visa, CB, Diners
(*See advertisement on p. 66*)

Seaford Lodge (Acclaimed), 2 Fellows Rd, Hampstead, NW3 3LP ☎071-722 5032 Fax: 071-586 8735 ♿
£ B&B £50–£70; [10% V w/e].

Rosslyn House, 2 Rosslyn Hill, NW3 1PH ☎071-431 3873
£ B&B £42·50–£52·50.

NW6
Dawson House, 72 Canfield Gdns, NW6 3ED ☎071-624 0079. *Hotel.* ⚒ De, Pl, Yu
£ B&B £19–£25; [10% V].

NW7
★★★ Welcome Break, Scratchwood Service Area, M1, nr Hendon, NW7 3HB ☎081-906 0611 Tx: 9413467
See Motor Lodge section

NW11
Croft Court (Highly Acclaimed), 44 Ravenscroft Av, Golders Green, NW11 8AY ☎081-458 3331. Fax: 081-455 9175. *Hotel.* ⚒ Fr, Po
£ B&B £44–£49; [10% V Sun–Thur]

Central, 35 Hoop La, Finchley Rd, Golders Green, NW11 8BS ☎081-458 5636 Fax: 081-455 4792. *Hotel.* ⚒Fr, De
£ B&B £35–£45; [10% V].
Hazelwood House, 865 Finchley Rd, Golders Green, NW11 8LX ☎081-458 8884. *Private Hotel.*
£ B&B £22–£26; [5% V Nov–Mar].
Regal, 170 Golders Green Rd, NW11 8BB ☎081-455 7025. *Guest House.*

SE3
★★ Bardon Lodge, 15 Stratheden Rd, Blackheath, SE3 7TH ☎081-853 4051 Fax: 081-858 7387
Two grey-brick Victorian residences linked by a modern extension in keeping.
⚒ Fr, De, Es
🛏 37 bedrs, 31 en suite, (9 sh), 3 ba; annexe 30 bedrs, 30 en suite; TV; tcf
🏠 lift, TV, ns; P 16, coach; child facs; con 20
✕ LD 9.30, Resid & Rest lic
£ B&B £54 (w/e £21); B&B (double) £75; D £14·30; WB
cc Access, Amex, B'card/Visa; dep.

Vanbrugh (Highly Acclaimed), St John's Park, SE3 7TD ☎081-853 4051 Fax: 081-858 7387. *Hotel.* ⚒ De
£ B&B £58–£65 (w/e £31).

Clarendon (Acclaimed), 8–16 Montpelier Row, Blackheath, SE3 0RW ☎081-318 4321 Tx: 896367. *Hotel.* ⚒ Es, Fn
£ B&B £40·15–£44.

Stonehall House, 35–37 Westcombe Park Rd, Blackheath, SE3 7RE ☎081-858 8706. *Hotel.*
£ B&B £21; [10% V].

SE9
Yardley Court (Acclaimed), 18 Court Yard, Eltham, SE9 5PZ ☎081-850 1850. *Private Hotel.*

SE10
★★ Ibis Greenwich, 30 Stockwell St, SE10 9JN ☎081-305 1177 Tx: 929647 Fax: 081-358 7139 ♿
Attractive 3-storey purpose-built hotel close to Cutty Sark and Maritime Museum. ⚒Fr
🛏 82 bedrs, 82 en suite; TV
🏠 lift, TV, dogs, ns; P 47; child facs
✕ LD 10.30
£ B&B £47, B&B (double) £52; L £8·50, D £10
cc Access, Amex, B'card/Visa, Diners

SE19
Crystal Palace Tower, 114 Church Rd, SE19 2UB ☎081-653 0176. *Guest House.* ⚒ Fr
£ B&B £18–£25; [5% V].

SW1
★★★★★ Berkeley, Wilton Pl, Knightsbridge, SW1X 7RL ☎071-235 6000 Tx: 919252 Fax: 071-235 4330

Five-storey modern building but retaining style and luxury of old Berkeley. Indoor swimming pool, sauna, solarium, gymnasium.
🛏 160 bedrs, 160 en suite; TV
🏠 lift, G 60 (£19); child facs; con 220
✕ LD 11
£ room £150–£215, double room £215–£265; L £17·50
cc Access, Amex, B'card/Visa, Diners; dep.
(*London street map 10B2*)

Licences

Establishments have a full licence unless shown as unlicensed or with the limitations listed on p 6.

★★★★★ **Hyatt Carlton Tower,** 2 Cadogan Place, SW1X 9PY ☎071-235 5411 Tx: 21944 Fax: 071-235 9129

Modern luxury hotel conveniently situated in Knightsbridge. Tennis, sauna, solarium, gymnasium. Fr, De, It, Es, Po
224 bedrs, 224 en suite; TV
lift, ns; G 55 (£16); child facs; con 150
LD 11
£ room £218·50–£241·50 (w/e £182·50); Bk £8·75, L £23·50, D £30·35
cc Access, Amex, B'card/Visa, CB, Diners.
(*London street map 10A1*)

★★★★★ **Hyde Park,** Knightsbridge, SW1Y 7LA ☎071-235 2000 Tx: 262057
Situated in Knightsbridge overlooking Hyde Park. Luxuriously modernised hotel. (THF)

★★★★★ **Sheraton Park Tower,** 101 Knightsbridge, SW1X 7RN ☎071-235 8050 Tx: 917222 Fax: 071-235 8231

Elegant circular tower block set in the heart of Knightsbridge. Luxuriously furnished. Fr, De, It, Es, Tu
295 bedrs, 295 en suite; TV
lift, ns; G 90 (£5·20), coach; child facs; con 80
LD 11.30
£ B&B £207–£287, B&B (double) £228·50–£299; L £18, D £26;
cc Access, Amex, B'card/Visa, Diners.

★★★★ **Belgravia Sheraton,** 20 Chesham Pl, SW1X 8HQ ☎071-235 6040 Tx: 919020 Fax: 071-259 6243
Luxury hotel in heart of Belgravia.
89 bedrs, 89 en suite; TV
lift, ns; child facs; con 25
(*London street map 10B1*)

Weekend breaks
Please consult the hotel for full details of weekend breaks; prices shown are an indication only. Many hotels offer mid week breaks as well.

★★★★ **Cavendish,** Jermyn St, SW1Y 6JF ☎071-930 2111 Tx: 263187 Fax: 071-839 2125

Purpose-built hotel with modern decor. Situated near Piccadilly. (THF)
254 bedrs, 254 en suite; TV
lift, dogs, ns; P 80; child facs; con 100
(*London street map 11B3*)

★★★★ **Chelsea,** 17 Sloane St, SW1X 9NU ☎071-235 4377 Tx: 91911 Fax: 071-235 3705
Modern, luxuriously furnished, tower-block hotel at the Knightsbridge end of Sloane Street.
225 bedrs, 225 en suite; TV; tcf
lift, dogs, ns; coach; child facs; con 120
(*London street map 10A1*)

★★★★ **Dukes,** St James's Place, SW1A 1NY ☎071-491 4840 Tx: 28283 Fax: 071-491 1264

Five-storey Edwardian building in quiet courtyard. Small luxury hotel. Fr, De, It
62 bedrs, 62 en suite; TV
lift; children over 10; con 10
LD 10.30
£ room £170, double room £198; Bk fr £8·50; L fr £18; D fr £25
cc Access, Amex, B'card/Visa, Diners.

★★★★ **Goring,** Beeston Pl, Grosvenor Gdns, SW1W 0JW ☎071-834 8211 Tx: 919166 Fax: 071-834 4393

Elegant 6-storey Edwardian building proprietor-run for three generations. Fr, De, It, Es, Po.
90 bedrs, 90 en suite; TV
lift; P 10 (£7·50), G 3 (£7·50); child facs; con 50
LD 10; bar meals only Sat lunch
£ room £105–£115, double room £155–£165; L £20, D £24
cc Access, Amex, B'card/Visa, Diners.
(*London street map 11A1*)

★★★★ C **Lowndes Thistle,** Lowndes St, SW1X 9ES ☎071-235 6020 Tx: 919065 Fax: 071-235 1154

Deluxe hotel in Belgravia with Adam styled interior. Near to Harrods. Fr, De, It, Da, Ja. (MtCh)
79 bedrs, 79 en suite; TV
lift, ns; coach; child facs
LD 10.30
£ room £138–£155·25, double room £161–£181; Bk £9·25, L £19·50, D £19·50; [V w/e low season]
cc Access, Amex, B'card/Visa, Diners.
(*London street map 10A1*)

★★★★ C R **Royal Horseguards Thistle,** Whitehall Court, SW1A 2EJ ☎071-839 3400 Tx; 917096 Fax: 071-925 2263

Impressive deluxe hotel overlooking River Thames. Near Trafalgar Square. (ThH)
376 bedrs, 376 en suite; TV; tcf
lift, ns; coach; child facs; con 60
LD 11.15
£ room £93, double room £99; Bk £8·95, L £15·75; D £15·75; WB
cc Access, Amex, B'card/Visa, CB, Diners; dep. (*London street map 12B3*)

★★★★ C **Royal Westminster Thistle,** Buckingham Palace Rd, SW1W 0QT ☎071-834 1821 Tx: 916821 Fax: 071-931 7542

Deluxe hotel near Victoria coach and rail terminus. (MtCh)
🛏 134 bedrs, 134 en suite; TV
🏠 lift, ns; coach; child facs; con 150
✕ LD 11.30
£ room £105, double room £130; Bk £9·25, L £15·95, D £15·95; WB
cc Access, Amex, B'card/Visa, CB, Diners
(*London street map 11B1*)

★★★★ **Scandic Crown,** 2 Bridge Pl, SW1V 1QA ☎071-834 8123 Tx: 914973
Fax: 071-828 1099
Modern hotel with sleek Scandinavian decor and furnishings. Just behind Victoria Station. Indoor swimming pool, sauna, solarium.
🛏 212 bedrs, 212 en suite; TV
🏠 lift, ns; coach; child facs; con 250
(*London street map 17B3*)

★★★★ **Stakis St Ermin's,** Caxton St, SW1H 0QW ☎071-222 7888 Tx: 917731
Fax: 071-222 6914
Carefully restored, elegant Victorian building with spectacular public rooms.
Fr, De, It, Es, Du, Ar (Sk).
🛏 290 bedrs, 290 en suite; TV; tcf
🏠 lift, dogs, ns; P 23 (£5), coach; child facs; con 250
✕ LD 11
£ L £14·50; D £15·50; WB £42 (min 2 nts)

★★★ H C **Royal Court,** Sloane Sq, SW1W 8EG ☎071-730 9191 Tx: 296818
Fax: 071-824 8381

Period building, recently refurbished in traditional style, overlooking Sloane Square.
Fr, De, It, Es. (QMH)
🛏 102 bedrs, 102 en suite; TV; tcf
🏠 lift; G 5 (£20), coach; child facs; con 40
✕ LD 10.30; bar meals only Sat lunch
£ B&B £128·50 (w/e £57), B&B (double) £162; [10% V w/d]
cc Access, Amex, B'card/Visa; dep.
(*London street map 16B3*)

★★★ **Grosvenor,** 101 Buckingham Palace Rd. SW1W 0SJ ☎071-834 9494 Tx: 916006
Fax: 071-630 1978
Stone-faced, 6-storey Victorian building next to Victoria Station. Fr, Es, It, Po
🛏 366 bedrs, 366 en suite; TV; tcf
🏠 lift, TV, ns; coach; child facs; con 200
✕ LD 10.30
£ B&B £95·45–£104·95 (w/e £44·50), B&B (double) £121·90–£131·90; HB weekly £521·15–£556·15. L £13·50, D £10·50; [5% V]
cc Access, Amex, B'card/Visa, Diners.

★★★ **Rubens,** Buckingham Palace Rd, SW1W 0PS ☎071-834 6600 Tx: 916577
Fax: 071-828 5401
Imposing building near Victoria and opposite mews entrance to Buckingham Palace. Fr, It, Po
🛏 191 bedrs, 191 en suite; TV; tcf
🏠 lift, ns; coach; child facs; con 80
✕ LD 10, nr Sat & Sun lunch

£ B&B £98·25–£113·25, B&B (double) £126·50–£141·50; L £14·95, D £15·50
cc Access, Amex, B'card/Visa, Diners
(*London street map 11B1*)

★ **Ebury Court,** 26 Ebury St, SW1W 0LV
☎071-730 8147 Fax: 071-823 5966
Quiet hotel with resident proprietor. Near Victoria Station. Closed 2 wks Xmas
🛏 45 bedrs, 13 en suite, (3 sh), 13 ba; TV; tcf
🏠 lift, dogs; child facs
✕ LD 9; Resid, Rest & Club lic
£ B&B £50–£55, B&B (double) £75–£95
cc Access, B'card/Visa; dep.
(*London street map 16B3*)

Caswell, 25 Gloucester St, SW1V 2DB
☎071-834 6345. *Hotel.* Fr
£ B&B £23–£34.
Diplomat, 2 Chesham St, Belgrave Sq, SW1X 8DT ☎071-235 1544. Tx: 926679
Fax: 071-259 6153. *Hotel.*
£ B&B £54·95–£64·95.
Easton, 36–40 Belgrave Rd, SW1V 1RG
☎071-834 5938 Fax: 071-976 6560. *Guest House.* Fr, De, It, Gr
Elizabeth, 37 Eccleston Sq, SW1V 1PB
☎071-828 6812. *Tennis. Hotel.* Fr
£ B&B £30–£50.
Executive, 57 Pont St, SW1X 0BD ☎071-581 2424 Tx: 9413498 Fax: 071-589 9456
£ B&B £62·19–£74·69.
Hamilton House, 60 Warwick Way, SW1V 1SA ☎071-821 7113 Tx: 262433. *Hotel.*
Fr, It, Da
£ B&B £35–£50; D £12; [10% V w/e].
Willett, 32 Sloane Gdns, Sloane Sq, SW1W 8DJ ☎071-824 8415 Tx: 926678
Fax: 071-824 8415. *Hotel.*
£ B&B £62·19–£68·94.
Winchester, 17 Belgrave Rd, SW1 1RB
☎071-828 2972. *Hotel.*

SW3

★★★★ **Capital,** Basil St, Knightsbridge, ♿ SW3 1AT ☎071-589 5171 Tx: 919042
Fax: 071-225 0011

Modern luxury hotel with stylish furnishings. Adjacent to Harrods. Fr, It, Es
🛏 48 bedrs, 48 en suite; TV
🏠 lift, dogs; G 13; child facs; con 22
✕ LD 11
£ B&B £157·50, B&B (double) £190, L £18·50, D £30
cc Access, Amex, B'card/Visa, CB, Diners.
(*London street map 10A1*)

★★★ H R **Basil Street,** Knightsbridge, SW3 1AH ☎071-581 3311 Tx: 28379
Fax: 071-581 3693

Elegant hotel with period furnishings. A few steps from Harrods. Fr, De, It, Es
🛏 92 bedrs, 72 en suite, 8 ba; TV
🏠 lift, dogs; child facs; con 50
✕ LD 9.45, coffee shop only Sat lunch

£ room £100, double room £133; Bk £9·50, L £13·50, D £23
cc Access, Amex, B'card/Visa, Diners.
(*London street map 10A2*)

Parkes, 41–43 Beaufort Gdns, SW3 1PW
☎071-581 9944 Tx: 922488
Fax: 071-225 3447
Hotel awaiting inspection.
🛏 30 bedrs, 30 en suite
£ B&B £90–£150, B&B (double) £185–£200.

Blair House, 34 Draycott Pl. SW3 2SA
☎071-581 2323 Fax: 071-823 7752.
Hotel. It, Es
£ room £35–£52.
Claverley, 13 Beaufort Gdns, SW3 1PS
☎071-589 8541. *Hotel.*
Knightsbridge, 10 Beaufort Gdns, SW3 1PT ☎071-589 9271 Fax: 071-823 9692.
Hotel.

SW5

★★★★ **Swallow International,** Cromwell Rd, SW5 0TH ☎071-973 1000 Tx: 27260
Fax: 071-244 8194
International hotel located in West End of London near Earls Court. Indoor swimming pool, sauna, solarium, gymnasium. Fr, De, It, Es, Du. (Sw)
🛏 417 bedrs, 417 en suite; TV; tcf
🏠 lift, dogs, ns; P 60 (£11·50), G 20 (£11·50), coach; child facs; con 200
✕ LD midnight
£ B&B £85, B&B (double) £100; L £10·50, D £13·95; WB £88 (HB)
cc Access, Amex, B'card/Visa, Diners.

Merlyn Court, 2 Barkston Gdns, SW5 0EN
☎071-370 1640 Fr, It, Es
B&B £20–£25; [10% V Oct–Apr].

SW6

★★★ **Ramada Inn,** Lillie Rd, SW6 1UQ
☎071-385 1255 Tx: 917728.
Fax: 071-381 4450
Large tower hotel close to Earls Court Exhibition Centre.
🛏 501 bedrs, 501 en suite; TV; tcf
🏠 lift, ns; P 130 (£5), coach; child facs; con 1750
✕ LD 10.30
cc Access, Amex, B'card/Visa, Diners.
(*See advertisement on p. 72*)

SW7

★★★★ **Gloucester,** 4–18 Harrington Gdns, SW7 4LH ☎071-373 6030
Tx: 917505 Fax: 071-373 0409
Seven-storey modern purpose-built hotel just off Cromwell Road. Fr, De, It, Es
🛏 550 bedrs, 550 en suite; TV; tcf
🏠 lift, ns, G 120 (£10), coach; child facs; con 600
✕ LD 10.30
£ B&B £129·75–£149·75 (w/e £58), B&B (double) £157·50–£187·50; L £15·50, D £18·50
cc Access, Amex, B'card/Visa, CB, Diners.

Please tell the manager if you chose your hotel through an advertisement in the guide.

★★★★ **Norfolk,** 2–10 Harrington Rd, SW7 3ER ☎071-589 8191 Tx: 268852 Fax: 071-581 1874

Built in 1888, a brick and sandstone building recently refurbished to retain its original charm and elegance. Sauna, solarium, gymnasium. Fr, De, It, Es, Du, Po. (QMH)
96 bedrs, 96 en suite; TV; tcf
lift, dogs; coach; child facs; con 60
LD 10.30; bar meals only Sat lunch
£ B&B £118 (w/e £44·50), B&B (double) £156–£176; L £14·50, D £16·75; [10% V]
cc Access, Amex, B'card/Visa, Diners.

★★★ C R **Forum,** Cromwell Rd, SW7 4DN ☎071-370 5757 Tx: 919663 Fax: 071-373 1448

Modern 27-storey building; "London Pub" bar a feature. Near Gloucester Rd tube.
Fr, De, It, Es, Ja
911 bedrs, 911 en suite; TV; tcf
lift, ns; G 90 (£6·50), coach; child facs; con 500
LD 11
£ B&B £110–£130 (w/e fr £32·50), B&B (double) £135–£155; L £14·50, D £14·50; [10% V]
cc Access, Amex, B'card/ Visa, Diners; dep.

★★★ H **Regency,** 100 Queen's Gate, SW7 5AG ☎071-370 4595 Tx: 267594 Fax: 071-370 5555

A well-decorated hotel in a row of tall Victorian houses in a tree-lined road. Sauna, solarium, gymnasium. Fr, De, It, Es.
210 bedrs, 210 en suite; TV
lift, ns; coach; child facs; con 200
LD 10·30
£ B&B £111–£115 (w/e £49·50), B&B (double) £139–£145; L £12, D £20; [10% V]
cc Access, Amex, B'card/Visa, Diners.

★★★ **Rembrandt,** 11 Thurloe Pl, SW7 2RS ☎071-589 8100 Tx: 295828 Fax: 071-225 3363
Ornate six-storey Victorian hotel close to V and A Museum and Harrods. Swimming pool, sauna, solarium, gymnasium. Fr, De, It, Es, Po, Du, Tu, Ma
200 bedrs, 200 en suite; TV
lift, ns; coach; child facs; con 220
LD 10
£ B&B £93·25, B&B (double) £121·50; L £14·95, D £14·95; WB £61
cc Access, Amex, B'card/Visa, Diners; dep.

★★★ **Vanderbilt,** 68–86 Cromwell Rd, SW7 5BT ☎071-589 2424 Tx: 946944 Fax: 071-225 2293

Large hotel off Cromwell Road, completely refurbished to high standard.
224 bedrs, 224 en suite; TV
lift, dogs; coach; child facs; con 120

Alexander, 9 Sumner Pl, SW7 3EE ☎071-581 1591 Tx: 917133 Fax: 071-589 5530
Hotel awaiting inspection.
60 bedrs, 60 en suite; TV; tcf
£ B&B £70, B&B (double) £90–£130.

Prince, 6 Sumner Pl, SW7 3AB ☎071-589 6488 Tx: 917133 Fax: 071-589 5530
Hotel awaiting inspection.
30 bedrs, 21 en suite
£ B&B £30–£40, B&B (double) £45–£55.

Number Eight, Emperors Gate, SW7 4HH ☎071-370 7516 Tx: 925975 Fax: 071-373 3163. *Private Hotel.* It, Pl
£ B&B £57·50–£69 [5% V].

SW15

Lodge, 52 Upper Richmond Rd, Putney, SW15 2RN ☎081-874 1598 Fax: 081-874 0910. *Hotel. Billiards.*

SW19

★★★★**Cannizaro House,** West Side, Wimbledon Common, SW19 4UF ☎081-879 1464 Tx: 9413837 Fax: 081-879 7338

Georgian mansion luxuriously furnished and equipped in garden and parkland on edge of Wimbledon Common.
51 bedrs, 51 en suite; TV
lift, dogs; P 60, coach; child facs; con 50
LD 10.30
£ room £85, double room £99; Bk £8, L £16·50, D £16·50; WB
cc Access, Amex, B'card/Visa, CB, Diners.

Worcester House (Acclaimed), 38 Alwyne Rd, Wimbledon, SW19 7AE ☎081-946 1300. *Hotel.*
£ B&B £40·50–£47·50

Trochee, 21 Malcolm Rd, Wimbledon, SW19 4AS ☎081-946 3924 Fax: 081-785 4058. *Hotel.*
£ B&B £32 (w/e £30); [5% V Sep–Mar].
Trochee, 52 Ridgway Pl, Wimbledon, SW19 4SW ☎081-946 1579 Fax: 081-785 4058. *Hotel.*
£ B&B £32–£64; [5% V Sep–Mar].
Wimbledon, 78 Worple Rd, SW19 4HZ ☎081-946 9265. *Hotel.*
£ B&B £38–£42.

W1

★★★★★ **Churchill,** 30 Portman Sq, W1A 4ZX ☎071-486 5800 Tx: 264831 Fax: 071-486 1255

Elegant purpose-built luxury hotel near Marble Arch. Tennis.
452 bedrs, 452 en suite; TV
lift, ns; G 48, coach; child facs; con 250
(*London street map 2A2*)

★★★★★ **Claridge's,** Brook St, W1A 2JQ ☎071-629 8860 Tx: 21872 Fax: 071-499 2210

Elegant, spacious luxury hotel with its own famous style and character.
190 bedrs, 190 en suite; TV
lift; child facs; con 200
£ room £190–£220, double room £245–£285
cc Access, Amex, B'card/Visa, Diners.
(*London street map 3A1*)

EC *early closing* **MD** *market day* *country house hotel* *ns (NS) no smoking areas* *tcf tea/coffee facilities*

★★★★★ Connaught, Carlos Pl, W1Y 6AL ☎071-499 7070

Beautifully-appointed luxury hotel in elegant Mayfair building. ✂ Fr, De, It, Es
🛏 90 bedrs, 90 en suite; TV
🏨 lift; child facs
✕ LD 10.15
£ L £20·45, D £24·70
cc Access

★★★★★ Dorchester, Park La, W1A 2HJ ☎071-629 8888 Tx: 887704
Famous international luxury hotel in distinctive building overlooking Hyde Park. Recently refurbished to the highest standards.
£ room £180–205, double room £215–£240

★★★★★ Grosvenor House, Park La, W1A 3AA ☎071-499 6363 Tx: 24871 Fax: 071-[illegible]

Overlooking Hyde Park, luxury hotel offering elegant accommodation. Indoor swimming pool, sauna, solarium, gymnasium. (THF)
🛏 454 bedrs, 454 en suite; TV
🏨 lift, ns; P 20, G 100 (£18); child facs; con 1,500
(*London street map 2B1*)

★★★★★ Inn on the Park, Hamilton Pl, Park La, W1A 1AZ ☎071-499 0888 Tx: 22771 Fax: 071-499 5572

Spacious luxury tower block situated beside Hyde Park. ✂ De, It, Es, Du
🛏 228 bedrs, 228 en suite; TV
🏨 lift, ns; G 80 (£10); child facs; con 250
✕ LD midnight
£ B&B £211·31–£237·48 (w/e £180), B&B (double) £257·31–£260·48; L fr £23·25, D fr £30
cc Access, Amex, B'card/Visa, Diners.
(*London street map 10B2*)

★★★★★ London Hilton on Park Lane, Park La, W1A 2HH ☎071-493 8000 Tx: 24873 Fax: 071-493 4957
Modern luxury tower block on Park Lane. Elegantly furnished. Sauna, solarium. (HI)
🛏 446 bedrs, 446 en suite; TV
🏨 lift, dogs, ns; child facs; con 1000
(*London street map 10B3*)

★★★★★ London Marriott, Grosvenor Sq, W1A 4AW ☎071-493 1232 Tx: 268101 Fax: 071-491 3201

Large modern luxury hotel, situated between Oxford Street and Grosvenor Square. ✂ Fr, De, It, Es, Du, Sw
🛏 223 bedrs, 223 en suite; TV
🏨 lift, ns; child facs; con 375
✕ LD 10pm; nr Sat lunch
£ B&B £190·50–£215·50 (w/e £78·37), B&B (double) £200–£237·25; WB
cc Access, Amex, B'card/Visa, CB, Diners.
(*London street map 2B1*)

★★★★★ Mayfair Inter-Continental, Stratton St, W1A 2AN ☎071-629 7777 Tx: 262526 ♿
Imposing large modern luxury hotel, situated in the heart of Mayfair.

★★★★★ Meridien Piccadilly, Piccadilly W1V 0BH ☎071-734 8000 Tx: 25795 Fax: 071-437 3574 ♿

Luxury hotel furnished with great style. Indoor swimming pool, squash, sauna, solarium, gymnasium, billiards. ✂ Fr, De
🛏 260 bedrs, 260 en suite; TV
🏨 lift, ns; G (£24); child facs; con 250
£ B&B £213–£236, B&B (double) £241–£264; WB £165 (2 nts)
(*London street map 4A1*)

> **Residents only**
> Some Listed hotels only serve meals to residents. It is always wise to make a reservation for a meal in a hotel.

★★★★★ Ritz, 150 Piccadilly, W1V 9DG ☎071-493 8181 Tx: 267200 Fax: 071-493 2687

Famous luxury hotel in Piccadilly. Elegant decor and furnishing. ✂ Fr, De, It, Es
🛏 130 bedrs, 130 en suite; TV
🏨 lift; child facs; con 60
✕ LD 11
£ B&B £197, B&B (double) £240; L £24·50, D £37·50; WB £180 (2 nts)
cc Access, Amex, B'card/Visa, Diners; dep.
(*London street map 11B3*)

★★★★ Athenaeum, 116 Piccadilly, W1V 0BJ ☎071-499 3464 Tx: 261589 Fax: 071-493 1860

Elegant modern hotel overlooking Green Park. Stylish furnishing. ✂ Fr, De, It, Es, Po.
🛏 112 bedrs, 112 en suite; TV
🏨 lift, ns; child facs; con 44
✕ LD 10.30
£ B&B £168 (w/e £75), B&B (double) £189–£204; L £22, D £29
cc Access, Amex, B'card/Visa, Diners.
(*London street map 11A3*)

★★★★ Berkshire, 350 Oxford St, W1N 0BY ☎071-629 7474 Tx: 22270 Fax: 071-629 8156

Purpose-built, eight storey hotel superbly furnished in traditional style, just off Oxford Street.

> **Discount vouchers**
> RAC discount vouchers are on p. 34. Hotels with a [V] shown at the end of the price information will accept them in part payment for accommodation bills on the full, standard rate, not against bargain breaks or any other special offers. Please note the limitations shown in the entry: w/e for weekends, w/d for weekdays, and which months they are accepted.

London SW6

London SE23

London W1

147 bedrs, 147 en suite; TV
lift, dogs, ns; coach; child facs; con 50
LD 10.30; bar meals only Sat lunch
£ room £142, double room £182; Bk £11·50, L £19·70
cc Access, Amex, B'card/Visa, Diners.

★★★★ C R **Britannia Inter-Continental,** Grosvenor Sq, W1A 3AN
071-629 9400 Tx: 23941
Fax: 071-629 7736

Elegant hotel in imposing Georgian-style block in Grosvenor Square. Fr, De, It, Es, Ar
326 bedrs, 326 en suite; TV
lift, ns; P 16, G 180; child facs; con 100
LD 10.30; coffee shop only Sat lunch & all Sun
£ B&B £154·25 (w/e £109·50) B&B (double) £222·25; L £18·95, D £25·50
cc Access, Amex, B'card/Visa, Diners.
(*London street map 2B1*)

★★★★ **Brown's,** Albemarle St, Dover St, W1A 4SW 071-493 6020
Tx: 28686
Fax: 071-493 9381
Luxury period hotel in elegant Mayfair terrace near Bond Street. (THF)
133 bedrs, 133 en suite; TV
lift, dogs, ns; child facs; con 80
(*London street map 3B1*)

★★★★ H C **Chesterfield,** 35 Charles St, W1X 8LX 071-491 2622 Tx: 269394
Fax: 071-491 4793
Luxury hotel in distinguished Georgian building in Mayfair. Fr, De, It, Es, Po, Du, Da, Ar.
110 bedrs, 110 en suite; TV
lift, ns; child facs; con 100
LD 10.30
£ B&B £111·75–£113·75 (w/e £45), B&B (double) £163·50–£317·50; L £16·50, D £22·50
cc Access, Amex, B'card/Visa, Diners.
(*London street map 11A3*)

★★★★ **Cumberland,** 1A Gt Cumberland Pl, Marble Arch, W1A 4RF 071-262 1234
Tx: 22215 Fax: 071-724 4621

Very large modern hotel situated at west end of Oxford Street. Sauna, solarium. (THF)
905 bedrs, 905 en suite; TV
lift, dogs, ns; coach; child facs; con 500
(*London street map 2A2*)

★★★★ **Green Park,** Half Moon St, W1Y 8BP 071-629 7522 Tx: 28856
Fax: 071-491 8971
Hotel in Georgian terrace just off Piccadilly. Near Green Park. Fr, De, It, Du, Ar.
161 bedrs, 161 en suite; TV
lift, ns; coach; child facs; con 65
LD 10.45
£ B&B £100·50, B&B (double) £142; L £14·85, D £14·85
cc Access, Amex, B'card/Visa, CB, Diners.
(*London street map 11A3*)

★★★★ **Holiday Inn Marble Arch,** 134 George St, W1H 6DN 071-723 1277
Tx: 27983 Fax: 071-402 0666
Twelve-storey modern luxury hotel, near Marble Arch. Indoor swimming pool, sauna, solarium, gymnasium. (CHIC)
241 bedrs, 241 en suite; TV
lift, dogs, ns; P 5, G 60; child facs; con 120
LD 10.30
£ room £136–£151, double room £162–£181; Bk £10·25, L £14·50, D £15; WB
cc Access, Amex, B'card/Visa, CB, Diners.
(*London street map 1B2*)

★★★★ **Holiday Inn Mayfair,** 3 Berkeley St, W1X 6NE 071-493 8282 Tx: 24561
Fax: 071-629 2827
In heart of central London, luxury hotel offering atmosphere of elegance. (HI)
186 bedrs, 186 en suite; TV; tcf
lift, ns; child facs; con 70
LD 10.30, nr Sat & Sun lunch
£ B&B £150·75, B&B (double) £191·50; L £13·75, D £18·50; WB £119 (2 nts); [5% V]
cc Access, Amex, B'card/Visa, Diners.
(*London street map 11B3*)

★★★★ **Park Lane,** Brick St, Piccadilly, W1Y 8BX 071-499 6321 Tx: 21533
Fax: 071-499 1965

Large period luxury hotel, modernised with style. Overlooking Green Park. Solarium, gymnasium. Fr, De, It, Es, Ja.
320 bedrs, 320 en suite; TV
lift, dogs, ns; G 180, coach; child facs; con 600
£ room £169–£200, double room £200–236; Bk £8, L £15, D £23; WB
cc Access, Amex, B'card/Visa, Diners.
(*London street map 11A2*)

Please tell the manager if you chose your hotel through an advertisement in the guide.

★★★★ R **Portman Inter-Continental,** Portman Sq, W1H 9FL 071-486 5844
Tx: 261526 Fax: 071-935 0537

In Portman Square, modern luxury hotel with pleasing decor. Tennis.
272 bedrs, 272 en suite; TV; tcf
lift; G 400, coach; child facs; con 420
LD 11, coffee shop only Sat lunch
£ B&B £172–£196 (w/e £109), B&B (double) £208–£221; HB weekly £826–£871·50; L £14, D £17; [10% V]
cc Access, Amex, B'card/Visa, CB, Diners.
(*London street map 2A2*)

★★★★ **Ramada,** Berners St, W1A 3BE
071-636 1629 Tx: 25759
Fax: 071-580 3972

Edwardian hotel with elegant public rooms, graced by marble columns and classical ceilings.
238 bedrs, 238 en suite; TV
lift, ns; coach; child facs; con 200
(*London street map 4A2*)

★★★★ **Regent Crest,** Carburton St, W1P 8EE 071-388 2300 Tx: 22453
Fax: 071-387 2806

Large modern luxury hotel near Tottenham Court Road. Fr, It, Es. (Cr/THF)

319 bedrs, 319 en suite; TV; tcf
lift, ns; G 80, coach; child facs; con 600
LD 10.30, nr Sat & Sun lunch
£ room £104–£114 (w/e £41), double room £119–£129; Bk £9·95; [10% V]
cc Access, Amex, B'card/Visa, Diners; dep.

★★★★ **St George's,** Langham Pl, W1N 8QS 071-580 0111 Tx: 27274
Fax: 071-436 7997

Modern luxury hotel in tower block adjacent to the BBC. Fr, De, It, Es. (THF)
86 bedrs, 86 en suite; TV; tcf
lift, ns; P 2, coach; child facs; con 35
LD 10, bar meals only Sat & Sun lunch
£ room £100–£110, double room £125–£135; Bk £7·25, L £18·50, D £18·50; WB £56
cc Access, Amex, B'card/Visa, CB, Diners.
(*London street map 3B3*)

★★★★ **Selfridge,** Orchard St, W1H 0JS
071-408 2080 Tx: 22361
Fax: 071-629 8849

Luxury hotel on Orchard Street, adjacent to Selfridge's store. (MtCh)
298 bedrs, 298 en suite; TV
lift, ns; coach; child facs; con 250
LD 11
£ room £124, double room £145; Bk £9·25, L £16·95, D £16·95; WB £49·50
cc Access, Amex, B'card/Visa, CB, Diners.
(*London street map 2B2*)

★★★★ **Washington,** 5 Curzon St, W1Y 8DT 071-499 7000 Tx: 24540
Fax: 071-495 6172
Seven-storey, purpose-built Mayfair hotel, with art-deco style. Fr, De, Es
173 bedrs, 173 en suite; TV
lift, dogs, ns; coach; child facs; con 70
LD 10
£ room £118 (w/e £40), double room £148; Bk £9·75, L £16, D £16
cc Access, Amex, B'card/Visa, Diners; dep.

★★★★ **Westbury,** Bond St at Conduit St, W1A 4UH 071-629 7755 Tx: 24378
Fax: 071-495 1163

Distinctive 8-storey modern luxury building in the heart of Mayfair. (THF)
243 bedrs, 243 en suite; TV
lift, dogs, ns; P 16; child facs; con 120
(*London street map 3B1*)

★★★ **Clifton-Ford,** Welbeck St, W1M 8DN
071-486 6600 Tx: 22569
Fax: 071-486 7492

Well-equipped hotel in Georgian terrace.
Fr, De, It, Es, Ca
213 bedrs, 213 en suite; TV, tcf
lift, dogs; G 20 (£16), coach; child facs; con 80
LD 11, bar meals only lunch
£ B&B £123 £146·50, B&B (double) £155 £218·25; D £19
cc Access, Amex, B'card/Visa, Diners.
(*London street map 2B3*)

★★★ **Flemings,** 7–12 Half Moon St, W1Y 8BQ 071-499 2964 Tx: 27510
Fax: 071-629 4063

A luxurious hotel in a Georgian terrace.
137 bedrs, 137 en suite; TV
lift, dogs; coach; child facs; con 25
(*London street map 11A3*)

★★★ **Londoner,** 57–59 Welbeck St, W1M 8HS 071-935 4442 Tx: 894630
Fax: 071-487 3782
Six-storey hotel in an Edwardian terrace close to Oxford Street. Fr, De, Es, Sw.
144 bedrs, 144 en suite; TV
lift, ns; coach; child facs; con 90
LD 10.30
£ room £126·50 (w/e £37·50), double room £143·75; Bk £8·75, L £13·95, D £13·95; WB
cc Access, Amex, B'card/Visa, Diners.
(*London street map 10B2*)

★★★ **Mandeville,** Mandeville Pl, W1M 6BE 071-935 5599 Tx: 269487
Fax: 071-935 9588
Modernised Victorian hotel conveniently placed just behind Oxford Street.
165 beds, 165 en suite; TV
lift; coach; child facs
£ B&B £85–£93·50 (w/e £45), B&B (double) £105–£115·50; L £15, D £15
cc Access, Amex, B'card/Visa, Diners; dep.
(*London street map 2B2*)
(*See advertisement on p. 72*)

★★★ **Mostyn,** Bryanston St, W1H 0DE
071-935 2361 Tx: 27656
Fax: 071-487 2759

Modernised hotel in quiet side road. Fr, De, It, Es, Sw
122 bedrs, 122 en suite; TV
lift, ns; coach; child facs; con 150
LD 11.45
£ B&B £91·25–£102·50, B&B (double) £113·50–£130; L £12·50, D £12·95; [10% V]
cc Access, Amex, B'card/Visa, CB, Diners
(*London street map 2A2*)

★★★ **Mount Royal,** 49 Bryanston St, W1A 4UR 071-629 8040 Tx: 23355
Fax: 071-499 7792

Large modernised hotel situated near Marble Arch. Fr, It, Es. (MtCh)
705 bedrs, 705 en suite; TV; tcf
lift, ns; coach; child facs; con 320
LD 11
£ B&B £88; B&B (double) £106; L £11·50, D £11·50; WB £35·50
cc Access, Amex, B'card/Visa, Diners.

★★ **Regent Palace,** Glasshouse St, Piccadilly Circus, W1A 4BZ 071-734 7000 Tx: 23740 Fax: 071-734 6435
Large hotel near Piccadilly Circus. Custom-built between the wars. (THF)

999 bedrs, 123 ba; TV; tcf
lift, dogs, ns; coach; child facs; con 120
(*London street map 4A1*)

Edward Lear, 28 Seymour St, W1H 5WD 071-402 5401 Fax: 071-706 3766. *Hotel.*
£ B&B £37·50–£39·50; [10% V w/e & Dec–Feb].

Georgian House, 87 Gloucester Pl, W1H 3PG 071-935 2211 Tx: 266079 Fax: 071-486 7335. *Hotel.*
£ B&B £45.

Hart House, 51 Gloucester Pl, W1H 3PE 071-935 2288. *Hotel.*
£ B&B £30; [10% V].

Montagu House, 3 Montagu Pl, W1H 1RG 071-935 4632. *Hotel.*

W2

★★★★ **Hospitality Inn,** Bayswater Rd, W2 3HL 071-262 4461 Tx: 22667 Fax: 071-706-7560
Modernised luxury hotel block with fine views over Kensington Gardens. (MtCh)
175 bedrs, 175 en suite; TV; tcf
lift, dogs; G 40, coach; child facs; con 40
LD 10.30
£ B&B £85·50–£94 (w/e £41); B&B (double) £109·50–£118; L £7·95, D £12
cc Access, Amex, B'card/Visa, Diners.

★★★★ **London Embassy,** 150 Bayswater Rd, W2 4RT 071-229 6871 Tx: 27727 Fax: 071-229 2623

Modern 7-floor luxury hotel opposite Kensington Gardens. De, It, Es, Sw, Ar. (Emb)
193 bedrs, 193 en suite; TV; tcf
lift, dogs, ns; P10, G 30, coach; child facs; con 30
LD 10.15
£ B&B £103–£116, B&B (double) £124–£148; L £12, D £12; WB £41·50
cc Access, Amex, B'card/Visa, Diners; dep.

★★★★ **London Metropole,** Edgware Rd, W2 1JU 071-402 4141 Tx: 23711 Fax: 071-724 8866

Luxury 23-storey purpose-built hotel near Marble Arch. Fr, De, It, Es, Ja
571 bedrs, 571 en suite; TV; tcf
lift, dogs, ns; G 120 (£5); coach; child facs; con 250
LD 11
£ B&B £125 (w/e £40), B&B (double) £165; L £12, D £13·75; WB; [10% V]
cc Access, Amex, B'card/Visa, Diners

★★★★ H C R **Royal Lancaster,** Lancaster Terr, W2 2TY 071-262 6737 Tx: 24822 Fax: 071-724 3191

Large modern luxury tower block enjoying fine views of Hyde Park. Fr, De
418 bedrs, 418 en suite; TV
lift, ns; P 50 (£6), G 48 (£6); child facs; con 1400
LD 11.30, coffee shop only Sun dinner
£ B&B £148–£223 (w/e £61), B&B (double) £156–£231; L £18·50, D £21·50
cc Access, Amex, B'card/Visa, CB, Diners.
(*London street map 1A1*)

★★★★ **Whites,** Lancaster Gate, W2 3NR 071-262 2711 Tx: 24771 Fax: 071-262 2147

A fine Victorian building by Kensington Gardens. Fr, De, It, Es. (MtCh)
54 bedrs, 54 en suite; TV
lift, ns; P 25; child facs; con 20
LD 10.30
£ B&B £150, B&B (double) £210; L £17·50, D £17·50; WB £119 (2 nts)
cc Access, Amex, B'card/Visa, Diners.

★★★ **Coburg,** Bayswater Rd, W2 4RJ 071-221 2217 Tx: 268235 Fax: 071-589 9526

Distinctive older style building with 3 domes. Near Kensington Palace.
142 bedrs, 142 en suite; TV; tcf
lift, dogs; child facs
£ B&B £69·50–£94·50; B&B (double) £94·50–£150
cc Access, Amex, B'card/Visa, Diners.

★★★ **Park Court,** 75 Lancaster Gate, W2 3NN 071-402 4272 Tx: 23922 Fax: 071-705 4156

Large Regency building with superb views over the Royal Park. Fr, De, It, Es (MtCh)
398 bedrs, 398 en suite; TV, tcf
lift, dogs, ns; coach; child facs; con 120
LD 11
£ B&B £78·25, B&B (double) £103; L £12, D £13; WB £36·50
cc Access, Amex, B'card/Visa, Diners

★★ H C **Delmere,** 130 Sussex Gdns, W2 1UB 071-706 3344 Tx: 8953857 Fax: 071-262 1863

Two completely refurbished Victorian town houses by Hyde Park. Fr, De, Es, Du
38 bedrs, 38 en suite; TV; tcf
lift, dogs; P 2
LD 10.30, nr lunch & Sun dinner. Resid lic
£ B&B £61·60–£68, B&B (double) £75·50–£83; D £10·75; WB £61 (HB, 2 nts); [10% V]
cc Access, Amex, B'card/Visa, Diners
(*See advertisement on p. 77*)
(*London street map 1A2*)

Byron (Highly Acclaimed), 36–38 Queensborough Terr, W2 3SH 071-723 3386 Tx: 266059 Fax: 071-723 3505. *Hotel.* Fr, De, It, Es
£ B&B £70 (w/e £56). [5% V]

Pembridge Court (Highly Acclaimed), 34 Pembridge Gdns, W2 4DX 071-229 9977 Tx: 298363 Fax: 071-727 4982. *Hotel.* Fr, It, Es
£ B&B £63·25–£92

Camelot (Acclaimed), 45–47 Norfolk Sq, W2 1RX ☎ 071-262 1980 Tx: 268312 Fax: 071-402 3412. *Hotel.* De, Es
£ B&B £35·50–£52; [10% V Dec–Mar]
Mitre House (Acclaimed), 178–180 Sussex Gdns, Lancaster Gate, W2 1TU ☎ 071-723 8040 Tx: 914113 Fax: 071-402 0990. *Hotel.* Fr, It, Es, Gr, Is
£ B&B £50–£55
(See advertisement on p. 77)
Westland (Acclaimed), 154 Bayswater Rd, W2 4HP ☎ 071-229 9191 Tx: 94016297. *Hotel.*

Ashley, 15 Norfolk Sq, W2 1RU ☎ 071-723 3375. Closed 24 Dec–4 Jan. *Hotel.*
£ B&B £19·50–£22; dep.
Commodore, 50–52 Lancaster Gate, Hyde Park, W2 3NA ☎ 071-402 5291 Tx: 298928. *Hotel.*
Dylan, 14 Devonshire Ter, W2 3DW ☎ 071-723 3280. *Hotel.* Es
£ B&B £25–£38; [5% V Nov–Feb].
Garden Court, 30–31 Kensington Gdns Sq, W2 4BG ☎ 071-727 8304 Fax: 071-727 2749. *Hotel.*
£ B&B £26–£38.
Kings, 60–62 Queensborough Terr, W2 3SH ☎ 071-229 6848 Tx: 24236 Fax: 071-792 8868. *Hotel.* Es
£ B&B £45; [10% V].
Norfolk Plaza, 29–33 Norfolk Sq, W2 1RX ☎ 071-723 0792. *Hotel.*
Parkwood, 4 Stanhope Pl, W2 2HB ☎ 071-402 2241 Fax: 071-402 1574. *Hotel*
£ B&B £38·50–£42; [10% V Nov–Apr].
Slavia, 2 Pembridge Sq, W2 4EW ☎ 071-727 1316 Tx: 917458. *Hotel.* Fr, De, It, Es, Pl, Ru, Sc, Cz
£ B&B £23–£42; [V].
Tregaron, 17 Norfolk Sq, Hyde Park, W2 1RU ☎ 071-723 9966. *Hotel.*
Coburg, 129 Bayswater Rd, ☎ 071-221 2217.
Hotel awaiting inspection.

W3

Acton Park, 116 The Vale, W3 7JT ☎ 081-743 9417. Fax: 081-743 9417. *Hotel.*
£ B&B £45·43 (w/e £39·85); [10% V].

W5

★★★ **Carnarvon,** Ealing Common, W5 3HN ☎ 081-992 5399 Tx: 935114

Modern brick-built hotel overlooking Ealing Common; convenient for M40.

Grange Lodge, 50 Grange Rd, Ealing, W5 5BX ☎ 081-567 1049. *Hotel.* Fr
£ B&B £25–£32; [5% V w/e].

> **Atlas Section**
> Consult the Atlas section at the back of the guide to find out which towns and villages have RAC Appointed and Listed hotels in them. They are shown on the maps by purple circles.

W8

★★★★★ **Royal Garden,** Kensington High St, W8 4PT ☎ 071-937 8000 Tx: 263151 Fax: 071-938 4532

Modern purpose-built luxury hotel on edge of Kensington Gardens.
380 bedrs, 380 en suite; TV
lift, dogs, ns; G 142 (£6), coach; child facs; con 800
LD 11.30, coffee shop only Sat/Sun lunch & Sun dinner
£ B&B £143·95–£173·95 (w/e £68), B&B (double) £185·90–£202·90; L £18·50, D £35
cc Access, Amex, B'card/Visa, CB, Diners.

★★★★ **London Tara,** Scarsdale Pl, Kensington, W8 5SR ☎ 071-937 7211 Tx: 918834 Fax: 071-937 7100 ♿

Modern 12-storey hotel in a quiet cul-de-sac off Kensington High Street. Fr, De, It, Es
831 bedrs, 831 en suite; TV
lift, ns; G 90 (£6), coach; child facs; con 650
LD 1am
£ B&B £93·40–£123·40, B&B (double) £114–£146; L £11·15, D £11·15; WB £51·50
cc Access, Amex, B'card/Visa, CB, Diners.

★★★ **Kensington Close,** Wrights La, Kensington, W8 5SP ☎ 071-937 8170 Tx: 23914 Fax: 071-937 8289

Large hotel in quiet location near Kensington High Street. Garden. Indoor swimming pool, squash, sauna, solarium, gymnasium. (THF)
522 bedrs, 522 en suite; TV; tcf
lift, dogs, ns; P 40 (£14), G 60 (£14), coach; child facs; con 300

★★ **Lexham** 32–38 Lexham Gdns, W8 5JU ☎ 071-373 6471 Tx: 268141 Fax: 071-244 7827

Quiet hotel in attractive terrace in a garden square. Closed 23 Dec–2 Jan. Fr, Ge, It
64 bedrs, 40 en suite, 11 ba; TV
lift, TV; child facs; con 20
LD 8. Unlic
£ B&B £32·50–£44·50, B&B (double) £41·50–£64·50; HB weekly £191–£265; L £5·50, D £8·25; WB £54·68 (HB, × 2nts)
cc Access, B'card/Visa; dep.

Observatory House (Acclaimed), 37 Hornton St, W8 7NR ☎ 071-937 1557 Tx: 914972 Fax: 071-938 3585. *Hotel.*
£ B&B £57·40–£62·90; [5% V]

Apollo, 18–22 Lexham Gdns, W8 5JE ☎ 071-835 1133 Tx: 264189 Fax: 071-370 4853. *Hotel.* Fr, Ge, It, Es, Po, Pl
£ B&B £30–£48; [5% V]
Atlas, 24–30 Lexham Gdns, W8 5JE ☎ 071-835 1155 Tx: 264189 Fax: 071-370 4853. *Hotel.* Fr, Ge, It, Es
£ B&B £30–£48; [5% V]

W9

Colonnade, 2 Warrington Cres, W9 1ER ☎ 071-286 1052. Tx: 298930 Fax: 071-286 1057. *Hotel.* Fr, Ge, It, Es
£ B&B £60·50–£66; [5% V w/e Mar–Oct, 10% V Oct–Mar]

W14

Centaur, 21 Avonmore Rd, W14 8RP ☎ 071-603 5973 Fr, Ge, It, Es
£ B&B £32; [5% V]

WC1

★★★★ **Marlborough,** Bloomsbury St, WC1B 3QD ☎ 071-636 5601 Tx: 298274 Fax: 071-636 0532 ♿
Attractively furnished Victorian 7-storey hotel near British Museum.
169 bedrs, 169 en suite; TV; tcf
lift, dogs, ns; child facs; con 200
(London street map 4B3)

★★★★ **Kenilworth,** Great Russell St, WC1B 3LB ☎ 071-637 3477 Tx: 25842 Fax: 071-631 3133
Turetted Edwardian building in the centre of Bloomsbury. Fr, Ge, It, Du, Ar
192 bedrs, 192 en suite; TV; tcf
lift, dogs; coach; child facs, con 120
LD 10.30
£ room £99–£115, double room £135–£165; Bk £7; L £15·95, D £15·95; [V]
cc Access, Amex, B'card/Visa, Diners.
(London street map 4B3)

> **Weekend breaks**
> Please consult the hotel for full details of weekend breaks; prices shown are an indication only. Many hotels offer mid week breaks as well.

London W2

The Delmere Hotel **

The Delmere is a quality Victorian town house hotel fashionably located along a tree lined avenue near Hyde Park, Park Lane and Oxford Street, ideal for West End shopping and theatres.

Traditional standards of comfort and courtesy still exist at the hotel with many guest facilities including the continental "La Perla" restaurant, Regency styled lounge and cocktail bar. Business services are available from reception.

130 Sussex Gardens, Hyde Park, London W2 1UB
Tel: 071-706 3344 Fax: 071-262 1863 Telex: 8953857

London W2

MITRE HOUSE HOTEL

RAC ACCLAIMED

Completely refurbished in 1990 · All seventy rooms with en-suite bathrooms, satellite television, radio and direct dial telephone.

● Junior suites available ●

● Free car park ● Licensed bar ● Lift ● English Breakfast ●

Centrally located to all major sights and shopping areas.
Close to Paddington Station and A2 Airbus to Heathrow

● Reasonable rates ●

CONTACT US NOW FOR FURTHER INFORMATION AND OUR BROCHURE

Tel: 071-723 8040
Fax: 071-402 0990
Tlx: 914113 MITRE G

178–184 SUSSEX GARDENS
HYDE PARK
LONDON W2 1TU

★★★★ **Hotel Russell,** Russell Sq, WC1B 5BE ☎071-837 6470 Tx: 24615

A modernised, grand detached Edwardian building overlooking Russell Square. (THF)

★★★★ **Waverley House,** 130 Southampton Row WC1B 5AG ☎071-833 3691 Tx: 296270 Fax: 071-837 3485
Exuberant Edwardian building on a corner in Bloomsbury. Fr, Gr
109 bedrs, 109 en suite; TV; tcf
lift; coach; child facs; con 24
LD 11
£ B&B £96·50 (w/e £35); B&B (double) £127·50; L fr £20, D fr £30; [5% V]
cc Access, Amex, B'card/Visa, Diners.

★★★ **Bloomsbury Crest,** Coram St, WC1N 1HT ☎071-837 1200 Tx: 22113 Fax: 071-837 5374

Large, modern purpose-built hotel, close to the British Museum. Fr, It, Es. (Cr/THF)
284 bedrs, 284 en suite; TV; tcf
lift, ns; coach; child facs; con 700
LD 11
£ room £104·50–£114·50, double room £119·50–£129·50 (w/e £96); L £14·50, D £16·50; WB £36
cc Access, Amex, B'card/Visa, CB, Diners.

★★★ **Bloomsbury Park,** 126 Southampton Row, WC1B 5AD ☎071-430 0434 Tx: 25757 Fax: 071-242 0665
Extensively refurbished Edwardian hotel close to Russell Square. (MtCh)
95 bedrs, 95 en suite; TV; tcf
lift, dogs, ns; coach, child facs; con 35
LD 10, nr lunch & Sat, Sun dinner
£ B&B £83·50–£91·50, B&B (double) £109–£120; D £13·50; WB £39·50
cc Access, Amex, B'card/Visa, Diners.

Hotel locations
Hotel locations are shown on the maps at the back of the guide. All towns and villages containing an RAC Appointed or Listed hotel are ringed in purple.

★★★ **Bonnington,** 92 Southampton Row, WC1B 4BH ☎071-242 2828 Tx: 261591 Fax: 071-831 9170

Purpose-built, six-storey hotel, furnished in traditional style. Fr, It, Es, Gr
215 bedrs, 215 en suite; TV; tcf
lift, dogs, ns; coach; child facs; con 120
LD 11.30
£ B&B £67–£76 (w/e £40), B&B (double) £88–£100; L£10, D £10; [10% V]
cc Access, Amex, B'card/Visa, Diners.
(*London street map 5A3*)

★★★ **Kingsley,** Bloomsbury Way, WC1A 2SD ☎071-242 5887 Tx: 21157 Fax: 071-831 0225

Impressive red-brick Victorian building. Easy access to City and West End. Fr, It, Es (MtCh)
145 bedrs, 145 en suite; TV; tcf
lift, dogs; coach; child facs; con 100

★★★ **London Ryan,** Gwynne Pl, Kings Cross Rd, WC1X 9QB ☎071-278 2480 Tx: 27728 Fax: 071-837 3776

Modern hotel situated between the City and West End. Fr, De, Es (MtCh)
211 bedrs, 211 en suite; TV; tcf
lift, dogs, ns; P 20, G 10, coach; child facs
LD 9.30; bar meals only lunch
£ B&B £64·50–£74·50, B&B (double) £74·50–£89; HB weekly £539–£609, D £12·50; WB £35; [5% V]
cc Access, Amex, B'card/Visa, Diners.

★★★ **Royal Scot,** 100 Kings Cross Rd, WC1X 9DT ☎071-278 2434 Tx: 27657

Modern hotel convenient for both the City and West End. Fr, De. (MtCh)
351 bedrs, 351 en suite; TV; tcf
lift, dogs, ns; P 35 (£3), coach; child facs; con 150
LD 10.30
£ room £63·50–£74·50, double room £79·50–£95; L £10·50, D £10·50; WB £32·50; [5% V]
cc Access, Amex, B'card/Visa, Diners.

Academy (Highly Acclaimed), 17–21 Gower St, WC1E 6HG ☎071-631 4115 Tx: 24634 Fax: 071-636 3442. *Hotel.* Fr, De, Da
£ B&B £72·95–£79·95; [10% V w/e]

Crescent, 49–50 Cartwright Gdns, WC1H 9EL ☎071-387 1515. *Hotel. Tennis.* Fr, It
£ B&B £26–£29

Haddon Hall, 39–40 Bedford Pl, WC1B 5JT ☎071-636 2474. *Hotel.*

WC2

★★★★★ **Savoy,** Strand, WC2R 0EU ☎071-836 4343 Tx: 24234 Fax: 071-240 6040

Famous luxury hotel on the Strand. Elegant and impressive decor.
200 bedrs, 200 en suite; TV
lift, ns; G 58 (£19); child facs; con 450
LD 11.30
£ room £170, double room £200–£265; L £24·50, D £38·50
cc Access, Amex, B'card/Visa, Diners; dep.

★★★★ **Drury Lane Moat House,** 10 Drury La, High Holborn, WC2B 5RE ☎071-836 6666 Tx: 8811395 Fax: 071-831 1548

Well-furnished modern luxury hotel near Covent Garden. ✂ Fr, De, It, Da (QMH)
🛏 153 bedrs, 153 en suite; TV
🏨 lift, dogs; P 7 (£8), coach; child facs; con 100
✕ LD 10.30
£ B&B £118–£128 (w/e £50), B&B (double) £157–£171; L £14, D £17·50; WB £104
cc Access, Amex, B'card/Visa, Diners.
(*London street map 4B2*)

★★★★ **H C R Mountbatten,** Monmouth St, Covent Gdn, WC2H 9HD ☎071-836 4300 Tx: 298087 Fax: 071-240 3540
Purpose-built hotel, furnished like a country house. ✂De, It
🛏 127 bedrs, 127 en suite; TV
🏨 lift, dogs, ns; child facs; con 75
✕ LD 11, nr Sat lunch
£ B&B £144–£154 (w/e £80), B&B (double) £183–£350; L £18·50, D £21·50; WB; [10% V]
cc Access, Amex, B'card/Visa, Diners.

★★★★ **R Waldorf,** Aldwych, WC2B 4DD ☎071-836 2400 Tx: 24574 Fax: 071-836 7244

Elegant, well established Edwardian hotel. (THF)
🛏 310 bedrs, 310 en suite; TV
🏨 lift, dogs, ns; coach; child facs; con 450
(*London street map 5A1*)

Discount vouchers
RAC discount vouchers are on p. 34. Hotels with a [V] shown at the end of the price information will accept them in part payment for accommodation bills on the full, standard rate, not against bargain breaks or any other special offers. Please note the limitations shown in the entry: w/e for weekends, w/d for weekdays, and which months they are accepted.

★★★ **Royal Trafalgar Thistle,** Whitcomb St, Trafalgar Square, WC2H 7HG ☎071-930 4477 Tx: 298564 Fax: 071-925 2149

Modern hotel next to National Gallery. Features a French style Brasserie. (MtCh)
🛏 108 bedrs, 108 en suite; TV; tcf
🏨 lift, dogs, ns; coach; child facs
✕ LD 11.30
£ room £87, double room £99; Bk £8·95, L £12·50, D £12·50; WB
cc Access, Amex, B'card/Visa, CB, Diners.
(*London street map 4B1*)

★★★ **Strand Palace,** Strand, WC2R 0JJ ☎071-836 8080 Tx: 24208

Grand-looking hotel with a lively atmosphere in the Strand close to Covent Garden. (THF)

LONDON AIRPORT – HEATHROW

Greater London.
Map 13B3
See also SLOUGH.
London 14, M4 (jn 4) ½, Ealing 8½, Harrow 9½, Kingston upon Thames 9½, Slough 7, Staines 5½, Watford 16, Windsor 7½, Uxbridge 5½.
Leaflet giving particulars of facilities at and in the vicinity of the Airport is available from any RAC Office.
ℹ Heathrow Station. ☎081-730 3488

★★★★ **Sheraton Skyline,** Bath Rd, Hayes, UB3 5BP ☎081-759 2535 Tx: 934254 Fax: 081-750 9150 ♿

Excellent modern 3-storey hotel opposite Heathrow. Indoor swimming pool in a tropical garden, sauna, solarium.
🛏 352 bedrs, 352 en suite; TV
🏨 lift, dogs, ns; P 425, coach; child facs; con 500

★★★★ **Excelsior,** Bath Rd, West Drayton, UB7 0DU ☎081-759 6611 Tx: 24525 Fax: 081-759 3421
Large modern hotel. Restaurant decor in stately home" style. Indoor swimming pool, sauna, solarium, gymnasium. (THF)
🛏 581 bedrs, 581 en suite; TV; tcf
🏨 lift, dogs, ns; P 500, coach; child facs; con 700

★★★★ **Holiday Inn Heathrow,** Stockley Rd, West Drayton, UB7 9NA ☎West Drayton (0895) 445555 Tx: 934518 Fax: (0895) 445122 ♿
Large modern hotel—2 minutes from Heathrow. Indoor swimming pool, golf, sauna, solarium, gymnasium. (HI)
✂ Fr, De, It
🛏 380 bedrs, 380 en suite; TV; tcf
🏨 lift, dogs, ns; P 400, coach; child facs; con 100
✕ LD 10
£ room £98–£118 (w/e £40), double room £114–£134; L £14, D £14
cc Access, Amex, B'card/Visa, CB, Diners

★★★ **Ariel,** Bath Rd, Hayes, UB3 5AJ ☎081-759 2552 Tx: 21777 Fax: 081-564 9265
Well known landmark with its circular design; on the Bath road. (THF)
🛏 177 bedrs, 177 en suite; TV; tcf
🏨 lift, dogs, ns; P 100, coach; child facs; con 60

★★★ **Berkeley Arms,** Bath Rd, Cranford, TW5 9QE ☎081-897 2121 Tx: 935728 Fax: 081-759 7154

Small luxury hotel with delightful garden just 10 minutes from Heathrow. ✂ Fr, It, Es, Po. (Emb)
🛏 56 bedrs, 56 en suite; TV; tcf
🏨 lift, dogs; P 150, coach; child facs; con 100
✕ LD 9.30
£ B&B £76 (w/e £31), B&B (double) £86; L £12, D £12; WB
cc Access, Amex, B'card/Visa, Diners.

★★★ **Heathrow Park,** Bath Rd, West Drayton, UB7 0EQ ☎081-759 2400 Tx: 934093 Fax: 081-759 5278 ♿

Large bustling airport hotel situated alongside Heathrow. Billiards. (MtCh)
🛏 306 bedrs, 306 en suite; TV; tcf
🏨 dogs, ns, P 300, coach; child facs; con 700

✕ LD 11.30
£ B&B £88·75–£110·75 (w/e £25), B&B (double) £110–£129; HB weekly £722·75–£873·25; L £11·95, D £14·50; WB £31
cc Access, Amex, B'card/Visa, Diners.

★★★ Post House, Sipson Rd, West Drayton, UB7 0JU ☎ 081-759 2323
Tx: 934280 Fax: 081-897 8659
Large and busy high-rise modern hotel conveniently near M4. (THF)
🛏 569 bedrs, 569 en suite; TV; tcf
ꟻ lift, dogs, ns; P 400, coach; child facs; con 200

★★ Ibis Heathrow, 112 Bath Rd, Hayes, UB3 5AL ☎ 081-759 4888 Tx: 929014
Fax: 081-564 7894 ♿
Five-storey purpose-built modern hotel on A4 opposite Airport. ✗ Fr.
🛏 244 bedrs, 244 en suite; TV
ꟻ lift, P 120; child facs; con 120
✕ LD 10.30
£ B&B £53, B&B (double) £59; L £8·50, D £8·50
cc Access, Amex, B'card/Visa, Diners; dep.

★★ Stanwell Hall, Town La, Stanwell, Staines, TW19 7PW ☎ Ashford (0784) 252292

Large Victorian house conveniently situated for airport. Family run. ✗ Es
🛏 18 bedrs, 18 en suite, TV; tcf
ꟻ dogs; P 30, coach; child facs; con 25
✕ LD 9.30, bar meals only Sat lunch & all Sun
£ B&B £70–£80, B&B (double) £90–£140; L £16·50, D £16·50; WB £80; [10% V Aug also w/e]
cc Access, Amex, B'card/Visa, Diners

Shepiston Lodge, 31 Shepiston Rd, Hayes, UB3 1LJ ☎ 081-573 0266
Fax: 081-569 2279. *Guest House.*
£ B&B £26·50–£29·50.

Heathrow Sterling, Terminal Four, Heathrow Airport, TW6 3AF ☎ 081-759 7755
Tx: 925094 Fax: 081-759 7579
New hotel linked to Terminal 4; opening November 1990.

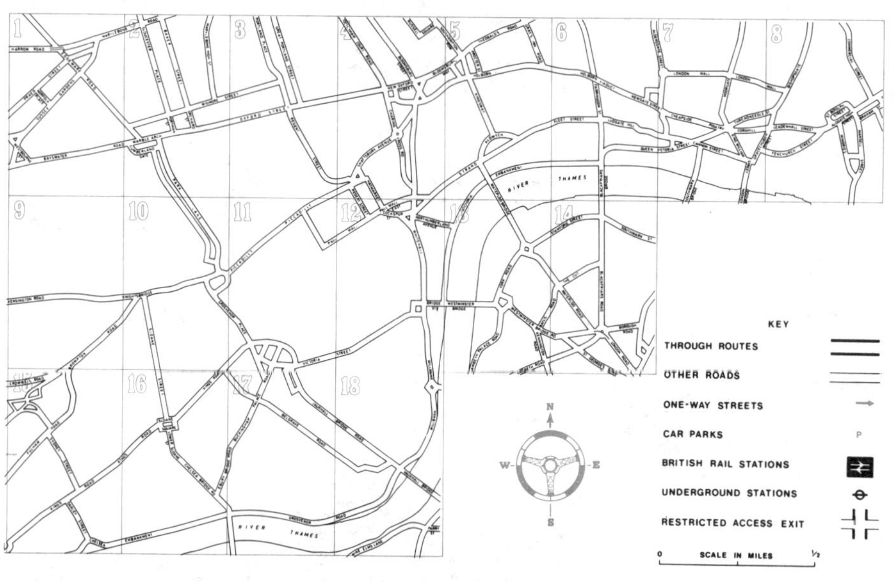

EC *early closing* **MD** *market day* ♣ *country house hotel* *ns (NS) no smoking areas* *tcf tea/coffee facilities*

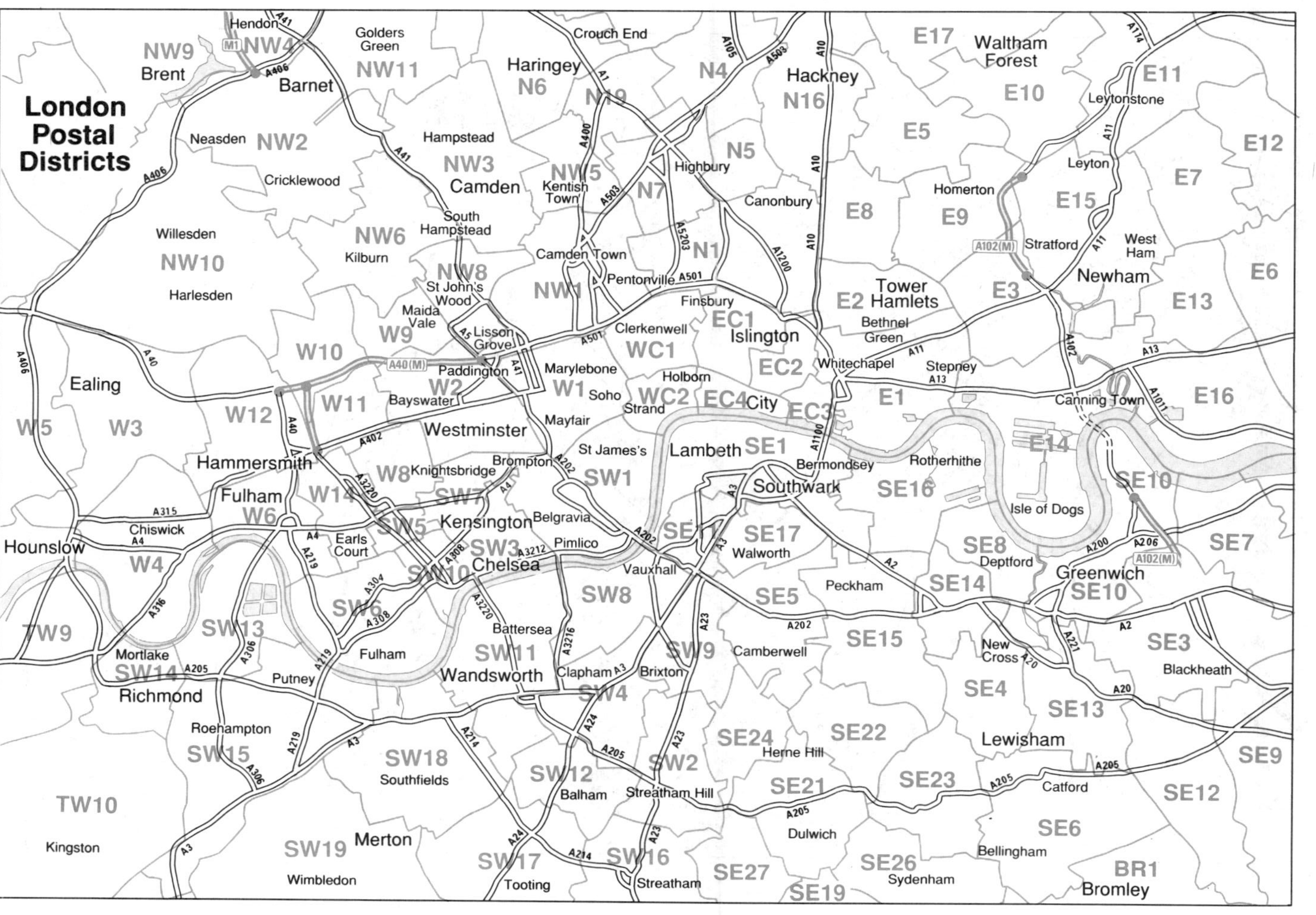
London Postal Districts
Hendon
NW9
Brent
NW4
Barnet
Golders Green
NW11
Haringey
N6
Crouch End
N4
Hackney
N16
E17
Waltham Forest
E10
E11
Leytonstone
E12
Neasden
NW2
Cricklewood
Hampstead
NW3
Camden
Kentish Town
N7
Highbury
N5
Canonbury
E5
E8
Homerton
E9
Leyton
E15
E7
Willesden
NW10
Harlesden
South Hampstead
NW6
Kilburn
St John's Wood
Camden Town
Pentonville
N1
Stratford
West Ham
Newham
E6
Tower Hamlets
E2
E3
E13
Maida Vale
W9
W10
Lisson Grove
Paddington
W2
Clerkenwell
Finsbury
EC1
Islington
WC1
Bethnel Green
Whitechapel
Stepney
Ealing
W5
W3
W12
W11
Bayswater
Marylebone
W1
Soho
Holborn
WC2
Strand
EC2
EC4
City
EC3
E1
Canning Town
E16
Hammersmith
Westminster
Mayfair
St James's
Lambeth
SE1
Rotherhithe
E14
Fulham
W6
W14
W8
Knightsbridge
Brompton
SW7
SW1
Bermondsey
Southwark
SE16
Isle of Dogs
SE10
Hounslow
Chiswick
W4
Earls Court
SW5
Kensington
Belgravia
SW3
Chelsea
Pimlico
SE11
SE17
Walworth
SE8
Deptford
Greenwich
SE7
TW9
SW13
SW6
SW10
Vauxhall
SW8
SE5
Peckham
SE14
Mortlake
SW14
Richmond
Putney
Fulham
Battersea
SW11
Wandsworth
Clapham
SW4
Brixton
SW9
Camberwell
SE15
New Cross
SE4
SE13
SE3
Blackheath
Roehampton
SW15
SW18
Southfields
SW12
Balham
Streatham Hill
SW2
SE24
Herne Hill
SE22
SE21
Lewisham
SE23
Catford
SE9
SE12
TW10
Kingston
SW19
Wimbledon
Merton
SW17
Tooting
SW16
Streatham
SE27
Dulwich
SE19
SE26
Sydenham
SE6
Bellingham
BR1
Bromley
M1
A1
A3
A4
A5
A10
A11
A13
A20
A23
A24
A40
A41
A102
A105
A114
A200
A202
A205
A206
A214
A219
A221
A304
A306
A308
A315
A316
A400
A402
A406
A501
A503
A1011
A1100
A1200
A3212
A3216
A3220
A5203
A40(M)
A102(M)

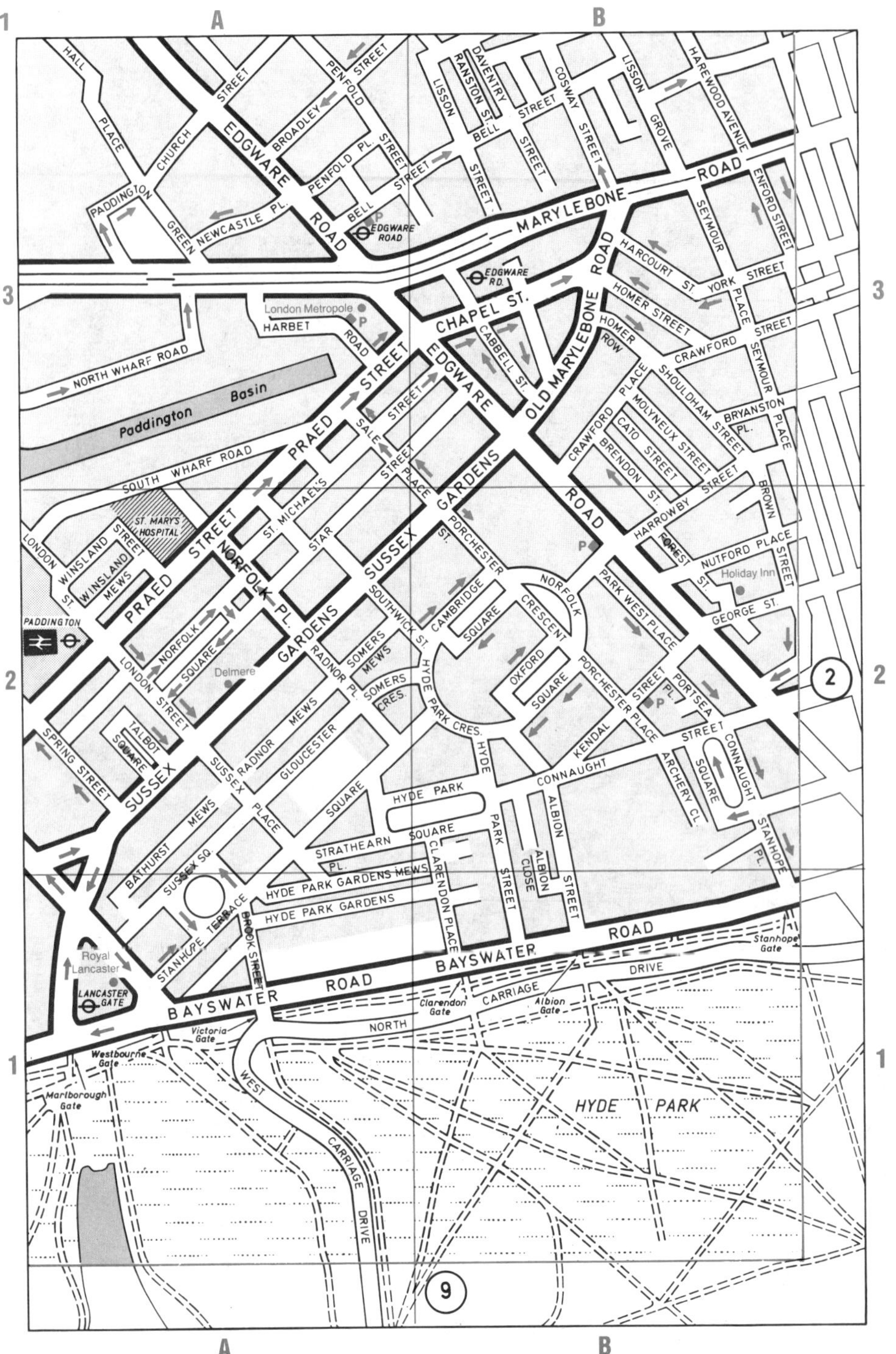
1
A
B
3
2
1
HALL PLACE
CHURCH STREET
EDGWARE ROAD
PENFOLD STREET
BROADLEY STREET
PENFOLD PL.
LISSON STREET
RANSTON ST.
DAVENTRY STREET
BELL STREET
COSWAY STREET
LISSON GROVE
HAREWOOD AVENUE
PADDINGTON GREEN
NEWCASTLE PL.
EDGWARE ROAD
MARYLEBONE ROAD
ENFORD STREET
SEYMOUR PLACE
HARCOURT ST.
YORK STREET
HOMER STREET
HOMER ROW
EDGWARE RD.
London Metropole
HARBET ROAD
CHAPEL ST.
CABBELL ST.
OLD MARYLEBONE ROAD
CRAWFORD STREET
CRAWFORD PLACE
SHOULDHAM STREET
MOLYNEUX STREET
CATO STREET
BRENDON ST.
BRYANSTON PL.
NORTH WHARF ROAD
Paddington Basin
SOUTH WHARF ROAD
PRAED STREET
SALE PLACE
ST. MICHAEL'S STREET
HARROWBY STREET
BROWN STREET
FOREST ST.
NUTFORD PLACE
Holiday Inn
GEORGE ST.
ST. MARY'S HOSPITAL
LONDON ST.
WINSLAND STREET
WINSLAND MEWS
NORFOLK PL.
STAR STREET
SUSSEX GARDENS
PORCHESTER ST.
NORFOLK CRESCENT
PARK WEST PLACE
PADDINGTON
NORFOLK SQUARE
LONDON STREET
Delmere
SOUTHWICK ST.
CAMBRIDGE SQUARE
RADNOR PL.
SOMERS MEWS
SOMERS CRES.
HYDE PARK CRES.
OXFORD SQUARE
PORCHESTER PLACE
PORTSEA PL.
KENDAL STREET
CONNAUGHT STREET
CONNAUGHT SQUARE
SPRING STREET
TALBOT SQUARE
SUSSEX PLACE
RADNOR MEWS
GLOUCESTER SQUARE
HYDE PARK STREET
HYDE PARK SQUARE
ALBION STREET
ALBION CLOSE
ARCHERY CL.
STANHOPE PL.
BATHURST MEWS
SUSSEX SQ.
STRATHEARN PL.
HYDE PARK GARDENS MEWS
CLARENDON PLACE
HYDE PARK GARDENS
STANHOPE TERRACE
BROOK STREET
Royal Lancaster
LANCASTER GATE
BAYSWATER ROAD
Stanhope Gate
NORTH CARRIAGE DRIVE
Clarendon Gate
Albion Gate
Victoria Gate
Westbourne Gate
Marlborough Gate
WEST CARRIAGE DRIVE
HYDE PARK
9
A
B

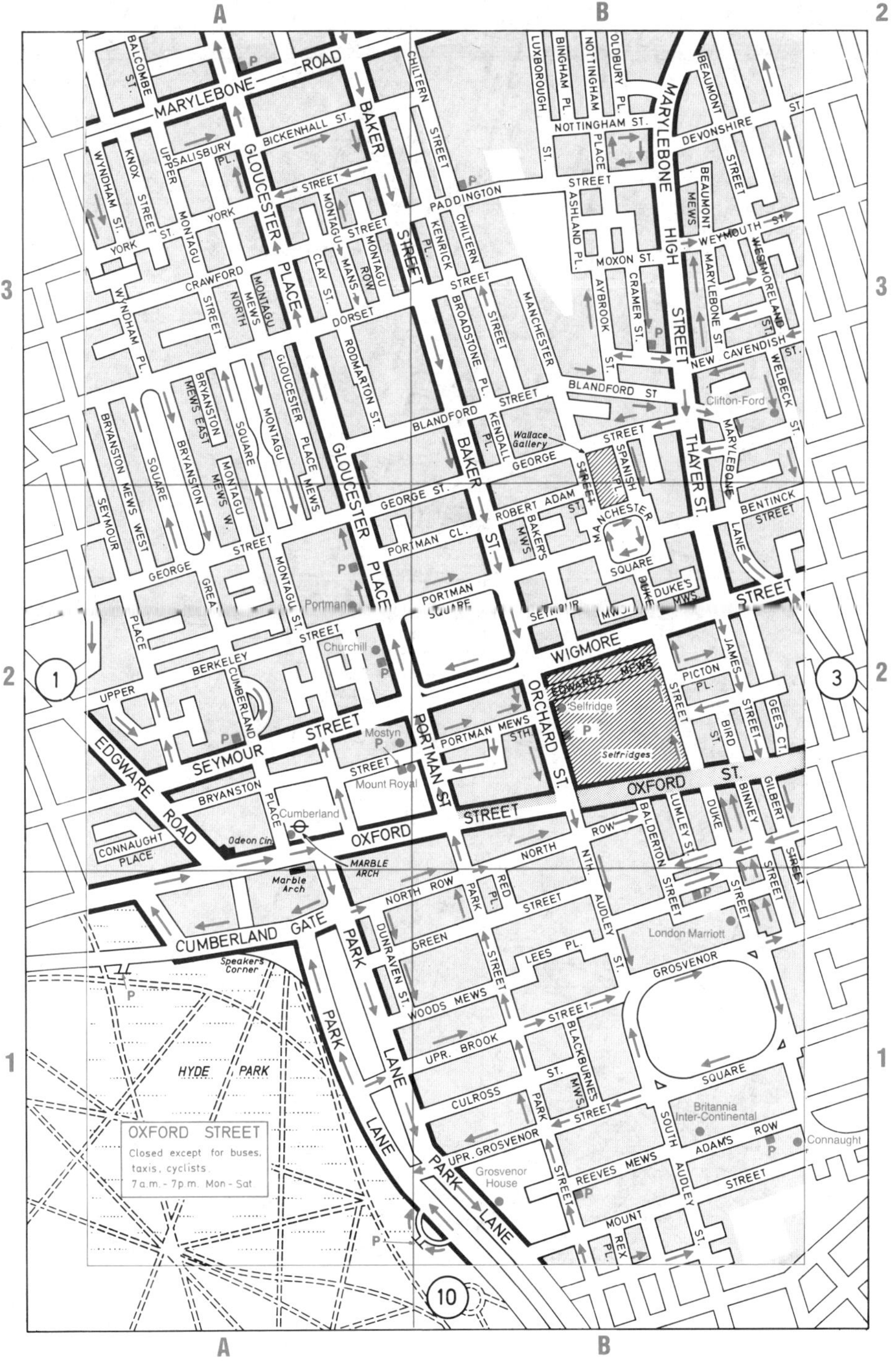
A
B
2
3
2
1
1
A
B
MARYLEBONE ROAD
BALCOMBE ST.
BAKER STREET
CHILTERN STREET
LUXBOROUGH ST.
BINGHAM PL.
NOTTINGHAM PLACE
OLDBURY PL.
MARYLEBONE HIGH STREET
BEAUMONT ST.
DEVONSHIRE ST.
NOTTINGHAM ST.
WYNDHAM ST.
KNOX STREET
UPPER MONTAGU STREET
SALISBURY PL.
GLOUCESTER PLACE
BICKENHALL ST.
YORK ST.
YORK
MONTAGU STREET
MONTAGU MANS
MONTAGU ROW
PADDINGTON STREET
KENRICK PL.
ASHLAND PL.
MOXON ST.
BEAUMONT MEWS
WEYMOUTH ST.
WESTMORELAND ST.
MARYLEBONE ST.
CRAWFORD STREET
NORTH MEWS
MONTAGU
CLAY ST.
DORSET
BROADSTONE PL.
MANCHESTER STREET
AYBROOK ST.
CRAMER ST.
NEW CAVENDISH ST.
WELBECK ST.
WYNDHAM PL.
BRYANSTON MEWS EAST
MONTAGU SQUARE
GLOUCESTER PLACE MEWS
RODMARTON ST.
BLANDFORD STREET
BLANDFORD ST
Clifton-Ford
BRYANSTON MEWS WEST
BRYANSTON SQUARE
MONTAGU MEWS W.
KENDALL PL.
Wallace Gallery
SPANISH PL.
THAYER ST.
MARYLEBONE LANE
SEYMOUR PLACE
GEORGE STREET
GEORGE ST.
ROBERT ADAM ST.
BAKERS MWS
MANCHESTER SQUARE
BENTINCK STREET
PORTMAN CL.
MONTAGU ST.
GREAT CUMBERLAND PLACE
Portman
PORTMAN SQUARE
SEYMOUR MWS
DUKE ST.
DUKE'S MWS
WIGMORE STREET
JAMES STREET
UPPER BERKELEY STREET
Churchill
CUMBERLAND
EDWARDS MEWS
PICTON PL.
1
3
Selfridge
P
Selfridges
SEYMOUR STREET
Mostyn
PORTMAN ST
PORTMAN MEWS STH.
ORCHARD ST.
BIRD ST.
GEES CT.
EDGWARE ROAD
BRYANSTON STREET
Mount Royal
OXFORD STREET
OXFORD ST.
PLACE
Cumberland
Odeon Cin.
CONNAUGHT PLACE
MARBLE ARCH
Marble Arch
NORTH ROW
PARK ST.
RED PL.
NTH. AUDLEY ST.
BALDERTON STREET
LUMLEY ST.
BINNEY STREET
GILBERT STREET
DUKE STREET
London Marriott
CUMBERLAND GATE
Speakers Corner
DUNRAVEN ST.
GREEN STREET
LEES PL.
GROSVENOR SQUARE
WOODS MEWS
UPR. BROOK STREET
BLACKBURNES MWS
HYDE PARK
PARK LANE
CULROSS ST.
PARK STREET
Britannia Inter-Continental
SOUTH AUDLEY ST.
ADAMS ROW
Connaught
OXFORD STREET
Closed except for buses, taxis, cyclists
7 a.m. - 7 p.m. Mon - Sat
UPR. GROSVENOR STREET
Grosvenor House
REEVES MEWS
MOUNT STREET
REX PL.
10

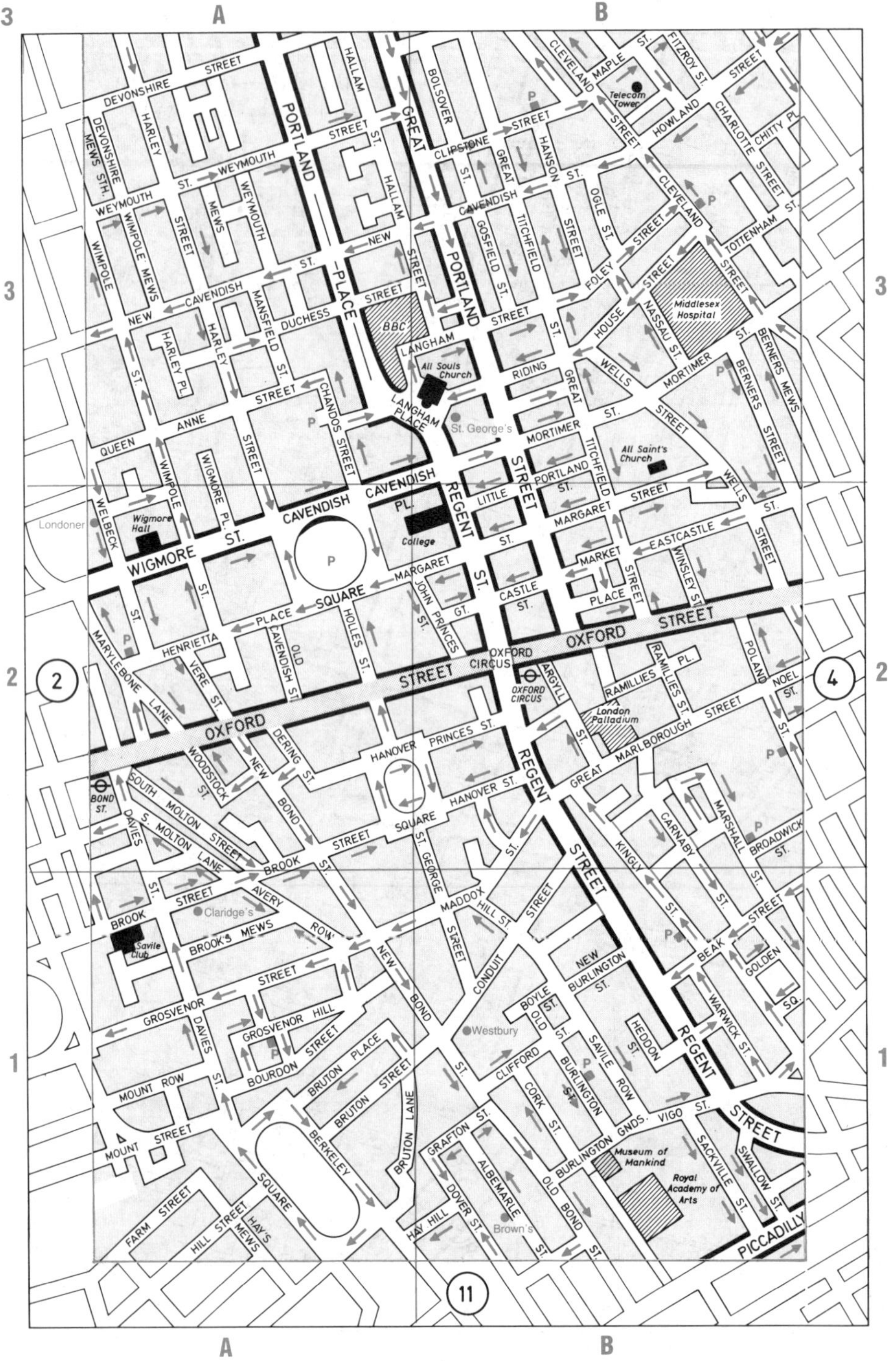
A
B
3
3
3
2
2
1
1
2
4
11
A
B
Telecom Tower
Middlesex Hospital
BBC
All Souls Church
St. George's
All Saint's Church
Londoner
Wigmore Hall
College
OXFORD CIRCUS
London Palladium
BOND ST.
Claridge's
Savile Club
Westbury
Museum of Mankind
Royal Academy of Arts
Brown's
OXFORD STREET
REGENT STREET
PORTLAND PLACE
WIGMORE ST.
CAVENDISH SQUARE
HANOVER SQUARE
BERKELEY SQUARE
PICCADILLY

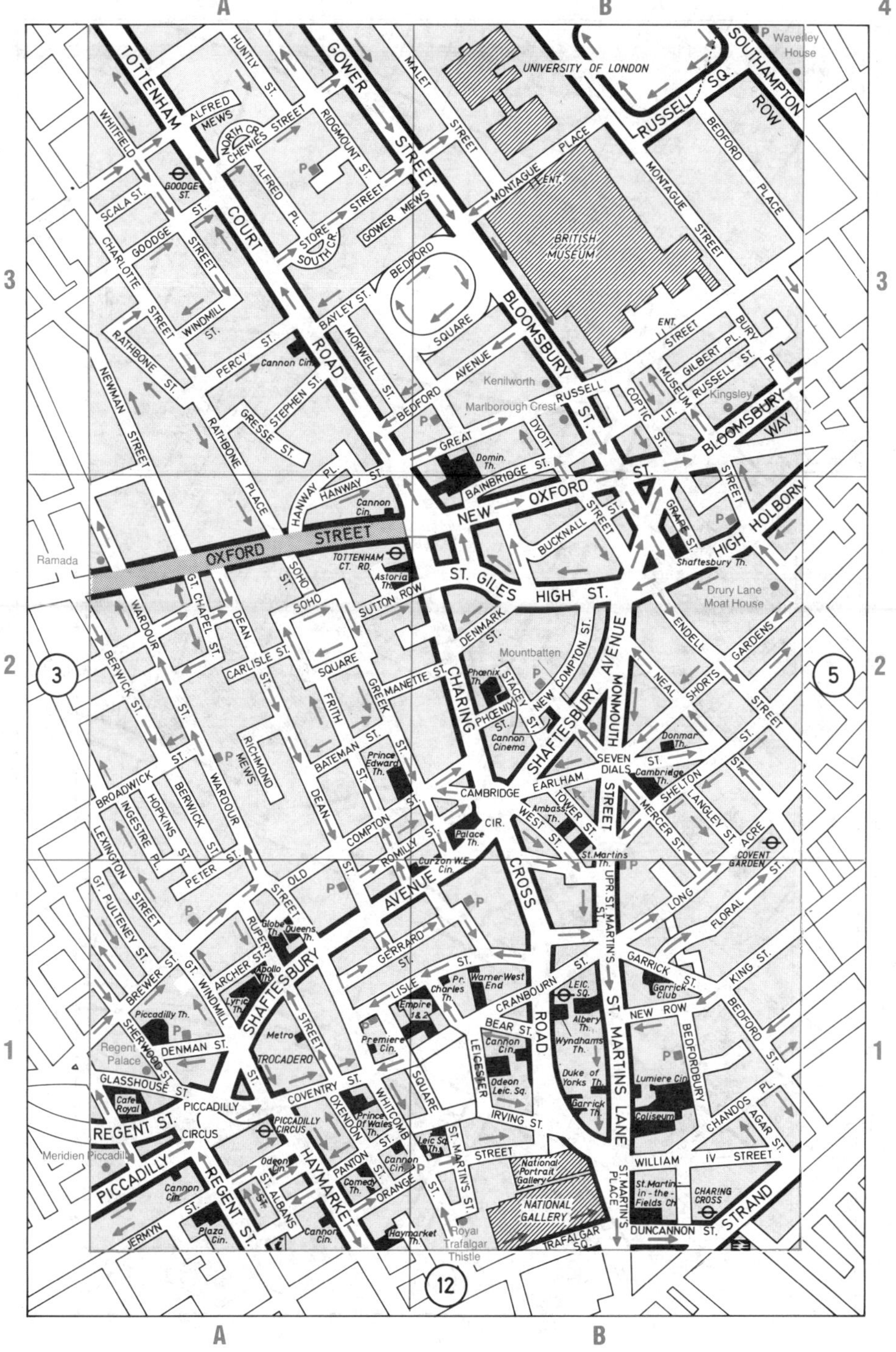

A
B
4
3
2
1
A
B
3
2
1
3
5
12
UNIVERSITY OF LONDON
Waverley House
SOUTHAMPTON ROW
RUSSELL SQ.
BEDFORD PLACE
MONTAGUE STREET
MONTAGUE PLACE
BRITISH MUSEUM
ENT.
TOTTENHAM COURT ROAD
HUNTLY ST.
GOWER STREET
MALET STREET
ALFRED MEWS
NORTH CR.
CHENIES STREET
RIDGMOUNT ST.
ALFRED PL.
STORE STREET
GOWER MEWS
STORE SOUTH CR.
WHITFIELD
GOODGE ST.
SCALA ST.
GOODGE STREET
CHARLOTTE STREET
WINDMILL ST.
RATHBONE ST.
PERCY ST.
Cannon Cin.
BAYLEY ST.
BEDFORD SQUARE
MORWELL ST.
BEDFORD AVENUE
BLOOMSBURY ST.
Kenilworth
Marlborough Crest
RUSSELL
GREAT
DYOTT
NEWMAN STREET
RATHBONE PLACE
GRESSE ST.
STEPHEN ST.
BEDFORD
HANWAY PL.
HANWAY ST.
Domin. Th.
BAINBRIDGE ST.
STREET
BURY PL.
GILBERT PL.
RUSSELL ST.
MUSEUM
COPTIC
LIT.
Kingsley
BLOOMSBURY WAY
NEW OXFORD ST.
BUCKNALL STREET
GRAPE ST.
HIGH HOLBORN
Shaftesbury Th.
Drury Lane Moat House
Ramada
OXFORD STREET
TOTTENHAM CT. RD.
Astoria Th.
ST. GILES HIGH ST.
SOHO ST.
SOHO SQUARE
SUTTON ROW
GT. CHAPEL ST.
WARDOUR
DEAN ST.
BERWICK ST.
CARLISLE ST.
FRITH ST.
GREEK ST.
MANETTE ST.
CHARING CROSS ROAD
DENMARK ST.
Mountbatten
Phœnix Th.
PHŒNIX ST.
STACEY ST.
NEW COMPTON ST.
SHAFTESBURY AVENUE
MONMOUTH STREET
ENDELL ST.
NEAL ST.
SHORTS GARDENS
Donmar Th.
SEVEN DIALS
Cambridge Th.
EARLHAM ST.
CAMBRIDGE CIR.
Cannon Cinema
BROADWICK ST.
RICHMOND MEWS
BATEMAN ST.
Prince Edward Th.
HOPKINS
BERWICK ST.
WARDOUR ST.
INGESTRE PL.
LEXINGTON STREET
PETER ST.
COMPTON ST.
ROMILLY ST.
Palace Th.
WEST ST.
Ambass. Th.
TOWER ST.
St. Martins Th.
SHELTON ST.
MERCER ST.
LANGLEY ST.
ACRE
COVENT GARDEN
GT. PULTENEY ST.
OLD COMPTON STREET
Curzon W.E. Cin.
UPR. ST. MARTIN'S LANE
LONG ACRE
FLORAL ST.
RUPERT ST.
Globe Th.
Queens Th.
GERRARD ST.
LISLE ST.
Warner West End
Pr. Charles Th.
CRANBOURN ST.
LEIC. SQ.
GARRICK ST.
Garrick Club
KING ST.
BREWER ST.
GT. WINDMILL ST.
ARCHER ST.
Apollo Th.
Lyric Th.
Piccadilly Th.
Empire 1 & 2
BEAR ST.
Albery Th.
NEW ROW
BEDFORD ST.
BEDFORDBURY
Regent Palace
SHERWOOD ST.
DENMAN ST.
Metro
TROCADERO
Premiere Cin.
Cannon Cin.
Wyndhams Th.
ST. MARTINS LANE
Lumiere Cin.
GLASSHOUSE ST.
Cafe Royal
PICCADILLY
COVENTRY ST.
OXENDON ST.
Prince Of Wales Th.
WHITCOMB ST.
LEICESTER SQUARE
Odeon Leic. Sq.
Duke of Yorks Th.
Garrick Th.
Coliseum
CHANDOS PL.
AGAR ST.
REGENT ST.
PICCADILLY CIRCUS
IRVING ST.
Leic Sq Th.
Meridien Piccadilly
Odeon Cin.
HAYMARKET
PANTON ST.
Cannon Cin.
ST. MARTIN'S STREET
National Portrait Gallery
WILLIAM IV STREET
Comedy Th.
ORANGE ST.
ST. MARTIN'S PLACE
St. Martin-in-the-Fields Ch.
CHARING CROSS
ST. ALBANS ST.
NATIONAL GALLERY
STRAND
JERMYN ST.
Plaza Cin.
Haymarket Th.
Royal Trafalgar Thistle
TRAFALGAR SQ.
DUNCANNON ST.
P

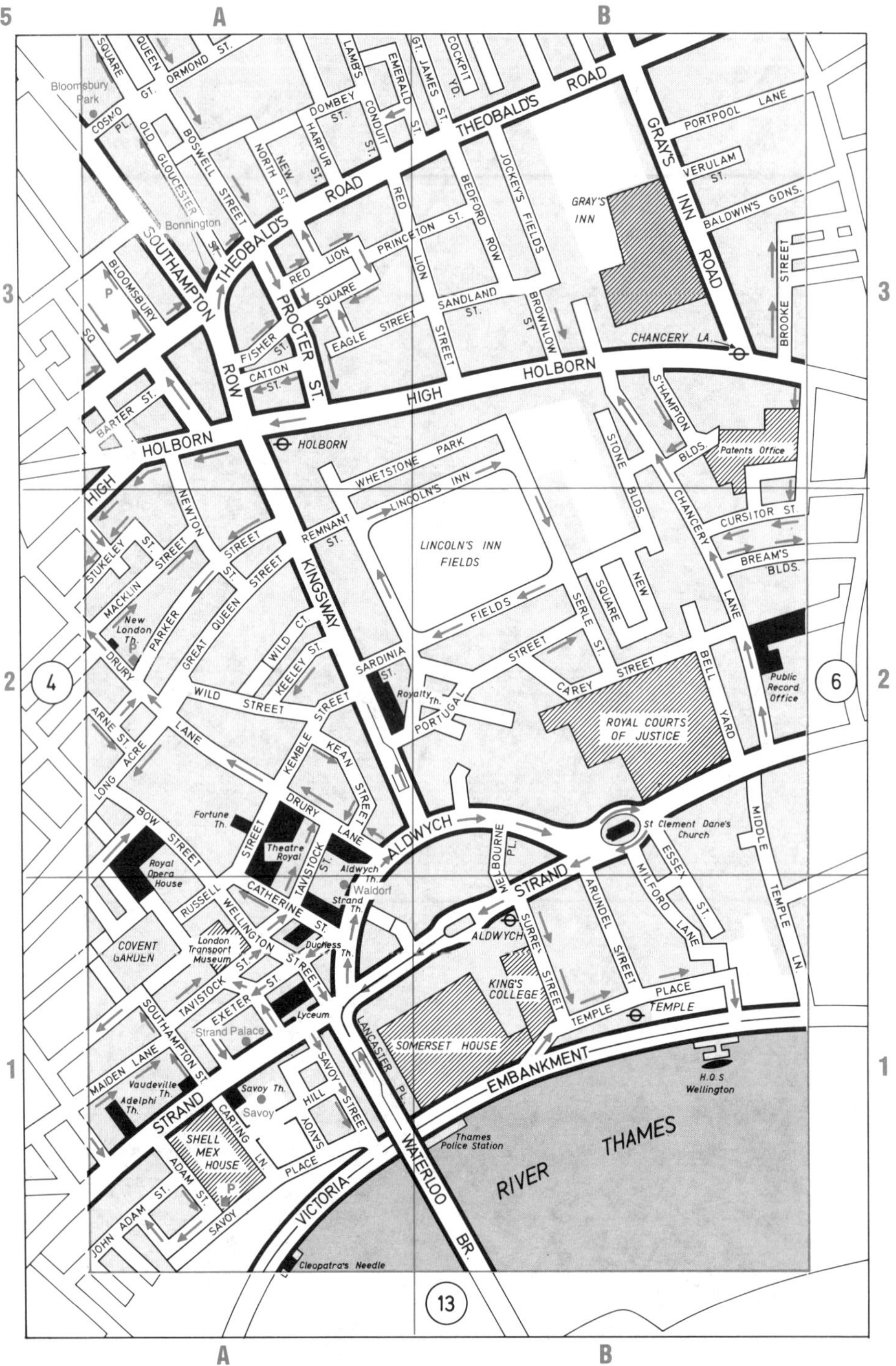

5
A
B
A
B
3
2
1
3
2
1
4
6
13
SQUARE
QUEEN
GT.
ORMOND ST.
LAMB'S
EMERALD
GT. JAMES ST.
COCKPIT YD.
DOMBEY ST.
HARPUR ST.
CONDUIT ST.
THEOBALD'S ROAD
GRAY'S INN ROAD
PORTPOOL LANE
VERULAM ST.
BALDWIN'S GDNS.
Bloomsbury Park
COSMO PL.
OLD GLOUCESTER ST.
BOSWELL STREET
NORTH ST.
NEW NORTH ST.
ROAD
RED LION ST.
BEDFORD ROW
JOCKEY'S FIELDS
GRAY'S INN
Bonnington
SOUTHAMPTON ROW
BLOOMSBURY SQ.
THEOBALD'S
RED LION SQUARE
PRINCETON ST.
BROOKE STREET
PROCTER ST.
EAGLE STREET
SANDLAND ST.
BROWNLOW ST.
FISHER ST.
CATTON ST.
CHANCERY LA.
HIGH HOLBORN
BARTER ST.
HOLBORN
HOLBORN
S'HAMPTON BLDS.
STONE BLDS.
Patents Office
WHETSTONE PARK
LINCOLN'S INN
NEWTON
STREET
REMNANT ST.
LINCOLN'S INN FIELDS
CHANCERY
CURSITOR ST.
BREAM'S BLDS.
STUKELEY ST.
MACKLIN STREET
PARKER
ST.
GREAT QUEEN STREET
KINGSWAY
FIELDS
NEW SQUARE
SERLE ST.
LANE
New London Th.
DRURY
WILD CT.
KEELEY ST.
SARDINIA ST.
Royalty Th.
STREET
CAREY STREET
BELL YARD
Public Record Office
WILD STREET
STREET
PORTUGAL
ROYAL COURTS OF JUSTICE
ARNE ST.
LANE
ACRE
LONG
KEMBLE
KEAN STREET
DRURY LANE
Fortune Th.
ALDWYCH
MELBOURNE PL.
St Clement Dane's Church
MIDDLE TEMPLE LN.
BOW STREET
Royal Opera House
STREET
Theatre Royal
TAVISTOCK ST.
Aldwych Th.
Waldorf
STRAND
ESSEX ST.
RUSSELL
CATHERINE ST.
Strand Th.
ARUNDEL STREET
MILFORD LANE
COVENT GARDEN
WELLINGTON
London Transport Museum
Duchess Th.
ALDWYCH
SURREY STREET
ST.
STREET
TAVISTOCK ST.
EXETER ST.
Lyceum
KING'S COLLEGE
TEMPLE
TEMPLE PLACE
SOUTHAMPTON ST.
Strand Palace
LANCASTER PL.
SOMERSET HOUSE
MAIDEN LANE
Vaudeville Th.
Savoy Th.
SAVOY HILL
SAVOY STREET
EMBANKMENT
H.Q.S. Wellington
Adelphi Th.
STRAND
Savoy
CARTING LN.
SHELL MEX HOUSE
WATERLOO BR.
Thames Police Station
RIVER THAMES
ADAM ST.
PLACE
JOHN ADAM ST.
SAVOY
VICTORIA
Cleopatra's Needle

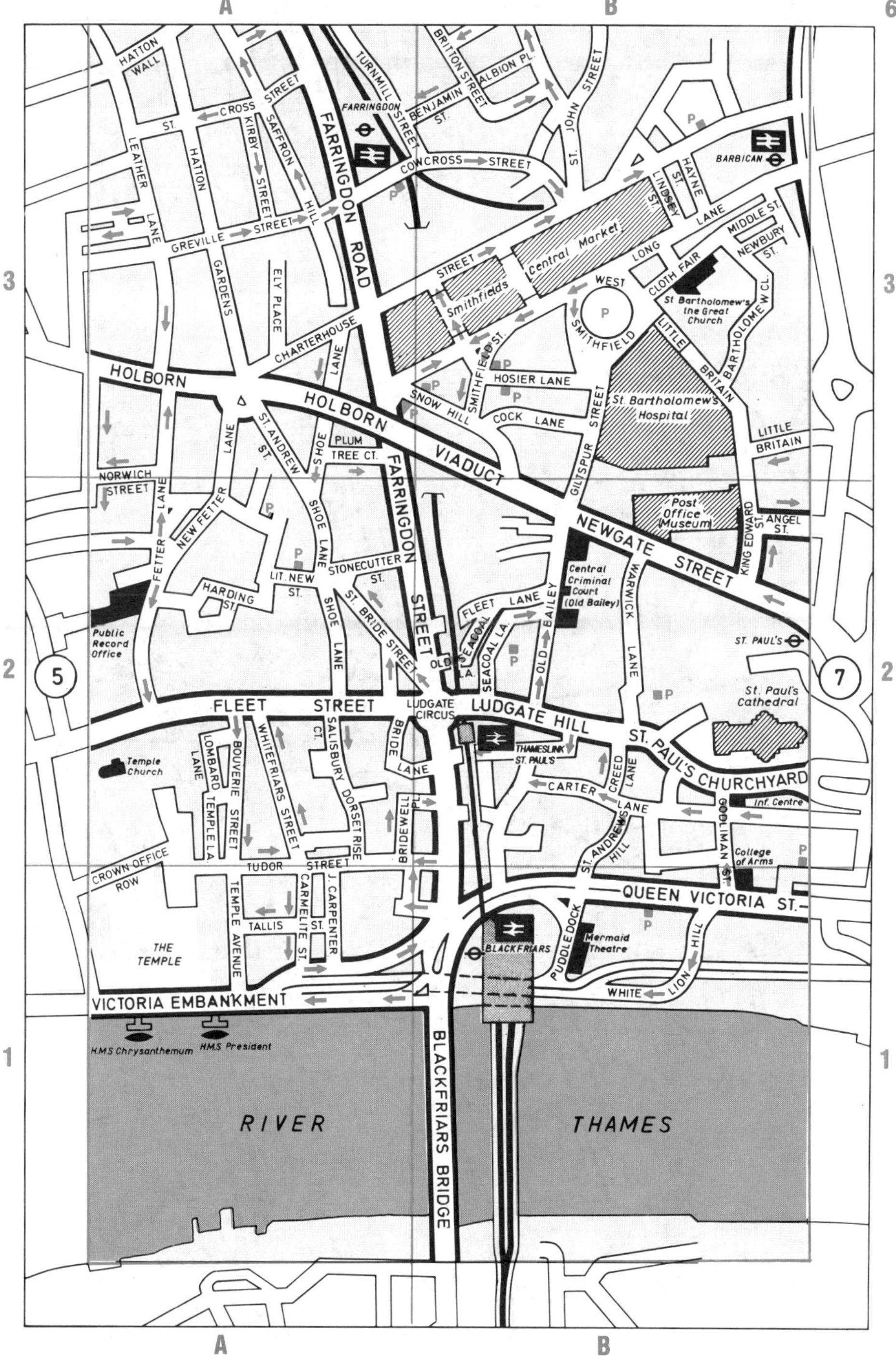

A
B
6
3
2
1
5
7
HATTON WALL
CROSS STREET
ST.
LEATHER LANE
HATTON
KIRBY STREET
SAFFRON HILL
FARRINGDON ROAD
FARRINGDON
TURNMILL STREET
BRITTON STREET
BENJAMIN ST.
ALBION PL.
ST. JOHN STREET
COWCROSS STREET
GREVILLE STREET
GARDENS
ELY PLACE
CHARTERHOUSE
LANE
Smithfields
Central Market
WEST SMITHFIELD
LONG LANE
CLOTH FAIR
LINDSEY ST.
HAYNE ST.
MIDDLE ST.
NEWBURY ST.
BARBICAN
St Bartholomew's the Great Church
LITTLE BRITAIN
BARTHOLOMEW CL.
HOLBORN
HOLBORN VIADUCT
SNOW HILL
SMITHFIELD ST.
HOSIER LANE
COCK LANE
GILTSPUR STREET
St. Bartholomew's Hospital
ST. ANDREW ST.
SHOE LANE
PLUM TREE CT.
FARRINGDON STREET
NORWICH STREET
FETTER LANE
NEW FETTER LANE
Post Office (Museum)
KING EDWARD ST.
ANGEL ST.
NEWGATE STREET
STONECUTTER ST.
LIT. NEW ST.
HARDING ST.
ST. BRIDE STREET
FLEET LANE
SEACOAL LA.
OLD SEACOAL LA.
OLD BAILEY
Central Criminal Court (Old Bailey)
WARWICK LANE
Public Record Office
ST. PAUL'S
St. Paul's Cathedral
FLEET STREET
LUDGATE CIRCUS
LUDGATE HILL
ST. PAUL'S CHURCHYARD
THAMESLINK ST. PAUL'S
Temple Church
LOMBARD LANE
BOUVERIE STREET
TEMPLE LA.
WHITEFRIARS STREET
SALISBURY CT.
DORSET RISE
BRIDE LANE
BRIDEWELL PL.
CARTER LANE
CREED LANE
ST. ANDREWS HILL
Inf. Centre
GODLIMAN ST.
College of Arms
CROWN OFFICE ROW
TUDOR STREET
J. CARPENTER
CARMELITE ST.
TEMPLE AVENUE
TALLIS ST.
QUEEN VICTORIA ST.
PUDDLE DOCK
Mermaid Theatre
BLACKFRIARS
LION HILL
WHITE
THE TEMPLE
VICTORIA EMBANKMENT
BLACKFRIARS BRIDGE
H.M.S Chrysanthemum
H.M.S President
RIVER
THAMES

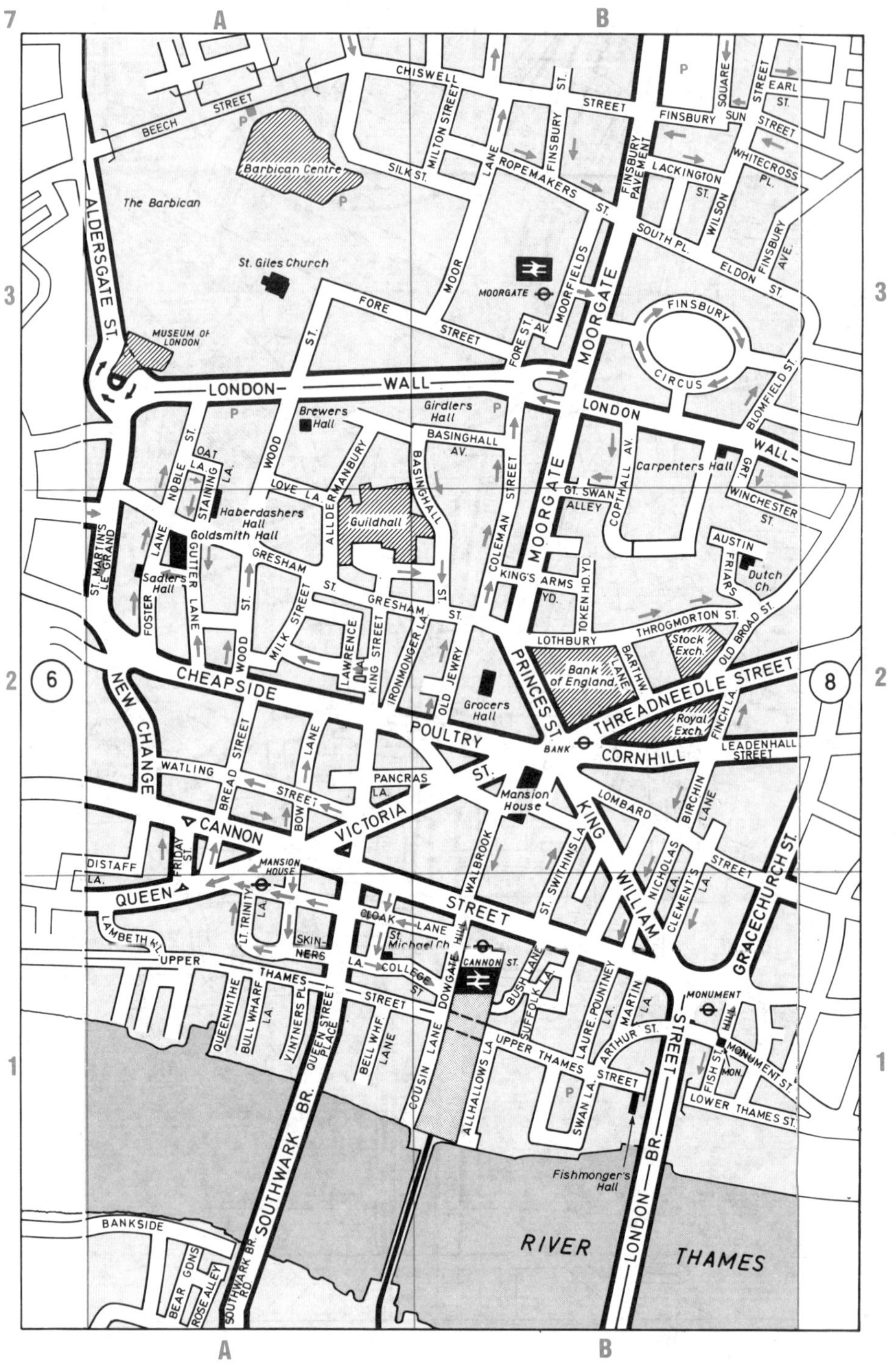

7
A
B
3
2
1
6
8
CHISWELL
STREET
BEECH
STREET
MILTON STREET
LANE
FINSBURY
ST.
FINSBURY
PAVEMENT
FINSBURY
SQUARE
SUN
STREET
EARL
ST.
LACKINGTON
ST.
WHITECROSS
PL.
WILSON
SOUTH PL.
ELDON
ST.
FINSBURY
AVE.
Barbican Centre
SILK ST.
ROPEMAKERS
ST.
The Barbican
ALDERSGATE ST.
St. Giles Church
MOOR
MOORGATE
MOORFIELDS
FORE
STREET
ST.
FORE ST. AV.
MUSEUM OF LONDON
FINSBURY
CIRCUS
BLOMFIELD ST.
LONDON
WALL
Brewers Hall
Girdlers Hall
BASINGHALL AV.
BASINGHALL
ST.
COLEMAN
STREET
NOBLE
OAT
LA.
STAINING
LA.
WOOD
ALDERMANBURY
LOVE LA.
Haberdashers Hall
Goldsmith Hall
Guildhall
Carpenters Hall
COPTHALL AV.
GT. SWAN ALLEY
GRT.
WINCHESTER
ST.
AUSTIN
FRIARS
Dutch Ch.
ST. MARTIN'S LE GRAND
FOSTER
LANE
GUTTER
LANE
Sadlers Hall
GRESHAM
ST.
MILK STREET
LAWRENCE
LA.
KING STREET
IRONMONGER LA.
OLD JEWRY
KING'S ARMS
YD.
TOKEN HD. YD.
LOTHBURY
THROGMORTON ST.
Stock Exch.
OLD BROAD ST.
Bank of England
BARTHW.
PRINCES ST.
CHEAPSIDE
NEW CHANGE
Grocers Hall
POULTRY
THREADNEEDLE STREET
Royal Exch.
FINCH LA.
BANK
CORNHILL
LEADENHALL STREET
WATLING
BREAD
STREET
BOW
PANCRAS
LA.
ST.
Mansion House
LOMBARD
BIRCHIN
CANNON
VICTORIA
KING
WILLIAM
FRIDAY
ST.
DISTAFF
LA.
QUEEN
MANSION HOUSE
WALBROOK
ST. SWITHINS LA.
NICHOLAS
LA.
CLEMENT'S
LA.
STREET
GRACECHURCH ST.
LAMBETH HL.
LT. TRINITY
LA.
CLOAK
LANE
SKINNERS
LA.
St. Michael Ch.
COLLEGE
DOWGATE HILL
CANNON ST.
BUSH LANE
SUFFOLK LA.
LAURE. POUNTNEY
LA.
MARTIN
LA.
MONUMENT
UPPER
THAMES
STREET
QUEENHITHE
BULL WHARF
LA.
VINTNERS PL.
QUEEN STREET PLACE
BELL WHF.
LANE
COUSIN LANE
ALLHALLOWS LA
UPPER THAMES
ARTHUR ST.
STREET
SWAN LA.
FISH ST.
HILL
MON.
MONUMENT ST.
LOWER THAMES ST.
Fishmonger's Hall
SOUTHWARK BR.
LONDON BR.
RIVER
THAMES
BANKSIDE
BEAR
GDNS
ROSE ALLEY
SOUTHWARK BR. RD
P

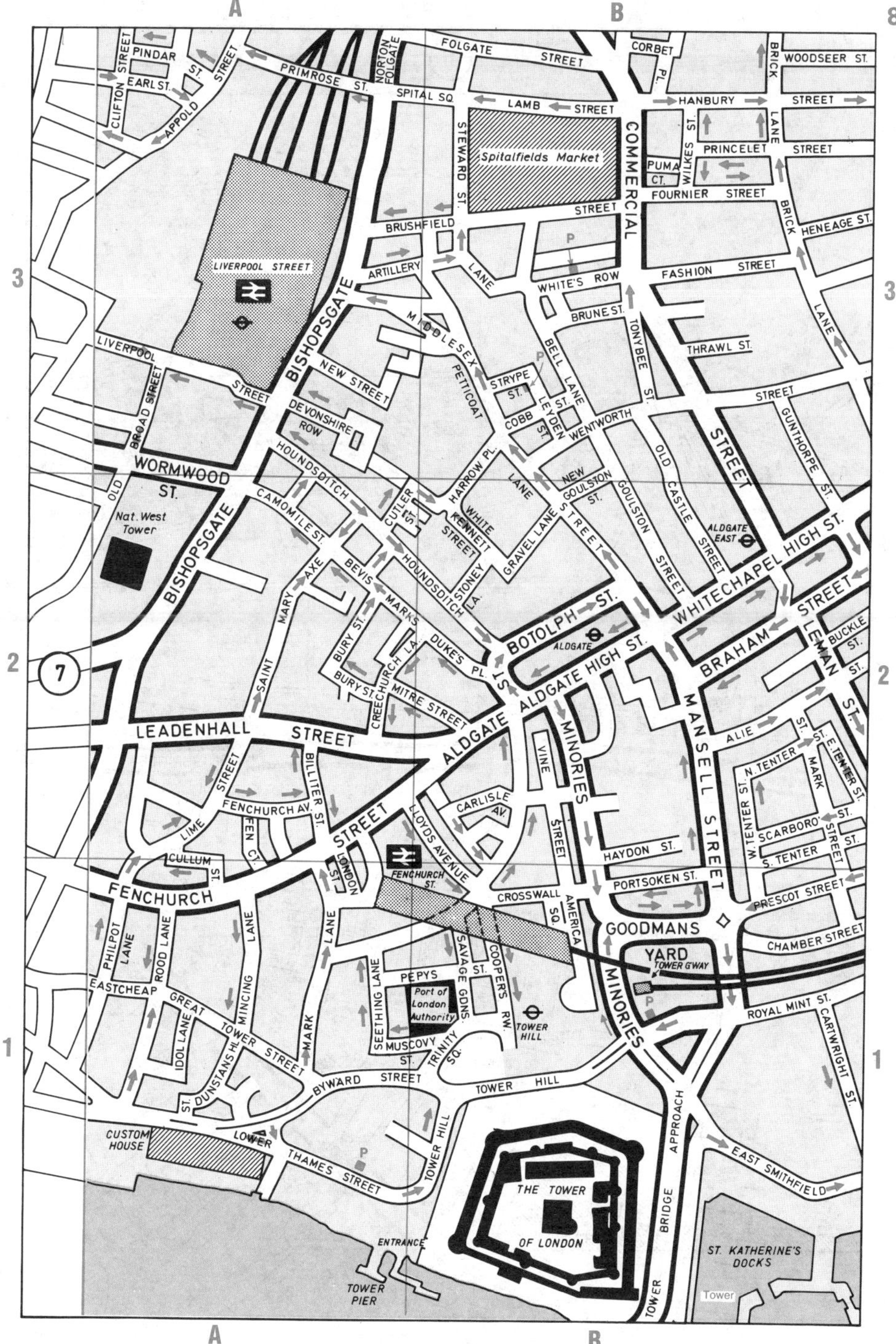

A
B
8
3
2
1
FOLGATE STREET
CORBET PL.
NORTON FOLGATE
PRIMROSE ST.
PINDAR
CLIFTON STREET
EARL ST.
APPOLD ST.
STREET
SPITAL SQ.
LAMB STREET
HANBURY STREET
BRICK LANE
WOODSEER ST.
Spitalfields Market
STEWARD ST.
COMMERCIAL
PUMA CT.
WILKES ST.
PRINCELET STREET
FOURNIER STREET
HENEAGE ST.
BRUSHFIELD STREET
LIVERPOOL STREET
ARTILLERY LANE
FASHION STREET
WHITE'S ROW
BRUNE ST.
TONYBEE ST.
THRAWL ST.
LANE
LIVERPOOL STREET
BROAD STREET
OLD
BISHOPSGATE
NEW STREET
MIDDLESEX
PETTICOAT
STRYPE ST.
BELL LANE
LEYDEN ST.
COBB ST.
WENTWORTH STREET
GUNTHORPE ST.
STREET
DEVONSHIRE ROW
WORMWOOD ST.
HOUNDSDITCH
HARROW PL.
LANE
NEW GOULSTON ST.
GOULSTON STREET
OLD CASTLE STREET
Nat. West Tower
CAMOMILE ST.
CUTLER ST.
WHITE KENNETT STREET
GRAVEL LANE
ALDGATE EAST
BISHOPSGATE
BEVIS MARKS
HOUNDSDITCH
STONEY LA.
WHITECHAPEL HIGH ST.
MARY AXE
BURY ST.
CREECHURCH LA.
DUKE'S PL.
BOTOLPH ST.
ALDGATE
BRAHAM STREET
LEMAN ST.
BUCKLE ST.
7
SAINT
BURY ST.
MITRE STREET
ST.
ALDGATE HIGH ST.
MINORIES
MANSELL STREET
LEADENHALL STREET
ALDGATE
VINE
ALIE ST.
N. TENTER ST.
E. TENTER ST.
MARK ST.
LIME STREET
BILLITER ST.
FENCHURCH AV.
STREET
LLOYDS AVENUE
CARLISLE AV.
STREET
W. TENTER ST.
SCARBORO' ST.
S. TENTER ST.
FEN CT.
CULLUM ST.
LONDON ST.
FENCHURCH ST.
HAYDON ST.
PORTSOKEN ST.
PRESCOT STREET
FENCHURCH
CROSSWALL
AMERICA SQ.
GOODMANS YARD
CHAMBER STREET
PHILPOT LANE
ROOD LANE
MINCING LANE
MARK LANE
SAVAGE GDNS.
COOPER'S RW.
TOWER G'WAY
EASTCHEAP
GREAT TOWER STREET
PEPYS ST.
SEETHING LANE
Port of London Authority
TOWER HILL
ROYAL MINT ST.
CARTWRIGHT ST.
IDOL LANE
ST. DUNSTANS HL.
MUSCOVY ST.
TRINITY SQ.
MINORIES
BYWARD STREET
TOWER HILL
APPROACH
CUSTOM HOUSE
LOWER THAMES STREET
TOWER HILL
EAST SMITHFIELD
THE TOWER OF LONDON
TOWER BRIDGE
ENTRANCE
TOWER PIER
ST. KATHERINE'S DOCKS
Tower

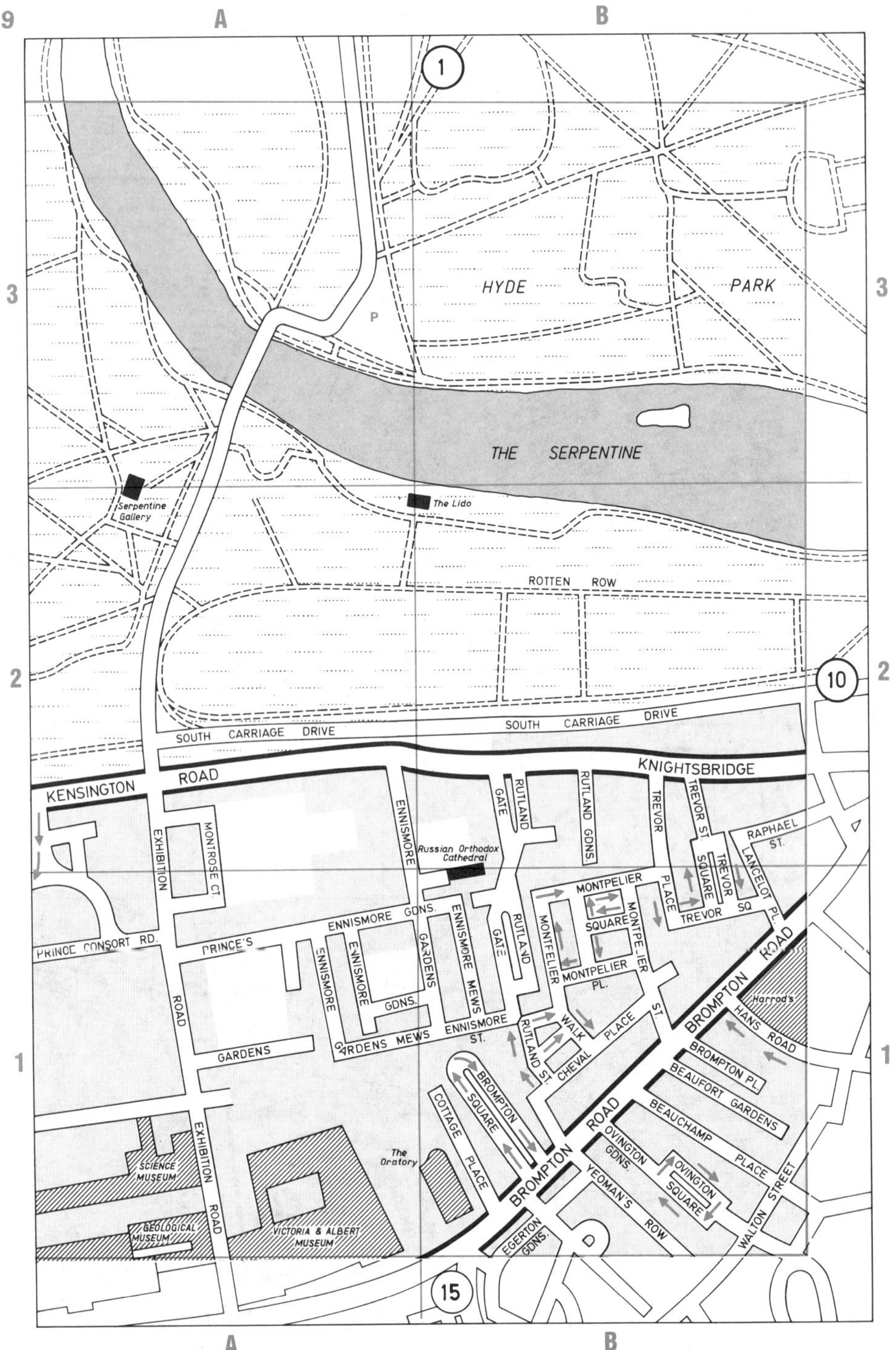
9
A
B
1
HYDE
PARK
3
P
THE SERPENTINE
Serpentine Gallery
The Lido
ROTTEN ROW
2
10
SOUTH CARRIAGE DRIVE
SOUTH CARRIAGE DRIVE
KENSINGTON ROAD
KNIGHTSBRIDGE
EXHIBITION
MONTROSE CT.
ENNISMORE
RUTLAND GATE
RUTLAND GDNS.
TREVOR
TREVOR ST.
RAPHAEL ST.
Russian Orthodox Cathedral
TREVOR SQUARE
TREVOR
LANCELOT PL.
MONTPELIER
MONTPELIER SQUARE
PLACE
TREVOR SQ
PRINCE CONSORT RD.
PRINCE'S
ENNISMORE GDNS.
ENNISMORE MEWS
RUTLAND GATE
MONTPELIER
MONTPELIER
MONTPELIER PL.
ENNISMORE
ENNISMORE GDNS.
GARDENS
ROAD
GARDENS
GARDENS MEWS
ENNISMORE ST.
RUTLAND ST.
WALK
CHEVAL PLACE
ST.
BROMPTON ROAD
Harrod's
HANS ROAD
BROMPTON PL.
BEAUFORT GARDENS
1
BROMPTON SQUARE
COTTAGE PLACE
The Oratory
EXHIBITION ROAD
SCIENCE MUSEUM
GEOLOGICAL MUSEUM
VICTORIA & ALBERT MUSEUM
BROMPTON
ROAD
OVINGTON GDNS.
BEAUCHAMP PLACE
OVINGTON SQUARE
YEOMAN'S ROW
WALTON STREET
EGERTON GDNS.
15
A
B

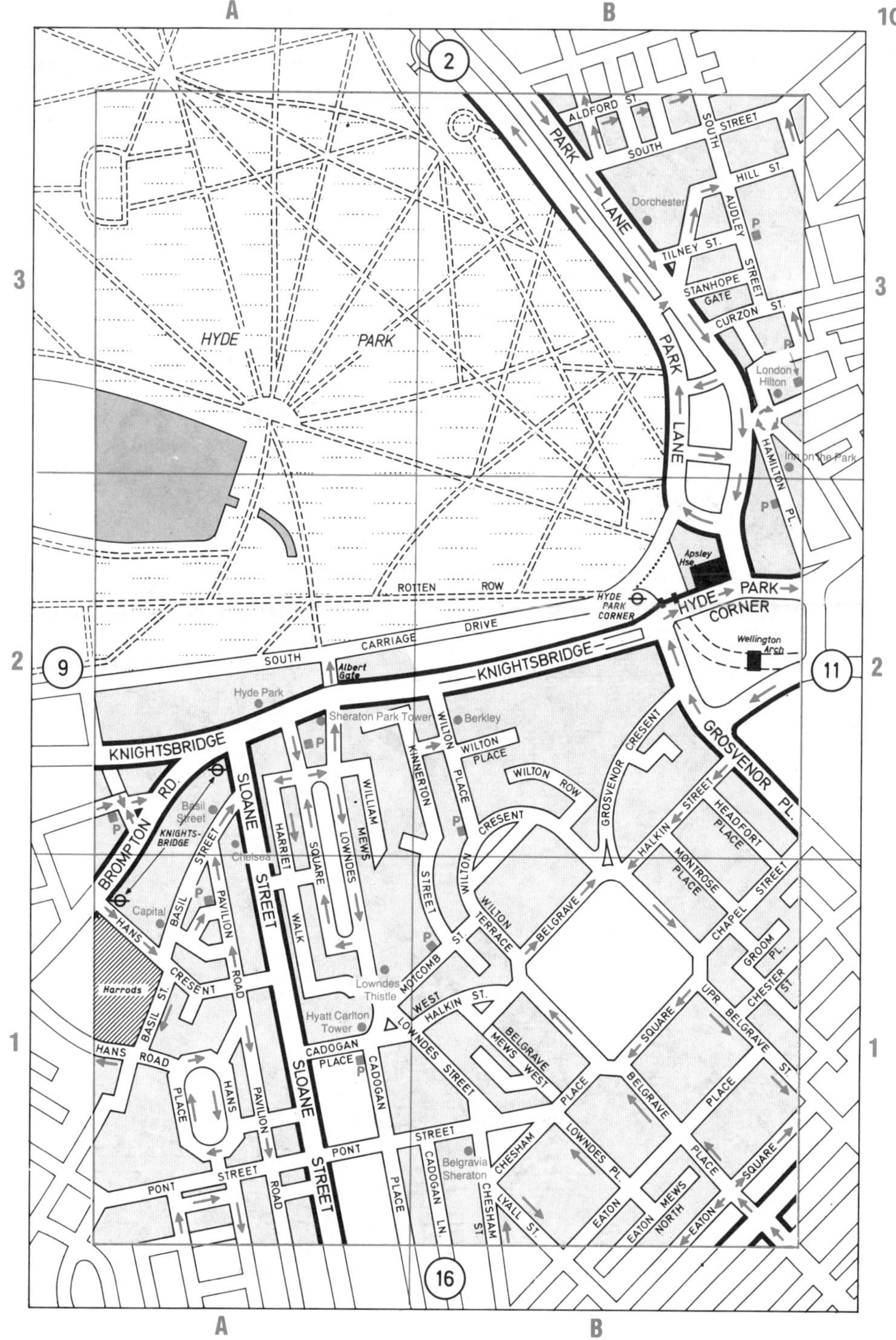

A
B
10
3
2
1
HYDE PARK
ROTTEN ROW
SOUTH CARRIAGE DRIVE
HYDE PARK CORNER
PARK LANE
ALDFORD ST.
SOUTH STREET
SOUTH AUDLEY STREET
HILL ST.
Dorchester
TILNEY ST.
STANHOPE GATE
CURZON ST.
London Hilton
HAMILTON PL.
Inn on the Park
Apsley Hse.
HYDE PARK CORNER
Wellington Arch
KNIGHTSBRIDGE
Albert Gate
Hyde Park
Sheraton Park Tower
Berkley
WILTON PLACE
WILTON ROW
WILTON CRESENT
GROSVENOR CRESENT
GROSVENOR PL.
HALKIN STREET
HEADFORT PLACE
MONTROSE PLACE
CHAPEL STREET
GROOM PL.
CHESTER ST.
KINNERTON STREET
WILLIAM MEWS
LOWNDES SQUARE
HARRIET WALK
BROMPTON RD.
KNIGHTS-BRIDGE
Basil Street
Chelsea
Capital
BASIL STREET
PAVILION ROAD
SLOANE STREET
HANS CRESENT
Harrods
BASIL ST.
HANS ROAD
HANS PLACE
Lowndes Thistle
Hyatt Carlton Tower
MOTCOMB ST.
WILTON TERRACE
BELGRAVE SQUARE
WEST HALKIN ST.
BELGRAVE MEWS WEST
BELGRAVE PLACE
UPR. BELGRAVE ST.
LOWNDES STREET
CADOGAN PLACE
PONT STREET
Belgravia Sheraton
CHESHAM PLACE
CHESHAM ST.
LYALL ST.
LOWNDES PL.
EATON PLACE
EATON MEWS NORTH
EATON SQUARE
CADOGAN LN.
P
2
9
11
16

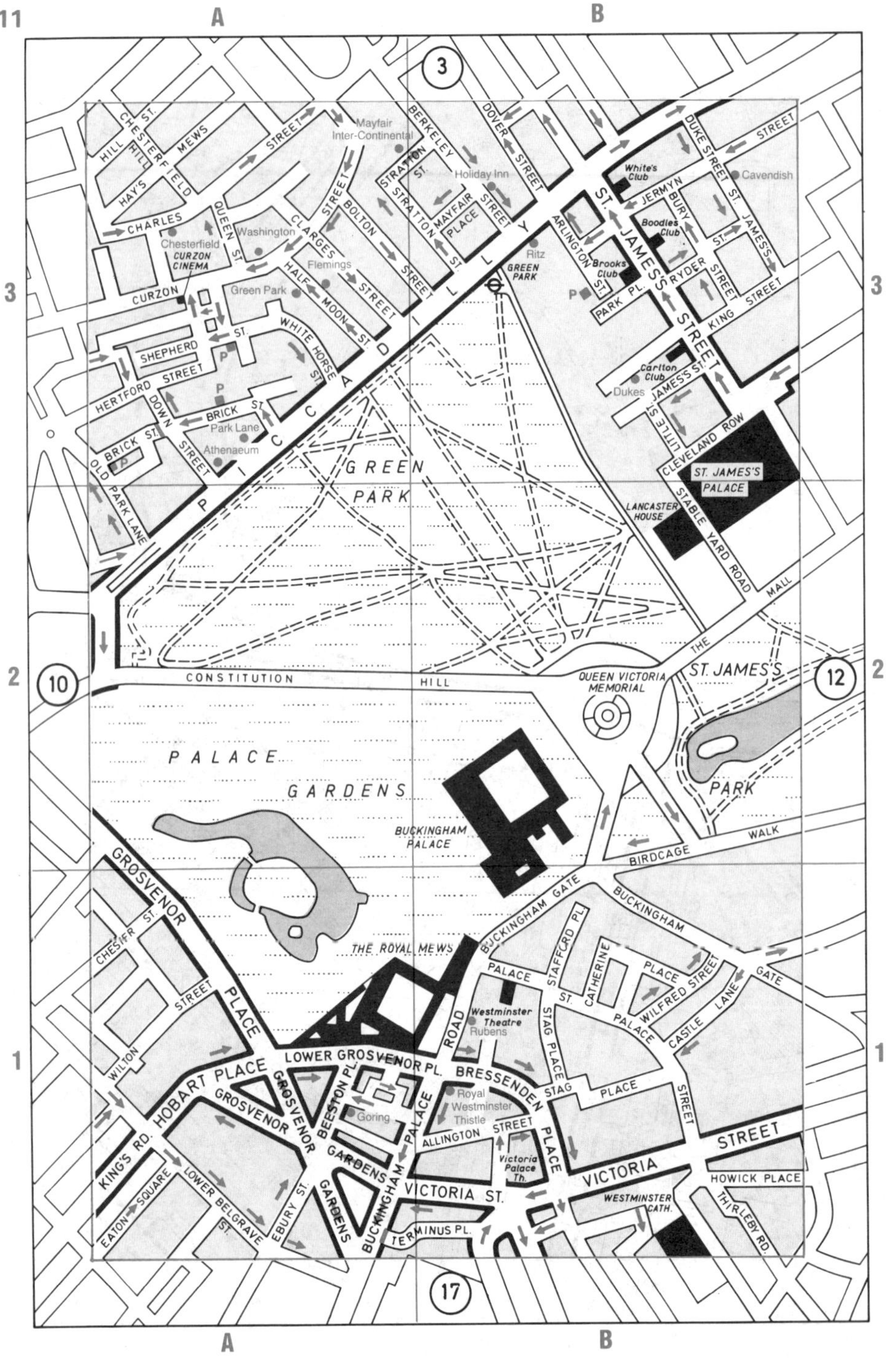
A
B
3
3
2
2
1
1
A
B
3
10
12
17
PICCADILLY
GREEN PARK
PALACE GARDENS
BUCKINGHAM PALACE
THE ROYAL MEWS
CONSTITUTION HILL
QUEEN VICTORIA MEMORIAL
THE MALL
ST. JAMES'S PARK
BIRDCAGE WALK
ST. JAMES'S PALACE
LANCASTER HOUSE
STABLE YARD ROAD
CLEVELAND ROW
ST. JAMES'S STREET
KING STREET
JERMYN STREET
DUKE STREET ST. JAMES'S
BURY ST.
RYDER ST.
PARK PL.
ARLINGTON ST.
LITTLE ST. JAMES'S ST.
DOVER STREET
BERKELEY STREET
STRATTON ST.
MAYFAIR PLACE
BOLTON STREET
CLARGES STREET
HALF MOON ST.
WHITE HORSE ST.
CURZON ST.
SHEPHERD STREET
HERTFORD STREET
BRICK ST.
DOWN STREET
OLD PARK LANE
QUEEN ST.
CHARLES STREET
HAY'S MEWS
CHESTERFIELD HILL
HILL ST.
White's Club
Boodles Club
Brooks Club
Carlton Club
Dukes
Cavendish
Ritz
Holiday Inn
Mayfair Inter-Continental
Washington
Chesterfield
CURZON CINEMA
Flemings
Green Park
Park Lane
Athenaeum
GREEN PARK
GROSVENOR PLACE
CHESTER ST.
WILTON STREET
HOBART PLACE
KING'S RD.
GROSVENOR GARDENS
LOWER GROSVENOR PL.
BEESTON PL.
Goring
BUCKINGHAM PALACE ROAD
BUCKINGHAM GATE
STAFFORD PL.
CATHERINE PLACE
WILFRED STREET
CASTLE LANE
PALACE ST.
STAG PLACE
BRESSENDEN PLACE
Westminster Theatre
Rubens
Royal Westminster Thistle
ALLINGTON STREET
Victoria Palace Th.
VICTORIA STREET
VICTORIA ST.
HOWICK PLACE
THIRLEBY RD.
WESTMINSTER CATH.
TERMINUS PL.
ESCOURT ST.
EBURY ST.
LOWER BELGRAVE ST.
EATON SQUARE
BUCKINGHAM GATE
P

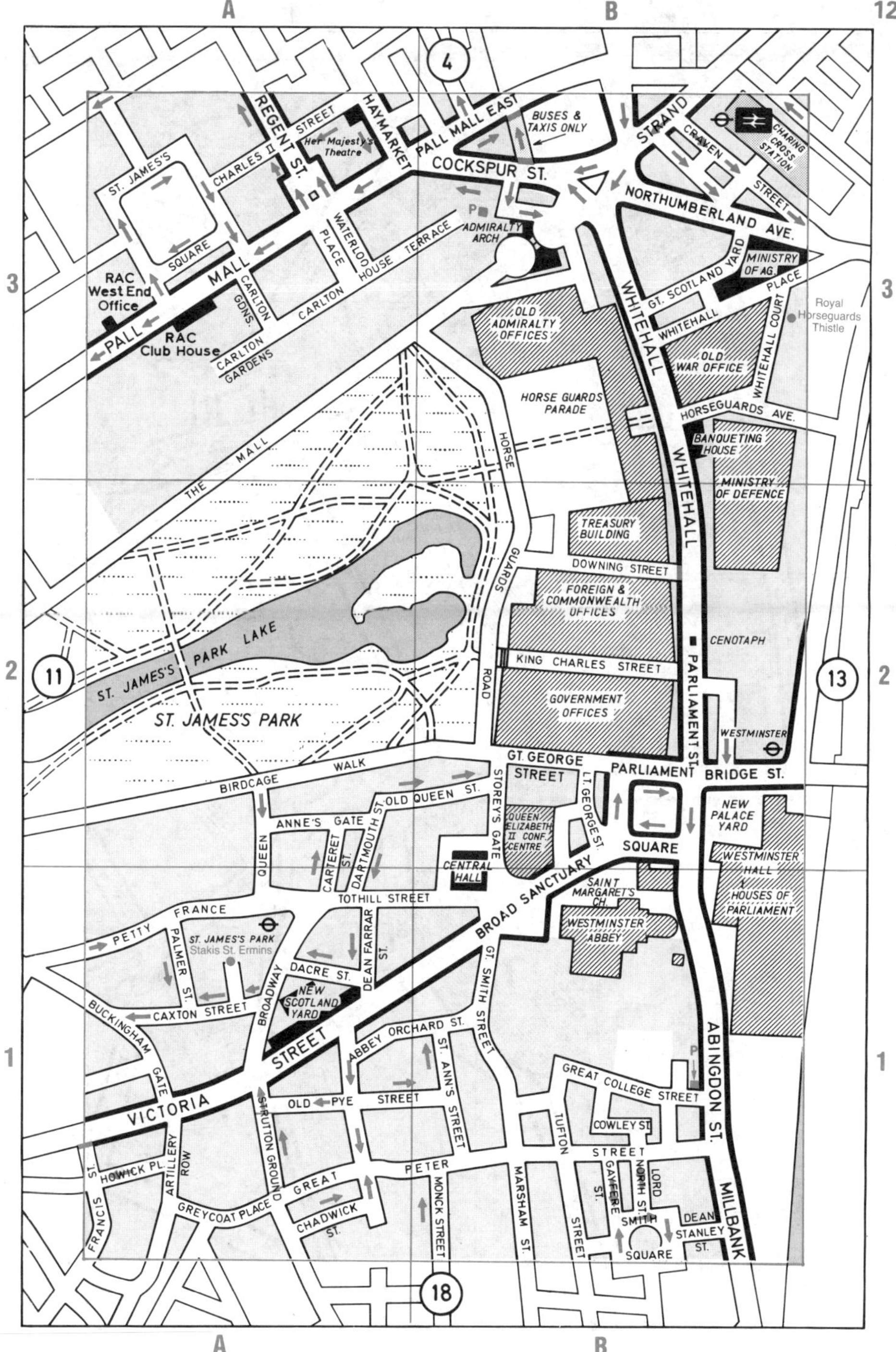
A
B
12
4
REGENT ST.
HAYMARKET
CHARLES II STREET
Her Majesty's Theatre
PALL MALL EAST
BUSES & TAXIS ONLY
STRAND
CRAVEN STREET
CHARING CROSS STATION
ST. JAMES'S SQUARE
COCKSPUR ST.
NORTHUMBERLAND AVE.
WATERLOO PLACE
ADMIRALTY ARCH
HOUSE TERRACE
CARLTON
MINISTRY OF AG.
GT. SCOTLAND YARD
WHITEHALL PLACE
RAC West End Office
PALL MALL
RAC Club House
CARLTON GDNS.
CARLTON GARDENS
OLD ADMIRALTY OFFICES
WHITEHALL
Royal Horseguards Thistle
WHITEHALL COURT
OLD WAR OFFICE
HORSE GUARDS PARADE
HORSEGUARDS AVE.
BANQUETING HOUSE
THE MALL
HORSE GUARDS ROAD
MINISTRY OF DEFENCE
TREASURY BUILDING
DOWNING STREET
FOREIGN & COMMONWEALTH OFFICES
CENOTAPH
ST. JAMES'S PARK LAKE
KING CHARLES STREET
PARLIAMENT ST.
11
13
GOVERNMENT OFFICES
ST. JAMES'S PARK
WESTMINSTER
BIRDCAGE WALK
GT. GEORGE STREET
PARLIAMENT SQUARE
BRIDGE ST.
STOREY'S GATE
OLD QUEEN ST.
LT. GEORGE ST.
NEW PALACE YARD
QUEEN ANNE'S GATE
CARTERET ST.
DARTMOUTH ST.
QUEEN ELIZABETH II CONF. CENTRE
CENTRAL HALL
BROAD SANCTUARY
WESTMINSTER HALL & HOUSES OF PARLIAMENT
TOTHILL STREET
SAINT MARGARET'S CH.
PETTY FRANCE
ST. JAMES'S PARK
Stakis St. Ermins
WESTMINSTER ABBEY
PALMER ST.
DEAN FARRAR ST.
DACRE ST.
BROADWAY
NEW SCOTLAND YARD
GT. SMITH STREET
BUCKINGHAM GATE
CAXTON STREET
ABINGDON ST.
VICTORIA STREET
ABBEY ORCHARD ST.
ST. ANN'S STREET
GREAT COLLEGE STREET
OLD PYE STREET
STRUTTON GROUND
TUFTON STREET
COWLEY ST.
HOWICK PL.
ARTILLERY ROW
FRANCIS ST.
GREAT PETER ST.
GAYFERE ST.
NORTH ST.
LORD NORTH ST.
MILLBANK
GREYCOAT PLACE
CHADWICK ST.
MONCK STREET
MARSHAM ST.
SMITH SQUARE
DEAN STANLEY ST.
18
3
2
1

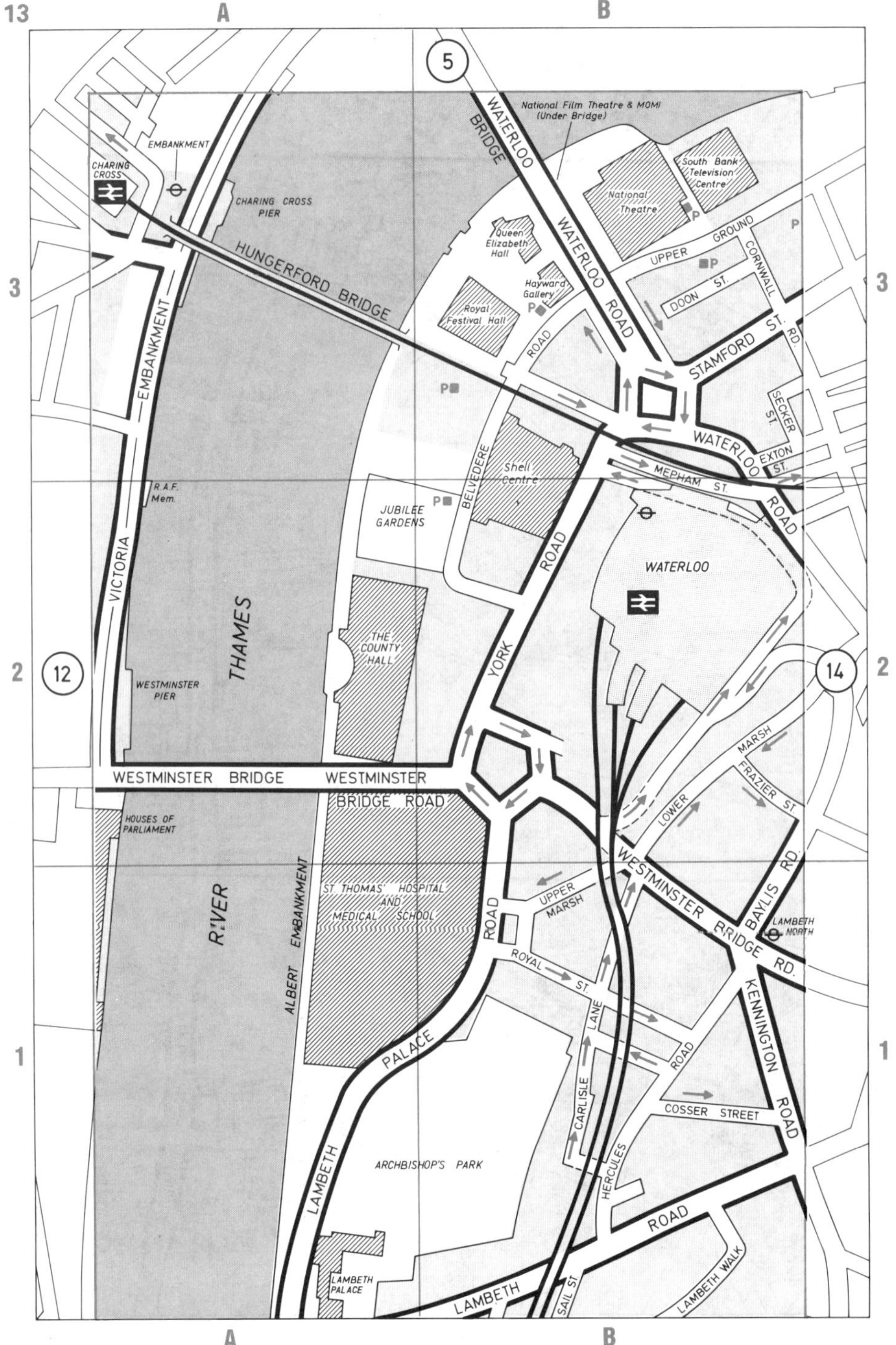
13
A
B
5
WATERLOO BRIDGE
National Film Theatre & MOMI (Under Bridge)
EMBANKMENT
CHARING CROSS
CHARING CROSS PIER
HUNGERFORD BRIDGE
South Bank Television Centre
National Theatre
Queen Elizabeth Hall
Hayward Gallery
Royal Festival Hall
WATERLOO ROAD
UPPER GROUND
CORNWALL RD.
DOON ST.
STAMFORD ST.
SECKER ST.
EXTON ST.
MEPHAM ST.
WATERLOO ROAD
3
EMBANKMENT
BELVEDERE ROAD
Shell Centre
R.A.F. Mem.
JUBILEE GARDENS
YORK ROAD
WATERLOO
VICTORIA
THAMES
THE COUNTY HALL
2
12
14
WESTMINSTER PIER
MARSH
LOWER
FRAZIER ST.
WESTMINSTER BRIDGE
WESTMINSTER BRIDGE ROAD
HOUSES OF PARLIAMENT
RIVER
ALBERT EMBANKMENT
ST. THOMAS' HOSPITAL AND MEDICAL SCHOOL
UPPER MARSH
ROAD
WESTMINSTER BRIDGE RD.
BAYLIS RD.
LAMBETH NORTH
ROYAL ST.
KENNINGTON ROAD
1
PALACE
LANE
CARLISLE
ROAD
COSSER STREET
ARCHBISHOP'S PARK
LAMBETH
HERCULES
ROAD
LAMBETH WALK
LAMBETH PALACE
LAMBETH
SAIL ST.
A
B

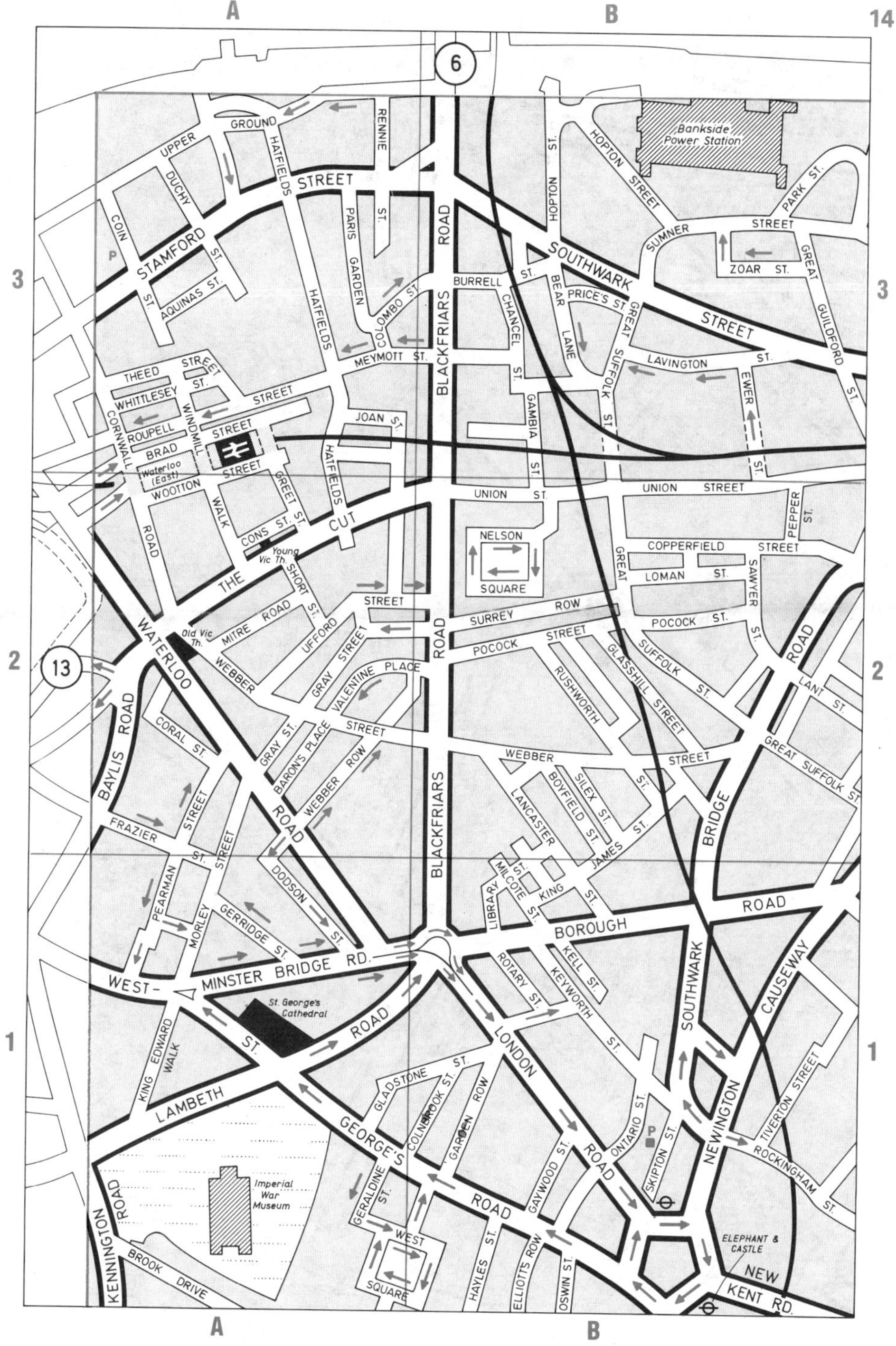
A
B
3
2
1
6
13
Bankside Power Station
HOPTON STREET
HOPTON ST.
PARK ST.
SUMNER STREET
ZOAR ST.
GREAT GUILDFORD ST.
SOUTHWARK STREET
UPPER GROUND
RENNIE
STAMFORD STREET
DUCHY ST.
COIN ST.
AQUINAS ST.
HATFIELDS
PARIS GARDEN
COLOMBO ST.
BLACKFRIARS ROAD
BURRELL ST.
CHANCEL ST.
BEAR LANE
PRICE'S ST.
GREAT SUFFOLK ST.
LAVINGTON ST.
EWER ST.
MEYMOTT ST.
JOAN ST.
GAMBIA ST.
THEED STREET
WHITTLESEY ST.
ROUPELL STREET
WINDMILL
BRAD STREET
CORNWALL ROAD
Waterloo (East)
WOOTTON STREET
GREET ST.
WALK
CONS ST.
THE CUT
Young Vic Th.
UNION ST.
UNION STREET
PEPPER ST.
NELSON SQUARE
COPPERFIELD STREET
LOMAN ST.
SAWYER ST.
POCOCK ST.
SURREY ROW
POCOCK STREET
SHORT ST.
MITRE ROAD
UFFORD
STREET
Old Vic Th.
WATERLOO ROAD
WEBBER ST.
GRAY STREET
VALENTINE PLACE
RUSHWORTH
GLASSHILL STREET
SUFFOLK ST.
ROAD
LANT ST.
BAYLIS ROAD
CORAL ST.
GRAY ST.
BARON'S PLACE
WEBBER ROW
WEBBER STREET
GREAT SUFFOLK ST.
SILEX ST.
BOYFIELD ST.
LANCASTER ST.
JAMES ST.
SOUTHWARK BRIDGE ROAD
FRAZIER ST.
STREET
PEARMAN ST.
MORLEY STREET
GERRIDGE ST.
DODSON ST.
LIBRARY ST.
MILCOTE ST.
KING ST.
BOROUGH ROAD
WESTMINSTER BRIDGE RD.
ROTARY ST.
KELL ST.
KEYWORTH ST.
SOUTHWARK
CAUSEWAY
St. George's Cathedral
ST. GEORGE'S ROAD
LONDON ROAD
KING EDWARD WALK
LAMBETH ROAD
GLADSTONE ST.
COLNBROOK ST.
GARDEN ROW
ONTARIO ST.
P
SKIPTON ST.
NEWINGTON
TIVERTON STREET
ROCKINGHAM ST.
Imperial War Museum
GERALDINE ST.
WEST SQUARE
GAYWOOD ST.
KENNINGTON ROAD
BROOK DRIVE
HAYLES ST.
ELLIOTT'S ROW
OSWIN ST.
ELEPHANT & CASTLE
NEW KENT RD.

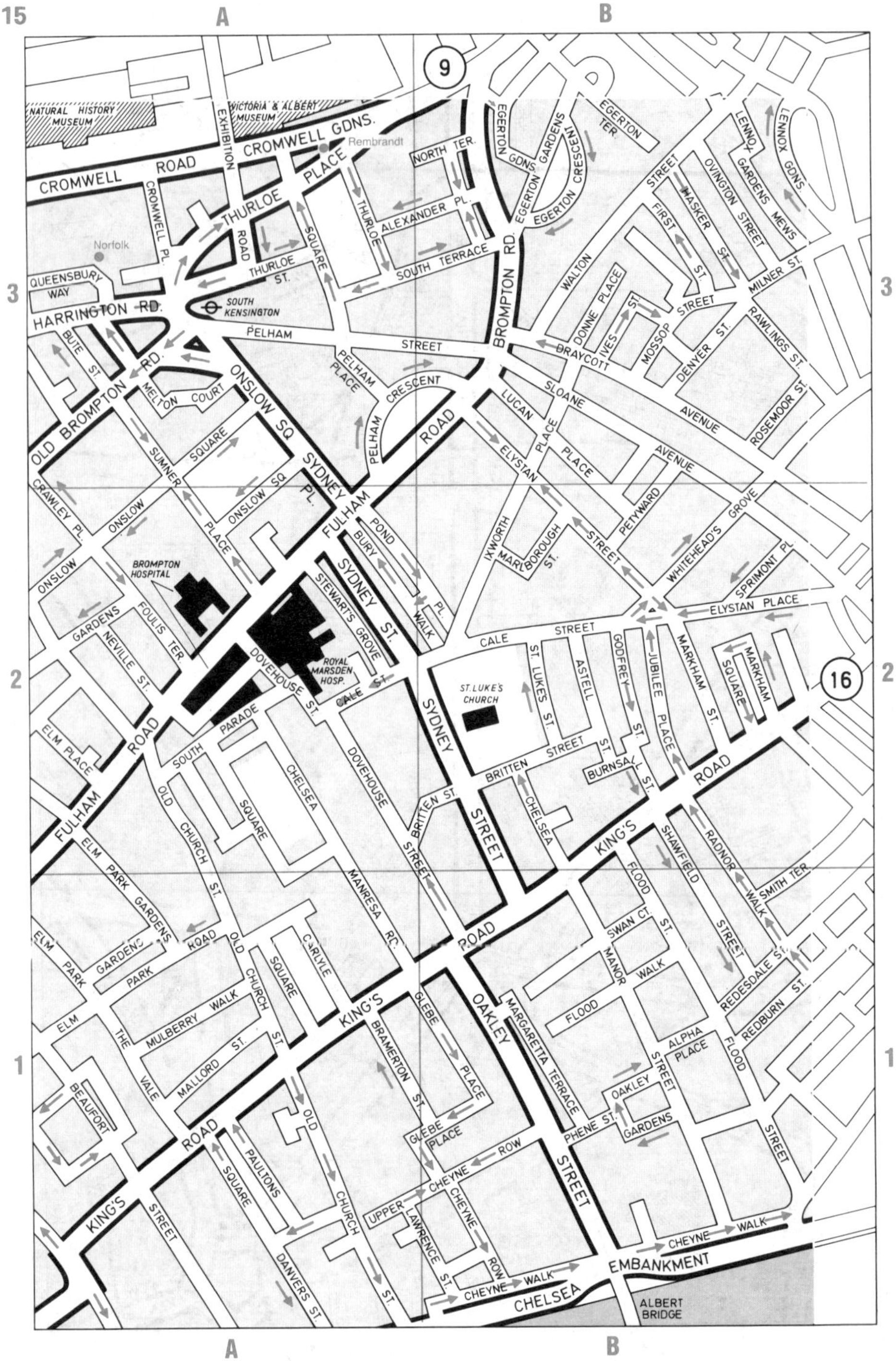

A B

9

NATURAL HISTORY MUSEUM
VICTORIA & ALBERT MUSEUM
EXHIBITION
CROMWELL GDNS.
Rembrandt
CROMWELL ROAD
CROMWELL PL.
THURLOE PLACE
THURLOE SQUARE
THURLOE ST.
THURLOE
ROAD
NORTH TER.
ALEXANDER PL.
SOUTH TERRACE
EGERTON GDNS
EGERTON GARDENS
EGERTON CRESCENT
EGERTON TER.
BROMPTON RD.
WALTON STREET
FIRST ST.
HASKER ST.
OVINGTON STREET
LENNOX GARDENS MEWS
LENNOX GDNS.
MILNER ST.
Norfolk
QUEENSBURY WAY
HARRINGTON RD.
SOUTH KENSINGTON
PELHAM STREET
DONNE PLACE
IVES ST.
MOSSOP STREET
DENYER ST.
RAWLINGS ST.
DRAYCOTT AVENUE
SLOANE AVENUE
ROSEMOOR ST.
BUTE ST.
OLD BROMPTON RD.
MELTON COURT
ONSLOW SQ.
PELHAM PLACE
PELHAM CRESCENT
ROAD
LUCAN PLACE
ELYSTAN PLACE
SUMNER PLACE
ONSLOW SQUARE
ONSLOW SQ.
SYDNEY PL.
FULHAM ROAD
CRAWLEY PL.
ONSLOW GARDENS
BROMPTON HOSPITAL
FOULIS TER.
NEVILLE ST.
POND PL.
BURY WALK
SYDNEY ST.
STEWART'S GROVE
ROYAL MARSDEN HOSP.
DOVEHOUSE ST.
CALE ST.
IXWORTH PL.
MARLBOROUGH ST.
ELYSTAN STREET
PETYWARD
WHITEHEAD'S GROVE
SPRIMONT PL.
ELYSTAN PLACE
CALE STREET
ST. LUKE'S CHURCH
ST. LUKES ST.
ASTELL ST.
GODFREY ST.
JUBILEE PLACE
MARKHAM ST.
MARKHAM SQUARE
MARKHAM

16

ELM PLACE
SOUTH PARADE
CHELSEA SQUARE
OLD CHURCH ST.
DOVEHOUSE STREET
BRITTEN ST.
BRITTEN STREET
SYDNEY STREET
CHELSEA MANOR ST.
BURNSALL ST.
KING'S ROAD
SHAWFIELD STREET
RADNOR WALK
SMITH TER.
FLOOD ST.
SWAN CT.
MANOR
ELM PARK GARDENS
MANRESA RD.
ELM PARK GARDENS
PARK ROAD
CARLYLE SQUARE
OLD CHURCH ST.
ROAD
KING'S ROAD
OAKLEY STREET
MARGARETTA TERRACE
WALK
FLOOD
FLOOD ST.
REDESDALE ST.
REDBURN ST.
ELM
THE VALE
MULBERRY WALK
MALLORD ST.
GLEBE PLACE
BRAMERTON ST.
ALPHA PLACE
OAKLEY STREET
BEAUFORT ST.
OAKLEY GARDENS
PHENE ST.
GLEBE PLACE
CHEYNE ROW
PAULTONS SQUARE
OLD CHURCH ST.
UPPER CHEYNE ROW
LAWRENCE ST.
CHEYNE ROW
KING'S ROAD
STREET
DANVERS ST.
CHEYNE WALK
CHELSEA EMBANKMENT
CHEYNE WALK
ALBERT BRIDGE
STREET

3 2 1

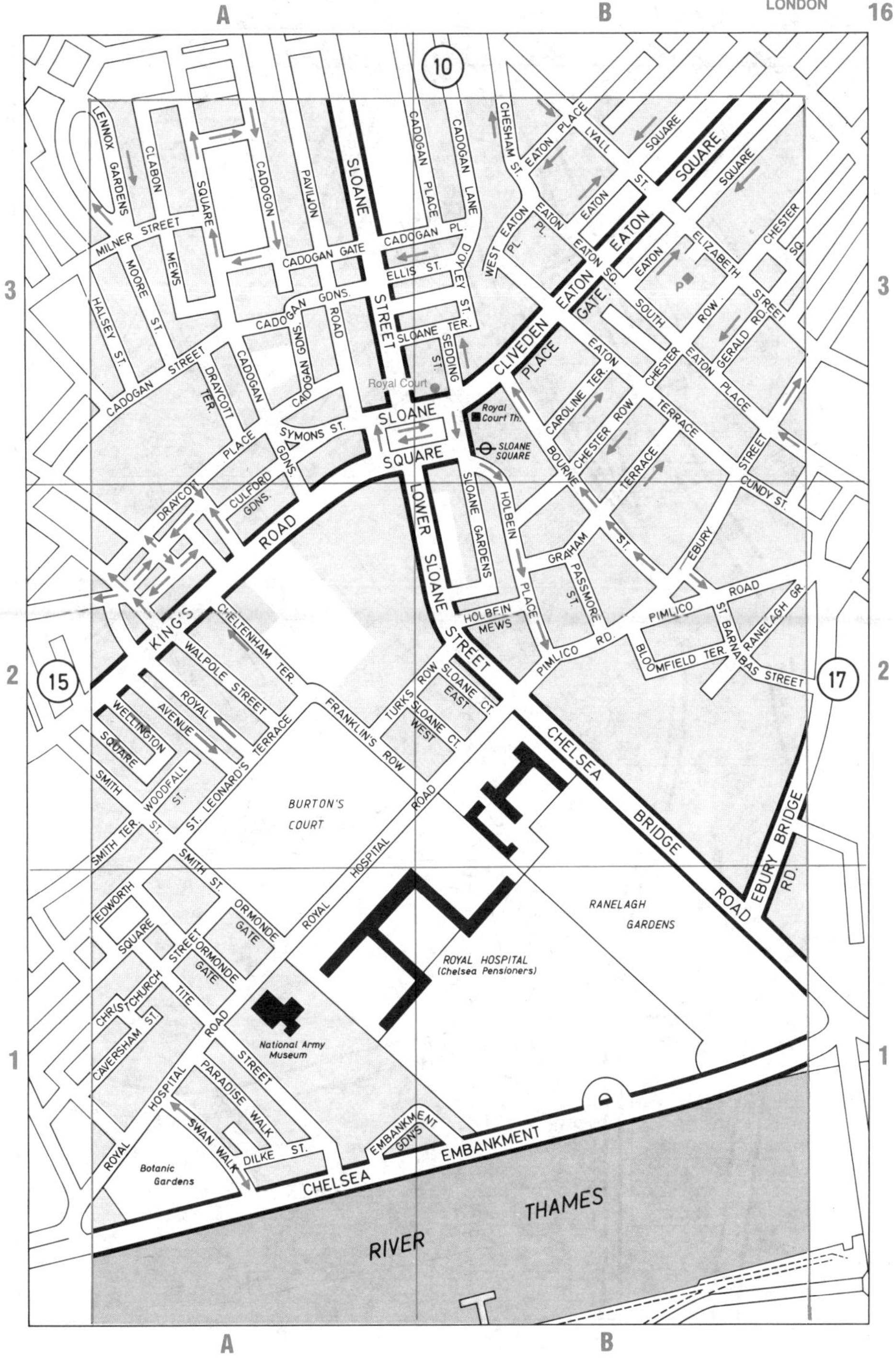
A
B
3
2
1
10
15
17
LENNOX GARDENS
CLABON
MILNER STREET
SQUARE
CADOGAN
PAVILION
SLOANE
CADOGAN PLACE
CADOGAN LANE
CHESHAM ST.
EATON PLACE
LYALL
SQUARE
EATON
CADOGAN GATE
CADOGAN PL.
ELLIS ST.
DOYLEY ST.
MOORE ST.
MEWS
HALSEY ST.
CADOGAN GDNS.
CADOGAN STREET
ROAD
STREET
SLOANE TER.
SEDDING
ST.
WEST EATON PL.
EATON PL.
EATON SQ.
EATON GATE
ELIZABETH
STREET
CHESTER SQ.
SOUTH
ROW
GERALD RD.
DRAYCOTT TER.
CADOGAN
CADOGAN GDNS.
Royal Court
CLIVEDEN PLACE
CHESTER EATON PLACE
TERRACE
Royal Court Th.
SLOANE SQUARE
SYMONS ST.
GDNS.
PLACE
CAROLINE TER.
CHESTER ROW
BOURNE
TERRACE
CUNDY ST.
DRAYCOTT
CULFORD GDNS.
LOWER SLOANE STREET
SLOANE GARDENS
HOLBEIN
GRAHAM
ST.
PASSMORE
EBURY
ROAD
KING'S
CHELTENHAM TER.
HOLBEIN MEWS
PLACE
PIMLICO RD.
PIMLICO
BLOOMFIELD TER.
ST BARNABAS STREET
RANELAGH GR.
WALPOLE STREET
ROYAL AVENUE
WELLINGTON SQUARE
TURKS ROW
SLOANE CT. EAST
SLOANE CT. WEST
FRANKLIN'S ROW
TERRACE
SMITH
WOODFALL ST.
ST. LEONARD'S
BURTON'S COURT
CHELSEA BRIDGE ROAD
EBURY BRIDGE RD.
SMITH TER.
SMITH ST.
ROYAL HOSPITAL ROAD
RANELAGH GARDENS
TEDWORTH SQUARE
ORMONDE GATE
STREET
ROYAL HOSPITAL
(Chelsea Pensioners)
CHRISTCHURCH ST.
CAVERSHAM ST.
TITE
National Army Museum
ROYAL HOSPITAL
PARADISE WALK
SWAN WALK
DILKE ST.
EMBANKMENT GDN'S
CHELSEA EMBANKMENT
Botanic Gardens
RIVER THAMES

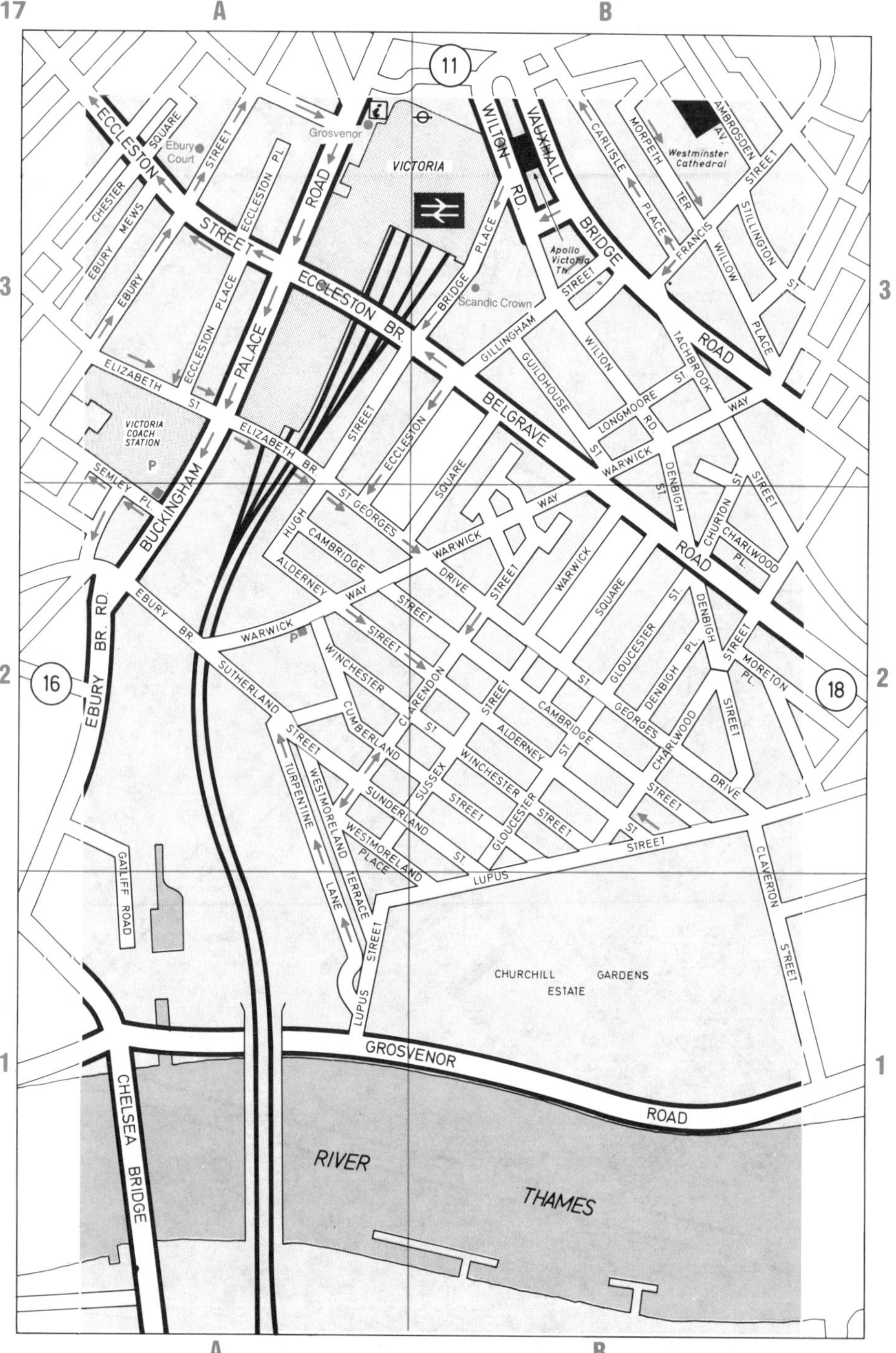
17
A
B
3
2
1
11
16
18
VICTORIA
Grosvenor
Ebury Court
Westminster Cathedral
Apollo Victoria Th.
Scandic Crown
VICTORIA COACH STATION
P
ECCLESTON SQUARE
CHESTER
EBURY MEWS
EBURY STREET
ECCLESTON STREET
ECCLESTON PL.
ECCLESTON PLACE
BUCKINGHAM PALACE ROAD
ECCLESTON BR.
ELIZABETH ST.
ELIZABETH BR.
SEMLEY PL.
WILTON RD.
VAUXHALL BRIDGE ROAD
BRIDGE PLACE
CARLISLE PLACE
MORPETH TER
AMBROSDEN AV.
FRANCIS STREET
STILLINGTON ST.
WILLOW PLACE
GILLINGHAM STREET
GUILDHOUSE ST.
WILTON
TACHBROOK ST.
LONGMOORE RD.
WARWICK WAY
BELGRAVE ROAD
ECCLESTON STREET
ECCLESTON SQUARE
DENBIGH ST.
CHURTON ST.
CHARLWOOD PL.
STREET
ST. GEORGES DRIVE
HUGH
CAMBRIDGE
ALDERNEY
WARWICK STREET
WARWICK SQUARE
GLOUCESTER ST.
DENBIGH PL.
MORETON PL.
MORETON STREET
EBURY BR. RD.
EBURY BR.
SUTHERLAND STREET
WINCHESTER STREET
CLARENDON ST.
CUMBERLAND
ST. GEORGES
CAMBRIDGE ST.
ALDERNEY STREET
CHARLWOOD STREET
DRIVE
TURPENTINE LANE
WESTMORELAND TERRACE
WESTMORELAND PLACE
SUNDERLAND ST.
SUSSEX STREET
WINCHESTER STREET
GLOUCESTER ST.
LUPUS STREET
CLAVERTON STREET
GATLIFF ROAD
CHURCHILL GARDENS ESTATE
GROSVENOR ROAD
CHELSEA BRIDGE
RIVER THAMES

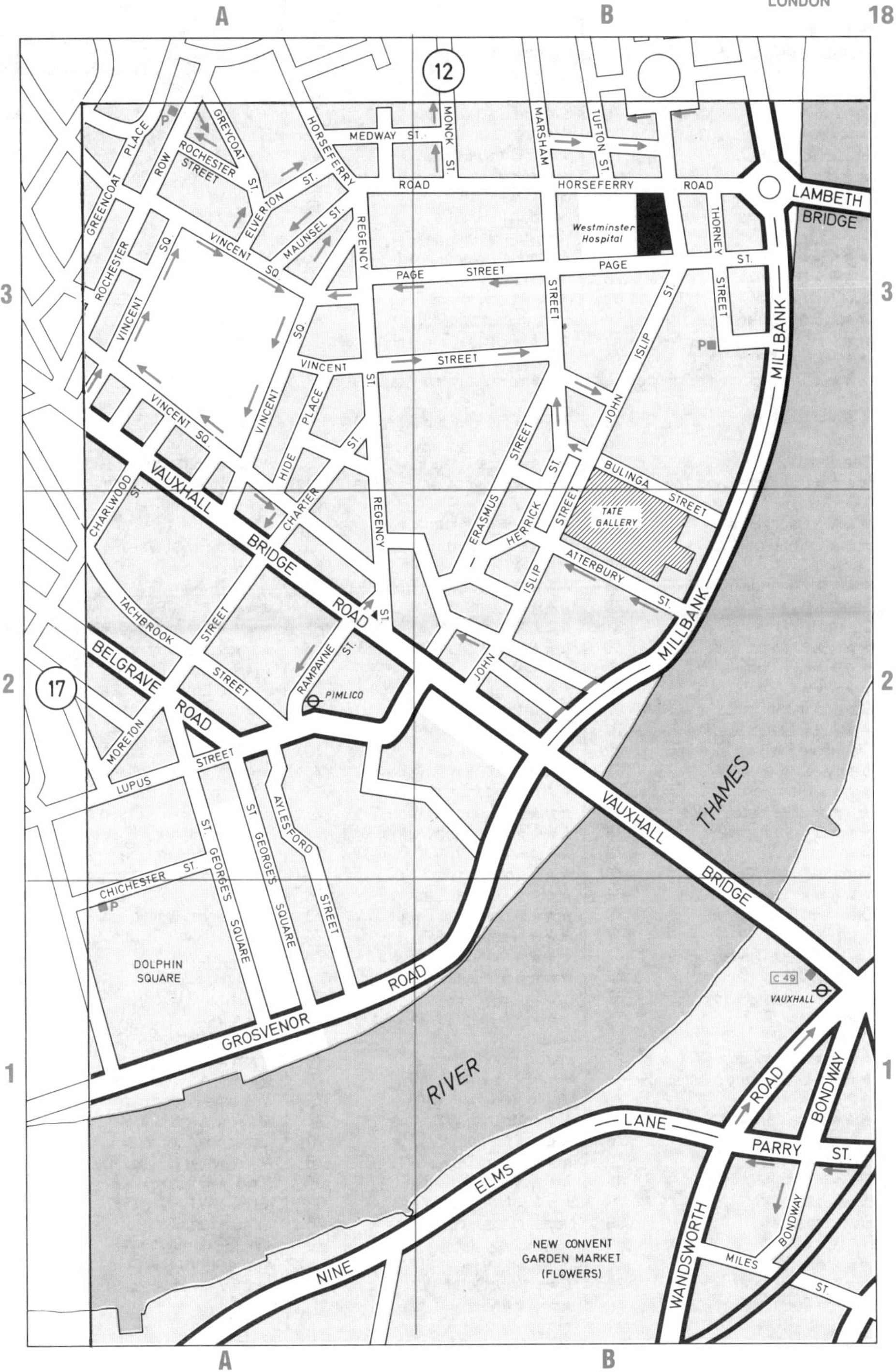
A
B
12
17
3
2
1
MEDWAY ST.
MONCK ST.
MARSHAM
TUFTON ST.
HORSEFERRY ROAD
HORSEFERRY ROAD
LAMBETH BRIDGE
GREYCOAT PLACE
ROCHESTER ROW
ROCHESTER STREET
GREYCOAT ST.
ELVERTON ST.
MAUNSEL ST.
REGENCY
Westminster Hospital
THORNEY STREET
PAGE STREET
PAGE ST.
GREENCOAT
ROCHESTER
VINCENT SQ.
VINCENT STREET
JOHN ISLIP ST.
MILLBANK
HIDE PLACE
REGENCY ST.
ERASMUS STREET
HERRICK ST.
BULINGA STREET
TATE GALLERY
VAUXHALL BRIDGE ROAD
CHARLWOOD ST.
CHARTER
ATTERBURY ST.
ISLIP
TACHBROOK STREET
BELGRAVE ROAD
RAMPAYNE ST.
PIMLICO
JOHN
MORETON
LUPUS STREET
ST. GEORGE'S SQUARE
ST GEORGES SQUARE
AYLESFORD STREET
THAMES
CHICHESTER ST.
DOLPHIN SQUARE
GROSVENOR ROAD
RIVER
C 49
VAUXHALL
ROAD
BONDWAY
LANE
PARRY ST.
NINE ELMS
NEW CONVENT GARDEN MARKET (FLOWERS)
WANDSWORTH
MILES ST.
P

Index of London Hotels

ENGLAND

ABBERLEY Hereford & Worcester (Worcestershire). Map 20B3
Pop 589. Worcester 12, London 126, Kidderminster 8, Ludlow 18, Bromyard 12.
See Clock Tower, Abberley Hill.

★★★ H R Elms, Stockton Rd, WR6 6AT Gt Witley (0299) 896666 Tx: 337105 Fax: (0299) 896804

Luxuriously appointed and newly refurbished Queen Anne residence, with fine gardens and views. Putting, tennis. Fr, Sw. (QMH)
16 bedrs, 16 en suite; annexe 9 bedrs, 9 en suite; TV
P 60, coach; child facs; con 60
LD 9.30
£ B&B £80, B&B (double) £95–£145; L £13·95, D £20; WB £65. [5% V]
cc Access, Amex, B'card/Visa, Diners.

Manor Arms at Abberley, WR6 6BN Gt Witley (0299) 896507 Tx: 335672

A 300-year-old inn with bedrooms in a modern extension. Situated in the village centre with rural views.

ABBOTS SALFORD Warwickshire. Map 20C3
Bidford-on-Avon 2, London 104, Birmingham 24, Evesham 6, Stratford-upon-Avon 9½

> **Atlas Section**
> Consult the Atlas section at the back of the guide to find out which towns and villages have RAC Appointed and Listed hotels in them. They are shown on the maps by purple circles.

★★★ Salford Hall, Nr Stratford-upon-Avon, WR11 5UT (0386) 871300 Tx: 336682 Fax: (0386) 871301

A magnificent, Grade I listed, Tudor manor in spacious grounds. Beams, oak panelling and log fires create the atmosphere, modern amenities add comfort. Tennis, sauna, solarium, snooker. Fr
15 bedrs, 14 en suite; annexe 19 bedrs, 19 en suite; TV; tcf
ns; P 50; child facs; con 70
LD 10
£ B&B £70–£100; B&B (double) £90–£140; L £13·25, D £18·95; WB £55 (HB); [10% V]
cc Access, Amex, B'card/Visa, Diners

ABINGDON Oxfordshire. Map 21A1
Pop 21,966. Henley-on-Thames 21, London 56, Faringdon 14, High Wycombe 29, Newbury 19, Oxford 6½, Swindon 25, Wallingford 10.
EC Thur. **MD** Mon. **Golf** Frilford Heath 18h.
See County Hall, 1677; containing Museum, 15th-18th cent Guildhall (portraits and plate), 14th cent Abbey ruins, Almshouses, 13th-15th cent St Helen's Church, St Nicholas' Church.
Old Gaol, Bridge St. (0235) 22711

★★★ Abingdon Lodge, Marcham Rd, OX14 1TZ (0235) 553456 Tx: 837750 Fax: (0235) 554117

A modern purpose-built hotel close to A34 with an attractive and unusual hexagonal building. Fr, De.
63 bedrs, 63 en suite; TV; tcf
dogs; P 85, coach; child facs; con 100
LD 10
£ B&B £55–£90 (w/e £30), B&B (double) £60–£95; L £9·50, D £9·50; WB £37·50. [10% V]
cc Access, Amex, B'card/Visa, Diners.

★★★ Upper Reaches, Thames St, OX14 3JA (0235) 522311 Fax: (0235) 555182

Attractive ancient converted Abbey cornmill close to River Thames. Fishing. Fr, De (THF)
20 bedrs, 20 en suite; annexe 6 bedrs, 6 en suite; TV; tcf
dogs, ns; P 60, coach; child facs; con 60
LD 9.30
£ B&B £83; B&B (double) £99–£109; L £10·75, D £15; WB £50
cc Access, Amex, B'card/Visa, CB, Diners.

★★ Crown and Thistle, Bridge St, OX14 3HS (0235) 522556

17th century coaching inn with attractive cobbled courtyard. Near Thames. Fr, De (BCB)
21 bedrs, 21 en suite; TV; tcf
ns; P 36, coach; child facs; con 50
LD 10.30
£ B&B £43–£54, B&B (double) £70–£75; L £8·15, D £8·15; WB £27·50
cc Access, Amex, B'card/Visa, Diners.

ADLINGTON Lancashire. Map 32C3
Pop 5,827. Wigan 6½, London 201, Bolton 8½, Preston 12.
EC Wed. **Golf** Duxbury Park 18h.
See Church.

★★ Gladmar, Railway Rd, Chorley PR6 9RH (0257) 480398 Fax: (0257) 482681

Pleasantly modernised and converted house with recent extension. Closed 25 & 26 Dec.
🛏 20 bedrs, 20 en suite; TV; tcf
🏠 P 35, coach; child facs; con 45.
✕ LD 8·30. Resid & Rest lic.
£ B&B £35–£46 (w/e £28); B&B (double) £56 (w/e £46); L fr £3·50; D £8·70

ALBRIGHTON Shropshire. Map 29B1
Pop 1030. Shrewsbury 3½, London 157, Newport 21, Oswestry 14, Whitchurch 22.

★★★★ **Albrighton Hall,** SY3 3AG
📞Bomere Heath (0939) 291000 Tx: 35726
Fax: (0939) 291123

Red-brick 17th century mansion set in 14 acres of grounds with a small lake. Indoor swimming pool, sauna, solarium, gymnasium, squash, billiards. ✈ Es, Po
🛏 28 bedrs, 28 en suite, annexe 10 bedrs, 10 en suite; TV; tcf
🏠 dogs; P 120, coach; child facs; con 260
✕ LD 10
cc Access, Amex, B'card/Visa, Diners.

ALCESTER Warwickshire. Map 20C3
Pop 5,287. Stratford-upon-Avon 7½, London 100, Birmingham 19, Bromsgrove 13, Evesham 9½, Worcester 17.
EC Thur. **See** No. 1 Malt Mill La (Shakespeare assns), Ragley Hall 1½ m SW.

★★ C R **Arrow Mill,** Arrow, B49 5NL
📞(0789) 762419 Tx: 312522
Fax: (0789) 765170

Attractively converted old mill house on River Arrow in 55 acres of grounds. Fishing.
✈ Fr. Closed 24 Dec–5 Jan
🛏 18 bedrs, 18 en suite; TV; tcf
🏠 dogs, P 200, U 2, coach; child facs; con 60
✕ LD 9.30
£ room £46–£56, double room £56–£84; HB weekly £252–£336; Bk £5·75, L £8·25, D £14·50; [10% V]
cc Access, Amex, B'card/Visa, Diners.

Changes made after July 1990 are not included.

★★ **Cherrytrees,** Stratford Rd, B49 6LN
📞(0789) 762505

Country motel with cedarwood chalet bedrooms. Convenient for Stratford.

ALDEBURGH Suffolk. Map 27C3
Pop 2,911. Ipswich 24, London 98, Lowestoft 27, Norwich 41, Saxmundham 7.
EC Wed. **Golf** Aldeburgh 18h. **See** Memorial to George Crabbe, poet, in Perp Church, 16th cent Moot Hall, Festival of Music and the Arts at Snape Maltings.
ℹ The Cinema, High St. 📞(0728) 453637

★★★ **Brudenell,** The Parade, IP15 5BU
📞(0728) 452071

Pleasant holiday hotel on seafront. Sea views from restaurant. ✈ Fr (THF)
🛏 47 bedrs, 47 en suite; TV; tcf
🏠 lift, dogs, ns; P 12, G 12, coach; child facs; con 50
✕ LD 9
£ B&B £45–£55, B&B (double) £55–£65; L £8·50, D £12·50; WB £46.
cc Access, Amex, B'card/Visa, CB, Diners.

Cotmandene (Acclaimed), 6 Park La, IP15 5HL 📞(0728) 453775. *Guest House.*

ALDERLEY EDGE Cheshire. Map 33B1
Pop 4,600. Congleton 11, London 172, Altrincham 9, Knutsford 6½, Macclesfield 6, Manchester 14, Middlewich 14.
EC Wed. **Golf** Alderley Edge 9h.
See The Edge (views), Chorley Hall, Alderley Old Mill 1½ m S (Nat Trust).

Hotel locations
Hotel locations are shown on the maps at the back of the guide. All towns and villages containing an RAC Appointed or Listed hotel are ringed in purple.

★★★ **De Trafford Arms,** Congleton Rd, SK9 7AA 📞(0625) 583881 Tx: 666741

A charming black and white country hotel in village setting. (DeV)
🛏 37 bedrs, 37 en suite; TV; tcf
🏠 lift, dogs; P 50, coach; child facs; con 40

ALDERMINSTER Warwickshire. Map 20C3
Shipston-on-Stour 4½, London 91, Banbury 19, Oxford 32, Stratford-upon-Avon 5½, Warwick 12.

♣♣ ★★★★ C **Ettington Park,** CV37 8BS
📞(0789) 740740 Fax: (0789) 87472

Beautifully restored listed building of chateau-appearance set in parkland. Indoor swimming pool, tennis, fishing, riding, sauna, solarium. ✈ Fr, Ge
🛏 48 bedrs, 48 en suite; TV
🏠 lift, dogs, ns; P 120, coach; children over 7; con 80
✕ LD 10
£ B&B £95–£185, B&B (double) £125–£185; L £17·50, D £30; WB £175 (HB 2 nts) [10% V]
cc Access, Amex, B'card/Visa, Diners
(*See advertisement on p. 000*)

ALDRIDGE West Midlands. Map 22C3
Pop 26,470. London 119, Birmingham 10, Lichfield 7, Sutton Coldfield 5½, Walsall 3½.
EC Thur. **Golf** Calderfields 18h.
See Barr Beacon, 14th cent Church, Manor Hse, Longwood Country Park.

Using RAC discount vouchers
Please tell the hotel when booking if you plan to use an RAC discount voucher (see p. 34) in part payment of your bill. Only one voucher will be accepted per party per stay. Discount vouchers will only be accepted in payment for accommodation, not for food.

★★★ **R** **Fairlawns,** Little Aston Rd, B91 1AT ☎(0922) 55122 Tx: 339873 Fax: (0922) 743210

An extended Victorian building set in own grounds. Good country views.
🛏 36 bedrs, 36 en suite; TV; tcf
🏨 dogs; P 85, coach; child facs; con 70
✕ LD 10, bar meals only Sat lunch
£ B&B £55–£65 (w/e £35); B&B (double) £69·50–£79·95 (w/e £42·50); D £16·50; WB £65 (Fri/Sat); [10% V]
cc Access, B'card/Visa, Diners.

ALFRISTON East Sussex. Map 6C1

Pop 712. Uckfield 16, London 60, Eastbourne 9½, Hastings 22, Hurst Green 24, Lewes 10, Newhaven 7½.
EC Wed. **Golf** Seaford Head 18h. **See** 14th cent Clergy House (Nat Trust), 14th cent Star Inn, Market Cross House, Church, George Inn, Charleston Manor 1½ m S, Drusillas (at Berwick—zoo, gardens, rly), High and Over (viewpoint S of the village), Litlington Church.

★★★ **Star Inn,** High St, BN26 5TA ☎(0323) 870495 Fax: (0323) 870922

Listed 14th century inn (with extension) in picturesque village. ⚒ Fr, De, Es (THF)
🛏 34 bedrs, 34 en suite; TV; tcf
🏨 dogs, ns; P 40; child facs; con 40
✕ LD 9.30
£ room £65–£75, double room £87–£97; HB weekly £245; Bk £7, L £11·50, D £13; WB £47
cc Access, Amex, B'card/Visa, CB, Diners.

♣♣ ★★★ **White Lodge Country House,** Sloe La, BN26 5UR ☎(0323) 870284 ♿
In 5 acres of gardens and paddocks, an elegant long white neo-Georgian building. Tennis, billiards.

Weekend breaks
Please consult the hotel for full details of weekend breaks; prices shown are an indication only. Many hotels offer mid week breaks as well.

★★ **George Inn,** High St, BN26 5SY ☎(0323) 870319 Tx: 957141

Picturesque half-timbered inn first licensed in 1397; in centre of village.
🛏 8 bedrs, 6 en suite, 1 ba; TV
🏨 dogs; coach; no children under 8
✕ LD 9.30 bar snacks only Mon–Sat lunch
£ B&B £42–£50, B&B (double) £62–£75; L £11, D £14; WB £78 (2 nts)
cc Access, Amex, B'card/Visa, Diners.

Riverdale, Seaford Rd, Alfriston, Polegate BN26 5TR ☎(0323) 870397. *Hotel.*

ALKMONTON Derbyshire. Map 30C2

Burton upon Trent 12, London 134, Ashbourne 6, Derby 11, Uttoxeter 10.

Dairy House Farm (Acclaimed), nr Longford DE6 3DG ☎(0335) 330359.
£ B&B £14–£17; HB weekly £148–£160.

ALLENDALE Northumberland. Map 44B2

Wearhead 10, London 286, Alston 14, Brampton 28, Hexham 10.

♣♣ ★★ **Bishopfield,** Hexham, NE47 9EJ ☎(0434) 683248 Fax: (0434) 683830

Charming old farmhouse converted into a friendly, family-run hotel. Fishing.
🛏 12 bedrs, 12 en suite; TV; tcf
🏨 dogs, ns; P 20; child facs; con 20
✕ LD 8.15. Resid & Rest lic
£ B&B £32, B&B (double) £54
cc Access; B'card/Visa; dep.
(See advertisement under Hexham)

ALNE North Yorkshire. Map 38C4

York 14, London 212, Boroughbridge 7, Easingwold 3, Thirsk 12.

★★★★ **Aldwark Manor** YO6 2NF ☎(034 73) 8146 Fax: (034 73) 8867
A splendid 19th century house with spacious rooms, elegantly furnished, set in 180 acres of wooded grounds. Golf, putting, fishing. ⚒ Fr, De
🛏 16 bedrs, 16 en suite; TV; tcf
🏨 dogs; P 75, coach; child facs; con 120
✕ LD 9
£ B&B £72–88, B&B (double) £99·50–£132; L £12·50, D £17·50; WB £62 (HB 2 nts min); [5% V]
cc Access, Amex, B'card/Visa, Diners.

ALNMOUTH Northumberland. Map 45A4

Pop 300. Alnwick 4½, London 309, Corbridge 45, Newcastle upon Tyne 35.
EC Wed. **Golf** Alnmouth 18h, Alnmouth Village 9h. **See** Alnmouth Bay.

Marine House (Highly Acclaimed), 1 Marine Rd, NE66 2RW ☎Alnwick (0665) 830349. *Private hotel.*
£ B&B & dinner £29–£33; HB weekly £200–£228

ALNWICK Northumberland. Map 45A4

Pop 7,000. Newcastle upon Tyne 34, London 307, Berwick-upon-Tweed 30, Coldstream 32, Hexham 44.
EC Wed. **MD** Sat. **Golf** Alnwick 9h.
See Castle, 15th cent Bondgate Tower.
ℹ The Shambles, Northumberland Hall.
☎(0665) 510665

★★★ **White Swan,** Bondgate Within, NE66 1TD ☎(0665) 602109 Fax: (0665) 510400

Former coaching inn located in centre of Alnwick near castle. ⚒ Fr, (Sw)
🛏 43 bedrs, 43 en suite; TV; tcf
🏨 dogs, ns; P 30, coach; child facs; con 150
✕ LD 9.30
£ L £7·50, D £13·95 [10% V]
cc Access, Amex, B'card/Visa.

★★ **Hotspur,** Bondgate Without, NE66 1PR ☎(0665) 510101 Fax: (0665) 605033

Sandstone former coaching inn with modern extensions standing by main road.
🛏 28 bedrs, 18 en suite, 3 ba; TV; tcf
🏨 TV, dogs; P 25, coach; child facs; con 50

Aln House (Acclaimed), South Rd, NE66 2NZ ☎(0665) 602265. *Guest house.*
£ B&B £11, B&B (double) £22–£26.
Bondgate House (Acclaimed), 20 Bondgate Without, NE66 1PN ☎(0665) 602025. Fax: (0665) 602554. *Private hotel.*
£ B&B (double) £26–£30; HB weekly £130–£144.

Alresford (Hampshire)

Alton (Hampshire)

Altrincham (Cheshire)

Aydon House, South Rd, NE66 2NT ☎(0665) 602218. *Hotel.*

ALSTON Cumbria. Map 44B2

Pop 1,931. Middleton-in-Teesdale 22, London 280, Brampton 19, Hexham 21, Penrith 19.
EC Tue. **MD** Sat.
ℹ Railway Station. ☎(0434) 381696

★★ H C R Lovelady Shield, CA9 3LF ☎(0434) 381203 Fax: (0434) 381515

Charming Regency country house in 2½ acres of sheltered secluded gardens. 2 miles east of Alston on A689. Tennis. Closed 2 Jan–23 Feb.
11 bedrs, 11 en suite; TV
dogs, ns; P 25; child facs; con 10
LD 8.30; bar meals only lunch. Resid & Rest lic
£ B&B £32, B&B (double) £58–£82; HB weekly £306–£307; L £10·50, D £15; WB [10% V]
cc Access, Amex, Diners; dep.

★★ Lowbyer Manor, Hexham Rd, CA9 3JX ☎(0434) 381230
Attractive 300 year old manor house in quiet area of outstanding natural beauty.
7 bedrs, 7 en suite; annexe 4 bedrs, 4 en suite; TV; tcf
dogs; P 14, coach; child facs; con 20
LD 8.30, bar meals only lunch. Resid & Rest lic
£ B&B £29, B&B (double) £50·50; HB weekly £245–£275; D £13·15 WB £75; [10% V]
cc Access, Amex, B'card/Visa, Diners; dep.

★★ Nent Hall, CA9 3LQ ☎(0434) 381584
Recently refurbished 18th century house with Victorian additions including an ornate tower. Set in spectacular fellside scenery on A689 2½ miles east of Alston. Swimming pool.
8 bedrs, 8 en suite; TV; tcf
TV, dogs; P 48, coach; child facs; con 50
LD 8.30, bar meals only lunch
£ B&B £25–£30, B&B (double) £40–£60; D £11·50; WB £55; [10% V]
cc Access, B'card/Visa.

ALTON Hampshire. Map 6A2

Pop 15,000. Farnham 9½, London 48, Basingstoke 12, Fareham 24, Haslemere 16, Petersfield 12, Winchester 17.
EC Wed. **MD** Tue. **Golf** Alton 9h.
See Jane Austen's Home at Chawton ½ m S.

> **Licences**
> Establishments have a full licence unless shown as unlicensed or with the limitations listed on p 6.

★★★ Alton House, Normandy St, GU34 1DW ☎(0420) 80033 Fax: (0420) 89222

Regency hotel in 2½ acres of gardens, close to town centre. Swimming pool, tennis, billiards.
38 bedrs, 38 en suite; TV; tcf
dogs; P 90, G 4, coach; child facs; con 180
LD 9.30
£ B&B £35–£50, B&B (double) £48–£56; L £9·25; D £10·25; WB £34·25–£45·25
cc Access, Amex, B'card/Visa.

★★★ Swan, High St, GU34 1AT ☎(0420) 83777 Tx: 859916 Fax: (0420) 87975

Attractive coaching inn dating from 16th century; in High Street. (THF)
38 bedrs, 38 en suite; TV; tcf
dogs, ns; P 50, coach; child facs; con 60
LD 9.30, bar meals only Sat lunch
£ room £65, double room £81–£87; Bk £7·55, L £11, D £14·50; WB £44
cc Access, Amex, B'card/Visa, CB, Diners.

★★ C R Grange, 17 London Rd, GU34 4EG ☎(0420) 86565 Fax: (0420) 541346
Two-storey country house style building with new wing of executive bedrooms. 9-hole golf; putting. Closed Xmas week.
28 bedrs, 28 en suite; annexe 6 bedrs, 6 en suite; TV; tcf
TV, dogs, ns; P 48, coach; con 45
LD 9; bar meals only Sat lunch
£ B&B £45, B&B (double) £49·50–£69·50; L £8·95, D £9·95
cc Access, Amex, B'card/Visa, Diners; dep.

ALTRINCHAM Gtr Manchester (Cheshire), Map 33B1

Pop 39,641. Knutsford 7½, London 180, M56 (jn 7) 2½, Macclesfield 15, Manchester 8, Northwich 13, Stockport 8½, Warrington 11.
EC Wed. **MD** Tue, Fri, Sat. **Golf** Municipal 18h. **See** Dunham Park, St George's Church.
ℹ Stamford New Road ☎061-926 8336

★★★ Ashley, Ashley Rd, Hale WA15 9SF ☎061-928 3794 Tx: 669406 Fax: 061-926 9046
Modern hotel situated in Cheshire village of Hale, 9 miles S of Manchester city centre. (DeV)
48 bedrs, 48 en suite; TV; tcf
lift, dogs, coach; child facs; con 240
LD 9.45, bar meals only Sat lunch
£ B&B £60 (w/e £22), B&B (double) £72; L £9, D £11·95; WB £49 (min 2 nts) [V]
cc Access, Amex, B'card/Visa, Diners.

★★★ Bowdon, Langham Rd, Bowdon, WA14 2HT ☎061-928 7121 Tx: 668208 Fax: 061-927 7560

Large Victorian building with modern extensions; in residential area convenient for motorway network.
82 bedrs, 82 en suite; TV; tcf
dogs; P 168, coach; child facs; con 150
LD 10
£ B&B £59 (w/e £32), B&B (double) £72 (w/e £44); HB weekly £365; L £11·50, D £11·50; WB £32 (HB)
cc Access, Amex, B'card/Visa, Diners.
(*See advertisement on p. 104*)

★★★ Cresta Court, Church St, WA14 4DP ☎061-927 7272 Tx: 667242 Fax: 061-926 9194
Large modern purpose-built hotel within easy reach of Manchester. Fr
139 bedrs, 139 en suite; TV; tcf
lift, dogs; P, coach; child facs; con 400
LD 11
£ B&B £55 (w/e £30), B&B (double) £66 (w/e £51·50)

★★★ C R Woodland Park, Wellington Rd, Timperley WA14 7RG ☎061-928 8631 Tx: 635091 Fax: 061-941 2821
In a residential area, a pleasant white faced building conveniently situated for Manchester Airport. Fr, De, Es
45 bedrs, 45 en suite; TV; tcf
P 150, U1, coach; child facs; con 200
LD 10; nr Sun
£ B&B £39, B&B (double) £54; L £8·95, D £11·95; WB; [10% V]
cc Access, Amex, B'card/Visa, Diners.

★★ George & Dragon, Manchester Rd, WA14 4PH ☎061-928 9933 Tx: 665051

Attractive hotel only minutes from motorway, airport and city centre. (DeV)
47 bedrs, 47 en suite; TV; tcf
lift, dogs; P 60, coach; child facs; con 20

> Changes made after July 1990 are not included.

★★ **Pelican,** Manchester Rd, WA14 5NH
☎061-962 7414 Tx: 668014

Black and white inn with quiet courtyard motel bedrooms. (DeV)
🛏 50 bedrs, 50 en suite; TV; tcf
🏨 dogs; P 150, coach; child facs; con 50

Beach Mount, Barrington Rd, WA14 1HN
☎051-928 4523. Closed 24 Dec–2 Jan
£ B&B fr £27·60.

ALVELEY Shropshire. Map 20B4

Pop 2,005. Kidderminster 7, London 130, Bridgnorth 7
EC Thur. **Golf** Bridgnorth 18h. **See** Coton Hall (1m E).

★★★★ **Mill,** WV15 6HL ☎Quatt (0746) 780437 Fax: (0746) 780850
An attractive old water mill, imaginatively developed with modern extensions, in gardens landscaped round the mill pond.
🛏 21 bedrs, 21 en suite; TV; tcf
🏨 lift; P 220, coach; child facs; con 200
✕ LD 10.15
£ room £49·50–£60, double room £60–£70 (w/e £50); Bk £3·50–£5·50, L £7; [10% V]
cc Access, Amex, B'card/Visa, Diners.

ALVESTON Avon. Map 20A1

Pop 2,500. M4 & M5 4, London 115, Bristol 10, Chepstow 9½, Gloucester 24.
EC Wed **Golf** Filton, Bristol 18h. **See** British Encampment, Tumuli, Church.

★★★ **H C R Alveston House,** BS12 2LJ ☎Thornbury (0454) 415050 Tx: 449212
Fax: (0454) 415425 ♿

Elegant Georgian residence with modern bedroom complex pleasantly situated with walled gardens.
🛏 30 bedrs, 30 en suite; TV; tcf
🏨 TV, dogs; P 75, coach; child facs; con 85
✕ LD 10
£ B&B £67·50–£72·50, B&B (double) £77·50–£85·50; L £12·75, D £14·25; WB £40·50; [V]
cc Access, Amex, B'card/Visa, Diners.

★★★ **Post House,** Thornbury Rd, BS12 2LL ☎Thornbury (0454) 412521 Tx: 444753
Fax: (0454) 413920
Wings of modern purpose-built rooms adjoin Tudor former coaching inn. Swimming pool, putting. ⚒ Fr, De, It (THF)
🛏 75 bedrs, 75 en suite; TV; tcf
🏨 dogs, ns; P 150, coach; child facs; con 100
✕ LD 10
£ B&B £69·50 (w/e £39·50 room only), B&B (double) £87; HB weekly £266; WB £38 (HB)
cc Access, Amex, B'card/Visa, CB, Diners.

AMBERLEY Gloucester. Map 20B1

Pop 680. Stroud 2½, London 100, Bath 25, Bristol 27, Cheltenham 17, Chepstow 28, Cirencester 12, Gloucester 12, Stow-on-the-Wold 30, Tetbury 7½.
Golf Minchinhampton 18h. **See** Old Houses, Church.

★★ **H C Amberley Inn,** GL5 5AF
☎(0453) 872565 Fax: (0453) 872738

Family-run, attractive hotel of Cotswold stone with excellent views.
🛏 10 bedrs, 10 en suite; annexe 4 bedrs, 4 en suite; TV; tcf
🏨 dogs; P 20; child facs; con 16
✕ LD 9.30
£ B&B £52–£60, B&B (double) £64–£72; HB weekly £315–£497; L £7·50, D £13·50; WB £36
cc Access, Amex, B'card/Visa.

AMBLESIDE Cumbria. Map 43C1

See also RYDAL, GREAT LANGDALE, LITTLE LANGDALE, ELTERWATER, SKELWITH BRIDGE, NEAR SAWREY, HAWKSHEAD, FAR SAWREY and GRIZEDALE
Pop 2,562. M6 (jn 36) 25, London 269, Broughton-in-Furness 16, Kendal 13, Keswick 16, Penrith 22, Windermere 5.
EC Thur. **MD** Wed. **Golf** Windermere 18h. **See** House on the Bridge, Stock Ghyll Force, Lake Windermere, Jenkin Crag (viewpoint), Borrans Field (remains of Roman Camp), Rush Bearing ceremony July, White Craggs Rock Garden 1 m W.
ⓘ Old Courthouse, Church St. ☎(053 94) 32582

★★★ **Regent,** Waterhead Bay, LA22 0ES
☎(053 94) 32254

Family-owned hotel in an attractive building only 20 yards from lake. Indoor swimming pool.
🛏 11 bedrs, 11 en suite; annexe 10 bedrs, 10 en suite; TV; tcf
🏨 dogs, ns; P 30; child facs
✕ LD 9
£ B&B £38–£43, B&B (double) £64–£84; HB weekly £239–£291·50; L £8, D £16·50; WB £79 (HB 2 nts)
cc Access, B'card/Visa; dep.

★★★ **H C Rothay Manor,** Rothay Bridge, LA22 0EH ☎(053 94) 33605
Fax: (053 94) 33607 ♿

Elegant Regency manor house in pleasant garden on edge of town. Closed 2 Jan–early Feb.
🛏 15 bedrs, 15 en suite; annexe 3 bedrs, 3 en suite; TV; tcf
🏨 ns; P 30; child facs
✕ LD 9. Resid & Rest lic
£ B&B £58–£63, B&B (double) £82–£94; L £6, D fr £17; WB £122 (2 nts Nov–Mar)
cc Access, Amex, B'card/Visa, Diners; dep.

★★★ **Salutation,** Lake Rd, LA22 9BX
☎(053 94) 32244 Fax: (053 94) 34157
Three-storey, stone-built hotel, painted white, conveniently situated in town centre.
🛏 32 bedrs, 32 en suite; TV; tcf
🏨 dogs; P 40, coach; child facs; con 50
✕ LD 9, bar meals only lunch
£ B&B £22–£31 (w/e £25), B&B (double) £44–£62; D £14; WB £37 (HB); [V w/d]
cc Access, B'card/Visa.

★★★ **H Wateredge,** Waterhead LA22 0EP
☎(053 94) 32332 Fax: (053 94) 32332

Two extended 17th century cottages of character right beside lake. Fishing. Closed mid Dec–early Feb.
🛏 18 bedrs, 18 en suite; annexe 5 bedrs, 5 en suite; TV; tcf
🏨 TV, dogs; P 25; no children under 7
✕ LD 8.30, bar meals only lunch. Resid & Rest lic
£ B&B & dinner (single) £48·50–£59·50 (w/e £47), B&B & dinner (double) £84–£140; HB weekly £294–£460; D £18·90; WB
cc Access, Amex, B'card/Visa; dep.
(*See advertisement on p. 107*)

★★★ **Waterhead,** Waterhead, LA22 0ER
☎(053 94) 32566 Tx: 65372
Two-storey stone-built hotel right on edge of Lake Windermere.
🛏 27 bedrs, 27 en suite; TV; tcf
🏨 dogs, ns; P 50, coach; child facs; con 40

EC *early closing* **MD** *market day* 👥 *country house hotel* *ns (NS) no smoking areas* *tcf tea/coffee facilities*

Ambleside (Cumbria)

Wateredge Hotel

Waterhead Bay, Ambleside, English Lake District

Delightfully situated on the shores of Windermere, these seventeeth century former fishermen's cottages have been skilfully converted.

Comfortable lounges overlook the garden and lake.

All of the bedrooms have private facilities. Exquisitely cooked food from an imaginative menu, served in an oak beamed dining room. Fishing: guests have the use of our rowing boat and private jetty.

Please telephone or write for our brochure
Ambleside (05394) 32332

EGON RONAY, SIGNPOST & ASHLEY COURTENAY RECOMMENDED.

Ambleside (Cumbria)

RAC ★★

Riverside Hotel

Nr. Rothay Bridge Under Loughrigg Ambleside Cumbria LA22 9LJ Tel: (05394) 32395

The Riverside enjoys its own river frontages with woodland walks leading on to Loughrigg Fell.

Exceptional standards of accommodation, each of our ten thoughtfully furnished bedrooms have en-suite facilities, hair-dryers, telephones, colour TV, and tea/coffee making facilities.

We have three Lounges (one of which overlooks the river), an elegant dining room to enjoy food in a candle-lit atmosphere.

English Lake District Hotels & Caterers Association Member

LES ROUTIERS **ASHLEY COURTENAY** **MICHELIN**

Ambleside (Cumbria)

Recommended by EGON RONAY, SIGNPOST and ASHLEY COURTENAY

Kirkstone Foot

Country House Hotel

Kirkstone Pass Road,
Ambleside, Cumbria LA22 9EH
Tel: Ambleside (05394) 32232

Imagine an attractive country house hotel set in the heart of the English Lake District with a friendly welcome, courteous and attentive service, the best of traditional English home cooking and all the comforts and convenience that you could hope for. Kirkstone Foot with its 15 bedrooms, studio apartments and cottages has just such a reputation. To find out why, Jane & Simon Bateman and family invite you to call for full details and a colour brochure on Ambleside (05394) 32232.

Ambleside (Cumbria)

Breakaway

Situated on a wooded private estate beside the sparkling waters of Great Langdale Beck, the Langdale Hotel and Country Club offers seclusion, luxurious accommodation and choice of activities in the Lake District National Park. Charming rooms – private bathrooms, direct dial phones, satellite TV – some with balcony, four poster bed, whirlpool bath. Free guest membership of the Country Club with indoor heated pool, sauna, solarium, hydro-spa, gymnasium and squash. A choice of restaurants, excellent food, and friendly, attentive staff. Telephone **Langdale 09667 302** for details of our special seasonal and activity breaks.

LANGDALE

The Langdale Hotel and Country Club, Great Langdale, near Ambleside, Cumbria, LA22 9JD

✕ LD 8.30, bar meals only Mon–Sat lunch
£ B&B £32–£73, B&B (double) £64–£102; D £15·50; WB £86 (HB)
cc Access, Amex, Diners; dep.

★★ **C** **R** **Borrans Park,** Borrans Rd, LA22 0EN ☎(053 94) 33454 ♿
Georgian house with modern extensions surrounded by trees and shrubs yet close to town. Fr
14 bedrs, 13 en suite, 1 ba; TV; tcf
ns, P 18; no children under 7
✕ LD 7.30, nr lunch. Resid & Rest lic
£ B&B £26–£64; B&B (double) £52–£64; HB weekly £260–£302; WB £70 (HB low season)
cc Access, B'card/Visa; dep.

★★ **H** **C** **Fisherbeck,** Lake Rd, LA22 0DH ☎(053 94) 33215

Three-storey stone-built hotel in southern outskirts of this attractive Lakeland town.
20 bedrs, 18 en suite, 2 ba; TV; tcf
TV; P 21; child facs; con 15
✕ LD 8
£ B&B £26·50–£29; B&B (double) £45–£59; HB weekly £190–£265; L £7·50, D £15
cc Access, B'card/Visa; dep.

★★ **H** **C** **Kirkstone Foot,** Kirkstone Pass Rd, LA22 9EH ☎(053 94) 32232

Charming 17th century house in 2 acres of landscaped gardens. Closed Jan.
15 bedrs, 15 en suite; TV; tcf
P 35; child facs
✕ LD 8.30, nr lunch. Resid lic
£ B&B & dinner £35–£48; HB weekly £253–£312; D £16; WB; [5% V]
cc Access, B'card/Visa, dep.
(*See advertisement on p. 107*)

Discount vouchers

RAC discount vouchers are on p. 34. Hotels with a [V] shown at the end of the price information will accept them in part payment for accommodation bills on the full, standard rate, not against bargain breaks or any other special offers. Please note the limitations shown in the entry: w/e for weekends, w/d for weekdays, and which months they are accepted.

★★ **C** **Riverside Hotel,** Nr Rothay Bridge, Under Loughrigg, LA22 9LJ ☎(053 94) 32395

Modernised 19th century house in extensive grounds beside river. Fishing. Closed Jan.
10 bedrs, 10 en suite; TV; tcf
TV; P 20; child facs; con 20
(*See advertisement on p. 107*)

★★ **White Lion,** Market Pl, LA22 9DB ☎(053 94) 33140
Three-storey white-painted stone building on main street through town.

Gables (Highly Acclaimed), Church Walk, LA22 9DJ ☎(053 94) 33272. *Hotel.*
£ B&B £17–£20; HB weekly £189.

Grey Friar Lodge Country House (Highly Acclaimed), Brathay LA22 9NE ☎(053 94) 33158. *Hotel.*
£ B&B & dinner £29–£37; HB weekly £195–£238.

Anchorage (Acclaimed), Rydal Rd, LA22 9AY ☎(053 94) 32046. *Guest House.* Open Mar–Nov.
£ B&B (double) £30–£40.

Lyndhurst (Acclaimed), Wansfell Rd, LA22 0EG ☎(053 94) 32421. *Hotel.*
£ B&B £17·50–£22; HB weekly £175–£205 [10% V Nov–May w/d]

Rysdale Hotel (Acclaimed), Rothay Rd, LA22 0EE ☎(053 94) 32140. *Hotel.* Fr
£ B&B £14–£20; HB weekly £160–£195; [10% V]

Smallwood House (Acclaimed), Compton Rd, LA22 9DJ ☎(053 94) 32330. *Hotel.*
£ B&B £14–£17·50; HB weekly £142–£165; [V Oct–Jun]

Hillsdale, Church St, LA22 0BT ☎(053 94) 33174. *Private hotel.*

AMERSHAM
Buckinghamshire. Map 13A4

Pop 17,512. Denham 9½, London 26, Aylesbury 15, Dunstable 19, High Wycombe 7½, Rickmansworth 8, Slough 12.
EC Thur. **MD** Tue. **Golf** Chesham 9h.
See Parish Church (brasses), 17th cent Almhouses, Market Hall (1682), 17th cent Bury Farm (Penn assns), Protestant Martyr's Memorial, Milton's Cottage 3 m S.

★★ **Crown,** High St, HP7 0DH ☎(0494) 721541 Fax: (0494) 431283
Half-timbered 16th-century inn with attractive courtyard. In centre of town. (THF)
25 bedrs, 14 en suite, (1 sh), 3 ba; TV; tcf
dogs, ns; P 30, child facs; con 25
✕ LD 9.30
£ room £75·60, double room £91·80; Bk fr £4·75; L £8·50–£10·50; D £14; WB £42
cc Access, Amex, B'card/Visa, Diners.

AMESBURY
Wiltshire. Map 5B3

Pop 5,500. Andover 14, London 79, Devizes 18, Pewsey 13, Salisbury 8, Shaftesbury 26, Wantage 37, Warminster 19, Wincanton 30.
EC Mon. **MD** Wed. **Golf** High Post, Salisbury 18h, Salisbury and S Wilts 18h.
See Fine Parish Church (formerly Abbey Church), Stonehenge 2½ m W.
ℹ Flower La. ☎(0980) 623255

★★ **Antrobus Arms,** Church St, SP4 7EY ☎(0980) 623163

Two-storey stone building of character close to town centre. Attractive gardens.
20 bedrs, 14 en suite, 2 ba; TV; tcf
dogs; P 60, coach; child facs; con 30
✕ LD 10
£ B&B £26–£34; B&B (double) £48·50–£55; L £9·45, D £12·50; [5% V Oct–Mar]
cc Access, Amex, B'card/Visa, Diners.

Druids Motel, 2 Countess Rd, SP4 7DW ☎(0980) 22800.

AMPFIELD
Hampshire. Map 5C2

Winchester 7, London 73, Romsey 3, Salisbury 19, Southampton 5.

★★★ **Potters Heron,** SO51 9ZF ☎(0703) 266611 Tx: 47459 Fax: (0703) 251 359 ♿
Thatched, 2-storey, cosy old inn with modern extensions, elegantly furnished and set in countryside. Sauna, gymnasium. (Lns)
60 bedrs, 60 en suite; TV; tcf
lift, ns; P 200, coach; con 100
✕ LD 10
£ B&B £77, B&B (double) £88; L £11, D £11; WB £35, [10% V]
cc Access, Amex, B'card/Visa, Diners.

ANDOVER
Hampshire. Map 5B3

Pop 29,840. Basingstoke 19, London 65, Amesbury 14, Devizes 27, Newbury 16, Romsey 17, Salisbury 18, Winchester 14.
EC Wed. **MD** Thur, Sat. **Golf** Andover 9h.
See Guildhall, 19th cent Church.
ℹ Town Mill Car Park, Bridge St. ☎(0264) 24320.

★★★ **Ashley Court,** Micheldever Rd, SP11 6LA ☎(0264) 57344 Fax: (0264) 56755 ♿

Two-storey, white-painted hotel in 3½ acres of well-tended garden. Conference centre. Snooker. Fr, De, Du
35 bedrs, 35 en suite; TV; tcf
TV, dogs, ns; P 100, coach; child facs, con 200
✕ LD 9.30, bar meals only Sat lunch

EC *early closing* **MD** *market day* *country house hotel* *ns (NS) no smoking areas* *tcf tea/coffee facilities*

£ B&B £62–£65 (w/e £22), B&B (double) £79–£82; L £9·50, D £12·50; WB; [10% V w/e]
cc Access, Amex, B'card/Visa.

★★ **White Hart,** 12 Bridge St, SP10 1BH ☎(0264) 52266

Former coaching inn with typical internal features. Close to town centre. (THF)
🛏 20 bedrs, 20 en suite; TV; tcf
🏨 dogs, ns; P 30, coach; child facs; con 60
✕ LD 9.30
£ B&B £42–£52 (w/e £31), B&B (double) £64–£74; D £12·95; WB
cc Access, Amex, B'card/Visa, CB, Diners.

ANDOVERSFORD
Gloucestershire, Map 20C2
Burford 16, London 91, Cheltenham 6, Cirencester 12, Gloucester 14, Stow-on-the-Wold 12

Old Comfort (Acclaimed), Dowdeswell, GL54 4LR ☎(0242) 820349. *Private Hotel.*
Fr, It, Es
£ B&B £35

APPLEBY-IN-WESTMORELAND
Cumbria. Map 44B1
Pop 2,339. Brough 8, London 272, Alston 26, Hawes 26, Kendal 24, Kirkby Lonsdale 30, Penrith 13.
EC Thur. **MD** Sat. **Golf** Appleby 18h. **See** Castle (not open), St Lawrence's Church, St. Michael's Church, Grammar School, High Cross, 16th cent Moot Hall, Bull Ring.
ℹ Moot Hall, Boroughgate. ☎(076 83) 51177

★★★ **Appleby Manor,** Roman Rd, CA16 6JD ☎(076 83) 51571 Tx: 94012971
Fax: (076 83) 52888 ♿

Victorian country house, recently extended. Extensive grounds with panoramic views. Indoor swimming pool, sauna, solarium.
🛏 23 bedrs, 23 en suite; annexe 7 bedrs, 7 en suite; TV; tcf
🏨 dogs, ns; P 40, U 3 (£1), coach; child facs; con 28
✕ LD 9
£ B&B £42·50–£56, B&B (double) £65–£90; HB weekly £270–£387; L £12·95, D £12·95; WB £42
cc Access, Amex, B'card/Visa, Diners; dep.

★★★ **Tufton Arms,** Market Sq, CA16 6XA ☎(076 83) 51593 Fax: (076 83) 52761
Refurbished 16th century posting house occupying one side of market square. Fishing.
🛏 19 bedrs, 19 en suite; TV; tcf
🏨 dogs; P 17, G 2, coach; child facs; con 50
✕ LD 9.30
£ B&B £30–£75; B&B (double) £45–£95; HB weekly £210–£385; L £9·50; D £11·50; WB £30; [10% V]
cc Access, B'card/Visa; dep.

★★ **Royal Oak,** Bongate, CA16 6UN ☎(076 83) 51463
Two-storey coaching inn with beams. Dates back at least to 17th century.

★**Courtfield,** Bongate, CA16 6UP ☎(076 83) 51394
Charming small residence in own grounds close to town centre.

APPLETON-LE-MOORS
North Yorkshire. Map 39A4
Pop 172. Pickering 7, London 220, Thirsk 23, York 33.
Golf Kirkbymoorside 9h.

★★ **H** **Dweldapilton Hall,** YO6 6TF ☎Lastingham (075 15) 227 Fax: (075 15) 540

Stone-built Victorian house in large gardens with moors as background. Closed 7 Jan–6 Feb.
🛏 12 bedrs, 12 en suite; TV; tcf
🏨 lift, dogs; P 30, no children under 12; con 40
✕ LD 8.15, bar meals only Mon–Sat lunch. Resid & Rest lic
£ B&B £40; HB weekly £345; D £18·50; WB £52·50 (HB); [10% V]
cc Access, Amex, B'card/Visa; dep.

APSLEY GUISE
Bedfordshire. Map 14A4
Dunstable 11, London 45, M1 (jn 13) 1, Bedford 12, Milton Keynes 6.

Hotel locations
Hotel locations are shown on the maps at the back of the guide. All towns and villages containing an RAC Appointed or Listed hotel are ringed in purple.

★★★ **C** **R** **Moore Place,** The Square, Nr Woburn MK17 8DW ☎(0908) 282000 Fax: (0908) 281888

A Georgian mansion with a restaurant and bedroom extension at rear. In village centre, close to junction 13 of M1.
🛏 39 bedrs, 39 en suite; annexe 15 bedrs, 15 en suite; TV; tcf
🏨 dogs; P 60, coach; child facs; con 50
✕ LD 9.45, nr Sat lunch
£ room £75, double room £90; Bk £6·50; L £15, D £19·50; WB £42·50 (HB); [V]
cc Access, Amex, B'card/Visa, Diners.

ARMATHWAITE
Cumbria. Map 44A2
Pop 420. Penrith 11, London 287, Brampton 11, Carlisle 9½.
Golf Penrith 18h. **See** Castle.

★★ **Fox & Pheasant Inn,** CA4 9PY ☎(069 92) 400

An 18th century inn in typical Lakeland style; across the river from the village. Fishing.

ARNSIDE
Cumbria. Map 36B4
Pop 1,865. M6 7, London 249, Ambleside 22, Broughton-in-Furness 31, Kendal 13, Kirkby Lonsdale 13, Lancaster 14, Ulverston 25.
EC Thur. **Golf** Silverdale 9h, Grange-over-Sands 18h. **See** Arnside Knott (viewpoint), ruins of Arnside and Hazelslack pele towers.

Willowfield, The Promenade, LA5 0AD ☎(0524) 761354. *Private Hotel.*

ARUNDEL
West Sussex. Map 6B1
Pop 2,162. Pulborough 9, London 56, Bognor Regis 9½, Brighton 20, Chichester 11, Littlehampton 4, Worthing 10.
EC Wed. **Golf** Goodwood 18h, Littlehampton 18h. **See** Castle, Maison Dieu ruins, Swanbourne Lake, 14th cent St Nicholas Church, R.C. Cathedral of Our Lady and St Philip Howard, Wildfowl Trust.
ℹ 61 High St. ☎(0903) 882268

Licences
Establishments have a full licence unless shown as unlicensed or with the limitations listed on p 6.

★★★★ **Avisford Park**, Yapton La, Walbeton, BN18 0LS ☎(0243) 551215 Tx: 86137 Fax: (0243) 552485

Georgian house, with later extensions, set in 62 acres of grounds including a walled garden, just off A27. Indoor and outdoor swimming pools, golf, putting, tennis, squash, sauna, solarium, snooker.
100 bedrs, 100 en suite; TV; tcf
ns; P 160, coach; child facs; con 200
LD 9.15, bar meals only Sat lunch
£ B&B £70, B&B (double) £106–£120; L £16·50, D £23·75; WB £114. [5% V w/d]
cc Access, Amex, B'card/Visa

★★★ **Amberley Castle.** Amberley, BN18 9ND ☎(0798) 831992 Fax: (0798) 831998

A lovely, genuine medieval castle, exquisitely decorated and furnished. Greystone crenellated walls surround a delightful garden, the whole secluded in extensive grounds. Fr
12 bedrs, 12 en suite; TV
P; child facs; con 30
LD 10
£ B&B £100–£130, B&B (double) £150–£220; L £17·50, D £23·50; WB £350 (for 2)
cc Access, Amex, B'card/Visa, Diners.

★★★ **Norfolk Arms,** High St, BN18 9AB ☎(0903) 882101 Tx: 878436 Fax: (0903) 884275

Elegant 18th century coaching inn set under battlements of the castle.
34 bedrs, 34 en suite; TV; tcf
dogs, ns; P 35, coach; child facs; con 100
£ B&B £44·50–£48·95, B&B (double) £65–£71·50; L £9, D £15·75; [10% V w/e]
cc Access, Amex, B'card/Visa, Diners.

★★ **Arundel Resort,** 16 Chichester Rd, BN18 0AD ☎(0903) 882 677 Fax: (0903) 884 154
Modern hotel built on to a 300 year old beamed inn on the A27. Fr, De.
16 bedrs, 16 en suite; TV; tcf
dogs, ns; P 70, coach; child facs; con 20
LD 10
£ B&B £50·50 (w/e £28), B&B (double) £67; L £7, D £10; [5% V]
cc Access, Amex, B'card/Visa, Diners.

★★ **Howards,** Crossbush, BN19 9PQ ☎(0903) 882655
Two-storey hotel built in Georgian style on corner site near Arundel.
10 bedrs, 10 en suite; TV; tcf
P 150; no children; con 80

★★ **Swan Inn,** High St, BN18 9AG ☎(0903) 882314
Listed 18th century inn on main street of town. Du
13 bedrs, 13 en suite; TV; tcf
ns; coach; child facs; con 40
LD 9.30
£ B&B £45, B&B (double) £60; L £8·50, D £12·50; WB £75 (HB, 2 nts)
cc Access, Amex, B'card/Visa, Diners.

ASCOT
Berkshire. Map 13A2

Pop 7,100. Staines 8, London 25, Bagshot 4½, Reading 14, Windsor 6½.
EC Wed. **Golf** Wentworth, Sunningdale and R Berkshire 18h.
See Racecourse founded 1711 by Queen Anne, Royal Meeting in June.

★★★★ **Berystede,** Bagshot Rd, Sunninghill SL5 9JH ☎(0344) 23311 Tx: 847707 Fax: (0344) 872301

Large luxury mansion converted with modern extensions; in woodland setting. Swimming pool, putting. (THF)
91 bedrs, 91 en suite; TV; tcf
lift, dogs, ns; P 150, coach; child facs; con 125
LD 9.45
£ B&B £96, B&B (double) £118; L £15, D £18; WB £50
cc Access, Amex, B'card/Visa, CB, Diners.

Discount vouchers
RAC discount vouchers are on p. 34. Hotels with a [V] shown at the end of the price information will accept them in part payment for accommodation bills on the full, standard rate, not against bargain breaks or any other special offers. Please note the limitations shown in the entry: w/e for weekends, w/d for weekdays, and which months they are accepted.

★★★★ **Royal Berkshire,** London Rd, Sunninghill SL5 0PP ☎(0344) 23322 Tx: 847280 Fax: (0344) 27100 ♿

Queen Anne mansion with later additions, in 15 acres of lawns, gardens and woods. Indoor swimming pool, putting, tennis, squash, sauna. (H. Int)
64 bedrs, 64 en suite; annexe 18 bedrs, 18 en suite; TV; tcf
dogs; P 150, coach; child facs; con 70
LD 9.30
£ B&B £100–£150, B&B (double) £120–£170
cc Access, Amex, B'card/Visa, Diners.
(*See advertisement on p. 112*)

★★ **Royal Foresters,** London Rd, SL5 8DR ☎(0344) 884747
White-faced building, originally a coaching inn but considerably altered over the years; motel-type bedrooms to the rear.

Highclere (Acclaimed), Kings Rd, SL5 9AD ☎(0344) 25220 Fax: (0344) 872528. *Hotel.*
£ B&B £55 (w/e £35); [5% V].

ASHBOURNE
Derbyshire. Map 30C2

Pop 5,971. Derby 13, London 139, Buxton 20, Matlock 13, Stoke-on-Trent 22, Uttoxeter 12.
i 13 The Market Pl ☎(0335) 43666

★★★★ **Ashbourne Lodge,** Derby Rd, DE6 1XH ☎(0335) 46666 Tx: 378560 Fax: (0335) 46549 ♿
Attractive, newly built, 2-storey hotel on A52 to east side of town. It, Es
51 bedrs, 51 en suite, TV, tcf
lift, ns; P 200, coach; child facs; con 170
LD 10
£ B&B £65–£90 (w/e £44), B&B (double) £80–£95; HB weekly £309–£329; L £10, D £15; WB; [10% V]
cc Access, Amex, B'card/Visa, Diners.

★★★ **Callow Hall,** Mappleton Rd, DE6 2AA ☎(0335) 43403 Fax: (0335) 43624

Substantial mid Victorian country house set in gardens and woodland. Lovely views of

EC *early closing* **MD** *market day* *country house hotel* *ns (NS) no smoking areas* *tcf tea/coffee facilities*

Dove Valley. Fishing. Fr, De. Closed 2 wks Jan/Feb.
12 bedrs, 12 en suite, TV; tcf
P 60; child facs; con 50
LD 9.30; nr Mon–Sat lunch & Sun dinner. Resid & Rest lic
£ B&B £60–£75, B&B (double) £80–£110; L £12, D £21; WB £110–£135; [5% V]
cc Access, Amex, B'card/Visa, Diners; dep.

ASHBURTON

Devon. Map 3B2

Pop 3,554. M5 17, London 187, Exeter 19, Newton Abbot 7½, Okehampton 27, Plymouth 24, Tavistock 20, Totnes 8.
EC Wed. **Golf** Newton Abbot (Stover) 18h.

★★★ **Holne Chase,** TQ13 7NS
(036 43) 471 Fax: (036 43) 453

Quiet and secluded hunting lodge, in 20 acres of woodland. Putting, fishing. Fr
12 bedrs, 12 en suite, TV; tcf
dogs, ns; P 40; child facs; con 40
LD 9. Resid & Rest lic
£ B&B £55–£70 (w/e £40), B&B (double) £72–£110; L £12·50, D £19·50; WB £56
cc Access, Amex, B'card/Visa, Diners.

★★ **Dartmoor,** Pear Tree Cross, TQ13 7JW
☎(0364) 52232

Off A38, in pleasant country on edge of Dartmoor, a purpose-built family-run motel.
18 bedrs, 18 en suite; annexe 14 bedrs, 14 en suite; TV; tcf
lift, dogs, ns; P 50, U 1 (£2·50), coach; child facs; con 70
LD 9.15
£ B&B £31, B&B (double) £37·50–£54; D £8·95, WB £89·95 (HB 2 people)
cc Access, Amex, B'card/Visa, dep.

★★ **Tugela House,** 68–70 East St, TQ13 7AX ☎(0364) 52206
Fax: (0364) 52206
Small hotel in attractive Georgian terrace building on main street.
7 bedrs, 5 en suite, (2 sh); TV
dogs; P 8; con 20
LD 9, nr lunch & Sun dinner. Rest lic
£ B&B £25, B&B (double) £40; D £11; [5% V]; dep.

Gages Mill (Acclaimed), Buckfastleigh Rd, TQ13 7JW ☎(0364) 52391. *Hotel.* Open Mar–end-Oct
£ B&B (double) £31–£37; HB weekly £152·50–£175.

ASHBY-DE-LA-ZOUCH

Leicestershire. Map 23B4

Pop 12,082. Hinckley 16, London 113, Atherstone 13, Burton-upon-Trent 9, Derby 14, Leicester 17, Loughborough 12, Nottingham 21, Nuneaton 17, Tamworth 13.
EC Wed. **MD** Sat. **Golf** Willesley Park 18h.
[i] North St. ☎(0530) 411767

★★★ **Royal Osprey,** Station Rd, LE6 5GP
☎(0530) 412833 Tx: 341629
Charming Regency-styled hotel situated on A453. Near centre of town.
31 bedrs, 31 en suite; TV; tcf
dogs, ns; P 100, coach; child facs; con 100

ASHFORD

Kent. Map 7B2

Pop 47,000. Maidstone 19, London 56, Canterbury 14, Folkestone 16, Rochester 27, Tenterden 12, Tunbridge Wells 32.
EC Wed. **MD** Tue, Wed, Sat. **Golf** Ashford 18h.
[i] Lower High St. ☎(0233) 37311

★★★★ **Ashford International**, Simone Weil Av, TN 24 8UX ☎(0233) 611444
Tx: 96498 Fax: (0233) 627708

Large, modern, red-brick hotel conveniently situated near Ashford north exit from M20. Indoor swimming pool, sauna, solarium, gymnasium. Closed 25–27 Dec. Fr, De
200 bedrs, 200 en suite; TV; tcf
lift, dogs, ns; P 400, coach; child facs; con 400
LD 10.45
£ B&B £89–£170, B&B (double) £95–£230; L £11·25, D £15·85; WB £56 (HB). [10% V w/d]
cc Access, Amex, B'card/Visa, Diners.

★★★★ [C] **Eastwell Manor,** Boughton Aluph, TN25 4HR ☎(0233) 635751
Tx: 966281 Fax: (0233) 635530

Superbly furnished, restored Tudor building commanding fine views over parkland. Tennis, fishing, billiards. Fr, De, It. (QMH)
23 bedrs, 23 en suite; TV
lift, dogs; P 100, G 4, coach; child facs; con 70
LD 9.30
£ B&B £94–£116 (w/e £62·50), B&B (double) £110–£138; L £15·50, D £22·50; WB £83
cc Access, Amex, B'card/Visa, Diners; dep.

★★★ **Post House,** Canterbury Rd, TN24 8QQ ☎(0233) 625790 Tx: 966685
Fax: (0233) 643176
A much-extended, 15th-century manor house with adjacent 17th-century timber-clad barn; on the A28 close to the M20.
60 bedrs, 60 en suite; TV; tcf
dogs, ns; P 90, coach; child facs; con 120
LD 10
£ room £67–£83 (w/e £39·50), double room £78–£92; Bk £8, L £9·95, D £14·95; WB £38
cc Access, Amex, B'card/Visa, Diners, dep.

★★★ **Master Spearpoint,** Canterbury Rd, Kennington, TN24 9QR ☎(0233) 636863
Tx: 965978 Fax: (0233) 610119
On outskirts of town, hotel in 5 acres of natural parkland with Downland views. It
36 bedrs, 32 en suite, (4 sh), 2 ba; TV; tcf
dogs; P 60, coach; child facs; con 60
LD 9.45
£ B&B £57–£70 (w/e £32); B&B (double) £75–£91; L fr £6, D fr £10; WB £40
cc Access, Amex, B'card/Visa, Diners.

Garden Court Holiday Inn, Maidstone Rd, Hothfield TN26 1AR ☎(0233) 713333
New hotel opening Autumn 1990.
£ room £37·50–£47·50.

Croft (Acclaimed), Canterbury Rd, Kennington, TN25 4DU ☎(0233) 622140. Fax: (0233) 622140. *Private hotel.* Fr
£ B&B £34–£44. [10% V].

Downsview, Willesborough Rd, Kennington TN24 9QP. ☎(0233) 621953. *Hotel. Putting.* (QMH)
£ B&B £32–£39; [10% V w/e].

ASHOVER

Derbyshire. Map 24A1

M1 (jn 28) 14, London 150, Alfreton 10, Belper 16, Chesterfield 7½, Matlock 4.

Old School Farm, Uppertown S45 0JF ☎(0246) 590813. Open Mar–Oct.
£ B&B £9–£12; FB weekly £98–£126

ASHTON-UNDER-LYNE

Gtr Manchester (Lancashire). Map 33C2
Pop 44,725. Buxton 22, London 181, Barnsley 30, Glossop 7½, Huddersfield 20, Manchester 6½, Oldham 4, Stockport 7½.
EC Tue. **MD** Daily (exc Tue). **Golf** Hyde 18h.

★★★ **York House,** York Pl, Richmond St, OL6 7TT ☎061-330 5899 Fax: 061-343 1613
Fine Victorian terrace house in tree lined street near town centre. Run by proprietor. Fr, It, Es
24 bedrs, 24 en suite, TV; tcf
dogs; P 34, coach; child facs; con 50
LD 9.30, nr Sat lunch & Sun dinner. Resid & Rest lic
£ B&B £45–£55 (w/e £25), B&B (double) £60; L £8·50, D £10
cc Access, Amex, B'card/Visa, Diners.

Welbeck House, 324 Katharine St, OL6 7BD. ☎061-344 0751. *Hotel.* Es
£ B&B £40 (w/e £20); [5% V].

Ascot (Berkshire)

Ashurst (Hampshire)

Bakewell (Derbyshire)

EC *early closing* **MD** *market day* ♣♣ *country house hotel* *ns (NS) no smoking areas* *tcf tea/coffee facilities*

ASHURST Hampshire. Map 5B2

Pop 2,200. Winchester 16, London 81, Lyndhurst 3, Romsey 9, Salisbury 19, Southampton 6½.
EC Wed. **Golf** New Forest, Lyndhurst 18h.

★★ **Busketts Lawn,** 174 Woodlands Rd, Woodlands, SO4 2GL (0703) 292272 Fax: (0703) 292487
Charming small country house hotel in quiet surroundings at edge of New Forest. Swimming pool, putting.
14 bedrs, 14 en suite; TV; tcf
TV, dogs; P 50, coach; child facs; con 100
LD 8·30, bar meals only lunch & Sun dinner. Resid & Rest lic
£ B&B £32·50–£65, B&B (double) £65–£95; HB weekly £245–£296; L £9·50, D £13; WB £78–£92
cc Access, Amex, B'card/Visa, Diners; dep.
(*See advertisement on p. 112*)

ASKRIGG North Yorkshire. Map 38A4

Leyburn 12, London 245, Brough 26, Hawes 5, Skipton 31.

★★ **Kings Arms,** DL8 3HQ Wensleydale (0969) 50258 Fax: (0969) 50635
A 3-storey 18th century building in typical Dales style in village centre.
14 bedrs, 14 en suite; TV; tcf
dogs, ns; P 14; no children under 6; con 10
LD 9; bar meals only Mon–Fri lunch
£ B&B £30–£38, B&B (double) £55–£60; HB weekly £250–£265; D £15; WB £75–£80 (HB); [10% V w/d]
cc Access, B'card/Visa, dep.

ASTBURY Cheshire. Map 30B3

Pop 760. M6 (jn 17) 8, London 164, Buxton 18, Congleton 1, Manchester 26, Sandbach 9, Stoke on Trent 12.

Egerton Arms, CW12 4RQ Congleton (0260) 273946
Period black and white inn opposite Norman church. Large gardens.
7 bedrs, (1 sh), 3 ba; TV; tcf
TV, dogs, ns; P 100, coach; child facs; con 30
LD 9.30
£ B&B £22, B&B (double) £38
cc Access, B'card/Visa, Diners.

ASTON CLINTON Buckinghamshire. Map 14A2
Pop 3,167. Watford 19, London 36, Aylesbury 4½, Denham 22, Dunstable 11, High Wycombe 15, St Albans 19.
Golf Chiltern Forest 18h. **See** Roman remains, Parish Church.

Atlas Section
Consult the Atlas section at the back of the guide to find out which towns and villages have RAC Appointed and Listed hotels in them. They are shown on the maps by purple circles.

★★★ **Bell Inn,** London Rd, HP22 5HP Aylesbury (0296) 630252
Tx: 83252 Fax: (0296) 631250

Charming 18th century mellow brick building with cobbled courtyard and lovely roses.
Fr, De
6 bedrs, 6 en suite; annexe 15 bedrs, 15 en suite; TV; tcf
dogs, ns; P 250; child facs; con 200
LD 9.45
£ B&B £86–£95, B&B (double) £100–£125; L £17, D £17; [10% V]
cc Access, B'card/Visa.

ATHERSTONE Warwickshire. Map 23B2

Pop 7,429. M1 24, London 104, Birmingham 19, Burton-upon-Trent 19, Hinckley 8½, Nuneaton 5½, Sutton Coldfield 14, Tamworth 8.
EC Thur. **MD** Tue, Fri. **Golf** Atherstone 9h. **See** Church, Shrove Tue Football in Main St, Milestone, Roman Roads.

Old Red Lion, Long St, CV9 1BB (0827) 713156 Fax: (0827) 711404

Historic inn conveniently situated in main street of town.
22 bedrs, 22 en suite; TV; tcf
P 22, coach; child facs; con 40
LD 9.45; bar meals only Sun dinner
£ B&B £45; B&B (double) £55–£65; L £8, D £10; [5% V w/e]
cc Access, Amex, B'card/Visa, Diners.

ATTLEBOROUGH Norfolk. Map 27B4

Pop 6,000. Thetford 14, London 96, East Dereham 14, Lowestoft 36, Norwich 15, Scole 14, Stowmarket 26, Swaffham 19.
EC Wed. **MD** Thur. **Golf** Thetford 18h. **See** Norm and Perp Parish Church of St Mary, Attleborough Hall, Earthworks.

★★ **Breckland Lodge,** London Rd, NR17 1AY (0953) 455202 Fax: (0953) 455202
Modern hotel of unusual design with ground-floor bedrooms and public rooms on first floor. Two miles west of town on A11.
15 bedrs, 15 en suite, 2 ba; TV; tcf
lift, dogs; P 100, coach; child facs; con 70
LD 9.30, nr Sun–Tue
£ B&B £28 (w/e £25); B&B (double) £44; [5% V].

AUSTWICK North Yorkshire. Map 36C4

Pop 250. Settle 4, London 233, Hawes 21, Kirkby Lonsdale 12, Lancaster 21.
Golf Bentham 9h.

★ **Traddock,** LA2 8BY Clapham (046 85) 224
Listed Georgian building with fine views and own gardens. In Dales village. Open Easter–end Sep. Fr.
12 bedrs, 11 en suite, 1 ba; TV; tcf
dogs; P 20; coach; no children under 5
LD 6; nr lunch. Resid. & Rest lic
£ B&B £26, B&B (double) £44; HB weekly £217–£245; D £12

AVON Hants. Map 5B2

Christchurch 4, London 98, Bournemouth 9½, Lymington 16, Ringwood 4½.

★★★ H R **Tyrrells Ford,** BH23 7BH Bransgore (0425) 72646 Fax: (0425) 72262

Small 18th century house in 10 acres of lawns and woodland.
16 bedrs, 16 en suite; TV; tcf
P 100; child facs; con 40
LD 10
£ B&B £45–£65, B&B (double) £65–£80; HB weekly £280–£455; L £8·95, D £14·95; WB £40
cc Access, B'card/Visa; dep.

AXBRIDGE Somerset. Map 4B3

Pop 1,525. Bath 27, London 131, M5 (jn 22) 9, Bristol 20, Wells 12, Weston-super-Mare 10.
EC Wed, Sat. **Golf** Burnham & Berrow 18h. **See** King John's Hunting Lodge (Museum), 14th cent Church, Manor House.

★★★ **Webbington,** Loxton, BS28 2XA (0934) 750100 Fax: (0934) 750100

Edwardian manor house, with attractive conservatories and a new wing, set in landscaped grounds. Extensive conference

facilities. Indoor swimming pool, tennis, sauna, solarium, gymnasium. ✂ Fr, De
🛏 59 bedrs, 59 en suite; TV; tcf
🏨 dogs; P 200, coach; child facs; con 1000
✕ LD 10; bar meals only Sat lunch.
£ B&B £58 (£32 w/e); B&B (double) £68 (£60 w/e); HB weekly £250; L £9·50, D £15; WB £39 (HB). [10% V]
cc Access, Amex, B'card/Visa, Diners.

AXMINSTER Devon. Map 4B2

Pop 4,909. Chard 7, London 147, Dorchester 27, Honiton 10, Lyme Regis 5½. **EC** Wed. **MD** Thur. **Golf** Axmouth 18h, Lyme Regis 18h. **See** Parish Church.
ℹ Old Courthouse, Church St. ☎(0297) 34386

★★★ H R Tytherleigh Cot, Chardstock, EX13 7BN ☎South Chard (0460) 21170 Fax: (0460) 21291

Cream-painted farmhouse and converted barn, with landscaped grounds, in village north of Axminster. Swimming pool, sauna, solarium. ✂ Es
🛏 15 bedrs, 15 en suite, annexe 14 bedrs, 14 en suite; TV; tcf
🏨 dogs; P 30; no children under 14; con 20
✕ LD 9.30. Resid & Rest lic
£ B&B £45–£58·50, B&B (double) £77–£102; HB weekly £301–£458; L £9·95, D £17·95; WB £90. [10% V w/d]
cc Access, B'card/Visa; dep.

♣ ★★ Woodbury Park, Woodbury Cross, EX13 5TL ☎(0297) 33010
Converted Georgian residence in 5½ acres of grounds with good views. Swimming pool, sauna.
🛏 8 bedrs, 6 en suite, 1 ba; TV; tcf
🏨 TV, dogs; P 30; child facs
✕ LD 9; nr Sun dinner
£ B&B £25–£28, B&B (double) £40–£46; HB weekly £175–£196; L £9, D £12; [5% V]
cc Access, Amex, B'card/Visa, Diners; dep.

AYLESBURY Buckinghamshire. Map 21B2

Pop 48,000. Watford 23, London 40, Bicester 16, Buckingham 16, Dunstable 15, High Wycombe 16, Oxford 22, St Albans 23. **EC** Thur. **MD** Wed, Fri, Sat. **Golf** West Turville 18h. **See** 15th cent EE Church of St Mary, King's Head Hotel, Statue of John Hampden, Bucks County Museum, Prebendal House (home of John Wilkes).
ℹ County Hall, Walton St. ☎(0296) 382308

★★★★ Forte, Aston Clinton Rd, HP22 5AA ☎(0296) 393388 Tx: 838820 Fax: (0296) 392211 ♿
Long low hotel in landscaped grounds in a rural area. Indoor swimming pool, sauna, solarium, gymnasium. ✂ Fr, De, Es (THF)
🛏 94 bedrs, 94 en suite; TV; tcf
🏨 dogs, ns; P 120, coach; child facs; con 80
✕ LD 9.50, nr Sat lunch
£ B&B £92·60–£100 (w/e £40); B&B (double) £110·20–£115·20; Bk £8·50, L £9·50, D £15·50; WB £40
cc Access, Amex, B'card/Visa, CB, Diners.

♣ ★★★★ Hartwell House, Oxford Rd, HP17 8NL ☎(0296) 747444 Tx: 837108 Fax: (0296) 747304

Superb hotel in a lovely part Jacobean, part Georgian mansion, lovingly restored and furnished in keeping, set in landscaped parkland. Swimming pool, fishing. ✂ Fr, It.
🛏 32 bedrs, 32 en suite; TV
🏨 lift; P 60; no children under 8; con 30
✕ LD 9.45
£ B&B £92·50–£124·50; B&B (double) £146–£294; L £17, D £29·50; WB £85 (HB)
cc Access, Amex, B'card/Visa, Diners.

★★ Bell, Market Sq, HP20 1TX ☎(0296) 89835

Originally a coaching inn. Fine Georgian building in market square. (THF)
🛏 17 bedrs, 17 en suite; TV; tcf
🏨 dogs, ns; child facs

BADMINTON, GREAT Avon. Map 5A4

M4 (jn 18) 5, London 111, Bristol 18, Chippenham 10, Chepstow 24, Swindon 26. **Golf** Chipping Sodbury 18h.

★★★ Petty France, Dunkirk, GL9 1AF (A46) ☎Didmarton (0454) 23361 Fax: (0454) 23768

18th century former coaching inn with annexe (converted stables); attractive gardens. ✂ De
🛏 8 bedrs, 8 en suite; annexe 12 bedrs, 12 en suite; TV; tcf
🏨 dogs; P 50, coach; child facs; con 16
✕ LD 10
£ B&B £55–£95, B&B (double) £75–£110; L £11, D £16, WB £96 (2 nts). [5% V]
cc Access, Amex, B'card/Visa, Diners.

Bodkin House (Highly Acclaimed), (A46), GL9 1AF ☎ Didmarton (045 423) 310 Fax: (0453) 843572. *Hotel.* Closed 25 & 26 Dec.
£ B&B £40–£45 (w/e £25); [10% V].

BAGSHOT Surrey. Map 13A2

Pop 4,255. M3 (jn 3) 1, London 27, Basingstoke 20, Farnham 12, Guildford 11, Reading 16, Windsor 10, Woking 7½. **EC** Wed. **Golf** Berkshire 18h (2). **See** Parish Church, 17th cent almshouses.

♣ ★★★★ Pennyhill Park, London Road, GU19 5ET ☎(0276) 71774 Tx: 858841 Fax: (0276) 73217
Luxuriously furnished Edwardian manor house in attractive parkland of 112 acres. Swimming pool, golf, tennis, fishing, riding, sauna, solarium. ✂ Fr, Es
🛏 54 bedrs, 54 en suite; TV
🏨 dogs; ns, P 150; child facs; con 30
✕ LD 10.30
£ room £105–£250, double room £130–£250; Bk £11, L £20, D £38; WB £180
cc Access, Amex, B'card/Visa, Diners; dep.

★★ The Cricketers, London Rd, GU19 5HR ☎(0276) 73196
Traditional inn—lawns to rear adjoin tree-lined cricket ground.

BAINBRIDGE North Yorkshire. Map 38A4

Pop 360, Leyburn 12, London 245, Hawes 4, Leeds 54, Skipton 31. **EC** Wed. **Golf** Catterick 18h. **See** Old Inn, Waterfalls, Semerwater Lake 1 m W.

★★ Rose and Crown, Wensleydale, DL8 3EE ☎Wensleydale (0969) 50225

Two-storey coaching inn of character in village centre overlooking green. Fishing. ✂ Fr, De
🛏 12 bedrs, 12 en suite; TV; tcf
🏨 dogs; P 65, coach; child facs; con 50
✕ LD 9.30, bar meals only Mon–Sat lunch
£ B&B £33, B&B (double) £58; HB weekly £280–£308; L £8·50, D £14·50; WB £72 (2 nts winter)
cc Access, B'card/Visa.

Riverdale House (Highly Acclaimed), DL8 3EW ☎Wensleydale (0969) 50311. *Hotel.* Open Mar–Nov.
£ B&B £24·50; [10% V] dep.

BAKEWELL Derbyshire. Map 30C3

See also HASSOP.
Pop 3,946. Matlock 8, London 153, Ashbourne 17, Buxton 12, Chapel-en-le-Frith 15, Chesterfield 12, Leek 19, Sheffield 16.
EC Thur. **MD** Mon. **Golf** Bakewell 9h. **See** Church (Vernon monuments), Saxon Cross in Churchyard, Old Bridge, Grammar School, Almshouses, Holme Hall, Old House Museum, Haddon Hall 2 m SE, Chatsworth House, Garden and Theatre Gallery, 3 m NE.
[i] Old Market Hall, Bridge St. ☎(0629) 813227

★★★ **Rutland Arms,** The Square, DE4 1BT ☎(062 981) 2812 Tx: 377077 Fax: (062 981) 4600

Imposing Georgian building in local stone, well-situated overlooking the town square.
Fr, Es
18 bedrs, 18 en suite; annexe 18 bedrs, 18 en suite; TV; tcf
dogs; P 34, G 2, coach; child facs; con 80
LD 9.45
£ B&B £42–£51, B&B (double) £59–£69; HB weekly £272–£282; L £7·95, D £15·95; WB £42
cc Access, Amex, B'card/Visa, Diners; dep.
(*See advertisement on p. 000*)

★★ **Milford House,** Mill St, DE4 1DA ☎(0629) 812130

Georgian residence standing in own grounds yet only 300 yards from town centre. Open Apr–Oct.
12 bedrs, 12 en suite, TV; tcf
P 10, G 9, U 2; children over 10
LD 7.30, nr Mon–Sat lunch & Sun dinner. Resid & Rest lic
£ B&B £28·75–£32, B&B (double) £50·60–£60; HB weekly £240–£285; L £11·50, D £12·50; dep.

Lathkil (Acclaimed), Over Haddon, DE4 1JE ☎(0629) 812501. *Hotel.*

Castle Cliff, Monsal Head, DE4 1NL ☎Gt Longstone (062 987) 258. *Private Hotel.*

BAMBURGH Northumberland. Map 51C2

Pop 458. Alnwick 16, London 324, Berwick-upon-Tweed 20, Coldstream 26.
EC Wed. **Golf** Bamburgh Castle 18h. **See** Castle, St Aidan's Church, Grace Darling Museum and boathouse, Farne Islands (Bird sanctuary).

★★ H **Lord Crewe Arms,** Front St, NE69 7BL ☎(066 84) 243
Late 18th century 2-storey stone-built hotel near village green. Fr. Open Mar–Nov.
25 bedrs, 20 en suite, 3 ba; TV; tcf
dogs, ns; P 34; no children under 5
LD 8.45, bar meals only lunch
£ B&B £30–£42, B&B (double) £40–£58; HB weekly £200–£260; D £15·50; WB £80 (2 nts)
cc Access, B'card/Visa.

★★ **Victoria,** Front St, NE69 7BP ☎(066 84) 431

Victorian stone-built hotel of 3 storeys in traditional style.
23 bedrs, 16 en suite, 2 ba; TV; tcf
dogs, ns; P 7, coach; child facs; con 50
LD 8.30, bar meals only Mon–Sat lunch
£ B&B £26·40–£34·10, B&B (double) £39·60–£66; HB weekly £246·40–£338·80; L £7·20, D £15·40; WB £30; [10% V]
cc Access, Amex, B'card/Visa, Diners; dep.

★ **Mizen Head,** Lucker Rd, NE69 7BS ☎(066 84) 254

Stone built 3-storey house with extensions, set in own grounds on edge of village.
15 bedrs, 5 en suite, 4 ba; TV; tcf
TV, dogs; P 30, coach; child facs; con 30
LD 8.15, bar meals only Mon–Sat lunch
£ B&B £16–£25, B&B (double) £26–£52; HB weekly £147–£197; L £5, D £9·75; WB £13; dep.

★ **Sunningdale,** Lucker Rd, NE69 7BS ☎(066 84) 334

Cheerful hotel, originally two private houses on edge of village.
19 bedrs, 6 en suite, 3 ba; TV; tcf
TV, dogs; P 16, coach; child facs
LD 7.30, bar meals only lunch
£ B&B £15–£25, B&B (double) £30–£48; HB weekly £240–£348; D £9; WB £13; [5% V]
cc Access, B'card/Visa; dep.

BAMPTON Devon. Map 3C4

Pop 1,447. Taunton 20, London 163, Dunster 19, South Molton 17, Tiverton 7½.
Golf Tiverton 18h. **See** Exmoor Pony Fair (last Thur in Oct), 13th cent Church, The Mount (castle site), 19th cent Town Hall.
[i] Station Rd Car Park. ☎(0398) 31854

Courtyard (Acclaimed), 19 Fore St, EX16 9NO ☎(0398) 31536. *Hotel.*

Bridge House, 24 Luke St, EX16 9NF ☎(0398) 31298. *Hotel.*

BANBURY Oxfordshire. Map 21A3

See also BLOXHAM
Pop 38,176. Bicester 15, London 72, Buckingham 17, Chipping Norton 13, Coventry 27, Daventry 16, Oxford 23, Stratford-upon-Avon 20, Warwick 20.
EC Tue. **MD** Thur, Sat. **Golf** Cherwell Edge 9h. **See** 19th cent Cross in Horse Fair, 16th cent Calthorpe Manor House, 18th cent Church, Broughton Castle 2½ m SW.
[i] Museum, 8 Horsefair. ☎(0295) 259855

★★★★ **Whately Hall,** Banbury Cross, OX16 0AN ☎(0295) 263451 Tx: 837149 Fax: (0295) 271736

17th century building of local stone with modern extension. Attractive gardens. (THF).
Fr, De, It, Da
74 bedrs, 74 en suite; TV; tcf
lift, dogs, ns; P 70, U 3 (£8), G 12; child facs; con 150
LD 9.30
£ B&B £84–£89, B&B (double) £114–£124; L £9·95, D £14·95; WB £50
cc Access, Amex, B'card/Visa, Diners, dep.

★★★ **Banbury Moat House,** Oxford Rd, OX16 9AH ☎(0295) 259361 Tx: 838967 Fax: (0295) 270954

Fine, well-modernised Georgian hotel in heart of town. (QMH).

Banbury (Oxfordshire)

The Banbury Moat House

The Banbury Moat House combines the elegance of a beautiful Georgian House with modern amenities, excellent food and a caring standard of service.

The Cotswolds, Stratford upon Avon, Warwick and Oxford are all on your doorstep whilst there are also many individual sites of interest including Blenheim Palace, Warwick Castle, Broughton Castle, Upton House and Sulgrave Manor.

The Moat House offers 48 tastefully decorated bedrooms, each with en-suite bathroom, remote control colour television and radio, hair dryer, individually controlled central heating, refreshment tray and direct dial telephone.

Private functions are a speciality at the Moat House, and it is a first class venue for residential or non-residential conferences, training courses and meetings, with a choice of four well-equipped rooms.

The Banbury Moat House
Oxford Road, Banbury, Oxon. OX16 9AH
Tel: (0295) 259361

Banbury (Oxfordshire)

Wroxton House Hotel

Wroxton St Mary, Near Banbury, Oxfordshire OX15 6QB
Tel: 0295 730777 Fax: 730800

The warmest welcome awaits you at this beautifully refurbished Cotswold Hotel. Superb cuisine. Log fires. Romance breaks, Stratford Theatre breaks and Antiques weekends. Fifteen historic houses & gardens within 30 minutes drive.

Barnstaple (North Devon)

The Park Hotel

RAC★★★

ENJOY LUXURY 3 STAR COMFORTS OVERLOOKING THE RIVER TAW

Superbly situated by Rock Park overlooking the river, yet only a short walk to Barnstaple bridge and town centre. Newly refurbished throughout offering excellent service and value. Very popular bar, entertainment and function rooms. All rooms with colour T.V., radio, telephone, en suite bathroom etc. First class cuisine in International Restaurant.

For free colour brochure please contact: Mr. R. Holtby, The Park Hotel, Taw Vale, Barnstaple, North Devon. Tel: (0271) 72166 Fax No: (0271) 78558

Barnstaple (Devon)

Barnstaple Motel

Braunton Road, Barnstaple, Devon EX31 1LE
Tel: (0271) 76221 Fax: (0271) 24101

We are a family owned and managed modern motel ideally situated for both business and holiday visits to North Devon, a short walk from Barnstaple town centre and main trading areas, together with ample parking facilities. All 60 double/twin en suite bedrooms have colour TVs, telephone, tea/coffee making and child listening facilities.
High quality restaurant and conference/banqueting facilities available.
Indoor heated swimming pool and other leisure facilities available to both residents and non-residents.
Special weekend breaks and reduction for children offered.
Please apply for colour brochure and tariff.

EC early closing MD market day ♣♣ country house hotel ns (NS) no smoking areas tcf tea/coffee facilities

🛏 50 bedrs, 50 en suite; TV; tcf
🏠 dogs; P 40, coach; child facs; con 65
✕ LD 9.30
cc Access, B'card/Visa, Diners.
(*See advertisement on p. 116*)

★★★ Wroxton House, Wroxton St Mary, OX15 6QB ☎ (0295) 730482 Tx: 83409 Fax: (0295) 730800

Attractive building of local stone with part thatched roof. Fr, De
🛏 29 bedrs, 29 en suite; annexe 3 bedrs, 3 en suite; TV; tcf
🏠 dogs, ns; P 48; child facs; con 45
✕ LD 10
£ B&B £75–£95 (w/e £32·50), B&B (double) £95–£120; L £16, D £24·50; WB £49 (HB)
cc Access, Amex, B'card/Visa, Diners.
(*See advertisement on p. 116*)

★★ Cromwell Lodge, North Bar, OX16 0TB ☎ (0295) 59781 Tx: 83343

Charming 17th century Cotswold stone building. Large walled private garden.
🛏 32 bedrs, 32 en suite; TV; tcf
🏠 dogs; P 25, coach; child facs; con 30

★★ Lismore, 61 Oxford Rd, OX16 9AJ ☎ (0295) 67661

A 3-storey red-brick Victorian building on main Oxford-Banbury road. Gardens to rear.

Please tell the manager if you chose your hotel through an advertisement in the guide.

🛏 14 bedrs, 11 en suite, 1 ba; TV; tcf
🏠 TV, dogs; P 19, coach; child facs; con 25

Easington House (Highly Acclaimed), 50 Oxford Rd, OX16 9AN ☎ (0295) 270181. *Hotel.* Closed Xmas wk. Fr, Es
£ B&B £28–£55, [5% V]

La Madonette (Highly Acclaimed), North Newington OX15 6AA ☎ (0295) 730212. *Guest House. Swimming pool.* Closed 21 Dec–1 Jan.
£ B&B £35–£37·50.

Kelvedon, 11 Broughton Rd, OX16 9QB ☎ (0295) 263028. *Guest House.*
£ B&B £16–£20.

Tredis, 15 Broughton Rd, OX16 9QB ☎ (0295) 264632. *Guest House.*

BARHAM

Kent. Map 7C3

Canterbury 6, London 64, Ashford 20, Dover 9, Margate 17.

★★ Old Coach House, Dover Rd, CT4 6JA ☎ (0227) 831218 Fax: (0227) 831932.
Small hotel in early 19th-century building just off the main Dover-Canterbury road. Convenient overnight stop en route to Dover. Fr.
🛏 5 bedrs, 5 en suite; TV; tcf

BARNARD CASTLE

Durham. Map 44C1

Pop 5,700 Bishop Auckland 15, London 248, Brough 18, Middleton in Teesdale 10.
ℹ 43 Galgate ☎ (0833) 690909

West Roods Farm, Boldron, DL12 9SW ☎ (0833) 690116. Open Easter–Oct.
£ B&B £13–£15, HB weekly £122–£149; [5% V].

BARNBY MOOR

Nottinghamshire. Map 31B3

Pop 227. Newark 23, London 150, A1 (M) 3½, Doncaster 14, Gainsborough 14, Rotherham 17, Sheffield 22, Worksop 9.
EC Wed. **Golf** Retford 9h. **See** Old Posting House.

★★★ Ye Olde Bell, Gt North Rd, DN22 8QS ☎ Retford (0777) 705121 Fax: (0777) 860464

Traditional coaching house with white-painted brickwork. On old Gt North Rd. (THF)
🛏 55 bedrs, 55 en suite; TV; tcf
🏠 dogs, ns; P 250, coach; child facs; con 250

BARNSDALE BAR

North Yorkshire. Map 38C2

A1 (M) 3, London 171, Barnsley 12, Doncaster 8, Goole 21, Pontefract 6½, Selby 15, Wakefield 13.
Golf Pontefract & District 18h.

★★★ Welcome Lodge, Gt North Rd, WF8 3JB ☎ Pontefract (0977) 620711 Tx: 557457
Main road motel with petrol, restaurant and shops complex. (THF)
See Motor Lodge section

BARNSLEY

South Yorkshire. Map 41A3

Pop 223,900 (Metropolitan Borough). M1 (jn 37) 1½, London 172, Doncaster 15, Huddersfield 17, Manchester 36, Pontefract 14, Sheffield 14, Wakefield 9½.
MD Mon, Wed, Fri, Sat. **Golf** Silkstone 18h. **See** Parish Church of St Mary, Town Hall, Cooper Art Gallery, Tower, Monk Bretton Priory, Cannon Hall Park and Museum, Quaker burial grounds.
ℹ 56 Eldon St. ☎ (0226) 206757

★★★★ Ardsley Moat House, Doncaster Rd, Ardsley, S71 5EH ☎ (0226) 289401 Tx: 547762 Fax: (0226) 205374
Attractive 18th century stone building with modern wings. Lovely views. Billiards. (QMH). Closed Xmas Day. Fr, Es, It
🛏 75 bedrs, 75 en suite; TV; tcf
🏠 dogs; P 200, coach; child facs; con 350
✕ LD 10.30, bar meals only Sat lunch
£ B&B £66·50 (w/e £38), B&B (double); L £11·50, D £14; WB £87; [10% V]
cc Access, Amex, B'card/Visa, Diners.

★★★ Queens, Regent St, S70 2HG ☎ (0226) 731010 Tx: 547348 Fax: (0226) 248719
Gracious Victorian building in town centre.
🛏 48 bedrs, 48 en suite; TV; tcf
🏠 dogs; P 500, coach; child facs; con 120
✕ LD 9.30
£ B&B £47·50 (w/e £32), B&B (double) £59; L £4, D £10·50; WB
cc Access, Amex, B'card/Visa, Diners.

★ Royal, 11 Church St, S70 2AD ☎ (0226) 203658

Handsome modernised 18th century building in town centre.

BARNSTAPLE

Devon. Map 3B4

Pop 18,500. South Molton 11, London 193, Bideford 9, Crediton 33, Ilfracombe 11, Lynmouth 19.
EC Wed. **MD** Tue, Fri. **Golf** Saunton 18h (2). **See** St Peter's Church, 13th cent Arched Bridge, Norm Castle, Almshouses, Queen Anne's Walk, St Anne's Chapel, Museum, New Civic Centre.
ℹ Library, Tuly St ☎ (0271) 47172

★★★ Barnstaple Motel, Braunton Rd, EX31 1LE ☎ (0271) 76221 Fax: (0271) 44251 ♿

Purpose-built motel in own grounds. Indoor swimming pool, sauna, solarium, gymnasium.
🛏 57 bedrs, 57 en suite; TV; tcf
🏠 TV, dogs; P 200, G 10, coach; child facs; con 200
✕ LD 10, nr Mon–Sat lunch
£ B&B £45–£50, B&B (double) £65–£70; HB weekly £275; L £7·25, D £10·50; WB £60
cc Access, B'card/Visa, CB, Diners; dep.
(*See advertisement on p. 116*)

★★★ Imperial, Taw Vale Par, EX32 8NB ☎(0271) 45861 Fax: (0271) 24448
18th century former private residence overlooking River Taw. (THF)
🛏 56 bedrs, 56 en suite; TV; tcf
🏠 lift, dogs, ns; P 60, coach; child facs; con 100
✕ LD 9, bar meals only Mon–Sat lunch
£ B&B £60–£64 (w/e £47), B&B (double) £70–£77; HB weekly £231–£280; D £13·25; WB
cc Access, Amex, B'card/Visa.

★★★ H Park, New Rd, EX32 9AE ☎(0271) 72166 Tx: 42551
Fax: (0271) 78558

Purpose-built motel convenient for town centre. Commanding view of river.
🛏 25 bedrs, 25 en suite; annexe 17 bedrs, 17 en suite; TV; tcf
🏠 dogs; P 80, coach; child facs; con 100
✕ LD 9
£ B&B £39·50–£49, B&B (double) £60–£75; HB weekly £245–£350; L £8, D £10·25; WB £77 (2 nts)
cc Access, Amex, B'card/Visa, Diners.
(*See advertisement on p. 116*)

★★ Royal & Fortescue, Boutport St, EX31 3HG ☎(0271) 42289 Tx: 42551
Fax: (0271) 78558

Former coaching inn conveniently set in the heart of town.
🛏 62 bedrs, 35 en suite, 7 ba; TV; tcf
🏠 lift, TV, dogs; P 20, G 4, coach; child facs
✕ LD 9
£ B&B £30–£39, B&B (double) £48–£55; HB weekly £210–£280; L £6, D £10; WB £60 (2 nts)
cc Access, Amex, B'card/Visa, Diners.
(*See advertisement on p. 119*)

★ Lynwood House, Bishops Tawton Rd, EX32 9DZ ☎ (0271) 43695
Fax: (0271) 79340
Hotel with popular restaurant in Victorian building of local stone, in residential area about 1 mile from town centre.
🛏 5 bedrs, 5 en suite; TV; tcf
🏠 dogs; P 35, coach; con 20
✕ LD 9.30, nr Sun lunch
£ B&B £47·50, B&B (double) £67·50; WB £195 (for 2)
cc Access, B'card/Visa

Muddlebridge House (Acclaimed), Freminton EX31 2NQ ☎(0271) 76073. *Guest House.*

Yeo Dale, Pilton Bridge, EX31 1PG ☎(0271) 42954. *Hotel.*
£ B&B £15–£18, HB weekly £150·50–£171·50; [10% V].

BARROW IN FURNESS Cumbria. Map 36A4

Pop 60,000. Ulverston 8½, London 280, Broughton-in-Furness 14.
EC Thur. **MD** Wed, Fri, Sat. **Golf** Barrow 18h, Furness 18h. **See** Parish Churches, Ruins of Furness Abbey, Piel Island and Castle, Two Nature Reserves on Walney Island, Biggar Village.
ℹ Town Hall, Duke St. ☎(0229) 870156

★★★★ Abbey House, Abbey Rd, LA13 0PA ☎(0229) 838282 Tx: 65357
Fax: (0229) 820403

Lutyens-designed mansion in 14 acres of gardens and woods, on A590 north of town. Putting. Fr
🛏 27 bedrs, 27 en suite; TV; tcf
🏠 lift, dogs; P60, coach; child facs; con 100
✕ LD 10, bar meals only Sat lunch
£ B&B £60·50–£70·50, B&B (double) £75·50–£85·50; L £9, D £16·50; WB £80·50 (2 nts); [5% V]
cc Access, Amex, B'card/Visa, Diners.

★ White House, Abbey Rd, LA13 9AE ☎(0229) 827303

Purpose-built hotel on main road to north of town. Adjacent to Barrow Park.
🛏 29 bedrs, 2 en suite, 6 ba; TV; tcf
🏠 dogs; P 80, G 10, coach; child facs; con 40
✕ LD 9.30, bar meals Mon–Sat lunch, Sun dinner
£ B&B £10–£21·50 (w/e £10–£15), B&B (double) £35–£42; L £6, D £11·50
cc Access, Amex, B'card/Visa, Diners.

BARTLE Lancashire. Map 36B2

Preston 5, London 217, M55 (jn 1) 2, Blackburn 14, Blackpool 15, Lancaster 22.

★★★ Bartle Hall, Lea La, Nr Preston, PR4 0HA ☎Catforth (0772) 690506
Fax: (0772) 690841

Former country residence standing in 16 acres of lawns and woodlands. Swimming pool, tennis. It, Es, Po
🛏 12 bedrs, 12 en suite; TV; tcf
🏠 P 120, coach, child facs; con 100
✕ LD 11. Resid & Rest lic
£ B&B £60, B&B (double) £75–£85
cc Access, Amex, B'card/Visa, CB, Diners.

BARTON ON SEA Hampshire. Map 5B1

Pop 3,600. Lyndhurst 13, London 97, Blandford Forum 26, Bournemouth 11, Lymington 7, Ringwood 12.
EC Wed. **Golf** Barton on Sea 18h.

★★ C R Cliff House, Marine Dr West, BH25 7QL ☎(0425) 619333 ♿

Gabled hotel, recently refurbished, in ½ acre of garden on cliff-tops overlooking Christchurch Bay. Po
🛏 9 bedrs, 8 en suite, 3 ba; TV; tcf
🏠 ns; P 50
✕ LD 9
£ B&B £30–£45, B&B (double) £66–£80, HB weekly £298–£345; L £8·50, D £12·95; WB £85 (2 nts). [5% V]
cc Access, Amex, B'card/Visa, Diners.

Old Coastguard (Acclaimed), 53 Marine Dr East, BH25 7DX ☎(0425) 612987. *Hotel.*

Licences
Establishments have a full licence unless shown as unlicensed or with the limitations listed on p 6.

Barnstaple (North Devon)

The Royal & Fortescue Hotel

RAC★★

ONE OF THE WEST COUNTRY'S TRULY TRADITIONAL MARKET TOWN HOTELS

Situated in the heart of this busy West Country market town, The Royal & Fortescue Hotel provides a friendly, congenial atmosphere and personal service. Many of the bedrooms have private bath, colour T.V., direct dial telephone and tea & coffee making facilities. The spacious restaurant provides a choice of à la carte and table d'hôte menus each day, also function rooms and entertainment.

For free colour brochure and tariff contact: Mr. R. Cawsey, Manager, The Royal & Fortescue Hotel, Boutport Street, Barnstaple, Devon. Tel: (0271) 42289 Fax No: (0271) 78558

Basildon (Essex)

THE CAMPANILE HOTEL – Basildon

A127 Southend Arterial Road, Pipps Hill, Basildon, Essex SS14 3AE

Tel: (0268) 530810 Telex: 995068

Part of the international budget hotel chain "Campanile", the hotel offers 100 comfortable double or twin rooms with en-suite bathrooms, and tea/coffee making facilities, radio alarm, remote control colour TV, Sky TV, and direct dial telephone at **competitive rates.** Our informal restaurant provides a variety of home-cooked French/ Continental cuisine, and personal service at **affordable prices.** Our seminar room is available for business meetings or small functions.

Your hosts: Carrine & Daniel Meys

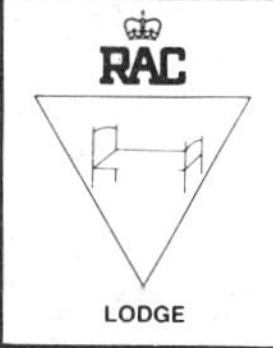

Bath (Avon)

The Gainsborough – Bath

Weston Lane, Bath, Avon. Tel: (0225) 311380

ETB ♛♛♛ RAC ★★

A spacious and comfortable country house hotel situated in its own grounds near the botanical gardens and Victoria Park. The Abbey, Roman Baths, and Pump Rooms are within easy walking distance via the Park. All our 16 bedrooms are en-suite, with colour TV, direct dial telephones, tea/coffee making facilities and full central heating. The Hotel has a small restaurant and cocktail bar overlooking the garden. We have our own car park, high recommended. Warm welcome by friendly staff.

BASILDON Essex. Map 17A2

Pop 101,200. Romford 13, London 30, Brentwood 9, Chelmsford 13, Dartford Tunnel 14, Southend 12.
MD Mon, Tue, Thur, Fri, Sat. **Golf** Basildon 18h. **See** St Martin's Church 'Basildon Christ' sculpture by T Huxley-Jones, Gloucester Park, Fairytale Clock.

★★★ **Crest,** Cranes Farm Rd, SS14 3DG
☎(0268) 533955 Tx: 995141
Fax: (0268) 530119

Modern hotel in own picturesque lakeside gardens. Putting, billiards. Fr (Cr/THF)
110 bedrs, 110 en suite; TV; tcf
lift, dogs, ns; P 150, coach; child facs; con 300
LD 10, bar meals only Sat lunch
£ B&B £78–£94 (w/e £33), B&B (double) £86–£102·50; L £10·25, D £14·25
cc Access, Amex, B'card/Visa, Diners; dep.

★★ **Campanile,** Mites Cray Rd, Pipps Hill, SS14 3AE ☎(0268) 530810 Tx: 995068
(See Motor Lodge section
(See advertisement on p. 119)

BASINGSTOKE Hampshire. Map 12B1

See also SILCHESTER.
Pop 81,700. M3 (jn 6) 1½, London 47, Alton 12, Andover 19, Farnham 15, Newbury 16, Reading 16, Salisbury 36, Winchester 18.
EC Thurs. **MD** Wed, Sat. **Golf** Basingstoke 18h. **See** 15th cent Church, Museum, War Memorial Park, The Vyne—early 16th cent house (Nat Trust) 3 m N. Willis Museum.
[i] Market Sq. ☎ (0256) 817618

★★★ **Crest,** Grove Rd, RG21 3EE
☎ (0256) 468181 Tx: 858501 Fax: (0256) 840081

Beside A30, modern hotel in own gardens. On outskirts of town. Billiards. Fr, Es (Cr/THF)
85 bedrs, 85 en suite; TV; tcf
dogs, ns; P 200, coach; child facs; con 150
LD 9.45, bar meals only Sat lunch
£ B&B £90·95 (w/e £45), B&B (double) £111·90; L £8·95, D £15·95
cc Access, Amex, B'card/Visa, CB, Diners.

★★★ **Hilton Lodge,** Old Common Rd, Black Dam, RG21 3PR ☎(0256) 460460
Tx: 859038 Fax: (0256) 840441

Long modern 1–2 storey hotel prominently placed on outer edge of town near M3. Indoor swimming pool, sauna, gymnasium. (H. Int) Fr, It
144 bedrs, 144 en suite; TV; tcf
dogs, n.s; P 100, coach; child facs; con 140
LD 10, nr Sat lunch
£ B&B £94·50–£106 (w/e £35), B&B (double) £113–£116; L £12·50
cc Access, Amex, B'card/Visa, Diners.

★★★ **Hilton National,** Aldermaston Roundabout, Northern Ringway, RG24 9NV
☎(0256) 20212 Tx: 858223
Fax: (0256) 842835

Large modern red brick hotel with open plan public areas. 1 mile from centre. Indoor swimming pool, sauna, gymnasium, snooker. Fr, De, Ca (HN)
135 bedrs, 135 en suite; TV; tcf
lift, dogs, ns; P 200, coach; child facs; con 160
LD 9.45; bar meals only Sat lunch
£ L £11·50, D £13·50
cc Access, Amex, B'card/Visa, Diners.

★★ **Red Lion,** London St, RG21 1NY
☎(0256) 28525 Fax: (0256) 844056

Town centre traditional coaching inn with beams. Large modern extensions. (THF)
62 bedrs, 62 en suite; TV; tcf
lift, dogs, ns; P 50, coach; child facs; con 30
LD 9.30, bar meals only Mon–Sat lunch & Sun dinner
£ B&B £83–£99 (w/e £22), B&B (double) £106; L £7·50, D £12·95; WB £32
cc Access, Amex, B'card/Visa, CB, Diners.

Centrecourt, Centre Dr, Chineham, RG24 0FY ☎(0256) 816664
Hotel awaiting inspection.
50 bedrs, 50 en suite
£ B&B £89–£102.

BASLOW Derbyshire. Map 30C3

Pop 1,204. Matlock 9, London 154, Ashbourne 21, Buxton 14, Chapel-en-le-Frith 15, Chesterfield 9, Leek 22, Sheffield 12.
Golf Bakewell 9h. **See** St Anne's Church, 17th cent bridge, Chatsworth (House, Garden and Theatre Gallery) 1½ m S.

★★★ **Cavendish,** Bakewell, DE4 1SP
☎(0246) 582311 Tx: 547150
Fax: (0246) 582312

On Chatsworth estate, 18th century fishing inn with elegant furnishings and decor. Putting, fishing.
23 bedrs, 23 en suite; TV; tcf
ns; P 40, coach; child facs; con 16
LD 10
cc Access, Amex, B'card/Visa, Diners.

BASSENTHWAITE Cumbria. Map 43C2

Pop 400. Keswick 7, London 292, Carlisle 21, Cockermouth 8, Penrith 23.
Golf Embleton, Cockermouth 18h. **See** Old Church by Lake.

★★★ **Castle Inn,** nr Keswick, CA12 4RG
☎(059 681) 401 Fax: (059 681) 604
Family-run hotel with lovely garden. Swimming pool, tennis, sauna, solarium, gymnasium, billards. Fr, De, Po
36 bedrs, 36 en suite; TV; tcf
dogs, ns; P 150, coach; child facs; con 200
LD 9.30
£ B&B £44–£54, B&B (double) £69–£79; HB weekly £295–£360; L £9·50, D £12·95. [10% V]
cc Access, Amex, B'card/Visa, Diners; dep.

Licences
Establishments have a full licence unless shown as unlicensed or with the limitations listed on p 6.

Overwater Hall, Ireby, CA5 1HH (059 681) 566 — ★★ [C] [R]

Family run country house hotel set in 20 acres of gardens and woodlands.
Closed Xmas–21 Feb.
13 bedrs, 13 en suite; TV; tcf
dogs; P 25; child facs
LD 8.30, nr lunch. Resid & Rest lic
£ B&B £31, B&B (double) £52; HB weekly £230; D £15; WB £70 (2 nts)
cc Access, B'card/Visa; dep.

Ravenstone (Highly Acclaimed), CA12 4QG (059 681) 240. *Hotel. Billiards.*
£ B&B £22–£25.

BATH
Avon. Map 4C4

See also FARMBOROUGH, HINTON CHARTERHOUSE and LIMPLEY STOKE
Pop 85,000. M4 (jn 18) 9, London 104, Bristol 12, Chippenham 13, Chepstow 25, Devizes 19, Frome 13, Radstock 8½, Tetbury 23, Warminster 16, Wells 19. See Plan p. 122.
MD Mon, Wed. **P** See Plan. **Golf** Sham Castle 18h, Lansdown 18h, Entry Hill 9h.
See Abbey Church, 18th cent Pump Room and Hot Springs, Roman Baths, Assembly Rooms and Museum of Costume, Guildhall, Victoria Art Gallery, Prior Park College, Royal Crescent (No 1 viewable), Pulteney Bridge, Holbourne of Menstrie Museum, The American Museum in Britain (Claverton Manor) 2 m E, Herschel House & Museum.
[i] Abbey Church Yard. (0225) 462831

★★★★★ **Bath Spa**, Sydney Rd, BA2 6JF (0225) 444424
An immaculately restored 19th century mansion which has the atmosphere of a country house yet is only a short distance from the city centre. Indoor swimming pool, sauna, solarium, gymnasium. (THF)
102 bedrs, 102 en suite; TV

★★★★ **Francis,** Queen Sq, BA1 2HH (0225) 424257 Tx: 449162
Fax: (0225) 319715
Traditional hotel built of Bath stone. Looking on to Queen Square. (THF) Fr, It
94 bedrs, 94 en suite; TV; tcf
lift, dogs, ns; P 35, coach; child facs; con 80
LD 10
£ B&B £84–£89, B&B (double) £119–£124; L £12·50, D £12·50; WB £52
cc Access, Amex, B'card/Visa, Diners; dep.

Atlas Section
Consult the Atlas section at the back of the guide to find out which towns and villages have RAC Appointed and Listed hotels in them. They are shown on the maps by purple circles.

★★★★**Hilton National,** Walcot St, BA1 5BJ (0225) 463411 Tx: 449519
Fax: (0225) 464393

Large purpose-built hotel offering modern accommodation. Near to city centre. Swimming pool, sauna, gymnasium. (HN)
150 bedrs, 150 en suite; TV; tcf
lift, dogs, ns; coach; child facs; con 240
LD 10
£ B&B £82·85–£98·95 (w/e £45); B&B (double) £102·95–£128·95; L £9·50, D £14·75; WB £45; [5% V]
cc Access, Amex, B'card/Visa, CB, Diners.

★★★★ [H] **Royal Crescent,** Royal Cres, BA1 2LS (0225) 319090 Tx: 444251
Fax: (0225) 339401

Luxuriously furnished hotel at centre of famous Georgian Royal Crescent. (QMH). Fr, Es
27 bedrs, 27 en suite; annexe 17 bedrs, 17 en suite; TV
lift; G 10 (£4), coach; child facs; con 40
LD 9.30
£ B&B $99–£105, B&B (double) £130–£195; L £21, D £33. [10% V]
cc Access, Amex, B'card/Visa, Diners; dep.

★★★ **Dukes,** Great Pulteney St, BA2 4DN (0225) 463512 Tx: 449227
Four-storey gracious Georgian town house in a wide boulevard in city centre. Fr
22 bedrs, 20 en suite, 1 ba; TV; tcf
dogs, ns; child facs; con 20
LD 8.30, bar meals only lunch
£ B&B £50–£60, B&B (double) £65–£95; D £15; WB £85
cc Access, Amex, B'card/Visa.

★★★ [H] [C] [R] **Lansdown Grove,** Lansdown Rd, BA1 5EH (0225) 315891
Tx: 444850 Fax: (0225) 448092

Elegant Georgian hotel set in own grounds on hilltop overlooking city. Fr, It
45 bedrs, 45 en suite; TV; tcf
lift, dogs, ns; P 38, G 4, coach; child facs; con 100
LD 9.30
£ B&B £54–£58, B&B (double) £80–£90; L £8·75; D £16; WB £46. [10% V]
cc Access, Amex, B'card/Visa, CB, Diners.

★★★ **Pratt's,** South Par, BA2 2AB (0225) 460441 Tx: 444827
Fax: (0225) 448807

Georgian stone terrace hotel in quiet area. Once home of Sir Walter Scott. Fr
46 bedrs, 46 en suite; TV; tcf
lift, dogs, ns; coach; child facs; con 50
LD 9.30
£ B&B £50–£55, B&B (double) £70–£77; D £13·75. [10% V]
cc Access, Amex, B'card/Visa, Diners.

★★★ **Priory,** Weston Rd, BA1 2XT (0225) 331922
Tx: 44612
Fax: (0225) 448276

Georgian building of Bath stone in country house style. Lovely garden. Swimming pool.
21 bedrs, 21 en suite; TV
ns; P 24, G 1, child facs; con 15
LD 9.15
£ B&B £85, B&B (double) £120; L £18, D £27·50
cc Access, Amex, B'card/Visa, Diners, dep.

Discount vouchers
RAC discount vouchers are on p. 34. Hotels with a [V] shown at the end of the price information will accept them in part payment for accommodation bills on the full, standard rate, not against bargain breaks or any other special offers. Please note the limitations shown in the entry: w/e for weekends, w/d for weekdays, and which months they are accepted.

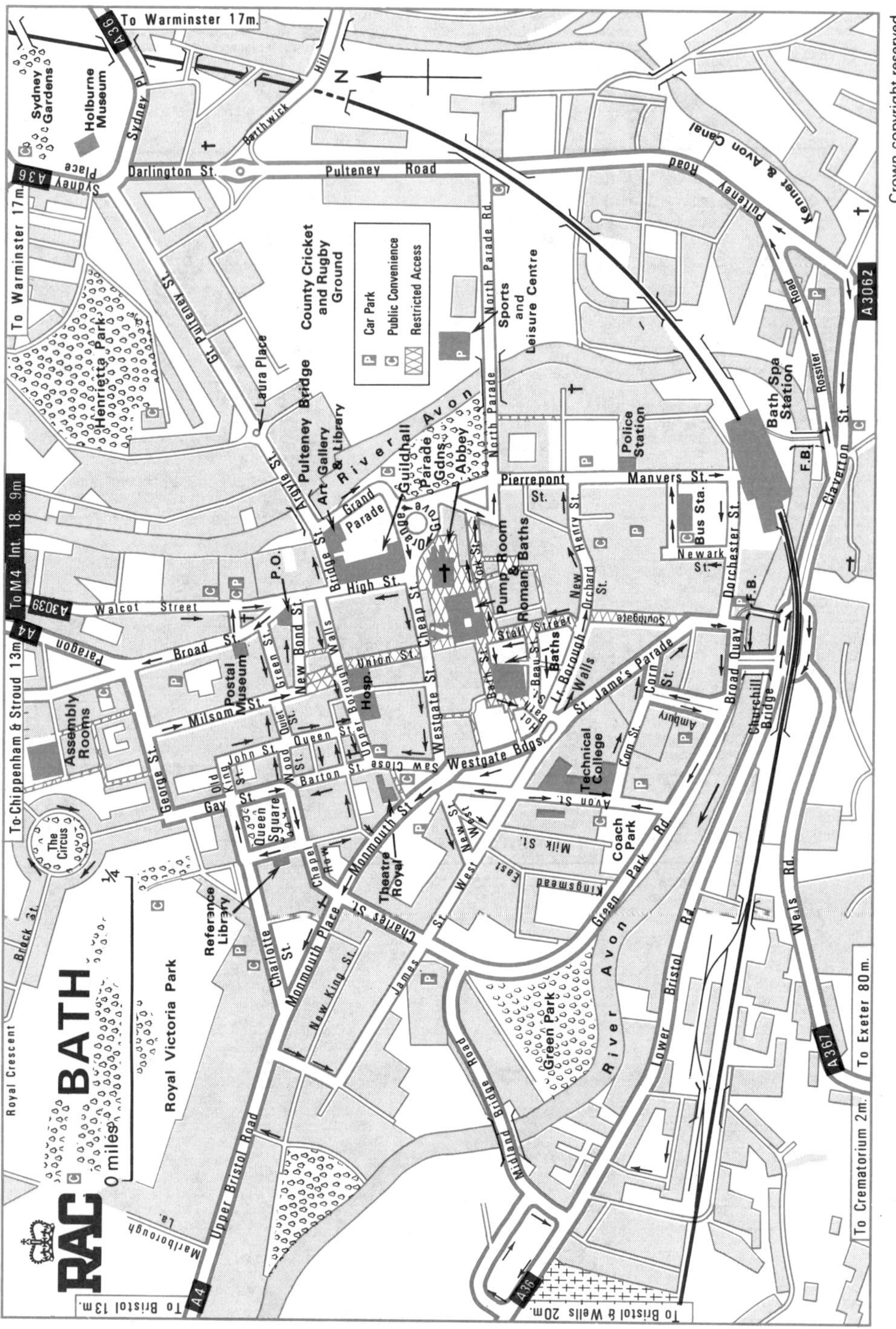

EC *early closing* **MD** *market day* ♣♣ *country house hotel* *ns (NS) no smoking areas* *tcf tea/coffee facilities*

★★★ **Redcar,** Henrietta St, BA2 6LR
☎(0225) 469151 Tx: 444842
Fax: (0225) 461424

Bath-stone terrace hotel in quiet area. Easy walk to town centre. ✂ Fr (MtCh]
🛏 31 bedrs, 22 en suite, (4 sh), 1 ba; TV; tcf
🏨 dogs; P 18, coach; child facs; con 100
✕ LD 10, bar meals only Mon–Sat lunch
£ B&B £66·96 (w/e £35), B&B (double) £85; D £14·50; WB £46; [10% V w/d]

★★ **Bailbrook Lodge**, 35–37 London Rd West, BA1 7HZ ☎ (0225) 859090
Bath-stone Georgian residence on A4, 1 mile east of Bath. Pleasantly furnished, with some antiques, and set in lovely gardens adjoining the grounds of Bailbrook House.
🛏 13 bedrs, 13 en suite; TV; tcf
🏨 TV, ns; P 13; child facs; con 24
✕ LD 8.30, nr lunch
£ B&B £30–£40, B&B (double) £40–£60; HB weekly £280–£490
cc Access, Amex, B'card/Visa, Diners; dep.
(*See advertisement on p. 124*)

★★ **Berni Royal,** Manvers St, BA1 1JP
☎ (0225) 463134

Four-storey Victorian building close to city centre and railway station. (BCB)
🛏 30 bedrs, 30 en suite; TV; tcf
🏨 lift, ns; coach; child facs
✕ LD 10.30
£ B&B £54–£63·50, B&B (double) £70; L £8·15, D £8·15; WB £27·50
cc Access, Amex, B'card/Visa, Diners.

★★ **Compass,** North Parade, BA1 1LG
☎(0225) 461603 Tx: 44812
Fax: (0225) 447758
Recently refurbished classical Georgian building in centre of Bath. Awaiting reclassification. ✂ Fr, De
🛏 54 bedrs, 54 en suite; TV; tcf
🏨 lift, dogs, ns; coach; child facs; con 40
✕ LD 9.15
£ B&B £65–£75; B&B (double) £75–£90; L £9·50, D £11·50; WB fr £87·50 (2 nts). [10% V]
cc Access, Amex, B'card/Visa, Diners.

★★ **Gainsborough,** Weston La, BA1 4AB
☎ (0225) 311380

In a residential area about a mile from the city centre, this mellow Bath stone Victorian house has a large, attractive garden.
Closed 24 Dec–4 Jan
🛏 16 bedrs, 16 en suite; TV; tcf
🏨 P 18; child facs
✕ LD 8.15, nr lunch, Resid & Rest lic
£ B&B £28–£35, B&B (double) £52–£66; D £10·50; WB
cc Access, Amex, B'card/Visa; dep.
(*See advertisement on p. 119*)

★★ **H** **Harington's,** 9 Queen St, BA1 1HE
☎(0225) 461728
A friendly, family-run hotel in an 18th-century, Bath-stone terrace in the city centre. ✂ Fr, De
🛏 12 bedrs, 10 en suite, 3 ba; TV; tcf
🏨 Coach; child facs; con 20
✕ LD 11 Resid & Rest lic
£ B&B £24–£28, B&B (double) £34–£40; L £3·95, D £5·95
cc Access, Amex, B'card/Visa; dep.

★★ **Old Mill,** Toll Bridge Rd, BA1 7DE (3 m NE A4) ☎(0225) 858476

Small riverside hotel in attractive surroundings. Off A4 in outskirts.
🛏 15 bedrs, 14 en suite, 2 ba; TV; tcf
🏨 P 30, coach; child facs; con 100

★ **Ashley Villa,** 26 Newbridge Rd, BA1 3TZ ☎(0225) 421683

Small villa hotel run by the proprietor. Off the A4. Swimming pool.
🛏 14 bedrs, 14 en suite; TV; tcf
🏨 TV, dogs, ns; P 10, coach; child facs
✕ Breakfast only. Resid lic
£ B&B £35–£40, B&B (double) £45–£60; [5% V]
cc B'card/Visa.

Bath Lodge (Highly Acclaimed), Norton St Philip, BA3 6NH ☎(0225 72) 3737.
Fax: (0225 72) 3193 *Hotel.*
£ B&B £65.
Brompton House (Highly Acclaimed), St Johns Rd, BA2 6PT ☎ (0225) 420972.
Closed 24–31 Dec. ✂ Fr, Es, It. ♿
£ B&B £30–£35.
Cheriton House (Highly Acclaimed), 9 Upper Oldfield Park, BA2 3JX ☎(0225) 429862. *Guest House.*
£ B&B £32–£35; [10% V].
Dorian House (Highly Acclaimed), 1 Upper Oldfield Pk, BA2 3JX ☎(0225) 426336.
Guest House. ✂ Fr
£ B&B £29–£35. [5% V]
Eagle House (Highly Acclaimed), Church St, Bathford BA1 7RS ☎(0225) 859946.
Hotel. ✂ Fr, De. Closed 21 Dec–5 Jan.
£ B&B £26·50–£34·50; [5% V]
Highways House (Highly Acclaimed), 143 Wells Rd, BA2 3AL ☎(0225) 421238. *Guest House.* Closed 24–28 Dec.
£ B&B £28–£36
Leighton House (Highly Acclaimed), 139 Wells Rd, BA2 3AL ☎(0225) 314769. *Guest House.*
Lord Nelson (Highly Acclaimed), Marshfield, SN14 8LP ☎(0225) 891820. *Inn.* ✂ Fr.
£ B&B £42; [5% V w/d].
Oakleigh House (Highly Acclaimed), 19 Upper Oldfield Pk, BA2 3JX ☎(0225) 315698. *Guest House.*
£ B&B £30–£45.
Orchard House (Highly Acclaimed), Warminster Rd, Bathampton, BA2 6XG ☎(0225) 466115. *Private Hotel. Sauna, solarium.*
£ B&B £41–£45; HB weekly £280. [5% V]
Bath Tasburgh (Highly Acclaimed), Warminster Rd, Bathampton, BA2 6SH ☎(0225) 425096. *Hotel.* Closed Xmas. ✂ It

---

Dorset Villa (Acclaimed), 14 Newbridge Rd, BA1 3JZ ☎(0225) 425975. *Guest House.*
£ B&B £26–£31; [10% V].
Kennard (Acclaimed), 11 Henrietta St, BA2 6LL
☎(0225) 310472 Fax: (0225) 442456.
Private Hotel.
£ B&B £25–£30.
Oldfields (Acclaimed), 102 Wells Road, BA2 3AL ☎(0225) 317984. *Guest House.* ✂ Fr.
£ B&B 125–£40.
Villa Magdala (Acclaimed), Henrietta Rd, BA2 6LX ☎(0225) 466329. *Guest House.*
£ B&B £50–£65
Wentworth House, (Acclaimed), 106 Bloomfield Rd, BA2 2AP ☎(0225) 339193.
Private Hotel. Swimming pool. Closed Xmas.
£ B&B £21–£30.

Arden, 73 Gt Pulteney St, BA2 4DL
☎(0225) 466601 Fax: (0225) 465548.
£ B&B £45–£55·60.
Arney, 99 Wells Rd, BA 2 3AN ☎(0225) 310020. *Guest House.*
Avon, Bathwick St, BA2 6NX
☎(0225) 446176 Fax: (0225) 447452. *Hotel.* ✂Fr, Es
£ B&B £35–£45; [5% V].
Cedar Lodge, 13 Lambridge, BA1 6BJ
☎(0225) 423468. Closed Xmas.
£ B&B 125.
Chequers, 50 Rivers St, BA1 2QA ☎(0225) 424246. *Inn.*
£ B&B £17·50–£19·50; [10% V].

Bath (Avon)

STREETS HOTEL

The Street, Farmborough, Nr Bath, BA3 1AR Telephone: 0761 71452

16th Century Hotel in picturesque village. 7 miles from Bath; 8 miles from Bristol; 10 miles from Wells

Bath (Avon)

The Rudloe Park Hotel & Restaurant

Leafy Lane, Corsham, Wiltshire Tel: 0225 810555

(On A4, half way between Bath & Chippenham). This Victorian Mansion, set in 4 acres of gardens, offers good fresh food with a vast choice of wines & drinks. A multi-award winning Hotel.

Bath (Avon)

Bailbrook Lodge Hotel

35/37 London Road West, Bath, BA1 7HZ
Telephone: (0225) 859090

A Georgian residence, 7 miles from the M4. Tastefully furnished accommodation. £40 per double room B&B to £60 in Regency four poster rooms.

Bath (Avon)

Hunstrete House

A classical English Country House Hotel set in its own 92 acre Deer Park, within 8 miles of Bristol and the elegance of Bath. All rooms enjoy a luxurious and individual style. Highly acclaimed award winning cuisine and extensive wine list have won The Terrace Restaurant an international reputation.

Hunstrete, Chelwood, Nr Bristol, Avon BS18 4NS
Telephone: 0761 490490 Fax: 0761 490732

Clipper Hotels

Enjoy standards you had forgotten existed

Bath (Avon)

LIMPLEY STOKE HOTEL

Lower Limpley Stoke, Bath BA3 6HZ
Tel: (0225) 723333 Fax: (0225) 722406

Delightful tranquil setting overlooking Avon Valley. Spacious lounges, bar, restaurant, billiard room. Large car park.
All rooms en-suite with TV, radio, telephone, tea & coffee. Family rooms available.
Rates from £49.50 single or £62.50 twin or double include English breakfast, service and VAT. Special rates for short breaks including dinner.

ETB 4 Crowns RAC ★★

Belford (Northumberland)

THE BLUE BELL HOTEL

Market Place, Belford
Tel: 0668 213543

Peaceful location. Perfect for heritage region. Internationally recommended providing comfort, style, good food and service for discerning guests.

RAC ★★★

County, 18 Pulteney Rd, BA2 4E2
☎(0225) 425003. *Hotel.*
£ B&B £42·50–£47·50.
Edgar, 64 Gt Pulteney St, BA2 4DN
☎(0225) 420619. *Private Hotel.*
Grove Lodge, 11 Lambridge, London Rd, BA1 6BJ ☎(0225) 310860. *Guest House.*
£ B&B £22–£25; [10% V].
Hotel St Clair, 1 Crescent Gds, Upper Bristol Rd, BA1 2NA ☎(0225) 425543. *Private Hotel.*
£ B&B £18–£24; HB weekly £91–£133.
Lynwood, 6 Pulteney Gdns, BA2 4HG
☎(0225) 426410. *Guest House.*
£ B&B £19·50.
Millers, 69 Gt Pulteney St, BA2 4DL
☎(0225) 465798. *Private Hotel.*
£ B&B £22–£24.
Oxford, 5 Oxford Row, Lansdown Rd, BA1 2QN ☎(0225) 314039. *Private Hotel.*
Tacoma, 159 Newbridge Hill, BA1 3PX
☎(0225) 310197. *Guest House.*
£ B&B £15·50–£17.
Waltons, 17 Crescent Gardens, Upper Bristol Rd, BA1 2NA ☎(0225) 426528. *Guest House.*

BATLEY West Yorkshire. Map 40C3

Pop 41,373. M62 (jn 27) 2, Dewsbury 2, London 189, Bradford 7½, Halifax 11, Huddersfield 9, Leeds 7.
EC Tue. **MD** Fri, Sat. **Golf** Howley Hall 18h. **See** Ancient Church, Oakwell Hall, Bagshaw Museum.

★★ **Alder House,** Towngate Rd, Healey La, WF17 7HR ☎(0924) 444777
Fax: (0484) 442644.
Handsome Georgian house quietly set in 2½ acres of garden on hill above town. ⚒ Fr
🛏 22 bedrs, 20 en suite, 2 ba; TV; tcf
🏠 TV, dogs; P 52, coach; child facs; con 80
✕ LD 9.30, bar meals only Sat lunch, Sun dinner. Resid lic
£ B&B £32–£47 (w/e £21), B&B (double) £58–£60; L £6·25, D £10·95; WB £21
cc Access, Amex, B'card/Visa.

BATTLE East Sussex. Map 7A2

Pop 5,000. Hurst Green 7½, London 57, Eastbourne 15, Hastings 6½, Lewes 24, Tenterden 18, Uckfield 20.
EC Wed. **MD** Fri. **Golf** Beauport Park 18h. **See** Abbey ruins, 15th cent Pilgrim's Rest, St Mary's Church, The Deanery, Bullring, Windmill, Langton House Museum.
ⓘ 88 High Street. ☎(042 46) 3721

♣♣ ★★★ **Burnt Wood,** Powdermill La, TN33 0SU ☎(042 46) 5151
Fax: (042 46) 2459
Red-brick Edwardian house in 18 acres of grounds 1½ miles west of Battle. Swimming pool, tennis, fishing, riding. ⚒ Fr
🛏 10 bedrs, 10 en suite; TV; tcf
🏠 dogs, ns; P 35, coach; child facs
✕ LD 10
£ B&B £45–£50, B&B (double) £60–£75; HB weekly £260–£300; L £11·50, D £16·25; WB £80
cc Access, Amex, B'card/Visa, Diners; dep.

Residents only
Some Listed hotels only serve meals to residents. It is always wise to make a reservation for a meal in a hotel.

♣♣ ★★★ **Netherfield Place,** Netherfield, TN33 9PP (4 miles NW on B2096)
☎(042 46) 4455
Tx: 95284
Fax: (042 46) 4024

Attractive 3-storey brick-built Georgian style manor in gardens and parkland. Tennis.
Closed 23 Dec–14 Jan. ⚒ Fr
🛏 14 bedrs, 14 en suite; TV
🏠 P 30, G 1; child facs; con 24
✕ LD 9.30
£ B&B £45, B&B (double) £75–£100; L £12·50, D £16·95; WB £110 (2 nts); [10% V]
cc Access, Amex, B'card/Visa, Diners.

★★ **George,** 23 High St, TN33 0EA
☎(042 46) 4466 Fax: (042 46) 4853

Privately-run historic coaching inn in town centre.
🛏 22 bedrs, 22 en suite; TV, tcf
🏠 dogs; P 30, coach; child facs; con 20
✕ LD 9.30
£ B&B (double) £42–£56; HB weekly £250; L £7·25, D £11·75; WB £45 (2 nts); [10% V]
cc Access, Amex, B'card/Visa, Diners; dep.

★★ **R** **La Vieille Auberge,** 27 High St, TN33 0EA ☎(042 46) 5171 Fax: (042 46) 4015
Enthusiastically run, small hotel in an attractive 17th-century stone building. ⚒ Fr
🛏 7 bedrs, 5 en suite, 1 ba; TV; tcf
🏠 con 14
✕ LD 10. Resid & Rest lic
£ B&B £29·50–£45, B&B (double) £45–£55; L £12·50, D £16; WB £80; [10% V]
cc Access, Amex, B'card/Visa; dep.

★★ **Abbey,** 84 High St, TN33 0AR
☎(042 46) 2755
Recently refurbished inn situated in town centre with garden behind.
🛏 8 bedrs, 8 en suite; TV; tcf
🏠 dogs; coach; child facs
✕ LD 10
£ B&B £34·50, B&B (double) £48·50; L £6·50, D £6·50; WB £62·50 (HB 2 nts); [10% V]
cc Access, B'card/Visa.

Little Hemingfold (Acclaimed), Telham, TN33 0TT ☎(042 46) 4338. *Farmhouse. Tennis, fishing.* ⚒ Fr
£ B&B £25–£30; HB weekly £244–£297.

BAWTRY South Yorkshire. Map 31A4

Pop 2,820. A1(M) 3½, London 155, Doncaster 9, Gainsborough 12, Rotherham 15, Thorne 13, Worksop 10.
EC Thur. **Golf** Doncaster 18h. **See** Georgian shops, old coaching inns.

★★★ **Crown,** Market Pl, DN10 6JW
☎Doncaster (0302) 710341 Tx: 547089
Fax: (0302) 711798

18th century posting inn with fine antiques and modern amenities. (THF)
🛏 57 bedrs, 57 en suite; TV; tcf
🏠 dogs, ns; P 50, coach; child facs; con 130
✕ LD 9.30, bar meals only Sat lunch
£ L £8·95, D £14; WB £37 (HB)
cc Access, Amex, B'card/Visa.

BEACONSFIELD Buckinghamshire. Map 13A4

Pop 11,300. M40 (jn 2) 1, London 24, Aylesbury 20, Henley-on-Thames 16, High Wycombe 6, Reading 21, Slough 7½.
EC Wed. **Golf** Beaconsfield 18h. **See** Church, The Old Rectory, Bekonscot Model Village.

★★★ **Bell House,** Oxford Rd, HP9 2XE
☎Gerrards Cross (0753) 887211
Tx: 848719 Fax: (0753) 888231

Modern low-built hotel set in peaceful countryside. Swimming pool, squash, sauna, solarium, gymnasium, billiards. (DeV) ⚒ Fr, De, It, Po, Gr
🛏 136 bedrs, 136 en suite; TV; tcf
🏠 lift, dogs, ns; P 400, coach; child facs; con 475
✕ LD 9.45
£ B&B £95–£105 (w/e £45), B&B (double) £135–£145; L £16, D £19·50
cc Access, Amex, B'card/Visa, CB, Diners.

★★ **White Hart Osprey,** Aylesbury End, HP9 1LW ☎(049 46) 71211 Tx: 837882
Attractive former coaching inn with modern extension. In town centre.

BEADLOW Bedfordshire. Map 14C4

Luton 12, London 43, Bedford 10, Bishop's Stortford 32.

★★ **Beadlow Manor,** SG17 5PH ☎(0525) 60800
Single storey extension to a golf and country club. Bars and restaurant in the club. Golf, putting, sauna, solarium, gymnasium.

BEAFORD Devon. Map 3B3

Pop 365. South Molton 18, London 199, Barnstaple 16, Bideford 12, Crediton 22, Okehampton 14.
EC Wed. **Golf** Torrington 9h. **See** Arts Centre, Green Warren House (Dartington Trust).

Beaford House, Winkleigh, EX19 8AB ☎(080 53) 305. *Private Hotel. Swimming pool, putting, tennis.*

BEANACRE Wiltshire Map 5A3

Chippenham 5, M4 (jn 17) 9, London 96, Bath 14, Devizes 9½, Melksham 2.

♣ ★★★ **H** **C** **R** **Beechfield House,** Nr Melksham, SN12 7PU ☎(0225) 703700
Fax: (0225) 790118 ♿

Fine Victorian house of ornate Bath stone in attractive gardens. Swimming pool, tennis, fishing. ⚒ Fr, Es.
🛏 16 bedrs, 16 en suite; annexe 8 bedrs, 8 en suite; TV
🏨 ns; P 50, coach; child facs; con 60
✕ LD 9.30; nr Sat lunch
£ B&B £78·50–£89·50, B&B (double) £103–£118; L £14·50, D £27·50; WB £115 (2 nts HB); [10% V w/d]
cc Access, Amex, B'card/Visa, Diners.

BEBINGTON Merseyside. Map 32A1

Pop 62,000. Chester 13, London 195, M53 (jn 4) 2, Bromborough 2, Birkenhead 3.
EC Wed. **Golf** Brackenwood 9h. **See** Garden village of Port Sunlight, Lady Lever Art Gallery.

★★ **Famous Old Bridge Inn,** Bolton Road, Port Sunlight Village, L62 4UQ
☎051-645 8441
Modern hotel in the style of an old coaching inn in the centre of the village. ⚒ Fr, De, It
🛏 16 bedrs, 16 en suite; TV; tcf
🏨 P 60, coach; child facs; con 100
✕ LD 10, nr Sat lunch
£ B&B £39·50 (w/e £22), B&B (double) £52·50; L £8·50, D £8·50; [10% V]
cc Access, Amex, B'card/Visa, Diners.

BECCLES Suffolk. Map 27C4

Pop 8,903. London 114, Great Yarmouth 14, Lowestoft 9½, Norwich 17, Scole 20.
EC Wed. **MD** Fri. **Golf** Beccles 9h. **See** Fine Perp Church with detached tower.
ⓘ The Quay, Fen La. ☎(0502) 713196

★★ **King's Head,** New Market, NR34 9HA ☎(0502) 712147

Traditional town centre hotel in market place.
🛏 12 bedrs, 12 en suite; TV; tcf
🏨 ns; P 18, coach; child facs; con 80
✕ LD 10
£ B&B £36·50–£41, B&B (double) £47·50; L £8, D £9; WB
cc Access, Amex, B'card/Visa, Diners.

★★ **Waveney House,** Puddingmoor, NR34 9PL ☎(0502) 712270
Listed building, delightfully located on banks of river with gardens. Fishing. ⚒ Fr, De
🛏 13 bedrs, 11 en suite (2 sh), 1 ba; TV; tcf
🏨 TV, dogs; P 80, coach; child facs; con 130
✕ LD 9.30
£ B&B £40, B&B (double) £50; HB weekly £280; L £9·60, D £11; WB £60
cc Access, Amex, B'card/Visa, CB, Diners; dep.

BECKERMET Cumbria. Map 43B1

Pop 4,022. Broughton-in-Furness 28, London 305, Egremont 3.
Golf Seascale 18h. **See** St Bridget's Church.

Royal Oak, CA21 2XB ☎(0946 84) 551. *Hotel.*
£ B&B £27·50 (w/e £14·50)

BEDFORD Bedfordshire. Map 26A3

Pop 74,000. Luton 19, London 50, M1 (jn 13) 10, Aylesbury 30, Biggleswade 11, Bletchley 16, Cambridge 30, Dunstable 19, Huntingdon 21, Northampton 22.
EC Thur. **MD** Wed, Sat. **Golf** Bedfordshire 18h, Bedford and County 18h. **See** Higgins Art Gallery, Museum, Bedford School, Churches, Bunyan Museum.
ⓘ St Paul's Sq. ☎(0234) 215226

★★★ **Barns,** Cardington Rd, MK44 3SA ☎(0234) 270044 Tx: 827748
Fax: (0234) 273102 ♿
Hotel developed from a 17th century manor house with extensions and an impressive 13th century tithe barn, overlooking the Great Ouse River. Sauna, solarium, gymnasium. (Lns). ⚒ De
🛏 49 bedrs, 49 en suite; TV; tcf
🏨 ns; P 120, coach; child facs; con 120
✕ LD 10, bar meals only Sat lunch
£ B&B £70, B&B (double) £82; L £11, D £15; WB £32; [10% V]
cc Access, Amex, B'card/Visa, Diners.

★★★ **Bedford Moat House,** St Mary's St, MK42 0AR ☎(0234) 55131 Tx: 825243
Fax: (0234) 40447 ♿

Modern hotel on banks of river; overlooking market square. Sauna. (QMH)
🛏 100 bedrs, 100 en suite; TV; tcf
🏨 lift, TV; P 72, coach; child facs; con 350
✕ LD 9.45
£ B&B £68 (w/e £32·50), B&B (double) £82·50 (w/e £49·74); L £12·50, D £14; WB £76
cc Access, Amex, B'card/Visa, Diners.

★★★ **Bedford Swan,** The Embankment, MK40 1RW ☎(0234) 46565 Tx: 827779
Historic hotel standing on riverside; near town centre. Indoor swimming pool. ⚒ De
🛏 122 bedrs, 122 en suite; TV; tcf
🏨 lift, dogs; P 90, coach; child facs; con 250
✕ LD 9.30
£ B&B £59–£65, B&B (double) £69 (w/e £40); L £9·85, D £9·85; WB £42; [10% V]
cc Access, Amex, B'card/Visa, Diners.

♣ ★★★ **H** **C** **Woodlands Manor,** Green La, Clapham, MK41 6EP
☎(0234) 63281 Tx: 825007
Fax: (0234) 272390

Late Victorian manor house in several acres of woods and gardens, 2½ miles N of town.
🛏 26 bedrs, 26 en suite; TV
🏨 P 100, coach; no children under 7; con 60
✕ LD 9.45
£ B&B £79–£85 (w/e £34), B&B (double) £79–£90; L £17·90, D £21; WB £82·50 (2 nts)
cc Access, Amex, B'card/Visa.

★★ **R** **Knife & Cleaver,** The Grove, Houghton Conquest, MK45 3LA ☎(0234) 740387 Fax: (0234) 740900
A country inn with a charming conservatory restaurant and bedrooms in a modern bungalow extension.
🛏 9 bedrs, 9 en suite; TV; tcf
🏨 dogs; P 40, coach; child facs; con 12
✕ LD 9.30, nr Sun dinner
£ B&B £44–£55, B&B (double) £57–£71;

HB weekly £420–£490; L £15, D £18
cc Access, Amex, B'card/Visa.

★★ **Queens Head,** 2 Rushden Rd, Milton Ernest, MK44 1RU ☎(0234) 272822
Fax: (023 02) 2337
Modernised and extended village inn on the A6, 5 miles north of city.
🛏 12 bedrs, 12 en suite; TV; tcf
🏠 P 30, coach; child facs, con 12
✕ LD 10, bar meals only Sun lunch
£ B&B £50 (w/e £35·40), B&B (double) £65·70; L £9, D £14·50; WB £60·70; [10% V]
cc Access, Amex, B'card/Visa.

★ **Embankment,** The Embankment, MK40 3PD ☎(0234) 261332 Tx: 82425
Fax: (0908) 690274
Victorian residence in mock Tudor style in residential suburbs overlooking river.
🛏 20 bedrs, 17 en suite; TV; tcf
🏠 dogs, ns; P 20; child facs

Linden View (Acclaimed), 16 Linden Rd, MK40 2DA ☎(0234) 52795. *Hotel.*

Kimbolton, 78 Clapham Rd, MK41 7PN ☎(0234) 54854. Closed 25–31 Dec
£ B&B £36·80–£39·10.

BEESTON Cheshire. Map 29B3

Pop 221. Nantwich 11, London 173, Chester 13, Middlewich 14, Northwich 13, Warrington 20, Whitchurch 9, Wrexham 17.
Golf Hill Valley 18h. **See** Castle ruins.

★★★ H C **Wild Boar,** CW6 9NW ☎(0829) 260309 Tx: 61222
Fax: (0829) 261081 ♿

Black and white timbered building with chalet bedrooms alongside. ✂ Fr, De, Es, Pl.
🛏 37 bedrs, 37 en suite; TV; tcf
🏠 TV, dogs; P 70, coach; child facs; con 50
✕ LD 10
£ B&B £50–£68, B&B (double) £65–£80; L £11, D £16·50; WB £60; [10% V]
cc Access, Amex, B'card/Visa, Diners.

BEESTON Nottinghamshire. Map 24C3

Pop 40,940. Long Eaton 3, London 124, M1 5, Ilkeston 5½, Nottingham 4.
MD Fri, Sat. **Golf** Bramcote Hills 18h, Chilwell Manor 18h. **See** St John's Church, Bramcote Hemlock Stone.

Brackley House, 31 Elm Av, NG9 1BU ☎Nottingham (0602) 251787. *Hotel.*

BEETHAM Cumbria. Map 36B4

Pop 1,657. London 247, M6 (jn 36) 5½, Ambleside 20, Kendal 8½, Kirkby Lonsdale 8½, Lancaster 12, Ulverston 23.
EC Sat. **Golf** Silverdale 9h. **See** Norman and EE Church, 14th–17th cent Beetham Hall, Fairy Steps (wooded ravine).

★ **Wheatsheaf,** A6 Road, LA7 7AL ☎(0539) 562123
Family-managed village inn in quiet area yet convenient for A6.
🛏 6 bedrs, 6 en suite, 1 ba; TV; tcf
🏠 TV, dogs; P 40, coach; child facs
✕ LD 8.30
£ B&B £27, B&B (double) £35; L £6, D £8; WB £42
cc Access, B/card/Visa.

BELFORD Northumberland. Map 51C2

Pop 460. Alnwick 15, London 322, Berwick-upon-Tweed 15, Coldstream 20.
EC Thur. **Golf** Bamburgh Castle 18h. **See** St Mary's Church.

★★★ C **Blue Bell,** Market Pl, NE70 7NE ☎(0668) 213543 Fax: (0668) 213787 ♿

Original coaching inn, modernised but retaining character; in centre of village.
🛏 15 bedrs, 15 en suite; annexe 2 bedrs, 2 en suite; TV; tcf
🏠 dogs, ns; P 10, G 2, coach; no children under 6
✕ LD 8.45
£ B&B £25–£40; HB weekly £245–£322; L £7, D £14·50; WB
cc Access, Amex, B'card/Visa, Diners; dep.
(*See advertisement on p. 124*)

♣ ★★★ **Waren House,** Waren Mill NE70 7EE ☎(066 84) 581 Fax: (066 84) 484 ♿

18th-century country house in 6 acres of wooded grounds on edge of Budle Bay. Two miles from A1. Tennis.
🛏 7 bedrs, 7 en suite; TV; tcf
🏠 ns; P 20; no children under 15
✕ LD 8.30; nr lunch
£ B&B £50–£70, B&B (double) £65–£95; HB weekly £225–£450; [10% V w/d Nov–Apr]
cc Access, Amex, B'card/Visa, Diners; dep.

BELLINGHAM Northumberland. Map 44B3

Pop 800. Corbridge 18, London 295, Brampton 33, Hawick 38, Newcastle upon Tyne 32.
EC Tue, Sat. **Golf** Bellingham 9h. See Kielder Forest and Water (largest reservoir in Britain).
ℹ Main St ☎ (0434) 220616

★★ H R **Riverdale Hall**, Hexham, NE48 2JT ☎(0434) 220254

Stone-built spacious 19th century mansion in 5 acres of grounds. Indoor swimming pool, putting, fishing, sauna. ✂ Fr, Da
🛏 20 bedrs, 20 en suite; TV; tcf
🏠 TV, dogs; P 50, coach; child facs; con 50
✕ LD 9.30
£ B&B £28–£34·50, B&B (double) £48–£58; HB weekly £225–£279; L £6·50, D £13·50; WB £34/£39 (2 nts)
cc Access, Amex, B'card/Visa, Diners; dep.

BERE FERRERS Devon Map 3A2

Tavistock 8, London 210, Liskeard 21, Plymouth 15.

Lanterna, Yelverton, PL20 7JL ☎Tavistock (0822) 840380. *Private Hotel.*
£ B&B £15·50–£18; HB weekly £123–£138.

BERKELEY Gloucestershire. Map 20B1

See also NEWPORT.
Pop 1,390. Tetbury 15, London 113, M5 (jn 14) 4, Bristol 20, Gloucester 16.
EC Wed. **Golf** Stinchcombe Hill 18h. **See** EE Parish Church (grave of Dr Jenner), Castle, Wildfowl Trust, Slimbridge 6 m NE.

★★ **Berkeley Arms,** GL13 9BG ☎Dursley (0453) 810291

Three-storey stone building—a former coaching inn of 15th century origins.
🛏 10 bedrs, 9 en suite, 1 ba; TV; tcf
🏠 dogs; P 20, coach; child facs; con 100
✕ LD 9.30
£ B&B £31, B&B (double) £42; HB weekly £280; L £9·95, D £9·95; WB £29; [10% V]
cc Access, Amex, B'card/Visa, CB, Diners; dep.

BERKELEY ROAD Gloucestershire. Map 20B1

2 m E of Berkeley. Tetbury 13, London 111, M5 (jn 14) 2.

★★ **Prince of Wales,** Berkeley Rd (A38) GL13 9HD ☎ Dursley (0453) 810474

Family-owned and run, mid-Victorian hotel on A38. Pleasant gardens.
🛏 10 bedrs, 8 en suite, 1 ba; TV; tcf
🏨 dogs; P 120, coach; child facs, con 120

BERKHAMSTED Hertfordshire. Map 14B2

Pop 15,549. Watford 11, London 27, Aylesbury 12, Dunstable 11, High Wycombe 15, St Albans 11.
EC Wed, Sat. **MD** Sat. **Golf** Berkhamsted 18h. **See** Castle ruins, St Peter's Church (Saxon doorway), 17th cent Almshouses, 15th cent house of Dean Incent (founder of Berkhamsted School), 16th cent Court House, Kings Arms.
ℹ Library, Kings Rd. ☎ (0442) 864545

★ **Swan Inn,** 129 High St, HP4 3HH ☎ (0442) 871451 Fax: (0442) 870885

Lovingly restored 15th century coaching inn retaining most of its originality.
🛏 17 bedrs, 17 en suite; TV; tcf
🏨 TV, dogs; P 9, coach
✕ LD 8.45, bar meals only Sun lunch, Fri–Sun dinner
£ B&B £40–£50 (w/e £25), B&B (double) £65–£75; L £2·50, D £5. [5% V]
cc Access, Amex, B'card/Visa.

BERWICK-UPON-TWEED Northumberland. Map 51B2

Pop 11,647. Alnwick 30, London 337, Coldstream 14, Haddington 39, Lauder 32.
EC Thur. **MD** Wed, Fri, Sat. **Golf** Berwick-on-Tweed 18h, Magdolene Fields 18h. **See** Elizabethan Ramparts, 18th cent Georgian Walls, Castle remains, 17th cent Jacobean Bridge and modern bridges.
ℹ Castlegate Car Park. ☎ (0289) 330733

En suite rooms
En suite rooms may be bath or shower rooms. If you have a preference, remember to state it when booking a room.

★★★ **King's Arms,** Hide Hill, TD15 1EJ ☎ (0289) 307454 Tx: 847938 Fax: (0289) 308867

Former Georgian coaching inn in traditional style, standing on main street.
🛏 36 bedrs, 36 en suite; TV; tcf
🏨 dogs; coach; child facs; con 160
✕ LD 10
£ B&B £42·50–£49·50, B&B (double) £64·50; L £4·85, D £15·50; WB £85 (2 nts)
cc Access, Amex, B'card/Visa, CB, Diners.

★★★ **Turret House,** Etal Rd, Tweedmouth, TD15 2EG ☎ (0289) 330808 Fax: (0289) 330467 ♿

Stone-built Victorian house, with modern extension, standing in its own wooded grounds on outskirts of town. Closed Jan.
🛏 13 bedrs, 13 en suite; TV; tcf
🏨 dogs; P 60; child facs; con 250
✕ LD 9
£ B&B £46·50; B&B (double) £63; HB weekly £290·50; D £14·50; WB £41·50 (HB). [5% V]
cc Access, Amex, B'card/Visa, Diners.

★ **Queen's Head,** Sandgate, TD15 1EP ☎ (0289) 307852

Town centre hotel converted from 2-storey stone-built terrace houses. Family-run.
🛏 6 bedrs, (6 sh), 1 ba; TV; tcf
🏨 TV, dogs; coach; child facs
✕ LD 8.30. Resid lic
£ B&B £19·50–£20; HB weekly £180; L £6·50, D £9·50. [5% V]
cc Access, B'card/Visa.

BEVERLEY Humberside (North Humberside). Map 39B3

Pop 17,180. Lincoln 46, London 179, Bridlington 22, Hull 8½, Malton 27, Market Weighton 10, Scarborough 33.
MD Wed, Sat. **Golf** Beverley and East Riding 18h. **See** Minster, 15th cent North Bar, Art Gallery and Museum, Market Cross.
ℹ Guildhall. ☎ Hull (0482) 867430

★★★ **Beverley Arms,** North Bar Within, HU17 8DD ☎ Hull (0482) 869241 Tx: 597568 Fax: (0482) 870907
Refurbished 18th century coaching inn situated in a quiet area. (THF)
🛏 57 bedrs, 57 en suite; TV; tcf
🏨 lift, dogs, ns; P 60, coach; child facs; con 60
✕ LD 9.30
£ room £65 (w/e £45), double room £80–£100; L £9·95, D £13·95; WB £45
cc Access, Amex, B'card/Visa, CB, Diners.

👥 ★★★ **Tickton Grange,** HU17 9SH ☎ Hornsea (0964) 543666 Tx: 527254 Fax: (0964) 542556
Georgian building—a country house in 4 acres of lawns and gardens. ⚒ Fr, De, Es
🛏 16 bedrs, 16 en suite; TV; tcf
🏨 dogs; P 65, coach; child facs; con 40
✕ LD 9.30
£ B&B £63 (w/e £32·50), B&B (double) £78 L £11·95, D £13·95. [10% V]
cc Access, Amex, B'card/Visa, Diners.

★★ **Lairgate,** 30 Lairgate, HU17 8EP ☎ Hull (0482) 882141
Stone-built Georgian listed building in narrow street in older part of town.

Manor House (Highly Acclaimed), Northlands, Walkington, HU17 8RT ☎ (0482) 881645 Fax: (0482) 866501. *Hotel.* ⚒ Fr
£ B&B £61·50–£81·50; [10% V].

BEWDLEY Hereford & Worcester (Worcestershire). Map 20B4

Pop 9,927. Kidderminster 3, London 126, Bridgnorth 15, Bromyard 19, Droitwich 13, Leominster 24, Ludlow 19, Worcester 15.
EC Wed. **MD** Tue, Sat. **Golf** Kidderminster 18h. **See** Forest of Wyre, St Anne's Church, old Tudor houses and inns, Georgian houses, fine bridge (1797, by Telford).
ℹ Library, Load St. ☎ (0299) 404740.

★★ **Black Boy,** 14 Kidderminster Rd, DY12 1AG ☎ (0299) 402119
A hotel of character (17th century inn) adjacent to River Severn. Closed Xmas Day.
🛏 17 bedrs, 5 en suite, (4 sh), 4 ba; annexe 8 bedrs, 2 en suite, (3 sh), 2 ba; TV; tcf
🏨 TV, dogs; P 30; child facs
✕ LD 9.30, nr Sun dinner
£ B&B £27·50–£41·80, B&B (double) £41·80–£59·40; L £7·50, D £9·75; WB £41·80 (2 nts)
cc Access, Amex, B'card/Visa.

★★ **George,** Load St, DY12 2AW ☎ (0299) 402117
Town centre coaching inn with attractive bow windows and a rear courtyard. ⚒ Fr
🛏 13 bedrs, 7 en suite, 2 ba; TV; tcf
🏨 dogs; P 60; child facs; con 60
✕ LD 10, bar meals only Sun & Mon dinner
£ B&B £22–£32, B&B (double) £35–£45; HB weekly £184–£245; L £5·50, D £10; WB £49·50. [5% V]
cc Access, Amex, B'card/Visa, Diners; dep.

BEXHILL-ON-SEA East Sussex. Map 7A1

See also COODEN BEACH
Pop 35,000. Hurst Green 14, London 64, Eastbourne 12, Hastings 5½, Lewes 23.

EC Wed. **Golf** Cooden Beach 18h. **See** St Peter's Church (1070), De La Warr Pavilion, Manor House Gardens (Old Town).
ℹ De La Warr Pavilion. ☎(0424) 212023

★★★ **Granville,** Sea Rd, TN40 1EE
☎(0424) 215437 Fax: (0424) 225028

Refurbished Victorian hotel with spacious public rooms and well-equipped bedrooms.
🛏 50 bedrs, 50 en suite; TV; tcf
🏨 lift, dogs; coach; child facs; con 150
✕ LD 9
£ B&B £39·50–£43·45, B&B (double) £59·50–£65·45; HB weekly £190–£275; L £7·50, D £11; WB £69·50 (2 nts). [10% V]
cc Access, Amex, B'card/Visa, Diners.

Dunselma, Marina, TN40 1BP ☎ (0424) 212988. *Hotel.*
Park Lodge, 16 Egerton Rd, TN39 3HH ☎(0424) 216547. *Hotel.*
Victoria, 1 Middlesex Rd, TN40 1LP ☎(0424) 210382. *Hotel.*

BEXLEY
Greater London (Kent). Map 9B2
London 15, Dartford 3½, Sidcup 2½.

★★★ **Crest,** The Black Prince, Southwold Rd, DA5 1ND ☎Crayford (0322) 526900 Tx: 8956539 Fax: (0322) 526113 ♿

Modern 3-storey motor hotel convenient for M2. Billiards. ⚒ Fr. (Cr/THF)
🛏 106 bedrs, 106 en suite; TV; tcf
🏨 lift, dogs, ns; P 130, coach; child facs; con 70
✕ LD 9.45, bar meals only Sat lunch
£ B&B £89·95–£102·95 (w/e £44), B&B (double) £110·95–£123·95; L £13, D £15·50. [10% V w/e]
cc Access, Amex, B'card/Visa, CB, Diners.

BIBURY
Gloucestershire. Map 20C2
Pop 568. Faringdon 14, London 84, Burford 10, Cirencester 7, Cheltenham 17, Stow-on-the-Wold 14.
EC Wed. **Golf** Cirencester 18h. **See** Interesting Church, Arlington Row (15th cent cottages), Arlington Mill Museum, picturesque old cottages, Wildfowl Reserve (Nat Trust), Trout Hatchery.

♣ ★★ R **Bibury Court,** GL7 5NT
☎(028 574) 337 Fax: (028 574) 660

Large 3-storey Jacobean country house of Cotswold stone. Fine gardens by River Coln. Fishing, squash. Closed 21–31 Dec. ⚒ Fr
🛏 18 bedrs, 18 en suite; TV
🏨 TV, dogs; P 100; child facs; con 20
✕ LD 9, bar meals only Mon–Sat lunch
£ B&B £45–£55, B&B (double) £60–£66; L £15, D £18; WB £90
cc Access, Amex, B'card/Visa, CB, Diners.

BICKLEY
Kent. Map 9A2
Bromley 1½, London 12, Bromley 2, Dartford 10, Orpington 5, Swanley 6½.

Glendevon House, 80 Southborough Rd, BR1 2EN ☎081-467 2183. *Guest House.*
£ B&B £18–£19·50; [10% V].

BIDEFORD
Devon. Map 3A4
Pop 12,210. Barnstaple 9, London 202, Bude 25, Holsworthy 18, Okehampton 26.
EC Wed. **MD** Tue. **Golf** Royal North Devon 18h. **See** Royal Hotel (assoc. with Kingsley), Kingsley Statue, Chudleigh Fort, Burton Art Gallery, St Mary's Church, Victoria Park (Armada guns).
ℹ The Quay. ☎(0237) 477676

★★★ C **Durrant House,** Heywood Rd, Northam, EX39 3QB ☎(0237) 472361
Purpose-built large hotel in own grounds. Within easy reach of coast. Swimming pool, sauna, solarium.
(See advertisement on p. 130)

♣ ★★★ **Portledge,** Fairy Cross, EX39 5BX (3½m W A39) ☎Horns Cross (023 75) 262 Telex: 9312132625 Fax: (023 75) 717 ♿

17th century country house in 60 acres of lovely parkland. Own private beach. Indoor swimming pool, putting, tennis. ⚒ De
🛏 26 bedrs, 26 en suite; annexe 9 bedrs, 9 en suite; TV; tcf
🏨 TV, dogs; P 100, coach; child facs; con 70
✕ LD 9.15
£ B&B £37–£62·50, B&B (double) £74–£105; D £18; WB £45–£50
cc Access, Amex, B'card/Visa, Diners; dep.

★★★ **Royal,** Barnstaple St, EX39 4AE
☎(0237) 472005 Tx: 42551 Fax: (0271) 78558

Refurbished Victorian building at East end of bridge. Charles Kingsley associations.
🛏 30 bedrs, 30 en suite; TV; tcf
🏨 dogs; P 60, coach; child facs; con 150
✕ LD 9
£ B&B £44–£50, B&B (double) £66–£77; HB weekly £245–£350; L £7·50, D £10; WB £75 (2 nts)
cc Access, Amex, B'card/Visa, Diners.
(See advertisement on p. 130)

★★ **Hoops Inn,** Horns Cross, EX39 5DL
☎(0237) 451222
Atmospheric old inn with thatched roof and white cob walls on A39 between Bideford and Clovelly in rural surroundings.
🛏 6 bedrs, 2 ba; annexe 8 bedrs, 8 en suite; TV; tcf
🏨 TV, dogs; P 50; no children under 6
✕ LD 9, bar meals only Mon–Sat lunch
£ B&B £25–£33, B&B (double) £40–£55; D £12·50; WB £45. [V w/d Oct–Mar]
cc Amex, B/card/Visa, Diners; dep.

♣ ★★ **Kenwith Castle,** Abbotsham, EX39 5BE ☎(0237) 473712

A neo-Gothic 'castle' added to an earlier manor house set in 9 acres of grounds with lake. Swimming pool, fishing, tennis, solarium.

★★ H **Riversford,** Limers La, EX39 2RG
☎(0237) 474239 Fax: (0237) 421661

Family-run hotel in 3 acres of secluded gardens sloping down to river. Putting, solarium. ⚒ Fr
🛏 16 bedrs, 13 en suite, (1 sh), 1 ba; TV; tcf
🏨 TV, dogs, ns; P 20, G 2, U 1, coach; child facs; con 50
✕ LD 9, bar meals only Mon–Sat lunch

Bexley (Kent)

BEXLEY MUSEUM

Hall Place, Bourne Road, Bexley, Kent.

Tel: 0322 526574

Historic house, permanent and temporary exhibitions. Open weekdays 10–5 (dusk in winter); Sundays (summer only) 2-6. Beautiful gardens open daily.

Bideford (North Devon)

Durrant House Hotel

Heywood Road, Northam, Bideford, North Devon EX39 3QB Tel: 0237 472361

Former Georgian residence now extended and modernised to provide the ultimate in comfort and a high standard of cuisine. Conveniently situated amidst the beauty of North Devon.

Bideford (North Devon)

The Royal Hotel

RAC★★★

OVERLOOKING THE HISTORIC PORT OF BIDEFORD

Enjoy the luxuries and comfort of this 3 star hotel, whilst savouring the first class cuisine and personal service of Bideford's traditional hotel. All rooms have private bathroom, colour T.V. and tea and coffee making facilities. Hotel facilities include spacious lounge bar and first class restaurant both offering À la Carte and Table d'hôte Menus. Open all year for accommodation and banquets.

For free colour brochure and tariff contact: The Manager, Mr. R. Maun, The Royal Hotel, Bideford, Devon. Tel: (0237) 472005 Fax No: (0271) 78558

Birmingham (West Midlands)

Midland Hotel, New Street,
Birmingham B2 4JT.
Tel: 021-643 2601 Telex: 338419
Fax: 021-643 5075
RAC ★★★★

Our four star luxury hotel enjoys an unrivalled situation in the centre of Birmingham, with road, rail and international air links only minutes away. We've 111 bedrooms, all with private en-suite bathroom, colour TV and 24 hour room service as well as a choice of four fully licensed bars in which to relax including the fashionable Burlingtons.

Our special weekend rates for overnight accommodation and breakfast, Friday, Saturday and Sunday starts from £45 per person per night. *Enjoy the Midland experience – whether you're wining, dining or staying overnight . . . We'll take better care of you.*

Birmingham (West Midlands)

Great Barr Hotel & Conference Centre

Peartree Drive, Newton Road, Great Barr, Birmingham B43 6HS

Telephone: 021-357 1141 Fax: 021-357 7557 Telex: 336406

114 Bedrooms all having en-suite facilities, colour television, radio, in-house video system, direct dial telephone & tea/coffee making facilities.

The Partridge Restaurant offers seasonal à la Carte and Table d'Hôte menus featuring fresh produce.

Conference and banqueting facilities for up to 120 guests, located in a peaceful suburb of Birmingham just 1 mile from junction 7 of the M6, the hotel is a convenient base for visitors to the NEC and the West Midlands.

£ B&B £24–£42, B&B (double) £64–£74; HB weekly £220–£310; L £7·70, D £16·80; WB £84 (2 nts). [10% V]
cc Access, Amex, B'card/Visa, Diners; dep.

★★ Sonnenheim, Heywood Rd, Northam, EX39 2QA ☎(023 72) 74989

Stone-built former private house in an acre of grounds just off A39, north of town.
🛏 9 bedrs, 9 en suite; TV; tcf

★★ Yeoldon House, Durrant La, Northam EX39 2RL ☎ (023 72) 74400
Georgian country residence in attractive grounds with panoramic view. Putting, sauna.
🛏 10 bedrs, 10 en suite; TV; tcf
🏠 dogs, ns; P 20, coach; child facs; con 80
✕ LD 8.30
£ B&B £40·75–£43·25; B&B (double) £75·50–£80; HB weekly £243–£258; L £10·75, D £20·75. [10% V]
cc Access, Amex, B'card/Visa, Diners; dep.

BIDFORD-ON-AVON Warwickshire. Map 20C3
Pop 3,196. Stratford-upon-Avon 7½, London 102, Birmingham 24, Bromsgrove 17, Droitwich 17, Evesham 7½.
Golf Stratford 18h. **See** 15th cent Bridge, 13th cent Church, Elizabethan house.

★★ H C White Lion, B50 4BQ ☎(0789) 773309 Fax: (0789) 490058

Pleasant country hotel on banks of the Avon in village centre. Fishing.
🛏 10 bedrs, 10 en suite, 2 ba; TV; tcf
🏠 dogs; P 16, coach; child facs; con 12

BIGBURY-ON-SEA Devon. Map 3B1
Pop 532. Ashburton 21, London 209, Kingsbridge 9, Plymouth 18, Totnes 18.
Golf Bigbury 18h. **See** Clematon Hill (Nat Trust), Burgh Island.

★ Henley, Folly Hill, TQ7 4AR ☎(0548) 810240

Small cliff-top hotel with terraced garden and steps to beach. Superb views over Bigbury Bay. Fr
🛏 8 bedrs, 6 en suite, 1 ba; TV; tcf
🏠 dogs, NS; P 8; child facs; con 12
✕ LD 9. Resid & Rest lic
£ B&B £16·65–£22·50; HB weekly £170·77–£214·75; L £4·90, D £11·50; WB £62 (2 nts). [10% V]
cc B'card/Visa; dep.

BILBROOK Somerset. Map 4A3
Williton 3, London 160, Minehead 5½.

★★ H C R Dragon House, Nr Washford TA24 6HQ ☎(0984) 40215
Privately-owned stone building with character. In the country house style.
🛏 8 bedrs, 8 en suite; annexe 2 bedrs, 2 en suite; TV; tcf
🏠 dogs; P 25; child facs
✕ LD 9.15. Resid & Rest lic
£ B&B £39–£43, B&B (double) £60–£72·50; D £15; WB £70 (2 nts)
cc Access, Amex, B'card/Visa, Diners; dep.

BILLINGHAM Teeside, Cleveland. Map 45A2
Pop 34,600. Stockton-on-Tees 2½, London 346, Darlington 13, Durham 20, Middlesbrough 4, Sunderland 23.
MD Mon. **Golf** Billingham 18h. **See** St Cuthbert's Church, Art Gallery, Billingham Forum.

★★★ Billingham Arms, The Causeway, TS23 2HD ☎Stockton-on-Tees (0642) 553661 Tx: 587746 Fax: (0642) 552104

Two-storey brick-built hotel in town square/shopping precinct of town. Solarium.
🛏 65 bedrs, 55 en suite, 5 ba; TV; tcf
🏠 lift, TV, dogs, ns; P 50, coach; child facs; con 450

BILLINGSHURST West Sussex. Map 6B2
Pop 5,570. Dorking 18, London 41, Guildford 18, Haywards Heath 18, Horsham 7, Petworth 8½, Pulborough 5½, Worthing 17.
EC Wed. **Golf** Pulborough 18h. **See** Old Church (15th cent wooden ceiling), Unitarian Church.

Old Wharf (Highly Acclaimed), Newbridge, Wisborough Green, RH14 0JG ☎(0403) 784096. *Farm.*

BINGLEY West Yorkshire. Map 40A2
Pop 13,300. Bradford 6, London 202, Halifax 12, Leeds 14, Skipton 13, Todmorden 18.
EC Tue. **MD** Wed, Fri, Sat. **Golf** Bingley (St Ives) 18h. **See** Stocks, Cross and Market House re-erected in Prince of Wales Park, All Saints' Church.

★★★ Bankfield, Bradford Rd, BD16 1TU ☎Bradford (0274) 567123
Fax: (0274) 551331 ♿

A much extended, Victorian building, set in 5½ acres of grounds. (Emb). Fr, It
🛏 103 bedrs, 103 en suite; TV; tcf
🏠 lift, dogs, ns; P 250, G 20; child facs; con 300
✕ LD 9.15, nr Thu–Sat lunch, Tue–Sun dinner
£ B&B £72–£85 (w/e £28), B&B (double) £86–£99; L £11·50, D £11·50; WB £38
cc Access, Amex, B'card/Visa, Diners.

Hallbank (Highly Acclaimed), Beck La, BD16 4DD ☎Bradford (0274) 565296. *Private Hotel.* Closed Xmas.
£ B&B £35 (w/e £20); HB weekly £260.

BIRDLIP Gloucestershire. Map 20B2
Cirencester 12, London 100, Cheltenham 8, Gloucester 5, Stroud 6.

★★★ C Royal George, GL4 8JH ☎Gloucester (0452) 862506 Tx: 437238 Fax: (0452) 862277 ♿
Traditional Cotswold coaching inn with a modern extension; on main Gloucester-Cirencester road. Putting, sauna, solarium. (Lns)
🛏 33 bedrs, 33 en suite; TV; tcf
🏠 dogs, ns; P 120, coach; child facs; con 80
✕ LD 10
£ B&B £67, B&B (double) £80; L £8·95, D £14; WB £70 [10% V]
cc Access, Amex, B'card/Visa, Diners.

BIRKENHEAD Merseyside. Map 32A1
See also WALLASEY.
Pop 95,000. Chester 15, London 197, M53 (jn 3) 3, Liverpool 2, Queensferry 14.
EC Thur. **MD** Daily. **Golf** Arrowe Park 18h. **See** Priory ruins, Town Hall, Williamson Art Gallery, Queen Victoria Memorial (styled in form of an Eleanor Cross).
ⓘ Library, Borough Rd. ☎051-652 6106

★★★ **Bowler Hat,** 2 Talbot Rd, Oxton, L43 2HH ☎051-652 4931 Tx: 628761

A large converted period residence, attractively gabled, overlooking the Wirral Peninsula. It, Es
29 bedrs, 29 en suite; TV; tcf
dogs; P 40, coach; child facs; con 100
LD 10, bar meals only Sat lunch
£ B&B £33–£51·50 (w/e £24), B&B (double) £48–£64; L £9·50, D £13·50. [10% V]
cc Access, Amex, B'card/Visa, Diners.

★★ R **Riverhill,** Talbot Rd, Oxton, L43 2HJ ☎051-653 3773 Fax: 051-653 7162
Former private house standing in own grounds in quiet residential area. Fr, It
16 bedrs, 16 en suite; TV; tcf
TV; P 30; child facs
LD 9.30
£ B&B £39·95 (w/e £29·95), B&B (double) £49·95; L £7·95; D £9·90
cc Access, Amex, B'card/Visa, Diners.

BIRMINGHAM West Midlands. Map 22C1/C2
See also HOPWOOD, SOLIHULL and SUTTON COLDFIELD.
RAC Office, *1059 Alcester Road South, Maypole, Birmingham, B14 5UH.* ☎021-430 8585.
RAC Office, *57 North Walk, The Pallasades, Birmingham B2 4JX.* ☎021-430 8585.
Pop 1,017,300. Coventry 18, London 111, A38(M) 1½, Bromsgrove 13, Droitwich 19, Kidderminster 17, Lichfield 15, Nuneaton 21, Sutton Coldfield 7, Walsall 8½, Warwick 21, Wolverhampton 13.
See Plan, p. 133.
EC Wed (suburbs). **MD** Daily. **P** See Plan. **Golf** Eight public courses and numerous others. **See** University Buildings at Edgbaston and Gosta Green, Cathedral Church of St Philip (Burne-Jones windows), Hall of Memory and Civic Centre, RC Cathedral of St Chad, St Martin's Church, Art Gallery and Museum, Town Hall, Museum of Science and Industry, Engineering and Building Centre, Botanical Gardens, Midlands Art Centre, Sarehole Mill, Aston Hall (Jacobean), 16th cent Blakesley Hall (Yardley), Weoley castle (site).
[i] National Exhibition Centre, ☎021-780 4321 and 2 City Arcade. ☎021-643 2514

★★★★★ **Swallow,** 12 Hagley Rd, B16 8SJ ☎021-452 1144
Once an office block, this neo-classical brick and sandstone building is now an elegant and luxurious hotel. (Sw)
98 bedrs, 98 en suite

★★★★ **Albany** Smallbrook, Queensway, B5 4EW ☎021-643 8171 Tx: 337031 Fax: 021-631 2528
Hotel under extensive refurbishment. Indoor swimming pool, squash, sauna, solarium, gymnasium, snooker. (THF)

★★★★ **Copthorne,** Paradise Circus, B3 3HJ ☎ 021-200 2727 Tx: 339026 Fax: 021-200 1197 ♿

Very modern city-centre hotel with black glass exterior. Indoor swimming pool, sauna, solarium, gymnasium.
212 bedrs, 212 en suite; TV; tcf
lift, dogs, ns; G 50, coach; child facs; con 200
LD 10.30
£ room £85, double room £95; Bk £5·65, L £10·95, D £12·95; WB £35
cc Access, Amex, B'card/Visa, CB, Diners; dep.

★★★★ **Holiday Inn,** Holliday St, B1 1HH ☎021-631 2000 Tx: 337272 ♿
Impressive, large, modern international hotel in city centre. Indoor swimming pool, sauna, solarium, gymnasium. (HI)

★★★★ **Midland,** New St, B2 4JT ☎021-643 2601 Tx: 338419 Fax: 021-643 5075

Modernised 19th century purpose-built city centre hotel. Snooker. Fr, It
111 bedrs, 111 en suite; TV; tcf
lift, dogs, coach; child facs; con 200
LD 10
£ B&B £93 (w/e £35), B&B (double) £115; L £12·50, D £15
cc Access, Amex, B'card/Visa, Diners; dep.
(*See advertisement on p. 130*)

Using RAC discount vouchers
Please tell the hotel when booking if you plan to use an RAC discount voucher (see p. 34) in part payment of your bill. Only one voucher will be accepted per party per stay. Discount vouchers will only be accepted in payment for accommodation, not for food.

★★★★ **Plough & Harrow,** Hagley Rd, B16 8LS ☎021-454 4111 Tx: 338074 Fax: 021-454 1868

Well-appointed, superbly furnished hotel in Victorian building. Sauna. Fr, De, It Es. (Cr/THF)
44 bedrs, 44 en suite; TV
lift, dogs, ns; P 80; child facs; con 65
LD 10.15
£ B&B £104·95 (w/e £35), B&B (double) £117·95; L £19, D £28, WB £62
cc Access, Amex, B'card/Visa, Diners.

★★★★ **Strathallan,** 225 Hagley Rd, B16 9RY ☎021-455 9777 Tx: 336680 Fax: 021–454 9432
Modern hotel of circular design with covered parking facilities. (MtCh)
167 bedrs, 167 en suite; TV; tcf
lift, dogs, ns; P 250, G 150, coach; child facs; con 200
LD 10
£ room £72, double room £82; Bk £7·75, L £12, D £15; WB
cc Access, Amex, B'card/Visa, CB, Diners.

★★★ **Grand,** Colmore Row, B3 2DA ☎021-236 7951 Tx: 338174 Fax: 021-233 1465

Modernised Victorian hotel situated opposite Cathedral. (QMH)
173 bedrs, 173 en suite, TV, tcf
lift, dogs; coach; child facs; con 500.

★★★ **Great Barr,** Pear Tree Dr, Newton Rd, Gt Barr, B43 6HS ☎021-357 1141 Tx: 336406 Fax: 021-357 7557

Mainly modern hotel in quiet leafy suburb.
114 bedrs, 114 en suite; TV; tcf
P 175, coach; child facs; con 120
LD 9.45
£ B&B £45·50, B&B (double) £59·50; L £9·50, D £12; WB
cc Access, Amex, B'card/Visa, CB, Diners.
(*See advertisement on p. 136*)

EC *early closing* **MD** *market day* *country house hotel* *ns (NS) no smoking areas* *tcf tea/coffee facilities*

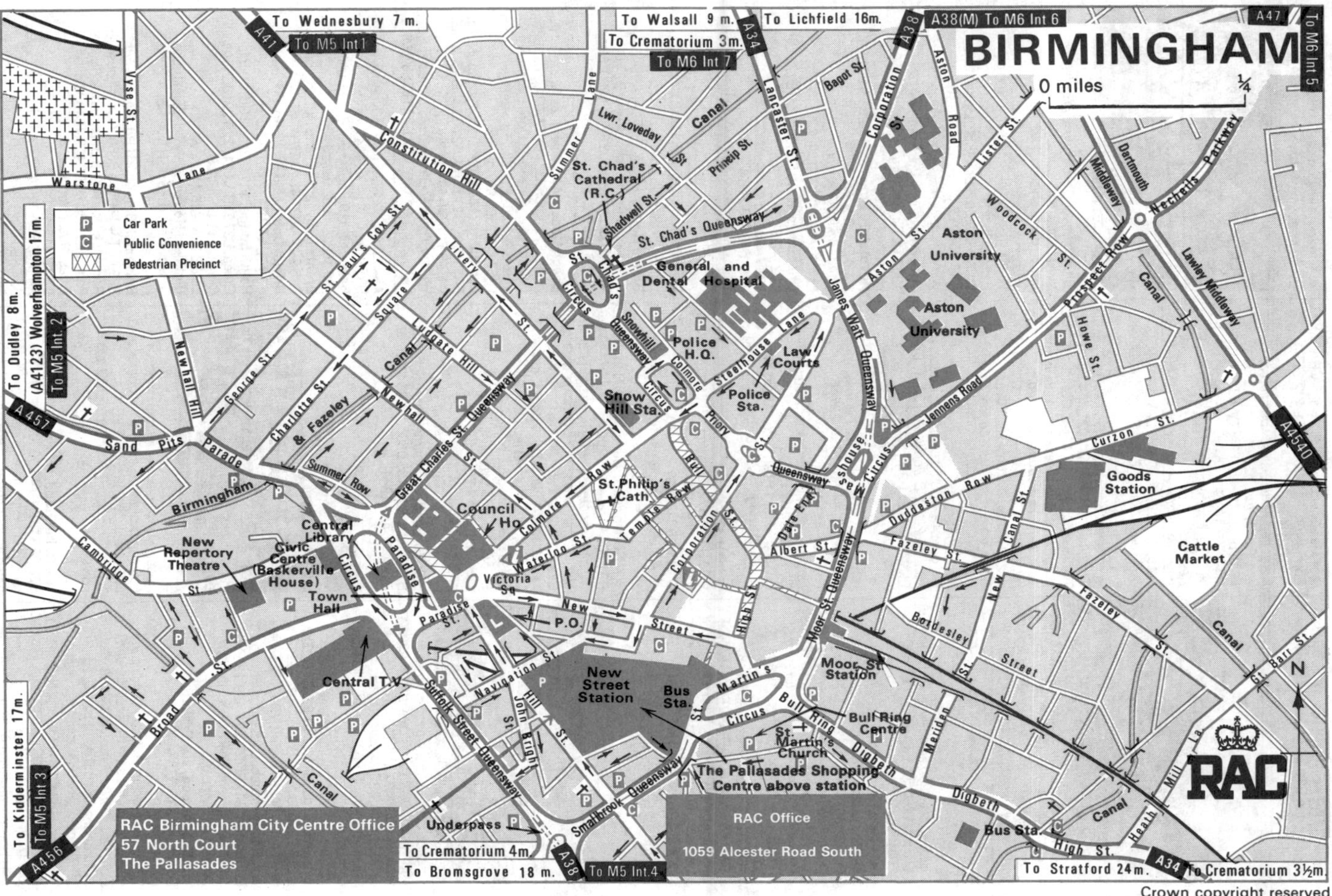

BIRMINGHAM
0 miles
¼
RAC
N
P Car Park
C Public Convenience
Pedestrian Precinct
RAC Office
1059 Alcester Road South
RAC Birmingham City Centre Office
57 North Court
The Pallasades
To M6 Int 5
A47
A38(M) To M6 Int 6
A38
To Lichfield 16m.
A34
To Walsall 9 m.
To Crematorium 3m.
To M6 Int 7
To Wednesbury 7 m.
To M5 Int 1
A41
To Dudley 8m.
(A4123) Wolverhampton 17m.
To M5 Int. 2
A457
To Kidderminster 17m.
To M5 Int 3
A456
To Crematorium 4m.
To Bromsgrove 18 m.
A38
To M5 Int.4
To Stratford 24m.
A34
To Crematorium 3½m.
A4540
Goods Station
Cattle Market
Aston University
St. Chad's Cathedral (R.C.)
General and Dental Hospital
Law Courts
Police Sta.
Police H.Q.
Snow Hill Sta.
St. Philip's Cath.
Council Ho
Victoria Sq.
P.O.
New Street Station
Bus Sta.
Moor St. Station
Bull Ring Centre
St. Martin's Church
The Pallasades Shopping Centre above station
Central Library
Town Hall
Central T.V.
Civic Centre (Baskerville House)
New Repertory Theatre
Underpass
Bus Sta.

B

★★★ H C **Norton Place,** 180 Lifford La, Kings Norton B30 3NT ☎021-433 5656 Fax: 021-433 3048 ♿

Low, brick-built hotel next to Patrick Motor Museum with a new wing of luxurious bedrooms and separate popular restaurant and bar, all surrounded by charming rock gardens and patio areas. Gymnasium. ⚒ Fr
🛏 10 bedrs, 10 en suite; TV
🏨 ns; P 300, G 20; no children, con 150
✕ LD 10
£ B&B £150–£250 (w/e £120), B&B (double) £170·50–£280·50; L £16·50, D £20·50; WB £120.

★★★ **Post House,** Chapel La, Gt Barr, B43 7BG ☎021-357 7444 Tx: 338497 Fax: 021-357 7503
Modern hotel adjacent to motorway. Indoor & outdoor swimming pools. (THF) ⚒ Fr, Es
🛏 204 bedrs, 204 en suite; TV; tcf
🏨 dogs, ns; P 300, coach; child facs; con 150
✕ LD 10.15, nr Sat lunch & Sun dinner
£ B&B £80–£86·50 (w/e £43), B&B (double) £98–£109; L £10, D £15; WB £43
cc Access, Amex, B'card/Visa, CB, Diners.

★★★ C **Royal Angus,** St Chads, Queensway, B4 6HY ☎021-236 4211 Tx: 336889 Fax: 021-233 2195

Modern city centre hotel with public parking facilities adjoining. (MtCh)
🛏 135 bedrs, 135 en suite; TV; tcf
🏨 lift, dogs, ns; P 600, coach; child facs; con 180
✕ LD 10
£ room £72, double room £82; Bk £7·75, L £10·25, D £13·50; WB
cc Access, Amex, B'card/Visa, CB, Diners.

★★ **Bailey House,** 21 Sandon Rd, Edgbaston, B17 8DR ☎021-429 1929
Small 2-storey privately owned hotel on western outskirts.

★★ **Beechwood,** 201 Bristol Rd, Edgbaston, B5 7UB ☎ 021-440 2133 Fax: 021-446 4549
White, slate-roofed Victorian building in a residential area. Large terraced garden with small lake. Set back from busy A38. Fishing.
🛏 18 bedrs, 16 en suite, 2 ba; TV; tcf
🏨 TV, dogs; P 25, coach; child facs; con

★★ **Campanile,** 55 Irving St, Lee Bank B1 1DH ☎021-622 4925 Tx: 333701 ♿
See Motor Lodge section
(See advertisement on p. 136)

★★ **Meadow Court,** 397 Hagley Rd, Edgbaston, B17 8BL ☎021-429 2377 Fax: 021-434 3140
Detached white 2-storey building on corner site. Family-run. ⚒ De
🛏 12 bedrs, 12 en suite; TV; tcf
🏨 TV; P 16, G 1, coach; child facs; con 22
✕ LD 9, bar meals only Sat & Sun lunch. Resid lic
£ B&B £43·70 (w/e £25), B&B (double) £58; L £10·75, D £10·75; WB £25; [5% V]
cc Access, Amex, B'card/Visa, CB, Diners.

★★ **New Cobden,** 166 Hagley Rd, Edgbaston, B16 9NZ ☎021-454 6621 Tx: 333851 Fax: 021-456 2935 ♿
Large hotel with pleasant garden. Indoor swimming pool, sauna, solarium, gymnasium. ⚒ Fr, De
🛏 250 bedrs, 250 en suite; TV; tcf
🏨 lift, dogs, ns; P 130, coach; child facs; con 100
✕ LD 9.45
£ room £49–£58·50 (w/e £32), double room £58·50–£66; HB weekly £60·25–£109·75; Bk £4·95, D £11·95. [10% V]
cc Access, Amex, B'card/Visa, Diners.

★★ **Norfolk,** Hagley Rd, Edgbaston, B16 9NA ☎021-454 8071 Tx: 339715 Fax: 021-454 1910
Large hotel on western approach to city. Gymnasium. ⚒ Fr, De
🛏 180 bedrs, 119 en suite, 40 ba; TV; tcf
🏨 lift, TV, dogs, ns; P 100, coach; child facs; con 90
✕ LD 9.30
£ B&B £49–£58·50 (w/e £32), B&B (double) £58·50–£66; HB weekly £421·75–£488·25; D £11·25. [10% V]
cc Access, Amex, B'card/Visa, Diners; dep.

★★ **Norwood,** 87 Bunbury Rd, Northfield B31 2ET ☎021-411 2202
Family-run hotel, recently converted from two 1920s houses, with landscaped garden. Closed Xmas. ⚒ Fr
🛏 17 bedrs, 11 en suite, 1 ba; TV; tcf
🏨 dogs; coach; child facs; con 25
✕ LD 9.30. Resid & Rest lic
£ B&B £25–£45 (w/e £20), B&B (double) £55–£65; L £13·75, D £13·75
cc B'card/Visa.

★★ **Portland,** 313 Hagley Rd, Edgbaston, B16 9LQ ☎ 021-455 0535 Tx: 334200 Fax: 021-456 1841

Recently extended, four-storey modern building beside the A456 in residential area.
🛏 64 bedrs, 64 en suite; TV; tcf
🏨 lift, TV, dogs; P 80, coach; child facs, con 90

★★ **Robin Hood,** Stratford Rd, Hall Green, B28 9ES ☎021-745 9900
Large public house with grill restaurant; motel accommodation adjoining.

★ **Wake Green Lodge,** 20 Wake Green Rd, Moseley, B13 9ER ☎021-449 4499

Gabled, mock-Tudor house in quiet residential area.
🛏 8 bedrs, 2 en suite, (4 sh), 3 ba; TV; tcf
🏨 P 10; child facs; con 16
✕ LD 10, nr Mon–Sat lunch & Sun dinner. Resid & Rest lic
£ B&B £16·50–£24, B&B (double) £25–£30; L £7·95, D £9·95
cc Access, Amex, B'card/Visa, Diners.

Arcade, Hurst St ☎(Central res) 071-621 1962 Tx: 8813608 Fax: 071-283 5752.
New hotel opening May 1991.

Novotel, 70 Broad St, B1 2HT ☎021-643 2000 Fax: 021-643 9796.
Hotel awaiting inspection.
🛏 148 bedrs, 148 en suite; TV; tcf

Oriental Pearl. 19 Sandon Rd, B17 8DP ☎021-429 1182
Hotel awaiting inspection.
🛏 12 bedrs, 12 en suite; TV; tcf
🏨 TV, ns; P 15, coach; no children under 5; con 40
✕ LD 11
£ B&B £40, B&B (double) £60; L £8·90, D £12·50; [5% V]

Bridge House (Highly Acclaimed), 49 Sherbourne Rd, Acocks Green, B27 6DX ☎021-706 5900 Fax: 021-706 5900. *Hotel.*
£ B&B £25·30.

Beech House (Acclaimed), 21 Gravelly Hill North, Erdington, B23 6BT ☎021-373 0620. *Private Hotel.* Closed 23 Dec–5 Jan
£ B&B £25·30–£32·20; HB weekly £257·60–£305·90.

Lyndhurst (Acclaimed), 135 Kingsbury Rd, Erdington, B24 8QT ☎021-373 5695. *Hotel.*
£ B&B £27·50–£34; [10% V].

Willow Tree (Acclaimed), 759 Chester Rd, Erdington, B24 0BY ☎021-373 6388. *Hotel.*

Alexander, 44 Bunbury Rd, Northfield, B31 2DW ☎021-475 4341. *Hotel.*

Belmont, 419 Hagley Rd, B17 8BL ☎ 021-429 1663. *Hotel. Billiards.*

Brentwood, 127 Portland Rd, Edgbaston, B16 9QX ☎021-454 4079

Bristol Court, 250 Bristol Rd, Edgbaston, B5 7SL ☎021-472 0078. *Hotel.*

Heath Lodge, 117 Coleshill Rd, Marston Green, B37 7HT ☎021-779 2218. *Hotel.* Closed 24 Dec–1 Jan.
£ B&B £26–£35; [10% V].

Highfield House, Holly Rd, Blackheath, Rowley Regis B65 0BH ☎021-559 1066. *Hotel.*

Holyhead, 6 Holyhead Rd, Handsworth, B20 0CT ☎021-554 8560. *Guest House.*

Remwick House, 13 Bournbrook Rd, Selly Park, B29 7BL ☎021-472 4640. Closed Xmas. *Guest House.*
£ B&B £15–£20.

Rollason Wood, Wood End Rd, Erdington, B24 8BJ ☎021-373 1230 Fax: 021-382 2578. *Hotel.*

EC *early closing* **MD** *market day* ♣♣ *country house hotel* *ns (NS) no smoking areas* *tcf tea/coffee facilities*

£ B&B £15·60–£32.
Tri-Star, Coventry Rd, Elmdon, B26 3QR ☎021-782 1010. *Hotel.*
£ B&B £27·60–£41·40.
Welcome House, 1641 Coventry Rd, Yardley, B26 1DD ☎021-707 3232. *Guest House.*
Wentworth, 103 Wentworth Rd, Harborne, B17 9SU ☎021-427 2839. *Hotel.*
£ B&B £35 (w/e £30).
Woodlands, 379 Hagley Rd, B17 8DL ☎021-429 3935. *Hotel.*

BIRMINGHAM AIRPORT & NATIONAL EXHIBITION CENTRE West Midlands. Map 23A1
Coventry 11, London 105, Atherstone 15, Birmingham 7, Sutton Coldfield 11.
[i] ☎021-767 5511

★★★★ **Birmingham Metropole,** B40 1PP ☎021-780 4242 Tx: 336129
Fax: 021-780 3923 ♿

Six-storey, purpose-built, red-brick building beside lake within the National Exhibition Centre complex. Squash. Fr, De, It
807 bedrs, 807 en suite; TV; tcf
lift, dogs; P 600, coach; child facs; con 2000
LD 10.30
£ B&B £95, B&B (double) £135–£145; L £15·95, D £15·95; WB £32
cc Access, Amex, B'card/Visa, Diners; dep.

★★★ **Excelsior,** Coventry Rd, B26 3QW ☎021-782 8141 Tx: 338005
Fax: 021-782 2476
Well-appointed large hotel at approach to Airport to SE of city. (THF)
141 bedrs, 141 en suite; TV; tcf
dogs, ns; P 120, coach; child facs; con 150
LD 10.15
£ B&B £75–£85 (w/e £39·50), B&B (double) £88–£93; L £10, D £15; WB
cc Access, Amex, B'card/Visa, CB, Diners.

BISHAMPTON Hereford & Worcester (Worcestershire). Map 20C3
Evesham 6, London 104, Alcester 9, Pershore 5, Worcester 11.

Nightingale Farm (Highly Acclaimed), Nr Pershore, WR10 2NH. ☎(038 682) 384. *Billiards.*

BISHOP AUCKLAND Durham. Map 45A2
Pop 15,839. West Auckland 3, London 251, Darlington 11, Durham 11, Middleton-in-Teesdale 19, Stockton-on-Tees 19.
EC Wed. **MD** Sat. **Golf** Bishop Auckland 18h. **See** 12th cent Church, Roman Heating Chamber at Vinovium (Binchester), Saxon Church (Escomb), Auckland Castle, residence of the Bishops of Durham since 12th cent (Chapel viewable by arr).

★★★ **Helme Park Hall,** Nr Fir Tree, DL13 4NW ☎(0388) 730970
Modernised 17th century house with Victorian additions in wooded gardens beside A68. Lovely views. Solarium. Fr
10 bedrs, 9 en suite (1 sh); TV; tcf
P 50; child facs; con 50
LD 10
£ B&B £39·50, B&B (double) £54·50–£75; L £13·95, D £13·95; WB £65. [10% V]
cc Access, Amex, B'card/Visa; dep.

Greenhead Country House (Highly Acclaimed), Greenhead, Fir Tree, Crook DL15 8BL ☎(0388) 763143. *Hotel.*
£ B&B £28.

BISHOPS CASTLE Shropshire. Map 19C4
Ludlow 17, London 160, Knighton 13, Newtown 16, Shrewsbury 23, Welshpool 17.
See Church.

Castle, SY9 5DG ☎(0588) 638403
Early 18th century stone-built hotel on high ground in market square.

BISHOP'S STORTFORD Hertfordshire. Map 1500
Pop 24,000. London 31, M11 (jn 8) 1½, Baldock 20, Cambridge 27, Chelmsford 18, Dunmow 9, Hoddesdon 14.
EC Wed. **MD** Thur, Sat. **Golf** Bishop's Stortford 18h. **See** Cecil Rhodes birthplace, Rhodes Memorial Museum, St Michael's Church, old inns, R. Stort – navigable waterway.
[i] The Causeway. ☎(0279) 655261

★★★ **Foxley,** Foxley Dr, Stanstead Rd, CM23 2EB ☎(0279) 653977
Fax: (0279) 507176
Large former residence set in quiet location. Owner-managed.
10 bedrs, 10 en suite, 1 ba, annexe 2 bedrs, 2 en suite; TV; tcf
TV, dogs; P 40, G 5; child facs; con 40

BISHOPS TAWTON Devon. Map 3B4
South Molton 11½, London 194, Barnstaple 1½, Bideford 9, Crediton 29.

★★ **Downrew House,** EX32 0DY ☎(0271) 42497 Fax: (0271) 23947

Charming, part Queen Anne house with beautiful country views. Swimming pool, golf, tennis, solarium, billiards.
6 bedrs, 6 en suite; annexe 6 bedrs, 6 en suite; TV; tcf
dogs, ns; P 20; children over 6; con 20
LD 9.15, nr Mon–Sat lunch. Resid & Rest lic
£ B&B & dinner (double) £109–£133; HB weekly £380–£403; D £16·50
cc Access, B'card/Visa; dep.
(*See advertisement on p. 136*)

BISHOPSTEIGNTON Devon. Map 3C2
Pop 2,025. Exeter 13, London 181, Newton Abbot 4, Torquay 9.
EC Thur. **Golf** Teignmouth 18h. **See** Old walls of 11th cent. Bishop of Exeter's Palace, Church.

★★ **Cockhaven Manor,** Cockhaven Rd, TQ14 9RF ☎Teignmouth (0626) 775252

16th century buildings with Georgian extension. Fine views from grounds.
12 bedrs, 11 en suite, 1 ba; TV; tcf
dogs, ns; P 60, coach; child facs; con 150
LD 9.45
£ B&B £31, B&B (double) £52; HB weekly £192; L £6, D £6; WB £26 (2 nts). [10% V]
cc Access, B/card/Visa; dep.
(*See advertisement on p. 136*)

BISPHAM Lancashire. Map 36A3
Blackpool 2, London 230, Fleetwood 6, Lancaster 24, Lytham St Annes 9.

Garville, 3 Beaufort Av, FY2 9HQ ☎Blackpool (0253) 51004. *Private Hotel.*
Langwood, 250 Queens Prom, FY2 9HA ☎(0253) 51370. Open Mar–Dec. Fr
£ B&B £18; HB weekly £148.

BLACKBURN Lancashire. Map 33A4
Pop 89,000. Bolton 13, London 208, Burnley 11, Bury 15, Chorley 10, Preston 10, Rochdale 18, Skipton 28, Whalley 7.
EC Thur. **MD** Wed, Fri, Sat. **Golf** Blackburn 18h. **See** Cathedral, Museum and Art Gallery, Lewis Textile Museum.
[i] Town Hall. ☎(0254) 53277

★★★ **Blackburn Moat House,** Yew Tree Dr, BB2 7BE ☎(0254) 64441 Tx: 63271

Attractive modern gabled building surrounded by lawns. (QMH)
98 bedrs, 98 en suite; TV, tcf
lift, dogs, ns; P 300, coach; child facs; con 380

Birmingham (West Midlands)

THE CAMPANILE HOTEL – Birmingham

55 Irving Street, Birmingham B1 1DH

Tel: (021) 622 4925 Telex: 333701

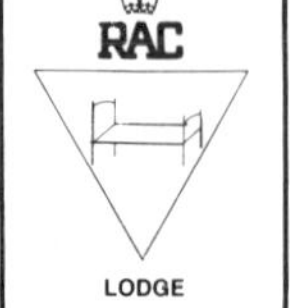

Part of the international budget hotel chain "Campanile", the hotel offers 100 comfortable double or twin rooms with en-suite bathrooms, and tea/coffee making facilities, radio alarm, remote control colour TV, Sky TV and direct dial telephone at **competitive rates.** Our informal restaurant provides a variety of home-cooked French/ Continental cuisine, and personal service at **affordable prices.** Our seminar room is available for business meetings or small functions.

Your hosts: Anne & Graeme Harley

Bishopsteignton (Devon)

ETB ♛♛♛ RAC ★★

Cockhaven Manor Hotel

Cockhaven Road, Bishopsteignton, S. Devon TQ14 9RF Tel: 0626 775252

Superb 16th century Manor House overlooking the Teign Estuary. Full en-suite accommodation with all facilities. Bar and Restaurant Meals available. Functions and Conferences catered for. *Proprietors P. J. & J. Patchett*

Bishops Tawton (Devon)

Downrew House Hotel

Bishops Tawton, Barnstaple,
Devon EX32 0DY

Tel: (0271) 42497/46673 Fax: (0271) 23947

This gracious Queen Anne Country House stands nestled in 12 acres of meadowland and gardens and overlooks the very splendid panoramic views of the Devon countryside. 12 bedrooms all en-suite and tastefully furnished, all with colour TV, Tea/Coffee making facilities, Trouser press with iron/ironing board. Our facilities include own golf, heated outdoor swimming pool, tennis court, solarium, croquet lawn and billiards table.

RAC ★★ EGON RONAY, JOHANSENS, ASHLEY COURTENAY, DEVON TOURISM, HOTELS OF DISTINCTION

Blackpool (Lancashire)

The hotel is situated perfectly for the Pleasure Beach, the Sandcastle, and the newly opened Ocean Boulevard shopping complex. All these are within 100 metres of the hotel. We also host a series of speciality weekends throughout the year. *All prices on application.*

Balmoral Road, South Shore, Blackpool, Lancs FY4 1HR.
Tel: (0253) 45432. Fax: (0253) 406058

EC *early closing* **MD** *market day* ♣♣ *country house hotel* *ns (NS) no smoking areas* *tcf tea/coffee facilities*

★★★ **Mytton Fold Farm,** Whalley Rd, Langho BB6 8AB ☎ (0254) 240662 Fax: (0254) 248119 ♿

Attractively built in local stone, a country hotel in delightful surroundings.
🛏 27 bedrs, 27 en suite; TV; tcf
ns; P 150, coach; children over 6; con 300
✕ LD 9.30, nr Sat lunch. Resid & Rest lic
£ B&B £42–£51 (w/e £23), B&B (double) £56–£73; L £7·50; WB £63; [10% V]
cc Access, B'card/Visa.

🍽🍽🍽 **C** **Millstone,** Church La, Mellor, BB2 7JR ☎ (0254) 813333 Tx: 635309 Fax: (0254) 812628
Traditional inn in village setting with all modern comforts.
🛏 20 bedrs, 20 en suite; TV; tcf
dogs, ns; P 40, coach; child facs; con 20
✕ LD 9.45, bar meals only Sat lunch
£ B&B £57–£66, B&B (double) £80; HB weekly £497–£560; L £11·50, D £14; WB £74 (HB 2 nts)
cc Access, Amex, B'card/Visa, Diners.

BLACKCROSS Cornwall. Map 2B2
Pop 25. Bodmin 13, London 246, Newquay 7, Penzance 37, Truro 13, Wadebridge 10.
Golf Newquay 18h.

Home Stake Farm, Nr Newquay, TR8 4LU ☎ St Austell (0726) 860423. *Swimming pool, tennis.* ♿

BLACKPOOL Lancashire. Map 36A3
See also THORNTON CLEVELEYS.
Pop 147,000. Preston 16, London 228, M55 (jn 4) 4, Lancaster 24.
See Plan, p. 138.
EC Wed. **P** See Plan. **Golf** Blackpool Park 18h, North Shore 18h. **See** Tower (518ft), Winter Gardens, International Circus, Zoo Park, Model Village (Stanley Park), Tussaud's Waxworks, Art Gallery, Autumn Illuminations.
ℹ 1 Clifton St. ☎ (0253) 21623

★★★★ **Imperial,** North Promenade, FY1 2HB ☎ (0253) 23971 Tx: 677376 Fax: (0253) 751784 ♿
Majestic hotel in commanding promenade position; elegant public rooms. Indoor swimming pool, sauna, solarium, gymnasium. (THF)
🛏 183 bedrs, 183 en suite; TV; tcf
lift, dogs, ns; P 200, coach; child facs; con 600
✕ LD 10
£ B&B £40–£75, B&B double £60–£100; L £9·50, D £12·50; WB £40 (HB)
cc Access, Amex, B'card/Visa, Diners; dep.

Changes made after July 1990 are not included.

★★★★ **Pembroke,** North Promenade, FY1 2JQ ☎ (0253) 23434 Tx: 677469 Fax: (0253) 28764 ♿

Large modern hotel on seafront in 4½ acres of own grounds. Indoor swimming pool, sauna, solarium.
🛏 278 bedrs, 278 en suite; TV; tcf
lift, dogs, ns; P 320, coach; child facs; con 900
✕ LD 10.30
£ B&B £85–£95, B&B (double) £107–£118; L £11·25, D £13·25; WB £46 (HB)
cc Access, Amex, B'card/Visa, Diners

★★★ **Savoy,** Queen's Promenade, FY2 9SJ ☎ (0253) 52561 Tx: 67570 Fax: (0253) 500735

Large and impressive well-equipped hotel on promenade, recently refurbished.
🛏 148 bedrs, 148 en suite; TV; tcf
lift; dogs; P 60, coach; child facs; con 400
✕ LD 10.30
£ B&B £55–£65 (w/e £40); B&B (double) £85–£95; L £9, D £12; [10% V, w/d, not Sep. Oct]
cc Access, Amex, B'card/Visa, Diners; dep.

★★ **Brabyns,** Shaftesbury Av, North Shore, FY2 9QQ ☎ (0253) 54263

Brick-built hotel with mullioned windows and a sun loggia. Close to North Shore Promenade.
🛏 22 bedrs, 22 en suite; annexe 3 bedrs, 3 en suite; TV; tcf
TV, dogs; P 12, coach; child facs
✕ LD 8. Resid & Rest lic
£ B&B £28–£32·50, B&B (double) £50–£59; HB weekly £193·50; L £5, D £8·50; WB £50
cc Access, B'card/Visa, Diners.

★★ **Carlton,** North Promenade, FY1 2EZ ☎ (0253) 28966 Fax: (0253) 752587
Prominent Victorian hotel overlooking quieter North Promenade; family-run. Fr
🛏 57 bedrs, 47 en suite, 6 ba; TV; tcf
lift, TV, dogs; P 45, coach; child facs; con 130
✕ LD 8.45
£ B&B £32–£42, B&B (double) £45–£55; L £4·50, D £8·50; [10% V, not Sep, Oct]
cc Access, Amex, B'card/Visa, Diners; dep.

★★ **Claremont,** 270 North Promenade, FY1 1SA ☎ (0253) 293122 Fax: (0253) 752409 ♿

Large modernised family-run hotel on sea front. Many facilities.
🛏 143 bedrs, 143 en suite, annexe 25 bedrs, 25 en suite; TV; tcf
lift, dogs, ns; P 50, coach; child facs; con 300
✕ LD 8.30, bar meals only Mon–Sat lunch
£ B&B £25–£37; B&B (double) £50–£74; HB weekly £170–£210; L £4·75, D £9·50; WB £55; [10% V, w/d; Nov–Apr]
cc Access, Amex, B'card/Visa.

★★ **Cliffs,** Queens Promenade, FY2 9SG ☎ (0253) 52388 Tx: 67191 Fax: (0253) 500394

Well-positioned on promenade, an updated 1930s hotel. Indoor swimming pool, squash, sauna, gymnasium, billiards. Fr, Es, Po.
🛏 165 bedrs, 165 en suite; TV; tcf
lift, dogs; P 70, coach; child facs; con 350
✕ LD 8.30, bar meals/coffee shop lunch
£ B&B £26·50–£90; B&B (double) £53–£90; HB weekly £175–£250; D £10·50; WB £52
cc Access, Amex, B'card/Visa.

★★ **Gables Balmoral,** Balmoral Rd, FY4 1HP ☎ (0253) 45432 Tx: 67178 Fax: (0253) 406058 ♿

B

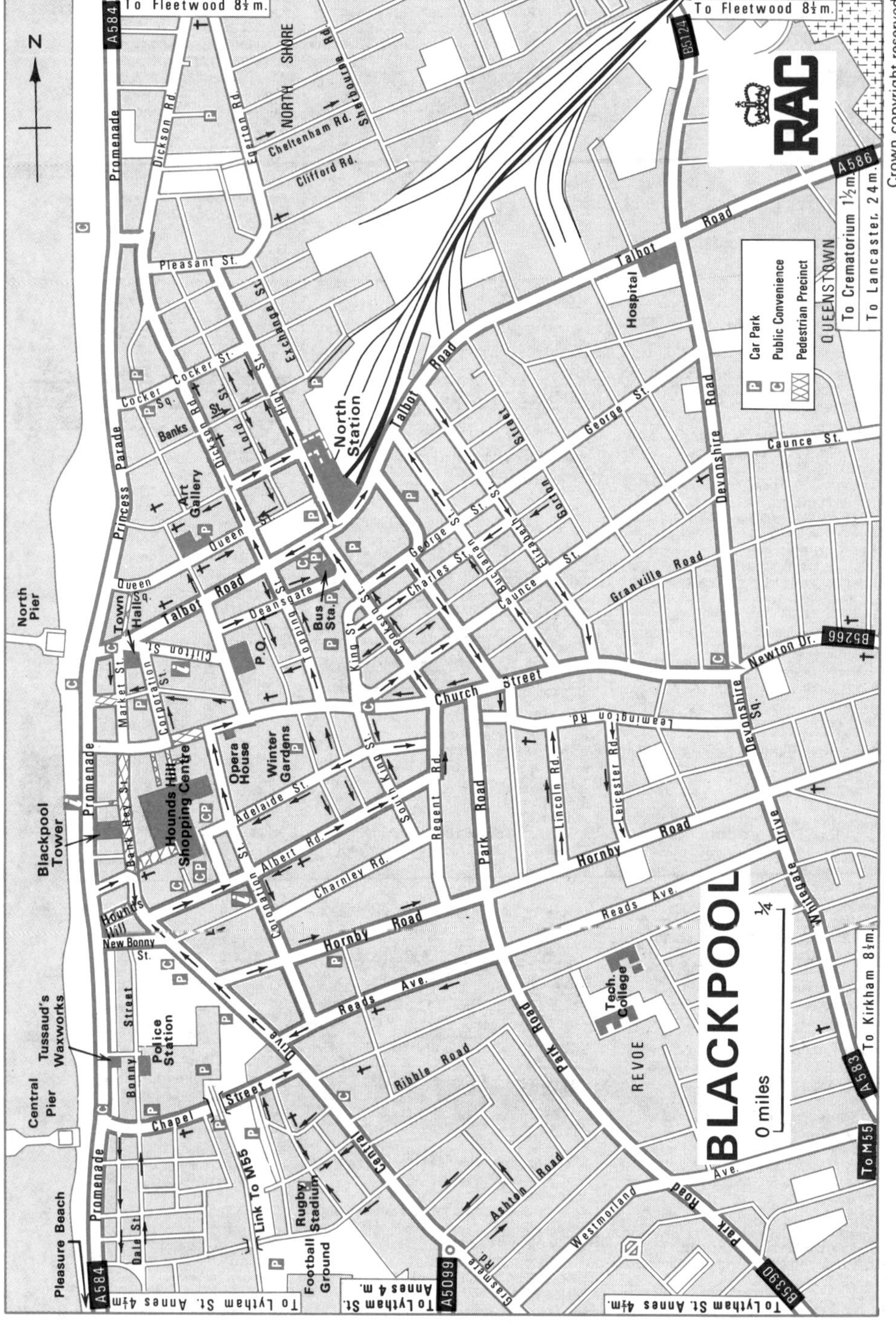

EC *early closing* **MD** *market day* *country house hotel* *ns (NS) no smoking areas* *tcf tea/coffee facilities*

Family-run hotel with distinctive façade. Conveniently near Promenade. Snooker.
70 bedrs, 70 en suite; TV; tcf
TV, dogs; P 5, U 2, coach; child facs; con 100
LD 8.30, bar meals only lunch
£ B&B £34·10–£48·40, HB weekly £176–£250; [10% V]
cc Access, Amex, B'card/Visa, Diners; dep.
(*See advertisement on p. 140*)

★★ **Headlands,** New South Promenade, FY4 1NJ ☎(0253) 41179
Privately-owned hotel on prominent corner site near beach with coastal views. Solarium. Closed 2–11 Jan. Fr, De
43 bedrs, 43 en suite; TV; tcf
lift, TV, dogs; P 38, G 8, coach; child facs; con 70
LD 7.30. Resid lic
£ B&B £27·50–£38·50, B&B (double) £55–£66; L £8, D £11·75; WB £35 (Nov–May); [5% V, Nov–Jun]
cc Access, B'card/Visa; dep.
(*See advertisement on p. 140*)

★★ **Kimberley,** New South Promenade, FY4 1NQ ☎(0253) 41184
Well-appointed, attractive terrace building with sun loggia in quiet area. Billiards.
Es. Closed 2–15 Jan.
54 bedrs, 37 en suite, 5 ba; TV; tcf
lift, TV, dogs; P 25, coach; child facs; con 130
LD 7.30. Resid lic
£ B&B £24–£27, B&B (double) £42–£48; HB weekly £168–£210; L £5·95, D £9·50; [5% V, not Sep, Oct]
cc Access, B'card/Visa; dep.
(*See advertisement on p. 140*)

★★ **Revill's,** 192 North Promenade, FY1 1RJ ☎(0253) 25768

Privately-owned family-run hotel on North Promenade. Near town centre. Billiards.
47 bedrs, 47 en suite; TV; tcf
lift, TV, ns; P 22, coach; child facs
LD 7.30, bar meals only lunch.
£ B&B £22–£24, B&B (double) £32–£41·80; D £6
cc Access, B'card/Visa; dep.

★★ **Ruskin,** 57 Albert Rd, FY1 4PW ☎(0253) 24063 Fax: (0253) 23571
Well-run hotel with elegant 'art-deco' style public rooms; close to Winter Gardens.
Fr, SGa.
80 bedrs, 80 en suite; TV; tcf.
lift, TV, dogs, ns; G 12(£5), coach; child facs; con 200
LD 8.30, bar meals only lunch
£ B&B £30, B&B (double) £50; HB weekly £240; D £10; WB £68 (HB 2 nts); [10% V, Mon–Thu]
cc Access, B'card/Visa

★★ **Sheraton,** 54 Queens Prom, FY2 9RP ☎(0253) 52723
Red-brick 4-storey hotel in central position on Queens Promenade; panoramic sea views. Indoor swimming pool, sauna, solarium.
119 bedrs, 119 en suite; TV; tcf.
lift, dogs, P 12; coach; child facs; con 200
LD 7.45, bar meals only lunch. Resid lic
£ B&B £31, B&B (double) £58; D £9·50; WB £50; [10% V, Jan–Jun]; dep.

★★ **Stretton,** 206 North Prom, FY1 1RU ☎(0253) 25688 Fax: (0253) 24075

Three-storey building with glass sun lounge overlooking sea near Tower. Solarium, snooker.
51 bedrs, 26 en suite, 3 ba; TV; tcf
TV, dogs; P 10, coach; child facs; con 150
LD 7, bar meals only Mon–Sat lunch
£ B&B £20–£32, B&B (double) £32–£53·50; D £6·50; WB
cc Access, Amex, B'card/Visa, Diners; dep.

★★ **Warwick,** 603 New South Promenade, FY4 1NG ☎(0253) 42192 Tx: 677334 Fax: (0253) 405776

Modern hotel enjoying panoramic sea views. Indoor swimming pool, solarium.
52 bedrs, 52 en suite; TV; tcf
dogs; P 30, coach; child facs; con 150
LD 8.30, bar meals only lunch
£ B&B £30·50–£38·50, B&B (double) £51·50–£65·50; HB weekly £455·52–£498·75; D £10·50; WB £33
cc Access, Amex, B'card/Visa, Diners; dep.

★ **Westmorland,** 256 Queens Prom, FY2 9HB ☎(0253) 54974
Purpose-built hotel, on Promenade overlooking sea.
20 bedrs, 20 en suite, 1 ba; TV; tcf
lift, TV, dogs, P 8; coach; child facs
LD 7.30, bar meals only lunch. Resid lic
£ B&B £16–£22, B&B (double) £32–£48; D £6; [5% V, w/d, Jan–Aug]; dep.

Clifton, Talbot Sq., FY1 1ND ☎(0253) 21481
Hotel trading but under refurbishment, completion 1991.

Metropole, Princes Par, FY1 1RQ ☎(0253) 28321
Hotel awaiting inspection.

Arosa (Highly Acclaimed), 18 Empress Dr, FY2 9SD ☎(0253) 52555. *Hotel.*
Cliff Head (Highly Acclaimed), 174 Queens Prom, Bispham, FY2 9JN ☎(0253) 591086. *Hotel.* Fr, De.
£ B&B £12·65–£17·25; HB weekly £97·75–£125; [10% V].
Lynstead (Highly Acclaimed), 40 King Edward Av, FY2 9TA ☎(0253) 51050. *Private Hotel.*
Old Coach House (Highly Acclaimed), 50 Dean St, PY4 1BP. ☎(0253) 44330. *Hotel.* Closed Nov, Dec.
£ B&B £18·40–£21; HB weekly £148·75–£168·75; [V, Jan–May]
Sunray (Highly Acclaimed), 42 Knowle Av, North Shore, FY2 9TQ ☎(0253) 51937. *Guest House.* Closed Xmas & New Year.
£ B&B £20–£27; HB weekly £158–£228; [10% V]

Brooklands (Acclaimed), 28 King Edward Av, North Shore, FY2 9TA ☎(0253) 51479. *Hotel.*
£ B&B £14–£18; HB weekly £115·50–£136·50; [5% V]
Burlees (Acclaimed), 40 Knowle Av, Queens Prom, North Shore, FY2 9TQ ☎(0253) 54535. *Hotel.*
£ B&B £14–£20; HB weekly £133–£177
Cliftonville (Acclaimed), 14 Empress Dr, FY2 9SE ☎(0253) 51052. *Hotel. Solarium.*
£ B&B £14·50–£17·50; HB weekly £105–£130
Derwent (Acclaimed), 8 Gynn Av, FY1 2LD ☎(0253) 55194. *Hotel.*
Hartshead (Acclaimed), 17 King Edward Av, FY2 9TA ☎(0253) 53133. *Private Hotel.*
Knowsley (Acclaimed), 68 Dean St, FY4 1BP ☎(0253) 43414. *Hotel.*
Mimosa (Acclaimed), 24A Lonsdale Rd, FY1 6EE ☎(0253) 41906. *Hotel.*
£ B&B £15–£35; [10% V, w/d]
Surrey House (Acclaimed), 9 Northumberland Av, FY2 9SB ☎(0253) 51743. *Hotel.*
£ B&B £11–£13·50; HB weekly £120.
Villa (Acclaimed), 9 Withnell Rd, FY4 1HF ☎(0253) 43314. *Private Hotel.* Open Easter–Nov, Xmas–New Year
£ B&B £13·50–£24; HB weekly £91–£125; [10% V]

Ashcroft, 42 King Edward Av, FY2 9TA ☎(0253) 51538. *Private Hotel.*
£ B&B £14; HB weekly £114
Denely, 15 King Edward Av, FY2 9TA ☎(0253) 52757. *Private Hotel.* Closed Dec.
£ B&B £12–£18; HB weekly £108·50–£147
Lyndale, 13 Northumberland Av, FY2 9SB ☎(0253) 54033
Lynwood, 38 Osborne Rd, FY4 1HG ☎ (0253) 44628. *Guest House.*
£ B&B £12–£17; HB weekly £112–£140; [5% V]
New Esplanade, 551 New South Prom, FY4 1NF ☎(0253) 41646. *Hotel.*
New Heathcot, 270 Queens Prom., Bispham FY2 9HD ☎(0253) 595130. *Hotel.* Open Easter–Nov
£ B&B £13·50–£16·50; HB weekly £112–£132·50; [10% V]
North Mount, 22 King Edward Av, FY2 9TD ☎(0253) 55937. *Hotel.*
£ B&B £11–£12·50; HB weekly £92–£110; [5% V Dec–Aug]
Roker, 563 New South Prom, FY4 1NF ☎(0253) 41853. *Hotel.* Open May–Oct, Xmas
£ B&B £12·50–£16, HB weekly £108–£125

Blackpool (Lancashire)

Headlands

SOUTH PROMENADE, BLACKPOOL FY4 1NJ
Phone: 0253 41179
RAC ★★

The Headlands has been renowned for more than fifty years for the quality of its cuisine, its atmosphere and its cleanliness. It is a family hotel situated on Blackpool's South Promenade with commanding views over the Irish Sea. It's one of the few remaining hotels offering completely inclusive terms comprising double glazed en-suite bedrooms with TV, tea & coffee maker, full English breakfast, 4-course luncheon, afternoon tea and 7-course dinner. Remarkable value. Lift and large car park. The Hotel is under the personal supervision of its resident proprietors and is noted for its quiet friendly and courteous service. The Hotel has a resident organist during the season and is open for both the Christmas and New Year periods. It also has **"THEME WEEKENDS"** featuring the British Counties, every weekend from 17th November 1990 to May 18th 1991 from £35. Also **4 DAY MID-WEEK SPECIALS** in APRIL and MAY from £97 incl. Half Board, Nightly Dancing, Coach trips, Games and Quizzes.

FOR ILLUSTRATED BROCHURE WRITE TO MR CHARLES SIMKIN, THE HEADLANDS, SOUTH PROMENADE, BLACKPOOL FY4 1NJ or Telephone 0253 41179

Blackpool (Lancashire)

RAC
2 STAR

2 Car Parks

KIMBERLEY PRIVATE HOTEL

NEW SOUTH PROMENADE

● FINEST CUISINE ● 120-FOOT SUN LOUNGE ● 55 BEDROOMS ● MOST WITH PRIVATE BATHS ● LIFT ● CENTRAL HEATING ● LICENSED TO RESIDENTS ● BALLROOM ● BILLIARDS AND GAMES ROOM ● COCKTAIL LOUNGE ● 22 BEDROOMS WITH SEA VIEW ● 2 CAR PARKS

Write for our illustrated Brochure

Under the Personal Supervision of the Resident Director: K. T. HOLLAND

Telephone: **41184** Management, **42500** Visitors *Telegrams:* KIMBERLEY, SOUTH PROM, BLACKPOOL

Sunny Cliff, 98 Queens Promenade, FY2 9NS ☎(0253) 51155. *Hotel.* Open Easter–Nov, Xmas
£ B&B £12–£14; HB weekly £110–£120
Woodleigh, 32 King Edward North Shore, FY2 9TA ☎(0253) 593624. *Private Hotel.*
£ B&B £10–£12.

BLACK TORRINGTON Devon. Map 3A3

Crediton 26, London 203, Bude 18, Exeter 34, Okehampton 13.

Hayne Farm (Acclaimed), Beaworthy, EX21 5QG ☎ (040 923) 449. *Farmhouse. Billiards.*

BLAKENEY Gloucestershire Map 20B2

Gloucester 15, London 119, M4 (jn 22) 12½, Chepstow 11, Monmouth 12.

Lower Viney (Acclaimed), Viney Hill, GL15 4LT ☎(0594) 516000. *Guest House.*
£ B&B £15–£18; [5% V]

BLAKENEY Norfolk. Map 35B2

Pop 835. Fakenham 13, London 125, Cromer 12, East Dereham 22, Norwich 27. **EC** Wed. **Golf** Sheringham 18h, Fakenham 9h. **See** 15th cent Guildhall, 14th cent Church, with two towers, Bird Sanctuary (Blakeney Point, Nat Trust).

★★★ **Blakeney,** Quayside, NR25 7NE ☎Cley (0263) 740797
Fax: (0263) 740795 ♿
Hotel right on the quay and enjoying fine sea views. Indoor swimming pool, sauna, gymnasium, snooker.
🛏 41 bedrs, 41 en suite; annexe 10 bedrs, 10 en suite; TV; tcf
🏠 TV, dogs; P 100, coach; child facs; con 110
✕ LD 9.30
£ B&B £39–£59; B&B (double) £78–£118; HB weekly £316–£456; L £6, D £15; WB £96 (2 nts)
cc Access, Amex, B'card/Visa, Diners; dep.

★★ **Manor,** Holt, NR25 7ND ☎Cley (0263) 740376 Fax: (0263) 741116
16th century manor house with pleasant walled courtyard patio. Overlooking the marshes. 🗣 De. Closed 4 Dec–28 Dec.
🛏 8 bedrs, 8 en suite; annexe 27 bedrs, 27 en suite; TV; tcf
🏠 dogs, ns; P 60, coach; children over 10, con 20
✕ LD 8.30
£ B&B £22–£28, B&B (double) £48–£66; D £12; dep.

Flintstones (Acclaimed), Wiveton, Holt, NR25 7TL ☎(0263) 740337. *Guest House.*

BLANCHLAND Northumberland. Map 44C2

Pop 150. West Auckland 27, London 276, Durham 24, Hexham 10, Middleton-in-Teesdale 24, Newcastle upon Tyne 24. **Golf** Hexham 18h. **See** Abbey Church (1165), Derwent Reservoir 3 m NE, Historic Inn.

★★ **Lord Crewe Arms,** DH8 9SP ☎(0434 675) 251 Fax: (0434 675) 337
Fascinating 3-storey stone-built 17th century hotel incorporating medieval Prior's residence.
🛏 6 bedrs, 6 en suite; annexe 4 bedrs, 4 en suite; TV; tcf
🏠 dogs; coach; child facs; con 24
✕ LD 9.15, bar meals only Mon–Sat lunch
£ B&B £60–£72, B&B (double) £84–£96; L £4·50; WB £102 (HB 2 nts); [5% V]
cc Access, Amex, B'card/Visa, Diners.

BLANDFORD FORUM Dorset. Map 5A2

Pop 7,309. Salisbury 23, London 106, Bournemouth 17, Dorchester 16, Shaftesbury 11, Sherborne 20, Wareham 14. **EC** Wed. **MD** Thur, Sat. **Golf** Ashley Wood 9h. **See** Parish Church, Georgian houses.
ℹ West St. ☎(0258) 451989

★★★ **Crown,** West St, DT11 7AJ ☎(0258) 456626 Fax: (0258) 451084

Well-modernised Georgian hotel overlooking water meadows. Fishing. Closed 25, 26 Dec.
🛏 29 bedrs, 29 en suite; TV; tcf
🏠 dogs; P 60, G 3 (£2·50), U 2 (£2·50), coach; child facs; con 150
✕ LD 9.15, bar meals only Sat lunch
£ B&B £54, B&B (double) £64; L £10, D £10; WB £75
cc Access, Amex, B'card/Visa, Diners.

★★ **Anvil,** Salisbury Rd, Pimperne, DT11 8UQ (2 m NE on A354) ☎(0258) 453431

Privately-owned thatched inn in Pimperne village adjoining Blandford.
🛏 9 bedrs, 9 en suite; TV; tcf
🏠 dogs; P 25, coach; child facs
✕ LD 9.45
£ B&B £37·50, B&B (double) £55; L £9·50, D £9·50
cc Access, Amex, B'card/Visa, Diners; dep.
(*See advertisement on p. 142*)

BLAWITH Cumbria. Map 36A4

(M6) 27, London 272, Broughton-in-Furness 8½, Coniston 6, Ulverston 7.

★★ **Highfield Country,** nr Ulverston, LA12 8EG ☎(0229 85) 238
Stone-built Victorian house in 2 acres of mature gardens. Fine views.
🛏 12 bedrs, 12 en suite; TV; tcf
🏠 TV, dogs; P 30; child facs; con 18

Please tell the manager if you chose your hotel through an advertisement in the guide.

BLOCKLEY Gloucestershire. Map 20C2

Pop 1,718. Moreton-in-Marsh 4, London 87, Banbury 22, Evesham 11, Stow-on-the-Wold 6½, Stratford-upon-Avon 15, Tewkesbury 20.
Golf Broadway 18h. **See** 12th cent Parish Church, 17th cent Porch House, Rock Cottage (home of Joanna Southcott).

★★★ **H C R** **Crown Inn,** High St, GL56 9EX ☎(0386) 700245 Fax: (0386) 700247

A 16th-century, Cotswold-stone inn with some bedrooms in attractively converted stables. In centre of village.
🛏 13 bedrs, 13 en suite; annexe 8 bedrs, 8 en suite; TV; tcf
🏠 dogs; P 50; child facs; con 20
✕ LD 9.45
£ B&B £49·50, B&B (double) £66·50–£106; HB weekly £280·90–£397·95; WB £46·50.
cc Access, Amex, B'card/Visa

★★ **Lower Brook House,** Lower St, GL56 9DS ☎(0386) 700286

Small hotel of Cotswold stone situated in quiet village.
🛏 8 bedrs, 8 en suite; TV; tcf
🏠 dogs; P 12; child facs; con 20

BLOXHAM Oxfordshire. Map 21A2

Pop 3,000. Bicester 15, London 72, Banbury 3½, Buckingham 18, Chipping Norton 9½, Moreton-in-Marsh 16, Oxford 20. **EC** Wed. **Golf** Tadmarton Heath 18h. **See** 14th cent Church. Museum.

★★ **R** **Olde School,** Church St, Nr Banbury, OX15 4ET ☎Banbury (0295) 720369
Fax: (0295) 721748 ♿
Cleverly converted old school house, built of local stone. 🗣 Fr, De, Es.
🛏 10 bedrs, 10 en suite, annexe 29 bedrs, 29 en suite; TV; tcf
🏠 TV, dogs, ns; P 150, coach; child facs; con 72
✕ LD 9.30
£ B&B £55–£60, B&B (double) £72–£78; L £11, D £15·50; WB £40; [10% V]
cc Access, Amex, B'card/Visa, Diners; dep.

Blandford (Dorset)

Boldon (Tyne & Wear)

Bolton Abbey (Yorkshire)

Boroughbridge (N Yorkshire)

EC *early closing* **MD** *market day* *country house hotel* *ns (NS) no smoking areas* *tcf tea/coffee facilities*

BODINNICK Cornwall. Map 2C1

Pop 200. Liskeard 15, London 229, Bodmin 13, Looe 10, St Austell 16 (Fy) 8. **Golf** Looe Bin Down 18h. **See** Old Chapel and cottages.

★ R **Old Ferry Inn,** PL23 1LX ☎ Polruan (0726) 870237

Beside the River Fowey, an historic inn in an attractive setting. Restricted Nov–Feb.
12 bedrs, 7 en suite, 3 ba; TV
dogs; P 8, G 2; child facs
LD 8.15, bar meals only lunch
£ B&B £27·50–£35, B&B (double) £55–£70; HB weekly £280–£324; D £17·50
cc Access, B'card/Visa; dep.

BODMIN Cornwall. Map 2C2

Pop 15,000. Launceston 22, London 233, Camelford 13, Liskeard 13, Newquay 19, St Austell 11, Truro 24, Wadebridge 7. **EC** Wed. **MD** Sat. **Golf** St Enodoc Rock 18h. **See** Parish Church of St Petroc, 14th cent chantry chapel ruins in churchyard, Guildhall, Respryn Bridge, DCLI Regimental Museum, Bodmin Beacon (obelisk), Lanhydrock House 2 m SE (Nat Trust).
i Shire House, Mount Folly Sq. ☎ (0208) 76616

★★ **Allegro,** 50 Higher Bore St. PL31 1JW ☎ (0208) 73480

Small, modern Spanish-style hotel round courtyard. In the town centre.
12 bedrs, 4 en suite, (2sh), 2 ba; TV
TV, dogs; P 12, coach; child facs
LD 8.30, bar meals only lunch & Sun dinner. Resid & Rest lic
£ B&B £20–£29, B&B (double) £35–£39·50; HB weekly £147–£219·45; D £5·25
cc Access, Amex, B'card/Visa, Diners.

★★ **Westberry,** Rhind St, PL31 2EL ☎ (0208) 2772
Two-storey modernised building in elevated position above ring road. Sauna, solarium, gymnasium, billiards.

BOGNOR REGIS West Sussex. Map 6B1

Pop 36,960. Pulborough 16, London 63, Arundel 9½, Chichester 6½, Haywards Heath 35, Littlehampton 7, Petworth 16. **EC** Wed. **MD** Fri. **Golf** Bognor 18h. **See** Hotham Park (Arboretum, Mansion and Children's Zoo), RC Church, Dome House.
i Belmont St. ☎ (0243) 823140

★★★ **Royal Norfolk,** Esplanade, PO21 2LH ☎ (0243) 826222 Tx: 477575 Fax: (0243) 826325
Enjoying good sea views, a distinctive Regency building with pleasant garden. Swimming pool, putting, tennis. Fr, De, Es, Du. (THF)
51 bedrs, 51 en suite; TV; tcf
lift, dogs, ns; P 100, coach; child facs; con 100
LD 9.30
£ B&B £55, B&B (double) £60; L £9·95, D £12·50; dep.
cc Access, Amex, B'card/Visa, Diners.

★ **Black Mill House,** Princess Av, Aldwick, West Bognor Regis PO21 2QU ☎ (0243) 821945 Fax: (0243) 821316

Family-run hotel near to Marine Park Gardens and close to sea. Putting. Fr.
22 bedrs, 18 en suite, 4 ba; annexe 4 bedrs, 1 ba; TV; tcf
TV, dogs, ns; P 13; child facs; con 45
LD 8
£ B&B £25–£38·50, B&B (double) £42–£68; HB weekly £160–£244; L £7·50, D £9; WB £52 (HB 2 nts); [10% V]
cc Access, Amex, B'card/Visa, Diners; dep.

Homestead, 90 Aldwick Rd, PO21 2PD ☎ (0243) 823443. *Private Hotel.*
£ B&B £10·50–£11; HB weekly £89·50–£92·50.

BOLDON Tyne & Wear Map 37C3

A1(M) 3, London 272, Newcastle 7, South Shields 5, Sunderland 4, Washington 4.

Friendly, Whitney Way (jn A1/A19), NE35 9PE ☎ 091-519 1999
Hotel awaiting inspection.
(See advertisement on p. 142)

BOLNEY West Sussex. Map 6C2

Pop 1,150. Crawley 9½, London 40, Brighton 13, East Grinstead 16, Haywards Heath 5½, Horsham 10, Petworth 21. **EC** Sat. **Golf** Mannings Heath 18h. **See** Parish Church.

★★★ **Hickstead Resort,** Jobs Lane, RH17 5PA ☎ (0444) 248023 Fax: (0444) 245280

Country mansion with Tudor-style fittings, plus a large modern extension offering well-equipped bedrooms. Indoor swimming pool, sauna, solarium, gymnasium, fishing.
Fr, De, Du.
49 bedrs, 49 en suite; TV; tcf
dogs; ns; P 150, coach; child facs; con 80
LD 9.15
£ B&B £61·50, B&B (double) £83; L £10, D £14; WB £56 (2 nts); [10% V]
cc Access, Amex, B'card/Visa, Diners.

BOLTON Gtr Manchester (Lancashire), Map 33A3. See also WESTHOUGHTON

Pop 148,000. Manchester 11, London 195, M61 3, Blackburn 13, Bury 6, Chorley 11, Walkden 4½, Wigan 10. **EC** Wed. **MD** Tue, Thur, Sat. **Golf** Bolton 18h, Bolton Municipal 18h. **See** 15th cent Hall i'th' Wood Museum, Civic Centre, Art Gallery, Aquarium and Museum, Smithills Hall, St Peter's Church.
i Town Hall. ☎ (0204) 36433

★★★ **Crest,** Beaumont Rd, BL3 4TA ☎ (0204) 651511 Tx: 635522

Modern hotel near Jn 5 of M61. (Cr/THF)
100 bedrs, 100 en suite; TV; tcf
dogs, ns; P 120, coach; child facs; con 120
LD 9.45, bar meals only Sat lunch
£ B&B £78·95–£90·95 (w/e £40), B&B (double) £97–£109; L £10·25, D £14·25; WB; [10% V w/e]
cc Access, Amex, B'card/Visa, Diners.

★★★ **Egerton House,** Blackburn Rd, BL7 9PL ☎ (0204) 57171 Fax: (0204) 593030

B

Attractive country house amongst 4½ acres of lawns, trees and shrubs; fine views.
33 bedrs, 33 en suite; TV; tcf
dogs; P 100, coach; child facs; con 150
LD 9.30, nr Sat lunch. Resid & Rest lic
£ B&B £67 (w/e £50), B&B (double) £80; L £8·95, D £14; WB £80
cc Access, Amex, B'card/Visa, Diners.

★★★ Last Drop Village, Bromley Cross, BL7 9PZ (0204) 591131 Tx: 635322 Fax: (0204) 54122

Unique stone-built hotel of character—hub of beautifully restored village. Indoor swimming pool, squash, sauna, solarium, gymnasium, billiards.
26 bedrs, 26 en suite; annexe 57 bedrs, 57 en suite; TV; tcf
dogs; P 400, coach; child facs; con 200
LD 10, bar meals only Sat lunch
£ B&B £69–£80 (w/e £55), B&B (double) £85–£95; L £10·50; WB £82
cc Access, Amex, B'card/Visa, CB, Diners.

★★★ Pack Horse, 60 Bradshawgate, BL1 1DP (0204) 27261 Tx: 635168 Fax: (0204) 364352

Traditional Georgian hotel in centre. Public car park adjacent. (DeV)
73 bedrs, 73 en suite; TV; tcf
lift, dogs, ns; coach; child facs; con 300
LD 9.45, bar meals only Sat lunch
£ B&B £65 (w/e £25), B&B (double) £80; L £8·50, D £14; WB £68; [10% V]
cc Access, Amex, B'card/Visa, Diners

BOLTON ABBEY N. Yorks. Map 38A3
Pop 500. Leeds 23, London 214. Harrogate 17, Keighley 11, Skipton 6.
EC Tue. **Golf** Skipton 18h. **See** Bolton Priory (12th cent).

Complaints

If you are dissatisfied with the facilities or service offered by a hotel, please take the matter up with the Manager WHILE YOU ARE AT THE HOTEL. In this way, any problems can usually be solved promptly and amicably.

The RAC will investigate matters if a personal approach has failed to resolve the problem. Please submit details of any discussion or correspondence when reporting the problem to the RAC.

★★★ H C R Devonshire Arms, BD23 6AJ (075 671) 441 Tx: 51218 Fax: 075-671 564

Carefully restored and enlarged coaching inn retaining its charm. Putting, fishing.
Fr, It.
40 bedrs, 40 en suite; TV; tcf
TV, dogs, ns; P 150, coach; child facs; con 150
LD 10
£ B&B £75–£80, B&B (double) £95–£110; L £15, D £25; WB £115; [5% V]
cc Access, Amex, B'card/Visa, Diners.
(See advertisement on p. 142)

BOREHAM STREET East Sussex. Map 7A1
Pop 442. Tunbridge Wells 27, London 59, Eastbourne 9, Hastings 11, Hurst Green 13, Lewes 18, Newhaven 20, Uckfield 17.
EC Wed. **Golf** Highwoods (Bexhill) 18h. **See** Smugglers Farm, Royal Observatory.

★★★ White Friars, BN27 4SE Herstmonceux (0323) 832355 Tx: 877440 Fax: (0323) 32072

Charming 18th century building, with beams, situated on the A271. Putting.
20 bedrs, 20 en suite; TV; tcf
dogs, ns; P 120, coach; child facs; con 50

BOREHAMWOOD Hertfordshire. Map 13C4
Pop 26,990. London 12, Barnet 4, Harrow 7½, Hatfield 10, St Albans 8, Watford 6½.
EC Thur. **Golf** Aldenham G & CC 18h. **See** Film and TV Studios.
Civic Offices, Elstree Way. 081-207 2277

Using RAC discount vouchers

Please tell the hotel when booking if you plan to use an RAC discount voucher (see p. 34) in part payment of your bill. Only one voucher will be accepted per party per stay. Discount vouchers will only be accepted in payment for accommodation, not for food.

★★★ Elstree Moat House, Barnet By-Pass, WD6 5PU 081-953 1622 Tx: 928581

Hotel being redeveloped. (QMH)

Grosvenor, 148 Shenley Rd, WD6 1EQ 081-953-3175 Fax: 081-207 5500
£ B&B £34–£48; [5% V w/d]

BOROUGHBRIDGE North Yorkshire. Map 38C3
Pop 2,500. Doncaster 44, London 208, Harrogate 10, Leyburn 26, Northallerton 19, Pontefract 31, Thirsk 12, York 17.
EC Thur, **MD** Mon. **Golf** Knaresborough 18h.
See "Devil's Arrows", millstone-grit monoliths, Roman Museum at Aldborough.
Fishergate. (0423) 323373

★★★ Crown, Horsefair, YO5 9LB (0423) 322328 Tx: 57906
Fine 17th century coaching inn refurbished to high standard.
42 bedrs, 42 en suite; TV; tcf
lift, dogs; P 60, coach; child facs; con 150
LD 9.15. Resid lic
£ B&B £42–£60 (w/e £37·50), B&B (double) £60–£82·50; L £9, D £14·50; WB £37·50; [5% V]
cc Access, Amex, B'card/Visa, Diners.
(See advertisement on p. 146)

★★★ Three Arrows, Horsefair, YO5 9LL (0423) 322245

Small but spacious hotel with extensive grounds; convenient for A1. (Emb)
17 bedrs, 17 en suite; TV; tcf
dogs; P 50, coach; child facs; con 50
LD 9. Resid lic
£ B&B £57, B&B (double) £70; L £8, D £15
cc Access, Amex, B'card/Visa, Diners.
(See advertisement on p. 142)

Crown Inn, Roecliffe YO5 9LY (0423) 322578
Small, busy country inn in tranquil setting overlooking village green. Excellent, well-equipped bedrooms.
6 bedrs, 6 en suite; TV, tcf

EC *early closing* **MD** *market day* *country house hotel* *ns (NS) no smoking areas* *tcf tea/coffee facilities*

Farndale (Acclaimed), Horsefair, YO5 9AH (0423) 323463. *Guest House.*

BORROWDALE Cumbria. Map 43C1
See also GRANGE IN BORROWDALE and KESWICK
Pop 736. Keswick 6½, London 286, Cockermouth 16, Egremont 24.
Golf Embleton 18h, Cockermouth 18h. **See** Bowder Stone, Lodore Falls.

★★★ **Borrowdale,** Borrowdale Rd, CA12 5UV (0596) 84224
Fax: (0596) 84338

19th century Lakeland stone building with beautiful hill and lake views. Fr.
34 bedrs, 34 en suite; TV; tcf
dogs; P 100, coach; child facs; con 40
LD 9.15
£ B&B £19·50–£34·50, B&B (double) £39–£69; HB £249–£336; D £15·50; WB £37 (HB)
cc Access, B'card/Visa.

★★★ **Scafell,** Rosthwaite, CA12 5XB
(059 684) 208 Fax: (059 684) 280
Former coaching inn in heart of Borrowdale valley amid spectacular mountain scenery. Closed Jan.
20 bedrs, 20 en suite; TV; tcf
dogs; P 50; child facs
LD 9.15, bar meals only Mon–Sat lunch
£ B&B £30, B&B (double) £60; HB weekly £294; D £15·80; WB £82
cc Access; dep.

BOSCASTLE Cornwall. Map 2C3
Pop 750. Launceston 18, London 229, Bude 14, Camelford 5.
Golf St Enodoc Rock 18h. **See** Harbour, Willapark Point, Museum of Witchcraft.

★★ **Bottreaux House,** PL35 0BG (084 05) 231

Georgian hotel in picturesque village. Enjoys uninterrupted sea views of harbour.
7 bedrs, 7 en suite, 1 ba; TV; tcf
dogs; P 10; children over 10

★★ **Wellington,** The Harbour, PL35 0AQ
(084 05) 202 Fax: (084 05) 621
An atmospheric old stone coaching inn, part dating to the 16th century; near the harbour.
Fr, De, Es. Open 8 Feb–24 Nov.
21 bedrs, 16 en suite, 2 ba; TV; tcf
dogs, ns; P 20, coach; no children under 10
LD 9.30, bar meals only lunch
£ B&B £17–£29, B&B (double) £48–£54; HB weekly £180–£243; D £15·50; WB £55 (HB 2 nts); [10% V]
cc Access, Amex, B'card/Visa, Diners; dep.
(*See advertisement on p. 146*)

Melbourne House, New Rd, PL35 0DH
(084 05) 650. *Hotel.*
£ B&B £12–£16; HB weekly £119–£145; [5% V]

Old Coach House, Tintagel Rd, PL35 0AS
(084 05) 398. *Hotel.* Closed Dec.
£ B&B £13–£20; HB weekly £132–£176

BOSHAM West Sussex. Map 6A1
Chichester 3½, London 64, Havant 8.

★★ **Millstream,** Bosham Lane, PO18 8HL
(0243) 573234 Fax: (0243) 573459

A 19th-century red brick and stone building on a stream, with a modern extension at the rear overlooking the mill pond. De.
29 beds, 29 en suite; TV; tcf
dogs; P 40, coach; child facs; con 20
LD 9.30. Resid & Rest lic
£ B&B £55, B&B (double) £85; L £10, D £14
cc Access, Amex, B'card/Visa, Diners; dep.

BOSTON Lincolnshire. Map 34B2
Pop 26,648. Spalding 16, London 117, Grantham 30, Horncastle 18, King's Lynn 34, Louth 30, Skegness 21, Sleaford 17.
EC Thur. **MD** Wed, Sat. **Golf** Boston 18h, Sleaford South Rauceby 18h. **See** 14th cent St Botolph's Church with 272 ft tower—"Boston Stump", 15th cent Guildhall.
28 South St. (0205) 56656

★★★ **New England,** Wide Bargate, PE21 6SH (0205) 365255 Fax: (0205) 310597

Well-maintained red brick hotel in town centre. (THF)
25 bedrs, 25 en suite; TV; tcf
dogs, ns; coach; child facs; con 50
LD 10
£ B&B £60, B&B (double) £66; L £9·25, D £12·50; WB £29
cc Access, Amex, B'card/Visa, CB, Diners.

★★★ **White Hart,** 1–5 High St, Bridgefoot, PE21 8SH (0205) 364877

Regency building close to the centre of town and overlooking the River Whitham.
23 bedrs, 19 en suite, 1 ba; TV; tcf
P 35, coach; child facs; con 70

BOSTON SPA West Yorkshire.
Map 40A4
Doncaster 30, London 194, Leeds 20, Otley 16, Selby 16, Wetherby 3, York 13.
Golf Boston Spa.

★★ **Royal,** 182 High St, LS23 6HT (0937) 842142

Attractive, cream-washed, 18th-century coaching inn in centre of village. (BCB).
Fr, Es.
13 bedrs, 13 en suite; TV; tcf
ns; P 65; coach, child facs; con 20
LD 10.30
£ B&B £38–£42, B&B (double) £50; L £8·15, D £8·15; WB £27·50
cc Access, Amex, B'card/Visa, Diners.

BOTLEY Hampshire. Map 5C2
Pop 5,300. M27 (jn 7) 2½, London 71, Cosham 11, Fareham 8, Petersfield 20, Southampton 6½, Winchester 11.
EC Wed. **MD** Sat. **Golf** Fleming Park 18h.

★★★★ **Botley Park,** Winchester Rd, Boorley Green, SO3 2LLA (0489) 780888
Fax: (0489) 789242.
Modern, long, low, rambling hotel in red brick and tile with well-equipped leisure centre. Indoor swimming pool, golf, putting, tennis, squash, sauna, solarium, gymnasium, snooker.
100 bedrs, 100 en suite; TV; tcf
TV, dogs, ns; P 250, coach; child facs, con 200
LD 10; nr Sat lunch
£ B&B £87–£120 (w/e £65), B&B (double) £105–£175; L £12·95, D £16·95; WB £115 (2 nts); [10% V]
cc Access, Amex, B'card/Visa, Diners.

Boroughbridge (North Yorks)

CROWN HOTEL

The Crown Hotel caters especially for those who seek excellence in cuisine and comfort. 42 bedrooms, all en suite with colour TV, radio, in-house video, telephone, courtesy tea and coffee. Antique and Executive Rooms. The Restaurant offers an extensive à la Carte menu and five course table d'hôte. Monthly dinner dances. Five Conference Suites. Excellent banquet and function facilities catering for up to 120. Ample parking.

Horsefair, Boroughbridge, North Yorkshire YO5 9LB
Telephone: (0423) 322328 Telex: 57906

Boscastle (Cornwall)

THE WELLINGTON HOTEL

Historic, listed c.16th Century Coaching Inn of real character. Set in glorious National Trust Country by Elizabethan Harbour. Very comfortable, full central heating, 21 bedrooms (16 en-suite), 4 poster bed, colour TV's, tea/coffee making, direct dial telephones. Antiques and Wellingtonia on display. Excellent Anglo French Georgian restaurant plus FREEHOUSE with real ales and buffet. Lots of atmosphere, log fires, beams and real hospitality. 10 acres private woodland walks. Pets always welcome. For FREE brochure write or phone.

RAC ★ ★

Victor & Solange Tobutt

The Harbour, BOSCASTLE, Cornwall PL35 0AQ
08405 202 ETB

Bournemouth (Dorset)

The Chesterwood Hotel

East Overcliff Drive, Bournemouth, BH1 3AR
Tel: 0202 558057

The Chesterwood Hotel is prominently sited on Bournemouth's East Cliff offering panoramic sea views. Entertainment during the summer season. Heated outdoor swimming pool (May to September). Special winter breaks available.

Please write for Brochure or phone (0202) 558057

★★★ **Botleigh Grange,** Grange Rd, Hedge End, SO3 2GA ☎(0489) 787700 Fax: (0489) 788535

16th century mansion set in pleasant grounds with lakes. Putting, fishing.
43 bedrs, 43 en suite; TV; tcf
dogs, P 120, coach; child facs; con 120
LD 10
£ B&B £60–£80, B&B (double) £73–£100; L £8, D £10; WB £78 (HB 2 nts); [10% V excl Sep]
cc Access, Amex, B'card/Visa, Diners.

BOURNE Lincolnshire. Map 34A1

Pop 8,218. Peterborough 15, London 98, Boston 26, Grantham 18, Melton Mowbray 25, Sleaford 18, Spalding 11, Stamford 11. **EC** Wed. **MD** Thur, **Golf** Stoke Rochford 18h, Stamford 18h. **See** Church (Abbey remains), School (1678), Elizabethan Red Hall and pleasure grounds, Roman Carr Dyke.

Angel, Market Place, PE10 9AE ☎(0778) 422346 Fax: (0778) 393065
Traditional coaching inn with its coach yard roofed to provide a small arcade of shops.
14 bedrs, 14 en suite; TV, tcf
P 75, coach; child facs

BOURNEMOUTH and BOSCOMBE

Dorset. Map 5B1
See also FERNDOWN & POOLE.
RAC Office, *9 Poole Road, Bournemouth, BH2 5QW.* ☎(0202) 765328.
Pop 144,800. Ringwood 12, London 104, Blandford Forum 17, Dorchester 27, Lymington 17, Wareham 13.
See Plan, p. 148.
P See Plan. **Golf** Two 18h Municipal Courses—Queen's Park and Meyrick Park, over which several clubs play. **See** Russell-Cotes Art Gallery and Museum, Winter Gardens, Pine Woods, Chines, St Peter's Church, Pavilion Entertainment Centre, Compton Acres Gardens 2 m SW, Hengistbury Head, Christchurch Priory Church, Poole Harbour and Brownsea Island (Nat. Trust).
i Westover Rd. ☎ (0202) 291715

Carlton, East Overcliff, BH1 3DN ☎(0202) 552011 Tx: 41244 Fax: (0202) 299573
Large luxury 3 and 4 storey Edwardian hotel on the cliff-top overlooking sea now undergoing extensive refurbishment. Swimming pool, sauna, solarium, gymnasium, billiards. Fr, De, It, Yu.
72 bedrs, 72 en suite, TV
lift; P 110, G 20, U 8; coach; child facs; con 180
LD 9.45
£ B&B £100–£165, B&B (double) £155–£195; L £17·50, D £25
cc Access, Amex, B'card/Visa, CB, Diners.

★★★★★ **Royal Bath,** Bath Rd, BH1 2EW ☎(0202) 555555 Tx: 41375 Fax: (0202) 554158 ♿
Magnificent hotel in own grounds only minutes from the town centre. Indoor swimming pool, putting, sauna, solarium, gymnasium. (DeV)
131 bedrs, 131 en suite; TV
lift; G 120 (£3·50); child facs; con 500
LD 10
£ B&B £85–£95, B&B (double) £125–£210; HB weekly £445–£665; L £15·10, D £21·10; WB £65 (HB); [5% V]
cc Access, Amex, B'card/Visa, Diners.

★★★★ **Highcliff,** 105 St Michael's Rd, BH2 5DU ☎(0202) 557702 Tx: 417153 Fax: (0202) 292734
Impressive 5-storey hotel in commanding cliff-top location overlooking the bay. Swimming pool, putting, tennis, sauna, solarium, billiards. Fr, Po.
96 bedrs, 96 en suite; annexe 14 bedrs, 14 en suite; TV; tcf
lift, ns; P 90, coach; child facs; con 500
LD 9
£ B&B £70, B&B (double) £110; L £10·50, D £15; WB £96
cc Access, Amex, B'card/Visa, Diners.

★★★★ **H C R Norfolk Royale,** Richmond Hill, BH2 6EN ☎(0202) 551521 Tx: 418474 Fax: (0202) 299729 ♿

Restored Edwardian hotel, elegantly furnished, set in attractive garden. Indoor swimming pool, sauna. Fr, De, Es.
95 bedrs, 95 en suite; TV; tcf
lift, ns; G 85, coach; child facs; con 80
LD 10·30
£ B&B £725–£300, B&B (double) £100–£300; L £12·95, D £14·50; WB £55; [10% V]
cc Access, Amex, B'card/Visa, CB, Diners.

★★★★ **Palace Court,** Westover Rd, BH1 3BZ ☎(0202) 557681 Tx: 418451 Fax: (0202) 24918

Large, attractively decorated, modern town centre hotel with sea views. Swimming pool, sauna, solarium, gymnasium, snooker.
103 bedrs, 103 en suite; TV; tcf
lift, ns, G 250 (£1·50); children over 6; con 300
LD 9
£ B&B £55, B&B (double) £82–£110; L £9·50; D £12·50; WB £45
cc Access, Amex, B'card/Visa, Diners; dep.

★★★ **Anglo-Swiss,** 16 Gervis Rd, East Cliff, BH1 3EQ ☎(0202) 554794 Fax: (0202) 299615

Large 4-storey hotel with spacious public rooms and delightful gardens. New leisure complex opening Easter 1991. Swimming pool, sauna, solarium, gymnasium. Es.
70 bedrs, 62 en suite; annexe 8 bedrs, 8 en suite; TV, tcf
lift, dogs; P 60, coach; child facs; con 160
LD 8.30, bar meals only lunch
£ B&B £33–£42, B&B (double) £66–£84; HB weekly £259–£312; L £6·50, D £9·50; WB £79 (HB 2 nts); [10% V]
cc Access, Amex, B'card/Visa, Diners; dep.

★★★ **Belvedere,** Bath Rd, BH1 2EU ☎(0202) 297556 Fax: (0202) 294699
Small modern hotel in central location with sea views. Walking distance of beach. De.
63 bedrs, 63 en suite; TV; tcf
lift; P 50, coach; child facs; con 50
LD 9
£ B&B £37–£42, B&B (double) £52–£57; HB weekly £238–£266; L £7·95, D £11·50–£13·50; WB £34 (till May)
cc Access, Amex, B'card/Visa, Diners; dep.

★★★ **Bournemouth Heathlands,** 12 Grove Rd, East Cliff, BH1 3AY ☎(0202) 553336 Tx: 8954665 Fax: (0202) 25937 ♿

Attractive building in pleasant garden. In popular East Cliff district overlooking beach. Swimming pool, sauna, solarium, gymnasium.
116 bedrs, 116 en suite; TV; tcf
lift, dogs; P 80, coach; child facs; con 270

★★★ **Bournemouth Moat House,** Knyveton Rd, BH1 3QQ ☎(0202) 293311 Tx: 417226 Fax: (0202) 292221

B

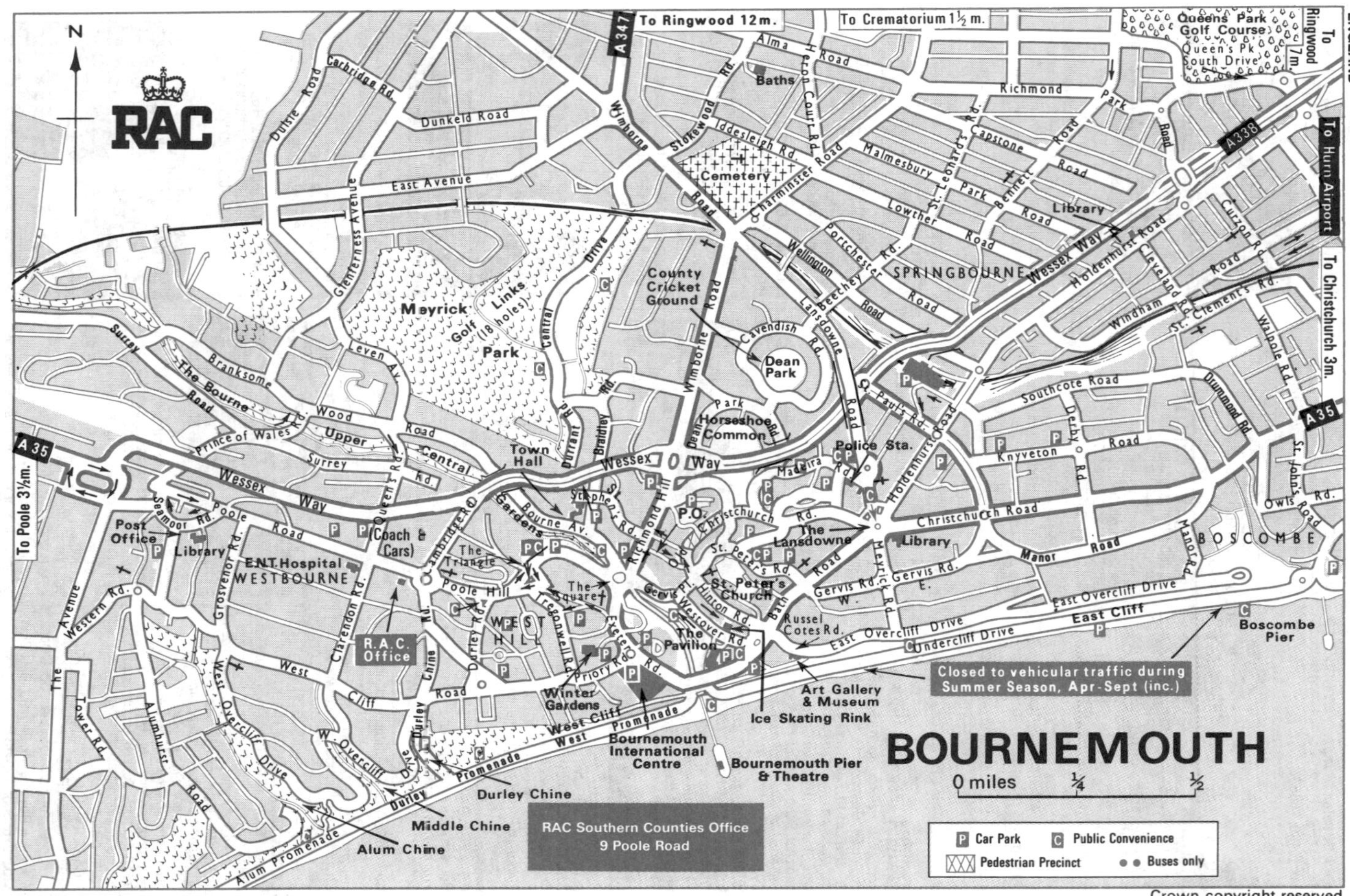

EC *early closing* **MD** *market day* *country house hotel* *ns (NS) no smoking areas* *tcf tea/coffee facilities*

Modern hotel in quiet tree-lined avenue. Convenient for sea and shops. Indoor swimming pool, sauna, gymnasium, billiards. ⚒ Fr, It, Es. (QMH)
🛏 147 bedrs, 147 en suite; TV; tcf
🏨 lift, dogs; P 100, coach; child facs; con 700
✕ LD 9.30
£ B&B £52·50–£60, B&B (double) £70–£80; HB weekly £297·50; L £9·50; D £13·50; WB £48 (HB); [10% V]
cc Access, Amex, B'card/Visa, Diners.

★★★ **H** **Burley Court,** Bath Rd, BH1 2NP
📞(0202) 552824 Fax: (0202) 298514

Two-storey white-painted hotel owned for more than 30 years by same family. Near sea. Swimming pool, solarium. ⚒ Fr, Po.
🛏 39 bedrs, 34 en suite, 2 ba; TV; tcf
🏨 lift, TV, dogs; P 35; child facs
✕ LD 8.30, bar meals only lunch. Resid & Rest lic
£ B&B £25–£38, B&B (double) £49·50–£76; HB weekly £177–£275; D £10; WB £59 (Nov–May); [5% V Oct–May]
cc Access, B'card/Visa; dep.

★★★ **Chesterwood,** East Overcliff Dr, BH1 3AR 📞(0202) 558057 Fax: (0202) 293457
Prominently sited large cliff-top hotel offering wide sea views. Swimming pool. ⚒ Fr, De.
🛏 49 bedrs, 47 en suite, 2 ba; annexe 3 bedrs, 3 en suite; TV; tcf
🏨 lift, TV, dogs (Oct–May only); P 39, G 8, coach; child facs; con 150
✕ LD 8.30, bar meals only Mon–Sat lunch.
£ B&B £32–£43, B&B (double) £60–£86; HB weekly £245–£315; L £8·50, D £12; [10% V Nov–May]
cc Access, Amex, B'card/Visa, Diners; dep.
(See advertisement on p. 146)

★★★ **Chine,** 25 Boscombe Spa Rd, Boscombe, BH5 1AX 📞(0202) 396234 Tx: 41338 Fax: (0202) 391737

Multi-gabled building in magnificent elevated location overlooking the bay. Indoor & outdoor swimming pools, putting, sauna, solarium, gymnasium. ⚒ Fr, It, Tu.
🛏 98 bedrs, 98 en suite; TV; tcf
🏨 lift; P 55, U 1 (£3), coach; child facs; con 120
✕ LD 8.30
£ B&B £35–£45; B&B (double) £70–£90; HB weekly £350–£400; L £12, D £15
cc Access, Amex, B'card/Visa, Diners; dep.

★★★ **Cliffeside,** East Overcliff Dr, BH1 3AQ 📞(0202) 555724 Tx: 418297 Fax: (0202) 294810
Large family-owned cliff-top hotel; enjoys panoramic sea views. Swimming pool. ⚒ It, Es, Eg.
🛏 62 bedrs, 62 en suite; TV; tcf
🏨 lift, TV, dogs; P 50, coach; child facs; con 200
✕ LD 8.30, bar meals only lunch
£ B&B £31·50–£49, B&B (double) £63–£98; L £8·25, D £14·95; [10% V]
cc Access, B'card/Visa; dep.
(See advertisement on p. 150)

★★★ **H** **C** **Connaught,** West Hill Rd, BH2 5PH 📞(0202) 298020 Fax: (0202) 298028 ♿
Refurbished and improved hotel in Victorian house with modern extensions. Indoor & outdoor swimming pools, sauna, solarium, gymnasium, billiards. ⚒ Fr, De, Es.
🛏 60 bedrs, 60 en suite; TV; tcf
🏨 lift, dogs, ns; P 40, coach; child facs; con 300
✕ LD 10, bar meals only Mon–Sat lunch
£ B&B £48, B&B (double) £94; D £16·50; WB £84 (HB 2 nts)
cc Access, Amex, B'card/Visa, Diners; dep.

★★★ **Courtlands,** 16 Boscombe Spa Rd, BH5 1BB 📞(0202) 302442 Tx: 41344 Fax: (0202) 309 880 ♿
Modern hotel in quiet location near Boscombe Pier and beach. Swimming pool, sauna, solarium.
🛏 60 bedrs, 60 en suite; TV; tcf
🏨 lift, dogs; P 50, coach; child facs; con 120
✕ LD 8.30, bar meals only Mon–Sat lunch
£ B&B £37–£43, B&B (double) £68–£76; HB weekly £280–£300; D £13; WB £73
cc Access, Amex, B'card/Visa, Diners; dep.

★★★ **Crest,** The Lansdowne, BH1 2PR 📞(0202) 553262 Tx: 41232 Fax: (0202) 557698

Distinctive modern round hotel conveniently located for town and sea. ⚒ Fr. (Cr/THF)
🛏 102 bedrs, 102 en suite; TV; tcf
🏨 lift, dogs, ns; P 80, G 80, coach; child facs; con 120
✕ LD 9.45
£ room £69–£79 (w/e £36), double room £81–£91, Bk £8·50; L £6·25, D £13·95; WB
cc Access, Amex, B'card/Visa, Diners; dep.

★★★ **Cumberland,** East Overcliff Dr, BH1 3AF 📞(0202) 290722 Tx: 418297 Fax: (0202) 294810
Thirties-style, purpose-built hotel with balconies and a sunken patio area with swimming pool. Fine sea views. ⚒ It, Es.
🛏 102 bedrs, 102 en suite; TV; tcf
🏨 lift, TV; P 65; child facs; con 100
✕ LD 8.30, nr Mon–Sat lunch
£ L £7·50, D £14·95; WB £70; [10% V]
cc Access, B'card/Visa; dep.

★★★ **Durley Hall,** Durley Chine Rd, BH2 5JS 📞(0202) 766886 Fax: (0202) 762236

Large imposing hotel set in own secluded gardens. Indoor & outdoor swimming pools, sauna, solarium, gymnasium, snooker. ⚒ Es, Po.
🛏 70 bedrs, 70 en suite; annexe 11 bedrs, 11 en suite; TV; tcf
🏨 lift, dogs; P 150, coach; child facs; con 200
✕ LD 8.45, coffee shop only Mon–Sat lunch
£ B&B £53–£58, B&B (double) £79–£84; HB weekly £276–£285; D £14·50; WB £79 (2 nts)
cc Access, Amex, B'card/Visa, Diners; dep.

★★★ **Durlston Court,** Gervis Rd, BH1 3DD 📞(0202) 291488 Fax: (0202) 299615
Modern hotel ideally set in quiet district yet near centre. Access to beach nearby. Guests may use sports facilities at sister hotel Anglo-Swiss. ⚒ It, Es.
🛏 55 bedrs, 55 en suite, annexe 5 bedrs, 5 en suite; TV; tcf
🏨 lift, dogs, ns; P 40, coach; child facs; con 120
✕ LD 8.30, bar meals only lunch
£ B&B £33–£42, B&B (double) £66–£84; HB weekly £259–£312; L £6·50, D £9·50; WB £79 (HB 2 nts); [10% V]
cc Access, Amex, B'card/Visa, Diners; dep.

★★★ **East Anglia,** 6 Poole Rd, BH2 5QX 📞(0202) 765163 Fax: (0202) 752949 ♿
Privately-owned hotel within walking distance of main shops. Swimming pool, sauna, solarium, gymnasium. ⚒ Fr, It.
🛏 49 bedrs, 49 en suite; annexe 24 bedrs, 24 en suite; TV; tcf
🏨 lift; ns, P 73, coach; child facs; con 150
✕ LD 8.30, bar meals only Mon–Sat lunch
£ B&B £35–£38, B&B (double) £64–£76; HB weekly £252–£294; L £7·25, D £13·50; WB £70
cc Access, Amex, B'card/Visa, Diners; dep.

★★★ **H** **C** **East Cliff Court,** East Overcliff Dr, BH1 3AN 📞(0202) 24545 Fax: (0202) 27456

Recently refurbished, white-painted hotel overlooking the sea. Sunken garden and

B

Bournemouth (Dorset)

Marsham Court Hotel

EAST CLIFF BOURNEMOUTH BH1 3AB
RAC★★★ 0202–552111

Overlooking Bournemouth Bay, in a quiet centrally located cliff top position, Marsham Court offers the ideal venue for your summer holiday or short break.
86 superior rooms, all with Satellite TV, many with sea view and balcony. Our restaurant serves imaginative and varied cuisine, both table d'hôte and à la carte. Snooker room. Relax on the sun terraces beside our heated outdoor pool. Large car park.
LEISURE BREAKS – from £41 DAILY HALF BOARD
FREE ACCOMMODATION FOR CHILDREN

Bournemouth (Dorset)

The Cumberland Hotel
EAST OVERCLIFF DRIVE
TEL. (0202) 290722

The Trouville Hotel
WESTCLIFF
TEL. (0202) 552262

Arthur Young Hotels

RAC *** RAC

BOURNEMOUTH

These outstanding sister hotels offer real comfort and relaxation. Situated on Bournemouth's prestigious East Cliff with superb views overlooking the bay, with its seven miles of sandy beach, yet near town centre & shops. Privately owned & managed by the Young family, all hotels offer Bargain Breaks, spacious accommadation, first class cuisine, recreation facilities, entertainment & dancing, a friendly, efficient staff and ample free parking.

PHONE AND BOOK NOW

The Cliffeside Hotel
EAST OVERCLIFF DRIVE
TEL. (0202) 555724

The Queens Hotel
MEYRICK ROAD
TEL. (0202) 554415

Bournemouth (Dorset)

Durley Grange Hotel

6 Durley Road, Westcliff, Bournemouth BH2 5JL ★★

Modern family managed hotel situated in the heart of Bournemouth.
50 en-suite bedrooms all with colour TV, radio, telephone and tea maker. Excellent food served in the lovely Grange Restaurant. Superb Lounge Bar, where Bar Lunches are available March–November. Entertainment twice weekly during season. Lift. Central heating. Car park. Sun patio. LET'S GO Bargain Breaks. October–May. Any two days dinner, room and breakfast from £56.00 inclusive of VAT. **EASTER, CHRISTMAS AND NEW YEAR PROGRAMME.**
NEW FOR SPRING '91 Heated Indoor pool, sauna and solarium.

Telephone: Reception 0202 554473/290743 Fax: 0202 293774

 EC *early closing* **MD** *market day* *country house hotel* *ns (NS) no smoking areas* *tcf tea/coffee facilities*

patio. Swimming pool, sauna, solarium. Es, Po, Ar.
68 bedrs, 68 en suite; TV; tcf
lift, dogs; P 75, coach; child facs; con 250
LD 9
£ B&B £35–£64 (w/e £32·50), B&B (double) £70–£115; HB weekly £170–£380; L £6·50, D £13·95; WB £75 (HB 2 nts); [10% V]

★★★ C **Elstead,** 12 Knyveton Rd, BH1 3QP (0202) 293071 Fax: (0202) 293827

Hotel located in tree-lined avenue in quiet residential area. Pleasant garden. Billiards. Open Apr–Sep.
51 bedrs, 46 en suite, 2 ba; TV, tcf
lift, dogs, ns; P 32, coach; child facs; con 50
LD 8.30, bar meals only lunch. Resid lic
£ B&B £22·50–£29, B&B (double) £45–£58; HB weekly £201–£241; L £5·50, D £10; WB £60 (2 nts)
cc Access, B'card/Visa; dep.

★★★**Embassy,** Meyrick Rd, BH1 3DW (0202) 290751 Fax: (0202) 557459
Hotel in pleasant tree-lined location within walking distance of cliff-top lift. Swimming pool. It.
39 bedrs; 39 en suite; TV, tcf
lift, dogs, P 75, coach, child facs, con 150
LD 8.30, bar meals only lunch. Resid lic
£ B&B £29·50–£41, B&B (double) £59–£82; L £6·50, D £10·50
cc Access, Amex, B'card/Visa; dep.

★★★ H **Grosvenor,** Bath Rd, BH1 2EX (0202) 28858 Tx: 417200
Compact modern hotel in elevated corner location close to centre. Indoor swimming pool, sauna, solarium, gymnasium.
40 bedrs, 40 en suite; TV; tcf
lift, TV, dogs, ns; P 40, coach; child facs; con 80

★★★ **Hermitage,** Exeter Rd, BH2 5AH (0202) 27363 Tx: 418316

Privately-run hotel in prime central site facing main pier and beach. Sauna, solarium.
78 bedrs, 75 en suite, 3 ba; TV; tcf
lift, TV, godgs, ns; P 60; coach; children over 9; child facs; con 100

★★★ H C R **Langtry Manor,** 26 Derby Rd, BH1 3QB (0202) 553887 Fax: (0202) 290115
Tudor style lovenest of Edward VII and Lillie Langtry. Fr.
14 bedrs, 14 en suite; annexe 13 bedrs, 13 en suite; TV; tcf
dogs, ns; P 30; coach; child facs; con 100
LD 9, bar meals only lunch. Resid & Rest lic
£ B&B £49·50–£64·50, B&B (double) £76–£142; HB weekly £346·50–£420; D £17·75; WB £49·50; [10% V]
cc Access, Amex, B'card/Visa, Diners; dep.

★★★ **Marsham Court,** Russell Cotes Rd, BH1 3AB (0202) 552111 Tx: 41420 Fax: (0202) 294744

Edwardian hotel overlooking the Bay, only minutes from town centre. Swimming pool, snooker.
86 bedrs, 86 en suite, TV; tcf
lift, P 100, coach; child facs; con 200
LD 9
£ B&B £47–£52, B&B (double) £84–£94; HB weekly £287–£322; L £9·50, D £13·50; WB £90 (HB 2 nts); [10% V]
cc Access, Amex, B'card/Visa, Diners; dep.
(*See advertisement on p. 150*)

★★★**Melford Hall,** St Peter's Rd, BH1 2LS (0202) 551516 Fax: (0202) 292533

Privately-owned hotel in own grounds. Quiet location though near centre. Indoor swimming pool, sauna, solarium, gymnasium.
60 bedrs, 58 en suite, 4 ba; annexe 3 bedrs; 3 en suite; TV; tcf
lift, dogs, P 75, coach; child facs; con 100
LD 8.30. Resid & Rest lic

Licences
Establishments have a full licence unless shown as unlicensed or with the limitations listed on p 6.

£ B&B £22–£34, B&B (double) £44–£68; HB weekly £150–£285; L £6·50, D £9; WB £22; [10% V]
cc Access, B'card/Visa, Diners; dep.

★★★ **Miramar,** East Overcliff Dr, BH1 3AL (0202) 556581 Fax: (0202) 299573

Large seafront hotel in ¾ acre of grounds. Good sea views. Putting. Fr, De, Po.
39 bedrs, 39 en suite, 1 ba; TV; tcf
lift, TV; P 50, U 2 (£4), coach; child facs; con 100
LD 8.30. Resid & Rest lic
£ B&B £41–£50, B&B (double) £80–£90; HB weekly £287–£315, L £5, D £13·50; WB £70 (til Mar); [10% V, not May, Jun, Sep, Oct]
cc Access, Amex, B'card/Visa; dep.

★★★ **New Durley Dean,** Westcliff Rd, BH2 5HE (0202) 557711 Fax: (0202) 292815

Victorian terrace near the cliff top walk. Recently refurbished and now a lively hotel with entertainment most nights. Indoor swimming pool, sauna, solarium, gymnasium, snooker. Fr, De, It, Es.
111 bedrs, 111 en suite; TV; tcf
lift, dogs, ns; P 40, coach; child facs; con 200
LD 9; bar meals only Mon-Sat lunch
£ B&B £32·50–£39, B&B (double) £65–£78; HB weekly £249–£299; D £12·50; WB £65 (HB 2 nts); [5% V]
cc Access, Amex, B'card/Visa.

★★★ **Pavilion,** Bath Rd, BH1 2NS (0202) 291266 Tx: 418253 Fax: (0202) 559264
Compact hotel with large front lawn. Set on tree-lined avenue. Fr, It, Es, Po.
44 bedrs, 44 en suite; TV; tcf
lift, TV, dogs, ns; P 30, coach; child facs; con 100
LD 8.30. Resid & Rest lic
£ B&B £38, B&B (double) £54; HB weekly £195–£210; L £4·50, D £14; WB £29; [5% V]
cc Access, Amex, B'card/Visa, Diners; dep.

Atlas Section
Consult the Atlas section at the back of the guide to find out which towns and villages have RAC Appointed and Listed hotels in them. They are shown on the maps by purple circles.

Bournemouth (Dorset)

RAC ★★★★

Set in 10 acres of scenic grounds, adjacent to the Ferndown Golf Course and located near Bournemouth and the New Forest. All guests have free use of the fully fitted exclusive Leisure Club, featuring indoor pool and squash courts. A la Carte and Table d'Hôte restaurant plus snack bar in addition to the 3 bars. Friday night Barbecue/ Dance (summer months) and Dinner Dance every Saturday. 130 de Luxe en suite bedrooms. Special Leisure Breaks all year and summer specials (August). Please telephone for brochure and tariff.

THE DORMY

NEW ROAD, FERNDOWN, DORSET BH22 8ES
TEL: BOURNEMOUTH (0202) 872121
FAX: (0202) 895388

Bournemouth (Dorset)

"The Country Setting by the Sea"

○ Personally run ○ RAC Two Merit Awards
○ Direct dial telephones ○ Conference and Function facilities
○ A la Carte Restaurant ○ ETB 4 Crowns

Studland Road, Alum Chine, Westcliff, Bournemouth
Tel: 0202 764583 5 lines

Bournemouth (Dorset)

Russell Court Hotel

Bath Road, Bournemouth BH1 2EP Tel: (0202) 295819

Situated in the heart of beautiful Bournemouth

★ 62 Bedrooms ★ Near to Pier, beach, shops, Shows ★ Excellent food, with choice of menu ★ Large car park ★ Lift ★ Ballroom ★ 2 Bars ★ Sea View Rooms ★ All rooms colour TV, radio, tea and coffee facilities ★ Direct Dial Telephones ★ Short stroll to International Conference and Leisure Centre ★ Bargain Breaks, early and late season ★ Open all year ★ Christmas and New Year Programmes.

Write or phone for Colour Brochure and Tariff

Bournemouth (Dorset)

Hinton Firs

BOURNEMOUTH

INDOOR AND OUTDOOR POOLS

In the heart of the East Cliff, set amongst rhododendrons and pine trees,our friendly family hotel has 4 lounges facing sheltered gardens and sun terrace.

- **All 52 Rooms incl. 12 Singles, with Bath or Shower**
- **TV, Radio, Tea-making and Direct-Dial Telephone in every room**
- **Dancing • Games Room • Sauna**
- **Indoor and Outdoor Pools • Spa Pool**
- **Bar Lunches • Children's Teas**
- **Lift • Car Parking • Night Porter**

ASHLEY COURTENAY RECOMMENDED

Colour Brochure from **Mr & Mrs R.J. Waters**

Hinton Firs (RAC 91), Manor Road, East Cliff, Bournemouth BH1 3HB
Tel: (0202) 555409

★★★ **Piccadilly,** Bath Rd, BH1 2NN
(0202) 552559 Fax: (0202) 298 235

Well-managed hotel in attractive Georgian-style building, recently refurbished.
45 bedrs, 45 en suite; TV
lift; P 30, coach; child facs; con 150
LD 9. Resid & Rest lic
£ B&B £35–£45, B&B (double) £50–£66; HB weekly £205–£225; L £7·50, D £10·95; WB £50; [10% V]
cc Access, Amex, B'card/Visa, Diners; dep.

★★★ **Queen's,** Meyrick Rd, East Cliff, BH1 3DL (0202) 554415 Tx: 418297
Fax: (0202) 294810
Large family-run hotel with balcony sea-views from some rooms. Billiards. Fr, De.
114 bedrs, 114 en suite; TV; tcf
lift, dogs, ns; P 80, G 12 (£1·50), coach; child facs; con 150
LD 9. Resid & Rest lic
£ B&B £34·50–£42·50, B&B (double) £69–£85; HB weekly £248·50–£315; L £8·25, D £14·95; WB £75·50; [10% V]
cc Access, B'card/Visa; dep.

★★★ **Savoy,** 36 West Hill Rd, BH2 5EJ
(0202) 294241 Fax: (0202) 298367
An elegant 5-storey Victorian building with gardens leading to the cliff-top promenade. Swimming pool, sauna.
91 bedrs, 91 en suite; TV; tcf
lift, dogs, ns; P 81; child facs; con 100
LD 8.45
£ B&B £39–£55, B&B (double) £66·50–£90; £6·95, D £10·95; WB £83 (2 nts); [10% V],
cc Access, Amex, B'card/Visa, Diners; dep.

★★★ **Suncliff,** East Overcliff Dr, BH1 3AG
(0202) 291711 Tx: 41363
Fax: (0202) 299182

Well-kept, 4-storey building painted pale green; fine sea views. Indoor swimming pool, squash, sauna, solarium, gymnasium. Fr, De, It, Es.
95 bedrs, 95 en suite; TV
lift, dogs, ns; P 60, coach; child facs; con 150
LD 8.30, bar meals only lunch
£ B&B £27–£53, B&B (double) £54–£106; HB weekly £188·10–£370; D £13·95
cc Access, Amex, B'card/Visa, Diners; dep.

Changes made after July 1990 are not included.

★★★ **Trouville,** 5 Priory Rd, BH2 5DH
(0202) 552262 Fax: (0202) 294810

Privately-run hotel near International Centre. Sauna, solarium, gymnasium. It, Es.
80 bedrs, 80 en suite, 1 ba; TV; tcf
lift, dogs; P 55, U 5; child facs; con 60
LD 8.30, bar meals only Sat & Sun lunch. Resid & Rest lic
£ B&B £32–£45, B&B (double) £64–£90; HB weekly £224–£280; L £7·50, D £13·95; [10% V Oct–Mar]
cc Access, B'card/Visa; dep.

★★★ **Wessex,** 11 West Cliff Rd, BH2 5EU
(0202) 551911 Fax: (0202) 297354
Extended Victorian building with modern facilities and accommodation. Own grounds. Indoor & outdoor swimming pools, sauna, solarium, gymnasium, billiards.
84 bedrs, 75 en suite, (9 sh); TV; tcf
lift, dogs, ns; P 200, coach; child facs; con 400
LD 9.15
£ B&B £49·50–£54·50, B&B (double) £67·50–£74·50; L £3·75, D £13; [10% V w/e]
cc Access, Amex, B'card/Visa, Diners.

★★ **Arlington,** Exeter Park Rd, Lower Gardens, BH2 5BD (0202) 552879
In quiet position yet central to all facilities, Victorian building overlooking delightful gardens.
28 bedrs, 28 en suite, 1 ba; TV; tcf
lift, TV, ns; P 21, coach; child facs
LD 8. Resid & Rest lic
£ B&B £23·50–£29, B&B (double) £47–£58; D £9·25; WB £54 (HB 2 nts); [5% V]
cc Access, B'card/Visa; dep.

★★ **H C Boltons,** 9 Durley Chine Rd, Westcliff, BH2 5JT (0202) 760907.
Attractive late-Victorian building set in own gardens in quiet residential area. Recently refurbished. Swimming pool.
12 bedrs, 12 en suite; TV; tcf
dogs; P 10, children over 5
LD 8.30. Resid & Rest lic
£ B&B £23; HB weekly £161; L £5·50; D £10·50; WB
cc Access, Amex, B'card/Visa, Diners; dep.

★★ **Cadogan,** 8 Poole Rd, BH2 5QU
(0202) 763006

Popular town-centre hotel in spacious grounds; personally run by proprietors. Es.

55 bedrs, 55 en suite; TV; tcf
lift, TV, dogs; P 60, coach; child facs; con 60
LD 8.15, nr Mon–Sat lunch. Resid lic
£ B&B £30–£34, B&B (double) £44–£58; L £5·50, D £9·50; WB £46; [5% V w/d Oct–May]
cc Access, B'card/Visa; dep.

★★ **Chequers,** 17 West Cliff Rd, BH2 5EX
(0202) 553900.
Family-run hotel in white-painted building convenient for West Cliff.
25 bedrs, 21 en suite, 1 ba; TV; tcf
TV, dogs; P 25, coach; child facs
LD 10. Resid & Rest lic
£ B&B £21–£32·50, B&B (double) £42–£65; HB weekly £150–£225; D £7·50; [10% V]
cc Access, B'card/Visa; dep.
(*See advertisement on p. 158*)

★★ **C R Chinehead,** 31 Alumhurst Rd, Westbourne, BH4 8EN (0202) 752777

Modern 2-storey building at a cross-roads in residential area on west side of town.
21 bedrs, 21 en suite; TV; tcf
ns; P 20; child facs
LD 8.30, bar meals only Mon–Sat lunch. Resid & Rest lic
£ B&B £24–£28, B&B (double) £48–£56; HB weekly £145–£192; L £6·25, D £9·25; WB £53 (2 nts); [10% V]
cc Access, B'card/Visa; dep.

★★ **H C Chinehurst,** Studland Rd, Westbourne, BH4 8JA (0202) 764583

Privately-run hotel within walking distance of Alum Chine. Snooker.
31 bedrs, 31 en suite; TV; tcf
dogs; P 14, coach; child facs; con 30
LD 8.30
£ B&B £18·50–£35; HB weekly £150–£175; L £6·50, D £9·50; WB £50 (2 nts)
cc Access, Amex, B'card/Visa, Diners; dep.
(*See advertisement on p. 152*)

★★ **Cliff End,** 99 Manor Rd, BH1 3EX
(0202) 309711
Red-brick Victorian building with modern extension. Swimming pool, solarium, gymnasium.
40 bedrs, 40 en suite; TV; tcf
lift, dogs; P 50, coach; child facs; con 30
LD 8.30; bar meals only Mon–Sat lunch
£ B&B £32·50; HB weekly £234·50; L £6, D £8·25; WB £57·50; [5% V Sep–May]

cc Access, Amex, B'card/Visa; dep.

★★ **County,** Westover Rd, BH1 2BT ☎(0202) 552385
Centrally-located hotel near shops and pier. Opposite conference centre.
🛏 51 bedrs, 46 en suite, 4 ba; TV; tcf
🏨 lift, dogs; U 12 (£1), coach; child facs; con 50
✕ LD 8, bar meals only lunch
£ B&B £20–£35, B&B (double) £40–£60; HB weekly £150–£220; D £8; WB £25
cc Access, Amex, B'card/Visa; dep.

★★ **H C Durley Chine,** 29 Chine Crescent, West Cliff, BH2 5LR ☎(0202) 551926.

A large Victorian house, with pleasant lawned garden to rear, within walking distance of town centre and sea front. ⚒ Fr
🛏 22 bedrs, 22 en suite; annexe 14 bedrs, 14 en suite; TV; tcf
🏨 dogs, ns; P 40, coach; no children under 5; con 45
✕ LD 8. Resid & Rest lic
£ B&B £28·50–£35; HB weekly £161–£199; D £9·95; [10% V, Oct–May]
cc Access, B'card/Visa; dep.

★★ **Durley Grange,** 6 Durley Rd, West Cliff, BH2 5JL ☎(0202) 554473 Fax: (0202) 293774
Family-run hotel in pleasant area close to West Cliff top. Indoor swimming pool, sauna, solarium. Closed Jan.
🛏 50 bedrs, 50 en suite; TV; tcf
🏨 lift, TV, dogs, ns; P 30, coach; no children under 5; con 50
(*See advertisement on p. 150*)

★★ **Fircroft,** Owls Rd, BH5 1AE ☎(0202) 309771

Large family-run hotel with modern extension. Squash. Guests may use swimming pool at sister hotel. ⚒ Es.
🛏 49 bedrs, 49 en suite; TV; tcf
🏨 lift, TV, dogs; P 50, coach; child facs; con 60
✕ LD 8, bar meals only lunch. Resid & Rest lic
£ B&B £22–£26; HB weekly £150–£203; D £11·50; WB £54 [10% V, Oct–Jun]
cc Access, B'card/Visa; dep.

★★ **Grange,** Overcliff Dr, Southbourne, BH6 3NL ☎(0202) 433093
Victorian building with later additions in pleasant grounds near sea.

★★ **Hazelwood,** 43 Christchurch Rd, BH1 3NZ ☎(0202) 298727 Fax: (0202) 28584

Purpose-built hotel with spacious lounges overlooking the garden; close to East Cliff promenade. Snooker.
🛏 59 bedrs, 59 en suite; TV; tcf
🏨 lift, TV, dogs; P 40, coach; children over 3

★★ **H C Hinton Firs,** Manor Rd, East Cliff, BH1 3HB ☎(0202) 555409 Fax: (0202) 299607

Privately-owned hotel in pleasant location with pine trees and rhododendrons. Indoor/outdoor swimming pool, sauna. ⚒ It, Es.
🛏 46 bedrs, 46 en suite; annexe 6 bedrs, 6 en suite; TV, tcf
🏨 lift, TV, ns; P 40; child facs; con 20
✕ LD 8.30, bar meals only Mon–Sat lunch, also Sun in summer. Resid & Rest lic
£ B&B £29·50–£50, B&B (double) £59–£88; HB weekly £241·50–£335; D £9·25; WB £59 (HB 2 nts)
cc Access, B'card/Visa; dep.
(*See advertisement on p. 152*)

Hotel locations
Hotel locations are shown on the maps at the back of the guide. All towns and villages containing an RAC Appointed or Listed hotel are ringed in purple.

★★ **Hotel Riviera,** West Cliff Gdns, BH2 5HL ☎(0202) 552845

Modern hotel with terrace in popular West Cliff area. Enjoys magnificent views. Open Mar–Nov.
🛏 34 bedrs, 34 en suite; TV; tcf
🏨 lift, TV, dogs; P 24; child facs
✕ LD 7.30, bar meals only lunch. Resid lic
£ B&B £27; HB weekly £190; D £8·50
cc Access, Amex, B'card/Visa.

★★ **Manor House,** 34 Manor Rd, East Cliff, BH1 3EZ ☎(0202) 396669
Traditional Victorian manorial house in peaceful garden setting. Open Xmas–Nov.
🛏 27 bedrs, 18 en suite, (1 sh), 3 ba; TV; tcf
🏨 TV, ns; P 21, coach; child facs; con 50
✕ LD 8, nr lunch. Rest lic
£ B&B £22–£27·50; B&B (double) £36–£40; HB weekly £150–£160; D £9; [V, Mar, Oct]
cc Access, B'card/Visa; dep.

★★ **Overcliff,** Overcliff Dr, Southbourne, BH6 3TA ☎(0202) 428300

Delightful, owner-run holiday hotel near the cliff top in Southbourne.
🛏 30 bedrs, 22 en suite, 2 ba; tcf
🏨 TV; P 16, coach; child facs

★★ **Pinehurst,** West Cliff Gardens, BH2 5HR ☎(0202) 556218
Large red-brick terraced building in side road near popular cliff-top walks. Solarium.
🛏 75 bedrs, 72 en suite, 2 ba; TV; tcf
🏨 lift, dogs; P 48, coach; child facs; con 180

Weekend breaks
Please consult the hotel for full details of weekend breaks; prices shown are an indication only. Many hotels offer mid week breaks as well.

★★ Riviera, Burnaby Rd, Alum Chine, BH4 8JF ☎(0202) 763653 Tx: 41363 Fax: (0202) 299182

Modern, family-run hotel in quiet location overlooking Alum Chine. Indoor and outdoor swimming pools, sauna, solarium, snooker. Es, Po. Closed Jan.
70 bedrs, 70 en suite; annexe 9 bedrs, 9 en suite; TV; tcf
lift, TV, dogs, ns; P 60, coach, child facs, con 40
LD 8.30, bar meals only lunch
£ B&B £20–£40, B&B (double) £50–£100; HB weekly £184·50–£270; D £14
cc Access, B'card/Visa; dep.

★★ Royal Exeter, Exeter Rd, BH2 5AG ☎(0202) 290566

Multi-gabled mansion near Bournemouth International Centre. Basement night club has own entrance. It. (BCB)
36 bedrs, 36 en suite; TV; tcf
lift, ns; P 65, coach; child facs; con 20
LD 10
£ B&B £46·50–£52·50, B&B (double) £61·50; L £8·15, D £8·15; WB £27·50

★★ Russell Court, Bath Rd, BH1 2EP ☎(0202) 295819 Fax: (0202) 293457

Family hotel in distinctive 1930s building, on elevated site with sea views.
62 bedrs, 54 en suite, 3 ba; TV; tcf
lift, P 60, coach; child facs; con 30
LD 8, bar meals only Mon–Sat lunch
£ B&B £40, B&B (double) £35–£84; HB weekly £175–£315; D £7·50; [5% V]
cc Access, Amex, B'card/Visa, Diners; dep.
(*See advertisement on p. 152*)

Please tell the manager if you chose your hotel through an advertisement in the guide.

★★ H St George, West Cliff Gardens, BH2 5HL ☎(0202) 556075
Compact, privately-owned hotel in side street. Near Winter Gardens and shops. Closed 3 Jan–mid-Mar.
22 bedrs, 22 en suite; TV; tcf
lift, dogs; P 4; coach; child facs; con 100
LD 7.15, bar meals only lunch. Resid & Rest lic
£ B&B £20–£24·50, B&B (double) £44–£56; D fr £7·50; dep.

★★ C Sun Court, West Hill Rd, BH2 5PH ☎(0202) 551343

Four-storey hotel with modern extension. In popular West Cliff area. Swimming pool, solarium, gymnasium. De, It, Es.
36 bedrs, 36 en suite; TV; tcf
lift, dogs; P 50, G 1, coach; child facs; con 25
LD 8.30, bar meals only Mon-Sat lunch. Resid lic
£ B&B £26·50–£35, B&B (double) £53–£70; D £13; WB £44
cc Access, Amex, B'card/Visa, Diners; dep.

★★ Ullswater, West Cliff Gdns, BH2 5HW ☎(0202) 555181

Four-storey terrace building in quiet road. Near cliff-top and within sight of sea. Billiards. Fr.
42 bedrs, 42 en suite; TV; tcf
lift; P 9, coach; child facs; con 35
LD 8, bar meals only lunch. Resid & Rest lic
£ B&B £21–£28, B&B (double) £42–£56; HB weekly £136–£210; D £8·50; WB £44; [10% V, Jan–Mar, Nov–22 Dec]
cc Access, B'card/Visa; dep.

Using RAC discount vouchers
Please tell the hotel when booking if you plan to use an RAC discount voucher (see p. 34) in part payment of your bill. Only one voucher will be accepted per party per stay. Discount vouchers will only be accepted in payment for accommodation, not for food.

★★ West Cliff Hall, 14 Priory Rd, BH2 5DN ☎(0202) 299715

Four-storey hotel on corner site close to cliff-top walk. Near International Centre.
49 bedrs, 49 en suite, 1 ba; TV; tcf
lift, dogs; P 36, coach; child facs; con 45
LD 8. Resid & Rest lic
£ B&B £18–£31, B&B (double) £36–£62; D £6; WB £24 (HB); [V]
cc Access, Amex, B'card/Visa, Diners; dep.
(*See advertisement on p. 158*)

★★ H Whitehall, Exeter Park Rd, BH2 5AX ☎(0202) 554682 Fax: (0202) 554682
Hotel in quiet side-road location close to town centre. Open 8 Mar–Nov.
49 bedrs, 48 en suite, (4 sh), 11 ba; TV, tcf
lift, TV, dogs, ns; P 25, coach; child facs;
LD 8, bar meals only lunch. Resid & Rest lic
£ B&B £22–£28, B&B (double) £44–£56; HB weekly £168–£210; D £8·50; WB £104
cc Access, Amex, B'card/Visa, Diners; dep.

★★ Winterbourne, 4 Priory Rd, BH2 5DJ ☎(0202) 296366 Tx: 417153

Centrally situated family run hotel in elevated location. Fine views of bay. Swimming pool. Fr, De. Closed 31 Dec–15 Jan.
41 bedrs, 41 en suite; TV, tcf
lift, dogs; P 32, G 1, coach; child facs; con 80
LD 8, bar meals only lunch. Resid lic
£ B&B £29–£37, B&B (double) £51–£60; HB weekly £170–£247; D £10; WB £49 (2 nts, Nov–Apr); [5% V]
cc Access, B'card/Visa; dep.

★★ Woodcroft Tower, 49 Gervis Rd, East Cliff, BH1 3DE ☎(0202) 558202

Hotel in own grounds in quiet tree-lined avenue. Few minutes to cliff lift.

🛏 40 bedrs, 40 en suite, 4 ba; TV; tcf
lift; P 60, coach; child facs; con 140
✕ LD 8.30. Resid & Rest lic
£ B&B £30–£40, B&B (double) £50–£70; D £10
cc Access, B'card/Visa; dep.

★ **Taurus Park,** 16 Knyveton Rd, BH1 3QN ☎(0202) 557374

Well-kept, 4-storey hotel, quietly situated in a tree-lined road. Fr, Es.
🛏 50 bedrs, 25 en suite, 9 ba; TV; tcf
lift, TV; P 25, coach; no children under 3
✕ LD 7.30, bar meals only lunch. Resid & Rest lic
£ B&B £18–£26, B&B (double) £34–£52; HB weekly £120–£175; D £5; WB £50–£75 (3 days); [5% V, Mar–Jun, Oct, Nov]; dep.

★ **Tree Tops,** 50 Christchurch Rd, BH1 3PE ☎(0202) 553157

Two-storey family hotel in heart of resort; close to beach.

Tudor Grange (Highly Acclaimed), 31 Gervis Rd, BH1 3EE ☎(0202) 291472. *Hotel.* Open Mar–Nov.
£ B&B £20–£26; HB weekly £175–£205; [5% V, w/d Mar–May, Nov]

Borodale (Acclaimed), 10 St John's Rd, Boscombe, BH5 1EL ☎(0202) 35285. *Hotel.*
Cransley (Acclaimed), 11 Knyveton Rd, East Cliff, BH1 3QG ☎(0202) 290067. *Private Hotel.* Open April–Nov.
£ B&B £12–£20; HB weekly £90–£139; [10% V, Apr–Jun, Sep, Oct]
Croham Hurst (Acclaimed), 9 Durley Rd Sth, West Cliff, BH2 5JH ☎(0202) 22353. *Hotel.*
East Cliff Cottage (Acclaimed), 57 Grove Rd, East Cliff, BH1 3AT ☎(0202) 22788 Fax: (0202) 26400
£ B&B £17·50–£20; HB weekly £120–£145; [10% V, Oct–Jun]
Golden Sands (Acclaimed), 83 Alumhurst Rd, Alum Chine, BH4 8HR ☎(0202) 763832. *Private Hotel.* Closed Dec & Jan.
£ B&B £28·80; HB weekly £140–£175
Highclere (Acclaimed), 15 Burnaby Rd, Alum Chine, BH4 8JF ☎(0202) 761350. *Private Hotel.* Open Easter–Oct.
£ B&B £15·75–£17; HB weekly £134–£150; [5% V, Mon–Thu; Apr–Jun, Oct]
Holmcroft (Acclaimed), 5 Earle Rd, Alum Chine, Westbourne, BH4 8JQ ☎(0202) 761289. *Hotel.*
£ B&B £20–£25; HB weekly £154–£175
Linwood House (Acclaimed), 11 Wilfred Rd, Boscombe, BH5 1ND ☎(0202) 397818. *Private Hotel.* Open mid-Mar–Oct
£ HB weekly £93·80–£114·50
New Dorchester (Acclaimed), 64 Lansdowne Rd, BH1 1RS ☎(0202) 551271. *Hotel.* Closed 20 Dec–4 Jan.
£ B&B £16–£30; HB weekly £150–£210
Ravenstone (Acclaimed), 36 Burnaby Rd, Alum Chine, Westbourne, BH4 8JG ☎(0202) 761047. *Hotel.* Open Mar–Oct.
£ B&B £18–£20; HB weekly £136–£165; [5% V, Mar–May, Oct]
Silver Trees (Acclaimed), 57 Wimborne Rd, BH3 7AL ☎(0202) 556040 Fax: (0202) 556040. *Hotel.*
£ B&B £23–£29
Tower House (Acclaimed), West Cliff Gdns, BH2 5HP ☎(0202) 290742. *Hotel.*
West Dene (Acclaimed), 117 Alumhurst Rd, Alum Chine, BH4 8HS ☎(0202) 764843. *Private hotel.* Open Feb–Nov.
£ B&B £22·50–£26·50; HB weekly £160–£214
Wood Lodge (Acclaimed), 10 Manor Rd, East Cliff, BH1 3EY ☎(0202) 290891. *Private Hotel.* Open Easter–mid-Oct
£ B&B £18–£27; HB weekly £145–£190
Wychcote (Acclaimed), 2 Somerville Rd, BH2 5LH ☎(0202) 557898. *Hotel.*
£ B&B £14·50–£21·50; HB weekly £120–£195

Albemarle, 123 West Hill Rd, Westcliff, BH2 5PH ☎(0202) 551351. *Private Hotel.*
£ B&B £14–£20; HB weekly £120–£160; [5% V, not July–Sept]
Alum Bay, 19 Burnaby Rd, Alum Chine, BH4 8JF ☎(0202) 761034. *Hotel.*
£ B&B £19–£25; HB weekly £147–£180; [5% V]
Bay Tree, 17 Burnaby Rd, Alum Chine, BH4 8JF ☎(0202) 763807. *Private Hotel.* Closed 29–31 Dec
£ B&B £13·75–£20·75; HB weekly £125·50–£155·25; [10% V].
Blinkbonnie Heights, 26 Clifton Rd, Southbourne, BH6 3PA ☎(0202) 426512. ♿
£ B&B £10–£18; HB weekly £84–£125
Braemar, 30 Glen Rd, Boscombe, BH5 1HS ☎(0202) 396054. *Private Hotel.* Open Mar–end Oct & 23–28 Dec.
£ B&B £14–£17; HB weekly £95–£130; [5% V]
Britannia, 40 Christchurch Rd, BH1 3PE ☎(0202) 26700. *Hotel.*
Chinebeach, 14 Studland Rd, Alum Chine, BH4 8JA ☎(0202) 767015. *Hotel.*
£ B&B £14–£21; HB weekly £130–£180; [5% V, not Jul, Aug]
Clifton Court, 30 Clifton Rd, Southbourne, BH6 3PA ☎(0202) 427753. *Hotel.*
Denby, 24 Southern Rd, Southbourne, BH6 3SR ☎(0202) 428958. *Private Hotel.*
Derwent House, 36 Hamilton Rd, Boscombe, BH1 4EH ☎(0202) 309102. *Private Hotel.*
£ B&B £12–£17; HB weekly £80–£132; [5% V]
Dorset Westbury, 62 Lansdowne Rd North, BH1 1RS ☎(0202) 551811. *Private Hotel.*
Closed 20 Dec–10 Jan.
£ B&B £14·50–£22; HB weekly £126–£170; [10% V, Oct–Mar]
Gervis Court, 38 Gervis Rd, BH1 3DH ☎(0202) 556871. *Hotel.* Open Mar–mid-Dec.
£ B&B £18; HB weekly £106–£180; [10% V]
Glen, 12 Rosemount Rd, Alum Chine, BH4 8HB ☎(0202) 763795. *Hotel.* Open Mar–Nov
£ B&B £13–£18; HB weekly £113–£135; [V, Apr–Jun, Sep–Nov]
Hawaiian, 4 Glen Rd, Boscombe, BH5 1BR ☎(0202) 393234. *Hotel.* Open Mar–Nov.
£ B&B £15–£18; HB weekly £120–£138; [10% V, Apr, May, Oct, Nov]
Holme Lacy, 32 Florence Rd, Boscombe, BH5 1HQ ☎(0202) 36933
Hotel Cavendish, 20 Durley Chine Rd, West Cliff, BH2 5LF ☎(0202) 290489. *Hotel.* Open Easter–Nov.
£ B&B £12–£17·50; HB weekly £100–£150
Hotel Sorrento, 16 Owls Rd, Boscombe, BH5 1AG ☎(0202) 394019. *Hotel.* Closed 29 Dec–15 Jan.
Hotel Washington, 3 Durley Rd, West Cliff, BH2 5JQ ☎(0202) 557023. *Hotel.*
£ B&B £17·25–£21·50; HB weekly £153–£180
Ingledene, 20 Derby Rd, BH1 3QA ☎(0202) 555433. *Guest House.*
£ B&B £11·40–£15·20; HB weekly £88–£121·50; [5% V, not July, Aug]
Langton Hall, 8 Durley Chine Rd, BH2 5JY ☎(0202) 25025. *Hotel.*
Mae Mar, 91 West Hill Rd, BH2 5PQ ☎(0202) 553167. *Hotel.*
£ B&B £15–£25·50; HB weekly £112·50–£168; [V, not 21 Jul–end Aug]
Naseby-Nye, Byron Rd, Boscombe Overcliff, BH5 1JD ☎(0202) 34079. *Hotel.*
Newlands, 14 Rosemount Rd, Alum Chine, BH4 8HB ☎(0202) 761922. *Private Hotel.* Open Mar–Oct.
£ B&B £10–£16; HB weekly £88–£133
Northover, 10 Earle Rd, Alum Chine, BH4 8JQ ☎(0202) 767349. *Hotel.* Open Mar–Oct & 23–28 Dec.
£ B&B £15–£20; HB weekly £120–£150; [5% V, Mar–May, Oct]
Oak Hall, 9 Wilfred Rd, Boscombe, BH5 1ND ☎(0202) 395062. *Hotel.* Open Nov–Sep.
£ B&B £16–£18·50; HB weekly £113–£152; [10% V, Jan–May]
Parklands, 4 Rushton Cres, BH3 7AF ☎(0202) 552529. *Hotel.*
£ B&B £17–£23
Pine Lodge, 12 Westbourne Pk Rd, BH4 8HG ☎(0202) 761872. *Private Hotel.*
St Johns Lodge, 10 Swithun's Rd South, BH1 3RQ ☎(0202) 290677. *Hotel.*
£ B&B £15·50–£18·50; HB weekly £115–£159
Sea Dene, 10 Burnaby Rd, Alum Chine, BH4 8JF ☎(0202) 761372. *Hotel.* Open Mar–Nov.
£ B&B £11–£16; HB weekly £110–£145
Sea View Court, 14 Boscombe Spa Rd, BH5 1AZ ☎(0202) 397197. *Private Hotel.*
£ B&B £12–£20; HB (weekly) £90–£145
Seaway, 30 St Catherines Rd, Southbourne, BH6 4AB ☎(0202) 423636. *Private Hotel.*
Shoreline, 7 Pinecliffe Ave, Southbourne, BH6 3PY ☎(0202) 429654. *Private Hotel.*
£ B&B £11–£15; HB weekly £95–£135; [10% V, not Jun–Sep]
Sunnylees, 231 Holdenhurst Rd, BH8 8DD ☎(0202) 35831. *Private Hotel.*

Valberg, 1a Wollenstonecraft Rd, Boscombe, BH5 1JQ ☎(0202) 394644. *Hotel.*
£ B&B £13; HB weekly £120–£144
Vine, 22 Southern Rd, Southbourne, BH6 3SR ☎(0202) 428309
Wenmaur House, 14 Carysfort Rd, Boscombe, BH1 4EJ ☎(0202) 395081. *Private Hotel.*
£ HB weekly £95–£140.
West Bay, West Cliff Gdns, BH2 5HL ☎(0202) 552261. *Hotel.* Open Jan–Nov.
£ B&B £20–£23·50; HB weekly £161–£184; [5% V, Jan–Jun, Oct]
Whitley Court, West Cliff Gdns, West Cliff, BH2 5HL ☎(0202) 21302. *Private Hotel.*
Wrenwood, 11 Florence Rd, Boscombe, BH5 1HH ☎(0202) 395086. *Private Hotel.*

BOURTON-ON-THE-WATER Glos.

Map 20C2
Pop 2,711. Burford 9½, London 84, Cheltenham 16, Cirencester 16, Gloucester 24, Stow-on-the-Wold 4, Tewkesbury 22.
EC Sat. **Golf** Burford 18h. **See** Model Village, Aquarium, Birdland.

★★★ **Old Manse,** Victoria St, GL54 2BX ☎(0451) 20082 Fax: (0451) 20642
Fine mid-18th century Cotswold stone house overlooking river. Fr, It.
12 bedrs, 12 en suite; TV; tcf
P 12, coach; child facs; con 30
LD 9·30
£ B&B £35, B&B (double) £55–£105; HB weekly £240·75; L £5·95, D £14·75; [5% V]
cc Access, B'card/Visa; dep.

★★ **Chester House,** GL54 2BU ☎(0451) 20286 Fax: (0451) 20471

Cotswold stone building with converted cottages to the rear. Open mid-Feb–mid-Dec.
13 bedrs, 13 en suite, 1 ba, annexe 10 bedrs, 10 en suite; TV; tcf
dogs; P 23, coach; child facs; con 12
LD 9.30, nr Fri lunch. Resid & Rest lic.
£ B&B £35–£38, B&B (double) £54–£66; L £9·50, D £14·95; WB £40·45
cc Access, Amex, B'card/Visa, Diners; dep.

★★ **H** **C** **Finden Lodge,** Whiteshoots Hill, Cirencester Rd, GL54 2LE ☎(0451) 20387

Newly developed, family-run hotel of Cotswold stone on outskirts of village on A429 Stow to Cirencester. Fine views to the rear. Fr, De, Ca.
12 bedrs, 12 en suite; TV; tcf
dogs, ns; P 34, coach; child facs; con 12
LD 9.30
£ B&B £35–£45, B&B (double) £56–£70; HB weekly £253–£290; L £8·50, D £12·50; WB £35; [5% V]
cc Access, B'card/Visa; dep.

★★ **Old New Inn,** High St, GL54 2AF ☎Cotswold (0451) 20467
Cotswold stone inn dating from 18th century. Charming model village in grounds. Closed Xmas.
17 bedrs, 8 en suite, 1 ba; annexe 6 bedrs, 1 en suite, 1 ba; TV
TV, dogs; P 25, U 6 (£1·50); child facs
LD 8.30
£ B&B £24–£30; L £9, D £13
cc Access, B'card/Visa.

The Ridge (Highly Acclaimed), Whiteshoots, GL54 2LE ☎Cotswold (0451) 20660. *Guest House.*
£ B&B £15–£20

BOVEYTRACEY Devon. Map 3B2

Pop 4,500. Exeter 14, London 181, Ashburton 8, Crediton 16, Newton Abbot 6, Okehampton 18, Tavistock 26.
EC Wed. **Golf** Newton Abbot (Stover) 18h.
Lower Car Park. ☎(0626) 832047

★★★ **Edgemoor,** Lowerdown Cross TQ13 9LE ☎(0626) 832466 Fax: (0626) 834760
Recently refurbished and improved Victorian grey-stone building, with extensive grounds, on edge of Dartmoor.
13 bedrs, 13 en suite; TV; tcf

★★ **Coombe Cross,** Coombe La, TQ13 9EY ☎(0626) 832476

Pleasant country house-style hotel with spectacular view. Gymnasium.
26 bedrs, 24 en suite, 2 ba; TV; tcf
dogs, ns; P 26; coach; child facs; con 60
LD 8, bar meals only lunch. Resid lic
£ B&B £33; HB weekly £217–£251·30; D £15·95; WB £64 (HB 2 days)
cc Access, Amex, B'card/Visa, Diners; dep.

★★ **Riverside,** Fore St, TQ13 9AF ☎(0626) 832295 Fax: (0626) 833880
A 17th-century inn in the middle of the village with river views. Fishing.
10 bedrs, 10 en suite; TV; tcf
dogs, P 150, coach; child facs; con 280
LD 9
£ B&B £30, B&B (double) £50; HB weekly £220; D £7·50; [10% V]
cc Access, B'card/Visa; dep.

BOWDON Greater Manchester (Cheshire).

See ALTRINCHAM.

BOWNESS-ON-WINDERMERE Cumbria.

See WINDERMERE.

B

BRACKLEY Northamptonshire.

Map 21B3
Pop 6,621. Buckingham 8, London 64, Banbury 10, Bicester 11, Chipping Norton 21, Oxford 22, Towcester 11.
EC Wed. **MD** Fri. **Golf** Buckingham 18h.

★★ **Crown,** 20 Market Place, NN13 5DP ☎(0280) 702210

This white-painted former coaching inn in the market place can trace its history back to the 13th century.
14 bedrs, 14 en suite; TV; tcf
TV; P 20, coach; child facs; con 100

BRACKNELL Berkshire. Map 13A2

Pop 51,552. Staines 11, London 28, Bagshot 5½, Basingstoke 21, Henley-on-Thames 13, Reading 11, Weybridge 14, Windsor 9.
EC Wed. **MD** Fri, Sat. **Golf** Downshire 18h.
Library, Town Sq. ☎(0344) 423149

★★★★ **Hilton National,** Bagshot Rd, RG12 3QJ ☎(0344) 424801 Tx: 848058 Fax: (0344) 487454

Large modern hotel on edge of woodland. Indoor swimming pool. Fr, De, It, Es, Po (HN)
167 bedrs, 167 en suite; TV; tcf
lift, dogs, ns; P 150, coach; child facs; con 200
LD 10, bar meals only Sat lunch

Bournemouth (Dorset)

CHEQUERS HOTEL

West Cliff Road, Bournemouth, Dorset BH2 5EX Tel: 0202 553900

Friendly family run hotel at the head of Durley Chine. A few minutes from the sea, shops, cinemas and Conference Centre. Large car park. *Highly recommended.*

Bournemouth (Dorset)

BOURNEMOUTH

West Cliff Hall Hotel

14 Priory Road, Bournemouth BH2 5DN

- Close to beaches and Bournemouth town centre.
- All 49 bedrooms have en suite, colour television, tea-making, direct dial telephone and radio intercom.
- Central heating throughout.
- Generous catering of a high standard, with plenty of fresh local produce. Good menu choice to appeal to all tastes.
- Full English Breakfast. Six course evening dinner.
- Residential Bar
- Free car parking (36 spaces).
- Tempting selection of bar snacks available each lunchtime.
- Dancing and live music three times weekly in season.
- Lift
- 4 day Christmas programme.

	Low Season	Mid Season	High Season
Room & B'fast daily	£20.00	£29.00	£31.00
with dinner	*£24.00*	*£35.00*	*£37.00*
Half board daily *(min 2 days)*	£22.00	£33.00	£35.00
Half board weekly	£132.00	£198.00	£210.00

ETB 4 Crowns
RAC ★★
☎ (0202) 299715
Fax: (0202) 552669

The Resident Proprietors will be delighted to welcome you to the West Cliff Hall, where cheerful friendly service is not a thing of the past.

Brent Knoll (Somerset)

Battleborough Grange Hotel

Brent Knoll, Somerset
Telephone: (0278) 760208

18 bedrooms, 14 with private WC and bath or shower.

Beautiful country hotel nestling at the foot of the historical Brent Knoll. 5 minutes Junction 22, M5.

Most rooms en-suite. Some 4 posters and spa baths.

Highly recognised restaurant. Large conference/ function suite. Licensed.

EC *early closing* **MD** *market day* *country house hotel* *ns (NS) no smoking areas* *tcf tea/coffee facilities*

£ room £86·50–£102·50 (w/e £40); double room £102·50–£120; Bk £8·50, L £11·25, D £16·50; WB £35
cc Access, Amex, B'card/Visa, Diners.

★★★ **Stirrups,** Maidens Green, RG12 6LD
☎(0344) 882284 Fax: (0344) 882300

A Tudor-style inn, extended in keeping, in the village of Maidens Green north east of Bracknell. Decorative details throughout echo the racing theme. It, Es
24 bedrs, 24 en suite; TV; tcf
lift, dogs; P 150, coach; child facs; con 70
LD 10
£ B&B £75–£90 (w/e £29·50); B&B (double) £87·50–£105 (w/e £59); L £14·95, D £14·95; WB £45
cc Access, Amex, B'card/Visa, Diners.

BRADFORD West Yorkshire. Map 40B2
See also BINGLEY.
Pop 303,622. M606 2, London 196, Halifax 8, Harrogate 18, Huddersfield 10, Leeds 9, Pontefract 22, Skipton 19.
EC Wed. **MD** All week (not Wed). **Golf** West Bowling 18h, Bradford Moor 9h, South Bradford 9h, West Bradford 18h. **See** Cathedral, City Hall, Cartwright Hall (Museum and Art Gallery), 15th cent Bolling Hall (Museum), Wool Exchange, Industrial Museum (Moorside Mills, Eccleshill), National Museum of Photography.
[i] Hall Ings/Channing Way. ☎(0274) 753678

★★★★ **Stakis Norfolk Gardens,** Hall Ings, BD1 5SH ☎(0274) 734734 Tx: 517573 Fax: (0274) 306146
A modern city centre hotel commanding views over town and gardens. (Sk)
126 bedrs, 126 en suite; TV; tcf
Lift, dogs, ns; coach; child facs; con 750
LD 10; nr Sat lunch
£ B&B £82·50–£92·50, B&B (double) £110–£120; L £8·50; D £14·50; WB £25
cc Access, Amex, B'card/Visa, Diners.

★★★ **Baron,** Highfield Rd, BD10 8QH
☎(0274) 611111 Tx: 517229
Fax: (0274) 613456
Modern hotel in residential area on northern outskirts of city. Indoor swimming pool, sauna, solarium, billiards.
44 bedrs, 44 en suite; TV; tcf
dogs; P 150, coach; child facs; con 120
cc Access, Amex, B'card/Visa, Diners.

★★★ **Novotel,** Merrydale Rd, BD4 6SA
☎(0274) 683683 Tx: 517312
Fax: (0274) 651342 ♿
Modern multi-storey French-operated hotel. On M606. Swimming pool.
132 bedrs, 132 en suite, 2 ba; TV; tcf
lift, dogs; P 140, coach; child facs; con 250
cc Access, Amex, B'card/Visa, Diners.

★★★ **Victoria,** Bridge St, BD1 1JX
☎(0274) 728706 Tx: 517456
Fax: (0274) 736358

Formerly a station hotel situated in the city centre. Elegant public rooms. (THF)
59 bedrs, 59 en suite; TV; tcf
lift, dogs, ns; P 50, coach; child facs; con 230
LD 10; bar meals only Sat lunch.
£ B&B £72 (w/e £38), B&B (double) £89; L £8·50, D £11·95; WB £38
cc Access, Amex, B'card/Visa, Diners.

BRADFORD-ON-AVON Wiltshire. Map 5A3
Corsham 6, London 101, Bath 7, Melksham 5, Trowbridge 3, Warminster 13.
[i] 34 Silver St ☎(022 16) 5797

★★★ **Leigh Park,** Leigh Rd West, BA15 2RA ☎(022 16) 4885 Fax: (022 16) 2315

Bath-stone Georgian house in 5 acres of gardens on north side of town. Lovely views. Tennis, snooker.
21 bedrs, 21 en suite; TV; tcf
dogs; P 80, coach; child facs; con 120
LD 9.15; nr Sat lunch
£ B&B £65–£75, B&B (double) £78–£98; HB weekly £350; L £16·50, D £19·50; WB £48 [10% V]
cc Access, Amex, B'card/Visa, Diners.

BRAINTREE Essex. Map 17B4
Pop 30,515. Chelmsford 11, London 44, Cambridge 32, Colchester 15, Great Dunmow 8½, Haverhill 18, Sudbury 14.
EC Thur. **MD** Wed, Sat. **Golf** Towerlands 9h. **See** Old Church, Bocking Windmill.
[i] Town Hall ☎(0376) 550066

★★★ **White Hart,** Bocking End, CM7 6AB
☎(0376) 21401 Tx: 988835
Fax: (0376) 552628
Charming 15th century, half-timbered coaching inn. Near town centre.
35 bedrs, 35 en suite; TV; tcf
ns; P 40, coach; child facs; con 40
LD 10.30
£ B&B £60, B&B (double) £72; L £8, D £13; WB £24
cc Access, Amex, B'card/Visa, Diners.

★★ **Old Court,** Bradford St, CM7 6AJ
☎(0376) 21444

Ancient half-timbered building with a Georgian facade.
12 bedrs, 12 en suite; TV; tcf
P 30, coach; child facs

BRAITHWAITE Cumbria. Map 43C2
Pop 500. Keswick 2½, London 288, Carlisle 30, Cockermouth 9½.
Golf Cockermouth 18h. **See** National Park.

★★★ H **Middle Ruddings,** CA12 5RY
☎(0768 778) 436

Well-equipped hotel enjoying magnificent views and spacious grounds. Fr
12 bedrs, 12 en suite, 1 ba; TV; tcf
dogs, ns; P 20, U 1, coach; child facs; con 25
LD 8.45, bar meals only Mon dinner
£ B&B £36, B&B (double) £63·80; HB weekly £258·50; D £15·50; [10% V]
cc Access, B'card/Visa.

BRAMHALL Greater Manchester (Cheshire). Map 33C1
Pop 31,595. Macclesfield 9½, London 177, Altrincham 10, Congleton 17, Knutsford 12, Middlewich 20, Sandbach 21, Stockport 4.
EC Wed. **Golf** Bramhall 18h. **See** Bramall Hall.
[i] 13 Bramhall Lane South. ☎061-440 8400

★★★ **Bramhall Moat House,** Bramhall Lane South, SK7 2EB ☎061-439 8116 Tx: 668464 Fax: 061-440 8071

B

Purpose-built modern hotel with conference facilities. Sauna, solarium. (QMH)
65 bedrs, 65 en suite; TV; tcf
lift; P 130, coach; child facs; con 125

BRAMHOPE West Yorks. Map 40A3

Pop 3,537. Leeds 8, London 199, Bradford 10, Harrogate 11, Skipton 19, York 28.
Golf Headingley 9h. **See** Puritan chapel.

★★★ R **Post House,** Otley Rd, LS16 9JJ
(0532) 842911 Tx: 556367
Fax: (0532) 843451

Modern hotel set amidst 16 acres of lawns and gardens. Indoor swimming pool, sauna, solarium, gymnasium. (THF)
129 bedrs, 129 en suite; TV; tcf
lift, dogs, ns; P 240, coach; child facs; con 180
LD 10.15; bar meals only Sat lunch
£ Bk £7·95, L £12·95, D £15·75; WB
cc Access, Amex, B'card/Visa, Diners.

BRAMPTON Cambridgeshire.

Map 26B3
Pop 4,525. Biggleswade 19, London 64, Huntington 1½, Kettering 24.
Golf St Neots 18h. **See** Church, Old Cottages, Watermill.

★★★ **Brampton,** A1 Roundabout, PE18 8NH Huntingdon (0480) 810434

A modern motor hotel situated outside the village at A1/A604 crossroads. (MtCh)

BRAMPTON Cumbria. Map 44A3

Pop 3,400. M6 (jn 43) 7, London 299, Alston 19, Carlisle 9, Gretna 15, Hexham 28.
EC Thur. **MD** Wed. Brampton 18h. **See** Church (Burne-Jones windows), Moot Hall, Stocks, Prince Charlie's House, Lanercost Priory 3 m NE, Roman Wall.
[i] Moot Hall. (069 77) 3433

Hotel locations
Hotel locations are shown on the maps at the back of the guide. All towns and villages containing an RAC Appointed or Listed hotel are ringed in purple.

★★ **Farlam Hall** CA8 2NG
Hallbankgate (069 76) 234
Fax: (069 76) 683

Lovely 17th century manor with lake in grounds. Closed Feb.
13 bedrs, 13 en suite; TV
dogs; P 35; no children under 5
LD 8, nr lunch. Resid & Rest lic
£ B&B & dinner £85–£95, B&B & dinner (double) £130–£190; D £24; WB
cc Access, Amex, B'card/Visa.

★★ **Howard Arms,** Front St, CA8 1NG
(069 77) 2357
Small town-centre hotel in typical Lakeland style. Completion of 1990 refurbishment expected by December. Es.
8 bedrs, 8 en suite; TV; tcf
dogs; coach; child facs
LD 9
£ B&B £20; L fr £6·90, D £10·50
cc Access, B'card/Visa.

★★ **Kirby Moor,** Longtown Road, CA8 2AB (069 77) 3893
A Victorian house set in 2 acres of grounds with views of open countryside; off the A6021, north west of town.
6 bedrs, 6 en suite, 1 ba; TV; tcf
P 30; child facs; con 12
LD 9.15. Resid & Rest lic
£ B&B £25, B&B (double) £32; HB weekly £168; L £3·25, D £6·85; WB £45 (2 nts); [10% V]
cc Access, B'card/Visa.

★★ R **Tarn End,** Talkin, CA8 1LS
(069 77) 2340
A 19th century farmhouse in quiet grounds on banks of 62-acre lake. Fishing. Fr, It.
Open 1 Mar–31 Jan.
6 bedrs, 6 en suite; TV; tcf
P 70; child facs; con 10
LD 8·45, bar meals only lunch & Sun dinner
£ B&B £40, B&B (double) £58; D £19; WB £90; [5% V]
cc Access, Amex, B'card/Visa, Diners.

Oakwood Park (Highly Acclaimed), Longtown Rd, CA8 2AP (069 77) 2436.
Hotel. Tennis.
£ B&B £20, B&B (double) £30–£36; HB weekly £126; D £8·50 [5% V]

BRANDON Suffolk. Map 27A4

Pop 6,960. Newmarket 18, London 81, Bury St Edmunds 15, East Dereham 24, Ely 22, King's Lynn 25, Swaffham 15, Thetford 6½.
EC Wed. **MD** Thur, Sat. **Golf** Thetford 18h.
See St Peter's Church, 15th cent bridge.

★★★ **Brandon House,** High St, IP27 0AX
(0842) 810171 Fax: (0842) 814859
A fine late Georgian residence on the edge of town. Fr.
15 bedrs, 15 en suite; TV, tcf
dogs; P 40; con 15
LD 9.15
£ B&B £33–£44·50 B&B (double) £44–£59; L £11·95, D £11·95; WB £33 (HB); [5% V]
cc Access, Amex, B'card/Visa dep.

BRANDSHATCH Kent. Map 9B2

See also FAWKHAM GREEN
Swanley 5½, London 30, M20/M25 3½, Dartford 7, Maidstone 7, Sevenoaks 8½.

★★★★ **Brands Hatch Thistle,** DA3 8PE
(0474) 854900 Tx: 966449
Fax: (0474) 853220

Recently built, two-storey hotel with a motoring theme in park-like gardens. (ThH)
140 bedrs, 140 en suite; TV; tcf
ns; P 178, coach; child facs; con 230
LD 9.30
£ room £75, room (double) £87; Bk £7·75, L £14, D £14
cc Access, Amex, B'card/Visa, Diners.

BRANSCOMBE Devon. Map 4B1

Pop 447. Axminster 10, London 157, Exeter 18, Honiton 10, Lyme Regis 12.

★★ **Masons Arms at Branscombe,** EX12 3DJ (029 780) 300 Fax: (0297 80) 500
Charming 2-storey stone-built 14th century inn set ¼ mile from sea.
8 bedrs, 5 en suite, 2 ba; annexe 13 bedrs, 13 en suite; TV
dogs; P 45; child facs; con 20

Bulstone (Highly Acclaimed), Higher Bulstone, EX12 3BL (029 780) 446.
Private Hotel.
£ B&B £15–£24; HB weekly £183–£215.

BRAUNTON Devon. Map 3A4

Pop 8,000. Barnstable 5½, London 108, Ilfracombe 8, Lynmouth 23.
EC Wed. **Golf** Saunton 18h (2). **See** 3 m of excellent sands at Saunton, 3 m, Museum.
[i] Car Park. (0271) 816400

Denham (Acclaimed), North Buckland, EX33 1HY (0271) 890297. *Farm.*
£ B&B (double) £34–£38; HB weekly £140–£150

BREDWARDINE Hereford & Worcester (Herefordshire). Map 19C3
Hereford 13, London 145, Builth Wells 26, Hay-on-Wye 6, Leominster 25.

Bredwardine Hall (Highly Acclaimed), HR3 6DB Moccas (098 17) 596. *Guest House.*
£ B&B £26–£28, HB weekly £198–£212.

BRENDON Devon. Map 3B4

Pop 80. Minehead 15, London 182, Lynmouth 3½, Tiverton 35.

EC *early closing* **MD** *market day* *country house hotel* *ns (NS) no smoking areas* *tcf tea/coffee facilities*

EC Thur. **Golf** Ilfracombe 18h. **See** Doone Valley.

★★ **Stag Hunters,** EX35 6PS
☎(059 87) 222
An attractive old country inn in the heart of Exmoor.

Millslade (Highly Acclaimed)
☎(059 87) 322. *Hotel.* Fishing
£B&B £22; HB weekly £224–£434

BRENT KNOLL Somerset. Map 4B3
Pop 1,148. M5 (jn 22) 2, Wells 15, London 137, Bridgwater 10, Bristol 24, Glastonbury 14, Weston-super-Mare 9.
Golf Burnham and Berrow 18h. **See** Brent Knoll, St Michael's Church, Iron Age Fort.
[i] Service Area, M5 Southbound. ☎ Edingworth (093 472) 466

★★ **Battleborough Grange,** Bristol Rd, TA9 4HJ ☎(0278) 760208
Fax: (0278) 760208

Small country hotel at foot of Brent Knoll convenient for M5.
🛏 18 bedrs, 14 en suite, (4 sh), 1 ba; TV; tcf
🏨 TV; P 60, coach; no children under 14; con 100
(*See advertisement on p. 158*)

BRENTWOOD Essex. Map 17A2
Pop 72,800. Romford 6, London 22, Bishop's Stortford 23, Chelmsford 11, Dartford-Purfleet Tunnel 13, Southend 21.
EC Thur. **Golf** Hartswood, Brentford 18h.
See "White Hart" Inn (old Coaching House), 16th cent Moat House (once Hunting Lodge, now motel), RC Cathedral.

★★★★ **Brentwood Moat House,** London Rd, CM14 4NR ☎(0277) 217974
Tx: 995182 Fax: (0277) 262809 ♿

Well-preserved hunting lodge of Henry VIII, with modern residential wings. (QMH)
🛏 33 bedrs, 33 en suite, 2 ba; TV
🏨 TV, dogs, ns; P 100, coach; child facs; con 40
(*See advertisement on p. 163*)

Changes made after July 1990 are not included.

★★★ **Post House,** Brook St, CM14 5NF
☎(0277) 260260 Tx: 995379
Fax: (0277) 264264

Modern hotel in attractive residential area near Jn 28 (M25). Indoor swimming pool, sauna, solarium, gymnasium. De (THF)
🛏 117 bedrs, 117 en suite; TV; tcf
🏨 lift, dogs, ns; P 130, coach; child facs; con 130
✕ LD 10.
£ B&B £81–£91 (w/e room £19·75), B&B (double) £91–£101; L £9·95, D £12·95; WB £38 (HB)
cc Access, Amex, B'card/Visa, CB, Diners.

BRERETON Staffordshire. Map 22C4
Lichfield 7, London 122, Burton-on-Trent 15, Stafford 9, Stone 15, Uttoxeter 12, Walsall 16, Wolverhampton 16.

★★ **Cedar Tree,** Main Rd, WS15 1DY
☎Rugeley (0889) 584241
Converted Georgian house with large cedar tree in front. Squash, solarium.
🛏 14 bedrs, 7 en suite, 3 ba; annexe 14 bedrs, 14 en suite, 1 ba; TV; tcf
🏨 TV; P 200; no children under 3; con 200
✕ LD 9.30, bar meals only Sun dinner
£ B&B £19–£25, B&B (double) £38–£42; L £6, D £8·50
cc Access, Amex, B'card/Visa, Diners.

BRIDESTOWE Devon. Map 3A3
Pop 400. Okehampton 6, London 198, Launceston 12, Tavistock 11.
See Parish Church.

Linden Glade, EX20 4NS ☎(083 786) 236.
Guest House.
£ B&B £12; HB weekly £80 (B&B)

BRIDGNORTH Shropshire. Map 20B4
Pop 11,126. Kidderminster 13, London 137. Birmingham 25, Ludlow 19, Shrewsbury 21, Wolverhampton 14.
EC Thur. **MD** Mon, Sat. **Golf** Bridgnorth 18h. **See** St Leonard's Church, St Mary's Church, 16th cent Bishop Percy's House, cliff railway, Town Hall 1652, Northgate Museum, remains of 12th cent Castle, Severn Valley Rly (steam engines) to Bewdley, Midland Motor Museum and Bird Garden.
[i] Library, Listley St. ☎(0746) 763358

En suite rooms
En suite rooms may be bath or shower rooms. If you have a preference, remember to state it when booking a room.

★★★ **Old Vicarage,** Worfield, WV15 5JZ ☎Worfield (074 64) 497
Fax: (074 64) 552 ♿

Attractive Victorian vicarage in 2 acres of lovely grounds. Family-run.
🛏 11 bedrs, 11 en suite; annexe 4 bedrs, 4 en suite; TV; tcf
🏨 dogs, ns; P 30; child facs; con 20
✕ LD 9. Resid & Rest lic
£ B&B £60–£70, B&B (double) £74·50–£82·50; L £17·50, D fr 17·50; WB £80
cc Access, Amex, B'card/Visa, Diners; dep.

★★ H C **Falcon,** St. John St, Low Town, WV15 6AG ☎(0746) 763134
Fax: (0746) 765401
17th century coaching inn in Low Town area of Bridgnorth.
🛏 15 bedrs, 13 en suite, (1 sh); TV, tcf
🏨 dogs; P 200, coach; child facs; con 50
✕ LD 10, bar meals only Sat lunch & Sun dinner
£ B&B £27·50–£38, B&B (double) £45–£48; L £10·50, D £12·50
cc Access, Amex, B'card/Visa.
(*See advertisement on p. 163*)

★★ **Parlors Hall,** Mill St, WV15 5AL
☎(0746) 761931 Fax: (0746) 767058

Red brick building dating to the 12th century with a walled garden, in Low Town of Bridgnorth. De, lt.
🛏 15 bedrs, 13 en suite, 1 ba; TV; tcf
🏨 P 25, coach; child facs; con 60
✕ LD 9.45
£ B&B £42, B&B (double) £50; L £7, D £7·75
cc Access, B'card/Visa.
(*See advertisement on p. 163*)

★ **Whitburn Grange,** 35 Salop St, WV16 5BH ☎(0746) 766786
Refurbished Victorian building in centre of town.
🛏 10 bedrs, 4 en suite, 3 ba; TV; tcf
🏨 TV, dogs; P 9, coach; child facs

Middleton Lodge, Middleton Priors, WV16 6UR ☎(0746 34) 228. *Guest House.*
£ B&B £20–£25.

BRIDGWATER Somerset. Map 4B3. *See* NORTH PETHERTON

BRIDLINGTON Humberside (North Humberside). Map 39B3
Pop 30,000. Beverley 22, London 201, Hull 30, Malton 28, Scarborough 17, York 41.
EC Thur. **MD** Wed, Sat. **Golf** Belvedere 18h. **See** Bayle Gate (museum), Priory Church, Flamborough Head and Lighthouse.
[i] Prince St. ☎(0262) 673474

★★★ **Expanse,** North Marine Drive, YO15 2LS ☎(0262) 675347 Fax: (0262) 604928

Modern family-run hotel in splendid situation with fine sea views.
48 bedrs, 48 en suite; TV; tcf
lift; P 8, G 15 (£1·50); child facs; con 40
LD 9
£ B&B £39–£42, B&B (double) £60–£67; HB weekly £230–£340; L £7·50, D £12·00; WB £67.
cc Access, Amex, B'card/Visa, Diners; dep.

★★**Monarch,** South Marine Drive, YO15 3JJ ☎(0262) 674447 Fax: (0262) 604928

Medium-sized hotel with 5 storeys. Overlooking beaches and bay. Closed 19 Dec–7 Jan.
40 bedrs, 36 en suite, 4 ba; TV, tcf
lift, TV, ns; P 10, coach; child facs; con 40
LD 8.30, bar meals only Mon–Sat lunch. Resid lic
£ B&B £38, B&B (double) £60; HB weekly £260–£292; L £6, D £11; WB £70; [10% V]
cc Access, Amex, B'card/Visa, Diners; dep.

★★ H C **New Revelstoke,** 1–3 Flamborough Rd, YO15 2HU ☎(0262) 672362 Fax: (0262) 672362

Two well-appointed large buildings on the north side of town.
29 bedrs, 29 en suite; TV; tcf
P 14; child facs; con 150
LD 8.30. Resid & Rest lic
£ B&B £35–£45, B&B (double) £55–£65; HB weekly £200–£240; WB £30 (HB)
cc Access, Amex, B'card/Visa, Diners; dep.

★ **Langdon,** Pembroke Terr. YO15 3BX ☎(0262) 673065
Small family-run hotel with fine views of sea and harbour entrance from most rooms.

Bay Ridge (Acclaimed), Summerfield Rd, YO15 3LF ☎(0262) 673425. *Hotel.* Closed Jan.
£ B&B £15; HB weekly £120

Norton Lodge (Acclaimed), 123 Promenade, YO15 2QN ☎(0262) 673489. *Private Hotel.*

Glencoe, 43 Marshall Ave, YO15 2DT ☎(0262) 676818. *Private Hotel.*

Park View, 9 Tennyson Av, YO15 2EH ☎(0262) 672140. *Private Hotel.* Open Feb–Oct.
£ B&B £10.

BRIDPORT Dorset. Map 4C1
Pop 6,800. Dorchester 15, London 137, Axminster 12, Crewkerne 13, Lyme Regis 10, Sherborne 26, Weymouth 19.
EC Thur. **MD** Wed, Sat. **Golf** West Bay 18h.
[i] 32 South St. ☎(0308) 24901

★★★ **Eype's Mouth Country,** Eype, DT6 6AL (2m SW). ☎(0308) 23300

Family-run Georgian hotel with spectacular views. Easy walking distance to sea.
18 bedrs, 18 en suite; TV; tcf
dogs; P 50, coach; con 30
LD 8.45
£ B&B £37·50, B&B (double) £52–£65; HB weekly £201·25; L £6·95, D £10·50; WB £69·50
cc B'card/Visa; dep.

★★★ **Haddon House,** West Bay, DT6 4EL ☎(0308) 23626 ♿

Family-run hotel in elegant Regency style building. Easy walking distance to sea.
13 bedrs, 13 en suite; TV; tcf
TV, dogs; P 60, G 4, coach; child facs; con 40
LD 9
£ L £8·95, D £13·50; WB [5% V]
cc Access, Amex, B'card/Visa, Diners; dep.
(*See advertisement on p. 163*)

★★ H C **Roundham House,** Roundham Gdns, West Bay Rd, DT6 4BD ☎(0308) 22753 Tx: 417182 Fax: (0308) 421145
Mellow stone-built residence with pleasant secluded garden few minutes from sea. Open mid Jan–mid Nov.
8 bedrs, 8 en suite; TV; tcf
dogs; ns; P12, coach; child facs
LD 8.15. bar meals only lunch. Resid & Rest lic
£ B&B £27·50–£34, B&B (double) £39·50–£51·50; HB weekly £192·50–£233·45; L £6.50, D £12; WB £33·75 (2 nts); [5% V Nov–Apr]
cc Amex, B'card/Visa, Diners; dep.

★ **Bridport Arms,** West Bay, DT6 4EN ☎(0308) 22994

Cottage style thatched roof inn near to harbour. Proprietor managed.
8 bedrs, 6 en suite, 1 ba; annexe 5 bedrs, 2 ba; TV; tcf
TV, dogs; ns; coach; child facs
LD 8.45, bar meals only Mon–Sat lunch
£ B&B £19·50–£27·50, B&B (double) £35–£55; HB weekly £185–£245; D £9·50; WB £27
cc Access, B'card/Visa; dep.

Britmead House (Acclaimed), 154 West Bay Road, DT6 4EG ☎(0308) 22941. *Guest House.*
£ B&B £18·50–£26; HB weekly £155·75–£196.

BRIGHOUSE West Yorkshire. Map 40C2
Huddersfield 5, London 185, Bradford 7, Dewsbury 8, Halifax 4.

★★★★ **Forte,** Clifton Village, HD6 4HW ☎(0484) 400400 Tx: 518204 Fax: (0484) 400068 ♿

Long, low building next to junction 25 of M62 motorway overlooking Calder Valley. Indoor swimming pool, sauna, solarium, gymnasium. (THF)
94 bedrs, 94 en suite; TV; tcf
dogs, ns; P 155, coach; child facs; con 200
LD 10
£ room £75–£92, double room £95–£108; Bk £8, L £12, D £17; WB £47–£50 (HB)
cc Access, Amex, B'card/Visa, Diners; dep.
(*See advertisement on p. 172*)

EC *early closing* **MD** *market day* *country house hotel* *ns (NS) no smoking areas* *tcf tea/coffee facilities*

Brentwood (Essex)

Bridgnorth (Shropshire)

Bridgnorth (Shropshire)

Bridport (Dorset)

Bristol (Avon)

Grove Inn Motel, 281 Elland Rd, Brookfoot, HD6 2RG (0484) 713049
Two-storied white-painted building, with motel-style bedrooms, in large garden and overlooking its own fishing and boating lake.

BRIGHTON East Sussex. Map 6C1
See also HOVE and ROTTINGDEAN.
RAC Office, *23 Churchill Square, Brighton, BN1 2DW.* Brighton (0273) 509253.
Pop 152,700. Crawley 22, London 53, Arundel 20, Haywards Heath 14, Horsham 23, Lewes 8½, Newhaven 9, Worthing 11. See Plan, p. 165.
EC Wed. **MD** Tue, Sat. **Golf** Dyke 18h, East Brighton 18h, Waterhall 18h, Hollingbury Park Municipal 18h. **See** Royal Pavilion, Aquarium and Dolphinarium, St Nicolas' Church, Booth Museum of British Birds, Preston Manor, Marina, St Peter's Church, The Lanes (narrow streets of shops formerly fishermen's cottages).
[i] Marlborough House, 54 Old Steine. (0273) 23755

★★★★★ **Grand,** King's Rd, BN1 2FW (0273) 21188 Tx: 877410
Fax: (0273) 202694

Elegantly reconstructed luxury hotel superbly situated facing the sea. Valet parking. Swimming pool, sauna, solarium, gymnasium. Fr, De (DeV)
163 bedrs, 163 en suite; TV; tcf
lift, dogs; coach; child facs; con 300
LD 10
£ B&B £60–£110, B&B (double) £88–£145; L £14·50, D £19·50; WB £70
cc Access, Amex, B'card/Visa, Diners.

★★★★★ **Hospitality Inn,** King's Rd, BN1 2GS (0273) 206700 Tx: 878555
Fax: (0273) 820692

Stylish hotel on seafront centered around the spacious 4-storey high Atrium lounge/reception area. Indoor swimming pool, sauna, solarium, gymnasium. Fr, De, It
204 bedrs, 204 en suite; TV
lift, dogs, ns; P 62, coach; child facs; con 300
LD 10.20
£ room £99 (w/e £45), double room £119, L £12; WB
cc Access, Amex, B'card/Visa, Diners.

Changes made after July 1990 are not included.

★★★★ **Bedford,** King's Rd, BN1 2JF (0273) 29744 Tx: 878397
Fax: (0273) 775877
Recently refurbished, tall modern hotel on the sea front. Guests may use leisure facilities of Metropole hotel.
127 bedrs, 127 en suite; TV; tcf
lift, ns; G 75 (£3·50), coach; child facs; con 400

★★★★ C R **Brighton Metropole,** King's Rd, BN1 2FU (0273) 775432
Tx: 877245 Fax: (0273) 207764

Imposing Victorian red brick seafront hotel with impressive decor. Car park adjacent. Indoor swimming pool, sauna, solarium, gymnasium. Es, Fr, It
328 bedrs, 328 en suite; TV, tcf
lift, dogs, ns; G 200 (£9); coach; child facs; con 1000
LD 10.30
£ B&B £110, B&B (double) £147; L £13·75, D £15·20; WB £48.
cc Access, Amex, B'card/Visa, Diners; dep.

★★★ **Granville,** 125 Kings Rd, BN1 2FA (0273) 26302

Small luxuriously furnished hotel on seafront. Near Brighton Centre. Solarium.
25 bedrs, 25 en suite; TV
lift, dogs; P 4, coach; child facs; con 30

Discount vouchers
RAC discount vouchers are on p. 34. Hotels with a [V] shown at the end of the price information will accept them in part payment for accommodation bills on the full, standard rate, not against bargain breaks or any other special offers. Please note the limitations shown in the entry: w/e for weekends, w/d for weekdays, and which months they are accepted.

★★★ **Norfolk Resort,** 149 King's Rd, BN1 2PP (0273) 738201 Tx: 877247
Fax: (0273) 821752

Fine Regency hotel attractively modernised. Well situated on seafront. Indoor swimming pool, sauna, solarium. Fr
121 bedrs, 121 en suite; TV; tcf
lift, dogs, ns; P 20, G 40 (£1), coach; child facs; con 180
LD 9·45
£ B&B £56·50–£68, B&B (double) £83–£93; HB weekly £210; L £8·50, D £16; WB £76. [V]
cc Access, Amex, B'card/Visa, Diners; dep.

★★★ **Old Ship,** King's Rd, BN1 1NR (0273) 29001 Tx: 877101
Fax: (0273) 820718

Well-known historic building overlooking seafront. Near Lanes.
150 bedrs, 150 en suite; TV; tcf
lift, dogs, G 80, coach; child facs; con 358

Ocean, Longridge Av, Saltdean BN2 8PR (0273) 32291
Awaiting inspection.

Preston Resort, 216 Preston Rd, BN1 6UU (0273) 507853 Tx: 877247
Fax: (0273) 540039.
Awaiting inspection.
34 bedrs, 34 en suite; TV; tcf
£ B&B £55–£66·50, B&B (double) £73–£90; HB weekly fr £360; L £9·50, D £15; WB £42 (HB)
cc Access, Amex, B'card/Visa, Diners.

Adelaide (Highly Acclaimed), 51 Regency Sq, BN1 2FF (0273) 205286
Fax: (0273) 220904. *Private Hotel.*
£ B&B £33–£60; HB weekly £285–£290
Ascott House (Highly Acclaimed), 21 New Steine, Marine Parade, BN2 1PD (0273) 688085. *Hotel.*
£ B&B £22–£30.
Kempton House (Highly Acclaimed), 33 Marine Par, BN2 1TR (0273) 570248
£ B&B £30–£50; HB weekly £126–£175

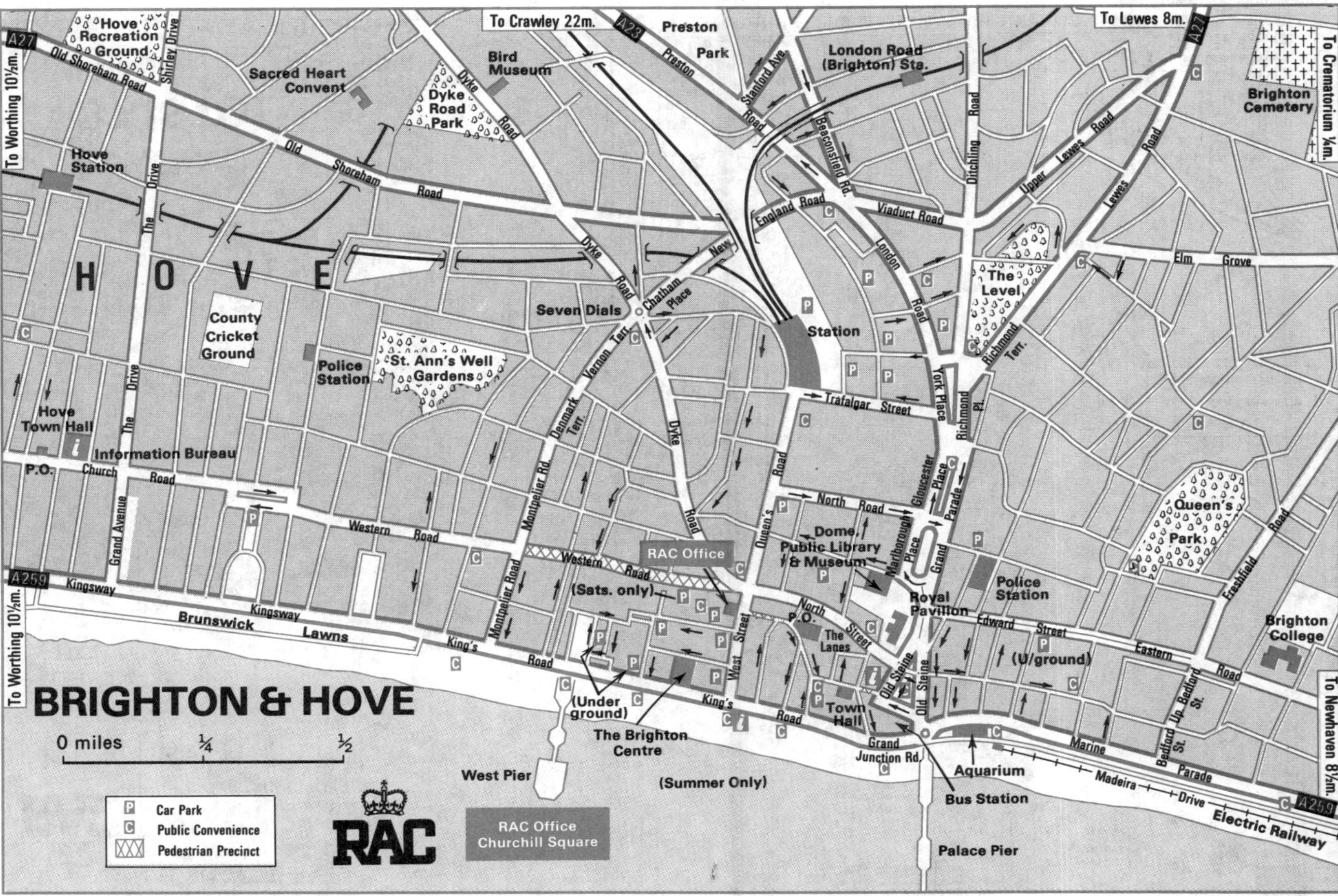
BRIGHTON & HOVE
0 miles
¼
½
Car Park
Public Convenience
Pedestrian Precinct
RAC
RAC Office Churchill Square
To Crematorium ¼m.
To Newhaven 8½m.
To Lewes 8m.
To Crawley 22m.
To Worthing 10½m.
Brighton Cemetery
Brighton College
Queen's Park
The Level
Police Station
Royal Pavilion
Dome, Public Library & Museum
Aquarium
Bus Station
Palace Pier
Town Hall
The Lanes
RAC Office
The Brighton Centre
West Pier
Station
London Road (Brighton) Sta.
Preston Park
Seven Dials
Bird Museum
Dyke Road Park
St. Ann's Well Gardens
Sacred Heart Convent
County Cricket Ground
Hove Recreation Ground
Hove Station
Hove Town Hall
Information Bureau
Brunswick Lawns
Madeira Drive
Electric Railway
(Summer Only)
(Sats. only)
(Under ground)
(U/ground)
H O V E

B

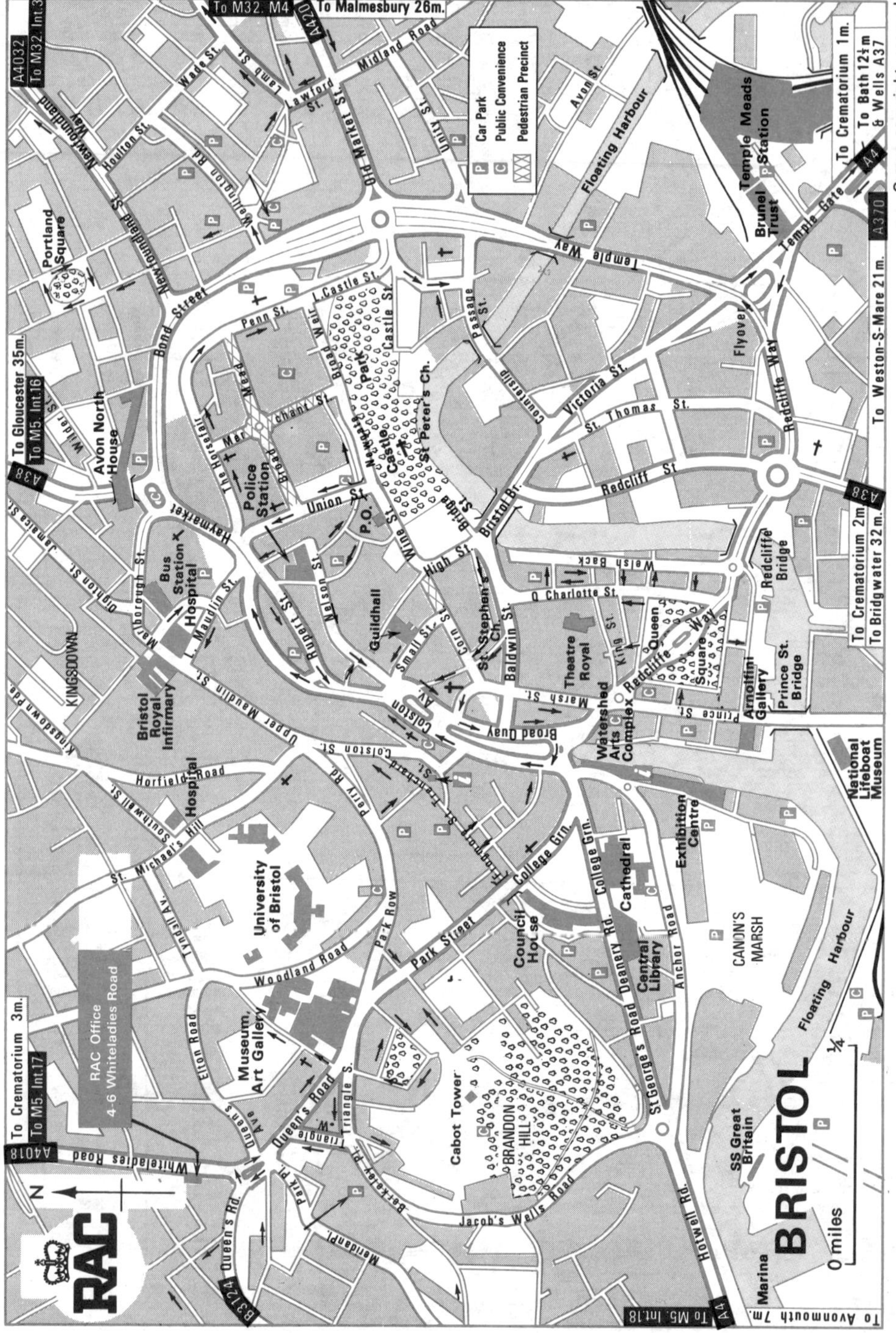

EC *early closing* **MD** *market day* *country house hotel* *ns (NS) no smoking areas* *tcf tea/coffee facilities*

Allendale (Acclaimed), 3 New Steine, BN2 1PB ☎(0273) 675436
£ B&B £24–£27
Amblecliff (Acclaimed), 35 Upper Rock Gdns, BN2 1QF ☎(0273) 681161. *Hotel.*
£ B&B £16–£30
Andorra (Acclaimed), 15–16 Oriental Pl, BN1 2LJ ☎(0273) 21787. *Hotel.*
£ B&B £18–£25
Arlanda (Acclaimed), 20 New Steine, BN2 1PD ☎(0273) 699300. *Hotel.*
£ B&B £30
Cavalaire House (Acclaimed), 34 Upper Rock Gdns, BN2 1QF ☎(0273) 696899. *Guest House.*
Gullivers (Acclaimed), 10 New Steine, BN2 1PB ☎(0273) 695415
£ B&B £20–£36
Le Fleming's (Acclaimed), 12A Regency Sq, BN1 2FG ☎(0273) 27539. *Hotel.*
£ B&B £30–£45
Malvern (Acclaimed), 33 Regency Sq, BN1 2GG ☎(0273) 24302. *Hotel.*
£ B&B £30–£38
Marina House (Acclaimed), 8 Charlotte St, Marine Par, BN2 1AG ☎(0273) 605349. *Hotel.*
£ B&B £12·50–£19, HB weekly £121–£163.
New Steine (Acclaimed), 12A New Steine, Marine Par, BN2 1PB ☎(0273) 681546. *Hotel.* Open Feb–Nov.
£ B&B £14–£25
Regency (Acclaimed), 28 Regency Square BN1 2FH ☎(0273) 202690. *Hotel.*
£ B&B £30–£37; HB weekly £210–£280
Sutherland (Acclaimed), 10 Regency Sq, BN1 2FG ☎(0273) 27055. *Hotel.* ♿
£ B&B £16–£38
The Twenty One (Acclaimed), 21 Charlotte St, Marine Par, BN2 1AG ☎(0273) 686450. *Hotel.*
£ B&B £30–£45; [10% V Sun–Thur]
Trouville (Acclaimed), 11 New Steine, Marine Par, BN2 1PB ☎(0273) 697384. *Hotel.* Open 1 Feb–Dec.
£ B&B £17

Ambassador, 22 New Steine, Marine Parade, BN2 1PD ☎(0273) 676869. *Hotel.*
£ B&B £23–£25
Fyfield House, 26 New Steine, BN2 1PP ☎(0273) 602770. *Guest House.*
£ B&B £14–£23
Paskins, 19 Charlotte St, BN2 1AG ☎(0273) 601203. *Hotel.*
£ B&B £15–£27·50.
Portland House, 55 Regency Sq, BN1 2FF ☎(0273) 820464. *Hotel.* Open Feb–Nov.
£ B&B £30–£35
Rowland House, 21 St George's Terr, Marine Par, BN2 1JJ ☎(0273) 603639. *Guest House.*

BRISTOL Avon. Map 4C4

See also WINTERBOURNE
RAC Office, *4–6 Whiteladies Rd, Bristol, BS8 1PE* ☎Bristol (0272) 732201. Pop 399,300. M32 (jn 3) 1, London 113, M5 (jn 18) 6, Bath 12, Chepstow 16, Tetbury 26, Wells 21, Weston-super-Mare 20.
See plan, p. 166.
EC Wed. **MD** Sun. **P** See Plan. **Golf** Bristol and Clifton 18h, Filton 18h, Knowle 18h, Long Ashton 18h, Shirehampton Park 18h. **See** Cathedral, Temple Church, Merchant Venturer's Almshouses, 17th cent Llandoger Trow Inn, Theatre Royal, Cabot Tower, Lord Mayor's Chapel, Zoo, Observatory, Clifton Suspension Bridge and Avon Gorge, The Georgian House, Red Lodge, Church of St Mary Redcliffe, John Wesley's Chapel, SS "Great Britain" (at Great Western Dock), Chatterton House, Blaise Castle House Folk Museum (Henbury), RC Cathedral (Clifton), Maritime Heritage Centre, Brunel exhibition (Temple Meads).
[i] 14 Narrow Quay ☎(0272) 260767

★★★★ **Crest,** Filton Rd, Hambrook, BS16 1QX ☎(0272) 564242 Tx: 449376
Fax: (0272) 569735

Purpose-built modern hotel offering conference facilities. Convenient for M32. Indoor swimming pool, sauna, solarium, gymnasium. (Cr)
🛏 197 bedrs, 197 en suite; TV; tcf
[FI] lift, dogs, ns; P 400, coach; child facs; con 400

★★★★ **Grand,** Broad St, BS1 2EL ☎(0272) 291645 Tx: 449889
Fax: (0272) 227619

Large traditional Victorian hotel with modern facilities. Near city centre. (MtCh)
🛏 178 bedrs, 178 en suite; TV; tcf
[FI] lift, dogs, ns; coach; child facs; con 700
✕ LD 10.30; nr Sat lunch
£ L £8·95, D £15; WB £38·50
cc Access, Amex, B'card/Visa, Diners.

★★★★ **Hilton International,** Redcliffe Way, BS1 6NJ ☎(0272) 260041 Tx: 449240
Fax: (0272) 230089 ♿

Purpose-built modern hotel with spacious public areas. Convenient for station. Indoor swimming pool, sauna, solarium, gymnasium. ⚒ Fr, De, It, Du (H. Int)
🛏 201 bedrs, 201 en suite; TV; tcf
[FI] lift, dogs, ns; P 150, coach; child facs; con 400
✕ LD 10.30, bar meals only Sat lunch
£ B&B £93·50–£113·50, B&B (double) £119–£144; L £15, D £15
cc Access, Amex, B'card/Visa, Diners.

★★★★ **Holiday Inn,** Lower Castle St, BS1 3AD ☎(0272) 294281 Tx: 449720
Fax: (0272) 225838 ♿
Purpose-built modern hotel in pleasant location. Indoor swimming pool, sauna, solarium, gymnasium. (CHIC)
🛏 284 bedrs, 284 en suite; TV; tcf
[FI] lift, dogs, ns; G 350, coach; child facs; con 600
✕ LD 11; nr Sat lunch
£ B&B £95, B&B (double) £115; L £15·95, D £17·25; WB £40
cc Access, Amex, B'card/Visa, Diners.

★★★ **Avon Gorge,** Sion Hill, Clifton, BS8 4LD ☎(0272) 738955 Tx: 444237
Fax: (0272) 238125
A traditional large Victorian terraced hotel overlooking Gorge. (MtCh)
🛏 76 bedrs, 76 en suite; TV; tcf
[FI] lift, dogs, ns; P 20, coach; child facs; con 100
✕ LD 10
£ B&B £72–£77, B&B (double) £88·50–£104; L £10·75, D £13; WB £39·50 (HB); [10% V]
cc Access, Amex, B'card/Visa, Diners.

★★★ [C] **Berkeley Square,** Berkeley Sq, Clifton BS8 1HB ☎(0272) 254000
Fax: (0272) 252970

Two newly refurbished terraced houses set in quiet square within walking distance of city centre.
🛏 43 bedrs, 43 en suite; TV; tcf
[FI] lift, dogs, ns; child facs; con
✕ LD 10.15
£ B&B £66–£76 (w/e £49), B&B (double) £94; L £12, D £18; WB £98
cc Access, Amex, B'card/Visa, Diners.

★★★ **Henbury Lodge,** Station Rd, Henbury, BS10 7QQ ☎(0272) 502615
Fax: (0272) 509532
A gracious white-painted, part Georgian house in a quiet residential suburb. Converted stable block with sauna, solarium, gymnasium. ⚒ Fr
🛏 11 bedrs, 11 en suite; annexe 7 bedrs, 6 en suite, 2 ba; TV; tcf
[FI] dogs, ns; P 25; child facs; con 30
✕ LD 9. Resid & Rest lic
£ B&B £64·50–£74·50, (w/e £29·50) B&B (double) £74·50–£84·50; L £12·80, D £14·80 [10% V]
cc Access, Amex, B'card/Visa, Diners.

★★★ Redwood Lodge & Country Club, Beggar Bush La, Failand, BS8 3TG ☎(0272) 393901 Tx: 444348 Fax: (0272) 392104

Hotel and country club with stylish modern accommodation close to Clifton suspension bridge. Indoor/outdoor swimming pools, tennis, squash, sauna, solarium, gymnasium, billiards. Fr, Es, Gr
112 bedrs, 112 en suite; TV; tcf
TV, P 1000, coach; child facs; con 175
LD 9.45, nr Sat lunch
£ B&B £80–£90 (w/e £50), B&B (double) £90–£105; D £16·35; WB £45; [10% V]
cc Access, Amex, B'card/Visa, Diners. dep.

★★★ St Vincent's Rocks, Sion Hill, BS8 4BB ☎(0272) 739251 Tx: 444932 Fax: (0272) 238139

Modernised Regency building with fine views of Clifton Suspension Bridge. Fr, De, Es (THF)
46 bedrs, 46 en suite; TV; tcf
dogs, ns; P 20, coach; child facs; con 50
LD 10, bar meals only Sat lunch
£ B&B £69–£87, B&B (double) £91–£102; L £8·50, D £14; WB £40 HB
cc Access, Amex, B'card/Visa, CB, Diners.

★★★ Stakis Leisure Lodge, Woodlands La, Patchway, BS12 4JF ☎(0454) 201144 Tx: 445774 Fax: (0454) 612022
Modern low-built hotel to north of city, convenient for the motorway network. Indoor swimming pool, sauna, solarium, gymnasium. (Sk)
112 bedrs, 112 en suite; TV; tcf
dogs, ns; P 136, coach; child facs; con 80
LD 10, nr Sat lunch
£ B&B £82–£96, B&B (double) £102–£116; L £10·50, D £14·50, WB £38
cc Access, Amex, B'card/Visa, Diners.

★★ Clifton, St Pauls Rd, BS8 1LX ☎(0272) 736882 Tx: 449075 Fax: (0272) 741082
Large stone-built terrace residence set in attractive part of Clifton.
63 bedrs, 45 en suite, (1 sh), 7 ba; TV; tcf
lift, dogs, ns; P 12, coach; child facs
LD 10.30, bar meals only Mon lunch & Sun dinner
£ B&B £28–£46, B&B (double) £46–£66; L £9·90, D £9·50 [V w/e]
cc Access, Amex, B'card/Visa, Diners.

★★ Parkside, 470 Bath Rd, BS4 3HQ ☎(0272) 711461 Fax: (0272) 715507

Stone-built, part Georgian building with an attractive conservatory in residential suburb. Separate night club. Billiards. It, Po
30 bedrs, 9 en suite, 11 ba; TV; tcf
dogs; P 300; coach; child facs; con 200
LD 10.30
£ £7·95; [10% V]
cc Access, Amex, B'card/Visa, Diners.

★★ Rodney, Rodney Pl, Clifton, BS8 4HY ☎(0272) 735422 Tx: 449075 Fax: (0272) 741082

Elegant, refurbished, Georgian terrace house in centre of Clifton village. Closed 24 Dec–4 Jan. Fr
31 bedrs, 31 en suite; TV; tcf
dogs, ns; coach; child facs; con 10
LD 10, bar meals only Mon–Sat lunch. Resid & Rest lic
£ B&B £53–£56, B&B (double) £79·50–£85; D £12·50; WB £60; [10% V]
cc Access, Amex, B'card/Visa, Diners.

★★ Seeley's, 17–27 St Paul's Rd, BS8 1LX ☎(0272) 738544 Fax: (0272) 732406
Terraced houses in Clifton converted to privately-owned hotel. Sauna, solarium. Es, Fr. Closed Xmas.
45 bedrs, 39 en suite, (1 sh), 4 ba, annexe 20 bedrs, 18 en suite, 1 ba; TV; tcf
ns; P 12, G 20, coach; child facs; con 100
LD 10.30, bar meals only Sun lunch & dinner. Resid & Rest lic
£ B&B £32–£40 (w/e £26), B&B (double) £52–£57; L £6·50, D £11; WB £71 (HB) [10% V]
cc Access, Amex, B'card/Visa.

★ Westbury Park, 37 Westbury Rd, BS9 3AU ☎(0272) 620465 Fax: (0272) 620465
Two-storey building with garden in a residential area on edge of Downs. Fr
9 bedrs, 5 en suite, 1 ba; TV; tcf
ns; P 4; child facs
LD 9, bar meals only Mon–Sun lunch, Sun dinner
£ B&B £26–35, B&B (double) £35–£46, HB weekly £243·25–£297·25; L £5, D £11·75
cc B'card/Visa.

Swallow Royal, College Rd, BS1 5TE ☎(0272) 255100 Tx: 449418 Fax: (0272) 251515
Hotel opening late summer 1991.

Alandale (Acclaimed), 4 Tyndall's Park Rd, Clifton BS8 1PG ☎(0272) 735407. *Hotel.*
£ B&B £35
Glenroy (Acclaimed), Victoria Square, Clifton, BS8 4EW ☎(0272) 739058 *Hotel.* Closed Christmas Week
£ B&B £40
Washington (Acclaimed), 11 St Paul's Rd, BS8 1LX ☎(0272) 733980 Tx: 449075 Fax: (0272) 211594. *Hotel.* Closed 21 Dec–4 Jan
£ B&B £26–£45.

Alcove, 508 Fishponds Rd, Fishponds, BS16 3DT ☎(0272) 653886. *Guest House.*
£ B&B £17–£25
Birkdale, 10–11 Ashgrove Rd, Redland, BS6 6LY ☎(0272) 733635
Cavendish House, 18 Cavendish Rd, Henleaze, BS9 4DZ ☎(0272) 621017. *Guest House.*
£ B&B £19
Chesterfield, 3 Westbourne Pl, BS8 1RZ ☎(0272) 734606. *Private Hotel.* Closed 16–29 Aug, 21 Dec–9 Jan, weekends
£ B&B £23
Downlands, 33 Henleaze Gdns, Henleaze, BS9 4HH ☎(0272) 621639. *Guest House.*
Downs View, 38 Upper Belgrave Rd, Clifton, BS8 2XN ☎(0272) 737046. *Guest House.*
£ B&B £20–£22
Kingsley, 93 Gloucester Rd North, Filton, BS12 7PT ☎(0272) 699947. *Guest House.*
Oakdene, 45 Oakfield Rd, Clifton, BS8 2BA ☎(0272) 735900. *Private Hotel.* Closed 25–31 Dec
£ B&B £22–£28
Oakfield, 52–54 Oakfield Rd, BS8 2BG ☎(0272) 735556. *Hotel.*
Pembroke, 13 Arlington Villas, St Paul's Rd, BS8 2EG ☎(0272) 735550. *Private Hotel.* Closed 2–14 Aug, 21 Dec–9 Jan, weekends
£ B&B £23
Westbourne, 40–44 St Pauls Rd, Clifton BS8 1LR ☎(0272) 734214

BRIXHAM Torbay, Devon. Map 3C2

Pop 11,900. Torquay 7½, London 197, Dartmouth (Fy) 4½, Totnes 9½.
EC Wed. **Golf** Churston 18h. **See** Wm of Orange statue, Museum, Aquarium, Cavern, replica of Drake's "Golden Hind", Parish Church of St Mary, All Saints Church, Berry Head (Napoleonic forts, coast guard station), Lighthouse.
ℹ Old Market House, The Quay. ☎(080 45) 2861

★★★ Quayside, King St, TQ5 9TJ ☎(080 45) 55751 Tx: 336682 Fax: (0803) 882733
On Inner Harbour with views over Torbay; converted 17th century fishermen's cottages.
30 bedrs, 30 en suite; TV; tcf
dogs; P 37, coach; child facs; con 20
LD 9.45
£ B&B £35·50, B&B (double) £68. HB weekly £280 L £7·95, D £13·95; WB £39·50
cc Access, Amex, B'card/Visa, Diners

Bristol (Avon)

Bristol (Avon)

★ **Ranscombe House,** Ranscombe Rd, TQ5 9UP ☎(0803) 882337
Charming 18th century building with attractive wrought-iron balconies; overlooking the outer harbour.

Fair Winds, New Rd, TQ5 8DA ☎(080 45) 3564
Harbour View, 65 King St, TQ5 9TH ☎(0803) 853052. *Private Hotel.*
£ B&B £14·50–£15·50; HB weekly £143·50–£166·25
Raddicombe Lodge, Kingswear Rd, TQ5 0EX ☎(0803) 882125. *Guest House.* Open May–Sep
£ B&B £14·30–£25·40
Sampford House, 57 King St, TQ5 9TH ☎(080 45) 7761. *Guest House.* Open Mar–15 Nov.
£ B&B £14

BROADSTAIRS Kent. Map 7C3

See also KINGSGATE
Pop 20,048. Canterbury 18, London 76, Dover 20, Folkestone 26, Margate 3½.
EC Wed. **Golf** North Foreland 18h & 9h. **See** St Peter's Church (12th cent), Bleak House where Dickens lived, 16th cent York Gate, Dickens Museum, North Foreland Lighthouse.
[i] Pierremont Hall, High St. ☎(0843) 68399

★★★ **Castle Keep,** Kingsgate, CT10 3PQ ☎Thanet (0843) 65222 ♿
Hotel standing in own grounds on cliff edge. Swimming pool, snooker.
🛏 29 bedrs, 29 en suite; TV; tcf

★★ **Castlemere,** Western Esplanade, CT10 1TD ☎Thanet (0843) 61566

Large detached red brick building overlooking Western Esplanade. Fr
🛏 37 bedrs, 31 en suite, 2 ba; TV; tcf
TV, dogs; P 30, G 2 (95p); coach; child facs; con 30
✕ LD 7.45, bar meals only lunch
£ B&B £32–£35·50, B&B (double) £60–£70·50; HB weekly £262–£350; D £12; WB £70·50–£77 HB
cc Access, B'card/Visa; dep.

★★ **Royal Albion,** Albion St, CT10 1LU ☎Thanet (0843) 68071 Fax: (0843) 61509

Terraced Georgian building overlooking Broadstairs Bay. Family-run. Fr, It
🛏 20 bedrs, 20 en suite; annexe 6 bedrs, 6 en suite; TV; tcf
TV; P 20, G 2, coach; child facs; con 50
✕ LD 9.15
£ B&B £55, B&B (double) £66, HB weekly £434–£470; L £14, D £15·50; [10% V]
cc Amex, B'card/Visa.

Devonhurst, 13 Eastern Esplanade, CT10 1DR ☎(0843) 63010
£ B&B (double) £33–£41; HB weekly £140–£160
East Horndon, 4 Eastern Esplanade, CT10 1DP ☎(0843) 68306. *Hotel.* Open Mar–Nov
£ B&B £15, HB weekly £125
Merriland, The Vale, CT10 1RB ☎Thanet (0843) 61064. *Guest House.*
Rothsay, 110 Pierremont Av, CT10 1NT ☎(0843) 62646. *Private Hotel.*
£ B&B £20–£22
Sunnydene, 10 Chandos Rd, CT10 1QP ☎Thanet (0843) 63347. *Guest House.*
£ B&B £14–£16; HB weekly £117–£130
White House, 59 Kingsgate Av, CT10 3LW ☎Thanet (0843) 63315. *Hotel.*
£ B&B £18–£25; HB weekly £135–£166·25

BROADSTONE Dorset. Map 5A1

Ringwood 12, London 105, Blandford Forum 11, Bournemouth 7½, Dorchester 24, Poole 4, Wimborne Minster 3½.

Fairlight (Acclaimed), 1 Golf Links Rd, BH18 8BE ☎(0202) 694316. *Private Hotel.*
£ B&B £26–£29; HB weekly £196–£238

BROADWAY Hereford & Worcester (Worcestershire). Map 20C3

Pop 2,389. Moreton-in-Marsh 8½, London 92, Banbury 27, Cheltenham 15, Evesham 5½, Stow-on-the-Wold 10, Stratford-upon-Avon 15, Tewkesbury 15.
EC Thur. **Golf** Broadway 18h.
[i] 1 Cotswold Court. ☎(0386) 852937

★★★★ [H] [R] **Lygon Arms,** WR12 7DU ☎(0386) 852255 Tx: 338260 Fax: (0386) 858611

World famous luxury 15th century inn of Cotswold stone with pleasant gardens. Indoor swimming pool, tennis, sauna, solarium, gymnasium.
🛏 61 bedrs, 61 en suite; TV
TV, dogs; P 100, U 4 (£7·50), coach; child facs; con 80
✕ LD 9.45
£ B&B £105–£115, B&B (double) £135–£190; L £17·50, D £27·50
cc Access, Amex, B'card/Visa, CB, Diners; dep.

★★★ **Broadway,** The Green, WR12 7AA ☎(0386) 852401 Fax: (0932) 232366
Old timber-framed building (mainly 16th century) with recent extensions. Putting.
🛏 12 bedrs, 11 en suite, 1 ba; annexe 10 bedrs, 9 en suite, 1 ba; TV; tcf
ns; P 18; coach; child facs; con 25
✕ LD 9.30, bar meals only Mon–Sat lunch
£ B&B £48·50, B&B (double) £74–£79; L £3·50, D £14·95
cc Amex, B'card/Visa, Diners.

★★★ **Dormy House,** Willersey Hill, WR12 7LF ☎(0386) 852711 Tx: 338275 Fax: (0386) 858636

Fine 17th century Cotswold stone country house overlooking Broadway. Da, De, Fr, It. Closed Xmas.
🛏 26 bedrs, 26 en suite; annexe 23 bedrs, 23 en suite; TV; tcf
dogs; ns; P 80, coach; child facs; con 200
✕ LD 9.30, bar meals only Sat lunch
£ B&B £54–£70, B&B (double) £108–£130; L £16·50, D £24·95; WB 144
cc Access, Amex, B'card/Visa, Diners.
(*See advertisement on p. 170*)

Leasow House (Highly Acclaimed), Laverton Meadows, WR12 7NA ☎(0386) 73526. *Guest House.* ♿
£ B&B (double) £42–£52
Old Rectory (Highly Acclaimed), Church Street, Willersey, WR12 7PN ☎(0386) 853729. *Guest House.* Open mid Jan–mid Dec.
£ B&B £48–£85

Whiteacres (Acclaimed), Station Rd, WR12 7DE ☎(0386) 852320. *Guest House.* Open Mar–Oct.
£ B&B (double) £36

Olive Branch, 78 High St, WR12 7AJ ☎(0386) 853440. *Guest House.* Closed Xmas & New Year
£ B&B £17·50

BROCKENHURST Hampshire. Map 5B2

Pop 3,305. Lyndhurst 4, London 88, Lymington 5, Ringwood 11.
EC Wed. **Golf** Brockenhurst Manor 18h. **See** Parish Church (Norman features), yew tree reputed to be 1,000 years old, New Forest.

★★★★ [C] **Balmer Lawn,** Lyndhurst Rd, SO42 7ZB ☎Lymington (0590) 23116 Tx: 477649 Fax: (0590) 23864

Splendid country house set in heart of New Forest but convenient for road and rail. Indoor/outdoor swimming pool, tennis, squash, sauna, gymnasium. Fr, It (H. Int)
🛏 58 bedrs, 58 en suite; TV; tcf

lift, dogs, ns; P 90, coach; child facs; con 90
LD 9.30, bar meals only Sat lunch
£ B&B £75, B&B (double) £95; L £8·50, D £14; WB £40
cc Access, Amex, B'card/Visa, Diners; dep.

★★★ H C **Carey's Manor,** Lyndhurst Rd, SO42 7RH Lymington (0590) 23551 Fax: (0590) 22799

Elegant manor house (modern additions), in heart of forest. Indoor swimming pool, putting, sauna, solarium, gymnasium. De, Fr, It
80 bedrs, 80 en suite; TV; tcf
dogs, ns; P 200; child facs; con 60
LD 10
£ B&B £69·90–£89·90, B&B (double) £89·90–£119·90; L £11·95, D £19·95; WB £107·70
cc Access, Amex, B'card/Visa, Diners; dep.
(See advertisement on p. 172)

★★★ **Forest Park,** Rhinefield Rd, SO42 7ZG Lymington (0590) 22844 Tx: 47572 Fax: (0590) 23948
Compact half-timbered hotel with immediate access to New Forest. Swimming pool, tennis, riding, sauna, billiards. Fr
38 bedrs, 38 en suite; TV; tcf
dogs, ns; P 60, coach; child facs; con 50
LD 10
£ B&B £55–£60·50, B&B (double) £70–£77; L £6·95 (£8·45 Sun); WB £62·50 (HB); [10% V w/e]
cc Access, Amex, B'card/Visa, CB, Diners.

C ★★★ **New Park Manor,** Lyndhurst Rd, SO42 7DH (0590) 23467 Fax: (0590) 22268
A lovely 17th-century manor house, with modern extension in keeping, set in six acres of gardens off the A337. Swimming pool, tennis, riding, solarium. Fr, De, Es
26 bedrs, 26 en suite; TV; tcf
dogs, ns; P 60; child facs; con 40
LD 9.30
£ B&B £50–£62, B&B (double) £80–£104; D £17·50; WB £50
cc Access, Amex, B'card/Visa; dep.

★★★ **Rhinefield House,** Rhinefield Rd, SO42 7QB (0590) 22922 Tx: 477617 Fax: (0590) 22800

Grand Victorian mansion set in lovely gardens, restored to their former glory. Indoor and outdoor swimming pool, putting, tennis, sauna, solarium, gymnasium.
34 bedrs, 34 en suite; TV; tcf
dogs; ns; P 100; coach, child facs; con 120
LD 9.30, bar meals only Sat lunch
£ B&B £75, B&B (double) £95; HB weekly £385; L £12, D £16; WB £55 (HB); [10% V]
cc Access, Amex, B'card/Visa, Diners.

★★ **Watersplash,** The Rise, SO42 7ZP Lymington (0590) 22344
Family-run, quietly situated Victorian house with a pleasant garden. Swimming pool.
23 bedrs, 23 en suite; TV; tcf
TV, dogs; P 25, U 4, coach; child facs; con 20

★ **Cloud,** Meerut Rd, SO4 7TD Lymington (0590) 22165

Small privately-owned hotel in quiet side street with open forest views.

The Cottage (Highly Acclaimed), Sway Rd, SO4 7SH Lymington (0590) 22296. *Private Hotel.*
£ B&B £38–£40; HB weekly £275–£295

BROMBOROUGH Merseyside. Map 32A1

Pop 30,000. M53 (jn 5) 2, London 193, Birkenhead 4½, Ellesmere Port 5.
EC Wed. **Golf** Bromborough 18h.

★★★ **Cromwell,** High St, L62 7HZ 051-334 2917 Tx: 628225 Fax: 051-346 1175
A modern brick-built hotel on the A41 in centre of village. Sauna, solarium, gymnasium. (Lnb)
31 bedrs, 31 en suite; TV; tcf
dogs, ns; P 92, coach; child facs; con 70
LD 11
£ B&B £64, B&B (double) £77; L £8·95, D £14; WB 50 [10% V]
cc Access, Amex, B'card/Visa, Diners.
(See advertisement on p. 170)

★★ **Dibbinsdale,** Dibbinsdale Rd, Wirral, L63 0HJ 051-334 5171

Former private residence with purpose-built extension. Quietly situated.
19 bedrs, 19 en suite; TV; tcf
TV, ns; P 50, coach; child facs

Dresden, 866 New Chester Rd, L62 7HF 051-334 1331. Closed 16 Feb–4 Mar.
£ B&B £22·50; HB weekly £199

BROME Suffolk. Map 27B4

Pop 260. Bury St Edmunds 23, London 97, Diss 3½, Eye 2.
EC Wed. **Golf** Diss 9h. **See** Church, Castle at Eye (2 m S).

★★★ **Oaksmere,** IP23 8AJ (0379) 870326
A 16th-century manor house down a tree-lined drive, well furnished with some Victorian pieces.
11 bedrs, 11 en suite; TV; tcf
£ B&B £46·50, B&B (double) £66·50; L £13·95, D £13·95

★★ **Brome Grange,** Eye, IP23 8AP Eye (0379) 870456 Fax: (0379) 870921
16th century main building with modern chalets around a courtyard.
22 bedrs, 22 en suite; TV; tcf
TV, dogs; P 60, coach; child facs; con 150
LD 9.30
£ B&B fr £38·50, B&B (double) fr £53; L fr £11·50, D fr £12·50; WB £70 HB
cc Access, Amex, B'card/Visa, Diners.

BROMLEY Greater London (Kent). Map 9A2

Pop 65,703. London 11, Croydon 6, Sevenoaks 14, Sidcup 4½, Westerham 11.
EC Wed. **MD** Thur. **Golf** Sundridge Park 18h. **See** Church of SS Peter and Paul (memorial Dr Johnson's wife, Norman Font).

★★★ **Bromley Court,** Bromley Hill, BR1 4JD 081-464 5011 Tx: 896310 Fax: 081-460 0899

Large detached hotel with conference facilities. Close to town centre. De, Fr, It
122 bedrs, 122 en suite; TV; tcf
lift, dogs; P 100, coach; child facs; con 150
LD 9.45
£ B&B £70 (w/e £50), B&B (double) £95 (w/e £60); L £11·25, D £12·75; WB £46·50 (HB)
cc Access, Amex, B'card/Visa, Diners; dep.

Grianan, 23 Orchard Rd, BR1 2PR 081-460 1795. *Hotel.*
Villa St. Philomena, 1 Lansdowne Rd 081-460 6311. *Hotel.*

BROMSGROVE Hereford & Worcester (Worcestershire). Map 20B4

Pop 35,000. M42 (jn 1) 1, London 113, M5 3, Birmingham 13, Droitwich 6, Evesham 21, Kidderminster 9½.

B

EC Thur. **MD** Tue, Fri, Sat. **Golf** Blackwell 18h. **See** Church of St John the Baptist, Valley House, Fockbury (birthplace of A E Housman), United Reform Church.
[i] 47 Worcester Rd. ☎(0527) 31809

★★★ **Perry Hall,** Kidderminster Rd, B61 7JN ☎(0527) 579976 Tx: 8813387 Fax: (0527) 575998

Renovated 17th century house, one-time home of A. E. Housman. (Emb)
55 bedrs, 55 en suite; TV; tcf
dogs; P 140, coach; child facs; con 70
LD 9.45, bar meals only Sat lunch
£ B&B £67·50–£78·50 (w/e £24), B&B (double) £84·50–£95·50; L £10·95, D £10·95; WB £30 HB
cc Access, Amex, B'card/Visa, Diners.

BROMYARD Hereford & Worcester (Herefordshire). Map 20A3
Worcester 14, London 128, Hereford 14, Ledbury 13, Leominster 9½.
[i] 1 Rowberry St ☎(0885) 482038

★★★ **Falcon,** Broad St, HR7 4BT ☎(0885) 483034
Refurbished and extended black and white Tudor building in town centre.
10 bedrs, 10 en suite; TV; tcf
dogs; P 30, coach; child facs; con 80
LD 9·15
£ B&B £39·50, B&B (double) £49·50 [10% V]

BROOK Hampshire. Map 5B2
Pop 100. Romsey 7, London 82, M27 1, Lyndhurst 5, Salisbury 13, Shaftesbury 30, Southampton 9.
Golf Bramshaw 18h.

★★★ C **Bell Inn,** SO43 7HE ☎Southampton (0703) 812214 Fax: (0703) 813958

An attractive inn set at the edge of New Forest. Golf, putting. Fr
20 bedrs, 20 en suite; TV; tcf
dogs, ns; P 50; child facs; con 12
LD 9.30; bar meals only lunch
£ B&B £51–£72; B&B (double) £72·50–£97·50; HB weekly £425–£575; L £13·95, D £16·95; [10% V Mon–Thur, Nov–Mar]
cc Access, Amex, B'card/Visa, Diners; dep.

BROSELEY Shropshire. Map 20A4
Wolverhampton 20, London 144, Bridgnorth 7, Shrewsbury 15.

Cumberland, Jackson Av, TF12 5NB ☎Telford (0952) 882301. *Hotel.*

BROUGH Cumbria. Map 44B1
Bowes 13, London 264, Appleby 9, Kirkby Stephen 6.
[i] Main St ☎(093 04) 260

★★ **Castle,** Main St, CA17 4AX ☎(093 04) 252
Substantial 3-storey stone period building with converted stables at rear.

BROUGHTON-IN-FURNESS Cumbria. Map 36A4
Pop 1,037. Lancaster 41, London 277, Ambleside 16, Barrow-in-Furness 14, Egremont 31, Kendal 30, Ulverston 9½.
EC Thur. **MD** Tue. **Golf** Ulverston 18h, Silecroft 9h. **See** St Mary Magdalene Church, John Gilpin Obelisk.

★★ **Eccle Riggs,** Foxfield Rd, LA20 6BN ☎(0229) 716398
Stone-built residence in quiet situation in own grounds. Indoor swimming pool, golf (9 hole), sauna.
12 bedrs, 12 en suite, ; TV; tcf
dogs; P 120, coach; child facs; con 120
LD 9, bar meals only lunch
£ B&B £39·50, B&B (double) £64·50, D £10·50; WB £41·50
cc Access, Amex, B'card/Visa, Diners; dep.

★ **Old King's Head,** Church St, LA20 6HJ ☎(065 76) 293
Charming old world country inn centrally placed in quiet village.

BROXTON Cheshire. Map 29B3
Whitchurch 8, London 171, Nantwich 6½, Tarporley 7, Wrexham 15.

★★★ **Broxton Hall,** CH3 9JS ☎(082 925) 321

Charmingly set in own grounds, a black and white part Jacobean building. Fr
12 bedrs, 12 en suite; TV; tcf
dogs, ns; P 30; no children under 12
LD 9.30 nr Sun dinner
£ B&B fr £50, B&B (double) fr £65–£85; L £8, D £16; WB; [10% V w/e]
cc Access, B'card/Visa; dep.

★★★ **Frogg Manor,** Fullersmoor, Nantwich Rd, CH3 9JH ☎(0829) 782629

White-painted country house with Georgian origins in delightful grounds by A534 off A41. Indoor swimming pool, tennis, sauna.
6 bedrs, 6 en suite, TV; tcf
dogs, ns; P 46; no children under 5; con 25
LD 10.30. Resid & Rest lic
£ B&B £44·70–£72, B&B (double) £56·75–£99; L £9·50, D £19·55; WB £ 80 [10% V]
cc Access, Amex, B'card/Visa, CB, Diners.

BRUTON Somerset. Map 4C3
Pop 1,731. Amesbury 33, London 112, Frome 10, Glastonbury 13, Shaftesbury 14, Shepton Mallet 7½, Wincanton 5.
EC Thu. **Golf** Tower Hill 9h, Mendip, Shepton Mallet 18h. **See** Perp Church, Packhorse Bridge, 16th cent roofless dovecote (Nat Trust), 17th cent Sexey's Hospital (Almshouses).

Fryerning, Burrowfield Frome Rd, BA10 0HH ☎(0749) 812343

BUCKDEN Cambridgeshire. Map 26B3
Pop 2,670. Biggleswade 16, London 62, Bedford 16, Huntingdon 4½, Kettering 25.
Golf St Neots 18h. **See** Perp Church, remains of Palace of Bishops of Lincoln, Grafham Water 1 m.

★★ **Lion,** High St, Nr Huntingdon, PE18 9XA ☎(0480) 810313 Fax: (0480) 811070
Early 15th century coaching inn which has retained its period atmosphere. De, Fr
11 bedrs, 11 en suite, annexe 4 bedrs, 4 en suite; TV; tcf
dogs, ns; P 32, coach; child facs; con 25
LD 9.15
£ B&B £52–£54, B&B (double) £65–£68; L £7·95, D £10; WB 55 [10% V w/e]
cc Access, Amex, B'card/Visa, Diners.

BUCKDEN North Yorkshire. Map 38A4
Skipton 18, London 222, Leyburn 16.
EC Wed. **Golf** Skipton 18h.

★★ **Buck Inn,** Upper Wharfedale, BD23 5JA ☎Kettlewell (075 676) 227

A traditional stone coaching inn, recently refurbished, facing old deer park.
15 bedrs, 15 en suite; TV; tcf
dogs; P 40, coach; child facs

✕ LD 9, bar meals only lunch
£ B&B £25–£35 (w/e £28), B&B (double) £50–£70; HB weekly £235–£275; D £15; WB; [10% V Nov–Mar]
cc Access, B'card/Visa; dep.

BUCKFAST Devon. Map 3B2

Ashburton 2½, London 189, Buckfastleigh ½, Plymouth 23, Totnes 7, Two Bridges 11.

Black Rock (Acclaimed), Buckfast Rd, TQ11 0EA ☎(0364) 42343. *Hotel.*
£ B&B £20; HB weekly £175

BUCKFASTLEIGH Devon. Map 3B2

Pop 3,000. Ashburton 3, London 190, Plymouth 21, Tavistock 22, Totnes 6.
EC Wed. **Golf** Newton Abbot (Stover) 18h. **See** Buckfast Abbey, Caves, EE and Perp Church, Farm Museum, Dart Valley Rly (standard gauge, steam engine) to Totnes.

Rockfield House (Acclaimed), Station Rd, TQ11 0BU ☎(0364) 43602. *Guest House.*

Royal Oak, 59 Jordan St, TQ11 0AX ☎(0364) 43611. *Guest House.*

BUCKHURST HILL Essex. Map 15B1

Pop 10,921. London 12, Enfield 6½, Epping 6½, Woodford 3.
EC Wed. **Golf** Theydon Bois 18h.

★★★ Roebuck, North End, IG9 5QY ☎081-505 4636 Fax: 081-504 7826

Small 18th century inn adjacent to Epping Forest. Much renovated. (THF)
🛏 29 bedrs, 29 en suite; TV; tcf
🏠 dogs, ns; P 40, coach; child facs; con 200
✕ LD 9.30
£ B&B £78·50, B&B (double) £100–£108; L £12, D £15·75; WB £40 (2 nts)
cc Access, Amex, B'card/Visa, Diners; dep.

BUCKLOW HILL Cheshire. Map 33A1

Pop 1,041. Knutsford 3½, London 177, M56 (jn 8) 2, M6 (jn 19) 3, Altrincham 4, Northwich 8½, Warrington 9.
Golf Mere G and CC 18h. **See** Tatton Park (Georgian house, gardens) (NT).

★★★ Swan, Chester Rd, WA16 6RD ☎(0565) 830295 Tx: 666911 Fax: (0565) 830614

Coaching inn steeped in history and with much local charm. On A556. ⚒ Fr (DeV)
🛏 70 bedrs, 70 en suite; TV; tcf
🏠 lift, dogs, ns; P 200, coach; child facs; con 24
✕ LD10, bar meals only Sat lunch
£ B&B £30–£70 (w/e £30), B&B (double) £60–£82; L £9, D £13·75; WB £70 [10% V w/e]
cc Access, Amex, B'card/Visa, Diners.

BUDE Cornwall. Map 2C3

Pop 4,624. Holsworthy 9½, London 220, Bideford 25, Camelford 17, Launceston 18.
EC Thur. **Golf** Bude and North Cornwall 18h. **See** Compass Hill (Tower), Poughill Church.
ℹ Crescent Car Park. ☎(0288) 4240

★★★ Hartland, Hartland Terr, EX23 8JY ☎(0288) 355661
Modern hotel on private road overlooking beach. Short walk to town. Swimming pool. Open Mar–Nov & Xmas.
🛏 29 bedrs, 29 en suite; TV
🏠 lift, dogs; P 30, coach; child facs
✕ LD 8.30
£ B&B £32·50–£36·80, B&B (double) £55·20–£62·10; HB weekly £235·75–£261·05; L £12·50, D £15; dep.

★★ Burn Court, Burn View, EX23 8DB ☎(0288) 352872
Modern 3-storey hotel on edge of golf course. Countryside views.

★★ Camelot, Downs View, EX23 8RE ☎(0288) 352361 Fax: (0288) 355470

Small hotel in former residence convenient for town and beach. Solarium.
🛏 21 bedrs, 21 en suite; TV; tcf
🏠 ns; P 18; child facs
✕ LD 8.30, nr lunch. Resid & Rest lic
£ B&B £22, B&B (double) £44; HB weekly £175–£195; D £10 [5% V]
cc Access, B'card/Visa; dep.

★★ St. Margaret's, Killerton Rd, EX23 8EN ☎(0288) 352252 Fax: (0409) 254351 ♿

Small hotel of character with attractive garden. Convenient for beach. ⚒ Fr
🛏 10 bedrs, 9 en suite, 1 ba; TV; tcf
🏠 TV, dogs; P 4; con 30
✕ LD 9, bar meals only Mon–Sat lunch. Resid & Rest lic
£ B&B £30, B&B (double) £44–£51; HB weekly £187·50–£222·50; D £9·20; [5% V]
cc Access, B'card/Visa; dep.

★ Edgcumbe, Summerleaze Cres, EX23 8HJ ☎(0288) 353846

Small 3-storey hotel surrounded by Downs and enjoying fine views of the beach.
🛏 15 bedrs, 8 en suite, (1 sh), 2 ba; TV; tcf
🏠 TV, dogs; P 7, coach; child facs; con 20
✕ LD 7.30, bar meals only lunch. Resid & Rest lic
£ B&B £13·50–£16, B&B (double) £27–£32; HB weekly £122·50–£146·85; D £7
cc Access, B'card/Visa; dep.

★ Maer Lodge, Maer Down, EX23 8NG ☎(0288) 353306

Two-storey 20th century building in attractive gardens. Putting. ⚒ Es, Fr. Open 23 Mar–12 Oct. & Xmas
🛏 19 bedrs, 15 en suite, 2 ba; TV; tcf
🏠 TV, dogs, ns; P 20, coach; child facs; con 30
✕ LD 7.30, bar meals only lunch
£ B&B £17·50–£26, B&B (double) £33–£48; HB weekly £164·50–£192·50; D £8 [10% V]
cc Access, B'card/Visa; dep.

★ Meva-Gwin, Upton, EX23 0LY ☎(0288) 352347

Purpose-built modern hotel with magnificent sea and country views. Open Apr–Oct.
🛏 12 bedrs, 11 en suite, 1 ba; TV; tcf
🏠 TV, ns; P 44, coach; child facs
✕ LD 7.30, bar meals only lunch. Resid & Rest lic
£ B&B £13–£18, B&B (double) £26–£36, HB weekly £116–£150; D £7·50; dep.

Pencarrol, 21 Downs View, EX23 8RF ☎(0288) 352478. *Guest House.*
£ B&B £11–£15; HB weekly £114·50–£127·50

B

BUDLEIGH SALTERTON Devon. Map 4A1
Pop 4,346. Honiton 16, London 169, Exeter 13, Lyme Regis 23, Tiverton 26.
EC Thur. **Golf** East Devon 18h. **See** Octagon'', location of Millais' picture of Boyhood of Raleigh'', Art Centre and Museum, Hayes Barton (birthplace of Sir Walter Raleigh) 2 m NW, Bicton Gardens.
ℹ Fore St. ☎(0395) 445275

Long Range (Acclaimed), Vales Rd, EX9 6HS ☎(039 54) 3321. *Hotel.* Open Mar–Oct.
£ B&B 19·50; HB weekly £175
Tidwell House, Knowle, EX9 7AG ☎(039 54) 2444. *Hotel.*

BULPHAN Essex. Map 17A2
Pop 700. London 25, Brentwood 7, Dartford Tunnel 9½, Romford 11, Southend 16.
EC Wed. **Golf** Orsett 18h. **See** 14th cent Church, 15th cent Old Plough House, 16th cent Garlesters.

★★★ **Ye Olde Plough House,** Brentwood Rd (off M25), RM14 3SR ☎Grays Thurrock (0375) 891592 Tx: 995088
Fax: (0375) 892256 ♿

Reconstructed 16th century barn beside modern motel chalets. Indoor swimming pool, putting, tennis, sauna, solarium, gymnasium.
🛏 79 bedrs, 79 en suite; TV, tcf
🏠 TV, dogs, P 180, coach; child facs; con 120
✕ LD 10, bar meals only lunch
£ B&B £55 (w/e £44), B&B (double) £64; D £10·50
cc Access, Amex, B'card/Visa, Diners

BUNWELL Norfolk. Map 27B4
Pop 831. Thetford 18, London 99, Bury St Edmunds 26, East Dereham 18, Lowestoft 31, Norwich 12, Scole 12, Swaffham 25.
EC Wed. **Golf** Diss 9h. **See** 15th cent Church.

👥 ★★ **Bunwell Manor,** NR16 1QU ☎(0953) 898304

Lovely part-Tudor manor house set in acres of grounds deep in rural Norfolk.
🛏 10 bedrs, 10 en suite; TV; tcf
🏠 dogs; P 30; child facs; con 20
✕ LD 9.30
£ B&B £40–£44, B&B (double) £55–£60; HB weekly £205–£225; L £9·90, D £9·90; WB £65 HB [5% V]
cc Access, B'card/Visa.

BURFORD Oxfordshire. Map 20C2
Pop 1,150. Oxford 20, London 75, Cheltenham 22, Chipping Norton 11, Cirencester 17, Stow-on-the Wold 10, Swindon 19.
EC Wed. **Golf** Burford 18h. **See** Church of St John, old Almshouses, small museum in 15th cent Tolsey, Old Houses, Cotswold Wild Life Park 2 m S.
ℹ The Brewery, Sheep St. ☎(0993) 823558

★★★ **Bay Tree,** Sheep St, OX8 4LW ☎(0933) 822791 Fax: (0993) 823008
A lovely 16th-century Cotswold-stone building, with a walled garden behind, just off the High Street. Recently refurbished with suitable furnishings and some antiques.
🛏 9 bedrs, 9 en suite; annexe 14 bedrs, 14 en suite; TV; tcf
🏠 dogs, ns; P 17, coach; child facs; con 12

★★ **Golden Pheasant,** High St, OX8 4RJ ☎(0993) 823223 Fax: (0993) 822621 ♿
Charming family-run hotel of Oxford stone situated in High Street. ✂ It
🛏 12 bedrs, 12 en suite; TV; tcf
🏠 dogs; ns; P 20; child facs; con 15
✕ LD 9.30
£ B&B £50, B&B (double) £69–£88; L £12·95, D £12·95; WB £45
cc Access, B'card/Visa.

★★ **Inn For All Seasons,** The Barringtons, OX8 4TN ☎Windrush (045 14) 324

Coaching inn of Cotswold stone with attractive walled gardens. Surrounded by woods.

🍷🍷 **Maytime Inn,** Asthall, OX8 4HW ☎(099 382) 2068 ♿

A centuries-old, Cotswold-stone inn in the little village of Asthall off A40. ✂ Fr
🛏 2 bedrs, 2 en suite; annexe 4 bedrs, 4 en suite; TV; tcf
🏠 dogs; P 100, coach; child facs; con 30
✕ LD 10
£ B&B £35; B&B (double) £48; L £12·50, D £12·50; WB £62·50 (HB)
cc Access, Amex, B'card/Visa.

Changes made after July 1990 are not included.

BURGH-HEATH Surrey. Map 8C1
Sutton 4, London 15, M25 (jn 8) 4½, Epsom 3, Dorking 8, Reigate 5½, Croydon 8.

★★ **Heathside,** Brighton Rd, KT20 6BW ☎(0737) 353355 Tx: 929908
Fax: (0737) 370857 ♿
Modern motel-type hotel with restaurants attached. Indoor swimming pool, sauna, gymnasium. ✂ De
🛏 73 bedrs, 73 en suite; TV; tcf
🏠 dogs; ns; P 150, coach; child facs; con 200
✕ LD 10
£ B&B £58–£70 (w/e rm £47·50), B&B (double) £71–£85; L £7, D £10; WB £80 [10% V]
cc Access, Amex, B'card/Visa, Diners.

BURLEY Hampshire. Map 5B2
Pop 1,400. Lyndhurst 7, London 91, Bournemouth 13, Lymington 9½, Ringwood 5.
Golf Burley 9h. **See** Cricket Green.

👥 ★★★ **Burley Manor,** BH24 4BS ☎(042 53) 3522 Tx: 41565
Fax: (042 53) 3227

19th century country house surrounded by gardens and parkland. Swimming pool, riding.
🛏 21 bedrs, 21 en suite; annexe 9 bedrs, 9 en suite; TV; tcf
🏠 dogs, ns; P 50, coach; child facs; con 90
✕ LD 10
£ B&B £60–£66, B&B (double) £75–£82·50; D £15·75 [10% V w/e]
cc Access, Amex, B'card/Visa, Diners.

👥 ★★★ **Moorhill House,** BH24 4AG ☎(042 53) 3285 Fax: (0703) 283719

Gabled Victorian house in 3 acres of well-tended garden in the Forest. Indoor swimming pool, sauna.
🛏 24 bedrs, 24 en suite; TV; tcf
🏠 TV, dogs, ns; P 35, G 2; child facs; con 54
✕ LD 8.45. Resid & Rest lic
£ B&B £59–£69, B&B (double) £85–£95
cc Access, Amex, B'card/Visa, Diners.

BURNHAM Buckinghamshire. Map 13A3
Slough 3½, London 24, M4 (jn 7) 2, Henley on Thames 12, High Wycombe 8½, Reading 16, Windsor 5½.

★★★ **Burnham Beeches Moat House,** Grove Rd, SL1 8DP ☎(0628) 603333 Fax: (0628) 603994

Former Royal hunting lodge in 10 acres of attractive grounds. Indoor swimming pool, tennis, sauna, solarium, gymnasium, billiards. Fr, De, It (QMH)
76 bedrs, 76 en suite; TV; tcf
lift, dogs, ns; P 150, coach; child facs; con 180
LD 10, nr Sat lunch
£ B&B £80–£85, B&B (double) £91–£95; L £13·50, D £16·50; WB £48 HB
cc Access, Amex, B'card/Visa, CB, Diners.

BURNHAM-ON-CROUCH Essex. Map 7B4
Pop 6,500. London 45, Braintree 25, Brentwood 24, Chelmsford 20, Southend 24.
EC Wed. **Golf** Burnham-on-Crouch 9h. **See** St Mary's Church (Norman Font).

★ **Ye Olde White Harte,** The Quay, CM0 8AS ☎Maldon (0621) 782106
Attractive waterside inn of character. Owner-managed.
15 bedrs, 11 en suite, 2 ba; TV
TV, dogs; P 15, coach; child facs
LD 9
£ B&B £18·15–£30·80, B&B (double) £31·90–£49·50; L £8, D £8·50; [5% V].

BURNHAM-ON-SEA Somerset. Map 4B3
Pop 15,000 (inc Highbridge). Wells 17, London 140, Bridgwater 9, Bristol 27, Glastonbury 18, Weston-super-Mare 11.
EC Wed. **MD** Mon. **Golf** Burnham and Berrow 18h. **See** St Andrew's Church with marble altarpiece by Inigo Jones, Gore Sands, Brean Down.
ℹ Berrow Rd. ☎(0278) 787852

★★ **Dunstan House,** 8–10 Love La, TA8 1EU ☎(0278) 784343
Georgian period house with gardens. Few minutes walk from sea.
7 bedrs, 4 en suite, 2 ba; TV; tcf
TV, dogs, ns; P 30; child facs; con 30
LD 10
£ B&B £22, B&B (double) £36–£38; L £3·50, D £5·50
cc Access, Amex, B'card/Visa, Diners.

★★ **Royal Clarence,** 31 The Esplanade, TA8 1BQ ☎(0278) 783138

Three-storey building, once a coaching inn. Fine sea views. Snooker.
15 bedrs, 13 en suite, 2 ba; TV; tcf
TV, dogs; P 18; child facs; con 100
LD 8.30, bar meals Mon–Sat lunch
£ B&B £25, B&B (double) £40; HB weekly £170; L £5·50, D £9; sc; WB
cc Access, Amex, B'card/Visa, Diners; dep.
(*See advertisement p. 178*)

★ **Pine Grange,** 27 Berrow Rd, TA8 2EY ☎(0278) 784214
Privately-owned, spacious semi-detached house. Near to sea and Championship links. Solarium.

BURNLEY Lancashire. Map 36C2
Pop 93,620. Rochdale 14, London 206, Blackburn 11, Bolton 19, Bury 15, Settle 23, Skipton 18, Todmorden 8½, Whalley 8.
EC Tue. **MD** Mon, Thur, Sat. **Golf** Towneley 18h. **See** St Peter's Church, 16th–17th cent Towneley Hall (now Art Gallery and Museum).
ℹ Burnley Mechanics, Manchester Rd ☎(0282) 30055

★★★ **Keirby,** Keirby Walk, BB11 2DH ☎(0282) 27611 Tx: 63119 Fax: (0282) 36370
Centrally-placed modern purpose-built hotel with ballroom, banqueting and conference facilities. Gymnasium. Fr, De
49 bedrs, 49 en suite; TV; tcf
lift, dogs, ns; P 50, G 15, coach; child facs; con 280
LD 9.30
£ B&B £49–£58·50 (w/e £32), B&B (double) £58·50–£66; D £11.25; [10% V]
cc Access, Amex, B'card/Visa, Diners; dep.
(*See advertisement on p. 178*)

★★★ **Oaks,** Colne Rd, Reedley, BB10 2LF ☎(0282) 414141 Tx: 635309 Fax: (0282) 33401
Modernised Victorian mansion in landscaped gardens. Indoor swimming pool, squash, sauna, solarium, gymnasium, billiards. Closed Xmas.
58 bedrs, 58 en suite; TV; tcf
dogs, ns; P 110, coach; child facs; con 120
LD 9.45, bar meals only Sat lunch
£ B&B £75–£85, B&B (double) £90–£100; HB weekly £623–£693; L £11·50, D £14; WB £124 (HB)
cc Access, Amex, B'card/Visa, Diners.

★★ **Rosehill House,** Rosehill Av, BB11 2PW ☎(0282) 53931
Secluded elegant stone-built manor retaining interesting original features. Fr
20 bedrs, 20 en suite; TV; tcf
TV, dogs; P 60, child facs; con 80
LD 9.30, Resid lic
£ B&B £34·50 (w/e £20), B&B (double) £50; L £6·50, D £10·25; WB £60
cc Access, Amex, B'card/Visa, Diners.

BURNSALL North Yorkshire. Map 38A3
Pop 110. Ilkley 12, London 219, Grassington 3, Pateley Bridge 10, Skipton 9.
EC Thur. **Golf** Skipton 12h. **See** Elizabethan School, Church, village green.

★★ **Fell,** BD23 6BT ☎(075 672) 209
Large stone building in elevated position overlooking village and river. Family-run.

★★ **Red Lion,** BD23 6BU ☎(0756) 72204

Small stone-built village hotel facing green and near river.
8 bedrs, 3 en suite,(2 sh), 2 ba; annexe 4 bedrs, 3 en suite; TV; tcf
TV, P 40, coach; child facs
LD 9, bar meals only Mon–Sat lunch
£ B&B £27, B&B (double) £38; L £7, D £10; dep.

BURNT YATES North Yorkshire. Map 38B3
Pop 400. Harrogate 7, London 211, Pateley Bridge 7½, Thirsk 21, York 25.
Golf Harrogate 18h.

Bay Horse Inn, HG3 3EJ ☎Harrogate (0423) 770230
Attractive Georgian coaching inn with motel-type bedrooms adjoining.
6 bedrs, 6 en suite; annexe 10 rooms, 10 en suite; TV, tcf
dogs; P 70, coach; child facs
LD 9.30; bar meals only Mon–Sat lunch
£ B&B £35–£38, B&B (double) £50–55; HB weekly £250–£275; L £8·95, D £12·95; WB £65 [5% V w/d]
cc Access, Amex, B'card/Visa.

BURRINGTON Devon. Map 3B3
Pop 384. Tiverton 23, London 186, Barnstaple 13, Chulmleigh 4, Okehampton 19, South Molton 10.
EC Sat. **Golf** Chulmleigh 18h.

★★★ H **Northcote Manor,** Umberleigh, EX37 9LZ ☎High Bickington (0769) 60501

Manor house in 12 acres of landscaped gardens overlooking Taw Valley.

BURSCOUGH Lancashire. Map 32B3
Pop 4,997 M6 (jn 27) 8½, London 198, Ormskirk 3, Southport 11, Preston 17.

★★★ **Beaufort,** High Lane, L40 7SN ☎(0704) 892655 Fax: (0704) 895135 ♿
Newly built, two-storey hotel, well furnished and equipped, in a rural area beside the A59. De, Es
21 bedrs, 21 en suite; TV; tcf
dogs; P 140, coach; child facs; con 40
LD 10
£ B&B £54 (w/e £35), B&B (double) £67; L £5·50, D £14·95; WB £35 (HB); [10% V]
cc Access, Amex, B'card/Visa.

Buckingham (Buckinghamshire)

Burford (Oxfordshire)

Burnham-on-Sea (Somerset)

Burnley (Lancashire)

BURSLEM Staffordshire. Map 30B2

Stoke-on-Trent 3½, London 156, Congleton 9½, Leek 9, Nantwich 15, Newcastle-under-Lyme 3½, Sandbach 10.
Golf Burslem 9h. **See** Old Town Hall, Wedgwood Institute, Royal Doulton Works.

★★ **George,** Swan Sq, ST6 2AE ☎ Stoke-on-Trent (0782) 577544 Fax: (0782) 577544
1920s building in the Georgian manner. In commercial town centre. Sauna, solarium, gymnasium. ⚒ Fr
🛏 39 bedrs, 39 en suite, 6 ba; TV; tcf
🏨 lift, dogs; P 10, coach; child facs; con 250
✕ LD 10, bar meals only Sat lunch
£ B&B £36 (w/e £24·50), B&B (double) £49; L £6·75, D £8·75; WB £44 (HB)
cc Access, Amex, B'card/Visa, Diners.

BURTON-UPON-TRENT Staffordshire.

Map 23A4
Pop 46,961. Ashby-de-la-Zouch 9, London 122, Ashbourne 19, Derby 11, Lichfield 13, Stafford 26, Tamworth 15, Uttoxeter 13.
MD Thur, Sat. **Golf** Bretby, Branston 18h.
See Parish Church, Abbey ruins.
ℹ Town Hall. ☎ (0283) 45454

♣ ★★★ **Newton Park,** Newton Solney, Derbys, DE15 0SS ☎ (0283) 703568
Fax: (0283) 703214 ♿

Stone-built country house hotel in Georgian manner. Pleasant gardens.
🛏 25 bedrs, 25 en suite; annexe 21 bedrs, 21 en suite; TV; tcf
🏨 lift, dogs, ns; P 150, coach; child facs; con 100
✕ LD 9.30
£ B&B £67–£77 (w/e £25), B&B (double) £84–£94; HB weekly £178·50; L £7·95, D £11·95; WB £31 (HB, 2 nts)
cc Access, Amex, B'card/Visa, CB, Diners.

★★★ R **Riverside Inn,** Riverside Dr, Branston, DE14 3EP ☎ (0283) 511234
Fax: (0283) 511441

White-painted Georgian house with modern extension in quiet setting. Lawns run down to River Trent. Fishing. ⚒ Es, Po
🛏 12 bedrs, 11 en suite; TV; tcf
🏨 dogs; P 100, coach; child facs; con 150
✕ LD 10, bar meals only Sat lunch
£ B&B £48, B&B (double) £58; L £8·95, D £11·95; WB £75.70
cc Access, Amex, B'card/Visa.
(*See advertisement on p. 180*)

★★★ **Stanhope,** Ashby Road East, DE15 0PU ☎ (0283) 217954 Tx: 347185
Fax: (0283) 226619
Gabled, red-brick hotel, recently refurbished, beside A50 two miles east of town. Sauna, solarium, gymnasium. (Lns)
🛏 28 bedrs, 28 en suite; TV; tcf
🏨 ns; P 150, coach; child facs; con 200
✕ LD 10 bar meals only Sat lunch
£ B%B £64, B&B (double) £76; L £8, D £14; WB £28 [10% V]
cc Access, Amex, B'card/Visa, Diners.

♣ ★★ **Needwood Manor,** Rangemore, DE13 9RS ☎ Barton under Needwood (028 371) 2932
Victorian manor house in 2 acres of grounds on edge of Needwood Forest.

Delter (Acclaimed), 5 Derby Rd, DE14 1RU ☎ (0283) 35115. *Hotel.*

BURWASH East Sussex. Map 7A2

Pop 2,000. Tunbridge Wells 12, London 49, Hastings 15, Hurst Green 4½, Uckfield 14.
EC Wed. **Golf** Dale Hill, Ticehurst 18h.

Admiral Vernon, Etchingham Rd, TN19 7BJ ☎ (0435) 882230. *Inn.*
£ B&B £22; HB weekly £115.

BURY Gtr Manchester (Lancashire).

Map 33B3
See also RAMSBOTTOM
Pop 69,000. Manchester 8, London 192, M66 (jn 2) 1½, Blackburn 15, Bolton 6, Burnley 15, Oldham 10, Rochdale 6.
EC Tue. **MD** Wed, Fri, Sat. **Golf** Bury 18h.
See Art Gallery and Museum, Regimental Museum, Statue of Sir Robert Peel.

★★ **Bolholt,** Walshaw Rd, BL8 1PS ☎ 061-764 3888 Fax: 061-763 1789
Historic building set in 3 acres of grounds, within 55 acres of parkland. Tennis, fishing, sauna, gymnasium. ⚒ De
🛏 38 bedrs, 36 en suite; TV; tcf
🏨 TV; P 250, coach; child facs; con 200
✕ LD 9.30
£ B&B £45, B&B (double) £56; L £7, D £10; WB £49; [10% V w/e]
cc Access, B'card/Visa.

★ **Woolfield House,** Wash La, BL9 6BJ ☎ 061-797 9775

Privately-owned and run town centre hotel convenient for M66.
🛏 16 bedrs, 10 en suite, 2 ba; TV; tcf
🏨 P 20, coach; con 12
✕ LD 8.30, bar meals lunch; Fri–Sun dinner by arr. only. Resid & Rest lic
£ B&B £25–£30, B&B (double) £38–£45
cc Access, B'card/Visa; dep.

BURY ST EDMUNDS Suffolk. Map 27A3

Pop 31,000. Sudbury 16, London 74, Ely 24, Harwich 41, Haverhill 19, Newmarket 14, Scole 22, Stowmarket 14, Thetford 12.
EC Thur. **MD** Wed, Sat. **Golf** Bury St Edmunds 18h. **See** Cathedral Church of St James, St Edmund's Abbey, St Mary's Church contains tomb of Mary Tudor.
ℹ Abbey Gdns, Angel Hill. ☎ (0284) 764667

★★★ R **Angel,** Angel Hill, IP33 1LT ☎ (0284) 753926 Tx: 81630
Fax: (0284) 700092

An elegant, historic creeper-covered Georgian hotel near Cathedral. ⚒ Fr, De
🛏 40 bedrs, 40 en suite; TV
🏨 dogs, ns; P 40, G 7, coach; child facs; con 120
✕ LD 9.30
£ B&B £68–£80 (w/e £39), B&B (double) £78–£164; L £11·50, D £11·50 [10% V]
cc Access, Amex, B'card/Visa, Diners.

★★★ **Butterfly,** A45 Bury East Exit, Moreton Hall, IP32 7BW ☎ (0284) 760884.
Tx: 818360 Fax: (0284) 755476

Modern, purpose-built hotel with rustic decor in rural setting.
🛏 50 bedrs, 50 en suite; TV; tcf
🏨 ns; P 70, coach; child facs; con 40
✕ LD 10
£ B&B £57–£61 (w/e £33·50), B&B (double) £62–£67; L £9·50, D £9·50
cc Access, Amex, B'card/Visa, Diners.
(*See advertisement on p. 180*)

★★★ **Suffolk,** Buttermarket, IP33 1DL ☎ (0284) 753995 Fax: (0284) 750973
An old coaching inn of character in the town centre. (THF)
🛏 33 bedrs, 33 en suite; TV; tcf
🏨 dogs, ns; P 20, G 13, coach; child facs; con 20
✕ LD 9.15
£ B&B £73–£78, B&B (double) £97–£107; L £10·50, D £13·50; WB £40
cc Access, Amex, B'card/Visa, CB, Diners.

White Hart (Acclaimed), 35 Southgate St, IP33 2AZ ☎ (0284) 755547
£ B&B £34–£38.

BUSHEY Hertfordshire. Map 13C4

Pop 23,017. London 14, M1 (jn 4) 3, Barnet 7½, Harrow 5, Hatfield 12, Watford 2½.

Burton on Trent (Staffordshire)

Riverside Drive, Branston, Burton on Trent, Staffordshire DE14 3EP
Tel: (0283) 511234 Fax: (0283) 511441

The Riverside has become one of the most flourishing hotels in the county with excellent all round comfort and a marvellous name for food, having recently gained an RAC merit award for the extensive à la carte menu as well as a good selection from the Table d'hôte menu. It stands on the outskirts of Burton half a mile from the A38 and has an attractive terraced garden stretching down to the river Trent which offers a fascinating view of the bird sanctuary on the opposite bank. The twenty one bedrooms, many of which have river views, are all provided with en-suite bathrooms, colour television, radios, baby listening and beverage making facilities.

Burton on Trent (Staffordshire)

Ye Olde Dog and Partridge Hotel

High Street, Tutbury, Nr Burton on Trent DE13 9LS Telephone: (0283) 813030

Hotel 3 beds. 3 en-suite rooms. Annexe with 19 beds. 19 en-suite rooms.
Carvery open 7 days a week, lunch and dinner. Restaurant open Tues/Sat evenings only.

Bury St. Edmunds (Suffolk)

SPECIAL WEEKEND RATES AVAILABLE

RAC ★★★

Butterfly – A new style of hotel we think you'll like! Where you will find all modern facilities today's travellers require in a rustic traditional setting, that's welcoming and friendly. Bedrooms fully equipped with private bathrooms/shower rooms, TV/radio, etc. Choose from Studio Singles, Twins, Doubles.

'Walt's Place' Restaurant & Bar – for good food, wines and friendly service at affordable prices.

A45 Bury East Exit, Moreton Hall, Bury St. Edmunds, Suffolk IP32 7BW. Tel: (0284) 760884. Fax: (0284) 755476.

Buxton (Derbyshire)

BUCKINGHAM HOTEL

1 Burlington Road, Buxton, Derbyshire SK17 9AS
Tel: 0298 70481

Set on a broad tree-lined avenue overlooking the Pavilion Gardens and Serpentine Walks. The Buckingham is a well-established owner-managed hotel offering excellent cuisine and generous hospitality. The Games Room includes a full size billiards table.

Outskirts of town on route A53.

Buxton (Derbyshire)

Sandringham Hotel RAC ★★

Broadwalk, Buxton, Derbyshire SK17 6JT Tel: (0298) 72257

A large, comfortable hotel overlooking the Pavillion Gardens in the centre of Buxton, the Sandringham makes an ideal jumping-off point for the whole Peak District.

EC Wed. **Golf** Bushey Hall 18h.

★★★★ **Hilton National,** Watford By-Pass, Elton Way, WD2 8HA ☎(0923) 35881 Tx: 923422 Fax: (0923) 220836

Purpose-built large modern hotel convenient for the M1. Indoor swimming, sauna, solarium, gymnasium. (HN)
🛏 196 bedrs, 196 en suite; TV; tcf
🏠 lift, dogs; P 350, coach; child facs; con 400
✕ LD 9.45
£ room £75–£90 (w/e £40), double room £90–£105; Bk £8·50, L £15, D £15·75; WB £35
cc Access, Amex, B'card/Visa, Diners.

BUTTERMERE Cumbria. Map 43B1

Pop 120. Keswick 8½, London 294, Cockermouth 10, Workington 16.
Golf Cockermouth 18h. **See** Crummock Water, Scale Force (120 ft fall).

★★ **Bridge,** CA13 9UZ ☎(059 685) 252
Small 18th century hotel in quiet Cumbrian village. ⚒ Fr
🛏 22 bedrs, 22 en suite; tcf
🏠 dogs; P 45; con 30
✕ LD 8.30, bar meals only lunch
£ B&B & dinner £35; D £15; dep.

BUXTON Derbyshire. Map 30C3

Pop 20,797. Ashbourne 20, London 159, Chapel-en-le-Frith 5½, Chesterfield 23, Congleton 17, Leek 13, Macclesfield 12, Matlock 20, Stockport 18.
EC Wed. **MD** Tue, Sat. **Golf** Buxton and High Peak 18h. Cavendish 18h. **See** The Crescent (18th cent houses, Pump Room), Pavilion Gdns, Peak Rail Steam Centre.
ℹ The Crescent. ☎(0298) 25106

★★★ **Buckingham,** 1 Burlington Rd, SK17 9AS ☎(0298) 70481 Fax: (0298) 72186
Substantial stone-built hotel overlooking the Pavilion Gardens. Billiards.
🛏 29 bedrs, 29 en suite; TV; tcf
🏠 lift; P 30, coach; child facs; con 30
✕ LD 9.30
£ B&B £48, B&B (double) £65, HB weekly £275; L £7.95, D £13·95; WB £86 [10% V]
cc Access, Amex, B'card/Visa, Diners.
(*See advertisement on p. 180*)

Using RAC discount vouchers
Please tell the hotel when booking if you plan to use an RAC discount voucher (see p. 34) in part payment of your bill. Only one voucher will be accepted per party per stay. Discount vouchers will only be accepted in payment for accommodation, not for food.

★★★ **Lee Wood,** Manchester Rd, SK17 6TQ ☎(0298) 23002 Tx: 669848 Fax: (0298) 23228

Fully modernised building of Georgian splendour, situated in own grounds. ⚒ Fr
🛏 37 bedrs, 37 en suite; TV; tcf
🏠 lift, TV, dogs, P 50, coach; child facs; con 100
✕ LD 9.30
£ B&B £56–£64, B&B (double) £64–£82; HB weekly £320–£340; L £6, D £15; WB £44 [10% V Sun]
cc Access, Amex, B'card/Visa, Diners.

★★★ **Palace,** Palace Rd, SK17 6AG ☎(0298) 22001 Tx: 668169 Fax: (0298) 72131
Stately hotel with elegant public rooms and sun lounge. Indoor swimming pool, putting, sauna, solarium, gymnasium, snooker.
⚒ Fr, De, Du (THF)
🛏 122 bedrs, 122 en suite; TV; tcf
🏠 lift, dogs; P 200, coach; child facs; con 250
✕ LD 9.30
£ B&B £78, B&B (double) £102; L £9, D £14; WB £45
cc Access, Amex, B'card/Visa, CB, Diners.

★★ **Grove,** Grove Pde, SK17 6AJ ☎(0298) 23804
Proprietor-run central hotel in 18th century building.
🛏 22 bedrs, 7 en suite, 6 ba; TV; tcf
🏠 TV, dogs, ns; P 10, coach; child facs; con 80
£ B&B £25–£40, B&B (double) £45–£50; L £7·95, D £12·50.

★★ **Portland,** 32 St Johns Rd, SK17 6XQ ☎(0298) 71493 Fax: (0298) 27464

Family-run, stone-built hotel facing park near town centre. Conservatory restaurant. ⚒ Fr
🛏 25 bedrs, 25 en suite; TV; tcf
🏠 dogs, ns; P 18, coach; child facs; con 100
✕ LD 9, bar meals only Sat lunch
£ B&B £42, B&B (double) £55; HB weekly £280; L £8, D £14·50; WB; [10% V Sun]
cc Access, Amex, B'card/Visa, Diners; dep.
(*See advertisement on p. 000*)

★★ **Sandringham,** Broad Walk, SK17 6JT ☎(0298) 72257
Hotel in attractive setting with views of Pavilion Gardens. Closed 24 Dec–2 Jan.
🛏 39 bedrs, 13 en suite, (8 sh), 5 ba; tcf
🏠 TV, dogs; P 8, coach; child facs; con 60
✕ LD 8·15
£ B&B £18–£30, B&B (double) £30–£45·50; L £6·50, D £9·50; WB £57·50
cc Access, B'card/Visa.
(*See advertisement on p. 180*)

★ **Hartington,** Broad Walk, SK17 6JR ☎(0298) 22638 ♿

Small privately-owned hotel in attractive residence overlooking gardens and lake. Closed mid Dec–Feb, mid July
🛏 17 bedrs, 7 en suite, 3 ba; TV; tcf
🏠 TV, ns; P 15, coach; child facs
✕ LD 8, nr lunch. Resid & Rest lic
£ B&B £25–£33, B&B (double) £38–£45; D £9; WB fr £25; [10% V]
cc Access, B'card/Visa; dep.

Thorn Heyes (Highly Acclaimed), 137 London Rd, SK17 9NW ☎(0298) 23539. *Private Hotel*. Closed 2 wks Nov
£ B&B £17·50, HB weekly £168
Westminster (Highly Acclaimed), 21 Broad Walk, SK17 6JR ☎(0298) 23929. *Private Hotel*. Open Feb–Nov & Xmas.
£ B&B £22; HB weekly £165

Netherdale (Acclaimed), 16 Green Lane, SK17 9DP ☎(0298) 23896 *Guest House*. Open Feb–Nov.
£ B&B £15–£17.50, HB weekly £165–£186
Old Hall (Acclaimed), The Square, SK17 6BD. ☎(0298) 22841 Fax: (0298) 72437. *Hotel.*

Buxton Lodge, 28 London Rd, SK17 9NX ☎(0298) 23522. *Hotel*. Closed Jan.
£ B&B £16·50–£24·50, HB weekly £157·50–£171·50
Buxton View, 74 Corbar Rd, SK17 6RJ ☎(0298) 79222. *Guest House*. Open Mar–Nov.
£ B&B £20
Hawthorn Farm, Fairfield Rd, SK17 7ED ☎(0298) 23230. *Guest House*. Open Apr–Oct.
£ B&B £14–£15
Swanleigh, 7 Grange Rd, SK17 6NH ☎(0298) 24588. *Guest House*.
£ B&B £13–£15

CADNAM Hampshire. Map 5B2

M27 ½, London 82, Lyndhurst 4, Ringwood 12, Salisbury 14, Southampton 8

Hotel locations
Hotel locations are shown on the maps at the back of the guide. All towns and villages containing an RAC Appointed or Listed hotel are ringed in purple.

♛ ★★★ Bartley Lodge, Lyndhurst Rd, SO4 2NR ☎(0703) 812248 Fax: (0703) 812075

Red-brick, 18th-century hunting lodge in 11 acres of mature grounds. Swimming pool, tennis.
🛏 19 bedrs, 19 en suite; TV
🏨 TV, dogs, ns; P 60; coach; child facs; con 80
✕ LD 8.45, bar meals only Mon–Sat lunch
£ B&B £59–£69, B&B (double) £85–£95; L £13, D £13; WB £105 (2 nts); [10% V]
cc Access, Amex, B'card/Visa, Diners.

CALDBECK Cumbria. Map 43C2

Penrith 16, London 292, Carlisle 14, Cockermouth 15, Wigton 8, Windermere 31.

High Greenrigg House (Highly Acclaimed), CA7 8HD ☎(06998) 430. *Hotel.* ♿ Open Mar–Oct.
£ B&B £19·50–£24·50; HB weekly £177–£207

Park End (Highly Acclaimed), CA7 8HH ☎(069 98) 494

Swaledale Watch, Whelpo, CA7 8HQ ☎(069 98) 409. *Farm.*

CALNE Wiltshire. Map 5A4

Pop 11,000. M4 (jn 16) 12, London 85, Chippenham 6, Devizes 8½, Marlborough 13, Swindon 16.
EC Wed. **MD** Fri. **Golf** North Wilts 18h. **See** Adam Church, 17th cent. Almshouses.

★★ Lansdowne Strand, The Strand, SN11 0JR ☎(0249) 812488 Fax: (0249) 812488

White 2-storey building. Former 16th century coaching inn with cobbled courtyard.
🛏 21 bedrs, 21 en suite, annexe 5 bedrs, 5 en suite; TV; tcf
🏨 dogs; P 25, coach; child facs; con 100
✕ LD 10
£ B&B £44, B&B (double) £52; HB weekly £320, L £8·50, D £9·50; WB £46·50 [10% V]
cc Access, Amex, B'card/Visa, Diners.

CAMBERLEY Surrey. Map 13A2

Pop 52,271 (inc Frimley). Bagshot 3, London 30, Basingstoke 17, Farnham 10, Guildford 12, Henley-on-Thames 18, Reading 15.
EC Wed. **Golf** Camberley Heath 18h. **See** St Michael's Church.

★★★ Frimley Hall, Portsmouth Rd, GU15 2BG ☎(0276) 28321 Tx: 858446 Fax: (0276) 691253

Converted manor house with pleasant terraces and lawns. (THF). ✻ Fr, It, Es
🛏 66 bedrs, 66 en suite; TV; tcf
🏨 dogs, ns; P 110; coach; child facs; con 130
✕ LD 10.30
£ room £75–£85, double room £100–£106; Bk £8·60, L £13·50, D £17·50; WB £52; [10% V]
cc Access, Amex, B'card/Visa, CB, Diners.

Camberley, 116 London Rd, GU15 3TJ. ☎(0276) 24410. *Guest House.* Closed 24–27 Dec. ✻ Fr, De, Es
£ B&B £30

CAMBORNE Cornwall. Map 2B1

Pop 13,000. Redruth 3½, London 267, Helston 9½, Penzance 14, St Ives 11.
EC Thur. **MD** Fri. **Golf** Tehidy Park 18h. **See** School of Mines, 15th cent Church.

Lowenac (Highly Acclaimed), Bassett Rd, TR14 8SL ☎(0209) 719295. *Hotel.* ✻ Es
£ B&B £45–£52·50, WB £75 (2 nts HB)

CAMBRIDGE Cambridgeshire. Map 26C3

Pop 101,000. M11 (jn 12) 1½, London 55, Biggleswade 22, Bishop's Stortford 27, Ely 16, Haverhill 18, Huntingdon 16, Newmarket 13, Royston 13.
See Plan, p. 183.
MD Daily. **P** See Plan. **Golf** Gog Magog 18h and 9h, Girton 18h. **See** Colleges and Gardens, The Backs', Churches, Mathematical Bridge, Bridge of Sighs (St John's), Fitzwilliam Museum, King's College Chapel, Botanic Garden.
ℹ Wheeler St. ☎(0223) 322640

★★★★ Cambridgeshire Moat House, Bar Hill, CB3 8EU ☎(0954) 780555 Tx: 817141 Fax: (0954) 780010

Large modern 2-storey building, set in parkland. On A604. Indoor swimming pool, golf, putting, tennis, squash, sauna, solarium, gymnasium. (QMH). Closed Xmas Day.
🛏 100 bedrs, 100 en suite; TV; tcf
🏨 dogs; P 200, coach; child facs; con 200
✕ LD 10, bar meals only Sat lunch
£ B&B £70–£77, B&B (double) £87–£95; L £15, D £15; WB £49
cc Access, Amex, B'card/Visa, Diners.

★★★★ Garden House, Granta Pl, Mill La, CB2 1RT ☎(0223) 63421 Tx: 81463 Fax: (0223) 316605

Luxurious modern hotel, set in secluded riverside gardens, near city centre. Fishing.
✻ Fr, De, It, Es, Pl
🛏 118 bedrs, 118 en suite; TV; tcf
🏨 lift, ns; P 180, coach; child facs; con 250
✕ LD 9.30
£ B&B £73–£125, B&B (double) £99–£150; L £15·75, D £18·50; WB £57; [10% V]
cc Access, Amex, B'card/Visa, Diners.
(*See advertisement on p. 184*)

★★★★ Post House, Bridge Rd, Impington, CB4 4PH ☎(0223) 237000 Tx: 817123 Fax: (0223) 233426 ♿

Modern Post House with many facilities. Indoor swimming pool, sauna, solarium, gymnasium, snooker. (THF) ✻ Fr
🛏 120 bedrs, 120 en suite; TV; tcf
🏨 dogs, ns; P 200, coach; child facs; con 80
✕ LD 10.30
£ B&B £91·20–£100·20 (w/e £52), B&B (double) £118·40–£124·40; HB weekly £364; L £11, D £16.40; WB £52
cc Access, Amex, B'card/Visa, CB, Diners.

★★★★ University Arms, Regent St, CB2 1AD ☎(0223) 351241 Tx: 817311 Fax: (0223) 315256 ♿

Victorian building in the Grand Hotel' style, with modern extensions. (DeV) ✻ Fr, Es
🛏 117 bedrs, 117 en suite; TV; tcf
🏨 lift, dogs; G 75, coach; child facs; con 300

EC *early closing* **MD** *market day* ♛ *country house hotel* *ns (NS) no smoking areas* *tcf tea/coffee facilities*

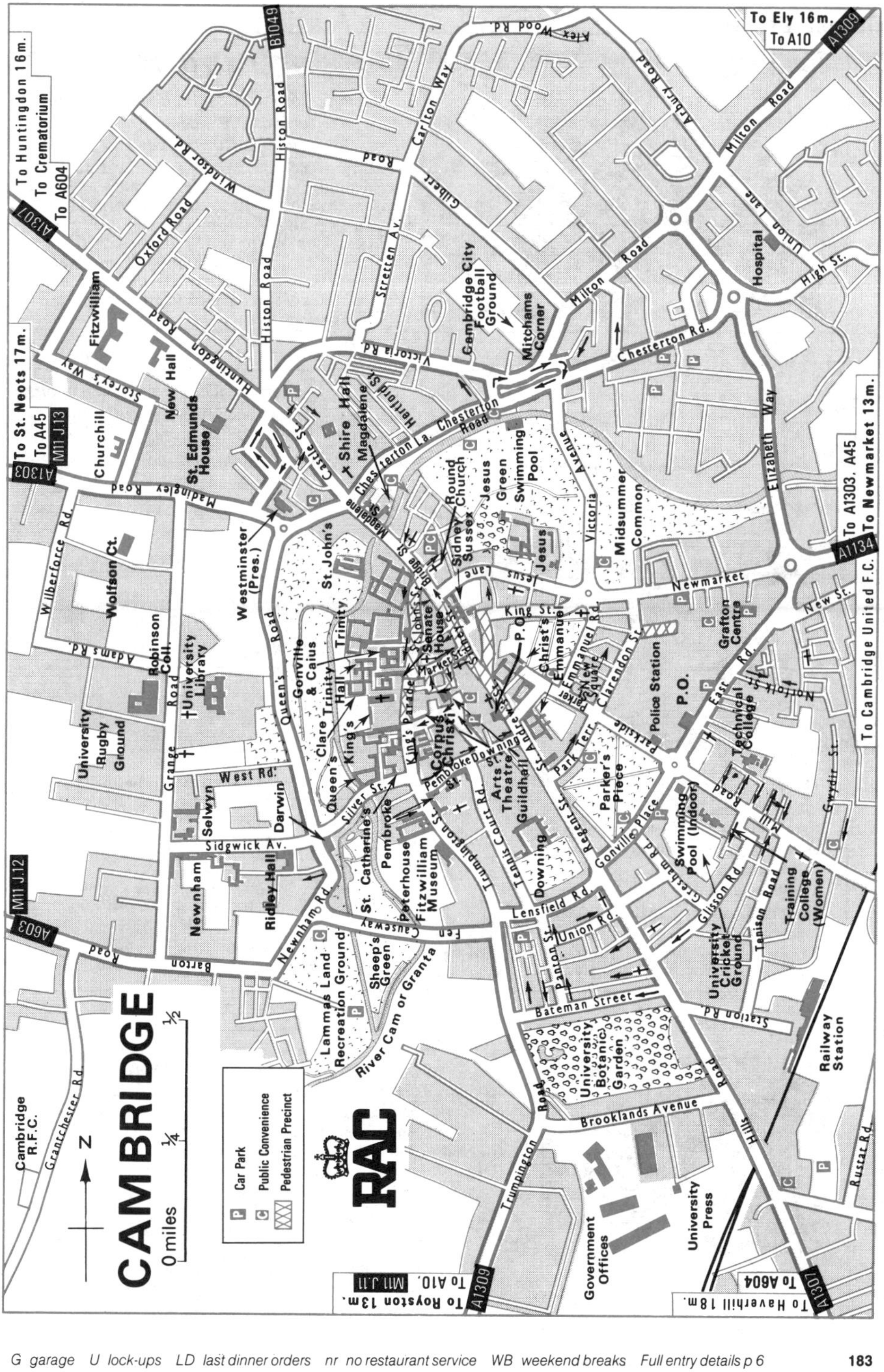

CAMBRIDGE

0 miles ¼ ½

N

RAC

P Car Park
C Public Convenience
Pedestrian Precinct

To Huntingdon 16m.
To Crematorium
To A604
A1307

B1049

To Ely 16m.
To A10
A1309

To St. Neots 17m.
To A45
M11 J.13
A1303

To A1303, A45
To Newmarket 13m.
A1134

To Cambridge United F.C.

M11 J.12
A603

To Royston 13m.
To A10. M11 J.11
A1309

To Haverhill 18m.
To A604
A1307

Cambridge R.F.C.
Grantchester Rd.
Barton Road
Newnham Rd.
Newnham
Ridley Hall
Sidgwick Av.
Selwyn
Darwin
West Rd.
Grange Road
University Rugby Ground
Robinson Coll.
University Library
Adams Rd.
Wilberforce Rd.
Wolfson Ct.
Madingley Road
Churchill
Storey's Way
Fitzwilliam
New Hall
St. Edmunds House
Huntingdon Road
Oxford Road
Windsor Rd.
Histon Road
Westminster (Pres.)
Queen's Road
Castle St.
Shire Hall
Magdalene
Magdalene St.
Chesterton La.
Chesterton Road
Hertford St.
Victoria Rd.
Stretten Av.
Gilbert Road
Carlton Way
Alex Wood Rd.
Arbury Road
Milton Road
Cambridge City Football Ground
Mitchams Corner
Chesterton Rd.
Union Lane
Hospital
High St.
Elizabeth Way
Midsummer Common
Victoria Avenue
Jesus Green
Swimming Pool
Jesus
Jesus Lane
Round Church
Sidney Sussex
Bridge St.
St. John's
St. John's St.
Trinity
Trinity Hall
Gonville & Caius
Senate House
Market St.
Sidney St.
Clare
King's
King's Parade
Queen's
Silver St.
St. Catharine's
Corpus Christi
Pembroke
Pembroke St.
Downing St.
Arts Theatre
Guildhall
St. Andrews St.
P.O.
Christ's
Emmanuel
Emmanuel Rd.
King St.
New Square
Parker St.
Park Terr.
Parker's Piece
Regent St.
Parkside
Clarendon St.
Police Station
P.O.
Grafton Centre
Newmarket Road
New St.
East Rd.
Norfolk St.
Technical College
Mill Road
Gwydir St.
Gonville Place
Swimming Pool (Indoor)
Gresham Rd.
Glisson Rd.
Tenison Road
Training College (Women)
University Cricket Ground
Station Rd.
Railway Station
Hills Road
Rustat Rd.
Peterhouse
Fitzwilliam Museum
Trumpington St.
Tennis Court Rd.
Downing
Lensfield Rd.
Union Rd.
Panton St.
Bateman Street
Fen Causeway
Sheep's Green
Lammas Land Recreation Ground
River Cam or Granta
University Botanic Garden
Trumpington Road
Brooklands Avenue
Government Offices
University Press

C

Crown copyright reserved

Buxton (Derbyshire)

The Portland Hotel RAC ★★

32 St John's Road, Buxton, Derbyshire SK17 6XQ
Telephone: (0298) 22462/71493
Facsimile: (0298) 27464

A warm welcome awaits you at our long established, family run hotel. New elegant conservatory "Park Restaurant" offering excellent cuisine and traditional service. All our 25 bedrooms enjoy en-suite facilities and have your comfort in mind. Rotary, Round Table, Freemasons and Soroptimists eat and meet with us. Ideally situated for touring the beautiful Peak District.

Cambridge (Cambridgeshire)

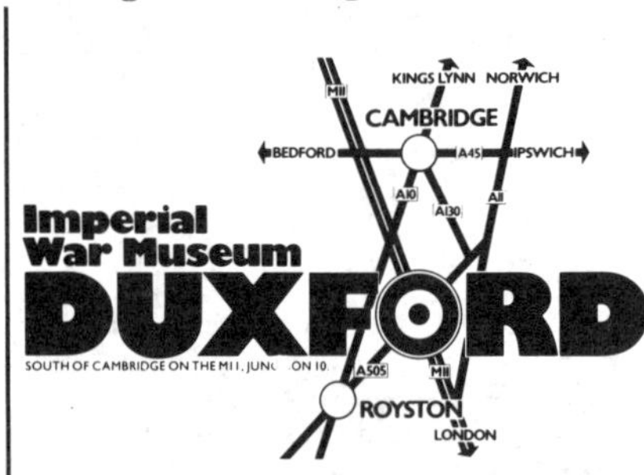

See the finest collection of civil and military aircraft in Britain. Tanks, guns, naval exhibits and many special exhibitions to suit all the family. Concorde open daily, adventure playground, ride simulator.

Open daily from 10.00am except for Christmas and New Year Bank Holidays. Admission charged. Ring 0223 835000 (recorded message) or 0223 833963/835075. Ample free parking, restaurant, shops. No dogs please.

Imperial War Museum, Duxford – 8 miles south of Cambridge, junction 10 of M11.

Cambridge (Cambridgeshire)

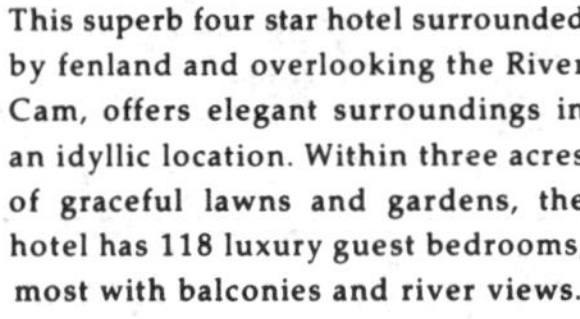

This superb four star hotel surrounded by fenland and overlooking the River Cam, offers elegant surroundings in an idyllic location. Within three acres of graceful lawns and gardens, the hotel has 118 luxury guest bedrooms, most with balconies and river views.

Le Jardin restaurant is renowned for its international cuisine, while the Lounge and conservatory serves an excellent and unusual selection of light meals including scrumptious afternoon teas.
Weekend break rates available throughout the year.
Open to non residents.

Granta Place, Mill Lane, Cambridge CB2 1RT
Telephone (0223) 63421 Fax (0223) 316605 Telex 81463

Canterbury (Kent)

Canterbury's four-star premier hotel first licensed in 1588. In the centre of the city and close to the Cathedral. Seventy-three bedrooms, some with Tudor and Colonial four-poster and Georgian half-tester beds, with private bathroom, direct-dial telephone and colour television. The Hotel features modern facilities with the charm of an old timbered building. The ideal base to explore Canterbury. Private car park. Gourmet restaurant. Coffee Shop. Full room service. ****

County Hotel Canterbury

High Street, Canterbury, Kent CT1 2RX
Telephone: **Canterbury (0227) 766266**
Telex: **965076** *Fax:* **(0227) 451512**

✕ LD 9.45
£ B&B £75, B&B (double) £90; L £12, D £14·50; WB £85; [10% V]
cc Access, Amex, B'card/Visa, CB, Diners.

★★★ **Gonville,** Gonville Pl, CB1 1LY
(0223) 66611 Fax: ext 301

Privately-owned Victorian building situated opposite Parkers Piece. Closed 24–28 Dec. Fr, De, It, Es
62 bedrs, 62 en suite; TV; tcf
lift, TV, dogs; P 100, coach; child facs; con 50
✕ LD 9·45
£ B&B £61·50, B&B (double) £77; L £8·75, D £10·75; WB £40
cc Access, Amex, B'card/Visa, CB, Diners.

★★★ **Royal Cambridge,** Trumpington St, CB2 1PY (0223) 351631 Tx: 329265
Fax: (0223) 352972
Grey-brick terrace building in Georgian style, close to colleges and The Backs: Entrance at back of terrace. Fr, Es, Po
16 bedrs, 12 en suite; TV; tcf
lift, dogs; P 80, coach; child facs; con 120
✕ LD 9.30
£ B&B £60, B&B (double) £72 (w/e £40) L £7·50, D £10·50; WB £42 (HB); [10% V]
cc Access, Amex, B'card/Visa, Diners.

★★ **Arundel House,** 53 Chesterton Rd, CB4 3AN (0223) 67701
Fax: (0223) 67721

Elegant Victorian building beautifully located by the River Cam. Fr, Es
66 bedrs, 53 en suite, 8 ba; annexe 22 bedrs, 22 en suite; TV; tcf
ns; P 70, coach; child facs; con 35
✕ LD 9.30
£ B&B £26·50–£47, B&B (double) £39·50–£65; L £7·50, D £11·75; WB £72·50 (2nts); [5% V w/e Nov–Apr]
cc Access, Amex, B'card/Visa, Diners.

Cambridge Lodge (Highly Acclaimed), 139 Huntingdon Rd, CB3 0DQ (0223) 352833
Fax: (0223) 355166. *Private Hotel.* Fr, De
£ B&B £45–£55

Lensfield (Highly Acclaimed), 53 Lensfield Rd, CR2 1GH (0223) 355017 Tx: 818183
Fax: (0223) 312022 *Hotel.* Closed 21 Dec–4 Jan. Fr, Es, Gr
£ B&B £30–£40.

Bon Accord House (Acclaimed), 20 St Margaret's Sq, CB1 4AP (0223) 411188.
Guest House.
£ B&B £18–£26

Suffolk House (Acclaimed), 69 Milton Rd, CB4 1XA (0223) 352016. *Private Hotel*
£ B&B £45

Centennial, 63–69 Hills Rd, CB2 1PG
(0223) 314652 Tx: 817019. *Private Hotel.*

CAMELFORD Cornwall. Map 2C2

Pop 1,800. Launceston 16, London 227, Bodmin 13, Bude 17, Wadebridge 11.
EC Wed. **Golf** Launceston 18h. **See** Church of St Thomas, Lanteglos Church, Slaughter Bridge (scene of King Arthur's last battle), 43rd Wessex Division Memorial at Roughtor, Cornwall's highest hill Brown Willy.
[i] North Cornwall Museum, The Clease. (0840) 212954

Countryman, 7 Victoria Rd, PL32 9XA
(0840) 212250. *Private Hotel.*

Warmington House, 32 Market Pl, PL32 9PD (0840) 213380. *Private Hotel.*

CANFORD CLIFFS Dorset.

See POOLE

CANTERBURY Kent. Map 7C3

See also BARHAM

Pop 33,000. M2 (jn 7) 8, London 58, Ashford 14, Dover 15, Folkestone 16, Maidstone 27, Margate 15.
See Plan, p. 186.
EC Thur. **MD** Wed, (cattle Mon). **P** See Plan. **Golf** Canterbury 18h. **See** Cathedral (site of Becket's murder), St Martin's and other old Churches, Christchurch Gate, King's School, Eastbridge Hospital (Almshouses), Beaney Institute Museum, The Weavers, City Walls, Dane John Gardens (Invicta Engine), Castle Keep, St Thomas's Hospital (almshouse), Museum (Poor Priests' Hospital).
[i] 34 St Margaret's St. (0227) 766567

★★★★ R **County,** High St, CT1 2RX
(0227) 766266 Tx: 965076
Fax: (0227) 451512

Gabled 16th century building on historic site. Luxury city centre hotel. Fr, It
73 bedrs, 73 en suite; TV; tcf
lift; P 40, G 20 (£2·50), coach; child facs; con 180
✕ LD 10
£ room £66, double room £79–£85; Bk £4·50, L £14, D £18; WB £32 (2nts)
cc Access, Amex, B'card/Visa, CB, Diners.
(*See advertisement on p. 184*)

★★★ **Chaucer,** Ivy La, CT1 1TU
(0227) 464427 Tx: 965096
Fax: (0227) 450397

Detached red-brick Regency building near town centre and Cathedral. (THF)
45 bedrs, 45 en suite; TV; tcf
dogs, ns; P 45, coach; child facs; con 80
✕ LD 9.45
£ B&B £77 (w/e £45), B&B (double) £100; HB weekly £364; L £10, D £14; WB £45
cc Access, Amex, B'card/Visa, Diners.

★★★ **Falstaff,** St Dunstan's St, CT2 8AF
(0227) 462138 Tx: 96394
Fax: (0227) 463525
18th century inn with a well-matched extension. In city centre. (Lns)
25 bedrs, 25 en suite; TV; tcf
ns; P 50; con 40
✕ LD 9.45
£ B&B £69, B&B (double) £85; L £11, D £11; WB £48; [10% V]
cc Access, Amex, B'card/Visa, Diners.

★★★ **Slatters,** St Margaret's St, CT1 1AA
(0227) 463271 Fax: (0227) 764117

16th century building with modern block added. In shopping centre. (QMH)
31 bedrs, 27 en suite, 4 ba; TV; tcf
lift, dogs; coach; child facs; con 100
✕ LD 9.15
£ B&B £50, B&B (double) £60; HB weekly £259; L £7·95, D 11·50; WB £37
cc Access, Amex, B'card/Visa, Diners.

★★ **Canterbury,** 71 New Dover Rd, CT1 3DZ (0227) 450551 Tx: 965809
Fax: (0227) 450873
Large detached Georgian-style house, half mile from city centre. Fr, It, Du
27 bedrs, 27 en suite; TV; tcf
lift, dogs; P 40, coach; child facs; con 20
✕ LD 10
£ B&B £40–£45, B&B (double) £50–£58; L £8·50, D £11·50; WB £62; [5% V]
cc Access, Amex, B'card/Visa, Diners.

★★ **Victoria,** 59 London Rd, CT2 8JY
(0227) 459333

Weekend breaks
Please consult the hotel for full details of weekend breaks; prices shown are an indication only. Many hotels offer mid week breaks as well.

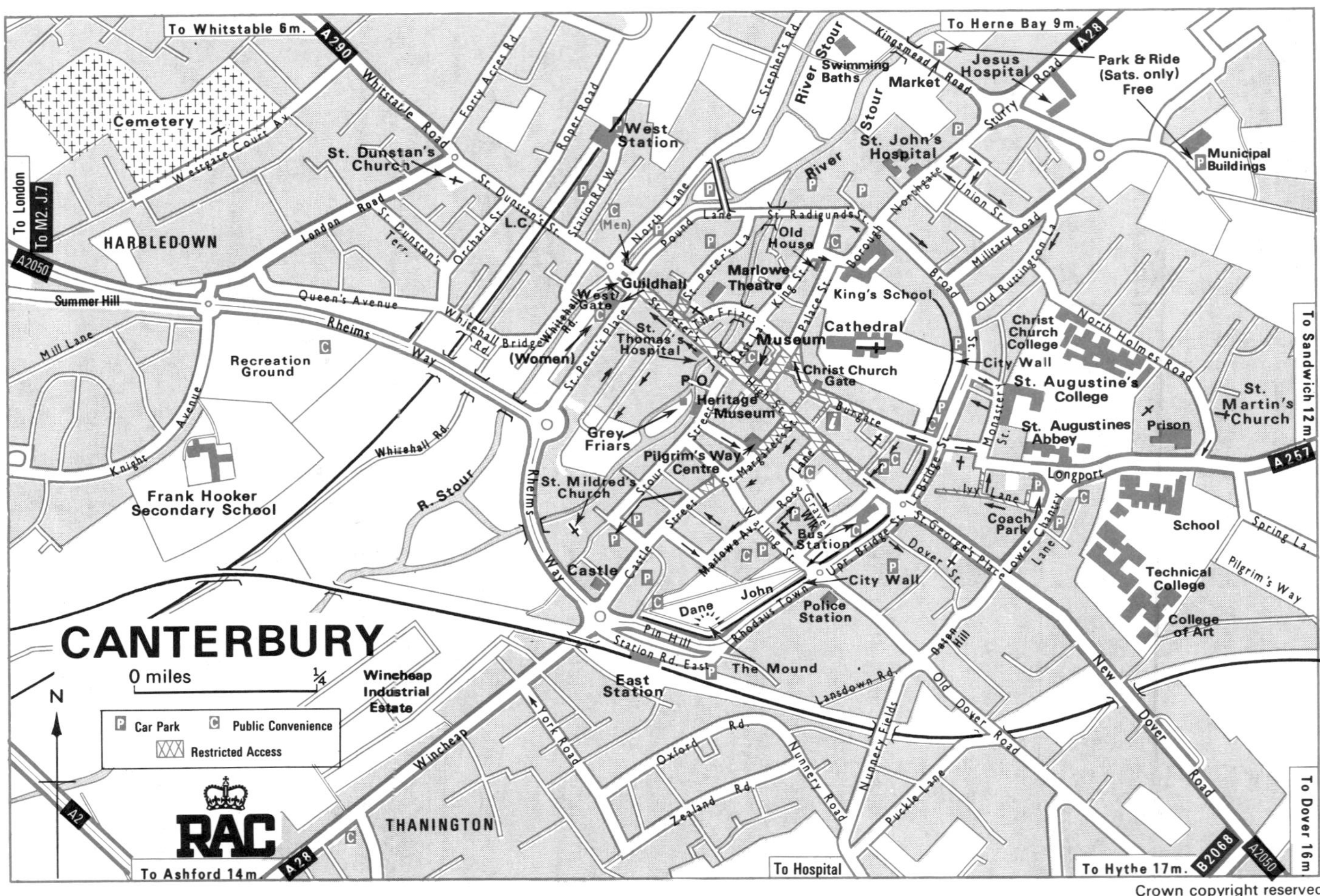

EC *early closing* **MD** *market day* *country house hotel* *ns (NS) no smoking areas* *tcf tea/coffee facilities*

Detached red brick residence with modern extension in attractive garden. (BCB)
🛏34 bedrs, 34 en suite; TV; tcf
🏨ns; P 26, coach; child facs; con 20
✕LD 10.30
£B&B £42–£54, B&B (double) £70; L £8·15, D £8·15; WB £27·50
cc Access, Amex, B'card/Visa, Diners.

★ **Three Tuns,** Watling St, CT1 2UD
☎(0227) 767371

Two-storey, white-painted, 18th century inn in centre of city. (BCB)
🛏7 bedrs, 4 en suite, 2 ba; TV; tcf
🏨ns; P 4, coach; child facs
✕LD 9
£ B&B £35·50–£41, B&B (double) £44·50–£51·50; L £8·15, D £8·15; WB £27·50
cc Access, Amex, B'card/Visa, Diners.

Ebury (Highly Acclaimed), 65 New Dover Rd, CT1 3DX ☎(0227) 768433
Fax: (0227) 459187. *Hotel. Indoor swimming pool.* Closed 25 Dec–Jan 13.
⚒ Fr, It
£B&B £35–£37, HB weekly £200–£220; [5% V w/d]
Thanington (Highly Acclaimed), 140 Wincheap, CT1 3RY ☎(0227) 453227. *Hotel.* ⚒ Fr, De
£ B&B £42–£48

Ersham Lodge (Acclaimed), 12 New Dover Rd, CT1 3AP ☎(0227) 463174
Fax: (0227) 455482. *Hotel.* Closed 7 Nov–Dec. ⚒ Fr, De, It
£B&B £39–£47·50; [5% V 15 Sep–Jun]

Abba, Station Rd West, CT2 8AN
☎(0227) 464771. *Hotel.*
£B&B £17·50–£20, HB weekly £150–£170.
Alexandra House, 1 Roper Rd, CT2 7EH
☎(0227) 767011. *Guest House.*
£B&B £14–£16; [5% V]
Castle Court, 8 Castle St, CT1 2QF
☎(0227) 463441. *Guest House.*
£B&B £15–£18; [10% V Nov–Mar]
Highfield, Summer Hill, CT2 8NH ☎(0227) 462772. *Guest House.* Open Feb–Nov.
£B&B £24
Pointers, 1 London Rd, CT2 8LR
☎(0227) 456846. *Hotel.* Closed 25 Dec–15 Jan. ⚒ Fr, De
£B&B £28–£35, HB weekly £168–£217, WB £48; [10% V Nov–Jun].

CARBIS BAY Cornwall. Map 2A1

Pop 2,500. Redruth 14, London 277, Helston 13, Penzance 8½, St Ives 2.
EC Thur. **Golf** West Cornwall, Lelant 18h. **See** North Cornwall Coast Path (view), sandy beach, St Ives Art Galleries and Old Mariners Church at St Ives (2 m NW).

★★ **Boskerris,** Boskerris Rd, TR26 2NQ
☎Penzance (0736) 795295
Three-storey white-painted building in attractive gardens overlooking bay. Swimming pool, putting.

★★ **St Uny,** Boskerris Rd, TR26 2NQ
☎Penzance (0736) 795011
Near superb beach, former private residence in sheltered gardens. Putting, billiards. Open Easter–Oct.
🛏30 bedrs, 19 en suite (1 sh), 4 ba
🏨TV, ns; P 28, G 4, coach; no children under 5; con 15
✕LD 8, nr lunch. Resid & Rest lic
£B&B £20–£26; HB weekly £154–£245; D £11·50
cc Access, B'card/Visa; dep.

Tregorran, Headland Rd, TR26 2NU
☎Penzance (0736) 795889. *Private Hotel. Swimming pool, solarium, gymnasium.* Open Easter–Oct. ⚒ Fr, De
£ B&B £13·50–£30; [5% V]
White House, The Valley, TR26 2QY
☎Penzance (0736) 797405. *Hotel.* Closed Nov.
£B&B £18–£25; HB weekly £145–£216

CARLISLE Cumbria. Map 43C3

See also DALSTON, WARWICK-ON-EDEN and WETHERAL.
Pop 70,000. M6 (jn 44) 1½, London 294, Brampton 9, Cockermouth 25, Gretna 9, Langholm 20, Penrith 18.
EC Thur. **MD** all expt Thur & Sun. **Golf** Stoneyholme 18h. **See** Cathedral and Monastic buildings, Castle (Border Regt Museum), Tullie House Museum and Art Gallery, 17th cent Market Cross, The Citadel.
[i] Old Town Hall, Green Market.
☎(0228) 512444

★★★ **Central,** Victoria Viaduct, CA3 8AL
☎(0228) 20256 Fax: (0228) 514657
Tall, Victorian brick-built hotel in the city centre. Two minutes from station.
🛏84 bedrs, 84 en suite; TV; tcf
🏨lift, TV, dogs; G 20, coach; child facs; con 100
✕LD 9, bar meals only Sun lunch
£B&B £55–£65, B&B (double) £66–£76; D £14·50; WB £90 (2nts); [5% V, Nov–Mar]
cc Access, Amex, B'card/Visa, CB, Diners; dep.

★★★ **Crest,** Kingstown, CA4 0HR
☎(0228) 31201 Tx: 64201
Fax: (0228) 43178

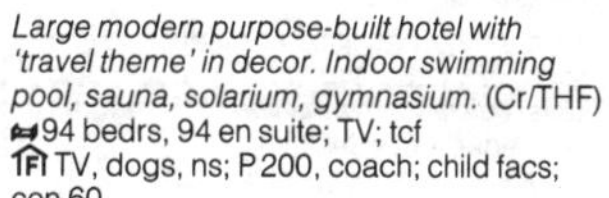

Large modern purpose-built hotel with 'travel theme' in decor. Indoor swimming pool, sauna, solarium, gymnasium. (Cr/THF)
🛏94 bedrs, 94 en suite; TV; tcf
🏨TV, dogs, ns; P 200, coach; child facs; con 60
✕LD 9.45, nr Sat lunch
£room £70–£84 (w/e £38), double room £82–£96; Bk £5·95, L £8·25, D £14·95; WB £43
cc Access, Amex, B'card/Visa, Diners.

★★★ **Crown and Mitre,** 4 English St, CA3 8HZ ☎(0228) 25491 Tx: 64183
Edwardian period hotel in centre of Carlisle, near the Cathedral. Indoor swimming pool.
🛏78 bedrs, 78 en suite; annexe 20 bedrs, 20 en suite; TV; tcf
🏨lift, TV, dogs, ns; P 45, coach; child facs; con 400

★★★ **Cumbrian,** Court Sq., CA1 1QY
☎(0748) 850445 Tx: 64287
Fax: (0228) 47799
Four-storey elegant Victorian building in the city centre.
🛏70 bedrs, 70 en suite; TV; tcf
🏨lift, dogs, ns; P 15, G 30, coach; child facs; con 275

★★★ **Cumbria Park,** 32 Scotland Rd, CA3 9DG ☎(0228) 22887
Fax: (0228) 514796 ♿

Family-managed hotel, set in beautiful gardens, between city centre and M6. Hadrian's Wall runs through grounds.
🛏51 bedrs, 51 en suite; TV; tcf
🏨lift, TV; P 40, coach; child facs; con 170
✕LD 9
£B&B £50–£70, B&B (double) £60–£95; L £10·25, D £13·50; [5% V]
cc Access, Amex, B'card/Visa; dep.

★★★ **Hayton Castle,** nr Wetheral, CA4 8QD ☎(0228) 70651 Fax: (0228) 70010
Castle-style mansion set in 68 acres of park and woodland. Fishing.
🛏13 bedrs, 13 en suite; TV; tcf
🏨P100, coach; child facs; con 300
✕LD 9.30, bar meals only Mon–Sat lunch
£ B&B £49, B&B (double) £65; D £14·95; WB £37
cc Access, Amex, B'card/Visa.

★★★ [H] [C] **String of Horses,** Heads Nook, Faugh, CA4 9EG ☎Hayton (0228) 70297 Fax: (0228) 70675

C

17th century coaching inn at Faugh to east of city. Easy access to M6. Swimming pool, sauna, solarium, gymnasium.
14 bedrs, 14 en suite; TV; tcf
dogs; P 50, coach; child facs; con 20
LD 10, bar meals only Sat lunch
£ B&B £55–£68, B&B (double) £62–£88; L £9·95, D £14·95; WB; [5% V]
cc Access, Amex, B'card/Visa, Diners; dep.

★★★ Swallow Hilltop, London Rd, CA1 2PQ (0228) 29255 Tx: 64292
Fax: (0228) 25238

Modern 2-storey hotel in own grounds by A6 link road. Indoor swimming pool, putting, tennis, sauna, solarium, gymnasium, billiards. (Sw)
97 bedrs, 97 en suite; TV; tcf
lift, dogs, ns; P 350, U 1, coach; child facs; con 500
LD 10
£ B&B £60, B&B (double) £70; WB £85–£90 (2nts)
cc Access, Amex, B'card/Visa, Diners.

★★ Carrow House, Carleton, CA4 0AD
(0228) 32073
Traditional detached red sandstone building with single storey extension.
10 bedrs, 10 en suite; TV; tcf
P 120, child facs

★★ Pinegrove, 262 London Rd, CA1 2QS
(0228) 24828
Small traditional stone-built house set in own grounds; convenient for town centre.
Closed Xmas. Po
28 bedrs, 18 en suite (3 sh), 2 ba; annexe 4 bedrs, 4 en suite; TV; tcf
TV, dogs, ns; P 32, coach; child facs con 120
LD 9, nr Sun
£ B&B £24–£34, B&B (double) £36–£46; L £2·50, D £9
cc Access, B'card/Visa.

★★ Woodlands, 264 London Rd, CA1 2QS (0228) 45643 Fax: (0228) 45643
Family-run hotel in two converted stone-built houses on A6, 2 miles S of town centre.
Closed 25 Dec–5 Jan.
15 bedrs, 7 en suite, 3 ba; TV; tcf
dogs; P 20; child facs; con 15
LD 9, bar meals only lunch. Resid lic
£ B&B £23, B&B (double) £42; D £11·50; [10% V]
cc Access, Amex, B'card/Visa, Diners; dep.

★ Vallum House, Burgh Rd, CA2 7NB
(0228) 21860
Small hotel in 2-storey red brick building in western outskirts.
9 bedrs, 5 en suite, 2 ba; TV; tcf
TV, dogs; P 10, coach; child facs; con 40
(*See advertisement on p. 189*)

Angus (Acclaimed), 14 Scotland Rd, CA3 9DG (0228) 23546. *Hotel.* Fr
£ B&B £17–£25
East View (Acclaimed), 110 Warwick Rd, CA1 1JU (0228) 22112. *Guest House.*

All Seasons, Park Broom, CA6 4QH
(0228) 73696. *Hotel.*
Royal, 9 Lowther St, CA3 8ES
(0228) 22103. *Private Hotel. Sauna.*
£ B&B £16·50–£26·50, HB weekly £140–£210; [10% V]

CARLTON COLVILLE Suffolk. Map 27C4
London 113, Beccles 6½, Lowestoft 3½, Southwold 10.

★★ Hedley House Park, Chapel Rd, NR33 8BL Lowestoft (0502) 560772
Fax: (0502) 573949
Attractive gabled house standing in 9 acres of own grounds. Fishing.
16 bedrs, 16 en suite; TV; tcf
dogs; P 180, coach; child facs; con 100
LD 10.30
£ B&B £36, B&B (double) £48; HB weekly £225; L £8·50, WB £65 (2nts); [10% V]
cc Access, Amex, B'card/Visa, Diners.

CARLYON BAY Cornwall
See ST AUSTELL

CARNFORTH Lancashire. Map 36B4
M6 (jn 35) 1, London 243, Kendal 15, Kirkby Lonsdale 10, Lancaster 7, Settle 24.

★★★ Pine Lake Lodge, LA6 1JZ
(0524) 736191 Tx: 65459
Fax: (0524) 736793
Hotel in a large leisure complex with 70-acre lake just off junction 35 of M6. Motel-style bedrooms or family-sized lodges. Indoor swimming pool, fishing, sauna, gymnasium.
Fr, It
23 bedrs, 23 en suite; TV; tcf
P; child facs; con 125
£ B&B £46·50, B&B (double) £63; D £13·50; WB £25; [10% V]
cc Access, Amex, B'card/Visa, Diners; dep.

★★ Royal Station, Market St, LA5 9BT
(0524) 733636
Prominent 3-storey Victorian building well-situated in the main street of town.
12 bedrs, 12 en suite; TV; tcf
dogs; P 7, G 15, coach; child facs; con
LD 8, bar meals only lunch
£ B&B £24·50, B&B (double) £42; [5% V]
cc Access, Amex, B'card/Visa, Diners.
(*See advertisement on p. 189*)

Holmere Hall (Acclaimed), Yealand Conyers, LA5 9SN (0254) 735353

CARPERBY North Yorkshire. Map 38B4
Leyburn 8, London 243, Grassington 16, Hawes 8, Richmond 15.
See Aysgarth Force.
Grayford, Nr Leyburn. DL8 4DW
(09693) 517

CASTERTON Cumbria. Map 36B4
Kirkby Lonsdale 1, London 247, Brough 28, Kendal 13, Lancaster 13, Settle 17.

★★ Pheasant, nr Kirkby Lonsdale, LA6 2RX (052 42) 71230

Charming old coaching inn in village centre.
Fr
10 bedrs, 10 en suite, annexe 4 bedrs, 4 en suite; TV; tcf
TV, dogs, ns; P 60; child facs
LD 9.15, bar meals only Mon–Sat lunch
£ B&B £30–£35, B&B (double) £50–£55; HB weekly £218·75–£245; D £11; WB £31·25–£35
cc Access, B'card/Visa; dep.

CASTLE BROMWICH West Midlands. Map 22C2
Pop 15,952. M6 (jn 5) 1, London 109, Birmingham 6, Nuneaton 16, Sutton Coldfield 5, Tamworth 11, Walsall 11, Warwick 21.
EC Wed, Thur. **Golf** Pype Hayes 18h. **See** Castle Bromwich Hall, Church of SS Mary and Margaret.

★★ Bradford Arms, Chester Rd, B36 0AG
021-748 7675
Former inn with adjoining modern motel accommodation.

CASTLE CARY Somerset. Map 4C3
Frome 10, London 117, Bruton 5, Shepton Mallet 8, Wincanton 6, Yeovil 15.

★★ George Inn, Market Pl, BA7 7AH
(0963) 50761.

Recently refurbished, thatched 15th-century inn on the Market Place.
12 bedrs, 12 en suite; annexe 4 bedrs, 4 en suite; TV
dogs; P 10, coach; child facs; con 22
LD 9; bar meals only Mon–Sat lunch
£ B&B £40–£45, B&B (double) £55–£65; D £15; WB £50–£60 (2nts)
(*See advertisement on p. 189*)

CASTLE COMBE Wiltshire. Map 5A4
Pop 347. M4 (jn 7) 6½, London 97, Bath 11, Bristol 18, Chippenham 6, Cirencester 22, Frome 22, Tetbury 12.
See Very picturesque village, Market Cross, Church.

★★★★ H C R Manor House, SN14 7HR (0249) 782206 Tx: 449931
Fax: (0249) 782159

Carlisle (Cumbria)

Carnforth (Lancashire)

Castle Cary (Somerset)

Castle Donington (Derbyshire)

Imposing 14th century house in 26 acres of woods and parkland. Swimming pool, tennis, fishing. ⚒ Fr, De, It, Es
🛏 12 bedrs, 12 en suite; annexe 24 bedrs, 24 en suite; TV
🏨 dogs, ns; P 100, child facs; con 60
✕ LD 9
£ B&B £90·50–£205·50; B&B (double) £106–£211; L £16·50, D £22·50; WB £75 (2nts)
cc Access, Amex, B'card/Visa, Diners; dep.

CASTLE DONINGTON Leicestershire.

Map 25A2
Pop 5,359. M1 (jn 24) 3, London 118, Ashby-de-la-Zouch 9½, Burton-upon-Trent 16, Derby 9½, Loughborough 9.
Golf Longcliffe 18h. **See** Donington Hall, King's Mill, Church, old Key House.

★★★ **Donington Manor,** DE7 2PP
📞 Derby (0332) 810253 Tx: 934999
Fax: (0332) 850330
Privately-owned former coaching inn, mainly of stone, set back from road. Closed 27 Dec–31 Jan.
🛏 34 bedrs, 34 en suite, annexe 3 bedrs, 1 en suite; TV; tcf
🏨 P 60, coach; child facs; con 80
✕ LD 9.15
£ B&B £53–£60 (w/e £29), B&B (double) £62–£71; L £6·70, D £8·50
cc Access, Amex, B'card/Visa, Diners.

Park Farmhouse (Acclaimed), Melbourne Rd, DE7 2RN 📞 (0332) 862409. *Hotel.*
£ B&B £26–£39, [10% w/e, winter]

Four Poster, 73 Clapgun St, DE7 2LF
📞 Derby (0332) 810335. *Guest House.*
£ B&B £15.

CATLOWDY Cumbria. Map 44A3

M6 14, London 310, Canonbie 5, Carlisle 16, Greenhead 19, Longtown 8, Newcastleton 8.

Bessiestown Farm, (Acclaimed), Penton CA6 5QP 📞 Nicholforest (022877) 219.
Indoor swimming pool.
£ B&B £22·50–£25 HB weekly £170–£190.

CATTERICK North Yorkshire. Map 45A1

Pop 2,824. Boroughbridge 22, London 230, Darlington 13, Leyburn 11, Northallerton 13, Scotch Corner 5, Stockton-on-Tees 23.
EC Wed. **Golf** Catterick Garrison 18h. **See** River Swale, 14th cent Church.

★★ **Bridge House,** Catterick Bridge, DL10 7PE 📞 Richmond (0748) 818331
15th century coaching inn attractively set on banks of River Swale opposite race course. Fishing.
🛏 15 bedrs, 13 en suite, 1 ba; TV; tcf
🏨 TV, dogs; P 70, coach; child facs; con 120
✕ LD 10, bar meals only Sun dinner
£ B&B £25–£40, B&B (double) £40–£52; L £7·50, D £12·50; [10% V]
cc Access, Amex, B'card/Visa, Diners; dep.

CAWSTON Norfolk. Map 35B2

East Dereham 13, London 118, Cromer 15, Fakenham 19, Norwich 13.

Grey Gables Country House, (Acclaimed), Norwich Rd, Eastgate NR10 4EY 📞 (0603) 871259. *Private Hotel. Tennis, riding.* Closed Xmas. ⚒ Fr
£ B&B £30–£42, HB weekly £178–£203; [10% V]

CHAGFORD Devon. Map 3B3

Pop 1,250. Exeter 16, London 186, Ashburton 13, Crediton 14, Newton Abbot 16, Okehampton 11, Tavistock 20.
EC Wed. **Golf** Okehampton 18h. **See** Dartmoor, St Michael's 13th cent Church, Old Inns.

♣ ★★★ **Gidleigh Park,** TQ13 8HH
📞 (0647) 432367 Tx: 42643
Fax: (0647) 432574

A substantial mock-Tudor house, elegantly furnished and appointed, with lovely gardens running down to the River Teign. Tennis, fishing. ⚒ Fr, De
🛏 12 bedrs, 12 en suite; annexe 2 bedrs, 2 en suite; TV
🏨 dogs; P 25; con 18
✕ LD 9. Resid & Rest lic
£ B&B & dinner £140–£255; B&B & dinner (double) £175–£290; L £30 or £40
cc Access, B'card/Visa.

♣ ★★★ **Great Tree,** nr Sandy Park, TQ13 8JS 📞 (0647) 432491 Tx: 9312132116

18th century hunting lodge situated in 25 acres of garden and woodland. Solarium. ⚒ De
🛏 12 beds, 12 en suite; TV; tcf
🏨 dogs, ns; P30; child facs; con 25
✕ LD 8.45
£ B&B £42·50–£55, B&B (double) £68–£88; HB weekly £310–£371; L £8·95, D £16·50; WB £96 (HB 2nts); [10% V Apr–Nov]
cc Access, Amex, B'card/Visa, Diners; dep.

♣ ★★★ **H C R** **Mill End,** Sandy Pk, TQ13 8JN 📞 (0647) 432283
Fax: (0647) 433106

Charmingly converted flour mill, retains mill wheel. Riverside setting. Fishing. Closed 13–21 Dec & 10–19 Jan.
🛏 17 bedrs, 15 en suite, 2 ba; TV; tcf
🏨 TV, dogs; P 17, U 4; child facs
✕ LD 9. Resid & Rest lic
£ room £30–£60, double room £55–£70; L £20–£25, D £20–£25
cc Amex, B'card/Visa, Diners; dep.
(*See advertisement on p. 191*)

★★ **Three Crowns,** High St. TQ13 8AJ
📞 (0647) 433444 Fax: (0647) 433117

13th century thatched stone-built inn situated opposite ancient church. Billiards.
🛏 13 bedrs, 13 en suite; annexe 5 bedrs, 4 en suite; TV; tcf
🏨 TV, dogs; P 16, coach; child facs; con 100
✕ LD 9.30
£ B&B £20–£28·50. HB weekly £180–£210; L £5·75, D £15; WB
cc Access, Amex, B'card/Visa.
(*See advertisement on p. 191*)

Thorworthy House (Highly Acclaimed), TQ13 8EY 📞 (0647) 433297. *Private Hotel. Putting, tennis.*
£ B&B £30, HB weekly £350.

Glendarah House, TQ13 8BZ 📞 (0647) 433270. *Private Hotel.* Open Mar–Dec. ⚒ De
£ B&B £14·50–£18·50; HB weekly £161–£189; [5% V]

CHARD Somerset. Map 4B2

Pop 9,384. Ilminster 5, London 141, Axminster 7, Crewkerne 8, Honiton 14, Taunton 13.
EC Wed. **MD** Sat. **Golf** Windwhistle 12h. **See** 15th cent Church, old Grammar School, Manor House (Judge Jeffreys assoc), Guildhall, Waterloo House, Choughs Inn, Cricket St Thomas Wild Life Park 3m E, Museum.

EC *early closing* **MD** *market day* ♣ *country house hotel* *ns (NS) no smoking areas* *tcf tea/coffee facilities*

Chagford (Devon)

Mill End Hotel

Sandy Park, Chagford, Devon TQ13 8JN
Tel: 0647 432282

This old flourmill with its wheel still turning in the peaceful courtyard, nestles in the Teign Valley on the edge of Dartmoor. Tea by the fire in winter, drinks on the lawns in Summer – it is a most relaxing place.

C

Chagford (Devon)

Three Crowns Hotel ★★

Chagford, Devon
Tel: (0647) 433444
Fax: (0647) 433117

* A 13th-century hostelry of character within Dartmoor National Park.
* Centrally heated with period furnishing including two classic four poster beds.
* An ideal touring centre; close to the scenic golf course at Moretonhampstead as well as riding, walking, swimming and fishing facilities.
* Fully licensed, free house. Open all year.
* Bar snacks and à la carte or table d'hôte menus.
* Resident proprietors of local birth.
* Weddings, conferences etc. catered for in our Cavalier Function Room.

Chester (Cheshire)

The Chester Court Hotel

The Chester Court is a quiet hotel approximately 1 mile from the City Centre on the Hoole Road.

We are ½ mile from the Railway Station, and there is a frequent bus service into town.

A characterful detached building. It is set in its own grounds with parking facilities.

There is full central heating throughout – Direct Dial Telephone – Colour TV – Tea-making Facilities – Trouser Press – Hair Drier – Radio/Alarm in all rooms.

Tel: (0244) 320779/311098
Fax: (0244) 344795

48 Hoole Road (A56), Chester, Cheshire CH2 3NL

[i] Guildhall, Fore St ☎(0460) 67463

George, Fore Street ☎(04606) 3413
A stone and brick inn with a courtyard in town centre opposite the Guildhall.

Watermead (Acclaimed), 83 High St, TA20 1QT ☎(0460) 62834. *Guest House.*
£ B&B £12·50–£15, HB weekly £150; [5% V]

CHARLBURY Oxfordshire. Map 21A2

Pop 2,637. Oxford 15, London 71, Banbury 15, Bicester 16, Burford 9, Chipping Norton 6½, Faringdon 19, Wantage 24.
EC Wed or Thur. **Golf** Chipping Norton 9h, Burford 18h.

★★ [R] **Bell,** Church St, OX7 3AP ☎(0608) 810278 Tx: 837883 Fax: (0608) 811447

17th century building of Cotswold stone situated in centre of village. Fr, Es,
10 bedrs, 10 en suite; annexe 4 bedrs, 4 en suite; TV; tcf
TV, dogs; P 30, coach; child facs; con 50
LD 9
£ B&B £50, B&B (double) £75; L £12·50, D £19; WB £49 (HB 2nts); [10% V]
cc Access, Amex, B'card/Visa, Diners.

CHARLECOTE Warwickshire. Map 20C3

Banbury 17, London 89, Moreton-in-Marsh 18, Stratford-upon-Avon 5, Warwick 6.

★★★ [C] **Charlecote Pheasant,** CV35 9EW ☎Stratford-upon-Avon (0789) 470333 Fax: (0789) 470222 ♿

17th century farmhouse, modernised and extended round a courtyard. Swimming pool, tennis, sauna, solarium, gymnasium. (QMH). Closed 21–31 Dec.
40 bedrs, 40 en suite; annexe 20 bedrs, 20 en suite; TV; tcf
dogs, ns; P 113, coach; child facs; con 130
LD 9.45
£ B&B £65, B&B (double) £80; L £9·95, D £12·95; WB £41·50 (HB); [5% V]
cc Access, Amex, B'card/Visa, Diners.

CHARLTON Oxfordshire. Map 21A2

Bicester 11, London 68, Banbury 6, Brackley 6.

Home Farm, OX7 3BR ☎Banbury (0295) 811683

CHARLWOOD Surrey. Map 10B1

Horley 2, London 27, Gatwick Airport 2, Crawley 3, Reigate 7.
See Gatwick Zoo.

Stanhill Court, Stanhill Rd, RH6 OEP ☎(0293) 862166
Hotel awaiting inspection.

CHARMOUTH Dorset. Map 4B1

Pop 1,122. Dorchester 22, London 144, Axminster 6, Crewkerne 13, Lyme Regis 3.
Golf Lyme Regis 18h.

★★ **Charmouth House,** The Street, DT6 6PH ☎(0297) 60319
Stone-built, thatched roof Elizabethan building overlooking gardens and sea. Swimming pool, sauna.
13 bedrs, 8 en suite, 2 ba; TV; tcf
dogs, ns; P 30, coach; child facs; con 30
LD 9, bar meals only Mon–Sat lunch
£ B&B £26·50–£28, B&B (double) £38–£44; HB weekly £170–£190; L £6, D £10
cc Access, B'card/Visa; dep.

★★ **Fernhill,** DT6 6BX ☎(0297) 60492
Set in 14 acres, a family-run hotel with fine views of coast and country. Swimming pool, squash.

★★ **Queen's Arms,** The Street, DT6 6QF ☎(0297) 60339
16–17th century building of character in main street. Family-run. Open Feb–Nov
11 bedrs, 11 en suite; TV; tcf
TV, dogs; P 20; no children under 5
LD 8, bar meals only lunch. Resid & Rest lic
£ B&B £23–£26; HB weekly £190–£230; D £7; WB £58 (HB 2 nts)
cc Access, B'card/Visa; dep.

★★ **White House,** The Street, DT6 6PJ ☎(0297) 60411

Attractive Regency house in the centre of town close to the sea front. Fr, It
7 bedrs, 6 en suite (1 sh); TV; tcf
dogs; P 15; no children under 14
LD 9. Resid & Rest lic
£ B&B £46–£48·50 B&B (double) £72–£77; HB weekly £287–£301; L £12, D £16·50; WB £43 (HB)
cc Access, B'card/Visa.

Newlands House (Acclaimed), Stonebarrow La, DT6 6RA ☎(0297) 60212. *Hotel.* Open Mar–Oct.
£ B&B £17·50–£20·50; HB weekly £171·60–£188.

CHARNOCK RICHARD Lancs. Map 32C3

Pop 1,947. Wigan 7, London 202, M6 (jn 27) 5, Chorley 3, Ormskirk 12, Preston 10, Southport 18.
EC Wed. **Golf** Leyland 18h.
[i] Service Area, M6 (Northbound) ☎(0257) 793773

★★★ **Hunters Lodge,** Preston Rd, PR7 5LH ☎Coppull (0257) 793011 ♿
Modern hotel in black and white style–convenient for M6.

★★★ **Park Hall,** PR7 5LP ☎(0257) 452090 Tx: 677604 Fax: (0257) 451838

Modern three-storey hotel with a conference centre, between junctions 27 and 28 of M6. Swimming pool, sauna, solarium, gymnasium, squash, tennis, snooker.
55 bedrs, 55 en suite; TV; tcf
lift, TV, dogs, ns; P 2500, coach; child facs; con 750

★★★ **Welcome Lodge,** Mill La, PR7 5LR (M6 Motorway) ☎Coppull (0257) 791746 Tx: 67315 Fax: (0257) 793596
See Motor Lodge Section

CHATHAM Kent. Map 11C3

Rochester 1, London 31, M2 (jn 3) 3½, Maidstone 3½, Sittingbourne 10.
EC Wed. **MD** Daily. **See** Almshouses, Heritage Centre, Napoleonic Fort.

★★★ **Crest,** Maidstone Rd, ME5 9SF ☎Medway (0634) 687111 Tx: 965933 Fax: (0634) 684512 ♿

Modern hotel built on to original old inn. Swimming pool, sauna, solarium, gymnasium. (Cr/THF)
105 bedrs, 105 en suite; TV; tcf
lift, dogs, ns; P 150, coach; child facs; con 110
LD 9.45
£ room £85–£93, double room £100–£116; Bk £6, L £8, D £16; WB £45
cc Access, Amex, B'card/Visa, CB, Diners.

CHATTERIS Cambridgeshire. Map 26C4

London 75, M11 (jn 14) 11, Huntingdon 16, Peterborough 21, Wisbech 17.

★ **Cross Keys,** 16 Market Hill, PE16 6BA ☎(03543) 3036
A fine, small 16th century inn situated in the town centre. Beams and open fires add character to the public rooms.
7 bedrs, 5 en suite, 1 ba; TV; tcf
TV, dogs; P 8, coach; child facs; con 40
LD 10
£ B&B £19·50–£32·50, B&B (double) £29·50–£42·50; L £6·95; WB £17·50; [10% V]
cc Access, Amex, B'card/Visa, Diners.

Bramley House (Acclaimed), 15 High St, PE16 6BE ☎(036 43) 5414. *Guest House.*
£B&B £15; [V]

CHEADLE Staffordshire. Map 30B2

Pop 10,876. Uttoxeter 9½, London 145, Ashbourne 13, Buxton 23, Stoke 9.
EC Wed. **MD** Fri, Sat. **Golf** Whiston 18h.
See Gothic Church (R.C.), 17th cent Market Cross.

Royal Oak, 69 High St, ST10 1AN
☎(0538) 753116

CHEDDAR Somerset. Map 4C3

Pop 3,500. Wells 8, London 130, Bath 23, Bridgwater 18, Bristol 17, Glastonbury 13, Radstock 17, Weston-super-Mare 12.
EC Wed. **MD** Wed. **Golf** Burnham and Berrow 18h. **See** Market Cross, Gorge, Caves, Jacob's Ladder, Motor and Transport Museum, Museum with prehistoric remains, Ambleside Water Gardens and Aviaries.
[i] The Gorge. ☎(0934) 744071

★ **Gordons,** Cliff St, BS27 3PT
☎(0934) 742497
Attractive stone-built house extended into a small hotel. Caves nearby. Swimming pool. Closed 16 Dec–31 Jan.
🛏11 bedrs, 3 en suite (3 sh), 2 ba; annexe 2 bedrs, 2 en suite; TV; tcf
🏨TV, dogs; P 10, coach; child facs
✕LD 8.45, bar meals only lunch. Resid & Rest lic
£B&B £16–£27·50, B&B (double) £32–£40; HB weekly £140–£175 D £6·50; [10% V]
cc Access, B'card/Visa; Diners; dep.

The Market Cross (Acclaimed), Church St, The Cross, BS27 3RA ☎(0934) 742264. *Hotel.* ✂Fr
£ B&B £16–£17, [5% V Mon–Wed, Feb–Apr & June]

CHELMSFORD Essex. Map 17B3

Pop 58,099. Brentwood 11, London 33, Bishop's Stortford 18, Braintree 11, Colchester 22, Epping 17, Great Dunmow 12, Southend 19.
EC Wed. **MD** Tue, Wed, Sat. **Golf** Chelmsford 18h (2). **See** Cathedral, Shire Hall, Chelmsford and Essex Museum.
[i] County Hall ☎(0245) 283400

♛ ★★★★ **Pontlands Park,** West Hanningfield Rd, Great Baddow, CM2 8HR
☎(0245) 76444 Tx: 995256
Fax: (0245) 478393

19th century manor house in 4 acres of grounds. Comprehensive fitness centre with two swimming pools, sauna, solarium. Closed 27 Dec–4 Jan.
🛏17 bedrs, 17 en suite; TV
🏨dogs; P 70; child facs; con 40
✕LD 10, nr Mon & Sat lunch, Sun dinner
£B&B £77·50–£90·50 (w/e £45·50), B&B (double) £111; L £20·90, D £29·70;
cc Access, Amex, B'card/Visa, Diners.

★★★ **Saracen's Head,** 3 High St, CM1 1BE ☎(0245) 262368 Fax: (0245) 262418
Sympathetically restored Victorian hotel set in town centre.
🛏18 bedrs, 18 en suite; TV; tcf
🏨dogs; coach; child facs; con 70
✕LD 10.30
£B&B £65·75 (w/e £60), B&B (double) £90·50; [5% V w/e]
cc Access, Amex, B'card/Visa, Diners

★★★ **South Lodge,** 196 New London Rd, CM2 0AR ☎(0245) 264564 Tx: 99452
Fax: (0245) 492897
Attractive Georgian town residence with small garden and mature trees. ✂Fr, De, It, Es, Da
🛏24 bedrs, 24 en suite; annexe 17 bedrs, 17 en suite; TV; tcf
🏨dogs, ns; P 50; child facs; con 50
✕LD 9.30
£B&B £40–£70, B&B (double) £50–£80; L £12, D £15; [10% V w/e]
cc Access, Amex, B'card/Visa, CB, Diners.

★★ **County,** 29 Rainsford Rd, CM1 2QA.
☎(0245) 491911
Traditional county town" hotel close to railway station. Closed 27–30 Dec.

Snows Oaklands (Highly Acclaimed), 240 Springfield Rd, CM2 6BP ☎(0245) 352004. *Hotel.*
£B&B £28·40; [5% V]

Boswell House (Acclaimed), 118 Springfield Rd, CM2 6LF ☎(0245) 287587. *Hotel.* Closed 25 Dec–5 Jan.
£B&B £33–£38, HB weekly £287–£301; [5% V]

Beechcroft, 211 New London Rd, CM2 0AJ ☎(0245) 352462. *Private Hotel.* Closed 25 Dec–1 Jan.
£B&B £24·85–£32, HB weekly £173·95–£224

Tanunda, 217 New London Rd, CM2 0AJ
☎(0245) 354295. *Private Hotel.* Closed 25 Aug–8 Sep & 2 wks Xmas.
£ B&B £22·75–£28·75

CHELTENHAM Gloucestershire. Map 20B2.

See also CLEEVE HILL, COLESBOURNE and SOUTHAM.
Pop 85,000. Burford 22, M5 (jn 11) 3½, London 97, Cirencester 14, Evesham 16, Gloucester 9, Tewkesbury 9.
See Plan, p. 194.
EC Wed. **MD** Thur. **Golf** Cleeve Hill 18h.
See Art Gallery and Museum, St Mary's Parish Church, Rotunda, Mineral Springs.
[i] The Promenade. ☎(0242) 522878

★★★★ **Golden Valley Thistle,** Gloucester Rd, GL51 0TS ☎(0242) 232691 Tx: 43410
Fax: (0242) 221846

Modern hotel in own grounds on the western outskirts of town. Indoor swimming pool, sauna, solarium, gymnasium. (MtCh)
🛏97 bedrs, 97 en suite; TV; tcf
🏨lift, dogs, ns; P 275, coach; child facs; con 220
✕LD 10
£room £69, double room £75; Bk £7·75, L £11·50, D £14·50
cc Access, Amex, B'card/Visa, CB, Diners.

★★★★ **Queen's,** Promenade, GL50 1NN
☎(0242) 514724 Tx: 43381
Fax: (0242) 224145
Elegant Regency building overlooking Imperial Gardens. (THF)
🛏77 bedrs, 77 en suite; TV; tcf
🏨lift, dogs, ns; P 50, coach; child facs; con 250
✕LD 9.45
£room £80–£90 (w/e £55), double room £100–£120; Bk £8; L £13·75, D £19·50; WB £55
cc Access, Amex, B'card/Visa, CB, Diners.

★★★ **Carlton,** Parabola Rd, GL50 3AQ
☎(0242) 514453 Tx: 43310
Fax: (0242) 226487
Fine Regency building centrally but quietly situated.
🛏68 bedrs, 68 en suite; TV; tcf
🏨lift, dogs; P 35, coach; child facs; con 240
✕LD 9.30
£B&B £50–£55, B&B (double) £72; HB weekly £280·50; L £9, D £11·50; WB £74 (HB 2 nts); [10% V]
cc Access, Amex, B'card/Visa, Diners.

★★★ **White House,** Gloucester Rd, Staverton, GL51 0ST ☎(0452) 713226
Tx: 437382 Fax: (0452) 857590

Peacefully located hotel on the outskirts of town, close to junction 11 of the M5.
🛏50 bedrs, 50 en suite; TV; tcf
🏨dogs, ns; P 100, coach; child facs; con 180
✕LD 9.30
£B&B £66–£105 (w/e £35); B&B (double) £83–£113; L £6, D £12·25
cc Access, Amex, B'card/Visa, Diners; dep.

★★ **George,** 41 St George's Rd, GL50 3DZ
☎(0242) 235751 Tx: 437304
Fax: (0242) 224359
Gracious Georgian building—a landmark close to the town centre. ✂Es
🛏40 bedrs, 40 en suite; TV; tcf
🏨dogs; P 30, coach; child facs; con 40
✕LD 9.15
£ B&B £45 (w/e £35), B&B (double) £55 (w/e £45); L £7·50, D £10·50; WB £60 (2 nts); [5% V w/e only]
cc Access, Amex, B'card/Visa, Diners.

★★ **Lansdown,** Lansdown Rd, GL50 2LB
☎(0242) 522700

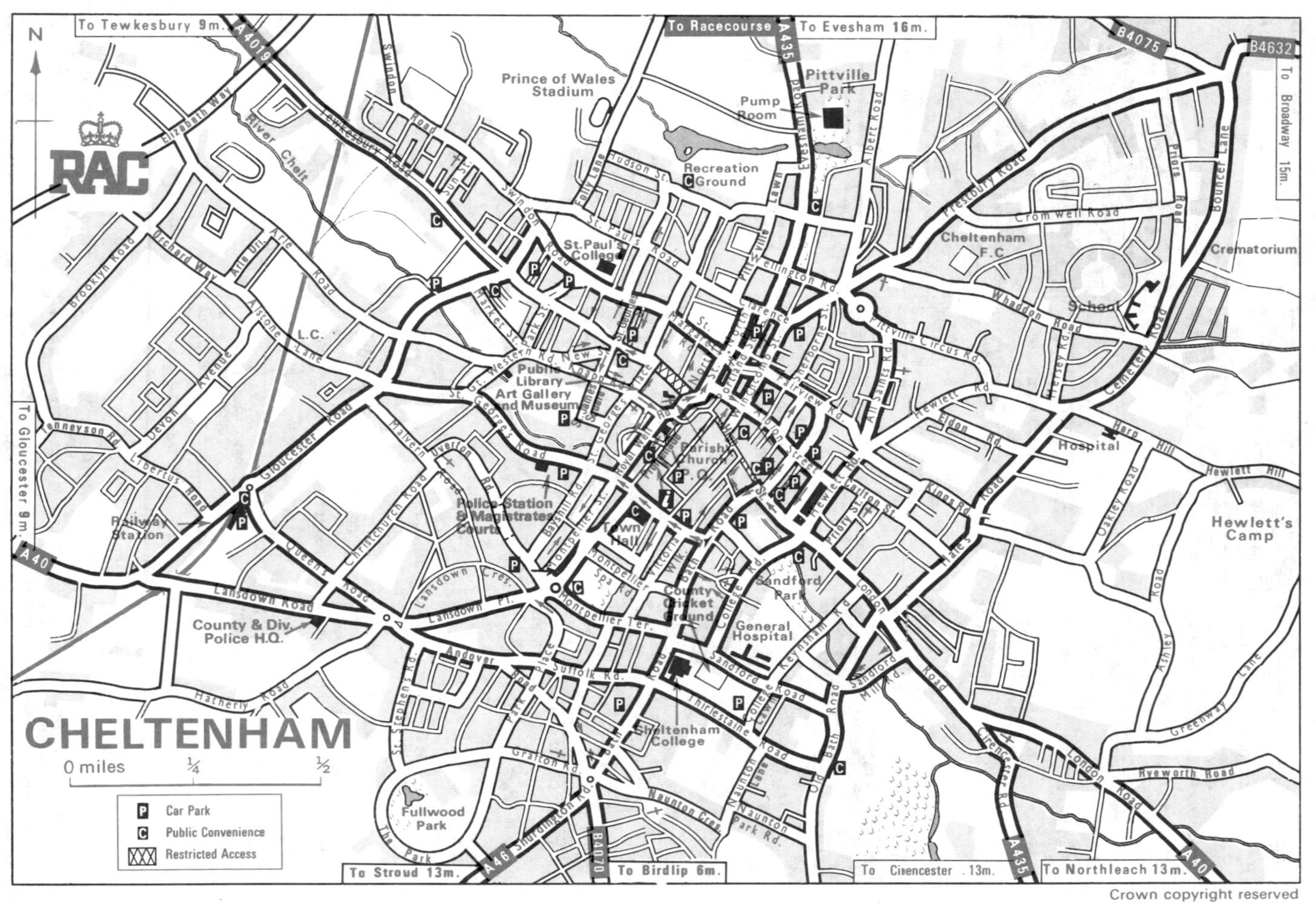

 EC *early closing* **MD** *market day* *country house hotel* *ns (NS) no smoking areas* *tcf tea/coffee facilities*

White stone Regency building with attractive gardens; a short way from town centre.
14 bedrs, 14 en suite; TV; tcf
ns: P 25, coach; child facs; con 204

★ Wellesley Court, Clarence Sq, GL50 4JR (0242) 580411 Tx: 67596
Fax: (0242) 224609

Pleasant Regency house hotel situated in a quiet square.
20 bedrs, 10 en suite, (2 sh), 2 ba; TV; tcf
lift, dogs; P 14, coach; children over 6; con 40

Allards (Highly Acclaimed), Shurdington GL51 5XA (0242) 862498. *Hotel.*
£ B&B £19–£20, [5% V]
Beaumont House (Highly Acclaimed), 56 Shurdington Rd, GL53 0JE (0242) 245986. *Hotel.*
£ B&B £16–£32 (w/e £19·50), HB weekly £175–£280; WB £19·50; [10% V]
Cotswold Grange (Highly Acclaimed), Pittville Circus Rd, GL52 2QH (0242) 515119. *Hotel.*
£ B&B £34, [10% V w/e]
Hannaford's (Highly Acclaimed), 20 Evesham Rd GL52 2AB (0242) 515181. *Hotel.* Fr, It
£ B&B £20; [10%]
Lypiatt House (Highly Acclaimed), Lypiatt Rd, GL50 2QW (0242) 224994 Fax: (0242) 224996. *Hotel.* Closed 23 Dec–2 Jan.
£ B&B £37–£52 (w/e £25) [10% V w/d]
On the Park (Highly Acclaimed), 38 Evesham Rd, GL52 2AH (0242) 518898. *Hotel.*
Regency House (Highly Acclaimed), 50 Clarence Sq, GL50 4JR (0242) 582718.
£ B&B £25.
Stretton Lodge (Highly Acclaimed), Western Rd, GL50 3RN (0242) 528724.
£ B&B £30–£40; HB weekly £230–£330.

Abbey (Acclaimed), 16 Bath Par. (0242) 516053 Tx: 437369 Fax: (0242) 227188
£ B&B £18–£22; [10% V w/e]
Hallery House (Acclaimed), 48 Shurdington Rd, GL53 0JE (0242) 578450. *Hotel.* It
£ B&B £15–£40, HB weekly £170–£350; [10% V]
Hollington House (Acclaimed), 115 Hales Rd, GL52 6ST (0242) 519718.
Fax: (0242) 570280 *Hotel.* Fr, De.
£ B&B £28; [10% V]
Milton House, (Acclaimed), 12 Royal Par. Bayshill Rd, GL50 3AY (0242) 582601.
Fax: (0242) 222326 *Hotel.*
£ B&B £28·75–£38
Willoughby (Acclaimed), 1 Suffolk Sq, GL50 2DR (0242) 522798. *Guest House.*

Bowler Hat, 130 London Rd, GL52 6HN (0242) 577362. *Hotel.*
Broomhill, 218 London Rd, GL52 6HW (0242) 513086. *Guest House.* Fr
£ B&B £17·50; [10% V]
Hilden Lodge, 271 London Rd, Charlton Kings GL52 6YL (0242) 583242. *Hotel.*
£ B&B £25; [10% V]
Ivy Dene, 145 Hewlett Rd, GL52 6TS (0242) 521726. *Guest House.* Closed 1–11 Jan.
£ B&B £12·50–£15; [10% V]
Leeswood, 14 Montpellier Dr, GL50 1TX (0242) 524813. *Hotel.*
£ B&B £16·50–£17·50.
Montpellier, 33 Montpellier Terr., GL50 1UX (0242) 526009. *Hotel.*
£ B&B £16–£26; WB £15; [5% V]
North Hall, Pittville Circus Rd, GL52 2PZ (0242) 520589. *Hotel.* Closed Xmas.
£ B&B £18–£27·50, HB weekly £165–£222; [5% V]
Old Vineyards, Timbercombe Lane, Charlton Kings, GL53 8EE (0242) 582893.

CHELWOOD Avon. Map 4C3

Bath 8, London 112, Bristol 7, Wells 14, Weston-super-Mare 23.

★★★ Chelwood House, BS18 4NH (0761) 490730 Tx: 44830

A gracious house delightfully furnished and set in an attractive garden. Conveniently placed on A37. Closed 26–31 Dec. De
11 bedrs, 11 en suite; TV; tcf
ns, P 15; children over 10
LD 9, nr Mon lunch, Sun dinner. Resid & Rest lic
£ B&B £59–£65, B&B (double) £69–£95; L £15·50, D £23; WB £107 (HB 2nts); [10% V; 5% Jul–Aug]
cc Access, B'card/Visa; dep.

Complaints

If you are dissatisfied with the facilities or service offered by a hotel, please take the matter up with the Manager WHILE YOU ARE AT THE HOTEL. In this way, any problems can usually be solved promptly and amicably.

The RAC will investigate matters if a personal approach has failed to resolve the problem. Please submit details of any discussion or correspondence when reporting the problem to the RAC.

CHENIES Buckinghamshire. Map 14B1

Pop 1,044. Rickmansworth 4, London 22, Aylesbury 18, High Wycombe 12.
Golf Gerrards Cross 18h. **See** Church, mill.

★★★ R Bedford Arms Thistle, WD3 6EQ (092 78) 3301 Tx: 893939
Fax: (092 78) 4825

Elizabethan-style former coaching inn in an historic village. (MtCh)
10 bedrs, 10 en suite; TV
dogs, ns; P 120, coach; child facs; con 25
LD 10
£ room £68, double room £80; Bk £7·90, L £12, D £15; WB
cc Access, Amex, B'card/Visa, CB, Diners.

CHERTSEY Surrey. Map 8A2

Pop 11,620. M25 (jn 11) 1½, London 19, Bagshot 9½, Staines 3½, Weybridge 3, Woking 3.
EC Wed. **MD** Sat. **Golf** Laleham 18h. **See** St Peter's Church founded 1310, Museum, 18th cent Bridge.

★ Bridge, Chertsey Bridge Rd, KT16 8JZ (0932) 564408

Pleasant riverside inn overlooking Thames. Easy access to Heathrow.

CHESTER Cheshire. Map 29B3

See also BROXTON and TATTENHALL
Pop 116,000 (City incl. surrounding district). Nantwich 21, London 183, M53 2, Birkenhead 15, Mold 11, Northwich 18, Queensferry 6½, Wrexham 11.
See Plan p. 196.
EC Wed. **MD** Daily exc Wed. **P** See Plan. **Golf** Vicars Cross 18h, Chester 18h. **See** Cathedral, The Rows, City Walls, Gates and Towers, High Cross, Roman amphitheatre, St John's Church and ruins.
i Town Hall, Northgate St. (0244) 324324 & Vicars Lane (0244) 351609

★★★★ Chester Grosvenor, 56 Eastgate St, CH1 1LT (0244) 324024 Tx: 61240 Fax: (0244) 313246

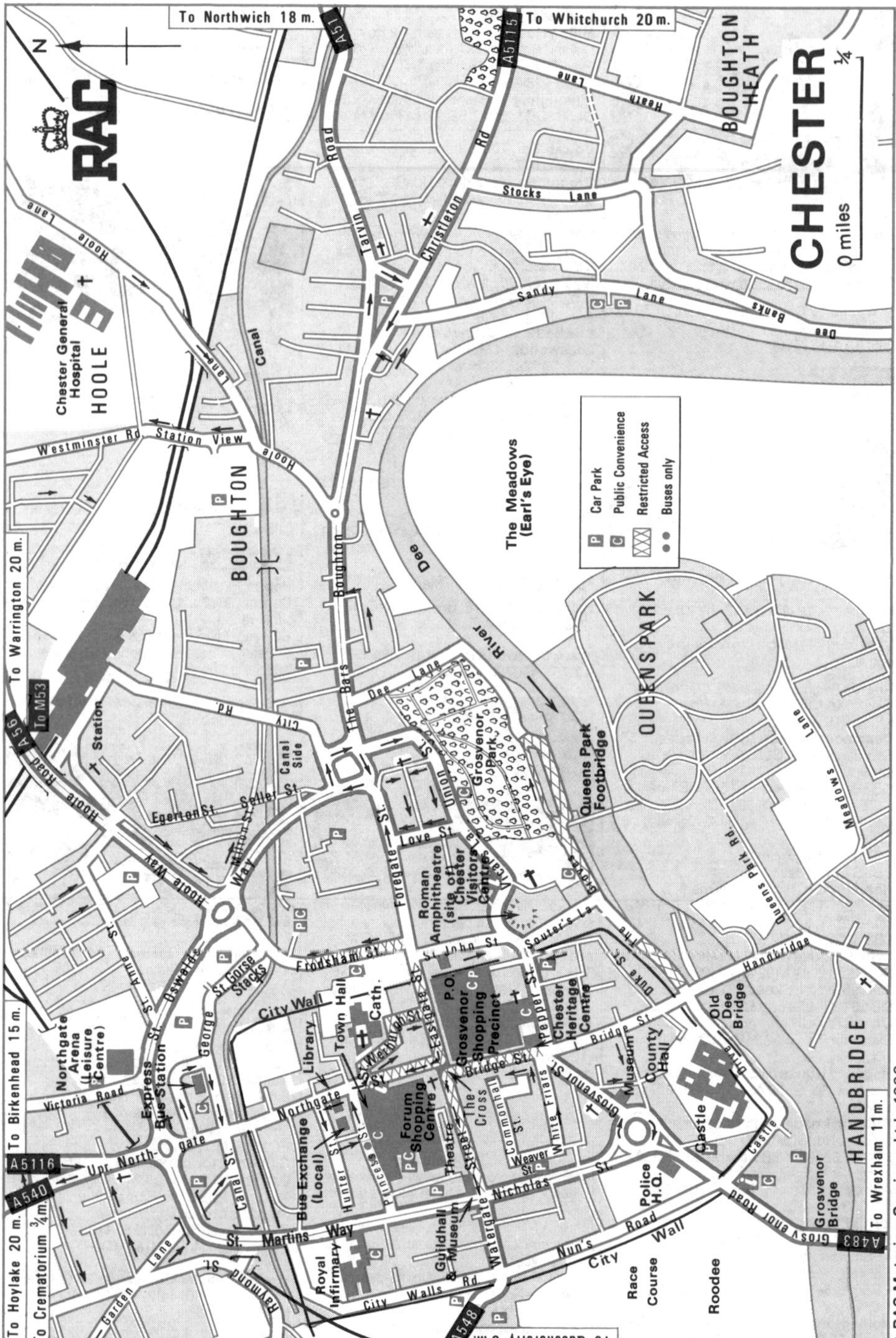

CHESTER
0 miles ¼
RAC
N
Car Park
Public Convenience
Restricted Access
Buses only
To Northwich 18 m.
To Whitchurch 20 m.
To Warrington 20 m.
To M53
To Birkenhead 15 m.
To Hoylake 20 m.
To Crematorium ¾ m.
To Queensferry 6 m.
To Wrexham 11 m.
BOUGHTON HEATH
HOOLE
Chester General Hospital
BOUGHTON
The Meadows (Earl's Eye)
QUEENS PARK
Queens Park Footbridge
River Dee
HANDBRIDGE
Roodee
Race Course
Crown copyright reserved
© RAC Motoring Services, Ltd., 1990

EC *early closing.* **MD** *market day* *country house hotel* *ns (NS) no smoking areas* *tcf tea/coffee facilities*

Elegant half-timbered mid-Victorian building with individually decorated luxury suites. Sauna, solarium, gymnasium. Closed Xmas.
⚒ Fr, De, It, Es
🛏 86 bedrs, 86 en suite; TV
lift, ns; P 600, coach; child facs; con 250
✕ LD 11
£ room £110, double room £165; Bk £9·50, L £12·50; D £17·50; WB £55
cc Access, Amex, B'card/Visa, CB, Diners.

★★★★ **Chester International**, Trinity St, CH1 2BD ☎ (0244) 322330 Tx: 61251
Fax: (0244) 316118 ♿

New, purpose-built hotel, decorated and furnished to a high standard, situated above a car park in the city centre. Good conference facilities and a leisure complex. Sauna, solarium, gymnasium. (QMH).
⚒ De, It, Es
🛏 152 bedrs, 152 en suite; TV; tcf
dogs, ns; P70, coach; child facs; con 500
✕ LD 10.45, bar meals only Sat lunch
£ B&B £94 (w/e £45), B&B (double) £135; L £15, D £18; WB £100 (2 nts); [10% V]
cc Access, Amex, B'card/Visa, Diners.

★★★★ **H** **C** **Crabwall Manor,** Mollington, CH1 6NE ☎ Great Mollington
☎ (0244) 851666 Tx: 61220
Fax: (0244) 851400 ♿

Gothic-style country mansion set in attractive grounds with helipad, 2 miles N of city. Snooker. ⚒ Fr, De, It, Es, Sw, Tu
🛏 48 bedrs, 48 en suite; TV
ns; P 115, coach; child facs; con 130
✕ LD 9.30
£ B&B £87·50–£102·50, (w/e £59·50), B&B (double) £115–£130; L £12·95, D £21; WB £59·50
cc Access, Amex, B'card/Visa, CB, Diners.

★★★★ **Mollington Banastre,** Parkgate Rd, CH1 6NN ☎ (0244) 851471 Tx: 61686
Fax: (0244) 851165 ♿

Set in gardens, 3-storey ornate Victorian building on A540. Indoor swimming pool, putting, squash, riding, sauna, solarium, gymnasium. ⚒ Fr
🛏 64 bedrs, 64 en suite; TV; tcf
lift, dogs, ns; P 260, coach; child facs; con 300
✕ LD 10.30, nr Sat lunch
£ B&B £73–£85 (w/e £51), B&B (double) £89–£100; L £9·25, D £16; WB
cc Access, Amex, B'card/Visa, Diners; dep.

★★★ **Abbots Well,** 107 Whitchurch Rd, Christleton, CH3 5QL ☎ (0244) 332121
Tx: 61561 Fax: (0244) 335287

Modern purpose-built hotel with spacious gardens enjoying fine views. Indoor swimming pool, sauna, solarium, gymnasium. (Emb) ⚒ De, It, Es
🛏 127 bedrs, 127 en suite; TV; tcf
dogs, ns; P150, coach; child facs; con 200
✕ LD 9.45, bar meals only Sat lunch
£ B&B £76 (w/e £28), B&B (double) £99; L £9, D £14; WB £38
cc Access, Amex, B'card/Visa, Diners.

★★★ **Blossoms,** St John St, CH1 1HL
☎ (0244) 323186 Tx: 61113
Fax: (0244) 346433

Large 300 year old city centre building of character. (THF). ⚒ Fr, De, It, Es, Ar
🛏 64 bedrs, 64 en suite; TV; tcf
lift, dogs; coach; child facs; con 100
✕ LD 9.45
£ B&B £77–£92 (w/e £50), B&B (double) £104–£124; HB weekly £280–£350; L £9, D £13·50; WB £50
cc Access, Amex, B'card/Visa, Diners; dep.

★★★ **C** **Hoole Hall,** Warrington Rd, Hoole, CH2 3PD ☎ (0244) 350011 Tx: 61292
Fax: (0244) 320251 ♿

Rambling Georgian-cum-Victorian building, with sympathetic modern extension and a conservatory, in landscaped grounds. ⚒ Fr, De, It
🛏 99 bedrs, 99 en suite; TV; tcf; lift
dogs, ns; P200, coach; child facs; con 150
✕ LD 9.45, bar meals only Sat lunch
£ B&B £76·45–£88·45 (w/e £27·50), B&B (double) £91–£103·30; L £8·95, D £13·25; WB £40 (HB); [10% V w/e]
cc Access, Amex, B'card/Visa, Diners.
(*See advertisement on p. 192*)

★★★ **Plantation Inn,** Liverpool Rd, CH2 1AG ☎ (0244) 374100 Tx: 61263
Fax: (0244) 379240

Attractive modern hotel with leisure centre. Just N of city centre. Solarium. ⚒ Fr, It
🛏 75 bedrs, 75 en suite; TV; tcf
lift, dogs; P 130, coach; child facs; con 200
✕ LD 10.30
£ B&B £64–£77 (w/e £28·50), B&B (double) £70–£105; L £6·50, D £11·50; WB £44 [10% V]
cc Access, Amex, B'card/Visa, CB, Diners; dep.

★★★ **Post House,** Wrexham Rd, CH4 9DL
☎ (0244) 680111 Tx: 61450
Fax: (0244) 674100 ♿
Modern purpose-built hotel in extensive grounds. Indoor swimming pool, sauna, solarium, gymnasium.(THF)
🛏 107 bedrs, 107 en suite; TV; tcf
dogs, ns; P 150, coach; child facs; con 150
✕ LD 9.45,
£ room £67–£77 (w/e £39·50), double room £77–£87; HB weekly £315–£385; L £8·95, D £14·10; WB £40
cc Access, Amex, B'card/Visa, CB, Diners.

★★★ **Rowton Hall,** Whitchurch Rd, Rowton, CH3 6AD ☎ (0244) 335262
Tx: 61172 Fax: (0244) 335464 ♿

Georgian manor house in attractive grounds. Indoor swimming pool, sauna, solarium, gymnasium. Closed Xmas. Fr, De
42 bedrs, 42 en suite; TV; tcf
dogs; P 150, coach; child facs; con 200
LD 9.30
£B&B £70–£80, B&B (double) £86–£96; L £11, D £14; WB £49
cc Access, Amex, B'card/Visa, Diners.

★★★ **Royal Oak,** Warrington Rd, Mickle Trafford CH2 4EX (0244) 301391 Tx: 61536
Attractive hotel building with motel extension. 1 mile from city centre.
36 bedrs, 36 en suite; TV; tcf
dogs; P 150, coach; child facs

★★ H C **Chester Court,** 48 Hoole Rd, CH2 3NL (0244) 20779
Black and white gabled building with purpose-built chalets.

★★ **Dene,** 95 Hoole Rd, CH2 3ND (0244) 321165

Family-owned hotel in its own grounds adjacent to Alexandra Park. Fr, De, Es
41 bedrs, 39 en suite, 2 ba; annexe 8 bedrs, 8 en suite; TV; tcf
TV, dogs; P 55, coach; child facs; con 12
LD 8.30, nr lunch. Resid & Rest lic
£B&B £35–£37, B&B (double) £46–£48; D £8; WB £54 (2nts); [5% V Oct–Jul]
cc Access, B'card/Visa; dep.
(*See advertisement on p. 200*)

★★ **Green Bough,** 60 Hoole Rd, CH2 3NL (0244) 326241 Fax: (0244) 326265

Small privately-owned and run hotel in residential district one mile from city centre. Closed 21 Dec–6 Jan.
14 bedrs, 14 en suite; TV; tcf
TV, dogs; P 21, coach; child facs; con 15
LD 8, nr Sat & Sun lunch. Resid & Rest lic
£B&B £34·50–£38, B&B (double) £43–£47; L £6·60, D £10; WB £31; [10% V Nov–Feb, w/e Mar–Oct]
cc Access, B'card/Visa; dep.

★ **City Walls,** City Walls Rd, CH1 2LU (0244) 313416
Overlooking the city walls, a red-brick period building close to the city centre. Sauna.

★ **Ye Olde King's Head,** 48 Lower Bridge St, CH1 1RS (0244) 24855
Historic black and white building (1520) near the famous old Rows.

Oaklands, Hoole Rd, CH2 3NB (0244) 45528.

Hotel under refurbishment.

Green Gables (Highly Acclaimed), 11 Eversley Pk (off Liverpool Rd), CH2 2AJ (0244) 372243. *Guest House.* It, Pol
£ B&B £20; [5% V Sun–Thu, winter]

Redland (Highly Acclaimed), 64 Hough Green, CH4 8JY (0244) 671024. *Hotel. Snooker, sauna, solarium.*
£ B&B £35; [5% V]

Weston (Acclaimed), 82 Hoole Rd, CH2 3NT (0244) 326735. *Hotel.*

Brookside, 12 Brook La, CH2 2AP (0244) 381943. Fax: (0244) 379701. *Hotel. Sauna/solarium.* Closed 25 Dec–1 Jan.
£B&B £27; [5% V]

Cavendish, 42–44 Hough Green, CH4 8JQ (0244) 675100. *Hotel.*

Devonia, 33–35 Hoole Rd, CH2 3NH (0244) 322236. *Hotel.*

Eaton, 29 City Rd, CH1 3AE (0244) 320840. *Hotel.*
£B&B £24·50–£29·50, HB weekly £171·50–£248·50; [10% V]

Egerton Lodge, 57 Hoole Rd, Hoole, CH2 3NJ (0244) 320712. *Hotel.* Closed Xmas.
£B&B £15–19·50; [5% V Apr–Oct]

Eversley, 9 Eversley Park, CH2 2AJ (0244) 373744. *Hotel.*
£B&B £20–£25.

Gables, 5 Vicarage Rd, Hoole CH2 3HZ (0244) 323969. *Guest House.* Closed 21 Dec–2 Jan.
£B&B £16, [10% V Jan–Jun].

Hamilton Court, 5 Hamilton St, Hoole CH2 3A (0244) 345387. *Hotel.* Closed 24 Dec–5 Jan.
£B&B £16

Riverside and Recorder, 22 City Walls (off Lower Bridge St), CH1 1SB (0244) 326580 Fax: (0244) 311567. *Hotel.*
£B&B £35–£42, HB weekly £220–£260; [5% V Nov–Feb]

Vicarage Lodge, 11 Vicarage Rd, Hoole CH2 3HZ (0244) 319533. *Guest House.* It
£ B&B £14–£20.

CHESTERFIELD Derbyshire. Map 31A3
Pop 97,000. M1 (jn 29) 5, London 149, Chapel-en-le-Frith 23, Derby 23, Mansfield 12, Matlock 10, Sheffield 12, Worksop 14. **EC** Wed (exc Town centre). **MD** Mon, Fri, Sat. **Golf** Tapton 18h. **See** 14th cent Parish Church ('crooked' spire), Trinity Church.
i Peacock Heritage Centre, Low Pavement. (0246) 207777

★★★ **Chesterfield,** Malkin St, S41 7UA (0246) 271141 Fax: (0246) 220719
Town centre Victorian hotel refurbished in 1920s art deco style. Indoor swimming pool, sauna, solarium, gymnasium, snooker. Fr
72 bedrs, 72 en suite; TV; tcf
lift, dogs; P 150, coach; child facs; con 250
LD 10
£B&B £36–£56, B&B (double) £56–£72; L £7·50; D £10·95; WB £36; [10% V w/e]
cc Access, Amex, B'card/Visa.

★★★ **Ringwood Hall**, Brimington, S43-1DQ (0246) 280077
Substantial, early 19th century stone building with elegant portico, recently refurbished to a high standard. Pleasant gardens with a bowling green.
24 bedrs, 24 en suite; TV; tcf
TV, dogs, ns; P170, coach; child facs; con 200
LD 11
£B&B £70–£85; B&B (double) £90–£100; L £7·50, D £10·50; [10% V w/e]
cc Access, Amex, B'card/Visa, Diners.

★★ **Abbeydale,** 1 Cobden Rd, S40 4TD (0246) 277849

Family-run hotel in a recently converted 3-storey Victorian house. Fr
11 bedrs, 9 en suite, 1 ba; TV; tcf
TV; P12; child facs; con 15
LD 8.30, nr lunch. Resid lic
£B&B £25–£41 (w/e £20), B&B (double) £46; HB weekly £215–£330; D £6; WB £54; [10% V]
cc Access, Amex, B'card/Visa; dep.

★★ **Portland,** West Bars, S40 1AY (0246) 234502 Fax: (0246) 550915

19th century medium-sized hotel with mock Tudor black and white gables.
27 bedrs, 17 en suite, 2 ba; TV; tcf
TV; P 30, coach; child facs; con 60
LD 9.30
£B&B £32–£43·50 (w/e £32), B&B (double) £43·50–£57; L £7·50, D £11; WB £35
cc Access, Amex, B'card/Visa; dep.

Olde House, Loudsley Green Rd, New Bold, S40 4RN ☎(0246) 274321

Hotel under refurbishment. (BCB)

Van Dyke, Worksop Rd, Clowne, S43 4TD ☎(0246) 810219

Hotel under refurbishment. (BCB)

CHICHESTER West Sussex. Map 6A1
See also GOODWOOD
Pop 24,000. Midhurst 12, London 61, Arundel 11, Bognor Regis 6½, Cosham 13, Petersfield 18, Pulborough 17.
EC Thur. **MD** Wed, Sat. **Golf** Goodwood 18h. **See** Cathedral, Market Cross, ancient Walls, Council House (Corporation plate), remains of Greyfriars Monastery, St Mary's Hospital Almshouses, Chichester Festival Theatre, The Roman Palace and Museum at Fishbourne, Goodwood House 3 m NE, Goodwood Racecourse, West Dean Gardens and House, Bosham Church and Harbour, The Trundle (viewpoint).
ⓘ St Peter's Market, West St. ☎(0243) 775888

★★★ **Chichester Resort,** Westhampnett, PO19 4UL ☎(0243) 786351 Tx: 86381 Fax: (0243) 782371 ♿

Recently extended, modern hotel in motel style conveniently situated at East end of by-pass. Indoor swimming pool, sauna, solarium. ✈ Fr, De
🛏76 bedrs, 76 en suite; TV; tcf
ⓕ dogs, ns; P 138, coach; child facs; con 300
✕ LD 9.30
£ B&B £56·50–£66·50 (w/e £38), B&B (double) £73–£83; L £10·50, D £13·50; [10% V]
cc Access, Amex, B'card/Visa, Diners.

★★★ **Dolphin & Anchor,** West St, PO19 1QE ☎(0243) 785121 Fax: (0243) 533408

Elegant hotel in city centre opposite Cathedral. Near shopping precinct. (THF)
🛏51 bedrs, 51 en suite; TV; tcf
ⓕ dogs, ns; P 6, G 20, coach; child facs; con 200
✕ LD 9.30
£ B&B £72–£78, B&B (double) £96–£107; HB weekly £406–£448; L £7·25, D £13; WB £46
cc Access, Amex, B'card/Visa, CB, Diners.

★★★ **Ship,** North St, PO19 1NH ☎(0243) 782028 Fax: (0243) 774254

Elegant 4-storey red-brick Georgian building with fine Adam staircase.
🛏37 bedrs, 32 en suite, 5 ba; TV; tcf
ⓕ lift, dogs; P 32, U 2 (£5), coach; child facs; con 70
(*See advertisement on p. 200*)

CHILDER THORNTON Cheshire. Map 32A1
Chester 8, London 191, M53 (jn 5) ½, Birkenhead 7, Ellesmere Port 3.

★★★ **Berni Royal**, Nr Ellesmere Port, Wirral, L66 1QW ☎051-339 8101
Red-brick Victorian mansion with modern extensions; in residential area by A41.
🛏47 bedrs, 47 en suite; TV; tcf
ⓕ TV, ns; P 180, coach; child facs; con

CHILHAM Kent. Map 7B3
Pop 1,500. M2 (jn 6) 8, London 56, Ashford 9, Canterbury 6½, Charing 8.
See 15th cent Church, Castle.

★★ **Woolpack,** High St, CT4 8DL ☎(0227) 730208 Fax: (0227) 731053 ♿
Picturesque village inn with modern en suite rooms built on at rear. ✈ Fr
🛏16 bedrs, 16 en suite; TV; tcf
ⓕ dogs; P 30; child facs
✕ LD 9

Atlas Section
Consult the Atlas section at the back of the guide to find out which towns and villages have RAC Appointed and Listed hotels in them. They are shown on the maps by purple circles.

£ B&B £37·50, B&B (double) £45–£60; D £20; WB £51 (2nts HB); [5% V w/d Oct–Mar]
cc Access, Amex, B'card/Visa, Diners; dep.

CHILLINGTON Devon. Map 3B1
Pop 1,715. Kingsbridge 4½, London 209, Dartmouth 10.
Golf Thurlestone 18h. **See** Church.

♣ ★★ **Oddicombe House,** TQ7 2JD ☎Frogmore (0548) 531234

Country house in 3 acres of attractive grounds. Swimming pool. Open Easter–Oct.
🛏8 bedrs, 6 en suite, 1 ba; annexe 2 bedrs, 2 en suite; tcf
ⓕ TV, dogs, ns; P 15; child facs
✕ LD 8.15, nr lunch
£ B&B £22–£31, B&B (double) £44–£54; HB weekly £200–£250; D £13; dep.

CHIPPENHAM Wiltshire. Map 5A4
Pop 21,000. M4 (jn 17) 4, London 91, Bath 13, Bristol 22, Cirencester 21, Devizes 11, Marlborough 19, Warminster 20.
EC Wed. **MD** Fri, Sat. **Golf** Chippenham 18h. **See** Maud Heath's Causeway' (1474), Yelde Hall Museum, Church.
ⓘ The Neeld Hall, High St. ☎(0249) 657733

★★ R **Angel,** Market Pl, SN15 3HD ☎(0249) 652615 Fax: (0249) 443210

Attractive 17th century coaching inn with modern motel complex to the rear. (QMH)
🛏44 bedrs, 44 en suite; TV; tcf
ⓕ dogs, ns; P 70, coach; child facs; con 100
✕ LD 9.30, bar meals only Sat lunch
£ B&B £56, B&B (double) £72·50; L £9, D £13·50; WB £30; [10% V]
cc Access, Amex, B'card/Visa, Diners.

★ **Bear,** 12 Market Place, SN15 3HJ ☎(0249) 653272
Stone-built, 17th-century inn just off the old Market Place in town centre.

Aarons Oxford (Acclaimed), 32–36 Langley Rd, SN15 1BX ☎(0249) 652542.
Hotel. ✈ De
£ B&B £22–£32 (w/e £20); HB weekly £190–£250; [10% V]

Chester (Cheshire)

The Dene Hotel

HOOLE ROAD (A56) CHESTER CH2 3ND
Telephone: Reception – Chester 321165
Fax: 0244 350277

Set in its own grounds and adjacent to Alexandra Park yet only 1 mile from the City Centre, this pleasant family run hotel has Residents' Bar, lounge and Elizabethan restaurant. All bedrooms have private bathrooms, colour TV, tea and coffee making facilities and direct dial telephones. Ample parking.

Bargain Breaks. Motel Suites available.

Chichester (West Sussex)

The Ship Hotel at Chichester

A charming hotel situated within the historic city of Chichester and just a few hundred yards from both the beautiful Cathedral and Festival Theatre. The hotel has recently had a major refurbishment, to bring alive the space and elegance of its Georgian origins. A warm welcome and good service awaits you at The Ship at Chichester. Free car parking.

Write or phone for a brochure today

THE SHIP HOTEL
NORTH STREET, CHICHESTER, WEST SUSSEX PO19 1NH
Telephone: (0243) 782028 Fax: (0243) 774254

Chipperfield (Hertfordshire)

The Two Brewers

The Common, Chipperfield, Kings Langley, Herts WD4 9BS.
Tel: (0923) 265266 Fax: (0923) 261884

Situated on a beautiful English village green, The Two Brewers Inn was built in the late 1700s and provides a lovely setting for your holiday.

Chipping Norton (Oxfordshire)

The Crown & Cushion Hotel

**RAC

Chipping Norton, Oxon OX7 5AD *General Enquiries* Tel 0608 642533
Reservations only Freephone 0800 585251 Fax 0608 642926

500 year old coaching inn. 39 excellent en-suite bedrooms, CTV, telephones etc. Some de-luxe rooms. Conference facilities for 2 to 200 delegates. Indoor pool, gym, squash court etc. Convenient new M40, London, Shakespeare country, Cotswolds.

CHIPPERFIELD Hertfordshire. Map 14B1
Watford 6, London 22, M25 (jn 20) 3.

★★★ **Two Brewers,** The Common, WD4 9BS ☎ KingsLangley (0923) 265266 Fax: (0923) 261884

Small historic country inn with a modern wing. Borders the village green. (THF)
🛏 20 bedrs, 20 en suite; TV; tcf
🏨 dogs, ns; P 26, G6; child facs
✕ LD 10
£ room £75–£80, double room £90–£95; HB weekly £525–£560; Bk £5, L £13·50, D £15·50; WB £42 (HB)
cc Access, Amex, B'card/Visa, Diners; dep.
(*See advertisement on p. 200*)

CHIPPING CAMPDEN Glos. Map 20C3
Pop 1,964. Moreton-in-Marsh 6½, London 90, Banbury 22, Cheltenham 21, Evesham 9, Stratford-upon-Avon 12.
EC Thur. **Golf** Broadway 18h. **See** 15th cent Parish Church, 14th cent Grevel's House, Market Hall, Almshouses, 17th cent Town Hall, Campden House ruins, Woolstaplers Hall, Hidcote Manor Gdns 2½ m NE.
ℹ Woolstaplers Hall Museum, High St. ☎ Evesham (0386) 840289

♛ ★★★ **Charingworth Manor,** GL55 6NS ☎ Paxford (038 678) 555 Tx: 333444 Fax: (038 678) 353

A 14th century, Cotswold-stone manor house set in 54 acres of lovely gardens and parkland, 3 miles E of Chipping Campden.
⚒ Fr, De, Es, Du
🛏 25 bedrs, 25 en suite; TV
🏨 dogs; P 50; child facs; con 34
✕ LD 10.30. Resid & Rest lic
£ B&B £80–£180, B&B (double) £95–£195; L £15·50; D £24·50
cc Access, Amex, B'card/Visa, Diners; dep.

★★★ **H C R Cotswold House,** The Square, GL55 6AN ☎ Evesham (0386) 840330 Fax: (0386) 840310

Town centre, Regency stone building with attractive 1½ acre garden. Closed Xmas.
⚒ Fr
🛏 15 bedrs, 15 en suite; TV
🏨 ns; P 12; no children under 8; con 20
✕ LD 9.30, nr Mon–Sat lunch
£ B&B £50–£60, B&B (double) £110–£142; D £22; WB £95; [10% V Sun]
cc Access, Amex, B'card/Visa, Diners.

★★★ **H C Seymour House**, High St, GL55 6AH ☎ (0386) 840429 Fax: (0386) 840369

Recently renovated, 17th century Cotswold stone building with charming secluded garden. In town centre. ⚒ Fr, It, Pu
🛏 12 bedrs, 12 en suite; TV; tcf
🏨 dogs; P28, coach; child facs; con 24
✕ Resid & Rest lic
£ B&B £51·50–£56·50, B&B (double) £78–£88; L £10·50, D £13·60; WB fr £37; [10% V]
cc Access, Amex, B'card/Visa.

★★ **Noel Arms,** High St, GL55 6AT ☎ (0386) 840317 Fax: (0386) 841136

14th century former coaching inn with open courtyard and attractive garden.
🛏 26 bedrs, 26 en suite; TV; tcf
🏨 P 40, coach; child facs; con 60
✕ LD 9
£ B&B £50–£55, B&B (double) £70–£90; HB weekly £280, L £6·50, D £10·50; WB £40 (HB)
cc Access, Amex, B'card/Visa.

CHIPPING NORTON Oxon. Map 21A2
Pop 5,200. Oxford 20, London 75, Banbury 13, Bicester 19, Burford 11, Moreton-in-Marsh 8½, Stratford-upon-Avon 21.
EC Thur. **MD** Wed. **Golf** Chipping Norton 9h. **See** 15th cent Parish Church, 17th cent Almshouses, Old Guildhall, old 'White Hart' Inn, 'Rollright Stones' and 'Whispering Knights' 3 m.
ℹ New St. Car Park ☎ (0608) 44379

★★ **Crown & Cushion,** 23 High St, OX7 5AD ☎ (0608) 642533 Fax: (0608) 642926

15th century building of local stone. Situated in town centre. Swimming pool, squash, solarium, gymnasium, snooker.
🛏 28 bedrs, 28 en suite; TV; tcf
🏨 dogs; P17, coach; child facs; con 200
✕ LD 9, bar meals only Mon–Sat
£ B&B £33–£56, B&B (double) £39–£85; HB weekly £220·50–£280; D £16·50; WB £31·50; [10% V w/d]
cc Access, Amex, B'card/Visa, Diners; dep.
(*See advertisement on p. 200*)

CHISLEHAMPTON Oxfordshire. Map 12A4
High Wycombe 18, London 48, Oxford 7.

Coach and Horses, Stadhampton Rd. OX9 7UX ☎ (0865) 890255

Three-storey, Oxford-stone, 16th-century inn of considerable character.
🛏 9 bedrs, 9 en suite; TV; tcf
🏨 dogs; P 34

CHITTLEHAMHOLT Devon. Map 3B4
South Molton 5, London 185, Barnstaple 10, Crediton 26, Great Torrington 11.

♛ ★★★ **High Bullen**, Umberleigh, EX37 9HD ☎ (076 94) 561 Fax: (076 94) 492

> **Residents only**
> Some Listed hotels only serve meals to residents. It is always wise to make a reservation for a meal in a hotel.

> Changes made after July 1990 are not included.

Edwardian gothic mansion with spacious, well-furnished accommodation. In 60 acres of parkland with marvellous views. Indoor/outdoor swimming pools, putting, golf, tennis, squash, sauna, solarium, billiards. Fr
12 bedrs, 12 en suite; annexe 23 bedrs, 23 en suite; TV; tcf
ns; P 60; no children under 10; con 20
LD 9, nr Mon–Sat lunch. Resid & Rest lic
£ B&B £40–£60, B&B (double) £60–£85; D £15.

CHOLDERTON Wiltshire. Map 5B3
Andover 11, London 76, Amesbury 5, Marlborough 19, Salisbury 11.

★★ **Cholderton Country**, Parkhouse Corner, SP4 0EG (0980) 64484
Attractive red-brick building set in 5 acres of gardens at junction of A338 and A303. Closed 24 Dec–2 Jan. Hi
14 bedrs, 14 en suite; TV; tcf
TV; P 25, coach; child facs; con
LD 8.30, bar meals only Sun lunch, Sat & Sun dinner
£ B&B £34, B&B (double) £44; L £8·50, D £15; WB £19; [10% V excl. w/e Mar–Sep]
cc Access, Amex, B'card/Visa, Diners; dep.

CHOLLERFORD Northumberland. Map 44C3
Hexham 5, London 285, Alston 24, Bellingham 11, Brampton 26, Corbridge 7½, Newcastle upon Tyne 22.

★★★ **George,** NE46 4EW Humshaugh (0434) 681611 Fax: (0434) 681727

Riverside country coaching inn, with leisure centre. Indoor swimming pool, putting, fishing, sauna, solarium. (Sw)
50 bedrs, 50 en suite; TV; tcf
dogs, ns; P 70, coach; child facs; con 60
LD 9.30
£ B&B £63–£73, B&B (double) £82–£97; L £8·75; D £14·95; WB £85 (HB)
cc Access, Amex, B'card/Visa, Diners.

CHORLEY Lancashire. Map 32C4
Pop 35,104. M61 (jn 8) 1, London 203, Blackburn 10, Bolton 11, Ormskirk 15, Preston 9, Southport 19, Wigan 8.
EC Wed. **MD** Fri, Sat. **Golf** Duxbury Chorley 18h. **See** Astley Hall and Park, St Mary's RC Church, St Laurence's Church, Art Gallery.

★★★ R **Shawhill Golf & Country Club**, Whittle-le-Woods, PR6 7PP (02572) 69221 Fax: (02572) 61223

Magnificent Georgian mansion in 110 acres of rolling parkland. Golf, putting, fishing, sauna, solarium, billiards. Fr, Es
18 bedrs, 18 en suite, 2 ba; TV; tcf
TV, dogs; P 200, coach; child facs; con 65
LD 9.45, bar meals only Sat lunch
£ B&B £44–£63·25, B&B (double) £53·90–£87·45; HB weekly £413–£547·75; L £10·95, D £17; WB £75 (HB); [5% V]
cc Access, Amex, B'card/Visa, Diners; dep.

★★ **Hartwood Hall**, Preston Rd, PR6 7AZ (02572) 69966 Fax: (02572) 41678
Privately-owned Georgian style hotel 1 mile from town centre.
12 bedrs, 5 en suite (4 sh); annexe 10 bedrs, 10 en suite; TV; tcf
TV, dogs; P 100, coach; child facs; con 120
LD 9, bar meals only Sat lunch. Resid lic
£ B&B £38–£50, B&B (double) £45–£60; L £7·50, D £11·50; WB; [10% V]
cc Access, Amex, B'card/Visa, Diners.

CHRISTCHURCH Dorset. Map 5B1
See also MUDEFORD
Pop 29,000. Lyndhurst 14, London 98, Blandford Forum 21, Bournemouth 5, Lymington 12, Ringwood 9.
EC Wed. **MD** Mon. **Golf** Highcliffe Castle 18h. **See** Priory Church, Red House Museum. Hengistbury Head.
30 Saxon Sq. (0202) 471780

★★★ H C **Waterford Lodge,** 87 Bure La, Friars Cliff, BH23 4DN Highcliffe (0425) 272948 Tx: 418120 Fax: (0425) 279130
Tudor-style building close to peacefully situated pleasant beaches.
20 bedrs, 20 en suite; TV; tcf
dogs; P 38; child facs; con 16
LD 8.30, bar meals only Mon lunch
£ B&B £50–£58 (w/e £35), B&B (double) £68–£76; HB weekly £250–£308; L £9·95, D £14·50; WB £42 (HB)
cc Access, Amex, B'card/Visa, Diners; dep.

★★ H **Fisherman's Haunt,** Winkton, BH23 7AS (0202) 477283
17th century 2-storey building of old-world charm on banks of Avon. Closed Xmas Day.
De, Pol
4 bedrs, 3 en suite, 1 ba; annexe 15 bedrs, 13 en suite, 1 ba; TV; tcf
dogs; P 100, coach; child facs
LD 10
£ room £25–£33, double room £52–£56; Bk £5·50, L £9, D £20
cc Access, Amex, B'card/Visa, Diners; dep.

★★ **Kings Arms,** Castle St, BH23 1DT (0202) 484117
Modernised, 18th century coaching inn with an extension; close to Priory and main shopping area.

Pines (Acclaimed), 39 Mudeford, BH23 3NQ (0202) 475121. *Private Hotel.*

Belvedere, 59 Barrack Rd, BH23 1PD (0202) 485978. *Hotel.*

CHURCH STRETTON Shropshire. Map 20A4
Pop 3,890. Bridgnorth 19, London 156, Ludlow 15, Newton 28, Shrewsbury 13.
EC Wed. **MD** Thur. **Golf** Church Stretton 18h. **See** Parish Church, The Longmynd 5,000 acres. (N.T.) Waterfall, Cardingmill Valley (N.T.), Acton Scott Farm Museum.
Church St. (0694) 723133

★★★ **Long Mynd,** Cunnery Rd, SY6 6AG (0694) 722244 Fax: (0694) 722718

Large, purpose-built hotel with panoramic views from hillside. Swimming pool, golf, sauna, solarium, gymnasium. Fr, De
52 bedrs, 52 en suite; TV; tcf
lift, dogs; P 100, coach; child facs; con 100
LD 9.30
£ B&B £35, B&B (double) £60–£90; L £7, D £10·50; WB £30 (HB); [10% Mon–Thu]
cc Access, Amex, B'card/Visa, Diners; dep.

★★ **Denehurst**, Shrewsbury Rd, SY6 6EU (0694) 722699 Fax: (0694) 724110
Victorian house, with modern extensions, in centre of village. Indoor swimming pool, sauna, solarium, gymnasium.
14 bedrs, 4 en suite, 1 ba; TV; tcf
TV; P70, coach; child facs; con 150
LD 9
£ B&B £30·35, B&B (double) £45·50; HB weekly £195–£215; L £7, D £9·50; WB £70
cc Access, B'card/Visa; dep.
(*See advertisement on p. 205*)

★★ C R **Mynd House,** Little Stretton, SY6 6RB (0694) 722212 Fax: (0694) 724180
Red-brick Edwardian house with modern extensions in 4 acres of gardens. At foot of Long Mynd Hill. Closed Jan.
8 bedrs, 8 en suite; TV; tcf
dogs, ns; P 12; child facs; con 15
LD 9.15, nr Sun lunch. Resid lic
£ B&B £30–£32, B&B (double) £42–£65; HB weekly £225–£270; L £2·50, D £14; WB £35; [10% V]
cc Access, B'card/Visa.

Paddock Lodge (Highly Acclaimed), Old Shrewsbury Rd, All Stretton SY6 6HG (0694) 723702. *Guest House.*

£B&B (double) £32; HB weekly £158; dep.

Belvedere (Acclaimed), Burway Rd, SY6 6DP ☎(0694) 722232. *Guest House*. Closed 18–31 Dec.
£B&B £15·50–£17; HB weekly £98–£107·10; [10% V]
Court Farm (Acclaimed), Gretton, SY6 7HU ☎Longville (06943) 219. Open Feb–Nov.
£B&B £14–£17; HB weekly £155–£168; [5% V]

CIRENCESTER Gloucestershire. Map 20C1. *See also* EWEN
Pop 15,535. M4 (jn 15) 19, London 88, Burford 17, Cheltenham 14, Chippenham 21, Gloucester 18, Stow-on-the-Wold 19, Swindon 15, Tetbury 10.
EC Thur. **MD** Mon, Tue, Fri. **Golf** Cirencester 18h.
ⓘ Corn Hall, Market Pl. ☎(0285) 654180

★★★ C R **Fleece,** Market Pl, GL7 4NZ ☎(0285) 658507 Tx: 437287
Fax: (0285) 651017

Black and white Tudor-style coaching inn in town centre. Fr
25 bedrs, 25 en suite; TV; tcf
dogs; P12, coach; child facs; con 60
LD 9.30, bar meals only Mon–Sat lunch
£B&B £64·50–£76·50, B&B (double) £79–£93; D £13·95; WB £64 (2 nts); [5% V Sun]
cc Access, Amex, B'card/Visa, Diners.

★★★ **King's Head,** Market Pl, GL7 2NR ☎(0285) 653322 Tx: 43470
Fax: (0285) 655103

14th century former coaching inn in square facing Parish Church. Closed 27–30 Dec.
Fr, It
70 bedrs, 70 en suite; TV; tcf
lift, dogs, ns; P 25, coach; child facs; con 100
LD 9
£B&B £45–£60 (w/e £36), B&B (double) £67–£79; L £10·50, D £14; WB £36; [10% V]
cc Access, Amex, B'card/Visa, Diners.

★★★ **Stratton House,** Gloucester Rd, GL7 2LE ☎(0285) 651761
Fax: (0285) 640024
Attractive Georgian manor house of Cotswold stone. Delightful garden. Fr
26 bedrs, 26 en suite; TV; tcf
dogs; P 70, coach; child facs; con 100
LD 9.45,
£B&B £43·50–£48, B&B (double) £56–£62; L £13·50, D £13·50; [10% V]
cc Access, Amex, B'card/Visa, Diners.

★★ H **Corinium Court,** Gloucester St, GL7 2DG ☎(0285) 659711
Fax: (0285) 885807
Originally a wool merchant's house (1595) converted to a small hotel. Fr
16 bedrs, 16 en suite; TV
dogs; P30, coach; child facs
LD 9.30, nr Sun dinner
£B&B £45–£55 (w/e £32), B&B (double) £48–£60; L £6·50, D £10; WB £32; [5% V]
cc Access, Amex, B'card/Visa, Diners; dep.

La Ronde (Highly Acclaimed), 52 Ashcroft Rd, GL7 1QX ☎(0285) 654611. Fr, Es
£B&B £39·50, HB weekly £299·25
Wimborne (Highly Acclaimed), 91 Victoria Rd, GL7 1ES ☎(0285) 653890 *Guest House*.
£B&B £20–£25; HB weekly £136–£149.

Raydon House (Acclaimed), 3 The Avenue, GL7 1 EB ☎(0285) 653485
£B&B £29–£35.

Arkenside, 44 Lewis La, GL7 1EB ☎(0285) 653072. *Hotel*.

CLACTON-ON-SEA Essex. Map 27B2
Pop 43,597. Colchester 15, London 71, Harwich 16, Ipswich 24, Stowmarket 35.
EC Wed. **MD** Tue, Sat. **Golf** Clacton-on-Sea.
ⓘ 23 Pier Av. ☎(0255) 423400

★★★ **King's Cliff,** King's Par, Holland-on-Sea, CO15 5JB ☎(0255) 812343
A modern hotel standing right on the seafront.

CLARE Suffolk. Map 27A3
Pop 2,025. Dunmow 19, London 57, Bishop's Stortford 27, Braintree 15, Bury St Edmunds 15, Haverhill 8, Newmarket 16, Sudbury 9.
EC Wed. **MD** Mon, Sat. **Golf** Bury 18h.

★ **Seafarer,** Nethergate St, CO10 8NP ☎(0787) 277449.

Small hotel set back from main road in village. Well-equipped bedrooms.
5 bedrs, 3 en suite, 1 ba; TV; tcf
TV, dogs; P 10, coach; no children under 10; con 10
LD 9.45
£B&B £31·95–£42·95, B&B (double) £43·95–£54·95; L £10, D £10; WB
cc Access, Amex, B'card/Visa, Diners.
(*See advertisement on p. 205*)

CLAUGHTON Lancashire. Map 36B3
Lancaster 7, London 245, M6 (jn 34) 5, Kendal 25, Kirby Lonsdale 9.

★★★ R **Old Rectory,** Nr Lancaster, LA2 9LA ☎(05242) 21455

Family-run hotel in Georgian house; some bedrooms in converted barn across stream running through grounds. Fishing.

CLAWTON Devon. Map 3A3
Pop 291. Holsworthy 3, London 213, Launceston 10.
Golf Holsworthy 18h. **See** 14th cent Church.

★★ R **Court Barn,** Holsworthy, EX22 6PS ☎North Tamerton (040 927) 219

An attractive Victorian country house in four acres of gardens. Putting, solarium, gymnasium. Closed 1–13 Jan. Fr
8 bedrs, 8 en suite, 1 ba; tcf
TV, dogs, ns; P 16, U 1, coach; child facs; con 30
LD 9. Resid & Rest & Club lic
£B&B £28–£37, B&B (double) £56–£66; HB weekly £235–£265; L £7·70, D £16·50; WB £78 (2 nts); [10% V w/d Nov–Jun]
cc Access, Amex, B'card/Visa, Diners; dep.

CLAYTON-LE-MOORS Lancs. Map 36C2
London 204, M65 (jn 7) ½, Accrington 1½, Blackburn 5, Burnley 6, Clitheroe 10.

★★★ H R **Dunkenhalgh,** BB5 5JP ☎Accrington (0254) 398021 Tx: 63282
Fax: (0254) 872230

Set in 17 acres of parkland, a mellow stone hotel close to junction 7 of M65. Indoor swimming pool, sauna, solarium, gymnasium, billiards.
67 bedrs, 67 en suite; TV; tcf
TV, dogs; P 400, coach; child facs; con 400

EC *early closing* **MD** *market day* *country house hotel* *ns (NS) no smoking areas* *tcf tea/coffee facilities*

Church Stretton (Shropshire)

Denehurst Hotel & Restaurant

Shrewsbury Road, Church Stretton, Shropshire SY6 6EU
Telephone: Office (0694) 722699 Guests (0694) 722825

A comfortable, friendly family atmosphere. (All rooms en-suite, colour TV, tea/coffee) with recently built leisure centre. Dinner dance/banqueting/wedding/conference facilities for up to 200.

Clare (Suffolk)

The Seafarer Hotel & Restaurant

K & A. Ross, The Seafarer Hotel, Nethergate st, Clare, Suffolk. CO10 8np Telephone (0787) 277449

Friendly 17th century hotel, centrally situated in beautiful large village, 1 minutes walk from Castle Country Park, River Walks, Market place and shops. Large garden (with garden restaurant), Les Routiers hotel restaurant and friendly bar (log fire) & excellent bedrooms with every modern comfort. THREE CROWN COMMENDED, TOURIST BOARD.

Clevedon (Avon)

WALTON PARK HOTEL

RAC ★★★ **CLEVEDON** ETB ♛♛♛♛

Competitive Conference rates, with the advantage of being only 2miles from Junction 20 on M5.
Recently refurbished to a high standard. Character Victorian building with panoramic views across the estuary.
Five conference/training rooms. 10 to 150 delegates.
37 en-suite rooms with ample car parking.

The Hotel that puts customer care FIRST

Please send for our brochure and conference package.
Walton Park Hotel, Wellington Terrace, Clevedon, Bristol, Avon BS21 7BL

Tel: 0272 874253 Fax: 0272 343577

Cockermouth (Cumbria)

TROUT HOTEL

Situated on the banks of the River Derwent, the hotel has a well deserved reputation for excellent food, comfortable surroundings and a friendly atmosphere.
All 22 bedrooms, many of which have river views, have en-suite facilities, hairdryers, direct dial telephone and satellite television.
For reservations please telephone:
0900 823591 or Fax: 0900 827514

Congleton (Cheshire)

Lion and Swan Hotel

Swan Bank, Congleton, Cheshire CW12 1JR

This charming 3 star 16th century Coaching Inn is situated in the heart of historic Congleton, and completed a major refurbishment in 1990.

The Hotel is proud of its many antiques, oak beams and original fixtures and fittings which have all been carefully combined with every modern day convenience.

Each of its luxurious bedrooms is en suite and equipped with colour TV, tea and coffee making facilities, direct dial telephone, hairdryer, and trouser press. The intimate Restaurant has earned a well deserved reputation for the consistently high standard of both service and cuisine, and the hotel's conference and banqueting facilities make it the perfect choice for business or pleasure.

Special short break rates are available throughout the year, please telephone Congleton (0260) 273115 for brochure.

LD 9.45, bar meals only Sat lunch
£ B&B £70–£82, B&B (double) £82–£94; L £9·50, D £16; WB £85 (2 nts)
cc Access, Amex, B'card/Visa, Diners.

CLAYTON-LE-WOODS Lancs. Map 32C4
Pop 8,929. M6 (jn 28) ½, London 207, Blackburn 9.
EC Wed. **Golf** Shaw Hill 18h. **See** RC Church of St Bedes, Convent, Clayton Hall.

★★★ C R **Pines,** Preston Rd, PR6 7ED
Preston (0772) 38551 Tx: 67308
A fine Victorian house set in 4 acres on A6 just south of Clayton Green. Closed Xmas.
25 bedrs, 25 en suite; TV; tcf
P 100, coach; child facs; con 160
LD 9.30
£ B&B £40–£60, B&B (double) £65–£80; L £10, D £10·85; WB £60; [5% w/e]
cc Access, Amex, B'card/Visa, Diners; dep.

CLAYWORTH Nottinghamshire. Map 31B4
Pop 275. East Retford 6, London 152, Doncaster 15, Gainsborough 8.
EC Wed. **See** 14th cent Church, Canal, Blacksmiths Arms.

★★★ **Royston Manor,** St Peters Lane, DN22 9AA Retford (0777) 817484

Well-preserved Elizabethan house in 4 acres of garden. Period furnishings.

CLEARWELL Gloucestershire Map 20A2
Gloucester 22, London 126, Chepstow 9, Monmouth 6, Ross on Wye 14.

★★★ **Wyndham Arms,** GL16 8JT
(0594) 33666 Fax: (0594) 36450

Characterful old inn, part dating to the 14th century, now a delightful, owner-run hotel.
5 bedrs, 5 en suite, annexe 12 bedrs, 12 en suite; TV; tcf
dogs; P 52; child facs; con 12

CLEETHORPES Humberside (South Humberside). Map 35C3
Pop 35,770. Louth 16, London 164, Grimsby 6½, Hull 34, Market Rasen 20.
EC Thur (winter). **MD** Wed. **Golf** Cleethorpes 18h. **See** Beacon, Leisure Park.

[i] 43 Alexandra Rd. (0472) 200220

★★★ R **Kingsway,** Kingsway, DN35 0AE
(0472) 601122 Tx: 527920

Seafront 3-storey hotel with pleasant roof garden. Closed 25 & 26 Dec. Es
50 bedrs, 50 en suite; TV; tcf
lift, ns; P 32, G 18 (£1·50); no children under 5; con 18
LD 9. Resid & Rest lic
£ B&B £59, B&B (double) £79; L £10, D £13·50; WB £80 (2nts HB)
cc Access, Amex, B'card/Visa, Diners.

★★ **Wellow,** Kings Rd, DN35 0AQ (0472) 695589
A small modern hotel situated on the fringe of town.

Mallow View, 9–11 Albert Rd, DN35 8LX
(0472) 691297. *Hotel.*

CLEEVE HILL Gloucestershire. Map 20C2
Cheltenham 4, London 101, Broadway 12, Evesham 14, Gloucester 12, Stow-on-the-Wold 17
Golf Municipal 18h. **See** ancient earthworks.

★★★ **The Rising Sun,** GL52 3PX
Bishop's Cleeve (0242) 676281
Tx: 437410 Fax: (0242) 673069
Refurbished stone-built inn on the edge of the Cotswolds affording outstanding views over the Severn Vale. Sauna, solarium. (Lns)
25 bedrs, 25 en suite; TV; tcf
dogs, ns; P 56, coach; child facs; con 55
LD 10
£ B&B £63, B&B (double) £76; L £8·95, D £14·50; WB £70; [10% V]
cc Access, Amex, B'card/Visa, Diners.

CLEOBURY MORTIMER Shropshire. Map 20A4
Pop 2,008. Kidderminster 11, London 134, Bridgnorth 13, Droitwich 20, Leominster 18, Ludlow 11, Worcester 20.
EC Thur. **Golf** Ludlow 18h.

★★ R **The Redfern,** Lower St, DY14 8AA
(0299) 270395 Tx: 335176
Fax: (0299) 271011

Attractive stone-built listed Georgian building with beams. In main street.

5 bedrs, 5 en suite; annexe 6 bedrs, 6 en suite; TV; tcf
dogs; P 20; child facs; con 30
LD 9.30. Resid & Rest lic
£ B&B £35–£38 (w/e £32), B&B (double) £50·50–£55; HB weekly £215–£235; L £7, D £13·50; WB £32; [10% V]
cc Access, Amex, B'card/Visa, Diners; dep.

CLEVEDON Avon. Map 4B4
Pop 20,983. M5 (jn 20) 1, Bristol 12, London 126, Bridgwater 28, Radstock 27, Wells 24, Weston-super-Mare 14.
EC Wed. **Golf** Clevedon 18h.

★★★ **Walton Park,** 1 Wellington Terr, BS21 7BL (0272) 874253
Fax: (0272) 343577

Converted residence with pleasant gardens, and fine Channel views.
36 bedrs, 36 en suite; TV; tcf
lift, dogs, ns; P40, coach; child facs; con 150
LD 9, bar meals only Mon–Fri lunch
£ B&B £49·50–£55 (w/e £30), B&B (double) £65–£70; HB weekly £267–£300; L £8·95, D £14·50; WB £83 (2nts HB); [5% V]
cc Access, Amex, B'card/Visa, Diners.
(*See advertisement on p. 205*)

★★ **Highcliffe,** Wellington Ter, BS21 7PU
(0272) 873250
Charming Victorian stone building in quiet area. Overlooks Severn estuary.
18 bedrs, 16 en suite (2 sh), 2 ba; TV; tcf
TV; P 14; child facs; con 80

CLIFTON HAMPDEN Oxfordshire. Map 12A4
Wallingford 6, London 52, M40 (Int. 7) 12, Abingdon 4, Didcot 12, Oxford 10.

Barley Mow, OX14 3EH (086 730) 7847. *Inn.*
£ B&B £34·50–£41.

CLIFTONVILLE Kent. Map 7C3
See also MARGATE.
Pop 6,284. Margate 1, London 74.
EC Thur. **Golf** North Foreland, Broadstairs 18h, Westgate and Birchington 18h, St Augustine's, Ramsgate 18h. **See** Winter Gardens, King Vortigern Caves, Grotto, Shell Temple.

Greswolde (Acclaimed), 20 Surrey Rd, CT9 2LA (0843) 223956. *Private Hotel.* Fr, Es
£ B&B £15–£19; [5% V]

Falcon, 4 Ethelbert Rd, CT9 1RY Thanet (0843) 223846. *Private Hotel. Swimming pool.* Open Apr–Nov & Xmas.
£ B&B £15·50–£18·50; HB weekly £106–£128; [10% V].

Riverdale, 40 Sweyn Rd, CT9 2DF
Thanet (0843) 223628. *Private Hotel.* Open Mar–Nov & 24 Dec–1 Jan.

£B&B £17·50–£24·50; HB weekly £118–£157; [10% V].

CLIMPING West Sussex. Map 6B1

Arundel 3, London 59, Bognor Regis 5½, Chichester 9, Littlehampton 2.
Golf Littlehampton 18h. **See** Church.

★★★ **Bailiffscourt,** BN17 5RW
Littlehampton (0903) 723511 Tx: 877870
Fax: (0903) 723107

Attractive country house built in 1930s in medieval style. Unspoilt coast nearby. Swimming pool, putting, tennis, riding.
20 bedrs, 20 en suite; TV
dogs, ns; P 40, coach; no children under 8; con 26
LD 9.30
£ B&B £65–£85, B&B (double) £85–£180; L £15·50, D £19·50; [10% V w/d]
cc Access, Amex, B'card/Visa, Diners; dep.

CLITHEROE Lancashire. Map 36C3

Pop 13,671. Whalley 4, London 214, Settle 19, Skipton 18.
EC Wed. **MD** Tue, Sat. **Golf** Clitheroe 18h. **See** Castle Keep, Pendle Hill 1,830 ft, Sawley Abbey.
[i] Council Offices, Church Walk. (0200) 25566

Harrop Fold (Highly Acclaimed), Harrop Fold, Bolton by Bowland, BB7 4PJ Bolton by Bowland (020 07) 600 Tx: 635562. *Farm.*

Brooklyn (Acclaimed), 32 Pimlico Rd, BB7 2AH (0200) 28268. *Guest House.*
£B&B £14–£15·50; HB weekly £140–£150·50; [10% V]

COALVILLE Leicestershire. Map 23C4

M1 (jn 22)½, London 113, Ashby de la Zouche 5, Castle Donington 12, Hinckley 16, Leicester 20.
[i] Library, High St (0530) 35951

Bardon Hall, Beveridge La, Bardon Hill (0530) 813644
A country inn situated on A50 west of jn 21 of M1. Several modern bedroom blocks surround the original building.
35 bedrs, 35 en suite; TV; tcf
(See advertisement under Leicester)

COBHAM Kent. Map 11C3

Dartford 10, London 27, Maidstone 13, Rochester 6, Sevenoaks 16, Tonbridge 19.

★★ **Ye Olde Leather Bottle,** High St, DA1 23B (0474) 814327

A 17th century inn with Dickens associations. (BCB)
7 bedrs, 2 en suite (3 sh); TV; tcf
ns; P 50, G 2, coach; child facs; con 20
LD 10
£ B&B £35·50–£41, B&B (double) £52; L £8·15, D £8·15; WB £27·50
cc Access, Amex, B'card/Visa, Diners.

COBHAM Surrey. Map 8B1

Pop 9,518. Kingston upon Thames 8, London 18, Epsom 7½, Leatherhead 5, Weybridge 5.
EC Wed. **Golf** Fairmile & Silvermere 18h. **See** Church of St Andrew, 15th–18th cent The Cedars', 17th cent White Lion Inn.

★★★ **Hilton International,** Seven Hills Rd, KT11 1EW (0932) 64471 Tx: 929196
Fax: (0932) 68017

Mostly modern, well-appointed hotel, in 27 acres of parkland, close to M25. Swimming pool, tennis, squash, sauna. (H. Int). Fr, De, It, Es, Po
140 bedrs, 140 en suite; TV; tcf
lift, dogs, ns; P 160, coach; child facs; con 250
LD 10, nr Sat lunch
£ room £95–£115, double room £108–£135; Bk £8·95, L £13·50, D £19·50; WB £40
cc Access, Amex, B/card/Visa, Diners.

★★★ [C] **Woodlands Park,** Woodlands La, Stoke D'Abernon KT11 3 QB (037284) 3933 Tx: 919246 Fax: (037284) 2704
Red-brick Victorian house with turrets and gables. Magnificent part-panelled, galleried Great Hall. Set in 10 acres of lawns and gardens. Putting, tennis. Fr, De
59 bedrs, 59 en suite; TV; tcf
lift; P 150, coach; child facs; con 300
LD 10.30, bar meals only Sat lunch
£ B&B £90–£115, B&B (double) £100–£120; L £13·95, D £20·50; WB £95, [10% V]
cc Access, Amex, B'card/Visa.

COCKERMOUTH Cumbria. Map 43B2

Pop 6,290, Keswick 11, London 297, Carlisle 25, Egremont 15, Maryport 7, Workington 8½.
Ec Thur. **MD** Mon. **Golf** Cockermouth 18h.
[i] Riverside Car Park, Market St. (0900) 822634

★★★ [C] **Broughton Craggs,** Gt Broughton, CA13 0XP (0900) 824400
19th century manor house in 3 acres overlooking river to west of town.
14 bedrs, 14 en suite; TV; tcf
P 60; child facs; con 50
LD 9.30
£ B&B £38, B&B (double) £50; L £14, D £14; [5% V]
cc Access, Amex, B'card/Visa.

★★★ **Trout,** Crown St, CA13 0EJ
(0900) 823591 Fax: (0900) 827514

White-painted 17th century building with lovely garden river. Fishing. It
22 bedrs, 22 en suite; TV; tcf
dogs, ns; P 60, coach; child facs; con 60
LD 9.30
£ B&B £49–£55, B&B (double) £59–£64; L £8·50, D £14·95; WB £70 (2 nts HB)
cc Access, B'card/Visa; dep.
(See advertisement on p. 205)

★★ **Globe,** Main St, CA13 9LE
(0900) 822126 Fax: (0900) 823705
Handsome 3-storey Georgian red brick building in centre of market town. Fr
30 bedrs, 17 en suite, 5 ba; TV; tcf
TV, dogs, ns; G 15, coach; child facs; con 80
LD 9.30, nr lunch
£ B&B £30, B&B (double) £50; D £13; WB £30 (HB); [10% V]
cc Access, Amex, B'card/Visa, Diners; dep.

CODSALL West Midlands. Map 22A3

Pop 9,640. Wolverhampton 4½, London 129, Newport 14, Stafford 16, Telford 15.
EC Wed. **Golf** Patshull 18h.

Moors Farm (Acclaimed), Chillington La, WV8 1QM (090 74) 2330. *Farm.*
£ B&B £21–£26, B&B (double) £34–£42; HB weekly £168–£230

COGGLESHALL Essex. Map 27A2

Chelmsford 15, London 48, Braintree 6, Colchester 9, Sudbury 15.
See Paycocke's House (NT.)

★★★ **White Hart**, Market End, CO6 1NH
(0376) 561789
Fascinating 15th century inn—the lounge was once part of the original Guildhall—sensitively renovated and restored to reveal its ancient beams to best advantage.
18 bedrs, 18 en suite; TV
dogs; P20, G4, coach; child facs; con 40
LD 9
£B&B £55–£100 (w/e £40), B&B (double) £80–£160; L £11·50, D £17·50; WB £80; [5% V w/e Aug]
cc Access, Amex, B'card/Visa, Diners.

COLCHESTER Essex. Map 27B2

Pop 140,000 (Borough inc surroundings).

Chelmsford 22, London 56, Braintree 15, Clacton 15, Harwich 18, Haverhill 28, Ipswich 18, Sudbury 14.
EC Thur. **MD** Tues, Sat. **Golf** Colchester 18h. **See** Colchester and Essex Museum (incorp the Castle, Hollytrees mansion and All Saints' Church), St. John's Abbey.
ℹ 1 Queen St. ☎(0206) 712233

★★★ **George,** 116 High St, CO1 1DT ☎(0206) 578494 Fax: (0206) 761732

Ancient town centre inn, modernised without loss of charm. Sauna, solarium, gymnasium. (QMH). Fr, It
47 bedrs, 47 en suite; TV; tcf
dogs, ns; P 50, coach; child facs; con 90
LD 10
£ B&B £57, B&B (double) £72; L £10·25, D £10·25; WB £64 (2 nts HB)
cc Access, Amex, B'card/Visa, Diners; dep.

★★★ **Marks Tey,** London Rd, Marks Tey, CO6 1DU ☎(0206) 210001 Tx: 987176 Fax: (0206) 212167
Modern 2-storey hotel situated well outside the town on A12. Tennis, gymnasium.
108 bedrs, 108 en suite; TV; tcf
dogs; P 160; child facs; con 200
LD 10
£ B&B £52–£59, B&B (double) £65 (w/e £40); L £9·85, D £9·85; WB £37·50 (HB); [10% V]
cc Access, Amex, B'card/Visa, Diners.

★★★ **Mill,** East St, CO1 2TS ☎(0206) 865022 Fax: (0206) 860851
Clever conversion of an imposing Victorian flour mill on the River Colne. Separate night club behind hotel. Fishing. Fr
59 bedrs; 59 en suite; TV; tcf
lift, dogs; P60, coach; child facs; con 80
LD 10, nr Sat lunch
£ B&B £59 (w/e £40 room); L £9, D £12.50; WB £38 (2nts HB); [10% V w/e]
cc Access, Amex, B'card/Visa, Diners; dep.

★★★ **Red Lion,** High St, CO1 1DJ ☎(0206) 577986

Historic town-centre coaching inn refurbished to a high standard. Closed 25 Dec–1 Jan.
24 bedrs, 24 en suite; TV; tcf
dogs; child facs; con 35
LD 9.30
£ B&B £59, B&B (double) £72–£85; L £9·85, D £10·85; WB £84
cc Access, Amex, B'card/Visa, CB, Diners.

Bovills Hall (Acclaimed), Ardleigh, CO7 7RT ☎(0206) 230217 *Guest House.* Open Feb–3 Nov. De
£ B&B £18–£23

COLDEN COMMON Hampshire Map 5C2.

Marwell Resort, SO21 1JY ☎(0800) 500100 (Central reservations)
New hotel awaiting inspection.
60 bedrs, 60 en suite; TV; tcf
£ B&B £71·50–£76·50

COLEFORD Gloucestershire, Map 20A2

Pop 4,363. M4 (jn 27) 14, London 124, Chepstow 13, Gloucester 20, Monmouth 5½, Ross-on-Wye 12.
EC Thur. **Golf** Coleford 18h. **See** Remains of 14th cent Church, Forest of Dean.
ℹ Market Pl ☎(0594) 36307

★★ **Bells,** Lords Hill, GL16 8BD ☎Dean (0594) 32583
Interesting modern hotel next to golf complex. Swimming pool, golf, putting, tennis, billiards.
32 bedrs, 32 en suite; TV; tcf
TV; P 200, coach; child facs; con 200

★★ **Speech House**, Forest of Dean, GL16 7EL (3 m E on B4226). ☎(0594) 22607
17th century Court House adapted to an hotel of great character. (THF)
14 bedrs, 3 en suite, 4 ba; TV; tcf
dogs, ns; P 40, coach; child facs; con 50

COLERNE Wiltshire. Map 5A4

Chippenham 7, London 98, M4 (jn 17) 11, Bath 6, Devizes 15.

★★★★ **Lucknam Park**, SN14 8AZ ☎Bath (0225) 742777 Tx: 445648 Fax: (0225) 743536
Stone-built Georgian mansion, beautifully decorated and furnished, in a 280-acre park. Indoor swimming pool, tennis, sauna, solarium, gymnasium, snooker. Fr, De, It
39 bedrs, 39 en suite; TV
P 70, coach; child facs; con 26
LD 10
£ B&B £90, B&B (double) £120–£275; L £16·50, D £31·50; WB £190 (HB)
cc Access, B'card/Visa, Diners.

COLESBOURNE Gloucestershire. Map 20C2

Cirencester 8, London 96, Cheltenham 6, Gloucester 12, Stow on the Wold 18.

Colesbourne Inn, nr Cheltenham, GL55 9NP ☎Coberley (024 287) 376 Fax: (024 287) 397

A 200-year-old, Cotswold-stone coaching inn on the A435, six miles south of Cheltenham. Bedrooms in a converted stable block.

10 bedrs, 10 en suite; TV; tcf
dogs; P 70; child facs
LD 10
£ B&B £25–£28, B&B (double) £44–£48; D £7; WB £75 (2nts); [10%]
cc Access, Amex, B'card/Visa, Diners.

COLESHILL Warwickshire. Map 23A2

Pop 6,470. M6 (jn 4) 2, London 106, Atherstone 10, Birmingham 9½, Coventry 12, Lichfield 15, Nuneaton 12, Sutton Coldfield 7½, Tamworth 10, Warwick 18.
EC Thur. **Golf** Maxstoke Park 18h. **See** Pillory, Whipping Post and Stocks on Church Hill, 14th cent Church.

★★★ **Coleshill,** High St, B46 3BG ☎(0675) 465527 Tx: 333868 Fax: (0675) 464013

Modern hotel in red brick and timbered buildings dating to 16th century. (Lns). Es
15 bedrs, 15 en suite; annexe 8 bedrs, 8 en suite; TV; tcf
ns; P 48, coach; child facs; con 150
LD 9.30, bar meals only Sat lunch
£ B&B £62, B&B (double) £74; L £8·75, D £15·50; WB £25; [10% V]
cc Access, Amex, B'card/Visa, Diners.

★★★ **Grimstock Country,** Gilson Rd, Gilson, B46 1AJ ☎(0675) 462369 Tx: 334256 Fax: (0675) 467646
Former private house with modern bedroom wing added, set in attractive gardens in rural situation.
44 bedrs, 44 en suite; TV; tcf
TV, dogs; P 80, coach; child facs; con 100
LD 9.15, nr Sat lunch & Sun dinner. Resid & Rest lic
£ B&B £55, B&B (double) £65; L £8, D £10·50;
cc Access, Amex, B'card/Visa, Diners.

COLWALL *see under* MALVERN

COLYTON Devon. Map 4B1

Pop 2,372. Lyme Regis 7, London 154, Honiton 8, Seaton 2½, Axminster 5.
EC Wed. **Golf** Axe Cliffe, Axmouth 18h.

★★ H R **Old Bakehouse,** Lower Church St, EX13 6ND ☎(0297) 52518
Charming 17th century bakehouse of character converted to an hotel. Set in main street.
6 bedrs, 6 en suite, 3 ba; TV; tcf
dogs; P 8; child facs
LD 9.30. Resid & Rest lic
£ B&B £22; HB weekly £196; L £10, D £16; WB £37; [5% V w/d, low season]
cc Access, B'card/Visa; dep.

★★ H R **White Cottage,** Dolphin St, EX13 6NA ☎(0297) 52401

EC *early closing* **MD** *market day* *country house hotel* *ns (NS) no smoking areas* *tcf tea/coffee facilities*

Thatched 15th-century former farm house in cottage garden close to village centre. Closed 21 Dec–27 Jan.
🛏 6 bedrs, 6 en suite; TV; tcf
🏠 dogs; P 15; child facs
✕ LD 9.15, nr Mon lunch. Resid & Rest lic
£ B&B £26–£27·50; HB weekly £235–£300; D £12·50; WB £37 (HB, Oct–Mar); [10% V Oct–Mar]
cc Access, B'card/Visa; dep.

Swallows Eaves (Highly Acclaimed), Colyford EX13 6QJ ☎(0297) 53184. *Hotel.*
£ B&B £22·50–£26·50; HB weekly £224–£245; [10% V Nov–Apr]

St Edmunds, Swan Hill Rd, Colyford EX13 6QQ ☎(0297) 52431. *Guest House.* Open Mar–Oct.
£ B&B £12·50–£14, HB weekly £150–£187.

COMBE MARTIN Devon. Map 3B4

Pop 2,500. Dunster 31, London 196, Barnstaple 10, Ilfracombe 5, Lynmouth 12.
EC Wed. **Golf** Ilfracombe 18h.
ⓘ Cross St. ☎(0271) 883319

★★★ **Higher Leigh Manor**, EX34 0HG ☎(027 188) 2486
Restored Victorian manor house overlooking the village and sea. Set in 20 acres of garden and woodland.
🛏 12 bedrs, 12 en suite; TV; tcf
🏠 P 20, coach; child facs

★★ **White Gates,** Woodlands, EX34 0AT ☎(027 188) 3511

Motel-by-name-only in quiet private road. Good views of coastline from all rooms. Indoor swimming pool.

Blair Lodge (Acclaimed), Moory Meadow, EX34 0DG ☎(0271) 882294
Channel Vista (Acclaimed), 2 Woodlands, EX34 0AT ☎(027 188) 3514. *Guest House.* Open Easter–Oct.
£ B&B £17–£18·50; HB weekly £120–£142.
Saffron House (Acclaimed), King St, EX34 0BX ☎(027 188) 3521. *Hotel. Swimming pool.*
£ B&B £13–£20, HB weekly £140–£175.
Wheel Farm (Acclaimed), Berrydown, EX34 0NT ☎(027 188) 2550 Fax: (027 188) 2550. *Guest House.*

Firs, Woodlands, Seaside, EX34 0AS ☎(027 188) 3404. *Hotel.*
Woodlands, 2 The Woodlands, EX34 0AT ☎(027 188) 2769. *Guest House.*

CONGLETON Cheshire. Map 30B3

Pop 24,700. M6 (jn 17) 6, London 161, Buxton 17, Leek 9½, Macclesfield 8½, Manchester 24, Middlewich 10, Newcastle-under-Lyme 12, Sandbach 7.
EC Wed. **MD** Tue, Sat. **Golf** Astbury 18h, Congleton 9h. **See** Town Hall, Little Moreton Hall (NT) 3 m SW, Capesthorne Hall 6½ m.
ⓘ Town Hall, High St. ☎(0260) 271095

★★ **Lion & Swan,** Swan Bank, CW12 1JR ☎(0260) 273115 Fax: (0260) 299270 ♿
Attractive 16th century coaching inn with timber frame and impressive porchway. Fr, De
🛏 21 bedrs, 21 en suite; TV; tcf
🏠 TV, dogs, ns; P 40, G 4, coach; child facs; con 150
✕ LD 9.30
£ B&B £55·50–£91 (w/e £37·50), B&B (double) £71·50–£102; HB weekly £350; L £7·95, D £12·50; WB £50; [5% V (Thu–Sun, Oct–May only)]
cc Access, Amex, B'card/Visa, Diners.
(*See advertisement on p. 205*)

CONISTON Cumbria. Map 43C1

Pop 1,063. Ambleside 7, London 275, Broughton-in-Furness 9, Ulverston 13.
EC Wed. **Golf** Ulverston 18h. **See** Brantwood (Ruskin Museum), Parish Church (Ruskin's grave), Donald Campbell Memorial, Tent Lodge (home of Tennyson), Coniston Old Man, 2,633 ft, Coniston Water.
ⓘ 16 Yewdale Rd, ☎(053 94) 41533

★★ **H** **Coniston Sun,** LA21 8HQ ☎(053 94) 41248

Small hotel in woodland garden with stunning mountain and forest views. Closed Jan.
🛏 11 bedrs, 11 en suite; TV; tcf
🏠 dogs; P 15, coach; child facs
✕ LD 8, bar meals only lunch
£ B&B £30–£35; D £15·50;
cc Access, B'card/Visa; dep.
(*See advertisement on p. 210*)

★★ **Yewdale,** Yewdale Rd, LA21 8LU ☎(053 94) 41280
Attractive 3-storey building, with green slate roof, set in centre of village.
🛏 10 bedrs, 8 en suite, 2 ba; TV; tcf
🏠 dogs, ns; P 6, coach; con 50
✕ LD 8.30
£ B&B £18·95–£26·95; HB weekly £169·40–£232·40, D £12·95
cc Access, B'card/Visa; dep.

Black Bull, Yewdale Rd, LA21 8DU ☎(053 94) 41335

Pleasantly situated 16th century coaching inn at foot of Old Man mountain. Fr
🛏 7 bedrs, 7 en suite, 1 ba; TV; tcf
🏠 TV, dogs, ns; P 15, U 1, child facs
✕ LD 9
£ B&B £25; L £6·95, D £9·75
cc Access, B'card/Visa; dep.

Coniston Lodge (Highly Acclaimed), Sunny Brow, LA21 8HH. ☎(05394) 41201. *Hotel.*
£ B&B £27·50–£35·50; [5% V w/d]

Crown, LA21 8EA ☎(053 94) 41243. *Inn.*
£ B&B £17–£18, HB weekly £250–£300; [10% V]

CONSTANTINE BAY Cornwall. Map 2B2

Pop 100. Wadebridge 11, London 250, Newquay 12.
Golf Trevose G and CC 18h and 9h. **See** Trevose Head (Lighthouse, Cliffs).

★★★ **H** **Treglos,** PL28 8JH ☎Padstow (0841) 520727 Tx: 45795 Fax: (0841) 521163 ♿

Modern 3-storey white building in attractive gardens. Magnificent sea view. Indoor swimming pool. Open 7 Mar–5 Nov.
🛏 44 bedrs, 44 en suite; TV
🏠 lift, dogs, ns; P 50, U 9; child facs; con 15
✕ LD 9.30. Resid & Rest lic
£ B&B £39·50–£59·50, B&B (double) £75–£114; HB weekly £250·50–£360; L £9·95, D £16·95
cc Access (rest only); dep.

COODEN BEACH East Sussex. Map 7A1

Hurst Green 15, London 65, Eastbourne 9, Hastings 7½, Lewes 21, Uckfield 23.
EC Wed. **Golf** Cooden Beach 18h.

★★★ **Cooden Resort,** nr Bexhill, TN39 4TT ☎(042 43) 2281 Fax: (042 43) 6142 ♿

Coniston (Cumbria)

Coventry (Warwickshire)

Coventry (West Midlands)

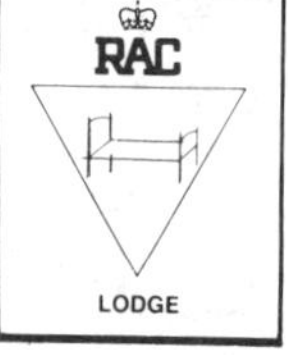

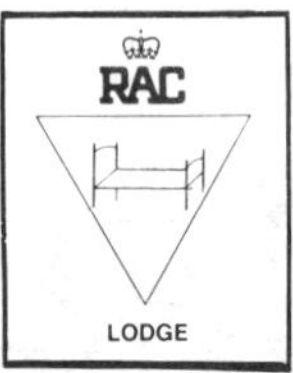

Crawley (West Sussex)

Crediton (Devon)

EC *early closing* **MD** *market day* *country house hotel* *ns (NS) no smoking areas* *tcf tea/coffee facilities*

Modernised 1930s holiday hotel situated on the beach. Indoor/outdoor swimming pools, golf, sauna, solarium, gymnasium. Es
36 bedrs, 34 en suite, 1 ba; TV; tcf
dogs; P 70, coach; child facs; con 100
LD 9.30
£ B&B £56·50, B&B (double) £78; HB weekly £336; L £11·50, D £16·50; WB £84 (2 nts); [10% V]
cc Access, Amex, B'card/Visa, Diners.

COPTHORNE West Sussex. Map 10C1

Pop 3,102. Redhill 8, London 28, M23 5, Crawley 4½, East Grinstead 6½, Godstone 12.
Golf Copthorne 18h.

★★★★ R **Copthorne,** RH10 3PG
(0342) 714971 Tx: 95500
Fax: (0342) 717375

Attractive hotel built around farmhouse. Extensive grounds. Convenient for Gatwick. Putting, squash, sauna, solarium, gymnasium, billiards. Fr, De, It, No.
224 bedrs, 224 en suite; TV; tcf
dogs, ns; P 400 (£2·95), coach; child facs; con 110
LD 10.45
£ B&B £96·25, B&B (double) £114·50–£121·50; L £13·50, D £13·50; WB £45; [10% V]
cc Access, Amex, B'card/Visa.

★★★★ **Effingham Park**, West Park Rd, RH10 3EU (0342) 714994 Tx: 95649
Fax: (0342) 716039

Superb hotel of Spanish appearance in 40 acres of parkland. Conference and leisure centre. Indoor swimming pool, golf, putting, sauna, solarium, gymnasium. Fr, De, It, Es, Po
122 bedrs, 122 en suite; TV; tcf
lift, dogs, ns; P 500, coach; child facs; con 500
LD 10·30
£ B&B £103·50–£113·50, (w/e £45), B&B (double) £127–£137; L £13·50, D £13·50; [10% V]
cc Access, Amex, B'card/Visa, Diners; dep.

CORBRIDGE ON TYNE

Northumberland. Map 44C3
Pop 2,200. West Auckland 31, London 280, Bellingham 18, Durham 25, Hexham 3½, Jedburgh 47, Newcastle upon Tyne 17.
EC Thur. **Golf** Hexham 18h & 9h. **See** St Andrew's Church, Market Cross, 17th cent bridge, 17th cent Angel Inn, ruins of Aydon and Dilston castles. Museum of Roman relics at Corstopitum.
[i] Vicars Pele, Market Pl. (0434) 632815

★★★ **Lion of Corbridge** Bridge End, NE45 5AX (0434) 632504
Fax: (0434) 632571
A late Victorian villa in local stone, with modern extensions, on outskirts of village south of the river.
14 bedrs, 14 en suite; TV; tcf
P30, coach; child facs, con 40

★★ **Angel Inn,** Main St, NE45 5LA
(0434) 632119
White-painted, Georgian coaching inn in centre of Corbridge. (ThH)

Tynedale (Acclaimed), Market Pl, NE45 5AW (0434) 632149. Hotel.
£ B&B £18·50, [10% V]

CORBY Northamptonshire. Map 21C4

Pop 47,600. Kettering 7½, London 82, Huntingdon 27, Market Harborough 12, Stamford 16.
[i] George St (0536) 402551

★★★ **Crest,** Rockingham Rd, NN17 1AE
(0536) 401348 Tx: 341752
Fax: (0536) 66383
Modern, well-appointed hotel with spacious public areas set in a quiet location. (Cr/THF)
70 bedrs, 70 en suite; TV; tcf
dogs, ns; P 200, coach; child facs; con 400
LD 9.45, nr Sat lunch
£ B&B £71·95 (w/e £31), B&B (double) £76–£91·90; L £8·45, D £14·95
cc Access, Amex, B'card/Visa, Diners.

CORNHILL-ON-TWEED

Northumberland. Map 51B2
Pop 320. Newcastle upon Tyne 59, London 333, Alnwick 30, Berwick-upon-Tweed 13, Coldstream 1½, Kelso 10.
EC Thur. **Golf** Coldstream 9h.

★★★ **Tillmouth Park,** TD12 4UU
Coldstream (0890) 2255

Imposing stone-built Victorian mansion of 4 storeys in parkland. Fishing.
12 bedrs, 12 en suite; TV; tcf
dogs; P 50, coach; child facs; con 35
LD 9.15
£ B&B £40–£45, B&B (double) £60–£70; HB weekly £231–£266; L £7·50, D £14·75; WB £38 (HB)
cc Access, Amex, B'card/Visa, Diners; dep.

★★ **Collingwood Arms**, TD12 4UH
(0890) 2424

A friendly hotel in an attractive stone-built Georgian coaching inn on the A697.
17 bedrs, 8 en suite, 3 ba; TV; tcf
TV, dogs, ns; P 40, coach; child facs; con 100
LD 8.45
£ B&B £23–£27, B&B (double) £38–£48; L £7, D £10
cc B'card/Visa.

CORSHAM Wiltshire. Map 5A4

Pop 11,000. Chippenham 4, London 95, Bath 9½, Bristol 21, Chepstow 31, Devizes 12, Frome 17, Westbury 14.
EC Wed. **MD** Tue. **Golf** Kingsdown 18h.
See Corsham Court, Flemish Houses & Almshouses.
[i] Arnold House, High St. (0249) 714660

★★★ H R **Rudloe Park,** Leafy La, SN13 0PA Bath (0225) 810555
Fax: (0225) 811412

Portland stone mansion in attractive grounds. Views down valley to Bath. Fr
11 bedrs, 11 en suite; TV; tcf
dogs, ns; P 70; children over 10; con 30
LD 10
£ B&B £55–£60, B&B (double) £80–£90; HB weekly £340–£375; L £13, D £15·50; WB £100 (2 nts HB); [10% V]
cc Access, Amex, B'card/Visa, Diners; dep.
(See advertisement on p. 124)

★★ C **Methuen Arms,** High St, SN13 0HB (0249) 714867 Fax: (0249) 712004

Privately-owned 17th century Cotswold stone building. Near the town centre. Fr
19 bedrs, 18 en suite, 1 ba; annexe 6 bedrs, 6 en suite; TV; tcf
P 80, coach; child facs; con 26
LD 9.30, bar meals only Sun dinner
£ B&B £37–£42, B&B (double) £53–£58 (w/e £42·66); L £14·75, D £14·75; [10% V]
cc Access, B'card/Visa; dep.

COTLEIGH Devon. Map 4B2

Taunton 16, London 159, Axminster 8, Honiton 3.

★★ **Snodwell Farm,** EX14 9HZ Upottery (040 486) 263
Small, stone-built manor house in beautiful country surroundings. Swimming pool.

COTTINGHAM Northamptonshire. Map 21B4

Kettering 8½, London 83, Corby 3, Leicester 22, Market Harborough 8½, Oakham 14.

★★ **Hunting Lodge,** High St, Nr Market Harborough LE16 8XN Rockingham (0536) 771370
Attractive 16th century building with motel accommodation.
23 bedrs, 23 en suite; TV; tcf
TV, dogs, ns; P 100, coach; child facs; con 200

COUNTISBURY Devon. Map 3B4

Minehead 16, London 183, Barnstaple 19, Ilfracombe 18.

★★ **Exmoor Sandpiper,** nr Lynton, EX35 6NE (059 87) 263 Fax: (059 87) 358
Atmospheric old coaching inn beside the A39 in lovely Exmoor countryside.
16 bedrs, 16 en suite; TV; tcf
TV, dogs; P70, coach; child facs
LD 9.30, bar meals only lunch
£ B&B £32·20; HB weekly £277·15; D £16·67; WB £91·54; dep.

COVENTRY West Midlands. Map 23B1

Pop 318,000. Daventry 19, London 94, M6 (jn 2) 4, Banbury 27, Birmingham 18, Leicester 25, Nuneaton 8½, Rugby 12, Warwick 10.
See Plan, p. 213.
MD Daily expt Thur. **P** See Plan. **Golf** Coventry 18h, Coventry Hearsall 18h, Grange 9h. **See** Cathedral remains and new Cathedral, St Mary's Hall, Holy Trinity Church, Lady Godiva Statue, Herbert Art Gallery and Museum, City Wall and Lady Herbert's Garden, new City centre, Ford's Hospital and Bonds Hospital (Almshouses).
i Central Library. (0203) 82311

★★★★ R **De Vere,** Cathedral Sq, CV1 5RP (0203) 633733 Tx: 31380 Fax: (0203) 225299

Impressive large modern city centre hotel adjacent to the Cathedral. (DeV)
190 bedrs, 190 en suite; TV; tcf
lift, dogs, ns; G 130, coach; child facs; con 500
LD 10.15
£ B&B £81·50–£98·50 (w/e £39·50), B&B (double) £98–£116; L £10·50, D £15; WB £50 (2 nts); [10% V]
cc Access, Amex, B'card/Visa, CB, Diners.

★★★ **Ansty Hall,** Ansty, CV7 9HZ (0203) 612222 Fax: (0203) 602155
A mellow, red-brick, 17th-century house in eight acres of grounds on edge of village only ½ mile from junction 2 of M6. Fr
13 bedrs, 13 en suite; TV
P 30, coach; child facs; con 100
LD 9.30, nr Sat lunch, Sun dinner. Resid & Rest lic
£ B&B £77, B&B (double) £104; L £12·50, D £15; WB £95 (HB); [5% V w/d]
cc Access, Amex, B'card/Visa, Diners.

★★★ **Brandon Hall,** Main St, Brandon, CV8 3FW (0203) 542571 Tx: 31472 Fax: (0203) 544909
Former country residence in peaceful surroundings. Putting, squash. Fr, De (THF)
60 bedrs, 60 en suite; TV; tcf
dogs, ns; P 200; child facs; con 100
LD 9.30, bar meals only Sat lunch
£ B&B £84–£95, B&B (double) £114–£124; L £9·20, D £13·50; WB £45
cc Access, Amex, B'card/Visa, CB, Diners.

★★★ H C **Brooklands Grange,** Holyhead Rd CV5 8HX (0203) 601601 Fax: (0203) 601277

A recently developed hotel in a 16th-century farmhouse with Victorian additions and modern extensions. Set in pleasant grounds in residential area. Closed 23 Dec–1 Jan.
30 bedrs, 30 en suite; TV; tcf
ns; P 54; child facs; con 12
LD 9.30, nr Sat lunch
£ B&B £75–£80, B&B (double) £90–£95; L £14·75, D £18·50; [10% V]
cc Access, Amex, B'card/Visa, Diners.

★★★ **Chace Crest,** London Rd, Willenhall, CV3 4EQ (0203) 303398 Tx: 311993 Fax: (0203) 301816

Former Victorian residence extended and developed; in suburbs. Fr. (Cr/THF)
67 bedrs, 67 en suite; TV; tcf
dogs, ns; P 100, coach; child facs; con 70
LD 10, bar meals only Sat lunch
£ B&B £76·95–£88·95, B&B (double) £96·90–£108·90; L £9·50, D 14·95; WB £44 (HB); [10% V w/e]
cc Access, Amex, B'card/Visa, CB, Diners.

★★★ **Crest,** (M6, Jn 2), Hinckley Rd, Walsgrave, CV2 2HP (0203) 613261 Tx: 311292 Fax: (0203) 621736

Large modern hotel situated in own grounds. Convenient to motorway. Indoor swimming pool, sauna, solarium, gymnasium. (Cr/THF). Fr, It, Es, Ja
147 bedrs, 147 en suite; TV; tcf
lift, dogs; P 250, coach; child facs; con 450
LD 10, nr Sat lunch
£ B&B £84·95–£96·95 (w/e £39), B&B (double) £105·90–£117·90; HB weekly £294–£329; L £9·50, D £14·50; WB £42; [10% V Jul–Aug]
cc Access, Amex, B'card/Visa, Diners.

★★★ **Novotel,** Wilsons La, Longford, CV6 6HL (0203) 365000 Tx: 31545
Motel-type modern hotel in pleasant garden. Swimming pool, sauna, solarium, gymnasium, squash, snooker.

★★★ **Old Mill,** Mill Hill, Baginton, CV8 2BS (0203) 303588

Converted mill house set in 5 acres of garden beside River Sowe. (BCB)
20 bedrs, 20 en suite; TV; tcf
ns; P 200, coach; child facs; con 20
LD 9.30

Licences
Establishments have a full licence unless shown as unlicensed or with the limitations listed on p 6.

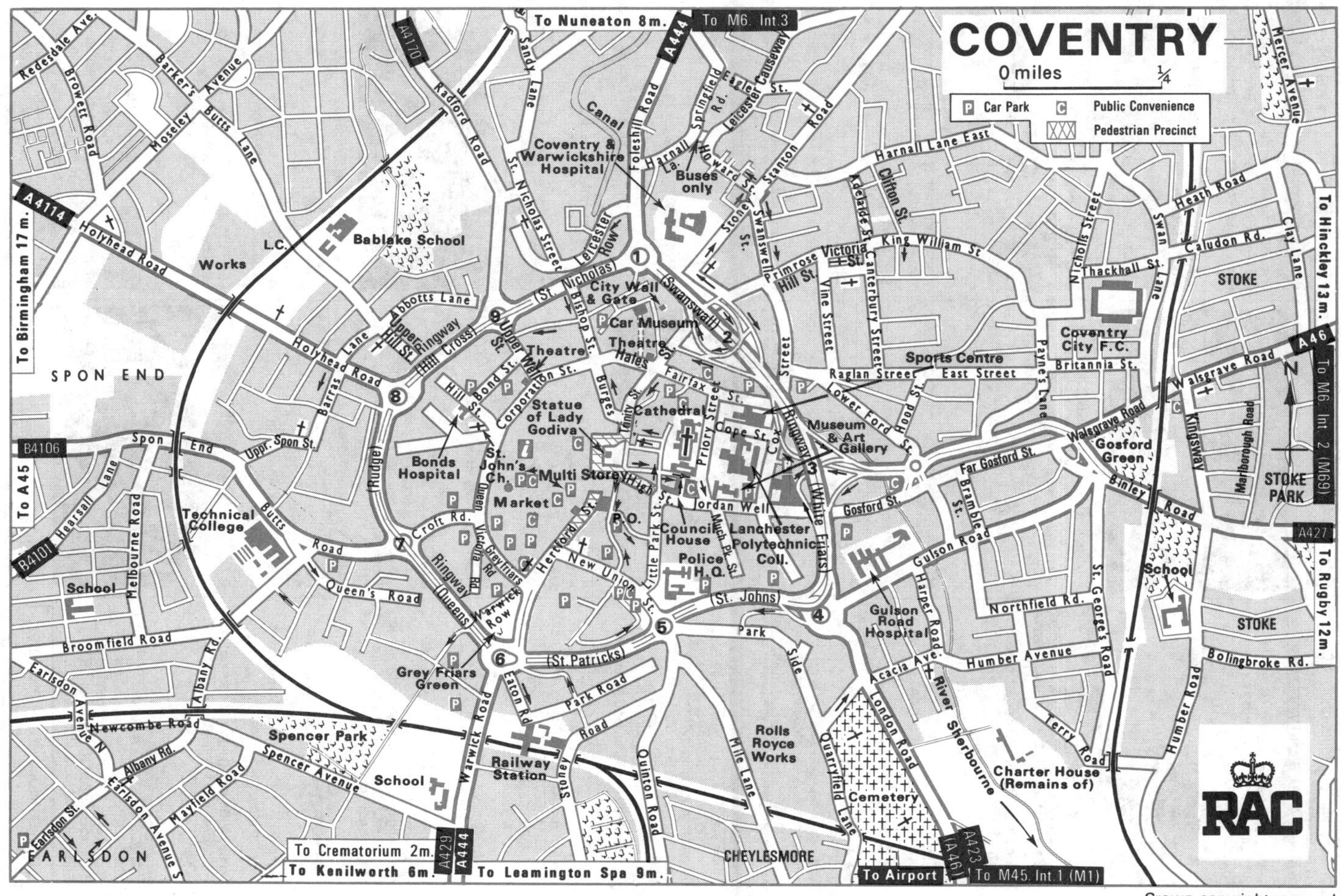

COVENTRY
0 miles 1/4
Car Park
Public Convenience
Pedestrian Precinct
RAC
To Nuneaton 8m.
To M6. Int.3
To Birmingham 17 m.
To A45
To Hinckley 13 m.
To M6. Int. 2 (M69)
To Rugby 12m.
To Crematorium 2m.
To Kenilworth 6m.
To Leamington Spa 9m.
To Airport
To M45. Int.1 (M1)
SPON END
STOKE
STOKE PARK
EARLSDON
CHEYLESMORE
Coventry & Warwickshire Hospital
Buses only
Bablake School
Works
City Wall & Gate
Car Museum
Theatre
Cathedral
Statue of Lady Godiva
Bonds Hospital
Multi Storey
Market
Council House
Police H.Q.
Lanchester Polytechnic Coll.
Museum & Art Gallery
Sports Centre
Coventry City F.C.
Gosford Green
Gulson Road Hospital
Technical College
Grey Friars Green
Spencer Park
Railway Station
Rolls Royce Works
Cemetery
Charter House (Remains of)
River Sherbourne

£B&B £58·50, B&B (double) £71; L £8·15, D £8·15; WB £27·50
cc Access, Amex, B'card/Visa, Diners.

★★★ **Post House,** Rye Hill, Allesley, CV5 9PH (0203) 402151 Tx: 31427 Fax: (0203) 402235

Modern hotel located on western outskirts of city. (THF)
184 bedrs, 184 en suite; TV; tcf
lift, dogs, ns; P 250, coach; child facs; con 130
LD 10
£B&B £75–£85 (w/e £43), B&B (double) £94–£104; L £9·50, D £14·50; WB £41 (HB)
cc Access, Amex, B'card/Visa, CB, Diners.

★★ **Anchor**, 7 Park Rd, CV1 2L (0203) 633366
Convenient city hotel adjacent to main railway station. A 1920s building with modern extension.
25 bedrs, 25 en suite; TV; tcf.

★★ **Beechwood,** Sandpits La, CV6 2FR (0203) 338662 Fax: (0203) 337080
Charming former farmhouse set in pleasant grounds 3 miles N of city.
24 bedrs, 24 en suite; TV; tcf
dogs; P 60, coach; child facs; con 14
LD 9.30. Resid & Rest lic
£B&B £39·50 (w/e £25), B&B (double) £51; D £10; [10% V w/e]
cc Access, Amex, B'card/Visa, Diners.

★★ **Campanile,** 4 Wigston Rd, Walsgrave, CV2 2SD (0203) 622311.
See Motor Lodge Section p. 00.
(*See advertisement on p. 210*)

Croft, 23 Stoke Green, CV3 1FP (0203) 457846. *Private Hotel. Billiards.*
£B&B £24–£28 (w/e £18)
Hearsall Lodge, 1 Broad La, CV5 7AA (0203) 074543. *Private Hotel.*
Northanger, 35 Westminster Rd, Earlsdon CV1 3GB (0203) 226780. *Guest House.*
£B&B £15–£16

COXLEY VINEYARD Somerset. Map 4C3
Glastonbury 4, London 130, Axbridge 11, Shepton Mallet 6½, Wells 2.

Coxley Vineyard (Highly Acclaimed), Nr Wells, BA5 1RQ Wells (0749) 73854. *Hotel.* ♿

CRACKINGTON HAVEN Cornwall. Map 2C3
Pop 1,800. Launceston 18, London 229, Bideford 35, Bude 10, Camelford 10.
Golf Bude and North Cornwall 18h.

Changes made after July 1990 are not included.

Coombe Barton, EX23 0JG St Gennys (084 03) 345

An extended Georgian building right by the beach in beautiful bay. Open 15 Mar–Oct.
7 bedrs, 3 en suite, 2 ba; TV; tcf
TV, dogs, ns; P 30; no children under 2
LD 9.30
£B&B £19–£31·50, B&B (double) £36–£45; [5% V]
cc Access, Amex; dep.

CRANBORNE Dorset. Map 5A2
Pop 592. Salisbury 14, London 97, Blandford Forum 14, Bournemouth 17, Southampton 26, Wimborne Minster 10.
Golf Ferndown 18h.

★★ H **Fleur de Lys,** 5 Wimborne St, BH21 5PP (072 54) 282

Attractive olde worlde inn in centre of this historic village. Closed Xmas.
8 bedrs, 7 en suite (1 sh); TV; tcf
TV, dogs; P35, coach; con 12
LD 9.30
£ B&B £22–£28, B&B (double) £33–£40; [10% V]
cc Access, Amex, B'card/Visa.

CRANBROOK Kent. Map 7A2
Pop 4,247. London 49, Ashford 18, Hawkhurst 4, Maidstone 14, Rye 17, Tenterden 8½, Tunbridge Wells 14½.
EC Wed. **Golf** Cranbrook 18h. **See** Church (15th cent), Angley House Gardens, Sissinghurst Castle 2½ NE, Sissinghurst Place Gardens 2 m NE.
i Vestry Hall, Stone St. (0580) 712538

★★ **Willesley,** Angley Rd, TN17 2LE (0580) 713555

Typical historic Kentish red-brick building in 4 acres of gardens.

CRANTOCK Cornwall. Map 2B2
Pop 914. Bodmin 21, London 254, Newquay 3½, Redruth 15, St Austell 17, Truro 12, Wadebridge 18.
EC Wed. **Golf** Newquay 18h. **See** 12th cent Church, St Ambrose Well, sandy beach.

★★ **Crantock Bay,** West Pentire, TR8 5SE (0637) 830229

Three-storey modern building in 4 acres of grounds with magnificent Atlantic views. Indoor swimming pool, putting, tennis, sauna, gymnasium. Open Mar–Nov.
36 bedrs, 36 en suite; TV; tcf
dogs, ns; P 35; child facs; con 20
LD 8
£B&B £20–£32; D £11·50; [10% V]
cc Amex, B'card/Visa, Diners; dep.

Crantock Cottage, West Pentire Rd, TR8 5SA (0637) 830232. *Hotel.*
£B&B £15·20–£20; HB weekly £122·50–£154·50.

CRATHORNE Cleveland. Map 45A1
Thirsk 16, London 236, Darlington 12, Middlesbrough 8, Stockton on Tees 8.

★★★★ **Crathorne Hall,** Yarm, nr Middlesbrough, TS15 0AR

Impressive Edwardian mansion in classical style with oak-panelled rooms and fine antiques; set in 15 acres of wooded grounds. Billiards. Fr, De, It
39 bedrs, 30 en suite; TV; tcf
dogs, ns; P157, coach; child facs; con 160
£B&B £75–£95, B&B (double) £90–£155; L £14·50, D £14·50; WB £95
cc Amex, B'card/Visa, Diners.

CRAWLEY West Sussex. Map 10B1
Pop 83,500. Redhill 10, London 31, M23 3, Brighton 22, Dorking 13, East Grinstead 9, Gatwick Airport 3½, Horsham 8.
EC Wed. **MD** Fri, Sat. **Golf** Tilgate Park 18h. **See** George Inn (16th cent Gallows' sign), 15th cent Parish Church, medieval Prior's House now cafe, Tilgate Park.

★★★ **Gatwick Concorde,** Church Rd, Lowfield Heath, RH11 0PQ ☎(0293) 775900 Tx: 878775 Fax: (0293) 785991

Close to Gatwick Airport; modern hotel running courtesy coach. (QMH)
🛏121 bedrs, 121 en suite; TV; tcf
🏠 lift, dogs; P 120, coach; child facs; con 60

★★★ **Gatwick Manor,** London Rd, Lowfield Heath, RH10 2ST ☎(0293) 26301

Attractive historic moated building with considerable modern extensions. (BCB)
🛏30 bedrs, 30 en suite; TV; tcf
🏠 TV, ns; P 250, coach; child facs; con 50
✕LD 10.30
£ B&B £70, B&B (double) £77·50; L £8·15, D £8·15; WB £27·50
cc Access, Amex, B'card/Visa, Diners.

★★★ **George,** High St, RH10 1BS ☎(0293) 24215 Tx: 87385 Fax: (0293) 548565
Carefully modernised timbered coaching inn with modern extension. (THF)
🛏86 bedrs, 86 en suite; TV; tcf
🏠 dogs, ns; P 90, coach; child facs; con 30
✕LD 9.30
£ B&B £81–£96 (w/e £40·75), B&B (double) £108–£113; L £9·95, D £13·95; WB £48 (HB)
cc Access, Amex, B'card/Visa, CB, Diners.

★★★ **Goffs Park,** Goffs Park Rd, RH11 8AX ☎(0293) 35447 Tx: 87415 Fax: (0293) 542050
Attractive red-brick building with modern extensions. ⚒ Fr
🛏37 bedrs, 37 en suite; annexe 28 bedrs, 28 en suite; TV; tcf
🏠 dogs; P 92, coach; child facs; con 120
✕LD 9.30, bar meals only Sat lunch
£ B&B £69·50, B&B (double) £89·50; L £9, D £12
cc Access, Amex, B'card/Visa, Diners.

Using RAC discount vouchers
Please tell the hotel when booking if you plan to use an RAC discount voucher (see p. 34) in part payment of your bill. Only one voucher will be accepted per party per stay. Discount vouchers will only be accepted in payment for accommodation, not for food.

★★★ **Holiday Inn,** Langley Dr, RH11 7SX ☎(0293) 529991 Tx: 877311 Fax: (0293) 515913

Tall, modern hotel by A23 conveniently situated for Gatwick Airport. Indoor swimming pool, sauna, solarium, gymnasium, billiards. (HI).
🛏226 bedrs, 226 en suite; TV; tcf
🏠 lift, dogs, ns; P 300, coach; child facs; con 200
✕LD 9.30
£ B&B £99·50, B&B (double) £124; L £15·50, D £15·50; WB £50 (HB)
cc Access, Amex, B'card/Visa, CB, Diners.

Barnwood (Acclaimed), Balcombe Rd, Pound Hill, RH10 4RU ☎(0293) 882709. *Hotel.*

CREDITON Devon. Map 3C3

Pop 6,169. Exeter 7½, London 177, Barnstaple 33, Holsworthy 34, Okehampton 17, Tiverton 12.
EC Wed. **Golf** Downes Credition 18h. **See** Restored 13th cent Lawrence's Chapel, Statue of St Boniface, Parish Church.

★★ **Coombe House,** Coleford, EX17 5BY ☎(0363) 84487

A family-run hotel in a Georgian manor house set in 5 acres of grounds. Swimming pool, putting, tennis. ⚒ Fr, De
🛏12 bedrs, 10 en suite, 1 ba; TV; tcf
🏠 dogs; P 100, coach; child facs; con 90
✕LD 9.30, bar meals only Mon & Sun dinner
£ B&B £25–£40, B&B (double) £45–55; HB weekly £210; L £10·50, D £10·50; WB £30 (HB); [10% V]
cc Amex, B'card/Visa, Diners.
(See advertisement on p. 210)

Thatched Cottage (Acclaimed), Barnstaple Cross, EX17 2EW ☎(036 32) 3115. *Guest House.*

CREWE Cheshire. Map 29C3

Pop 45,000. Newcastle-under-Lyme 12, London 162, Middlewich 7½, Nantwich 4½, Newport 27, Sandbach 6.
MD Mon, Fri, Sat. **Golf** Crewe 18h.
[i] Market Hall, Earle St. ☎(0270) 583191

★★★ **Crewe Arms,** Nantwich Rd, CW1 1DW ☎(0270) 213204 Fax: (0270) 588615

Imposing hotel in Victorian style. (Emb). ⚒ Fr
🛏53 bedrs, 53 en suite; TV; tcf
🏠 dogs, ns; P 150, coach; child facs; con 100
✕LD 9.30, bar meals only Sat
£ B&B £59–£75 (w/e £21), B&B (double) £79–£99; HB weekly £336–£436; L £9·75, D £11·75; WB £29 (HB)
cc Access, Amex, B'card/Visa, Diners.

CRICK Northamptonshire. Map 21B4

M1 (jn 18) ½, London 80, Daventry 8, Leicester 22, Northants 14, Rugby 5½.

★★★★ **Post House,** NN6 7XR ☎(0788) 822101 Tx: 311107 Fax: (0788) 823955
Modern purpose-built hotel in gardens adjacent to junction 18 of M1. Indoor swimming pool, sauna, solarium, gymnasium. (THF)
🛏96 bedrs, 96 en suite; TV; tcf
🏠 dogs, ns; P 150, coach; child facs; con
✕LD 10.30, nr Sat lunch
£ room £73 (w/e £39·50), double room £84; L £10, D £15; WB £40
cc Access, Amex, B'card/Visa, Diners.

CRICKLADE Wiltshire. Map 20C1

Pop 4,000. Wantage 22, London 83, Swindon 8, Cirencester 7½, Faringdon 14, Burford 17.
EC Wed & Sat. **Golf** Swindon 18h. **See** Church, Inglesham Church nearby, Museum, North Meadow nature reserve.

★★ **White Hart,** High St, SN6 6AA ☎Swindon (0793) 750206

A 3-storey, gabled building in the town centre. Closed 25 Dec–1 Jan. ⚒ Fr
🛏16 bedrs, 14 en suite, 1 ba; TV; tcf
🏠 TV, dogs; P 20, G 4, coach; child facs
✕LD 9.30, bar meals only Mon lunch, Sun dinner
£ B&B £40 (w/e £22·50), B&B (double) £52; L £9·95, D £9·95
cc Access, Amex, B'card/Visa, Diners.

CROMER Norfolk. Map 35B2

Pop 6,206. Fakenham 22, London 133, Great Yarmouth 34, Norwich 23.
EC Wed. **Golf** Royal Cromer 18h. **See** 14th cent Church, Lighthouse, Lifeboat Stations and Museum, Felbrigg Hall 3 m SW.
[i] Town Hall, Prince of Wales Rd. ☎(0263) 512497

★★ **Cliftonville,** Runton Rd, NR27 9AS ☎(0263) 512543 Fax: (0263) 511764
Imposing Victorian building—traditional style hotel overlooking sea. Billiards. Fr, De, It
44 bedrs, 23 en suite, 9 ba; TV; tcf
lift, TV, dogs; P 20, U 3, coach; child facs; con 200
LD 9
£ B&B £22·50–£36·50, B&B (double) £43–£61; HB weekly £215·50–£316·25; L £7·50, D £11·50; WB £65 (2 nts)
cc Access, Amex, B'card/Visa, Diners; dep.
(*See advertisement on p. 217*)

★ **Anglia Court,** 5 Runton Rd, NR27 9AR ☎(0263) 512443

Modernised Victorian seaside hotel situated on the front. Facing delightful gardens.

Westgate Lodge (Highly Acclaimed), Macdonald Rd, NR 27 9AP ☎(0263) 512840. *Private Hotel*. Open Easter–Oct.
£ B&B (double) £42·55; HB weekly £157·55

Chellow Dene (Acclaimed), 23 Macdonald Rd, NR27 9AP ☎(0263) 513251. *Guest House*. Open Apr–Oct.
£ B&B £14; HB weekly £104

Sandcliff, Runton Rd, NR27 0HJ ☎(0263) 512888. *Private Hotel*. Closed 22–31 Dec.
£ B&B £18·20–£22·40.

CROOK Cumbria

See WINDERMERE.

CROOKLANDS Cumbria. Map 36B4

London 249, M6 (jn 36) 1, Kendal 6, Kirkby Lonsdale 6, Lancaster 15.
Golf Kendal 18h.

★★★ **H** **R** **Crooklands,** LA7 7NW ☎(044 87) 432 Tx: 94017303 Fax: (044 87) 525

Attractive 2-storey stone-built 16th century hotel with oak beams. De

30 bedrs, 30 en suite; TV; tcf
dogs; P 150, coach; child facs; con 100
LD 9.30, bar meals only lunch, Sun dinner
£ B&B £60–£80, B&B (double) £80–£100; HB weekly £250; D £16·50; WB £96
cc Access, Amex, B'card/Visa, Diners; dep.

CROSBY Merseyside. Map 32A2

London 201, M58/M57 (jn 7) 5, Formby 5, Liverpool 6.

★★★ **Blundellsands,** The Serpentine, Blundellsands, L23 6TE ☎051-924 6515 Tx: 626270 Fax: 051-931 5364

Striking Edwardian mansion quietly situated in a suburban area. (Lns)
41 bedrs, 41 en suite; TV; tcf
lift, dogs, ns; P 350, coach; child facs; con 400
LD 11
£ B&B £63, B&B (double) £76; L £8·95, D £14; WB £48; [10% V]
cc Access, Amex, B'card/Visa, Diners.

CROWBOROUGH East Sussex. Map 6C2

Pop 17,000, Tunbridge Wells 7, London 44, Eastbourne 25, East Grinstead 12, Hastings 28, Hurst Green 16, Uckfield 7½.
EC Wed. **Golf** Crowborough Beacon 18h.

★★★ **Winston Manor,** Beacon Rd, TN6 1AD ☎(0892) 652772 Fax: (0892) 665537
Small detached hotel on A26 at southern edge of town. Privately-owned. Indoor swimming pool, sauna, gymnasium. Fr
50 beds, 50 en suite; TV; tcf
lift, dogs, ns; P90, coach; child facs; con 300
LD 9.45; nr Sat lunch
£ B&B £61·50, B&B (double) £88; L £10·50, D £14·50; WB £80 (2nts HB); [10% V w/e, w/d 2 nts]
cc Access, Amex, B'card/Visa, Diners.

CROWTHORNE Berkshire. Map 12C2

Pop 5,465. Staines 15, London 32, Bagshot 6½, Basingstoke 17, Farnham 13, Henley-on-Thames 15, Reading 12, Windsor 13.
EC Fri. **Golf** Downshire 18h.

★★★ **Waterloo,** Duke's Ride, RG11 7NW ☎(0344) 777711 Tx: 848139 Fax: (0344) 778913

In tree-lined corner of village, this period hotel has a modern extension. (THF). Fr, It, Du
58 bedrs, 58 en suite; TV; tcf
dogs, ns; P, coach; child facs; con 50
LD 9.30
£ B&B £77–£97 (w/e £35), B&B (double) £89·75–£109·75; L £9·95, D £13·95; WB £40 (2nts HB)
cc Access, Amex, B'card/Visa, Diners.

CROYDE Devon. Map 3A4

Barnstaple 10, London 203, Ilfracombe 9.

★★ **Croyde Bay House,** Braughton EX33 1PA ☎(0271) 890270

Pleasing Victorian brick building enjoying panoramic views of quiet beach. Open Mar–15 Nov.
7 bedrs, 7 en suite; TV; tcf
dogs, ns; P 8; child facs
LD 8, nr lunch. Resid lic
£ B&B £27–£43, B&B (double) £54–£70; HB weekly £230–£260; D £15
cc Access, B'card/Visa; dep.

★★ **C** **R** **Kittiwell,** St Mary's Rd, EX33 1PG ☎(0271) 890247

Lovely thatched 16th century Devon longhouse converted to hotel. Set in centre of village.
12 bedrs, 12 en suite; TV; tcf
TV, dogs, ns; P 20, coach; child facs
LD 9.30, nr Mon–Sat lunch. Resid & Rest lic
£ B&B £46–£52, B&B (double) £80–£90; HB weekly £250–£270; L £8, D £13; WB £80 (2 nts)
cc Access, Amex, B'card/Visa, Diners; dep.
(*See advertisement on p. 217*)

Whiteleaf at Croyde (Highly Acclaimed), EX33 1PN ☎(0271) 890266. *Guest House*. It
£ B&B £27–£29; HB weekly £235–£255.

CROYDE BAY Devon. Map 3A4

Barnstaple 10, London 203, Blackmoor Gate 6, Ilfracombe 8½, Woolacombe 5.

Moorsands House (Acclaimed), Moor La, EX33 1NP ☎Croyde (0271) 890781. *Private Hotel*. Open Mar–Oct. Fr
£ B&B £18–£20; HB weekly £150·50–£164·50; [10% V]

 EC *early closing* **MD** *market day* *country house hotel* *ns (NS) no smoking areas* *tcf tea/coffee facilities*

Cromer (Norfolk)

CLIFTONVILLE HOTEL

RAC ** **CROMER**

On the West Cliff – Facing Sea – 40 rooms with sea view – Lift to all floors

FULLY LICENSED

Radio & direct dial Telephones, and Televisions in all rooms. Wing with private suites. Specially reduced terms for children sharing rooms with parents, also out of season periods October to May.

OPEN ALL YEAR **SPECIAL 2 & 4 DAY "LET'S GO" BREAKS AVAILABLE**

Brochure and Terms available on request.

Tel: CROMER 0263 512543 Fax: 0263 511764 *Under personal supervision of Proprietor:* **T. A. Bolton**

C

Croyde (North Devon)

Magnificent 16th century thatched roof Devon long house within walking distance of the sea. Interior has considerable character with its wealth of beamed ceilings and walls creating an old world charm. the 12 well appointed bedrooms, all ensuite, some with 4 poster beds have all been recently renovated. Restaurant offers à la Carte and table d'Hôte menus prepared by our Chef de Cuisine using fresh vegetables. Wide choice of local and international wines. Walking, golf, fishing, surfing and touring minutes from the hotel. Midweek/ weekend breaks. Christmas & New Year House Parties.

16th Century

Kittiwell House Hotel & Restaurant

Croyde, N. Devon. (0271) 890247

Croydon (Surrey)

CLEAN, COMFORTABLE, QUIET

THAT'S THE

CENTRAL HOTEL

3-5 SOUTH PARK HILL ROAD, CROYDON CR2 7DY

081-688 5644 RAC ** 081-688 0840

Ideal for the businessman to put his feet up after a hard day, or as a base while visiting friends, or London. Informal, but good service from our staff, in both our bar and the dining-room, serving well cooked English food, à la carte. Weddings, parties and private functions catered for.

All rooms have: Colour TV, teasmade, telephone, trouser press, hair dryer.

Also available: Four poster and self-catering apartments.

CROYDON Greater London (Surrey). Map 8C2
RAC Office, *PO Box 8, Marco Polo House, 3–5 Lansdowne Rd, Croydon, CR9 2JH* ☎081-686 2314.
Pop 320,500. Thornton Heath 2, London 10, Bromley 6, Epsom 8½, Mitcham 4, Purley 2½, Westerham 12.
See Plan, p 219.
MD Daily. **P** See Plan. **Golf** Addington Palace 18h. Addington Court Public Courses 18h and 9h, Shirley Park 18h, Selsdon Park Hotel Course 18h, Croham Hurst 18h. **See** Parish Church, Archbishop's Palace.
ℹ Katharine St. ☎081-688 3627 ext 45

★★★★ **Holiday Inn,** 7 Altyre Rd, CR9 5AA ☎081-680 9200 Tx: 8956268 Fax: 081-760 0426 ♿
Modern hotel in central position. Indoor swimming pool, squash, sauna, solarium, gymnasium. Fr, It, Gr
214 bedrs, 214 en suite; TV; tcf
lift, dogs, ns; P 12, G 100, coach; child facs; con 300
LD 10.15
£ B&B £103·50 (w/e £37), B&B (double) £127; L £14·95, D £15·95; WB
cc Access, Amex, B'card/Visa, Diners.

★★★★ **Selsdon Park,** Sanderstead, South Croydon, CR2 8YA ☎081-657 8811 Tx: 945003 Fax: 081-651 6171

Greatly enlarged Tudor mansion in 200 acres. Outstanding sports facilities. Indoor/outdoor swimming pools, golf, putting, tennis, squash, sauna, solarium, gymnasium, billiards. Fr, De, It, Es, Du
170 bedrs, 170 en suite; TV; tcf
lift, dogs, ns; P 250, U 6 (£2), coach; child facs; con 150
LD 9.15
£ B&B £115–£129 (w/e £95), B&B (double) £138–£170; HB weekly £637–£742; L £17·50, D £20; WB
cc Access, Amex, B'card/Visa, CB, Diners; dep.
(See advertisement on p. 220)

★★★ **Post House,** Purley Way, CR9 4LT ☎081-688 5185 Tx: 893814 Fax: 081-681 6438

Modernised hotel, reconstructed from former Airport reception building. (THF)
85 bedrs, 85 en suite; TV; tcf
dogs, ns; P 80, coach; child facs; con 200
LD 10, bar meals only Sat lunch
£ room £81–£91 (w/e £39·50), double room £91–£101; Bk £7·50, L £9·95, D £13·95; WB £38
cc Access, Amex, B'card/Visa, Diners.

★★ **Briarley** 8 Outram Rd, CR0 6XE ☎081-654 1000 Fax: 081-656 6084

Three-storey hotel in quiet road; Victorian building with modern facilities. Fr, De
18 bedrs, 18 en suite; annexe 20 bedrs, 20 en suite; TV; tcf
TV, dogs, ns; P 30, coach; child facs; con 40
LD 10, bar meals only Mon–Sat lunch, Sun dinner
£ B&B £55 (w/e £40), B&B (double) £65 (w/e £50); [10% V]; D £10·50; [10% V]
cc Access, Amex, B'card/Visa, Diners; dep.

★★ **Central,** 3–5 South Park Hill Rd, CR2 7DY ☎081-688 5644 Fax: 081-760 0861
Owner-run hotel, in former private residences in quiet street. Convenient for station. De
23 bedrs, 19 en suite, 1 ba; TV; tcf
TV, dogs; P 30, coach; child facs; con 40
LD 8, bar meals only Mon–Thu lunch & Fri–Sun dinner.
£ B&B £38–£48 (w/e £33), B&B (double) £60; HB weekly £350–£420; L £6·50, D £12; WB £104 (3 nts)
cc Access, B'card/Visa; dep.
(See advertisement on p. 217)

★ **Oakwood,** 69–71 Outram Rd, CR0 6XJ ☎081-654 2835 Fax: 081-656 6084
Small hotel in quiet side street; run by proprietors. Sauna, solarium.
16 bedrs, 16 en suite; TV; tcf
TV, dogs; P 8; child facs

⑨⑨ **Windsor Castle,** 415 Brighton Rd, CR2 6EJ ☎081-680 4559 Fax: 081-680 4559
Modernised Queen Anne coaching inn with recent extensions of red brick.
30 bedrs, 30 en suite; TV; tcf
TV, dogs, ns; P 65, coach; child facs

Kirkdale (Acclaimed) 22 St Peter's Rd, CR0 1HD ☎081-688 5898 Fax: 081-667 0817. Closed Xmas. *Hotel.*
£ B&B £23–£28

Markington (Acclaimed), 9 Haling Park Rd, South Croydon, CR2 6NG ☎081-681 6494 Fax: 081-688 6530. *Hotel.* Closed 23 Dec–2 Jan.
£ B&B £30–£48; [10% w/e]

Alpine, 16 Moreton Rd, South Croydon CR2 7DL ☎081-688 6116. Fax: 081-667 1822. *Hotel.*
£ B&B £33–£42, HB weekly £260–£324

Beech House, 7–11 Beech House Rd, CR0 1JQ ☎081-688 4385 Fax: 081-760 0861. *Private Hotel.*

Lonsdale, 158 Lower Addiscombe Rd, CR0 6AG ☎081-654 2276. *Hotel. Billiards.* Fr
£ B&B £32–£37 HB weekly £285·50–£321·50; [10% V w/d, 5% V w/e].

CRUDWELL Wiltshire. Map 20B1
Pop 910. Swindon 19, London 96, Bristol 30, Chippenham 13, Cirencester 7½.

★★ **H** **C** **Crudwell Court,** SN16 9EP ☎(066 67) 7194 Fax: (066 67) 7853

A stone-built, 17th century rectory with restful decor and some fine furnishings. The graceful rooms look out over the lovely walled gardens. Swimming pool. Fr
15 bedrs, 15 en suite; TV; tcf
dogs, ns; P50; child facs; con 47
LD 9.30
£ B&B £37–£60, B&B (double) £70–£90; HB weekly £280–£335; L £15·50, D £15·50; WB £95; [10% V]
cc Access, Amex, B'card/Visa, Diners; dep.

★★ **Mayfield House,** nr Malmesbury SN16 9EW ☎(066 67) 409 Fax: (066 67) 7977
Small Victorian former private house with sympathetic extension. Attractive garden. Fr
20 bedrs, 20 en suite; TV; tcf
TV, dogs; P 50, coach; child facs; con 15
LD 9. Resid & Rest lic
£ B&B £40–£42, B&B (double) £53–£56; L £6·95, D £10
cc Access, Amex, B'card/Visa; dep.

CUCKFIELD West Sussex. Map 6C2
Pop 4,000. Redhill 17, London 37, Brighton 14, Crawley 9½, Haywards Heath 2, Horsham 11, Worthing 22.
EC Wed. **Golf** Haywards Heath 18h.

★★★ **H** **C** **R** **Ockenden Manor,** Ockenden La, RH17 5LD ☎Haywards Heath (0444) 416111 Fax: (0444) 415549

16th century manor house with lovely beamed and panelled public rooms. Fr, Du.
22 bedrs, 22 en suite; TV; tcf
P 40; child facs; con 25
LD 9.15. Resid & Rest lic
£ B&B £60–£90, B&B (double) £90–£150; L £15·50, D £21·95; WB £120
cc Access, Amex, B'card/Visa, Diners; dep.

★★ **Hilton Park,** RH17 5EG ☎Haywards Heath (0444) 454555
Family-run country house in 3 acres with fine views of Downs.

 EC *early closing* **MD** *market day* *country house hotel* *ns (NS) no smoking areas* *tcf tea/coffee facilities*

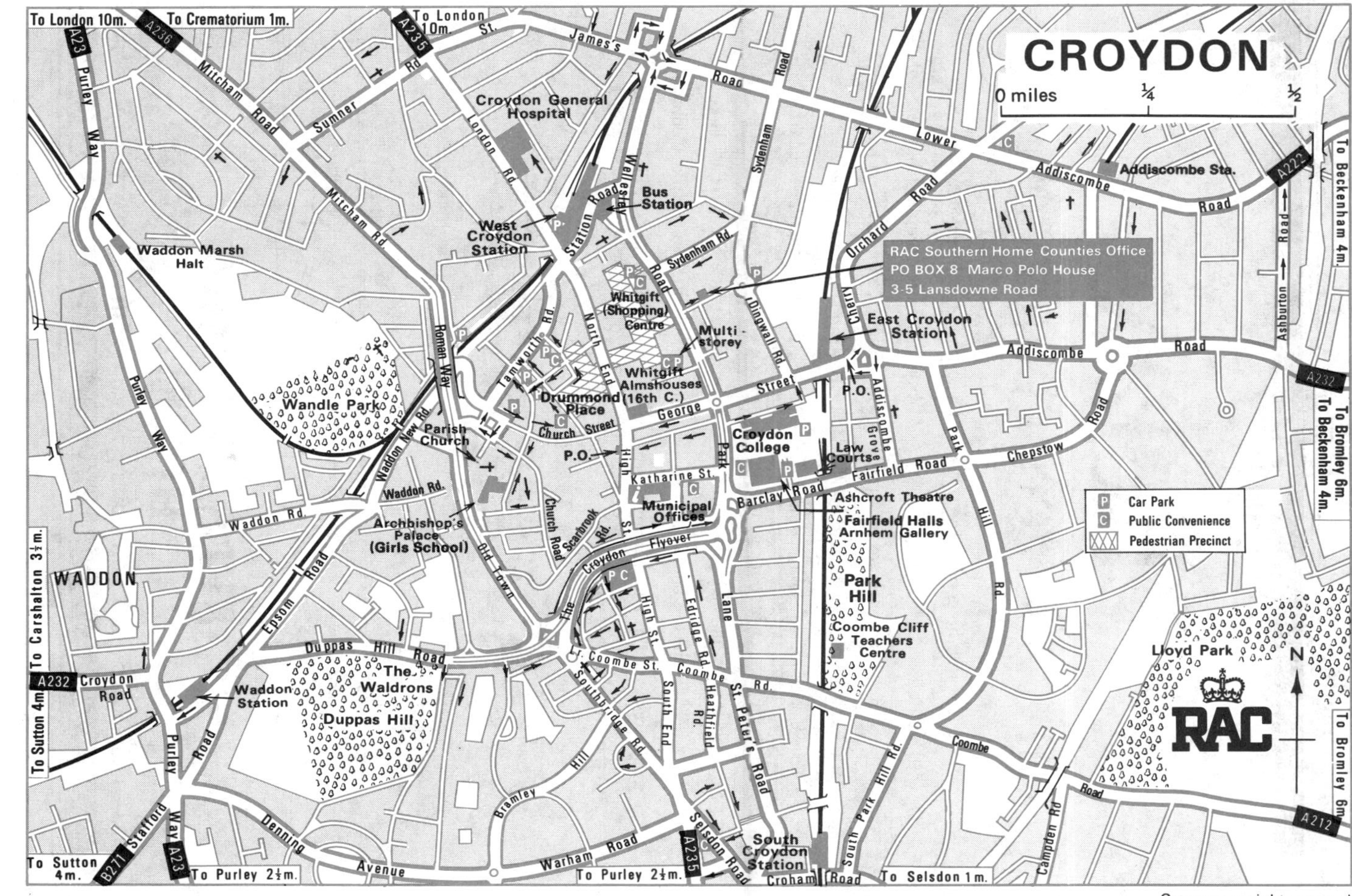
CROYDON
0 miles
1/4
1/2
RAC Southern Home Counties Office
PO BOX 8 Marco Polo House
3-5 Lansdowne Road
Car Park
Public Convenience
Pedestrian Precinct
RAC
N
To London 10m.
To Crematorium 1m.
To London 10m.
To Beckenham 4m.
To Bromley 6m.
To Beckenham 4m.
To Bromley 6m.
To Selsdon 1m.
To Purley 2½m.
To Purley 2½m.
To Sutton 4m.
To Sutton 4m.
To Carshalton 3½m.
East Croydon Station
West Croydon Station
South Croydon Station
Waddon Station
Waddon Marsh Halt
Addiscombe Sta.
Croydon General Hospital
Bus Station
Whitgift (Shopping) Centre
Whitgift Almshouses (16th C.)
Multi-storey
Drummond Place
Croydon College
Law Courts
Municipal Offices
Ashcroft Theatre
Fairfield Halls
Arnhem Gallery
Parish Church
Archbishop's Palace (Girls School)
Wandle Park
The Waldrons
Duppas Hill
Park Hill
Coombe Cliff Teachers Centre
Lloyd Park
WADDON
Crown copyright reserved

C

🛏13 bedrs, 9 en suite, 3 ba; TV; tcf
🏨 dogs, ns; P 50, U 3; child facs; con 30
✕ LD 8.30. Resid & Rest lic
£ B&B £48, B&B (double) £66; L £7·50, D £14·50
cc Access, Amex, B'card/Visa, CB, Diners.

DALSTON Cumbria. Map 43C2

M6 (jn 43) 5½, Penrith 20, London 296, Brampton 13, Carlisle 4½, Wigton 8½.

★★★ Dalston Hall, CA5 7JX
☎(0228) 710271 Tx: 94017266
Fax: (0228) 711273
Magnificent 15th century fortified mansion set in 7 acres of landscaped gardens. Putting.
🛏14 bedrs, 13 en suite, 2 ba; TV; tcf
🏨 TV, dogs; P 40; child facs; con 120

DARESBURY Cheshire. Map 32C1

Pop 1,399. Northwich 10, London 183, Chester 15, Knutsford 13, Liverpool 17, St Helens 13, Warrington 5.
EC Wed. **Golf** Runcorn 18h. **See** Church.

★★★ H C Lord Daresbury, WA4 4BB
☎Warrington (0925) 67331 Tx: 629330
Fax: (0925) 65615

Well-situated modern hotel. Indoor swimming pool, squash, sauna, solarium, gymnasium, billiards. Fr, De. (DeV)
🛏141 bedrs, 141 en suite; TV; tcf
🏨 lift, dogs, ns; P 400, coach; child facs; con 300
✕ LD 9.45
£ B&B £80 (w/e £55); B&B (double) £90 (w/e £80); L £14·95, D £14·95; WB £95 (HB 2nts)
cc Access, Amex, B'card/Visa, Diners.

DARLASTON West Midlands. Map 22B2

Dudley 6, London 126, M6 (junc. 9) 3, Cannock 10, Wolverhampton 5.

Hotel Petite, (Acclaimed) Stafford Rd WS10 8UA ☎021-526 5482. *Hotel.*

DARLEY DALE Derbyshire. Map 24A1

Matlock 3, London 147, Chesterfield 10.

★★ Red House, Old Rd, DE4 2ER
☎Matlock (0629) 734854.
Gabled Victorian house in an acre of attractive gardens just off the A6. Fr
🛏7 bedrs, 7 en suite; annexe 2 beds, 2 en suite; TV; tcf
🏨 dogs; P 14; child facs
✕ LD 9, nr Sat lunch. Resid & Rest lic
£ B&B £43, B&B (double) £60–£70; L £10·95, D £16·50
cc Access, Amex, B'card/Visa, Diners.

DARLINGTON Durham. Map 45A1

Pop 97,219. A66(M) 2, London 244, Barnard Castle 19, Durham 18, Leyburn 24, Northallerton 16, Stockton-on-Tees 11, West Auckland 10.
EC Wed. **MD** Mon, Thur, Sat. **Golf** Darlington 18h, Blackwell 18h. **See** Stephenson's Locomotion No 1' on view at North Rd Rail Museum, St Cuthbert's Church (12th–15th cent), Museum and Art Gallery.
ℹ Library, Crown St. ☎(0325) 469858

★★★★ Blackwell Grange Moat House, Blackwell Grange, DL3 8QH ☎(0325) 380898 Tx: 587272 Fax: (0325) 380899

Imposing brick-built 17th century mansion with later extensions in pleasant grounds. Indoor swimming pool, golf, putting, tennis, sauna, solarium, gymnasium. De, Hu (QMH)
🛏99 bedrs, 99 en suite; TV; tcf
🏨 lift, dogs, ns; P 250, G 3, coach; child facs; con 300
✕ LD 9.45, bar meals only Sat lunch
£ B&B £75–£120 (w/e £52), B&B (double) £100–£148; L £9·75, D £13·75; WB
cc Access, Amex, B'card/Visa, Diners; dep.

★★★ St. George, Tees-side Airport, DL2 1RH ☎(0325) 332631 Tx: 587623
Fax: (0325) 333851

Modern building conveniently set just 200 yards from the airport. Squash, sauna, solarium. (MtCh)
🛏59 bedrs, 59 en suite; TV; tcf
🏨 dogs, ns; P 200, U 10 (£2), coach; child facs; con 200
✕ LD 9.45; bar meals only Sat lunch & Sun dinner
£ B&B £55–£65; B&B (double) £65–£75 HB weekly £227·50; L £7·50, D £11·75; WB £32·50; [10%V w/e, 5%V w/d]
cc Access, Amex, B'card/Visa, Diners; dep.

★★★ Stakis White Horse, Harrowgate Hill, DL1 3AD ☎(0325) 382121 Tx: 778704
Fax: (0325) 355953
Two-storey red-brick former inn with 4-storey modern accommodation extension. (Sk)
🛏40 bedrs, 40 en suite; TV; tcf
🏨 lift, dogs, ns; P 150, coach; child facs; con 100

★★★ Swallow Kings Head, Priestgate, DL1 1NW ☎(0325) 380222 Tx: 587112
Fax: (0325) 382006

Victorian building of character in the centre of the town. (Sw)
🛏60 bedrs, 60 en suite; TV; tcf
🏨 lift, dogs; ns; P 30, coach; child facs; con 250
✕ LD 9.45, coffee shop only lunch
£ B&B £58, B&B (double) £75; L £9·75, D £11·50; WB £75 (HB); [10% V]
cc Access, Amex, B'card/Visa, Diners.

DARRINGTON West Yorkshire. Map 38C2

Pop 1,125. A1 (M) 8, London 176, Barnsley 14, Doncaster 13, Goole 19, Leeds 16, Pontefract 2½, Selby 13.
EC Thur. **Golf** Pontefract 18h. **See** Old Windmill, Church.

★★ Darrington, Great North Rd, WF8 3BL
☎Pontefract (0977) 791458
1930s brick-built hotel with easy access to nearby trunk road. Sauna, solarium. (SN)
🛏28 bedrs, 28 en suite; TV; tcf
🏨 dogs; P 120, coach; child facs; con 70
✕ LD 9.30, bar meals only Mon & Sat lunch, nr Sun dinner
£ B&B £42, B&B (double) £52; D £6·50 [V w/e]
cc Access, Amex, B'card/Visa, Diners.

DARTMOUTH Devon. Map 3C1

Pop 5,541. Totnes 13 (Fy 11), London 205, Kingsbridge 15, Plymouth 28, Torquay (Fy) 10.
EC Wed. **MD** Tue, Fri. **Golf** Churston 18h. **See** St Pyrroc's Church, Butterwalk, Castle, St Saviour's Church (14th cent), Mayflower Stone, Newcomen Engine House.
ℹ 11 Duke St. ☎(080 43) 4224

★★★ Dart Marina, Sandquay, TQ6 9PH
☎(0803) 832580
Modern hotel near yacht marina; panoramic views over River Dart. (THF)
🛏31 bedrs, 31 en suite; annexe 4 bedrs, 4 en suite; TV; tcf
🏨 dogs, ns; P 100, child facs
✕ LD 9
£ B&B £65–£75, B&B (double) £86–£116; HB weekly £272–£340; L £8·50, D £15
cc Access, Amex, B'card/Visa, Diners.

★★★ **Royal Castle,** 11 The Quay, TQ6 9PS ☎(0803) 833033 Fax: (0803) 835445

16th century coaching inn of historic interest. Situated on quayside. Fr, It
25 bedrs, 25 en suite; TV; tcf
dogs, ns; P 3 (£1), G 8, coach; child facs; con 60
LD 9·45, bar meals only Mon/Sat lunch
£ B&B £31–£44, B&B (double) £55–£88; L £8·75 D £13·50; WB £89
cc Access, Amex, B'card/Visa; dep.

DARWEN Lancashire. Map 33A4

Pop 29,769. Bolton 9, London 204, Blackburn 4, Preston 14.
EC Tue. **MD** Mon, Fri, Sat. **Golf** Darwen 18h.

★★★ **Whitehall,** Springbank, Whitehall, BB3 2JU ☎(0254) 701595
Fax: (0254) 773426
Attractive stone-built hotel in secluded grounds one mile from town centre. Indoor swimming pool, sauna, solarium, snooker.
Fr, Es.
18 bedrs, 14 en suite, 2 ba; TV; tcf
dogs; P 60, coach; child facs; con 50
LD 9.30; Resid & Rest & Club lic
£ B&B £50 (w/e £22·50), B&B (double) £60; L £8, D £10; [10% V]
cc Access, Amex, B'card/Visa, Diners.

DATCHET Berkshire. Map 13A3

M4 (jn 5) 2, London 19, Reading 20, Slough 2, Staines 5, Windsor 2.

★★ **Manor,** The Village Green, SL3 9EA
☎(0753) 43442 Tx: 41363
Fax: (0202) 299182

A gabled, half-timbered building, part 18th century, in village overlooking the Green.
Fr, Es.
30 bedrs, 30 en suite; TV; tcf
dogs; P 20, coach; child facs; con 120
LD 9.45, bar meals only lunch
£ B&B £59–£79, (w/e £34·50) L £10, D £18; WB £34·50
cc Access, Amex, B'card/Visa, Diners.

DAVENTRY Northamptonshire. Map 21A3

M1 (jn 16) 9, London 78, Banbury 17, Royal Leamington Spa 18, Rugby 13.
ℹ Moot Hall, Market Sq. ☎(0327) 300277

★★★ **Staverton Park**, Staverton, NN1 6JT
☎(0327) 705911
A new hotel in rural surroundings, 1 mile west of Daventry. Well-furnished spacious rooms. Golf.
52 bedrs, 52 en suite; TV; tcf
(*See advertisement on p. 223*)

DAWLISH Devon Map 3C2

Pop 10,000. Honiton 26, London 179, Exeter 13, Newton Abbot 9, Okehampton 30, Torquay 11.
EC Thur. **Golf** Dawlish Warren 18h.
ℹ The Lawn. ☎ (0626) 863589

★★★ **Langstone Cliff,** Dawlish Warren, EX7 0NA ☎(0626) 865155
Fax: (0626) 867166

A rambling, white-painted hotel overlooking the sea, set in 12 acres of lawns and woods north of Dawlish. Indoor & outdoor swimming pools, tennis, solarium, snooker.
64 bedrs, 64 en suite; TV; tcf
lift, TV, dogs; P 200, coach; child facs; con 400
LD 9
£ B&B £40–£45, B&B (double) £70–£90; HB weekly £280; L £9, D £11; WB £80 [5% V]
cc Access, Amex, B'card/Visa, Diners.

West Hatch (Acclaimed), 34 West Cliff, EX7 9DN ☎(0626) 864211. *Private Hotel.*
£ B&B £24–£31·50, HB weekly £138·50–£172; dep.

Mimosa, 11 Barton Terr, EX7 9QH
☎(0626) 863283. *Guest House.*
£ B&B £10–£11; HB weekly £97–£103; dep.

DEAL Kent. Map 7C3

Canterbury 16, London 74, Dover 8, Ramsgate 13.
ℹ Town Hall, High St ☎(0304) 369576

Sutherland House, 186 London Rd, CT14 9PT ☎(0304) 362853. *Private Hotel.*
£ B&B £38; HB weekly £350–£504.

DEDDINGTON Oxfordshire. Map 21A2

Oxford 17, London 73, Banbury 7, Bicester 8½, Chipping Norton 12.

★★ C **Holcombe,** High St, OX5 4SL
☎(0869) 38274 Tx: 83147
Fax: (0869) 37167

Cotswold-stone, 17th-century hotel in centre of village. Fr, De, Es, Ar
17 bedrs, 16 en suite; TV; tcf
dogs; ns, P 50, coach; child facs; con 30
LD 10
£ B&B £54–£68; B&B (double) £66–£80; HB weekly £210–£252; L fr £12·95, D fr £16·95; WB £45 (HB) [10% V]
cc Access, Amex, B'card/Visa, Diners; dep.

DEDHAM Essex. Map 27B2

Pop 1,500. Colchester 7, London 63, Clacton 17, Harwich 15, Ipswich 11, Sudbury 14.
EC Wed. **Golf** Stoke by Nayland 18h. **See** 15th cent Church, Castle House, Flatford Mill & Dedham Vale (Constable country).
ℹ Countryside Centre, Duchy Barn, The Drift. ☎(0206) 323447

★★★ H C R **Dedham Vale,** Stratford Rd, CO7 6HW ☎Colchester (0206) 322273 Tx: 987083 Fax: (0206) 322752
Sumptuously appointed 19th century country house overlooking Dedham Vale.
Fr, De, Du
6 bedrs, 6 en suite; TV
P 100; child facs; con 16
LD 9.30, nr Sat lunch & Sun dinner. Rest lic
£ B&B £70–£75, B&B (double) £85–£95; L £10, D £20; [5% V Oct–Apr]
cc Access, B'card/Visa.

★★★ **Maison Talbooth,** Stratford Rd, CO7 6HN ☎Colchester (0206) 322367
Tx: 987083 Fax: (0206) 322752

Luxuriously furnished Victorian country house in gardens overlooking Dedham Vale.
10 bedrs, 10 en suite; TV
P 20; child facs
LD 9. Resid & Rest lic
£ B&B £80–£105, B&B (double) £100–£135; HB weekly £560–£735; L £16; WB £200
cc Access, B'card/Visa.

DELPH Lancashire. Map 30C4

Oldham 5, London 188, Glossop 15, Huddersfield 13, Rochdale 6.

Old Bell, Huddersfield Rd, Saddleworth, OL3 5EG ☎Saddleworth (0457) 870130
Well-restored 18th-century stone-built inn on edge of village on A62. Fr
10 bedrs, 9 en suite, (1 sh); TV; tcf
dogs; P 25; child facs; con 20
LD 9.30
£ B&B £38·50–£45·50 (w/e £21·80), B&B (double) £54·50; L £7·50, D £10·50; [10%V]
cc Access, B'card/Visa.

EC *early closing* **MD** *market day* *country house hotel* *ns (NS) no smoking areas* *tcf tea/coffee facilities*

Darlington (Co Durham)

D

Daventry (Northamptonshire)

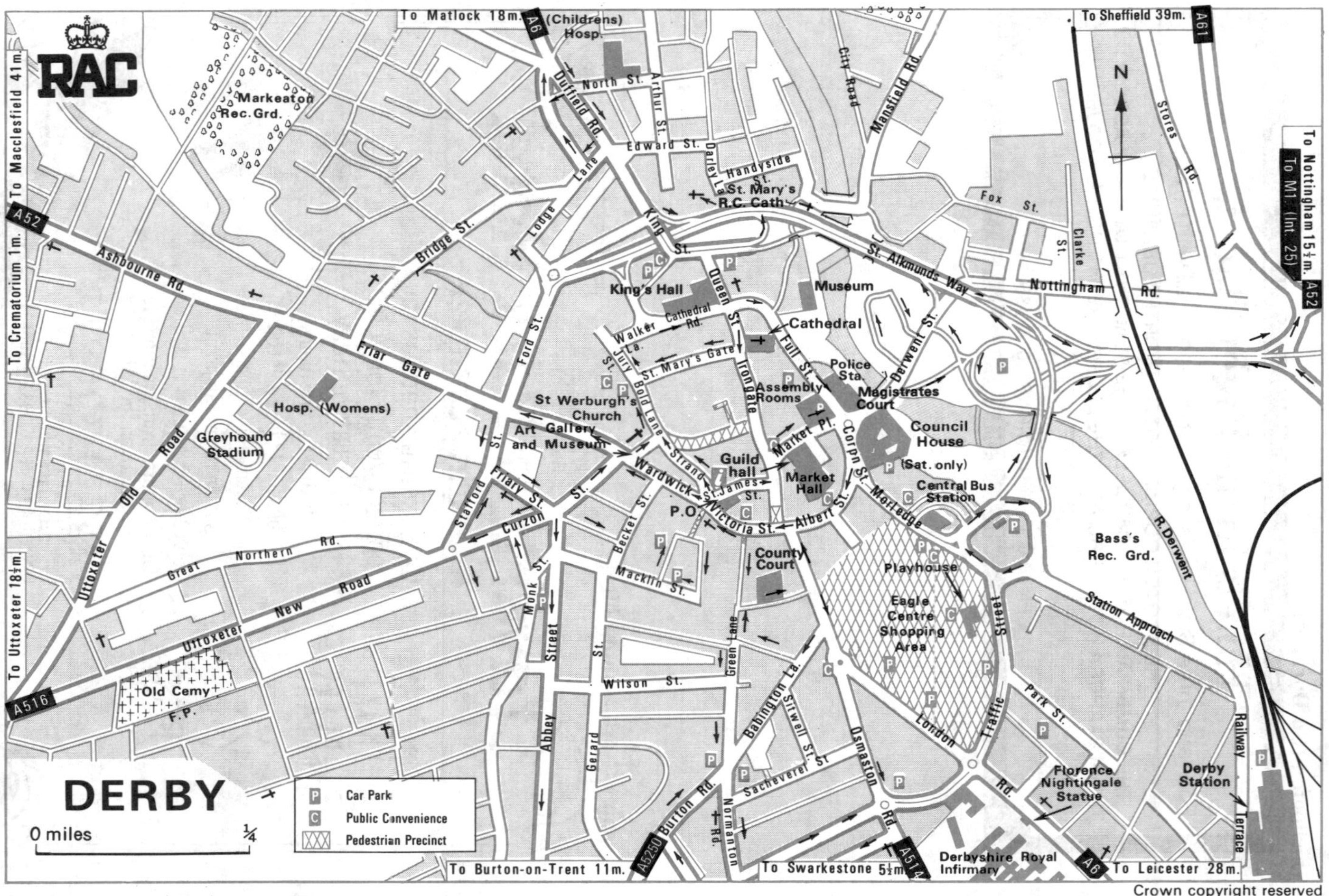

EC *early closing* **MD** *market day* *country house hotel* *ns (NS) no smoking areas* *tcf tea/coffee facilities*

DERBY Derbyshire. Map 24C1

Pop 217,000. M1 (jn 25) 10, London 126, Ashbourne 13, Ashby-de-la-Zouch 14, Burton-upon-Trent 11, Loughborough 16, Mansfield 23, Matlock 18, Nottingham 15. See Plan, p. 224.
MD Tue, Thur, Fri, Sat. **P** See Plan. **Golf** Allestree Park 18h. Sinfin 18h, Mickleover 18h. **See** Cathedral, St Werburgh's Church, RC Church of St Mary by Pugin, St Mary's Bridge, St Peter's Church, Sadler Gate.
ℹ Central Library, The Wardwick. ☎(0332) 290664

★★★ Breadsall Priory, Moor Rd, Morley DE7 6DL ☎(0332) 832235 Tx: 37409 Fax: (0332) 833509 ♿

Large stone-built mansion in parkland setting. Indoor swimming pool, golf, putting, tennis, squash, sauna, solarium, gymnasium, billiards. Completion of refurbishment expected August 1990.
🛏 15 bedrs, 15 en suite; annexe 79 bedrs, 79 en suite; TV; tcf
🏨 lift, ns; P 200, coach; child facs; con 80.

★★★ Crest, Pastures Hill, Littleover, DE3 7BA ☎(0332) 514933 Tx: 377081 Fax: (0332) 518668 ♿

Traditional hotel with modern bedrooms. In country setting yet handy for town. (Cr/THF)
🛏 64 bedrs, 64 en suite; TV; tcf
🏨 dogs, ns; P 200, coach; child facs; con 45
£ B&B £80·95–£94·95 (w/e £35), B&B (double) £100·90–£114·90; L £5·95; D £14·30
cc Access, Amex, B'card/Visa, Diners.

★★★ Gables, 119 London Rd, DE1 2QR ☎(0332) 40633 Fax: (0332) 293502

Brick-built city centre hotel near to station. Closed 24 Dec–2 Jan
🛏 101 bedrs, 101 en suite, 1 ba; TV; tcf
🏨 P 90, coach; con 170
✕ LD 9.45
£ B&B £32–£57 (w/e £22), B&B (double) £44–£66; L £7·50, D £10·50; [5% V w/e]
cc Access, Amex, B'card/Visa.

★★★ H C R International, Burton Rd, DE3 6AD ☎(0332) 369321 Tx: 377759 Fax: (0332) 294430
Privately owned hotel in well-modernised Victorian house close to city centre. Fr, It
🛏 61 bedrs, 61 en suite, annexe 10 bedrs, 10 en suite; TV; tcf
🏨 lift, dogs; P 70, coach; child facs; con 60
✕ LD 10.30. Resid & Rest lic
£ B&B £25–£50 (w/e £25), B&B (double) £35–£70; L £6·95, D £11·25; WB £30
cc Access, Amex, B'card/Visa, Diners; dep.

★★★ Midland, Midland Rd, DE1 2SQ ☎(0332) 45894 Tx: 378373 Fax: (0332) 293522

Dignified and spacious 3-storey mid-19th century hotel next to station. Fr, De, Closed 25 & 26 Dec, 1 Jan
🛏 60 bedrs, 60 en suite, TV; tcf
🏨 dogs; P 95, G 15, coach; child facs; con 150
✕ LD 10, bar meals only Sat lunch
£ B&B £57·50–£74, B&B (double) £69·50–£86; HB weekly £402·50–£598·50; L £9·50, D £11·50; WB
cc Access, Amex, B'card/Visa, Diners.

★★★ Pennine, Macklin St, DE1 1LF ☎(0332) 41741 Fax: (0332) 294549

Large modern hotel in city centre with conference facilities. (DeV)
🛏 94 bedrs, 94 en suite; TV; tcf
🏨 lift, dogs; P 24, coach; child facs; con 450
✕ LD 9.45, nr Sat, Sun lunch
£ B&B £60 (w/e £44), B&B (double) £75–£85; L £7, D £12; WB £60 (HB) [V]
cc Access, Amex, B'card/Visa, Diners.

★★ Aston Court, Midland Rd, DE1 2SL ☎(0332) 42716
Medium-sized hotel adjacent to station to south of city centre.

★★ Clarendon, Midland Rd, DE1 2SL ☎(0332) 365235 Fax: (0332) 293522
Pleasant city centre hotel constructed at end of the Victorian era.
🛏 50 bedrs, 20 en suite, (8 sh), 6 ba; TV; tcf
🏨 TV, dogs; P 100, coach; child facs; con 50
✕ LD 9.30, bar meals only Sat lunch & Sun dinner
£ B&B £19·50 (w/e £15·50), B&B (double) £45 (w/e £38·50); L fr £3·95, D fr £8·95 [10% V]
cc Access, Amex, B'card/Visa, Diners; dep.

★★ R Kedleston, Kedleston Rd, DE6 4JD ☎(0332) 559202 Fax: (0332) 558822 ♿
A mid-18th century listed building situated in delightful countryside NW of Derby.
🛏 14 bedrs, 14 en suite; 2 ba; TV; tcf
🏨 child facs
✕ LD 9.30; bar meals only Sun dinner
£ L £8·25, D £11·95
cc Access, Amex, B'card/Visa, Diners; dep.

Rollz, (Acclaimed) 684 Osmaston Rd, DE2 8GT ☎(0332) 41026. *Hotel*
£ B&B £18·40; HB weekly £169

Rangemoor, 67 Macklin St, DE1 1LF ☎(0332) 47252. *Hotel.*
£ B&B £21·50.

DEREHAM Norfolk.

See EAST DEREHAM

DERSINGHAM Norfolk. Map 34C2

Pop 3,268. King's Lynn 9, London 108, East Dereham 25, Fakenham 16, Swaffham 17.
EC Thur. **Golf** Hunstanton 18h. **See** Church, Tithe Barn, Sandringham Gdns 2 m SE.

Westdene House (Acclaimed), 60 Hunstanton Rd, PE31 6HQ ☎(0485) 540395. *Hotel*
£ B&B £16–£18; HB weekly £148–£160.

DEVIZES Wiltshire. Map 5A3

Pop 11,000. Marlborough 14, London 86, Amesbury 18, Bath 19, Chippenham 11, Pewsey 12, Swindon 15, Warminster 15.
EC Wed. **MD** Thur, Sat.
Golf Bishops Cannings 18h. **See** Market Cross, St John's Church, Wiltshire Archaeological Society Museum, Town Hall.

★★ Bear, Market Pl, SN10 1HS ☎(0380) 722444 Fax: (0380) 722450

A 16th century former coaching inn overlooking attractive market square. Closed 25 & 26 Dec.
🛏 24 bedrs, 24 en suite, 1 ba; TV; tcf
🏨 TV, dogs, ns; P 18 (50p), G 6 (50p), coach; child facs; con 120
✕ LD 10, bar meals only Sun dinner
£ B&B £45, B&B (double) £60–£80; L £10·75, D £14; WB £80 (2 nts HB); [10% V]
cc Access, B'card/Visa.

Doncaster (Yorkshire)

THE CAMPANILE HOTEL – Doncaster

Doncaster Leisure Park, Bawtry Road, Doncaster DN4 7PD

Tel: (0302) 370770 Telex: 547942

Restaurant Hotel

Campanile

Part of the international budget hotel chain "Campanile", the hotel offers 50 comfortable double or twin rooms with en-suite bathrooms, and tea/coffee making facilities, radio alarm, remote control colour TV, Sky TV and direct dial telephone at **competitive rates.**

Our informal restaurant provides a variety of home-cooked French/Continental cuisine, and personal service at **affordable prices.**

Our seminar room is available for business meetings or small functions.

Your hosts: Caroline & Richard Summers

Dovedale (Derbyshire)

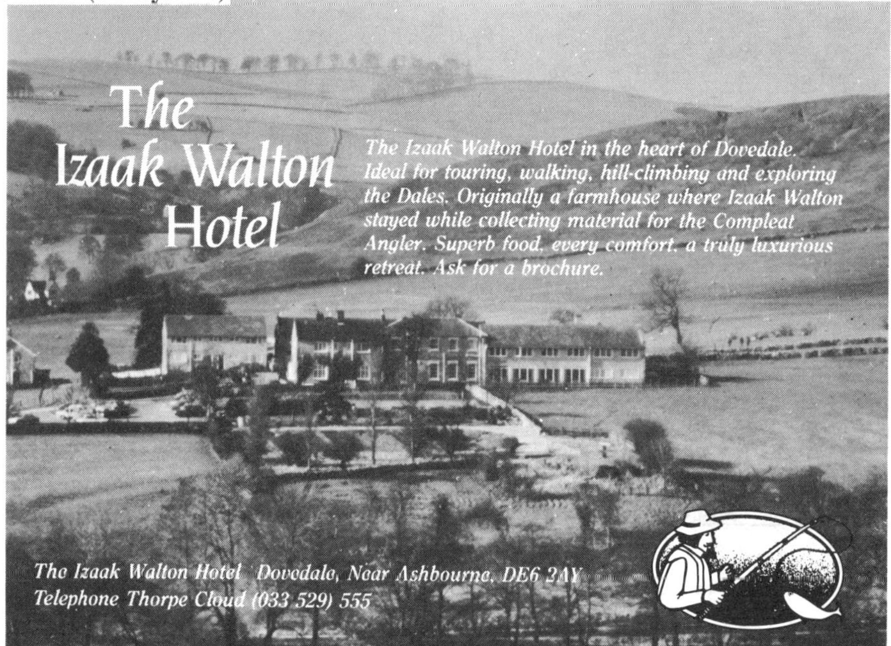

Dover (Kent)

Cliffe Court Hotel

East Cliff, Dover. Tel: (0304) 211001/206000

STOPPING IN DOVER?

Visit our elegant Regency Hotel in Dover's most convenient position on the historic seafront opposite the car ferry entrance. Spacious modern single, double and family rooms – all with radio/colour TV & DIRECT DIAL TELEPHONES.

The RENDEZVOUS RESTAURANT on the first floor serves a discerning clientèle and offers magnificent sea views.

SPECIAL PACKAGE OFFER – All year round – ANY TWO NIGHTS with Dinner, Bed & Breakfast and a FREE DAY TRIP to FRANCE from £65 inclusive. Please ask for details. ALSO CONFERENCE AND GROUP Facilities.

A Hotel in the Bressingham Holdings Ltd Group

DIDDLEBURY Shropshire. Map 20A4

Ludlow 8, London 151, Bridgnorth 16, Craven Arms 5.

Glebe Farm (Acclaimed), Nr Craven Arms, SY7 9DH ☎ Munslow (058 476) 221. ⚒ Fr, De
£ B&B £36–£50

DINNINGTON South Yorkshire. Map 31A4

M1 (jn 31) 4½, London 149, Bawtry 10½, Doncaster 13, Rotherham 8, Worksop 6½.

★★★ **Dinnington Hall,** Falcon Way, S31 7NY ☎ (0909) 569661
Fax: (0909) 569661 ♿

Charming Georgian house with spacious rooms and 3 acres of gardens.
🛏 10 bedrs, 10 en suite; TV; tcf
🏠 dogs, P 30; child facs; con 60
✕ LD 9.30, nr Sun dinner. Resid & Rest lic
£ B&B fr £46·75, B&B (double) fr £58·50; D £15·95
cc Access, Amex, B'card/Visa.

DISLEY Cheshire. Map 41C1

Pop 4,500. Buxton 11, London 170, Chapel-en-le-Frith 7½, Glossop 9½, Knutsford 17, Macclesfield 10, Oldham 15, Stockport 7. **EC** Wed. **Golf** Disley 18h. **See** Lyme Park (Elizabethan) (Nat Trust).

★★★ **Moorside,** Higher Disley, SK12 2AP ☎ (0663) 64151 Tx: 665170
Fax: (0663) 627994

Spacious, elegant hotel on open moorland commanding superb views. Indoor swimming pool, golf, squash, sauna, solarium, gymnasium, billiards. ⚒ Fr
🛏 96 bedrs, 96 en suite; TV; tcf
🏠 dogs; P 200, coach; child facs; con 300
£ B&B £77·50 (w/e £40), B&B (double) £109; L £12, D £18; WB £60 [10%V]
cc Access, Amex, B'card/Visa, Diners; dep.

En suite rooms
En suite rooms may be bath or shower rooms. If you have a preference, remember to state it when booking a room.

DISS Norfolk Map 27B4

Pop 5,694. London 97, Bury St Edmunds 19, Ipswich 24, Scole 2½, Thetford 19. **EC** Tue. **MD** Fri. **Golf** Diss 9h. **See** Diss Mere, St Mary's Church.
ℹ Meresmonth, Mere St ☎ (0379) 650523

★★ **Park,** 29 Denmark St, IP22 3LE ☎ (0379) 642244

Low-built modern hotel near centre of town.
🛏 17 bedrs, 17 en suite; TV; tcf
🏠 P 60, coach; child facs; con 200
✕ LD 10
£ B&B £35·50, B&B (double) £47·50; L £8, D £8; WB
cc Access, Amex, B'card/Visa, Diners.

DONCASTER South Yorkshire. Map 31A4

Pop 81,611. A1(M) 2½, London 164, Barnsley 15, Bawtry 9, Pontefract 14, Rotherham 11, Thorne 9½, Worksop 16. **EC** Thur. **MD** Tue, Fri, Sat. **Golf** Doncaster 18h. Wheatley 18h, Doncaster Town Moor 18h. **See** St George's Church, Christ Church, Art Gallery, Mansion House.
ℹ Library, Waterdale. ☎ (0302) 734309

★★★ **Danum Swallow,** High St, DN1 1DN ☎ (0302) 342261 Tx: 547533
Fax: (0302) 329034

An impressive town centre hotel, 5 minutes from the station. (Sw)
🛏 66 bedrs, 66 en suite; TV; tcf
🏠 lift, dogs, ns; P 100, G 24, coach; child facs; con 300
✕ LD 9.45, nr Sat lunch
£ L £7·95, D £10·95; WB
cc Access, Amex, B'card/Visa, Diners.

Residents only
Some Listed hotels only serve meals to residents. It is always wise to make a reservation for a meal in a hotel.

★★★ **Doncaster Moat House,** Warmsworth, DN4 9UX ☎ (0302) 310331
Tx: 547963 Fax: (0302) 310197 ♿

Modern hotel in grounds of 17th century Warmsworth Hall which contains the hotel's conference suites. Convenient for A1(M).
🛏 70 bedrs, 70 en suite; TV; tcf
🏠 dogs, ns; P 250, coach; child facs, con 300
✕ LD 10, nr Sat lunch
£ B&B £54, B&B (double) £66; L £9·50, D £11·50; WB
cc Access, Amex, B'card/Visa, Diners.

★★★ **Mount Pleasant,** Gt North Rd, (A638), Rossington, DN11 0HP ☎ (0302) 868219 Fax: (0302) 865130 ♿

Interesting period hotel in open country, with lawns and country garden. Closed 25 Dec.
🛏 36 bedrs, 31 en suite, 1 ba; TV; tcf
🏠 P 100, U 2 (£1), coach; child facs; con 60
✕ LD 9.30. Resid & Rest lic
£ B&B £39·50, B&B (double) £49·50; L £7·50, D £10; WB £55 (2 nts)
cc Access, B'card/Visa.

★★ **Regent,** Regent Sq, DN1 2DS ☎ (0302) 364180 Tx: 54480
Modernised fine Regency building in central square of stone Victorian houses. Sauna.
🛏 34 bedrs, 34 en suite; TV; tcf
🏠 lift, dogs; P 20, U 1, coach; child facs; con 30

Almel, 20 Christchurch Rd, DN1 2QL ☎ (0302) 365230. *Hotel.* ⚒ De
£ B&B fr £17.
Campanile, Bantry Rd, DN4 7PH
(*See Motor Lodge section*)
(*See advertisement on p. 226*)

DORCHESTER Dorset. Map 4C1

Pop 14,000. Blandford Forum 16, London 122, Bournemouth 27, Crewkerne 21, Lyme Regis 24, Sherborne 18, Wareham 16, Weymouth 8, Yeovil 18.
EC Thur. **MD** Wed. **Golf** Carie Down 18h. **See** Membury Rings, Poundbury Camp,

Hangman's Cottage, Dorset County Museum, Thomas Hardy Monument, Barnes' Monument, Judge Jeffrey's Lodgings (now Restaurant), St Peter's Church, Nappers Mite Almshouses, Hardy's House, Maiden Castle earthworks 1½ m SW. [i] 7 Acland Rd. ☎(0305) 67992

★★★ **King's Arms,** High St, DT1 1HF ☎(0305) 265353 Fax: (0305) 262069
18th century coaching inn with distinctive bow windows.
31 bedrs, 31 en suite; annexe 2 bedrs, 2 en suite; TV; tcf
lift, dogs; P 32, coach; child facs; con 80
LD 9.30; bar meals only Sat lunch
£ B&B £54; B&B (double) £77–£88; L £6·50, D £12·50; WB £82·50 (HB)
cc Access, Amex, B'card/Visa; dep.

★★★ R **Yalbury Cottage,** Lower Bockhampton, DT2 8PZ ☎(0305) 262382

Beautifully kept, thatched cottage with sympathetic bedroom extension to rear. De
8 bedrs, 8 en suite; TV; tcf
P 19; no children under 16
LD 9.30, nr lunch. Rest lic
£ B&B £65, B&B (double) £100; HB weekly £385–£483; D £25; WB £59 (HB)
cc Access, B'card/Visa; dep.

DORCHESTER-ON-THAMES

Oxfordshire. Map 12A4
Pop 995. Wallingford 4, London 50, Aylesbury 20, Burford 28, Faringdon 20, Oxford 9.
Golf Frilford Heath 18h. **See** Dec. Abbey Church, Museum.

★★★ R **George,** High St, OX9 8HH ☎(0865) 340404 Tx: 83147

An ancient, heavily beamed inn with an attractive courtyard and garden. Closed 24 Dec–31 Dec.
9 bedrs, 9 en suite, annexe 9 bedrs, 9 en suite; TV; tcf
TV, dogs; P 50; coach, con 40
LD 9.45
£ B&B £54, B&B (double) £72; L £14, D £17; WB £90 (HB 2 nts)
cc Access, Amex, B'card/Visa, Diners.

★★★ C **White Hart,** 26 High St, OX9 8HN ☎Oxford (0865) 340074 Fax: (0865) 341082

Privately-owned attractive 18th-century coaching inn at village centre. It
20 bedrs, 20 en suite; TV; tcf
TV, ns; P 24; child facs; con 24
LD 9, nr Sun dinner
£ B&B £60–£65, B&B (double) £85–£90; L £8, D £12; WB £85
cc Access, Amex, B'card/Visa, Diners.

DORKING

Surrey. Map 13C1
Pop 23,010. Leatherhead 5, London 23, Crawley 13, Guildford 12, Horsham 13, Reigate 6.
EC Wed. **MD** Fri. **Golf** Betchworth Park 18h, Dorking 18h. **See** Old Inns, Parish Church of St Martin, Box Hill, Polesden Lacey 2½ m NW.

★★★★ **Burford Bridge,** Burford Bridge, Box Hill, RH5 6BX (2 m N on A24) ☎(0306) 884561 Tx: 859507 Fax: (0306) 880386

Large hotel at bottom of Box Hill; pleasant gardens. Swimming pool. (THF)
48 bedrs, 48 en suite; TV; tcf
dogs, ns; P 80; con 200
LD 9.30.
£ B&B £90–£106 (w/e £57), B&B (double) £117–£139; HB weekly £378–£434; L £15, D £18; WB £57
cc Access, Amex, B'card/Visa, Diners.

★★★ **White Horse,** High St, RH4 1BE ☎(0306) 881138 Fax: (0306) 887241
Modernised coaching inn, with new block at rear. Swimming pool. (THF)
68 bedrs, 68 en suite (3 sh); TV; tcf
dogs, ns; P 70; coach; child facs; con 60
LD 9.30
£ room £65–£80, double room £80–£88; Bk £5–£8, L £10, D £15; WB £30
cc Access, Amex, B'card/Visa, CB, Diners.

DORSINGTON

Warwickshire. Map 20C3
Pop 90. Stratford-upon-Avon 7, London 100, Evesham 10, Redditch 17, Stow on the Wold 18.

Church Farm, CV37 8AX ☎Stratford-upon-Avon (0789) 720471

DOVEDALE

Derbyshire. Map 30C2
Pop 225. Ashbourne 4½, London 143, Buxton 17, Leek 13, Matlock 15, Stoke-on-Trent 21.
Golf Clifton 9h. **See** Dale (explorable on foot), Pike Pool (Beresford Dale), Thorpe Cloud, Lion's Head Rock, Ilam Hall.

★★★ H C R **Izaak Walton,** DE6 2AY Thorpe Cloud (033 529) 555 Tx: 378406 Fax: (033 529) 539
Extended and modernised 17th century farmhouse set in picturesque area. Putting, fishing. Es, Po, Fr
34 bedrs, 34 en suite; TV, tcf
ns; P 100, coach; child facs; con 40
LD 9
£ B&B £45, B&B (double) £68·50, HB weekly £406–£668·50; L £9, D £13·50; WB £52·50 (HB); [10% V w/d]
cc Access, Amex, B'card/Visa, Diners.
(*See advertisement on p. 226*)

★★★ **Peveril of the Peak,** Thorpe, DE6 2AW ☎Thorpe Cloud (033 529) 333 Fax: (033529) 507
Charming converted and extended former rectory, overlooking Dovedale in pleasant gardens. Tennis. (THF)
47 bedrs, 47 en suite; TV; tcf
dogs, ns; P 65, coach; child facs; con 65
LD 9.30; bar meals only Sat lunch
£ room £65–£80, room (double) £80–£96, HB weekly £315–£385; Bk £8; L £9·50, D £15·50; WB £50
cc Access, Amex, B'card/Visa, CB, Diners.

DOVER

Kent. Map 7C2
RAC Port Office, *Terminal Building, Eastern Docks, Dover Harbour, CT16 1JA* ☎(0304) 204256
Pop 33,000. Canterbury 15, London 74, Folkestone 7, Margate 20.
See Plan, p. 229.
EC Wed. **MD** Sat. **P** See Plan. **Golf** Walmer and Kingsdown 18h. **See** Castle and Roman Pharos (lighthouse), Keep and underground passages, Church, Town Hall incorp 13th cent Maison Dieu, Museum, Bleriot Memorial, Roman Painted House.
[i] Townwall St. ☎(0304) 205108

★★★★ **Dover Moat House,** Townwall St, CT16 1SZ ☎(0304) 203270 Tx: 96458 Fax: (0304) 213230

Modern purpose-built 6-storey hotel convenient for ferry terminal. Indoor swimming pool. Es, Fr (QMH)
79 bedrs, 79 en suite; TV; tcf
lift, dogs, ns; P 8, coach; child facs; con 80
LD 10.15
£ B&B £70·25–£80·50, B&B (double) £86·50–£99; L £15, D £15; WB £43 (HB) [10%V]
cc Access, Amex, B'card/Visa, Diners.

★★★ **Crest,** Singledge La, Whitfield, CT16 3LF ☎(0304) 821222 Tx: 965866

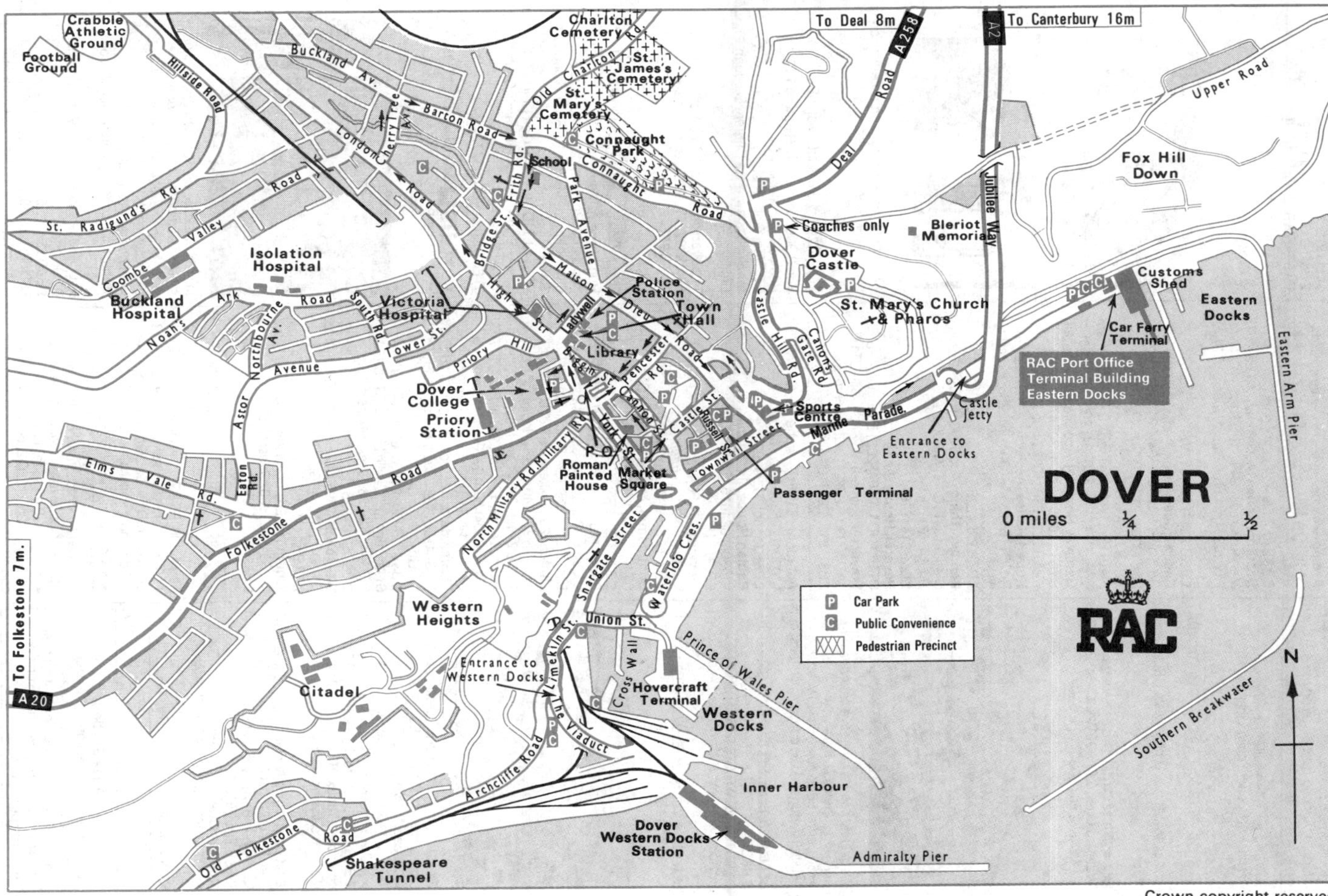

DOVER
RAC
0 miles
¼
½
N
Car Park
Public Convenience
Pedestrian Precinct
To Deal 8m
A258
A2
To Canterbury 16m
To Folkestone 7m.
A20
Crabble Athletic Ground
Football Ground
Hillside Road
Buckland Av.
Cherry Tree Av.
Barton Road
London Road
Charlton Cemetery
Old Charlton Rd.
St. James's Cemetery
St. Mary's Cemetery
Connaught Park
Connaught Road
School
Frith Rd.
Park Avenue
Upper Road
Fox Hill Down
Deal Road
Jubilee Way
Coaches only
Bleriot Memorial
Dover Castle
St. Mary's Church & Pharos
Castle Hill Rd.
Canons Gate Rd
Customs Shed
Eastern Docks
Car Ferry Terminal
RAC Port Office Terminal Building Eastern Docks
Eastern Arm Pier
St. Radigund's Rd.
Valley Road
Coombe
Buckland Hospital
Noah's Ark Road
Isolation Hospital
Northbourne Av.
South Rd.
Victoria Hospital
Tower St.
Avenue
Astor
Bridge St.
High St.
Maison Dieu Road
Police Station
Town Hall
Ladywell
Library
Pencester Rd.
Priory Hill
Biggin St.
Cannon St.
Dover College
Priory Station
Castle St.
Russell St.
Sports Centre
Marine Parade
Castle Jetty
Entrance to Eastern Docks
Townwall Street
York St.
P.O.
Roman Painted House
Market Square
Passenger Terminal
Military Rd.
North Military Rd.
Elms Vale Rd.
Eaton Rd.
Road
Folkestone
Snargate Street
Waterloo Cres.
Western Heights
Union St.
Citadel
Entrance to Western Docks
Limekiln St.
The Viaduct
Cross Wall
Hovercraft Terminal
Prince of Wales Pier
Western Docks
Archcliffe Road
Inner Harbour
Southern Breakwater
Dover Western Docks Station
Admiralty Pier
Old Folkestone Road
Shakespeare Tunnel
Crown copyright reserved
D

Fax: (0304) 825576 ♿
Modern purpose-built motel on the A2. Short drive from ferry terminal. Fr, De, Du (Cr/THF)
67 bedrs, 67 en suite; TV; tcf
ns; P 90, coach; child facs; con 45
LD 10.30
£ B&B £76·95–£88·95, B&B (double) £101·90–£113·90; L £9·90, D £10·70; WB £39 (HB)
cc Access, Amex, B'card/Visa, CB, Diners; dep.

★★★ **White Cliffs,** The Esplanade, Waterloo Cres, CT17 9BW (0304) 203633 Tx: 965422 Fax: (0304) 216320

Traditional hotel in attractive seafront terrace enjoying superb Harbour view.
56 bedrs, 56 en suite, 5 ba; TV; tcf
lift, TV, dogs; G 25, coach; child facs; con 30
LD 9.30, bar meals only Mon–Sat lunch
£ B&B £45–£55, B&B (double) £70–£75; L £8, D £9·50; WB £36 (HB); [10% V]
cc Access, Amex, B'card/Visa, Diners; dep.

★★ **Cliffe Court,** 25 East Cliffe, CT16 1LU (0304) 211001

Pleasant small hotel very close to Eastern Docks terminal. Fr, It, Es
25 bedrs, 15 en suite; TV
TV; P 18, coach; child facs; con 40
LD 9. Resid & Rest lic
£ B&B £28, B&B (double) £39; D £8·75
cc Access, Amex, B'card/Visa, Diners; dep.
(*See advertisement on p. 226*)

East Lee (Highly Acclaimed), 108 Maison Dieu Rd, CT16 1RT
(0304) 210176. *Guest House.*
£ B&B £25; [5% V].
Number One (Highly Acclaimed), 1 Castle St, CT16 1QH (0304) 202007. *Guest House.*
£ B&B (double) £26–£35; [10% V]

Atlas Section
Consult the Atlas section at the back of the guide to find out which towns and villages have RAC Appointed and Listed hotels in them. They are shown on the maps by purple circles.

Ardmore (Acclaimed), 18 Castle Hill Rd, CT16 1QW (0304) 205895. *Private Hotel.* Fr
£ B&B (double) £25–£40; dep.
Beaufort House (Acclaimed), 18 Eastcliff Marine Parade, CT16 1LU (0304) 216444 Fax: (0304) 211100 *Guest House.* Fr, De, Es.
£ B&B £24–£29; [5% V]
Castle House (Acclaimed), 10 Castle Hill Rd, CT16 1QW (0304) 201656 Fax: (0304) 210197. *Guest House.*
£ B&B £23–£26
Fleur de Lis (Acclaimed), 9–10 Effingham Cres, CT17 9RH (0304) 206142. *Hotel.*
Gateway Hovertel (Acclaimed), Snargate St, CT17 9BL (0304) 205479. *Hotel.*
£ B&B £25–£30 [10% V not July/Aug]
Hubert House (Acclaimed), 9 Castle Hill Rd, CT16 1QW (0304) 202253. *Hotel.* Fr.
£ B&B £22–£25
Pennyfarthing (Acclaimed), 109 Maison Dieu Rd, CT16 1RT (0304) 205563. *Guest House.* Fr, It
£ B&B £14–£16.
Peverell House (Acclaimed), 28 Park Av, CT16 1HD (0304) 202753. *Private Hotel.*
Tower (Acclaimed), 98 Priory Hill, CT17 0AD (0304) 208212. *Guest House.*
£ B&B £18–£25 [10% V Thurs–Sat].

Ashmohr, 331 Folkestone Rd, CT17 9JG (0304) 205305. *Guest House.*
£ B&B (double) £20–£24.
Beulah House, 94 Crabble Hill, CT17 0SA (0304) 824615. *Guest House.*
£ B&B £18.
Byways, 247 Folkestone Rd, CT17 9LL (0304) 204514. *Hotel.*
£ B&B £14–£20; [5% V]
Continental, Marine Par, East Cliff, CT16 1LZ (0304) 201669. *Hotel.*
£ B&B £30–£35; HB (weekly) £231–£266
Elmo, 120 Folkestone Rd, CT17 9SP (0304) 206236. *Guest House.*
£ B&B £13–£16; [5% V Nov–Mar]
Linden, 231 Folkestone Rd, CT17 9SL (0304) 205449. *Guest House.* De
£ B&B £14; [10% V Oct–May]
Palma Nova, 126 Folkestone Rd, CT17 9SP (0304) 208109. *Guest House.*
£ B&B £14–£18 [10% V Dec–Apr]
St Brelade's, 82 Buckland Av, CT16 2NW (0304) 206126. *Guest House.* Fr, Es, Ur, Gu
£ B&B £14·50–£18 [5% V Nov–Apr]
St Martins, 17 Castle Hill Rd, CT16 1QW (0304) 205938. *Guest House.* Fr
£ B&B £18–£25.
Westbank, 239 Folkestone Rd, CT17 9LL (0304) 201061. *Guest House.*
£ B&B £14–£16.
Whitmore, 261 Folkestone Rd, CT17 9LL (0304) 203080. *Guest House.*
£ B&B £12–£15.

DOWNHAM MARKET
Norfolk. Map 34C1
Pop 4,600. Ely 17, London 88, King's Lynn 11, Swaffham 15, Thetford 22, Wisbech 13. **EC** Wed. **MD** Fri, Sat. **Golf** Ryston 9h. **See** St Edmund's Parish Church.

★★ **Castle,** High St, PE38 9HF (0366) 384311 Tx: 817787 Fax: (0366) 384740
Stone-built 17th-century coaching inn situated near to town centre. De, Fr, Es
11 bedrs, 9 en suite, 1 ba; TV; tcf
dogs, P 25, U 1, G 2, coach; child facs; con 40
LD 9
£ B&B £33, B&B (double) £42; L £8·50, D £9·90; WB (£28); [10% V]
cc Access, Amex, B'card/Visa, Diners; dep.

★ **Crown,** Bridge St, PE38 9DH (0366) 382322

17th-century coaching inn with interesting staircase. Privately-owned.

DOWNTON
Wiltshire. Map 5B2
Pop 2,900. London 88, Ringwood 12, Romsey 13, Salisbury 6½.
EC Wed. **Golf** Salisbury & S. Wilts 18h & 9h. **See** St Lawrence Church, Borough Cross.

The Warren, High St, Nr Salisbury, SP5 3PG (0725) 20263. *Guest House.*
£ B&B £25–£30; dep.

DRIFFIELD, GREAT
Humberside (North Humberside). Map 39B3
Pop 9,400. Beverley 13, London 192, Bridlington 11, Malton 19, Scarborough 21, York 29.
EC Wed. **MD** Thur, Sat. **Golf** Driffield 9h. **See** All Saints Church, St Mary's Church (Little Driffield).
[i] 60 Market Pl. (0377) 47644

★★★ **H C R Bell,** Market Pl, YO25 7AP (0377) 46661 Tx: 52341 Fax: (0377) 43228 ♿

In market-place, 18th-century coaching inn; modern bedrooms built on. Indoor swimming pool, squash, sauna, solarium, gymnasium billiards. Du
14 bedrs, 14 en suite; TV; tcf
ns; P 50, coach; children over 12; con 300
LD 9.30, bar meals only Mon–Sat lunch & Sun dinner
£ B&B £54–£59·50, B&B (double) £70–£82·50; L £6·75; D £12; WB (£100)
cc Access, Amex, B'card/Visa, Diners.

 EC *early closing* **MD** *market day* *country house hotel* *ns (NS) no smoking areas* *tcf tea/coffee facilities*

🏞 ★★ Wold House, Nafferton, YO25 0LD ☎(0377) 44242

Large country house on hillside; fine views over open countryside. Swimming pool, putting, billiards. Closed 23 Dec–2 Jan.
🛏 10 bedrs, 9 en suite, 2 ba; TV; tcf
🏨 TV, dogs; P 40, coach; child facs; con 20
✕ LD 8.30, nr Mon–Sat lunch. Resid & Rest lic
£ B&B £30–£37, B&B (double) £40–£52; HB weekly £190–£220; L £6·75, D £12·50; [5%V Nov–Mar]
cc Access, B'card/Visa.

DRONFIELD

Derbyshire. Map 41C4

Pop 25,000. Chesterfield 5½, London 154, Buxton 23, Sheffield 6½, Worksop 16.
EC Wed. **Golf** Hallowes 18h. **See** Corn Memorial, Parish Church, Old buildings.

★★ Manor, High St, S18 6PY ☎(0246) 413971
Stone-built 18th-century building with bedrooms added at rear. ⚒ Gr
🛏 10 bedrs, 10 en suite; TV; tcf
🏨 dogs; P 16, coach; child facs; con 34
✕ LD 10, bar meals only Sun dinner. Resid & Rest lic
£ B&B £45–£47 (w/e £33), B&B (double) £58–£60; L £7·50, D £13·25; [5% V w/e]
cc Access, Amex, B'card/Visa, Diners; dep.

DROXFORD

Hampshire. Map 5C2

Pop 600. Alton 16, London 62, Cosham 10, Fareham 8½, Petersfield 11, Southampton 14, Winchester 11.
EC Wed. **Golf** Corhampton 18h. **See** Church.

★★ Coach House Motel, Brockbridge SO3 1QT ☎(0489) 877812
Converted coach house in rural surroundings
🛏 8 bedrs, 8 en suite; TV; tcf
🏨 P 15
✕ Breakfast only. Unlic.
£ B&B £27·50–£31·50, B&B (double) £37·50–£45
cc Access, Amex, B'card/Visa, Diners; dep.

Little Uplands (Highly Acclaimed), Garrison Hill, Little Uplands, SO3 1QL ☎(0489) 878507 Fax: (0489) 877853. *Motel.*
£ B&B £30; HB weekly £300; [10% V].

DUDLEY

West Midlands. Map 22B2

See also HIMLEY
Pop 190,000. Birmingham 8½, London 120, Bridgnorth 17, Kidderminster 12, Walsall 7½, Wolverhampton 6.
EC Wed. **MD** Daily. **Golf** Dudley 18h. **See** Castle ruins, remains of 12th cent Cluniac Priory, Art Gallery, Geological Museum, Zoo, Black Country Museum.
ℹ 39 Churchill Precinct. ☎(0384) 50333

★★★ Ward Arms, Birmingham Rd, DY1 4RN ☎(0384) 458070 Fax: (0384) 457502.

Extended and refurbished 2-storey hotel beside main road to Birmingham. ⚒ Fr, Es
🛏 48 bedrs, 48 en suite; TV; tcf
🏨 dogs
✕ LD 9.30
£ B&B £56·65, B&B (double) £71·50; L £9·95, D £10·95; WB £25
cc Access, Amex, B'card/Visa.

★★ Station, Castle Hill, Birmingham Rd, DY1 4RA ☎(0384) 253418 ♿
Fax: (0384) 457503
Victorian town-centre hotel near the Castle.
🛏 38 bedrs, 38 en suite; TV; tcf
🏨 lift, dogs; P 75, coach; child facs; con 200
✕ LD 10, bar meals only Sat lunch
£ B&B £51·70, B&B (double) £65·45.

DULVERTON

Somerset. Map 3A4

Pop 1,293. Taunton 25, London 168, Dunster 14, South Molton 12, Tiverton 18.
EC Thur. **Golf** Tiverton 18h. **See** 12th cent Church Tower, Tarr Steps 5 m NW.

🏞 ★★ H C Tarr Steps, Hawkridge, TA22 9PY ☎ Winsford (064 385) 293 ♿

Attractive 2-storey stone building in 8 acres overlooking Barle Valley. Fishing, riding.
🛏 12 bedrs, 6 en suite, 2 ba; annexe 3 bedrs, 2 en suite
🏨 dogs; P 20; child facs; con 12

DUNMOW, GREAT

Essex. Map 17A4

Pop 4,529. M11 (jn 8) 7½, London 38, Bishop's Stortford 9, Braintree 8½, Chelmsford 12, Saffron Walden 13.
EC Wed. **Golf** Bishop's Stortford 18h, Braintree 18h.

★★★ Saracen's Head, High St, CM6 1AG ☎ Gt Dunmow (0371) 873901
Fax: (0371) 075743
Modernised 18th century coaching inn, opposite the Tudor Town Hall. ⚒ Fr, It, Es (THF)
🛏 24 bedrs, 24 en suite; TV; tcf
🏨 dogs, ns; P 45, coach; child facs; con 50
✕ LD 9.30
£ B&B £78; L £8·95; D £12·95; WB £40
cc Access, Amex, B'card/Visa, CB, Diners.

Spicer (Acclaimed), Brick End, Broxted, CM6 2BL ☎(0279) 850047. *Guest House.*

DUNSTABLE

Bedfordshire. Map 14B3

Pop 35,716. M1 (jn 11) 2½, London 34, Aylesbury 15, Bedford 19, Bletchley 12, Luton 5, St Albans 13.
EC Thur. **MD** Wed, Fri, Sat. **Golf** Dunstable Downs 18h. **See** Priory Church of St Peter, Chew's Almshouses, Dunstable Downs (Nat Trust), Whipsnade Zoo, Luton Hoo.
ℹ Vernon Pl. ☎(0582) 471012

★★ Highwayman, London Rd, LU6 3DX ☎(0582) 601122 Tx: 825562
Fax: (0582) 471131

Two-storey modern hotel conveniently situated on main A5.
🛏 38 bedrs, 38 en suite; TV; tcf
🏨 dogs; P 66, coach; child facs; con 40
✕ LD 9, bar meals only Mon–Sat lunch
£ B&B £45 (w/e £32·50), B&B (double) £56
cc Access, Amex, B'card/Visa, Diners.

DUNSTER

Somerset. Map 4A3

See also BILBROOK
Pop 786. Taunton 22, London 165, Bridgwater 24, Minehead 2, South Molton 24, Tiverton 26.
EC Wed. **Golf** Minehead and West Somerset 18h. **See** Historic Castle, Yarn Market, Church with 15th cent font and rood screen, Dovecote (unique revolving ladder), Nunnery (pantiled cottages), old Grist Mill with double wheel, old Buttercross, ancient packhorse bridge, Cleeve Abbey 4 m SE, West Somerset Rly (steam engines).

★★★ H C Luttrell Arms, High St, TA24 6SG ☎(0643) 821555
Former guest house of Cleeve Abbey, large stone-built hotel of character. (THF)
🛏 27 bedrs, 27 en suite; TV; tcf
🏨 dogs, ns; P 3 (£1); child facs
✕ LD 9.30
£ Bk £7, L £7·95, D £15
cc Access, B'card/Visa, CB.

★★ H C Exmoor House, 12 West St, TA24 6SN ☎(0643) 821268

D

Dudley (West Midlands)

HIMLEY COUNTRY CLUB & HOTEL
School Road, Himley, Nr. Dudley DY3 4LG
Tel: 0902 896716 Fax: 0902 896668
Telex: 333688 HIMLEY G

2 miles from Wolverhampton, 2 miles from Dudley in a country setting.
A friendly, privately owned hotel. 76 bedrooms all with private bathrooms, including four poster suites.
Our 2 restaurants, which are open to non-residents, include an excellent à la Carte and a carvery restaurant. Conference facilities available.

RAC ★★★ ETB 👑👑👑

Durham (Co Durham)

WHERE A WARM WELCOME AWAITS YOU

82 BEDROOMS – ALL EN-SUITE WITH COLOUR T.V.
FREE IN-HOUSE VIDEO – TROUSER PRESS – TELEPHONES
TEA AND COFFEE MAKING FACILITIES

- LIVE MUSIC 7 NIGHTS A WEEK
- THE PEMBERTON CARVERY
- SUPERB NEW RESTAURANT
- STEAK BAR SERVING THE FINEST ANGUS STEAKS
- TWO PRESIDENTIAL SUITES
- LARGE BALLROOM
- CONFERENCE FACILITIES
- NEW LARGE CAR PARK
- COCKTAIL AND LOUNGE BARS
- SUNDAY LUNCHEONS
- SPECIAL WEEKEND RATES
- WEDDING RECEPTIONS A SPECIALITY

DURHAM (091) 386 5282 FAX NO. (091) 386 0399

CARRVILLE, DURHAM, DH1 1TD
LOCATION: WE'RE JUST OFF THE A1M–A690 MOTORWAY INTERCHANGE. FOLLOW THE DUAL CARRAGEWAY TOWARDS SUNDERLAND FOR 400 METRES, TURN RIGHT UNDER THE BRIDGE ... AND YOU'RE IN OUR DRIVE

 EC *early closing* **MD** *market day* ♣ *country house hotel* *ns (NS) no smoking areas* *tcf tea/coffee facilities*

Attractive Grade II listed Georgian building with a well-maintained garden to the rear. Closed Dec–Jan. ⚒ De, It
🛏 7 bedrs, 7 en suite; TV
🏨 TV, dogs, NS; no children under 12
✕ LD 6.30 nr lunch. Resid & Rest lic
£ B&B £29·50–£31·50, B&B (double) £44–£48, HB weekly £210–£231; L £5·50, D £14; WB £32 (HB)
cc Access, Amex, B'card/Visa, Diners; dep.

Bilbrook Lawns (Acclaimed), Bilbrook, TA24 6HE ☎ Washford (0984) 40331. *Hotel.* ⚒ De, Fr
£ B&B £21·50–£25; HB weekly £150–£185

DURHAM Durham. Map 37B1

Pop 24,777. A1(M) 3, London 260, Corbridge 24, Darlington 19, Newcastle upon Tyne 14, Stockton-on-Tees 19, Sunderland 13, West Auckland 13.
EC Wed. **MD** Sat. **Golf** Durham City 18h. **See** Cathedral, Norman Castle, St Giles and St Margaret's Churches (both 12th cent), St Oswald's Church, remains of 14th cent Almshouses, Art Gallery, Gulbenkian Museum of Oriental Art and Archaeology.
ℹ Market Pl. ☎ 091-384 3720

★★★★ Royal County, Old Elvet, DH1 3JN ☎ 091-386 6821 Tx: 538238
Fax: 091-386 0704 ♿

Luxury hotel in centre of Durham. Indoor swimming pool, sauna, solarium, gymnasium. ⚒ Es, It, Fr (Sw)
🛏 152 bedrs, 152 en suite; TV; tcf
🏨 lift, dogs, ns; P 120, coach; child facs; con 140
✕ LD 10.15
£ B&B £70–£85, B&B (double) £85–£95; L £10·50, D £16·50; WB £95 (HB)
cc Access, Amex, B'card/Visa, Diners.

★★★ Bridge, Croxdale, DH1 3SP (3¾ m S on A167). ☎ 091-378 0524 Tx: 538156
Fax: 091-378 9981
Two-storey hotel with modern motel accommodation units around it.
🛏 46 bedrs, 46 en suite; TV; tcf
🏨 dogs, ns; P 150, coach; child facs

★★★ Hallgarth Manor, Pittington, DH6 1AB ☎ 091-372 1188 Tx: 537023
Fax: 091-372 1249
Grade II listed Victorian country house set in grounds of 4 acres on edge of village.
🛏 23 bedrs, 23 en suite; TV; tcf
🏨 dogs; P 110, coach; child facs; con 350
✕ LD 9.15, bar meals only Mon–Sat lunch
£ B&B £60, B&B (double) £77; L £10·75, D £16
cc Access, Amex, B'card/Visa, Diners.

★★★ Ramside Hall, Carrville, DH1 1TD ☎ 091-386 5282 Tx: 537681
Fax: 091-386 0399 ♿
Largely Victorian (part-Tudor) castle-like mansion, in extensive grounds.
🛏 84 bedrs, 82 en suite, (2 sh), 2 ba; TV; tcf
🏨 lift, TV, dogs, ns; P 600, coach; child facs; con 400
(*See advertisement on p. 232*)

★★★ Three Tuns, New Elvet, DH1 3AQ ☎ 091-386 4326 Tx: 538238
Fax: 091-386 1406

Historic hotel with many Tudor features, in centre of Durham. Guests may use facilities at Royal County Hotel. (Sw)
🛏 48 bedrs, 48 en suite; TV; tcf
🏨 dogs, ns; P 50, coach; child facs; con 300
✕ LD 9.45, bar meals only Sat lunch
£ B&B £59–£65, B&B (double) £76; L £7·50, D £12·50; WB £82–£85 (HB 2nts)
cc Access, Amex, B'card/Visa, Diners.

DUXFORD Cambridgeshire. Map 26C3

Pop 1,690. M11 (jn 10) 1, London 48, Bishop's Stortford 18, Cambridge 9, Haverhill 15, Newmarket 16, Royston 9½.
Golf Gog Magog 9h and 18h. **See** 15th cent St Peter's Church, Duxford Chapel, Imperial War Museum (RAF).

★★★ C R Duxford Lodge, Ickleton Rd, CB2 4RU ☎ Cambridge (0223) 836444
Fax: (0223) 832271

Three-storey former private residence with impressive portico. Attractively set near village centre. ⚒ Fr, De
🛏 11 bedrs, 11 en suite; annexe 5 bedrs, 5 en suite; TV; tcf
🏨 dogs; ns; P 34; child facs; con 30
✕ LD 9.30, nr Sat lunch. Resd & Rest lic
£ B&B £45–£60, B&B (double) £65–£85; L £13·50, D £17·25; WB £30
cc Access, Amex, B'card/Visa, Diners.

DYMCHURCH Kent. Map 7B2

Pop 5,600. M20 (jn 11) 7, London 68, Ashford 12, Folkestone 9½, Rye 16, Tenterden 17.
EC Wed. **Golf** Littlestone 9h & 18h. **See** Romney, Hythe & Dymchurch Railway, 12th cent Church, Smugglers Inn, Martello Towers.

Chantry, Sycamore Gdns, TN29 0LA ☎ (0303) 873137. *Hotel.*
£ B&B £15–£21; HB weekly £128–£157·50; WB £42.

EAGLESCLIFFE Cleveland. Map 45A1

Pop 8,160. Thirsk 20, London 239, Darlington 9, Helmsley 28, Northallerton 16, Stockton-on-Tees 4, Whitby 35.
Golf Eaglescliffe 18h. **See** Preston Park.

★★★ Parkmore, 636 Yarm Rd, TS16 0DH ☎ (0642) 786815 Tx: 58298
Fax: (0642) 790485 ♿

Two-storey red-brick former private residence with later extensions. Indoor swimming pool, sauna, solarium, gymnasium, billiards.
🛏 55 bedrs, 55 en suite; TV; tcf
🏨 TV, dogs, ns; P 100, coach; child facs; con 80
✕ LD 9.30, bar meals only Sat lunch. Resid & Rest Lic.
£ B&B £46–£56 (w/e £25), B&B (double) £58–£74; L £9·75·75, D £13·95; WB £80
cc Access, Amex, B'card/Visa, Diners.

★★ Claireville, 519 Yarm Rd, TS16 9BG ☎ (0642) 780378 Fax: (0642) 784109

Large 3-storey late Victorian villa set in own grounds. Family-run hotel.
🛏 19 bedrs, 16 en suite, 2 ba; TV, tcf
🏨 TV, dogs; P20, coach; child facs; con 30
✕ LD 8.30, nr Mon–Sat lunch. Resid & Rest Lic
£ B&B £27–£34 (w/e £14), B&B (double) £35–£45; L £6·95, D £9·75; [5% V]
cc Access, B'card/Visa, Diners.

★ Sunnyside, 580–582 Yarn Road, TS16 0DF ☎ (0642) 780075
A family run hotel in a pair of substantial, stone built houses sympathetically joined, set back from A135.
🛏 25 beds, 11 en suite, 4 ba; TV, tcf
🏨 TV, dogs; P 15; child facs; con 30
✕ LD8; nr lunch. Resid lic
£ B&B £18·50–£25, B&B (double) £31–£40; D £10; WB £33; [5% V].

EASINGWOLD North Yorkshire. Map 38C4

Pop 3,640. York 13, London 211, Boroughbridge 11, Helmsley 13, Leeds 31, Malton 19, Pontefract 36, Thirsk 10.
MD Fri. **Golf** Easingwold 18h. **See** Church, Market Cross, Byland Abbey.
ℹ Chapel La ☎ (0347) 21530

★★ Garth, York Road, YO6 3PG
☎(0347) 22988
Extended private house on A19 set in 2 acres of gardens.
🛏 10 bedrs, 10 en suite, TV; tcf

★★ George, Market Pl, YO6 3AD ☎(0347) 21698
Stone-built hotel with Georgian-style windows; focal point in this country town. Solarium.

EASTBOURNE East Sussex. Map 7A1
Pop 79,000. Uckfield 19, London 63, Hastings 20, Hurst Green 23, Lewes 16, Newhaven 12, Tunbridge Wells 29.
See Plan, p. 235.
EC Wed. **MD** Wed, Sat. **P** See Plan. **Golf** Royal Eastbourne 18h and 9h. Eastbourne Downs, 18h, Willingdon 18h. **See** Beachy Head and Lighthouse, Towner Art Gallery, Wish Tower, Redoubt Tower, St Mary's Church, Pevensey Castle 4 m NE.
ℹ 3 Cornfield Ter. ☎(0323) 411400

★★★★★ Grand, King Edward's Par, BN21 4EQ ☎(0323) 412345 Tx: 87332
Fax: (0323) 412233

Luxury hotel overlooking sea. Indoor & indoor swimming pools, putting, sauna, solarium, gymnasium, billiards. Fr, De (DeV)
🛏 164 bedrs, 164 en suite; TV
Lift, dogs; P 75; child facs; con 300
✕ LD 9.30
£ B&B £85–£100; B&B (double) £110–£135; HB weekly £420–£540; L £17, D £23; WB £60
cc Access, Amex, B'card/Visa, Diners.
(See advertisement on p. 236)

★★★★ Cavendish, Grand Par, BN21 4DH
☎(0323) 410222 Tx: 87579
Fax: (0323) 410941

Elegant and impressive hotel, opposite the bandstand on the sea front. Billiards. Fr, It. Po. (DeV)
🛏 114 bedrs, 114 en suite; TV; tcf
lift, dogs; P 50, coach; child facs; con 220
✕ LD 9.30
£ B&B £70–£80, B&B (double) £115–£140; HB weekly £405–£460; L £10, D £16; WB £120; [5% V]
cc Access, Amex, B'card/Visa, CB, Diners; dep.

★★★★ Queen's, Marine Par, BN21 3DY
☎(0323) 22822 Tx: 877736
Fax: (0323) 31056

Elegant Victorian hotel well-situated on sea front overlooking pier. Billiards. (DeV) Fr, De, It, Es, Po.
🛏 108 bedrs, 108 en suite; TV; tcf
lift, dogs; P 85, coach; child facs; con 300
✕ LD 8.45
£ B&B £65–£70, B&B (double) £115–£120; HB weekly £360; L £10·50, D £14; WB £110 (2 nts HB) [10% V w/e Jul & Aug]
cc Access, Amex, B'card/Visa, Diners.

★★★ Chatsworth, Grand Par, BN21 3YR
☎(0323) 411016 Fax: (0323) 643270
Pleasant 4-storey family-run hotel on seafront. Sun terrace. De, It
🛏 46 bedrs, 46 en suite, 1 ba; TV
lift, dogs; child facs; con 46
✕ LD 8.30, bar meals only Mon–Sat lunch. Resid lic
£ B&B £32–£47, B&B (double) £64–£94, L £11, D £12·50; WB £85 (2 nts); [5% V]
cc Access, B'card/Visa.

★★★ Cumberland, Grand Par, BN21 3YT
☎(0323) 30342 ♿

Large pleasant, family run hotel on seafront opposite bandstand.
🛏 70 bedrs, 70 en suite, 7 ba; TV; tcf
lift, TV, dogs; coach; child facs; con 150

★★★ Lansdowne, King Edward's Par, BN21 4EE ☎(0323) 25174 Tx: 878624
Fax: (0323) 39721

In attractive terrace, large family hotel on Western end of seafront. Billiards. Closed 1–14 Jan.
🛏 130 bedrs, 130 en suite, 4 ba; TV; tcf
lift, TV, dogs, ns; U 22 (£2·80), coach; child facs; con 130
✕ LD 8.30
£ B&B £43–£57, B&B (double) £68–£88; HB weekly £231–£469; L £8, D £13·50; WB £36; [5% V 6 May–26th Oct]
cc Access, Amex, B'card/Visa, Diners.
(See advertisement on p. 236)

★★★ Princes, Lascelles Terr, BN21 4BL
☎(0323) 22056 Fax: (0323) 27469

Family-run Victorian terrace hotel in quiet area just off seafront. Open Feb–Dec. Fr
🛏 46 bedrs, 46 en suite; TV; tcf
lift; coach; child facs; con 60
✕ LD 8.15
£ B&B £38·50–£40·50, B&B (double) £67–£94; HB weekly £330; L £9, D £12·50; WB £75
cc Access, Amex, B'card/Visa, Diners.

★★★ Wish Tower, King Edward's Par, BN21 4EB ☎(0323) 22676
Fax: (0323) 21474
Family hotel near Winter Gardens and Devonshire Theatre. (THF) Fr, Es, Po
🛏 67 bedrs, 59 en suite, 3 ba; TV; tcf
lift, dogs, ns; U4; coach; child facs; con 100
✕ LD 8.45. bar meals only Mon–Sat lunch
£ B&B £59·50 B&B (double) £80; D £13·50; WB £38; [V Nov–Feb]
cc Access, Amex, B'card/Visa, Diners.

Residents only
Some Listed hotels only serve meals to residents. It is always wise to make a reservation for a meal in a hotel.

En suite rooms
En suite rooms may be bath or shower rooms. If you have a preference, remember to state it when booking a room.

Licences
Establishments have a full licence unless shown as unlicensed or with the limitations listed on p 6.

 EC *early closing* **MD** *market day* *country house hotel* *ns (NS) no smoking areas* *tcf tea/coffee facilities*

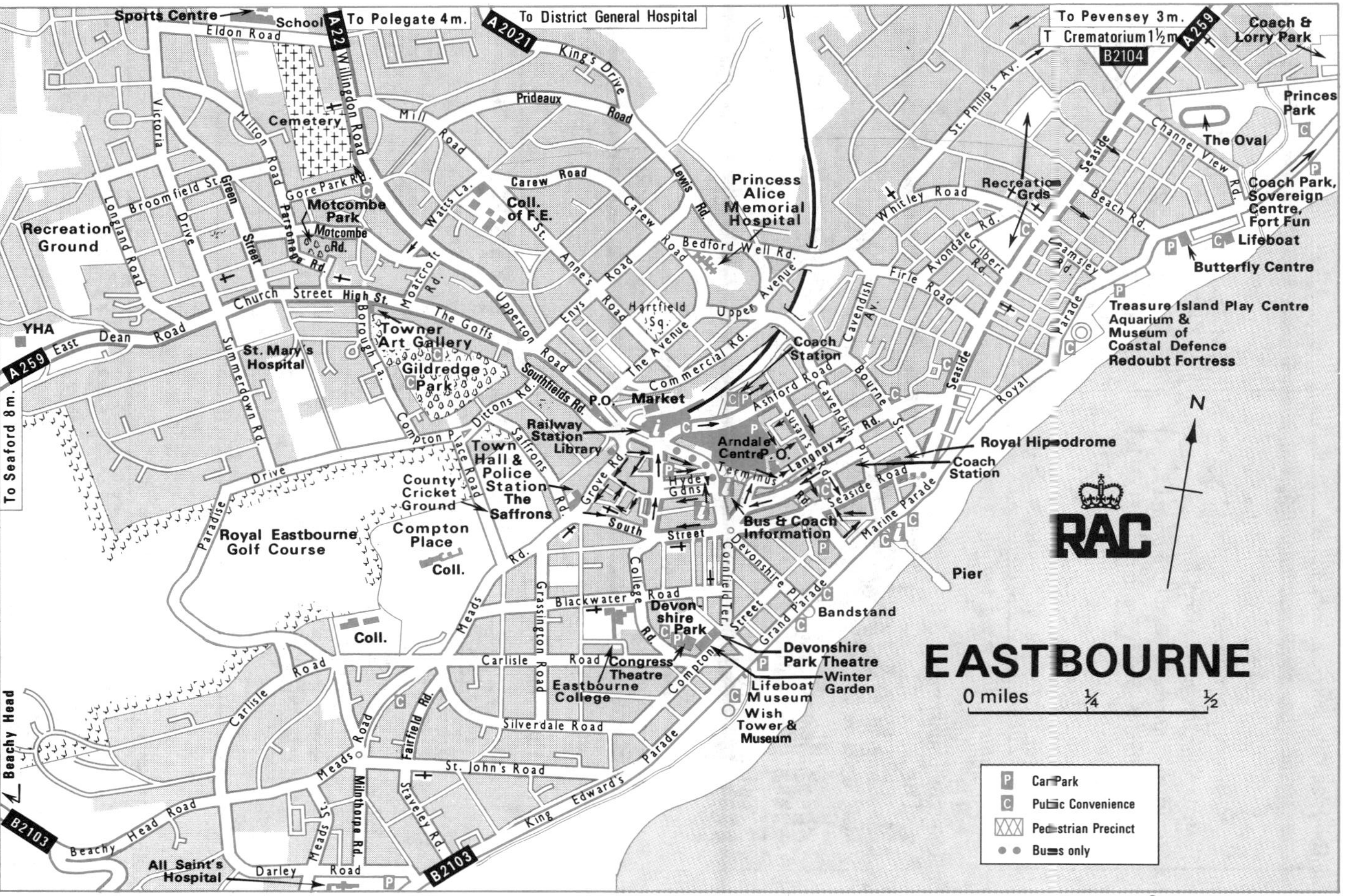
EASTBOURNE
RAC
0 miles
¼
½
N
Car Park
Public Convenience
Pedestrian Precinct
Buses only
Sports Centre
School
To Polegate 4 m.
A22
To District General Hospital
A2021
To Pevensey 3 m.
T Crematorium 1½m
B2104
A259
Coach & Lorry Park
Princes Park
The Oval
Coach Park, Sovereign Centre, Fort Fun
Lifeboat
Butterfly Centre
Treasure Island Play Centre
Aquarium & Museum of Coastal Defence
Redoubt Fortress
Royal Hippodrome
Coach Station
Pier
Bandstand
Devonshire Park Theatre
Winter Garden
Lifeboat Museum
Wish Tower & Museum
Bus & Coach Information
Arndale Centre
P.O.
Market
Coach Station
Railway Station
Library
Town Hall & Police Station
The Saffrons
County Cricket Ground
Compton Place
Coll.
Princess Alice Memorial Hospital
Recreation Grds
Coll. of F.E.
Motcombe Park
Cemetery
Recreation Ground
YHA
Towner Art Gallery
Gildredge Park
St. Mary's Hospital
Royal Eastbourne Golf Course
Devonshire Park
Congress Theatre
Eastbourne College
To Seaford 8 m.
Beachy Head
B2103
All Saint's Hospital
Eldon Road
Willingdon Road
King's Drive
Prideaux Road
Mill Road
Carew Road
Lewis Rd.
Bedford Well Rd.
Upper Avenue
Whitley Road
St. Philip's Av.
Seaside
Channel View Rd.
Beach Rd.
Ramsay Rd.
Avondale Rd.
Gilbert Rd.
Firle Road
Cavendish Av.
Royal Parade
Victoria Drive
Milton Road
Gore Park Rd.
Watts La.
St. Anne's Road
Enys Road
Hartfield Sq.
The Avenue
Commercial Rd.
Longland Road
Broomfield St.
Green Street
Parsonage Rd.
Motcombe Rd.
Moatcroft Rd.
Upperton Road
The Goffs
Church Street
High St.
East Dean Road
Summerdown Rd.
Borough La.
Southfields Rd.
Ditton's Rd.
Compton Place Road
Saffrons Rd.
Ashford Road
Susan's Rd.
Cavendish Pl.
Bourne St.
Langney Rd.
Terminus Rd.
Seaside Road
Marine Parade
Grove Rd.
Hyde Gdns.
South Street
Cornfield Ter.
Devonshire Pl.
Grand Parade
College Road
Blackwater Road
Grassington Road
Carlisle Road
Meads Rd.
Compton St.
Paradise Drive
Silverdale Road
Fairfield Rd.
St. John's Road
Meads Road
Milnthorpe Rd.
Staveley Rd.
Meads St.
Darley Road
Beachy Head Road
King Edward's Parade
Crown copyright reserved

Eastbourne (Sussex)

take a look at our entry in this guide . . . it tells only part of the story. For here are standards of personal service and gracious comfort that, to many people, elevate the Grand Hotel beyond its five-star classification.

Eastbourne East Sussex
Tel. (0323) 412345

Eastbourne (Sussex)

The
Lansdowne RAC RSAC ★ ★ ★

the hotel for you!

. . . because The Lansdowne is the hotel that has everything – in the resort that has everything!

* Premier sea front location close to theatres and shops * 130 bedrooms, all with private bath/shower, colour TV, radio, direct-dial telephone, tea/coffee making facilities * Attractive Regency Bar * Light lunches served daily * Spacious lounges facing sea * Snooker/Games/Card rooms * Hotel entertainment June – September * 22 lock-up garages * Conference facilities * Bargain Breaks November to May including Golf, Bridge Weekends and Rambling holidays

Colour brochure/tariff from R. A. Hazel, Lansdowne Hotel, King Edward's Parade, Eastbourne BN21 4EE. Tel: (0323) 25174 Telex: 878624

Eastbourne (East Sussex)

FARRAR'S HOTEL RAC★★

Wilmington Gardens, Eastbourne, Sussex BN21 4JN
Telephone: (0323) 23737 *Open All Year*

A well-established family-run hotel where hospitality means so much. Excellent cuisine. 200 yards from sea-front. Close to theatres & conference centre. Full central heating. All 45 bedrooms have private bath/shower, remote control colour TV, radio, direct dial telephone, tea & coffee making facilities. Day/Night Porters. Large private car park.

Eccleshall (Staffordshire)

The St George Hotel

Castle Street, Eccleshall, Staffs. ST21 6DF. Tel: 0785 850300 Fax: 0785 851452
Family run 16th century hotel in historic market town. Ten luxury bedrooms all en-suite. Olde Worlde bar serving traditional beers. Log Fires. 50 seater à la carte restaurant.

EC *early closing* **MD** *market day* *country house hotel* *ns (NS) no smoking areas* *tcf tea/coffee facilities*

★★ **Congress,** 31 Carlisle Rd, BN21 4JS ☎(0323) 32118 ♿

Pleasant, family-run hotel, in white-painted Victorian terrace. Sea nearby.

★★ **Croft,** 18 Prideaux Rd, BN21 2NB ☎(0323) 642291

In quiet residential area, mock Tudor building with attractive acre of garden. Swimming pool, tennis.
🛏 11 bedrs, 10 en suite; TV; tcf
🏨 TV; P 18; child facs; con 12

★★ **R** **Downland,** 37 Lewes Rd, BN21 2BU ☎(0323) 32689
Conveniently situated 2-storey family hotel in gardens in residential area. Closed Jan. ✗ Fr, De.

🛏 15 bedrs, 15 en suite, TV; tcf
🏨 TV; P 12; child facs
✕ LD 9. Resid & Rest lic
£ B&B £27·50–£37·50; B&B (double) £55–£75; HB weekly £187·50–£240
cc Access, Amex, B'card/Visa, dep.

Atlas Section
Consult the Atlas section at the back of the guide to find out which towns and villages have RAC Appointed and Listed hotels in them. They are shown on the maps by purple circles.

★★ **Farrar's,** 3 Wilmington Gdns, BN21 4JN ☎(0323) 23737 Fax (0323) 32902

Victorian hotel 200 yards from seafront, overlooking Winter Gardens. ✗ Es, Po, Gr.
🛏 45 bedrs, 45 en suite; TV; tcf
🏨 lift, TV, dogs, ns; P 26, coach; child facs; con 60
✕ LD 8, bar meals only lunch. Resid & Rest lic
£ B&B £25–£33; HB weekly £206–£275; L £7, D £12; WB £62 (2 nts Nov–Apr)
cc Access, Amex, B'card/Visa; dep.
(*See advertisement on p. 236*)

★★ **Langham,** Royal Par, BN22 7AH ☎(0323) 31451
Four-storey modernised family hotel in Victorian terrace on the Eastern esplanade. Open 22 Mar–12 Nov. ✗ Fr.
🛏 87 bedrs, 87 en suite, 4 ba; TV; tcf
🏨 lift, TV, dogs; U 3, coach; child facs; con 60
✕ LD 7.30
£ B&B £26–£29, B&B (double) £40–£52; HB weekly £179–£239; L £5·95, D £8·75. [5% V]
cc Access, B'card/Visa; dep.

★★ **Lathom,** Howards Sq, BN21 4BG ☎(0323) 641986 ♿
Victorian building overlooking gardens just off the sea front. Open Apr–Nov, 23 Dec–3 Jan.
🛏 45 bedrs, 41 en suite, 4 ba; TV; tcf
🏨 lift; P 5, coach; child facs
✕ LD 8
£ B&B £22–£28, B&B (double) £44–£56; HB weekly £150–£160; L £4, D £6·50
cc Access, Visa/B'card; dep.

★★ **New Wilmington,** 25 Compton St, BN21 4DU ☎(0323) 21219

Pleasant 4-storey family hotel. Two minutes walk from sea front. Open 1 Mar–28 Dec.
🛏 41 bedrs, 41 en suite; TV; tcf
🏨 lift, TV, dogs, ns; U 3 (£2), coach; child facs; con 20
✕ LD 8, bar meals only lunch.
£ B&B £35–£39·50, B&B (double) £58–£74; HB weekly £197–£260; L £6; D £10; WB [5% V]
cc Access, Amex, B'Card/Visa; dep.

★★ **Sussex Toby,** Cornfield Terr, BN21 4NS ☎(0323) 27681 Fax: (0323) 646077
Modernised hotel conveniently situated in centre of town.
🛏 27 bedrs, 27 en suite, 1 ba; TV; tcf
🏨 lift, TV, dogs, ns; coach; child facs; con 50

★★ **West Rocks,** Grand Parade, BN21 4DL ☎(0323) 25217
White-painted, 5-storey hotel formed from 3 Victorian houses on the sea front. Open mid Mar–mid Nov. ✗ De, Es, Po, Sw.
🛏 54 bedrs, 40 en suite, 6 ba; TV; tcf
🏨 lift, TV; ns coach; no children under 3; con 30
✕ LD 7.30.
£ B&B £20–£38, B&B (double) £36–£80; HB weekly £140–£300; [5% V Mar–May, Jul–Aug, Oct–Nov]
cc Access, Amex, B'card/Visa, Diners; dep.

★★ **York House,** 14 Royal Par, BN22 7AP ☎(0323) 412918

Family hotel in elegant Victorian terrace on Eastern esplanade. Indoor swimming pool. Open Mar–Nov. ✗ Fr, De
🛏 103 bedrs, 93 en suite, 8 ba; TV; tcf
🏨 lift, dogs; coach; child facs; con 100
✕ LD 7.30
£ B&B £22–£27; HB weekly £168–£231; L £7·50, D £9; WB; [10% V]
cc Access, B'card/Visa; dep.

★ **Oban,** King Edward's Par, BN21 4DS ☎(0323) 31581
White Victorian building on seafront facing lawns and Wish Tower. Open Mar–Nov.
🛏 31 bedrs, 31 en suite, 1 ba; TV; tcf
🏨 lift, TV, dogs; coach; child facs
✕ LD 7.30
£ B&B £24–£30; B&B (double) £48–£60; HB weekly £150–£260; L £5, D £8·50; WB £22; [5% V]

Bay Lodge (Acclaimed), 61 Royal Par, BN22 7AQ ☎(0323) 32515. *Hotel.* Open 1 Mar–15 Oct. ✗ Fr.
£ B&B £16–£21; HB weekly £147–£174; [10% V excl Jul–Aug]
Beachy Rise (Acclaimed), 20 Beachy Head Rd, BN20 7QN ☎(0323) 639171. *Guest House.*
£ B&B (double) £28–£40; HB weekly £138–£170; [5% V]
Flamingo (Acclaimed), 20 Enys Rd, BN21 2DN ☎(0323) 21654. *Private Hotel.*
Hanburies (Acclaimed), 4 Hardwick Rd, BN21 4HY ☎(0323) 30698. *Private Hotel.* Open Feb–Dec.
£ B&B £18·50–£20·50; HB weekly £138–£160; [10% V]
Mandalay (Acclaimed), 16 Trinity Trees, BN21 3LE ☎(0323) 29222. *Hotel.*

Alfriston, 16 Lushington Rd, BN21 4LL ☎(0323) 25640. *Hotel.* Open Mar–Oct.
£ B&B £16·50–£17·50; D £5; dep.
Courtlands, 68 Royal Par, BN22 7AQ ☎(0323) 26915. ✗ Fr, We. *Hotel.*

E

£B&B £16; [10% V]
Falcondale, 5 South Cliffe Av, BN20 7AH ☎(0323) 643633. *Private Hotel.* Open Apr–Oct
£B&B £15; HB weekly £127–£138
Gilday, 1 Marine Par, BN21 3DX ☎(0323) 21818. *Hotel.*
Meridale, 91 Royal Par, BN22 7AE ☎(0323) 29686 *Guest House.*
Oakwood, 28 Jevington Gdns, BN21 4HN ☎(0323) 21900. *Private Hotel.*
£ B&B £13–£21; HB Weekly £95–£149; [10% V Nov–Mar; 5% V April, May, Oct]
Sherwood, 7 Lascelles Terr, BN21 4BJ ☎(0323) 24002. *Hotel.*
£ B&B £14·50–£19·50; HB weekly £120–£150; [5% V Oct–Mar]
Sovereign View, 93 Royal Par, BN22 7AE ☎(0323) 21657. *Guest House.* Open Apr–Sep.
£B&B (double) £30–£34; HB weekly £125–£137; [5% V Apr, May, Sep]
Stirling House, 5 Cavendish Pl, BN21 3EJ ☎(0323) 32263. *Hotel.* Fr De
£B&B £16; B&B (double) £30–£34; HB weekly £99–£149; [5% V].

EAST DEREHAM Norfolk. Map 35A1

Pop 12,364. Newmarket 43, London 105, Cromer 27, Fakenham 12, Norwich 16, Scole 28, Swaffham 12, Thetford 24.
EC Wed. **MD** Tue, Fri. **Golf** Dereham 9h.
See Fine EE and Perp Church (Cowper's tomb), St Withburga's Well.

★★★ **Phoenix,** Church St, NR19 1DL ☎(0362) 692276

1960s red-brick hotel quietly situated just off the town centre. (THF)
22 bedrs, 22 en suite; TV; tcf
dogs, ns; P 30, coach; child facs; con 180
LD 9.30
£ B&B £40; B&B (double) £45; L £8·25, D £10·25; WB £36 (HB)
cc Access, Amex, B'card/Visa, CB, Diners.

★★ **George,** Swaffham Rd, NR19 2AZ ☎(0362) 696801

Picturesque 17th-century coaching inn with original oak panelling. (BCB)
8 bedrs, 8 en suite; TV; tcf
P 40, coach; child facs

★★ **Kings Head,** Norwich St, NR19 1AD ☎(0362) 693842

Attractive 2-storey 18th-century hotel, thoroughly modernised. Garden.
10 bedrs, 6 en suite, 2 ba; annexe 5 bedrs, 5 en suite; TV; tcf
dogs; P 30, G 3, coach; child facs; con 40
LD 9
£B&B £33, B&B (double) £48; L £7·25, D £8; WB £28·50; [5% V]
cc Access, Amex, B'card/Visa, Diners; dep.

EAST GRINSTEAD West Sussex. Map 10C1

Pop 22,395. Godstone 10, London 30, Crawley 9, Lewes 21, Redhill 13, Reigate 14, Tunbridge Wells 13, Uckfield 13.
EC Wed. **MD** Sat. **Golf** Copthorpe 18h. **See** Sackville College (17th cent almshouses), Museum, old buildings in High St, St Swithin's Church.

★★★ **Gravetye Manor,** Nr East Grinstead, RH19 4LJ ☎Sharpthorne (0342) 810567 Tx: 957239 Fax: (0342) 810080

Lovely 16th century mansion, appropriately furnished. Gardens are justly famous. Fishing. Fr, De
14 bedrs, 12 en suite, TV, tcf
ns; P35; con 14
LD 9.30, Resid lic.
£ B&B £93·15–£98·90, B&B (double) £117–£218·50; L £21·85; D £25·30; dep.

★★★ **Woodbury House**, Lewes Rd, RH19 3UD ☎(0342) 313657
Two-storey multi-gabled 19th-century residence. Charming grounds.
14 bedrs, 14 en suite; TV; tcf
dogs; P 38; child facs; con 20

Acorn Lodge (Acclaimed), Turners Hill Rd, RH19 4LX ☎(0342) 23207. *Hotel.*

Cranfield, Maypole Rd, RH19 1HW ☎(0342) 410371. *Hotel.*
£ B&B £27–£35; HB weekly £200–£250; WB £30 (2 nts); [5% V w/e Dec–Mar]

EAST HORSLEY Surrey. Map 8B1

Pop 4,300. Leatherhead 6, London 24, Cobham 4½, Dorking 8, Guildford 8.
EC Thur. **Golf** East Horsley 18h.

Licences
Establishments have a full licence unless shown as unlicensed or with the limitations listed on p 6.

★★★ **Thatchers,** Epsom Rd, KT24 6TB ☎(048 65) 4291 Fax: (048 65) 4222

Half-timbered hotel with modern extension in attractive grounds. Swimming pool. Fr, De, It, Ar, Ma.
36 bedrs, 36 en suite; annexe 23 bedrs, 23 en suite; TV; tcf
dogs; P 80, coach; child facs; con 60
LD 9.30, bar meals only Sat lunch
£B&B £71·50–£81·50; B&B (double) £88–£98; L £13·75; D £16·50; WB £121 (3 nts HB)
cc Access, Amex, B'card/Visa, Diners.

EASTLEIGH Hampshire. Map 5C2

Pop 94,000. Winchester 7½, London 72, Fareham 12, Ringwood 24, Southampton 5.
EC Wed. **MD** Thur. **Golf** Fleming Park 18h.
[i] Town Hall Centre. ☎(0703) 614646

★★★ **Crest,** Leigh Rd, SO5 5PG ☎(0703) 619700 Tx: 47606 Fax: (0703) 643945

Light and pleasant modern purpose-built hotel conveniently situated. Indoor swimming pool, sauna, solarium, gymnasium, snooker. Fr, De, It, Es, Po. (Cr/THF)
120 bedrs, 120 en suite; TV; tcf
lift, dogs, ns; P200,; coach; child facs; con 200
LD 9.45, bar meals only Sat lunch
£ B&B £93–£107 (w/e £45); B&B (double) £114–£128; L £10·95; D £15·95.
cc Access, Amex, B'card/Visa, CB, Diners.

EAST RETFORD Nottinghamshire

See RETFORD.

EASTWOOD Nottinghamshire. Map 24B2

Pop 11,665. M1 (jn 26) 3½, London 131, Ashbourne 21, Chesterfield 18, Derby 11, Mansfield 12, Matlock 17, Nottingham 8½.
MD Wed. **Golf** Alfreton 9h.

Sun Inn, Market Pl, NG16 3NR ☎Langley Mill (0773) 712940
Well-established hotel adjacent to the D H Lawrence centre.
15 bedrs, 12 en suite, 1 ba; tcf
TV, dogs; coach; child facs
LD 8.30, nr Sun dinner
£ D £6·75.

EC *early closing* **MD** *market day* *country house hotel* *ns (NS) no smoking areas* *tcf tea/coffee facilities*

EBBERSTON North Yorkshire. Map 39A4
Pop 432. Malton 12, London 217, Bridlington 25, Pickering 7, Scarborough 11, Whitby 24.
EC Wed. **Golf** Ganton 18h. **See** Church.

Foxholm, YO13 9NJ ☎Scarborough (0723) 85550. *Hotel*. Open March–30 Nov.
£B&B £20–£22, B&B (double) £30–£36; HB weekly £184–£190; D £8; WB £82 (3 nts); dep.

EBCHESTER Durham. Map 37A2
Consett 3, London 246, Corbridge 10, Durham 15, Newcastle upon Tyne 15.

★★★ **Raven**, Broomhill, DH8 6RY ☎(0207) 560367. Fax: (0207) 560262.
Stone building situated high up on the south side of Derwent valley with spectacular views over unspoilt countryside.
28 bedrs, 28 en suite; TV; tcf.

ECCLESHALL Staffordshire Map 29 C2
M6 (jn 14) 5, London 148, Market Drayton 11½, Newport 8½, Stoke on Trent 12.

★★ H C **St George,** Castle St, ST1 6DF ☎(0785) 850300 Fax: (0785) 851452
Town-centre hotel, created from several 18th-century buildings. Beams and open fires give period atmosphere to the public rooms.
10 bedrs, 10 en suite; TV; tcf
TV; P 16; child facs; con 18
LD 9.45, nr Sun, Mon dinner
£B&B £54·25 (w/e £33), B&B (double) £72; L £5·95, D £10·50; WB £37; [10% V]
cc Access, Amex, B'card/Visa, Diners.
(*See advertisement on p. 237*)

Glenwood, Croxton, ST21 6PF ☎(063 082) 238. *Guest House*
£ B&B £12; [10% V].

EDENHALL Cumbria. Map 44B2
Pop 667. M6 (jn 40) 5, London 286, Alston 16, Brough 22, Carlisle 19, Penrith 4.
Golf Penrith 18h. **See** St. Cuthbert Church.

★★★ **Edenhall,** Penrith, CA11 8SX ☎Langwathby (076881) 454 ♿
Two-storey red brick building with modern extensions. Pleasant gardens.
22 bedrs, 22 en suite; annexe 8 bedrs, 8 en suite; TV; tcf
TV; P40; U3 (£1), G2; coach; child facs; con 50
LD 9.00; Resid & Rest lic.
£ B&B £30, B&B (double) £45; WB £75·50.
cc Access, B'card/Visa.

EGGESFORD Devon. Map 3B3
Tiverton 16, London 179, Barnstaple 19, Exeter 14, Okehampton 16.

★★ **Eggesford House,** Chumleigh, EX18 7JZ ☎(0769) 80345 ♿
Rambling old coaching inn, the Fox and Hounds, in lovely countryside off A377. Fishing, putting, snooker.
20 bedrs, 20 en suite, annexe 2 bedrs, 2 en suite; TV; tcf
dogs; ns; P 200, G 3, coach; child facs; con 200
LD 9
£ B&B £27·50; HB weekly £225; L £10, D £13·50; WB £75; [5% V]
cc Access, B'card/Visa; dep.

EGHAM Surrey. Map 8A2
Pop 15,733. Staines 1½, London 18, M25 (jn 13) ½, Bagshot 8½, Reading 21, Weybridge 7, Windsor 6, Woking 10.
EC Thur. **Golf** Wentworth 18h (2) and 9h.

★★★★ **Great Fosters,** Stroude Rd, TW20 9UR ☎(0784) 33822 Tx: 944441 Fax (0784) 472455
Elizabethan manor house with antique furniture. Extensive gardens and parkland. Swimming pool, tennis, sauna.
23 bedrs, 23 en suite; TV; tcf
TV; P 200; con 100
LD 9.15
£ B&B £55–£57·50; B&B (double) £70–£130; L £13·50–£14·50; D £19·50–£23·50.
cc Access, Amex, B'card/Visa, Diners; dep.

★★★★ **Runnymede**, Windsor Rd, TW20 0AG ☎(0784) 436171 Tx: 934900 Fax: (0784) 436340
Modern custom-built hotel with fine views overlooking Thames close to Runnymede.
125 bedrs, 125 en suite; TV; tcf
lift, dogs; P 250, child facs; con 400
LD 9.45, bar meals only Sat lunch
£B&B £88·25–£103·25 (w/e £41·25), B&B (double) £111·50–£126·50; L £14·75, D £16·95
cc Access, Amex, B'card/Visa.
(*See advertisement on p. 240*)

EGREMONT Cumbria. Map 43B1
Pop 8,035. Broughton-in-Furness 31, London 308, Cockermouth 15, Keswick 25, Workington 13.
ℹ 12 Main St ☎(0946) 820693

★★★ **Blackbeck Bridge,** Beckermet CA22 2NY ☎(094 684) 661
A white-washed inn in typical Lakeland style beside the A595. ⚒ It
20 bedrs; 2 en suite; TV, tcf.
dogs; P50; coach; child facs; con 40
LD 9.30
£ B&B £23–£43·50, (w/e £23); B&B (double) £35–£55; L £4, D £10; [5% V]
cc Access, Amex, B'card/Visa, Diners.

ELLESMERE PORT Cheshire. Map 32A1
Chester 7, London 190, Birkenhead 10, Queensferry 8½, Runcorn 14.

★★ **Woodhey**, Berwick Road, Welsh Road, Little Sutton, L66 4PS ☎051-339 5121 Fax: 051-339 3214.

Pleasant Georgian residence, greatly extended, in 4½ acres of grounds.
53 bedrs, 53 en suite; TV; tcf
dogs; P 195, coach; child facs; con 225
LD 10.30
£ B&B £55–£65, B&B (double) £70–£85; D £10; WB £55; [10% V w/e]
cc Access, Amex, B'card/Visa, Diners.

ELSTREE Hertfordshire. Map 8B4
Edgware 3, London 12, Brentford 8, Chiswick 13, Harrow 8, St Albans 8.

★★★ **Edgwarebury,** Barnet La, WD6 3RE ☎081-953 8227 Tx: 918707 Fax: 081-207 3668 ♿
Tudor-style mansion with modern extension set in 10 acres of woodland, lawns and gardens. Tennis, sauna, solarium, gymnasium. (Lns)
50 bedrs, 50 en suite; TV; tcf
ns; P 120; child facs; con 80
LD 10
£ B&B £88, B&B (double) £97; L £11; D £11; WB £33; [10% V]
cc Access, Amex, B'card/Visa, Diners.

ELTERWATER Cumbria. Map 43C1
3 m W of Ambleside. M6 (jn 37) 28, London 272, Broughton-in-Furness 15, Kendal 16, Keswick 15, Ulverston 19.

★★ **Britannia Inn,** Langdale, LA22 9HP ☎Langdale (096 67) 382

Attractive old world traditional inn on the green in a quiet village.

★★ R **Eltermere,** LA 22 9HY ☎Langdale (096 67) 207
Surrounded by lawns and trees, a family-managed country house hotel.
18 bedrs, 15 en suite; 3 ba; TV; tcf
LD 8, nr lunch. Resid & Rest lic.
£ B&B £32–£39·50, B&B (double) £64–£79; HB weekly £210–£250; D £14·95; WB £68 (winter); dep.

ELY Cambridgeshire. Map 26C4
Pop 10,268. Cambridge 16, London 71, Huntingdon 21, King's Lynn 28, Newmarket 13, Swaffham 26, Wisbech 23.
EC Tue. **MD** Thur. **Golf** Ely 18h. **See** Cathedral, Bishop's Palace, Prior Crauden's Chapel and Ely Porta (King's School), 15th cent Monk's Granary, 13th cent St Mary's Church, Goldsmith Tower, Museums, Brass Rubbing Centre.
ℹ 29 St Mary's St ☎(0353) 662062

★★★ **Fenlands Lodge,** Soham Rd, Stuntney, CB7 5TR ☎(0353) 667047
Attractively converted former farm buildings set 2 miles outside city.
9 bedrs, 9 en suite; TV; tcf
dogs; P 50, coach; child facs; con 50
LD 9; nr Sun dinner
£ B&B £45, B&B (double) £57; HB weekly £280; L £11·50, D £11·50
cc Access, Amex, B'card/Visa, Diners

★★★ **Lamb,** Lynn Rd, CB7 4EJ ☎(0353) 663574

E

Egham (Surrey)

Centrally situated coaching inn with pleasant courtyard, close to Cathedral. (QMH)
🛏 32 bedrs, 32 en suite; TV; tcf
🏨 dogs; P 20, U1, coach; child facs; con 100
✕ LD 9.45
£ B&B £52–£60, B&B (double) £68–£85; L £8·95, D £12·50; WB £35; [10% V]
cc Access, Amex, B'card/Visa, Diners.

★ **Nyton,** 7 Barton Rd, CB7 4HZ ☎ (0353) 662459.
White painted house in mature gardens overlooking a golf course. ♿
🛏 9 bedrs, 9 en suite; annexe 4 bedrs, 4 en suite; TV; tcf
🏨 P 25, coach; child facs
✕ LD 8.30.
£ B&B £30–£35, B&B (double) £40–£45; HB weekly £210–£315; L £12; D £12; [5% V]
cc Access, Amex, B'card/Visa, Diners; dep.

EMBLETON Northumberland. Map 51C1

Pop 300. Alnwick 7½, London 315, Berwick-upon-Tweed 30, Coldstream 36.
EC Wed. **Golf** Embleton Village 18h. **See** Dunstanburgh Castle ruins, old Church, Vicarage with Pele Tower.

★★ **Dunstanburgh Castle,** Nr Alnwick, NE66 3UN ☎ (066 576) 203
Retaining much original character, a stone-built village inn.

EMSWORTH Hampshire. Map 6A1

Petersfield 13, London 66, A3 (M) 3, Chichester 7, Cosham 6.
EC Wed. **Golf** Rowlands Castle 18h. **See** St James's Church. Oyster beds.

★★★ **Brookfield,** Havant Rd, PO10 7LF ☎ (0243) 373363 Fax: (0243) 376342
Modern conversion of 2 former residences in landscaped gardens. On A27.
🛏 41 bedrs, 41 en suite; TV; tcf
🏨 P 85; coach; child facs; con 50
✕ LD 9.30. Resid & Rest lic
£ B&B £53, B&B (double) £63; D £11·50; WB £70.
cc Access, Amex, B'card/Visa, Diners.

Jingles (Acclaimed), 77 Horndean Rd, PO10 7PU ☎ (0243) 372233. *Hotel.*
Merry Hall (Acclaimed), 73 Horndean Rd, PO10 7PU ☎ (0243) 372424. *Hotel. Putting.* ♿
🍴 Fr.
£ B&B £35; [V].

Chestnuts, 55 Horndean Rd, PO10 7PU ☎ (0243) 372233. *Guest House. Swimming pool.*
£ B&B (double) £25–£30.
Queensgate, 80 Havant Rd, PO10 7LH ☎ (0243) 371960. *Hotel.*
£ B&B £19·50; [5% V].

ENFIELD Greater London (Middx). Map 8C4

Pop 109,543. London 12, Barnet 6, Epping 11, Hatfield 12, Hoddesdon 9, Woodford 6½.
EC Wed. **MD** Sat. **Golf** Enfield 18h, Bush Hill Park 18h.

> Changes made after July 1990 are not included.

★★★ R **Royal Chace,** The Ridgeway, EN2 8AR ☎ 081-366 6500 Tx: 266628 Fax: 081-367 7191

Three-storey gabled hotel with helipad. Adjoins open countryside. Swimming pool. 🍴 Fr, It, Gr.
🛏 92 bedrs, 92 en suite; TV; tcf
🏨 TV; dogs; P30; child facs; con 300
✕ LD 10, bar meals only. Sat lunch & Sun dinner.
£ B&B £71·50–£156·50; B&B (double) £98–£163; L £15·50; D £12·75; WB £32; [10% V]
cc Access, Amex, B'card/Visa, Diners.

★★ **Holtwhites,** 92 Chase Side, EN2 0QN ☎ 081-363 0124 Fax: 081-366 9089
Large converted Victorian house with a modern extension. Owner run. 🍴 Fr, De
🛏 30 bedrs, 27 en suite, (2 sh), 1 ba; TV; tcf
🏨 TV, ns; P 20, G4, coach; no children under 5; con 20
✕ LD 8.30, bar meals only lunch & Fri–Sun dinner. Resid & Rest lic
£ B&B £65–£70 (w/e £50), B&B (double) £97; [5% V]
cc Access, Amex, B'card/Visa, Diners; dep.

EPPING Essex. Map 9A4

Pop 12,336. Woodford 8½, London 18, M11 (jn 27) 3½, Bishop's Stortford 13, Chelmsford 17, Hoddesdon 9.
EC Wed. **MD** Mon. **Golf** Theydon Bois 18h. **See** Epping Forest–5,000 acres.

★★★ **Post House,** Bell Common, High Rd, CM16 4DG ☎ (0378) 73137 Tx: 81617 Fax: (0378) 560402

Modernised 16th-century former coaching inn with residential annexes. (THF)
🛏 82 bedrs, 82 en suite; TV; tcf
🏨 dogs, ns; P 130, coach; child facs; con 100
✕ LD 10.15
£ B&B £79·50–£89·50 (w/e £39·50), B&B (double) £98–£109; Bk £7·50, L £9·75, D £14·50; WB; [V]
cc Access, Amex, B'card/Visa, CB, Diners.

EPSOM Surrey. Map 8B1

RAC Country Club, *Woodcote Park, Epsom, KT18 7EW* ☎ Ashtead (037 22) 76311
Pop 69,300 (inc Ewell). Mitcham 7½, London 14, Croydon 8½, Leatherhead 4, Reigate 9.
EC Wed. **MD** Sat. **Golf** Epsom 18h, Cuddington, Banstead 18h, the RAC Country Club (Members to accompany all visitors) 18h (2).

★★ **Drift Bridge,** Reigate Rd, KT17 3JZ ☎ Burgh Heath (073 73) 52163
Large detached public house convenient for Epsom race course.

Epsom Downs (Acclaimed), 9 Longdown Rd, KT17 3PT ☎ (037 27) 40643 Fax: (037 27) 23259. *Hotel.* 🍴 Fr.
£ B&B £65; WB (£23).

ERMINGTON Devon. Map 3B2

Pop 881. Ashburton 15, London 203, Plymouth 11, Totnes 12.

★★ C R **Ermewood House,** Totnes Rd, Nr Ivybridge, PL21 9NS ☎ Modbury (0548) 830741
In attractive countryside, a Georgian rectory of great charm. Spacious garden. Closed 24 Dec–15 Jan. 🍴 Fr.
🛏 12 bedrs, 12 en suite; TV; tcf
🏨 dogs, ns; P 15; child facs; con 12
✕ LD 8.30, Resid & Rest Lic
£ B&B £45, B&B (double) £60; D £16·50; WB £80.
cc Access, B'card/Visa.

ESHER Surrey. Map 8B2

Pop 113,800 (Elmbridge District). Kingston 3½, London 13, Guildford 15, Leatherhead 6½, Chertsey 6½, M3 6; M25 (jn 9) 5.
EC Wed. **Golf** Moore Place 9h.

★★ **Haven,** Portsmouth Rd, KT10 9AR ☎ 081-398 0023 Fax: 081-398 9463

Privately-run detached Edwardian house lying back on main Surbiton–Esher road.
🛏 16 bedrs, 16 en suite, 1 ba; annexe 4 bedrs, 4 en suite; TV; tcf
🏨 TV; dogs; P 20, U 1; child facs; con 40
✕ LD 8.30, bar meals only lunch, Sat dinner. Resid & Rest lic
£ B&B £55–£62, B&B (double) £65–£72; L £3·50, D £8; WB £53 (2nts).
cc Access, Amex, B'card/Visa, Diners.

ETON Berkshire. Map 13A3

M4 (jn 6) ½, London 18, Beaconsfield 7, Maidenhead 7, Slough 1½, Windsor ½.

★★ **Christopher,** 110 High St, SL4 6AN ☎ (0753) 852359
Brick-built hotel in town centre with motel-type bedrooms in annexes behind.
🛏 32 bedrs, 32 en suite; TV; tcf.

ETWALL Derbyshire. Map 25A1

Burton upon Trent 6, London 128, Ashbourne 15, Derby 5, Uttoxeter 13.
Blenheim House (Acclaimed), 56 Main St, DE6 6LP ☎ (028 373) 2254. *Hotel.*

EVERCREECH Somerset. Map 4C3

Pop 1,900. Frome 11, London 116, Shepton Mallet 4, Sherborne 15, Wincanton 8.
EC Wed. **Golf** Mendip 18h.

Pecking Mill Inn, A371, BA24 6PG (0749) 830336
A characterful 16th century inn with a modern extension; one mile SW of village, on A371.

EVESHAM Hereford & Worcester (Worcestershire). Map 20C3

Pop 15,271. Moreton-in-Marsh 14, London 98, Birmingham 30, Cheltenham 16, Stratford-upon-Avon 14, Tewkesbury 13, Worcester 16.
EC Wed. **Golf** Broadway 18h, Evesham 9h. **See** Abbey ruins, All Saints' Church, St Lawrence Church, Walker Hall, Abbey Almonry (now local history museum), Old Town Hall, Abbey Park and Gardens.
i Almonry Museum, Abbey Gate. (0386) 44 6944

★★★ R **Evesham,** Coppers La, off Waterside, WR11 6DA (0386) 765566 Tx: 339342 Fax: (0386) 765443

Tudor and Georgian mansion set in a quiet, pleasant 2½ acre garden. Indoor swimming pool, putting. Closed 25–26 Dec.
40 bedrs, 40 en suite; TV; tcf
dogs; P 50; child facs; con 15
LD 9.30
£ B&B £50–£54, B&B (double) £72–£80; L £9, D £15; WB £33.
cc Access, Amex, B'card/Visa, Diners.

★★★ **Northwick Arms**, Waterside, WR11 6BT (0386) 40322 Tx: 333686 Fax: (0386) 41070
Refurbished 3-storey Victorian building overlooking River Avon. (Lns)
25 bedrs, 25 en suite; TV; tcf
dogs, P 60, coach; child facs; con 50
LD 9
£ B&B £45 (w/e £22), B&B (double) £55; D £11; WB £32
cc Access, Amex, B'card/Visa, Diners.

★★ C **Mill at Harvington**, Anchor La, WR11 5NR. (0386) 870688. Fr

An 18th century mill, sensitively converted and in a superb location by the River Avon. Fishing. Closed 23–29 Dec.
15 bedrs, 15 en suite; TV; tcf;
P 30; no children under 16; con 14
LD 9, nr Mon–Sat lunch. Resid & Rest lic
£ B&B £54–£57; B&B (double) £78–£83; L £14; D £17·50; WB £70
cc Access, B'card/Visa.

★★ **Riverside**, The Parks, Offenham Rd, WR11 5JP. (0386) 446200. Fax: (0386) 40021. Fr, Es.
Large, cottage style house looking down over a 3 acre garden to the River Avon. Well appointed individually decorated bedrooms.
7 bedrs, 7 en suite; TV; tcf
P 40; coach; child facs
LD 9. Resid & Rest lic.
£ B&B £45–£50; B&B (double) £60–£75; L £11·95, D £15·95, WB £65 (HB); [10% V]
cc Access, B'card/Visa.

★ **Park View,** Waterside, WR11 6BS (0386) 442639

Small hotel facing river and gardens. Carefully updated, turn-of-century building.
29 bedrs; 6 ba
TV; dogs: P40; coach; child facs
LD 7; bar snacks only Mon–Sat lunch & Sun dinner, Resid & Rest lic
£ B&B £16–£20; B&B (double) £30·50–£33·50; D £7·75; [5% V]
cc Access, B'card/Visa; dep.

EWEN Gloucestershire. Map 20C1

Pop 150. Cirencester 3½, London 91, Chippenham 18, Swindon 16, Tetbury 9.
Golf Cirencester 18h.

★★★ **Wild Duck Inn,** Cirencester, GL7 6BY (0285) 770310

An attractive 16th century village inn of great character.
10 bedrs, 10 en suite; TV; tcf
dogs; P 50; child facs
£ B&B £48, B&B (double) £65–£75; [5% V]
cc Access, B'card/Visa.

EXEBRIDGE Somerset. Map 3C4

Taunton 22, London 166, Dunster 17, Lynmouth 25, South Molton 14, Tiverton 10.

★★ **Anchor Inn,** Dulverton (0398) 23433
Small 300 year old inn in pleasant setting by the River Exe. Fishing, snooker.
6 bedrs, 6 en suite; TV; tcf
TV, dogs; P 100, coach; child facs; con 40
LD 9
£ B&B £40, B&B (double) £54–£60; HB weekly £215–£225; L £8·25, D £12·95
cc Access, B'card/Visa, dep.

EXETER Devon. Map 3C3

See also STOKE CANON
RAC Office, *188 Sidwell St, Exeter, EX4 6RD* (0392) 58333
Pop 98,800. Honiton 17, London 169, M5 Motorway 3, Ashburton 19, Crediton 7½, Okehampton 22, Tiverton 15.
See Plan, p. 243.
MD Daily. **P** See Plan. **Golf** Exeter G and CC 18h. **See** Cathedral, Museum and Art Gallery, Northernhay Gardens, Southernhay (old houses and fine gardens), Customs House, Mol's Coffee House, Tucker's Hall, Rougemont, Castle ruins, Maritime Museum, Guildhall, St Nicholas' Priory (16th-cent), remains of City Walls, ancient underground passage, Museum (Rougemont House), Wynard's Almshouses.
i Civic Centre. (0392) 72434

★★★★ **Forte**, Southern Way East, EX1 1QF (0392) 412812. Tx 42712 Fax: (0329) 413549.

Modern hotel with a mock Georgian facade close to the Cathedral in the city centre. Set in landscaped gardens with a Health and Fitness Centre.
110 bedrs, 110 en suite; TV; tcf
lift; dogs; ns; P 115; coach; child facs; con 80
LD 10.00
£ B&B £98; B&B (double) £108; HB weekly £371; L £13, D £17; WB £61
cc Amex, Access, B'card/Visa, CB, Diners.

★★★★ **Royal Clarence,** Cathedral Yard, EX1 1HD (0392) 58464 Tx: 42919 Fax: (0392) 439423.

Weekend breaks
Please consult the hotel for full details of weekend breaks; prices shown are an indication only. Many hotels offer mid week breaks as well.

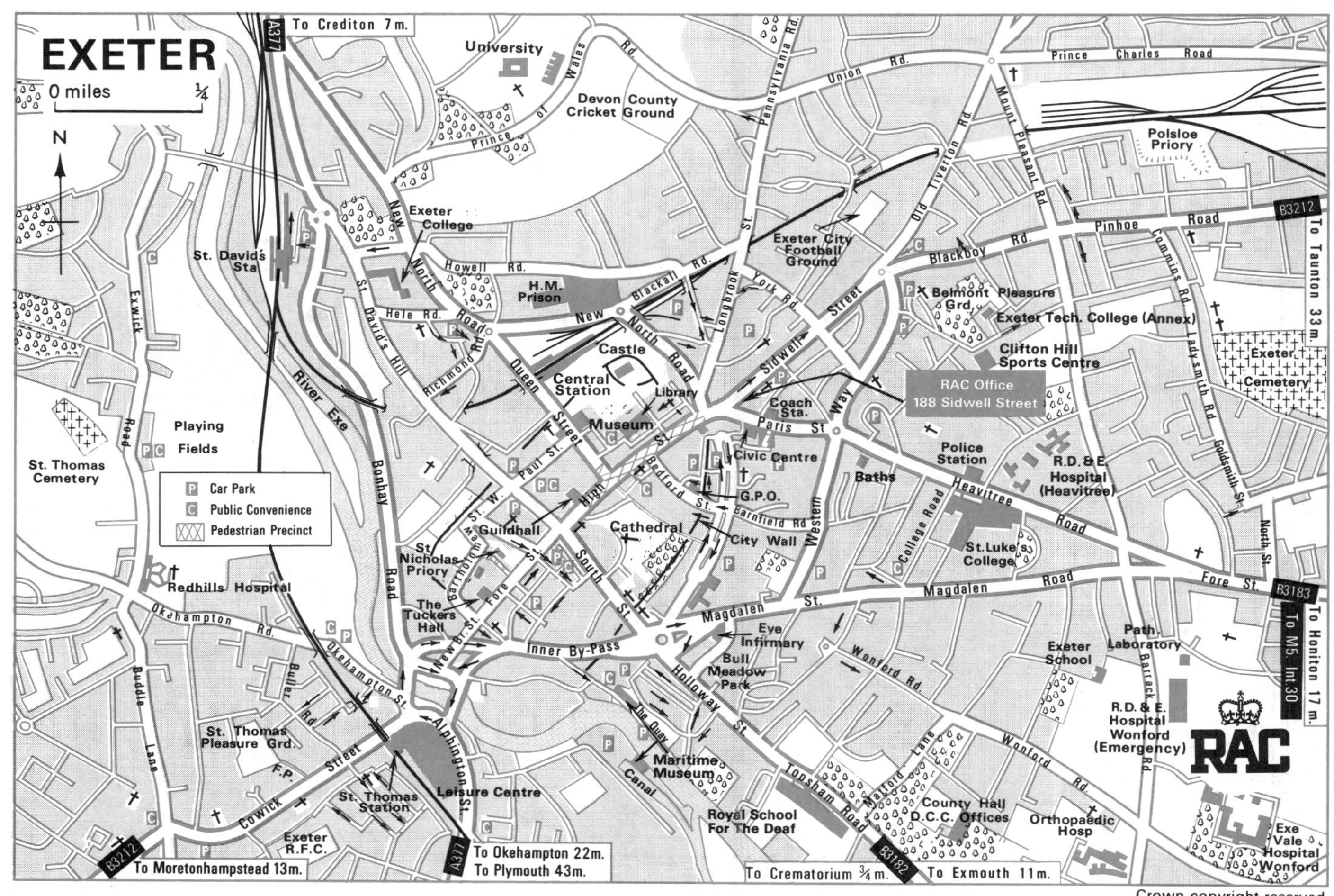

EXETER
0 miles
1/4
N
To Crediton 7 m.
A377
University
Devon County Cricket Ground
Exeter College
St. David's Sta
H.M. Prison
Castle
Central Station
Library
Museum
Guildhall
St Nicholas Priory
The Tuckers Hall
Cathedral
City Wall
G.P.O.
Civic Centre
Coach Sta.
Exeter City Football Ground
Polsloe Priory
Belmont Pleasure Grd.
Exeter Tech. College (Annex)
Clifton Hill Sports Centre
RAC Office
188 Sidwell Street
Exeter Cemetery
Police Station
Baths
R.D.& E. Hospital (Heavitree)
St.Luke's College
Eye Infirmary
Bull Meadow Park
Maritime Museum
Canal
Royal School For The Deaf
County Hall D.C.C. Offices
Orthopaedic Hosp
Exe Vale Hospital Wonford
R.D.& E. Hospital Wonford (Emergency)
Exeter School
Path. Laboratory
RAC
Leisure Centre
St. Thomas Station
Exeter R.F.C.
St. Thomas Pleasure Grd.
Redhills Hospital
Playing Fields
St. Thomas Cemetery
River Exe
Car Park
Public Convenience
Pedestrian Precinct
To Taunton 33 m.
B3212
To Honiton 17 m.
To M5. Int.30
B3183
To Moretonhampstead 13m.
To Okehampton 22m.
To Plymouth 43m.
To Crematorium 3/4 m.
B3182
To Exmouth 11 m.
Crown copyright reserved

Exeter (Devon)

★★★ *RAC Appointed*

THE WHITE HART HOTEL

SOUTH STREET EXETER DEVON

Telephone EXETER (0392) 79897

FOR TARIFF SOUVENIR

Visitors to The White Hart today, will enjoy the wide and varied menus that are offered from the Dining Room, the Grill Room or the Bars. Traditional meals, excellently prepared, cooked and served in the proper manner are available for your choice, together with the finest Wines, Port, Sherry, Madeira, etc. — All to be savoured in an atmosphere, and with such service, you may think belongs to bygone days.

The White Hart is one of the City's most ancient Inns. It is situated in a central position within the old city wall and a few yards from the site of the South Gate, through which Henry VI entered the city in 1452. The gate, together with its mediaeval prison, was demolished in 1819, by which time The White Hart had been in existence for nearly four hundred years, originating it is thought, as a resting house for monks. Two of the more notable features are the XV century Wine Room and an adjoining wall with an early English stone fireplace, now incorporated in the Bar. This fireplace was discovered during restoration work in 1955 and is one of the finest examples of its type in the West of England. It was probably constructed between 1440 and 1460. Much too, of the original structure of the Stables, where Cromwell rested his horses during the Civil War is in evidence in the reception area.

THE COURTYARD

During the XVII and XVIII centuries The White Hart became a coaching Inn. The coaches drove through the courtyard to the stables, horses snorting and hooves clattering on the cobbles. Travellers with the coachmen, would call for their half gallon jugs of Ale to be passed through the windows of the Wine Room. Today The White Hart still offers half gallon jugs of real ale and still maintains the old world atmosphere and comfort of the traditional English Inn.

SPECIAL WEEKEND TERMS

Distinguished Georgian building, with modern bedrooms; facing Cathedral.
56 bedrs, 56 en suite; TV; tcf
lift, ns; P 15, child facs; con 120
LD 9.45
£ B&B £80 (w/e £35), B&B (double) £101–£137; HB weekly £350; L £9·95, D £17·50
cc Access, Amex, B'card/Visa, CB, Diners.

★★★ C R **Buckerell Lodge,** Topsham Rd, EX2 4SQ (0392) 52451
Tx: 42410
Villa-type building with a modern extension set in pleasant grounds.

★★★ **Countess Wear Lodge,** 398 Topsham Rd, EX2 6HE Topsham (039 287) 5441 Tx: 42551
Fax: (039 287) 6174

Modern motor hotel with purpose built accommodation in annexe. Tennis. (QMH)
Fr, It
annexe 44 bedrs, 44 en suite; TV; tcf
dogs, ns; P 120, coach; child facs; con 200
LD 9.45. Resid & Rest lic
£ B&B £49–£59 (w/e £30), B&B (double) £60–£65 (w/e £48); L £9·10, D £14·50; WB £36; [10% V]
cc Access, Amex, B'card/Visa, Diners.

★★★ **Devon,** Exeter By-pass, Matford, EX2 8XU (0392) 59268 Tx: 42551
Fax: (0392) 413142

Adjacent to by-pass, building of Georgian origin with motel accommodation.
41 bedrs, 41 en suite; TV; tcf
dogs, P 300, coach; child facs; con 160
LD 9
£ B&B £42–£50, B&B (double) £52–£72; HB weekly £245–£340; L £9, D £12; WB £72 (2 nts HB)
cc Access, Amex, B'card/Visa, Diners.
(*See advertisement on p. 246*)

★★★ **Exeter Arms,** Rydon La, Middlemoor, EX2 7HL (0392) 435353 Fax: (0392) 420826
Modern purpose-built motor hotel conveniently situated on ring road.
37 bedrs, 37 en suite; TV; tcf
ns; P 380, coach; child facs; con 80

Changes made after July 1990 are not included.

★★★ **Exeter Court,** Kennford Service Area, EX6 7UX (0392) 832121 Tx: 42443
Fax: (0392) 833590

Purpose-built motor hotel on the A38, at Kennford. Golf, tennis, billiards. Fr
63 bedrs, 63 en suite; TV; tcf
dogs; P 200, coach; child facs; con 160
LD 9.30
£ B&B £41–£49, B&B (double) £54–£59; HB weekly £165–£220; L £10·95, D £10·95; WB; [5% V Jan–Oct]
cc Access, Amex, B'card/Visa, Diners.

★★★ **Gipsy Hill Country House,** Gipsy Hill La, Pinhoe, EX1 3RN (0392) 65252
Fax: (0392) 64302
Family-run, brick-built house in attractive gardens. Modernised and extended. Fr, Es, Po
20 bedrs, 20 en suite; annexe 8 bedrs, 8 en suite; TV; tcf
dogs, ns; P 80, coach; child facs; con 120
LD 9.15
£ B&B £47–£55, B&B (double) £58–£70; L £8, D £13; WB £77 (2 nts); [V]
cc Access, Amex, B'card/Visa.
(*See advertisement on p. 246*)

★★★ R **Imperial,** New North Rd, EX4 4JX (0392) 211811 Tx: 42551
Fax: (0392) 420906

Privately-owned, well-appointed hotel in Queen Anne house in attractive grounds. Putting.
27 bedrs, 23 en suite, 3 ba; TV
dogs; P 70, U 3, coach; child facs; con 220

★★★ H C **Lord Haldon,** Dunchideock, EX6 7YF (0392) 832483
Pleasant country house, originally one wing of a Georgian mansion, six miles SW of Exeter. Riding.
20 bedrs, 20 en suite; TV; tcf
TV, dogs; P 60, coach; child facs; con 150
LD 9
£ B&B £32·50–£38·50, B&B (double) £49·50–£64·50; HB weekly £220–£248; WB £70 (2 nts HB)
cc Access, B'card/Visa; dep.

★★★ **Rougemont,** Queen St, EX4 3SP (0392) 54982 Tx: 42455

City centre hotel—an imposing Victorian building opposite Central station. (MtCh)
90 bedrs, 90 en-suite; TV; tcf
lift; dogs; P 40; coach; child facs; con 300
LD 10
£ B&B £60; B&B (double) £69·50; WB £36·50 (HB) L £7·50, D £12·50
cc Access, Amex, B'card/Visa, Diners.

★★★ **St Olaves Court,** Mary Arches St, EX4 3AZ (0392) 217736
Fax: (0392) 413054
A fine 2-storey Georgian building built around a pretty courtyard set in secluded gardens in city centre. Fr
13 bedrs, 11 en suite, annexe 4 bedrs, 4 en suite, 1 ba; TV; tcf
TV, dogs; P 15, G 2; child facs; con 30
LD 9.30
£ B&B £33–£59, B&B (double) £46–£70; L £10·95, D £14·95; WB £30 (HB); [10% V]
cc Access, Amex, B'card/Visa, Diners.

★★★ C R **White Hart,** South St, EX1 1EF (0392) 79897 Tx: 42521
Fax: (0392) 50159

Inn of great character (14th century) with large hotel extension. In city centre.
64 bedrs, 64 en suite; TV
lift, TV; P 55; child facs; con 60
LD 10
£ B&B £48–£52; B&B (double) £64; L £7·50; WB £36
cc Access, Amex, B'card/Visa, Diners.
(*See advertisement on p. 244*)

E

Exeter (Devon)

The Devon Motel

RAC★★★

ENJOY LUXURY 3 STAR COMFORTS IN DEVON'S HEARTLAND

Conveniently situated close to Exeter by-pass and town centre with easy access to the M5 – yet surrounded by beautiful countryside.

Family owned and managed offering excellent service and value. Very popular bar, entertainments and function rooms. All rooms with colour T.V., radio, direct dial telephones, tea & coffee making facilities, en suite shower/bath etc. First class menu and wine list.

For free colour brochure contact: Mr. R. Towl, Devon Motel, Matford, Exeter, Devon EX32 8XU. Tel: (0392) 59268 Fax No: (0392) 413142

Exeter (Devon)

Gipsy Hill Hotel and Restaurant

R.A.C. ★★★

GIPSY HILL LANE (Nr. Sowton Ind. Estate)
PINHOE, EXETER, DEVON EX1 3RN

* Country House Hotel in lovely gardens with views over Devon countryside.
* Close to Exeter Airport and City Centre.
* Convenient to M5 junction 30 (1 mile).
* All the centrally heated rooms have private bathroom, colour TV, telephone (direct dial), radio, tea and coffee making, trouser press and hair dryer.
* Excellent cuisine from our Table d'Hôte and à la Carte.
* A variety of meeting rooms and function suites for up to 120 guests.
* Personally managed by proprietor Geoffrey Stockman, MHCIMA.

Telephone: 0392 65252

Exeter (Devon)

The Barton Cross Hotel

xvii century

17th Century Charm – 20th Century Luxury

RAC ★★★ Comfort, Restaurant and Hospitality Awards
British Tourist Authority Commended Hotel

International Standard Accommodation with superb cuisine. Set in glorious Devon countryside yet only five miles from Exeter. Easy access to Dartmoor, Exmoor and the coast.
Relaxing Weekend and Midweek Breaks. Christmas House Party.

BARTON CROSS HOTEL AND RESTAURANT
at HUXHAM, Exeter, EX5 4EJ
Phone (0392) 841245 Telex: 42603 Fax: (0392) 50402

★★ **Bystock,** Bystock Ter, EX4 4HY
☎(0392) 72709

Family-run, Gothic style stone-built hotel in quiet location.

★★ **Ebford House,** Exmouth Rd, Ebford EX3 0QH ☎(0392) 877658
Fax: (0392) 874424

In spacious and attractive gardens, a charming Georgian residence just off A37. Sauna, solarium, gymnasium. ✗ Fr, De
🛏9 bedrs, 9 en suite; annexe 9 bedrs, 9 en suite; TV; tcf
ns; P 45, child facs
✕LD 9.30, bar meals only Sat lunch & all Sun & Mon. Resid & Rest lic.
£ B&B £45–£52, B&B (double) £60–£75; L £12·25, D £17
cc Access, Amex, B'card/Visa.

★★ **Gt Western,** St David's Station Approach, EX4 4NU ☎(0392) 74039
Tx: 42551
Privately-owned, 3-storey hotel adjacent to St David's station.
🛏 42 bedrs, 20 en suite, 10 ba; TV; tcf
dogs; P 30, coach; child facs; con 40

★★ **Red House,** 2 Whipton Village Rd, EX4 8AR ☎(0392) 56104

Brick-built turn-of-century building, just off the B3212 in quiet residential area.
🛏12 bedrs, 12 en suite; TV; tcf
dogs; P 28, coach, child facs
✕LD 9.30
£ B&B £35 (w/e £27); B&B (double) £48; WB £50 (2 nts); L £7·50, D £10·50; [5% V]
cc Access, B'card/Visa.

★★ H C **St Andrews,** 28 Alphington Rd, EX2 8HN ☎(0392) 76784 ♿

Family-run, brick-built hotel with modern facilities. Five minutes from city centre. Closed 23 Dec–2 Jan.
🛏17 bedrs, 17 en suite, 2 ba; TV; tcf
dogs; P 20; child facs
✕LD 8.15, bar meals only lunch. Resid & Rest lic
£ B&B £35–£44, B&B (double) £54–£63; D £11; WB £38
cc Access, Amex, B'card/Visa.

Park View (Acclaimed), 8 Howell Rd, EX4 4LG ☎(0392) 71772. *Hotel.* ✗ De
£ B&B £16–£28

Braeside, 21 New North Rd, EX4 4HF ☎(0392) 56875. *Hotel.*
Cre-Ber, 32 Heavitree Rd, EX1 2LQ ☎(0392) 76102. *Guest House.*
Regents Park, Polsloe Rd, EX1 2NU ☎(0392) 59749. *Hotel.*
£ B&B £15.
Rowhorne House, Rowhorne, Whitestone, EX4 2LQ ☎(0392) 74675. *Farm.* Open Mar–Oct
£ B&B £11; HB weekly £112; [V].
Telstar, 77 St David's Hill, EX4 4DW ☎(0392) 72466. *Private Hotel.* Closed 24 Dec–2 Jan
£ B&B £12–£20; HB weekly £110–£140; [5% V]
Trees Mini, 2 Queen's Cres, York Road, EX4 6AY ☎(0392) 59531. Hotel.
£ B&B £14–£15.

EXFORD Somerset. Map 3C4

Dunster 11, London 177, Barnstaple 22, Ilfracombe 24, Lynmouth 14, South Molton 13, Taunton 35, Tiverton 22.

★★★ **Crown,** Minehead, TA24 7PP ☎(064 383) 554

17th-century coaching inn in 3 acres of gardens. Riding.
(*See advertisement on p. 248*)

EXMOOR

See Dulverton, Exford, Wheddon Cross, Winsford.

EXMOUTH Devon. Map 4A1

Pop 28,319. Honiton 17, London 170, Axminster 26, Exeter 11, Lyme Regis 27. **EC** Wed. **Golf** East Devon, Budleigh Salterton 18h. **See** A La Ronde–18th cent house with Shell Gallery.
ℹ Alexandra Ter. ☎(0395) 263744

★★★ **Devoncourt,** Douglas Av, EX8 2EX ☎(0395) 272277
Purpose-built pleasant 1930s hotel in 4 acres of sub-tropical gardens. Indoor/outdoor swimming pool, putting, tennis, sauna, solarium, gymnasium, snooker.
🛏47 bedrs, 47 en suite; TV; tcf
lift; TV; P 60; child facs
✕LD 9.45, bar meals only Sat lunch
£ B&B £34–£57, B&B (double) £68–£104; L £7·60, D £10·95
cc Access, Amex, B'card/Visa, Diners; dep.
(*See advertisement on p. 000*)

★★★ **Imperial,** Esplanade, EX8 2SW ☎(0395) 274761

Purpose-built hotel with fine sea views. Swimming pool, tennis. (THF)
🛏57 bedrs, 57 en suite; TV; tcf
lift, dogs, ns; P 50; child facs; con 61
✕LD 9, bar meals only Mon–Sat lunch
£ B&B £67; B&B (double) £94–£104; HB weekly £280–£343. L £7·50, D £13·50; WB £47
cc Access, Amex, B'card/Visa, Diners.

★★★ **Royal Beacon,** The Beacon, EX8 2AF ☎(0395) 264886 Fax: (0395) 268890

Terraced Georgian hotel on high ground with good sea views. Billiards. ✗ Fr
🛏30 bedrs, 30 en suite, TV; tcf
lift, TV, dogs, ns; P 20, U10, coach; child facs; con 100
✕LD 9.30
£ B&B £39–£42·35, B&B (double) £67·30–£72·60; L £7·25, D £12·50
cc Access, B'card/Visa; dep.

Please tell the manager if you chose your hotel through an advertisement in the guide.

E

Exford (Somerset)

THE CROWN HOTEL

Exford, Somerset TA24 7PP

Tel: (064 383) 554/5

17th Century Hotel situated in the heart of Exmoor, 17 bedrooms comfortably furnished with private bathrooms. Dine by candlelight and enjoy our award winning cuisine and fine wines. Bargain breaks available all year. Pets welcome. Ashley Courtenay/Egon Ronay recommended.

Exmoor (Somerset)

The Royal Oak Inn

Winsford

14th Century, oak-beamed, cosy, residential Inn and first-class Restaurant situated in prettiest Somerset village in Exmoor National Park.

Winsford, Exmoor National Park
Somerset TA24 7JE
Tel: Winsford (064385) 455 (4 lines)
Fax: (064385) 388

Exmouth (Devon)

Devoncourt Hotel

16 Douglas Avenue, Exmouth, Devon EX8 2EX. Tel: 0395 272277

Purpose-built pleasant 1930s hotel in four acres of sub-tropical gardens. Indoor/outdoor swimming pool, putting, tennis, sauna, solarium, gymnasium.

Fairford (Gloucestershire)

Hyperion House Hotel

London Road, Fairford, Glos. GL7 4AH Tel: 0285 712349

Situated in the historic town of Fairford in the Cotswolds, The Hyperion, with 30 bedrooms en-suite, offers good food and wine in a warm, friendly and relaxing atmosphere.

★★ **Balcombe House,** 7 Stevenstone Rd, EX8 2EP ☎(0395) 266349

Spacious brick-built hotel with agreeable garden in residential area. Open Apr–Oct.
12 bedrs, 12 en suite; TV; tcf
ns; P 14; children over 10
LD 6, bar meals only lunch. Resid lic
£ B&B £22·10–£25·50; HB weekly £197–£207; B&B (double) £44·20–£48; D £9·85; dep.

★★ **Barn,** Foxholes, off Marine Dr, EX8 2DF ☎(0395) 274411

Listed stone-built hotel in peaceful garden with good sea views. Swimming pool, tennis.
11 bedrs, 9 en suite, (1 sh), TV; tcf
ns; P 30, G 3 (£1), coach; child facs; con 100
LD 8, bar meals only Mon–Sat lunch. Resid & Rest lic
£ B&B £24·50–£33·50, B&B (double) £49–£57; HB weekly £216–£240; L £7·25, D £12
cc Access, B'card/Visa; dep.

★★ **Manor,** The Beacon, EX8 2AG ☎(0395) 272549
Terraced hotel with modern facilities. Easy walk to town and sea. Fr, De.
42 bedrs, 40 en suite; TV; tcf
lift; dogs; P 8; coach; child facs; con 100
LD 8; nr lunch.
£ B&B £24–£27; B&B (double) £40–£52; L £4·50, D £6·50
cc Access, Amex, B'card/Visa; dep.

★ **Aliston House**, 58 Salterton Sq, EX8 2EW ☎(0395) 274119

Small hotel pleasantly situated in own grounds 1 mile from the sea front.
12 bedrs, 6 en suite; 2 ba; annexe 2 bedrs, 2 en suite; TV; tcf
TV; dogs; P 16; coach; child facs; con 60
LD 8.30; nr lunch Mon–Fri. Resid lic
£ B&B £18–£23; B&B (double) £36–£44; HB weekly £170–£190; L £6; D £7·25; WB £52 (2 nts); [5% V Nov–May]; dep.

Carlton Lodge (Acclaimed), Carlton Hill, EX8 2AJ ☎(0395) 263314. *Hotel.*
£ B&B £21–£26·50; HB weekly £135–£175; WB £42·50; [5% V Nov–Mar]

Blenheim, 39 Morton Rd, EX8 1BA ☎(0395) 264230. *Guest House.*
St. Aubyns, 11 Hartley Rd, EX8 2SG ☎(0395) 264069. *Guest House.*

EYNSFORD Kent. Map 9B2

Pop 1,800. Sidcup 7½, London 20, M20/M25 2½, Dartford 6½, Dartford Tunnel 9½, Rochester 16, Sevenoaks 7½.
EC Wed. **Golf** Lullingstone Park 18h. **See** Norm and EE Church, Castle ruins, Tudor Cottages. At Lullingstone–Roman Villa & Castle.

Castle, High St, DA4 0AB ☎Farningham (0322) 863162. *Inn.*

FAIRFORD Gloucestershire. Map 20C1

Pop 2,308. Faringdon 10, London 80, Burford 13, Cirencester 9, Swindon 15.
EC Thur. **Golf** Cirencester 18h. **See** Perp St Mary's Church.

★★★ **Hyperion House,** London St, GL7 4AH ☎Cirencester (0285) 712349
Fax: (0285) 713126
Extensively modernised Cotswold vicarage (partly Tudor) set in pleasant gardens.
30 bedrs, 30 en suite; TV; tcf
dogs; P 30, child facs; con 50
LD 9.30, bar meals only lunch
£ B&B £60–£70; B&B (double) £70–£80; L £10, D £20; WB £100 (HB)
cc Access, Amex, B'card/Visa, Diners.
(*See advertisement on p. 248*)

FAKENHAM Norfolk. Map 35A2

Pop 5,803. Swaffham 16, London 113, Cromer 22, East Dereham 12, King's Lynn 22, Norwich 26.
EC Wed. **MD** Thur. **Golf** Fakenham 9h. **See** Parish Church, Walsingham Abbey ruins.
ℹ 37 Market Pl. ☎(0328) 51981

★★ **Crown,** 37 Market Pl, NR21 9BP ☎(0328) 51418

A 17th-century town-centre inn with many beams and a 'listed' fireplace.
11 bedrs, 11 en suite; TV; tcf
P 25, coach; child facs
LD 9.30
£ B&B £36, B&B (double) £48; L £8, D £8; WB
cc Access, Amex, B'card/Visa, Diners.

FALMOUTH Cornwall. Map 2B1

See also MAWNAN SMITH
Pop 18,000. Truro 11, London 266, Helston 13, Redruth 10.
Golf Falmouth 18h.
ℹ 28 Killigrew St, ☎(0326) 312300

★★★ **Falmouth,** Cliff Road, TR11 4NZ ☎(0326) 312671 Tx: 45262.
Modernised Victorian hotel on seafront set in prize-winning gardens. Swimming pool, putting, billiards.

★★★ **Greenbank,** Harbourside, TR11 2SR ☎(0326) 312440 Tx: 45240
Fax: (0326) 211362
Historic Georgian building right on the quayside. Fishing, solarium. Fr.
43 bedrs, 43 en suite, 1 ba; TV; tcf
lift, dogs; P 40, G 24, coach; child facs; con 100
LD 9.45
£ B&B £33–£65, B&B (double) £80–£115; HB weekly £325–£450; L £9, D £15·50; WB £90 (2 nts)
cc Access, Amex, B'card/Visa, Diners.

★★★ **Green Lawns,** Western Terr, TR11 4QJ ☎(0326) 312734 Tx: 45169
Fax: (0326) 211427
In lovely gardens, a distinctive building with French château features. Indoor swimming pool, tennis, sqaush, sauna, solarium, gymnasium. Fr. Closed 24–30 Dec.
40 bedrs, 40 en suite, 2 ba; TV; tcf
dogs; P 60, G 9; coach; child facs; con 200
LD 10
£ B&B £42·55–£60·20, B&B (double) £58·64–£89·70; HB weekly £278·30–£404·80; L £8·50 (Sun), D £15·50; WB fr £52; [10% V w/d]
cc Access, Amex, B'card/Visa, CB, Diners; dep.

★★★ **Gyllyngdune Manor,** Melvill Rd, TR11 4AR ☎(0326) 312978

Old Georgian manor house in 2 acres of gardens. Indoor swimming pool, sauna, solarium.
35 bedrs, 35 en suite, TV; tcf
dogs; P 25, G 3, coach; child facs
LD 9, bar meals only Mon–Sat lunch
£ B&B £28–£40; HB weekly £259–£350; L £8, D £12
cc Access, Amex, B'card/Visa, Diners; dep.

Residents only
Some Listed hotels only serve meals to residents. It is always wise to make a reservation for a meal in a hotel.

F

Falmouth (Cornwall)

Falmouth (Cornwall)

Falmouth (Cornwall)

★★★ H C Meudon, Maenporth Road, TR11 5HT ☎(0326) 250541 Tx: 45478 Fax: (0326) 250543

Country-house hotel in 10 acres of sub-tropical gardens descending to private beach and the sea. Fishing, riding. Closed Jan. Fr, It.
32 bedrs, 32 en suite, TV;
dogs, ns; P 50, U 2; children over 5
LD 9. Resid & Rest lic
£ B&B £60–£70, B&B (double) £100–£170; HB weekly £409·50–£535·50; L £12, D £22·50; WB fr £55 (HB)
cc Access, B'card/Visa, Diners; dep.

★★★ H C Penmere Manor, Mongleath Rd, TR11 4PN ☎(0326) 211411 Tx: 45608 Fax: (0326) 317588
Two-storey white-faced fine Georgian mansion in secluded gardens. Indoor & outdoor swimming pools, sauna, solarium, gymnasium. Closed 24–27 Dec.
39 bedrs, 39 en suite; TV; tcf
dogs, ns; P 60; child facs; con 18
LD 9, bar meals only lunch
£ B&B £45–£86, B&B (double) £68–£97; HB weekly £292–£430; D £17; WB £43.
cc Access, Amex, B'card/Visa, Diners; dep.

★★★ Royal Duchy, Cliff Rd, TR11 4NX ☎(0326) 313042 Tx: 42551 Fax: (0326) 319420

Surrounded by own garden, 3-storey gabled hotel with views of the Bay. Indoor swimming pool, sauna, solarium.
50 bedrs, 50 en suite; TV; tcf
lift, TV, dogs; P 45, G 9, coach; child facs; con 150
LD 9
£ B&B £44–£50, B&B (double) £77–£125; HB weekly £240–£470; L £7·50, D £13·50; WB £80 (2 nts HB)
cc Access, Amex, B'card/Visa, Diners.
(See advertisement on p. 250)

Changes made after July 1990 are not included.

★★★ St Michaels of Falmouth, Gyllyngvase Beach, TR11 4ND ☎(0326) 312707 Tx: 45540 Fax: (0326) 319147

Substantial hotel in exceptional gardens enjoying fine sea views. Indoor swimming pool, sauna, solarium, gymnasium. Fr, De.
60 bedrs, 60 en suite; TV; tcf
dogs, ns; P 100, coach; child facs; con 200
LD 9.30, bar meals only Mon–Sat lunch
£ L £8·50, D £13; WB £42 (HB Nov–May)
cc Access, Amex, B'card/Visa, Diners; dep.
(See advertisement on p. 250)

★★ Carthion, Cliff Rd, TR11 4AP ☎(0326) 313669

Small family-managed hotel with panoramic view over the sea. Open Mar–Oct
18 bedrs, 18 en suite; TV; tcf
dogs; ns; P 14; no children under 10
LD 8, bar snacks only lunch. Resid & Rest lic
£ B&B £25–£30, B&B (double) £50–£60; D £11·50
cc Access, Amex, B'card/Visa, Diners; dep.

★★ Crill Manor, Budock Water, TR11 5BL ☎(0326) 312994. Fax: (0326) 211229

Small family-run hotel in quiet countryside with attractive garden. Swimming pool, sauna, solarium. De.
11 bedrs, 11 en suite; TV; tcf
dogs; P 25; child facs
LD 9.30, Resid & Rest lic
£ B&B £32·50–£52·50; HB weekly £276–£416·50; L £9; D £13·50; [10% V Nov–Mar]
cc Access, B'card/Visa; dep.

★ Tresillian House, Stracey Rd, TR11 4DW ☎(0326) 312425
Three-storey white-faced hotel just off the main sea front road. Closed Nov–Feb.
12 bedrs, 12 en suite; TV; tcf
ns; P 8; child facs
LD 7.30, bar snacks only lunch. Resid & Rest lic
£ B&B £18·50–£19·50; HB weekly £136·50–£157·50; D £11; WB £61·50; [V Mar–May, Oct]; dep.

Chellowdene (Acclaimed), Gyllyngvase Hill, TR11 4DN ☎(0326) 314950. *Guest House.* Open 28 Apr–3 Oct.
£ B&B (double) £28; [V Apr–May]
Hawthorne Dene (Acclaimed), 12 Pennance Rd, TR11 4EA ☎(0326) 311427. *Private Hotel.* Open Easter–Oct
£ B&B £14–£17; HB weekly £124–£149
Rathgowry (Acclaimed), Gyllyngvase Hill, TR11 4DN ☎(0326) 313482. *Hotel.* Open Mar–end Oct.
Trevaylor (Acclaimed) 8 Pennance Rd, TR11 4EA ☎(0326) 313041. *Hotel.* Open Easter–Oct
£ B&B (double) £24–£28; HB weekly £112–£126

Cotswold House, 49 Melvill Rd, TR11 4DF ☎(0326) 312077. *Private Hotel.* Fr, Ge.
£ B&B £16·50; HB weekly £256–£280; [5% V]
Dolvean, 50 Melvill Rd, TR11 4DQ ☎(0326) 313658. *Hotel.* Open Easter–15 Oct.
£ B&B £13·20–£22; HB weekly £110–£165
Dunmede, 11 Melvill Rd, TR11 4AS ☎(0326) 313429. *Guest House.* De.
£ B&B £11; HB weekly £79; [10% V]
Gyllyngvase House, Gyllyngvase Rd, TR11 4DJ ☎(0326) 312956. *Hotel.* Fr
£ B&B £15·50–£29; HB weekly £142–£159
Penty Bryn, 10 Melvill Rd, TR11 4AS ☎(0326) 314988. *Guest House.* Closed Easter–Oct.
£ B&B £13·50

F

FAREHAM Hampshire. Map 5C2

Pop 84,200. Cosham 5, London 72, M27 (jn 10) 1, Alton 24, Portsmouth 9, Romsey 20, Southampton 12, Winchester 19.
MD Mon. **Golf** Lee-on-the-Solent 18h. **See** St Peter's Church. Titchfield Abbey 2 m W, Portchester Castle, Church and Roman Fort 3 m E, Titchfield Abbey 2 m W.
[i] Ferneham Hall, Osborn Rd. ☎(0329) 221342

★★ Maylings Manor, Highland Rd, PO16 7XJ ☎(0329) 286451 Fax: (0329) 822584
Attractive Georgian manor house set in 3 acres of landscaped gardens.
24 bedrs, 24 en suite, 1 ba; TV; tcf
dogs; P 87, coach; child facs; con 100
LD 9.30, bar meals only Sat lunch and Sun dinner
£ B&B £48, B&B (double) £58; L £9·50, D £9·50; WB £28 (HB)
cc Access, Amex, B'card/Visa, Diners; dep.
(See advertisement on p. 255)

★★ Red Lion, East St, PO16 0BP ☎(0329) 822640 Tx: 86204 Fax: (0329) 823579 ♿
A 16th-century former coaching inn in town centre. (Lns).
44 bedrs, 44 en suite; TV; tcf
ns; P 136, con 120
£ B&B £69, B&B (double) £83; L £11, D £11; WB £31; [10% V]
cc Access, Amex, B'card/Visa, Diners.

Avenue House (Acclaimed), 22, The Avenue, PO14 1NS ☎(0329) 232175. *Private Hotel.* ♿
£ B&B £29–£40; [10% V]

Seven Sevens, Hillhead Rd, Hillhead, PO14 3JL ☎ Stubbington (0329) 662408. *Guest House.*

FARINGDON Oxfordshire. Map 21A1

Pop 5,107. Wantage 9, London 70, Burford 12, Cirencester 18, Oxford 17, Swindon 12. **EC** Thur. **MD** Tue. **Golf** Bremhill Park, Shrivenham 18h. **See** Gothic Church, old arcaded Town Hall (now Library), Folly Tower, Pusey House Gardens, Buscot Park. ℹ Pump House, 5 Market Pl. ☎ (0367) 22191

★★ **Bell,** Market Pl, SN7 4HP ☎ (0367) 20534 Tx: 83343

Attractive 16th century inn situated in town square; privately owned.
🛏 11 bedrs, 7 en suite, 1 ba; TV
🏠 TV, dogs; P 11, G 4, coach; child facs, con 20
(*See advertisement on p. 255*)

★★ **Faringdon,** Market Pl, SN7 7HL ☎ (0367) 20536
Family run hotel in modernised and refurbished 19th century building.
🛏 17 bedrs, 17 en suite; annexe 5 bedrs, 5 en suite; TV; tcf
🏠 dogs; child facs; con 20
✕ LD 8.30, nr lunch & w/e dinner
£ B&B £38, B&B (double) £48; D £10
cc Access, Amex, B'card/Visa, Diners; dep.

FARMBOROUGH Avon. Map 5A3.

Bath 6, London 114, Bristol 7, Frome 12, Shepton Mallet 11.

★★ **Streets,** The Streets, BA3 1AR ☎ (0761) 71452 Tx: 44830 Fax: (0761) 52695
Stone-built, 17th-century house, charmingly furnished and set in an acre of landscaped gardens. Swimming pool. Open 2 Jan–22 Dec. ✗ Es.
🛏 8 bedrs, 8 en suite; TV; tcf
🏠 TV; P 8; children over 5
✕ LD 8.50, nr lunch & Sun dinner. Resid lic
£ B&B £39–£44, B&B (double) £46–£53; cc Access, Amex, B'card/Visa.
(*See advertisement on p. 126*)

FARNBOROUGH Hampshire. Map 13A1

Pop 79,400 (with Aldershot). Bagshot 7, London 34, M3 (jn 4) 3, Basingstoke 18, Farnham 5½, Guildford 11, Henley-on-Thames 22, Reading 19, Woking 10. **EC** Wed. **MD** Tue. **Golf** Southwood 9h. ℹ Library, Pinehurst Av. ☎ (0252) 513838 **See** St Michael's Abbey and Benedictine Monastery.

Licences
Establishments have a full licence unless shown as unlicensed or with the limitations listed on p 6.

★★★ **Queen's,** Lynchford Rd, GU14 6AZ ☎ (0252) 545051 Tx: 859637 Fax: (0252) 377210

Imposing hotel with an Edwardian facade on the A325. Indoor swimming pool, sauna, solarium, gymnasium. ✗ Fr, De, Es, Da (THF)
🛏 110 bedrs, 110 en suite; TV; tcf
🏠 dogs, ns; P 170, coach; child facs; con 100
✕ LD 10, nr Sat lunch
£ room £85 (w/e £39·50); double room £90; Bk £8, L £15, D £15; WB £38
cc Access, Amex, B'card/Visa, Diners.

★★ **Falcon,** 68 Farnborough Rd, GU14 6TH ☎ (0252) 545378 Fax: (0252) 522539

Modernised hotel situated on A325 south of town opposite the aerospace centre, 3 miles from M3 junction 4. Closed 26 Dec–2 Jan. ✗ Du
🛏 30 bedrs, 30 en suite; TV; tcf
🏠 ns; P 30; child facs; con 20
✕ LD 9.30, bar meals only Sat & Sun lunch.
£ B&B £57 (w/e £37), B&B (double) £67; (w/e £57); L £12·50, D £15·50
cc Access, B'card/Visa.

FARNHAM Surrey. Map 6A2

Pop 35,160. Guildford 10, London 38, Alton 9½, Bagshot 12, Basingstoke 15, Hindhead 8½, Reading 25, Woking 14. **EC** Wed. **Golf** Farnham 9h. **See** 12th cent Castle Keep, 14th cent Church, "The William Cobbett" (birthplace of William Cobbett). ℹ South St ☎ (0483) 861111.

★★★ **Bush,** The Borough, GU9 7NN ☎ (0252) 715237 Tx: 858764 Fax: (0252) 733530

Well-known 17th–18th century coaching inn with modern block; pleasant gardens. (THF)
🛏 68 bedrs, 68 en suite; TV; tcf
🏠 dogs, ns; P 80, coach; child facs; con 70
✕ LD 9.30, nr Sat lunch
£ B&B £78–£90 (w/e £35), B&B (double) £101–£112; L £10·50, D £14·50; WB £45 (HB)
cc Access, Amex, B'card/Visa, CB, Diners.

★★★ **Frensham Pond,** Bacon Rd, Churt, GU10 2QB ☎ Frensham (025 125) 5161. Fax: (025 125) 2631

Delightful detached house overlooking pond; in a rural setting. Indoor swimming pool, squash, sauna, solarium, gymnasium.
🛏 41 bedrs, 41 en suite; annexe 12 bedrs, 12 en suite; TV; tcf
🏠 dogs; ns; P150; child facs; con 150
✕ LD 9.30
£ B&B £73–£83; B&B (double) £81–£121; HB weekly £616–£690; L £15·75; D £18·75; WB £50
cc Access, Amex, B'card/Visa, Diners.

★★ **H C R Bishop's Table,** 27 West St, GU9 7DR ☎ (0252) 710222 Tx: 94016743 Fax: (0252) 733494
18th century terrace house, furnished to a very high standard. Large garden. Closed 24 Dec–7 Jan
🛏 9 bedrs, 9 en suite; annexe 9 bedrs, 9 en suite, TV; tcf
🏠 ns; child facs; con 20
✕ LD 9.45
£ B&B £65–£79, B&B (double) £79; L £12·50, D £15; WB £45; [10% V w/e]
cc Access, Amex, B'card/Visa, Diners.

★★ **Pride of the Valley,** Tilford Rd, GU10 2LE ☎ Hindhead (0428) 605799 Tx: 858893 Fax: (0428) 605875

Small, detached country inn, beside lovely woods and commonland. ✗ Gr.
🛏 12 bedrs, 12 en suite; TV; tcf
🏠 dogs; P 40; child facs; con 20
✕ LD 10
£ B&B £57, B&B (double) £58; L £12·50, D £12·50; WB £45 (HB); [10% V]
cc Access, Amex, B'card/Visa, Diners.

🏰 ★★ **Trevena House,** Alton Rd, GU10 5ER ☎ (0252) 716908 Fax: (0252) 722583
Mock Tudor detached building in quiet grounds off main A31. Swimming pool, tennis. Open 4 Jan–24 Dec.
🛏 20 bedrs, 20 en suite; TV; tcf

 EC *early closing* **MD** *market day* 🏰 *country house hotel* *ns (NS) no smoking areas* *tcf tea/coffee facilities*

🏛 P 30; child facs; con 45
✕ LD 9.15, nr lunch, Sun dinner. Resid & Rest lic
£ B&B £45–£55, B&B (double) £55–£65. WB £33 (2 nts); [5% V w/e Oct–Apr]
cc Access, Amex, B'card/Visa, Diners; dep.

FAR SAWREY
Cumbria. Map 43C1

Ambleside 6, M6 (jn 36) 29, London 269, Coniston 6, Windermere 11 (Fy 3).
Golf Windermere 18h. **See** Hill Top (NT).

★★ **Sawrey,** Nr Ambleside, LA22 0LQ
📞 Windermere (096 62) 3425

Attractive 2-storey 18th century inn in traditional Lake District style.
🛏 17 bedrs, 13 en suite, 2 ba; TV
🏛 dogs; P 30; child facs; con 35
✕ LD 8.45
£ B&B £17·50–£21·50; B&B (double) £50–£59; HB weekly £160–£185; L £7·50, D £11·75; WB £44 (HB, 2nts)

West Vale (Acclaimed), Nr Hawkshead, LA22 0LQ 📞 Windermere (096 62) 2817.
Guest House.
£ B&B £15–£17; HB weekly £147–£161.

FARTHING CORNER
Kent. Map 7A3

Gillingham 4, London 37, Canterbury 26, Maidstone 6, Sittingborne 11.

★★ **Rank Motor Lodge,** M2, nr Gillingham, ME8 8PW 📞 Medway (0634) 377337 ♿
See *Motor Lodge Section*

FAUGH
Cumbria

See CARLISLE.

FAVERSHAM
Kent. Map 7B3

Pop 16,000. Rochester 18, London 49, M2 (jn 6) 1, Ashford 13, Canterbury 10, Maidstone 20, Margate 24.
EC Thurs. **MD** Wed, Fri, Sat. **Golf** Belmont 18h. **See** Town Hall, restored period houses in Abbey St, Parish Church, Davington Priory, Globe House (formerly Globe Inn), 16th cent Grammar School, 15th cent Maison Dieu 1 m SW.
ℹ Fleur de Lis Heritage Centre, Preston St 📞 (0795) 534542.

Atlas Section
Consult the Atlas section at the back of the guide to find out which towns and villages have RAC Appointed and Listed hotels in them. They are shown on the maps by purple circles.

★★★ H C **Throwley House** (formerly Barons), Ashford Rd, Sheldwich, ME13 0LT
📞 (0795) 539168 Fax: (0795) 535086 ♿

Charming Georgian manor house with Regency additions standing in 16 acres of parkland close to M2 junction 6. Fr, It, Es.
🛏 6 bedrs, 6 en suite; TV
🏛 dogs; ns; P 30; child facs; con 20
✕ LD 9, nr Mon lunch & Sun dinner. Resid & Rest lic
£ B&B £89–£129, B&B (double) £109–£149; L £16·50, D £25·50; WB £75
cc Access, Amex, B'card/Visa, Diners.

FAWKHAM GREEN
Kent Map 9B2

Swanley 5, London 30, M20/M25 3½, Dartford 6½, Maidstone 20, Sevenoaks 9

★★★ **Brandshatch Place,** DA3 8NQ
📞 (0474) 872239 Fax: (0474) 879652

Red-brick Georgian mansion with good views and 12 acres of parkland. Indoor swimming pool, tennis, squash, sauna, solarium, gymnasium, billiards. Fr.
🛏 29 beds, 29 en suite; TV
🏛 ns; P 70; child facs; con 150
✕ LD 9.45; nr Sat lunch
£ B&B £77, B&B (double) £100; L £17·50; WB £190; [5% V, w/d]
cc Access, Amex, B'card/Visa, Diners; dep.

FELIXSTOWE
Suffolk. Map 27C2

Pop 20,858. Ipswich 12, London 86, Aldeburgh 29, Saxmundham 25, Scole 36.
EC Wed. **MD** Thur. **Golf** Felixstowe Ferry 18h. **See** St Peter's Church, St Andrew's Church.
ℹ Sea Front. 📞 (0394) 276770

Complaints
If you are dissatisfied with the facilities or service offered by a hotel, please take the matter up with the Manager WHILE YOU ARE AT THE HOTEL. In this way, any problems can usually be solved promptly and amicably.
The RAC will investigate matters if a personal approach has failed to resolve the problem. Please submit details of any discussion or correspondence when reporting the problem to the RAC.

★★★★ **Orwell Moat House,** Hamilton Rd, IP11 7DX 📞 (0394) 285511 Tx: 987676
Fax: (0394) 670687

Spacious red-brick hotel in the grand tradition. Fr, De, It. (QMH)
🛏 58 bedrs, 58 en suite; TV; tcf
🏛 lift, dogs, ns; P 90, coach; child facs; con 200
✕ LD 10
£ B&B £61·50, B&B (double) £83–£88; HB weekly £350; L £12·50, D £15; WB £80 (2 nts); [10% V]
cc Access, Amex, B'card/Visa, Diners.

★★ **Marlborough,** Sea Rd, IP11 8BJ
📞 (0394) 285621 Tx: 987047
Fax: (0394) 670724 ♿

Large four-storey hotel in commanding position on sea-front. De.
🛏 45 bedrs, 45 en suite, 2 ba; TV; tcf
🏛 lift, TV, dogs; P 19, coach; child facs; con 100
✕ LD 9.45
£ B&B £42·45–£52, B&B (double) £63·50–£65·50; HB weekly £245–£280; L £8·95, D £11·95; WB £33; [10% V]
cc Access, Amex, B'card/Visa, Diners.

★★ **Waverley,** 2 Wolsey Gdns, IP11 7DF
📞 (0394) 282811 Tx: 987568
Fax: (0394) 670185

Victorian building in high position overlooking sea. Fr
🛏 20 bedrs, 20 en suite; TV; tcf
🏛 dogs; P 26, coach; child facs; con 90
✕ LD 10.30
£ B&B £44·25–£51·25 (w/e £24·75), B&B (double) £64; L £8·50, D £10·50; WB £28·75
cc Access, Amex, B'card/Visa, Diners; dep.
(*See advertisement on p. 255*).

F

FENNY BRIDGES Devon. Map 4A1

Pop 300. Honiton 3, London 156, Exeter 13, Tiverton 20.
Golf Honiton 9h.

★★ Greyhound, EX14 0BJ ☎Honiton (0404) 850380

A thatched roof and oak beams give period charm to this fine old inn on the A30. (BCB)
🛏 10 bedrs, 10 en suite; TV; tcf
🏠 ns; P 60, coach; child facs
✕ LD 10
£ B&B £36·50, B&B (double) £49·50; L £8·15, D £8·15; WB £27·50
cc Access, Amex, B'card/Visa, Diners.

★ Fenny Bridges, EX14 0BQ ☎Honiton (0404) 850218
Small inn beside the A30 in Devon country surroundings. Fishing.

FENTON Staffordshire.

See STOKE-ON-TRENT.

FERNDOWN Dorset. Map 5B2

Pop 15,474. Ringwood 6, London 99, Blandford Forum 14, Bournemouth 7, Dorchester 28, Wareham 15.
EC Wed. **Golf** Ferndown 18h. **See** Church.

★★★★ Dormy, New Rd, BH22 8ES ☎(0202) 872121 Tx: 418301 Fax: (0202) 895388
Country style hotel in 12 acres of grounds next to a golf course. Indoor swimming pool, putting, tennis, squash, sauna, solarium, gymnasium, billiards. ✻ Fr, It, Po. (DeV)
🛏 100 bedrs; 100 en suite, annexe 29 bedrs, 29 en suite; TV; tcf
🏠 lift, TV, dogs; P 220, coach; child facs; con 250
✕ LD 9.20, bar meals only Sat lunch
£ B&B £90–£115 (w/e £60), B&B (double) £120–£145 (w/e £90); HB weekly £300–£600; L £12·50, D £17·50; WB £130
cc Access, Amex, B'card/Visa, Diners.
(*See advertisement on p. 152*)

★★ Welcome Lodge, Ringwood Rd, BH22 9AL ☎(0202) 874221

White painted hotel with touches of half-timbering, on the A31 east of Ferndown. Motel-type bedrooms. ✻ De.
🛏 28 bedrs, 28 en suite; TV; tcf
🏠 dogs; P 70, coach; child facs; con 100
✕ LD 9.15; bar meals only Mon–Sat lunch
£ B&B £35; B&B (double) £50; HB weekly £260; WB £65 (2 nts); [10% V]
cc Access, B'card/Visa.

FILEY North Yorkshire. Map 39B4

Pop 5,480. Gt Driffield 21, London 213, Bridlington 10, Malton 23, Scarborough 7½.
EC Wed. **Golf** Filey 18h.
ℹ John St. ☎(0723) 512204

★★★ White Lodge, The Crescent, YO14 9JX ☎Scarborough (0723) 514771
Elegant white building with sun lounge enjoying fine sea views.
🛏 19 bedrs, 19 en suite; TV; tcf
🏠 lift, dogs; P 10, coach; child facs; con 60

Southdown, The Beach, YO14 9LA ☎Scarborough (0723) 513392. *Hotel.*

FINDON West Sussex. Map 6B1

Horsham 15, London 51, Bognor Regis 19, Pulborough 11, Worthing 5.

♣ ★★ Findon Manor, BN14 0TA ☎(090 671) 2733
Sixteenth-century stone and flint rectory, in grounds of 1¼ acres in middle of village.

FINEDON Northamptonshire. Map 21C4

Bedford 18, London 68, Kettering 6, Northampton 20, Thrapston 9.

★★ Tudor Gate, 35 High St, NN9 5JN ☎(0933) 680408 Fax: (0933) 680745
Family run hotel in a fine converted 17th-century farmhouse, with a modern extension, just off the A6.
🛏 16 bedrs, 16 en suite; TV
🏠 dogs, ns; P 20, child facs; con 40
✕ LD 9.45
£ B&B £48–£65, B&B (double) £57–£75; L £12·50, D £20.
cc Access, Amex, B'card/Visa, Diners.

FITTLEWORTH West Sussex. Map 6B2

Billingshurst 7½, London 49, Arundel 12, Midhurst 8½.

★★ Swan, Lower St, RH20 1EW ☎(079 882) 429

Traditional tile-hung inn, dating from the 14th century, heavily beamed and furnished in country style. Golf, riding. (BCB)
🛏 10 bedrs, 6 en suite; TV; tcf
🏠 ns; P 25, coach; child facs; con 20

FLEET Hampshire. Map 12C1

Pop 25,993. Bagshot 10, London 37, M3 (jn 4) 6½, Alton 12, Basingstoke 12, Farnham 6, Reading 15, Woking 14.
EC Wed. **MD** Sat. **Golf** North Hants 18h.
See Fleet Pond (nature reserve).
ℹ Fleet Rd ☎(0252) 811151

♣ ★★★ Lismoyne, Church Rd, GU13 8NA ☎(0252) 628555 Fax: (0252) 811761

Substantial Victorian country house set in attractive gardens and grounds.
🛏 44 bedrs, 44 en suite; TV; tcf
🏠 dogs; P 80, coach; child facs; con 80
✕ LD 9.30
£ B&B £62–£70 (w/e £50–£54), B&B (double) £80 (w/e £56); L £11·75, D £12·75; WB; [10% V w/e]
cc Access, Amex, B'card/Visa, Diners.

FLEETWOOD Lancashire. Map 36A3

Pop 28,600. Preston 22, London 223, Blackpool 8½, Lancaster 25.
EC Wed. **MD** Tue, Fri. **Golf** Fleetwood 18h.
See Large market.
ℹ Marine Hall, Esplanade. ☎(039 17) 71141

★★★ North Euston, Esplanade, FY7 6BN ☎(039 17) 6525 Fax: (039 17) 77842
Mid-Victorian crescent-shaped building, overlooking the sea. ✻ Fr.
🛏 60 bedrs, 60 en suite; TV; tcf
🏠 lift, P 60, coach; child facs; con 100
✕ LD 9.30; nr Sat lunch
£ B&B £37–£48, B&B (double) £53–£58; L £8, D £11·50; WB £65 (2 nts)
cc Access, Amex, B'card/Visa, Diners.

FLITWICK Bedfordshire. Map 14B4

M1 (jn 12) 3½, London 41, Bedford 10.

♣ ★★★ Flitwick Manor, Church Rd, MK45 1AE, ☎(0525) 712242 Tx: 825562 Fax: (0525) 712242 ♿

Substantial 18th century house attractively set in a 50 acre park. Putting, tennis, fishing.
🛏 16 bedrs, 16 en suite; TV
🏠 P 70, coach; child facs; con 20

FOLKESTONE Kent. Map 7C2

RAC Port Office, *West Side Terminal, Folkestone Harbour, CT20 1QG* ☎(0303) 58560
Pop 46,500. Ashford 16, London 71, M20 (jn 13) 2, Canterbury 16, Dover 7, Margate 26, Rye 25, Tenterden 23.
See Plan, p. 256.
EC Wed. **MD** Thur, Sun. **P** See Plan. **Golf** Sene Valley 18h. **See** Church of St Mary and

EC *early closing* **MD** *market day* ♣ *country house hotel* *ns (NS) no smoking areas* *tcf tea/coffee facilities*

Fareham (Hampshire)

Faringdon (Oxfordshire)

Felixstowe (Suffolk)

Forest Row (Sussex)

Fowey (Cornwall)

Gatwick (Surrey)

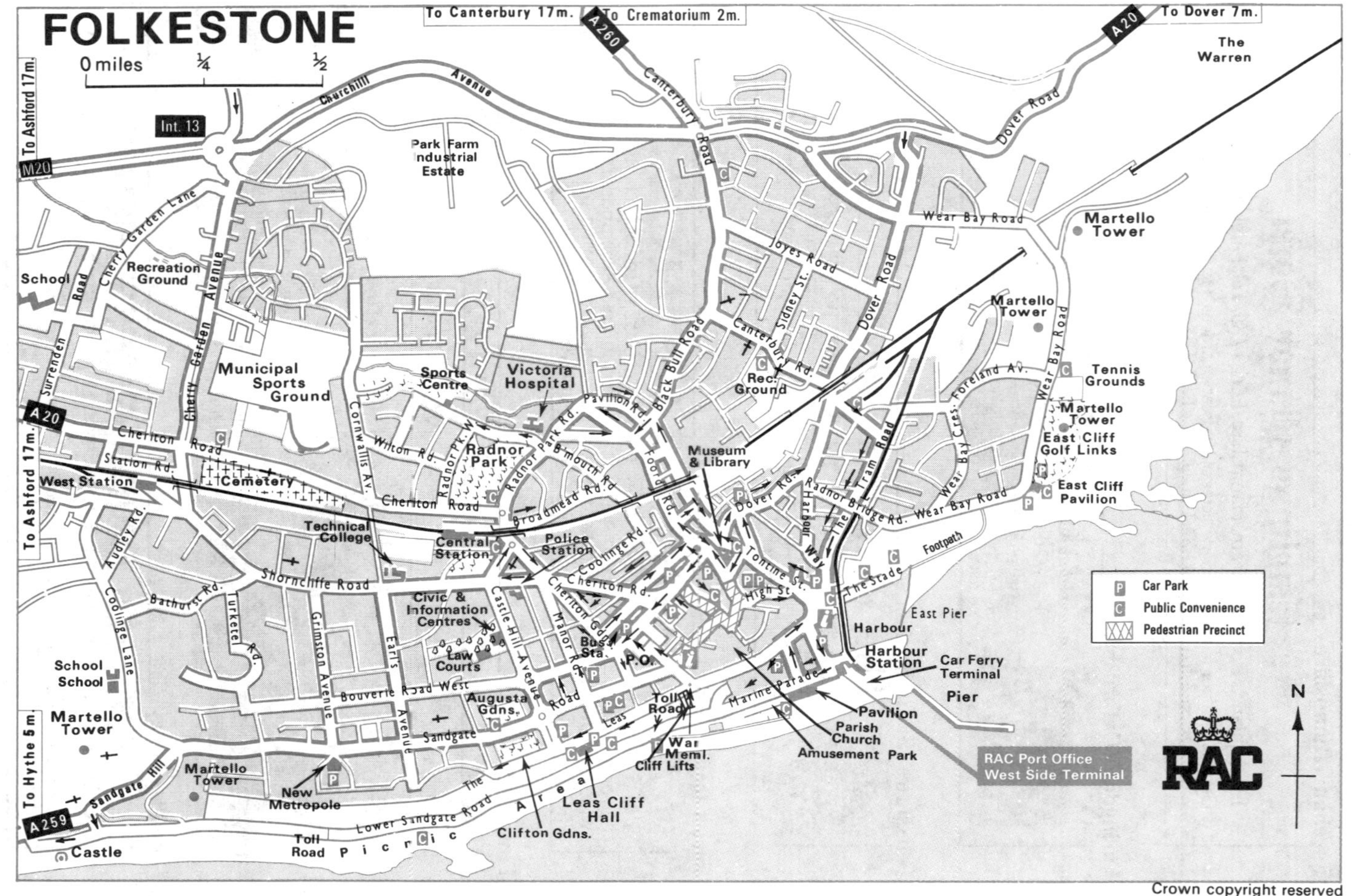

EC *early closing* **MD** *market day* *country house hotel* *ns (NS) no smoking areas* *tcf tea/coffee facilities*

St Eanswythe, Kingsnorth Gdns, The Leas, The Arts Centre (New Metropole).
[i] Harbour St. ☎(0303) 58594

★★★ **Burlington,** Earls Av, The Leas, CT20 2HR ☎(0303) 55301 Tx: 966389 Fax: (0303) 51301
Large detached building on West end of the Leas overlooking sea. ⚘ It, Es
🛏 59 bedrs, 59 en suite; TV
🏨 lift, dogs; P 14, coach; child facs; con 160
£ B&B £39–£43, B&B (double) £60–£66; HB weekly fr £207; L £7·50, D £13; WB £37·50 (HB); [10% V]
cc Access, Amex, B'card/Visa, Diners, dep.

★★★ **Clifton,** The Leas, CT20 2EB ☎(0303) 851231 Tx: 57515 Fax: (0303) 851231

Large Edwardian corner building on the Leas overlooking the sea. Solarium. ⚘ Fr, It, Es.
🛏 84 bedrs, 80en suite, 1 ba; TV; tcf
🏨 lift, dogs; coach; child facs; con 100
✕ LD 9
£ B&B £42·50–£54·50; B&B (double) £59–£69; HB weekly £245–£283·50; L £10·25, D £15·95; WB £37·75.
cc Access, Amex, B'card/Visa, Diners.

★★★ **Garden House,** 142 Sandgate Rd, CT20 2TE ☎(0303) 52278 Fax: (0303) 41376
Georgian building conveniently situated close to sea and town centre. ⚘ Fr.
🛏 42 bedrs, 42en suite; TV; tcf
🏨 lift, dogs; P 17, coach; child facs; con 80
✕ LD 9.45
£ B&B £41·25, B&B (double) £60·50; D £12·50; WB £30·25; [10% V]
cc Access, Amex, B'card/Visa, Diners; dep.

Beaumont, 5 Marine Ter, CT20 1PZ ☎(0303) 52740. *Guest House.*
Belmonte, 30 Castle Hill Av, CT20 2RE ☎(0303) 54470. *Private Hotel.*
Gresham, 18 Clifton Cres, The Leas, CT20 2EP ☎(0303) 53906. Fax: (0303) 220746. Hotel. ⚘ Fr, De, Hi
£ B&B £16–£22; HB (weekly) £143–£163
Wearbay, 23 Wear Bay Cres, CT19 6AX ☎(0303) 52586. *Hotel.* ⚘ Fr, Ge, It, Es.
£ B&B £21; HB weekly £196–£202·65.
Westward Ho, 13 Clifton Cres, CT20 2EL ☎(0303) 52663. *Hotel.*
£ B&B £17·50–£20, HB weekly £132–£145; [10% V Oct–May]

FORD Wiltshire. Map 5A4

Pop 248. M4 (jn 17) 7, Chippenham 5, London 96, Bath 10, Bristol 16, Chipping Sodbury 11, Melksham 9.
Golf Kingsdown 18h.

★★ **White Hart Inn,** Nr. Chippenham, SN14 8RP ☎Castle Combe (0249) 782213
16th century building of Cotswold stone by beautiful trout stream. Swimming pool.
🛏 3 bedrs, 3 en suite; annexe 8 bedrs, 8 en suite; TV; tcf
🏨 TV, dogs; P 80, coach; con 10

FORDINGBRIDGE Hampshire. Map 5B2

Pop 5,075. Romsey 15, London 91, Blandford Forum 21, Lyndhurst 13, Ringwood 6, Salisbury 10, Shaftesbury 23, Southampton 19.
EC Thur. **Golf** Bramshaw 18h. **See** Modernised 14th cent 7-arch bridge, EE and Dec Church, Augustus John statue. Breamore House 3 m N.

★★ **Ashburn,** Station Rd, SP16 1JP ☎(0425) 652060

Substantial brick-built hotel in pleasant grounds with swimming pool.
🛏 22 bedrs, 22 en suite; TV; tcf
🏨 TV, dogs, ns; P 60, coach; child facs; con 150
✕ LD 9, bar meals only Mon–Sat lunch
£ B&B £35–£41, B&B (double) £62–£71; HB weekly £236; L £7·25; D £11·50; WB £73 (HB); [10% V]
cc Access, B'card/Visa.

FORDWICH Kent. Map 7C3

Pop 175. Canterbury 2½, London 61, Dover 16, Folkestone 17, Margate 13.
Golf Canterbury 18h. **See** Old Town Hall, Ducking Stool, Stocks, Church.

★★ **George & Dragon,** Nr Canterbury, CT2 0BN ☎Sturry (0227) 710661
Attractive modernised 16th-century inn set in small village.
🛏 8 bedrs, 3 en suite, 2 ba; annexe 4 bedrs, 4 en suite; TV; tcf
🏨 dogs, ns; P 40, coach; child facs
£ B&B £25–£30, B&B (double) £35–£40; L £6·50, D £6·50; WB; [5% V]
cc Access, Amex, B'card/Visa, Diners.

FOREST OF DEAN Gloucestershire

See COLEFORD.

FOREST ROW East Sussex. Map 11A1

Pop 4,246. East Grinstead 3, London 33, Haywards Heath 10, Lewes 17, Tunbridge Wells 12, Uckfield 10.
EC Wed. **Golf** Royal Ashdown Forest 18h (2). **See** Ruins of Brambletye Castle.

★★★ **Roebuck,** Wych Cross, RH18 5JL (2 m S A22) ☎(0342) 823811 Fax: (0342) 824790
Detached red-brick Georgian building in pleasant gardens. Just off A22. (Emb)
🛏 28 bedrs, 28 en suite; TV; tcf
🏨 dogs; P 100, coach; child facs; con 100
✕ LD 9.15
£ B&B £67–£77, B&B (double) £84–£94; L £12·50, D £12·50; WB £34·50 (HB)
cc Access, Amex, B'card/Visa, Diners.

★★ **Brambletye,** The Square, RH18 5EZ ☎(0342) 824144 Fax: (0342) 824833

Pleasing late Victorian-Edwardian style residence with modern extension. ⚘ Fr, De.
🛏 22 bedrs, 22 en suite; TV; tcf
🏨 dogs, TV; P 40, coach; child facs; con 12
✕ LD 9.30, bar meals only Mon–Sat lunch
£ B&B £48–£52, B&B (double) £55–£65; L £8·50, D £11·50; WB £70 (HB 2nts)
cc Access, Amex, B'card/Visa, Diners; dep.
(*See advertisement on p. 255*)

★★ **Chequers Inn,** The Square, RH18 1ES ☎(0342) 823333 Fax: (0342) 825454
An ancient tile-hung inn with modern bedroom accommodation. ⚘ Fr, It.
🛏 17 bedrs, 17 en site; TV; tcf
🏨 P 2, G 6 coach; child facs, con 30
✕ LD 9.15
£ B&B £45 (w/e £40), B&B (double) £59·50–£75; HB weekly £300; L £5·45, D £15
cc Access, Amex, B'card/Visa, Diners.

F

FOWEY Cornwall. Map 2C1

Pop 2,393. Liskeard 18, London 239 (Fy 236), Bodmin 8, Looe 19 (Fy 10), St Austell 7½.
EC Wed. **Golf** St Austell 18h, Carlyon Bay 18h. **See** Parish Church, Museum, Aquarium, St Catherine's Castle ruins, St Catherine's and St Saviour's Point (Nat Trust).
[i] 4 Custom House Hill. ☎(0726) 833308

★★★ **Fowey,** PL23 1HX ☎(0726) 832551 Fax: (0726) 832125

Family hotel with sun terrace enjoying panoramic views of Fowey Estuary. Fishing.
🛏 30 bedrs, 26 en suite; 4 ba; TV; tcf
🏨 lift, dogs; P24; child facs; con 25
✕ LD 9
£ B&B £33·75–£37·50; B&B (double) £62·55–£69·50; HB weekly £263·70–£293; D £12·95; WB £140 (for 2); [5% V Nov–Feb]
cc Access, Amex, B'card/Visa, Diners; dep.

★★ **Cormorant,** Golant, PL23 1LL ☎(072683) 3426.
Perched high above the river, a family-run hotel with breathtaking views. Swimming pool.

★★ **Marina,** Esplanade, PL23 1HY ☎(0726) 833315

Georgian building with charming balconies. Garden with own quay. Fishing. Open Mar–Oct.
🛏 11 bedrs, 11 en suite; TV; tcf
🏠 dogs, child facs
✕ LD 8.30, bar meals only lunch. Resid & Rest lic
£ B&B £23; B&B (double) £46–£68; HB weekly £230–£300; D £14; WB £66 (HB 2 nts)
cc Access, Amex, B'card/Visa, Diners; dep.
(*See advertisement on p. 255*)

★ **Old Quay House,** Fore St, PL23 1AQ ☎(072 683) 3302
Three-storey white-faced hotel charmingly set right on the water's edge.

Carnethic House (Highly Acclaimed), Lambs Barn, PL23 1HQ ☎(072 683) 3336. *Private Hotel. Swimming pool, tennis, putting.* Open 1 Feb–30 Nov. ✈ De. ♿
£ B&B £23–£30; HB weekly £180–£225; [10% V].

FOWNHOPE Hereford & Worcester (Herefordshire). Map 20A2
Gloucester 21, London 125, Abergavenny 27, Bromyard 16, Hereford 6½, Ledbury 13, Ross-on-Wye 8½, Worcester 24.

★★ C **Green Man,** HR1 4PE ☎(043 277) 243. Fax: (0432 77) 207 ♿
Attractive, 15th-century black and white building in landscaped gardens. ✈ Es.
🛏 11 bedrs, 11 en suite; annexe 5 bedrs, 5 en suite; TV; tcf
🏠 dogs, ns; P 75, coach; child facs; con 30
✕ LD 9, bar meals only Mon–Sat lunch
£ B&B £28, B&B (double) £39·50, HB weekly £194·50; D £12; WB £54
cc Access, B'card/Visa; dep.

FRADLEY Staffordshire. Map 23A4
Tamworth 10, London 154, Burton-on-Trent 19, Litchfield 6, Stafford 22.

★★ **Fradley Arms,** WS13 8RD ☎Burton-on-Trent (0283) 790186 Fax: (0283) 791464
A white-painted hotel in a rural area on the A38. Family run.
🛏 6 bedrs, 6 en suite; TV; tcf
🏠 TV, dogs; P 200, coach; child facs; con 200
✕ LD 9
£ B&B £36–£40, B&B (double) £48–£52; D £10·95; WB £42; [10% V Thurs–Fri, Jan, May, Aug]
cc Access, Amex, B'card/Visa, Diners; dep.

FRAMLINGHAM Suffolk. Map 27B3
Pop 2,190. Ipswich 15, London 89, Aldeburgh 13, Lowestoft 29, Norwich 33, Saxmundham 7, Scole 15, Stowmarket 17. **EC** Wed. **MD** Sat. **Golf** Woodbridge 18h. **See** Norman Castle ruins, Parish Church.

★★★ **Crown,** Market Hill, IP13 9AN ☎(0728) 723521 Fax: (0728) 724274

16th-century inn with magnificent oak beams. Situated in town centre. (THF)
🛏 14 bedrs, 14 en suite; TV; tcf
🏠 dogs, ns; P 12; coach; child facs
✕ LD 9.30
£ B&B £67 (w/e £47); B&B (double) £89–£99; L £14, D £14; WB £57
cc Access, Amex, B'card/Visa, CB, Diners; dep.

FRAMPTON Dorset. Map 4C1
Pop 390. Dorchester 5½, London 128, Crewkerne 15, Lyme Regis 22, Shaftesbury 27, Sherborne 17, Weymouth 12. **Golf** Dorchester 18h. **See** Parish Church.

Wessex Barn, DT2 9NB ☎Maiden Newton (0300) 20282. *Guest House.* ✈ Fr
£ B&B £15–£18; dep.

FRIMLEY-GREEN Surrey. Map 13A1
M3 (jn 4) 1, London 32, Basingstoke 18, Farnborough 2, Reading 17, Woking 10

★★★ **Lakeside International,** Wharf Rd, nr Camberley, GU16 6JR ☎(0252) 83800, Tx: 858 095 Fax: (0252) 837857
Large, red-brick, modern hotel, overlooking lake to rear. Squash, snooker. ✈ Fr, Es, Po, Cz.
🛏 97 bedrs, 97 en suite; TV; tcf
🏠 lift; P 250, child facs; con 200
✕ LD 10.30
£ B&B £78 (w/e £45), B&B (double) £96; L £12·50, D £12·50
cc Access, Amex, B'card/Visa, Diners.

FRINTON-ON-SEA Essex. Map 27B2
Pop 4,586. Colchester 17, London 73, Bury St Edmunds 43, Clacton 7, Harwich 14, Ipswich 23, Stowmarket 35. **EC** Wed. **Golf** Frinton 18h and 9h. **See** Old Parish Church.

★★ **Maplin,** Esplanade, CO13 9EL ☎(0255) 673832

On commanding site, by greensward, with bow windows overlooking the sea. Swimming pool. Closed Jan.
🛏 12 bedrs, 10 en suite, 1 ba; TV; tcf
🏠 TV, dogs; P 12, coach, children over 10
✕ LD 9. Resid & Rest lic
£ B&B £35, B&B (double) £72–£82; HB weekly £245; L £14·75, D £16·50; WB £25
cc Access, Amex, B'card/Visa, Diners; dep.

★★ **Rock,** Esplanade, CO13 9EO ☎(0255) 675173
Large Victorian building situated in own grounds on sea front. Solarium. Closed Jan
🛏 6 bedrs, 5 en suite; 2 ba; TV; tcf
🏠 TV, dogs; P 12; child facs; con 20
✕ LD 9. Resid & Rest lic
£ B&B £40·50–£43; B&B (double) £53·50–£56·50; L £7·50, D £11·50; [10% V]
cc Access, Amex, B'card/Visa, Diners.

Montpellier (Highly Acclaimed), Harold Grove, CO13 9BD ☎(0255) 674462
£ B&B £32·50–£34·50

FRODSHAM Cheshire. Map 32C1
Pop 8,965. Northwich 10, London 184, M56 4½, Chester 11, Ellesmere Port 10, Runcorn 5, Warrington 9. **EC** Wed. **MD** Thur. **Golf** Helsby 18h.

★★ C **Old Hall,** Main St, WA6 7AB ☎(0928) 32052 Fax: (0928) 39046
A Tudor building which blends antiquity with modern comforts. Swimming pool.
🛏 19 bedrs, 19 en suite; TV; tcf
🏠 dogs; P 20, coach; child facs; con 30
✕ LD 10
£ L £10·50; WB £45–£80
cc Access, Amex, B'card/Visa, Diners.

FROGMORE Devon. Map 3B1
Kingsbridge 3, London 206, Dartmouth 11, Plymouth 23

Globe Inn, Nr Kingsbridge, TQ7 2NR ☎(054 853) 351

FROME Somerset. Map 5A3
Pop 25,000. Warminster 7, London 105, Bath 13, Chippenham 21, Devizes 18, Radstock 8, Shaftesbury 19, Shepton Mallet 11, Wincanton 15. **EC** Thur. **MD** Wed. **Golf** W Wilts, Warminster 18h. **See** Church (14th cent), Blue House. ℹ Cattle Market Car Park. ☎(0373) 67271

★★★ **Mendip Lodge,** Bath Rd, BA11 2HP ☎(0373) 63223 Tx: 44832 Fax: (0373) 63990

Modern motel-style hotel adjoining Edwardian house in quiet position. ✈ Fr
🛏 40 bedrs, 40 en suite; TV; tcf
🏠 dogs, P 60; coach; child facs; con 90
✕ LD 9.30
£ B&B £55, B&B (double) £80; L £18, D £18; WB £48 (HB); [10% V]
cc Access, Amex, B'card/Visa, Diners.

EC *early closing* **MD** *market day* 🏠 *country house hotel* *ns (NS) no smoking areas* *tcf tea/coffee facilities*

★★ **George,** 4 Market Pl, BA11 1AF
☎(0373) 62584 Fax: (0373) 51945

Privately-owned former coaching inn in the Market Place. Solarium.
🛏 20 bedrs, 20 en suite; TV; tcf
🏨 dogs; G 17, coach; child facs; con 40

★★ **Portway,** Portway, BA11 1QP ☎(0373) 63508
A corner building of Georgian origin, with a pleasant garden. Closed Xmas.
🛏 19 bedrs, 19 en suite, 1 ba; TV; tcf
🏨 dogs; P 30, coach; child facs; con 60

Keyford Elms, 92 Locks Hill, BA11 1NG
☎(0373) 63321. *Hotel.*

GAINSBOROUGH Lincolnshire. Map 31B4
Pop 18,715. Newark 24, London 150, Doncaster 20, Grimsby 35, Hull 38, Lincoln 18, Market Rasen 20, Scunthorpe 16.
EC Wed. **MD** Mon, Tue, Sat. **Golf** Thonock 18h, Torksey 18h. **See** Model Railway, Elswitha Hall, Trinity Arts Centre.

★★ **Hemswell Cliff**, Lancaster Green, Hemswell Cliff, DN21 5TU ☎(042 773) 8181
Fax: (042 773) 483
A two-storied building standing in its own grounds off the Market Rasen road. RAF memorabilia in the bar recall its origins as an Officers' Mess. Extensive function facilities.
🛏 22 bedrs, 22 en suite; TV; tcf
🏨 P 100, G 20, coach; child facs; con 200
✕ LD 9.30
£ B&B £35, B&B (double) £60; HB weekly £215; L £8·50, D £10·50; [5% V]
cc Access, Amex, B'card/Visa; dep.

★★ **Hickman-Hill,** Cox's Hill, DN21 1HH
☎(0427) 613639

Interesting 16th-century former school building in own grounds. Solarium.
🛏 8 bedrs, 6 en suite, (2 sh), 1 ba; TV; tcf
🏨 TV, dogs, ns; P 30; child facs; con 50
✕ LD 9, bar meals only Sat lunch & Sun dinner

£ B&B £35, B&B (double) £47·50; L £5·95, D £9·50; [10% V w/e]
cc Access, B'card/Visa.

GARBOLDISHAM Norfolk. Map 27B4
Bury St Edmunds 15, London 89, Diss 7½, Norwich 24, Swaffham 24, Thetford 9½.

Ingleneuk Lodge (Highly Acclaimed), Hopton Rd, Diss, IP22 2RQ ☎(095 381) 541.
£ B&B £18–£26; HB weekly £166–£241

GARSTANG Lancashire. Map 36B3
Preston 10, London 221, M55 (jn 33) 7½, Blackpool 15, Lancaster 10.
EC Wed. **MD** Thur. **Golf** Lancaster 18h.
ℹ High Street ☎(099 52) 4430

★★★ **Crofters,** A6 Cabus, PR3 1PH
☎(0995) 604128
Modern purpose-built hotel with conference facilities. Convenient for M6 and A6.
🛏 19 bedrs, 19 en suite; TV; tcf
🏨 dogs; P 200, coach; child facs; con 200
✕ LD 10, bar meals only Sat lunch
£ B&B £44·50–£57, B&B (double) £49·50–£62; L £8, D £13; WB £33 (HB); [5% V]
cc Access, Amex, B'card/Visa, Diners.

GATESHEAD Tyne & Wear. Map 37B2
See also NEWCASTLE UPON TYNE.
Pop 76,969. Durham 14, London 272, Newcastle upon Tyne 1, Sunderland 11.
EC Wed. **Golf** Ravensworth 18h. **See** Shipley Art Gallery, St Mary's Church, Holy Trinity Church, Saltwell Towers and Park.
ℹ Library, Prince Consort Rd. ☎091-477 3478

★★★ **Springfield,** Durham Rd, NE9 5BT
☎091-477 4121 Tx: 538197
Fax: 091-477 7213 ♿

1930s building with modern bedrooms; large car park on A1. (Emb)
🛏 60 bedrs, 60 en suite; TV; tcf
🏨 lift, TV, dogs, ns; P 80, coach; child facs; con 110
✕ LD 9.30, bar meals only Sat lunch
£ B&B £55·50–£76, (w/e £25), B&B (double) £80–£93; HB weekly £400; L £8·95, D £11·95; WB £35 (HB)
cc Access, Amex, B'card/Visa, Diners.

★★★ **Swallow,** High West St, NE8 1PE
☎091-477 1105 Tx: 53534
Fax: 091-478 7214

Modern hotel located off A1(M), 2 miles from Newcastle city centre. Indoor swimming pool, sauna, solarium, gymnasium. (Sw)
🛏 103 bedrs, 103 en suite; TV; tcf
🏨 lift, dogs, ns; P 85, G 60, coach; child facs; con 350
✕ LD 10, nr Sat lunch
£ B&B £65, B&B (double) £75; L £10·95, D £10·95; WB £85 (HB)
cc Access, Amex, B'card/Visa, Diners.

GATWICK AIRPORT West Sussex. Map 10B1
See also COPTHORNE, CRAWLEY, and HORLEY.
M23 (jn 9) 1, London 28, Crawley 3½, Redhill 6½, Reigate 7.
ℹ ☎(293) 560108

★★★★ **Gatwick Hilton International,** RH6 0LL ☎(0293) 518080 Tx: 877021
Fax: (0293) 28980 ♿
Modern hotel within the airport complex; direct access to terminal building via covered walkway. Parking adjacent. Indoor swimming pool, sauna, gymnasium. (H. Int)
🛏 552 bedrs, 552 en suite; TV
🏨 lift, TV, dogs, ns; coach; child facs; con 450
£ room £105, room (double) £115; Bk £9·95, L £13·95, WB £53
cc Access, Amex, B'card/Visa, CB, Diners.

Gatwick Sterling, RH6 0PH ☎(0293) 567070 Tx: 87202 Fax: (0293) 567739
New hotel opening September 1990. Linked to Gatwick North Terminal.

G

GERRARDS CROSS Bucks. Map 13B4
Pop 6,900. Denham 3, London 20, M40 (jn 1a) & M25 (jn 16) 3. Aylesbury 22, High Wycombe 10, Slough 6.
EC Wed. **Golf** Gerrards Cross 18h.

★★★ **Bull,** Oxford Rd. SL9 7PA ☎(0753) 885995 Tx: 847747 Fax: (0753) 885504 ♿
Delightful 17th-century coaching inn set in Buckinghamshire countryside. ✠ De, Fr (DeV)
🛏 95 bedrs, 95 en suite; TV; tcf
🏨 lift, dogs, P 200, child facs, con 200
✕ LD 9.30
£ B&B £90 (w/e £30), B & B (double) £135; L £15·75, D £17·50; WB £30 (2 nts)
cc Access, Amex, B'card/Visa, Diners.

★★ **Ethorpe,** Packhorse Rd, SL9 8MX
☎(0753) 882039

Small hotel in a Georgian mansion standing in landscaped grounds close to town. ✠ Fr, It. (BCB)
🛏 29 bedrs, 29 en suite; TV; tcf

🏠 ns; P 80, coach; child facs; con 50
✕ LD 10.30
£ B&B £69·50–£77·50, B&B (double) £84; L £8·15, D £8·15; WB £27·50
cc Access, Amex, B'card/Visa, Diners.

GILLAN Cornwall. Map 2B1

Pop 180. Truro 24, London 279, Falmouth 17, Helston 11.
Golf Mullion 18h. **See** Gillan Cove.

★★ **Tregildry,** Manaccan, TR12 6HG
📞 Manaccan (032 623) 378
Overlooking a lovely cove, small hotel with private access to beach. Open Easter–Oct.
🛏 10 bedrs, 10 en suite; TV; tcf
🏠 TV, dogs, P 20; child facs
✕ LD 7.30, bar meals only lunch
£ B&B £30–£45, HB weekly £220–£280; D £15
cc Access, B'card/Visa; dep.

GILLINGHAM Dorset Map 5AZ

Pop 5,514. Shaftesbury 4½, London 108, Frome 15, Sherborne 14, Warminster 14, Wincanton 7.
EC Thur. **Golf** Sherborne 18h. **See** St Mary's Church, Museum.

♣ ★★ **H** **C** **Stock Hill House**, Wyke SP8 5NR 📞 (0747) 823626

Stone-built Victorian manor house, elegantly furnished, set in 12 acres of beautiful gardens and grounds. 🏸 Fr, De.
🛏 8 bedrs, 8 en suite; TV
🏠 ns; P 20; no children under 7
✕ LD 8·45
£ B&B £70–£80; L £20, D £28
cc Access, B'card/Visa; dep.

GILLINGHAM Kent. Map 7A3

Pop 94,100. Rochester 3, London 33, Canterbury 26, Maidstone 10, Margate 41.
EC Wed. **MD** Mon. **Golf** Gillingham 18h.
See St Mary's Church Clock Tower.

★ **Park,** Nelson Rd, ME7 4NA 📞 Medway (0634) 51546 Fax: (0634) 575455
Public house with a restaurant and letting rooms. Conveniently situated.
🛏 7 bedrs, 3 en suite; 3 ba, TV; tcf
🏠 dogs, P 6, G 1, coach; child facs
✕ LD 10
£ B&B £25–£35, B&B (double) £35–£45 L £10, D £11; [5% V]
cc Access, B'card/Visa; dep.

GISBURN Lancashire. Map 36C3

Pop 356. Nelson 8, London 218, Clitheroe 7, Preston 23, Settle 12, Skipton 11.
MD Thur. **Golf** Clitheroe 18h.

★★★ **Stirk House,** Gisburn, BB7 4LJ
📞 0200 445581 Tx: 635238
Fax: 0200 445744

Attractive 16th-century manor house set in pleasant grounds. Indoor swimming pool, squash, sauna, solarium, gymnasium. 🏸 Fr, Es
🛏 36 bedrs, 36 en suite; annexe 12 bedrs, 12 en suite; TV; tcf
🏠 ns; P 100, coach; child facs; con 300
✕ LD 9.30
£ B&B £60–£80, (w/e £50), B&B (double) £75–£80; L £9; D £16; WB £75; [10% V w/d]
cc Access, Amex, B'card/Visa, Diners.

GISLINGHAM Suffolk. Map 27B4

Stowmarket 9½, London 86, Bury St Edmunds 16, Diss 8.

Old Guildhall (Highly Acclaimed), Mill St, nr Eye, IP23 8JT 📞 Mellis (037 983) 361.
Private Hotel.. Open Feb–Dec.
£ B&B £37·50; HB weekly £175

GLASTONBURY Somerset. Map 4C3

Pop 7,362. Shepton Mallet 9, London 126, Bridgwater 15, Ilminster 23, Sherborne 20, Taunton 22, Wells 5½, Wincanton 23.
EC Wed. **MD** Tue. **Golf** Wells (Somerset) 9h.
See Ruins of Benedictine Abbey, Weary-all Hill (site of "Glastonbury Thorn"), Ye Olde Pilgrim's Inn (15th cent), Abbot Bere's Almshouses, St Michael's Tower.
ℹ 1 Marchant's Buildings, Northload St. 📞 (0458) 32954

★★★ **George and Pilgrims,** High St, BA6 9DP 📞 (0458) 31146 Fax: (0458) 32252

Lovely stone-built 15th-century building. Historic bedrooms with 4-poster beds.
🛏 14 bedrs, 14 en suite; TV; tcf
🏠 dogs; P 4, G 6; child facs
✕ LD 9
£ B&B £42–£55, B&B (double) £60–£80; L £7·50, D £13·50; WB £44 (2 nts); [5% V]
cc Access, Amex, B'card/Visa, Diners

Red Lion, West Pennard, BA6 8NN
📞 (0458) 32941
A 17th-century stone-built inn on A361, 3 miles out of town. Bedrooms in converted stone barn to one side.

Cradlebridge, BA16 9SD 📞 (0458) 31827 *Farm.* Closed Xmas. ♿
Dower House, Butleigh, BA6 8TG
📞 Baltonsborough (0458) 50354. *Farm.* Open Feb–Nov
£ B&B £15
Hawthorns, Northload St, BA6 9JJ 📞 (0458) 31255. *Hotel.*
Tor Down, Ashwell La, BA6 4BG 📞 (0458) 32287

GLENRIDDING Cumbria. Map 43C1

Pop 444. Ambleside 9, London 277, Kendal 21, Keswick 16, Penrith 13.
Golf Penrith 18h. **See** Ullswater, Helvellyn (3,118 ft), Aira Force.
ℹ Car Park. 📞 (085 32) 414

★★★ **Ullswater**, CA11 0PA 📞 (085 32) 444
Tx: 58164 Fax: (085 36) 303 ♿

Three-storey stone building in own grounds with lawns stretching down to lakeside. Putting, fishing.
🛏 47 bedrs, 47 en suite; TV, tcf
🏠 lift, dogs, ns; P 200, coach; child facs; con 80

★★ **Glenridding,** CA11 0PB 📞 (076 84) 82228 Fax: (076 84) 82555
Hotel with spectacular views of lake. Offers special interest breaks. Closed 3–31 Jan.
🛏 43 bedrs, 43 en suite; TV; tcf
🏠 lift, dogs, ns, P 25, coach; child facs
✕ LD 9.30, bar meals only lunch
£ B&B £41, B&B (double) £65; HB weekly £282; WB £47 (HB); [10% V]
cc Access, Amex, B'card/Visa, Diners.

GLOSSOP Derbyshire. Map 41B1

Pop 24,147. Chapel-en-le-Frith 9, London 174, Barnsley 24, Huddersfield 19, Macclesfield 19, Manchester 14, Oldham 12, Sheffield 24, Stockport 11.
EC Tue. **MD** Thur, Fri, Sat. **Golf** Glossop 9h.
See Dinting Rly Centre (steam trains), Saxon Cross, Snake Pass, Peak National Park.
ℹ Station Forecourt, Norfolk St. 📞 (045 74) 5920

Wind in the Willows (Highly Acclaimed), Derbyshire Level, off Sheffield Rd, SK13 9PT 📞 (0457) 868001. *Hotel.*
£ B&B £48–£65

Hotel Winston, 34 Norfolk St. 📞 (045 74) 5449. *Hotel.*

GLOUCESTER Gloucestershire. Map 20B2

RAC Office, ***Kings Square, Gloucester, GL1 1RP*** 📞 (0452) 20460
Pop 92,000. Cheltenham 9, London 104, M5 (jn 11) 4½, Bristol 35, Chepstow 28,

EC *early closing* **MD** *market day* ♣ *country house hotel* *ns (NS) no smoking areas* *tcf tea/coffee facilities*

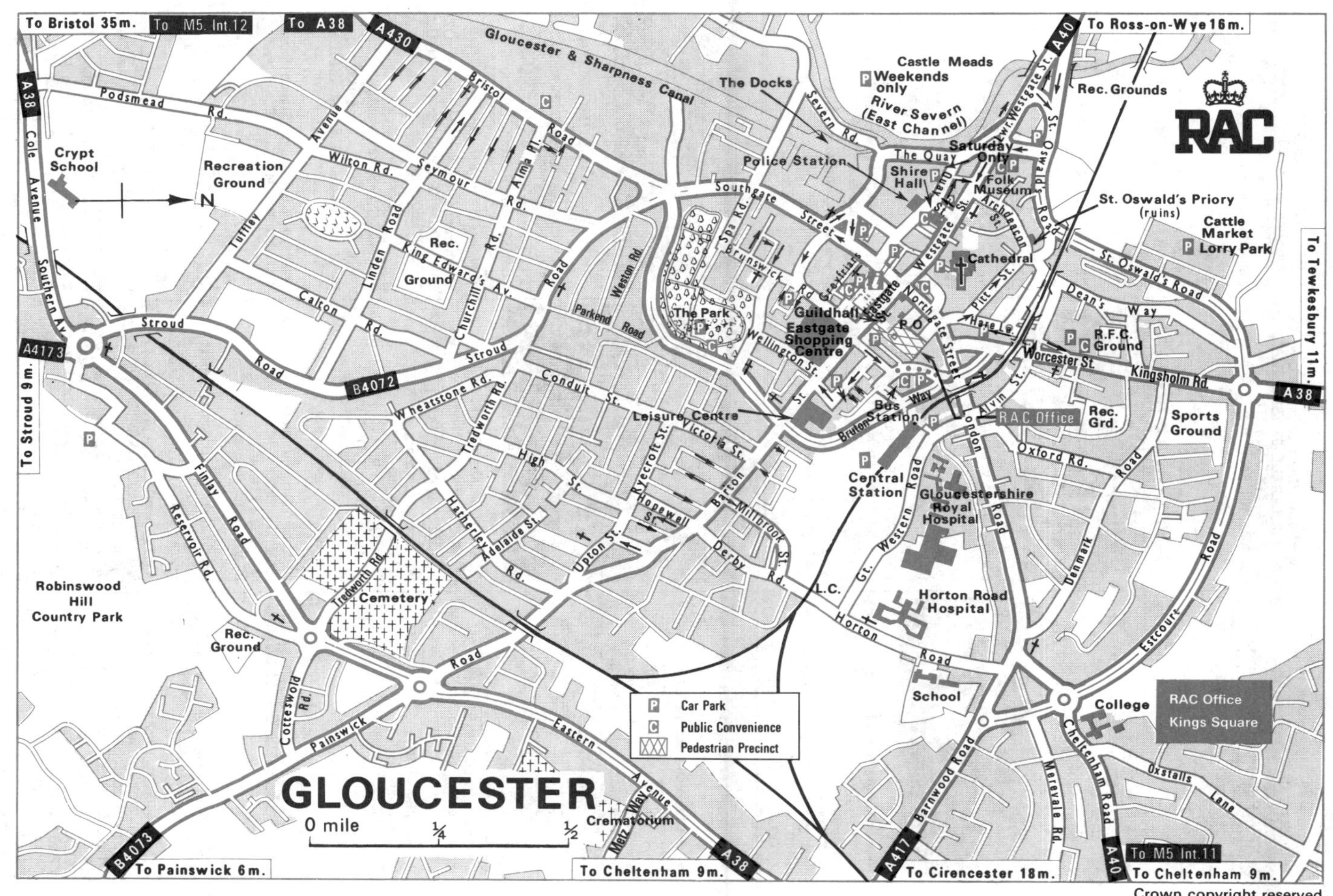
To Bristol 35m.
To M5. Int.12
To A38
To Ross-on-Wye 16m.
RAC
GLOUCESTER
0 mile
1/4
1/2
Car Park
Public Convenience
Pedestrian Precinct
Castle Meads
Weekends only
River Severn (East Channel)
The Docks
Gloucester & Sharpness Canal
Rec. Grounds
St. Oswald's Priory (ruins)
Cattle Market Lorry Park
Police Station
Shire Hall
Folk Museum
Saturday Only
Cathedral
Guildhall
Eastgate Shopping Centre
The Park
Leisure Centre
Bus Station
R.A.C. Office
R.F.C. Ground
Rec. Grd.
Sports Ground
Central Station
Gloucestershire Royal Hospital
Horton Road Hospital
School
College
RAC Office
Kings Square
Crypt School
Recreation Ground
Rec. Ground
Robinswood Hill Country Park
Cemetery
Crematorium
To Stroud 9m.
To Tewkesbury 11m.
To Painswick 6m.
To Cheltenham 9m.
To Cirencester 18m.
To M5 Int.11
To Cheltenham 9m.
Crown copyright reserved

G

Cirencester 18, Ross-on-Wye, 16, Tewkesbury 10.
See Plan p. 261.
MD Daily. **P** See Plan. **Golf** Gloucester G.C. 18h & 9h. **See** Cathedral (fine cloisters), St Mary de Crypt Church, Bishop Hooper's Lodging, St Oswald's Priory.
[i] St Michael's Tower, The Cross. (0452) 421188

★★★ **H** **C** **Crest,** Crest Way, Barnwood, GL4 7RX (0452) 613311 Tx: 437273 Fax: (0452) 371036

Modern purpose-built hotel situated on the outskirts of the city. Indoor swimming pool, sauna, solarium, gymnasium. (Cr/THF)
123 bedrs, 123 en suite; TV; tcf
dogs, ns; P 177, coach; child facs; con 100
LD 9.45, bar meals only Sat lunch
£ B&B £81·95 (w/e £46), B&B (double) £101·90; L £10·25, D £15·75; WB
cc Access, Amex, B'card/Visa, Diners.

★★★ **Gloucester Hotel and Country Club,** Robinswood Hill GL4 9EA (0452) 25653 Tx: 43571 Fax: (0452) 307212
Converted 16–17th century farmhouse with modern leisure complex added. Swimming pool, golf, putting, tennis, squash, sauna, solarium, gymnasium, billiards.
97 bedrs, 97 en suite; annexe 10 bedrs, 10 en suite; TV; tcf
TV, dogs, ns; P 300, coach; child facs; con 80
LD 9.30, nr Sat lunch
£ B&B £85–£95, B&B (double) £102·50–£112·50; L £11·50, D £15; WB £49·50
cc Access, Amex, B'card/Visa, Diners; dep.

★★★ **Hatherley Manor,** Down Hatherley La, Down Hatherley (0452) 730217 Tx: 437353 Fax: (0452) 731032

In 35 acres of grounds, an attractive manor house, completely refurbished. Fr, De
55 bedrs, 55 en suite: TV; tcf
dogs, ns; P 250, coach; child facs; con 280
LD 9.30, bar meals only Sat lunch
£ B&B £70–£83 (w/e £40), B&B (double) £88–£100; L £11·50, D £16·25; WB £55; [10% V w/e]
cc Access, Amex, B'card/Visa, Diners.

★★★ **Hatton Court,** Upton Hill, Upton St Leonards, GL4 8DE (3½m SE on B4073) (0452) 617412 Tx: 437334 Fax: (0452) 612945

Lovely old 17th-century Cotswold-stone building. Attractive grounds of seven acres. Swimming pool.
16 bedrs, 16 en suite; annexe 30 bedrs, 30 en suite; TV; tcf.
P 70, coach; child facs; con 60
LD 10
£ B&B £72–£84, B&B (double) £92–£110; L £14, D £19·50; WB £105–£120 (2 nts)
cc Access, Amex, B'card/Visa, Diners, dep.

★★ **New County,** 44 Southgate St, GL1 2DU (0452) 307000 Fax: (0452) 500487

Attractive four-storey Georgian building situated in the city centre. Closed Xmas/New Year.
31 bedrs, 31 en suite, TV; tcf
nc; coach; child facs; con 200
LD 9.30, nr Sun dinner
£ B&B £46·75, B&B (double) £56·50; L £5, D £10, WB £50 (HB); [10% V]
cc Access, Amex, B'card/Visa, Diners.

★★ **New Inn,** Northgate St, GL1 1SF (0452) 22177
Interesting old inn built around a charming cobbled courtyard in the centre of the city.
24 bedrs, 13 en suite, 3 ba; TV; tcf
coach; child facs; con 60
LD 10.30
£ B&B £25–£45, B&B (double) £40–£65; L £6, D £10; WB
cc Access, Amex, B'card/Visa, Diners.

★★ **Twigworth Lodge,** Tewkesbury Rd, Twigworth, GL2 9PG (0452) 730266 Fax: (0452) 730099
Delightful Regency building in 3 acres of grounds on the A38 about 2 miles north east of Gloucester. Indoor swimming pool, billiards.
30 bedrs, 30 en suite; TV; tcf
dogs; P 60, coach; child facs; con 20
LD 10, nr Sat lunch
£ B&B fr £45 (w/e room fr £23), B&B (double) fr £59; WB £33
cc Access, Amex, B'card/Visa, Diners.

Gilbert's (Acclaimed), Gilbert's La, Brookthorpe, GL4 0UH (0452) 812364. *Guest House.*
£ B&B £19–£30
Lulworth (Acclaimed), 12 Midland Rd, GL1 4UF (0452) 21881. *Guest House.* Closed 25 Dec–1 Jan
£ B&B £13–£16
Rotherfield House (Acclaimed), 5 Horton Rd, GL1 3PX (0452) 410500. *Hotel.*
£ B&B £16·95–£26·95

Pembury, 9 Pembury Rd (0452) 21856. *Guest House.*
£ B&B £15–£25
Westville, 255 Stroud Rd, GL1 5JZ (0452) 301228. *Guest House.*

GOATHLAND North Yorkshire. Map 45C1

Pop 394. Pickering 14, London 227, Whitby 9.
EC Thur. **Golf** Whitby 18h. **See** Church, Moors, Waterfalls, Roman Road.

★★★ **Inn on the Moor,** YO22 5LZ (0947) 86296

Attractive country house in own gardens in popular moors village.
24 bedrs, 22 en suite; 3 ba; TV; tcf
TV, dogs; P 30, coach; child facs; con 5
LD 8.30, bar meals only Mon–Sat lunch
£ B&B £27–£80; B&B (double) £54–£90; HB weekly £210–£260; L £7·50, D £13·50
cc Access, B'card/Visa; dep.

Heatherdene (Acclaimed), Nr Whitby YO22 5AN Whitby (0947) 86334. Open Apr–Oct.
£ B&B £13·50

GODALMING Surrey. Map 6B2

Pop 18,209. Guildford 4, London 32, Dorking 15, Farnham 9, Haslemere 8½, Hindhead 8, Horsham 18, Petworth 16.
EC Wed. **MD** Fri. **Golf** West Surrey 18h, Bramley 18h. **See** Church, Church House, Winkworth Arboretum 2m SE.
[i] South St (048 64) 4104

Meads, 65 Meadow Row, GU7 3HS (048 68) 21800. *Hotel.*
£ B&B £24–£38

GOODRINGTON Devon

See PAIGNTON.

GOODWOOD West Sussex. Map 6A1

Midhurst 9, London 58, Chichester 4½.
Golf Goodwood 18h. **See** Goodwood House, Boxgrove Priory 1 m SE, Weald and Downland Open Air Museum at Singleton (2m N), West Dean Gardens.

G

★★★ [R] **Goodwood Park,** PO18 0QB ☎Chichester (0243) 775537 Tx: 869173 Fax: (0243) 533802 ♿

An ancient inn, refurbished and expanded, standing on the Goodwood estate. Indoor swimming pool, golf, putting, tennis, squash, sauna, solarium, gymnasium, billiards.
89 bedrs, 89 en suite; TV; tcf
dogs, ns; P 200, coach; child facs; con 100
LD 9.30
£ B&B £85–£95 (w/e £50); B&B (double) £95–£110; L £10·95, D £17·25; WB £50
cc Access, Amex, B'card/Visa; dep.

GOOLE Humberside. Map 39A2
Pop 18,602. M62 (jn 36) 1, London 190, Beverley 23, Hull 33, Pontefract 20, Scunthorpe 21, Selby 12, York 24.
EC Thur. **MD** Mon, Wed, Fri. **Golf** Boothferry 18h. **See** Port.
[i] Central Library ☎(0405) 762187

★★ **Clifton,** 1 Clifton Gdns, Boothferry Rd, DN14 6AR ☎(0405) 761336
Fax: (0405) 762350
Three-storey, brick-built hotel on main road close to town centre.
10 bedrs, 8 en suite, (1 sh), 1 ba; TV; tcf
TV, dogs; P 8, coach; con 40
LD 9, bar meals only Sat lunch & all Sun. Resid & Rest lic
£ B&B £35, B&B (double) £42; [10% V]
cc Access, Amex, B'card/Visa, Diners

GORLESTON-ON-SEA Norfolk. Map 35C1
Lowestoft 8, London 125, Gt Yarmouth 2, Scole 32.
EC Wed. **Golf** Gorleston 18h. **See** St Andrew's Parish Church, Lifeboat Station.

★★★ [C] **Cliff,** Cliff Hill, NR31 6DH ☎Gt Yarmouth (0493) 662179 Tx: 987129

Three-storey white building with attractive balconies. Superb cliff-top setting.
30 bedrs, 30 en suite, 1 ba; TV; tcf
dogs, ns; P 50; child facs; con 125

★★ **Pier,** Harbour Mouth, NR31 6PL ☎Gt Yarmouth (0493) 662631
Fax: (0493) 440263
Small owner-managed hotel, standing between beach and harbour mouth.
20 bedrs, 20 en suite; TV; tcf
dogs; P 20, coach; child facs; con 100
LD 9,
£ B&B £35–£45, B&B (double) £60; HB weekly £300; L £6, D £10·50; WB £47·50 (2 nts), [10% V]
cc Access, Amex, B'card/Visa; dep.

Squirrel's Nest (Acclaimed), 71 Avondale Rd, NR31 6DJ ☎(0493) 662746. *Hotel*
£ B&B £20–£30; HB weekly £160–£225; [10% V w/d]

Balmoral, 65 Avondale Rd, NR31 6DJ ☎Gt Yarmouth (0493) 662538. *Hotel.*
£ B&B £15–£22; HB weekly£95–£140

GOSFORTH Tyne & Wear.
See NEWCASTLE-UPON-TYNE.

GOSPORT Hampshire. Map 5C2
Pop 80,000. Fareham 5, London 81, Romsey 23, Southampton 16.
EC Wed. **MD** Tue. **Golf** Gosport and Stokes Bay 18h, Lee-on-the-Solent 18h. **See** Holy Trinity Church (1696), Submarine Museum.
[i] Falkland Gardens. ☎(0705) 522944

★★ **Anglesey,** Crescent Rd, Alverstoke, PO12 2DH ☎(0705) 582157
Regency building in an attractive quiet terrace.
18 bedrs, 18 en suite; TV; tcf
dogs; G 2 (£1·50), coach; child facs; con 65

Bridgemary Manor, Brewers Lane, PO13 0JY ☎Fareham (0329) 232946
£ B&B £30; HB weekly £345.

GOUDHURST Kent. Map 11C1
Pop 2,663. Tonbridge 12, London 44, Ashford 21, Canterbury 33, Hawkhurst 6, Hurst Green 7, Tunbridge Wells 10.
EC Wed. **Golf** Lamberhurst 18h. **See** Parish Church, Bedgebury National Pinetum 2½ m.

★★ [H] [C] [R] **Star & Eagle,** High St, TN17 1AL ☎(0580) 211512
In centre of Goudhurst, attractive 16th century inn with modern extension.
11 bedrs, 9 en suite, 1 ba; TV; tcf
dogs; P 25, coach; child facs; con 25

GRANGE-IN-BORROWDALE Cumbria. Map 43C1
Pop 50. Keswick 4, London 289.
EC Sat. **Golf** Keswick 9h.

★★★ **Borrowdale Gates,** CA12 5UQ ☎Borrowdale (0596 84) 204 ♿
Country house hotel enjoying pleasant Lakeland hill view. Fr
23 bedrs, 23 en suite, 1 ba; TV; tcf
P 40
LD 8.45, bar meals only Mon–Sat lunch. Resid & Rest lic
£ B&B £27·50–£42·50; B&B (double) £51–£85; L £8·50, D £15·50; WB fr £100 (HB 3 nts)
cc Access, Diners; dep.

GRANGE-OVER-SANDS Cumbria. Map 36A4
Pop 3,474. Lancaster 24, London 259, Ambleside 19, Kendal 13, Kirkby Lonsdale 20, Ulverston 15.
EC Thur. **Golf** Grange-over-Sands 18h. **See** 12th century Cartmel Priory Gatehouse. 1½m W, Holker Hall 3m SW.
[i] Victoria Hall, Main St. ☎(053 95) 34026

★★★ **Cumbria Grand,** Lindale Rd, LA11 6EN ☎(044 84) 2331

Grand grey-stone Victorian hotel with breathtaking views and extensive grounds. Putting, tennis, billiards.

★★★ **Grange,** Lindale Rd, LA11 6EJ ☎(053 95) 33666 ♿

Spacious stone-built mid-Victorian hotel in prominent position overlooking sea.
40 bedrs, 40 en suite; TV; tcf
TV, dogs; P 100; child facs; con 150

★★ [R] **Graythwaite Manor,** Fernhill Rd, LA11 7JE ☎(053 95) 32001 ♿

Attractive, well-appointed country house hotel. Eight acres of delightful gardens. Putting, tennis, billiards. Fr, De.
22 bedrs, 22 en suite; TV; tcf
P 20; child facs; con 25
LD 8.30
£ B&B & dinner £37·50–£55; B&B (double) & dinner £74–£104; HB weekly £241·50–£350; L £8·50, D £17; [5% V]

Hotel locations
Hotel locations are shown on the maps at the back of the guide. All towns and villages containing an RAC Appointed or Listed hotel are ringed in purple.

★★ H **Netherwood,** Lindale Rd, LA11 6ET ☎(053 95) 32552 ♿

Lovely Victorian house, in "Jacobean" style, with oak panelling. Own grounds. Indoor swimming pool, gymnasium.
🛏 33 bedrs, 27 en suite, 2 ba; TV; tcf
🏨 TV, dogs, ns; P 100, coach; child facs; con 150
✕ LD 8.30
£ B&B £32·75–£33·75; B&B (double) £65·50–£67·50; HB weekly £292–£299; L £7·50, D £10; WB £60; dep.

Elton (Highly Acclaimed), Windermere Rd, LA11 7BB ☎(053 95) 32838. *Private Hotel.*

Corner Beech, Methven Ter, Kents Bank Rd, LA11 7DP ☎(053 95) 33088. *Guest House.*
£ B&B £12·50; HB weekly £115.
Holme Lea, 90 Kentsford Rd, LA11 7BB ☎(053 95) 32545. *Guest House.* Open Mar–Oct.
£ B&B £12; HB weekly £113.

GRANTHAM Lincolnshire. Map 31B2

Pop 30,502. Stamford 21, London 111, Boston 30, Lincoln 25, Melton Mowbray 16, Newark 15, Nottingham 24, Sleaford 14.
EC Wed. **MD** Thur, Sat. **Golf** Belton Park18h. **See** Market Cross, Isaac Newton statue, Belton House.
ℹ The Museum, St Peters Hill. ☎(0476) 66444

★★★ **Angel & Royal,** High St, NG31 6PN ☎(0476) 65816 Fax: (0476) 67149

13th-century building with unique stonework in bar. Situated in town centre. (THF)
🛏 30 bedrs, 30 en suite; TV; tcf
🏨 dogs, ns; P 50, coach; child facs; con 25
✕ LD 9.45
£ room £70–£85 (w/e £37), room (double) £87–£95; Bk £7·50, L £9·75, D £14·95; WB £37
cc Access, Amex, B'card/Visa, Diners, dep.

Weekend breaks
Please consult the hotel for full details of weekend breaks; prices shown are an indication only. Many hotels offer mid week breaks as well.

★★★ **George,** High St, NG31 6NN ☎(0476) 63286 Tx: 378121

Imposing historic hotel (1760) situated in main thoroughfare. Under refurbishment, completion expected early 1991.

★★ **Kings,** North Par, NG31 8AU ☎(0476) 590800 Fax: (0476) 590800 ♿

Pleasant brick building, former private residence, set back from road. Tennis. Es, Fr
🛏 22 bedrs, 22 en suite, 2 ba; TV; tcf
🏨 dogs; P 60, coach; child facs; con 100
✕ LD 10.30
£ B&B £25–£40, B&B (double) £55; L £9·25, D £9·25; WB £27·50 (HB)
cc Access, Amex, B'card/Visa, Diners.

Lanchester (Acclaimed), 84 Harrowby Rd, NG31 9DS ☎(0476) 74169 *Guest House.*
£ B&B £16–£22·50, HB weekly £161–£206·50

Garden, 86 Harrowby Rd, NG31 9AF ☎(0476) 62040
Hawthornes, 51 Cambridge St, NG31 9EZ ☎(0476) 73644 *Guest House.*
£ B&B £16–£18

GRAPPENHALL Cheshire. Map 33A1

Pop 8,468. Knutsford 9½, London 181, Altrincham 10, Chester 21, Northwich 11, Warrington 3.
Golf Lymm 18h. **See** St Wilfrid's Church.

★ **Rockfield,** Alexandra Rd, WA4 2EL ☎Warrington (0925) 62898
Small, quietly situated hotel with pleasant garden. 2 miles from town centre.

Kenilworth, 2 Victoria Rd, WA4 2EN ☎Warrington (0925) 62323. *Hotel.*
£ B&B £18–£30.

GRASMERE Cumbria. Map 43C1

Pop 1,029. Ambleside 4, London 273, Keswick 12, Penrith 25.
EC Thur. **Golf** Windermere 18h. **See** Dove Cottage and Wordsworth Museum, St Oswald's Church, graves of Wordsworth and Coleridge. Grasmere Sports Aug.
ℹ Red Bank Road. ☎(096 65) 245

★★★★ H R **Wordsworth,** LA22 9TA ☎(096 65) 592 Tx: 65329 Fax: (096 65) 765 ♿
Modernised traditional building with own grounds in village. Indoor swimming pool, sauna, solarium, gymnasium. Fr, De, Es
🛏 37 bedrs, 37 en suite; TV
🏨 lift; P 56, coach; child facs; con 100
✕ LD 9
£ B&B £44–£58, B&B (double) £88–£116; WB £60 (HB)
cc Access, Amex, B'card/Visa; dep.
(See advertisement on p. 266)

★★★ R **Gold Rill,** LA22 9PU ☎(096 65) 486

Attractive stone-built hotel with magnificent views from pleasant gardens. Swimming pool, putting, fishing.

★★★ **Prince of Wales,** LA22 9PR ☎(096 65) 666 Tx: 65364

Stone-built hotel with mature gardens on lakeside. (MtCh) Fr, It, Es.
🛏 77 bedrs, 77 en suite; TV; tcf
🏨 dogs; P 120, coach; child facs; con 100
✕ LD 9, bar meals only lunch
£ D £12·50
cc Access, Amex, B'card/Visa, diners.

★★★ **Red Lion,** Red Lion Sq, LA22 9SS ☎(096 65) 456 Fax: (05394) 34157
A 200 year-old coaching inn enlarged and transformed into a modern hotel.
🛏 36 bedrs, 36 en suite; TV; tcf
🏨 lift, dogs, ns; P 40, coach; child facs; con 50
✕ LD 9, bar meals only lunch
£ B&B £25–£33; B&B (double) £50–£66; D £14; WB £39 (HB); [10% V]
cc Access, Amex, B'card/Visa, Diners.

★★★ H R **Swan,** LA22 9RF ☎(096 65) 551 Fax: (096 65) 741

A former 17th-century coaching inn at side of A591. (THF)

G

Grange-over-Sands (Cumbria)

Cark-in-Cartmel, Grange-over-Sands, Cumbria LA11 7PL
Tel: (05395) 58328
Cumbria's premier stately home with magnificent gardens. Exhibitions, Deer Park, Café and Gift Shop. Open every day (excl. Saturdays) Easter Sunday to last Sunday in October.

Grasmere (Cumbria)

Everything at the Garden is Beautiful

ROTHAY GARDEN HOTEL Grasmere Village Heart of the Lakes

Restaurant and residential licence; 21 bedrooms, all with private bathrooms; children and dogs welcome; car park (30); London 280 miles, Keswick 13, Windermere 9, Ambleside 4.
Our warm-welcoming country house hotel is set in two acres of riverside gardens, and offers quiet, well appointed rooms (the majority of which offer the most attractive views), some having four-poster beds and whirlpool baths. With our comfortable bar and lounge, our very elegant conservatory Restaurant, serving a wide variety of traditional and international cuisine, our friendly and attentive staff, we can assure you that your stay with us will be a memorable and enjoyable experience. Wordsworth said of Grasmere, "The loveliest spot that man hath ever known . . ." We look forward to meeting you.

Proprietors: Chris and Wendy Carss

ROTHAY GARDEN HOTEL, Grasmere, Ambleside LA22 9RJ

Grasmere (Cumbria)

Four-Star Luxury in the heart of English Lakeland . . .

The WORDSWORTH HOTEL
and "PRELUDE RESTAURANT"
Grasmere, Cumbria

All bedrooms and suites have bathrooms, TV, radio, direct-dial telephone and intercom. There are spacious lounges, cocktail bar, terrace and garden, heated indoor pool, jacuzzi, sauna, sunbed and mini-gym.
In the delectable "Prelude Restaurant" the finest fresh produce is skilfully presented on an à la carte menu. Non-residents most welcome. Exceptional conference and banqueting facilities.

Tel: Grasmere (09665) 592 Fax: (09665) 765

Hadley Wood (Hertfordshire)

RAC ★★★★

West Lodge Park

The nearest country hotel to London – only 12 miles from the West End, and one mile from exit 24 on the M25, but set in 35 acres of parkland and fields. Country house atmosphere with antiques and log fire. Individually decorated bedrooms with carefully chosen fabrics and furnishings. Some four poster bedrooms and whirlpool baths. Ask for colour brochure and details of weekend breaks.

West Lodge Park, Hadley Wood, Barnet, Herts.
Tel: 081-440 8311 Telex: 24734 Fax: 081-449 3698

36 bedrs, 36 en suite; TV; tcf
dogs, ns; P 40; child facs; con 30
LD 9
£ B&B £78–£88(w/e £50), B&B (double) £104–£124; HB weekly £315–£455; L £10·50, D £18; WB £55
cc Access, Amex, B'card/Visa, CB, Diners.

★★ **Grasmere,** LA22 9TA (096 65) 277
Three-storey Victorian stone building with own garden. Putting. Fr. Open Feb–Dec.
12 bedrs, 12 en suite, 1 ba; TV; tcf
dogs, ns; P 14; no children under 7
LD 8, bar meals only lunch. Resid & Rest lic
£ B&B £30–£40, B&B (double) £56–£80; HB weekly £210–£294; D £14; [10% V w/d, Nov–Apr]
cc Access, B'card/Visa; dep.

★★ **Moss Grove,** LA22 9SW (096 65) 251
Fax: (096 65) 691

Centrally-situated refurbished Victorian house. Sauna. Open Feb–Dec.
14 bedrs, 13 en suite, 2 ba; TV; tcf
P 17, coach; child facs; con 10
LD 8.30, bar meals only lunch. Resid & Rest lic
£ B&B £25·25–£32, B&B (double) £44–£63·75; D £13·50; [10% V w/d]
cc Access, B'card/Visa; dep.

★★ H R **Oak Bank,** Broadgate, LA22 9TA (096 65) 217

Attractive stone-built family-managed hotel. Pleasant garden. Open Feb–Xmas.
15 bedrs, 15 en suite; TV; tcf
TV, dogs, ns; P 15, coach; child facs; con 10

★★ **Rothay Garden,** LA22 9RH (096 65) 334 Fax: (09665) 723

Charming mid-19th century building with lawns and gardens. Fishing.

21 bedrs, 21 en suite, 1 ba; TV; tcf
dogs, ns; P 30; child facs; con 20
(*See advertisement on p. 266*)

Bridge House (Highly Acclaimed), Stock Lane, LA22 9SN (096 65) 425. *Hotel.* Open mid-Mar–mid Nov.
£ B&B £23–£30; HB weekly £200–£230

Ben Place, 2 Ben Place, LA22 9RL (09665) 581 *Guest House.* Open Easter–Nov.
£ B&B £16–£18

GRASSINGTON North Yorkshire. Map 38A3

Pop 1,300. Leeds 31, London 222, Harrogate 25, Hawes 26, Leyburn 26, Settle 18, Skipton 9, Thirsk 34.
EC Thur. **Golf** Skipton 18h, Ilkley 18h.
See old lead mines on Moor, Linton Church, Museum.
National Park Centre, Hebden Rd (0756) 752748

★★★ **Wilson Arms,** Threshfield, BD23 5EL (0756) 752666 Tx: 57515
Fax: (0756) 752666
Attractive white-painted building in 2 acres of landscaped garden in Dales.
14 bedrs, 14 en suite; TV; tcf
lift, TV, dogs; P 40, coach; child facs; con 120
LD 9.30
£ B&B £36; B&B (double) £72; HB weekly £290; L £9·50, D £14·95
cc Access, Amex, B'card/Visa.

Black Horse, Garrs La, BD23 5AT (0756) 752770
Stone-built former coaching inn on edge of market square.
11 bedrs, 11 en suite; TV; tcf
TV, dogs; coach

GRAVESEND Kent. Map 9C2

Pop 52,303. Dartford 8, London 24, Dartford Tunnel 8½, Rochester 7, Sevenoaks 18.
EC Wed. **MD** Daily. **Golf** Mid Kent 18h. **See** Chapel of Milton Chantry, Princess Pocahontas Memorial Church and Statue.
10 Parrock St. (0474) 337600

★★ **Clarendon Royal,** Royal Pier Rd, DA12 2BE (0474) 363151

Typical Georgian building overlooking Thames estuary. (BCB)
24 bedrs, 14 en suite, 3 ba; TV; tcf
ns; P 140, coach; child facs
LD 10.30
£ B&B £42–£59·50, B&B (double) £54–£65; L £8·15, D £8·15; WB £27·50
cc Access, Amex, B'card/Visa, Diners.

★★ **Tollgate Motel,** Watling St, DA13 9RA (0474) 357655 Tx: 966227
Fax: (0474) 567543
Modern motel units adjoin restaurant and bars. Convenient for A2. Closed Xmas. Fr.

114 bedrs, 114 en suite; TV; tcf
dogs; ns; P 250, coach; child facs; con 100
LD 10.30, bar meals only Mon–Sat lunch.
£ B&B £51–£65 (w/e £36), B&B (double) £63–£75; L £5, D £8·55; [5% V w/e]
cc Access, Amex, B'card/Visa, Diners.

Sunnyside, 3 Sunnyside, off Windmill St, DA12 1LG (0474) 365445. *Guest House.*

GREAT AYTON North Yorkshire. Map 45B1

Pop 5,160. Thirsk 22, London 241, Darlington 19, Helmsley 21, Middlesbrough 8½, Northallerton 18, Whitby 26.
EC Wed. **Golf** Nunthorpe 18h. **See** Captain Cook's Obelisk, All Saints' Church.
High Green (0642) 722835

★★★ H C **Ayton Hall,** Low Green, TS9 6BW (0642) 723595
Fax: (0642) 722149

Lovely country house, largely Georgian, in 6 acres of gardens. Tennis.
9 bedrs, 9 en suite; TV
ns; P 35; coach; con 20
LD 9.45. Resid & Rest lic
£ B&B £77–£89, B&B (double) £95–£115; L £10·95, D £20·50; WB £95; [10% V]
cc Access, Amex, B'card/Visa, Diners.

GREAT BRICKHILL Buckinghamshire. Map 14A4

Leighton Buzzard 4, London 45, Bedford 17, Buckingham 15, Dunstable 10, Milton Keynes 6, Newport Pagnell 10.

Duncombe Arms, 32 Lower Way, MK17 9AG (0525) 261226. *Inn. Putting.*
£ B&B £32–£35; HB weekly £276·50–£297·50

GREAT LANGDALE Cumbria. Map 43C1

6 miles west of Ambleside, Windermere 9½, London 274, Coniston 6, Grasmere 4½.
See Langdale, Langdale Fell & Pikes.

★★★★ **Langdale,** Langdale Estate, Nr Ambleside, LA22 9JB Langdale (096 67) 302 Fax: (09667) 694
Modern hotel and country club in forest setting. Indoor swimming pool, putting, tennis, fishing, squash, sauna, solarium, gymnasium, billiards.
10 bedrs, 10 en suite; annexe 43 bedrs, 43 en suite; TV; tcf
ns; P 100, coach; child facs; con 100
(*See advertisement on p. 107*)

Residents only
Some Listed hotels only serve meals to residents. It is always wise to make a reservation for a meal in a hotel.

G

GREAT MILTON Oxfordshire. Map 21B1

M40 (jn 7), London 49, Abingdon 12, Oxford 8, Thame 5.

★★★ Le Manoir aux Quat' Saisons, OX9 7PD (0844) 27881 Tx: 837552 Fax: (0844) 278847

Exquisite 15th century manor house in honey-coloured stone, luxuriously decorated and furnished and set in 27 acres of gardens and parkland. Swimming pool, tennis. Fr, De.
19 bedrs, 19 en suite; TV
kennels, ns; P50; child facs; con 46
LD 10.45
£ double room £150–£250; Bk £12, L £24·50, D fr £54
cc Access, Amex, B'card/Visa, Diners; dep.

GREAT WITCHINGHAM Norfolk. Map 35B1

Pop 400. Norwich 11, London 122, Cromer 19, East Dereham 9½, Fakenham 14.
EC Sat. **Golf** Royal Norwich 18h.

★★★ Lenwade House, NR9 5QP Norwich (0603) 872288

Tudor-style country house in 18 acres of grounds with river frontage. Swimming pool, putting, tennis, fishing, squash, riding, solarium.

GRETA BRIDGE Durham. Map 44C1

Pop 90. Boroughbridge 37, London 244, Brough 19, Darlington 16, Leyburn 23, Middleton-in-Teesdale 13, West Auckland 13.
Golf Barnard Castle 18h.

★★ Morritt Arms, Rokeby, DL12 9SE Teesdale (0833) 27232 Fax: (0833) 27570

Three-storey stone-built former coaching inn with an "olde worlde" atmosphere. Fishing.
17 bedrs, 17 en suite, 4 ba; TV; tcf
TV, dogs; P 100, G 3; child facs; con 150
LD 8.45, bar meals only Mon–Sat lunch
£ B&B £42, B&B (double) £65; D £18; WB fr £45 (HB)
cc Access, Amex, B'card/Visa, Diners.

GRIMSBY Humberside (South Humberside). Map 35C3
See also CLEETHORPES.
Pop 92,000. Louth 16, London 164, Hull 31, Gainsborough 36, Market Rasen 20, Scunthorpe 30.
EC Thur. **MD** Tue, Fri, Sat. **Golf** Great Grimsby 18h, Cleethorpes 18h. **See** Fish Docks, Market Hall, Churches.
[i] Library, Town Hall (0472) 240410

★★★★ Humber Royal Crest, Littlecoates Rd, DN34 4LX (0472) 350295 Tx: 527776 Fax: (0472) 241354

A medium-sized modern hotel, in quiet area overlooking golf course. (Cr/THF)
52 bedrs, 52 en suite; TV; tcf
lift, dogs, ns; P 200, coach; child facs; con 260
LD 9.45, bar meals only Sat lunch
£ B&B £75·95–£82·95, B&B (double) £102·90; Bk £7·95; L £9·50, D £14·50; WB fr £41
cc Access, Amex, B'card/Visa, Diners.

★★★ Crest, St James Sq, DN 31 1EP (0472) 359771 Tx: 527741 Fax: (0472) 241427

Modern hotel conveniently situated in town centre. Sauna. (Cr/THF) Closed 25 Dec–1 Jan.
125 bedrs, 125 en suite; TV; tcf
lift, dogs, ns; P 85, coach; child facs; con 70
LD 10
£ B&B £71·45–£76·45 (w/e £29), B&B (double) £91·90–£96·90; L £7·95, D £13·65; WB £34 (HB)
cc Access, Amex, B'card/Visa, Diners.

★★★ Oaklands, Barton St, Laceby, DN37 7LF (0472) 72248
Traditional brick building, in 5 acres of pleasant gardens. Swimming pool, putting, sauna, solarium, gymnasium.
46 bedrs, 46 en suite; TV; tcf
dogs, ns; P 200, coach; child facs; con 100

★★★ Yarborough, Bethlehem St, DN31 1LY (0472) 242266
A grand, Victorian, red-brick station hotel in centre of town, updated, but keeping its character.
52 bedrs, 52 en suite; TV; tcf

GRIMSTON Norfolk. Map 35A2

Pop 1,763. King's Lynn 7, London 106, East Dereham 21, Fakenham 16, Swaffham 12.
EC Tue. **Golf** King's Lynn 18h.

★★★ Congham Hall, King's Lynn, PE32 1AH Hillington (0485) 600250 Tx: 81508 Fax: (0485) 601191

Luxury owner-managed hotel in Georgian mansion in lovely rural setting. Swimming pool, tennis.
14 bedrs, 14 en suite, 1 ba; TV
ns; P 50, children over 12; con 12
LD 9.30, nr Sat lunch. Resid & Rest lic
£ B&B £70–£75, B&B (double) £95–£110; L £14·50, D £27·50; WB £150
cc Access, Amex, B'card/Visa, Diners; dep.

GRINDLEFORD Derbyshire. Map 30C3

Pop 411. Matlock 13, London 158, Buxton 15, Chapel-en-le-Frith 14, Chesterfield 13, Glossop 20, Sheffield 10.
Golf Bakewell 9h. **See** Padley Chapel.

★★★ Maynard Arms, Main Rd, S30 1HP Hope Valley (0433) 30321 Fax: (0433) 30445

Attractive "olde worlde" hotel in well-kept garden. Four-poster beds available.
13 bedrs, 11 en suite, 2 ba; TV; tcf
dogs; P 60, coach; child facs; con 50

EC *early closing* **MD** *market day* *country house hotel* *ns (NS) no smoking areas* *tcf tea/coffee facilities*

✕ LD 9.30
£ B&B £50, B&B (double) £60; L £8·95, D £14·95; WB £37·50
cc Access, Amex, B'card/Visa, Diners.

GRINTON IN SWALEDALE North Yorkshire. Map 44C1

Leyburn 10, Richmond 11, London 246, Brough 20, Darlington 17, Hawes 17.

Bridge, Nr Richmond, DL11 6HH
Richmond (N Yorks) (0748) 84224 *Hotel.*
Open Mar–Oct
£ B&B £19·50; HB weekly £185

GRIZEDALE Cumbria. Map 43C1

M6 (jn 36) 22, London 269, Ambleside 8, Broughton-in-Furness 12, Kendal 17, Windermere 8.

★★ H R **Grizedale Lodge,** LA22 0QL
(096 66) 532

Typical Lakeland building in quiet setting close to forest. Open mid Feb–beg Jan.
6 bedrs, 4 en suite; TV; tcf
ns; P 20
✕ LD 8.30, bar meals only lunch. Resid & Rest lic
£ B&B & dinner £40–£46, B&B & dinner (double) £68–£80; HB weekly £250; D £15·50; WB
cc Access, B'card/Visa; dep.

GROBY Leicestershire. Map 25C3

Pop 5,399. Leicester 5, London 102, Burton-on-Trent 21, Coventry 27.
Golf Charnwood Forest 9h. **See** Charnwood Forest.

★★ **Brant Inn,** Leicester Rd, LE6 0DU
Leicester (0533) 872703
Fax: (0533) 875292

A 2-storey modern inn located in quiet situation with gardens.
10 bedrs, (8 sh), 1 ba; TV; tcf
dogs, ns; P 100, coach; child facs; con 160
✕ LD 9.30, bar meals only Sat lunch, Sun dinner
£ B&B £29·50 (w/e £21·50); B&B (double) £49·50; L £7·75, D £11
cc Access, B'card/Visa, Diners.

GUILDFORD Surrey. Map 13B1

Pop 60,000. Ripley 6, London 28, Bagshot 11, Dorking 13, Farnham 10, Haslemere 12, Horsham 19, Leatherhead 12, Woking 6½.
See Plan, p. 270.
MD Tue, Fri, Sat. **P** See Plan. **Golf** Guildford 18h. **See** Cathedral, Castle ruins, Abbot's Hospital (1619), Guildhall, St Mary's Church.
i 155 High St, (0483) 444007

★★★★ **Forte,** Egerton Road, GU2 5XZ
(0483) 574444 Tx: 858572
Fax: (0483) 302960 ♿

Newly built, long, low red-brick building just off the A3. Indoor swimming pool, sauna, solarium, gymnasium. Fr, De, Du. (THF)
121 bedrs, 121 en suite; TV; tcf
dogs, ns; P 190, coach; child facs; con 120
✕ LD 9.45, nr Sun dinner
£ B&B £106–£160, B&B (double) £126–£170; L £14·50, D £16·50; WB £47
cc Access, Amex, B'card/Visa, CB, Diners.

★★★ C **Manor at Newlands,** Newlands Corner, GU4 8SE (0483) 222624 Fax: (0483) 211389

Gabled stucco manor house in 9 acres of parkland and gardens just off A25 E of city.
20 bedrs, 20 en suite; TV
P 100, U 6, coach; no children under 7; con 100

★★★ **White Horse,** Upper High St, GU1 3JG (0483) 64511 Fax: (0483) 31160

Georgian building with modern rooms attached. Near centre. (Emb)
42 bedrs, 42 en suite; 2 ba; TV; tcf
G 14, coach; child facs
✕ LD 9.15, bar meals only Mon–Sat lunch
£ B&B £64·50 (w/e £28·50), B&B (double) £71·50; HB weekly £470·75; L £8·50, D £10·50
cc Access, Amex, B'card/Visa, CB, Diners.

★★ **Clavadel,** Epsom Rd, GU1 2JH
(0483) 69066
Converted Edwardian gabled house, well furnished and decorated in style.
20 bedrs, 20 en suite; TV; tcf

Blanes Court, Albury Rd, GU1 2BT
(0483) 573171. *Hotel.*
Carlton, 36 London Rd, GU1 2AF (0483) 576539. *Hotel.*
£ B&B £26–£36, HB weekly £217–£287

GUISBOROUGH Cleveland. Map 45B1

Pop 19,100. Thirsk 27, London 246, Helmsley 27, Stockton-on-Tees 13, Whitby 20.
EC Wed. **MD** Thur, Sat. **Golf** Saltburn 18h. **See** Upleathen Church.
i Fountain St (0287) 33801

Fox & Hounds, Slapewith, TS14 6PX
(0287) 632964
Typical white-painted inn with some very well-furnished bedrooms.
16 bedrs, 16 en suite; TV; tcf
dogs, ns; P 150; coach; no children under 8; con 100
✕ LD 10
£ B&B £25–£35, B&B (double) £35–£45; L £5, D £7
cc Access, Amex, B'card/Visa.

GUNNISLAKE Cornwall. Map 3A2

Pop 1,200. Tavistock 4½, London 207, Launceston 14, Liskeard 13, Saltash 13.
EC Wed. **Golf** St. Mellion 18h. **See** Morwell Rocks, Weir Head.

★ **Cornish Inn,** The Square, PL18 9BW
Tavistock (0822) 832475
Attractive 2-storey white-faced inn of character in the square.

Hingston Country House, St Anns Chapel, PL18 9HB Tavistock (0822) 832468. *Hotel. Putting.*

HACKNESS North Yorkshire. Map 39A4

Scarborough 5, London 212, Pickering 17, Whitby 17.

★★★ **Hackness Grange,** nr Scarborough, YO13 0JW (0723) 82345
Fax: (0723) 82391
Victorian sandstone country house in 11 acres of grounds beside the River Derwent. Indoor swimming pool, golf, tennis, fishing.
26 bedrs, 26 en suite; TV; tcf
TV, ns; P 50; child facs
✕ LD 9
£ B&B £50–£60; L £7·50, D £15·50; WB £106; [10% V Nov–Apr]
cc Access, Amex, B'card/Visa, Diners; dep.

HADLEY WOOD Greater London (Middx.). Map 15A1

Barnet 1½, London 13, Enfield 5, Hatfield 9, St Albans 11.
EC Thur. **Golf** Hadley Wood 18h.

H

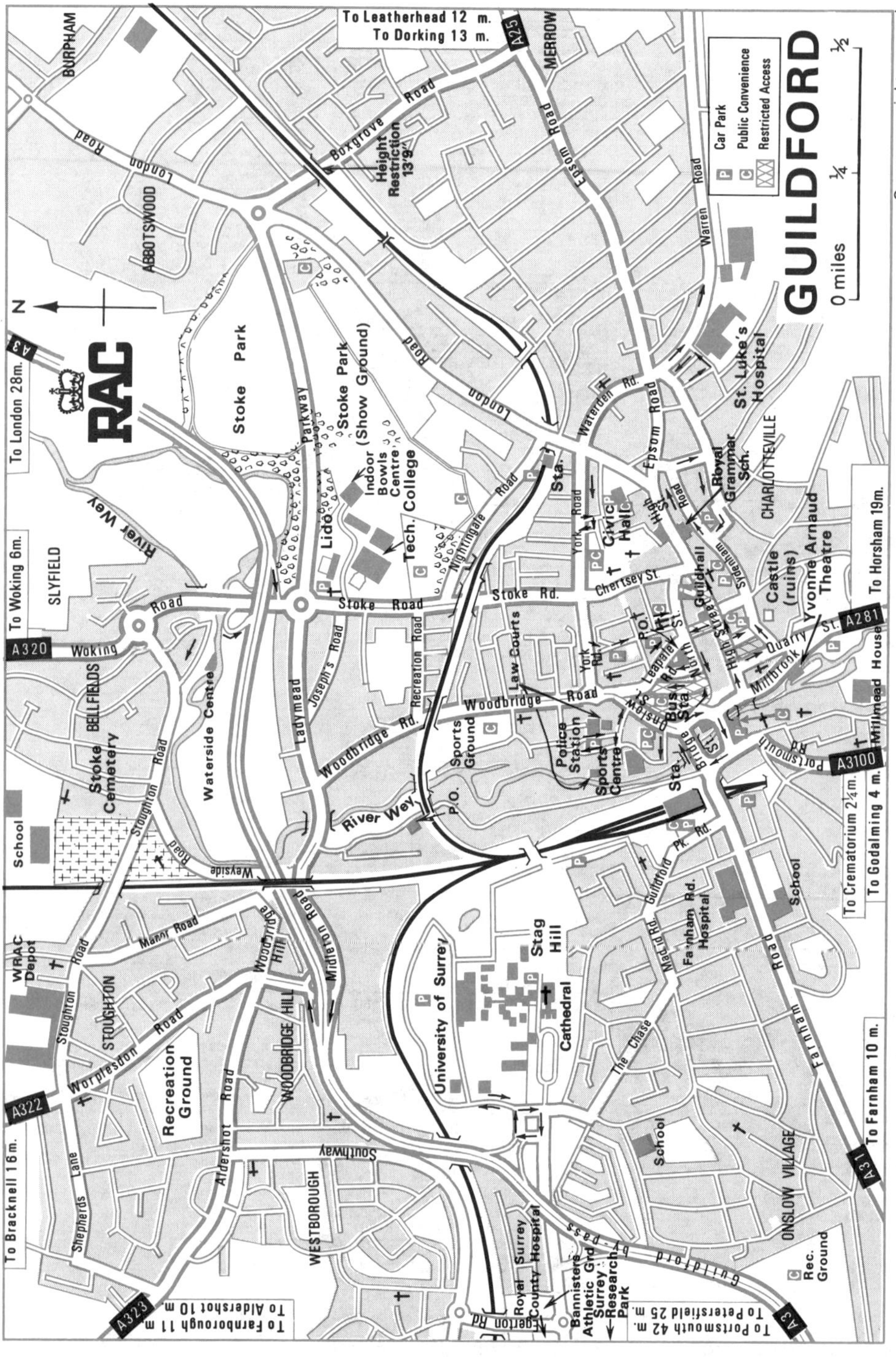

GUILDFORD

0 miles ¼ ½

P	Car Park
C	Public Convenience
XXX	Restricted Access

To Bracknell 16 m.
A322
To Woking 6m.
A320
To London 28m.
A3
To Leatherhead 12 m.
To Dorking 13 m.
A25
To Farnborough 11 m.
To Aldershot 10 m.
A323
To Portsmouth 42 m.
To Petersfield 25 m.
A3
To Farnham 10 m.
A31
To Crematorium 2¼ m.
To Godalming 4 m.
A3100
To Horsham 19m.
A281

BURPHAM
ABBOTSWOOD
SLYFIELD
BELLFIELDS
STOUGHTON
WOODBRIDGE HILL
WESTBOROUGH
ONSLOW VILLAGE
CHARLOTTEVILLE
MERROW
Stoke Park
Stoke Park (Show Ground)
Stoke Cemetery
Waterside Centre
Recreation Ground
University of Surrey
Stag Hill
Cathedral
Royal Surrey County Hospital
Bannisters Athletic Grd
Surrey Research Park
Farnham Rd. Hospital
St. Luke's Hospital
Royal Grammar Sch.
Castle (ruins)
Yvonne Arnaud Theatre
Millmead House
Guildhall
Civic Hall
Law Courts
Police Station
Sports Centre
Sports Ground
Tech. College
Indoor Bowls Centre
Lido
WRAC Depot
School
Rec. Ground
Height Restriction 13'9"

EC *early closing* **MD** *market day* ♣♣ *country house hotel* *ns (NS) no smoking areas* *tcf tea/coffee facilities*

♚ ★★★★ R **West Lodge Park,** EN4 0PY
☎081-440 8311 Tx: 24734
Fax: 081-449 3698 ♿

Luxurious Georgian country house hotel in 35 acres of grounds with small lake. Putting.
🛏 48 bedrs, 48 en suite; annexe 2 bedrs, 2 en suite; TV; tcf
🏠 lift; P 100; child facs; con 40
✕ LD 9.30. Resid & Rest lic
£ B&B £75, B&B (double) £99·50; WB £72·50
cc Access, Amex, B'card/Visa.
(*See advertisement on p. 266*)

HAILSHAM East Sussex. Map 7A1
Pop 17,000. Uckfield 12, London 56, Eastbourne 8, Hastings 17, Lewes 13.
EC Thur. **MD** Wed. **Golf** Willingdon, Eastbourne 18h. **See** Restored Perp. Church, Michelham Priory 2 m.
ℹ Library, Western Rd. ☎(0323) 840604.

★★ **Old Forge,** Magham Down, BN27 1PN
☎(0323) 842893

Originally a 16th century forge, now a charming tile-hung, cottage-style hotel on A271 at edge of village. Closed Dec 25–Jan 1.
🛏 8 bedrs, 8 en suite; TV; tcf
🏠 dogs; P 10; G 4; child facs
✕ LD 9.30, nr lunch. Resid & Rest lic
£ B&B £25–£30, B&B (double) £38–£46; HB weekly £200–£225; L £8·50, D £9·50; WB fr £55; [10% V]
cc Access, Amex, B'card/Visa, Diners.

HALIFAX West Yorkshire. Map 40C2
See also SOWERBY BRIDGE
Pop 87,488. Huddersfield 7, London 187, M62 (jn 24) 4½, Bradford 8, Leeds 15, Oldham 19, Rochdale 17, Skipton 17.
MD Daily. **Golf** Halifax 18h, West End 18h. **See** St John's Parish Church, Piece Hall, Shibden Hall Folk Museum and Park, Bankfield Museum, Wainhouse Tower.
ℹ Piece Hall. ☎(0422) 368725

★★★ H R **Holdsworth House,** Holdsworth, HX2 9TG ☎(0422) 240024
Tx: 51574 Fax: (0422) 245174 ♿
Attractive Jacobean stone-built hotel in 2 acres of landscaped gardens. ✈ Fr, Gr. Closed 25 Dec–1 Jan.
🛏 40 bedrs, 40 en suite; TV
🏠 dogs; P 40; child facs; con 100
✕ LD 9.30, nr Sat & Sun lunch
£ B&B £65–£80, B&B (double) £80–£95; L £18, D £18; WB £37·50; [10% V w/e]
cc Access, Amex, B'card/Visa, Diners.

★★★ **Imperial Crown,** 42 Horton St, HX1 1BR. ☎(0422) 342342 Fax: (0422) 349866.
Two early Victorian stone buildings, restored and rebuilt into an appealing hotel with 30s styling. In central situation. ✈ Pl, Ru
🛏 42 bedrs, 42 en suite; TV; tcf
🏠 TV; P 16; child facs; con 250
✕ LD 10, nr lunch
£ B&B £52 (w/e £37), B&B (double) £62 (w/e £47); L £7·50, D £9·75; WB £95; [5% V w/e]
cc Access, Amex, B'card/Visa, Diners.
(*See advertisement on p. 272*)

★★★ **Wool Merchants,** 5 Mulcture Hall Rd, HX1 1SP ☎(0422) 368783
Converted from a restored woollen warehouse close to the centre of town. ✈ It, Ar
🛏 25 bedrs, 25 en suite; TV; tcf
🏠 lift, TV; P 200, coach; child facs; con 60
✕ LD 10.30
£ B&B £30–£46 (£22·50 w/e), B&B (double) £45–£57; HB weekly £325; L £5, D £8·75; WB £22·50
cc Access, Amex, B'card/Visa.

Fleece Inn (Acclaimed), Elland Rd, Bankisland, HX4 ODJ ☎(0422) 822598
£ B&B £30–£45

HALLAND East Sussex. Map 6C2
Pop 780. Uckfield 3½, London 47, Eastbourne 15, Hastings 25, Hurst Green 17, Lewes 7½.
Golf Piltdown, Uckfield 18h.

★★★ **Halland Forge,** Nr Lewes, BN8 6PW
☎(082 584) 456 Fax: (082 584) 773
Attractive timbered building set in lawns and flowerbeds, motel units attached. ✈ Fr, De.
🛏 20 bedrs, 20 en suite; TV; tcf
🏠 dogs; P 70, coach; children over 5; con 70
✕ LD 9.30
£ B&B £45·45– £55·45; B&B (double) £62·40; HB weekly £226·50; L £8·95, D £14·50; WB £73 (2 nts HB); [10% V w/d Nov–May]
cc Access, Amex, B'card/Visa, Diners.

HALSTEAD Essex. Map 27A2
Pop 9,385. Braintree 6½, London 50, Colchester 13, Haverhill 15, Sudbury 8.
EC Wed, **MD** Tues, Fri, **Golf** Braintree 18h. **See** St Andrews Church, Gosfield Hall.

★★ **Judges,** 53 High St, Earls Colne, CO6 2PB. ☎(0787) 222484 Fax: (0787) 224668
Red-brick, bay windowed coaching inn with a history dating back to the 13th century.
🛏 8 bedrs, 8 en suite; annexe 2 bedrs, 2 en suite; TV; tcf.
🏠 P 20, coach; child facs
✕ LD 10
£ B&B £38–£45, B&B (double) £56; L £14·95, D £14·95; [5% V]
cc Access, Amex, B'card/Visa.

HALTWHISTLE Northumberland. Map 44B3
Brompton 12, London 311, Carlisle 21, Hexham 17.
ℹ Sycamore St ☎(0434) 302351

Ashcroft, NE49 0DA ☎(0434) 320213.
Guest House. Closed 22 Dec–5 Jan.
£ B&B £13–£15; [10% V]

HAMPSON GREEN Lancashire. Map 36B3
M6 (jn 33) 1, Preston 17, London 230, Blackpool 20, Lancaster 5.
Golf Lancaster 18h.

♚ ★★ **Hampson House,** Galgate, LA2 0JB ☎(0524) 751158
Hotel built around Tudor farmhouse and set in mature gardens.

HAMPTON COURT Greater London. (Middx). Map 8B2
Kingston upon Thames 2, London 11, Epsom 7, Leatherhead 8½, Ripley 10, Staines 8, Uxbridge 13, Weybridge 6½.
EC Wed. **Golf** Home Park 18h, Fulwell 18h, Strawberry Hill 9h, Thames Ditton and Esher 9h, Surbiton 18h. **See** Palace, Maze and Gardens, Bushy Park.

★★★ **Lion Gate,** Hampton Court Rd, KT8 9BZ ☎081-977 8121 Tx: 928412
Attractive Georgian building with later annexe, near Hampton Court Palace. (Lns)

HANDFORTH Cheshire. Map 33B1
Pop 6,843. Congleton 14, London 175, Altrincham 9, Knutsford 9, Macclesfield 9, Manchester 10, Stockport 6.
EC Wed. **Golf** Wilmslow 18h. **See** Handforth Hall.

★★★★ **Belfry,** Stanley Rd, SK9 3LD
☎061-437 0511 Tx: 666358
Fax: 061-499 0597 ♿

Family-run luxury modern hotel; with small beamed building attached. ✈ Fr, It, Es, Po
🛏 82 bedrs, 82 en suite; TV; tcf
🏠 lift, dogs; P 150, coach; child facs; con 150
✕ LD 10. Resid & Rest lic
£ B&B £84–£101(£25 w/e), B&B (double) £105·50–£120; L £10·25.
cc Access, Amex, B'card/Visa, Diners.

HANLEY Staffordshire. Map 30B2
See also STOKE-ON-TRENT.
Stoke-on-Trent 2, London 154, M6 (jn 15) 4½, Congleton 11, Leek 10, Nantwich 16, Newcastle-under-Lyme 2, Sandbach 12.
See Museum and Art Gallery.

★★★ **Stakis Grand,** 66 Trinity St, ST1 5NB
☎(0782) 202361 Tx: 367264
Fax: (0782) 286464 ♿
Substantial Victorian hotel in centre. Indoor swimming pool, sauna, solarium, gymnasium. ✈ Fr, De, Es, Po, Yu, Ur. (Sk)
🛏 128 bedrs, 128 en suite; TV; tcf
🏠 lift, dogs, ns; P 150, coach; child facs; con 275

Halifax (Yorkshire)

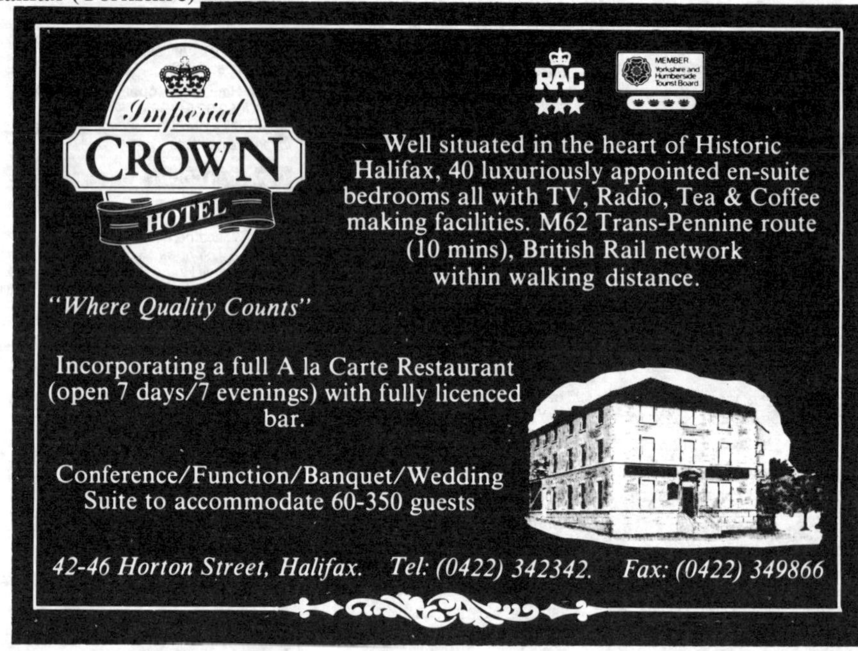

Harrogate (North Yorkshire)

HOB GREEN
Hotel & Restaurant

Most tastefully restored Country House Hotel set in award winning gardens and enjoying magnificent views of the rolling Yorkshire countryside. Peaceful yet only 10 minutes drive from Harrogate, Hob Green provides everything the most exacting guest could demand, resulting in the award of highest rated hotel in the Harrogate district by Egon Ronay, HCR award from the RAC.

The Hotel is an ideal venue for small private parties and business meetings up to 12.

During your stay in the district why not dine out in our Restaurant which, under manager Gary Locker, has earned a fine reputation locally.

Hob Green, Markington, Harrogate HG3 3PJ.
Tel: (0423) 770031 Telex: 557780

Harrogate (Yorkshire)

RAC Acclaimed

Ashley House *36–40 Franklin Road, Harrogate HG1 5EE. Tel: 0423 507474*

Alan & Carole Thompson welcome you to Ashley House. Three charming townhouses built in the elegant Victorian era and tastefully converted to a 17 bedroom hotel. With a reputation for personal and friendly service we offer: *most bedrooms en-suite *colour TV *tea/coffee facilities *direct dial telephone and radio clock alarms *quiet reading lounge *residents' lounge with colour TV *cosy 'Olde Worlde Bar'. A 4-course dinner is offered in our elegant and inviting dining room. B&B from £16. Bargain off season breaks available. Only 3 minutes Conference Centre – Town.

✕ LD 9.45, bar meals only Sat lunch
£ B&B £77·50–£87·50 (w/e £45), B&B (double) £89·50–£99·50; L £7·50, D £12·50; WB £41 (HB); [10% V]
cc Access, Amex, B'card/Visa, Diners.
(*See advertisement on p. 000*)

HARBERTONFORD Devon Map 3B2

Totnes 5, London 196, Dartmouth 10, Kingsbridge 10, Modbury 13.

★★★ Old Mill, Totnes, TQ7 7SU ☎ (080 423) 349.
Well-converted old mill buildings, furnished in cottagey style, in lawned gardens with pond and stream. Fishing.
7 bedrs, 7 en suite; TV; tcf.

HAREWOOD West Yorkshire. Map 40A3

Leeds 7, London 214, Harrogate 5½, Otley 17, Wetherby 3½.

★★ C Harewood Arms, Harrogate Rd, LS17 9LH ☎ (0532) 886566
Fax: (0532) 886064
Traditional stone-built inn with a sympathetic extension. Opposite entrance to Harewood House.
24 bedrs, 24 en suite; TV; tcf
dogs, P 100, coach; child facs; con 16
✕ LD 9.45
£ B&B £59–£62 (w/e £45), B&B (double) £75–£78; L £6·50, D £11·95
cc Access, Amex, B'card/Visa, Diners.

HARLOW Essex. Map 15C2

Pop 79,000. Epping 6, London 25, M11 (jn 7) 3, Bishop's Stortford 6½, Chelmsford 18, Dunmow 14, Hoddesdon 8.
EC Wed. **MD** Tue, Thur, Fri, Sat. **Golf** Canons Brook 18h.

★★★ Churchgate Manor, Churchgate St, CN17 0JT ☎ (0279) 420246 Tx: 818289
Fax: (0279) 437720

Enlarged Jacobean chantry house of great charm. Indoor swimming pool, sauna, solarium, gymnasium.
85 bedrs, 85 en suite; TV; tcf
dogs; P 110, coach; child facs; con 170
✕ LD 9.45, bar meals only Sat lunch
£ B&B £72–£85 (w/e £32), B&B (double) £79–£95. L £15, D £14·95; WB £39 (HB)
cc Access, Amex, B'card/Visa, Diners.

★★★ Green Man, Mulberry Green, CM17 0ET ☎ (0279) 442521 Tx: 817972
Fax: (0279) 626113

Much modernised old coaching inn with added residential wing. Fr, De, Es. (THF)
55 bedrs, 55 en suite; TV; tcf
dogs, ns; P 75, coach; child facs; con 60
✕ LD 9.30, nr Sat lunch
£ B&B £75–£86 (w/e £45), B&B (double) £94–£105; L £12·50, D £14·50
cc Access, Amex, B'card/Visa, CB, Diners.

★★★ Harlow Moat House, Southern Way, CM18 7BA ☎ (0279) 422441 Tx: 81658
Fax: (0279) 635094
Large modern hotel situated on A11 at edge of New Town. Convenient for M25. Fr, De. Closed 25 Dec–1 Jan (QMH)
120 bedrs, 120 en suite; TV; tcf
dogs, ns; P 180, coach; child facs; con 150
✕ LD 10, bar meals only Sat lunch
£ B&B £70–£75 (w/e £40–£45), B&B (double) £80–£85 (w/e £56–£60); L £13·50, D £13·50; WB £35–£38 (HB); [10% V]
cc Access, Amex, B'card/Visa, Diners.

HAROME North Yorkshire. Map 38C4

York 27, London 225, Helmsley 3, Malton 13, Scarborough 29, Thirsk 17.

★★★ C Pheasant, YO6 5JG ☎ Helmsley (0439) 71241
Interesting historic building with walled garden and courtyard. Open Mar–Dec.
11 bedrs, 11 en suite; annexe 4 bedrs, 4 en suite; TV; tcf
dogs, ns; P 20; children over 12
✕ LD 8.15, bar meals only lunch. Resid & Rest lic
£ B&B £18–£25, B&B (double) £36–£50; HB weekly £273–£350; D £16·50; WB £39 (Nov–May); dep.

HARPENDEN Hertfordshire. Map 14C2

Pop 27,896. St Albans 5, London 25, M1 (jn 9) 4½, Aylesbury 25, Baldock 17, Hatfield 8, High Wycombe 26, Luton 5½.
EC Wed. **Golf** Harpenden 18h, Harpenden Common 18h. **See** Church with 15th cent tower, Luton Hoo 3 m N.

★★★★ Harpenden Moat House, 18 Southdown Rd, AL5 1PE ☎ (0582) 764111
Tx: 826938 Fax: (0582) 769858

A 300-year-old, red-brick building overlooking Harpenden Common. Closed 25 Dec–1 Jan. (QMH)
17 bedrs, 17 en suite; annexe 36 bedrs, 36 en suite; TV; tcf
dogs, ns; P 120, coach; child facs; con 120
✕ LD 10, nr Sat lunch
£ B&B £78·50–£98·75 (w/e £39·50), B&B (double) £97·50–£110; L £12·50, D £16; WB £42
cc Access, Amex, B'card/Visa, Diners.

★★★ Glen Eagle, Luton Rd, AL5 2PX ☎ (0582) 760271. Fax: (0582) 460819
Attractive former country house with additional wings, at edge of town centre.
Fr, De, Es, It
50 bedrs, 50 en suite; TV; tcf
lift, dogs; P 100, coach; child facs; con 80
✕ LD 10
£ B&B £70–£86 (£22 w/e), B&B (double) £86–£96; L £14, D £16·25; [5% V]
cc Access, Amex, B'card/Visa, Diners.

HARROGATE North Yorkshire. Map 38B3

See also BURNT YATES & NIDD
Pop 65,000. Wetherby 10, London 204, Leeds 15, Ripon 10, Skipton 22, York 22.
See Plan p. 000.
EC Wed. **MD** Daily. **Golf** Harrogate 18h, Pannal 18h, Oakdale 18h. **See** Valley Gardens, The Stray, Harlow Car Gardens, Pump Room Museum, Moors and Dales.
i Royal Bath Assembly Rooms, Crescent Rd. ☎ (0423) 525666

★★★★ Crown, Crown Pl, HG1 2RZ ☎ (0423) 502284 Tx: 57652
Fax: (0423) 502284
Large traditional stone-built hotel in pleasant surroundings in town centre. Fr, De, It, Es, Du, Yu. (THF)
121 bedrs, 121 en suite; TV; tcf
lift, dogs, ns; P 80, coach; child facs; con 400
✕ LD 9.30
£ room £76, room (double) £92–£98; Bk fr £5·30, L £9, D £14·50; WB £47 (HB)
cc Access, Amex, B'card/Visa, CB, Diners.

★★★★ Majestic, Ripon Rd, HG1 2HU ☎ (0423) 568972 Tx: 57918
Fax: (0423) 502283
Elegant domed 6-storey Victorian hotel set amidst extensive gardens. Indoor swimming pool, tennis, squash, sauna, solarium, gymnasium, billiards. Fr. (THF)
156 bedrs, 156 en suite; TV; tcf
lift, dogs, ns; P 250, coach; child facs; con 450
✕ LD 9.30, bar meals only Sat lunch
£ room £81–£99, double room £114–£125; WB £57 (HB)
cc Access, Amex, B'card/Visa, CB, Diners.

★★★★ Moat House International, Kings Rd, HG1 1XX ☎ (0423) 500000 Tx: 57575
Fax: (0423) 524435

Large modern hotel linked to the Harrogate Conference Centre. (QMH)
214 bedrs, 214 en suite; TV; tcf
lift, dogs, ns, P 125, coach; child facs; con 400
✕ LD 10.30
£ B&B £90, B&B (double) £108; L fr £15, D fr £14·50; WB £42; [10% V]
cc Access, Amex, B'card/Visa, Diners, dep.

H

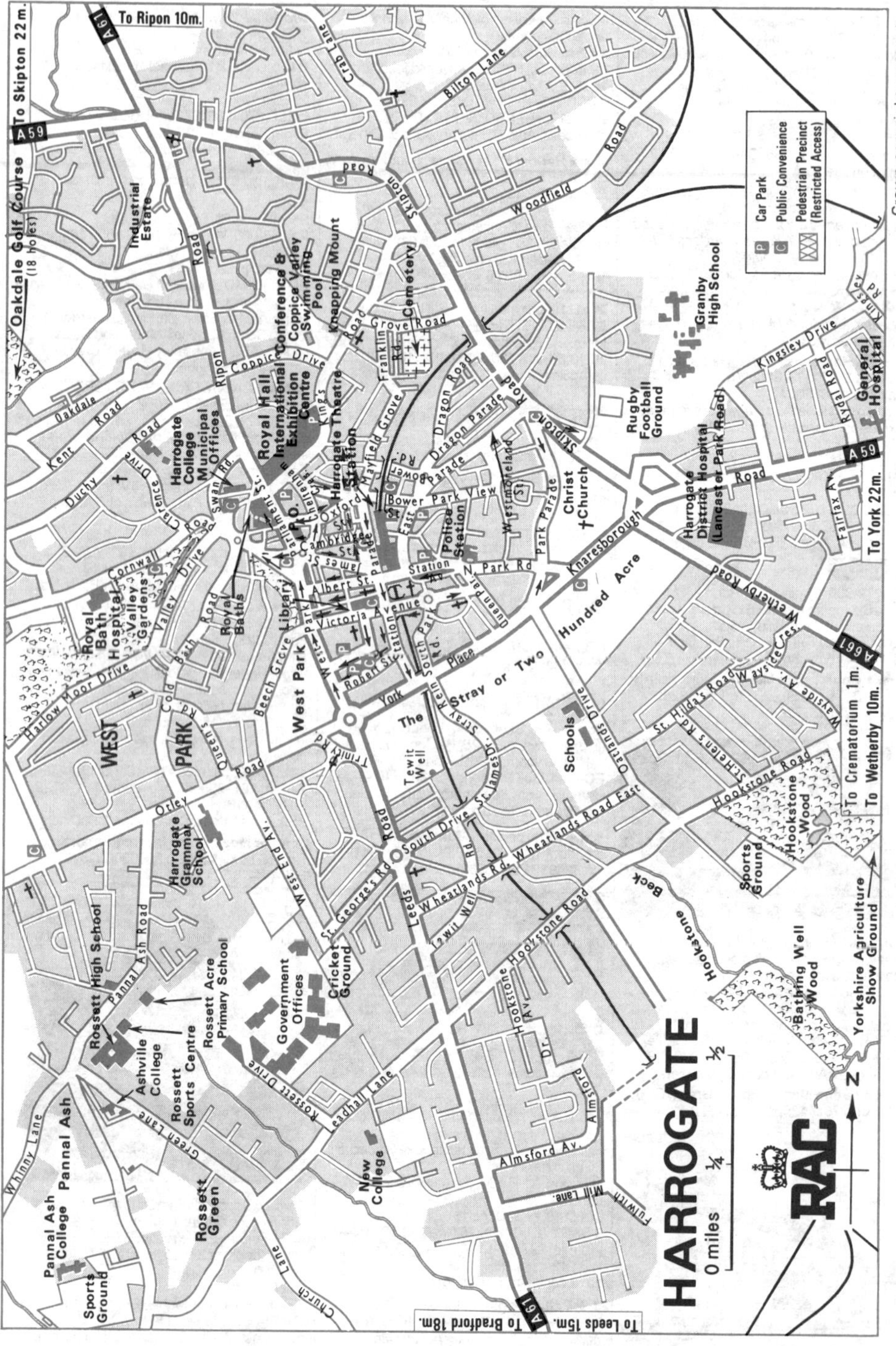

 EC *early closing* **MD** *market day* *country house hotel* *ns (NS) no smoking areas* *tcf tea/coffee facilities*

★★★★ **Old Swan,** Swan Rd, HG1 2SR
☎(0423) 500055 Tx: 57922
Fax: (0423) 501154 ♿

Elegant stone-built hotel, circa 1770, in 4 acre garden. Near conference centre. Putting, tennis.
🛏 137 bedrs, 137 en suite; TV; tcf
🏨 lift, dogs; P 200, coach; child facs; con 300

★★★ **Cairn,** Ripon Rd, HG1 2JD ☎(0423) 504005 Tx: 57992 Fax: (0423) 500056
Modernised late Victorian hotel close to conference centre.
🛏 134 bedrs, 134 en suite; TV; tcf
🏨 lift, dogs, ns; P 180, coach; child facs; con 450

★★★ **Fern,** Swan Rd, HG1 2SS ☎(0423) 523866 Tx: 57583 Fax: (0423) 501825
Stone-built hotel in elegant corner of town. Easy access to shops.
🛏 27 bedrs, 27 en suite, annexe 8 bedrs, 8 en suite; TV; tcf
🏨 coach; child facs, con 40

★★★ **H** **Grants,** 3/11 Swan Rd, HG1 2SS ☎(0423) 560666 Fax: (0423) 502550 ♿

Proprietor-run hotel in stone building of charm near town centre.
🛏 37 bedrs, 37 en suite; TV; tcf
🏨 lift, dogs; P 20, coach; child facs; con 20
✕ LD 9.30, bar meals only Mon–Sat lunch
£ B&B £37·50–£75, B&B (double) £42·50–£95; HB weekly £262·50–£430·15; L £10·50, D £13·95
cc Access, Amex, B'card/Visa, Diners.

♣ ★★★ **H** **C** **R** **Hob Green,** Markington, HG3 3PJ ☎(0423) 770031 Tx: 57780 Fax: (0423) 771589

Changes made after July 1990 are not included.

Former private residence, now converted to a pleasing country-house hotel.
🛏 12 bedrs, 12 en suite; TV; tcf
🏨 dogs; P 65; child facs; con 10
✕ LD 9.30, nr lunch Mon–Sat. Resid lic
£ B&B £59–£65, B&B (double) £78–£85; L £10·95, D £16·50; WB (£110)
cc Access, Amex, B'card/Visa, Diners.
(*See advertisement on p. 272*)

★★★ **Hospitality Inn,** West Park, HG1 1LB ☎(0423) 564601 Tx: 57530
Fax: (0432) 507508

Splendid Victorian stone buildings overlooking West Stray and gardens. (MtCh)
🛏 71 bedrs, 71 en suite; TV; tcf
🏨 lift, dogs; P 40, coach; child facs; con 200
✕ LD 9.30, bar meals only Mon–Sat lunch
£ B&B £72–£84, B&B (double) £ 89·50–£101; L £3, D £13·75; WB £35
cc Access, Amex, B'card/Visa, Diners.

★★★ **Hotel St George,** Ripon Rd, HG1 2SY ☎(0423) 561431 Tx: 57995
Fax: (0423) 530037

Fine 19th century building with spacious public rooms. Indoor swimming pool, sauna, solarium, gymnasium. (Sw)
🛏 93 bedrs, 93 en suite; TV; tcf
🏨 lift, dogs; P 60, coach; child facs; con 150
✕ LD 9.30
£ B&B £72–£97, B&B (double) £95–£104; L £11·25, D £16·50; WB £92 (HB 2 nts)
cc Access, Amex, B'card/Visa, Diners.

★★★ **Russell,** Valley Dr, HG2 0JN ☎(0423) 509866. Fax: (0423) 506185
Imposing hotel overlooking Valley Gardens. Distinctive turreted Victorian building.
Closed 29–31 Dec.
🛏 35 bedrs, 35 en suite; TV; tcf
🏨 lift, ns; coach; child facs; con 16
✕ LD 10, bar meals only lunch
£ B&B £47·50, B&B (double) £58–£73; D £14·95; WB £84 (HB 2 nts); [10% V Jan–Jun]
cc Access, Amex, B'card/Visa, Diners.

Please tell the manager if you chose your hotel through an advertisement in the guide.

★★ **Ascot House,** 53 King's Rd, HG1 5HJ
☎(0423) 531005 Fax: (0432) 503523

Attractive Victorian house, recently refurbished, near conference centres. ✂ Fr, De
🛏 24 bedrs, 13 en suite, (11 sh), 1 ba; TV; tcf
🏨 dogs; P 14, coach; child facs; con 80
✕ LD 9, bar meals only lunch.
£ B&B £35–£49·50, B&B (double) £47·50–£76·50; HB weekly £196·50– £229·25; D £11·50; WB £32·75 (HB); [5% V]
cc Access, Amex, B'card/Visa, Diners.

★★ **Caesars,** 51 Valley Dr, HG2 0JH
☎(0423) 565818

Stone Victorian building with spacious ground floor rooms. Terraced garden.
🛏 10 bedrs, 10 en suite; TV; tcf
🏨 TV; ns; child facs
✕ LD 8.30, nr lunch. Resid & Rest lic
£ B&B £42·50, B&B (double) £60; HB weekly £280; D £14·50; WB £40 (min 2 nts)
cc Access, B'card/Visa; dep.

★★ **H** **Gables,** 2 West Grove Rd, HG1 2AD ☎(0423) 505625

Turreted, stone-built hotel; easy access to conference centre and exhibition halls.
✂ De
🛏 9 bedrs, 8 en suite, (1 sh); TV; tcf
🏨 dogs, P 9, coach; child facs; con 30
✕ LD 8.30, nr lunch
£ B&B £22–£25; HB weekly £210–£215; D £10; WB £62 (HB, 2 nts); [5% V]
cc Access, B'card/Visa.

H

★★ **Green Park,** Valley Dr, HG2 0JT
☎(0423) 504681. Fax: (0423) 530811

Late Victorian stone building with fine views over public gardens.
🛏 43 bedrs, 43 en suite; TV; tcf
🏨 lift, dogs, ns; P 8, coach; child facs; con 40

★★ **White House,** 10 Park Par, HG1 5AH
☎(0423) 501388
A "mock Venetian" villa, built in 1836, overlooking the famous Stray.
🛏 13 bedrs, 13 en suite; TV; tcf
🏨 TV, dogs; P 10; child facs; con 40

★ **Alvera Court,** 76 Kings Rd, HG1 5JX
☎(0423) 505735
Fine stone building on corner site, adjacent to conference centre.
🛏 12 bedrs, 12 en suite; TV; tcf
🏨 P 4; child facs; con 21
✕ LD 7.30, nr lunch
£ B&B £26–£30, HB weekly £217–£280; D £11
cc Access, B'card/Visa, dep.

★ **Croft,** 42–46 Franklin Rd, HG1 5EE
☎(0423) 563326
A Victorian sandstone terraced building conveniently situated close to the conference centre and exhibition hall. ⚒ Fr, De.
🛏 14 bedrs, 12 en suite; 1 ba; TV; tcf
🏨 dogs; P 10, coach; child facs
✕ LD 9.30, nr lunch. Rest lic
£ B&B £25–£30, B&B (double) £40–£48; HB weekly £196–£224; D £8; WB £19; [10% V]
cc Access, B'card/Visa.

Glenayr (Highly Acclaimed), 19 Franklin Mount, HG1 5EJ ☎(0423) 504259 *Hotel.*
£ B&B £17·50–£19·50; HB weekly £175–£210; [5% V Nov–Mar]
Shannon Court (Highly Acclaimed), 65 Dragon Av, HG1 5DS ☎(0423) 509858. *Hotel.* Closed 21 Dec–1 Jan.
£ B&B £18–£22·50; HB weekly £175–£200; [5% V]

Abbey Lodge (Acclaimed), 31 Ripon Rd, HG1 2JL ☎(0423) 569712. *Hotel.*
£ B&B £19; [5% V, Oct–Apr]
Arden House (Acclaimed), 69/71 Franklin Rd, HG1 5EH ☎(0423) 509224. *Hotel.*
Ashley House (Acclaimed), 36–40 Franklin Rd, HG1 5EE ☎(0423) 507474. *Hotel.*
£ B&B £18·75–£25
(*See advertisement on p. 272*)
Aston (Acclaimed), 7–9 Franklin Mount, HG1 5EJ ☎(0423) 564262. *Hotel.* ⚒ De, Pl
£ B&B £22–£24
cc Access, B'card/Visa; dep.
Delaine (Acclaimed), 17 Ripon Rd, HG1 2JL ☎(0423) 567974. *Private Hotel.*
£ B&B £18–£25; [10% V Nov–Feb]
Grafton (Acclaimed), 1–3 Franklin Mount, HG1 5EJ ☎(0423) 508491. *Private Hotel.*
⚒ De
£ B&B £20·50–£23·50
Rosedale (Acclaimed), 86 Kings Rd, HG1 5JX ☎(0423) 566630. *Private Hotel.*
£ B&B £25; HB weekly £197·75
Scotia House (Acclaimed), 66 Kings Rd, HG1 5JR ☎(0423) 504361. *Hotel.*
£ B&B £25–£28, HB weekly £195–£216; [5% V w/e, & Nov–Mar]
Wharfedale House (Acclaimed), 28 Harlow Moor Drive, HG2 0JY ☎(0423) 522233. *Private Hotel.*
£ B&B £24; HB weekly £207–£378; [10% V]

Alexa House, 26 Ripon Rd, HG2 2JJ ☎(0423) 501988. *Hotel.* Closed 21 Dec–5 Jan
£ B&B £21
Cavendish, 3 Valley Dr, HG2 0JJ ☎(0423) 509637. Fax: (0423) 504429. *Hotel.*
£ B&B £22–£28
Craigleigh, 6 West Grove Rd, HG1 2AD ☎(0423) 64064. *Guest House*
£ B&B £25–£30; HB weekly £196–£224; [10% V]
Cumbria, 4 Studley Rd, HG1 5JU ☎(0423) 508356. *Guest House.*
Gillmore, 98 Kings Rd, HG1 5HH ☎(0423) 503699. *Guest House.* ⚒ It
£ B&B £18–£22·50; HB weekly £160–£175; [5% V]
Hadleigh, 33 Ripon Rd, HG1 2JL ☎(0423) 522994. *Hotel.* ⚒ Fr.
£ B&B £22–£25; [5% V]
Lamont House, 12 St Mary's Walk, HG2 0LW ☎(0423) 567143. *Guest Housel.* Closed Xmas.
£ B&B £16–£18; [5% V]
Mrs Murray's, 67 Franklin Rd, HG1 5EH ☎(0423) 505857. *Guest House.*
Princes, 7 Granby Rd, HG1 4ST ☎(0423) 883469. *Hotel.*
Roan, 90 Kings Rd, HG1 5JX ☎(0423) 503087. *Guest House.*
£ B&B £15; [5% V]
Young's, 15 York Rd, off Duchy Rd, HG1 2QL ☎(0423) 567336. *Hotel.*
£ B&B £28–£46; HB weekly £200

HARROW Greater London (Middx). Map 13C4

Pop 208,963. London 10, Barnet 9½, Denham 8½, Ealing 5½, Hatfield 16, Rickmansworth 7½, St Albans 13, Uxbridge 8, Watford 7.
EC Wed. **MD** Thur. **See** Harrow School, St Mary's Church, 16th cent King's Head.

★★ **Cumberland,** St Johns Rd, HA1 2EF
☎ 081-863 4111 Tx: 917201
Fax: 081-861 5668

Three-storey hotel with easy access to M1, M4. Near Underground station. ⚒ Fr, De, It
🛏 30 bedrs, 30 en suite; annexe 51 bedrs, 51 en suite; TV; tcf
🏨 ns; P 55, coach; child facs
✕ LD 9.30 (10 Sat)
£ B&B £62 (w/e £22·50), B&B (double) £73; L £6·50, D £10·95
cc Access, Amex, B'card/Visa, Diners.

★★ **Harrow,** 12–22 Pinner Rd, HA1 4HZ
☎081-427 3435 Tx: 917898
Fax: 081-861 1370
Converted from several terrace houses, a refurbished hotel conveniently close to the Underground station. ⚒ Fr, De, Es
🛏 65 bedrs, 63 en suite, (1 sh), 1 ba; annexe 35 bedrs, 35 en suite; TV; tcf
🏨 TV, ns; P 50, coach; child facs; con 150
✕ LD 9.45, Resid lic
£ B&B £55–£75 (w/e £26), B&B (double) £70–£90; D £16·95
cc Access, Amex, B'card/Visa, Diners.
(*See advertisement on p. 280*)

★★ **Monksdene,** 2–12 Northwick Park Rd, HA1 2NT ☎081-427 2899 Tx: 919171
Fax: 081-863 2314
Several houses have been joined together to form this conveniently placed hotel on a corner site in a residential area. ⚒ It, Gu, Ur
🛏 70 bedrs, 70 en suite; annexe 20 bedrs, 20 en suite; TV; tcf
🏨 TV; P 65, coach; child facs; con 100
✕ bar meals only Sun lunch. Resid lic
£ B&B £58 (w/e £38), B&B (double) £75 (w/e £48); D £14·95; [10% V]
cc Access, Amex, B'card/Visa, Diners.
Lindal (Highly Acclaimed), 2 Hindes Rd, HA1 1SJ ☎081-863 3164. *Hotel.*
£ B&B £33–£43

Cresent Lodge (Acclaimed), 58 Welldon Cresc, HA1 1QR ☎081-863 5491
Fax: 081-427 5965. *Private Hotel.*
£ B&B £26–£42; HB weekly £280–£476; [5% V]

Central, 6 Hindes Rd, HA1 1SJ ☎081-427 0893. *Private Hotel.*
Hindes, 8 Hindes Rd, HA1 1SJ ☎081-427 7468. *Hotel.* ⚒ Fr, De
£ B&B £28

HARTINGTON Derbyshire. Map 30C3

Pop 343. Ashbourne 12, London 151, Buxton 12, Chesterfield 20, Leek 12, Matlock 13.
Golf Buxton 18h. **See** Dovedale and Beresford Dale (explorable on foot).

★ **Minton House,** Market Pl, SK17 0AL
☎(029 884) 368
Family-run hotel in 3-storey stone building in village centre. Fishing.

HARTLAND Devon. Map 3A4

Pop 1,420. Bideford 14, London 216, Bude 15, Holsworthy 16, Launceston 29.
EC Tue. **Golf** Westward Ho! 18h.

★ **Hartland Quay,** EX39 6DU ☎(02374) 41218
Stone-built hotel on lower slopes of cliff; views of rugged coastline. Swimming pool. Open Easter–end Oct.
🛏 16 bedrs, 8 en suite, 3 ba; tcf
🏨 TV, dogs; P 100, coach; child facs
✕ LD 8, bar meals only lunch
£ B&B £15–£16·50; HB weekly £130–£150; D fr £7
cc Access, B'card/Visa.

HARTLEPOOL Cleveland. Map 45B2

See also PETERLEE.
Pop 95,000. Stockton-on-Tees 9½, London 253, Durham 17, Middlesbrough 8, Newcastle-upon-Tyne 29, Sunderland 18.
EC Wed. **MD** Thur. **Golf** Hartlepool 18h, Seaton Carew 18h. **See** St Hilda's Church, Fish Quay and Market, H.M.S. Warrior.

EC *early closing* **MD** *market day* 🏠 *country house hotel* *ns (NS) no smoking areas* *tcf tea/coffee facilities*

ℹ Civic Centre, Victoria Rd. ☎(0429) 266522, H.M.S. Warrior, Coal Dock ☎(0429) 266522

★★★ **Grand,** Swainson St, TS24 8AA ☎(0429) 266345 Fax: (0429) 265217 ♿
Large red sandstone Victorian hotel, in town centre; overlooking the sea. Fr. Closed 24–26 Dec, 31 Dec–1 Jan.
48 bedrs, 40 en suite; TV; tcf
lift; TV; dogs, ns; P 6, coach; child facs; con 150
LD 10, bar meals only Sat lunch
£ B&B £39·50–£51·50, (w/e £22·50) B&B (double) £51·50–£72·50; L £5·25, D £7·45; [10% V]
cc Access, Amex, B'card/Visa, Diners; dep.

HARWELL Oxfordshire. Map 21A1

Wallingford 9, London 55, M4 (jn 13) 10, Newbury 22, Oxford 12, Wantage 5.

★★★ **Kingswell,** Reading Rd, OX11 0LZ ☎(0235) 833043 Tx: 83173 Fax: (0235) 833193 ♿

16th-century farmhouse tastefully extended to provide accommodation. On eastern outskirts of village, near A34.
19 bedrs, 19 en suite; TV; tcf
coach; no children under 10; con 20
LD 9.30
£ B&B £60, B&B (double) £80
cc Access, Amex, B'card/Visa, Diners; dep.

HARWICH Essex. Map 27B2

RAC Port Office, Parkeston Quay, CO12 4SH. ☎(0255) 503567.
Pop 15,000. Colchester 18, London 74, Bury St Edmunds 41, Clacton 16, Ipswich 22.
EC Wed. **MD** Fri. **Golf** Dovercourt 18h. **See** Guildhall, Redoubt (Napoleonic Fort).
ℹ Parkeston Quay ☎(0255) 506139

★★ **Cliff,** Marine Par, Dovercourt, CO12 3RE ☎(0255) 503345 Tx: 987372 Fax: (0255) 242111
Attractive white-faced Victorian hotel in sea-front position overlooking bay.
27 bedrs, 26 en suite, (1 sh); 2 ba; TV; tcf
dogs; P 70, coach; child facs; con 150
LD 9
£ B&B £40; B&B (double) £50; L £8, D £9; WB £75
cc Access, Amex, B'card/Visa, Diners.

★★ R **Pier at Harwich,** The Quay, CO12 3HH ☎(0255) 241212 Tx: 987083 Fax: (0206) 322752
Right on the waterfront, a turn-of-the-century building with stunning views of the Stour and Orwell estuaries.
6 bedrs, 6 en suite; TV; tcf
P 10.

★★ **Tower,** Main Rd, Dovercourt, CO12 3PJ ☎(0255) 504952 Fax: (0255) 504952
Hotel featuring Grade I listed Italian ceilings and friezes. Close to shops.
15 bedrs, 15 en suite; TV; tcf
dogs; P 60, coach; child facs; con 60
LD 10
£ B&B £38–£45, B&B (double) £49–£55; L £8·50; [10% V]
cc Access, Amex, B'card/Visa, Diners.

HASLEMERE Surrey. Map 6A2

Pop 14,022 (inc Hindhead). Guildford 12, London 41, Dorking 23, Hindhead 3½, Horsham 20, Midhurst 8, Petersfield 12.
EC Wed. **Golf** Hindhead 18h. **See** Educational Museum, Dolmetsch Workshops (early musical instruments).

★★★ **Georgian,** High St, GU27 2JY ☎(0428) 51555

Red-brick Georgian house, in High Street. Pleasant portico at rear. Squash, sauna.

★★★ C R **Lythe Hill,** Petworth Rd, GU27 3QB ☎(0428) 651251 Tx: 858402 Fax: (0428) 644131

Lovely extended Elizabethan timbered building set in 14 acres including Italian garden. Tennis, putting, fishing. Fr, De, It
29 bedrs, 29 en suite; annexe 11 bedrs, 11 en suite; TV
dogs; P 200, coach; child facs; con 100
LD 9.15
£ B&B £81–£135, B&B (double) £99–£164; L £16, D £16; WB £99 (2 nts)
cc Access, Amex, B'card/Visa; dep.

HASSOP Derbyshire. Map 30C3

Pop 104. Chesterfield 10, London 159, Ashbourne 20, Buxton 12, Chapel-en-le-Frith 15, Matlock 11, Sheffield 14.
Golf Bakewell 18h. **See** Church.

★★★ H C R **Hassop Hall,** Nr. Bakewell, DE4 1NS ☎ Gt Longstone (062 987) 488 Tx: 378485 Fax: (062 987) 577

Stately country house, largely 17th century, in magnificent parkland setting. Tennis. Closed Xmas. Fr
12 bedrs, 12 en suite; TV
lift, dogs, ns; P 60, coach; child facs; con 30
LD 9.30, nr Mon lunch & Sun dinner. Resid & Rest lic
£ B&B £66–£86, B&B (double) £82–£102; L £11·50, D £19·95
cc Access, Amex, B'card/Visa, CB, Diners; dep.

HASTINGS AND ST LEONARDS East Sussex. Map 7A1

Pop 73,622. Hurst Green 13, London 63, Eastbourne 20, Hawkhurst 15, Lewes 29, Rye 11, Tenterden 20, Uckfield 26.
See Plan p. 278.
EC Wed. **MD** Wed, Sat. **P** See Plan. **Golf** Hastings Municipal 18h. **See** Ruins of Castle, Museum and Art Gallery, Hastings Historical Embroidery, Fishermen's Museum.
ℹ 4 Robertson Ter. ☎(0424) 718888

★★★★ H C R **Royal Victoria,** Marina, St Leonards-on-Sea, TN38 0BD ☎(0424) 445544 Tx: 95529 Fax: (0424) 721995

A splendid hotel in the grand style built in 1829, and refurbished in 1988, on the seafront. Fr
52 bedrs, 52 en suite; TV
lift, dogs; P 10; coach; child facs; con 100
LD 10
£ B&B £69–£98; B&B (double) £98–£126; HB weekly £320; L £14·50, D £17; WB £102·50 (2 nts HB); [10% V w/e]
cc Access, Amex, B'card/Visa, Diners; dep.

★★★ **Beauport Park,** Beauport Park (On A2100 3 m S. Battle), TN38 8EA ☎(0424) 851222 Tx: 957126 Fax: (0424) 852465

Attractive converted Georgian manor house, in gardens and parkland. Swimming pool, golf, putting, tennis, riding.
23 bedrs, 23 en suite; TV; tcf
dogs; P 60, U 4 (£1·20), G 4 (£1·20); child facs; con 120
LD 9.30
£ B&B £50–£55, B&B (double) £68–£75; HB weekly £219–£270, L £14, D £16; WB £80
cc Access, Amex, B'card/Visa, Diners.

H

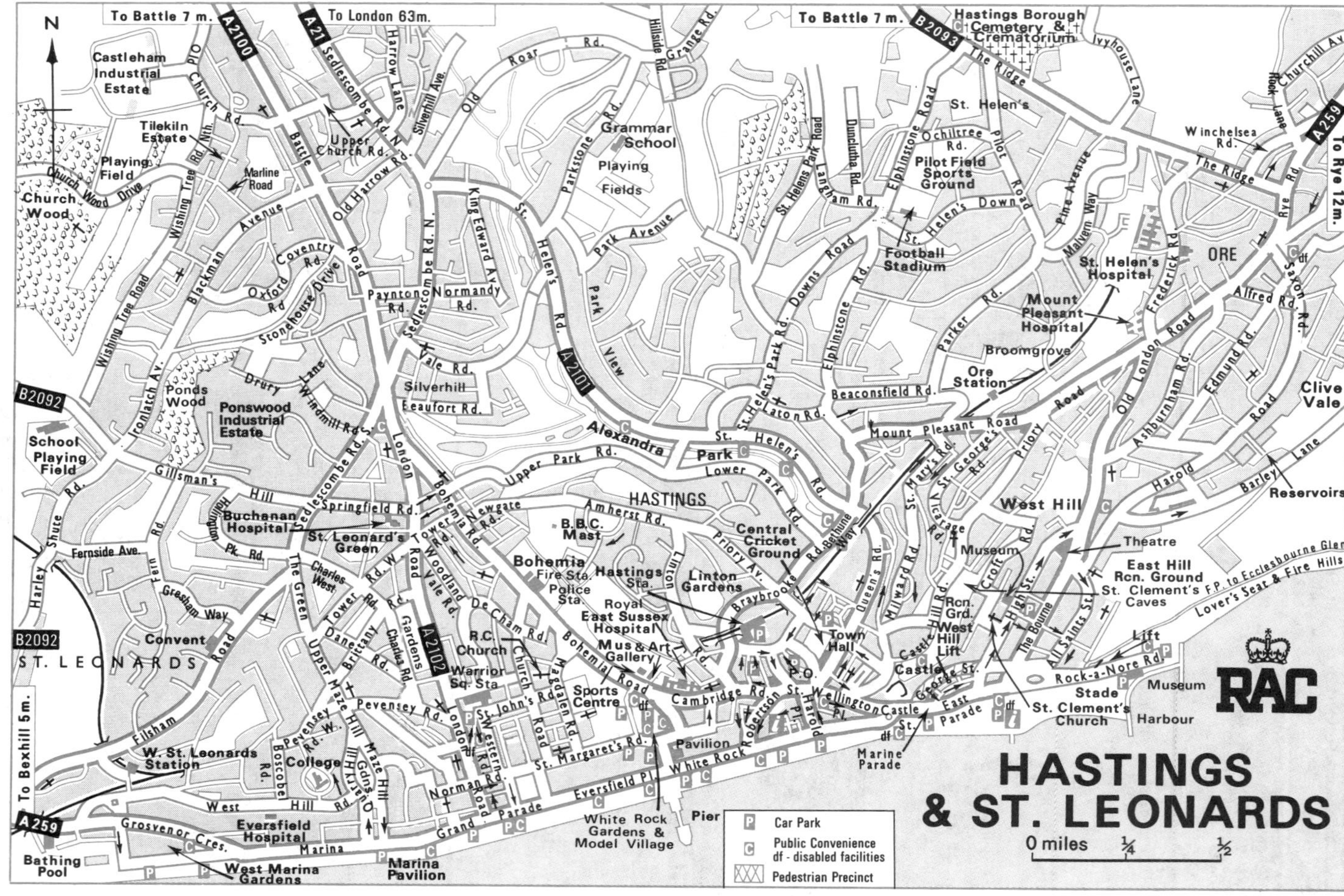

HASTINGS & ST. LEONARDS
RAC
0 miles 1/4 1/2
Car Park
Public Convenience
df - disabled facilities
Pedestrian Precinct
Crown copyright reserved
To Battle 7 m.
To London 63m.
To Battle 7 m.
To Rye 12m.
To Bexhill 5m.
A2100
A21
B2093
A259
A2101
A2102
B2092
Hastings Borough Cemetery & Crematorium
Castleham Industrial Estate
Tilekiln Estate
Playing Field
Church Wood
Grammar School
Playing Fields
St. Helen's
Pilot Field Sports Ground
Football Stadium
ORE
St. Helen's Hospital
Mount Pleasant Hospital
Broomgrove
Ore Station
Clive Vale
Reservoirs
West Hill
Ponds Wood
Ponswood Industrial Estate
School Playing Field
Alexandra Park
HASTINGS
B.B.C. Mast
Central Cricket Ground
Bohemia
Fire Sta.
Police Sta.
Hastings Sta.
Linton Gardens
Royal East Sussex Hospital
Mus & Art Gallery
Town Hall
P.O.
Museum
Theatre
East Hill Rcn. Ground
St. Clement's Caves
Rcn. Grd.
West Hill Lift
Castle
Lift
Stade
St. Clement's Church
Harbour
Marine Parade
Buchanan Hospital
St. Leonard's Green
R.C. Church
Warrior Sq. Sta
Sports Centre
Pavilion
Convent
ST. LEONARDS
W. St. Leonards Station
College
Eversfield Hospital
White Rock Gardens & Model Village
Pier
Bathing Pool
West Marina Gardens
Marina Pavilion

★★★ **Cinque Ports,** Summerfields, ☎(0424) 439222 Tx: 957584 Fax: (0424) 437277 ♿

A Spanish-style, purpose-built new hotel in a woodland setting.
🛏 40 bedrs, 40 en suite; TV
🏨 P 80, coach; no children under 8; con 300
✕ LD 10
£ B&B £58–£68, B&B (double) £84–£96; WB £90 (2 nts)
cc Access, Amex, B'card/Visa, Diners.

Eagle House (Highly Acclaimed), 12 Pevensey Rd, St Leonards, TN38 0JZ ☎(0424) 430535. *Hotel.*
£ B&B £27–£31, HB weekly £237·65–£262·15; [10% V]
(See advertisement on p. 000)

Norton Villa (Acclaimed), Hill St, Old Town, TN3Y 3H21 ☎(0424) 428168. *Guest House.*
£ B&B fr £16; HB weekly fr £224; [5% V w/d]

Argyle, 32 Cambridge Gdns, TN34 1EN ☎(0424) 421294. *Guest House.*
£ B&B £13 (£11 w/e)
Beechwood, 59 Baldslow Rd, TN34 2EY ☎(0424) 420078. *Private Hotel.* ⚒ De.
£ B&B £12–£23, HB weekly £120–£180; [5% V, Sep–May].
French's, 24 Robertson St. ☎(0424) 421195 Tx: 957141. *Inn.*
£ B&B £40–£45
Gainsborough, 5 Carlisle Par, TN34 1JG ☎(0424) 434010. *Hotel.* Closed Xmas.
£ B&B £13–£19; HB weekly £136·50–£178·50; [5% V].
Waldorf, Seafront, 4 Carlisle Par. TN34 1JG ☎(0424) 422185. *Hotel.*
£ B&B £18–£22; HB weekly £132–£157

HATFIELD

Hertfordshire, Map 15A2

Pop 29,000. Barnet 9, London 20, A1 (M) 2, Baldock 17, Enfield 12, Hoddesdon 11, Luton 13, St Albans 6.
EC Thur. **MD** Wed, Sat. **Golf** Panshanger 18h. **See** Church, Hatfield House.

★★★ **Comet,** 301 St Albans Rd West, AL10 9RH (jn A1/A414) ☎(0707) 265411 Fax: (0707) 264019

Red-brick hotel situated on A1 on the edge of town. ⚒ Fr, It. (Emb)
🛏 57 bedrs, 57 en suite; TV; tcf
🏨 dogs, ns; P 150, coach; child facs; con 40
✕ LD 9.55
£ B&B £36–£69·50 (w/e £29), B&B (double) £84–£94; HB weekly £463; L £10·95, D £10·95; WB £31·50 (HB)
cc Access, Amex, B'card/Visa, Diners.

★★★ **Hazel Grove,** Roehydo Way, AL10 9AF ☎(0707) 262338 Tx: 916580 Fax: (0707) 266033. ♿
Purpose-built modern hotel just off the A1M. Well-appointed and spacious bedrooms. Gymnasium. ⚒ Fr, De, Es
🛏 76 bedrs, 76 en suite; TV; tcf
🏨 dogs, ns; P 140, coach; child facs; con 120
✕ LD 9.30
£ B&B £70–£90 (w/e £30–£50), B&B (double) £80–£90; L £11 (Sun), D £17, WB fr £55 (HB 2 nts)
cc Access, Amex, B'card/Visa, Diners.

HATFIELD HEATH

Essex. Map 15C2

Harlow 5, London 30, M11 (jn 8) 8, Bishop's Stortford 5, Chelmsford 15½.

♛ ★★★★ **H C Down Hall,** CM22 7AS ☎(0279) 731441 Tx: 81609 Fax: (0279) 730416 ♿

An elegantly furnished Victorian Italianate mansion set in 20 acres of parkland and gardens. Golf course planned for 1991. Indoor swimming pool, putting, tennis, sauna, billiards. ⚒ Fr, De, It
🛏 103 bedrs, 103 en suite; TV; tcf
🏨 lift; dogs; P 200, coach; child facs; con 320
✕ LD 9.45
£ B&B £76·50–£97, B&B (double) £100–£143; L £14·50, D £16; WB £39 (HB); [5% V w/e]
cc Access, Amex, B'card/Visa, Diners.

HATHERLEIGH

Devon. Map 3A3

Pop 974. Crediton 20, London 197, Bideford 19, Holsworthy 13, Okehampton 7.
EC Wed. **MD** Mon, Tue. **Golf** Okehampton 18h. **See** Church (1184).

★★ **George,** Market St, EX20 3JN ☎Okehampton (0837) 810454
15th century coaching inn with 'olde worlde' atmosphere. Panelled restaurant. Swimming pool.

HATHERN

Leicestershire. Map 25A3

M1 (jn 23) 3, London 109, Loughborough 2, Melton Mowbray 17, Nottingham 13.

Leys, Loughborough Rd, LE12 5JB ☎(0509) 844373. *Guest House.*
£ B&B £13

HATHERSAGE

Derbyshire. Map 41C3

Pop 1,426. Matlock 19, London 163, Chesterfield 15, Glossop 18, Sheffield 11.
Golf Chapel-en-le-Frith 18h. **See** Iron Age Fort, Norman Castle (earthworks), 14th cent Church, assns with Robin Hood.

★★★ **George,** Main St, S30 1BB ☎Hope Valley (0433) 50436 Tx: 547196 Fax: (0433) 50099

Modernised 16th century coaching inn with Brontë connections. ⚒ It. (Lns)
🛏 18 bedrs, 18 en suite; TV; tcf
🏨 ns; P 40, coach; child facs; con 30
✕ LD 10
£ B&B £64, B&B (double) £78; L £8·25, D £14·25; WB £48 (HB); [10% V]
cc Access, Amex, B'card/Visa; Diners.

★★ **Hathersage Inn,** Main Rd, S30 1BB ☎Hope Valley (0433) 50259 Tx: 34619 Fax: (0433) 51199

Hotel of character built in local stone by the village squire. Welcoming log fires.
🛏 11 bedrs, 11 en suite; annexe 4 bedrs, 4 en suite; TV; tcf
🏨 dogs, ns; P 20, coach; child facs; con 12
✕ LD 9.30, bar meals only Mon–Sat lunch
£ B&B £45–£50; B&B (double) £60–£70; L £7·95, D £12·50; WB £41
cc Access, Amex, B'card/Visa, Diners; dep.

HATT

Cornwall. Map 3A2

Saltash 3, London 215, Callington 6, Liskeard 11, Looe 13.

Holland Toby Inn, nr Saltash, PL12 6PJ ☎Saltash (0752) 844044
£ B&B £28·50

HAVANT

Hampshire. Map 6A1

Pop 115,900. A3(M) 1, London 64, Chichester 8½, Portsmouth 6½, Petersfield 12.
EC Wed. **MD** Tue, Sat. **Golf** Crookham 18h.
ℹ 1 Park Rd South. ☎(0705) 480024

★★★ **Bear,** East St, PO9 1AA ☎(0705) 486501 Tx: 869136 Fax: (0705) 470551
An ancient coaching inn, extended through the years, and recently refurbished. In town centre.

Harrow (Middlesex)

Hawkhurst (Kent)

Hawkshead (Cumbria)

🛏 42 beds, 42 en suite; TV; tcf
🏠 ns; P 90; con 100
✕ LD 10
£ B&B £72, B&B (double) £85; L £11, D £11; WB £36; [10% V]
cc Access, Amex, B'card/Visa, Diners.

HAVERTHWAITE Cumbria. Map 36A4
Newby Bridge 6, London 268, Broughton in Furness 10, Ulverston 5.

Dicksons Arms, nr Ulverston, LA12 8AA ☎ Greenodd (022 9861) 384
Two-storey, white-painted Lakeland inn on the A590.
🛏 10 bedrs, 7 en suite, 1 ba, annexe 6 bedrs, 3 ba; TV; tcf
🏠 dogs; P 35, coach
✕ LD 10, bar meals only lunch & Sun dinner
£ B&B £20–£28, B&B (double) £30–£39
cc Access, Amex, B'card/Visa.

HAWES North Yorkshire. Map 36C4
Pop 1,300. Leyburn 16, London 250, Brough 21, Kendal 26, Kirkby Lonsdale 23, Settle 22, Skipton 36.
EC Wed. **MD** Tue. **Golf** Catterick 18h.
ℹ National Park Centre, Station Yard.
☎ (0969) 667450

★★ **Simonstone Hall,** DL8 3LY ☎ (0969) 667255

On hillside with panoramic views, attractive Georgian manor. Fr
🛏 10 bedrs, 10 en suite; TV; tcf
🏠 dogs; P 24; child facs
✕ LD 8.30, bar meals only Mon–Sat lunch
£ B&B (double) £90–£115; HB weekly £385–£490; L fr £9·75, D fr £18·50; WB £46; [10% V w/d Nov–May]
cc Access, B'card/Visa, dep.

HAWKCHURCH Devon. Map 4B2
Pop 418. Crewkerne 9, London 143, Axminster 6, Ilminster 11, Lyme Regis 7, Taunton 18.
Golf Axe Cliff 18h.

★★★ H C R **Fairwater Head,** EX13 5TX ☎ (029 77) 349
Attractive flint and stone residence with views across the Axe valley. Open late Feb–1 Dec
🛏 14 bedrs, 14 en suite; annexe 6 bedrs, 6 en suite; TV; tcf
🏠 dogs, ns, P 30
✕ LD 8.30, bar meals only Mon–Sat lunch
£ B&B £48–£52, B&B (double) £80–£84; HB weekly £320–£335; L £8·75
cc Access, Amex, B'card/Visa, Diners; dep.

HAWKHURST Kent. Map 7A2
Pop 3,908. Tonbridge 16, London 50, Hastings 15, Hurst Green 3, Maidstone 17, Rye 13, Tenterden 10, Tunbridge Wells 15.
EC Wed. **Golf** Hawkhurst 9h. **See** Church, Bodiam Castle 3 m S.

★★ **Tudor Court,** Rye Rd, TN18 5DA
☎ (0580) 752312 Tx: 957565
Fax: (0580) 753966

Georgian building situated in pleasant rural setting. Lovely garden. Putting, tennis.
Es.
🛏 18 bedrs, 18 en suite; TV; tcf
🏠 dogs, ns, P 50, coach; child facs; con 60
✕ LD 9.15
£ B&B £51·50, B&B (double) £82–£87; HB weekly £374; L £11, D £12·50; [5% V]
cc Access, Amex, B'card/Visa, Diners; dep.
(*See advertisement on p. 280*)

HAWKSHEAD Cumbria. Map 43C1
Pop 684. M6 (jn 36) 24, London 271, Ambleside 5, Broughton-in-Furness 13, Kendal 17, Lancaster 36, Ulverston 14.
EC Thur. **Golf** Windermere 18h. **See** 12th-14th cent Church, Court House Tarn Hows, Quaker Meeting House, Grizedale Forest Nature Reserve.
ℹ ☎ (096 66) 525

★★★ **Tarn Hows,** LA22 0PR ☎ (096 66) 696 Fax: (096 66) 294
Attractive country house in quiet situation on hill. 25 acres of grounds. Swimming pool, fishing, putting, solarium.
🛏 16 bedrs, 16 en suite, annexe 6 bedrs, 6 en suite; TV; tcf
🏠 TV; dogs, ns; P 40; coach; child facs; con 30
✕ LD 8.45
£ B&B £35–£40; HB weekly £245–£350; L £8·50, D £16·50; WB £45
cc Access, Amex, B'card/Visa, Diners; dep.
(*See advertisement on p. 280*)

★★ **Highfield House,** Hawkshead Hill, LA22 0PN ☎ (096 66) 344
Three-storey building in local stone set in a large garden overlooking the village. Closed 24–26 Dec
🛏 11 bedrs, 8 en suite, 2 ba; TV; tcf
🏠 dogs, ns; P 12; child facs
✕ LD 8, bar meals only lunch. Rest lic
£ B&B £19–£27, B&B (double) £36–£56; HB weekly £210–£266; D £12; dep.

Atlas Section
Consult the Atlas section at the back of the guide to find out which towns and villages have RAC Appointed and Listed hotels in them. They are shown on the maps by purple circles.

Queens Head, LA22 0NS
☎ (096 66) 271

Family-run 17th century inn of character in centre of village. Fr
🛏 10 bedrs, 6 en suite; 2 ba; TV; tcf
🏠 coach; children over 10
✕ LD 9.30, bar meals only lunch
£ B&B £23·50–£30, B&B (double) £39–£46; WB £67 (3 nts); [5% V Nov–Mar, Mon–Thurs]
cc Access, Amex, B'card/Visa; dep.

Red Lion, The Square, LA22 0NS
☎ (096 66) 213
Stone-built 15th century inn in village centre. Friendly, old world atmosphere.
🛏 9 bedrs, 9 en suite; TV; tcf
🏠 TV; P 12, coach; child facs

Greenbank Country House (Acclaimed), nr Ambleside, LA22 0NS ☎ (096 66) 497.
Private Hotel.
£ B&B £16–£20; HB weekly £150–£180; [5% V]

Ivy House (Acclaimed), LA22 0NS
☎ (096 66) 204. *Private Hotel. Fishing.* Open Mar–Nov
£ B&B £17·25–£21·75; HB weekly £155·75–£187·25

HAWORTH West Yorkshire. Map 40B1
Halifax 9½, London 203, Bradford 9, Keighley 3½, Todmorden 8. **See** Old Vicarage–home of Bronte Sisters, Keighley & Worth Valley Steam Railway.
ℹ 2 West Lane. ☎ (0535) 42329

★★ **Old White Lion,** 6 West La, BD22 8DU
☎ (0535) 42313

Attractive stone-built 300 year old coaching inn in historic small town.

H

🛏 14 bedrs, 14 en suite; TV; tcf
🏠 TV; P 10, coach; child facs; con 100
✕ LD 9.30, bar meals only Mon–Sat lunch
£ B&B £29·50, B&B (double) £42·50; D £8; WB £40 (HB)
cc Access, Amex, B'card/Visa, Diners; dep.
(*See advertisement on p. 284*)

★★ **Rydings Country,** Bridgehouse La, BD22 8QE ☎(0535) 45206
Fax: (0535) 46997 ♿
Traditional two storied house of character in valley below Haworth village. Fr
🛏 10 bedrs, 10 en suite, TV; tcf
🏠 TV; ns; P 20, coach; child facs; con 20
✕ LD 10. Resid & Rest lic.
£ B&B £22–£32, B&B (double) £36–£42; HB weekly £182–£252; L £5·95, D £9·95; WB £26; [10% V w/e]
cc Access, Amex, B'card/Visa, Diners.

Moorfield (Acclaimed), 80 West La, BD22 8EN ☎(0535) 43689. *Guest House.* Open Feb–Dec. De
£ B&B £15–£18

Ferncliffe, Hebden Rd, BD22 8RS ☎(0535) 43405. *Private Hotel.*
£ B&B £19–£21; HB weekly £192·50–£206·50

HAYDOCK Merseyside Map 32C2

(jn 23) 1½, London 194, Newton-le-Willows 2½, St Helens 4½, Wigan 6.

★★★★ **Haydock Thistle,** Penny La, WA11 9SG ☎(0942) 272000 Tx: 67304
Fax: (0942) 711092 ♿

Modern Georgian-style building with an attractive courtyard set in 11 acres of gardens next to the racecourse. Indoor swimming pool, sauna, solarium, gymnasium, snooker. Fr, De, Es
🛏 139 bedrs, 139 en suite; TV; tcf
🏠 dogs, ns; P 180, coach; child facs, con 250
✕ nr Sat lunch
£ room £75–£95 (w/e £32·50), double room £90–£110; L £9·50, D £16; WB £42 (HB); [10% V]
cc Access, Amex, B'card/Visa, Diners.

★★★★ **Post House,** Lodge La, WA12 0JG ☎Wigan (0942) 717878 Tx: 677672
Fax: (0942) 718419 ♿

Changes made after July 1990 are not included.

Purpose-built hotel with modern decoration and furnishings. Indoor swimming pool, sauna, solarium, gymnasium. (THF)
🛏 142 bedrs, 142 en suite; TV; tcf
🏠 lift, dogs, ns; P 200, coach; child facs; con 60
✕ LD 10
£ B&B £74·50 (w/e room £39·50), B&B (double) £87; D £10·50; WB £38
cc Access, Amex, B'card/Visa, Diners.

HAYDON BRIDGE Northumberland. Map 44B3

Pop 1,800. Hexham 6, London 288, Alston 17, Corbridge 10, Haltwhistle 9
EC Wed. **Golf** Hexham 9h & 18h.

★★ **Anchor,** John Martin St, NE47 6AB ☎(0434) 684227

Charming riverside 17th century courthouse with atmosphere of village inn. Fishing.
🛏 12 bedrs, 10 en suite, 1 ba; TV; tcf
🏠 dogs; P 25, coach; child facs; con 20
✕ LD 8.30, bar meals only lunch
£ B&B £23–£29, B&B (double) £40–£46; L £7, D £13; [10% V]
cc Access, Amex, B'card/Visa, Diners; dep.

HAYLING ISLAND Hampshire. Map 6A1

Pop 12,225. Petersfield 18, London 71, Chichester 14, Cosham 9.
EC Wed. **Golf** Hayling 18h.
ℹ 32 Seafront. ☎(0705) 467111

★★★ **Post House,** Northney Rd, PO11 0NQ ☎(0705) 465011 Tx: 46620
Fax: (0705) 466468
Modern hotel located close to bridge linking Havant to the Island. Indoor swimming pool, sauna, solarium, gymnasium. (THF)
🛏 96 bedrs, 96 en suite; TV; tcf
🏠 dogs; P 200, coach; child facs; con 180
✕ LD 10, coffee shop only Sat lunch
£ WB £45
cc Access, Amex, B'card/Visa, Diners.

★★ **Newtown House,** Manor Rd, PO11 1QR ☎(0705) 466131 Fax: (0705) 461366

Attractive early 19th century farmhouse in own grounds, ¼ mile from the sea. Indoor swimming pool, tennis, sauna, solarium, gymnasium, snooker. De
🛏 21 bedrs, 19 en suite, 2 ba; annexe 7 bedrs, 7 en suite; TV; tcf
🏠 dogs, P 50, coach; child facs; con 40
✕ LD 9.30
£ B&B £38–£45 (w/e £28), B&B (double) £50–£67·50; HB weekly £210–£245; L £7·75, D £10·75; WB £60 (HB 2 nts); [10% V]
cc Access, Amex, B'card/Visa, Diners.

Please tell the manager if you chose your hotel through an advertisement in the guide.

Cockle Warren Cottage (Highly Acclaimed), 36 Seafront, PO11 9HL. ☎(0705) 464961
£ B&B £30–£45; [10% V]

Rook Hollow (Acclaimed), 84 Church Rd, PO11 0NX ☎(0705) 467080. *Hotel.*
£ B&B £20–£23; [10% V Jan–Mar, Jun, Sep–Nov]

HAYTOR VALE Devon. Map 3B2

Exeter 17, London 185, Ashburton 5½, Newton Abbot 7½, Okehampton 21.
EC Wed. **Golf** Newton Abbot (Stover) 18h.

★★★ **H C R Bel Alp House,** nr Bovey Tracey, TQ13 9XX ☎(0364) 661217
Fax: (0364) 661292

Elegant, Edwardian mansion in own secluded grounds. Billiards. Fr, De. Closed Dec.
🛏 9 bedrs, 9 en suite; TV; tcf
🏠 lift, dogs, ns; P 20; child facs
✕ LD 8.30, nr lunch. Resid & Rest lic
£ B&B £66–£78, B&B (double) £108–£132; HB weekly £546–£735; D £30
cc Access, B'card/Visa; dep.

HEACHAM Norfolk. Map 34C2

King's Lynn 11, London 88, Fakenham 13, Hunstanton 3.

St Annes, 53 Neville Rd, PE31 7HB ☎(0485) 70021. *Guest House.* ♿
£ B&B £13–£16

HEADLAM Durham. Map 45A1

Scotch Corner 10, London 246, Barnard Castle 10, Bishop Auckland 9, Darlington 8½, Durham 19.

Complaints

If you are dissatisfied with the facilities or service offered by a hotel, please take the matter up with the Manager WHILE YOU ARE AT THE HOTEL. In this way, any problems can usually be solved promptly and amicably.

The RAC will investigate matters if a personal approach has failed to resolve the problem. Please submit details of any discussion or correspondence when reporting the problem to the RAC.

★★★ Headlam Hall, nr Gainford, DL2 3HA Darlington (0325) 730238 Fax: (0325) 730238

In 4 acres of grounds amidst quiet farmland, lovely 3-storey 17th century mansion. Indoor swimming pool, putting, tennis, fishing, billiards, sauna, gymnasium. Fr. Closed Xmas week.
17 bedrs, 17 en suite; 2 ba; TV; tcf
dogs, ns; P 60, coach; child facs; con 40
LD 9.30, nr Mon–Sat lunch. Resid & Rest lic
£ B&B £43–£50, B&B (double) £55–£62; L £8·50 (Sun); [10% V w/e]
cc Access, Amex, B'card/Visa.

HEBDEN BRIDGE West Yorkshire. Map 38A2
Halifax 8, London 195, Keithley 11, Rochdale 12.
1 Bridge Gate (0422) 843831

★★★ Carlton, Albert St, HX7 8ES (0422) 844400 Tx: 518176

Restored Victorian sandstone building with hotel situated above shops in centre of town.
18 bedrs, 18 en suite; TV; tcf
lift; coach; child facs; con 150

HELMSLEY North Yorkshire. Map 38C4
Pop 1,460. York 24, London 222, Malton 16, Middlesbrough 28, Pickering 13, Thirsk 14.
EC Wed. **MD** Fri. **Golf** Kirbymoorside 9h. **See** Castle ruins, Rievaulx Terrace frescoes 2 m NW, Rievaulx Abbey 3 m NW.
Town Hall. (0439) 70173

★★★ H C R Black Swan, Market Pl, YO6 5BJ (0439) 70466 Fax: (0439) 70174
Attractive old building, partly Tudor, situated in market place. Fr. (THF)
44 bedrs, 44 en suite; TV; tcf
TV, dogs, ns; P 60; coach; child facs; con 15
LD 9.30
£ B&B £89–£104, B&B (double) £100–£115; HB weekly £490–£595; L £12·50, D £28; WB £82 (HB)
cc Access, Amex, B'card/Visa, Diners.

Weekend breaks
Please consult the hotel for full details of weekend breaks; prices shown are an indication only. Many hotels offer mid week breaks as well.

★★★ Feversham Arms, YO6 5AG (0439) 70766 Tx: 57966 Fax: (0439) 70346

Attractive stone building on corner by church and market place. Swimming pool, tennis. Fr, Es
18 bedrs, 18 en suite; TV; tcf
dogs; P 30, coach; child facs; con 24
LD 9.30, bar meals only Tue–Sat lunch
£ B&B £45–£55, B&B (double) £70–£80; L £12, D £18; WB fr £43 (HB)
cc Access, Amex, B'card/Visa, Diners; dep.
(See advertisement on p. 284)

★★ Crown, Market Pl, YO6 5BJ (0439) 70297
Charming ivy-covered old building of character, at the head of market place.
14 bedrs, 12 en suite, (1 sh), 1 ba; TV; tcf
TV, dogs, ns; P 20, G 4; con 16
LD 8
£ B&B £24–£26; HB weekly £245–£259; L £7·10, D £12·25; WB £65 (HB Oct–May)
cc Access, B'card/Visa; dep.

★★ Feathers, Market Pl, YO6 5BH (0439) 70275

Lovely stone-built hotel with Georgian façade but dating to 15th century. Closed 24 Dec–31 Jan
17 bedrs, 13 en suite, 2 ba; TV; tcf
TV, dogs; P 8, coach; child facs
LD 9
£ B&B £24–£29, HB weekly £231–£262; L £7·50, D £13; WB £75
cc Access, Amex, B'card/Visa, Diners; dep.

Beaconsfield, Bondgate, YO6 5BW (0439) 71346. *Guest House.*
£ B&B £23; dep.

HELSTON Cornwall. Map 2B1
Pop 7,975. Truro 16, London 271, Falmouth 13, Penzance 13, Redruth 10, St Ives 15.
EC Wed. **MD** Mon, Sat. **Golf** Mullion 18h, Praa Sands 9h. **See** Furry Day' celebrations (May), Museum, St Michael's Church, Godolphin House 4½ m NW.

★★ Gwealdues, Falmouth Rd, TR13 8JX (0326) 572808

On main Falmouth Road, a small, modern hotel. Swimming pool.
12 bedrs, 9 en suite, 2 ba; TV; tcf
TV, dogs; P 60, coach; child facs; con 225
LD 9, bar meals only lunch
£ B&B £25–£35, B&B (double) £30–£40; HB weekly £140–£175; D £9·50; WB £50 (HB 2 nts); [10% V winter w/e]
cc Access, B'card/Visa; dep.

★★ Nansloe Manor, Meneage Rd, TR13 0SB (0326) 574691

Part-Georgian house in 4½ acres of parkland on the outskirts of town. Closed Dec 25–30.
7 bedrs, 6 en suite, 1 ba; TV; tcf
dogs; P 40; children over 10; con 20
LD 9.30. Rest lic
£ B&B £28–£45, B&B (double) £60–£84; WB £80 (Nov–Mar)
cc Access, B'card/Visa; dep.

Hillsdale, Polladras, Breage, TR13 9NT Penzance (0736) 763334. *Hotel.*
£ B&B £16·65; HB weekly £113·85–£132·25; dep.

HEMEL HEMPSTEAD Herts. Map 14B2
Pop 79,585. Watford 7½, London 24, M1 (jn 8) 2½, Aylesbury 17, Barnet 16, Bletchley 22, Dunstable 12, St Albans 7.
The Pavilion, The Marlowes. (0442) 64451

★★★ Post House, Breakspear Way, HP2 4UA (0442) 51122 Tx: 826902 Fax: (0442) 211812
Modern purpose-built hotel with pleasant motel-style bedrooms. (THF)
107 bedrs, 107 en suite; TV; tcf
lift, dogs, ns; P 100, coach; child facs; con 120
LD 10, nr Sat lunch
£ room £72 (w/e £42), double room £94; Bk £7·50, L £9·95, D £11·95
cc Access, Amex, B'card/Visa, Diners.

H

Haworth (West Yorkshire)

THE OLD WHITE LION HOTEL

HAWORTH, WEST YORKSHIRE. BD22 8DU

Nearly 300 years old, the Old White Lion is situated at the centre of this famous village close to the Bronte Museum. 14 rooms, all with facilities. Full central heating throughout. Open all year round with weekend bargain breaks. Catering for the businessman as well as visitors from all over the world. Candlelit restaurant recommended in major guides. Brochure sent on request.

TELEPHONE HAWORTH (0535) 42313

Helmsley (North Yorkshire)

COMMENDED

The Feversham Arms Hotel

RAC ★★★

Helmsley, North Yorkshire YO6 5AG *Tel: (0439) 70766*
Situated in the unique North York Moors National Park *Fax: (0439) 70346*

Rebuilt by the Earl of Feversham in 1855, now luxuriously modernised retaining its old charm, this friendly Inn has 18 bedrooms all with bathroom, hairdryer, trouser press, telephone, safe, radio, colour TV and tea-coffee facilities. Some bedrooms have four poster bed and de-luxe bathroom. Central heating throughout. Own tennis court, swimming pool and gardens. The Goya Restaurant is well known for the shellfish and game specialities. The hotel is central to over 20 golf courses and for touring the Moors, Dales, East Coast and York. Attractive bargain breaks all year round and an incredible super-bargain break in winter. Six ground floor bedrooms available for guests with walking difficulties. Brochure on request.

Helston (Cornwall)

Hexham (Northumberland)

RAC ★★

Bishop Field Country House Hotel & Restaurant

ETB

Allendale, Hexham, Northumberland NE47 9EJ. Tel: (0434) 683248 Fax: (0434) 683830

Bishop Field is situated in an area of outstanding natural beauty. All rooms en-suite, renowned for its English to French cooking. High standard of accommodation.

Hitchin (Hertfordshire)

Firs Hotel & CLASSICO ITALIAN RESTAURANT

83 Bedford Road, Hitchin, Hertfordshire SG5 2TY Tel: (0462) 422322 Fax: (0462) 432051

30 bedrooms, majority en-suite with colour TV, direct dial telephone, tea/coffee making facilities. Italian Restaurant, conference up to 40, function for 85. Ample parking.

HOTELIERS FOR

★ **Midland,** Midland Rd, HP2 5BH ☎(0442) 53218

A 2-storey brick built hotel on the edge of the old town next to former station. (GMR)
🛏 6 bedrs, 6 en suite; TV; tcf
🏠 P 75; child facs

Southville, 9 Charles St, HP1 1JH ☎(0442) 51387. *Private Hotel.*
£ B&B £18·50–£26, (w/e £16·50); [10% V]
cc B'card/Visa; dep.

HENLEY-IN-ARDEN Warwicks. Map 20C3
Pop 1,640. Stratford-upon-Avon 8, London 101, Birmingham 15, Bromsgrove 14, Coventry 19, Evesham 18, Warwick 9.
EC Thur. **MD** Mon. **Golf** Redditch 18h.

Ashleigh House (Highly Acclaimed), Whitley Hill, B95 5DL ☎(056 42) 2315. *Hotel.*
£ B&B £35–£45; [5% V, 2 nts]
cc Access, B'card/Visa; dep.

Lapworth Lodge (Acclaimed), Bushwood La, Lapworth, B94 5PJ ☎(0564) 783038. *Guest House.* ✗ Fr
£ B&B £30–£40

Spinney (Acclaimed), Stratford Rd, Wootton Wawen, B95 6DG ☎(0564) 792534. *Guest House. Swimming pool, putting.*

HENLEY ON THAMES Oxon. Map 12C3
Pop 12,000. Slough 14, London 35, A423 (M) (jn 9) 6½, Bagshot 19, High Wycombe 12, Reading 8, Wallingford 11.
EC Wed. **MD** Thur. **Golf** Henley 18h.
ℹ Town Hall, Market Pl. ☎(0491) 578034

★★ **Edwardian,** Station Rd, RG9 1AT ☎(0491) 578678 Fax: (0491) 572295

A flamboyant 1890 half-timbered building, with balconies and oriel windows, close to town centre and river. ✗ Fr.
🛏 22 bedrs, 22 en suite; TV; tcf
🏠 coach; child facs; con 80
✗ LD 9.45, bar meals only Sat lunch
£ B&B £58 9w/e £32), B&B (double) £74; HB weekly £493·50; L £12·50, D £12·50; WB; [10% V w/e]
cc Access, Amex, B'card/Visa.

★ **R** **Flohr's,** 15 Northfield End, RG9 2JG ☎(0491) 573412
Small, unspoilt Georgian, family-run hotel conveniently situated close to town centre.

HEREFORD Hereford & Worcester (Herefordshire). Map 20A3
See also MUCH BIRCH
Pop 48,700. London 132, Abergavenny 23, Ledbury 14, Leominster 12, Monmouth 17, Ross-on-Wye 14, Worcester 25.
EC Thur. **MD** Mon, Wed, Thur, Fri, Sat. **Golf** Wormsley 18h, Belmont 18h. **See** Cathedral, The Old House, Museum and Art Gallery.
ℹ Town Hall. ☎(0432) 268430

★★★ **Green Dragon,** Broad St, HR4 9BG ☎(0432) 272506 Tx: 35491 Fax: (0432) 352139

Large former coaching inn in city centre near Cathedral. (THF)
🛏 88 bedrs, 88 en suite; TV; tcf
🏠 lift, dogs, ns; G 72, coach; child facs; con 200

★★★ **Hereford Moat House,** Belmont Rd, HR2 7BP ☎(0432) 354301 Fax: (0432) 275114 ♿

A modern hotel on outskirts of city. Bedrooms set by quiet garden. (QMH)
🛏 28 bedrs, 28 en suite; annexe 32 bedrs, 32 en suite; TV; tcf
🏠 dogs; P 200, coach; child facs; con 300
✗ LD 9.45, bar meals only Sat lunch
£ B&B £48–£60 (w/e £45), B&B (double) £58–£70; HB weekly £315; L £10, D £17·50; WB
cc Access, Amex, B'card/Visa, Diners.

Changes made after July 1990 are not included.

★★ **Castle Pool,** Castle St, HR1 2NR ☎(0432) 356321 Fax: (0432) 356321
Quietly placed city centre Georgian building with lawned garden overlooking castle moat. ✗ Es
🛏 26 bedrs, 26 en suite; TV; tcf
🏠 TV, dogs; P 14, coach; child facs; con 25
✗ LD 9.30
£ B&B £44, B&B (double) £60·50; HB weekly £280–£385; L £7·50, D £15; WB £78
cc Access, Amex, B'card/Visa, Diners.

★★ **R** **Merton,** Commercial Rd, HR1 2BD ☎(0432) 265925 Fax: (0432) 354983

Three-storey Georgian building of character, conveniently near town centre. Sauna, solarium, gymnasium. ✗ Fr, De, It
🛏 15 bedrs, 15 en suite; TV
🏠 TV; dogs, ns; P 6, coach; child facs, con 60
✗ LD 9.30, nr Sun
£ B&B £41·50, B&B (double) £64; HB weekly £366; L £12·50, D £15; WB £40 (HB); [10% V]
cc Access, Amex, B'card/Visa, Diners.

★★ **Munstone House,** Munstone, HR1 3AH. ☎(0432) 267122
Charming early Victorian house in 2 acres of garden. views over Hereford, 2 miles to south east.
🛏 6 bedrs, 3 en suite; 1 ba; TV; tcf
£ B&B £21–£26, B&B (double) £38–£43

★★ **Netherwood,** Tupsley, HR1 1UT ☎(0432) 272388

An attractive early Victorian house in 2 acres of grounds on eastern edge of the city.
🛏 7 bedrs, 7 en suite; TV; tcf
🏠 TV, dogs; P 30, coach; child facs; con 40

★★ **New Priory,** Stretton Sugwas, HR4 7AR ☎(0432) 760264
In 3pi½ acres of lawns, a charming red-brick Victorian building with mock Tudor features. *Tennis.*
🛏 8 bedrs, 7 en suite, 1 ba; TV; tcf
🏠 TV, dogs, ns; P 100, coach; child facs; con 150
✗ LD 9.30
£ B&B £25–£30, B&B (double) £40–£50; L £10, D £9
cc Access, B'card/Visa; dep.

Collins House (Highly Acclaimed), 19 St Owens St, HR1 2JB ☎(0432) 272416

H

Fax: (0432) 341867. *Private Hotel.*
£ B&B £65; HB weekly £455

Hopbine, Roman Rd, HR1 1LE ☎(0432) 268722. *Hotel.*
£ B&B £16–£20; HB weekly £150·50–£192·50; [5% V]

HERNE BAY Kent. Map 7C3
Pop 26,050. Rochester 30, London 62, Canterbury 8½, Maidstone 31, Margate 12.
EC Thur. **MD** Sat. **Golf** Herne Bay 18h.
ℹ Central Parade. ☎(0227) 361911

Beauvalle, 92 Central Parade, CT6 5JJ ☎(0227) 375330

HERSTMONCEUX East Sussex. Map 7A1
Pop 1,400. Lower Dicker 5½, London 58, Battle 8, Bexhill 9, Eastbourne 11.
EC Wed. **Golf** Willingdon 18h. **See** Castle.

★★ **Horse Shoe Inn,** Windmill Hill, BN27 4RU ☎(0323) 833265 Fax: (0323) 832001
Neo-Tudor inn with a tiled roof and beams, situated on A27 on outskirts of Herstmonceux.
15 bedrs, 15 en suite, TV; tcf
dogs; P100, coach; child facs; con 180
LD 10
£ B&B £44, B&B (double) £59; HB weekly £160–£208; L fr £6·25, D fr £6·25; WB £44; [V]
cc Access, Amex, B'card/Visa, Diners.

Cleavers Lyng, Church Rd, nr Hailsham, BN27 1QJ ☎(0323) 833131. *Hotel.* Closed 24–31 Dec.
£ B&B £15·25–£17·25; HB weekly £150–£172·50; [5% V]

HERTFORD Hertfordshire. Map 15B2
Pop 25,000. Hoddesdon 4½, London 24, Baldock 17, Barnet 13, Bishop's Stortford 13, Epping 13, Hatfield 7, Royston 19.
EC Thur. **MD** Sat. **Golf** Chadwell Springs 9h. **See** Municipal buildings (once castle), St Leonard's Church, All Saints' Church.
ℹ The Castle ☎(0992) 584322.

★★★ **White Horse Inn,** Hertingfordbury, SG14 2LB (1½ m W A414) ☎(0992) 586791 Fax: (0992) 550809

Beautifully-preserved coaching inn situated off the Hertford/Hatfield road. Pleasant garden. Fr, It. (THF)
42 bedrs, 42 en suite; TV; tcf
dogs, ns; coach; child facs; con 60
LD 9.15
£ B&B £72–£77, B&B (double) £99; L £10·95, D £13·95; WB £42 (HB)
cc Access, Amex, B'card/Visa, CB, Diners.

★★ **Salisbury Arms,** Fore St, SG14 1BZ ☎(0992) 583091 Fax: (0992) 552510
Attractive old town centre hotel–3-storey building of ornate design. Solarium.
29 bedrs, 29 en suite; TV; tcf
dogs; P 40, coach; child facs; con 35
LD 9
£ B&B £49·50 (w/e £31·50), B&B (double) £69·50; L £6·50, D £9·50; WB
cc Access, B'card/Visa, Diners.

HESWALL Merseyside. Map 32A1
Pop 16,325. Chester 13, London 197, Birkenhead 7, Queensferry 11.
EC Wed. **Golf** Arrow Park 18h.

★★ **Hill House,** Mount Av, L60 4RH ☎051-342 5535

A converted and extended former mill-owner's house with attractive views over River Dee.

HEVERSHAM Cumbria. Map 36B4
Pop 703. M6 (jn 36) 3½, London 253, Ambleside 18, Kendal 6½, Kirkby Lonsdale 9, Lancaster 15, Ulverston 22.
Golf Kendal 18h. **See** Church, Old Hall.

★★★ **Blue Bell at Heversham,** Prince's Way, LA7 7EE ☎(053 95) 62018

Extended 17th century vicarage in a delightful rural setting.
24 bedrs, 24 en suite; 3 ba; TV; tcf
TV; dogs, ns; P 100, coach; child facs; con 30
LD 9
£ B&B £35–£45, B&B (double) £63; HB weekly £294; L £7·50, D £11·95; WB £74 (2 nts)
cc Access, Amex, B'card/Visa.

HEWISH Avon. Map 4B4
Pop 252. 2½ m W of Congresbury. Bristol 14, London 128, M5 (jn 21) 3, Bath 25, Glastonbury 22, Radstock 24, Shepton Mallet 23, Wells 18, Weston-super-Mare 6.
EC Wed. **Golf** Worlebury, Weston-super-Mare 18h.

Kara, BS24 6RQ ☎Yatton (0934) 834442. *Guest House.*

HEXHAM Northumberland. Map 44C3
Pop 10,000. West Auckland 33, London 282, Alston 21, Bellingham 17, Brampton 28, Corbridge 3½, Durham 27, Jedburgh 48.
EC Thur. **MD** Tue, Fri. **Golf** Hexham 18h. **See** Abbey Church, 15th cent Moot Hall, Roman Wall, Housesteads Roman Camp, Chesters Roman Camp, Brunton Turret (Roman Milecastle), Vindolanda excavations, Kielder Water.
ℹ Manor Office, Hallgate. ☎(0434) 605225

★★★ **Beaumont,** Beaumont St, NE46 3LT ☎(0434) 602331 Fax: (0434) 602331
Three-storey brick-built traditional style hotel, in town centre near Abbey.
23 bedrs, 23 en suite; TV; tcf
lift; ns; child facs; con 80
LD 9.45, bar meals only Mon–Sat lunch
£ B&B £42, B&B (double) £66; L £10, D £12
cc Access, Amex, B'card/Visa, Diners.

★★ H **County,** Priestpopple, NE46 1PS ☎(0434) 602030

Privately-owned stone-built 15th century hotel on main street in town centre.
9 bedrs, 8 en suite (1 sh), 1 ba; TV; tcf
dogs; P 2, coach; child facs; con 60
LD 9.30.
£ B&B £38, B&B (double) £53; L £8·25, D £11; WB (£60)
cc Access, Amex, B'card/Visa.

★★ R **Langley Castle,** Langley-on-Tyne, NE47 5LU ☎(0434) 688888 Fax: (0434) 684019
A 14th-century castle with 7-feet thick walls, lovingly rebuilt and restored around 1900, recently converted to a hotel.
8 bedrs, 8 en suite; TV
lift; dogs; P120, coach; child facs; con 120
LD 9.30, nr Mon–Sat lunch. Rest lic
£ B&B £49–£72, B&B (double) £70–£94; L £7·50, D £14·95; WB £80
cc Access, Amex, B'card/Visa, Diners.

★★ **Royal,** Priestpopple, NE46 1PQ ☎(0434) 602270

On main street in town centre an extended stone-built coaching inn. Near Abbey.
24 bedrs, 22 en suite, (2 sh); TV; tcf
TV, dogs; P 20, coach; child facs; con 100
LD 9.30
£ B&B £37–£40, B&B (double) £57–£60; L fr £4, D fr £9; WB £72 (HB 2 people)
cc Access, Amex, B'card/Visa, Diners.

Westbrooke, Allendale Rd, NE46 2DE ☎(0434) 603818. *Hotel.*.
£ B&B £18–£20; HB weekly £179–£196; [5% V]

EC *early closing* **MD** *market day* *country house hotel* *ns (NS) no smoking areas* *tcf tea/coffee facilities*

HIGH WYCOMBE Bucks. Map 12C4

Pop 60,800. London 30, M40 (jn 4) 1½, Aylesbury 16, Henley-on-Thames 12, Oxford 26, Reading 18, Rickmansworth 15. **EC** Wed. **MD** Tue, Fri, Sat. **Golf** Flackwell Heath 18h. **See** All Saints Church, Guildhall, Art Gallery and Museum, The Priory (now shops), Little Market House, Hughenden Manor, home and burial place of Disraeli (Nat Trust), West Wycombe Park.
ℹ Cornmarket ☎(0494) 421892.

★★★ Crest, Crest Rd, HP11 1TL ☎(0494) 442100 Tx: 83626 Fax: (0494) 439071 ♿

Modern, purpose-built hotel close to Jn. 4 of M40. (Cr/THF)
🛏 110 bedrs, 110 en suite; TV; tcf
🏨 dogs, ns; P 178; coach; child facs; con 100
✕ LD 10.30
£ B&B £82–£130 (w/e £40); B&B (double) £94–£130; L £8·95, D £15·95
cc Access, Amex, B'card/Visa, Diners.

Clifton Lodge (Acclaimed), 210 West Wycombe Rd, (A40), HP12 3AR ☎(0494) 440095. *Private Hotel. Sauna.* ✈ Fr, Du ♿
£ B&B £28–£44 (w/e £20); [5% V w/e]

Drake Court, 141 London Rd, HP11 1BT ☎(0494) 23639. *Private Hotel. Swimming pool.*
£ B&B £25·30–£40; [10% V w/e]

HILGAY Norfolk. Map 34C1

Pop 1,125. Ely 14, London 85, Downham Market 3, King's Lynn 15, Thetford 22, Wisbech 16.
EC Wed. **Golf** Ryston 9h.

Crosskeys Riverside (Highly Acclaimed), nr Downham Market, PE38 0LN ☎Downham Market (0366) 387777. *Private Hotel. Fishing.*
£ B&B £29·10; HB weekly £171

HILLINGDON Greater London (Middx). Map 10A4

Ealing 7, London 15, Harrow 8, Kingston upon Thames 12, Rickmansworth 9.
EC Wed. **Golf** Hillingdon, Uxbridge 9h. **See** 13th cent Church.

★★★ Master Brewer, Western Av, Hillingdon Circus, UB10 9NX ☎(0895) 51199 Tx: 946589 Fax: (0895) 810330 ♿

Low-rise motel-type hotel set in attractive gardens. Near Underground station.
🛏 106 bedrs, 106 en suite; TV; tcf
🏨 P 200, coach; child facs; con 200

HIMLEY Staffordshire. Map 22A2

Pop: 849. Birmingham 13, London 124, Bridgnorth 13, Kidderminster 10, Wolverhampton 6.
Golf Himley 18h. **See** Himley Hall, Church.

★★★ Himley Country Club, School Rd, DY3 4LG ☎Wombourne (0902) 896716 Tx: 333688 Fax: (0902) 896668
A converted Victorian school house, with large modern extensions, set in pleasant gardens.
🛏 76 bedrs, 76 en suite; TV; tcf
🏨 P 140, coach; child facs; con 110
✕ LD 10
£ B&B £54·50–£59·50 (w/e £43), B&B (double) £63·50; L £13, D £13
cc Access, Amex, B'card/Visa, Diners.
(*See advertisement on p. 232*)

★★ Himley House, nr, Dudley, DY3 4QD ☎Wombourne (0902) 892468

Elegant Georgian building set in pleasant grounds. Closed Xmas. (BCB)
🛏 24 bedrs, 24 en suite; TV; tcf
🏨 ns; P 120, coach; child facs; con 50
✕ LD 10.30
£ B&B £50·50, B&B (double) £69; L £8·15, D £8·15; WB £27·50
cc Access, Amex, B'card/Visa, Diners.

HINCKLEY Leicestershire. Map 23C2

Pop 38,999. London 97, M69 (jn 1) 2, Ashby-de-la-Zouch 16, Atherstone 8½, Daventry 23, Leicester 13, Market Harborough 24, Nuneaton 4½, Rugby 15.
EC Thur. **MD** Mon, Sat. **Golf** Hinckley 18h. **See** Church (13th-14th cent), Bosworth Field 4 m NNW.
ℹ Library, Lancaster Rd. ☎(0455) 635106

★★★ Hinckley Island, (A5), LE10 3JA ☎(0455) 631122 Tx: 34691 Fax: (0455) 634536 ♿
Modern low-built hotel with leisure complex and conference facilities. Situated beside a small lake near junction of A5 and M69. Indoor swimming pool, fishing, sauna, solarium, gymnasium, billiards.
🛏 380 bedrs, 380 en suite; TV; tcf
🏨 dogs; P 500, coach; child facs; con 450

★★★ Sketchley Grange, Burbage, LE10 3HU ☎(0455) 634251
Former private residence in quite siuation in 4 acres of parkland.
🛏 34 bedrs, 34 en suite; TV; tcf
🏨 ns; P 200, coach; child facs; con 250

★★ Fernleigh, 32 Wood St, Earl Shilton, LE9 7ND ☎(0455) 847011
Modern hotel set beside A47 right in the middle of Earl Shilton. ✈ It
🛏 27 bedrs, 27 en suite; 1 ba; TV; tcf
🏨 TV, dogs; P 100, G 12; child facs; con 100
✕ LD 9.30
£ B&B £25–£45 (w/e £25), B&B (double) £50–£55; L £5·95, D £8·50
cc Access, B'card/Visa.

Kings (Acclaimed) 13 Mount Rd, LE10 1AD ☎(0455) 637193 Fax: (0455) 636201. *Hotel.* ✈ Hu.
£ B&B £54·50–£64·50 (w/e £45); HB weekly £350–£370; [5% V]

HINDHEAD Surrey. Map 6A2

Pop 3,000. Guildford 12, London 41, Alton 13, Dorking 23, Farnham 8½, Haslemere 3½, Midhurst 10, Petersfield 12.
Golf Hindhead 18h. **See** Devil's Punch Bowl, Waggoners Wells (Nat Trust). Greensand Way footpath, Frencham Common (3 m N).

★★★ Devils Punchbowl, London Rd, GU26 6AG ☎(042 873) 6565

Gabled, cream and black building with modern bedroom accommodation. On A3.
🛏 17 bedrs, 17 en suite, annexe 20 bedrs, 20 en suite; TV; tcf
🏨 dogs; P 90, coach; child facs; con 70

HINDON Wiltshire. Map 5A3

Pop 600. Amesbury 17, London 97, Frome 14, Salisbury 16, Shaftesbury 7½, Warminster 9½, Wincanton 14.
Golf W Wilts. Warminster 18h.

★★ R Lamb, High St, SP3 6DP ☎(074 789) 573 Fax: (074 789) 605
A 17th century stone-built hotel of character and tradition.
🛏 16 bedrs, 11 en suite, 3 ba; TV; tcf
🏨 TV, dogs; P 22, coach; child facs; con 50

HINTON CHARTERHOUSE Avon. Map 5A3

Bath 5, London 109, M4 (jn 18) 14, Bristol 16, Frome 8, Warminster 11.

★★★ Homewood Park, nr Bath, BA3 6BB ☎(0225) 723731 Fax: (0225) 723820 ♿
Bath-stone country mansion, 18th century with 19th century additions, beautifully decorated and set in 10 acres of gardens. Tennis. ✈ Fr.
🛏 15 bedrs, 15 en suite; TV
🏨 ns; P 40, coach; child facs; con 40
✕ LD 9.30. Resid & Rest lic
£ B&B £87·50–£102·50, B&B (double) £120–£163; L £19; D £32·50
cc Access, Amex, B'card/Visa, Diners.

HITCHIN Hertfordshire. Map 14C3

Pop 30,317. Hatfield 14, London 35, A1 (M) (jn 8) 3, Baldock 5, Bedford 16, Hoddesdon 19, Luton 8, St Albans 16.

H

EC Wed. MD Tue, Sat. Golf Letchworth 18h. See Priory, St Mary's Church, The Biggin. [i] The Library, Paynes Park. (0462) 434738

★★ **Firs,** 83 Bedford Rd, SG5 2TY (0462) 422322 Fax: (0462) 432051. It

Recently refurbished, family-run hotel on A606 in residential area on northern outskirts of town.
30 bedrs, 25 en suite, 2 ba; TV; tcf
TV, dogs; P 33, coach; con 40
LD 9.30, nr lunch & Sun dinner
£ B&B £29–£46, B&B (double) £45·50–£56; D £15
cc Access, Amex, B'card/Visa, Diners.
(*See advertisement on p. 284*)

★★ **Sun,** Sun St, SG5 1AF (0462) 36411
Renovated 14th-century coaching inn in town centre.
32 bedrs, 32 en suite; TV; tcf
ns; P 32, coach; child facs; con 150

HOAR CROSS Staffordshire. Map 22C4

Hoar Cross Hall, nr Yoxall, DE13 8QS (028 375) 224.
Hotel awaiting inspection.

HODNET Shropshire. Map 29C2

Telford 13, London 180, Market Drayton 5, Shrewsbury 12, Whitchurch 10.

★★ **Bear,** nr Market Drayton, TF9 3NM (063 084) 214 Fax: (063 084) 351
An ancient inn, refurbished but retaining its beams and period atmosphere, opposite the church in village centre. Closed Xmas.
6 bedrs, 6 en suite; TV; tcf
ns; P 80; coach; child facs; con 100
LD 10
£ B&B £37·50, B&B (double) £57·50; L £7·50, D £10; [5% V]
cc Access, B'card/Visa, dep.

HOG'S BACK Surrey. Map 6A3

Guildford 6½, London 35, Bagshot 11, Basingstoke 18, Farnham 3½, Haslemere 13.

Discount vouchers

RAC discount vouchers are on p. 34. Hotels with a [V] shown at the end of the price information will accept them in part payment for accommodation bills on the full, standard rate, not against bargain breaks or any other special offers. Please note the limitations shown in the entry: w/e for weekends, w/d for weekdays, and which months they are accepted.

★★★ **Hog's Back,** nr Seale, Farnham, GU10 1EX Runfold (025 18) 2345 Tx: 859352 Fax:(025 18) 3113

On top of Hog's Back, large red-brick hotel with modern extension. Indoor swimming pool, sauna, solarium, gymnasium, snooker. Fr, Es, Po. (Emb)
75 bedrs, 75 en suite; TV; tcf
dogs, ns; P 140, coach; child facs; con 120
LD 9.30
£ B&B £77–£87 (w/e £30), B&B (double) £94–£114; L £8·50, D £8·50; WB £39·50
cc Access, Amex, B'card/Visa, Diners.

HOLBEACH Lincolnshire. Map 34B2

Pop 4,760. Peterborough 23, London 106, Boston 15, Grantham 34, King's Lynn 19, Sleaford 26, Spalding 8, Wisbech 14.
EC Wed. MD Thur. Golf Holbeach 9h.

Crown, 5 West End, PE12 1LW (0406) 23941. *Hotel.*

HOLFORD Somerset. Map 4B3

Pop 265. Bridgwater 11, London 152, Dunster 13, Taunton 15, Tiverton 31.
Golf Enmore Park 18h. See Holford Glen, Holford Combe, Hodder's Combe, Alfoxton House (home of Wordsworth).

★★ C R **Alfoxton Park,** TA5 1SG (027 874) 211
Attractive Georgian country house set in own grounds. Swimming pool, tennis.

★★ H C R **Combe House,** TA5 1RZ (027 874) 382

Attractive 17th century country house hotel with lovely gardens. Indoor swimming pool, tennis, sauna, solarium. Fr, Da. Open Mar–Nov.
20 bedrs, 15 en suite, 3 ba; TV; tcf
dogs, ns; child facs
LD 8.30, bar meals only lunch. Resid & Rest lic
£ B&B £27–£39, B&B (double) £51–£80; HB weekly £217–£287; D £12·75; WB £62
cc Access, B'card/Visa; dep.

HOLKHAM Norfolk. Map 35A2

Pop 241. Fakenham 11, London 124, Cromer 23, King's Lynn 25, Norwich 35.
EC Wed. Golf Fakenham 9h. See Holkham Hall Gardens and Pottery.

★ **Victoria,** NR23 1RG Fakenham (0328) 710469
Cosy inn-type hotel in truly rural setting on the Leicester estate.
8 bedrs, 2 ba; tcf
TV, dogs; P 50, coach; child facs; con 80

HOLLINGBOURNE Kent. Map 7B3

Pop 1,000. Maidstone 6, London 42, M20 (jn 8) 1½, Ashford 16, Canterbury 23, Dartford Tunnel 27, Hawkhurst 19.
EC Wed. Golf Leeds Castle 18h. See Eyhorne Manor, Leeds Castle.

★★★ **Great Danes,** Ashford Rd, ME17 1RE Maidstone (0622) 30022 Tx: 96198 Fax: (0622) 35290

Large hotel built around Georgian manor house in 20 acres of parkland. Indoor swimming pool, putting, tennis, fishing, sauna, solarium, gymnasium, snooker. It, Fr, De. (Emb)
126 bedrs, 126 en suite; TV; tcf
lift, dogs, ns; P 500, coach; child facs; con 600
LD 11, nr Sat lunch
£ B&B £82, B&B (double) £99, L £11·25, D £12·25; WB £44·50 (HB min 2 nts)
cc Access, Amex, B'card/Visa, Diners.

HOLMES CHAPEL Cheshire. Map 30B3

Newcastle under Lyme 16, London 165, M6 (jn 18) 1½, Chester 24, Manchester 23.

★★★ **Old Vicarage,** Knutsford Rd, Cranage, CW4 8EF (0477) 32041 Fax: (0477) 35728

A 17th-century house, much extended and renovated but retaining its traditional character. On A50. Es, It, De
22 bedrs, 22 en suite; TV; tcf
P 60, coach; child facs; con 30
LD 10, bar meals only Sat lunch & Sun dinner

£ B&B £54 (w/e £27), B&B (double) £66; L £10·50, D £14·50; WB £68
cc Access, Amex, B'card/Visa.

HOLMFIRTH West Yorkshire. Map 41A2

Pop 20,800. Sheffield 21, London 181, Barnsley 14, Huddersfield 6½, Oldham 15.
EC Tue. **MD** Tue, Thur. **Golf** Meltham 18h.
[i] 49 Huddersfield Rd. ☎(0484) 687603

White Horse, Jackson Bridge, HR7 7HF ☎(0484) 683940. *Inn.* Closed 31 Dec.
£ B&B £17; [10% V]

HOLMROOK Cumbria. Map 43B1

Pop 296. Broughton-in-Furness 21, London 299, Ambleside 21, Egremont 9.
EC Wed. **Golf** Seascale 18h.

★★ **Bridge Inn,** Santon Bridge, CA19 1UY ☎Wasdale (09406) 221
Two-storey traditional Cumbrian Inn with extension; situated beside river and bridge.

★★ **Lutwidge Arms,** CA19 1UH ☎(094 04) 230

White-painted hotel with trout river flowing close by.
18 bedrs, 18 en suite; 2 ba; TV; tcf
P 40; coach; con 50
LD 8.30
£ B&B £32·50, B&B (double) £40; WB £15 (min 2 nts)
cc Access, Amex, B'card/Visa.

HOLNE Devon. Map 3B2

Pop 234. Ashburton 3, London 194, Plymouth 26, Tavistock 18.
Golf Stover 18h. **See** Church, 14th cent inn

Church House Inn, TQ13 7SJ ☎Poundsgate (036 43) 208
Traditional inn in centre of picturesque village.

Wellpritton Farm (Acclaimed), TQ13 7RX ☎Poundsgate (036 43) 273. *Swimming pool, snooker.* Closed 25–26 Dec.
£ B&B £13–£15; HB weekly £119–£154; [5% V]

HOLSWORTHY Devon. Map 3A3

Pop 1,645. Crediton 34, London 210, Bideford 18, Bude 9½, Launceston 13, Okehampton 20, South Molton 31.
EC Tue. **MD** Wed, Thur. **Golf** Holsworthy 18h. **See** Perp Church, Museum, St Peter's Fair (July), Agricultural Show (May).

Coles Mill (Acclaimed), EX22 6LX ☎(0409) 253313. *Private Hotel.* Open Mar–Oct
£ B&B £15–£16·50; HB weekly £138–£150

Leworthy, EX22 6SJ ☎(0409) 253488.
Farm. Putting, tennis, fishing, snooker.

HOLT Norfolk. Map 35B2

Pop 3,197. Fakenham 12, London 123, Cromer 10, East Dereham 18, Great Yarmouth 40, Norwich 22.
EC Thur. **Golf** Sheringham 18h. **See** Parish Church.

★★ **Feathers,** 6 Market Pl, NR25 6BW ☎(026 371) 2318

A traditional inn with a rear courtyard situated in the centre of town. Riding.
13 bedrs, 10 en suite (3 sh); TV; tcf
P 50, coach; child facs; con 20
LD 9.30
£ B&B £35·50, B&B (double) £47·50; L £8, D £8; WB
cc Access, Amex, B'card/Visa, Diners.

Lawn's (Highly Acclaimed), 26 Station Rd, NR25 6BS ☎(0263) 713390. *Hotel.*
£ B&B £30; HB weekly £250–£275; [5% V w/d)

HONILEY Warwickshire. Map 20C4

Warwick 7, London 99, Coventry 10, M42 (jn 5) 7.

★★★ **Honiley Court,** Honiley Rd, nr Kenilworth, CV8 1NP ☎(0926) 484234
A large new red-brick development carefully designed to blend with the original early Victorian inn. Situated in rural area.
64 bedrs, 64 en suite; TV; tcf

HONITON Devon. Map 4B2

See also WILMINGTON
Pop 6,490. Ilminster 17, London 153, Axminster 10, Crewkerne 13, Exeter 17, Taunton 18, Tiverton 19.
EC Thur. **MD** Tue, Sat. **Golf** Honiton 18h.
[i] Angel Hotel, High St. ☎(0404) 43716.

★★★ [C] [R] **Deer Park,** Weston, EX14 0PG (2½ m W off A30). ☎(0404) 41266
Georgian mansion in 26 acres of beautiful countryside. Swimming pool, putting, tennis, fishing, squash, sauna, solarium, billiards.

Colestocks House (Highly Acclaimed), Colestocks, EX14 0JR ☎(0404) 850633. *Hotel. Putting.* Fr, Ha, Ar
£ B&B £22·95–£29; HB weekly £189–£225

HOOK Hampshire. Map 12 B1

M3 (jn 5) 1, London 41, Basingstoke 6, Camberley 11, Farnham 11, Reading 13.

Cedar Court, Reading Rd, RG27 9DB ☎(0256) 762178. *Guest House.*
£ B&B £17–£20; [5% V Jun–Aug]

HOPE COVE Devon. Map 3B1

Pop 500. Kingsbridge 5, London 209, Plymouth 23, Tavistock 33.
Golf Thurlestone 18h.

★★ **Cottage,** TQ7 3HJ ☎Kingsbridge (0548) 561555

Former residence in pleasant grounds enjoying spectacular sea views. Closed 2–31 Jan.
35 bedrs, 19 en suite, 7 ba; TV
TV, dogs, ns; P 50; child facs; con 50
LD 8.45, bar meals only Mon–Sat lunch
£ B&B £26·70, B&B (double) £52·80–£93·50; HB weekly £261·80–£404·25; WB £54 (2 nts Nov–Easter); dep.

★★ **Sun Bay,** TQ7 3HH ☎Kingsbridge (0548) 561371
Small, modern hotel with a fine view of the bay. Open Apr–Oct.
14 bedrs, 12 en suite, 1 ba; TV; tcf
TV, dogs; P 10; child facs

★ **Greystone,** TQ7 3HH ☎Kingsbridge (0548) 561233

Two-storey modern hotel in pleasant garden above the bay. Fine views. De
8 bedrs, 8 en suite; annexe 2 bedrs, 2 en suite; tcf
TV; dogs; P15; G4; children over 7, child facs.
LD 8.30; nr Mon–Sat lunch, Resid lic
£ B&B £27–£35, B&B (double) £54–£70; L £5·75, D £9·50; WB £52
cc Access, B'card/Visa; dep.

HOPWOOD West Midlands. Map 22C1

Redditch 8, London 116, M42 (jn 2) 1½, Birmingham 8, Bromsgrove 7.

★★★ **Westmead,** Redditch Rd, B48 7AL ☎021-445 1202 Tx: 335956
Fax: 021-445 6163
Modern hotel developed from a pre-war building in a rural area on the busy A441 8 miles from Birmingham.
60 bedrs, 60 en suite; TV; tcf
ns; P 250, coach; child facs; con 300
LD 10
£ B&B £74, B&B (double) £87; L £8·95

D £14; WB £50; [10% V]
cc Access, Amex, B'card/Visa, Diners.

HORLEY Surrey. Map 10B1

Pop 21,000. Redhill 5, London 25, Gatwick Airport 2, M23 (jn 9) 3, Crawley 5½, East Grinstead 8½.
EC Wed. **Golf** Earlswood 18h. **See** EE Church, 15th cent 'Six Bells' Inn.

★★★★ **Gatwick Penta,** Povey Cross Rd, RH6 0BE ☎Crawley (0293) 820169 Tx: 87440 Fax: (0293) 820259 ♿

Modern 5-storey, red-brick hotel with large car park. Near Gatwick. Indoor swimming pool, squash, sauna, solarium, gymnasium.
🛏 260 bedrs, 260 en suite; TV; tcf
🏨 lift, dogs, ns; P 500, coach; child facs; con 150
✕ LD 10.45, bar meals only Sat lunch
£ B&B £110 (w/e £35), B&B (double) £130; L £16, D £20
cc Access, Amex, B'card/Visa, CB, Diners; dep.

★★★ **Chequers Thistle**, Brighton Rd, RH6 8PH ☎Crawley (0293) 786992 Tx: 877550 Fax: (0293) 820625

A mock Tudor building with large modernised extension. Convenient for Gatwick. Swimming pool. (ThH)
🛏 78 bedrs, 78 en suite; TV; tcf
🏨 lift; ns; P 190, coach; child facs; con 70
✕ LD 10.15
£ room £72, double room £85; Bk £7·75, L £7·95, D £14·50; WB
cc Access, Amex, B'card/Visa, CB, Diners.

Complaints

If you are dissatisfied with the facilities or service offered by a hotel, please take the matter up with the Manager WHILE YOU ARE AT THE HOTEL. In this way, any problems can usually be solved promptly and amicably.

The RAC will investigate matters if a personal approach has failed to resolve the problem. Please submit details of any discussion or correspondence when reporting the problem to the RAC.

★★★ **Gatwick Moat House,** Longbridge Roundabout, RH6 0AB ☎Crawley (0293) 785599 Tx: 877138 Fax: (0293) 785991

Large modern hotel with underground car park. Convenient for Gatwick. (QMH)
🛏 121 bedrs, 121 en suite; TV; tcf
🏨 lift, dogs,ns; P 120, coach; child facs; con 160

★★★ **Gatwick Post House,** Povey Cross Rd, RH6 0BA ☎Crawley (0293) 771621 Tx: 877351 Fax: (0293) 771054

Large modern hotel with garden and large car park. Near Gatwick. Swimming pool.
✗ Fr, De, Es. (THF)
🛏 216 bedrs, 216 en suite; TV; tcf
🏨 lift, dogs, ns; P 300, coach; child facs; con 100
✕ LD 10.30, coffee shop only Sat lunch
£ room £80–£90 (w/e £55), room (double) £90–£100; L £11, D £15; WB £45 (min 2 nts)
cc Access, Amex, B'card/Visa, CB, Diners.

Langshott Manor (Highly Acclaimed), Langshott, RH6 9LN ☎(0293) 786680 Fax: (0293) 783905. *Private Hotel.*
£ B&B £84·50–£92·50; HB weekly £630–£693; [5% V]

Cumberland House (Acclaimed), 39 Brighton Rd, RH6 7HH ☎(0293) 784379 Fax: (0293) 772001. *Hotel.*
£ B&B £25–£33; [10% V]
Gainsborough Lodge (Acclaimed), 39 Massetts Rd, RH6 7DT ☎(0293) 783982. *Guest House.*
Massetts Lodge (Acclaimed), 28 Massetts Rd, RH6 7DE ☎(0293) 782738. *Guest House.*
£ B&B £21–£32; HB weekly £141·75–£169·75; [10% V]
Mill Lodge (Acclaimed), 25 Brighton Rd, RH1 6PP ☎Horley (0293) 771170. *Guest House.*

Lawns, 30 Massetts Rd, RH6 7DE ☎(0293) 775751. *Guest House.*
£ B&B (double) £39; [10% V]
Melville Lodge, 15 Brighton Rd, RH6 7HH. *Guest House.* ☎(0293) 784951. ✗ Fr
£ B&B £20
Woodlands, 42 Massetts Rd, RH6 7DS ☎(0293) 782994. *Guest House.* Closed 23–31 Dec.
£ B&B £26; [10% V]
(*See advertisement on p. 255*)

HORNCASTLE Lincolnshire. Map 34B3

Pop 4,207. Sleaford 23, London 134, Boston 18, Lincoln 21, Louth 13, Skegness 21.
EC Wed. **MD** Thur, Sat. **Golf** Woodhall Spa 18h. **See** St Mary's Church.

★ **Bull,** Bull Ring, LN9 5HU ☎(065 82) 3331
Town-centre hotel of character. Focal point of this market town. Closed 24–26 Dec.
🛏 7 bedrs, 7 en suite; TV; tcf
🏨 dogs; P 30, coach; child facs; con 100

HORNCHURCH Greater London. Map 9B3

Pop 84,000. London 18, Brentwood 6½, Dartford Tunnel 8, Rainham 4, Romford 2½.
EC Thur. **See** Parish Church.

★★★★ **Hilton National Hornchurch,** Southend Arterial Rd, RM11 5UT ☎Ingrebourne (040 23) 46789 Tx: 897315 Fax: (040 23) 41719

A modern purpose-built hotel just off the M25. (HN)
🛏 137 bedrs, 137 en suite, TV; tcf
🏨 dogs, ns; P 170, coach; child facs; con 250
✕ LD 10
£ room £90–£120 (w/e £35), double room £100–£120, Bk £7·50, L £10, D £15
cc Access, Amex, B'card/Visa, Diners; dep.

HORNING Norfolk. Map 35C1

Pop 1,116. Norwich 10, London 122, Cromer 19, Fakenham 32, Great Yarmouth 17.
EC Wed. **Golf** Royal Norwich 18h, Mundesley 9h. **See** St Benet's Abbey ruins.

♣♣ ★★★ **C** **Petersfield House,** Lower St, NR12 8PF ☎(0692) 630741 Fax: (0692) 630745

Enlarged country house with water frontage and 2 acres of gardens. Putting.

H

🛏 18 bedrs, 18 en suite; TV; tcf
🏠 dogs; P 70; child facs; con 70
✕ LD 9.30
£ B&B £52–£58, B&B (double) £65–£75; L £12, D £14; WB £43 (HB)
cc Access, Amex, B'card/Visa, Diners; dep.

★★ Swan, NR12 8AA ☎(0692) 630316

A half-timbered, mock-Tudor building on the River Bure. Fishing.
🛏 11 bedrs, 11 en suite; TV; tcf
🏠 P 150, coach; child facs

HORNS CROSS Devon. Map 3A4

Pop 147. Bideford 5½, London 207, Bude 20, Holsworthy 14.
Golf Westward Ho! 18h.

♣ ★★★ H R Foxdown Manor, nr Bideford, EX39 5PJ ☎(023 75) 325
Well-appointed stone-built country house in secluded woodland. Attractive public rooms. Swimming pool, putting, tennis, sauna, solarium. Closed Feb 1–Mar 10.
🛏 6 bedrs, 6 en suite; 1 ba; TV; tcf
🏠 dogs; P 30; child facs; con 12
✕ LD 8.45, bar meals only Mon–Sat lunch. Resid & Rest lic
£ B&B £34–£42, B&B (double) £53–£68; HB weekly £240–£350; L £9, D £16; WB £80 (HB 2 nts)
cc Access, Amex, B'card/Visa; dep.

HORNSEA Humberside (North Humberside). Map 39B3

Pop 7,270. Beverley 13, London 192, Bridlington 15, Hull 17, Malton 36.
EC Wed. **MD** Sun. **Golf** Hallgate Park 18h.
See Church, Market Cross, Hornsea Potteries, Hornsea Mere.
ℹ Floral Hall. ☎(0964) 532919

Merlstead, 59 Eastgate, HU18 1NB ☎(0964) 533068. *Private Hotel.*
£ B&B £14–£22; HB weekly £120–£165; [5% V]

HORRABRIDGE Devon. Map 3A2

Pop 2,155. Exeter 34, London 203, Ashburton 20, Plymouth 11, Tavistock 4½.
EC Wed. **Golf** Tavistock 18h. **See** Dartmoor.

Overcombe (Acclaimed), nr Yelverton, PL20 7RN ☎Yelverton (0822) 853501. *Hotel.* ♿
£ B&B £18–£23; HB weekly £178–£205; [5% V]

HORSHAM West Sussex. Map 6B2

Pop 26,000. Dorking 13, London 36, Brighton 23, Crawley 8, Guildford 19, Haslemere 20, Haywards Heath 13, Pulborough 12.
EC Thur. **Golf** Mannings Heath 18h. **See** St Mary's Church, 16th cent North Chapel, Museum, Leonardslee Gardens 4½ m SE.
ℹ Museum, The Causeway ☎(0403) 211661

★★ Ye Olde King's Head, Carfax, RH12 1EG ☎(0403) 53126
Attractive 15th-century former coaching inn in the town centre. ⚒ De
🛏 43 bedrs; 42 en suite (1 sh), 1 ba; TV; tcf
🏠 dogs, ns; P 40, coach; child facs; con 50
✕ LD 9.45, bar meals only Sun dinner
£ B&B £49·50–£59·50 (w/e £32), B&B (double) £72; L £9·50, D £13·50
cc Access, Amex, B'card/Visa, Diners.

Blatchford House (Acclaimed), 52 Kings Rd, RH13 5PR ☎(0403) 65317. *Guest House. Sauna.*

Horsham Wimblehurst, 6 Wimblehurst Rd, RH12 2ED ☎(0403) 62319. Fax: (0403) 211212. *Hotel.*
£ B&B £39·50–£49·50; [5% V w/d]

HORTON Dorset. Map 5A2

Ringwood 9, London 102, Blandford Forum 11, Salisbury 21, Wimborne Minster 9½.

Northill House (Acclaimed), BH21 7HL ☎(0258) 840407. ⚒ De. *Hotel.* Open 14 Feb–20 Dec. ♿
£ B&B £28; HB weekly £233·10–£245·70

HORTON-CUM-STUDLEY

Oxfordshire. Map 21B2
Pop 458. M40 10, London 56, Aylesbury 17, Bicester 8½, Oxford 7½.
Golf North Oxford 18h.

♣ ★★★ Studley Priory, OX9 1AZ ☎Stanton St John (086 735) 203 Tx: 262433 Fax: (086 735) 613

Former 12th century nunnery and Elizabethan manor in 13 acres of attractive grounds. Tennis. ⚒ Fr
🛏 19 bedrs, 19 en suite; TV; tcf
🏠 coach; child facs; con 35
✕ LD 9.30
£ B&B £75–£100, B&B (double) £88–£135; L £28, D £28; WB £100
cc Access, Amex, B'card/Visa, Diners; dep.

HORTON-IN-RIBBLESDALE

North Yorkshire. Map 36C4
Pop 508. Settle 6, London 235, Hawes 16, Kirkby Lonsdale 18, Lancaster 26.
EC Wed. **See** Craven Caves, Church.
ℹ Pen-y-ghent Cafe. ☎(072 96) 333

Crown, nr Settle, BD24 0HF ☎(072 96) 209.
£ B&B £15·75–£19·80; HB weekly £164·50–£183·50

HORWICH Greater Manchester (Lancashire). Map 33A3

Pop 18,000. Wigan 6, London 201, M61 (jn 6) 3, Bolton 6, Manchester 18, Preston 14.
EC Wed. **MD** Tue, Fri. **Golf** Bolton 18h.

★★ Swallowfield, Chorley New Rd, BL6 6HN ☎(0204) 697914 Fax: (0204) 68900

Converted, modernised and extended late Victorian house in pleasant grounds. Closed 21 Dec–1 Jan.
🛏 31 bedrs, 31 en suite; TV; tcf
🏠 dogs; P35, coach; child facs; con 20
✕ LD 8.30, nr Sat–Sun lunch. Resid & Rest lic
£ B&B £37–£42 (w/e £32), B&B (double) £52–£57; HB weekly £322–£357; L £9, D £9; WB £45
cc Access, B'card/Visa; dep.

HOUNSLOW Greater London (Middx.), Map 8B2

Pop 105,000. M4 (jn 3) 2, London 10, Harrow 8½, Kingston upon Thames 6, Slough 11, Staines 7, Uxbridge 8½, Weybridge 9½.
EC Wed.

★★★ Master Robert, Great West Rd, TW5 0BA ☎081-570 6261 Tx: 9413782 Fax: 081-569 4016 ♿

Hotel with extensive modern motel-type accommodation. Near Heathrow.
🛏 63 bedrs, 63 en suite; TV; tcf
🏠 ns; P 160, coach; child facs; con 135
✕ LD 10.45
£ room £69–£75 (w/e £52), room double £85; Bk £4·25–£6·40; WB £45
cc Access, Amex, B'card/Visa, Diners.

HOVE East Sussex. Map 6C1

See also BRIGHTON.
Pop 89,000. Brighton 1½, London 54, Arundel 18, Pulborough 21, Worthing 9½.
See Plan of Brighton p. 000.
EC Wed. **P** See Plan for Brighton. **Golf** West Hove 18h. **See** All Saints' Church, Floral Clock, Brocke Scented Garden for the Blind, King Alfred Leisure Centre, British Engineerium, Hove Museum.
ℹ Town Hall. ☎(0273) 775400.

★★★★ Dudley, Lansdowne Pl, BN3 1HQ ☎Brighton (0273) 736266 Tx: 87537 Fax: (0273) 729802
Large Edwardian building in side road off seafront. Under refurbishment. ⚒ Fr. (THF)

 EC *early closing* **MD** *market day* ♣ *country house hotel* *ns (NS) no smoking areas* *tcf tea/coffee facilities*

Horsham (West Sussex)

Ghyll Manor Hotel

High Street, Rusper, Sussex RH12 4PX
Tel: 0293 871571 Fax: 0293 871419

Once an Ancestral Home, this beautiful hotel, with its beamed ceilings and open fires, offers elegant accommodation. The unique ambience of the library and restaurant provide the perfect setting to enjoy the excellent English cuisine.

Hull (North Humberside)

Humberside's Premier Hotel Complex

- 109 luxury bedrooms with every modern amenity
- Exclusive executive suites
- Fully equipped conference, seminar and exhibition facilities for 10 to 700 delegates
- 'The Cedars' country-style pub with Italian Restaurant
- French Gourmet Restaurant L'Eau Vive
- 'Club Tamarisk' leisure, health and beauty centre including large indoor swimming pool, sauna, whirlpool and modern gymnasium
- Parking for over 600 cars and helicopter landing site
- 12 acres of beautiful landscaped grounds

Best Western WORLDWIDE HOTELS

GRANGE PARK HOTEL

Beverly Road, Willerby, Hull
North Humberside HU10 6EA

Telephone (0482) 656488
Fax: (0482) 655848 Telex 592773

Hull (Humberside)

The *Award Winning* WATERFRONT HOTEL, CLUB & RESTAURANT

Dagger Lane, Old Town, Kingston upon Hull HU1 2LS

Situated in the heart of the old town, these Victorian Warehouses have been luxuriously converted and now offer first class accommodation, excellent food in beautiful surroundings, and the best Nightclub in Town. Winner of six national and international awards for its style and originality. Perfect for Weddings, Conferences, Functions, etc.
Egon Ronay recommended

80 bedrs, 80 en suite; TV; tcf
lift, dogs, ns; P 10, U 3 (£3·50), G 20 (£1·50) coach; child facs; con 150
LD 9.45
£ B&B £60–£63, B&B (double) £75–£79; HB weekly £260–£275; L £9·50, D £15·50; WB £40
cc Access, Amex, B'card/Visa, Diners.

★★★ Alexandra, 42 Brunswick Terr, BN3 1HA (0273) 202722 Tx: 877579
Fax: (0273) 204018
Large modernised Regency corner building on seafront on Hove–Brighton border. Sauna, solarium. De
61 bedrs, 61 en suite; TV; tcf
lift, dogs; coach; child facs; con 30
LD 9.30, bar meals only Mon–Sat lunch
£ B&B £59·50–£86·50 (w/e £25), B&B (double) £79·50–£95; HB weekly £393·50–£606·50; L £8, D £11; [10% V]
cc Access, Amex, B'card/Visa, Diners; dep.

★★★ Courtlands, 19 The Drive, BN3 3JE (0273) 731055 Tx: 87574
Fax: (0273) 28295
Former private residences, with terrace and garden. Indoor swimming pool, solarium.
53 bedrs, 53 en suite; annexe 5 bedrs, 5 en suite; TV; tcf
lift, TV, dogs, ns; P 26, coach; child facs; con 80

★★★ St Catherine's Lodge, Kingsway, BN3 2RZ (0273) 778181 Tx: 877073
Fax: (0273) 774949

A large Victorian detached building on main seafront road. Fr, Es, Gr
50 bedrs, 40 en suite, 5 ba; TV
lift, TV, dogs; P 4, U 4 (£4), coach; child facs; con 60
LD 9
£ B&B £36–£45 (w/e £30), B&B (double) £54–£65; HB weekly £190–£240; D £13·50; WB £40 (HB); [10% V]
cc Access, Amex, B'card/Visa, Diners; dep.

★★ R Whitehaven, 34 Wilbury Rd, BN3 3JP Brighton (0273) 778355 Tx: 877159
Fax: (0273) 731177

Yellow brick Victorian residence with secluded walled garden. Solarium.
17 bedrs, 17 en suite; TV; tcf
ns; coach; no children under 8; con 20
LD 9.45, nr Sat & Sun lunch, Sun dinner. Resid & Rest lic
£ B&B £42–£51, B&B (double) £56–£69; HB weekly £250–£370; L £13·50, D £13·50; WB £37·50 (HB min 2 nts)
cc Access, Amex, B'card/Visa, Diners.

Claremont House (Highly Acclaimed), Second Av, BN3 2LL (0273) 735161
Fax: (0273) 24764

Albany, St Catherine Terr, Kingsway, BN3 2RR (0273) 773807. *Private Hotel.*
£ B&B £19·50–£29·50.
Cornerways, 18 Caburn Rd, BN3 6EF (0273) 731882. *Private Hotel.* Fr
£ B&B £15; HB weekly £145
Croft, 24 Palmeria Av, BN3 3GB (0273) 732860. Fax: (0273) 820775. *Private Hotel.* Fr.
£ B&B £20–£25; [10% V]

HOVINGHAM North Yorkshire. Map 38C4

Pop 334. York 16, London 214, Helmsley 7½, Malton 8, Pickering 15, Thirsk 19.
EC Thur. **Golf** Gilling 18h. **See** Parish Church (Saxon tower).

★★★ Worsley Arms, High St, YO6 4LA (0653) 628234 Fax: (0653) 628130

Attractive 2-storey Georgian coaching inn in centre of peaceful village. Putting. Fr, De, It
14 bedrs, 14 en suite; annexe 9 bedrs, 9 en suite; TV
dogs; P 50; G 3; coach; child facs; con 40
LD 9
£ B&B £47–£52; B&B (double) £66–£74; L £8, D £16·50
cc Access, B'card/Visa; dep.

HOW CAPLE Hereford and Worcester. Map 20A2

Gloucester 19, London 123, Hereford 11.

★★ How Caple Grange, HR1 4TF (098 986) 208
Charming 2-storey stone building. Large garden. Swimming pool, putting, sauna, solarium, gymnasium.
26 bedrs, 18 en suite, 4 ba; TV; tcf
TV, dogs; P 100, coach; child facs; con 100
LD 8.30
£ B&B £37·75, B&B (double) £61·50; HB weekly £225; L £7·50, D £9·75; WB £74·75

HOWDEN Humberside (N. Humberside). Map 39A2

Pop 3,250. Goole 4, London 183, M62 (jn 37) 1, Beverley 19, Hull 23, Market Weighton 12, Selby 10, York 20.
EC Wed. **Golf** Spaldington 18h. **See** Church of St Peter, Shire Hall.

★★★ Bowmans, Bridgegate, DN14 7JG (0430) 430805

Three-storey stone-built former coaching inn of character. In town centre.
13 bedrs, 10 en suite, 3 ba; TV; tcf
dogs, ns; P 80; child facs; con 12

HOWTOWN Cumbria. Map 44A1

Windermere 23, London 264, M6 (jn 40) 9, Keswick 22, Penrith 8.

★★★ Sharrow Bay, Sharrow Bay, CA10 2LZ Pooley Bridge (076 84) 86483
Fax: (076 84) 86349

Lovely stone-built lakeside hotel renowned for its furnishings. Open early Mar– late Nov.
12 bedrs, 8 en suite, 2 ba; annexe 18 bedrs, 18 en suite; TV; tcf
ns; P 30, G 2; no children under 13; con 12
LD 8.45. Resid & Rest lic
£ B&B & dinner £77–£125; L £23, D £35

HUBBERHOLME North Yorkshire. Map 38A4

Skipton 14, London 218, Bainbridge 18, Grassington 8.

Kirkgill Manor (Highly Acclaimed), BD23 5JE (075 676) 800. *Guest House.* Closed Dec.

HUDDERSFIELD West Yorkshire. Map 40C2

See also MARSDEN
Pop 123,168. Sheffield 26, London 180, M62 (jn 24) 2½, Barnsley 17, Bradford 10, Halifax 7, Leeds 15, Oldham 18.
EC Wed. **MD** Mon, Thur. **Golf** Bradley Park 18h. **See** Town Hall, Art Gallery, Roman remains, Museum, Castle Hill Tower, Kirklees Hall, Scammonden Dam.
i 3 Albion St. (0484) 430808

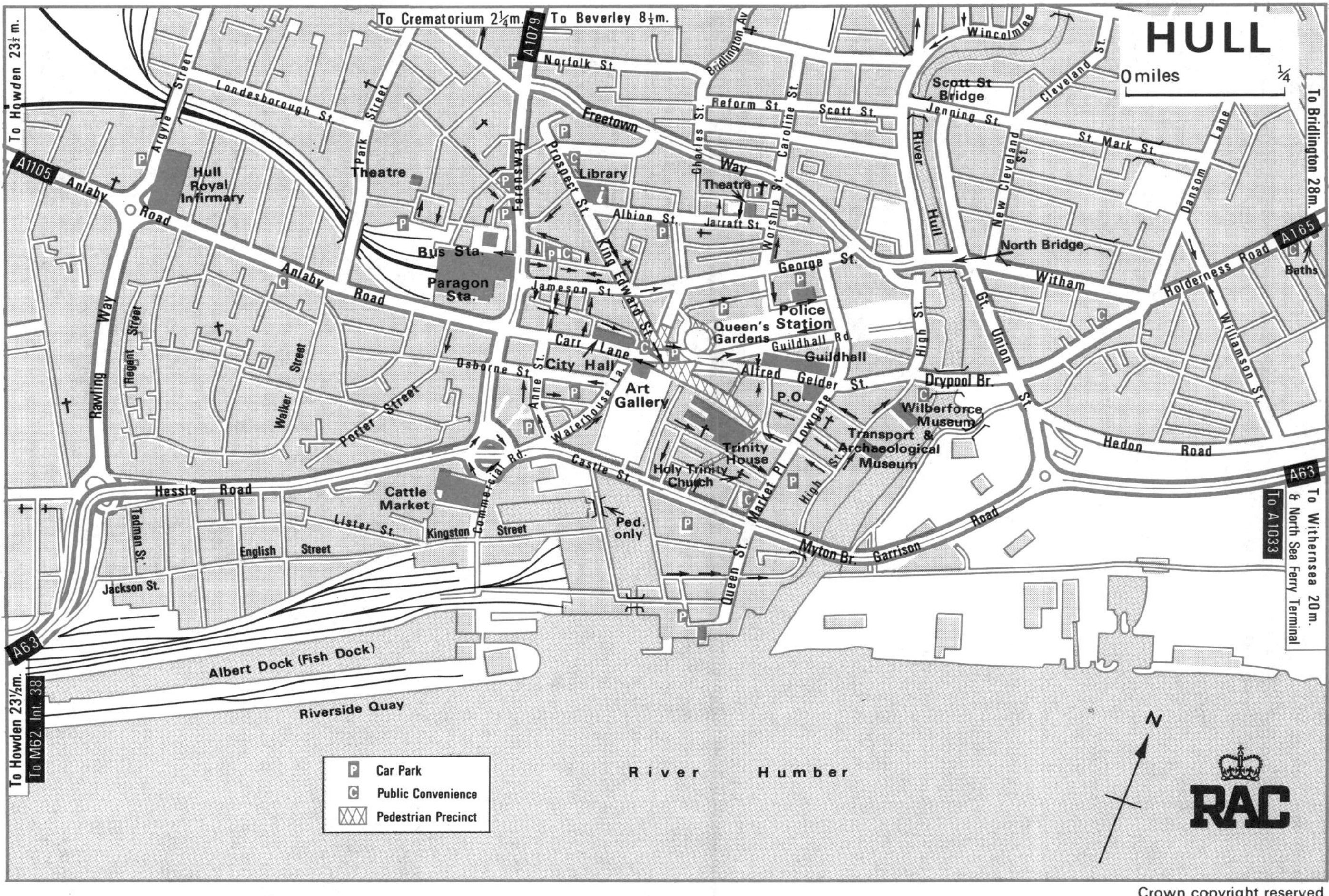
HULL
0 miles
1/4
To Crematorium 2¼m.
A1079
To Beverley 8½m.
To Bridlington 28m.
A165
Baths
To Howden 23¼m.
A1105
To Withernsea 20m.
& North Sea Ferry Terminal
A63
To A1033
To Howden 23½m.
To M62. Int. 38
Wincolmlee
Norfolk St.
Bridlington Av.
Scott St Bridge
Cleveland St.
Jenning St.
Londesborough St.
Argyle Street
Street
Park Street
Freetown
Reform St.
Scott St.
Charles St.
Caroline St.
River Hull
New Cleveland St.
St. Mark St.
Dansom Lane
Hull Royal Infirmary
Anlaby Road
Theatre
Ferensway
Prospect St.
Library
Way
Theatre
Worship St.
Albion St.
Jarratt St.
North Bridge
Witham
Holderness Road
Bus Sta.
Paragon Sta.
George St.
King Edward St.
Jameson St.
Police Station
Queen's Gardens
Guildhall Rd.
Guildhall
High St.
Gt. Union St.
Williamson St.
Rawling Way
Regent Street
Walker Street
Carr Lane
City Hall
Osborne St.
Anne St.
Art Gallery
Alfred Gelder St.
Drypool Br.
P.O.
Lowgate
Wilberforce Museum
Transport & Archaeological Museum
Hedon Road
Porter Street
Waterhouse La.
Trinity House
Holy Trinity Church
Commercial Rd.
Castle St.
Market Pl.
High St.
Hessle Road
Cattle Market
Lister St.
Kingston Street
Ped. only
Queen St.
Myton Br.
Garrison Road
Tadman St.
English Street
Jackson St.
Albert Dock (Fish Dock)
Riverside Quay
Car Park
Public Convenience
Pedestrian Precinct
River Humber
N
RAC
Crown copyright reserved

★★★ Briar Court, Halifax Rd, Birchencliffe, HD3 3NT ☎(0484) 519902 Tx: 518260 Fax: (0484) 431812
A modern, stone-fronted building set back from the A629 some 2 miles from M62. It, Es
48 bedrs, 48 en suite; TV; tcf
P 140, coach; child facs; con 90
LD 10.45
£ B&B £60 (w/e £35), B&B (double) £75; L £8·50, D £11·50
cc Access, Amex, B'card/Visa, Diners.

★★★ Flying Horse, Nettleton Hill Rd, Scapegoat Hill, HD7 4NY ☎(0484) 642368 Fax: (0484) 642866
Much extended stone-built moorland farmhouse in spectacular position with views over Huddersfield and surrounding valleys.
33 bedrs, 33 en suite; TV; tcf
£ B&B £54·80 (w/e £25), B&B (double) £68·50 (w/e £30); D £10·50.

★★★ George, St George's Sq, HD1 1JA ☎(0484) 515444
Five-storey stone-built hotel of character situated in town centre. Fr, It. (THF)
60 bedrs, 60 en suite; TV; tcf
lift, dogs, ns; P 12, coach; child facs; con 200
LD 10, bar meals only Sat lunch
£ B&B £66·95 (w/e £22·50), B&B (double) £81·75; L £6·50, D £12·95; WB £35 (HB)
cc Access, Amex, B'card/Visa, Diners.

★★★ Old Golf House, New Hey Rd, Outlane, HD3 3YP ☎(0422) 379311 Tx: 51324 Fax: (0422) 372694
Three-storey, stone-built hotel with modern extensions, once the club house of a golf course. Situated next to M62, at junction 23. Sauna, solarium, gymnasium. (Lns)
50 bedrs, 50 en suite; TV; tcf
ns; P 70, coach; child facs; con 70
LD 10
£ B&B £65–£75, B&B (double) £77–£88; L £9·50, D £13·75; WB £23; [10% V]
cc Access, Amex, B'card/Visa, Diners.

★★★ Pennine Hilton National, Ainley Top, HD3 3RH ☎Elland (0422) 377822 Tx: 517346 Fax: (0422) 310067
Modern hotel of striking design adjacent to M62. Fine Pennine views. Indoor swimming pool, sauna, gymnasium. (HN) Fr.
118 bedrs, 118 en suite; TV; tcf
lift, dogs, ns; P 170, coach; child facs; con 400
LD 10, nr Sat lunch
£ B&B £85·95–£105 (w/e £35), B&B (double) £106·90–£109; D £15·50; [10% V]
cc Amex, B'card/Visa, Diners.

★★ Huddersfield, 34 Kirkgate, HD1 1QT ☎(0484) 512111 Tx: 51575 Fax: (0484) 435262
Pleasant modern conversion of a Georgian building in town centre. Sauna, solarium. It
37 bedrs, 37 en suite, 1 ba; TV; tcf
lift, TV, dogs; P 40, coach; child facs; con 50
LD 12 midnight, bar meals only Sun
£ B&B £36–£46 (w/e £17·50); L £3·50, D £7·50; [10% V]
cc Access, Amex, B'card/Visa, CB, Diners.

HULL
Humberside (North Humberside). Map 35B4
Pop 271,000. Lincoln 42, London 175, Beverley 8½, Bridlington 30, Goole 33, Scunthorpe 26, Grimsby 31.
See Plan, p. 295.
EC Thur. **MD** Tue, Fri, Sat. **P** See Plan. **Golf** Springhead 18h, Sutton 18h. **See** Wilberforce House Museum, Holy Trinity Church, St Mary's Church.
Library, Albion St. ☎(0482) 223344

★★★★ Marina Post House, Castle St, HU1 2BX ☎(0482) 225221 Tx: 592777 Fax: (0482) 213299
Four-storey hotel overlooking the yacht marina in the old dock area. Indoor swimming pool, putting, sauna, solarium, gymnasium. (THF)
99 bedrs, 99 en suite, 2 ba; TV; tcf
lift; dogs, ns; P 150, coach; child facs; con 120
LD 10.30
£ room £67–£77 (w/e £39·50), room double £77–£87; Bk £5·50–£7·50, L £10·95, D £14·50; WB £38 (HB)
cc Access, Amex, B'card/Visa, CB, Diners.

★★★ Crest Hull-Humber Bridge, Ferriby High Rd, North Ferriby, HU14 3LG ☎(0482) 645212 Tx: 592558 Fax: (0482) 643332

Modern hotel in own grounds overlooking river and Humber Bridge. (Cr/THF)
102 bedrs, 102 en suite; TV; tcf
dogs, ns; P 100, coach; child facs; con 100

★★★ C R Grange Park, Main St, Willerby, HU10 6EA ☎(0482) 656488 Tx: 592773 Fax: (0482) 655848
Substantial early Victorian house in large garden next to A164. Indoor swimming pool, sauna, solarium, gymnasium. It, Fr, Es
109 bedrs, 109 en suite; TV; tcf
lift, dogs; P 600, coach; child facs; con 600
LD 10.30
£ B&B £58·50–£88·50 (w/e £41), B&B (double) £78·50–£99·50; L £9·50, D £12·50; WB £85; [5% V]
cc Access, Amex, B'card/Visa.
(*See advertisement on p. 293*)

★★★ Pearson Park, Pearson Park, HU5 2TQ ☎(0482) 43043 Fax: (0482) 447679

Large Victorian building situated in public park north of city centre. Closed 24 Dec–1 Jan.
35 bedrs, 29 en suite, (4 sh), 1 ba; TV; tcf
dogs; P 30, coach; child facs; con 36
LD 9, nr Sun dinner. Resid & Rest lic
£ B&B £26–£42 (w/e £19·50), B&B (double) £39–£54; L £5, D £9·50; WB; [5% V]
cc Access, Amex, B'card/Visa, Diners.
(*See advertisement on p. 297*)

★★★ Rowley Manor, Little Weighton, HU20 3XR ☎(0482) 848248 Fax: (0482) 849900
Attractive Georgian country house set in lawns and rose gardens. Solarium.
16 bedrs, 16 en suite; TV; tcf
dogs; P 100, coach; child facs; con 60

★★★ Stakis Paragon, 65 Paragon St, HU1 3JP ☎(0482) 26462 Tx: 592431
A modern 6-storey hotel situated near station in centre. Car parking service. (Sk)
124 bedrs, 124 en suite; TV; tcf
lift, dogs, ns, coach; child facs; con 220

★★★ Waterfront, Dagger La, Old Town, HU1 2LS ☎(0482) 227222 Fax: (0482) 22722
Fine Victorian warehouse, successfully converted into luxury hotel of character. Fr, De, Es
30 bedrs, 30 en suite; TV; tcf
dogs; P 16, G 7; coach; child facs; con 100
LD 10.15, coffee shop only Mon-Sat lunch & Sun dinner
£ B&B £63·95 (w/e £25·50), B&B (double) £79·90 (w/e £40); D £8·95; [10% V w/d]
cc Access, B'card/Visa.
(*See advertisement on p. 293*)

★★★ H C R Willerby Manor, Well La, Willerby, HU10 6ER (4½ m W on A164). ☎(0482) 652616 Tx: 592629 Fax: (0482) 653901
Large attractive manorial building in 3 acres of gardens. Lesuire complex planned. Fr, De
36 bedrs, 36 en suite; TV; tcf
dogs; P 200; child facs; con 500
LD 9.30, coffee shop only Sat lunch & Sun dinner
£ B&B £56–£59 (w/e £35), B&B (double) £69–£75 (w/e £45); L £9, D £12·50; [10% V]
cc Access, Amex, B'card/Visa.

★★ Maxim's, 394 Anlaby Av, HU3 6PB ☎(0482) 509660 Fax: (0482) 51606
Victorian building in Dutch colonial style on main road, west of city centre.
14 bedrs, 14 en suite; TV; tcf
TV; P 30, coach; child facs; con 100
LD 9.30, nr Sun dinner
£ B&B £32 (w/e £28), B&B (double) £44 (w/e £36); [10% V]
cc Access, B'card/Visa.
(*See advertisement on p. 297*)

Earlsmere (Acclaimed), 76 Sunnybank, off Spring Bank West, HU3 1LQ ☎Hull City (0482) 41977 Tx: 592729 Fax: (0482) 214121. *Hotel.*

Roseberry, 86 Marlborough Av, HU5 3JJ. ☎(0482) 445256. Fr, De. *Guest house.*
£ B&B £17

HUNGERFORD
Berkshire. Map 5B4
Pop 3,900. Newbury 9, London 63, M4 (jn 14) 3, Marlborough 10, Pewsey 14, Salisbury 30, Swindon 17, Wantage 14.
EC Thur. **Golf** Newbury and Chaddleworth 18h. **See** Church, old Bear Inn.

Hull (Humberside)

PEARSON PARK HOTEL

The Hotel in the Park ***

PEARSON PARK, HULL HU5 2TQ
Telephone: (0482) 43043

Proprietors: D.A. & I. Atkinson

Situated in a public park with rose gardens, bowling greens and conservatory, the hotel has extensive open views. All 35 rooms have telephone, radio, television, tea making facilities and most have private bathrooms. There are comfortable lounges, an excellent restaurant, all-day coffee shop and good conference facilities.

Hull (North Humberside)

THE CAMPANILE HOTEL – Hull

Beverley Road, Freetown Way, Kingston-upon-Hull HU2 9AN

Tel: (0482) 25530 Telex: 592840

Restaurant Hotel

Campanile

Part of the international budget hotel chain "Campanile", the hotel offers 50 comfortable double or twin rooms with en-suite bathrooms, and tea/coffee making facilities, radio alarm, remote control colour TV, Sky TV and direct dial telephone at **competitive rates.**

Our informal restaurant provides a variety of home-cooked French/ Continental cuisine, and personal service at **affordable prices.**

Our seminar room is available for business meetings or small functions.

Your hosts: Helen & Jonathan Kinghorn

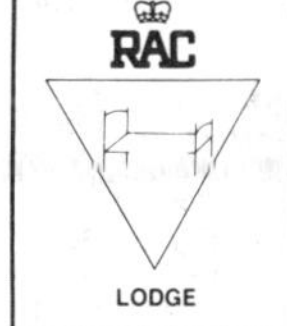

Hull (Humberside)

Maxim's

Hotel & Restaurant

394 Anlaby Road, Hull HU3 6PB
Telephone: (0482) 509660 Fax: (0482) 51606

Independently owned, friendly, town centre hotel, close to all amenities. Cocktail bar, à la carte restaurant. All rooms en-suite, TV, phone and tea making facilities.

Huntingdon (Cambridgeshire)

Alconbury House Hotel,
Alconbury Weston,
Huntingdon, Cambs PE17 5JG
Telephone: 0480 890807 Fax: 0480 891259
MANAGED BY PEAK HOTELS

RAC ★★

PEAK

Alconbury House Hotel

Enjoy the warm welcome and charming surroundings of the Alconbury House Hotel. This delightful 18th century house has been tastefully refurbished to offer first class facilities.

Set in 2½ acres of grounds Alconbury House is just off the A1, 5 miles from the centre of Huntingdon.

Enjoy a drink in the attractive Garden Room lounge bar. Bar meals are available and the hotel's restaurant serves the very best cuisine.

All 26 bedrooms are en-suite, decorated to a high standard, with colour t.v., telephone and tea and coffee making facilities.

For your added enjoyment, we have 3 squash courts, sauna, solarium and snooker room.

The Courthills Suite is available for banquets of up to 80 people.

Car parking is excellent.

★★★ R **Bear**, Charnham St, RG17 0EL ☎(0488) 682512 Tx: 477575 Fax: (0488) 684357

13th century former coaching inn, with Civil War connections. On A4. Es, Fr, Pol, Du
32 bedrs, 32 en suite; annexe 9 bedrs, 9 en suite; TV; tcf
dogs, ns; P 80; child facs; con 100
LD 9.30
£ B&B £66·50–£81·50, B&B (double) £79–£101·50; HB weekly £456; L £13·95, D £17·95; WB £84 (HB 2 nts); [5% V w/e]
cc Access, Amex, B'card/Visa, Diners.

Marshgate Cottage (Acclaimed), Marsh La, RG17 0QX ☎(0488) 682307. *Private hotel.* Fr, De, Sw, No, Da. Open 25 Jan–24 Dec.
£ B&B £23·50–£33; [5% V Nov–Apr]

HUNSTANTON Norfolk. Map 34C2

Pop 3,990. King's Lynn 16, London 115, Cromer 37, Fakenham 19, Swaffham 24. **EC** Thur. **MD** Wed. **Golf** Hunstanton 18h. **See** Church of St Mary the Virgin, St Edmunds Chapel ruins, Lighthouse.
[i] The Green. ☎(048 53) 2610

★★★ **Le Strange Arms,** Old Hunstanton, PE36 6JJ ☎(048 53) 34411 Tx: 817403 Fax: (04853) 34724
By the sea, a large 19th century building with fine views across the Wash. Tennis, billiards. De
26 bedrs, 26 en suite; TV; tcf
dogs; P 120, coach; child facs; con 200
LD 9
£ B&B £45–£50, B&B (double) £62–£67; L £12·50, D £12·50
cc Access, Amex, B'card/Visa, Diners; dep.

★★ **Caley Hall Motel**, Old Hunstanton, PE36 6HH ☎(0485) 533486

A 17th century manor house plus modern bedroom blocks set round a patio. Snooker. Closed 1 Jan–1 Mar
28 bedrs, 28 en suite; TV, tcf
dogs; P50, coach; child facs; con 70
LD 9; nr Mon–Sat lunch & Sun dinner, Resid & Rest lic
£ B&B £33–£36; B&B (double) £46–£52; HB weekly £206·50–£227·10; L £10·50, D £10·50; WB £64 (HB 2 nts); [5% V]
cc Access, B'card/Visa.

★★ **Lodge,** Cromer Rd, Old Hunstanton, PE36 6WX ☎(048 53) 2896

Owner-run 17th century former Dower House, 2 miles from town centre. Billiards.
16 bedrs, 16 en suite, TV; tcf
dogs; P 70, coach; child facs; con 20
LD 9.30
£ B&B £30, B&B (double) £48–£60, L £8·95, D £8·95; WB
cc Access, Amex, B'card/Visa.

Sunningdale (Highly Acclaimed), 3 Avenue Rd, PE36 5BW ☎(0485) 532562. *Hotel.*
£ B&B £25–£26·50; [10% V]

Deepdene (Acclaimed), 29 Avenue Rd, PE36 5BW ☎(048 53) 2460 Fax: (048 53) 2460. *Hotel, Indoor swimming pool, sauna, solarium, gymnasium, billiards:* Closed Oct.
£ B&B £22·50; HB weekly £252

Linksway (Acclaimed), Golf Course Rd, Old Hunstanton PE36 6JE ☎(048 53) 2209. *Private Hotel. Indoor swimming pool.*
£ B&B £27·50; [5% V]

HUNSTRETE Avon Map 4C3

Bath 10, London 114, Bristol 11, Shipham 17, Shepton Mallet 17

★★★★ H C **Hunstrete House**, BS18 4NS ☎(0761) 490490 Tx: 449540 Fax: (0761) 490732
A beautifully furnished and professionally run 18th-century stone house set in 90 acres of parkland with very attractive gardens. Swimming pool, tennis. Fr, De
24 bedrs, 24 en suite; TV
ns, P 40; children over 9; con 40
LD 10, Resid lic
£ B&B fr £95, B&B (double) fr £170; L £15, D £32
cc Access, B'card/Visa.
(See advertisement on p. 124)

HUNTINGDON Cambridgeshire. Map 26B4

Pop 18,155 (inc Godmanchester). Royston 21, London 62, Biggleswade 20, Cambridge 16, Ely 21, Kettering 26, Peterborough 19, Stamford 27, Wisbech 33. **EC** Wed. **MD** Sat. **Golf** St Ives (Hunts) 9h. **See** All Saints' Church, Cromwell Museum, Town Hall, Bridge, Cowper's House.
[i] Library, Princes St. ☎(0480) 425831

Atlas Section
Consult the Atlas section at the back of the guide to find out which towns and villages have RAC Appointed and Listed hotels in them. They are shown on the maps by purple circles.

★★★ **George,** George St, PE18 6AB ☎(0480) 432444 Fax: (0480) 453130

Historic old posting inn with attractive galleried inner courtyard. Fr. (THF)
24 bedrs, 24 en suite; TV; tcf
dogs, ns; P 70, coach; child facs; con 120
LD 9.30
£ B&B £79, B&B (double) £103; L £9, D £14; WB £40 (2 nts min)
cc Access, Amex, B'card/Visa, CB, Diners.

★★★ R **Old Bridge,** High St, PE18 6TQ ☎(0480) 52681 Tx: 32706 Fax: (0480) 411071
A renovated 18th century Georgian hotel on the river bank. Fishing. Fr, It
26 bedrs, 26 en suite; TV
dogs; P 50, coach; child facs; con 50
LD 10.30
£ B&B £65–£80 (w/e £42), B&B (double) £88–£100; L £16·95, D £19·95; WB £49·50 (HB)
cc Access, Amex, B'card/Visa, Diners.

★★ **Alconbury House,** Alconbury Weston, PE17 5JG ☎(0480) 890807 Fax: (0480) 891259
Three-storey grey-brick hotel in rural area on A1. Squash, sauna, solarium, snooker. Fr
22 bedrs, 22 en suite; TV; tcf
dogs, ns; P 60, coach; child facs; con 100
LD 9.30
£ B&B £25–£49·50 (£20 w/e), B&B (double) £40–£60·50; L £10·95, D £10·95; WB £30 (HB); [10% V w/e]
cc Access, Amex, B'card/Visa, Diners.
(See advertisement on p. 296)

HURLEY Berkshire. Map 12C3

Maidenhead 5, London 31, High Wycombe 8½, Reading 12, Oxford 28, Wantage 30.

★★★ R **Ye Olde Bell,** nr Maidenhead, SL6 5LX ☎Littlewick Green (062 882) 5881 Fax: (062 882) 5939
White-faced gabled building dating from 12th century. Large attractive garden. (THF)
10 bedrs, 10 en suite; annexe 15 bedrs, 8 en suite; TV; tcf
dogs, ns; P 90, coach; con 140
LD 9.30
£ B&B £76·50–£91·50, B&B (double) £98–£103; L £14·50 (£17·50 Sun), D £16·50; WB £64 (2 nts min)
cc Access, Amex, B'card/Visa, CB, Diners.

★★ **East Arms,** Henley Rd, Nr Maidenhead, SL6 5LS ☎Littlewick Green (062 882) 3227
Privately-owned former coaching inn in pleasant surroundings. Fr
7 bedrs, 7 en suite; annexe 4 bedrs, 1 ba; TV; tcf
dogs; P120, coach; child facs; con 100
LD 10
£ B&B £35–£60 (w/e £20); B&B (double) £45–£70; WB £61 (HB 2 nts); [10% V, not Dec 24–31]
cc Access, Amex, B'card/Visa.

EC *early closing* **MD** *market day* *country house hotel* *ns (NS) no smoking areas* *tcf tea/coffee facilities*

HURSTBOURNE TARRANT Hampshire

Map 5C3
Newbury 11, London 65, Andover 7, Marlborough 22, Whitchurch 10.

★★ **H C Esseborne Manor,** SP11 0ER ☎(0264) 76444 Fax: (0264) 76473 ♿
Charming Victorian house in lovely countryside near the A 343, now a delightful, owner-run hotel. Putting, tennis. Fr
12 bedrs, 12 en suite; TV
P 50; children over 12; con 12
LD 9.30. Resid & Rest lic
£ B&B £77, B&B (double) £95–£125; L £12·80, D £27·59; WB £170 (HB, 2 nts); [10% V]
cc Access, Amex, B'card/Visa, Diners.

HURST GREEN Lancashire. Map 36B3

Pop 800. Whalley 4½, London 215, Blackburn 9, Blackpool 26, Preston 12, Settle 24.
Golf Whalley 9h.

★★★ **Shireburn Arms,** Whalley Rd, BB6 9QJ ☎Stonyhurst (025 486) 518

Privately-owned and run 17th century hotel in quiet countryside. Putting, fishing. Fr. *Closed New Year.*
14 bedrs, 14 en suite; TV; tcf
dogs; P 120, coach; con 75
LD 9.30
£ B&B £39–£42·50, B&B (double) £57·50–£62·50; L £7·25, D £12·50; WB £87·50
cc Access; B'card/Visa; dep.
(*See advertisement on p. 296*)

HYDE Gtr Manchester. Map 33C2

Stockport 7, London 186, M67 (jn 3) 1, Ashton under Lyne 4, Glossop 6, Manchester 8.

Needhams Farm (Acclaimed), Uplands Rd, Werneth Low, Gee Cross, SK14 3AQ ☎061-368 4610 Fax: 061-367 9160
£ B&B £15–£16·50; HB weekly £140–£150; [5% V]

HYTHE Kent. Map 7C2

Pop 12,200. Ashford 11, London 66, Canterbury 17, Folkestone 5, Rye 21.
EC Wed. **Golf** Hythe Imperial 9h. **See** St Leonard's Church and Crypt, Romney, Hythe and Dymchurch Light Rly, Royal Military Canal, Port Lympne Zoo Park.
Prospect Rd. ☎(0303) 267799.

★★★★ **Imperial,** Prince's Par, CT21 6AE ☎(0303) 267441 Tx: 965082 Fax: (0303) 264610 ♿
Impressive seafront hotel set in 52 acres, with splendid sea views. Indoor swimming pool, golf, putting, tennis, squash, sauna, solarium, gymnasium, billiards. Fr, De
100 bedrs, 100 en suite; TV; tcf
lift, ns; P 200, coach; child facs; con 200
LD 9.15 (Fri/Sat 10)
£ B&B £70–£90, B&B (double) £200–£260; WB £100 (2 nts HB)
cc Access, Amex, B'card/Visa, Diners; dep.

★★★ **Fredericks,** 95 Seabrook Rd, CT21 5QY ☎(0303) 67279
Elegant small hotel in a beamed and gabled Edwardian building overlooking the sea. On A259 between Hythe and Folkestone.

★★★ **Stade Court,** West Par, CT21 6DT ☎(0303) 268263 Tx: 965082 Fax: (0303) 264610
Modernised hotel with dramatic sea views. Shares sports facilities with Imperial Hotel.
43 bedrs, 43 en suite; TV; tcf
lift, dogs, P 20, U 3 (£3), coach; child facs; con 35
LD 9
£ B&B £48–£55, B&B (double) £75; L £10, D £15
cc Access, Amex, B'card/Visa, Diners; dep.

ILFORD Greater London (Essex). Map 9A3

Pop 178,024. London 11, Epping 11, Rainham 7, Romford 5, Woodford 4.
EC Thur. Golf Ilford 18h.

Cranbrook, 24 Coventry Rd, IG1 4QR ☎01-081-554 6544. *Hotel.* ♿
Park, 327 Cranbrook Rd, IG1 4UE ☎081-554 5010. Fax: 081-518 2700. *Hotel.* Fr, De, It
£ B&B £27·50–£37

ILFRACOMBE Devon. Map 3A4

Pop 10,000. Dunster 36, London 201, Barnstaple 11, Lynmouth 18.
EC Thur. **MD** Sat. **Golf** Ilfracombe 18h. **See** Holy Trinity Church, Museum, 14th cent Chapel of St Nicholas on Lantern Hill.
The Promenade. ☎(0271) 63001

★★★ **Trimstone Manor,** Trimstone, EX34 8NR ☎(0271) 62841

Two-storey manor house with adjacent leisure centre set in 50 acres of grounds, 3 miles south of Ilfracombe. Indoor swimming pool, putting, tennis, fishing, squash, sauna, solarium, gymnasium, billiards.
17 bedrs, 17 en suite, 1 ba; TV; tcf
TV; NS; P 60; child facs; con 80
LD 8.30, bar meals only Mon–Sat lunch, Sun dinner. Resid lic
£ B&B & dinner £28–£35, B&B (double) & dinner £160–£190; D £10·25; [5% V excl. July & Aug and cc payments]
cc Access, B'card/Visa; dep.

★★ **Arlington,** Sommors Cres, EX34 9DT ☎(0271) 862002. Fax: (0271) 862015
Bay-windowed, 5-storey hotel overlooking harbour and coast. Family run. Swimming pool, sauna, solarium. Open Mar–Oct & Xmas–New Year.
29 bedrs, 29 en suite; TV; tcf
lift, dogs; P 30; coach, child facs; con 70
LD 8.30, nr lunch. Resid & Rest lic
£ B&B £29·70–£40·70; HB weekly £192·50–£256·10; D £12·50; WB £50
cc Access, Amex, B'card/Visa; dep.

★★ **Carlton,** Runnacleave Rd, EX34 8AR ☎(0271) 62446 Fax: (0271) 865379

Large Victorian building in own grounds close to sea.
50 bedrs, 40 en suite, 7 ba; TV; tcf
lift, dogs; P 18, coach; child facs; con 50
LD 8.30, bar meals only lunch
£ B&B £17·50–£23·50, HB weekly £160–£195; D £10·50; [5% V]
cc Access, Amex, B'card/Visa; dep.

★★ **Elmfield,** Torrs Park, EX34 8AZ ☎(0271) 63377
Brick-built Victorian mansion with a terraced garden. Indoor swimming pool, sauna, solarium, gymnasium. Open Easter–Nov.
12 bedrs, 11 en suite, 1 ba; TV; tcf
ns; P 14; no children under 8
LD 7.30, bar meals only lunch. Resid & Rest lic
£ B&B £30–£33; HB weekly £185–£200; D £9·50; WB £87.
cc Access, Amex, B'card/Visa; dep.

★★ **Imperial,** Wilder Rd, EX34 9AL ☎(0271) 862536 Fax: (0271) 862571
Privately-owned Victorian building on main road with Bay views. Open Apr–Oct.
105 bedrs, 105 en suite; TV; tcf
lift, TV, dogs; P 12, coach; child facs
LD 7.45. Resid & Rest lic
£ B&B £20–£30; HB weekly £155–£190; D £9
cc Access, B'card/Visa.

★★ **Langleigh,** Langleigh Rd, EX34 8EA ☎(0271) 62629
In very attractive garden with stream, a substantial former manor house. Solarium.

★★ **St Helier,** Hillsborough Rd, EX34 9QQ ☎(0271) 864906

Modern family-run hotel in a terrace overlooking the sea. Fr, De. Open May–Oct.
23 bedrs, 17 en suite, 2 ba; TV; tcf
TV, dogs; P 20, G 9; child facs

✕ LD 8, nr lunch
£ B&B £18–£20, B&B (double) £34–£38; HB weekly £140–£170; D £6·50
cc Access, B'card/Visa; dep.

★★ **Tracy House,** Belmont Rd, EX34 8DR ☎(0271) 863933

In quiet area, stone-built Victorian residence in acre of walled garden. Putting. Open Apr–Sep.
🛏 11 bedrs, 9 en suite, 1 ba; TV; tcf
⌂ dogs; P 11, U 1; child facs
✕ LD 8, nr lunch. Resid & Rest lic
£ B&B £20–£26, B&B (double) £35·50–£53; HB weekly £157–£194; D £8·50; WB £70 (3 nts HB); [5% V]
cc Access, Amex, B'card/Visa; dep.

★ **Torrs,** Torrs Park, EX34 8AY ☎(0271) 862334

Victorian house with grounds in a quiet part of town. Solarium. Open 9 Mar–Oct.
🛏 14 bedrs, 14 en suite; TV; tcf
⌂ dogs, ns; P 12; no children under 5
✕ LD 7.30. Resid & Rest lic
£ B&B £18–£19·50; HB weekly £164·50–£182; L £6·50, D £8·50; [10% Mar–May, Sep–Oct]
cc Access, Amex, B'card/Visa, Diners; dep.

Avalon (Acclaimed), 6 Capstone Cres, EX34 9BT ☎(0271) 863325. *Hotel.*
£ B&B £16·50; HB weekly £112–£127; [10% V]

Avoncourt (Acclaimed), Torrs Walk Av, EX34 8AU ☎(0271) 862543. *Hotel.*

Cairngorm (Acclaimed), 43 St Brannocks Rd, EX34 8EH ☎(0271) 863911. *Hotel.* Open Mar–Nov.
£ B&B £19–£22; HB weekly £168–£175; [10% V]

Gables (Acclaimed), 1 Belmont Rd, EX34 8DR ☎(0271) 862475. *Private Hotel.* Open Apr–Oct.
£ B&B £16; HB weekly £143·50–£164·50; [10% V]

Rosslyn (Acclaimed), 15 St Brannocks Rd, EX34 8EG ☎(0271) 862643. Open Mar–Dec. *Guest House.* ⚒ Fr
£ B&B £14; HB weekly £140–£175; [5% V Mar–May, Oct–Dec]

Southcliffe (Acclaimed), Torrs Park, EX34 8AZ ☎(0271) 862958. *Hotel.* Open May–15 Sep.
£ HB weekly £153–£159

South Tor (Acclaimed), Torrs Park, EX34 8AZ ☎(0271) 863750. *Hotel.*

Strathmore (Acclaimed), 57 St Brannocks Rd, EX34 8EQ ☎(0271) 862248. *Private Hotel.* Open Easter–Sep.
£ B&B £15; HB weekly £159·50

Trafalgar (Acclaimed), Larkstone Terr, EX34 9NU ☎(0271) 862145. *Hotel.*
£ B&B £25–£27·50; HB weekly £150–£175; [10% V]

Wildercombe House (Acclaimed), St Brannocks Rd, EX34 8EP ☎(0271) 862240 *Hotel.* ⚒ Fr, De
£ B&B £18·50–£20; HB weekly £170–£185; [10% V]

Avenue, Greenclose Rd, EX34 8BT ☎(0271) 863767. *Hotel.*
£ B&B £14–£18·50; HB weekly £140–£180; [5% V]

Beaufort, Torrs Park, EX34 8AY ☎(0271) 865483. *Hotel. Swimming pool, solarium, gymnasium.*
£ B&B £15–£21, HB weekly £120–£160; [10% V]

Collingdale, Larkstone Terr, EX34 9NU ☎(0271) 863770. *Hotel.* Open Mar–Oct.
£ £15–£16; HB weekly £120–£135

Cresta, Torrs Park, EX34 8AY ☎(0271) 863742. *Hotel. Putting.* Open May–Oct.
£ B&B £16·50–£20·50, HB weekly £136·50–£161; [5% V]

Earlsdale, 51 St Brannocks Rd, EX34 8EQ ☎(0271) 862496. *Private Hotel.*
£ B&B £10–£12·50; HB weekly £105–£125; [5% V]

Excelsior, Torrs Park, EX34 8AZ ☎(0271) 862919. *Hotel.* Open Apr–Oct.
£ B&B £15–£18; HB weekly £122–£145

Glendower, Wilder Rd, EX34 9AW ☎(0271) 865711.

Goodrest, 45 St Brannocks Rd, EX34 8EH ☎(0271) 863865. *Hotel.*
£ B&B £12; HB weekly £119; [5% V]

Laston House, Hillsborough Rd, EX34 9NT ☎(0271) 862627. *Hotel.*

Lympstone, 14 Cross Park, EX34 8BJ ☎(0271) 863038. *Private Hotel.* Open Mar–Oct. ⚒ Fr
£ B&B £13–£16; HB weekly £120–£135

Lyncott, 56 St Brannocks Rd, EX34 8EQ ☎(0271) 862425. *Guest House.* Open Mar–Oct.
£ B&B £10–£11·50; HB weekly £90–£105; [5% V]

Merlin Court, Torrs Court, EX 34 8AY ☎(0271) 862697. *Private Hotel.* Open Mar–Nov.
£ B&B £19–£21; HB weekly £168–£182

St Brannocks House, 61 St Brannocks Rd. EX34 8EQ ☎(0271) 863873 *Private Hotel.*
£ B&B £13–£17; HB weekly £115–£147; [10% V]

Sunnyhill Country House, Lincombe, Lee, EX34 8LL ☎(0271) 862953. *Hotel.*

Wentworth House, Belmont Rd, EX34 8DR ☎(0271) 863048. *Hotel.* Open Apr–Xmas.
£ B&B £12·50–£14·50; HB weekly £105–£126

Westwell Hall, Torrs Park, EX34 8AZ ☎(0271) 862792. *Hotel. Billiards.*
£ B&B £20; HB weekly £154–£175; [5% Oct–Mar]

> Changes made after July 1990 are not included.

ILKLEY
West Yorkshire. Map 40A2

Pop 17,069. Leeds 16, London 207, Bradford 13, Harrogate 17, Skipton 9½, Todmorden 26.
EC Wed. **Golf** Ilkley 18h.
ℹ Station Rd. ☎(0943) 602319

★★★ **Cow & Calf,** Moor Top, LS29 8BT ☎(0943) 607335

Fine example of a Yorkshire stone-built hotel. On Ilkley Moor. ⚒ Fr
🛏 17 bedrs, 17 en suite; TV; tcf
⌂ dogs, ns; P 50; child facs
✕ LD 9
£ B&B £52·50–£65, B&B (double) £65–£75; L £7·50, D £13·50; WB £37·50 (HB)
cc Access, Amex, B'card/Visa, CB, Diners.

★★★ H R **Rombalds,** West View, Wells Rd, LS29 9JG ☎(0943) 603201 Tx: 51593 Fax: (0943) 816586

Attractive early Victorian building situated on fringe of Ilkley Moor. Closed 28–30 Dec.
🛏 16 bedrs, 16 en suite; TV; tcf
⌂ dogs; P 30; child facs; con 50
✕ LD 9.30. Resid & Rest lic
£ B&B £55–£76, B&B (double) £80–£95; HB weekly £344–£455; L £8·75, D £22·50; WB £58; [10% V]
cc Access, Amex, B'card/Visa, Diners.

★★ **Greystones,** 1 Ben Rhydding Rd, LS29 8RJ ☎(0943) 607408
Large stone house of quality, now a family-run hotel.
🛏 10 bedrs, 8 en suite, (1 sh), 1 ba; tcf
⌂ TV, dogs; P 16, coach; child facs

ILMINSTER
Somerset. Map 4B2

Yeovil 10, London 135, Crewkerne 8, Honiton 17, Taunton 12.
See church, 16th cent. Grammar school.
ℹ Shrubbery Hotel Car Park ☎(0460) 57294

★★ **Shrubbery,** Station Rd, TA19 9AR ☎(0460) 52108 Tx: 43679 Fax: (0460) 53660
A substantial, stone-built residence in 2½ acres of gardens on A303 in town centre. Swimming pool, tennis.

EC *early closing* **MD** *market day* ♣ *country house hotel* *ns (NS) no smoking areas* *tcf tea/coffee facilities*

🛏 12 bedrs, 12 en suite; TV; tcf
TV, dogs; P 100, coach; child facs; con 280

INGATESTONE Essex. Map 17A3

Pop 5,000. Brentwood 5, London 27, Bishop's Stortford 23, Chelmsford 6, Epping 15, Southend-on-Sea 21.
EC Wed. **Golf** Brentwood 18h. **See** 15th cent Church, Ingatestone Hall.

★★★★ **Heybridge Moat House,** Roman Rd, CM4 9AB (0277) 355355 Tx: 995186 Fax: (0277) 353288

A rambling building part dating back to 1494 with modern bedroom accommodation. (QMH) Fr, Es, Gr
🛏 22 bedrs, 22 en suite; TV
TV; P 200, coach; child facs; con 500
LD 10.30
£ B&B £72·25, B&B (double) £85·50; L £12, D £12; [5% V]
cc Access, Amex, B'card/Visa, Diners.

INGLETON North Yorkshire. Map 36B4

Pop 1,930. Settle 11, London 240, Hawes 16, Kirkby Lonsdale 6, Lancaster 18.
EC Thur. **MD** Fri. **Golf** Bentham 9h.
Community Centre. (052 42) 41049

Pines Country House (Highly Acclaimed), nr Carnforth, LA6 3HN (052 42) 41252. *Hotel.*
£ B&B £16–£18; HB weekly £185·50–£192

Oakroyd (Acclaimed), Main St, Via Carnforth, LA6 3HJ (052 42) 41258. *Hotel.* Fr
£ B&B £15; HB weekly £145; [10% V]
Springfield (Acclaimed), Main St, LA6 3HJ (052 42) 41280. *Hotel.* Closed Nov & Dec.
£ B&B £14–£16; HB weekly £140–£156; [5% V]

Langber, LA6 3DT (052 42) 41587. *Guest House.* Closed 24 Dec–2 Jan.

INSTOW Devon. Map 3A4

Pop 721, Barnstaple 6, London 199, Bideford 3.
EC Wed. **Golf** Royal North Devon 18h.

★★★ H R **Commodore,** Marine Par, EX39 4JN (0271) 860347
Fax: (0271) 861233
Purpose-built hotel in spacious grounds overlooking beach.
🛏 20 bedrs, 20 en suite; TV; tcf
P 150; child facs; con 100
LD 9.30

Licences
Establishments have a full licence unless shown as unlicensed or with the limitations listed on p 6.

£ B&B £47–£49, B&B (double) £70–£80; HB weekly £278–£312; L £9·50, D £16
cc Access, Amex, B'card/Visa; dep.

IPSWICH Suffolk. Map 27B3

Pop 123,000. Colchester 18, London 74, Aldeburgh 24, Harwich 22, Saxmundham 21, Scole 23, Stowmarket 12, Sudbury 21.
MD Tue, Wed, Fri, Sat. **Golf** Ipswich 18h.
See Wolsey's Gate, Christchurch Mansion and Wolsey Art Gallery.
Town Hall, Princes St. (0473) 258070

★★★★ **Hintlesham Hall,** Hintlesham, IP8 3NS Hintlesham (047 387) 334 Tx: 98340 Fax: (047 387) 463

Fine Elizabethan manor with Georgian façade set in 18 acres of parkland 6 miles W of town. Golf, putting, tennis, fishing, billiards. Fr
🛏 22 bedrs, 22 en suite; annexe 11 bedrs, 11 en suite; TV
dogs, ns; coach; con 100
LD 9.30, nr Sat lunch
£ B&B £80–£95, B&B (double) £90–£140; L £20, D £25; WB £165 (2 nts); [10% V]
cc Access, Amex, B'card/Visa, Diners.

★★★ **Belstead Brook,** Belstead Rd, IP2 9HB (0473) 684241 Tx: 987674
Fax: (0473) 681249

Converted period farmhouse with modern residential wing. Seven acres of grounds.
🛏 26 bedrs, 26 en suite; annexe 7 bedrs, 7 en suite; TV; tcf
ns; P 100, coach; child facs; con 60

★★★ **Ipswich Moat House,** London Rd, (3½ m SW on A12) IP8 3JD Copdock (047 386) 444 Tx: 987207
Fax: (047 386) 801

Modern hotel with extensive function facilities outside town. Indoor swimming pool, sauna, solarium, gymnasium. (QMH)
🛏 74 bedrs, 74 en suite; TV; tcf
lift; dogs; P 500, coach; child facs; con 500
LD 9.50
£ B&B £77–£82·50 (w/e £38), B&B (double) £88–£102·50; L £12, D £13; WB £39; [10% V]
cc Access, Amex, B'card/Visa, CB, Diners, dep.

★★★ R **Marlborough,** 73 Henley Rd, IP1 3SP (0473) 257677
Fax: (0473) 226927

Delightfully situated luxury hotel. Set in residential area opposite park. Fr, De, It
🛏 22 bedrs, 22 en suite; TV; tcf
dogs; P 60; child facs; con 24
LD 9.30, bar meals only Sat lunch
£ B&B £70–£84 (w/e £35), B&B (double) £99–£109;, L £13·50, D £16; WB £37·50
cc Access, Amex, B'card/Visa, Diners; dep.

★★★ **Novotel,** Greyfriars Rd, IP1 1UP (0473) 232400 Tx: 987684
Fax: (0473) 232414
Well-kept modern hotel in city centre with attractive open-plan public areas.
🛏 101 bedrs, 101 en suite; TV; tcf
lift, dogs, ns; P 50, coach; child facs; con 200

★★★ **Post House,** London Rd, IP2 0UA (0473) 690313 Tx: 987150
Fax: (0473) 680412
Modern purpose-built hotel. Swimming pool. (THF)
🛏 118 bedrs, 118 en suite; TV; tcf
dogs, ns; P 300, coach; child facs; con 100
LD 10, bar meals only Sat lunch
£ room £62–£72, (w/e £39·50), room (double) £89–£97; Bk £7·50, L £7·95, D £13·50; WB £38 (HB 2 nts)
cc Access, Amex, B'card/Visa, CB, Diners.

★★ **Great White Horse,** Tavern St, IP1 3AH (0473) 256558 Fax: (0473) 253396
Famous old coaching inn with covered courtyard. Dickensian associations. Closed Xmas.
🛏 57 bedrs, 45 en suite (5 sh), 7 ba; TV; tcf
lift; TV; P 10, G 20, coach; child facs; con 150
LD 9.30, bar meals only lunch & Fri–Sun dinner
£ B&B £23–£43 (w/e £23), B&B (double) £23–£48; HB weekly £370·65; D £9·95
cc Access, Amex, B'card/Visa, Diners.

Anglesea (Acclaimed), Oban St, IP1 3PH (0473) 255630. *Private Hotel.*
£ B&B £38
Highview House (Acclaimed), 56 Belstead Rd, IP2 8BE (0473) 688659. *Hotel.*
£ B&B £28–£33; [10% V w/e]

Graham Court, Anglesea Rd, IP1 3PW (0473) 53583. *Hotel.*

ISLE OF WIGHT

BEMBRIDGE Map 5C1
Pop 3,183. Portsmouth (Fy) 9, London 80, Newport 11, Ryde 6, Sandown 7.
EC Thur. **Golf** Sandown 18h. **See** Ruskin Art Gallery and Museum at Bembridge School (by appmt), picturesque harbour, Old Windmill (Nat Trust), Pottery.

★★ **Birdham,** 1 Steyne Rd, PO35 5UH ☎(0983) 872875
Small inn-type hotel convenient for the picturesque harbour. Pleasant garden. Fr
14 bedrs, 12 en suite; 2 ba; TV; tcf
TV, dogs, ns; P 100, coach; child facs; con 28
LD 10
£ B&B £24; L £7·50, D £12·50
cc Amex; dep.

CHALE Map 5C1
Pop 576. Portsmouth (Fy) 16, London 90, Cowes 14, Ryde 16, Shanklin 8½, Ventnor 6½.
EC Wed. **Golf** Ventnor 9h.

★★ **Clarendon & Wight Mouse Inn,** PO38 2HA ☎(0983) 730431. *Billiards.*

A 17th century coaching inn delightfully set in rural area overlooking Chale Bay. Popular Wight Mouse pub next door.
14 bedrs, 9 en suite, 3 ba; TV; tcf
dogs; P 150, coach; child facs
LD 10
£ B&B £24–£36, B&B (double) £48–£52; HB weekly £190–£207; L £5, D £15; [10% V Oct–May]; dep.

COWES Map 5C1
Pop 16,255. Ferry service to Southampton. London 76, Newport 4½, Ryde (Fy) 8, Yarmouth 13.
EC Wed. **Golf** Cowes 9h. **See** Osborne House (Royal Apartments, Swiss Cottage, Museum, Gardens), 16th cent Cowes Castle.
[i] 1 Bath Rd. ☎Isle of Wight (0983) 291914

★★ **Cowes,** 260 Arctic Rd, PO31 7PJ ☎(0983) 291541 Tx: 86284
2-storey former inn with good views of Marina and River Medina. Swimming pool, sauna, solarium.

★★ **Fountain,** High St, PO31 7AW ☎(0983) 292397
A Georgian inn in a narrow street near the waterfront. An archway leads to the hotel's restaurant and bar and the ferry concourse.

Weekend breaks
Please consult the hotel for full details of weekend breaks; prices shown are an indication only. Many hotels offer mid week breaks as well.

FRESHWATER BAY Map 5B1
Pop 4,197. Portsmouth (Fy) 16, London 77, Newport 11, Ventnor 18, Yarmouth 2½.
EC Thur. **Golf** Freshwater 18h. **See** Tennyson's Home and Memorial, All Saints Church, St Agnes thatched Church.

★★★ **Albion,** PO40 9RA ☎(0983) 753631 Fax: (0983) 755295

Attractive white building on water's edge. Most rooms with sea views and balconies.
43 bedrs, 43 en suite, 3 ba; TV; tcf
TV, dogs; P 75, coach; child facs; con 50

★★★ **Farringford,** PO40 9PE ☎(0983) 752500 Tx: 477575
Gothic style mansion, once belonging to Tennyson, set in lovely grounds. Swimming pool, golf, putting, tennis, billiards. Fr, It, Es
16 bedrs, 15 en suite, 1 ba; annexe 4 bedrs, 4 en suite; TV; tcf
TV, dogs; P 150, coach; child facs; con 20
LD 9.30, bar meals only Mon–Sat lunch
£ B&B £25–£40; HB weekly £195–£300; D £14; WB £75; [10% V w/d Nov–Mar]
cc Access, Amex, B'card/Visa, Diners; dep.

Blenheim House (Highly Acclaimed), Gate La, PO40 9QD ☎(0983) 752858. *Hotel. Swimming pool.* Open May–Oct.
£ B&B £17·50; HB weekly £175

RYDE Map 5C1
See also SEAVIEW.
Pop 22,957. London (Fy) 74, Cowes 8, Newport 7, Sandown 5½.
EC Thur. **Golf** Ryde 9h. **See** Shell Museum and Albert Cottage, long pier, St Helen's Abbey, Quarr Abbey nearby.
[i] Western Esplanade. ☎(0983) 62905

★★★ **Ryde Castle,** Esplanade, PO33 1JA ☎(0983) 63755 Fax: (0983) 616436

Attractive building on seafront enjoying good views of Solent. Fr, De
17 bedrs, 17 en suite; TV; tcf
dogs, ns; P 90, coach; child facs; con 175
LD 9.45
£ B&B £49·50–£64·90, B&B (double) £65·90–£88; HB weekly £410–£470; L £8·75, D £15·35; WB £64·90
cc Access, B'card/Visa; dep.

★★ **Yelf's,** Union St, PO33 2LG ☎(0983) 64062

Former coaching inn–in busy street near ferry pier and beach. (THF)
21 bedrs, 21 en suite; TV; tcf
dogs, ns; coach; child facs; con 45

Dorset, 31 Dover Rd, PO33 2BW ☎(0983) 64327. *Hotel. Swimming pool.*
Georgian, 22 George St, PO33 2EW ☎(0983) 63989. *Private Hotel.*

ST LAWRENCE Map 5C1
Pop 700. Ventnor 2, London (Fy) 88, Newport 9.
EC Wed. **Golf** Ventnor 9h.

★★ **Old Park,** nr Ventnor, PO38 1XS ☎(0983) 852583

Three-storey granite building with extension in attractive gardens. Quiet location. Indoor swimming pool, putting, sauna, solarium, billiards. Open Easter–Oct
37 bedrs, 37 en suite; TV; tcf
TV; dogs; P 80; child facs
LD 8.30, bar meals only lunch. Resid & Rest lic
£ B&B £22–£31; D £10; [10% V]
cc Access, B'card/Visa; dep.

★★ **Rocklands,** PO38 1XH ☎(0983) 852964

EC *early closing* **MD** *market day* *country house hotel* *ns (NS) no smoking areas* *tcf tea/coffee facilities*

Country house family hotel attractively set in peaceful situation. Swimming pool, sauna, solarium, billiards. Open 16 May–Nov
16 bedrs, 16 en suite; TV
TV; dogs; P 20, coach; child facs
LD 8.30, bar meals only lunch
£ B&B £37·20–£39·50, B&B (double) £64·40–£69; HB weekly £305·90–£322; D £11·50; [10% V]; dep.

★ **Lawyers Rest,** Undercliff Dr, PO38 1XF (0983) 852610.
Attractive early Victorian country house with terraced gardens to the sea. Fr. Open Mar–Oct & w/e Dec–Feb
8 bedrs, 8 en suite, 1 ba
dogs, ns; P 12; no children under 10; con 25
LD 7 nr Mon lunch
£ B&B £33·35, B&B (double) £57·50–£69; D £13·50 (bookings only)
cc Access, Amex, B'card/Visa, Diners; dep.

SANDOWN Map 5C1

Pop 3,943. Ryde 6, London (Fy) 80, Newport 8½, Shanklin 2.
EC Wed. **MD** Mon. **Golf** Sandown and Shanklin 18h. **See** Geological Museum, Yaverland Church and Manor House, Snake & Reptile Centre.
Esplanade. (0983) 403886

★★★ **Broadway Park,** Melville St, PO36 9DJ (0983) 405214
Charming country house set in 7 acres of gardens and parkland. Swimming pool, putting, tennis, billiards.

★★★ **Melville Hall,** Melville St, PO36 9DH (0983) 406526

Large former residence in attractive gardens. Swimming pool, putting.
33 bedrs, 33 en suite; TV; tcf
P 30, coach; child facs
LD 9.30
£ B&B £25–£36; HB weekly £195–£265; L £6·50, D £11·95; [10% V]
cc Access, B'card/Visa, Diners; dep.

★ **Rose Bank,** High St, PO36 8DA (0983) 403854

Small hotel with pleasant garden, enjoying sea views. Closed 16–31 Dec.
6 bedrs, 1 en suite (2 sh), 1 ba
TV, dogs; no children under 6
LD 7.30, bar meals, only lunch
£ B&B £12–£15; HB weekly £96–£102; D £7·50; dep.

St Catherine's (Highly Acclaimed), 1 Winchester Park Rd. PO36 8HJ (0983) 402392. *Hotel.* Closed 25 Dec–1 Jan.
£ B&B £17·50–£20·50; HB weekly £159·25–£191·75; [10% V]
cc Access, B'card/Visa; dep.

Chester Lodge (Acclaimed), 7 Beachfield Rd, PO36 8NA (0983) 402773. *Private Hotel.* Open Feb–Nov.
£ B&B £13·80–£16·10; HB weekly £138–£150

Braemar, 5 Broadway, PO36 9DQ. (0983) 403358. *Private Hotel.*
£ B&B £24; HB weekly £172–£218; [10% V]
cc Access, B'card/Visa; dep.

SEAVIEW Map 5C1

Pop 3,537 (inc St Helens). Ryde 2½, London (Fy) 77, Newport 9, Sandown 6.
EC Thur. **Golf** Ryde 9h. **See** Flamingo Park.

★★ H R **Seaview,** High St, PO34 5EX (0983) 612711 Fax: (0983) 613729

Small privately-owned hotel close to seafront in sailing village.
16 bedrs, 16 en suite; TV
dogs, ns; P 14; child facs; con 20
LD 9.30, bar meals only Sun dinner
£ B&B £44–£65; B&B (double) £66–£72; HB weekly £325–£485; L £15·85, D £15·85
cc Access, Amex, B'card/Visa.

SHANKLIN Map 5C1

Pop 7,436. Sandown 2, London (Fy) 82, Newport 9, Ventnor 3½.
EC Wed. **Golf** Sandown and Shanklin 18h.
67 High St. (0983) 862942

★★★ **Cliff Tops,** Park Rd, PO37 6BB (0983) 863262 Tx: 869441 Fax: (0983) 867139

Large resort type hotel with spacious public rooms. Panoramic views of Sandown Bay. Indoor swimming pool, solarium, gymnasium, snooker.
88 bedrs, 88 en suite; TV; tcf
lift, dogs; P 38, coach; child facs; con 220

★★★ **Holliers,** Church Rd, Old Village, PO37 6NU (0983) 862764
17th-century coaching inn in centre of Shanklin Old Village. Indoor/outdoor swimming pools, sauna, solarium.
33 bedrs, 33 en suite; TV; tcf
P 40, coach; child facs
LD 8.30, bar meals only lunch
£ B&B £30–£33; HB weekly £245–£280; D £11·75; WB £108 (3 dys)
cc Access, Amex, B'card/Visa; dep.
(See advertisement on p. 305.)

★★ **Belmont,** Queen's Rd, PO37 6AN (0983) 862864
Attractive small hotel in quiet location. Easy walk to seafront. Swimming pool, solarium.
15 bedrs, 15 en suite; TV; tcf
dogs; P 12; coach
LD 9.30, bar meals only Mon–Sat lunch. Resid & Rest lic
£ B&B £23–£27; HB weekly £169–£236; L £7, D £9; [5% V excl, Jul–Sep]
cc Access, B'card/Visa; dep.

★★ **Brunswick House,** Queen's Rd, PO37 6AN Isle of Wight (0983) 863245
Attractive, conveniently-situated building facing the sea. Indoor and outdoor swimming pools, sauna. Open Mar–Nov.
29 bedrs, 29 en suite; TV; tcf
TV, dogs; P 25; child facs

★★ **Fernbank,** Highfield Rd, PO37 6PP Isle of Wight (0983) 862790

Small hotel run by owner. Pleasantly situated. Indoor swimming pool, sauna, solarium. Closed Xmas.
30 bedrs, 30 en suite; TV; tcf
dogs, ns; P 24, coach; no children under 7
LD 10.30, bar meals only Mon–Sat lunch. Rest lic
£ B&B £20·30–£28·70; HB weekly £173–£223; D £8·50; WB; [10% V Oct–May]
cc Access, B'card/Visa; dep.

★★ **Keats Green,** Queens Rd, PO37 6AN (0983) 862742.

En suite rooms
En suite rooms may be bath or shower rooms. If you have a preference, remember to state it when booking a room.

Three-storey, holiday hotel by Keats Green with lovely views of Sandown Bay. Swimming pool. Open Mar–Oct.
🛏 34 bedrs, 33 en suite, 2 ba; TV; tcf
🏨 dogs, ns; P 30, coach; child facs
✕ LD 7.45, bar meals only lunch. Resid lic
£ B&B £20–£24; HB weekly £130–£195; D £8·50; WB £40; [10% V]
cc Access, B'card/Visa; dep.

★★ Luccombe Hall, Luccombe Rd, PO37 6RL 📞(0983) 862719 Fax: (0983) 867482 ♿

Substantial building in 2 acres of lovely terraced gardens. Fine views. Indoor/ outdoor swimming pools, tennis, squash, sauna, solarium, gymnasium.
🛏 30 bedrs, 30 en suite, TV; tcf
🏨 TV, dogs, ns; P 30, coach; child facs; con 40
✕ LD 8.30, bar meals only lunch. Club lic
£ B&B £26–£33, HB weekly £198–£276; D £13·25; [5% V]
cc Access, B'card/Visa; dep.

★★ Melbourne-Ardenlea, Queens Rd, PO37 6AP 📞(0983) 862283

Attractive rambling 2-storey 19th century building in gardens. Indoor swimming pool, sauna, solarium. Open Mar–Oct.
🛏 51 bedrs, 51 en suite, TV
🏨 lift, TV, dogs, P 20, coach, child facs
✕ LD 8, Resid & Rest lic
£ B&B £18–£30; HB weekly £161–£252; D £9; [10% V]
cc Access, B'card/Visa; dep.

★★ Monteagle Priory Rd, PO37 6RJ 📞 Isle of Wight (0983) 862854

Charming 2-storey 19th century building in own grounds. Swimming pool, billiards.

★★ Ocean View, Esplanade, PO37 6BG 📞 Isle of Wight (0983) 862602

Substantial hotel in prime seafront position. Near pier.
🛏 36 bedrs, 33 en suite, 3 ba; TV; tcf
🏨 TV, dogs, ns; P 25, coach; child facs

★★ Shanklin Manor House, Church Rd, Old Village, PO37 6QX 📞(0983) 862777

Stone-built 19th century manor house in attractive gardens on outskirts of town. Indoor swimming pool, putting, tennis, sauna, solarium, gymnasium. Open Feb–Nov & Xmas.
🛏 33 bedrs, 33 en suite, annexe 5 bedrs, 5 en suite; TV; tcf
🏨 P 50, coach; child facs; con 60
✕ LD 8, nr lunch. Resid & Rest lic
£ B&B £26–£29, B&B (double) £48–£54; HB weekly £195–£230; D £13·50; [5% V excl. Jun–Sep]; dep.

Apse Manor Country House (Highly Acclaimed), Apse Manor Rd, PO37 7NP 📞(0983) 866651. *Hotel.*
Bay House (Highly Acclaimed), 8 Chine Av, Keats Green, PO37 6AN 📞(0983) 863180. *Hotel. Indoor swimming pool, sauna, solarium.*
Luccombe Chine House (Highly Acclaimed), Luccombe, PO37 6RH 📞(0983) 862037. *Hotel.*
Open Feb–Nov.
£ B&B £39–£45; HB weekly £210–£252
Osborne House (Highly Acclaimed), Esplanade, PO37 6BN 📞(0983) 862501. *Hotel.* Open Jan–Oct. ⚒ Es
£ B&B £26·50

Hambledon (Acclaimed), 11 Queens Rd, PO37 6AW 📞(0983) 862403. *Hotel.*
Pulboro (Acclaimed), 6 Park Rd, PO37 6AZ 📞(0983) 862740. Open 1 Feb–1 Dec
Soraba (Acclaimed), 2 Paddock Rd, PO37 6NZ 📞(0983) 862367. *Hotel.* Closed Dec.
£ B&B £12–£15; HB weekly £95–£131; [5% V Sep–May]; dep.

Aqua, Esplanade, PO37 6BN 📞(0983) 863024. *Hotel.* Open Mar–Nov.
£ B&B £19–£23; HB weekly £135–£185; [10% V]
Culver Lodge, Culver Rd, PO37 6ER 📞(0983) 863515. *Hotel.*
La Turbie, Culver Rd, PO37 6ER 📞(0983) 862767. *Hotel. Swimming pool.*
Overstrand, Howard Rd, PO37 6HD 📞(0983) 862100. *Private Hotel. Putting, tennis.*
Victoria Lodge, Alexandra Rd, PO37 6AF 📞(0983) 862361. *Hotel.* Open Easter–Oct
£ B&B £14–£19; HB weekly £115–£154; [5% V w/d Apr–May & Oct]

TOTLAND BAY Map 5B1

Pop 2,083. Portsmouth (Fy) 17, London 78, Newport 10, Ventnor 18, Yarmouth 2½.
EC Wed. **Golf** Freshwater Bay 18h.

★★★ Country Garden, Church Hill, PO39 0ET 📞(0983) 754521 Tx: 94017218

Country residence (built 1883) set in attractive gardens. Overlooks the Solent.
🛏 16 bedrs, 16 en suite; annexe 2 bedrs, 2 en suite; TV; tcf
🏨 dogs; P 40, coach; child facs; con 20
✕ LD 9. Resid & Rest lic
£ B&B £29–£43, B&B (double) £58–£78; HB weekly £215–£335; L £8·45, D £13·50; WB £63 (2 nts HB); [10% V Sun & Nov–Feb]
cc Access, Amex, B'card/Visa, Diners; dep.
(*See advertisement on p. 305*)
Lismore (Acclaimed), The Avenue, PO39 0DH 📞(0983) 752025. *Private Hotel.* Closed Dec.
£ B&B £15·50; HB weekly £127–£157·50; [10% V]

Hermitage, Cliff Rd, PO39 0EW 📞(0983) 752518. *Hotel. Swimming pool.* Open Mar–Oct.
£ B&B £21–£23; HB weekly £200–£220
Nodes, Alum Bay Rd, PO39 OHZ 📞(0983) 752859 Fax: (0705) 201621. *Private Hotel.*
⚒ De, Es
£ B&B £15·50–£18·50; HB weekly £150–£189; [10% V Oct–Apr]

VENTNOR Map 5C1

Pop 4,386. Shanklin 3½, London (Fy) 86, Newport 9½, Yarmouth 20.
EC Wed. **Golf** Ventnor 9h. **See** Ventnor Botanic Garden, old Church at Bonchurch (grave of Swinburne), St Boniface Down.
ℹ 34 High St. 📞(0983) 853625

★★★ Royal, Belgrave Rd, PO38 1JJ 📞(0983) 852186

Hotel stands in beautiful gardens in elevated position facing the sea. Swimming pool, solarium, billiards. (THF) ⚒ Fr, It
🛏 54 bedrs, 54 en suite; TV; tcf
🏨 lift, TV, dogs, ns; P 100, coach; child facs; con 33
✕ LD 9
£ B&B £40 (w/e £36); B&B (double) £45; HB weekly £217; D £13·25; [5% V]
cc Access, Amex, B'card/Visa, CB, Diners.

Shanklin (Isle of Wight)

HOLLIERS HOTEL

The first and original hotel in Shanklin, superbly situated in the Old Village, this 17th Century Coaching Inn retains its historic charm combined with the latest facilities.

The Restaurant offers a bar for your Aperitif and an extensive dinner menu. There are also a Piano Bar and Disco within the Hotel.

Well appointed bedrooms all en suite with colour TV/radio, direct dial telephones, tea and coffee making facilities, hairdryers. Children welcome. Indoor pool, sauna/solarium, outdoor pool and children's play area.

Excellent facilities in picturesque surroundings only minutes from the Chine, beach and country walks.

RAC ★★★
Shanklin

ETB 4 Crowns
Open all Year

Totland Bay (Isle of Wight)

Country Garden Hotel & Restaurant

Church Hill, Totland Bay, Isle of Wight, PO39 0ET. Tel: (0983) 754521

Country House set in beautiful landscaped gardens overlooking Solent and Dorset coastline. Superb cuisine, elegant relaxation. Bedrooms luxurious – suites also available. Brochure upon request.

St Marys (Isles of Scilly)

Atlantic Hotel

St Marys, Isles of Scilly TR21 0PL Tel: (0720) 22417 Fax: (0720) 23009

The only hotel in the Scillies which sits on the water's edge, overlooking the harbour and town beach. 23 bedrooms – all with private facilities, CH, TV and telephone. Panoramic views.

★★★ **Ventnor Towers,** Madeira Rd, PO38 1QT ☎(0983) 852277

Fine Victorian white-faced house in 4 acres of cliff top gardens. Swimming pool, putting, tennis. ✂ Fr, De, It, Es, Du.
🛏 29 bedrs, 26 en suite, 1 ba; TV; tcf
🏠 TV, dogs; P 20, G 1, coach; child facs; con 80
✕ LD 8.30
£ B&B £29–£35; HB weekly £245–£283·50; L £8·95, D £12·95; [10% V excl. Aug]
cc Access, Amex, B'card/Visa, Diners.

⚘ ★ **Madeira Hall,** Trinity Rd, PO38 1NS ☎(0983) 852624

Lovely country house built of local stone (1800) in 2 acres of gardens. Swimming pool, putting.
🛏 12 bedrs, 9 en suite, 1 ba; TV; tcf
🏠 TV, dogs; P 12; child facs

Ap. Lake, Bonchurch, PO38 1RF ☎(0983) 852613

Attractive 2-storey building in 2½ acres of gardens opposite Bonchurch Pond. Open Mar–Oct.
🛏 11 bedrs, 9 en suite, 2 ba; annexe 10 bedrs, 10 en suite, 3 ba; tcf
🏠 TV, dogs, ns; P 20; children over 3
✕ LD 7, nr lunch. Resid lic
£ B&B £15–£17; HB weekly £139·50–£157·50; D £6; [5% V]

Hillside (Acclaimed), Mitchell Ave, PO38 1DR ☎Isle of Wight (0983) 852271. *Private Hotel.*
£ B&B £16–£18; HB weekly £154–£175
Richmond (Acclaimed), Esplanade, PO38 1JX ☎Isle of Wight (0983) 852496.
£ B&B £14·95–£17·45; HB weekly £135–£151·50

Channel View, Hambrough Rd, PO38 1SQ ☎(0983) 852230. *Hotel.*
Llynfi, 23 Spring Hill, PO38 1PF ☎(0983) 852202. *Private Hotel.* Open Easter–Sept.
£ B&B £14·50–£19; HB weekly £136–£170; [10% V]
Macrocarpa, Mitchell Av, PO38 1DP ☎(0983) 852428. *Hotel.*
£ B&B £15·50–£33·50 (w/e £12·50); HB weekly £126·50–£200·10; [10% V]
Picardie, Esplanade, PO38 1JX ☎(0983) 852647. Open 16 Mar–Oct.
£ B&B £15; HB weekly £135.
St Maur, Castle Rd. PO38 1LG ☎(0983) 852570 *Hotel.*
Under Rock, Shore Rd, Bonchurch, PO38 1RF ☎(0983) 852714.

ISLES OF SCILLY

ST MARY'S Map 2B3/4

Pop 1,960. Steamer Service to Penzance. London 281.
EC Wed. **Golf** St Mary's 9h.
ℹ Town Hall, St Mary's ☎(0720) 22536

★★ **Atlantic,** TR21 0PL ☎(0720) 22417

Family hotel right by the beach. Sun lounge enjoys harbour views. ✂ Fr. Open 21 Mar–21 Oct.
🛏 23 bedrs, 23 en suite; TV; tcf
🏠 TV; dogs, ns; child facs
✕ LD 9, bar meals only lunch
£ B&B £37·50–£38·50, B&B (double) £38·50–£46; D £15
cc Access, B'card/Visa; dep.
(*See advertisement on p. 305*)

★★ **Godolphin,** Church St, Hughtown, TR21 0JR ☎(0720) 22316 Fax: (0720) 22252

Large stone-built hotel in quiet situation yet central to Hughtown. Sauna.
🛏 31 bedrs, 27 en suite, 1 ba; TV; tcf
🏠 ns; child facs

★★ **Tregarthen's,** Hughtown, TR21 0PP ☎(0720) 22540
Historic building enjoying magnificent views of harbour and other islands.

Brantwood (Highly Acclaimed), Rocky Hill, TR21 0NW ☎Scillonia (0720) 22531
Tx: 45117 Fax: (0736) 64293. *Hotel.* Open May–Sep. ✂ De
£ HB weekly £378; [10% V May & Sep]

TRESCO Map 2 A/B 4

Pop 180. Steamer Service, St Mary's to Penzance. London 281.
Dogs banned from island.

★★★ **H** **R** **Island,** TR24 0PU ☎(0720) 22883

Attractive stone and timber hotel in glorious garden beside the sea. Swimming pool, fishing. ✂ Fr. Open Mar–Oct.
🛏 40 bedrs, 40 en suite; TV; tcf
🏠 TV; child facs
✕ LD 8.30, bar meals only Mon–Sat lunch
£ B&B & dinner £72–£85, B&B & dinner (double) £132–£220; D £22
cc Access, B'card/Visa; dep.

ISLEWORTH Greater London

(Middlesex). Map 10A4
Brentford & Chiswick 5½, London 12, M3 (jn 3) 4½, Richmond 5½, Staines 7, Uxbridge 8, Wembley 10.

★★★ **Osterley,** 764 Great West Rd, TW7 5NA ☎081-568 9981 Tx: 915059 Fax: 081-569 7819

A Tudor-style converted pub with bedroom accommodation in a separate block. ✂ Fr
🛏 56 bedrs, 56 en suite; TV; tcf
🏠 dogs, P 120, coach; child facs; con 250
✕ LD 10
£ B&B £70·75 (w/e £20), B&B (double) £82·50; L £8·50, D £9·50; [10% V Fri–Sun]
cc Access, Amex, B'card/Visa, Diners; dep.

Kingswood, 33 Woodlands Rd, TW7 6NR ☎081-560 5614. *Hotel.* ✂ Fr
£ B&B £25–£30; [10% V]

KEGWORTH Leicestershire

(Derbyshire). Map 25A2
Pop 3,300. Loughborough 6, London 116, M1 (jn 24) 1, Ashby-de-la-Zouch 11, Derby 11, Melton Mowbray 18, Nottingham 11.

★★★ **Yew Lodge,** DE7 2DF ☎(0509) 672518 Tx: 341995 Fax: (0509) 674730

A brick-built modern hotel in village centre. Situated on A6. Fr
54 bedrs, 54 en suite; TV; tcf
lift, dogs; P 100, coach; child facs; con 100
LD 10
£ B&B £49·70 (w/e £28), B&B (double) £67; L £7, D £11·50; [10% V]
cc Access, Amex, B'card/Visa, Diners.

KEIGHLEY West Yorkshire. Map 40A1
Pop 47,614 (Inc Haworth). Halifax 12, London 199, Bradford 10, Skipton 9½, Todmorden 14.
EC Tue. **MD** Wed, Fri, Sat. **Golf** Keighley 18h. **See** Cliffe Castle Museum and Art Gallery, Keighley–Worth Valley Rly.

★★ **Dalesgate,** 406 Skipton Rd, Utley ☎(0535) 664930 Fax: (0535) 611253

Stone-built Victorian house, once a manse, with a modern extension. Closed 24 Dec–3 Jan
21 bedrs, 21 en suite; TV; tcf
TV; dogs; P 30, coach; child facs
LD 9, nr lunch & Sun dinner. Resid & Rest lic
£ B&B £24·50–£32·50, B&B (double) £38–£44; D £10; WB £37; [10% V w/e Dec–Apr]
cc Access, Amex, B'card/Visa, Diners; dep.
(*See advertisement on p. 308*)

KENDAL Cumbria. Map 44A1
See also CROOKLANDS.
Pop 21,596. London 257, M6 (jn 37) 5½, Ambleside 13, Brough 28, Kirkby Lonsdale 12, Penrith 25, Ulverston 24.
MD Sat. **Golf** Kendal 18h. **See** 13th cent Parish Church, Castle ruins, Abbot Hall Art Gallery and Museum, Sandes Hospital.
Town Hall, Highgate. ☎(0539) 725758

★★★ **County,** Station Rd, LA9 6BT ☎(0539) 722461 Fax: (0539) 732644
Classic early 19th century building near station and town centre.
31 bedrs, 28 en suite, (3 sh), 3 ba; TV; tcf
lift, dogs, ns; P 10, coach; child facs; con 75
LD 9.45
£ B&B £47 (w/e £30), B&B (double) £63; HB weekly £315; L £7·50, D £10·50; [5% V]

★★★ **Riverside,** Stramongate Bridge, LA9 4BZ ☎(0539) 724707 Fax: (0539) 740274

A sympathetic conversion of a 17th-century stone-built tannery beside the River Kent.
Fr, It, Es
47 bedrs, 47 en suite; TV; tcf
lift, ns; P 40, coach; child facs; con 200
LD 10, bar meals only Sat lunch
£ B&B £35–£50, B&B (double) £48–£66; HB weekly £318·50; L £8·50, D £13·50; WB £40; [10% V]
cc Access, Amex, B'card/Visa, Diners.
(*See advertisement on p. 308*).

★★★ **Woolpack,** Stricklandgate, LA9 4ND ☎(0539) 723852 Fax: (0539) 728608 ♿

Coaching inn in centre of Kendal, retaining 'old worlde' charm. (Sw) Fr, De, Es
53 bedrs, 53 en suite; TV; tcf
TV; dogs, ns; P 60, coach; child facs; con 100
LD 9.30, bar meals only Mon–Sat lunch.
£ B&B £62–£75 (w/e £75), B&B (double) £75–£90; L £7·50, D £13·50; WB £75
cc Access, Amex, B'card/Visa.

★★ **R** **Garden House,** Fowl-Ing La, LA9 6PH ☎(0539) 731131 Fax: (0539) 740064

En suite rooms
En suite rooms may be bath or shower rooms. If you have a preference, remember to state it when booking a room.

Attractive Regency house in two acres of formal gardens and lawns.
10 bedrs, 10 en suite; TV; tcf
ns, P 40; child facs; con 18
LD 9, bar meals only lunch & Sun dinner. Resid & Rest lic
£ B&B £42–£47, B&B (double) £59–£64; D £14·75; WB £37 (HB)
cc Access, Amex, B'card/Visa, Diners; dep.

Martindales (Acclaimed), 9–11 Sandes Av, LA9 4LL ☎(0539) 24028. *Guest House.*

Garnett House, Burneside, LA9 5SF ☎(0539) 724542. *Farm.*
£ B&B (double) £22–£23
Gateside, Windermere Rd, LA9 5SE ☎(0539) 722036. *Farm.* Closed Xmas.
£ B&B £15; [5% V]
Plough Inn, Selside, LA8 9LD ☎Selside (053 983) 687. *Inn.*
£ B&B £17·50

KENILWORTH Warwickshire. Map 21A4
Pop 19,315. Warwick 4½, London 96, Birmingham 19, Coventry 6, Tamworth 23.
EC Mon, Thur. **MD** Thur. **Golf** Kenilworth 18h. **See** Castle ruins, Parish Church of St Nicholas, Old houses, Augustine Priory (remains), National Agricultural Show Centre.
11 Smalley Pl. ☎ (0926) 52595

★★★★ **De Montfort,** The Square, CV8 1ED ☎(0926) 55944 Tx: 311012 Fax: (0926) 57830

Modern hotel close to the historical Kenilworth Castle. Snooker. (DeV). Fr, De, It
96 bedrs, 96 en suite; TV; tcf
lift, dogs, ns; P 89, coach; child facs; con 300
LD 9.45, nr Sat lunch
£ B&B £88, B&B (double) £98; L £13·50, D £15; WB £65 (2 nts HB); [5% V]
cc Access, Amex, B'card/Visa, CB, Diners.

★★★ **Chesford Grange,** Chesford Bridge, CV8 2LD ☎(0926) 59331 Tx: 311918 Fax: (0926) 59075

K

Keighley (Yorkshire)

Kendal (Cumbria)

Keswick (Cumbria)

EC *early closing* **MD** *market day* *country house hotel* *ns (NS) no smoking areas* *tcf tea/coffee facilities*

Attractive rambling Victorian house with landscaped gardens. In rural setting.
130 bedrs, 130 en suite; TV; tcf
lift, dogs, ns; P 500, coach; child facs; con 750
LD 10, nr Sat lunch
£ B&B £40–£61·75 (w/e £34), B&B (double) £50–£89; L £9·25, D £10·50
cc Access, Amex, B'card/Visa, Diners; dep.

★★★ **Clarendon House,** Old High St, CV8 1LZ (0926) 57668 Tx: 311240 Fax: (0926) 50669

Ancient inn with restaurant. Located in older part of town. Fr, De
31 bedrs, 31 en suite; TV; tcf
dogs; P 30; child facs; con 120
LD 9.30, bar meals only Mon–Sat lunch
£ B&B £50–£55, B&B (double) £75–£80; L £8·50, D £11·50; WB £40; [10% V]
cc Access, B'card/Visa.

★★★ **Kenilworth Moat House,** Chesford Bridge, CV8 2LN (0926) 58331 Fax: (0926) 58153
Modern purpose-built hotel. 1990 Closed for redevelopment.

Nightingales, 95 Warwick Rd, CV8 1HP (0926) 53594. *Hotel.* It, Es
£ B&B £19

KESWICK

Cumbria. Map 43C3

See also BASSENTHWAITE, BORROWDALE and THORNTHWAITE.
Pop 4,850. Ambleside 16, London 285, Carlisle 31, Cockermouth 11, Egremont 25, Penrith 16.
EC Wed. **MD** Sat. **Golf** Keswick (Threlked) 18h. **See** Derwentwater, Friar's Crag, School of Industrial Arts, Castlerigg prehistoric stone circle.
[i] Moot Hall, Market Sq. (076 87) 72645

Hotel locations
Hotel locations are shown on the maps at the back of the guide. All towns and villages containing an RAC Appointed or Listed hotel are ringed in purple.

★★★★ **Stakis Lodore Swiss,** Borrowdale Rd, CA12 5UX Borrowdale (059 684) 285 Tx: 64305 Fax: (059 684) 343
Modernised, largely Victorian, impressive hotel with grounds overlooking lake. Indoor/outdoor swimming pools, tennis, squash, sauna, solarium, gymnasium. Closed 4 Jan–12 Feb.
70 bedrs, 70 en suite; TV; tcf
lift; ns; P 80, U 23 (£2·50); child facs; con 80
LD 9.30
£ B&B £55, B&B (double) £110; HB weekly £350–£455; D £22
cc Access, Amex, B'card/Visa, Diners.
(*See advertisement on p. 311*)

★★★ **Brundholme,** Brundholme Rd, CA12 4NL (076 87) 74495

Regency villa, described by Coleridge as being 'in a delicious situation'. Closed 21 Dec–31 Jan.
11 bedrs, 11 en suite; TV; tcf
dogs, ns; P 20; children over 11
LD 8.45
£ B&B £35–£45, B&B (double) £70–£90; HB weekly £301–£366; L £8·50, D £17·50; WB £94·50; [10% V excl Sep–Oct]
cc B'card/Visa; dep.

★★★ **Derwentwater,** Portinscale, CA12 5RE (076 87) 72538 Fax: (07687) 71002

Pleasant white-painted 3-storey hotel in 15 acres of grounds by lake. Putting, fishing. Fr, It.
52 bedrs, 52 en suite, annexe 31 bedrs, 31 en suite; TV; tcf
lift, dogs, ns; P 120, coach; child facs; con 70
LD 9.30, bar meals only lunch
£ B&B £45–£52·50, B&B (double) £77–£83·50; HB weekly £149·50–£289·50; D £13·50; WB £35·50 (HB); [10% V]
cc Access, Amex, B'card/Visa; dep.
(*See advertisement on p. 310*)

★★★ H C **Grange Country House,** Manor Brow, CA12 4BA (076 87) 72500
Attractive small hotel with garden, on hill to south of town. Open 22 Mar–3 Nov. De
11 bedrs, 11 en suite; TV; tcf
dogs, ns; P12, G1; no children under 5
LD 8, nr lunch. Resid & Rest lic.
£ B&B £34·50–£39·50, B&B (double) £54–£62; HB weekly £228–£249; D £12·75; WB £102 (HB 3 nts); [10% V]
cc B'card/Visa; dep.

★★★ **Keswick,** Station Rd, CA12 4NQ (076 87) 72020 Tx: 64200

Majestic, turreted Victorian hotel in quiet situation within own grounds. Putting. (THF)
66 bedrs, 66 en suite; TV; tcf
lift, dogs; P 60, coach; child facs; con 80

★★★ **Queen's,** Main St, CA12 5JF (076 87) 73333 Fax: (076 87) 71144

Modernised early 19th century posting house pleasantly situated in town centre.
36 bedrs, 36 en suite; TV; tcf
lift, G 16, coach; child facs; con 20
LD 9.30
£ B&B £22–£31, B&B (double) £38–£60;

L £4·50, D £12; WB £25 (HB); [10% V]
cc Access, Amex, B'card/Visa, Diners; dep.

★★ Chaucer House, Derwentwater Pl, CA12 4DR ☎ (076 87) 72318

Four-storey stone-built family-managed hotel in quiet street near town centre. Open Mar–Nov. ⚒ De
🛏 35 bedrs, 28 en suite, 4 ba; TV; tcf
🏠 TV, dogs, ns; P 27, coach; child facs
✕ LD 7.30, nr lunch. Resid & Rest lic
£ B&B £19·50–£25·50 (w/e £24), B&B (double) £28–£49; HB weekly £172·50–£216; D £10·25
cc Access, Amex, B'card/Visa; dep.

★★ Crow Park, The Heads, CA12 5ER ☎ (076 87) 72208

Tall Lakeland stone 19th century building enjoying panoramic views of Derwentwater.
🛏 26 bedrs, 26 en suite; TV; tcf
🏠 dogs, ns; P 26, coach; child facs
✕ LD 8, nr lunch
£ B&B £19–£25, B&B (double) £38–£50; HB weekly £203–£242; D £10; WB £55 (2 nts HB); [10% V Nov–Mar]
cc Access, B'card/Visa; dep.
(*See advertisement on p. 309*)

♣ ★★ Dale Head Hall, Thirlmere Lake, CA12 4TN ☎ (076 87) 72478
Charming manor house in 4 acres of lovely wooded gardens beside Lake Thirlmere. Tennis, fishing. ⚒ Fr, De, Du
🛏 9 bedrs, 9 en suite; tcf
🏠 ns; P20; no children under 12; con 18
✕ LD 8.30, nr lunch. Resid & Rest lic
£ B&B £47·50, B&B (double) £65–£85, HB weekly £301–£364; D £13·75; WB £42·50 (HB); [5% V]
cc Access, B'card/Visa; dep.

★★ Daleview, Lake Rd, CA12 5DQ ☎ (076 87) 72666
Small family-run hotel near to the town centre. Open Mar–15 Nov.
🛏 15 bedrs, 10 en suite, 2 ba; TV; tcf
🏠 P 17; child facs
✕ LD 8, bar meals only Mon–Fri lunch. Resid & Rest lic
£ B&B £21–£26·50, B&B (double) £38–£51; HB weekly £178–£222; D £8; WB £53 (2 nts HB)
cc Access, B'card/Visa; dep.

★★ Hazeldene, The Heads, CA12 5ER ☎ (076 87) 72106
Three-storey stone terrace houses at south end of town. Lovely views to Derwentwater. Open Feb–Nov.
🛏 22 bedrs, 17 en suite; TV; tcf
🏠 TV; dogs, ns; P 18; child facs
✕ LD 4, nr lunch. Rest lic
£ B&B £15·50–£20·50; HB weekly £182·50–£219·50; dep.

★★ Highfield, The Heads, CA12 5ER ☎ (076 87) 72508

Enjoying magnificent hill views, a 3-storey building of local slate and stone to south of town. Open Apr–Oct.
🛏 19 bedrs, 15 en suite, 1 ba; tcf
🏠 TV, dogs, ns; P 19; no children under 5
✕ LD 6, nr lunch. Resid & Rest lic
£ B&B £15·50–£23, B&B (double) £38–£46; HB weekly £182–£234·50; D £10·50; dep.

★★ Lairbeck, Vicarage Hill, CA12 5QB ☎ (076 87) 73373

Fine house of Lakeland stone in secluded garden with mountain views.
🛏 15 bedrs, 10 en suite, 3 ba; TV; tcf
🏠 ns; P 25; child facs
✕ LD 8, nr lunch. Resid & Rest lic
£ B&B £16–£23; HB weekly£168–£224; D £10
cc Access, B'card/Visa; dep.

♣ ★★ H C Lyzzick Hall, Underskiddaw, CA12 4PY ☎ (076 87) 72277
In spacious grounds on southern foot of Skiddaw, a country house with fine views. Swimming pool. ⚒ Es. Open Mar–Jan.
🛏 19 bedrs, 19 en suite, 1 ba; annexe 1 bedr, 1 en suite; TV; tcf
🏠 ns; P 45; child facs; con 15
✕ LD 9.30
£ B&B £24–£25; HB weekly £215–£230; D £10
cc Access, Amex, B'card/Visa, Diners.

Weekend breaks
Please consult the hotel for full details of weekend breaks; prices shown are an indication only. Many hotels offer mid week breaks as well.

♣ ★★ Red House, Underskiddaw, CA12 4QA ☎ (076 87) 72211

Country mansion (1840) of red stone and brick with lawns and woodland. Swimming pool, putting. Closed Jan. ⚒ Fr, De
🛏 22 bedrs, 22 en suite; TV; tcf
🏠 dogs, ns; P 25; child facs; con 30
✕ LD 8.30, nr lunch . Resid & Rest lic
£ B&B £26–£30; HB weekly £250–£295; D £14·50; [5% V Feb–15 May & Nov–20 Dec]
cc Access; B'card/Visa, dep.

★ George, St John St, CA12 5AZ ☎ (076 87) 72076
A 16th century coaching inn right in the heart of Keswick. (MtCh)
🛏 17 bedrs, 5 ba; tcf
🏠 TV; dogs; P4; coach; child facs; con 14
✕ LD 9
£ B&B £17·50; D £11; [10% V]
cc. Access, Amex, B'card/Visa, Diners.

★ Linnett Hill, 4 Penrith Rd, CA12 4HF ☎ (076 87) 73109

Well-appointed hotel in listed 19th century building near town centre.
🛏 9 bedrs, 9 en suite; TV; tcf
🏠 dogs, ns; P 12; no children under 5
✕ LD 7. Resid & Rest lic
£ B&B £20, B&B (double) £36; HB weekly £178·50; L £5·50, D £8·50; WB £24 (2 nts); [10% V]
cc Access, B'card/Visa, dep.

★ Priorholm, Borrowdale Rd, CA12 5DD ☎ (076 87) 72745

Small hotel in town, quietly situated on road to Borrowdale.
🛏 8 bedrs, 6 en suite, 1 ba; TV; tcf

Keswick (Cumbria)

King's Lynn (Norfolk)

K

King's Lynn (Norfolk)

TV, ns; P 7; child facs
LD 7.30, nr lunch. Resid & Rest lic
£ B&B £18; B&B (double) £36–£46; HB weekly £175–£220; D £14; [10% V]
cc Access, B'card/Visa; dep.

Allerdale House (Highly Acclaimed), 1 Eskin St, CA12 4DH (076 87) 73891. *Guest House*. Closed Dec.
£ B&B £17·50; HB weekly £175.
Dalegarth House (Highly Acclaimed), Portinscale, CA12 5RQ (07687) 72817. *Hotel*.
£ B&B £20–£22; HB weekly £190–£210
Gales Country House (Highly Acclaimed), Applethwaite, CA12 4PL (07687) 72413. *Private Hotel. Putting, bowling*.
Greystones (Highly Acclaimed), Ambleside Rd, CA12 4DP (076 87) 73108. *Private Hotel*. Open Feb–Nov.
£ B&B £17·50; HB weekly £231–£333
Ravensworth (Highly Acclaimed), 29 Station St, CA12 5HH (076 87) 72476. *Hotel*. Closed Jan.
£ B&B (double) £30–£36; HB weekly £154–£175
Shemara (Highly Acclaimed), 27 Bank St, CA12 5JZ (076 87) 73936. *Guest House*. Open Feb–Nov.
£ B&B (double) £32–£39; [10% V]
Stonegarth (Highly Acclaimed), 2 Eskin St, CA12 4DH (076 87) 72436. *Private Hotel*.
£ B&B £14·60; HB weekly £165–£167·80
Swiss Court (Highly Acclaimed), 25 Bank St, CA12 5JZ (076 87) 72637
Thornleigh (Highly Acclaimed), 23 Bank St, CA12 5JZ (076 87) 72863. *Guest House*.
£ B&B (double) £34–£39; HB weekly £165–£185

Acorn House (Acclaimed), Ambleside Rd, CA12 4DL (076 87) 72553. Open Feb–Nov.
£ B&B (double) £30–£40
Charnwood (Acclaimed), 6 Eskin St, CA12 4DH (076 87) 74111. *Guest House*.
£ B&B (double) £24–£32; HB weekly £124–£152; [5% V]
Fell House (Acclaimed), 28 Stanger St, CA12 5JU (076 87) 72669. *Guest House*.
£ B&B £11·50–£14·25; HB weekly £110–£138
Heights, Rakefoot La, Castlerigg CA12 4TE (076 87) 72251. *Hotel*.
£ B&B £19, HB weekly £105; D £9; [10% V]
Silverdale (Acclaimed), Blencathra St, CA12 4HT (076 87) 72294. *Hotel*.
£ B&B £13–£14·50; HB weekly £128–£155; [5% V]

Greta View, 2 Greta St, CA12 4HS (076 87) 73102. *Private Hotel*. Fr, De
£ B&B £20; HB weekly £155·50–£193·50; [5% V Oct–Jul]
Greystoke House, Leonard St, CA12 4EL (076 87) 72603. *Guest House*.
£ B&B £15; D £6
Hazelgrove, 4 Ratcliffe Pl, CA12 4DZ (076 87) 73391. *Guest House*.
£ B&B (double) £11–£27; HB weekly £110–£136·50; dep.
Holmwood House, The Heads, CA12 5ER (076 87) 73301. *Guest House*.
Leonard's Field, 3 Leonard's St, CA12 4EJ (076 87) 74170. *Guest House*.
£ B&B £12–£16·50; HB weekly £133–£164·50; [10% V Mar, May, Jun]
Sunnyside, 25 Southey St, CA12 4EF (076 87) 72446. *Guest House*.

KETTERING Northamptonshire.

Map 21B4
Pop 45,000. Bedford 25, London 75, Huntingdon 26, Market Harborough 11, Northampton 14, Peterborough 28½.
EC Thur. **MD** Wed, Fri, Sat. **Golf** Kettering 18h. **See** Church with 177ft spire, art gallery and museum, The Mission House.
Coach House, Sheep St. (0536) 410266

★★★ **Kettering's Royal,** Market Pl, NN16 0AJ (0536) 520732
Former 18th century coaching inn–a fine stone building set in the market square.
39 bedrs, 39 en suite; TV; tcf
dogs; G 35, coach; child facs; con 200

★★ **George,** Sheep St, NN16 0AN (0536) 518620 Fax: (0536) 410787
16th century coaching inn on main road into town centre.
45 bedrs, 33 en suite, 12 ba; TV; tcf
TV; dogs; P36, coach; child facs; con 150
LD 11
£ B&B £34·50–£67·50 (w/e £19·75), B&B (double) £40–£70; L £6·50, D £12; WB £27·50 (HB); [10% V]
cc Access, Amex, B'card/Visa, CB, Diners.

KETTLEWELL North Yorkshire. Map 38A4

Pop 320. Leeds 37, London 228, Hawes 22, Leyburn 20, Settle 19, Skipton 14.
EC Thur. **Golf** Skipton 18h. **See** 12th century church, caves.

★★ **Race Horses,** BD23 5QZ (075 676) 233
White painted building of character in picturesque village beside river. Fishing.

★ **Bluebell,** Middle La, BD23 5QX (075 676) 230
A small village inn in Yorkshire Dales National Park.

Langcliffe (Highly Acclaimed), BD23 5RJ (075 676) 243. *Guest House*.

KEXBY North Yorkshire. Map 39A3

Howden 23, London 206, Great Driffield 25, Malton 14, Market Weighton 13, York 5½.

★★★ **Kexby Bridge,** Hull Rd, YO4 5LD (07595) 8223

Modern hotel with pretty decor in light and airy style. Fishing.
32 bedrs, 32 en suite; TV; tcf
TV, ns; P65, coach; child facs; con 100
LD 9.30, nr Sun lunch. Resid & Rest lic
£ B&B £50, B&B (double) £75; L £3·50, D £10·95; WB £70; [10% V]
cc Access, B'card/Visa; dep.

Ivy House, Hull Rd, YO4 5LQ York (0904) 489 368. *Farm*.

KEYNSHAM Avon. Map 4C4

Pop 20,433 (inc Saltford). Bath 7, London 111, Bristol 5½, Radstock 12, Shepton Mallet 16, Tetbury 30, Wells 17.
EC Wed. **Golf** Saltford 18h. **See** Museum, Roman Villa, St John's Church.

★★ **Grange,** 42 Bath Rd, BS18 1SN (0272) 869181
Privately-owned former Georgian farmhouse with modern bedrooms in annexe.
Grasmere Court (Acclaimed), 22 Bath Rd, BS18 1SN (0272) 862662. *Hotel. Swimming pool.*
£ B&B £27–£40 (w/e £20); [5% V]

KIDDERMINSTER Hereford & Worcester

(Worcestershire). Map 22A1
See also STONE
Pop 50,603. Bromsgrove 9, London 122, Birmingham 17, Bridgnorth 13, Leominster 25, Wolverhampton 15, Worcester 14.
EC Wed. **MD** Tue, Thur, Fri, Sat. **Golf** Kidderminster 18h. **See** St Mary's Church, Statue of Sir Rowland Hill, Caldwell Tower.
Severn Valley Railway. (0562) 829400

★★★ H **Gainsborough House,** Bewdley Hill, DY11 6BS (0562) 820041 Tx: 333058 Fax: (0562) 66179

Modern 2-storey hotel, personally managed by the proprietor.
42 bedrs, 42 en suite, 1 ba; TV; tcf
dogs, ns; P 130, coach; child facs; con 250
LD 9.45, bar meals only Sat lunch
£ B&B £54·50–£66 (w/e £34·50), B&B (double) £72·50–£88; L £7·50, D £12·75; WB £69; [10% V w/e]
cc Access, Amex, B'card/Visa, Diners.

Cedars (Highly Acclaimed), Mason Rd, DY11 6AL (0562) 515595 Fax: (0562) 751103. *Hotel*. Fr
£ B&B £42·50–£47·50 (w/e £22·60); [5% V]

KIDLINGTON Oxfordshire. Map 21A2

Pop 12,888. Oxford 5, London 63, Banbury 17, Bicester 8, Chipping Norton 14.
EC Mon, Wed. **MD** Fri. **Golf** North Oxford 18h. **See** Church (spire).

Bowood House (Highly Acclaimed), 238 Oxford Rd, OX5 1EB (0865) 842288 Fax: (0865) 841858. *Private Hotel*.
£ B&B £32–£55

KILBURN North Yorkshire. Map 38C4

York 20, London 213, Helmsby 10, Thirsk 7. **See** Byland Abbey, Shandy Hall & Sterne Museum, Sutton Bank.

★★ **Foresters Arms,** YO6 4AH (034 76) 386
Attractive stone-built inn between the church and 'Mouseman' furniture workshops in a quiet village.

🛏 8 bedrs, 8 en suite; TV; tcf
🏨 dogs; P 12; child facs

KILDWICK West Yorkshire. Map 40A1

Pop 100. Keighley 6, London 211, Burnley 15, Ilkley 8, Skipton 8.
EC Tue. **Golf** Keighley 18h. **See** Church, 14th cent bridge.

★★★ **Kildwick Hall,** BD20 9AE ☎ Cross Hills (0535) 32244
A handsome, Jacobean stone building on hillside overlooking Aire Valley. Solarium.

KILNSEY North Yorkshire. Map 38A3

Ilkley 17, London 224, Hawes 24.

★★ **Tennant Arms,** nr Grassington, BD23 5PS ☎ Grassington (0756) 752301
17th century Yorkshire stone hotel situated beneath dramatic Kilnsey Crag. Fishing, riding.
🛏 10 bedrs, 10 en suite; TV; tcf
🏨 P 40, coach; child facs; con 40
✕ LD 9
£ B&B (double) £50; D £10·95; WB £66·50
cc Access, B'card/Visa; dep.

KINGHAM Oxfordshire. Map 20C2

Pop 570. Oxford 23, London 79, Burford 9, Chipping Norton 4½, Moreton-in-Marsh 7½, Stow-on-the-Wold 5½.

★★★ H C R **Mill House,** OX7 6UH
☎ (060 871) 8188 Tx: 849041
Fax: (060 871) 492 ♿
Charming converted 17th century Cotswold stone mill house. Fishing. Fr, De
🛏 21 bedrs, 21 en suite; TV; tcf
🏨 P 60, coach; no children under 5; con 30
✕ LD 9.30
£ B&B £45–£56, B&B (double) £70–£107; L £12·95, D £16·95; WB £63·50
cc Access, Amex, B'card/Visa, CB, Diners; dep.

KINGSBRIDGE Devon. Map 3B1

Pop 4,236. Totnes 12, London 203, Dartmouth 13, Plymouth 20.
EC Thur. **MD** Wed, Fri.
i The Quay. ☎ (0548) 7340

★★★ **Buckland Tout Saints,** Goveton, TQ7 2DS ☎ (0548) 853055 Tx: 42513
Fax: (0548) 856261

Elegant 17th century country house set in gardens and parkland. Putting. Closed 3 Jan–2 Feb.
🛏 12 bedrs, 12 en suite; TV
🏨 ns; P 20; children over 8; con 20
✕ LD 9.30. Resid & Rest lic
£ B&B £75–£95, B&B (double) £95–£165; L £17·50, D £27·50; WB £160
cc Access, Amex, B'card/Visa; dep.

★ **Crabshell Motor Lodge,** Embankment Rd, TQ7 1JZ ☎ (0548) 3301

Modern purpose-built hotel beautifully situated on the waters-edge.
🛏 24 bedrs, 24 en suite; TV; tcf
🏨 dogs, ns; P 31, G 8, coach; child facs; con 20

KINGSDOWN Kent. Map 7C3

Pop 250. Canterbury 18, London 76, Dover 6, Margate 17, Ramsgate 15.

Blencathra, Kingsdown Hill, CT14 8EA
☎ Deal (0304) 37252. *Private Hotel.* Fr
£ B&B £14–£15

KING'S LYNN Norfolk. Map 34C1

Pop 33,346. Ely 29, London 99, Fakenham 22, Spalding 28, Swaffham 15, Thetford 27, Wisbech 13.
EC Wed. **MD** Tue, Fri, Sat. **Golf** King's Lynn 18h. **See** Guildhall of St George, Old Guildhall, Custom House, Hampton Court, Thoresby College, St Nicholas' Chapel, Red Mount Chapel, Museum and Art Gallery.
i Old Gaol House, Saturday Market.
☎ (0553) 763044

★★★ **Butterfly,** Beveridge Way, Hardwick Narrows Estate, PE30 4NB ☎ (0553) 771707
Tx: 818313 Fax: (0553) 768027 ♿

Ultra modern 2-storey hotel on the eastern outskirts of town on the A47/A10 junction.
Fr, De, It
🛏 50 bedrs, 50 en suite; TV; tcf
🏨 TV; ns; P 70, coach; child facs; con 55
✕ LD 10
£ B&B £54·50 (w/e £30), B&B (double) £59·50; HB weekly £451·50; L £8·75, D £8·75; [10% V]
cc Access, Amex, B'card/Visa, Diners.
(See advertisement on p. 310)

★★★ **Duke's Head,** Tuesday Market Pl, PE30 1JS ☎ (0553) 774996 Tx: 817349
Fax: (0553) 763556
Hotel with beautifully preserved Regency façade, on 'Tuesday Market' place. (THF)
🛏 72 bedrs, 72 en suite; TV; tcf
🏨 lift, dogs, ns; P 40, coach; child facs; con 230
✕ LD 10
£ B&B £73–£86, B&B (double) £97–£102; HB weekly £227; L £7, D £13; WB £43
cc Access, Amex, B'card/Visa, CB, Diners.

★★★ C R **Knights Hill Village,** South Wootton, PE30 3HQ ☎ (0553) 675566
Tx: 818118 Fax: (0553) 675568
Hotel complex containing accommodation ranging from country house to motel, a restaurant, conference rooms and a sports club. Indoor swimming pool, tennis, sauna, solarium, gymnasium, billiards.
🛏 40 bedrs, 40 en suite; annexe 18 bedrs, 18 en suite; TV; tcf
🏨 dogs, ns; P 350, coach; child facs; con 400
✕ LD 10
£ B&B £62, B&B (double) £78; D £15; WB £45 (HB); [10% V Fri–Sun only]
cc Access, Amex, B'card/Visa, Diners.

★★ **Globe,** Tuesday Market Pl, PE30 1EZ
☎ (0553) 772617

A Georgian-style building overlooking the river Ouse and close to town centre. (GMR)
🛏 40 bedrs, 40 en suite; TV; tcf
🏨 ns; P 15, G 8, coach; child facs; con 50
✕ LD 10.30
£ B&B £42–£50·50, B&B (double) £59·50; L £8·15, D £8·15; WB £27·50
cc Access, Amex, B'card/Visa, Diners.

★★ **Grange,** Willow Park, off South Wootton La, PE30 3BP ☎ (0553) 673777
Fax: (0553) 671222

Refurbished Edwardian house quietly set on edge of town with some bedrooms in a separate modern block.
🛏 5 bedrs, 5 en suite; annexe 4 bedrs, 4 en suite; TV; tcf
🏨 dogs, ns; P 15, U 1; child facs; con 20
✕ LD 8.30. Resid & Rest lic
£ B&B £35–£38, B&B (double) £48–£50; L £6·95, D £8·95; WB £20
cc Access, Amex, B'card/Visa.

K

★★ Stuart House, Goodwins Rd, PE30 5QX ☎(0553) 772169 Tx: 817209

Set back from residential road, 2-storey house in own grounds.
19 bedrs, 15 en suite, (1 sh), 2 ba; TV; tcf
TV, dogs; P 30; child facs

★★ R Tudor Rose, St Nicholas St, Tuesday Market Place, PE30 1LR ☎(0553) 762824 Fax: (0553) 764894
Town centre hotel formed from three attractive period houses.
14 bedrs, 11 en suite, 2 ba; TV; tcf
dogs, ns; coach; child facs
LD 8.30, bar meals only lunch
£ B&B £19·95–£30, B&B (double) £45; HB weekly £200; D £8·50; WB £30
cc Access, Amex, B'card/Visa, Diners; dep.

Russet House (Highly Acclaimed), 53 Goodwins Rd, Vancouver Av, PE30 5PE ☎(0553) 773098. *Hotel.* Closed 1–14 Jan.
£ B&B £30–£39

Havana (Acclaimed), 117 Gaywood Rd, PE30 2PU ☎(0553) 772331. *Guest House.*
£ B&B £15

Beeches, 2 Guannock Terr, PE30 5QT ☎(0553) 766577. *Guest House.* Closed 25 Dec–1 Jan.
£ B&B £17–£20
Guanock, South Gates, PE30 5JG ☎(0553) 772959. *Hotel. Billiards.*
£ B&B £20
Maranatha, 115 Gaywood Rd, PE30 2PU ☎(0553) 774596. *Guest House.*
£ B&B £12–£15; HB £112–£133

KINGSTON Devon. Map 3B1

Pop 317. Ashburton 20, London 208, Kingsbridge 8½, Plymouth 14, Tavistock 23, Totnes 17.
Golf Bigbury 18h.

Trebles Cottage (Acclaimed), nr Kingsbridge, TQ7 4PT ☎Bigbury-on-Sea (0548) 810268. *Hotel.*
£ B&B £33–£36; HB weekly £225–£250; [5% V excl Apr–Sep]

KINGSTON-UPON-HULL

See HULL.

KINGSTON UPON THAMES Greater London (Surrey). Map 13C2

Pop 140,210. London 10, Croydon 11, Epsom 6½, Leatherhead 8½, Staines 9½, Uxbridge 15, Woking 14.
EC Wed. **MD** Daily. **Golf** Home Park 18h, Surbiton 18h, Richmond Park 18h (2).
See Saxon Coronation Stone, All Saint's Church, Ham House.
ℹ Fairfield West. ☎081–546 5386

★★★ Kingston Lodge, Kingston Hill, KT2 7NP ☎081-541 4481 Fax: 081-541 1013
Two-storey white stucco hotel built around a pleasant central courtyard. Attractive conservatory-style restaurant. (THF)
61 bedrs, 61 en suite; TV; tcf
dogs, ns; P 65; child facs; con 60
LD 9.45, nr Sat lunch. Resid lic
£ B&B £99·60 (w/e £40), B&B (double) £121·21–£129·21; HB weekly £697·20; L £15·50, D £15·50
cc Access, Amex, B'card/Visa, CB, Diners.

Antoinette, 26 Beaufort Rd, KT1 2TQ ☎081-546 1044. Tx: 928180
Fax: 081-547-2595 *Hotel.* Fr, It, Es, Hu
£ B&B £42
Whitewalls, 12 Lingfield Av, KT1 2TN ☎081-546 2719. *Guest House.*

KINGSWINFORD West Midlands. Map 22A2

Dudley 4, London 124, Birmingham 12, Bridgnorth 13, Stourbridge 3, Wolverhampton 7.

Kingfisher, Kidderminster Rd, Wall Heath, DV6 OEN ☎(0384) 273763
Fax: (0384) 277094
A flamboyant thatched frontage identifies this popular modern inn on the A449.
23 bedrs, 23 en suite; TV; tcf

KINGTON Hereford & Worcester (Herefordshire). Map 19C3

Pop 2,040. Hereford 19, London 151, Brecon 28, Builth Wells 20, Knighton 13, Leominster 13.
EC Wed. **MD** Tue. **Golf** Kington 18h. **See** Parish Church, 15th cent Farmhouse, Offa's Dyke gardens.
ℹ Council Offices, Mill St ☎(0544) 230202

★★ Burton, Mill St, HR5 3BQ ☎(0544) 230323 Fax: (0544) 230323
Refurbished 3-storey Victorian building, with modern extensions, in town centre. Es
15 bedrs, 15 en suite; TV; tcf
dogs; P 45, coach; child facs; con 150
LD 9.30
£ B&B £36·50, B&B (double) £48; HB weekly £227·50–£311·50; L £12·50, D £12·50; WB £65
cc Access, Amex, B'card/Visa, Diners.

Penrhos Court, HR5 3LH ☎(0544) 230720
Fax: (0544) 230754.
Hotel being developed, opening March 1991.
19 bedrs, 19 en suite; TV; tcf

KINTBURY Berkshire. Map 5C3

Newbury 5, London 59, Andover 14, Hungerford 5.

★★★ Elcot Park, nr Newbury, RG16 8NJ ☎Kintbury (0488) 58100 Tx: 846448
Fax: (0488) 58288

Attractively furnished Georgian mansion in 16 acres of landscaped gardens and woodland. Swimming pool planned for June 91. Tennis. Fr, De.
16 bedrs, 16 en suite; annexe 18 bedrs, 18 en suite; TV; tcf
dogs, ns; P60; child facs; con 40
LD 9.30
£ B&B £76·50–£91·50, B&B (double) £98–£104·50; L £15, D £19·50; WB £104
cc Amex, B'card/Visa, Diners.

KIRBY MISPERTON North Yorkshire.

Map 39A4
Malton 7, London 212, Pickering 4, Scarborough 22, Thirsk 28.

★★ Bean Sheaf, Malton Rd, YO17 0UE ☎(065 386) 614 ♿
Purpose-built modern motel type hotel conveniently situated. Sauna, solarium.
20 bedrs, 20 en suite, annexe 5 bedrs, 5 en suite; TV; tcf
dogs, ns; P 60, coach; child facs; con 50
LD 9.30, bar meals only Mon lunch
£ B&B £24·50–£26·50, B&B (double) £40–£42; HB weekly £196; L £6·50, D £9·50; WB £57; [10% V w/d]
cc Access, B'card/Visa; dep.
(*See advertisement on p. 310*)

KIRKBY LONSDALE Cumbria. Map 36B4

Pop 1,506. Settle 16, London 246, Brough 29, Kendal 12, Lancaster 12.
EC Wed. **MD** Thur. **Golf** Kirkby Lonsdale 9h.
See Church, Devil's Bridge.
ℹ 18 Main St. ☎(052 42) 71437

★★★ H R Royal, The Market Sq, LA6 2AE ☎(052 42) 71217 Fax: (05242) 72228
Attractive old stone-built 3-storey hotel overlooking the town square. Billiards. Fr, De, Es
19 bedrs, 16 en suite, 3 ba; TV; tcf
TV; dogs; P 20, G 6, coach; child facs; con 60
LD 10, bar meals only Mon–Sat lunch
£ B&B £25–£35, B&B (double) £45–£55; D £11·50; WB £80; [10% V]
cc Access, B'card/Visa; dep.

★★ Whoop Hall, Skipton Rd ☎(052 42) 71284 Fax: (052 42) 72154
Beamed 17th-century inn sympathetically modernised to retain character. On A65.
15 bedrs, 15 en suite; TV; tcf
ns; P 200, coach; child facs; con 100
LD 10
£ B&B £32, B&B (double) £44–£55; WB fr £55; [10% V excl. w/e]
cc Access, B'card/Visa; dep.

Cobwebs (Highly Acclaimed), Leck, Cowan Bridge, LA6 2HC ☎(052 42) 72141
Fax: (052 42) 72141. *Hotel.* Open Mar–Dec.
£ B&B £30; HB weekly £261; [5% excl. Sat]

Capernwray House, Capernwray, LA6 1AE ☎(0524) 732363. *Farm.*
£ B&B (double) £34–£40

KIRKBY STEPHEN Cumbria. Map 44B1

Pop 1,523. Hawes 16, London 265, Brough 4, Kendal 24, Kirkby Lonsdale 24.
EC Thur. **MD** Mon. **Golf** Appleby 18h. **See** Church, Wharton Hall, Stenkrith Park.
ℹ 22 Market St. ☎(07683) 71199

★★ King's Arms, Market St, CA17 4QN ☎(076 83) 71378

EC *early closing* **MD** *market day* *country house hotel* *ns (NS) no smoking areas* *tcf tea/coffee facilities*

Modernised 17th century posting inn with dignified Georgian entrance. Closed Xmas Day.
🛏 10 bedrs, 4 en suite, 3 ba; tcf
🏨 TV, dogs; P 4, G 6, coach; child facs; con 120
✕ LD 8.45
£ B&B £24·50–£29, B&B (double) £40–£47·50; L £6, D £16·50
cc Access, B'card/Visa; dep.

Thrang (Acclaimed), Mallerstang, CA17 4JX ☎(076 83) 71889
£ B&B £19–£20; HB weekly £224; [10% V w/d]

Town Head House, High St, CA17 4SH, ☎(076 83) 71044 Fax: (076 83) 72128. *Private Hotel. Putting.* Fr, De
£ B&B £31–£39, HB weekly £275–£360; [10% V]

KNARESBOROUGH North Yorkshire. Map 38B3
Pop 13,000. Harrogate 3, London 201, Boroughbridge 7, Leeds 19, York 18.
EC Thur. **MD** Wed. **Golf** Knaresborough 18h. **See** 14th cent Knaresborough Castle ruins, St Robert's Chapel, Dripping Well, Mother Shipton's Cave, Nidderdale.
ℹ Market Pl. ☎Harrogate (0423) 866886

★★★ Dower House, Bond End, HG5 9AL ☎Harrogate (0423) 863302 Tx: 57202 Fax: (0423) 867665

A fine modern building overlooking private gardens. Indoor swimming pool, sauna, solarium, gymnasium. Fr, Po
🛏 28 bedrs, 28 en suite; TV; tcf
🏨 dogs, ns; P 100; child facs; con 70
✕ LD 9.30, nr Sat lunch. Resid & Rest & Club lic
£ B&B £47·50–£63, B&B (double) £66–£80; L £8, D £14; WB £43 (2 nts)
cc Access, Amex, B'card/Visa, Diners; dep.

Yorkshire Lass, High Bridge, Harrogate Rd HG5 8DA ☎(0423) 862962
Typical country inn with verandah at front in superb situation on River Nidd over looking Nidd Valley.
🛏 6 bedrs, 6 en suite; TV; tcf
🏨 P 32, coach
✕ LD 10
£ B&B £30–£36, B&B (double) £40–£45; Hb weekly £210–£230; L £5, D £10; WB £32 (HB); [10% V]
cc Access, Amex, B'card/Visa.
(*See advertisement on p. 317*)

Newton House (Highly Acclaimed), 5 York Pl, HG5 OAD ☎(0432) 863539 Fax: (0423) 869614. *Private Hotel.*
£ B&B £30–£35; [5% V]

Ebor Mount, 18 York Pl, HG5 0AA ☎Harrogate (0423) 863315 *Guest House.*
£ B&B £16·50–£35

KNUTSFORD Cheshire. Map 33B1
Pop 13,751. Newcastle-under-Lyme 24, London 173, M6 (jn 19) 3, Altrincham 7½, Congleton 14, Northwich 7, Warrington 11, Stockport 14, Macclesfield 11.
EC Wed. **MD** Fri, Sat. **Golf** Knutsford 9h. **See** 17th cent Unitarian Chapel (grave of Mrs Gaskell), Gaskell Memorial Tower, The Sessions House, Georgian Church (1744).
ℹ Council Offices, Toft Rd. ☎(0565) 2611

★★★ H C Cottons, Manchester Rd, WA16 0SU ☎(0565) 50333 Tx: 669931 Fax: (0565) 55351 ♿
Beautifully designed and appointed hotel reminiscent of New Orleans. Indoor swimming pool, tennis, sauna, solarium, gymnasium.
🛏 86 bedrs, 86 en suite; TV; tcf
🏨 lift, dogs, ns; P 200, coach; child facs; con 200
✕ LD 9.45, bar meals only Sat lunch
£ B&B £94–£104, B&B (double) £110–£118; HB weekly £756–£826; L £11·50, D £14; WB £102 (2 nts HB)
cc Access, Amex, B'card/Visa, Diners.

★★★ Royal George, King St, WA16 6EE ☎(0565) 4151

Historic Georgian-fronted hotel with panelled interior and minstrel gallery. (BCB). Fr, Es
🛏 31 bedrs, 31 en suite; TV; tcf
🏨 lift, ns; P 40, coach; child facs; con 40
✕ LD 10.30
£ B&B £59–£65·50; B&B (double) £73·50; L £8·15, D £8·15
cc Access, Amex, B'card/Visa, Diners.

Longview (Highly Acclaimed), Manchester Rd, WA16 0LX ☎(0565) 2119. *Hotel.*
£ B&B £29–£42

LAMORNA COVE Cornwall. Map 2A1
Pop 150. Penzance 4, London 285.
EC Wed. **Golf** West Cornwall Lelant 18h.

★★★ Lamorna Cove, TR19 6XH ☎(0736) 731411
Family-run hotel in attractive gardens with views of the Cove. Swimming pool, sauna, solarium.

LANCASTER Lancashire. Map 36B3
See also CLAUGHTON
Pop 45,126. M6 (jn 34) 4½, London 238, Blackpool 24, Kendal 22, Kirkby Lonsdale 16, Preston 22, Settle 25.
EC Wed. **MD** daily. **Golf** Castle, RC Cathedral, John of Gaunt's Gateway, Royal Grammar School, St Mary's Church, Town Hall Gardens, old Town Hall (now museum), 18th cent Custom House, Williamson Park.
ℹ 7 Dalton Sq. ☎(0524) 32878

★★★★ Post House, Caton Rd, Waterside Park, LA1 3RA ☎(0524) 65999 Tx: 65363 Fax: (0524) 841265 ♿
Modern hotel standing in 10 acres of grounds. Indoor swimming pool, sauna, solarium, gymnasium. (THF)
🛏 117 bedrs, 117 en suite; TV; tcf
🏨 lift, dogs, ns; P 200, coach; child facs; con 120
✕ LD 10
£ B&B £80–£91 (w/e £39·50 Dec–Feb), B&B (double) £83–£94; Bk £8, L £10, D £14; WB £49 (2 nts)
cc Access, Amex, B'card/Visa, Diners.

★★★ Royal King's Arms, Market St, LA1 1HP ☎(0524) 32451 Tx: 65481 Fax: (0524) 841698

A substantial, town-centre hotel recently refurbished to a high standard. Fr, Da
🛏 55 bedrs, 55 en suite; TV; tcf
🏨 lift; dogs; P25, coach; child facs; con 70
✕ LD 9.30
£ B&B £49–£75, B&B (double) £65–£75; Bk £5·50, L £5·95, D £11; WB £35; [10% V Jul, Aug]
cc Access, Amex, B'card/Visa, Diners

Lancaster House, Green La, Ellel, LA1 4GT ☎(0524) 844822 Fax: (0524) 844766
Hotel under construction, completion expected August 1991.
🛏 80 bedrs, 80 en suite.

LANCING West Sussex. Map 6B1.
Pop 17,940. Horsham 20, London 59, Brighton 8½, Crawley 23, Worthing 2.
EC Wed **Golf** Worthing 18h (2), Worthing Municipal 18h **See** Lancing College, Church, Widewater.

Sussex Pad, Old Shoreham Rd, BN1 5RH ☎(0273) 454647
Modernised period inn on the A27, opposite Shoreham airport, just below Lancing College.
🛏 6 bedrs, 6 en suite; TV; tcf
🏨 dogs; P60; coach; child facs
✕ LD 10
£ B&B £39, B&B (double) £52; Bk £4·45, L £11·50; D £11·50; WB £60
cc Access, Amex, B'card/Visa

LANGPORT Somerset. Map 4B2
Pop 940. Wincanton 22, London 130, Bridgwater 12, Glastonbury 14, Ilminster 9½, Taunton 13.
EC Wed. **Golf** Taunton 18h. **See** 15th cent All Saints' Parish Church, Hanging Chapel.

L

★★ Langport Arms, Cheapside, TA10 9PD ☎(0458) 250530

An historic hotel, dating back to 15th century, in centre of village.
🛏 8 bedrs, 6 en suite, 2 ba; TV; tcf
🏨 dogs; P 5, coach; child facs; con 180
✕ LD 10, bar meals only lunch; Resid & Rest lic
£ B&B £30, B&B (double) £45; [10% V Mon–Thurs]; D £10
cc Access, Amex, B'card/Visa, Diners.

Hillards Farm (Highly Acclaimed), High St, Curry Rivel, TA10 0EY ☎(0458) 251737

LANREATH Cornwall. Map 2C2

Pop 300. Liskeard 9½, London 230, Bodmin 15, Looe 6.
Golf Bin Down, Looe 18h. **See** Backabarrow Downs, Parish Church, Farming Museum.

★★ Punch Bowl, PL13 2NX ☎(0503) 20218
"Olde world" 17th century coaching inn with smuggling associations.
🛏 14 bedrs, 10 en suite, (2 sh), 1 ba; TV; tcf
🏨 TV, dogs; ns; P 50, coach; child facs
✕ LD 9, bar meals only Mon–Sat lunch
£ B&B £15–£24, B&B (double) £30–£48; HB weekly £133–£189; L £5·95, D £8·50; WB £55·50
cc Access, B'card/Visa, Diners; dep.

LARKFIELD Kent. Map 11C3

M20 (jn 4) 2, London 34, Maidstone 4, Sevenoaks 12, Tonbridge 11.

★★★ Larkfield, London Rd, ME20 6HJ ☎West Malling (0732) 846858 Tx: 957420 Fax: (0732) 846786

Large custom-built modern brick building attached to earlier hotel. (THF) ⚒ Fr.
🛏 44 bedrs, 44 en suite; annexe 8 bedrs, 8 en suite; TV; tcf
🏨 dogs, ns; P 80, coach; child facs; con 80
✕ LD 10, bar meals only Sat lunch
£ B&B £72–£82, B&B (double) £94–£99; L £8·95, D £14·50; WB £40
cc Access, Amex, B'card/Visa, CB, Diners.

LASTINGHAM North Yorkshire. Map 39A4

Pop 112. Pickering 9, London 233, Helmsley 11, Scarborough 25.
Golf Kirkbymoorside 9h.

♣♣ ★★★ H C R Lastingham Grange, YO6 6TH ☎(075 15) 345
Peacefully located, family-run country house hotel set in own grounds. Open Mar–Dec.
🛏 12 bedrs, 12 en suite; TV; tcf
🏨 dogs; ns; P 30, U2; child facs
✕ LD 8.30; Resid & Rest lic
£ B&B £45·50–£50, B&B (double) £84·50–£93; HB weekly £385–£423·50; L £10·75, D £17·25; WB £46
cc Amex, Diners

LAUNCESTON Cornwall. Map 3A2

Pop 5,000. Okehampton 19, London 211, Bodmin 22, Camelford 16, Holsworthy 13, Liskeard 15, Tavistock 13.
EC Thur. **MD** Tue. **Golf** Launceston 18h.
See Castle ruins, Southgate Arch.
ℹ Market House Arcade, Market Street. ☎(0566) 2321

★★★ Eagle House, Castle St, PL15 8QZ ☎(0566) 772036 Fax: (0566) 776056
Georgian, red-brick building on edge of town near castle ruins. Recently refurbished in period style.
⚒ Fr, Es, It, Po, Du
🛏 10 bedrs, 10 en suite; TV; tcf
🏨 dogs; P 20, coach; child facs; con 170
✕ LD 9·30. Resid & Rest lic
£ B&B £37·50–£41·25, B&B (double) £49·50–£54·50; L £9·95, D £9·95; WB £70; [10% V]
cc Access, Amex, B'card/Visa.

★★White Hart, Broad St, PL15 8AA ☎(0566) 772013 Fax: (0566) 773668
Three-storey former coaching inn set in town centre. Billiards.
🛏 27 bedrs, 22 en suite, 5 ba; TV; tcf
🏨 TV, dogs; P 25, coach; child facs; con 200
✕ LD 9.30
£ B&B £25–£29, B&B (double) £45–£48; L £9·50, D £9·50; WB £56 (2nts)
cc Access, Amex, B'card/Visa, Diners; dep.

Hurdon Farm, PL15 9LS ☎(0566) 772955
Open May–Oct.
£ B&B £12–£14·50; HB weekly £110–£127

LAVENHAM Suffolk. Map 27A3

Pop 1,725. Sudbury 6½, London 65, Aldeburgh 41, Bury St Edmunds 11, Clacton-on-Sea 33, Harwich 31, Haverhill 19, Ipswich 19, Saxmundham 37, Stowmarket 15.
Golf Newton Green, Sudbury 9h. **See** 16th cent half-timbered Guildhall (with Museum), mainly Perp Church, Market Cross.
ℹ Market Pl ☎(0787) 248207

★★★★ Swan, High St, CO10 9QA ☎(0787) 247477 Fax: (0787) 248286

Amalgam of splendidly preserved Elizabethan house, inn and woolhall. (THF). ⚒ Fr, Es, De
🛏 47 bedrs, 47 en suite, TV; tcf
🏨 dogs, ns; P 50, coach; child facs; con 40
✕ LD 9.30
£ room £81–£85·50, double room £103–£107; Bk £6–£8, L £10·75–£14, D £19·50; WB £62
cc Access, Amex, B'card/Visa, Diners.

LEA MARSTON Warwickshire.

Map 23 A2
M42 (jn 9) 1½, London 108, Birmingham 12, Nuneaton 12, Sutton Coldfield 7, Tamworth 9

★★★ Lea Marston, Haunch Lane, B76 0BY ☎(0675) 470468
Fax: (0675) 470871 ♿

Low-built modern hotel in 20 acres of landscaped grounds. Golf, putting, tennis, sauna, solarium, gymnasium. ⚒ Fr, Es
🛏 19 bedrs, 19 en suite; TV; tcf
🏨 TV, dogs; P165, coach; child facs; con 120
✕ LD 10, bar meals only Sat lunch, Mon & Sun dinner
£ B&B £60–£80 (w/e £40), B&B (double) £65–£90; L £9·30, D £9·30; WB £69 (2nts); [10% V]
cc Access, Amex, B'card/Visa.

LEAMINGTON SPA Warwickshire.

Map 21A3
See also EATHORPE
Pop 56,538. Banbury 20, London 93, Coventry 8½, Daventry 18, Rugby 14, Tamworth 28, Warwick 2.
MD Wed, Fri. **Golf** Newbold Comyn 18h.
See Royal Pump Room, Jephson Gardens, All Saint's Church, Museum and Art Gallery.
ℹ Royal Pump Room, The Parade. ☎(0926) 311470

★★★ Falstaff, 20 Warwick New Rd, CV32 5JG ☎(0926) 312044 Fax: (0926) 450574
In residential area, a hotel converted from fine Regency residences.
🛏 65 bedrs, 65 en suite; TV; tcf
🏨 lift; dogs; P60; coach; child facs; con 60
✕ LD 10
£ B&B £57 (w/e £18), B&B (double) £67; D £14; WB £32
cc Access, B'card/Visa, Diners.

★★★ Garden Court Holiday Inn, Olympus Av, Tachbrook Park, CV34 6RJ ♿

 EC *early closing* **MD** *market day* ♣♣ *country house hotel* *ns (NS) no smoking areas* *tcf tea/coffee facilities*

Kirby Misperton (Yorkshire)

RAC ★★

Bean Sheaf Restaurant and Hotel

ETB 4 Crowns

Kirby Misperton, Pickering, Nr Malton, N. Yorks. Telephone: (065386) 614 or 488

Heart of North Yorkshire Moors, family run hotel. Chef/proprietor. 16th century building with hotel and wine bar addition. Half hour from York and coast; fine food, large wine list.

Knaresborough (N. Yorkshire)

A real country pub and Restaurant

Restaurant open 7 days a week serving traditional Yorkshire food. Excellent selection of wines.

★

Fantastic 40s character bar where bar meals, a wide choice of malt whiskies and traditional hand pulled ales are the order of the day.

6 luxurious en-suite bedrooms some with beautiful views of the river Nidd.

★

Historical Knaresborough is ideally situated for Harrogate (2 miles), York (17 miles), the Dales (30 min. drive). Numerous golf courses, race courses galore, & fishing all nearby.

Bridget & Derek assure you of a very warm welcome and an enjoyable stay at

HIGH BRIDGE, KNARESBOROUGH (opp. Mother Shipton's). TELEPHONE (0423) 862962

Leeds (North Yorkshire)

100 Bedrooms with en-suite bathrooms, tea and coffee facilities and colour television. Excellent restaurant, bar lunches and cocktail bar. Conference facilities for 2 to 400, Weddings, Exhibitions, Seminars and Dinner Dances. Extensive car parking, easy access to all major routes and services. THE STAFF ARE HERE TO CARE FOR YOU.

Tel: 0532—732323

STAKIS

Windmill Hotel

LEEDS

Modern red-brick hotel with conservatory entrance situated in development park between Leamington and Warwick. Views of Warwick Castle.
🛏 98 bedrs, 98 en suite; TV; tcf
✕ LD 10; bar meals only Sat lunch
£ B&B £58·95–£72·95, B&B (double) £65·90–£79·90 (w/e £35); L £12·50, D £14·50
cc Access, Amex, B'card/Visa, Diners.

★★★ **Manor House,** Avenue Rd, CV31 3NJ ☎(0926) 423251 Fax: (0926) 425933

Attractive former manor house. The first lawn tennis club was founded here. (THF).
Fr, Es
🛏 53 bedrs, 53 en suite; TV; tcf
lift, TV, dogs, ns; P 100; coach; child facs; con 100
✕ LD 10
£ B&B £65 (w/e £42, B&B (double) £85; L £7·50–£9·50, D £14·50
cc Access, Amex, B'card/Visa, CB, Diners; dep.

★★★ **Regent,** The Parade, CV32 4AX ☎(0926) 427231 Tx: 311715 Fax: (0926) 450728

Named by permission of Prince Regent, an elegant Regency hotel.
🛏 80 bedrs, 80 en suite; TV; tcf
lift, TV, dogs; P 70, G 30, coach; child facs; con 100
✕ LD 10.45
£ B&B £55–£72, B&B (double) £75–£90; L £9·75, D £14; WB £86 (2nts)
cc Access, Amex, B'card/Visa, CB, Diners.

★★ C R **Abbacourt,** 40 Kenilworth Rd, CV32 6JF ☎(0926) 451775 Fax: (0926) 450330. Es
Former private residence, now a hotel situated on town outskirts.
🛏 26 bedrs, 17 en suite; 3 ba; TV; tcf
TV, dogs; P30, coach; child facs; con 30
✕ LD 9.30, nr Sun
£ B&B £45 (w/e £35), B&B (double) £65; Bk £4, D £10
cc Access, Amex, B'card/Visa, Diners.

★★ **Adams,** 22 Avenue Rd, CV31 3PQ ☎(0926) 450742 Fax: (0926) 313110
Privately-owned early 19th century hotel, refurbished but retaining its period charm. Solarium. De, Du
🛏 11 bedrs, 11 en suite; TV
dogs, ns; P 14; child facs; con 14
✕ LD 8.30, nr Sat & Sun. Resid & Rest lic
£ B&B £34–£45 (w/e £22), B&B (double) £46–£52
cc Access, Amex, B'card/Visa, Diners; dep.

★★ **Angel,** 143 Regent St, CV32 4NZ ☎(0926) 881296 Fax: (0926) 881296
Attractive 3-storey Georgian building painted white. Conveniently sited for shops. Fr, De ♿
🛏 36 bedrs, 35 en suite, 2 ba; TV; tcf
lift, dogs; P 50, coach; child facs; con 90
✕ LD 9. Unlic
£ B&B £25·50–£49·50, B&B (double) £39–£59·50; L £7·95, D £11·50; WB £30
cc Access, Amex, B'card/Visa.

★★ **Beech Lodge,** 28 Warwick New Rd, CV32 5JJ ☎(0926) 422227
Former private house converted to hotel in residential area. Closed 24 Dec–2 Jan.
🛏 12 bedrs, 9 en suite, (1 sh), 2 ba, TV; tcf
TV, dogs; P 16; child facs; con 20
✕ LD 9. Resid & Rest lic
£ B&B £29·50–£39·50 (w/e £33, B&B (double) £50–£55; L £3·95, D £8·50; [10% V]
cc Access, Amex, B'card/Visa.

★★ **Berni Royal,** 2 Kenilworth Rd, CV32 5TE ☎(0926) 883561
Refurbished, cream-painted, four-storey Georgian building in town centre. (BCB)
🛏 22 bedrs, 22 en suite; TV; tcf
lift, ns; P 30, coach; child facs

★★ H C **Tuscany,** 34 Warwick Pl, CV32 5DE ☎(0926) 332233
Small country-house-style hotel in Regency building, elegantly furnished and with excellent bedrooms. No smoking throughout.
🛏 8 bedrs, 8 en suite; TV; tcf
NS; P8, coach; child facs; con 18
✕ LD 9.30; nr lunch. Resid lic
£ B&B £65–£85 (w/e £39), B&B (double) £75–£95; L £9·55, D £16·95; WB £22·50; [10% V]
cc Access, Amex, B'card/Visa, Diners.

★ **Lansdowne,** Clarendon St, CV32 4PF ☎(0926) 450505 Fax: (0675) 463699

Small hotel in elegant Regency building with some period furnishings. Fr, It, De
🛏 15 bedrs, 12 en suite, 1 ba; TV; tcf
TV; dogs; P 11; no children under 5
✕ LD 8.30, nr lunch. Resid & Rest lic
£ B&B £27·85–£44·95, B&B (double) £39·30–£53·90; D £14·95; WB £36·95 (2 nts)
cc Access, B'card/Visa; dep.

Buckland Lodge, 35 Avenue Rd, CV31 3PG ☎(0926) 23843. *Hotel.* ♿
Charnwood House, 47 Avenue Rd, CV31 3PF ☎(0926) 831074. *Guest House.* Closed Xmas.
£ B&B £14–£28; HB weekly £120–£222 [5% V]
Milverton House, 1 Milverton Terr, CV32 5BE ☎(0926) 428335. *Hotel.*

LEDBURY Hereford & Worcester

(Herefordshire). Map 20B3
Pop 4,517. Tewkesbury 14, London 119, M50 (jn 2) 4½, Bromyard 13, Gloucester 16, Hereford 14, Ross-on-Wye 12, Worcester 16.
EC Wed. **MD** Tue, Wed. **Golf** Ross 18h.
ℹ St Katherines, High St. ☎(0531) 2641

★★ **Royal Oak,** 5 The Southend, HR8 2EY ☎(0531) 2110 Fax: (0531) 4761

Family-run old coaching inn situated near town centre. Panelled lounge. Billiards. Fr, De, Gr
🛏 10 bedrs, 7 en suite, 3 ba; TV; tcf
P 10, G 6, coach; child facs; con 140
✕ LD 8.30
£ B&B £19·50–£32·50, B&B (double) £32·50–£45·50; L £8·65, D £8·65; WB £65
cc Access, Amex, B'card/Visa, Diners; dep.

LEE Devon. Map 3A4

Pop 100. Blackmoor Gate 14, London 205, Barnstaple 13, Croyde 8, Ilfracombe 3½.

★★ H **Lee Manor,** Lee Bay, Nr Ilfracombe, EX34 8LR ☎(0271) 863920
Elizabethan manor in gardens and woodland. Great hall has minstrel gallery. Open Easter–Oct. Fr, De
🛏 11 bedrs, 11 en suite; TV; tcf
ns; P 15; no children under 14
✕ LD 8, nr lunch
£ HB weekly £196–£226; D £9·95; dep.

LEEDS West Yorkshire. Map 40B3

See also SOUTH MILFORD
RAC Office, *34 Regent St, Leeds, LS2 7QL* ☎(0532) 436091.
Pop 450,000. Pontefract 13, London 191, M1 (jn 46) 1½, Bradford 9, Halifax 15, Harrogate 15, Huddersfield 15, York 24. See Plan, p. 319.
MD Daily. **P** See Plan. **Golf** Armley 18h, Temple Newsam 18h and others. **See** RC Cathedral, Town Hall, Art Gallery, Museum, Churches, Kirkstall Abbey, Armley Mills.
ℹ 19 Wellington St. ☎(0532) 462454

EC *early closing* **MD** *market day* *country house hotel* *ns (NS) no smoking areas* *tcf tea/coffee facilities*

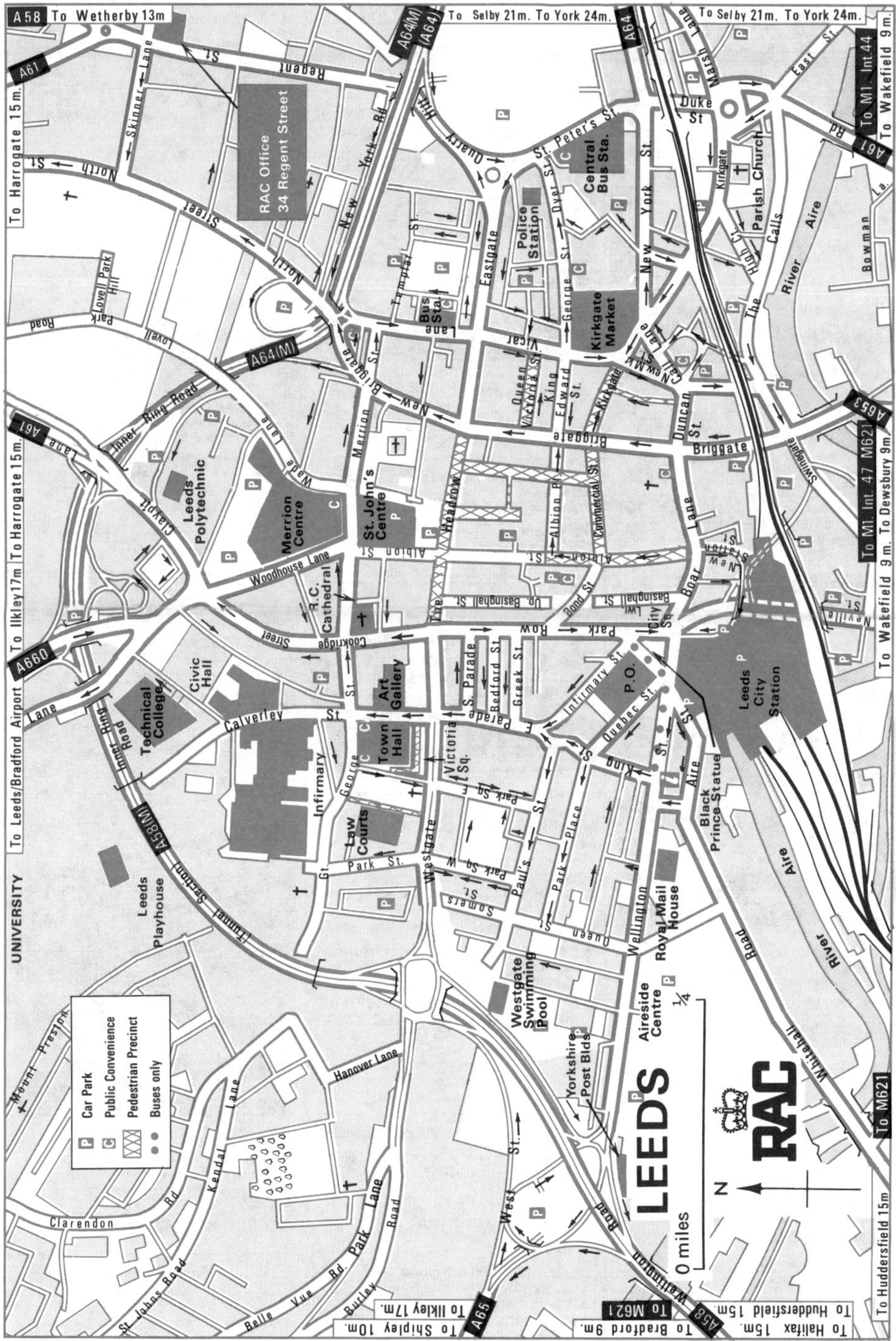

LEEDS
RAC
Car Park
Public Convenience
Pedestrian Precinct
Buses only
0 miles
1/4
N
A58 To Wetherby 13m
To Selby 21m. To York 24m.
To Selby 21m. To York 24m.
A64(M) (A64)
A64
To Harrogate 15m.
To Harrogate 15m.
To Harrogate 15m.
To Ilkley 17m
To Leeds/Bradford Airport
To Shipley 10m.
To Ilkley 17m.
To Bradford 9m.
To M621
To Halifax 15m.
To Huddersfield 15m.
To Huddersfield 15m
To M621
To Wakefield 9m. To Dewsbury 9m
To M1 Int. 47 M621
To Wakefield 9m.
To M1 Int. 44
To Wakefield 9m.
A61
A653
A660
A65
A58
A58(M)
RAC Office 34 Regent Street
Central Bus Sta.
Police Station
Kirkgate Market
Parish Church
Merrion Centre
St. John's Centre
Leeds Polytechnic
R.C. Cathedral
Civic Hall
Technical College
Art Gallery
Town Hall
Law Courts
Leeds City Station
P.O.
Black Prince Statue
Royal Mail House
Aireside Centre
Westgate Swimming Pool
Yorkshire Post Blds
Leeds Playhouse
UNIVERSITY
River Aire
Crown copyright reserved

★★★★ Hilton International Leeds, Neville St, LS1 4BX ☎(0532) 442000 Tx: 557143 Fax: (0532) 433577
Fr, Es, De, It ♿

A large modern high-rise city hotel with conference facilities. Near station. (H. Int)
210 bedrs, 210 en suite; TV; tcf
lift, dogs, ns; P 10, G 70, coach; child facs; con 400
LD 10
£ room £98–£150, double room £110–150; Bk £9·75, L £11·50, D £16·50
cc Access, Amex, B'card/Visa, Diners, dep.

★★★★ Queen's, City Sq, LS1 1PL ☎(0532) 431323 Tx: 55161 Fax: (0532) 425154 ♿

An imposing listed building (c. 1937) in neo-classic style. Fr, De, It, Es (THF)
188 bedrs, 188 en suite; TV; tcf
lift, dogs, ns; coach; child facs; con 700
LD 10
£ B&B £95–£116, B&B (double) £114–£124; L £12·50, D £13·60; WB £45
cc Access, Amex, B'card/Visa, CB, Diners.

Complaints
If you are dissatisfied with the facilities or service offered by a hotel, please take the matter up with the Manager WHILE YOU ARE AT THE HOTEL. In this way, any problems can usually be solved promptly and amicably.

The RAC will investigate matters if a personal approach has failed to resolve the problem. Please submit details of any discussion or correspondence when reporting the problem to the RAC.

★★★ Golden Lion, Briggate, LS1 4AL ☎(0532) 436454 Tx: 557934 Fax: (0532) 429327 ♿

Modernised hotel close to shopping centre and motorway links. (MtCh)
89 bedrs, 89 en suite; TV, tcf
dogs; coach; child facs; con 100
LD 9.45; bar meals only lunch
£ B&B £65, B&B (double) £75; D £11·25; WB £30
cc Access, Amex, B'card/Visa, Diners

★★★ Haley's, Shire Oak Rd, Headingley LS6 2DE ☎(0532) 784446 Fax: (0532) 753342

Stone-built, Victorian town house in quiet, tree-lined cul-de-sac in suburb north west of centre. Fr, De
22 bedrs, 22 en suite; TV; tcf
P 16; child facs, con 20
LD 9.45. Resid & Rest lic
£ B&B £92–£110 (w/e £35), B&B (double) £110–£125; L £17, D £19·50
cc Access, Amex, B'card/Visa.

★★★ Hilton National, Wakefield Rd, Garforth, LS25 1LH ☎(0532) 866566 Tx: 556324 Fax (0532) 868326
Large modern hotel with spacious grounds. Swimming pool, sauna, gymnasium. (HN)
144 bedrs, 144 en suite; TV; tcf
dogs, ns; P 250, coach; child facs; con 300
LD 10, nr Sat lunch
£ B&B £96·50–£109 (w/e £35), B&B (double) £117–£132; L £11, D £16
cc Access, Amex, B'card/Visa, Diners; dep.

★★★ Merrion, Merrion Centre, LS2 8NH ☎(0532) 439191 Tx: 55459 Fax: (0532) 423527
High-rise city centre hotel with access from multi-storey car park. (MtCh)

Hotel locations
Hotel locations are shown on the maps at the back of the guide. All towns and villages containing an RAC Appointed or Listed hotel are ringed in purple.

120 bedrs, 120 en suite; TV; tcf
lift, dogs, ns; G, coach; child facs; con 80
LD 10.30
£ room £64·50 (w/e £37·50), double room £69·50; Bk £7·85, L £12·25, D £12·25
cc Access, Amex, B'card/Visa, Diners.

★★★ Parkway, Otley Rd, LS16 8AG ☎(0532) 672551 Tx: 556614 Fax: (0532) 674410 ♿

Large 1930s building set in 2 acres of grounds and overlooking country park. Swimming pool, tennis, sauna, solarium, gymnasium, billiards. Fr (Emb)
103 bedrs, 103 en suite; TV; tcf
lift, dogs, ns; P 350, coach; child facs; con 250
LD 10
£ B&B £92·70–£102·70 (w/e £34), B&B (double) £114·40–£124·40; L £10·95, D £14; WB £41
cc Access, Amex, B'card/Visa, Diners; dep.

★★★ Stakis Windmill, Ring Rd, Seacroft, LS14 5QP ☎(0532) 732323 Tx: 55452 Fax: (0532) 323018
A modern hotel with original windmill an integral feature of building. (Sk)
100 bedrs, 100 en suite; TV, tcf
lift, dogs, ns; P 100, coach; child facs; con 250
£ L £7·95
(*See advertisement on p. 317*)

★★ Wellesley, Wellington St, LS1 4HJ ☎(0532) 430431 Fax: (0532) 436

Elegant Victorian city centre hotel close to main railway station. (MtCh)
54 bedrs, 22 en suite; 8 ba; TV; tcf
lift; dogs; P25, coach; child facs; con 200
LD 9.30, nr lunch Sat, Sun

En suite rooms
En suite rooms may be bath or shower rooms. If you have a preference, remember to state it when booking a room.

£ B&B £35·50, B&B (double) £46·50; L £6, D £10; WB £24
cc Access, Amex, B'card/Visa, Diners

★ **Hartrigg,** 10 Shire Oak Rd, Headingley, LS6 2DL (2 m NW A660). ☎ (0532) 751568
A stone building, pleasantly situated in gardens, in quiet suburb.

Pinewood (Acclaimed), 78 Potternewton La, LS7 3LW ☎ (0532) 622561. *Private Hotel.* Closed 20 Dec–7 Jan.
£ B&B £25–£31

Aragon (Acclaimed), 250 Stainbeck La, LS7 2PS ☎ (0532) 759306. *Hotel.* Closed 24 Dec–2 Jan.
£ B&B £23·40–£33·92; [V]

Broomhurst, 12 Chapel La, Cardigan Rd, LS6 3BW ☎ (0532) 786836. *Hotel.*
£ B&B £17·50–£27, HB weekly £150·50–£217

Clock, 317 Roundhay Rd, LS8 4HT ☎ (0532) 490304. *Hotel.*

Merevale, 16 Wetherby Rd, LS8 2QD ☎ (0532) 658933. *Hotel.*
£ B&B £17–£25; [5% V]

LEEK Staffordshire. Map 30B3
Pop 19,504, Ashbourne 15, London 154, Buxton 13, Congleton 9½, Macclesfield 13, Matlock 28, Nantwich 25, Newcastle-under-Lyme 11, Stoke-on-Trent 11.
EC Thur. **MD** Wed. **Golf** Leek 18h. **See** Parish Church, Nicholson Institute.
[i] Market Pl ☎ (0538) 381000

★ **Peak Weavers,** 21 King St, ST13 5NW ☎ (0538) 383729
Red-brick mansion in garden 5 minutes walk from town centre.
🛏 11 bedrs, 4 en suite, (2 sh), 2 ba; TV; tcf
🏨 TV, dogs; P 8, G 4, coach; child facs; con 25

LEEMING BAR N. Yorkshire. Map 38B4
Pop 670. Boroughbridge 16, London 224, Northallerton 6, Scotch Corner 11, Leyburn 13, Ripon 14.
EC Thur. **Golf** Bedale 18h.
[i] Leeming Service Area, A1/A684, Bedale. ☎ Bedale (0677) 23611

★★★ **Leeming,** Bedale, DL8 1DT ☎ Bedale (0677) 23611 Fax: (0677) 24507
Small modern family-run motor hotel standing near to A1 motorway. ✱ Fr, De
🛏 40 bedrs, 40 en suite; TV; tcf
🏨 dogs, ns; P100, U3 (£2), G7; coach; child facs; con 90
✕ LD 9.45. Resid lic
£ B&B £25–£35, B&B (double) £35; L £5·95, D £7·95; WB £44; [10% V]
cc Access, Amex, B'card/Visa, CB, Diners; dep.

★★ **White Rose,** Northallerton, DL7 9AY ☎ Bedale (0677) 22707 Fax: (0677) 25123 ♿
A modern purpose-built hotel near A1 with large car park. On edge of village. ✱ Fr
🛏 18 bedrs, 18 en suite; TV; tcf
🏨 TV, dogs; P 40, coach; child facs; con 40
✕ LD 9
£ B&B £25, B&B (double) £40; L £5·10, D £9·50; WB £48; [10% V]
cc Access, Amex, B'card/Visa, Diners; dep.

Hotel locations
Hotel locations are shown on the maps at the back of the guide. All towns and villages containing an RAC Appointed or Listed hotel are ringed in purple.

LEE ON THE SOLENT Hampshire Map 5C2
Fareham 4, London 76, Romsey 20, Southampton 13, Winchester 21.
EC Thur **Golf** Lee on the Solent 18h.

★★★ **Belle Vue,** 39 Marine Parade East, PO13 9BW ☎ (0705) 550258
Fax: (0705) 552624

Two-storey, white-painted hotel on seafront with lovely views over the Solent. ✱ Fr
🛏 24 bedrs, 24 en suite, annexe 3 bedrs, 3 en suite; TV; tcf
🏨 dogs; P 55, coach; child facs, con 175
✕ LD 9.45
£ B&B £60 (w/e £27·50); B&B (double) £72; L £8·25, D £15; WB £82·50 (HB, 2 nts); [10% V]
cc Access, B'card/Visa.

LEICESTER Leicestershire. Map 25C3
See also NEWTON LINFORD and ROTHLEY
Pop 282,300. London 97, M1 (jn 21) 4, Ashby-de-la-Zouch 17, Coventry 25, Hinckley 13, Loughborough 11, Market Harborough 15, Melton Mowbray 15, Nottingham 26, Rugby 20, Stamford 32. See Plan, p. 323.
MD Daily. **P** See Plan. **Golf** Leicestershire 18h, Birstall 18h, Rothley Park 18h, Scraptoft 18h, Glen Gorse 18h. **See** Cathedral, St Mary de Castro Church, St Nicholas' and other churches, Jewry Wall Museum, Leicester Castle remains, Guildhall, Newarke Gateway (with Regimental Museum), Town Hall, Museum of Technology.
[i] 2–6 St Martin's Walk ☎ (0533) 511300

Complaints
If you are dissatisfied with the facilities or service offered by a hotel, please take the matter up with the Manager WHILE YOU ARE AT THE HOTEL. In this way, any problems can usually be solved promptly and amicably.
The RAC will investigate matters if a personal approach has failed to resolve the problem. Please submit details of any discussion or correspondence when reporting the problem to the RAC.

★★★★ **Grand,** Granby St, LE1 6ES ☎ (0533) 555599 Tx: 342244
Fax: (0533) 544736

Traditional city centre hotel with large foyer and modern decorations. (Emb) ✱ Fr, It, Po, Gr
🛏 92 bedrs, 92 en suite; TV; tcf
🏨 lift, dogs; P 120, G 7, coach; child facs; con 450
✕ LD 10, nr Sat lunch
£ B&B £77–£87 (w/e £30), B&B (double) £96–£106; L £10·95, D £10·95; WB £38
cc Access, Amex, B'card/Visa, Diners.

★★★★ **Holiday Inn,** St Nicholas Circle, LE1 5LX ☎ (0533) 531161 Tx: 341281
Fax: (0533) 513169 ♿
Modern purpose-built hotel with 8 storeys. Indoor swimming pool, sauna, solarium, gymnasium. (HI)
🛏 188 bedrs, 188 en suite; TV; tcf
🏨 lift, dogs, ns; P 700, coach; child facs; con 300
✕ LD 10.15, nr Sat lunch
£ room £72–£87, double room £80–£95; L £9·50, D £14·75; WB £40
cc Access, Amex, B'card/Visa, Diners.

★★★ **C** **R** **Belmont,** De Montfort St, LE1 7GR ☎ (0533) 544773 Tx: 34619
Fax: (0533) 470804

In quiet tree-lined street, several houses combined into an imposing hotel. ✱ Fr, It, Cr
🛏 46 bedrs, 46 en suite; annexe 22 bedrs, 22 en suite; TV; tcf
🏨 lift, dogs, ns; P 41, coach; child facs; con 120
✕ LD 9.50, nr Sat lunch
cc Access, Amex, B'card/Visa, Diners.

L

★★★ Leicester Forest Moat House, Hinckley Rd, LE3 3GH (0533) 394661 Fax: (0533) 394952.

Modern hotel of brick construction. Set in own grounds in suburbs. (QMH) Fr, Es
34 bedrs, 34 en suite; TV; tcf
dogs; P 200, coach; child facs; con 100
LD 9.45, bar meals only Sat lunch
£ B&B £61 (w/e £25), B&B (double) £76; L £8, D £10·50; WB £30
cc Access, Amex, B'card/Visa, Diners.

★★★ Leicestershire Moat House, Wigston Rd, Oadby, LE2 5QE (0533) 719441 Fax: (0533) 720559

Light modern 4-storey hotel attached to older building near racecourse. (QMH)
Fr, De, It, Gr
57 bedrs, 57 en suite; TV; tcf
lift, TV, dogs, ns; P 160, coach; child facs; con 250
LD 9.45, bar meals only Sat lunch
£ B&B £66–£73·50, B&B (double) £82; L £9·20, D £11·50; WB £30 (HB); [5% V]
cc Access, Amex, B'card/Visa, Diners; dep.

★★★ Park International, Humberstone Rd, LE5 3AT (0533) 620471 Tx: 341460 Fax: (0533) 514211
A large modern purpose-built hotel in the city centre.
209 bedrs, 209 en suite; TV; tcf
lift, dogs, ns; P 20, G 25, coach; child facs; con 400
LD 10.30
£ B&B £32·95–£73·95, B&B (double) £49·90–£90·90; HB weekly £444·50–£514·50; L £7·95, D £12·50; WB £18; [10% V]
cc Access, Amex, B'card/Visa, Diners.

Weekend breaks
Please consult the hotel for full details of weekend breaks; prices shown are an indication only. Many hotels offer mid week breaks as well.

★★★ Post House, Braunstone Lane East, LE3 2FW (0533) 630500 Tx: 341009 Fax: (0533) 823623

A modern hotel situated south of Leicester city centre. (THF)
172 bedrs, 172 en suite; TV; tcf
lift, dogs, ns; P 250, coach; child facs; con 120
LD 10, nr Sat lunch
£ room £67–£72·50, room (double) £78–£89; Bk £7·50, L £9·95, D £12·95; WB £38 (w/e £39·50 per room)
cc Access, Amex, B'card/Visa, Diners.

★★★ St James, Abbey St, LE1 3TE (0533) 510666 Tx: 342434 Fax: (0533) 515183
Modern city centre hotel above public car park. Sauna, solarium, gymnasium. Es
72 bedrs, 72 en suite; TV; tcf
lift, TV, dogs; P 200, coach; child facs; con 150
bar snacks only, Sat & Sun lunch
£ B&B £63–£66 (w/e £30·50), B&B (double) £79–£82; L £9, D £12; WB £35
cc Access, Amex, B'card/Visa, Diners

★★★ Stage, 299 Leicester Rd, Wigston Fields LE8 1JW (0533) 886161 Fax: (0533) 811874
Low-built modern hotel with adjacent bedroom block. On A50 just south of outer ring road. Fr, De
78 bedrs, 78 en suite; TV; tcf
dogs; ns; P 180, coach; child facs; con 250
LD 10
£ B&B £42–£52, B&B (double) £52–£62; HB weekly £396·65; L £6·95, D £8·95; [5% V]
cc Access, Amex, B'card/Visa, Diners
(See advertisement on p. 324)

Red Cow, Hinckley Rd, Leicester Forest East, LE3 3PG (0533) 387878 Fax: (0533) 387878
Attractive old thatched pub with separate modern bedroom block. On A47 on west side of Leicester Forest East.
31 bedrs, 31 en suite; TV; tcf
dogs; P 120, coach; child facs
LD 10.30
£ B&B £38 (w/e £19), B&B (double) £46; L £9, D £9
cc Access, Amex, B'card/Visa, Diners
(See advertisement on p. 324)

Burlington, Elmfield Av, LE2 1RB (0533) 705112. Fax: (0533) 550548. *Hotel.*
Daval, 292 London Rd, Stoneygate, LE2 2AG (0533) 708234. *Hotel.* Es
£ B&B £18·50; [10% V w/e]
Old Tudor Rectory, Main St, Glenfield, LE3 8DG (0533) 320220. *Hotel.*
£ B&B £28·75–£33·35; HB weekly £251–£281·36; [5% V]
Scotia, 10 Westcotes Dr, LE3 0QR (0533) 549200. *Hotel.*
£ B&B £20–£21
Stoneycroft, 5–7 Elmfield Ave, LE2 1RB (0533) 707605 Fax: (0533) 543788
£ B&B £22–£33; [10% V]

LEIGH Gtr Manchester (Lancashire). Map 33A2

Pop 45,626. M6 (jn 23) 5½, London 194, Bolton 7, Chorley 12, Manchester 12, St. Helens 10, Warrington 10, Wigan 6.
EC Wed. **MD** Thur, Fri, Sat. **Golf** Leigh 18h.

★★★ Greyhound, Warrington Rd, WN7 3XQ (0942) 671256 Fax: (0942) 261949

Former public house with modern hotel extension. On East Lancs Road. (Emb) Fr
48 bedrs, 48 en suite; TV; tcf
lift, dogs, ns; P 90, G 8, coach; child facs; con 60
LD 9.45, bar meals only Sat lunch
£ B&B £59–£65 (w/e £21), B&B (double) £76–£82; L £8·95, D £10·75; WB £57 (2nts)
cc Access, Amex, B'card/Visa, Diners.

LEIGH-ON-SEA Essex. Map 17C2

Basildon 9, London 39, Chelmsford 18, Southend-on-Sea 3½.

★ Manor House, 24–26 Nelson Dr, SS9 1DA (0702) 75127. Fax: (0702) 77161
Large, two-storied building with attractive bay windows. Fr, It, Gr
15 bedrs, 13 en suite, 1 ba; TV; tcf
TV, dogs, ns; P 5, coach; child facs, con 80
LD 9.30. Resid & Rest lic
£ B&B £17·25–£35, B&B (double) £35–£50; L £7·25, D £8·95; [10% V]
cc Access, Amex, B'card/Visa.

LEIGHTON BUZZARD Beds. Map 14A3

Pop 30,625. Dunstable 7½, London 41, Aylesbury 10, Bedford 18, Bletchley 6½, Buckingham 17.
EC Thur **MD** Tue, Thur, Sat. **Golf** Leighton Buzzard 10h. **See** EE Church (spire). Ascott House, Wing (2m SW).

★★★ Swan, High St, LU7 7EA (0525) 372148 Fax: (0525) 370444

Carefully restored 18th century posting house in centre of market town.

EC *early closing* **MD** *market day* *country house hotel* *ns (NS) no smoking areas* *tcf tea/coffee facilities*

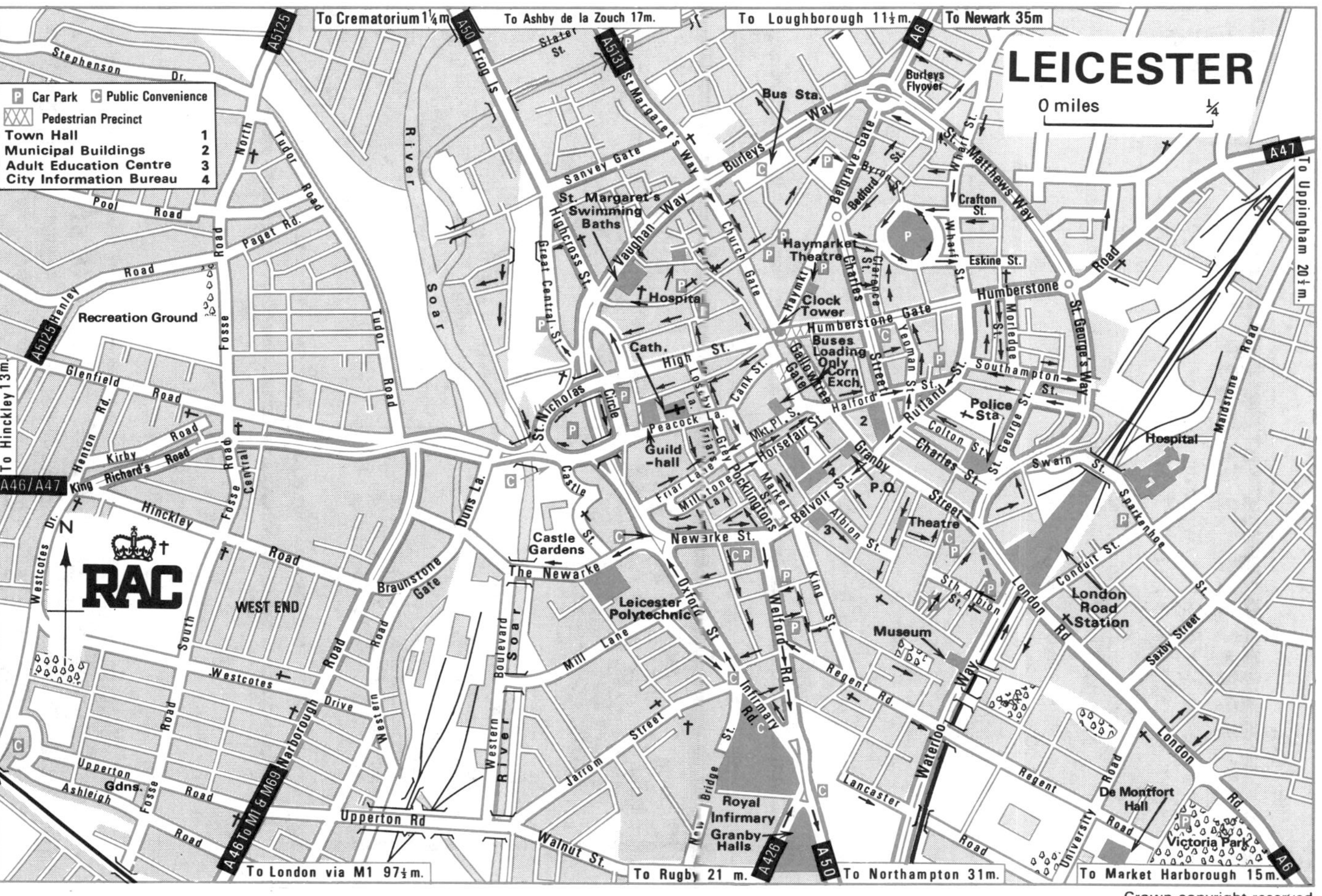

LEICESTER
0 miles
¼
To Crematorium 1¼ m
To Ashby de la Zouch 17m.
To Loughborough 11½ m.
To Newark 35m
To Uppingham 20½ m.
To Hinckley 13m.
To London via M1 97½ m.
To Rugby 21 m.
To Northampton 31m.
To Market Harborough 15m.
Crown copyright reserved
A5125
A50
A5131
A6
A47
A46/A47
A46 To M1 & M69
A426
P Car Park
C Public Convenience
Pedestrian Precinct
Town Hall 1
Municipal Buildings 2
Adult Education Centre 3
City Information Bureau 4
St. Matthews Way
St. George's Way
Humberstone Gate
Charles St.
London Rd
London Road Station
Belgrave Gate
Burleys Way
Bus Sta.
Haymarket Theatre
Clock Tower
Gallowtree Gate
Buses Loading Only
Corn Exch.
Granby St.
Police Sta.
Hospital
Museum
Welford Rd.
Infirmary Rd.
Royal Infirmary
Granby Halls
Oxford St.
Leicester Polytechnic
Newarke St.
Guild-hall
Cath.
High St.
Church Gate
St. Margaret's Way
Vaughan Way
St. Margaret's Swimming Baths
Highcross St.
Great Central St.
St. Nicholas Circle
Castle Gardens
The Newarke
River Soar
Western Boulevard
Braunstone Gate
Narborough Road
Tudor Road
Fosse Road
Hinckley Road
WEST END
Recreation Ground
King Richard's Road
Westcotes Dr.
Upperton Rd
Walnut St.
Jarrom Street
Mill Lane
Regent Rd.
University Road
De Montfort Hall
Victoria Park
Waterloo Way
RAC
N

Leicester (Leicestershire)

THE STAGE HOTEL

299 Leicester Road (A50), Wigston Fields, Leicester LE8 1JW
Phone: (0533) 886161 Fax: (0533) 811874

All 38 newly built bedrooms have en-suite bathroom with bath and shower, heated towel rail, direct dial phone. Remote Control Colour TV with teletext, Radio with wake-up alarm clock. Complimentary tea and coffee making facilities. Trouser Press, Hair Drier. Bedroom adapted for disabled use.
The Restaurant offers extensive cuisine including à la Carte, table d'hôte and a Carvery.
Conference facilities for up to 200 people.
Easy access from Motorways and major trunk roads.
NEC Birmingham only 30 minutes drive.

Member of the CONSORT HOTEL GROUP

Leicester (Leicestershire)

The Red Cow

Hinckley Road, Leicester Forest East, Leicester LE3 3PG. Telephone: 0533 387878
* 31 Ensuite Bedrooms, TV, Tea & Coffee making facilities, Hair Dryer, Trouser Press, Direct Dial Telephone * A la Carte Restaurant * Conservatory * Childrens Play Area * Fine Traditional Ales.

Bardon Hall

Beveridge Lane, Bardon Hill, Nr Coalville, Leicestershire. Telephone: 0530 813644.
* 35 Ensuite Bedrooms, TV, Tea & Coffee making facilities, Hair Dryer, Trouser Press, Direct Dial Telephone * A la Carte Restaurant * Lounge Bar & Bar Meals * Fine Traditional Ales * Childrens Play Area.

FOR FURTHER DETAILS OF EVERARDS ORIGINAL INNS.
PLEASE WRITE TO EVERARDS BREWERY LTD. CASTLE ACRES, NARBOROUGH, LEICESTER LE9 5BY.
Tel: 0533 630900

Lenham (Kent)

Dog & Bear Hotel

RAC ★★

The Square, Lenham, Nr Maidstone, Kent ME17 2PG. Tel: (0622) 858219

16th-century coaching inn retaining its olde worlde character and serving good Kent ale and lagers, fine wines and home cooking. 21 bedrooms, all en-suite. Large car park and function room.

🛏 34 bedrs, 34 en suite; annexe 4 bedrs, 4 en suite; TV; tcf
ns, P 12; child facs; con 30
✕ LD 9.30
£ B&B £72·50–£78 (w/e £50), B&B (double) £85–£120; HB weekly £576–£625; L £13·50, D £18·50; WB £110 (2nts); [10% V]
cc Access, Amex, B'card/Visa, Diners.

LELANT Cornwall. Map 2A1
Hayle 2, London 277, Helston 11, Penzance 7, St Ives 2½.

Badger Inn, Fore St, TR26 3JT (0736) 752181
Two-storey inn on corner of main street in village centre. Attractive garden behind with lawns and flowers.
🛏 6 bedrs, 4 en suite, 1 ba; TV; tcf
£ B&B £30, B&B (double) £39
cc Access, B'card/Visa.

LENHAM Kent. Map 7B3
Pop 3,600. Maidstone 9, London 45, Ashford 10, Canterbury 18, Tenterden 16. **Golf** Leeds Castle 9h.

★★ **Dog & Bear,** The Square, ME17 2PG (0622) 858219 Fax (0622) 859415
An early 17th century inn with modern extension in keeping, in centre of village.
🛏 21 bedrs, 21 en suite; TV; tcf
dogs; P 40, coach; child facs; con 60
(*See advertisement on p. 324*)

Harrow Inn (Acclaimed), Warren St, ME17 2ED Maidstone (0622) 858727. *Private Hotel.*

LEOMINSTER Hereford & Worcester (Herefordshire). Map 20A3
Pop 9,079. Bromyard 9½, London 148, Hereford 12, Knighton 18, Ludlow 11. **EC** Thur. **MD** Fri. **Golf** Ford Bridge 9h. **See** Priory Church, 17th cent Butter Cross, 17th cent Grange Court, Museum.
[i] School La. (0568) 6460.

★★ **Royal Oak,** South St, HR6 8JA (0568) 2610

Georgian coaching inn–a family-run hotel in town centre.
🛏 17 bedrs, 17 en suite, annexe 1 bedr, 1 en suite; TV; tcf
TV, dogs; P 24, G 1, coach; child facs; con 250
✕ LD 9 (9.30 Fri & Sat). Rest lic
£ B&B £28·50, B&B (double) £42·50; L £13, D £13; WB fr £29·50; [5% V]
cc Access, Amex, B'card/Visa, Diners; dep.

★★ **Talbot,** West St, HR6 8EP (0568) 6347 Tx: 35332
Old coaching inn dating from 15th century; well appointed bedrooms.
🛏 23 bedrs, 23 en suite; TV; tcf
dogs; P 20, coach; child facs; con 150
✕ LD 9.30
£ B&B £43–£50, B&B (double) £70–£84; HB weekly £250–£278; L £9, D £14; WB £44, (w/e £40); [10% V]
cc Access, Amex, B'card/Visa, Diners.

Withenfield (Highly Acclaimed), South St, HR6 8JN (0568) 2011. *Hotel.* Fr, Es
£ B&B £39–£45; HB weekly £263–£282; WB fr £65; [5% V]

Marsh, Eyton, HR6 0AG (0568) 3952
Wharton Bank Farm, Wharton Bank, HR6 0NX (0568) 2575. *Swimming pool.*

LETCHWORTH Hertfordshire. Map 15A4
Pop 31,835. Hatfield 16, London 36, A1(M) 2, Baldock 1½, Luton 11.
EC Wed. **Golf** Letchworth 18h.

★★★ **Broadway Toby,** The Broadway, SG6 3NZ (0462) 685651 Tx: 82425
Modern hotel in 'Georgian' style, part of original Garden City development.

LEVENS Cumbria. Map 36B4
Pop 895. M6 (jn 36) 5, London 252, Ambleside 16, Kendal 5, Kirkby Lonsdale 10, Lancaster 16, Ulverston 18.
EC Thur. **Golf** Kendal 18h. **See** Levens Hall, Sizergh Castle.

★★ **Heaves,** LA8 8EF Sedgwick (053 95) 60396
A quiet, temperance country house; convenient for A6. Putting, billiards.
🛏 15 bedrs, 9 en suite, 2 ba; TV; tcf
TV, dogs; P 24, coach; child facs
✕ Resid & Rest lic
£ B&B £22–£24; B&B (double) £42–£44; HB weekly £180–£200; L £5·50, D £8
cc Access, Amex, B'card/Visa, Diners.

LEWDOWN Devon. Map 3A3
Pop 62. Okehampton 10, London 202, Holsworthy 18, Launceston 8, Tavistock 9½.

Stowford House (Acclaimed), Stowford, EX20 4BP (056 683) 415. *Private Hotel.* Open Mar–Dec
£ B&B £17–£24·50; HB weekly £160–£212·50; [10% V]; dep.

LEWES East Sussex. Map 6C1
Pop 14,725. East Grinstead 21, London 51, Brighton 8½, Eastbourne 16, Hastings 29, Haywards Heath 13, Uckfield 8.
EC Wed. **MD** Mon. **Golf** Lewes 18h. See Castle and Museum, Anne of Cleves House.
[i] 32 High St. (0273) 471600

★★★ **Shelleys,** High St, BN7 1XS (0273) 472361
In High Street, a modernised Georgian building, of character. (MtCh)
🛏 21 bedrs, 21 en suite; TV
dogs; P 25, U 3, coach; child facs; con 50
✕ LD 9.15, Resid lic
£ B&B £65·50–£80·50, B&B (double) £100–£131; L £12·50, D £15·50; WB £49·50
cc Access, Amex, B'card/Visa, Diners

★★ **White Hart,** High St, BN7 1XE (0273) 473794 Tx: 878468 Fax: (0273) 474676

Georgian coaching inn with modern development, situated in High Street. Fr
🛏 19 bedrs, 14 en suite, annexe 21 bedrs, 21 en suite, 1 ba; TV; tcf
dogs; P 40, coach; child facs; con 200
✕ LD 10
£ B&B £51, B&B (double) £72; L £10·50, D £10·50; WB £86 (2nts); [5% V]
cc Access, Amex, B'card/Visa, Diners.

LEYBURN North Yorkshire. Map 38B4
Harrogate 31, London 235, Boroughbridge 26, Darlington 24, Hawes 16, Northallerton 18, Skipton 34, Thirsk 24.
[i] Thornboroug Hall (0969) 23069

★ C **Golden Lion,** Market Place, DL8 5AS Wensleydale (0969) 22161

Fine traditional Yorkshire stone building overlooking the market square. Closed 25 & 26 Dec.
🛏 14 bedrs, 11 en suite, 2 ba; TV; tcf
lift, dogs; child facs; con 20

LEYLAND Lancashire. Map 32C4
Pop 26,640. M6 (jn 28) ½, London 207, Blackburn 10, Chorley 4½, Ormskirk 13, Preston 6, Southport 14, Wigan 11.
EC Wed. **MD** Tue, Fri, Sat. **Golf** Leyland 18h.

★★★ **Penguin,** Junc 28 (M6), Leyland Way, PR5 2JX (0772) 422922 Tx: 677651 Fax: (0772) 622282

A luxurious modern motorway hotel.
🛏 93 bedrs, 93 en suite; TV; tcf
🏠 TV, dogs, ns; P 150, coach; child facs; con 300
✕ LD 10
£ B&B £56·50–£61·50 (w/e £21), B&B (double) £73–£79; L £7·95, D £11·25; WB £42; [10% V]
cc Access, Amex, B'card/Visa, Diners.

LICHFIELD Staffordshire. Map 22C3

Pop 26,310. Coventry 25, London 116, Ashbourne 26, Burton-on-Trent 13, Stafford 16, Stoke-on-Trent 29, Stone 21, Sutton Coldfield 8, Tamworth 7, Uttoxeter 17, Walsall 9½, Wolverhampton 14.
EC Wed. **MD** Mon, Fri, Sat. **Golf** Whittington Barracks 18h. **See** Cathedral, Birthplace of Dr Samuel Johnson (Statue adjacent), Museum, St John's Hospital (Almshouses).
ⓘ Donegal Ho, Bore St. ☎(0543) 252109

★★★ George, Bird St, WS13 6PR ☎(0543) 414822 Fax: (0543) 415817

Modernised coaching inn in city centre near Cathedral. ⚒ Fr (Emb)
🛏 38 bedrs, 38 en suite; TV; tcf
🏠 dogs, ns; P 40, coach; child facs; con 100
✕ LD 9.30
£ B&B £66·50–£76·50 (w/e £21), B&B (double) £81–£91; HB weekly £178·50; L £9·95, D £13·50; WB £24·50
cc Access, Amex, B'card/Visa, CB, Diners.

★★★ Little Barrow, Beacon St, WS13 7AA ☎(0543) 414500
Modern purpose-built hotel in city centre convenient for Cathedral.
🛏 24 bedrs, 24 en suite; TV; tcf
🏠 TV; P 70, coach; child facs; con 100
✕ LD 9.30
£ B&B £55, B&B (double) £65; L £7·50, D £10·50; WB £30
cc Access, Amex, B'card/Visa, Diners.
(*See advertisement on p. 327*)

Discount vouchers
RAC discount vouchers are on p. 34. Hotels with a [V] shown at the end of the price information will accept them in part payment for accommodation bills on the full, standard rate, not against bargain breaks or any other special offers. Please note the limitations shown in the entry: w/e for weekends, w/d for weekdays, and which months they are accepted.

★★ C Angel Croft, Beacon St, WS13 7AA ☎(0543) 258737 Fax: (0543) 415605

A brown brick 18th century residence situated near the Cathedral. ⚒ De
🛏 11 bedrs, 9 en suite, annexe 8 bedrs, 8 en suite; 1 ba; TV; tcf
🏠 P 60, coach; child facs; con 20
✕ LD 8.45, bar meals only Sun dinner
£ B&B £35–£60 (w/e £20), B&B (double) £50–£70; L £8·75, D £11·75
cc Access, B'card/Visa, Diners.

Oakleigh House (Highly Acclaimed), 25 St Clad's Rd, WS13 7LZ ☎(0543) 262688. *Hotel.*

Coppers End, Walsall Rd, Muckley Corner, WS14 0BG ☎Brownhills (0543) 372910. *Guest House.* ♿
£ B&B £18·40–£21·85

LIFTON Devon. Map 3A2

Pop 967. Okehampton 14, London 206, Holsworthy 13, Launceston 3½, Tavistock 9½.

★★★ H C R Arundell Arms, PL16 0AA ☎(0566) 84666 Fax: (0566) 84494

Stone-built former coaching inn of character specialising in fishing and shooting. ⚒ Fr. Closed Xmas.
🛏 24 bedrs, 20 en suite (4 sh); annexe 5 bedrs, 3 en suite, (2 sh); TV; tcf
🏠 dogs, ns; P 80, coach; child facs; con 60
✕ LD 9
£ B&B £46–£51, B&B (double) £75–£83; HB weekly £364–£399; L £13, D £22; WB £88 (2nts)
cc Access, Amex, B'card/Visa, Diners.

Weekend breaks
Please consult the hotel for full details of weekend breaks; prices shown are an indication only. Many hotels offer mid week breaks as well.

★★ Lifton Cottage, PL16 0DR ☎(0566) 84439 ♿

Attractive stone-built Gothic-style hotel in pleasant gardens. On A30.
🛏 13 bedrs, 12 en suite, (1 sh), 2 ba; TV; tcf
🏠 TV, dogs; P 25; child facs
✕ LD 9
£ B&B £19·50–£24, B&B (double) £45; L £6·50, D £9·50; WB £55
cc Access, Amex, B'card/Visa, Diners; dep.

Thatched Cottage (Acclaimed), Sprytown, PL16 0AY ☎(0566) 84224. *Hotel.*
£ B&B £27·50; [5% V Jan–Mar]

LIMPLEY STOKE Wiltshire. Map 5A3

Pop 633. Bath 3½, London 108, Devizes 13, Frome 9, Radstock 9½, Warminster 12.
EC Wed. **Golf** Kingsdown, Box 18h.

★★ Limpley Stoke, Nr Bath, Avon, BA3 6HZ ☎(0225) 723333 Fax: (0225) 722406

A substantial Victorian house in 3 acres of grounds overlooking the Avon Valley. Snooker. ⚒ Fr, De.
🛏 55 bedrs, 55 en suite; TV; tcf
🏠 dogs; P 80, coach; child facs; con 120
✕ LD 8.30, nr lunch
£ B&B £49·50–£55, B&B (double) £62·50–£69·50; D £12·95; WB £72·50; [10% V]
cc Access, Amex, B'card/Visa, Diners; dep.
(*See advertisement on p. 124*)

LINCOLN Lincolnshire. Map 34A3

Pop 78,000. Sleaford 17, London 133, Gainsborough 18, Grantham 25, Horncastle 21, Louth 26, Market Rasen 15, Newark 17.
EC Wed. **MD** Daily. **Golf** Carholme 18h. **See** Cathedral, Castle (1069) and Court House, Jew's House, The Stonebow (15th–16th cent) with Guildhall above.
ⓘ 9 Castle Hill. ☎(0522) 29828 & 21 Cornhill ☎(0522) 512971

Atlas Section
Consult the Atlas section at the back of the guide to find out which towns and villages have RAC Appointed and Listed hotels in them. They are shown on the maps by purple circles.

Lichfield (Staffordshire)

THE LITTLE BARROW HOTEL

Beacon Street, Lichfield, Staffordshire
Tel: (0543) 414500 Fax: (0543) 415734

The Little Barrow Hotel offers old world charm combined with every comfort you would expect of a first class hotel. All bedrooms have private bath, shower, WC, radio, telephone and colour TV, tea/coffee making facilities, hairdrier, trouser press. The air conditioned restaurant is famous for its international cuisine.

Lichfield Cathedral, Dr Johnson's birthplace and many other places of interest are within easy walking distance of the hotel.

Lincoln (Lincolnshire)

RAC
Highly
Acclaimed

An elegant Victorian house offering luxuriously appointed en-suite bedrooms, complete with direct dial telephones.
Just three minutes walk from the Cathedral and Castle in the heart of old Lincoln.

☆Residential Licence☆
☆Private Car Park☆
☆Terraced garden☆

MINSTER LODGE HOTEL

3 Church Lane, Lincoln LN2 1QJ Tel and Fax: (0522) 513220

Liverpool (Merseyside)

THE CAMPANILE HOTEL – Liverpool

Wapping and Chaloner Street, Albert Docks, Liverpool
Tel: (081) 569 6969 Fax: (081) 569 4888

Restaurant
Hotel

Campanile

Part of the international budget hotel chain "Campanile", the hotel offers 83 comfortable double or twin rooms with en-suite bathrooms, and tea/coffee making facilities, radio alarm, remote control colour TV, Sky TV and direct dial telephone at **competitive rates.**
Our informal restaurant provides a variety of home-cooked French/Continental cuisine, and personal service at **affordable prices.**
Our seminar room is available for business meetings or small functions.

Your hosts: Lesley & John MacCanney

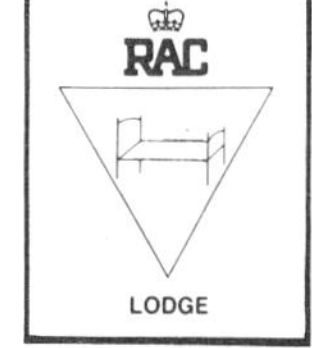

The Lizard (Cornwall)

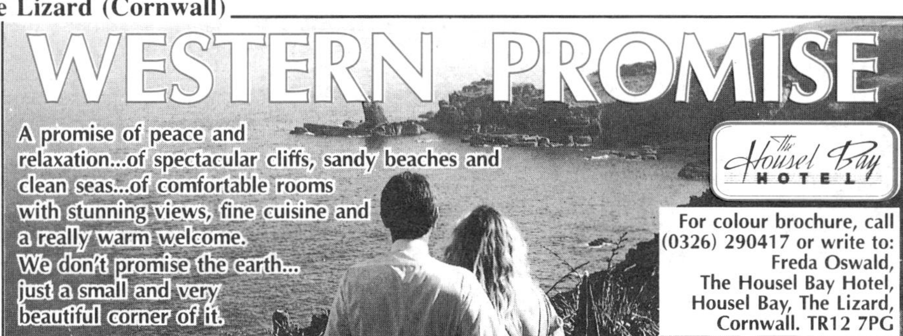

WESTERN PROMISE
A promise of peace and relaxation...of spectacular cliffs, sandy beaches and clean seas...of comfortable rooms with stunning views, fine cuisine and a really warm welcome.
We don't promise the earth... just a small and very beautiful corner of it.
The Housel Bay HOTEL
For colour brochure, call (0326) 290417 or write to: Freda Oswald, The Housel Bay Hotel, Housel Bay, The Lizard, Cornwall. TR12 7PG

★★★★ **White Hart,** Bailgate, LN1 3AR
☎(0522) 26222 Tx: 56304
Fax: (0522) 531798

Historic hotel, dating to c 1750, and boasting charming modern orangery. (THF) ✗ Fr, De, Es, It
🛏 50 bedrs, 50 en suite; TV; tcf
🏨 lift, dogs, ns; P 60, G 60, coach; child facs; con 70
✗ LD 10
£ B&B £82·50, B&B (double) £110; L £9·50, D £14·95
cc Access, Amex, B'card/Visa, CB, Diners.

★★★ **Eastgate Post House,** Eastgate, LN2 1PN ☎(0522) 520341 Tx: 56316
Fax: (0522) 510780

Modern hotel in old city in elevated position near to Cathedral. (THF) ✗ Es, It
🛏 71 bedrs, 71 en suite; TV; tcf
🏨 lift, dogs, ns; P 120, G 3; coach; child facs; con 90
✗ LD 10
£ B&B £75 (w/e £39·50), B&B (double) £95; Bk £8, L £12, D £14; WB £38
cc Access, Amex, B'card/Visa, CB, Diners.

★★★ **Four Seasons**, Scothern La, Dunholme, LN2 3QP ☎Market Rasen (0673) 60108 Fax: (0673) 62784
Modern hotel situated in rural area 5½ miles NE of Lincoln.
🛏 annexe 24 bedrs, 24 en suite; TV; tcf
🏨 TV, dogs; P 130, coach; child facs; con 250
✗ LD 9.45. Resid, Rest & Club lic
£ B&B £35, B&B (double) £50–£55; L £8·95, D £8·95; WB £40
cc Access, Amex, B'card/Visa.

★★★ **Moor Lodge,** Branston, LN4 1HU
☎(0522) 791366 Fax: (0522) 794389 ♿

Medium-sized early 20th century hotel in attractive village setting. 4½ m SE of city.
🛏 25 bedrs, 25 en suite; TV; tcf
🏨 dogs; P 150, coach; child facs; con 180
✗ LD 9.15, bar meals only Sat lunch, nr Sun dinner
£ B&B £57·20–£64·90, B&B (double) £74·80–£85·80; L £12·60, D £15·30; WB £73 (2nts); [10% V]
cc Access, Amex, B'card/Visa, Diners.

♣♣ ★★★ **Washingborough Hall,** Church Hill, Washingborough, LN4 1BE ☎(0522) 790340

Dignified Georgian mansion standing in 3 acres of fine grounds near to Lincoln. Swimming pool.
🛏 12 bedrs, 12 en suite; TV; tcf
🏨 dogs, ns; P 50; child facs; con 50
✗ LD 9, bar meals only Mon–Sat lunch
£ B&B £42–£55, B&B (double) £59–£75; HB weekly £230–£266; D £12; WB £33
cc Access, Amex, B'card/Visa, Diners; dep.

★★ **Barbican,** St Mary's St, LN5 7EQ
☎(0522) 543811 Fax: (0522) 540436
An early Victorian city-centre hotel furnished in period style.
🛏 19 bedrs, 12 en suite, (2 sh), 2 ba; TV; tcf
🏨 TV, dogs; coach; child facs; con 40
✗ LD 9.30, nr Sun
£ B&B £29–£34, B&B (double) £41–£46; [V w/e]
cc Access, Amex, B'card/Visa, Diners

★★ **Castle,** Westgate, LN1 3AS ☎(0522) 538801
17th century stone-built hotel situated on elevated ground adjacent to castle.

★★**Hillcrest,** 15 Lindum Terr, LN2 5RT
☎(0522) 510182 Fax: (0522) 510182

High up, close to the Cathedral, a Victorian former rectory with splendid views over the lower town. Closed 20 Dec–2 Jan.
🛏 17 bedrs, 17 en suite; TV; tcf
🏨 dogs, ns; P 8, U 1; child facs; con 20
✗ LD 8.45, bar meals only lunch & Sun dinner. Resid & Rest lic
£ B&B £36·50, B&B (double) £49·50; WB £64; [5% V w/e]
cc Access, B'card/Visa.

★★ **Loudor,** 37 Newark Rd, North Hykeham, LN6 8RB ☎(0522) 680333
Fax: (0522) 680403

Conveniently situated on A1434 in North Hykeham, west of Lincoln, a large house pleasantly converted into a hotel.
🛏 10 bedrs, 10 en suite; TV; tcf
🏨 dogs, ns; P 14; child facs; con 20
✗ LD 8.30, nr lunch, bar meals. Resid & Rest lic
£ B&B £28–£33, B&B (double) £40–£42; D £8·45; [5% V]
cc Access, Amex, B'card/Visa, Diners.

★ **Tennyson,** 7 South Park Av, LN5 8EN
☎(0522) 521624

Two-storey pleasant traditional building. On main road half mile from city centre. ✗ Fr, De, It
🛏 8 bedrs, 8 en suite; TV; tcf
🏨 P 8; child facs
✗ LD 7.45, bar meals only lunch & Sun dinner. Resid lic
£ B&B £25–£27, B&B (double) £38–£40; WB £50; [V]
cc Access, Amex, B'card/Visa; dep.

D'Isney Place (Highly Acclaimed), Eastgate, LN2 4AA ☎(0522) 538881. Fax: (0522) 511321. *Hotel.* ✗ Fr
£ B&B £38–£46

Minster Lodge (Highly Acclaimed), 3 Church La, LN2 1QJ ☎(0522) 513220. *Hotel.*
£ B&B (double) £48
(*See advertisement on p. 327*)

Brierley House (Acclaimed), 54 South Park, LN5 8ER ☎(0522) 526945. *Hotel* Closed 24 Dec–14 Jan.
£ B&B £16–£18, HB weekly £137–£151

Carline (Acclaimed), 3 Carline Rd, LN1 1HN ☎0522 530422. *Guest House.* Closed Xmas and New Year.

Hollies, 65 Carholme Rd, LN1 1RT ☎(0522) 22419. *Private Hotel.*

LIPHOOK Hampshire Map 6A2

Guildford 16, London 45, Alton 12, Haslemere 4, Petersfield 8.

EC *early closing* **MD** *market day* ♣♣ *country house hotel* *ns (NS) no smoking areas* *tcf tea/coffee facilities*

🏰 C ★★★ **Milland Place**, GU30 7JW
☎(042 876) 633

Gabled Edwardian house, elegantly furnished. Lovely public rooms, including a creeper-hung conservatory, look out over the well-tended gardens. Just off A3 south of Liphook. Fr, It, Es
18 bedrs, 18 en suite; TV
P 55; child facs; con 40
LD 9.30. Resid & Rest lic
£ B&B £88·50, B&B (double) £97–£147; L £15, D £20; WB £135
cc Access, Amex, B'card/Visa, Diners

LISKEARD Cornwall. Map 3A2

Pop 6,500. Tavistock 18, London 214, Bodmin 13, Fowey 17, Launceston 14, Looe 7½, St Austell 18, Saltash 13.

🏰 ★★ **Country Castle,** Lemellion Hill, PL14 4EB ☎(0579) 42694

Imposing mid-Victorian house with beautiful views. Landscaped gardens. Swimming pool. Fr
11 bedrs, 10 en suite, (1 sh), 1 ba; TV; tcf
dogs, ns; P 40, coach; child facs; con 40
LD 7.45. Resid & Rest lic
£ B&B £36, B&B (double) £50–£60; Bk £6·75, D £12·50; [5% V]
cc Access, B'card/Visa.

★★ **Webb's,** The Parade, PL14 6AG
☎(0579) 43675
Attractive 3-storey Georgian building conveniently situated in the town centre.

Old Rectory Country House, St Keyne, PL14 4RL ☎(0579) 42617. *Hotel.* ♿
Trewint Farm, Menheriot, PL14 3RE
☎(0579) 47155
£ B&B £11–£13, HB weekly £105–£112

LITTLEHAMPTON West Sussex. Map 6B1

See also RUSTINGTON
Pop 21,974. Arundel 3½, London 60, Bognor 6½, Chichester 12, Horsham 22, Worthing 8½.
EC Wed. **MD** Fri, Sat. **Golf** Littlehampton 18h. **See** Miniature Railway, Museum.
[i] Windmill Theatre, Coastguards Rd.
☎(0903) 713480

★★ **Beach,** Seafront, BN17 5NT ☎(0903) 717277
Large hotel in pleasant grounds right on the seafront. Swimming pool, snooker.

Colbern (Acclaimed), South Terr, BN17 5LQ ☎(0903) 714270. *Hotel.*
£ B&B £20–£25; HB weekly £180–£211; [5% V]

Regency, 85 South Terr, BN17 5LJ
☎(0903) 717707. *Hotel.*
£ B&B £18–£20
Sharoleen, 85 Bayford Rd, BN17 5HW
☎(0903) 713464. *Private Hotel.*

LITTLE LANGDALE Cumbria. Map 43C1

6 miles West of Ambleside. Windermere 9½, London 274, Coniston 9, Grasmere 4½.

★★ **Three Shires Inn,** LA22 9NZ
☎Langdale (096 67) 215

Charming Lakeland inn (1872) with 'olde worlde' atmosphere. Lovely views. Open mid Feb–mid Nov & New Year. Fr
11 bedrs, 7 en suite, 2 ba; tcf
TV, ns; P 22, U 2
LD 8, bar meals only lunch
£ B&B £22–£30; B&B (double) £44–£60; HB weekly £220–£300; D £15; dep.

LITTLE TORRINGTON Devon. Map 3A3

South Molton 17, London 197, Bideford 8½, Holsworthy 18, Okehampton 17.

Smytham Manor, EX38 8PU ☎Torrington (0805) 22110. *Private Hotel. Swimming pool, putting.* Open 1 Mar–24 Dec.
£ B&B £11–£17; HB weekly £120–£160; [10% V]

LITTLE WEIGHTON Humberside (North Humberside) *See* HULL.

LIVERPOOL Merseyside. Map 32A2

See also BIRKENHEAD
RAC Office, (*changing in 1991*)
☎051-709 7979.
Pop 503,700. London 198, M62 (jn 4) 3½, Birkenhead 1, Ormskirk 13, St Helens 11, Southport 18, Warrington 17.
See Plan, p. 330.
P See Plan. **EC** Wed. **MD** Daily. **Golf** Municipal courses: Allerton Park 18h and 9h, Bowring Park 9h, Liverpool (Kirkby) 18h. **See** Anglican Cathedral, Metropolitan Cathedral, Walker Art Gallery, City Museum, St George's Hall, University, Town Hall, Philharmonic Hall, Building and Design Centre, Planetarium, Bluecoat Chambers, Garden Festival Hall and Promenade.
[i] 29 Lime St. ☎051-709 3631

★★★★ **Atlantic Tower,** Chapel St, L3 9RE
☎051-227 4444 Tx: 627070
Fax: 051-236 3973

Distinctive modern hotel with luxury suites. Fine river views. (MtCh) De, Es, Po, Ru, Yu
226 bedrs, 226 en suite; TV; tcf
lift, dogs, ns; P 60, U 45, coach; child facs; con 120
LD 10.15, bar meals only Sat lunch
£ B&B £40–£69 (w/e £28); B&B (double) £80
cc Access, Amex, B'card/Visa, CB, Diners.

★★★★ **Liverpool Moat House,** Paradise St, L1 8JD ☎051-709 0181 Tx: 627270
Fax: 051-709 2706 ♿

Modern 9-storey city centre hotel. Indoor swimming pool, sauna/solarium, gymnasium. (QMH) Fr, De, Es, It
251 bedrs, 251 en suite; TV; tcf
lift, dogs; ns; P 25, coach; child facs; con 450
LD 10.30, nr Sat lunch
£ B&B £77·50, B&B (double) £99; HB weekly £652·75; L £12, D £17·50
cc Access, Amex, B'card/Visa, Diners.

★★★★ **St George's,** St John's Precinct, Lime St, L1 1NQ ☎051-709 7090
Tx: 627630 Fax: 051-709 0137

High rise purpose-built central hotel with all modern facilities. (THF)
155 bedrs, 155 en suite; TV; tcf
lift, dogs, ns; P 30, G 20, coach; child facs; con 250
LD 10

L

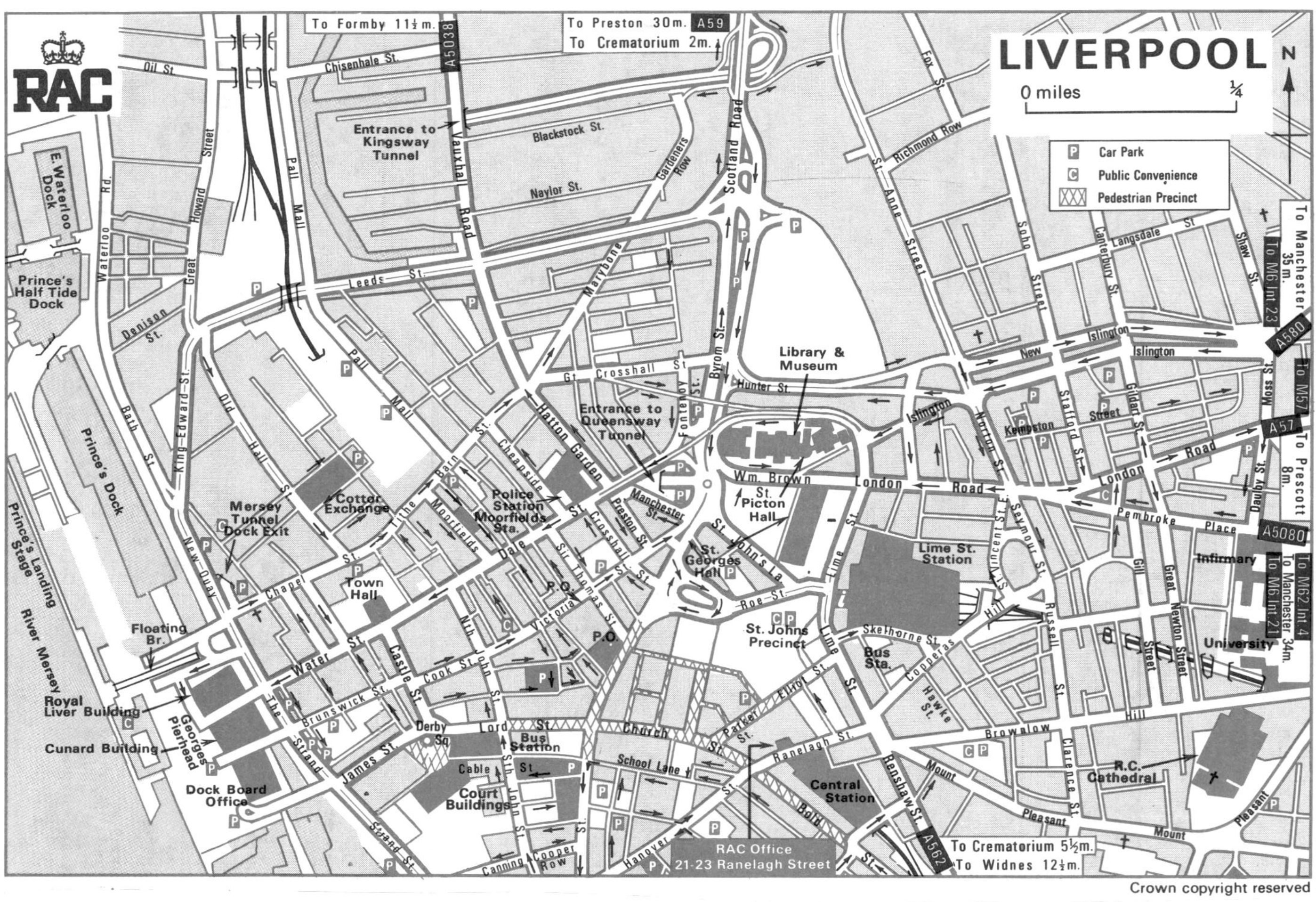

 EC *early closing* **MD** *market day* ♣♣ *country house hotel* *ns (NS) no smoking areas* *tcf tea/coffee facilities*

£ room £56–£62 (w/e £26), double room £71; L £10·45, D £10·45; WB £31
cc Access, Amex, B'card/Visa, CB, Diners.

★★★ **Cherry Tree,** East Lancs Rd, Knowsley, Prescot, L34 9HA ☎ 051-546 7531 Tx: 629769 Fax: 051-549 1069
Purpose-built 2-storey hotel with modern bedroom wings to rear.
🛏 50 bedrs, 50 en suite; TV; tcf
🏨 dogs; ns; P 150, coach, child facs; con 130
✕ LD 9.30
£ B&B £30–£48, B&B (double) £35–£58; L £7·50, D £10; WB £35; [10% V]

★★★ **Crest,** Lord Nelson St, L3 5QB ☎ 051-709 7050 Tx: 627954 Fax: 051-709 2193

Centrally situated modern hotel with many amenities. Billiards. (Cr/THF)
🛏 150 bedrs, 150 en suite; TV; tcf
🏨 lift, dogs, ns; P 200, coach; child facs; con 600
✕ LD 9.45, nr Sat & Sun lunch
£ B&B £75·50, B&B (double) £96; L £8, D £15; WB £36
cc Access, Amex, B'card/Visa, Diners.

★★★ **Park,** Dunnings Bridge Rd, Netherton, L30 3SU ☎ 051-525 7555 Tx: 629772 Fax: 051-525 2481
Modern purpose-built hotel with well-equipped bedrooms. Near Aintree. (DeV)
🛏 60 bedrs, 60 en suite; TV; tcf
🏨 lift, dogs; P 250, coach; child facs; con 100
✕ LD 9.15
£ B&B £53, B&B (double) £65; L £6·50, D £9·95; WB £60 (w/e £22·50); [V]
cc Access, Amex, B'card/Visa, Diners.

★★★ **Royal,** Bath St, L22 5PS ☎ 051-928 2332
Cream-faced historic Georgian building offering modern facilities. Views of Mersey.

★★★ **Trials,** 56 Castle St, L2 7LQ ☎ 051-227 1021
A luxury hotel in a fine Victorian city-centre building originally a bank.

★★ **Grange,** Holmfield Rd, Aigburth, L19 3PG ☎ 051-427 2950 Fax: 051-427 9055

An extended large and elegant cream-faced building set in own grounds.

🛏 25 bedrs, 25 en suite, 2 ba; TV; tcf
🏨 TV, ns; P 40, coach; child facs; con 30
✕ LD 9, nr Mon–Sat lunch & Sun dinner. Resid & Rest lic
£ B&B £31·60–£48·80, B&B (double) £50·20–£65·25; L £7·95, D £11·95; WB £38·05; [V w/e]
cc Access, Amex, B'card/Visa, Diners.

★★ **Green Park,** Greenbank Dr, L17 1AN ☎ 051-733 3382

Well-equipped privately-run hotel two miles from city centre. Attractive frontage.
🛏 23 bedrs, 16 en suite, 4 ba; TV
🏨 TV, dogs; P 25, coach; child facs; con 80
✕ LD 9. Resid & Rest lic
£ B&B £26–£30, B&B (double) £35–£40; L £4·80, D £5·95; [V]
cc Access, Amex, B'card/Visa, Diners.

Aachen, 91 Mount Pleasant, L3 5TB ☎ 051-709 3477. ⚒ De *Private Hotel. Billiards.*
£ B&B £18–£24, HB weekly £166·25; [V]
New Manx, 39 Catherine St, L8 7NE ☎ 051-708 6171. *Hotel.*
£ B&B £12·50–£15; HB weekly £70

LIZARD Cornwall. Map 2C1

Pop 810. Helston 11, London 282, Falmouth 19.
Golf Mullion, Helston 18h. **See** Lighthouse.

★★ **Housel Bay,** Housel Cove, TR12 7PG ☎ (0326) 290417 Fax: (0326) 290359

Victorian hotel in extensive grounds with magnificent sea views. ⚒ Fr. Open 11 Feb–31 Dec.
🛏 23 bedrs, 23 en suite; TV; tcf
🏨 lift, TV, dogs, ns; P 25, G 4, coach; child facs; con 20
✕ LD 9, bar meals only Mon–Sat lunch
£ B&B £20–£40, B&B (double) £40–£72; HB weekly £201–£311; D £12·50; WB £60; [10% V]
cc Access, Amex, B'card/Visa; dep.
(*See advertisement on p. 327*)

Please tell the manager if you chose your hotel through an advertisement in the guide.

★ **Kynance Bay House,** Penmenner Rd, TR12 7NR ☎ (0326) 290498

Family-run hotel in Victorian stone-built house. Panoramic sea views across National Trust land. Closed 3 Jan–mid. Feb.
🛏 9 bedrs, 7 en suite, (1 sh), 1 ba; tcf
🏨 TV, dogs, ns; P 9; coach; child facs
✕ LD 9. Resid & Rest lic
£ B&B £15–£22; HB weekly £150–£192·50; L £6·50, D £10; [V, Oct–Jun]
cc Access, Amex, B'card/Visa, Diners; dep.

Mounts Bay House, Penmenner Rd, TR12 7NP ☎ (0326) 290305. *Hotel.* Closed Nov.
£ B&B £16·50–£22·50; HB weekly £160–£204; [V, Dec–Jun, Oct]
Parc Brawse House, Penmenner Rd, TR12 7NR ☎ (0326) 290466. *Private Hotel.* Open Mar–Nov.
£ B&B £12–£19·50; HB weekly £126–£171·50; [5% V, Oct–May]
Penmenner House, Penmenner Rd, TR12 7NR ☎ (0326) 290370. *Hotel.*
£ B&B £19–£21; HB weekly £185·50–£199·50; [5% V]

LONDON See pp 65–100

LONG BUCKBY Northamptonshire. Map 21B3

M1 (jn 17) 3, London 75, Daventry 7½, Market Harborough 16, Northampton 9½.

★★ **Rockhall House,** Market Sq, NN6 7BW ☎ (0327) 843625
A 17th-century stone building, once a farmhouse, recently renovated and converted into a pleasant hotel in town centre.
🛏 10 bedrs, 10 en suite; TV

LONG EATON Derbyshire. Map 24C3

Pop 32,895. M1 (jn 25) 5, London 121, Ashby-de-la-Zouch 15, Derby 9½, Loughborough 12, Nottingham 7.
EC Thur. **MD** Wed, Fri, Sat. **Golf** Chilwell Manor 18h. **See** Church, Trent Lock.
ℹ Library, Tamworth Rd. ☎ (0602) 735426.

★★★ **Novotel,** Bostock La, NG10 4EP ☎ Nottingham (0602) 720106 Tx: 377585 ♿
A large modern complex near M1. Swimming pool.
🛏 110 bedrs, 110 en suite; TV; tcf
🏨 lift, dogs; P 180, coach; child facs; con 300

★★ **Europa,** Derby Rd, NG10 1LW ☎ Nottingham (0602) 728481 Tx: 377494
Victorian building–a privately-run hotel which has been extensively refurbished.
🛏 19 bedrs, 14 en suite, (5 sh), 1 ba; TV; tcf
🏨 TV, dogs; P 22; child facs; con 20
✕ LD 8.30, nr Sat lunch & Sun. Resid lic
£ B&B £28–£35, B&B (double) £45; L £5, D £8·95; [10% V]
cc Access, Amex, B'card/Visa, Diners.

L

The RAC Motoring Atlas Europe

- An indispensable aid to European Travel
- Clear and accurate mapping, Western Europe at 1:1,000,000 (1 inch to 16 miles) and Eastern Europe at 1:2,750,000 (1 inch to 43 miles)
- 16 pages of essential touring information
- 45 city approach maps
- Comprehensive index of over 85,000 names

THE ULTIMATE ROAD TO EUROPE

Price: £7.95 paperback (£9.95 incl. p&p).
Hardback: £12.95 (£14.95 incl. p&p).

LONGHAM Dorset. Map 5B2

Ringwood 7, London 100, Bournemouth 5½, Christchurch 8, Wimborne Minster 4

★★★ C R **Bridge House,** 2 Ringwood Rd (A348), BH22 9AN ☎ Bournemouth (0202) 578828 Tx: 418484 Fax: (0202) 572620
Privately-owned modern riverside hotel. Fishing. Closed 25 & 26 Dec.
37 bedrs, 37 en suite; TV; tcf
ns; P 200, coach; child facs; con 120
LD 10, bar meals only Mon–Sat lunch
£ B&B £50–£65, B&B (double) £60–£80; L £7·50, D £14·50
cc Access, Amex, B'card/Visa.

LONGHORSLEY Northumberland. Map 44C4

Morpeth 7, London 295, Alnwick 14, Newcastle-upon-Tyne 21, Rothbury 8½, Wooler 25.

★★★★ C **Linden Hall,** NE65 8XG ☎ Morpeth (0670) 516611 Tx: 538224 ♿

Fully restored Georgian mansion in large secluded grounds. Elegant public rooms. Putting, tennis, sauna, solarium, billiards.

LONG MELFORD Suffolk. Map 27A3

Pop 3,267. Sudbury 3, London 61, Bury St Edmunds 13, Haverhill 14, Stowmarket 19. **Golf** Newton Green 9h. **See** 15th cent Bull Hotel, Church with detached 15th cent Lady Chapel, Kentwell Hall, Melford Hall (N.T.).

★★★ **Bull,** CO10 9JG ☎ Sudbury (0787) 78494 Fax: (0787) 880307

Fine timbered mid-15th century house, once a busy posting house. (THF) Fr
25 bedrs, 25 en suite; TV; tcf
dogs, ns; P 30, coach; child facs; con 60
LD 9.30
£ B&B £77·50–£84·50 (w/e £51), B&B (double) £102–£110; Bk £7·50, L £10·75, D £15·25
cc Access, Amex, B'card/Visa, CB, Diners; dep.

★★ **Black Lion,** CO10 9DN ☎ Sudbury (0787) 312356
Restored 17th century coaching inn on a corner of the green. Owner-run.
10 bedrs, 10 en suite; TV; tcf
dogs; P 10; child facs; con 20

★★ **Crown Inn,** Hall St, CO10 9JL ☎ Sudbury (0787) 77666 Fax: (0787) 881883 ♿
Owner-run old English pub hotel, much enhanced, with attractive garden. Fr, Es
9 bedrs, 8 en suite, 1 ba; annexe 5 bedrs, 5 en suite; TV; tcf
TV, dogs, P6, coach; child facs
LD 9.30, bar meals only Mon–Sat lunch
£ B&B £39·50, B&B (double) £45–£55 D £8·50; WB £55; [10% V]
cc Access, Amex, B'card/Visa, Diners; dep.

LONGTON Staffordshire.

See STOKE-ON-TRENT.

LONGTOWN Cumbria. Map 43C3

Pop 2,200. M6 (jn 44) 6, Carlisle 8, London 302, Brampton 11, Canonbie 6, Gretna 5. **EC** Wed. **Golf** Carlisle 18h. **See** Arthuret Church, St Michael's Well
i Memorial Hall ☎ Carlisle (0228) 791876

★★ **Graham Arms,** English St, CA6 5SE ☎ Carlisle (0228) 791213
Attractive 3-storey building with pillared entrance overlooking wide main street.
13 bedrs, 6 en suite, 3 ba; TV; tcf
TV, dogs; P 10, G 2, coach; child facs; con 70

LOOE Cornwall. Map 3A2

Pop 4,700. Saltash 15, London 227, Bodmin 13, Fowey 19 (Fy 10), Liskeard 7½, Plymouth (Fy) 18, St Austell 24. **EC** Thur. **Golf** Looe Bin Down 18h.
i The Guildhall, Fore St. ☎ (050 36) 2072

★★★ **Hannafore Point,** Marine Dr, PL13 2DG ☎ (050 36) 3273 Tx: 45604 Fax: (050 36) 3272

Modern hotel with unspoilt views of glorious coastline. Indoor swimming pool, squash, sauna, solarium, gymnasium.
38 bedrs, 38 en suite, 5 ba; TV
lift, dogs; P 35, coach; child facs; con 40
LD 9, bar meals only Mon–Sat lunch
£ B&B £45·50–£66, B&B (double) £72–£100, HB weekly £291–£375; D £14; WB £43 (HB)
cc Access, Amex, B'card/Visa, Diners; dep.

★★★ H **Talland Bay,** Talland Bay, nr Looe, PL13 2JB ☎ Polperro (0503) 72667 Fax: (0503) 72940 ♿

Attractive country house in lovely garden with sea view. Swimming pool, putting, sauna, solarium, gymnasium. Fr. Closed Jan.
22 bedrs, 22 en suite, 1 ba; annexe 2 bedrs, 2 en suite; TV
dogs, ns; P 20; child facs; con 50
LD 9, bar meals only Mon–Sat lunch. Resid & Rest lic
£ B&B £37–£70, B&B (double) £74–£140; HB weekly £315–£490; D £16·50
cc Access, Amex, B'card/Visa, Diners; dep.

★★ **Commonwood Manor,** St Martin's Rd, PL13 1LP ☎ (050 36) 2929

Manor house set in 3 acres of grounds with lovely views of the river valley and town. Swimming pool. Open Mar–Oct.
10 bedrs, 10 en suite, 3 ba; TV
TV, dogs; P 20; no children under 8
LD 8, bar meals only lunch. Resid & Rest lic
£ B&B £27–£32, B&B (double) £48–£56; D £12·50
cc Access, Amex, B'card/Visa; dep.

★★ **Fieldhead,** Portuan Rd, Hannafore, PL13 2DR ☎ (050 36) 2689

In elevated position with good sea views, an attractive Victorian building in gardens. Swimming pool. Open Feb–Nov.
13 bedrs, 12 en suite, (1 sh); TV; tcf
dogs; P 13; no children under 5
LD 8.30, bar meals only lunch. Resid & Rest lic
£ B&B £28–£35, B&B (double) £44–£59; HB weekly £219–£250; D £10·75; WB £60 (HB 2 nts)
cc Access, Amex, B'card/Visa; dep.

★★ **Klymiarven,** Barbican Hill, PL13 1BH ☎ (050 36) 2333
Originally the manor house of East Looe set in extensive gardens. Swimming pool, solarium. Open Feb–Dec.
14 bedrs, 14 en suite; TV; tcf
TV, dogs; P 20; child facs

Polraen Country House (Highly Acclaimed), Sandplace, Morval, PL13 1PJ ☎ (050 36) 3956
£ B&B £25–£27; [5% V, excl Jul, Aug]

Bodrigan, Hannafore Rd, PL13 2DD ☎ (050 36) 2065

Coombe Farm, Widegates, PL13 1QN ☎ Widegates (050 34) 223. Open Mar–Oct.

L

£ B&B £14·50–£18·50; HB weekly £160–£186

Deganwy, Station Rd, PL13 1HL ☎(050 36) 2984. *Hotel.* Closed 24 Dec–1 Jan.

Panorama, Hannafore Rd, West Looe, PL13 2DE ☎(050 36) 2123. *Hotel.* Open Mar–Nov.
£ B&B £15–£24; HB weekly £135–£189; [5% V, Apr, May, Sep, Oct]

Pixies Holt, Shutta, East Looe, PL13 1JD ☎(050 36) 2726. *Private Hotel.* Closed Nov–Feb
£ B&B £11–£20

LORTON Cumbria. Map 43B2

Keswick 7½, London 293, Cockermouth 4, Penrith 24, Whitehaven 16.

Low Hall (Acclaimed), Lorton Vale, CA13 0RE ☎(0900) 826654. *Hotel.* Open Easter–end Oct
£ HB weekly £234·50–£248·50

LOSTWITHIEL Cornwall. Map 2C2

Pop. 2,242. Liskeard 11, London 232, Bodmin 5½, Fowey 7, St Austell 8½.
EC Wed. **Golf** Carlyon Bay 18h.
ⓘ Community Centre, Liddicoat Rd. ☎Bodmin (0208) 872207

★★ **Restormel Lodge**, 6 Edgcumbe Rd, PL22 0DD ☎Bodmin (0208) 872223 Tx: 873568

Purpose-built motel in convenient situation on A38. Swimming pool. Fr
34 bedrs, 34 en suite; TV; tcf
dogs; P 40, coach; child facs; con 80
LD 9.30, bar meals only lunch. Resid & Rest lic
£ B&B £34·50–£38, B&B (double) £49–£54; HB weekly £220–£240; D £12; WB £35; [10% V]
cc Access, Amex, B'card/Visa, Diners; dep.

Royal Oak, Duke St, PL22 1AH ☎(0208) 872552
Sympathetically modernised 13th century inn situated in town centre.
6 bedrs, 4 en suite, 1 ba; TV; tcf
dogs; P 20; no children
£ B&B £26·95; B&B (double) £46·20; L £5, D £8
cc Access, Amex, B'card/Visa, Diners.

LOUGHBOROUGH Leics. Map 25B2

Pop 49,081. Leicester 11, London 109, M1 (jn 23) 3, Ashby-de-la-Zouch 12, Derby 16, Melton Mowbray 15, Nottingham 15.
EC Wed. **MD** Thur. **Golf** Longscliffe 18h.
See War Memorial with Carillon Tower (47 bells), restored remains of 13th cent Rectory, University of Technology, Parish Church, Great Central Railway (steam trains).
ⓘ John Storer House, Wards End. ☎(0509) 230131.

★★★ **Cedars,** Cedar Rd, LE11 2AB ☎(0509) 214459 Fax: (0509) 233573

Attractive 2-storey building with modern bedroom wing. Situated off A6. Swimming pool, sauna, solarium. Closed 25–27 Dec.
37 bedrs, 37 en suite; TV; tcf
dogs; P 50, coach; child facs; con 30
LD 9.30, bar meals only Sat lunch, Sun dinner. Resid lic
£ B&B £45 (w/e £28), B&B (double) £55; WB £55
cc Access, Amex, B'card/Visa, Diners.

★★★ **King's Head,** High St, LE11 2QL ☎(0509) 233222 Fax: (0509) 262911

Large Georgian style hotel of brick and stone in town centre. Snooker. (Emb)
78 bedrs, 78 en suite; TV; tcf
lift, dogs, ns; P 80, coach; child facs; con 120
LD 9.30, bar meals only Sat lunch
£ B&B £59·50–£69·50 (w/e £19), B&B (double) £79–£89; L £10·50, D £11·50; WB £24·50
cc Access, Amex, B'card/Visa, Diners.

★★ **Great Central,** Gt Central Rd, LE11 1RW ☎(0509) 263405 Fax: (0509) 264130

Victorian hotel of character—"railway hotel" furnished with railway memorabilia.
18 bedrs, 18 en suite; TV
dogs; P 40, coach; child facs; con 80
LD 9, bar meals only Sat lunch
£ B&B £27·50–£40, B&B (double) £37·50–£60; L £7·50, D £10; WB £25; [10% V]
cc Access, Amex, B'card/Visa, Diners.

De Montfort, 88 Leicester Rd, LE11 2AQ ☎(0509) 216061. *Hotel.*
£ B&B £17·50; HB weekly £143; [10% V]

Sunnyside, 5 The Coneries, LE11 1DZ ☎(0509) 216217. *Hotel.*
£ B&B £16

LOUTH Lincolnshire. Map 34B4

Pop 13,296. Horncastle 13, London 148, Boston 30, Hull (Fy) 32, Lincoln 26, Grimsby 16, Market Rasen 14, Skegness 23.
EC Thur. **MD** Wed, Fri, Sat. **Golf** Louth 18h.
See St James's Church, Town Hall, Market Hall.

Priory (Acclaimed), Eastgate, LN11 9AJ. ☎(0507) 602930. *Hotel.*

LOWER BEEDING West Sussex Map 6B2

M23 5, London 38, Brighton 19, Crawley 7, Haywards Heath 10, Horsham 5.

★★★★ **South Lodge**, Brighton Rd, RH13 6PS ☎(0403) 891711 Tx: 877765 Fax: (0403) 891253

Grey-stone Victorian mansion set in 90 acres of grounds with magnificent gardens. Spacious well-furnished rooms with some fine antiques. Tennis. Fr, It
39 bedrs, 39 en suite; TV
ns, P 120; child facs; con 85
LD 10.30
£ B&B £79–£119, B&B (double) £118–£153; L £15, D £23; WB £80; [10% V, w/e]
cc Access, Amex, B'card/Visa, Diners.
(See advertisement on p. 335)

LOWER DICKER East Sussex. Map 7A1

Pop 5,070. Uckfield 9½, London 53, Eastbourne 10, Hailsham 1½, Lewes 11.

★★★ **Boship Farm,** BN27 4AT (on A22 at Hailsham Roundabout) ☎Eastbourne (0323) 844826 Tx: 878400 Fax: (0323) 843945

Modern purpose-built hotel attached to old farmhouse and barn. Swimming pool, tennis, sauna, solarium, gymnasium, snooker.
annexe 46 bedrs, 46 en suite; TV; tcf
dogs, ns; P 150, coach; child facs; con 40
LD 10

Lower Beeding (West Sussex)

Lowestoft (Suffolk)

£ B&B £55–£60·50, B&B (double) £65–£71·50; L £10·45, D £15; WB £65 (HB); [10% V, w/e]
cc Access, Amex, B'card/Visa, Diners.

LOWER SLAUGHTER Gloucestershire. Map 20C2
Pop 206. Stow-on-the-Wold 3, London 87, Burford 11, Cheltenham 15, Cirencester 17, Evesham 18.
Golf Burford 18h. **See** Brick Mill, Cotswold stone cottages, attractive riverside setting.

★★★ H C R Lower Slaughter Manor, GL54 2HP Cotswold (0451) 20456 Tx: 437287 Fax: (0451) 22150
Imposing 17th century house set in five acres of attractive gardens. Indoor swimming pool, putting, tennis, fishing, sauna, solarium.
11 bedrs, 11 en suite; annexe 8 bedrs, 8 en suite; TV
dogs; P 60, coach; children over 8; con 16

LOWESTOFT Suffolk. Map 27C4
See also CARLTON COLVILLE
Pop 58,000. Saxmundham 23, London 117, Aldeburgh 27, Great Yarmouth 10, Norwich 27, Scole 29, Stowmarket 45.
EC Thur. **MD** Fri, Sat, Sun. **Golf** Lowestoft 18h. **See** St Margaret's Church, Sparrow's Nest, Lighthouse, Somerleyton Hall.
Esplanade. (0502) 565989

★★★ Victoria, Kirkley Cliff Rd, NR33 0BZ (0502) 574433 Fax: (0502) 501529
In traditional Grand Hotel style, occupying a commanding position overlooking beach. Swimming pool. Fr, De, It
35 bedrs, 35 en suite, (2 sh); TV; tcf
lift, TV, dogs, ns, P, coach; child facs; con 200
LD 9.30
£ B&B £45·50 (w/e £33), B&B (double) £65·50; L £8·50, D £10; [V]
cc Access, Amex, B'card/Visa, CB, Diners.

Lodge (Highly Acclaimed), London Rd, Pakefield, NR33 7AA (0502) 69805. *Hotel.*

Albany (Acclaimed), 400 London Rd South, NR33 0BQ (0502) 574394. *Private Hotel.*
Rockville House (Acclaimed), 6 Pakefield Rd, NR33 0HS, (0502) 581011. *Private Hotel.*
£ B&B £16·50–£30; HB weekly £153–£175; [5% V, w/e; Oct–Apr]

Katherine, 49 Kirkley Cliff Rd, NR33 0DF (0502) 567858. *Hotel. Solarium.*
Kingsleigh, 44 Marine Parade, NR 33 0QN (0502) 572513
£ B&B £16–£18; [5% V]
Seavilla, 43 Kirkley Cliff Rd, NR33 0DF (0502) 574657. *Hotel.*
£ B&B £18·40; HB weekly £148–£159·85

LOWESWATER Cumbria. Map 43B1
Pop 180. Keswick 11, London 296, Cockermouth 11, Workington 10.
EC Mon. **Golf** Embleton Cockermouth 18h. **See** Loweswater, Crummock Water, Scale Force–120 ft waterfall.

★★ H Scale Hill, CA13 9UX Lorton (090 085) 232
Former 17th century inn, an attractive white building in glorious countryside. Open Mar–Nov.
15 bedrs, 15 en suite; annexe 2 bedrs, 2 en suite
dogs, ns; P 25; child facs
LD 7.45, nr lunch
£ B&B £33–£42, B&B (double) £44–£76; HB weekly £208–£345; D £16

★ Grange Country House, CA13 0SU Lamplugh (0946) 861211
Small 300-year old Lakeland building of charm close to lake.
7 bedrs, 6 en suite, (1 sh), 2 ba; annexe 5 bedrs, 4 en suite, 1 ba; TV; tcf
TV, dogs; P 20, U 2; child facs

LUDLOW Shropshire. Map 20A4
Pop 8,130. Worcester 29, London 143, Bridgnorth 19, Kidderminster 25, Knighton 15, Leominster 11, Shrewsbury 27.
EC Thur. **MD** Mon, Fri, Sat. **Golf** Ludlow 18h. **See** Castle ruins, remains of Norman circular chapel, St Laurence's Church, Old Inns, Reader's House, Butter Cross, Broad Gate, Museum, Craft Centre.
Castle St. (0584) 875053

★★★ Dinham Hall, SY8 1EJ (0584) 876464 Fax: (0584) 876019
Sandstone building with attractive bow windows; in walled garden next to Ludlow Castle. Sauna, gymnasium. Fr
12 bedrs, 12 en suite; TV; tcf
P 17, no children under 6; con 24
LD 9.30, nr Mon–Wed lunch. Resid & Rest lic
£ B&B £55, B&B (double) £70; L £14·95, D £22·50; [V, Mon–Thu]
cc Access, Amex, B'card/Visa.

★★★ H C Feathers, Bull Ring, SY8 1AA (0584) 875261 Tx: 35637 Fax: (0584) 876030

A famous timbered hotel; well-appointed bedrooms. Billiards.
40 bedrs, 40 en suite; TV; tcf
lift, dogs, ns; P 36, coach; child facs; con 100
LD 9
£ B&B £60–£80, B&B (double) £86–£102; L £11·50, D £18; WB £116; [V]
cc Access, Amex, B'card/Visa, CB, Diners; dep.

★★★ Overton Grange, SY8 4AD (0584) 873500 Fax: (0584) 873524
An Edwardian house with pleasant grounds in open country; 1½ miles S of town. Fr, It, Es
16 bedrs, 13 en suite, 2 ba; TV; tcf
ns; P 80, coach; child facs; con 120
LD 9.15
£ B&B £35–£55 (w/e £42), B&B (double) £55–£90; HB weekly £250–280; L £13·95, D £15; WB £42; [5% V]
cc Access, Amex, B'card, Visa, Diners; dep.

★★ Angel, Broad St, SY8 1NG (0584) 2581

Ancient coaching inn with Lord Nelson connections.

Church Inn (Acclaimed), Church St, Buttercross, SY8 1AP (0584) 872174 *Inn.*
£ B&B £25

Cecil, Sheet Rd, SY8 1LR (0584) 2442. *Hotel*

LULWORTH Dorset. Map 5A1
Wareham 8½, London 120, Blandford Forum 18, Dorchester 16, Weymouth 14.
Golf Wareham 9h, Lakey Hill 18h. **See** Cove, Durdle Door, Lulworth Castle & RC Church, Worbarrow Bay, Ringstead Bay.

★ Bishop's Cottage, West Lulworth, BH20 5RQ West Lulworth (092 941) 261

Cottage type holiday hotel with pleasant garden. Swimming pool.
11 bedrs, 6 en suite, 3 ba; annexe 3 bedrs, 2 en suite; tcf
TV, dogs; P 8, coach; child facs; con 25
LD 9.30. Resid & Rest lic
£ B&B £17·50–£19·50, B&B (double) £35–£39; HB weekly £175–£190; L £6·25, D £9
cc Access, B'card/Visa; dep.

LUTON Bedfordshire. Map 14C3
Pop 165,000. St Albans 10, London 31, M1 (jn 10) 1½, Baldock 13, Bedford 19, Biggleswade 19, Dunstable 5, Hatfield 13.
MD Daily. **Golf** Stockwood Park 18h. **See** Church of St Mary, Museum (Wardown Park), Luton Hoo (Fabergé collection).
45 Alma St. (0582) 401579

★★★★ Strathmore Thistle, Arndale Centre, LU1 2TR (0582) 34199 Tx: 825763 Fax: (0582) 402528
Modern purpose-built centre of town hotel adjacent to shopping centre. (MtCh)
150 bedrs, 150 en suite; TV; tcf
lift, ns; P 44, coach; child facs; con 200
LD 11
£ room £70, double room £84; Bk £7·75, L £12·50, D £16; WB
cc Access, Amex, B'card/Visa, CB, Diners.

 EC *early closing* **MD** *market day* *country house hotel* *ns (NS) no smoking areas* *tcf tea/coffee facilities*

★★★ Chiltern, Dunstable Rd/Waller Ave, LU4 9RU ☎(0582) 575911 Tx: 825048 Fax: (0582) 581859

Near M1, large modern hotel with some executive rooms. (Cr/THF)
93 bedrs, 93 en suite; TV; tcf
lift, dogs, ns; P 250, coach; child facs; con 250
✕9.45; nr Sat lunch
£ room £43–£90 (w/e £21·50); double room £43–£102; Bk £7·95, L £13, D £15; WB £35
cc Access, Amex, B'card/Visa, Diners.
(*See advertisement on p. 338*)

★★★ Luton Crest, Dunstable Rd, LU4 8RQ ☎(0582) 575955 Tx: 826283 Fax: (0582) 490065

Modern purpose-built hotel adjacent to junction 11 of the M1. (Cr/THF)
117 bedrs, 117 en suite; TV; tcf
lift, dogs, ns; P 117, coach; child facs; con 100
✕LD 9.45, nr Sat lunch
£ B&B £81, B&B (double) £107; L £11·95, D £14·95; WB £40; [10% V]
cc Access, Amex, B'card/Visa, Diners.

★★★ Red Lion, Castle St, LU1 3AA ☎(0582) 413881 Tx: 51324 Fax: (0582) 23864
A refurbished town-centre inn with a rear courtyard. Near Arndale Centre. (Lns)
24 bedrs, 24 en suite; annexe 15 bedrs, 15 en suite; TV; tcf
ns; P 50, coach; child facs; con 50
✕LD 10.30, bar meals only Sat lunch
£ B&B £72, B&B (double) £84; L £8·25, D £13·25; [V]
cc Access, Amex, B'card/Visa, Diners.

★★ Leaside, 72 New Bedford Rd, LU13 1BT ☎(0582) 417643 Fax: (0582) 598646

Small, owner-managed hotel close to town centre. Billiards. Fr. Closed 24, 25 & 26 Dec.
13 bedrs, 13 en suite; TV
TV, dogs; P 40; child facs; con 25
✕LD 9.45, bar meals only Sat lunch & Sun dinner.
£ B&B £40–£55 B&B (double) £53–£63; HB weekly £390–£400; L £13, D £18
cc Access, Amex, B'card/Visa, Diners.

★ C Central, 100 Park St, LU1 3EY ☎(0582) 421371
Small hotel above a tandoori restaurant in centre of Luton.
16 bedrs, 16 en suite
(*See advertisement on p. 338*)

Ambassador (Acclaimed), 31 Lansdowne Rd, LU3 1EE ☎(0582) 451656. *Hotel.*
£ B&B £51·75

LUTTERWORTH Leicestershire. Map 21A4

Pop 6,758. M1 (jn 20) ½, London 89, Coventry 14, Hinckley 10, Leicester 13, Market Harborough 12, Rugby 7.
EC Wed. **MD** Thur. **Golf** Lutterworth 18h, Ullesthorpe 18h. **See** St Mary's Church, Stanford Hall.

★★★ Denbigh Arms, High St, LE17 4AD ☎(0455) 553537 Tx: 342545 Fax: (0455) 556627

Completely refurbished, an old building of great character set in centre of town. Fr. Closed 25, 31 Dec & 1 Jan.
34 bedrs, 34 en suite; TV; tcf
P 35; child facs; con 60
✕LD 9.30; nr Sat lunch & Sun dinner
£ B&B £66·50–£76 (w/e £35), B&B (double) £80–£90; L £12, D £16; [5% V]
cc Access, Amex, B'card/Visa, Diners.

★★★ Greyhound Inn, 9 Market St, LE17 4EJ ☎(0455) 553307 ♿

A typical 18th century coaching inn with carefully restored courtyard. No lounge but two bars. Excellent bedrooms. Fr, De
20 bedrs, 20 en suite; annexe 9 bedrs, 9 en suite; TV; tcf
ns; coach; child facs; con 64
✕LD 9.45
£ B&B £35–£59 (w/e £30), B&B (double) £49–£59; L £9·95, D £12·95; [10% V w/e, 5% w/d]

★★ Moorbarns, A5 Trunk Rd, LE17 4HU ☎(045 55) 2237
Modern complex with motel style bedrooms, lounges and restaurant. Swimming pool.

LYDFORD Devon. Map 3A2

Pop 321. Okehampton 8½, London 200, Launceston 12, Tavistock 8½.
Golf Tavistock 18h. **See** Gorge, St Petroc's Church, Lydford Gorge (& waterfall), Castle ruins.

★★ Lydford House, EX20 4AU ☎(082 282) 347 Fax: (082 282) 442

Late Victorian country house in 3 acres of attractive grounds. Riding.
13 bedrs, 13 en suite, 1 ba; TV; tcf
dogs, ns; P 30; no children under 5
✕LD 7.45, bar meals only Mon–Sat lunch
£ B&B £26, B&B (double) £52; HB weekly £215–£229; D £11
cc Access, Amex, B'card/Visa, Diners; dep.

Dartmoor Inn (Acclaimed), EX20 4AY ☎(082 282) 221
£ B&B £25

LYME REGIS Dorset. Map 4B1

See also HAWKCHURCH
Pop 3,500. Dorchester 26, London 147, Axminster 5, Crewkerne 15, Exeter 28.
EC Thur. **Golf** Charmouth 18h. **See** Parish Church, The Cobb (Harbour) Museum, 250-year-old Umbrella Cottage, Charton Bay.
ℹ Guildhall, Bridge St. ☎(029 74) 2138

★★★ H Alexandra, Pound St, DT7 3HZ ☎(029 74) 2010

Large white 18th century building. Fine sea view from gardens. Closed 22 Dec–31 Jan.
23 bedrs, 23 en suite; annexe 1 bedr, 1 en suite; TV; tcf
dogs; P 20; child facs
✕LD 8.30
£ B&B £30–£40, B&B (double) £70–£90; HB weekly £270–£330; L £7·95, D £14·50; WB £40
cc Access, B'card/Visa; dep.
(*See advertisement on p. 338*)

★★★ H Devon, Uplyme, DT7 3TQ ☎(029 74) 3231 Tx: 42513

L

Luton (Bedfordshire)

CHILTERN CREST HOTEL
LUTON

Waller Avenue, Luton LU4 9RU.
Tel: (0582) 575911. Fax: (0582) 581859. Telex: 825048
One mile from M1 junction 11, close to Luton Hoo and Airport. 93 bedrooms. Restaurant. Meeting rooms maximum 250. Ample car parking.

Luton (Bedfordshire)

100 Park Street, Luton LU1 3EY
Tel: (0582) 421371
Fax: (0582) 411427
Telex: 825562 CHACOM G
CENTRAL HOTEL

Is ideally situated in the centre of town, within walking distance of the Arndale Shopping Centre, bus and train stations and Vauxhall Motors.
Only five minutes drive from Luton International Airport, M1 (Junction 10), A505 and A6.

★ Each room is equipped with en-suite bath/shower room, WC, hand wash basin
★ Colour TV ★ Tea/coffee making facilities
★ Direct dial telephone ★ Hair dryer
Hotel has its own bar and restaurant
★ 24 hour service
★ Breakfast served until 9am
★ Lunch 12–2.00pm ★ Dinner 6pm to 12 midnight

Lyme Regis (Dorset)

Alexandra Hotel

Pound Street, Lyme Regis, Dorset Tel: (029 74) 2010
Built as a Dower House in 1735, tastefully modernised and set in its peaceful garden overlooking the Cobb, the Alexandra occupies a prime position in Lyme Regis.

Lyme Regis (Dorset)

THE DOWER HOUSE HOTEL

ROUSDON, Nr LYME REGIS, DORSET. Tel: 0297 21047
Beautiful Olde Worlde country mansion set in acres of tree fringed ground with no parking problems. Indoor heated swimming pool and sauna. All rooms en-suite. Excellent cuisine. Short breaks available throughout the year.

Lyme Regis (Dorset)

Comfort, good food and friendly service

The Mariners Hotel RAC ★★★

Silver Street, Lyme Regis, Dorset DT7 3HS Tel: (02974) 2753

350th Anniversary! Former 17th century coaching hotel, scheduled as of historical interest and illustrated by Beatrix Potter in *Tales of a Little Pig Robinson*. Superbly preserved to include all the modern comforts with en-suite bathrooms. Retaining the charm and ambience of the period with its crooked rooms. A 325 year old tulip tree in the garden from where there are spectacular views of the Dorset coast. Finest cuisine with local fish specialities. Bargain Breaks available. **For colour brochure please telephone or write.**

Lymington (Hampshire)

Georgian Town House Hotel with rooms overlooking traditional English walled garden close to the Quay. Ideal for visiting New Forest and Beaulieu. 10 miles from M27. All rooms recently refurbished. Weekend Breaks and Christmas programme.
Egon Ronay & Michelin recommended.

High Street, Lymington, Hants SO41 9AA. Telephone: 0590 677123 Telex: 477463 G.
Fax: 0590 677756.

Clipper Hotels
Enjoy standards you had forgotten existed

EC *early closing* **MD** *market day* *country house hotel* *ns (NS) no smoking areas* *tcf tea/coffee facilities*

Originally the old rectory in Uplyme, with attractive grounds. Swimming pool, putting, solarium, gymnasium. ⚒ Da. Open Mar–Nov.
🛏 21 bedrs, 21 en suite; TV; tcf
🏠 dogs; P 30; child facs
✕ LD 8.30
£ B&B £38·50–£40·50, B&B (double) £77–£81; L £6·50, D £10·95; WB £80 (2 days); [10% V]
cc Access, Amex, B'card/Visa, Diners; dep.

★★★ **Mariners,** Silver St, DT7 3HS
📞 (029 74) 2753 Tx: 46491
Fax: (02974) 2431
A building of old world charm in delightful garden. ⚒ De
🛏 16 bedrs, 14 en suite; TV; tcf
🏠 dogs; P 23, coach; child facs; con 20
✕ LD 9, nr lunch. Resid & Rest lic
£ B&B £31–£44, B&B (double) £62–£90; HB weekly £280–£350; D £13·50; WB £74; [10% V, 1 Nov–30 Mar]
cc Access, Amex, B'card/Visa, Diners; dep.
(See advertisement on p. 338)

★★ **H** **Bay,** Marine Par, DT7 3JQ
📞 (029 74) 2059
Purpose-built hotel on Marine Parade with fine sea views. Privately owned. Sauna, solarium, gymnasium, snooker. ⚒ De. Open Mar–Nov.
🛏 22 bedrs, 13 en suite, 4 ba; TV; tcf
🏠 dogs; G 20; child facs
✕ LD 8, bar meals only lunch
£ B&B £24–£29·50, B&B (double) £48–£59; HB weekly £198–£249; D £14
cc Access, B'card/Visa; dep.

★★ **Buena Vista,** Pound St, DT7 3HZ
📞 (029 74) 2494

Privately-owned Regency house with garden and sea views. On main street.
🛏 19 bedrs, 19 en suite, 2 ba; TV; tcf
🏠 dogs, ns; P 20; coach; child facs; con 55
✕ LD 8, nr lunch. Resid & Rest lic
£ B&B £30–£34, B&B (double) £52–£78; HB weekly £204–£282; D £10·50
cc Access, Amex, B'card/Visa, Diners; dep.

★★ **Dorset,** Silver St, DT7 3HX 📞 (029 74) 2482.

An extended Georgian building in quiet residential area. Privately owned. Open Apr–Oct.
🛏 14 bedrs, 12 en suite, 3 ba; TV; tcf
🏠 dogs; P 13; coach; child facs
✕ LD 7.45, bar meals only lunch. Resid & Rest lic
£ B&B £22, B&B (double) £44; HB weekly £189·50; WB £62·75 (BB 3nts)
cc Access, B'card/Visa; dep.

★★ **H** **C** **Dower House,** Rousdon, DT7 3RB 📞 Seaton (0297) 21047
Substantial country residence in rural surroundings at Rousdon. Privately owned. Indoor swimming pool, sauna. Closed Nov.
🛏 10 bedrs, 10 en suite, 1 ba; TV; tcf
🏠 TV, dogs; P 50, coach; child facs
✕ LD 9
£ B&B £28–£30, B&B (double) £48–£52; HB weekly £175–£230; L £10·95, D £12·95; WB £58
cc Access, Amex, B'card/Visa, Diners; dep.
(See advertisement on p. 338)

★★ **H** **C** **R** **Kersbrook,** Pound Rd, DT7 3HX 📞 (029 74) 2596

An attractive stone built hotel with thatched roof. Pleasant garden to rear. ⚒ Fr, De. Open 1 Feb–8 Dec.
🛏 10 bedrs, 10 en suite; TV; tcf
🏠 dogs, ns; P 14, coach; child facs
✕ LD 9, bar meals only Mon–Sat lunch & Sun dinner. Resid & Rest lic
£ B&B £39–£45, B&B (double) £50–£55; HB weekly £250–£285; D £16·50; WB £75 (2dys); [10% V, w/d]
cc Access, B'card/Visa; dep.

★★ **Orchard Country,** Rousdon, DT7 3XW 📞 (029 74) 2972 ♿
Pleasant hotel set in gardens in the countryside. ⚒ Fr, Es. Open 28 Mar–27 Oct.
🛏 12 bedrs, 12 en suite; TV; tcf
🏠 TV, dogs, ns; P 25, coach; no children under 8; con 20
✕ LD 8.15, bar meals only lunch. Resid & Rest lic
£ B&B £27–£34, B&B (double) £50–£59, HB weekly £195–£215; D £12·50; WB £58 (HB 2 nts)
cc Access, B'card/Visa; dep.

★★ **Royal Lion,** Broad St, DT7 3QF
📞 (029 74) 5622

Privately-owned coaching inn of character; in main street. Indoor swimming pool, sauna, gymnasium, billiards.
🛏 30 bedrs, 30 en suite, 1 ba; TV; tcf
🏠 dogs, ns; P 38; child facs
✕ LD 9, bar meals only Mon–Sat lunch
£ B&B £30–£33, B&B (double) £60–£66; HB weekly £215–£237; D £12·50; WB £60
cc Access, Amex, B'card/Visa, Diners; dep.

★★ **St Michaels,** Pound St, DT7 3HZ
📞 (029 74) 2503
Pleasantly modernised family-run Regency hotel in central location.
🛏 13 bedrs, 12 en suite; TV; tcf
🏠 dogs, ns; P 12, G 1; child facs; con 10
✕ LD 7.30, bar meals only lunch. Resid lic.
£ B&B £25–£30·50, B&B (double) £50–£61
cc Access, B'card/Visa; dep.

★ **Tudor House,** Church St, DT7 3BU
📞 (029 74) 2472
Privately-owned, terraced building, a stone's throw from sea. Near main street. Open mid-Mar–mid-Oct.
🛏 17 bedrs, 4 en suite, 4 ba; tcf
🏠 TV, dogs; P 12, coach; child facs
✕ LD 7.30, nr lunch. Resid & Rest lic
£ B&B £11·50, B&B (double) £23; HB weekly £125–£185; D £5·50
cc Access, B'card/Visa; dep.

White House (Acclaimed), 47 Silver St, DT7 3HR 📞 (029 74) 3420. *Guest House.* Open Easter–Oct.
£ B&B (double) £27–£34

LYMINGTON Hampshire. Map 5B1

Pop 12,500. Lyndhurst 8, London 92, Bournemouth 16, Ringwood 13.
EC Wed. **MD** Sat. **Golf** Barton-on-Sea 18h. **See** Beaulieu Abbey, Palace House and National Motor Museum 5½ m NE.
ℹ St Thomas St car park 📞 (0590) 672422

★★★ **C** **Passford House,** Mount Pleasant, SO41 8LS 📞 (0590) 682398
Tx: 47502 ♿

Lovely white-faced country house, partly 17th century, in attractive grounds. Indoor & outdoor swimming pools, putting, tennis, sauna, solarium, gymnasium.
🛏 54 bedrs, 54 en suite, 2 ba; TV; tcf
🏠 TV, dogs; P 100, U 2 (£3); child facs; con 40
✕ LD 9
£ B&B £55–£60, B&B (double) £86–£95; WB
cc Access, Amex, B'card/Visa; dep.

Hotel locations
Hotel locations are shown on the maps at the back of the guide. All towns and villages containing an RAC Appointed or Listed hotel are ringed in purple.

L

★★★ **Stanwell House,** 15 High St, SO41 9AA ☎(0590) 677123 Tx: 477463 Fax: (0590) 677756

Converted charming Georgian terrace houses with well-furnished bedrooms.
🛏35 bedrs, 35 en suite; TV; tcf
🏠child facs; con 20
✕LD 9.30
£ B&B fr £62·50, B&B (double) fr £80; L £10·50, D £17·50; WB £98·50
cc Access, B'card/Visa.
(*See advertisement on p. 338*)

LYMM Cheshire. Map 33A1

Pop 10,496. M6 (jn 20) 2, London 181, Altrincham 6½, Bolton 17, Manchester 13, Northwich 11, Warrington 4½.
EC Wed. **MD** Thur. **Golf** Lymm 18h. **See** Parish Church, Stocks, Market Cross.

★★★ **Lymm,** Whitbarrow Rd, WA13 9AQ ☎(092 575) 2233 Tx: 629455 Fax: (0925 75) 6035

Quiet hotel in pleasant Cheshire village. 15 minutes from motorways and airport. (DeV)
🛏22 bedrs, 22 en suite, annexe 47 bedrs, 47 en suite; TV; tcf
🏠dogs, ns; P 160, coach; child facs; con 120
✕LD 9.45, bar meals only Sat lunch
£ B&B £75 (w/e £30), B&B (double) £92; L £11, D £14; WB £70; [10% V, Fri–Sun; Jul, Aug]
cc Access, Amex, B'card/Visa, Diners.

LYMPSHAM Somerset. Map 4B3

Pop 686. M5 (jn 22) 4, Axbridge 7, London 139, Bridgwater 13, Wells 18, Weston-super-Mare 6.
Golf Burnham 18h. **See** Perp Church.

Changes made after July 1990 are not included.

♣♣ ★★ R **Batch Farm Country,** Batch La, BS24 0EX ☎Weston-super-Mare (0934) 750371

Converted and extended farm house with pleasant garden in country surroundings. Fishing, billiards. Closed Xmas.
🛏8 bedrs, 8 en suite; TV; tcf
🏠TV, ns; P 50; child facs; con 80
✕LD 8, bar meals only lunch. Resid & Rest lic
£ B&B £28–£30, B&B (double) £46–£48; HB weekly £185–£195; D £10; WB £64; [5% V]
cc Access, Amex, B'card/Visa, Diners; dep.

LYNDHURST Hampshire. Map 5B2

Pop 2,900. London 84, M27 (jn 1) 3, Bournemouth 19, Lymington 8, Ringwood 14, Salisbury 19, Southampton 9½.
EC Wed. **Golf** Lyndhurst 18h. **See** Church, 14th cent Queen's House.
ℹ New Forest Visitor Centre. ☎(0703) 282269

★★★ **Beaulieu,** Beaulieu Rd, SO4 7YQ ☎(0703) 293344 Fax: (0703) 293719

Recently refurbished hotel in gabled Victorian building on B2056 between Lyndhurst and Beaulieu. Set in 2½ acres of gardens.
🛏13 bedrs, 12 en suite; TV; tcf
🏠TV, dogs, ns; P 50, coach; child facs; con 80
✕LD 8.45, bar meals only lunch
£ B&B £59–£69, B&B (double) £85–£95; HB weekly £326·67; D £10; WB £105 (HB)
cc Access, Amex, B'card/Visa, Diners.

★★★ **Crown,** High St, SO43 7NF ☎(0703) 282922 Tx: 9312110733 Fax: (0703) 282751

Fine black and white building set in town centre. ⚒ Fr
🛏40 bedrs, 40 en suite; TV; tcf
🏠lift, TV, dogs; P 60, coach; child facs; con 70
✕LD 9.30, bar meals only Sat lunch
£ B&B £46–£55, B&B (double) £70–£88; HB weekly £315–£385; L £14, D £14; WB £96 (HB 2nts)
cc Access, Amex, B'card/Visa, Diners.

★★★ **Forest Lodge,** Pikes Hill, Romsey Rd, SO43 7AS ☎(0703) 283677

Modernised and extended 1830s former Royal hunting lodge. Swimming pool, putting.
🛏19 bedrs, 19 en suite; TV; tcf
🏠TV, dogs, ns; P 20, coach; child facs; con 120
✕LD 8.45, nr Mon–Sat lunch, Resid & Rest lic
£ B&B £59–£69, B&B (double) £85–£95; L £9·95, D £13; [10% V]
cc Access, Amex, B'card/Visa, Diners

★★★ **Lyndhurst Park,** High St, SO43 7NL ☎(0703) 283923 Tx: 477802 Fax: (0703) 283019

Set in own grounds, an imposing Georgian building. Swimming pool, tennis, snooker, sauna. ⚒ Fr
🛏59 bedrs, 59 en suite; TV; tcf
🏠lift, dogs, ns; P 100, coach; child facs; con 150
✕LD 10
£ B&B £55–£60, B&B (double) £70–£77; L £6, D £13; [10% V, w/e]
cc Access, Amex, B'card/Visa, Diners.

♣♣ ★★★ **Parkhill,** Beaulieu Rd, SO43 7FZ ☎(0703) 282944
Charming, largely 18th-century house in parkland and gardens, down a long drive from B3056, south east of Lyndhurst. Well-furnished rooms with some antique pieces.
🛏20 bedrs, 20 en suite; TV; tcf

★★ **Evergreens,** Romsey Rd, SO43 7AR ☎(0703) 282175
Small hotel, with attractive garden, in a rural setting. Swimming pool. ⚒ De
🛏18 bedrs, 16 en suite, 1 ba; annexe 2 bedrs, 2 en suite; TV; tcf
🏠dogs; P 40, coach; child facs; con 50
✕LD 9, bar meals only lunch. Resid & Rest lic
£ B&B £35–£42, B&B (double) £51–£64; D £12·50
cc Access, B'card/Visa.

★ **Forest Point,** Romsey Rd, SO43 7AR ☎(0703) 282944

EC *early closing* **MD** *market day* ♣♣ *country house hotel* *ns (NS) no smoking areas* *tcf tea/coffee facilities*

Family-owned hotel in attractive Georgian building close to forest.

Knightwood Lodge (Acclaimed), Southampton Rd, SO43 7BU ☎(0703) 282502 Fax: (0703) 283730
£ B&B £26–£32; [V, 1 Nov–1Apr]

Ormonde House (Acclaimed), Southampton Rd SO43 7BT ☎(0703) 282806 Fax: (042 128) 3775. *Hotel.*

LYNMOUTH Devon. Map 3B4

Pop 1,600 (with Lynton). Minehead 16, London 184, Barnstaple 17, Ilfracombe 17, South Molton 20.
Golf Ilfracombe 18h. **See** Valley of Rocks, Watersmeet, Glen Lyn, Doone Valley and Oare Church, Shelley's Cottage, Countisbury Church (16th cent), Exmoor, Culbone Church (16th cent) reputed smallest in England.
ℹ Lee Rd, Lynton. ☎Lynton (0598) 52225

★★★ Tors, EX35 6NA ☎Lynton (0598) 53236

Stone-built hotel with commanding views. Swimming pool. Closed 4 Jan–9 Mar.
🛏35 bedrs, 33 en suite; TV; tcf
lift, TV, dogs, ns; P 40, coach; child facs; con 80

★★ Bath, Sea Front, EX35 6EL ☎Lynton (0598) 52238

Family-run hotel overlooking harbour in a picturesque setting. Open Mar–end Oct.
🛏24 bedrs, 24 en suite; TV; tcf
dogs; P 10, U 4 (£1·50); child facs
✕LD 8.30
£ B&B £27·50, B&B (double) £48–£63; HB weekly £190–£260; L £6·75, D £13; [10% V, Mar–Oct]
cc Access, Amex, B'card/Visa, Diners; dep.

★★ Beacon, Countisbury Hill, EX35 6ND ☎Lynton (0598) 53268

Attractive stone building in 27 acres of grounds; overlooking Lynmouth Bay. ⚒ De. Open Easter–15 Oct.
🛏7 bedrs, 5 en suite, 2 ba; TV; tcf
P 10; children over 12
✕LD 7.30. Resid & Rest lic
£ B&B £26·50, B&B (double) £51; HB weekly £238; D £12; dep.

★★ H C R Rising Sun, Harbourside, Mars Hill, EX35 6EQ ☎Lynton (0598) 53223

14th century thatched inn on waterfront with attractive beamed bar. Fishing. ⚒ Fr, De, Es. Closed Jan.
🛏11 bedrs, 11 en suite; annexe 5 bedrs, 5 en suite; TV; tcf
dogs, ns; no children under 5
✕LD 9
£ B&B £35–£45, B&B (double) £70, L £10, D £16·50; WB £42; [5% V]
cc Access, Amex, B'card/Visa; dep.

★ H Rock House, EX35 6EN ☎Lynton (0598) 53508
Elegant Regency house, graciously furnished. On water's edge overlooking harbour.
🛏6 bedrs, 4 en suite, 1 ba; TV; tcf
TV, dogs; P 7; child facs
✕LD 9. Resid & Rest lic
£ B&B £21–£28, B&B (double) £42–£56; HB weekly £190–£235; L £4·50, D £11; WB £59 (2 nts)
cc Access, Amex, B'card/Visa, Diners; dep.

★ Shelley's Cottage, Watersmeet Rd, EX35 6EP ☎Lynton (0598) 53219
Cottage-style stone building in centre of village by the Gorge.

Countisbury Lodge (Acclaimed), 6 Tors Park, EX35 6NB ☎Lynton (0598) 52388. *Hotel.*
£ B&B £14·40–£19, HB weekly £161

East Lynn House, (Acclaimed) 17 Watersmeet Rd, EX35 6EP ☎Lynton (0598) 52540. *Private Hotel.*
£ HB weekly £168–£182; [5% V]

Heatherville (Acclaimed), Tors Park, EX35 6NB ☎Lynton (0598) 52327. *Hotel.* Open Easter–Oct.
£ B&B £17; HB weekly £162–£174

LYNTON Devon. Map 3B4

Pop 1,600 (inc Lynmouth). Lynmouth ½, London 185, Barnstaple 16, Ilfracombe 16
EC Sat (win). **Golf** Ilfracombe 18h.
ℹ Lee Rd. ☎(0598) 52225

Hotel locations
Hotel locations are shown on the maps at the back of the guide. All towns and villages containing an RAC Appointed or Listed hotel are ringed in purple.

★★★ H R Lynton Cottage, North Walk, EX35 6ED ☎(0598) 52342 Fax: (0598) 52597

Attractive row of 17th century cottages in grounds with panoramic views. Open Feb–Dec.
🛏17 bedrs, 17 en suite; TV; tcf
dogs; P 26; no children under 10; con 20
✕LD 8.45, bar meals only Sun lunch
£ B&B £40·50–£49·50, B&B (double) £81–£99; HB weekly £327–£389; L £12·50, D £18·50; WB £52·50; [5% V]
cc Access, Amex, B'card/Visa, Diners; dep.

★★ Castle Hill House, Castle Hill, EX35 6JA ☎(0598) 52291

Small attractive stone and brick building in centre of village. ⚒ Fr
🛏9 bedrs, 9 en suite; TV; tcf
dogs, ns; child facs
✕LD 9.30, nr lunch Resid & Rest lic
£ B&B £19·50–£21·50, B&B (double) £35–£40; D £6·95; [10% V]
cc Access, B'card/Visa; dep.

★★ Crown, Sinai Hill, EX35 6AG ☎(0598) 52253
18th century coaching inn with attractive dining room. Near spectacular scenery. Closed Jan.
🛏16 bedrs, 16 en suite; TV; tcf
dogs; P 25, coach; child facs; con 50
✕LD 8.30, bar meals only lunch
£ B&B fr £35·50, B&B (double) fr £60; HB weekly fr £225; D £13·50; WB £35·50
cc Access, Amex, B'card/Visa, Diners; dep.

Using RAC discount vouchers
Please tell the hotel when booking if you plan to use an RAC discount voucher (see p. 34) in part payment of your bill. Only one voucher will be accepted per party per stay. Discount vouchers will only be accepted in payment for accommodation, not for food.

L

★★ **Sandrock,** Longmead, EX35 6DH
(0598) 53307

Privately-owned south-facing, Edwardian house in own pleasant grounds. Es. Open 1 Feb–30 Nov.
9 bedrs, 7 en suite, 1 ba; TV; tcf
dogs; P 9; child facs
LD 7.45, bar meals only lunch
£ B&B £17·50–£21, B&B (double) £37–£45; HB weekly £185·50–£214; D £10·50; WB £43; [10% V]
cc Access, Amex, B'card/Visa; dep.

★ H **Chough's Nest,** North Walk, EX35 6HJ (0598) 53315

Attractive stone-built hotel in quiet elevated position offering panoramic view. Fr. Open Easter–20 Oct.
11 bedrs, 11 en suite; TV; tcf
ns; P 10; no children under 2
LD 7.30, bar meals only lunch. Rest lic
£ B&B £21; HB weekly £195–£218; D £9; dep.

★ **Fairholme**, North Walk, EX35 6ED
(0598) 52263

Stone-built former residence in grounds giving panoramic views of coastline. Indoor swimming pool. Open May–Oct.
12 bedrs, 7 en suite, 4 ba; TV
TV; P 12; no children under 10
LD 7.30. Resid lic
£ B&B £16·50–£17·50; HB weekly £165; D £7; dep.

★ **North Cliff,** North Walk, EX35 6HJ
(0598) 52357
Originally 2 Victorian residences, in own grounds, on wooded cliffside.
16 bedrs, 13 en suite, 6 ba; TV; tcf
TV, dogs, P 13; child facs

★ H **Rockvale,** Lee Rd, EX35 6HW
(0598) 52279

Attractive stone-built Victorian house near centre of village. Fr, De. Open Mar–mid-Nov.
8 bedrs, 7 en suite, 2 ba; TV; tcf
dogs; P 9; no children under 4
LD 7, bar meals only lunch. Resid & Rest lic
£ B&B £17·50–£20; HB weekly £190–£200; D £10; WB £55 (HB 2nts)
cc Access, B'card/Visa; dep.

★ H **Seawood,** North Walk, EX35 6HJ
(0598) 52272
Early Victorian stone-built house in grounds on wooded cliffs. Open Mar–Nov.
12 bedrs, 12 en suite, 2 ba; TV; tcf
dogs, ns; P 10; child facs
LD 7.30, nr lunch. Resid & Rest lic
£ B&B £22–£26, B&B (double) £22–£48; D £12; [5% V] dep.

Gordon House (Highly Acclaimed), 31 Lee Rd, EX35 6BS (0598) 53203. *Hotel.* Open Mar–Nov,
£ B&B £18–£21; HB weekly £172–£193 [10% V]

Millslade (Highly Acclaimed), Brendon, EX35 6PS Brendon (059 87) 322. *Private Hotel. Fishing, riding.*

Alford House (Acclaimed), 3 Alford Terr, EX35 6AT (0598) 52359. *Private Hotel.*
£ B&B £23–£25, HB weekly £145–£165; [5% V]

Gable Lodge (Acclaimed), 35 Lee Rd, EX35 6BS (0598) 52367. *Private Hotel.*

Hazeldene (Acclaimed), 27 Lee Rd, EX35 6BP (0598) 52364. *Private Hotel.*

Ingleside (Acclaimed), Lee Rd, EX35 6HW (0598) 52223. *Hotel.* Open Mar–Oct.
£ B&B £21–£23; HB weekly £210–£214; [5% V]

Kingford House (Acclaimed), Longmead, EX35 6DQ (0598) 52361. *Private Hotel.*

Waterloo House (Acclaimed), Lydiate La, EX35 6AT (0598) 53391. *Hotel.*

Longmead House, Longmead, EX35 6DQ (0598) 52523. *Private Hotel.* Open Mar–Oct.
£ B&B £14; HB weekly £142–£152; [5% V]

Mayfair, Lynway, EX35 6AY (0598) 53227. *Private Hotel.* Fr
£ B&B £21–£23; HB weekly £162–£183

St Vincent, Castle Hill, EX35 6JA (0598) 52244. *Guest House.*

LYTHAM ST ANNES Lancs. Map 32A4

Pop 42,150. Preston 14, London 224, Blackpool 4½.
EC Wed. **Golf** Fairhaven 18h. Royal Lytham and St Annes 18h, Lytham (Green Drive) 18h, St Annes Old Links 18h.
See Parish Church, St Annes Pier, Lifeboat Memorial, Motive Power Museum.
i St Annes Square. (0253) 725610

★★★★ **Clifton Arms,** West Beach, FY8 5QJ (0253) 739898 Tx: 677463
Fax: (0253) 730657

Handsome building, largely 19th century, overlooking the Green. Fine sea view. Sauna, solarium. (Lns)
41 bedrs, 41 en suite; TV; tcf
lift, dogs, ns; P 50; child facs; con 150
LD 10
£ B&B £79–£87, B&B (double) £92–£100; L £8·95, D £15; WB £74; [V]
cc Access, Amex, B'card/Visa, Diners.

★★★ **Bedford,** 307–311 Clifton Dr South, FY8 1HN (0253) 724636
Fax: (0253) 729244

Three converted residences form pleasant family-run hotel enjoying central position. Sauna, solarium, gymnasium.
36 bedrs, 36 en suite; TV; tcf
lift, TV, dogs, ns; P 20, coach; child facs; con 150
LD 8.30. Resid & Rest lic
£ B&B £27·50–£30, B&B (double) £50–£60; HB weekly £220–£230; L £5·50, D £12·50; WB £65 (HB)
cc Access, B'card/Visa; dep.

★★★ H **Chadwick**, South Prom, FY8 1NP (0253) 720061 Fax: (0253) 714455

Converted dwelling houses, modernised with extensive sun lounges facing estuary. Indoor swimming pool, sauna, solarium. Es
70 bedrs, 70 en suite; TV; tcf
lift, ns; P 40, coach; child facs; con 70
LD 8.30. Resid & Rest lic
£ B&B £29·50–£34, B&B (double) £39·50–£44; HB weekly £205·80–£239·60; L £6·80, D £11·50; WB £58·80
cc Access, Amex, B'card/Visa, Diners.
(See advertisement on p. 344)

★★★ **Dalmeny,** 19–33 South Prom, FY8 1LX (0253) 712236
Fax: (0253) 724447
An ultra-modern glass-fronted extension to this hotel overlooks the sea. Indoor swimming pool, squash, sauna, solarium.
Fr, Es. Closed 24–26 Dec.
99 bedrs, 99 en suite; TV; tcf
lift, ns; P 90, G 10, coach; child facs; con 200
LD 10
£ B&B £29·75–£49·75, B&B (double) £41·50–£67·50; L £9·50, D £9·75; WB; [10% V]
cc Access, B'card/Visa; dep.

★★★ **Grand Osprey,** South Prom, FY8 1NB ☎(0253) 721288 Tx: 67481

Splendidly restored impressive hotel situated on South Promenade overlooking bay.
🛏 40 bedrs, 38 en suite, (2 sh); TV; tcf
🏨 lift, dogs, ns; P 200, coach; child facs; con 250

★★ **Fernlea,** 15 South Prom, FY8 1LU ☎(0253) 726726 Tx: 677150 Fax: (0253) 721561 ♿

Spacious 3-storey modern hotel on seafront. Indoor swimming pool, squash, sauna, solarium, gymnasium, billiards.
🛏 100 bedrs, 100 en suite, 2 ba; TV; tcf
🏨 lift, TV, dogs, ns; P 70, coach; child facs; con 300

★★ **Glendower,** North Prom, FY8 2NQ ☎(0253) 723241 Fax: (0253) 723241
Privately-owned Victorian style building situated on North Promenade. Indoor swimming pool, sauna, solarium.
🛏 60 bedrs, 60 en suite; TV; tcf
🏨 TV, dogs; P 45, coach; child facs; con 100
✕ LD 7.45, bar meals only lunch
£ B&B £27·50–£33; D £11·95
cc Access, Amex, B'card/Visa, Diners; dep.

★★ **St Ives,** 7 South Prom, FY8 1LS ☎(0253) 720011
Light modern 2-storey family hotel, offering entertainment. Indoor swimming pool, sauna, solarium, billiards.

★ **Lindum,** 63–67 South Prom, FY8 1LZ ☎(0253) 721534 Fax: (0253) 721364
Pleasant family hotel situated on the promenade. Sauna/solarium.
🛏 80 bedrs, 80 en suite, 3 ba; TV; tcf
🏨 lift, TV, dogs; P 20, coach; child facs; con 70
✕ LD 7, bar meals only Mon–Sat lunch. Resid & Rest lic
£ B&B £24–£30, B&B (double) £38–£40; HB weekly £189; L £6·25 (Sun), D £8·50; WB £47 (HB 2 nts); [5% V]
cc Access, Amex, B'card/Visa; dep.

Endsleigh (Acclaimed), 315 Clifton Drive South, FY8 1HN ☎(0253) 725622. *Private Hotel.*
£ B&B £16·75, HB weekly £125–£135

Strathmore (Acclaimed), 305 Clifton Dr South, FY8 1HN ☎(0253) 725478. *Hotel.*
£ B&B £15·75–£17·75; HB weekly £131·25–£138·25

Beaumont, 11 All Saints Rd, FY8 1PL ☎(0253) 723958. *Private Hotel.*
£ B&B £10–£12; HB weekly £105–£125

MACCLESFIELD Cheshire. Map 30B3

See also WINCLE.
Pop 33,600. Leek 12, London 167, Altrincham 14, Buxton 11, Congleton 8, Knutsford 11, Stockport 11.
EC Wed. **MD** Daily. **Golf** Macclesfield 9h. **See** Museum (silk industry), Glacial Stone, Market Stone, St Michael's Church, Unitarian Chapel.
ℹ Town Hall, Market Pl. ☎(0625) 21955

★★★★ R **Shrigley Hall,** Shrigley Park, Pott Shrigley, SK10 5SB ☎Bollington (0625) 575757 Fax: (0625) 573323 ♿

Early 19th century mansion restored to former elegance, set in 260 acres of parkland. Indoor swimming pool, golf, putting, tennis, fishing, squash, sauna, solarium, gymnasium, snooker. Fr, De, It
🛏 58 bedrs, 58 en suite; TV; tcf
🏨 lift, dogs, ns; P 600, coach; child facs; con 165
✕ LD 9.45
£ B&B £50–£85 (w/e £30) B&B (double) £60–£100; HB weekly £475–£720; L £14·50, D £17·50; WB £79·50; [10% V w/e]
cc Access, Amex, B'card/Visa.

★★ **Park Villa,** Park La, SK11 8AE ☎(0625) 511428 Fax: (0625) 614637
Victorian house on busy A34 in suburban area. Garden with lawns and rock garden.
🛏 7 bedrs, 7 en suite, 1 ba; TV; tcf
🏨 lift, TV, dogs, ns; P 14; child facs; con 25
✕ LD 8·45. Resid & Rest lic
£ B&B £38·50–£54, B&B (double) £55–£77; L £6·30, D £11; WB £135; [5% V w/d]
cc Access, Amex, B'card/Visa, Diners.

Moorhayes House, 27 Manchester Rd, SK10 2JJ ☎(0625) 33228. *Private Hotel.*
£ B&B £26–£38; dep.

MADELEY Staffordshire Map 30B2

Newcastle-under-Lyme 5, London 154, Market Drayton 11, Nantwich 11, Whitchurch 16.

Wheatsheaf Inn at Onneley, Barhill Rd, Onneley CW3 9QF ☎(0782) 751581 Fax: (0782) 751499

18th-century country inn next to golf course, six miles west of Newcastle-under-Lyme. Fr, Es
🛏 5 bedrs, 5 en suite; TV; tcf
🏨 dogs; P 150, coach; child facs; con 24
✕ LD 9.30, bar meals only Mon–Sat lunch
£ B&B £37–£42, B&B (double) £42–£52, D £12·95; WB £42; [10% V]
cc Amex, B'card/Visa.

MAIDENCOMBE Devon.

See Torquay

MAIDENHEAD Berkshire. Map 13A3

Pop 50,000. Slough 6, London 26, A308(M) 1½, Henley-on-Thames 8½, High Wycombe 9½, Reading 12, Windsor 6½.
EC Thur. **MD** Fri, Sat. **Golf** Maidenhead 18h. **See** Brunel's Viaduct, Oldfield House (Henry Reitlinger bequest), 18th cent Bridge, Cliveden 3 m NE, Courage Shire Horse Centre 1½ m W, Stanley Spencer Gallery (Cookham).
ℹ Library, St Ives Rd. ☎(0628) 781110

★★★★ H C R **Fredrick's,** Shoppenhangers Rd, SL6 2PZ ☎(0628) 35934 Tx: 849966 Fax: (0628) 771054

Former private residence with a modern extension in 2 acres of attractive landscaped gardens. De, Fr, It, Es. Closed 24–31 Dec.
🛏 37 bedrs, 37 en suite; TV
🏨 P 90; child facs; con 160
✕ LD 9.45, nr Sat lunch
£ B&B £79·50–£110, B&B (double) £135–£145; L £19·50, D £32·50
cc Access, Amex, B'card/Visa, Diners.

★★★★ **Holiday Inn,** Manor La, SL6 2RA ☎(0628) 23444 Tx: 847502 Fax: (0628) 770035
Modern purpose-built 3-storey hotel with restaurant and conference facilities in 13th century manor house, Shoppenhangers Manor. Indoor swimming pool, sauna, solarium, gymnasium, billiards. (HI)
🛏 189 bedrs, 189 en suite; TV; tcf
🏨 lift, dogs, ns; P 400, coach; child facs; con 400
✕ LD 10
£ B&B fr £103·50, B&B (double) fr £132; L £15·50, D £17; WB fr £52 (HB)
cc Access, Amex, B'card/Visa, CB, Diners.

★★★★ **Monkey Island,** Bray-on-Thames, SL6 2EE ☎(0628) 23400 Tx: 846589 Fax: (0628) 784732

M

Lytham St Annes (Lancashire)

Enjoy the luxury of this modern family run, seventy bedroom hotel. The Hotel is renowned for good food and comfortable bedrooms, all of which have private facilities, colour televisions, in-house movies, radio and direct dial telephone.

Other facilities include an indoor swimming pool designed on an Ancient Greek theme and also a Spa Bath, Sauna, Turkish room, Solarium and Games room.

Maidenhead (Berkshire)

Set in sweeping parkland on an island in one of the loveliest reaches of the Thames stands the historic Monkey Island Hotel, now proudly restored to its former elegance and style.

Tastefully appointed accommodation, a sumptuous Regency style restaurant, and unparalleled riverside surroundings combine to give Monkey Island a special place in the heart and mind of the discerning guest. This idyllic and romantic hotel is within easy reach of Windsor, Ascot, Marlow and Henley, and only 30 minutes from London.

Stay on our island – Make it one of your special memories.

Monkey Island Hotel

Bray-on-Thames, Maidenhead, Berkshire SL6 2EE.
Tel: (0628) 23400. Telex 846589 MONTEL. Fax (0628) 784732

Maidenhead (Berkshire)

Courage Shire Horse Centre

Cherry Garden Lane, Maidenhead Thicket, Maidenhead, Berkshire SL6 3QD
Tel. Littlewick Green 4848

Spend a family day out with lots to see. **Free parking, free guided tours.** Open 1st March – 31st October 10am – 5pm. ● Dray rides ● Farrier ● Aviaries ● Gift Shop ● Tea Rooms ● Audio visual ● Mare & Foal ● Bygones. *Disabled facilities.* On A4 between Maidenhead & Reading. Junction 8/9 M4.

EC *early closing* **MD** *market day* *country house hotel* *ns (NS) no smoking areas* *tcf tea/coffee facilities*

This famous hotel in an extended 18th century 'temple' is on an island in the Thames reached by footbridge. Fr, It, Es, Da, Ar, Du. Closed Dec 26–Jan 6
27 bedrs, 27 en suite; TV; tcf
P 200, coach; child facs; con 100
LD 9.45 Resid & Rest lic
£ B&B £72·50–£82·50, B&B (double) £100–£155; L £15·50, D £21·75; WB fr £120
cc Access, Amex, B'card/Visa, Diners.
(*See advertisement on p. 344*)

★★★ R **Boulters Lock,** Boulters Island, SL6 8PE (0628) 21291
Built as a mill in 1726, an enchanting inn by a lock on the Thames. All bedrooms in two riverside cottages.
19 bedrs, 19 en suite; TV; tcf

★★★ **Taplow House,** Berry Hill, Taplow, SL6 0DA (0628) 70056
Fax: (0628) 773625

Former Georgian manor house in 6 acres of attractive grounds. Putting.
30 bedrs, 30 en suite; TV; tcf
dogs; P 100, coach; child facs; con 60
LD 9.30, nr Sat lunch
£ B&B £75–£85, B&B (double) £95–£110; L £12·75 D £17·50; WB £85 (2 nts HB)
cc Access, Amex, B'card/Visa, Diners.

★★ H C R **Norfolk House,** Bath Rd, Taplow, SL6 0AP (0628) 784031
Tx: 849462 Fax: (0628) 23687
Georgian listed building in 3 acres of wooded grounds close to the river on A4. Swimming pool. Fr, Es, Po. Closed 25–29 Dec.
10 bedrs, 10 en suite, 1 ba; TV; tcf
dogs; P 40; child facs; con 25
LD 10.30, nr Sat lunch & Sun dinner
£ B&B £55·95–£75·95 (w/e £40), B&B (double)£96·90–£101·90; L £15·50, D £18·50;
cc Access, Amex, B'card/Visa, CB, Diners; dep.

★★ **Thames,** Ray Mead Rd, SL6 8NR (0628) 28721 Fax: (0628) 773921

Victorian red brick building overlooking Thames near Maidenhead Bridge.
34 bedrs, 34 en suite; TV; tcf
dogs; P 38, coach; child facs; con 65
LD 9.30, bar meals only lunch & Sun dinner
£ B&B £60·25, B&B (double) £79·50; D £15; WB £85; [5% V w/e]
cc Access, Amex, B'card/Visa, Diners.

Clifton, 21 Crauford Rise, SL6 7LR (0628) 23572. *Guest House.*
£ B&B £26·45

MAIDEN NEWTON Dorset. Map 4C1

Pop 763. Dorchester 8, London 130, Crewkerne 13, Lyme Regis 19, Sherborne 15.
Golf Came Down 18h.

Maiden Newton House (Highly Acclaimed), DT2 0AA (0300) 20336. Tx: 417182 *Private Hotel. Fishing.* Closed Jan.
£ B&B £44–£69; [5% V]

MAIDSTONE Kent. Map 11C2

See also HOLLINGBOURNE
Pop 71,800. M20 (jn 6) 2, London 36, Ashford 18, Canterbury 27, Rochester 8½, Sevenoaks 16, Tenterden 18, Tonbridge 13, Tunbridge Wells 16.
EC Wed. **MD** Mon, Tue. **Golf** Cobtree Manor 18h. **See** Archbishop's Palace, All Saints' Church, St Peter's Church, Carriage Museum, Art Gallery and Museum.
i The Gatehouse, Old Palace Gardens. (0622) 673581

★★★★ **Tudor Park,** Ashford Rd, Bearsted, ME14 4NQ (0622) 34334
Tx: 966655 Fax: (0622) 35360

Long, low modern hotel on east side of Maidstone, close to junction 8 of M20. Indoor swimming pool, golf, tennis, squash, sauna, solarium, gymnasium, snooker. Fr, De, It, Du. (Lns)
120 bedrs, 120 en suite; TV; tcf
dogs, ns; P 240, coach; child facs; con 250
LD 9.30, coffee shop only Sat lunch
£ B&B £90–£100 (w/e £55), B&B (double) £105–120; L £11·50, D £15; WB £55; [10% V]
cc Access, Amex, B'card/Visa, Diners; dep.

★★★ **Wateringbury,** Tonbridge Rd, Wateringbury ME18 5NS (0622) 812632
Tx: 96265 Fax: (0622) 812720
Long 2-storey building forming hotel, inn and restaurant complex. Attractive Kent peg tiling upper storey. (Lns)
28 bedrs, 28 en suite; TV; tcf
ns; P 60, con 80
LD 10
£ B&B £75, B&B (double) £88; L £11, D £11; WB £31; [10% V]
cc Access, Amex, B'card/Visa, Diners.

★★ **Grange Moor,** St Michaels Rd, ME16 8BS (0622) 677623 Fax: (0622) 678246
Family-run hotel with pleasant garden. Set in quiet residential area.
36 bedrs, 33 en suite, 2 ba; TV; tcf
TV, dogs; P 60, coach; child facs; con 150
LD 10
£ B&B £30–£48 (w/e £21), B&B (double) £42–£60; HB weekly £280–£364; L £8·50, D £11·50
cc Access, B'card/Visa.
(*See advertisement on p. 344*)

Russell, Boxley Rd, ME14 2EA (0622) 692221
Hotel awaiting inspection.
43 bedrs, 43 en suite
£ B&B £49·40, B&B (double) £75; D £9·50

Carval, 56 London Rd, ME16 8QL (0622) 762100. *Private Hotel.*
Howard, 22 London Rd, ME16 8QL (0622) 58778. *Private Hotel.* Fr
£ B&B £18
Kingsgate, 85 London Rd, ME16 0DX (0622) 753956 *Hotel.*
£ B&B £29–£32 (w/e £24); HB weekly £245–£266; [10% V]

MALBOROUGH Devon. Map 3B1

Pop 983. Kingsbridge 3½, London 208, Plymouth 21.
Golf Thurlestone 18h. **See** Bolt Head, Bolt Tail, Bolberry (Nat Trust), All Saints' Church.

★★★ H R **Soar Mill Cove,** Soar Mill Cove, Salcombe, TQ7 3DS Kingsbridge (0548) 561566 Fax: (0548) 561223

Single storey airy modern hotel in attractive surroundings. Sea views. Indoor & outdoor swimming pools, putting, tennis. Closed 29 Dec–6 Feb.
14 bedrs, 14 en suite; TV; tcf
dogs, ns; P 30; child facs
LD 9. Resid & Rest lic
£ B&B £54–£68, B&B (double) £98–£119, HB weekly £344–£450; L £15, D £25; WB fr £163 (HB 3 nts)
cc Access, B'card/Visa; dep.

MALDON Essex. Map 17C3

Pop 15,500. Chelmsford 10, London 43, Braintree 13, Colchester 16, Southend 20.
EC Wed. **MD** Thur, Sat. **Golf** Maldon 9h, Warren 18h. **See** All Saints' Church, St Peter's Church, Plume Library, old Inns, Moot Hall, Beeleigh Abbey.
i The Hythe. (0621) 856503

Please tell the manager if you chose your hotel through an advertisement in the guide.

M

★★ Blue Boar, Silver St, CM9 7QE ☎(0621) 852681

Old coaching inn in town centre, modernised yet retains much originality. (THF)

Swan, 73 High St, CM9 7EP ☎(0621) 853170. *Private Hotel.* De
£ B&B £24; HB weekly £200; [5% V]

MALMESBURY Wiltshire. Map 20B1

Pop 2,593. Swindon 15, London 92, M4 (jn 17) 5½, Bath 24, Bristol 26, Chippenham 9, Cirencester 11, Tetbury 4½.
EC Thur. **Golf** Minchinhampton 18h. **See** Abbey, Market Cross, St John's Almshouses, Old Bell Museum; Athelston Museum (local history).
ⓘ Town Hall, Cross Hayes. ☎(0666) 823748

★★★ Old Bell, Abbey Row, SN16 0BW ☎(0666) 822344 Fax: (0666) 825145

A 3-storey stone building of 12th century origins. Pleasant walled gardens.
37 bedrs, 37 en suite; TV; tcf
P 40, coach; child facs; con 25
LD 9.30
£ B&B fr £65, B&B (double) fr £80; L fr £10·50, D fr £17·50; WB fr £98·50
cc Access, B'card/Visa.
(*See advertisement on p. 348*)

★★★ C R **Whatley Manor,** Easton Grey, SN16 0RB (2½ m W on B4040)
☎(0666) 822888 Tx: 840394
Fax: (0666) 826120

Imposing 18th century manor house in 12 acres of attractive gardens. Swimming pool, tennis, fishing, sauna, solarium. Fr
15 bedrs, 15 en suite; annexe 11 bedrs, 11 en suite; TV, tcf
dogs; P 60; child facs; con 40
LD 9. Resid & Rest lic
£ B&B £70–£80, B&B (double) £98–£116; L £14, D £26; WB £117 (2 nts HB)
cc Access, Amex, B'card/Visa, Diners.

MALTON North Yorkshire. Map 39A4

Pop 4,325. Beverley 26, London 205, Bridlington 28, Helmsley 16, Pickering 8, Scarborough 24, Thirsk 25, York 17.
EC Thur. **MD** Tue, Fri, Sat. **Golf** Malton and Norton 18h. **See** Relic of Gilbertine Priory, Town Hall, 17th cent Malton Lodge, St Michael's Church, Roman Museum, Old Malton Priory, Flamingoland Zoo.
ⓘ Old Town Hall, Market Pl ☎(0653) 600048

★★ Leat House, Welham Rd, Norton, YO17 9DS ☎(0653) 692027
Friendly hotel in a modernised 18th century manor house, part brick, part stone, with an attractive conservatory.

★★ Talbot, Yorkersgate, YO17 0AA
☎(0653) 694031
A fine old stone inn situated in centre of market town.

★ Wentworth Arms, Town St, Old Malton, YO17 0HD ☎(0653) 692618

Pleasant small country hotel, originally 18th century coaching inn.
6 bedrs, 2 en suite, 1 ba, TV, tcf
P 30; children over 6
LD 8.45
£ B&B £18–£20; L £6, D £8
cc Access, B'card/Visa.

Greenacres, Amotherby, YO17 0TG
☎(0653) 693623. *Guest House.*
£ B&B £20

MALVERN Hereford & Worcester (Worcestershire). Map 20B3

Pop 30,162. Tewkesbury 13, London 118, Hereford 19, Ledbury 7, Worcester 8
EC Wed. **MD** Fri. **Golf** Worcestershire 18h. **See** College, Priory Church and Gateway, St Anne's Well, Priory remains and St Wulstan's Church, Little Malvern (Priory and grave of Sir Edward Elgar), Malvern Hills (views).
ⓘ Winter Gardens, Grange Rd. ☎(0684) 892289

★★★ Abbey, Abbey Rd, WR14 3ET
☎(0684) 892332 Tx: 335008
Fax: (0684) 892662

Splendid ivy clad country hotel adjoining an old Benedictine Priory. (DeV)
107 bedrs, 107 en suite; TV; tcf
lift, dogs; P 120, coach; child facs; con 350
LD 8.30
£ B&B £62, B&B (double) £88; L £10, D £15; WB £70 (2 nts HB)
cc Access, Amex, B'card/Visa, Diners.

★★★ H R **Foley Arms,** 14 Worcester Rd, WR14 4QS ☎(0684) 573397 Tx: 437287

Former coaching inn (1810) near town centre. Family-run hotel.
28 bedrs, 28 en suite; TV; tcf
dogs, ns; P 40, coach; child facs; con 120
LD 9.30, bar meals only lunch
£ B&B £56, B&B (double) £72; L 8·50, D £13·50; WB £40; [5% V Jan, Feb, Nov, Dec]
cc Access, Amex, B'card/Visa, Diners; dep.

★★ Mount Pleasant, Belle Vue Terr, WR14 4PZ ☎(0684) 561837

Georgian building in centre of town. Overlooks the Abbey. Es. Closed 25–26 Dec.
15 bedrs, 15 en suite, 1 ba; TV; tcf
P 20, coach; children over 7; con 90
LD 9.30, bar meals only, Sun dinner
£ B&B £40–£47, B&B (double) £57·50–£63;

EC *early closing* **MD** *market day* *country house hotel* *ns (NS) no smoking areas* *tcf tea/coffee facilities*

HB weekly £225–£305; L £8·50, D £10·50; WB £32·50–£45 (2 nts), [5% V]
cc Access, Amex, B'card/Visa, Diners.

★★ Royal Malvern, Graham Rd, WR14 2HN ☎(0684) 563411 Fax: (0684) 560514

A large Victorian building right in the centre of Great Malvern. ✻ Fr. Closed Xmas.
🛏 14 bedrs, 12 en suite, 1 ba; TV; tcf
🏨 lift, dogs, ns; P 9, coach; child facs; con 12
✕ LD 9.30, bar meals only lunch, Sun dinner
£ B&B £43–£60, B&B (double) £55–£65; L £7·50, D £9·75; WB £45; [10% V]
cc Access, Amex, B'card/Visa, Diners.

★★ Thornbury House, Avenue Rd, WR14 3AR ☎(0684) 572278
Former Victorian house in quiet residential area. Convenient for trains.
🛏 15 bedrs, 7 en suite, 2 ba; TV; tcf
🏨 dogs; P 10, coach; child facs; con 20

Sidney House (Acclaimed), Worcester Rd, WR14 4AA ☎(0684) 574994. *Private Hotel.*
£ B&B £17–£35; [5% V]

COLWALL
★★★ Colwall Park, WR13 6QG ☎Colwall (0684) 40206 Fax: (0684) 40847

An Edwardian hotel, with well-appointed bedrooms.
🛏 20 bedrs, 20 en suite; TV; tcf
🏨 dogs; P 30, coach; child facs; con 100
✕ LD 9
£ B&B £46·50–£52·50, B&B (double) £65–£75; HB weekly £265–£297·50 L £8·50, D £16·50; WB £42·50 (HB); [10% V]
cc Access, Amex, B'card/Visa; dep.

Hotel locations
Hotel locations are shown on the maps at the back of the guide. All towns and villages containing an RAC Appointed or Listed hotel are ringed in purple.

MALVERN WELLS
♔ ★★★ Cottage in the Wood, Holywell Rd, WR14 4LG ☎(0684) 573487 Tx: 339342 Fax: (0684) 560662

Charming, white-painted hotel in a dramatic wooded setting high on the Malvern hills. Breathtaking views across the Severn Valley and Cotswolds.
🛏 8 bedrs, 8 en suite; annexe 12 bedrs, 12 en suite; TV; tcf
🏨 dogs; P 40; child facs; con 14
✕ LD 8.30, Resid & Rest lic
£ B&B £60, B&B (double) £78–£115; HB weekly £241·50–£367·50; L £11·50; WB £69 (2 nts HB); [10% V Sun/Mon]
cc Access, B'card/Visa.

★★ Essington, Holywell Rd, WR14 4LQ ☎Malvern (0684) 561177
Family-run Victorian hotel in 2 acres of terraced garden.
🛏 9 bedrs, 9 en suite; TV; tcf
🏨 dogs, ns; P 30; child facs

Mellbreak, 177 Wells Rd, WR14 4HE ☎(068 45) 61287. *Guest House.* ✻ Fr
£B&B £14

WELLAND
♔ ★★ Holdfast Cottage, WR13 6NA ☎Hanley Swan (0684) 310288
Small 17th century country house in 2 acres of beautiful gardens. ✻ Fr
🛏 8 bedrs, 8 en suite; 1 ba; TV; tcf
🏨 dogs ns; P16; child facs; con 8
✕ LD 9, nr lunch. Resid & Rest lic
£ B&B £36–£54; B&B (double) £68–£76; D £19·50; WB £80 (2 nts); [5% V]
cc Access, B'card/Visa; dep.

WEST MALVERN
★★ Broomhill, WR14 4AY (2 m W B4232). ☎Malvern (0684) 564637

Family-run, modernised Victorian hotel, high in hills with panoramic views.
🛏 9 bedrs, 5 en suite; 4 ba; tcf
🏨 TV, dogs, P 9
✕ LD 8.30. Resid lic
£B&B £20–£22·50; HB weekly £180–£195; WB £52·50 (HB, Sept–May); [5% V]; dep.

Please tell the manager if you chose your hotel through an advertisement in the guide.

WYNDS POINT
★★ Malvern Hills, WR13 6DW. ☎Colwall (0684) 40237 Fax: (0684) 40327

Attractive country hotel with panoramic views; close to British Camp.
🛏 16 bedrs, 16 en suite, TV; tcf
🏨 dogs, P 40, coach; child facs; con 60
✕ LD 9.15, bar meals only Mon–Sat lunch
£ B&B £40 B&B (double) £55; L £4, D £11·60; WB £85
cc Access, B'card/Visa; dep.

MANCHESTER

Gtr Manchester. Map 33B2
See also ALTRINCHAM, ASHTON-UNDER-LYNE, SALFORD and STOCKPORT.
Pop 458,600. Stockport 6, London 184, M602 6, Altrincham 8, Bolton 11, Bury 8, Oldham 7, Rochdale 10, Walkden 7, Warrington 16.
See Plan, pp. 350–51.
P See Plan. **Golf** Bramhall 18h, Ringway 18h, Heaton Park Municipal 18h, Northenden 18h etc. **See** Cathedral, John Ryland's Library, City Art Gallery, Museum, Heaton Hall, Platt Hall Gallery of English Costume, Museum of Science and Technology.
ℹ Town Hall, Lloyd St. ☎061-234 3157

★★★★ Britannia, Portland St, M1 3LA ☎061-228 2288 Tx: 665007 Fax: 061-236 9154
A grand Victorian building in city centre, originally a famous cotton warehouse, lavishly restored. Indoor swimming pool, sauna, solarium, gymnasium.
🛏 360 bedrs, 360 en suite; TV; tcf
🏨 lift, TV, dogs; coach; child facs; con 280

★★★★ Copthorne, Clippers Quay, Salford Quays, Salford, M5 3DL ☎061-873 7321 Tx: 669090 Fax: 061-873 7318 ♿

Modern red-brick building in traditional style set beside a yacht marina on the Manchester Ship Canal. Indoor swimming pool, sauna, solarium, gymnasium.
🛏 166 bedrs, 166 en suite; TV; tcf
🏨 lift, dogs, ns; P 120, coach; child facs; con 150
✕ LD 10

Changes made after July 1990 are not included.

M

Maidstone (Kent)

The Grangemoor Hotel

RAC ★★

St Michaels Road, (off A26 Tonbridge Road), Maidstone, Kent

47 bedrooms, most en-suite. A la Carte. Bar meals. Weddings. Parties. Business meetings. Reduced weekend B&B. Open to non-residents. Ample parking.

Telephone: Maidstone 677623

Malmesbury (Wiltshire)

THE OLD BELL HOTEL
★★★

Wisteria clad hotel dating from 1210, possibly the oldest in the country, adjacent to Malmesbury Abbey. Old English comfort and hospitality with every modern amenity. 5 miles from Junction 17 on the M4 on the edge of the Cotswolds. All rooms recently refurbished. Weekend Breaks and Christmas programme. Egon Ronay & Michelin recommended.

Clipper Hotels

Enjoy standards you had forgotten existed

Abbey Row, Malmesbury, Wiltshire SN16 0BW. Telephone: 0666 822344. Fax No: 0666 825145.

Manchester (Greater Manchester)

RAC ★★
Les Routiers
ETB
commended
CRESCENT
GATE HOTEL

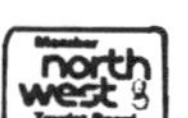

Park Crescent, Victoria Park, Rusholme, Manchester M14 5RE
Tel: 061 224 0672 Fax: 061 257 2822

A 26 bedroom hotel ideally situated in a tree-lined crescent only 2 miles from the city centre. Most rooms with en-suite bathrooms, and all have colour TV, direct dial telephones, tea makers. Private car park.

ONE OF MANCHESTER'S MOST POPULAR INDEPENDENT HOTELS.

Please write or telephone for further details and brochure.

Manchester (Greater Manchester)

ROYALS HOTEL

Close to Manchester Airport

Situated at the heart of Manchester's motorway network, Royals is minutes from both Manchester International Airport and the thriving city centre. Privately owned, of mock-Tudor design and set in its own grounds, this 34 bedroomed licensed hotel boasts all the creature comforts you could wish for. En-suite bathrooms, colour TV, direct-dial telephone and tea/coffee making facilities. There is an excellent restaurant, welcoming bars and ample car parking.

ROYALS HOTEL

Altrincham Road (J2, M56), Manchester M22 4BJ
Telephone: 061-998 9011

★★★★ Holiday Inn Crowne Plaza Midland, Peter St, M60 2DS ☎ 061-236 3333 Tx: 667550 Fax: 061-228 2241 ♿

A splendid Edwardian building, restored and refurbished to luxury standards. Next to GMex Exhibition Centre. Indoor swimming pool, squash, sauna, solarium, gymnasium. (HI)
🛏 303 bedrs, 303 en suite, TV
🏨 lift, dogs, ns; coach; child facs; con 500
✕ LD 10.30
£ B&B £105·95–£111·95 (w/e £60), B&B (double) £122·95–£129·95; L £14·95, D £14·95
cc Access, Amex, B'card/Visa, Diners.

★★★★ Hotel Piccadilly, PO Box 107, Picadilly, M60 1QR ☎ 061-236 8414 Tx: 668765 Fax: 061-228 1568 ♿

Large modern luxury hotel with many facilities; in city centre. Indoor swimming pool, sauna, solarium, gymnasium. ✈ Fr, It, Po. (Emb)
🛏 271 bedrs, 271 en suite; TV; tcf
🏨 lift, dogs, ns; P 80, coach; child facs; con 900
✕ LD 10.30
£ room £95–£100 (w/e £42·50), room (double) £115–£120, Bk £6, L £12, D £18·50; WB £34·60
cc Access, Amex, B'card/Visa, CB, Diners; dep.

★★★★ Portland Thistle, Portland St, M1 6DP ☎ 061-228 3400 Tx: 669157 Fax: 061-228 6347

Modern luxury hotel with Victorian façade and elegant decor. Indoor swimming pool, sauna, solarium, gymnasium. (ThH)
🛏 205 bedrs, 205 en suite; TV; tcf
🏨 lift, dogs, ns; coach; child facs; con 300
✕ LD 10.30
£ room £79, room (double) £95; Bk £8·50, L £11·95, D £13·95; WB
cc Access, Amex, B'card/Visa, CB, Diners.

★★★★ Sachas, Tie St, Piccadilly, M4 1PQ ☎ 061-228 1234 Tx: 6685504 Fax: 061-236 9202
Converted from a department store, a stylish hotel in the heart of the city, close to the Exhibition Centre and shopping area. Swimming pool, sauna, solarium, gymnasium. ✈ Fr, It
🛏 223 bedrs, 223 en suite; TV; tcf
🏨 lift, TV, dogs; coach; child facs; con 700
✕ LD 11
£ B&B £32·75–£97·75 (w/e £17·50), B&B (double) £50–£115; HB weekly £300–£500; L £4·95, D £11·50–£18·50; WB £29·50; [10% V]
cc Access, Amex, B'card/Visa, Diners.

★★★ Britannia Ringway, Palatine Rd, Didsbury, M20 8UF ☎ 061-434 3411
A bustling hotel with two bedroom wings leading off the central public areas.

★★★ Gardens, 55 Piccadilly, M1 2AP ☎ 061-236 5155 Fax: 061-228 7287
In the heart of the city, overlooking Piccadilly Gardens, an ultra-modern hotel inside a tall old building
🛏 85 bedrs, 85 en suite; TV; tcf
£ B&B £63·50–£76·50, B&B (double) £80–£93; L £8, D £10·50

★★★ Novotel, Worsley Brow, M28 4YA ☎ 061-799 3535 Tx: 669586 ♿
Modern hotel set in own grounds, ½ mile from M62. Swimming pool.

★★★ Post House, Palatine Rd, Northenden, M22 4FH ☎ 061-998 7090 Tx: 669248 Fax: 061-946 0139

Modern purpose-built hotel with well-equipped bedrooms. Easy access to motorways. (THF)
🛏 200 bedrs, 200 en suite; TV; tcf
🏨 lift, dogs, ns; P 200, coach; child facs; con 150
✕ LD 10.30, coffee shop only Sat
£ room £68–£79 (w/e £39·50), room (double) £79–£90; Bk £7·50, L £10·50, D £13·50; WB £38
cc Access, Amex, B'card/Visa, Diners.

★★★ Willow Bank, 340 Wilmslow Rd, Fallowfield, M14 6AF ☎ 061-224 0461 Tx: 668222 Fax: 061-257 2561

A former Edwardian private house with modern extensions. ✈ Es, Po, De
🛏 122 bedrs, 122 en suite; TV; tcf
🏨 TV, ns; P 75, G 35, coach; child facs; con 50
✕ LD 10.15, nr Sat & Sun lunch. Resid & Rest lic
£ B&B £53–£56 (w/e £15), B&B (double) £70–£75; HB weekly £225; L £6·50, D £9; [10% V]
cc Access, Amex, B'card/Visa, Diners.

★★ Cornish House, 122 Withington Rd, M16 8FB ☎ 061-226 2235 Tx: 362 74 Fax: 061-226 0141
Gabled, cream-painted building recently refurbished, on main road a mile south of city centre. Close to M63. ✈ Ar, Fr
🛏 34 bedrs, 34 en suite; 1 ba; TV; tcf
🏨 TV, dogs; P70, U3; coach, child facs; con
✕ LD 9.30. Resid & Rest lic
£ B&B £44 (w/e £25); B&B (double) £60 (w/e £35); L £5, D £7·50; [10% V]
cc Access, Amex, B'card/Visa, Diners.

★★ Crescent Gate, Park Crescent, Victoria Park, M14 5RE ☎ 061-224 0672 Fax: 061-257 2822

Family-run hotel in Victorian house set in quiet, residential park, not far from the city centre. Closed Xmas.
🛏 15 bedrs, 5 en suite, 2 ba; annexe 11 bedrs, 11 en suite; TV; tcf
🏨 TV, dogs, ns; P 18, coach; child facs
✕ LD 8, bar meals only lunch. Resid & Rest lic
£ B&B £25–£30, B&B (double) £45; L £2, D £8; [10% V]
cc Access, Amex, B'card/Visa, Diners.
(*See advertisement on p. 348*)

★★ Royals, Altrincham Rd, M22 4BJ ☎ 061-998 9011 Fax: 061-998 4641
Privately owned mock-Tudor hotel on outskirts adjacent to junction 2 of M56. Courtesy transport to airport. Billiards.
🛏 34 bedrs, 34 en suite; TV; tcf
🏨 P 100, coach; child facs; con 100
✕ LD 9.45
£ B&B £41·40 (w/e £20), B&B (double) £59·80; L £7, D £9·45; [10% V]
cc Access, Amex, B'card/Visa, Diners.
(*See advertisement on p. 348*)

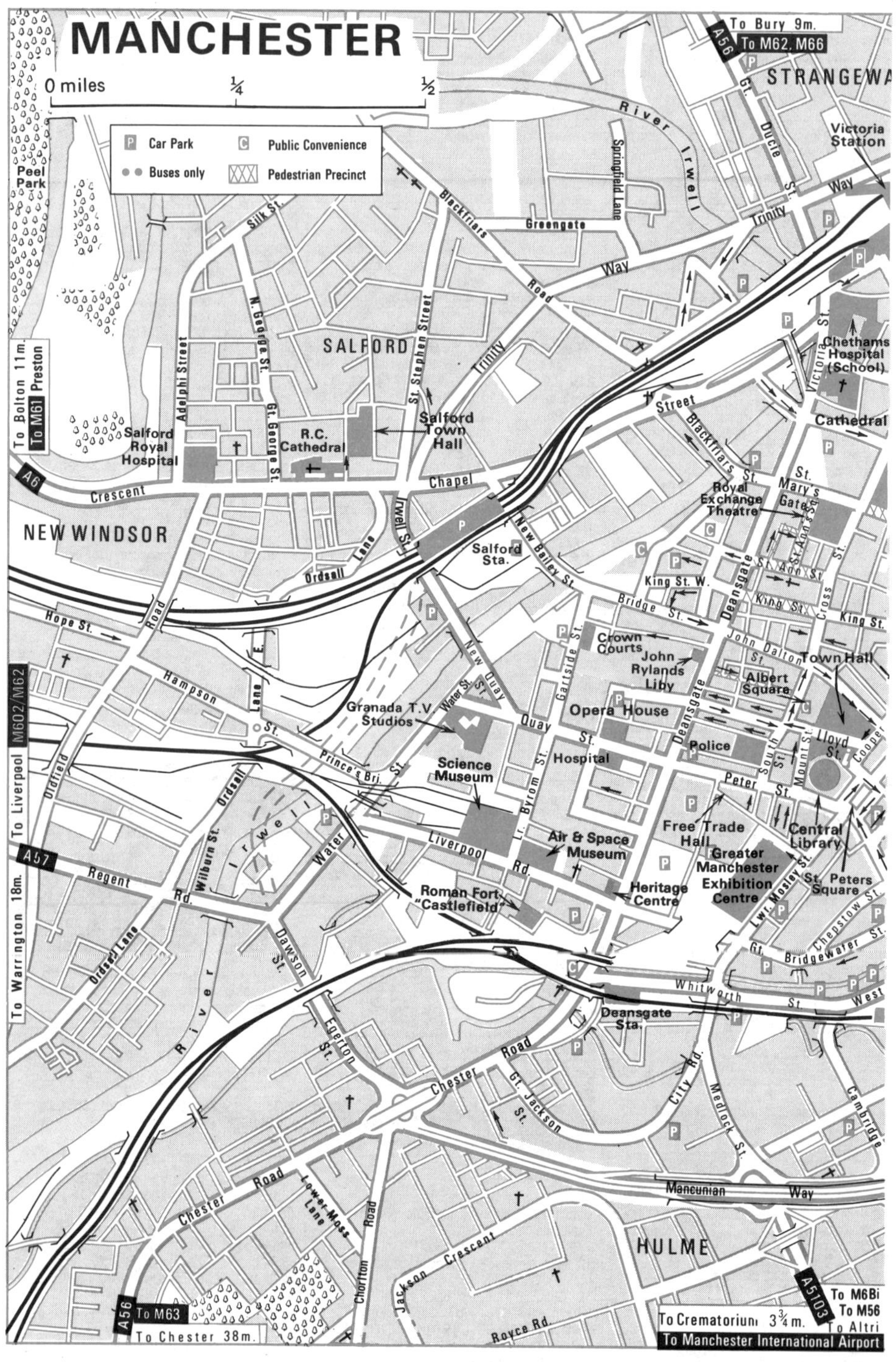
MANCHESTER
0 miles
¼
½
Car Park
Public Convenience
Buses only
Pedestrian Precinct
To Bury 9m.
A56
To M62, M66
STRANGEWA
Victoria Station
River Irwell
Springfield Lane
Gt. Ducie St.
Way
Trinity
Peel Park
Silk St.
Blackfriars
Greengate
Way
Road
SALFORD
N. George St.
St. Stephen Street
Trinity
Chethams Hospital (School)
Victoria St.
Cathedral
To Bolton 11m.
To M61 Preston
Adelphi Street
Gt. George St.
Salford Royal Hospital
R.C. Cathedral
Salford Town Hall
Street
Blackfriars St.
A6
Crescent
Chapel
St. Mary's Gate
Royal Exchange Theatre
NEW WINDSOR
Irwell St.
Salford Sta.
New Bailey St.
St. Ann's Sq.
St. Ann St.
Cross St.
Ordsall Lane
King St. W.
Deansgate
Bridge St.
King St.
King St.
Hope St.
Road
Crown Courts
John Rylands Liby
John Dalton St.
Town Hall
Gartside St.
New Quay St.
Albert Square
M602/M62
Hampson
Lane
Water St.
Granada T.V Studios
Quay St.
Opera House
Deansgate
St.
Prince's Bri. St.
Police
Lloyd St.
Cooper
Science Museum
Hospital
South St.
Mount St.
To Liverpool
Oldfield
Ordsall
Byrom St.
Peter St.
Irwell
Free Trade Hall
Central Library
Wilburn St.
Water
Liverpool
Air & Space Museum
A57
Regent
Lr. Rd.
Greater Manchester Exhibition Centre
St. Peters Square
Lwr. Mosley St.
Rd.
Roman Fort "Castlefield"
Heritage Centre
Chepstow St.
To Warrington 18m.
Ordsall Lane
Dawson St.
Gt. Bridgewater St.
River
Whitworth St.
West
Deansgate Sta.
Egerton St.
Road
City Rd.
Chester
Gt. Jackson St.
Medlock St.
Cambridge
Road
Chester
Lower Moss Lane
Road
Mancunian Way
HULME
Chorlton
Crescent
Jackson
A5103
A56
To M63
To Chester 38m.
Royce Rd.
To Crematorium 3¾m.
To M6Bi
To M56
To Altri
To Manchester International Airport

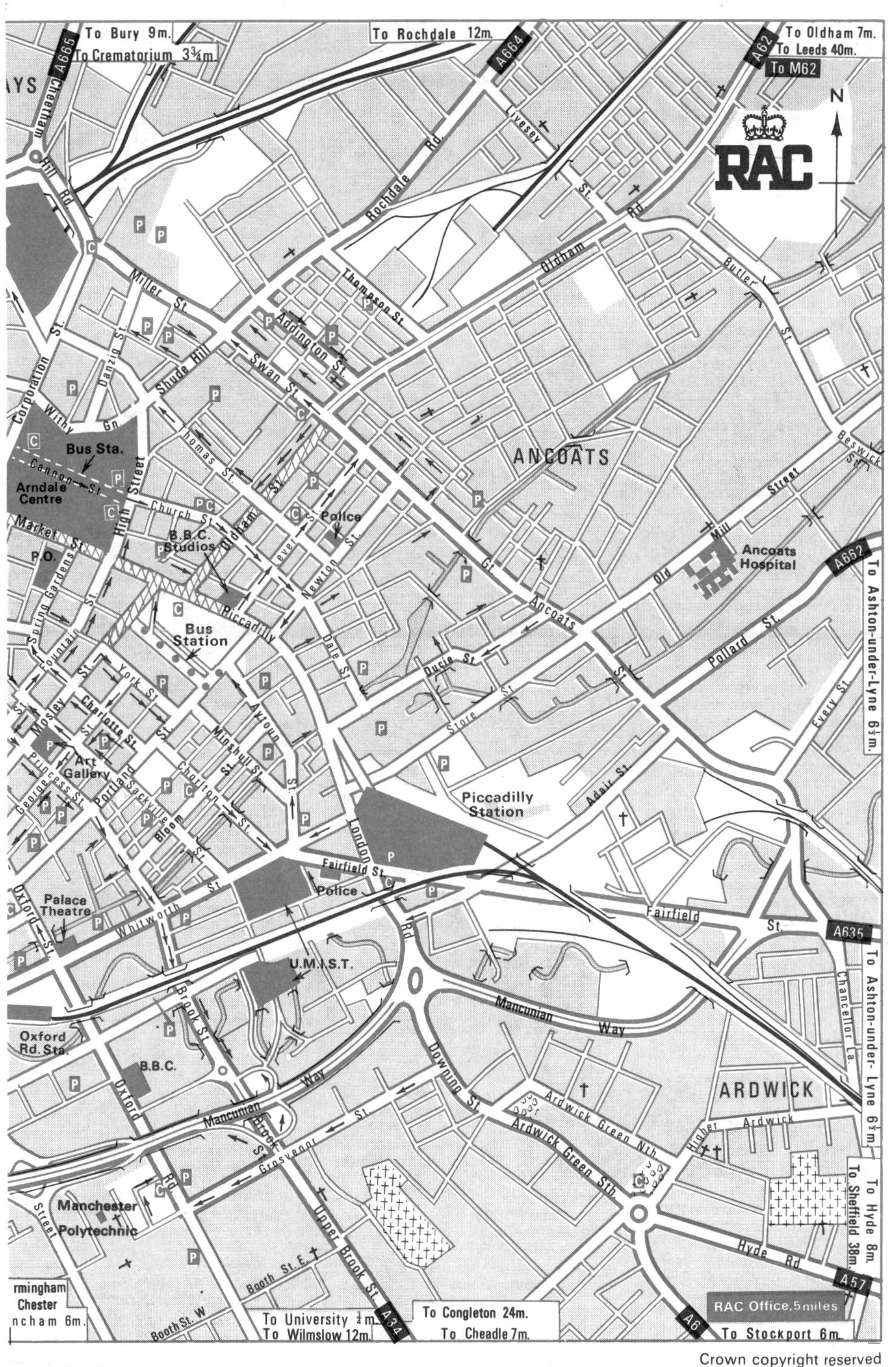
To Bury 9m.
To Crematorium 3¾m.
To Rochdale 12m.
A665
A664
A62
To Oldham 7m.
To Leeds 40m.
To M62
N
RAC
Cheetham Hill Rd.
Rochdale Rd.
Livesey St.
Oldham Rd.
Butler St.
Miller St.
Thompson St.
Addington St.
Shude Hill
Swan St.
Corporation St.
Danzig St.
Withy Gn
Bus Sta.
Cannon St.
Arndale Centre
High Street
Market St.
Thomas St.
Church St.
B.B.C. Studios
Oldham St.
Police
Newton St.
ANCOATS
Beswick St.
Mill Street
Old Mill Street
Ancoats Hospital
A662
To Ashton-under-Lyne 6½m.
P.O.
Spring Gardens
Fountain St.
Piccadilly
Bus Station
Gt. Ancoats St.
Ducie St.
Dale St.
Pollard St.
Every St.
Store St.
Mosley St.
York St.
Charlotte St.
Aytoun St.
Minshull St.
Art Gallery
Portland St.
Sackville St.
Chorlton St.
Princess St.
George St.
Bloom St.
London Rd.
Piccadilly Station
Adair St.
Fairfield St.
Police
Oxford St.
Palace Theatre
Whitworth St.
U.M.I.S.T.
Fairfield St.
A635
To Ashton-under-Lyne 6¾m.
Chancellor La.
Oxford Rd. Sta.
Brook St.
Mancunian Way
B.B.C.
Oxford Rd.
Downing St.
ARDWICK
Ardwick Green Nth
Ardwick Green Sth
Higher Ardwick
Grosvenor St.
Manchester Polytechnic
Street
Upper Brook St.
Booth St. E.
Booth St. W
Hyde Rd
To Hyde 8m.
To Sheffield 38m.
A57
rmingham
Chester
ncham 6m.
To University ¼m.
To Wilmslow 12m.
A34
To Congleton 24m.
To Cheadle 7m.
A6
RAC Office, 5 miles
To Stockport 6m.
M

★ **Baron,** 116 Palatine Rd, West Didsbury, M20 9ZA ☎061-434 3688

A converted Victorian yellow-brick house, between Manchester city centre and airport.
🛏 16 bedrs, 16 en suite; TV; tcf
🏨 TV, ns; P 25, coach; child facs; con 30
✕ LD 4, nr lunch, Fri–Sun dinner. Unlic
£ B&B £20–£27 (w/e £15), B&B (double) £30–£39; D £7·50; WB £30 (2nts); [5% V w/e]
cc Access, B'card/Visa, Diners; dep.

Grand, Aytoun St, M1 3DR ☎061-236 9559 Tx: 667580
Hotel closed for refurbishment. Open June 1991. (THF)

Horizon (Acclaimed), 69 Palatine Rd, West Didsbury, M20 9LJ ☎061-445 4705. *Hotel.*
£ B&B £23 (w/e £20); [5% V]

Ebor, 402 Wilbraham Rd, Chorlton-cum-Hardy, M21 1UA ☎061-881 1911. *Hotel.* Closed 24 Dec–1 Jan.
£ B&B £20–£26, HB weekly £164·50–£201·50; [10% V w/e], D £7·50; WB; dep.
Imperial, 157 Hathersage Rd, M13 0HY ☎061-225 6500. *Private Hotel.* ♿
£ B&B £24–£30, WB
New Central, 144 Heywood St, M8 7PD ☎061-205 2169. *Hotel.*
£ B&B £19·50; [5% V]

MANCHESTER AIRPORT

Gtr Manchester (Lancashire). Map 33B1
See also WILMSLOW.
Congleton 16, London 177, M56 (jn 5) ½, Altrincham 5, Macclesfield 12, Manchester 9½, Stockport 6½.
ℹ 061-436 3344

★★★★ **Excelsior,** Ringway Rd, Wythenshawe, M22 5NS ☎061-437 5811 Tx: 668721 Fax: 061-436 2340

Large modern purpose-built hotel with spacious bedrooms. Indoor swimming pool, sauna, solarium, gymnasium. (THF)
🛏 300 bedrs, 300 en suite; TV; tcf
🏨 lift, dogs, ns; P, coach; child facs; con 220
✕ LD 10.15, coffee shop only Sat lunch.
£ B&B £101, B&B (double) £123; L £14·95, D £16·95; WB £46
cc Access, Amex, B'card/Visa, CB, Diners.

★★★★ **Hilton International,** Outwood La, Ringway, M22 5WP ☎061-436 4404 Tx: 668361 Fax: 061-436 1521 ♿

A large 5-storey modern red-brick hotel five minutes walk from the airport. Indoor swimming pool, sauna. ⚒ Fr. (H. Int)
🛏 223 bedrs, 223 en suite; TV; tcf
🏨 lift, dogs, ns; P 200, coach; child facs; con 160
✕ LD 11
£ room £95–£150 (w/e £65), room (double) £115–£150; Bk £7·50, L £14, D £16·50; WB £42
cc Access, Amex, B'card/Visa, CB, Diners.

MANSFIELD

Nottinghamshire. Map 24A3
Pop 100,000. Nottingham 14, London 138, M1 (jn 28) 6½, Chesterfield 12, Derby 23, Matlock 18, Newark 18, Sheffield 22.
EC Wed. **MD** Mon, Thur, Fri, Sat. **Golf** Mansfield 18h. **See** Parish Church of SS Peter and Paul, Moot Hall, Bentinck Memorial, Clumber Park, Newstead Abbey 4½ m S, Sherwood Forest and "Major Oak".

★★ **Midland,** Midland Pl, NG18 1DP ☎(0623) 24668
Situated on fringe of central area, a completely refurbished hotel.

★★ **Pine Lodge,** 281 Nottingham Rd, NG18 4SE ☎(0623) 22308 Fax: (0623) 656819

Two, stone-faced Victorian houses with a modern extension to the rear. Close to junction 27 of the M1. Sauna.
🛏 21 bedrs, 16 en suite, (5 sh), TV; tcf
🏨 P 50, coach; child facs; con 50
✕ LD 9.30, nr lunch. Resid lic
£ B&B £32·50–£46 (w/e £32·50), B&B (double) £48–£56; HB weekly £244·65–£398·65; D £10·95, WB £38; [5% V w/d]
cc Access, Amex, B'card/Visa; dep.

Atlas Section
Consult the Atlas section at the back of the guide to find out which towns and villages have RAC Appointed and Listed hotels in them. They are shown on the maps by purple circles.

Fringe, Briar La, NE18 3HS ☎(0623) 641337

Hotel under refurbishment. Completion expected Autumn 1989. (GMR)

MARAZION

Cornwall. Map 2A1
Pop 1,385. Helston 9, London 280, Penzance 4, Redruth 15, St Ives 8.
EC Wed. **Golf** Praa Sands 18h & Lelant 18h. **See** St Michaels Mount, Castle, Age of Steam (steam engines).

★★ **Mount Haven,** Turnpike Rd, TR17 0DQ ☎Penzance (0736) 710249

200 year-old coaching house with modern extension. Enjoys fine sea views. ⚒ Fr, De
🛏 17 bedrs, 17 en suite; TV; tcf
🏨 dogs, ns; P 40, child facs; con 20
✕ LD 9
£ B&B £21–£35; B&B (double) £42–£52; HB weekly £196–£280; L £7·95, D £13
cc Access, Amex, B'card/Visa.

Chymorvah-Tolgarrick (Acclaimed), TR17 0DQ ☎Penzance (0736) 710497. *Hotel.* ♿
£ B&B £15–£18; HB (weekly) £145–£212; [5% V Oct–Easter]

MARCH

Cambridgeshire. Map 26C4
Pop 14,630. Cambridge 30, London 85, Ely 18, Huntingdon 23, Peterborough 16, Wisbech 11.
EC Tue. **MD** Wed, Sat. **Golf** March 9h.

Olde Griffin, High St, PE15 9EJ ☎(0354) 52517. *Hotel.*

MARGARETTING

Essex. Map 17A3
Pop 933. Brentwood 7, London 29, Bishop's Stortford 20, Chelmsford 3½.
Golf Chelmsford 18h. **See** 15th cent Church.

En suite rooms
En suite rooms may be bath or shower rooms. If you have a preference, remember to state it when booking a room.

★★★ **Ivy Hill,** Ivy Barn La, CM4 0EW
☎ Ingatestone (0277) 353040
Fax: (0277) 355038

A restored and extended Victorian mansion standing in about 4 acres of parklike grounds. Swimming pool, tennis. Fr, Es, De
18 bedrs, 18 en suite; TV; tcf
TV; P 60, coach; child facs; con 10
LD 9.30, bar meals only Sun lunch
£ B&B £70·95 (w/e £44), B&B (double) £81·95 (w/e £55); D £12·50–£15·50; [10% V w/d]
cc Access, Amex, B'card/Visa, Diners; dep.

MARGATE Kent. Map 7C3
See also CLIFTONVILLE and WESTGATE-ON-SEA.
Pop 50,347. Rochester 42, London 69, Canterbury 15, Dover 20.
EC Thur. **Golf** North Foreland, Broadstairs 18h, Westgate and Birchington 18h. **See** The Grotto (shell mosaics), Powell-Cotton Big Game Museum (Birchington), St John's Church, Caves, Tudor Cottage (Hosking Memorial Museum) in King St.
[i] Marine Ter. ☎ Thanet (0843) 220241

Cliftonville, Eastern Esplanade CT9 2LE
☎ (0843) 221444
Hotel awaiting inspection.

Beachcomber, 3 Royal Esplanade, Westbrook, CT9 5DL ☎ Thanet (0843) 221616. *Private Hotel.* Es
£ B&B £13·50–£16·50; HB weekly £125–£140

Charnwood, 20 Canterbury Rd, Westbrook, CT9 5BW. ☎ Thanet (0843) 224158. *Private Hotel.*
£ B&B £15–£18; HB weekly £110–£120; [5% V]

MARKET DRAYTON Shropshire. Map 30A2
Pop 8,937. Newport 11, London 153, Nantwich 14, Newcastle-under-Lyme 13, Shrewsbury 19, Whitchurch 13.
EC Thur. **MD** Wed. **Golf** Sutton 11h. **See** Parish Church (Norman west door), Grammar School (assoc Robert Clive).

★★★ **Goldstone Hall**, Goldstone, TF9 2NA ☎ (063 086) 202

Early Victorian house incorporating building from previous centuries. Five acres of mature gardens. Fishing, billiards.
8 bedrs, 8 en suite; TV; tcf
dogs; P 40, coach; child facs; con 80
LD 10.30. Resid & Rest lic
£ B&B £54·50, B&B (double) £66·50–£76·50; L £13·25, D £20; WB £107·50 (2 nts)

★★ **Corbet Arms,** High St, TF9 1PY
☎ (0630) 2037 Fax: (0630) 2961

Ivy-clad former coaching inn situated in the town centre.
12 bedrs, 10 en suite, 1 ba; TV; tcf
dogs, ns; P 60, coach; child facs; con 180
LD 9.30
£ B&B £38, B&B (double) £55, L £7·25, D £9·50; WB £32·50
cc Access, Amex, B'card/Visa, Diners.

MARKET HARBOROUGH
Leicestershire. Map 21B4.
See also MARSTON TRUSSEL
Pop 15,965. Northampton 17, London 82, Coventry 28, Kettering 11, Leicester 15, Melton Mowbray 22.
EC Wed. **MD** Tue, Sat. **Golf** Market Harborough 9h.
[i] Library, Adam and Eve St.
☎ (0858) 62649

★★★ **Three Swans,** High St, LE16 7NJ
☎ (0858) 466644 Tx: 342375
Fax: (0858) 33101

16th century hotel in town centre, recently enlarged and refurbished. Fr, De, Es
21 bedrs, 21 en suite; annexe 16 bedrs, 16 en suite; TV; tcf
ns; P 40, G 8, coach; child facs; con 75
LD 10
£ B&B £67–£71 (w/e £40), B&B (double) £77–£81; L £10·95, D £16·75; WB £39 (HB)
cc Amex, B'card/Visa, Diners.

MARKET RASEN Lincolnshire. Map 34A4
Pop 2,786. Lincoln 16, London 149, Gainsborough 19, Grimsby 20, Horncastle 18, Hull 25, Louth 14, Scunthorpe 22.
EC Thur. **MD** Tue, Wed. **Golf** Market Rasen 18h. **See** St Thomas's Church, Racecourse.

★★★ **Limes,** Gainsborough Rd, LN8 3JW ☎ (0673) 842357

Victorian building with modern extension for bedrooms; pleasant gardens. Squash.

MARKYATE Hertfordshire. Map 14B2
Pop 2,591. London 30, M1 (jn 9) 2, Dunstable 4, Luton 4, St Albans 8.
EC Wed. **Golf** Redbourn 18h.

★★★ **Hertfordshire Moat House,** London Rd, AL3 8HH ☎ (0582) 840840 Tx: 83343
Fax: (0582) 842282

A modern purpose-built hotel set in its own grounds 1 mile from junction 9 of M1. Courtesy service to Luton airport. (QMH)
95 bedrs, 95 en suite; TV; tcf
dogs; P 300, coach; child facs; con 250
LD 10, bar meals only Sat lunch
£ B&B £50–£85, B&B (double) £60–£95; L £14, D £14; WB £90 (2 nts HB); [10% V]
cc Access, Amex, B'card/Visa, Diners; dep.

MARLBOROUGH Wiltshire. Map 5B4
Pop 7,000. Newbury 19, London 72, M4 (jn 15) 8, Andover 21, Chippenham 18, Devizes 14, Faringdon 21, Swindon 11.
EC Wed. **MD** Wed, Sat. **Golf** Marlborough.
[i] High St. ☎ (0672) 53989

★★★ **Castle and Ball,** High St, SN8 1LZ
☎ (0672) 515201 Fax: (0672) 515895

17th century hotel of considerable character; carefully modernised. (THF)
36 bedrs, 36 en suite; TV; tcf
dogs; P 50, coach; child facs; con 30
LD 9
£ B&B £83–£89, B&B (double) £99–£110; HB weekly £266–£301; L £11, D £15; WB £40
cc Access, Amex, B'card/Visa, Diners.

M

★★★ **H** **C** **R** **Ivy House,** SN8 1HJ
☎(0672) 515333 Fax: (0672) 515338

Three-storey Georgian former coaching inn, with attractive walled garden.
🛏 14 bedrs, 14 en suite; annexe 16 bedrs, 16 en suite; TV; tcf
🏠 dogs, ns; P 30; no children under 8; con 100

Merlin, 36–39 High St, SN8 1LW ☎(0672) 512151. *Hotel.*
£ B&B £30–£35; [5% V]

MARLEY HILL Tyne & Wear. Map 37B3

Consett 14, London 263, Chester-le-Street 10, Durham 16, Newcastle-upon-Tyne 6.
See Beamish Museum.

★★★ **Beamish Park,** Beamish Burn Rd, NE16 5EU ☎(0207) 230666
Fax: (0207) 281260
Modern hotel with motel-style bedrooms round a courtyard. In rural area.
🛏 47 bedrs, 47 en suite; TV; tcf
🏠 TV, dogs; P 80, coach; child facs; con 80
✕ LD 10, nr Mon–Sat lunch, Sun dinner.
£ B&B £44–£54 (w/e £24·50) B&B (double) £59–£69; HB weekly £418·50–£624; L fr £7, D £12·50; WB £34·50 (HB); [5% V]
cc Access, Amex, B'card/Visa, Diners; dep.

MARLOW Bucks. Map 12C3

Pop 14,590. Slough 11, London 31, M40 (jn 4) 3, Henley-on-Thames 7½, High Wycombe 4½, Oxford 27, Reading 13.
EC Wed. **Golf** Temple 18h. **See** RC Church by Pugin, Marlow Pl, Bisham Abbey.
ℹ Court Garden, Pound La, ☎(062 84) 3597

★★★★ **Compleat Angler,** Marlow Bridge, SL7 1RG ☎(0628) 484444 Tx: 848644
Fax: (0628) 486388

Imposing Georgian hotel with delightful verandah. Lawns and gardens beside Thames. Tennis, fishing. ⚒ It, Fr, De. (THF)
🛏 46 bedrs, 46 en suite; TV
🏠 dogs, ns; P 100, coach; child facs; con 125
✕ LD 10
£ B&B £117·50–£139·50, B&B (double) £149–£164; L £21; WB £75
cc Access, Amex, B'card/Visa, CB, Diners.

MARPLE Greater Manchester (Cheshire). Map 33C1

Buxton 16, London 175, Glossop 12, Manchester 11

★★ **West Towers,** Church La, SK6 7LB
☎061-427 7133 Tx: 614277133
Fax: 061-449 0733
Family-owned hotel converted and extended from a former private residence, in a quiet, semi-rural area.
🛏 28 bedrs, 28 en suite; TV; tcf.
🏠 dogs, ns; P 70, coach; child facs; con 100
✕ LD 10. Resid & Rest lic
£ B&B £28–£42; B&B (double) £50; HB weekly £269·50–£423·50; L 6·95, D £10·50; WB
cc Access, Amex, B'card/Visa; Diners; dep.

★ **Springfield,** Station Rd, SK6 6PA
☎061-449 0721

Attractive 19th century building with bay windows. On corner site in residential area.

MARSDEN West Yorkshire. Map 41A1

Sheffield 28, London 182, Huddersfield 7, Manchester 18.

♣♣ ★★★ **Hey Green,** Waters Rd, HD7 6NJ
☎Huddersfield (0484) 844235
Stone-built early Victorian house with modern extension in keeping. Situated in large garden on edge of moors.
🛏 10 bedrs, 10 en suite; TV; tcf
£ B&B £50–£55, B&B (double) £65

MARSTON TRUSSEL Northants. Map 21B4

Pop 140. Northampton 18, London 84, Coventry 24, Leicester 15, Market Harborough 3, Rugby 15.
Golf Market Harborough 9h. **See** Church.

★★ **Sun Inn,** LE16 9TY ☎Market Harborough (0858) 65531

Former village inn with modern extension, in quiet surroundings. Refurbished to give cheerful public rooms and pretty bedrooms.
🛏 20 bedrs, 20 en suite; TV; tcf
£ B&B £40, B&B (double) £50–£70; WB fr £30 (HB)

MARTINHOE Devon. Map 3B4

Pop 110. Lynmouth 5, London 189, Barnstaple 15, Ilfracombe 11, South Molton 19.
Golf Ilfracombe 18h. **See** 11th cent Church.

♣♣ ★ **H** **C** **Old Rectory,** Nr Barnstaple, EX31 4QT ☎Parracombe (059 83) 368 ♿

Former Georgian rectory with grounds. Dining room furnished with fine antiques. Putting. Open Mar–Nov.
🛏 9 bedrs, 9 en suite, 2 ba; TV
🏠 dogs, ns; P 14; children over 12
✕ LD 7.45, nr lunch, Sat dinner. Resid lic
£ B&B £33–£35; B&B (double) £60–£66; HB weekly £231–£239; D £12·50; dep.

MARTOCK Somerset. Map 4C2

Pop 3,723. Wincanton 18, London 126, Bridgwater 18, Crewkerne 7, Glastonbury 14, Ilminster 8½, Sherborne 10.
EC Thur. **Golf** Yeovil 18h. **See** All Saints' Church, Treasurer's House (NT), 17th cent Church House.

★ **White Hart,** East St, TA12 6JQ
☎(0935) 822005
Privately-owned stone-built former coaching inn situated in the main street.
🛏 10 bedrs, (1 sh), 3 ba; TV; tcf
🏠 TV, dogs; P 12, G 3, coach
✕ LD 9.30, nr Sun dinner
£ B&B £19·10, B&B (double) £33·60; L £4·25, D £7·50
cc Access, B'card/Visa.

MARYPORT Cumbria. Map 43B2

Pop 11,300. Cockermouth 6½, London 305, Carlisle 27, Workington 5½.
EC Wed. **MD** Fri. **Golf** Maryport 9h. **See** Christ Church, Maritime Museum.
ℹ 1 Senhouse St. ☎(0900) 813738

★★ **Ellenbank,** Birkby, CA5 6RE ☎(0900) 815233 ♿
Fine 3-storey sandstone building set in own grounds to N of town. ⚒ Fr, De
🛏 26 bedrs, 26 en suite; TV; tcf
🏠 TV, dogs; P 50, coach; child facs; con 300
✕ LD 9.15, bar meals only Mon–Sat lunch
£ B&B £28–£35, B&B (double) £45–£55; D £11·50; WB £30·50
cc Access, B'card/Visa.

★★ **Waverley,** Curzon St, CA15 6LW
☎(0900) 812115
Corner terraced building on main street. Family-managed. Billiards.
🛏 20 bedrs, 4 en suite, (6 sh), 3 ba; TV; tcf

 EC *early closing* **MD** *market day* ♣♣ *country house hotel* *ns (NS) no smoking areas* *tcf tea/coffee facilities*

TV, dogs; coach; child facs; con 50
LD 9·30
£ B&B £15, B&B (double) £27; L £5, D £8; [10% V]
cc Access, B'card/Visa.

MARY TAVY Devon. Map 3A2

Pop 731. Okehampton 12, London 204, Exeter 34, Launceston 17, Plymouth 17, Tavistock 4½. **See** Wheal Betsy (Cornish beam engine house).

★★ **Moorland Hall,** Brentor Rd, PL19 9PY (082 281) 466

Victorian stone-built country house in 4 acres of quiet grounds. Fr, De
8 bedrs, 7 en suite, 1 ba; TV; tcf
dogs, ns; P 20; child facs
LD 8, nr lunch. Resid & Rest lic
£ B&B £30, B&B (double) £46–52; HB weekly £220; D £15
cc Access, B'card/Visa; dep.

MASHAM North Yorkshire. Map 38B4

Pop 1,000. Harrogate 17, London 222, Boroughbridge 13, Darlington 26, Leyburn 9½, Northallerton 13, Thirsk 13.
EC Thur. **MD** Wed. **Golf** Masham 9h. **See** Norman Church with Saxon Cross.

Bank Villa, Nr Ripon, HG4 4DB Ripon (0765) 89605. *Guest House.* Fr, Du. Open Easter–end Oct.
£ B&B £17; HB weekly £175

MATLOCK Derbyshire. Map 24A1

See also MATLOCK BATH.
Pop 19,565. Derby 18, London 144, Ashbourne 13, Buxton 20, Chesterfield 10.
EC Thur. **MD** Tue, Fri. **Golf** Matlock 18h. **See** High Tor (673ft), Hall Leys Park, Riber Castle, Fauna Reserve, Artists Corner.

★★★ **H R Riber Hall,** DE4 5JU (0629) 582795 Fax: (0629) 580475

A luxurious Elizabethan house with antique 4-poster beds. Superb views. Tennis. De
11 bedrs, 11 en suite; 1 ba; TV; tcf
P 50; children over 10; con 34
LD 9.30. Resid & Rest lic
£ B&B £58–£75, B&B (double) £78–£120; L £12·50; WB £115 (2 nts); [5% V]
cc Access, Amex, B'card/Visa, Diners; dep.

Parkfield (Acclaimed), 115 Lime Tree Rd, DE4 3NP (0629) 57221

Jackson Tor, 76 Jackson Rd, DE4 3JQ (0629) 582348. *Hotel.* Closed 24–31 Dec
£B&B £16–£18
Packhorse, Tansley, DE4 5LF (0629) 582781. *Farm.*
£ B&B £15

MATLOCK BATH Derbyshire. Map 24A1

See also MATLOCK.
Pop 3,566. Derby 17, London 143, Ashbourne 12, Leek 27, Matlock 1.
EC Thur. **Golf** Matlock 18h. **See** Petrifying Well, Heights of Abraham (Rutland and Masson Caverns), Aquarium, Lovers' Walks, Illuminations and Venetian Fête Nights (Sept).
The Pavilion. (0629) 55082

★★★ **New Bath,** New Bath Rd, DE4 3PX (0629) 583275 Fax: (0629) 580268

Elegant Georgian white-faced spa hotel, with gardens. Swimming pool, putting, tennis, sauna, solarium, billiards. Fr, It, Po. (THF)
55 bedrs, 55 en suite; TV; tcf
dogs, ns; P 100, coach; child facs; con 250
LD 9.30
£ L £8·50, D £13·50.
cc Access, Amex, B'card/Visa, CB, Diners.

★★★ **Temple,** Temple Walk, DE4 3PG (0629) 583911 Fax: (0629) 580851
A small hotel in attractive Georgian building in own grounds. De
14 bedrs, 14 en suite; TV; tcf
TV, ns; P40, coach; child facs; con 80
LD 9.30, bar meals only Sun
£ B&B £43, B&B (double) £53–£56; L £6, D £11; dep.
cc Access, Amex, B'card/Visa, Diners.

MAWGAN PORTH Cornwall. Map 2B2

Pop 1,208 (inc St Mawgan-in-Pydar). Bodmin 18, London 251, Newquay 5, St Austell 18, Wadebridge 13.
Golf Newquay 18h, Trevose 18h.

★★ **Tredragon,** Nr Newquay, TR8 4DQ St Mawgan (0637) 860213 Fax: (0637) 860269

Modern hotel with fine sea view. Indoor swimming pool, sauna, solarium. Fr, De
27 bedrs, 27 en suite, 1 ba; TV; tcf
TV, dogs; P 35, coach; child facs; con 55
LD 7.55, nr Mon–Sat lunch & Sun dinner. Resid & Rest lic
£ B&B £29–£41, B&B (double) £50–£66; HB weekly £185·50–£265; D £10; [10% V Oct–Jun]
cc Access, B'card/Visa; dep.

Trenance Farm House, Trenance, TR8 4BY St Mawgan (0637) 860515
White Lodge, Nr Newquay, TR8 4BN St Mawgan (0637) 860512. *Hotel.*

MAWNAN SMITH Cornwall. Map 2B1

Pop 1,185. Truro 13, London 259, Falmouth 5, Helston 8, Redruth 12.
Golf Falmouth 18h.

★★★ **Budock Vean,** TR11 5LG, Falmouth (0326) 250288 Fax: (0326) 250892

Extended 18th century country house in mature gardens. Indoor swimming pool, golf, putting, tennis, fishing, billiards. Open end Feb–early Jan.
59 bedrs, 59 en suite; TV
lift, dogs; P 60; child facs; con 60
(*See advertisement on p. 250*)

MAYFIELD East Sussex. Map 7A2

Tunbridge Wells 8½, London 45, Eastbourne 20, Haywards Heath 19, Hurst Green 12.

★★ **Middle House,** High St TN20 6AB (0435) 872146
Superb listed Tudor building heavily beamed and furnished in appropriate style. Garden with fine views.

MEALSGATE Cumbria. Map 43B2

Keswick 14, London 299, Carlisle 15, Cockermouth 9, Maryport 12, Penrith 22.

★★ **C Pink House,** Nr Wigton, CA5 1JP Low Ireby (096 57) 229
Small proprietor-managed residence at side of A595 in rural setting.
6 bedrs, 6 en suite; TV; tcf
TV, dogs; P 40, coach; child facs
LD 9, bar meals only Mon lunch. Resid & Rest lic
£ B&B £30 (w/e £16), B&B (double) £42; D £7
cc Access, B'card/Visa, Diners.

MEIR Staffordshire.
See STOKE-ON-TRENT.

Residents only
Some Listed hotels only serve meals to residents. It is always wise to make a reservation for a meal in a hotel.

M

MELKSHAM Wiltshire. Map 5A3

Pop 10,000. Marlborough 20, London 93, Bath 12, Chippenham 7, Devizes 7½, Frome 14, Radstock 17, Warminster 13.
EC Wed. **MD** Sat. **Golf** Kingsdown Box 9h. **See** Parish Church, Georgian houses, Lacock Abbey 3 m N (Nat Trust).
ℹ Round House, Church St. ☎ (0225) 707424

★★ H R **Conigre Farm,** Semington Rd, SN12 6BZ ☎ (0225) 702229
Ivy clad 17th century stone farmhouse. Near town centre.
🛏 4 bedrs, 1 en suite, 1 ba; annexe 5 bedrs, 5 en suite; TV; tcf
🏨 P 20; child facs; con 40

★★ **King's Arms,** Market Pl, SN12 6EX ☎ (0225) 707272 Fax: (0225) 702085

16th century former coaching inn in town centre. Family owned. 🗣 Es, Fr
🛏 14 bedrs, 10 en suite, 2 ba; TV; tcf
🏨 dogs, ns; P 50, coach; child facs; con 50
✕ LD 9, nr Tue lunch
£ B&B £30–£40, B&B (double) £50; L £8·50, D £9·50; WB £63 (HB 2 nts); [5% V]
cc Access, Amex, B'card/Visa, Diners.

★★ **Shaw Country,** Bath Rd, Shaw, SN12 8EF ☎ (0225) 702836 Fax: (0225) 790275
Reputedly 400 years old, this vine-covered farmhouse with modern extensions has attractive gardens. Swimming pool. Closed 24–27 Dec.
🛏 10 bedrs, 10 en suite; TV; tcf
🏨 P 30; coach; child facs; con 20

Regency, (Acclaimed), 10 Spa Rd, SN12 7NS ☎ (0225) 702971. *Hotel.*
£ B&B £18–£28; HB weekly £196–£216

MELTHAM W Yorkshire. Map 41A2

Pop 7,000. Sheffield 24, London 184, Barnsley 16, Huddersfield 4½, Oldham 14.
EC Wed. **Golf** Meltham 18h.

★★★ **Durker Roods,** Nr Huddersfield, HD7 3AG ☎ Huddersfield (0484) 851413 Tx: 517429
Hotel in spacious Victorian building set in own pleasant grounds.
🛏 13 bedrs, 13 en suite; TV; tcf
🏨 dogs; P 90, coach; child facs; con 100

Complaints
If you are dissatisfied with the facilities or service offered by a hotel, please take the matter up with the Manager WHILE YOU ARE AT THE HOTEL. In this way, any problems can usually be solved promptly and amicably.
The RAC will investigate matters if a personal approach has failed to resolve the problem. Please submit details of any discussion or correspondence when reporting the problem to the RAC.

MELTON MOWBRAY Leics. Map 25B4

Pop 23,500. Kettering 29, London 104, Grantham 16, Leicester 15, Loughborough 15, Nottingham 18, Stamford 20.
EC Thur. **MD** Tue, Sat. **Golf** Melton Mowbray 9h. **See** Church (13th cent, enlarged 1550), 17th cent Bede House, Anne of Cleves House.
ℹ Carnegie Museum, Thorpe End. ☎ (0664) 69946

♣ ★★★★ **Stapleford Park,** Stapleford, LE14 2EF ☎ Wymondham (057 284) 522 Tx: 342319 Fax: (057 284) 651

An elegant hotel in a large, mainly 18th century country house set in 500 acres of park with a lake. Marvellous views. Putting, tennis, fishing, riding.
🛏 35 bedrs, 35 en suite; TV
🏨 lift, dogs, ns; P 100, coach; children over 10; con 300
✕ LD 9.45
£ B&B £105; L £19·95, D £27·50; [5% V w/d Jan–Feb]
cc Access, Amex, B'card/Visa, Diners; dep.

★★ **Sysonby Knoll,** Asfordby Rd, LE13 0HP ☎ (0664) 63563 Fax: (0664) 410364 ♿
Large early 20th century red-brick house with modern bedroom wing. Swimming pool. Closed Dec 25–Jan 1
🛏 26 bedrs, 23 en suite, 2 ba; TV; tcf
🏨 TV, dogs; P 30; child facs; con 24
✕ LD 9, bar meals only Sat lunch & Sun dinner. Resid & Rest lic
£ B&B £24–£33 (w/e £14–£21), B&B (double) £33–£42; L £5·50, D £8·50; WB £37·50 (HB 2 nts)
cc Access, B'card/Visa; dep.

Westbourne House, 11A–15 Nottingham Rd, LE13 0NP ☎ (0664) 69456. *Hotel.* 🗣 Fr. Open Jan 3–Oct 24.
£ B&B £18 (w/e £16·50)

MERE Wiltshire. Map 5A3

Pop 1,800. Amesbury 24, London 103, Frome 12, Salisbury 22, Shaftesbury 9, Shepton Mallet 18, Warminster 10, Wincanton 7½.
EC Wed. **Golf** West Wilts Warminster 18h, Bruton 9h. **See** Church, medieval Chantry House, Stourhead 3 m NW.
ℹ The Square, Church St. ☎ (0747) 860341

Using RAC discount vouchers
Please tell the hotel when booking if you plan to use an RAC discount voucher (see p. 34) in part payment of your bill. Only one voucher will be accepted per party per stay. Discount vouchers will only be accepted in payment for accommodation, not for food.

★★ **Old Ship,** Castle St, BA12 6JE ☎ (0747) 860258 Fax: (0747) 860501

A former 17th century coaching inn of tradition and character. 🗣 Fr, Es
🛏 13 bedrs, 6 en suite, 3 ba; annexe 10 bedrs, 10 en suite; TV; tcf
🏨 dogs; P 40, G 3, coach; child facs; con 40
✕ LD 9.30
£ B&B £28–£33, B&B (double) £40–£48; HB weekly £210; WB £34 (HB, min 2 nts); [10% V]
cc Access, B'card/Visa; dep.

MERIDEN West Midlands. Map 23A1

Pop 2,432. Coventry 6, London 100, Birmingham 12, Nuneaton 11, Solihull 6, Tamworth 16, Warwick 13.
EC Wed. **Golf** North Warwickshire, Hampton in Arden 9h. **See** St Lawrence's Church, Cross (reputedly marking centre of England), Cyclists War Memorial.

★★★★ **Forest of Arden,** Maxstoke La, CV7 7HR ☎ (0676) 22335 Tx: 312604 Fax: (0676) 23711 ♿
New purpose-built hotel, beside a golf course in rural area. Central courtyard and lake views. Indoor swimming pool, golf, putting, tennis, fishing, squash, sauna, solarium, gymnasium. 🗣 Fr, De, It, Es, Gr, Sw, No, Fi
🛏 153 bedrs, 153 en suite; TV; tcf
🏨 lift, ns; P500, coach; child fac; con 150
✕ LD 9.45, bar meals only Sat lunch
£ B&B £95–£105 (w/e £60), B&B (double) £110–£125; L £15, D 15; WB £55

★★★ H C **Manor,** Main Rd, CV7 7NH ☎ (0676) 22735 Tx: 311011 Fax: (0676) 22186 ♿
Picturesque Georgian residence set in the countryside. Swimming pool. (DeV)
🛏 74 bedrs, 74 en suite; TV; tcf
🏨 dogs; P 250, coach; child facs; con 300
✕ LD 10, buttery only Sat lunch
£ B&B £75, B&B (double) £90; L £15, D £15; WB £36 (HB)
cc Access, Amex, B'card/Visa, Diners.

MEVAGISSEY Cornwall. Map 2C1

Pop 2,271. St Austell 5½, London 244, Truro 14.
Golf Carlyon Bay 18h, St Austell 18h.

★★ **Spa,** Polkirt Hill, PL26 6UY ☎ (0726) 842244
Attractive white building surrounded by trees and lawns. Sea views. Putting.
🛏 12 bedrs, 11 en suite, 3 ba; TV; tcf
🏨 TV, dogs; P 14, coach; child facs
✕ LD 7.30, bar meals only lunch. Resid & Rest lic
£ B&B £22–£26·50; HB weekly £189–£219
cc Access, Amex, B'card/Visa; dep.

★★ **Tremarne,** Polkirt Hill, PL26 6UY
☎(0726) 842213

In peaceful surroundings, white building enjoying fine sea views. Swimming pool. Open Mar–mid Nov.
🛏 14 bedrs, 14 en suite, 1 ba; TV; tcf
🏨 dogs; P 14; no children under 3
✕ LD 8, nr lunch. Resid lic
£ B&B £21·50–£26·50, B&B (double) £36–£44; HB weekly £168–£203; D £13·50; [5% V Mar–Jun, Sept–Nov]
cc Access, B'card/Visa; dep.

★★ **Trevalsa Court,** Polstreath, PL26 6TH
☎(0726) 842468 ♿
Small hotel in clifftop position with direct access to beach. Beautiful views.
🛏 10 bedrs, 10 en suite; TV; tcf
🏨 dogs; P 30; child facs; con 40
✕ LD 9
£ B&B £20–£27; HB weekly £203–£252; D £6; WB fr £10
cc Access, Amex, B'card/Visa, Diners, dep.

Mevagissey House (Acclaimed), Vicarage Hill, PL26 6SZ ☎(0726) 842427. *Guest House.* Open Mar–Oct.
£ B&B £20–£25; HB weekly £192–£213.

Headlands, Polkirt Hill, PL26 6UX ☎(0726) 843453. *Private Hotel.* Open Mar–Oct.
£ B&B £14–£22; HB weekly £161–£217
Sharksfin, The Quay, PL26 6QU ☎(0726) 843241. *Hotel.* Open Feb–Nov.
£ B&B £21–£26; [10% V]
Ship Inn, Fore St, PL26 6TU ☎(0726) 843324. *Inn.*
Treleaven, PL26 6RZ ☎(0726) 842413. *Farm. Swimming pool, putting.* Open Jan–mid Dec.
£ B&B (double) £32–£44; HB weekly £145–£220; [5% V, Oct–May]
Valley Park, Valley Park, PL26 6RS ☎(0726) 842347

MICKLETON

Gloucestershire. Map 20C3
Pop 1,343. Moreton-in-Marsh 9½, London 93, Banbury 25, Cheltenham 22, Evesham 9½, Stratford-upon-Avon 9, Tewkesbury 21. **Golf** Broadway 18h. **See** Church, Hidcote Manor Gardens 4 m.

★★★ H **Three Ways,** Chipping Campden, GL55 6SB ☎(0386) 438 429 Fax: (0386) 438118 ♿

Cotswold-stone building of character, over 200 years old. Walled garden. Fr
🛏 40 bedrs, 40 en suite; TV; tcf
🏨 dogs; P 35, coach; child facs; con 80
✕ LD 9, bar meals only Mon–Sat lunch
£ B&B £35–£45 (w/e £31), B&B (double) £56–£66; D £15; WB £29 (Jan, Feb); [10% V w/d]
cc Access, Amex, B'card/Visa, Diners.

MIDDLEHAM

North Yorkshire. Map 38B4
Pop 800. Masham 7½, London 230, Bedale 10, Hawes 17, Leyburn 2, Richmond 12. **EC** Thur. **Golf** Catterick 18h.

★★ **Millers House,** Market Pl, DL8 4NR
☎Wensleydale (0969) 22630

Small stone building—owner-run hotel in quiet corner of village. Closed Jan 3–31
🛏 7 bedrs, 6 en suite, (1 ba); TV; tcf
🏨 ns; P 10; children over 10
✕ LD 8.30, nr lunch
£ B&B £32·50–£35·50, B&B (double) £71–£77; HB weekly £300–£350; D £16; WB £37·50 (HB, 1 Feb–Easter)
cc Access, B'card/Visa; dep.

MIDDLESBROUGH

Cleveland. Map 45B1
See also CRATHORNE and THORNABY-ON-TEES
Pop 149,100. Stockton-on-Tees 4, London 247, Helmsley 28, Pickering 38, Sunderland 27, Whitby 30.
MD Daily. **Golf** Middlesbrough 18h. **See** Municipal Art Gallery, Dorman Museum, Parks, Bridges, RC Cathedral, Ormesby Hall 3 m SE, Newham Grange (farm museum), Captain Cook's Birthplace Museum, Preston Hall Museum and Stockton Transport Museum (4 m W).
ⓘ 51 Corporation Rd ☎(0642) 243425

★★★★ **Hospitality Inn,** Fry St, TS1 1JH
☎(0642) 232000 Tx: 58266
Fax: (0642) 232655 ♿

Ten-storey modern hotel in the centre of Middlesbrough. Solarium. (MtCh)
🛏 159 bedrs, 159 en suite; TV; tcf
🏨 lift, dogs, ns; P 43, G 36, coach; child facs; con 400

★★★ **Marton Way,** Marton Way, TS4 3BS
☎(0642) 817651 Tx: 587783
Modern hotel in motel style on main road south of town. Closed Xmas night
🛏 53 bedrs, 53 en suite; TV; tcf
🏨 dogs, ns; P 500, coach; child facs; con 90

★★ C **Highfield,** Marton Rd, TS4 2PA
☎(0642) 817638

Turn-of-the-century private residence with modern extensions. On outskirts. (BCB)
🛏 23 bedrs, 23 en suite; TV; tcf
🏨 TV, ns, P 100, coach, child facs; con 50
✕ LD 10.30
£ B&B £41–£47·50, B&B (double) £54; L £8·15 D £8·15; WB £27·50
cc Access, Amex, B'card/Visa, Diners.

Grey House (Highly Acclaimed), 79 Cambridge Rd, Linthorpe, TS5 5NL
☎(0642) 817485. *Hotel.*
£ B&B £27

MIDDLETON IN TEESDALE

Co. Durham. Map 44C2
Pop 1,200. Barnard Castle 10, London 258, Alston 22, Brough 14, Darlington 24.

★★ **Teesdale,** Market Pl, DL12 0QG
☎Teesdale (0833) 40264
Attractive stone-built 3-storey former coaching inn in centre of town.
🛏 13 bedrs, 7 en suite, 1 ba; TV
🏨 TV, dogs; P 20; child facs

MIDDLETON-ON-SEA

West Sussex. Map 6B1
Pop 3,070. Pulborough 15, London 62, Arundel 7½, Bognor Regis 3, Littlehampton 4½, Petworth 17.

Ancton (Acclaimed), Ancton La, PO22 6NH
☎(0243) 692482. *Private Hotel.*

MIDDLETON STONEY

Oxon. Map 21A2
Bicester 3½, London 61, Banbury 14, Chipping Norton 16, Oxford 12, Witney 16.

★★ **Jersey Arms,** OX6 8SE
☎(086 989) 505 Fax: (086 989) 565

Former staging inn (some 300 years old). An attractive Oxford stone building.

🛏 6 bedrs, 6 en suite; annexe 10 bedrs, 10 en suite; TV
🏨 P 55; child facs; con 20

MIDDLE WALLOP Hampshire. Map 5B3

Andover 7, London 72, Amesbury 10, Salisbury 12, Stockbridge 5½.

♣ ★★★ R Fifehead Manor, Nr Stockbridge, SO20 8EG ☎ Andover (0264) 781565 Fax: (0264) 781400 ♿
Manor house dating from Middle Ages. Pleasant grounds near river. ☧ Fr, De, Du. Closed 10 days Xmas.
🛏 10 bedrs, 10 en suite, annex 6 bedrs, 6 en suite; TV
🏨 dogs; P 50, coach; child facs; con 10
✕ LD 9.30
£ B&B £45, B&B (double) £65–£85; HB weekly £450; L £16, D £22; WB £100 (2 days, 1 Feb–Good Fri)
cc Access, Amex, B'card/Visa, Diners.

MIDHURST West Sussex. Map 6A2

See also TROTTON
Pop 4,148. Haslemere 8, London 49, Alton 18, Chichester 12, Cosham 21, Hindhead 10, Petersfield 10, Petworth 6½.
EC Wed. **Golf** Cowdray Park 18h.

★★★ C Spread Eagle, South St, GU29 9NH ☎ (073 081) 6911 Tx: 86853 Fax: (0730) 815668

Fine historic (1430) building of great character. Individually styled bedrooms. ☧ Fr, De, It
🛏 37 bedrs, 37 en suite, TV
🏨 dogs, ns; P 50; child facs; con 35
✕ LD 9·30
£ B&B £70–£90; B&B (double) £80–£175; L £15·50, D £24·50; WB £60 (HB); [5% V, 2nd week Aug–Jun]
cc Access, Amex, B'card/Visa, Diners.

★★ Angel, North St, GU29 9UJ ☎ (073 081) 2421
Former 16th century coaching inn, a white fronted building set in main street of town. Modern hotel in farmhouse style in the grounds of a country club. Indoor swimming pool, golf, squash, sauna, billiards. ☧ Es
🛏 44 bedrs, 44 en suite; TV; tcf
🏨 P 150, coach; child facs; con 100
✕ LD 10
£ B&B £48 (w/e £30), B&B (double) £66; L £7·50, D £15; WB £50
cc Access, Amex, B'card/Visa, Diners.

MIDSOMER NORTON Somerset. Map 4C3

Frome 7, London 112, Bath 9, Bristol 12, Glastonbury 16.
ℹ Rackvernal Rd ☎ (0761) 417510

★★★ Centurion, Charlton La, BA3 4BD ☎ (0761) 417711 Fax: (0761) 418357 ♿

MILDENHALL Suffolk. Map 27A4

Pop 12,040. Newmarket 9, London 71, Bury St Edmunds 12, Ely 15, King's Lynn 35, Thetford 11.
EC Thur. **MD** Fri. **Golf** Royal Worlington 9h, Newmarket 18h. **See** St Mary's Church, 15th cent Market Cross.

★★★ Riverside, Mill St, IP28 7DP ☎ (0638) 717274 Fax: (0638) 715997

Large Georgian building with gardens down to the river. Putting, fishing.
🛏 19 bedrs, 15 en suite; TV; tcf
🏨 lift, dogs; P 45, coach; child facs; con 50
✕ LD 9.30
£ B&B £42–£49, B&B (double) £60–£64; HB weekly £225; L £9·50, D £12; WB £81; [10% V]
cc Access, Amex, B'card/Visa, Diners; dep.

★★★ Smoke House Inn, Beck Row, IP28 8DH ☎ (0638) 713223 Fax: (0638) 712202 ♿
16th century building with exposed beams. Bedrooms in new wings.
🛏 100 bedrs, 100 en suite; annexe 10 bedrs, 10 en suite; TV; tcf
🏨 TV, P 200, coach; child facs; con 120
✕ LD 10
£ B&B £60–£65, B&B (double) £70–£80; L £7·50, D £12·50; WB £65 (HB); [10% V]
cc Access, Amex, B'card/Visa; dep.

★★ Bell, High St, IP28 7EA ☎ (0638) 717272 Fax: (0638) 717057

Family-owned and managed, well-preserved old coaching inn in town centre. ☧ Fr
🛏 17 bedrs, 16 en suite, 2 ba; TV; tcf
🏨 dogs; P 25, coach; child facs; con 120
✕ LD 9
£ B&B £40–£48 (w/e £23), B&B (double) £55–£60; L £10·25, D £10·25; WB £65 (HB 2 nts)
cc Access, Amex, B'card/Visa, Diners, dep.

★★ Bird in Hand, Beck Row, IP28 8ES ☎ (0638) 713247

Large modernised pub with bedroom accommodation in separate chalets. (BCB)

MILFORD ON SEA Hampshire. Map 5B1

Pop 4,350. Lymington 4½, London 96, Bournemouth 14, Ringwood 15.
Golf Barton-on-Sea 18h. **See** Norman Parish Church, Hurst Castle 3 m SE.

★★★ Westover Hall, Park La, SO4 0PT ☎ Lymington (0590) 643044 Fax: (0590) 644490

Victorian manor house with rich decor. Outstanding sea views. ☧ Fr, De, Es, It
🛏 15 bedrs, 15 en suite; TV; tcf
🏨 dogs; P 50, U3 (£5), coach; child facs; con 45
✕ Rest & Club lic
£ B&B £35–£45, L fr £12·95, D fr £12·95; WB £45; [10% V, May–Jun, Sept–Oct]
cc Amex, B'card/Visa, Diners; dep.

MILTON ABBAS Dorset. Map 5A2

Pop 732. Blandford Forum 8, London, 113, Bournemouth 21, Dorchester 11, Ringwood 26, Sherborne 17, Wareham 13.
Golf Ashley Wood 9h.

♣ ★★ C Milton Manor, Blandford Forum, DT11 0AZ ☎ (0258) 880254

Stone manor house with wooded grounds and attractive garden. Putting.
🛏 12 bedrs, 9 en suite (1 sh), 2 ba; TV; tcf
🏨 P 20; children over 12

MILTON COMMON Oxfordshire. Map 21B1

London 46, M40 (jn 7) ½, Aylesbury 13, High Wycombe 16, Oxford 10, Wallingford 18.

★★★ **Belfry,** Brimpton Grange, OX9 2JW
☎ Gt Milton (0844) 279381 Tx: 837968
Fax: (0844) 279624 ♿

Large half-timbered house with modern extensions in own grounds. Indoor swimming pool, sauna, solarium, gymnasium. Fr. Closed 24–31 Dec.
57 bedrs, 57 en suite; TV; tcf
dogs, ns; P 150, coach; child facs; con 250
LD 9.30, bar meals only Sat lunch
£ B&B £65–£75, B&B (double) £75·50–£90; L £13, D £16; WB £85
cc Access, Amex, B'card/Visa, Diners; dep.
(*See advertisement on p. 388*)

Three Pigeons, OX9 2NS ☎ Milton (0844) 279247. *Inn.*
£ B&B £28·75; [5% V]

MILTON DAMEREL Devon. Map 3A3

Pop 450. South Molton 30, London 211, Bideford 13, Bude 12, Holsworthy 6.
Golf Holsworthy 18h.

★★★ **Woodford Bridge,** EX22 7LL (A 388)
☎ (040 926) 481 Fax: (040 926) 585

Stone-built 15th century inn with thatched roof. Indoor swimming pool, fishing, squash, sauna, solarium, gymnasium, billiards. Fr, Es
12 bedrs, 12 en suite; TV; tcf
dogs, ns; P 75, coach; child facs
LD 10
£ B&B £45–£50, B&B (double) £70–£75; L £7·95, D £7·95; WB £80; [10% V]
cc Access, Amex, B'card/Visa; Diners; dep.

MILTON KEYNES Buckinghamshire.

Map 14A4
See also NEWPORT PAGNELL
Pop 95,900 (New City designated area). London 56, M1 (jn 14) 1, Bedford 13, Bletchley 5½, Buckingham 13, Newport Pagnell 4, Towcester 13.
MD Tue, Sat. **Golf** Abbey Hill 18h. **See** Modern town centre, Broughton Church, Bradwell Abbey, Stacey Hill Collection.
ℹ Saxon Court, 502 Avebury Boulevard.
☎ (0908) 691995

★★★★ **Post House,** 500 Saxon Gate West, Central Milton Keynes, MK9 2HQ
☎ (0908) 667722 Tx: 826842
Fax: (0908) 674714 ♿
Modern 5-storey hotel with stylish open plan public areas. Indoor swimming pool, sauna, solarium, gymnasium. (THF)
163 bedrs, 163 en suite; TV; tcf
lift, TV, dogs, ns; P 80, coach; child facs; con 150
LD 10.30
£ room £85 (w/e £39·50), room (double) £95; Bk £7·50, L £10·95, D £14·50; WB £37
cc Access, Amex, B'card/Visa, CB, Diners.

★★★ **Broughton,** Broughton Village, MK10 9AA ☎ (0908) 667726
Fax: (0908) 604844 ♿
A well-furnished, red-brick hotel in country surroundings but close to junction 14 of M1. Putting. Fr
30 bedrs, 30 en suite; TV; tcf
P 58; child facs; con 60
LD 9·45, bar meals only Sun dinner
£ B&B £55 (w/e £22·50), B&B (double) £70; [5% V w/d, 10% V w/e]
cc Access, Amex, B'card/Visa, Diners.

★★★ **Friendly,** Monks Way, Two Mile Ash, MK8 8LY ☎ (0908) 561666 Tx: 826152
Fax: (0908) 568303 ♿
A modern red-brick complex in landscaped grounds next to a golf course on the A5.
Fr, De
50 bedrs, 50 en suite; TV; tcf
dogs, ns; P 60, coach; child facs; con 120
LD 9.30
£ B&B £52–£62·50 (w/e £36), B&B (double) £68·50–£73; HB weekly £442·75–£516·25; D £11·25; [10% V]
cc Access, Amex, B'card/Visa, Diners; dep.
(*See advertisement on p. 361*)

★★★ **C** **H** **Hatton Court,** Bullington End, Hanslope, MK19 7BQ ☎ (0908) 510044
Victorian mansion in gothic style, elegantly decorated and furnished with many antiques. Set in 7½ acres of gardens in quiet countryside.
12 bedrs, 12 en suite, annexe 8 bedrs, 8 en suite; TV; tcf
£ B&B £40–£80, B&B (double) £80–£110; L £13·50, D £23·50
(*See advertisement on p. 361*)

★★★ **Moorings Toby,** Milton Keynes Marina, Waterside, Peartree Bridge, MK6 3PE ☎ (0908) 691515 Tx: 826244
Fax: (0908) 690274 ♿
Modern low-built brick hotel on east side of city. Damaged by fire in 1990, Limited facilities open while refurbishment underway, completion expected December 1990.
40 bedrs, 40 en suite; TV; tcf
ns; P 120; child facs; con 25

★★★ **Welcome Lodge,** Service Area 3, M1, Newport Pagnell, MK16 8DS ☎ (0908) 610878 Tx: 826186 Fax: (0908) 617226
See Motor Lodge section

Linford Lodge (Highly Acclaimed), Wood Lane, Great Linford, MK14 5AZ ☎ (0908) 605879. Fax: (0908) 667998. *Private Hotel. Indoor swimming pool.*
£ B&B £43·45–£52·95; [5% V]

MILTON UNDER WYCHWOOD

Oxfordshire. Map 21A2
Shipton under Wychwood 1, London 80, Burford 5, Chipping Norton 7½, Stow-on-the-Wold 8½.

Hillborough (Highly Acclaimed), The Green, OX7 6JH ☎ (0993) 830501. *Hotel.* Closed Jan. ♿

MINEHEAD Somerset. Map 3C4

Pop 8,722. Taunton 24, London 167, Bridgwater 26, Dunster 2, Lynmouth 16.
EC Wed. **Golf** Minehead and West Somerset 18h. **See** Parish Church (14th cent), 17th cent Quirke's Almshouses, 14th cent Fishermen's Chapel, West Somerset Rly.
ℹ Market House, The Parade.
☎ (0643) 702624

★★★ **Benares,** Northfield Rd, TA24 5PT
☎ (0643) 704911

Spacious hotel with attractive garden, in quiet residential area. Open Mar 23–Nov 5.
20 bedrs, 19 en suite; TV; tcf
dogs, ns; P 20, U 2 (£1·75); child facs
LD 8.30, bar meals only lunch. Resid & Rest lic
£ B&B £32·50–£36·50, B&B (double) £58·50–£68; HB weekly £254–£276·50; L £6·25, D £14·85
cc Access, Amex, B'card/Visa, Diners; dep.

★★★ **H** **Northfield,** Northfield Rd, TA24 5PU ☎ (0643) 705155 Tx: 42513 ♿

Pleasant hotel with gardens in residential area. Indoor swimming pool, putting, sauna, gymnasium.
24 bedrs, 24 en suite; TV; tcf
lift, dogs, ns; P 42, coach; child facs; con 100
LD 8.30
£ B&B £39–£49, B&B (double) £68–£98; HB weekly £252–£378; D £12·50
cc Access, Amex, B'card/Visa, Diners; dep.

★★ **C** **Beaconwood,** Church Rd, North Hill, TA24 5SB ☎ (0643) 702032

Villa-style hotel with pleasant garden. Away from town on high ground with spectacular views. Swimming pool, tennis. Open Mar–Oct.
16 bedrs, 12 en suite, 2 ba; TV; tcf

M

dogs, ns; P 25, coach; child facs
LD 7·30, nr lunch. Resid lic
£ B&B £25–£35, B&B (double) £40–£55; HB weekly £190–£220; D £11; [10% V]
cc Access, B'card/Visa; dep.

★★ H C R **Remuera,** Northfield Rd, TA24 5QH (0643) 702611

A spacious residence with attractive garden and views of coast. Putting. Fr, De. Open Apr–Oct.
8 bedrs, 5 en suite (1 sh), 1 ba; TV; tcf
dogs, ns; P 9
LD 8. Resid & Rest lic
£ B&B £23–£30, B&B (double) £44–£56; HB weekly £189–£224; D £13
cc Access, B'card/Visa; dep.

★★ C **Winsor,** The Avenue, TA24 5AW (0643) 702171
Spacious hotel, near to sea and shops. Privately-owned and run.
33 bedrs, 11 en suite (4 sh), 7 ba; TV; tcf
TV, dogs, ns; P 24, coach; child facs

★★ **York,** The Avenue, TA24 5AN (0643) 705151
Main street hotel with an attractive Spanish type long bar. Closed Xmas week.
18 bedrs, 18 en suite, TV; tcf
TV; P 12, coach; children over 5
LD 9, bar meals only lunch
£ B&B £19–£21; HB weekly £161–£189; L £5·75, D £5·75
cc Access, Amex, B'card/Visa, Diners; dep.

★ H **Kingsway,** Ponsford Rd, TA24 5DY (0643) 702313
Pleasant privately-run hotel; two minutes drive to the sea.
8 bedrs, 8 en suite; TV; tcf
TV, dogs, ns; P 8; children over 3

Alcombe House (Highly Acclaimed), Bircham Rd, Alcombe, TA24 6BG (0643) 705130. *Hotel.*
Dorchester (Highly Acclaimed), TA24 5AZ (0643) 702052
£ B&B £19–£22; HB weekly £140–£150
Mayfair (Highly Acclaimed), The Avenue, TA24 5AY (0643) 702719. *Hotel.* Open Easter–Nov. Fr, De, Du
£B&B £19–£22; HB weekly £140–£150.

Carbery (Acclaimed), Western La, The Parks, TA24 8BZ (0643) 702941. *Private Hotel.* Open Mar–Oct.
£B&B £22; HB weekly £160
Gascony (Acclaimed), 50 The Avenue, TA24 5BB (0643) 705939. *Hotel.* Open Mar–Oct.
£ B&B £19·50; HB weekly £148; [5% V]

Marshfield (Acclaimed), Tregonwell Rd, TA24 5DU (0643) 702517. *Private Hotel.* Open Mar–Nov.
£B&B £13; HB weekly £119
Marston Lodge (Acclaimed), St Michael's Rd, North Hill, TA24 5JP (0643) 7025 10. *Private Hotel.* Open Feb–Dec.
£ B&B £15–£19; HB weekly £165–£189.
Poplars (Acclaimed), 10 Townsend Rd, TA24 5RG (0643) 704289. *Hotel.*
£ B&B £15·50; HB weekly £154–£168

Woodbridge, 12 The Parks, TA24 8BS (0643) 704860. *Private Hotel.*

MINSTER-ON-SEA Kent. Map 7B3

Rochester 18, London 50, Ashford 29, Canterbury 25, Maidstone 18, Sheerness 2.

★★ **Abbey,** The Broadway, Sheerness ME12 2DX (0795) 872873
Fax: (0795) 874728

Close to the sea, a modern motel with a quadrangle of single-storey bedroom accommodation round a garden.
50 bedrs, 50 en suite; TV; tcf
dogs; P 70, coach; child facs; con 70
LD 9.15
£ B&B £30–£40, B&B (double) £42·50–£60; L £3·75, D 9·50
cc Access, Amex, B'card/Visa, Diners.

MOLESWORTH Cambridgeshire.

Map 26A4
Bedford 19, London 69, Cambridge 28, Corby 16, Kettering 15,Northampton 27.

Cross Keys, Huntingdon, PE11 0QF Bythorn (080 14) 283. *Inn.*
£ B&B £19·25

MONK FRYSTON North Yorkshire.

Map 38C2
Pop 695. Doncaster 20, London 184, Castleford 7, Selby 7, Tadcaster 9, Leeds 14.
Golf Selby 18h.

★★★ H C R **Monk Fryston Hall,** Selby Rd, LS25 5DU South Milford (0977) 682369 Tx: 556634 Fax: (0977) 683544

Grey stone manor, of medieval origin, set in attractive gardens and grounds.
29 bedrs, 29 en suite; TV, tcf
dogs, ns; P 60; child facs; con 50
LD 9.30
£ B&B £54–£68, B&B (double) £76–£90; L £9·60, D £15; WB £82–£92 (HB, 2 nts)
cc Access, Amex, B'card/Visa.

MORCHARD BISHOP Devon. Map 3B3

Tiverton 16, London 179, Barnstaple 25, Exeter 15, Okehampton 16

Wigham Farm (Highly Acclaimed), Wigham, EX17 6RJ (036 37) 350. *Swimming pool, billiards.* Fr, De
£ B&B and dinner (double) £72–£106

MORECAMBE Lancashire. Map 36B3

Pop 40,661 (inc. Heysham). Lancaster 3½, London 242, Ambleside 33, Broughton-in-Furness 42, Kendal 22, Kirkby Lonsdale 17.
EC Wed. **MD** Tue, Sat. **Golf** Morecambe 18h, Heysham 18h.
[i] Marine Road Central. (0524) 414110

★★★ **Elms,** Bare, LA4 6DD (0524) 411501 Fax: (0524) 831979

White-painted hotel with spacious lounge and dining room; own pleasant grounds. Fr, De. It
40 bedrs, 40 en suite; TV; tcf
lift, TV, dogs; P 70, coach; child facs; con 200
LD 8.45
£ B&B £45–£50, B&B (double) £65–£70; L £6·75, D £10·25; WB £85; [5% V, w/e]
cc Access, Amex, B'card/Visa, Diners.

★★★ **Headway,** East Promenade, LA4 5AN (0524) 412525

On promenade with sea view, attractive hotel specialising in family holidays.
53 bedrs, 53 en suite; TV; tcf
lift; P 20, coach; child facs; con 50

★★★ **Midland,** Marine Rd West, LA4 4BZ (0524) 417180 Fax: (0524) 832827
Hotel of outstanding 1930s architecture, commanding panoramic view of bay.
46 bedrs, 46 en suite; TV; tcf
lift, dogs, ns; P 100, coach; child facs; con 150
£ B&B £39–£45, B&B (double) £52–£70; L £7·95, D £12·50; WB £75 (min 2 nts)

Milton Keynes (Buckinghamshire)

Morecambe (Lancashire)

Moreton (Merseyside)

cc Access, Amex, B'card/Visa, Diners. (*See advertisment on p. 361*)

★★★ **Strathmore,** Marine Rd East, LA4 5AP ☎(0524) 421234 Tx: 65452 Fax: (0524) 414242 ♿

Attractive hotel overlooking Morecambe Bay and facing Lakeland hills.
🛏 51 bedrs, 51 en suite; TV; tcf
🏨 lift, ns; P 24, coach; child facs; con 200

★★ **Clarendon,** Marine Rd West, LA4 4EP ☎(0524) 410180

19th century building of character in central position overlooking bay. Closed 24 Dec–1 Jan
🛏 31 bedrs, 29 en suite, (2 sh), 3 ba; TV; tcf
🏨 lift, TV, dogs; coach; child facs; con 60
✕ LD 9
£ B&B £28, B&B (double) £39; HB weekly £180; L £5, D £7·50; WB £46 (2 nts); [5% V, Nov–Mar, w/e]
cc Access, Amex, B'card/Visa, Diners; dep.

★ **Channings,** 455 Marine Rd East, Bare, LA4 6AD ☎(0524) 417925
Small hotel on promenade with outstanding view across Morecambe Bay.
🛏 20 bedrs, 18 en suite, 1 ba; TV; tcf
🏨 dogs; coach; child facs; con 30
✕ LD 7, nr lunch. Resid & Rest lic
£ B&B £16–£23, B&B (double) £37–£40, D £7; [10% V]
cc Access, B'card/Visa; dep.

Beach Mount (Highly Acclaimed), 395 Marine Rd East, LA4 5AN ☎(0524) 420753. *Hotel.* Open Mar–Oct.
£ B&B £16·50–£19·50; HB weekly £129–£147
Prospect (Highly Acclaimed), 363 Marine Rd, LA4 5AQ ☎(0524) 417819. *Hotel.* Open Easter–Nov
£ B&B £17–£20; HB weekly £115–£125
Warwick (Highly Acclaimed), 394 Marine Rd East, LA4 5AN ☎(0524) 418151. *Hotel.* ⚒ De
£ B&B £16·50–£20·50; HB weekly £150–£164; [5% V]

Ashley (Acclaimed), 371 Marine Rd East, LA4 5AH ☎(0524) 412034. *Private Hotel.* Closed 24–31 Dec
£ B&B £17–£18, HB weekly £140–£147.
New Hazelmere (Acclaimed), 391 Marine Rd East, LA4 5AN ☎(0524) 417876. ⚒ Fr *Hotel.* Open 1 May–1 Nov.
£ B&B £15; HB weekly £135; [5% V]
Wimslow (Acclaimed), 374 Marine Rd East, LA4 5AH ☎(0524) 417804. *Private Hotel.*

Carr Garth, 18 Bailey La, Heysham Village, LA3 2PS ☎(0524) 51175. *Guest House.* Open Easter–mid Oct.
£ B&B £12; HB weekly £88–£97
Ellesmere, 44 Westminster Rd, LA4 4JD ☎(0524) 411881. *Guest House.*
Stresa, 96 Sandylands Prom, LA3 1DP ☎(0524) 412867. *Private Hotel.*
York, Lancaster Rd, LA4 5QR ☎(0524) 418226. *Hotel.*

MORETON

Wirral, Merseyside. Map 29A4
Pop 15,040. Birkenhead 4, London 201, Chester 18, Queensferry 17.
EC Wed. **Golf** Wallasey 9h.

★★★ **Leasowe Castle,** Leasowe, L46 3RF ☎051-606 9191 Tx: 627189 Fax: 051-678 5551

Elizabethan castle, now a hotel offering range of leisure facilities. Golf, sauna, solarium, gymnasium.
🛏 41 bedrs, 41 en suite, TV; tcf
🏨 TV, dogs; P 200, coach; child facs; con 300
(*See advertisement on p. 361*)

MORETON HAMPSTEAD

Devon. Map 3B3
Pop 1,620. Exeter 13, London 182, Ashburton 13, Crediton 11, Okehampton 13, Plymouth 29, Tavistock 21.
EC Thur. **Golf** Manor House Hotel 18h.

★★ **White Hart,** The Square, TQ13 8NF ☎(0647) 40406 Fax: (0647) 40565

A listed building–Georgian stone-built posting house in village centre. Billiards.
🛏 20 bedrs, 20 en suite, 2 ba; TV; tcf
🏨 dogs, ns; P 12, coach; children over 10; con 50
✕ LD 8.30, bar meals only lunch
£ B&B £33–£36, B&B (double) £53–£56; D £10·95; WB £73; [10% V, not Aug & Fri]
cc Access, Amex, B'card/Visa, Diners.

Cookshayes (Acclaimed), 33 Court St, TQ13 8LG ☎(0647) 40374. *Guest House. Putting.* Open mid Mar–end Oct.
£ B&B £18, HB weekly £175–£203; [10% V, May–Sep]

MORETON-IN-MARSH

Gloucestershire. Map 20C2
Pop 2,572. Chipping Norton 8½, London 83, Banbury 19, Evesham 14, Stow-on-the-Wold 4½, Stratford-upon-Avon 16.
EC Wed. **Golf** Broadway 18h.
ℹ Council Offices, High St. ☎(0608) 50881

★★★ **H C Manor House,** High St, GL56 0LJ ☎(0608) 50501 Tx: 837151 Fax: (0608) 51481

A 16th century manor with well-furnished rooms. Indoor swimming pool, tennis, putting, sauna.
🛏 35 bedrs, 34 en suite, 1 ba; annexe 3 bedrs, 3 en suite; TV
🏨 lift; P 30, coach; child facs; con 60
✕ LD 9.30
£ B&B £50–£55, B&B (double) £65–£70; L £10·95, D £19; WB £49·50 (HB); [5% V w/d]
cc Access, Amex, B'card/Visa, Diners; dep.

★★ **Redesdale Arms,** High St, GL56 0AW ☎(0608) 50308 Fax: (0608) 51843

18th century former coaching inn of Cotswold stone in the centre of town. ⚒ Fr
🛏 9 bedrs, 9 en suite, 2 ba; annexe 8 bedrs, 8 en suite; TV; tcf
🏨 ns; P 20, coach; child facs; con 80
✕ LD 9.30
£ B&B £44·50, B&B (double) £65; HB weekly £292; L £9·95, D £13·95; WB £85; [10% V]
cc Access, B'card/Visa; dep.

★★ **White Hart Royal,** High St, GL56 0BA ☎(0608) 50731
Former coaching inn opposite town market square. Interesting cobbled hallway. (THF)
🛏 18 bedrs, 9 en suite, 2 ba; TV; tcf
🏨 TV, dogs, ns; P 6, coach; child facs; con 75
✕ LD 9.30, bar meals only Mon–Sat lunch
£ B&B £33–£44, B&B (double) £44–£60; HB weekly £252–£272; D £13; WB £84 (HB 2 nts)
cc Access, Amex, B'card/Visa, Diners.

Moreton House (Acclaimed), High St, GL56 0LQ ☎(0608) 50747. *Guest House.*
£ B&B £18·50

MORTEHOE Devon. Map 3A4

Pop 500. Dunster 39, London 204, Barnstaple 13, Ilfracombe 6, Lynmouth 21. **EC** Wed (win). **Golf** Ilfracombe 18h. **See** Parish Church, Morte Stone, Morte Point.

Baycliffe, Chapel Hill, EX34 7DZ
☎ Woolacombe (0271) 870393

MOTTRAM ST ANDREW Cheshire. Map 33C1

Pop 503. Prestbury 2½, London 73, Buxton 16, Congleton 13, Knutsford 10, Macclesfield 5½, Stockport 10. **Golf** Alderley Edge 9h.

★★★ Mottram Hall, Prestbury, SK10 4QT
☎ Prestbury (0625) 828135 Tx: 668181
Fax: (0625) 829284 ♿

Gracious Georgian country house, set in 120 acres of parkland. Indoor swimming pool, golf, putting, tennis, fishing, squash, sauna, solarium, gymnasium, snooker. (DeV)
🛏 95 bedrs, 95 en suite; TV; tcf
🏨 ns; P 250; child facs; con 220
✕ LD 9.45
£ B&B £90 (w/e £39), B&B (double) £100; L £12·50, D £17·50
cc Access, Amex, B'card/Visa, Diners.

MOULSFORD-ON-THAMES

Oxfordshire. Map 12A3
Reading 11, London 49, Henley-on-Thames 12, Newbury 14, Wallingford 4, Wantage 15.

★★ Beetle & Wedge, Ferry La, OX10 9JF
☎ Cholsey (0491) 651381

Privately-owned riverside hotel of some character with attractive gardens. Fishing.
🛏 8 bedrs, 8 en suite; annexe 4 bedrs, 4 en suite; TV; tcf
🏨 dogs; P 46, coach; child facs; con 25

MOUSEHOLE Cornwall. Map 2A1

Pop 2,000. Penzance 3, London 284. **EC** Wed. **Golf** West Cornwall, Lelant 18h.

★★ The Lobster Pot, South Cliff, TR19 6QX ☎ Penzance (0736) 731251
Fax: (0736) 731140
Charming historic hotel with verandah overhanging the harbour. Closed Jan.
🛏 13 bedrs, 13 en suite; TV; tcf
🏨 dogs; coach; child facs
✕ LD 9·45, bar meals only Mon–Sat lunch. Resid & Rest lic
£ B&B £23–£35·50, B&B (double) £46–£85; HB weekly £218–£297; D £14·50; WB £67·50
cc Access, Amex, B'card/Visa; dep.

Tavis Vor, The Parade, TR19 6PR
☎ Penzance (0736) 731306. *Guest House.*
✈ Fr, De, It
£ B&B £37·20–£41·20; HB weekly £196·70–£217·70

MUCH BIRCH Hereford and Worcester

(Herefordshire). Map 20A2
Ross-on-Wye 8½, London 129, Abergavenny 20, Hereford 6½, Ledbury 18.

★★★ Pilgrim, Hereford, HR2 8HJ
☎ Golden Valley (0981) 540742 Tx: 35332
Fax: (0981) 540620

Modern well-appointed hotel on main road in country area. Fine views. Putting. ✈ Fr
🛏 20 bedrs, 20 en suite; TV; tcf
🏨 dogs, ns; P 50; child facs; con 45
✕ LD 9.45, bar meals only Mon–Fri lunch
£ B&B £39·50–£54, B&B (double) £54–£68; L £8·75, D £16·75; WB £45 (HB); [10% V]
cc Access, Amex, B'card/Visa, Diners; dep.

MUDEFORD Dorset. Map 5B1

Pop 3,846. Lyndhurst 13, London 97, Bournemouth 7, Christchurch 2, Lymington 10, Ringwood 9½.
EC Wed. **Golf** Highcliffe Castle 18h.

★★★ Avonmouth, Christchurch, BH23 3NT ☎ Bournemouth (0202) 483434
Hotel in pleasant grounds running down to Christchurch Harbour. Swimming pool, putting. (THF)
🛏 41 bedrs, 41 en suite; TV; tcf
🏨 dogs, ns; P 60, coach; child facs; con 25
✕ LD 9
£ B&B £72·30, B&B (double) £102–£114; HB weekly £378–£511, L £8·10, D £14·50
cc Access, Amex, B'card/Visa, CB, Diners.

MULLION Cornwall. Map 2C1

Pop 1,995. Helston 6½, London 277, Falmouth 15.
EC Wed. **Golf** Mullion 18h. **See** Mullion Cove, 16th cent Church, Marconi Memorial.

★★★ Polurrian, Polurrian Rd, TR12 7EN
☎ (0326) 240421 Fax: (0326) 240083
Impressive 3-storey white building in 12 acres with panoramic sea views. Indoor/outdoor swimming pool, putting, tennis, squash, sauna, solarium, gymnasium, billiards. ✈ Es. Open Mar–Dec.
🛏 40 bedrs, 38 en suite, 1 ba; TV;
🏨 dogs, ns; P, coach; child facs.
✕ LD 9.30
£ B&B £41·50–£55·50; B&B (double) £107–£131; D £13; WB £144; [5% V, Mar–May, Oct–Dec]
cc Access, Amex, B'card/Visa, Diners; dep.

★★ Mullion Cove, Helston, TR12 7EP
☎ (0326) 240328
Substantial building overlooking whole sweep of Mount's Bay. Swimming pool, tennis, sauna, solarium..
🛏 36 bedrs, 21 en suite, 5 ba; TV; tcf
🏨 TV, dogs; P 25, G 6 (£1), coach; child facs; con 70

Henscath House, Mullion Cove, TR12 7EP
☎ (0326) 240537. *Guest House.*
£ HB weekly £162–£176

MUNGRISDALE Cumbria. Map 43C2

M6 (jn 40) 12, Windermere 24, London 288, Kendal 38, Keswick 9½, Penrith 13.

★ H C R The Mill CA11 0XR ☎ (076 87) 79659

Beautiful 17th century white-painted stone mill house in quiet country situation. Fishing. Open Feb–Nov.
🛏 7 bedrs, 5 en suite, 1 ba; TV; tcf
🏨 TV, dogs, ns; P 15; child facs
✕ LD 7, nr lunch. Resid & Rest lic
£ B&B £26·50–£30·50, B&B (double) £43–£46; HB weekly £214–£245; D £15; dep.

Mill Inn, CA11 0XR ☎ (059 683) 632 [changing to (076 87) 79632].
Picturesque 16th century inn beside a river.
🛏 7 bedrs, 3 en suite, (1 sh), 1 ba; tcf
🏨 TV, dogs; P 20, coach
✕ LD 7, bar meals only lunch
£ B&B ££15·50–£16·50; B&B (double) £31–£39; D £9·75; WB £31–£39
cc B'card/Visa; dep.
(*See advertisement on p. 392.*)

Near Howe (Acclaimed), Near Howe, CA11 0SH ☎ (059 683) 678. [changing to (076 87) 79678] *Farm. Snooker.*

MURTON North Yorkshire. Map 38C3

York 3, London 196, Harrogate 25, Leeds 27, Malton 16, Selby 14, Thirsk 24.

Dray Lodge (Acclaimed), Moor La, YO1 3UH ☎ (0904) 489591 Fax: (0904) 488587. *Private Hotel.* ✈ Fr
£ B&B £26·45–£29·90; HB weekly £215–£246; [5% V]

MYLOR BRIDGE Cornwall. Map 2B1

Truro 8, London 252, Falmouth 4, Helston 11, Redruth 9.

Penmere, Rosehill, TR11 5LZ ☎ Falmouth (0326) 74470. *Guest House.*

NANTWICH Cheshire. Map 29C2

Pop 11,500. London 162, Chester 18, Middlewich 9½, Newcastle-under-Lyme 13, Sandbach 9½, Whitchurch 10, Wrexham 18. **EC** Wed. **MD** Thur, Sat. **Golf** Crewe 18h. **See** Churche's Mansion, Sweet Briar Hall. [i] Beam St. ☎(0270) 623914

♛ ★★★ **Alvaston Hall,** Middlewich Rd, CW5 6PD ☎(0270) 624341 Tx: 36311 Fax: (0270) 623395

Mock-Tudor Victorian country house 2 miles north of town. Some bedrooms in converted stables. Indoor swimming pool, tennis, squash, sauna, solarium, gymnasium. Fr
36 bedrs, 36 en suite; annexe 52 bedrs, 52 en suite; TV; tcf
dogs; P 250, coach; child facs; con 300
LD 9.45, nr Sat lunch
£ B&B £75–£109 (w/e £49), B&B (double) £90–£135 (w/e £66); L £12·50, D £15; WB £90 (2 nts); [10% V Jan & Jun–Aug]
cc Access, Amex, B'card/Visa, Diners.

♛ ★★★ **Rookery Hall,** Worleston, CW5 6DQ ☎(0270) 626866 Tx: 367169 Fax: (0270) 626027 ♿

Continental-style baronial building in 28 acres of ground. Panelled dining room. Putting, tennis, fishing. Fr
30 bedrs, 30 en suite; annexe 15 bedrs, 15 en suite; TV
TV; ns; P 150; children over 10; con 60
LD 9.30. Resid & Rest lic
£ B&B £92·50–£235, B&B (double) £140–£260; L £16·50, D £27·50; WB £109·83
cc Access, Amex, B'card/Visa, Diners.

★★ **Cedars,** 134–136 Crewe Rd, CW5 6NB ☎(0270) 626455
Converted and extended former private house of character in a residential area.

★★ **Crown,** High St, CW5 5AS ☎(0270) 625283
Historic black and white Tudor hotel in town centre. Modern extensions at rear.

★★ **Lamb,** Hospital St, CW5 5RH ☎(0270) 625286
A Georgian family-run hotel in centre of market town. Fr
16 bedrs, 13 en suite, 2 ba; TV; tcf
TV, ns; P 15, G 10, coach; child facs; con 15
LD 9.30, bar meals only Mon lunch
£ B&B £22–£33, B&B (double) £40–£50; L £6, D £11·50; WB £50
cc Access; dep.

NARBOROUGH Leicestershire. Map 25C3

Pop 6,333. M1 (jn 21) 3, London 101, Coventry 19, Leicester 6, Lutterworth 11, Market Harborough 18. **EC** Wed. **Golf** Kirby Muxloe 18h.

★★ **Charnwood,** Leicester Rd, LE9 5DF ☎Leicester (0533) 862218 Fax: (0533) 750119

Detached Victorian building with 2 upper storeys situated in residential village. Closed 26 Dec–1 Jan.
20 bedrs, 20 en suite; TV; tcf
dogs; P 40, coach; child facs
LD 9.30, nr Sat lunch & Sun dinner. Resid & Rest lic
£ B&B £30–£46 (w/e £30), B&B (double) £40–£55 (w/e £40); L £6·50, D £10·50; WB; [10% V]
cc Access, Amex, B'card/Visa.

NEAR SAWREY Cumbria. Map 43C1

M6 (jn 36) 29, London 269, Coniston 5½, Windermere 10 (Fy 3½). **See** Hill Top.

Garth (Acclaimed), LA22 0JZ ☎Hawkshead (096 66) 373. *Guest House.*

High Green Gate (Acclaimed), LA22 0LF ☎Hawkshead (096 66) 296. *Guest House.* Open Apr–Oct & Xmas–New Year
£ B&B £13·75–£16·50; HB weekly £137·50–£148·50

Sawrey House (Acclaimed), LA22 0LF ☎Hawkshead (096 66) 387. *Hotel.* Open Mar–Nov.
£ B&B £18·75; HB weekly £180–£200

NEEDHAM MARKET Suffolk. Map 27B3

Pop 3,890. Colchester 23, London 79, Ipswich 8, Stowmarket 4, Sudbury 18. **EC** Tue. **Golf** Stowmarket 18h.

Pipps Ford (Acclaimed), IP6 8LJ ☎Coddenham (044 979) 208. *Guest House. Swimming pool.* ♿

NELSON Lancashire. Map 38A3

Pop 30,000. Burnley 4, London 210, Settle 17, Skipton 13. **EC** Tue. **MD** Wed, Fri, Sat. **Golf** Nelson 18h. **See** St Mary's Church, Roughlee Hall, Packhorse bridge, Museum. [i] 20a Scotland Rd. ☎(0282) 692890

★★ **Great Marsden,** Barkerhouse Rd, BB9 9NL ☎(0282) 64749 ♿

Impressive Edwardian style stone building set in its own grounds.

NETHER WASDALE Cumbria. Map 43B1

Pop 273. Ravenglass 7, London 304, Broughton-in-Furness 16, Whitehaven 16. **Golf** Seascale 18h. **See** Wastwater Lake, nature trail.

★★ **Low Wood Hall,** CA20 1ET ☎Wasdale (094 67) 26289.

Victorian mansion sympathetically modernised to retain many original features. Magnificent views.
7 bedrs, 7 en suite; annexe 6 bedrs, 6 en suite; TV; tcf
ns; P 24; child facs
LD 8.45, nr lunch. Resid & Rest lic
£ B&B £26–£29, B&B (double) £40–£44; HB weekly £175–£196; D £10; dep.

NEWARK ON TRENT Notts. Map 31B2

Pop 24,600. Grantham 15, London 126, Doncaster 37, Leicester 35, Lincoln 17, Mansfield 18, Nottingham 19, Sleaford 18. **EC** Thur. **MD** Wed, Fri, Sat. **Golf** Newark 18h. **See** Castle ruins, Church of St Mary Magdalene (14th cent), Beaumond Cross, Town Hall, Museum and Art Gallery, Governor's House, old inns, interesting old buildings in Market Square, Folk Museum. [i] The Ossington, Beast Market Hall. ☎(0636) 78962

★★ **Grange,** London Rd, NG24 1RZ ☎(0636) 703399 Fax: (0636) 702328
Attractive stone building originally a Victorian house. Closed 24 Dec–1 Jan.
9 bedrs, 9 en suite; TV; tcf
ns; P 9; con 20
LD 9. Resid & Rest lic
£ B&B £40–£45, B&B (double) £50–£65; L £7·50, D £10; WB £60
cc Access, B'card/Visa; dep.

★★ **Ram,** Castle Gate, NG24 1AZ ☎(0636) 702255
A stone building in town centre; opposite the Castle.

NEW BRIGHTON Merseyside.

See WALLASEY.

EC *early closing* **MD** *market day* ♛ *country house hotel* *ns (NS) no smoking areas* *tcf tea/coffee facilities*

NEWBURY Berkshire. Map 5C4

Pop 29,000. Reading 15, London 54, M4 (jn 13) 3½, Andover 16, Basingstoke 16, Marlborough 19, Oxford 26, Winchester 24. **EC** Wed. **MD** Thur, Sat. **Golf** Newbury 18h, Donnington Valley 18h. **See** Church (1510), 16th cent Cloth Hall (now museum). St Bartholomew's Hospital (almshouses), Sandleford Priory, 18th cent bridge.
ℹ The Wharf. ☎(0635) 30267

★★★★ R Foley Lodge, Stockcross, RG16 8JU ☎(0635) 528770
Fax: (0635) 528398

Victorian hunting lodge, modernised and extended, in landscaped grounds off B4000 between Newbury and Hungerford. Indoor swimming pool, snooker. Fr, Es
70 bedrs, 70 en suite; TV; tcf
lift, ns; P 140, coach; no children under 7; con 200
LD 9.30, nr Sun
£ B&B £89–£130, B&B (double) £110–£180; HB weekly £585–£820; L £12·50, D £12·50; WB £57·50 (HB)
cc Access, Amex, B'card/Visa, Diners

★★★★ Regency Park, Bowling Green Rd, Thatcham, RG13 3RP ☎(0635) 71555
Tx: 847844 Fax: (0635) 71571
Four-storey mansion with a large modern extension giving spacious and tastefully furnished accommodation. Set in 5 acres of parkland. Fr
50 bedrs, 50 en suite; TV; tcf
lift, dogs; P 120; child facs; con 65
LD 10.30
£ B&B £79·50–£94·25 (w/e £54), B&B (double) £99–£114·50, L £14·25, D £17·50; WB £49·50; [10% V]
cc Amex, B'card/Visa, Diners.
(*See advertisement on p. 366*)

★★★ Chequers, Oxford St, RG13 1JB
☎(0635) 38000 Fax: (0635) 37170

Former 3-storey coaching inn with later wing. Near town centre. (THF)
56 bedrs, 56 en suite; TV; tcf
dogs, ns; P 60, coach; child facs; con 70
LD 9.45, nr Sat lunch
£ room £76–£82 (w/e £40), double room £92–£102; Bk £7·50, L £11·50, D £14·95; WB £50
cc Access, Amex, B'card/Visa, CB, Diners.

★★★ C Millwaters, London Rd, RG13 2BY ☎(0635) 528838 Tx: 83343
Fax: (0635) 523406
Charming 2-storey Georgian house in lovely grounds with two rivers running by. Fishing.
32 bedrs, 31 en suite, 1 ba; TV; tcf
dogs, ns; P 50, coach; children by arrangement; con 40

★★ Enborne Grange, Essex St, Wash Common, RG14 6RP ☎(0635) 40046
Fax: (0635) 580246
Family-run hotel converted from a private house in 5 acres of attractive gardens. On south-west edge of town. Closed 25 Dec–14 Jan.
25 bedrs, 25 en suite; TV; tcf
TV; P 60, coach; child facs; con 60

★★ Hare & Hounds, Bath Rd, Speen, RG13 1QY ☎(0635) 521152 Tx: 847662

Conveniently situated on A4 west of town, a red-brick 17th-century former coaching inn.
7 bedrs, 7 en suite; annexe 23 bedrs, 23 en suite; TV; tcf
dogs; P 72, coach; child facs

NEWBY BRIDGE Cumbria. Map 36A4

M6 16, London 262, Ambleside 12, Broughton-in-Furness 13, Kendal 15, Kirkby Lonsdale 22, Ulverston 7½.
Golf Ulverston 18h. **See** Stott Park Bobbin Mill, Lakeside–Haverthwaite Rly.

★★★ Lakeside on Windermere, LA12 8AT ☎(053 95) 31207 Tx: 65149 Fax: (053 95) 31699
Impressive buildings beside the pier, with good lake views. Putting.
79 bedrs, 79 en suite; TV; tcf
lift, dogs; P 100, coach; child facs; con 100
LD 9.30, bar meals only Mon–Sat lunch
£ B&B £60–£65, B&B (double) £90–£100; HB weekly £525–£630; L £9.50, D £17·50; WB £45; [10% V]
cc Access, Amex, B'card/Visa, Diners; dep.
(*See advertisement on p. 370*)

★★★ Whitewater, The Lakeland Village, LA12 8PX ☎(053 95) 31133
Fax: (05395) 31881

Very modern hotel in what was the local mill. Swimming pool, putting, tennis, squash, sauna, solarium, gymnasium.
35 bedrs, 35 en suite; TV; tcf
lift; P 50, coach; child facs; con 70
LD 9, bar meals only Mon–Sat lunch
£ B&B £60, B&B (double) £85; D £14·95; WB £36 (HB); [5% V]
cc Access, Amex, B'card/Visa, Diners.

Furness Fells, LA12 8ND ☎(053 95) 31260. *Guest House.*

NEWCASTLE-UNDER-LYME

Staffordshire. Map 30B2
See also ONNELEY
Pop 73,000. Stone 8½, London 149, M6 (jn 15) 2½, Congleton 12, Leek 11, Nantwich 13, Stoke-on-Trent 2.
EC Thur. **MD** Mon, Fri, Sat. **Golf** Newcastle 18h, Wolstanton 18h, Keele 18h. **See** Museum, Guildhall, Castle Mound.
ℹ Library, Ironmarket. ☎(0782) 711964

★★★ Clayton Lodge, Clayton Rd, Clayton, ST5 4AF ☎(0782) 613093
Tx: 36547 Fax: (0782) 711896
Early Victorian building with extensions and conference facilities; M6 nearby. (Emb)
50 bedrs, 50 en suite; TV; tcf
dogs, ns; P 300, G 5, coach; child facs; con 300
LD 9.45
£ B&B £25–£73, B&B (double) £50–£83, L £10·30, D £11·30; WB £32 (HB)
cc Access, Amex, B'card/Visa, CB, Diners.

★★★ Post House, Clayton Rd, ST5 4DL
☎(0782) 717171 Tx: 36531
Fax: (0782) 717138

Modern well-designed hotel set in landscaped gardens. Close to M6. Indoor swimming pool, sauna, solarium, gymnasium. (THF)
126 bedrs, 126 en suite; TV; tcf
dogs, ns; P 150, coach; child facs; con 60
LD 10.30, nr Sat lunch
£ room £72 (w/e £39·50), double room £83; Bk £7·50, L £10·50, D £14·95; WB £41
cc Access, Amex, B'card/Visa, CB, Diners.

★★ Borough Arms, King St, ST5 1HX
☎(0782) 629421 Fax: (0782) 712388

Privately-run hotel in an 18th century listed building. Es
30 bedrs, 30 en suite; annexe 15 bedrs, 15 en suite; TV; tcf
P 40, coach; child facs; con 90
LD 10, bar meals only Sat lunch
£ B&B £43 (w/e £24), B&B (double) £57; L £5·75, D £10·25; WB; [5% V]
cc Access, Amex, B'card/Visa, Diners; dep.

N

Newbury (Berkshire)

★ **Deansfield,** 98 Lancaster Rd, ST5 1DS
(0782) 619040

Small Victorian hotel with garden set in quiet residential area. Fr
6 bedrs, 6 en suite; TV; tcf
TV, dogs, ns; P 35, U 1; child facs; con 30
LD 8.30 Rest lic
£ B&B £27·90 (w/e £19·25), B&B (double) £34 (w/e £32); L £5, D £8·50; WB £16; [5% V]
cc Access, Amex, B'card/Visa, Diners; dep.

NEWCASTLE UPON TYNE Tyne & Wear. Map 37B3
See also GATESHEAD, MARLEY HILL and WALLSEND.
RAC Office, *2 Granville Rd, Jesmond Rd, Newcastle upon Tyne, NE2 1UB.* 091-281 5714
Pop 267,600. Durham 14, London 273, Alnwick 34, Coldstream 60, Corbridge 17, Hawick 62, Jedburgh 57, Sunderland 12. See Plan p. 368.
EC Wed (suburbs) **MD** Tue, Thur, Sat, Sun. **P** See Plan. **Golf** Newcastle United 18h. **See** St Nicholas' Cathedral, St Mary's RC Cathedral, Castle, Civic Centre, Laing Art Gallery, Hancock Museum, Museum of Science and Engineering, John George Joicey Period Museum, Guildhall, Scotswood Bridge, Jesmond Dene.
i Library, Princess Sq. 091-261 0691

★★★★ **Holiday Inn,** Great North Rd, Seaton Burn, NE13 6BP 091-236 5432 Tx: 53271 Fax: 091-236 8091
Modern purpose-built 2-storey hotel, near A1. Indoor swimming pool, sauna, solarium, gymnasium. (CHIC). Fr, De
150 bedrs, 150 en suite; TV; tcf
dogs, ns; P 200, coach; child facs; con 400
LD 10.30
£ B&B £92·30–£108·80 (w/e £41), B&B (double) £118·60–£135·10; L £15·95, D £17; [5% V]
cc Access, Amex, B'card/Visa, CB, Diners.

★★★★ H ★★★ **Swallow Gosforth Park,** High Gosforth Park, Gosforth, NE3 5HN 091 236 4111 Tx: 53655 Fax: 091-236 8192

Modern hotel in grounds adjacent to Racecourse. Indoor swimming pool, tennis, squash, sauna, solarium, gymnasium. (Sw)
178 bedrs, 178 en suite; TV; tcf
lift, dogs, ns; P 300, coach; child facs; con 600
LD 11
£ B&B £98 (w/e £40), B&B (double) £118, L £13·50, D £17·50; WB £135 (HB)
cc Access, Amex, B'card/Visa, Diners

★★★ **Airport Moat House,** (formerly Stakis Airport), Woolsington, NE13 8DJ
Ponteland (0661) 24911 Tx: 537121
Fax: (0661) 860 157

Three-storey brick-built modern hotel within airport area. Many function facilities. (QMH)
100 bedrs, 100 en suite; TV; tcf
life, TV, dogs, ns; P200; coach; child facs; con 400
LD 9.45
£ B&B £45–£75, B&B (double) £55–£85; L £12·95, D £12·95, WB £37·50 (HB); [10% V w/e]
cc Access, Amex, B'card/Visa, CB, Diners.

★★★ C **County Thistle,** Neville St, NE99 1AH 091-232 2471 Tx: 537873 Fax: 091 232 1285

In city centre opposite the station, a modernised Victorian hotel. (MtCh)
115 bedrs, 115 en suite; TV; tcf
lift, dogs, ns; P 25, coach; child facs; con 120
LD 11
£ room £65, double room £75, Bk £7·75, L £8·45, D £12; WB £33
cc Access, Amex, B'card/Visa, CB, Diners.

★★★ **Crest,** New Bridge St, NE1 8BS
091-232 6191 Tx: 53467
Fax: 091-261 8529

Modern brick-built 8-storey hotel in city centre. (Cr/THF)
166 bedrs, 166 en suite; TV; tcf
lift, dogs, ns; G 130, coach; child facs; con 500
LD 10
£ room £74–£87 (w/e £32), double room £86–£99; Bk £7·95, L £12·50, D £14·50; WB £32; [5% V] (w/e only)
cc Access, Amex, B'card/Visa, Diners, dep.

★★★ **Hospitality Inn,** Osborne Rd, NE2 2AT 091-281 7881 Tx: 53636
Fax 091-281 6241

Attractive modernised hotel 1 mile from city centre, Sauna. (MtCh)
89 bedrs, 89 en suite; TV; tcf
lift, ns; P 80, G 5 (£3), coach; child facs; con 120
LD 9.30
£ room £60–£90 (w/e £28), double room £70–£120; Bk £4·50, L £6·75, D £12·75; WB £28; [10% V]
cc Access, Amex, B'card/Visa, CB, Diners.

★★★ **Imperial Swallow,** Jesmond Rd, Jesmond, NE2 1PR 091-281 5511
Tx: 537972 Fax: 091-281 8472

Traditional building efficiently modernised; includes leisure centre and choice of restaurants. Indoor swimming pool, sauna, solarium, gymnasium. (Sw)
129 bedrs, 129 en suite; TV; tcf
lift, dogs, ns; G 130, coach; child facs; con 130
LD 10, nr Sat lunch
£ B&B £65, B&B (double) £75; L £7·50, D £12·50; WB £80 (HB)
cc Access, Amex, B'card/Visa, Diners.

Hotel locations
Hotel locations are shown on the maps at the back of the guide. All towns and villages containing an RAC Appointed or Listed hotel are ringed in purple.

N

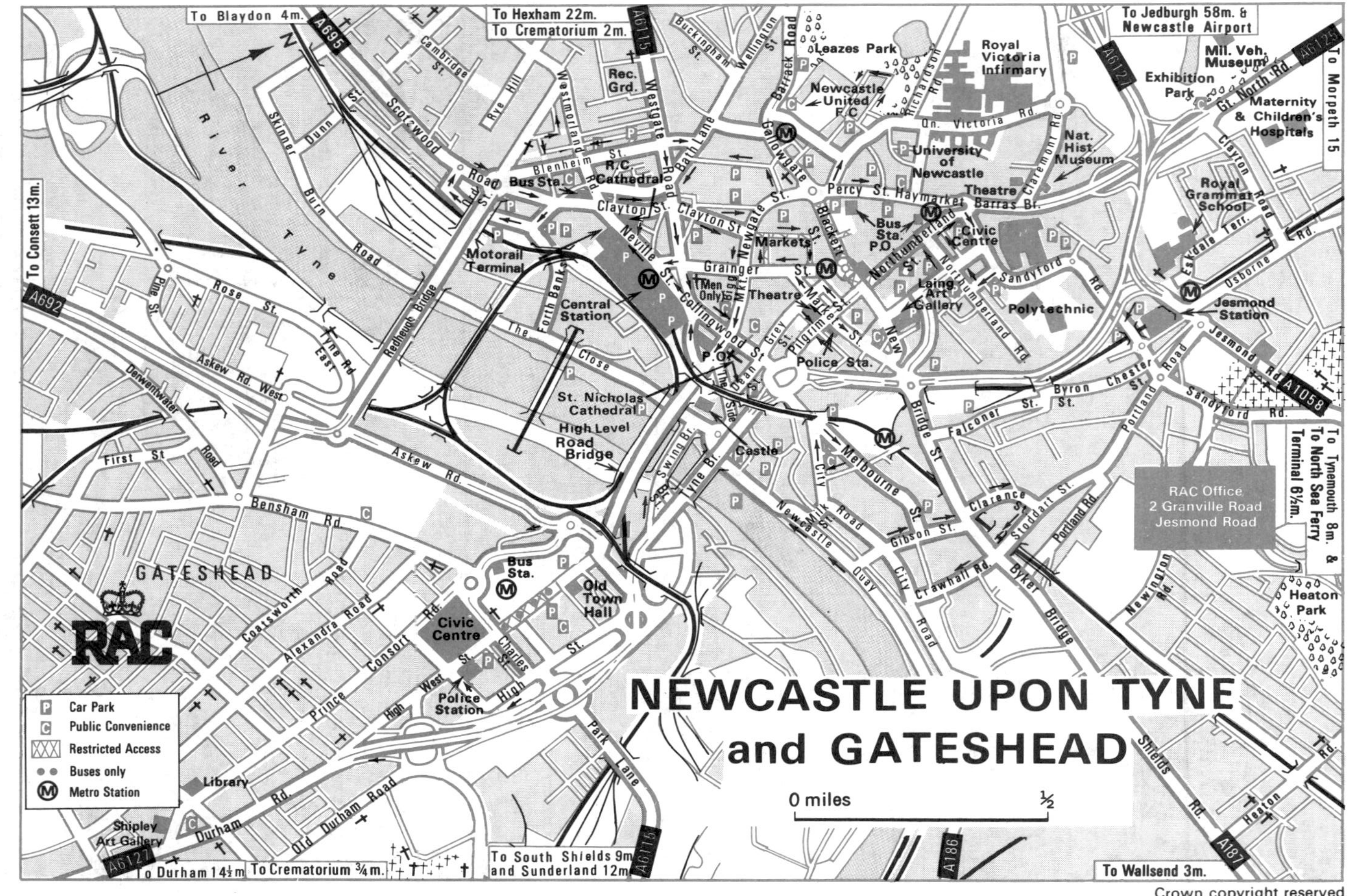

EC *early closing* **MD** *market day* ♣♣ *country house hotel* *ns (NS) no smoking areas* *tcf tea/coffee facilities*

★★★ **Northumbria,** Osborne Rd, Jesmond. NE2 2BR ☎ 091-281 4961 Tx: 53636 Fax: 091-281 6241

Modernised hotel, 1 mile north-east of city centre. Sauna. (MtCh)
🛏 70 bedrs, 70 en suite; TV; tcf
🏨 lift; P40, coach; child facs; con 60
✕ LD 9.30
£ B&B £46·50–£57·50 (w/e £33), B&B (double) £57·50–£67·50; L £6·75, D £12·50; WB £33
cc Access, Amex, B'card/Visa, CB, Diners.

★★★ **Swallow,** Newgate Arcade, NE1 5SX ☎ 091-232 5025 Tx: 538230 Fax: 091-232 8428

Modern city centre hotel near to Newcastle central station. Indoor swimming pool, sauna, solarium, gymnasium. (Sw)
🛏 93 bedrs, 93 en suite; TV; tcf
🏨 lift, dogs, ns; P 120, coach; child facs; con 100

★★ **Cairn,** 97 Osborne Rd, NE2 2TA ☎ 091-281 1358 Fax: 091-281 9031

Converted from a terrace of houses; situated 1 mile from city centre on main road north.
🛏 51 bedrs, 51 en suite; TV; tcf
🏨 dogs; P 20, coach; child facs; con 120
✕ LD 9.15
£ B&B £42–£45 (w/e £23·50), B&B (double) £59·50–£65, L £5·50, D £11; [10% V]
cc Access, Amex, B'card/Visa, Diners; dep.
(*See advertisement on p. 370*)

★★ **Osborne,** 15 Osborne Rd, NE2 2AE ☎ 091-281 3385
Three-storey hotel, in residential area 1 mile from city centre on bus/metro routes.
🛏 26 bedrs, 10 en suite, 4 ba; TV; tcf
🏨 TV, dogs; P 6, U 1 (£1); child facs
✕ LD 8.30, nr lunch. Resid lic
£ B&B £30–£38, B&B (double) £48–£58; D £7·50; WB £20
cc B'card/Visa.

Copthorne, Close Gate, Quayside ☎ (0800) 414741 (central reservations).
Stylish new hotel on the bank of the Tyne in City Centre, opening February 1991. Indoor swimming pool, sauna, solarium, gymnasium.
🛏 156 beds, 156 en suite; TV; tcf
🏨 lift, dogs, ns; P160, coach; child facs, con 220
✕ LD 10.30
£ room £90–£100; Bk £7·50, L £10, D £12·50; WB
cc Access, Amex, B'card/Visa, CB, Diners; dep.

Novotel, Ponteland Rd, Kenton NE3 3HZ ☎ 091-214 0303 Tx: 53675 Fax: 091-214 0633 ♿
New hotel north west of city next to western by-pass. Hotel awaiting inspection. Indoor swimming pool, sauna.
🛏 126 bedrs, 126 en suite; TV; tcf
£ room £56 (w/e £35), double room £60 (w/e £50); Bk £6·50

Chirton House (Acclaimed), 46 Clifton Rd, NE4 6XH ☎ 091-273 0407. *Hotel.*
£ B&B £20–£30; HB weekly £170–£230; [5% V]

Portland, 134 Sandyford Rd, NE2 1DD ☎ 091-232 7868. *Guest House.*

NEWHAVEN East Sussex. Map 6C1

Pop 11,000. Lewes 6½, London 58, Brighton 8, Eastbourne 12.
EC Wed. **See** St Michael's Church, Fort (incl. Museum).

Old Volunteer, 1 South Rd, BN9 9QL ☎ (0273) 515204. *Guest House.* Closed 22–31 Dec. ♿
£ B&B £16·50–£30

NEWINGREEN Kent. Map 7B2

Ashford 8½, London 64, M20 (jn 11) 1, Canterbury 14, Folkestone 6½, Rye 20, Tenterden 16.
Golf Sene Valley 18h, Hythe 9h.

★★ **Royal Oak,** Ashford Rd, CT21 4JA ☎ Hythe (0303) 264663

Situated on main A20, refurbished period inn with motel block adjoining. (BCB)

🛏 28 bedrs, 28 en suite; TV; tcf
🏨 ns; P 150, coach; child facs; con 20+

NEWLYN Cornwall

See PENZANCE

NEWMARKET Suffolk. Map 26C3

See also SIX MILE BOTTOM.
Pop 16,650 (inc Exning). Bishop's Stortford 32, London 63, Bury St Edmunds 14, Cambridge 13, Ely 13, Thetford 18.
EC Wed. **MD** Tue, Sat. **Golf** Links 18h. **See** Devil's Dyke' (prehistoric earthworks), Cooper Memorial, Nell Gwynne's House, racecourses.

★★★ **Newmarket Moat House,** Moulton Rd, CB8 8DY ☎ (0638) 667171 Fax: (0638) 666533 ♿

Well-adapted modern building, originally flats. Adjoins town and Heath. (QMH). Fr, It
🛏 45 bedrs, 45 en suite; TV; tcf
🏨 lift, TV, dogs; P 50, G 10, coach; child facs; con 120
✕ LD 9.45, bar meals only Sat lunch
£ B&B £65–£85, B&B (double) £85–£95; L £15, D £15; WB £40 (HB)
cc Access, Amex, B'card/Visa, Diners.

★★★ **Rutland Arms,** High St, CB8 8NB ☎ (0638) 664251 Tx: 329265 Fax: (0638) 666298
Former coaching inn with modern residential wings. In town centre.
🛏 45 bedrs, 45 en suite; TV; tcf
🏨 dogs; P 50, coach; child facs; con 90
✕ LD 9
£ B&B £49–£55, B&B (double) £59·50 (w/e £40); L £9·85, D £9·85; WB £39·50 (HB); [10% V]
cc Access, Amex, B'card/Visa, Diners.

★★★ **White Hart,** High St, CB8 8JP ☎ (0638) 663051 Fax: (0638) 667284

Attractive gabled modern hotel in town centre. Associations with horse racing.
🛏 23 bedrs, 23 en suite; TV; tcf
🏨 dogs; P 60, coach; child facs; con 120

★★ **Bedford Lodge**, Bury Rd, CB8 7BX ☎ (0638) 663175
Pleasing white 18th century building in mature gardens one mile north of town centre. Some bedrooms in attractive converted stable courtyard.

N

Windermere (Cumbria)

Newcastle upon Tyne (Tyne & Wear)

🛏 11 bedrs, 11 en suite; annexe 7 bedrs, 7 en suite; TV; tcf

NEW MILTON Hampshire. Map 5B1

Pop 18,300. Lyndhurst 10, London 94, Bournemouth 11, Lymington 6.
EC Wed. **Golf** Barton-on-Sea 18h. **See** 16th cent Parish Church.

★★★★ Chewton Glen, Christchurch Rd, BH25 6QS ☎ Highcliffe (0425) 275341 Tx: 41456 Fax: (0425) 272310 ♿

Elegant country house–a luxury hotel surrounded by woodland. Indoor & outdoor swimming pools, golf, putting, tennis, sauna, solarium, gymnasium, billiards. Fr, De, It, Es, Ja, Da
🛏 56 bedrs, 56 en suite; TV
P 100; no children under 7; con 80
✕ LD 9.30
£ B&B (double) £187–£440; L £22, D £42
cc Access, Amex, B'card/Visa, CB, Diners.

NEWPORT Gloucestershire. Map 20B1

Pop 250. Tetbury 14, London 112, M5 (jn 14) 3½, Bristol 19, Gloucester 16.
Golf Stinchcombe Hill 18h. **See** Dissenters Chapel.

★★ Newport Towers, GL13 9PX ☎ Dursley (0453) 810575 Fax: (0222) 704785
Modern, purpose built motel on main A38, privately owned. Sauna, solarium, gymnasium.
🛏 56 bedrs, 56 en suite; TV; tcf
dogs; P 250, coach; child facs; con 240

NEWPORT Shropshire. Map 30A1

Pop 9,000. Wolverhampton 18, London 142, Newcastle-under-Lyme 20, Shrewsbury 18, Stafford 12, Whitchurch 21.
EC Thur. **MD** Mon, Fri, Sat. **Golf** Lilleshall 18h. **See** 12th cent St Nicholas Church, 13th cent Pulestone Cross, Old Guildhall.
ℹ 9 St Mary's St. ☎ (0952) 814109

★★ Royal Victoria, St Marys St, TF10 7AB ☎ (0952) 820331 Fax: (0952) 820209

Refurbished Victorian hotel conveniently situated in town centre.
🛏 24 bedrs, 24 en suite; TV; tcf
dogs, ns; P80; child facs; con 110
✕ LD 9.30, bar meals only Sun dinner
£ B&B £46·75 (w/e £20), B&B (double) £63·80; L £10·55, D £10·55; WB £26
cc Access, Amex, B'card/Visa

NEWPORT PAGNELL

Buckinghamshire. Map 21B3
See also MILTON KEYNES.
Pop 10,670. London 52, M1 (jn 14) 2½, Bedford 12, Bletchley 6½, Buckingham 14, Northampton 15, Towcester 14.
EC Thur. **Golf** Abbey Hill 18h.

★★★ Coach House, London Rd, Moulsoe, MK16 0JA ☎ (0908) 613688 Tx: 825341 Fax: (0908) 617335 ♿
A Georgian coach house extended in keeping round a courtyard. Next to a farm on A509, one mile from M1. Sauna, solarium, gymnasium. (Lns)
🛏 49 bedrs, 49 en suite; TV, tcf
ns; P 160, coach; child facs, con 220
✕ LD 10; bar meals only Sat lunch
£ B&B £75–£90 (w/e £28), B&B (double) £90; L £10·25, D £14·75; WB £35
cc Access, Amex, B'card/Visa, Diners.

★★ Swan Revived, High St, MK16 8AR ☎ (0908) 610565 Tx: 826801 Fax: (0908) 210995

Privately-owned, 15th century former coaching inn, situated in town centre. It, Es
🛏 40 bedrs, 40 en suite; TV; tcf
lift, dogs; P 15, G 3, coach; child facs; con 80
✕ LD 10
£ B&B £25–£56 (w/e £19); B&B (double) £40–£60; L £10, D £10
cc Access, Amex, B'card/Visa, Diners.

Thurstons, 90 High St, MK16 8EH ☎ (0908) 611377. *Private Hotel.*
£ B&B £25–£38 ♿

NEWQUAY Cornwall. Map 2B2

Pop 15,465. Bodmin 18, London 252, Redruth 15, St Austell 14, Truro 18, Wadebridge 14.
EC Wed (win). **Golf** Newquay 18h.
ℹ Cliff Rd. ☎ (0637) 871345

★★★ Barrowfield, Hilgrove Rd, TR7 2QY ☎ (0637) 878878 Fax: (0637) 879490
Large 4-storey modern hotel just off the seafront. Indoor/outdoor swimming pool, sauna, solarium, gymnasium, billiards.
🛏 81 bedrs, 81 en suite; TV; tcf
lift, TV, dogs; P 50, G 14, coach; child facs; con 100
✕ LD 8.30, nr Mon–Sat lunch. Resid & Rest lic
£ B&B £33–£39; HB weekly £141–£272; D £11; WB £69
cc Access, B'card/Visa; dep.

★★★ Bristol, Narrowcliff, TR7 2PQ ☎ (0637) 875181 Fax: (0637) 879347

Large building with distinctive turrets–a family-run hotel overlooking beach. Indoor swimming pool, sauna, solarium, billiards.
De
🛏 83 bedrs, 66 en suite, 16 ba; TV
lift, TV, dogs; P 100, U 5, coach; child facs; con 150
✕ LD 8.30
£ B&B £42–£46, B&B (double) £68–£82; HB weekly £343–£679; L £9·50, D £15; WB £80
cc Access, Amex, B'card/Visa, Diners; dep.

★★★ Edgcumbe, Narrowcliff, TR7 2RR ☎ (0637) 872061 Fax: (0637) 879490

Four-storey white hotel with fine sea views. Offers entertainment programme. Indoor/ outdoor swimming pools, sauna, solarium.
🛏 86 bedrs, 86 en suite; TV; tcf
lift, TV, dogs; P 60, coach; child facs
✕ LD 8.30, nr lunch. Resid & Rest lic
£ B&B £27·60; HB weekly £138–£169·05; [5% V]
cc Access, B'card/Visa; dep.

★★★ Euro, 9 Esplanade Rd, Pentire, TR7 1PS ☎ (0637) 873333 Fax: (0637) 878717

Large white-painted hotel overlooking Fistral beach. Night club on lower ground floor. Swimming pool, sauna, solarium.
🛏 76 bedrs, 76 en suite, 2 ba; TV; tcf
lift, dogs; P36, coach; child facs; con 100
✕ LD 8.30, bar meals only lunch
£ B&B £22–£46, B&B (double) £40–£88, HB weekly £148–£289; D £13·50; [10% V]; dep.
(*See advertisement on p. 372*)

N

Newquay (Cornwall)

All 76 rooms en suite, colour satellite TV, baby listening, direct dial telephones.
•
Many family rooms. Children's creche & playground.
•
Outdoor & heated indoor pool, spa, sauna, solarium.
•
Cocktail bar with sun patio.
•
Disco and live entertainment.
•
Excellent food. Vegetarians catered for.
•
Lift, full central heating, ample parking.
•
Christmas, New Year and Easter Programme.

Directly overlooking beautiful Fistral Bay, Newquay

The Euro is set in a magnificent position. The rolling surf and golden sands extend for nearly a mile in front of the hotel. As you enter the reception, you will know this hotel is where your comfort matters – you can relax in a happy, cheerful atmosphere, surrounded by a wide range of amenities to make your stay enjoyable.
•
Write or telephone NOW for Brochure & Tariff.

ESPLANADE ROAD · PENTIRE
NEWQUAY · CORNWALL TR7 1PS
•
TELEPHONE: (0637) 873333

Tariff: Wkly £148-289 also 2, 3, 4 day breaks. D, B & B or B & B

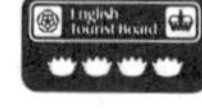

★★★ **Kilbirnie,** Narrowcliff, TR7 2RS
☎(0637) 875155

Three-storey cliff-top building with excellent sea views. Easy access to beach. Indoor swimming pool, sauna, solarium, billiards.
🛏 73 bedrs, 73 en suite; TV; tcf
🏨 lift dogs; P 60, G 10, coach; child facs; con 180
✕ LD 8.30, bar meals only lunch
£ B&B £25; D 10·50
cc Access, B'card/Visa.

★★★ **Riviera,** Lusty Glaze Rd, TR7 3AA
☎(0637) 874251 Tx: 42513

Owner-run cliff-top hotel set in grounds. Swimming pool, squash, sauna, billiards.
🛏 50 bedrs, 50 en suite; TV
🏨 lift, TV, dogs; P 60, coach; child facs; con 100
✕ LD 8.30
£ B&B £34·75–£41·75, B&B (double) £65–£79·50; L £7·50, D £12·50; WB £55; [5% V]
cc Access, Amex, B'card/Visa; dep.

★★★ **St Brannocks,** Narrowcliff Promenade, TR7 2PN ☎(0637) 872038
Four-storey hotel in commanding position with magnificent seascape views. Indoor swimming pool, sauna, solarium.

★★★ **Trebarwith,** Trebarwith Cres, TR7 1BZ ☎(0637) 872288
Cliff-top hotel with subtropical secluded gardens and commanding sea views. Indoor swimming pool, fishing, sauna, solarium, billiards. Open 28 Mar–2 Nov.
⚒ Fr
🛏 42 bedrs, 42 en suite; TV; tcf
🏨 TV, P 40, coach; child facs
✕ LD 8.30, bar meals only lunch. Resid & Rest lic
£ B&B £27–£39·50, B&B (double) £46–£79; HB weekly £161–£276·50; D £12
cc Access, B'card/Visa; dep.

★★★ **Windsor,** Mount Wise, TR7 2AY
☎(0637) 875188
Large hotel with modern extension. Secluded sun trap garden. Indoor and outdoor swimming pools, putting, squash, sauna, solarium, gymnasium.

★★ **Beachcroft,** Cliff Rd, TR7 1SW
☎(0637) 873022 ♿
Large hotel in 2½ cliff-top acres; private steps to beach. Swimming pool, putting, tennis, sauna, solarium.
🛏 69 bedrs, 60 en suite, (5 sh), 3 ba; TV; tcf
🏨 lift, TV, dogs; P 70, coach; child facs

★★ **Bewdley,** Pentire Rd, TR7 1NX
☎(0637) 872883
Modern owner-run hotel in outskirts. Overlooks Fistral Beach. Swimming pool.

★★ **Corisande Manor,** Riverside Av, Pentire, TR7 1PL ☎(0637) 872042

Hotel of unique turreted design; in secluded grounds by tidal estuary. Putting, solarium. Open 11 May–12 Oct.
🛏 11 bedrs, 9 en suite, 3 ba; annexe 8 bedrs, 6 en suite, 4 ba; TV; tcf
🏨 dogs; P 19; no children under 3
✕ LD 8, bar meals only lunch. Resid & Rest lic
£ B&B £15–£23·50; HB weekly £120–£165; D £10; WB £38
cc Access, B'card/Visa; dep.

★★ **Cross Mount,** Church St, St Columb Minor, TR7 3EX ☎(0637) 872669
Charming 2-storey white-painted 17th century building with beamed restaurant.

★★ **Great Western,** Cliff Rd, TR7 2PT
☎(0637) 872010 ♿
Imposing white building convenient for town and enjoying fine sea views. Indoor swimming pool, sauna, solarium.
🛏 72 bedrs, 72 en suite; TV; tcf
🏨 lift, dogs; P 40, U 10, coach; child facs; con 60

★★ **Newgarth,** Narrowcliff, TR7 2PG
☎(0637) 873250
A four-storey, stone-built hotel, a short way from the town centre.
🛏 49 bedrs, 32 en suite, 4 ba; TV; tcf

★★ **Porth Veor Manor,** Porth Way, St Columb Porth, TR7 3LW ☎(0637) 873274

Small hotel with manor house appearance. Fine sea views. Putting, tennis.

★★ **Sandy Lodge,** Hillgrove Rd, TR7 2QY
☎(0637) 872851
Owner-run pleasant hotel conveniently situated by the sea front. Indoor & outdoor swimming pools, sauna, solarium, billiards.

★★ **Tregurrian,** Watergate Bay, TR8 4AB
☎St Mawgan (0637) 860280
Attractive white building 100 yards from a mile-long sandy beach. Swimming pool, solarium.

★★ **Waters Edge,** Esplanade Rd, Pentire, TR7 1QA ☎(0637) 872048
Small hotel in own grounds. Picture windows give panoramic sea views. Open May–15 Oct.
🛏 18 bedrs, 17 en suite, 2 ba; TV; tcf
🏨 P 18; child facs
✕ LD 8. Resid & Rest lic
£ B&B £22·50–£35; HB weekly £175–£250; [5% V excl. Aug]
cc Access, B'card/Visa; dep.

Porth Enodoc (Highly Acclaimed), 4 Esplanade Rd, Pentire, TR7 1PY ☎(0637) 872372. *Private Hotel.* Open Easter–30 Oct.
£ B&B £15·50–£18; HB weekly £106–£146; [5% V Easter–27 May & 20 Sept–31 Oct]

Arundell, 86 Mount Wise, TR7 2BS ☎(0637) 872481. *Hotel. Indoor swimming pool, billiards, sauna, solarium.*
Copper Beech, 70 Edgcumbe Av, TR7 2NN ☎(0637) 873993 [changing to (0637) 850626]. *Hotel.* Open Easter–Oct.
£ B&B £16·10–£18·40; HB weekly £126·50–£160
Fistral Beach, Esplanade Rd, Pentire, TR7 1QA ☎(0637) 850626. *Hotel. Indoor swimming pool, billiards.* Open Feb–Nov & Xmas. ⚒ Fr
£ B&B £25–£35; HB weekly £140–£160.
Jonel, 88–90 Crantock St, TR7 1JW ☎(0637) 875084. *Hotel.*
Kellsboro, 12 Henver Rd, TR7 3BJ ☎(0637) 874620. *Hotel. Indoor swimming pool.*
Links, Headland Rd, TR7 1HN ☎(0637) 873211
Pendeen, 7 Alexandra Rd, Porth, TR7 3ND ☎(0637) 873521. *Private Hotel.*
Philema, Esplanade Rd, Pentire, TR7 1PY ☎(0637) 872571. Fax: (0637) 873188. *Hotel. Indoor swimming pool, sauna, solarium.*
£ B&B £18·50–£28; HB weekly £120–£190.
Priory Lodge, 30 Mount Wise, TR7 2BH ☎(0637) 874111. *Hotel. Swimming pool, sauna, solarium.*
Quies, 84 Mount Wise, TR7 2BS ☎(0637) 872924. *Private Hotel.* Open Mar–Dec.
£ B&B £14–£22; HB weekly £115·50–£163·50; [10% V excl. Jul & Aug]
Rolling Waves, Alexandra Rd, Porth, TR7 3NB ☎(0637) 873236. *Private Hotel.* Closed Xmas.
£ B&B £19·20–£22·65 (w/e £37·96); HB weekly £138–£160; WB £37·96; [5% V excl. Jul–Sep]
Wheal Treasure, 72 Edgcumbe Av, TR7 2NN ☎(0637) 874136. *Guest House.*
Windward, Alexandra Rd, Porth, TR7 3NB ☎(0637) 873185. *Private Hotel.* Open Easter–Oct
£ B&B £15–£25; HB weekly £133–£210; [5% V May & June, Sept & Oct]

NEW ROMNEY Kent. Map 7B2

Pop 4,100. Tenterden 15, London 69, Ashford 14, Folkestone 14, Hastings 24. EC Wed. **Golf** Littlestone 18h.

N

★ **Broadacre,** North St, TN28 8DR (0679) 62381

Small hotel in Georgian house set in a quiet back street.
10 bedrs, 4 en suite, 3 ba; TV; tcf
dogs; P 10, coach; child facs

NEWTON ABBOT Devon. Map 3C2

Pop 20,500. London 183, Ashburton 7½, Exeter 15, Torquay 6, Totnes 8.
EC Thur. **MD** Wed, Sat. **Golf** Newton Abbot (Stover) 18h.
8 Sherborne Rd. (0626) 67494

★★★ **Passage House,** Hackney La, Kingsteignton, TQ12 3QH (0626) 55515 Fax: (0626) 63336

New hotel, cream painted with a pitched roof, in a stunning position overlooking the Teign estuary. Indoor swimming pool, fishing, sauna, solarium, gymnasium.
39 bedrs, 39 en suite; TV; tcf
lift, dogs; P 200, coach; child facs; con 150
LD 9.30. Resid & Rest lic
£ B&B £55–£65, B&B (double) £85–£95; L £8·50, D £13·75; WB £45; [10% V w/e]
cc Access, Amex, B'card/Visa, Diners; dep.
(See advertisement on p. 375)

★★ R **Queen's,** Queen St, TQ12 2EZ (0626) 63133 Fax: (0626) 55179
Privately-owned, stone-built Victorian hotel opposite station and motorail terminus.
24 bedrs, 20 en suite, 2 ba; TV; tcf
dogs, P 10, coach; child facs; con 125
LD 8.30, nr Mon–Sat lunch & Sun dinner
£ B&B £42, B&B (double) £56; HB weekly £379·75; L £4·95, D £12·25; WB £66; [5% V]
(See advertisement on p. 375)

Hazelwood House (Acclaimed), 33a Torquay Rd, TQ12 2LW (0626) 66130. *Private Hotel.*
£ B&B £25–£33; [10% V]

Lamorna, Ideford Coombe, TQ13 0AR (0626) 65627. *Guest House. Indoor swimming pool.*
£ B&B £16–£18

NEWTON AYCLIFFE Durham. Map 45A1

A1(M) 2, London 251, Barnard Castle 20, Darlington 7, Durham 11, Stockton-on-Tees 15.

★★★ **Redworth Hall,** Redworth, DL5 6NL (0388) 772442 Fax: (0338) 775112

Extended, stone-built, 17th-century manor house in 25 acres of parkland in rural area. Swimming pool, squash, sauna, solarium, gymnasium, billards. Fr
100 bedrs, 100 en suite; TV; tcf
lift, dogs, ns; P100, coach; child facs; con 300
LD 10
£ B&B £64·50–£69·50 (w/e £38), B&B (double) £76·50–£81·50 (w/e £33); L £8·95, D £12·95; WB £45 (HB); [10% V] (w/e only)
cc Access, Amex, B'card/Visa, Diners.

NEWTON FERRERS Devon. Map 3B1

Pop 1609. Ashburton 21, London 208, Kingsbridge 16, Plymouth 10, Totnes 19.
Golf Staddon Heights 18h.

★★ **River Yealm,** Yealm Rd, PL8 1BL Plymouth (0752) 872419
Attractive building set in gardens beside estuary. Own quay.
19 bedrs, 5 en suite, (4 sh), 3 ba; tcf
TV, dogs; P 60, U 1, coach; child facs; con 60
LD 8.30, bar meals only lunch
£ B&B £25, B&B (double) £45; D £10.

NEWTON SOLNEY Derbyshire.
See BURTON-UPON-TRENT

NEWTOWN LINFORD Leicestershire. Map 25B3

Pop 1200. M1 (jn 22) 3, Leicester 6½, London 104, Burton-on-Trent 26, Nottingham 25, Peterborough 47.
Golf Nanpantan 18h, Rothley 18h. **See** Bradgate Park, All Saints Church.

★★ **Johnscliffe,** 73 Main St, LE6 0AF Markfield (0530) 242228
A small country hotel with restaurant. Closed 24 Dec–4 Jan.
15 bedrs, 9 en suite, (1 sh); TV; tcf
TV, dogs; P 50, coach; child facs; con 25
LD 9.30, nr Sat lunch. Rest lic
£ B&B £30·50–£36·50 (w/e £24·50), B&B (double) £49·50–£59·50; L £7, D £10·50
cc Access, Amex, B'card/Visa; dep.

NIDD North Yorkshire. Map 38B3

Harrogate 5, London 209, Knaresborough 6, Ripon 8, Skipton 23.

★★★★ H C **Nidd Hall,** nr Harrogate, HG3 3BN (0423) 771598
Listed Victorian Yorkstone mansion in fine terraced gardens. Luxuriously furnished and with a wealth of fine architectural features. Indoor swimming pool, tennis, squash, sauna, solarium, gymnasium.
38 bedrs, 38 en suite; annexe 4 bedrs, 4 en suite; TV
£ B&B £85–£145, B&B (double) £125–£145; L £14, D £22

NINFIELD East Sussex. Map 7A1

Battle 5, London 62, Bexhill 5½, Eastbourne 11, Hailsham 8.

Moonshill Farm, The Green, TN33 9LN (0424) 892645

NORMAN CROSS Cambridgeshire. Map 31C1

Pop 12,000. Alconbury 8, London 77, Kettering 22, Peterborough 5½, Stamford 13.
Golf Peterborough 18h. **See** Elton Hall, Iron Post in Holme Fen.

★★★ **Crest,** Great North Rd, PE7 3TB Peterborough (0733) 240209 Tx: 32576 Fax: (0733) 244455

Large modern motor hotel conveniently situated alongside A1 and A15. (THF)
Fr, It
96 bedrs, 96 en suite; TV; tcf
dogs, ns; P 130; child facs; con 35
LD 10
£ B&B £73–£86 (w/e £41, HB), B&B (double) £93–£105; L £9·25, D £12·95
cc Access, Amex, B'card/Visa, CB, Diners.

NORTHALLERTON North Yorkshire. Map 45A1

Pop 10,300. Boroughbridge 19, London 227, Darlington 16, Leyburn 18, Stockton-on-Tees 19, Thirsk 9½.
EC Thur. **MD** Wed, Sat. **Golf** Thirsk and Northallerton 9h. **See** Church (12th–14th cent), Porch House (1584), Market Cross.
The Applegarth (0609) 776864

★★★ **Solberge Hall,** Newby Wiske, DL7 9ER (0609) 779191

Substantial stone-built Victorian country mansion situated in parkland. Billiards.
30 bedrs, 30 en suite; TV
dogs, ns; P 100, coach; child facs; con 100

★★★ **Sundial,** Darlington Rd, DL6 2PN (0609) 780525 Fax: (0609) 780491
Two-storey modern hotel in 3½ acres of grounds on A167, ½ mile from town centre.
28 bedrs, 28 en suite; TV; tcf
dogs, ns; P 100; coach; child facs; con 150
(See advertisement on p. 375)

Newton Abbot (Devon)

Queens Street · Newton Abbot · Devon TQ12 2EZ Telephone: (0626) 63133

The Queens Hotel, situated adjacent to Courtney Park offers 26 comfortably furnished bedrooms, en-suite, all with colour TV, tea making facilities and direct dial telephones.

The Queens Restaurant is open to residents and non residents and offers table d'hôte and à la carte menus.

The Queens Hotel is situated halfway between Dartmoor and the English Riviera, making it an ideal situation for touring.

Newton Abbot (Devon)

PASSAGE HOUSE

HOTEL

Newton Abbot, Devon TQ12 3QH
Tel 0626 55515 Fax 0626 63336

DEVON'S NEW HOTEL

- ★ 40 luxurious bedrooms
- ★ Superb in-house leisure complex
- ★ Excellent cuisine & service
- ★ Idyllic Riverside setting
- ★ Extra Special Break prices

Northallerton (North Yorkshire)

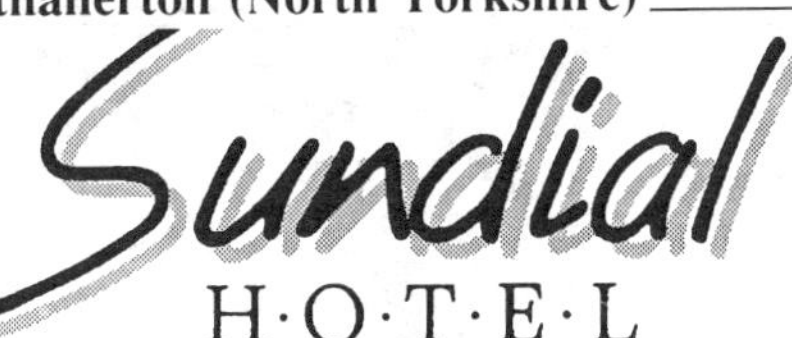

SUNDIAL HOTEL
NORTHALLERTON
North Yorkshire, DL6 2XF

Telephone (0609) 780525 Fax (0609) 780491

In Herriot country, yet close to Teesside, A peaceful Hotel with all executive guest rooms. Purpose built Conference and Banquet Centre. 24 hour service. Full facilities for Handicapped.

NEW FOR 1991

RAC Guide to Small Hotels, Guest Houses & Inns

- full details of over 2,000 RAC approved establishments
- pictures of Highly Acclaimed and Acclaimed hotels
- colour section of regional award winners

Great Value! — only £4.95

N

★★ **Golden Lion,** Market Pl, DL7 8PP
☎(0609) 777411

A 17th century building in centre of pleasant market town. (THF)
🛏 28 bedrs, 15 en suite, 3 ba; TV; tcf
🏨 TV, dogs, ns; P 100, coach; child facs; con 150
✕ LD 9.30
£ room £65 (w/e £45), double room £81, HB weekly £315; Bk £7, L £8, D £12·50; WB £45
cc Access, Amex, B'card/Visa, CB, Diners.

Alverton (Acclaimed), 26 South Par, DL7 8SG ☎(0609) 776207. *Guest House.*
£ B&B £16; HB weekly £145; [5% V]; dep.

Station, 2 Boroughbridge Rd, DL7 8AN ☎(0609) 772053. *Hotel.*
Windsor, 56 South Par, DL7 8SL ☎(0609) 774100. *Guest House.* Closed 25 Dec–4 Jan. ✗ Fr, De
£ B&B £18; dep.

NORTHAMPTON Northamptonshire.

Map 21B3
Pop 162,200 (inc Weston Favell). M1 (jn 15) 4, London 66, Bedford 22, Buckingham 21, Daventry 12, Kettering 14, Market Harborough 17, Rugby 20, Towcester 8½.
EC Thur. **MD** Wed, Fri, Sat. **Golf** Northampton 18h. **See** Abingdon Park Museum, Church of Holy Sepulchre (12th cent interior, rare round church), St John's Church (former medieval Hospital), Museum and Art Gallery, County Hall, Guildhall, Queen Eleanor Cross 2 m S, Althorp House 5 m NW.
ℹ 21 St Giles St. ☎(0604) 22677

★★★★ **Swallow,** Eagle Dr, NN4 0HW
☎(0604) 768700 Tx: 31562
Fax: (0604) 769011 ♿

An ultra-modern hotel in landscaped grounds overlooking a lake. Indoor swimming pool, sauna, solarium, gymnasium.
🛏 122 bedrs, 122 en suite; TV; tcf
🏨 dogs, ns; P 200, coach; child facs; con 200
✕ LD 10
£ B&B £75, B&B (double) £95; L £11·25, D £12·50; WB £90 (2 nts HB)
cc Access, Amex, B'card/Visa, Diners.

★★★ **Grand,** 15 Gold St, NN1 1RE
☎(0604) 250511 Tx: 311198
Fax: (0604) 234534
Red brick building situated in town centre. Privately-owned.
🛏 62 bedrs, 62 en suite; TV; tcf
🏨 lift, dogs; P 65, G 10; coach; child facs; con 120
✕ LD 9.30
£ B&B £50–£55, B&B (double) £60–£65; L £7·50, D £10; WB £30; [10% V]
cc Amex, B'card/Visa, Diners.

★★★ **Heyford Manor,** Flore, NN7 4LP
☎Weedon (0327) 349022 Tx: 312437
Fax: (0327) 349017 ♿

Long, low modern hotel in rural surroundings 1 mile from jn 16 of M1. Sauna, gymnasium. ✗ Fr. (Lns)
🛏 56 bedrs, 56 en suite; TV; tcf
🏨 ns; P 100, coach; child facs; con 60
✕ LD 10; bar meals only Sat lunch
£ B&B £76, B&B (double) £88; L £12, D £16·25; [10% V]
cc Access, Amex, B'card/Visa, Diners; dep.

★★★ **Northampton Moat House,** Silver St, NN1 2TA ☎(0604) 22441 Tx: 311142
Fax: (0604) 230614

Large, modern purpose-built hotel in town centre. Conference facilities. Sauna. (QMH)
✗ Fr, De, It
🛏 140 bedrs, 140 en suite; TV; tcf
🏨 lift, dogs, ns; P 150, coach; child facs; con 500
✕ LD 10.30
£ B&B £64·50 (w/e £34), B&B (double) £79·50; L £10·50, D £12; WB
cc Access, Amex, B'card/Visa, CB, Diners.

★★★ **Westone Moat House,** Ashley Way, NN3 3EA (Weston Favell 3 m E A45)
☎(0604) 406262 Tx: 312587
Fax: (0604) 415023

Large and handsome house with modern extensions. Putting, sauna, solarium, gymnasium. (QMH). Closed 27 Dec–1 Jan.
✗ Es
🛏 66 bedrs, 66 en suite; TV; tcf
🏨 lift, TV, dogs, ns; P 100, coach; child facs; con 150
✕ LD 9.45
£ B&B £64 (w/e £25), B&B (double) £74; L £9·50, D £10·50
cc Access, B'card/Visa, Diners.

★★ **Lime Trees,** 8 Langham Pl, Barrack Rd, NN1 6AA ☎(0604) 32188
Fax: (0604) 233012
Originally two Victorian terrace houses; additional accommodation in converted mews. On A508 not far from city centre.
🛏 17 bedrs, 16 en suite, 2 ba; annexe 2 bedrs, 2 en suite; TV; tcf
🏨 TV, dogs; P 21, G 2; child facs; con 16

★★ **Queen Eleanor,** London Rd, Wootton, NN4 0JJ ☎(0604) 762468

A 1930s pub with modern bedroom accommodation set in a large garden. 1 mile from junction 15 of M1. (BCB)
🛏 19 bedrs, 19 en suite; TV; tcf
🏨 ns; P 120, coach; child facs; con 50
✕ LD 10
£ B&B £53, B&B (double) £60·50; L £8·15, D £8·15; WB £27·50
cc Access, Amex, B'card/Visa, Diners.

★ **Fish Inn,** 11 Fish St, NN1 2AA
☎(0604) 234040

Town-centre hotel, originally an inn in the town's fish market.
🛏 12 bedrs, 2 en suite (8 sh), 2 ba; TV; tcf
🏨 P 3, coach; child facs; con
✕ LD 10
£ B&B £32–£42, B&B (double) £46–£58; L £8·15, D £8·15; WB £27·50
cc Access, Amex, B'card/Visa, Diners.

Poplars (Acclaimed), Cross St, Moulton, NN3 1RZ ☎(0604) 643983. *Private Hotel.*
£ B&B £16–£30 (w/e £16); WB £16; [5% V w/d]

Simpson's, 13 Leicester Par, Barrack Rd, NN2 6AA ☎(0604) 32127. *Private Hotel.*

NORTHBOURNE Dorset.

See BOURNEMOUTH.

EC *early closing* **MD** *market day* ♣ *country house hotel* *ns (NS) no smoking areas* *tcf tea/coffee facilities*

NORTH BOVEY Devon. Map 3B2

Pop 620. Moretonhampstead 1½, London 184, Bovey Tracey 7½, Exeter 14, Okehampton 14, Plymouth 27.

Blackaller House (Acclaimed), TQ13 8QY ☎Moretonhampstead (0647) 40322 *Guest House*. Open Apr–Oct.
£ B&B £17–£20; [10% V]

NORTHLEACH Gloucestershire. Map 20C2

Pop 1,043. Burford 9, London 75, Cheltenham 13. Cirencester 10, Gloucester 20, Stow-on-the-Wold 9.
EC Wed. **Golf** Burford 18h.
ℹ Cotswold Countryside Collection. ☎(0451) 60715

★ **Wheatsheaf,** West End, GL54 3EZ ☎Cotswold (0451) 60244

Small 2-storey Cotswold stone hotel situated in centre of town.
🛏 9 bedrs, 6 en suite, (1 sh), 1 ba; TV; tcf
🏨 dogs; P 20, G 3; child facs
✕ LD 9.30
£ B&B £15–£25, B&B (double) £30–£40; HB weekly £150–£160; L £6, D £10·25; WB £25 (HB, Oct–Mar)
cc Access, Amex, B'card/Visa, Diners.

NORTH NEWINGTON Oxfordshire. Map 21A3

Banbury 2½, London 75, Coventry 29, Buckingham 19, Chipping Norton 13, Oxford 25, Stratford upon Avon 20.

Mill House, Nr Banbury, OX15 6AA ☎Banbury (0295) 730212. *Guest House. Swimming pool.*

NORTH NIBLEY Gloucestershire. Map 20B1

Tetbury 12, London 108, Bath 25, Bristol 20, Severn Bridge 14, Wotton under Edge 3.

Burrows Court (Acclaimed), Nibley Green, Dursley, GL11 6AZ ☎Dursley (0453) 546230. *Private Hotel*. Closed 28–31 Dec.
£ B&B £26–£34, HB weekly £189–£220

Black Horse Inn, GL11 6DT ☎(0453) 46841. *Inn.*

NORTH PETHERTON Somerset. Map 4B3

★★★ **Walnut Tree Inn,** TA6 6QA ☎(0278) 662255 Tx: 46529 Fax: (0278) 663946
Attractive coaching inn in village. Some motel-type accommodation. Solarium.
🛏 28 bedrs, 28 en suite; TV; tcf
🏨 TV, dogs; P 70, coach; child facs; con 70
✕ LD 10
£ B&B £44–£60, B&B (double) £64–£80; L £7·50, D £12; WB £45; [10% V]
cc Access, Amex, B'card/Visa, Diners.

Quantock View House, Bridgwater Rd, JA6 6PR ☎(0278) 663309. *Guest House.*
£ B&B £11–£12·50; HB weekly £105–£119; [5% V]

NORTH STIFFORD Essex. Map 17A1

Pop 395. M25 (jn 30) 2, London 21, Brentwood 10, Chelmsford 21, Dartford Tunnel 3, Romford 11, Southend-on-Sea 20.
EC Wed. **Golf** Belhus Park 18h.

★★★ **Stifford Moat House,** High Rd, RM16 1UE ☎Grays Thurrock (0375) 390909 Tx: 995126 Fax: (0375) 390426 ♿

Elegant Georgian house in 6 acres of woodland gardens with modern extension. Tennis. (QMH) ⚒ Fr, De
🛏 98 bedrs, 98 en suite; TV; tcf
🏨 dogs, ns; P 130, coach; child facs; con 120
✕ LD 9.50, nr Sat lunch
£ B&B £68·25–£73·25, B&B (double) £92·50–£97·50; L £14·50, D £14·50; WB £35; [10% V w/e]
cc Access, Amex, B'card/Visa, Diners; dep.

NORTH STOKE Oxon. Map 12A3

Henley-on-Thames 13, London 48, Newbury 19, Oxford 16, Reading 14.

♣ ★★★ **C** **R** **Springs,** Wallingford Rd, OX9 6BE ☎Wallingford (0491) 36687 Tx: 849794
Mock-Tudor country house in secluded grounds with attractive lake.

NORTH WALSHAM Norfolk. Map 35B2

Pop 8,292. Norwich 14, London 126, Cromer 8½, Fakenham 24, Great Yarmouth 24.
EC Wed. **MD** Thur. **Golf** Mundesley 9h. **See** Perp Church, Market Cross, Paston School.

♣ ★★★ **Felmingham Hall,** Felmingham, NR28 0LP ☎ (0692) 69631 Fax: (0692) 69320

Charming 16th century manor house in wooded parkland next to tributary of River Bure. Swimming pool.
🛏 12 bedrs, 12 en suite; annexe 6 bedrs, 5 en suite; TV; tcf
🏨 ns; P 30, coach; child facs; con 15
✕ LD 9.30, lunch by arrangement. Rest lic
£ B&B £40–£45; HB weekly £297–£351; L fr £12, D £22·95; WB fr £49·50 (HB)
cc Access, Amex, B'card/Visa; dep.

NORTH WALTHAM Hampshire. Map 5C3

Basingstoke 6, London 53, M3 (jn 8) 2, Andover 15, Overton 4, Winchester 12.

★★★ **Wheatsheaf,** RG25 2BB ☎(0256) 398282 Tx: 859775 Fax: (0256) 398253
A red-brick inn, sympathetically extended. On A30 in rural surroundings, close to M3 junction 7. (Lns)
🛏 28 bedrs, 28 en suite; TV; tcf
🏨 ns; P 70; con 80
✕ LD 10.30
£ B&B £72, B&B (double) £85; L £11, D £11, WB £31; [10%/5% V]
cc Access, Amex, B'card/Visa, Diners.

NORTHWICH Cheshire. Map 29C3

Pop 17,098. Middlewich 6, London 173, M6 (jn 19) 6, Altrincham 13, Chester 18, Knutsford 7, Warrington 11, Whitchurch 24.
EC Wed. **MD** Tue, Fri, Sat. **Golf** Sandiway 18h. **See** Parish Church, Memorial Hall, Anderton Lift (connecting R Weaver to the Trent and Mersey Canal) 2½ m.

★★★ **Hartford Hall,** School La, CW8 1PW ☎(0606) 75711 Fax: (0606) 782285
17th century building set in beautiful gardens.
🛏 21 bedrs, 21 en suite; TV; tcf
🏨 dogs, ns; P 50, coach; child facs; con 26

★★★ **Nunsmere Hall,** Tarporley Rd, Sandiway, CW8 2ES ☎(0606) 889100 Fax: (0606) 889055 ♿

Spacious Victorian mansion beautifully set on a wooded peninsula in a lake.
🛏 15 bedrs, 15 en suite; TV; tcf
🏨 lift, ns; P 70; no children under 12; con 60
✕ LD 9.30. Resid & Rest lic
£ B&B £80 (w/e £59), B&B (double) £90; L fr £12, D £25; WB £59; [10% V]
cc Access, Amex, B'card/Visa; dep.

★★ **Blue Cap,** Chester Rd, Sandiway, CW8 2DN ☎(0606) 883006

White painted, part 18th century inn with distinctive diamond leaded windows. On busy A559. (BCB). ⚒ Es
🛏 12 bedrs, 12 en suite; TV; tcf
🏨 ns; P 200, coach; child facs; con 50

N

✕ LD 9.30
£ B&B £42–£45, B&B (double) £53; L £8·15, D £8·15; WB £27·50
cc Access, Amex, B'card/Visa, Diners.

★★ Woodpecker, London Rd, Leftwich Green, CW9 8EG ☎ (0606) 45524 Tx: 668025

Victorian country residence. 20 minutes from motorways and Chester city centre. (GW)
🛏 33 bedrs, 33 en suite, 1 ba; TV; tcf
🏛 dogs; P 80, coach; child facs; con 40

NORWICH Norfolk. Map 35B1
See also BUNWELL.
RAC Office, (*changing in 1991*) ☎ (0603) 628255
Pop 121,000. Scole 19, London 111, Cromer 23, East Dereham 16, Great Yarmouth 18, Lowestoft 27, Thetford 28. See Plan, p. 379.
EC Thur. **MD** Daily. **P** See Plan. **Golf** Royal Norwich 18h. Eaton 18h. **See** Cathedral (mainly Norman, entire length 461 ft with many notable items), 40 City Churches, King Edward VI School, Erpingham Gate with archway built 1420, remains of city wall.
ℹ Guildhall, Gaol Hill. ☎ (0603) 666071

★★★★ Airport Ambassador, Norwich Airport, Cromer Rd, NR6 6JA ☎ (0603) 410544 Fax: (0603) 789935 ♿
Large modern red-brick hotel at entrance to airport. Indoor swimming pool, sauna, solarium, gymnasium. ⚒ Fr, De
🛏 108 bedrs, 108 en suite; TV; tcf
🏛 lift, TV, dogs, ns; P 320, coach; child facs; con 400
✕ LD 10.30
£ B&B £50–£60 (w/e £30), B&B (double) £60–£72·50; L £7·95; D £7·95
cc Access, Amex, B'card/Visa, Diners.

★★★ Arlington, 10 Arlington La, off Newmarket Rd, NR2 2DA ☎ (0603) 617841 Fax: (0603) 663708

Expanded building in residential suburbs. Extensive non-residents facilities. ⚒ Fr
🛏 44 bedrs, 44 en suite; TV; tcf
🏛 P 60, coach; child facs
✕ LD 10
£ B&B £49·95–£55, B&B (double) £65–£75; L 7·50, D £11·50; WB £70
cc Access, Amex, B'card/Visa, CB, Diners.

★★★ R Barnham Broom, Honingham Rd, Barnham Broom, NR9 4DD ☎ (060 545) 393 Tx: 975711 Fax: (060 545) 8224

Modern complex of hotel with leisure and conference centre. Indoor swimming pool, golf, tennis, squash, sauna, putting, solarium, gymnasium. ⚒ Fr, De
🛏 52 bedrs, 52 en suite; TV; tcf
🏛 dogs; P200, coach; child facs; con 250
✕ LD 9.30
£ B&B £55–£60, B&B (double) £70–£75; HB weekly £312–£320; L £7·50, D £12; WB £96 (2 nts); [10% V w/d]
cc Access, Amex, B'card/Visa, Diners; dep.

★★★ Friendly Lodge, 2 Barnard Rd, Bowthorpe NR5 9JB ☎ (0603) 741161
Low-built modern hotel on Western outskirts of city. Indoor swimming pool, sauna, solarium, gymnasium.
🛏 80 bedrs, 80 en suite; TV; tcf.
(*See advertisement on p. 380*)

★★★ Maid's Head, Tombland, NR3 1LB ☎ (0603) 761111 Tx: 975080 Fax: (0603) 613688

The Maid's Head is an example of 13th century architecture. (QMH). ⚒ Es
🛏 81 bedrs, 81 en suite; TV; tcf
🏛 lift, dogs, ns; P 45; coach; child facs; con 120
✕ LD 9.30
£ B&B £72–£80 (w/e £42), B&B (double) £87–£91; L £9·95, D £14; WB £47
cc Amex, B'card/Visa, Diners.

★★★ Nelson, Prince of Wales Rd, NR1 1DX ☎ (0603) 760260 Tx: 975203 Fax: (0603) 620008 ♿

Modern hotel with garden beside the River Wensum. Near station. Sauna. ⚒ Fr, De, Du
🛏 121 bedrs, 121 en suite; TV; tcf
🏛 lift, ns; P 180, G 20, coach; child facs; con 90
✕ LD 9.45, bar meals only Sat lunch
£ B&B £66·50–£70·50, B&B (double) £77·50–£81·50; L £9·75, D £11·50; WB £39
cc Access, Amex, B'card/Visa, Diners.

★★★ Norwich, Boundary Rd (A47), NR3 2BA ☎ (0603) 787260 Tx: 975337 Fax: (0603) 400466 ♿
Large modern hotel on the city ring road.
🛏 102 bedrs, 102 en suite; TV; tcf
🏛 ns; P, coach; child facs; con 300
✕ LD 10, nr Sat lunch
£ B&B £57, B&B (double) £67; D £11; WB £35 (HB); [10% V w/e]
cc Access, Amex, B'card/Visa, Diners.

★★★ Norwich Sport Village, Drayton High Rd, Hellesdon, NR6 5DU ☎ (0603) 788898 Tx: 975550 Fax: (0603) 406845 ♿
Modern, Swiss-designed village incorporating hotel, sports and leisure centre. Indoor swimming pool, tennis, squash, sauna, solarium, gymnasium, billiards.
🛏 53 bedrs, 53 en suite; TV; tcf
🏛 lift, ns; P 600, coach; child facs, con 900

★★★ Post House, Ipswich Rd, NR4 6EP ☎ (0603) 56431 Tx: 975106 Fax: (0603) 506400
Typical Post House with an all-day coffee shop. Indoor swimming pool, sauna, solarium, gymnasium. (THF). ⚒ Fr
🛏 116 bedrs, 116 en suite; TV; tcf
🏛 dogs, ns; P 150, coach; child facs; con 100
✕ LD 9.45, nr Sat lunch
£ room £72–£83, double room £83–£89; L £9·95, D £13·95; WB £35
cc Access, Amex, B'card/Visa, Diners.

🏠 ★★★ Sprowston Manor, Wroxham Rd, NR7 8RP ☎ (0603) 410871.
Recently refurbished, red-brick, Tudor manor house in ten acres of parkland next to a golf course. New adjoining wing of bedrooms.
🛏 24 bedrs, 24 en suite; annexe 11 bedrs, 11 en suite

★★ R Annesley, Newmarket Rd, NR2 2LA ☎ (0603) 624553

Two Georgian-style buildings joined by a fully glazed covered way. Situated on the A11 in a residential area. New bedrooms planned for 1991. ⚒ Fr
🛏 19 bedrs, 13 en suite, 4 ba; TV; tcf
🏛 P 18, U 1; child facs
✕ LD 9, bar meals only lunch. Resid & Rest lic
£ B&B £35–£50, B&B (double) £45–£65; L £7, D £13·50; WB £60 (2 nts); [10% V w/e]
cc Access, Amex, B'card/Visa, Diners.

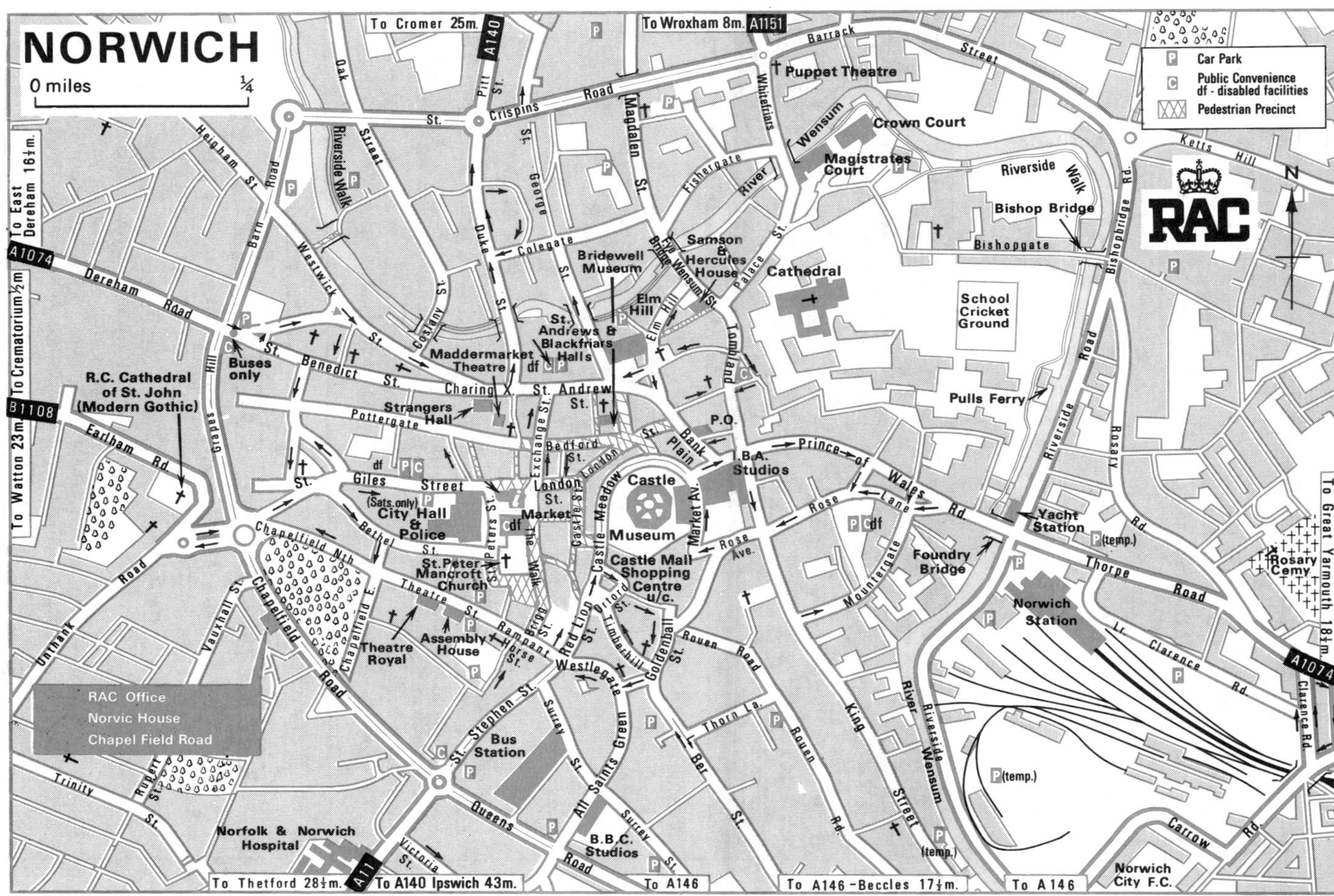
NORWICH
0 miles
1/4
Car Park
Public Convenience
df - disabled facilities
Pedestrian Precinct
RAC
N
To Cromer 25m.
A140
To Wroxham 8m.
A1151
Barrack Street
Puppet Theatre
Crown Court
Wensum
Magistrates Court
Riverside Walk
Bishop Bridge
Bishopgate
Ketts Hill
Bishopbridge Rd.
Oak Street
Pitt St.
Crispins Road
Magdalen St.
Whitefriars
Fishergate
River
Heigham St.
Barn Road
Riverside Walk
Duke St.
St. George St.
Colegate
Coslany St.
Westwick St.
Bridewell Museum
Samson & Hercules House
Fye Bridge
Wensum St.
Palace St.
Cathedral
School Cricket Ground
Elm Hill
St. Andrews & Blackfriars Halls
Maddermarket Theatre
Tombland
Buses only
St. Benedict St.
Charing X
St. Andrew St.
Pulls Ferry
Riverside Road
Rosary Rd.
To East Dereham 16½m.
A1074
Dereham Road
To Crematorium ½m.
To Watton 23m.
B1108
R.C. Cathedral of St. John (Modern Gothic)
Earlham Rd.
Grapes Hill
Strangers Hall
Pottergate
Exchange St.
Bedford St.
London St.
P.O.
Bank Plain
I.B.A. Studios
Prince of Wales Rd.
Giles Street
St.
(Sats. only)
City Hall & Police
Castle Meadow
Castle Museum
Market Av.
Rose Lane
Yacht Station
(temp.)
Market
St. Peters St.
The Walk
Castle St.
Rose Ave.
Castle Mall Shopping Centre u/c.
Foundry Bridge
Thorpe Road
To Great Yarmouth 18½m.
Rosary Cemy
Chapelfield Nth
Bethel St.
St. Peter Mancroft Church
Theatre St.
Theatre Royal
Assembly House
Rampant Horse St.
Brigg St.
Red Lion St.
Orford St.
Timberhill
Goldenball St.
Westlegate
Mountergate
Norwich Station
Lr. Clarence Rd.
A1074
Clarence Rd.
Road
Unthank
Vauxhall St.
Chapelfield Road
Chapelfield E.
Rouen Road
RAC Office
Norvic House
Chapel Field Road
St. Stephen St.
Bus Station
Surrey St.
All Saints Green
Thorn La.
Ber St.
Rouen Rd.
King Street
River Riverside Wensum
(temp.)
Trinity St.
Rupert St.
Queens Road
Norfolk & Norwich Hospital
Victoria St.
B.B.C. Studios
Surrey St.
Carrow Rd.
Norwich City F.C.
To Thetford 28½m.
A11
To A140 Ipswich 43m.
To A146
To A146 - Beccles 17½m.
To A146

N

Norwich (Norfolk)

Nottingham (Nottinghamshire)

Nuneaton (Warwickshire)

★★ **Lansdowne,** Thorpe Rd, NR1 1RU
☎(0603) 620302 Fax: (0603) 761706

Three-storey modern hotel, outside city centre. (Emb)
🛏39 bedrs, 38 en suite, 1 ba; annexe 6 bedrs, 6 en suite; TV; tcf
🏨 lift, TV, dogs, ns; P 60, coach; child facs; con 120
✕ LD 9.15, bar meals only Sat lunch. Resid, Rest & Club lic
£ B&B £54·50 (w/e £26), B&B (double) £71·50; L £7·50, D £8·95; WB £34 (HB)
cc Access, Amex, B'card/Visa, Diners.

★★ **Oaklands,** 89 Yarmouth Rd, NR7 0HH
☎(0603) 34471 Fax: (0603) 700318

Privately-owned hotel sited in pleasant outskirts of city overlooking River Yare.
🛏39 bedrs, 39 en suite; TV; tcf
🏨 TV, dogs; P 70, coach; child facs; con 140
✕ LD 9.30.
£ B&B £53·50, B&B (double) £71·50; L £7, D £12; WB £75 (2 nts HB)
cc Access, Amex, B'card/Visa, Diners.

Belmont (Highly Acclaimed), 60–62 Prince of Wales Rd, NR1 1LT ☎(0603) 622533. *Private Hotel.*
Cavalier (Highly Acclaimed), 244 Thorpe Road, NR1 1TP ☎(0603) 34291
Fax: (0603) 31744 *Hotel.*
£ B&B £33–£38 (w/e £17·50); [10% V w/e]
Wedgewood (Highly Acclaimed), 42 St Stephens Rd, NR1 3RE ☎(0603) 625730. *Private Hotel.* Closed 25–31 Dec
£ B&B £15–£16·50

NOTTINGHAM Nottinghamshire. Map 24C3
See also BEESTON, TOTON and WHATTON.
RAC Office, *Gregory Boulevard, Nottingham, NG7 6NY* ☎(0602) 623331
Pop 271,000. Leicester 26, London 123, M1 (jn 26) 5, Ashby-de-la-Zouch 21, Derby 15, Grantham 24, Mansfield 14, Melton Mowbray 18, Newark 19.
See Plan, p. 382.
EC Mon (large stores) **MD** Daily. **P** See Plan. **Golf** Bulwell 18h, Wollaton 18h. **See** Parish Church (15th cent), Castle (now art gallery and museum), Statue of Robin Hood, Council House, Willoughby House, Bromley House, Newdigate House, Arboretum, Wollaton Hall (Natural History and Industrial Museum).
ℹ 14 Wheeler Gate. ☎(0602) 470661

★★★★ **Albany,** St James's St, NG1 6BN
☎(0602) 470131 Tx: 37211
Fax: (0602) 484366
A modern high-rise building situated in centre of city. (THF)
🛏139 bedrs, 139 en suite; TV; tcf
🏨 lift, dogs, ns; coach; child facs; con 600
✕ LD 10.15
£ B&B £95, B&B (double) £119, L 13·50, D £13·50; WB £42 (HB)
cc Access, Amex, B'card/Visa, Diners.

★★★★ **Nottingham Moat House** (formerly Savoy), Mansfield Rd, NG5 2BT
☎(0602) 602621 Tx: 377429
Fax: (0602) 691506 ♿

A large modern hotel to the north of city centre. (QMH) ⚒ Fr, It, Eg, Gr, We
🛏172 bedrs, 172 en suite; TV; tcf
🏨 lift, ns; P 300, G 100, coach; child facs; con 200
✕ LD 11
£ B&B £61·50 (w/e £23), B&B (double) £83, L £4·50, D £6·50, WB £23
cc Access, Amex, B'card/Visa, Diners.

★★★★ **Royal Moat House,** Wollaton St, NG1 5RH ☎(0602) 414444 Tx: 37101
Fax: (0602) 475667

Large modern city centre hotel, attractively furnished. Winter garden. Squash, solarium, gymnasium. (QMH). Closed 25–31 Dec.
⚒ Fr, De, It, Es
🛏201 bedrs, 201 en suite; TV; tcf
🏨 lift, ns; P 600, coach; child facs; con 550
£ room £64·90 (w/e £28·60), double room £82·50; Bk £5·50, L £2·95, D £5·95; WB £45·10
cc Access, Amex, B'card/Visa, CB, Diners; dep.

★★★★ **Stakis Victoria,** Milton St, NG1 3PZ ☎(0602) 419561 Tx: 37401
Fax: (0602) 484736 ♿
A large Victorian style hotel ideally located in city centre. (Sk)
🛏166 bedrs, 166 en suite; TV; tcf
🏨 lift, dogs, ns; P 20, coach; child facs; con
✕ LD 9.45, bar meals only lunch
£ B&B £45–£70 (w/e £25), B&B (double) £65–£90; HB weekly £245–£350; D £12·50; [10% V]
cc Access, Amex, B'card/Visa, Diners.

★★★ **Bestwood Lodge,** Bestwood Lodge Dr, Arnold, NG5 8NE ☎(0602) 203011
Fax: (0602) 670409

Former Victorian hunting lodge set in a country park. Tennis, riding, solarium. ⚒ Fr, De
🛏39 bedrs, 39 en suite; TV; tcf
🏨 dogs; P 80; child facs; con 150
✕ LD 9.30, bar meals only Sat lunch & Sun dinner
£ B&B £44–£60 (w/e £24), B&B (double) £54–£75; D £8·95; [10% V w/e]
cc Access, Amex, B'card/Visa, CB, Diners.

★★★ **Strathdon Thistle,** Derby Rd, NG1 5FT ☎(0602) 418501 Tx: 377185
Fax: (0602) 483725

A modern purpose-built city centre hotel with conference and function facilities. (MtCh)
🛏69 bedrs, 69 en suite; TV; tcf
🏨 lift, dogs, ns; P 10, G 5, coach; child facs; con 130
✕ LD 9
£ room £75, double room £87, Bk £7·75, L £10, D £13
cc Access, Amex, B'card/Visa, CB, Diners.

★★★ **Walton's,** North Lodge, North Rd, The Pk, NG7 1AG ☎(0602) 475215
Fax: (0602) 475053
Stone-built former lodge to Park with modern extension. Swimming pool, sauna, solarium. ⚒ Fr
🛏15 bedrs, 15 en suite; annexe 3 bedrs, 3 en suite; TV; tcf
🏨 TV, dogs; P14; child facs; con 20
✕ LD 9.30, bar meals only Sat lunch & Sun
£ B&B £42–£55, B&B (double) £65–£75; L £12, D 15
cc Access, B'card/Visa.

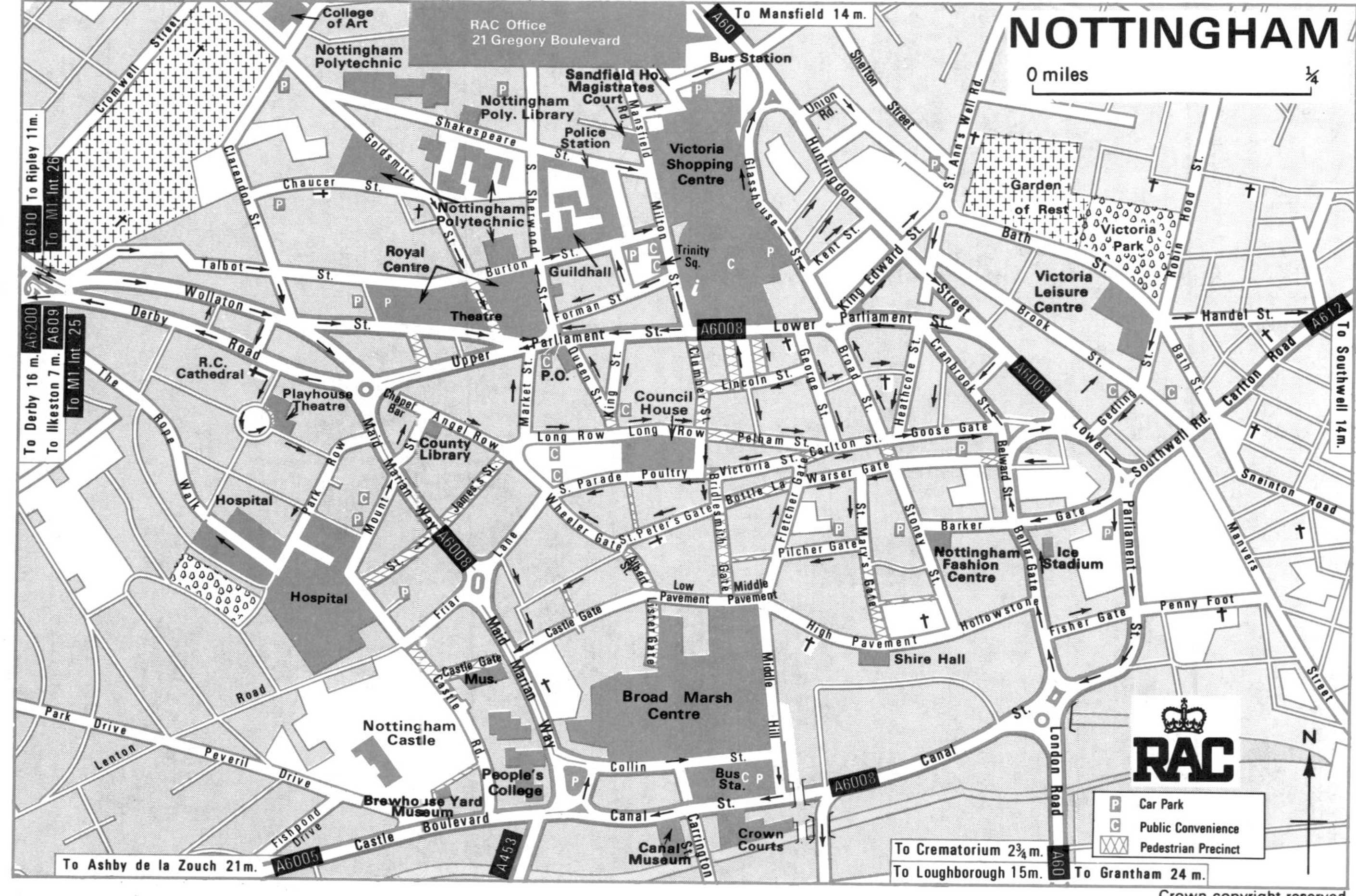

EC *early closing* **MD** *market day* ♣♣ *country house hotel* *ns (NS) no smoking areas* *tcf tea/coffee facilities*

★★ **Rufford,** Melton Rd (A606), West Bridgford, NG2 7NE ☎(0602) 814202 Fax: (0602) 455801

Pleasant 1920s style residence conveniently near to Test cricket ground. Closed Xmas.
🛏 35 bedrs, 35 en suite; TV; tcf
🏠 TV; P 35, coach; child facs
✕ LD 8, nr lunch & Fri–Sun dinner. Resid & Rest lic
£ B&B £39·10 (w/e £23), B&B (double) £52·90; D £10·35
cc Access, Amex, B'card/Visa, Diners.
(*See advertisement on p. 380*)

★★ **Sherwood,** Gregory Boulevard, NG7 6LB ☎(0602) 603261
White-painted hotel on inner ring road. Facing large open park.

★★ **Westminster,** Mansfield Rd, NG5 2EF ☎(0602) 623023 Fax: (0602) 691156
Two Edwardian houses, linked together, conveniently situated on main northern approach to the city.
🛏 60 bedrs, 60 en suite; TV; tcf
🏠 lift; P 40, coach; child facs; con 20
✕ LD 9.15, nr lunch & Sun dinner. Resid & Rest lic.
£ B&B £40–£44; B&B (double) £48–£52; D £11·95
cc Access, B'card/Visa.

★★ **H C Windsor Lodge,** 116 Radcliffe Rd, West Bridgford, NG2 5HG ☎(0602) 813773 Fax: (0602) 819405.
Three adjoining houses sympathetically joined with new wings to rear, on main road south east of city. Snooker.
🛏 52 bedrs, 48 en suite, (4 sh); TV; tcf
🏠 TV, dogs; P 60; child facs
£ B&B £32–£38 (w/e £27); B&B (double) £45–£52; [5% V]
cc Access, Amex, B'card/Visa, Diners

Balmoral (Highly Acclaimed), 55 Loughborough Rd, West Bridgford, NG2 7LA ☎(0602) 455020 Fax: (0602) 455683. *Hotel.* Closed Xmas.
£ B&B £26·50–£34·50; [5% V]

Fairhaven (Acclaimed), 19 Meadow Rd, Beeston Rylands, NG9 1JP ☎(0602) 227509. *Private Hotel.* Closed 25–31 Dec.
£ B&B £16–£19·50; HB weekly £364–£434

Crantock, 480 Mansfield Rd, Sherwood, NG5 2EL ☎(0602) 623294. *Hotel.*
£ B&B £24–£39; [5% V]
Park, 7 Waverley St, NG7 4HF ☎(0602) 786299 Fax: (0602) 424358. *Private Hotel.*
£ B&B £48 (w/e £35); HB weekly £400; [5% V]
P & J, 277 Derby Rd, Lenton, NG7 2DP ☎(0602) 783998. *Private Hotel.*
£ B&B £22–£32 (w/e £18); [10% V]; dep.
Royston, 326 Mansfield Rd, NG5 2EF ☎(0602) 622947. *Private Hotel.*
£ B&B £28; [10% V Oct–Apr]

NUNEATON
Warwickshire. Map 23B2

Pop 72,000. London 99, M6 (jn 3) 5, Ashby-de-la-Zouch 16, Birmingham 21, Coventry 8½, Hinckley 4½, Rugby 16.
MD Sat. **Golf** Nuneaton 18h. **See** EE and Perp Church of St Nicolas, St Mary's Church, 13 cent All Saints Church, Council House.
ℹ Library, Church St. ☎(0203) 384027

★★ **Longshoot,** Watling St, CV11 6JH ☎Coventry (0203) 329711 Tx: 311100
Modern purpose-built red brick hotel with attractive, distinctive roof.
🛏 46 bedrs, 46 en suite; TV; tcf
🏠 dogs, ns; P 120, coach; child facs; con 35

Ambion Court (Highly Acclaimed), The Green, Dadlington ☎(0455) 212292 Fax: (0455) 213141. *Hotel.* ✗ Fr
£ B&B £30–£45; [10% V w/e]
(*See advertisement on p. 380*)

OAKFORD BRIDGE
Devon. Map 3C4

Taunton 20, London 163, Minehead 21, South Molton 14, Tiverton 8.

★★ **H C Bark House,** Bampton, EX16 9HZ ☎(039 85) 236
An attractive stone building, once a tannery, in a lovely wooded valley. Charming garden. Open 1 Mar–20 Dec. ✗ Fr
🛏 6 bedrs, 4 en suite, 1 ba; TV
🏠 dogs; P 12, U 2 (£1); no children under 5
✕ LD 8.30. Resid & Rest lic
£ B&B £18, B&B (double) £38–£54; HB weekly £210–£254; D £13
cc Access, B'card/Visa.

OAKHAM
Leicestershire. Map 31B1

Pop 8,859. Kettering 20, London 95, Grantham 20, Leicester 19, Melton Mowbray 9, Stamford 10.
EC Thur. **MD** Wed, Sat. **Golf** Luffenham Heath 18h. **See** Castle ruins with fine Norman banqueting hall, unique collection of horseshoes, Rutland County Museum.
ℹ Library, Catmos St. ☎(0572) 724329

★★ **H C Boultons,** 4 Catmose St, LE15 6HW ☎(0572) 722844 Fax: (0572) 724473 ♿

Once a medieval hunting lodge and part Georgian, a listed building in a pleasant garden on south side of town. Hotel recently extended; new bedrooms, bar, restaurant and function room.
🛏 25 bedrs, 25 en suite; TV; tcf
🏠 dogs; P 15, coach; con 180
✕ LD 9.30, bar meals only Sun dinner
£ B&B £50 (w/e £62·50, 2 nts), B&B (double) £60; L £7·95, D £12·50; WB £62·50 (2 nts)
cc Access, Amex, B'card/Visa, Diners.

OCKLEY
Surrey Map 10A1

Dorking 9, London 32, Billingshurst 10, Crawley 16, Guildford 16, Horsham 10.

★★★ **Gatton Manor,** RH5 5PQ ☎(0306) 79 555 Fax: (0306) 79713

A gabled 18th century house with modern extension set in 200 acres of parkland. Golf, putting, tennis, fishing. ✗ Fr, Es
🛏 10 bedrs, 10 en suite; 1 ba; TV; tcf
🏠 dogs; P 150, coach; child facs; con 60
✕ LD 9.45
£ B&B £45–£50, B&B (double) £70–£80; D £12·50; WB £68 (min 2 nts)
cc Access, B'card/Visa; dep.

OKEHAMPTON
Devon. Map 3B3

Pop 4,000. Exeter 22, London 192, Ashburton 27, Bideford 26, Crediton 17, Launceston 19, Tavistock 16.
EC Wed. **MD** Sat. **Golf** Okehampton 18h. **See** Castle ruins. 17th cent Town Hall, All Saints Parish Church, Fitz Well, St James's Church (14th cent tower).
ℹ 3 West St. ☎(0837) 53020

ꝏ ★★★ **H C R Collaven Manor,** Sourton, EX20 4HH ☎Bridestowe (083 786) 522 Fax: (083 786) 570

Mellow stone country manor, some parts dating back to 15th century, standing in 5 acres of grounds. Putting.
🛏 9 bedrs, 9 en suite; TV; tcf
🏠 P 25; children over 12; con 20
✕ LD 9.30. Resid & Rest lic
£ B&B £50, B&B (double) £77–£95; L £13·95, D £19·95; WB £40
cc Access, B'card/Visa; dep.

OLDHAM
Gtr Manchester (Lancashire). Map 33C3

Pop 103,690. Glossop 12, London 186, A 627(M) 1½, Barnsley 29, Bury 10, Huddersfield 18, Manchester 7, Rochdale 5½.
EC Tue. **MD** Mon, Fri, Sat. **Golf** Oldham 18h. **See** Art Gallery, Parish Church (crypt), Town Hall, Bluecoat School.
ℹ 84 Union St. ☎061-678 4654

Licences
Establishments have a full licence unless shown as unlicensed or with the limitations listed on p 6.

★★★ **Avant,** Windsor Rd, Manchester St, OL8 4AS ☎ 061-627 5500 Tx: 668264 Fax: 061-627 5896 ♿

Purpose built, two-storey hotel on A62 west of town. Good modern design in furnishings and fittings.
🛏 103 bedrs, 103 en suite; TV; tcf
🏨 lift, dogs, ns; P 150, coach; child facs; con 300
✕ LD 10
£ B&B £56 (w/e £45), B&B (double) £62 (w/e £50); HB weekly £442; L £6·50, D £12·95; WB £98 (HB); [10% V]
cc Access, Amex, B'card/Visa, Diners.

★★★ **Bower,** Hollinwood Av, Chadderton, OL9 8DE ☎ 061-682 7254 Tx: 666883 Fax: 061-683 4605

Former private house with picturesque gardens, near local beauty spots. (DeV)
🛏 65 bedrs, 65 en suite; TV; tcf
🏨 dogs; P 140, coach; child facs; con 220
✕ LD 9.30, nr Sat lunch
£ B&B £65 (w/e £26), B&B (double) £75; HB weekly £350; L £10·75, D £10·75; WB £70; [10% V]
cc Access, Amex, B'card/Visa, Diners; dep.

★★★ C **Smokies Park,** Ashton Rd, Bardsley, OL8 3HX ☎ 061-624 3405 Tx: 667490 Fax: 061-627 5262
Modern, almost E-shaped, two-storey hotel, elegantly decorated in Art Nouveau style. Sauna, solarium, gymnasium. Fr, Gr, Pol
🛏 47 bedrs, 47 en suite; TV; tcf
🏨 P 120, coach; child facs; con 450
✕ LD 10, nr Sat lunch
£ B&B £52–£70 (w/e £25), B&B (double) £60–£80; L £12, D £11·50; [5% V w/e]
cc Access, Amex, B'card/Visa, Diners.

★★ **High Point,** Napier St, OL8 1TR ☎ 061-624 4130 Fax: 061-627 2757

Large Victorian mansion within easy reach of the town centre. Fr
🛏 18 bedrs, 16 en suite, 1 ba; TV; tcf
🏨 dogs; P 35, G2, coach; child facs; con 30
✕ LD 9.45, nr Sat lunch
£ B&B £32–£42 (w/e £19), B&B (double) £42–£52·50; L £6·50, D £9·50
cc Access, Amex, B'card/Visa; Diners.

OLD SODBURY Avon. Map 20B1

Pop 400. Swindon 27, London 104, M4 (jn 18) 3, Bristol 13, Tetbury 10.
EC Thur. **Golf** Chipping Sodbury 18h. **See** Church.

★★★ **Cross Hands,** Tetbury Rd, BS17 6RJ ☎ Chipping Sodbury (0454) 313000 Fax: (0454) 324409

Three-storey former posting house of Cotswold stone. Steak house restaurant. Fr, It, Es
🛏 24 bedrs, 20 en suite, 2 ba; TV; tcf
🏨 dogs, ns; P 200; child facs; con 100
✕ LD 10.30
£ B&B £38·50–£60·50, B&B (double) £65·50–£92·50; L 11, D 11; WB £55·50 (3 nts)
cc Amex, B'card/Visa, Diners.

Dornden (Acclaimed), Church La, BS17 6NB ☎ Chipping Sodbury (0454) 313325. *Guest House. Tennis.* Closed Xmas & New Year. Es
£ B&B £23–£32; WB £18·50; [5% V]; dep.

OLLERTON Nottinghamshire. Map 24A4

Pop 7,000. Newark 13, London 139, Doncaster 25, Gainsborough 22, Lincoln 23, Mansfield 8½, Nottingham 18, Worksop 9.
EC Wed. **MD** Fri, Sat. **Golf** Sherwood Forest 18h. **See** Sherwood Forest, Major Oak, Ollerton Hall, Thoresby Hall 2 m N.
ℹ Sherwood Heath ☎ (0623) 824545

Old Rectory, Main St, Kirton, NG22 9LP ☎ Mansfield (0623) 861540 Fax: (0623) 860751. *Hotel.*
£ B&B £21

ORFORD Suffolk. Map 27C3

Pop 662. Ipswich 20, London 94, Aldeburgh 11, Saxmundham 9, Stowmarket 29.
EC Wed. **Golf** Woodbridge 18h. **See** Castle, 14th cent Church, forest and river walks.

Residents only
Some Listed hotels only serve meals to residents. It is always wise to make a reservation for a meal in a hotel.

★★ **Crown & Castle,** IP12 2LJ ☎ (0394) 450205

Attractive historic building, reputed to have been a haunt of smugglers. (THF)
🛏 9 bedrs, 1 en suite, 2 ba; annexe 11 bedrs, 11 en suite; TV; tcf
🏨 dogs, ns; P 19, coach; child facs

King's Head, Front St, IP12 2LW. ☎ (0394) 450271. *Inn.*
£ B&B £20; [5% V w/d]

ORMESBY ST MARGARET Norfolk. Map 35C1

Pop 2,000. Norwich 18, London 129, Caister 3, Cromer 27, Great Yarmouth 4½.
EC Wed. **Golf** Caister 18h. **See** Church.

♣♣ ★★ **Ormesby Lodge,** Decoy Rd, NR29 3LG ☎ Gt Yarmouth (0493) 730910
Owner-managed former country residence in a quiet rural setting.
🛏 8 bedrs, 7 en suite, (1 sh); TV; tcf
🏨 dogs, P 40; child facs; con 30
✕ LD 10.30, nr lunch, Sun dinner. Resid & Rest lic
£ B&B £34·50 (w/e £30), B&B (double) £46; L £15, D £15; WB £30; [10% V]
cc Access, Amex, B'card/Visa, Diners; dep.

OSSETT West Yorkshire. Map 40C3

Pop 17,183. Wakefield 4, London 186, M1 (jn 40) 1, Barnsley 12, Bradford 12, Halifax 14, Huddersfield 11, Leeds 9½.
EC Mon, Wed. **MD** Tue, Fri. **Golf** Low Laithes 18h. **See** Parish Church.

★★★ **Post House,** Queens Dr, WF5 9BE ☎ Wakefield (0924) 276388 Tx: 55407 Fax: (0924) 280277
A modern hotel with well designed accommodation. (THF)
🛏 99 bedrs, 99 en suite; TV; tcf
🏨 lift, dogs, ns; P 220, coach; child facs; con 160
✕ LD 10·30, nr Sat lunch
£ B&B £75–£85 (w/e £39·50), B&B (double) £94–£104; L £9·50, D £13·50; WB £38
cc Access, Amex, B'card/Visa, CB, Diners.

OSWESTRY Shropshire. Map 29A2

Pop 13,210. Shrewsbury 17, London 173, Bala 32, Llangollen 12, Welshpool 15, Whitchurch 19, Wrexham 16.
EC Thur. **MD** Wed. **Golf** Oswestry 18h, Llanymynech 18h. **See** Parish Church of St Oswald, King Oswald's Well, Llwyd Mansion, 16th cent Croeswylan Stone, Castle Bank (traces of ancient castle), Offa's Dyke, Iron Age earthworks at Old Oswestry.
ℹ Library, Arthur St. ☎ (0691) 662753

O

★★★ Wynnstay, Church St, SY11 2SZ ☎(0691) 655261 Fax: (0691) 670606

Three-storey Georgian town centre hotel with elegant porch. Ancient bowling green. Fr, It, We
26 bedrs, 26 en suite; TV; tcf
dogs, ns; P 80, coach; child facs; con 200
LD 10
£ B&B £60·50–£63·50 (w/e £41), B&B (double) £78–£88; L £10·50, D £12·50; WB £47; [10% V]
cc Access, Amex, B'card/Visa, CB, Diners.

★★ Sweeney Hall, SY10 9EU ☎(0691) 652450

Gracious country house, largely Georgian, quietly situated in 100 acre park. Putting.
9 bedrs, 6 en suite, 3 ba; tcf
TV, dogs; P 50, coach; child facs; con 60
LD 9.30
£ B&B £30–£35, B&B (double) £49–£59; L £11, D £11
cc Access, B'card/Visa.

OTLEY West Yorkshire. Map 40A2

Leeds 12, London 203, Harrogate 12, Skipton 15, York 29.
[i] 8 Boroughgate, ☎(0943) 465151

★★★ Chevin Lodge, Yorkgate, LS21 3NU ☎(0943) 467818 Tx: 51538 Fax: (0943) 850335
Scandinavian-style hotel with residents' cabins in 50 acres of birchwood. Tennis, fishing, sauna, solarium. Fr
27 bedrs, 27 en suite; annexe 25 bedrs, 25 en suite; TV; tcf
dogs; P 120, coach; child facs; con 120
LD 9.30, nr Sat lunch. Resid & Rest lic
£ B&B £55–£80 (w/e £34), B&B (double) £68–£92·50; L £9·50, D £14·75; WB £89·50 (2 nts HB)
cc Access, Amex, B'card/Visa.
(See advertisement on p. 388)

OTTERY ST MARY Devon. Map 4A1

Pop 6,946. Honiton 5½, London 158, Exeter 12, Lyme Regis 18, Tiverton 19.
EC Wed, Sat. **Golf** Honiton 18h. **See** St Mary's Church (14th cent clock), Cadhay (16th cent manor house) 1 m NW, Circular Tumbling Weir.
[i] The Flexton. ☎(0404) 813964

★★ Coach House, Southerton, EX11 1SE ☎Colaton Raleigh (0395) 68577 Fax: (0395) 68946

A family-run hotel, converted from the coach house of a country estate, set in 2½ acres of landscaped gardens. Closed 4–31 Jan
6 bedrs, 6 en suite; TV; tcf
TV, ns; P 16; no children under 14
LD 9, nr Mon–Sat lunch. Resid & Rest lic
£ B&B £35–£45, B&B (double) £50–£80; HB weekly £180–£240; D £11·50; [10% V]
cc Access, B'card/Visa; dep.

★★ Tumbling Weir, EX11 1AO ☎(0404) 812752 Fax: (0404) 812752

Charming thatched white cottage-style hotel, with tactful extension, on edge of town. A mill stream separates the hotel from car park; approach on foot over a little bridge. Fishing.
12 bedrs, 12 en suite; TV; tcf
TV, dogs; P3, coach; con 120
LD 9.30, nr Mon & Sat lunch, Sun dinner. Resid & Rest lic
£ B&B £30–£33, B&B (double) £48–£50; L £7·50, D £15; WB £99 (3 nts); [5% V]
cc Access, B'card/Visa.

Venn Ottery Barton (Acclaimed), EX11 1RZ ☎(040 481) 2733. *Private Hotel.*
£ B&B £18–£24, HB weekly £150·50–£192·50, WB £21·50 (3 nts)

OULTON West Yorkshire. Map 40B4

Pop 4,500. Pontefract 8½, London 186, Halifax 19, Huddersfield 18, Leeds 5, Wakefield 5½, York 23.
EC Mon, Wed. **Golf** Temple Newsam 18h (2). **See** St John's Church, The Nookin (17th cent house).

★★★ Grove Crest, The Grove, Aberford Rd, LS26 8EJ ☎Leeds (0532) 826201 Tx: 557646 Fax: (0532) 829243
Modern purpose-built hotel strategically placed for Leeds and M62. (Cr)
40 bedrs, 40 en suite; TV; tcf
dogs, ns; P 100, coach; child facs; con 8

OULTON BROAD Suffolk. Map 27C4

Saxmundham 23, London 118, Great Yarmouth 10, Lowestoft 2, Norwich 25.
EC Thur. **Golf** Lowestoft 18h.

★★★ Broadlands, Bridge Rd, NR32 3LN ☎Lowestoft (0502) 516031 Tx: 975621 Fax: (0502) 501454

A 3-storey modern hotel over shops and a bank in the town centre. Indoor swimming pool, sauna, solarium, billiards.
52 bedrs, 52 en suite; TV; tcf
TV, ns; P 100, coach; child facs; con 80

★★★ Wherry, Bridge Rd, NR32 3LN ☎Lowestoft (0502) 573521 Tx: 975788 Fax: (0502) 501350
Red-brick building with charming verandah overlooking Broad. Own boathouse. Fishing.
30 bedrs, 30 en suite; TV; tcf
lift, dogs, ns; P 100, coach; child facs; con 250
LD 10
£ B&B £45–£48·50, B&B (double) £55; L £6·25, D £9·25, WB £18·75; [5% V w/d]
cc Access, Amex, B'card/Visa, CB, Diners.
(See advertisement on p. 335)

OUNDLE Northamptonshire. Map 26A4

Pop 3,450. London 80, Bedford 30, Huntingdon 23, Kettering 17, Market Harborough 21, Peterborough 13.
EC Wed. **MD** Thur. **Golf** Oundle 18h. **See** St Peter's Church (200 ft spire), 17th cent Talbot Inn, Paines Almshouses.
[i] Market Pl. ☎(0832) 274333

★★★ Talbot, New St, PE8 4EA ☎(0832) 273621 Tx: 32364 Fax: (0832) 274545

17th century stone building of character, with modern extensions. (THF)
39 bedrs, 39 en suite; TV; tcf
dogs, ns; P 100, coach; child facs; con 80
LD 10
£ room £70–£80, double room £85–£120; L 8·50, D £15; WB £35
cc Access, Amex, B'card/Visa, CB, Diners.

OWER Hampshire. Map 5B2

Pop 500. M27 (jn 2) 1, London 79, Ringwood 14, Romsey 3½, Salisbury 15, Southampton 7.
Golf Lyndhurst 18h, Bramshaw 18h (2).

Changes made after July 1990 are not included.

★★★ **New Forest Heathlands,** Romsey Rd, SO51 6ZJ ☎ Southampton (0703) 814333 Tx: 8954665 Fax: (0703) 812123

A modern hotel built onto a 16th century inn. Putting. ⚒ Fr
🛏 52 bedrs, 52 en suite; TV; tcf
🏠 dogs, ns; P 150, coach; child facs; con 200
✕ LD 9.15 (Fri & Sat 10), bar meals only Sat lunch
£ B&B £60–£75 (w/e £40), B&B (double) £75–£90, HB weekly £280–£332·50; L £7·50, D £14·75; WB £40; [10% V excl. Sep]
cc Access, Amex, B'card/Visa, Diners; dep.

OXFORD Oxfordshire. Map 21A2
See also GREAT MILTON, HORTON-CUM-STUDLEY & MILTON COMMON
RAC Office, *226 Banbury Road, Oxford, OX2 7DN* ☎ (0865) 53443
Pop 116,400. High Wycombe 26, London 56, M40 (jn 7) 8½, Aylesbury 22, Banbury 23, Bicester 12, Burford 20, Chipping Norton 20, Faringdon 17, Wallingford 12, Wantage 15.
See Plan, p. 387.
MD Wed. **P** See Plan. **Golf** North Oxford 18h, Southfield 18h. **See** Colleges, Cathedral, Bodleian Library, Sheldonian Theatre, Ashmolean, History of Science and University Museums, Botanic Garden, many churches, Martyrs Memorial, Carfax Tower.
ℹ St Aldates. ☎ (0865) 726871

★★★★ **Randolph,** Beaumont St, OX1 2LN ☎ (0865) 247481 Tx: 83446 Fax: (0865) 726871

Large, Gothic-style, Victorian building with elegant furnishings; centrally situated. (THF). ⚒ Fr, De, Es
🛏 109 bedrs, 109 en suite; TV; tcf
🏠 lift, dogs, ns; G 80, coach; child facs; con 200
✕ LD 10
£ room £101–£113, double room £132–£144; Bk £9·50; L £16, D £21; WB £72
cc Access, Amex, B'card/Visa, Diners.

Licences
Establishments have a full licence unless shown as unlicensed or with the limitations listed on p 6.

★★★ **Cotswold Lodge,** Banbury Rd, OX2 6JP ☎ (0865) 512121 Tx: 837127 Fax: (0865) 512490

Large and attractive stone-built Victorian house, with rear extension; ½ mile north of city centre. Closed 26–31 Dec. ⚒ Gk
🛏 50 bedrs, 50 en suite; TV
🏠 dogs; P 50, coach; child facs; con 100
✕ LD 10
£ B&B £79·50–£95·50, B&B (double) £102·50–£122·50, L £13·75, D £19·25; WB £110
cc Access, Amex, B'card/Visa, Diners.
(See advertisement on p. 388)

★★★ **Eastgate,** Merton St, OX1 4BE ☎ (0865) 248244 Tx: 83302 Fax: (0865) 791681

Victorian stone building in keeping with surrounding colleges. In city centre. (THF). ⚒ Fr
🛏 43 bedrs, 43 en suite; TV; tcf
🏠 lift, dogs, ns; P 40, coach; child facs; con 15
✕ LD 9.30
£ B&B £82·60–£92·60 (w/e £52), B&B (double) £120·20–£140·20
cc Access, Amex, B'card/Visa, Diners.

★★★ **Linton Lodge,** Linton Rd, OX2 6UJ ☎ (0865) 53461 Tx: 837093 Fax: (0865) 310365

Former private house with modern extension in Victorian residential area. (H. Int)
🛏 71 bedrs, 71 en suite; TV; tcf
🏠 lift, dogs, ns; P 40, coach; child facs; con 120
✕ LD 9.30, bar meals only Sat lunch
£ B&B £94–£124 (w/e £38), B&B (double) £118–£140; L £11, D £15; [5% V Fri–Sun]
cc Amex, B'card/Visa, Diners.

★★★ **Oxford Moat House,** Godstow Rd, Wolvercote Roundabout, OX2 8AL ☎ (0865) 59933 Tx: 837926 Fax: (0865) 310259

Large, modern hotel on outskirts of city. Indoor swimming pool, putting, squash, sauna, solarium, gymnasium, billiards. (QMH)
🛏 155 bedrs, 155 en suite; TV; tcf
🏠 dogs, ns; P 200, coach; child facs; con 150
✕ LD 9.45, nr Sat lunch
£ B&B £85, B&B (double) £105; L £12·50, D £18; WB £48·50
cc Access, Amex, B'card/Visa, Diners.

★★★ **Welcome Lodge,** (formerly Travelodge), Peartree Roundabout, Woodstock Rd, OX2 8JZ ☎ (0865) 54301 Tx: 83202 Fax: (0865) 513474
Modern motel-type hotel with purpose-built accommodation in outskirts of Oxford. Meals served in adjacent service area. Swimming pool. (THF)
See Motor Lodge section

★★ **Foxcombe Lodge,** Fox La, Boars Hill, OX1 5DP ☎ (0865) 730746 Tx: 837744 ♿
A gabled former private house set in attractive gardens on Boars Hill overlooking Oxford (3 miles away).

★★ **Royal Oxford,** Park End St, OX1 1HR ☎ (0865) 248432 Fax: (0865) 250049

Traditional stone building situated close to railway station. (Emb). ⚒ Fr, Es
🛏 25 bedrs, 12 en suite, 5 ba; TV; tcf
🏠 P 60, coach; child facs; con 50
✕ LD 9.15, nr lunch
£ B&B £65–£75, B&B (double) £82–£92; D £13·50; WB £40 (HB)
cc Access, Amex, B'card/Visa, CB, Diners.

★★ **C** **Tree,** Church Way, Iffley, OX4 4EY ☎ (0865) 775974
Red-brick Victorian house in village of Iffley. Attractive gardens.
🛏 7 bedrs, 7 en suite; TV; tcf
(See advertisement on p. 390)

★★ **Victoria,** 180 Abingdon Rd, OX1 4RA ☎ (0865) 724536 Tx: 837031
Well-modernised converted private house with modern facilities. In residential area. Closed 21 Dec–19 Jan.

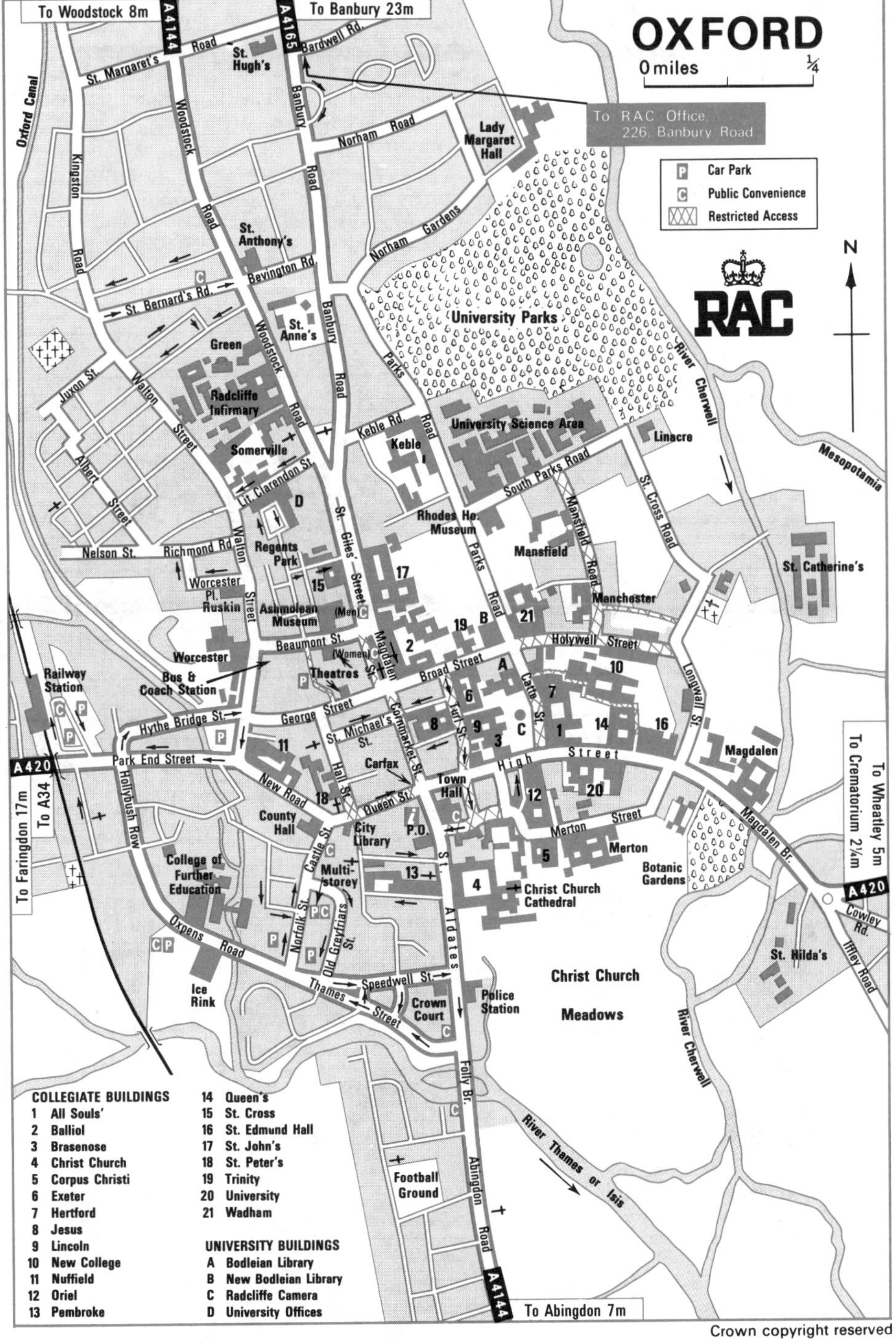
OXFORD
0 miles ¼
To RAC Office, 226, Banbury Road
Car Park
Public Convenience
Restricted Access
N
RAC
To Woodstock 8m
A4144
A4165
To Banbury 23m
St. Hugh's
Lady Margaret Hall
University Parks
River Cherwell
Mesopotamia
Linacre
University Science Area
Keble
St. Anne's
St. Anthony's
Green
Radcliffe Infirmary
Somerville
Rhodes Ho. Museum
Mansfield
Manchester
St. Catherine's
Regents Park
Ashmolean Museum
Worcester
Railway Station
Bus & Coach Station
Theatres
Carfax
Town Hall
County Hall
City Library
P.O.
Multi-storey
College of Further Education
Ice Rink
Crown Court
Police Station
Magdalen
Merton
Botanic Gardens
Christ Church Cathedral
Christ Church Meadows
St. Hilda's
Football Ground
River Thames or Isis
To Wheatley 5m
To Crematorium 2¼m
A420
To Faringdon 17m
To A34
To Abingdon 7m
COLLEGIATE BUILDINGS
1 All Souls'
2 Balliol
3 Brasenose
4 Christ Church
5 Corpus Christi
6 Exeter
7 Hertford
8 Jesus
9 Lincoln
10 New College
11 Nuffield
12 Oriel
13 Pembroke
14 Queen's
15 St. Cross
16 St. Edmund Hall
17 St. John's
18 St. Peter's
19 Trinity
20 University
21 Wadham
UNIVERSITY BUILDINGS
A Bodleian Library
B New Bodleian Library
C Radcliffe Camera
D University Offices

Otley (West Yorkshire)

CHEVIN LODGE HOTEL

Yorkgate, Nr Otley, West Yorkshire LS21 3NY

In the heart of Emmerdale Farm country situated in 50 acres of Birchwood forest and private lakes. Sauna, jacuzzi, solarium and all-weather tennis court are all available to guests. Also fishing, jogging and cycling trails through the woods.
Lodges deep in the woods can be booked as alternatives to Hotel bedrooms and all have en-suite Bathroom.
Beverage making facilities, in-house video etc.
Places to visit are The Dales, Brontë Country, Harrogate and York.

Oxford (Oxfordshire)

Cotswold Lodge Hotel

Beautiful Victorian house – 52 berooms all en-suite, TV, CH, tea & coffee facilities and hairdryers.
Restaurant open 7 days a week.
Lunch 12 – 2.30.
Dinner 6.30 – 10.30.
Table d'Hôte and à la Carte.
Conference and banqueting up to 150.

AMPLE PARKING ■ NON-RESIDENTS WELCOME

OXFORD (0865) 512121/30

66A, BANBURY ROAD, OXFORD.

Oxford (Oxfordshire)

Touring, Walking, **COTSWOLDS** · Golfing, Cycling, **OXFORD** · Dreaming Spires, Colleges, Museums, River Thames, Punting, Boating, **LONDON** · Sightseeing, Shops, Theatres, **CHILTERN HILLS** · Villages, Photography, Stately Homes, Horse Riding, Special Weekend Breaks, **Leisure Complex,** Relaxation, Care, Sauna, Solarium, Gym.

THE

BELFRY HOTEL

Brimpton Grange
Milton Common
Oxford OX9 2JW
Great Milton
(0844) 279381
RAC ★★★

🛏 23 bedrs, 14 en suite, 3 ba; TV; tcf
🏨 dogs; P 20, coach; child facs
✕ LD 9. Resid & Rest lic
£ B&B £37·50–£48·50, B&B (double) £49·50–£62·50; L £8·50, D £12·95; [5% V]
cc Access, B'card/Visa; dep.

★★ Westwood Country, Hinksey Hill Top, OX1 5BG ☎(0865) 735408
Fax: (0865) 736536 ♿
Attractive country house set in lawns and woods, in rural setting near Oxford. Sauna, gymnasium.
🛏 27 bedrs, 27 en suite; TV; tcf
🏨 dogs, ns; P 30, G2, coach; child facs; con 50
✕ LD 8.30, bar meals only lunch
£ B&B £38–£55, B&B (double) £60–£80; D £13; WB £40
cc Access, Amex, B'card/Visa, CB, Diners; dep.
(See advertisement on p. 390)

Chestnuts (Highly Acclaimed), 45 Davenant Rd, OX2 8BU ☎(0865) 53375. *Guest House.*
£ B&B £44–£54; [5% V excl Apr–Sep & Nov]
Cotswold House (Highly Acclaimed), 363 Banbury Rd, OX2 7PL ☎(0865) 310558. *Guest House.*
£ B&B £24–£27
Gables (Highly Acclaimed), 6 Cumnor Hill, OX2 9HA ☎(0865) 862153. *Guest House.* Closed 24–31 Dec. ✗ Fr
£ B&B £17–£18; dep.
Tilbury Lodge (Highly Acclaimed), 5 Tilbury La, Eynsham Rd, Botley, OX2 9NB ☎(0865) 862138. *Private Hotel.*
£ B&B £27–£30

Courtfield (Acclaimed), 367 Iffley Rd, OX4 4DP ☎(0865) 242991. *Private Hotel.*
£ B&B £24–£32; [10% V Oct–Apr only, 2 nts min]

Ascot, 283 Iffley Rd, OX4 4AQ ☎(0865) 240259. *Guest House.* ✗ Fr
£ B&B £20–£30
Bedford House, 19 Polstead Rd, OX2 6TW ☎(0865) 54107. *Guest House.*
£ B&B £17–£18; [10% V Jan–Mar]
Bravalla, 242 Iffley Rd, OX4 1SE ☎(0865) 241326. *Guest House.*
£ B&B £20–£30; [10% V]
Brown's, 281 Iffley Rd, OX4 4AQ ☎(0865) 246822. *Guest House.*
Conifer, 116 The Glade, Headington OX3 7DX ☎(0865) 63055. *Guest House. Swimming pool.*
£ B&B £20; dep.
Galaxie, 180 Banbury Rd, OX2 7BT ☎(0865) 515688. *Private Hotel.*
£ B&B £28–£42 (w/e £28); [5% V w/e]
Kings, 363 Iffley Rd, OX4 4DP ☎(0865) 241363. *Guest House.*
Melcombe House, 227 Iffley Rd, OX4 1SQ ☎(0865) 249520. *Guest House.* Closed Xmas.
£ B&B £18
Pickwick, 17 London Rd, Headington OX3 7SP ☎(0865) 750487. *Private Hotel.*
Pine Castle, 290 Iffley Rd, OX4 4AE ☎(0865) 241497. *Guest House.* Closed Xmas. ✗ Fr, De
£ B&B £16–£19; WB £16; [10% V w/e Sep–May, 2/3 nts only)
Portland House, 338 Banbury Rd, OX2 7PR ☎(0865) 52076. *Guest House.*
£ B&B £17–£18
River, 17 Botley Rd, OX2 0AA ☎(0865) 24375 Fax: (0865) 724306. *Hotel.* Closed 21 Dec–1 Jan
£ B&B £33–£45
Willow Reaches, 1 Wytham Street, OX1 4SU ☎(0865) 721545. Fax: (0865) 251139 *Hotel.*
£ B&B £36–£48; HB weekly £357
Windrush, 11 Iffley Rd, OX4 1EA ☎(0865) 247933. *Guest House.* ✗ Hi, Pu, Ur
£ B&B £17·50–£21

OXTED Surrey. Map 9A1

Purley 9½, London 21, M25 (jn 6) 3, Crawley 17, East Grinstead 10, Redhill 8, Westerham 3½.

★★ Hoskins, Station Rd West, RH8 9EE ☎(0883) 712338 Fax: (0883) 716456
Round modern brick-built public house with letting rooms.
🛏 11 bedrs, 11 en suite; TV; tcf
🏨 TV, dogs; P 23, coach; child facs; con 35
✕ LD 9, nr Sun
£ B&B £53·75 (w/e £33·50), B&B (double) £65 (w/e £42); [10% V]
cc Access, Amex, B'card/Visa, Diners.

PADSTOW Cornwall. Map 2B2

See also CONSTANTINE BAY & TREYARNON BAY.
Pop 3,000. Wadebridge 7½, London 246, Newquay 14, St Austell 18, Truro 23.
EC Wed. **MD** Thur. **Golf** Trevose Gold and CC 18h. **See** 13th–15th cent St Petroc's Church, Tropical Bird and Butterfly Garden, Trevose Head.

★★★ Metropole, Station Rd, PL28 8DB ☎(0841) 532486 Fax: (0841) 532867

Hotel above the town overlooking the Camel estuary. Swimming pool, putting. (THF)
🛏 44 bedrs, 44 en suite; TV; tcf
🏨 lift, dogs, ns; P 35, coach; child facs; con 40
✕ LD 9, bar meals only Mon–Sat lunch
£ B&B £73, B&B (double) £85; D £15; WB £50
cc Access, Amex, B'card/Visa, Diners.

★★ Old Custom House, South Quay, PL28 8BY ☎(0841) 532359
Delightful inn with views of busy harbour and Camel Estuary.
🛏 24 bedrs, 24 en suite, 1 ba; TV; tcf
🏨 TV; coach; child facs; con 30

Green Waves (Highly Acclaimed), Trevone Bay, PL28 8RD ☎(0841) 520114. *Private Hotel.* Open Apr–Sep.
£ B&B £15–£20; HB weekly £120–£150
Woodlands (Highly Acclaimed), Treator, PL28 8RU ☎(0841) 532426. *Private Hotel.* Open Mar–Oct.
£ B&B £23·50–£25·50; WB £78 (3 nts); [5% V Mar–31 May & Sep–31 Oct]; dep.

Old Mill (Acclaimed), Little Petherick, PL27 7QT ☎Rumford (0841) 540388. *Hotel.*
£ B&B (double) £37–£46; HB weekly £188–£219.

Bay House, Porthcothan Bay, PL28 8LW ☎(0841) 520472. *Hotel.*
£ B&B £15–£17; HB weekly £114–£143.
Dower House, Fentonluna La, PL28 8BA ☎(0841) 532317. *Private Hotel.*
£ B&B £18–£26·50; HB weekly £150–£210; dep.
Tregea, 16 High St, PL28 8BB ☎(0841) 532455. *Hotel.*

PAIGNTON Torbay. Devon. Map 3C2

Pop 35,100. Torquay 3, London 191, Dartmouth (Fy) 7½, Totnes 6.
EC Wed. **Golf** Churston 18h.
ℹ Esplanade. ☎(0803) 558383

★★★ Palace, Esplanade Rd, TQ4 6BJ ☎(0803) 555121 Fax: (0803) 527974

Early Victorian spacious building on sea front. Swimming pool, tennis, squash, sauna, solarium, gymnasium. (THF)
🛏 52 bedrs, 52 en suite; TV; tcf
🏨 lift, dogs, ns; P 60, coach; child facs; con 45
✕ LD 9, bar meals only Mon–Sat lunch
£ B&B £65 (w/e £51), B&B (double) £86; Bk £7·50, D £11·50
cc Access, Amex, B'card/Visa, CB, Diners.

★★★ H Redcliffe, Marine Drive, TQ3 2NL ☎(0803) 526397
Fax: (0803) 528030

18th century 'castle' in grounds on water's edge with fine view. Swimming pool, putting, fishing.
🛏 63 bedrs, 63 en suite, 2 ba; TV; tcf
🏨 lift, TV; P 80, coach; child facs; con 150
(See advertisement on p. 390)

★★ Dainton, 95 Dartmouth Rd, Three Beaches, Goodrington, TQ4 6NA ☎(0803) 550067
Early 20th century residence, now a privately owned hotel. Sauna.
🛏 11 bedrs, 10 en suite; 1 ba; TV; tcf
🏨 TV, dogs, ns; P 20; child facs
✕ LD 9.30
£ L £5·50, D £9
cc Access, B'card/Visa; dep.

★★ Sunhill, Alta Vista Rd, Goodrington Sands, TQ4 6DA ☎(0803) 557532
Fax: (0803) 663850

Iffley (Oxford)

The Tree Hotel

Iffley Village, Oxford OX4 4EY

Tel: (0865) 775974 Fax: (0865) 747554

A small family hotel situated within 1½ miles Oxford city centre. All rooms en suite, with licensed bar and traditional home cooked food

Proprietors: A. & D. Bowman FBII

Oxford (Oxfordshire)

Westwood Country Hotel ETB 4 Crowns

Hinksey Hill Top, OX1 5BG

Tel: (0865) 735408

Fax: (0865) 736536

Proprietor: Mr & Mrs A.J. and M. Parker

A family run hotel with 26 bedrooms, all with private facilities, radio, intercom, colour TV, hairdryer, video and tea/coffee making facilities. Three acres of gardens and woodland. Excellent food, log fires in cold weather. Intimate bar. For Hotel guests, sauna, jacuzzi and mini gym available.

AWARDED HOTEL OF THE YEAR 1987 BY BOOKER (FOODS)

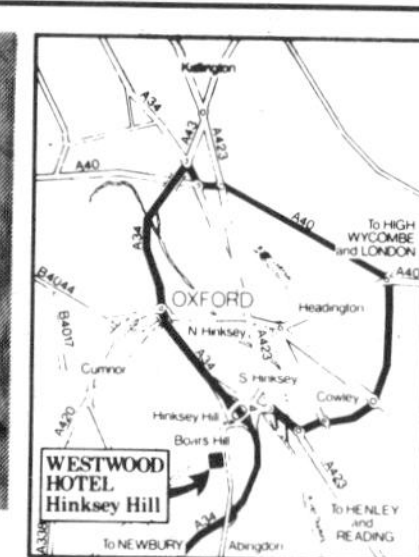

Paignton (Devon)

REDCLIFFE HOTEL

RAC ***

MARINE DRIVE, PAIGNTON

A superbly situated 63 bedroomed hotel standing in 4 acres of attractive grounds directly adjoining the beach in the centre of beautiful Torbay.

* All rooms with private bathroom, radio, telephone and colour TV.
* Sea-view Restaurant offering first class cuisine and service.
* Heated outdoor pool
* Ballroom with regular dancing during the season.
* Putting, table tennis, pool.
* Ample parking in grounds.
* Conference Facilities.

Telephone: (0803) 526397

Fax: (0803) 528030

Extended former private house recently refurbished. Lovely views of Paignton sands, half a mile away.
🛏 29 bedrs, 29 en suite; TV; tcf
🏠 lift, dogs, ns; P 29, coach; no children under 4; con 50
★★ Torbay Holiday, Totnes Rd, TQ4 7PP ☎(0803) 558226
Purpose built motel on A385. Indoor & outdoor swimming pools, sauna, solarium, gymnasium. Closed 24–31 Dec.
🛏 16 bedrs, 16 en suite; TV; tcf
🏠 dogs; P 120; child facs
✕ LD 9, bar meals only lunch
£ B&B £23–£26, B&B (double) £36–£42; D £8·50
cc Access, B'card/Visa; dep.
(*See advertisement on p. 392*)
★ H Oldway Links, Southfield Rd, TQ2 2LZ ☎(0803) 559332

Square building with a partly terraced garden, high up in a residential area. Good views.
🛏 13 bedrs. 10 en suite, (1 sh), 3 ba; TV; tcf
🏠 dogs; P 40, coach; child facs
✕ LD 8, bar meals only lunch. Resid & Rest lic
£ B&B £20–£23; HB weekly £213·50–£234·50; D £11·50; [10% V]
cc Access, B'card/Visa; dep.
★ Preston Sands, Marine Par, TQ3 2NU ☎(0803) 558718

Family-run holiday hotel situated on the sea front.
🛏 26 bedrs, 26 en suite, 1 ba; TV; tcf
🏠 TV, dogs; P 24; coach; no children under 10
✕ LD 7.30. Resid & Rest lic
£ B&B £18–£24; B&B (double) £36–£48; HB weekly £140–£210; D £8·50; [10% V]
Channel View (Acclaimed), 8 Marine Par, Sea Front, TQ3 2NU ☎(0803) 522432. *Private Hotel.*
Hotel Retreat (Acclaimed), 43 Marine Dr, TQ3 2NS ☎(0803) 550596. *Hotel.* Open Apr–Sep.
£ B&B £16–£20; HB weekly £144–£185
St. Weonards (Acclaimed), 12 Kernou Rd, TQ4 6BA ☎(0803) 558842. *Private Hotel.*
£ B&B £13–£18; HB weekly £120–£135; dep.
Sea Verge (Acclaimed), Marine Dr, Preston, TQ3 2NJ ☎(0803) 557795. *Hotel.* Closed Dec.
Sealawn (Acclaimed), 20 Esplanade, TQ4 6BE ☎(0803) 559031. *Private Hotel. Solarium.*
£ B&B £21–£27; HB weekly £147–£189; [V Oct–May]

Bayview, 6 Cleveland Rd, TQ4 6EN ☎(0803) 557400. *Hotel. Putting, billiards.*
Beresford, Adelphi Rd, TQ4 6AW ☎(0803) 551560. *Private Hotel.*
£ B&B fr £14
Blue Seas, 4 St Andrews Rd, TQ4 6HA ☎(0803) 558348. *Hotel.* Open Mar–Oct
£ B&B £10·95–£15; HB weekly £109·55–£117·95; WB £30 (2 nts); [10% V Mar–Jun].
Florida, 9 Colin Rd, Preston, TQ3 2NR ☎(0803) 551447. *Guest House.*
Palm Sands, 21 Morin Rd, Preston, TQ3 2PL ☎(0803) 523226. *Private Hotel.*
£ B&B £13–£15; HB weekly £80–£95; dep.
Sattva, 29 Esplanade, TQ4 6BL ☎(0803) 557820. *Private Hotel.* Open Mar–Oct.
£ B&B £20–£28; HB weekly £120–£170; [5% V Mar–May, Sep–Oct]
Sunnybank, 2 Cleveland Rd, TQ4 6EN ☎(0803) 525540. *Private Hotel.*
Torbay Sands, 16 Marine Par, Preston, TQ3 2NU ☎(0803) 525568. *Private Hotel.*
£ B&B £12–£15; HB weekly £95–£120; [10% V Oct–May].

PAINSWICK Gloucestershire. Map 20B2

Pop 3,154. Stroud 3½, London 103, Cheltenham 10, Gloucester 6.
EC Wed. **MD** Fri. **Golf** Painswick 18h.
See 14th cent Church, Painswick House.
ℹ The Library, Stroud Rd. ☎(0452) 813552

★★★ Painswick, Kemps La, GL6 6YB ☎(0452) 812160
Georgian house with well-furnished rooms. In town centre. Billiards.
🛏 15 bedrs, 15 en suite; TV; tcf
🏠 dogs, ns; P 20, coach; child facs
✕ LD 9.30, bar meals only lunch Mon–Sat lunch, Sun dinner. Resid & Rest lic
£ B&B £60, B&B (double) £80; L £10, D £25
cc Access, Amex, B'card/Visa, Diners; dep.

★★ Falcon, New St, GL6 6YB ☎(0452) 812189
16th century former inn rebuilt in Queen Anne's time. ⚒ Es
🛏 10 bedrs, 10 en suite, 1 ba; TV; tcf
🏠 dogs; P 50, coach; child facs
✕ LD 9.30; bar meals only Sun dinner
£ B&B £35, B&B (double) £49·50; L £5, D £11·95; [5% V]
cc Access, Amex, B'card/Visa; dep.

PANGBOURNE Berkshire, Map 12B3

Pop 2,460. Reading 6, London 45, M4 (jn 12) 5, Basingstoke 18, Newbury 13, Wallingford 10, Wantage 18.
Golf Calcot Park 18h.

★★★ Copper Inn, Church Rd, RG8 7AR ☎(0734) 842244 Tx: 849041 Fax: (0734) 845542

Half-timbered, former coaching inn with well-furnished extension. Pleasant gardens. ♿
⚒ Fr, It, Th
🛏 14 bedrs, 14 en suite; annexe 8 bedrs, 8 en suite; TV; tcf
🏠 dogs; P 30; child facs; con 60
✕ LD 9.30
£ B&B £65–£75, B&B (double) £85–£90; L £13·50, D £16·95; WB £42 (2 nts)
cc Access, Amex, B'card/Visa, Diners.
★★ George, The Square, RG8 7AJ ☎(0734) 842237 Tx: 849910 Fax: (0734) 844354

A 3-storey half-timbered inn with a history going back to 13th century. Situated in centre of village. ⚒ Fr, Ma, Ar
🛏 16 bedrs, 8 en suite, (9 sh); TV; tcf
🏠 dogs; P 17, coach; child facs; con 100
✕ LD 10
£ B&B £34·25–£54·25 (w/e £25), B&B (double) £59·50; L £8·50, D £10·50
cc Access, Amex, B'card/Visa, Diners.
(*See advertisement on p. 392*)

PAR Cornwall. Map 2C1

Pop 1,187. Liskeard 16, London 237, Bodmin 9½, Fowey 3½, Launceston 30, St Austell 4½.
EC Thur. **Golf** Carlyon Bay 18h, St Austell 18h. **See** 10th cent monolith in churchyard.
Elmswood, 73 Tehidy Rd, Tywardreath, PL24 2QD ☎(072 681) 4221. *Private Hotel.*

PARBOLD Lancashire. Map 32B3

Pop 4,236. M6 (jn 27) 3, London 199, Ormskirk 6½, Preston 15, Skelmersdale 4½, Southport 13, Wigan 8.
Golf Beacon Park 18h.
★★ C Lindley, Lancaster Lane, WN8 7AB ☎(025 76) 2804
Former private house with wooded lawned grounds on slopes of hill.

PARKGATE Cheshire. Map 32A1

12 m NW of Chester. London 195, Birkenhead 10, Northwich 29, Queensferry 10, Warrington 28.
★★★ Ship, The Parade, L64 6SA ☎051-336 3931

Paignton (Devon)

TORBAY HOLIDAY MOTEL

IDEAL FOR A SUMMER HOLIDAY OR OVERNIGHT ACCOMMODATION

● Heated Pool ● Sauna ● Solarium ● Restaurant ● Bar ● Shop ● 35-acre Picnic Area ●

Brochure from: Dept RAC, Torbay Holiday Model, Totnes Road, Paignton.
Tel: 0803-558226

★★ *RAC* *4 Crowns ETB*

Pangbourne (Berkshire)

THE GEORGE HOTEL & RESTAURANT

The Square, Pangbourne RG8 7AJ
Tel: (0734) 842237 Fax: (0734) 844354 Telex: 849910

This privately owned hotel is situated just 5 miles from M4 J12, has 17 bedrooms, 8 en-suite. Weddings, conferences and parties are catered for.

Penrith (Cumbria)

EDENHALL HOTEL

Edenhall, Penrith, Cumbria CA11 8SX Tel: 076881 454

The Edenhall Hotel is situated in the picturesque village of Edenhall, 3½ miles from M6 motorway. All rooms en-suite, excellent dining room, extensive wine list.

Penrith (Cumbria)

THE MILL INN

Mungrisdale, near Penrith, Cumbria CA11 0XR Tel: 059 683 632

16th Century Inn, situated at foot of Blencathra (Saddleback). A real 'get away from it all' holiday. 2 miles A66. Real ale, home cooking, warm friendly atmosphere.

Penzance (Cornwall)

THE QUEENS HOTEL

SPACIOUS AND ELEGANT VICTORIAN HOTEL

Enjoying spectacular views of Mounts Bay from it's promenade location. Excellent cuisine specializes in freshest sea food, and only best local produce used. Extensive wine cellar and choice of beers. Good value is a tradition at this genuinely charming hotel.

- *STROLLERS Fabulous brasserie bar and restaurant*
- *Free Health Club Membership* • *Fresh Seafood a Speciality*
- *Art and Antique Furnishings Throughout*
- *Spectacular Sea Views* • *Choice of Special Breaks*

RAC★★★

THE PROMENADE · PENZANCE · CORNWALL TR18 4HG · TEL (0736) 62371

Attractive early 19th century building with beautiful views across Dee Estuary. (THF) ⚒ Fr, Es
🛏 26 bedrs, 26 en suite; TV; tcf
🏨 dogs; P 60, coach; child facs; con 20
✕ LD 9.30; bar snacks only Mon–Fri lunch
£ B&B £60, B&B (double) £65–£76; D £12·50; WB £29
cc Access, Amex, B'card/Visa, Diners.

★★ Parkgate, Boathouse La, L64 6RD ☎051-336 5001 Tx: 629469 Fax: 051-336 8504
Fine period house set in own grounds on edge of Dee. (Lns)
🛏 27 bedrs, 27 en suite; TV; tcf
🏨 dogs, ns; P 150, coach; child facs; con 110
✕ LD 11
£ B&B £63, B&B (double) £76; L £8·95, D £14; WB £50; [V]
cc Access, Amex, B'card/Visa, Diners.

PARKHAM Devon. Map 3A4

Bideford 6, London 208, Bude 17, Holsworthy 13, Great Torrington 8.

★★★ C R Penhaven Country House, Nr Bideford, EX39 5PL ☎Horns Cross (023 75) 711 Fax: (023 75) 878
Attractive former Victorian rectory in 11 acres of woodland and garden.
🛏 12 bedrs, 12 en suite; TV; tcf
🏨 dogs; P 40; children over 10; con 15
✕ LD 9, Resid & Rest lic
£ B&B £36·50–£42·50, B&B (double) £75–£97; D £12·95; WB £79·50; [10% V Oct–Mar]
cc Access, Amex, B'card/Visa, Diners; dep.

PARKSTONE Dorset

See POOLE

PATELEY BRIDGE North Yorkshire. Map 38B3

Pop 1,900. Harrogate 14, London 217, Leeds 27, Leyburn 31, Skipton 20.
EC Thur. **Golf** Ripon 9h.
ℹ Southlands Car Park, off High St. ☎(0423) 711147

★★ Harefield Hall, HG3 5QE ☎ (0423) 711429
Manorial style stone house on fringe of town overlooking river. Fishing.
🛏 16 bedrs, 16 en suite; annexe 10 bedrs, 10 en suite, 2 ba; TV; tcf
🏨 TV, dogs; P 50, coach; child facs; con 60
✕ LD 9.30, bar meals only Mon–Fri lunch
£ B&B £29, B&B (double) £47; L £6, D £8·50
cc Access, Amex, B'card/Visa, Diners; dep.

Roslyn House, King St, HG3 5AT ☎(0423) 711374. *Private Hotel.*
Talbot, High St, HG3 5AL ☎(0423) 711597. *Private Hotel.* Open Feb–Oct.
£ B&B £16–£18·50; HB weekly £150·50–£175

PATTERDALE Cumbria. Map 43C1

Pop 444. M6 (jn 36) 28, London 276, Ambleside 8, Kendal 20, Penrith 14.
Golf Penrith 18h. **See** Quaint Church, old Spinning Gallery, Aira Force, Ullswater, Helvellyn 3,118 ft.

★★ Patterdale, CA11 0NN ☎Glenridding (076 84) 82231 Fax: (076 84) 82440
Stone-built 3-storey hotel close to shores of Ullswater. Fishing. Open Mar–Nov.
🛏 57 bedrs, 57 en suite, 6 ba; TV; tcf
🏨 TV, dogs; P 40, coach; child facs
✕ LD 8
£ B&B £20–£27, B&B (double) £40–£54; HB weekly £250; D £12·50; [5% V Apr–Jun, Sep–Oct]
cc Access, B'card/Visa.

PEASLAKE Surrey, Map 10A1

Pop 1,241. Leatherhead 10, London 29, Dorking 6½, Guildford 8½, Haslemere 19, Horsham 12, Woking 12.
Golf Merrow 18h. **See** Old Cottages.

★★ Hurtwood Inn, Walking Bottom, GU5 9RR ☎Dorking (0306) 730851

A picturesque timbered building, situated in a Surrey country lane. (THF) ⚒ Fr, Gr
🛏 10 bedrs, 2 en suite; annexe 8 bedrs, 8 en suite, 2 ba; TV; tcf
🏨 TV, ns; P 30, coach; child facs; con 30
✕ LD 9.30
£ B&B £42, B&B (double) £49; HB weekly £280–£329; L £11, D £13; WB £49
cc Access, Amex, B'card/Visa, CB, Diners; dep.

PELYNT Cornwall. Map 2C2

Pop 700. Looe 4, London 231, Bodmin 16, Fowey 19 (Fy 6), Liskeard 11, St Austell 20.
EC Wed. **Golf** Looe Bin Down 18h. **See** 15th cent Church, (Trelawney's Grave).

★★ Jubilee Inn, Jubilee Hill, PL13 2JZ ☎Lanreath (0503) 20312
Two-storey Cornish country inn with old world charm.

PENCRAIG Hereford & Worcester (Herefordshire). Map 20A2

Ross-on-Wye 4, London 125, M50 (jn 4) 5, Monmouth 7.
Golf Monmouth 18h. Ross 18h.

★★ Pencraig Court, nr Ross-on-Wye, HR9 6HR ☎Llangarron (098 984) 306
A small family-run country house in pleasant grounds. Riding. Open Apr–Oct. ⚒ Fr
🛏 11 bedrs, 11 en suite; TV
🏨 P 25, coach; child facs; con 25
✕ LD 9, bar meals only lunch. Resid & Rest lic
£ B&B £31–£35, B&B (double) £40–£48; HB weekly £217; D £12·50; WB £66
cc Access, Amex, B'card/Visa, Diners; dep.

PENDOGGETT Cornwall. Map 2C2

Camelford 6½, London 234, Bodmin 10, Wadebridge 6½.
EC Thur. **Golf** St Endoc, Rock 18h.

★★ Cornish Arms, St Kew, PL30 3HH ☎Bodmin (0208) 880263
Old 2-storey stone-built Cornish inn with modern bedroom extension.
🛏 7 bedrs, 5 en suite, 1 ba; TV; tcf
🏨 TV; dogs, ns; P 55, coach

PENRITH Cumbria. Map 44A2

See also EDENHALL
Pop 12,093. Kendal 25, London 276, M6 (jn 40) ½, Alston 19, Ambleside 22, Brough 21, Carlisle 18, Keswick 16.
EC Wed. **MD** Tue. **Golf** Penrith 18h.
ℹ Middlegate. ☎(0768) 67466

★★★★ North Lakes, Ullswater Rd, CA11 8QT ☎(0768) 68111 Tx: 64257 Fax: (0768) 68291 ♿

Modern stone-built 3-storey hotel near M6. Impressive foyer-lounge featuring massive fireplace. Indoor swimming pool, squash, sauna, solarium, gymnasium, billiards.
🛏 85 bedrs, 85 en suite; TV; tcf
🏨 lift, dogs, ns; P 150, coach; child facs; con 200
✕ LD 9.45, bar meals only Sat lunch
£ B&B £84–£100, B&B (double) £108–£124; HB weekly £686–£798; L £11·50, D £14; WB £122 (2 nts)
cc Access, Amex, B'card/Visa, Diners; dep.

★★★ George, 23 Devonshire St, CA11 7SU ☎(0768) 62696 Fax: (0768) 68223
Substantial well-appointed former coaching house; stone-built in Georgian style. ⚒ Fr, De. Closed 25 & 26 Dec & 1 Jan.
🛏 32 bedrs, 31 en suite, 2 ba; TV; tcf
🏨 dogs; P 30, coach; child facs; con 100
✕ LD 8.30, nr Sun dinner
£ B&B £37, B&B (double) £49·50; L £6·50, D £10·50; WB £70; [10% V]
cc Access, B'card/Visa; dep.

★★ Clifton Hill, Clifton, CA10 2EJ (2¾ m S A6) ☎(0768) 62717
Modernised hotel in charming Edwardian style building south of the town.

★★ Glen Cottage, Corney Sq, CA11 7PX ☎(0768) 62221
Attractive cottage-style building situated close to town centre.
🛏 7 bedrs, 4 en suite, 1 ba; TV; tcf
🏨 dogs, ns; U 3; child facs
✕ LD 9
£ B&B £19·50–£25, B&B (double) £31–£37; L £3·95, D £5·50; [V Nov–Feb]
cc Access, Amex, Diners; dep.

Grotto (Acclaimed), Yanwath, CA10 2LF ☎(0768) 63288. *Hotel.*
£ B&B £20; HB weekly £200
Woodland House (Acclaimed), Wordsworth St, CA11 7QY ☎(0768) 64177. *Private Hotel.*
£ B&B £15–£18; HB weekly £152–£172; dep.

Barco, Carleton Rd, CA11 8LR ☎(0768) 63176. *Guest House.*
Limes Country, Redhills, Stainton, CA11 0DT ☎(0768) 63343. *Hotel.*
£ B&B £14–£20; HB weekly £140–£180; WB £17·50 (Oct–Mar).
Voreda View, 2 Portland Pl, CA11 7QN ☎(0768) 63395. *Guest House.*
£ B&B £14–£18; [V Sun]

PENRYN
Cornwall. Map 2B1

Pop 5,090. Truro 8½, London 263, Falmouth 2, Helston 10, Redruth 8.
EC Thur. **Golf** Falmouth 18h. **See** St Gluvias Church, Museum, Town Hall, Queen Ann Cottage.

Prospect House (Acclaimed), 1 Church Rd, TR10 8DA ☎(0326) 73198. *Guest House.* Fr, De
£ B&B £15–£25; HB weekly £178·50–£248·50; [5% V Oct–Apr]; dep.

PENSHURST
Kent. Map 11B1

Pop 1,633. Westerham 9, London 32, East Grinstead 10, Sevenoaks 8, Tonbridge 5, Tunbridge Wells 5.
EC Mon. **Golf** Tunbridge Wells, Knole Park 18h. **See** Penshurst Place, Church.

★★ **Leicester Arms,** TN11 8BT ☎(0892) 870551
An attractive old timbered coach house in a picturesque village.
7 bedrs, 7 en suite; TV; tcf
TV, dogs, ns; P 30, coach; child facs
LD 9.30, bar meals only Mon & Sun dinner. Rest lic
£ B&B £40, B&B (double) £55; L £10·50, D £10·50; [10% V]
cc Acess, Amex, B'card/Visa, Diners.

PENZANCE
Cornwall. Map 2A1

Pop 19,579. Redruth 17, London 281, Helston 13, St Ives 8.
EC Wed. **MD** Tue, Thur, Sat. **Golf** West Cornwall Lelant 18h. **See** Penlee Memorial Park, with Museum, Market Cross, Nautical Museum, Geological Museum, Gulval Church, Madron Church.
i Station Rd. ☎(0736) 62207

★★★ **Mount Prospect,** Britons Hill, TR18 3AE ☎(0736) 63117 Fax: (0736) 50970
Attractive stone-built hotel with breathtaking views of Mount's Bay. Swimming pool.
Fr, De
26 bedrs, 26 en suite, 1 ba; TV; tcf
TV, dogs, ns; P 14; child facs; con 100
LD 9, bar meals only lunch. Resid & Rest lic
£ B&B £34·50, B&B (double) £55·20; HB weekly £234·60; D £11·50
cc Access, Amex, B'card/Visa, Diners; dep.

★★★ **Queen's,** Promenade, TR18 4HG ☎(0736) 62371
Large white hotel with fine views over Mount's Bay. Sauna, solarium, gymnasium.
71 bedrs, 71 en suite, 6 ba; TV; tcf
lift, dogs; P 70, coach; child facs
LD 8.45, bar meals only Mon–Sat lunch
£ B&B £33–£44, B&B (double) £60–£80; L £5·90, D £14; [10% V]
cc Access, Amex, B'card/Visa, Diners; dep.
(*See advertisement on p. 392*)

Beechfield, The Promenade, TR18 4NW ☎(0736) 62067
Under refurbishment, completion expected March 1991.

Estoril (Highly Acclaimed), 46 Morrab Rd, TR18 4EX ☎(0736) 62468. *Hotel.* Open Feb–Nov.
£ B&B £23–£24; HB weekly £192·50–£220; [10% V]
Tarbert (Highly Acclaimed), 11 Clarence St, TR18 2NU ☎(0736) 63758. *Hotel.* Open 15 Jan–30 Nov. Fr, Es
£ B&B £22·50–£25·50, HB weekly £180–£216.

Sea and Horses (Acclaimed), 6 Alexandra Terr, TR18 4NX ☎(0736) 61961. *Hotel.* Open Feb–Nov.
£ B&B £16–£19; HB weekly £166–£185

Alexandra, Alexandra Terr, TR18 4NX ☎(0736) 62644. *Hotel.*
Blue Seas, Regent Ter, TR18 4DW ☎(0736) 64744
Camilla House, 12 Regent Terr, TR18 4DE ☎(0736) 63771. *Private Hotel.* Fr, De, It, Du
£ B&B £14·50–£17·50; HB weekly £135–£150
Carlton, Promenade, TR18 4NW ☎(0736) 62081. *Private Hotel.* Open Mar–Oct.
£ B&B £14–£15; [5% V]
Carnson House, 2 East Terr, TR18 2TD ☎(0736) 65589. *Hotel.* Fr, De
£ B&B £13·50–£15·50; HB weekly £120–£162·50; [5% V]
Dunedin, Alexandra Rd, TR18 4LZ ☎(0736) 62652. *Hotel.*
£ B&B £12–£14; HB weekly £124–£132.
Georgian House, 20 Chapel St, TR18 4AW ☎(0736) 65664. *Hotel.*
£ B&B £16·10–£20·70.
Keigwin, Alexandra Rd, TR18 4LZ ☎(0736) 63930. *Private Hotel.* Closed Xmas.
£ B&B £10·50; HB weekly £105–£133
Kimberley House, 10 Morrab Rd, TR18 4EZ ☎(0736) 62727. *Guest House.* Open Feb–Dec.
£ B&B £12–£13; HB weekly £114–£124
Lynwood, 41 Morrab Rd, TR18 4EX ☎(0736) 65871. *Guest House.*
£ B&B £11–£12; [5% V]
Mount Royal, Chyandour Cliff, TR18 3LQ ☎(0736) 62233. *Private Hotel.* Open Apr–Oct.
£ B&B £24–£26; [10% V].
Panorama, Chywoone Hill, Newlyn, TR18 5AR ☎(0736) 68498. *Private Hotel.*
£ B&B £16–£19; HB weekly £166–£186; [5% V]
Penmorvah, Alexandra Rd, TR18 4LZ ☎(0736) 63711. *Private Hotel.*
Southern Comfort, Alexandra Terr, Sea Front, TR18 4NX ☎(0736) 66333. *Hotel.*
Trevelyan, 16 Chapel St, TR18 4AW ☎(0736) 62494. *Hotel.* Closed Xmas.
£ B&B £11–£12; HB weekly £115–£120; [5% V Dec–May].
Trewella, 18 Mennaye Rd, TR18 4NG ☎(0736) 63818. *Guest House.* Open Mar–Oct.
£ B&B £10·25–£12·75; HB weekly £106·75–£124·25; [5% V 3 days min, Mar–Jun, Sep–Oct].
Woodstock, 29 Morrab Rd, TR18 4EL ☎(0736) 69049. *Guest House.*
£ B&B £9·50–£13·50; HB weekly £66·50–£94·50; [10% V Jan, Feb, Oct, Nov]

PERRANPORTH
Cornwall. Map 2B2

Pop 1,750. Bodmin 24, London 257, Newquay 8, Redruth 10, Truro 9.
Golf Perranporth 18h. **See** Remains of 6th cent Church, Piran Round (open air theatre), Perran Bay, St Agnes Head.

Villa Margarita Country (Acclaimed), Bone Mill Rd, Bolingey, TR6 0AS ☎Truro (0872) 572063. *Hotel. Swimming pool.*
£ B&B £18·50; HB weekly £176–£185; dep.

Beach Dunes, Ramoth Way, Reen Sands, TR6 0BY ☎(0872) 572263 Fax: (0872) 572263. *Hotel. Indoor swimming pool, squash.*
Cellar Cove, Droskyn Way, TR6 0DS ☎(0872) 572110. *Hotel. Swimming pool.*
Fairview, Tywarnhayle Rd, TR6 0DX ☎(0872) 572278. *Hotel.* Open Mar–Oct.
£ B&B £12·60–£14·50; HB weekly £110–£126·50

PERSHORE
Hereford & Worcester (Worcestershire). Map 20B3

Pop 5,767. Evesham 6½, London 104, M5 (jn 7) 6, Cheltenham 17, Stratford-upon-Avon 20, Tewkesbury 10, Worcester 9½.
EC Thur. **Golf** Evesham (Hadbury) 9h. **See** Abbey Church, St Andrew's Church.
i 19 High St. ☎(0386) 554262

★★★ **Angel Inn,** High St, WR10 1AF ☎(0386) 552046 Fax: (0386) 552581
Old posting house in town centre. Gardens beside river.
16 bedrs, 16 en suite; TV; tcf
dogs; P 30, coach; child facs

PETERBOROUGH
Cambridgeshire. Map 31C1

See also NORMAN CROSS
Pop 110,000. Alconbury 13, London 83, Kettering 28, Leicester 42, Spalding 17, Stamford 14, Wisbech 20.
EC Thur. **MD** Wed, Fri, Sat. **Golf** New Milton, Peterborough 18h. **See** Cathedral, Bishop's Palace, Museum, Old Guildhall, 15th cent St John's Church.
i 45 Bridge St. ☎(0733) 317336

★★★★ C **Swallow,** Alwalton Village, Lynch Wood, PE2 0GB ☎(0733) 371111 Tx: 32422 Fax: (0733) 236725
Long low hotel, 6 miles south of Peterborough on A605, opposite East of England showground. Indoor swimming pool, sauna, solarium, gymnasium.
163 bedrs, 163 en suite; TV; tcf
TV, dogs, ns; P 180, coach; child facs; con 300
LD 10.30
£ B&B £74, B&B (double) £92; L £11, D £14; WB £92 (2 nts)
cc Access, Amex, B'card/Visa, Diners.

★★★ **Bull,** Westgate, PE1 1RB ☎(0733) 61364 Tx: 329265 Fax: (0733) 557304
Much enlarged and extensively altered old coaching inn in city centre.
112 bedrs, 112 en suite; TV; tcf
dogs; P 85, coach; child facs; con 200
LD 10.30
£ B&B £59·50–£66·50, B&B (double) £72; L £10·45, D £10·45; WB £39·50; [10% V]
cc Access, Amex, B'card/Visa, Diners.

EC *early closing* **MD** *market day* *country house hotel* *ns (NS) no smoking areas* *tcf tea/coffee facilities*

★★★ **Butterfly,** Thorpe Meadows, off Longthorne Parkway, PE3 6GA ☎(0733) 64240 Tx: 818360 Fax: (0733) 65538

Low-built modern hotel on edge of city centre. Pleasant country aspect with mature trees.
🛏 70 bedrs, 70 en suite; TV; tcf
🏨 ns; P 80, coach; child facs; con 80
✕ LD 10
£ B&B £57–£61 (w/e £33·50), B&B (double) £62–£67; L £9·50, D £9·50
cc Access, Amex, B'card/Visa, Diners.
(See advertisement on p. 396)

★★★ **R** **Peterborough Moat House,** Thorpe Wood, PE3 6SG ☎(0733) 260000 Tx: 32708 Fax: (0733) 262737 ♿

Luxury hotel situated well outside the City. Indoor swimming pool, sauna, solarium, gymnasium. (QMH). ⚒ Fr, De, Es, It, Pol, Tu
🛏 125 bedrs, 125 en suite; TV; tcf
🏨 lift, dogs, ns; P 200, coach; child facs; con 400
✕ LD 10, bar meals only Sat lunch
£ B&B £73·25 (w/e £46), B&B (double) £90·50; L £12·95, D £12·95; WB £74 (2 nts)
cc Access, Amex, B'card/Visa, Diners.

Hawthorn House (Acclaimed), 89 Thorpe Rd, PE3 6JQ ☎(0733) 40608. *Hotel.*
£ B&B £38·25–£43·25 (w/e £19·99; [10% V]

Thorpe Lodge (Acclaimed), 83 Thorpe Rd, PE3 6JQ ☎(0733) 48759. *Hotel.* ⚒ De, It, Pl, Ru
£ B&B £36·50–£48·50 (w/e £20)

Aaron Park, 109 Park Rd, PE1 2TR ☎(0733) 64849. *Private Hotel.*
£ B&B £22–£40 (w/e £19); [10% V]

Dalwhinnie Lodge, 31 Burghley Rd, PE1 2QA ☎(0733) 65968
£ B&B £19–£27

PETERLEE Durham. Map 37C1

Pop 24,168. Stockton-on-Tees 17, London 260, Darlington 23, Durham 11, Newcastle upon Tyne 20, Sunderland 11.
EC Wed. **Golf** Castle Eden 18h.
ℹ The Upper Chase. ☎091-586 4450

★★★ **Norseman,** Bede Way, SR8 1BU ☎091-586 2161
Four-storey brick-built modern hotel, in recently developed area of town.

♛ ★★ **Hardwicke Hall,** Heslenden Rd, Blackhall, TS27 4PA ☎Wellfield (0429) 836326

A 3-storey stone-built historic mansion in 8 acres of grounds.
🛏 11 bedrs, 11 en suite; TV; tcf
🏨 P 100, U 3, coach; child facs; con 50
✕ LD 9.30, nr Sun dinner
£ B&B £35–£50, B&B (double) £45–£60; L £6·50; [10% V w/e]
cc Access, Amex, B'card/Visa.

PETTY FRANCE See BADMINTON.

PEVENSEY East Sussex. Map 7A1

Pop 2,656, Uckfield 19, London 65, Eastbourne 4, Hastings 12, Lewes 17.
EC Thur. **Golf** Royal Eastbourne 18h and 9h. **See** Castle ruins, Martello Towers.

★★ **Priory Court,** Pevensey Castle, BN24 5LG ☎Eastbourne (0323) 763150
Hotel in an attractive converted Georgian building opposite Pevensey Castle.
🛏 9 bedrs, 6 en suite; 1 ba; TV; tcf
🏨 TV; dogs; P 60; child facs
✕ LD 9
£ B&B £23–£28, B&B (double) £38–£56
cc Access, B'card/Visa.
(See advertisement on p. 396)

PEVENSEY BAY East Sussex. Map 7A1

Uckfield 20, London 66, Eastbourne 5, Hastings 13, Lewes 18.
See Castle ruins, Martello towers.

Napier, The Promenade, BN24 6HD ☎(0323) 768875. *Guest House.* Open Mar–Nov.
£ B&B £15–£17; HB weekly £110–£125; [5% V Mar, Apr, Sep, Oct]

PICKERING North Yorkshire. Map 39A4

Pop 6,205. Malton 8, London 213, Bridlington 31, Helmsley 13, Scarborough 16, Whitby 20.
EC Wed. **MD** Mon. **Golf** Malton & Norton 18h. **See** Castle ruins, Church (15th cent mural paintings), Steam Railway.
ℹ Eastgate Car Park. ☎(0751) 73791

Discount vouchers

RAC discount vouchers are on p. 34. Hotels with a [V] shown at the end of the price information will accept them in part payment for accommodation bills on the full, standard rate, not against bargain breaks or any other special offers. Please note the limitations shown in the entry: w/e for weekends, w/d for weekdays, and which months they are accepted.

★★ **Crossways**, Eastgate, YO18 7DW ☎(0751) 72804

Stone built hotel with a slate roof and pillared entrancein a residential area at crossing of A170 and A169. ⚒ Fr
🛏 10 bedrs, 7 en suite, 2 ba; TV; tcf
🏨 dogs; P 12, coach; child facs
✕ LD 8.30. Resid lic
£ B&B £18–£20, B&B (double) £20–£27·50; L £7·50, D £15; [10% V w/d]
cc Access, B'card/Visa; dep.

★★ **Forest & Vale,** Malton Rd, YO18 7DL ☎(0751) 72722

Hotel in Yorkshire stone situated in centre of market town.
🛏 12 bedrs, 12 en suite; annexe 5 bedrs, 5 en suite; TV; tcf
🏨 dogs; P 70, coach; child facs; con 120
✕ LD 9
£ B&B £45–£58, B&B (double) £70–£82; HB weekly £290–£315; L £7·80, D £14·50
cc Access, Amex, B'card/Visa, Diners.

★★ **H** **C** **White Swan,** Market Place, YO18 7AA ☎(0751) 72288
Ancient inn set in market place of pleasant Yorkshire town. ⚒ Fr
🛏 13 bedrs, 13 en suite; TV; tcf
🏨 dogs, ns P 35, coach; child facs; con 12
✕ LD 9
£ B&B £35–£38·50, B&B (double) £55–£60; L £8·50, D £15; [5% V w/d Nov–May]
cc Access, B'card/Visa; dep.

PICKHILL North Yorkshire. Map 38B4

A1 1, London 219, Boroughbridge 11, Ripon 9, Scotch Corner 18, Thirsk 8.

★★ **R** **Nags Head,** nr Thirsk, YO7 4JG ☎Thirsk (0845) 567570 Fax: (0845) 567212
Georgian coaching inn of character, with adjacent cottage and modern annexe, in peaceful village.
🛏 8 bedrs, 8 en suite; annexe 7 bedrs, 7 en suite; TV; tcf
🏨 TV; dogs, ns; P 50, coach; child facs; con 34

En suite rooms

En suite rooms may be bath or shower rooms. If you have a preference, remember to state it when booking a room.

Peterborough (Cambridgeshire)

SPECIAL WEEKEND RATES AVAILABLE

Butterfly

RAC
★★★

Situated at the water's edge, in the heart of Hereward Country, this Hotel has been purpose built to meet the needs of the modern traveller and an informal, friendly ambience has been created to help you relax and feel at home. All bedrooms have private bathrooms, TVs, telephone, etc.
'Walt's Place' Restaurant & Bar – for good food, wines and friendly service at affordable prices.

Thorpe Meadows, Off Longthorpe Parkway, Peterborough, Cambridgeshire PE3 6GA. Tel: (0733) 64240. Fax: (0733) 65538.

Pevensey (East Sussex)

Priory Court Hotel

Pevensey, East Sussex BN24 5LG
Telephone (0323) 763150

16th century hotel, situated in 2½ acres opposite Pevensey Castle, offers 9 well equipped bedrooms and two oak beamed à la Carte restuarants featuring fresh local produce. 4 poster bedroom. Free house. Car park.

Pickhill (Yorkshire)

NAGS HEAD HOTEL & RESTAURANT

PICKHILL, Nr THIRSK YO7 4JG. Telephone: (0845) 567391

Residential country inn, family owned. Renowned cuisine, Good Beer Guide. One mile off A1. Bedale, Ripon, Thirsk, Masham and Catterick Golf Courses within 12 miles.

Plymouth (Devon)

Strathmore
Hotel

RAC
★★★

Elliot Street, The Hoe, Plymouth PL1 2PP
Tel: (0752) 662101 Fax: (0752) 223690

APPROVED

Ideally situated on Plymouth's historic Hoe, only 5 minutes' walk from city centre, Barbican and ferry port.
54 well appointed rooms, all en-suite and refurbished to a high standard. Unique canopied restaurant offering English and Continental cuisine, local seafood fresh from the day's catch our speciality.
Distinct lounge bar with Drake theme. Exclusive nightclub in basement. Celebration suite available for weddings, parties, banquets, conferences and exhibitions. Special weekend breaks available.

Plymouth (Devon)

****RAC** **Invicta Hotel** **RAC****

11/12 OSBORNE PLACE, LOCKYER STREET
THE HOE, PLYMOUTH PL1 2PU Tel (0752) 664997

This modern, licensed family-run hotel and conference suite, is directly opposite the gateway to the world famous Plymouth Hoe and is also in direct line of a minute's walk from the City Centre and historical Barbican. The Hotel is also ideally suited to travellers using Britanny Ferries.

* 23 bedrooms, 20 with private facilities. Colour TV, telephone, C/Heating, tea/coffee making facilities in all rooms.
* Excellent restaurant food * Licensed Bar & Lounge * Car Parking
* Private conference or party suite with bar for 10–100 persons

For full Colour Brochure & Tariff –
Telephone (0752) 664997 or write to 'Invicta Hotel'

✕ LD 9.30, bar meals only Sun dinner. Resid & Rest lic
£ B&B £26, B&B (double) £44; L £9, D £12
cc Access, B'card/Visa.
(See advertisement on p. 396)

PIDDLETRENTHIDE Dorset. Map 4C2
Pop 594. Blandford Forum 15, Dorchester 7, Wareham 18, Sherborne 13.
Golf Came Down 18h.

★★★ **Poachers Inn,** DT2 7QX
(030 04) 358
An attractive, 16th century inn with bedroom extension; garden to the river. Swimming pool.
10 bedrs, 10 en suite; TV; tcf
dogs; P 40; child facs
✕ LD 9
£ B&B £18, B&B (double) £32–£34; L fr £6, D fr £8; WB £25; [5% V]

★★ H R **Old Bakehouse,** DT2 7QR
(030 04) 305
Attractive old world building with modern annexe. In the village street. Swimming pool. Closed Jan.
3 bedrs, 3 en suite; annexe 7 bedrs, 7 en suite; TV; tcf
dogs; P 16; no children under 12
✕ LD 9, nr lunch. Rest lic
£ B&B £24·50, B&B (double) £44–£50; D £12·75; WB
cc Access, B'card/Visa; dep.

PILSLEY Derbyshire. Map 24A2
Alfreton 5, London 143, Chesterfield 6½, Mansfield 9, Matlock 10.

Shoulder of Mutton Inn, Hardstoft, S4S 8AF Chesterfield (0246) 850276.
Private Hotel.

PLYMOUTH Devon. Map 3A2
RAC Office, *RAC House, 15–17 Union St, Plymouth, PL1 2SZ* (0752) 669301
Pop 255,200. Ashburton 24, London 211, Kingsbridge 20, Saltash 4, Tavistock 14, Totnes 22.
See Plan, p. 398.
P See Plan. **Golf** Yelverton 18h. **See** Citadel, The Hoe (Drake's Statue), Elizabethan House, Museum and Art Gallery, Smeaton's Tower (Aquarium), RC Cathedral, Brunel's Rly Bridge, Tamar Road Bridge, Barbican (curio shops, tiny alleys), St Andrew's Church, Civic Centre, Guildhall, Devonport Dockyard, Saltram House 3 m E.
i Civic Centre, Royal Par. (0752) 264849

★★★★ **Copthorne Plymouth,** Armada Way, PL1 1AR (0752) 224161 Tx: 45756
Fax: (0752) 670688 ♿

Five-storey custom-built hotel in heart of city. Indoor swimming pool, sauna, solarium, gymnasium, billiards. Fr, De, Es
135 bedrs, 135 en suite; TV; tcf
lift, dogs, ns; P 46, coach; child facs; con 75
✕ LD 10
£ B&B £79–£89 (w/e £31), B&B (double) £96–£106; L £16·95, D £18·95; [5% V]
cc Access, Amex, B'card/Visa, Diners.
(See advertisement on p. 400)

★★★★ **Plymouth Moat House,** Armada Way, PL1 2HJ (0752) 662866 Tx: 45637
Fax: (0752) 673816 ♿

Purpose-built modern 10-storey hotel. Adjacent to the Hoe. Indoor swimming pool, sauna, solarium, gymnasium. (QMH)
213 bedrs, 213 en suite; TV; tcf
lift, dogs, ns; P 50, G 120, coach; child facs; con 425
✕ LD 10
£ B&B £77·95–£102·95 (w/e £39·50), B&B (double) £95·90–£120·90; L £14·75; D £13·50
cc Access, Amex, B'card/Visa, Diners.

★★★ **Astor,** 14 Elliot St, PL1 2PS (0752) 225511 Tx: 45652

Elegant late Victorian traditional hotel situated on the Hoe. (MtCh)

★★★ **Duke of Cornwall,** Millbay Rd, PL1 3LG (0752) 266256 Tx: 45424
Fax: (0752) 600062

Near city centre, splendid Victorian stone building in Gothic style. Fr, De

Weekend breaks
Please consult the hotel for full details of weekend breaks; prices shown are an indication only. Many hotels offer mid week breaks as well.

70 bedrs, 70 en suite; TV; tcf
lift, dogs; P 40, coach; child facs; con 300
✕ LD 9.30
£ B&B £55 (w/e £45), B&B (double) £68·50–£125; L £7·95, D £10·45; WB £32·50; [10% V w/e Oct–Apr]
cc Access, Amex, B'card/Visa, Diners.

★★★ **Mayflower Post House,** The Hoe, PL1 3DL (0752) 662828 Tx: 45442
Fax: (0752) 660974

P

Modern high-rise hotel standing on the Hoe. Swimming pool. (THF). Es
106 bedrs, 106 en suite; TV; tcf
lift, dogs, ns; P 157, coach; child facs; con
✕ LD 10, bar meals only Sat lunch
£ B&B £69·50 (w/e £39·50), B&B (double) £87–£97; L £10·50, D £13; WB £45
cc Access, Amex, B'card/Visa, Diners.

★★★ **New Continental,** Mill Bay Rd, PL1 3LD (0752) 220782 Tx: 45193
Fax: (0752) 227013
Large prominent building in open elevated site. Leisure facilities.
99 bedrs, 99 en suite; TV; tcf
lift, dogs; P 80, coach; child facs; con
✕ nr Sat lunch
£ B&B £50–£55 (w/e £43), B&B (double) £63–£68 (w/e £53); L £8·50, D £12·75; [10% V]
cc Access, B'card/Visa.

★★★ **Novotel,** Marsh Mills Roundabout, 270 Plymouth Rd, PL6 8NH (0752) 221422 Tx: 45711 Fax: (0752) 221422 ♿
Modern purpose-built hotel with open-plan reception. In city outskirts. Swimming pool.
101 bedrs, 101 en suite; TV; tcf
lift, dogs; P 140, coach; child facs; con 170

★★★ **Strathmore House,** Elliot St, The Hoe, PL1 2SP (0752) 662101
Fax: (0752) 223690

Three-storey hotel on the historic Hoe. Conveniently near shopping centre. Es, Gr

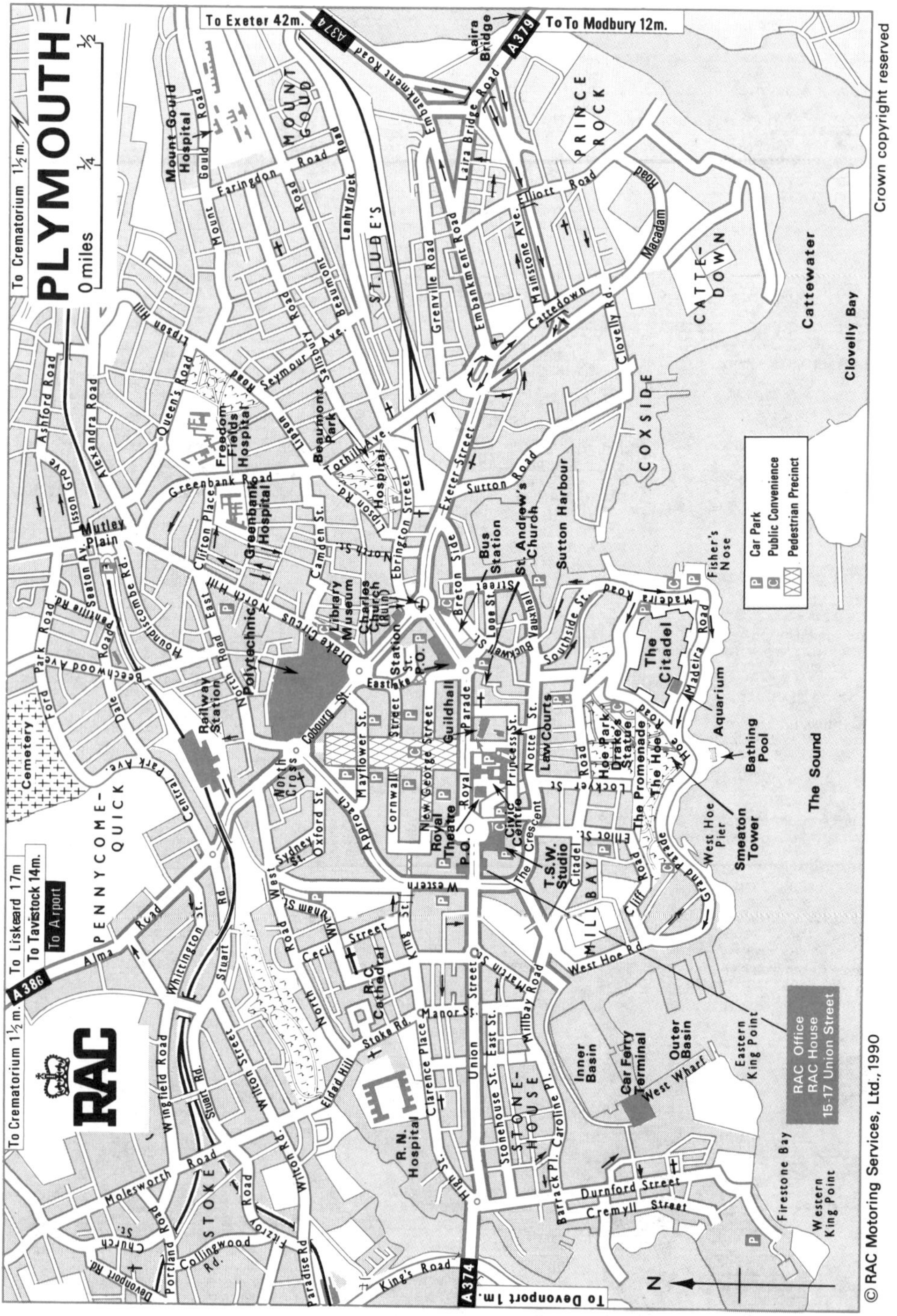

PLYMOUTH

0 miles ¼ ½

RAC

To Crematorium 1½ m.
To Exeter 42m. A374
A379 To Modbury 12m.
To Liskeard 17m
To Tavistock 14m.
To Airport
A386
To Crematorium 1½ m.
A374 To Devonport 1m.

Car Park
Public Convenience
Pedestrian Precinct

RAC Office
RAC House
15-17 Union Street

Pennycomequick, Mutley Plain, Mount Gould Hospital, Mount Gould, St. Jude's, Prince Rock, Cattedown, Coxside, Cattewater, Clovelly Bay, Freedom Fields Hospital, Beaumont Park, Greenbank Hospital, Railway Station, Polytechnic, Library Museum, Charles Church (Ruin), Bus Station, St. Andrew's Church, Sutton Harbour, Fisher's Nose, The Citadel, Aquarium, Bathing Pool, The Sound, Smeaton Tower, West Hoe Pier, The Hoe, Drake's Statue, Hoe Park, The Promenade, Law Courts, Guildhall, Station P.O., North Cross, Royal Theatre, P.O., Civic Centre, T.S.W. Studio, Millbay, R.C. Cathedral, Stoke, R.N. Hospital, Stonehouse, Inner Basin, Car Ferry Terminal, Outer Basin, West Wharf, Eastern King Point, Firestone Bay, Western King Point, Laira Bridge

N

🛏 54 bedrs, 54 en suite; TV; tcf
🏠 lift, dogs; coach; child facs; con 90
✕ LD 10
£ B&B fr £45, B&B (double) fr £55; L £6, D £11·50; [10% V]
cc Access, Amex, B'card/Visa, Diners.
(See advertisement on p. 396)

★★ **Camelot,** 5 Elliott St, PL1 2PP
📞 (0752) 221255 Fax: (0752) 603660
Small hotel conveniently situated on the Hoe. Easy access to city. Fr
🛏 17 bedrs, 17 en suite; TV; tcf
🏠 TV, dogs; coach; con 80
✕ LD 9.30
£ B&B £34, B&B (double) £47; L £7·50, D £10; WB £32; [V]
cc Access, Amex, B'card/Visa, Diners.

★★ **Grosvenor,** 9 Elliot St, PL1 2PP
📞 (0752) 260411 Fax: (0752) 668878
Tall terraced house conveniently placed just below the Hoe.
🛏 12 bedrs, 12 en suite; TV; tcf
🏠 TV
✕ LD 9.45, bar meals only Fri. Resid & Rest lic
£ B&B £33, B&B (double) £46; D £9·75; WB £54
cc Access, Amex, B'card/Visa.

★★ **Invicta,** 11 Osborne Pl, Lockyer St, The Hoe, PL1 2PU 📞 (0752) 664997
Three-storey cream-painted corner building just below the Hoe. Closed 24 Dec–5 Jan. Fr.
🛏 23 bedrs, 20 en suite, 2 ba; TV; tcf
🏠 TV, dogs; P 10, coach; child facs; con 80
✕ LD 9, bar meals only lunch & Sun dinner. Resid lic
£ B&B £26–£38, B&B (double) £50; D £8·75
cc Access, B'card/Visa; dep.
(See advertisement on p. 396)

★★ **Langdon Court,** Down Thomas, Wembury, PL9 0DY 📞 (0752) 862358
Fax: (0752) 863428
Lovely stone-built Elizabethan manor set in gardens, 4 miles SE of Plymouth.
🛏 15 bedrs, 15 en suite; TV; tcf
🏠 dogs; P 100, coach; no children under 5; con 25
✕ LD 9.30, bar meals only Mon–Sat lunch & Sun dinner
£ B&B £27–£42, B&B (double) £51–£62; D £14
cc Access, Amex, B'card/Visa, CB, Diners; dep.

★ **Drake,** 1 Windsor Villas, Lockyer St, The Hoe, PL1 2QD 📞 (0752) 229730

Small hotel conveniently located on the Hoe. Closed 22 Dec–1 Jan. Fr, De
🛏 36 bedrs, 25 en suite, (6 sh), 4 ba; TV; tcf
🏠 dogs; P 25; child facs
✕ LD 9. Resid & Rest lic
£ B&B £23–£35, B&B (double) £40–£45, HB weekly £175–£200; L £8·50, D £8·50; WB £25·50 (min 2 nts)
cc Access, Amex, B'card/Visa, Diners; dep.

★ **Imperial,** Lockyer St, The Hoe, PL1 2QD
📞 (0752) 227311

Modernised Victorian hotel in convenient position between the Hoe and city centre. Closed Xmas week. Fr
🛏 22 bedrs, 16 en suite, 3 ba; TV; tcf
🏠 TV; P 16; child facs; con 25
✕ LD 8.15, bar meals only lunch & Sun dinner. Resid & Rest lic
£ B&B £28–£38, B&B (double) £38–£48; HB weekly £249–£329; D £11·75; WB £75 (2 nts); [10% V]
cc Access, Amex, B'card/Visa, Diners; dep.

Campanile
See Motor Lodge section

Georgian House (Highly Acclaimed), 51 Citadel Rd, The Hoe PL1 3AQ 📞 (0752) 663237. *Hotel.*
£ B&B £28–£30

Alexander, 20 Woodland Terr, Greenbank, PL4 8NL 📞 (0752) 663247. *Hotel.*
£ B&B £11–£15; HB weekly £115–£140; [5% V]
Benvenuto, 69 Hermitage Rd, Mannamead, PL3 4RZ 📞 (0752) 667030. *Private Hotel.* Closed Xmas.
Bowling Green, 9 Osborne Pl, Lockyer St, PL1 2PU 📞 (0752) 667485. Closed 23–31 Dec.
£ B&B £20–£27
(See advertisement on p. 400)
Carnegie, 172 Citadel Rd, The Hoe, PL1 3BD 📞 (0752) 225158. *Hotel.*
Devonia, 27 Grand Par, West Hoe, PL1 3DQ 📞 (0752) 665026. *Guest House.* Closed Jan.
£ B&B £15–£20; [V]; dep.
Dudley, 42 Sutherland Rd, Mutley, PL4 6BN 📞 (0752) 668322. *Guest House.*
£ B&B £14; HB weekly £122
Gables End, 29 Sutherland Rd, Mutley, PL4 6BW 📞 (0752) 220803. *Hotel.*
Glendevon, 20 Ford Park Rd, Mutley, PL4 6RB 📞 (0752) 663655. *Hotel.*
Headland, 1a Radford Rd, West Hoe, PL1 3BY 📞 (0752) 660866. *Hotel.*
Lockyer House, 2 Alfred St, The Hoe, PL1 2RP 📞 (0752) 665755. *Hotel.*
Merville, 73 Citadel Rd, The Hoe, PL1 3AX 📞 (0752) 667595. *Hotel.*
£ B&B £11
Oliver's, 33 Sutherland Rd, Mutley, PL4 6BN 📞 (0752) 663923. *Hotel.*
Phantele, 176 Devonport Rd, Stoke, PL1 5RD 📞 (0752) 561506. *Guest House.*
£ B&B £10·50–£15·50; HB weekly £94·50–£114
Riviera, 8 Elliott St, The Hoe, PL1 2PP 📞 (0752) 667379. *Hotel.*
Russell Lodge, 9 Holyrood Pl, The Hoe, PL1 2BQ 📞 (0752) 667774. *Private Hotel.* Open 1 Mar–1 Oct.
£ B&B £16–£18; [5% V 2 nts or more]
St James, 49 Citadel Rd, The Hoe, PL1 3AU 📞 (0752) 661950. *Hotel.*
£ B&B £26
Swinton, 43 Sutherland Rd, Mutley, PL4 6BN 📞 (0752) 660887. *Private Hotel.*
Trillium, 4 Alfred St, The Hoe, PL1 2RP 📞 (0752) 670452. *Guest House.* Fr, De, Es, It, Po
£ B&B £16–£20·50
Victoria Court, 62 North Rd East, PL4 6AL 📞 (0752) 668133. *Hotel.* Closed Xmas–New Year.
£ B&B £18–£28; [10% V w/e Oct–Apr]

PLYMPTON
★★★ C **Elfordleigh,** Colebrook, Shaugh Prior Rd, PL7 5EB 📞 (0752) 336428
Fax: (0752) 344581

Privately-owned country hotel set in gardens, lawns and woodland. Indoor & outdoor swimming pools, golf, putting, tennis, fishing, squash, sauna, solarium, gymnasium, billiards.
🛏 18 bedrs, 18 en suite; TV; tcf
🏠 TV; P 250, coach; child facs; con 100
✕ LD 9, nr Mon–Sat lunch
£ B&B £52–£57, B&B (double) £85–£95; D £14·95; WB £109 (2 nts)
cc Access, Amex, B'card/Visa; dep.

POCKLINGTON Humberside. Map 39A3

Pop 5,750. Market Weighton 6, London 191, Bridlington 28, York 13.
EC Wed. **MD** Tue. **Golf** Fulford (York) 18h.

★★ **Feathers,** Market Pl, YO4 2AH 📞 (0759) 303155 Fax: (0759) 302099

Town centre former coaching inn retaining some Tudor beams.
🛏 6 bedrs, 6 en suite; annexe 6 bedrs, 6 en suite; TV; tcf
🏠 TV; P 40, G 3, coach; child facs; con 20
✕ LD 9.30
£ B&B £31·50–£35, B&B (double) £45–£50; L £6·50, D £6·50; WB £140 (for 2)
cc Access, Amex, B'card/Visa, Diners.

POLBATHIC Cornwall. Map 3A2

Pop 100. St Germans 1½, London 219, Liskeard 9, Looe 8, Saltash 7½, Seaton 3½, Torpoint 8.

Plymouth (Devon)

THE
COPTHORNE
PLYMOUTH
★★★★

NOTHING CAN COMPARE WITH COPTHORNE CARE

The Copthorne Plymouth, an excellent four star hotel providing the very highest standards of service, accommodation and cuisine for business or pleasure.

For details and reservations:- The Copthorne Plymouth, The Armada Centre, Armada Way, Plymouth, Devon, PL1 1AR Tel (0752) 224161.

Plymouth (Devon)

Bowling Green Hotel

9-10 Osborne Place, Lockyer St., The Hoe,
Plymouth, Devon PL1 2PU
Telephone (0752) 667485

Rebuilt Victorian property with views of Dartmoor on the horizon. Overlooking Sir Francis Drake's Bowling Green on beautiful PLYMOUTH HOE.
All rooms showers, colour TV, tea and coffee facilities, direct dial telephone. En-suite rooms available.

Plymouth (Devon)

THE CAMPANILE HOTEL – Plymouth

Marsh Mills, Longbridge Road, Forder Valley, Plymouth PL6 8LD
Tel: (0752) 601087 Telex: 45544

Restaurant Hotel
Campanile

Part of the international budget hotel chain "Campanile", the hotel offers 50 comfortable double or twin rooms with en-suite bathrooms, and coffee making facilities, radio alarm, remote control colour TV, Sky TV and direct dial telephone at **competitive rates.**
Our informal restaurant provides a variety of home-cooked French/ Continental cuisine, and personal service at **affordable prices.**
Our seminar room is available for business meetings or small functions.

Your hosts: Murielle & Denis Rabine

RAC
LODGE

Poole (Dorset)

SEA-WITCH HOTEL

Haven Road, Canford Cliffs, Poole BH13 7LH Tel: 0202 707697

Small hotel in light, attractive 20th century building situated in quiet village.
8 bedrooms, Prices from £25.

Porlock Harbour (Somerset)

EXMOOR
PORLOCK HARBOUR
SOMERSET TA24 8PB
Telephone: Porlock (0643) 862753

Lovely part 15th century thatched hotel 10 yds from picturesque harbour surrounded by Exmoor's magnificent scenery.

- Michelin & Egon Ronay recommended
- Special reduced rates for inclusive terms for stays of 2-5 days.

Old Mill House, Torpoint, PL11 3HA ☎ St Germans (0503) 30596. *Guest House.*
£ B&B £10–£12; HB weekly £100–£150; [10% V]

POLPERRO Cornwall. Map 2C1

Pop 920. Looe 4, London 231, Fowey (Fy) 9.
EC Sat. **Golf** Looe Bin Down 18h.

★ Claremont, The Coombes, PL13 2RG ☎ (0503) 72241

Small 3-storey hotel in sheltered position in attractive village. ✱ Fr
🛏 11 bedrs, 10 en suite, 1 ba; TV; tcf
🏨 dogs; P 16; child facs
✕ LD 8.30. Resid & Rest lic
£ B&B £18–£23, B&B (double) £26–£46; L £7, D £10·95; [5% V]
cc Access, B'card/Visa; dep.

Landaviddy Manor, Landaviddy Lane, PL13 2RT ☎ (0503) 72210

Lanhael House, Langreek Rd, PL13 2PW ☎ (0503) 72428. *Guest House. Swimming pool.* Open Mar–Oct.
£ B&B £18–£20

Mill House, Mill Hill, PL13 2RP ☎ (0503) 72362. *Hotel.*

Penryn House, The Coombes, PL13 2RG ☎ (0503) 72157. *Hotel.*

POLZEATH Cornwall. Map 2C2

Pop 250. Camelford 12, London 240, Wadebridge 6.
Golf St Endoc Rock 18h.

White Lodge, Old Polzeath, PL27 6TJ ☎ Trebetherick (020 886) 2370. *Hotel.* Closed Jan. ✱ Fr ♿
£ B&B £22·50–£30; HB weekly £280–£385

POOLE Dorset. Map 5A1

Pop 123,000. Ringwood 12, London 106, Blandford Forum 13, Bournemouth 4, Dorchester 23, Sandbanks 4½, Wareham 9.
EC Wed. **MD** Tue, Sat. **Golf** Broadstone (Dorset) 18h, Parkstone 18h. **See** Old Town House (orig Guildhall), Pottery, 14th cent Gateway and walls, Guildhall (1761).
ℹ Poole Quay. ☎ (0202) 673322

★★★★ Hospitality Inn, The Quay, BH15 1HD ☎ (0202) 666800 Tx: 418374 Fax: (0202) 684470

Modern purpose-built hotel, on quay with fine views of harbour. (MtCh)
🛏 68 bedrs, 68 en suite; TV; tcf
🏨 lift, dogs; P 150, coach; child facs; con 60
✕ LD 9.45
£ room £72 (w/e £46), room (double) £85; L £14; D £15; WB £92 (min 2 nts)
cc Access, Amex, B'card/Visa, Diners.

★★★ Dolphin, High St, BH15 1DU ☎ (0202) 673612 Tx: 417205 Fax: (0202) 674197

Modern purpose-built hotel in built-up area. High rise parking available. ✱ Fr
🛏 66 bedrs, 66 en suite; TV; tcf
🏨 lift, dogs, ns; P 50, coach; child facs; con 60
✕ LD 10.30
£ B&B £48–£66, B&B (double) £66–£76; L £7·50, D £9·95 (w/e £25)
cc Access, Amex, B'card/Visa, Diners.

★★★ C Harbour Heights, Haven Rd, BH13 7LW ☎ (0202) 707272 Fax: (0202) 708594

Modern family-run hotel with fine views of the harbour.
🛏 49 bedrs, 49 en suite; TV; tcf
🏨 lift, dogs; P 84, coach

★★★ C Haven, Sandbanks, BH13 7QL ☎ (0202) 707333 Tx: 41338 Fax: (0202) 708796
Large holiday hotel with modern facilities; at edge of sea. Indoor/outdoor swimming pool, fishing, squash, sauna, solarium, gymnasium. ✱ Fr, It
🛏 96 bedrs, 96 en suite; TV; tcf
🏨 lift, ns; P 150, coach; child facs; con 175
✕ LD 8.30
£ B&B £50–£70; L £12, D fr £18; [10% V]
cc Access, Amex, B'card/Visa, Diners; dep.
(*See advertisement on p. 402*)

★★★ H C R Salterns, 38 Salterns Way, Lilliput, BH14 8JR ☎ (0202) 707321 Tx: 41259 Fax: (0202) 707488
Large attractive brick-built modern hotel at water's edge. Pleasant grounds. Fishing, squash, billiards. ✱ Fr
🛏 16 bedrs, 16 en suite; TV; tcf
🏨 P 150; child facs; con 50
✕ LD 10. Resid, Rest & Club lic
£ B&B £64·25–£78·25, B&B (double) £87·25–£128·50; L £11·50, D £15; WB £41 [10% V]
cc Access, Amex, B'card/Visa, Diners.

★★★ Sandbanks, Banks Rd, Sandbanks, BH13 7PS ☎ (0202) 707377 Tx: 41338 Fax: (0202) 708796

Purpose-built holiday hotel on seashore. Indoor swimming pool, putting, sauna, solarium, gymnasium. ✱ Fr, De, Po
🛏 105 bedrs, 105 en suite; TV; tcf
🏨 lift, ns; P 200, coach; child facs; con 170
✕ LD 8.30
£ B&B £40–£50; B&B (double) £80–£100; L £10, D £15; [10% V]
cc Access, Amex, B'card/Visa, Diners; dep.
(*See advertisement on p. 402*)

★★ Norfolk Lodge, 1 Flaghead Rd, Canford Cliffs, BH13 7JL ☎ (0202) 708614
Red-brick Victorian house in a quiet residential area. Garden with aviary. ✱ Fr
🛏 19 bedrs, 15 en suite, (2 sh), 2 ba; TV; tcf
🏨 dogs, ns; P 16; child facs; con 40
✕ LD 8, bar meals only Mon–Sat lunch. Rest lic
£ B&B £32–£38; B&B (double) £50–£55; HB weekly £140–£170; L £7, D £8·50; WB £70 (2 nts)
cc Access, Amex, B'card/Visa; dep.

★★ R Quarterdeck, 2 Sandbanks Rd, BH14 8AQ ☎ (0202) 740066
Family-run hotel in modern brick building opposite the Law Courts. ✱ Fr
🛏 15 bedrs, 14 en suite, 1 ba; TV; tcf
🏨 P 34, U 2; child facs
✕ LD 9, bar meals only Mon–Fri lunch. Resid & Rest lic
£ B&B £38, B&B (double) £50; HB weekly £296; L £7·95, D £10·95; WB £29
cc Access, B'card/Visa; dep.

★★ Sea-Witch, 47 Haven Rd, Canford Cliffs, BH13 7LH ☎ (0202) 707697

Small hotel in attractive 20th century building in quiet residential area.
🛏 10 bedrs, 10 en suite; TV; tcf
🏨 P 45; child facs
✕ LD 9.30, bar meals only Mon lunch
£ B&B £40, B&B (double) £56; HB weekly £235; L £8, D £10; WB fr £45
cc Access, B'card/Visa.
(*See advertisement on p. 400*)

Sheldon Lodge (Acclaimed), 22 Forest Rd, Branksome Park, BH13 6DA ☎ (0202) 761186. *Private Hotel. Billiards.* ✱ Fr
£ B&B £22–24; HB weekly £210–224

Poole (Dorset)

Avoncourt, 245 Bournemouth Rd, Parkstone, BH14 9HX ☎(0202) 732025. *Private Hotel.* Open 1 Jan–14 Dec

Bays, 82 Bournemouth Rd, Parkstone, BH14 0HA ☎(0202) 740116. *Guest House.* Closed Jan.
£ B&B £15–£17

Lewina Lodge, 225 Bournemouth Rd, Parkstone, BH14 9HU ☎(0202) 742295

POOLEY BRIDGE Cumbria. Map 44A2

Pop 265. Kendal 28, London 285, Ambleside 16, Keswick 19, Penrith 5½, Ulverston 35.
Golf Penrith 18h. **See** Ullswater.
[i] The Square. ☎(076 84) 86530

★★ **Swiss Chalet Inn,** Lake Ullswater, CA10 2NN ☎(076 84) 86215
Swiss-style building in Cumbrian village. Proprietor-managed hotel with well-appointed bedrooms.
8 bedrs, 8 en suite; TV; tcf
dogs; P 40, coach; child facs
LD 9.30
£ B&B £24–£30, B&B (double) £40–£48; L £4·90, D £15·20; [10% V w/d Sep–Jun]
cc Access, B'card/Visa; dep.

PORLOCK Somerset. Map 3C4

Pop 1,374. Minehead 5½, London 173, Lynmouth 11.
EC Wed. **Golf** Minehead & West Somerset 18h.

★★ H C R **Oaks,** TA24 8ES ☎(0643) 862265

With good views of the coast, a pleasant former residence with secluded gardens.
11 bedrs, 11 en suite; TV; tcf
dogs, ns; P 12
LD 8.30, nr lunch. Resid & Rest lic
£ B&B £33·50–£37, B&B (double) £52–£58; HB weekly £240–£265; D £14; [5% V]

★ **Ship Inn,** High St, TA24 8QD ☎(0643) 862507

Privately-owned old world inn to west side of attractive village. Fr
11 bedrs, 7 en suite, 2 ba; TV
dogs; P 40; child facs
LD 9
£ room £11·50–£18·50, B&B (double) £31–£35; HB weekly £161–£175; D £9·50
cc Access, Amex, B'card/Visa; dep.

Lorna Doone (Acclaimed), High St, TA24 8PS ☎(0643) 862404. *Private Hotel.* Fr
£ B&B £15–£16·50; [5% V]

PORLOCK WEIR Somerset. Map 3C4

Pop 1,374. Minehead 7½, London 175, Lynmouth 13.

★★★ R **Anchor & Ship,** TA24 8PB ☎(0643) 862636 Fax: (0643) 862843
Complex of two hotels (one 13th century) near to harbour.
26 bedrs, 20 en suite, 4 ba; TV; tcf
dogs; P 28, coach; child facs; con 40
LD 9
£ B&B £38·50–£62·45, B&B (double) £65–£99·90; HB weekly £315–£385; D £13·75; WB £85–£115
cc Access, Amex, B'card/Visa; dep.
(*See advertisement on p. 400*)

PORTESHAM Dorset. Map 4C1

Dorchester 11, London 133, Weymouth 7, Bridport 12.

Millmead (Acclaimed), DT3 4HE ☎Abbotsbury (0305) 871432. *Hotel.* Fr
£ B&B £19·50–£30·25; HB weekly £203–£275; [5% V Oct–May]

PORTHLEVEN Cornwall. Map 2B1

Pop 3,200. Helston 2½, London 274, Lizard 14, Penzance 13, Redruth 13, St Ives 14.
EC Wed. **Golf** Mullion 18h, Praa Sands 9h.

★ **Tye Rock,** Looe Bar Rd, Helston, TR13 9EW ☎Helston (0326) 572695
Small hotel in 3 acres of natural cliff-top land with uninterrupted sea views. Swimming pool. Open Easter–Dec.
7 bedrs, 4 en suite, 3 ba; tcf
TV, dogs; P 20; child facs
LD 7.30, nr lunch. Resid lic
£ B&B £17·75; B&B (double £35·50–£44; HB weekly £172–£193; D £10·50; [10% V Oct–Mar]
cc Access, B'card/Visa; dep.

PORT ISAAC Cornwall. Map 2C2

Pop 900. Camelford 7½, London 235, Wadebridge 10.
Golf St Enodoc Rock 18h (2). **See** Harbour, Smugglers' caves, 17th cent Golden Lion.

★★ **Castle Rock,** 4 New Rd, PL29 3SB ☎Bodmin (0208) 880300

Cliff-top building with magnificent views over Port Isaac Bay. Open 1 Mar–5 Jan.
17 bedrs, 13 en suite, 2 ba; TV; tcf
TV, dogs, ns; P 20, coach; child facs; con 30
LD 8.30, bar meals only Mon–Sat lunch. Resid & Rest lic
£ B&B £22–£28; HB weekly £215–£245; D £12; [10% V Sep–Jun]
cc Access, B'card/Visa; dep.

Bay, 1 The Terrace, PL29 3SC ☎Bodmin (0208) 880380. *Hotel.* Open Apr–Oct.
£ B&B £15·50–£23·50; HB weekly £161–£190

Fairholme, 30 Trewetha La, PL29 3RW ☎Bodmin (0208) 880397. *Guest House.* Open Easter–Oct.
£ B&B £12–£17·50; HB weekly £133–£164; [5% V w/d Mar–May]

St Andrews, The Terrace, PL29 3SG ☎Bodmin (0208) 880240. *Hotel.*

PORTLAND Dorset. Map 4C1

Pop 12,000. Weymouth 6, London 137.
EC Wed. **Golf** Weymouth 18h. **See** Portland Castle, Museum, Portland Bill and Lighthouse, Chesil Bank.
[i] St George's Centre, Reforne. ☎(0305) 823406

★★★ **Portland Heights,** Yeates Corner, DT5 2EN ☎(0305) 821361 Fax: (0305) 860081 ♿
Long, low modern hotel built of Portland stone. Superb views of Chesil Beach and Weymouth Bay. Swimming pool, squash, sauna, solarium, gymnasium.
66 bedrs, 66 en suite; TV; tcf
dogs, ns; P 180, coach; child facs; con 130
LD 9.30
£ B&B £50, B&B (double) £66; HB weekly £286; L £8·50, D £13; WB £44; [10% V]
cc Access, Amex, B'card/Visa, Diners.

PORTSCATHO Cornwall. Map 2B1

Pop 500. St Austell 15, London 255, Falmouth (Fy) 14, Newquay 25, Truro (Fy) 10.
Golf Truro 18h. **See** Quay.

★★★ **Rosevine,** Porthcurnick Beach, TR2 5EW ☎(087 258) 206
Lovely Georgian manor house in 3½ acres of gardens overlooking the sea. Open Easter–Oct. Fr
14 bedrs, 12 en suite, (1 sh), 2 ba; TV; tcf
TV, dogs, ns; P 40; child facs; con 130
LD 8.30, bar meals only lunch
£ B&B £23·50–£47; HB weekly £248–£400; D £18·50; WB £33 (min 3 nts)
cc Access, B'card/Visa; dep.

★★ **Gerrans Bay,** Gerrans, TR2 5ED ☎(087 258) 338

Attractive large Victorian house with extensive modern additions. Fine views. Open April–Oct & Xmas.
14 bedrs, 14 en suite; tcf
TV, dogs; P 16; child facs
LD 8, bar meals only Mon–Sat lunch. Resid & Rest lic
£ B&B £23–£25; HB weekly £205–£220; D £13·50
cc Access, Amex, B'card/Visa; dep.

★★ Roseland House, Rosevine, TR2 5EW ☎(087 258) 644 ♿

White painted country house in lovely terraced gardens. Private beach with fishing.
18 bedrs, 18 en suite
TV, dogs, ns; P 25, G 3; child facs; con 50
✕ LD 8; Resid & Rest lic
£ B&B £20–£30; B&B (double) £40–£60; HB weekly £189–£217; L £5, D £13; WB £28 (3 days min); dep.

PORTSMOUTH AND SOUTHSEA

Hampshire. Map 5C2
RAC Port Office, *Wharf Road, PO2 8HB* ☎(0705) 697713
Pop 175,382. Cosham 4, London 71, M275 1½.
See Plan, pp. 405.
MD Thur, Fri, Sat. **P** See Plan. **Golf** Gt Salterns 18h. **See** Cathedral, Dickens's Birthplace and Museum, Dockyard (Nelson's flagship 'Victory' and Museum), HMS 'Mary Rose' War Memorial, Point Battery and Round Tower. Southsea: D-Day Memorial, Castle, Royal Naval Museum, Royal Marines Museum.
[i] Clarence Esp, Southsea. ☎(0705) 832464
The Hard ☎(0705) 826722 and Continental Ferry Port ☎(0705) 698111

★★★★ Holiday Inn, North Harbour, PO6 4SH ☎(0705) 383151 Tx: 86611 Fax: (0705) 388701 ♿
Modern 'Holidome' hotel. Leisure and conference facilities. Indoor swimming pool, squash, sauna, solarium, gymnasium. (CHIC). Fr
170 bedrs, 170 en suite; TV; tcf
lift, dogs, ns; P 200, coach; child facs; con 300
✕ LD 10.30
£ B&B £104·95–£134·95, B&B (double) £123·90–£153·90; L £12·50, D £14·95
cc Access, Amex, B'card/Visa, CB, Diners.

★★★ Crest, Pembroke Rd, PO1 2TA ☎(0705) 827651 Tx: 86397 Fax: (0705) 756715 ♿
Modern purpose-built hotel overlooking Southsea Common. Centrally situated. Indoor swimming pool, sauna, solarium, gymnasium. (Cr/THF)
163 bedrs, 163 en suite; TV; tcf
lift, dogs, ns; P 80, coach; child facs; con 250

Atlas Section
Consult the Atlas section at the back of the guide to find out which towns and villages have RAC Appointed and Listed hotels in them. They are shown on the maps by purple circles.

★★★ Pendragon, Clarence Par, Southsea, PO5 2HY ☎(0705) 823201 Tx: 86376

Traditional hotel facing Southsea Common and near sea front. (THF)

★★★ Hospitality Inn, South Par, PO4 0RN ☎(0705) 731281 Tx: 86719 Fax: (0705) 812572
Large white sea front hotel with superb views across the Solent. (MtCh) Fr
115 bedrs, 115 en suite; TV; tcf
lift, dogs, ns; P 25, G 15; coach; child facs; con 250
✕ LD 9.45
£ room £60 (w/e £36·50), double room £69·50; L £10·50, D £11·95
cc Access, Amex, B'card/Visa, Diners.

★★ Arcade, Winston Churchill Av, PO1 2DG ☎(0705) 821992 Tx: 869429 Fax: (0705) 863460 ♿

Ultra-modern French-owned hotel situated in city centre.
144 bedrs, 144 en suite; TV; tcf
lift, dogs; P 50, coach; child facs; con 70
✕ LD 10, Sat, Sun lunch. Resid lic
£ B&B £42, B&B (double) £52 (w/e £35); L £10·75, D £10·75; [5% V Mon–Thur]
cc Access, Amex, B'card/Visa, CB.

★★ Keppel's Head, 24 The Hard, PO1 3DT ☎(0705) 833231 Tx: 86376

A hotel with a maritime flavour set on the Portsmouth Hard. (THF). Fr, De
27 bedrs, 27 en suite; TV; tcf
lift, dogs, ns; P 18, coach; child facs; con 60
✕ LD 9
£ B&B £55–£60 (w/e £38), B&B (double) £70–£80; HB weekly £217–£280; L £8·50, D £12·50
cc Access, Amex, B'card/Visa, CB, Diners.

Seacrest (Highly Acclaimed), 12 South Par, PO5 2JB ☎(0705) 733192. *Hotel*
£ B&B £30–£35; HB weekly £360–£420; [10% V Nov–Apr]

Hamilton House (Acclaimed), 95 Victoria Rd North, PO5 1PS ☎(0705) 823502. *Guest House.*
£ B&B £12·50–£14; HB weekly £119–£129·50; [V Nov–Feb]
Rock Gardens (Acclaimed), Clarence Rd, PO5 2LQ ☎(0705) 833018. *Hotel.*
£ B&B £20–£25; HB weekly £110–£125
Turret (Acclaimed), Clarence Par, PO5 2HZ ☎(0705) 291810 *Private Hotel.*
£ B&B £30
Westfield Hall (Acclaimed), 65 Festing Rd, PO4 0NQ ☎(0705) 826971 *Private Hotel.*
£ B&B £22–£34; HB weekly £177–£198; [10% V low season]

Abbeville, 26 Nettlecombe Av, PO4 0QW ☎(0705) 826209
Amberley Court, 97 Waverley Rd, PO5 2PL ☎(0705) 735419. *Guest House.*
Annaley, 63 Clarendon Rd, PO5 2JX ☎(0705) 825525. *Guest House.*
£ B&B £15; HB weekly £126; [5% V]
Aquarius Court, 34 St Ronan's Rd, PO4 0PT ☎(0705) 822872. *Private Hotel.*
£ B&B £13–£14; HB weekly £115–£125; [10% V]
Ashwood, 10 St Davids Rd, PO5 1QN ☎(0705) 816228. *Guest House.* Closed Xmas.
Birchwood, 44 Waverley Rd, PO5 2PP ☎(0705) 811337. *Guest House.*
Bristol, 55 Clarence Par, PO5 2HX ☎(0705) 821815. *Hotel.*
£ B&B £15·50–£32; [10% V]
Collingham, 89 St Ronan's Rd, PO4 0PR ☎(0705) 821549. *Guest House.*
£ B&B £12·50; [V]
Dolphins, 10 Western Par, PO5 3JF ☎(0705) 820833. *Hotel.* Fr, Tu
£ B&B £22–£30; HB weekly £200–£260; [10% V Jan–Apr & Nov]
Dorcliffe, 42 Waverley Rd, PO5 2PP ☎(0705) 828283. *Guest House.* ♿
£ B&B £11–£14; HB weekly £102–£111
Gainsborough House, 9 Malvern Rd, PO5 2LZ ☎(0705) 822604. *Guest House.* Closed Xmas–New Year.
£ B&B £12–£13·50
Goodwood House, 1 Taswell Rd, Southsea, PO5 2RG ☎(0705) 824734. *Guest House.*
£ B&B £11–£14; HB weekly £102–£102.
Saville, 38 Clarence Par, PO5 2EU ☎(0705) 822491. *Private Hotel. Billiards.* De, Ar.
£ B&B £19–£28; HB weekly £145–£190; [10% V]
Upper Mount House, The Vale, Clarendon Rd, PO5 2EQ ☎(0705) 820456. *Hotel.*
£ B&B £19–£28; HB weekly £120–£160; [V Oct–May]

POWBURN

Northumberland. Map 44C4
Pop 150. Newcastle upon Tyne 37, London 310, Alnwick 9, Berwick-upon-Tweed 24, Coldstream 22.
Golf Wooler 9h.

Changes made after July 1990 are not included.

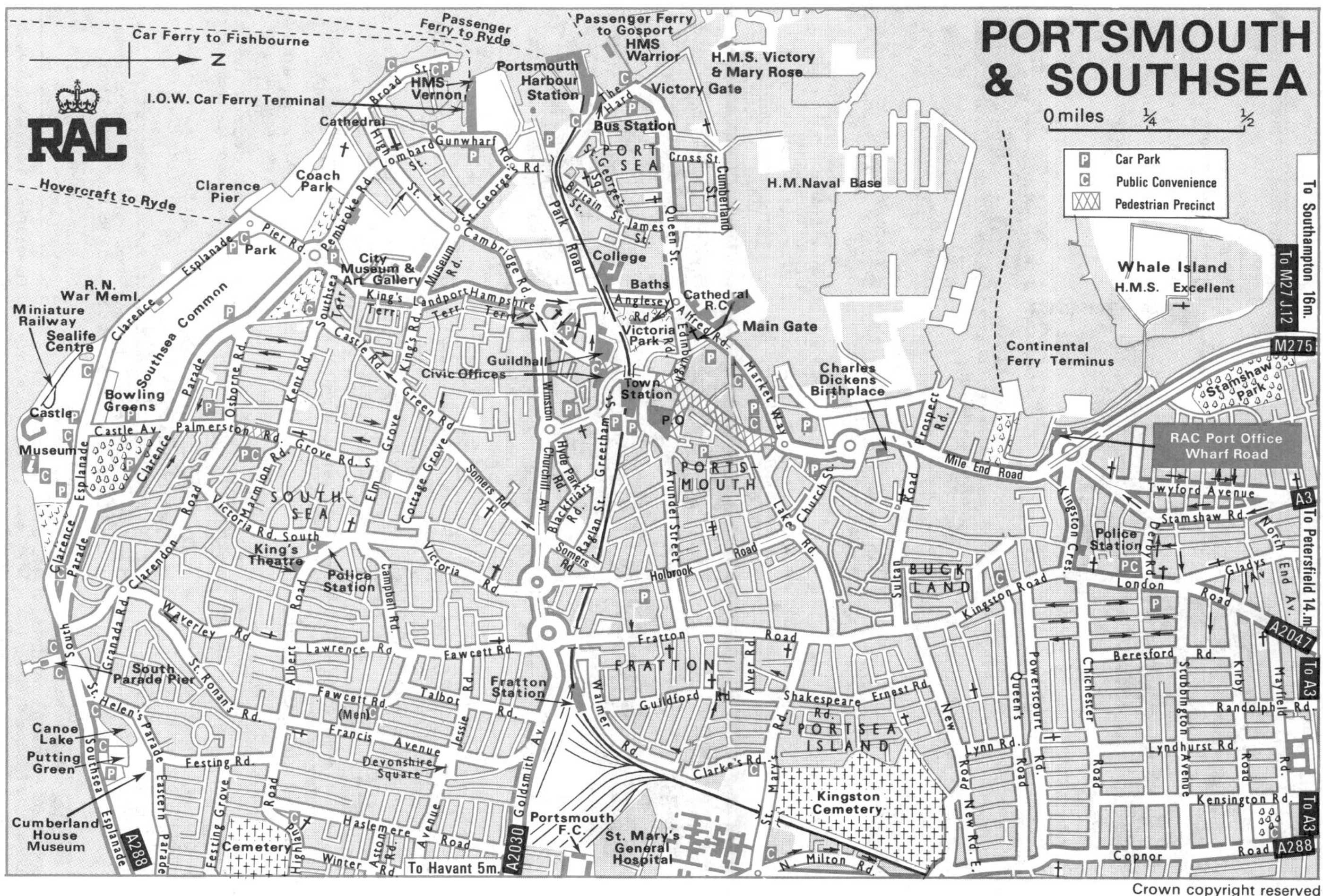
PORTSMOUTH & SOUTHSEA
0 miles ¼ ½
Car Park
Public Convenience
Pedestrian Precinct
To Southampton 16m.
To M27 J.12
M275
A3
To Petersfield 14.m.
A2047
To A3
To A3
A288
RAC Port Office Wharf Road
Whale Island H.M.S. Excellent
Continental Ferry Terminus
H.M.Naval Base
H.M.S. Victory & Mary Rose
Victory Gate
Main Gate
Cathedral R.C.
Charles Dickens Birthplace
Passenger Ferry to Gosport
HMS Warrior
Portsmouth Harbour Station
Bus Station
College
Baths
Town Station
PO
Guildhall
Civic Offices
City Museum & Art Gallery
Cathedral
HMS Vernon
Passenger Ferry to Ryde
Car Ferry to Fishbourne
I.O.W. Car Ferry Terminal
Hovercraft to Ryde
Coach Park
Clarence Pier
Park
R.N. War Meml.
Miniature Railway
Sealife Centre
Castle
Museum
Bowling Greens
Southsea Common
South Parade Pier
Canoe Lake
Putting Green
Cumberland House Museum
King's Theatre
Police Station
Fratton Station
Portsmouth F.C.
St. Mary's General Hospital
Kingston Cemetery
Cemetery
A2030
To Havant 5m.
PORTSEA
PORTSMOUTH
SOUTHSEA
FRATTON
BUCKLAND
PORTSEA ISLAND
RAC
N
Crown copyright reserved
P

Breamish House, NE66 4LL (066 578) 266 Fax: (066 578) 500 — ★★ H C R, country house hotel

Stone-built Georgian mansion in 5 acres of gardens and woodland in rural surroundings. Open Feb–Dec.
10 bedrs, 10 en suite; TV; tcf
dogs; P 30, G 2; children over 12
LD 8, bar meals only Mon–Sat lunch. Resid & Rest lic
£ B&B £40–£45, B&B (double) £64–£94; L £12, D £18·50; dep.

PRAA SANDS Cornwall. Map 2A1

Pop 785. Helston 6, London 277, Penzance 7½, St Ives 13.
Golf Praa Sands 9h. **See** Restored 16th cent Pengersick Castle, St Michael's Mount.

★★ **Prah Sands,** TR20 9SY Penzance (0736) 762438

Two-storey hotel in 4 acres of attractive grounds. 300 yards from sea. Swimming pool, tennis, billiards.
20 bedrs, 12 en suite, 4 ba; TV; tcf
TV; P 20; child facs
LD 8.30, bar meals only lunch. Resid & Rest lic
£ B&B £20, B&B (double) £40–£76; D £10·20; WB £70
cc Access, B'card/Visa; dep.

PRESTBURY Cheshire Map 30B3

Macclesfield 4, London 170, Buxton 14, Stockport 8, Wilmslow 5.

★★★ **Bridge,** SK10 4DQ (0625) 829326 Fax: (0625) 827557
Converted row of charming 17th century cottages with an extension providing good modern bedrooms and conference facilities.
Fr, It, Es, Gr
23 bedrs, 23 en suite; TV; tcf
TV; P 52; child facs; con 60
LD 9.45, nr Sun dinner. Resid & Rest lic
£ B&B £80–£85 (w/e £30), B&B (double) £100–£110; L £8·45, D £11·75
cc Access, Amex, B/card/VIsa, Diners.

PRESTON Lancashire. Map 32C4

Pop 126,000. M6 (jn 30) 4, London 211, Blackburn 10, Blackpool 16, Chorley 9, Lancaster 22, Ormskirk 17, Southport 17.
MD Daily (excl. Thur). **Golf** Preston 18h.
Town Hall, Lancaster Rd. (0772) 53731

★★★★ **Broughton Park,** Garstang Rd, Broughton, PR3 5JB (0772) 864087 Tx: 67180 Fax: (0772) 861728

Edwardian country house with purpose-built extension including leisure complex. Indoor swimming pool, sauna, solarium, gymnasium. Fr, Es, Yu
98 bedrs, 98 en suite; TV; tcf
lift, TV, dogs, ns; P 200, coach; child facs; con 252
LD 10, nr Sat lunch
£ B&B £78–£88 (w/e £50), B&B (double) £88–£98; L £9·20, D £15·35; WB £45; [10% V]
cc Access, Amex, B'card/Visa, Diners.

★★★ **Barton Grange,** Barton, PR3 5AA (5½m N on A6) (0772) 862551 Tx: 67392 Fax: (0772) 861267

Unique combination of modern purpose-built hotel with international garden centre. Indoor swimming pool.
56 bedrs, 56 en suite; annexe 10 bedrs, 10 en suite; TV; tcf
lift, TV, dogs; P 250, coach; child facs; con 300
LD 10, nr Sat lunch
£ B&B £45–£75, B&B (double) £53–£87; L £9, D £14·85; (w/e £45)
cc Access, Amex, B'card/Visa, Diners.

★★★ **Crest,** The Ringway, PR1 3AU (0772) 59411 Tx: 677147 Fax: (0772) 201923

Centrally placed modern hotel with conference facilities. (Cr/THF)
126 bedrs, 126 en suite; TV; tcf
lift, dogs, ns; P 26, coach; child facs; con 120

★★★ **Novotel Summit,** Reedfield Pl, Walton Summit, (M6 Jn 29), PR5 6AB (0772) 313331 Tx: 677164
Modern purpose-built hotel (French chain) conveniently near motorway junction. Swimming pool, billiards.

★★★ **Swallow Trafalgar,** Preston New Rd, Samlesbury, PR5 0UL (0772) 877351 Tx: 677362 Fax: (0772) 877424

Modern hotel situated in open countryside close to Ribble valley. Indoor swimming pool, squash, sauna, solarium, gymnasium. (Sw)
78 bedrs, 78 en suite; TV; tcf
lift, dogs, ns; P 300, coach; child facs; con 250
LD 9.45, bar meals only Sat lunch
£ B&B £62, B&B (double) £75; L £8·25, D £12·50; WB £84 (2 nts)
cc Access, Amex, B'card/Visa, Diners.

★★★ R **Tickled Trout,** Preston New Rd, Samlesbury, PR5 0UJ (M6) (0772) 877671 Tx: 677625 Fax: (0772) 877463

Modern purpose-built hotel halfway between London and Glasgow. Indoor swimming pool, sauna, solarium.
72 bedrs, 72 en suite; TV; tcf
dogs, ns; P 150, G 10, coach; child facs; con 150
LD 9.45
£ B&B £68–£70 (w/e £50), B&B (double) £80 (w/e £65); L £8, D £14; WB £60
cc Access, Amex, B'card/Visa; dep.

★★ H C R **Dean Court,** Brownedge La, Bamber Bridge, PR5 6TB (0772) 35114
Well-maintained hotel in a converted private house with an attractive Italian patio garden.
9 bedrs, 9 en suite, 2 ba; TV; tcf
TV; P 35, coach; children over 10
LD 10, bar meals only Sat lunch. Resid & Rest lic
£ B&B £35–£45 (w/e £25), B&B (double) £37–£60; L £5·95, D £8·75; WB £50; [10% V]
cc Access, B'card/Visa; dep.

Tulketh (Highly Acclaimed), 209 Tulketh Rd, PR2 1ES (0772) 728096. *Hotel.* Closed 23 Dec–2 Jan
£ B&B £26–£36, HB weekly fr £133·95; [5% V min. 2 nts]

Fulwood Park, 49 Watling St Rd, Fulwood, PR2 4EA (0772) 718067. *Hotel.*

PRINCES RISBOROUGH

Buckinghamshire. Map 6A4
Pop 8,200. High Wycombe 8, London 38, Aylesbury 8, Dunstable 18, Oxford 20, Rickmansworth 18, Wallingford 17.
EC Wed. **MD** Sat. **Golf** Whiteleaf 9h. **See** Parish Church, Manor, Market House.

★★ **Rose & Crown,** Wycombe Rd, Saunderton, HP17 9NP (084 44) 5299
In rural setting, 2-storey white Georgian inn. Modern extension. Closed 23Dec–1 Jan
17 bedrs, 14 en suite, 1 ba; TV; tcf
con 25
LD 9.30, bar meals only Mon/Sat lunch & Sun dinner
£ B&B £43–£72 (w/e £30), B&B (double) £72–£77; L £15, D £15; WB £75·50
cc Access, Amex, B'card/Visa.

PRINCETHORPE Warwickshire.

Map 21A3
Pop 556. Daventry 12, London 86, Banbury 20, Coventry 6½, Rugby 7, Warwick 7½.
Golf Rugby 18h. **See** Manor House.

★★ **Woodhouse,** Leamington Rd, CV23 0PZ Marton (0926) 632303
Attractive converted farmhouse in a rural location. Swimming pool, tennis, riding.
Fr, De, It, Es
7 bedrs, 5 en suite; annexe 10 bedrs, 10 en suite, 2 ba; TV; tcf
ns; P 100, coach; child facs; con 60
LD 8.15, carvery only Sun dinner
£ B&B £40–£45, B&B (double) £60–£70; L £8·75; WB £75; [V]
cc Access, Amex, B'card/Visa, Diners.

PULBOROUGH West Sussex. Map 6B2

Billingshurst 5½, London 47, Arundel 8½, Bognor Regis 16, Petworth 5, Worthing 14.
Golf West Sussex 18h. **See** Church, medieval Stopham Bridge, Hardham Church.

★★ **Chequers,** Church Place, RH20 1AD (079 82) 2486 Fax: (079 82) 2715

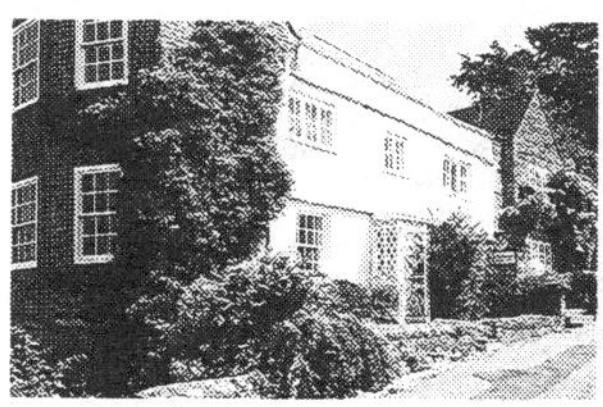

Small period house—a 2-storey listed building now family-run hotel. Fr
11 bedrs, 11 en suite; TV; tcf
dogs; P 14; child facs; con 16
LD 8.30, bar meals only lunch. Resid & Rest lic
£ B&B £39·50–£44·50, B&B (double) £53–£63; D £13·50; WB £65; [5% V Sun–Thur]
cc Access, Amex, B'card/Visa, Diners; dep.

★★ **H** **Arun Cosmopolitan,** 87 Lower St, RH20 2BP (079 82) 2162
Fax: (079 82) 2935
Flower-decked, 3-storey 18th century building with well-tended garden on A283.
6 bedrs, 6 en suite; TV; tcf
dogs; P 5, G 10, coach; child facs; con 50
LD 9, bar meals only all Mon & Sun dinner
£ B&B £38·40–£40, B&B (double) £55–£60; HB weekly £200–£238; L £9·95, D £9·95; WB £58 (2 nts); [5% V]
cc Access, Amex, B'card/Visa, Diners

PULFORD Cheshire. Map 29B3

Wrexham 6½, London 184, Chester 5½, Mold 11, Whitchurch 20.

★★★ **Grosvenor Arms,** Wrexham Rd, CH4 9DG Rossett (0244) 570560
Tx: 61313 Fax: (0244) 570809
Converted farmhouse of Victorian origins but of lovely Elizabethan design.
42 bedrs, 42 en suite, 6 ba; TV; tcf
dogs; P 200, coach; child facs; con 100

PURFLEET Essex. Map 11B4

Pop 1,270. Rainham 3½, London 21, Dartford Tunnel 2½, Southend 22.
EC Wed. **Golf** Belhus Park 18h.

★★ **Royal,** High St, RM16 1QA (0708) 865432 Fax: (0708) 860582
Riverside inn with a more recently built residential annexe alongside. Fishing.
22 bedrs, 22 en suite; annexe 9 bedrs, 9 en suite; TV; tcf
P 50, coach; child facs; con 70
LD 10.30
£ B&B £45, B&B (double) £55, L £6, D £7; WB £25 (single), £35 (twin)
cc Access, Amex, B'card/Visa, Diners.

QUORN or QUORNDON

Leicestershire. Map 25B3
Leicester 8½, London 107, Coalville 10, Loughborough 2½, Melton Mowbray 14.

★★★★ **H** **C** **R** **Quorn Country,** Charnwood House, 66 Leicester Rd, LE12 8BB (0509) 415050 Tx: 347166
Fax: (0509) 415557

A modern extension blends well with the original mansion. Set in 4 acres of landscaped grounds. Fishing. Fr, De, Du
19 bedrs, 19 en suite; TV; tcf
dogs; P 100; child facs; con 50
LD 9.45, nr Sat lunch
£ B&B £75·50 (w/e £48), B&B (double) £97; L £11·95, D £15·95
cc Access, Amex, B'card/Visa, Diners.

RADFORD Avon. Map 4C3

Radstock 2, London 112, Bath 8, Bristol 12, Wells 12.

Old Malt House, Timsbury, BA3 1QF Timsbury (0761) 70106. *Hotel.*
£ B&B £29, B&B (double) £30·50; HB weekly £234·50–£252; [5% V]

RAMSBOTTOM Greater Manchester

(Lancashire). Map 33B4
Pop 16,000. Bury 4½, London 196, M66 (jn 1) 1, Blackburn 11, Bolton 7½, Burnley 10, Rochdale 8, Todmorden 12.
EC Wed. **MD** Sat. **Golf** Greenmount 9h. **See** Peel Tower on Holcombe Hill, ruins of 16th cent New Hall (Edenfield), Grant's Tower.

★★★ **Old Mill,** Springwood St, BL0 9DS (0706) 822991 Fax: (0706) 822291

A unique black and white timbered building incorporating a mill wheel. Indoor swimming pool, sauna, solarium, gymnasium. It, Es, Po
36 bedrs, 36 en suite; TV; tcf
P 97, coach; child facs; con 30
LD 10.30
£ B&B £41–£47·50 (w/e £28·50), B&B (double) £58; L £7·25, D £11·95; WB £34
cc Access, Amex, B'card/Visa, CB, Diners; dep.

RAMSGATE Kent. Map 7C3

Pop 39,561. Canterbury 16, London 74, Dover 18, Margate 4.
EC Thur. **MD** Fri. **Golf** St Augustine's 18h, North Foreland, Broadstairs 18h & 9h. **See** St Augustine's RC Church, St Laurence's Church, Model Tudor Village, replica of Viking Ship 'Hugin' on clifftop, St Augustine's Cross (Ebbsfleet).
i Argyle Centre, Queen St. (0843) 591086

★★ **Marina Resort,** Harbour Par, CT11 8LJ (0843) 588276
Contemporary brick-built hotel overlooking the harbour. Indoor swimming pool, sauna, solarium.
59 bedrs, 59 en suite; TV; tcf
£ B&B £59·50–£64·50, B&B (double) £78–£83; D £14·50; WB £56

★★ **Savoy,** 43 Grange Rd, CT11 9NA Thanet (0843) 592637
Small hotel in former terraced houses; offers modern amenities.
14 bedrs, 7 en suite, (3 sh), 4 ba; annexe 11 bedrs, 11 en suite; TV; tcf
P 15, U 2 (£3), coach; child facs; con 100

Goodwin View, 19 Wellington Cres, CT11 8JD (0843) 591419. *Guest House.*
£ B&B £19–£25; HB weekly £154–£205; [5% V, not Jul–Sep]

Residents only
Some Listed hotels only serve meals to residents. It is always wise to make a reservation for a meal in a hotel.

G garage U lock-ups LD last dinner orders nr no restaurant service WB weekend breaks Full entry details p 6

St Hilary, 21 Crescent Rd, CT11 9QU
Thanet (0843) 591427. *Private Hotel.*
£ B&B £14–£16; HB weekly £68–£80;
[V, w/d; not Aug]

RANGEWORTHY Avon. Map 20B1

Pop 320. Chippenham 20, London 111, M4 (jn 19) 9½, M5 (jn 14) 5, Bath 19, Bristol 11, Cirencester 29, Gloucester 27, Severn Road Bridge 10.
EC Thur. **Golf** Cotswold Edge 18h.

★★ Rangeworthy Court, Bristol, BS17 5ND (045 422) 347 Fax: (045 422) 8945

Large 3-storey stone mansion of 14th century origin. Attractive gardens. Swimming pool.
14 bedrs, 14 en suite; TV; tcf
dogs; P 50; child facs; con 15
LD 9. Resid & Rest lic
£ B&B £44–£52, B&B (double) £60–£68; L £9·50, D £15; WB £35 (HB); [10% V, Fri–Sun]
cc Access, Amex, B'card/Visa, Diners; dep.
(*See advertisement on p. 168*)

RAVENGLASS Cumbria. Map 43B1

Pop 266. Broughton-in-Furness 20, London 297, Egremont 11.
EC Sat. **Golf** Seascale 18h. **See** Muncaster Castle and Gardens, Nature Reserve, Roman Villa ruins, Ravenglass and Eskdale Narrow Gauge Rly, Museum.
[i] Ravenglass & Eskdale Railway Stn.
(065 77) 278

★ Pennington Arms, Main St, CA18 1SD
(0229) 717222.

Family-managed country inn in small village close to sea overlooking estuary.
17 bedrs, 9 en suite, (1 sh); 3 ba; annexe 12 bedrs, 3 en suite, 3 ba; tcf
TV; dogs; P 24, G 1, U 1, coach; child facs; con 60
LD 8.30
£ B&B £15·50–£28·50, B&B (double) £26·50–£44; L £7, D £8·25; WB £15·50; dep.

St Michael's, Muncaster, CA18 1RD
(06577) 362

RAVENSCAR North Yorkshire. Map 45C1

Pop 250. Scarborough 9½, London 222, Whitby 14.
Golf Raven Hall Hotel 9h & 18h.

★★★ Raven Hall, YO13 0ET
Scarborough (0723) 870353
Fax: (0723) 870012

Large stone-built hotel with gardens on cliff top with magnificent views. Swimming pool, golf, putting, tennis, billiards. Du
54 bedrs, 54 en suite; TV; tcf
dogs, ns; P 200, coach; child facs; con 100
LD 9
£ B&B £42–£52, B&B (double) £73–£82·50; L £9·50, D £13; WB £85 (HB 2 nts)
cc Access, Amex, B'card/Visa, Diners; dep.

RAVENSTONEDALE Cumbria. Map 44B1

Kirkby Lonsdale 21, London 267, Brough 9, Hawes 21, Kendal 18, Penrith 28.
See Parish Church, Scandal Beck Valley.

★★ Black Swan, Kirkby Stephen, CA17 4NG Newbiggin-on-Lune (058 73) 204
Attractive Lakeland stone country inn in small village. Family-run. Fishing.
16 bedrs, 16 en suite, 1 ba; TV; tcf
TV, dogs, ns; P 26; child facs; con 20
LD 9.30
£ B&B £36·50, B&B (double) £49; L £8·50, D £16; WB £82
cc Access, Amex, B'card/Visa; dep.

RAWTENSTALL Lancs. Map 33B4

Pop 64,500. Bury 8½, London 201, Blackburn 10, Bolton 11, Burnley 6½, Rochdale 9.
EC Tue. **MD** Thur, Sat. **Golf** Rossendale 18h.
[i] 41–45 Kay St. (0706) 217777

Lindau, 131 Haslingden Old Rd, nr Rossendale, BB4 8RR (0706) 214592. *Guest House.*

READING Berkshire. Map 12B2

See also TILEHURST.
Pop 138,000. Slough 18, London 38, A329 (M) 1½, Bagshot 16, Basingstoke 16, Farnham 25, Henley-on-Thames 8, Newbury 15, Staines 22, Wallingford 14.
MD Mon, Wed, Fri, Sat. **Golf** Calcott 18h, Emmer Green 18h. **See** Art Gallery and Museum (Roman collection from Silchester). Town Hall, remains of Norman Abbey, Churches-St Laurence's, St Mary's, St Matthew's, St Giles, Greyfriars.
[i] Town Hall. (0734) 566226

★★★★ Caversham, Caversham Bridge, Richfield Av, RG1 8BD (0734) 391818
Tx: 846933 Fax: (0734) 391665

Well-designed modern hotel with landscaped gardens and terraces beside the river. Indoor swimming pool, sauna, solarium, gymnasium. Fr, De, It, Es, Po, Du. (QMH)
114 bedrs, 114 en suite; TV; tcf
lift, dogs; P 175; child facs; con 250
LD 10
£ B&B (double) £111·90, L £14·50, D £18; WB £58 (HB)
cc Access, Amex, B'card/Visa, Diners; dep.

★★★★ Ramada, Oxford Rd, RG1 7RH
(0734) 586222 Tx: 847785
Fax: (0734) 597842

Purpose-built modern town centre hotel. Indoor swimming pool, sauna, solarium, gymnasium. Fr, De, It, Da, Du
196 bedrs, 196 en suite; TV; tcf
lift, ns; G 75, coach; child facs; con 220
LD 11.30
£ B&B £45–£100, B&B (double) £60–£120; L £8·50, D £14; WB £30
cc Access, Amex, B'card/Visa, CB, Diners.

★★★★ Reading Moat House, Mill La, Sindlesham, Wokingham, RG11 5DF
(0734) 351035 Tx: 846360
Fax: (0734) 666530

Modern hotel based on a 19th century mill beside the River Loddon 4 miles south east of Reading. Sauna, gymnasium. Fr. (QMH)
96 bedrs, 96 en suite; TV; tcf

En suite rooms
En suite rooms may be bath or shower rooms. If you have a preference, remember to state it when booking a room.

🏠 lift, dogs; P 350, coach; child facs; con 80
✕ LD 10.30
£ B&B £105–£109, B&B (double) £119–£125; L £16·50, D £20·25; WB £42·50; [10% V]
cc Access, Amex, B'card/Visa, Diners.

★★★ **Mill House,** Old Basingstoke Rd, Swallowfield, RG7 1PY ☎(0734) 883124. Tx: 847423

Set in attractive gardens, 3-storey Georgian house in quiet location to S of Reading. Fishing. ⚒ Fr. Closed 25 Dec–30 Dec.
🛏 10 bedrs, 10 en suite; TV; tcf
🏠 P 30, coach; child facs; con 30
✕ LD 10, bar meals only Sat lunch, Sun dinner
£ B&B £72·50 (w/e £24), B&B (double) £92–£103; L £14·50, D £16·95; WB £34·50 (HB)
cc Access, Amex, B'card/Visa, Diners.

★★★ **Post House,** Basingstoke Rd, RG2 0SL ☎(0734) 875485 Tx: 849160
Fax: (0734) 311958

Modern red-brick hotel constructed round central garden. Indoor swimming pool, sauna, solarium, gymnasium. (THF)
🛏 143 bedrs, 143 en suite; TV; tcf
🏠 dogs, ns; P 250; child facs; con 120
✕ LD 11
£ B&B £100–£110, B&B (double) £119–£129; L £12·50, D £19; WB £43 (HB)
cc Access, Amex, B'card/Visa, CB, Diners.

★★★ **Ship,** 4 Duke St, RG1 4RY ☎(0734) 583455
Four-storey hotel with Georgian features conveniently situated in town centre.
(See advertisement on p. 410)

★★**George,** King St, RG1 2HE ☎(0734) 573445

Centrally placed former coaching inn with charming Georgian cobbled courtyard.
⚒ Fr, De. (BCB)
🛏 68 bedrs, 68 en suite; TV; tcf
🏠 ns; coach; child facs; con 50
✕ LD 10.30
£ B&B £59·50–£65, B&B (double) £70; L £8·15, D £8·15; WB £27·50
cc Access, Amex, B'card/Visa, Diners.

★★ **Rainbow Corner,** 132 Caversham Rd, RG1 8AY ☎(0734) 588140
Fax: (0734) 586500
Four Victorian terrace houses make up this family-run hotel. 100 yards from the river and not far from the city centre.
🛏 22 bedrs, 22 en suite; TV; tcf
🏠 TV; P 15, G 2, coach; child facs; con 40
✕ LD 9.30, nr Mon–Sat lunch, Sun dinner. Resid & Rest lic.
£ B&B £62·95–£79·50 (w/e £41), B&B (double) £71·90–£84; D £13·75; WB £20; [10% V]
cc Access, Amex, B'card/Visa, Diners; dep.
(See advertisement on p. 410)

REDBOURN Hertfordshire. Map 14C2

Pop 5,154. St Albans 4½, London 25, M1 (jn 9) 2, Aylesbury 22, Dunstable 8½, High Wycombe 24, Luton 6.
Golf Redbourn 18h & 9h.

★★★ **Aubrey Park,** Hemel Hempstead Rd, AL3 7AF ☎(058 285) 2105 Tx: 82195
Fax: (058285) 2001

Peaceful hotel set in 7 acres of grounds 25 miles north of London. Swimming pool. ⚒ Fr
🛏 119 bedrs, 119 en suite; TV; tcf
🏠 P 160, coach; child facs; con 75
✕ LD 10
£ B&B £94–£104 (w/e £40), B&B (double) £104–£120; L £13, D £15; WB £50; [5% V w/e]
cc Access, Amex, B'card/Visa, Diners.

REDCAR Cleveland. Map 45B2

Pop 36,700. London 254, Middlesbrough 8½, Northallerton 31, Pickering 36, Whitby 22. **EC** Wed. **Golf** Redcar 18h.
ℹ Regent Cinema Building, Newcomen Terr. ☎(0642) 471921

★★★ **Hotel Royal York,** 27 Coatham Rd, TS10 1RP ☎(0642) 486221
A modern purpose-built hotel close to sea front. Billiards. ⚒ Fr, It, Es, Po
🛏 51 bedrs, 51 en suite; TV
🏠 lift; P 300, coach; child facs; con 300
✕ LD 10
£ B&B £19·50–£26·50, B&B (double) £28·50–£35·50; HB weekly £213·50; L £5·55, D £7·25; WB £58·50; [10% V, w/d]
cc Access, Amex, B'card/Visa, Diners.

REDDITCH Hereford & Worcester (Worcestershire). Map 20C3

Pop 73,200. Stratford-upon-Avon 15, London 108, Bromsgrove 6, Birmingham 13, Evesham 16.
EC Wed. **MD** Tue, Wed, Thur, Fri, Sat. **Golf** Redditch 18h.
ℹ Civic Sq, Alcester St. ☎(0527) 60806

★★★ **Southcrest,** Pool Bank, Mount Pleasant, B97 4JG ☎(0527) 541511
Tx: 338455 Fax: (0527) 402600 ♿
Modernised 19th century residence in parklands. ⚒ Fr, It. Closed Xmas–New Year.
🛏 58 bedrs, 58 en suite; TV; tcf
🏠 dogs, ns; P 100, coach; child facs; con 80
✕ LD 9.15, bar meals only Sat lunch & Sun dinner
£ B&B £60–£75 (w/e £24), B&B (double) £70–£85; L £10, D £12; WB £32 (HB); [5% V, w/d; 10% V, w/e]
cc Access, Amex, B'card/Visa, Diners; dep.
(See advertisement on p. 410)

Campanite
(See Motor Lodge section)

REDHILL Surrey. Map 10B2

Pop 22,100. Purley 7½, London 20, Crawley 9½, East Grinstead 13, Godstone 4½, Haywards Heath 18, Mitcham 12, Reigate 1½.
EC Wed. **Golf** Earlswood Common 18h.

♣ ★★★ **C** **Nutfield Priory,** Nutfield, RH1 4EN ☎(0737) 822066 Fax: (0737) 823321

Vast neo-Gothic mansion, complete with a tower, stained glass and gargoyles, set in 40 acres of grounds. Indoor swimming pool, squash, sauna, solarium, gymnasium, billiards. ⚒ Fr. Closed 27–30 Dec.
🛏 34 bedrs, 34 en suite; TV
🏠 lift, ns; P 150, coach; child facs; con 100
✕ LD 10.15, nr Sat lunch. Resid lic
£ B&B £70, B&B (double) £85–£105; L £15·50, WB; [5% V, w/d]
cc Access, Amex, B'card/Visa, Diners; dep.

Ashleigh House, 39 Redstone Hill, RH1 4BG ☎(0737) 764763. *Hotel. Swimming pool.* Closed Xmas.
£ B&B £22·24

REDMILE Leicestershire (Notts). Map 31B2

Grantham 8, London 118, Melton Mowbray 17, Newark 16, Nottingham 17.
See Belvoir Castle.

Peacock Farm (Acclaimed), NG13 0GQ ☎(0949) 42475. *Guest House.*
£ £16·50; HB weekly £166–£220; [V]

REDRUTH Cornwall. Map 2B1

Pop 10,180. Bodmin 30, London 263, Falmouth 10, Helston 10, Newquay 15, Penzance 17, St Ives 14, Truro 9.
EC Thur. **MD** Fri. **Golf** Tehidy Park 18h.

Reading (Berkshire)

Ship Hotel

RAC ★★★

4-8 DUKE STREET, READING, BERKSHIRE RG1 4RY
Telephone: (0734) 583455 Facsimile: (0734) 504450

Usefully situated in the town centre with its own car park and completely re-furbished, the Ship offers a new standard of accommodation and convenience. Comfortable, fully equipped bedrooms (all en-suite); the superb Captain's Carvery; Captain's Cabin bar; a range of excellent meeting rooms; business facilities; and Lesters Wine Bar, plus many other facilities ensure guest and visitors' needs are well catered for.

Reading (Berkshire)

Rainbow Corner Hotel

132-138 Caversham Road, Reading RG1 8AY Tel: (0734) 588140 *Proprietor: D. J. Staples*

Within ½ mile's walking distance from Reading town centre. 22 en-suite bedrooms with Colour TV, Direct Dial Phone, Tea/Coffee making facilities. Restaurant and Bar. Conference facilities also available.
Double/twin room £64. Single £59. Presidential Room £74. These prices are exclusive of Breakfast but inclusive of service and VAT.
Special Weekend Rates of Double/twin £49. Single £38. Presidential £58. Inclusive of Breakfast and VAT. All major credit cards accepted.

Redditch (Worcestershire)

A Residential Hotel, situated in seven acres of landscaped gardens, with surrounding woodlands and walks. 58 bedrooms all with private facilities. Easy access to all Midland Motorways. Wedding and conference facilities. Licensed French Restaurant.

Pool Bank, Redditch
Worcs. B97 4JG
☎ (0527) 541511
Telex 338455
Fax (0527) 402600

R.A.C. ★★★

Redditch (Worcestershire)

THE CAMPANILE HOTEL – Redditch

Far Moor Lane, Winyates Green, Redditch B98 0SD
Tel: (0527) 510710 Telex: 339608

Restaurant
Hotel

Part of the international budget hotel chain "Campanile", the hotel offers 50 comfortable double or twin rooms with en-suite bathrooms, and tea/coffee making facilities, radio alarm, remote control colour TV, Sky TV and direct dial telephone at **competitive rates.**
Our informal restaurant provides a variety of home-cooked French/Continental cuisine, and personal service at **affordable prices.**
Our seminar room is available for business meetings or small functions.
Your hosts: Alison & Eric Godard

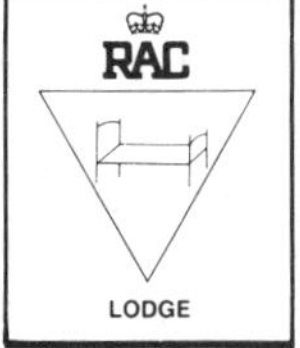

★★★ **Penventon,** TR15 1TS ☎ (0209) 214141 Fax: (0209) 219164

Georgian manor situated in pleasant grounds. Modern extensions. Indoor swimming pool, sauna, gymnasium, billiards. Fr, De, It, Es, Po
55 bedrs, 55 en suite; 4 ba; TV; tcf
dogs; P 100, coach; child facs; con 300
LD 9.30
£ £19–£39 (w/e £19), B&B (double) £35–£70; L £7·95, D £11·95; [V min 2 nts]
cc Access, Amex, B'card/Visa; dep.

★★ **Aviary Court,** Mary's Well, Illogan, TR16 4QZ ☎ Portreath (0209) 842256.
Charming 300-year-old Cornish house in 2 acres of grounds on the edge of woodland.
6 bedrs, 6 en suite; TV; tcf
P 25; children over 3; con 25
LD 8.45, nr Mon–Sat lunch, Sun dinner. Resid & Rest lic
£ B&B £36·50, B&B (double) £51; HB weekly £210; L £7·50
cc Amex, Diners; dep.

★★ **Crossroads,** Scorrier, TR16 5BP ☎ St Day (0209) 820551

Modern purpose-built motel conveniently situated in village off A30.

Lyndhurst, 80 Agar Rd, TR15 3NB ☎ (0209) 215146. *Guest House.*
£ B&B £11

REETH North Yorkshire. Map 44C1

Pop 650. Leyburn 11, London 247, Brough 21, Darlington 18, Hawes 16, Middleton-in-Teesdale 24, West Auckland 26.
EC Wed, Thur. **Golf** Catterick 18h.
[i] Swaledale Folk Museum. ☎ Richmond, N. Yorks (0748) 84517

★ **Arkleside,** Richmond, DL11 6SG ☎ Richmond, N. Yorks (0748) 84200.
A delightful small Dales hotel just off the village green; magnificent views over Swaledale. Closed Jan & Feb
8 bedrs, 6 en suite, 1 ba; TV; tcf
dogs, ns; P 6, G 2; children over 12
LD 8, bar meals only lunch. Resid & Rest lic
£ B&B £30–£35, B&B (double) £44–£50; HB weekly £260–£290; D £13·50
cc Access, Amex, B'card/Visa; dep.

REIGATE Surrey. Map 10B2

Pop 22,900. Purley 8½, London 21, M25 (jn 8) 2, Crawley 10, Dorking 6, East Grinstead 14, Epsom 9, Haywards Heath 18, Leatherhead 8½, Mitcham 12, Redhill 1½.
EC Wed. **Golf** Reigate Heath 9h, Earlswood Common 18h. **See** Castle grounds and Baron's Cave, St Mary's Church.

★★★ **Bridge House,** Reigate Hill, RH2 9RP ☎ (0737) 244821 Tx: 268810 Fax: (0737) 223756

Modern two-storey hotel built on top of Reigate Hill. Fr, De, It, Es
40 bedrs, 40 en suite; TV; tcf
P 110; child facs; con 40
LD 10.30. Resid lic
£ B&B £63–£68·50 (w/e £40), B&B (double) £81–£87·50 (w/e £50); L £15·75, D £20·81; WB; [V]
cc Access, Amex, B'card/Visa, Diners.

★★★ **Reigate Manor,** Reigate Hill, RH2 9PF ☎ (0737) 240125 Tx: 927845 Fax: (0737) 223883
Refurbished Georgian manor house, with modern additions, on Reigate Hill. Sauna, solarium, gymnasium. Fr, De, Es
51 bedrs, 51 en suite; TV; tcf
P 130, coach; child facs; con 200
LD 10, bar meals only Sat lunch
£ room £55–£76, room (double) £76–£84; Bk £6·50, L £10·50, D £14·50; WB £92
cc Access, Amex, B'card/Visa, Diners; dep.

Cranleigh (Acclaimed), 41 West St, RH2 9BL ☎ (0737) 223417 Fax: (0737) 223734. *Hotel.*
£ B&B £44–£59; [5% V, Mon–Wed; 10% V Fri–Sun]

RENISHAW Derbyshire. Map 31A3

Mansfield 13, London 151, M1 (jn 30) 2, Chesterfield 7, Doncaster 22, Sheffield 9, Worksop 9.

★★★ **Sitwell Arms Osprey,** Renishaw Village, Sheffield, S. Yorks, S31 9WE (1½ m W of M1 (jn 30) on A616) ☎ Eckington (0246) 435226 Tx: 547303
Stone-built hotel situated in historic village.
30 bedrs, 30 en suite; TV; tcf
dogs, ns; P 150, coach; child facs; con 175

RETFORD, EAST Nottinghamshire. Map 31B3

Pop 18,402. Newark 20, London 146, Doncaster 16, Gainsborough 10, Ollerton 11, Rotherham 19, Worksop 8.
EC Wed. **MD** Thur, Sat. **Golf** Retford 9h.
[i] 40 Grove St ☎ (0777) 860780

★★★ **West Retford,** North Rd, DN22 7XG ☎ (0777) 706333 Tx: 56143 Fax: (0777) 709951 ♿

Historic 18th century manor house set in extensive grounds. Modern extensions. Fr, De, Es
annexe 63 bedrs, 63 en suite; TV; tcf
dogs, ns; P 120, coach; child facs; con 120
LD 10
£ B&B £40–£67 (w/e £35), B&B (double) £55–£82; L £9·50, D £15·50; WB £74 (2 nts)
cc Access, Amex, B'card/Visa, Diners.

RICHMOND North Yorkshire. Map 45A1

Pop 7,245. Boroughbridge 25, London 233, Brough 32, Darlington 12, Leyburn 10, Middleton-in-Teesdale 28, Northallerton 14.
EC Wed. **MD** Sat. **Golf** Richmond (Yks) 18h. **See** Holy Trinity Church, St Mary's Church, Green Howards' Museum, Castle ruins.
[i] Friary Garden, Victoria Rd. ☎ (0748) 850252

★★ **Frenchgate,** 59–61 Frenchgate, DL10 7AE ☎ (0748) 2087
Small hotel in stone terrace in quaint cobbled street near town centre. Open mid Feb–mid Dec.
13 bedrs, 7 en suite, 3 ba; TV; tcf
dogs; P 6; no children under 7
LD 8.30, nr lunch. Resid & Rest lic
£ B&B £24–£32, B&B (double) £44–£50·50; HB weekly £363–£405·50; D £10; WB £54
cc Access, Amex, B'card/Visa, Diners; dep.

★★ **Kings Head,** Market Pl, DL10 4HS ☎ (0748) 850220 Fax: (0748) 850635
Attractive listed Georgian hotel in famous cobbled market square. Recently refurbished. Fr, De
22 bedrs, 22 en suite; annexe 4 bedrs, 4 en suite; TV; tcf
dogs, ns; P 25, coach; child facs; con 150
bar meals only Mon–Sat lunch & Sun dinner
£ B&B £42–£45, B&B (double) £65–£85; D £11·95; WB £75 (HB 2 nts); [10% V]
cc Access, Amex, B'card/Visa, Diners.

RICHMOND-UPON-THAMES Greater London (Surrey). Map 8B2

Pop 41,024. London 8½, Kingston upon Thames 3½, Mitcham 9, Slough 13, Staines 16, Weybridge 10.
EC Wed. **Golf** Richmond 18h, Royal Mid Surrey 18h. **See** Remains of Palace on the Green, Maids of Honour Row, Almshouses.
[i] Library, Little Green. ☎ 081-940 9125

Please tell the manager if you chose your hotel through an advertisement in the guide.

R

★★★★ R **Petersham,** Nightingale La, TW10 6UZ ☎081-940 7471 Tx: 928556 Fax: 081-940 9998

An impressive 5-storey Victorian Gothic building with fine views of river Thames. Fr, De, It, Es
56 bedrs, 56 en suite; TV
lift; P 50; child facs; con 50
LD 9.45
£ B&B £85–£100 (w/e £65–£80), B&B (double) £95–£120; L £14·50, D £19; WB £110 (2 nts)
cc Access, Amex, B'card/Visa, CB, Diners.

★★★ **Richmond Hill,** 144 Richmond Hill, TW10 6RW ☎081-940 2247 Tx: 21844 Fax: 081 940 5424
Large Georgian hotel, situated at the top of Richmond Hill. Squash. Fr, De, Es, Po, Ar, Fil
125 bedrs, 125 en suite; TV; tcf
lift, dogs, P 125, coach; child facs; con 120
LD 8.45
£ B&B £71·50–£82·50, B&B (double) £88–£99; L £12·50, D £16·50; WB £38 (HB); [10% V]
cc Access, Amex, B'card/Visa, Diners.

Richmond Gate (Highly Acclaimed), Richmond Hill, TW10 6RP ☎081-940 0061. *Hotel.*

Kew, 339 Sandycombe Rd, TW9 3NA ☎081-948 2902. *Hotel.*

RINGWOOD Hampshire. Map 5B2

Pop 11,900. Romsey 17, London 93, Bournemouth 12, Dorchester 32, Lymington 13, Salisbury 16, Southampton 18.
EC Thur. **MD** Wed. **Golf** Burley 9h.
[i] The Furlong ☎(0425) 470896

★★ **Struan,** Horton Rd, Ashley Heath, BH24 2EG ☎(0425) 473553 Fax: (0425) 480529
Privately-owned modern hotel with a pleasant garden. Quiet location. Fr
10 bedrs, 10 en suite; TV; tcf
dogs; P 75, coach; child facs
LD 10
£ B&B £50–£55, B&B (double) £65–£80; L £10, D £12; WB £46 (2 nts)
cc Access, Amex, B'card/Visa, Diners.

Moortown Lodge (Acclaimed), 244 Christchurch Rd, BH24 3AS ☎(0425) 471404. *Private Hotel.* Closed 24 Dec–14 Jan
£ B&B £28–£37; HB weekly £217–£322

RIPLEY Derbyshire. Map 24B2

Pop 18,691. M1 (jn 28) 13, London 135, Ashbourne 16, Chesterfield 10, Derby 12, Mansfield 12, Matlock 10, Nottingham 13.
EC Wed. **MD** Fri, Sat. **Golf** Codnor 18h.

Britannia, 243 Church St, Waingroves, DE5 9TF ☎(0773) 43708. *Guest House.* ♿

RIPON North Yorkshire. Map 38B4

Pop 12,500. Harrogate 11, London 216, Boroughbridge 6, Darlington 35, Leyburn 20, Northallerton 18, Skipton 29, Thirsk 11.
EC Wed. **MD** Thur. **Golf** Ripon 18h. **See** Cathedral, St Wilfrid's Church, Wakeman's House (13th cent), Wakeman's Horn blown nightly at 9 pm. Fountains Abbey 3 m SW, Newby Hall, 3½ m SE.
[i] Minster Rd, ☎(0765) 4625

★★★ **Ripon Spa,** Park St, HG4 2BU ☎(0765) 2172 Tx: 57780 Fax: (0756) 690770
Traditional Edwardian style hotel with own grounds and pleasant gardens.
40 bedrs, 40 en suite; TV; tcf
lift, TV, dogs; P 60, coach; child facs; con 160
LD 9
£ B&B £48–£60, B&B (double) £66–£90; L £9, D £12·95; WB £110
cc Access, Amex, B'card/Visa, Diners; dep.

★★ **Bridge,** Magdalen Rd, HG1 4HX ☎(0765) 3687 ♿

Red-brick, well-furnished hotel on edge of city near River Ure.
15 bedrs, 15 en suite; TV; tcf
dogs, ns; P 15, coach; child facs

★★ **Unicorn,** Market Pl, HG4 1BP ☎(0765) 2202 Tx: 57515 Fax: (0765) 700321

Historic posting house with white-painted Georgian façade.
33 bedrs, 33 en suite; TV; tcf
dogs; P 15, G 4, coach; child facs; con 60
LD 9.30
£ B&B £39–£43, B&B (double) £45–£53, HB weekly £180–£230; L £5·50, D £12·50; [10% V, Jan–Mar, Oct–21 Dec]
cc Access, Amex, B'card/Visa, Diners.

Crescent Lodge, 42 North St, HG4 1EN ☎(0765) 2331. *Guest House.*

ROCHDALE Greater Manchester (Lancashire). Map 33C3

Pop 94,119. Oldham 5½, London 192, A627(M) 2, Burnley 14, Bury 6, Halifax 17, Manchester 10, Todmorden 7½.
EC Tue. **MD** Daily (exc Tue). **Golf** Rochdale 18h, Springfield Park 18h. **See** St Chad's Church, Town Hall, Art Gallery and Museum, John Bright's grave (Friends' Graveyard), original Co-op Shop in Toad Lane (now Co-op Museum).
[i] Town Hall ☎(0706) 356592

★★★ **Norton Grange,** Manchester Rd, Castleton, OL11 2XZ ☎(0706) 30788 Fax: (0706) 49313 ♿

Turreted and gabled Victorian building standing in 14 acres of pleasant grounds. New bedroom extension. It
50 bedrs, 50 en suite; TV; tcf
lift, dogs; P 150, coach; child facs; con 180
LD 9.45, bar meals only Sat lunch
£ B&B £68 (w/e £40), B&B (double) £80–£105; L £14·50, D £14·50; WB £63
cc Access, Amex, B'card/Visa, Diners.

ROCHESTER Kent. Map 11C3

Pop 144,700. London 30, Canterbury 26, Maidstone 8, Tonbridge 19.
EC Wed. **MD** Fri. Deangate Ridge 18h. **See** Castle (open to public), Cathedral, 17th cent Guildhall, Corn Exchange.
[i] Eastgate Cottage, High St, ☎(0634) 43666

★★★★ **Bridgewood Manor,** Maidstone Rd, ☎(0634) 201333 Tx: 965864 Fax: (0634) 201330 ♿

Modern hotel, built round a courtyard, with gothic-style interior. Indoor swimming pool, tennis, sauna, solarium, gymnasium, billiards. Fr, De, Du
100 bedrs, 100 en suite; TV; tcf
lift, dogs; P 175, coach; child facs; con 200
LD 10
£ B&B £70–£115 (w/e £30), B&B (double) £90–£135; L £10, D £17·50; WB £90 (HB 2 nts)
cc Access, Amex, B'card/Visa, Diners.

★★ **Royal Victoria and Bull,** 16–18 High St, ME1 1PT ☎Medway (0634) 846266 Fax: (0634) 832312.
400-year old coaching inn. An attractive building with Dickens associations. Fr, It
28 bedrs, 21 en suite, (1 sh), 5 ba; TV; tcf

TV, dogs, ns; P 25, coach; child facs; con 100
LD 11, bar meals only Sat lunch
£ B&B £43·75–£75, B&B (double) £56·50–£66·50; L 9·95, D £9·95
cc Access, Amex, B'card/Visa, Diners.

ROCHESTER Northumberland. Map 44B4
Pop 150. Corbridge 25, London 308, Alnwick 32, Bellingham 12, Hawick 26, Jedburgh 21
Golf Bellingham 18h. **See** Roman Fort with Pele Tower.

★ **Redesdale Arms,** NE19 1TA Otterburn (0830) 20668
Stone-built roadside former coaching inn in rural surroundings among hills. Billiards.

ROCHFORD Essex. Map 17C2
Pop 7,315. Romford 26, London 42, Brentwood 21, Chelmsford 18, Colchester 36, Dartford Tunnel 26, Southend-on-Sea 3.
EC Wed. **MD** Tue. Rochford 18h.

★★★ **Renouf,** Bradley Way, SS4 1BU
Southend (0702) 541334 Tx: 995158
Fax: (0702) 549563

Purpose-built modern hotel set in its own gardens.
24 bedrs, 24 en suite; TV; tcf
dogs, P 25; child facs; con 50
LD 8.30, nr Tue–Sat lunch. Resid lic
£ B&B £56–£80 (w/e £32), B&B (double) £64–£90; L £15·60, D £15·60
cc Access, Amex, B'card/Visa, Diners.

ROCK Cornwall. Map 2C2
Pop 1,650. Camelford 14, London 241, Wadebridge 6½.
EC Wed. **Golf** St Enodoc 18h (2).

★★ **Mariners,** Slipway, PL27 6LD
Trebetherick (020 886) 2312
Modern hotel with motel-style bedrooms in two separate buildings; overlooking the Camel estuary. Open Easter–1 Nov
15 bedrs, 15 en suite; TV
dogs; P 36; coach; child facs
LD 9.30, bar meals only lunch
£ B&B £25–£28, B&B (double) £44–£50; HB weekly £245–£270; D £6;
cc Access, B'card/Visa; dep.

★★**Roskarnon House,** PL27 6LD
Trebetherick (020 886) 2329
Overlooking the sea, attractive Edwardian house set in gardens. Fr. Open Mar–Oct.
12 bedrs, 6 en suite, (3 sh), 2 ba; TV
TV; dogs; P 16, G 2; child facs
LD 8, bar meals only lunch. Resid & Rest lic
£ B&B £16, B&B (double) £32; HB weekly £150–£220; D £12·50; WB £30 (HB 2 nts); [5% V]

ROMALDKIRK Durham. Map 44C1
Pop 190. Boroughbridge 47, London 254, Brough 16, Darlington 21, Durham 26, Middleton-in-Teesdale 4, West Auckland 14.
Golf Barnard Castle 18h. **See** Bowes Museum, 12th–14th cent Cathedral of the Dales', Market Cross, Barnard Castle.

★★ **Rose and Crown,** DL12 9EB
Teesdale (0833) 50213 Fax: (0833) 50828

Stone-built pub and restaurant in centre of delightful Durham village. Fr
6 bedrs, 6 en suite; annexe 5 bedrs, 5 en suite; TV; tcf
dogs; P 40, coach; child facs; con 14
LD 9.30, bar meals only Mon–Sat lunch & Sun dinner
£ B&B £44, B&B (double) £55; HB weekly £203; L £8·50, D £15·50; WB £75; [10% V, Nov–Apr]
cc Access, B'card/Visa, dep

ROMNEY *see* NEW ROMNEY.

ROMSEY Hampshire. Map 5B2
Pop 13,150. Winchester 10, London 75, M27 (jn 2) 3, Andover 17, Lyndhurst 9½, Ringwood 17, Salisbury 15, Southampton 8.
EC Wed. **Golf** Romsey 18h. **See** Abbey Church, Palmerston's Statue, King John's House (13th cent).
Bus Sta. Car Park, Broadwater Rd. (0794) 512987

★★★ **White Horse,** Market Pl, SO5 8NA
(0794) 512431 Fax: (0794) 517485

Town-centre hotel with traces of Mummers' Gallery and Tudor wall-paintings. (THF)
33 bedrs, 33 en suite; TV; tcf
dogs, ns; P 60, coach; child facs; con 30
LD 9.30
£ B&B £69·75–£77, B&B (double) £84–£94; L £7, D £10·95; WB £47
cc Access, Amex, B'card/Visa, Diners.

ROSEDALE ABBEY North Yorkshire. Map 45B1
Pickering 10, London 233, Helmsley 13, Stokesley 18, Whitby 14.

★★★ **Blacksmith's Arms,** Hartoft End, Pickering, YO18 8EN Lastingham (075 15) 331

Typical Yorkshire Dales inn and restaurant. Situated on country road.
14 bedrs, 14 en suite; TV; tcf
TV, ns; P 80, coach
LD 8.30
£ B&B £45–48, B&B (double) £70–£76; HB weekly £260–£310; L £11·50, D £18·50; WB £42 (HB, Nov–Mar); [5% V]
cc Access, B'card/Visa; dep.

★★ **White Horse Farm,** Pickering, YO18 8SE Lastingham (075 15) 239

Converted farm house of stone construction with magnificent views of Rosedale. Closed 24 & 25 Dec.
11 bedrs, 11 en suite, 1 ba; annexe 4 bedrs, 4 en suite; TV; tcf
dogs; P 40; child facs; con 25
LD 8.45, bar meals only Mon–Sat lunch
£ B&B £28–£47; HB weekly £277–£302; D £16; WB £40·50 (min 2 nts)
cc Access, Amex, B'card/Visa, Diners; dep.

ROSS-ON-WYE Hereford & Worcester (Herefordshire). Map 20A2
See also PENCRAIG
Pop 8,000. Gloucester 16, London 121, M50 (jn 4) 1½, Chepstow 24, Hereford 14, Ledbury 12, Monmouth 10, Tewkesbury 24.
EC Wed. **MD** Thur, Sat. **Golf** Ross-on-Wye.
20 Broad St. (0989) 62768

★★★ **Chase,** Gloucester Rd, HR9 5LH
(0989) 763161 Tx: 35658
Fax: (0989) 768330

R

Lovely Georgian house with extensions in pleasant grounds.
40 bedrs, 40 en suite; TV
P 200, coach; child facs; con 200
LD 9.30
£ B&B £65, B&B (double) £93; HB weekly £367·50; L £15, D £15; WB £55 (HB); [10% V]
cc Access, Amex, B'card/Visa, Diners.

★★★ H Pengethley, HR9 6LL (4 m W on A49) Harewood End (098 987) 211 Tx: 35332 Fax: (098 987) 238

Elegant Georgian house with extensive grounds, and pleasant views. Swimming pool, putting, fishing, billiards. Fr, De, Du
11 bedrs, 11 en suite; annexe 11 bedrs, 11 en suite; TV; tcf
dogs; P 50; child facs; con 60
LD 9.30
£ B&B £60–£110 (w/e £60), B&B (double) £100–£150; L £13·75, D £18·50; WB £60; [V]
cc Access, Amex, B'card/Visa, Diners; dep.

★★★ Royal, Palace Pound, HR9 5HZ (0989) 65105 Fax: (0989) 768058

Modernised Victorian hotel in elevated situation above river. Fine views. (THF)
38 bedrs, 38 en suite; TV; tcf
dogs, ns; P 40, coach; child facs; con 85
LD 9.30
£ B&B £77–£87, B&B (double) £105–£110; HB weekly £378–£448; L £9·75, D £14·95; WB £47
cc Access, Amex, B'card/Visa, Diners.

★★ Bridge House, Wilton, HR9 6AA (0989) 62655
White-painted Georgian house with garden running down to the River Wye. On A40, ½ mile west of town.
7 bedrs, 7 en suite; 1 ba; TV; tcf
TV; P 12; no children under 10
LD 9, nr Mon–Sat lunch. Resid & Rest lic
£ B&B £29–£31, B&B (double) £48–£52; HB weekly £200–£215; L £9·50, D £9·50; WB £30
cc Access, B'card/Visa; dep.

★★ Castle Lodge, Wilton, HR9 6AD (0989) 62234 Fax: (0989) 768306

Historic house in rural setting. Family-run hotel enjoying wonderful views. .
10 bedrs, 10 en suite; TV; tcf
TV, dogs, ns; P 5, coach; no children under 5; con 20
LD 9.15
£ B&B £30, B&B (double) £50; HB weekly £230; D £10; WB £70
cc Access, B'card/Visa; dep.

★★ Chasedale, Walford Rd, HR9 5PQ (0989) 62423

Small country house, quietly situated on outskirts of town. Fr. Closed 1–15 Jan.
11 bedrs, 9 en suite, 1 ba; TV; tcf
dogs, ns; P 15; child facs; con 40
LD 9, bar meals only Mon–Sat lunch
£ B&B £29–£31, B&B (double) £35–£50, HB weekly £167–£250; L £7·50, D £9·75; WB £63 (2 nts); [10% V]
cc Access, B'card/Visa, Diners; dep.

★★ Hunsdon Manor, Weston-under-Penyard, HR9 7PE (0989) 62748
14 bedrs, 14 en suite, annexe 10 bedrs, 10 en suite; TV; tcf
dogs; P 50; child facs; con 24
(*See advertisement below*)

★★ Kings Head, 8 High St, HR9 5HL (0989) 763174
14th century coaching inn in town centre. Attractive rear courtyard.
11 bedrs, 11 en suite; annexe 13 bedrs, 13 en suite; TV; tcf
dogs, P 20; child facs
LD 9.30, bar meals only lunch
£ B&B £34, B&B (double) £50; D £15; WB £70
cc Access, B'card/Visa; dep.

★★ Orles Barn, Wilton, HR9 6AE (0989) 62155
Small family-run hotel set in a pleasant garden. Swimming pool. Es. Closed Nov.
9 bedrs, 9 en suite; TV; tcf
dogs, ns; P 20, coach; child facs; con 12
LD 9.30, nr Mon–Sat lunch. Resid & Rest lic
£ B&B £27·50–£45 (w/e £30), B&B (double) £50–£70; HB weekly £195–£220; L £8·25, D £9·25; WB £30; [5% V w/d]
cc Access, Amex, B'card/Visa, Diners; dep.

★ Rosswyn, High St, HR9 5BZ (0989) 62733
A small pleasant inn situated in town centre.
8 bedrs, 7 en suite, 1 ba; TV; tcf
TV, dogs; P 6; child facs

Arches Country House (Acclaimed), Walford Rd, HR9 5PT (0989) 63348. *Hotel.*
£ B&B £16–£18; [5% V]
Edde Cross House (Acclaimed), Eddie Cross St, HR9 7BZ (0989) 65088. *Guest House.* Open Feb–Nov.
£ B&B £16–£18
Ryefield House (Acclaimed), Gloucester Rd, HR9 5NA (0989) 63030 *Hotel.*

Brookfield House, Overross, HR9 7AT (0989) 62188. *Guest House.* Closed Dec.
£ B&B £15; [5% V]
Radcliffe, Wye St, HR9 7BS (0989) 63895. *Guest House.* Open Mid Jan–Mid Dec.
£ B&B £14; HB weekly £130–£150; [10% V, Sun–Thu, Oct–Jun]
Sunnymount, Ryefield Rd, HR9 5LU (0989) 63880. *Hotel.* Closed 21–31 Dec.
£ B&B £16–£29; HB weekly £195; [10% V, Nov–May]
Vaga House, Wye St, HR9 7BS (0989) 63024. *Guest House.*

ROTHERHAM South Yorkshire. Map 41B4
Pop 82,000. Mansfield 23, London 161, M1 (jn 34) 2½, Barnsley 11, Chesterfield 16, Doncaster 11, Sheffield 5½, Worksop 14. **EC** Thur. **MD** Mon, Fri, Sat. **Golf** Grange Park 18h. **See** Ancient Bridge with Chapel, All Saints' Church, Museum and Art Gallery.
ℹ Library, Walker Pl. ☎(0709) 823611

★★★★ **Rotherham Moat House,** 102–104 Moorgate Rd, S60 2BG ☎(0709) 364902 Tx: 547810 Fax: (0709) 368960 ♿

In residential area, attractive modern hotel with two restaurants. Sauna, solarium, gymnasium. Fr, De, It, Es, Po, Sw, Fin. (QMH)
83 bedrs, 83 en suite; TV; tcf
lift, TV, dogs, ns; P 95, coach; child facs; con 250
LD 9.45, bar meals only Sat lunch
£ B&B £63·95 (w/e £26), B&B (double) £75·90; L £6·25, D £11·50; WB £32·50
cc Access, Amex, B'card/Visa, Diners.

★★★ **Consort,** Brampton Rd, Thurcroft, S66 9JA ☎(0709) 530022
Fax: (0709) 531529
Well-placed near M1/M18 junction. Single storey original building has public rooms with newly built bedroom block adjoining. Extensive function facilities.
18 bedrs, 18 en suite; TV; tcf
£ B&B £40–£48, B&B (double) £56–£62
cc Access, B'card/Visa.

★★★ **Earl of Stafford,** Doncaster Rd, Hooton Roberts, S65 4PF ☎(0709) 852737
Fax: (0709) 851903
Lovely old stone building of 15th century origins with modern extension containing bedrooms and leisure centre at rear. Indoor swimming pool, suana, solarium, gymnasium, snooker. Es
27 bedrs, 27 en suite; TV; tcf
dogs; P 96, coach; con 80
LD 9.45, nr Sun dinner
£ B&B £60–£65, B&B (double) £70–£75; L £7·95, D £10·95; WB £75; [5% V w/e]
cc Access, Amex, B'card/Visa, Diners.

★★ **Brecon,** Moorgate Rd, S60 2AY
☎(0709) 828811 Fax: (0709) 820213
In a quiet residential area, pleasant original hotel building with modern annexe.
13 bedrs, 4 en suite, 2 ba; annexe 12 bedrs, 12 en suite; TV; tcf

★★ **Brentwood,** Moorgate Rd, S60 2TY
☎(0709) 382772 Fax: (0709) 820289 ♿
A well-established privately-owned hotel in residential area. Close to town. Es
36 bedrs, 31 en suite, 2 ba; annexe 10 bedrs, 10 en suite; TV; tcf
dogs, P 60, coach; child facs; con 50
LD 9.30
£ B&B £30–£44 (w/e £19), B&B (double) £60; L £8·50, D £13·95; WB £19; [V]
cc Access, Amex, B'card/Visa, Diners.

★★ **Elton,** Main St, Bramley, S66 0SF
☎(0709) 545681 Fax: (0709) 549100

Modernised farmhouse built in traditional stone. Near M18.
15 bedrs, 5 en suite, (2 sh), 3 ba; annexe 16 bedrs, 16 en suite; TV; tcf
dogs, ns; P 36, coach; child facs; con 10
LD 9.30
£ B&B £29–£46 (w/e £20), B&B (double) £40–£54; L £9·25, D £13·75
cc Access, Amex, B'card/Visa, Diners.

Regis, 1 Hall St, S60 2BP ☎(0709) 376666
£ B&B £20–£29

ROTHERWICK Hampshire. Map 12B1
Camberley 13, London 43, Basingstoke 7, Farnham 13, Reading 12

★★★★ **H C R Tylney Hall,** Hook, RG27 9AJ ☎Hook (0256) 764881
Tx: 859864 Fax: (0256) 728141

In large well-kept parkland, fine ornate 3-storey Victorian mansion in Elizabethan style. Indoor swimming pool, tennis, sauna, gymnasium, billiards. Fr, Es
91 bedrs, 91 en suite; 1 ba; TV
lift; P 120, coach; child facs; con 100
LD 9.30
£ B&B £85–£220, B&B (double) £99–£220; L £17, D £23·50; WB £88 (HB); [10% V]
cc Access, Amex, B'card/Visa, Diners.

ROTHLEY Leicestershire. Map 25B3
M1 (jn 22) 6½, Leicester 6, London 115, Ashby-de-la-Zouch 18, Loughborough 6, Melton Mowbray 13.
EC Wed. **Golf** Rothley Park 18h. **See** Ancient Temple, Church.

★★★ **H C R Rothley Court,** Westfield La, LE7 7LG ☎Leicester (0533) 374141 Tx: 342811 Fax: (0533) 374483

Medieval manor in parkland with temple. Modern rooms in annexe. (THF)
15 bedrs, 15 en suite; annexe 21 bedrs, 21 en suite; TV; tcf
dogs, ns; P 100, coach; child facs; con 100
LD 9.30
£ B&B £83·80, B&B (double) £105·20–£125·20; L £10·95, D £18·50; WB £47
cc Access, Amex, B'card/Visa, Diners.

ROTTINGDEAN East Sussex. Map 6C1
Brighton 3½, London 56, Lewes 8½, Newhaven 4½.
EC Wed. **Golf** East Brighton Ltd 18h. **See** Burne-Jones grave, Windmill, Cliffs.

★★ **Olde Place,** High St, BN2 7HE
☎Brighton (0273) 31051
Detached Georgian building with modern motel block added at rear.

★★ **White Horse,** Marine Dr, BN2 7HR
☎Brighton (0273) 300301

A detached building overlooking the sea in pleasant cliff top site. (GMR)
17 bedrs, 17 en suite; TV; tcf
lift, ns; P 45, coach; child facs; con 45

Braemar House, Steyning Rd, BN2 7GA
☎Brighton (0273) 304263. *Guest House.*
£ B&B £12–£13

ROWLEY REGIS Warley, West Midlands. Map 22B2
Birmingham 7½, London 118, Bridgnorth 19, Bromsgrove 11, Kidderminster 12, Sutton Coldfield 13, Walsall 9, Wolverhampton 8.
EC Thur. **MD** Wed, Sat. **Golf** Dudley 18h.

Highfield House, Holly Rd, Blackheath, B65 0BH ☎021-559 1066. *Hotel.* Closed 24 Dec–1 Jan.
£ B&B £24–£35

ROWSLEY Derbyshire. Map 24A1
Pop 199. Matlock 4, London 148, Buxton 14, Chapel-en-le-Frith 16, Chesterfield 11, Glossop 29, Sheffield 16.
Golf Bakewell 9h, Matlock 18h. **See** 17th cent Peacock Hotel, Haddon Hall 1½ m NW, Chatsworth House, (Garden and Theatre Gallery) 4½ m N.

★★★ **H R Peacock,** nr Matlock, DE4 2EB ☎Matlock (0629) 733518
Fax: (0629) 732671

17th century building with antique furniture and riverside gardens. Fishing. ✖ Fr. (Emb)
🛏 14 bedrs, 14 en suite; annexe 6 bedrs, 1 en suite, 2 ba; TV; tcf
🏨 dogs, ns; P 45, U 5, coach; child facs; con 20
✕ LD 9
£ B&B £36–£73, B&B (double) £64–£91; L £9·50; WB £55
cc Access, Amex, B'card/Visa, Diners.

ROYAL LEAMINGTON SPA *See* LEAMINGTON SPA

ROYAL TUNBRIDGE WELLS *See* TUNBRIDGE WELLS

RUAN HIGH LANES Cornwall. Map 2B1

Pop 215. St Austell 11, London 243, Falmouth (Fy) 14, Newquay 21, Truro 11, Wadebridge 28.
Golf Truro 18h. **See** 14th cent Church.

★★ **Hundred House,** nr Truro, TR2 5JR
📞 Truro (0872) 501336
Attractive family-run hotel, set in 3 acres of grounds. ✖ Fr. Open 1 March–31 Oct.
🛏 10 bedrs, 10 en suite; TV; tcf
🏨 dogs, ns; P 15, children over 6
✕ LD 6, snacks only lunch. Resid & Rest lic
£ B&B £26·50–£29·50, B&B (double) £53–£59; HB weekly £192·50–£259; D £16; [5% V, Mar, Apr, Oct]
cc Access, B'card/Visa; dep.

RUGBY Warwickshire. Map 23C1

Pop 60,380. London 81, M1 (jn 18) 2½, Banbury 25, Coventry 12, Daventry 10, Leicester 20, Nuneaton 16, Warwick 14.
MD Mon, Fri, Sat. **Golf** Rugby 18h. **See** Rugby School, Art Gallery, Percival Guildhouse, Town Hall.
ℹ Library, St Matthews St. 📞 (0788) 71813

★★★★ **Post House,** Crick, NN6 7XR
📞 Crick (0788) 822101 Tx: 311107

Modern purpose-built hotel in gardens adjacent to junction 18 of M1. Billiards, gymnasium. (THF)

Avondale, 16 Elsee Road, CV21 3BA
📞 (0788) 578639. *Guest House.*
£ B&B £18–£25; [5% V]

RUISLIP Greater London (Middx). Map 13B4

Pop 72,791 (inc Northwood), London 13, Denham 4, Ealing 7, Harrow 3½, Rickmansworth 6, Uxbridge 3.
EC Wed. **Golf** Ruislip 18h, Northwood 18h, Haste Hill 18h, Pinner Hill 18h, Hillingdon 9h.

Barn, West End Rd, HA4 6JB 📞 (0895) 636057 Tx: 892514 Fax: (0895) 638379. *Hotel.*

RUNCORN Cheshire. Map 32C1

Pop 64,600 (inc Halton Village). Northwich 11, London 184, M56 (jn 12) 5, Chester 14, Liverpool 13, Nantwich 23, St Helens 8½, Warrington 8½, Whitchurch 27.
EC Wed. **MD** Tue, Thur, Sat. **Golf** Runcorn 18h. **See** Rebuilt All Saints' Church, Castle Inn, Runcorn–Widnes High Level Road Bridge, Norton Priory & Museum open to public (excavation).
ℹ 57 Church St. 📞 (0928) 569656

★★★ 🅷 **Crest,** Wood La, Beechwood, WA7 3HA (at jn 12, M56). 📞 (0928) 714000 Tx: 627426 Fax: (0928) 714611

Modern purpose-built red brick hotel; conveniently near M62. Indoor swimming pool, sauna, solarium, gymnasium. (THF)
🛏 134 bedrs, 134 en suite; TV; tcf
🏨 lift, dogs, ns; P 200, coach; child facs; con 450
✕ LD 10, bar meals only Sat lunch
£ B&B £83·95–£96·95 (w/e £39), B&B (double) £103·90–£116·90; L £11·50, D £15·95; WB £39
cc Access, Amex, B'card/Visa, Diners.

Campanite
(See Motor Lodge section)

RUSHDEN Northamptonshire. Map 21C3

Pop 22,700. Bedford 14, London 64, Huntingdon 23, Kettering 11, Northampton 15, Peterborough 28, Stamford 29.
EC Thur. **MD** Sat. **Golf** Rushden 9h. **See** 13th cent Church, Rushden Hall, Hinwick House nearby.

★★ **Rilton,** High St, NN10 9BT 📞 (0933) 312189 Fax: (0933) 58593
Small hotel conveniently situated a short distance from town centre.
🛏 22 bedrs, 22 en suite, 1 ba; TV; tcf
🏨 dogs; P 80; coach; child facs; con 100
✕ LD 10, nr Sun dinner
£ B&B £32·50; B&B (double) £42·50

★ **Westward,** Shirley Rd, NN10 9BY
📞 (0933) 312376
Family-run pleasant hotel close to town centre. Swimming pool. Closed Xmas.
🛏 15 bedrs, 6 en suite, (3 sh), 2 ba; annexe 10 bedrs, (8 sh), 3 ba; TV; tcf
🏨 TV; dogs; P 15, coach; child facs; con 80
✕ LD 9, nr Mon–Sat lunch & Sun dinner. Resid lic
£ B&B £21·50–£27·50 (w/e £15), B&B (double) £34·50–£39·50; HB weekly £140; L £8·50, D £6·95; [V]
cc Access, B'card/Visa.

RUSHYFORD Durham. Map 45A2

Pop 226. Darlington 9, London 253, A1(M) 2, Alston 41, Durham 8½, Middleton-in-Teesdale 14, West Auckland 7½.
Golf Bishop Auckland 18h. **See** Auckland Castle and Deer House (4½m W).

★★★ **Eden Arms,** DL17 0LL 📞 Bishop Auckland (0388) 720541 Tx: 53168 Fax: (0388) 721871 ♿
18th century building of long low frontage; modern extensions. Indoor swimming pool, sauna, solarium and gymnasium. (Sw)
🛏 46 bedrs, 46 en suite; TV; tcf
🏨 TV, dogs, ns; P 200, coach; child facs; con 100
✕ bar meals only Sat lunch
£ B&B £58 (w/e £40), B&B (double) £78; L £8·25, D £11·50; WB £85 (HB)
cc Access, Amex, B'card/Visa, Diners.

RUSPER West Sussex. Map 10B1

Dorking 9, London 32, Crawley 5, Guildford 18, Horsham 5, Petworth 22, Reigate 11.

♣ ★★★★ **Ghyll Manor,** RH12 4PX
📞 (0293) 871 571 Fax: (0293) 871419
Beautifully-restored Elizabethan manor attractively furnished and set in pleasant gardens. Swimming pool, tennis, sauna, solarium. (THF)
🛏 7 bedrs, 7 en suite; 21 annexe bedrs, 21 en suite; TV; tcf
🏨 dogs, ns; P 150, coach; child facs; con 100
✕ LD 10
£ B&B £95 (w/e £62), B&B (double) £126–£146; L £17, D £22; WB £62
cc Access, Amex, B'card/Visa, Diners; dep.
(See advertisement on p. 293)

RUSTINGTON West Sussex. Map 6B1

Pop 8,650. Horsham 21, London 57, Arundel 4½, Littlehampton 2, Worthing 6½.
EC Wed. **Golf** Littlehampton 18h.

Kenmore, Claigmar Rd, BN16 2NL
📞 (0903) 784634. *Guest House.*

RUTLAND WATER Leicestershire. Map 31B1.

Stamford 5, London 95, Corby 16, Oakham 6.

♣ ★ **Normanton Park,** Rutland Water South Shore, LE15 8RP 📞 Stamford (0780) 720315 ♿

Elegant hotel in converted Georgian Clock Tower, Coach House, and stables in 4 acres of grounds next to Rutland Water. ✖ Fr
🛏 8 bedrs, 7 en suite, 1 ba; annexe 8 bedrs, 8 en suite; TV; tcf
🏨 TV, dogs, P 100; child facs; con 60
✕ LD 9.45, bar meals only Sun dinner. Resid & Rest lic
£ B&B £46–£56, B&B (double) £57–£66; L £11·75, D £16; WB £78

RYDAL Cumbria. Map 43C1

M6 (jn 36) 27, Ambleside 1½, London 271, Broughton-in-Furness 18, Kendal 15, Keswick 15, Penrith 24, Windermere 6½.
Golf Cleabarrow 18h. **See** Nab Cottage, Rydal Mount, Rydal Fell, Rydal Water.

EC *early closing* **MD** *market day* ♣ *country house hotel* *ns (NS) no smoking areas* *tcf tea/coffee facilities*

St Austell (Cornwall)

The Carlyon Bay Hotel

RAC★★★★

In a world of its own on the Cornish Riviera

The exceptionally mild climate and wealth of firstclass facilities combine to provide the perfect location for your family or golfing holiday. Situated within its own 250 acres of grounds, overlooking this unspoilt bay with its golden beaches, you are assured the highest standards of comfort, cuisine and personal service. Excellent facilities include large indoor and outdoor heated pools, sauna, solarium, spa bath, 2 full size snooker tables, tennis courts, children's play area and amusement room. *FREE GOLF IS AVAILABLE to residents on our new 9 hole approach course in the grounds and 18 hole, 6,500 yard course adjacent to the hotel, with resident professional and clubhouse facilities available.* All bedrooms have private bath, colour TV with video facility, radio and telephone, most having panoramic seaviews. Open all year round.

For free brochure, tariff and child reductions please contact The Manager, The Carlyon Bay Hotel, Nr. St. Austell, Cornwall.

Phone Par (072 681) 2304
Fax: (072 681) 4938

R

Runcorn (Merseyside)

THE CAMPANILE HOTEL – Runcorn

Restaurant Hotel

Campanile

Low Lands Road, Runcorn, Merseyside WA7 5TP

Tel: (081) 569 6969 Fax: (081) 569 4888

Part of the international budget hotel chain "Campanile", the hotel offers 83 comfortable double or twin rooms with en-suite bathrooms, and tea/coffee making facilities, radio alarm, remote control colour TV, Sky TV and direct dial telephone at **competitive rates.** Our informal restaurant provides a variety of home-cooked French/ Continental cuisine, and personal service at **affordable prices.** Our seminar room is available for business meetings or small functions.

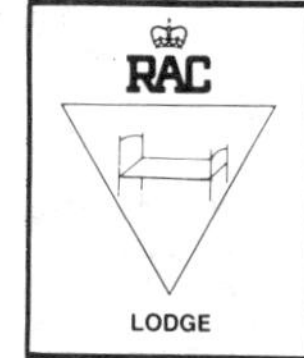

St Austell (Cornwall)

PORTH AVALLEN HOTEL

SEA ROAD, CARLYON BAY,
ST AUSTELL

A Country House Hotel. Quiet, Friendly, Well Appointed. Excellent Cuisine. Overlooking the Bay for a restful holiday with many local amenities. Weekend Breaks.

Tel: Par (072-681) 2802

★★ Glen Rothay, nr Ambleside, LA22 9LR
☎Ambleside (053 94) 32524

Beautiful 17th century country house with beamed ceilings; close to lake. Du. Closed 1–24 Jan.
12 bedrs, 12 en suite, 1 ba;TV; tcf
dogs, ns; P 45; child facs
LD 8, bar meals only lunch. Resid lic
£ B&B £25–£35, B&B (double) £50–£110; HB weekly £231–£500; D £16·95; WB £124 (HB 3 nts); [10% V, Mon–Thu]
cc Access, B'card/Visa; dep.

★ H C R Rydal Lodge, LA22 9LR
☎Ambleside (053 94) 33208

Pleasant family-run hotel, with secluded walled garden. Closed Jan.
8 bedrs, 2 en suite, 3 ba
TV, dogs; P 12, coach; child facs
LD 7, nr lunch. Rest lic
£ B&B £19–£21, B&B (double) £46–£50; HB weekly £150–£55; D £11
cc Access, B'card/Visa.

RYE East Sussex. Map 7B2

Pop 5,000. Hawkhurst 13, London 63, Folkestone 25, Hastings 11, Hurst Green 16, Tenterden 10.
EC Tue. **MD** Thur. **Golf** Camber 18h. **See** Cinque Port, 12th cent Ypres Tower (museum), Flushing Inn (15th cent), Mermaid Inn (15th cent), Land Gate, Town Hall, St Mary's Church (quarter-boys clock), George Hotel, Lamb House (Nat Trust).
ℹ 48 Cinque Ports St. ☎(0797) 222293

★★★ Flackley Ash, Peasmarsh, TN31 6YH ☎Peasmarsh (079 721) 651 Tx: 957210 Fax: (079 721) 510

Georgian mansion in own grounds. Indoor swimming pool, sauna, solarium, gymnasium.
30 bedrs, 30 en suite; TV; tcf
dogs; P 70, coach; child facs; con 100
LD 9.45
£ B&B £52·50–£66·50, B&B (double) £79·50–£94·50; L £10·95, D £15·50; WB £84
cc Access, Amex, B'card/Visa, Diners; dep.

★★★ George, High St, TN31 7JP ☎(0797) 222114 Fax: (0797) 224068

In centre of town, modernised coaching inn with oak beams. Fr, It. (THF)
22 bedrs, 22 en suite; TV; tcf
dogs, ns; G 17, coach; child facs; con 120
LD 9
£ B&B £73, B&B (double) £96; HB weekly £308; L £6·95, D £11·95; WB £51
cc Access, Amex, B'card/Visa, Diners; dep.

★★★ Mermaid Inn, Mermaid St, TN31 7EY ☎(0797) 223065 Tx: 957141 Fax: (0797) 226995

One of the oldest inns in England. Antique furniture, linenfold panelling. Tucked away among cobbled streets.
28 bedrs, 25 en suite, 2 ba; TV
TV; P 25, coach; no children under 8; con 50
LD 9.15
£ B&B £52–£56, B&B (double) £80–£96; L £12, D £16; WB £90 (2 nts)
cc Access, Amex, B'card/Visa, Diners.

Atlas Section
Consult the Atlas section at the back of the guide to find out which towns and villages have RAC Appointed and Listed hotels in them. They are shown on the maps by purple circles.

★★ Hope Anchor, Watchbell St, TN31 7HA ☎(0797) 222216

Small, 18th century hotel in quiet backwater, commanding fine views.
14 bedrs, 8 en suite, 3 ba; TV; tcf
coach; child facs
LD 9, bar meals only Mon–Sat lunch
£ B&B £36–£40, B&B (double) £53–£63; HB weekly £250–£280; L £7·50, D £10; WB £72
cc Access, B'card/Visa; dep.

★★ Ship Inn, Strand Quay, TN31 7DB ☎(0797) 222233 Tx: 957141

Historic small inn set between warehouses on Strand Quay.
12 bedrs, 8 en suite, 3 ba; TV
dogs; P 6, coach; children over 8
LD 9.30, bar meals only Mon–Sat lunch
£ B&B £42–£50, B&B (double) £62–£75; L £11, D £14; WB £74 (2 nts)
cc Access, Amex, B'card/Visa, Diners.

Jeakes House (Highly Acclaimed), Mermaid St, TN31 7ET ☎(0797) 222828 Fax: (0797) 225 758. *Guest House.*
Old Vicarage (Highly Acclaimed), 15 East St, TN31 7JY ☎(0797) 225131
£ B&B £39–£44; HB weekly £259–£287

Aviemore, 28 Fishmarket Rd, TN31 7LP ☎(0797) 223052. *Guest House.*
£ B&B £15–£18; HB weekly £147–£161; [10% V, w/d Oct–Feb]
Cliff Farm, Iden Lock, Nr Rye, TN31 7QE ☎Iden (079 78) 331.
£ B&B (double) £12–£13·50.
Old Borough Arms, The Strand, TN31 7DB ☎(0797) 222128. *Hotel.*
£ B&B £22
Playden Oasts, Playden, TN31 7UL ☎(0797) 223502. *Hotel.*

Licences
Establishments have a full licence unless shown as unlicensed or with the limitations listed on p 6.

SAFFRON WALDEN Essex. Map 15C4

Pop 9,971. Bishop's Stortford 11, London 43, M11 (jn 9) 4½, Braintree 19, Cambridge 15, Dunmow 13, Haverhill 12, Royston 13. **EC** Thur. **MD** Tue, Sat. **Golf** Saffron Walden 18h. **See** Audley End Mansion.
[i] Market Sq. ☎(0799) 24282

★★ **Queens Head Inn,** Littlebury CB 11 4TD ☎(0799) 22251

A 16th-century coaching inn sympathetically modernised. Beamed restaurant and bar.
6 bedrs, 6 en suite; TV; tcf
dogs; P 30, coach; child facs
LD 9, nr all Mon & Sun dinner
£ B&B £35, B&B (double) £40; HB weekly £210; L £6·50, D £9; WB £30; [10% V]

★★ H R **Saffron,** 10 High St, CB10 1AY ☎(0799) 22676 Tx: 81653
Fax: (0799) 513979

Family-run former coaching inn with many delightfully developed features. De, Es, Fr
21 bedrs, 16 en suite, (2 sh), 2 ba; TV; tcf
TV, dogs; P 10, coach; child facs; con 100
LD 9.15, bar meals only Sat & Sun lunch, Sun dinner
£ B&B £31–£48 (w/e £42·75), B&B (double) £56–£66; L £7·50, D £15·95; WB £42·75; [10% V w/e]
cc Access, B'card/Visa.

ST AGNES Cornwall. Map 2B1

Pop 2,000. Bodmin 26, London 269, Newquay 11, Redruth 7½, Truro 8. **EC** Wed. **Golf** Truro 18h. **See** Church, Ancient Cross, St Agnes Head, Beacon.

Discount vouchers

RAC discount vouchers are on p. 34. Hotels with a [V] shown at the end of the price information will accept them in part payment for accommodation bills on the full, standard rate, not against bargain breaks or any other special offers. Please note the limitations shown in the entry: w/e for weekends, w/d for weekdays, and which months they are accepted.

★★ **Rose-in-Vale,** Mithian, TR5 0QD ☎(087 255) 2202

Georgian country house in sheltered wooded valley near the coast. Swimming pool, solarium. De, Fr. Open Mar–Oct.
15 bedrs, 15 en suite; TV; tcf
TV, dogs, ns; P 20; child facs
LD 8, bar meals only lunch. Resid & Rest lic
£ B&B £24·95; B&B (double) £49·90; HB weekly £209·65; D £13·95; WB £54·90 (any 2 nts)
cc Access, B'card/Visa; dep.

★★**Rosemundy House,** 8 Rosemundy, TR5 0UF ☎(087 255) 2101
Set in large wooded garden, an attractive historic building. Swimming pool, putting. Open Easter wk & 4 May–5 Oct.
44 bedrs, 44 en suite; TV; tcf
TV, dogs, ns; P 50; child facs; con 100
LD 8. Resid & Rest lic
£ B&B £18–£29; B&B (double) £36–£58; HB weekly £140–£200; D £10; dep.

★ **Sunholme,** Goonvrea Rd, TR5 0NW ☎(087 255) 2318

High up, with good country and sea views, a 2-storey building pleasantly set in garden and paddock. De, Fr. Open Mar–Oct.
10 bedrs, 10 en suite, 2 ba; TV; tcf
TV, dogs, ns; P 20, coach; child facs
LD 7.30, bar meals only lunch. Resid & Rest lic
£ B&B £19·50–£21; B&B (double) £39–£42; D £9; [10% V]
cc Access, B'card/Visa; dep.

Penkerris, Penwinnick Rd, (B3277), TR5 0PA ☎(087 255) 2262. *Guest House.*
£ B&B £15–£20; HB weekly £105–£140

Porthvean, Churchtown, TR5 0QP ☎(087 255) 2581. *Hotel.* Open Mar–Dec.
£ B&B £24·15–£31·05

St Agnes, Churchtown, TR5 0QP ☎(087 255) 2307.
£ B&B £18·50–£27·50

Hotel locations

Hotel locations are shown on the maps at the back of the guide. All towns and villages containing an RAC Appointed or Listed hotel are ringed in purple.

ST ALBANS Herts. Map 14C2

Pop 72,344. London 19, M10 (jn 1) 1½, Aylesbury 23, Barnet 9½, Dunstable 13, Hatfield 6, Luton 10, Watford 7. **EC** Thur. **MD** Wed, Sat. **Golf** Batchwood Hall 18h. **See** 11th cent Cathedral—massive tower faced with Roman tiles, Abbey Gateway, St Michael's Church (effigy of Sir Francis Bacon), 'Fighting Cocks' Inn, 'Verulamium'—Roman excavations, Museum, Hypocaust (in Verulamium Park).
[i] Town Hall, Market Pl. ☎(0727) 64511

★★★ **Noke Thistle**, Watford Rd, AL2 3DS (2½ m S at junc of A405/B4630/A414). ☎(0727) 54252 Tx: 893834
Fax: (0727) 41906

Elegant country-house style hotel outside St Albans. (ThH)
111 bedrs, 111 en suite; TV; tcf
dogs, ns; P 150, coach; child facs; con 60
LD 10
£ room £75, double room £85; Bk £7·75, L £14·50, D £17·50
cc Access, Amex, B'card/Visa, CB, Diners.

★★★ **Lake Holidays,** 237 London Rd, AL1 1JQ ☎(0727) 40904 Tx: 266020
Fax: (0727) 62750
Modern brick-built, mostly 2-storey hotel set back from the main road into the city from the south. Fr, De, Es, Ar
43 bedrs, 43 en suite; TV; tcf
TV; dogs; P; child facs; con 250
LD 9.30, bar meals only lunch & Sat & Sun dinner
£ B&B £50·90–£55·90 (w/e £42·90); B&B (double) £69·80–£76·80; L £8·50, D £10·50; [10% V]
cc Access, Amex, B'card/Visa, Diners.

★★★ H **St Michael's Manor,** Fishpool St, AL3 4RY ☎(0727) 64444 Tx: 917647
Fax: (0727) 48909

Elizabethan manor house in 5 acres of attractive gardens. Closed 27–30 Dec.
26 bedrs, 26 en suite; TV
dogs; P 80; no children under 10; con 30
LD 9
£ B&B £65–£80, B&B (double) £80–£100; L £14·50, D £19
cc Access, Amex, B'card/Visa, Diners.

S

***** Sopwell House,** Cottonmill La, AL1 2HQ (0727) 864477 Tx: 927823 Fax: (0727) 44741
Owner-managed beautifully maintained elegant country residence, set in parkland. Fr
65 bedrs, 65 en suite; TV; tcf
lift, dogs; P 150, coach; child facs; con 400
LD 9.30, nr Sat lunch
£ B&B £79–£85 (w/e £64), B&B (double) £101–£114; HB weekly £380–£400; L £13·50, D £15·75; WB £44; [5% V]
cc Access, Amex, B'card/Visa, Diners.

Ardmore House, 54 Lemsford Rd. (0727) 59313. *Private Hotel.*
£ B&B £28·75–£43·70.
Haven, 234 London Rd, AL1 1JQ (0727) 40904. *Hotel.*
£ B&B £66
Melford, 24 Woodstock Rd North, AL1 4QQ (0727) 53642. *Private Hotel.*
£ B&B £24·15–£43·70

ST ANNES ON SEA Lancashire.

See LYTHAM ST ANNES.

ST AUSTELL Cornwall. Map 2C1

Pop 19,862. Liskeard 18, London 232, Bodmin 11, Fowey 7½, Newquay 14, Truro 14.
EC Thur. **Golf** St Austell 18h, Carlyon Bay 18h. **See** Church (12th–15th cent), China Clay quarries (tours), Market House (1791), Mengu Stone.

****** H Carlyon Bay,** PL25 3RD Par (072 681) 2304 Tx: 42551 Fax: (072 681) 4938

Large 1930s hotel with lovely cliff-top views. Indoor & outdoor swimming pools, golf, putting, tennis, sauna, solarium, billiards.
69 bedrs, 69 en suite; TV; tcf
lift, TV; P 100; child facs; con 150
LD 9
£ B&B £56–£69, B&B (double) £106–£150; HB weekly £309–£560; L £11, D £16; WB £100 (2 nts HB)
cc Access, Amex, B'card/Visa, Diners.
(*See advertisement on p. 417.*)

***** Cliff Head,** Sea Rd, Carlyon Bay, PL25 3RB Par (072 681) 2345 Fax: (072 681) 5511
In its own pleasant grounds, family-run hotel enjoying sea views. Swimming pool.
48 bedrs, 48 en suite, 2 ba; TV; tcf
TV, dogs, ns; P 60, U 6, coach; child facs; con 100
LD 9
£ B&B £37·03, B&B (double) £64·80; HB weekly £215·90–£229·70; L £6·50, D £10·95; WB £63·25
cc Access, Amex, B'card/Visa, Diners; dep.

***** Porth Avallen,** Sea Rd, Carlyon Bay, PL25 3SG Par (072 681) 2802 Fax: (072 681) 7097
Overlooking the bay, an attractive mid-20th century building. Closed 23 Dec–2 Jan.
24 bedrs, 22 en suite; TV; tcf
TV; P 50, U, G; child facs; con 100
LD 8.30, bar meals only Sat lunch. Resid lic
£ B&B £43–£49·30, B&B (double) £60·50–£69·50; HB weekly (share) £250–£280; L £6·80, D £11·10; WB £67·50 (HB)
cc Access, Amex, B'card/Visa, Diners.
(*See advertisement on p. 417.*)

**** H C R Boscundle Manor,** Tregrehan, PL25 3RL Par (072 681) 3557 Fax: (072 681) 4997

Charming stone-built 18th century manor house in secluded grounds. Swimming pool, gymnasium. Open mid Apr–mid Oct.
9 bedrs, 9 en suite; annexe 2 bedrs, 2 en suite, 1 ba; TV
dogs; P 15; child facs
LD 8.30, nr lunch. Sun dinner residents only. Resid & Rest lic
£ B&B £52·50, B&B (double) £80–£95; HB weekly £360–£435; D £20
cc Access, B'card/Visa; dep.

**** White Hart,** Church St, PL25 4AT (0726) 72100
Georgian hotel conveniently situated in town centre. Fr. Closed 25 & 26 Dec.
18 bedrs, 18 en suite; TV; tcf
dogs; child facs; con 50
LD 8.30
£ B&B £38–£45 (w/e £95), B&B (double) £55–£65; HB weekly £200–£300; L £6·50, D £9·50; WB £95; [10% V]
cc Access, Amex, B'card/Visa, Diners.

Nanscawen House (Highly Acclaimed), Prideaux Rd, PL24 2SR. (072 681) 4488. *Hotel.* Closed 21 Dec–5 Jan.
£ B&B £30–£45; HB weekly £297·50.
Alexandra, 52 Alexandra Rd, PL25 4QN (0726) 74242. *Hotel.* Closed 24–31 Dec.
£ B&B £14–£20; HB weekly £130–£149
Lynton House, 48 Bodmin Rd, PL25 5AF (0726) 73787. *Hotel.*
£ B&B £11.
Selwood House, 60 Alexandra Rd, PL25 4QN (0726) 65707. *Hotel.*
£ B&B £27·50–£31·50; HB weekly £249–£280

ST EVAL Cornwall. Map 2B2

Pop 1,280. Wadebridge 9½, London 248, Newquay 10, St Austell 18, Truro 24.
Golf St Enodoc 18h. Trevose 18h.

Bedruthan House, Bedruthan Steps, PL27 7UW St Mawgan (0637) 860346. *Private Hotel.* Closed Nov & Xmas.
£ B&B £12–£14; HB weekly £115·50–£130

ST IVES Cambridgeshire. Map 26B4

Pop 13,500. Royston 20, London 61, Biggleswade 19, Cambridge 13, Ely 18, Huntingdon 5½, Peterborough 23.
EC Thur. **MD** Mon, Fri. **Golf** St Ives 9h. **See** All Saints' Church, Stone Bridge (with Chapel), Norris Museum and Library.

***** Dolphin,** Bridge Foot, London Rd, PE17 4EP (0480) 66966 Fax: (0480) 495597
Modern hotel in attractive 'period' style on banks of R Ouse. Fishing.
22 bedrs, 22 en suite; TV; tcf
dogs; P 150, coach; child facs; con 150
LD 9.45
£ B&B £48 (w/e £36·50), B&B (double) £58; L £11·50, D £11·50; WB £36·50
cc Access, Amex, B'card/Visa, Diners.

***** R Slepe Hall,** Ramsey Rd, PE17 4RB (0480) 63122 Fax: (0480) 300706

Elegantly adapted Victorian mansion near the town centre. Closed Xmas.
16 bedrs, 15 en suite, 1 ba; TV; tcf
dogs, ns; P 70; child facs; con 220
LD 9.45
£ B&B £57, B&B (double) £70–£75; L £12·25, D £12·25; WB £30 (HB)
cc Access, Amex, B'card/Visa, Diners.

**** St Ives,** London Rd, PE17 4EX (0480) 63857 Fax: (0480) 492027
Small but typical motel—privately-owned and purpose-built.
16 bedrs, 16 en suite; TV; tcf
dogs; P 80, coach; child facs; con 60
LD 9.30
£ B&B £39·50 (w/e £27·50), B&B (double) £55; L £9·50, D £10·50; WB £60 (HB)
cc Access, Amex, B'card/Visa, Diners.

ST IVES Cornwall. Map 2A1

See also CARBIS BAY
Pop 6,000. Redruth 14, London 277, Helston 15, Penzance 8.
EC Thur. **Golf** West Cornwall Lelant 18h.
i Street-an-Pol. Penzance (0736) 796297

***** Chy-an-Drea,** The Terrace, TR26 2BP Penzance (0736) 795076

Extended granite buildings overlooking Porthminster Beach. Solarium, gymnasium. Open mid Mar–end Nov.
33 bedrs, 31 en suite, 1 ba; TV; tcf
dogs, ns; P 5, G 20, coach; no children under 5
LD 8.30, bar meals only lunch. Resid lic
£ B&B £26·95–£36·50; D £13; [10% V Mar–Jun & Oct]
cc Access, Amex, B'card/Visa, Diners; dep.

 EC *early closing* **MD** *market day* *country house hotel* *ns (NS) no smoking areas* *tcf tea/coffee facilities*

★★★ **Porthminster,** The Terrace, TR26 2BN ☎ Penzance (0736) 795221 Fax: (0736) 797043

Large and imposing building with views across Bay. Indoor & outdoor swimming pools, sauna, solarium, gymnasium. ⚒De
🛏 50 bedrs, 50 en suite; TV; tcf
🏨 lift, TV, dogs; P 32, G 9, coach; child facs
✕ LD 8.30
£ B&B £38–£44; B&B (double) £76–£88, HB weekly £316–£373·45; D £13·50; WB £74; [5% V B&B Oct–May]
cc Amex, B'card/Visa, CB, Diners; dep.

★★ **Chy-an-Albany,** Albany Ter, TR26 2BS ☎ Penzance (0736) 796759

Privately-owned 3-storey hotel with fine view of Bay and beach.

★★ **Chy-an-Dour,** Trelyon Ave, TR26 2AD ☎ Penzance (0736) 796436
Fine granite building, with extension, enjoying panoramic views of Bay.
🛏 23 bedrs, 23 en suite, 3 ba; TV; tcf
🏨 lift, TV; ns; P 23, coach; child facs; con 100
✕ LD 8, nr lunch. Resid & Rest lic
£ B&B (double) £66–£72; HB weekly £175–£215; D £9–£11·50; WB £61; [10% V Jan–June, 13 Sep–23 Dec]
cc B'card/Visa; dep.

★★ **Pedn Olva,** Porthminster Beach, TR26 2EA ☎ Penzance (0736) 796222
Attractive white building almost surrounded by sea. Sun terraces overlooking beach. Swimming pool.
🛏 31 bedrs, 29 en suite, 1 ba; annexe 4 bedrs, 4 en suite; TV; tcf
🏨 dogs; P 22, coach; child facs
✕ LD 9.30, Resid & Rest lic
£ B&B £32–£36, B&B (double) £60–£68; HB weekly £208–£223; D £12·50; WB £65 (HB); [10% V Oct–Apr]
cc Access, B'card/Visa; dep.

Dean Court (Highly Acclaimed), Trelyon Av, TR26 2AD ☎ Penzance (0736) 796023. *Hotel.* Open Mar–31 Oct.
£ B&B £25–£32; HB weekly £180–£220

Blue Mist, 6 The Warren, TR26 2EA ☎ (0736) 795209. *Guest House.* Open Easter–end Oct.
£ B&B £15·40–£22·27; HB weekly £138·05–£144·65

Dunmar, 1 Pednolver Terr, TR26 2EL ☎ (0736) 796117. *Private Hotel.*
£ B&B £14·50–£20

Hollies, Talland Rd, TR26 2DF ☎ Penzance (0736) 796605. *Hotel.*
£ B&B £16–£20; HB weekly £130–£180

Longships, 2 Talland Rd, TR26 2DF ☎ Penzance (0736) 798180. *Hotel.*
£ B&B £14·50–£20; HB weekly £129–£187

Lyonesse, Talland Rd, TR26 2DF ☎ Penzance (0736) 796315. *Private Hotel.* Open Mar–Oct.
£ B&B £18–£25

Porth-Dene, Primrose Valley, TR26 2ED. ☎ (0736) 796713. *Guest House.* Open Apr–Oct.
£ £12–£14

Primrose Valley, Primrose Valley, TR26 2ED ☎ Penzance (0736) 794939. *Hotel.* Open Mar–Dec.
£ B&B £16–£25; HB weekly £137·50–£210.

St Margaret's, 3 Parc Av, TR26 2DN ☎ Penzance (0736) 795785

St Merryn, Trelyon, TR26 2PF ☎ Penzance (0736) 795767. *Hotel. Putting.*

ST JUST-IN-PENWITH
Cornwall. Map 2A1
Pop 4,020. Penzance 7, London 288, St Ives 12.
EC Thur. **Golf** West Cornwall, Lelant 18h.

Boswedden House, Cape Cornwall, TR19 7NJ ☎ Penzance (0736) 788733. *Hotel. Indoor swimming pool.* Open Mar–Nov.

ST JUST-IN-ROSELAND
Cornwall. Map 2B1
Pop 1,200. St Austell 17, London 249, Newquay 22, Truro 8.
Golf Truro 18h. **See** 13th cent Church.

Rose-da-Mar (Acclaimed), TR2 5JB ☎ St Mawes (0326) 270450. *Hotel.* Open Apr–Oct.
£ B&B £21; HB weekly £214·99–£254·23

ST LEONARDS
Dorset. Map 5B2
Ringwood 2, London 95, Bournemouth 10, Dorchester 30, Lymington 15, Salisbury 18.
ℹ Avon Forest Park Centre ☎ (0425) 478470

★★★ **St Leonards,** Ringwood Rd, BH24 2NP ☎ (0425) 471220 Tx: 418215 Fax: (0425) 480274 ♿
Modern hotel built at side of 18th century inn on A31. Excellently furnished bedrooms. Sauna, gymnasium. (Lns)
🛏 33 bedrs, 33 en suite; TV; tcf
🏨 ns; P 250; con 175
£ B&B £65, B&B (double) £78; L £11, D £11; WB £33; [10% V]
cc Access, Amex, B'card/Visa, Diners.

ST LEONARDS-ON-SEA
East Sussex
See HASTINGS.

ST MAWES
Cornwall. Map 2B1
Pop 1,100. St Austell 18, London 251, Falmouth (Fy) 15, Truro 18 (Fy 9½).

★★★ **Idle Rocks,** Sea Front, TR2 5AN ☎ (0326) 270771

Privately owned 3-storey building attractively situated on seafront overlooking harbour.
🛏 16 bedrs, 16 en suite; annexe 6 bedrs, 6 en suite; TV; tcf
🏨 dogs, ns; child facs; con 30
✕ bar meals only lunch
£ B&B £19–£54, B&B (double) £38–£108; D £15·95; dep.

★★ **St Mawes,** The Seafront, TR2 5DW ☎ (0326) 270266
Charming 3-storey terraced building with wrought iron balcony. Picturesque site near pier. ⚒Fr. Open Feb–Nov.
🛏 7 bedrs, 7 en suite, 1 ba; TV; tcf
🏨 dogs; children over 5
✕ LD 8.15
£ B&B £40, B&B (double) £56–£70; HB weekly £210–£250; L £9, D £14; WB
cc Access, B'card/Visa; dep.

ST MELLION
Cornwall. Map 3A2
Saltash 5, London 217, Callington 4, Liskeard 10, Tavistock 12.

★★★ **St Mellion,** Saltash, PL12 6RN ☎ Liskeard (0579) 50101 Fax: (0579) 50116
Attractive modern complex, hotel and sports club house, set in countryside. Indoor swimming pool, golf, putting, tennis, squash, sauna, solarium, gymnasium, billiards. Closed 24–26 Dec.
🛏 24 bedrs, 24 en suite; TV; tcf
🏨 ns; P 500; child facs; con 220
✕ LD 9.15, grill room only Mon–Sat lunch
£ B&B £25–£72; B&B (double) £50–£115; L £8, D £16·25
cc Access, Amex, B'card/Visa, Diners

ST NEOTS
Cambridgeshire. Map 26B3
Pop 12,500. Biggleswade 11, London 57, Bedford 10, Cambridge 19, Huntingdon 10.

★★ **Old Falcon,** Market Sq, PE19 2AW ☎ Huntingdon (0480) 72749

An inn since the 15th century, this riverside hotel was a stagecoach stop on the old Great North Road.
🛏 8 bedrs, 8 en suite; TV; tcf
🏨 dogs; P 4; coach; child facs; con 90
✕ LD 9.30, bar meals only Mon, Sun dinner
£ B&B £40, B&B (double) £50
cc Access, Amex, B'card/Visa, Diners.

S

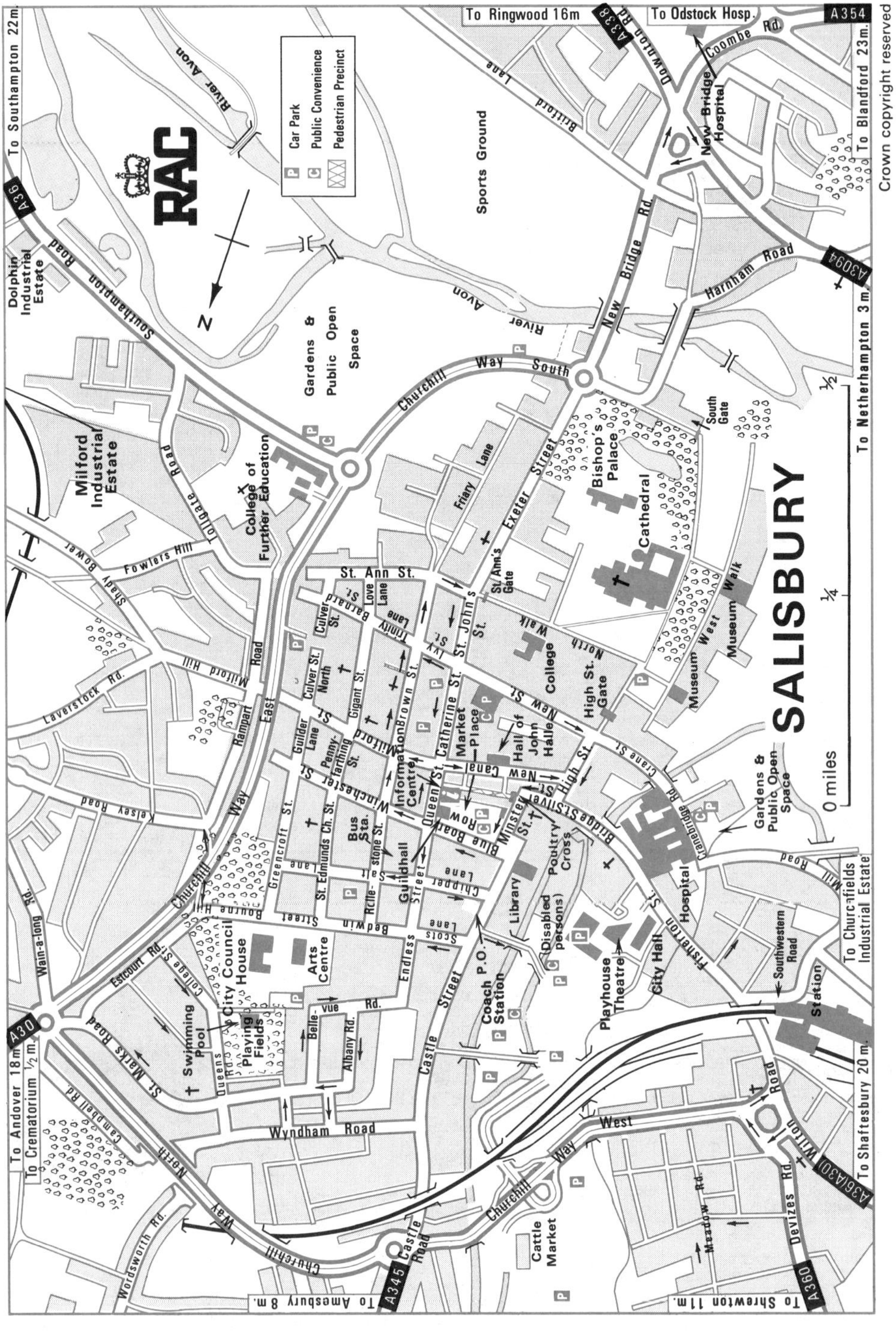

SALISBURY

RAC

Car Park
Public Convenience
Pedestrian Precinct

0 miles ¼ ½

To Southampton 22m.
To Ringwood 16m
To Odstock Hosp.
To Blandford 23m.
To Netherhampton 3 m.
To Churchfields Industrial Estate
To Shaftesbury 20 m.
To Shrewton 11m.
To Amesbury 8 m.
To Crematorium ½ m.
To Andover 18m.

A36
A338
A354
A3094
A36(A30)
A360
A345
A30

Dolphin Industrial Estate
Southampton Road
River Avon
Sports Ground
Britford Lane
Downton Rd.
Coombe Rd.
New Bridge Hospital
New Bridge Rd.
Harnham Road
Gardens & Public Open Space
Churchill Way South
Milford Industrial Estate
College of Further Education
Tollgate Road
Fowlers Hill
Shady Bower
Milford Hill
Laverstock Rd.
Rampart Road
Churchill Way East
Kelsey Road
Wain-a-long Rd.
Friary Lane
Exeter Street
Bishop's Palace
South Gate
Cathedral
St. Ann's Gate
St. Ann St.
Love Lane
Barnard St.
Culver St.
Trinity Lane
Ivy St.
St. John's St.
North Walk
College
High St. Gate
New St.
Museum West Walk
Culver St. North
Gigant St.
Brown St.
Catherine St.
Market Place
Hall of John Halle
Guilder Lane
Penny-farthing St.
Milford St.
Winchester St.
Information Centre
Queen St.
New Canal
Crane St.
High St.
Silver St.
Bridge St.
Crane Bridge Rd.
Gardens & Public Open Space
Mill Road
Greencroft St.
St. Edmunds Ch. St.
Bus Sta.
Rollestone St.
Guildhall
Blue Boar Row
Minster St.
Poultry Cross
Salt Lane
Chipper Lane
Bourne Hill
Bedwin Street
Scots Lane
Endless Street
Library
Disabled persons
Hospital
Fisherton St.
City Hall
Playhouse Theatre
Southwestern Road
Station
Estcourt Rd.
College St.
City Council House
Arts Centre
Swimming Pool
Playing Fields
Queens Rd.
Bellevue Rd.
Albany Rd.
Castle Street
Coach Station
P.O.
St. Marks Road
Campbell Rd.
Wyndham Road
Churchill Way West
Churchill Way North
Wordsworth Rd.
Castle Road
Cattle Market
Meadow Rd.
Devizes Rd.
Wilton Road

★★ **Wyboston Lakes,** Great North Rd, Wyboston, MK44 3AL ☎ Huntingdon (0480) 219 949 Tx: 826303 Fax: (0480) 407349

Modern motel by a golf and leisure park alongside the River Ouse 3 miles S. of town. Golf, putting, fishing. Closed 24–26 Dec.
🛏 38 bedrs, 38 en suite; TV; tcf
🏨 dogs; P 70, coach; child facs; con 25

SALCOMBE Devon. Map 3B1

Pop 2,451. Kingsbridge 6½, London 211, Plymouth 22.
EC Wed. **Golf** Thurlestone 18h.
ℹ 66 Fore St. ☎ Salcombe (054 884) 3927

★★★ **H** **Bolt Head,** Cliff Rd, TQ8 8LL ☎ (054 884) 3751 Fax: (054 884) 3060

Attractive building overlooking estuary and sea in peaceful setting. Swimming pool. Fr. Open 24 Mar–9 Nov.
🛏 28 bedrs, 28 en suite; TV; tcf
🏨 dogs; P 30; child facs
✕ LD 9
£ B&B £43–£63, B&B (double) £86–£126; HB weekly £329–£483; L £9·50, D £19·50; [10% V]
cc Access, Amex, B'card/Visa, Diners; dep.

★★★ **H** **C** **R** **Tides Reach,** Cliff Rd, TQ8 8LJ ☎ (054 884) 3466 Fax: (054 884) 3954
Modern hotel in attractive gardens on small cove. Swimming pool, squash, sauna, solarium, gymnasium, billiards. Da, De, Es, Fr. Open Mar–Nov.
🛏 41 bedrs, 41 en suite, TV
🏨 lift, dogs; P 100; children over 8
✕ LD 10, bar meals only lunch
£ B&B £41, B&B (double) fr £76; HB weekly £294–£462; D £19·75; WB £99 (HB)
cc Access, Amex, B'card/Visa, Diners; dep.

★★ **Grafton Towers,** Moult Rd, TQ8 8LG ☎ (054 884) 2882

Distinctive building with attractive tower. Magnificent sea views. Open Apr–Oct.
🛏 13 bedrs, 11 en suite, 1 ba; TV; tcf
🏨 dogs, ns; P 11; child facs
✕ LD 8.30, nr lunch. Resid & Rest lic
£ B&B £25–£33, B&B (double) £52–£65; HB weekly £220–£280; D £12·50
cc Access; B'card/Visa; dep.

★ **Sunny Cliff,** Cliff Rd, TQ8 8JX ☎ (054 884) 2207
Attractive 3-storey hotel enjoying panoramic views of estuary. Swimming pool, fishing.
🛏 15 bedrs, 3 en suite, (2 sh), 5 ba; annexe 4 bedrs, 4 en suite; tcf
🏨 TV, dogs, ns; P 14, G 1, coach; child facs
✕ LD 8, bar meals only lunch. Resid & Rest lic
£ B&B £23–£27·50; B&B (double) £46–£55 HB weekly £200–£250; D £10·50; WB £60
cc Access, B'card/Visa; dep.

Lyndhurst (Highly Acclaimed), Bonaventure Rd, TQ8 8BG ☎ (054 884) 2481. *Hotel.* Open Jan–Nov.
£ B&B £18·50–£22; HB weekly £196–£210

Devon Tor, Devon Rd, TQ8 8HJ ☎ (054 884) 3106. *Private Hotel.*
Old Porch House, Shadycombe Rd, TQ8 8DJ ☎ (054 884) 2157. *Guest House.* Closed 23–28 Dec.
£ B&B (double) £35–£50
Penn Torr, Herbert Rd, TQ8 8HN ☎ (054 884) 2234. *Hotel.* Open Easter–Oct.
£ B&B £16·50–£21
Terrapins, Buckley St, TQ8 8DD ☎ (054 884) 2861. *Hotel.* Open Mar–Nov & winter weekends.
£ B&B £21·85–£30·90; HB weekly £190·75–£255
Torre View, Devon Rd, TQ8 8HJ ☎ (054 884) 2633. *Hotel.* Open Feb–Nov.
£ B&B £23–£29; HB weekly £179–£199

SALE Greater Manchester. Map 33B2

Pop 57,824. Altrincham 3, London 183, Macclesfield 17, Manchester 5, Stockport 8.

★★★ **Amblehurst,** 44 Washway Rd, M33 1QZ ☎ (061-973) 8800 Tx: 668871 Fax: 061-905 1697 ♿
Brick-built gabled building on A56. Modern bedroom extension round an attractive sunken garden. De, Es, It, Po
🛏 39 bedrs, 39 en suite; TV; tcf
🏨 P 50, coach; child facs; con 70
✕ LD 10, bar meals only Sat lunch, all Sun
£ B&B £50 (w/e £15), B&B (double) £60; L £7·95, D £9·95; [10% V]
cc Access, Amex, B'card/Visa.

SALFORD Greater Manchester (Lancashire). Map 33B2

Pop 246,400. Manchester 2, London 186, M602 4, Altrincham 7, St Helens 21, Walkden 6½, Warrington 15, Wigan 16.
ℹ Museum, The Crescent ☎ 061-745 8773

★★ **Hazeldean,** 467 Bury New Rd, Kersall, M7 0NX ☎ 061-792 6667 Fax: 061-792 6668
Many-gabled hotel set back from road in residential area half way between town centre and M62.
🛏 21 bedrs, 17 en suite, 2 ba; annexe 3 bedrs, 1 en suite, 1 ba; TV; tcf
🏨 TV, dogs; P 21, coach; child facs; con 30

★★ **Racecourse,** Littleton Rd, M7 0TN ☎ 061-792 1420 Fax: 061-708 9227
Convenient hotel with modern facilities. 10 minutes from Manchester city centre.
🛏 19 bedrs, 18 en suite; TV; tcf
🏨 dogs; P 40, coach; child facs; con 150
✕ LD 9.30
£ B&B £33, B&B (double) £43

★ **Beaucliffe,** 254 Eccles Old Rd, M6 8ES ☎ 061-789 5092 Fax: 061-787 7739

Family-owned and run, small hotel in former private house. Fr, It
🛏 21 bedrs, 17 en suite, 1 ba; TV; tcf
🏨 TV; P 24; con 30
✕ LD 8.45, bar meals only lunch & Fri, Sat & Sun dinner. Resid & Rest lic
£ B&B £34 (w/e £22), B&B (double) £47; HB weekly £280; L £8, D £9
cc Access, Amex, B'card/Visa, Diners; dep.

SALFORDS Surrey. Map 10C2

Redhill 3, London 23, Crawley 6½, East Grinstead 10, Gatwick Airport 4.

Mill Lodge (Acclaimed), 25 Brighton Road, RH1 6PP. ☎ (0293) 771170.
£ B&B £25

SALISBURY Wiltshire. Map 5B2

Pop 36,000. Basingstoke 36, London 83, Amesbury 8, Andover 18, Blandford Forum 23, Ringwood 16, Shaftesbury 20, Southampton 22, Winchester 23.
See Plan, p. 422.
EC Wed. **MD** Tue, Sat. **P** See Plan. **Golf** High Post 18h, South Wilts 18h. **See** Cathedral (404 ft spire), the North Canonry, Bishop's Palace (now Choir School), Mompesson House (Nat Trust), Old Sarum 2 m N.
ℹ Fish Row. ☎ (0722) 334956.

★★★ **Red Lion,** Milford St, SP1 2AN ☎ (0722) 23334 Tx: 477674 Fax: (0722) 25756 ♿

Three-storey former coaching inn, originally 13th century. Attractive courtyard.
🛏 57 bedrs, 56 en suite, (1 sh); TV; tcf
🏨 lift; P 20, coach; child facs; con 100
✕ LD 9
£ B&B £55, B&B (double) £80; L £7·50, D £12·50; WB £85
cc Access, Amex, B'card/Visa, Diners; dep.

S

Salisbury (Wiltshire)

Sandbach (Cheshire)

Saunton (Devon)

 EC *early closing* **MD** *market day* *country house hotel* *ns (NS) no smoking areas* *tcf tea/coffee facilities*

★★★ **Rose and Crown,** Harnham Rd, SP2 8JQ ☎(0722) 27908 Tx: 47224 Fax: (0722) 339816 ♿

Charming 2-storey timber framed building, dating from 14th century. By river. Fr (QMH)
40 bedrs, 40 en suite; TV; tcf
dogs, ns; P 44, coach; child facs; con 80
LD 9.30
£ B&B £70·50–£75·50, B&B (double) £90·50–£95·50; L £9·50, D £10·50; WB £49·25
cc Access, Amex, B'card/Visa, Diners; dep.

★★★ **White Hart,** St John St, SP1 2SD. ☎(0722) 27476 Fax: (0722) 412761

City centre hotel of some character, close to Cathedral. (THF)
68 bedrs, 68 en suite; TV; tcf
dogs, ns; P 80, G10; coach; child facs; con 80
LD 9.30
£ room £65–£73 (w/e £50), double room £80–£91; Bk £4·75, L £8·50, D £12·95; WB £50
cc Access, Amex, B'card/Visa, CB, Diners.

★★ **Cathedral,** 7 Milford St, SP1 2AJ ☎(0722) 20144

4-storey terraced hotel in city centre. Family owned and run.

★★ **County,** Bridge St, SP1 2ND ☎(0722) 20229
Early Victorian sandstone building beside River Avon in city centre. (BCB)
31 bedrs, 31 en suite; TV; tcf
ns; P 31, coach; child facs; con 100
LD 10
£ B&B £53–£62·50, B&B (double) £70; L £8·15, D £8·15; WB £27·50
cc Access, Amex, B'card/Visa, Diners.

★★ **King's Arms,** 9 St Johns St, SP1 2SB ☎(0722) 27629

Attractive 16th century half-timbered former coaching inn close to Cathedral.
15 bedrs, 15 en suite; TV; tcf
coach; child facs; con

★★ **Trafalgar,** 33 Milford St, SP1 2AP ☎(0722) 338686 Fax: (0722) 414496

Charming 14th century inn close to city centre.
16 bedrs, 16 en suite; TV; tcf
dogs; coach; child facs
LD 9.30
£ B&B £40, B&B (double) £58; L £6·95, D £8·95; WB £44
cc Access, Amex, B'card/Visa, Diners.

★★ **White Horse,** 38 Castle St, SP1 1BN ☎(0722) 27844 Fax: (0722) 27844
Three-storey red brick Victorian building, short distance from city centre. Fr, Es, Po
11 bedrs, 7 en suite, 2 ba; TV; tcf
G 10, coach; child facs; con 20
LD 9, bar meals only lunch
£ B&B £27–£36, B&B (double) £45–£49; L (Sun) £5·95, D £8·95
cc Access, B'card/Visa, Diners; dep.
(*See advertisement on p. 000*)

Byways (Acclaimed), 31 Fowler's Rd, SP1 2QP ☎(0722) 328364. *Guest House.* ♿
£ B&B £16–£25; HB weekly £175–£210

Glen Lyn, 6 Bellamy La, Milford Hill, SP1 2SP ☎(0722) 327880. *Guest House.* Closed 24–25 Dec.
£ B&B £16–£20
Hayburn Wyke, 72 Castle Rd, SP1 3RL ☎(0722) 412627. *Guest House.*
£ B&B £18–£23
Holmhurst, Downton Rd, SP2 8AR ☎(0722) 323164. *Guest House.* Open Apr–Nov.
£ B&B £15–£32
Leena's, 50 Castle Rd, SP1 3RL ☎(0722) 335419
£ B&B £17–£22
Old Mill, Town Path, West Harnham, SP2 8EU ☎(0722) 27517. *Hotel.* Open 1 Apr–30 Nov.
Richburn, 23 Estcourt Rd, SP1 3AP ☎(0722) 325189. *Guest House.*
£ B&B £15

Changes made after July 1990 are not included.

SALTBURN-BY-THE-SEA Cleveland. Map 45B1
Guisborough 6, London 252, Darlington 29, Middlesbrough 12, Scarborough 35.
EC Wed. **Golf** Saltburn 18h. **See** Guisborough Priory, Chapel Beck Gallery Guisborough.
ℹ Station Sq. ☎(0287) 22422

★★★ **Grinkle Park,** Easington, TS13 4UB ☎Guisborough (0287) 40515 Fax: (0287) 41278

Stone-built manorial style building in tranquil parkland with extensive gardens. Tennis, fishing, billiards.
20 bedrs, 20 en suite; TV; tcf
dogs; P 130, U 2 (£2); coach; child facs; con 50
LD 9
£ B&B £55·50, B&B (double) £72; L £7·50, D £14·50; WB £48; [10% V Sun–Thur]
cc Access, Amex, B'card/Visa, Diners.

SANDBACH Cheshire. Map 30B3
Pop 15,500. London 161, M6 (jn 17) 1, Congleton 7, Knutsford 12, Middlewich 5, Nantwich 9½, Newcastle-under-Lyme 11.
EC Tue. **MD** Thur. **Golf** Sandbach 9h, Malkins Bank 18h. **See** Remarkable sculptured Saxon Crosses in Market Sq, 17th cent Old Hall, now hotel, Church.
ℹ Sandbach Service Area M6 (northbound). ☎Crewe (0270) 760460

★★★ **Chimney House,** Congleton Rd, CW11 0ST ☎Crewe (0270) 764141 Tx: 367323 Fax: (0270) 768916
Attractive converted Tudor-style country rectory. Sauna, solarium.
50 bedrs, 50 en suite; TV; tcf
dogs, ns; P 110, coach; child facs; con 92
LD 10, bar meals only Sat lunch
£ B&B £74, B&B (double) £87; L £8·95, D £15; WB £54; [10% V]
cc Access, Amex, B'card/Visa, Diners.

★★★ **Saxon Cross,** Holmes Chapel Rd, CW11 9SE (M6 Junction 17). ☎Crewe (0270) 763281 Tx: 367169 Fax: (0270) 768723 ♿

Modern purpose-built hotel in quiet country.
52 bedrs, 52 en suite; TV; tcf
dogs; P 150, coach; child facs; con 80
LD 9.30, bar meals only Sat lunch, Sun dinner. Resid lic

S

£ B&B £33–£54 (w/e £33), B&B (double) £45–£68; L £8·50, D £13·50; [10% V Mon–Thur]
cc Access, Amex, B'card/Visa, Diners.
(*See advertisement on p. 424.*)

★★ Old Hall, Newcastle Rd, CW11 0AL ☎(0270) 761221 Fax: (0270) 762551

Jacobean building of character offering all modern comforts.
🛏 12 bedrs, 12 en suite; annexe 3 bedrs, 3 en suite; TV; tcf
🏨 dogs, ns; P50, coach; child facs; con 30
✕ LD 9, nr Sun dinner
£ B&B £52 (w/e £30), B&B (double) £72–£82; L £10, D £15; WB £75
cc Access, Amex, B'card/Visa.

SANDBANKS Dorset

See POOLE.

SANDIACRE Derbyshire. Map 24C2

Pop 7,879. M1 (jn 25) 1, London 123, Ashby-de-la-Zouch 17, Derby 8, Loughborough 12, Mansfield 20, Nottingham 6½.
EC Thur. **Golf** Erewash, Stanton 18h. **See** Parish Church.

★★★ Post House, Bostocks La, NG10 5NJ ☎Nottingham (0602) 397800 Tx: 399378 Fax: (0602) 490469
Modern hotel strategically placed at M1/A52 junction. (THF)
🛏 107 bedrs, 107 en suite; TV; tcf
🏨 dogs, ns; P 250, coach; child facs; con 80
✕ LD 10, nr Sat lunch. Resid lic
£ B&B £67 (w/e £39·50), B&B (double) £78; L £8·50, D £13
cc Access, Amex, B'card/Visa, CB, Diners.

SANDWICH Kent. Map 7C3

Pop 4,500. Canterbury 12, London 70, Dover 10, Folkestone 15, Margate 8½.
EC Wed. **MD** Thur. **Golf** Prince's 27h. **See** Cinque Port, The Barbican (Tudor), Guildhall, Fisher Gate, old Town Walls, Richborough Castle & Roman fort 1½ m NW.
ℹ St Peter's Church, Market St. ☎(0304) 613565.

★★★ Bell, The Quay, CT13 9EF ☎(0304) 613388 Fax: (0304) 615308
Brick-built, 17th century building, with modern extension, picturesquely set by Quay. Golf, putting, fishing.
🛏 29 bedrs, 29 en suite; TV; tcf
🏨 dogs, ns; P 60, coach; child facs; con 120

SARRE Kent. Map 7C3

Canterbury 8, London 66, Herne Bay 8, Margate 7, Ramsgate 8.

★★ Crown Inn, nr Birchington, CT7 0LF ☎(0843) 47808

A 16th Century inn, tactfully modernised and with a recent extension providing bedrooms and restaurant facilities. Noted for cherry brandy, made here for over 400 years.
🛏 12 bedrs, 12 en suite; TV; tcf
£ B&B £38·50, B&B (double) £55–£60

SAUNTON Devon. Map 3A4

Barnstaple 7, London 200, Dunster 39, Ilfracombe 10, Lynmouth 23.
Golf Saunton 18h. **See** Five miles of sands.

★★★★ C R Saunton Sands, EX33 1LQ ☎Croyde (0271) 890212 Tx: 42551 Fax: (0271) 890145

Purpose-built hotel with fine view of sands. Indoor swimming pool, putting, tennis, squash, sauna, solarium, billiards.
🛏 92 bedrs, 92 en suite; TV; tcf
🏨 lift, TV, dogs; P 140; child facs; con 200
✕ LD 9
£ B&B £56–£69, B&B (double) £104–£138; HB weekly £250–£520; L £11·50, D £15·50; WB £80 (HB)
cc Access, Amex, B'card/Visa, Diners.
(*See advertisement on p. 424*)

SAVERNAKE Wiltshire. Map 5B4

Pop 240. Newbury 18, London 72, Amesbury 20, Andover 18, Marlborough 5, Pewsey 7

★★ Savernake Forest, Marlborough, SN8 3AY ☎Marlborough (0672) 810206
Old-established stone building in rural surroundings on edge of forest. Fishing.
🗣 De, No
🛏 10 bedrs, 10 en suite, 1 ba; annexe 6 bedrs, 6 en suite; TV; tcf
🏨 TV, dogs; P 50, coach; child facs; con 50
✕ LD 9.15, buttery Mon–Sat lunch, Sun dinner
£ B&B £50, B&B (double) £70; L £5, D £12·50; WB £40; [5% V]
cc Access, Amex, B'card/Visa, Diners; dep.

Please tell the manager if you chose your hotel through an advertisement in the guide.

SCALBY North Yorkshire. Map 39B4

Pop 9,138. Scarborough 2½, London 216, Bridlington 20, Pickering 18, Whitby 17.

🏠 ★★★ C Wrea Head, Barnoor La, YO11 0PB ☎Scarborough (0723) 378211 Fax: (0723) 363457
Large sandstone residence in elevated position. 14 acres of parkland. Putting, riding.
🛏 21 bedrs, 21 en suite; TV
🏨 ns ; P 50, G 3 (£5); child facs; con 36
✕ LD 9. Resid & Rest lic
£ B&B £37·50–£47·50, B&B (double) £75–£130; HB weekly £315–£455; L £12·50, D £18·50; WB £95; [10% V]
cc Amex, B'card/Visa.

SCARBOROUGH N. Yorkshire. Map 39B4

See also TROUTSDALE
Pop 41,770. Driffield 21, London 213, Beverley 33, Bridlington 17, Malton 24, Pickering 16, Whitby 18.
See Plan, p. 427.
EC Wed. **MD** Thur. **P Golf** North Cliff 18h, South Cliff 18h. **See** Spa, Castle ruins, St Mary's Church (Anne Brontë's grave).
ℹ St Nicholas Cliff. ☎(0723) 373333

🏠 ★★★★ Holbeck Hall, Seacliff Rd, South Cliff, YO11 2XX ☎(0723) 374374 Fax: (0723) 351114

Fine brick building, in commanding position on South Cliff.
🛏 30 bedrs, 30 en suite; TV
🏨 P 50; child facs; con 175
£ B&B £45–£50, B&B (double) £90–£100; L £9·50, D £17·50; WB £107; [10% V]
(*See advertisement on p. 428*)

★★★★ Royal, St Nicholas St, YO11 2HE ☎(0723) 364333 Tx: 527609 Fax: (0723) 500618

A beautiful example of the best of Regency architecture and luxury. Indoor swimming pool, sauna, solarium, gymnasium, billiards.
🗣 De, Es, Fr, Po

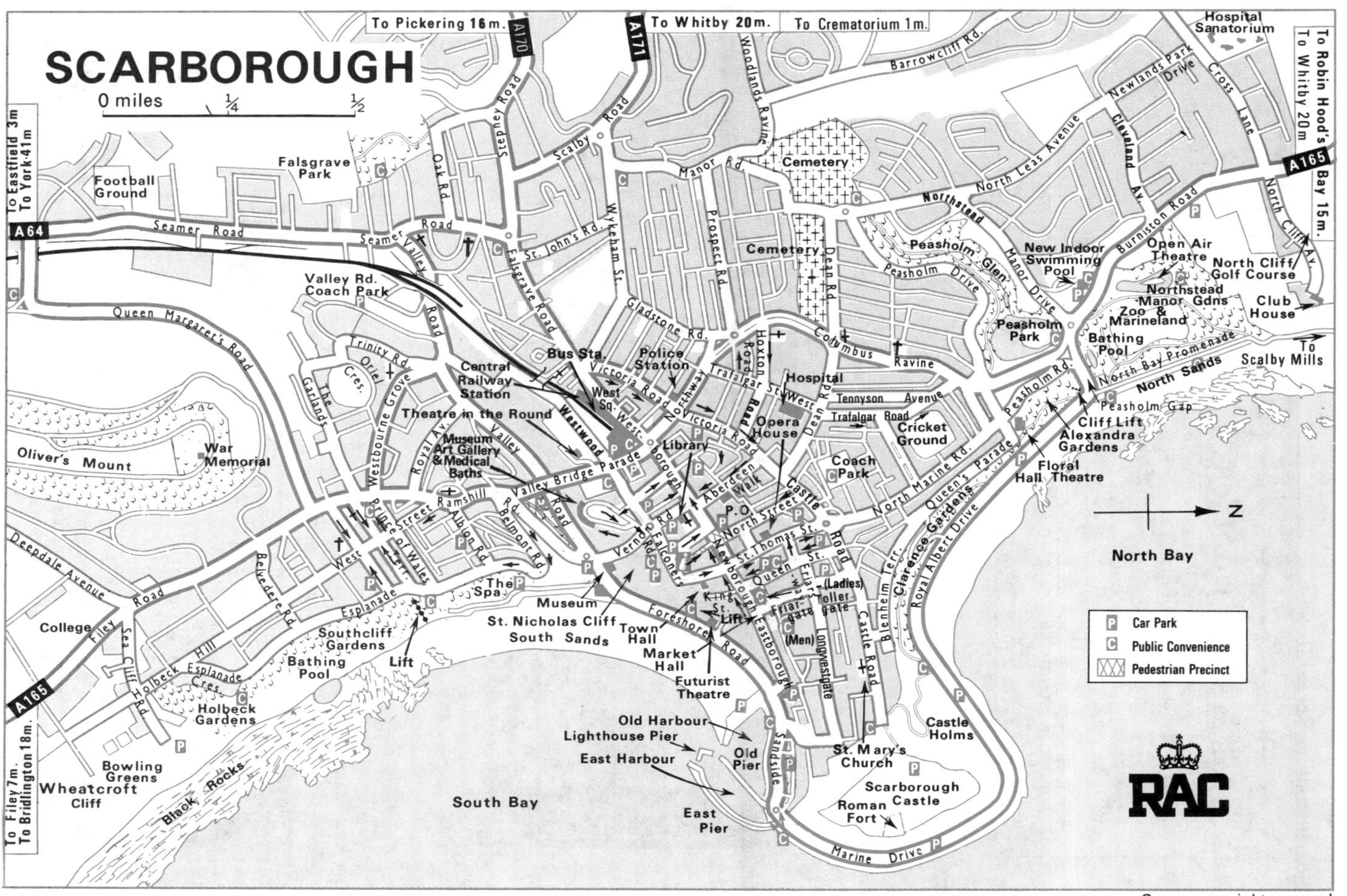
SCARBOROUGH
0 miles
¼
½
To Pickering 16m.
A170
To Whitby 20m.
A171
To Crematorium 1m.
Hospital Sanatorium
To Robin Hood's Bay 15m.
To Whitby 20m
A165
To Eastfield 3m
To York 41m
A64
To Filey 7m.
To Bridlington 18m.
A165
Football Ground
Falsgrave Park
Seamer Road
Oak Rd.
Stepney Road
Scalby Road
Woodlands Ravine
Barrowcliff Rd.
Newlands Park Drive
Cross Lane
Cemetery
Manor Rd.
North Leas Avenue
Cleveland Av.
Northstead
Burniston Road
North Cliff Av.
Valley Road
Falsgrave Road
St. John's Rd.
Wykeham St.
Prospect Rd.
Cemetery
Dean Rd.
Peasholm Glen
Peasholm Drive
Manor Drive
New Indoor Swimming Pool
Open Air Theatre
North Cliff/ Golf Course
Northstead Manor Gdns
Zoo & Marineland
Club House
Valley Rd. Coach Park
Queen Margaret's Road
Gladstone Rd.
Hoxton Road
Columbus Ravine
Peasholm Park
Bathing Pool
North Bay Promenade
To Scalby Mills
North Sands
Trinity Rd.
Oriel Cres.
The Garlands
Bus Sta.
Police Station
Hospital
Peasholm Rd.
Peasholm Gap
Central Railway Station
Victoria Road
Northway
Trafalgar St. West
Road
Dean Rd.
Tennyson Avenue
Trafalgar Road
Cliff Lift
Alexandra Gardens
Theatre in the Round
West Sq.
Westwood
Westborough
Opera House
Cricket Ground
Westbourne Grove
Royal Av.
Museum Art Gallery & Medical Baths
Valley
Library
Aberdeen Walk
Coach Park
Floral Hall Theatre
Oliver's Mount
War Memorial
Valley Bridge Parade
Ramshill Rd.
Albion Rd.
Belmont Rd.
Valley Road
P.O.
North Street
Castle Road
North Marine Rd.
Queen's Parade
Clarence Gardens
Royal Albert Drive
N
North Bay
Prince of Wales Terr.
Street
West
Vernon Rd.
Falconers Rd.
Newborough
St. Thomas St.
Queen St.
Friars-way
(Ladies)
Toller gate
Friargate
Blenheim Terr.
Deepdale Avenue
Road
Belvedere Rd.
Esplanade
The Spa
Museum
King St.
Lift
(Men)
Longwestgate
Castle Road
Car Park
Public Convenience
Pedestrian Precinct
College
Filey
Sea Cliff Rd.
Holbeck Hill
Esplanade Cres.
Holbeck Rd.
Southcliff Gardens
Bathing Pool
Lift
St. Nicholas Cliff
South Sands
Town Hall
Foreshore Road
Eastborough
Market Hall
Futurist Theatre
Holbeck Gardens
Old Harbour
Lighthouse Pier
East Harbour
Old Pier
Sandside
St. Mary's Church
Castle Holms
Bowling Greens
Wheatcroft Cliff
Black Rocks
South Bay
East Pier
Scarborough Castle
Roman Fort
Marine Drive
RAC
Crown copyright reserved
S

Scarborough (Yorkshire)

Holbeck Hall — Hotel & Restaurant

Elegant Country House Hotel situated in superb cliff top position in own grounds overlooking Scarborough's South Bay. Panelled Baronial Hall with Minstrels Gallery, and log fire. All bedrooms with private bathroom, colour TV, radio, hairdrier, trouser-press and direct dial telephone, many with panoramic sea views. Some suites available. Candlelit restaurant serving English and Continental Cuisine. Ample free car parking. Nearest hotel to the South Cliff Golf Club.

Please write or telephone for brochure and details from: Holbeck Hall Hotel, Seacliff Road, South Cliff, Scarborough YO11 2XX. Telephone 0723 374374.

Scarborough's only BTA commended Hotel

ENGLISH ROSE HOTELS

Scarborough (Yorkshire)

PERIOD ELEGANCE WITH EVERY MODERN COMFORT

You can have the best of both worlds at the Esplanade – and one of the finest views in Scarborough. Our colour brochure gives the full picture; please write or 'phone:

THE ESPLANADE HOTEL

Belmont Road, Scarborough YO11 2AA

Telephone: (0723) 360382

Sevenoaks (Kent)

MAIDSTONE/SEVENOAKS Post House Hotel

thf

Fax No.: (0732) 885850

THE PERFECT LOCATION AT WROTHAM HEATH.

This luxury Hotel is ideally situated close to the M20 and M26. Built in a new, fresh style, the Post House Hotel offers sumptuous accommodation and also offers a choice of luxury suites and executive rooms. The superb Restaurant, featuring the 'Traders Table', offers exquisite cuisine with authentic dishes from all around the World. The Hotel is also equipped with a magnificent Health and Fitness Club with heated indoor swimming pool, jacuzzi, sauna, solarium and multi-gym.

For more information/reservations,

Telephone: (0732) 883311

London Road, Wrotham Heath, Kent, TN15 7RS

Telex No: 957309

🛏 134 bedrs, 134 en suite; TV; tcf
lift; dogs; coach; child facs; con 260
✕ LD 11.30
£ B&B £55–£60 (w/e £98–£120), B&B (double) £85–£96; HB weekly £287–£300; L £8, D £17; WB £98–£120; [10% V]
cc Access, Amex, B'card/Visa, Diners.

★★★ Clifton, Queens Parade, YO12 7HX. (0723) 375691 Fax: (0723) 364203
Substantial Victorian building with corner turret and many bay windows. Marvellous views over North Bay. Recently refurbished to a high standard. Sauna, solarium.
🛏 70 bedrs, 70 en suite; TV; tcf
P 40, coach; child facs; con 180
✕ LD 8.45, bar meals only Mon–Sat lunch
£ B&B £28·50–£33, B&B (double) £57–£66; HB weekly £245–£266; L £6·50, D £12·50; WB £75–£85; [5% V]
cc Access, Amex, B'card/Visa.

★★★ Esplanade, Belmont Rd, YO11 2AA (0723) 360382 Fax: (0723) 376137

Traditional resort hotel with 4 storeys. Fine views over South Bay.
🛏 73 bedrs, 73 en suite, 7 ba; TV; tcf
lift, TV, dogs; P 24, coach; child facs; con 150
✕ LD 9
£ B&B £33–£40, B&B (double) £61–£67·50; HB weekly £239–£246·50; L £8, D £11; WB £66 (HB)
cc Access, Amex, B'card/Visa; dep.
(*See advertisement on p. 428*)

★★★ Hotel St Nicholas, St Nicholas Cliff, YO11 2EU (0723) 364101
Recently refurbished period hotel on cliff-top, close to main shopping area. Indoor swimming pool, sauna, solarium, gymnasium.
🛏 138 bedrs, 138 en suite; TV; tcf.

★★★ Palm Court, St Nicholas Cliff, YO11 2ES (0723) 368161 Tx: 527579 Fax: (0723) 371547

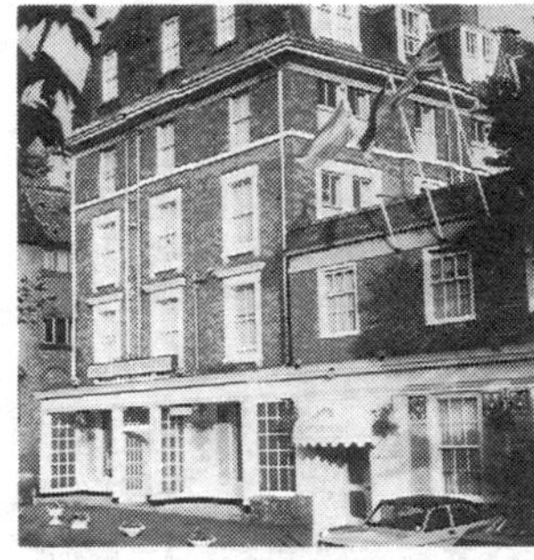

Pleasantly modernised town centre hotel. Swimming pool, sauna.
🛏 50 bedrs, 50 en suite; TV; tcf
lift, TV; P6, G100 (£3); child facs; con 200
✕ LD 9, buttery Mon–Sat lunch, Resid lic
£ B&B £34–£50, B&B (double) £55–£70; HB weekly £239–£274; L £8, D £10·50; WB £79; [5% V]
cc Access, Amex, B'card/Visa, Diners; dep.

★★ Bradley Court, 7 Filey Rd, YO11 2SE. (0723) 360476
Recently refurbished Victorian building on main road south from town, half a mile from town centre, 500 yards to Esplanade and South Bay.
🛏 38 bedrs, 38 en suite; TV; tcf
£ B&B £25–£30, B&B (double) £50–£70; L £6·95, D £8·95

★★ Brooklands, Esplanade Gdns, YO11 2AW (0723) 376576

Family-run hotel in 4-storey Victorian building overlooking gardens on South Cliff. Open Mar–Nov.
🛏 61 bedrs, 52 en suite, 10 ba; TV; tcf
lift; coach; child facs; con 120
✕ LD 8.30. Rest lic
£ B&B £22·50–£34·50, B&B (double) £41·50–£51·50; HB weekly £206–£259; L £6, D £9; [10% V]
cc Access, B'card/Visa; dep.

★★ Central, 1–3 The Crescent, YO11 2PW (0723) 365766
A stately Georgian building overlooking gardens in centre of Scarborough. Fr
🛏 39 bedrs, 21 en suite, 5 ba; TV; tcf
lift, dogs; P 15, coach; child facs; con 30
✕ LD 9.30, bar meals only Mon–Sat lunch, nr Sun
£ B&B £26·75–£31; B&B (double) £47–£55; HB weekly £208–£235; D £8; [5% V Nov–May]
cc Access, Amex, B'card/Visa, Diners; dep.

★★ Crescent, 1, Belvoir Terr, YO11 2PP (0723) 360929 Fax: (0723) 354126

A late Victorian stone building overlooking gardens in town centre. De, Fr, It
🛏 20 bedrs, 20 en suite; TV; tcf
lift, ns; no children under 6; con 25
✕ LD 10, carvery Mon–Sat lunch
£ B&B £35·75–£46·75, B&B (double) £60–£70; HB weekly £255–£285; L £8·25, D £12·50; WB £50
cc Access, B'card/Visa; dep.

★★ East Ayton Lodge, Moor La, East Ayton YO13 9EW. (0723) 864227
Early 19th-century house with attractive bay windows in 3 acres of gardens off the A170. Further bedrooms planned in redevelopment scheduled for early 1991.
🛏 11 bedrs, 11 en suite; annexe 6 bedrs, 6 en suite; TV; tcf
TV; dogs; P 50, coach; child facs; con 30
✕ LD 9, nr Mon lunch. Resid & Rest lic
£ B&B £30–£45; B&B (double) £40–£70; HB weekly £250–£300; L £9·50, D £15; WB £60; [10% V]
cc Access, Amex, B'card/Visa, Diners.

★★ Red Lea, Prince of Wales Terr, South Cliff, YO11 2AJ (0723) 362431 Fax: (0723) 371230

Large established hotel in terrace of elegant Victorian houses overlooking South Bay. Indoor swimming pool, sauna, solarium, gymnasium. Fr
🛏 67 bedrs, 67 en suite; TV; tcf
lift, TV, ns; coach; child facs; con 100
✕ LD 8.30, bar meals only Mon–Sat lunch. Resid & Rest lic
£ B&B £26–£27; B&B (double) £52–£54; HB weekly £242–£250; L £7, D £9·50; WB £74
cc Access, B'card/Visa.

★★ Southlands, 15 West St, YO11 2QW (0723) 361461 Tx: 57515 Fax: (0723) 376035 ♿

Large, mainly brick building, situated in South Cliff residential area. Solarium.
🛏 58 bedrs, 10 en suite; TV; tcf
lift; TV; dogs; P 30, coach; child facs; con 100
✕ LD 8.30, bar meals only lunch
£ B&B £25–£35, B&B (double) £40–£60; D £11; WB £70; [5% V]
cc Access, Amex, B'card/Visa, Diners; dep.

★ Commodore, Prince of Wales Terr, Southcliff, YO11 2AN (0723) 361001

Owner-run hotel in tall Victorian terrace on outskirts of town.
🛏 50 bedrs, 32 en suite, (2 sh), 6 ba; TV; tcf
🏨 lift, TV, dogs, ns; coach; child facs

Pickwick Inn, Huntriss Row, YO11 2ED ☎(0723) 375787 Fax: (0723) 374284

Busy inn on edge of pedestrianised area. Well-furnished bedrooms some with partial sea views.
🛏 11 bedrs, 11 en suite; TV; tcf
🏨 lift; con 50
✕ LD 10.15
£ B&B £24–£30, B&B (double) £40–£60; HB weekly £188–£209; L £5·95, D £9; WB £59
cc Access, Amex, B'card/Visa, Diners; dep.

Grand, St Nicholas Cliff, YO11 2ET ☎(0273) 375371. *Hotel awaiting inspection.*

Bay (Highly Acclaimed), 67 Esplanade, South Cliff, YO11 2UZ ☎(0723) 373926. *Hotel.*
Premier (Highly Acclaimed), 66 Esplanade, South Cliff, YO11 2UZ ☎(0723) 361484. *Hotel.* Open Mar–Dec.
£ B&B £28–£30; HB weekly £210–£224

Anatolia (Acclaimed), 21 West St, YO11 2QR ☎(0723) 360864
£ B&B £11–£15
Crawford (Acclaimed), 8–9 Crown Terr, YO11 2BL ☎(0723) 361494. *Hotel.* Open Apr–Nov
£ B&B £17; HB weekly £143·50
Glen Grant (Acclaimed), 18 West Sq, YO11 1UY ☎(0723) 364291. *Hotel.*
Parade (Acclaimed), 29 Esplanade, YO11 2AQ ☎(0723) 361285 *Hotel.* Open Mar–Dec
£ B&B £19·50–£22; HB weekly £168–£178·50
Parmella (Acclaimed), 17 West St, South Cliff, YO11 2QN ☎(0723) 361914. *Private Hotel.* Open Mar–Nov.

Geldenhuis, 143 Queen's Par, YO12 7HU ☎(0723) 361677. *Hotel.* Open Easter–Oct.
£ B&B £19·55; HB weekly £128·80
Glenville, 8 Blenheim St, North Bay, YO12 7HB ☎(0723) 372681. *Hotel.*
£ B&B £12·75–£16·25; HB weekly £105–£133
Paragon, 123 Queen's Par, YO12 7HU ☎(0723) 372676. *Hotel*
£ B&B £21–£23; HB weekly £196–£210
Saint Margaret's, 16 Weydale Ave, YO12 6AX ☎(0723) 373717. *Hotel.*
Scalby Manor, Burniston Coast Rd, YO13 ODA. ☎(0723) 375716
£ B&B £20, HB weekly £96–£120

Sefton, 18 Prince of Wales Terr, South Cliff, YO11 2AL ☎(0723) 372310. *Hotel.* Open Mar–Oct.
£ B&B £13·50; HB weekly £108·50–£122·50
Valley Lodge, 51 Valley Rd, YO11 2LX ☎(0723) 375311
West Lodge, 38 West St, YO11 2QP ☎(0723) 500754
£ B&B £10; HB weekly £87·50–£105
Weydale, Weydale Av, YO12 6BA ☎(0723) 373393. *Hotel.* Open Mar–22 Oct.
£ B&B £14–£17; HB weekly £133–£161

SCILLY ISLES

See ISLES OF SCILLY

SCOLE

Norfolk. Map 27B4
Pop 1,139. Colchester 40, London 96, Bury St Edmunds 22, East Dereham 28, Ipswich 23, Norwich 19, Thetford 18.
EC Wed. **Golf** Diss 9h.
★★ **Scole Inn,** Diss, IP21 4DR ☎Diss (0379) 740481 Fax: (0379) 740762

17th century former coaching inn which has been modernised.
🛏 12 bedrs, 12 en suite; annexe 11 bedrs, 11 en suite; TV; tcf
🏨 TV, dogs, ns; P 60; child facs; con 36
✕ LD 9.45, bar meals only Sat lunch
£ B&B £45–£55, B&B (double) £65–£75; L £10·95, D £11·95; WB £65 (HB); [5% V]
cc Access, Amex, B'card/Visa, Diners; dep.

SCOTCH CORNER

North Yorkshire. Map 45A1
Boroughbridge 28, London 230, A1 (M) 1½, Brough 24, Darlington 7½, Leyburn 15, Middleton-in-Teesdale 21.
EC Wed. **Golf** Richmond 18h.
ℹ Rank Motorway Service Area, A1 ☎(0325) 377677
★★★ **Scotch Corner,** Gt North Rd, DL10 6NR ☎Richmond (N. Yorks) (0748) 850900 Tx: 587447 Fax: (0748) 5417

Large traditional 1930s hotel situated at junction of A1 and A66.
🛏 90 bedrs, 90 en suite; TV; tcf
🏨 lift, dogs; P 250, G 5, coach; child facs; con 350
✕ LD 10
£ B&B £59 (w/e £60 2 nts), B&B (double) £74–£96 (suite); L £3·75, D £12·50; [8% V]
cc Access, Amex, B'card/Visa.
★★ **Vintage,** DL10 6NP. ☎Richmond (N Yorks) (0748) 4424
Small family-run modern hotel at junction of A1 and A66.

SCUNTHORPE

Humberside (South Humberside). Map 39A2
Pop 66,047. Lincoln 28, London 161, M181 2, Doncaster 22, Gainsborough 16, Goole 21, Grimsby 30, Hull 26.
MD Fri, Sat. **Golf** Scunthorpe 18h. **See** Church of St Laurence, Normandy Hall.
ℹ Library, Carlton St. ☎(0724) 860161
★★★ **Royal,** Doncaster Rd, DN15 7DE ☎(0724) 282233 Tx: 527479 Fax: (0724) 281826

Modernised traditional hotel on western fringe of town. (THF)
🛏 33 bedrs, 33 en suite; TV; tcf
🏨 TV; dogs, ns; P 25, coach; child facs; con 250
✕ LD 9.15, bar meals only Sat lunch.
£ B&B £55 (w/e £22·50), B&B (double) £60; L £5, D £10·50; WB £29
cc Access, Amex, B'card/Visa, CB, Diners.
★★★ **Wortley House,** Rowland Rd, DN16 1SU ☎(0724) 842223 Tx: 527837 Fax: (0724) 280646
Large brick building on fringe of town. Banqueting suite and ballroom. De, Fr, It
🛏 38 bedrs, 38 en suite; TV; tcf
🏨 dogs, ns; P 120, coach; child facs; con 300
✕ LD 9.30
£ B&B £54–£57 (w/e £35), B&B (double) £64–£67; L £8, D £8; WB £66; [10% V]
cc Access, Amex, B'card/Visa, Diners.

SEAHOUSES

Northumberland. Map 51C1
Pop 1,709. Alnwick 14, London 321, Berwick-upon-Tweed 22, Coldstream 29.
EC Wed. **Golf** Seahouses 18h. **See** Bamburgh Castle, Sand Dunes, Farne Islands–Bird Sanctuary and Seal Colony.
ℹ Seafield Rd. ☎(0665) 720884
★★ **C** **Beach House,** Seafront, NE68 7SR ☎(0665) 720337

Two-storey detached villa with extension overlooking the sea. ⚒ Fr. Open Mar–Nov
🛏 14 bedrs, 14 en suite, 2 ba; TV; tcf
🏨 TV; dogs, ns; P 16; child facs
✕ LD 8, nr lunch. Resid & Rest lic
£ B&B £24–£32·50; B&B (double) £48–£59; D £14·75; [10% V, Apr, May, Oct].
cc Access, B'card/Visa; dep.

★★ Olde Ship, 9 Main St, NE68 7RD
📞 (0665) 720200

Two-storey stone-built inn, with modern extension, on street near harbour. Putting. Open Feb–Nov.
🛏 10 bedrs, 10 en suite, 2 ba; annexe 4 bedrs, 4 en suite; TV; tcf
🏨 TV; P 14; child facs
✕ LD 8.15
£ B&B £25·50; B&B (double) £51; HB weekly £220; WB £62 (HB)
cc Access, B'card/Visa; dep.

★ St Aidan's, Sea Front, NE68 7SR
📞 (0665) 720355

Three-storey former private villa on edge of town facing sea. Open Feb–Nov.

SEASCALE Cumbria. Map 43B1
See also EGREMONT, HOLMROOK and BECKERMET.
Pop 2,134. Broughton-in-Furness 37, London 314, Egremont 8.
EC Wed. **Golf** Seascale 18h.

Cottage (Highly Acclaimed), Black How CA20 1LQ 📞 (094 67) 28416. *Guest House.*

SEATON Cornwall. Map 3A2
Pop 260. Plymouth 17, London 228, Liskeard 9, West Looe 5½.
Golf Looe Bin Down 18h.

Blue Haven, Looe Hill, PL11 3JQ
📞 Downderry (050 35) 310. *Hotel.*
£ B&B £12–£14; HB weekly £119·50–£134

SEATON Devon. Map 4B1
Pop 4,890. Axminster 6½, London 153, Exeter 22, Honiton 11, Lyme Regis 7½.
EC Thur. **MD** Mon. **Golf** f1Axecliffe 18h.
ℹ The Esplanade. 📞 (0297) 21660

Mariners (Acclaimed), East Walk, Esplanade, EX12 2NP 📞 (0297) 20560. *Hotel.* Open Mar–Dec.
£ B&B £20·50–£24·50; HB weekly £132–£156

SEDBERGH Cumbria. Map 36B4
M6 (jn 37) 4, London 256, Brough 19, Hawes 15, Kendal 9½, Kirkby Lonsdale 10.
ℹ 72 Main St 📞 (053 96) 20125

★★ Oakdene, Garsdale Rd, LA10 5JN
📞 (053 96) 20280

Victorian stone-built house of character with views of the Yorkshire dales. Open Mar–Dec.
🛏 6 bedrs, 6 en suite; TV; tcf
🏨 P 10, no children under 8
✕ LD 9.15, bar meals only lunch. Resid & Rest lic
£ B&B £27–£33, B&B (double) £45–£54; D £9·50
cc Access, B'card/Visa; dep.

SEDGEFIELD Cleveland. Map 45A2
Pop 6,072. Stockton-on-Tees 8, London 252, A1 (M) 2½, Durham 9, Darlington 13.
EC Wed. **MD** Tue. **Golf** Castle Eden 18h.

★★★ Hardwick Hall, TS21 2EH 📞 (0740) 20253 Fax: (0740) 22771
Attractive 18th century former mansion in own grounds near the town.
🛏 17 bedrs, 17 en suite; TV; tcf
🏨 P 300, coach; child facs; con 100
✕ LD 9.45
£ B&B £65–£75 (w/e £55), B&B (double) £80–£90; L £9
cc Access, Amex, B'card/Visa, Diners; dep.

★★ Crosshill, TS21 2AB 📞 (0740) 20153
Part of a block on town green, a two-storey stone-built hotel. ⚒ Po
🛏 8 bedrs, 8 en suite; TV; tcf
🏨 dogs, ns; P 9, coach; child facs; con 25
✕ LD 9.45, nr Sun dinner
£ B&B £40–£45, B&B (double) £50–£61; HB weekly £380–£427; L £7·25, D £15; WB £76; [5% V]
cc Access, Amex, B'card/Visa.

SEDLESCOMBE East Sussex. Map 7A2
Pop 1,400. Hurst Green 6½, London 56, Eastbourne 15, Hastings 7, Hawkhurst 7½, Lewes 21, Rye 10.
EC Wed. **Golf** Beauport Park 18h.

★★ R Brickwall, The Green, TN33 0QA
📞 (042 487) 0253
Hotel in attractive red-brick building in quiet Sussex village. Swimming pool, putting.
🛏 24 bedrs, 24 en suite; TV; tcf
🏨 dogs; P 25; child facs; con 50

SELBY North Yorkshire. Map 38C2
See also SOUTH MILFORD
Pop 10,960. Thorne 12, London 180, Doncaster 20, Goole 12, Hull 34, Leeds 21, Pontefract 13, York 13.
EC Thur. **MD** Mon, Fri. **Golf** Selby 18h. **See** Abbey Church, 18th cent Market Cross.
ℹ Park St. 📞 (0757) 703263

★★ Londesborough Arms, Market Pl, YO8 0NS 📞 (0757) 707355

Refurbished traditional inn in centre of town next to Abbey church. (BCB)
🛏 27 beds, 23 en suite, 1 ba; TV; tcf
🏨 TV; ns, P 18, G 6, coach; child facs; con 50
✕ LD 9.30
£ B&B £40–£49, B&B (double) £52–£54; L £8.15, D £8.15; WB £27·50.
cc Access, Amex, B'card/Visa, Diners.

SENNEN Cornwall. Map 2A1
Pop 772. Penzance 9½, London 291.
Golf Lelant 18h. **See** Cove.

★★ Old Success Inn, Sennen Cove, TR19 7DG 📞 Penzance (0736) 871232
White-painted, 17th-century fisherman's inn just above the beach.
🛏 10 bedrs, 9 en suite; TV; tcf
🏨 TV; P 15, coach; con 50
✕ LD 8.45, bar meals only lunch
£ B&B £25–£30; B&B (double) £50–£60; HB weekly £240–£270; L £7·50; D £11; WB £75
cc B'card/Visa; dep.

Sunny Bank, Seaview Hill, TR19 7AR
📞 (0736) 871278. *Hotel.* Closed Dec.
£ B&B £11–£16; HB weekly £115–£150

SETTLE North Yorkshire. Map 36C3
Pop 2,312. Burnley 23, London 229, Hawes 22, Kirkby Lonsdale 16, Skipton 16.
EC Wed. **MD** Tue. **Golf** Settle 9h.
ℹ Town Hall, Cheapside. 📞 (072 92) 5192

★★★ H Falcon Manor, Skipton Rd, BD24 9BD 📞 (072 92) 3814
Fax: (072 92) 2087
Large stone-built manor situated on outskirts of town. Open views to South-east.
🛏 15 bedrs, 15 en suite, 1 ba; annexe 5 beds, 5 en suite; TV; tcf
🏨 dogs; P 80, coach; child facs; con 40

★★ Royal Oak, Market Pl, BD24 9ED
📞 (072 92) 2561
Dating from 17th century, charming 2-storey hotel in town centre.

S

6 bedrs, 6 en suite; TV; tcf
P 20, coach; child facs; con 20
LD 10, bar meals only Mon–Sat lunch
£ B&B £34·50, B&B (double) £60; L £7·50; D £11·95; dep.

SEVENOAKS Kent. Map 9B1

Pop 20,000. London 25, M25 (jn 5) 3½, Dartford Tunnel 16, Maidstone 16, Tonbridge 7, Westerham 6.
EC Wed. **MD** Mon, Wed. **Golf** Knole Park 18h. **See** Perp Church, Knole (Nat Trust).
Buckhurst La. (0732) 450305

★★ H C **Royal Oak,** Upper High St, TN14 5PG (0732) 451109
Fax: (0732) 740187

Pleasant mellow stone building of medium size. In old part of town. Fr
24 bedrs, 24 en suite; TV; tcf
dogs; P 21, coach; child facs; con 30
LD 9.30
£ B&B £68 (w/e £30), B&B (double) £80; L £13·95, D £18·95; WB £42·50 (min 2 nts); [10% V]
cc Access, Amex, B'card/Visa, Diners.

★★ **Sevenoaks Park,** 4 Seal Hollow Rd, TN13 3SH (0732) 454245
Fax: (0732) 457468

Quiet hotel with pleasant gardens in side road. Near to Knole. Swimming pool. Fr, It. Closed 27 Dec–2 Jan.
15 bedrs, 6 en suite, 3 ba; annexe 10 bedrs, 10 en suite; TV; tcf
TV; P 30, U1; coach; child facs
LD 9, nr Mon–Sat lunch, Sun dinner. Resid & Rest lic
£ B&B £30–£55, B&B (double) £45–£70; L £8·95; D £10·50
cc Access, Amex, B'card/Visa, Diners; dep.

Moorings, 97 Hitchen Hatch La, TN13 3BE (0732) 452589. *Hotel.*
£ B&B £30–£45.

SHAFTESBURY Dorset. Map 5A2

Pop 5,213. Salisbury 20, London 103, Blandford Forum 11, Sherborne 16, Warminster 15, Wincanton 11.
EC Wed. **MD** Thur. **Golf** Sherborne 18h. **See** Abbey ruins, Castle Hill, Gold Hill.
Bell St. (0747) 53514

★★★ **Grosvenor,** The Commons, SP7 8JA (0747) 52282
Large town centre hotel with character of an old world inn. (THF)
41 bedrs, 35 en suite, 1 ba; TV; tcf
dogs, ns; coach; child facs; con 150
LD 9.30
£ B&B £43 (w/e £39), B&B (double) £49; D £10·95; WB £39
cc Access, Amex, B'card/Visa, CB, Diners.

★★★ **Royal Chase,** Royal Chase Roundabout, SP7 8DB (0747) 53355
Tx: 418414 Fax: (0747) 51969

A period building in country house style on outskirts of town. Indoor swimming pool, putting, sauna, solarium. Fr
35 bedrs, 35 en suite; TV; tcf
dogs, ns; P 100, coach; child facs; con 150
LD 10
£ B&B £54–£65 (w/e £44), B&B (double) £64–£99; HB weekly £264; L £12, D £16; WB £44
cc Access, Amex, B'card/Visa, Diners; dep.

★★ **Grove House,** Ludwell, SP7 9ND Donhead (0747) 828365

Small privately-owned hotel in extended modern house with pleasant gardens. Open Feb–Nov
11 bedrs, 10 en suite, 1 ba; TV; tcf
dogs, ns; P 12; children over 5
LD 7.30, bar meals only lunch. Resid & Rest lic
£ B&B £24·50–£27; B&B (double) £49–£54; HB weekly £222–£245; L £7·50, D £15; WB
cc Access, B'card/Visa; dep.

SHALDON Devon. Map 3C2

Pop 1,500. Exeter 16, London 183, Newton Abbot 5, Torquay 6.
EC Thur. **Golf** Teignmouth 18h.

★★ **Ness House,** Marine Dr, TQ14 0HP (0626) 873480 Fax: (0626) 873486
Built in 1810 in Colonial style, a delightful hotel overlooking the Teign estuary. Fr, Es
7 bedrs, 7 en suite; annexe 5 bedrs, 5 en suite; TV; tcf
TV; P 20; child facs; con 12
LD 10
£ B&B £24·50–£42·50, B&B (double) £57–£65; L £12, D £12; WB
cc Access, Amex, B'card/Visa; dep.

★ **Glenside,** Ringmore Rd, TQ14 0EP (0626) 872448

Small stone-built Victorian cottage style hotel with fine river views. Closed Nov.
10 bedrs; 7 en suite, 1 ba; TV; tcf
dogs; P 10; child facs
LD 6.30, bar meals only lunch. Resid & Rest lic
£ B&B £16–£19·65, B&B (double) £32–£39·50; HB weekly £152–£174; D £10; WB £53; dep.

SHAP Cumbria. Map 44B1

Pop 1,117. Kendal 16, London 273, M6 (jn 39) 3, Penrith 9.
Golf Appleby 18h.

★★ **Shap Wells,** CA10 3QU (093 16) 628
Fax: (093 16) 377

Modernised 150 years old hotel set in large secluded grounds. Tennis, billiards. Open 14 Feb–2 Jan.
90 bedrs, 82 en suite, 4 ba; TV; tcf
TV, dogs, ns; P 200, coach; child facs; con 200
LD 8.30
£ B&B £32–£45, B&B (double) £48–£65; HB weekly £175–£210; L £5·50, D £11·50
cc Access, Amex, B'card/Visa, Diners.

SHAWBURY Shropshire. Map 29B2

Pop 2,403. Wellington 9½, London 153, Newport 15, Newcastle-under-Lyme 26, Shrewsbury 7, Whitchurch 15.

New Farm (Acclaimed), Muckleton, Telford, TF6 6RJ (0939) 250358
£ B&B £15–£18

SHEDFIELD Hampshire. Map 5C2

Wickham 1½, London 69, Portsmouth 13, Southampton 10, Winchester 14.

★★★ **Meon Valley,** Sandy La, SO3 2HQ
📞Wickham (0329) 833455 Tx: 86272
Fax: (0329) 834411

Modern accommodation is offered by this country hotel. Indoor swimming pool, golf, putting, tennis, squash, sauna, solarium, gymnasium, billiards.
🛏 84 bedrs, 84 en suite; TV; tcf
🏨 TV; P, coach; child facs; con 60
✕ LD 9.45, grill room only Sat lunch
£ B&B £85–£95 (w/e £50), B&B (double) £95–£100; D £15; WB £50; [10% V]
cc Access, Amex, B'card/Visa, Diners; dep.

SHEERNESS Kent. Map 7B3
Pop 13,141. Rochester 18, London 50, Ashford 29, Canterbury 25, Maidstone 18
EC Wed. **MD** Tue. **Golf** Sheerness 18h.
ⓘ Bridge Rd Car Park. 📞(0795) 665324

Victoriana, 103–109 Alma Rd, ME12 2PD
📞(0795) 665555. *Hotel.*
£ B&B £16·50–£30

SHEFFIELD South Yorkshire. Map 41C4
See also SPINKHILL
RAC Office, *137 The Moor, Sheffield, S1 4PH.* 📞(0742) 737944
Pop 544,200. Mansfield 22, London 154, M1 30, 10, Barnsley 14, Buxton 25, Chesterfield 12, Glossop 24, Huddersfield 26, Rotherham 5½, Worksop 18.
See Plan, pp. 000–00.
EC Thur. **MD** Daily exc Thur. **P** See Plan.
Golf Abbeydale 18h, Beauchief 18h, Dore and Totley 18h, etc. **See** Cathedral, University, City Museum and Mappin Art Gallery, Graves Art Gallery, Cutlers Hall.
ⓘ Town Hall Extension, Union St. 📞(0742) 734671

★★★★ **Grosvenor House,** Charter Sq, S1 3EH 📞(0742) 720041 Tx: 54312
Fax: (0742) 757199

A modern city centre hotel with attractive decor and furnishings. (THF)
🛏 103 bedrs, 103 en suite; TV; tcf
🏨 lift, dogs, ns; G 89 (£3), coach; child facs; con 400
✕ LD 10
£ B&B £89, B&B (double) £109; L £10, D £16; WB £45
cc Access, Amex, B'card/Visa, CB, Diners; dep.

★★★★ **Hallam Tower Post House,** Manchester Rd, S10 5DX 📞(0742) 670067
Tx: 547293 Fax: (0742) 682620
Modern high-rise hotel in residential area. Indoor swimming pool, sauna, solarium, gymnasium. ⚒ Fr, De, It. (THF)
🛏 136 bedrs, 136 en suite; TV; tcf
🏨 lift, dogs, ns; p 120, coach; child facs; con 230
✕ LD 10.15
£ room £72 (w/e £39·50), double room £83–£94; Bk £7·50, L £9·95, D £14·25; WB £38 (HB)
cc Access, Amex, B'card/Visa, CB, Diners.

★★★★ **Swallow,** Kenwood Rd, S7 1NQ
📞(0742) 583811 Tx: 547030
Fax: (0742) 500138

A country club hotel set in 11 acres of grounds. Indoor swimming pool, fishing, sauna, solarium, gymnasium. (Sw)
🛏 141 bedrs, 141 en suite; TV; tcf
🏨 lift, dogs; P 200, coach; child facs; con 100
✕ LD 10
£ B&B £69, B&B (double) £86; L £11, D £14; WB £90 (HB)
cc Access, Amex, B'card/Visa, Diners.

★★★ **Beauchief,** 161 Abbeydale Rd, S7 2QW 📞(0742) 620500 Tx: 54164
Fax: (0742) 350197
A 3-storied stone building, with a modern bedroom wing, on south west edge of city. Sauna, solarium, gymnasium. ⚒ Fr. (Lns)
🛏 41 bedrs, 41 en suite; TV; tcf
🏨 ns; P 200, coach; child facs; con 100
✕ LD 10
£ B&B £76, B&B (double) £88; L £9·75, D £14·75; WB £28; [10% V]
cc Access, Amex, B'card/Visa, Diners.

★★★ **H C R Charnwood,** 10 Sharrow La, S11 8AA 📞(0742) 589411
Fax: (0742) 555107

Attractive converted Georgian house in city centre. Undergoing improvements to public rooms. Privately-owned and managed.
⚒ De, Fr
🛏 26 bedrs, 26 en suite; TV; tcf
🏨 lift, ns; P 22; child facs; con 100
✕ LD 12 midnight. Resid & Rest lic
£ B&B £70–£80, B&B (double) £80–£90; L £12·50, D £19·50; [10% V w/e]
cc Access, Amex, B'card/Visa, Diners.

★★★ **Rutland,** 452 Glossop Rd, S10 2PY
📞(0742) 664411 Tx: 547500
Fax: (0742) 670348

Substantial series of buildings forming large hotel in city centre.
🛏 73 bedrs, 69 en suite, 3 ba; annexe 17 bedrs, 17 en suite; TV; tcf
🏨 lift, dogs; P 80, coach; child facs; con 70
✕ LD 9.30
£ B&B £53–£59, B&B (double) £70; L £6·50, D £9·95; WB £70; [10% V]
cc Access, Amex, B'card/Visa, Diners.

★★★ **Saint James,** George St, S1 2PF
📞(0742) 739939 Tx: 54361
Fax: (0742) 768332
Situated in the heart of Sheffield, luxuriously converted former gentlemans' club.
🛏 32 bedrs, 32 en suite; TV; tcf
🏨 lift, dogs; coach; child facs; con 80

★★★ **Sheffield Moat House,** Chesterfield Rd South, S8 8BW 📞(0742) 375376
Tx: 547890 Fax: (0742) 378140 ♿

Modern, purpose-built hotel on ring road to south of city. Indoor swimming pool, sauna, solarium, gymnasium. Closed 24–26 Dec.
🛏 95 bedrs, 95 en suite; TV; tcf
🏨 lift, dogs, ns; P 250, coach; child facs; con 500
✕ LD 10, bar meals only Sat lunch
£ B&B £78 (w/e £45), B&B (double) £99; L £11·30, D £13; WB £38
cc Access, Amex, B'card/Visa, Diners.

★★ **Andrews Park,** 48 Kenwood Rd, Nether Edge, S7 1NQ 📞(0742) 500111
Fax: (0742) 555423
Substantial Victorian house with well-kept gardens in pleasant wooded inner suburb. Attentive service by proprietor and family.
⚒ Hu, Cz
🛏 11 bedrs, 6 en suite, (1 sh), 1 ba; annexe 2 bedrs, 2 en suite; TV; tcf
🏨 TV; dogs; P 12; child facs; con 30
✕ LD 8.45, nr Fri–Sun. Resid lic.
£ B&B £30–£35, B&B (double) £40–£48; L £6·95, D £9·50
cc Access, Amex, B'card/Visa.

★★ **Roslyn Court,** 180 Psalter La, S11 8US 📞(0742) 666188 Fax: (0742) 684279
Two large houses joined by central reception and restaurant area.
🛏 31 bedrs, 31 en suite; TV; tcf
🏨 TV, dogs; P 30, coach; child facs; con 35
✕ LD 8.45, nr Mon–Sat lunch, Fri–Sun dinner

S

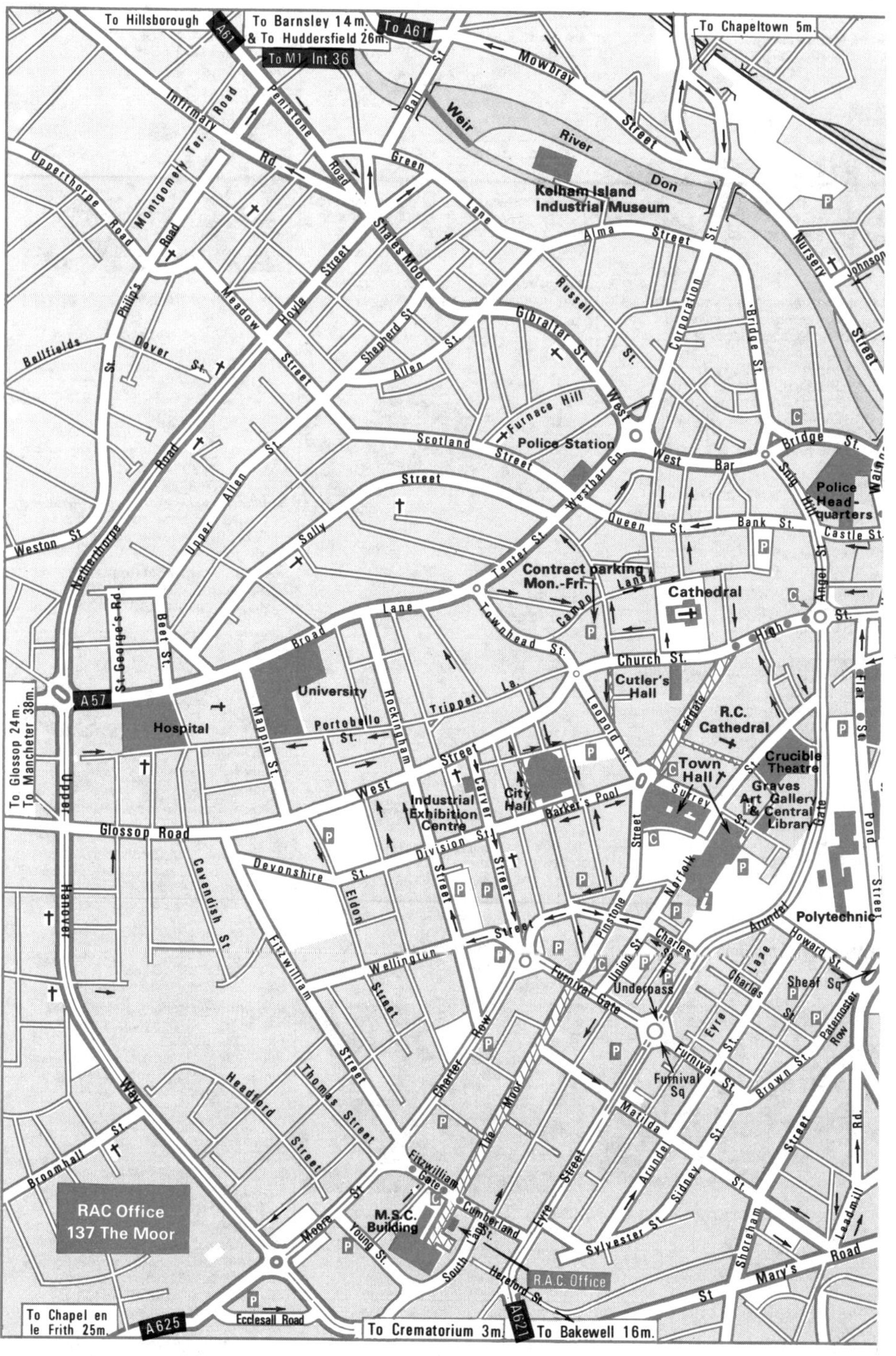

To Hillsborough
A61
To Barnsley 14m.
& To Huddersfield 26m.
To M1 Int.36
To A61
To Chapeltown 5m.
Mowbray Street
Weir
River Don
Kelham Island
Industrial Museum
Infirmary Road
Penistone Road
Ball St.
Green Lane
Upperthorpe Road
Montgomery Ter. Road
Shales Moor
Alma Street
Nursery Street
Russell St.
Corporation St.
Bridge St.
Philip's St.
Meadow Street
Hoyle Street
Shepherd St.
Gibraltar St.
Allen St.
Bellfields
Dover St.
Furnace Hill
West
Scotland Street
Police Station
West Bar
Bridge St.
Snig Hill
Police Head-quarters
Westbar Gn.
Queen St.
Bank St.
Castle St.
Street
Solly
Upper Allen St.
Weston St.
Netherthorpe Road
Tenter St.
Contract parking
Mon.-Fri.
Campo Lane
Cathedral
Angel St.
St. George's Rd
Beet St.
Broad Lane
Townhead St.
High St.
Church St.
University
Rockingham
Trippet La.
Cutler's Hall
Leopold St.
Fargate
R.C. Cathedral
Flat St.
A57
Hospital
Mappin St.
Portobello St.
To Glossop 24m.
To Manchester 38m.
West Street
Town Hall
Crucible Theatre
Graves Art Gallery & Central Library
Surrey St.
Industrial Exhibition Centre
Carver
City Hall
Barker's Pool
Norfolk St.
Pond Street
Upper Hanover
Glossop Road
Division St.
Cavendish St.
Devonshire St.
Eldon
Street
Pinstone
Arundel Gate
Polytechnic
Howard St.
Charles St.
Union St.
Fitzwilliam
Wellington
Furnival Gate
Underpass
Sheaf Sq
Lane
Charles St.
Eyre St.
Paternoster Row
Furnival Sq
Furnival St.
Brown St.
Charter Row
The Moor
Matilda St.
Thomas Street
Headford Street
Hanover Way
Broomhall St.
Arundel St.
Sidney St.
Eyre Street
Shoreham Street
Leadmill Rd.
Fitzwilliam Gate
Cumberland St.
RAC Office
137 The Moor
Moore St.
M.S.C. Building
Young St.
South Lane
Sylvester St.
Hereford St.
R.A.C. Office
St Mary's Road
To Chapel en le Frith 25m.
A625
Ecclesall Road
To Crematorium 3m.
A621
To Bakewell 16m.

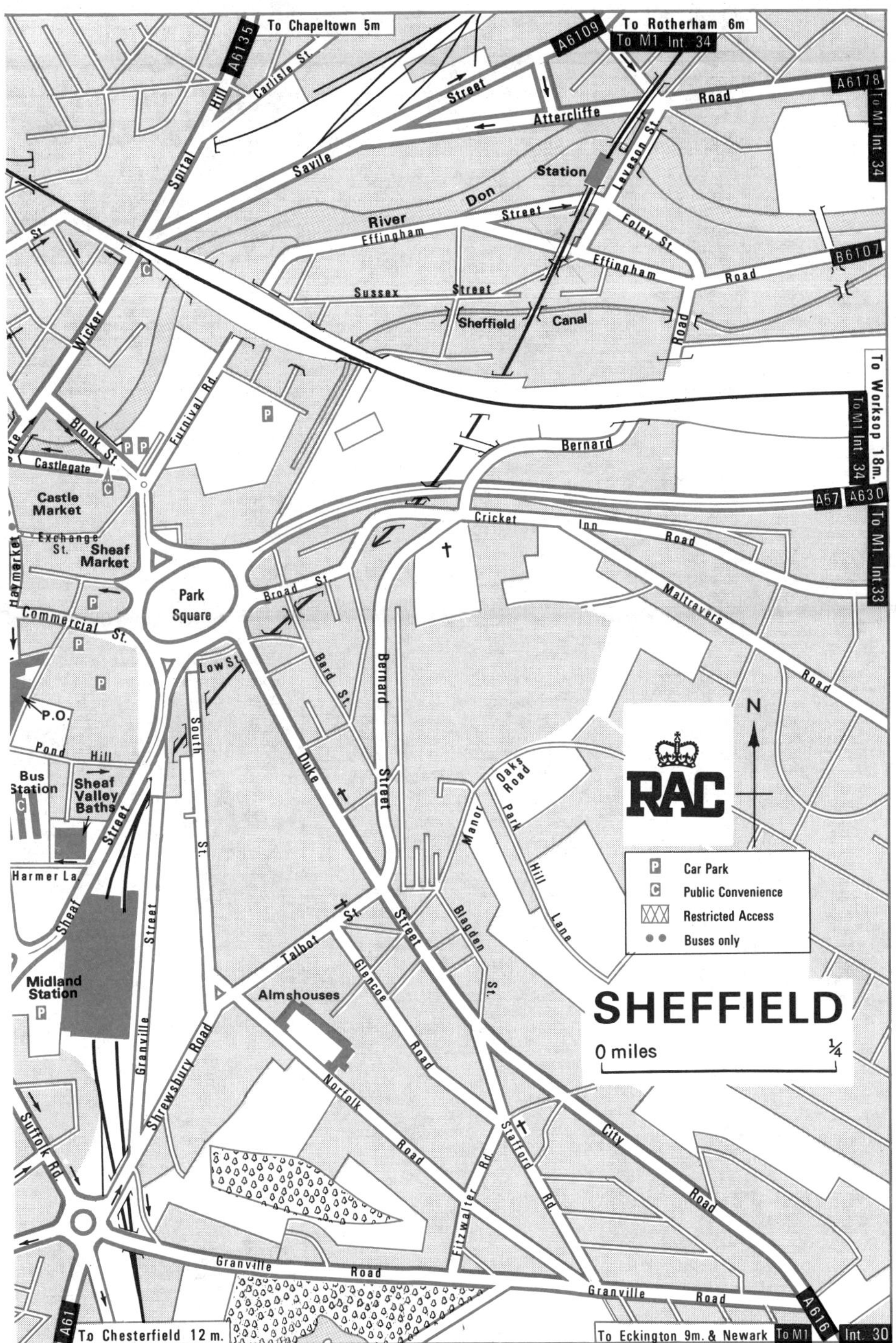

To Chapeltown 5m
A6135
To Rotherham 6m
A6109
To M1 Int. 34
A6178
To M1 Int. 34
Carlisle St.
Street
Savile
Attercliffe
Road
Spital
Hill
Station
Leveson St.
River
Don
Street
Effingham
Foley St.
B6107
Effingham
Road
Wicker
Sussex
Street
Sheffield
Canal
Road
To Worksop 18m.
To M1 Int. 34
Furnival Rd
Blonk St.
Castlegate
Castle Market
Bernard
Exchange St.
Sheaf Market
Haymarket
A57
A630
To M1 Int. 33
Cricket
Inn
Road
Park Square
Broad St.
Maltravers
Road
Commercial St.
Low St.
Bard St.
Bernard
Street
P.O.
Pond
Hill
South
St.
Duke
Bus Station
Sheaf Valley Baths
Street
Oaks Road
Manor
Park
Hill
Lane
RAC
N
Car Park
Public Convenience
Restricted Access
Buses only
Harmer La.
Sheaf
Street
Talbot
St.
Street
Bladen
St.
Glencoe
Road
Midland Station
Granville
Almshouses
SHEFFIELD
0 miles
¼
Shrewsbury Road
Norfolk
Road
Suffolk Rd.
Stafford
Rd.
City
Road
Fitzwalter Rd.
Granville
Road
Granville
Road
A61
To Chesterfield 12 m.
To Eckington 9m. & Newark
To M1
A616
Int. 30

£ B&B £36–£42 (w/e £28), B&B (double) £56 (w/e £42); L £5, D £7; [10% V]
cc Access, Amex, B'card/Visa, Diners.

Etruria House, 91 Crookes Road, Broomhill, S10 5BD ☎ (0742) 662241
£ B&B £22–£27

Lindum, 91 Montgomery Rd, Nether Edge, S7 1LP ☎ (0742) 552356. *Hotel.* Closed Xmas.
£ B&B £15·50–£25

Millingtons, 70 Broomgrove Rd, S10 2NA ☎ (0742) 669549. *Guest House.*

Westbourne House, 25 Westbourne Rd, Broomhill, S10 2QQ ☎ (0742) 660109. *Private Hotel.*

SHEPPERTON

Surrey. Map 10A3

Richmond upon Thames 9, London 17, Chertsey 4, Esher 5, Kingston upon Thames 8, Staines 4.

★★★ **Shepperton Moat House,** Felix La, TW17 8NP ☎ Walton-on-Thames (0932) 241404 Tx: 928170 Fax: (0932) 245231

Close to marina, a modern 3-storey brick building in own grounds. Sauna, solarium, gymnasium, billiards. Fr, De, It, Ar. Closed Xmas. (QMH)
185 bedrs, 185 en suite; TV; tcf
lift, TV; P 225, coach; child facs; con 300
LD 10, nr Sat lunch
£ B&B £68·50–£78 (w/e £36), B&B (double) £86·50–£94 (w/e £50); L £13·75, D £14; WB £60; [10% V w/e]
cc Access, Amex, B'card/Visa, Diners.
(*See advertisement on p. 438*)

SHEPTON MALLET

Somerset. Map 4C3

Pop 6,600. Frome 11, London 118, Bristol 20, Glastonbury 9, Radstock 9, Sherborne 25, Wells 5½, Wincanton 12.
EC Wed. **MD** Fri. **Golf** Mendip 18h.
[i] 2 Petticoat La. ☎ (0749) 5258

★★★ **Charlton House,** Charlton Rd, BA4 4PR ☎ (0749) 342008
Fax: (0749) 346362

17th century manor house in extensive grounds, to east of town. Indoor swimming pool, tennis, sauna. Fr
12 bedrs, 12 en suite; annexe 5 bedrs, 5 en suite; TV; tcf
dogs; P 50, coach; child facs; con 90
LD 9.30. Resid & Rest lic
£ B&B £50–£75, B&B (double) £75–£90; L £11, D £17; [5% V]
cc Access, Amex, B'card/Visa, Diners; dep.

Belfield, 34 Charlton Rd, BA4 5PA ☎ (0749) 4353. *Guest House.*
£ B&B £15·50–£17.

SHERBORNE

Dorset. Map 4C2

Pop 7,500. Shaftesbury 16, London 120, Blandford Forum 20, Crewkerne 14, Dorchester 18, Wincanton 9.
EC Wed. **MD** Thur, Sat. **Golf** Sherborne 18h.
See Abbey Church, Sherborne School (incorp Abbey remains), 16th cent Chapel, ruins of Sherborne Old Castle, Sherborne Castle, Museum, Almshouses.
[i] Hound St. ☎ (0935) 815341

★★★ [H] [R] **Eastbury,** Long St, DT9 3BY ☎ (0935) 813131 Tx: 46644
Fax: (0935) 817296
Georgian town house in a quiet street. Pleasant garden. Fr
15 bedrs, 15 en suite; TV; tcf
P 20; child facs; con 80
LD 9.30
£ B&B fr £62·50, B&B (double) fr £80; L fr £10·50, D fr £17·50; WB £98·50
cc Access, B'card/Visa.
(*See advertisement on p. 438*)

★★★ **Post House,** Horsecastles La, DT9 6BB ☎ (0935) 813191 Tx: 46522
Fax: (0935) 816493
Modern purpose-built hotel situated in outskirts of town. Putting. (THF)
60 bedrs, 60 en suite; TV; tcf
dogs, ns; P 150, coach; child facs; con 100
LD 10
£ B&B £69·50–£79·50 (w/e £39·50), B&B (double) £87–£97; HB weekly £266; L £7·50, D £12·75; WB
cc Access, Amex, B'card/Visa, Diners.

★★ **Half Moon,** Half Moon St, DT9 3LN ☎ (0935) 812017
Near to Abbey, a substantial brick and stone building with attractive high gables.
15 bedrs, 15 en suite; TV; tcf
dogs, ns; P 44; child facs

SHERINGHAM

Norfolk. Map 35B2

Pop 5,263. Cromer 4, London 137, Fakenham 18.
EC Wed. **MD** Sat. **Golf** Sheringham 18h.
See Upper Sheringham Church, Beeston Priory ruins at Beeston Regis, North Norfolk Railway (Preserved Steam Trains).
[i] Station Approach. ☎ (0263) 824329

Beacon (Highly Acclaimed), 1 Nelson Rd, NR26 8BT ☎ (0263) 822019. *Hotel.* Open May–Sep.
£ HB weekly £165

Fairlawns (Highly Acclaimed), 26 Hooks Hill Rd, NR26 8NL ☎ (0263) 824717. *Guest House.* Open Easter–end Oct. Fr
£ B&B £22·50; HB weekly £158

Melrose (Acclaimed), 9 Holway Rd, NR26 8HN ☎ (0263) 823299. *Hotel.*
£ B&B £15·50–£21; HB weekly £152·50–£177·50; [5% V Sep–Jun]

SHIFNAL

Shropshire. Map 30A1

Pop 6,045. Wolverhampton 12, London 136, M54 (jn 4) 3, Bridgnorth 10, Lichfield 24, Newport 8, Wellington 6.
EC Thur. **Golf** Shifnal 18h. **See** 12th cent Parish Church, 19th cent RC Church.

★★★★ [H] [R] **Park House,** Park St, TF11 9BA ☎ Telford (0952) 460128 Tx: 35438
Fax: (0952) 461658 ♿

Two tastefully converted 19th century houses joined by a new extension in keeping. In own grounds. Indoor swimming pool, sauna, solarium.
38 bedrs, 38 en suite; annexe 16 bedrs, 16 en suite; TV; tcf
lift, dogs, ns; P 150, coach; child facs; con 250
LD 10, bar meals only Sat lunch
£ B&B £73, B&B (double) £85; L £10·50, D £11·95; WB
cc Access, Amex, B'card/Visa, Diners.

Old Bell, Church St. ☎ Telford (0952) 460475. *Private Hotel.*

SHIPHAM

Somerset. Map 4B3

Pop 1,050. M5 (jn 22) 7, Axbridge 3, London 135, Bath 24, Bristol 15, Bridgwater 18, Wells 11, Weston-super-Mare 9.
Golf Wells 18h.

★★ [H] [C] [R] **Daneswood House,** Cuck Hill, BS25 1RD ☎ Winscombe (093 484) 3145 Fax: (093 484) 3824 ♿

Imposing Edwardian house set high up in attractive gardens with good views over Bristol Channel to Wales.
9 bedrs, 9 en suite; annexe 3 bedrs, 3 en suite; TV; tcf
dogs, ns; P 35, G 2; child facs; con 20
LD 9.30, nr Sat lunch & Sun dinner. Resid lic
£ B&B £55, B&B (double) £70; L £14·95, D £19·95; WB £47·50 (HB); [10% V w/e]
cc Access, Amex, B'card/Visa, Diners.

★ **Penscot Farmhouse,** Winscombe, BS25 1TW ☎ Winscombe (093 484) 2659

EC *early closing* **MD** *market day* *country house hotel* *ns (NS) no smoking areas* *tcf tea/coffee facilities*

Farmhouse-style hotel with a separate restaurant. In village centre. Open 7 Jan–29 Nov.
🛏 18 bedrs, (12 sh), 3 ba; tcf
🏨 TV, dogs, ns; P 40, coach; child facs; con 30
✕ LD 9, nr Mon–Sat lunch. Resid & Rest lic
£ B&B £23·75–£27·50, B&B (double) £37·50–£45; HB weekly £166·50–£197·50; D £8; WB £49·75; [10% V]
cc Amex, B'card/Visa, Diners; dep.

SHIRLEY West Midlands. Map 22C1

Pop 30,400. Warwick 15, London 108, Birmingham 6, Bromsgrove 16, Coventry 15, Evesham 24, Stratford-upon-Avon 17, Sutton Coldfield 12.
EC Wed. **Golf** Shirley 18h.

★★★ **Regency,** Stratford Rd, B90 4EB
📞 Birmingham 021-745 6119 Tx: 334400
Fax: 021-733 3801

Cream-rendered Regency building with modern extensions situated in spacious grounds. Indoor swimming pool, sauna, solarium, gymnasium. Fr, De, Gr, Ar
🛏 112 bedrs, 112 en suite; TV; tcf
🏨 lift; dogs, ns; P 300, coach; child facs; con 150
✕ LD 10, bar meals only Sat lunch
£ B&B £76·45 (w/e £58), B&B (double) £91·30; L £9·50, D £13·25; WB £40 (2nts HB)
cc Access, Amex, B'card/Visa.

SHRAWLEY Hereford and Worcester (Worcestershire). Map 20B3

Worcester 8, London 122, Bromsgrove 13, Kidderminster 9½, Stratford-upon-Avon 28.

★★★ **Lenchford,** WR6 6TB 📞 Worcester (0905) 620229 Fax: (0905) 621125
Charming 2-storey Georgian building with lawns down to R Severn. Own moorings. Swimming pool, fishing.
🛏 16 bedrs, 15 en suite, 1 ba; TV; tcf
🏨 P 80, coach; child facs; con 80
✕ LD 9.15, bar meals only lunch, Sun dinner
£ B&B £47, B&B (double) £62; WB £35
cc Access, Amex, B'card/Visa, Diners; dep.

SHREWLEY Warwickshire. Map 20C3

Warwick 5, London 98, Birmingham 19, Coventry 15, Redditch 13, Stratford-upon-Avon 11.

Shrewley House (Highly Acclaimed), Hockley Rd, CV35 7AT 📞 (092 684) 2549

SHREWSBURY Shropshire. Map 29B1

See also WESTON UNDER REDCASTLE
Pop 87,300. Wellington 11, London 154, Bridgnorth 21, Ludlow 27, Newport 18, Welshpool 18, Whitchurch 18, Wrexham 29.
EC Thur. **MD** Tue, Wed, Fri, Sat. **Golf** Meole Brace 9h. **See** Castle (regimental museum), Council House, Abbey Church, old Market Hall, Statue of Charles Darwin, Owens Mansions, Butcher Row.
ℹ The Square. 📞 (0743) 50761

★★★ **Lion,** Wyle Cop, SY1 1UY 📞 (0743) 53107

An ancient coaching inn with Dickensian connections. (THF)
🛏 59 bedrs, 59 en suite; TV; tcf
🏨 lift, dogs, ns; P 36, G 36, coach; child facs; con 200

★★★ **Prince Rupert,** Butcher Row, SY1 1UQ 📞 (0743) 236000 Tx: 35100
Fax: (0743) 57306

Black and white 15th century building with oak beams and modern comforts. Fr, De, It
🛏 65 bedrs, 65 en suite; TV; tcf
🏨 lift, dogs, ns; P 60, coach; child facs; con 90
✕ LD 10.15
£ B&B £58–£64 (w/e £42), B&B (double) £72–£78; L £10·50, D £15·50; [5% V]
cc Access, Amex, B'card/Visa, Diners.

★★★ **Radbrook Hall,** Radbrook Rd, SY3 9BQ 📞 (0743) 236676

Former country house on outskirts of town. Squash, sauna, billiards. (BCB)
🛏 28 bedrs, 28 en suite; TV; tcf
🏨 TV, ns; P 250; child facs; con 50
✕ LD 10.30
£ B&B £48–£56, B&B (double) £62; L £8·15, D £8·15; WB £27·50
cc Access, Amex, B'card/Visa, Diners.

★★ **Beauchamp,** The Mount, SY3 8PJ
📞 (0743) 3230
Large modernised and extended house overlooking the Severn. Sauna, solarium.

★★ **Shelton Hall,** Shelton, SY3 8BH
📞 (0743) 3982

A red-brick Victorian country house in pleasant grounds.
🛏 10 bedrs, 9 en suite, 1 ba; TV; tcf
🏨 P 50; child facs; con 50
✕ LD 8.30, nr Mon–Sat lunch, Sun dinner
£ Bk £7, L £10, D £15.
cc Access, B'card/Visa.

★★ **Shrewsbury,** Mardol, SY1 1TU
📞 (0743) 231246 Fax: (0743) 247701

'Olde worlde' 19th century hotel, at the foot of the Welsh Bridge. Billiards. Closed 25 & 26 Dec.
🛏 24 bedrs, 24 en suite; TV; tcf
🏨 TV, dogs; P 36, coach; child facs; con 50
✕ LD 9, bar meals only lunch, Sun dinner.
£ B&B £40–£50 (w/e £30), B&B (double) £50–£60; HB weekly £245–£315; L £6·50; D £9·65; [10% V w/e]
cc Access, Amex, B'card/Visa, Diners; dep.

Abbots Mead (Highly Acclaimed), 9–10 St Julians Friars 📞 (0743) 235281. *Hotel.*

SIBSON Leicestershire. Map 23B3

Leicester 16, London 113, Ashby-de-la-Zouch 12, Nuneaton 6, Tamworth 12

★★ **Millers,** Main Rd, nr Nuneaton, Warwicks, CV13 6LB 📞 Tamworth (0827) 880223 Fax: (0827) 880223 ♿
Converted water mill with modern extensions on main road in rural area.
🛏 40 bedrs, 40 en suite; TV; tcf
🏨 TV, dogs; P 100, coach; child facs; con 40
✕ LD 9.45, bar meals only Mon & Sat lunch
£ B&B £49·50, B&B (double) £59·50; HB weekly £400; L £12·95, D £19·95; [5% V]
cc Access, Amex, B'card/Visa, Diners.
(See advertisement on p. 000)

SIDMOUTH Devon. Map 4A1

Pop 11,826. Honiton 9½, London 162, Axminster 14, Exeter 16, Lyme Regis 16.
EC Thur. **Golf** Sidmouth 18h.
ℹ The Esplanade. 📞 (0395) 516441

S

Shepperton (Middlesex)

Sherborne (Dorset)

Sidmouth (Devon)

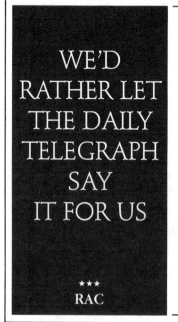

★★★★ C R **Belmont,** Esplanade, EX10 8RX ☎(0395) 512555 Tx: 42551 Fax: (0395) 579154 ♿

Large hotel, near to Promenade; easy walk to town centre. Putting.
🛏 54 bedrs, 54 en suite; TV; tcf
🏨 lift; P 50; child facs; con 100
£ B&B £60–£66, B&B (double) £90–£145; HB weekly £250–£490; L £9·50, D £15; WB £72 (2 nts HB)
cc Access, Amex, B'card/Visa, Diners.
(*See advertisement on p. 440*)

★★★★ H C R **Victoria,** Esplanade, EX10 8RY ☎(0395) 512651 Tx: 42551 Fax: (0395) 579154 ♿

Large hotel with fine sea views; quiet surroundings. Indoor & outdoor swimming pools, putting, tennis, sauna, solarium, billiards.
🛏 61 bedrs, 61 en suite; TV
🏨 lift; P 100, U 3, G 4; child facs; con 100
✕ LD 9
£ B&B £60–£69, B&B (double) £99–£150; HB weekly £280–£560; L £10, D £16; WB £86 (2 nts HB)
cc Access, Amex, B'card/Visa, Diners.
(*See advertisement on p. 440*)

★★★ **Bedford,** Esplanade, EX10 8NR ☎(0395) 513047 ♿
Terraced hotel, situated on the Promenade. Easy walk to town centre.

★★★ **Fortfield,** Station Rd, EX10 8NU ☎(0395) 512403

Large brick-built hotel in extensive grounds overlooking sea. Indoor swimming pool, putting, sauna, solarium.
🛏 52 bedrs, 52 en suite, 3 ba; TV; tcf
🏨 lift, TV, dogs, ns; P 60; child facs
✕ LD 8.30, bar meals only lunch
£ B&B £30–£50; HB weekly £245–£385; D £12·50; WB £70 (2 nts HB)
cc Access, Amex, B'card/Visa; dep.

★★★ H C R **Riviera,** Esplanade, EX10 8AY ☎(0395) 515201 Tx: 42551 Fax: (0395) 577775 ♿

Promenade hotel, with fine sea views. Easy walk to town centre, golf. ☧ Fr
🛏 34 bedrs, 29 en suite, 3 ba; TV
🏨 lift, dogs; P 12, U 3, G 6; child facs; con 85
✕ LD 9
£ B&B £41–£57, B&B (double) £82–£114; HB weekly £329–£441; L £10·50, D £17·50; WB £83·50 (2 nts HB)
cc Access, Amex, B'card/Visa, Diners; dep.
(*See advertisement on p. 438*)

★★★ H C **Royal Glen,** Glen Rd, EX10 8RW ☎(0395) 513221
Privately-run country house style hotel near sea. Convenient for town centre. Indoor swimming pool, putting.
🛏 34 bedrs, 32 en suite, 2 ba; TV
🏨 TV, dogs; P 16, G 8 (£1); children over 8
✕ LD 8. Resid & Rest lic
£ B&B £20·90–£38·10, B&B (double) £31·36–£47·05; HB weekly £173·75–£349·45; L £5·25, D £9·50
cc Access, Amex, B'card/Visa; dep.

★★★ **Salcombe Hill House,** Beatlands Rd, EX10 8JQ ☎(0395) 514697
Spacious Georgian house in secluded surroundings. Swimming pool, putting, tennis. Open Mar–Oct.
🛏 33 bedrs, 29 en suite, 3 ba; TV; tcf
🏨 lift, dogs, ns; P 35, U 5 (£2·50); no children under 3
✕ LD 8.30
£ B&B £22·50–£36; HB weekly £182–£290·50; L £7·50, D £10·50; WB £28·80 (HB)
cc Access, B'card/Visa, Diners.

★★★ C R **Westcliff,** Manor Rd, EX10 8RU ☎(0395) 513252 Fax: (0395) 578203

Brick-built hotel with spacious gardens and sea views. Swimming pool, putting, solarium, gymnasium. Open 15 Mar–31 Oct.
🛏 40 bedrs, 40 en suite; TV
🏨 lift, ns; P 40; child facs; con 80
✕ LD 8.30, bar meals only Mon–Sat lunch
£ B&B £31·75–£46·25; HB weekly £267·75–£418·60; L £9·50, D £16·50; WB £31·75
cc Access, B'card/Visa.

★★ H C R **Abbeydale,** Manor Rd, EX10 8RP ☎(0395) 512060 ♿

Brick-built hotel in sheltered garden. Fine views of the sea. ☧ De, Es. Open Mar–Nov, Xmas.
🛏 18 bedrs, 18 en suite; TV; tcf
🏨 lift, ns; P 24; no children under 4
✕ LD 8, bar meals only lunch. Resid & Rest lic
£ B&B £30–£35; HB weekly £250–£285; L £4·75; D £13; dep.

★★ H C **Brownlands,** Sid Rd, EX10 9AG ☎(0395) 513053
Country house hotel in delightful grounds with fine sea views. Putting, tennis. ☧ It. Open Mar–Oct.
🛏 15 bedrs, 15 en suite; TV; tcf
🏨 TV, dogs, ns; P 25; no children under 8
✕ LD 8, nr Mon–Sat lunch
£ B&B £28·60–£33, B&B (double) £57·20–£84; HB weekly £215–£295; L £8; D £14·95; WB £33·50

★★ **Byes Links,** Sid Rd, EX10 9AA ☎(0395) 513129
Brick-built hotel in own grounds. Few minutes from local amenities.

★★ **Elizabeth,** Esplanade, EX10 8AT ☎(0395) 513503
Right on the sea front, a white-painted late Victorian building with lovely sea views. Family run.
🛏 28 bedrs, 28 en suite, 1 ba; TV; tcf
🏨 lift, ns; P 2 (£1–£3), G 8 (£1–£3), coach; child facs
✕ LD 7.15, nr lunch. Resid & Rest lic
£ B&B £23–£52, B&B (double) £46–£72; HB weekly £167–£252; D £8·50; WB £21; [10% V Nov–Apr]. dep.

★★ C **Little Court,** Seafield Rd, EX10 8HF ☎(0395) 515279
Regency hotel with secluded garden. Easy walk to sea and town. Swimming pool.
🛏 21 bedrs, 18 en suite, 1 ba; TV; tcf
🏨 TV, dogs, ns; P 17, coach; child facs; con 45
✕ bar meals only Mon–Sat lunch. Resid lic
£ B&B £17–£36, B&B (double) £40–£74; HB weekly £168–£272; L £6·95, D £9·50
cc Access, B'card/Visa; dep.

★★ **Royal York & Faulkner,** Esplanade, EX10 8AZ ☎(0395) 513043 Fax: (0395) 577472 ♿

S

Sidmouth (Devon)

Large terraced hotel on the promenade with fine sea views. Sauna, solarium, gymnasium.
68 bedrs, 68 en suite, 5 ba; TV; tcf
lift, TV, dogs, ns; P 7, G2, coach; child facs; con 50
LD 8
£ B&B £18–£38; HB weekly £140–£315; L £5·50, D £9·50; WB £46 (2 nts Oct–Mar)
cc Access, B'card/Visa; dep.

★★ **Torbay,** Station Rd, EX10 8NW
(0395) 513456
Privately-owned terraced hotel, near to promenade. Easy walk to sea.
30 bedrs, 26 en suite, 3 ba; TV
lift, TV, dogs; P 10; child facs
LD 7.45. Resid & Rest lic
£ B&B £18–£30; HB weekly £155–£225; L £4·50, D £8·50; WB
cc Access, B'card/Visa; dep.

★★ **Westbourne,** Manor Rd, EX10 8RR
(0395) 513774
A Victorian residence set in pleasant garden in a residential area. Open Mar–Oct.
13 bedrs, 9 en suite, 4 ba; TV; tcf
dogs; P 14; child facs
LD 7.30, bar meals only lunch. Resid lic.
£ B&B & dinner, £31·35–£35·75, B&B & dinner (double) £62·70–£80·50; HB weekly £208·75–£244·35; D £10·50; [10% V]
cc Access, B'card/Visa; dep.

★★ H C **Woodlands,** Cotmaton Cross, EX10 8HG (0395) 513120
Privately-owned period hotel with attractive garden. Convenient for sea. Putting.

Groveside (Acclaimed), Vicarage Rd, EX10 8UQ (0395) 513406. *Guest House.* Open Apr–Oct.
£ B&B £12·65–£16·45; HB weekly £133·40–£165; [5% V]
Willow Bridge (Acclaimed), 1 Millford Rd, EX10 8DR (0395) 513599. *Hotel.*

Canterbury House, Salcombe Rd, EX10 8PR (0395) 513373 *Guest House.* Open Mar–Nov.
£ B&B £15·50–£18·50; HB weekly £140–£165; [5% V]

SILCHESTER Hampshire. Map 12A2
M4 (jn 11) 10, London 44, Basingstoke 9½, Newbury 14, Reading 8.

★★★ **Romans,** Little London Rd, RG7 2PN (0734) 700421
Lutyens-designed house, skilfully converted with appropriate decor and furnishings, now a family-owned and run hotel set in well-tended formal gardens. Swimming pool, tennis.
11 bedrs, 11 en suite, annexe 13 bedrs, 13 en suite; TV; tcf
dogs; P 40; child facs; con 25
LD 9.30
£ B&B £60–£80, B&B (double) £70–£90; L £13·50, D £18·50; WB £40 (HB); [10% V]

SILLOTH Cumbria. Map 43B2
Pop 2,585. Penrith 33, London 309, Cockermouth 17, Maryport 13.
The Green. (069 73) 31944.

★★★ **Golf,** Criffel St, CA5 4AB (069 73) 31438 Fax: (069 73) 32582

Pleasant 19th century building, overlooking grass and trees to sea. Closed 24 & 25 Dec.
Fr, It, Es
22 bedrs, 22 en suite, 2 ba; TV; tcf
TV, dogs; coach; child facs
LD 9.15
£ B&B £34–£40, B&B (double) £48–£62; L £6·75, D £12·50; WB £35·50
cc Access, Amex, B'card/Visa, Diners.

★★★ **Skinburness,** CA5 4QY (069 73) 32332

Refurbished hotel in a peacefully situated, large Victorian house. Sauna, solarium, gymnasium, billiards.
25 bedrs, 25 en suite; TV; tcf
P 65, coach; child facs; con 180

SITTINGBOURNE Kent. Map 7B3
Pop 53,250 (inc. Milton). Rochester 11, London 42, M2 (jn 5) 3½, Ashford 20, Canterbury 17, Maidstone 13, Margate 31. **EC** Wed. **MD** Fri. **Golf** Sittingbourne 18h. **See** St Michael's Church (Easter Sepulchre), Dolphin Sailing Barge Museum, 15th cent Old Court Hall (Milton).

★★★ **Coniston,** London Rd, ME10 1NT (0795) 472131 Fax: (0795) 428056
Situated on the A2, a red brick hotel with modern extension. De, Fr, It, Es
60 bedrs, 52 en suite, 4 ba; TV; tcf
TV, dogs; P 100, U 2, coach; child facs; con 200
LD 10
£ B&B £58·50, B&B (double) £70; L £13, D £13
cc Access, Amex, B'card/Visa, Diners.

SIX MILE BOTTOM Cambridgeshire. Map 26C3
London 56, Cambridge 9, Haverhill 17, Newmarket 6, Saffron Walden 14.

★★★ C R **Swynford Paddocks,** Newmarket, CB8 0UE (063 870) 234 Fax: (063 870) 283

Elegant country house surrounded by 40 acre stud farm. Tennis. Fr, De
15 bedrs, 15 en suite; TV; tcf
dogs, ns; P 120; child facs; con 30
LD 9.30, bar meals only Sat lunch
£ B&B £60–£70, B&B (double) £90–£140; L £13·50, D £18·50; WB £55 (HB)
cc Access, Amex, B'card/Visa, Diners.

S

SKEGNESS Lincolnshire. Map 34C3
Pop 14,553. Boston 21, London 139, Horncastle 21, Louth 23, Sleaford 38. **EC** Thur (Oct–May). **MD** Daily (sum). **Golf** North Shore 18h, Seacroft 18h. **See** St Clement's Church, Natureland (Aquarium and marine Zoo).
Embassy Centre, Grand Par. (0754) 4821

★★★ **Crown,** Drummond Rd, PE25 3AB (0754) 610760
Recently refurbished hotel in large, white pebble-dash building standing in own grounds. Indoor swimming pool. Fr
27 bedrs, 27 en suite; TV; tcf
lift, TV; P 80, coach; child facs; con 150
LD 9.30
£ B&B £40, B&B (double) £60; L £10·50, D £10·50; [10% V w/d]
cc Access, B'card/Visa; dep.

★★ **County,** North Par, PE25 2UB (0754) 2461

A large, modernised hotel in commanding position overlooking beach. Sauna.

★★ **Vine,** Vine Rd, PE25 3DB (0754) 3018

Building of character in pleasant residential area with gardens to rear

🛏 20 bedrs, 17 en suite, 2 ba; TV
🏠 dogs; P 70–80, coach; child facs; con 100

★ **Crawford,** South Par, PE25 3HR ☎ (0754) 4215
Double-fronted early 20th century brick building with views of dunes and sea. Swimming pool.

South Lodge, 147 Drummond Rd, PE25 3BT ☎ (0754) 5057. *Hotel.*

SKELWITH BRIDGE Cumbria. Map 43C1

2½ miles W of Ambleside, London 271, Kendal 15.

★★ **Skelwith Bridge,** LA22 9NJ
☎ Ambleside (05394) 32115
Fax: (053 94) 34254

Attractively set former coaching inn (17th century). Woodlands nearby. Fishing. ✂ Fr
🛏 23 bedrs, 23 en suite; annexe 6 bedrs, 6 en suite; TV; tcf
🏠 dogs, ns; P 60; child facs; con 50
✕ LD 9, bar meals only Mon–Sat lunch
£ B&B £20–£37, B&B (double) £38–£65; HB weekly £175–£300; L £7·95, D £15·50; WB £68; [10% V]
cc Access, B'card/Visa; dep.

SKIPTON North Yorkshire. Map 38A3

Pop 13,000. Halifax 17, London 204, Bradford 19, Burnley 18, Harrogate 22, Leeds 26, Leyburn 34, Settle 16.
ℹ Victoria Sq. ☎ (0756) 792809

Skipton Park (Acclaimed), 2 Salisbury St, BD23 1NQ ☎ (0756) 700640
£ B&B £35

Highfield, 58 Keighley Rd, BD23 2NB
☎ (0756) 793182. *Hotel.*
£ B&B £17–£18

SLAIDBURN Lancashire. Map 36C3

Pop 318. Clitheroe 9, London 223, Kirkby Lonsdale 21, Preston 22, Settle 14.

♣ ★★ **C** **Parrock Head Farm,** Woodhouse La, BB7 3AH ☎ (020 06) 614

Modernised 17th century farm at foot of Bowland Fells. Some bedrooms in two modern bungalows. ✂ Fr. Closed Xmas, New Year.

🛏 3 bedrs, 3 en suite; annexe 6 beds, 6 en suite; TV; tcf
🏠 dogs; ns; P 20; child facs; con 12
✕ LD 8.30, bar meals only lunch. Resid & Rest lic
£ B&B £35–£38, B&B (double) £50–£55; HB weekly £500–£525; [5% V]
cc Access, Amex, B'card/Visa; dep.

SLEAFORD Lincolnshire. Map 34A2

Pop 8,895. Peterborough 33, London 116, Boston 17, Grantham 14, Horncastle 23, Lincoln 17, Newark 18, Spalding 19.
EC Thur. **MD** Mon, Fri, Sat. **Golf** Sleaford 18h. **See** Church of St Denys.
ℹ Money's Yard, Carre St ☎ (0529) 414294

★ **Whichcote Arms,** London Rd, Osbournby, NG34 0DG ☎ Culverthorpe (052 95) 239.
Ivy clad, mid Victorian house now a popular inn situated in a village on the A15 south of Sleaford.
🛏 7 bedrs, 7 en suite; TV; tcf
🏠 dogs; P 40, coach; child facs; con 50
✕ LD 10
£ B&B £25, B&B (double) £34; L £6·75; WB £15 (min 2 nts); [10% V]
cc Access, B'card/Visa; dep.

Cross Keys (Acclaimed), Cross Keys Yard, Eastgate ☎ (0529) 305463
Fax: (0529) 414495. *Hotel.*
£ B&B £22–£28 (£14 w/e); [5% V w/e]

SLOUGH Berkshire. Map 13A3

ℹ RAC Motor Sports Association, Motor Sports House, Riverside Park, Colnbrook, SL3 0HG ☎ (0753) 681736.
Pop 96,715. London 20, M4 (jn 5) 2½, Henley-on-Thames 14, High Wycombe 13, Reading 18, Uxbridge 6, Windsor 2.
EC Wed. **MD** Daily. **Golf** Stoke Poges 18h.
See 12th cent Church of St Laurence.

★★★★ **Holiday Inn,** Ditton Rd, Langley, SL3 8PT ☎ (0753) 44244 Tx: 848646
Fax: (0753) 40272 ♿

Purpose-built modern hotel in red-brick. Indoor swimming pool, golf, tennis, sauna, solarium, gymnasium. ✂ Fr, De, Du, It (CHIC)
🛏 302 bedrs, 302 en suite; TV; tcf
🏠 lift, dogs, ns; P 375, coach; child facs; con 350
✕ LD 10.30
£ B&B £109–£125 (w/e £41), B&B (double) £128–£168; L £18, D £18
cc Access, Amex, B'card/Visa, Diners; dep.

★★ **King William,** Bath Rd, Langley, SL3 8P3 ☎ (0753) 44253 ♿

Please tell the manager if you chose your hotel through an advertisement in the guide.

Traditional hotel with substantial modern extension for bedrooms.
🛏 38 bedrs, 38 en suite; TV; tcf
🏠 dogs, ns; P 88, coach; child facs; con 12

Copthorne, Cippenham La, SL1 2YE
☎ (0753) 516222 Fax: (0753) 516237
Striking new hotel close to junction 6 of M4. Indoor swimming pool, solarium, gymnasium. Awaiting inspection.
🛏 219 bedrs, 219 en suite; TV; tcf
🏠 lift, dogs, ns; P 250, coach; child facs; con 300
✕ LD 10.30
£ room £90–£100; Bk £7·50, L £10, D £12·50; WB
cc Access, Amex, B'card/Visa, Diners; dep.

Colnbrook Lodge, Bath Rd, Colnbrook, SL3 0NZ. Guest House. ✂ Es, Sw
£ B&B £25–£38 (w/e £17·50); [10% V]

SMALLWAYS North Yorkshire. Map 44C1

Boroughbridge 35, London 242, Brough 21, Darlington 14, Harrogate 45, Leyburn 21, Middleton-in-Teesdale 15, Northallerton 23, Thirsk 32, West Auckland 13.

★ **A66 Motel,** Nr Richmond, DL11 7QW
☎ Teesdale (0833) 27334
Small motel adjacent to A66 trunk road in open country. Privately owned.
🛏 6 bedrs, 1 en suite, 1 ba; TV; tcf
🏠 dogs; P 30, coach; child facs; con 20
✕ LD 10.30
£ B&B £18, B&B (double) £25–£35; L £6·80, D £12·50; [10% V]; dep.

SNAINTON North Yorkshire. Map 39A4

Pop 744. London 222 (Fy 217), Bridlington 23, Malton 11, Pickering 7½, Scarborough 9.

★★ **Coachman Inn,** Pickering Rd West, YO13 9PL ☎ Scarborough (0723) 85231
Medium-sized country inn in small village with pleasant views.

SOHAM Cambridgeshire. Map 26C4

Newmarket 7½, London 70, Cambridge 21, Ely 6, Mildenhall 8.

Brook House (Acclaimed), 49 Brook St, CB7 5AD ☎ (0353) 721522. *Hotel.*

SOLIHULL West Midlands. Map 22C1

Pop 107,095. Warwick 13, London 105, Birmingham 7½, Bromsgrove 18, Coventry 12, Evesham 27, Stratford-upon-Avon 19.
EC Wed. **Golf** Olton Ltd 18h. **See** Church, timbered houses.
ℹ Library, Homer Rd. ☎ 021-704 6130.

★★★ **Arden,** Coventry Rd, Bickenhill, B92 0EH ☎ Hampton-in-Arden (067 55) 3221
Tx: 334913 Fax: (067 55) 3225 ♿
Modern hotel, well situated for airport, station and NEC. Indoor swimming pool, sauna, solarium, gymnasium, snooker. ✂ It, Fr, Po, De
🛏 76 bedrs, 76 en suite; TV; tcf
🏠 lift, dogs; P 150, coach; child facs; con 130
✕ LD 10, bar meals only Sat lunch
£ B&B £66, B&B (double) £84; L £11, D £11
cc Access, Amex, B'card/Visa, Diners.

★★★ **George,** High St, B91 3RF ☎ 021-711 2121 Tx: 334134 Fax: 021-711 3374
Former coaching inn with modern extension. Near town centre. (Emb)

Skipton (Yorkshire)

Pamela and Robert Heseltine invite you to the

Wilson Arms Country House Hotel

Station Road, Threshfield

RAC
★★★

ETB

Set in the heart of the Yorkshire Dales National Park. Ideal base for touring and walking holidays. Close to Dalesway Walk, Kilnsey Crag and historic Skipton.

Excellent bar meals – traditional beers. Restaurant open every day for lunch and dinner. Extensive wine cellar – luxurious lounges – log fires.

Adjoining Threshfield Court Nursing Care where those requiring 24-hour attention can also have a break in a home from home atmosphere.

Enquiries and reservations telephone and fax
0756 752666

Street (Somerset)

The Shoe Museum

(C. & J. Clark Ltd)

High Street, Street, Somerset
Tel: (0458) 43131

The museum is housed in the oldest part of the factory and contains shoes from Roman times to the present. Georgian shoe buckles, caricatures and engravings of shoemakers, costume illustrations and fashion plates, shoe machinery, hand tools, advertising material and 19th century documents and photographs illustrating the early history of the firm from the founding in 1825 by Cyrus Clark.

Open Easter Monday-Oct, Mon-Fri 10 – 4.45, Sat 10 – 4.30. Winter months by appointment only.
Admission FREE *P (200 yards); disabled (main floor only); shop.*

Southampton (Hampshire)

● Stunning displays of Rhododendrons, Azaleas, Camellias and Magnolias in Spring and early Summer. ● Visit later in the year and enjoy the rich autumn colours. ● 200 acre woodland setting by the Beaulieu River and New Forest. ● Expert advice available on acid soil gardening. ● Dogs on leads welcome. ● Plant Centre, Gift Shop and Tea Rooms.

Open 1991 Season: Gardens: March 2 to July 7 and Autumn: Sept 7 to Oct 20. 10.00 am to 5.30 pm (Or dusk) Plant Centre and Gift Shop: Open all year except Christmas Day and Boxing Day.

A delightful drive through the enchanting NewForest and just 3 Miles past Beaulieu, Hampshire. Easily reached by M3 from London.

🛏 74 bedrs, 74 en suite; TV; tcf
lift, dogs, ns; P 120, coach; child facs; con 200
✕ LD 10, nr Sun dinner
£ B&B £75–£89 (w/e £26), B&B (double) £93–£108; L £12, D £15·50; WB £36
cc Access, Amex, B'card/Visa, Diners; dep.

★★★ **H** **C** **St John's Swallow,** 651 Warwick Rd, B91 1AT ☎ 021-711 3000 Tx: 339352 Fax: 021-456 3442

Large modern red brick hotel with conference facilities. Indoor swimming pool, sauna, solarium, gymnasium. (Sw)
🛏 206 bedrs, 206 en suite; TV; tcf
lift, TV, dogs; P 380, coach; child facs; con 800
✕ LD 9.45, bar meals only Sat lunch
£ B&B £72–£90, B&B (double) £86–£100; L £13·50, D £16·50; WB £85
cc Access, Amex, B'card/Visa, CB, Diners.

★★ **Flemings,** 141 Warwick Rd, Olton, B92 7HW ☎ 021-706 0371 Fax: 021-706 4494

Four large linked Victorian houses in a part residential, part business area. Billiards.
🛏 84 bedrs, 84 en suite; TV; tcf
TV, dogs; P 84, coach; child facs; con 30

Cedarwood House (Acclaimed), 347 Lyndon Rd, Sheldon, B92 7QT ☎ 021-743 58443. *Guest House.*
£ B&B £30–£40 (w/e £18·50); [5% V w/d]

Richmond House, 47 Richmond Rd, Olton, B92 7RP ☎ 021-707 9746. *Hotel.*

SOMERTON
Somerset. Map 4C2

Pop 4,376. Wincanton 16, London 126, Bridgwater 16, Crewkerne 14, Glastonbury 8, Sherborne 13, Taunton 18.
EC Wed. **Golf** Yeovil 18h.

★★★ **Red Lion,** Broad St, TA11 7NJ ☎ (0458) 72339

Handsome building–a former coaching inn set centrally in town.

Lynch Country House (Highly Acclaimed), 4 Behind Berry, TA11 7PD ☎ (0458) 72316. Fax: (0458) 74370. *Hotel.*
£ B&B £30–£60; [5% V w/d]

Church Farm, School La, Compton Dundon, TA11 6PE ☎ (0458) 72927. *Guest House.* ♿

SONNING-ON-THAMES
Berkshire.

Map 12C3
Pop 1,750. Slough 14, London 35, A423 (M) 7, Bagshot 14, Farnham 23, Henley-on-Thames 6, Reading 3.

★★★ **Great House at Sonning** (formerly White Hart), Thames St, RG4 0UT ☎ Reading (0734) 692277 Tx: 849031 Fax: (0734) 441296

Former 16th century inn with converted cottages. Beautiful riverside gardens. Tennis, fishing. Fr
🛏 12 bedrs, 12 en suite; annexe 24 bedrs, 24 en suite; TV; tcf
dogs, ns; P 100, coach; child facs; con 80
✕ LD 10.15, bar meals only Sat lunch.
£ B&B £79–£89, B&B (double) £104–£114; L £15·50; WB £110; [10% V]
cc Access, Amex, B'card/Visa, Diners.

SOUTHAM
Gloucestershire. Map 20C2

Pop 699. Cheltenham 3, London 100, Gloucester 11, Stow-on-the-Wold 16.

★★★ **De la Bere,** Cheltenham, GL52 3NH ☎ Cheltenham (0242) 237771 Tx: 43232 Fax: (0242) 236016
Large Tudor mansion in attractive grounds. Swimming pool, putting, tennis, squash, sauna, solarium, snooker. (THF)
🛏 32 bedrs, 32 en suite; annexe 25 bedrs, 25 en suite; TV; tcf
dogs, ns; child facs; con 100
✕ LD 10
£ room £70·20, double room £91·80; L £10·50, D £15·50; WB £50
cc Access, Amex, B'card/Visa, Diners.

SOUTHAMPTON
Hampshire. Map 5C2

See also BOTLEY.
RAC Office, *West Quay Road Car Park, Southampton, SO1 0NY* ☎ (0703) 224244
Pop 204,400. Winchester 12, London 77, M271 (jn 4) 3, Fareham 12, Lyndhurst 9½, Ringwood 18, Romsey 8, Salisbury 22.
See Plan p. 445.
MD Thur, Fri, Sat. **P** See Plan. **Golf** Municipal 18h. **See** Old Gates, Towers and Town Walls, Docks, Museums: Tudor House, Bargate, Pilgrim Fathers' Memorial.
ℹ Above Bar Precinct. ☎ (0703) 221106

★★★★ **Polygon,** Cumberland Pl, SO9 4GD ☎ (0703) 330055 Tx: 47175 Fax: (0703) 332435

Modern hotel near Watts Park in town centre. Near station. Fr, De, It. (THF)
🛏 120 bedrs, 120 en suite; TV; tcf
lift, dogs, ns; P 120, coach; child facs; con 500
✕ LD 10
£ B&B £84 (w/e £33·50), B&B (double) £110; L £14, D £18·50; WB £40
cc Access, Amex, B'card/Visa, Diners.

★★★ **Dolphin,** High St, SO9 2DS ☎ (0703) 339955 Tx: 477735 Fax: (0703) 333650

Charming city centre Georgian building with bay windows. (THF)
🛏 72 bedrs, 72 en suite; TV; tcf
lift, dogs, ns; P 80; child facs; con 100
✕ LD 9.45
£ B&B £71–£78, B&B (double) £96–£107; L fr £9·50, D fr £13; WB £40 (HB)
cc Access, Amex, B'card/Visa, CB, Diners.

★★★ **Novotel,** 1 West Quay Rd, SO1 0RA ☎ (0703) 330550 ♿

New, purpose built, six storey hotel close to city centre. Indoor swimming pool, sauna, gymnasium. Fr, De
🛏 121 bedrs, 121 en suite; TV; tcf

Licences
Establishments have a full licence unless shown as unlicensed or with the limitations listed on p 6.

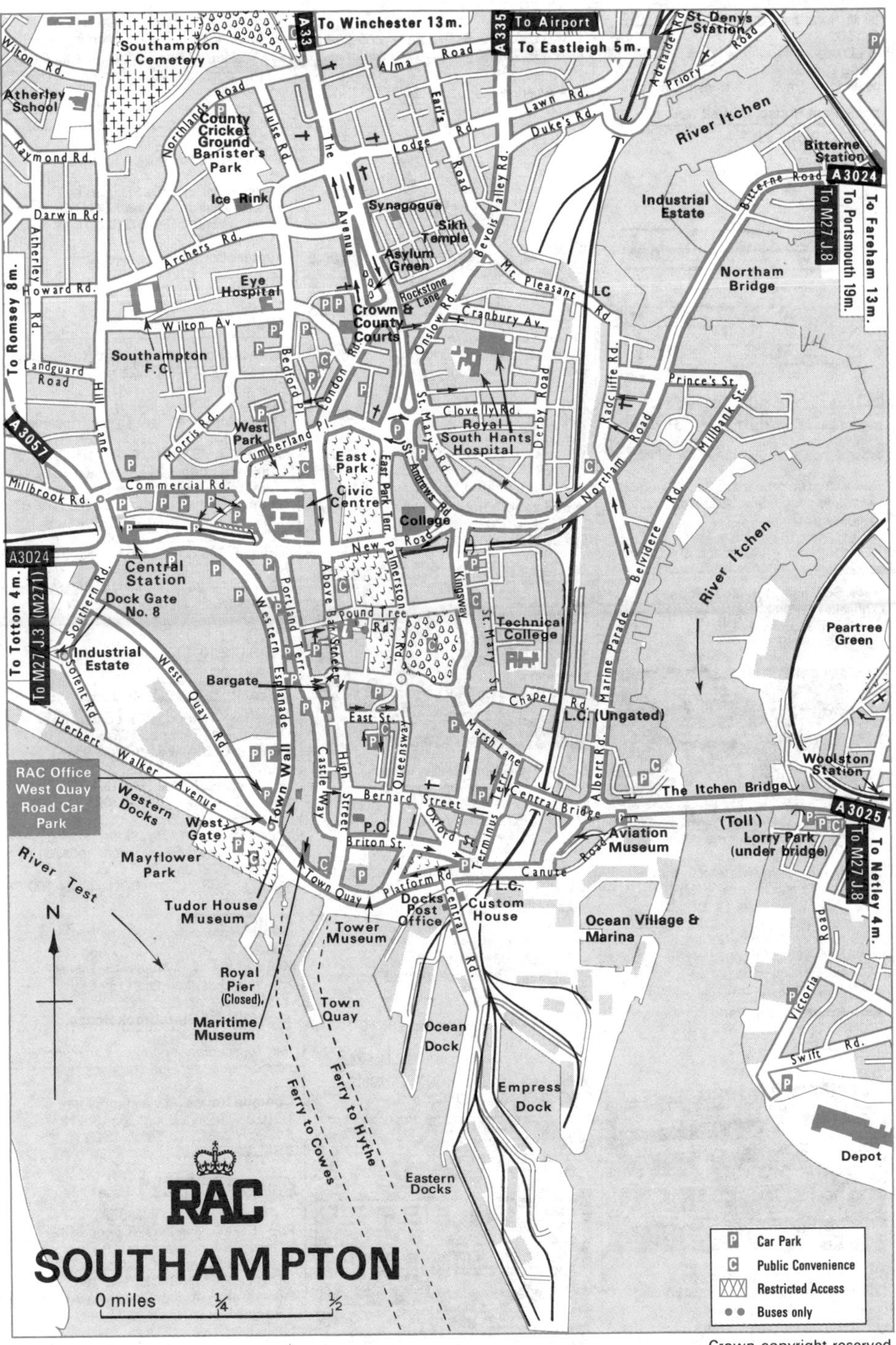

Crown copyright reserved

lift, dogs, ns; P 300, coach; child facs; con 500
LD midnight
£ B&B £65, B&B (double) £72
cc Access, Amex, B'card/Visa, Diners.

★★★ **Post House,** Herbert Walker Av, SO1 0HJ (0703) 330777 Tx: 477368 Fax: (0703) 332510

Tall modern hotel near the Docks. Indoor swimming pool, sauna, solarium, gymnasium. (THF)
132 bedrs, 132 en suite; TV; tcf
lift, dogs, ns; P 250, coach; child facs; con 200

★★★ **Southampton Moat House,** Highfield La, Portswood, SO9 1YQ (0703) 559555 Tx: 47186 Fax: (0703) 583910

Modern purpose-built hotel of 3 storeys situated in Portswood area. (QMH)
70 bedrs, 70 en suite; TV; tcf
dogs; P 100, coach; child facs; con 200
LD 10, bar meals only Sat lunch
£ B&B £55–£65, B&B (double) £80; L £9·50, D £12·50; WB £34 (HB); [10% V]
cc Access, Amex, B'card/Visa, Diners.

★★★ **Southampton Park,** Cumberland Pl, SO9 4NY (0703) 223467 Tx: 47439 Fax: (0703) 332538

City centre hotel overlooking park. Convenient for station. Indoor swimming pool, sauna, solarium, gymnasium.
71 bedrs, 71 en suite; TV; tcf
lift, dogs, ns; coach; child facs; con 200
LD 11
£ B&B £60–£66, B&B (double) £75–£82·50; L £8·50; WB £30 (HB); [10% V w/e]
cc Access, Amex, B'card/Visa, Diners.

★★ **Avenue,** Lodge Rd, SO2 0QR (0703) 229023 Fax: (0703) 334569

Seven-storey modern hotel set back from main road out of city to North.
48 bedrs, 48 en suite; TV; tcf
lift, TV, dogs, ns; P 48; coach; child facs; con 100
LD 9.15
£ room £55, double room £75; HB weekly £393·75; Bk £5·75; L £9·50, D £11·25; WB £40; [5% V]
cc Access, Amex, B'card/Visa, Diners.

★★ **Elizabeth House,** 43–44 The Avenue, SO1 2SX (0703) 224327 Fax: (0703) 224327

Elegantly modernised Victorian house close to the common and city centre.
24 bedrs, 20 en suite, 2 ba; TV; tcf
dogs; P 22; child facs; con 30
LD 9.15. Rest lic
£ B&B £40, B&B (double) £54; WB £20
cc Access, Amex, B'card/Visa, Diners; dep.

★★ **Ibis,** West Quay Rd, SO1 0RA (0703) 634463 Tx: 477698 Fax: (0703) 223273
New purpose-built hotel in city centre opposite Central Station.
93 bedrs, 93 en suite; TV
lift, dogs; P 125, coach; child facs; con 80
LD 11
£ B&B £44·25, B&B (double) £55·50; L £8·50, D £8·50
cc Access, Amex, B'card/Visa, Diners.

★★ **Star,** High St, SO9 4ZA (0703) 339939 Fax: (0703) 335291

Former coaching inn, modernised into pleasant hotel. Close to station.
45 bedrs, 37 en suite, 2 ba; TV; tcf
lift, dogs, ns; P 30, coach; child facs; con 70
LD 9, bar meals only Sun dinner
£ B&B £30–£65 (£15 w/e), B&B (double) £45–£75; L £5·75, D £9·95
cc Access, Amex, B'card/Visa, Diners.

Dormy (Acclaimed), 21 Barnes La, Sarisbury Green, Warsash, SO3 6DA Locks Heath (0489) 572626. *Hotel.*
£ B&B £20–£32; [10% V w/e]
Hunters Lodge (Acclaimed), 25 Landguard Rd, Shirley, SO1 5DL (0703) 227919 Fax: (0703) 230913. *Hotel.* Closed 24 Dec–13 Jan
£ B&B £23·58 (w/e £16)

Banister House, 11 Brighton Rd, Banister Park, SO1 2JJ (0703) 221279. *Hotel.* Closed Xmas.
£ B&B £21–£26·50; [5% V]
Earley House, 46 Pear Tree Av, Bitterne, SO2 7JP (0703) 448117. *Hotel.*
£ B&B £25; HB weekly £325; [10% V]
Languard Lodge, 21 Languard Rd, SO1 5DL (0703) 636904. *Guest House.*
Linden, 51 The Polygon, SO1 2BP (0703) 225653. *Guest House.*
£ B&B £12·50–£13·50; [5% V]
Nirvana, 386 Winchester Rd, Bassett, SO1 7DH (0703) 790087. *Private Hotel.*
£ B&B £24–£26; HB weekly £235; [5% V]
Villa Capri, 50 Archers Rd, SO1 2LU (0703) 632800. *Guest House. Sauna.*
Fr, It, Es
£ B&B £12·10–£15

SOUTHBOROUGH Kent. Map 11B1

Pop 9,994. Tonbridge 2½, London 35, Godstone 18, Tunbridge Wells 2.
EC Wed. **Golf** Tunbridge Wells 9h.

★★ **Sceptre,** London Rd, TN4 0RL Tunbridge Wells (0892) 37055 Fax: (0892) 515535
Greatly extended 17th century posting house offering modern accommodation.
27 bedrs, 27 en suite; TV; tcf
dogs; P 38, coach; child facs; con 100

SOUTH BRENT Devon. Map 3B2

Pop 2,166. Ashburton 8, London 195, Kingsbridge 11, Plymouth 15, Totnes 7.
EC Wed. **Golf** Wrangaton 18h.

★★ H R **Glazebrook House,** TQ10 9JE (036 47) 3322
Part 16th century – part Victorian manor house in quiet secluded grounds.

Coombe House (Acclaimed), North Huish, TQ10 9NJ Gara Bridge (054 882) 277. *Private Hotel.* Open 1 Mar–15 Dec.
£ B&B £25; [5% V]

SOUTHEND-ON-SEA Essex. Map 17C2

See also WESTCLIFF-ON-SEA.
Pop 157,600. Romford 25, London 42, Brentwood 21, Chelmsford 19, Colchester 37, Dartford Tunnel 21, Rainham 26.
MD Thur, Fri, Sat. **Golf** Belfairs 18h. **See** Pier—over 1¼ m long, Civic House (formerly 16th cent Manor House), 13th cent Southchurch Hall.
i High Street Precinct. (0702) 355120

EC *early closing* **MD** *market day* *country house hotel* *ns (NS) no smoking areas* *tcf tea/coffee facilities*

★★★ **Airport Moat House,** Aviation Way, SS2 6UL ☎(0702) 546344 Tx: 996866 Fax: (0702) 541961

Modern purpose-built hotel with all rooms on ground floor. Fr. (QMH)
65 bedrs, 65 en suite; TV; tcf
dogs; P 300, coach; child facs; con 300
LD 9.45, bar meals only Mon–Sat lunch & Sun dinner
£ B&B £55 (w/e £22·50); B&B (double) £72 D £11; WB £38; [5% V]
cc Access, Amex, B'card/Visa, Diners; dep.

★★ **Tower,** 146 Alexandra Rd, SS1 1HE ☎(0702) 348635 Fax: (0702) 431076
Large house, with distinctive tower, in corner position. Recently refurbished and redecorated.
16 bedrs, 16 en suite; TV; tcf
TV, dogs; coach; child facs; con 45
LD 9.30, Resid & Rest lic
£ B&B £33–£39·50 (w/e £20–£25), B&B (double) £46–£55; HB weekly £250–£330; L £2·95, D £6·50; WB £25; [5% V]
cc Access, Amex, B'card/Visa, Diners; dep.

Ilfracombe (Highly Acclaimed), 11 Wilson Rd, SS1 1HG ☎(0702) 351000. *Private Hotel.* It
£ B&B £28·75–£35·65; HB weekly £297·10; [5% V]

Argyle, 12 Cliff Town Par, SS1 1DP ☎(0702) 339483. *Hotel.* Fr. Closed Xmas.
£ B&B fr £17
The Bay, 187 Eastern Esplanade, Thorpe Bay, SS1 3AA ☎(0702) 588415. *Guest House.*
£ B&B £15–£18
Mayflower, 6 Royal Terr, SS1 1DY ☎(0702) 340489. *Hotel.*
£ B&B £18–£30
Regency, 18 Royal Terr, SS1 1DU ☎(0702) 340747. *Hotel.*
Terrace, 8 Royal Terr, SS1 1DY ☎(0702) 348143. *Hotel.*
£ B&B £16

SOUTH MILFORD North Yorkshire.

Map 38C2
Pop 1,645. Doncaster 20, London 184, Leeds 13, York 17.
Golf Selby 18h. **See** Steeton Gateway.

Discount vouchers
RAC discount vouchers are on p. 34. Hotels with a [V] shown at the end of the price information will accept them in part payment for accommodation bills on the full, standard rate, not against bargain breaks or any other special offers. Please note the limitations shown in the entry: w/e for weekends, w/d for weekdays, and which months they are accepted.

★★★ **Post House** (formerly Selby Fork), Junction A1/A63, LS25 5LF ☎(0977) 682711 Tx: 550574 Fax: (0977) 685462

Modern purpose-built hotel conveniently situated on the A1. Indoor swimming pool, 9 hole golf, tennis, sauna. (THF)
103 bedrs, 103 en suite; TV; tcf
dogs, ns; P 200, coach; child facs; con 200
LD 10
£ B&B £74·50–£84·50 (w/e £47), B&B (double) £92–£102; L £10·50, D £14·10; WB £38
cc Access, Amex, B'card/Visa, Diners.

SOUTH MIMMS Hertfordshire. Map 15A1

Barnet 3½, London 15, A1(M) M25 1, Ealing 15, Enfield 8, Harrow 11, Hatfield 7, Hoddesdon 14, St Albans 6½, Watford 9½.
EC Thur. **Golf** Potters Bar 18h.
[i] M25 Service Area ☎(0707) 43233

★★★ **Crest,** Jn 23 M25/A1(M), EN6 3NH ☎Potters Bar (0707) 43311 Tx: 299162 Fax: (0707) 46728

At motorway service area, purpose-built motel. Indoor swimming pool, sauna, solarium, gymnasium, snooker. Fr, De, It. (Cr/THF)
123 bedrs, 123 en suite; TV; tcf
dogs, ns; P 220, coach; child facs; con 200
LD 9.45, nr Sat lunch
£ room £82–£94, double room £94–£106; Bk £8·45, L £11, D £16; WB £45 (HB)
cc Access, Amex, B'card/Visa, CB, Diners.

SOUTH MOLTON Devon. Map 3B4

Pop 3,600. Tiverton 17, London 180, Barnstaple 11, Crediton 26, Great Torrington 15, Okehampton 29.
EC Wed. **MD** Thur. **Golf** Saunton 18h (2).
[i] 1 East St. ☎(076 95) 4122

Hotel locations
Hotel locations are shown on the maps at the back of the guide. All towns and villages containing an RAC Appointed or Listed hotel are ringed in purple.

★★★ **H C R** **Whitechapel Manor,** EX36 3EG ☎(076 95) 3377 Fax: (076 95) 3797

Elizabethan manor house in 14 acres of gardens and grounds quietly set on the edge of Exmoor. Putting.

★★ **H C R** **Marsh Hall,** EX36 3HQ ☎(076 95) 2666
Elegant red-brick Victorian house in 3 acres of well-tended gardens in lovely country.
7 bedrs, 7 en suite; TV; tcf
dogs; P 15; children over 12; con 12
LD 8.45, bar meals only lunch. Resid & Rest lic
£ B&B £28–£35, B&B (double) £56–£70; HB weekly £259–£280; D £15·95; WB £37 (3 nts)
cc Access, B'card/Visa; dep.

Heasley House, Heasley Mill, EX36 3LE ☎North Molton (059 84) 213. *Private Hotel.* Open Mar–Oct.
£ B&B £16–£17·50; HB weekly £170–£180

SOUTH NORMANTON Derbyshire.

Map 24B2
Pop 7,130. M1 (jn 28) 1, London 140, Ashbourne 19, Chesterfield 12, Derby 16, Mansfield 7, Matlock 12, Nottingham 14.
EC Wed. **Golf** Coxmoor 18h.

★★★★ **Swallow,** Jn 28 (M1), DE55 2EH ☎Ripley (0773) 812000 Tx: 377264 Fax: (0773) 580032

Large modern red-brick hotel adjacent to M1 motorway. Indoor swimming pool, sauna, solarium, gymnasium. (Sw)
161 bedrs, 161 en suite; TV; tcf
dogs, ns; P 200, coach; child facs; con 200
LD 10.30
£ B&B £72 (w/e £45), B&B (double) £86 (w/e £60); L £6·95, D £11·50; WB £90 (HB 2 nts); [10% V]
cc Access, Amex, B'card/Visa, Diners.

SOUTHPORT Merseyside. Map 32A4

Pop 89,756. Ormskirk 8, London 211, Chorley 19, Liverpool 18, Preston 17.
Golf Royal Birkdale 18h. Southport and Ainsdale 18h. **See** St Cuthbert's Church, Atkinson Art Gallery, Floral Hall.
[i] 112 Lord St. ☎(0704) 33133

S

Southport (Merseyside)

RAC
★★

English Tourist Board COMMENDED

Balmoral Lodge Hotel

Queens Road, Southport
Tel: (0704) 544298 & 530751

A small select hotel for those requiring a higher than usual standard. All bedrooms have en suite bathrooms, TV, radio, tea/coffee facilities, direct dial telephones, hair dryers and trouser presses. The Tudor style bar has access to picturesque garden for sunbathing or open air lunch. A newly built garden wing offers deluxe twin rooms with garden balconies. A sauna bath is available to all guests free of charge. Comprehensive menu and wine list makes candlelight dining a delight. Short breaks and weekly rates quoted.

Southport (Merseyside)

22 Bedrooms all ensuite. Popular Bars. A la Carte Restaurant. Raphaels Bar/Café. Finest Foods in the Area.
Renowned for Fresh Fish and Gourmet Meals.
Fine wines to traditional Oysters and Aberdeen Angus Meats to Home-made Steak and Kidney Pie.
Excellent value for money.

4 Crowns ★★ RAC Egon Ronay

Southport (Lancashire)

STUTELEA HOTEL & Leisure Club

ALEXANDRA ROAD SOUTHPORT PR9 0NB TEL (0704) 544220

R.A.C.
★★

18 De-Luxe Bedrooms (Single to Family Suites) all with Private Bathroom.
9 Apartments (Studio to 2 Bedroomed) all with Private Bathroom and fitted Kitchen.
All Accommodation has Colour TV, Radio, Direct Dial Telephone, Hair Dryers, Trouser Press, and Tea/Coffee Making Facilities.
Heated Indoor Swimming Pool, Jacuzzi, Scandinavian Sauna, Solarium, Gymnasium, Games Room, Gardens and Car Park, 2 Licensed Bars, Restaurant, Lounge with Library. Lift.

FAX: 0704 500232

Stockport (Cheshire)

CHURCH LANE
MARPLE · STOCKPORT
CHESHIRE SK6 7LB

OFFERS a quiet semi-rural elevated location, central for the many attractions of the Greater Manchester, Cheshire and Derbyshire areas. Delightful local walks to the famous Marple locks and canal system, and to the Ridge with its spectacular panoramic views.

PROVIDES an excellent restaurant with Table d'Hôte and à la Carte menus. Thirty four well appointed bedrooms (24 singles). Reasonable tariffs, with discounts for Mini-breaks, weekend, long term and block bookings. Private car parking. Family owned and managed. Brochures sent with pleasure.

Tel: 061-426 0086
061-427 7133
Fax: 061-449 0733

EC *early closing* **MD** *market day* *country house hotel* *ns (NS) no smoking areas* *tcf tea/coffee facilities*

★★★★ **Prince of Wales,** Lord St, PR8 1JS
📞(0704) 36688 Tx: 67415 Fax: (0704) 43488
Large, gracious Victorian classic hotel. Under refurbishment. 🗣 De, Fr, Es
🛏 104 bedrs, 104 en suite; TV; tcf
🏨 lift, dogs, ns; P 90, coach; child facs; con 450
✕ LD 10
£ room £70–£80, double room £80–£90; L £10, D £12; WB £40 (HB)
cc Access, Amex, B'card/Visa, CB, Diners; dep.

★★★ **Royal Clifton,** Promenade, PR8 1RB
📞(0704) 533771 Tx: 677191
Fax: (0704) 500657 ♿
Striking white-faced hotel in central position. Well-equipped bedrooms. Indoor swimming pool, sauna, solarium, gymnasium.
🛏 107 bedrs, 107 en suite; TV; tcf
🏨 lift, dogs, ns; P 42, coach; child facs; con 300
✕ LD 9.30
£ B&B £64–£70, B&B (double) £75–£85; HB weekly fr £245; L fr £7·50, D fr £12·50; WB fr £90 (HB); [10% V]
cc Access, Amex, B'card/Visa, Diners; dep.

★★★ **Scarisbrick,** 239 Lord St, PR8 1NZ
📞(0704) 43000 Fax: (0704) 33335
Centrally-placed hotel with attractive arcade frontage. Facilities include disco bars. 🗣 Po, It, Es
🛏 66 bedrs, 66 en suite; 1 ba; TV; tcf
🏨 lift, dogs; P 35, G 7, coach; child facs; con 180
✕ LD 9.30
£ B&B £52–£65, B&B (double) £65–£95; HB weekly £233–£303; L £6·20, D £11; WB £65 (HB, 2 nts); [10% V]
cc Access, Amex, B'card/Visa; Diners; dep.

★★ **Balmoral Lodge,** 41 Queens Rd, PR9 9EX 📞(0704) 44298
Fax: (0704) 501224

Edwardian residence with well-equipped bedrooms. Close to town centre. Sauna.
🛏 15 bedrs, 15 en suite; 1 ba; TV; tcf
🏨 TV; P 10; child facs
✕ LD 8.30, bar meals only lunch. Resid & Rest lic
£ B&B £25–£50, B&B (double) £50–£60; HB weekly £215–£250; D £11; WB £65–£74; [10% V]
cc Access, Amex, B'card/Visa, Diners; dep.
(*See advertisement on p. 448*)

Atlas Section
Consult the Atlas section at the back of the guide to find out which towns and villages have RAC Appointed and Listed hotels in them. They are shown on the maps by purple circles.

★★ **Lockerbie House,** 11 Trafalgar Rd, Birkdale, PR8 2EA 📞(0704) 65298

Converted brick-built villa in quiet residential area. Billiards.
🛏 14 bedrs, 14 en suite, 1 ba; TV; tcf
🏨 TV, dogs; P 14, U 2, coach; child facs
✕ LD 8. Resid & Rest lic
£ B&B £25, B&B (double) £46; D £8·50; [10% V]
cc Access, Amex, B'card/Visa, Diners; dep.

★★ **Metropole,** Portland St, PR8 1LL
📞(0704) 536836
Attractive former private house under proprietor's personal supervision. Billiards.
🛏 25 bedrs, 18 en suite, 4 ba; TV; tcf
🏨 TV, dogs; P 12, coach; child facs
✕ LD 8.30
£ B&B £22–£30, B&B (double) £39·50–£53; L £4·25, D £8·50; WB £44 (2 nts)
cc Access, Amex, B'card/Visa; dep.

★★ **New Bold,** 583 Lord St, PR9 0BE
📞(0704) 32578

Victorian commerical hotel set on attractive tree-lined Lord Street.
🛏 22 bedrs, 22 en suite; TV; tcf
🏨 dogs; P 14–16, coach; child facs; con 25–30
✕ LD 10
£ B&B £45–£50, B&B (double) £50–£55; HB £184–£190; L £6·50, D £9; WB £60 (2 nts)
cc Access, Amex, B'card/Visa, CB, Diners.
(*See advertisement on p. 448*)

Discount vouchers
RAC discount vouchers are on p. 34. Hotels with a [V] shown at the end of the price information will accept them in part payment for accommodation bills on the full, standard rate, not against bargain breaks or any other special offers. Please note the limitations shown in the entry: w/e for weekends, w/d for weekdays, and which months they are accepted.

★★ **Stutelea,** Alexandra Rd, PR9 0NB
📞(0704) 544220 Fax: (0704) 500232

Pleasant 3-storey Victorian building with ½ acre garden. Indoor swimming pool, sauna, solarium, gymnasium.
🛏 18 bedrs, 18 en suite; 4 ba; TV; tcf
🏨 lift; ns; P 18, coach; child facs; con 40
✕ LD 8.30, bar meals only lunch. Resid & Rest lic
£ B&B £35–£40, B&B (double) £55–£63; L £4·50, D £9·90; WB £67 (HB 2 nts); [10% V]
cc Access, Amex, B'card/Visa, Diners; dep.
(*See advertisement on p. 448*)

★ **Talbot,** Portland St, PR8 1LR 📞(0704) 533975

Three-storied hotel in a mainly residential area near to town centre and sea front.
Closed 24 Dec–14 Jan.
🛏 24 bedrs, 18 en suite, 2 ba; TV; tcf
🏨 TV, dogs; P 30, coach; child facs; con 60
✕ LD 8, bar meals only lunch, Sat & Sun dinner. Resid & Rest lic
£ B&B £27·50–£37·40, B&B (double) £38·50–£50·60; HB weekly £180·40–£202·40; D £10·50; WB £54
cc Access, Amex, B'card/Visa; dep.

Merlwood (Acclaimed), 22 Portland St, PR8 1HU 📞(0704) 531247. *Private Hotel.* Open Mar–Oct.
£ B&B £12–£16; HB weekly £105–£119; [10% V]

Ambassador, 13 Bath St, PR9 0DP
📞(0704) 43998. *Private Hotel.* 🗣 It. Closed 1–15 Jan.
£ B&B £30; HB weekly £165
Brae-Mar, 4 Bath St, PR9 0DA 📞(0704) 35838. *Private Hotel.*
Crimond, 28 Knowsley Rd, PR9 0HN
📞(0704) 536456. Fax: (0704) 548643 *Hotel. Indoor swimming pool, sauna.*
£ B&B £37; [5% V]
Fairways, 106 Leyland Rd, PR9 0DQ
📞(0704) 542069. *Private Hotel.* Open Feb–Nov
£ B&B £15–£19; HB weekly £154

Residents only
Some Listed hotels only serve meals to residents. It is always wise to make a reservation for a meal in a hotel.

Lake, 55 Promenade, PR9 0DY ☎(0704) 30996. *Hotel.*
£ B&B £20–£21; HB weekly £147·20–£155; [10% V Oct–Easter]
Lyndhurst, 101 King St, PR8 1LQ ☎(0704) 537520. *Guest House.*
£ B&B £13; HB weekly £116; [10% V, 5% V]
Oakwood, 7 Portland St, PR8 1LJ ☎(0704) 31858. *Private Hotel.*
Rosedale, 11 Talbot St, PR8 1HP ☎(0704) 30604. *Hotel.*
£ B&B £14–£16; HB weekly £110–£130; [5% V Oct–Apr]
Sidbrook, 14 Talbot St, PR8 1HP ☎(0704) 30608. *Hotel. Sauna, solarium.* Closed Xmas & New Year.
£ B&B £15–£18; HB weekly £95–£145; [5% V]
Sunningdale, 85 Leyland Rd, PR9 0NJ ☎(0704) 538673. *Hotel.*
£ B&B £18–£20; HB weekly £168–£182
White Lodge, 12 Talbot St, PR8 1HP ☎(0704) 36320. *Private Hotel.*
£ B&B £13–£18; HB weekly £120–£135; [10% V]
Whitworth Fall, 16 Latham Rd, PR9 0JL ☎(0704) 530074. *Hotel.*
£ B&B £13·50; HB weekly £120; [5% V Nov–May]
Windsor Lodge, 37 Saunders St, PR9 0HJ ☎(0704) 30070. *Hotel.*

SOUTHSEA Hampshire

See PORTSMOUTH and SOUTHSEA.

SOUTH SHIELDS Tyne & Wear. Map 37C3

Pop 87,187. Sunderland 7, London 277, Durham 19, Newcastle upon Tyne 9½.
EC Wed. **MD** Mon, Sat. **Golf** South Shields 18h. **See** Roman Fort and Museum.
[i] Museum, Ocean Road. ☎091-456 6612

★★★ **Sea,** Sea Rd, NE33 2LD ☎091-427 0999 Tx: 53533 Fax: 091-454 0500
In 1930s style, 3-storey red-brick purpose-built hotel on seafront. Near to town centre.
33 bedrs, 33 en suite; TV; tcf
dogs; P 34, coach; child facs; con 120
LD 9.30
£ B&B £43·80–£49·80, B&B (double) £54·80 £60·80 (w/e £44·80); L £5·60, D £7·77
cc Access, Amex, B'card/Visa, Diners.

★★ **New Crown,** Mowbray Rd, NE33 3NG ☎091-455 3472
Stone-built hotel located on seafront with views of harbour and beaches.
11 bedrs, 10 en suite, (1 sh), 2ba; TV; tcf
TV; P40, coach; child facs
LD 9, bar meals only Mon–Sat lunch, Sun dinner
£ B&B £28–£31, B&B (double) £47–£51; L £7·45, D £7·45; WB £20; [10% V w/e]
cc Access, Amex, B'card/Visa, Diners; dep.

SOUTHWELL Nottinghamshire. Map 24B4

Mansfield 11, Melton Mowbray 25, Newark 7, Nottingham 12, Ollerton 12.
EC Wed. **MD** Sat. **Golf** Oxton 18h. **See** Minster (earliest part 12th cent), Bishop's Manor, Prebend's Walk.

★★★ **Saracen's Head,** Market Pl, NG25 0HE ☎(0636) 812701 Tx: 377201 Fax: (0636) 815408

A modernised historic hotel with Stuart associations. Near the Minster. (THF)
27 bedrs, 27 en suite; TV; tcf
dogs, ns; P 80, coach; child facs; con 150
LD 9.45
£ B&B £73–£88 (w/e £45), B&B (double) £95–£106; L £9·95, D £15
cc Access, Amex, B'card/Visa, CB, Diners.

Upton Fields (Acclaimed), Upton Rd, NG25 0QA ☎(0636) 812303. *Guest House.*
£ B&B £25; [5% V Nov–Mar]

SOUTHWOLD Suffolk. Map 27C4

Pop 1,795. Saxmundham 14, London 109, Aldeburgh 17, Lowestoft 11, Norwich 29.
EC Wed. **MD** Mon, Thur. **Golf** Southwold 9h.
[i] Town Hall, High St. ☎(0502) 722366

★ **Pier Avenue,** Station Rd, IP18 6LB ☎(0502) 722632

A small owner-run hotel attractively located on the edge of town.
14 bedrs, 9 en suite, 2 ba; TV; tcf
TV, dogs; P 10, coach; child facs; con 25

SOUTH WOODHAM FERRERS Essex. Map 17B2

Pop 12,002. London 38, Brentwood 16, Chelmsford 12, Dartford Tunnel 24, Southend-on-Sea 14.

★★ **Oakland,** Merchant St, CM3 5XE ☎Chelmsford (0245) 322811 Fax: (0245) 329201

Attractive modern hotel built as part of the New town development. Billiards.
41 bedrs, 41 en suite; TV; tcf
TV; P 20, coach; child facs
LD 9.30, bar meals only Sun dinner
£ B&B £37, B&B (double) £48; L £7·50, D £7·50
cc Access, Amex, B'card/Visa, Diners.

SOUTH ZEAL Devon. Map 3B3

Exeter 18, London 188, Ashburton 19, Crediton 14, Okehampton 5.
EC Wed. **Golf** Okehampton 18h.

★★ **Oxenham Arms,** EX20 2JT ☎Okehampton (0837) 840244

Granite pillar supports beam in restaurant of this ancient (12th century) inn. Fr
8 bedrs, 8 en suite; annexe 2 bedrs, 2 en suite; TV; tcf
TV; dogs; P12; child facs
LD 9
£ B&B £34·50–£40, B&B £45–£60; L £7·50, D £14·50; WB £35 (2 nts, Nov–Mar); [10% V]
cc Access, Amex, B'card/Visa, Diners; dep.

SOWERBY BRIDGE West Yorkshire. Map 40C1

Huddersfield 7½, London 188, M62 (jn 24) 5, Bradford 9, Burnley 18, Rochdale 14.
[i] 40 Town Hall St ☎(0422) 835326

★★ **H C R** **Hobbit,** Hob La, Norland, HX6 3QL ☎Halifax (0422) 832202 Fax: (0422) 835381

Sympathetically extended stone-built inn set high up with panoramic views of the Calder Valley and moors.
18 bedrs, 18 en suite; TV; tcf
P 106, coach; child facs; con 80
LD 11, bar meals only Mon, Tues, Sat lunch & Mon dinner
£ B&B £44–£52 (w/e £20), B&B (double) £55–£66; L £7·95, D £9·95; WB £59 (2 nts HB); [5% V, Mon–Thu]
cc Access, Amex, B'card/Visa; dep.

SPALDING Lincolnshire. Map 34B2

Pop 19,000. Peterborough 17, London 101, Boston 16, Grantham 30, King's Lynn 28, Sleaford 19, Stamford 19, Wisbech 20.
EC Thur. **MD** Tue. **Golf** Surfleet 18h. **See** Church (13th cent), Ayscoughfee Hall.
[i] Ayscoughfee Hall, Churchgate. ☎(0775) 725468

★★ **Cley Hall,** 22 High St, PE11 1TX
☎(0775) 725157 Fax: (0775) 710785
A ship-owner's Georgian house of character on banks of River Welland near town centre.
🛏 11 bedrs, 11 en suite; TV; tcf
🏠 dogs; P 24, coach; child facs; con 40
✕ LD 9.30–10, bar meals only Sat/Sun lunch & Sun dinner
£ B&B £25–£47 (w/e £25), B&B (double) £38–£52 (w/e £38); L £9·25, D £9·25; [5% V Mon–Thurs]
cc Access, Amex, B'card/Visa, Diners; dep.

★★ **C** **R** **Woodlands,** 80 Pinchbeck Rd, PE11 1QF ☎(0775) 769933
Fax: (0775) 711369 ♿

A large Victorian house converted into well-appointed hotel.
🛏 17 bedrs, 17 en suite; TV; tcf
🏠 dogs, ns; P 60; child facs; con 60

Stables (Highly Acclaimed), Cowbit Rd, PE11 2RJ ☎(0775) 767290
Fax: (0775) 767716. *Motel.* ⚒ Fr
£ B&B £29·50–£46·50; HB weekly £308–£360·50; [5% V]

SPARSHOLT Hampshire.
See WINCHESTER.

SPINKHILL Derbyshire. Map 38C1
M1 (jn 30) 2, London 156, Chesterfield 7, Rotherham 7½, Sheffield 8½, Worksop 10.

♣ ★★★ **Park Hall,** S31 9YD ☎(0246) 434897 Tx: 342239 Fax: (0246) 436282

Listed 16th-century manor house in extensive wooded grounds in rural surroundings.
🛏 8 bedrs, 8 en suite; TV; tcf
🏠 P100, coach; child facs; con 50
✕ LD 9.45, nr Sat lunch & Sun dinner
£ B&B £57, B&B (double) £80; L £8·90, D £14·50; WB £92; [5% V w/e]

STAFFORD Staffordshire. Map 22B4
Pop 54,530. Lichfield 16, London 132, M6 (jn 14) 2, Nantwich 22, Newport 12, Stone 7½, Uttoxeter 14, Wolverhampton 15.
EC Wed. **MD** Tue, Fri, Sat. **Golf** Stafford Castle 9h. **See** Churches of St Mary and St Chad, Art Gallery and Museum, Izaak Walton cottage at Shallowford, Shugborough Hall 5½ m E.

ℹ Ancient High House, Greengate St.
☎(0785) 40204

★★★ **Tillington Hall,** Eccleshall Rd, ST16 1JJ ☎(0785) 53531 Tx: 36566
Fax: (0785) 59223

Country house type hotel, in its own grounds, near motorway. Indoor swimming pool, tennis, gymnasium, billiards. ⚒ Fr, It. (DeV)
🛏 90 bedrs, 90 en suite; TV; tcf
🏠 lift, dogs, ns; P 200, coach; child facs; con 200
✕ LD 9.45, bar meals only Sat lunch
£ B&B £75–£95 (w/e £35), B&B (double) £90–£120; L £8, D £10; WB £78 (2 nts HB)
cc Access, Amex, B'card/Visa, Diners.

★★ **Abbey,** 65 Lichfield Rd, ST14 4LW
☎(0785) 58531
Pleasant hotel close to town centre. ⚒ De, Fr
🛏 21 bedrs, 7 en suite, 1 ba; TV; tcf
🏠 TV, dogs; P 21; U4; child facs
✕ LD 8.30, bar meals only lunch, Sun dinner. Resid & Rest lic
£ B&B £19–£28, B&B (double) £30–£40; L £3, D £5·50
cc Access, B'card/Visa; dep.

★★ **Albridge,** Wolverhampton Rd, ST17 4AW ☎(0785) 51400
Two-storey late Victorian building set beside A449 in the suburbs. Closed 25 Dec.
🛏 19 bedrs, 7 en suite, 2 ba; annexe 8 bedrs, 2 en suite, 2 ba; TV; tcf
🏠 TV, dogs; P 20, coach; child facs
✕ LD 9.45, bar meals only Sun lunch & dinner
£ B&B £21·95, B&B (double) £31·95; L £3·60, D £7·25; WB; [5% V]
cc Access, Amex, B'card/Visa, Diners.

★★ **Garth,** Moss Pit, ST17 9JR ☎(0785) 56124 Tx: 36479 Fax: (0785) 55152

On outskirts of town convenient for M6, hotel with modern bedrooms. ⚒ Fr
🛏 60 bedrs, 60 en suite; TV; tcf
🏠 dogs, ns; P 200, coach; child facs; con 50
✕ LD 10, bar meals only Sat lunch
£ B&B £52·25 (w/e £35), B&B (double) £69·30; L £6·95, D £10·55; WB £32 (3 nts)
cc Access, Amex, B'card/Visa.

★★ **Swan,** Greengate St, ST16 2JA
☎(0785) 58142

Old coaching house, in town centre, with modernised bedrooms. (BCB)
🛏 32 bedrs, 32 en suite; TV; tcf
🏠 ns; P 50, coach; child facs
✕ LD 10
£ B&B £43–£47, B&B (double) £61; L £8·15, D £8·15; WB £27·50.
cc Access, Amex, B'card/Visa, Diners.

★★ **Vine,** Salter St, ST16 2JU ☎(0785) 44112 Fax: (0785) 46612

An old inn of character in the centre of the town.
🛏 27 bedrs, 27 en suite; TV; tcf
🏠 dogs; P 30; child facs; con 8

Leonards Croft, 80 Lichfield Rd, ST17 4LP ☎(0785) 223676. *Private Hotel. Putting.* Closed Dec 21–Jan 1.
£ B&B £16·50

STAINES Surrey. Map 8A2
Pop 19,000. London 17, M25 (jn 13) 1, Bagshot 10, Kingston upon Thames 9½, Reading 22, Uxbridge 11, Woking 9.
EC Thur. **MD** Wed & Sat. **Golf** Ashford Manor 18h.

★★★ **C** **Thames Lodge,** Thames St, TW18 4SJ ☎(0784) 464433 Tx: 8812552
Fax: (0784) 454858

Large building attractively set on the banks of the River Thames. (THF)
🛏 44 bedrs, 44 en suite; TV; tcf

S

🏠 dogs, ns; P 50, coach; child facs; con 55
✕ LD 9.45, bar meals only Sat lunch
£ room £80–£88 (w/e £47), double room £95–£103; Bk £7·60, L £10·75, D £15
cc Access, Amex, B'card/Visa, Diners.

Angel, 24 High St, TW19 5NT ☎ (0784) 452509 Fax: (0784) 458338. *Hotel.*
£ B&B £30; [5% V]
Swan, The Hythe, TW18 3JB ☎ (0784) 452494 Fax: (0784) 461593. *Inn.* De
£ B&B £33

STALHAM Norfolk. Map 35C2
Norwich 14, London 125, Cromer 17, Great Yarmouth 17.

★★ **Kingfisher,** High St, NR12 9AN ☎ (0692) 81974 Fax: (0692) 82544
Modern two-storey converted hotel just off village High St. Fr, It, Du
16 beds, 16 en suite; TV; tcf
🏠 TV, dogs; P 50, coach; child facs; con 100
✕ LD 9
£ B&B £35, B&B (double) £40–£50; HB weekly £220·50–£227·50; WB £60; [10% V]
cc Access, B'card/Visa.

STAMFORD Lincolnshire. Map 31C1
Pop 16,656. London 91, Grantham 21, Kettering 23, Leicester 32, Melton Mowbray 20, Peterborough 14, Spalding 19.
See Burghley House 1½ m SE.
ℹ Museum, Broad St. ☎ (0780) 55611

★★★ **Garden House,** St Martins, PE9 2LP ☎ (0780) 63359 Tx: 329230
Fax: (0780) 63339
18th century terraced hotel with spacious accommodation. Fr
20 bedrs, 20 en suite; TV; tcf
🏠 dogs; P 25, G 5, coach; child facs; con 50
✕ LD 9.30, bar meals only Sun dinner
£ B&B £59·75, B&B (double) £75; L £15, D £15; WB £40 (HB); [10% V]
cc Access, Amex, B'card/Visa.

★★★ H C R **George of Stamford,** St Martins, PE9 2LB ☎ (0780) 55171 Tx: 32578
Fax: (0780) 57070

Famous 16th century coaching inn offering modern amenities. Business centre. It, De, Fr
47 bedrs, 47 en suite; TV
🏠 dogs; P 190, coach; child facs; con 50
✕ LD 10.30
£ B&B £59·50–£67, B&B (double) £86–£130; L £9–£17, D £24; WB £85 (2 nts min)
cc Access, Amex, B'card/Visa.

★★★ **Lady Anne's,** 37–38 High St, St Martins, PE9 1FG ☎ (0780) 53175
Tx: 32376
A dignified stone-built hotel situated in residential area of town. Tennis. Closed 28–30 Dec.
28 bedrs, 26 en suite, (2 sh), 1 ba; TV; tcf
🏠 dogs; P 150, coach; child facs; con 120
✕ LD 9.30
£ £39–£45·50, B&B (double) £65–£80; L £9·50, D £9·50; WB £50 (Nov–Apr)
cc Access, Amex, B'card/Visa, Diners

★★ **Crown,** All Saints Pl, PE9 2AG ☎ (0780) 63136
Stone building of character situated in centre of this ancient town. Closed 25 Dec.
18 bedrs, 15 en suite, 3 ba; TV; tcf
🏠 dogs, ns; P 40, coach; child facs; con 60
✕ LD 9.30
£ B&B £35, B&B (double) £45; L £7·50, D £11
cc Amex, B'card/Visa, Diners; dep.

STANDISH Greater Manchester (Lancashire). Map 32C3
Pop 12,317. Wigan 3, London 198, M6 (jn 27) 1½, Chorley 5, Ormskirk 10.
EC Wed. **Golf** Haigh Hall Municipal 18h.

★★★ **Almond Brook,** Almond Brook Rd, WN6 0SR ☎ (0257) 425588 Tx: 677662
Fax: (0257) 427327 ♿

Modern purpose-built family-owned and managed hotel. Indoor swimming pool, sauna, solarium, gymnasium. Fr, De, It.
Closed 25–31 Dec.
102 bedrs, 102 en suite; TV; tcf
🏠 lift, dogs, ns; P 400, coach; child facs; con 150
✕ LD 10
£ B&B £60–£95 (w/e £27); B&B (double) £70–£95; L 7·25, D £9·75; WB £30; [5% V]
cc Access, Amex, B'card/Visa, CB, Diners.

★★ **Beeches,** School La, Wigan, WN6 0TD ☎ (0257) 426432. Fax: (0257) 427503
Victorian mansion with elegant public rooms, set in own grounds, 1½ miles from M6, junction 27.
11 bedrs, 11 en suite; TV; tcf
🏠 ns; P 75, coach; child facs
✕ LD 10, brasserie only Sat lunch, Sun dinner
£ B&B £36–£44, B&B (double) £44–£54; L £9, D £9; [5% V w/e]
cc Access, Amex, B'card/Visa, Diners.

STANNERSBURN Northumberland. Map 44B3
Bellingham 8, London 303, Brampton 41, Corbridge 26, Hawick 46.

Pheasant, Falstone, Hexham, NE48 1DD ☎ (0434) 240382
Stone-built inn dating back 350 years, set in rural surroundings amidst fine scenery.
11 bedrs, 2 en suite, 2 ba; TV; tcf
🏠 dogs, ns; P 40, coach; child facs
✕ LD 9, bar meals only Mon–Sat lunch
£ B&B £18–£24, B&B (double) £34–£42; HB weekly £176·40–£186·40; L £7·50, D £10·50; WB £24 (HB); dep

STANSTEAD ABBOTTS Hertfordshire. Map 15B2
Hoddesdon 2½, London 23, Bishops Stortford 11, Chelmsford 24, Harlow 5½, Hatfield 12, Royston 23.
Golf East Herts 18h. **See** Marina.

★★★★ R **Briggens House,** Ware, SG12 8LD ☎ Roydon (027 979) 2416
Tx: 817906 Fax: (027 979) 3685

Large elegant country house in 45 acres of parkland. Swimming pool, golf, putting, tennis, fishing. Fr, De, It
22 bedrs, 22 en suite; annexe 32 bedrs; 32 en suite; TV; tcf
🏠 lift; ns; P 100, coach; child facs; con 100
✕ LD 10
£ B&B £85·50 (w/e £39), B&B (double) £108·50–£126; L £18·50, D £21·50; [5% V]
cc Access, Amex, B'card/Visa, Diners; dep.

STANSTED AIRPORT Essex, Map 15C3
M11 (jn 8) ½, London 32, Bishop's Stortford 2, Braintree 15½, Harlow 12, Saffron Walden 12.

★★★ **Stansted Harlequin,** Round Coppice Rd, CM24 8SE ☎ (0279) 680800
Tx: 818840 Fax: (0279) 680890
New purpose-built hotel in 13 acres of grounds by the airport. Modern decor and furnishings; triple glazing to bedrooms. Indoor swimming pool, sauna, solarium, gymnasium. Fr, De, It, Ar
249 bedrs, 249 en suite; TV; tcf
🏠 lift, dogs; ns; P 250, coach; child facs; con 350
✕ LD 11.45
£ B&B £65–£68, B&B (double) £75–£78; L £10·50, D £12·50; WB £34·50
cc Access, Amex, B'card/Visa, Diners.

STANSTED MOUNTFITCHET Essex. Map 15C3
Pop 4,974. Bishop's Stortford 2½, London 34, Cambridge 24, Dunmow 9, Haverhill 22.

★★★ **Old Bell,** Pines Hill, CM24 8EY ☎ Bishop's Stortford (0279) 816555

Much-renovated old inn, with modern residential block; situated outside town.

STARBOTTON N. Yorkshire. Map 38A4
Kettlewell 2, London 230, Leyburn 17½, Skipton 16½.

Hilltop (Highly Acclaimed), nr Skipton, BD23 5HY ☎ Kettlewell (075 676) 321. *Guest House*. De. Open Mar–mid Nov.
£ B&B (double) £48; [5% V, Mar–May, Oct–Nov]

STAVERTON Devon. Map 3B2
Pop 100. Newton Abbot 8, London 217, Ashburton 5, Plymouth 23, Totnes 3.

★ H R **Sea Trout Inn,** TQ9 6PA
☎ (080 426) 274
Attractive 15th century 'olde worlde' inn with beamed ceilings. Fr
10 beds, 10 en suite; TV; tcf
dogs; P 50, coach, child facs
LD 9.45, bar meals only Mon–Sat lunch, Sun dinner
£ B&B £35–£50, B&B (double) £44–£60; L £7, D £12; WB £33 (HB); [10% V]
cc Access, B'card/Visa; dep.

STEEPLE ASTON Oxfordshire. Map 21A2
Pop 872. Bicester 9, London 66, Banbury 10, Brackley 14, Chipping Norton 12, Oxford 13½.
Golf North Oxford 18h.

★★★ **Hopcrofts Holt,** Banbury Rd, OX5 3QQ ☎ (0869) 40259 Fax: (0869) 40865
Privately-owned 15th century former coaching inn in attractive village. Putting.
88 bedrs, 88 en suite; TV; tcf
dogs; P 150, coach; child facs; con 175
LD 9.45, bar meals only Sat lunch.
£ B&B £76, B&B (double) £98; L £12·50, D £17; WB £48
cc Access, B'card/Visa, Diners.

Westfield Farm, The Fenway, OX5 3SS ☎ (0869) 40591. *Motel. Riding.*
£ B&B £28–£33; [10% V w/e]

STEVENAGE Hertfordshire. Map 15A3
Pop 75,000. Hatfield 10, London 31, A1(M) (jn 7) 1½, Baldock 6, Bedford 20, Bishop's Stortford 21, Luton 12.
EC Wed. **MD** Thur, Fri, Sat. **Golf** Stevenage 18h. **See** Early 12th cent St Nicholas' Church, Knebworth House 3 m S.
i Library Southgate. ☎ (0438) 369441

★★★ **Blakemore Thistle,** Little Wymondley, SG4 7JJ ☎ (0438) 355821 Tx: 825479 Fax: (0438) 742114

Georgian-style mansion with modern wing; in 5 acres of attractive gardens. Swimming pool, sauna, solarium. (MtCh)
82 bedrs, 82 en suite; TV; tcf
lift, dogs; P 200, coach; child facs; con 150
LD 9.30
£ B&B £64, B&B (double) £75, L £11·25, D £13·50; WB
cc Access, Amex, B'card/Visa, CB, Diners.

★★★ **Hertford Park,** Danestrete, SG1 1EJ ☎ (0438) 350661 Tx: 825697 Fax: (0438) 741880

Modern tower block hotel on edge of the new town shopping centre. Es, It, Fr. (QMH)
100 bedrs, 100 en suite; TV; tcf
lift, dogs, ns; coach; child facs; con 200
LD 9.45, bar meals only, Sat & Sun lunch
£ B&B £62, (w/e £30), B&B (double) £72; L £10·75, D £10·75; WB £35 (HB)
cc Access, Amex, B'card/Visa, Diners.

★★★ **Novotel,** Knebworth Park, SG1 2AX ☎ (0438) 742299 Tx: 826132
Fax: (0438) 723872 ♿
Modern hotel with open-plan public areas conveniently situated just off A1M (junction 7). Swimming pool.
101 bedrs, 101 en suite; TV; tcf
lift, dogs, ns; P120, coach; child facs; con 130

★★★ **Roebuck Inn,** Old London Rd, Broadwater, SG2 8DS ☎ (0438) 365444 Tx: 825505 Fax: (0438) 741308

A thoroughly modernised period country inn with up-to-date residential wing. Fr, Es, Po. (THF)
54 bedrs, 54 en suite; TV; tcf
dogs, ns; P 60, coach; child facs; con 65
LD 9.45, bar meals only Sat lunch
£ B&B £47–£79·50, B&B (double) £54·50–£97, L £8·95, D £14·25, WB £38
cc Access, Amex, B'card/Visa, CB, Diners; dep.

★★★ **Stevenage Moat House,** High St, Old Town, SG1 3AZ ☎ (0438) 359111 Fax: (0438) 359111

17th century building in old high street. Modernised but retains much charm. (QMH)
60 bedrs, 60 en suite; TV, tcf
dogs, ns; P 100, coach, child facs; con 200
LD 9.45
£ B&B £57·75–£62·75 (w/e £35), B&B (double) £70 (w/e £45); L £9·50, D £9·50
cc Access, Amex, B'card/Visa, Diners.

STEYNING West Sussex. Map 6B1
Pop 4,385. Crawley 20, London 50, Brighton 11, Haywards Heath 18, Horsham 16, Pulborough 11, Worthing 7.
EC Thur. **Golf** Hill Barn, Worthing 18h.

Nash Country (Acclaimed), Horsham Rd, BN4 3AA ☎ (0903) 814988. *Hotel. Swimming pool, tennis.*
£ B&B £25; [10% V]
Springwells, High St, BN4 3GG ☎ (0903) 812446. *Hotel. Swimming pool, sauna.*

STOCKBRIDGE Hampshire. Map 5B3
Pop 490. Basingstoke 21, London 68, Amesbury 16, Andover 7½, Romsey 10, Salisbury 15, Winchester 9.
EC Wed. **Golf** Leckford 9h.

★★★ **Grosvenor,** High St, SO20 6EU ☎ (0264) 810606 Tx: 477677
Fax: (0264) 810747
Attractive inn, popular with fishermen. Set in broad street. Sauna, billiards. (Lns)
25 bedrs, 25 en suite; TV; tcf
ns; P 60, con 70
LD 9.45
£ B&B £65, B&B (double) £75; L £11, D £11; WB £36; [10% V]
cc Access, Amex, B'card/Visa, Diners.

Carbery (Acclaimed), Salisbury Hill, SO20 6EZ ☎ (0264) 810771. *Guest House. Swimming pool.*
£ B&B £17·25–£25; HB weekly £177·34–£230·34
Old Three Cups (Acclaimed), High St, SO20 6HB ☎ (0264) 810527. *Hotel.* Closed Jan.
£ B&B £22–£32 [5% V]

STOCKPORT Greater Manchester (Cheshire). Map 33C2
See also BRAMHALL.
RAC Office, *65–81 St Petersgate, Stockport, SK1 1DS* ☎ 061-477 6500
Pop 289,000. Buxton 18, London 179, M63 ½, Altrincham 8½, Glossop 11, Huddersfield 27, Knutsford 14, Macclesfield 12, Manchester 6, Oldham 11.
See Plan pp. 454.
EC Thurs. **MD** Tue, Fri, Sat. **P** See Plan. **Golf** Stockport 18h. **See** Art Gallery Museum, Bramall Hall, Bramhall 2½ m S.
i 9 Princes St. ☎ 061-474 3320

★★★ **Alma Lodge,** 149 Buxton Rd, SK2 6EL ☎ 061-483 4431 Tx: 665026 Fax: 061-483 1983

S

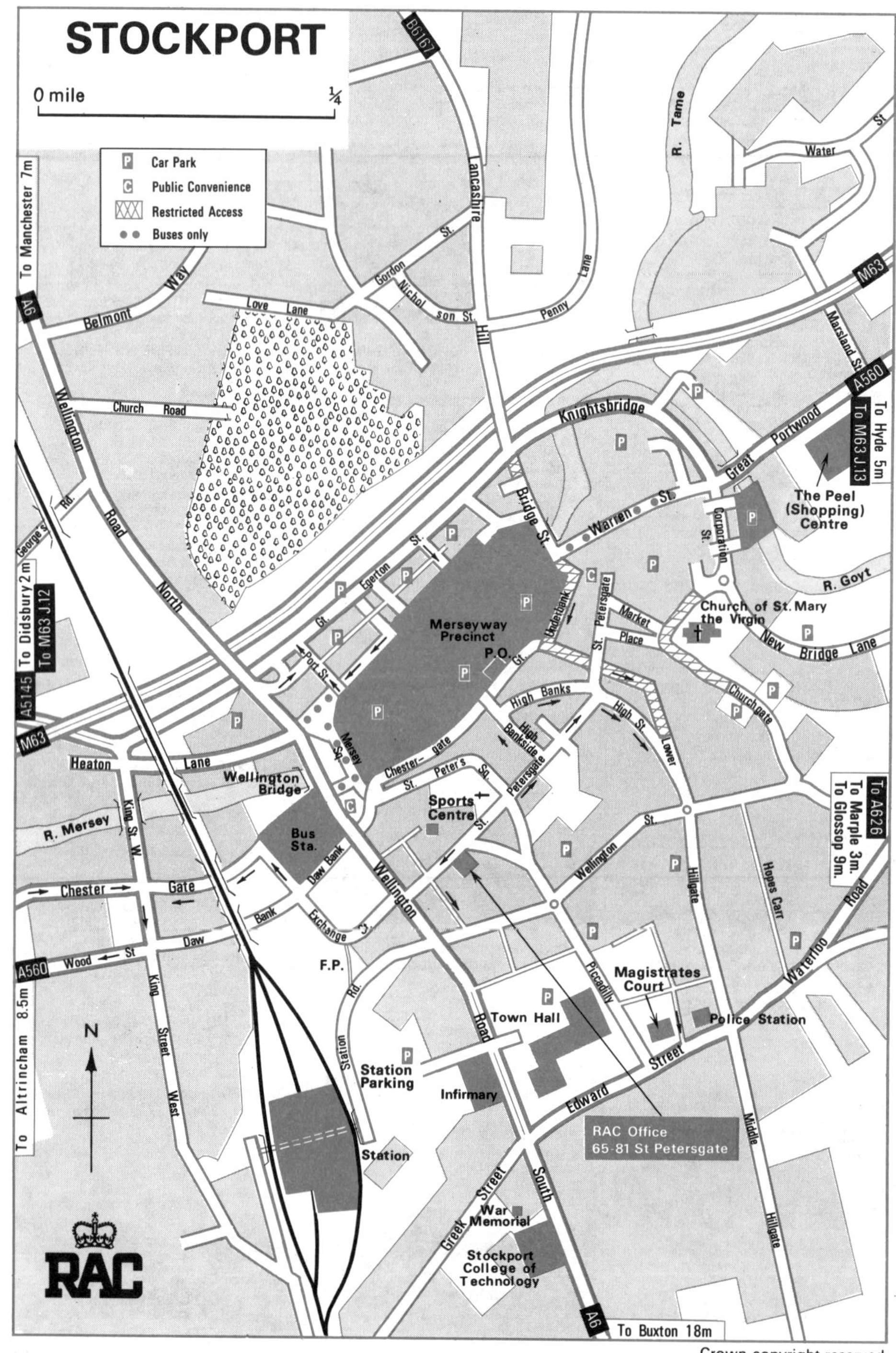
STOCKPORT
0 mile
¼
Car Park
Public Convenience
Restricted Access
Buses only
To Manchester 7m
A6
Belmont
Way
Love Lane
Gordon
St.
Nicholson St.
Lancashire
Hill
Penny
Lane
B6167
R. Tame
Water
St
M63
Marsland St.
A560
To Hyde 5m
To M63 J.13
Church Road
Wellington
Road
North
George's Rd.
To Didsbury 2m
To M63 J.12
A5145
Knightsbridge
Great
Portwood
The Peel
(Shopping)
Centre
Warren
St.
Bridge St.
Corporation
St.
R. Goyt
Egerton
St.
Gt.
Port St.
Merseyway
Precinct
P.O.
Underbank
St. Petersgate
Market
Place
Church of St. Mary
the Virgin
New Bridge Lane
Churchgate
High Banks
High St.
Lower
High
Bankside
Petersgate
Mersey
Sq.
Chester-
gate
St. Peter's
Sq.
Sports
Centre
St.
Heaton
Lane
Wellington
Bridge
King St. W
R. Mersey
Bus
Sta.
Daw Bank
Wellington
Chester
Gate
Bank
Exchange
Daw
Wood
St
A560
King
Street
West
To Altrincham 8.5m
F.P.
Station
Rd.
Road
Wellington
St.
Hillgate
Hopes Carr
Waterloo
Road
To A626
To Marple 3m.
To Glossop 9m.
Piccadilly
Magistrates
Court
Police Station
Town Hall
Station
Parking
Infirmary
Edward
Street
RAC Office
65-81 St Petersgate
Station
Greek Street
South
War
Memorial
Stockport
College of
Technology
Middle
Hillgate
A6
To Buxton 18m
N
RAC

On A6, a red-brick building with purpose-built extension. Fr, De, It, Es, Po (Emb)
58 bedrs, 52 en suite, 2 ba; TV; tcf
dogs, ns; P 200, coach; child facs; con 250
LD 9.30, bar meals only Sat lunch
£ B&B £66·50–£76·50 (w/e £24·50), B&B (double) £86–£97; L £11, D £11, WB £29 (HB, 2 nts min)
cc Access, Amex, B'card/Visa, CB, Diners.

★★ Rudyard Toby, 271 Wellington Rd North, SK4 5BP 061-432 2753
Off A6, pleasant hotel in converted residences with attractive pillared and stepped entrances.
21 bedrs, 21 en suite; TV; tcf
dogs, ns; P 82, coach; child facs; con 100

★ Acton Court, 187 Buxton Rd, SK2 7AB 061-483 6172 Fax: 061-483 0147

Well-established hotel ideally positioned near A6.
37 bedrs, 28 en suite, 3 ba; TV; tcf
TV, dogs; P 200; coach; child facs; con 180
LD 10, bar meals only Sat lunch
£ B&B £35–£46 (w/e £26), B&B (double) £49–£60; L £5·95, D £9·50
cc Access, Amex, B'card/Visa, Diners.

Ascot House, 195 Wellington Rd North, SK4 2PB 061-432 2380 Tx: 666514; Fax: 061-443 1936. *Hotel.*
£ B&B £25–£33 (w/e £15)

STOCKTON-ON-TEES Teesside, Cleveland. Map 45A1

Pop 86,800. Thirsk 22, London 243, Darlington 11, Durham 19, Middlesbrough 4, Northallerton 19, Sunderland 26.
EC Thur. **MD** Wed, Fri, Sat. **Golf** Eaglescliffe 18h. **See** 18th cent Town Hall, Preston Hall, Darlington and Stockton Rly Museum.
Theatre Yard, off High Street (0642) 615080

★★★★ Swallow, 10 John Walker Sq, TS18 1AQ (0642) 679721 Tx: 587895 Fax: (0642) 601714

Six-storey purpose-built luxury hotel in centre of town redevelopment. Indoor swimming pool, sauna, solarium, gymnasium. (Sw)
124 bedrs, 124 en suite; TV; tcf
lift, dogs, ns; P 400, coach; child facs; con 300
LD 10.30, coffee shop only Sat lunch
£ B&B £68, B&B (double) £86; L £10·50, D £14·75; WB £85 (HB)
cc Access, Amex, B'card/Visa, CB, Diners.

★ Claireville, 519 Yarm Rd, Eaglescliffe, TS16 9BG Eaglescliffe (0642) 780378
Large 3-storey late Victorian villa set in own grounds.

STOKE CANON Devon. Map 3C3

Tiverton 10, London 173, M 5 (jn 29) 4, Crediton 8, Exeter 5.

★★★ H C R Barton Cross, Huxham, EX5 4EJ (0392) 841245 Tx: 42603 Fax: (0392) 50402

Attractive part thatched cottage, with new extension in keeping, in well-tended garden.
6 bedrs, 6 en suite; TV; tcf
dogs; P 24; child facs; con 10
LD 9.30. Resid & Rest lic
£ B&B £63–£69 (w/e £47); B&B (double) £77–£83; HB weekly £315; D £18·50; WB
cc Access, Amex, B'card/Visa, Diners.
(See advertisement on p. 246)

STOKE FLEMING Devon. Map 3C1

Pop 992. Dartmouth 3, London 208 (Fy 202), Kingsbridge 12.
Golf Churston 18h.

★★★ Stoke Lodge, nr. Dartmouth, TQ6 0RA (0803) 770523
Small hotel in Devon village enjoying fine sea and country views. Indoor and outdoor swimming pool, putting, tennis, sauna, solarium, gymnasium.
24 beds, 24 en suite; TV; tcf
dogs, ns; P 60; child facs; con 100
LD 9. Resid & Rest lic
£ B&B £37, B&B (double) £59–£62; L £7·25, D £12·50; WB £64; [10% V w/d Oct–May]; dep.

STOKE GABRIEL Devon. Map 3C2

Pop 1,169. Torquay 6, London 221, Dartmouth 7, Totnes 4.
Golf Churston 18h.

★★★ H Gabriel Court, Stoke Hill, TQ9 6SF (080 428) 206

Attractive white-faced country house in Elizabethan garden. Fine views. Swimming pool. Closed Feb.
18 bedrs, 18 en suite, 1 ba; annexe 2 bedrs, 2 en suite; TV; tcf
TV, dogs; child facs; con 20
LD 8.30, nr Mon–Sat lunch. Resid lic
£ B&B £40–£50, B&B (double) £70–£80; HB weekly £350–£400; L £10, D £18·75
cc Access, Amex, B'card/Visa, Diners.

STOKE-ON-TRENT Staffordshire. Map 30B2

Comprising BURSLEM, FENTON, HANLEY, LONGTON, STOKE-UPON-TRENT and TUNSTALL and *including* BUCKNALL, CORBRIDGE, HANFORD, MEIR and TRENTHAM.
See also NEWCASTLE-UNDER-LYME.
Pop 250,000. Lichfield 29, London 152, M6 (jn 15) 3, Ashbourne 22, Congleton 13, Leek 11, Newcastle-under-Lyme 2, Newport 21, Sandbach 13, Stone 8, Uttoxeter 15.
See Plan, p. 456.
EC Thur. **MD** Wed, Fri, Sat. **Golf** Burslem 9h, Trentham Park 18h. **See** STOKE-UPON-TRENT: Josiah Wedgwood and Colin Minton Monuments, St Peter's Church, Town Hall. BURSLEM: St John's Church part 16th cent, Royal Doulton Works (viewable by appt). HANLEY: Museum and Art Gallery. SMALLTHORNE: Ford Green Hall. TRENTHAM: Trentham Gdns.
1 Glebe St. (0782) 411222

★★★ H C Hanchurch Manor, Hanchurch, ST4 8SD (0782) 643030 Fax: (0782) 643035
19th-century Tudor-style manor house with tall chimneys and stone-mullioned windows, set on high ground overlooking a lake. Fishing. It, Es
7 bedrs, 7 en suite, annexe 5 bedrs, 5 en suite; TV; tcf.
ns; P 30, coach, con 14
LD 9.30. Rest lic
£ B&B £71–£85 (w/e £55), B&B (double) £105–£125, L £11–£13, D £19; [10% V]
cc Access, Amex, B'card/Visa, Diners.

★★ Crown, Times Sq, Longton, ST3 1HD (0782) 599343, Fax: (0782) 598062

Recently developed hotel in red-brick Victorian building on corner opposite railway station. De
40 bedrs, 40 en suite; TV; tcf
P 38, coach, child facs; con 120
LD 10
£ B&B £39·50 (w/e £22·50), B&B (double) £51, L fr £5, D fr £6·50; [5% V]
cc Access, Amex, B'card/Visa, Diners; dep.

★ Central, 86 Wellesley St, Shelton (0782) 272380

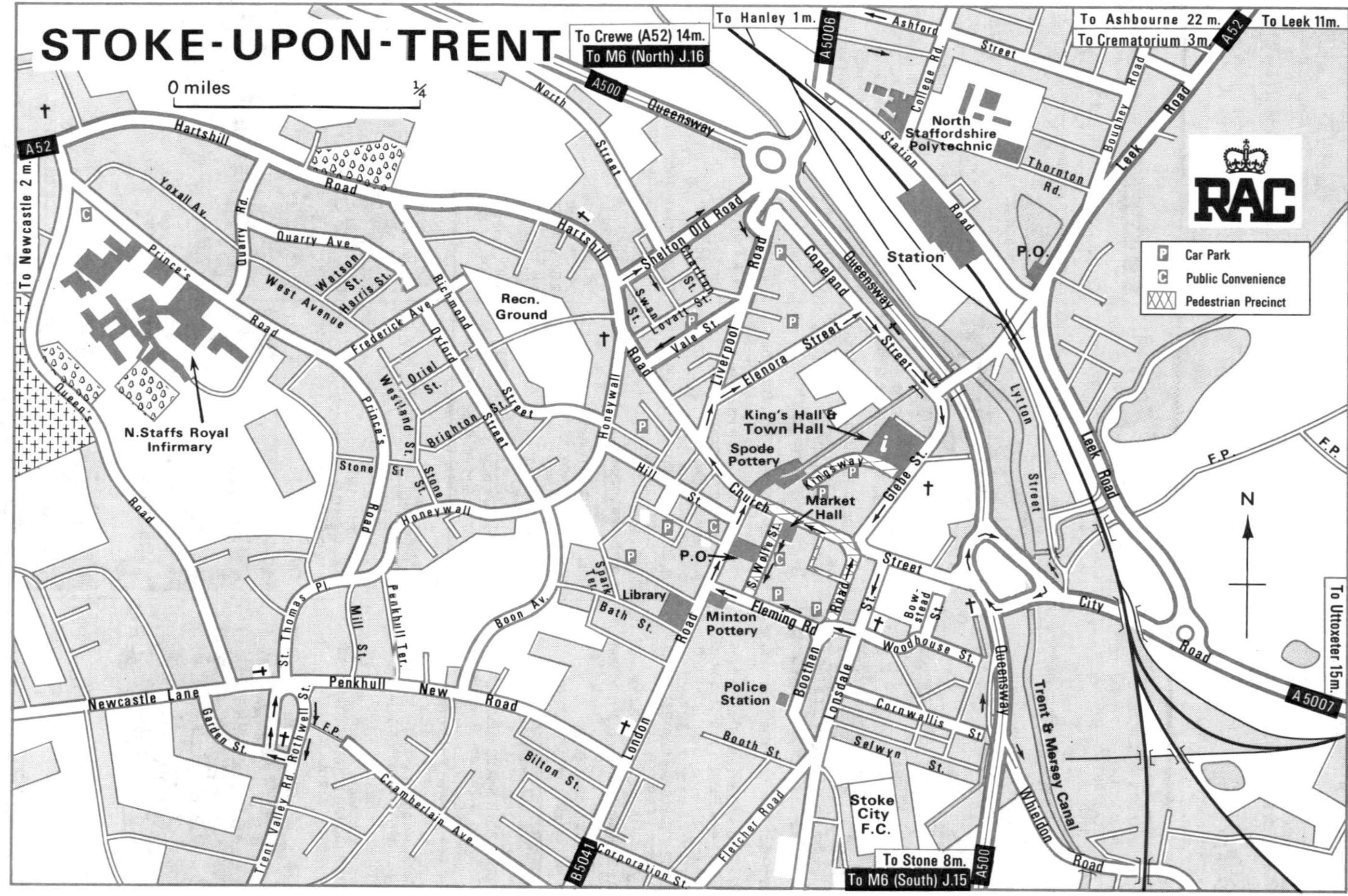

STOKE-UPON-TRENT
0 miles
1/4
To Crewe (A52) 14m.
To M6 (North) J.16
To Hanley 1m.
A5006
To Ashbourne 22 m.
To Crematorium 3m.
A52
To Leek 11m.
A500
RAC
Car Park
Public Convenience
Pedestrian Precinct
N
To Uttoxeter 15m.
A5007
To Stone 8m.
To M6 (South) J.15
A500
B5041
To Newcastle 2 m.
A52
Leek Road
Trent & Mersey Canal
Queensway
Whieldon Road
City Road
Lytton Street
Station
Station Road
North Staffordshire Polytechnic
Thornton Rd.
Boughey Road
College Rd.
Ashford Street
P.O.
Copeland Street
Glebe St.
Kingsway
King's Hall & Town Hall
Market Hall
Spode Pottery
Church Street
Liverpool Road
Shelton Old Road
Elenora Street
Vale St.
Lovatt St.
Charlton St.
Swan St.
Hill St.
S. Wolfe St.
Fleming Rd
Minton Pottery
Library
Bath St.
Spark Ter.
Bow-stead St.
Woodhouse St.
Cornwallis St.
Selwyn St.
Lonsdale
Boothen Road
Stoke City F.C.
Police Station
Booth St.
Fletcher Road
Corporation St.
London Road
Honeywall
Hartshill Road
North Street
Recn. Ground
Richmond Street
Oxford St.
Oriel St.
Brighton Street
Westland St.
Stone St.
Boon Av.
Bilton St.
Penkhull New Road
Cramberlain Ave.
Penkhull Ter.
Mill St.
Prince's Road
Frederick Ave.
Harris St.
Watson St.
Quarry Ave.
West Avenue
Quarry Rd.
Yoxall Av.
St. Thomas Pl.
Rothwell St.
Trent Valley Rd.
Garden St.
Newcastle Lane
N.Staffs Royal Infirmary
Queen's Road
F.P.
Crown copyright reserved

Converted from a terrace of red-brick Victorian houses close to centre of town.

STONE Hereford & Worcester. Map 22A1

Pop 609. Bromsgrove 7, London 120, Kidderminster 2½, Stourbridge 8. **Golf** Kidderminster 18h. **See** Church.

★★★★ **Stone Manor,** nr Kidderminster, DY10 4PJ ☎Chaddesley Corbett (056 283) 555 Tx: 335661 Fax: (056 283) 834
Large country residence in pleasant grounds near Kidderminster. Swimming pool, putting, tennis. Es, It, Po
53 bedrs, 53 en suite; TV; tcf
TV, dogs; P 400, coach; child facs; con 150
LD 10
£ B&B £67·75–£77·90 (w/e £50), B&B (double) £88–£100·50; L £19·25; WB £95·90 (min 2 nts); [10% V]
cc Access, Amex, B'card/Visa, Diners.

STONE Staffordshire. Map 30B2

Pop 13,600. Lichfield 21, London 138, Nantwich 20, Newcastle-under-Lyme 8½, Newport 14, Stafford 7½, Stoke-on-Trent 8, Uttoxeter 13, Whitchurch 24.
EC Wed. **MD** Tue, Sat. **Golf** Stone 9h.

★★★ **Stone House,** ST15 0BQ ☎(0785) 815531 Tx: 367404 Fax: (0785) 814764 ♿

Regency country house in landscaped garden converted into hotel. Swimming pool, putting, tennis, sauna, solarium, gymnasium. (Lns)
50 bedrs, 50 en suite; TV; tcf
ns; P 100, coach; child facs; con 250
LD 10
£ B&B £74, B&B (double) £87; L £8·95, D £14; WB £54; [10% V]
cc Access, Amex, B'card/Visa, Diners.

★★★ **Crown Osprey,** High St, ST15 8AS ☎(0785) 813535
18th century coaching inn with oak panelled restaurant and modern facilities.
13 bedrs, 13 en suite; annexe 16 bedrs, 16 en suite; TV; tcf
dogs; P 200, coach; child facs

STONEHOUSE Gloucestershire. Map 20B2

Stroud 2½, London 102, M5 (jn 13) 2½, Bristol 28, Gloucester 10.

★★★ C **Stonehouse Court,** Bristol Rd, GL10 3RA (2 miles W on A419) ☎(0453) 825155 Fax: (0453) 824611

17th century manor of Cotswold stone in attractive and secluded gardens. Snooker.
37 bedrs, 37 en suite; TV; tcf
P 150; coach; child facs; con 150
LD 9.30
£ B&B fr £67·50, B&B (double) fr £80; L £10·50, D £17·50; WB £98·50
cc Access, B'card/Visa.
(*See advertisement on p. 458*)

STONY STRATFORD

Buckinghamshire. Map 21B3
Pop 5,270. Bletchley 7½, London 54, Aylesbury 18, Bedford 19, Buckingham 8, Northampton 14, Towcester 7½.
EC Thur. **Golf** Abbey Hill 18h.

★★ **Cock,** High St, Milton Keynes, MK11 1AH ☎Milton Keynes (0908) 567733 Fax: (0908) 562109
Historic former coaching inn, rebuilt in Georgian times, and famed in folklore. Fr
20 beds, 9 en suite, 2 ba; annexe 8 bedrs, 8 en suite, TV; tcf
dogs; P 50, coach; child facs; con 30
LD 9.45, bar meals only Mon–Sat lunch & Sun dinner.
£ B&B £35–£60 (w/e £25), B&B (double) £45–£65; L £7·95, D £12·50
cc Access, Amex, B'card/Visa, Diners.

STORRINGTON West Sussex. Map 6B2

Pop 5,000. Horsham 15, London 51, Arundel 8½, Bognor Regis 15, Brighton 17, Chichester 16, Pulborough 5, Worthing 9½.
EC Wed. **Golf** West Sussex 18h.

★★★ H R **Abingworth Hall,** Thakeham, RH20 EF ☎(0798) 813636. Tx: 877835 Fax: (0798) 813914

Edwardian country house set in lovely grounds including a lake. Swimming pool, golf, putting, tennis, fishing. Closed 1–15 Jan.
21 bedrs, 21 en suite; TV
ns; P 40; children over 10, con 40
LD 9
£ B&B £58–£70, B&B (double) £80–£135; HB weekly £395–£551; L £14·50, D £25; WB £120
cc Access, Amex, B'card/Visa, Diners; dep.

★★★ **Little Thakeham,** Merrywood La, RH20 3HE ☎(0903) 744416, Fax: (0903) 745022
Beautiful Lutyens house set in a lovely Jekyll garden. Swimming pool, tennis. Closed 24 Dec–4 Jan.
9 bedrs, 9 en suite, TV
P 40, coach, con 15
LD 9, nr Sun dinner.
£ B&B £75–£100, B&B (double) £140–£155, L £18·50, D £27·50
cc Access, Amex, B'card/Visa, Diners; dep.

STOURBRIDGE W. Midlands. Map 22A1

Pop 55,000. Birmingham 11, London 122, Bridgnorth 13, Bromsgrove 9½, Kidderminster 7, Wolverhampton 10.

★★ **Talbot,** High St, DY8 1DW ☎(0384) 394350 Tx: 335464 Fax: (0384) 371318

Attractive former coaching inn situated in the town centre. Fr, Es
25 bedrs, 25 en suite; TV; tcf
dogs, P 25; coach; child facs; con 150
LD 9.30, nr Sun dinner
£ B&B £53·35 (w/e £25), B&B (double) £69·30; L £4·95, D £11·75; WB £28; [10% V w/e]
cc Access, Amex, B'card/Visa.

Limes, 260 Hagley Rd, Pedmore, DY9 0RW ☎Hagley (0562) 882689. *Hotel.*

STOURPORT-ON-SEVERN Hereford & Worcester (Worcestershire). Map 20B4

Pop 19,054. Bromsgrove 11, London 124, Birmingham 20, Bromyard 17, Kidderminster 3½, Leominster 31, Ludlow 21, Worcester 11.
EC Wed. **MD** Fri. **Golf** Littlelakes 9h.
i Library County Buildings, Worcester St. ☎Stourport (029 93) 2866

★★★ **Stourport Moat House,** 35 Hartlebury Rd, DY13 9LT ☎(0299) 827733 Tx: 333676 Fax: (0299) 378520

Former residence of Stanley Baldwin, now a modernised and extended hotel.

Stow-on-the-Wold (Gloucestershire)

WYCK HILL HOUSE
Country Hotel and Restaurant

This lovely 18th Century Manor House is set in almost 100 acres of grounds in this area of outstanding natural beauty in the heart of the Cotswolds. The hotel has over thirty de-luxe bedrooms and the elegant lounges and restaurant provide a gracious atmosphere in which to relax and enjoy Ian Smith's fine classical cuisine.

Prices – Lunch from £7.50; Dinner from £27.50. TDH and ALC available. Accommodation from £65 single/£80 double. Children are welcome over 6 years of age. *Dogs by arrangement only.*

Stow-on-the-Wold Gloucestershire GL54 1HY
Tel: 0451 31936 Fax: 0451 32243 Telex: 43611

Stow-on-the-Wold (Gloucestershire)

STOW LODGE HOTEL
The Square, Stow-on-the-Wold
Nr Cheltenham GL54 1AB Tel: 0451 30485

Privately owned, family run, Cotswold Manor House Hotel, set back in its own gardens in a secluded corner of the Market Square. Comfortable bedrooms with private baths and showers, colour TV, radio and tea/coffee making facilities. Restaurant with a Table d'Hôte and A la Carte Menu featuring traditional English cooking. Light meals and snacks are served in the Hotel bar or on the Hotel lawns, weather permitting, every lunchtime and evening. Full central heating throughout the Hotel with log fires in the bar and lounge. Car Park.

Stratford-upon-Avon (Warwickshire)

ETTINGTON PARK HOTEL
Alderminster, Stratford-upon-Avon CV37 8BS
Tel: (0789) 740740

There are few hotels in England to match the grandeur of Ettington Park. The 48 luxury bedrooms including 9 suites have been carefully created within the Grade 1 neo-Gothic Stately Home. The Dining Room offers some of the finest English and French cuisine and overlooks the Victorian Gardens which are incorporated within the 40 acres of outstanding parkland and meadows.

To shake off the rigours of everyday life, relax within the hotel's indoor swimming pool, spa bath, sauna and sunbed; whilst for those whose thoughts turn to outdoors, the hotel offers fishing, tennis, croquet, horse-riding and clay pigeon shooting.

Situated 5 miles south of Stratford-upon-Avon, off the A34.

Swimming pool, putting, tennis, squash, sauna, gymnasium, billiards. Pol, Fr, De, Yu. (QMH)
68 bedrs, 68 en suite; TV; tcf
dogs; ns; P 400, coach; child facs; con 350
LD 9 45, bar meals only Sat lunch
£ B&B £60–£70, B&B (double) £70–£80; HB weekly £315–£385, L £10·50, D £12·50; WB £40; [5% V]
cc Access, Amex, B'card/Visa, Diners.

STOW-ON-THE-WOLD Gloucestershire. Map 20C2
Pop 1,652. Chipping Norton 9, London 84, Burford 10, Cheltenham 18, Cirencester 19, Evesham 16, Moreton-in-Marsh 4½.
EC Wed. **Golf** Broadway 18h. **See** Town Hall, St Edward's Church, St Edward's Hall, Cotswold Farm Park (Guiting Power).
ℹ Talbot Court (0451) 31082

★★★★ Wyck Hill House, Burford Rd, GL54 1HY Cotswold (0451) 31936 Tx: 43611 Fax: (0451) 32243

Gracious 2-storey Cotswold stone manor in acres of woods, lawns and gardens. Fr
16 bedrs, 16 en suite, annexe 15 bedrs, 15 en suite; TV.
lift, dogs, TV, P 100, coach, children over 6; con 40
LD 9.30
£ B&B £85–£100, B&B (double) £100–£175, L fr £8, D £29, WB £135; [10% V w/e]
cc Access, Amex, B'card/Visa, Diners.
(*See advertisement on p. 458*)

★★★ Unicorn Crest, Sheep St, GL54 1HQ Cotswold (0451) 30257 Tx: 437186 Fax: (0451) 31090
A 16th century former coaching inn of Cotswold stone in town centre. (Cr/THF) Fr, Du
20 bedrs, 20 en suite; TV; tcf
TV, dogs, ns; P 50, child facs; con 12
LD 9.30
£ B&B £66·95–£78·95, B&B (double) £86·90–£98·90; L £9·95, D £14·95, WB £44; [5% V w/d]
cc Access, Amex, B'card/Visa, Diners.

★★ Fosse Manor, Fosseway GL54 1JX Cotswold (0451) 30354 Fax: (0451) 32486.
Attractive manor house peacefully set in its own grounds. Solarium. De, Es, Gr. Closed 12 Dec–5 Jan
14 bedrs, 14 en suite, 2 ba; annexe 6 bedrs, 5 en suite, 2 ba; TV; tcf.
dogs, ns; P 60+, coach, child facs, con 36.
LD 9.30
£ B&B £45, B&B (double) £76–£96; HB weekly £320; L fr £16·95, D fr £16·95; [5% V w/d]
cc Access, Amex, B'card/Visa, Diners; dep.

★★ Grapevine, Sheep St, GL54 1AU Cotswold (0451) 30344, Fax: (0451) 32278

Charming 17th century small hotel with a live grapevine in the restaurant. Fr. Closed 25 Dec–10 Jan
17 bedrs, 17 en suite; TV; tcf
dogs, ns; P 17; child facs; con 10
LD 9.30
£ B&B £57–£72, B&B (double) £78–£106; HB weekly fr £269·50; L £7·25, D £16·95, WB £89 (2 nts HB); [10% V]
cc Access, Amex, B'card/Visa, Diners; dep.

★★ C Stow Lodge, The Square, Cheltenham, GL54 1AB Cotswold (0451) 30485

A house of Cotswold stone in own pleasant grounds overlooking the square. Closed 21 Dec–31 Jan
12 bedrs, 10 en suite, 1 ba; annexe 10 bedrs, 10 en suite; TV; tcf
ns; P 30; no children under 5
LD 9, bar meals only lunch
£ B&B £33–£45, B&B (double) £47–£75; D £12·50
cc Amex, Diners; dep.
(*See advertisement on p. 458*)

Cross Keys Cottage (Acclaimed), Park St, GL54 1AQ Cotswold (0451) 31128. *Guest House.*
Limes (Acclaimed), Tewkesbury Rd, GL54 1EN Cotswold (0451) 30034. *Guest House.* Closed Xmas & New Year.
£ B&B (double) £26–£32

Royalist, Digbeth St, GL54 1BN Cotswold (0451) 30670
£ B&B £25–£35

STRATFORD-UPON-AVON
Warwickshire. Map 20C3
See also ABBOTS SALFORD & CHARLECOTE
Pop 21,220. Oxford 39, London 93, Banbury 20, Birmingham 23, Chipping Norton 21, Evesham 14, Moreton-in-Marsh 16, Warwick 8, Worcester 27.
See Plan, p. 460.
EC Thur. **MD** Tue, Fri. **P** See Plan. **Golf** Stratford-upon-Avon 18h. **See** Shakespeare's birthplace (Henley St), (tomb in Holy Trinity Church), Royal Shakespeare Theatre and Museum, New Place (foundations of Shakespeare's last home preserved in an Elizabethan garden, Nash's House, New Place Museum, adj), Hall's Croft, Elizabethan Garrick Inn and other old inns, Town Hall, Grammar School (in Guildhall), Anne Hathaway's Cottage (Shottery), Charlecote Park, 4 m E.
ℹ Judith Shakespeare's House, 1 High St. (0789) 293127

★★★★ Moat House International, Bridgefoot, CV37 6YR (0789) 414411 Tx: 311127 Fax: (0789) 298589

Overlooking the river Avon, a modern hotel situated in centre of town. Indoor swimming pool, sauna, solarium, gymnasium, billiards. De. (QMH)
249 bedrs, 249 en suite; TV; tcf
lift, TV, dogs; ns; P 350, coach; child facs; con 420
LD 11
£ B&B £75 (w/e £52·50, £42·50 Jul–Aug), B&B (double) £99, L £10·75, D £12·95; [10% V]
cc Access, Amex, B'card/Visa, Diners.

★★★★ Shakespeare, Chapel St, CV37 6ER (0789) 294771 Tx: 311181 Fax: (0789) 415411

Ancient timbered building convenient for theatre. Open fires in winter. (THF)
70 bedrs, 70 en suite; TV; tcf
lift, dogs, ns; P 45, coach; child facs; con 100
LD 10
£B&B £83·50, B&B (double) fr £118; HB weekly fr £375; L £11, D £16, WB £62 (2 nts min)
cc Access, Amex, B'card/Visa, CB, Diners.

Changes made after July 1990 are not included.

S

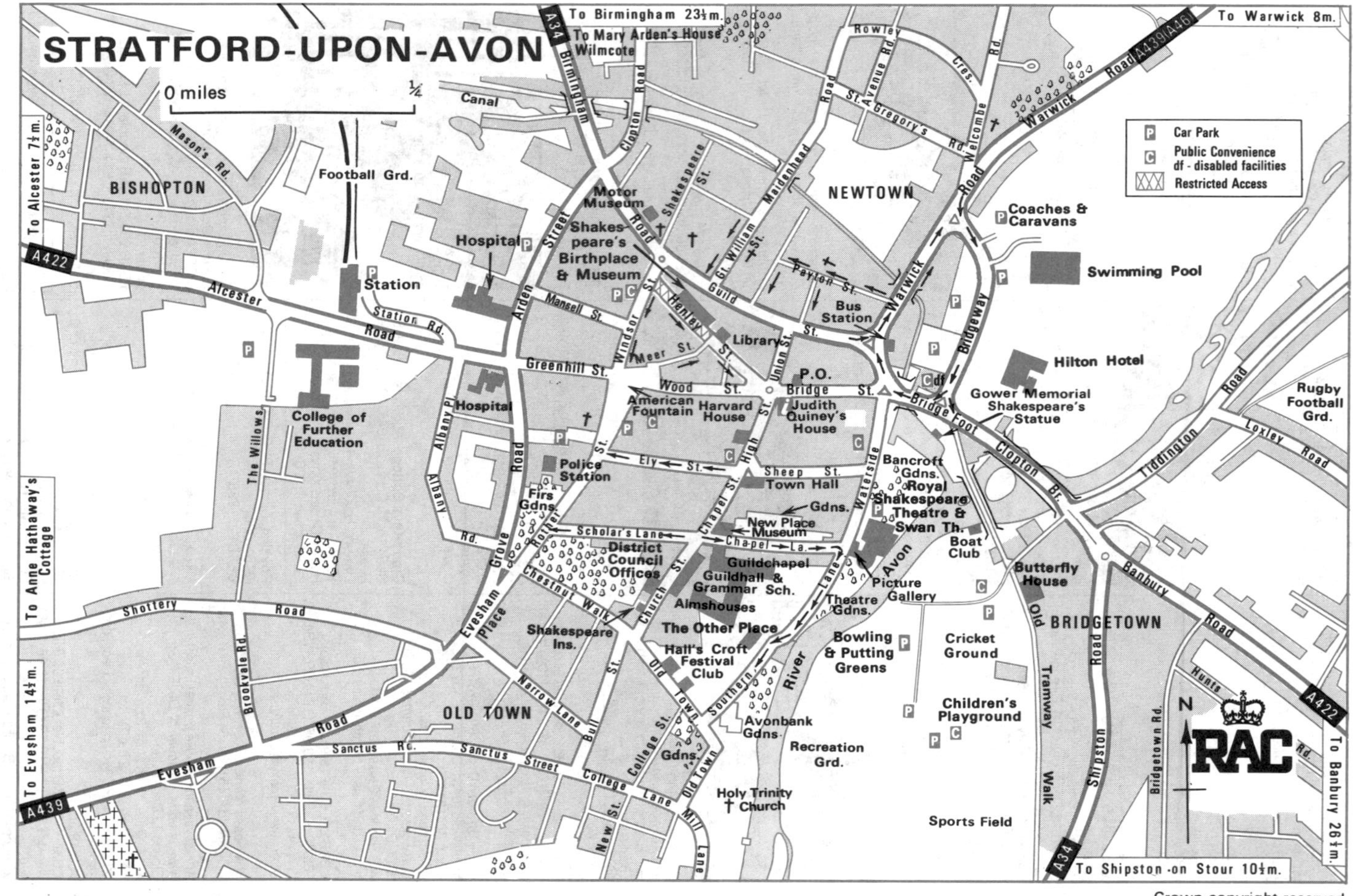

EC *early closing* **MD** *market day* *country house hotel* *ns (NS) no smoking areas* *tcf tea/coffee facilities*

★★★★ R Welcombe, Warwick Rd, CV37 0NR (0789) 295252 Tx: 31347 Fax: (0789) 414666

Fine large country mansion in extensive grounds. Two golf courses. Putting, tennis, fishing, billiards. Fr, De, Es, It. Closed Dec 28–Jan 2
76 bedrs, 76 en suite; TV
dogs; P 100, U 5, coach; child facs; con 150
LD 9.30
£ B&B £85–£190, B&B (double) £120–£190; L £15, D £27; WB £160 (2nts HB)
cc Access, Amex, B'card/Visa, Diners; dep.

★★★ Alveston Manor, Clopton Bridge, CV37 7HP (0789) 204581 Tx: 31324 Fax: (0789) 414095

Well-furnished timbered manor house with modern extensions, pleasant grounds. Putting. Fr, De. (THF)
108 bedrs, 108 en suite; TV; tcf
dogs, ns; P 200, coach; child facs; con 200
LD 9.30
£ B&B £84–£100 (w/e £56), B&B (double) £105–£135; L £12, D £17·75
cc Access, Amex, B'card/Visa, CB, Diners.

★★★Arden, 44 Waterside, CV37 6BA (0789) 294949 Tx: 3117269

A hotel, partly Regency, with modern extensions. Opposite the theatre.

Atlas Section
Consult the Atlas section at the back of the guide to find out which towns and villages have RAC Appointed and Listed hotels in them. They are shown on the maps by purple circles.

★★★ R Billesley Manor, Billesley, nr Alcester, B49 6NF (0789) 400888. Tx: 312599 Fax: (0789) 764145

Elizabethan country house with elegant furnishings. Indoor swimming pool, putting, tennis. Fr (QMH)
41 bedrs, 41 en suite, TV; tcf
P 100, coach, child facs; con 100
LD 9.30
£ B&B £95 (w/e £49), B&B (double) £117; L £17, D £23
cc Access, Amex, B'card/Visa, Diners.

★★★ Falcon, Chapel St, CV37 6HA (0789) 205777 Tx: 312522 Fax: (0789) 414260

An ancient black and white inn with modern extensions. Fr, De. Closed 23–30 Dec.
73 bedrs, 73 en suite; TV; tcf
lift, ns; dogs; P 95, G 25, coach; child facs; con 200
LD 9
£ B&B £60–£75, B&B (double) £85–£95; L £15, D £16; WB £46; [10% V]
cc Access, Amex, B'card/Visa, Diners; dep.

★★★ Grosvenor House, Warwick Rd, CV37 6YT (0789) 269213 Tx: 311699 Fax: (0789) 266089

A hotel in 2-storey white Georgian buildings. Closed 24–26 Dec.
51 bedrs, 51 en suite; TV; tcf
P 50, coach; child facs; con 70
LD 8.45
£ B&B £50–£60, B&B (double) £72–£82; HB weekly £280–£350; L £7, D £10·50
cc Access, Amex, B'card/Visa, Diners; dep.

★★★ Swan's Nest, Bridgefoot, CV37 7LT (0789) 66761 Fax: (0789) 414547
Located by riverside, an ancient inn with modern extensions. Fr, De. (THF)
60 bedrs, 60 en suite; TV; tcf
dogs, ns; P 80+, coach; child facs; con 150
LD 9.30. Resid lic
£ B&B £47·50–£108, B&B (double) £97·20–£153; HB weekly £273, L £8·95, D £14; WB £45 (HB)
cc Access, Amex, B'card/Visa, Diners.

★★★ White Swan, Rother St, CV37 6NH (0789) 297022. Fax: (0789) 68773
Ancient timbered building near American fountain. Interesting public rooms. (THF)
42 bedrs, 42 en suite; TV; tcf
dogs, ns; P10, coach; child facs; con 30
LD 9
£ B&B £78 (w/e £36), B&B (double) £102–£125; L fr £8·50, D fr £13·95
cc Access, Amex, B'card/Visa, Diners; dep.

★★★ H C Windmill Park, Warwick Rd, CV37 OPE (0789) 731173
New hotel, purpose-built in contemporary style round three sides of a square with a centre fountain. Two miles north east of Stratford just off A439. Indoor swimming pool, tennis, sauna, solarium, gymnasium. Fr, De
100 bedrs, 100 en suite, TV; tcf
lift, dogs, P220, coach, child facs; con 350
£ B&B £65–£75, B&B (double) £80–£88, L £8·50, D £11·50; WB £38·50 (HB)
cc Access, Amex, B'card/Visa, Diners.

★★ Coach House, 16–17 Warwick Rd, CV37 6YW (0789) 204109.
Two substantial early Victorian houses on edge of town. Fr
10 bedrs, 10 en suite, annexe 13 bedrs, 8 en suite, 2 ba; TV; tcf
dogs; ns; P 30, coach; child facs
LD 10. Resid & Rest lic
£ B&B £19–£33·40, B&B (double) £35–£79; L £10·25, D £10·25; WB £31·50; [10% V w/d]
cc Access, B'card/Visa; dep.
(*See advertisement on p. 462*)

★★ Swan House, The Green, Wilmcote, CV37 XJ (0789) 67030 Fax: (0789) 204875

Attractive building (Georgian and 19th century) adjacent to Mary Arden's house. Billiards. Es. Closed 24–28 Dec.
12 bedrs, 12 en suite; TV; tcf
P 35, coach; child facs; con 20
LD 9.30, bar meals only Mon–Sat lunch
£ B&B £32–£42, B&B (double) £52–£62, WB £62; [10% V]
cc Access, Amex, B'card/Visa.

Melita (Highly Acclaimed) 37 Shipston Rd, CV37 7LN (0789) 292432. *Private Hotel.* It
£ B&B £27–£37 [5% V w/d, Jan–May]

Twelfth Night (Highly Acclaimed), Evesham Pl, CV37 6HT (0789) 414595. *Guest House.*

Ambleside (Acclaimed), 41 Grove Rd, CV37 6PB (0789) 297239. *Guest House.*
£ B&B £14–£16; [10% V]

Stratford-upon-Avon (Warwickshire)

The Coach House Hotel

RAC ★★

16-17 Warwick Road, Stratford-upon-Avon CV37 6YW Tel: (0789) 204109 or 299468

Warm friendly hotel of Regency and Victorian period – 4 poster. CELLAR RESTAURANT.
7 min. walk Royal Shakespeare Theatre. Ideal touring Cotswolds. 2 day breaks.

Street (Somerset)

THE

wessex hotel

and

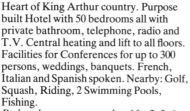

The Knight's Tavern

Grill, Carvery, Restaurant and Bar Snacks.

*** RAC

STREET SOMERSET

Telephone: Street (0458) 43383
Glastonbury – 2 miles
Wells – 8 miles
Bath – 25 miles

Heart of King Arthur country. Purpose built Hotel with 50 bedrooms all with private bathroom, telephone, radio and T.V. Central heating and lift to all floors. Facilities for Conferences for up to 300 persons, weddings, banquets. French, Italian and Spanish spoken. Nearby: Golf, Squash, Riding, 2 Swimming Pools, Fishing.

Reduced terms every weekend for 2, 3, 4 or 5 nights.

Stroud (Gloucestershire)

17th Century Manor House situated in 6 acres of secluded gardens just 1 mile from Junction 13 on the M5 mid way from Bath to Stratford on the edge of the Cotswolds. Excellent function facilities.
All rooms recently refurbished. Weekend Breaks and Christmas programme.
Egon Ronay & Michelin recommended.

Bristol Road, Stonehouse, Gloucestershire GL10 3RA. Telephone: 0453 825155
Fax: 0453 824611.

Clipper Hotels

Enjoy standards you had forgotten existed

Sutton Coldfield (West Midlands)

A luxury moated country house hotel, dating back to the 12th Century, New Hall on the edge of Sutton Coldfield is just seven miles from the centre of Birmingham and close to the NEC and international airport. With a restaurant recognised as one of the best outside London and tastefully furnished accommodation, New Hall will appeal to those who appreciate service which is discreet and exacting. The place for memorable meetings and private dining for up to 40 guests.

New Hall, Walmley Road, Sutton Coldfield, England B76 8QX
Telephone: 021-378 2442 Telex: 333580 Fax: 021-378 4637

EC *early closing* **MD** *market day* *country house hotel* *ns (NS) no smoking areas* *tcf tea/coffee facilities*

Avon View (Acclaimed) 121 Shipston Rd, CV37 7LW ☎(0789) 297542 Fax: (0789) 294550. *Private Hotel.*
Hardwick House (Acclaimed), 1 Avenue Rd, CV37 6UY ☎(0789) 204307. *Guest House.* Closed 24–26 Dec
£ [10% V]
Nando's (Acclaimed), 18 Evesham Pl, CV37 6HT ☎(0789) 204907. *Guest House.*
Victoria Spa Lodge (Acclaimed), Bishopton La, Bishopton, CV37 9QY ☎(0789) 67985. *Guest House.* Fr
£ B&B (double) fr £30
Virginia Lodge (Acclaimed), 12 Evesham Pl, CV37 6HT ☎(0789) 292157. *Guest House.*
£ B&B £14; [10% V]
Woodburn House (Acclaimed) 89 Shipston Rd, CV37 7LW ☎(0789) 204453. *Hotel.*

Cymbeline House, 24 Evesham Pl, CV37 6HT ☎(0789) 292958.
Dylan, 10 Evesham Pl, CV37 6HT ☎(0789) 204819. *Guest House.*
£ B&B £13–£19, HB weekly £151–£182
Glenavon, 6 Chestnut Walk, CV37 6HG ☎(0789) 292588. *Guest House.* Closed Xmas
£ B&B £12–£15; dep.
Marlyn, 3 Chestnut Walk, CV37 6HG ☎(0789) 293752. *Guest House.*
£ B&B £16
Parkfield, 3 Broad Walk, CV37 6HS ☎(0789) 293313. *Guest House.*
Penryn, 126 Alcester Rd, CV37 9DP ☎(0789) 293718. *Guest House.*
£ B&B £18–£30
Penshurst, 34 Evesham Pl, CV37 6HT ☎(0789) 205259. *Guest House.*
Ravenhurst, 2 Broad Walk, CV37 6HS ☎(0789) 292515. *Guest House.*

STREATLEY Berkshire. Map 12A3

Reading 9½, London 48, Basingstoke 21, Newbury 12, Wallingford 6, Wantage 14.

★★★ **H C R Swan Diplomat,** RG8 9HR ☎Goring-on-Thames (0491) 873737 Tx: 848259 Fax: (0491) 872554 ♿

With extensive riverside terraces, lawns and gardens, a lovely 300 year old building right beside the Thames. Indoor swimming pool, sauna, solarium, gymnasium. Fr, Es, Sw
46 beds, 46 en suite; TV; tcf
TV, dogs; P 145, coach; child facs; con 100
LD 9.30
£ B&B £89–£107, B&B (double) £124–£147; L £17·50, D £20·50; WB £126 (min 2 nts); [10% V]
cc Access, Amex, B'card/Visa, Diners.

STREET Somerset. Map 4C3

Pop 9,557. Glastonbury 2, London 128, Bridgwater 13, Crewkerne 23, Ilminster 21, Taunton 20, Wincanton 23.
EC Wed. **Golf** Wells (Somerset) 18h.

★★★ **Bear,** High St, BA16 0EF ☎(0458) 42021
Victorian stone-built hotel with modern bedrooms. In main street. Fr
10 bedrs, 10 en suite; annexe 5 bedrs, 5 en suite; TV; tcf
dogs, ns; P 40, coach; child facs; con 100
LD 9.30
£ B&B £30–£45 (w/e £30), B&B (double) £60–£120; L £7, D £15; WB £67·50
cc Access, Amex, B'card/Visa.

★★★ **Wessex,** High St, BA16 0EA ☎(0458) 43383 Fax: (0458) 46581 ♿
Privately-owned purpose-built modern hotel, with large bar and restaurant.
50 bedrs, 50 en suite, TV; tcf
lift, dogs; P 90, coach, child facs, con 250
LD 9.30
£ B&B £54·45 (w/e £37·50), B&B (double) £76·45; HB weekly £250, L £7·70, D £13·25, WB £68·75; [10% V]
cc Amex, B'card/Visa, Diners.
(*See advertisement on p. 462*)

STROUD Gloucestershire. Map 20B2

Pop 20,569. Cirencester 12, London 100, M5 (jn 13) 5, Bath 27, Bristol 30, Cheltenham 13, Chepstow 29, Gloucester 9, Tetbury 8½.
EC Thur. **MD** Sat. **Golf** Minchinhampton 18h. **See** 16th cent Town Hall, Museum, Art Gallery, St Lawrence's Church
Subscription Rooms ☎(0453) 765768

★★★ **Bear of Rodborough,** Rodborough Common, GL5 5DE ☎(0453) 878522 Tx: 437130 Fax: (0453) 872523

Cotswold stone building in own attractive grounds enjoying fine views. (THF)
47 bedrs, 47 en suite; TV; tcf
dogs, ns; P 200, G 12, coach; child facs; con 80
LD 9.30, bar meals only Sat lunch
£ B&B £77–£87, B&B (double) £94–£114; HB weekly £315, L £7·50, D £14; WB £45 (HB)
cc Access, Amex, B'card/Visa, CB, Diners.

★★★ **H C Burleigh Court,** Minchinhampton, GL5 2PF (2½ miles SE off A419) ☎(0453) 883804 Fax: (0453) 886870 ♿
A large country house of local Cotswold stone set in pleasant grounds. Swimming pool, putting. Fr, De, Closed 25 Dec–3 Jan.
11 bedrs, 11 en suite; annexe 6 bedrs, 6 en suite; TV; tcf
ns; P 40, G 1; coach; child facs; con 20
LD 8.45, bar meals only Sun dinner. Resid & Rest lic
£ B&B £54–£59, B&B (double) £70–£80; HB weekly £332·50–£367·50; L £10·95, D £17·25; WB £47·50 (HB)
cc Access, Amex, B'card/Visa, Diners.

Alpine lodge, Stratford Rd, GL5 4AJ ☎(045 36) 4949.

Situated near town centre. A 3-storey building with some Alpine' features.
10 bedrs, 8 en suite, (2 sh), 2 ba; TV; tcf

★★ **Bell,** Wallbridge, GL5 3JA ☎(0453) 763556
Attractive small hotel in mainly Victorian red-brick building close to town centre.
12 bedrs, 10 en suite, 1 ba, TV; tcf

★★ **Imperial,** Station Rd, GL5 3AP ☎(0453) 764077

Stone-built hotel in town centre; close to railway station. (BCB)
25 bedrs, 25 en suite; TV; tcf
ns; P 15, coach; child facs
LD 10.30
£ B&B £42–£46, B&B (double) £58; L £8·15, D £8·15; WB £27·50
cc Access, Amex, B'card/Visa, Diners.

★★ **London,** 30 London Rd, GL5 2AJ ☎(0453) 759992
Attractive, small hotel close to town centre. Well-furnished rooms.
12 bedrs, 8 en suite, 1 ba; TV; tcf
ns; P 10; no children under 2
LD 9.30, nr Sun. Resid & Rest lic
£ B&B £23–£42, B&B (double) £36–£56; HB weekly £206·50–£374·50, L £5·50, D £11·50; WB £26; dep.
cc Access, B'card/Visa; dep.

Downfield (Acclaimed), 134 Cainscross Rd, GL5 4HN ☎(0453) 764496. *Private Hotel.* Closed 25 Dec–7 Jan ♿
£ B&B £18–£28, HB weekly £189; [5% V]
cc Access, B'card/Visa; dep.

STUDLAND Dorset. Map 5A1

Pop 432. Wareham 9½, London 126 (Fy 111), Sandbanks (Fy) 3.
Golf Isle of Purbeck 18h.

★★★ **Knoll House,** Swanage Rd, BH19 3AH ☎(092 944) 251

Modern country house hotel with direct access to beach. Swimming pool, golf, putting, tennis, sauna, solarium, gymnasium. Open 28 Mar–28 Oct.
🛏 57 bedrs, 42 en suite, 10 ba; annexe 22 bedrs, 15 en suite, 3 ba
🏨 TV, dogs; P 100; child facs
✕ LD 8.15. Resid lic
£ B&B £38–£61; B&B (double) £76–£122, L £12, D £14; dep.

★★ Manor House, BH19 3AU
📞 (092 944) 288

An 18th century manor house in secluded gardens overlooking the sea. Tennis. Closed 18 Dec–31 Jan.
🛏 18 bedrs, 18 en suite; 1 ba; TV; tcf
🏨 dogs; P 40; no children under 5
✕ LD 8.30, bar meals only lunch. Resid & Rest lic
£ B&B £32–£35, B&B (double) £50·50–£60·50; HB weekly £247–£305, L £5–£7, D £16·50
cc Access, B'card/Visa; dep.

SUDBURY Suffolk. Map 27A3

Pop. 10,067, Braintree 14, London 60, Bury St. Edmunds 16, Colchester 14, Harwich 30, Haverhill 16, Ipswich 21.
EC Wed. **MD** Thur, Sat **Golf** Newton Green.
ℹ Library, Market Hill. 📞 (0787) 72092

★★★ Mill, Walnut Tree La, CO10 6BD
📞 (0787) 75544 Tx: 987623
Fax: (0787) 310033

Beautifully converted water mill and granary. Modern extension near river. Fishing. Fr
🛏 49 bedrs, 49 en suite; TV; tcf
🏨 dogs, P 60, coach; child facs; con 70
✕ LD 9.30
£ B&B £50–£60, B&B (double) £60–£75; HB weekly £267–£297; L £11, D £15·95; WB £89 (2 nts); [10% V]
cc Access, Amex, B'card/Visa, Diners.

SUMMERCOURT Cornwall. Map 2B2

Bodmin 12, London 245, Newquay 5, Redruth 14, St Austell 8, Truro 8.

Goonhoskyn Farm, TR8 4PP 📞 (0872) 510226

SUNDERLAND Tyne & Wear. Map 37C2

Pop 210,000. Stockton-on-Tees 26, London 269, Durham 13, Middlesbrough 27, Newcastle upon Tyne 12.
Golf Wearside 18h. **See** St Peter's Church.
ℹ Crowtree Leisure Centre. 📞 091-565 0960

★★★ Puffin Billy, Ocean Park, Whitburn Rd, Seaburn, SR6 8AA 📞 091-529 2020 ♿

Unusual hotel on a railway theme – the restaurant and bar are in two genuine Pullman railway carriages! Separate accommodation block.
🛏 16 bedrs, 16 en suite; TV; tcf
🏨 dogs; P, coach; child facs; con 200

★★★ Mowbray Park, Borough Rd, SR1 1PR 📞 091-567 8221
4-storey brick-built town centre hotel, with public park at rear. Fr, De, It, Es, Po
🛏 50 bedrs, 42 en suite, 6 ba; TV; tcf
🏨 lift, TV, dogs, G 26, coach; child facs; con 100
✕ LD 9.30, bar meals only lunch
£ [10% V]

★★★ Swallow (formerly Seaburn), Queen's Par, SR6 8DB 📞 091–529 2041
Tx: 53168 Fax: 091-529 4227. ♿

On seafront, 1930s hotel with modern extension. Hotel closed during major refurbishment. Completion expected February 1991. (Sw)
🛏 65 bedrs, 65 en suite; TV; tcf
🏨 lift, TV, dogs, P 100, coach; child facs; con 300
✕ LD 9.30, bar meals only Sat lunch
£ B&B £70–£75, B&B (double) £80–£100; L £9·50, D £14·50; WB £80 (2 nts HB)
cc Access, Amex, B'card/Visa, Diners.

★★ Roker, Roker Terr, SR6 0PH 📞 091-567 1786

White-painted terraced hotel overlooking the sea front. Fr. (BCB)
🛏 45 beds, 45 en suite; TV; tcf
🏨 ns; P 200, coach; child facs; con 50
✕ LD 10.30
£ B&B £42–£48, B&B (double) £54; L £8·15, D £8·15, WB £27·50
cc Access, Amex, B'card/Visa, Diners.

★ Gelt House, 23 St Bede's Terr, Christchurch, SR2 8HS 📞 091-567 2990.
Fax: 091-510 0724
Modernised victorian hotel in quiet side street near centre. Closed 25 Dec & 1 Jan.
🛏 14 bedrs, 9 en suite, (1 sh), 2 ba; annexe 8 bedrs, 8 en suite; TV; tcf
🏨 dogs; P 14; child facs
✕ LD 8.30, bar meals only lunch & Fri–Sun dinner. Resid & Rest lic
£ B&B £34 (w/e £17), B&B (double) £40, D £8; WB
cc Access, Amex, B'card/Visa, Diners.

SURBITON Greater London (Surrey). Map 8B2

See also KINGSTON UPON THAMES.
Pop 63,150. Kingston upon Thames 1½, London 11, Croydon 10, Epsom 5, Leatherhead 7, Mitcham 7, Purley 11, Ripley 11, Weybridge 7½, Woking 14.
EC Wed. **Golf** Home Park, Hampton Wick 18h, Surbiton 18h.

Amber Lodge, 54 The Avenue, KT5 8JL
📞 081-390 7360, 081-399 3058. *Guest House.*
Pembroke Lodge, 35 Cranes Park, KT5 8AB 📞 081-390 0731. *Guest House.*
£ B&B £25·30; [10% V]

SUTTON Greater London (Surrey). Map 8C1

Pop 170,000. Mitcham 3½, London 11, Croydon 4, Epsom 4½, Kingston upon Thames 6½, Purley 5, Reigate 9½.
EC Wed. **Golf** Banstead Downs 18h.

Thatched House (Acclaimed), 135 Cheam Rd, SM1 2BD 📞 081-642 3131.
Fax: 081-770 0684. *Hotel.* Fr
£ B&B £32·50–£47·50; [10% V w/e]

Ashling Tara, 50 Rosehill, SM1 3EU
📞 081-641 6142. *Hotel*
Dene, 39 Cheam Rd, SM1 2AT 📞 081-642 3170. *Hotel.*
Eaton Court, 49 Eaton Rd, SM2 5ED 📞 081-643 6766. *Hotel.* Closed 23 Dec–1 Jan.
£ B&B £30; [10% V]

SUTTON BENGER Wiltshire. Map 5A4

Swindon 16, London 93, Bristol 26, Chippenham 4, Cirencester 17.

★★★ Bell House, SN15 4RH 📞 Seagry (0249) 720401 Fax: (0249) 720401

2-storey white stone building (15th century origin) set in attractive garden. It, Ch

 EC *early closing* **MD** *market day* *country house hotel* *ns (NS) no smoking areas* *tcf tea/coffee facilities*

🛏 14 bedrs, 14 en suite; TV; tcf
🏠 dogs, ns; P 40, coach; child facs; con 40
✕ LD 10.30
£ B&B £48–£59·95, B&B (double) £74–£96, L £10, D £10; WB £55 (2 nts); [5% w/e]
cc Access, Amex, B'card/Visa, Diners.

SUTTON COLDFIELD West Midlands.
Map 22C2
See also LEA MARSTON
Pop 83,550. Coventry 19, London 113, M6 (jn 6) 4, Birmingham 7, Lichfield 8½, Newport 31, Stafford 21, Tamworth 7, Walsall 9, Warwick 23.
Golf Sutton Coldfield 18h. **See** Parish Church, Sutton Park.

★★★★ **H** **C** **Belfry,** Lichfield Rd, Wishaw, B76 9BR ☎ Curdworth (0675) 470301 Tx: 338848 Fax: (0675) 470178 ♿

Lovely Victorian house with extensions. Outstanding leisure facilities include 2 golf courses, indoor swimming pool, putting, tennis, squash, sauna, solarium, gymnasium, billiards. Fr
🛏 219 bedrs, 219 en suite; TV; tcf
🏠 lift; dogs; P 1,000; coach, child facs; con 300
✕ LD 10.30
£ B&B £99–£210 (w/e £82), B&B (double) £135–£210; L £13·75, D £18; WB £70
cc Access, Amex, B'card/Visa, Diners, dep.

★★★★ **H** **R** **New Hall,** Walmley Rd, B76 8QX ☎ 021-378 2442 Tx: 333580 Fax: 021-378 4637

Crenellated medieval manor house, reputed to be the oldest inhabited moated house in England, with extension in keeping, all lavishly refurbished. In 26 acres of grounds.
🛏 65 bedrs, 65 en suite; TV
🏠 ns; P 100, coach; no children under 8; con 50
✕ LD 10
£ room £79, double room £95; Bk £8, L £12·50, D £19·50; WB
cc Access, Amex, B'card/Visa, CB, Diners.
(*See advertisement on p. 462*)

★★★★ **Penns Hall,** Penns La, Walmley, B76 8LH ☎ 021-351 3111 Tx: 335789 Fax: 021-313 1297
Considerably extended 17th century residence in spacious grounds with lake. Indoor swimming pool, fishing, squash, sauna, solarium, gymnasium, billiards. It, Es. (Emb)
🛏 114 bedrs, 114 en suite; TV; tcf
🏠 lift, dogs, ns; P 500, coach; child facs; con 400
✕ LD 9.45
£ B&B £93–£105 (w/e £30), B&B (double) £110–£124; L £18, D £18; WB £41 (HB)
cc Access, Amex, B'card/Visa, CB, Diners.

★★★ **H** **Moor Hall,** Moor Hall Dr, B75 6LN ☎ 021-308 3751 Tx: 335127 Fax: 021-308 8974
Attractive former residence greatly extended. Adjacent to golf course. Sauna, solarium, gymnasium. Indoor swimming pool. Fr
🛏 75 bedrs, 75 en suite; TV; tcf
🏠 lift, dogs, ns; P 160, coach; child facs; con 320
✕ LD 10.30, bar meals only Sat lunch & Sun dinner
£ B&B £70–£95, B&B (double) £80–£110; L £7·95, D £16·95; WB £40 (2 nts min)
cc Access, Amex, B'card/Visa, Diners.

★★★ **Sutton Court,** 66 Lichfield Rd, B74 2NA ☎ 021-355 6071 Tx: 334175 Fax: 021-355 0083
Charming red-brick turreted Victorian building–managed by owner.
🛏 56 bedrs, 56 en suite; TV; tcf
🏠 dogs, ns; P 90, coach; child facs; con 90
✕ LD 10, bar meals only Sat lunch. Resid & Rest lic
£ B&B £75–£81, B&B (double) £98–£104 (w/e £50); L £5·95, D £13·95; WB £78 (HB 2 nts); [10% V]
cc Access, Amex, B'card/Visa, Diners.

★★ **Berni Royal,** High St, B72 1UD ☎ 021-355 8222

Refurbished, red-brick Georgian building in town centre. (BCB)
🛏 22 bedrs, 22 en suite; TV; tcf
🏠 ns; P 80; coach, child facs; con 50
✕ LD 10.50
£ B&B £48·50–£53, B&B (double) £64; L £8·15, D £8·15; WB £27·50
cc Access, Amex, B'card/Visa, Diners.

SUTTON IN THE ELMS Leicestershire.
Map 31A1
M1 (jn 20) 6, London 95, Coventry 15, Hinchly 6, Leicester 9.

Mill on the Soar, Coventry Rd, LE9 6QD. (099) (0455) 282419 Fax: (0455) 282419
Hotel awaiting inspection
🛏 20 bedrs, 20 en suite, TV, tcf.
🏠 P 120, coach; child facs, con 180
✕ LD 10
£ B&B £38, B&B (double) £46; L £12, D £12
cc Access, Amex, B'card/Visa, Diners.

SUTTON-ON-SEA Lincolnshire. Map 34C3
Pop 6,156 (inc Mablethorpe). Skegness 15, London 154, Boston 32, Grimsby 30, Horncastle 22, Louth 16.

★★★ **Grange & Links,** Sea La, Sandilands, LN12 RA ☎ (0507) 441334 Fax: (0507) 443033
1930s style building situated in quiet suburb. Golf, putting, tennis, billiards.
🛏 23 bedrs, 23 en suite; annexe 7 bedrs, 7 en suite, 1 ba; TV; tcf
🏠 TV, dogs; P 60, coach; child facs; con 300

★★ **Bacchus,** High St, LN12 2ET ☎ (0521) 41204
Hotel with painted brick frontage. Has gardens and bowling green. Putting.

Athelstone Lodge, 25 Trusthorpe Rd, LN12 2LR ☎ (0507) 441521. *Hotel.* Open Mar–Oct.
£ B&B £14–£15·50, HB weekly £216–£238; WB £38; [5% V Mar–Jun, Sep–Oct]; dep.

SWAFFHAM Norfolk. Map 35A1
Pop 4,776. Newmarket 33, London 96, East Dereham 12, Ely 26, Fakenham 16, King's Lynn 15, Thetford 18, Wisbech 26.

★★★ **George,** Station Rd, PE37 7LJ ☎ (0760) 721238 Fax: (0760) 721238
Charming William & Mary period building with modern luxury residential wing.
🛏 28 bedrs, 28 en suite, 1 ba; TV; tcf
🏠 dogs; P 100, coach; child facs; con 150
✕ LD 9.30
£ B&B £45, B&B (double) £59–£65; L 11·50, D £11·50; WB £68 (2 nts); [10% V w/e]
cc Access, Amex, B'card/Visa, Diners.

★★ **Grady's Country House,** Norwich Rd, PE37 7QS ☎ (0760) 23355
Attractive red-brick Georgian building in pleasant grounds close to town centre.
🛏 11 bedrs, 11 en suite; TV; tcf
🏠 dogs; P 80; child facs; con 200

Horse & Groom (Highly Acclaimed), 40 Lynn St, PE37 7AY ☎ (0760) 721567 ♿

SWANAGE Dorset. Map 5A1
Pop 8,647. Wareham 9½, London 126 (Fy 115), Sandbanks (Fy) 6½.
ℹ White House, Shore Rd, ☎ (0929) 422885

★★★ **Grand,** 12 Burlington Rd, BH19 1LU ☎ (0929) 423353 Tx: 94014967 Fax: (0929) 427968

Large refurbished Victorian hotel, of red brick, in secluded area. Fine sea views. Indoor swimming pool, fishing, sauna, solarium, gymnasium, snooker. Fr, It, Es
🛏 30 bedrs, 30 en suite; TV; tcf
🏠 lift, dogs; ns; P 15, coach; child facs
✕ LD 9.30
£ B&B £35–£40; L fr £6·50; D £12·95; WB £76 (HB 2 nts); [10% V w/d Oct–May]
cc Access, Amex, B'card/Visa, Diners; dep.
(*See advertisement on p. 467*)

S

★★★ **C** **R** **Pines,** Burlington Rd, BH19 1LT ☎(0929) 425211 Tx: 418297 Fax: (0929) 422075 ♿

Family-run large modern hotel in secluded position. Fine sea views. ✗ Fr
🛏 51 bedrs, 49 en suite, 1 ba; TV
🏨 lift, dogs; P 60; child facs; con 100
✕ LD 9
£ Bk £5, L £8·50, D £15; WB £38·50
cc Access, B'card/Visa; dep.
(*See advertisement on p. 467*)

★ **Suncliffe,** Burlington Rd, BH19 1LR ☎(0929) 423299
Privately-owned small residential hotel in quiet location. Near to sea.

Havenhurst (Acclaimed), 3 Cranborne Rd, BH19 1EA ☎(0929) 424224. *Hotel.*
£ B&B £17–£23·50; HB weekly £150–£186; [10% V Oct–Mar]
Sandringham (Acclaimed), 20 Durlston Rd, BH19 2HX ☎(0929) 423076. *Hotel.* Open Jan–Nov.
Seychelles (Acclaimed), Burlington Rd, BH19 1LR ☎(0929) 422794. *Private Hotel.* Open May–Sept.
£ B&B £16 [5% V May, Jun, Sep]

Bella Vista, 14 Burlington Rd, BH19 1LS ☎(0929) 422873. *Private Hotel.* Open Feb–Nov.
£ B&B (double) £32–£36
Chines, 9 Burlington Rd, BH19 1LR ☎(0929) 422457. *Hotel.* Open Apr–Nov.
£ B&B £20·13–£21·85; HB weekly £172·50–£202·40
Eversden, 5 Victoria Rd, BH19 1LY ☎(0929) 423276. *Hotel.*
Firswood, 29 Kings Rd, BH19 9HF ☎(0929) 422306. *Hotel.* Closed Xmas.
£ B&B £12·50; HB weekly £130
Glenlee, 6 Cauldon Av, BH19 1PQ ☎(0929) 425794. *Hotel.*
Monsal, 32 Victoria Ave, BH19 1AP ☎(0929) 422805 ♿
£ B&B £14·38–£24·15, HB weekly £131·10–£194·35; [5% V w/d]
Oxford, 3–5 Park Rd, BH19 2AA ☎(0929) 422247. *Hotel.* Open Feb–Nov.
£ B&B £18–£19; HB weekly £175–£182; [5% V]
St Michaels, 31 Kings Rd, BH19 1HF ☎(0929) 422064. *Guest House.*
£ B&B (double) £14–£17; HB weekly £130–£142

SWINDON Wiltshire. Map 5B4

Pop 133,000. Wantage 17, London 77, M4 (jn 15) 4½, Burford 19, Cirencester 15, Devizes 15, Faringdon 12, Marlborough 11, Oxford 29, Tetbury 19.
MD Mon, Wed, Sat. **Golf** Brome Manor 18h. **See** Railway Works, Railway Museum.
ℹ 32 The Arcade. ☎(0793) 530328

★★★★ **H** **Blunsdon House,** The Ridge, Blunsdon, SN2 4AD (4 m N A419) ☎(0793) 721701 Tx: 444491 Fax: (0793) 721701 ♿

In attractive gardens, this hotel has been greatly modernised and extended. Indoor swimming pool, putting, tennis, squash, sauna, solarium, gymnasium, snooker. ✗ Fr
🛏 89 bedrs, 89 en suite; TV; tcf
🏨 lift; P 300, coach; child facs; con 300
✕ LD 10
£ B&B £82·50–£90, B&B (double) £92·50–£100; L £10·50, D £10·50; WB £54 (HB 2 nts min); [10% V w/e]
cc Access, Amex, B'card/Visa, Diners.

★★★★ **Holiday Inn,** Pipers Way, SN3 1SH. ☎(0793) 512121 Tx: 445789 Fax: (0793) 513114

New purpose-built hotel on south-west edge of Swindon. Spacious bedrooms. Indoor swimming pool, tennis, squash, sauna, solarium, gymnasium. ✗ Fr, De. (CHIC)
🛏 158 bedrs, 158 en suite; TV; tcf
🏨 lift, dogs, ns; P 190, coach, child facs; con 250
✕ LD 10.15; bar meals only Sat lunch
£ B&B £97·50–£129·50, B&B (double) £115–£143; L £14·25, D £16·50; WB £37
cc Access, Amex, B'card/Visa, Diners; dep.

★★★ **Crest,** Oxford St, Stratton St Margaret, SN3 4TL ☎(0793) 831333 Tx: 444456 Fax: (0793) 831401 ♿

Spacious, modern purpose-built hotel in own grounds in the outskirts. (Cr/THF)
🛏 94 bedrs, 94 en suite; TV; tcf
🏨 dogs, ns; P 120, coach; child facs; con 80
✕ LD 9.45, nr Sat lunch
£ B&B £83–£96, B&B (double) £103–£117; L £12·50, D £14·95; WB
cc Access, Amex, B'card/Visa, CB, Diners.

★★★ **Goddard Arms,** High St, SN1 3EW ☎(0793) 692313 Tx: 444764 Fax: (0793) 512984

Attractive, old established inn set in the older part of the town. (THF)
🛏 65 bedrs, 65 en suite; TV; tcf
🏨 P 120, coach; child facs; con 150
✕ LD 9.30, bar meals only Sat lunch
£ B&B £79, B&B (double) £103; L £12·50, D £12·50; WB £45 (HB)
cc Access, Amex, B'card/Visa, Diners.

★★★ **H** **C** **Peartree at Purton,** Church End, Purton, SN5 9ED ☎(0793) 772100. Fax: (0793) 772369. ♿

Cotswold–stone former Vicarage, tactfully extended and set in 7½ acres of attractive lawned gardens. Three miles west of Swindon.
🛏 18 bedrs, 18 en suite; TV
🏨 P 70, child facs, con 50
✕ LD 9.30, nr Sat lunch. Resid & Rest lic
£ B&B (double) £85–£120; L £14·50, D £20·50; WB £85 (HB); [5% V w/e Aug]
cc Access, Amex, B'card/Visa, Diners.

★★★ **Post House,** Marlborough Rd, Coate, SN3 6AQ ☎(0793) 524601 Tx: 444464 Fax: (0793) 512887

Conveniently situated away from centre; modern hotel with conference facilities.

Swanage (Dorset)

Swanage (Dorset)

S

Taunton (Somerset)

Taunton (Somerset)

Indoor swimming pool, sauna, solarium, gymnasium. (THF)
104 bedrs, 104 en suite; TV; tcf
dogs, ns; P 150, coach; child facs; con 100
LD 10
£ room £73–£83 (w/e £43), double room £84–£94, Bk £8, L £10, D £13·50; WB £42 (HB)
cc Access, Amex, B'card/Visa, Diners.

★★★ **South Marston**, South Marston, SN3 4SH (0793) 827777 Tx: 444634 Fax: (0793) 827879
On outskirts of Swindon, modern purpose-built hotel. Indoor/outdoor swimming pool, squash, sauna, solarium, gymnasium, billiards.
41 bedrs, 41 en suite; TV; tcf
TV, ns; P 200, coach; child facs; con 150

★★★ **Wiltshire,** Fleming Way, SN1 1TN (0793) 528282 Tx: 444250, Fax: (0793) 541283

In town centre, a modern tall purpose-built hotel.
93 bedrs, 93 en suite; TV; tcf
lift, dogs; coach, child facs, con 200
LD 10, bar meals only Sat lunch
£ B&B £77·50–£92 (w/e £28), B&B (double) £93·50–£106; L £14·50, D £14·50; [10% V]
cc Access, Amex, B'card/Visa, Diners.

★★ **Ibis,** Delta Business Park, Gt Western Way, SN5 7XG (0793) 514777 Tx: 449310 Fax: (0793) 514570
Modern, 4-storey red-brick hotel situated in business park on western edge of Swindon. Fr
120 bedrs, 120 en suite; TV; tcf
lift, dogs, P 120, coach, child facs, con 120
LD 10.30
£ B&B £42; B&B (double) £47, L £8·75, D £8·75

★★ **Kings Arms,** Wood St, SN1 4AB (0793) 22156 Fax: (0793) 617415
Modernised and extended period coaching inn situated in the Old Town.
18 bedrs, 14 en suite; TV; tcf
dogs; P 40, coach; child facs; con 70

★★ H C **School House,** Hook St, Hook, SN4 8EF (0793) 851198 Tx: 449703 Fax: (0793) 851025

Stone-built, listed Victorian school in village on outskirts of Swindon. Fr, De, Du
10 bedrs, 10 en suite; TV; tcf
ns; P 30; child facs, con 10
LD 10, bar meals only Sat lunch
£ B&B £78, B&B (double) £86; L £13·75, D £16·50; WB £43 (HB); [10% V]
cc Access, Amex, B'card/Visa, Diners.

SYMONDS YAT Hereford & Worcester (Herefordshire). Map 20A2
Pop 350. Gloucester 20, London 125, Chepstow 17, Hereford 17, Monmouth 7, Ross-on-Wye 6½.
Golf Monmouth 18h.

★★ **Old Court,** Symonds Yat West, HR9 6DA (0600) 890367 Fax: (0600) 890964

Hotel set in pleasant garden and developed from historic building. Swimming pool.
20 bedrs, 14 en suite, 2 ba; TV; tcf
dogs, ns; P 50, coach; children over 12; con 100
LD 9.30, bar meals only lunch
£ B&B £36–£43, B&B (double) £52–£66; D £16; WB £40; [10% V]
cc Access, Amex, B'card/Visa, Diners.

★★ **Paddocks,** Symonds Yat West, HR9 6BL (0600) 890246 Fax: (0600) 890964
Largely modern hotel in pleasant grounds. River views through picture windows. Putting, tennis.
26 bedrs, 24 en suite, 1 ba; TV; tcf
dogs; coach; children over 12; con 200
LD 9.45
cc Access, B'card/Visa, Diners.

★★ **Royal,** Symonds Yat East, HR9 6JL (0600) 890238

Attractive 3-storey building with large dormers. Quiet grounds beside river. Fishing, sauna, solarium. Fr, De, It, Es
Closed Jan.
20 bedrs, 20 en suite; tcf
dogs; P 80; children over 12; con 50
LD 9.30, bar meals only Mon–Sat lunch
£ B&B £29·50, B&B (double) £59–£69; HB weekly £241·50–£276·50; L £8·75, D £15·50; WB £34·50
cc Access, Amex, B'card/Visa; dep.

Saracens Head (Highly Acclaimed), Symonds Yat East, HR9 6JL (0600) 890435. *Hotel.* Closed Xmas.

Garth Cottage (Acclaimed), Symonds Yat East, HR9 6JL (0600) 890364. *Hotel. Fishing.*

Woodlea (Acclaimed), Symonds Yat West, HR9 6BL (0600) 890206. *Hotel. Swimming pool.* Closed 16 Dec–14 Feb
£ B&B £18·50–£19·50; HB weekly £179–£199

SYWELL Northamptonshire. Map 21B3
Pop 758. M1 (jn 15) 10, London 69, Bedford 23, Bletchley 25, Kettering 9, Market Harborough 16, Northampton 6.
EC Thur. **Golf** Northampton 18h.

★★ **Sywell,** Sywell Airport, NN6 0BT Northampton (0604) 491594
Privately-owned, purpose-built motel complex in country setting.
58 bedrs, 58 en suite; TV; tcf
dogs, ns; P 100, coach; child facs; con 120
LD 9.30
£ B&B £29·50–£31·50, B&B (double) £40–£43; L £8·50, D £10
cc Access, Amex, B'card/Visa, Diners.

TAPLOW Buckinghamshire. Map 13A3
Pop 2,270. M4 (jn 7) 3, London 24, Bagshot 17, Henley-on-Thames 10, High Wycombe 9, Reading 14, Slough 4½.
EC Wed. **Golf** Burnham Beeches 18h.

★★★★★ **Cliveden,** SL6 0JF (0628) 668561 Tx: 846562 Fax: (0628) 661837

Historic house, successively the home of a Prince of Wales, three dukes and the Astor family, now the ultimate in luxurious hotels. Superb garden and parkland setting beside the Thames. Swimming pool, tennis, squash, fishing, riding, sauna. Fr, De, Es
31 bedrs, 31 en suite; TV
lift; dogs, ns; P 40; child facs; con 28
LD 9. Resid lic
£ B&B £150, B&B (doublé) fr £185; L £27, D £39·80
cc Access, B'card/Visa, Diners; dep.

TARPORLEY Cheshire. Map 29B3
Pop 1,774. Nantwich 10, London 172, Chester 11, Middlewich 13, Northwich 11, Warrington 19, Whitchurch 14
EC Wed. **Golf** Delamere Forest 18h. **See** Medieval Church, Castle ruins.

★★★ **Willington Hall,** Willington, CW6 0NB (3 miles NW of Tarporley) Kelsall (0829) 52321

EC *early closing* **MD** *market day* *country house hotel* *ns (NS) no smoking areas* *tcf tea/coffee facilities*

Early 19th century mansion built in Elizabethan style. Parkland with superb views.

TATTENHALL Cheshire. Map 29B3

Pop 1,055. Nantwich 15, London 177, Chester 9, Tarporley 6, Whitchurch 14, Wrexham 16.

Pheasant Inn, Higher Burwardsley, CH3 9DF Fax: (0829) 71097
A 300-year-old timber and sandstone inn with smart bedrooms mostly in a converted barn. Magnificent views.
2 bedrs, 2 en suite; annexe 6 bedrs, 6 en suite; TV; tcf
dogs; P 60; no children under 14
LD 9.30, bar meals only lunch
£ B&B £35 (w/e £30 2 nts min), B&B (double) £45; HB weekly £256; L £6·50, D £12; [5% V Fri–Sun]
cc Access, Amex, B'card/Visa, Diners; dep.

TAUNTON Somerset. Map 4B2

Pop 36,146. London 143, M5 (jn 25) 1½, Bridgwater 10, Dunster 22, Exeter 33, Glastonbury 22, Honiton 18, Ilminster 12. **Golf** Vivary Park 18h. Pickeridge 18h. **See** Castle, St Mary Magdalene Church, St James's Church, Priory Gatehouse, West Somerset Rly.
Library, Corporation St. (0823) 274785

★★★★ **Castle,** Castle Green, TA1 1NF (0823) 272671 Tx: 46488 Fax: (0823) 336066

Once part of a Norman fortress, an imposing hotel with interesting garden. Fr, It
35 bedrs, 35 en suite; TV
lift, dogs; P 30, G 5 (£5), coach; child facs; con 90
LD 9. Resid lic
£ L £13·90, D £24·50
cc Access, Amex, B'card/Visa, CB, Diners; dep.

★★★ **County,** East St, TA1 3LT (0823) 337651 Tx: 46484 Fax: (0823) 334517
A large Georgian hotel of character, set in centre of town. (THF)
66 bedrs, 66 en suite; TV; tcf
lift, dogs, ns; P 100, coach; child facs; con 400
LD 9.30
£ room £70 (w/e £40), room (double) £81; Bk £7; L £9·95, D £12·95
cc Access, Amex, B'card/Visa, CB, Diners.

★★★ **Crest,** Deane Gate Av, TA1 2UA (0823) 332222 Tx: 46703 Fax: (0823) 332266
New purpose-built hotel just off junction 25 of M5 overlooking countryside. Sauna, gymnasium. (Cr)
101 bedrs, 101 en suite; TV; tcf
lift, dogs, ns; P 300, coach; child facs; con 200
LD 9.45, bar meals only Sat lunch
£ room £68 (w/e £38); double room £80; D £14·60; [5% V w/e]

★★★ **Rumwell Manor,** Wellington Rd, Rumwell TA4 1EL (0823) 461902 Fax: (0823) 254861

Recently refurbished Georgian building, spacious and elegantly furnished. Situated in 5 acres of grounds on the A38 west of town. Swimming pool.
10 bedrs, 10 en suite; annexe 10 bedrs, 10 en suite; TV; tcf
TV, dogs, ns; P 30; child facs; con 40
LD 8.30. Resid & Rest lic
£ B&B £44·50–£49·50, B&B (double) £60–£75; HB weekly £250–£300; L £8·50, D £14·50
cc Access, Amex, B;card/Visa, Diners.
(See advertisement on p.467)

★★ **Corner House** R, Park St, TA1 4DQ (0823) 284683 Tx: 46288 Fax: (0823) 332276
Victorian brick-built house in Gothic style. West from town centre.
30 bedrs, 25 en suite, 3 ba; TV; tcf
(See advertisement on p. 467)

★★ H C **Falcon,** TA3 5DH (0823) 442502

Privately-owned, spacious residence standing in its own grounds. Near A358.
11 bedrs, 11 en suite; TV; tcf
dogs, ns; P 25, coach; child facs; con 40
LD 9.30, bar meals only Mon–Sat lunch & Sun dinner. Resid & Rest lic
£ B&B £39·50, B&B (double) £55; D £9·50; WB
cc Access, B'card/Visa.

★★ **Heatherington Grange,** Bradford on Tyne, TA4 1ET (0823) 461777
Modernised and extended 18th century coaching inn on the A38 between Taunton and Wellington.
17 bedrs, 17 en suite, 1 ba; TV; tcf

Meryan House (Highly Acclaimed), Bishops Hull, TA1 5EG (0823) 337445. *Private Hotel. Solarium.*
£ B&B £32–£36 (w/e £20); HB weekly £283–£290; [5% V w/e Nov–Mar]

Old Manor Farmhouse (Acclaimed), Norton Fitzwarren, TA2 6RZ (0823) 289801. *Private Hotel.* Fr, De
£ B&B £30–£32; HB weekly £273–£286

Brookfield, 16 Wellington Rd, TA1 4EQ (0823) 272786. *Guest House.*
£ B&B £13–£15, HB weekly £126–£140

White Lodge, 81 Bridgwater Rd, TA1 2DU (0823) 321112. *Hotel.*
£ B&B £27·50

TAVISTOCK Devon. Map 3A2

Pop 9,188. Exeter 33, London 202, Ashburton 20, Launceston 13, Liskeard 18, Okehampton 16, Plymouth 14, Saltash 14. **EC** Wed. **MD** Fri. **Golf** Tavistock 18h. **See** Abbey ruins (10th cent), Parish Church.
Bedford Sq. (0822) 612938

★★★ **Bedford,** Plymouth Rd, PL19 8BB (0822) 613221 Fax: (0822) 618034

Castle-like hotel, parts dating from Middle Ages. In centre of town. (THF)
31 bedrs, 30 en suite, 1 ba; TV; tcf
dogs, ns; P 34, G 6, coach; child facs; con 80
LD 9.15, bar meals only Mon–Sat lunch
£ B&B £73 (w/e £40), B&B (double) £102; L £9·50, D £13·50

TEBAY Cumbria. Map 44B1

Pop 585. Kirkby Lonsdale 18, London 264, Brough 16, Hawes 25, Kendal 12, Penrith 18.
Golf Appleby 18h.

★★★ **Tebay Mountain Lodge,** Orton, CA10 3SB Orton (058 74) 351

Light and airy modern hotel of striking design. Enjoys wide views.
30 bedrs, 30 en suite; TV; tcf
TV, dogs; P 50, coach; child facs; con 12
LD 8.30, nr lunch. Resid lic
£ B&B £27·50–£32·50 (w/e £27·50), B&B (double) £32·50–£37·50; D £9·50; [5% V first nt only]
cc Access, Amex, B'card/Visa, Diners; dep.

Carmel House (Acclaimed), Mount Pleasant, CA10 3TH (05874) 651
£ B&B £14·50–£16·50

TEDBURN ST MARY Devon. Map 3B3
Pop 690. Exeter 7, London 176, Ashburton 21, Crediton 4, Okehampton 15.
EC Thur. **Golf** Exeter 18h. **See** Church.

★ **King's Arms,** EX6 6EG (064 76) 1224

Small 17th century coaching inn in centre of village.
8 bedrs, 1 en suite (1 sh), 2 ba; TV; tcf.
dogs, P 50, coach; child facs; con 70
LD 10, bar meals only Mon–Sat lunch. Resid & Rest lic
£ B&B £17·50, B&B (double) £27; L £4·95, D £8; [5% V Mon–Wed]
cc Amex, B;card/Visa.

TEIGNMOUTH Devon. Map 3C2
See also BISHOPSTEIGNTON.
Pop 13,500 (inc Shaldon). Exeter 15, London 184, Newton Abbot 6.
EC Thur. **Golf** Teignmouth (Haldon) Ltd 18h.
[i] The Den, Sea Front. (0626) 779769

★ **Belvedere,** Barnpark Rd, TQ14 8PJ (0626) 774561

Family-run hotel in elevated position giving fine view of town and bay.
13 bedrs, 9 en suite, 2 ba; TV; tcf
TV; P 12; child facs
LD 10. Resid lic
£ B&B £15·50–£18·50; HB weekly £136·50–£157·50; L £4·60, D £6; WB
cc Access, B'card/Visa; dep.

Using RAC discount vouchers
Please tell the hotel when booking if you plan to use an RAC discount voucher (see p. 34) in part payment of your bill. Only one voucher will be accepted per party per stay. Discount vouchers will only be accepted in payment for accommodation, not for food.

★ **Coombe Bank,** Landscore Rd, TQ14 9JL (0626) 772369

Stone-built family-run hotel with grounds; in quiet area of town.
11 bedrs, 4 en suite, 2 ba; TV; tcf
TV, dogs, ns; P 10; child facs
LD 7.30, bar meals only lunch. Resid & Rest lic
£ B&B £15·50–£18, B&B (double) £31–£36; HB weekly £121–£154; D £6·50; [5% V]
cc Access, B'card/Visa; dep.

Cotteswold, Second Drive, Landscore Rd, TQ14 9JS (0626) 774662. *Hotel. Swimming pool, sauna.*
Glen Devon, 3 Carlton Pl, TQ14 8AB (0626) 772895. *Hotel.*
£ B&B £11–£12; HB weekly £90–£112; [10% V Sep–Jun]; dep.

TELFORD Shropshire. Map 29C1
See also WELLINGTON.
Pop 103,000. Wolverhampton 17, London 167, M54 (jn 6) 1, Wellington 3, Bridgnorth 12, Shrewsbury 14.
Golf Wrekin 18h. **See** Ironbridge Gorge.
[i] Shopping Centre (0952) 291370

★★★ **Buckatree Hall,** The Wrekin, Wellington, TF6 5AL (0952) 641821 Tx: 35701 Fax: (0952) 47540

Well-appointed former manor house in quiet grounds at foot of Wrekin. De
37 bedrs, 37 en suite; TV; tcf
dogs; P 110, coach; child facs; con 110
LD 10
£ B&B £59–£69, B&B (double) £69–£79; L £8·50, D £10·50; WB £72–£75 (2 nts HB); [5% V]
cc Access, Amex, B'card/Visa, Diners.

★★★ H **Madeley Court,** TF7 5DW (0952) 680068 Fax: (0952) 684275

A sandstone Tudor manor house, with beams and a turreted gatehouse, carefully restored and sympathetically furnished. In gardens and woods next to a lake. Fishing. Fr
30 bedrs, 30 en suite; TV; tcf
ns; P 120, coach; child facs; con 80
LD 10
£ B&B £65–£85, B&B (double) £90–£110; L £15·50, D £22; WB £98; [10% V w/e]

★★★ **Telford Hotel, Golf and Country Club,** Great Hay, Sutton Hill, TF7 4DT (0952) 587878 Tx: 35481 Fax: (0952) 586602

Modern hotel developed about 18th century red brick country house. Overlooks golf course and gorge. Indoor swimming pool, golf, putting, squash, sauna, snooker. (QMH) Fr
50 bedrs, 50 en suite; annexe 9 bedrs, 9 en suite; TV; tcf
dogs; P 150, coach; child facs; con 240
LD 10, nr Sat lunch
£ B&B £67·50–£77·50 (w/e £41·50), B&B (double) £78·50–£88·50; L £7·25, D £12
cc Access, Amex, B'card/Visa, Diners.

★★★ **Telford Moat House,** Foregate, Telford Centre, TF3 4NA (0952) 291291 Tx: 35588 Fax: (0952) 292012

Adjacent to Jn 5 of M54, spacious modern purpose-built hotel. Indoor swimming pool, sauna, solarium, gymnasium. Fr, De. Closed 24 Dec–2 Jan (QMH)
148 bedrs, 148 en suite; TV; tcf
lift, TV, dogs, ns; P 300, coach; child facs; con 500
LD 10, bar meals only Sat lunch
£ B&B £66–£89, B&B (double) £70–£108; L £14·75, D £14·75, WB £41 (HB)
cc Access, Amex, B'card/Visa, Diners.

Weekend breaks
Please consult the hotel for full details of weekend breaks; prices shown are an indication only. Many hotels offer mid week breaks as well.

EC *early closing* **MD** *market day* *country house hotel* *ns (NS) no smoking areas* *tcf tea/coffee facilities*

★★ **White House,** Wellington Rd, Donnington, TF2 8NG ☎(0952) 604276

2-storey white-faced building, a pleasant family-run small hotel. Fr
30 bedrs, 30 en suite; TV; tcf
dogs; P 100; child facs
LD 9.30, bar meals only Sat lunch
£ B&B £45–£55, B&B (double) £60–£65; L £7·50, D £10·50; [V]
cc Access, Amex, B'card/Visa.

C **Hundred House,** Norton TF11 9EE ☎(095 271) 353
Fax: (095 271) 355
Stylishly refurbished 18th-century inn with Tudor out-buildings forming a rear courtyard. On main A442, 5 miles SE of Telford.
9 bedrs, 9 en suite; TV; tcf
dogs; P 30, coach; child facs; con 20
LD 9.30
£ B&B £59–£65; B&B (double) £65–£75; L £16·50, D £16·50; WB £42·50 (HB); [V]
cc Access, Amex, B'card/Visa; dep

Holiday Inn, St Quentin Gate, TF3 4EH ☎(0952) 292500 Tx: 359126
Fax: (0952) 291949.
Hotel awaiting inspection. Fr
100 bedrs, 100 en suite; tcf
lift, dogs, ns; P 150, coach; child facs; con 250
LD 10
£ B&B £76–£101 (w/e £33), B&B (double) £96–£117; HB weekly £315–£500; L £10·50, D £14·75; [V w/e]
cc Access, Amex, B'card/visa, Diners.

TEMPLE SOWERBY

Cumbria. Map 44B2
M6 (jn 40) 6½, London 285, Brough 14, Kendal 28, Penrith 6.

★★★ **H** **R** **Temple Sowerby House,** CA10 1RZ ☎(076 83) 61578
Old Cumbrian farmhouse beside the A66 with landscapedgardens to rear. Solarium.
8 bedrs, 8 en suite; annexe 4 bedrs, 4 en suite; TV; tcf
dogs, ns; P 30; coach; child facs; con 20
LD 9. Resid & Rest lic
£ B&B £41·50, B&B (double) £56; D £17·50; WB (£39·50); [5% V]
cc Access, B'card/Visa; dep.

TEMPSFORD

Bedfordshire. Map 26B3
Biggleswade 6, London 51, Bedford 10, Cambridge 13, Huntingdon 29, St Neots 5.

En suite rooms
En suite rooms may be bath or shower rooms. If you have a preference, remember to state it when booking a room.

★★ **Anchor,** Gt North Rd, SG19 2AS ☎(0767) 40233

Red-brick period inn on West side of A1 standing in 11 acres of grounds beside the River Ouse. Fishing. (BCB) Fr
10 bedrs, 8 en suite, 1 ba
ns; P 150, coach; child facs; con 50
LD 10
£ B&B £38–£43 (w/e £27·50), B&B (double) £56; L £8·15, D £8·15
cc Access, Amex, B'card/Visa, Diners.

TENBURY WELLS

Hereford & Worcester (Worcestershire). Map 20A3
Pop 2,461. Worcester 20, London 134, Bridgnorth 23, Bromsgrove 10, Droitwich 20, Kidderminster 18, Leominster 9½, Ludlow 8.
EC Thur. **MD** Tue, Fri. **Golf** Ludlow 18h.

★ **Royal Oak,** Market St, WR15 8BQ ☎(0584) 810117
An ancient black and white inn with olde worlde' atmosphere.
6 bedrs, (4 sh), 2 ba; TV; tcf
TV, dogs; P 100, coach; con 100

TENTERDEN

Kent. Map 7B2
Pop 6,250. Maidstone 18, London 54, Ashford 12, Folkestone 23, Hastings 20, Hawkhurst 10, Rye 10, Tonbridge 24.
EC Wed. **MD** Fri. **Golf** Tenterden 18h.
[i] Town Hall, High St. ☎(058 06) 3572

★★ **C** **White Lion Inn,** High St, TN30 6BD ☎(058 06) 5077 Fax: (058 06) 4157
Attractive old inn, in centre of picturesque market town. Fr, Du
15 bedrs, 15 en suite; TV; tcf
dogs, ns; P 20, coach; child facs; con 50
LD 10
£ B&B £50–£55, B&B (double) £65–£75; L £9·50, D £12·50; WB £64 (2 nts HB)
cc Access, Amex, B'card/Visa, Diners.

TETBURY

Gloucestershire. Map 20B1
Pop 4,353. Swindon 19, London 96, Bath 23, Bristol 26, Cheltenham 24, Chippenham 14, Cirencester 10, Gloucester 19.
EC Thur. **Golf** Westonbirt 9h. **See** 'Chipping Steps', Market Hall, St Mary's Church, Jacobean and Georgian Houses in Long St, Police bygones Museum, Westonbirt Arboretum 3½ m SW.
[i] Old Court House, Long St. ☎(0666) 53552

Weekend breaks
Please consult the hotel for full details of weekend breaks; prices shown are an indication only. Many hotels offer mid week breaks as well.

★★★ **H** **C** **R** **Calcot Manor,** GL8 8YJ ☎(0666) 890391 Fax: (0666) 890394

Cotswold-stone manor house and barn dating to 1300 surrounded by lawns and gardens. Swimming pool. Fr
7 bedrs, 7 en suite, annexe 9 bedrs, 9 en suite; TV
P 30, no children under 12; con 20
LD 9.30; nr Sun dinner
£ B&B £80–£90, B&B (double) £100–£130; L £11·50; D £25
cc Access, Amex, B'card/Visa, Diners.

★★★ **Close,** Long St, GL8 8AQ ☎(0666) 502272

15th century stone building built for wool merchant. Attractive walled garden. Fr, De
15 bedrs, 15 en suite; TV
ns; P 20; children over 10; con 36
LD 9.45. Resid & Rest lic
£ B&B £82·50–£132·50, B&B (double) £110–£169; HB weekly £700–£980; L £14·95, D £27·50, WB £110 (HB); [10% V w/d]
cc Access, Amex, B'card/Visa, Diners.

★★★ **H** **C** **R** **Snooty Fox,** Market Pl, GL8 8DD ☎(0666) 502436
Fax: (0666) 503479

Former 16th century coaching inn of Cotswold stone; in town centre. Fr
12 bedrs, 12 en suite; TV
ns; coach; child facs: con 25
LD 9.45
£ B&B £66–£72, B&B (double) £84–£110; L £14, D £18; WB £98; [5% V w/d]
cc Access, Amex, B'card/Visa, CB, Diners.

TETFORD

Lincolnshire. Map 34B3
Horncastle 6, London 140, Louth 8½, Skegness 17.

White Hart, East Rd, nr Horncastle, LN9 6QQ (065 883) 255
Picturesque 16th century inn opposite the church.

TEWKESBURY Gloucestershire. Map 20B2
Pop 9,554. Stow-on-the-Wold 20, London 104, M5 (jn 9) 1½, Cheltenham 9, Evesham 13, Gloucester 10, Ledbury 14, Ross-on-Wye 24, Worcester 15.
EC Thur. **MD** Wed, Sat. **Golf** Tewkesbury Park 18h. **See** Fine Norman Abbey.
[i] Museum, 64 Barton St. (0684) 295027

★★★ **Bell,** 52 Church St, GL20 5SA (0684) 293293 Tx: 43535

17th century inn opposite Abbey, attractive black and white building. Fr
25 bedrs, 25 en suite; TV; tcf
dogs; P 55, coach; child facs; con 45
LD 9.15, bar meals only Mon–Sat lunch
£ B&B £53–£75 (w/e £40); B&B (double) £66–£120; HB weekly £280–£350; L £5, D £16·95; [10% V]
cc Access, Amex, B'card/Visa, Diners

★★★ **Royal Hop Pole Crest,** Church St, GL20 5RT (0684) 293236 Tx: 437176 Fax: (0684) 296680

Three-storey white-faced building, originally a 15th century inn. (Cr/THF)
29 bedrs, 29 en suite; TV; tcf
dogs, ns; P 35, coach; child facs; con 12
LD 10
£ B&B £71–£74 (w/e £42), B&B (double) £91–£111; L £9·95, D £14·95; [5% V]
cc Access, Amex, B'card/Visa, CB, Diners.

★★★ **Tewkesbury Hall,** Puckrup, GL20 6EL (0684) 296200 Fax: (0684) 850788

Charming white-painted Georgian house, elegantly furnished and set in 40 acres of parkland. Fishing, putting. Fr
16 bedrs, 16 en suite; TV; tcf
dogs, ns; P 80, coach; child facs; con 200
LD 9.30
£ B&B £70–£85 (w/e £45), B&B (double) £90–£125; L £12, D £19·50
cc Access, Amex, B'card/Visa, CB, Diners.

★★★ **Tewkesbury Park,** Lincoln Green La, GL20 7DN (0684) 295405 Tx: 43563 Fax: (0684) 292386

18th century mansion with outstanding recreational facilities and sports complex. Enjoys panoramic views. Indoor swimming pool, golf, putting, tennis, squash, sauna, solarium, gymnasium, billiards. Fr
78 bedrs, 78 en suite; TV; tcf
P 200, coach; child facs; con 150
LD 9.45, bar meals only Sat lunch
£ B&B £84–£94 (w/e £50), B&B (double) £94–£110; L £10·50, D £15; WB £45; [10% V]
cc Access, Amex, B'card/Visa, CB, Diners; dep.

★★ **Tudor House,** High St, GL20 5BH (0684) 297755
Attractive 3-storey building of Tudor origin situated in town centre.
16 bedrs, 12 en suite, 2 ba, annexe 3 bedrs, 3 en suite; TV; tcf
dogs, ns; P 25, G 1; coach; child facs; con 40
LD 9.30–10.30
£ B&B £45–£55, B&B (double) £55–£65; L £7·50, D £12·25; WB £64 (2 nts HB) [10% V w/e]
cc Access, Amex, B'card/Visa, Diners; dep.

THAKEHAM West Sussex.
See STORRINGTON.

THAME Oxfordshire. Map 21B2
Pop 10,000. High Wycombe 15, London 45, M40 (jn 7) 4, Aylesbury 9, Bicester 13, Oxford 13, Reading 23, Wallingford 17.
EC Wed. **MD** Tue. **Golf** Princes Risborough 9h. **See** Parish Church, Old Grammar School (John Hampden educated here).
[i] Town Hall. (084 421) 2834

Discount vouchers
RAC discount vouchers are on p. 34. Hotels with a [V] shown at the end of the price information will accept them in part payment for accommodation bills on the full, standard rate, not against bargain breaks or any other special offers. Please note the limitations shown in the entry: w/e for weekends, w/d for weekdays, and which months they are accepted.

★★★ H R **Spread Eagle,** 16 Cornmarket, OX9 2BR (084 421) 3661 Tx: 83343 Fax: (0844) 261380

Georgian former coaching inn of repute situated opposite market square. Fr
33 bedrs, 33 en suite; TV
dogs, ns; P 80, coach; child facs; con 250
LD 10, bar meals only Sat lunch
£ B&B £72·50–£79·05, B&B (double) £85·65–£95·55; HB weekly £618·80–£664·90; L £14·80, D £17; WB £93·50 (2 nts); [10% V]
cc Access, Amex, B'card/Visa, Diners.
(*See advertisement on p. 476*)

Essex House (Highly Acclaimed), Chinnor Rd, OX9 3LS (084 421) 7567. Fax: (084 421) 6420. *Hotel.*
£ B&B £30–£40 (w/e £22·50); [V]
cc Access, B'card/Visa; dep

THAXTED Essex Map 26C2
M11 (jn 8) 10, London 42, Bishop's Stortford 10, Braintree 13, Haverhill 16, Saffron Walden 7. **See** Church, Guildhall.

★★★ **Swan,** Bull Ring, Whatling St., CB10 1AE (0371) 830321 Fax: (0371) 831186
Charming old inn, recently refurbished, opposite the church; two adjacent period buildings form annexes. Fr, De
21 bedrs, 21 en suite; TV; tcf
dogs; P 25, coach; child facs; con 30
LD 10
£ B&B £65, B&B (double) £70; L £13·50, D £21·50; WB £75 (2 nts)
cc Access, Amex, B'card/Visa.

Farmhouse Inn, Monk St, (0371) 830864 Fax: (0371) 831196

Original white-washed farmhouse with bedroom extensions forming a small courtyard. It
11 bedrs, 11 en suite; TV; tcf
dogs, ns; P 48, coach; child facs
LD 10

EC *early closing* **MD** *market day* *country house hotel* *ns (NS) no smoking areas* *tcf tea/coffee facilities*

£ B&B £42, B&B (double) £55; HB weekly £275; L £7·50, D £7·50; WB £99; [10% V]
cc Access, Amex, B'card/Visa.

THELBRIDGE Devon Map 3B3

Tiverton 12, London 175, Crediton 8, South Molton 13.

Thelbridge Cross Inn, EX17 4SQ (0884) 860316 Fax: (0884) 860316
Charming country inn developed from an 18th century farmhouse and barn with views of Dartmoor and Exmoor.
8 bedrs, 8 en suite; TV; tcf
P 70; child facs
LD 9.30
£ B&B £25–£30; L fr £6·50, D fr £10
cc Access, B'card/Visa; dep.

THETFORD Norfolk. Map 27A4

Pop 20,000. Newmarket 18, London 81, Bury St Edmunds 12, East Dereham 24, King's Lynn 27, Norwich 28, Scole 18, Stowmarket 21, Swaffham 18.
EC Wed. **MD** Tue, Sat. **Golf** Thetford 18h. **See** Cluniac Priory ruins, St Peter's, St Mary the Less and St Cuthbert's Churches, Guildhall Art Gallery, King's House.
Ancient House Museum, White Hart St. (0842) 752599

★★★ **Bell,** King St, IP24 2AZ (0842) 754455 Tx: 818868 Fax: (0842) 755552

Well-preserved coaching inn, in part 15th century. Modern bedroom wing. (THF)
47 bedrs, 47 en suite; TV; tcf
dogs, ns; P 48, coach; child facs; con 80
LD 9.45
£ room £65–£92 (w/e £51), room (double) £81–£92; Bk £7·75, L £9·45, D £16·75
cc Access, Amex, B'card/Visa, CB, Diners; dep.

★★ **Anchor,** Bridge St, IP24 3AE (0842) 763925

Traditional old coaching inn beside the river in centre of town.
17 bedrs, 17 en suite; TV; tcf
ns; P 60, coach; child facs; con 20

THEYDON BOIS Essex Map 15C1

Pop 4,008. Woodford 7½, London 17, Enfield 8½, Epping 2, Romford 10.
EC Wed. **Golf** Theydon Bois 18h *See* 17th Century Bull Inn, Theydon Hall.

Parsonage Farm House, Abridge Rd, CM16 7NN 037 881 4242.
£ B&B £28; [5 % V]

THIRSK North Yorkshire. Map 38C4

Pop 6,830. Boroughbridge 12, London 220, Helmsley 14, Leyburn 24, Malton 25, Northallerton 8½, Stockton-on-Tees 22, York 23.
EC Wed. **MD** Mon, Thur, Sat. **Golf** Thirsk and Northallerton 9h. **See** Church (ancient statue of Madonna and Child), Thirsk Hall.
Museum, 16 Kirkgate. (0845) 22755

★★ **Golden Fleece,** Market Pl, YO7 1LL Fax: (0845) 523996

Creeper-clad town centre inn, furnished in early 19th century tradition. (THF)
22 bedrs, 6 en suite, 5 ba; TV; tcf
dogs, ns; P 50, coach; child facs; con 120
LD 9.30
£ B&B £52 (w/e £30), B&B (double) £69; L £8·50, D £11·50
cc Access, Amex, B'card/Visa, Diners; dep.

★★ **Nevison's,** Sutton Rd, YO7 2ER (0845) 522293
Recently refurbished hotel on east side of town. Leisure facilities planned for completion end 1990.

★★ H R **Sheppard's,** Church Farm, Front St, Sowerby, YO7 1JF (0845) 523655 Fax: (0845) 524720

18th century Georgian building in picturesque village on outskirts of Thirsk.
8 bedrs, 8 en suite; TV; tcf
ns; P 35; no children under 10; con 50
LD 9.30. Resid & Rest lic
£ B&B £45–£50, B&B (double) £55–£65; WB (10% reduction)
cc Access, B'card/Visa; dep.

Old Red House, Station Rd, Carlton Miniott, YO7 4LT (0845) 524383
Red-brick roadside pub on the A61 south west of Thirsk.
6 beds, 6 en suite; annexe 6 bedrs, 6 en suite; TV
dogs, ns; P 30, coach; child facs; con 50
LD 9.30
£ B&B £16, B&B (double) £26; L £4·50, D £6·50
cc Amex, B'card/Visa.

THORALBY North Yorkshire Map 38A4

Leyburn 9, London 244, Ashrigg 6, Buckden 8, Howes 10.

High Green House (Highly Acclaimed), DL8 3SU (0969) 663420. Open 1 Apr–31 Oct
£ B&B fr £25·50, HB weekly fr £185·50

THORNABY-ON-TEES Teesside, Cleveland. Map 45A1

Pop 28,000. Thirsk 20, London 242, Middlesbrough 3, Northallerton 17, Stockton-on-Tees 1½.
MD Thur. **Golf** Teesside 18h. **See** Church of St Peter ad Vincula.

★★★ **Post House,** Low La, Stainton Village, TS17 9LW Middlesbrough (0642) 591213 Tx: 58426 Fax: (0642) 594989

Modern motel-style hotel conveniently situated in outskirts. Sauna, solarium. (THF)
135 bedrs, 135 en suite; TV; tcf
dogs, ns; P 350, coach; child facs; con 120
LD 10.15
£ B&B £75–£85 (w/e £51), B&B (double) £94–£104; L £7·50, D £15; WB £41
cc Access, Amex, B'card/Visa, Diners.

THORNBURY Avon. Map 20A1

Pop 12,488. Chippenham 25, London 117, Bath 23, Bristol 12, Chepstow 10, Gloucester 23, Tetbury 20.
EC Thur, **MD** Thur, Sat. **Golf** Filton 18h. **See** Castle (begun 1511, never completed), Church.

★★★ **Thornbury Castle,** BS12 1HH (0454) 418511
Tx: 449986 Fax: (0454) 416188

A beautifully furnished Tudor castle set in magnificent formal gardens. Fr, De, Es, Du
18 bedrs, 18 en suite; TV; tcf
ns; P 50; children over 12; con 24
LD 9.30. Resid & Rest lic

£ B&B £80–£85, B&B (double) £125–£190; L £17·50, D £29
cc Access, Amex, B'card/Visa, Diners.
(*See advertisement on p. 168*)

THORNE South Yorkshire. Map 39A2

Pop 11,741. Newark 40, London 166, M18 (jn 6) 1, Doncaster 9½, Gainsborough 26, Goole 11, Pontefract 20, Scunthorpe 14, Selby 12.
EC Thur. **MD** Tue, Fri, Sat. **Golf** Doncaster 18h. **See** Parish Church.

★★ **Belmont,** Horse Fair Green, DN4 5EE
(0405) 812320 Tx: 54480
Fax: (0405) 740508 ♿

Small modern hotel and restaurant in centre of quiet market town. Fr
23 bedrs, 23 en suite; TV; tcf
dogs; P 30, coach; child facs; con 60
LD 9.30
£ B&B £36·50–£38·50, B&B (double) £48·50–£50·50; L £8·95, D £8·95; WB; [V]
cc Access, B'card/Visa.

THORNLEY Co. Durham. Map 37C1

Stockton on Tees 18, London 261, Bishop Auckland 13, Durham 7, Newcastle upon Tyne 22.

★★ **Crossways,** Dunelm Rd, D6 3HT
Wellfield (0429) 821248
Fax: (0429) 820034 ♿
Small cream-washed hotel with red-brick extension standing at road junction in rural area. Solarium, billiards. Fr, De
23 bedrs, 23 en suite; TV; tcf
TV, dogs, ns; P 150, coach, child facs; con 150
LD 9.45
£ B&B £42·50–£55, B&B (double) £55–£85; L £4·50, D £8·50; WB £60 (2 nts HB)
cc Access, Amex, B'card/Visa, Diners.

THORNTHWAITE Cumbria. Map 43C2

Pop 150. Keswick 3½, London 289, Carlisle 27, Cockermouth 8.
Golf Cockermouth 18h.

★★ **Ladstock,** CA12 5RZ
Braithwaite (059 682) 210
18th century hotel with modern extension in 12 acres of wooded grounds, lawns, and terraces. Closed Feb.
22 bedrs, 18 en suite, (4 sh), 2 ba; TV; tcf
TV; P 80, coach; child facs; con 150
LD 8.30, nr Mon–Sat lunch
£ B&B £24–£30, B&B (double) £36–£64; HB weekly £199–£290; L £7·50, D £12·50; [5% V]
cc Access, B'card/Visa; dep.

★★ R **Swan,** CA12 5SQ. Braithwaite (059 682) 256

Attractive white-faced 17th century former coaching inn in quiet village. Open Mar–Nov.
14 bedrs, 8 en suite, 2 ba; TV
TV, dogs, ns; P 60, U 3 (£2), coach; child facs
LD 8.30, bar meals only lunch
£ B&B £19·50, B&B (double) £39–£52·60; HB weekly £195·85–£241·75; L £6, D £14·50; WB £57·75; [V w/d]
cc Access, B'card/Visa; dep.

★★ **Thwaite Howe,** CA12 5SA
Braithwaite (059 682) 281

Family-managed Victorian house in own grounds facing Skiddaw. Open Mar–Oct.
Fr
8 bedrs, 8 en suite; TV; tcf
dogs, ns; P 12; children over 12
LD 7.30, nr lunch. Resid lic
£ B&B (double) £44–£50; HB weekly £199·50–£330; D £10·50; WB £57; [5% V May, Jun, Sep, Oct]; dep.

THORNTON CLEVELEYS Lancashire.

Map 36A3
Pop 27,060. Preston 19, London 230, Blackpool 4½, Lancaster 22.
EC Wed. **Golf** Fleetwood 18h. **See** Windmill
Victoria Sq. (0253) 853378

★★ **Regal,** Victoria Road West, FY5 1AG
(0253) 852244
Three-storey 1930s hotel with imposing double entrance. Near promenade.
41 bedrs, 41 en suite; TV; tcf
lift, TV, dogs, P 15, coach, child facs, con 70

Victorian House (Highly Acclaimed), Trunnan Rd, FY5 4HF (0253) 860619. *Private Hotel.* Fr
£ B&B £37·50; [5% V]

Beachview, 67–69 Beach Rd, FY5 1EG
(0253) 854003

THORNTON HEATH Greater London

(Surrey). Map 8C2
Pop 14,500. Bromley 6½, London 8½, Croydon 1½, Mitcham 3, Purley 4.
EC Wed. **Golf** See Croydon.

Cresta House, 601 London Rd, CR4 6AY
081-684 3947

Norfolk House, 587 London Rd, CR4 6AY
081 689 8989 Fax: 081-689-0335. *Hotel.*
Fr, Es
Hotel being refurbished; awaiting inspection.

THORNTON HOUGH Merseyside

(Cheshire). Map 32A1
Pop 800. M53 (jn 4) 2, Chester 16, London 199, Birkenhead 8, Ellesmere Port 8.
EC Thur. **Golf** Bromborough 18h.

★★★ **Thornton Hall,** Neston Road, Wirral, L63 1JF 051-336 3938 Tx: 628678
Fax: 051-336 7864 ♿
Victorian house with magnificent interior carving. In 7 acres of parkland.
11 bedrs, 11 en suite, annexe 27 bedrs, 27 en suite; TV ; tcf
P 100, coach; child facs; con 250

THORPENESS Suffolk Map 27C3

Woodbridge 17, London 98, Aldeburgh 2, Lonestoft 26, Saxmundham 7.

Dolphin, Peace Pl, Nr Leiston (0728) 452681. *Hotel.*
£ B&B £12·50–£22·50; HB weekly £301–£402·50; [10% V not w/e Jul–Aug]

THURLESTONE Devon. Map 3B1

Pop 928. Kingsbridge 3½, London 207, Plymouth 20.
Golf Thurlestone 18h. **See** Perp Church.

★★★★ H C **Thurlestone,** TQ7 3NN
Kingsbridge (0548) 560382
Fax: (0548) 561069

Impressive white building set in gardens and parkland. Indoor and outdoor swimming pools, golf, putting, tennis, squash, sauna, solarium, gymnasium, billiards. Fr, De, It. Closed Jan 4–21.
68 bedrs, 68 en suite; TV
lift, dogs; P 100, G 19; child facs; con 100
LD 9
£ B&B £43–£69, B&B (double) £86–£138; HB weekly £363–£575; L £8·50, D £21; WB £118 (2 HB)

TILEHURST Berkshire. Map 12B2

Pop 9,825. Reading 3, London 41, Abingdon 22, Basingstoke 20, Newbury 16, Oxford 26.
EC Wed. **Golf** Calcot 18h.

Aeron, 191 Kentwood Hill, RG3 6JE
Reading (0734) 424119. *Private Hotel.*

TINTAGEL Cornwall. Map 2C3

Pop 1,600. Launceston 19, London 230, Bude 17, Camelford 5.
EC Wed. **MD** Thur. **Golf** St Enodoc Rock 18h and 9h. **See** 'King Arthur's Castle', 'King Arthur's Hall', Saxon Church.

★★ **Atlantic View,** Treknow, PL34 OEJ
☎Camelford (0840) 770221

Substantial 3-storey house set in landscaped garden with large lawn. Indoor swimming pool, solarium.
🛏8 bedrs, 8 en suite; TV; tcf
🏨 TV, dogs, ns; P 12, child facs
✕LD 9. Resid & Rest lic
£ B&B £16·50–£22·50, B&B (double) £33–£45; HB weekly £180–£223; L £1·50–£6·50, D £11·50; WB £27 (HB)
cc Access, B'card/Visa; dep.

★★**Bossiney House,** Bossiney, PL34 0AX
☎ Camelford (0840) 770240
In 2½ acres above lovely cove, white building with large extensions. Indoor swimming pool, putting, sauna, solarium, gymnasium. Open 1 Mar–31 Oct and Xmas
🛏17 bedrs, 17 en suite, annexe 1 bedrs, 1 en suite, 2 ba; tcf
🏨 TV, dogs; P 30, coach; child facs
✕LD 8.15, bar meals only lunch. Resid lic.
£ B&B £28–£33, B&B (double) £46–£51; HB weekly £195–£230; D £11; WB £75 (3 nts HB); [10% V Mar–Jun, Sep, Oct]
cc Access, Amex, B'card/Visa, Diners; dep.

Belvoir House, Tregatta, PL34 0DY
☎Camelford (0840) 770265. *Guest House.*

TITCHWELL Norfolk. Map 35A2

Pop 94. King's Lynn 22, London 119, Cromer 31, Fakenham 15, Swaffham 24.
Golf Hunstanton 18h.

★★ H **Titchwell Manor,** Main Rd, PE31 8BB ☎Brancaster (0485) 210221 Tx: 32376 ♿

Isolated converted manor house overlooking coastal salt marshes.
🛏12 bedrs, 10 en suite; annexe 4 bedrs, 4 en suite, TV; tcf
🏨 dogs; P 50; child facs; con 20
✕LD 9.30, bar meals only Mon–Sat lunch
£B&B £34–£40, B&B (double) £60–£70; HB weekly £240–£280; L £5, D £14·50; WB £72; [5% V Nov–Apr]
cc Access, Amex, B'card/Visa, Diners; dep.
(*See advertisement on p. 310*)

TIVERTON Devon. Map 3C3

Pop 16,539. Taunton 20, London 163, Crediton 12, Dunster 26, Exeter 15, Honiton 19, South Molton 21.
EC Thur. **MD** Tue, Fri, Sat. **Golf** Tiverton 18h. **See** Castle remains, 17th cent Blundells School, Great House of St George (now Council Offices), St Peter's Church, Museum, Almshouses, Knighthayes Court Gardens 1½ m N.
ℹ Phoenix La. ☎(0884) 255827

★★★ **Tiverton,** Blundells Rd, EX16 4DB
☎(0884) 256120 Tx: 42551
Fax: (0884) 258101 ♿
Modern purpose-built hotel set on edge of town. Owner-run. Fr
🛏75 bedrs, 75 en suite; TV; tcf
🏨 dogs, ns; P 130, coach; child facs; con 250
✕LD 9.15
£ B&B £28–£37, B&B (double) £46–£64; HB weekly £196–£217; L £7·50, D £14·50; [10% V]
cc Access, Amex, B'card/Visa, Diners; dep.
(*See advertisement on p. 476*)

Bridge (Acclaimed), 23 Angel Hill, EX16 6PE ☎(0884) 252804. *Guest House.*
£ B&B £14·50–£17·50; HB weekly £135–£165; [5% V]

Lodge Hill Farm, Ashley, EX16 5PA
☎(0884) 252907. *Guest House.*
£ B&B £13–£15; [10% V]

TODMORDEN West Yorkshire (Lancashire) Map 33C4

M62 (jn 21) 10, London 197, Burnley 9, Halifax 11½, Rochdale 9½
ℹ 15 Burnley Rd ☎(0706) 818181

★★★ **Scaitcliffe Hall,** Burnley Rd, OL14 7DQ ☎(0706) 818888
Fax: (0706) 818825 ♿

17th-century sandstone house, with attractive mullioned windows, set in 16 acres of grounds on A646. Fr, It, Ar, Ma
🛏13 beds, 13 en suite; TV; tcf
🏨 TV, dogs, ns; P 200; child facs; con 200
🏨 LD 10, bar meals only lunch Sat
£ room £29·95–£42·50, double room £42·50–£52·50; Bk 5·95, L £7·95, D £13·95; WB £69 (2 nts HB); [10% V]
cc Access, Amex, B'card/Visa, Diners; dep.

TODWICK South Yorkshire. Map 31A3

Mansfield 17, London 155, Chesterfield 13, Doncaster 17, Rotherham 8, Sheffield 10, Worksop 8

★★★ **Red Lion,** Worksop Rd, S31 0DJ
☎(0909) 771654 Tx: 54120
Fax: (0909) 773704 ♿
Stone-faced hotel situated close to the M1 in rural surroundings. (Lns)
🛏29 bedrs, 29 en suite; TV; tcf
🏨 ns; P 90, coach; child facs; con 80
✕LD 10, bar meals only Sat lunch
£ B&B £70 (w/e £28), B&B (double) £82; L £9·25, D £14·25; [V]
cc Access, Amex, B'card/Visa, Diners.

TONBRIDGE Kent. Map 11B2

Pop 30,000. Sevenoaks 7, London 32, Maidstone 13, Rochester 19, Tenterden 24, Tunbridge Wells 4, Westerham 14.
EC Wed. **MD** Sat. **Golf** Poult Wood 18h. **See** 16th cent Chequers Inn, Port Reeve's House, remains of 12th cent castle.
ℹ Castle, Castle St ☎(0732) 770929

★★★ **Rose & Crown,** High St, TN9 1DD
☎(0732) 357966 Fax: (0732) 357194
A modernised coaching inn retaining oak beams; later extension at rear. (THF)
🛏30 bedrs, 30 en suite; annexe 20 bedrs, 20 en suite; TV; tcf
🏨 dogs, ns; P 50, coach; child facs; con 100
✕LD 9.45, bar meals only Thur dinner
£ B&B £78, B&B (double) £92–£99; L £8·50, D £12·95; WB £37
cc Access, Amex, B'card/Visa, CB, Diners.

Tonbridge, 18–20 London Rd, TN10 3DA
☎(0732) 353311
Hotel awaiting inspection.
🛏8 bedrs, 8 en suite; TV; tcf
🏨 dogs; P
£ B&B £52·50

TORCROSS Devon. Map 3B1

Pop 100. Kingsbridge 6, London 211 (Fy 207), Dartmouth 7½.
Golf Thurlestone 18h

★ **Greyhomes,** TQ7 2TH ☎Kingsbridge (0548) 580220
Small family-run hotel in elevated position enjoying fine sea views. Open Mar–Nov.
🛏7 bedrs, 7 en suite; TV; tcf
🏨 dogs; P 15, G 2; no children under 2
✕LD 7.30, nr lunch. Resid & Rest lic
£ B&B £25–£28, B&B (double) £50–£56; D £9·85; WB £60; [5% V Apr, May, Sep, Oct]
cc Access, B'card/Visa; dep.

TORMARTON Avon. Map 5A4

M4 (jn 18) 1½, London 102, Bath 11, Bristol 15, Chippenham 11, Stroud 20.

★★ **Compass Inn,** Badminton, GL9 1JB
☎Badminton (045 421) 242
Fax: (045 421) 741

18th century stone-built former coaching inn in pleasant gardens. Fr
🛏33 bedrs, 33 en suite; TV; tcf
🏨 dogs, ns; P 160, coach; child facs; con 80
✕LD 9.30, bar meals only lunch
£ B&B £49·95–£59·50, B&B (double) £64·90–£74·50; L £5·75, D £15; WB £37 (HB); [V]
cc Access, Amex, B'card/Visa, Diners.

TORPOINT Cornwall. Map 3A2

Pop 7,000. Saltash 13½, London 243 (Fy 215), Liskeard 15, Looe 15½, Plymouth (Fy) 4.

T

Thame (Oxford)

SPREAD EAGLE

Come & be spoilt ... by us!

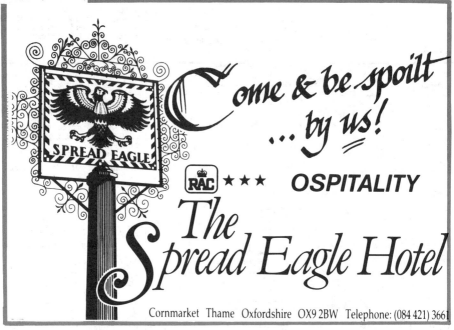

RAC ★★★ OSPITALITY

The Spread Eagle Hotel

Cornmarket Thame Oxfordshire OX9 2BW Telephone: (084 421) 3661

Tiverton (Devon)

★★★*RAC* *Mid Devon is Beautiful All Year Round* *ETB 4 Crowns*

THE TIVERTON HOTEL

Blundell's Road, Tiverton, Devon EX16 4DB Tel: (0884) 256120

Ashley Courtenay Recommended

Situated 6 miles from Junction 27 on the M5. This modern Hotel has 75 spacious en-suite bedrooms, all with sitting areas, colour televisions, direct dial telephones, trouser presses, irons, hairdryers and courtesy tea and coffee trays. Ideal base for businessmen, holiday makers and tourists. Special low cost breaks including superb à la Carte candlelit dinner all year round. Reduced entry vouchers at local National Trust houses and gardens, local Country Houses, Castles and Mid Devon attractions.

Kindly telephone Tiverton (0884) 256120 for Brochures and Menus.

Torquay (Devon)

Everything you expect of a fine 4-Star hotel – plus friendly and caring service.

Our colour brochure gives all the details – phone for your copy now.

The Grand Hotel, The Seafront, Torquay, Devon.
Tel: 0803 296677 Fax: 0803 213462

EC Wed. **Golf** Whitsand Bay 18h. **See** Anthony House (Nat Trust).

Ap. Whitsand Bay, Portwinkle, Crafthole, PL11 3BU ☎(0503) 30276 ⚒ Fr, De

Stone-built house in cliff-top grounds. Panoramic sea views. Indoor swimming pool, golf, putting, sauna, solarium, gymnasium.
£ B&B £15–£20; HB weekly £155–£190; WB £60 (2 nts min); [5% V w/d Nov–Apr]; dep.

TORQUAY Torbay, Devon. Map 3C2

Pop 120,000. Newton Abbot 6, London 189, Dartmouth (Fy) 10, Totnes 8.
See Plan, p. 478.
EC Wed, Sat. **P** See Plan. **Golf** Torquay 18h.
[i] Vaughan Par. ☎(0803) 297428

★★★★★ **Imperial,** Park Hill Rd, TQ1 2DG ☎(0803) 294301 Tx: 42849 Fax: (0803) 298293

Luxury hotel in sub-tropical gardens. Period decor in public rooms. Indoor and outdoor swimming pools, putting, tennis, squash, sauna, solarium, gymnasium, billiards. (THF) ⚒ Fr, De, It
🛏 167 bedrs, 167 en suite, 2 ba; TV
🏠 lift, dogs, ns; P 100, G 50; coach; child facs; con 400
✕ LD 9.30
£ B&B £86–£104, B&B (double) £150–£186; L £15, D £28; WB £106 (2 nts)
cc Access, Amex, B'card/Visa, CB, Diners.

★★★★ **Grand,** Sea Front, TQ2 6NT ☎(0803) 296677 Tx: 42891 Fax: (0803) 213462

Spacious and imposing Victorian building at Western end of seafront. Indoor/outdoor swimming pools, tennis, sauna, solarium, gymnasium. ⚒ Fr, De, It, Du
🛏 112 bedrs, 112 en suite; TV; tcf
🏠 lift, dogs; G 40, coach; child facs; con 300
✕ LD 9.30
£ B&B £50–£76, B&B (double) £100–£152; HB weekly £371–£553; L £13·50, D £16·50; WB £40 (2 nts min)
cc Access, B'card/Visa, Diners.
(*See advertisement on p. 476*)

★★★★ **Palace,** Babbacombe Rd, TQ1 3TG. ☎(0803) 200200 Tx: 42606 Fax: (0803) 299899

Large hotel with splendid decor. Extensive Italian grounds leading to the sea. Indoor and outdoor swimming pools, golf, putting, tennis (indoor and outdoor), squash, sauna, billiards.
🛏 140 bedrs, 140 en suite; TV; tcf
🏠 lift, TV; P 130, G 50; child facs; con 2000
✕ LD 9.15
£ B&B £50–£95, B&B (double) £100–£190; HB weekly £342–£700; L £12, D £18; WB £55 (HB); [5% V]
cc Access, B'card/Visa, Diners.
(*See advertisement on p. 480*)

★★★ [H] [C] **Abbey Lawn,** Scarborough Rd, TQ2 5UQ ☎(0803) 299199 Fax: (0803) 291460

Refurbished, large, white-painted hotel in central position. Swimming pool, tennis, sauna, solarium, gymnasium.
🛏 65 bedrs, 65 en suite; TV; tcf
🏠 lift, dogs, ns; P 45; no children under 13; con 120
✕ LD 8.30. Resid & Rest lic
£ B&B £55–£65, B&B (double) £110–£130; L £8·50, D £15; WB £78; [10% V]
cc Access, Amex, B'card/Visa, Diners; dep.

★★★ **Belgrave,** Belgrave Rd, TQ2 5HE ☎(0803) 296666 Fax: (0803) 211308

A large modern hotel at the centre of seafront. Swimming pool. ⚒ Fr, Es, Po
🛏 68 bedrs, 68 en suite; TV; tcf
🏠 lift, dogs; P 80, U 4 (£2); child facs; con 150
✕ LD 8.30, bar meals only lunch
£ B&B £32–£45, B&B (double) £64–£90; HB weekly £238–£336; D £9·50; WB £66
cc Access, B'card/Visa, Diners.

★★★ [H] [C] **Corbyn Head,** Sea Front, Torbay Rd, TQ2 6RH ☎(0803) 213611 Fax: (0803) 296152 ♿

A modern hotel built on high ground on main seafront. Swimming pool. ⚒ De
🛏 50 bedrs, 50 en suite; TV; tcf
🏠 dogs; P 40, coach; child facs; con 40
✕ LD 9.30, bar meals only lunch
£ B&B £26–£40; B&B (double) £52–£80; HB weekly £180–£260; L £6·95, D £12·50
cc Access, Amex, B'card/Visa, Diners; dep.

★★★ **Gleneagles,** Asheldon Rd, TQ1 2QS ☎(0803) 293637 Fax: (0803) 295106

Modern-style hotel in quiet surroundings overlooking cove and near golf course. Swimming pool, solarium.
🛏 40 bedrs, 40 en suite; TV; tcf
🏠 TV, dogs; P 40; child facs
✕ LD 8.30, bar meals only lunch. Resid & Rest lic
£ B&B £23–£33·50, B&B (double) £46–67; HB weekly £185–£236
cc Access, Amex, B'card/Visa, Diners.
(*See advertisement on p. 480*)

★★★ **Homer's,** Warren Rd, TQ2 5TN ☎(0803) 213456

Victorian-style building high up in quiet road with panoramic views.

★★★ **Kistor,** Belgrave Rd, TQ2 5HF ☎(0803) 212632 Fax: (0803) 293219
A large hotel in its own grounds just off sea front. Indoor and outdoor swimming pools, putting, sauna, solarium, gymnasium.
🛏 59 bedrs, 59 en suite; TV; tcf

T

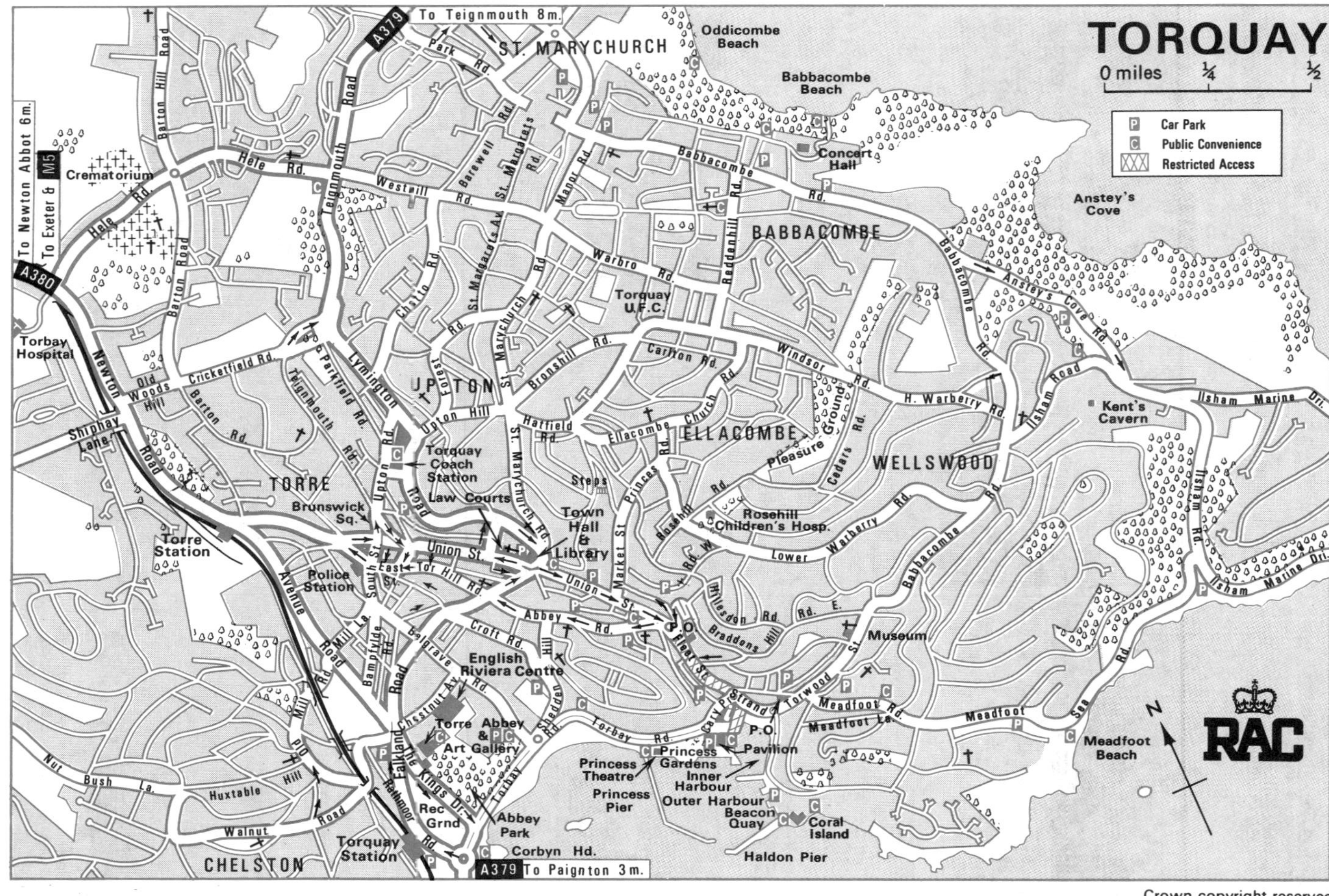
TORQUAY
0 miles ¼ ½
Car Park
Public Convenience
Restricted Access
RAC
N
Anstey's Cove
Kent's Cavern
Meadfoot Beach
Oddicombe Beach
Babbacombe Beach
Concert Hall
BABBACOMBE
WELLSWOOD
ELLACOMBE
ST. MARYCHURCH
UPTON
TORRE
CHELSTON
Torquay U.F.C.
Pleasure Ground
Rosehill Children's Hosp.
Museum
Town Hall & Library
Torquay Coach Station
Law Courts
Police Station
Brunswick Sq.
English Riviera Centre
Torre Abbey & Art Gallery
Abbey Park
Rec Grnd
Torquay Station
Torre Station
Torbay Hospital
Crematorium
Princess Theatre
Princess Gardens
Princess Pier
Pavilion
P.O.
Inner Harbour
Outer Harbour
Beacon Quay
Coral Island
Haldon Pier
Corbyn Hd.
To Teignmouth 8m.
To Newton Abbot 6m.
To Exeter & M5
To Paignton 3 m.
A379
A380

🏛 lift, TV, dogs; P 45, coach; child facs; con 100
✕ LD 8.30
cc Access, Amex, B'card/Visa, Diners; dep.
(*See advertisement on p. 480*)

★★★ **Lincombe Hall,** Meadfoot Rd, TQ1 2JX ☎ (0803) 213361
Two fine Georgian buildings linked and extended. In 5 acres of attractive grounds. Swimming pool, putting, tennis, sauna, solarium.

★★★ **H** **R** **Livermead Cliff,** Sea Front, TQ2 6RQ ☎ (0803) 299666 Tx: 42424 Fax: (0803) 294496 ♿

Large red stone building in pleasant grounds. Private steps to beach. Swimming pool, fishing, solarium. Use of facilities at Livermead House. Fr, De, It
64 bedrs, 64 en suite; TV; tcf
🏛 lift, dogs; P 65, G 20, coach; child facs; con 80
✕ LD 8.30
£ B&B £27·50–£44, B&B (double) £54–£82; HB weekly £231–£315; L £7·25, D £13·50; WB £62 (2 nts HB); [V Nov–Mar]
cc Access, Amex, B'card/Visa, Diners.

★★★ **Livermead House,** Sea Front, TQ2 6QJ ☎ (0803) 294361 Tx: 42918 Fax: (0803) 200758

Large red stone hotel on seafront enjoying good view. Swimming pool, putting, tennis, squash, sauna, solarium, gymnasium, billiards. Fr
62 bedrs, 62 en suite; TV; tcf
🏛 lift, dogs; P 90, coach; child facs; con 80
✕ LD 8.30
£ B&B £29–£41, B&B (double) £58–£82; HB weekly £234·50–£315; L £6·25, D £11; WB £36 (HB 2 nts min); [10% V]
cc Access, Amex, B'card/Visa, Diners; dep.
(*See advertisement on p. 484*)

★★★ **Nepaul,** 27 Croft Rd, TQ2 5UB ☎ (0803) 28457
4-storey purpose-built hotel with grounds high up overlooking Torbay.

Hotel locations
Hotel locations are shown on the maps at the back of the guide. All towns and villages containing an RAC Appointed or Listed hotel are ringed in purple.

★★★ **H** **Orestone Manor House,** Rockhouse La, Maidencombe, TQ1 4SX ☎ (0803) 328098 Fax: (0803) 328336

Built in 1800, a hotel in grounds on hillside with good views. Swimming pool, putting. Fr
20 bedrs, 20 en suite, 1 ba; TV; tcf
🏛 TV; dogs; P 35, coach; child facs; con
✕ LD 8.45, Resid & Rest lic
£ B&B £34·50–£52, B&B (double) £68–£94; L £7·50, D £17·50; WB £74 (2 nts HB); [10% V w/d]
cc Access, B'card/Visa; dep.

★★★ **Overmead,** Daddyhole Rd, TQ1 2EF ☎ (0803) 295666 Fax: (0803) 211175 ♿

A large Victorian building in its own grounds, overlooking the sea. Swimming pool, putting, sauna, solarium, gymnasium. billiards. Fr.
55 bedrs, 55 en suite; TV; tcf
🏛 lift, dogs; P 13, coach; child facs; con 130
✕ LD 9, bar meals only Mon–Sat lunch
£ B&B £24–£41, B&B (double) £48–£100; L £6, D £14; WB £48 (2 nts); [10% V w/e Oct–Feb]
cc Access, Amex, B'card/Visa; dep.

★★★ **Rainbow House,** Belgrave Rd, TQ2 5HP ☎ (0803) 213232
A modern hotel 400 yards from seafront. Indoor and outdoor swimming pools, squash, sauna, solarium, gymnasium, billiards.
118 bedrs, 118 en suite; TV; tcf
🏛 lift, TV, dogs; P 80, coach; child facs; con 350

★★★ **Toorak,** Chestnut Av, TQ2 5JS ☎ (0803) 291444 Tx: 42885 Fax: (0803) 291666

Brick-built hotel in 4 acres of pleasant grounds; near seafront. Swimming pool, tennis, billiards. Es, It
90 bedrs, 90 en suite; TV; tcf
🏛 lift, TV, dogs; P 90, coach; child facs; con 200
✕ LD 8.30, bar meals only lunch Mon–Sat
£ L £7·50, D £12·50
cc Access, Amex, B'card/Visa, Diners; dep.

★★ **Anstey's Lea,** Babbacombe Rd, TQ1 2QJ ☎ (0803) 294843
Attractive Victorian house in grounds. Swimming pool, solarium, billiards. Fr
24 bedrs, 15 en suite, 2 ba; TV; tcf
🏛 TV, dogs; P 18, coach; child facs
✕ LD 7.30, bar meals only lunch. Resid & Rest lic
£ B&B £17–£26, B&B (double) £31–£49; HB weekly £132–£198; WB £49 (HB off season); [10% V Sep–Jun]
cc Access, B'card/Visa; dep.

★★ **Apsley,** Torwood Gardens Rd, TQ1 1EG ☎ (0803) 292058
Pleasant hotel converted from two houses of character. Close to Harbour. Closed Nov.
31 bedrs, 27 en suite, 1 ba; TV; tcf
🏛 dogs; P 20, coach; child facs

★★ **Balmoral,** Meadfoot Beach, TQ1 2LQ ☎ (0803) 23381

Attractive Victorian residence in grounds high up in quiet residential area.

★★ **Bancourt,** Avenue Rd, TQ2 5LE ☎ (0803) 295077
In row of detached houses, large hotel with spacious dining room. Indoor swimming pool, putting, billiards. Fr
46 bedrs, 30 en suite, 3 ba; TV; tcf
🏛 TV, dogs, ns; P 50, coach; child facs; con 25
✕ LD 7.45, bar meals only lunch. Resid & Rest lic
£ B&B £25–£32·50, B&B (double) £50–£65; HB weekly £99–£235; D £10·50
cc Access, Amex, B'card/Visa; dep.

★★ **Bowden Close,** Teignmouth Rd, Maidencombe, TQ1 4TJ ☎ (0803) 328029

An attractive house in grounds midway between Teignmouth and Torquay.
20 bedrs, 16 en suite, (1 sh), 1 ba; TV; tcf
🏛 TV, dogs, ns; P 25, G 2, coach; child facs; con 25
✕ LD 8, bar meals only lunch. Resid & Rest lic

T

Torquay (Devon)

Our name says it all!

Easy access M5
9 hole golf course, squash, saunas, etc., indoor & outdoor swimming & tennis, 5 Resident sports professionals, Resident Children's Nanny.
Set in 25 acres of colourful gardens & woodland.
On the edge of the sea.

Simply write or telephone

THE PALACE, TORQUAY TQ1 3TG

Torquay (0803) 200200

Torquay (Devon)

RAC
★★★

RAC
★★★

Modern 42 bedroom luxury hotel overlooking one of the most beautiful beaches in South Devon, Anstey's Cove and Redgate Beach, access to both through the hotel grounds. All bedrooms en-suite with sun balcony, colour TV, telephone, baby listening, room service.
For your enjoyment, poolside restaurant, cocktail lounge, jacuzzi, solarium, games room, cabaret.
Why chance where you stay, Gleneagles is recommended by Ashley Courtenay, Egon Ronay, Signpost, to mention just a few. This is a family run hotel which has a renowned reputation as one of the leading hotels in the South Devon area. Reservations: (0803) 293637/297011

Torquay (Devon)

A relaxed 3 Star Hotel, open all year; it is levelly situated close to Beach, Parks and Country walks. Nearby, is the Leisure Centre, many sports activities; and it's level to Theatre, Harbour, Marina and Shops. All Rooms en-suite, with Tea Making, TV, Radio and Telephone. There is an Indoor Pool, Spa Bath, Sauna and Solarium. Music/Dancing up to 3 nights during most weeks of the year. Bookings from any day to any day, all fully inclusive. Full Board, Dinner Room and Breakfast or Room and Breakfast Terms. Short Breaks and Residential Conference/Meeting Terms.

Four Poster 'Celebration' Room at this 4 Crown Hotel.

Please contact: KISTOR HOTEL, Belgrave Road, Torquay
Tel: 0803 212632 Fax: 0803 293219

£ B&B £18·50–£20, B&B (double) £37–£40; HB weekly £150·50–£178·50; D £8·50; [5% V]
cc Access, B'card/Visa; dep.

★★ **Burlington,** 462 Babbacombe Rd, TQ1 1HN (0803) 294374
Fax: (0803) 200189

Privately-owned and run, stone and brick-built hotel in pleasant location. Indoor swimming pool, putting, sauna, solarium.
55 bedrs, 45 en suite; TV; tcf
TV, dogs; P 20, coach; child facs
LD 8, bar meals only lunch. Resid & Rest lic
£ B&B £21·50–£27·50, B&B (double) £38–£50; D £12; WB; [10% V Oct–May]
cc Access, B'card/Visa; dep.

★★ H **Bute Court,** Belgrave Rd, TQ2 5HQ (0803) 293771

Large Victorian building in own gardens on main road close to sea and shops. Swimming pool, billiards. Fr
46 bedrs, 42 en suite, 4 ba; TV; tcf
lift, TV, dogs; P 35, coach; child facs; con 50
LD 8, nr lunch. Resid & Rest lic
£ B&B £18·50–£30 (w/e £24), B&B (double) £37–£60; D £8; [10% V]
cc Access, Amex, B'card/Visa, Diners; dep.

★★ **Chelston Towers,** Rawlyn Rd, TQ2 6PQ (0803) 607351
Attractive country house set in 2 acres of woodland and garden. Swimming pool. Open Feb–Dec
24 bedrs, 11 en suite, 4 ba
dogs; P 40, coach; child facs
LD 8, bar meals only lunch. Resid lic
£ B&B £17·50–£28, B&B (double) £35–£56; HB weekly £150–£219; D £12; [10% V Feb–May; Oct–Dec]; dep.

★★ H **Conway Court,** Warren Rd, TQ2 5TS (0803) 299699
A Victorian building high up in quiet road overlooking sea front. Swimming pool.
38 bedrs, 35 en suite, 1 ba; TV; tcf
TV, dogs, ns; coach; child facs; con 50
LD 8, bar meals only lunch. Resid lic
£ D £10
cc Access, Amex, B'card/Visa, Diners; dep.

★★ **Coppice,** Barrington Rd, TQ1 2QJ (0803) 27786
Victorian house standing in grounds above main road to Babbacombe. Swimming pool, putting, solarium. Open Apr–Oct
38 bedrs, 36 en suite, 1 ba; TV; tcf
TV, dogs, ns; P 30, coach; child facs
LD 7.30, bar meals only lunch. Resid lic
£ B&B £16·50–£21·75, B&B (double) £33–£43·50; HB weekly £138–£182; D £8; dep.

★★ **Crofton House,** Croft Rd, TQ2 5TZ (0803) 23761

Cream-painted, Edwardian building with pleasant garden, close to seafront. Swimming pool, solarium, snooker.
37 bedrs, 30 en suite, 2 ba; TV; tcf
dogs, ns: P 13, coach; child facs; con 50

★★ H **Elmington,** St Agnes La, TQ2 6QE (0803) 605192

Originally a Victorian residence attractively set in quiet residential area. Swimming pool.
22 bedrs, 16 en suite, 2 ba; TV; tcf
TV, dogs; P 8, coach; child facs
LD 8, bar meals only lunch. Resid & Rest lic
£ B&B £22–£33, B&B (double) £44–£66; HB weekly £159–£232; D £9·95; [V Oct–May]
cc Access, B'card/Visa; dep.

★★ C **Gresham Court,** Babbacombe Rd, TQ1 1HG (0803) 293007
A large Victorian building close to sea and shops. Open Mar–Nov.
30 bedrs, 30 en suite; TV; tcf
lift, TV, dogs; P 12, coach; child facs
LD 8, bar meals only lunch. Resid lic
£ B&B £19–£25, B&B (double) £38–£50; HB weekly £140–£177; D £7
cc Access, B'card/Visa; dep.

★★ **Howden Court,** 23 Croft Rd, TQ2 5UD (0803) 294844
Sea front approached by private path through grounds of this Victorian house. Open May–Oct.
32 bedrs, 32 en suite, 1 ba; TV; tcf
TV, dogs; P 28, coach; child facs
LD 8, bar meals only lunch & Fri dinner. Resid & Rest lic
£ B&B £20·50–£23·50, B&B (double) £36·50–£41; HB weekly £164·50–£187·25; D £12·50; dep.

★★ **Hunsdon Lea,** Hunsdon Rd, TQ1 1QB (0803) 26538
Victorian house in its own grounds in quiet residential area. Swimming pool, solarium.

★★ **Lansdowne,** Babbacombe Rd, TQ1 1PW (0803) 299599
Edwardian building in own pleasant grounds; on main road. Swimming pool, solarium.
27 bedrs, 27 en suite; TV; tcf
TV, dogs, ns; P 32, coach; child facs; con 100
LD 7.45, bar meals only lunch. Resid & Rest lic
£ B&B £21; HB weekly £139·50; D £9·50, WB £47·50 (2 nts); [10% V Oct–May]
cc Access; dep

★★ **Meadfoot Bay,** Meadfoot Sea Rd, TQ1 2LQ (0803) 294722
Fax: (0803) 292871

A Victorian-built house in attractive gardens on high ground. Open Feb–Nov & Xmas.
25 bedrs, 20 en suite, 2 ba; TV; tcf
TV, dogs; P 17, coach; child facs
LD 8, bar meals only lunch. Resid & Rest lic
£ B&B £19–£26, B&B (double) £32–£46; HB weekly £130–£200, D £8·50, WB £55
cc Access, Amex, B'card/Visa; dep.

★★ **Morningside,** Sea Front, Babbacombe, TQ1 3LG (0803) 327025
Two-storey residence with modern extension well situated overlooking Oddicombe and Babbacombe beaches.
14 bedrs, 14 en suite; TV, tcf
TV, ns; P 14, coach; no children under 10
LD 8.30, bar meals only lunch; Resid & Rest lic
£ B&B £20–£29; B&B (double) £40–£58; HB weekly £178–£248; D £9; WB £81 (3 nts HB); [10% V]
cc Access, B'card/Visa; dep.

★★ C **Mount Nessing**, St Luke's Rd North, TQ2 5PD (0803) 292970
Three-storey Victorian building with attractive Victorian-style conservatory extension.
12 bedrs, 12 en suite; TV; tcf
TV, ns; P 10; no children under 7
LD 8.30, nr lunch. Resid & Rest lic
£ B&B £16–£21, B&B (double) £32–£42; HB weekly £165–£200; D £9; WB £48; [10% V Sep–Jun]
cc Access, B'card/Visa; dep.
(*See also advertisement on p. 484*)

★★ **Nethway,** Falkland Rd, TQ2 5JR (0803) 297630

T

Victorian building in own grounds in quiet situation near shops. Swimming pool.
27 bedrs, 24 en suite, 1 ba; TV; tcf
TV; dogs, P 20, coach; child facs
LD 7.30, bar meals only lunch. Resid & Rest lic
£ B&B £18–£21, B&B (double) £36–£42; HB weekly £160–£200; D £8·50
cc Access, Amex, B'card/Visa, Diners; dep

★★ Norcliffe, Babbacombe Downs Rd, TQ1 3LF (0803) 328456
A modern hotel on Downs with commanding view of Bay.
20 bedrs, 20 en suite, 2 ba; TV; tcf
lift, dogs; P 16, coach; child facs; con 80

★★ Palm Court, Torbay Rd, Sea Front, TQ2 5HD (0803) 294881
A large seafront hotel. Attractive dining room with minstrel gallery. Fr, Es
70 bedrs, 53 en suite, 17 ba; TV; tcf
lift, dogs; coach; child facs; con 200
LD 8.45, bar meals only lunch
£ B&B £26–£28·50, B&B (double) £52–£57; HB weekly £242·55–£261·80; L £6·50, D £10·50
cc Access, B'card/Visa, Diners; dep.

★★ Regina, Victoria Par, TQ1 2BE (0803) 292904 Tx: 9312102425
Fax: (0803) 214014

Large hotel in seafront terrace overlooking harbour. Close to main shops.
70 bedrs, 61 en suite, (1 sh), 6 ba; TV; tcf
lift, TV, dogs; G 12, coach; child facs; con 50
LD 8
£ B&B £16·50–£19·50; HB weekly £130–£175; L fr £4·50, D fr £6·95; WB £17·50; [5% V Oct–Apr]
cc Access, Amex, B'card/Visa, Diners; dep.

★★ Roseland, Warren Rd, TQ2 5TT (0803) 213829 Fax: (0803) 291266
Mid-Victorian residence in quiet road with panoramic view of Torbay.
34 bedrs, 34 en suite; TV; tcf
lift, dogs, ns; G 2 (£2), coach; child facs; con 100

★★ Sefton, Babbacombe Downs Rd, TQ1 3LH (0803) 328728
Cream-washed Victorian house with later additions—gardens at rear. Good views. Billiards.
47 bedrs, 47 en suite; TV; tcf
lift, dogs; P 47, coach; child facs; con 100
LD 8.45, bar meals only Mon–Sat lunch
£ B&B £30·50–£36·50, B&B (double) £61–£73; HB weekly £269·50–£311·50; L £6·50, D £9·95; WB £30 (off season); [10% V]
cc Access, Amex, B'card/Visa; dep.

Changes made after July 1990 are not included.

★★ Shedden Hall, TQ2 5TY (0803) 292964

A Victorian built hotel on hill just off main seafront. Swimming pool, solarium.
29 bedrs, 26 en suite, 2 ba; TV; tcf
dogs; P 29, coach; child facs
LD 8, nr Mon–Sat lunch. Resid & Rest lic
£ B&B £21–£32, B&B (double) £42–£50; HB weekly £188–£216; L £6·50, D £10·95; WB £40; [10% V]
cc Access, Amex, B'card/Visa, Diners; dep.

★★ Sunray, Aveland Rd, Babbacombe, TQ1 3PT (0803) 328285
A purpose-built, family-run hotel pleasantly set in residential area. Open Apr–Nov & Xmas.
21 bedrs, 21 en suite, 2 ba; TV; tcf
TV, dogs; P 16, coach, child facs
LD 8, nr lunch, Resid lic
£ B&B £15–£16, B&B (double) £30–£32; D £7·50; [5% V Mar–Jun, Sep–Oct]
cc Access, B'card/Visa, dep.

★★ Sydore, Meadfoot Rd, TQ1 2JP (0803) 294758

A Georgian residence, in its own grounds, close to sea. Fr
13 bedrs, 13 en suite; TV; tcf
TV, dogs, ns; P 20, coach; child facs
LD 8.30. Resid & Rest lic
£ B&B £22–£27, B&B (double) £50–£64; L £5·50, D £7; [10% V]
cc Access, B'card/Visa; dep.

★★ Templestowe, Tor Church Rd, TQ2 5UU (0803) 299499
Fax: (0803) 295101
Large 3-storey hotel just off town centre. Swimming pool, tennis, solarium.
87 bedrs, 87 en suite, 2 ba; TV; tcf
lift, TV, dogs; P 50, coach; child facs
LD 8.30, bar meals only lunch
£ B&B £24·50–£37·50, B&B (double) £41–£67; HB weekly £172·10–£264·60; L £5, D £8
cc Access, B'card/Visa; dep.

En suite rooms
En suite rooms may be bath or shower rooms. If you have a preference, remember to state it when booking a room.

★★ Vernon Court, Warren Rd, TQ2 5TR (0803) 292676

Hotel with spacious public rooms; in terrace with panoramic seafront views. Open Mar–Nov & Xmas. Fr
21 bedrs, 9 en suite; TV; tcf
TV, dogs; P 9, coach; child facs
bar meals only lunch; Resid & Rest lic
£ B&B £20·50–£31, B&B (double) £43–£62; D £10; [10% V Mar–Nov]
cc Access, Amex, B'card/Visa, Diners; dep.

★ Ashley Rise, Babbacombe Rd, TQ1 3SJ (0803) 327282

Modern hotel on main road and in its own pleasant grounds. Open Mar–Nov.
28 bedrs, 11 en suite, 5 ba; tcf
TV, dogs; P 14, coach; child facs
LD 7.30, bar meals only lunch. Resid & Rest lic
£ B&B £16–£20; HB weekly £136–£168; D £8·75; [10% V]; dep.

★ Belvedere House, Braddon Hill West, TQ1 1BG (0803) 293313
South facing, 19th century mansion high up with good views over Torbay.
10 bedrs, 10 en suite; TV; tcf
TV, dogs, ns; P 9; no children under 10

★ Fairmount House, Herbert Rd, Chelston, TQ2 6RW (0803) 605446

Victorian house situated in own grounds; small attractive dining room. Open Mar–6 Nov.
8 bedrs, 8 en suite, 2 ba; tcf

⌂ TV, dogs; P 9, coach; child facs
✕ LD 7.30, bar meals only Mon-Sat lunch, Sun dinner. Resid lic
£ B&B £20–£24, B&B (double) £40–£48; L £7·50, D £9; WB £56·50 (2 nts); [5% V]
cc Access, Amex, B'card/Visa; dep.

★ **Fluela,** 15 Hatfield Rd, TQ1 3BW ☎ (0803) 297512

White-painted Victorian building in quiet area towards Marychurch village.
🛏 13 bedrs, 13 en suite, 1 ba; TV; tcf
⌂ TV, ns; P 18; child facs
✕ LD 7.30, bar meals only lunch
£ B&B £14·50–£21·50, B&B (double) £24–£36; HB weekly £110–£160
cc Access, B'card/ Visa.

★ **Palm Grove,** Meadfoot Sea Rd, TQ1 2LQ ☎ (0803) 23027
Privately-owned Victorian hotel in grounds close to sea and shops.

★ **Shelley Court,** Croft Rd, TQ2 5UD ☎ (0803) 23042
Large Victorian house with modern extension, in its own grounds.

★ **Sunleigh,** Livermead Hill, TQ2 6QY ☎ (0803) 607137

Victorian house built of stone in own grounds overlooking Bay. Open 22 Mar–2 Nov & Xmas/New Year
🛏 21 bedrs, 21 en suite, 1 ba; TV; tcf
⌂ TV, dogs; P 18, coach; child facs
✕ LD 7.00, nr lunch. Resid & Rest lic
£ B&B £16·50–£22; HB weekly £139–£180; D £8·75; [10% V Easter–Nov]; dep.

★ **Tormohun,** Newton Rd, TQ2 5BZ ☎ (0803) 23681
A small, family-run hotel. Swimming pool.

★ **Windsurfer,** St Agnes La, TQ2 6QE ☎ (0803) 606550

Victorian building in its own grounds. Small attractive restaurant.
🛏 10 bedrs, 10 en suite; TV; tcf
⌂ ns; P 11; child facs
✕ LD 7.15. Resid lic
£ B&B (double) £16–£19; [5% V Oct–Mar]; dep.

Glenorleigh (Highly Acclaimed), 26 Cleveland Rd, TQ2 5BE ☎ (0803) 292135. *Hotel. Swimming pool, solarium.* Open Jan–Oct. ⚒ De, Sw
£ B&B £14·50–£25; HB weekly £119–£161
cc Access, B'card/Visa; dep.
Haldon Priors (Highly Acclaimed), Meadfoot Sea Rd, TQ1 2LQ ☎ (0803) 213365
Robin Hill (Highly Acclaimed), Braddons Hill Rd East, TQ1 1HF ☎ (0803) 214518. *Hotel.*
£ B&B £20–£25; HB weekly £151–£183.

Barn Hayes (Acclaimed), Brim Hill, Maidencombe TQ1 4TR ☎ (0803) 327980. *Private Hotel.*
£ B&B £14·50–£22; HB weekly £135–£198; [10% V]
Belmont (Acclaimed), 66 Belgrave Rd, TQ2 5HY ☎ (0803) 295028. *Hotel.*
£ B&B £12–£20; HB weekly £105–£164
Chesterfield (Acclaimed), 62 Belgrave Rd, TQ2 5HY ☎ (0803) 292318. *Hotel.*
£ B&B £12–£17; HB weekly £99–£146; [10% V Sep–Jun]
Concorde, 26 Newton Rd, TQ2 5BZ ☎ (0803) 22330. *Private Hotel. Swimming pool.*
Cranborne (Acclaimed), 58 Belgrave Rd, TQ2 5HY ☎ (0803) 298046. *Hotel.* Closed Dec.
£ B&B £13–£17·50; HB weekly £97–£130; [10% V excl Jul, Aug]
Cranmore (Acclaimed), 89 Avenue Rd, TQ2 5LH ☎ (0803) 298488. *Private Hotel.*
£ B&B £10–£12; HB weekly £108·50–£136·50
Daphne Court (Acclaimed), Lower Warberry Rd, TQ1 1QS ☎ (0803) 212011. *Hotel. Swimming pool.* Open Mar–Oct.
£ B&B £19–£25; HB weekly £150–£200; [5% V]
Elmdene (Acclaimed), Rathmore Rd, TQ2 6NZ ☎ (0803) 294940. *Hotel.*
£ B&B £15–£22; HB weekly £150·50–£160
Exmouth View (Acclaimed), St Alban's Rd, Babbacombe, TQ1 3LJ ☎ (0803) 327307. *Hotel.*
£ B&B £10·95–£21·95; HB weekly £100·50–£177; [V]
Fairways (Acclaimed), 72 Avenue Rd, TQ2 5LF ☎ (0803) 298471. *Hotel.*
£ B&B £12; HB weekly £122–£142; [5% V Nov–Apr]
Glenwood (Acclaimed), Rowdens Rd, TQ2 5AZ ☎ (0803) 296318. *Private Hotel.*
Ingoldsby (Acclaimed), 1 Chelston Rd, TQ2 6PT ☎ (0803) 607497. *Hotel.*
£ B&B £12·50–£17; HB weekly £102–£146
Lindens (Acclaimed), 31 Bampfylde Rd, TQ2 5AY ☎ (0803) 212281. *Hotel.* ⚒ Fr
£ B&B 15–£20; HB weekly £149–£184; [10% V Sep–May]
Lindum (Acclaimed), Abbey Rd, TQ2 5ND ☎ (0803) 292795. *Private Hotel.* Open Easter–Oct.
£ B&B £10·50–£18·50; HB weekly £104·50–£154·50; [5% V Apr–Oct]
Mapleton (Acclaimed), St Luke's Rd North, TQ2 5PD ☎ (0803) 292389. *Hotel.* ⚒ Fr, De
£ B&B £13·75–£19; HB weekly £120–£161
Norwood (Acclaimed), 60 Belgrave Rd, TQ2 5HY ☎ (0803) 294236. *Hotel.*
£ B&B £12·50; HB weekly £108–£152; [5% V Sep–Jun]
Patricia (Acclaimed), Belgrave Rd, TQ2 5HY ☎ (0803) 293339. *Hotel.*
£ B&B £18–£22; [V]
Rawlyn House (Acclaimed), Rawlyn Rd, Chelston, TQ2 6PL ☎ (0803) 605208. *Hotel. Swimming pool.* Open Apr–Oct & Xmas.
£ B&B £19–£26; HB weekly £144–£195; [5% V]
Red Squirrel Lodge (Acclaimed), Chelston Rd, TQ2 6PU ☎ (0803) 605496. *Hotel.*
£ B&B £14·50–£20·50; HB weekly £121–£155·65; [10% V Oct–Apr]
Seaway (Acclaimed), Chelston Rd, TQ2 6PU ☎ (0803) 605320. *Private Hotel.* ⚒ Fr
£ B&B £16–£24; HB weekly £114–£160; [V]
Sherwood (Acclaimed), Belgrave Road, TQ2 5HP ☎ (0803) 294534. *Hotel.*
£ B&B £20–£28; HB weekly £156–£214; [5% V Oct–Apr]
White Gables (Acclaimed), Rawlyn Rd, Chelston TQ2 6PQ ☎ (0803) 605233. *Hotel. Swimming pool.*

Ascot House, 7 Tor Church Rd, TQ2 5UR ☎ (0803) 295142. *Private Hotel.* ⚒ Ma
£ B&B £12·50–£15·50; HB weekly £133–£169·50; [5% V Jan–May]
Ashwood, 2 St Margaret's Rd, St Marychurch, TQ1 4NW ☎ (0803) 328173. ♿
£ B&B £12–£20; HB weekly £108–£156; [5% V Sep–May]
Avron, 70 Windsor Rd, TQ1 1QZ ☎ (0803) 294182. *Hotel.* Open May–Sep.
£ HB weekly £98–£122
Briarfields, 84–86 Avenue Rd, TQ2 5LF ☎ (0803) 297844. *Hotel.* Open 14 Jan–14 Nov.
£ B&B £14–£28; HB weekly £115–£150; [V Jan–May]
Colindale, 20 Rathmore Rd, TQ2 6NZ ☎ (0803) 293947. *Hotel.*
£ B&B £14–£16; HB weekly £120–£139; [5% V Oct–Mar]
Courthouse, Rock House Lane, Maidencombe, TQ1 4SU ☎ (0803) 328335. *Hotel.* Open Apr–Oct
£ B&B £13·50–£16·50; HB weekly £140–£161; [5% V Apr–Jun, Sep–Oct]
Craig Court, 10 Ash Hill Rd, TQ1 3HZ ☎ (0803) 294400. *Private Hotel.* Open Easter–Oct.
£ B&B £15–£18; HB weekly £140–£161
Devon Court, Croft Rd, TQ2 5UE ☎ (0803) 293603. *Hotel. Swimming pool.* Open Easter–Oct
£ B&B £12–£20; HB weekly £98–£154; [10% V Easter–May, Sep, Oct]
Durlstone, 156 Avenue Rd, TQ2 5LQ ☎ (0803) 212307. *Guest House.*
£ B&B £10–£12; HB weekly £97–£110
Hart Lea, 81 St Marychurch Rd, TQ1 3HG ☎ (0803) 312527. *Guest House.*
Melba House, 62 Bampfylde Rd, TQ2 5AY ☎ (0803) 292331. *Private Hotel.*
Olivia Court, Braddons Hill Rd, TQ1 1HD ☎ (0803) 292595. *Hotel.* ⚒ Fr ♿
£ B&B £15–£31·50; HB weekly £133·50–£180; [10% V Oct–Apr]
Pencarrow, 64 Windsor Rd, TQ1 1SZ ☎ (0803) 293080. *Hotel.*
Richwood, 20 Newton Rd, TQ2 5BZ ☎ (0803) 293729. *Swimming pool.*
£ B&B £12–£21; HB weekly £84–£144; [5% V]
St Kilda, 49 Babbacombe Rd, TQ1 3SJ ☎ (0803) 327238. *Hotel.* Open Easter–Oct

T

Torquay (Devon)

Livermead House Hotel

Seafront, Torquay. Tel: (0803) 294361 Telex: 42918

Right on the seafront at sea level, the Livermead House Hotel is situated in three acres of garden and has ample parking. The 62 en-suite rooms all have colour TV, 'phone, hair dryer, radio, tea and coffee trays. Extensive leisure facilities. Restaurant and Bar also open to non-residents for lunch, dinner, bar meals and teas. Conference and function facilities.

Proprietors: The Rew Family

Colour Brochure on Request

Torquay (Devon)

Mount Nessing Hotel

ST. LUKES ROAD NORTH
TORQUAY DEVON TQ2 5PD
Telephone: (0803) 292970

Mount Nessing Hotel is a fine detached Victorian House situated in an elevated position overlooking Torbay in a tranquil tree lined road, yet enjoying a central position to the harbour, beach and town.

The hotel has 12 elegantly decorated bedrooms all with private facilities, colour TV, tea/coffee making, some with views over Torbay.

The dining room creates a relaxing atmosphere to enjoy commendable cuisine where the style is classical French/ English with modern presentation.

The large Victorian Conservatory bar offering beers and fine wines.

★ 3 Night Breaks Available.
★ Christmas 4 Night Programme.
★ Gourmet Weekends.
★ Sorry No Children Under 10 years.
★ Four Poster Suite with Whirlpool Bath.
★ Direct Dial Telephones.
★ Complimentary Toiletries.
★ Private Parking.

Good Bedroom Award

Uppingham (Leicestershire)

The Crown Hotel

RAC

High Street East, Uppingham, Leicester LE15 9PY Tel: 0572 822302

All rooms en suite, colour TV, telephone and tea/coffee making facilities.
Single £30; Double £40; restaurant and bar.

£ B&B £13·50–£16·50; HB weekly £102–£125
Sandpiper, Rowdens Rd, TQ2 5AZ ☎(0803) 292779
Skerries, 25 Morgan Av, TQ2 5RR ☎(0803) 293618. *Hotel.*
£ B&B £10·50–£14·50; HB weekly £98·50–£115·50; [5% V Oct–Jun]
Southbourne, 9 Cleveland Rd, TQ2 5BD ☎(0803) 297609. *Hotel.*
£ B&B £15–£20; HB weekly £128; [V Oct–Mar]
Torbay Rise, Old Mill Rd, TQ2 6HL ☎(0803) 605541. *Hotel. Swimming pool.* Open Easter–Oct.
£ B&B £15–£24; HB weekly £140–£175; [5% V Sep–Jun]
Torcroft, 28 Croft Rd, TQ2 5UE ☎(0803) 298292. *Hotel.*
Trafalgar House, 30 Bridge Rd, TQ2 5BA ☎(0803) 292486. *Hotel.*
Villa Marina, Cockington Lane, Livermead, TQ2 6QU ☎(0803) 605440

TOTNES
Devon. Map 3B2

Pop 5,524. Newton Abbot 8, London 191, Ashburton 8, Dartmouth 13 (Fy 11), Kingsbridge 12, Plymouth 22, Torquay 8. **EC** Thur. **MD** Tue, Fri. **Golf** Churston 18h. **See** Church (15th cent), Castle ruins, Butterwalk, Guildhall (16th cent) and Museum, Totnes Museum, East Gate.
ℹ The Plains. ☎(0803) 863168

★★ Royal Seven Stars, The Plains TQ9 5DD ☎(0803) 862125
Fax: (0803) 867925

Fine former coaching inn with unusual porch. In town centre.
🛏 18 bedrs, 12 en suite, 4 ba; TV; tcf
🏠 TV, dogs, ns; P 20, coach; child facs; con 60
✕ LD 9.30
£ B&B £36–£46, B&B (double) £48–£58; HB weekly £213–£335; L £7·50, D £15; WB fr £65
cc Access, B'card/Visa, Diners; dep.

TOTON
Nottinghamshire. Map 24C3

M1 (jn 25) 3, London 119, Ashby-de-la-Zouch 14, Derby 10, Loughborough 13, Nottingham 6.

Manor, Nottingham Rd, NG9 6EF ☎Long Eaton (0602) 733487. *Private Hotel.*

TOTTENHILL
Norfolk. Map 34C1

Pop 237. Downham Market 6, London 94, King's Lynn 6½, Swaffham 14, Wisbech 13.

Oakwood House (Acclaimed), PE33 0RH ☎King's Lynn (0553) 810256. *Hotel.* ♿
£ B&B £23–£35; HB weekly £161–£280; WB £46–£64

TRICKETTS CROSS
Dorset. Map 5B2

Ringwood 6, London 99, Bournemouth 7, Poole 8, Wimborne Minster 7.

★★ Coach House, Ferndown, BH22 9NW ☎(0202) 861222 Fax: (0202) 894130

A complex of modern buildings with motel-style bedrooms; set amongst pine trees on edge of New Forest. ⚒ Fr, De, It
🛏 44 bedrs, 44 en suite; TV; tcf
🏠 TV, dogs; P 200, G 20, coach; child facs; con 200
✕ LD 9.30
£ B&B £37, B&B (double) £53; L £6, D £7·75; WB £62 (2 nts HB)
cc Access, Amex, B'card/Visa, Diners.

TRING
Hertfordshire. Map 14A2

Pop 10,610. Watford 16, London 32, Aylesbury 7, Dunstable 10, High Wycombe 16, Rickmansworth 15, St Albans 15. **EC** Wed. **MD** Mon, Fri. **Golf** Wendover 9h.

★★★ Rose & Crown, High St, HP23 5AH ☎(0442) 824071 Tx: 826538
Fax: (0442) 890735
20th century town centre inn built in the mock Tudor style. (Lns)
🛏 28 bedrs, 28 en suite; TV; tcf
🏠 ns; P 50, coach; child facs; con 80
✕ LD 10
£ B&B £76 (w/e £34), B&B (double) £88; L £8·25, D £13·25; [V]
cc Access, Amex, B'card/Visa, Diners.

Pendley Manor, Cow La, HP23 5QY ☎(0442) 891891 Fax: (0442) 890687

Hotel awaiting inspection. Indoor swimming pool, tennis, sauna, solarium, gymnasium, snooker.
🏠 lift, dogs; P 100, coach; con 160
✕ LD 9.30
£ B&B £100, B&B (double) £125; L £11, D £17·50
cc Access, Amex, B'card/Visa, Diners.

TROTTON
West Sussex. Map 6A2

Haslemere 11, London 52, Chichester 16, Petersfield 6, Petworth 10.

Licences
Establishments have a full licence unless shown as unlicensed or with the limitations listed on p 6.

★★★ Southdowns, Rogate, GU31 5JN ☎Rogate (073 080) 774 Tx: 86658
Fax: (0730 80) 790 ♿

Large country house set in attractive grounds. Indoor swimming pool, fishing, sauna, solarium, gymnasium. ⚒ Fr, De, Es
🛏 22 bedrs, 22 en suite; TV; tcf
🏠 ns, P 80, coach; child facs; con 120
✕ LD 10
£ B&B £45–£60 (w/e £37·50), B&B (double) £60–£80; L £9·95, D £15; [10% V]
cc Access, Amex, B'card/Visa; dep.

TROWBRIDGE
Wiltshire. Map 5A3

Pop 24,000. Devizes 7, London 93, Bath 11, Chippenham 12, Frome 8, Warminster 9. **EC** Wed. **MD** Tue, Fri, Sat. **Golf** West Wilts 18h. **See** Parish Church, Town Hall (bust of Pitman), 18th cent Lock-up (Blind House), The Courts, Holt 3 m N.
ℹ St Stephen's Pl ☎(0225) 777054

★★ Polebarn, Polebarn Rd, BA14 7EW ☎(0225) 777006 Fax: (0225) 754164
Two-storey Georgian house situated close to town centre. Family-owned. ⚒ De
🛏 13 bedrs, 12 en suite, 1 ba; TV; tcf
🏠 P 8, G 3; coach; child facs; con 25
✕ LD 9; nr Sun dinner
£ B&B £40, B&B (double) £53; L £6, D £8·50; [10% V w/e]
cc Access, B'card/Visa.

★ C Hilbury Court, Hilperton Rd, BA14 7JW ☎(0225) 752949

Two-storey Victorian building in outskirts. Attractive well-laid-out gardens.
🛏 13 bedrs, 7 en suite, (3 sh), 1 ba; TV; tcf
🏠 TV; P 14; child facs; con 20

Gordons, 65 Wingfield Rd, BA14 9EG ☎(0225) 752072

TRURO
Cornwall. Map 2B1

Pop 16,500. St Austell 14, London 246, Bodmin 24, Falmouth 11, Helston 16, Newquay 18, Redruth 8, Wadebridge 23. **MD** Wed. **Golf** Truro 18h. **See** Cathedral, County Museum and Art Gallery, Trelissick Gdns 4 m S.
ℹ Municipal Buildings, Boscawen St. ☎(0872) 74555

★★★ H **Brookdale,** Tregolls Rd, TR1 1JZ ☎(0872) 73513

Large modern hotel of impressive design set in grounds off A39. Closed Xmas. ✗ Fr, Es, De, It
🛏 22 bedrs, 22 en suite; TV; tcf
🏨 P 50, G 10, coach; child facs
✕ LD 8.45, bar meals only lunch. Resid lic
£ B&B £46 (w/e £42); B&B (double) £62 (w/e £55); HB weekly £350; D £15
cc Access, Amex, B'card/Visa, Diners.

★★ **Carlton,** Falmouth Rd, TR1 2HL ☎(0872) 72450 Fax: (0872) 223938

Attractive Victorian building with large modern bedroom extension. Sauna, solarium, gymnasium.
🛏 31 bedrs, 28 en suite, 1 ba; TV; tcf
🏨 dogs; P 32, coach; child facs
✕ LD 8, nr lunch. Resid & Rest lic
£ B&B £26–£36·20, B&B (double) £39·20–£48·50; HB weekly £195–£211; D £7·95
cc Access, B'card/Visa.

★★ **Royal,** Lemon St, TR1 2QB ☎(0872) 70345 Fax: (0872) 72453

Established hotel in the old tradition—a dignified city centre building. ✗ Fr, De, Es
🛏 34 bedrs, 34 en suite; TV; tcf
🏨 TV, dogs; P 18, G 18, coach; child facs; con 50
✕ LD 9.30, bar meals only Sun lunch
£ B&B £38·50–£42·50 (w/e £24·75), B&B (double) £50; L £6·50, D £6·50; [10% V]
cc Access, Amex, B'card/Visa.

Marcorrie, 20 Falmouth Rd, TR1 2HX ☎(0872) 77374. *Private Hotel.*

TUNBRIDGE WELLS Kent. Map 11B1

See also SOUTHBOROUGH.
Pop 44,821. Tonbridge 4, London 36, Eastbourne 29, East Grinstead 13, Maidstone 16, Uckfield 16.
EC Wed. **MD** Wed. **Golf** Nevill 18h (2). **See** The Pantiles, 17th cent King Charles the Martyr Church, Holy Trinity Church.
ℹ Town Hall. ☎(0892) 515675

★★★★ **Spa,** Langton Rd, Mount Ephraim, TN4 8XJ ☎(0892) 20331 Tx: 957188 Fax: (0892) 510575 ♿

Impressive Georgian building in own grounds. Indoor swimming pool, tennis, sauna, solarium, gymnasium. ✗ Fr, It
🛏 76 bedrs, 76 en suite; TV; tcf
🏨 lift, dogs, ns; P 120, coach; child facs; con 300
✕ LD 9.30, bar meals only Sat lunch
£ B&B £70, B&B (double) £93; L £15, D £20; WB £50 (HB); [10% V]
cc Access, Amex, B'card/Visa, Diners.

★★★ **Calverley,** Crescent Rd, TN1 2LY ☎(0892) 26455 Tx: 957565 Fax: (0892) 512044
Fine early 19th century building overlooking Calverley Gardens at the rear. ✗ Fr
🛏 46 bedrs, 35 en suite, (2 sh), 9 ba; TV; tcf
🏨 lift, TV, dogs; P 50, coach; child facs; con 130
✕ LD 8.30
£ B&B £40–£44, B&B (double) £58–£67; L £9, D £11; [5% V]
cc Access, B'card/Visa, Diners.

★★★ **Royal Wells Inn,** Mount Ephraim, TN4 8BE ☎(0892) 511188 Fax: (0892) 511908

Small detached hotel in lovely listed building. Overlooks the town.

Licences
Establishments have a full licence unless shown as unlicensed or with the limitations listed on p 6.

🛏 25 bedrs, 25 en suite; TV; tcf
🏨 lift, dogs; P 25; child facs; con 75
✕ LD 10
£ B&B £60, B&B (double) £80; L £13·50, D £15·50; WB £100 (2 nts); [5% V]
cc Access, Amex, B'card/Visa, Diners.

★★ **Mount Edgcumbe House,** The Common, TN4 8BX ☎(0892) 31123
Attractive Victorian house built on an outcrop of sandstone on the Common. ✗ Fr
🛏 6 bedrs, 6 en suite; TV; tcf
🏨 P 20; con 28
✕ LD 10
£ B&B £40–£50, B&B (double) £65–£80; L £10·20, D £10·20; [5% V]

★★ **Russell,** 80 London Rd, TN1 1DZ ☎(0892) 544833 Tx: 95177 Fax: (0892) 515846

Well-appointed small hotel, situated close to shopping centre.
🛏 21 bedrs, 21 en suite, annexe 5 bedrs, 5 en suite; TV; tcf
🏨 ns; P 20, coach; child facs; con 20
✕ LD 9.30, bar meals only lunch
£ B&B £56–£97·50 (w/e £40), B&B (double) £62–£105; D £14; [V w/e]
cc Access, Amex, B'card/Visa, Diners; dep.

★★ **Wellington,** Mount Ephraim, TN4 8BU ☎(0892) 542911 Tx: 23152
Regency style hotel overlooking the Common. Sauna, solarium, gymnasium.
🛏 65 bedrs, 50 en suite, (1 sh), 4 ba; TV
🏨 lift, TV, dogs, P 35, coach; child facs; con 100

TURNERS HILL West Sussex. Map 10C1

M23 (jn 10) 4½, London 34, Crawley 7½, East Grinstead 4, Haywards Heath 8, Horsham 13.

🏠 ★★★★ **Alexander House,** Fen Place, RH10 4QD ☎Copthorne (0342) 714914 Tx: 95611

A luxury hotel in a fine red-brick mansion set in a secluded park. Putting, tennis, fishing, billiards.

EC *early closing* **MD** *market day* 🏠 *country house hotel* *ns (NS) no smoking areas* *tcf tea/coffee facilities*

TURVEY Bedfordshire. Map 21C3

Pop 950. Bedford 7, London 57, Buckingham 21, Huntingdon 25, Kettering 19, Northampton 13.
EC Tue. **Golf** Bedford 18h.

★★ **Laws,** High St, MK43 8DB (023 064) 213
Attractive 2-storey period building; owner-run. Gr, Du
11 bedrs, 11 en suite; TV; tcf
dogs, P 40, coach; child facs; con 100
LD 9.30, nr Sat lunch, Sun dinner
£ B&B £42, B&B (double) £55; L £10·50, D £16·50
cc Access, B'card/Visa; dep.

TUTBURY Staffordshire. Map 30C2

Pop 3,048. Burton-on-Trent 4, London 125, Ashbourne 15. Derby 11, Uttoxeter 10.
EC Wed. **Golf** Burton-on-Trent 18h. **See** 15th cent Castle, Norman Church, N. Staffs Traction Engines.

★★★ R **Ye Olde Dog & Partridge,** High St, DE13 9LS Burton-on-Trent (0283) 813030 Fax: (0283) 813178

Old black and white inn of character. Fr, Du. Closed Xmas.
3 bedrs, 3 en suite; annexe 19 bedrs, 19 en suite; TV; tcf
dogs, ns; P 100; no children under 8
LD 10, carvery lunch & Mon & Sun dinner. Resid lic
£ B&B £54–£60 (w/e £36); B&B (double) £66–£72 (w/e £49); L £8·50, D £8·50; [V w/e]
cc Access, Amex, B'card/Visa.
(See advertisement on p. 180)

TUXFORD Nottinghamshire. Map 31B3

Pop 2,600. Newark 13, London 138, Doncaster 24, Gainsborough 17, Lincoln 18, Ollerton 6, Thorne 29, Worksop 12.
EC Wed. **Golf** Retford 9h. **See** Parish Church, old Grammar School, old lock-up.

★★ R **Newcastle Arms,** Market Pl, NG22 0LA (0777) 870208

A hotel of character (18th century) situated in centre of village.
11 bedrs, 11 en suite; TV; tcf
dogs; P 50, U 2, coach; child facs; con 70
LD 9.15
£ B&B £49–£64, B&B (double) £57–£62; HB weekly £418·25–£552·65; L £10·75, D £14·95
cc Access, Amex, B'card/Visa, Diners.

TWO BRIDGES Devon. Map 3B2

Exeter 24, London 193, Ashburton 11, Okehampton 9, Plymouth 17, Tavistock 9.

★★★ **Prince Hall,** PL20 6SW
(082 289) 403 Fax: (082 289) 676
Stone-built country house in 5 acres of gardens in the middle of moorland. Fishing, riding. Fr, De
7 bedrs, 7 en suite; TV
dogs; P 15; child facs; con 20
LD 8.30. Resid & Rest lic
£ B&B £34, L £3·50, D £16·50
cc Access, Amex, B'card/Visa, Diners; dep.

★★ **Two Bridges,** Yelverton, PL20 6SW
Princetown (082 289) 581
Fax: (082 289) 575

18th century coaching inn on the West Dart River. Fishing, riding, billiards.
25 bedrs, 23 en suite, 3 ba; TV; tcf
dogs, ns; P, coach; child facs; con 60
LD 8.45
£ B&B £21–£40, B&B (double) £36–£60; L £7·50, D £10·50
cc Access, Amex, B'card/Visa, Diners; dep.

Cherrybrook (Acclaimed), PL20 6SP
Tavistock (0822) 88260. *Hotel.* Closed Xmas & New Year.
£ B&B £21·50; HB weekly £210

TYNEMOUTH Tyne & Wear. Map 37C3

Pop 50,014. Tyne Tunnel 2½, London 280, Alnwick 36, Coldstream 54, Newcastle upon Tyne 8, Sunderland 11.
EC Wed. **Golf** Tynemouth 18h. **See** Ancient Gatehouse and ruins of 11th cent Priory, Collingwood Monument, Lighthouse.

★★★ **Park,** Grand Parade, NE30 4JQ
091-257 1406 Fax: 091-257 1716
1930s style brick-built hotel in residential area on seafront. Solarium, gymnasium.
49 bedrs, 43 en suite, 3 ba; TV; tcf
dogs, ns; P 400, coach; child facs; con 350

Weekend breaks
Please consult the hotel for full details of weekend breaks; prices shown are an indication only. Many hotels offer mid week breaks as well.

UCKFIELD East Sussex. Map 6C2

Pop 9,200. East Grinstead 13, London 43, Eastbourne 19, Haywards Heath 12, Lewes 8, Tunbridge Wells 16.
EC Wed. **Golf** Piltdown 18h.

★★ **Ye Maiden's Head,** High St, TN22 1RJ
(0825) 762019 Tx: 957141

Pleasant old coaching inn. Conveniently situated in High Street.
13 bedrs, 10 en suite, 2 ba; TV
dogs; P 70, coach, no children under 8; con 75
LD 9.30
£ B&B £40–£50, B&B (double) £60–£72; L £5, D £12; WB £74 (2 nts HB)
cc Access, Amex, B'card/Visa, Diners.

Hooke Hall (Highly Acclaimed), 250 High St, TN22 1EN (0825) 61578 Tx: 95228
Fax: (0825) 768025. *Private Hotel.* Fr, De, It, Es
£ B&B £42·50–£65·50

ULLSWATER Cumbria

See GLENRIDDING, HOWTOWN, PATTERDALE, POOLEY BRIDGE, WATERMILLOCK.

ULVERSTON Cumbria. Map 36A4

Pop 11,976. M6 (jn 36) 24, London 270, Ambleside 21, Broughton-in-Furness 9½, Kendal 24, Lancaster 34, Penrith 43.
EC Wed. **MD** Thur. **Golf** Ulverston 18h.
i Coronation Hall, County Sq. Ulverston (0229) 57120

★★★ **Lonsdale House,** Daltongate, LA12 7BD (0229) 52598
Fax: (0229) 581260

3-storey 18th century building in quiet street. Pleasant garden at rear. Fr, It
20 bedrs, 20 en suite; TV; tcf
dogs, ns; P 1, coach; child facs; con 20
LD 9, nr lunch. Resid & Rest lic
£ B&B £19·55–£37·95 (w/e £19·55), B&B (double) £46–£57·50; D £9·15; [10% V]
cc Access, Amex, B'card/Visa, Diners; dep.

U

★★ Sefton House, Queen St, LA12 7AF ☎(0229) 52190

Small pleasant proprietor-managed hotel in 3-storey Georgian town house.
🛏 14 bedrs, 10 en suite, 2 ba; TV; tcf
🏠 TV; P 15, G 3; child facs
✕ LD 8.30, bar meals only Sun. Resid & Rest lic
£ B&B £27·50–£40 (w/e £27·50), B&B (double) £40–£60; D £12·50; WB £38·50
cc Access, B'card/Visa; dep.

★ Railway, Prince's St, LA12 7NQ ☎(0229) 52208
Small 3-storey white-faced building. Quiet situation yet near town centre.

UMBERLEIGH Devon. Map 3B4

Pop 138. South Molton 7, London 188, Barnstaple 7½, Bideford 14, Crediton 24, Holsworthy 22, Okehampton 20.
Golf Saunton 18h.

★★ Rising Sun Inn, EX37 9DU ☎High Bickington (0769) 60447

Small country inn (500 years old) by the River Taw. Fishing. (BCB)
🛏 6 bedrs, 6 en suite; TV; tcf
🏠 TV; P 20; no children under 16

UPHOLLAND Lancs. Map 32C3

Pop 7,780. M6 (jn 26) 1½, London 193, Ormskirk 7½, St Helens 7, Wigan 4½.
Golf Beacon Park 18h. **See** Church, Beacon Park.

Using RAC discount vouchers
Please tell the hotel when booking if you plan to use an RAC discount voucher (see p. 34) in part payment of your bill. Only one voucher will be accepted per party per stay. Discount vouchers will only be accepted in payment for accommodation, not for food.

★★ Holland Hall, 6 Lafford La, Wigan, WN8 0QZ ☎(0695) 624426
Fax: (0695) 622433

Attractive building offering all the comforts of a country hotel. ⚒ Fr
🛏 29 bedrs, 29 en suite; annexe 5 bedrs, 5 en suite; TV; tcf
🏠 P 200, coach; child facs; con 150
✕ LD 10, bar meals only Mon–Sat lunch & Sun dinner
£ B&B £42·50–£52, B&B (double) £49–£63; D £10; [5% V w/e]
cc Access, Amex, B'card/Visa, Diners.

UPPER AFFCOT Shropshire. Map 20A4

Craven Arms 3, London 155, Bridgnorth 23, Ludlow 11, Shrewsbury 17, Welshpool 24.

Travellers Rest Inn, nr Church Stretton, SY6 6RL ☎Church Stretton (0694) 6275.

UPPER SLAUGHTER Gloucestershire. Map 20C2
See also LOWER SLAUGHTER.
Pop 188. Stow-on-the-Wold 3, London 87, Burford 11, Cheltenham 15, Cirencester 17, Evesham 18.
Golf Broadway 18h. **See** Church, Bridge, Well nearby.

♣ ★★★ H C R Lords of the Manor, GL54 2JD ☎Cotswold (0451) 20243
Tx: 83147 Fax: (0451) 20696

In 7½ acres of attractive grounds, an imposing 17th century manor house. Fishing. ⚒ Fr, Es
🛏 29 bedrs, 29 en suite; TV
🏠 P 50, coach; child facs; con 20
✕ LD 9.30
£ B&B (double) £65–£135; L £13·25, D £28·50; WB £125 (HB); [10% V Nov–Mar]
cc Access, Amex, B'card/Visa, CB, Diners; dep.

UPPINGHAM Leicestershire. Map 21B4

Pop 2,761. Kettering 14, London 89, Leicester 18, Market Harborough 12, Melton Mowbray 15, Peterborough 21.
EC Thur. **MD** Fri. **Golf** Luffenham Heath 18h. **See** Uppingham School (apply to Porter), Church.

★★★ Falcon, High St East, LE15 9PY ☎(0572) 823535 Fax: (0572) 821620

An attractive traditional coaching house in centre of market town. ⚒ Fr
🛏 22 bedrs, 22 en suite; annexe 5 bedrs, 5 en suite; TV
🏠 dogs; P 25, coach; child facs; con 50
✕ LD 10
£ B&B £60–£75, B&B (double) £70–£85; L £10·50, D £16; WB £89
cc Access, Amex, B'card/Visa, CB, Diners.

★★★ Marquess of Exeter, Main St, Lyddington/Oakham, LE15 9LT ☎(0572) 822477 Fax: (0572) 821343

Pleasant village inn in attractive setting. All bedrooms in annexe.
🛏 17 bedrs, 17 en suite; TV; tcf
🏠 P 70, coach; child facs; con 50
✕ LD 9.30, bar meals only Sat lunch & Sun dinner
£ B&B £55–£66, B&B (double) £70–£76; L £11·95, D £11·95; WB £72; [5% V w/e Jan & Feb only]
cc Access, Amex, B'card/Visa, CB, Diners.

★★ H Garden, High St West, LE15 9QD ☎(0572) 822352 Fax: (0572) 821156
Small family-run hotel with an attractive walled garden.
🛏 12 bedrs, 10 en suite, 1 ba; TV; tcf
🏠 TV, dogs, ns; coach; child facs
✕ LD 9, nr Sun
£ B&B £25–£40, B&B (double) £35–£55; L £8·50, D £11·75
cc Access, Amex, B'card/Visa.

★★ H C R Lake Isle, High St East, LE15 9PZ ☎(0572) 822951
Fax: (0572) 822951
A 17th-century building in town centre sympathetically restored to an elegantly fitted small hotel.
🛏 10 bedrs, 10 en suite; TV; tcf
🏠 dogs; P 4, U 1; con 10
✕ LD 9.30, nr Sun dinner, Mon lunch. Resid lic
£ B&B £38–£42, B&B (double) £54–£62; L £10·75, D £16
cc Access, Amex, B'card/Visa, Diners.

EC *early closing* **MD** *market day* ♣ *country house hotel* *ns (NS) no smoking areas* *tcf tea/coffee facilities*

Crown, High St East, LE15 9PY
(0572) 822302
Refurbished, 17th century inn of great character in town centre.
7 bedrs, 7 en suite; TV; tcf
dogs; P 20, coach; child facs
LD 9.30, nr Sun dinner
£ B&B £30, B&B (double) £40, L £5, D £10
cc B'card/Visa; dep.
(*See advertisement on p. 484*)

Old Rectory (Highly Acclaimed), Belton-in-Rutland, LE15 9LE Belton (057 286) 279 Fax: (057 286) 343. *Guest House. Riding.*
£ B&B £17·50–£20; HB weekly £132·50–£165

Rutland House, 61 High St, LE15 9QD (0572) 822497. *Hotel.*
£ B&B £25

UPTON-UPON-SEVERN Hereford & Worcester (Worcestershire). Map 20B3
Pop 2,267. Tewkesbury 6, London 111, M50 4, Bromyard 17, Evesham 13, Ledbury 10, Worcester 10.
EC Thur. **Golf** Malvern 18h. **See** Church, Bridge, old houses.
[i] The Pepperpot, Church St. (068 46) 4200

★★★ **White Lion,** High St, WR8 0HJ
(068 46) 2551

Hotel near river combining impressive Georgian façade and Tudor beams. Closed Xmas.
10 bedrs, 10 en suite; TV; tcf
dogs; P 20, coach; child facs; con 12
LD 9.15
£ B&B £46, B&B (double) £62; HB weekly £262·50; L £13·25, D £13·50; WB £75–£80
cc Access, Amex, B'card/Visa, Diners; dep.

UTTOXETER Staffordshire. Map 30C2
Pop 11,275. Burton-on-Trent 13, London 135, Ashbourne 12, Derby 18, Leek 19, Lichfield 17, Stafford 14, Stoke-on-Trent 15, Stone 13.
EC Thur. **MD** Wed, Sat. **Golf** Uttoxeter 9h. **See** Parish Church, Racecourse.

★★★ **White Hart,** Carter St, ST14 8EU
(088 93) 2437
16th century coaching inn modernised and extended but retaining many attractive original features.

★★ **Bank House,** Church St, ST14 8AG
(0889) 566922 Fax: (0889) 567565
Traditional red-brick Georgian town house opposite church.
16 bedrs, 16 en suite; TV; tcf
dogs; P 16, coach; child facs; con 22

Hillcrest, 3 Leighton Rd, ST14 8BL.
(0889) 564627. *Guest House.* Closed 25 Dec.
£ B&B £14–£23; [10% V]

VERYAN Cornwall. Map 2C1
Pop 500. St Austell 12, London 245, Falmouth (Fy) 16, Newquay 20, Truro 12 (Fy 11).
Golf Truro 18h. **See** 15th cent Church, Carne Beacon (Ancient Burial Place).

★★★ **Nare,** Carne Beach, TR2 5PF
(0872) 501279 Fax: (0872) 501856
Refurbished hotel of attractive design in Nat. Trust land overlooking Gerrans Bay. Swimming pool, tennis, sauna, solarium, gymnasium, snooker.
39 bedrs, 39 en suite, 3 ba; TV; tcf
dogs; P 70; child facs; con 50
LD 9.30, nr Mon–Sat lunch. Resid & Rest lic
£ B&B £43–£83; B&B (double) £72–£136; HB weekly £325–£550; D £19; [5% V Nov–Mar]
cc Access, B'card/Visa; dep.

★★ **Elerkey House,** TR2 5QA Truro (0872) 501261

Small hotel with attractive gardens, in village.

Treverbyn House, Pendower Rd, TR2 5QL Truro (0872) 501201. *Hotel.*

VOWCHURCH Hereford & Worcester (Herefordshire). Map 19C2
Ross-on-Wye 28, London 147, Abergavenny 20, Hay-on-Wye 12, Hereford 13.

Croft Country House (Highly Acclaimed), HR2 0QE Peterchurch (0981) 550226. *Private Hotel.* Fr, Es
£ B&B £20–£30; HB weekly £199·50

WADEBRIDGE Cornwall. Map 2C2
Pop 4,800. Camelford 11, London 238, Bodmin 7, Newquay 14, Truro 23.
EC Wed. **MD** Mon. **Golf** St Enodoc 18h.
[i] Town Hall. (020 881) 3725

★★ **Molesworth Arms,** Molesworth St, PL27 7DP (020 881) 2055
Fax: (020 881) 4254
16th century inn of attractive design. Conveniently situated.
14 bedrs, 12 en suite; 1 ba; TV; tcf
TV, dogs, P 14, coach; child facs; con 80
LD 9.30
£ B&B £21–£25, B&B (double) £36–£40; WB £120
cc Access, B'card/Visa.

Hendra Country (Acclaimed) St Kew Highway, PL30 3EQ (020 884) 343. *Guest House.*

WADESMILL Hertfordshire. Map 15B3
Cheshunt 10, London 25, Bishops Stortford 11, Buntingford 8½, Hertford 5.

★ **Feathers Inn,** SG12 0TN (0920) 462606

An old coaching inn in the village centre; bedrooms in converted stables.
22 bedrs, 15 en suite, 3 ba; TV; tcf
P 100, coach; child facs; con 100+

WAKEFIELD West Yorkshire. Map 40C3
See also OSSETT.
Pop 76,296. Barnsley 9½, London 182, M1 2½, Bradford 14, Doncaster 19, Huddersfield 13, Leeds 9, Pontefract 9.
EC Wed. **MD** Mon, Tue, Thur, Fri, Sat. **Golf** City of Wakefield 18h, Wakefield Woodthorpe 18h. **See** Cathedral, Ancient Bridge with Chantry Chapel, Museum, City Art Gallery, St Helen's Church.
[i] Town Hall, Wood St. (0924) 295000

★★★★ **Cedar Court,** Denby Dale Rd, WF4 3QZ (0924) 276310 Tx: 557647
Fax: (0924) 280221
Large modern hotel with bedrooms on ground and first floor. Fr, De, Es, Gr
151 bedrs, 151 en suite; TV; tcf
lift, dogs, ns; P 450, coach; child facs; con 400
LD 11
£ B&B £79·50–£89·50 (w/e £55), B&B (double) £86–£96; L £11·50, D £13·50; WB £79·50; [10% V]
cc Access, Amex, B'card/Visa, Diners.

★★★ **Stoneleigh,** Doncaster Rd, WF1 5HA (0924) 369461 Tx: 51458

Several stone-built large attractive houses converted into hotel and restaurant.

Using RAC discount vouchers
Please tell the hotel when booking if you plan to use an RAC discount voucher (see p. 34) in part payment of your bill. Only one voucher will be accepted per party per stay. Discount vouchers will only be accepted in payment for accommodation, not for food.

W

★★★ **Swallow,** Queens St, WF1 1JU ☎(0924) 372111 Tx: 557464 Fax: (0924) 383648

Modern brick-built hotel of distinctive design; in city centre. (Sw)
🛏 63 bedrs, 63 en suite; TV; tcf
🏨 lift, dogs, ns; P 40, coach; child facs; con 150
✕ LD 9.15
£ B&B £60, B&B (double) £78
cc Access, Amex, B'card/Visa, Diners.

WALKERINGHAM Nottinghamshire. Map 31B4

Pop 872. Gainsborough 4, London 154, Doncaster 18, Grimsby 39, Humber Bridge 36, Rotherham 24, Thorne 20, Worksop 17. **EC** Wed.

Brickmakers Arms, Fountain Hill Rd, DN10 4LT ☎Gainsborough (0427) 890375 *Pleasant inn, converted from cottages and a barn, with spacious beer garden; on edge of quiet village.*
🛏 17 bedrs, 17 en suite; TV; tcf
🏨 TV; P 20; child facs

WALL Northumberland. Map 44C3

Pop 200. Hexham 3½, London 285, Alnwick 40, Bellingham 13, Hawick 49, Jedburgh 44. **Golf** Hexham 18h & 9h. **See** Hadrian's Wall, Chester Fort.

★★ **Hadrian,** NE46 4EE ☎Humshaugh (043 481) 232
Two-storey stone-built country hotel overlooking river and standing at roadside.
🛏 9 bedrs, 3 en suite, (5 sh), 2 ba; TV; tcf
🏨 TV, dogs, ns; P 40, G 3, coach; no children under 12

WALLASEY Merseyside. Map 32A2

Pop 92,987. Birkenhead 3, London 201. **MD** Daily (except Wed). **Golf** Warren Pk 18h.
ℹ Bathing Pool, Marine Promenade, New Brighton ☎051-638 7144

Clifton, 293 Seabank Rd, L45 5AF ☎051-639 6505. *Guest House.*
Sea Level, 126 Victoria Rd, New Brighton, L45 9LD ☎051-639 3408. *Private Hotel.*

WALLINGFORD Oxfordshire. Map 12A4

See also NORTH STOKE.
Pop 6,500. Henley-on-Thames 11, London 46, Aylesbury 25, Basingstoke 28, High Wycombe 21, Newbury 18, Oxford 12, Reading 14, Wantage 14.
EC Wed. **MD** Fri. **Golf** Streatley 18h.
ℹ 9 St Martin's St. ☎(0491) 35351

★★★ **George,** High St, OX10 0BS ☎(0491) 36665 Tx: 847468 Fax: (0491) 25359

Refurbished Tudor hotel with attractive courtyard. (MtCh)
🛏 39 bedrs, 39 en suite; TV; tcf
🏨 dogs, ns; P 45, coach; child facs; con 100
✕ LD 10.30
£ B&B £67·50 (w/e £40), B&B (double) £92·50; HB weekly £280; L £13·75, D £16·50; WB £40; [5% V] (Fri–Sun only)
cc Access, Amex, B'card/Visa, Diners; dep.

★★★ **Shillingford Bridge,** Shillingford Rd, OX10 8LZ ☎Warborough (086 732) 8567 Fax: (086 732) 8636

Attractive white-painted hotel, beautifully situated in large garden on banks of Thames. Swimming pool, fishing, squash, riding. Closed 25–31 Dec. ⚒ Fr, Es
🛏 26 bedrs, 26 en suite, annexe 12 bedrs, 12 en suite; TV; tcf
🏨 dogs; P 100, coach; child facs; con 60
✕ LD 10
£ B&B £55–£65, B&B (double) £75–£90; L £12·50, D £12·50
cc Access, Amex, B'card/Visa, CB, Diners; dep.

WALLSEND Tyne & Wear. Map 37B3

Pop 41,604. Newcastle 3½, London 276, Durham 18, Tynemouth 5, Morpeth 16. **EC** Wed. **Golf** Wallsend 18h. **See** Holy Cross Church.

> **Using RAC discount vouchers**
> Please tell the hotel when booking if you plan to use an RAC discount voucher (see p. 34) in part payment of your bill. Only one voucher will be accepted per party per stay. Discount vouchers will only be accepted in payment for accommodation, not for food.

★★★ **Newcastle Moat House,** Coast Rd, NE28 9HP ☎091-262 8989 Tx: 53583 Fax: 091-263 4172

Modern 3-storey brick-built hotel at A1 junction in outskirts. Indoor swimming pool, sauna, solarium, gymnasium. (QMH)
🛏 151 bedrs, 151 en suite; TV; tcf
🏨 lift; TV; dogs, ns; P 400, coach; child facs; con 500
✕ LD 9.45, bar meals only Sat lunch
£ B&B £65–£75, B&B (double) £75–£90; L £11·95, D £11·95; WB £36
cc Access, Amex, B'card/Visa, CB, Diners.

WALSALL West Midlands. Map 22B2

Pop 265,922. Birmingham 8½, London 120, M6 (jn 9) 1, Lichfield 9½, Stafford 17, Sutton Coldfield 9, Wolverhampton 6½.
EC Thur. **MD** Mon, Tue, Fri, Sat. **Golf** Walsall 18h. **See** St Matthew's Parish Church, Art Gallery and Museum, Arboretum.

★★★ **Baron's Court,** Walsall Wood, WS9 9AH ☎Brownhills (0543) 452020 Tx: 333061 Fax: (0543) 361276
Mock Tudor style hotel with well-appointed bedrooms. Indoor swimming pool, sauna, solarium, gymnasium.
🛏 100 bedrs, 100 en suite; TV; tcf
🏨 lift, dogs, ns; P 180, coach; child facs; con 120
(*See advertisement on p. 491*)

★★★ **Crest,** Birmingham Rd, WS5 3AB ☎(0922) 35727 Tx: 335479 Fax: (0922) 612034

Large modern purpose-built hotel with three bars. (THF).
🛏 101 bedrs, 101 en suite; TV; tcf
🏨 lift; TV; dogs, ns; P 250, coach; child facs; con 45
✕ LD 9.45, bar meals only Sat lunch
£ B&B £79·95–£91·95, B&B (double) £99·90–£111·90; L £8·95, D £14·50; WB £31 (2 nts)
cc Access, Amex, B'card/Visa, Diners.

★★★ **Friendly,** Wolverhampton Rd West, Bentley, WS2 0BS ☎(0922) 724444 Tx: 334854 Fax: (0922) 723148
New long low hotel with large picture windows, conveniently placed by junction 10 of M6. Indoor swimming pool, sauna, solarium, gymnasium. ⚒ Fr, De
🛏 125 bedrs, 125 en suite; TV; tcf

Walsall (West Midlands)

Baron's Court Hotel

A461 Lichfield to Walsall Road, Walsall Wood, Walsall, West Midlands

Tel: (0543) 452020
Fax: (0543) 361276

Arrive and relax in the old world charm that makes your visit, whether on business or holiday, a pleasure. 100 well appointed bedrooms, including many enchanting bridal suites, complete with four poster beds, all bedrooms have private bathroom, shower, radio, colour television, direct dial telephones.
Leisure Club with indoor swimming pool, whirlpool, saunas, steam rooms and gymnasium.
The Barons Restaurant is romantic and relaxing. Dinner dances are normally held each Saturday.
Milady's Carvery offers an informal atmosphere with popular prices. Five individual Conference Suites are available for business functions. Weddings and banquets for up to 180 on selected occasions.

We look forward to welcoming you to Baron's Court – A Fine English Hotel

W

Walsall (West Midlands)

Friendly

WALSALL

Friendly Hotel, 20 Wolverhampton Road West, Bentley, Walsall, West Midlands WS2 0BS.

RAC ★★★

· Premier Plus Rooms · Own Hotel Parking · Superb Leisure Centre · Conveniently situated off junction 10 of the M6, guarantees you an ideal base for the West Midlands and the NEC.

FOR RESERVATIONS **(office hours)**
TELEPHONE FREEPHONE

0800 591910

or call direct on 0922 724444
FAX: 0922 723148 TELEX: 334854

Friendly
HOTELS PLC

IT'S BEST TO STAY FRIENDLY

Walsall (West Midlands)

RAC **RAC**

The BESCOT Hotel

Private & Commercial

BESCOT ROAD, WALSALL. Tel: 0922 22447 Telex: 339929 Fax: 0922 30256

All rooms have private bath, shower and WC, television and tea/coffee making facilities. Drinks cabinet. Single: £35; Double or Twin £50, as a single £45.

Walsall (West Midlands)

ROYAL HOTEL

Ablewell Street, Walsall, West Midlands Tel: (0922) 24555

This delightful half-timbered building is only five minutes from Walsall and fifteen minutes from Birmingham. All rooms en-suite and offers a warm and friendly service.

dogs, ns, P 145, coach; child facs; con 180
LD 10
£ B&B £52–£62·50 (w/e £36), B&B (double) £68·50–£73; HB weekly £442·75–£516·25; D £11·25; [10% V]
cc Access, Amex, B'card/Visa, Diners.
(*See advertisement p. 491*)

★★ **Abberley,** 29 Bescot Rd, WS2 9AD (0922) 27413 Fax: (0922) 720933
Detached white 2-storey building adjacent to the ring road. Fr, It, Es
29 bedrs, 29 en suite; TV; tcf
dogs, ns; P 29, coach; child facs; con 40
LD 8.30. Resid lic
£ B&B £36·80 (w/e £25), B&B (double) £48·30–£59·80 (w/e £35); L £5, D £6·50; [5% V]
cc Access, B'card/Visa.

★★ **Bescot,** Bescot Rd, WS2 9DG (0922) 22447 Tx: 339929 Fax: (0922) 30256
Converted red-brick 1930s house in garden. Close to junction 9 of M6.
13 bedrs, 13 en suite; TV; tcf
TV; P 25, coach; child facs; con 30
LD 9.30, nr Sun dinner
£ B&B £35, B&B (double) £50; L £2, D £8·50; [5% V Fri & Sun]
cc Access, Amex, B'card/Visa, Diners.
(*See advertisement on p. 491*)

★★ **County,** 45 Birmingham Rd, WS1 2NG (0922) 32323 Tx: 333639
A small traditional hotel quietly set in a residential area. (QMH).
43 bedrs, 21 en suite, (18 sh); TV; tcf
dogs; coach; child facs; con 28

★★ **Royal,** Ablewell St, WS1 2EL (0922) 24555 Fax: (0922) 30028
Bright modern hotel with 5-storey extension. Continental style café and restaurant.
32 bedrs, 16 en suite (14 sh), 2 ba; TV; tcf
lift, dogs; P 40, coach; child facs; con 240
LD 9.30, nr Sun dinner
£ B&B £30–£50, B&B (double) £40–£65; L £5, D £9
cc. Access, Amex, B'card/Visa, Diners.
(*See advertisement on p. 491*)

WALTHAM ABBEY
Essex. Map 15B1
London 14, M25 (jn 26) 1½, Cheshunt 3, Epping 6, Hertford 10, Potters Bar 11

★★★★ **Swallow,** Old Shire La, EN9 3LX (0992) 717170 Tx: 916596 Fax: (0992) 711 841

Stylish low-built modern red-brick hotel just off junction 26 of M25. Indoor swimming pool, sauna, solarium, gymnasium. (Sw)
163 bedrs, 163 en suite; TV; tcf
dogs; P 240, coach; child facs; con 250
LD 11
£ B&B £82, B&B (double) £92
cc Access, Amex, B'card/Visa, Diners.

WALTHAM-ON-THE-WOLDS
Leicestershire. Map 31B2
Pop 591. Melton Mowbray 5, London 109, Grantham 10.
Golf Melton Mowbray 9h. **See** 14th cent Church.

Royal Horseshoes, LE14 4AJ (066 478) 289. *Inn.* Closed 25 & 26 Dec.
£ B&B £30

WANSFORD
Cambridgeshire. Map 31C1
Pop 410. Alconbury 16, London 83, Kettering 22, Peterborough 7½, Stamford 5.
Golf Burghley Park, Stamford 18h.

★★★ **Haycock,** at Wansford, PE8 6JA Stamford (0780) 782223 Tx: 32710

A 17th-century coaching inn with gardens, a stone courtyard and terraces on the banks of the River Nene. Fr, De, It, Da
17 bedrs, 17 en suite, 4 ba; annexe 34 bedrs, 34 en suite, 1 ba; TV
dogs, ns; P 300, coach; child facs; con 200
LD 10
£ B&B £60–£85, B&B (double) £85–£120; D £7·95; WB £85; [10% V w/e]
cc Access, Amex, B'card/Visa, Diners

WANTAGE
Oxfordshire. Map 21A1
Pop 9,071. Wallingford 14, London 60, M4 (jn 14) 10, Faringdon 9, Marlborough 23, Newbury 14, Oxford 15, Swindon 17.
EC Thur. **MD** Wed, Sat. **Golf** Frilford Heath 18h (2). **See** King Alfred's Statue, Parish Church, old Bear Hotel, Styles Almshouses.

★★ **Bear,** Market Pl, OX12 8AB (023 57) 66366 Tx: 41363 Fax: (0202) 299182
Former coaching inn with well-appointed bedrooms. In town centre. Fr, De
37 bedrs, 37 en suite; TV; tcf
lift, dogs; coach; child facs; con 60
LD 9.30
£ B&B £32–£49, B&B (double) £46–£72; L £7·95, D £12·95; WB £34·50 (HB); [10% V Dec–Feb]
cc Access, Amex, B'card/Visa, Diners.

WARE
Hertfordshire. Map 15B2
Pop 14,203. Hoddesdon 4, London 24, Baldock 16, Bishop's Stortford 10, Hatfield 8½, Royston 17.
EC Thur. **MD** Tue. **Golf** Chadwell Spring 9h, East Herts 18h. **See** Parish Church.

En suite rooms
En suite rooms may be bath or shower rooms. If you have a preference, remember to state it when booking a room.

★★★ **Ware Moat House,** Baldock St, SG12 9DR (0920) 465011 Tx: 817417 Fax: (0920) 468016

Medium-size modern hotel, on the Northern edge of the town. (QMH)
50 bedrs, 50 en suite; TV; tcf
lift, dogs, ns; P 100, coach; child facs; con 180

WAREHAM
Dorset. Map 5A1
Pop 7,943. Bournemouth 13, London 117, Blandford Forum 14, Dorchester 16, Ringwood 21, Weymouth 17.
EC Wed (win). **MD** Thur. **Golf** Wareham 9h, Lakey Hill 18h. **See** Parish Church, St Martin's Church (Lawrence of Arabia).
[i] Town Hall, East St (0929) 552740

★★★★ C R **Priory,** Church Green, BH20 4ND (0929) 552772 Tx: 41143 Fax: (0929) 554519

Privately-owned 16th century stone building with a lovely garden on River Frome. Fishing.
15 bedrs, 15 en suite; annexe 4 bedrs, 4 en suite; TV
P 20; coach; no children; con 20
LD 10. Resid lic
£ B&B £60–£95, B&B (double) £75–£160; L £12·50, D £19·50; WB
cc Access, Amex, B'card/Visa, Diners

★★★ **Springfield Country,** Grange Rd, Stoborough, BH20 5AL (0929) 552177 Fax: (0929) 551862

Attractive 2-storey house in secluded grounds. Swimming pool, tennis, solarium, billiards.
32 bedrs, 32 en suite; TV; tcf
lift, dogs; P 100; no children under 2; con 140
LD 9, bar meals only lunch. Resid lic

£ B&B £60–£65, B&B (double) £89–£96; HB weekly £376–£390; D £13·50; WB £101 (2 nts HB)
cc Access, Amex, B'card/Visa; dep.

★★ **Worgret Manor,** Worgret, BH20 6AB ☎(092 95) 2957

A privately-owned attractive manor house converted into an hotel. Closed 25–27 Dec.
9 bedrs, 4 en suite, 2 ba; TV; tcf
TV, dogs; coach; child facs; con 40

★ **Black Bear,** 14 South St, BH20 4LT ☎(0929) 553339
Near the river, an 18th century coaching inn in main street.
15 bedrs, 15 en suite; TV; tcf
dogs; coach; child facs; con 30
LD 10
£ B&B £25, B&B (double) £40; HB weekly £175; L £4·50, D £5·50
cc Access, B'card/Visa.

WARKWORTH Northumberland. Map 45A4

Morpeth 18, London 298, Alnwick 9, Newcastle-upon-Tyne 32, Rothbury 21.

Warkworth House, 16 Bridge St, NE 65 0XB ☎(0665) 711276
Recently refurbished Georgian house in local stone; on main street of picturesque village.
14 bedrs, 14 en suite; TV; tcf
dogs, ns; P 14, coach; child facs; con 40
LD 9.30, bar meals only Mon–Sat lunch
£ B&B £32, B&B (double) £48; L £6·95, D £11·95
cc Access, B'card/Visa; dep.

WARMINSTER Wiltshire. Map 5A3

Pop 16,000. Amesbury 19, London 99, Bath 16, Chippenham 20, Devizes 15, Frome 7, Salisbury 20, Shaftesbury 15, Wincanton 16. **EC** Wed. **MD** Fri. **Golf** Warminster 18h. **See** Church, old inns, old Meeting House at Horningsham, Longleat House 4 m W.
Car Park, Three Horseshoes Mall. ☎(0985) 218548

★★★★ H C **Bishopstrow House,** Boreham Rd (A36), BA12 9HH ☎(0985) 212312 Tx: 444829 Fax: (0985) 216769

Swimming pool, tennis, fishing, sauna, solarium. Fr, De
32 bedrs, 32 en suite; TV; tcf
dogs; P 60; child facs; con 70
LD 9
£ B&B £80–£140; B&B (double) £110–£160; L £16, D £28
cc Access, Amex, B'card/Visa, Diners.

★★ **Old Bell,** Market Pl, BA12 9AN ☎(0985) 216611 Fax: (0985) 217111

Old-established former coaching inn with colonnaded arcade in town centre. Closed Xmas Eve & Day. Fr, De, It, Es
16 bedrs, 11 en suite, 2 ba; annexe 8 bedrs, 5 en suite, 2 ba; TV; tcf
dogs; P 24, coach; child facs; con 100
LD 10.30
£ B&B £45, B&B (double) £55; L £9, D £9; WB £50; [10% V]
cc Access, Amex, B'card/Visa, Diners.

Lane End Cottage (Acclaimed), 72 Lane End, Corsley, BA12 7PG ☎ (037 388) 392. *Guest House.*

WARRINGTON Cheshire. Map 32C1

Pop 176,000. M6 (jn 21) 4, London 183, M62 Motorway 2½, Chester 20, Liverpool 17, Manchester 16, Northwich 11, Wigan 12.
EC Thur. **MD** Every day exc Thur. **Golf** Warrington 18h. **See** Parish Church, Holy Trinity Church, Museum and Library.
Rylands St. ☎(0925) 36501

★★★ **Fir Grove,** Knutsford Old Rd, Grappenhall, WA4 2LD ☎(0925) 67471 Tx: 628117 Fax: (0925) 601092

Well-appointed small hotel in former private residence in wooded surroundings. Es, Gr, We
40 bedrs, 40 en suite; TV; tcf
dogs; P 84; child facs; con 200
LD 10, bar meals only Sat lunch
£ B&B £30–£48 (w/e £20), B&B (double) £40–£68; L £10·75, D £10·75
cc Access, Amex, B'card/Visa, Diners.

★★ **Old Vicarage,** Stretton Rd, Stretton, WA4 4NS (3½ m SE B5356). ☎Norcott Brook (0925 73) 706 Fax: (0925 73) 740

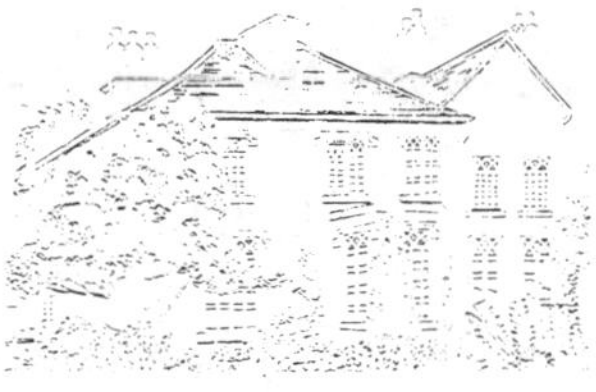

Former vicarage, modernised and extended.
26 bedrs, 26 en suite; TV; tcf
lift, dogs, ns; P 150; child facs; con 60
LD 9.30
£ B&B £60 (w/e £30), B&B (double) £70–£80; L £9·50, D £14·50; WB £70
cc Access, Amex, B'card/Visa.

★★ **Paddington House,** 514 Manchester Rd, WA1 3TZ ☎(0925) 816767
Former large residence with modern wing in landscaped garden with sweeping lawn.
38 bedrs, 38 en suite; TV; tcf
dogs; P 50; coach; child facs; con 180
LD 9.30
£ B&B £42·50, B&B (double) £55; L £12·50, D £12·50
cc Access, Amex B'card/Visa, Diners.
(*See advertisement below*)

W

★★ Patten Arms, Parker St, WA1 1LS ☎(0925) 36602

Yellow brick Victorian building close to town centre. Convenient for railway station. (DeV)
🛏 43 bedrs, 43 en suite; TV; tcf
TV, dogs; P 25, coach; child facs; con 50

★★ Ribblesdale, Balmoral Rd, Grappenhall, WA4 2EB ☎(0925) 601197
Conveniently placed hotel in ¼ acre of grounds.
🛏 14 bedrs, 11 en suite, 1 ba; TV; tcf
P 20; child facs
✕ LD 9. Resid & Rest lic
£ B&B £29–£35 (w/e £17·50), B&B (double) £35–£45; D £10; [10% V w/d]
cc Access, Amex, B'card/Visa.

★★Rockfield, Alexandra Rd, Grappenhall, WA4 2EL ☎(0925) 62898
Small quietly situated hotel with pleasant garden. 2 miles from town centre. Closed 25–31 Dec.
🛏 6 bedrs, 6 en suite; annexe 7 bedrs, 5 en suite, 1 ba; TV; tcf
TV, dogs; P 30, coach; child facs; con 25
✕ LD 9, nr Sun dinner. Rest lic
£ B&B £35–£45 (w/e £20), B&B (double) £50–£55; L £8·50, D £11; WB £20; [10% V w/e]
cc Access, B'card/Visa, Diners.

Birchdale (Acclaimed), Birchdale Rd, Appleton, WA4 5AW ☎(0925) 63662. Fax: (0925) 860607. *Private Hotel.* Closed 24 Dec–1 Jan.
£ B&B £28–£36.

WARSASH Hampshire.

See under SOUTHAMPTON

WARWICK Warwickshire. Map 21A3

See also LEAMINGTON SPA.
Pop 21,936. Banbury 20, London 92, Birmingham 21, Coventry 10, Rugby 14, Stratford-upon-Avon 8.
EC Thur. **MD** Sat. **Golf** Leamington and County 18h. **See** Castle, St Mary's Church, St Nicholas' Church, St John's House (Museum), Lord Leycester Hospital.
[i] Court House, 2 Jury St. ☎(0926) 492212

> **Atlas Section**
> Consult the Atlas section at the back of the guide to find out which towns and villages have RAC Appointed and Listed hotels in them. They are shown on the maps by purple circles.

★★★★ Hilton National, Longbridge, CV34 6RE ☎(0926) 499555 Tx: 312468 Fax: (0926) 410020 ♿

Spacious modern brick-built hotel. Indoor swimming pool, sauna, gymnasium. (H.Int). Fr, It
🛏 180 bedrs, 180 en suite; TV; tcf
lift, dogs, ns; P 200, coach; child facs; con 450
✕ LD 10, bar meals only Sat lunch
£ room £73–£99 (w/e £47), room (double) £100–£115; Bk £8·95, L £12·95, D £15·95; WB £42
cc Access, Amex, B'card/Visa, Diners.

★★★ Glebe, Church St, Barford, CV35 8BS ☎(0926) 624218 Tx: 312440

Attractive former vicarage converted to hotel with restaurant.

★★ Lord Leycester, Jury St, CV34 4EJ ☎(0926) 491481 Tx: 41363 Fax: (0202) 299182
Modernised Georgian coaching inn; located close to town centre. Fr
🛏 53 bedrs, 53 en suite; TV; tcf
lift, dogs; P 40, coach; child facs; con 200
✕ LD 8.30
£ B&B £42 (w/e £69), B&B (double) £59; L £13·50, D £13·50
cc Access, Amex, B'card/Visa, Diners, dep.

★★ Warwick Arms, High St, CV34 4AT ☎(0926) 492759 Fax: (0926) 410587

An 18th century former coaching inn now modernised; located near to castle.
🛏 35 bedrs, 35 en suite; TV; tcf
dogs; P 24, coach; child facs; con 95
✕ LD 9.30, bar meals only Mon–Sat lunch, Sun dinner
£ B&B £42, B&B (double) £60; L £8·50, D £12·50; [10% V]
cc Access, Amex, B'card/Visa, Diners.

North Leigh (Highly Acclaimed), Five Ways Rd, Hatton, CV35 7HZ ☎(0926) 484203. *Guest House.* Closed 16 Dec–15 Jan.
£ B&B £26–£33

Park Cottage (Highly Acclaimed), 113 West St, CV34 6AH. ☎(0926) 410319 Fax: (0926) 410319
£ B&B £35

Croft (Acclaimed), Haseley Knob, CV35 7NL ☎(0926) 484 447. *Guest House.* Fr
£ B&B £13–£18; [5% V Fri–Sun only]

Avon, 7 Emscote Rd, CV34 4PH ☎(0926) 491367. *Guest House.*
£ B&B £13
cc B'card/Visa.

Westham, 76 Emscote Rd, CV34 5QG ☎(0926) 491756. *Guest House.*
£ B&B £15

WARWICK-ON-EDEN Cumbria. Map 44A3

Wetheral 2, London 295, M6 (jn 43) 2, Brampton 6, Carlisle 5.

Queen's Arms, CA4 8PA ☎(0228) 60699
White-painted inn close to River Eden in quiet village. Bedrooms in adjoining modern building.
🛏 8 bedrs, 8 en suite, TV; tcf
dogs; P 60; child facs
✕ 9.30
£ B&B £28 (w/e £44 2 nts), B&B (double) £36; L £6, D £10; WB £44 (2 nts)
cc Access, Amex, B'card/Visa, Diners

WASDALE HEAD Cumbria. Map 43B1

Ravenglass 12, London 309, Broughton-in-Furness 21, Eskdale 10, Nether Wasdale 5½, Whitehaven 21.
Golf Seascale 18h. **See** Wastwater Lake, Climbing Centre.

★★ R Wasdale Head Inn, Wasdale Head, Gosforth, CA20 1EX ☎(09467) 26229
Quiet detached stone building beautifully situated at head of lake.
🛏 11 bedrs, 11 en suite; tcf
dogs, ns; P 50; child facs
✕ LD 7.30, bar meals only lunch
£ B&B £32, B&B (double) £71; HB weekly £269·50; D £13·50
cc Access, B'card/Visa; dep.

WASHINGTON Tyne & Wear. Map 37B2

Pop 50,000. Durham 11, London 271, Newcastle upon Tyne 6, Sunderland 6½.
Golf Wearside 18h. **See** Washington Old Hall, Holy Trinity Church, Waterfowl Park.

★★★ Post House, Emerson, District 5, NE37 1LB ☎091-416 2264 Tx: 537574 Fax: 091-415 3371

Six-storey purpose-built modern hotel convenient for A1 (M) (THF)

EC *early closing* **MD** *market day* *country house hotel* *ns (NS) no smoking areas* *tcf tea/coffee facilities*

138 bedrs, 138 en suite; TV; tcf
lift, dogs; P 200, coach; child facs; con 100
LD 10
£ B&B £69·50 (w/e £39·50), B&B (double) £87; WB £38 (HB)
cc Access, Amex, B'card/Visa, CB, Diners.

★★★ **Washington Moat House,** Stone Cellar Rd, District 12, Usworth Village, NE37 1PH ☎091-417 2626 Tx: 537143 Fax: 091-415 1166

Modern purpose-built hotel in red brick, in own landscaped grounds. Indoor swimming pool, golf, putting, squash, sauna, solarium, gymnasium, billiards. (QMH) Fr
106 bedrs, 106 en suite; TV; tcf
dogs, ns; P 150, coach; child facs; con 250
LD 10
£ room £65–£85 (w/e £42·50), B&B double room £75–£105; Bk £7·50, L £8, D £13·25; WB £105 (2 nts HB); [5% V Mon–Thurs]
cc Access, Amex, B'card/Visa, Diners

WATCHET Somerset. Map 4A3

Pop 3,050. Taunton 15, London 159, Bridgwater 18, Dunster 6, Tiverton 24.
EC Wed. **Golf** Minehead and West Somerset 18h. **See** St Decuman's Well and Church, West Somerset Rly (Steam Engines).
i 2 Market St. ☎(0984) 31824

★★ H C R **Downfield,** 16 St Decuman's Rd, TA23 0HR ☎(0984) 31267 Fax: (0984) 34369

Victorian residence with a pleasant garden. Views of harbour.
6 bedrs, 6 en suite; TV; tcf
dogs; P 22, coach; child facs; con 20
LD 9.15
£ B&B £30, B&B (double) £40; L £8, D £9 WB £35; [5% V]
cc Access, Amex, B'card/Visa, Diners; dep.

West Somerset, Swain St, TA23 0AB ☎(0984) 34434 De
£ B&B £12·50; [10% V]

WATERHEAD Cumbria

See under AMBLESIDE

WATERMILLOCK Cumbria. Map 44A1

Pop 466. M6 (jn 40) 6, London 281, Ambleside 15, Kendal 26, Keswick 17, Penrith 7¼.
Golf Penrith 18h.

★★★ R **Leeming House,** Ullswater, CA11 0JJ ☎(076 84) 86622 Tx: 64111 Fax: (076 84) 86443

Gracious early Victorian manor with elegant decor. Lovely garden and views. Fishing.
17 bedrs, 15 en suite; annexe 8 bedrs, 8 en suite; TV
TV, dogs, ns; P 50; child facs; con 12
LD 8.45
£ B&B £75·75–£105·75 (w/e £75), B&B (double) £111·50–£136·50; HB weekly £525–£630; L £15; D £29·50; WB £75
cc Access, Amex, B'card/Visa, CB, Diners; dep.

★★★ R **Rampsbeck,** Ullswater, CA11 0LP ☎(076 84) 86442

Late 18th century mansion standing in 14 acres of grounds on shores of Lake Ullswater. Fishing. Closed 7 Jan–23 Feb.
19 bedrs, 18 en suite, 1 ba; TV; tcf
dogs; P 30; no children under 5; con 60
LD 8.45, bar meals only Mon–Sat lunch
£ B&B £32–£48, B&B (double) £60–£85; HB weekly £385–£425; D £25; WB £80
cc Access, B'card/Visa; dep.

WATFORD Hertfordshire. Map 13B4

See also BUSHEY.
RAC Office, *130 St Albans Rd, Watford,* WD2 4AH ☎Watford (0923) 33543.
Pop 76,000. Aylesbury 23, London 16, M1 (jn 5) 3, Barnet 10, Dunstable 18, Harrow 7, Hatfield 13, Rickmansworth 3, St Albans 7.
See Plan, p. 496.
MD Tue, Fri, Sat. **P** See Plan. **Golf** West Herts 18h. **See** St Mary's Church, Bedford Almshouses, Cassiobury Park.

Using RAC discount vouchers
Please tell the hotel when booking if you plan to use an RAC discount voucher (see p. 34) in part payment of your bill. Only one voucher will be accepted per party per stay. Discount vouchers will only be accepted in payment for accommodation, not for food.

★★★ **Dean Park,** 30 St Albans Rd, WD1 1RN ☎(0923) 229212 Tx: 8813610 Fax: (0923) 54638

Modern high rise block close to station and town centre. Closed 26–29 Dec. (QMH).
90 bedrs, 90 en suite; TV; tcf
lift; P 12, coach; child facs; con 200
LD 10, nr Sat lunch
£ B&B £30–£80, B&B (double) £60–£83; L £12, D £14; WB £40
cc Access, Amex, B'card/Visa, Diners.

The White House, 29 Upton Rd, WD1 2EL ☎(0923) 37316 Tx: 8955439 Fax: (0923) 33109. *Hotel.* Fr, De, Es, Po
£ B&B £60–£100 (w/e £40); HB weekly £465–£705

WATTON Norfolk. Map 35A1

Pop 4,800. Newmarket 31, London 94, East Dereham 10, Norwich 21, Thetford 12.
EC Thur. **MD** Wed. **Golf** Dereham 9h. **See** Wayland Wood 1 m S, the traditional site of 'The Babes in the Wood'.

★★ **Clarence House,** 78 High St, IP25 6AH ☎(0953) 884252 Fax: (0953) 881323

Near town centre, an interesting Victorian residence. Fr
6 bedrs, 6 en suite; TV; tcf
dogs; P 25; child facs
LD 9. Resid & Rest lic
£ B&B £38–£40, B&B (double) £50–£54; HB weekly £224; L £14, D £17; WB £32; [5% V Oct–Mar only]
cc Access, Amex, B'card/Visa, Diners.

WEDMORE Somerset Map 4C3

Wells 7½, London 129, Bridgewater 15, Cheddar 4, Glastonbury 8, Weston-super-Mare 16.

Yew Tree (Acclaimed), Sand, BF28 4XF ☎(0934) 712520
£ B&B £25–£35; HB weekly £198–£262.

W

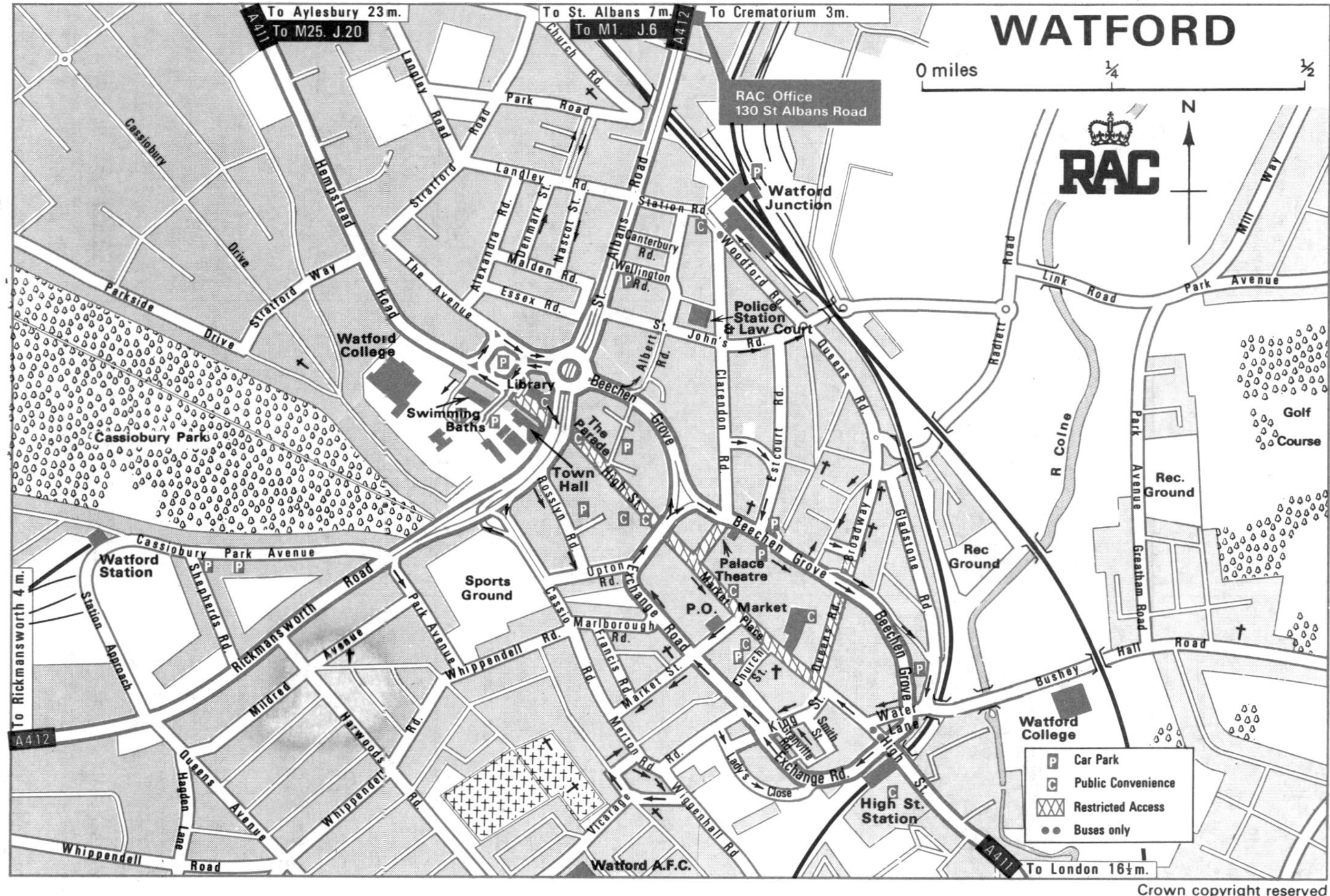

EC *early closing* **MD** *market day* *country house hotel* *ns (NS) no smoking areas* *tcf tea/coffee facilities*

WEEDON BEC Northamptonshire. Map 21B3
Pop 2,450. Towcester 8½, London 69, M1 (jn 16) 3, Daventry 4, Hinckley 26, Leicester 30, Market Harborough 21, Northampton 8½, Nuneaton 29, Rugby 13.
Golf Woodlands 18h. **See** Parish Church.

★★★ Crossroads, NN7 4PX ☎(0327) 40354 Tx: 312311 Fax: (0327) 40849 ♿

Originally a 19th century toll house, with modern well-appointed annexe. Tennis.
🛏 10 bedrs, 10 en suite; annexe 38 bedrs, 38 en suite; TV; tcf
🏨 P 100, coach; child facs; con 50
✕ LD 10.15
£ B&B £50–£66, B&B (double) £65–£80; L £16, D £16; WB £40
cc Access, Amex, B'card/Visa, CB, Diners.

★★ Globe, High St (A45), NN7 4QD ☎(0327) 40336 Fax: (0327) 349058

An old posting house at A5/A45 junction, refurbished to a family-run hotel. ✡ Fr
🛏 15 bedrs, 15 en suite; TV; tcf
🏨 dogs; P 40, coach; child facs; con 20
✕ LD 10, bar meals only Sun dinner
£ B&B £30–£42, B&B (double) £39·50–£52 (w/e £19·75); L £6·50, D £8·95; WB £18·75; [5% V]
cc Access, Amex, B'card/Visa, Diners; dep.

★★ Heart of England, Daventry Rd, NN7 4QD ☎(0327) 40335

White-faced 18th century coaching inn with attractive gardens. On A45.
🛏 12 bedrs, 3 en suite, (7 sh), 1 ba; TV; tcf
🏨 P 70; child facs; con 20

WELLAND *See* under MALVERN

WELLINGBOROUGH Northamptonshire. Map 21C3
Pop 39,600. Bedford 17, London 67, Huntingdon 27, Kettering 7, Northampton 10, Peterborough 30.
EC Thur. **MD** Wed, Fri, Sat. **Golf** Wellingborough 18h.
ℹ Library, Pebble La ☎(0933) 228101

★★★ Hind, Sheep St, NN8 1BY ☎(0933) 222827 Fax: (0933) 441921

17th century stone-built hotel located in town centre. ✡ Fr (QMH). Closed 25 Dec–1 Jan.
🛏 34 bedrs, 34 en suite; TV; tcf
🏨 dogs; ns; P 13, G 3, coach; child facs; con 100
✕ LD 9.30
£ B&B £55–£58 (w/e £36), B&B (double) £70–£74; HB weekly £322–£336; L £8·95, D £10·95; WB £35; [10% V Jul–Aug, 5% V]
cc Access, Amex, B'card/Visa, Diners

★★ Columbia, Northampton Rd, NN8 3HG ☎(0933) 229333 Fax: (0933) 440418

Two houses joined by a modern extension in pleasant tree-lined road. Closed 25–27 Dec.
🛏 29 bedrs, 29 en suite; TV; tcf
🏨 TV; P 18, coach; child facs; con 24
✕ LD 9.30
£ B&B £43 (w/e £28), B&B (double) £54 (w/e £40); L £6·95, D £9·50; WB £56 (2 nts)
cc Access, Amex, B'card/Visa.

★★ High View, 156 Midland Rd, NN8 1NG ☎(0933) 78733 (changing to (0278) 278733 Spring 1991). Fax: (0933) 225948

Attractive well maintained Victorian building in quiet situation.
🛏 14 bedrs, 14 en suite; TV; tcf
🏨 dogs, ns; P 9, U 1, coach; child facs
✕ LD 8.30. Resid & Rest lic
£ B&B £20–£44 (w/e £15), B&B (double) £30–£50; L £8·10, D £8·10
cc Amex, B'card/Visa, Diners.

Oak House, 9 Broad Green, NN8 4LE ☎(0933)271133. *Hotel.* Closed Xmas
£ B&B £30; [5% V]

WELLINGTON Shropshire. Map 29C1
See also TELFORD and DONNINGTON.
Pop 16,000. Wolverhampton 18, London 143, M54 1, Bridgnorth 14, Lichfield 29, Newport 8, Shrewsbury 11, Whitchurch 21.
EC Wed. **MD** Mon, Tue, Thur, Sat. **Golf** Wrekin 18h. **See** Wrekin College, All Saints' Parish Church, old houses and inns, the Wrekin 1,335 ft.
ℹ 9 Walker St. ☎(0952) 48295

★★ Charlton Arms, Church St, Telford TF1 1DG ☎Telford (0952) 251351 Fax: (0952) 222077

Characteristic old coaching inn in the heart of the Shropshire countryside. (DeV)
🛏 26 bedrs, 23 en suite, 3 ba; TV; tcf
🏨 dogs; P 120, coach; child facs; con 200

★★ Falcon, Holyhead Rd, TF1 2DD ☎Telford (0952) 255011
Off M54, a family-run hotel once an 18th century inn.
🛏 13 bedrs, 7 en suite, 2 ba; TV
🏨 TV, dogs; P 30
✕ LD 9, bar meals only Mon–Sat lunch & Sun dinner
£ B&B £27–£38, B&B (double) £35–£49; D £10; WB
cc Access, B'card/Visa.

WELLINGTON Somerset. Map 4A2
Pop 10,534. Taunton 6½, London 150, M5 (jn 26) 2, Dunster 22, Exeter 25, Honiton 20, Tiverton 14.
EC Thur. **Golf** Taunton and Vivary 18h. **See** 15th cent Parish Church, Wellington Monument, Wellington School.
ℹ The Museum, Fore St. ☎(0823) 664737

Blue Mantle, 2 Mantle St, TA21 8AW ☎(082 66) 2000. *Hotel. Swimming pool.*
£ B&B £18; [10% V]
Gamlins Farmhouse, Greenham, TA21 0LZ ☎(0823) 672596

W

Wellington (Herefordshire)

DINMORE MANOR Nr Hereford (R. G. Murray)

Spectacular hillside location. A range of impressive architecture dating from 14th–20th century, Chapel, Cloisters, Great Hall (Music Room) and extensive roof walk giving panoramic views of the countryside and beautiful gardens below. Large collection of stained glass. Interesting and unusual plants for sale in plant centre. *Location:* 6m N of Hereford on A49. *Opening Times:* 9.30–5.30 daily – all year. Admission £2, OAPs £1, children under 14 free when accompanied. *Refreshments:* Occasional teas served during summer.

Wells (Somerset)

OPPOSITE THE FAMOUS WEST FRONT OF WELLS CATHEDRAL

15th-century Coaching Inn with original four-poster beds and log fires providing good food and comfort in a relaxed atmosphere. All rooms are attractively furnished and have colour TV, private bathroom or shower. Car park. For brochure/tariff and details of our Bargain Breaks and conference facilities please write or phone (Ref. CH2):

SWAN HOTEL

WELLS, SOMERSET BA5 2RX Tel: (0749) 78877

A BEST WESTERN HOTEL *RAC****

Westgate-on-Sea (Kent)

SEA FRONT OPEN ALL YEAR RAC ★★

IVYSIDE HOTEL

Westgate-on-Sea, Kent

68 bedrooms – with bath/WC & TV, full central heating, telephones. For families – interconnecting family suites, baby sitting, mothers' kitchen, playroom.

Tariff – B&B from £22 per person. Special children's rates. Hotel facilities – indoor heated swimming pool and whirlpool spa, outdoor heated pool, sauna & steam room, 2 squash courts, solarium, sun bed, masseuse, full-size snooker table & games room, night porter, cocktail bar.

Reservations – **Ring Thanet (0843) 31082** – for brochure and enquiries

AS SEEN ON ITV'S "WISH YOU WERE HERE"

West Witton (North Yorkshire)

The Wensleydale Heifer

RAC**
Egon Ronay, Michelin
Les Routiers, Johansens

West Witton · Wensleydale · North Yorkshire · DL8 4LS
Telephone: Wensleydale (0969) 22322 Fax: (0969) 24183

A 17th Century Inn of character and distinction offering, quite simply, Wensleydale's best, together with the finest of Yorkshire Innkeeping traditions. Situated amidst spectacular James Herriot countryside and in the magnificent Yorkshire Dales National Park.

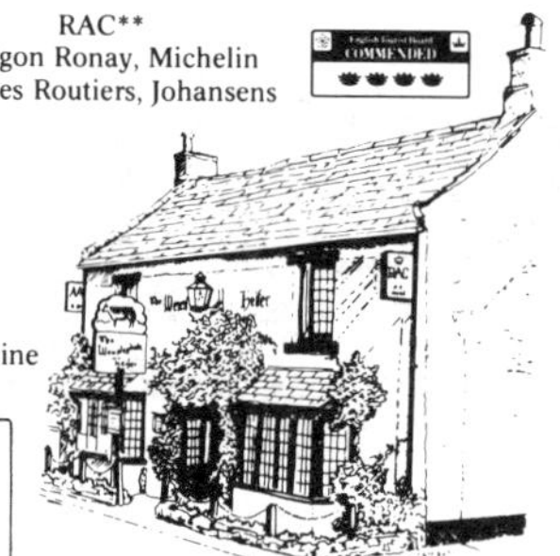

- Candlelit Restaurant
- 3 Four Poster Suites
- Finest Yorkshire Cuisine
- 19 'En Suite' Bedrooms
- Real Ales and Fine Wines
- Bistro

ACTIVITY BREAKS
- TROUT FISHING
- GOLFING
- JAMES HERRIOT TRAIL
- ROMANTIC
- WALKING
- CHRISTMAS AND NEW YEAR HOUSE PARTY

WELLS Somerset. Map 4C3
Pop 9,129. Shepton Mallet 5½, London 122, Bath 19, Bristol 21, Glastonbury 5½, Radstock 12, Weston-super-Mare 19.
EC Wed. **MD** Wed, Sat. **Golf** Wells (Somerset) 9h, Mendip 18h.
See Cathedral, Bishop's Palace, Browne's Gate, Old Deanery, Almshouse, Town Hall, medieval Tithe Barn, Museum, St Cuthbert's Church, Vicar's Close (14th cent St).
[i] Town Hall, Market Pl. ☎(0749) 72552

★★★ R Swan, Sadler St, BA5 2RX
☎(0749) 78877 Tx: 449658
Fax: (0749) 77647

Attractive 15th century coaching inn with fine view of Cathedral. Squash Fr, De, It
32 bedrs, 32 en suite; TV; tcf
dogs; P 32, coach; child facs; con 70
LD 9.30
£ B&B £55–£62·50, B&B (double) £75–£82·50; L £10·50, D £14·50; WB £95 (2 nts HB); [5% V Jul & Aug]
cc Access, Amex, B'card/Visa, Diners.
(*See advertisement on p. 498*)

★★ White Hart, 19 Sadlers St, BA5 2RR
☎(0749) 72056
Privately-owned 15th century attractive former coaching inn in main street.
8 bedrs, 8 en suite; annexe 8 bedrs, 8 en suite; TV; tcf
dogs; P 12, G 3, coach; child facs; con 20

★ Worth House, Worth, BA5 1LW ☎(0749) 72041
Grey stone building, parts reputed to be 400 years old, 2 miles west of town.
8 bedrs, 8 en suite; tcf
TV, dogs; P 18, coach

Bekynton (Acclaimed), 7 St Thomas St, BA5 2UU ☎(0749) 72222. *Guest House.*
£ B&B £17–£21; [5% V w/d Nov–May]

Tor, 20 Tor St, BA5 2US ☎(0749) 72322. *Guest House.*
£ B&B £16–£25; HB weekly £164–£210; [5% V]

WELLS-NEXT-THE-SEA Norfolk. Map 35A2
Pop 2,523. Fakenham 10, London 123, Cromer 19, King's Lynn 27, Norwich 31.
EC Thur. **Golf** Fakenham 9h. **See** Quay, Holkham Hall 2 m W.
[i] Staithe St ☎(0328) 710885

★★ R Crown, The Buttlands, NR23 1EX
☎Fakenham (0328) 710209
Typical old coaching inn on village green.
15 bedrs, 9 en suite, 1 ba; TV; tcf
TV; dogs, ns; child facs
LD 9
£ B&B £38–£45, B&B (double) £48–£55; L £9·50, D £13·50; WB £67 (2 nts)
cc Access, Amex, B'card/Visa, Diners; dep.

WELWYN GARDEN CITY Hertfordshire. Map 15A2
Pop 47,000. Hatfield 2½, London 23, Baldock 14, Bishop's Stortford 18, Hoddesdon 10, Luton 13.
EC Wed. **Golf** Panshanger 18h.
[i] Campus, West. ☎(0707) 332880

★★★ Crest, Homestead La, AL7 4LX
☎(0707) 324336 Tx: 261523
Fax: (0707) 326447

Modern hotel, purpose-built in red brick. To south of town centre. (THF) Fr
58 bedrs, 58 en suite; TV; tcf
lift, dogs, ns; P 60, coach; child facs; con 80
LD 9.45, nr Sat lunch
£ B&B £68, B&B (double) £81; L £11·95, D £15; WB £39 (HB); [10%]
cc Access, Amex, B'card/Visa, CB, Diners.

WEMBLEY Greater London (Middx). Map 13C3
Pop 124,892. Denham 9, London 7, Ealing 3, Harrow 3½, Uxbridge 8½.
EC Wed. **See** Empire Stadium, Empire Pool and Sports Arena.

★★★★ Hilton National, Empire Way, HA9 8DS ☎081-902 8839 Tx: 24837
Fax: 081-900 2201
Modern tower block building, part of the Wembley Stadium complex. (H Int) Fr, De, It, Ar
300 bedrs, 300 en suite; TV; tcf
lift, dogs, ns; P 300, coach; child facs; con 300
LD 10
£ room £93–£120, room (double) £125–£150; Bk £8·95, L £15, D £16·50; WB £36 (B&B) £150
cc Access, Amex, B'card/Visa, Diners.

Brookside, 32 Brook Ave, Wembley Park ☎081-904 0019.
£ B&B £23; [V]

Elm, Elm Rd, HA9 7JA ☎081-902 1764
Fax: 081-903 8365. *Hotel.*
£ B&B £32–£42

WENTBRIDGE North Yorkshire. Map 38C2
Pop 150, Doncaster 11, London 176, A1(M) 6, Barnsley 6, Pontefract 4½, Selby 17, Tadcaster 18, Wakefield 12.
EC Thur. **Golf** Pontefract 18h.

★★★ H C R Wentbridge House, WF8 3JJ ☎Pontefract (0977) 620444
Fax: (0977) 620148
Stone-built house of character in own grounds in village centre. Closed 25 Dec eve. Fr, De
12 bedrs, 12 en suite; TV
P 100, child facs; con 60
LD 9.30
£ B&B £60–£85, B&B (double) £73–£100; L £14·50
cc Access, Amex, B'card/Visa, Diners.

WEOBLEY Hereford & Worcester (Herefordshire). Map 19C3
Pop 1,067. Hereford 12, London 144, Brecon 29, Builth Wells 29, Knighton 22, Leominster 9, Rhayader 34.
EC Wed. **Golf** Wormsley 18h.

Tudor, Broad St, HR4 8SA ☎(0544) 318201. *Guest House.* Fr, It
£ B&B £15–£16·50; HB £154–£175; [5% V Nov–Mar]

Unicorn House, High St, HR4 8SL ☎(0544) 318230
£ B&B £16–£18; HB weekly £209·65; [5% V Sun & Wed]

WEST BROMWICH West Midlands. Map 22B2
Pop 166,000. Birmingham 4½, London 116, M5 (jn 1) 1½, Kidderminster 15, Walsall 5½, Wolverhampton 8.
EC Wed. **MD** Mon, Fri, Sat. **Golf** Sandwell Park 18h. **See** Restored 12th cent Manor House, Bishop Asbury Cottage (founder of Methodist Church in USA), Oak House.

★★★ West Bromwich Moat House, Birmingham Rd, B70 6RS ☎021-553 6111
Tx: 336232 Fax: 021-525 7403

This modern motorway hotel is alongside the M5 overlooking Sandwell Valley. (QMH)
170 bedrs, 170 en suite, TV; tcf
lift, dogs, ns; P 200, coach; child facs; con 160

WESTBURY Wiltshire. Map 5A3
Pop 8,000. Pewsey 22, London 98, Bath 15, Chippenham 15, Devizes 13, Frome 7, Warminster 3½.
EC Wed. **MD** Fri. **Golf** West Wilts, Warminster 18h. **See** Parish Church, White Horse-turf cutting on Downs.
[i] Library, Edward St. ☎(0373) 827158

★★ Cedar, 114 Warminster Rd, BA13 3PG ☎(0373) 822753
Three-storey white building on the outskirts. Attractive and well kept gardens.

Complaints
If you are dissatisfied with the facilities or service offered by a hotel, please take the matter up with the Manager WHILE YOU ARE AT THE HOTEL. In this way, any problems can usually be solved promptly and amicably.
The RAC will investigate matters if a personal approach has failed to resolve the problem. Please submit details of any discussion or correspondence when reporting the problem to the RAC.

W

WEST CHILTINGTON West Sussex. Map 6B2
See also PULBOROUGH.
Pop 2,075. Dorking 23, London 46, Arundel 11, Brighton 20, Haywards Heath 17, Horsham 14, Worthing 12.
Golf West Sussex, Pulborough 18h.

★★★ Roundabout, Monkmead La, RH20 2PF ☎(0798) 813838 Tx: 94013840 Fax: (0798) 812962
Three-storey hotel of considerable charm offering modern facilities and four posters.
Fr
17 bedrs, 17 en suite; annexe 6 bedrs, 6 en suite; TV; tcf
dogs, ns; P 45, coach; no children under 3; con 22
LD 9
£ B&B £60·75–£64·75 (w/e £84), B&B (double) £76·75–£83·25; HB weekly £318–£340; L £11·50, D £16·95; WB £84
cc Access, Amex, B'card/Visa, Diners; dep.

WESTCLIFF-ON-SEA Essex. Map 17C2
See also SOUTHEND-ON-SEA.
Romford 24, London 41, Brentwood 20, Chelmsford 20, Dartford Tunnel 20, Rainham 25, Southend-on-Sea 1.
EC Wed. **Golf** Thorpe Hall 18h, Rochford Hundred 18h. **See** Beecroft Art Galleries.

★★ Balmoral, Valkyrie Rd, SS0 8BU ☎Southend (0702) 342947 Fax: (0702) 337828

Owner-managed pleasant hotel in converted residential buildings. Closed 24–26 Dec. Es
22 bedrs, 22 en suite, TV; tcf
TV, dogs; P 22; child facs; con 25
LD 7.45, bar meals only Mon & Sat lunch nr Sun. Resid & Rest lic
£ B&B £35–£38, B&B (double) £45–£55; D £8·50; WB
cc Access, B'card/Visa.

West Park (Highly Acclaimed), 11 Park Rd, SS0 7PQ ☎(0702) 330729. Fax: (0702) 338162. *Private Hotel.*
£ B&B £29–£32; [5% V]

Cobham Lodge (Acclaimed), 2 Cobham Rd, SS0 8EA ☎(0702) 346438. *Private Hotel. Billiards.*
£ B&B £29·50; HB weekly £180

Rose House, 21–23 Manor Rd, SS0 7SR ☎(0702) 341959. *Private Hotel.*
£ B&B £19·50–£22·50; [10% V]

WEST DIDSBURY
See MANCHESTER.

WESTERHAM Kent. Map 9A1
Pop 4,255. Bromley 11, London 23, M25 (jn 5) 4½, Croydon 12, East Grinstead 13, Godstone 6½, Sevenoaks 6.
EC Wed. **Golf** Limpsfield Common 18h. **See** General Wolfe's birthplace 1727, Quebec House, Wolfe's Statue, Statue of Sir Winston Churchill, Chartwell 1½ m SE.

★★★ King's Arms, Market Sq, TN16 1AN ☎(0959) 62990 Fax: (0959) 61240
Old coaching inn, well-appointed and modernised. Situated in centre of town.
18 bedrs, 18 en suite; TV; tcf
dogs, ns; P 30, G 4, coach; child facs
LD 10
£ B&B £65–£75, B&B (double) £75–£95; L £13, D £15·75
cc Access, Amex, B'card/Visa, Diners.

WESTGATE-ON-SEA Kent. Map 7C3
Pop 6,512. Rochester 40, London 67, Canterbury 13, Dover 21, Margate 2.
EC Wed. **Golf** Westgate and Birchington 18h.

★★ Ivyside, 25 Sea Rd, CT8 8SB ☎Thanet (0843) 31082
A family seaside hotel attractively situated on seafront. Indoor & outdoor swimming pools, squash, sauna, solarium, gymnasium, billiards. Fr, Es
67 bedrs, 65 en suite, 3 ba; TV; tcf
P 25, coach; child facs; con 120
LD 8.30
£ B&B £19–£35, B&B (double) £44–£70; HB weekly £196–£231; L £6·50, D £8·50
cc Access, B'card/Visa; dep.
(*See advertisement on p. 498*)

WEST HOUGHTON Lancashire. Map 33A3
London 197, M61 (jn 5) 1½, Bolton 4½, Chorley 9½, Wigan 5½, Warrington 14.

★★★ Mercury, Manchester Rd, Bolton, BL5 3JP ☎(0942) 813270 Fax: (0942) 814366
Established motel conveniently situated on A6, at junction 5, M61/A58. Fr, De
21 bedrs, 21 en suite; TV; tcf
TV; P 85, coach; child facs; con 200
LD 10.30
£ B&B £39·50–£45 (w/e £35), B&B (double) £45–£55 (w/e £40); L £6·95, D £7·95; WB £49·95; [10% V]
cc Access, Amex, B'card/Visa, CB, Diners.

WEST LULWORTH Dorset
See LULWORTH

WESTONBIRT Gloucestershire. Map 5A4
Pop 439 (inc Lasborough). Swindon 20, London 97, Bath 19, Bristol 22, Tetbury 3.
Golf Westonbirt 9h. **See** Arboretum (150 acres of forest trees and shrubs).

★★★ Hare & Hounds, Tetbury, GL8 8QL ☎(066 688) 233 Tx: 94012242 Fax: (066 688) 241

Early 19th century building of Cotswold stone with later additions. Set in ten acres of garden & woodland. Tennis, squash.
Fr
22 bedrs, 22 en suite; annexe 8 bedrs, 8 en suite; TV; tcf
dogs; P 70, G 5, coach; child facs; con 150
LD 9
£ B&B £48–£60, B&B (double) £72–£85; L £10, D £16; WB £84
cc Access, Amex, B'card/Visa.

WESTON-SUPER-MARE Avon. Map 4B3
Pop 59,613. Bath 31, London 136, M5 (jn 21) 4, Bridgwater 18, Bristol 20, Glastonbury 24, Radstock 26, Wells 19.
EC Thur. **MD** Sun. **Golf** Weston-super-Mare 18h. **See** Floral Clock, Winter Gdns, Model Village, Museum, Model Rly, Mini-Zoo and Aquarium, Steepholm and Flatholm Islands.
[i] Beach Lawns. ☎(0934) 626838

★★★ Berni Royal, South Par, BS23 1JN ☎(0934) 623601

Regency-style hotel in attractive garden. Overlooks the promenade. (BCB)
37 bedrs, 37 en suite; TV; tcf
lift, ns; P 150, coach; child facs; con 200
LD 10.30
£ B&B £48·50–£59·50, B&B (double) £70; L £8·15, D £8·15; WB £27·50
cc Access, Amex, B'card/Visa, Diners.

★★★ H R Commodore, Beach Rd, Sand Bay, Kewstoke, BS22 9UZ ☎(0934) 415778 Fax: (0934) 636483

Traditional hotel by unspoilt bay.
12 bedrs, 12 en suite; annexe 8 bedrs, 4 en suite, 2 ba; TV; tcf
ns; P 80, coach; child facs; con 120
LD 9.30, nr Sat lunch
£ B&B £45, B&B (double) £60; HB weekly £255·50; L £8·50, D £11; WB £67; [10% V]
cc Access, Amex, B'card/Visa, CB, Diners; dep.

Atlas Section
Consult the Atlas section at the back of the guide to find out which towns and villages have RAC Appointed and Listed hotels in them. They are shown on the maps by purple circles.

★★★ **Grand Atlantic,** Beach Rd, BS23 1BA ☎(0934) 626543 Fax: (0934) 415048

A large conventional stone-built hotel with fine sea views. Swimming pool, tennis. (THF)
🛏 76 bedrs, 76 en suite; TV; tcf
🏨 lift, dogs, ns; P 200, coach; child facs; con 230
✕ LD 9.30
£ room £60–£70 (w/e £48), room (double) £81–£91 (w/e £76); Bk £7, L £9, D £12; WB £48–£76
cc Access, Amex, B'card/Visa, CB, Diners.

★★★ **Royal Pier,** Birnbeck Rd, BS23 2EJ ☎(0934) 626644 ♿
Large purpose-built hotel in dominant position overlooking the Estuary. Fine views.
🛏 40 bedrs, 36 en suite, 3 ba; TV; tcf
🏨 lift, TV; P 100, coach; child facs; con 60

★★★ **Rozel,** Madeira Cove, BS23 2BU ☎(0934) 415268 Fax: (0934) 415268
Bay-windowed Victorian building well-positioned at western end of town with good views of the bay. Swimming pool.
🛏 48 bedrs, 48 en suite, 2 ba; TV; tcf
🏨 lift, dogs; P 45, G 40, coach; child facs; con 180

★★ **Arosfa,** Lower Church Rd, BS23 2AG ☎(0934) 419523 Fax: (0934) 636084

Centrally situated, 4-storey white building, close to shops and sea front.
🛏 47 bedrs, 46 en suite, 1 ba; TV; tcf
🏨 lift, ns; P 6, coach; child facs; con 100
✕ LD 8.30
£ B&B £35–£45, B&B (double) £55–£65; HB weekly £190–£250; L £6·50, D £10·50; WB £60; [10% V w/e]
cc Access, Amex, B'card/Visa, Diners; dep.

★★ **Beachlands,** Uphill Rd North, BS23 4NG ☎(0934) 621401 ♿

Substantial former residence extended into hotel. Set in pleasant well-cared-for garden.
🛏 18 bedrs, 18 en suite; TV; tcf
🏨 TV, dogs; P 15, G 3; child facs; con 80
✕ LD 8.30 bar meals only lunch. Resid & Rest lic
£ B&B £25·75–£27·75; HB weekly £197·75–£213·57; D £9·75; WB £55·50
cc Access, Amex, B'card/Visa, Diners; dep.

★★ **Dauncey's,** Claremont Cres, Birnbeck Rd, BS23 2EE ☎(0934) 621144

Family-run, terraced hotel with fine sea views and pleasant gardens.
🛏 50 bedrs, 44 en suite, 4 ba; tcf
🏨 lift, TV, dogs; coach; child facs; con 50
✕ LD 6.45
£ B&B £23–£25·75; HB weekly £159–£180; L £6·50, D £8; WB £60 (FB); dep.

★★ **Dorville,** Madeira Rd, BS23 2EX ☎(0934) 21522

Spacious modern hotel offering fine sea views. Near town centre. Billiards. Open Easter–Nov. 🎀 De
🛏 40 bedrs, 22 en suite, 5 ba; TV
🏨 lift, TV, dogs, ns; P 2, G 4, coach; no children under 5
✕ LD 7.30
£ B&B £21·80, B&B (double) £36·70; HB weekly £129·40; L £5·95, D £6·95; WB £35; dep.

★★ **Old Manor,** Queensway, Nr Kewstoke Worle, BS22 9LP ☎(0934) 515143
Charming farmhouse in village, now a family-run hotel. Sauna, solarium, gymnasium, billiards.

★★ **H** **Queenswood,** Victoria Pk, Upper Church Rd, BS23 2HZ ☎(0934) 416141 Fax: (0934) 621759
Attractive privately-run hotel with modern facilities and sea views. 🎀 De
🛏 18 bedrs, 16 en suite, 2 ba; TV; tcf
🏨 dogs, ns; P 6, coach; child facs
✕ LD 8. Resid & Rest lic
£ B&B £27; HB weekly £210; L £7·50, D £10·50; WB
cc Access, Amex, B'card/Visa, Diners; dep.

Braeside (Highly Acclaimed), 2 Victoria Park, BS23 2HZ ☎(0934) 626642. *Private Hotel.*
£ B&B £18–£20; HB weekly £147–£166
Milton Lodge (Highly Acclaimed), 15 Milton Rd, BS23 2SH ☎(0934) 623161. *Hotel.* Open Easter–end Sep.
£ B&B £21; HB weekly £123–£134
Wychwood (Highly Acclaimed), 148 Milton Rd, BS23 2UZ ☎(0934) 627793. *Hotel. Swimming pool.* Open 10 Jan–24 Dec.
£ B&B £19; HB weekly £175; [5% V]

Ashcombe Court (Acclaimed), 17 Milton Rd, BS23 2SH ☎(0934) 625104. *Hotel.*
£ B&B £14–£17; HB weekly £85–£90; [5% V]

Accueil, 193 Locking Rd, BS23 3HE ☎(0934) 626797. *Guest House.*
Baymead, 19–23 Longton Grove Rd, BS23 1LS ☎(0934) 622951. *Hotel.*
£ B&B £15–£22; HB weekly £160
Denewood, 8 Madeira Rd, BS23 2EX ☎(0934) 620694
L'Arrivee, 75 Locking Rd, BS23 3DW ☎(0934) 625328. *Guest House.* ♿
Newton House, 79 Locking Rd, BS23 3DW ☎(0934) 629331. *Guest House.* Closed 24 Dec–2 Jan.
£ B&B £15– £17·50; HB weekly £144–£161·50; [V Sep–Mar]
Sandringham, 1 Victoria Sq, BS23 1AA ☎(0934) 624891. *Private Hotel.*
Shire Elms, 71 Locking Rd, BS23 3DQ ☎(0934) 628605
Vaynor, 346 Locking Rd, BS22 8PD ☎(0934) 632332. *Guest House.*
£ B&B £10–£10·50; HB weekly £98–£101·50; [10% V Oct–May]

WESTON TURVILLE Buckinghamshire.

Map 14A2
Watford 21, London 38, Aylesbury 4, Denham 22, Dunstable 13, High Wycombe 15, St Albans 21.
EC Thur. **Golf** Weston Turville 18h.

★★ **Five Bells,** 40 Main St, HP22 5RW ☎Stoke Mandeville (029 661) 3131
19th century inn with modernised and well-appointed bedrooms.

WESTON UNDER REDCASTLE Shropshire.

Map 29B2
Pop 241. Telford (Wellington) 15, London 158, Market Drayton 8½, Shrewsbury 11. **Golf** Hawkstone Park 18h. **See** Church.

🏆 ★★★ **Hawkstone Park,** SY4 5UY ☎Lee Brockhurst (093 924) 611 Tx: 35793 Fax: (093 924) 311 ♿

Elegant Georgian country house, in large park. Swimming pool, golf, putting, tennis, fishing, sauna, solarium, gymnasium, billiards. 🎀 De
🛏 43 bedrs, 43 en suite; annexe 16 bedrs, 16 en suite; TV; tcf

W

TV; P 300, coach; child facs; con 200
LD 10
£ B&B £60–£68, B&B (double) £88–£122; L £8·95, D £13; WB £55 (FB); [10% V Sun]
cc Access, Amex, B'card/Visa, Diners; dep.

WESTWARD HO! Devon. Map 3A4

See also BIDEFORD.
Pop 2,098. Bideford 2½, London 204, Bude 26.
EC Wed. **Golf** Royal North Devon 18h.

★★ **Culloden House,** Fosketh Hill, EX39 1JA Bideford (0237) 479421

Three-storey stone building attractively set in grounds on hillside overlooking Atlantic. Open Mar–Oct.
9 bedrs, 7 en suite, 2 (sh), 1 ba; TV
TV, dogs; P 9
LD 8.45, bar meals only lunch. Resid & Rest lic
£ B&B £30–£40, B&B (double) £48–£60; HB weekly £245–£310; D £15; [5% V Mar, Apr & Oct]
cc Access, Amex, B'card/Visa, Diners; dep.

Buckleigh Lodge (Acclaimed), Bay View Rd, EX39 1BJ Bideford (0237) 475988.
Guest House.
£ B&B £14–£17; [10% V]

WEST WITTON North Yorkshire. Map 38A4

Harrogate 35, London 239, Boroughbridge 30, Darlington 28, Hawes 12, Leyburn 4, Northallerton 22, Skipton 30, Thirsk 28.

★★ **Wensleydale Heifer,** nr Leyburn, DL8 4LS Wensleydale (0969) 22322
Fax: (0969) 24183

Picturesque 17th century former coaching inn with oak beams and antique furniture.
9 bedrs, 9 en suite; annexe 10 bedrs, 10 en suite; TV; tcf
dogs; P 30, coach; child facs
LD 10, bar meals only Mon–Sat lunch.
£ B&B £45–£60, B&B (double) £60–£80; HB weekly £280–£355; L £9·50, D £17·50; [10% V]
cc Access, Amex, B'card/Visa, Diners; dep.
(*See advertisement on p. 498*)

WEST WOODBURN Northumberland. Map 44C3

Pop 250. Corbridge 16, London 296, Alnwick 31, Bellingham 4, Hexham 16, Jedburgh 36.
Golf Bellingham 9h.

★ **Fox & Hounds,** NE48 2RA Bellingham (0660) 70210
Stone-built 2-storey inn with later additions; in elevated position in village. Billiards.

Bay Horse, NE48 2RX Bellingham (0660) 70218
£ B&B £18–£20

WETHERAL Cumbria. Map 44A2

Pop 4,081. Penrith 17, London 293, M6 (jn 42) 3½, Brampton 6½, Carlisle 4½.
Golf Carlisle 18h.

★★★ **Crown,** nr Carlisle, CA4 8ES (0228) 61888 Tx: 64175
Fax: (0228) 61637
Attractive 3-storey Georgian building in own grounds. Indoor swimming pool, squash, sauna, solarium, gymnasium, billiards.
49 bedrs, 49 en suite; TV; tcf
dogs, ns; P 80, coach; child facs; con 175
LD 9.30, bar meals only Sat lunch
£ B&B £83–£97, B&B (double) £100–£114; HB weekly £679–£777; L £11·50, D £14; WB £100–£134 (2 nts)
cc Access, Amex, B'card/Visa, Diners.

WETHERBY West Yorkshire. Map 40A4

Pop 10,200. Doncaster 31, London 195, Boroughbridge 13, Harrogate 8½, Leeds 12, Skipton 29, Tadcaster 6½, York 12.
EC Wed. **MD** Mon, Thur. **Golf** Linton Road 18h. **See** Bridge, Branham Park 4 m S.
[i] Council Offices, 24 Westgate. (0937) 62706

★★★★ **H C R** **Wood Hall,** Linton, LS22 4JA (0937) 67271 Fax: (0937) 64353

Stately Georgian mansion in 100 acres of parkland and woods running down to River Wharfe. Lovely views. Fishing, billiards.
Fr, Es
16 bedrs, 16 en suite; annexe 6 bedrs, 6 en suite; TV
dogs, ns; P 60, coach; child facs; con 40
LD 9.30, nr Sat lunch. Resid & Rest lic
£ B&B £85–£105, B&B (double) £105–£115; L £14·95, D £29·50; WB £75 (HB)
cc Access, Amex, B'card/Visa.

★★★ **Penguin,** Leeds Rd, LS22 5HE (0937) 63881 Tx: 556428
Fax: (0937) 580062
Modern hotel with attractive flagstone-floored public area. At junction A1/A58.
72 bedrs, 72 en suite; TV; tcf
dogs, ns; P 150, coach; child facs; con 160
LD 9.45
£ B&B £72–£77 (w/e £30), B&B (double) £94–£99; L £8, D £13; WB £30; [5% V]
cc Access, Amex, B'card/Visa, CB, Diners.

WEYBOURNE Norfolk. Map 35B2

Pop 512. Fakenham 15, London 128, Cromer 7, East Dereham 21, Norwich 25.
EC Wed. **Golf** Sheringham 9h.

★★ **Maltings,** The Street, NR25 7SY (026 370) 731

Originally a priory and maltings, with adapted outbuildings. Near clifftop.
11 bedrs, 11 en suite, 1 ba; annexe 11 bedrs, 9 en suite, 1 ba; TV
dogs; P 150, coach; child facs; con 40
LD 9
£ B&B £35–£40; B&B (double) £54–£60; HB weekly £368·20–£434; L £5, D £15; WB £37 (HB)
cc Access, Amex, B'card/Visa, Diners.

WEYBRIDGE Surrey. Map 8A2

Pop 51,820 (inc Walton), Kingston upon Thames 8, London 18, Bagshot 11, Ealing 14, Epsom 12, Leatherhead 9½, Woking 7.
EC Wed. **Golf** St George's Hill 18h and 9h, Burhill 18h. **See** St James's Church (Chantrey Monument), Museum.

★★★ **C** **Oatlands Park,** Oatlands Dr, KT13 9HB (0932) 847242 Tx: 915123
Fax: (0932) 842252

Large Victorian-Edwardian building with magnificent entrance portico. Recently refurbished, spacious rooms are elegantly furnished. In extensive grounds. Tennis.
131 bedrs, 117 en suite; TV; tcf
lift, dogs; P 100; child facs; con 200
LD 10, nr Sat lunch
£ B&B £90–£95, B&B (double) £110–£125; L £13, D £14; WB £104; [10% V w/e]
cc Amex, B'card/Visa, Diners.

Licences
Establishments have a full licence unless shown as unlicensed or with the limitations listed on p 6.

★★★ **Ship Thistle,** Monument Green, KT13 8BQ ☎(0932) 848364 Tx: 894271 Fax: (0932) 857153

Modernised old coaching inn with extension at rear. In town centre. (MtCh)
🛏 39 bedrs, 39 en suite; TV; tcf
🏨 dogs, ns; P 50, G 20, coach; child facs; con 150
✕ LD 10
£ room £79, room (double) £90; Bk £7·75, L £9·95, D £13·75; WB
cc Access, Amex, B'card/Visa, CB, Diners.

WEYMOUTH Dorset. Map 4C1
See also PORTLAND.
Pop 45,000 (inc Melcombe Regis). Dorchester 8, London 130, Axminster 30, Lyme Regis 28, Wareham 17.
See Plan. p. 504
EC Wed. **MD** Thur. **P** See Plan. **Golf** Weymouth 18h. **See** St Mary's Church, King George III Statue, Guildhall.
ℹ Pavilion Complex. ☎(0305) 772444

★★ **Central,** Maiden St, DT4 8BB ☎(0305) 760700 Fax: (0305) 760300
Modernised hotel conveniently placed for town centre and the beach. ✗ Es
🛏 29 bedrs, 9 en suite, 7 ba; tcf
🏨 lift, TV; P 10, coach; child facs
✕ LD 8
£ B&B £18·50–£20·50, B&B (double) £38·50; HB weekly £90–£143; L £5, D £5·50
cc Access, B'card/Visa; dep.

★★**Crown,** St Thomas St, DT4 8EQ ☎(0305) 760800 Fax: (0305) 760300

Centre of town, imposing purpose-built hotel. Convenient for harbour. ✗ Fr, Es
🛏 79 bedrs, 44 en suite, 14 ba; tcf
🏨 lift, TV; G 8, coach; child facs; con 120
✕ LD 8
£ B&B £23–£29, B&B (double) £42–£52; HB weekly £107–£182; L £5·50, D £8; WB £48 (2 nts); [10%/5% V]
cc Access, Amex, B'card/Visa, Diners; dep.

Weekend breaks
Please consult the hotel for full details of weekend breaks; prices shown are an indication only. Many hotels offer mid week breaks as well.

★★ **Glenburn,** Preston Rd, DT3 6PZ ☎(0305) 832353

Small family-run hotel in extended modern residence. Near to sea. Closed 27–31 Dec.
🛏 13 bedrs, 13 en suite; TV; tcf
🏨 P 25; no children under 3; con 75
✕ LD 9.30. Resid & Rest lic
£ B&B £30, B&B (double) £56; HB weekly £210; L £5·50, D £11·50; WB £75 (2 nts HB); [5% V Oct–May]
cc Access, B'card/Visa; dep.

★★ **Moonfleet Manor,** Moonfleet, DT3 4ED ☎(0305) 786948 Fax: (0305) 774395 ♿
Large Georgian manor house 5 miles west of Weymouth overlooking sea and Chesil Beach. Indoor swimming pool, squash, tennis, gymnasium. ✗ Fr, De
🛏 37 bedrs, 37 en suite; TV; tcf
🏨 lift; P 100, coach; child facs; con 50
£ B&B £30·50–£49, B&B (double) £74; HB weekly £235–£260; L £6·75, D £10; WB £72; [10% V w/d]

★★ **Prince Regent,** The Esplanade, DT4 7NR ☎(0305) 771313 Tx: 94011219

Hotel within a Regency terrace with fine sea views. Closed 25 Dec–1 Jan. ✗ Es
🛏 50 bedrs, 45 en suite, 3 ba; TV; tcf
🏨 lift, ns; P 5, G 13; child facs; con 200
✕ LD 8.30, bar meals only lunch
£ B&B £49·50, B&B (double) £66; HB weekly £292; D £11·75; WB £75 (2 nts)
cc Access, Amex, B'card/Visa, Diners; dep.

★★ **Rex,** The Esplanade, DT4 8DN ☎(0305) 760400

Georgian terraced hotel near to the sea. Easy walk to shops.
🛏 31 bedrs, 31 en suite, TV; tcf
🏨 lift, TV, dogs; G 8 (£1), coach; child facs; con 20
✕ LD 10.30, bar meals only lunch. Resid lic
£ B&B £32–£40, B&B (double) £52–£72; HB weekly £190–£225; D £6·50; WB £68 (2 nts); [10%/5% V]
cc Access, Amex, B'card/Visa, Diners; dep.

★★ **Streamside,** 29 Preston Rd, DT3 6QB ☎(0305) 833121

Two-storey black and white modern hotel with considerable charm.
🛏 15 bedrs, 9 en suite, (5 sh), 1 ba; TV; tcf
🏨 dogs; P 40, coach; child facs

★ **Alexandra,** 27–28 Esplanade, DT4 8DN ☎(0305) 785767
Recently refurbished Georgian building on sea front. ✗ Fr, He
🛏 20 bedrs, 14 en suite,;TV; tcf
🏨 dogs; P 7, coach; child facs
✕ LD 7; bar meals only lunch. Resid & Rest lic
£ B&B £19·50–£30, B&B (double) £39–£60; D £6·50
cc Access, B'card/Visa.

★ **Frensham,** 70 Abbotsbury Rd, DT4 0BJ ☎(0305) 786827

Substantial former residence with modern extension. Pleasantly set in suburbs. ✗ Fr
🛏 10 bedrs, 6 en suite, 1 ba; TV; tcf
🏨 TV, dogs; P 5, coach; child facs
✕ LD 7.30, bar meals only Mon–Sat lunch. Resid lic
£ B&B £14–£19 (w/e £12·50, 2 nts); HB weekly £115–£165; D £6; WB £12·50 (2 nts); [10% V excl. Jun–Sep]; dep.

Kenora (Acclaimed), 5 Stavordale Rd, Westham, DT4 0AD ☎(0305) 771215. *Private Hotel.* Open May–end Sep.
£ B&B £14·50–£22·50; HB weekly £130–£153·50
Tamarisk (Acclaimed), 12 Stavordale Rd, DT4 0AB ☎(0305) 786514. *Hotel.* Open Easter–Oct.
£ B&B £15–£17; HB weekly £122–£139
Westwey (Acclaimed), 62 Abbotsbury Rd, DT4 0BJ ☎(0305) 784564. *Private Hotel.*

Bay View, 35 The Esplanade, DT4 8DH ☎(0305) 782083. *Private Hotel.*

W

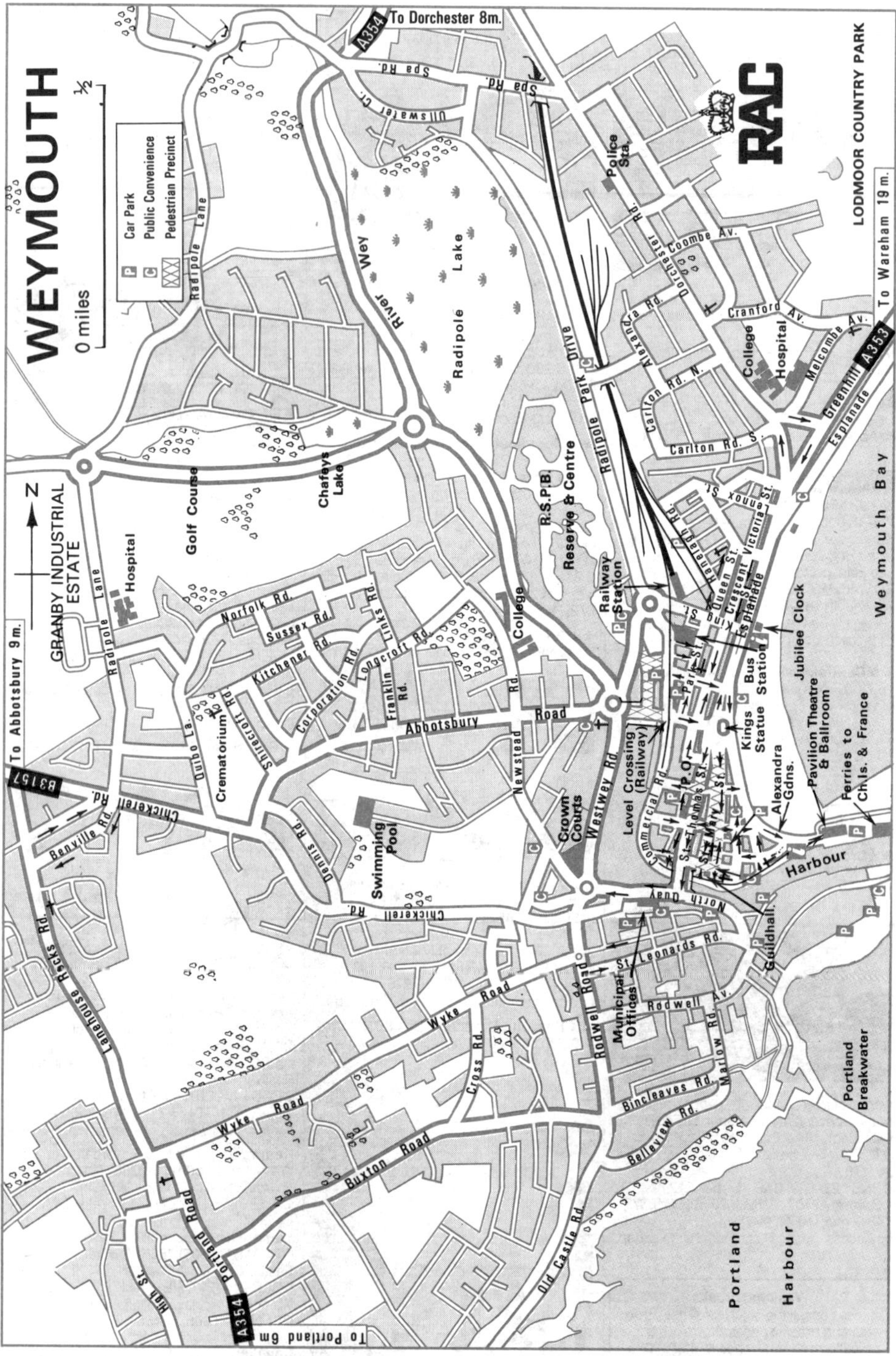

WEYMOUTH

0 miles ½

P Car Park
C Public Convenience
Pedestrian Precinct

RAC

To Dorchester 8m.
A354
Spa Rd.
Ullswater Cr.
Radipole Lane
River Wey
Radipole Lake
Police Sta.
Dorchester Rd.
Coombe Av.
Alexandra Rd.
Radipole Park Drive
Cranford Av.
College
Hospital
Melcombe Av.
Carlton Rd. N.
Carlton Rd. S.
Greenhill
A353
Esplanade
To Wareham 19 m.
LODMOOR COUNTRY PARK
Crown copyright reserved
Weymouth Bay
Chafeys Lake
Golf Course
R.S.P.B. Reserve & Centre
GRANBY INDUSTRIAL ESTATE
N
Hospital
To Abbotsbury 9m.
B3157
Norfolk Rd.
Sussex Rd.
Kitchener Rd.
Links Rd.
Longcroft Rd.
Corporation Rd.
Franklin Rd.
College
Railway Station
Lennox St.
Victoria St.
Ranelagh Rd.
Queen St.
Crescent St.
King St.
Park St.
Jubilee Clock
Bus Station
Kings Statue
Pavilion Theatre & Ballroom
Ferries to Ch.Is. & France
Alexandra Gdns.
Quibo La.
Crematorium Rd.
Shirecroft Rd.
Abbotsbury Road
Newstead Rd.
Westwey Rd.
Level Crossing (Railway)
Commercial Rd.
P.O.
St. Thomas St.
St. Mary St.
Chickerell Rd.
Benville Rd.
Dennis Rd.
Swimming Pool
Crown Courts
North Quay
Harbour
Guildhall
St. Leonards Rd.
Rocks Rd.
Lanehouse Rocks Rd.
Wyke Road
Rodwell Road
Municipal Offices
Rodwell Av.
Cross Rd.
Marlow Rd.
Bincleaves Rd.
Belleview Rd.
Portland Breakwater
Buxton Road
Portland Road
Old Castle Rd.
High St.
A354
To Portland 6m.
Portland Harbour

Beechcroft, 128–129 The Esplanade, DT4 7EH ☎(0305) 786608. *Private Hotel.* Open Apr–Oct.
£ B&B £13·28–£16·10; HB weekly £120·75–£138

Birchfields, 22 Abbotsbury Rd, DT4 0AE ☎(0305) 773255. *Hotel.*
£ B&B £12–£17; HB weekly £95–£122; [5% V Sep–Jun]

Cavendale, 10 The Esplanade, DT4 8EB ☎(0305) 786960. *Private Hotel.*

Concorde, 131 The Esplanade, DT4 7RY ☎(0305) 776900. *Hotel.*

Greenhill, 8 Greenhill, DT4 7SQ ☎(0305) 786026. *Private Hotel. Sauna, solarium.* ♿

Hazeldene, 16 Abbotsbury Rd, DT4 0AE ☎(0305) 782579. *Guest House.*
£ B&B £13–£16; HB weekly £75–£115

Kings Acre, 140 The Esplanade, DT4 7NH ☎(0305) 782534. Open Jan–Nov. Fr, De
£ B&B £17–£30; HB weekly £133–£175

Redcliff, 18–19 Brunswick Terr, DT4 7SE ☎(0305) 784682. *Hotel.*
£ B&B £14·50–£18·50; HB weekly £146·50–£175; [5% V w/d]

Sandcombe, 8 The Esplanade, DT4 4EB ☎(0305) 786833. *Hotel.*
£ B&B £12–£17; HB weekly £120–£135

Sou'West Lodge, Rodwell Rd, DT4 8QT ☎(0305) 783749. Closed 22 Dec–2 Jan.
£ B&B £17·60–£22; HB weekly £140–£167; [V]

Sunningdale, 52 Preston Rd, DT3 6QA ☎(0305) 832179. *Hotel. Swimming pool, putting.* Open Easter–Oct.
£ B&B £17·75–£22; HB weekly £139–£177; [5% V mid Sep–mid July]

WHATTON Nottinghamshire. Map 31B2

Nottingham 14, London 133, Grantham 14, Leicester 28, Newark on Trent 11.

★★ **Haven,** Grantham Rd, NG13 9EU ☎(0949) 50800
Two-storey house with modern extension in 5 acres of grounds off A52 south of Whatton.
17 bedrs, 17 en suite; TV; tcf
dogs; P 72; child facs; con 200
LD 9.45, bar meals only Sun dinner
£ B&B £25–£35, B&B (double) £42–£50 L £10; D £10
cc Access, Amex, B'card/Visa; dep.

WHEDDON CROSS Somerset. Map 3C4

Dunster 6½, London 172, Bampton 13, Ilfracombe 29, Minehead 9½.

Higherley, Nr Minehead, TA24 7EB ☎(064 384) 582. *Guest House.*

WHICKHAM Tyne & Wear. Map 37A2

A1(M) 6, London 269, Consett 9½, Newcastle upon Tyne 4½.

★★★ **Gibside Arms,** Front St, NE16 4JG ☎091-488 9292 Fax: 091-488 8000 ♿

Modern brick-built hotel in main street next to shopping precinct.
45 bedrs, 45 en suite; TV; tcf
P 18, G 8; coach; child facs; con 100
LD 10, bar meals only Sat lunch
£ B&B £44–£54 (w/e £24·50), B&B (double) £59–£69; HB weekly £418·50–£642; L £7·95, D £10·50; WB £34·50 (HB); [5% V]
cc Access, Amex, B'card/Visa, Diners.

WHITBY North Yorkshire. Map 45C1

See also GOATHLAND
Pop 13,403. Scarborough 19, London 232, Middlesbrough 30, Pickering 20.
EC Wed. **MD** Sat. **Golf** Whitby 18h. **See** Abbey ruins, St Mary's Church, Pannett Park, Town Hall, Capt Cook's house.
[i] New Quay Rd. ☎(0947) 602674

★★ **Old West Cliff,** 42 Crescent Av, YO21 3EQ ☎ (0947) 603292
A Victorian terrace building with bay windows and balcony. Closed 24 Dec–1 Jan.
12 bedrs, 8 en suite, 2 ba; TV; tcf
TV, dogs, ns; coach; child facs; con 25
LD 8; bar meals only lunch. Resid & Rest lic
£ B&B £22–£26, B&B (double) £32–£36; D £9; [5% V Oct–Feb]
cc Access, Amex, B'card/Visa; dep.

★★ **Royal,** West Cliff, YO21 3HA ☎(0947) 602234 Fax: (0947) 820355

Impressive large white-faced hotel overlooking sea and Esk estuary.
134 bedrs, 67 en suite, 16 ba; tcf
lift, TV, dogs; coach; child facs; con 250

★★ **Saxonville,** Ladysmith Av, YO21 3HX ☎(0947) 602631
Three-storey family-run hotel in quiet area on West Cliff. Open 16 May–15 Oct.
24 bedrs, 24 en suite; TV; tcf
P 20, coach; child facs; con 120
LD 8.30, bar meals only lunch
£ B&B £27·50; HB weekly £262·50; D £12·50; [5% V Jun–Sep]
cc Access, Amex, B'card/Visa; dep.

★★ **Sneaton Hall,** Sneaton, YO22 5HP (3 m S on the B1416). ☎(0947) 605929
A stone-built hotel in village. Fine views over countryside.
8 bedrs, 8 en suite; TV; tcf
dogs; P 30, coach; child facs; con 30
LD 8.30, bar meals only lunch
£ B&B £29, B&B (double) £45; HB weekly £210; D £10; WB £60
cc B'card/Visa; dep.

Kimberley (Highly Acclaimed), 7 Havelock Pl, YO21 3ER ☎(0947) 604125. *Hotel.* Closed Jan.

York House (Highly Acclaimed), High Hawsker, YO22 4LW ☎(0947) 880314. *Private Hotel.* Open Mar–Nov.
£ B&B (double) £37; HB weekly £192·50

Corra Lynn (Acclaimed), 28 Crescent Ave, YO21 3EW ☎(0947) 602214. Open Mar–Oct
£ B&B £16·50–£19·50; HB weekly £185–£199

Oxford (Acclaimed), West Cliff, YO21 3EL ☎(0947) 603349. *Solarium.* Open Feb–Dec.
£ B&B £26

Seacliffe (Acclaimed), North Promenade, YO21 3JX ☎(0947) 603139. *Hotel.*
£ B&B £37·50–£41·50; D £8·50
cc Access, Amex, B'card/Visa, Diners; dep.

Sandbeck (Acclaimed), 2 Crescent Terr, West Cliff, YO21 3EL ☎(0947) 604012

Banchory, 3 Crescent Terr, West Cliff, YO21 3EL ☎(0947) 603513. *Private Hotel.*
£ B&B £15–£20; HB weekly £161; [5% V w/d low season]

Corner, 3 Crescent Place, YO21 3HE ☎(0947) 602444. *Guest House.*
£B&B £9–£14

Europa, 20 Hudson St, West Cliff, YO21 3EP ☎(0947) 602251. *Private Hotel.* Open Feb–Nov.
£ B&B £12

Glendale, 16 Crescent Ave, YO21 3ED ☎(0947) 604242. *Guest House.*

Waverley, 17 Crescent Ave, YO21 3ED ☎(0947) 604389. Open Mar–Oct.
£B&B £12·50–£14·50; HB weekly £112·50–£126·50; [10%V]

WHITCHURCH Hampshire. Map 5C3

Pop 3,700. Basingstoke 12, London 59, Andover 8, Newbury 14, Winchester 13.
EC Wed. **MD** Fri. **Golf** Overton 9h.

★★ **White Hart,** Newbury St, RG28 7DN ☎(0256 89) 2900

Attractive 2-storey Georgian coaching inn on corner site.
10 bedrs, 3 en suite (4 sh), 2 ba; annexe 8 bedrs, 6 en suite, 1 ba; TV; tcf
dogs; P 18;
LD 9.30
£ B&B £29–£39, B&B (double) £43–£56; D £10·50
cc Access, Amex, B'card/Visa, Diners.

WHITCHURCH Hereford & Worcestershire

(Herefordshire). Map 20A2
M50 8, Ross-on-Wye 7, London 128, Gloucester 20, Hereford 16.

Crown, HR9 6DB ☎ (0600) 890234
An old inn, cream painted with red shutters, on busy A40 road.
5 bedrs, 5 en suite; TV; tcf
TV, dogs; P 40, coach; child facs; con 20
LD 9.45
£ B&B £25–£30, B&B (double) £40–£48; HB weekly £150–£170; L £6, D £8; WB £22 (2nts); [10%V w/d]
cc Access, Amex, B'card/Visa, Diners; dep.

W

Portland, HR9 6DB ☎ (0600) 890757. *Guest House.* Open Feb–Nov.
£ B&B £15·50–£17·50; HB weekly £140–£155

WHITCHURCH Shropshire. Map 29B2
Pop 7,246. Newport 21, London 163, Chester 20, Nantwich 10, Shrewsbury 18, Wrexham 15.
EC Wed. **MD** Fri. **Golf** Hill Valley 18h. **See** Parish Church, Higginson's Almshouses.
[i] Civic Centre, High St. ☎ (0948) 4577

★★★ **Dodington Lodge,** Dodington, SY13 1EN ☎ (0948) 2539

An attractive Georgian house on southern approach to town. Family-run.
10 bedrs, 8 en suite (2 sh); TV; tcf
dogs; P 70, coach; child facs; con 65
LD 9.30
£ B&B £37·50, B&B (double) £47·50; L £9·75, D £9·75; WB £24; [10%V w/e]
cc Access, B'card/Visa; dep.

★★★ **Terrick Hall,** Hill Valley, SY13 4JZ ☎ (0948) 3031

Attractive white-faced Victorian country house in secluded woodlands. Golf, putting, tennis, squash, sauna, billiards.
10 bedrs, 10 en suite; annexe 12 bedrs, 12 en suite; TV; tcf
TV, dogs; P 60, coach; con 40
LD 8.45
£ B&B £31·50–£36, B&B (double) £50–£55; HB weekly £290–£322; L £7·50, D £10
cc Access, Amex, B'card/Visa, Diners; dep.

★★ **Redbrook Hunting Lodge,** Wrexham Rd, SY13 3ET ☎ Redbrook Maelor (0948 73) 204 Fax: (0948 73) 533

An attractive former hunting lodge on Welsh borders. Set in 2½ acres. Fr
13 bedrs, 13 en suite; TV; tcf
dogs; P 100, coach; child facs; con 70
LD 9.30
£ B&B £40, B&B (double) £55; HB weekly £230; L £7, D £9·25; [10% V]
cc Access, Amex, B'card/Visa; dep.

WHITEHAVEN Cumbria. Map 43B1
Pop 26,714. Cockermouth 13, London 311, Egremont 5, Workington 7½.
EC Wed. **MD** Thur, Sat.
Golf St Bees 9h. **See** St Nicholas Church tower and remains, Pottery Craft Centre, Museum in 19th cent Market Hall, St Bees Head.
[i] Civic Centre, Lowther St. ☎ (0946) 695678

★★ **Chase,** Inkerman Terr, Corkickle, CA28 8AA ☎ (0946) 693656
Substantial 3-storey 19th century residence in 2½ acre grounds to south of town.
10 bedrs, 8 en suite, 1 ba; TV; tcf
dogs; P 40, coach; child facs; con 40
LD 9, nr Sun dinner
£ B&B £23–£31 (w/e £20), B&B (double) £36–£42; L £5, D £8; [10% V]
cc Access, B'card/Visa.

WHITESTONE Devon. Map 3C3
Pop 1,000. Exeter 4, London 173, Crediton 8, Moretonhampstead 13, Okehampton 19.
EC Tue. **Golf** Exeter G and CC 18h.

Rowhorne House, Rowhorne, EX4 2LQ ☎ Exeter (0392) 74675

WHITLEY BAY Tyne & Wear. Map 37C3
Pop 37,288. Tyne Tunnel 5, London 282, Alnwick 34, Coldstream 52, Sunderland 14.
MD Daily. **Golf** Whitley Bay Ltd 18h. **See** Seaton Delaval Hall 4 m NW, St Mary's Island, Lighthouse.
[i] Park Road. ☎ 091-252 4494

★★ **Ambassador,** South Pde, NE26 2RQ ☎ North Tyneside 091-253 1218 Fax: 091-297 0089
A pleasant 3-storey hotel, converted from terraced houses, near seafront. De
28 bedrs, 14 en suite (2sh), 12 ba; TV; tcf
TV, dogs; P 14, coach; child facs; con 15
LD 9.30
£ B&B £28–£44 (w/e £20), B&B (double) £39–£55; L £9·50, D £9·50
cc Access, Amex, B'card/Visa, Diners.

★★ **Windsor,** South Pde, NE25 8UT ☎ 091-252 3317 Fax: 091-297 0272.
Attractively modernised 3-storey hotel conveniently placed between the town and sea front. De
50 bedrs, 40 en suite (4 sh), 7 ba; TV; tcf
lift, TV, dogs, ns; P 22, coach; child facs; con 120
LD 9.30, bar meals only lunch
£ B&B £25–£48 (w/e £20), B&B (double) £40–£60; D £10; [10% V]
cc Access, Amex, B'card/Visa, Diners.

York House (Acclaimed), 30 Park Parade, NE26 1DX ☎ 091-252 8313. *Hotel.* ♿
£ B&B £18; HB weekly £147

Cherrytree House, 35 Brook St. NE26 1AF ☎ 091-251 4306. *Guest House.*
Lindisfarne, 11 Holly Av, NE26 1ER ☎ 091-251 3954. *Private Hotel.*
White Surf, 8 South Pde, NE26 2RG ☎ 091-253 0103. *Guest House.*
£ B&B £12·50–£14·50; HB weekly £122·80–£136·50; [5% V Jul–Sep]

WHITTINGTON Shropshire. Map 29B2
Pop 2,114. Shrewsbury 18, London 172, Llangollen 12, Oswestry 3, Whitchurch 17, Wrexham 16.
EC Thur. **Golf** Oswestry 18h.

★ **Ye Olde Boote Inn,** Castle St, SY11 4DF ☎ Oswestry (0691) 662250

A modernised inn of character; adjacent to the castle.
6 bedrs, 6 en suite; TV; tcf
dogs; P 100, coach
LD 10
£ B&B £19, B&B (double) £34·50; L £4·75, D £7·50
cc Access, B'card/Visa.

WHITWELL-ON-THE-HILL North Yorkshire Map 39A3
Pop. 135. York 12, London 205, Helmsley 17, Malton 6, Pickering 14.
Golf Malton 18h. **See** Kirkham Priory, Castle Howard.

★★★ **Whitwell Hall**, nr York, YO6 7SS ☎ (065 381) 551 Fax: (065 381) 554
Fine stone-built mansion with spacious rooms. Modern extension. Set in extensive grounds. Indoor swimming pool, tennis, sauna. Fr, Es
12 bedrs, 12 en suite; annexe 11 bedrs, 11 en suite; TV; tcf
ns; P 30; no children; P 70
LD 8.30. Resid lic
£ B&B £45–£49, B&B (double) £59–£95; L £6, D £19·50; WB
cc Access, B'card/Visa; dep.

WICKFORD Essex Map 17A2
Basildon 4, London 33, Brentwood 11, Chelmsford 12, Southend 13

★★★ **Chichester,** Old London Rd, Rawreth, SS11 8UE ☎ (0268) 560555 ♿
Tudor-style hotel round courtyard designed to complement the stable bar and function rooms which were converted from old farm buildings with notable beams.
34 bedrs, 34 en suite; TV; tcf
P 150, coach; con 100
LD 9.15; bar meals only Sat lunch. Resid lic
£ B&B £52–£55 (w/e £31), B&B (double) £62–£65; L £7·95, D £12·50; [10%V w/e]
cc Access, Amex, B'card/Visa, Diners.

WIDNES Cheshire. Map 32C1
Pop 54,900. Northwich 12, London 185, Chester 16, Liverpool 12, Nantwich 24, St Helens 7, Warrington 7, Whitchurch 28.
EC Thur. **MD** Mon, Fri, Sat. **Golf** Widnes 18h.
[i] Municipal Buildings, Kingsway. ☎ 051-424 2061

EC *early closing* **MD** *market day* *country house hotel* *ns (NS) no smoking areas* *tcf tea/coffee facilities*

Winchcombe (Gloucestershire)

Sudeley Castle and Gardens

Sudeley, the lovely Cotswold home of Lord and Lady Ashcombe, is rich in Tudor history, art treasures, antiques, arms and armour. The dungeon tower houses craft workshops. The tomb of Queen Katherine Parr lies in the 15th Century chapel. Award winning Gardens and Adventure Playground for children.

Open daily from April to October.
Sudeley Castle Holiday Cottages are available all the year round.

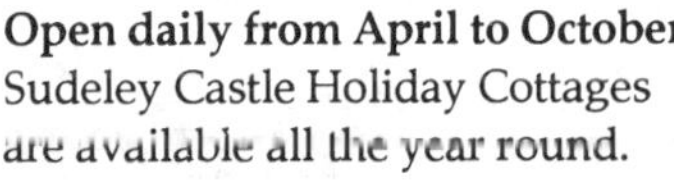

Winchcombe, Gloucestershire GL54 5JD Tel: Cheltenham (0242) 602308

W

Winchester (Hampshire)

LAINSTON HOUSE HOTEL

SPARSHOLT, WINCHESTER, HAMPSHIRE SO21 2LT. Tel: (0962) 863588

Lainston House is a beautiful William and Mary House, elegantly furnished, standing in 63 acres of spectacular Hampshire countryside.
Winchester City, once the capital of England, with many interesting places to visit is just 2½ miles away.
Lainston House has 32 bedrooms, all with private bathrooms, 4 conference rooms and a converted 16th century barn which accommodates 60 delegates.
Gourmet food, all freshly prepared and a high level of service, make Lainston House the ideal retreat to sample the luxuries of an English Country House.

★★★ **Hillcrest,** Cronton La, WA8 9AR
☎051-424 1616 Tx: 627098
Fax: 051-495 1348
Modernised dwelling house with purpose-built extension. Restaurant and buttery bar. It, Es
57 bedrs, 57 en suite; TV; tcf
dogs; P 300; child facs; con 120
✕ LD 11, bar meals only Sat lunch
£ B&B £45–£60 (w/e £30·50), B&B (double) £46·50–£67·50; L £9·25, D £10·50; [10% V w/e, Sep–Feb]
cc Access, Amex, B'card/Visa.

WIGAN Greater Manchester (Lancashire). Map 32C3
See also STANDISH and UPHOLLAND.
Pop 81,674. London 195, M6 (jn 26) 3, Bolton 10, Chorley 8, Manchester 19, Ormskirk 11, Preston 17, St Helens 8, Walkden 10, Warrington 12.
EC Wed. **MD** Daily exc Wed. **Golf** Haigh Hall Municipal 18h.
i Trencherfield Mill, Wigan Pier ☎(0942) 825677

★★★ **Brocket Arms,** Mesnes Rd, WN1 2DD ☎(0942) 46283 Tx: 628117
Well-appointed modern purpose-built red brick hotel in pleasant suburban surroundings.

★★★ C **Kilhey Court,** Chorley Rd, Worthington, Standish, WN1 2XN ☎Standish (0257) 423083 Tx: 67460
Fax: (0257) 422401
Victorian mansion of character set in 10 acres of grounds with many rhododendrons.
20 bedrs, 20 en suite; TV; tcf
dogs; P 210, coach; child facs; con 180

★★ H R **Bel Air,** Wigan La, WN1 2NU
☎(0942) 41410 Fax: (0942) 43967

On A49, privately-owned and run former private house.
12 bedrs, 11 en suite, 1 ba; TV; tcf
TV, dogs; P 10; child facs; con 30
✕ LD 9, bar meals only Sat lunch
£ B&B £36, B&B (double) £46; L £5·50, D £8·50
cc Access, B'card/Visa; dep.

★★ **Bellingham,** Wigan La, WN1 1NB
☎(0942) 43893 Fax: (0942) 821027 ♿
On A49, in a residential area, a former private house. Fr, De, It, Es
30 bedrs, 30 en suite; TV; tcf
lift, dogs, ns; P 35, coach; child facs; con 150
✕ LD 9.45
£ B&B £45–£60, B&B (double) £60–£70; L £8·95, D £9·95
cc Access, Amex, B'card/Visa, Diners.

★★ **Grand,** Dorning St, WN1 1ND ☎(0942) 43471 Tx: 57515 Fax: (0942) 824583

Black and white commercial hotel near town centre. Privately-owned. Es
38 bedrs, 38 en suite; TV; tcf
dogs; P 40, coach; child facs; con 125
✕ LD 9.30, bar meals only lunch, nr Sun dinner
£ B&B £34 (w/e £31), B&B (double) £50 (w/e £44); D £9·95; WB £59 (2nts HB); [10% V]
cc Access, Amex, B'card/Visa, Diners; dep.

Aalton Court (Acclaimed), 23 Upper Dicconson St, WN1 2AG ☎(0942) 322220. *Private Hotel.* Es
£ B&B £23

Charles Dickens, 14 Upper Dicconson St, WN1 2AD ☎(0942) 323263. *Inn.*
£ B&B £21

WIGGLESWORTH N. Yorkshire. Map 36C3
Skipton 13, London 223, Clitheroe 15, Settle 6½, Slaidburn 7½

Plough Inn, BD23 4RJ ☎(072 94) 243 ♿
Delightful 18th-century inn, with beams and open fires, set in beautiful countryside.

WIGTON Cumbria. Map 43C2
Pop 4,720. Penrith 22, London 298, Carlisle 11, Cockermouth 15, Keswick 20.
EC Wed. **MD** Tue. **Golf** Silloth 18h.

★★ **Greenhill Lodge,** Red Dial, CA7 8LS ☎(069 73) 43304
Elegant 2-storey 18th century mansion in 10 acres of parkland.
7 bedrs, 7 en suite; TV; tcf
dogs; P 100, coach; no children; con 80
✕ LD 8.45
£ B&B £30, B&B (double) £44; HB weekly £200–£300; L £5·95, D £15; WB £22·50; [5% V]
cc Access, B'card/Visa; dep.

WILLITON Somerset. Map 4A3
Pop 2,463. Taunton 14, London 157, Bridgwater 16, Dunster 6½, Tiverton 24.
EC Sat. **Golf** Minehead and W Somerset.

★★ H C R **White House,** Long St, TA4 4QW ☎(0984) 32306 ♿
Privately-run small and attractive hotel of character. Open 16 May–Nov.
8 bedrs, 5 en suite, 2 ba; annexe 4 bedrs, 4 en suite; TV
dogs, ns; P 17; child facs
✕ LD 8.30, nr lunch. Resid & Rest lic
£ B&B £29–£42, B&B (double) £52–£66; HB weekly £275–£333; D £25; WB £120 (3 nts); [5%V Sun–Thu, May–Nov only]; dep.

Fairfield House, 51 Long St, TA4 4QY ☎(0984) 32636. *Hotel.* Open Mar–Oct.
£ B&B £23; HB weekly £192·50

WILMINGTON Devon. Map 4B2
Pop 250. Ilminster 16, London 152, Axminster 6, Honiton 4, Taunton 18.
Golf Honiton 18h.

★★ **Home Farm,** Nr Honiton, EX14 9JR ☎(040 483) 278
Stone-built former farmhouse with pleasant garden in countryside.
14 bedrs, 8 en suite, 2 ba; annexe 5 bedrs, 5 en suite; TV; tcf
TV, dogs; P 20, coach; child facs

WILMSLOW Cheshire. Map 33B1
Pop 30,055. Congleton 12, London 173, Altrincham 7, Knutsford 6½, Macclesfield 7½, Manchester 12, Sandbach 16, Stockport 7.
EC Wed. **MD** Fri. **Golf** Wilmslow 18h.

★★★★ **Stanneylands,** Stanneylands Rd, SK9 4EY ☎(0625) 525225 Tx: 8950511

Family-run luxury hotel in red-brick building of character. Attractive gardens.
33 bedrs, 33 en suite, 2 ba; TV
P 80; child facs; con 90

★★★ **Wilmslow Moat House** (formerly Valley Lodge), Altrincham Rd, SK9 4LR
☎(0625) 529201 Tx: 666401
Fax: (0625) 531876

Purpose-built hotel in Tyrolean style. Under refurbishment. Indoor swimming pool, squash, sauna, solarium, gymnasium, billiards. (QMH). It, Es
125 bedrs, 125 en suite; TV; tcf
lift, dogs, ns; P 400, coach; child facs; con 300
LD 10.30
£ room £70–£75 (w/e £25), double room £80–£85; L £10, D £18; WB £40; [5% V]
cc Access, Amex, B'card/Visa, Diners.

WIMBORNE MINSTER Dorset. Map 5A2
Pop 5,531. Ringwood 10, London 103, Blandford Forum 9, Bournemouth 9, Dorchester 22, Salisbury 26, Wareham 12.
EC Wed. **MD** Fri. **Golf** Broadstone (Dorset) 18h. **See** Minster (11th cent astronomical clock and chained Library), St Margaret's Chapel and Hospital, Priest's House Museum, Julians' Bridge, Model of town (off West Row), Badbury Rings 3 m NW.
[i] 29 High St. ☎(0202) 886116.

★★★ **King's Head,** The Square, BH21 1JA ☎(0202) 880101 Fax: (0202) 881667

A hotel of character situated in centre of town. (THF).
27 bedrs, 27 en suite; TV; tcf
lift, dogs, ns; P 24, coach; child facs; con 40
LD 9, bar meals only Thu lunch
£ B&B £71·25–£77·25 (w/e £50), B&B (double) £94·50–£99·50; L £9·50, D £12·50; WB
cc Access, Amex, B'card/Visa, Diners.

Beech Leas (Highly Acclaimed), 17 Poole Rd, BH21 1QA ☎(0202) 841684. *Hotel.* Closed Jan
£ B&B £46·50–£66·50; HB weekly £430·50–£570·50

Riversdale, 33 Poole Rd, BH21 1QB ☎(0202) 884528. *Guest House.*

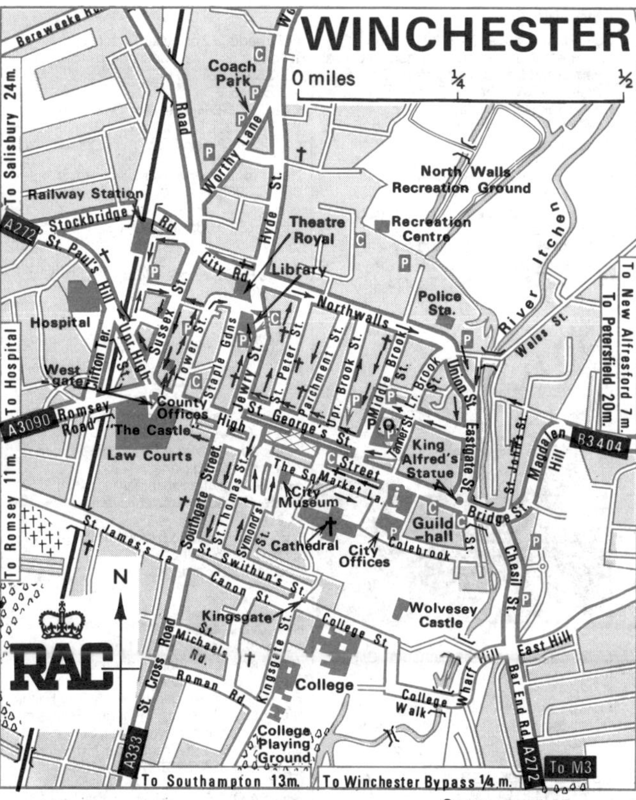

WINCANTON Somerset. Map 4C2
See also HORSINGTON
Pop 3,800. Amesbury 30, London 110, Frome 15, Glastonbury 23, Ilminster 25, Shaftesbury 11, Sherborne 9, Warminster 16.
EC Thur. **MD** Tue. **Golf** Sherborne 18h.
[i] The Library, 7 Carrington Way. ☎(0963) 32173
★★ [H] **Holbrook House,** Holbrook, BA9 8BS ☎(0963) 32377

17th century house of character set in attractive grounds with woods. Swimming pool, tennis, squash.
20 bedrs, 16 en suite, 4 ba; tcf
TV, dogs; P 30, G 3; child facs; con 30
LD 8.30
£ B&B £38–£48, B&B (double) £65–£72; HB weekly £320; L £8, D £13·50; WB £40 (HB); [10% V]
cc Access, B'card/Visa; dep.
(*See advertisement on p. 508*)

WINCHCOMBE Gloucestershire. Map 20C2
Pop 4,792. Stow-on-the-Wold 11, London 96, Cheltenham 7, Evesham 10, Stratford-upon-Avon 22, Tewkesbury 11.
EC Thur. **Golf** Cleeve Hill 18h. **See** St Peter's Church, Belas Knap (Neolithic Long Barrow), Sudeley Castle.
[i] Town Hall, High St. ☎(0242) 602925

★★ **George,** High St, GL54 5LT ☎(0242) 602331
Old established former coaching inn of historical interest. In town centre.

WINCHELSEA East Sussex. Map 7B2
Rye 3, London 66, Battle 12, Folkestone 14, Hastings 8

Strand House, A259, TN36 4JT ☎Rye (0797) 226276. *Guest House.*
£ B&B £18–£20

WINCHESTER Hampshire. Map 5C2
Pop 33,221. Basingstoke 18, London 65, Alton 17, Andover 14, Fareham 19, Newbury 24, Petersfield 19, Romsey 10, Salisbury 23, Southampton 12.
See Plan above.
MD Mon, Wed, Fri, Sat. **P** See Plan. **Golf** Royal Winchester 18h, Hockley 18h. **See**

Cathedral, Guildhall (with Art Gallery), Winchester College (apply porter), St Cross Hospital and Church (Wayfarer's Dole), Great Hall of Winchester Castle (legendary Round Table of King Arthur and his Knights), West Gate (Museum), King Alfred's Statue, City Museum, 14th cent Kingsgate (City Gateway, with St Swithin's Church built over), Hampshire Regt Museum (Serle's House), Royal Greenjackets Museum, The Weirs (City Wall), Wolvesey Castle ruins.
[i] Guildhall. ☎(0962) 840500

★★★★ R **Wessex**, Paternoster Row, SO23 9LQ ☎(0962) 61611 Tx: 47419 Fax: (0962) 841503

Modern hotel facing the Cathedral. Offers restaurant and coffee shop. Fr, De, It (THF)
94 bedrs, 94 en suite; TV; tcf
lift, dogs, ns; P 48, coach; child facs; con 80
LD 10
£ B&B £94–£105, B&B (double) £114–£125; L £14, D £19; WB £51
cc Access, Amex, B'card/Visa, CB, Diners.

★★★ H C **Lainston House,** Sparsholt (3 miles W on the A272), SO21 2LT ☎(0962) 63588 Tx: 477375 Fax: (0962) 72672

Fine 17th century red-brick mansion with attractive furnishings. Tennis, fishing. Fr, De, It
14 bedrs, 14 en suite; annexe 18 bedrs, 18 en suite; TV
dogs; P 100, coach; child facs; con 100
LD 10
£ B&B £97, B&B (double) £124–£164; L £16·50, D £30; WB £180; [10% V]
cc Access, Amex, B'card/Visa, CB, Diners.
(See advertisement on p. 507)

★★★ **Winchester Moat House** (formerly Saxon Court), Worthy La, SO23 7AB ☎(0962) 68102 Fax: (0962) 840862
Long, low, red-brick modern hotel in a quiet road about ½ mile from city centre. Indoor swimming pool, sauna, solarium, gymnasium. Fr (QMH)
72 bedrs, 72 en suite; TV; tcf
dogs, ns; P 72, coach; child facs; con 250
LD 9.45
£ B&B £79–£84 (w/e £48), B&B (double) £103–£113; L £11·50, D £16·50; WB £54·50
cc Access, Amex, B'card/Visa, Diners.

Harestock Lodge, Harestock Rd, SO22 6NX ☎(0962) 881870. *Hotel. Swimming pool.*
£ B&B £33–£38; HB weekly £294–£329; [5% V]

Kings Head, Hursley Village, SO21 2JW ☎(0962) 75208. *Hotel.*

WINCLE Cheshire. Map 30B3

Leek 8, London 162, Buxton 9, Congleton 10, Macclesfield 6.

★ **Fourways Diner Motel,** Cleulow Cross, SK11 0QL ☎(0260) 227228.
Small family-run motel in remote area on A54 overlooking Dane Valley.
11 bedrs, 11 en suite; TV
dogs; P 50, coach; child facs
LD 7.30. Rest lic
£ B&B £25–£28, B&B (double) £35–£38; L £5, D £7; [5% V]
cc Access, B'card/Visa; dep.

WINDERMERE Cumbria. Map 43C1

Pop 7,328. M6 (jn 36) 16, London 264, Ambleside 5, Kendal 8, Lancaster 28, Penrith 26, Ulverston 17.
EC Thur. **Golf** Windermere 18h. **See** Lake, Steamboat Museum, Aquarium, Belle Isle, Orrest Head (extensive views), St Martin's Church Townend (Troutbeck) 2 m N.
[i] Victoria St. ☎(096 62) 6499

★★★★ **Old England,** Bowness, LA23 3DF ☎(096 62) 2444 Tx: 65194 Fax: (096 62) 3432

Imposing 4-storey Victorian hotel (modern extension). Fine views from garden. Swimming pool, billiards.(THF)
82 bedrs, 82 en suite; TV; tcf
lift, dogs, ns; P 90, coach; child facs; con 120
LD 9.15
£ room £75–£80, double room £110–£120; HB weekly £350–£441; Bk £7·25, L £7·95, D £16·95
cc Access, Amex, B'card/Visa, CB, Diners.

★★★ **Beech Hill,** Newby Bridge Rd, LA23 3LR ☎(096 62) 2137 Tx: 65156 Fax: (096 62) 3745
Light modern hotel with terrace garden offering fine lake views. Indoor swimming pool, sauna, solarium. (THF)
46 bedrs, 46 en suite, TV, tcf
dogs, ns; P 50, coach; child facs; con 80
LD 9.30, bar meals only lunch
£ B&B £40–£43, B&B (double) £80–£86; HB weekly £297–£320; L £7, D £12·50; WB £42 (HB)
cc Access, Amex, B'card/Visa, CB, Diners; dep.

★★★ **Belmont Manor,** Ambleside Rd, LA23 1LN ☎(053 94) 33316
Stone-built villa, completely refurbished, with modern extensions in 7 acres of delightful gardens.
13 bedrs, 13 en suite; TV; tcf
ns; P 100, coach; child facs; con 100
LD 8
£ B&B £45; B&B (double) £66; L £7·95, D £13·95; [10% V]

★★★ **Belsfield,** Kendal Rd, Bowness, LA23 3EL ☎(096 62) 2448 Tx: 65238 Fax: (09662) 6397

Elegant early 19th century hotel in lovely grounds overlooking lake. Indoor swimming pool, putting, tennis, sauna, solarium, snooker. Fr, De. (THF)
66 bedrs, 66 en suite; TV; tcf
lift, dogs, ns; P 80, coach; child facs; con 150
LD 9.30, bar meals only Mon–Sat lunch
£ B&B £68–£79 (w/e £56), B&B (double) £97–£104; D £14; WB £56–£62
cc Access, Amex, B'card/Visa, CB, Diners; dep.

★★★ **Burn How,** Belsfield Rd, Bowness, LA23 3HH ☎(096 62) 6226

Modern chalets adjoin 19th century building in peaceful, secluded gardens. Sauna, solarium, gymnasium. Fr
26 bedrs, 26 en suite; TV; tcf
ns; P 35, coach; child facs; con 30
LD 9. Resid & Rest lic
£ B&B £39–£43, B&B (double) £58–£81; HB weekly £190–£290; D £15; [10% V]
cc Access, Amex, B'card/Visa; dep.

Discount vouchers
RAC discount vouchers are on p. 34. Hotels with a [V] shown at the end of the price information will accept them in part payment for accommodation bills on the full, standard rate, not against bargain breaks or any other special offers. Please note the limitations shown in the entry: w/e for weekends, w/d for weekdays, and which months they are accepted.

★★★ **Burnside,** Kendal Rd, Bowness, LA23 3EP ☎(096 62) 2211 Tx: 65430 Fax: (096 62) 3824

Attractive white-faced Victorian building with extensive lake view from garden. Swimming pool, squash, sauna, solarium, gymnasium, snooker.
🛏 45 bedrs, 45 en suite, 1 ba; TV; tcf
🏨 lift, dogs; P 60, coach; child facs; con 200

★★★ **Damson Dene Cottage,** Lyth Valley, LA8 8JE ☎Crosthwaite (044 88) 676 Fax: (044 88) 227
Charming 2-storey white-painted stone building set in country. Swimming pool, squash, sauna, solarium, gymnasium, snooker.
🛏 36 bedrs, 36 en suite; TV; tcf
🏨 dogs; P 100, coach; child facs; con 40

♔ ★★★ **H** **Langdale Chase,** LA23 1LW ☎Ambleside (053 94) 32201 Fax: (053 94) 32604
A stone-built Victorian country house with superb lake views from gardens. Putting, tennis.
🛏 26 bedrs, 23 en suite, 2 ba; annexe 7 bedrs, 7 en suite; TV; tcf
🏨 dogs; P 36; child facs; con 20
✕ LD 8.45
£ B&B £42–£50, B&B (double) £80–£110; L £9·25, D £19; WB £47
cc Access, Amex, B'card/Visa, Diners.

★★★ **Low Wood,** LA23 1LP (3¼ m N A591). ☎Ambleside (053 94) 33338 Tx: 65273 Fax: (053 94) 34072
Large white-faced building of character. With lake and mountain views. Indoor swimming pool, putting, fishing, squash, sauna, solarium, gymnasium, billiards.
🛏 98 bedrs, 98 en suite; TV; tcf
🏨 lift, TV, dogs, ns; P 200, coach; child facs; con 340

♔ ★★★ **Merewood,** Ecclerigg, LA23 1LH ☎(096 62) 6484 Fax: (096 62) 2128
Impressive Lakeland country house standing in 20 acres of grounds on a hill overlooking Lake Windermere. Putting. Closed 2 weeks Jan.
🛏 20 bedrs, 20 en suite; TV; tcf
🏨 dogs, ns; P 80; child facs; con 50+
✕ LD 9. Resid & Rest lic
£ B&B £30–£65; L £5·95, D £16·50; WB £47·50 (HB); [10% V w/d]
cc Access, Amex, B'card/Visa, Diners; dep.

★★★ **Royal,** Royal Sq, Bowness, LA23 3DB ☎(096 62) 3045 Tx: 65273 Fax: (053 94) 34072
Elegantly-furnished white-faced Georgian and 19th century building in town centre.
🛏 29 bedrs, 29 en suite; TV; tcf
🏨 dogs, ns; P 16, G 5, coach; child facs; con 60
✕ LD 8.30
£ B&B £29·50–£39·50; HB weekly £227·50–£294; L fr £4, D fr £13
cc Access, Amex, B'card/Visa, CB, Diners; dep.

★★★ **R** **Wild Boar,** Crook Rd, LA23 3NF (3½ m E B5284). ☎(096 62) 5225 Tx: 65464 Fax: (096 62) 2498

A well-appointed hotel east of Windermere and convenient for M6.
🛏 36 bedrs, 36 en suite; TV; tcf
🏨 dogs, ns; P 100, coach; child facs; con 40
✕ LD 8.45
£ B&B £40–£50; HB weekly £287–£378; L fr £7·25, D £18·50; WB £98 (2nts HB)
cc Access, Amex, B'card/Visa, Diners; dep.

★★★ **Windermere Hydro,** Helm Rd, Bowness, LA23 3BA ☎(096 62) 4455 Tx: 65196 Fax: (09662) 88000

Large modernised Victorian hotel overlooking the village. Fr, It. (MtCh)
🛏 96 bedrs, 96 en suite; TV; tcf
🏨 lift, TV, dogs, ns; P 70; child facs
✕ LD 9, bar meals only lunch
£ B&B £42·50, B&B (double) £64·50; L £8·50, D £11·50; [10% V]

♔ ★★ **C** **Bordriggs Country House,** Longtail Hill, LA23 3LD ☎(096 62) 3567 Fax: (096 62) 6949 ♿

A 2-storey white-faced house in 1½ acres of gardens. Swimming pool. Open Feb–Nov.
🛏 11 bedrs, 11 en suite; TV
🏨 ns; P 20; children over 10
✕ nr lunch. Resid lic
£ B&B £30, B&B (double) £55; HB weekly £301; WB; dep.

★★ **H** **Cedar Manor,** Ambleside Rd, LA23 1AX ☎(096 62) 3192

Pretty, Victorian stone-built house in 1½ acres of garden in residential area.
🛏 10 bedrs, 10 en suite; annexe 2 bedrs, 2 en suite; TV; tcf
🏨 dogs, ns; P 15; child facs
✕ LD 8.30, nr lunch. Resid & Rest lic
£ B&B £32·50–£39, B&B (double) £51–£64; HB weekly £196–£252; D £14·50; WB fr £68 (2 nts HB); [5% V]
cc Access, B'card/Visa; dep.

★★ **C** **R** **Crag Brow Cottage,** Helm Rd, LA23 3BU ☎(096 62) 4080

Early 19th century house, recently extended, in attractive garden with views over the town.
🛏 11 bedrs, 11 en suite; TV; tcf
🏨 P 30, child facs
✕ LD 9.30; bar meals only Mon–Sat lunch. Resid & Rest lic
£ B&B £35–£40, B&B (double) £47–£70: HB weekly £245–£325; L £8·95, D £16·95; WB £85 (2 nts HB); [10% V w/d Nov–Apr].

★★ **Ellerthwaite Lodge,** New Rd, LA23 2LA ☎(096 62) 5115 ♿
Town centre hotel with garden; a Victorian residence.
🛏 12 bedrs, 12 en suite; TV; tcf
🏨 TV, dogs; P 20, coach; child facs, con 25

★★ **Greywalls,** Elleray Rd, LA23 1AG ☎(096 62) 3741

Family-managed hotel in stone-built Victorian house overlooking fells.
🛏 14 bedrs, 12 en suite; TV; tcf

W

Wheatley (Oxfordshire)

Wheatley, Nr Oxford. Tel. 084-433 9226/9254

Lovely gardens, magnificent trees, a river to walk by, a quiet Saxon church – these delightful features, set in 83 acres of unspoilt Oxfordshire, makes Waterperry Gardens memorable.

High quality Plant Centre and Garden shop offering a wide choice of excellent produce direct from their own nurseries. Teashop open for morning coffee, light lunches and afternoon tea.

Open all year except Christmas and New Year holidays. Open only to visitors to ART IN ACTION 18–21 July.

Windermere (Cumbria)

Grey Walls Hotel

Windermere, Cumbria LS23 1AG
Tel: (09662) 3741 or 221

Family run, village centre hotel. Most bedrooms en-suite, all with colour TV, radio, tea making facilities, hair dryers and telephone. Lounge bar. Close to railway and bus station.

Windermere (Cumbria)

THE LINTHWAITE HOUSE HOTEL 

A classic country house with unobtrusive personal service, good food and fine wines

THE LINTHWAITE HOUSE HOTEL, BOWNESS-ON-WINDERMERE, CUMBRIA LA23 3JA TELEPHONE 09662 88600

Only 30 minutes from junction 36 on the M6, yet at the heart of the South Lakes

Windermere (Cumbria)

LAKESIDE HOTEL on WINDERMERE

Newby Bridge, Cumbria LA12 8AT Tel: 05395 31207

Peaceful setting with superb lake frontage, new conservatory and refurbished lakeview restaurant. Majority of bedrooms enjoy lake views. Suites, four posters, de luxe rooms with patio doors.

Completely refurbished while maintaining the character of a traditional Lakeland Hotel.

15 minutes from M6 exit 36.

★★★ RAC

Windsor (Berkshire)

SAVILL GARDEN

IN WINDSOR GREAT PARK

The home of good plants – and truly a garden for all seasons. Licensed Self Service Restaurant. Also our well stocked Plant – Gift – Book Shop is open throughout the season.

TV, dogs; P 14; child facs; con 4
LD 9.30
£ D £8; dep.
(See advertisement on p. 510)

★★ **Hideaway,** Phoenix Way, LA23 1DB
(096 62) 3070 Fax: (09662) 3070

A 19th century stone-built small house quietly set in own garden.
11 bedrs, 11 en suite, 1 ba; annexe 5 bedrs, 5 en suite; TV; tcf
dogs, ns; P 16; child facs
LD 7.30, bar meals only lunch. Resid lic
£ room £35–£45; HB weekly £210–£280; D £12·50; [10% V] dep.

★★ **Hillthwaite House,** Thornbarrow Rd, LA23 2DF (096 62) 3636
Family-run hotel on hill above Bowness with marvellous views of lake and hills. Indoor swimming pool, sauna, solarium.

★★ **Holbeck Ghyll,** Holbeck Lane, LA23 1LU Ambleside (053 94) 32375

Hotel in delightful hillside position outside town. Good lake views. Putting, billiards. Fr, De. Closed Jan.
14 bedrs, 14 en suite; TV; tcf
dogs, ns; P 20; child facs; con 20
LD 8.45, bar meals only Mon–Sat lunch. Resid & Rest lic
£ B&B & dinner £60, B&B & dinner (double) £90–£120; L £9·50, D £20; WB £40 (2nts min)
cc Access, B'card/Visa; dep.

★★ **Knoll,** Lake Rd, Bowness, LA23 2JF
(096 62) 3756

Attractive stone-built 19th century residence in wooded grounds. It. Open Mar–Dec.
12 bedrs, 9 en suite, 1 ba; TV; tcf
TV, ns; P 20, coach; no children under 3
LD 7.30–8, nr lunch. Resid & Rest lic
£ B&B £27; HB weekly £280; D £13·25; [10% V]
cc Access, B'card/Visa; dep.

★★ C R **Lindeth Fell,** LA23 3JP
(096 62) 3286

Charming lakeland house in magnificent gardens on the hills above Lake Windermere. Putting, tennis, fishing, Open mid Mar–early Nov. 14 bedns, 14 en suite; TV; tcf
P 20; no children under 7
LD 8.30; nr lunch. Resid & Rest lic
£ B&B & dinner £44–£49·50, B&B & dinner (double) £82–£99; HB weekly £265–£325; D £16·50
cc Access, B'card/Visa; dep.

★★ C **Lindeth Howe,** Longtail Hill, Storrs Park, LA23 3JF (096 62) 5759
Small country house, once home of Beatrix Potter; in beautiful grounds.

★★**Linthwaite,** Oaks Dr, LA23 3JA
(096 62) 3688
2-storey country house with lake views from grounds. Putting, fishing. Open Mar–Nov.
11 bedrs, 11 en suite; TV; tcf
ns; P 20; no children under 8
LD 8, nr lunch. Resid & Rest lic
£ B&B & dinner £43·50, B&B & dinner (double) £80; D £15; dep.
(See advertisement on p. 510)

★★ **Ravensworth,** Ambleside Rd, LA23 1BA (096 62) 3747

Family-managed hotel in 3-storey 19th century stone building.
12 bedrs, 12 en suite, TV; tcf
dogs, ns; P 15, coach; child facs; con 24
LD 8.30, nr lunch. Resid & Rest lic
£ B&B £24–£28·50, B&B (double) £48–£64; HB weekly £210–£235; D £11·50
cc Access, B'card/Visa; dep.

Albert, Queen's Sq, Bowness, LA23 3BY (096 62) 3241
Fax: (096 62) 88067
Family-run inn in centre of town.
6 bedrs, 6 en suite; TV; tcf
dogs; P 5, coach; child facs

Changes made after July 1990 are not included.

Blenheim Lodge (Highly Acclaimed), Brantfell Rd, LA23 3AE (096 62) 3440
£ B&B £16·50–£25; HB weekly £189–£234; [10% V, Thur]
Cranleigh (Highly Acclaimed), Kendal Rd, LA23 3EW (096 62) 3293. *Hotel.* Open Mar–Nov.
£ B&B £31–£35; HB weekly £190–£240; [10% V, w/d]
Fir Trees (Highly Acclaimed), Lake Rd, LA23 2EQ (096 62) 2272. *Guest House.* Es
£ B&B £22·50–£26·50; [10% V]
Glenburn (Highly Acclaimed), New Rd, LA23 2EE (096 62) 2649. De
£ B&B (double) £34–£54; HB weekly £179–£239
Glencree (Highly Acclaimed), Lake Rd, LA23 2EQ (096 62) 5822. *Private Hotel.* Open Feb–Nov.
£ B&B (double) £39–£55; [5% V w/d]
Hawksmoor (Highly Acclaimed), Lake Rd, LA23 2EQ (096 62) 2110. *Guest House.* Open Jan–Nov.
£ B&B £21–£27; HB weekly £175–£205
Holly Park (Highly Acclaimed), 1 Park Rd, LA23 2AW (096 62) 2107. *Guest House.* Open mid Mar–Oct 31.
£ B&B (double) £27–£34; [10% V Mar–May]
St John's Lodge (Highly Acclaimed), Lake Rd, LA23 2EQ (096 62) 3078. *Private Hotel.* Open Jan–end Nov.
£ B&B £16–£20; HB weekly £168–£187
West Lake (Highly Acclaimed), Lake Rd, LA23 2EQ (096 62) 3020. *Hotel.*
£ B&B (double) £32–£42; HB weekly £180–£205
Woodlands (Highly Acclaimed), New Rd, LA23 2EE (096 62) 3915. *Guest House.*
£ B&B £16–£25

Brendan Chase (Acclaimed), College Rd, LA23 1BU (096 62) 5638. *Guest House*
£ B&B £12·50–£20; [5% V]
Glenville (Acclaimed), Lake Rd, LA23 2EQ (096 62) 3371. Open Feb–Nov.
£ B&B £15–£19·50; HB weekly £135
Kirkwood (Acclaimed), Prince's Rd, LA23 2DD (096 62) 3907. *Guest House.*
Montford (Acclaimed), Prince's Rd, LA23 2DD (096 62) 5671. *Guest House.*
Mylne Bridge (Acclaimed), Brookside Lake Rd, LA23 2BX (096 62) 3314. *Guest House.* Open Mar–Oct.
£ B&B £15·50–£18·50; [10% V]
Newstead (Acclaimed), New Rd, LA23 2EE (096 62) 4485. *Guest House.*
£ B&B (double) £30–£40
Oakthorpe (Acclaimed), High St, LA23 1AF (096 62) 3547. *Hotel.*
£ B&B £18–£26; HB weekly £180–£220
Rockside (Acclaimed), Ambleside Rd, LA23 1AQ (096 62) 5343. *Guest House.* Closed 25 & 26 Dec.
£ B&B £13·50–£18·50; [10% V w/d]
Rosemount (Acclaimed), Lake Rd, LA23 2EQ (096 62) 3739. *Guest House*
£ B&B £16·50–£21; [5% V Oct–Mar]
Winbrook House (Acclaimed), 30 Ellerthwaite Rd, LA23 2AH (096 62) 4932. Open Mar–Nov & 27 Dec–6 Jan.
£ B&B £15–£24; [10 % V w/d]

Elim Bank, Lake Rd, LA23 2JJ (096 62) 4810. *Hotel.*
Field House, Kendal Rd, LA23 3EQ (096 62) 2476. *Guest House.*
Green Gables, 37 Broad St, LA23 2AB (096 62) 3886. *Guest House.*
£ B&B £12–£15

Lynwood, Broad St, LA23 2AB ☎(096 62) 2550. *Guest House.*
£ B&B £12–£20; [10% V]
Melbourne, 2 Biskey Howe Rd, LA23 2JP ☎(096 62) 3475. *Guest House.*
Oakfield, 46 Oak St, LA23 1EN ☎(096 62) 5692. *Guest House.*
£ B&B £12–£18; [10% V]
Thornleigh, Thornbarrow Rd, LA23 2EW ☎(096 62) 4203. Open Jan–Nov.
£ B&B £13–£16; [5% V]

WINDSOR Berkshire. Map 13A3

Pop 30,000. London 21, M4 (jn 6) 3, Bagshot 10, Ealing 15, Henley-on-Thames 14, High Wycombe 17, Reading 17, Slough 2, Staines 6.
See Plan, p. 515.
EC Wed. **MD** Sat. **P** See Plan. **Golf** Maidenhead 18h. **See** Castle (State Apartments, Albert Memorial Chapel, St George's Chapel, Queen Mary's Doll's House, etc), Royal Mausoleum (Frogmore, Home Park), Guildhall, Nell Gwynne's House (Church St), St John's Church, Great Park and Savill Gdn, Safari Park (Zoological Gardens) off Windsor–Bracknell Rd, Eton College, Windsor Forest, Virginia Water Valley Gardens.
[i] Central Station. ☎(0753) 852010

country house ★★★★ H C R **Oakley Court,** Windsor Rd, (A308) SL4 5UR ☎ Maidenhead (0628) 74141 Tx: 849958 Fax: (0628) 37011

Extended Victorian mansion in large riverside grounds. Fine public rooms. Putting, fishing, billiards.
92 bedrs, 92 en suite; TV
ns; P 150, coach; child facs; con 120;
LD 9.30
£ B&B £119·50–£224·50 (w/e £70); B&B (double) £144–£234; L £20, D £31·50; WB
cc Access, Amex, B'card/Visa, Diners; dep.

★★★ **Castle,** High St, SL4 1LJ ☎(0753) 851011 Tx: 849220 Fax: (0753) 830244
Large Georgian hotel with modern extensions. In town centre. Fr, Da. (THF)
103 bedrs, 103 en suite; TV; tcf
lift, dogs, ns; P 150, coach; child facs; con 420
LD 9.45
£ B&B £98–£178, B&B (double) £124–£206; L £14, D £19; WB £57 (HB)
cc Access, Amex, B'card/Visa, CB, Diners.

★★★ **Sir Christopher Wren's House,** Thames St, SL4 1PX ☎(0753) 861354 Tx: 847938 Fax: (0753) 860172

Elegant residence built by Wren for himself. Overlooking Thames. Fishing.
37 bedrs, 37 en suite; TV; tcf
dogs; P 14, coach; child facs; con 80

★★ H C **Aurora Garden,** Bolton Ave, SL4 3JF ☎(0753) 868686 Tx: 849462

Attractive converted residence–a small hotel conveniently sited on edge of Windsor.

★★ **Royal Adelaide,** Kings Rd, SL4 2AG ☎(0753) 863916 Tx: 848522 Fax: (0628) 773625
Privately-owned, modernised 3-storey Victorian building overlooking Home Park.
40 bedrs, 40 en suite; TV; tcf
dogs; P 25, coach; child facs; con 50
LD 9.30, bar meals only lunch
£ [10% V]
cc Access, Amex, B'card/Visa, Diners.

★★ **Ye Harte & Garter,** High St, SL4 1PH ☎(0753) 863426

Fine Georgian building with a steak-house restaurant. Opposite castle. Fr, Du. (BCB)
50 bedrs, 43 en suite, 2 ba; TV; tcf
lift, ns; coach; child facs; con 50;
LD 10.30
£ B&B £52–£68, B&B (double) £70–£85; L £8·15, D £8·15; WB £27·50
cc Access, Amex, B'card/Visa, Diners.

Dorset (Highly Acclaimed), 4 Dorset Rd, SL4 3BA ☎(0753) 852669. *Private Hotel.*
£ B&B £50–£55

Melrose (Acclaimed), 53 Frances Rd, SL4 3AQ ☎(0753) 865328. *Hotel.* Fr, Es
£B&B £32–£36

Clarence, 9 Clarence Rd, SL4 5AE ☎(0753) 864436. *Hotel.*
£ B&B £26–£28; [10% V]

WINSFORD Somerset. Map 3A4

Pop 340. Taunton 29, London 172, Dunster 9, Lynmouth 19, South Molton 20, Tiverton 18.
Golf Minehead and W Somerset 18h. **See** Devil's Punch Bowl.

★★★ C R **Royal Oak,** TA24 7JE ☎(064 385) 455 Tx: 46529 Fax: (064 385) 388

Old world thatched roof inn with high quality bedrooms and facilities. Fishing.
8 bedrs, 8 en suite; annexe 6 bedrs, 6 en suite; TV
dogs; P 18, G 2, coach; child facs
LD 9.30, bar meals only Mon–Sat lunch
£ B&B £60, B&B (double) £70; L £12·50, D £22·50; WB; [10% V w/d]
cc Access, Amex, B'card/Visa, Diners; dep.
(*See advertisement under Exmoor*)

WINSLOW Buckinghamshire. Map 21B2

Pop 3,500. Aylesbury 10, London 50, Bicester 14, Bletchley 9, Buckingham 5½.
EC Thur. **MD** Mon/Tue.

★★ **Bell,** Market Sq, MK18 3AB ☎(029 671) 2741

Historic former coaching inn—a 2-storey white-faced building in village centre.
15 bedrs, 14 en suite, (1 sh), 1 ba; TV; tcf
TV, dogs; P 70; child facs; con 140
(*See advertisement on p. 517*)

WINSTER Derbyshire. Map 24A1

Pop 670. Matlock 4½, London 148, Ashbourne 11, Buxton 18, Chesterfield 13, Mansfield 22, Newcastle under Lyme 32.

Winster Hall, DE4 2DE ☎(062 988) 204

WINTERBOURNE Avon. Map 4C4

M4 (junc 19) 1, London 120, Bristol 6, Chipping Sodbury 6, M5 (junc 15) 4, Wotton under Edge 11.

EC *early closing* **MD** *market day* *country house hotel* *ns (NS) no smoking areas* *tcf tea/coffee facilities*

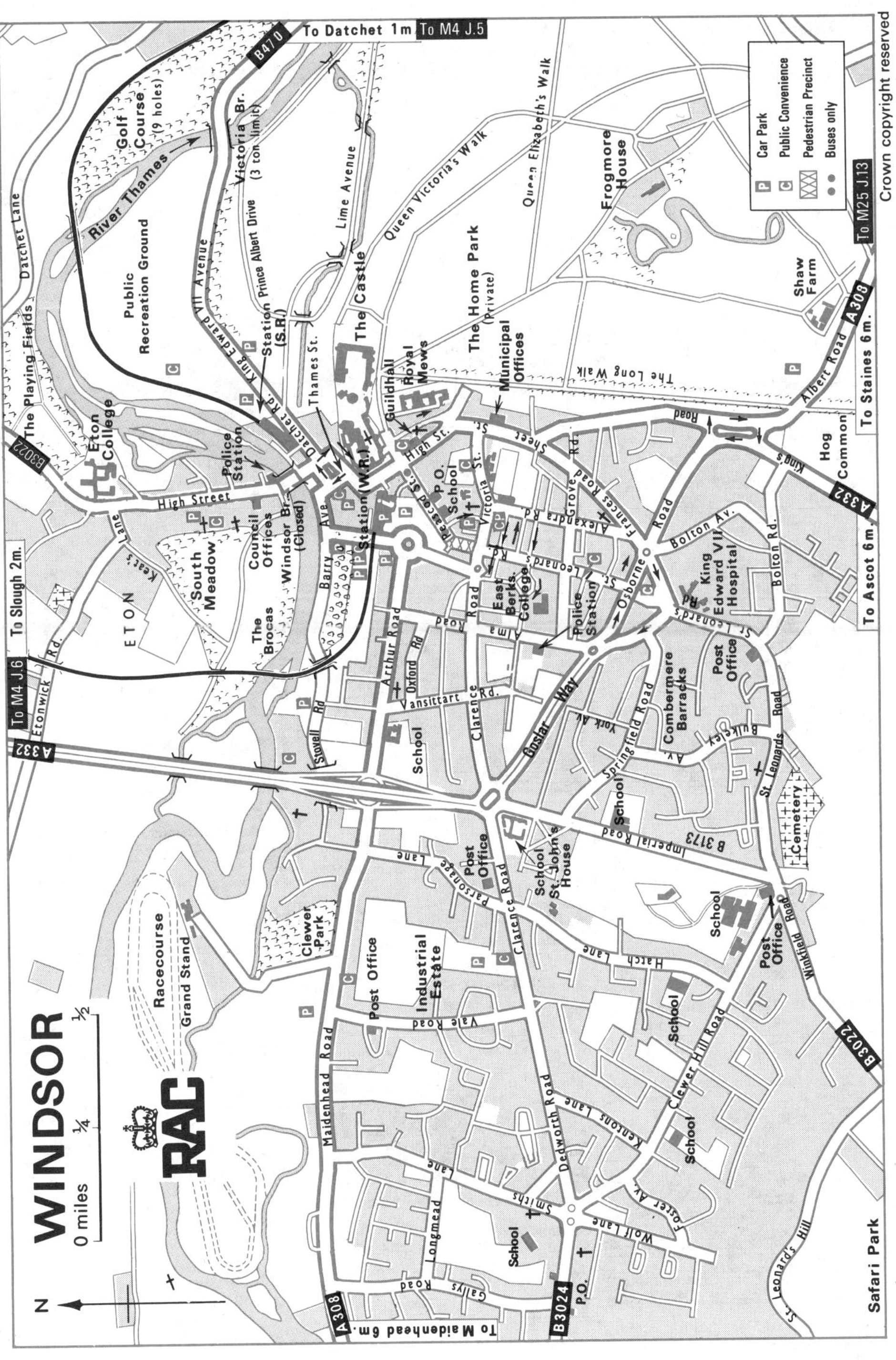
WINDSOR
0 miles
¼
½
RAC
N
To Datchet 1m
To M4 J.5
B470
To Slough 2m.
To M4 J.6
A332
B3022
To Maidenhead 6m.
A308
B3024
To M25 J.13
A308
To Staines 6m.
To Ascot 6m.
Safari Park
Car Park
Public Convenience
Pedestrian Precinct
Buses only
Crown copyright reserved
River Thames
Golf Course (9 holes)
Victoria Br. (3 ton limit)
Public Recreation Ground
The Playing Fields
Datchet Lane
Eton College
Police Station
High Street
Council Offices
Windsor Br. (Closed)
South Meadow
Keat's Lane
ETON
The Brocas
Eltonwick Rd.
King Edward VII Avenue
Prince Albert Drive
Station (S.R.)
Datchet Rd.
Thames St.
Lime Avenue
The Castle
Queen Victoria's Walk
The Home Park (Private)
Queen Elizabeth's Walk
Frogmore House
Shaw Farm
The Long Walk
Royal Mews
Guildhall
Municipal Offices
High St.
Sheet St.
Station (W.R.)
Barry Ave.
Peascod St.
P.O.
School
Victoria St.
Alexandra Rd.
Frances Road
Grove Rd.
St. Leonards Rd.
Osborne Road
King Edward VII Hospital
Bolton Av.
Bolton Rd.
Hog Common
King's Road
Albert Road
East Berks. College
Police Station
Alma Road
Arthur Road
Oxford Rd
Vansittart Rd.
Clarence Rd.
Goslar Way
Combermere Barracks
Springfield Road
York Av.
Bulkeley Av.
Post Office
Cemetery
St. Leonards Road
Imperial Road
B 3173
School
St. John's House
Stovell Rd
Parsonage Lane
Post Office
Clarence Road
Clewer Park
Racecourse
Grand Stand
Post Office
Industrial Estate
Vale Road
Hatch Lane
Winkfield Road
Clewer Hill Road
Maidenhead Road
Dedworth Road
Kentons Lane
Smiths Lane
Wolf Lane
Foster Av.
Longmead
Gallys Road
St. Leonard's Hill
P.O.

W

★★★ H C **Grange Resort**, Northwoods, BS17 1RP ☎(0454) 777333 Fax: (0454) 777447
Victorian residence with new extension, set in 18 acres of gardens and grounds. Indoor swimming pool, sauna, solarium, gymnasium. Fr
52 bedrs, 52 en suite; TV; tcf
dogs, ns; P 100, coach; child facs; con 150
LD 9·30
£B&B fr £66·50 (w/e £32), B&B (double) fr £83; L £13, D £15·50
cc Access, Amex, B'card/Visa, Diners.

WINTERSLOW Wiltshire. Map 5B3
Pop 1,500. Basingstoke 20, London 78, Andover 13, Amesbury 9½, Lyndhurst 20, Romsey 14, Salisbury 6½, Winchester 18.
Golf High Post, Salisbury 18h.

★★ **Pheasant,** London Rd, SP5 1BN
☎(0980) 862374

Pleasant 17/18th century coaching inn situated on A30 London–Salisbury road.
10 bedrs, 2 en suite, 2 ba; TV; tcf
P 100, coach

WISBECH Cambridgeshire. Map 34C1
Pop 17,740. Ely 23, London 94, Boston 29, Huntingdon 33, King's Lynn 13, Peterborough 20, Spalding 20, Swaffham 26.
EC Wed. **MD** Thur, Sat. **Golf** Sutton Bridge 9h. **See** Church, Peckover House.
Library, Ely Place. ☎(0945) 583263

★★ **Queens,** South Brink, PE13 1JJ
☎(0945) 583933 Tx: 329197
Fax: (0945) 474250
Georgian hotel overlooking river, near town centre. Fr
18 bedrs, 18 en suite; TV; tcf
dogs; P 40, coach; child facs; con 120
LD 9.45
£ room £37·50–£42·50, double room £47·50–£60; Bk £4·75, L £9·95, D £9·95; WB £60 (2nts HB)
cc Access, Amex, B'card/Visa, Diners.

★★ **White Lion,** 5 South Brink, PE13 1JD
☎(0945) 584813

Owner-managed old town hotel overlooking river and main road.
18 bedrs, 16 en suite, 1 ba; TV; tcf
dogs; P 25, coach; child facs; con 80
LD 9.30, bar meals only Sat lunch, Sun dinner
£ B&B £35–£45, B&B (double) £46–£59·95; L £11, D £11; WB £68 (2nts HB) [10% V w/d]
cc Access, Amex, B'card/Visa, Diners; dep.

WITHAM Essex. Map 17B4
Pop 25,681. Chelmsford 9, London 42, Braintree 7, Colchester 13, Southend-on-Sea 49.
EC Wed. **MD** Sat. **Golf** Braintree 18h. **See** St Nicholas' Church, Faulkbourne Hall 1½ m.

★★★ **Rivenhall Resort,** Rivenhall End, CM8 3BH ☎(0376) 516969
Fax: (0376) 513674
Beside A12, a converted farm house with adjoining motel-style chalets. Indoor swimming pool planned for 1991. Squash.
6 beds, 6 en suite; annexe 48 bedrs, 48 en suite; TV; tcf
dogs, ns; P 200, coach; child facs; con 200
LD 9.30, bar meals only Sat lunch
£ B&B £57·50–£67·50, B&B (double) £75–£85; L £12·95, D £14
cc Access, Amex, B'card/Visa, Diners.

★★ **White Hart,** Newland St, CM8 2AF
☎(0376) 512245

15th century coaching inn retaining much atmosphere in the public rooms.
18 bedrs, 18 en suite; TV; tcf
ns; P 43, coach; child facs; con 90

WITHYPOOL Somerset. Map 3C4
Pop 232. Taunton 33, London 176, Dunster 14, Lynton 17, South Molton 11, Tiverton 20.

★★ C R **Royal Oak,** TA 24 7QP
☎ (064 383) 506 Tx: 46529

An attractive old inn in the centre of the village. Riding. Fr. Closed 25 & 26 Dec.
8 bedrs, 6 en suite. 2 ba; TV; tcf
dogs; P 20; children over 10
LD 9
£ B&B £27–£40, B&B (double) £44–£60; L £8·50 (Sun), D £16
cc Access, Amex, B'card/Visa, Diners; dep.

★★ H C R **Westerclose Country House,** Nr Minehead, TA24 7QR
☎(064 383) 302

Pleasant privately-owned gabled country house in peaceful surroundings.
10 bedrs, 9 en suite, (1 sh); TV; tcf
dogs, P 10; child facs

WITNEY Oxfordshire. Map 21A2
Pop 17,500. Oxford 11, London 69, Bicester 18, Burford 7½, Chipping Norton 13, Faringdon 12, Wantage 17.
EC Tue. **MD** Thur, Sat. **Golf** Burford 18h. **See** Early 18th cent Blanket Hall with one-hand clock, 17th cent Butter Cross, Church.
Town Hall, Market Sq. ☎(0993) 775802

★★ **Marlborough,** 28 Market Sq, OX8 7BB
☎(0993) 776353
Fine stone building in keeping with this Cotswold stone town.
17 bedrs, 17 en suite; annexe 6 bedrs, 6 en suite;TV; tcf
dogs; P 18, coach; child facs; con 100
LD 9, nr Sun lunch
£ B&B £46–£55, B&B (double) £50–£60; L £9, D £12·50; WB £40; [10% V]
cc Access, B'card/Visa, Diners.

WIVELISCOMBE Somerset. Map 4A2
Pop 1,319. Taunton 9½, London 153, Dunster 14, South Molton 26, Tiverton 15.
EC Thur. **Golf** Vivary 18h.

Hurstone Farmhouse (Highly Acclaimed), Waterrow, TA4 2AT ☎(0984) 23441. *Private Hotel.*
£ B&B £43–£48·50, HB weekly £345–£378

WIX Essex. Map 27B2
Pop 630. Colchester 12, London 68, Clacton 10, Harwich 6, Ipswich 14.
EC Wed. **Golf** Harwich and Dovercourt 9h.

New Farm (Acclaimed), Spinnels La, Manningtree, CO11 2UJ ☎(0255) 870365. *Guest House.*
£ B&B £15·50–£18·50; HB weekly £145·65–£164·55; [10% V]

WOBURN Bedfordshire. Map 14B4
Pop 850. Dunstable 9, London 43, M1 (jn 13) 4, Aylesbury 16, Baldock 22, Bedford 13, Bletchley 5, Northampton 22.
Golf Millbrook 18h. **See** St Michael's Church, Woburn Abbey, Park and Wild Animal Kingdom.
Heritage Centre, 12 Bedford St

★★★★ **Bedford Arms,** George St, MK17 9PX ☎(0525) 290441 Tx: 825205
Fax: (0525) 290432
A modernised Georgian coaching inn with much old world charm. Fr, De, It
55 bedrs, 55 en suite; TV; tcf

EC *early closing* **MD** *market day* *country house hotel* *ns (NS) no smoking areas* *tcf tea/coffee facilities*

Winslow (Buckinghamshire)

** **The Bell Hotel** **

Market Square, Winslow, Bucks. ***Tel: (029671) 2741***

15th century former coaching inn. Friendly atmosphere, log fires, delightful restaurant, à la Carte, Table d'Hôte and Carvery menus. 15 bedrooms en suite bathroom/shower, TV, telephones. *Weekend Breaks; Functions; Real Ales.* Bar food, Sunday luncheon. Large à la Carte restaurant daily.

Wolverhampton (West Midlands)

HIMLEY COUNTRY CLUB & HOTEL

School Road, Himley, Nr. Dudley DY3 4LG
Tel: 0902 896716 Fax: 0902 896668
Telex: 333688 HIMLEY G

2 miles from Wolverhampton, 2 miles from Dudley in a country setting.
A friendly, privately owned hotel. 76 bedrooms all with private bathrooms, including four poster suites.
Our 2 restaurants, which are open to non-residents, include an excellent à la Carte and a carvery restaurant. Conference facilities available.

RAC ★★★ ETB 👑👑👑

Wolverhampton (West Midlands)

The Fox Hotel

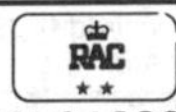

School Street, Wolverhampton, West Midlands WV3 0NR Tel: (0902) 21680

Situated in the town centre at the Penn Road (A449) island. Private parking. All rooms with en-suite shower/bathrooms. Colour TV, satellite programmes, direct dialling, tea/coffee making facilities. Bar and Restaurant. Function and Conference Room. Pool table. Nearby shopping, restaurants and night club.

W

Woodford (Essex)

The Prince Regent Hotel

☆ ☆ ☆ ☆

For the ultimate in comfort, elegance and service, just 20 minutes from central London. The finest English & European cuisine is available in Dukes, our intimate yet airy restaurant, whilst our conference & banqueting facilities will accommodate from 4–400 in air-conditioned comfort.

Manor Road, Woodford Bridge, Essex IG8 8AE Tel: 081 505 9966 Fax: 081 506 0807

🏨 dogs, ns; P 80, coach; child facs; con 60
✕ LD 10.30
£ B&B £76–£90 (w/e £38), B&B (double) £96–£108; L £12·75, D £16; WB £47·50
cc Access, Amex, B'card/Visa, Diners.

WOKING Surrey. Map 8A1

Pop 18,161; Borough (inc Byfleet) 93,200. Kingston upon Thames 14, London 24, Bagshot 7½, Farnham 14, Guildford 6½, Ripley 5, Staines 9, Weybridge 7.
EC Wed. **MD** Tue, Fri, Sat. **Golf** Woking 18h.

★★ **Northfleet,** Claremount Av, GU22 7SG ☎(048 62) 22971
A long, 2-storey building of 1920s appearance conveniently situated just off the Woking–Guildford road.
🛏 24 bedrs, 24 en suite; TV; tcf

★★ **Wheatsheaf,** Chobham Rd, GU21 4AL ☎(048 62) 73047
Completely refurbished hotel pleasantly situated close to town centre.

WOLVERHAMPTON West Midlands. Map 22B2

Pop 255,400. Birmingham 13, London 124, M6 (jn 10) 5, Bridgnorth 14, Kidderminster 15, Lichfield 14, Stafford 15, Walsall 6½.
MD Mon, Fri, Sat. **Golf** Penn 18h. S Staffordshire 18h. **See** St Peter's Collegiate Church, Museum and Art Gallery, St John's Church, Bantock House, Moseley Old Hall.
ℹ 16 Queen's Square ☎(0902) 312051

★★★ **Connaught,** Tettenhall Rd, WV1 4SW ☎(0902) 24433 Tx: 338490 Fax: (0902) 710353

Light and pleasant modern hotel conveniently situated on the A41. Sauna, solarium. ✂ It, Po
🛏 61 bedrs, 60 en suite, 3 ba; annexe 20 bedrs, 20 en suite; TV; tcf
🏨 lift, dogs; P 100, coach; child facs; con 250
✕ LD 10, bar meals only Sun dinner
£ B&B £49·50–£55 (w/e £30), B&B (double) £70–£75; L £8, D £10·25; [10% V]
cc Access, Amex, B'card/Visa, Diners; dep.

★★★ **Goldthorn,** Penn Rd, WV3 0ER ☎(0902) 29216 Tx: 339516 Fax: (0902) 710419
Pleasantly extended 19th century former private residence.
🛏 66 bedrs, 66 en suite; annexe 27 bedrs, 27 en suite; TV tcf
🏨 dogs; P 150, coach; child facs; con 120
✕ LD 9.30
£ B&B £57·50–£71·50, B&B (double) £88; L £8·95, D £10·95; WB £29·50; [10% V]
cc Access, Amex, B'card/Visa, Diners.

★★★ **Mount,** Mount Rd, Tettenhall Wood, WV6 8HL (2½ m W off A454). ☎(0902) 752055 Tx: 333546 Fax: (0902) 745263

Former residence now much extended and set in lovely gardens. ✂ Fr, De, It, Es, Po. (Emb)
🛏 58 bedrs, 58 en suite, 1 ba; TV; tcf
🏨 dogs, ns; P 250, coach; child facs; con 200
✕ LD 9.45, bar meals only Sat lunch
£ B&B £73 (w/e £30), B&B (double) £90·50; HB weekly £466; L £9·50, D £12; WB £36·50 (HB)
cc Access, Amex, B'card/Visa, CB, Diners.

★★★ **Park Hall,** Park Dr, Goldthorn Park, WV4 5AJ (Sedgley 3 m S A459). ☎(0902) 331121 Tx: 333546 Fax: (0902) 344760

Georgian style hotel set on a hill, overlooking countryside. (Emb)
🛏 57 bedrs, 57 en suite; TV; tcf
🏨 dogs, ns; P 350, coach; child facs; con 400
✕ LD 9.30, bar meals only Sat lunch
£ B&B £62, B&B (double) £79, L £10, D £10·50; WB £29·50
cc Access, Amex, B'card/Visa, Diners.

♣♣ ★★★ **Patshull Park Hotel,** Pattingham, WV6 7HR ☎Pattingham (0902) 700100 Tx: 334849 Fax: (0902) 700874

Modern hotel overlooking trout lakes in peaceful surroundings. Indoor swimming pool, golf, fishing, sauna, solarium, gymnasium, billiards.
🛏 48 bedrs, 48 en suite; TV; tcf
🏨 dogs; P 300, coach; child facs; con 120
✕ LD 9.30
£ B&B £60–£70, B&B (double) £74–£85; L £7·75, D £11·75; WB £140 (incl. golf); [10% V, Nov–Jan]
cc Access, Amex, B'card/Visa, Diners.

★★ **Castlecroft,** Castlecroft Rd, WV3 8NA ☎(0902) 764040

Attractive 2-storey late Victorian building overlooking cricket ground. Solarium.
🛏 20 bedrs, 17 en suite, (2 sh), 2 ba; TV; tcf
🏨 dogs; P 100, G 6, coach; child facs; con 60

★★ **Fox,** 118 School St, WV3 0NR ☎(0902) 21680

Town-centre hotel, popular with business people. Attractive bedrooms.
🛏 33 bedrs, 33 en suite; TV; tcf
🏨 P 25, coach; con 75
✕ LD 9.45, nr Sun dinner & all Sat
£ B&B £29·50–£34·50 (w/e £23·50), B&B (double) £34·50–£44·50; [10% V]
cc Access, Amex, B'card/Visa, Diners.
(*See advertisement on p. 517*)

★★ **York,** 138 Tettenhall Rd, WV6 0BQ ☎(0902) 758211
Small hotel conveniently situated near town centre. Owner-run.
🛏 16 bedrs, 16 en suite; TV; tcf
🏨 TV, dogs; P 20, coach; child facs; con 12

WOMENSWOLD Kent. Map 7C3

Canterbury 7, London 65, Dover 10, Folkestone 11, Margate 17, Ramsgate 17.
Golf Canterbury 18h. **See** Church.

Woodpeckers Country, CT4 6HB ☎Canterbury (0227) 831319. *Hotel. Swimming pool, putting, snooker.* ♿
£B&B £24; HB weekly £203; [5%V]

WOODBRIDGE Suffolk. Map 27B3

Pop 7,224. Ipswich 7½, London 81, Aldeburgh 17, Saxmundham 13, Scole 23, Stowmarket 18.
EC Wed. **MD** Thur. **Golf** Woodbridge 18h.

Atlas Section

Consult the Atlas section at the back of the guide to find out which towns and villages have RAC Appointed and Listed hotels in them. They are shown on the maps by purple circles.

★★★ C R Seckford Hall, Great Bealings, IP13 6NU (0394) 385678 Tx: 987446 Fax: (0394) 380610

Beautifully preserved and enlarged Tudor mansion set in 34 acres. Indoor swimming pool, fishing, solarium, gymnasium. Fr, It, Es. Closed Xmas Day.
23 bedrs, 23 en suite; annexe 10 bedrs, 10 en suite; TV; tcf
dogs, ns; P 100, coach; child facs; con 100
LD 9.30
£ B&B £69–£90, B&B (double) £75–£120; L £10·50; WB £105–£140
cc Access, Amex, B'card/Visa, Diners; dep.

★★ Crown, 2 Thorofare, IP12 1AD (039 43) 4242 Fax: (039 43) 7192

Pleasant town centre former coaching inn with chalet accommodation in annexe. (THF)
10 bedrs, 10 en suite; annexe 10 bedrs, 10 en suite; TV; tcf
dogs, ns; P 30, coach; child facs
LD 9
£ B&B £70 (w/e £50), B&B (double) £85; HB weekly £350; L £8, D £15
cc Access, Amex, B'card/Visa, CB, Diners; dep.

WOODFORD BRIDGE Greater London

(Essex). Map 9B4
London 11, Enfield 7½, Epping 8½, Rainham 11, Romford 8½.

★★★ Prince Regent, Manor Rd, IG8 8AE 08-505 9966 Fax: 08-506 0807
Georgian mansion with outbuildings converted to a luxury hotel.
61 bedrs, 61 en suite; TV; tcf
lift, ns; P 85, G 15, coach; child facs; con 400
(*See advertisement on p. 517*)

WOODFORD GREEN Greater London

(Essex). Map 16B2
1½ m N of Woodford. London 11, Enfield 5, Epping 7, Rainham 12, Romford 9½.
EC Thur. **Golf** Woodford 9h. **See** Statue of Sir Winston Churchill.

★★★ Woodford Moat House, Oak Hill, IG8 9NY 081-505 4511 Tx: 264428 Fax: 081-506 0941

Large modern hotel situated on the edge of Epping Forest. Fr, De, It. (QMH)
99 bedrs, 99 en suite; TV; tcf
lift; P 150, coach; child facs; con 150
LD 10.15, bar meals only Sat lunch
£ B&B £79 (w/e £69), B&B (double) £92; L £14·50, D £14·50; WB £42·50
cc Access, Amex, B'card/Visa, Diners.
(*See advertisement on p. 521*)

WOODHALL SPA Lincolnshire. Map 34B3

Pop 2,445. Spalding 30, London 129, Boston 14, Horncastle 6½, Lincoln 18, Sleaford 17.
EC Wed. **Golf** Woodhall Spa 18h. **See** Springs and Mineral Baths, Wellington Monument, Tower on the Moor, Tattershall Castle 3 m SE.
i Jubilee Park, Stixwould Rd. (0526) 52448

★★★ Golf, The Broadway, LN10 6SG (0526) 53535 Tx: 56448 Fax: (0526) 53096

Hotel in picturesque situation in own grounds adjacent to golf course. Tennis, snooker.
50 bedrs, 50 en suite; TV; tcf
TV, dogs, ns; P 150, coach; child facs; con 150
LD 9.30, bar meals only Mon–Sat lunch
£ B&B £65–£70, B&B (double) £80–£90; D £12·95; WB £47·50 (HB)
cc Access, Amex, B'card/Visa, CB, Diners.

★★★ Petwood, Stixwould Rd, LN10 6QF (0526) 52411 Fax: (0526) 53473

Superb Edwardian building in black and white timber. Extensive grounds. Putting, billiards.
46 bedrs, 46 en suite; TV; tcf
lift, ns; P 70, coach; child facs; con 160
LD 9.15, bar meals only Mon–Sat lunch
£ B&B £73–£83 (w/e £48), B&B (double) £89–£109; HB weekly £336–£406; L £7·95, D £11·50; WB; [5% V]
cc Access, Amex, B'card/Visa, Diners.

WOODSTOCK Oxfordshire. Map 21A2

Pop 3,000. Oxford 8, London 64, Banbury 15, Bicester 11, Burford 15, Chipping Norton 12.
EC Wed. **Golf** North Oxford 18h. **See** Blenheim Palace and Garden Centre, Grave of Sir Winston Churchill (Bladon Church).
i Hensington Rd. (0993) 811038.

★★★ C R Bear, Park St, OX7 1SZ (0993) 811511 Tx: 837921 Fax: (0993) 813380

16th–17th century hotel of character built round attractive courtyard. It, Es. (THF)
45 bedrs, 45 en suite; TV; tcf
dogs, ns; P 30, coach; child facs; con 70
LD 10
£ B&B £93–£108 (w/e £65), B&B (double) £136–£186; L £16·50, D £19·50; WB
cc Access, Amex, B'card/Visa, Diners.

★★ Kings Arms, Market St, OX7 1ST (0993) 811592 Tx: 837921 Fax: (0993) 813380
Former coaching inn situated in town centre. (THF)
9 bedrs, 9 en suite; TV; tcf
dogs, ns; coach; child facs; con 50

Gorseland, Boddington La, Nr North Leigh, OX8 6PU (0993) 881895. *Guest House. Billiards.* Fr, De, Es. Open early Jul–late Sep & most w/ends June & Oct
£ B&B £25–£30; HB weekly £125; [10% V]

WOODY BAY Devon. Map 3B4

Lynton 3, London 188, Barnstaple 15, Ilfracombe 12, South Molton 18.

★★ H Woody Bay, Parracombe, EX31 4QX Parracombe (059 83) 264

Attractive building in woodland on cliffside with panoramic view. Closed early Jan–late Feb.
14 bedrs, 13 en suite, 1 ba; tcf
dogs; P 15; no children under 8
LD 8.30, bar meals only lunch

W

£ B&B £24–£34, B&B (double) £44–£74; HB weekly £224–£308; D £14·50
cc Access, B'card/Visa; dep.

The Red House (Acclaimed), EX31 4QX
Parracombe (05983) 255. *Hotel.* Open Apr–Oct.
£ B&B (double) £33–£37; HB weekly £175–£190; [5% V]

WOOLACOMBE Devon. Map 3A4
See also MORTEHOE.
Pop 1,255. Dunster 38, London 203, Barnstaple 13, Ilfracombe 5½, Lynmouth 20.
EC Wed. **Golf** Ilfracombe 18h.
Hall '70', Beach Rd. (0271) 870553

★★★ H C R **Watersmeet,** Mortehoe, EX34 7EB (0271) 870333
Fax: (0271) 870890

Attractive hotel on cliff edge; commanding view of bay. Swimming pool, tennis. Open mid Feb–end Nov & Xmas.
25 bedrs, 25 en suite; TV
ns; P 30, G 20; child facs; con 30
LD 8.30, bar meals only lunch
£ B&B & dinner £35–£60; HB weekly £230–£382; D £19·50
cc Access, Amex, B'card/Visa, Diners; dep.

★★★ **Woolacombe Bay,** EX34 7BN
(0271) 870388 Tx: 46761
Fax: (0271) 870388

Spacious hotel in extensive grounds with level approach to sands. Indoor/outdoor swimming pool, putting, tennis, squash, sauna, solarium, gymnasium, billiards.
Fr. Closed Jan.
59 bedrs, 59 en suite; TV; tcf
lift, TV; P 70; child facs; con 100
LD 9.45, bar meals only Mon–Sat lunch
£ B&B & dinner £43–£95; B&B & dinner (double) £86–£190; L £8, D £16; WB £82·50
cc Access, Amex, B'card/Visa, Diners; dep.

★★ **Atlantic,** Sunnyside Rd, EX34 7DG
(0271) 870469
Brick-built family hotel with commanding view of three miles of sands. Sauna, solarium, gymnasium.

★★ H **Devon Beach,** The Esplanade, EX34 7DJ (0271) 870449
Well-appointed hotel on esplanade with uninterrupted view of sands and bay. Indoor swimming pool, solarium. Fr. Open Easter–mid Oct.
36 bedrs, 24 en suite, 4 ba; TV; tcf
dogs, ns; P 28, U 3 (£4), coach; child facs
LD 8.15 for 8.30, bar meals only lunch. Resid & Rest lic
£ B&B £30–£40; HB weekly £180–£250; D £9
cc Access, B'card/Visa; dep.

★★ H **Headlands,** Beach Rd, EX34 7BT
(0271) 870320

Modern hotel in own grounds with good view of bay. Open Mar–Nov & Xmas.
14 bedrs, 10 en suite, 2 ba; TV; tcf
TV, dogs, ns; P 14, coach; child facs
LD 8.30, bar meals only lunch. Resid & Rest lic
£ B&B £16–£25; HB weekly £140–£190; D £7·50; [5% V Mar–May, Sep–Oct]
cc Access, B'card/Visa; dep.

★★ **Little Beach,** The Esplanade, EX34 7DJ (0271) 870398

Edwardian house in pleasant grounds on hillside overlooking bay. Sauna. Open Feb–Oct.
10 bedrs, 8 en suite, 1 ba; TV; tcf
dogs, ns; P 7; no children under 7
LD 8; bar meals only lunch. Resid & Rest lic
£ B&B £22–£24·75, B&B (double) £38·50–£60; HB weekly £180–£240; WB £27·50
cc Access, B'card/Visa; dep.

★★ H **Waters Fall,** Beach Rd, EX34 7AD
(0271) 870365

Owner-run hotel in own grounds facing south and the sea. Open Mar–Oct & Xmas.
17 bedrs, 15 en suite, 1 ba; tcf
TV, dogs; P 20; no children under 5

★★ **Whin Bay,** Bay View Rd, EX34 7DQ
(0271) 870475

In a quiet road overlooking sea, a pleasant modern hotel.
18 bedrs, 14 en suite, 2 ba; TV; tcf
TV, dogs; P 12, coach; child facs

★ H **Crossways,** The Esplanade, EX34 7DJ (0271) 870395
Modern residence in own grounds with superb views all round. Open Mar–Oct.
9 bedrs, 5 en suite, (2 sh), 1 ba; TV; tcf
dogs, ns; P 9; child facs
LD 6.30, bar meals only lunch. Resid lic
£ B&B £14·75–£20·25; HB weekly £135–£170; D £7·50; dep.

Sunnycliff (Highly Acclaimed), Mortehoe, EX34 7EB (0271) 870597. *Hotel.*
£ B&B £22–£26; HB weekly £176–£208

Caertref (Acclaimed), Beach Rd, EX34 7BT
(0271) 870361. *Hotel.* Open Easter–end Oct.
£ B&B fr £12·50; HB weekly fr £120

Combe Ridge (Acclaimed), The Esplanade, EX34 7DJ (0271) 870321. *Hotel.* Open Apr–Sep.

Sunnyside, Sunnyside Rd, EX34 7DG
(0271) 870267. Open Easter–Sep.
£ B&B £13–£18; HB weekly £125–£165

WOOLER Northumberland. Map 51B1
Pop 1,833. Newcastle upon Tyne 47, London 321, Alnwick 16, Berwick-upon-Tweed 17, Coldstream 13, Corbridge 38, Hexham 37.
EC Thur. **MD** Mon, Wed, Sat. **Golf** Wooler 9h. **See** Ancient British Camps.
Bus Station Car Park. (0668) 81602

★★ **Tankerville Arms,** Cottage Rd, NE71 6AD (0668) 81581

Stone-built 17th century former coaching inn. Privately-owned.
14 bedrs, 8 en suite; TV; tcf
TV, dogs; P 100, coach; child facs; con 50
LD 9, bar meals only lunch
£ B&B £22–£31·50, B&B (double) £44–£57; D £14·75; WB fr £35
cc Access, B'card/Visa; dep.

Woodford Green (Essex)

Woodford Moat House ★★★

INTERNATIONAL HOTELIERS

Oak Hill, Woodford Green, Essex IG8 9NY
Telephone: 081-505 4511

The Woodford Moat House is a modern three star hotel providing comprehensive facilities for both business and pleasure. Here you can enjoy peace and quiet in comfortable surroundings, designed to make your stay as pleasant and as enjoyable as possible.

All 99 rooms have private shower or bath en suite, hair dryer, trouser press, colour TV, radio, telephone, and tea, coffee making facilities.

The Churchill Restaurant with its beautiful wood panelling enjoys a high reputation for serving fresh produce, a comprehensive wine list and friendly and attentive staff. An ideal venue for conferences, exhibitions, training courses, meetings, business interviews also specialists in banquets, dinner dances, wedding receptions and private parties.

Woodstock (Oxfordshire)

BLENHEIM PALACE

Home of the Eleventh Duke of Marlborough
Birthplace of Sir Winston Churchill

Open daily 10.30am-5.30pm (last admission 4.45pm) Mid March to 31st October

Inclusive Ticket: Palace Tour, Churchill Exhibition, Park, Gardens, Butterfly House, Aventure Play Area, Motor Launch, Train and Parking.
Gift Shops, Garden Centre, Restaurant & Cafeteria. NEW: Maze & Boat Hire.

Further detail from: The Administrator, Blenheim Palace, Woodstock, Oxford OX7 1PX
Telephone (0993) 811325

THE RIGHT TO CLOSE THE PARK & PALACE WITHOUT NOTICE IS RESERVED

WOOLFARDISWORTHY

Devon. Map 3A4
Pop 782. Bideford 9, London 211, Bude 17.

♠ ★★ **Manor House,** EX39 5QS ☎ Clovelly (023 73) 380
Tudor manor house, with Georgian additions, retaining its attractive beams.

WOOTTON BASSETT

Wiltshire. Map 5B4
Pop 10,000. Swindon 7, London 84, Avebury 10, Chippenham 13, Cricklade 8. **Golf** Swindon 18h.

Angel, 47 High St, SN4 7AQ ☎ Swindon (0793) 852314. *Hotel.*

WORCESTER

Hereford & Worcester (Worcestershire). Map 20B3
Pop 75,000. Evesham 16, London 114, M5 (jn 7) 2½, Bromyard 14, Droitwich 6½, Hereford 25, Kidderminster 14, Ledbury 16. **EC** Thur. **MD** Wed, Fri, Sat. **Golf** Worcester G and CC 18h. **See** Cathedral, Greyfriars, Worcester Royal Porcelain Works.
[i] Guildhall. ☎ (0905) 726311

★★★ **H** **C** **Fownes,** Clare St, City Wall Rd, WR1 2AP ☎ (0905) 613151 Tx: 335021 Fax: (0905) 23742 ♿

An elegant town hotel converted from a large Victorian building, once a glove factory. Fishing, sauna, gymnasium.
🛏 61 bedrs, 61 en suite; TV; tcf
🏨 lift; P 93, coach; child facs; con 120

★★★ **Giffard,** High St, WR1 2QR ☎ (0905) 726262 Tx: 338869 Fax: (0905) 723458

Modern city centre hotel opposite Cathedral. Billiards. (THF)
🛏 103 bedrs, 103 en suite; TV; tcf
🏨 lift, dogs, ns; coach; child facs; con 140
✕ LD 9.45, coffee shop only Sat lunch
£ B&B £60, B&B (double) £76; HB weekly £274; L £8·15, D £15·35; WB £46 (HB)
cc Access, Amex, B'card/Visa, CB, Diners.

> **En suite rooms**
> En suite rooms may be bath or shower rooms. If you have a preference, remember to state it when booking a room.

★★★ **Star,** Foregate St, WR1 1EA ☎ (0905) 24308 Tx: 335075 Fax: (0905) 23440 ♿
A former coaching inn of character. Near railway station. ✱ It, Du. Closed 24–26 Dec.
🛏 46 bedrs, 46 en suite; TV; tcf
🏨 lift, dogs; P 66, coach; child facs; con 100
✕ LD 9.45, coffee shop only lunch; nr Sun
£ B&B £56·65 (w/e £25), B&B (double) £69·30; L £8, D £12; WB £32
cc Access, Amex, B'card/Visa.

★★ **Ye Olde Talbot,** Friar St, WR1 2NA ☎ (0905) 23573 Tx: 333315 Fax: (0905) 612760

Near Cathedral, a modernised inn with well-appointed bedrooms. (Lns)
🛏 29 bedrs, 29 en suite; TV; tcf
🏨 dogs, ns; P 8, coach; child facs
✕ LD 10
£ B&B £63, B&B (double) £76; L £8·95, D £14; WB £54; [10% V]
cc Access, Amex, B'card/Visa, Diners.

★ **Maximillian,** Cromwell St, Shrub Hill, WR4 9EF ☎ (0905) 23867

Three-stoned building with basement bar and pillared porchway. Car park at rear reached via an archway. Near Shrub Hill station.
🛏 17 bedrs, 13 en suite; 1 ba; TV; tcf
🏨 ns; P 15, coach; child facs; con 50
✕ LD 10; bar meals only lunch
£ B&B £34·75–£45·50; B&B (double) £45·50; HB weekly £299·33; D £9·50; [10% V w/e]
cc Access, B'card/Visa; dep.

★ **Park House,** 12 Droitwich Rd, WR3 7LJ ☎ (0905) 21816 Fax: (0905) 612178
Pleasant small family-run hotel in the outskirts of city.
🛏 7 bedrs, 3 en suite, 1 ba; TV
🏨 TV, dogs, ns; P 10; child facs
✕ LD 7.30, nr lunch. Resid lic
£ B&B £20–£25, B&B (double) £28–£30

Loch Ryan, 119 Sidbury, WR5 2DH ☎ (0905) 351143. *Hotel.* ✱ Fr
£ B&B £25–£30; [5% V]

WORKINGTON

Cumbria. Map 43B2
Pop 29,600. Cockermouth 8½, London 306, Egremont 13, Maryport 5½. **EC** Thur. **MD** Wed, Sat. **Golf** Workington 18h. **See** St Michael's Church.

★★★ **Washington Central,** Washington St, CA14 3AW ☎ (0900) 65772 Fax: (0900) 68770 ♿
Four-storey purpose-built modern hotel in town centre with public rooms on first floor. ✱ Fr
🛏 40 bedrs, 40 en suite; TV; tcf
🏨 lift, ns; P 20, coach; child facs; con 250
✕ LD 9.30
£ B&B £38·50, B&B (double) £59·50; HB weekly £346; L £7·50, D £11·95; WB £60 (HB); [10 %V]
cc Access, Amex, B'card/Visa.

★★★ **Westland,** Branthwaite Rd, CA14 4SS ☎ (0900) 604544 Tx: 64229 Fax: (0900) 68830
Purpose-built hotel to south of town. Convenient for A595. Golf, fishing. ✱ Fr, De, No
🛏 110 bedrs, 110 en suite; 2 ba; TV; tcf
🏨 dogs; P 240, coach; child facs; con 750
✕ LD 10
£ B&B £40·50, B&B (double) £59·50; L £6·50; WB; [10% V]
cc Access, Amex, B'card/Visa, Diners.
(*See advertisement on p. 000*)

★★ **Crossbarrow,** Little Clifton, CA14 1XS ☎ (0900) 61443 Fax: (0900) 61443
Lovely old stone farm building with adjoining motel units.
🛏 37 bedrs, 37 en suite; TV; tcf
🏨 dogs; P 50, coach; child facs; con 25

Morven (Highly Acclaimed), Siddick Rd, CA14 1LE ☎ (0900) 602118. *Hotel.*
£ B&B £16–£19

WORKSOP

Nottinghamshire. Map 31A3
Pop 36,382. Newark 25, London 151, Chesterfield 14, Doncaster 16, Lincoln 28, Mansfield 13, Sheffield 18. **EC** Thur. **MD** Wed, Fri, Sat. **Golf** Worksop 18h. Lindrick 18h. Kilton Forest 18h, Serlby 9h. **See** Priory Church, 13th cent Lady Chapel, 14th cent Gatehouse, ancient Market Cross.
[i] Library, Memorial Av. ☎ (0909) 501148

★★★ **Charnwood,** Sheffield Rd, Blyth, S81 8HF ☎ Blyth (0909) 591610 Fax: (0909) 591429
Modern purpose-built hotel in 3 acres of landscaped gardens with picturesque pond. ✱ Es
🛏 20 bedrs, 20 en suite; TV; tcf
🏨 dogs; P 70, coach; con 80
✕ LD 9.45
£ B&B £44–£60, B&B (double) £55–£75; L £7·95, D £13·50
cc Access, Amex, B'card/Visa, Diners.

EC *early closing* **MD** *market day* ♠ *country house hotel* *ns (NS) no smoking areas* *tcf tea/coffee facilities*

WORTHING West Sussex. Map 6B1

Pop 93,400. Horsham 20, London 56, Arundel 10, Brighton 11, Littlehampton 8½, Pulborough 14.
EC Wed. **MD** Sat. **Golf** Worthing 18h (2), Worthing Hill Barn 18h. **See** Museum and Art Gallery, Salvington Mill, Cissbury Ring, Sompting Church (Saxon) 1½ m, Trans-Norman Church at Broadwater, Tarring Cottages and Parsonage Row Cottages at West Tarring (late 15th cent).
[i] Town Hall, Chapel Rd. & Marine Parade ☎(0903) 210022

★★★ **Burlington,** Marine Pde, BN11 3QL ☎(0903) 211222

Splendid Victorian hotel on the seafront, well equipped and tastefully furnished. Fr, Es
26 bedrs, 26 en suite; TV; tcf
lift; coach; child facs; con 50
LD 8.45, nr Sun dinner
£B&B £42, B&B (double) £64, HB weekly £310; L £10·50, D £10·50; WB £72; [5% V]
cc Access, Amex, B'card/Visa; dep.

★★★ **Chatsworth,** Steyne, BN11 3DU ☎(0903) 36103 Tx: 877046
Fax: (0903) 823726
Fine 4-storey Georgian building beside a garden square by seafront. Sauna, solarium, gymnasium, billiards. Fr, It, Es
105 bedrs, 105 en suite; TV; tcf
lift, dogs, ns; coach; child facs; con 120
LD 8.30
£ B&B £52–£64, B&B (double) £71·50–£75; HB weekly £308–£339·50; L £9·85, D £13·75; WB £70
cc Access, Amex, B'card/Visa, Diners; dep.

★★★ **Kingsway,** Marine Pde, BN11 3QQ ☎(0903) 37542 Fax: (0903) 204173

Owner-run hotel facing the sea. Most convenient for shops. Fr
28 bedrs, 28 en suite, 1 ba; TV; tcf
lift, dogs, ns; P 12; child facs; con 30
LD 9, bar meals only Mon lunch
£ B&B £38–£42, B&B (double) £52–£64; HB weekly £220–£303; L £8·95, D £14; WB £70; [10% V]
cc Access, Amex, B'card/Visa, Diners; dep.

★★ **Ardington,** Steyne Gdns, BN11 3DZ ☎(0903) 30451

Attractive building by a garden square just off the seafront.

★★ **Beechwood Hall,** Park Cres, Richmond Rd, BN11 4AH ☎(0903) 32872
Charming early 19th century building of character set in own wooded grounds.
18 bedrs, 16 en suite, (2 sh); TV; tcf
dogs; P 60, coach; child facs; con 100

★★ **Cavendish,** 115 Marine Par, BN11 3QG ☎(0903) 36767

A bay-windowed Victorian building on the sea front. Privately owned and run.
17 bedrs, 13 en suite; 1 ba; TV; tcf
P4; child facs; con 36
LD 9.15; nr Mon lunch & Sun dinner
£ B&B £23–£37, B&B (double) £55–£62; L £7·50, D £9·50; WB £72·50 (2nts)
cc Access, Amex, B'card/Visa, Diners; dep.

★★ **Windsor House,** 14 Windsor Rd, BN11 2LX ☎(0903) 39655
Fax: (0903) 39655
Family-run hotel in a double-fronted Victorian building with an attractive sun lounge, close to seafront.
33 bedrs, 30 en suite, 1 ba; TV; tcf
TV, ns; P 18, coach; child facs; con 120
LD 9.30, bar meals only lunch, Mon dinner
£ B&B £25·75–£39·75, B&B (double) £51·50–£62; HB weekly £212; L £7·50, D fr £10; WB £52 (2nts HB); [10% V 24 Sep–1 May]
cc Access, B'card/Visa; dep.

Bonchurch House (Acclaimed), 1 Winchester Rd, BN11 4DJ ☎(0903) 202492. *Hotel.*
£ B&B £13–£16; HB weekly £130–£145
Delmar (Acclaimed), 1 New Parade, BN11 2BQ ☎(0903) 211834. *Hotel.*
£ B&B £20·70–£22·43; HB weekly £228·83–£240·94
Moorings (Acclaimed), 4 Selden Rd, BN11 2LL ☎(0903) 208882.
Fax: (0903) 823872 *Private Hotel.* Fr, Es
£ B&B £19; HB weekly £152; [5% V]

Mayfair, Heene Ter, BN11 3NS ☎(0903) 201943. *Hotel.*
Meldrum House, 8 Windsor Rd, BN11 2LX ☎(0903) 33808. *Guest House.*
Osborne, 175 Brighton Rd, BN11 2EX ☎(0903) 35771. *Private Hotel.*
£ B&B £13·50–£17

WOTTON-UNDER-EDGE

Gloucestershire. Map 5A4
Pop 5,285. Tetbury 10, London 106, Bath 21, Bristol 17, Chippenham 16, Gloucester 21.
EC Wed. **MD** Fri. **Golf** Cotswold Edge 18h.

★★ **Swan,** Market St, GL12 7AE ☎Dursley (0453) 842329

Traditional coaching inn with attractive period features. In town centre. De, It, No
16 bedrs, 16 en suite; TV
dogs; coach
LD 10.15
£ B&B £51–£61, B&B (double) £72–£77; HB weekly fr £245; L £12·50, D £12·50; WB £37·50 (HB)
cc Access, Amex, B'card/Visa; Diners.

WRIGHTINGTON Lancashire. Map 32C3

M6 (jn 27) 2, London 201, Preston 11, Southport 18, Wigan 8.

★★★ **Wrightington**, Moss La, Nr Wigan, WN6 9PB ☎(0257) 425803
Purpose-built, white painted hotel surrounded by farm land yet only ¼ mile from junction 27 of M6. Indoor swiming pool, squash, sauna, solarium, gymnasium.
47 bedrs, 47 en suite; TV; tcf

WROTHAM HEATH Kent. Map 9C1

Swanley 11, London 29, M26 (jn 2) 1½, Maidstone 8½, Sevenoaks 9.

★★★★ **Post House,** London Rd, TN15 7RS ☎West Malling (0732) 883311
Fax: (0732) 885850
Modern hotel of distinctive design at junction of M20 and M26. Indoor swimming pool, sauna, solarium, gymnasium. Fr, De, It, Es, Gr. (THF)
120 bedrs, 120 en suite; TV; tcf
TV, dogs, ns; P 100, coach; child facs; con 60
LD 11
£ B&B £90–£95 (w/e £47), B&B (double) £105–£110; L £13·50, D £18·50
cc Access, Amex, B'card/Visa, CB, Diners; dep.
(*See advertisement on p. 428*)

W

Worcester (Worcestershire)

STEP INSIDE AND DISCOVER OVER 200 YEARS OF ENGLISH ARTISTRY, THE TREASURES OF THE DYSON PERRINS MUSEUM, SECRETS OF CRAFTSMEN AT WORK, SOUVENIRS, BARGAINS, ROYAL WORCESTER PORCELAIN AND FINE BONE CHINA AND A FAMILY RESTAURANT.

ROYAL
WORCESTER

For further details telephone 0905-23221. Royal Worcester Limited, Severn Street, Worcester WR1 2NE.

Yeovil (Somerset)

The Four Acres Hotel

West Coker, Yeovil BA22 9AJ. Tel: West Coker (0935 86) 2555/6 Fax: (0935 86) 3929

Charming comfortable, elegantly furnished Victorian house set within its own grounds and gardens. 24 beautifully furnished en suite rooms with colour TV, radio, tea/coffee making facilities, direct dial telephones, hospitality tray, trouser press, hair dryers.

Ample parking facilities available.

Open round the year and to non-residents.

We cater for conferences and social functions.

York (Yorkshire)

Take a Break with Tradition

For further details call 0904 653681

Reminiscent of an age of past elegance, this 148 bedroomed Victorian Hotel with a unique atmosphere of romantic splendour is delightfully set within its own private grounds overlooking the city walls, close to York city centre. Luxury accommodation is available and there is a choice of superb restaurants and bars.

Bygone Breakaways – Enjoy a luxury break inclusive of dinner, bed, full English breakfast and free admission to many of York's historic attractions. From £45 per person per night.

Conferences and Meetings – The Royal York Hotel offers a superb range of meeting and conference rooms. Technical and audio visual facilities are available and a guest liaison manager is on hand to assist conference organisers. There is a large car park within the hotel grounds and the main line railway station is close at hand.

The Royal York Hotel ★★★★ Station Road, York YO2 2AA

Telephone (0904) 653681 Telex 657912 Fax (0904) 623503

WROXHAM Norfolk. Map 35B1

Pop1,300. Norwich 7, London 118, Cromer 18, Fakenham 29, Great Yarmouth 19.
EC Wed. **Golf** Norwich 18h.

★★ **Broads,** Station Rd, NR12 8UR
☎(0603) 782869.
Family-managed, two-storied hotel with canopied picture windows and colourful window boxes.
🛏 21 bedrs, 20 en suite, (1 sh), 1 ba; annexe 7 bedrs, 7 en suite; TV; tcf
🏨 dogs, ns; P 40, coach; child facs
£ B&B £28–£30, B&B (double) £38–£48; L £6·95, D £8; WB
cc Access, Amex, B'card/Visa, Diners.

★★ R **Wroxham,** Broads Centre, NR12 8AJ ☎(0603) 782061 Fax: (0603) 784279

Attractive modern 2-storey building on North bank of River Bure. Fishing.
🛏 18 bedrs, 14 en suite, 1 ba; TV; tcf
🏨 TV, dogs, ns; P 60, coach; child facs; con 150
✕ LD 10
£ B&B £28–£39 (w/e £30), B&B (double) £42–£57; HB weekly £185–£233; L £6·85, D £9·50; WB
cc Access, Amex, B'card/Visa, Diners; dep.

🍺🍺 **King's Head,** Station Rd, Hoveton, NR12 8UR ☎(0603) 782429

Remodelled traditional pub on the bank of the River Bure in town centre. (BCB)
🛏 6 bedrs, 6 en suite; TV; tcf
🏨 P 50, coach; child facs

WYE Kent. Map 7B3

Pop 2,100. Ashford 4, London 59, Canterbury 10, Folkestone 14.
EC Wed. **Golf** Ashford (Kent) 18h. **See** Parish Church, Wye Downs Nature Reserve.

New Flying Horse, Upper Bridge St, TN25 5AN ☎(0233) 812297. *Inn.*

WYMONDHAM Norfolk. Map 35B1

Pop 9,500. Thetford 19, London 101, East Dereham 11, Lowestoft 31, Norwich 9½, Scole 18.
EC Wed. **MD** Fri. **Golf** Eaton, Norwich 18h.
See Abbey Church, Market Cross.

★★ **Abbey,** 10 Church St, NR18 0PH
☎(0953) 602148 Fax: (0953) 606247

Historic building in quiet street overlooking the Abbey.
🛏 25 bedrs, 25 en suite; TV; tcf
🏨 lift, dogs; P 4, coach; child facs; con 50
✕ LD 9.30
£ B&B £40–£45, B&B (double) £60–£65; L fr £6·50, D £11·50; WB £76 (2nts HB); [10% V]
cc Access, Amex, B'card/Visa, Diners; dep.

★★ **Sinclair,** 28 Market St, NR18 0BB
☎(0953) 606721 Fax: (0953) 601361
Red-brick 3-storey hotel in main street with cheerful family atmosphere. Sauna. ⚒ Fr, De, It
🛏 20 bedrs, 20 en suite; TV; tcf
🏨 TV, ns; P 8, coach; child facs; con 35
✕ LD 9.30, Sun dinner. Resid lic
£ B&B £39–£43, B&B (double) £49–£65; L £9·50, D £9·50; WB £60
cc Access, Amex, B'card/Visa.

WYNDS POINT

See under MALVERN

YARMOUTH, GREAT Norfolk. Map 35C1

See also GORLESTON-ON-SEA & ORMESBY ST MARGARET
Pop 52,000. Lowestoft 10, London 127, Cromer 34, Norwich 18, Scole 34.
EC Thur. **MD** Wed, Sat. **Golf** Gt Yarmouth and Caister 18h, Gorleston 18h. **See** The Rows', Old Merchant's House (museum), Nelson Monument, St Nicholas Parish Church, restored medieval Tollhouse, 17th cent Fisherman's Hospital, Caister Castle ruins (with Motor Museum adj).
ℹ Marine Par. ☎(0493) 842195

★★★★ **Carlton,** Marine Pde South, NR30 3JE ☎(0493) 855234 Tx: 975692 Fax: (0493) 852220

Large hotel of traditional style standing in prominent seafront position.
🛏 95 bedrs, 95 en suite; TV; tcf
🏨 lift, dogs, ns; P 30, G 40 (£3), coach; child facs; con 150
✕ LD 10; bar meals only Mon–Sat lunch
£ B&B £50, B&B (double) £70·£150; L fr £13·50, D £15·95; [10% V Oct–May]
cc Access, Amex, B'card/Visa, Diners; dep.

★★★ **Embassy,** Camperdown, NR30 3JB
☎(0493) 843135 Fax: (0493) 331064

Recently refurbished hotel, originally a row of Victorian houses, with attractive, balconied façade. Solarium.
🛏 24 bedrs, 24 en suite, 2 ba; TV; tcf
🏨 lift, TV; coach; child facs; con 50
✕ LD 10. Resid & Rest lic.
£ B&B £35–£40, B&B (double) £54–£65; HB weekly £172·50–£195·50; L £9·50, D £12·95; WB £60 (2nts HB); [5% V]
cc Access, Amex, B'card/Visa.

★★★ **Star,** Hall Quay, NR30 1HG ☎(0493) 842294 Fax: (0493) 330215

400 year-old building overlooking River Yare and quaysin town centre. ⚒ Fr. (QMH)
🛏 40 bedrs, 40 en suite; TV; tcf
🏨 lift, dogs; P 24, coach; child facs; con 140
✕ LD 9.45
£ B&B £43·50–£72, B&B (double) £55–£78; L £8·50, D £8·50; WB £35; [5% V Oct–Mar]
cc Access, Amex, B'card/Visa, Diners.

★★ **Burlington,** North Dr, NR30 1EG
☎(0493) 844568 ♿

Pleasant hotel with fine views of sea and beach. Indoor swimming pool, sauna, gymnasium. Open Mar–Nov.
🛏 30 bedrs, 29 en suite, 1 ba; TV; tcf
🏨 lift, TV, ns; P 40, coach; child facs; con 100
✕ LD 8. Resid lic
£ B&B £27·50–£37·50, B&B (double) £40–£46; L £7·50, D £9; WB £58
cc Access, B'card/Visa; dep.

★★ **Imperial,** North Dr, NR30 1EQ ☎(0493) 851113
Fine Victorian-style building in own grounds overlooking sea. ⚒ Fr
🛏 41 bedrs, 41 en suite; TV; tcf
🏨 lift, dogs; P 41, coach; child facs; con 140

Y

✕ LD 10, bar meals only Sat lunch. Resid lic
£ B&B £46–£50, B&B (double) £60–£65; HB weekly £227·50–£250; L £9·50, D £13·50; WB £34
cc Access, Amex, B'card/Visa, Diners.

★★ **Linwood,** 74–75 Marine Pde, NR30 3JH ☎(0493) 852427 Tx: 975037
Prominent yellow-brick 19th century building in town centre.

★★ **Palm Court,** North Dr, NR30 1EF ☎(0493) 844568 ♿

Large hotel conveniently situated and with good sea views. Indoor swimming pool, sauna, solarium, gymnasium. Open Mar–Nov.
🛏 47 bedrs, 34 en suite, 6 ba; TV; tcf
🏠 lift, TV, dogs, ns; P 50, coach; child facs; con 120
✕ LD 8; bar meals only Mon–Sat lunch. Resid & Rest lic
£ B&B £42·50–£50, B&B (double) £52–£62; HB weekly £170–£220; L £8·50, D £10; WB £62 (2nts HB)
cc Access, B'card/Visa; dep.

★★ **Royal,** Marine Par, NR30 3AE ☎(0493) 844215 ♿

Both Edward VII and Charles Dickens are said to have visited this large white 18th-century building on the sea front. Sauna, snooker. ⚒ Fr
🛏 69 bedrs, 39 en suite; TV; tcf
🏠 lift, TV, dogs; coach; child facs; con 120
✕ LD 8
£ B&B £22–£26, B&B (double) £40–£46; HB weekly £120–£180; L £6, D £8; dep.

★★ **Two Bears,** South Town Rd, NR31 0HV ☎(0493) 603198

Just across the River Yare from the business centre of town, an early 20th century building, once a station hotel.
🛏 11 bedrs, 11 en suite; TV; tcf
🏠 ns; P 120, coach; child facs

Trotwood (Highly Acclaimed), 2 North Dr, NR3D 1ED ☎(0493) 843971
£ B&B £21–£37

Georgian House (Acclaimed), 17 North Dr, NR30 4EW ☎(0493) 842623. *Hotel.*
£ B&B £20–£30

Bradgate, 14 Euston Rd, NR30 1DY ☎(0493) 842578. *Private Hotel.*
Woburn, 3 Sandown Rd, NR30 1EY ☎(0493) 844661.
£ B&B £12–£14; HB weekly £84–£98

YATTENDON Berkshire. Map 12A3

Pop 240. Reading 11, London 49, M4 (jn 13) 5½, Newbury 8.
Golf Streatley 18h.

★★ **H C R** **Royal Oak,** Nr Newbury, RG16 0UF ☎(0635) 201325
16th century inn in attractive village setting. Family owned.

YELVERTON Devon. Map 3A2

Pop 673. Exeter 33, London 204, Ashburton 18, Kingsbridge 22, Plymouth 9½, Saltash 10, Tavistock 5.
Golf Yelverton 18h.

🏡 ★★★ **Moorland Links,** PL20 6DA ☎(0822) 852245 Tx: 45616
Fax: (0822) 855004
Purpose-built hotel in nine acres of grounds. Billiards.
🛏 30 bedrs, 30 en suite; TV; tcf
🏠 dogs, ns; P 120, coach; child facs; con 80
✕ LD 10
£ B&B £57·50–£63·20, B&B (double) £77–£84·70; L £12, WB £55 (HB); [10% V w/e]
cc Access, Amex, B'card/Visa, Diners.

🍺🍺 **Burrator Inn,** Dousland, PL20 6NP ☎(0822) 854370

Harrabeer Country House (Acclaimed), Harrowbeer La, PL20 6EA ☎(0822) 853302. *Hotel. Swimming pool.*

Manor, (Acclaimed) Tavistock Rd, PL20 6JD (0822) 852099. *Hotel.*

YEOVIL Somerset. Map 4C2

Pop 27,265. Sherborne 5, London 125, Crewkerne 8½, Dorchester 18, Glastonbury 17, Ilminster 13, Wincanton 14.
EC Thur. **MD** Mon, Fri. **Golf** Yeovil 18h. **See** Church, Wymondham (Hendford Manor Hall), Montacute House 4 m W.
ℹ Petter's House, Petter's Way. ☎(0935) 71279

★★★ **Four Acres,** High St, West Coker, BA22 9AJ ☎West Coker (093 586) 2555
Tx: 46666 Fax: (093 586) 3929 ♿
Victorian stone manor house with modern extension. Pleasantly set in spacious grounds.
🛏 90 bedrs, 70 en suite, (2 sh); annexe 15 bedrs, 15 en suite; TV; tcf
🏠 dogs; P 70, G 6; child facs; con 80
✕ LD 9.45
£ B&B £56–£60, B&B (double) £66–£70; HB weekly £260; L fr £15·95, D fr £15·95; WB £74 (2 nts HB); [5% V w/e]
cc Access, Amex, B'card/Visa, Diners; dep.
(See advertisement on p. 524)

★★★ **Manor Crest,** Hendford, BA20 1TG ☎(0935) 23116 Tx: 46580
Fax: (0935) 706607

Large attractive 18th century hotel, in easy reach of town centre.
🛏 19 bedrs, 19 en suite; annexe 20 bedrs, 20 en suite; TV; tcf
🏠 dogs, ns; P 50, coach; child facs; con 60

★★ **Three Choughs,** Hendford, BA20 1TW ☎(0935) 74886 Fax: (0935) 33580
Stone-built inn with character. Situated in centre of Yeovil.
🛏 35 bedrs, 32 en suite, (3 sh), 2 ba; TV; tcf
🏠 dogs; coach; child facs; con 45

★ **Preston,** 64 Preston Rd, BA20 2DL ☎(0935) 74400 ♿

Spacious brick-built Victorian residence on main Taunton Rd. Modern extension.
🛏 7 bedrs, 5 en suite, 1 ba; annexe 10 bedrs, 6 en suite, 1 ba; TV; tcf
🏠 dogs; P 20, coach; child facs
✕ LD 9
£ B&B £22–£38, B&B (double) £40–£52; D £8·50
cc Access, B'card/Visa.

Manor Farm, Chiselborough, Stoke-sub-Hamdon, TA14 6TQ ☎(0935 88) 203.
Wyndham, 142 Sherborne Rd, BA21 4HQ ☎(0935) 21468. *Guest House.* Closed 24–27 Dec.
£ B&B £15

YORK North Yorkshire. Map 38C3

See also KEXBY and MURTON
Pop 97,240. Selby 13, London 193, Boroughbridge 17, Harrogate 22, Helmsley 24, Leeds 24, Malton 17, Market Weighton 19, Pontefract 25, Thirsk 23.
See Plan, p. 527.
EC Wed. **MD** Daily. **P** See Plan. **Golf** Fulford (York) 18h. **See** Minster, Walls and Gates, St Mary's Abbey ruins, Clifford's Tower, All Saints' Church (North St), Holy Trinity

EC *early closing* **MD** *market day* 🏡 *country house hotel* *ns (NS) no smoking areas* *tcf tea/coffee facilities*

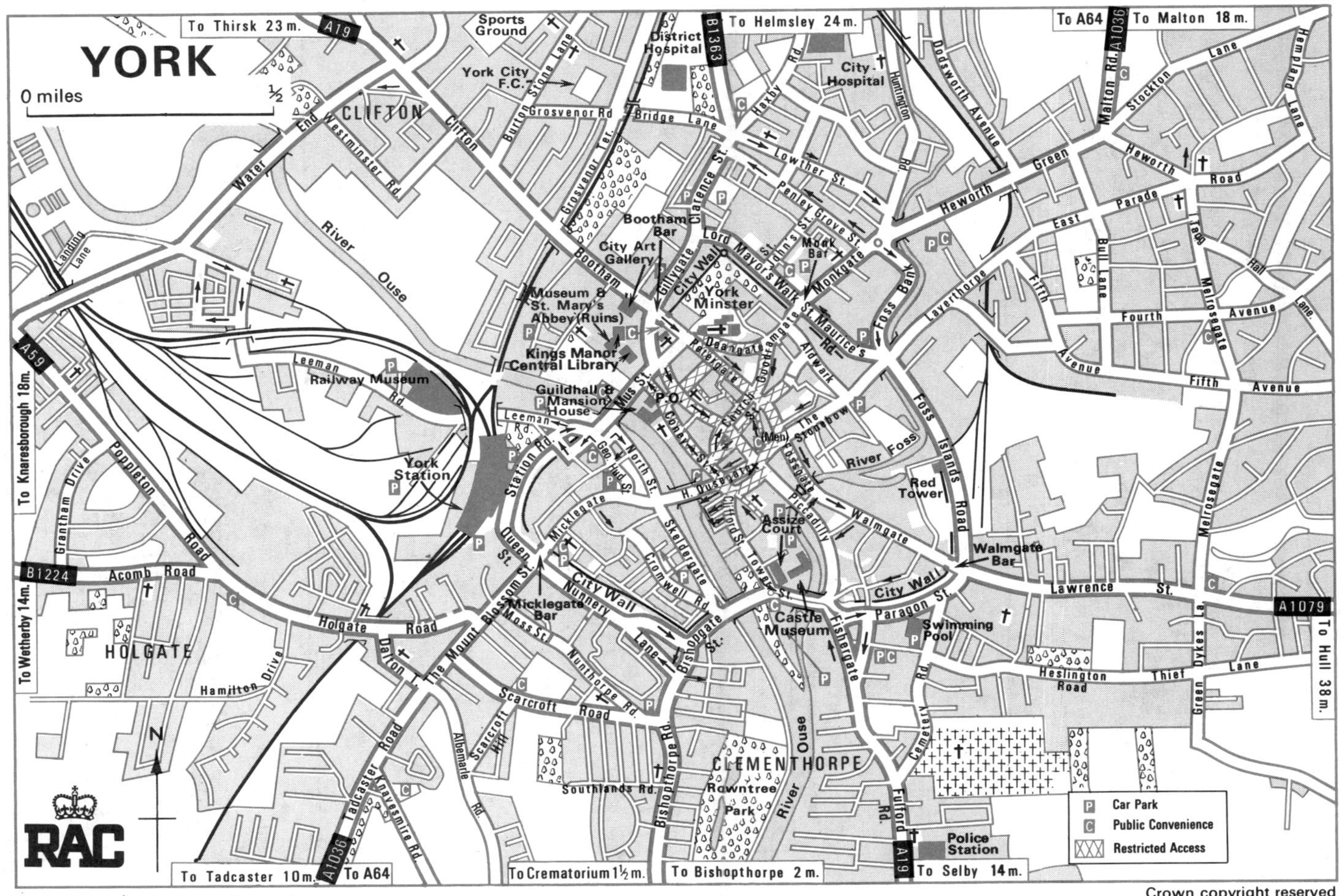
YORK
0 miles
½
To Thirsk 23 m.
A19
Sports Ground
District Hospital
B1363
To Helmsley 24 m.
City Hospital
To A64
A1036
To Malton 18 m.
York City F.C.
CLIFTON
Water End
Westminster Rd.
Clifton
Burton Stone Lane
Grosvenor Rd
Bridge Lane
Grosvenor Ter.
Haxby Rd
Huntington Rd
Dodsworth Avenue
Malton Rd.
Stockton Lane
Hempland Lane
Heworth Green
Heworth Road
East Parade
Bull Lane
Tang Hall Lane
Lowther St.
Penley Grove St.
Clarence St.
Bootham Bar
City Art Gallery
Lord Mayors Walk
Monk Bar
Monkgate
Foss Bank
Layerthorpe
Fifth Avenue
Fourth Avenue
Melrosegate
River Ouse
Landing Lane
Bootham
Gillygate
City Wall
York Minster
Museum & St. Mary's Abbey (Ruins)
Kings Manor Central Library
Deangate
Petergate
Goodramgate
St. Maurice's Rd.
Aldwark
A59
Leeman Rd.
Railway Museum
Guildhall & Mansion House
P.O.
Coney St.
Church St.
The Stonebow
(Men)
River Foss
Foss Islands Road
Red Tower
To Knaresborough 18m.
Poppleton Road
Grantham Drive
York Station
Station Rd.
Geo. Hud. St.
North St.
H. Ousegate
Clifford St.
Fossgate
Piccadilly
Assize Court
Walmgate
Walmgate Bar
Micklegate
Skeldergate
Tower St.
Queen St.
Blossom St.
Micklegate Bar
Nunnery Lane
Cromwell Rd.
City Wall
Lawrence St.
A1079
To Hull 38 m.
B1224
Acomb Road
To Wetherby 14m.
HOLGATE
Holgate Road
Dalton T.
The Mount
Moss St.
Nunthorpe Rd.
Bishopgate St.
Castle Museum
Fishergate
Paragon St.
Swimming Pool
Heslington Road
Thief Lane
Green Dykes La.
Hamilton Drive
Scarcroft Road
Scarcroft Hill
Albemarle Rd.
Bishopthorpe Rd.
Southlands Rd.
CLEMENTHORPE
Rowntree Park
River Ouse
Cemetery Rd.
Fulford Rd.
Police Station
N
Tadcaster Road
Knavesmire Rd.
RAC
To Tadcaster 10m.
To A64
To Crematorium 1½ m.
To Bishopthorpe 2 m.
To Selby 14 m.
P Car Park
C Public Convenience
Restricted Access
Crown copyright reserved

Y

York (Yorkshire)

York (Yorkshire)

York (Yorkshire)

Church, Guildhall, Mansion House (by apptm), The Shambles, City of York Art Gallery, Railway Museum, Viking Centre, Wax Museum, Fairfax House.
[i] De Grey Rooms, Exhibition Sq. ☎(0904) 621756

★★★★ Holiday Inn (formerly Crest), Tower St, YO1 1SB ☎(0904) 648111 Tx: 57566 Fax: (0904) 610317 ♿

Built of charming rustic brick, a dignified modern building in centre of city. (HI)
🛏 128 bedrs, 128 en suite; TV; tcf
🏨 lift, dogs, ns; G 45, coach; child facs; con 180
✕ LD 10.30 bar meals only Sat lunch
£ B&B £88·50, B&B (double) fr £112; L £10·50, D £15·50; WB fr £55 (HB)
cc Access, Amex, B'card/Visa, CB, Diners.

★★★★ Middlethorpe Hall, Bishopthorpe Rd, YO2 1QB ☎(0904) 641241 Tx: 57802 Fax: (0904) 620176

Handsome Queen Anne mansion beautifully furnished. Set in large park. Fr, Es
🛏 11 bedrs, 11 en suite; annexe 19 bedrs, 19 en suite; TV
🏨 lift; P 70; no children under 8; con 40
✕ LD 9.45
£ B&B £89–£102, B&B (double) £126–£138; L fr £13·90, D £26·90; WB £48 (Nov–Apr)
cc Access, Amex, B'card/Visa, Diners; dep.

★★★★ Royal York, Station Rd, YO2 2AA ☎(0904) 653681 Tx: 57912

A gracious Victorian building situated in pleasant gardens. Fine views. Putting.
(*See advertisement on p. 524*)

★★★★ Viking, North St, YO1 1JF ☎(0904) 659822 Tx: 57937 Fax: (0904) 641793 ♿

A modern hotel situated in centre of city overlooking River Ouse. Sauna, solarium, gymnasium. (QMH)
🛏 188 bedrs, 188 en suite; TV; tcf
🏨 lift, ns; P 10, G 50 coach; child facs; con 300
✕ LD 9.45
£ B&B £69–£80, B&B (double) £90–£105; HB weekly £350; L £9·50, D £13; WB £50 (HB); [5% V]
cc Access, Amex, B'card/Visa, Diners.

★★★ Ambassador, 123 The Mount, YO2 2DA ☎(0904) 641316 Tx: 57476 Fax: (0904) 611896
A stately listed building in spacious gardens on main road on south side of city.
🛏 19 bedrs, 19 en suite; TV; tcf
🏨 lift, dogs; P 30, coach; child facs; con 60
✕ LD 9.15. Resid lic
£ B&B £54, B&B (double) £70–£86; HB weekly £308–£686; L £7·95, D £12·75; WB £44; [5% V, Oct–Apr]
cc Access, B'card/Visa; dep.
(*See advertisement on p. 528*)

★★★ Dean Court, Duncombe Pl, YO1 2EF ☎(0904) 625082 Tx: 57584 Fax: (0904) 620305

Large mellow brick building, with new wing, beneath West Towers of Minster.
🛏 41 bedrs, 41 en suite; TV; tcf
🏨 lift, dogs, ns; P 20; child facs; con 16
✕ LD 9.30
£ B&B £50–£60, B&B (double) £85–£120; HB weekly £385; L £9, D £16
cc Access, Amex, B'card/Visa, Diners.

★★★ Disraelis, 140 Acomb Rd, YO2 4HA ☎(0904) 781181
Hotel in own grounds conveniently situated for the city centre. Closed Xmas.
🛏 9 bedrs, 9 en suite; annexe 4 bedrs, 4 en suite; TV; tcf
🏨 TV; P 40; child facs
✕ LD 9.30, nr Mon–Sat lunch. Rest lic
£ B&B £47–£52, B&B (double) £58–£64; L £5·90, D £14·50; WB £34 (HB)
cc Access, Amex, B'card/Visa; dep.
(*See advertisement on p. 528*)

★★★ Fairfield Manor, Shipton Rd, Skelton, YO3 6XW ☎(0904) 625621

Large building of Yorkshire brick in own grounds; 4 miles north of York. Putting.

★★★ H C Grange, Bootham, Clifton, YO3 6AA ☎(0904) 644744 Tx: 57210 Fax: (0904) 612453
Listed Regency building elegantly furnished in country-house style. Within walking distance of Minster and city centre.
🛏 29 bedrs, 29 en suite; TV; tcf
£ B&B £74, B&B (double) £88–£110, L £12·50, D 17·50

★★★ Hudsons, 60 Bootham, YO3 7BZ ☎(0904) 621267
Hotel complex of a converted Victorian house with an attractive new wing.
🛏 28 bedrs, 28 en suite; TV; tcf
🏨 lift; P 34; child facs; con 60
(*See advertisement on p. 528*)

★★★ Kilima, 129 Holgate Rd, YO2 4DE ☎(0904) 625787 Tx: 57928 Fax: (0904) 612083 ♿

Detached brick hotel on fringe of city. Pleasant garden at rear.
🛏 15 bedrs, 15 en suite; TV; tcf
🏨 dogs, ns; P 20; child facs
✕ LD 9.30
£ B&B £38, B&B (double) £56; HB weekly £240; L £14·75, D £14·75; WB £38; [5% V]
cc Access, Amex, B'card/Visa, Diners; dep.

Weekend breaks
Please consult the hotel for full details of weekend breaks; prices shown are an indication only. Many hotels offer mid week breaks as well.

Y

York (Yorkshire)

Abbots Mews Hotel

Marygate Lane
Bootham
York YO3 7DE

Telephones: 634866
622395
Telex: 57777 Abbots G
Fax: 0904 612848
RAC**

Proprietors:
Mr & Mrs N. F. Dearnley

Luxury hotel in city centre only few minutes walk from York Minster and historic attractions. All rooms have private bathrooms, Colour TV, radio and telephone.

Restaurant serving a la carte and table d'hote meals every evening.

Tea & coffee making facilities in rooms, licensed bar, car park and solarium.

Credit cards and cheques welcomed.

Enquire about our reduced winter rates.

Conferences, functions and weddings quoted for.

York (Yorkshire)

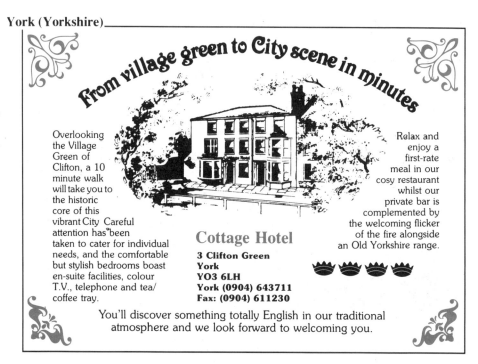

From village green to City scene in minutes

Overlooking the Village Green of Clifton, a 10 minute walk will take you to the historic core of this vibrant City Careful attention has been taken to cater for individual needs, and the comfortable but stylish bedrooms boast en-suite facilities, colour T.V., telephone and tea/ coffee tray.

Relax and enjoy a first-rate meal in our cosy restaurant whilst our private bar is complemented by the welcoming flicker of the fire alongside an Old Yorkshire range.

Cottage Hotel

3 Clifton Green
York
YO3 6LH
York (0904) 643711
Fax: (0904) 611230

You'll discover something totally English in our traditional atmosphere and we look forward to welcoming you.

★★★ **Novotel,** Fishergate, YO1 4AD
☎(0904) 611660 Tx: 57556
Fax: (0904) 610925 ♿

Purpose-built 4-storied hotel on riverside at edge of walled city. Boat landing and riverside terrace. Indoor swimming pool.
🛏 124 bedrs, 124 en suite; TV; tcf
🏨 lift, dogs, ns; P 150, coach; child facs; con 200

★★★ **Penguin Abbey Park,** The Mount, YO2 2BN ☎(0904) 658301 Tx: 57993
Fax: (0904) 621224
Modern hotel behind mellow brick Georgian façade. Fringe of city centre.
🛏 85 bedrs, 84 en suite, 1 ba; TV; tcf
🏨 lift, dogs, ns; P 32, coach; child facs; con 100
✕ LD 9.30, bar meals only lunch
£ B&B £60–£70, B&B (double) £85–£100; HB weekly £241·50; D £11·50; WB £36·50 (HB); [10% V]
cc Access, Amex, B'card/Visa, Diners; dep.

★★★ **Post House,** Tadcaster Rd, YO2 2QF ☎(0904) 707921 Tx: 57798
Fax: (0904) 702804

Modern stone building outside city walls and adjacent to York racecourse. Putting. (THF)
🛏 147 bedrs, 147 en suite; TV; tcf
🏨 lift, dogs, ns; P 180, coach; child facs; con 100
✕ LD 10
£ B&B £75–£80, B&B (double) £94–£99; L £11, D £13·50; WB £49
cc Access, Amex, B'card/Visa, Diners.

Discount vouchers

RAC discount vouchers are on p. 34. Hotels with a [V] shown at the end of the price information will accept them in part payment for accommodation bills on the full, standard rate, not against bargain breaks or any other special offers. Please note the limitations shown in the entry: w/e for weekends, w/d for weekdays, and which months they are accepted.

★★★ **Swallow Chase,** Tadcaster Rd, Dringhouses, YO2 2QQ ☎(0904) 701000
Tx: 57582 Fax: (0904) 702308 ♿

Hotel in traditional style with modern extensions, overlooking York racecourse. Indoor swimming pool, putting, sauna, solarium, gymnasium. ⚒ Fr. (Sw)
🛏 112 bedrs, 112 en suite; TV; tcf
🏨 lift, TV, dogs; P 200, coach; child facs; con 180
✕ LD 10
£ B&B £78, B&B (double) £95; L £12, D £17·50; WB £120 (2 nts HB)
cc Access, Amex, B'card/Visa, Diners.

★★★ **York Pavilion,** 45 Main St, Fulford, YO1 4PJ ☎(0904) 622099 Tx: 57305
Fax: (0904) 626939 ♿

Charming Georgian house with well-proportioned rooms; on main A19 to south of city. ⚒ Fr, Es
🛏 11 bedrs, 11 en suite; annexe 10 bedrs, 10 en suite; TV; tcf
🏨 P 45, coach; child facs; con 30
✕ LD 9.30
£ B&B £63·50, B&B (double) £83; WB £105 (2 nts)
cc Access, Amex, B'card/Visa, Diners.

★★ **Abbots Mews,** Marygate La, Bootham, YO3 7DE ☎(0904) 634866
Tx: 57777 Fax: (0904) 612848

Converted and enlarged Victorian cottage and coach house, now an attractive hotel in a central position.
🛏 12 bedrs, 12 en suite; 1 ba; annexe 36 bedrs, 36 en suite; TV; tcf
🏨 P 30, coach; child facs; con 50
✕ LD 9.30, bar meals only Mon–Sat lunch. Resid & Rest lic
£ B&B £35–£40, B&B (double) £60–£70; L £7, D £12; WB £75 (2 nts HB)
cc Access, Amex, B'card/Visa, Diners; dep.
(*See advertisement on p. 530*)

★★ **Alhambra Court,** 31 St Marys, Bootham, YO3 7DD ☎(0904) 628474
Close to the old walled city, a family-run hotel in a substantial 3-storied brick building.
🛏 25 bedrs, 25 en suite; TV; tcf
🏨 lift, TV; coach; child facs
(*See advertisement on p. 533*)

★★ **Ashcroft,** 294 Bishopthorpe Rd, YO2 1LH ☎(0904) 659286
Fax: (0904) 640107

Spacious hotel with annexe. In the country near to racecourse. Closed 25 Dec–1 Jan.
🛏 11 bedrs, 11 en suite; annexe 4 bedrs, 4 en suite; TV; tcf
🏨 TV, dogs; P 40, coach; child facs; con 60
✕ bar meals only Sun lunch
£ B&B fr £33, B&B (double) fr £55; D £9·50; WB fr £31
cc Access, Amex, B'card/Visa, Diners; dep.

★★ **Beechwood Close,** 19 Shipton Rd, YO3 6RE ☎(0904) 658378
Fax: (0904) 647124

Brick-built hotel situated in attractive area on northern edge of city. Family owned. Putting. Closed Xmas.
🛏 14 bedrs, 14 en suite; TV; tcf
🏨 P 36; child facs
✕ LD 9, bar meals only Mon–Sat lunch. Resid & Rest lic
£ B&B £34·65, B&B (double) £60; HB weekly £274·75; L £6, D £10·50; WB £65 (2 nts HB); [10% V Nov–Jun]
cc Access, Amex, B'card/Visa; dep.

★★ **Cottage,** 3 Clifton Green, YO3 6LH
☎(0904) 643711 Fax: (0904) 611230
Two connected stone-built Victorian houses overlooking village green, 15 minutes from city centre.
🛏 16 bedrs, 16 en suite; annexe 4 bedrs, 4 en suite; TV; tcf
🏨 dogs, P 12, coach; child facs
✕ LD 9, nr lunch. Resid lic
£ B&B £35–£45, B&B (double) £55–£70; HB weekly £504–£574; D fr £8
cc Access, Amex, B'card/Visa, Diners; dep.
(*See advertisement on p. 530*)

★★ **Elmbank,** The Mount, YO2 2DD
☎(0904) 610653 Tx: 57476
Fax: (0904) 627139
Refurbished, stone-built hotel with some fine original art nouveau decor. Sauna, solarium. ⚒ Fr
🛏 48 bedrs, 46 en suite; TV; tcf

Y

🏨 dogs; P 15, coach; child facs; con 100
✕ LD 9, bar meals only Mon–Sat lunch
£ B&B £54–£60, B&B (double) £77–£85; HB weekly £243–£267·30; L £6·95, D £12·50; WB £81; [10% V]
cc Access, Amex, B'card/Visa, Diners.

★★ H R Heworth Court, 76 Heworth Green, YO3 7TQ ☎(0904) 425156 Tx: 57571 Fax: (0904) 415290

Pleasantly set in a suburb with some rooms charmingly designed around a courtyard.
🛏 8 bedrs, 8 en suite, 1 ba; annexe 9 bedrs, 9 en suite, 1 ba; TV; tcf
🏨 P 25; children over 5; con 14
✕ LD 9.30. Resid & Rest lic
£ B&B £36–£39·50 (w/e £25), B&B (double) £56–£62; HB weekly £238–£265·50; L £8·50, D £12·50; WB £34 (HB); [10% V]
cc Access, Amex, B'card/Visa, Diners; dep.
(*See advertisement on p. 533*)

★★ Hilbra Court, York Rd, Haxby, YO3 8HB ☎(0904) 768335
A small modern hotel 4 miles north of city.

★★ Knavesmire Manor, 302 Tadcaster Rd, YO2 2HE ☎(0904) 702941 Fax: (0904) 709274

Sympathetically converted early 19th century mansion, once home of Rowntree family, overlooking the race course. Indoor swimming pool, sauna.
🛏 13 bedrs, 9 en suite, (1 sh), 1 ba; annexe 9 bedrs, 9 en suite; TV; tcf
🏨 lift, dogs; P 26, U1, coach; child facs; con 24
✕ LD 9, nr lunch. Resid & Rest lic
£ B&B £25–£49·50, B&B (double) £39–£65; D £12·75; WB £65; [5% V]
cc Access, Amex, B'card/Visa, Diners; dep.

Hotel locations

Hotel locations are shown on the maps at the back of the guide. All towns and villages containing an RAC Appointed or Listed hotel are ringed in purple.

★★ Newington, 147 Mount Vale, YO2 2DJ ☎(0904) 625173 Tx: 65430

Pleasant medium-size hotel on the fringe of city. Indoor swimming pool, sauna, solarium.
🛏 25 bedrs, 25 en suite; annexe 15 bedrs, 15 en suite; TV; tcf
🏨 lift; coach; child facs; con 25
✕ LD 8.30, bar meals only lunch. Resid & Rest lic
£ B&B £30–£38, B&B (double) £48–£58; HB weekly £219–£231; D £11; WB £66; [10% V]
cc Access, Amex, B'card/Visa, Diners; dep.

★★ Savages, St Peters Grove, Clifton, YO3 6AQ ☎(0904) 610818 Fax: (0904) 627729 ♿

Attractive Victorian building in residential area on fringe of city. Solarium, gymnasium. Closed Xmas.
🛏 18 bedrs, 18 en suite, 2 ba; TV; tcf
🏨 TV, ns; P 15, coach; child facs; con 30
✕ LD 9, bar meals only Sun lunch. Resid & Rest lic
£ B&B £32–£36, B&B (double) £52–£64; HB weekly £255·50–£332·50; L £6·50, D £11; WB £68 (2 nts HB); [10% V]
cc Access, Amex, B'card/Visa, Diners; dep.
(*See advertisement on p. 534*)

★★ Sheppard, 63 Blossom St, YO2 2BD ☎(0904) 620500 Tx: 57950
Small hotel in early 19th century building near city centre.

★★ H R Town House, 100 Holgate Rd, YO2 4BB ☎(0904) 636171 Fax: (0904) 623044

Attractive listed Victorian brick building with modern amenities. ✈ Fr
🛏 23 bedrs, 21 en suite, 1 ba; TV; tcf
🏨 dogs; P 30, coach; child facs; con
✕ LD 9.30, bar meals only lunch. Resid & Rest lic
£ B&B £20–£40, B&B (double) £38–£54; D £9·50; WB £60; [5% V, Dec–Feb]
cc Access, B'card/Visa; dep.
(*See advertisement on p. 533*)

Arndale (Highly Acclaimed), 290 Tadcaster Rd, YO2 2ET ☎(0904) 702424. *Hotel.* Closed Dec 24–Jan 1.
£ B&B (double) £45–£56; HB weekly £171·50–£280; [5% V w/d]

Acer (Acclaimed), 52 Scarcroft Hill, The Mount, YO2 1DE ☎(0904) 653839. *Guest House.*
£ B&B £25–£30; HB weekly £175–£215; [5% V]
Avimore House (Acclaimed), 78 Stockton La, YO3 0BS ☎(0904) 425556. *Hotel.*
£ B&B £17–£22; HB weekly £100–£130; [5% V Nov–Mar]
Barmby Moor (Acclaimed), Hull Rd, Barmby Moor, YO4 5ES ☎ Pocklington (0759) 302700. *Hotel. Swimming pool.*
£ B&B £40; HB weekly £244; [5% V w/d]
Bedford (Acclaimed), 108 Bootham, YO3 7DG ☎(0904) 624412. *Hotel.*
£ B&B £24–£32; HB weekly £175–£280
Curzon Lodge (Acclaimed), 23 Tadcaster Rd, Dringhouses, YO2 2QG ☎(0904) 703157. *Guest House.*
£ B&B £27–£32
Derwent Lodge (Acclaimed), Low Catton, YO4 1EA ☎(0759) 71468. *Guest House.* ♿ Open Feb–Nov.
£ B&B (double) £31–£35; HB weekly £273–£301
Fairmount (Acclaimed), 230 Tadcaster Rd, YO2 2ES ☎(0904) 638298 Tx: 557720 Fax: (0904) 627626. *Hotel.* ♿
£ B&B £30
Fourposter Lodge (Acclaimed), 68 Heslington, Barbican Rd, YO1 5AU ☎(0904) 651170. *Private Hotel.*
£ B&B £22–£24 (w/e £16·50); HB weekly £182–£217; [5% V w/d Nov–Feb]
Grasmead House (Acclaimed), 1 Scarcroft Hill, YO2 1DF ☎(0904) 629996. *Hotel.*
£ B&B (double) £45; [10% V]
Hazelwood, 24 Portland St, Gillygate, YO3 7EH ☎(0904) 626548 Fax: (0904) 628032.
Holgate Bridge (Acclaimed), 106 Holgate Rd, YO2 4BB ☎(0904) 635971. *Private Hotel.* Closed 24–26 Dec.
£ B&B £18–£35; [10% V, Dec–Jun, 5% V Jul–Nov]
Holmwood House (Acclaimed), 114 Holgate Rd, YO2 4BB ☎(0904) 626183. *Hotel.* ✈ Fr, It, Es
£ B&B £35–£38; [5% V w/d Nov–Mar]
Le Petit (Acclaimed), 103 The Mount, YO2 2AX ☎(0904) 647339. ✈ Fr. *Hotel.*
£ B&B £50; [5% V Nov–Mar]
Limes (Acclaimed), 135 Fulford Rd, YO1 4HE ☎(0904) 624548. *Private Hotel.*
£ B&B £16–£28; [5% V]
Midway House (Acclaimed), 145 Fulford Rd, YO1 4HG ☎(0904) 659272. *Hotel.*
£ B&B £27–£40
Priory (Acclaimed), 126 Fulford Rd, YO1 4BE ☎(0904) 625280. Closed Xmas week.
£ B&B £20–£22
Railway King (Acclaimed), George Hudson St, YO1 1JL ☎(0904) 645161. *Hotel.*
Skeldergate House, 56 Skeldergate, YO1 1DS ☎(0904) 35521. *Hotel.*

Abbingdon, 60 Bootham Cres, YO3 7AH ☎(0904) 621761. *Guest House.*

York (Yorkshire)

The Alhambra Court Hotel

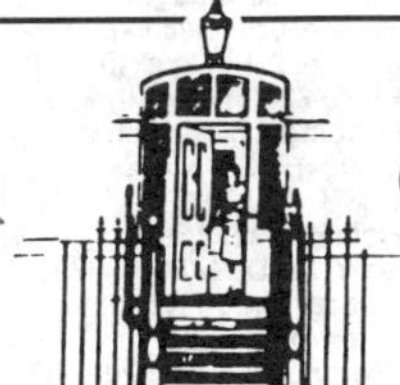

ETB 4 Crown

RAC ★★

31 St. Mary's York YO3 7DD Telephone: York (0904) 628474 Proprietors: Mr & Mrs L. S. Secchi

Situated in one of the most popular locations. A Georgian town residence in a quiet cul-de-sac, near city centre. All 25 rooms, (one four poster) with en-suite bathrooms, tea/coffee making, colour TV, direct dial telephone. Radio & baby listening. Lift, Bar, licensed restaurant open to non-residents. Winter & Summer breaks. Large car park for resident guests.

York (Yorkshire)

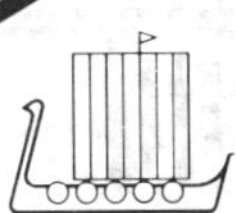

Heworth Court Hotel

RESTAURANT

76/78 HEWORTH GREEN, YORK YO3 7TQ.
Telephone: (0904) 425156/425157

Comfortable 2 star hotel within easy walking distance of the city centre. All rooms are en-suite with colour TV and tea/coffee makers. Cosy bar and restaurant offering the finest English cuisine and an extensive wine list featuring some superb wines. Enquire for Christmas & New Year and other special breaks. Phone for brochure and reservations.

York (Yorkshire)

Visit the Jorvik Viking Centre in York and a time car will whisk you back 1,000 years to a reconstruction of an actual street in Viking Age Jorvik. Complete with sights, sounds and smells, it's an unforgettable experience.

(Commentaries in English, French, German and Japanese.)

JORVIK VIKING CENTRE, COPPERGATE, YORK. TEL: (0904) 643211

York (Yorkshire)

The Town House Hotel

Holgate Road, York YO2 4BB Telephone: 0904 636171

A fine example of early Victorian town houses, an ideal family run hotel for the tourist, holidaymaker or businessman.

First class cuisine and an excellent selection of wines which will compliment your stay with us.

The Town House is a short walk from the city centre, York's famous Minster and other historical landmarks. The Racecourse is also close by. *Private car park*

RAC ★★

Z

£ B&B £16–£17; [10% V]
Acres Dene, 87 Fulford Rd, YO1 4BD ☎(0904) 637330. Open Easter–Oct.
£ B&B £14–£15
Ascot House, 80 East Par, YO3 7YH ☎(0904) 426826. *Guest House. Sauna.*
Beckett, 58 Bootham Cres, YO3 7AH ☎(0904) 644728. *Guest House.*
£ B&B £12·50–£17; [5% V Nov–Feb]
Beech House, 6 Longfield Terr, YO3 7DJ ☎(0904) 634581. *Guest House.*
Bootham Bar, 4 High Petergate, YO1 2EH ☎(0904) 658516. *Hotel.*
£ B&B (double) £40–£58
City, 68 Monkgate, YO3 7PF ☎(0904) 622483. *Guest House.* ✠ No, Sw
£ B&B £20–£22
Crescent, 77 Bootham, YO3 7DQ ☎(0904) 623216. *Guest House.* ✠ Fr, De
£ B&B £15–£18; HB weekly £168–£203; [10% V Nov–end May]
Duke of Connaught, Copmanthorpe Grange, Copmanthorpe YO2 3TN ☎Appleton Roebuck (090 484) 318. *Hotel.*
£ B&B £25; HB weekly £200; [10% V]
Farthings, 5 Nunthorpe Av, YO2 1PF ☎(0904) 653545. *Hotel.*
£ B&B (double) £26–£32; [10% V Nov–Mar]
Field House, 2 St George's Pl, Tadcaster Rd, YO2 2DR ☎(0904) 639572. *Hotel.*
Fleece, Bishop Wilton, YO4 1RU ☎Bishop Wilton (075 96)251
Heworth, 126 East Pde, YO3 7YG ☎(0904) 426384. *Guest House.* ✠ Fr
£ B&B £11·50–£14·50; [5% V Nov–Apr]
Inglewood, 7 Clifton Green, Clifton, YO3 6LH ☎(0904) 653523. *Guest House.* *(See advertisement on p. 000)*
Linden Lodge, 6 Nunthorpe Av, Scarcroft Rd, YO2 1PF ☎(0904) 620107. *Hotel.*
£ B&B £15; [10% V w/d Oct–Mar]
Marina, Naburn, YO1 4RL ☎(0904) 627365. *Guest House.* Open Mar–Nov.
£ B&B £13–£14·50.
Minster View, 2 Grosvenor Terr, Bootham, YO3 7AG ☎(0904) 655034
St Denys, St Denys Rd, YO1 1QD ☎(0904) 622207. *Hotel.*
St Raphael, 44 Queen Anne's Rd, Bootham, YO3 7AF ☎(0904) 645028. *Guest House.*

ZELAH Cornwall. Map 2B2.
Bodmin 20, London 253, Newquay 7, Redruth 10, Truro 5.

Nanteague Farm, Marazanvose, TR4 9DH ☎(0872) 540351. Open end Mar–early Oct
£ B&B £12—£15: HB weekly £129·50–£150; [5% V Apr–May, Sep]

 EC *early closing* **MD** *market day* ♣♣ *country house hotel* *ns (NS) no smoking areas* *tcf tea/coffee facilities*

Motor Lodges

Motor Lodges provide comfortable places to stay overnight at or near service areas on motorways or restaurants on main roads.

They aim to provide comfortable rooms at a modest price; many charge by the room, whether for single, double or family occupancy. Most provide at least one room with full facilities for disabled visitors. All accept Access and B'card/Visa credit cards, most accept all major cards.

Entries in this section are shown under the road they are on, then under the nearest junction number or place. For the convenience of readers we include brief details of Lodges to be opened in the next few months and indicate locations of lodges not appointed by the RAC.

M 1

Junction 1 or 2 via A4006
Travellers Rest Travel Inn, Kenton Rd, Kenton HA3 8AT 081-907 1671
40 bedrs steak house (meal times)
£ room £27·50

Between junctions 2 and 3
★★★ Welcome Lodge, Scratchwood Service Area, nr Hendon, 081-906 0611
100 bedrs cafeteria (24 hours)
£ B&B £49 (w/e £19·50), B&B (double) £59

Junction 13 – 3m northeast via A421
Travelodge, Beancroft Rd junc, Marston Moretaine, MK43 0PQ (0234) 766755
32 bedrs restaurant (7am–10pm)
£ room £24, double £29·50

Between junctions 14 and 15
★★★Welcome Lodge, Newport Pagnell Service Area, (0908) 610878
98 bedrs restaurant (24 hours)
£ B&B £42·50 (w/e £19·50), B&B (double) £52·50 (w/e £29·50)

Junction 16 via A45
Turnpike Travel Inn, Harpole Turn, Weedon Road, Harpole, (0604) 832340
51 bedrs restaurant (meal times)
£ room £27·50

Junction 24
Junction 24, Packington Hill, Kegworth, DE7 2DF (0509) 672427
44 bedrs restaurant (meal times)
£ B&B £40 (£25 w/e), B&B (double) £50

M 2

Between junctions 4 and 5
★★Rank Motor Lodge, Farthing Corner Service Area, Gillingham, ME8 9PW (0634) 377337
58 bedrs cafeteria (24 hours)
£ B&B £27·50, B&B (double) £34·50

M 3

Junction 6, 2 m south via A30
Travelodge, Stag & Hounds Harvester, Winchester Rd, Basingstoke RG22 6HN
32 bedrs restaurant (w/days: meal times, w/ends noon–11pm)
£ room £24, room (double) £29·50

Junction 6 or 7
Spruce Goose Travel Inn, Basingstoke Leisure Park, Worting Rd, Basingstoke
49 bedrs steak house (meal times)
£ room £27·50

M 4

Between junctions 2 and 3 (westbound)
Granada Lodge, Heston Service Area

Junction 3 or 4
Grapes Travel Inn, 362 Uxbridge Rd, Hayes, UB4 0HF 081-573 7479.
steak house (meal times)
£ room £27·50

Junction 11, 1 m south via A33
Travelodge, 387 Basingstoke Rd, Reading RG2 0JE (0734) 750618
36 bedrs restaurant (w/days meal times, w/ends nooon–11pm)
£ room £24, room (double) £29·50

Between junctions 17 and 18
Granada Lodge, Leigh Delamere Service Area

Junction 21
Rank Motor Lodge, Aust Service Area, BS12 3BJ Pilning (045 45) 3313
50 bedrs restaurant (24 hours)
£ B&B £27·50, B&B (double) £34·50

Junction 29 via A48
Campanile, Caxton Pl, Pentwyn, CF2 7HA (0222) 549044 Tx: 497553
50 rooms grill (meal times)
£ room £31 (single or double occupancy).

Junction 29 via A48/M
Travelodge, Circle Way East, Llandeyrn, Cardiff CF3 7ND (0222) 549564
32 bedrs restaurant (meal times)
£ room £24, (double) £29·50

Coach & Horses Travel Inn, Newport Road, Castleton, nr Cardiff CF3 8UQ (0633) 680070
49 rooms steak house (meal times)
£ room £27·50

Junction 33
Rank Motor Lodge, Pontyclun, CF7 8SB (0222) 892255
£ B&B £27·50, B&B (double) £34·50.

Junction 35 1 m north on A473
Travelodge, Old Mill Harvester, Felindre, Pencoed, CF3 5HU
40 bedrs restaurant
£ room £24, room (double) £29·50

Junction 36
Travelodge, Sarn Park Service Area, Bridgend CF32 9RW (0656) 59218
40 bedrs cafeteria (24 hours)
£ room £24, room (double) £29·50.

Junction 40
Bagle Brook Travel Inn, Baglan Rd, Port Talbot, SA12 8ES (0639) 813017
Opening Spring 1991.

Junction 42 via A48 and A483
Campanile, St Thomas Station, Pentre Guinea Rd, Swansea.
50 bedrs, grill (meal times)
£ room £31 (single or double occupancy).

M 5

Junction 2, 2m north on A4123
Travelodge, Wolverhampton Rd, Oldbury, Warley B69 2BH 021-552 2967
33 bedrs restaurant (7am–10pm)
£ room £24, room (double) £29·50.

Junction 3, 3m east via A456
Wharf Travel Inn, Bridge Road, Ladywood, Birmingham 021-633 4820
54 bedrs steak house (meal times)
£ room £27·50

Junction 3, 8m west via A456 and A491
Badgers Sett Travel Inn, Birmingham Rd, Hagley, Stourbridge (0562) 883120
£ room £27·50

Between junctions 4 and 5
Granada Lodge, Frankley Service Area

Junction 5, ½m west on A38
Travelodge, A38 Rashwood Hill, Droitwich WR9 8DA (052 786) 545
32 bedrs restaurant (7am–10pm)
£ room £24, room (double) £29·50.

Junction 10 via A4019
Cross Hands Travel Inn, Tewkesbury Rd, Uckington, Cheltenham (0242) 233847
40 rooms restaurant (meal times)
£ room £27·50

Junction 11 via A40
Longford Inn Travel Inn, Tewkesbury Rd, Longford (0452) 23519
40 bedrs steak house (meal times)
£ room £27·50

Junction 11 via A436
Twelve Bells Travel Inn, Witcombe, Gloucester GL3 4SS (0452) 862521
39 bedrs steak house (meal times)
£ room £27·50

Junction 19
Travelodge, Gordano Service Area, Portbury, nr Bristol (027 581) 3709
40 rooms cafeteria (24 hours)
£ room £24, room (double) £29·50

Between junctions 21 & 22 (northbound only)
Travelodge, Sedgemoor Service Area, nr Weston-super-Mare (0934) 750831
40 bedrs cafeteria (24 hours)
£ room £24, room (double) £29·50

Between junctions 26 & 27 (southbound only)
Roadchef Lodge, Taunton Deane Service Area, Trull, nr Taunton (0823) 332228 Fax: (0823) 338131
39 bedrs restaurant (24 hours)
£ room £29, room (double) £35

Junction 27
Travelodge, Sampford Peverell Service Area, nr Tiverton (0884) 821087
40 bedrs cafeteria (7am–10pm)
£ room £24, room (double) £29·50

Junction 30
Granada Lodge, Moor Lane, Sandygate, Exeter

M 6

Junction 2 via A46
Campanile, 4 Wigston Rd, Walsgrave, Coventry (0203) 622311
50 bedrs grill room (meal times)
£ room £31 (single or double occupancy)

Junction 3, 1 mile north via A444
Travelodge, Bedworth, Coventry.
40 bedrs family restaurant opposite (dual carriageway) – 1 mile journey.
£ room £24, room (double) £29·50

Junction 3, via A444, 3 miles north
Griff House Travel Inn, Coventry Rd, Nuneaton (0203) 343584
38 bedrs steak house (meal times)
£ room £27·50

Between junctions 10A and 11
Rank Motor Lodge, Hilton Park Services, nr Wolverhampton (0922) 414100
60 bedrs restaurant (24 hours)
£ B&B £27·50, B&B (double) £34·50

Junction 11 via A460 or junction 12 via A5
Longford House Travel Inn, Watling St, Cannock (0543) 572721
38 bedrs steak house (meal times)
£ room £27·50

Junction 19, ½ mile east on A556
Travelodge, Chester Rd, Tabley, Knutsford (0565) 52187
32 bedrs restaurant (7am–10pm)
£ room £24, room (double) £29·50

Junction 23, 2 miles west via A580 westbound
Travelodge, Piele Rd, Haydock, WA11 9TL (0942) 272055
40 bedrs cafeteria (7 am–10 pm)
£ room £24, (double) £29·50.

Between junctions 27 and 28

★★★ **Welcome Lodge,** Charnock Richard Service Area (0257) 791746
103 bedrs restaurant (7am–10pm), cafeteria (24 hours)
£ B&B £32 (w/e £24), B&B (double) £42 (w/e £31)

Between junctions 32 & 33
Rank Motor Lodge, Forton Service Area, nr Lancaster (0524) 792227
40 bedrs self-service restaurant
£ B&B £27·50, B&B (double) £34·50

Between junctions 38 and 39
★★★**Tebay Mountain Lodge,** Tebay Service Area (058 74) 351
30 bedrs restaurant (meal times)
£ B&B £36·50, B&B (double) £49·50

Junction 40, ½ mile west on A66
Travelodge, Redhills, Penrith (0768) 66958
32 bedrs restaurant (7am–10pm)
£ room £24, room (double) £29·50

Between junctions 41 and 42
Granada Lodge, Southwaite Service Area

M 11

Junction 7 via A414
Harlow Mill Travel Inn, Cambridge Rd, Harlow (0279) 442545 Fax: (0279) 452169
38 rooms steak house (meal times)
£ room £27·50

Junction 7, 8 miles east on A127
Campanile, Pipps Hill, Basildon SS14 3AE (0268) 530810
100 bedrs grill (meal times)
£ room £31 (single or double occupancy).

M 23

Junction 27, via A212
Coombe Lodge Travel Inn, Coombe Rd, Croydon CR0 5RB 081-686 2030
39 bedrs steak house (meal times)
£ room £27·50

M 25

Junction 9, via A243
Monkey Puzzle Travel Inn, Leatherhead Rd, Chessington KT9 2NE (0372) 744060
42 bedrs steak house (meal times)
£ room £27·50

Junction 29, 3 miles east via A127
Travelodge, East Horndon, CM13 3LL (0277) 810819
22 bedrs restaurant (7am–10pm)
£ room £24, (double) £29·50.

Junction 29, 9 miles east via A127 and A132
Watermill Travel Inn, Felmores, East Mayne, Basildon SS13 1BW (0268) 522227. Fax. (0268) 530092
32 bedrs steak house (meal times)
£ room £27·50

M 26

Royal Oak Travel Inn, London Rd, Wrotham Heath, TN15 7RS (0732) 884214
steak house (meal times)
£ room £27·50

M 53

Junction 5 on A41 northbound
Travelodge, New Chester Rd, Eastham, Bebington, L62 9AQ 051-327 2489
31 bedrs restaurant (7am–10pm)
£ room £24, (double) £29·50.

M 54

Junction 6 via A442
Travelodge, Whitchurch, Shawbirch
Opening Autumn 1990

M 55

Junction 1
Lea Gate Travel Inn, Blackpool Rd, Lea, Preston, PR4 0XL (0772) 720476
38 rooms steak house (meal times)
£ room £27·50.

M 56

Junction 4 or 5
Travel Inn, Finney Lane, Heald Green, Cheadle, SK8 2QH. *Opening Spring 1991.*

M 62

Junction 38 east on A63
Travelodge, South Cave by-pass, Hull
40 bedrs restaurant (7am–10pm)
£ room £24, room (double) £29·50.

M 65

Junction 10, ¼ m south on A671
Travelodge, Cavalry Barracks, Barracks Rd, Burnley, BB11 4AS (0282) 416039
32 bedrs restaurant (7am–10pm)
£ room £24, room (double) £29·50.

M 73

Junction 3 via A80
Dovecote Travel Inn, 4 South Muirhead Rd, Cumbernauld, Glasgow G67 1AX (0236) 725339 *Opening Spring 1991.*

M 74

Between junctions 5 and 6 northbound
Roadchef Lodge, Hamilton Service Area, ML3 6JW (0698) 891904
restaurant (24 hours)
£ room £29, room (double) £35

M 90

Junction 6 via A977
Granada Lodge, Kincardine Rd, Kinross

A1 (M)

Between junctions 2 and 4
★★★ **Welcome Lodge,** Scratchwood Service Area, nr Hendon 081-906 0611
100 bedrs restaurant (24 hours)
£ room £52 (w/e £24), room (double) £62

North of Baldock on southbound side
Travelodge, Hinxworth, SG7 5EX (0462) 835329
40 bedrs restaurant (7am–10pm)
£ room £24, room (double) £29·50.

Southbound, 3 miles west of Peterborough
Travelodge, Alwalton (0733) 231109
32 bedrs restaurant (7am–10pm)
£ room £24, room (double) £29·50.

Northbound, 9 m south of Grantham
Travelodge, New Fox, South Witham, Colsterworth, LE15 8AU (057 283) 586
32 bedrs restaurant (7am–10pm)
£ room £24, room (double) £29·50.

4 m north of Grantham
Travelodge, Grantham Service Area, NG32 2AB (0476) 77500
41 bedrs, cafeteria (24 hours)
£ room £24, room (double) £29·50.

Southbound, 3 m north of Newark
Travelodge, North Muskham, NG23 6HT (0636) 703635
30 bedrs restaurant (7am–10pm)
£ room £24, room (double) £29·50.

Northbound, 14 m north of Newark
Travelodge, Markham Moor, nr Tuxford DN22 0QU (0777) 838091
40 bedrs restaurant (7am–10pm)
£ room £24, room (double) £29·50.

Doncaster via A630 and A638
Campanile, Doncaster Leisure Park, Bawtry Rd, Doncaster
50 bedrs grill (meal times).
£ room £31 (single or double occupancy).

Northbound, 6 miles north of Doncaster
Travelodge, Carcroft, nr Doncaster (0302) 330841
bedrs cafeteria (7am–10pm)
£ room £24, (double) £29·50

6 m south of junction 33 with M62
Travelodge, Barnsdale Bar, Wentbridge, nr Pontefract, WS8 3JB
56 bedrs cafeteria (7am–10pm)
£ room £24, room (double) £29·50.

Northbound, ½ m south of Scotch Corner
Travelodge, Skeeby, nr Richmond DL10 5GQ (0748) 3768
40 bedrs restaurant (7am–10pm)
£ room £24, room (double) £29·50.

At Scotch Corner (junction of A1 and A66)
Rank Motor Lodge, Middleton Tyas Lane, nr Richmond (0325) 377177
50 bedrs restaurant (7.15am–10pm)
£ B&B £27·50, B&B (double) £34·50.

Junction A194, 4 m southeast of Newcastle
Travelodge, Lean La, Wardley, Whitemare Pool, nr Gateshead 091-438 3333
41 bedrs restaurant (7am–10pm)
£ room £24, room (double) £29·50.

Northbound, at junction with A189
Travelodge, Cromlington, North Tyneside
Opening winter 1990.

A 6

Soutbound, 4 miles southwest of Market Harborough
Travelodge, Harborough Rd, Desborough
Opening Autumn 1990.

A 11

8 m north east of Newmarket
Travelodge, Barton Mills, IP28 6AE (0638) 717675
32 bedrs restaurant (7am–10pm)
£ room £24, room (double) £29·50.

A 20

Between Dover and Folkestone
Plough Travel Inn, Hougham, CT15 7DF (0304) 213339 Fax: (0304) 214504
£ room £27·50

A 23

4 m north of Gatwick
Mill House Travel Inn, Brighton Rd, Salfords, Redhill RH1 5BS (0737) 767277
21 bedrs steak house (meal times)
£ room £27·50

A 25

Dorking, ½ m east of town centre
Travelodge, Reigate Rd, Dorking, RH4 1QB (0306) 740361
29 bedrs restaurant (7am–10pm)
£ room £24, room (double) £29·50.

A 27

5 m north of Bognor Regis
Travelodge, Fontwell, (0243) 548973
32 bedrs restaurant (7am–10pm)
£ room £24, (double) £29·50.

A 29

Northbound, 5 m southwest of Horsham
Travelodge, Five Oaks, Billingshurst RH14 9AE (0403) 812711
26 bedrs restaurant (7am–10pm)
£ room £24, room (double) £29·50.

A 30

4 miles west of Okehampton
Travelodge, Sourton Cross, nr Okehampton EX20 4LY (0837) 2124
32 bedrs restaurant (7am–10pm)
£ room £24, (double) £29·50.

A 31

Northbound, 6 miles north of New Alresford
Travelodge, Four Marks, 156 Winchester Road, Alton GU34 5HZ (0420) 62659
31 bedrs restaurant (7am–10pm)
£ room £24, (double) £29·50.

A 34

8 m north of Winchester
Travelodge, Sutton Scotney Service Area, nr Winchester, SO21 3JY

31 bedrs cafeteria (7am–10pm)
£ room £24, room (double) £29·50.

A 35

via A3059
Somerford Travel Inn, Somerford Rd, Christchurch, BH23 3QG (0202) 485376
38 bedrs steak house (meal times)
£ room £27·50

A 38

Northbound, 7 m north of Lichfield
Travelodge, Barton under Needwood, nr Burton-upon-Trent, (028 371) 6343
20 bedrs restaurant (7am–10pm)
£ room £24, room (double) £29·50.

Southbound, 7 m south of Burton-on-Trent
Travelodge, Rykneld St, Alrewas
32 bedrs restaurant (7am–10pm)
£ room £24, room (double) £29·50.

Taunton Travel Inn, 81 Bridgwater Rd, Taunton TA1 2DU (0823) 321112
40 bedrs steak house (meal times)
£ room £27·50

Plymouth, Longbridge roundabout
Campanile, Marsh Hills, Longbridge Rd, Forder Valley, Plymouth (0752) 601087
50 bedrs grill (meal times)
£ room £31 (single or double occupancy).

A 303

Junction with A345, Amesbury
Travelodge, Amesbury (0980) 624966
32 bedrs restaurant (7am–10pm)
£ room £24, room (double) £29·50.

4 m east of Andover
Travelodge, Barton Stacey, nr Winchester, SO21 3NP (026 472) 260
20 bedrs restaurant (7am–10pm)
£ room £24, room (double) £29·50.

Junction of A36, 6 m north of Yeovil
Travelodge, Podimore, nr Yeovil, BA22 8JG (0935) 840074
31 bedrs restaurant (7am–10pm)
£ room £24, room (double) £29·50.

A 335

Travelodge, Twyford Rd, Eastleigh
32 bedrs restaurant (meal times)
£ room £24, (double) £29·50

A40

Travelodge, London Rd, Wheatley (0800) 850950
24 bedrs restaurant (meal times)
£ room £24, (double) £29·50.

Travelodge, Ilminster (0800) 850950
32 bedrs cafeteria (7am–10pm)
£ room £24, (double) £29·50.

A 41

Crows Hill Travel Inn, Tring Hill, Tring, HP23 4LD (044 282) 4819
30 bedrs steak house (meal times)
£ room £27·50.

A 43

8 m south of Northampton
Travelodge, east Towcester by-pass, Northants, NN12 0DD (0327) 359105
33 bedrs restaurant (7am–10pm)
£ room £24, room (double) £29·50.

A 45

Westbound, 12 miles west of Ipswich
Travelodge, Stowmarket, IP14 3PY
40 bedrs restaurant (7am–10pm)
£ room £24, room (double) £29·50.

Eastbound, 9 miles west of Ipswich
Highway Lodge *Opening winter 1991*

On ring road, just west of Northampton
Travelodge, Upton Way, Northampton, NN5 6EG (0604) 758395
40 bedrs restaurant (7am–10pm)
£ room £24, (double) £29·50.

8 m east of Coventry
Travelodge, London Rd, Thurlaston, Dunchurch, CV23 9LG (0788) 521538
40 bedrs restaurant (7am–10pm)
£ room £24, (double) £29·50.

Eastbound, 4 miles east of Wellingborough
Highway Lodge, Rushden
Opening winter 1991

A 46

3 miles from Lincoln
Highway Lodge *Opening winter 1991*

Southbound, 8 m north of Leicester
Travelodge, Green Acres Filling Station, Thrussington, LE7 8TF (066 474) 525
32 bedrs restaurant (7am–10pm)
£ room £24, room (double) £29·50.

Junction with A423, 1 m south of Coventry
Campanile, Abbey Rd, Coventry
50 bedrs grill (meal times).
£ room £31 (single or double occupancy)

A 461

Travelodge, Dudley Rd, Dudley (0384) 481579
32 bedrs No restaurant
£ room £24, (double) £29·50.

A 47

Travelodge, Acle By Pass, (0493) 751970
40 bedrs restaurant (7am–10pm)
£ room £24, double £29·50

Travelodge, Morcott, Nr Uppingham
Opening Autumn 1990

A 48

20 m northwest of Swansea
Travelodge, Cross Hands, Llanelli (0269) 845700
32 rooms restaurant (7am–10pm)
£ room £24, (double) £29·50.

A 49

1 m north of Hereford
Starting Gate Travel Inn, Holmer Rd, Holmer, HR4 9RS (0432) 274853.
41 bedrs steak house (meal times)
£ room £27·50.

A 483

At A5152 roundabout, Wrexham by-pass
Travelodge, Rhostyllen, Wrexham, (0978) 365705
31 bedrs restaurant (7am–10pm)
£ room £24, room (double) £29·50.

A 5

At A483 roundabout
Travelodge, Mile End Service Area, Oswestry, SY11 4JA (0691) 658178
40 bedrs restaurant (7am–10pm)
£ room £24, room (double) £29·50.

A 50

At junction with A5030
Travelodge, Ashbourne Rd, Uttoxeter, ST14 5AA (0889) 502043
32 bedrs restaurant (7am–10pm)
£ room £24, room (double) £29·50.

A 51

3 miles north of Nantwich
Travelodge, Nantwich Rd, Calveley
Opening winter 1990

Junction with B5013
Travelodge, Western Springs Road, Rugeley, WS15 2AS (088 95) 70096
32 bedrs restaurant (7am–10pm)
£ room £24, room (double) £29·50.

A 523

Between Stockport and Macclesfield
Travelodge, Adlington nr Macclesfield
Opening Autumn 1990.

A 55

Eastbound, 3 miles north east of Mold
Travelodge, Northrop Hall
Opening autumn 1990

13 m west of Chester
Travelodge, Halkyn, (0352) 780952
31 bedrs restaurant (7am–10pm)
£ room £24, room (double) £29·50.

A 556

Travelodge, Chester Rd, Tabley Knutsford, WA16 0PP (0565) 52187
£ room £24, (double) £29·50

A 65

Junction with A59, northwest of Skipton
Travelodge, Gargrave Rd, Skipton, BD23 1UD (0756) 68091
32 bedrs restaurant (7am–10pm)
£ room £24, room (double) £29·50.

A 604

5 m northwest of Cambridge
Travelodge, Huntingdon Rd, Lolworth, CB3 8DR (0954) 81335
20 bedrs restaurant (7am–10pm)
£ room £24, room (double) £29·50.

10 m northwest of Cambridge
Travelodge, Huntingdon Rd, Fenstanton
40 bedrs restaurant (7am–10pm)
£ room £24, room (double) £29·50.

A 74

Northbound, 8 m north of Carlisle
Travelodge, Gretna Green, CA6 5HQ (0461) 37566
41 bedrs cafeteria (7am–10pm)
£ room £24, room (double) £29·50

A 720

Edinburgh ring road south
Travelodge, Dreghorn, Edinburgh
40 bedrs restaurant (7am–10pm)
£ room £24, room (double) £29·50.

A 82

1 m east of Dumbarton
Travelodge, Milton, Dumbarton, G82 2TY (0389) 65202
32 bedrs restaurant (7am–10pm)
£ room £24, room (double) £29·50.

Barnstaple

Cedar Lodge, Bickington Rd, EX31 2HP (0271) 71784
20 rooms restaurant (meal times)
£ B&B £27·50; B&B (double) £40.

Birmingham

Campanile, 55 Irving St, 021-622 4925
50 rooms grill (meal times)
£ room £31 (single or double occupancy).

Hull

Campanile, Beverley Rd/Freetown Way, HU2 9AN (0482) 25530 Tx: 592840
50 bedrs grill (meal times)
£ room £31 (single or double occupancy).

Liverpool

Campanile, Wapping St, Albert Dock
83 bedrs grill (meal times)
£ room £31 (single or double occupancy).

Redditch

Campanile, Far Mile Lane, Winyates Green, B98 0SD (0527) 510710 25 bedrs grill (meal times)
£ room £31 (single or double occupancy).

Wrexham

Travelodge, Wrexham By-Pass, Rhostyllen LL14 4EJ (0978) 365705
32 bedrs cafeteria (7am–10pm)
£ room £24, (double) £29·50.

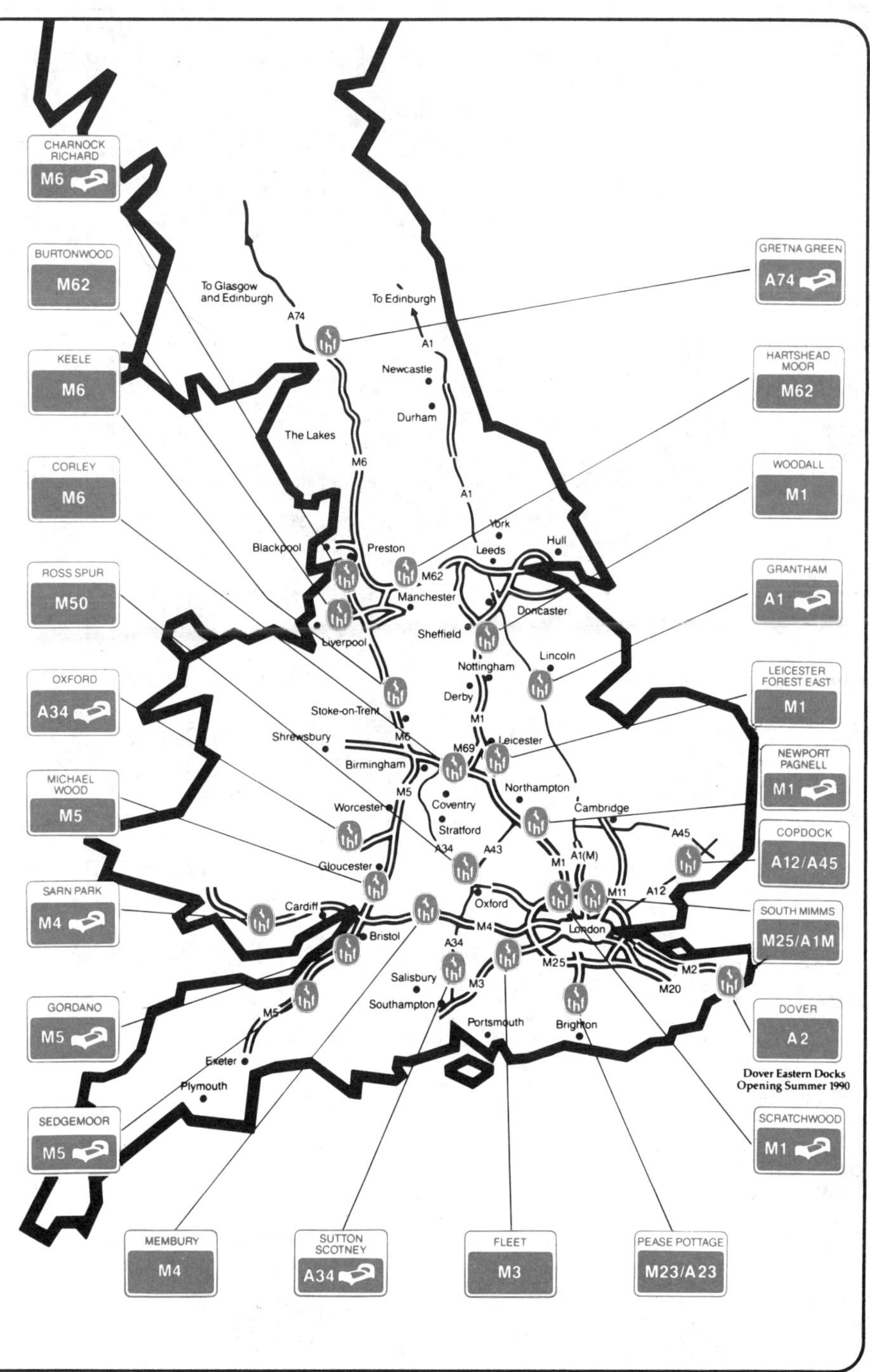

CHARNOCK RICHARD
M6
BURTONWOOD
M62
KEELE
M6
CORLEY
M6
ROSS SPUR
M50
OXFORD
A34
MICHAEL WOOD
M5
SARN PARK
M4
GORDANO
M5
SEDGEMOOR
M5
MEMBURY
M4
SUTTON SCOTNEY
A34
FLEET
M3
PEASE POTTAGE
M23/A23
GRETNA GREEN
A74
HARTSHEAD MOOR
M62
WOODALL
M1
GRANTHAM
A1
LEICESTER FOREST EAST
M1
NEWPORT PAGNELL
M1
COPDOCK
A12/A45
SOUTH MIMMS
M25/A1M
DOVER
A2
Dover Eastern Docks
Opening Summer 1990
SCRATCHWOOD
M1
To Glasgow and Edinburgh
To Edinburgh
A74
A1
Newcastle
Durham
The Lakes
M6
A1
York
Hull
Leeds
Blackpool
Preston
M62
Manchester
Doncaster
Liverpool
Sheffield
Lincoln
Nottingham
Derby
Stoke-on-Trent
M1
Shrewsbury
M6
M69
Leicester
Birmingham
Northampton
M5
Coventry
Cambridge
Worcester
Stratford
A45
A34
A43
Gloucester
M1
A1(M)
Cardiff
Oxford
M11
A12
Bristol
M4
London
A34
M25
M2
Salisbury
M3
M20
Southampton
M5
Portsmouth
Brighton
Exeter
Plymouth

SCOTLAND Town	Hotel	No. of conf. rooms	Seating capacity of main room	Total seating of additional rooms	No. of smaller rooms	Maximum capacity of smaller rooms	No. of bedrooms	Exhibition hall space	Photocopying	Projection/Video	Closed circuit TV	Audio	Interpreting	Sporting facilities available at the Hotel	Use of fax
ABERDEEN	★★★★Altens Skean Dhu	7	400	250	30	15	221	✓	✓	✓		✓	✓	⊃	✓
	★★★★Bucksburn Moat House	3	180	45	2	10	98		✓	✓	✓	✓		▤	✓
	★★★★Copthorne	1	220	15	2	15	89		✓	✓		✓		–	✓
	★★★★Dyce Skean Dhu	3	400	102	8	12	220	✓	✓	✓		✓		🏸 G	✓
	★★★★Holiday Inn	3	400	40	4	40	154	✓	✓	✓		✓		▤ G	✓
	★★★Ardoe House	3	200	120	4	60	19	✓	✓	✓	✓	✓	✓	▤ G-from April 1991	✓
	★★★Stakis Tree Tops	4	600	500	5	25	113	✓	✓	✓	✓	✓		▤ 🎾 G	✓
	★★★Westhill	3	300	60	2	35	52	✓	✓	✓		✓		–	✓
	★★Imperial	6	70	50	3	6	108		✓	✓				–	✓
	★★Kilspindie	2	60	10	1	10	26	✓	✓	✓				–	
ANSTRUTHER	★★★Craws Nest	3	750	70	4	40	50	✓	✓	✓		✓		–	✓
ARDEONAIG	★★Ardeonaig	1	20	–	3	10	12		✓	✓				–	
AUCHTERARDER	★★★★★Gleneagles	9	360	360	3	190	236		✓	✓	✓	✓		▤ ⛳ 🎾 🏸 G	✓
AVIEMORE	★★★★Stakis Four Seasons	–	–	–	–	–	88		✓	✓		✓		▤ G	✓
	★★★Aviemore Highlands	2	100	100	4	10	103		✓	✓		✓		–	✓
	★★★Red McGregor	3	250	20	3	20	30	✓	✓	✓				▤ G	✓
	★★★Stakis Coylumbridge Resort	2	1500	76	16	310	175	✓	✓	✓		✓		▤ 🎾 G	✓
AYR	★★★Caledonian	5	200	–	4	125	114	✓	✓	✓		✓		▤ G	✓
	★★★Kylestrome	1	30	–	1	30	12		✓	✓	✓			–	
	★★★Savoy Park	3	100	100	–	–	16		✓	✓		✓		–	✓
	★★Gartferry	2	200	70	2	100	16		✓	✓		✓		–	
	★★Old Racecourse	2	40	80	2	2	12		✓		✓			–	
BALLACHULISH	★★★Ballachulish	2	90	50	3	10	30		✓	✓		✓		–	✓
BALLATER	★★★★Craigendarroch	1	100	12	1	12	50		✓	✓		✓		▤ 🎾 🏸 G	✓
	★★★Glen Lui	2	25	–	2	18	19		✓	✓		✓		⛳	✓
	★★Monaltrie	2	100	25	1	25	25		✓	✓		✓		–	✓
BALLOCH	Cameron House	5	220	153	4	153	68	✓	✓	✓	✓	✓	✓	▤ ⛳ 🎾 🏸 G	✓
BALMACARA	★★Balmacara	5	80	150	2	20	29	✓	✓	✓	✓	✓		–	✓
BANAVIE	★★★Moorings	2	20	30	2	12	24	✓	✓	✓				–	✓
BANCHORY	★★★Raemoir House	2	60	30	2	22	–	✓	✓	✓				⛳ 🎾 G	✓
	★★★Tor-na-Coille	2	161	145	4	10	24	✓	✓	✓	✓	✓		🏸	✓
	★★Burnett Arms	2	150	50	1	10	18	✓	✓	✓		✓		–	✓
BANFF	★★★Banff Springs	2	200	100	2	25	30	✓	✓	✓		✓		–	✓
BARRHILL	★★★★Kildonan	6	100	60	8	10	31	✓	✓	✓		✓		▤ ⛳ 🎾 🏸 G	✓
BIGGAR	★★★★Shieldhill Country House	4	32	25	4	14	11		✓	✓				–	✓
BIRNAM	★★★Birnam	2	50	28	1	28	28	✓	✓					–	✓
BLACKWATER FOOT	★★Kinloch	3	150	50	2	50	49	✓	✓	✓		✓		▤ 🏸 G	✓
BLAIRGOWRIE	★★Angus	3	240	300	3	40	86	✓	✓	✓		✓	✓	▤ 🏸	✓
	★★Rosemount Golf	1	60	–	2	10	12							–	
BOTHWELL	★★★Bothwell Bridge	1	300	65	2	65	80	✓		✓				–	
	★★Silvertrees	3	200	90	2	90	26	✓	✓					–	✓
BRIDGE OF ALLAN	★★★Royal	5	150	–	3	20	32	✓	✓	✓		✓		–	✓
BRODICK	★★★Auchrannie Country House	1	50	50	2	50	43	✓	✓	✓		✓		–	✓
	★★Douglas	1	150	–	3	60	30	✓		✓		✓		–	
BRORA	★★★Links	2	120	60	4	8	22		✓	✓		✓		⛳ 🎾	
BUCKIE	★★Cluny	1	140	–	1	30	16	✓						–	
CASTLE DOUGLAS	★★Douglas Arms	3	100	70	1	20	25		✓	✓		✓		–	
	★★Imperial	2	45	20	1	20	13							–	
COLLISTON	★★★Letham Grange	2	25	20	3	6	20	✓	✓	✓				⛳	✓
CONNEL	★★Falls of Lora	1	50	–	1	–	30		✓	✓				–	✓
CRAIGELLACHIE	★★★Craigellachie	1	50	50	3	25	30		✓	✓	✓	✓	✓	G	✓
CRIEFF	★★Crieff	1	120	150	2	50	9		✓					G	✓
	★★Murray Park	1	52	–	1	6	13	✓	✓					–	✓
CRINAN	★★★Crinan	1	50	–	3	10	22	✓	✓					–	✓
CROSSMICHAEL	★★Culgruff House	1	160	55	1	55	17							–	
DALRY	★★Dalry Inn	3	200	80	2	80	6	✓		✓		✓	✓	–	
DINGWALL	★★National	1	220	–	1	–	42		✓	✓		✓		–	✓
DOLPHINTON	★★★Dolphinton House	2	14	6	1	6	12		✓	✓				–	✓
DORNOCH	★★★Royal Golf	1	120	50	2	60	34			✓				⛳	
DRYMEN	★★★Buchanan Highland	1	130	–	2	20	51	✓	✓	✓		✓		▤ 🏸 G	
	★★Winnock	2	160	20	4	10	29	✓	✓	✓		✓		–	✓
DUMBARTON	★★Dumbuck	2	150	30	1	30	2	✓	✓	✓		✓		–	✓

▤=indoor swimming pool; ⊃=outdoor swimming pool; ⛳=golf; 🎾=tennis; 🏸=squash; G=gymnasium

SCOTLAND Town	Hotel	No. of conf. rooms	Seating capacity of main room	Total seating of additional rooms	No. of smaller rooms	Maximum capacity of smaller rooms	No. of bedrooms	Exhibition hall space	Photocopying	Projection/Video	Closed circuit TV	Audio	Interpreting	Sporting facilities available at the Hotel	Use of fax
DUMFRIES	★★★Cairndale	5	100	133	3	10	60	✓	✓	✓		✓		–	✓
	★★★Hetland Hall	3	200	30	3	30	26	✓	✓	✓		✓		[squash] G	✓
	★★★Station	1	60	15	1	15	32		✓	✓		✓		–	✓
DUNDEE	★★★★Stakis Earl Grey	4	200	100	3	20	104	✓	✓	✓	✓	✓	✓	[indoor pool] G	✓
	★★★Invercarse	2	200	40	1	12	39	✓	✓	✓		✓		–	✓
	★★★Swallow	1	60	–	6	6	110		✓	✓				[indoor pool] G	✓
DUNDONELL	★★★Dundonell	1	50	15	2	15	24		✓	✓				–	✓
DUNFERMLINE	★★★Elgin	–	–	–	2	37	13		✓					–	✓
	★★★Keavil House	2	150	35	3	30	32	✓	✓	✓					✓
	★★★Pitfirrane Arms	2	100	40	–	–	38	✓	✓	✓		✓		–	✓
DUNTOCHER	★★Duntocher	–	–	–	1	30	–		✓					–	
EAST KILBRIDGE	★★★Bruce	6	200	175	2	6	79	✓	✓	✓				–	✓
	★★★Stuart	5	200	125	5	129	39	✓	✓	✓		✓		–	✓
ELGIN	★★★Eight Acres	4	280	190	2	80	53	✓	✓	✓		✓		[indoor pool] [squash] G	✓
	★★Hotel St. Leonards	2	150	–	2	20	16	✓		✓		✓		–	
EDINBURGH	★★★★★Caledonian	8	250	250	5	15	237		✓	✓	✓	✓	✓	–	✓
	★★★★★Sheraton Edinburgh	2	485	120	5	10	263	✓	✓	✓	✓	✓	✓	[indoor pool] G	✓
	★★★★Carlton Highland	11	350	500	6	12	207	✓	✓	✓	✓	✓	✓	[indoor pool] [squash] G	✓
	★★★★George	2	220	60	–	195		✓	✓		✓		–	✓	
	★★★★Hilton	–	120	–	–	–	144	✓	✓	✓	✓			–	✓
	★★★★Scandic Crown	5	200	337	11	45	238	✓	✓	✓	✓	✓	✓	[indoor pool] G	✓
	★★★★Swallow Royal Scot	2	350	180	4	30	259		✓	✓		✓		[indoor pool] G	✓
	★★★Braid Hills	2	140	200	4	9	69		✓	✓		✓		–	✓
	★★★Capital Moat House	1	300	–	5	30	98	✓	✓					[indoor pool] G	✓
	★★★Crest	3	180	194	1	14	120	✓	✓	✓		✓		–	✓
	★★★Ellersly House	2	77	10	1	10	54		✓	✓				–	✓
	★★★Mount Royal	3	50	20	3	10	159	✓	✓	✓					✓
	★★★Old Waverley	1	50	–	1	–	66		✓	✓				–	✓
	★★★Post House	1	120	10	10	10	208		✓	✓				–	✓
	★★★Roxburghe	2	200	270	2	15	75	✓	✓					–	✓
	★★Clarendon	1	50	20	2	12	51		✓	✓				–	✓
	★★Iona	1	20	–	1	21	–							–	✓
EDZELL	★★★Glenesk	2	100	–	2	30	25	✓	✓					[indoor pool] G	✓
ERSKINE	★★★Crest, Erskine Bridge	5	600	150	14	24	166	✓	✓	✓	✓	✓	✓	[indoor pool] G	✓
FALKIRK	★★★Stakis Park	3	300	120	6	6	55		✓	✓	✓	✓		–	✓
FORRES	★★Ramnee	3	220	60	2	60	20	✓	✓	✓				–	
FREUCHIE	★★Lomond Hills	–	150	2	1	25	25		✓	✓		✓		–	✓
GAIRLOCH	★★Old Inn	2	60	25	1	25	14	✓	✓					–	
GALASHIELS	★★Abbotsford Arms	1	150	–	–	–	13		✓					–	
GATEHOUSE OF FLEET	★★★★Cally Palace	1	80	12		12	54		✓	✓		✓		[indoor pool] [tennis]	✓
GIRVAN	★★Kings Arms	1	100	75	3	30	25	✓	✓	✓				–	
	★Hamilton Arms	1	120	–	–	20	11							–	
GLASGOW	★★★★Forte Albany	10	800		10		254		✓	✓		✓	✓	–	✓
	★★★★Holiday Inn	3	800	135	12	255	298	✓	✓	✓	✓	✓		[indoor pool] [squash] G	✓
	★★★Crest – Glasgow City	2	80	40	4	5	121		✓	✓	✓	✓		–	✓
	★★★Ewington	3	35	32	3	–	44		✓	✓		✓		–	✓
	★★★Swallow	4	380	160	13	12	119	✓	✓	✓		✓		[indoor pool] G	✓
	★★Sherbrooke Castle	2	140	40	2	14	25		✓	✓	✓	✓	✓	–	✓
	Town House	5	140	170	60	6	34		✓	✓				G	✓
GLENBORRODALE	★★★★Glenborrodale Castle	1	8	–	1	8	15		✓	✓				[tennis] G	✓
GLENROTHES	★★★Balgeddie House	2	50	40	2	37	18	✓	✓	✓				–	✓
GOUROCK	★★★Stakis Gantock	3	200	100	2	8	100		✓	✓		✓		[indoor pool] [tennis]	✓
GRANTOWN-ON-SPEY	★★Seafield Lodge	3	40	30	2	30	14	✓	✓					–	✓
HAWICK	★★Mansfield House	–	40	–	1	25	10		✓	✓				–	✓
INVERNESS	★★★Bunchrew	4	100	30	3	16	6		✓	✓				–	
	★★★Caledonian	5	200	230	4	230	100	✓	✓	✓	✓	✓	✓	[indoor pool] G	✓
	★★★Kingsmills	3	80	60	3	–	84		✓	✓		✓		[indoor pool] G	✓
	★★★Mercury	–	200	–	3	12	118		✓	✓		✓		–	✓
	★★★Station	2	120	95	2	40	65	✓	✓	✓		✓		–	✓
	★★Cummings	1	200	60	2	30	34	✓	✓	✓		✓		–	✓
	★★Glen Mhor	2	30	20	1	20	31		✓	✓		✓		–	
	★★Lochardil House	3	130	180	2	24	11	✓	✓	✓				–	
INVERURIE	★★Gordon Arms	1	220	20	1	20	11	✓	✓	✓		✓		–	✓
IRVINE	★★★★Hospitality Inn	6	320	110	5	50	128	✓	✓	✓		✓		[indoor pool]	✓
	★★★Montgreenan Mansion House	2	40	20	2	20	21		✓	✓	✓	✓		[golf] [tennis]	✓
	★★Redburn	3	200	90	2	50	20	✓		✓		✓	✓	–	
I. OF ARRAN, Kilmory	★★Lagg	2	120	20	1	20	15	✓	✓					–	
I. OF MULL, Tobermozy	★★★Western Isles	1	50	–	1	10	23							–	✓

[indoor pool]=*indoor swimming pool;* [outdoor pool]=*outdoor swimming pool;* [golf]=*golf;* [tennis]=*tennis;* [squash]=*squash;* **G**=*gymnasium*

SCOTLAND Town	Hotel	No. of conf. rooms	Seating capacity of main room	Total seating of additional rooms	No. of smaller rooms	Maximum capacity of smaller rooms	No. of bedrooms	Exhibition hall space	Photocopying	Projection/Video	Closed circuit TV	Audio	Interpreting	Sporting facilities available at the Hotel	Use of fax
I. OF SKYE, Broadford	★★Broadford	2	60	60	–	–	29	✓	✓	✓		✓		G	
Uig	★★Uig	1	10	–	1	–	17		✓					–	✓
KEITH	★★Royal	3	300	47	2	47	12	✓	✓					–	
KELSO	★★★Cross Keys	2	280	40	2	40	25	✓	✓	✓		✓		G	✓
	★Bellevue House	1	20	20	1	20	9							–	
KENMORE	★★★Kenmore	2	60	54	1	24	38		✓					[tennis]	✓
KILCHRENAN	★★★Ardanaiseig	2	25	–	–	15	14							[tennis]	✓
KILDRUMMY	★★★Kildrummy Castle	1	20	10	2	10	16		✓	✓				–	✓
KILFINAN	★★Kilfinan	1	50	–	1	50	11	✓	✓	✓		✓		–	✓
KINGSEAT	★★Halfway House	2	150	30	1	30	12	✓	✓	✓				–	✓
KINLOCH RANNOCH	★★★Loch Rannoch	3	150	90	85	12	17	✓	✓					[indoor pool] [tennis] [squash] G	✓
KINROSS	★★★Green	2	100	30	3	20	40	✓	✓	✓		✓		[indoor pool] [tennis] [golf] [squash] G	✓
	★★★Windlestrae	4	60	55	3	65	19	✓	✓	✓	✓	✓		–	✓
	★★Kirklands	1	40	–	1	20	10		✓					–	
KIRKCALDY	★★★Parkway	2	180	85	3	5	36	✓	✓	✓				–	✓
KIRKNEWTON	Dalmamoy	9	260	155	7	10	116	✓	✓	✓				[indoor pool] [golf] [tennis] [squash] G	✓
LAGGAN	★★★Gaskmore House	2	40	8	1	8	11		✓	✓	✓	✓		–	✓
LANGBANK	★★★Gleddoch House	2	50	40	3	6	33		✓	✓				[golf] [squash]	✓
LARGS	★★Elderslie	2	30	24	2	2	25		✓	✓	✓			–	
	★★Springfield	1	60	–	–	–	47	✓	✓	✓				–	
LERWICK	★★★Shetland	2	350	–	2	20	66	✓	✓	✓		✓		[indoor pool]	✓
LETHAM	★★★Fernie Castle	4	150	30	3	30	16	✓	✓	✓				–	✓
LOCHGILPMEAD	★★Stag	1	50	–	1	15	19							–	
LOCHMABEN	★★Balcastle	3	150	20	2	65	10	✓						–	
LOCKERBIE	★★★Dryfesdale	3	40	20	1	10	18		✓	✓				–	✓
	★★★Lockerbie House	4	150	210	2	30	27		✓	✓				–	✓
	★★★Queens	1	300	14	1	14	21	✓	✓	✓		✓		[indoor pool] G	✓
NEWTON STEWART	★★★★Kirroughtree	2	30	12	1	12	22	✓	✓					[tennis]	✓
NORTH BERWICK	★★★Marine	5	250	160	4	40	83	✓	✓	✓	✓	✓		[outdoor pool] [golf] [tennis] [squash]	✓
	★★Nether Abbey	1	50	20	1	–	16		✓	✓	✓	✓		–	✓
OBAN	★★★Alexandra	1	15	–	1	–	55		✓					–	✓
ONICH	★★★Lodge on the Loch	1	50	15	1	15	18		✓	✓				–	✓
PEEBLES	★★★Peebles Hydro	8	450	255	–	–	134		✓	✓		✓		[indoor pool] [tennis] [squash] G	✓
	★★★Park	2	70	35	–	–	25		✓	✓		✓		–	✓
PERTH	★★★Lovat	2	300	50	1	40	28	✓	✓	✓		✓		–	✓
	★★★Newton House	3	40	40	3	80	10		✓	✓	✓		✓	–	✓
	★★★Queen's	3	300	90	1	30	50	✓	✓	✓		✓		[indoor pool] G	✓
	★★★Royal George	2	100	20	–	–	43	✓	✓	✓		✓		–	✓
	★★★Salutation	1	300	–	5	60	70	✓	✓	✓		✓		–	✓
	★★★Stakis City Mills	2	200	50	–	–	78		✓	✓			✓	–	✓
PITLOCHRY	★★★Atholl Palace	3	300	300	3	30	84	✓	✓	✓		✓		[outdoor pool] [golf] [tennis]	✓
	★★★Pitlochry Hydro	2	90	60	2	6	64		✓	✓				[indoor pool] [golf] G	✓
	★★★Scotland's	4	200	160	4	20	80	✓	✓	✓		✓		[indoor pool] G	✓
	★★Dundarach	2	30	20	–	–	27		✓					–	
POLMONT	★★★Inchyra Grange	3	220	70	2	40	33	✓	✓	✓		✓		[indoor pool] G	✓
PORTPATRICK	★★★Fernhill	2	20	20	–	–	20		✓	✓				–	✓
	★★Portpatrick	3	140	60	3	14	57		✓	✓				[outdoor pool] [tennis] [golf]	
PORT WILLIAM	★★Monreith Arms	2	50	40	–	–	12	✓						–	
RENFREW	★★★★Excelsior	10	450	30	10	6	305	✓	✓	✓		✓		–	✓
	★★★Dean Park	9	350	140	8	20	120		✓	✓	✓	✓	✓	–	✓
	★★★Glenhill	3	220	300	5	60	125	✓	✓	✓		✓		[indoor pool] G	✓
	★★★Stakis Normandy	8	1000	400	4	15	141	✓	✓	✓		✓		–	✓
ST ANDREWS	★★★★Rusack's	2	100	70	4	30	50		✓	✓		✓		–	✓
	★★★St Andrews Golf	2	200	50	4	20	23	✓	✓	✓		✓		[golf]	✓
	★★★Scores	1	120	–	1	40	30		✓					–	✓
ST BOSWELLS	★★★Dryburgh	4	200	120	4	70	29		✓	✓		✓		–	✓
SCONE	★★★Murrayshall	2	50	30	2	10	19		✓					[golf] [tennis]	✓
STANLEY	★★Tayside	1	120	–	1	30	17		✓	✓		✓		–	✓
STIRLING	★★★Golden Lion	5	250	160	2	15	69	✓	✓	✓		✓		–	✓
	★★Terraces	3	100	35	1	12	15		✓	✓				–	✓
STRACHUR	★★★Creggans Inn	1	60	–	3	10	21		✓	✓				–	✓
STRATHAVEN	★★★Strathaven	1	180	–	–	–	10	✓	✓	✓		✓		–	✓
SYMINGTON	★★★Wyndales	1	50	–	2	25	14	✓	✓	✓				–	✓
	★★★Tinto	2	200	40	1	20	38	✓	✓	✓	✓	✓		–	✓

[indoor pool]=indoor swimming pool; [outdoor pool]=outdoor swimming pool; [golf]=golf; [tennis]=tennis; [squash]=squash; G=gymnasium

Town	Hotel	No. of conf. rooms	Seating capacity of main room	Total seating of additional rooms	No. of smaller rooms	Maximum capacity of smaller rooms	No. of bedrooms	Exhibition hall space	Photocopying	Projection/Video	Closed circuit TV	Audio	Interpreting	Sporting facilities available at the Hotel	Use of fax
SCOTLAND															
TAIN	★★★Mansfield	4	40	60	3	15	18		✓	✓	✓	✓		[tennis]	
	★★★Morangie House	1	25	–	–	–	11		✓					–	✓
TARBERT	★★★Stonefield Castle	2	120	60	3	20	32	✓	✓	✓	✓	✓		[outdoor pool]	✓
TAYNUILT	★★Brander Lodge	1	50	–	13	20	20		✓	✓		✓		–	✓
TROON	★★★★Marine Highland	4	220	60	4	10	72	✓	✓	✓		✓	✓	[indoor pool] [squash] G	✓
	★★★Piersland House	3	60	40	–	–	19	✓	✓						✓
	★★South Beach	1	120	–	1	20	27	✓	✓			✓		–	
TURNBERRY	★★★★★Turnberry	1	130	–	4	10	115	✓	✓	✓		✓	✓	[indoor pool] [tennis] [golf]	✓
	★★★Malin Court	1	120	–	1	20	8	✓	✓	✓				–	✓
ULLAPOOL	★★★Royal	2	100	50	2	25	58		✓	✓				–	✓
UPHALL	★★★Houstoun House	1	30	–	3	16	30		✓	✓				–	✓
WALKERBURN	★★★Tweed Valley	1	40	–	2	12	15		✓	✓			✓	G	✓
WEST WEMYSS	★★Belvedere	1	20	–	1	12	21		✓					–	
WORMIT	★★Sandford Hill	2	30	30	2	10	15		✓	✓			✓	[tennis]	✓
WALES															
ABERGELE	★★Kinmel Manor	3	100	70	3	30	25	✓	✓	✓		✓		[indoor pool] G	✓
ABERPORTH	★★Penbontbren	1	30	–	–	–	10	✓		✓				–	
ABERYSTWYTH	★★★Conrah Country House	1	50	–	1	8	22		✓					[indoor pool]	✓
	★★Bay	2	50	50	1	20	32		✓	✓		✓		–	✓
	★★Belle Vue Royal	1	60	–	–	–	42		✓	✓				–	✓
	★★Groves	1	20	–	–	–	11		✓	✓		✓		–	
BANGOR	★★★Menai Court	1	60	–	2	20	12		✓	✓	✓			[tennis] [squash]	
BARMOUTH	★★Panorama	1	50	–	1	20	20			✓		✓		–	
	★Bryn Melyn	1	30	–	2	10	10							–	
BARRY	★★★Mount Sorrel	4	150	120	2	10	50	✓	✓	✓				[indoor pool]	✓
BEAUMARIS	★★Henllys Hall	4	120	80	2	15	22	✓	✓	✓		✓	✓	[outdoor pool] [golf] [tennis] G	✓
BEDDGELERT	★★★Royal Goat	4	120	100	8	16	31	✓	✓	✓		✓	✓	–	✓
BETWS-Y-COED	★★★Plas Hall	1	50	–	2	20	20		✓					–	✓
BLACKWOOD	★★★Maes Manor	2	250	40	3	20	22	✓	✓			✓		–	
BONTDDU	★★★Bontddu Hall	2	120	20	3	6	20		✓	✓		✓		–	✓
BRECON	★★Aberclydach	1	12	–	2	8	11		✓	✓				–	✓
	★★Wellington	1	150	–	1	35	21	✓	✓					–	
BRIDGEND	★★★Coed-y-Mwstyr	3	40	–	3	16	28		✓					[outdoor pool] [tennis]	✓
BUILTH WELLS	★★The Lion	3	50	25	–	–	20	✓	✓	✓				–	✓
	★★Pencerrig Country House	4	100	–	3	10	20	✓	✓	✓				–	✓
CARDIFF	★★★★Angel	8	300	306	–	–	91	✓	✓	✓		✓	✓	G	✓
	★★★★Holiday Inn	2	30	60	2	20	182	✓	✓	✓		✓		[indoor pool] [squash] G	✓
	★★★★Stakis Inn on the Avenue	4	250	240	12	10	143	✓	✓	✓		✓		[indoor pool] G	✓
	★★★★Park	10	300	400	4	20	119	✓	✓			✓	✓	–	✓
	★★★Crest	8	140	160	7	40	157		✓	✓				–	✓
	★★★Manor Parc	1	120	–	1	12	12	✓	✓					[tennis]	✓
	★★★Post House	1	140	–	3	35	140		✓	✓		✓		[indoor pool] G	✓
	★★★St Mellons	4	250	260	3	18	31	✓	✓	✓	✓	✓		[indoor pool] [tennis] [squash] G	✓
	★★★Wentloog Resort	1	100	–	4	50	55		✓	✓		✓		–	✓
	★★Phoenix	1	110	–	1	22	24		✓	✓				–	✓
	★★Sandringham	1	80	–	–	–	28	✓		✓				–	
	★★Riverside	3	80	85	2	20	36	✓	✓	✓		✓		–	✓
CARMARTHEN	★★★Ivy Bush Royal	1	200	–	3	40	77	✓	✓	✓		✓		–	✓
CHEPSTOW	★★★St Pierre	12	220	140	5	10	150	✓	✓	✓				[indoor pool] [golf] [tennis] [squash] G	✓
	★★Beaufort	1	35	–	1	10	18		✓	✓				–	✓
	★★George	1	40	–	1	10	15		✓	✓				–	✓
COLWYN BAY	★★★Norfolk House	2	35	30	2	12	25			✓				–	
	★★★Hotel Seventy Degrees	1	150	–	1	10	43		✓	✓		✓		–	✓
	★★Edelweiss	3	–	–	–	–	25			✓				–	
	★★Hopeside	2	50	30	–	–	17	✓	✓	✓		✓		–	
CONWY	★★★Sychnant	1	20	–	–	–	13							–	
	★★Lodge	2	60	30	–	–	10		✓	✓				–	
CRICCIETH	★★Plas Gwyn	2	120	60	2	40	14	✓	✓	✓		✓		–	✓
CRICKHOWELL	★★Gliffaes	1	15	–	–	–	22							[tennis]	
CWMBRAN	★★★Consort Commodore	4	200	40	3	10	60	✓	✓	✓	✓	✓	✓	–	✓
DOLGELLAU	★★Dolsereau Hall	1	50	–	3	15	14		✓	✓				–	
	★★George III	1	6	–	–	–	12		✓					–	✓
DYFFRYN (Valley)	★★Bull	1	60	–	–	–	13					✓		–	
FISHGUARD	★★Cartref	1	40	–	3	10	12						✓	–	

[indoor pool]=*indoor swimming pool;* [outdoor pool]=*outdoor swimming pool;* [golf]=*golf;* [tennis]=*tennis;* [squash]=*squash;* G=*gymnasium*

WALES Town	Hotel	No. of conf. rooms	Seating capacity of main room	Total seating of additional rooms	No. of smaller rooms	Maximum capacity of smaller rooms	No. of bedrooms	Exhibition hall space	Photocopying	Projection/Video	Closed circuit TV	Audio	Interpreting	Sporting facilities available at the Hotel	Use of fax
GLYN CEIRIOG	★★★Golden Pheasant	2	60	10	1	15	18		✓	✓				–	
LAMPETER	★★★Falcondale	2	150	30	1	30	21		✓	✓		✓		♀	✓
LANGLAND BAY	★★★Osborne	1	50	–	–	8	36		✓	✓				–	✓
	★★Langland Court	3	150	60	–	–	21	✓	✓	✓		✓		–	✓
LLANARMON	★★West Arms	1	30	30	4	10	14			✓				–	✓
LLANDRINDOD WELLS	★★★Metropole	10	400	200	8	100	122	✓	✓	✓		✓		▣	✓
	★★Glen Usk	2	150	162	2	70	79		✓	✓		✓		–	
LLANDUDNO	★★★Bodysgallen Hall	1	80	30	–	–	28	✓	✓	✓		✓		♀	✓
	★★★Gogarth Abbey	3	80	60	4	12	40	✓	✓	✓		✓		▣ G	✓
	★★★Imperial	3	350	60	6	15	100		✓	✓		✓		▣ G	✓
	★★★Risboro	4	200	60	4	12	65	✓	✓	✓		✓		▣ G	✓
	★★Castle	4	80	100	4	20	56	✓	✓	✓				–	
	★★Esplanade	2	120	60	3	60	59	✓	✓	✓		✓		–	✓
	★★Ormescliffe	2	120	30	–	–	60	✓	✓	✓		✓		–	✓
	★★Royal	1	80	–	2	12	40	✓	✓					–	✓
	★Sandringham	2	80	120	–	–	18	✓						–	
LLANELLI	★★★Diplomat	2	250	–	1	25	31	✓	✓	✓				▣ G	✓
	★★★Stradey Park	4	400	130	14	96	80	✓	✓	✓		✓		–	
LLANGAMMARCH WELLS	★★★Lake Country House	2	60	20	3	3	19			✓				♀	✓
LLANGEFNI	★★★Tre-Ysgawen Hall	4	60	20	2	12	19	✓	✓	✓				▣	✓
LLANGOLLEN	★★★Hand	2	100	50	–	–	59	✓	✓	✓		✓		–	
	★★★Royal	1	60	–	–	20	33		✓	✓				–	✓
LLANRUG	★★★Seiont Manor	1	100	20	3	20	28	✓	✓	✓				▣ G	✓
LLANRWST	★★★Plas Maenan	6	100	80	4	20	15	✓		✓				–	
LLANTWIT	★★West House	3	70	20	1	20	20		✓	✓				–	
LLANWNDA	★★★Stables	3	100	30	2	30	14							⊃	
LLANWDDYN	★★★Lake Vyrnwy	1	30	15	5	–	30		✓	✓				♀	
LLECHRYD	★★★Castel Malgwyn	1	200	–	2	30	23	✓	✓					⊃	
MACHYNLLETH	★★Dolguog Hall	2	70	20	1	15	9	✓						–	
MERTHYR TYDFIL	★★★Baverstock	4	450	–	1	–	53	✓	✓	✓		✓		–	✓
	★★Tregenna	2	60	20	2	20	23		✓	✓		✓		–	✓
MILFORD HAVEN	★★Lord Nelson	1	40	10	1	10	31		✓					–	✓
MISKIN	★★★Miskin Manor	5	150	100	1	10	32		✓	✓				▣ ♀ G	✓
MOLD	★★Bryn Awel	1	50	–	1	35	17		✓					–	✓
MONMOUTH	★★★Kings Head	2	200	60	–	–	29		✓	✓		✓		–	✓
	★★Crown at Whitebrook	1	24	–	1	8	12		✓	✓				–	✓
MORFA NEFYN	★★Woodlands Hall	3	90	90	4	50	13		✓	✓		✓		–	
NEATH	★★Castle	3	160	50	2	20	28	✓	✓	✓		✓		–	✓
NEWPORT	★★★★Celtic Manor	6	350	267	4	117	73		✓	✓		✓		▣ G	✓
	★★★Hilton National	4	500	140	8	120	119	✓	✓	✓	✓	✓	✓	▣ G	✓
	★★★Kings	5	200	200	4	60	47	✓	✓	✓		✓		–	✓
	★★Westgate	7	150	60	2	15	69	✓	✓	✓		✓		–	✓
NORTHOPHALL	★★Chequers	2	120	20	1	10	27	✓	✓	✓	✓	✓		–	✓
OLD COLWYN	★★Lyndale	2	50	16	2	20	14	✓		✓				–	
PEMBROKE	★★★Court	3	100	190	?	–	30	✓	✓	✓	✓	✓	✓	▣ G	✓
	★★Coach House Inn	9	20	8	1	–	14		✓	✓				–	✓
	★★Hollyland Country House	1	60	20	1	20	12		✓	✓				–	
PENMAEN	★★Nicholaston House	2	120	45	2	45	11	✓		✓		✓		–	
PENYBONT	★★Severn Arms	–	20	–	1	20	10							–	
PORT TALBOT	★★★Aberafan Beach	5	500	–	3	20	66	✓	✓	✓		✓		–	
PORTHCAWL	★★★Sea Bank	5	250	200	–	–	62		✓	✓		✓		G	✓
PORTHKERRY	★★★Egerton Grey	2	30	14	3	30	10		✓	✓			✓	♀	✓
PRESTEIGNE	★★Radnorshire Arms	1	30	–	2	15	16		✓	✓				–	✓
REYNOLDSTON	★★Fairyhill Country House	1	22	–	–	–	11			✓				–	
RHYL	★★Grange	4	120	45	3	15	24	✓	✓			✓		–	
ROSSETT	★★★Llyndir Hall	14	140	70	8	10	38							▣ G	✓
RUTHIN	★★★Ruthin Castle	5	140	80	2	20	58	✓	✓	✓		✓		–	✓
	★★Castle	1	40	12	1	12	–	✓	✓	✓				–	✓
ST ASAPH	★★★Oriel House	3	250	100	1	12	19	✓	✓	✓		✓		–	✓
ST DAVID'S	★★★Warpool Court	3	100	50	–	20	25		✓	✓		✓		▣ ♀ G	✓
SAUNDERSFOOT	★★★St Brides	3	150	140	2	30	45	✓	✓	✓	✓	✓		⊃	✓
	★★Glen Beach	1	100	–	2	12	13	✓	✓	✓		✓		–	
	★★Rhodewood House	1	150	–	–	–	34	✓	✓	✓		✓		–	✓
SWANSEA	★★★Fforest	4	200	120	–	–	34		✓	✓		✓		–	✓
	★★★Hilton National	8	225	200	3	25	120	✓	✓	✓				▣ G	✓
	★★★Norton House	1	20	–	1	–	15		✓	✓				–	✓
	★★Beaumont	2	30	–	–	6	17							–	✓
	★Old School House	2	75	20	2	20	7		✓	✓		✓		–	

▣=indoor swimming pool; ⊃=outdoor swimming pool; ⊡=golf; ♀=tennis; ⚲=squash; G=gymnasium

Town	Hotel	No. of conf. rooms	Seating capacity of main room	Total seating of additional rooms	No. of smaller rooms	Maximum capacity of smaller rooms	No. of bedrooms	Exhibition hall space	Photocopying	Projection/Video	Closed circuit TV	Audio	Interpreting	Sporting facilities available at the Hotel	Use of fax
WALES															
TALYLLYN	★★Tynycornel	1	30	20	2	12	15		✓	✓				⊐	
TENBY	★★★Imperial	3	250	100	4	12	46	✓	✓	✓		✓		–	✓
	★★Atlantic	3	70	20	3	20	35	✓	✓	✓				⊟	✓
	★★Fourcroft	3	50	30	3	30	38	✓	✓					–	✓
	★★Milton Manor	2	40	16	2	6	18	✓	✓	✓				–	✓
	★★Royal Gate House	3	250	100	3	–	62	✓	✓			✓		⊟ ⚵ G	
TINTERN	★★★Beaufort	3	60	90	2	6	24		✓	✓				–	✓
TREARDDUR BAY	★★★Beach	3	100	30	2	15	26	✓	✓	✓		✓		⚵ ⚲ G	✓
TREFRIW	★★Hafod House	1	24	–	–	–	6		✓	✓				–	✓
USK	★★★★Cwrt Bleddyn	5	200	80	4	25	36	✓	✓	✓		✓		⊟ G ⚵ ⚲	✓
	★★Glen-yr-Afon House	3	40	20	2	30	17	✓	✓	✓		✓		–	
WELSHPOOL	★★Royal Oak	1	120	40	3	25	24	✓	✓	✓		✓		–	
	★★Golfa Hall	1	60	40	1	40	10		✓					–	✓
WOLFSCASTLE	★★Wolfscastle Country	1	180	220	1	10	15		✓			✓		⚵	✓
WREXHAM	★★★Llwyn Onn Hall	1	37	–	–	–	13		✓					–	✓
	★★Cross Lanes	3	100	50	2	6	18		✓					⊟	✓
ISLE OF MAN															
CASTLETOWN	★★★Castletown Golf Links	3	200	75	4	90	58	✓	✓	✓		✓		⊟ ⊡ G	✓
DOUGLAS	★★★Empress	1	180	–	2	25	102		✓	✓	✓	✓		⊟ G	✓
	★★★Sefton	1	100	–	1	25	75	✓	✓	✓		✓		⊟ G	✓
	★★★Palace	4	319	250	4	20	135	✓	✓	✓		✓		⊟ G	✓
	★★Ascot	1	100	–	2	60	45		✓	✓				–	✓
RAMSEY	★★★★Grand Island	3	200	200	4	10	54	✓	✓	✓		✓	✓	⊟ ⊡ ⚲ ⚵ G	✓
GUERNSEY															
CASTEL	★★Hogue du Pommier	1	25	–	–	–	39		✓					⊐ ⊡ G	✓
FERMAIN BAY	★★La Favorita	1	20	–	1	20	30		✓	✓				–	✓
ST PETER PORT	★★★★Old Government House	1	110	–	2	30	73		✓	✓		✓		⊐	✓
	★★★★St Pierre Park	1	220	–	5	50	134		✓	✓		✓		⊟ ⊡ ⚲ G	✓
	★★★De Havelet	1	20	–	–	–	34		✓	✓				⊟ G	✓
JERSEY															
GOREY	★★★Les Arches	2	150	120	3	30	54	✓	✓	✓		✓		⊐ ⊡ ⚲ G	✓
ST BRELADE	★★★★Atlantic	2	50	50	–	–	50		✓					⊟ ⊐ ⚲ G	✓
ST BRELADES BAY	★★★★L'Horizon	1	180	–	2	40	104	✓	✓	✓				⊟ G	✓
ST HELIER	★★★Apollo	1	180	–	2	35	85	✓	✓	✓		✓		⊟ G	✓
	★★★Beaufort	4	120	90	2	20	54		✓	✓		✓		⊟	✓
	★★★★Grand	6	200	200	7	60	115		✓	✓		✓		⊟ G	✓
	★★★Pomme D'Or	3	400	270	3	40	150	✓	✓	✓	✓	✓	✓	–	✓
ST LAWRENCE	★★★Little Grove	1	20	–	1	5	13		✓	✓				⊐ ⊡ ⚲ ⚵ G	✓
ST PETERS	★★★Mermaid	2	150	50	2	10	68	✓	✓	✓		✓		⊟ ⚲ G	✓
N. IRELAND															
BALLYMERA	★★★Adair Arms	4	300	230	4	30	38		✓	✓		✓		–	✓
BELFAST	★★★Europa	11	1100	326	4	20	198	✓	✓	✓		✓		–	✓
	★★★Stormont	6	300	50	–	–	67		✓	✓		✓		–	✓
BUSHMILLS	★★★Bushmills Inn	1	100	–	1	12	11	✓	✓				✓	–	✓
CARNLOUGH	★★Londonderry Arms	3	80	88	2	2	20	✓	✓	✓				–	✓
CARRICKFERGUS	★Dobbin's Inn	1	20	–	–	–	13			✓				–	
CRAWFORDSBURN	★★★Old Inn	3	120	35	–	–	32	✓						–	✓
CUSHENDALL	★★Thornlea	2	170	25	1	10	13	✓						–	
DUNADRY	★★★★Dunadry Inn	3	350	235	3	12	64	✓	✓	✓		✓	✓	⊟	✓
DUNGANNON	★★★Inn on the Park	4	400	190	–	–	–	✓	✓	✓	✓	✓		⚲	✓
ENNISKILLEN	★★★Killyherlin	3	550	400	3	25	23	✓	✓	✓		✓		–	✓
HOLYWOOD	★★★★Culloden	4	550	270	2	70	91	✓	✓	✓		✓	✓	⊟ ⚲ ⚵ G	✓
IRVINESTOWN	★★Mahon's	3	300	100	1	40	18	✓	✓					–	✓
KILKEEL	★★Kilmorey Arms	1	30	–	2	15	12	✓	✓					–	✓
NEWCASTLE	★★★Slieve Donard	7	800	510	2	20	100	✓	✓	✓		✓		⊟ ⚲ G	✓
OMAGH	★★Royal Arms	5	250	–	3	35	21	✓	✓	✓		✓		–	✓
PORTBALLINTRAE	★★Bayview	6	150	40	6	16	16	✓	✓	✓		✓		⊟	✓
STRABANE	★★★Fir Trees	3	200	100	3	30	30		✓	✓		✓	✓	–	✓

⊟=indoor swimming pool; ⊐=outdoor swimming pool; ⊡=golf; ⚲=tennis; ⚵=squash; **G**=*gymnasium*

SCOTLAND

ABERDEEN Grampian (Aberdeenshire). Map 55C3
Pop 214,100. Stonehaven 14, London 491, Banff 46, Braemar 58, Edinburgh 117, Glasgow 136, Huntly 38, Peterhead 32. See Plan, p. 547.
EC Wed. **MD** Fri. **P,** See Plan. **Golf** Royal Aberdeen 18h (2) and 9h, Bon-Accord 18h, etc. **See** Cathedral of St Machar, St Andrew's Episcopal Cathedral, St Mary's RC Cathedral, University (Marischal and King's Colleges), 17th cent Mercat Cross, Art Gallery and Regional Museum.
[i] St Nicholas House, Broad St. ☎(0224) 632727

★★★★ **Bucksburn Moat House,** Old Meldrum Rd, Bucksburn, AB2 9LN ☎(0224) 713911 Tx: 73108 Fax: (0224) 714020

Based on a converted 17th century grain mill 2 miles from Airport. Indoor swimming pool. (QMH)
🛏 98 bedrs, 98 en suite; TV; tcf
fn lift, dogs, ns; P 150, coach; child facs; con 180
✕ LD 10.30, bar meals only Sat & Sun lunch
£ B&B £77·75 (w/e £38), B&B (double) £93·40 (w/e £56); HB weekly £425; L fr £9, D £12; WB £81; [10% w/e]
cc Access, Amex, B'card/Visa, Diners.

★★★★ **Caledonian Thistle,** Union Terr, AB9 1HE ☎(0224) 640233 Tx: 73758 Fax: (0224) 641627 ♿

A traditional city-centre hotel refurbished to high standard. Sauna, solarium. (MtCh)
🛏 80 bedrs, 80 en suite; TV; tcf
fn lift, dogs, ns; P 25, coach; child facs; con 60
✕ LD 11.45
£ room £80, room (double) £85; Bk £7·75, L £9, D £14·95; WB
cc Access, Amex, B'card/Visa, CB, Diners.

★★★★ **Copthorne,** 122 Huntly St, AB1 1SU ☎(0224) 630404 Tx: 739707 Fax: (0224) 640573

Traditional stone building, completely redesigned internally into a smart modern hotel, in business part of city. ✈ It
🛏 89 bedrs, 89 en suite; TV; tcf
fn lift, dogs, ns; G 22, coach; child facs; con 220
✕ LD 10
£ B&B £87·50–£112·50 (w/e £32), B&B (double) £115–£130; L £4·50, D £12·95; WB; [10% V w/e]
cc Access, Amex, B'card/Visa, Diners.

★★★★ **Skean Dhu,** Souterhead Rd, Altens, AB1 4LE ☎(0224) 877000 Tx: 739631♿ Fax: (0224) 896964

Purpose-built 5-storey hotel just outside city. Swimming pool. ✈ Fr, De. (MtCh)
🛏 221 bedrs, 221 en suite, TV; tcf
fn lift, dogs, ns; P 300, coach; child facs; con 400
✕ LD 9.45, brasserie only Sat lunch & all Sun
£ B&B £77·50–£82·50 (w/e £26·50), B&B (double) £95–£100; L £11·50, D £14; [10% V w/e Jul–Aug]
cc Access, Amex, B'card/Visa, Diners.

♣ ★★★ **Ardoe House,** Blairs, South Deeside Rd, AB1 5YP ☎(0224) 867355 Tx: 739413 Fax: (0224) 861283

Scottish Baronial mansion set in wooded grounds in the lovely Dee Valley, 4 miles west of Aberdeen on B9077. Putting. ✈ Fr, De
🛏 19 bedrs, 19 en suite; TV; tcf
fn P 300, coach; child facs; con 200
✕ LD 9.30
£ B&B £80 (w/e £25), B&B (double) £90; L £10, D £17; WB £38 (HB)
cc Access, Amex, B'card/Visa, Diners.

★★★ **Dyce Skean Dhu,** Farburn Ter, AB2 0DW ☎(0224) 723101 Tx: 73473 Fax: (0224) 722965

Modern purpose-built hotel conveniently situated for city centre. Squash, sauna, solarium, gymnasium. ✈ Fr. (MtCh)
🛏 220 bedrs, 220 en suite; TV; tcf
fn dogs, ns; P 300, coach; child facs; con 400
✕ coffee shop only Sun dinner
£ B&B £64–£71·50 (w/e £32·50); B&B (double) £80·50–£88; D £13·45; WB (£25)
cc Access, Amex, B'card/Visa, Diners.

★★★ **Stakis Tree Tops,** 161 Springfield Rd, AB9 2QH ☎(0224) 313377 Tx: 73794 Fax: (0224) 312028
Long modern building in attractive wooded grounds. Indoor swimming pool, tennis, sauna, solarium, gymnasium. ✈ Fr, It. (Sk)
🛏 113 bedrs, 113 en suite; TV; tcf
fn lift, TV, dogs, ns; P 250, coach; child facs; con 600
✕ LD 9.30
£ B&B £42–£95, B&B (double) £55–£120; L £7·50, D £12·50; WB £40 (HB)
cc Access, Amex, B'card/Visa, Diners.

★★★ **Westhill,** Westhill, AB3 6TT ☎(0224) 740388 Tx: 739925 Fax: (0224) 744354

Purpose-built hotel beside a shopping centre close to A944 about 7 miles west of city. Sauna, solarium. ✈ Fr, De, It, Es
🛏 38 bedrs, 38 en suite; annexe 14 bedrs, 14 en suite; TV; tcf

EC *early closing* **MD** *market day* ♣ *country house hotel* *ns (NS) no smoking areas* *tcf tea/coffee facilities*

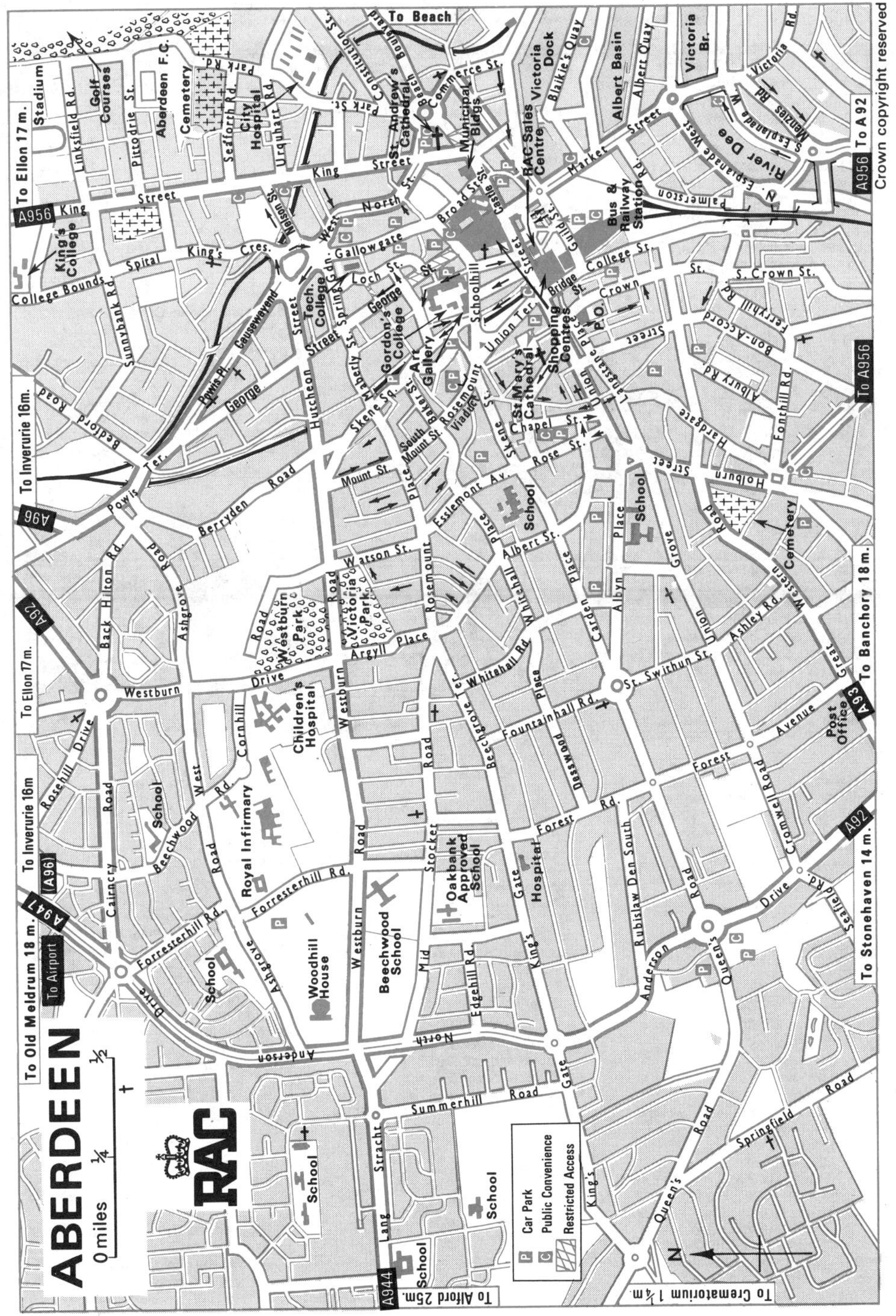

ABERDEEN
0 miles 1/4 1/2
RAC
Car Park
Public Convenience
Restricted Access
N
To Beach
To Ellon 17 m.
To Inverurie 16m.
To Ellon 17m.
To Inverurie 16m
To Old Meldrum 18 m.
To Airport
A956
A96
A92
A947
(A96)
A944
To Alford 25m.
To Crematorium 1¼ m.
To Stonehaven 14 m.
To Banchory 18 m.
To A956
To A92
A93
Crown copyright reserved
Stadium
Golf Courses
Aberdeen F.C.
Cemetery
City Hospital
King's College
St. Andrew's Cathedral
Municipal Bldgs
Victoria Dock
Albert Basin
Victoria Br.
River Dee
RAC Sales Centre
Bus & Railway Station
Tech. College
Gordon's College
Art Gallery
Shopping Centres
St. Mary's Cathedral
P.O.
School
Westburn Park
Victoria Park
Children's Hospital
Royal Infirmary
Woodhill House
Beechwood School
Oakbank Approved School
Hospital
Cemetery
Post Office

lift, dogs; P 350, coach; child facs; con 300
LD 9.45; bar meals only lunch
£ B&B £48 (w/e £25), B&B (double) £65
cc Access, Amex, B'card/Visa, Diners.

★★ **Ferryhill House,** Bon Accord St, AB1 2UA (0224) 590867
In residential area of city, stone-built 2-storey villa with small grounds. Fr
11 bedrs, 7 en suite, 2 ba; TV; tcf
TV, dogs; P 48, coach; child facs
LD 8.30; nr Fri & Sat dinner & all Sun
£ B&B £36 (w/e £20), B&B (double) £62; L 5·90, D £5·90; [10% V w/e]
cc Access, Amex, B'card/Visa, Diners.

★★ **Swallow Imperial,** Stirling St, AB9 2JY (0224) 589101 Tx: 73365
Fax: (0224) 574288

Traditional city centre hotel 100 yards from station. Fr. (Sw)
108 bedrs, 106 en suite; TV; tcf
lift, dogs, ns; coach; child facs; con 70
LD 9.30, bar meals only Mon–Sat lunch
£ B&B £68 (w/e £29), B&B (double) £78; D £12·95; WB £69 (2 nts HB)
cc Access, Amex, B'card/Visa, Diners.

Cedars (Acclaimed), 339 Great Western Rd, AB1 6NW (0224) 583225. *Private Hotel.*
£ B&B £25–£30

Fourways (Acclaimed), 435 Great Western Rd, AB1 6NJ (0224) 310218. *Guest House.*

Alelanro, 272 Holburn St, AB1 6DD (0224) 575601. *Guest House.*
Bimini, 69 Constitution St, AB2 1ET (0224) 646912. *Guest House.*
£ B&B £14–£16
Craiglynn, 36 Fonthill Rd, AB1 2UJ (0224) 584050 Fax: (0224) 584050. *Hotel.*
£ B&B £27–£35
Dunromin, 75 Constitution St, AB2 1ET (0224) 647995. *Guest House.*
Jays, 422 King St, AB2 3BR (0224) 638295
£ B&B £15–£16
Klibreck, 410 Great Western Rd, AB1 6NR (0224) 316115. *Guest House.*
Strathboyne, 26 Abergeldie Terr, AB1 6EE (0224) 593400. *Guest House.*

ABERDEEN AIRPORT

Grampian (Aberdeenshire). Map 55C3
Aberdeen 5½, London 497, Edinburgh 122, Fraserburgh 43, Glasgow 141, Huntly 35, Peterhead 33.

★★★★ **Holiday Inn,** Riverview Dr, Farburn, Dyce AB2 0AZ (0224) 770011 Tx: 739651 Fax: (0224) 722347
Modern purpose-built 2-storey hotel near Airport. Indoor swimming pool, sauna, solarium, gymnasium. Fr. (CHIC)
154 bedrs, 154 en suite; TV; tcf
dogs, ns; P 180, coach; child facs; con 400
LD 10.30
£ B&B £97·95–£128·95 (w/e £37), B&B (double) £121·90–£125·90; L £13·50; [5% V]
cc Access, Amex, B'card/Visa, CB, Diners; dep.

★★★★ **Skean Dhu,** Argyll Rd, AB2 0DU (0224) 725252 Tx: 739239
Fax: (0224) 723745
Large, modern hotel of two storeys next to airport terminal. Swimming pool. Fr, It, Po. (MtCh)
148 bedrs, 148 en suite; TV; tcf
dogs, ns; P 450, coach; child facs; con 500
LD 9.45
£ B&B £71·95–£81·95 (w/e £25); B&B (double) £78·90–£88·90; L £9, D £14·50; [10% V]
cc Access, Amex, B'card/Visa, Diners.

ABERDOUR

Fife. Map 47A3
Pop 1,200. South Queensferry 7½, London 392, Dunfermline 7½, Edinburgh 17, Kincardine 17, Kinross 13, Kirkcaldy 8.
EC Wed. **Golf** Aberdour 18h.

★★★ **Woodside,** High St, KY3 0SW (0383) 860328 Tx: 721656
Fax: (0383) 860920

Traditional style stone-built hotel with unique 'Orient Line' cocktail bar. Sauna.
21 bedrs, 21 en suite; TV; tcf
dogs; P 30, coach; child facs; con 90
LD 9.30
£ B&B £48·50 (w/e £30), B&B (double) £63·50; HB weekly £428·50; L £13·50, D £15·50; WB
cc Access, Amex, B'card/Visa, Diners.

ABERFELDY

Tayside (Perthshire). Map 54B1
Pop 1,500, Crieff 22, London 438, Blairgowrie 29, Crainlarich 37, Edinburgh 68, Perth 31, Pitlochry 14.
EC Wed. **Golf** Aberfeldy 9h. **See** Black Watch Monument, Gen. Wade's Bridge.
i 8 Dunkeld St. (0887) 20276

★★★ **Moness House,** PH15 2DY (0887) 20446 Fax: (0887) 20062
Attractive, white-painted, 18th-century house in 35 acres of grounds. Indoor swimming pool, squash, sauna, solarium, gymnasium, billiards.
12 bedrs, 12 en suite; TV; tcf
ns; P 60, coach; child facs; con 200
LD 9.30
£ B&B £31·50–£33·50, B&B (double) £53–£57; HB weekly £210–£240; L £3, D £12·50; WB £60; [5% V Nov–Mar]
cc Access, Amex, B'card/Visa, Diners; dep.

★★ **Weem,** Weem, PH15 2LD (0887) 20381
Stone-built 17th century former coaching inn of character. Quiet location. Fishing.
14 bedrs, 14 en suite; TV; tcf
TV, dogs, ns; P 20, coach; child facs; con 50
LD 8.30
£ B&B £24–£34, B&B (double) £40·50; L £6·50, D £12·50; [5% V] WB
cc Access, Amex, B'card/Visa, Diners; dep.

Guinach (Highly Acclaimed), Urlar Rd, PH15 2ET (0887) 20251. *Private Hotel.*
£ B&B £29·50, HB weekly £285·50; [10% V w/d May–Oct, all week Oct–Apr]

Balnearn, Crieff Rd, PH15 2BJ (0887) 20431. *Private Hotel.*
Caber-Feidh, 56 Dunkeld St, PH15 2AF (0887) 20342. *Guest House.* Fr
£ B&B £11·50; HB weekly £129·50; [5% V w/d]
Nessbank House, Crieff Rd, PH15 2BJ, (0887) 20214. *Hotel.*

ABERLADY

Lothian (East Lothian). Map 51A3
Pop 1,214. Haddington 5, London 374, Edinburgh 15, Glasgow 60, Peebles 32.
Golf Gullane 18h (3). **See** Parish Church, Mercat Cross, Nature Reserve.

★★ **Kilspindie House,** Main St, EH32 0RE (087 57) 682

Two-storey stone-built hotel in picturesque village. Interesting "golf addicts" bar. Fr, Es
26 bedrs, 26 en suite; TV; tcf
dogs; P 30; child facs; con 60
LD 8.30; bar meals only Mon–Sat lunch
£ B&B £27–£37, B&B (double) £50–£56; HB weekly £230–£250; L £7, D £11; WB £60 (2 nts HB); [10% V]
cc Access, B'card/Visa; dep.

ACHNASHEEN

Highland (Ross & Cromarty). Map 57C1
Pop 50. Garve 16, London 568, Beauly 31, Edinburgh 193, Gairloch 29, Glasgow 207, Kyle of Lochalsh (Fy) 39, Ullapool 48.
EC Wed. **Golf** Gairloch 9h.

★★ H **Ledgowan,** IV22 2EJ (044 588) 252 Tx: 75431
Fax: (044 588) 240
Family-run country house hotel set amidst rugged Highland scenery. Open 31 Mar–31 Oct.
13 bedrs, 13 en suite; TV; tcf
dogs; P 25; child facs
LD 8.45
£ B&B £38·50–£42·50, B&B (double) £57–£70; HB weekly £322–£350; L £5, D £17·50 [10% V]
cc Access, Amex, B'card/Visa, Diners; dep.

AIRDRIE

Strathclyde (Lanarkshire). Map 46B4
Pop 37,528. M8 (jn 8) 3½, Lanark 17, London 385, Edinburgh 33, Glasgow 11, Kincardine 21, Peebles 40, Stirling 19.
EC Wed. **MD** Tue, Fri. **Golf** Airdrie 18h.

★★ **Tudor,** 39 Alexandra St, ML6 0BA
(0236) 64144 Fax: (0236) 47589
Town centre hotel conveniently situated– pleasant white-washed appearance.
19 bedrs, 11 en suite; 6 ba; TV; tcf
dogs; P 100, coach; child facs; con 180
LD 9.30
£ B&B £37·50–£49·50, B&B (double) £56; L fr £8·50, D fr £8·50; [10% V]
cc Access, Amex, B'card/Visa, Diners.

ANNAN Dumfries & Galloway (Dumfriesshire). Map 43B3
Pop 8,952. Eastriggs 3½, London 311, Beattock 24, Carlisle 17, Dumfries 15, Edinburgh 76, Glasgow 79, Langholm 18.
EC Wed. **MD** Fri, Sat. **Golf** Powfoot 18h.

★ **Corner House,** 78 High St, DG12 6DL
(046 12) 2754

Town centre hotel (with 2 storeys over shops). Ornate exterior. (MtCh)

Ravenswood, St John's Rd, DG12 6AW
(046 12) 2158. *Private Hotel.*
£ B&B £15

ANSTRUTHER Fife. Map 51A4
Pop 3,260. Largo 10, London 422, Edinburgh 48, Kirkcaldy 22, Perth 38, St Andrews 9.
EC Wed. **Golf** Anstruther 9h.
[i] Scottish Fisheries Museum, St Ayles. (0333) 310628

★★★ **Craw's Nest,** Bankwell Rd, KY10 3DA (0333) 310691 Tx: 727049
Fax: (0333) 312216
Large pleasant white-painted 2-storey building on edge of town. Solarium.
31 bedrs, 31 en suite; annexe 19 bedrs, 19 en suite; TV; tcf
TV; P 180, coach; child facs; con 350
£ B&B £32–£46, B&B (double) £54–£80; L £8·50, D £15; WB £90 (HB)
cc Access, Amex, B'card/Visa, Diners; dep.

★★ **Smugglers Inn,** High St East, KY10 3DQ (0333) 310506
Long attractive 2-storey stone-built former inn with origins in 14th century. Fr
9 bedrs, 9 en suite; TV; tcf
TV, dogs, P 15, coach; no children
LD 9.30, bar meals only lunch
£ £22–£23·50; HB weekly £206·50–£217; D £11·50
cc Access, Amex, B'card/Visa, Diners.

Royal, 20 Rodger St, KY10 3DU (0333) 310581. *Hotel.*
£ B&B £17·50–£20·50; HB weekly £140–£175

ARBROATH Tayside (Angus). Map 55B1
Pop 24,093. Dundee 16, London 445, Brechin 12, Edinburgh 71, Forfar 15, Glasgow 95, Montrose 13.
EC Wed. **Golf** Arbroath 18h. **See** Abbey ruins, St Vigean's Church and Museum.
[i] Market Place. Arbroath (0241) 72690

★★ **Seaforth,** Dundee Rd, DD11 1QF
(0241) 72232
Red sandstone 1930s-style building with later extension. In outskirts. Indoor swimming pool, sauna, solarium, gymnasium, snooker.
20 bedrs, 20 en suite; TV; tcf
dogs; P 50, coach; child facs; con 120
LD 9.30
£ B&B £29·50–£34, B&B (double) £42·50–£45; L £6·50, D £8·50; [5% V w/e]
cc Access, Amex, B'card/Visa, Diners; dep.

Kingsley House, 29 Market Gate, DD11 1AU (0241) 73933. *Guest House. Snooker.* Fr, It, Es
£ B&B £12–£13, HB weekly £100; [10% V]

ARDEONAIG Central (Perthshire). Map 54B1
Lochearnhead 14, London 441, Aberfeldy 16, Crianlarich 20, Edinburgh 77, Glasgow 61.
Golf Killin 18h.

★★ **Ardeonaig,** FK21 8SU Killin (056 72) 400

Attractive former droving inn at lochside in isolated rural area. Fishing, riding. Closed Dec. Fr
12 bedrs, 12 en suite; tcf
TV, dogs; P 40; child facs; con 25
LD 9, bar meals only lunch
£ B&B £25; HB weekly £240; D £15; WB £70 (2 nts HB)
cc Access, Amex, B'card/Visa, Diners; dep.

ARDLUI Strathclyde (Dunbartonshire). Map 49B4
Pop 36. Glasgow 42, London 429, Arrochar 9½, Crianlarich 8½, Dumbarton 28.
Golf Helensburgh 18h, Killin 9h. **See** Rob Roy's Cave, Pulpit Rock.

★★ **Ardlui,** G83 7EB Inveruglas (030 14) 243 Fax: (030 14) 268

19th century building attractively set beside road at head of Loch Lomond. Fishing, billiards. Fr
11 bedrs, 7 en suite, 1 ba; TV; tcf
dogs; P 50, coach; child facs
LD 8.45, bar meals only lunch
£ B&B £25·30–£35·40, B&B (double) £43·70–£60·70; HB weekly £132·25–£166·75
cc Access, B'card/Visa; dep.

ARDROSSAN Strathclyde (Ayrshire). Map 49B2
Kilmarnock 18, London 401, Edinburgh 89, Glasgow 44, Largs 15.

★★ **Blair Lodge,** 20 South Cres, KA20 8EA
(0294) 68436
Pleasant, white-painted building on sea front.
7 bedrs, 7 en suite; TV, tcf

AUCHENCAIRN Dumfries & Galloway (Kirkcudbrightshire). Map 43A2
Pop 170. Dalbeattie 7, London 348, Edinburgh 91, Dumfries 21, Gatehouse of Fleet 19, Glasgow 90, New Galloway 22.
EC Wed. **Golf** Kirkcudbright 18h.

★★★ R **Balcary Bay,** DG7 1QZ
(055 664) 217

Fine country house in 4 acres of parkland. Good sea views. Open Mar–early Nov.
13 bedrs, 11 en suite, 1 ba; TV; tcf
dogs; P 50; child facs
LD 9
£ B&B £40, B&B (double) £54–£80; D £16; WB
cc Access, B'card/Visa; dep.

AUCHTERARDER Tayside (Perthshire). Map 50B4
Dunfermline 23, London 414, Crieff 9, Edinburgh 39, Glasgow 45, Kincardine 24, Kinross 19, Perth 14, Stirling 20.
[i] High St. (0764) 63450

★★★★★ **The Gleneagles,** PH3 1NF
(0764) 62231 Tx: 76105
Fax: (0764) 62134

Famous luxury hotel in large mansion house set in magnificent countryside. Indoor swimming pool, golf, putting, tennis, fishing,

Sc

By Achnasheen (Wester Ross)

Aviemore (Inverness-shire)

Ayr (Ayrshire)

squash, riding, sauna, solarium, gymnasium, billiards. Fr, De
236 bedrs, 236 en suite; TV
lift, dogs; P 250, coach; child facs; con 360
LD 10
£ B&B £97–£107, B&B (double) £164–£194; HB weekly £1256·50–£1466·50, WB £185 (2 nts HB)
cc Access, Amex, B'card/Visa, Diners; dep.

★★★ **Duchally,** PH3 1PN (0764) 63071

Converted and extended mansion situated in well-kept grounds in quiet wooded countryside. Billiards.
16 bedrs, 14 en suite, 2 ba; TV; tcf
TV, dogs, ns; P 30, coach; child facs; con 80

Cairn Lodge (Highly Acclaimed), Orchil Rd, PH3 1LX (0764) 62634. *Hotel. Putting.*
Fr, De, It, Es
£ B&B £45–£65; [5% V w/d]

AUCHTERMUCHTY Fife. Map 50C4

Kinross 10, London 411, Edinburgh 37, Glasgow 55, Kirkcaldy 15, Perth 16, St Andrews 19.

Ardchoille Farmhouse (Acclaimed), Woodmill Farm, KY14 7ER (0337) 28414. *Riding.*

AULTBEA Highland (Ross & Cromarty). Map 57B2

Pop 500. Dundonnell 20, London 602, Beauly 68, Edinburgh 228, Gairloch 12, Glasgow 238, Ullapool 50.
EC Wed. **Golf** Gairloch 9h. **See** Inverewe Gardens 4 m S.

★★ **Aultbea,** IV22 2HX (044 582) 201
Fax: (044 582) 214

Small stone-built family-run hotel attractively set on loch shore. Fr, De
8 bedrs, 7 en suite, 1 ba; TV; tcf
TV, dogs; P 25, coach; child facs
LD 9
£ B&B £18–£32, B&B (double) £36; L £10, D £16·50; WB £30 (HB winter)
cc Access, B'card/Visa; dep.

★★ **Drumchork Lodge,** IV22 2HU
(044 582) 242

An attractive converted lodge with panoramic views over Loch Ewe. Sauna, solarium, billiards.
9 bedrs, 9 en suite; TV; tcf
TV, dogs; P 50, coach; child facs

AVIEMORE Highland (Inverness-shire). Map 54B3

Pop 1,960. Kingussie 11, London 499, Carrbridge 7, Edinburgh 124, Glasgow 135, Grantown-on-Spey 14.
EC Wed. **Golf** Boat of Garten 18h. **See** reindeer herd, Ben Macdhui 4,296 ft, Rock of Craigellachie, Loch-an-Eilean, 3 m S, Wildlife Park 7 m, Larig Ghru Pass 7½ m SE.
[i] Grampian Rd. (0479) 810363

★★★★ **Stakis Four Seasons,** Aviemore Centre, PH22 1PF (0479) 810681
Tx: 75213 Fax: (0479) 810862
Modern 7-storey hotel set on a hill overlooking Aviemore Centre. Spectacular mountain views. Indoor swimming pool, putting, sauna, solarium, gymnasium. (Sk).
88 bedrs, 88 en suite; TV; tcf
lift, dogs, ns; P, coach; child facs; con 100
LD 9.30
£ L 8·50, D £15
cc Access, Amex, B'card/Visa, Diners; dep.
(See advertisement on p. 550)

★★★ **Aviemore Highlands** (formerly Post House), Aviemore Centre, PH22 1PJ
(0479) 810771 Tx: 57643
Fax: (0479) 811473
Custom-built hotel in holiday centre. Solarium.
103 bedrs, 103 en suite; TV; tcf
lift, dogs, ns; P 200, coach; child facs; con 100
LD 9; bar meals only lunch
£ B&B £27, WB £36 (HB)
cc Access, Amex, B'card/Visa, Diners.

★★★ **Red MacGregor,** Main Rd, PH22 1RH (0479) 810256
Fax: (0479) 810685
Modern, low built hotel in centre of village. Indoor swimming pool, sauna, solarium, gymnasium. Fr, It
30 bedrs, 30 en suite; TV; tcf
ns; P 75, coach; child facs; con 250
LD 10, bar meals only lunch
£ B&B & dinner £52, B&B (double) & dinner £89; HB weekly £311·50; D £10; WB £76 (HB); [10% V]
cc Access, Amex, B'card/Visa, Diners; dep.

★★★ **Stakis Coylumbridge,** PH22 1QN
(0479) 810661 Tx: 75272
Fax: (0479) 811309
Large modern hotel in 65 acres of heatherland. Indoorswimming pool, putting, tennis, sauna, solarium, gymnasium. (Sk)
Fr, De
175 bedrs, 175 en suite; TV; tcf
dogs, ns; P 175, coach; child facs; con 500
LD 9.30
£ B&B £75·50–£85·50, B&B (double) £107·50–£129; HB weekly £217–£441; L £7·95, D £14·50; WB £92 (2 nts); [10% V]
cc Access, Amex, B'card/Visa, Diners.

Balavoulin (Highly Acclaimed), Grampian Rd, PH22 1RL (0479) 810672
Fax: (0479) 810672. *Hotel.*
£ B&B (double) £36–£45; HB weekly £252–£315; [10% V]

Ravenscraig, Grampian Rd, PH22 1RP
(0479) 810278. *Guest House*
£ B&B (double) £29–£34; [10% V Feb–Jun, Sep–Oct]

AYR Strathclyde (Ayrshire). Map 49B1

See also PRESTWICK.
Pop 49,481. Dalmellington 14, London 381, Girvan 21, Glasgow 33, Kilmarnock 12.
EC Wed. **MD** Mon, Tue. **Golf** Ayr, Belleisle and Seafield Municipal Courses 18h (2).
See Burns' Cottage, Monument, Statue House and gardens (Alloway), The Twa Brigs, Tam o' Shanter Inn (museum), Burns Statue.
[i] 39 Sandgate (0292) 284196

★★★★ **Fairfield House,** 12 Fairfield Rd, KA7 2AS (0292) 267461 Tx: 778833
Fax: (0292) 261456

Victorian Glasgow merchant's house on seafront, recently restored to its original elegance. Indoor swimming pool, sauna, solarium, gymnasium.
22 bedrs, 22 en suite; annexe 8 bedrs, 8 en suite; TV; tcf
TV, dogs, ns; P 80; children over 12; con 40

★★★ **Belleisle House,** Doonfoot, KA7 4DU (0292) 42331 Fax: (0292) 45325
Country house in public park area. Golf, putting.
17 bedrs, 14 en suite, 1 ba; TV; tcf
dogs; P 50, coach; child facs; con 300

★★★ **Caledonian,** Dalblair Rd, KA7 1UG
(0292) 269331 Tx: 776611
Fax: (0292) 610722

Modern hotel, close to shops, harbour and sea. Indoor swimming pool, sauna, solarium, gymnasium, billiards. Fr. (Emb)
114 bedrs, 114 en suite; TV; tcf
lift, dogs, ns; P 70, coach; child facs; con 200
LD 9.45; coffee shop only Sat lunch

Sc

£ B&B £76–£82, B&B (double) £103–£113; HB weekly £252–£315; L £8·95, D £14·50; WB £36 (HB)
cc Access, Amex, B'card/Visa, Diners.

★★★ **Kylestrome,** Miller Rd, KA7 2AX ☎(0292) 262474

Refurbished hotel, conveniently situated between town centre and the seafront. Fr, De, It, Es
12 bedrs, 12 en suite; TV; tcf
dogs; P 50, coach; child facs; con 30
LD 10.30
£ B&B £50–£55, B&B (double) £70–£75; L 8·50; [10% V Oct–Apr]
cc Access, Amex, B'card/Visa, Diners; dep.

★★★ **Pickwick,** 19 Racecourse Rd, KA7 2TD ☎(0292) 260111 Fax: (0292) 43174

Well-furnished stone-built Victorian hotel, close to sea. Putting. Fr, De
15 bedrs, 15 en suite; TV; tcf
TV, dogs; P 80, coach; child facs; con 40
LD 9.45
£ B&B £40–£47·50, B&B (double) £70–£80; HB weekly £302–£334; L £7·25, D £12·95; WB £85 (2 nts HB)
cc Access, Amex, B'card/Visa, Diners.

★★★ **Savoy Park,** 16 Racecourse Rd, KA7 2UT ☎(0292) 266112
Fax: (0292) 611488

An interesting turreted residence with a pleasant garden. Fr
16 bedrs, 16 en suite; TV; tcf
dogs; P 80, coach; child facs; con 100
LD 9
£ B&B £35–£45, B&B (double) £50–£70; L £8, D £18; WB
cc Access, Amex, B'card/Visa; dep.

★★★ **Station,** Burns Statue Sq, KA7 3AT ☎(0292) 263268
Three-storey hotel in the traditional Scottish style; beside station.

★★ **Annfield,** 49 Maybole Rd, KA7 4SF ☎(0292) 41986 Fax: (0292) 43174

Modern tastefully decorated hotel in extensive grounds ½ mile from Ayr town centre. Fr
7 bedrs, 7 en suite; TV; tcf
TV; P 80, coach; child facs; con 40
LD 9.45
£ B&B £20–£35, B&B (double) £40–£50; HB weekly £202–£271; L £7·95, D £11·95; WB £60; [10% V]
cc Access, Amex, B'card/Visa, diners; dep.

★★ **Ayrshire and Galloway,** 1 Killoch Pl, KA7 2AE ☎(0292) 262626
Centrally situated traditional hotel, which overlooks town centre square.
25 bedrs, 8 en suite, 5 ba; TV
TV, dogs; P 20, coach; child facs
LD 8.30, bar meals only lunch
£ B&B £18–£20, D £10
cc Access, B'card/Visa; dep.

★★ R **Burns Monument,** Monument Rd, Alloway, KA7 4PQ ☎(0292) 42466
Fax: (0292) 611295
Historic (1829) riverside hotel set amongst own magnificent gardens. Fishing.
9 bedrs, 9 en suite; TV; tcf
TV, dogs; P 12, coach; child facs; con 150

★★ **Chestnuts,** 52 Racecourse Rd, KA7 2UZ ☎(0292) 264393 Fax: (0292) 264393

Family-run Georgian-style hotel with small garden; on coast road. Putting.
14 bedrs, 11 en suite, (1 sh), 2 ba; TV; tcf
TV, dogs; P 30; child facs
LD 9.45
£ B&B £28, B&B (double) £50; HB weekly £195; WB £58 (2 nts HB)
cc Access, Amex, B'card/Visa.

★★ **Gartferry,** 44 Racecourse Rd, KA7 2UY ☎(0292) 262768
Substantial 19th century building set in attractive award-winning garden.
8 bedrs, 8 en suite; 1 ba; TV, tcf
P 200, coach; child facs; con 200
LD 9.30, bar meals only lunch
£ B&B £35, B&B (double) £50
cc Access, Amex, B'card/Visa, Diners; dep.

★★ **Old Racecourse,** 2 Victoria Park, KT7 1HT ☎(0292) 262873
Large Victorian house in own grounds; convenient for beach and town centre.
10 bedrs, 7 en suite, 2 ba; TV; tcf
dogs; P 30, coach; child facs
LD 10
£ B&B £30–£32, B&B (double) £55–£60; L £7·50, D £12; [5% V Nov–May]
cc B'card/Visa; dep.
(*See advertisement on p. 550*)

Windsor (Highly Acclaimed), 6 Alloway Pl, KA7 2AA ☎(0292) 264689. *Hotel.*
£ B&B £16–£20, B&B (double) £30–£36; HB weekly £137–£156

Parkhouse, 1A Ballantine Dr, KA7 2RG ☎(0292) 264151. *Hotel.*
£ B&B £18–£30; HB weekly £150–£164; [10% V]

BALLACHULISH Highland (Argyll). Map 53C2
Pop 1,254. Crianlarich 39, London 475, Dalmally 38, Edinburgh 118, Fort William 14, Glasgow 85, Mallaig (Fy) 57, Oban 37.
EC Wed. **Golf** Fort William 18h.
i ☎(085 52) 296

★★★ **Ballachulish,** PA39 4JY ☎(085 52) 606 Tx: 94013696 Fax: (085 52) 629

Stone-built traditional hotel beautifully set on Loch. Panoramic views. Fishing. Fr
30 bedrs, 30 en suite, 2 ba; TV; tcf
dogs; P 75, G 1, U 1, coach; child facs; con 60
LD 9.30
£ B&B £39·50–£45, B&B (double) £59–£90; HB weekly £255–£395; D £16·50; WB £29·50 (HB); [5% V]
cc Access, B'card/Visa; dep.

Lyn Leven (Acclaimed), West Laroch ☎(085 52) 392. *Guest House.*
£ B&B (double) £26–£34; HB weekly £140–£155.

BALLATER Grampian (Aberdeenshire). Map 55A3
Pop 1,180. Braemar 16, London 479, Aberdeen 41, Edinburgh 104, Grantown-on-Spey 37, Huntly 40.
EC Thur. **Golf** Ballater 18h. **See** Falls of Muick, Lochnagar 3,786 ft, Loch Kinord 4 m NE, Balmoral Castle grounds and Crathie Church 8 m W, Highland Games in Aug.
i Station Sq. ☎(033 97) 55306

★★★★ H C R **Craigendarroch,** Braemar Rd, Royal Deeside, AB3 5XA ☎(033 97) 55858 Tx: 739952
Fax: (033 97) 55447

EC *early closing* **MD** *market day* *country house hotel* *ns (NS) no smoking areas* *tcf tea/coffee facilities*

Victorian house with modern extension situated in 29 acres of woodlands, overlooking the River Dee. Indoor swimming pool, tennis, squash, sauna, solarium, gymnasium, billiards.
50 bedrs, 50 en suite; TV; tcf
lift, ns; P 100, coach; child facs; con 100
LD 9. Resid lic
£ B&B £85, B&B (double) £115; L £10·95, D £20
cc Access, Amex, B'card/Visa, Diners; dep.

★★★ **Darroch Learg,** Braemar Rd, AB3 5UX (033 97) 55443 Fax: (033 97) 55443

Scottish style granite-built hotel on hillside enjoying fine views. Open Feb–Oct.
15 bedrs, 15 en suite; annexe 8 bedrs, 5 en suite, 2 ba; TV; tcf
dogs, ns; P 25; child facs
LD 8.30. Restrict lic
£ B&B £24–£30, B&B (double) £41·60–£70; HB weekly £201·60–£315; D £15·50
cc Access, B'card/Visa.
(See advertisement on p. 554)

★★★ **Glen Lui,** Invercauld Rd, AB3 5RP (033 97) 55402 Fax: (033 97) 55545
Much extended house quietly situated and with lovely views over golf course to hills beyond.
10 bedrs, 10 en suite; TV; tcf
TV, dogs; P 15, coach; child facs
LD 9.30, bar meals only Mon–Sat lunch
£ B&B £30–£50, B&B (double) £50–£70; L £4·50, D £13·50; WB £75 (HB); [10% V]
cc Access, Amex, B'card/Visa; dep.

★★ **Monaltrie** (formerly Invercauld Arms), 5 Bridge Sq, AB3 5QJ (033 97) 55417 Fax: (033 97) 55180

Standing on river bank on edge of village, a fully modernised Victorian building.
25 bedrs, 25 en suite; TV; tcf
dogs, ns; P40, coach; child facs; con 100
LD 8.30; bar meals only lunch
£ B&B £32–£38, B&B (double) £48–£58; HB weekly £224–£266; D £15·50; [10% V]
cc Access, Amex, B'card/Visa, Diners; dep.

Moorside (Acclaimed), Braemar Rd, AB3 5RL (033 97) 55492. *Guest House.*
£ B&B £21; HB weekly £146

Morvada (Acclaimed), Braemar Rd, AB3 5RL (033 97) 55501. *Guest House.* Open May–Oct.
£ B&B (double) £30–£32

Aspen, 44 Braemar Rd, AB2 5RQ (033 97) 55486

Ballater, 34 Victoria Rd, AB3 5QX (033 97) 55346. *Guest House.*

BALLOCH Strathclyde (Dunbartonshire).

Map 46A2
Pop 1,740. Glasgow 18, London 406, Arrochar 18, Crianlarich 33, Dumbarton 5, Edinburgh 60, Lochearnhead 41, Stirling 29.
EC Wed. **Golf** Vale of Leven, Bonhill 18h. **See** Loch Lomond, Cameron Estate Gardens, Wildlife & Leisure Park.
[i] Balloch Rd (0389) 53533

★★ **Balloch,** G83 8LQ Alexandria (0389) 52579 Fax: (0389) 55604
Old-established traditional stone-built tourist hotel near end of Loch Lomond.
13 bedrs, 12 en suite, (1 ba); TV; tcf
dogs; P 40, coach; child facs
LD 9.30, bar meals only lunch
£ B&B £34·50, B&B (double) £56; D £10; [10% V]
cc Access, Amex, B'card/Visa, Diners.

Cameron House, Alexandria, Loch Lomond, G83 8QZ. (0389) 55565 Fax: (0389) 59906
Hotel opened late summer 1990; awaiting inspection. Fr
68 bedrs, 68 en suite; TV; tcf
lift, ns; P 150, coach; child facs; con 220
LD 10
£ B&B £100–£110; B&B (double) £125–£135; L £14, D £25
cc Access, Amex, B'card/Visa, Diners.

BALMACARA Highland (Ross & Cromarty).

Map 53B4
Pop 300. Invergarry 45, London 559, Achnasheen 34, Edinburgh 193, Invermoriston 51, Kyle of Lochalsh 5½.

★★ **Balmacara,** IV40 8DH (059 986) 283 Fax: (059 986) 329

Privately-owned stone-built hotel at lochside. Superb mountain and sea views.
29 bedrs, 29 en suite, 2 ba; TV; tcf
dogs; P 60, coach; child facs; con 80
LD 9.45, bar meals only lunch
£ B&B £33–£39, B&B (double) £53–£65; L £3·65, D £16; [10% V]
cc Access, Amex, B'card/Visa, Diners; dep.

BANAVIE Highland (Inverness-shire).

Map 53C2
Pop 150. Fort William 3½, London 493, Edinburgh 136, Mallaig 40, Newtonmore 44, Oban 50.
Golf Fort William 18h.

★★★ **Moorings,** Fort William, PH3 7LY Corpach (0397) 772 797 Fax: (0397) 772 797
Modern family-run hotel in charming situation beside Caledonian Canal. De, Fr. Closed Xmas
21 bedrs, 21 en suite; annexe 3 bedrs, 3 en suite; TV; tcf
dogs, ns; P 60, coach; children over 10; con 70
LD 9.30, bistro only lunch
£ B&B £48–£65 (w/e £24), B&B (double) £56–£76; HB weekly £294–£364; L £7·90, D £17; WB £132 (HB); [5% V Oct–May]
cc Access, Amex, B'card/Visa, Diners; dep.

BANCHORY Grampian

(Kincardineshire). Map 55B3
Pop 5,320. Fettercairn 17, London 480, Aberdeen 18, Braemar 40, Edinburgh 105, Huntly 42, Stonehaven 16.
EC Thur. **Golf** Banchory 18h. **See** Bridge of Feugh, Crathes Castle 2 m E.
[i] Dee Street Car Park. (033 02) 2000

★★★★ H C R **Invery House,** Feughside, AB3 3NJ (0224) 321371 Tx: 73225 Fax: (0224) 311162
An attractive, well-modernised mansion, furnished in keeping with its country-house character, set in wooded grounds. Putting, tennis, fishing, billiards. Fr
17 bedrs, 17 en suite; annexe 10 bedrs, 10 en suite, TV, tcf
P 70, child facs
LD 9.45, bar meals only Sat & Sun lunch
£ B&B £33–£66, B&B (double) £38–£76; L £12·50, D £17·50
cc Access, Amex, B'card/Visa, Diners.

★★★ **Banchory Lodge,** Dee St, AB3 3HS (033 02) 2625 Fax: (033 02) 5019

Lovely riverside mansion, 16th century with later extensions, in own grounds. Fishing, sauna, pool. Fr. Open Feb–Dec 12.
23 bedrs, 23 en suite; TV; tcf
TV, dogs; P 50; child facs; con 30
LD 9.30
£ B&B £63·25, B&B (double) £92–£103·50; L £9·50, D £15; [10% V]
cc Amex, B'card/Visa, Diners; dep
(See advertisement on p. 554)

★★★ H C **Raemoir,** AB3 4ED (033 02) 4884 Tx: 73315 Fax: (033 02) 2171
Elegant Georgian stone-built mansion in quiet attractive grounds. Golf, tennis, fishing, sauna, solarium, gymnasium.
17 bedrs, 17 en suite, annexe 11 bedrs, 11 en suite; TV; tcf
TV, dogs, ns; P 200, coach; child facs; con 60
LD 9, bar meals Mon–Sat lunch
£ B&B £50–£75, B&B (double) £90–£100; L Sun £11·50, D £19·50; WB £95 (HB); [10% V]
cc Access, Amex, B'card/Visa, Diners.

★★★ **Tor-na-Coille,** Inchmarlo Rd, AB3 4AB (033 02) 2242 Fax: (033 02) 4012

Sc

Ballater (Grampian)

DARROCH LEARG HOTEL

BALLATER, GRAMPIAN AB35 5UX
Telephone and Fax: 03397 55443

The Darroch Learg, less than ten minutes walk from the centre of Ballater, sits high in five acres of grounds on the slopes of the Craigendarroch. The views over the golf course and River Dee to the Grampian mountains are superb.

The hotel has a relaxed atmosphere, with bedrooms individually decorated and equipped to a high standard. Predominantly fresh, local produce is served in the dining room, complemented by an interesting and varied wine list.

Banchory (Kincardineshire)

BANCHORY LODGE HOTEL

Banchory, Kincardineshire AB31 3HS
Telephone: (033 02) 2625

This former Georgian mansion is within easy reach of the centre of Banchory and 18 miles from Aberdeen. It overlooks the confluence of the River Feugh into the Dee and there is fishing on the hotel's own stretch of the river. The hotel has a leisured and hospitable atmosphere, whilst providing the guests with high standards of service, cuisine and comfort.

Barrhill (Ayrshire)

YOU CAN ONLY VISIT COUNTRY MANSIONS
FOR A FEW HOURS

HERE'S ONE WHERE YOU CAN STAY FOR AS LONG AS YOU LIKE

That's because we've transformed an Edwardian home into a luxury hotel, set in 83 acres of picturesque countryside. Facilities include a recently constructed 9 hole golf course, indoor pool, all weather tennis court, sauna, trimnasium and conference suite. Shooting, fishing and horse riding can be arranged.

RAC 4-Star, Egon Ronay Recommended

The Kildonan Hotel, Dept Z13, Barrhill, Ayrshire KA26 0PU
Tel. (0465) 82360 Fax: (0465) 82292

Fine granite-built Victorian residence on hillside on edge of town. Billiards, squash. Fr
24 bedrs, 24 en suite; TV; tcf
lift, dogs; P 250, coach; child facs; con 70
LD 9.45
£ B&B £44·50–£72·50 (w/e £49·50), B&B (double) £72·50–£85·50; L £5, D £16·50; WB £49·50; [10% V Oct–May]
cc Access, Amex, B'card/Visa, Diners.

★★ Burnett Arms, 25 High St, AB3 3TD (033 02) 4944 Tx: 739925
Fax: (0224) 744354
Traditional stone-built hotel standing on main street in town centre.
18 bedrs, 16 en suite, 2 ba; TV; tcf
TV, dogs; P 40, coach; child facs; con 150
LD 9
£ B&B £24–£28, B&B (double) £36–£44; HB weekly £210–£234; L £5, D £11; WB £62 (HB)
cc Access, Amex, B'card/Visa, Diners.

BANFF Grampian (Banffshire). Map 59B1
Pop 4,234. Huntly 20, London 532, Aberdeen 46, Craigellachie 36, Edinburgh 157, Elgin 33, Fraserburgh 23, Peterhead 35.
EC Wed. **Golf** Duff House Royal 18h. **See** Biggar Fountain, Mercat Cross, Duff House.
Collie Lodge. (026 12) 2419

★★★ Banff Springs, Golden Knowes Rd, AB4 2JE (026 12) 2881 Fax: (026 12) 5546
Modern 2-storey hotel on hillside on edge of town.
30 bedrs, 30 en suite; TV; tcf
dogs; P 120, coach; child facs; con 200
LD 9, bar meals only lunch
£ B&B £35–£40 (w/e £27·50), B&B (double) £55–£60; L £6·50, D £12·50; [10% V]
cc Access, Amex, B'card/Visa, Diners.

BARRHEAD Strathclyde (Renfrewshire). Map 46C2
Pop 20,000. East Kilbride 10, London 393, Glasgow 8, Irvine 18, Paisley 4.
EC Tue. **Golf** Fereneze 18h.

★★ Dalmeny Park, Lochlibo Rd, G78 1LE 041-881 9211
Extended modernised 19th century house in own grounds. Countryside views.
18 bedrs, 13 en suite, 4 ba; TV; tcf
dogs; P 100, coach; child facs; con 150

BARRHILL Strathclyde (Ayrshire). Map 42B3
Newton Stewart 18, London 385, Girvan 12, Glasgow 65, Stranraer 28.

★★★★ R Kildonan, KA26 0PU (046 582) 360 Fax: (046 582) 292
A splendid Edwardian mansion set in 83 acres of landscaped gardens and woodlands on A714. Indoor swimming pool, golf, tennis, fishing, squash, sauna, solarium, gymnasium, billiards. De
31 bedrs, 31 en suite; TV; tcf
lift, dogs, ns; P 70, coach; child facs; con 100
LD 9.30
£ B&B £75–£140, B&B (double) £105–£140; HB weekly £350–£500; L £13·50, D £21·95; WB £100; [5% V]
cc Access, Amex, B'card/Visa, Diners; dep.
(See advertisment on p. 554)

BATHGATE Lothian (West Lothian). Map 47C1
Pop 14,527. Lanark 19, London 387, M8 Motorway 2½, Edinburgh 18, Glasgow 25, Kincardine 15, Peebles 38, Stirling 22.
EC Wed. **MD** Fri. **Golf** Bathgate 18h.

★★★ Golden Circle, Blackburn Rd, EH48 2EL (0506) 53771 Tx: 72606

Modern two-storey purpose-built hotel near Edinburgh–Glasgow road.
75 bedrs, 75 en suite; TV; tcf
lift, dogs; P 100, coach; child facs; con 150

BEARSDEN Strathclyde (Dunbartonshire). Map 46B3
Glasgow 4, London 392, Dumbarton 10, Edinburgh 48, Gourock 22, Stirling 28.

★★ Burnbrae, Milngavie Rd, G61 3TA 041-942 5951

Purpose-built hotel on sloping ground with public rooms on first floor and bedrooms above. On A81. (BCB)
18 bedrs, 18 en suite; TV; tcf
ns; P 100, coach; child facs; con 200
LD 10
£ B&B £58–£60·50, B&B (double) £68; L £8·15, D £8·15; WB £27·50
cc Access, Amex, B'card/Visa, Diners.

BEATTOCK Dumfries & Galloway (Dumfriesshire). Map 43B4
Carlisle 39, London 333, Abington 19, Dumfries 19, Edinburgh 52, Glasgow 55, Langholm 32, Selkirk 36.
EC Wed. **Golf** Moffat 18h.

★★★ Auchen Castle, DG10 9SH (068 33) 407
Stone-built Victorian mansion in lovely grounds on a hillside with spectacular views. One mile north of town with access from A74. Fishing.
15 bedrs, 15 en suite; annexe 10 bedrs, 10 en suite; TV; tcf
dogs; P 35; child facs; con 40

★★ Beattock House, DG10 9QB (068 33) 402

Large, ornate country house amidst lawns and mature trees with river flowing through grounds. Fishing.
7 bedrs, 3 en suite, 2 ba; TV; tcf
TV, dogs; P 30, coach; child facs; con 25
LD 9.30
£ B&B £23·50, B&B (double) £45; L fr £7, D £14·50; WB £60 (2 nts HB)
cc Access, Amex, B'card/Visa, Diners; dep.

BEAULY Highland (Inverness-shire). Map 54A4
Pop 3,650. Inverness 11, London 539, Achnasheen 31, Dingwall 8½, Edinburgh 164, Glasgow 162, Invermoriston 26, Ullapool 48.
EC Thurs. **Golf** Muir of Ord 18h.

★★ Lovat Arms, Main Street, IV4 7BS (0463) 782313 Fax: (0463) 782313
Substantial, family-owned hotel in the main street of this small town. Some rooms have views of the Beauly Firth. Fr
22 bedrs, 22 en suite; TV, tcf
TV, dogs; P 15, coach; child facs
LD 9
£ B&B £24·75–£32·50, B&B (double) £41–£54; L , D £10; WB £55; [10% V Jan–May, Sep–Dec]
cc Access, B'Card/Visa; dep.

★★ Priory, The Square, IV4 7BX (0463) 782309 Fax: (0463) 782531

Small modern family-run hotel in main square beside Priory.
12 bedrs, 12 en suite; TV; tcf
dogs; coach; child facs
LD 9
£ B&B £26·95–£29·95, B&B (double) £47·50–£49·50; HB weekly £185–£235; L £5·50, D £9·50; WB £26·50 (HB); [10% V]
cc Access, Amex, B'card/Visa.

Chrialdon, Station Rd, IV4 7EH (0463) 782336. *Hotel.*
£ B&B £14–£18·50; HB weekly £185·50–£217
Heathmount, Station Rd, IV4 7EQ (0463) 782411. *Guest House.* Open Feb–Nov.
£ B&B £12–£12·50

Sc

BIGGAR Strathclyde (Lanarkshire). Map 50B2
Pop 1,931. Abington 12, London 363, Edinburgh 28, Glasgow 36, Kincardine 37, Lanark 13, Peebles 17.
EC Wed. **MD** Sat. **Golf** Biggar 18h. **See** Boghall Castle ruins, Old Church (1545), Cadger's Bridge, Gladstone Court Museum, Biggar Motte 12th cent.
ⓘ 155 High St. ☎(0899) 21066

★★★★ Shieldhill, Quothquan, ML12 6NA ☎(0899) 20035 Tx: 777308 Fax: (0899) 21092

Based on a 12th-century keep, an historic mansion, elegantly furnished. Fr
11 bedrs, 11 en suite; TV; tcf
ns; P 22; no children under 12; con 32
LD 9.30
£ B&B £81–£126, B&B (double) £91–£137; L £12, D £24; WB £61; [10% V]
cc Access, Amex, B'card/Visa, Diners; dep.

BIRNAM Tayside (Perthside). Map 54C1
Perth 14, London 430, Edinburgh 55, Glasgow 67, Dunkeld 1.

★★★ Birnam, PH8 0BQ ☎(035 02) 462 Tx: 57515 Fax: (03502) 8979

Large grey stone Victorian hotel in centre of village.
28 bedrs, 28 en suite; TV; tcf
lift, dogs; P 50, coach; child facs; con 50
LD 8.30, bar meals only lunch
£ B&B £39–£70, B&B (double) £60–£85; HB weekly £238; L £7·50, D £15–£16; WB £37 (HB); [10% V]
cc Access, Amex, B'card/Visa, Diners.

Waterbury, Dunkeld, PH8 0BG ☎Dunkeld (035 02) 324. *Guest House.*
£ B&B £12–£12·50; HB weekly £122·50–£129·50

BLACKWATERFOOT *See* Isle of Arran

BLAIRGOWRIE Tayside (Perthshire). Map 54C1
Pop 5,760. Perth 15, London 431, Aberfeldy 29, Braemar 34, Brechin 29, Dundee 18, Edinburgh 56, Forfar 20, Pitlochry 23.
EC Thur. **Golf** Rosemount 18h (2) & 9h. **See** Ardblair Castle, Newton Castle, Craighall Mansion.
ⓘ Wellmeadow. ☎(0250) 2960

★★ H C Altamount House, Coupar Angus Rd, PH10 6JN ☎(0250) 3512
Stone-built former private house in own grounds on outskirts of town. Closed 5 Jan–13 Feb.
7 bedrs, 7 en suite; TV; tcf
dogs; P 40, coach; con 20
LD 9, nr Sun dinner
£ B&B £28·50, B&B (double) £55; L £9·50, D £15·50
cc Access, B'card/Visa, dep.

★★ Angus, Wellmeadow, PH10 6NQ ☎(0250) 2838 Tx: 76526 Fax: (0250) 5289
Attractive, three-storied hotel, much extended and modernised, overlooking the Town Square and its gardens. Indoor swimming pool, fishing, squash, sauna, solarium, billiards. Fr
86 bedrs, 86 en suite; TV; tcf
lift, dogs; P 12, coach; child facs; con 200
LD 8.30
£ B&B £23–£30, B&B (double) £46–£60; HB weekly £215–£308; D £13·50; WB £66; [10% V]
cc Access, Amex, B'card/Visa, dep.

★★ Rosemount Golf, Golf Course Rd, PH10 6LJ ☎(0250) 2604

A 3-storey former private house with modern extensions in pleasant gardens. Fr
8 bedrs, 8 en suite; annexe 4 bedrs, 4 en suite; TV; tcf
P 60; child facs; con 60
LD 9.45, bar meals only lunch
£ B&B £27·50–£30, B&B (double) £45; HB weekly £198; D £11·50
cc Access, B'card/Visa; dep.

Rosebank House (Highly Acclaimed), Balmoral Rd, PH10 7AF ☎(0250) 2912. *Guest House.* Open Jan–Oct.
£ B&B £20–£22; HB weekly £172–£188

Glenshieling, Hatton Rd, PH10 7HZ ☎(0250) 4605. *Guest House.*
£ B&B £15·85–£19·80; HB weekly £170–£230

Ivy Bank House, Boat Brae, Rattray, PH10 7BH ☎(0250) 3056.
£ B&B £14·50

BOAT OF GARTEN Highland (Inverness-shire). Map 54B3
Pop 550. Aviemore 6, London 504, Carrbridge 4½, Edinburgh 129, Glasgow 141, Grantown-on-Spey 9, Kingussie 18.
EC Thur. **Golf** Boat of Garten 18h. **See** Loch Garten (Osprey nest), Steam Railway.
ⓘ Boat Hotel Car Park. ☎(047 983) 307

★★★ The Boat, PH24 3BH ☎(047 983) 258 Tx: 9401 3436 Fax: (047 983) 414

Substantial stone-built fully modernised hotel. Fishing.
32 bedrs, 32 en suite; TV; tcf
dogs, ns; P 30, coach; child facs

Moorfield House (Acclaimed), Deshar Rd, PH24 3BN ☎(047 983) 646. *Hotel.* Closed Nov.
£ B&B £14–£20; HB weekly £182–£224

BONAR BRIDGE Highland (Sutherland). Map 58A2
Pop 600. Alness 18, London 566, Edinburgh 191, Glasgow 198, Helmsdale 38, Lairg 10, Ullapool 47.
EC Wed. **Golf** Bonar Bridge and Ardgay 12h. **See** Stone Age Burial Cairns.
ⓘ ☎(086 32) 333

★★ Bridge, Ardgay, IV24 3EB ☎(086 32) 204

Stone-built village centre hotel with "olde worlde" bar. Fine views.

BO'NESS Central (West Lothian). Map 47B1
Pop 14,641. Abington 43, London 394, Dunfermline 17, Edinburgh 19, Glasgow 13, Kincardine 11, Kirkcaldy 25, Stirling 18.
EC Wed. **Golf** West Lothian 18h. **See** Kinneil House, Railway Museum.

Kinglass, Borrowstoun Rd, EH51 9RP ☎(0506) 822861. *Farm.*

BOTHWELL Strathclyde (Lanarkshire). Map 46C4
Pop 5,713. M74 Motorway ½, Hamilton 2, London 380, East Kilbride 6½, Glasgow 10.
MD Wed. **Golf** Bothwell Castle 18h. **See** 14th cent Church & Castle.

★★★ Bothwell Bridge, 89 Main St, G71 8LN ☎(0698) 852246 Tx: 776838
Red sandstone building close to centre of Bothwell and only 1½ miles from M 74.
De, Fr, It
80 bedrs, 80 en suite; TV; tcf
P 90, coach; child facs; con 300
LD 10.45
£ B&B £40–£55, B&B (double) £50–£65; L £5·50, D £15·50; [10% V w/e]
cc Access, Amex, B'card/Visa, Diners.

★★ **Silvertrees,** Silverwells Cres, G71 8DP ☎(0698) 852311 Fax: (0698) 852311

Attractive 19th century building with modern annexes; in quiet residential area.
🛏 7 bedrs, 7 en suite; annexe 19 bedrs, 19 en suite; TV; tcf
🏠 dogs; P 100, coach; child facs; con 200
✕ LD 8.45, high tea only Sun
£ B&B £52·50, B&B (double) £70–£80; L £9, D £11·50
cc Access, Amex, B'card/Visa, Diners.
(*See advertisement on p. 559*)

BOWMORE *See* Isle of Islay

BRAEMAR Grampian (Aberdeenshire). Map 54C3
Pop 400. Perth 47, London 463, Aberdeen 58, Blairgowrie 34, Edinburgh 88, Glasgow 104, Grantown-on-Spey 46, Huntley 57.
EC Thur. **Golf** Braemar 18h. **See** Balmoral Castle grounds 7 m NE, Crathie Church 7 m ENE, Braemar Castle.
ℹ Balnellan Rd. ☎(033 97) 41600

Callater Lodge, 9 Glenshee Rd, AB3 5YQ ☎(033 97) 41275. *Hotel.*

BRIDGE OF ALLAN Central (Stirlingshire). Map 50A3
Pop 4,314. M9 (jn 11) 2, Stirling 3, London 398, Crieff 19, Dunfermline 21, Edinburgh 37, Glasgow 29, Lochearnhead 26, Perth 31.
EC Wed. **Golf** Bridge of Allan 9h. **See** Wallace Monument.

★★★ **Royal,** Henderson St, FK9 4HL ☎(0786) 832284 Fax: (0786) 834377

Completely modernised, traditional style 3-storey stone-built hotel in town centre.
🛏 32 bedrs, 32 en suite; TV; tcf
🏠 lift, dogs; P 60, coach; child facs; con 150
✕ LD 9.30, bar meals only Sat lunch
£ B&B £46–£55, B&B (double) £69–£80; L £9·60, D £15·25; WB £35 (HB)
cc Access, Amex, B'card/Visa, Diners.

> Please tell the manager if you chose your hotel through an advertisement in the guide.

BRIDGE OF CALLY Tayside (Perthshire). Map 54C1
Pop 202. Blairgowrie 5½, London 437, Braemar 29, Edinburgh 62, Pitlochry 18.
EC Thur. **Golf** Blairgowrie 18h (2) & 9h.

★★ **Bridge of Cally,** PH10 7JJ ☎(025 086) 231

Traditional 2-storey Victorian hotel, in attractive setting in hills. Fishing. Closed Nov.
🛏 9 bedrs, 6 en suite, 2 ba
🏠 TV, dogs; P 40, no children under 12
✕ LD 8.45, bar meals only lunch
£ B&B £22–£23·50, B&B (double) £42–£45; HB weekly £210–£225; D £12
cc Access, B'card/Visa, Diners, dep.

BRIDGE OF EARN Tayside Map 50B4
M 90 (jn 9) 1, London 412, Edinburgh 38, Glasgow 57, Perth 4, St Andrews 29, Stirling 34

Rockdale, Dunning St, PH2 9AA ☎(0738) 812281. *Guest House.*
£ B&B £14; HB weekly £133–£152·95

BROADFORD *See* Isle of Skye

BRODICK *See* Isle of Arran

BRORA Highland (Sutherland). Map 58B2
Pop 1,800. Golspie 5, London 592, Brora Bridge 27, Edinburgh 217, Glasgow 224, Helmsdale 11, Lairg 24.
EC Wed. **Golf** Brora 18h. **See** Wool Mills.

★★★ **Links,** KW9 6QS ☎(0408) 21225 Tx: 75242 ♿

Modernised hotel overlooking sandy beach. Particularly attractive public rooms. Golf, fishing. Fr. Open Feb–24 Dec
🛏 22 bedrs, 22 en suite, TV; tcf
🏠 dogs, ns; P 50, coach; child facs; con 120
✕ LD 9, bar meals only lunch
£ B&B £39–£43, B&B (double) £72–£80; HB weekly £295–£330; L £6·50, D £15; WB £48–£53 (HB); [10% V]
cc Access, Amex, B'card/Visa, Diners; dep.

★★★ **Royal Marine,** KW9 6QS ☎(0408) 21252 Tx: 76165 Fax: (08212) 446

Former stately house in own grounds close to golf course. Indoor swimming pool, putting, fishing, sauna, billiards.
🛏 11 bedrs, 11 en suite; TV; tcf
🏠 TV, dogs; P 40, U 6 coach; child facs; con 100
✕ LD 9
£ B&B £45–£65, B&B (double) £70–£95; L £8·50, D £16; WB £55
cc Access, Amex, B'card/Visa, Diners; dep.

BRUICHLADDICH *See* Isle of Islay

BUCKIE Grampian (Banffshire). Map 59A1
Pop 7,950. Keith 12, London 534, Banff 19, Craigellachie 18, Edinburgh 159, Elgin 16, Glasgow 176, Huntly 22.
EC Wed. **Golf** Strathlene 18h. **See** Church (twin towers).
ℹ High St ☎(0542) 34853

★★ **Cluny,** 2 High St, AB5 1AL ☎(0542) 32922

A 3-storey stone-built town centre hotel in town square. Closed Jan.
🛏 10 bedrs, 10 en suite; annexe 6 bedrs, 4 en suite; TV; tcf
🏠 dogs; P 16, coach; child facs; con 140
✕ LD 8, bar meals only Sun lunch
£ B&B £19–£23, B&B (double) £34–£39; HB weekly £196; L £5, WB £17; [10% V]
cc Access, Amex, B'card/Visa, Diners.

BUSBY Strathclyde (Lanarkshire). Map 46C3
East Kilbride 4, London 387, Abington 35, Edinburgh 45, Glasgow 5½, Kilmarnock 18, Lanark 24, Paisley 8, Stirling 32.

★★ **Busby,** Field Rd, G76 8RX ☎041-644 2661
Small hotel located in an attractive setting.
🛏 14 bedrs, 14 en suite; TV; tcf
🏠 lift, dogs; P 40, coach; child facs; con 100

Sc

BUTE, ISLE OF *See* Isle of Bute

CALLANDER Central (Perthshire). Map 50A4
Pop 1,768. M9 (jn 11) 10, Doune 7½, London 413, Arrochar 46, Dumbarton 32, Dunfermline 34, Edinburgh 50, Glasgow 33, Lochearnhead 13, Perth 34, Stirling 16.
EC Wed. **Golf** Callander Municipal 9h. **See** The Trossachs, Falls of Bracklinn.
ℹ Ancaster Sq. ☎(0877) 30342

♣ ★★★ **Roman Camp,** off Main St, FK17 8BG ☎(0877) 30003 Tx: 9312132123 Fax: (0877) 31533 ♿

17th century stone-built former hunting lodge set in beautiful gardens. Fishing.
🛏 14 bedrs, 14 en suite, TV; tcf
🏨 dogs, ns; P 30; child facs; con 25
✕ LD 9
£ B&B £65–£80, B&B (double) £75–£110; HB weekly £819–£1039·50; L £15, D £25
cc Access, Amex, B'card/Visa, Diners; dep.

★★ **Dalgair House,** Main St, FK17 8BQ ☎(0877) 30283
Small hotel, above a popular restaurant in town. ⚒ Da, De, Es, No, Sw
🛏 9 bedrs, 9 en suite; TV; tcf
🏨 dogs; P 20, coach;
✕ LD 9.30
£ B&B £38, B&B (double) £48; L £4·50, D £9·50; [10% V Jan–May, Nov]
cc Access, Amex, B'card/Visa, Diners; dep.

★★ **Glenorchy,** Leny Rd, FK17 8AL ☎(0877) 30329
Stone-built villa with an extension in own grounds beside main road to west of town. Closed Jan
🛏 9 bedrs, 5 en suite, 1 ba; annexe 2 bedrs, 2 en suite; TV; tcf
🏨 P 16, child facs
✕ LD 9
£ B&B £16–£38, B&B (double) £32–£52; [10% V]
cc Access, B'card/Visa; dep.
(*See advertisement on p. 559*)

★ **H** **C** **R** **Lubnaig,** Leny Feus, FK17 8AS ☎(0877) 30376
In own grounds on edge of town, a 2-storey stone-built villa. Open Easter–Oct.
🛏 8 bedrs, 8 en suite, annexe 2 bedrs, 2 en suite; tcf
🏨 TV, dogs, ns; P 14, no children under 7
✕ LD 7, nr lunch. Resid & Rest lic
£ B&B & dinner £39–£46·50, B&B (double) & dinner £64–£72; HB weekly £203–£224; D £12; dep.

Arden House (Acclaimed), Bracklinn Rd, FK17 8EQ ☎(0877) 30235. *Guest House.* Open Feb–Nov.
£ B&B £12–£16; HB weekly £120–£145
Highland House (Acclaimed), South Church St, FK17 8BN ☎(0877) 30269. *Hotel.* Open Mar–Nov and Xmas/New Year
£ B&B £15–£27·50; HB weekly £167–£210

Rock Villa (Acclaimed), 1 Bracklinn Rd, FK17 8EH ☎(0877) 30331. *Guest House* open Mar–Oct
£ B&B £14

Annfield House, 18 North Church St, FK17 8EG ☎(0877) 30204.
Riverview House, Leny Rd, FK17 8AL ☎(0877) 30635. *Private Hotel.*

CAMPBELTOWN Strathclyde (Argyll). Map 48C1
Pop 5,500. Tarbert 26, London 517, Edinburgh 171, Glasgow 130, Lochgilphead 51.
EC Wed. **MD** Mon. **Golf** Machrihanish 18h.
ℹ ☎(0586) 52056

★★ **Royal,** Main St, PA28 6AG ☎(0586) 52017
Fine red sandstone building prominently situated at pierhead. Views over loch.
🛏 16 bedrs, 12 en suite, 2 ba; TV; tcf
🏨 lift, TV, dogs; coach; child facs

★★ **R** **Seafield,** Kilkerran Rd, PA28 6JL ☎(0586) 54385
Small traditional hotel looking out over the loch across the road.
🛏 3 bedrs, 3 en suite, 1 ba; annexe 6 bedrs, 6 en suite; TV; tcf
🏨 dogs; P 11; child facs
✕ LD 9. Restrict lic
£ B&B £27·50–£30, B&B (double) £44–£48; L £6·50, D £10·95; [10% V w/e Oct–Easter]
cc Access, B'card/Visa; dep

★ **Ardshiel,** Kilkerran Rd, PA28 6JL ☎(0586) 52133
Former large private Victorian house built by local whisky baron.
🛏 11 bedrs, 4 en suite, 1 ba; TV; tcf
🏨 dogs; P 20, coach; child facs; con 60
✕ LD 8.30
£ B&B £20–£30, B&B (double) £40–£50; L £5, D £9; WB £100, (HB 3 nts); [5% V]
cc Access, Amex, B'card/Visa, Diners.

CANONBIE Dumfries & Galloway (Dumfriesshire). Map 43C3
Pop 1,350. Carlisle 14, London 308, Edinburgh 76, Glasgow 88, Dumfries 30, Langholm 6.
Golf Carlisle 18h & Langholm 18h.

♠♠ **Cross Keys,** DG14 03Y ☎(054 15) 382
Old coaching inn, with modern restaurant. Set in a village.

CARDROSS Strathclyde. Map 46A1
Dumbarton 4, London 406, Crianlarich 39, Edinburgh 63, Glasgow 18, Helensburgh 5.

Kirkton House (Highly Acclaimed), Darleith Rd, G82 5EZ (0389) 841 951
££ B&B £20–£29·50

CARFRAEMILL Borders (Berwickshire). Map 51A2
Lauder 4, London 352, Berwick-upon-Tweed 35, Coldstream 25, Edinburgh 23, Glasgow 65, Haddington 17, Kelso 21.
Golf Lauder 9h.

★★ **Carfraemill,** Oxton by Lauder, TD2 6RA ☎(057 85) 200 Tx: 336587
Two-storey stone-built coaching inn at junction of A68/A697. In rural area.
🛏 11 bedrs, 2 en suite, 3 ba; TV; tcf
🏨 dogs; P 60, U 1, coach; child facs; con 100

CARNOUSTIE Tayside (Angus). Map 55B1
Pop 9,217. Dundee 11, London 439, Brechin 20, Edinburgh 65, Forfar 14, Montrose 21.
EC Tue. **Golf** Carnoustie 18h.
ℹ 24 High St. ☎(0241) 52258

★★ **Glencoe,** Links Parade, DD7 7JF ☎(0241) 53273. Closed New Year

Overlooking golf course and sea, a former villa with modern extensions. ⚒ Fr
🛏 11 bedrs, 8 en suite, 3 ba; TV
🏨 TV, dogs; P 10; child facs
✕ LD 9, bar meals only lunch
£ B&B £19·50, B&B (double) £46; HB weekly £231; L £7·50 D £10·50
cc Access, Amex, B'card/Visa, Diners.

CARRBRIDGE Highland (Inverness-shire). Map 54B4
Pop 533. Aviemore 7, London 506, Edinburgh 131, Elgin 41, Grantown-on-Spey 10, Inverness 24, Kingussie 19.
EC Thurs. **Golf** Carrbridge 9h.
ℹ Main St. ☎(047 984) 630

Fairwinds (Acclaimed), PH23 3AA ☎(047 984) 240. *Hotel.* Closed 2 Nov–mid Dec.
£ B&B £20–£21, HB weekly £180–£187

CASTLE DOUGLAS Dumfries & Galloway (Kirkcudbrightshire). Map 43A3
Pop 3,500. Crocketford 8½, London 344, Dumfries 18, Edinburgh 89, Gatehouse-of-Fleet 14, Glasgow 82, New Galloway 14.
EC Thur. **MD** Tue. **Golf** Castle Douglas 9h.
See 13th cent Threave Castle ruins 1½ m W, Threave Estate Gardens 1½ m SW.
ℹ Markethill. ☎(0556) 2611

★★ **Douglas Arms,** King St, DG7 1DB ☎(0556) 2231

Large 200-year-old coaching house in town centre. Fully modernised.
🛏 22 bedrs, 15 en suite, 3 ba; TV; tcf
🏨 dogs, ns; P 6, G 12, coach; child facs; con 100
✕ LD 9, bar meals only lunch

Bothwell (Strathclyde)

Callander (Perthshire)

Castle Douglas (Kirkcudbrightshire)

Sc

Dingwall (Ross-shire)

Dolphinton (Strathclyde)

£ B&B fr £20, B&B (double) fr £40; WB [10% V]
cc Access, B'card/Visa.

♣♣ ★★ **Urr Valley** (formerly Ernespie House), Ernespie Rd, DG7 3JG ☎ (0556) 2188 Fax: (0556) 2188
Red sandstone country house set amongst rolling hills ½ mile off A75.
🛏 14 bedrs, 12 en suite, 2 ba; TV; tcf
🏨 dogs; P 100, coach; child facs; con 240
(*See advertisement on p. 559*)

★★ **Imperial,** King St, DG7 1AA ☎ (0556) 2086

2-storey stone-built hotel in the Scottish style. On main street. ⚒ Fr
🛏 13 bedrs, 9 en suite, 2 ba; TV; tcf
🏨 dogs, ns; P 15, G 10, coach; child facs; con 45
✕ LD 8
£ B&B £18·50–£23·50, B&B (double) £34–£42; HB weekly £161–£189; L £3·30, D £5·25; WB £22; [10% V]
cc Access, B'card/Visa; dep.

CLARENCEFIELD Dumfries & Galloway. Map 43B3
Carlisle 21, London 317, Dumfries 10, Moffat 23, Edinburgh 61, Glasgow 63.

Comlongon Castle (Acclaimed), nr Annan, DG1 4NA ☎ (0387) 87283.
Hotel. Fishing. Open Mar–Nov.
£ B&B £27

CLYDEBANK Strathclyde. Map 46B3
Glasgow 5, London 393, Dunbarton 8, Edinburgh 50, Paisley 8.

★★★ **Patio,** 1 South Av, Clydebank Business Park, G81 2RW ☎ 041-951 1133 Fax: 041-952 3713 ♿

New hotel built round a central atrium, situated in Business Park. ⚒ Fr, It
🛏 80 bedrs, 80 en suite; TV; tcf
🏨 lift, dogs, ns; P100, child facs; con 150
✕ LD 10
£ B&B £57 (w/e £29·50), B&B (double) £74·50; L £9·75, D £10·75
cc Access, Amex, B'card/Visa, Diners.

COATBRIDGE Strathclyde (Lanarkshire). Map 46B4
Pop 48,301. M73 (jn 2) 3, Motherwell 6, London 384, Edinburgh 35, Glasgow 9½, Kincardine 22, Lanark 19, Stirling 20.
EC Wed. **Golf** Drumpellier 18h.

★★★ **Coatbridge,** Glasgow Rd, ML5 1EL ☎ (0236) 24392

Purpose-built hotel west of town. Easy access to A74 and Glasgow.

COLLISTON Tayside (Angus). Map 55B1
Arbroath 3½, London 449, Brechin 11, Edinburgh 74, Forfar 12, Glasgow 98.

♣♣ ★★★ **Letham Grange,** Arbroath DD11 4RL ☎ Gowanbank (024 189) 373 Fax: (024 189) 414

Imposing country house in extensive grounds. Golf, putting.
🛏 20 bedrs, 18 en suite, 1 ba; TV; tcf
🏨 P 150, coach; child facs; con 200
✕ LD 9.30
£ B&B £57–£67, B&B (double) £88–£135; L £9·50, D £16
cc Access, Amex, B'card/Visa, Diners; dep.

COLMONELL Strathclyde (Ayrshire). Map 42B3
Newton Stewart 25, London 392, Ayr 30, Edinburgh 104

★ **Boar's Head,** Main St, KA26 0RY ☎ (0468 588) 272

Attractive stone building at west end of Ayrshire hill village. ⚒ De, Es, It, Ru
🛏 6 bedrs, (1 sh), 2 ba; tcf
🏨 TV, dogs; coach; child facs
✕ LD 10
£ B&B £15–£16, B&B (double) £26–£27; L £5; D £8; WB £36

COMRIE Tayside (Perthshire). Map 50A4
Pop 1,406. Dunblane 17, London 418, Crieff 6½, Edinburgh 53, Glasgow 58, Lochearnhead 12, Stirling 23.
EC Wed. **Golf** Comrie 9h.

★★ **Comrie,** Drummond St, PH6 2DY ☎ (0764) 70239
Detached villa with later extensions. At end of main village street. Open Apr–Oct.
🛏 3 bedrs, 3 en suite, 2 ba; annexe 2 bedrs, 2 en suite; TV; tcf
🏨 dogs; P 24; no children under 5

CONNEL Strathclyde (Argyll). Map 53B1
Pop 250. Taynuilt 6½, London 473, Ballachulish 33, Dalmally 19, Edinburgh 114, Glasgow 85, Inveraray 33, Oban 5.
EC Wed. **Golf** Glencruitten 18h.

★★ **Falls of Lora,** PA37 1PB ☎ (063 171) 483 Fax: (063 171) 694

19th century building; elevated situation affords fine mountain and sea views. ⚒ Fr. Closed Xmas/New Year
🛏 30 bedrs, 30 en suite, 2 ba
🏨 TV, dogs, ns; P 40, G 9; child facs; con 50
✕ LD 8, bar meals only lunch
£ B&B £24·50–£47·50, B&B (double) £35–£91; L £6·75, D £14·50; [10% V]
cc Access, Amex, B'card/Visa, Diners; dep.
(*See advertisement on p. 602*)

Ards House (Acclaimed), PA37 1PT ☎ (063 171) 255. Open Mar–Nov.
£ B&B £20

Loch Etive (Acclaimed), PA37 1PH ☎ (063 171) 400. *Hotel.* Open Easter, May–Oct.
£ B&B £19·75–£22·25; HB weekly £164–£179·55

CONTIN Highland (Ross & Cromarty). Map 58A1
Pop 1,129. Muir of Ord 6, London 546, Achnasheen 22, Beauly 9, Dingwall 7½, Edinburgh 171, Glasgow 175, Ullapool 40.
EC Thur. **Golf** Strathpeffer 18h. **See** Falls of Rogie, Shell Shop, Forest Walk, Church.

♣♣ ★★ **Craigdarroch Lodge,** Strathpeffer, IV14 9EH ☎ Strathpeffer (0997) 21265 ♿

A former shooting lodge set in 12 acres of wooded grounds in a sheltered valley. Indoor swimming pool, tennis, fishing, sauna, solarium, billiards. ⚒ Fr. Open Mar–Dec

 EC *early closing* **MD** *market day* ♣♣ *country house hotel* *ns (NS) no smoking areas* *tcf tea/coffee facilities*

17 bedrs, 14 en suite, 1 ba; TV; tcf
dogs; P30, coach; child facs
LD 9.30, bar meals only lunch
£ B&B £21–£38, B&B (double) £42–£56; D £15·50; WB £25; [10% v Nov–Apr]
cc Amex;dep.

Coul House, IV14 9EY Strathpeffer (0997) 21487 *Hotel.*
£ B&B £28·50–£43·50; HB weekly £231–£329

CRAIGELLACHIE Grampian. Map 55A4

Grantown-on-Spey 26, London 534, Dufftown 5½, Edinburgh 157, Elgin 16, Glasgow 173.

★★★ **Craigellachie House,** AB3 9SS (0340) 881 204 Fax: (0340) 881253

Large, white-painted hotel, recently refurbished in country-house style. In own grounds next to A95. Sauna, solarium, gymnasium, snooker Fr, Da
30 bedrs, 30 en suite; TV; tcf
dogs; P 50, child facs; con 50
LD 9.30
£ B&B £53–£70, B&B (double) £77–£99; L £13·50, D £19·50; [10% V Nov–Feb]
cc Access, Amex, B'card/Visa, Diners.

CRAIGHOUSE *See* Isle of Jura

CRAIGNURE *See* Isle of Mull

CRAIL Fife. Map 51A4

Pop 1,200. Largo 14, London 426, Edinburgh 51, Glasgow 78, Kinross 36, Kirkcaldy 26, Perth 39, St Andrews 10.
EC Wed. **Golf** Balcomie Links 18h.
Museum, Marketgate (0333) 50869

★ **Croma,** 33 Nethergate Rd, KY10 3TU (0333) 50239

Traditional style stone-built hotel fronting on to village street. Open Apr–Nov.
8 bedrs, 5 en suite, 1 ba; TV; tcf
TV, dogs; child facs
LD 10
£ B&B £12·60–£17, B&B (double) £25–£34; HB weekly £120–£140; L £10, D £10; [5% V Apr, Sep, Oct]

Caiplie House, 53 High St, KY10 3RA (0333) 50564. *Guest House.* Open Mar–Oct.
£ B&B £11·50–£14·50; HB weekly £143·50–£164·50

CRAWFORD Strathclyde (Lanarkshire). Map 43B4

Pop 328. Beattock 15, London 348, Abington 4, Edinburgh 44, Glasgow 40.
EC Wed. **Golf** Leadhills 9h. **See** Crawford Castle, Roman Forts & Cairns.

Field End, The Loaning, ML12 6TN (086 42) 276. *Guest House.*
£ B&B £12.

CREETOWN Dumfries & Galloway (Kirkcudbrightshire). Map 42C3

Gatehouse of Fleet 12, London 375, Edinburgh 111, Girvan 36, Glasgow 91, New Galloway 25, Stranraer 32.

★★ **Ellangowan,** DG8 7JF (067 182) 201
Striking 3-storey late Victorian hotel built of granite. In main street. Fishing.
6 bedrs, 3 en suite, 1 ba; TV; tcf
TV; P 2, G 8, coach; child facs; con 40

CRIANLARICH Central (Perthshire). Map 49B4

Tarbet 17, Glasgow 52, London 437, Fort William 51, Lochearnhead 16, Oban 40.

Portnellan (Highly Acclaimed) FK208QS (083 83) 284. *Guest House. Fishing.*

Glenardran, FK20 8QS (083 83) 236. *Guest House.*
£ B&B £16·50; HB weekly £185

CRIEFF Tayside (Perthshire). Map 50B4

Pop 5,100. Dunblane 15, London 416, Aberfeldy 23, Dunfermline 30, Edinburgh 47, Glasgow 47, Kinross 26, Kincardine 30, Lochearnhead 19, Perth 18, Pitlochry 35, Stirling 21.
EC Wed. **Golf** Crieff 18h & 9h. **See** 10th cent Market Cross, Old Stocks, 17th cent Drummond Cross, Glass Works, Pottery, Drummond Castle Gardens 2½ m SW. Glenturret Distillery (conducted tours).
High St. (0764) 2578

★★ **Crieff,** 45 East High St, PH7 3JA (0764) 2632 Tx: 779980 Fax: (0786) 50034
An attractive-looking hotel well situated near town centre. Sauna, solarium, gymnasium.
8 bedrs, 8 en suite; TV; tcf
dogs; P 9, coach; child facs; con 100
LD 8, bar meals only lunch
£ B&B £22·75–£24·75, B&B (double) £42·50–£46·50; WB £32 (HB); [10% V]
cc Access, Amex, B'card/Visa; dep.

★★ **H** **Cultoquey House,** PH7 3NE (0764) 3253
Fine 2-storey stone-built late Georgian house set in 6 acres of grounds. Putting, tennis, fishing, riding, billiards. Closed Feb–Mar.
12 bedrs, 10 en suite, 1 ba; TV; tcf
dogs, ns; P 50; child facs

★★ **Locke's Acre,** Comrie Rd, PH7 4BP (0764) 2526
Small hotel set in its own grounds with magnificent views.
7 bedrs, 4 en suite, 2 ba; TV; tcf
ns; P 25; child facs
LD 8.45
£ B&B £30–£36, B&B (double) £40–£52; L £16·50, D £16·50; WB £32
cc Access, B'card/Visa; dep.

★★ **H** **R** **Murray Park,** Connaught Terr, PH7 3DJ (0764) 3731 Fax: (0764) 5311
Former private villa, built of stone, set in small grounds. Fr
13 bedrs, 13 en suite; TV; tcf
dogs; P 50; child facs; con 30
LD 9.30
£ B&B £35·75–£36·75, B&B (double) £53–£58; L £9·50, D £16·95; [10% V]
cc Access, Amex, B'card/Visa

★ **H** **Gwydyr House,** Comrie Rd, PH7 4BP (0764) 3277
Former private residence on edge of town. Pleasant views. Fr. Open Easter–Oct.
10 bedrs, 3 ba; TV; tcf
TV, dogs; P 15, coach; child facs
LD 8, bar meals only lunch. Resid & Rest lic
£ B&B £12·25–£14·50, B&B (double) £24·50–£29; HB weekly £145·25; L £4·30, D £8·50; [10% V]

Keppoch House (Acclaimed), Perth Rd (0764) 4341. Private Hotel. Closed Jan

---

Heatherville, 29 Burrell St, PH7 4DT (0764) 2825. *Guest House.*
Leven House, Comrie Rd, PH7 4BA (0764) 2529
£ B&B £14–£20; HB weekly £150–£190
Sydney Villa, 67 Burrell St, PH7 4DG (0764) 2757. *Guest House.* Closed Jan
£ B&B £12

CRINAN Strathclyde (Argyll). Map 48C3

Pop 70. Lochgilphead 6½, London 475, Edinburgh 128, Glasgow 87, Tarbert 20, Inveraray 31, Oban 34.
EC Sat. **Golf** Lochgilphead 9h.

★★★ **R** **Crinan,** PA31 8SR (054 683) 261 Fax: (054 683) 292

Charming white building overlooking canal and enjoying good views. Fr. Closed Xmas
22 bedrs, 22 en suite, 4 sh; TV
lift, dogs; P22, coach, child facs; con 50
LD 9, bar meals only lunch
£ B&B £55, B&B (double) £85; D £23·50–£35; [10% V Oct–Apr]
cc Access, B'card/Visa; dep.

CROCKET FORD Dumfries & Galloway (Kirkcudbrightshire). Map 43A3

Pop 100. Dumfries 9, London 336, Edinburgh 80, Gatehouse of Fleet 23, Glasgow 82, New Galloway 15.
EC Thur. **Golf** Castle Douglas 9h.

★★ **Galloway Arms,** Stranraer Rd, DG2 8KA (055 669) 240
Carefully modernised 16th-century inn retaining its 'olde-worlde' charm. Putting, snooker.

Sc

CROMARTY Highland (Ross & Cromarty). Map 58B1
Fortrose 9, London 550, Beauly 25, Dingwall 19, Edinburgh 175, Inverness 22.
Golf Fortrose & Rosemarkie 18h.

★★ Royal, Marine Ter, IV11 8YN ☎(038 17) 217
Traditional stone-built hotel in pleasant seafront setting. Good views. Billiards.
🛏 10 bedrs, 10 en suite; TV; tcf
🏠 TV, dogs; P 20, G 3, U 3, coach; child facs; con 40
✕ LD 8, nr Sun dinner
£ B&B £22, B&B (double) £44; L £7·75, D £13·95; [10% V Nov–Apr]
cc Access, Amex, B'card/Visa

CROSSMICHAEL Dumfries & Galloway (Kirkcudbrightshire). Map 43A3
Pop 440. Crocketford 9, London 345, Dumfries 19, Edinburgh 89, Gatehouse of Fleet 18, Glasgow 78, New Galloway 10.
Golf Castle Douglas 9h.

★★ Culgruff House, DG7 3BB ☎(055 667) 230

Prominent distinguished stone building in quiet setting above small village. Restricted Oct–Easter.
🛏 15 bedrs, 4 en suite, 4 ba; TV
🏠 TV, dogs, ns; P 50, U 8 (70p), coach; child facs; con 90
✕ LD 7.30
£ B&B £13–£15, B&B (double) £23–£34; L £4·20, D £11; [10% V]
cc Access, Amex, B'card/Visa, Diners.

CULLEN Grampian (Banffshire). Map 59A1
Pop 1,300. Keith 12, London 534, Banff 13, Craigellachie 28, Edinburgh 159, Elgin 21, Glasgow 177, Huntly 23.
EC Wed. **Golf** Cullen 18h. **See** Mercat Cross, Church, Deskford Church 3 m S.
ℹ 20 Seafield St. ☎(0542) 40757

★★★ Seafield Arms, Seafield St, AB5 2SG ☎(0542) 40791
Early 19th century stone-built former coaching inn on main street.
🛏 24 bedrs, 21 en suite, (1 sh), 2 ba; TV; tcf
🏠 TV, dogs; P 28, coach; child facs; con 25

★★ Cullen Bay, AB5 2XA ☎(0542) 40432
Fax: (0542) 40900

Long 2-storey hillside building above main road—fine sea views.
🛏 17 bedrs, 4 en suite, (5 sh), 3 ba; TV; tcf
🏠 TV, dogs; P 150, G 6, coach; child facs; con 200
✕ LD 9
£ B&B £15·50–£24·50, B&B (double) £31–£49; L £6·50, D £9·50; [5% V Oct–Jun]
cc Access, Amex, B'card/Visa, Diners; dep.

Bayview (Highly Acclaimed), 57 Seafield St, AB5 2SU ☎(0542) 41031. *Hotel.* Closed Nov
£ B&B £24–£30; HB weekly £274.

CUMNOCK Strathclyde (Ayrshire). Map 49C1
Pop 9,616. New Cumnock 6, London 370, Ayr 15, Dalmellington 13, Edinburgh 59, Glasgow 33, Kilmarnock 15, Lanark 31.
EC Wed. **MD** Fri. **Golf** Ballochmyle, Mauchline 18h. **See** Mercat Cross (1703), Peden Monument, Home of Kier Hardie.
ℹ Glaisnock St. ☎(0290) 23058

★★ Dumfries Arms, 54 Glaisnock St, KA18 1BY ☎(0290) 20282
Three-storey, grey stone hotel, pleasantly refurbished.
🛏 8 bedrs, 6 en suite, 1 ba; TV; tcf
🏠 dogs; P 40, coach; child facs; con 60
✕ LD 9
£ B&B £18–£28, B&B (double) £36–£42; HB weekly £140–£252; L £4, D £11·50; [10% V]
cc Access, Amex, B'card/Visa; dep.

★★ Royal, 1 Glaisnock St, KA18 1BP ☎(0290) 20822

Centrally situated Victorian building constructed of warm red sandstone. ⚒ Fr
🛏 11 bedrs, 3 en suite, 3 ba; TV; tcf
🏠 TV, dogs; P 10, coach; child facs
✕ LD 9
£ B&B £20–£22, B&B (double) £40–£44; L £6, D £10; [5% V w/d]
cc Access, B'card/Visa; dep.

CUPAR Fife. Map 50C4
Pop 7,370. M90 16, Kirkcaldy 17, London 417, Dundee 12, Dunfermline 29, Edinburgh 42, Glasgow 55, Kinross 19, Perth 22, St Andrews 10, Stirling 41.
EC Thur. **MD** Tue. **Golf** Cupar 9h. **See** Parish Church, County Hall, Town Hall, Douglas Bader Garden for the Disabled.
ℹ Fluthers Car Park ☎(0334) 55555

Redlands (Highly acclaimed), By Ladybank, KY7 7SH ☎ Ladybank (0337) 31091. *Guest House.* Closed Feb.
£ B&B £23·50; HB weekly £206·50

DALRY Dumfries & Galloway (Kirkcudbrightshire). Map 43A3
Pop 6,400. Crocketford 16, London 352, Dalmellington 19, Dumfries 26, Edinburgh 81, Glasgow 66, New Galloway 3.
EC Wed. **See** St John's Stone, Covenanters' Graves in Churchyard, Blair Castle.

DALRY Strathclyde. Map 49B2
London 397, Glasgow 20, Irvine 7, Largs 10.

Dalry, Kilbirnie Rd, KA24 5JS ☎(029 483) 5135
White-painted building situated in rural surroundings on the A284. ⚒ It
🛏 6 bedrs, 6 en suite; TV; tcf
🏠 dogs, coach;
✕ LD 10
£ B&B £20–£25, B&B (double) £40–£45; L £5, D £8·50; [10% V]
c Access, Amex, B'card/Visa.

DENNY Central (Stirlingshire). Map 50A3
M73 (jn 3) 10, London 385, Edinburgh 34, Glasgow 26, Stirling 10.

Topps Farm (Highly Acclaimed), Fintry Rd, FK6 5JF ☎(0324) 822471. *Guest House.*
£ B&B £22, HB weekly £170

DERVAIG *See* Isle of Mull

DINGWALL Highland (Ross & Cromarty). Map 58A1
Kessock Bridge 11, London 540, Achnasheen 30, Beauly 8½, Bonar Bridge 27, Edinburgh 167, Glasgow 178, Inverness 15.
EC Thur. **MD** Wed. **Golf** Strathpeffer 18h.

★★ National, High St, IV15 9HA ☎(0349) 62166 Fax: (0349) 65178
Substantial, stone-built, traditional hotel beside main street. ⚒ Fr, It
🛏 42 bedrs, 42 en suite; TV
🏠 dogs; P 40, coach; child facs; con 220
✕ LD 10
£ B&B fr £27·50, B&B (double) fr £22·50; L £6·50, D £12·50
cc Access, Amex, B'card/Visa, Diners
(*See advertisement on p. 559*)

DOLPHINTON Strathclyde (West Lothian). Map 50B2
Peebles 14, London 375, Biggar 7, Edinburgh 20, Lanark 16.

★★★ H C R Dolphinton House, West Linton, EH46 7AB ☎(0968) 82286 Fax: (0899) 20456

Early 19th-century red sandstone mansion in 186 acres of parkland and woods with magnificent specimen trees. Tennis.

 EC *early closing* **MD** *market day* *country house hotel* *ns (NS) no smoking areas* *tcf tea/coffee facilities*

🛏 12 bedrs, 12 en suite; TV; tcf
🏨 dogs, ns; P 40; child facs; con 14
✕ LD 9
£ B&B £50, B&B (double) £70; L £11·95, D £24·95; WB £109·95 (2 nts); [10% V]
cc Access, Amex, B'card/Visa, Diners.
(*See advertisement on p. 559*)

DORNOCH Highland (Sutherland). Map 58B2
Pop 1,100. Bonar Bridge 13, London 576, Edinburgh 204, Glasgow 211, Helmsdale 28, Lairg 21.
EC Thur. **Golf** Royal Dornoch 18h and 9h.
ℹ The Square. ☎(0862) 810400

★★★ **Royal Golf,** Grange Rd, IV25 3LG
☎(0862) 810283 Tx: 75300
A stone-built tourist hotel situated beside golf course. Golf, putting, solarium. Open Easter–Mid-Oct.
🛏 24 bedrs, 24 en suite; annexe 8 bedrs, 8 en suite; TV; tcf
🏨 dogs; P 14, coach; child facs; con 120
✕ LD 9.30, bar meals only lunch
£ B&B £48–£54, B&B (double) £80–£92; D £16; [10% V]
cc Access, Amex, B'card/Visa, Diners; dep.

★★ **Burghfield House,** IV25 3HW ☎(0862) 810212 Fax: (0862) 810404

Traditional Victorian turreted mansion house in a peaceful situation. Putting, fishing. Open 1 Apr–31 Oct.
🛏 14 bedrs, 14 en suite; annexe 28 bedrs, 15 en suite, TV; tcf
🏨 TV, dogs; P 80; child facs; con 150
✕ LD 9, bar meals only lunch
£ B&B £18–£38, B&B (double) £36–£66; HB weekly £238–£310; L £6, D £13; [5% V w/d]
cc Access, Amex, B'card/Visa, Diners.

★★ **Dornoch Castle,** Castle St, IV25 3SD
☎(0862) 810216
Fine 450 year old castle in centre of tourist and golfing town. ⚒ Fr, De, Du. Open mid-Apr–Oct.
🛏 19 bedrs, 17 en suite, 2 ba; TV; tcf
🏨 lift, TV, dogs; P 16, child facs
✕ LD 8.30
£ B&B £30, B&B (double) £52–£68; HB weekly £262·50–£318·50; L £7, D £14·50
cc Access, Amex, B'card/Visa; dep.

DOUNE Central (Perthshire). Map 50A4
Pop 741. M9 (jn 11) 3, Bridge of Allan 5, London 406, Crieff 19, Edinburgh 42, Glasgow 32, Lochearnhead 21, Perth 31, Stirling 8.
EC Wed. **Golf** Dunblane 18h. **See** 15th cent Doune Castle, Motor Museum.

★★ **Woodside,** Stirling Rd, FK16 6AB
☎(0786) 841237
Stone-built 2-storey former coaching inn, re-built 1868, standing at roadside.
🛏 11 bedrs, 11 en suite, TV; tcf
🏨 TV, dogs; P 100, coach; child facs; con 40
✕ LD 9
£ B&B £30·80, B&B (double) £50·60; L £8, D £10
cc Access; B'card/Visa.

DRUMMORE Dumfries & Galloway (Wigtownshire). Map 42B2
Pop 390. Glenluce 16, London 398, Edinburgh 135, Gatehouse of Fleet 52, Glasgow 97, Stranraer 17.
EC Wed. **Golf** Dunskey 18h & 9h. **See** Mull of Galloway (Lighthouse), 18th cent Church, St Medan Chapel ruins.

★ **Queen's,** Mill St, DG9 9PS ☎(077 684) 300
Attractive 3-storey building, with view over bay, situated in main village street. Snooker.

DRYMEN Central (Stirlingshire). Map 49C3
Pop 659. Bearsden 12, London 410, Crianlarich 44, Dumbarton 12, Edinburgh 54, Glasgow 17, Lochearnhead 32, Stirling 22.
EC Wed. **Golf** Buchanan Castle 18h.

★★★ **Buchanan Arms,** Main St, G63 0BQ
☎(0360) 60588 Fax: (0360) 60943

18th century building near to Loch Lomond. Enjoys fine views. Indoor swimming pool, squash, sauna, solarium, gymnasium. (SH)
🛏 51 bedrs, 51 en suite; TV; tcf
🏨 dogs; P 120, coach; child facs; con 130
✕ LD 9.30
£ B&B £60–£65, B&B (double) £85–£95; HB weekly £315; L £10, D £16; WB £80 (2 nts HB)
cc Access, Amex, B'card/Visa, Diners.

★★ **Winnock,** The Square, G63 0BL
☎(0360) 60245 Fax: (0360) 60267
Two-storied traditional building all along one side of village square. ⚒ Fr
🛏 29 bedrs, 22 en suite, TV; tcf
🏨 dogs, ns; P 60, coach; child facs; con 60
✕ LD 9.30
£ B&B £28–£37 (w/e £25), B&B (double) £44–£58; HB weekly £195; L £5·50, D £10·75; WB £25; [10% V]
cc Access, Amex, B'card/Visa, Diners.

DULNAIN BRIDGE Highland (Moray). Map 54C4
Pop 400. Aviemore 11, London 510, Carrbridge 6½, Edinburgh 135, Glasgow 146, Grantown-on-Spey 3.
EC Wed. **Golf** Carrbridge 9h. **See** Castle.

★★★ **Muckrach Lodge,** PH26 3LY
☎(047 985) 257
Former shooting lodge attractively situated in own grounds.
🛏 10 bedrs, 10 en suite; TV; tcf
🏨 P 50, G 2; child facs
✕ LD 8.45
£ B&B £28; HB weekly £300; L £8, D £18; [5% V Oct–Dec]
cc Access, Amex, B'card/Visa, Diners, dep.

DUMBARTON Strathclyde (Dunbartonshire). Map 46A2
Pop 23,559. M898 5, Glasgow 14, London 402, Crianlarich 37, Edinburgh 59, Lochearnhead 46, Paisley 16, Stirling 34.
EC Wed. **MD** Fri. **Golf** Dumbarton 18h, Broadmead Estate 18h. **See** Castle.
ℹ Milton ☎(0389) 42306

★★ **Dumbuck,** Glasgow Rd, G82 1EG
☎(0389) 34336 Tx: 778303
Fax: (0389) 34336
Family-run stone-built hotel in quiet position East of town. Billiards.
🛏 22 bedrs, 22 en suite; TV; tcf
🏨 TV, dogs; P 200, coach; child facs; con 150
✕ LD 9.30
£ B&B £38, B&B (double) £50; HB weekly £322–£337·75; L £8, D £10·25
cc Access, Amex, B'card/Visa, Diners.

DUMFRIES Dumfries & Galloway (Dumfriesshire). Map 43B3
Pop 31,000. Annan 16, Carlisle 33, London 327, Beattock 19, Edinburgh 71, Glasgow 73, Langholm 28, New Galloway 23, Thornhill 14.
EC Thur. **MD** Wed. **Golf** Dumfries and Galloway 18h, Dumfries and County 18h.
See Burns House, Burns Mausoleum, Burns Statue, Burgh Museum, The Auld Bridge, Greyfriars Church, St Michael's Church, Globe Inn, Lincluden Abbey 2 m NW, Sweetheart Abbey 6 m S, Caerlaverock Castle ruins and Wildfowl centre 7 m SE.
ℹ Whitesands. ☎(0387) 53862

★★★ **Cairndale,** English St, DG1 2DF
☎(0387) 54111 Tx: 777530
Fax: (0387) 50555

Red-brick Victorian building conveniently situated near town centre.
🛏 60 bedrs, 60 en suite; TV; tcf
🏨 Lift, TV, dogs; P 60, coach; child facs; con 100
✕ LD 9.30
£ B&B £54 (w/e £30), B&B (double) £66; HB weekly £250; L £7, D £12·95; WB £40 (HB); [10% V]

♛ ★★★ **Hetland Hall,** Carrutherstown, DG1 4JX ☎(0387) 84201 Tx: 776819
Fax: (0387) 84211 ♿

Sc

Dundee (Tayside)

RAC ★★★

The Queen's
HOTEL
DUNDEE

A prestigious City Centre Hotel of elegance and charm

47 tastefully appointed en-suite bedrooms. 8 channel TV. 24 hour room service.

Brasserie Restaurant
serving interesting and innovative cuisine

Conference and Banqueting facilities. Special weekend rates. Car Parking.

Tel: (0382) 22515 – Fax (0382) 202668

Dundee (Scotland)

Stakis Earl Grey Hotel, a prestigious hotel set along Dundee's rejuvenated waterfront, enjoying excellent views.

The hotel's superb leisure club includes swimming pool, sauna, jacuzzi and exercise area.

All bedrooms have T.V., radio, fresh fruit bowl and tea/coffee making facilities.

Tel: 0382—29271

STAKIS
Earl Grey Hotel
DUNDEE

Dunkeld (Perthshire)

Grand Country House Hotel standing in private estate on the banks of the River Tay. Now one of Scotland's finest leisure hotels, this historic house boasts an extensive array of leisure facilities. 92 luxury ensuite bedrooms. Excellent dining room with a wide ranging variety of international cuisine. The perfect place for a highland holiday.

Telephone: 03502 — 771

STAKIS
Dunkeld House Hotel
DUNKELD

East Linton (East Lothian)

The Harvesters Hotel

. . . in pursuit of excellence

Georgian House of character, offering good food, fine wines, and extremely comfortable en suite accommodation at attractive rates.

Special weekly and weekend terms

We're a touch better!

EAST LINTON, JUST OFF THE A1

Telephone: (0620) 860395

RAC ★★ STB 👑👑👑👑 Commended

Impressive country house set in fine grounds to SE of Dumfries. Putting, sauna, solarium, gymnasium, billiards.
🛏 26 bedrs, 26 en suite, 2 ba; TV; tcf
🏨 TV, dogs, ns; P 60, coach; child facs; con 200
✕ LD 9.30
£ B&B £40–£49, B&B (double) £62–£76; HB weekly £270; L £8·50, D £14; WB £80 (HB); [10% V]
cc Access, Amex, B'card/Visa, Diners; dep.
★★★ Station, Lovers Walk, DG1 1LT
☎ (0387) 54316 Tx: 778654
Fax: (0387) 50388

Large and handsome Victorian stone building of character.
🛏 32 bedrs, 32 en suite, 1 ba; TV; tcf
🏨 lift, dogs, ns; P 30, coach; child facs; con 60
✕ LD 9.30, bar meals only lunch
£ B&B £55–£65, B&B (double) £70–£80; L £8·50, D £17·50; WB £75 (2 nts HB); [10% V]
cc Access, Amex, B'card/Visa, Diners.
★★ Skyline, 123 Irish St, DG1 2NP
☎ (0387) 62416
Small hotel; well-situated in town centre.
★ Swan, Kingholm Quay, DG1 4SU
☎ (0387) 53756
Attractive inn set in village with interesting quay.
Embassy (Acclaimed), Newbridge, DG2 0HZ ☎ (0387) 720233. *Hotel.*
£ B&B £25

DUNBAR Lothian (East Lothian). Map 51A3
Pop 5,614. Cockburnspath 8½, London 365, Berwick-upon-Tweed 29, Coldstream 32, Edinburgh 29, Haddington 11, Lauder 32.
EC Wed. **Golf** Dunbar 18h, Winterfield Municipal 18h. **See** Castle ruins, 17th cent Town House, 16th cent dovecote, Parish Church
ℹ Town House, High St. ☎ (0368) 63353
★★ Bayswell, Bayswell Park, EH42 1AE
☎ (0368) 62225 Fax: (0368) 62225

Victorian resort hotel on clifftop on town outskirts. Fine sea views. Putting.
🛏 13 bedrs, 13 en suite; TV; tcf
🏨 dogs; P 20, coach; child facs
✕ LD 9
£ B&B £36·30, B&B (double) £54; L £8·50, D £12·50; WB £65 (2 nts); [10% V Sep–Mar]
cc Access, Amex, B'card/Visa; dep.
★★ Redheugh, Bayswell Park, EH42 1AE
☎ (0368) 62793
Victorian building in red sandstone situated in a quiet area of the town. ⚒ It
🛏 10 bedrs, 10 en suite; TV; tcf
🏨 TV, dogs; no children under 12
✕ LD 8.45, nr lunch except Thu. Restrict lic
£ B&B £35–£45, B&B (double) £44–£55; [10% V]
cc Access, Amex, B'card/Visa; dep.
Bay View (Acclaimed), Bayswell Rd, EH42 1AB ☎ (0368) 62778
£ B&B £15–£19; HB weekly £168–£196

Marine, 7 Marine Rd, EH42 1AR ☎ (0368) 63315. *Guest House.*
£ B&B £12
Overcliffe, 11 Bayswell Park, EH42 1AE
☎ (0368) 64004. *Guest House.*
£ B&B £12; HB weekly £140
St Beys, 2 Bayswell Rd, EH42 1AB ☎ (0368) 63571. *Guest House.*
Springfield, 42 Belhaven Rd, EH42 1NH
☎ (0368) 62502. *Guest House.* Open Mar–Oct
£ B&B £15, HB weekly £145

DUNDEE Tayside (Angus). Map 55A1
Pop 180,000. Glenrothes 24, London 429, Blairgowrie 18, Edinburgh 55, Forfar 14, Glasgow 78, Kinross 30, Montrose 30, Perth 21, St Andrews 12.
EC Wed. **MD** Tue. **Golf** Monifieth 18h (2). **See** Tay Road Bridge, Museum and Art Gallery, St Andrew's Church (1772), Law Hill (viewpoint), Claypotts Castle, Broughty Castle, Camperdown Park (Zoo).
ℹ City Sq. ☎ (0382) 27723
★★★★ Stakis Earl Grey, Earl Grey Pl, DD1 4DE ☎ (0382) 29271 Tx: 76569
Fax: (0382) 200072 ♿
Recently opened 5-storey hotel on northern side of River Tay with landscaped gardens to river. Indoor swimming pool, sauna, solarium, gymnasium. ⚒ De, Du, Fr (SH)
🛏 104 bedrs, 104 en suite; TV; tcf
🏨 lift, ns; P 100, coach; child facs; con 200
✕ LD 10
£ B&B £75·50–£85·50, B&B (double) £92–£102; L £8·75, D £14·50; WB £29; [10% V]
cc Access, Amex, B'card/Visa, Diners.
(*See advertisement on p. 564*)
★★★ Angus Thistle, 101 Marketgait, DD1 1QU ☎ (0382) 26874 Tx: 76456
Fax: (0382) 22564 ♿

Large modern purpose-built hotel in city centre. (ThH)
🛏 58 bedrs, 58 en suite; TV; tcf
🏨 lift, dogs, ns; P 20; child facs; con 450
✕ LD 10
£ room £60, double room £70; Bk £7·75, L £7·75, D £12·95
cc Access, Amex, B'card/Visa, CB, Diners.
★★★ Invercarse, 371 Perth Rd, DD2 1PG
☎ (0382) 69231 Tx: 76608
Fax: (0382) 644112

Victorian house, with extensive modern additions, in pleasant grounds. River views.
🛏 39 bedrs, 39 en suite; TV; tcf
🏨 dogs; P 150, coach; child facs; con 200
✕ LD 9.45, bar meals only Sat lunch, high tea only Sun dinner
£ B&B £48–£62·50 (w/e £25), B&B (double) £49–£80; L £9·95, D £14·95
cc Access, Amex, B'card/Visa, Diners.
★★★ Queen's, Nethergate, DD1 4DU
☎ (0382) 22515 Fax: (0382) 202668
A 5-storey stone-built traditional Victorian style hotel in city centre.
🛏 31 bedrs, 31 en suite; TV; tcf
🏨 lift; P 40, coach; child facs; con 180
(*See advertisement on p. 564*)
★★★ Swallow, Kingsway West, DD2 5JT
☎ (0382) 641122 Tx: 76694
Fax: (0382) 568340 ♿

Historic colonial' mansion extended to include indoor swimming pool, putting, sauna, solarium, gymnasium. (Sw)
🛏 110 bedrs, 110 en suite; TV; tcf
🏨 dogs, ns; P 80, coach; child facs; con 80
✕ LD 9.45, bar meals only Sat lunch
£ room £70, double room £95; Bk £6·50, L £9·25, D £14·50; WB £80 (HB); [10% V]
cc Access, Amex, B'card/Visa, CB, Diners.
Beach House (Acclaimed), 22 Esplanade, Broughty Ferry ☎ (0382) 76614
Fax: (0382) 480241. *Hotel.*
£ B&B £38–£44

Kemback, 8 Mcgill St, DD4 6PH ☎ (0382) 461273. *Guest House.*
£ B&B £15–£19

DUNDONNELL Highland (Ross & Cromarty). Map 57C2
Pop 70. Garve 31, London 583, Edinburgh 208, Gairloch 33, Glasgow 212, Ullapool 24.
Golf Gairloch 9h.
★★★ C Dundonnell, IV23 2QS
☎ (085 483) 204 Fax: (085 483) 366
Attractive coaching inn, carefully adapted into modern hotel.
🛏 24 bedrs, 24 en suite; TV; tcf
🏨 dogs; P 60, coach; child facs; con 50
✕ LD 8.15, bar meals only lunch

Sc

£ B&B £29·50–£37, B&B (double) £53–£68; L £5, D £15
cc Access, B'card/Visa; dep.

DUNFERMLINE Fife. Map 47A2

Pop 53,000. Queensferry 7, London 391, A823(M) 2½, Crieff 30, Edinburgh 16, Glasgow 38, Kincardine 10, Kinross 12, Kirkcaldy 12, St Andrews 39, Stirling 22.
EC Wed. **Golf** Dunfermline 18h, Canmore 18h, Pitreavie 18h. **See** Royal Palace ruins, Abbey Church (Bruce's Tomb, St Margaret's Shrine), Andrew Carnegie Birthplace Memorial (Moodie St).
ℹ Glen Bridge Car Park. ☎ (0383) 720999

★★★ **Elgin,** Charlestown, KY11 3EE
☎ (0383) 872257

Family owned and run hotel in Edwardian house with modern extensions. Fine views over village green and Firth of Forth.
🛏 13 bedrs, 13 en suite; TV; tcf
🏨 P 75; child facs; con 25
✕ LD 9
£ B&B £38–£41 (w/e £21·50), B&B (double) £48–£56; L £6, D £10
cc Access, B'card/Visa.

★★★ **Keavil House,** Crossford, KY12 8QW ☎ (0383) 736258 Tx: 728227
Fax: (0383) 621600 ♿

Mansion house with modern extensions in own grounds. Good public rooms. ✂ Fr, It
🛏 32 bedrs, 32 en suite; TV; tcf
🏨 dogs; P 80, coach; child facs; con 150
✕ LD 10, bar meals only lunch
£ B&B £40–£65, B&B (double) £50–£80; L £6·50, D £14·50; [10% V Thu–Sun]
cc Access, Amex, B'card/Visa, Diners.

★★★ **King Malcolm Thistle,** Queensferry Rd, KY11 5DS ☎ (0383) 722611 Tx: 727721
Fax: (0383) 730865 ♿

Light 2-storey modern purpose-built hotel in outskirts of town. (ThH)
🛏 48 bedrs, 48 en suite; TV; tcf
🏨 lift, dogs, ns; P 60, coach; child facs; con 120
✕ LD 9.30
£ room £49, double room £58; Bk £7·75, D £11·95
cc Access, Amex, B'card/Visa, CB, Diners.

★★★ **Pitbauchlie House,** Aberdour Rd, KY11 4PB ☎ (0383) 722282 Tx: 727756
Fax: (0383) 620738 ♿
Early 20th century 2–3 storey stone-built residence in own grounds. Solarium.
🛏 32 bedrs, 32 en suite; TV; tcf
🏨 dogs; P 75, coach; child facs; con 35

★★★ **Pitfirrane Arms,** Main St, Crossford, KY12 8NJ ☎ (0383) 736132 Tx: 728255
Fax: (0383) 621760 ♿
Modernised and extended stone-built former coaching inn in centre of village. Sauna, solarium.
🛏 38 bedrs, 38 en suite; TV; tcf
🏨 dogs; P 72, coach; child facs; con 100
✕ LD 10.15
£ B&B £35–£42 (w/e £24), B&B (double) £47–£54; WB £30
cc Access, Amex, B'card/Visa.

DUNKELD Tayside (Perthshire). Map 54C1

Pop 600. Bankfoot 6, London 432, Blairgowrie 11, Crieff 21, Dundee 28, Edinburgh 57, Glasgow 69, Perth 15, Pitlochry 13.
EC Thur. **Golf** Dunkeld and Birnam 9h.
ℹ The Cross. ☎ (035 02) 688

♣ ★★★★ **Stakis Dunkeld House,** PH8 0HX ☎ (035 02) 771 Tx: 76657
Fax: (035 02) 8924 ♿
Originally built for the 7th Duke of Atholl, a graceful, white-painted country house on the banks of the River Tay. Indoor swimming pool, putting, tennis, fishing, sauna, solarium, gymnasium. ✂ Fr, De (Sk)
🛏 92 bedrs, 92 en suite; TV; tcf
🏨 lift, ns; P 80, coach; child facs; con 100
✕ LD 10
£ B&B fr £90–£100, B&B (double) fr £100; L £15, D £22·50; WB £65
cc Access, Amex, B'card/Visa; Diners.
(*See advertisement on p. 564*)

★★ **Atholl Arms,** Bridge St, PH8 0AQ
☎ (035 02) 219
Traditional 16th century inn extended to 3 storeys. On main street.

Kinnaird, PH8 0LB ☎ (079 682) 440
Fax: (079 682) 289
Fine 18th century house with views of moors and River Tay, 4 miles north of Dunkeld. Awaiting inspection.
£ B&B (double) £95–£130

DUNNET Highland (Caithness). Map 58C4

Castletown 3, London 652, Edinburgh 277, Glasgow 284, Helmsdale 49, Thurso 8, Wick 18.
EC Thur.

★★ **Northern Sands,** KW14 8XD
☎ Barrock (084 785) 270

Family-run stone-built hotel in centre of village overlooking Dunnet Bay. ✂ It
🛏 9 bedrs, 9 en suite, 1 ba; TV; tcf
🏨 TV; P 50, coach; child facs
✕ LD 8.30
£ B&B £20, B&B (double) £36; L £5·50, D £12; [10% V]
cc B'card/Visa; dep.

DUNOON Strathclyde (Argyll). Map 49B3

Pop 8,759. Arrochar 39, London 466 (Fy 412), Edinburgh 118 (Fy 69), Glasgow 76 (Fy 24), Inveraray 39.
EC Wed. **Golf** Cowal 18h.
ℹ 7 Alexandra Par. ☎ (0369) 3785

★★ **Abbeyhill,** Dhalling Rd, PA23 8EA
☎ (0369) 2204
Family-run hotel in a pleasant garden overlooking Firth of Clyde. Open Apr–Mar
🛏 14 bedrs, 14 en suite; TV; tcf
🏨 dogs; P 40; child facs
✕ LD 8.30, bar meals only lunch
£ B&B £25, B&B (double) £38; HB weekly £160; D £8; [10% V]
cc Amex, B'card/Visa; dep.

★★ **Argyll,** Argyll St, PA23 7NE ☎ (0369) 2059
Traditional hotel in town centre with view of pier.
🛏 32 bedrs, 17 en suite, (11 sh), 6 ba; TV; tcf
🏨 lift, dogs; coach; child facs; con 80
✕ LD 8.30
£ B&B £25–£28, B&B (double) £44–£50; HB weekly £195–£210; L £5·50, D £8·50
cc Access, B'card/Visa, Diners; dep.

★★ **Esplanade,** West Bay, PA23 7HU
☎ (0369) 4070 Fax: (0369) 4070

Prominent white-painted building pleasantly situated overlooking lawns down to West Bay. Putting, sauna. Open 15 Apr–15 Oct.
🛏 51 bedrs, 51 en suite, 1 ba; TV; tcf
🏨 lift, dogs, ns; P 20, U 2 (£4), coach; child facs
✕ LD 8. Restrict lic
£ B&B £21, B&B (double) £40–£50; HB weekly £153–£168; L £5, D £9·50; dep.

Cedars (Acclaimed), 51 Alexandra Parade, PA23 8AF ☎ (0369) 2425. *Private Hotel.*
£ B&B £19

Rosscairn (Acclaimed), 51 Hunter St, Kirn, PA23 8JR ☎ (0369) 4344. *Private Hotel.* Open Mar–Oct
£ B&B £18–£20; HB weekly £155–£175

DUNTOCHER Strathclyde (Dunbartonshire). Map 46B2

Pop 3,032. Glasgow 8½, London 396, Arrochar 28, Crianlarich 43, Dumbarton 6½, Edinburgh 53, Greenock 14, Paisley 6½.
EC Wed. **See** Roman wall.

★★ **Duntocher** (formerly Maltings), Dumbarton Rd, G81 6DP ☎ (0389) 75371

EC *early closing* **MD** *market day* ♣ *country house hotel* *ns (NS) no smoking areas* *tcf tea/coffee facilities*

Modern brick and timber faced building situated close to A82.
🛏 28 bedrs, 28 en suite; TV; tcf
TV; P 200, coach; child facs; con 30
✕ LD 9.45
£ B&B £27, B&B (double) £42; L £5·50, D £8
cc Access, Amex, B'card/Visa.

DYCE Grampian (Aberdeenshire).
See ABERDEEN AIRPORT.

EAST KILBRIDE Strathclyde (Lanarkshire). Map 46C3
Pop 76,000. Hamilton 6½, London 383, Edinburgh 41, Glasgow 8, Kilmarnock 18, Kincardine 33, Lanark 20, Largs 33, Paisley 12, Peebles 46, Stirling 31.
EC Wed. **Golf** East Kilbride 18h. **See** Church with crown tower, Mains Castle, Museum.

★★★ **Bruce,** Cornwall St, G74 1AF
☎(035 52) 29771 Tx: 778428
Fax: (035 52) 42216

A modern hotel centrally located in town. (Sw).
🛏 79 bedrs, 79 en suite; TV; tcf
lift, dogs, ns; G 25, coach; child facs; con 200
✕ LD 9.45, bar meals only Sat/Sun lunch
£ B&B £60, B&B (double) £75; L £4·95, D £12·95; WB £66 (HB)
cc Access, Amex, B'card/Visa, Diners.

★★★ **R** **Crutherland,** Strathaven Rd, G75 0Q2 ☎(035 52) 37633
Country house in quiet rural situation, convenient for New Town and Glasgow. Putting, fishing.
🛏 19 bedrs, 19 en suite; TV; tcf
dogs; P 60, coach; child facs; con 40

★★★ **Stuart,** Cornwall Way, G74 1JS
☎(035 52) 21161 Tx: 778504
Fax: (035 52) 64410
Conveniently situated modern purpose-built hotel in town centre. Closed 25 & 26 Dec
🛏 39 bedrs, 39 en suite; TV; tcf
lift, TV, dogs; coach; child facs; con 200
✕ LD 9.30
£ B&B £46–£49 (w/e £16·50), B&B (double) £60–£64; L £6·50, D £11·50
cc Access, Amex, B'card/Visa, Diners.

Craigendarroch, Philipshill, Queen's Way
☎041-644 5564 Fax: 041-644 5511
Hotel due to open April 1991.

EAST LINTON Lothian (East Lothian). Map 51A3
Pop 1,394. Cockburnspath 13, London 367, Berwick-upon-Tweed 34, Coldstream 34, Edinburgh 23, Glasgow 68, Haddington 5½.
EC Wed. **Golf** Dunbar 18h.

★★ **C** **The Harvesters,** EH40 3DP
☎(0620) 860395
Attractive stone-built 2-storey Georgian building. Fishing.
🛏 5 bedrs, 5 en suite; annexe 7 bedrs, 4 en suite, 2 ba; TV; tcf
dogs; P 40; child facs; con 20
✕ LD 9, dinner Tues–Sat only
£ B&B £25–£38 (w/e £33), B&B (double) £50–£56; HB weekly £200–£250; L £6·50, D £6·50; WB £33; [10% V]
cc Access, Amex, B'card/Visa, Diners; dep.
(*See advertisement on p. 564*)

EDINBURGH Lothian (Midlothian). Map 47B3
See also UPHALL
RAC Office, *35 Kinneard Park, EH15 3SO*
☎031-657 1122
Pop 444,741. Dalkeith 7, London 375, Beattock 54, Coldstream 48, Dunfermline 16, Galashiels 32, Glasgow 45, Haddington 15, Kinross 26, Kirkcaldy 25, Lanark 33, Peebles 23, Stirling 36.
See Plan, p. 568.
P See Plan. **Golf** Six Corporation courses and numerous others. **See** Castle and War Memorial, Palace of Holyroodhouse, St Giles' Cathedral, National Museum of Antiquities, Royal Scottish Museum, 17th cent White Horse Close, Outlook Tower, Parliament House, John Knox's House (Museum), National Gallery, 17th cent Gladstone's Land, Royal Botanic Gdn, Lady Stair's House (Literary Museum), Canongate, Tolbooth, Zoo.
ℹ Waverley Market. ☎031-557 1700

★★★★★ **Caledonian,** Princes St, EH1 2AB ☎031-225 2433 Tx: 72179
Fax: 031-225 6632 ♿

Large, elegant, luxury hotel of 6 storeys in prime position at West End of Princes St.
Fr, De, It, Es
🛏 237 bedrs, 237 en suite; TV
lift, ns; P 80; coach, child facs; con 300
✕ LD 10.30
£ B&B £120·50, B&B (double) £176; L £16·50, D £19·50; WB £130
cc Access, Amex, B'card/Visa, Diners; dep.

Using RAC discount vouchers
Please tell the hotel when booking if you plan to use an RAC discount voucher (see p. 34) in part payment of your bill. Only one voucher will be accepted per party per stay. Discount vouchers will only be accepted in payment for accommodation, not for food.

★★★★★ **Edinburgh Sheraton,** 1 Festival Sq, Lothian Rd, EH3 9SR ☎031-229 9131
Tx: 72398 Fax: 031-228 4510 ♿

Opposite the Usher Hall, a custom-built modern 7-storey luxury hotel. Indoor swimming pool, sauna, gymnasium. Fr, De, It, Es
🛏 263 bedrs, 263 en suite; TV
lift, ns; P 150, coach; child facs; con 485
✕ LD 10.30
£ B&B £120·25–£125·25 (w/e £90), B&B (double) £170·25–£175·50; L £15·75, D £19·50; [10% V]
cc Access, Amex, B'card/Visa, CB, Diners.
(*See advertisement on p. 570*)

★★★★ **Carlton, Highland,** North Bridge, EH1 1SD ☎031-556 7277 Tx: 727001
Fax: 031-556 2691 ♿

Large and impressive hotel conveniently near station. Indoor swimming pool, squash, sauna, solarium, gymnasium, billiards.
De, Es, Fr, It (SH)
🛏 207 bedrs, 207 en suite; TV; tcf
lift; P 200, coach; child facs; con 350
✕ LD 10.30
£ B&B £82–£90 (w/e £42), B&B (double) £116–£125; L £15, D £15; WB £84 (2 nts HB)
cc Access, Amex, B'card/Visa, CB, Diners.

★★★★ **George,** George St, EH2 2PB
☎031-225 1251 Tx: 72570
Fax: 031-226 5644

Sc

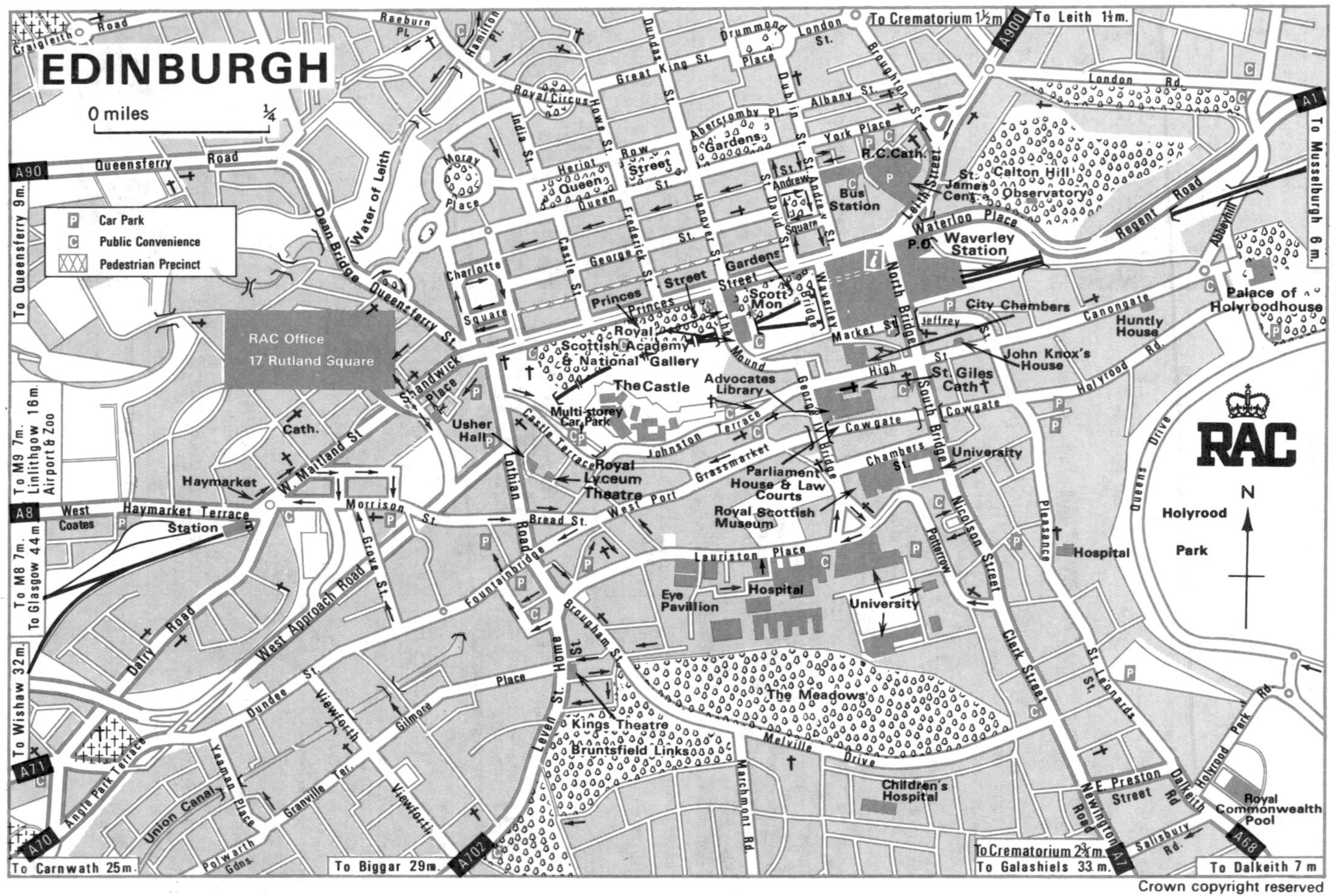

EC *early closing* **MD** *market day* *country house hotel* *ns (NS) no smoking areas* *tcf tea/coffee facilities*

Modernised, impressive city centre hotel with Georgian façade. Spacious public areas. Fr, De, It, Ar
195 bedrs, 195 en suite, TV; tcf
lift, dogs, ns; P 24, coach; child facs; con 220
LD 10
£ room £85–£105, double room £120–£132; Bk £9·50, L £13, D £13; WB
cc Access, Amex, B'card/Visa, CB, Diners.
(See advertisment on p. 570)

★★★★ **Hilton International,** Belford Rd, EH4 3DG 031-332 2545 Tx: 727979 Fax: 031-332 3805

Modern purpose-built luxury hotel on a beautiful woodland river bank. (H. Int)
144 bedrs, 144 en suite; TV; tcf
lift, dogs, ns; P120 G 15, coach; child facs; con 120
LD 10
£ room £90–£105 (w/e £45), double room £120–£135; L £11·75, D £14·75
cc Access, Amex, B'card/Visa, Diners.

★★★★ **Scandic Crown,** 80 High St, EH1 1TH 031-557 9797 Tx: 727298 Fax: 031-557 9789
A nine-storey, stone-built hotel designed to blend with the historic buildings of the old town, Indoor swimming pool, sauna, solarium, gymnasium. Fr, De, Da, Sw
238 bedrs, 238 en suite; TV; tcf
lift, dogs, ns; G 152, coach; child facs, con 200
24 hrs rest
£ room £46–£79, double room £92–£115; Bk £6·25, D £9·95
cc Access, Amex, B'card/Visa, Diners.

★★★★ **Swallow Royal Scot,** 111 Glasgow Rd, EH12 8NF 031-334 9191 Tx: 727197 Fax: 031-316 4507

Recently refurbished luxury hotel on outskirts of city. Indoor swimming pool, putting, sauna, solarium, gymnasium. Fr, De, It, Es, Po, Ar. (Sw)
259 bedrs, 259 en suite; TV; tcf
lift, dogs, ns; P 300, coach; child facs; con 350
LD 10
£ B&B £82, B&B (double) £110; L £15, D £16; WB £85 (2 nts HB); [10% V]
cc Access, Amex, B'card/Visa, Diners.

★★★ **Albany,** 39 Albany St, EH1 3QY 031-556 0397 Tx: 727079
Handsome terraced houses converted to hotel on fringe of elegant New Town area.
20 bedrs, 20 en suite; TV; tcf
dogs; coach; child facs; con 25

★★★ **Barnton Thistle,** 562 Queensferry Rd, EH4 6AS 031-339 1144 Tx: 727928 Fax: 031-339 5521

Victorian hotel with modern bedrooms. At cross roads in outskirts. Sauna. (ThH)
50 bedrs, 50 en suite; TV; tcf
lift, dogs, ns; P 100, coach; child facs; con 100
LD 10
£ room £65, double room £75; Bk £7·75, L £8·95
cc Access, Amex, B'card/Visa, CB, Diners.

★★★ **Braid Hills,** 134 Braid Rd, EH10 6JD (2½ m S on A702). 031-447 8888 Tx: 72311 Fax: 031-452 8477
Victorian hotel on hillside in residential outskirts of city. Fine views.
67 bedrs, 67 en suite; annexe 3 bedrs, 3 en suite; TV; tcf
dogs, ns; P 30, coach; child facs; con 200
LD 9.30
£ B&B £55 (w/e £35), B&B (double) £70; L £7·95, D £14·95; [10% V]
cc Access, Amex, B'card/Visa

★★★ **Capital Moat House,** Clermiston Rd, EH12 6UG 031-334 3391 Tx: 728284 Fax: 031-334 9712

Modern hotel on outskirts of city, towards airport. Indoor swimming pool, sauna, solarium, gymnasium. Fr, Es
98 bedrs, 98 en suite; TV; tcf
lift, dogs, ns; P 150, coach; child facs; con 300
LD 9.45, bar meals only lunch
£ B&B £58–£68, B&B (double) £78–£110; L £8·50, D £13·95; WB £37·50 (HB); [10% V]
cc Access, Amex, B'card/Visa, Diners.

Hotel locations
Hotel locations are shown on the maps at the back of the guide. All towns and villages containing an RAC Appointed or Listed hotel are ringed in purple.

★★★ **Crest,** Queensferry Rd, EH4 3HL 031-332 2442 Tx: 72541 Fax: 031-332 3408

Large light modern purpose-built hotel on main road into city. (Cr/THF)
120 bedrs, 120 en suite; TV; tcf
lift, dogs, ns; P 80, coach; child facs; con 180
LD 10
£ B&B fr £93·50, B&B (double) fr £127; L £10, D £15·50; WB £50 (HB)
cc Access, Amex, B'card/Visa, CB, Diners.

★★★ **Ellersly House,** Ellersly Rd, Murrayfield, EH12 6HZ 031-337 6888 Tx: 727239 Fax: 031-313 2543

Early 20th century house in own small grounds in residential suburbs. (Emb)
54 bedrs, 54 en suite; TV; tcf
lift, dogs, P 50, coach; child facs; con 50
LD 9.30, bar meals only Sat lunch
£ B&B £79, B&B (double) £101; L £8·95, D £14·25; WB
cc Access, Amex, B'card/Visa, Diners.

★★★ **C R Howard,** 36 Great King St, EH3 6QH 031-557 3500
In several Georgian terraced houses in Edinburgh's 'new town', a recently refurbished hotel of charm and style.
16 bedrs, 16 en suite; TV
£ B&B £95, B&B (double) £145–£185

★★★ **King James Thistle,** St James Centre, EH1 3SW 031-556 0111 Tx: 727200 Fax: 031-557 5333

Modern city centre hotel. Convenient for sightseeing and shopping. (ThH)

Sc

Edinburgh (Lothian)

Why our hotel runs more smoothly on five-star.

It's all about people, really. That's what makes the Sheraton Edinburgh so popular.

The doorman means it when he smiles. Waiters wait and never rush you. Managers mingle. And there's always someone close by if you should need anything.

Next time you're in town, pull into the Sheraton Edinburgh for a little five star treatment.

1 FESTIVAL SQUARE, LOTHIAN ROAD, EDINBURGH, SCOTLAND EH3 9SR
PHONE: 031 229 9131 FAX: 031 228 4510 TELEX: 72398 SHERED G

ITT Sheraton

Sheraton with a smile

Edinburgh (Lothian)

THE
GEORGE
HOTEL
EDINBURGH

George Street, Edinburgh EH2 2PB
Telephone: 031-225 1251 Telex: 72570
Fax: 031-226 5644

Listed amongst Edinburgh's premier hotels, The George enjoys one of the finest reputations in Europe. Centrally situated, close to the Castle, shopping and financial districts, the hotel offers 195 bedrooms, all with private facilities and many with superb views over the City.

Intercontinental Hotel Reservations:
London Reservations Tel: (081) 847 3711 (toll free)

Edinburgh (Lothian)

★★★★

King James Thistle Hotel 5 Crown Highly Commended

St James Centre, Edinburgh EH1 3SW Tel: 031-556 0111 Telex: 727200 Fax: 031-557 5333

Located just off world famous Princes Street. 147 tastefully designed en-suite bedrooms. Stylish French restaurant, American Theme Saloon, Cocktail bar and diner. Car Parking adjacent.

147 bedrs, 147 en suite; TV; tcf
lift, dogs, ns; P 21, G 10, coach; child facs; con 250
LD 10.20
£ room £65, double room £85; Bk £7·75, L £8·25, D £12·75
cc Access, Amex, B'card/Visa, CB, Diners.
(See advertisement on p. 570)

★★★ Mount Royal, 53 Princes St, EH2 2DG 031-225 7161 Tx: 727641
Fax: 031-220 4671

Large Victorian hotel, greatly modernised. Fine aspect on Princes Street. De, Fr (Emb)
159 bedrs, 150 en suite, 3 ba; TV; tcf
lift, dogs, ns; coach; child facs; con 50
LD 9.30
£ B&B £82–£102·50, B&B (double) £109–£130; L £8·50, D £13·50; WB £33
cc Access, Amex, B'card/Visa, Diners.

★★★ Old Waverley, 43 Princes St, EH2 2BY 031-556 4648 Tx: 727050
Fax: 031-557 6316

A large 5-storey stone-built hotel above shops in Princes Street. De, Fr (SH)
66 bedrs, 66 en suite; TV; tcf
lift, dogs; coach; child facs; con 50
LD 9.30
£ B&B £60–£65, B&B (double) £90–£98; L £5·75, D £11·25; WB £72 (2 nts HB)
cc Access, Amex, B'card/Visa, Diners; dep.

★★★ Post House, Corstorphine Rd, EH12 6UA 031-334 0390 Tx: 727103
Fax: 031-334 9237

Pleasing 5-storey concrete modern hotel with good views to countryside. Fr, De, Es (THF)
208 bedrs, 208 en suite; TV; tcf
lift, dogs, ns; P 160, coach; child facs; con 120
LD 10, bar meals only Sat lunch
£ room £67, double room £78; Bk £8, L £8·50, D £14·50; WB £41 (HB)
cc Access, Amex, B'card/Visa, CB, Diners.

★★★ H C Roxburghe, 38 Charlotte Sq, EH2 4HG 031-225 3921 Tx: 727054
Fax: 031-220 2518

Handsome 4-storey stone-built hotel of traditional style in an Adam square. Es, Fr
75 bedrs, 75 en suite; TV; tcf
lift, dogs; coach; child facs; con 200
LD 10, buttery only Sat lunch
£ B&B £55–£85, B&B (double) £70–£130; L £10, D £15·50
cc Access, Amex, B'card/Visa, Diners; dep.

★★ Clarendon, 18 Grosvenor St, EH12 5EG 031-337 7033 Tx: 72450
Fax: 031-346 7606

Attractive converted terraced houses in row of similar buildings. Fr, De, Gr (SH)
51 bedrs, 51 en suite; TV; tcf
lift, TV, dogs; coach; child facs; con 50
LD 9.30
£ B&B £50–£56, B&B (double) £75–£85; HB weekly £280; WB £62 (2 nts HB)
cc Access, Amex, B'card/Visa, Diners; dep.

★★ Hailes, 2 Wester Hailes Centre, EH1 2SW 031-442 3382
Modern 2-storey hotel adjoining high rise suburban shopping complex.

Complaints

If you are dissatisfied with the facilities or service offered by a hotel, please take the matter up with the Manager WHILE YOU ARE AT THE HOTEL. In this way, any problems can usually be solved promptly and amicably.

The RAC will investigate matters if a personal approach has failed to resolve the problem. Please submit details of any discussion or correspondence when reporting the problem to the RAC.

★★ Harp, St John's Rd, Corstorphine, EH12 8AX (3½ m W A8). 031-334 8235

Modernised and extended village inn on main road in city suburb.
25 bedrs, 25 en suite; TV; tcf
dogs, ns; P 50, coach; child facs; con 120

★★ Iona, 17 Strathearn Pl, EH9 2AL 031-447 5050 Fax: 031-452 8574
3-storey stone-built Georgian-style former private residence with modern extensions.
17 bedrs, 4 en suite, (11 sh), 5 ba; TV; tcf
TV, dogs; P 16; child facs; con 20
LD 9
£ B&B £28·85–£42·50, B&B (double) £51·50–£58·80; L £5·90, D fr £9; [5% V]
cc Access, B'card/Visa.

★★ Lady Nairne, 228 Willowbrae Rd, EH8 7NG 031-661 3396
Fax: 031-652 2789

Two-storey, grey stone building set back from road in pleasant gardens. (BCB)
33 bedrs, 33 en suite; TV; tcf
lift, ns; P 100; coach; child facs, con 120
LD 10
£ B&B £48–£56·50, B&B (double) £74·50; L £8·15, D £8·15; WB £27·50
cc Access, Amex, B'card/Visa, Diners.

★★ Murrayfield, 18 Corstorphine Rd, EH12 6HN 031-337 1844
Fax: 031-346 8159
Stone-built Edwardian-style former private residence with later extension.
23 bedrs, 23 en suite; TV; tcf
dogs; P 30, coach; child facs
LD 9.30, bar meals only lunch
£ B&B £30–£51, B&B (double) £44–£70; D fr £10; [10% V not Aug]
cc Access, Amex, B'card/Visa, Diners.

★★ Royal Ettrick, 13 Ettrick Rd, EH10 5BJ 031-228 6413 Fax: 031-229 7330
Two-storey sandstone villa in quiet residential area.
12 bedrs, 8 en suite, (2 sh), 2 ba; TV; tcf
TV, dogs; P 14; child facs
LD 8.30

Edinburgh (Lothian)

ROYAL ETTRICK HOTEL

13 Ettrick Road, Edinburgh EH10 5BJ
Tel: 031-228 6413 RAC ★★

The hotel is situated in a residential area close to the City Centre. All bedrooms have been modernised to a high standard with telephone, colour TV and tea/coffee making facilities. There is a very attractive garden and large private car parking facilities.

Elgin (Moray)

R.A.C. ★★★

EIGHT ACRES HOTEL

Sheriffmill, Elgin IV30 3UN Tel: 543077 Fax: 540001

Situated in spacious landscaped grounds. Ideal touring base and excellent centre for golfing. 54 rooms with private facilities – Restaurant – 2 Bars and extensive leisure facilities.

Falkirk (Scotland)

An ideal base from which to explore the nearby cities of Edinburgh and Stirling.
Travel east to the Firth of Forth coastline and explore the charming seaside villages.

Well appointed modern bedrooms, some family rooms, all ensuite with Col TV, telephone, tea/coffee maker and complimentary bowl of fruit.

Telephone: 0324 — 28331.

STAKIS

Park Hotel

FALKIRK

Fort William (Inverness-shire)

Allt-nan-Ros Hotel

Onich, by Fort William PH33 6RY. Tel. Onich (08553) 210

Proprietors: Lachlan, Fiona & James MacLeod

Family run country house hotel overlooking the loch. Highly commended cuisine. All bedrooms overlook the loch and have all facilities. Phone to book or for brochure, menus etc.

Fort William (Inverness-shire)

Nevis Bank Hotel

Belford Road, Fort William, Inverness-shire PH33 6BY
Telephone: (0397) 705721 (4 lines)
Telex: 94016892
Fax: 0397 706275

For colour brochure and tariff Contact Jim Lee, Manager

A member of Best Western Hotels

£ B&B £25–£30, B&B (double) £36–£46; cc Access, B'card/Visa; dep.
(*See advertisement on p. 572*)

Cumberland (Highly Acclaimed), 1 West Coates, EH12 5JQ ☎031 337 1198. Hotel.
£ B&B £35–£40
Lodge (Highly Acclaimed), 6 Hampton Terr, West Coates, EH12 5JD ☎031-337 3682. *Private Hotel.*
£ B&B £35–£45
Thrums (Highly Acclaimed), 14 Minto St, EH9 1RQ ☎031-667 5545. *Private Hotel.* Closed Xmas & New Year.
£ B&B £22–£35; HB weekly £315–£392

Allison House (Acclaimed), 15–17 Mayfield Gdns, EH9 2AX ☎031-667 8049
Arthur's View (Acclaimed), 10 Mayfield Gdns, EH9 2B2 ☎ 031-667 3468
£ B&B £18–£25
Ashdene House (Acclaimed), 23 Fountainhall Rd, EH9 2LN ☎031-667 6026. *Guest House.*
£ B&B (double) £28–£36
Ashlyn (Acclaimed), 42 Inverleith Row, EH3 5PY ☎031-552 2954. *Guest House.*
£ B&B £16–£18; HB weekly £168–£189
Boisdale (Acclaimed), 9 Coates Gdns, EH12 5LG ☎031-337 1134. *Hotel.*
£ B&B £20–£28
Brunswick (Acclaimed), 7 Brunswick St, EH7 5JB ☎031-556 1238. *Guest House.*
£ B&B (double) £20–£30
Buchan (Acclaimed), 3 Coates Gdns, EH12 5LG ☎031-337 1045. *Guest House.*
£ B&B £18
Dorstan (Acclaimed), 7 Priestfield Rd, EH16 5HJ ☎031-667 6721. *Private Hotel.*
£ B&B £16–£20
Galloway (Acclaimed), 22 Dean Park Cres, EH4 1PH ☎031-332 3672 *Guest House.*
£ B&B £18–£28
Glenora (Acclaimed), 14 Rosebery Cres, EH12 5JY ☎031-337 1186. *Private Hotel.*
£ B&B £25–£30
Heriott Park (Acclaimed), 256 Ferry Rd, EH5 3AN ☎031-552 6628. *Guest House.*
£ B&B £16–£17
Lovat (Acclaimed), 5 Inverleith Terr, EH3 5NS ☎031-556 2745
£ B&B £28; HB weekly £250
Marvin (Acclaimed), 46 Pilrig St, EH6 5AL ☎031-554 6605. *Guest House.* Open Feb–Nov
£ B&B (double) £23–£32.
Newington, (Acclaimed), 18 Newington Rd, EH9 1QS ☎031-667 3356. *Guest House.*
£ B&B £20–£22
Rockville (Acclaimed), 2 Joppa Pans, EH15 2HF ☎031-669 5418. *Private Hotel.*
£ B&B £30–£45
Roselea (Acclaimed), 11 Mayfield Rd, EH9 2NG ☎031-667 6115. *Guest House.*
£ B&B £13–£22
Salisbury (Acclaimed), 45 Salisbury Rd, EH16 5AA ☎031-667 1264. *Guest House.*
£ B&B £15–£20
Stra'ven (Acclaimed), 3 Brunstane Rd North, EH15 2DL ☎031-669 5580. *Guest House.*
£ B&B £15–£18

Amaragua, 10 Kilmaurs Terr, EH16 5DR ☎031-667 6775. *Guest House.*
Haven, 180 Ferry Rd, EH6 4NS ☎031-554 6559. *Guest House.*
£ B&B £18–£25
Kariba, 10 Granville Terr, EH10 4PQ ☎031-229 3773. *Guest House.*
Kildonan Lodge, 27 Craigmillar Park, EH16 5PE ☎031-667 2793. *Private Hotel.*
£ B&B £15–£25
Lindsay, 108 Polwarth Terr, EH11 1NN ☎031-337 1580. *Guest House.*
£ B&B £15–£18
Lygon, 4 Lygon Rd, EH16 5QE ☎031-667 1374. *Hotel.*
Marchhall, 14 Marchhall Cres, EH16 5HL ☎031-667 2743. Fax: 031-662 0777. *Hotel.*
£ B&B £17–£25
Shalimar, 20 Newington Rd, EH9 1QS ☎031-667 2827. *Guest House.*
Sherwood, 42 Minto St, EH9 2BR ☎031-667 1200. *Guest House.*
£ B&B (double) £20–£30
Southdown, 20 Craigmillar Park, EH16 5PS ☎031-667 2410. *Guest House.*
£ B&B £17·50–£25
Turret, 8 Kilmaurs Terr, EH16 5DR ☎031-667 6704. *Guest House.*
£ B&B £14–£16

EDZELL Tayside (Angus). Map 55B2

Pop 751. Brechin 6, London 459, Edinburgh 85, Montrose 12, Stonehaven 22.

★★★ **Glenesk,** High St, DD9 7TF ☎(035 64) 319 Fax: (035 64) 7333
Red sandstone Victorian style hotel adjacent to golf course. Indoor swimming pool, sauna, solarium, gymnasium, billiards. Fr
25 bedrs, 25 en suite, 1 ba; TV; tcf
dogs; P 150, U 2; child facs; con 100
LD 8.45
£ B&B £34, B&B (double) £60
cc Amex, B'card/Visa, Diners.
★★ **Panmure Arms,** 52 High St, DD9 7TA ☎(035 64) 420

Stone-built hotel, with appearance of a village inn. Indoor swimming pool, fishing, squash, sauna, solarium, billiards.

EILEAN IARMAIN See Isle of Skye

ELGIN Grampian (Moray). Map 58C1

Pop 19,245. Rothes 9½, London 527, Banff 33, Edinburgh 152, Glasgow 170, Grantown-on-Spey 34, Huntly 27, Inverness 39.
EC Wed. **Golf** Hard Hillock 18h. **See** Ruins of Cathedral (13th cent), St Giles Church.
[i] 17 High St. ☎(0343) 543388
★★★ **Eight Acres,** Sheriff Mill, IV30 3UL ☎(0343) 543077 Fax: (0343) 540001

Modern hotel on outskirts of town. Indoor swimming pool, squash, sauna, solarium, gymnasium, billiards. Fr, It
53 bedrs, 53 en suite, TV; tcf
TV, dogs; P 200, coach; child facs; con 280
LD 9
£ B&B £43·95–£48·95 (w/e £34·95), B&B (double) £60–£75; L £5·35, D £12·95; WB £34·95; [10% V]
cc Access, Amex, B'card/Visa, Diners.
(*See advertisement on p. 572*)

★★ **St Leonards,** Duff Av, IV30 1QS ☎(0343) 547350

Late Victorian stone building in Scottish style with later extensions.
16 bedrs, 11 en suite, 2 ba; TV; tcf
dogs, ns; P 40, coach; child facs; con 150

Park House (Highly Acclaimed), South St, IV30 1JB ☎(0343) 547695. *Hotel.*
£ B&B £35; HB weekly £300–£350

City, 191–193 High St, IV30 1DJ ☎(0343) 547055. *Hotel.*
£ B&B £25; HB weekly £192·50

ERSKINE Strathclyde (Renfrewshire). Map 46B2

Pop 8,977. Glasgow 10, London 397, M8 Motorway ½, Dumbarton 6, Edinburgh 55, Largs 24, Paisley 6.
EC Wed. **Golf** Erskine 18h.

★★★ **Crest,** PA8 6AN ☎041-812 0123 Tx: 776877 Fax: 041-812 7642

Large modern hotel situated near River Clyde. Indoor swimming pool, sauna, solarium, gymnasium, billiards. (THF)
166 bedrs, 166 en suite; TV; tcf
lift, dogs, ns; P 400, coach; child facs; con 600
LD 9.45, bar meals only Sat lunch
£ B&B £80·45–£93·45, B&B (double) £93·45–£101·90; L £12·50, D £15·50; WB £45; [5% V w/e]
cc Access, Amex, B'card/Visa, Diners.

ETTRICKBRIDGE Borders (Selkirkshire). Map 50C1

Pop 150. Langholm 35, London 348, Edinburgh 44, Glasgow 76, Selkirk 6.
EC Thur. **Golf** Selkirk 9h.

Sc

★★★ Ettrickshaws Country House, TD7 5HW ☎(0750) 52229

Large 3-storey Edwardian house in own grounds above river. In rural area. Fishing. Fr. Closed Dec & Jan.
6 bedrs, 6 en suite; TV; tcf
TV, dogs, ns; P 20; no children under 9
LD 8.30; bar meals only lunch
£ B&B £42–£55, B&B (double) £60–£70; HB weekly £270–£300; D £16; [V]
cc Access, B'card/Visa, Diners; dep.

FALKIRK Central (Stirlingshire). Map 47B1
See also POLMONT
Pop 36,881. Armadale 7½, London 394, M9 (jn 6) 2, Dumbarton 35, Edinburgh 25, Glasgow 23, Kincardine 7, Stirling 11.
EC Wed. **Golf** Falkirk 18h. **See** Falkirk Town Steeple, Old Parish Church, Mausoleum (Callendar Park), Roman remains (Antonine Wall, etc).
[i] The Steeple, High St ☎(0324) 20244

★★★ Stakis Park, Camelon Rd, Arnothill, FK1 5RY ☎(0324) 28331 Tx: 776502 Fax: (0324) 611593
Modern purpose-built hotel on outskirts of town. (SK)
55 bedrs, 55 en suite; TV; tcf
lift, dogs, ns; P 200, coach; child facs; con 200
LD 9.45, bar meals only Sat lunch
£ room £63, room (double) £72; Bk £7·50, L £7·50, D £13; WB £35; [5% V, w/e]
cc Access, Amex, B'card/Visa, Diners.
(*See advertisement on p. 572*)

FALKLAND Fife. Map 50C4
Glenrothes 5, London 410, M90 (junc. 8) 8, Cupar 9, Edinburgh 35, Kirkcaldy 11, Perth 18.

Covenanter (Acclaimed), The Square, KY7 7BU ☎(0337) 57224 Fax: (0337) 57272
Hotel.
£ B&B £35; [5% V]

FOCHABERS Grampian (Moray). Map 59A1
Pop 1,550. Keith 7½, London 529, Banff 24, Craigellachie 13, Edinburgh 154, Elgin 9.
EC Wed. **Golf** Spey Bay 18h. **See** Church.

★★ Gordon Arms, 80 High Street, IV32 7DH ☎(0343) 820508 Fax: (0343) 820300

Two-storey stone-built former coaching inn, fronting on to main street.
11 bedrs, 11 en suite 1 ba; annexe 2 bedrs, 2 en suite; TV; tcf
TV, dogs; P 50, G 2, coach; child facs; con 60
LD 9.30
£ B&B £38–£40, B&B (double) £50–£55; L £6·50; WB; [10% V, Oct–Apr]
cc Access, Amex, B'card/Visa.

FORRES Grampian (Moray). Map 58C1
Pop 7,440, Grantown-on-Spey 21, London 527, Carrbridge 26, Edinburgh 152, Elgin 12, Glasgow 169, Inverness 27.
EC Wed. **Golf** Muiryshade 18h.
[i] Falconer Museum. ☎(0309) 72938

★★ Park, Victoria Rd, IV36 0BN ☎(0309) 72328
Victorian-style 3-storey stone-built former mansion in small grounds.

★★ [H] Ramnee, Victoria Rd, IV36 0BN ☎(0309) 72410

Former private villa in small grounds. A stone-built hotel in outskirts. Fr
20 bedrs, 19 en suite; 1 ba; TV; tcf
dogs; P 50, coach; child facs; con 100
LD 9
£ B&B £34·50–£45, B&B (double) £49·50–£65; HB weekly £315–£388·50; L £7·25, D £12·50; WB £21·75; [V w/e, Nov–Mar]
cc Access, Amex, B'card/Visa, Diners

FORT AUGUSTUS Highland (Inverness). Map 54A3
Pop 1,000. Fort William 31, London 521, Carrbridge 49, Edinburgh 155, Glasgow 130, Invergarry 7, Invermoriston 6.
EC Wed. **Golf** Inverness 18h.
[i] Car Park. ☎(0320) 6367

★★★ Lovat Arms, Main Rd, PH32 4BE ☎(0320) 6206

A family-run traditional hotel with large rooms. Putting. Fr
23 bedrs, 23 en suite, 4 ba; TV; tcf
dogs; P 50, coach; child facs; con 45
LD 8.30, bar meals only Mon–Sat lunch
£ B&B £23·50–£29·50, B&B (double) £47–£59; HB weekly £225–£280; L £7·50, D £16; [5% V]
cc B'card/Visa; dep.

★★ Inchnacardoch Lodge, PH32 4BL ☎(0320) 6258

19th century hunting lodge charmingly set in elevated position. Fr, De, Es. Open 1 Apr– 30 Nov.
17 bedrs, 16 en suite, 1 ba; TV; tcf
TV, dogs, ns; P 40, coach; child facs
LD 8.30, bar meals only lunch
£ B&B (double) £40–£65; D £16·50; WB £60 (HB); [10% V]
cc Access, Amex, B'card/Visa, Diners; dep.

FORTINGALL Tayside (Perthshire). Map 54B1
Killin 16, London 451, Edinburgh 76, Glasgow 70, Aberfeld 8½.

★★ Fortingall, By Aberfeldy, PH15 2NQ ☎Kenmore (088 73) 367
Amid beautiful rural surroundings, a stone-built traditional hotel in centre of village. Fishing.
9 bedrs, 7 en suite, 2 ba; TV; tcf
TV, dogs; P 15, U 2, G 4, coach; child facs
LD 8.45, bar meals only lunch
£ B&B £22–£25; HB weekly £250–£270; D £15; WB £37·50 (HB); [5% V]
cc Access, Amex, B'card/Visa; dep.

Rose Villa (Highly Acclaimed), Nr Aberfeldy, PH15 2LL ☎Kenmore (088 73) 335. *Guest House.*

FORT WILLIAM Highland (Inverness-shire). Map 53C2
Pop 4,270. Ballachulish 14, London 490, Crianlarich 51, Edinburgh 132, Glasgow 99, Invergarry 25, Mallaig 44, Oban 48.
EC Wed (win). **Golf** Fort William 18h. **See** Ben Nevis 4,418 ft, Inverlochy Castle ruins.
[i] Cameron Sq ☎(0397) 3781

★★★★ Inverlochy Castle, Torlundy, PH33 6SN ☎(0397) 2177 Tx: 776229

Impressive Victorian building now a luxury hotel. In 500 acres of grounds stretching down to River Lochy. Tennis, billiards.
16 bedrs, 16 en suite; TV

★★★ **Mercury,** Achintore Rd, PH33 6RW ☎(0397) 3117 Tx: 778454

Modern custom-built motel overlooking Loch to south of town. Sauna. (MtCh)
🛏 86 bedrs, 86 en suite; TC; tcf
🏠 lift, dogs, ns; P 50, coach; child facs
✕ LD 9, bar meals only lunch
£ B&B £35–£50, B&B (double) £50–£65; D 12·95; WB £38
cc Access, Amex, B'card/Visa, Diners

★★ **Grand,** Gordon Sq. PH33 6DX ☎(0397) 2928 Fax: (0397) 5060

Fully modernised 3-storey 20th century building conveniently set in town centre.
🛏 33 bedrs, 33 en suite; TV; tcf
🏠 dogs; P 20, coach; child facs; con 120
✕ LD 8.30, bar meals only Mon, Tues & Thu–Sat lunch
£ B&B £25, B&B (double) £45; L £6·95, D £13·95 [5% V, Thu–Sat; Oct–Feb]
cc Access, Amex, B'card/Visa, Diners; dep.
(*See advertisement on p. 597*)

★★ **Nevis Bank,** Belford Rd, PH33 6BY ☎(0397) 705721 Tx: 94016892 Fax: (0397) 706275

White painted hotel close to Ben Nevis foothills. Sauna, solarium, gymnasium.
🛏 35 bedrs, 35 en suite; annexe 7 bedrs, 7 en suite; TV; tcf
🏠 dogs; P 35, G 35; coach; child facs; con 50
✕ LD 9, bar meals only lunch
£ [10% V]
cc Access, Amex, B'card/Visa, Diners; dep.
(*See advertisement on p. 572*)

Charlecote House, Alma Rd, PH33 6HB ☎(0397) 3288
£ B&B (double) £20–£28

FRASERBURGH Grampian (Aberdeenshire). Map 59C1
Pop 12,990. Mintlaw 13, London 534, Aberdeen 42, Banff 23, Edinburgh 160, Glasgow 179, Huntly 39, Peterhead 17. **EC** Wed. **Golf** Fraserburgh 18h. **See** Lighthouse, 16th cent Wine Tower.
ℹ Saltoun Sq. ☎(0346) 28315.

★★ **Alexandra,** High St, AB4 5HE ☎(0346) 28249
Traditional style late Victorian granite-built hotel set in town centre. Sauna.

FREUCHIE Fife. Map 50C4
Pop 869. Glenrothes 4, London 409, Cupar 8, Dundee 20, Edinburgh 34, Glasgow 59, Kirkcaldy 9½, Perth 19.
Golf Falkland 9h.

★★ **Lomond Hills,** High St, KY7 7EY ☎Falkland (0337) 57329 Fax: (0337) 58180
Former coaching inn with later extensions–an attractive stone building. Indoor swimming pool sauna, solarium, gymnasium, opening 1/1/91. ⚒ Du
🛏 24 bedrs, 24 en suite, TV;
🏠 dogs; P 30, coach; child facs; con 150
✕ LD 9.15, bar meals only Mon lunch
£ B&B £33–£37, B&B (double) £47–£52; L £6, D £17; WB £71 (2 nts); [5% V, not Aug]
cc Access, Amex, B'card/Visa, Diners; dep.

GAIRLOCH Highland (Ross & Cromarty). Map 57B1
Pop 1,000. Achnasheen 28, London 596, Edinburgh 221, Glasgow 225, Ullapool 57. **EC** Wed. **Golf** Gairloch 9h. **See** Loch Maree, View points at Gairloch, Crask and Red Point, Victoria Falls, Inverewe Gardens 5 m NE.
ℹ Achtercairn. ☎(0445) 2130

★★★ **Creag Mor,** Charleston, 1V21 2AH ☎(0445) 2068 Fax: (0445) 2044

Modern, two-storey hotel, recently extended, in elevated position with views over Gairloch harbour, Fishing. ⚒ Fr
🛏 17 bedrs, 17 en suite; TV; tcf
🏠 dogs; P 30; child facs
✕ LD 9.45
£ B&B £35·50–£41, B&B (double) £51–£61; HB weekly £264–£290; L £6·50, D £16; WB £30 (HB); [10% V Nov–Apr]
cc Access, B'card/Visa; dep

★★ **Old Inn,** IV21 2BD ☎(0445) 2006

Modernised 19th century hotel situated in own grounds beside harbour.
🛏 14 bedrs, 14 en suite; TV; tcf
🏠 dogs, P 50, coach; child facs; con 60
✕ LD 9, bar meals only lunch
£ B&B £22·50–£29·50, B&B (double) £45–£59; HB weekly £259–£294; D £14·50; [10% V, Oct–Apr]
cc Access, Amex, B'card/Visa; dep.

GALASHIELS Borders (Selkirkshire). Map 51A2
Pop 13,450. Melrose 4, London 344, Edinburgh 31, Glasgow 67, Jedburgh 17, Kelso 18, Lauder 13, Peebles 18, Selkirk 6½. **EC** Wed. **Golf** Ladhope 18h. **See** Old Gala House, Abbotsford 2 m SE.
ℹ Bank St. ☎(0896) 55551

♣ ★★★ **C** **Kingsknowes,** Selkirk Rd, TD1 3HY ☎(0896) 58375

Three-storey red sandstone Victorian style mansion. Putting, tennis.
🛏 11 bedrs, 10 en suite, 1 ba; TV; tcf
🏠 dogs; P 50; child facs

★★ **Abbotsford Arms,** 63 Stirling St, TD1 1BY ☎(0896) 2517
19th century stone-built inn in residential area of town. Fishing.
🛏 13 bedrs, 9 en suite, 2 ba; TV; tcf
🏠 TV; P 14, coach; child facs, con 120
✕ LD 9, bar meals only lunch
£ £20–£24, B&B (double) £34–£40; D £8; [5% V]
cc Access, B'card/Visa; dep.

GARVE Highland. Map 58A1
Pop 149. Contin 6, London 553, Achnasheen 16, Beauly 15, Dingwall 13, Edinburgh 182, Glasgow 177, Inverness 26.

★★ **Garve,** IV23 2PR ☎(099 74) 205
Family-owned tourist hotel beneath Ben Wyvis. Close to railway station. Fishing.

Residents only
Some Listed hotels only serve meals to residents. It is always wise to make a reservation for a meal in a hotel.

★★ **Inchbae Lodge,** Inchbae, IV23 2PH
☎ Aultguish (099 75) 269

Family-run hotel, formerly a hunting lodge, in rugged mountain scenery. Fishing. ✂ Fr. Closed 25 & 26 Dec.
🛏 6 bedrs, 3 en suite, 2 ba; annexe 6 bedrs, 6 en suite; tcf
🏠 dogs, P 50; child facs
✕ LD 8.30, bar meals only lunch
£ B&B £26·50–£28·50, B&B (double) £45–£49; D £15·75; WB £70; [5% V]; dep.

GATEHOUSE-OF-FLEET Dumfries & Galloway (Kirkcudbrightshire). Map 42C3
Pop 894. Castle Douglas 14, London 358, Dumfries 35, Edinburgh 102, Girvan 47, Glasgow 89, New Galloway 19, Stranraer 44.
ℹ Car Park. ☎ (055 74) 212

♛ ★★★★ **Cally Palace,** DG7 2DL
☎ (055 74) 341 Fax: (055 74) 522

Former stately home with imposing classical portico; set in fine scenery. Swimming pool, putting, tennis, fishing, sauna, solarium. Open Mar–3 Jan.
🛏 55 bedrs, 55 en suite; TV; tcf
🏠 lift, dogs, ns; P 100, child facs; con 80
✕ LD 9.30
£ B&B £30–£45, B&B (double) £60–£90, HB weekly £280–£336; L £7·50, D £16; WB £90 (2 nts)
cc B'card/Visa; dep.

★★★ **Murray Arms,** Main St, DG7 2HY
☎ (055 74) 207 Fax: (055 74) 370

One-time coaching house at side of quiet main street of small town.
🛏 12 bedrs, 12 en suite, 2 ba; annexe 1 bedr, 1 en suite; TV; tcf
🏠 TV, dogs; P 30, coach; child facs; con 100
✕ LD 8.45
£ B&B £32–£35, B&B (double) £64–£70; L £4·50, D £15; [10% V, Nov–Mar]
cc Access, Amex, B'card/Visa, Diners.

Bank o'Fleet, 47 High St, DG7 2HR
☎ (055 74) 302. *Hotel.*
Bobbin, 36 High St, DG7 2 HP ☎ (055 74) 229. *Guest House.*

GIFFNOCK Strathclyde. Map 46C3
Pop 13,000. Strathaven 13, London 387, Edinburgh 50, Glasgow 4½, Kilmarnock 17, Lanark 27, Paisley 6½.

★★★ R **MacDonald Thistle,** Eastwood Toll, G46 6RA ☎ 041-638 2225 Tx: 779138 Fax: 041-638 6231

Large modern hotel conveniently situated for Glasgow city centre and Airport. Sauna, solarium, gymnasium. (MtCh)
🛏 56 bedrs, 56 en suite; TV; tcf
🏠 lift, dogs, ns; P 200, coach; child facs; con 200
✕ LD 10
£ room £65, double room £75; Bk £7·75, L £7·50, D £12·95; WB
cc Access, Amex, B'card/Visa, CB, Diners.

★★ **Redhurst,** Eastwood Mains Rd, G46 6QE ☎ 041-638 6465
Fax: 041-620 0419

Two-storey, purpose-built hotel in residential area. ✂ It. (BCB).
🛏 17 bedrs, 17 en suite, TV; tcf
🏠 ns; P 50, coach; child facs; con 250
✕ LD 10
£ B&B £53–£59·50, B&B (double) £74·50; L £8·15, D £8·15; WB £27·50
cc Access, Amex, B'card/Visa, Diners.

GIRVAN Strathclyde (Ayrshire). Map 42B4
Pop 7,698. Pinwherry 8, London 395, Ayr 21, Dalmellington 22, Edinburgh 91, Gatehouse of Fleet 47, Glasgow 53, Stranraer 30.
EC Wed. **Golf** Girvan 18h, Turnberry Hotel courses, 18h (2).
ℹ Bridge St. ☎ (0465) 4950

★★ **Kings Arms,** Dalrymple St, KA26 0DU
☎ (0465) 3322

Attractive 4-storey former coaching inn. Close to beach. Billiards.
🛏 25 bedrs, 25 en suite, 2 ba; TV; tcf
🏠 dogs, P 100, coach; child facs; con 100
✕ LD 9.30
£ B&B £33, B&B (double) £48; WB £28 (HB); [10%]
cc Access, B'card/Visa; dep.

★★ **Westcliffe,** Louisa Dr, KA26 9AH
☎ (0465) 2128
Part of a seafront terrace, close to shops and harbour. Solarium. Closed 31 Dec.
🛏 annexe 21 bedrs, 9 en suite, (8 sh), 4 ba; TV; tcf
🏠 TV; coach; child facs; con 50
✕ LD 6
£ B&B £18, B&B (double) £32; HB weekly £132; L £7, D £8; [V]
cc Access, B'card/Visa; dep.

★ **Hamilton Arms,** 12 Bridge St, KA26 9KH
☎ (0465) 2182
Small hotel close to shops and harbour.
🛏 11 bedrs, 2 ba, TV; tcf
🏠 TV, dogs; P 4, coach; child facs; con 120
✕ LD 7.30
£ B&B £14·50, B&B (double) £27; L £3·75, D £7; [10% V]; dep.

GLAMIS Tayside. Map 55A1
Dundee 1, London 441, Edinburgh 66, Forfar 5, Glasgow 82, Perth 26.

★★★ **Castleton House,** Forfar, DD8 1SJ
☎ (030 784) 340 Fax: (030 784) 506
Edwardian house, with fine ornamental stairway, in wooded grounds beside A94. Putting.
🛏 6 bedrs, 6 en suite; TV; tcf
🏠 ns; P 20; child facs
✕ LD 9.30
£ B&B £45–£55, B&B (double) £75–£85; L £9·75, D £19·50; [5% V]
cc Access, Amex, B'card/Visa; dep.

GLASGOW Strathclyde (Lanarkshire). Map 46B3
See also BARRHEAD, GIFFNOCK, MILNGAVIE, PAISLEY and RUTHERGLEN.
RAC Office, *200 Finnieston Street, Glasgow G3 8NZ.* ☎ 041-248 4444
Pop 753,000. Hamilton 11, London 388, M8 1, Dumbarton 15, Edinburgh 45, Gourock 25, Kilmarnock 20, Kincardine 28, Lanark 25, Paisley 6½, Stirling 26.
See Plan, pp. 578–9.
P See Plan. **Golf** Eight public courses and numerous others. **See** Glasgow Cathedral, University, Art Gallery and Museum (Kelvingrove Park), Old Glasgow Museum, Transport Museum, Burrell Collection, Tolbooth Steeple, Iron Steeple, St Andrew's Church, Botanic Gardens, Kelvin Hall.
ℹ 35–39 St Vincent Place. ☎ 041-204 4400

EC *early closing* **MD** *market day* ♛ *country house hotel* *ns (NS) no smoking areas* *tcf tea/coffee facilities*

Glasgow (Strathclyde)

Holiday Inn®

Argyle Street, Anderston, Glasgow G3 8RR
Telephone: 041 226 5577. Telex: 776355. Fax: 041 221 9202
All of Holiday Inn Glasgow's 298 bedrooms are spacious with private facilities. Offering two excellent restaurants, cocktail bar, extensively equipped leisure club and conference/banqueting facilities.

Glasgow (Strathclyde)

Behind the magnificent Victorian style facade, this elegant hotel boasts a luxurious interior. The hotel's 96 ensuite bedrooms are all beautifully furnished and offer every comfort - Col TV/in-house movies/radio/telephone and bowl of fruit. Fully equipped suites available for any size of conference or meeting. Ideal touring base for visiting the Clyde coast, Loch Lomond and the Trossachs.

Telephone: 041 339 8811.

STAKIS
Grosvenor Hotel
GLASGOW

Glasgow (Strathclyde)

Friendly
GLASGOW
Central Hotel, Gordon Street, Glasgow G1 3SF.
RAC ★★★
· Premier Plus Rooms · Parking nearby ·
Located in the heart of the city, with superb communication links. The ideal location for business or pleasure.

FOR RESERVATIONS (office hours)
TELEPHONE FREEPHONE
0800 591910
or call direct on 041-221 9680
FAX: 041-226 3948 *TELEX:* 777771
Friendly
HOTELS PLC
IT'S BEST TO STAY FRIENDLY

Sc

Innerleithen (Peeblesshire)

TRAQUAIR

The Oldest Inhabited and most Romantic House in Scotland. Visited by 27 Scottish Monarchs. Rich in associations with Mary Queen of Scots and the Jacobites.

Open Easter week. Sundays and Mondays in May. June – September Daily. Times: 1.30pm – 5.30pm except July and August 10.30am – 5.30pm.

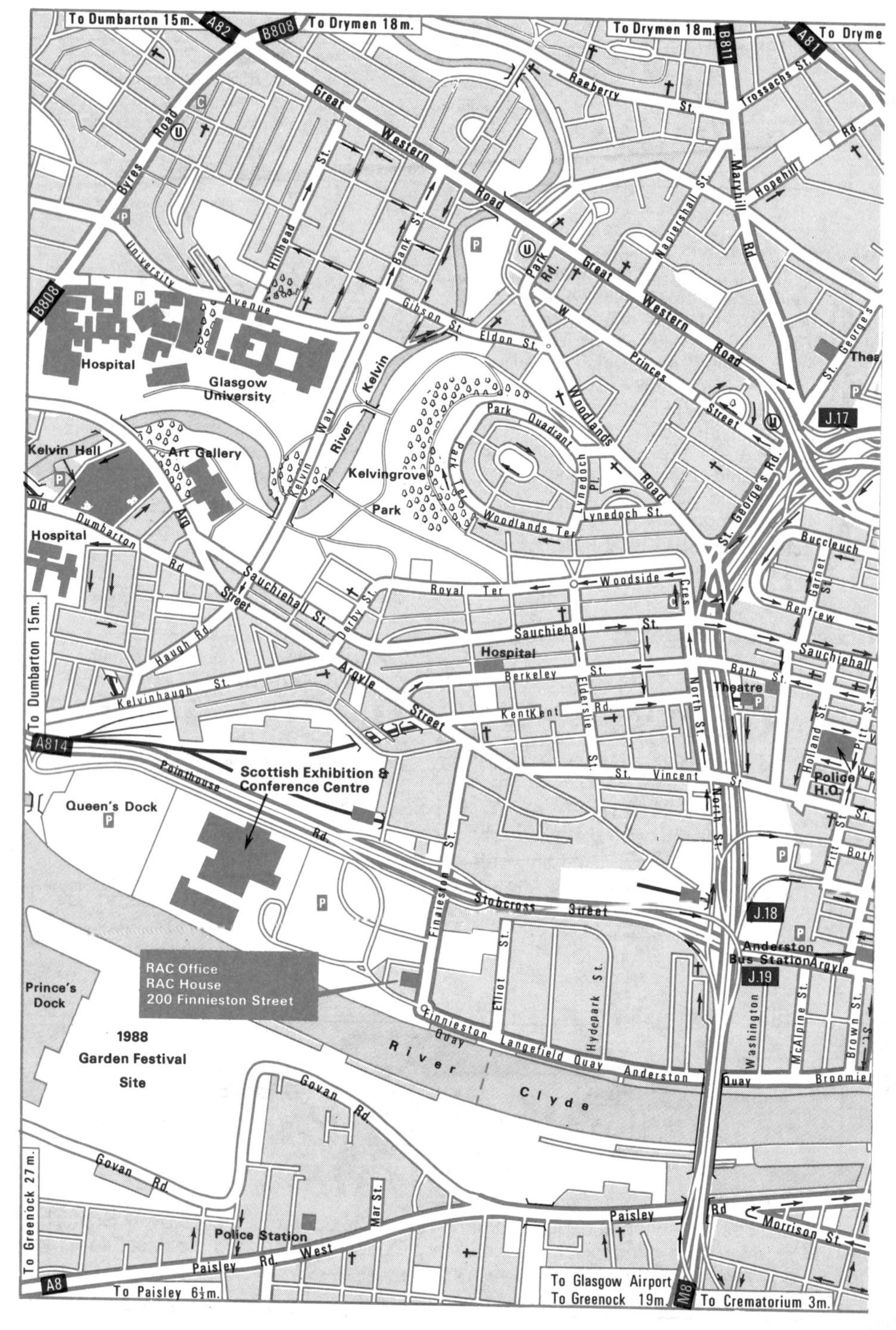

EC *early closing* **MD** *market day* ♣♣ *country house hotel* *ns (NS) no smoking areas* *tcf tea/coffee facilities*

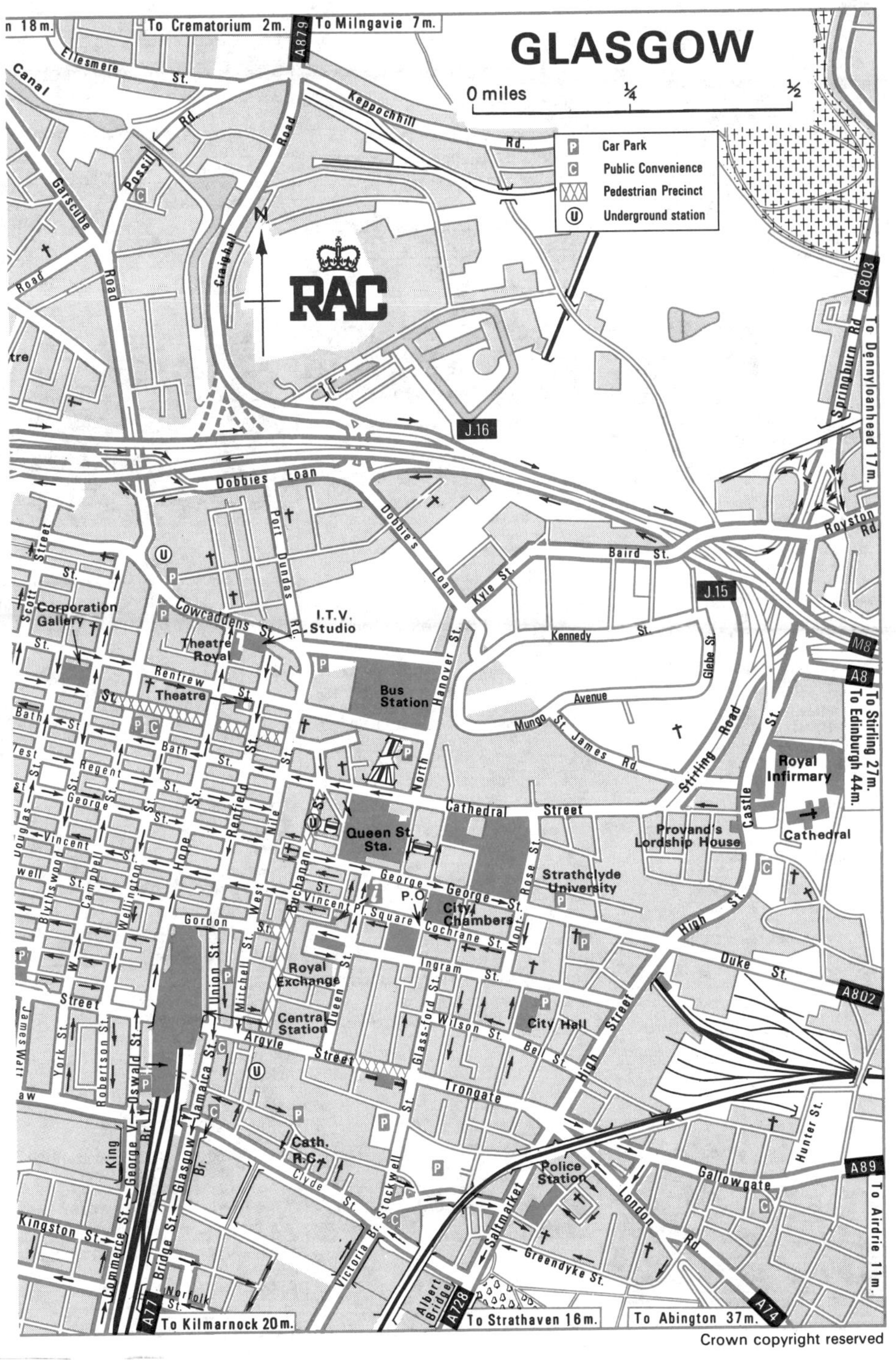
GLASGOW
0 miles 1/4 1/2
Car Park
Public Convenience
Pedestrian Precinct
Underground station
RAC
To Crematorium 2m.
To Milngavie 7m.
To Dennyloanhead 17m.
To Stirling 27m.
To Edinburgh 44m.
To Airdrie 11m.
To Kilmarnock 20m.
To Strathaven 16m.
To Abington 37m.
J.16
J.15
Corporation Gallery
Theatre Royal
Theatre
I.T.V. Studio
Bus Station
Queen St. Sta.
Royal Infirmary
Cathedral
Provand's Lordship House
Strathclyde University
P.O.
City Chambers
Royal Exchange
Central Station
City Hall
Cath. R.C.
Police Station
Crown copyright reserved

★★★★ **Albany,** Bothwell St, G2 7EN
☎041-248 2656 Tx: 77440
Fax: 041-221 8986
Large city centre hotel. Spacious and luxurious. Fr, De, It, Ja. (THF)
254 bedrs, 254 en suite; TV; tcf
lift, dogs; ns, P 70, coach; child facs; con 800
LD 10.45
£ B&B £93·50–£104·50, B&B (double) £122–£134; L £15·50, D £15·50; WB £57·75
cc Access, Amex, B'card/Visa, CB, Diners.

★★★★ **Holiday Inn,** Anderston, Argyle St, G3 8RR ☎041-226 5577 Tx: 776355
Fax: 041-221 9202

Luxurious modern central hotel with spacious bedrooms and leisure facilities. Indoor swimming pool, squash, sauna, solarium, gymnasium. Fr, It. (CHIC)
298 bedrs, 298 en suite; TV; tcf
lift, dogs, ns; P 180, coach; child facs; con 800
LD 11
£ B&B £98·75–£113·75, B&B (double) £124·50; L £16·25, D £16·25; WB £40
cc Access, Amex, B'card/Visa, CB, Diners.
(*See advertisement on p. 577*)

★★★★ **Hospitality Inn,** Cambridge St, G2 3HN ☎041-332 3311
Modern 9-storey building on a corner site in the city centre.
306 bedrs, 306 en suite; TV

★★★★ **Stakis Grosvenor,** Grosvenor Terr, Great Western Rd, G12 0TA ☎041-339 8811 Tx: 776247 Fax: 041-334 0710
Traditional Victorian style luxurious city hotel overlooking famous Botanic Gardens. (Sk)
95 bedrs, 95 en suite, TV; tcf
lift, dogs, ns; P 12, G 50; child facs; con 250
(*See advertisement on p. 577*)

★★★ **Central,** Gordon St, G1 35F ☎041-221 9680
A large flamboyant Victorian railway hotel in city centre beside Central Station.
221 bedrs, 221 en suite; TV; tcf
(*See advertisement on p. 577*)

★★★ **Crest,** Argyle St, G2 8LL ☎041-248 2355 Tx: 779652 Fax: 041-221 1014

Large custom-built modern hotel in city centre; close to railway station. (Cr/THF)
121 bedrs, 121 en suite; TV; tcf
lift, dogs, ns; coach; child facs; con 80
LD 9.45, bar meals only Wed dinner & Sat & Sun lunch
£ B&B £72–£82 (w/e £39); L £9·25, D £13·95; [V]
cc Access, Amex, B'card/Visa, CB, Diners.

★★★ **Ewington** 132 Queen's Dr, G42 8QW ☎041-423 1152 Fax: 041-422 2030

Family-run traditional hotel in terrace building overlooking Queen's Park. Billiards. Fr
44 bedrs, 36 en suite, 2 ba; TV; tcf
lift, dogs; P 12, coach; child facs; con 35
LD 8.45. Resid, Rest & Restrict lic
£ B&B £45–£65, B&B (double) £55–£75; L £5·50, D £11·50; WB; [10% V, w/e]
cc Access, Amex, B'card/Visa, Diners.

★★★ **Stakis Ingram,** 201 Ingram St, G1 1DQ ☎ 041-208 4401 Fax: 041-226 5149
Business and tourist hotel in 8-storey building part original stonework, part cement-faced. Close to George Square in city centre. Es. (Sk)
90 bedrs, 90 en suite; TV; tcf
lift, dogs, ns; coach; child facs; con 150
LD 10, bar meals only Sun lunch
£ room £76·50, double room £90; L £6·50, D £11·95
cc Access, Amex, B'card/Visa, Diners.

★★★ **Swallow,** 517 Paisley Rd, G51 1RN
☎041-427 3146 Tx: 778795
Fax: 041-427 4059
Modern hotel minutes from the M8. Glasgow Airport 5 miles. Indoor swimming pool, sauna, solarium, gymnasium. (Sw)
119 bedrs, 119 en suite; TV; tcf
lift, dogs, P 150, coach; child facs; con 250
LD 9.30
£ B&B £72–£75, B&B (double) £82–£85; L £10, D £14; WB £45 (HB)
cc Access, Amex, B'card/Visa, Diners.

★★★ **Tinto Firs Thistle,** 470 Kilmarnock Rd, G43 2BB ☎041-637 2353 Tx: 778329
Fax: 041-633 1340

Attractive refurbished hotel in residential area, close to the city centre. (MtCh)
28 bedrs, 28 en suite; TV; tcf
dogs, ns; P 46, G 1, coach; child facs; con 150
LD 9.45
£ room £65, double room £75; Bk £7·75, L £12·50, D £12·50
cc Access, Amex, B'card/Visa, CB, Diners.

★★ **Newlands,** 290 Kilmarnock Rd, G43 2XS ☎041-632 9171
Stone-built modernised small hotel situated in south of city.

★★ **Sherbrooke,** 11 Sherbrooke Av, G41 4PG ☎041-427 4227
Fax: 041-427 5685

Privately-owned small red sandstone "castle" building in quiet residential area.
11 bedrs, 11 en suite; annexe 14 bedrs, 14 en suite; TV; tcf
TV, dogs, ns; P 50, coach; child facs; con 140
LD 9.15
£ B&B £58·90–£90 (w/e £20), B&B (double) £69·50–£95; L £7·50, D £15; [10% V]
cc Access, Amex, B'card/Visa, Diners.

★ **Dunkeld** 10–12 Queen's Dr, G42 8BS
☎041-424 0160

Stone building set back from residential street overlooking playing fields. Snooker.

Town House, West George St, ☎041-332 3320 Fax: 041-332 9756
Hotel awaiting inspection
Sauna, solarium, gymnasium.
34 bedrs, 34 en suite; TV
lift, ns; coach; child facs; con 140
LD 9.45
£ B&B £73·50–£83·50, B&B (double) £102–£112; L £19·50, D £29; [5% V w/d]
cc Access, Amex, B'card/Visa, Diners.

Marie Stuart, 46–48 Queen Mary Av, G42 8DT ☎041-424 3939. *Hotel.*
£ B&B £17–£38; [5% V]

Smith's, 963 Sauchiehall St, G3 7TQ ☎041-339 6363. *Hotel.*
£ B&B £18–£21; [5% V]

GLASGOW AIRPORT (Abbotsinch)
See RENFREW.

GLENBORRODALE Highland (Argyll). Map 53A2
Ballachulish 66 (Fy 34), London 544 (Fy 509), Edinburgh 186 (Fy 152), Fort William 54 (Fy 37), Glasgow 153 (Fy 115), Mallaig 44.

★★★★ Glenborrodale Castle, Ardnamurchan, Acharacle, PH36 4JP
(097 24) 266 Tx: 778815 Fax: (097 24) 224
Imposing castellated building standing in 130 acres on shores of loch. Putting, tennis, fishing, sauna, solarium, gymnasium. Open Easter–31 Oct.
13 bedrs, 13 en suite; annexe 2 bedrs, 2 en suite; TV; tcf
TV; P 18, G 4; con 8
LD 9
£ B&B £110, B&B (double) fr £165; D £30
cc Access, Amex, B'card/Visa.

GLENCAPLE Dumfries & Galloway (Dumfriesshire). Map 43B3
Pop 270. Cummertrees 10, London 325, Brampton 37, Carlisle 31, Dumfries 5, Edinburgh 76, Glasgow 78, Langholm 31.
Golf Dumfries 18h.

★★ Nith, DG1 4RE (038 777) 213
Attractive village inn beside river, close to popular wildfowl area. Fishing.
10 bedrs, 7 en suite, 2 ba; TV, tcf
dogs; P 20, coach; child facs; con 130
LD 9
£ B&B £25, B&B (double) £40
cc Access; B'card/Visa, dep.

GLENCOE Highland (Argyll). Map 53C2
Pop 357. Crianlarich 35, London 472, M85 4, Dalmally 36, Edinburgh 115, Fort William 17, Glasgow 85, Oban 39.

★★ King's House, PA39 4HY (12 m SE A82), Kingshouse (085 56) 259
Reputed to be Scotland's oldest licensed inn; in rugged mountain scenery. Fishing.

GLENROTHES Fife. Map 50C4
Pop 36,200. M90 (jn 7) 10, Queensferry 21, London 405, Dundee 23, Dunfermline 17, Edinburgh 30, Glasgow 55, Kinross 13, Kirkcaldy 6, Perth 22, St Andrews 21.
EC Tue. **Golf** Glenrothes 18h.
North St (0592) 756684

★★★ Balgeddie House, Balgeddie Way, KY6 3ET (0592) 742511
Fax: (0592) 621702

Former mansion on hillside above New Town–own small grounds. Closed Jan.
18 bedrs, 18 en suite; TV, tcf
P 100; child facs; con 50
LD 9.30
£ B&B £54·25–£74·25 (w/e £30), B&B (double) £74·25–£79·25; L £11, D £12·50; WB £42·50 (HB)
cc Access, Amex, B'card/Visa

★★ Albany, 1 North St, KY7 5NA (0592) 752292 Fax: (0592) 756451
Purpose-built, six-storey hotel in town centre. (BCB)
29 bedrs, 29 en suite; TV; tcf.
lift, ns; P 200, coach; child facs; con 150
LD 10
£ B&B £40–£48·50; B&B (double) £60·50; L £8·15, D £8·15; WB £27·50
cc Access, Amex, B'card/Visa, Diners

GLENSHIEL Highland (Ross & Cromarty) Map 53B3
Invergarry 44, London 557, Edinburgh 192, Glasgow 168, Kyle of Lochalsh 12.

★★ Kintail Lodge, IV40 8HL.
(059 981) 275
Former shooting lodge in 4 acres of walled gardens at the head of Loch Duich. Fr. Closed 24 Dec–2 Jan.
12 bedrs, 10 en suite; TV; tcf
dogs, ns; P 20; child facs
LD 8.30, nr lunch
£ B&B £23–£32, B&B (double) £42–£58; HB weekly £216–£320; D £15·50; WB £66 (HB 2 nts, Oct–May); [5% V]
cc Access, B'card/Visa; dep.

GOLSPIE Highland (Sutherland). Map 58B2
Pop 1,400. Bonar Bridge 21, London 587, Edinburgh 212, Glasgow 219, Helmsdale 17, Lairg 18.

★★ Golf Links, Church St, KW10 6TT
(040 83) 3408
Small stone-built hotel. Convenient for beach and golf course. Putting.
9 bedrs, 9 en suite; TV; tcf
TV, dogs; P 10, coach; child facs
LD 8.30
£ B&B £20–£25, B&B (double) £40–£44; HB weekly £245; D £13

★★ Sutherland Arms, Main St, KW10 6SA
(040 83) 3234

Reputedly oldest inn in Sutherland, pleasantly modernised.
15 bedrs, 12 en suite, 4 ba; TV; tcf
TV, dogs; P 30, coach; child facs
LD 9
£ B&B £25–£30, B&B (double) £45–£55, HB weekly £250; L £6, D £12·50
cc Access, B'card/Visa.

GOUROCK Strathclyde. Map 49B3
Pop 11,071. Glasgow 24, London 411, Dumbarton 22, Edinburgh 69, Kilmarnock 34, Largs 14, Paisley 19.
EC Wed. **Golf** Gourock 18h.
Pierhead (0475) 39467

★★★ Stakis Gantock, Cloch Rd, PA19 1AR (0475) 34671 Tx: 778584
Fax: (0475) 32490
Modern hotel overlooking Firth of Clyde and Argyll hills. Indoor swimming pool, tennis, sauna, solarium, gymnasium. Fr. (Sk)
101 bedrs, 101 en suite; TV; tcf
lift, dogs, ns; P 200, coach; child facs, con 200
LD 9.30
£ B&B £73–£80, B&B (double) £96; L £7·50, D £15; WB £40 (HB); [V]
cc Access, Amex, B'card/Visa, Diners.

GRANTOWN-ON-SPEY Highland (Moray). Map 54C4
Pop 1,403. Tomintoul 13, London 508, Braemar 46, Carrbridge 10, Edinburgh 131, Elgin 34, Glasgow 147, Kingussie 26.
EC Thur. **Golf** Grantown 18h. **See** Parish Church, Bridge, Granite Buildings.
54 High St. (0479) 2773

★★★ Garth, Castle Rd, PH26 3HN
(0479) 2836 Fax: (0479) 2116

Privately-owned stone-built house with modern extensions. Putting. Fr
17 bedrs, 17 en suite; TV; tcf
ns; P 16, coach; child facs
LD 8.30, bar meals only lunch
£ B&B £28, B&B (double) £56; D £16; [5% V]
cc Access, B'card/Visa, dep.

★★ Seafield Lodge, Woodside Av, PH26 3JN (0479) 2152 Fax: (0479) 2340

In quiet street, 2-storey stone-built Edwardian former private house. Fr, No, Ja. Closed Nov–mid Dec.
14 bedrs, 14 en suite; TV; tcf
dogs; P 15, coach; child facs; con 50
LD 9, bar meals only lunch
£ B&B £26·50–£64, B&B (double) £38–£98; HB weekly £195–£385; [10% V, not Apr, May, 17–31 Aug]
cc Access, B'card/Visa; dep.

★ Dunvegan, Heathfield Rd, PH26 3HX
(0479) 2301

Stone-built 2-storey house, with additions, in residential outskirts of town. Fine views. Closed 16–31 Oct & 24–26 Dec.

Sc

🛏 9 bedrs, 2 en suite, 2 ba
TV, dogs; P 9, G 1; child facs
✕ LD 7.30, bar meals only lunch
£ B&B £12–£14; D £10; [10% V]; dep.
Ravenscourt House (Highly Acclaimed), Seafield Av, PH26 3JG ☎ (0479) 2286 Fax: (0479) 3260. *Private Hotel.* Open 1 Feb–31 Oct.
£ B&B £24–£31·50, HB weekly £300–£318; [10% V]

Culdearn House (Acclaimed), Woodlands Terrace PH26 3JU ☎ (0479) 2106 Open 1 Mar–31 Oct.
£ B&B £19·95–£25; HB weekly £194·65–£225; [V]
Garden Park (Acclaimed), Woodside Av, PH26 3JN ☎ (0479) 3235
£ B&B (double) £35–£37; HB weekly £160–£165
Kinross House (Acclaimed), Woodside Av, PH26 3JR ☎ (0479) 2042. *Guest House.* Open 1 Mar–31 Oct.
£ B&B £13·50–£14; HB weekly £145–£163

Umaria Highland, Woodlands Terr, PH26 3JD ☎ (0479) 2104. *Private Hotel.*

GREENLAW Borders (Berwickshire). Map 51A2
Pop 600. Kelso 9, London 343, Berwick-upon-Tweed 20, Coldstream 10, Edinburgh 37, Galashiels 18, Lauder 12, Selkirk 22.
♚ ★★ **H** **Purves Hall,** TD10 6UJ ☎ Leitholm (089 084) 558
Privately-owned Edwardian stone-built mansion in 13 acres of grounds. Swimming pool, putting, tennis, riding.
🛏 8 bedrs, 8 en suite, 1 ba; TV, tcf
dogs; P 20; child facs
✕ LD 9.15, bar meals only lunch
£ B&B £30, B&B (double) £55; HB weekly £248–£297·50; D £15; [V]
cc Access, Amex, B'card/Visa; dep.

GREENOCK Strathclyde (Renfrewshire). Map 46A1
Pop 56,194. Glasgow 21, London 408, Dumbarton 19, Edinburgh 66, Gourock 3½, Kilmarnock 31, Largs 14, Paisley 16.
EC Wed. **Golf** Greenock 18h and 9h.
[i] Municipal Buildings, 23 Clyde St. ☎ (0475) 24400
★★★ **Tontine** 6 Ardgowan Sq, PA16 8MG ☎ (0475) 23316
Modernised 19th century building on quiet square in town centre.
🛏 28 bedrs, 28 en suite; TV; tcf
dogs; P 25, coach; child facs; con 150

GRETNA Dumfries & Galloway. Map 43C3
Pop 2,200. Carlisle 9, London 303, Beattock 30, Brampton 15, Dumfries 24, Edinburgh 82, Glasgow 85, Langholm 15.
[i] Annan Rd. ☎ (0461) 37834
★★ **Gretna Chase,** CA6 5JB ☎ (0461) 37517

Modernised Georgian building surrounded by beautiful gardens. Open Feb–Dec.
🛏 9 bedrs, 6 en suite, (3 sh); TV; tcf
P 40, coach; child facs; con 30
✕ LD 8.30, bar meals only Sun
£ B&B £33–£50, B&B (double) £42–£80; L £10·50, D £12·50; [V, w/e; Feb–Dec]
cc Access, Amex, B'card/Visa, Diners; dep.

★★ **Royal Stewart,** Glasgow Rd, CA6 5DT ☎ (0461) 38210

Bright and airy modern motel in quiet situation close to A74.

★★ **Solway Lodge,** CA6 5DN ☎ (0461) 38266 Fax: (0461) 37791
Pleasing white building with motel accommodation. Family run.
🛏 3 bedrs, 3 en suite; annexe 7 bedrs, 7 en suite; TV; tcf
dogs, P 30; child facs
✕ LD 9, bar meals only lunch
£ B&B £29–£40, B&B (double) £40–£54; D £10
cc Access, Amex, B'card/Visa, Diners; dep.

Surrone House (Highly Acclaimed), Annan Rd, CA6 5DL ☎ (0461) 38341. *Guest House.*
£ B&B £20

GULLANE Lothian (East Lothian). Map 51A3
Pop 2,254. Haddington 7½, London 377, Berwick-upon-Tweed 45, Edinburgh 18, Glasgow 62, Peebles 35.
EC Wed. **Golf** Gullane 18h (3) and 9h, Muirfield 18h–home of oldest club in world.
See St Andrew's Church ruins, slight remains of Saltcoats Castle.

★★ **Queen's,** Main St, EH31 2AS ☎ (0620) 842275
Large 18th century stone-built mansion in centre of village. Putting.
🛏 35 bedrs, 16 en suite, (19 sh), 9 ba; tcf
TV, dogs; P 70, coach; child facs; con 80

HADDINGTON Lothian. Map 51A3
Gifford 4½, London 372, Aberlady 5, Dunbar 6, Edinburgh 16.

Browns' (Highly Acclaimed), 1 West Rd, EH41 3RD ☎ (062 082) 2254. *Private Hotel.*
£ B&B £47·50

HARRIS, ISLE OF *See* Isle of Harris.

HAWICK Borders. Map 44A4
Pop 16,500. Corbridge 50, London 330, Edinburgh 48, Glasgow 80, Jedburgh 15, Kelso 21, Langholm 23, Selkirk 12.
[i] Common Haugh Car Park. ☎ (0450) 72547

★★ **Elm House,** 17 North Bridge St, TD9 9BD ☎ (0450) 2866
Late Victorian house near town centre, now a family-run hotel.
🛏 7 bedrs, 7 en suite; annexe 8 bedrs, 8 en suite; TV

★★ **C** **Kirklands,** West Stewart Pl, TD9 8BH ☎ (0450) 72263

Hillside Victorian villa in own small grounds overlooking town.
🛏 6 bedrs, 3 en suite, annexe 7 beds, 7 en suite; TV; tcf
dogs; P 20, coach; child facs
✕ LD 9.30
£ B&B £36, B&B (double) £50; L £5, D £11·95; WB £50; [10% V]
cc Access, Amex, B'card/Visa, Diners.

♚ ★★ **Mansfield House,** Weensland Rd, TD9 9EL ☎ (0450) 73988 Fax: (0450) 72007

A stone-built former mansion (1878) in 10 acres of grounds. Family owned.
🛏 5 bedrs, 5 en suite, 1 ba, annexe 5 bedrs, 5 en suite; TV; tcf
TV, dogs; P 20, coach; child facs; con 25
✕ LD 9.30, bar meals only Sun dinner
£ B&B £34–£46, B&B (double) £52–£72; L £9, D £12·50; WB £42; [5% V]
cc Access, Amex, B'card/Visa, Diners; dep.

HELENSBURGH Strathclyde (Dunbartonshire). Map 46A1
Pop 14,460. Dumbarton 8, London 410, Arrochar 17, Crianlarich 34, Edinburgh 65, Glasgow 22, Lochearnhead 49, Stirling 38.
[i] Clock Tower. ☎ (0436) 72642

★★★ **Commodore,** 112 West Clyde St, G84 8ES ☎ (0436) 76924 Tx: 778740
Modern hotel overlooking sea at West end of town.

HUNTLY Grampian. Map 55A4
Pop 4,250. Kildrummy 15, London 512, Aberdeen 38, Banff 21, Braemar 57, Edinburgh 137, Glasgow 154.
[i] ☎ (0466) 2255

♚ ★★ **Castle,** AB5 4SH ☎ (0466) 2696 Fax: (0466) 2641
Stone-built mansion in 5 hillside acres. Fine views. Putting, fishing. ⚒ Fr, Da.
🛏 24 bedrs, 9 en suite, (3 sh), 6 ba; TV; tcf
TV, dogs; P 50, G 4, U 4, coach; child facs; con 50
✕ LD 10.30
£ B&B £27·50–£32·50, B&B (double) £38·50–£43·50; HB weekly £210–£250; L £7·50, D £9·50; WB £35 (HB); [10% V]
cc Access, Amex, B'card/Visa.

 EC *early closing* **MD** *market day* ♚ *country house hotel* *ns (NS) no smoking areas* *tcf tea/coffee facilities*

INCHNADAMPH Highland. Map 57C3
Ledmore 6, London 607, Bonar Bridge 36, Durness 46, Edinburgh 232, Glasgow 236, Lairg 33, Ullapool 24.
★★ **Inchnadamph,** IV27 4HN ☎ Assynt (057 12) 202
Modernised hotel in rugged countryside. A paradise for anglers. Fishing. Open Mar 15–Oct 31.
27 bedrs, 10 en suite, 7 ba
dogs; P 25, G 3 (£1·50); child facs
LD 7.30
£ B&B £24·75–£27·75, B&B (double) £49·50–£55·50; L £7·85, D £11·25
cc Access, B'card/Visa, Diners.

INNELLAN Strathclyde (Argyll). Map 49B3
Pop 1,306. Dunoon 5½, London 467 (Fy 417), Edinburgh 121 (Fy 74), Glasgow 79 (Fy 35).
Osborne (Acclaimed), Shore Rd, PA23 7TJ ☎ (036 983) 445. *Private Hotel.*
£ B&B £20·50; HB weekly £170; [10% V, Oct–Mar]

INVERARAY Strathclyde (Argyll). Map 49A4
Pop 450. Arrochar 21, London 444, Crianlarich 39, Edinburgh 99, Glasgow 57, Lochgilphead 24, Oban 38. **EC** Wed. **Golf** Lochgilphead 9h **See** Inveraray Castle, Bell Tower, Crarae Gardens (9½ in SW).
[i] Front St ☎ (0499) 2063
★★ **Great Inn,** PA32 8XB ☎ (0499) 2466
Fax: (0499) 2421

Typical Scottish inn, dating from the 18th century, at the gates of Inveraray Castle, overlooking Loch Fyne. Snooker. Fr, Es
25 bedrs, 19 en suite, 2 ba; TV; tcf
dogs; P 30, coach; child facs; con 100
LD 9
£ B&B £19·50–£33·50, B&B (double) £39–£67; HB weekly £185–£275; L £9·95, D £15; [10% V]
cc Access, B'card/Visa; dep.

INVERGARRY Highland (Inverness-shire) Map 53C3
Pop 150. Spean Bridge 15, London 513. Edinburgh 148, Fort William 25, Glasgow 124, Invermoriston 14, Kyle of Lochalsh 54.
★★ **Glengarry Castle,** PH35 4HW ☎ (080 93) 254 Fax: (080 93) 207

Fine Victorian mansion in extensive wooded grounds beside Loch Oich. Tennis, fishing. Open 28 Mar–21 Oct.
27 bedrs, 24 en suite, 2 ba; TV; tcf
TV, dogs; P 27, G 1, coach; child facs
LD 8.15. Restrict lic
£ B&B £30–£45, B&B (double) £52–£66; HB weekly £241·50–£314·50; L £8, D £13·50
cc Access, B'card/Visa; dep.

Ardgarry, Faichem, PH35 4HG ☎ (080 93) 226. *Farm.*
£ B&B (double) £21; HB weekly £112

Lundie View, Aberchalder, PH35 4HN ☎ (080 93) 291. *Guest House.*
£ B&B £14–£20; HB weekly £60–£100

INVERMORISTON Highland. Map 54A3
Pop 400. Fort Augustus 6, London 526, Beauly 26, Edinburgh 161, Glasgow 136, Invergarry 14, Inverness 28.
★★ **Glenmoriston Arms,** Glenmoriston, IV3 6YA ☎ Glenmoriston (0320) 51206

Small stone-built hotel set back from road close to Loch Ness. Fishing. Closed 25 Dec.
8 bedrs, 8 en suite; TV; tcf
TV, dogs; P 25, coach; child facs
LD 8.30
£ B&B £32–£38, B&B (double) £45–£51; HB weekly £295–£314; L £6, D £14; WB £66 (HB); [5% V]
cc Access, B'card/Visa; dep.

INVERNESS Highland. Map 54B4
Pop 41,000. Carrbridge 23, London 529, Achnasheen 42, Beauly 12, Dingwall 14, Edinburgh 154, Elgin 39, Glasgow 165, Invermoriston 28, Ullapool 55.
EC Wed. **MD** Mon, Tue. **Golf** Inverness 18h. **See** Episcopal Cathedral, Castle, Town House, Town Steeple, Abertarff House, Museum and Art Gallery, Castle Stewart.
[i] 23 Church St. ☎ (0463) 234353
★★★ **Bunchrew House,** Bunchrew, IV3 6TA ☎ (0463) 234917 ♿

Restored 17th-century house with turrets and gables set in 15 acres of grounds on shores of Beauly Firth. Fishing. Fr
6 bedrs, 6 en suite; TV
ns; P 50, U 2; child facs; con 100
LD 9
£ B&B £45–£55, B&B (double) £65–£95; L £9·50, D £19·50; WB £120 (HB 3 days); [10% V]
cc Access, Amex, B'card/Visa; dep.

★★★ **Caledonian,** 33 Church St, IV1 1DX ☎ (0463) 235181 Tx: 75232
Fax: (0463) 711206

Large modern town centre hotel catering for tourists and businessmen alike. Swimming pool, sauna, solarium, gymnasium, billiards. Fr, De. (Emb)
100 bedrs, 100 en suite; TV; tcf
lift, dogs, ns; P 80, coach; child facs; con 200
LD 9.30
£ room £63–£84, double room £84–£99, Bk £7·75, L £8·25, D £15·75; WB £37
cc Access, Amex, B'card/Visa, Diners.

★★★ [C] **Kingsmills,** Culcabock Rd, IV2 3LP ☎ (0463) 237166 Tx: 75566
Fax: (0463) 225208 ♿

Modernised hotel beside the golf course on south side of town. Indoor swimming pool, putting, sauna, solarium, gymnasium. (Sw)
78 bedrs, 78 en suite; annexe 6 bedrs, 6 en suite; TV; tcf
lift, dogs, ns; P 100, coach; child facs; con 80
LD 9.45
£ B&B £64–£81, B&B (double) £86–£104; L £8, D £15·75; WB £95 (2 nts HB)
cc Access, Amex, B'card/Visa, Diners.

★★★ **Mercury,** Millburn Rd, IV2 3TR ☎ (0463) 239666 Tx: 75377
Fax: (0463) 711145

Large modern custom-built hotel, conveniently situated to east of town (MtCh).
118 bedrs, 118 en suite; TV; tcf
lift, dogs, ns; P 150, coach; child facs;

Sc

con 200
✕ LD 9.30
£ B&B £59–£74 (w/e £28), B&B (double) £83–£92·50; L £6·50, D £12·50
cc Access, Amex, B'card/Visa, Diners.

★★★ **Palace,** Ness Walk, IV3 5NE ☎(0463) 223243 Tx: 777210

Modernised hotel in terraced property on riverside near town centre.

★★★ **Station,** Academy St, IV1 1LG ☎(0463) 231926 Tx: 75275 Fax: (0463) 710705 ♿
Large Victorian building with ornate stairway. Centrally situated near station.
🛏 67 bedrs, 58 en suite, 4 ba; TV; tcf
🏨 lift, ns; P 20, coach; child facs; con 120
✕ LD 9.15, bar meals only lunch
£ B&B £62, B&B (double) £95; HB weekly £378–£448; D £14·95; WB; [10% V]
cc Access, Amex, B'card/Visa, Diners.

★★ **Cumming's,** Church St, IV1 1EN ☎(0463) 232531 Fax: (0463) 236541

Stone-built terrace building conveniently situated for rail and coach terminals. Closed 31 Dec–2 Jan.
🛏 34 bedrs, 19 en suite (1 sh), 6 ba; TV; tcf
🏨 lift, TV; P 25, coach; child facs; con 200
✕ LD 8
£ B&B £30–£38, B&B (double) £42–£54; L £4·50, D £7; [10% V]

★★ **Drumossie,** Old Perth Rd, IV1 2BE ☎(0463) 236451 Tx: 75138

Busy tourist hotel in elevated position overlooking Moray Firth.
🛏 75 bedrs, 75 en suite; TV; tcf
🏨 TV, dogs; P 200, coach; child facs; con 170

★★ **Glen Mhor,** 10 Ness Bank, IV2 4SG ☎(0463) 234308 Tx: 75114 ♿

19th century mansion on banks of River Ness; convenient for town centre. ⚒ Fr. Open Jan 3–Dec 30.
🛏 20 bedrs, 18 en suite, 1 ba, annexe 11 bedrs, 10 en suite; TV; tcf
🏨 dogs, ns; P 25, coach; child facs; con 30
✕ LD 9.30, bar meals only Mon–Sat lunch
£ B&B £26–£50, B&B (double) £64–£80; L £7·95, D £16·50; WB £19·50; [V, w/e; not May–Sep]
cc Access, Amex, B'card/Visa, Diners; dep.

★★ **Lochardil,** Stratherrick Rd, IV2 4LF ☎(0463) 235995
Castellated Victorian building with impressive staircase set in 5 acres of grounds on south side of town. ⚒ Fr. Closed 1–3 Jan.
🛏 11 bedrs, 11 en suite; TV; tcf
🏨 P 100, G 2, coach; child facs; con 150
✕ LD 9, bar meals only lunch
£ B&B £45, B&B (double) £75; D £9·50; [5% V]
cc Access, Amex, B'card/Visa, Diners.

★★ **Loch Ness House**, Glenurquhart Rd, IV3 6JL ☎(0463) 231248

19th century mansion beside A82. ⚒ Fr, De
🛏 23 bedrs, 17 en suite, 2 ba; TV; tcf
🏨 dogs, ns; P 60; child facs; con 100
✕ LD 9, bar meals only lunch
£ B&B £35–£52·50, B&B (double) £50–£80; HB weekly £220–£295; L £6, D £12·50; WB £29·50 (HB); [5% V]
cc Access, Amex, B'card/Visa; dep.

★★ **Muirtown,** 11 Clachnaharry Rd, IV3 6LT ☎(0463) 234860 ♿
Small purpose-built chalet motel situated in the outskirts of town.
🛏 20 bedrs, 20 en suite; TV; tcf
🏨 TV, dogs; P 65, coach; child facs; con 120

Brae Ness (Acclaimed), Ness Bank, IV2 4SF ☎(0463) 712266. *Private Hotel.* Open Feb–Nov.
£ B&B £22–£29; HB weekly £173–£215; [5% V 15 Sep–25 May]

St Ann's House (Acclaimed), 37 Harrowden Rd, IV3 5QN ☎(0463) 236157. *Guest House.* Open Nov–Sep.
£ room £11–£12

Four Winds, 42 Old Edinburgh Rd, IV2 3PG ☎(0463) 30397. *Guest House.*

INVERSHIN Highland. Map 58A2

Pop 40. Bonar Bridge 7½, London 573, Edinburgh 198, Glasgow 205, Lairg 7½.

★★ **Invershin,** IV27 4ET ☎(054 982) 202

Attractive former coaching inn (built 1808); modernised by present owners. Fishing.
🛏 11 bedrs, 7 en suite, 4 ba; annexe 6 bedrs, 4 en suite; TV; tcf
🏨 dogs; P 50; child facs

INVERURIE Grampian. Map 55B4

Pop 6,150. Kintore 4, London 500, Aberdeen 15, Edinburgh 125, Glasgow 145, Huntly 22.
ℹ Town Hall, Market Place. ☎(0467) 20600.

★★★ **Strathburn,** Burghmuir Dr, AB5 9GY ☎(0467) 24422 Fax: (0467) 25133
Modern, purpose-built hotel overlooking park at west end of town. ⚒ De
🛏 15 bedrs, 15 en suite; TV; tcf
🏨 ns; P 40; child facs
✕ LD 9.30
£ B&B £43 (w/e £34), B&B (double) £58; HB weekly £308; L £6·75, D £14·75; WB [10% V, w/d]
cc Access, Amex, B'card/Visa.

★★ **Gordon Arms,** Market Pl, AB5 9SA ☎(0467) 20314 Fax: (0467) 21792
Three-storey stone-built hotel in traditional market-town style. In town centre. ⚒ Fr
🛏 11 bedrs, 6 en suite, 2 ba; TV; tcf
🏨 TV, dogs; coach; child facs; con 220
✕ LD 8
£ B&B £21·95, B&B (doublo) £32·50; L £4·50, D £7·95; [10% V, w/e]
cc Access, Amex, B'card/Visa, Diners.

IRVINE Strathclyde (Ayrshire). Map 49B2

Pop 54,000. Kilmarnock 7, London 390, Ayr 11, Glasgow 26, Largs 18, Paisley 21.
EC Wed. **Golf** Irvine 18h, Ravenspark 18h.

★★★★ **Hospitality Inn,** Roseholme, Annick Water, KA11 4LD ☎(0294) 74272 Tx: 777097 Fax: (0294) 77287 ♿

Modern purpose-built hotel on edge of New Town. Golf course being built. (MtCh) Fr, De
128 bedrs, 128 en suite; TV, tcf
dogs, ns; P 250, coach; child facs; con 320
LD 11
£ B&B £72·30–£82·30 (w/e £32·50); B&B (double) £95–£105·60; L £9·25, D £19·25; WB £41·50 (HB)
cc Access, Amex, B'card/Visa, Diners.
(See advertisement on p. 588).

★★★ **H C R Montgreenan Mansion House,** Montgreenan Estate, KA13 7QZ Kilwinning (0294) 57733 Tx: 778525 Fax: (0294) 85397
Attractive country house set in extensive grounds situated 4 miles N of Irvine off A736. Tennis, putting, billiards. Fr
21 bedrs, 21 en suite; TV; tcf
lift; P 40; child facs; con 40
LD 9.30
£ B&B £53·50–£61, B&B (double) £74–£87; L £13·75, D £21; WB £95; [10% V]
cc Access, Amex, B'card/Visa, Diners.
(See advertisement on p. 586)

★★ **Redburn,** 65 Kilwinning Rd, KA12 8SU (0294) 76792
Modern purpose-built hotel on outskirts of town. It
20 bedrs, 5 en suite, 5 ba; TV; tcf
dogs; P 100, coach; con 200
LD 10
£ B&B £20–£24·50, B&B (double) £33–£38; L £5, D £8·50; [10% V]
cc Access, Amex, B'card/Visa.

ISLE OF ARRAN

BLACKWATERFOOT Strathclyde (Bute). Map 49A1
Brodick 11, Fy to Ardrossan, London 409, Ayr 29, Glasgow 40, Kilmarnock 25, Largs 22.
Golf Blackwater Front 18h.

★★★ **Kinloch,** Brodick, KA27 8ET Shiskine (077 086) 444 Fax: (0770 86) 447

Small modern hotel in own grounds overlooking sea. Indoor swimming pool, squash, sauna, solarium, gymnasium, billiards.
49 bedrs, 49 en suite; TV; tcf
dogs; P 50, coach; child facs; con 150
LD 8.30, bar meals only lunch
£ B&B £29·90–£37·40, B&B (double) £49·80–£74·80; D £13·50; [5% V]
cc Access, B'card/Visa; dep.

BRODICK Strathclyde (Bute). Map 49A2
Pop 816. Fy to Ardrossan, London 398, Ayr 18, Edinburgh 74, Glasgow 29, Kilmarnock 14, Largs 11, Paisley 22.
EC Wed. **MD** Thur. **Golf** Brodick 18h.
The Pier. (0770) 2140

★★★ **R Auchrannie Country House,** KA27 8BZ (0770) 2234 Fax: (0770) 2812

Traditional Scottish mansion set in wooded grounds. Indoor swimming pool, leisure and conference facilities should be completed in Spring 1991.
12 bedrs, 12 en suite; TV; tcf
P 50, coach; child facs; con 40
LD 9.30
£ B&B £27·50–£55, B&B (double) £45–£95; HB weekly £245–£445; L £7·50, D £15·50; WB £67·50 (3 nts)
cc Access, B'card/Visa; dep.

★★ **Douglas,** KA27 8AW (0770) 2155
19th century red sandstone building in wooded grounds overlooking bay. Sauna, solarium.
30 bedrs, 18 en suite, 8 ba; TV; tcf
TV, dogs; P 20, coach; child facs; con 150
£ B&B £15–£29·50, B&B (double) £35–£73; D £10·95

KILMORY Strathclyde (Bute). Map 49A1
Pop 4,100. Brodick 16 , London Fy to Ardrossan 414, Edinburgh 90, Glasgow 45.
EC Wed. **Golf** Blackwater Front 12h.

★★ **H Lagg,** KA27 8PQ Sliddery (077 087) 255

Modernised extended 18th century coaching inn in attractive grounds. Fishing.
15 bedrs, 15 en suite; tcf
TV, dogs; P 50, coach; child facs; con 120
LD 9.30
£ B&B £23–£35, B&B (double) £46–£70; HB weekly £209–£290; L £5·50, D £14·50; [5% V]

ISLE OF BARRA

BARRA, ISLE OF Western Isles (Inverness-shire). Map 52A3
Fy to Oban, London 477, Edinburgh 121, Glasgow 90.

★★ **Isle of Barra,** Tangusdale Beach, Castlebay, PA80 5XW Castlebay (087 14) 383 Fax: (087 14) 385
Modern, attractively angular building situated on a rocky and sandy slope to nearby beach. Open May–Sept.
36 bedrs, 36 en suite, 2 ba; TV; tcf
TV, dogs; P 30; child facs; con 30

ISLE OF BUTE

ROTHESAY Strathclyde (Bute). Map 49A2
Pop 5,000. Fy to Wemyss Bay, Largs 6, London 415, Edinburgh 80, Glasgow 29, Inveraray 51 via Colintraive fy.
EC Wed. **Golf** Rothesay 18h.
The Pier. (0700) 542151

Ardyne (Highly Acclaimed), 38 Mount Stewart Rd, PA20 9EB (0700) 542052 Fax: (0700) 545129
£ B&B £15–£18·50; HB weekly £135–£162·50; [5% V]

St Ebba (Highly Acclaimed), 37 Mount Stuart Rd, Craigmore, PA20 9EB (0700) 542683. *Private Hotel.*
£ B&B fr £21; HB weekly fr £187

ISLE OF COLL

ARINAGOUR Strathclyde (Argyll). Map 52C2 Fy to Oban, Dalmally 22, London 79, Ballachulish 37, Edinburgh 121, Fort William 48, Glasgow 90, Inveraray 38, Lochgilphead 36.
EC Thur. **See** Views.

Tigh-na-Mara (Acclaimed), PA78 6SY (087 93) 354. *Guest House. Putting, fishing.*

ISLE OF HARRIS

Western Isles (Inverness-shire). Map 56B2
Fy to Uig, London 607, Edinburgh 246, Glasgow 218, Kyleakin 46, Mallaig 56, Stornoway 34.
EC Thur. **See** Quay.
Harris (0859) 2011

★★ **Harris,** Tarbert, PA85 3DL Harris (0859) 2154 Fax: (0859) 2281

Old established family-run hotel specialising in family holidays. Close to ferries.
25 bedrs, 15 en suite, 5 ba
TV, dogs, ns; P 30; child facs; con 100
LD 8
£ B&B £25·90, B&B (double) £48·90; HB weekly £226·80–£256·90; L £7·50, D £15; WB £32 (HB); [5% V]
cc Access, B'card/Visa.

Changes made after July 1990 are not included.

Sc

Irvine (Ayrshire)

ISLE OF ISLAY

BOWMORE Strathclyde (Argyll). Map 48B2
Port Askaig 11, Fy to Loch Tarbert, London 491, Edinburgh 144, Glasgow 103.
[i] ☎(049 681) 254

★★ **Lochside,** Shore St, PA43 7LB ☎(049 681) 244
Small stone-built family run hotel situated on seashore in town centre.

PORT ASKAIG Strathclyde (Argyll). Map 48B3
Fy to Loch Tarbert, London 480, Edinburgh 134, Glasgow 92.
EC Tue. **Golf** Islay, Machrie 18h.

★★ **Port Askaig,** PA46 7RD ☎(049 685) 245

Small family-run hotel beautifully situated in sheltered position beside harbour.
🛏 9 bedrs, 4 en suite, 3 ba; TV; tcf
🏨 TV, dogs; P 6, G 6; no children under 5; child facs

ISLE OF JURA

CRAIGHOUSE Strathclyde. Map 48C3
Pop 200. Feolin 8½, Fy to West Tarbert. London 488, Edinburgh 142, Glasgow 101, Lochgilphead 14.

★★ **Jura,** PA60 7XU ☎Jura (049 682) 243

Stone-built hotel with fine view overlooking Sound of Jura. Fishing.
🛏 17 bedrs, 5 en suite, 6 ba; tcf
🏨 TV, dogs; P 10, coach; child facs.

ISLE OF LEWIS

STORNOWAY Western Isles (Ross & Cromarty). Map 56C3
Pop 5,500. Fy to Ullapool, London 584, Edinburgh 209, Glasgow 213.
EC Wed. **Golf** Stornoway 18h. **See** Lewis Castle, Chapel of Eye, Callanish Stones, Dun Carloway Pictish tower, Lighthouse.
[i] South Beach St. ☎(0851) 3088

★ **Royal,** Cromwell St, PA87 2DG ☎(0851) 2109
Terrace building on main street near town centre and busy harbour.

ISLE OF MULL

CRAIGNURE Strathclyde. Map 53A1
Pop 50. Fy to Oban. London 478, Edinburgh 121, Glasgow 90.
EC Wed. **Golf** Tobermory 9h. **See** Church.

★★★ **Isle of Mull,** PA65 6BB ☎(068 02) 351 Tx: 778215 Fax: (068 02) 462

Modern hotel in which all bedrooms have sea and mountain views. (SH). Open 25 Mar–1 Nov.
🛏 60 bedrs, 60 en suite; TV; tcf
🏨 dogs; P 50, coach; child facs
✕ LD 8.30, bar meals only lunch
£ B&B £48, B&B (double) £78; HB weekly £273; D £13; WB £82 (2 nts HB)
cc Access, Amex, B'card/Visa, Diners.

DERVAIG Strathclyde. Map 52C1
Tobermory 7, Craignure 29, Fy to Oban, London 505, Edinburgh 148, Glasgow 118.

Druimard Country House (Highly Acclaimed), Druimard, PA75 6QW ☎(068 84) 345. *Guest House.* ✗ Fr, Sw. Open Easter–Oct.
£ B&B fr £37·50; [10% V Mar–Apr, Sep–Oct]

TOBERMORY Strathclyde (Argyll). Map 53A2
Pop 800. Craignure 21 Fy to Oban, London 498, Edinburgh 141, Glasgow 111.
EC Wed. **Golf** Western Isles 9h.
[i] 48 Main St. ☎(0688) 2182

★★★ **Western Isles,** PA75 6PR ☎(0688) 2012 Fax: (0688) 2297

Large stone-built hotel on clifftop overlooking town and Tobermory Bay. Solarium. Open 15 Mar–2 Jan. ✗ Fr, De
🛏 23 bedrs, 23 en suite; TV; tcf
🏨 dogs, ns; P 20, coach; no children under 8; con 50
✕ LD 8.30, bar meals only lunch
£ B&B £25·50–£45; D £16; [10% V Mar–May, Oct–Dec]

★ **Mishnish,** PA75 6NU ☎(0688) 2009 Fax: (0688) 2462
Family-run traditional hotel–at waters' edge in main street.
🛏 12 bedrs, 12 en suite, 4 ba; TV; tcf
🏨 dogs; coach; child facs
✕ LD 9.30
£ B&B £25–£30; HB weekly £210–£220; dep.
(*See advertisement on p. 588*)

Harbour House (Acclaimed), 59 Main St ☎(0688) 2209. *Guest House.*

ISLE OF SKYE

ARDVASAR Highland (Inverness-shire). Map 53A3
Armadale fy to Mallaig ½, London 533, Edinburgh 176, Glasgow 146, Kyleakin fy to Kyle of Lochalsh 22.

★★ [H] **Ardvasar,** IV48 8RS ☎(047 14) 223
Charming modernised 18th century coaching inn by harbour. ✗ Fr, De. Open Mar–Dec.
🛏 10 bedrs, 10 en suite; TV; tcf
🏨 TV, dogs, ns; P 30; child facs
✕ LD 8.30
£ B&B £30, B&B (double) £50–£60; D £16; WB (3 nts HB)
cc Access, B'card/Visa; dep.

BROADFORD Highland (Inverness-shire). Map 53A4
Pop 800. Armadale fy to Mallaig 16, London 549, Dunvegan 42, Edinburgh 192, Glasgow 162, Kyleakin fy to Kyle of Lochalsh 8, Portree 28.
Golf Sconser 9h.
[i] ☎(047 12) 361

★★ **Broadford,** IV49 9AB ☎(047 12) 204/5
Attractive modernised and extended inn (built 1611) on shore of Broadford Bay. Fishing, gymnasium. ♿
🛏 20 bedrs, 20 en suite, 1 ba; annexe 9 bedrs, 9 en suite; TV; tcf
🏨 dogs; P 100, coach; child facs, con 60
✕ LD 9, bar meals only lunch
cc Access, B'card/Visa; dep.

EILEAN IARMAIN or **ISLE ORNSAY** Highland (Inverness-shire). Map 53A3
Pop 200. Armadale fy to Mallaig 8, London 541, Broadford 9½, Edinburgh 174, Glasgow 154, Kyleakin fy to Kyle of Lochalsh 14.

★★ **Duisdale,** Isle Ornsay, Sleat, IV43 8QW ☎(047 13) 202

Sc

Irvine (Ayrshire)

Tobermory (Isle of Mull)

Sleat (Isle of Skye)

Kingseat (Fife)

Kinross (Tayside)

Surrounded in lovely countryside, a former shooting lodge set in own grounds. Putting. Fr, De, Es. Open Mar–4 Jan.
20 bedrs, 14 en suite; tcf
TV, dogs; P 20, coach; child facs
LD 8.30
£ B&B £26–£38; L £7·25, D £15·70; WB £84 (2 nts HB); [5% V]
cc Access, B'card/Visa; dep.

★ **Eilean Iarmain,** Camus Croise, IV43 8QR (047 13) 332 Tx: 75252

Old world country inn situated at beach on private harbour. Fishing.

PORTREE Highland (Inverness-shire). Map 53A4
Pop 1,800. Broadford 27, fy to Mallaig, London 573, Dunvegan 21, Edinburgh 216.
EC Wed. **Golf** Portree 9h.
Meall House. (0478) 2137

★★ **Rosedale,** Quay Brae, IV51 9DB (0478) 3131

Hotel in attractive modernised terrace situated beside harbour. Open May–Sep.
20 bedrs, 20 en suite; annexe 3 bedrs, 3 en suite; TV; tcf
dogs; P 12; child facs
LD 8.30; bar meals only lunch
£ B&B £30–£35, B&B (double) £56–£66; D £15; WB £129 (3 nts HB)

★★ **Royal,** Bank St, IV51 9LU (0478) 2525

Modern stone-built hotel in town centre. Fine sea views from many rooms.
25 bedrs, 25 en suite; TV; tcf
dogs; P 14, coach; child facs; con 120
LD 9
£ B&B £35–£38, B&B (double) £50–£53; HB weekly £224; D £13·50; WB £32; [10% V Sep–Jun]
cc Access, Amex, B'card/Visa, Diners.

★ H **Isles,** Somerled Sq, IV51 9EH (0478) 2129
Substantial stone-built hotel well situated overlooking town square. Open Apr–Oct.
9 bedrs, 7 en suite, 1 ba; TV; tcf
TV, dogs; coach
LD 8.30; nr Sat lunch
£ B&B £20–£22

SKEABOST BRIDGE Highland (Inverness-shire). Map 52C4
Broadford 32, fy to Mallaig London 580, Dunvegan 16, Edinburgh 223, Glasgow 193, Portree 6.

★★★ **Skeabost House,** IV51 9NR (047 032) 202
Family-run country house hotel in extensive grounds including small golf course. Golf, fishing, billiards. Open Apr–Oct.
21 bedrs, 20 en suite, 2 ba; annexe 5 bedrs, 4 en suite, 1 ba; TV; tcf
dogs, ns; P 40, coach; child facs
LD 8.30
£ B&B £29–£36, B&B (double) £70–£80; D £18
cc Access, B'card/Visa; dep.

TEANGUE Highland (Inverness-shire). Map 53A3
Pop 50. Armadale fy to Mallaig 4½, London 537, Edinburgh 180, Glasgow 150, Kyleakin fy to Kyle of Lochalsh 17.

★★ **Toravaig,** IV44 8RJ Isle of Ornsay (047 13) 231

Traditional Scottish house now a hotel in extensive gardens. Fishing. Open Mar–Oct.
9 bedrs, 9 en suite; TV; tcf
dogs, ns; P 20; child facs
(*See advertisement on p. 588*)

UIG Highland (Inverness-shire). Map 56C1
Pop 200. Portree 16, London 590, Dunvegan 26, Edinburgh 233, Glasgow 203.
Golf Portree 9h. **See** Quay.

★★ **Uig,** IV51 9YE (047 042) 205
Attractive modernised coaching inn overlooking Uig Bay. Own grounds. Riding. Open mid April–mid Oct. Fr
11 bedrs, 11 en suite; annexe 6 bedrs, 6 en suite; TV; tcf
dogs; P 20; no children under 12; con 10
LD 8
£ B&B £30–£38, D £15

★ **Ferry Inn,** IV51 9XP (047 042) 242
Small family-run inn in village centre. Convenient for ferries.
6 bedrs, 1 en suite, 2 ba; tcf
TV, dogs, P 12; child facs
LD 8.30
£ B&B £16, B&B (double) £29; D fr £8
cc Access, B'card/; dep.

ISLE OF SOUTH UIST

LOCHBOISDALE Western Isles, (Inverness-shire). Map 52A3
Pop 697. Fy to Oban, London 477, Edinburgh 121, Glasgow 90.
EC Wed. **Golf** Askernish 9h.
(087 84) 286.

★★ **Lochboisdale,** PA81 5TH (087 84) 332
Traditional Highland hotel overlooking harbour. Popular area for fishing and ornithology. Fishing. Fr
20 bedrs, 11 en suite, (9 sh), 2 ba; tcf
TV, dogs; P 50, coach; child facs
LD 9.30, bar meals only lunch
£ B&B £18·50–£33, B&B (double) £37–£66; D £14·50
cc Access, B'card/Visa.

ISLE OF WHITHORN Dumfries & Galloway
See WHITHORN.

JEDBURGH Borders (Roxburghshire). Map 44B4
Pop 4,134. Corbridge 46, London 327, Bellingham 33, Edinburgh 47, Galashiels 17, Glasgow 81, Hawick 15, Hexham 47, Kelso 11, Lauder 26, Selkirk 16.
EC Thur. **Golf** Jedburgh 9h, Minto 18h. **See** Abbey, Queen Mary's House.
Murray's Green. (0835) 63435

Ferniehirst Mill Lodge (Acclaimed), TD8 6PQ (0835) 63279. Fax: (0835) 63749 *Hotel.*
£ B&B £15–£18·50; HB weekly £300–£325; [5% V]

Froylehurst, Friars, TD8 6BN (0835) 62477. *Guest House.* Open 1 Apr–mid-Nov.
£ B&B £13·50

JURA, ISLE OF *See* Isle of Jura.

KEITH Grampian (Banffshire). Map 59A1
Pop 4,460. Huntly 10, London 522, Banff 21, Craigellachie 15, Edinburgh 147, Elgin 16, Glasgow 164.
EC Wed. **Golf** Keith 18h.
Church Rd. (054 22) 2634

★★ **Royal,** Church Rd, AB5 3BR (054 22) 2528
Three-storey stone-built traditional style market town hotel; centrally situated.
12 bedrs, 3 en suite, 2 ba; TV; tcf
TV; ns, P 20, coach; child facs; con 300
LD 8.30, bar meals only lunch
£ B&B £12·50–£17·50, B&B (double) £25–£35; HB weekly £140; L £5·50, D £9·50; [10% V]
cc Access, Amex, B'card/Visa.

KELSO Borders (Roxburghshire). Map 51A2
Pop 5,213. Jedburgh 11, London 338, Coldstream 9, Edinburgh 44, Galashiels 18, Hawick 21, Lauder 18, Selkirk 19.

Sc

EC Wed. Golf Kelso 18h. See 12th cent Abbey remains, Bridge, Roxburgh Castle. [i] Turret Ho. ☎(0573) 23464

★★★ **Cross Keys,** 36 The Square, TD5 7HL ☎(0573) 23303 Fax: (0573) 25792 *Completely modernised 4-storey hotel with Georgian facade. Dominates town square. Sauna, solarium, gymnasium.* Fr, De, It
25 bedrs, 25 en suite, 1 ba; TV; tcf
lift, dogs; coach; child facs; con 280
LD 9.15
£ B&B £34·50–£39, B&B (double) £44–£52; L £6·40, D £12·50; WB £30 (HB); [5% V]
cc Access, Amex, B'card/Visa, Diners; dep.

★★★ **Ednam House,** Bridge St, TD5 7HT ☎(0573) 24168

Fine Georgian house in town centre with rear facing River Tweed.
32 bedrs, 32 en suite; TV
TV, dogs; P 100, child facs.
LD 9, bar meals only Mon–Sat lunch
£ B&B £36, B&B (double) £53–£73; D £15·50
cc Access, B'card/Visa

★ **Bellevue House,** Bowmont St, TD5 7DZ ☎(0573) 24588.
Owner-managed hotel, in stone-built house between town square and gates of Floor Castle.
9 bedrs, 5 en suite, 1 ba; TV; tcf
TV, dogs; P 10, coach; child facs; con 20
LD 9
£ B&B £19·50–£21·50, B&B (double) £39–£43; HB weekly £189–£206·50; L £6, D £9·50; [10% V]
cc Access, B'card/Visa; dep.

KENMORE Tayside (Perthshire). Map 54B1
Pop 600. Aberfeldy 5½, London 444, Crianlarich 31, Edinburgh 74, Glasgow 74, Lochearnhead 25.
EC Wed. Golf Taymouth Castle 18h.

★★★ **Kenmore,** Village Sq, PH15 2NU ☎(088 73) 205 Fax: (088 73) 262
Charming 3-storey stone-built former inn (1570) on banks of Tay. Golf, putting, tennis, fishing.
24 bedrs, 24 en suite; annexe 14 bedrs, 14 en suite; TV; tcf
lift, dogs, ns; P 25, coach; child facs; con 60
LD 9.15, bar meals only Mon–Sat lunch
£ B&B £25–£40, B&B (double) £45–£75; HB weekly £240–£310; L £6·75, D £17·50; [5% V, Nov–Mar]
cc Access, Amex, B'card/Visa; dep.

KILCHRENAN Strathclyde (Argyll). Map 49A4
Dalmally 18, London 473, Edinburgh 115, Glasgow 85, Inveraray 32, Oban 19.

★★★ H C R **Ardanaiseig,** Taynuilt, 020PA35 1HE ☎(086 63) 333
Fax: (086 63) 222

Elegant country house in well-kept shrub and woodland garden, near Loch Awe. Tennis, fishing, billiards. Fr. Open Apr–Oct.
14 bedrs, 14 en suite; TV
dogs; P 15; no children under 8; con 25
LD 9
£ B&B & dinner £90–£125, B&B & dinner (double) £136–£175; L £12·50, D £28·50
cc Access, Amex, B'card/Visa, Diners; dep.

★★★ **Taychreggan,** Lochaweside by Taynuilt, PA35 1HQ ☎(086 63) 211

Modernised country house in peaceful setting by Loch Awe. Open Easter–Nov.
15 bedrs, 15 en suite, 1 ba
TV, dogs; P 30, coach; child facs
LD 9
£ B&B £22·50–£27·50, B&B (double) £64–£94; L £15
cc Access, Amex, B'card/Visa, Diners.

Cuil Na Sithe (Acclaimed), PA35 1HF ☎(086 63) 234. *Private Hotel. Putting, tennis, fishing, boating, riding.*

KILDRUMMY Grampian (Aberdeenshire). Map 55A3
Pop 220. Glenkindie 3½, London 497, Aberdeen 33, Braemar 34, Edinburgh 122, Elgin 38, Glasgow 139.
Golf Aboyne 18h.

★★★ H C **Kildrummy Castle,** AB3 8RA ☎(097 55) 71288 Tx: 94012529 Fax: (097 55) 71345

A stone-built mansion (1900) in isolated location in lovely scenery. Fishing, billiards.
16 bedrs, 16 en suite; TV; tcf
dogs, ns; P 30; child facs; con 20
LD 9
£ B&B £49, B&B (double) £84–£90; HB weekly £315–£399; L £12, D £19·50
cc Access, Amex, B'card/Visa.

KILFINAN Strathclyde. Map 49A3
Auchebreck 12, Glasgow 102 (Fy 50), London 492 (Fy 438), Dunoon 26, Edinburgh 144 (Fy 95), Strachur 19.

★★ H R **Kilfinan,** Tighnabruaich, PA21 2EP ☎(070 082) 201 Fax: (070 082) 205
Modernised and extended 19th-century coaching inn beside country road in a remote village. Fishing, snooker.
11 bedrs, 11 en suite; TV
dogs; P 50, coach; child facs; con 40
LD 9.30, bar meals lunch time
£ B&B £42, B&B (double) £62; D £20
cc Access, Amex, B'card/Visa, dep.

KILLEARN Central (Stirlingshire). Map 49C3
Pop 1,086. Glasgow 16, London 405, Dumbarton 15, Edinburgh 49, Stirling 21.
EC Wed. Golf Buchanan Castle.

★★ **Black Bull,** 2 The Square, G63 9NG ☎(0360) 50215
Stone-built hotel in village square.
13 bedrs, 6 en suite, 3 ba; TV, tcf
dogs; P 50, coach; child facs
LD 9
£ B&B £26·50–£31, B&B (double) £40–£47; L £10; D £10; [10% V]
cc Access, Amex, B'card/Visa, Diners.

KILLIECRANKIE Tayside (Perthshire). Map 54B2
Pop 100. Pitlochry 4, London 448, Dalwhinnie 27, Edinburgh 72, Glasgow 84.
Golf Pitlochry 18h. See Pass of Killiecrankie.

★★ **Killiecrankie,** PH16 5LG ☎(0796) 3220 Fax: (0796) 2451

Former villa amid lovely scenery–2-storey stone building in own grounds. Putting.
12 bedrs, 8 en suite, 2 ba
TV, dogs, ns; P 30; child facs

Dalnasgadh House, PH16 5LN ☎(0796) 3237. Open Easter–Oct.
£ £14·50–£15

KILLIN Central (Perthshire). Map 54A1
Pop 600. Lochearnhead 8, London 435, Aberfeldy 22, Crianlarich 14, Edinburgh 71, Glasgow 55.
Golf Killin 9h.
[i] Main St. ☎(056 72) 254

★★ **Bridge of Lochay,** Bridge of Lochay, FK21 8TS ☎(056 72) 272
Old 2-storey coaching inn on river bank on edge of village. Fishing.

EC *early closing* **MD** *market day* *country house hotel* *ns (NS) no smoking areas* *tcf tea/coffee facilities*

KILMARNOCK Strathclyde (Ayrshire). Map 49C2
Pop 47,518. Mauchlin 8, London 383, Ayr 12, Edinburgh 61, Glasgow 21, Lanark 31, Largs 26, Paisley 20, Thornhill 48.
EC Wed. **MD** Wed, Thur, Fri, Sat. **Golf** Annanhill 18h. **See** Burns Monument and Museum (Kay Park), Laigh Kirk, Dick Institute and Museum, remains of Dean Castle, 15th cent Church.
[i] 62 Bank St. (0563) 39090

★★★ Howard Park, 136 Glasgow Rd, KA3 1UT (0563) 31211 Tx: 53168 Fax: (0563) 27795 ♿

Modern 4-storey building in outskirts of town. On main A77 road.
46 bedrs, 46 en suite; TV; tcf
lift, dogs, ns; P 200, coach; child facs; con 150

KILMELFORD Strathclyde (Argyll). Map 49A4
Oban 14, London 491, Glasgow 104, Edinburgh 135, Lochgilphead 15.

★★ Cuilfail, Oban, PA34 4XA (085 22) 274

An old coaching inn of 3 storeys. Open Mar–Dec.
12 bedrs, 7 en suite, 3 ba; tcf
TV, ns; P 30; child facs
LD 9, bar meals only lunch
£ B&B £23–£29, B&B (double) £36–£50
cc Access, B'card/Visa.

KILMORY *See* Isle of Arran

KINCLAVEN Tayside (Perthshire). Map 54C1
Perth 12, London 428, Aberfeldy 25, Blairgowie 5, Dundee 17, Edinburgh 53, Forfar 21, Glasgow 69, Pitlochry 20.
Golf Perth 18h (3). **See** Kinclaven Bridge.

Licences
Establishments have a full licence unless shown as unlicensed or with the limitations listed on p 6.

★★★ C Ballathie House, Kinclaven by Stanley, PH1 4QN Meikleour (025 083) 268 Tx: 76216 Fax: (025 083) 396 ♿

Mansion standing on riverside in extensive grounds. Putting, tennis, fishing. De. Open 1 Mar–15 Feb.
28 bedrs, 28 en suite; TV; tcf
dogs; P 50; child facs; con 12
LD 8.30
£ B&B £42–£64, B&B (double) £75–£150; HB weekly £335–£510; L £11, D £21
cc Access, Amex, B'card/Visa, Diners; dep.

KINGHOLM QUAY *See under* DUMFRIES

KINGSEAT Fife. Map 47A2
M90 (jn 3) 1½, London 394, Cowdenbeath 2½, Dunfermline 2½, Perth 24, Rosyth 6½, Edinburgh 18, Glasgow 40.

★★ Halfway House, Main St, KY12 0TG (0383) 731661 Fax: (0383) 621274
Original single-storey pub with modern two-storey extension. In centre of village.
12 bedrs, 12 en suite; TV; tcf
TV; P 100, coach, child facs; con 150
LD 9, bar meals only Sun dinner
£ B&B £35, B&B (double) £45; WB £30
cc Access, Amex, B'card/Visa.
(*See advertisement on p.588*)

KINGUSSIE Highland (Inverness-shire). Map 54B3
Pop 1,300. Newtonmore 3, London 488, Carrbridge 19, Edinburgh 112, Fort William 47, Glasgow 124, Grantown-on-Spey 26.
EC Wed. **Golf** Kingussie 18h. **See** Highland Folk Museum, China Studios, Wildlife Park (5m).
[i] King St 054 02) 297

★★ H Columba House, Manse Rd, PH21 1JF (0540 661) 402

Former manse, converted and extended, situated in 2 acres of grounds at northern end of village. Putting, tennis.
5 bedrs, 5 en suite, 1 ba; annexe 2 bedrs, 2 en suite; TV; tcf
dogs, ns; P 10; child facs
LD 8.30. Restrict lic
£ B&B £18–£24, B&B (double) £36–£48; L £7·50, D £12; [10% V]; dep.
(*See advertisement on p. 592*)

★★ Royal, 29 High St, PH21 1HX (0540) 661898, 661236
Family-run hotel in much extended building in the main street.
52 bedrs, 37 en suite, 4 ba; TV; tcf
dogs, ns; P 12, coach; child facs; con 50

Craig an Darach, PH21 1JE (0540) 661235. Open Jan–Oct.
£ B&B £12–£15

KINLOCH RANNOCH Tayside. Map 54B2
Pop 300. Tummel Bridge 6½, London 457, Aberfeldy 20, Dalwhinnie 31, Edinburgh 88, Glasgow 88, Lochearnhead 40, Pitlochry 20.
EC Wed. **Golf** Strathtay 9h. **See** The Barracks, Rannoch Moor.

★★★ Loch Rannoch, PH16 5PS (088 22) 201 Fax: (088 22) 203

Substantial white Victorian building set in 250 acres beside the Loch. Indoor swimming pool, tennis, fishing, squash, sauna, solarium, gymnasium, billiards.
17 bedrs, 16 en suite, 1 ba; TV; tcf
dogs, ns; P 40, coach; child facs; con 150
LD 9.30, bar meals only Mon–Sat lunch
£ B&B £30–£36·50; HB weekly £260–£280; D £12·50; [5% V, Mon–Thu; not Jul–Sep]
cc Access, Amex, B'card/Visa, Diners; dep.

KINROSS Tayside. Map 50B4
Pop 4,500. S. Queensferry 17, London 401, M90 (jn 6) 1, Dundee 30, Dunfermline 12, Edinburgh 27, Glasgow 45, Kincardine 17, Kirkcaldy 16, Perth 16, St Andrews 35, Stirling 23.
EC Thur. **Golf** Kinross 18h.
[i] Turfhills Service Area, M90. (0577) 63680

★★★ Green, KY13 7AS (0577) 63467 Tx: 76684 Fax: (0577) 63180
16th century coaching inn with later extension. Indoor swimming pool, golf, putting, fishing, squash, sauna, solarium, gymnasium.
40 bedrs, 40 en suite; TV, tcf
dogs; P 60, coach; child facs; con 100
LD 9.30, bar meals only lunch
£ B&B £53–£60, B&B (double) £72–£80; HB weekly £320–£360; L £8·25, D £15·50; WB £45 (HB); [10% V]
cc Access, Amex, B'card/Visa, Diners; dep.

★★★ Windlestrae, KY13 7AS (0577) 63217 Fax: (0577) 64733
Small country residence of 2-storeys set in own grounds. Sauna. Fr
19 bedrs, 19 en suite; TV; tcf
TV, dogs; P 60, coach; child facs; con 60
LD 9.30
£ B&B £47·50, B&B (double) £65–£105; HB weekly £308–£433·50; L £10·50, D £17·50; WB; [10% V]
cc Access, Amex, B'card/Visa; dep.

★★ Bridgend, 253 High St, KY13 7EN (0577) 63413 Fax: (0577) 64769

Sc

Kingussie (Inverness-shire)

★★

Manse Road, Kingussie,
Inverness-shire PH21 1JF
Tel: 0540 661402

Ian & Myra invite you to visit their home at COLUMBA HOUSE, a small welcoming family run hotel, offering you the best in Highland hospitality and home cooking. Enjoy the comfort of the luxury bedrooms in this elegant 19th century former Manse. All rooms have private bathroom, colour TV, tea making, telephone, mini bar and magnificent views of the surrounding mountains. Sample a delicious meal made with fresh homegrown produce and local meat, fish and game. Relax in the secluded walled garden, stroll along our woodland path or have a friendly game of tennis, putting or croquet in the extensive grounds. Licensed. Open all year. Ample parking. Also luxury holiday cottages available. Send now for our colour brochure.
YOUR COMFORT AND ENJOYMENT IS OUR PRIORITY

Kirkcudbright (Dumfries & Galloway)

KIRKCUDBRIGHT, GALLOWAY
Whoro Robert Burnc wroto 'Tho Solkirk Grooo'
**RAC Ashley Courtenay recommended

Selkirk Arms Hotel

Historic 18th century Hotel, now newly refurbished in picturesque town. Ideal for business or family holidays.

Golf, squash, sailing, fishing, sea-angling all nearby.

Exciting à la carte menu prepared using finest fresh local ingredients.

All rooms with private facilities. TV, Radio and telephone. Large secluded gardens.

Kyle of Lochalsh (Ross-shire)

A FINE HOTEL OVERLOOKING THE ISLE OF SKYE
A HAVEN OF COMFORT AND HOSPITALITY
38 ROOMS WITH EN SUITE
Kyle of Lochalsh, Ross-shire IV40 8AF
Telephone: Kyle (0599) 4202 Telex: 75318

Lockerbie (Dumfries-shire)

The Dryfesdale Hotel

Lockerbie, Dumfries-shire Tel: (05762) 2427

Country House Hotel on rising ground with panoramic views close to A74, north of Lockerbie but quietly situated. *Ideal centre for curling, shooting and fishing.*

EC *early closing* **MD** *market day* *country house hotel* *ns (NS) no smoking areas* *tcf tea/coffee facilities*

Recently modernised former private house, much extended over the years.
🛏 15 bedrs, 14 en suite; TV; tcf
🏨 dogs; P 40; child facs; con 250

★★ Kirklands, 20 High St, KY13 7AN
📞(0577) 63313
Refurbished 18th-century coaching inn. Family run.
🛏 9 bedrs, 9 en suite; TV; tcf
🏨 P 15; child facs; con 40
✕ LD 9, bar meals only lunch
£ B&B £28·50, B&B (double) £42; D £12
cc Access, B'card/Visa.
(*See advertisement on p. 588*)

KIRKBEAN Dumfries & Galloway. Map 43B3
New Abbey 5, London 338, Dalbeattie 12, Edinburgh 82, Glasgow 84.

Cavens (Highly Acclaimed), DG2 8AA
📞(038 788) 234. *Guest House.*
£ £25–£30; HB weekly £220

KIRKCALDY Fife. Map 47A4
Pop 49,820. M90 9, S. Queensferry 16, London 400, Dundee 29, Dunfermline 12, Edinburgh 25, Kinross 16, St Andrews 23.
EC Wed. **Golf** Dunnikier Municipal 18h. **See** Sailor's Walk (Nat Trust Scot), Ravenscraig Castle ruins, Art Gallery and Museum, Royal Palace of Falkland 9½ m NW.
ℹ Esplanade. 📞(0592) 267775

★★★ Dean Park, Chapel Level. 📞(0592) 261635 Tx: 727071
Stone-built former private mansion with modern extensions; edge of town. Billiards.

★★★ Parkway, Abbotshall Rd, KY2 5DG
📞(0592) 262143 Tx: 728256
Fax: (0592) 200433
Three-storey modern purpose-built hotel standing at road junction in town.
🛏 32 bedrs, 32 en suite; annexe 4 bedrs, 4 en suite; TV; tcf
🏨 dogs; P 80; child facs; con 180
✕ LD 9.30
£ B&B £45, B&B (double) ££60; L £8, D £11·50; WB £30 (HB; Oct–Mar); [10% V w/e]
cc Access, Amex, B'card/Visa.

KIRKCUDBRIGHT Dumfries & Galloway (Kirkcudbrightshire). Map 43A2
Pop 3,406. Dalbeattie 13, London 354, Dumfries 25, Edinburgh 97, Glasgow 88, New Galloway 18.
EC Thur. **Golf** Kirkcudbright 9h. **See** Tolbooth, Mercat Cross, Museum, Broughton House, McLellans Castle ruins.
ℹ Harbour Sq. 📞(0557) 30494

★★ Selkirk Arms, Old High St, DG6 4JG
📞(0557) 30402 Fax: (0557) 31639

Hotel of 18th century origins. Sheltered garden with spacious lawn. ⚒ Fr, De
🛏 14 bedrs, 14 en suite; annexe 1 bedr, 1 en suite; TV; tcf
🏨 dogs; G 16, coach; child facs
✕ LD 9.30
£ B&B £37, B&B (double) £58; HB weekly £295; L £7, D £14
cc Access, Amex, B'card/Visa, Diners.
(*See advertisement on p. 592*)

KIRKMICHAEL Tayside (Perthshire). Map 54C2
Pop 780. Blairgowrie 12, London 443, Edinburgh 68, Glasgow 84, Pitlochry 12.
EC Thur. **Golf** Pitlochry 18h.

★★ Aldchlappie, PH10 7NS 📞Strathardle (025 081) 224

Victorian stone-built former lodge in attractive countryside near village. Fishing.
🛏 7 bedrs, 7 en suite, 1 ba; tcf
🏨 TV, dogs, ns; P 20, coach; child facs
✕ LD 9.30
£ B&B £17–£20·50, B&B (double) £34–£41; D £12; WB £26 (HB); [10% V]
cc Access, Amex, B'card/Visa; dep.

★★ Log Cabin, PH10 7NB 📞Strathardle (025 081) 288 ♿
Single-storey Norwegian timber-built hotel in beautiful isolated location. Fishing.
🛏 13 bedrs, 13 en suite; tcf
🏨 TV, dogs; P 16; child facs
✕ LD 8.45, bar meals only lunch
£ B&B £25–£32, B&B (double) £39–£43
cc Access, Amex, B'card/Visa, Diners; dep.

KIRKNEWTON Lothian Map 47C2
Edinburgh 11, London 382, M8 (Jn 3) 4, Lanark 24.

Dalmahoy, EH27 8EB 📞031-333 1845
Fax: 031-335 3203 ♿
New hotel opening September 1990, awaiting inspection. Indoor swimming pool, golf, putting, tennis, squash, sauna, solarium, gymnasium, snooker.
🛏 116 bedrs, 116 en suite; TV; tcf
🏨 lift, ns; P 250, coach; child facs; con 260
✕ LD 10
£ B&B £90–£100 (w/e £50), B&B (double) £105–£115; L £12, D £18; [10% V]
cc Access, Amex, B'card/Visa, Diners.

KYLE OF LOCHALSH Highland (Ross & Cromarty). Map 53B4
Pop 900. Invergarry 48, London 561 (fy 570), Achnasheen 35, Broadford 8 (fy to Kyleakin), Edinburgh 196, Glasgow 174, Invermoriston 56.
EC Thur. **Golf** Kyle 9h. **See** Harbour, Eilean Donan Castle, Castle Moil across Kyle Akin on Isle of Skye, Balmacara House (4 m E).
ℹ 📞(0599) 4276

★★★ Lochalsh, Ferry Road, IV40 8AF
📞(0599) 4202 Tx: 75318 Fax: (0599) 4881
Modern white-painted building, on promontory giving magnificent sea and mountain views. ⚒ Fr
🛏 38 bedrs, 38 en suite; TV; tcf
🏨 lift, TV, dogs, ns; P 20, coach; child facs; con 50
✕ LD 9
£ B&B £51–£68, B&B (double) £75–£105; L £9·75, D £18·75
cc Access, Amex, B'card/Visa, Diners.
(*See advertisement on p. 592*)

Retreat, Main St, IV40 8BY 📞Kyle (0599) 4308. *Guest House.*
£ B&B £11·50–£15

LAGGAN Highland (Inverness-shire). Map 54B3
Pitlochry 38, London 482, Fort William 38, Newtonmore 7.

★★★ Gaskmore House, by Newtonmore, PH20 1BS 📞(052 84) 250 ♿

Modernised and extended turreted mansion in pleasant gardens just off A86. ⚒ De, No
🛏 9 bedrs, 9 en suite; TV; tcf
🏨 dogs, ns; P 40, coach; child facs; con 40
✕ LD 9, bar meals only lunch
£ B&B £27·50; D £17·50; [10% V, excl. Jun–Sep]
cc Access, Amex, B'card/Visa; dep.

LAIDE Highland (Ross & Cromarty). Map 57B2
Dundonnell 18, London 600, Edinburgh 230, Gairloch 14, Glasgow 240, Ullapool 48.

★ Ocean View, Achnasheen, 1V22 2ND
📞 (044 582) 385
Friendly, owner-run hotel in spectacular scenery with views over Gruinard Bay to the Summer Isles.
🛏 9 bedrs, 9 en suite; TV; tcf
🏨 TV, dogs; P 50; child facs
✕ LD 9
£ B&B £25–£35, B&B (double) £50–£60; HB weekly £230–£260; L £5·50, D £13·50; WB £60; [10% V]
cc Access, B'card/Visa; dep.
(*See advertisement on p. 550*)

LAIRG Highland (Sutherland). Map 58A2
Pop 950. Bonar Bridge 11, London 577, Bettyhill 46, Durness 56, Edinburgh 202, Glasgow 209, Helmsdale 50, Ullapool 44.
EC Wed. **Golf** Royal Dornoch 18h and 9h.

★★★ Sutherland Arms, Main Rd, IV27 4AT 📞(0549) 2291 Fax: (0549) 2261

Sc

A traditional hotel overlooking Loch Shin, set in picturesque scenery. Open Apr–Oct.
Fr, De. (SH)
27 bedrs, 22 en suite, 4 ba; TV; tcf
dogs; P 30, coach; child facs
LD 8.30, bar meals only lunch
£ B&B £45–£48, B&B (double) £72–£78; HB weekly £273; D £15; WB £82 (2nts HB)
cc Access, Amex, B'card/Visa, Diners; dep.

LANGBANK Strathclyde (Renfrewshire). Map 46A1
Pop 804. Glasgow 14, London 402, M8 (jn 31) 1½, Dumbarton (via toll bridge) 10, Edinburgh 59, Glasgow 14, Greenock 7, Paisley 9½.
EC Wed. **Golf** Erskine 18h.

★★★ R **Gleddoch House,** PA14 6YE
(047 554) 711 Tx: 779801
Fax: (047 554) 201

Elegant country house in 250-acre estate with own golf course. Golf, putting, squash, riding, sauna, billiards. Fr, Po, Ar
33 bedrs, 33 en suite; TV; tcf
dogs; P 100, coach; child facs; con 50
LD 9
£ B&B £85–£100, B&B (double) £105–£150; L £15, D £30; WB £66 (HB)

LANGHOLM Dumfries & Galloway (Dumfriesshire). Map 43C3
Pop 2,500. Carlisle 20, London 314, Beattock 32, Brampton 20, Dumfries 28, Edinburgh 71, Glasgow 86, Hawick 23.
EC Wed. **Golf** Langholm 9h. **See** Remains of Castle, Common Riding, bnlast Fri in July, Gilnockie Tower 4 m S.
High St. (038 73) 80976

★★ **Eskdale,** Market Pl, DG13 0JH
(038 73) 80357

Three-storey stone-built coaching house set in town centre.
16 bedrs, 10 en suite, 4 ba; TV; tcf
TV, dogs; P 12, coach; child facs; con 70

LARGS Strathclyde (Ayrshire). Map 49B2
Pop 10,000. Irvine 17, London 408, Ayr 31, Edinburgh 74, Glasgow 29, Gourock 14, Kilmarnock 26, Paisley 23.
EC Wed. **Golf** Routenburn 18h, Kelburn.
Promenade. (0475) 673765

★★ **Elderslie,** Broomfields, KA30 8DR
(0475) 686460

Victorian building on seafront, commanding fine views of Firth of Clyde.
25 bedrs, 13 en suite, 4 ba; TV; tcf
TV, dogs, ns; P 30, coach; child facs; con 30
LD 8.30
£ B&B £25–£30; L £8·50, D £12·50; [10% May–Sep]
cc Access, Amex, B'card/Visa, Diners; dep.

★★ **Glen Eldon,** 2 Barr Cres, KA30 8PX
(0475) 673381
Two-storey building with a pleasant garden. At northern end of Largs.

★★ **Queen's,** North Promenade, KA30 8QW (0475) 675311 Fax: (0475) 675313
Small family-run hotel fronted by well-kept lawn. Good sea views. Putting.
16 bedrs, 3 en suite, (1 sh), 3 ba; TV; tcf
TV, dogs; P 50, coach; child facs; con 10

★★ **Springfield,** North Bay, KA30 8QL
(0475) 673119

Overlooking seafront, a 3-storey building with pleasant views of Firth of Clyde. Putting.
47 bedrs, 41 en suite, 6 ba; TV; tcf
lift, TV, dogs, ns; P 65, coach; child facs; con 60
LD 8.30
£ B&B £23–£35, B&B (double) £40–£48; HB weekly £180–£207; L £5, D £12·50
cc Access, Amex, B'card/Visa, Diners.

Carlton, 10 Aubrey Cres, KA30 8PR
(0475) 672313. *Guest House.* Open Easter–Oct.
£ B&B £12–£13; HB weekly £115·50–£122·50

LARKHALL Strathclyde (Lanarks). Map 46C4
M74 (jn 10) 6, London 373, Edinburgh 37, Glasgow 15, Hamilton 4, Kilmarnock 25, Lanark 12.

Fleming Crest, Ayr Rd, ML9 2TZ (0698) 791711 *Private Hotel. Snooker.*
£ B&B £23; [10% V]

LENNOXTOWN Strathclyde (Dunbartonshire). Map 46A3
Pop 5,000. Glasgow 8, London 396, Dumbarton 19, Edinburgh 46, Lochearnhead 36, Stirling 21.
Golf Campsie 18h.

Glazertbank, Main St, G65 7DJ (0360) 310790. *Private Hotel.*

LERWICK
See SHETLAND ISLANDS.

LESLIE Fife. Map 50C4
Pop 3,760. M90 (jn 7) 13, London 403, Glenrothes 3, Edinburgh 28, Glasgow 53, Kinross 11, Kirkcaldy 8, Perth 20.
EC Wed. **Golf** Leslie 18h. **See** Strathendry Castle, Falkland Palace 4 m N, Loch Leven.

★★ **Rescobie,** Valley Dr, KY6 3BQ
Glenrothes (0592) 742143.

Secluded country house in 2 acres of gardens. Putting. Fr, De
8 bedrs, 8 en suite; TV; tcf
P 20; child facs
LD 9
£ B&B £43–£50, B&B (double) £60–£65; HB weekly £259–£350; L £8·50, D £13·50
cc Access, Amex, B'card/Visa; dep.

LETHAM Fife. Map 50C4
Pop 170. Glenrothes 9, London 414, Dundee 15, Edinburgh 40, Glasgow 59, Kinross 16, Kirkcaldy 14, Perth 21, St Andrews 15.
Golf Ladybank 18h.

★★★ **Fernie Castle,** Ladybank, nr Cupar, KY7 7RU (033 781) 381
Fax: (033 781) 422

Lovely 14th century stone-built castle in own secluded grounds in rural area. Putting.
16 bedrs, 16 en suite; TV; tcf
dogs; P 70, coach; child facs; con 150
LD 9.30
£ B&B £46, B&B (double) £57–£108; HB weekly £420; D £19·50

LEWIS, ISLE OF *See* ISLE OF LEWIS

LINWOOD Strathclyde (Renfrewshire). Map 46B2
Pop 13,697. Paisley 3, London 396, Edinburgh 56, Glasgow 11, Gourock 17, Kilmarnock 21, Largs 21.
EC Tue. **Golf** Elderslie 18h.

★★ **Golden Pheasant,** Moss Rd, PA3 3HP ☎ Johnstone (0505) 21266
Modern hotel with easy access to motorway and Glasgow Airport.

LOCHBOISDALE
See ISLE OF SOUTH UIST.

LOCHEARNHEAD Central (Perthshire). Map 50A4
Callander 14, London 427, Crianlarich 16, Edinburgh 64, Glasgow 47, Stirling 30.
See Edinample falls, Rob Roy tomb.

★★ **Clachan Cottage,** FK19 8PU ☎ (056 73) 247

Converted 250-year-old cottages in a lochside setting. Fishing. Closed Feb.
19 bedrs, 14 en suite, 2 ba; tcf
TV, dogs; P 50, coach; child facs; con 60
LD 9. Restrict lic
£ B&B £18–£25, B&B (double) £36–£40; HB weekly £213·50–£227·50; WB £53 (2 nts HB); [10% V Apr & Oct–Dec]

LOCHGILPHEAD Strathclyde (Argyll). Map 49A3
Pop 1,900. Inveraray 23, London 468, Edinburgh 122, Glasgow 80, Oban 36.
EC Tue. **Golf** Lochgilphead 9h. **See** St Mary's Church.
[i] ☎ (0546) 2344

★★ **Stag,** PA31 8NE ☎ (0546) 2496
Three-storey building in centre of town with well-known corner turret. Sauna, solarium.
19 bedrs, 19 en suite; TV; tcf
dogs; coach; child facs; con 50
LD 8.30
£ B&B £27·50–£35, B&B (double) £49·50–£60; HB weekly £240–£300; L £6, D £10·50; WB £20
cc Access, B'card/Visa.

LOCHINVER Highland (Sutherland). Map 57C3
Pop 350. Inchnadamph 13, London 620, Dingwall 74, Durness 52, Edinburgh 245, Glasgow 249, Lairg 44, Ullapool 34.
EC Tue. **MD** Fri.
[i] ☎ (057 14) 330

★★★ **H** **C** **Inver Lodge,** IV27 4LU ☎ (057 14) 496 Tx: 75206 Fax: (057 14) 395
Modern, two-storey hotel in own grounds in an elevated situation overlooking village, harbour and Loch Inver. Fishing, sauna, solarium, snooker. Open May–18 Oct. Fr
20 bedrs, 20 en suite; TV; tcf
dogs; P 30; child facs
LD 9, bar meals only Mon–Sat lunch
£ B&B £62–£88, B&B (double) £94–£176
cc Access, Amex, B'card/Visa, Diners; dep.

Ardglas, Inver, IV27 4LI ☎ (057 14) 257.
Guest house Open Mar–Nov.
£ B&B £11–£11·50

LOCHMABEN Dumfries and Galloway (Dumfries-shire). Map 43B3
Carlisle 28, London 322, Beattock 13, Dumfries 8½, Edinburgh 65, Glasgow 68.

★★ **Balcastle,** High St, nr Lockerbie, DG11 1NG ☎ (0387) 810239

Red sandstone building well-situated in outskirts of this small town.
6 bedrs, 5 en suite; annexe 4 bedrs, 2 en suite, (1 sh); TV; tcf
TV, dogs; P 100, coach; child facs; con 150
LD 9
£ B&B £12–£15, L £3·50, D £6.

LOCKERBIE Dumfries & Galloway (Dumfriesshire). Map 43B3
Pop 3,000. Carlisle 24, London 318, Beattock 14, Brampton 30, Dumfries 12, Edinburgh 66, Glasgow 69, Langholm 18.
EC Tue. **MD** Tue, Thur, Fri. **Golf** Lockerbie 9h. **See** Old Tower, Roman Camp.

★★★ **Dryfesdale,** DG11 2SF ☎ (057 62) 2427 ♿

Carefully converted 18th-century manse with splendid panoramic views in 5 acres of mature gardens. Fr
16 bedrs, 14 en suite, 1 ba; TV; tcf
dogs; P 50, coach; child facs; con 40
LD 9.30
£ B&B £40, B&B (double) £60; L £9, D £12·50; WB £36 (2 nts HB, winter)
cc Access, Amex, B'card/Visa.
(*See advertisement on p. 592*)

★★★ **Lockerbie House,** DG11 2RG ☎ (057 62) 2610 Fax: (057 62) 3046

Beautiful Georgian country house in 78 acres of park and woodland. Fr, De, Ma.
26 bedrs, 26 en suite, 1 ba; TV; tcf
TV, dogs; P 80, U 1, coach; child facs; con 150
LD 9.30, bar meals only lunch
£ B&B £37–£46·50, B&B (double) £55–£70·50; HB weekly £238·50–£262·50; L £6·50, D £10·50; WB; [10% V]
cc Access, Amex, B'card/Visa; dep.

★★★ **Queens,** Annan Rd, DG11 2RB ☎ (057 62) 2415 Fax: (057 62) 3901
Small Victorian mansion in local stone in own pleasant grounds. Indoor swimming pool, putting, sauna, solarium, gymnasium, billiards.
21 bedrs, 21 en suite; TV; tcf
dogs; P 200, coach; child facs; con 300
LD 9.30
£ B&B £32·50, B&B (double) £52; D £11·25; WB £38 (HB)
cc Access, B'card/Visa.

★★ **Somerton House,** Carlisle Rd, DG11 2DR ☎ (057 62) 2583

Red sandstone building at southern edge of town. Near A74. Closed 25 Dec & 1 Jan
7 bedrs, 7 en suite; TV; tcf
dogs, ns; P 100, coach; child facs; con
LD 9, bar meals only lunch
£ B&B £28–£32·25, B&B (double) £45–£52; L £6·95, D £11·95
cc Amex, B'card/Visa.

LUNDIN LINKS Fife. Map 50C4
South Queensferry 27, London 411, Dundee 21, Edinburgh 36, Glasgow 63, Kinross 24, Kirkcaldy 11, St Andrews 11
EC Thur. **Golf** Lundin Links 18h. **See** Alexander Selkirk's birthplace, Robinson Crusoe statue (Lower Largo).

★★ **Lundin Links,** Leven Road, KY8 6AP ☎ (0333) 320207 Fax: (0333) 320930

Mock Tudor-style early 20th century building in own small grounds.
20 bedrs, 18 en suite; TV; tcf
TV, dogs; P 50, coach; child facs; con

MACDUFF Grampian. Map 59B1
Pop 4,028. Huntly 21, London 533, Aberdeen 47, Banff 1, Edinburgh 158, Fraserburgh 22, Glasgow 175.
EC Wed. **Golf** Royal Tarlair 18h.

Sc

★★ **Highland Haven,** Shore St, AB4 1UB ☎(0261) 32408 Fax: (0261) 33652

Overlooking harbour and sea. 4-storey stone-built hotel with first-floor sun lounge. Sauna, solarium, gymnasium, billiards. Fr
16 bedrs, 16 en suite; TV; tcf
dogs; P, coach; child facs; con 50
LD 9
£ B&B £19·95–£29·95, B&B (double) £38–£49·50; HB weekly £180–£210; L £4·95, D £11·65; WB £50 (2 nts HB); [10% V w/e]
cc Access, Amex, B'card/Visa; dep.

MALLAIG Highland (Inverness-shire). Map 53A3
Pop 1,050. Fort William 43, London 533, Edinburgh 175, Glasgow 142.
EC Wed. **Golf** Traig, Arisaig 9h.
Station Buildings. ☎(0687) 2170

★★ **Marine,** Station Rd, PH41 4PY ☎(0687) 2217

Family-owned hotel in terrace building beside railway station. Near harbour. Restricted Nov–Mar.
23 bedrs, 10 en suite, 4 ba; TV; tcf
TV, dogs; P 6, coach; child facs
LD 8.30, bar meals only lunch
£ B&B £18–£24; D £13; WB
cc Access, Amex, B'card/Visa; dep.

★★ **West Highland,** PH41 4QZ ☎(0687) 2210 Fax: (0687) 2130

Privately-owned stone-built hotel on high ground, overlooking Sound of Sleat. Open Apr–Oct.
26 bedrs, 26 en suite; tcf
TV, dogs; P 40, coach; child facs
LD 8.30
£ B&B £25–£27; L £6, D £13
cc Access, B'card/Visa; dep.
(*See advertisement on p. 597*)

MARKINCH Fife. Map 50C4
Kirkcaldy 10, London 410, Edinburgh 35, Freuchie 5, Kinross 15, Lundin Links 9½.

★★★★ **Balbirnie House,** KY7 6NE ☎(0592) 610066

A classical grade A listed mansion, built in 1777, has been rescued from dereliction to become a superb hotel, furnished in keeping with oil paintings and some good antiques. Set in 14 acres of gardens or the edge of a park. Golf.
30 bedrs, 30 en suite; TV; tcf

MARYCULTER Grampian. Map 55B3
Stonehaven 15, London 493, Aberdeen 11, Banchory 14, Edinburgh 118, Glasgow 137.

★★★ **Maryculter House,** Southdeeside Rd, AB1 0BB ☎(0224) 732124 Tx: 739579 Fax: (0224) 735510

Recently refurbished historic house, part dating to the 13th century, attractively furnished and set in wooded grounds by the Dee. Fishing. Fr, Po
11 bedrs, 11 en suite; TV; tcf
P 50, child facs; con 25
LD 9.30, bar meals only lunch
£ B&B £65, B&B (double) £75 (w/e £40); D £20·50
cc Access, Amex, B'card/Visa, Diners.

MAYBOLE Strathclyde (Ayrshire). Map 42B4
Dalmellington 17, London 392, Ayr 11, Edinburgh 82, Girran 13, Glasgow 44.

★★★ R **Ladyburn,** Ladyburn, KA19 7SG ☎(065 54) 585
Stone-built 17th century country house, beautifully furnished with some fine antiques and adorned with pictures and flowers, set in 23 acres of grounds. It. Ru
8 bedrs, 8 en suite; TV; tcf
dogs; ns; P 12; no children under 12; con 20
8.45. Restrict lic
£ B&B £55–£95, B&B (double) £115–£150; [10% V w/d excl Jul–Sep]
cc Access, Amex, B'card/Visa.

Changes made after July 1990 are not included.

MELROSE Borders (Roxburghshire). Map 51A2
Pop 2,000. St Boswells 2½, London 340, Edinburgh 35, Galashiels 4, Glasgow 71, Hawick 14, Jedburgh 12, Lauder 11, Kelso 13, Selkirk 6½.
EC Thur. **Golf** Melrose 9h. **See** Abbey ruins, Abbey Museum, 17th cent Cross, Timontium (site of Roman Camp), Dryburgh Abbey.
Priorwood Gardens, nr Abbey.
☎(089 682) 2555

★★ C **Burt's,** Market Sq, TD6 9PN ☎(089 682) 2285 Fax: (089 682) 2870

Traditional family run hotel amidst beautiful countryside. Billiards. Fr, De
21 bedrs, 21en suite; TV; tcf
dogs; P 36; child facs
LD 9
£ B&B £36–£38, B&B (double) £56–£62; HB weekly £280–£336; L £11, D £14; WB £40
cc Access, Amex, B'card/Visa, Diners.
(*See advertisement on p. 598*)

★★ **George & Abbotsford,** High St, TD6 9PD ☎(089 682) 2308 Fax: (089 682) 3363
Stone-built 3-storey coaching inn set in middle of town.
31 bedrs, 30 en suite, 1 ba; TV; tcf
TV, dogs, ns; P 150, U 2, coach; child facs; con 150
LD 9, bar meals only Mon–Sat lunch
£ B&B £38, B&B (double) £58; HB weekly £265–£280; D £13; WB £75 (2 nts); [5% V excl Aug & Sep]
cc Access, Amex, B'card/Visa, Diners.

MELVICH Highland (Sutherland). Map 58B4
Helmsdale 39, London 642, Edinburgh 267, Glasgow 274, Thurso 18, Tongue 25.

★★ **Melvich,** nr Thurso, KW14 7YJ ☎(06413) 206

Former 17th century hostelry in own grounds enjoying fine sea views. Fishing, billards. Fr, De, Du
14 bedrs, 14 en suite; TV; tcf
TV, dogs, ns; P 14; child facs; con 60
LD 8, bar meals only lunch
£ B&B £22·50–£25, B&B (double) £42–£46·50; D £12·50; [5% V]
cc Access, B'card/Visa.

 EC *early closing* **MD** *market day* *country house hotel* *ns (NS) no smoking areas* *tcf tea/coffee facilities*

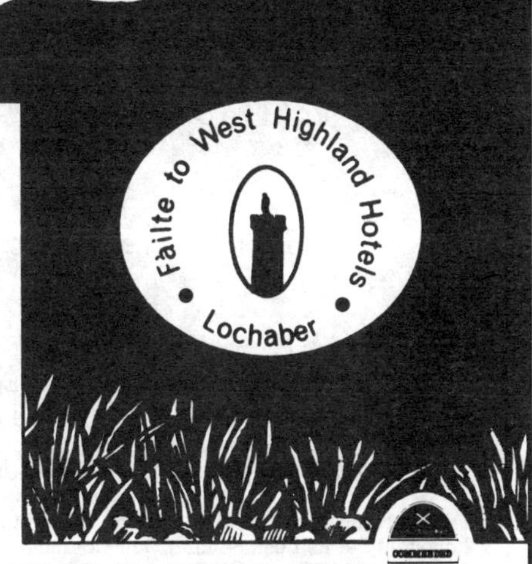

MORAR

Morar Hotel, Morar, PH40 4PA.
Reservations: (0687) 2346.

A friendly family-run Hotel on the romantic 'Road to the Isles'; 50 metres from Railway Station; 42 miles from Fort William and 3 miles from Mallaig – the Southern Gateway to Skye. The Hotel overlooks the superb Silver Sands and all the bedrooms have private bathrooms, hospitality trays, electric blankets, heaters, etc.

MALLAIG

West Higland Hotel, Mallaig, PH41 4QZ
Reservations: (0687) 2210.

Personally run 30 bedroom Hotel on the 'Road to the Isles', overlooking the famous fishing port of Mallaig – the ideal base for day touring to the Isle of Skye, Inner Hebrides, etc. The apartments all have private facilities, heating, electric blankets, hospitality tray, etc. Ferry & Rail terminals less than 100 metres from Hotel.

FORT WILLIAM

Grand Hotel, Fort William, PH33 6DX.
Reservations: (0397) 702928.

Centre of Fort William – gateway to the romantic and scenic West Highlands. 33 bedrooms all with bathrooms en suite. In-room facilities include: hospitality tray, colour TV, heating, radio/intercom/baby listening console, electric blankets, etc. The ideal base for day touring the Highlands.

Group Enquiry Fax: (0397) 705060

Sc

Melrose (Roxburghshire)

BURTS HOTEL

MELROSE ROXBURGHSHIRE

RAC ★★ STB ♛♛♛♛ commended Egon Ronay 'Taste of Scotland' commended

Friendly, family-run hotel, tastefully furnished with 21 recently refurbished bedrooms, all en-suite. All with telephones, colour TV, radio, tea and coffee making facilities and hair dryers. Elegant A la Carte Restaurant also Lounge Bar serving Lunches and Suppers daily. Billiard Room and Residents' Lounge. Private Car Park.

Burts Hotel is the ideal centre for touring the beautiful Border Country and enjoying Scottish hospitality at its best. Several Golf Courses are within easy reach and Salmon and Trout Fishing can be arranged. Game shooting on local estates also available with prior notice.

For brochure write to:

Graham and Anne Henderson – Proprietors

Phone (089 682) 2285 Fax No (089 682) 2870

Moffat (Dumfriesshire)

Moffat House Hotel

High Street, Moffat, Dumfriesshire

Tel: (0683) 20039 4 Crown Commended

MOFFAT HOUSE is a gracious 18th-century Adam mansion, centrally situated in 2½ acres of our own gardens. The charming village of Moffat is just off the A74 and provides an ideal stopping-off point for breaking your journey north/south.

The hotel is fully licensed and we provide a wide range of bar lunches/suppers together with a widely acclaimed à la carte dinner menu. All our rooms have private bath/shower with WC, central heating, colour TV, radio, telephone, hairdryer and tea/coffee tray.

We offer a 3-day, D,B&B break throughout the season for only £114.50 per person (until mid-May £105.00). Please send for a full colour brochure to 'The Reid Family', Moffat House Hotel, Moffat, Dumfriesshire quoting ref. no. MHH5. (Tel: 0683 20039; Fax: 0683 21288)

Muir of Ord (Ross-shire)

RAC ★★ Scottish Tourist Board

Egon Ronay, Les Routiers and the Chefs Golden Scroll of Excellent Awards

Great North Road, Muir of Ord, Ross-shire IV6 7XR.

Tel: 0463 870286 Fax: 0463 870048

Our bedrooms with private facilities are tastefully decorated and have their own colour TV, direct-dial telephone, radio and tea and coffee making facilities. The Ord Arms offers an escape for those looking for a relaxing holiday amongst unspoilt countryside.

MILNGAVIE Strathclyde (Dunbartonshire). Map 46A3
Pop 12,000. Glasgow 7, London 395, Dumbarton 11, Edinburgh 49, Gourock 23, Kincardine 29, Paisley 10, Stirling 27
★★★ **Black Bull Thistle,** Main St, G62 6BH ☎041-956 2291 Tx: 778323 Fax: 041-956 1896

Traditional hotel in town centre catering for both tourists and business people. (MtCh)
27 bedrs, 27 en suite; TV; tcf
dogs, ns; P 120, coach; child facs; con 150
LD 9.30
£ room £55, double room £60; Bk £7·75, L £6·75, D £12·75; WB
cc Access, Amex, B'card/Visa, CB, Diners.

MOFFAT Dumfries & Galloway (Dumfriesshire). Map 43B4
Pop 2,200. Beattock 2, London 335, Edinburgh 51, Glasgow 53, Hawick 44, Peebles 33, Selkirk 34, Thornhill 31.
EC Wed. **Golf** Coateshill 18h.
[i] Church Gate. ☎Moffat (0683) 20620
★★★ **Moffat House,** High St, DG10 9HL ☎(0683) 20039 Fax: (0683) 21288 ♿

Stone-built Georgian manor house in landscaped gardens. Close to town.
16 bedrs, 16 en suite; annexe 4 bedrs, 4 en suite; TV; tcf
dogs, ns; P 40, G 2, coach; child facs; con 80
LD 8.45, bar meals only lunch
£ B&B £30–£37, B&B (double) £54–£60; HB weekly £240–£270; L £8, D £13; WB £105 (3 nts HB); [5% V]
cc Access, Amex, B'card/Visa, Diners.
(*See advertisement on p. 598*)
★★ **Annandale Arms,** High St, DG10 9HF ☎(0683) 20013

Family-managed hotel in fine 4-storey building in town centre.
24 bedrs, 11 en suite (3 sh), 2 ba; TV; tcf
dogs; P 70, coach; child facs; con 40
LD 9, bar meals only lunch
£ B&B £26–£40, B&B (double) £40–£60; D £11; [10% V]
cc Access, B'card/Visa.

★★ **Balmoral,** High St, DG10 9DL ☎(0683) 20288
Distinguished 3-storey building of traditional style. Facing wide main street.
16 bedrs, 6 en suite, 3 ba; TV; tcf
TV, dogs; P 12, coach; child facs
LD 9.30, bar meals only Mon–Sat lunch, Mon–Wed & Sun dinner
£ B&B £25–£30, B&B (double) £42–£48; L £5·85, D £6·10
cc Access, B'card/Visa.

★★ **Star,** 44 High St, DG10 9EF ☎(0683) 20156

Interesting listed building–reputedly 'narrowest hotel in Scotland'.
8 bedrs, 8 en suite; TV; tcf
dogs; coach; child facs; con 50
LD 9
£ B&B £28–£30, B&B (double) £38–£42; L £6, D £8; WB £85 (3 nts HB)
cc Access, B'card/Visa; dep.

Well View (Highly Acclaimed), Ballplay Rd, DG10 9JU ☎(0683) 20184. *Private Hotel.*
De
£ B&B £20–£37; HB weekly £210–£322; [5% V]

Arden House (Acclaimed), High St, DG10 9HG ☎(0683) 20220. Open Mar–Oct. *Guest House.*
£ B&B £14–£16; HB weekly £125–£150.
Bridge (Acclaimed), Well Rd, DG10 9JT ☎(0683) 20383. *Guest House.*
Merkland House (Acclaimed), Buccleuch Pl, DG10 9AN ☎(0683) 20957. *Guest House.* Open Feb–Nov.
£ B&B £14–£20; [10% V Feb, Oct & Nov–Wed & Thu only]

Hartfell House, Hartfell Cres, DG10 9AL ☎(0683) 20153. *Putting.*
Ivy Cottage, High St, DG10 9HG ☎(0683) 20279. *Guest House.*
£ B&B £14·50

MONIAIVE Dumfries & Galloway (Dumfriesshire). Map 43A4
Pop 430. Dunscore 7, London 343, Dumfries 16, Edinburgh 69, Glasgow 67, New Galloway 14, Thornhill 8½.
EC Thur. **Golf** Thornhill 18h.

★★ **Woodlea,** DG3 4EN ☎(084 82) 209

Attractive turreted building set in country. Indoor swimming pool, golf, putting, tennis, fishing, riding, sauna, solarium. Open Feb–Oct. Fr, Fi
12 bedrs, 10 en suite, 1 ba; TV; tcf
TV, dogs, ns; P 20, coach; child facs
LD 8.30, nr lunch
£ B&B £28–£30; HB weekly £215–£250; D £13; WB £110 (3 nts); dep.

MONTROSE Tayside (Angus). Map 55B2
Pop 12,286. Arbroath 14, London 458, Brechin 8½, Dundee 30, Edinburgh 85, Forfar 17, Glasgow 105, Stonehaven 23.
EC Wed. **Golf** Montrose 18h, Broomfield Course 18h. **See** 18th cent Church, Statue of Sir Robert Peel, Museum, William Lamb Memorial Studio, 18th cent Town Buildings.
[i] 212 High St. ☎(0674) 72000

Linksgate, 11 Dorward Rd, DD10 8SB ☎(0674) 72273. *Guest House.*

MONYMUSK Grampian (Aberdeenshire). Map 55B3
Pop 278. Torphins 10, London 498, Aberdeen 19, Banff 34, Edinburgh 123, Glasgow 142, Huntly 23, Peterhead 39.

★★ **Grant Arms,** AB3 7HJ ☎(046 77) 226
A 3-storey granite-built former coaching inn in centre of village. Fishing. ♿
9 bedrs, 1 en suite, 3 ba; annexe 6 bedrs, 6 en suite; tcf
TV, dogs; coach; child facs; con 40
LD 9.45, bar meals only lunch
£ B&B £27–£35, B&B (double) £45–£49; HB weekly £250–£290; D £16; [5% V]
cc Access, Amex, B'card/Visa; dep.

MORAR Highland (Inverness-shire). Map 53A3
Fort William 39, London 528 (Fy 532), Edinburgh 171, Fort Augustus 67, Glasgow 141, Mallaig 3, Spean Bridge 45.
See Loch Morar (deepest in Europe).

★★ **Morar,** PH40 4PA ☎Mallaig (0687) 2346 Fax: (0687) 2130

Stone-built hotel in small village. Close to popular white sands. Fishing. Open Apr–Nov.

🛏 27 bedrs, 27 en suite; TV
🏨 TV, dogs; P 50, coach; child facs; con 150
✕ LD 8.30
£ B&B £24–£26; HB weekly £210–£238; L £7, D £13; WB
(*See advertisement on p. 597*)

MOTHERWELL Strathclyde (Lanarkshire) Map 46C4
See also WISHAW.
Pop 32,500 (inc Wishaw). London 378, M74 (jn 6) 1½, Edinburgh 35, Glasgow 13, Kilmarnock 27, Kincardine 28, Lanark 14, Peebles 38, Stirling 26.
EC Wed. **Golf** Colville Park 18h. **See** Dalzell House with 15th cent tower, RC Cathedral, Strathclyde Country Park.
ℹ Library, Hamilton Rd. ☎(0698) 51311

★★★ **Garrion,** 73 Merry St, ML1 1JN ☎(0698) 64561
Purpose-built hotel, situated in the town centre. Sauna.
🛏 52 bedrs, 37 en suite, 15 ba; TV; tcf
🏨 lift, dogs; coach; child facs; con 200

MUIR OF ORD Highland. Map 54A4
Beauly 3½, London 542, Dingwall 8, Edinburgh 167, Glasgow 165, Inverness 15.

★★ **Ord Arms,** Great North Rd, IV6 7XR ☎(0463) 870286 Fax: (0463) 870048
Red sandstone mansion, much extended over the years, beside the A862. Billiards.
🛏 12 bedrs, 7 en suite, 2 ba; TV; tcf
🏨 dogs; P 50, coach; child facs; con 130
✕ LD 9
£ B&B £24·50–£27·50, B&B (double) £38·50–£44; L £6·50, D £8; [5% V]
cc Access, B'card/Visa, Diners.
(*See advertisement on p. 598*)

MULL, ISLE OF *See* ISLE OF MULL.

NAIRN Highland (Nairnshire). Map 58B1
Pop 9,997. Grantown-on-Spey 23, London 529, Carrbridge 24, Edinburgh 154, Elgin 21, Glasgow 171, Inverness 15.
EC Wed. **Golf** Nairn 18h and 9h, Nairn Dunbar 18h.
ℹ King St. ☎(0667) 52753

★★★ **Newton,** Inverness Rd, IV12 4RX ☎(0667) 53144 Tx: 739248 Fax: (0667) 54026

Overlooking Moray Firth, splendid stone mansion in extensive grounds. Putting, tennis, sauna, solarium.
🛏 30 bedrs, 30 en suite; annexe 14 bedrs, 14 en suite; TV; tcf
🏨 lift, TV, dogs; P 100, coach; child facs; con 60

★★★ **Windsor,** Albert St, IV12 4HP ☎(0667) 53108 ♿

Stone-built hotel, formerly 3 charming houses, now linked and modernised. Riding.
🛏 60 bedrs, 52 en suite, (2 sh), 7 ba; TV; tcf
🏨 lift, TV, dogs; P 30, coach; child facs; con 200

★★ **Alton Burn,** Alton Burn Rd, IV12 5ND ☎(0667) 52051
Stone-built hotel, with extensions, on edge of town; views over Moray Firth. Swimming pool, putting, tennis, riding.

★★ **Carnach House,** Delnies, IV12 5NT ☎(0667) 52094
Attractive mansion in 8 acres of wooded grounds overlooking Moray Firth, 2 miles west of town.
🛏 14 bedrs, 11 en suite; TV; tcf
🏨 dogs, ns; P20, U2; child facs
✕ LD 8.45
£ B&B £31·50; HB weekly £294; L £4·50, D £13·50; WB £20 (Nov–Feb); [5% V Oct–May]
cc Access, Amex, B'card/Visa.

★ **Blenheim House,** Crescent Rd, IV12 4NB ☎(0667) 52019
A 3-storey stone-built late Victorian house in residential area of town.
🛏 8 bedrs, 2 ba; TV; tcf
🏨 TV, dogs; P 20; child facs

Ardgour, Seafield St, IV12 4HN ☎(0667) 54230. *Private Hotel.* Open Mar–30 Oct.
✕ Γr
£ B&B £13, HB weekly £107, dep.

NETHY BRIDGE Highland (Inverness-shire). Map 54C3
Pop 825. London 509, Braemar 47, Carrbridge 8½, Edinburgh 134, Glasgow 146, Grantown-on-Spey 5, Kingussie 22.
EC Thur. **Golf** Nethybridge 9h.

★★★ **Nethybridge,** PH25 3DP ☎(047 982) 203 Fax: (047 982) 686 ♿
Large traditional Victorian hotel situated in heart of Spey Valley. Billiards.
🛏 62 bedrs, 62 en suite; TV; tcf
🏨 lift, dogs, ns; P 180, coach; child facs; con 180

NEW ABBEY Dumfries & Galloway (Kirkcudbrightshire). Map 43B3
Pop 400. Dumfries 6½, London 333, Edinburgh 77, Gatehouse of Fleet 33, Glasgow 79, New Galloway 27.
Golf Southerness 18h. **See** Sweetheart Abbey, 13th cent remains, Kirkconnel Tower, Waterloo Monument, Corn Mill, Shambellie Ho Museum of costume.

★ **Abbey Arms,** DG2 8BU ☎(038 785) 215
A 3-storey stone-built hotel in quiet village. Popular with fishermen.

NEW GALLOWAY Dumfries & Galloway (Kirkcudbrightshire). Map 43A3
Pop 300. Crocketford 13, London 349, Dalmellington 21, Dumfries 23, Edinburgh 83, Gatehouse of Fleet 19, Glasgow 69, Stranraer 44, Thornhill 22.
EC Thur. **Golf** New Galloway 9h. **See** Kells Church, Kenmure Castle, Loch Ken.

★ **Ken Bridge,** DG7 3PR ☎(064 42) 211

Attractive 2-storey building on banks of River Ken; out of town. Fishing.
🛏 10 bedrs, 1 en suite, 3 ba
🏨 TV, dogs; P 30, coach; child facs
✕ LD 8.30
£ B&B £13·50; D £9; [5% V]; dep.

★ **Kenmure Arms,** High St, DG7 3RL ☎(064 42) 240
Modernised family-managed hotel in 3-storey stone building with distinctive gables.
🛏 9 bedrs, 1 en suite, 3 ba
🏨 TV, dogs; P 8, G 6, coach; child facs

NEWTONMORE Highland. Map 54B3
Pop 1,070 (with Dalwhinnie). Blair Atholl 34, London 485, Dalwhinnie 10, Edinburgh 109, Fort William 45, Glasgow 121, Kingussie 2½.
EC Wed. **Golf** Newtonmore 18h.
ℹ ☎(054 03) 274

★★ **Mains,** Main St, PH20 1DE ☎(054 03) 206

Substantial stone-built hotel in main street of town. Family-owned. Closed Jan.
🛏 30 bedrs, 30 en suite; TV; tcf
🏨 TV, ns; P 100, coach; child facs; con 20
✕ LD 10.30, bar meals only lunch
£ B&B £19–£22, B&B (double) £38–£40; HB weekly £170–£185; D £9·25; [10% V]
cc Access, B'card/Visa.

★★ **Weigh Inn,** Main St, PH20 1DD ☎(054 03) 203
Two-storey stone-built hotel in centre of village. Billiards.

NEWTON STEWART Dumfries & Galloway (Wigtownshire). Map 42C3
Pop 2,000. New Galloway 17, London 367, Edinburgh 101, Gatehouse of Fleet 18, Girvan 30, Glasgow 82, Stranraer 22.
EC Wed. **MD** Thur. **Golf** Wigtown 9h.
[i] Dashwood Sq. ☎(0671) 2431

♣♣ ★★★★ R **Kirroughtree,** DG8 6AN ☎(0671) 2141 ♿

Early 18th century picturesque country house with distinctive tower. Putting, tennis. Closed 2 Jan–mid Feb.
🛏 22 bedrs, 22 en suite; TV
🏨 dogs, ns; P 40, coach; children over 10; con 30
✕ LD 9.30
£ B&B £52–£96, B&B (double) £95–£130; HB weekly £365–£480; L £14·50, D £27·50
cc Access, Amex, B'card/Visa, Diners; dep.

★★★ **Bruce,** Queen St, DG8 6JL ☎(0671) 2294
Modern hotel on outskirts of town and convenient for A75. Solarium, gymnasium. Open Feb–Nov. ⚒ Fr
🛏 18 bedrs, 18 en suite; TV; tcf
🏨 dogs; P 20, coach; child facs
✕ LD 8.30
£ B&B £35–£40, B&B (double) £55–£60; HB weekly £250–£275; L £6, D £15; WB £40
cc Access, Amex, B'card/Visa, Diners; dep.

★★ **Crown,** Queen St, DG8 6JW ☎(0671) 2727

Imposing 3-storey 19th century building. On outskirts of town.
🛏 10 bedrs, 5 en suite, 3 ba; TV; tcf
🏨 dogs, ns; P 20, coach; child facs
✕ LD 8, bar meals only lunch
£ B&B £19–£25, B&B (double) £38–£42; HB weekly £185–£198; L £5, D £11
cc Access, B'card/Visa; dep.

NEWTON WAMPHRAY Dumfries & Galloway (Dumfries-shire). Map 43B4
Lockerbie 9, London 327, Moffat 7, Edinburgh 60, Glasgow 62.
Golf Moffat 18h.

Red House, DG10 9NF ☎Johnstone Bridge (057 64) 214. *Hotel.*

NORTH BERWICK Lothian (East Lothian) Map 51A3
Pop 5,229. East Linton 6, London 377, Berwick-upon-Tweed 41, Edinburgh 22, Glasgow 67, Haddington 11.
EC Thur. **Golf** West Links 18h, East Links 18h. **See** Ruins of Pre-Reformation Church Burgh Museum, 12th cent St Andrew's Kirk.
[i] Quality St. ☎(0620) 2197

★★★ **Marine,** Cromwell Rd, EH39 4LZ ☎(0620) 2406 Tx: 72550 Fax: (0620) 4480

Large 4-storey sandstone-built Victorian style hotel with extensions overlooking sea. Indoor swimming pool, putting, tennis, squash, sauna, solarium, billiards. (THF)
⚒ Fr, De
🛏 83 bedrs, 83 en suite; TV; tcf
🏨 lift, dogs, ns; P 80, coach; child facs; con 200
✕ LD 9.30
£ B&B £83–£85 (w/e £42), B&B (double) £99–£110; L £8·50, D £17·50; WB £55 (HB)
cc Amex, B'card/Visa, Diners; dep.

★★ **Nether Abbey,** Dirleton Av, EH39 4BQ ☎(0620) 2802
Two-storey red sandstone former private mansion (1890) in town centre.
🛏 16 bedrs, 16 en suite; TV; tcf
🏨 dogs; P 60, coach; child facs; con 50
✕ LD 9
£ B&B £24 (w/e £20), B&B (double) £50; D £7; [5% V]
cc Access, B'card/Visa.

★★ **Point Garry,** West Bay Rd, EH39 4AW ☎(0620) 2380

In quiet residential area, stone-built Victorian house in terrace. Billiards.

OBAN Strathclyde (Argyll). Map 53B1
Pop 7,000. Dalmally 23, London 477, Ballachulish 37, Edinburgh 121, Fort William 48, Glasgow 90, Lochgilphead 36.
EC Thur. **Golf** Glencruitten 18h. **See** RC Cathedral, McCaig Tower, St John's Episcopal Cathedral, Museum.
[i] Argyll Sq. ☎(0631) 63122

★★★ **Alexandra,** Corran Esplanade, PA34 5AA ☎(0631) 62381 Fax: (0631) 64497
Traditional holiday hotel overlooking harbour. Open 26 Mar–2 Nov. (SH)
🛏 55 bedrs, 55 en suite; TV; tcf
🏨 lift, dogs, ns; P 40, coach; child facs; con 15
✕ LD 9, bar meals only lunch
£ B&B £50, B&B (double) £80; HB weekly £273; D £12; WB £82 (2 nts HB)
cc Access, Amex, B'card/Visa, Diners.

★★★ **Caledonian,** Station Sq, PA34 5RT ☎(0631) 63133 Tx: 777210

An extensive Victorian style building with good sea views.

★★★ **Columba,** North Pier, Esplanade, PA34 5QD ☎(0631) 62183 Tx: 728256 Fax: (0631) 64683

Stone-built hotel dominating the North Pier with fine sea, mountain and island views.
🛏 49 bedrs, 49 en suite, 2 ba; TV; tcf
🏨 lift, dogs; P 10, coach; child facs; con 70

★★ **Lancaster,** Corran Esplanade, PA34 5AD ☎(0631) 62587

Family-run stone-built hotel overlooking Oban Bay at North end of town. Indoor swimming pool, sauna, solarium.
🛏 27 bedrs, 24 en suite, 4 ba; TV; tcf
🏨 dogs; P 20; child facs
✕ LD 8
£ B&B £27, B&B (double) £48; HB weekly £220; L £5·50, D £9; dep.

★★ **Rowan Tree,** George St, PA34 5NX ☎(0631) 62954
Modern town-centre hotel convenient for ferries to islands.
🛏 24 bedrs, 24 en suite; TV; tcf
🏨 dogs; P 15, coach; child facs
✕ LD 8.30, bar meals only lunch
£ B&B £22·50, B&B (double) £39
cc Access, Amex, B'card/Visa, Diners; dep.

★ **King's Knoll,** Dunollie Rd, PA34 5JH ☎(0631) 62536
Family-run stone-built hotel on high ground alongside A85 overlooking town.

Sc

Oban (Argyll)

**
RAC
RSAC
Taste of Scotland
STB 3 crowns commended

THE FALLS OF LORA HOTEL

CONNEL FERRY, By OBAN, ARGYLL PA 37 1PB
Telephone: 0631-71 483
Fax: 0631-71 694

Oban 5 miles, overlooking Loch Etive – an ideal centre for a touring, walking, sailing or fishing holiday. Only 2½-3 hours drive north-west of Edinburgh or Glasgow. The resident owners offer a warm welcome, good food, service and comfort. Most rooms have Central Heating, Private Bathrooms, Radio/Intercoms, TVs and telephones. From Luxury rooms – one with 'Four Poster' bed and king size round bath, another with round bed and 'Jacuzzi', bathroom en-suite to inexpensive family rooms with bunk beds. FREE accommodation for children sharing parents' room.

Relax in the super Cocktail Bar with open log fire. There are 100 brands of whisky to tempt you and an extensive bar/bistro menu. Out of season mini-breaks. Ashley Courtenay recommended

OPEN ALL YEAR *A FINE OWNER-RUN SCOTTISH HOTEL*

Stromness (Orkney)

STROMNESS HOTEL

Victoria Street, Stromness, Orkney, Scotland.
Tel: (0856) 850298

42 bedrooms, all en suite. Lift to all floors. Close to main ferry terminal between Orkney and the mainland of Scotland. Excellent cuisine – seafood specialities.

Peebles (Peeblesshire)

Venlaw Castle Hotel

Peebles, Scotland EH45 8QG Tel: 0721 20384

Venlaw Castle Hotel offers all the comforts of a modern hotel, with excellent cuisine, while retaining the atmosphere of gracious living of a bygone age.

Perth (Perthshire)

RAC★★★
QUEENS HOTEL & LEISURE CLUB PERTH **Tel: 0738 25471 Telex: 76531**
(55 Bedrooms)

All bedrooms in both hotels have private facilities - Colour TV - Radio/Alarm - D/D Telephone - Trouser Press - Hair Dryer - Tea/Coffee facilities

★ ★ ★

Swimming Pool - Sauna
Jacuzzi - Solarium
Gymnasium - Steam
Room - Jet Shower

Scottish Tourist Board
COMMENDED
Facilities

3 Restaurants serving Bar Meals to A La Carte Dinner and Fine Wines

LOVAT HOTEL, PERTH
Tel: 0738 36555 Telex: 76531
(30 Bedrooms)

PERTHS FINEST HOTELS

Both perfectly situated at the gateway to the Highlands in central Perth
Ideal for all types of Business including:
Conferences - Banquets - Exhibitions - Weddings - Meetings.

"AMPLE CAR PARKING"

LOVAT HOTELS LTD. - A winning combination

EC *early closing* **MD** *market day* *country house hotel* *ns (NS) no smoking areas* *tcf tea/coffee facilities*

15 bedrs, 8 en suite, 3 ba; TV; tcf
TV, dogs; P 9, coach
LD 7.30, bar meals only lunch
£ B&B £18·50–£22·50; D £10
cc Access, B'card/Visa; dep.

Foxholes (Acclaimed), Cologin, PA34 4SE (0631) 64982. *Private Hotel.* Open Mar–Oct.
£ HB weekly £200–£210; dep.
Glenburnie (Acclaimed), Esplanade, PA34 5AQ (0631) 62089. Open Apr–Sep. *Hotel* Es
£ B&B £13·50–£14·50.

Ardblair, Dalriach Rd, PA34 5JB (0631) 62668. *Guest House.* Open Easter & May–Oct.
£ B&B £12–£15; HB weekly £115–£132·50; D £7.
Craigvarran House, Ardconnel Rd, PA34 5DJ (0631) 62686. *Guest House.* Closed 16 Dec–14 Jan.
£ B&B £11; HB weekly £119; dep.
Roseneath, Dalriach Rd, PA34 5EQ (0631) 62929. *Guest House.*
£ B&B £12–£15.
Sgeir Mhaol, Soroba Rd, PA34 4JF (0631) 62650. *Guest House.*
£ B&B £12–£20

OLD RAYNE

Grampian (Aberdeenshire). Map 55B4
Inverurie 8½, London 508, Aberdeen 25, Edinburgh 133, Glasgow 153, Huntly 14, Insch 4, Peterhead 37.

★ **Lodge,** AB5 6RY (046 45) 205
Two-storey granite-built former private villa with modern extensions.

ONICH

Highland (Inverness-shire). Map 53B2
Pop 280. Ballachulish 4, London 478, Crianlarich 53, Edinburgh 121, Fort William 10, Glasgow 89, Oban 48.
EC Thur. **Golf** Fort William 9h.

★★★ H **Lodge on the Loch,** Creag Dhu, PH33 6RY (085 53) 237 Tx: 94013696 Fax: (085 53) 463

Traditional Highland hotel in tranquil situation with spectacular views. Open Feb–Oct & Xmas–New Year. Fr
18 bedrs, 18 en suite; TV; tcf
dogs, ns; P 25, coach; child facs; con 40
LD 9.30
£ B&B £29·50–£47·50, B&B (double) £59–£105; HB weekly £297·50–£458·50; L £4·50, D £16·50; WB (Feb–Apr & Oct); [10% V Feb–May & Oct]
cc Access, B'card/Visa; dep.

Changes made after July 1990 are not included.

★★★ **Onich,** PH33 6RY (085 53) 214 Fax: (085 53) 484

19th century building, progressively modernised. Overlooking loch. Solarium.
27 bedrs, 27 en suite; TV; tcf
dogs; P 50, coach; child facs; con 30
LD 8.30, bar meals only lunch
£ B&B £30–£37·50, B&B (double) £50–£65; HB weekly £245–£315; D £16·50; [10% V]
cc Access, Amex, B'card/Visa, Diners; dep.

★★ R **Allt-Nan-Ros,** PH33 6RY (085 53) 210 Fax: (085 53) 462

Family-owned former mansion house at roadside overlooking the sea. Fr
Open Easter–Oct.
19 bedrs, 19 en suite; annexe 2 bedrs, 2 en suite; TV; tcf
dogs, ns; P 50, coach; child facs
LD 8.30
£ B&B £32·75–£48; HB weekly £299–£380; D £16; [5% V]
cc Access, Amex, B'card/Visa, Diners; dep.
(*See advertisement on p. 572*)

★★ **Loch Leven,** PH33 6SA (085 53) 236

Attractive 19th century coaching inn overlooking the loch. Fr
12 bedrs, 5 en suite, 3 ba; TV
TV, dogs; P 100; child facs
LD 9, bar meals only lunch
£ B&B £20–£25; HB weekly £233–£268; D £14
cc Access, B'card/Visa; dep.

Tigh-a-Righ, PH33 6SE (085 53) 255. *Guest House.*

ORKNEY ISLANDS

An archipelago of 50 islands, about 30 inhabited.
See Antiquities (Skara Brae, Earl's Palace, etc), cliff scenery. In Kirkwall, St Magnus Cathedral, Bishop's Palace, Earl Patrick's Palace, 18th cent Tankerness House, Scapa Flow 'Royal Oak' memorial.
i Broad St. Kirkwall (0856) 2856

STROMNESS

Map 59A2
Pop 1,500. London via Scrabster 655, Kirkwall 15.
EC Thur. **MD** Wed. **Golf** Ness 18h.
i Ferry Terminal Building. (0856) 850716

★★ **Stromness,** 15 Victoria St, KW16 3AA (0856) 850298
Large stone-built privately-owned hotel in town centre overlooking harbour.
42 bedrs, 42 en suite, 2 ba; TV; tcf
lift, TV, dogs; P 15, coach; child facs; con 80
(*See advertisement on p. 602*)

OUTER HEBRIDES

See ISLES OF LEWIS, HARRIS and SOUTH UIST.

PAISLEY

Strathclyde (Renfrewshire). Map 46B2
See also LINWOOD.
Pop 85,855. Strathaven 19, London 393, M8 Motorway 1, Dumbarton 12, Edinburgh 52, Glasgow 7, Gourock 19, Kilmarnock 20.
EC Tue. **MD** Mon. **Golf** Barshaw Municipal.
i Town Hall, Abbey Clo. 041-889 0711

★★ **Rockfield,** 125 Renfrew Rd, PA3 4EA 041-889 6182 Fax: 041-389 9526
Popular hotel conveniently situated for Glasgow Airport and M8.
20 bedrs, 20 en suite; TV; tcf
dogs, ns; P 60, coach; child facs; con 40
LD 9.30, bar meals only lunch
£ B&B £41, B&B (double) £62; D £10·50; [10% V]
cc Access, Amex, B'card/Visa, Diners.

★★ **Stakis Watermill,** Lonend, PA1 1SR 041-889 3201
Converted mill, dating from 1580, by the side of the White Cart Water in the town centre.
51 bedrs, 51 en suite; TV; tcf
£ B&B £49·55–£67, B&B (double) £68·25–£87; L £5·50, D £7·50

Ashburn, Milliken Pk Rd, Kilbarchan, PA10 2DB (050 57) 5477. *Hotel.*
£ B&B £18·50–£25·50; [5% V w/e]

PEEBLES

Borders (Peeblesshire). Map 50C2
Pop 6,000. Walkerburn 8½, London 361, Beattock 36, Edinburgh 22, Galashiels 18, Glasgow 49, Lanark 27, Lauder 26.
EC Wed. **MD** Fri. **Golf** Peebles Municipal 18h. **See** Old Parish Church, Neidpath Castle, ruins of 12th cent Church, Mercat Cross, St Andrew's Church Tower (ruins).
i Chambers Institute, High St. (0721) 20138

★★★ **Hydro,** EH45 8LX (0721) 20602 Fax: (0721) 22999

Sc

Perth (Scotland)

THE NEWTON HOUSE HOTEL

RAC ★★★

Glencarse, By Perth,
Perthshire PH2 7LX

Tel: 073 886 250 Fax: 073 886 717

This former Dower House is only 4 miles from Perth, 13 from Dundee and an ideal base to explore the dramatic countryside and numerous places of interest such as Glamis Castle, Scone Palace and world famous golf courses. All 10 en-suite bedrooms overlook the gardens and daily change menus utilise fresh local produce.

Perth (Perthshire)

This converted mill has 78 bedrooms all with en suite bathrooms, colour television, tea and coffee facilities. Our two restaurants offer excellent cuisine. Conference facilities from 2 to 150, Weddings, Dinner Dances and Seminars. Easy access by road and rail.

Tel: 0738-28281

STAKIS

City Mills Hotel

PERTH

Prestwick (Ayrshire)

ST NICHOLAS HOTEL PRESTWICK LTD

41 Ayr Road, Prestwick, Scotland.
Telephone: (0292) 79568

Hotel centrally heated throughout. 16 bedrooms, most having private facilities and all with direct telephone, colour TV, tea and coffee making facilities. Bar and dining room meals with varied menus. Children catered for. Function suite available for conferences etc.

STB♛♛♛commended **RAC★★**

Glasgow Airport (Renfrew)

★★★ RAC

THE Glynhill HOTEL & LEISURE CLUB

The Hotel of the Nineteen Nineties

Glasgow Centre 7 miles. Adjacent M8 (J27 300 yards).

Paisley Road, Renfrew (Glasgow Airport 1 mile)
Tel: 041-886 5555 Fax: 041-885 2838 Telex: 779536

EC *early closing* **MD** *market day* *country house hotel* *ns (NS) no smoking areas* *tcf tea/coffee facilities*

A very large hotel in the grand style set in 30 acres of grounds on hill above town. Fine views. Indoor swimming pool, putting, tennis, squash, riding, sauna, solarium, gymnasium, billiards. ⚒ Fr, De, Po, Du
🛏 134 bedrs, 134 en suite; TV; tcf
lift, ns; P 200, coach; child facs; con 450
✕ LD 9
£ B&B £43–£49·50, B&B (double) £62–£106; L £9·50, D £14·50; [5% V]
cc Access, Amex, B'card/Visa, Diners; dep.

★★★ **Park,** Innerleithen Rd, EH45 8BA ☎(0721) 20451 Tx: 72568 Fax: (0721) 22999

Traditional Scottish-style private house which has been extended. Putting.
🛏 24 bedrs, 24 en suite; TV; tcf
dogs; P 50, coach; child facs; con 70
✕ LD 9.30
£ B&B £38–£41, B&B (double) £51·50–£83·50; HB weekly £218–£285; D £12·75; [10% V]
cc Access, Amex, B'card/Visa, Diners; dep.

★★★ **Tontine,** High St, EH45 8AJ ☎(0721) 20892

19th century inn with later extensions and elegant public rooms. (THF)
🛏 37 bedrs, 37 en suite; TV; tcf
dogs, ns; P 30, coach; child facs; con 45

★★ H C R **Cringletie House,** EH45 8PL ☎(072 13) 233

Large Victorian mansion in quiet location with magnificent views from all rooms. Putting, tennis. ⚒ Fr
🛏 13 bedrs, 13 en suite; TV; tcf
lift, dogs, ns; P 40; child facs
✕ LD 8.30
£ B&B £39–£50, B&B (double) £72; L £12·50, D £20
cc Access, B'card/Visa.

★★ **Venlaw Castle,** Edinburgh Rd, EH45 8OG ☎(0721) 20384
Handsome 18th century residence in Scottish baronial style. Own grounds. Open Apr–Oct. ⚒ Fr
🛏 12 bedrs, 9 en suite, 2 ba; TV; tcf
dogs, ns; P 20; child facs
✕ LD 8, nr lunch
£ B&B £20–£22; HB weekly £200–£220; D £12·50; WB £65; [5% V]
cc Access, Amex, B'card/Visa, Diners; dep.
(*See advertisement on p. 602*)

PERTH Tayside (Perthshire). Map 50B4

Pop 40,091. Bridge of Earn 4, London 416, M90 (jn 10) 2, Blairgowrie 15, Dundee 21, Edinburgh 41, Glasgow 57.
EC Wed. **MD** Fri. **Golf** King James VI 18h. North Inch 18h.
ℹ Round House, Marshall Pl. ☎(0738) 38353

★★★ **Huntingtower,** Crieff Rd, PH1 3JT ☎(0738) 83771 Tx: 76204

Late Victorian house, ½ mile from A85, set in 3½ acres of gardens. Putting.
🛏 14 bedrs, 14 en suite; TV; tcf
dogs, ns; P 40; child facs; con 50
✕ LD 9.30
£ B&B £39–£53; B&B (double) £72–£82; L £10, D £16·50; [5% V]
cc Access, Amex, B'card/Visa, Diners.

★★★ **Isle of Skye Osprey,** Dundee Rd, PH2 7AB ☎(0738) 24471 Tx: 76185

Formerly 4 separate Victorian buildings, now linked, extended and modernised.
🛏 56 bedrs, 56 en suite; TV; tcf
lift, ns; P 70, coach; child facs; con 140

Residents only
Some Listed hotels only serve meals to residents. It is always wise to make a reservation for a meal in a hotel.

★★★ **Lovat,** Glasgow Rd, PH2 0LT ☎(0738) 36555 Tx: 76531 Fax: (0738) 43123

Two-storey stone-built former private houses with linking extension in residential area.
🛏 28 bedrs, 28 en suite; TV; tcf
ns; P 60, coach; child facs; con 300
✕ LD 9.30
£ B&B £44–£48, B&B (double) £60–£64; L £6·75, D £10; WB £30 (HB); [5% V excl Jun–Sep]
cc Access, Amex, B'card/Visa.
(*See advertisement on p. 602*)

★★★ **Newton House,** Glencarse, PH2 7LX ☎(073 886) 250 Fax: (073 886) 717

Two-storey stone-built former private residence in own small grounds. ⚒ Fr, De
🛏 10 bedrs, 10 en suite; TV; tcf
dogs; P 60, coach; child facs; con 40
✕ LD 9
£ B&B £44–£50, B&B (double) £64; HB weekly £308; L £13·50, D £19; WB £44
cc Access, B'card/Visa, Diners; dep.
(*See advertisement on p. 604*)

★★★ **Queen's,** Leonard St, PH2 8HB ☎(0738) 25471 Tx: 76531 Fax: (0738) 38496
Traditional style 6-storey stone and brick-built hotel. Indoor swimming pool, sauna, solarium, gymnasium.
🛏 50 bedrs, 50 en suite; TV; tcf
lift; P 40, coach; child facs; con 300
✕ LD 9.30
£ B&B £52–£56, B&B (double) £68–£72; L £7·75, D £11·75; WB £34 (HB); [5% V excl Jul–Sep]
cc Access, Amex, B'card/Visa.
(*See advertisement on p. 602*)

★★★ **Royal George,** Tay St, PH1 5LD ☎(0738) 24455 Fax: (0738) 30345

Large Georgian stone-built hotel with fine river views. (THF)

Sc

🛏 43 bedrs, 43 en suite; TV; tcf
🏛 dogs, ns; P 17, coach; child facs; con 100
✕ LD 9.30, bar meals only lunch
£ B&B £67, B&B (double) £89–£99; HB weekly £280–£420; D £11·50; WB £40 (HB)
cc Access, Amex, B'card/Visa, Diners.

★★★ **Salutation,** South St, PH2 8PH ☎(0738) 30066 Tx: 76357 Fax: (0738) 33598

Traditional hotel on main street; dating from 16th century. (Emb) ✈ Fr, De, It
🛏 70 bedrs, 60 en suite, 4 ba; TV; tcf
🏛 TV, dogs, ns; coach; child facs; con 300
✕ LD 9.30, bar meals only lunch
£ B&B £39–£43, B&B (double) £50–£58; D £9·95; WB £24
cc Access, Amex, B'card/Visa, Diners.

★★★ **Stakis City Mills,** West Mill St, PH1 5QP ☎(0738) 28281 Tx: 778704 Fax: (0738) 43423
Original old mill buildings converted to modern hotel with extensions. (Sk)
🛏 78 bedrs, 78 en suite; TV; tcf
🏛 dogs, ns; P 50, coach; child facs; con 200
✕ LD 10
£ room £66–£77·50, room (double) £86–£96; L £8, D £11; WB £36; [5% V Oct–Mar]
cc Access, Amex, B'card/Visa, Diners.
(See advertisement on p. 604)

★★ **Station,** Leonard St PH2 8HE ☎(0738) 24141 Tx: 76481 Fax: (0738) 39912 ♿
A grand Victorian railway hotel, refurbished to a good standard, right in the city centre. Gymnasium. ✈ Fr, De, It, Gr, Ru
🛏 70 bedrs, 70 en suite; TV; tcf
🏛 lift, dogs, ns; P 60, coach; child facs; con 550
✕ LD 9.30; bar meals only Sun
£ B&B £43·50–£53 (w/e £32); B&B (double) £53–£63·50; L £8·75, D £11·25
cc Access, Amex, B'card/Visa, Diners.

Clunie (Acclaimed), 12 Pitcullen Cres, PH2 7HT ☎(0738) 23625
Pitcullen (Acclaimed), 17 Pitcullen Cres, PH2 7HT ☎(0738) 26506. *Guest House.*
£ B&B £15–£20

Rowanbank, 3 Pitcullen Cres, PH2 7HT ☎(0738) 21421. *Guest House.*
£ B&B (double) £25–£31; [5% V]

PETERHEAD

Grampian (Aberdeenshire). Map 55C4
Pop 17,960. Aberdeen 31, London 523, Banff 35, Edinburgh 148, Fraserburgh 17. **EC** Wed. **Golf** Peterhead 18h. **See** Museum and Art Gallery, 12th cent St Peter's Kirk, Harbour, Ravenscraig Castle, Inverugie Castle.
ℹ 54 Broad St ☎(0779) 71904

★★★ **Waterside Inn,** Fraserburgh Rd, AB4 7BN ☎(0779) 71121 Tx: 739413 Fax: (0779) 70670
Modern 2-storey building with an unusual slate roof, beside main road on north side of town. Indoor swimming pool, sauna, solarium, gymnasium, snooker. ✈ De, No
🛏 110 bedrs, 110 en suite; TV; tcf
🏛 dogs; P 200, coach; child facs; con 200
✕ LD 10
£ B&B £50–£65 (w/e £36·50 HB), B&B (double) £59–£74; L £8, D £12·75; WB £46·50 (HB); [10% V]
cc Access, Amex, B'card/Visa, Diners.

PITLOCHRY

Tayside (Perthshire). Map 54B2
Pop 2,500. Dunkeld 12, London 444, Aberfeldy 14, Blairgowrie 23, Braemar 41, Dalwhinnie 31, Edinburgh 69, Glasgow 80. **EC** Thur (win). **Golf** Pitlochry 18h. **See** Loch Faskally and Dam (Fish Ladder').
ℹ 22 Atholl Rd. ☎(0796) 2215

★★★ **Atholl Palace,** Atholl Rd, PH16 5LY ☎(0796) 2400 Tx: 76406 Fax: (0796) 3036

Vast Victorian hotel in the grand style—spacious beautiful grounds. Swimming pool, golf, putting, tennis, sauna, solarium, billiards. (THF)
🛏 84 bedrs, 84 en suite; TV; tcf
🏛 lift, dogs, ns; P 120, coach; child facs; con 300
✕ LD 9, bar meals only Mon–Sat lunch
£ B&B £38–£68 (w/e £42 HB), B&B (double) £66–£96; HB weekly £264–£350; D £13·95
cc Access, Amex, B'card/Visa, Diners.

🏠 ★★★ **Pine Trees,** Strathview Terr, PH16 5QR ☎(0796) 2121 Fax: (0796) 2460

White-painted 19th-century mansion carefully converted to retain much of its original character. Set in peaceful wooded grounds. Putting. Closed Jan. ✈ Fr
🛏 18 bedrs, 18 en suite; TV; tcf
🏛 P 40; child facs
✕ LD 8.30, bar meals only lunch
£ B&B £35–£40, B&B (double) £70; D £16
cc Access, B'card/Visa.

★★★ **Pitlochry Hydro,** Knockard Rd, PH16 5JH ☎(0796) 2666

Substantial granite-built Victorian hotel in attractive grounds on hillside. Indoor swimming pool, putting, sauna, solarium, gymnasium, billiards. Closed Jan. (SH) ✈ Fr
🛏 64 bedrs, 64 en suite; TV; tcf
🏛 lift, TV; P 100, coach; child facs; con 90
✕ LD 9, bar meals only lunch
£ B&B £48–£52 (w/e £38), B&B (double) £78–£85; HB weekly £302; D £13·50; WB £76 (2 nts HB)
cc Access, Amex, B'card/Visa, Diners; dep.

★★★ **Scotland's,** Bonnethill Rd, PH16 5BT ☎(0796) 2292 Tx: 76392 Fax: (0796) 3284 ♿
Refurbished, 4-storey stone-fronted hotel with extensions to rear. Indoor swimming pool, sauna, solarium, gymnasium. ✈ De
🛏 60 bedrs, 60 en suite; TV; tcf
🏛 lift, TV, dogs; P 80, coach; child facs; con 200
✕ LD 9
£ B&B £33–£49, B&B (double) £54–£78; HB weekly £262–£416; L £9·50, D £12·50; [10% V]
cc Access, Amex, B'card/Visa, Diners; dep.

★★ **Acarsaid,** Atholl Rd, PH16 5BX ☎(0796) 2389

Converted large private house with modern extensions overlooking main road. Putting. Closed Feb.
🛏 18 bedrs, 18 en suite; TV; tcf
🏛 ns; P 20, coach; child facs
✕ LD 8. Restrict lic
£ B&B £21–£25; HB weekly £185–£225; L £7·50, D £12·50; WB
cc Access, B'card/Visa; dep.

★★ **Airdanlar,** Atholl Rd, PH16 5QL ☎(0796) 2266
Converted 2-storey private house with modern extensions. On main road through town.
🛏 9 bedrs, 9 en suite; TV; tcf
🏛 dogs, ns; P 18; child facs
✕ LD 9.30, bar meals only lunch
£ B&B £36·50–£37·50, B&B (double) £53–£55; HB weekly £269·50–£276·50; D £14
cc Access, B'card/Visa; dep.

★★ Birchwood, East Moulin Rd, PH16 5DW ☎(0796) 2477

Victorian house with later additions set in small grounds. Open Mar–Nov. ⚒ Fr, Es
🛏 12 bedrs, 12 en suite; annexe 5 bedrs, 5 en suite; TV; tcf
🏨 dogs, ns; P 25, coach; child facs
✕ LD 8. Restrict lic
£ B&B £32–£36·50, B&B (double) £56–£65; HB weekly £230–£256; WB £105 (3 nts HB)
cc Access, B'card/Visa; dep.

★★ Castlebeigh, Knockard Rd, PH16 5HJ ☎(0796) 2925
On hill overlooking town, 3-storey stone-built house in small grounds.

★★ Claymore, Atholl Rd, PH16 5AR ☎(0796) 2888
Detached 2-storey house, extended and modernised. On edge of town. Closed Nov & Jan.
🛏 7 bedrs, 7 en suite; TV; tcf
🏨 dogs, ns; P 26; child facs
✕ LD 9, bar meals only lunch
£ B&B £19–£27·50; HB weekly £209·75–£252; D £14·50; [5% V Feb–Apr, Oct, Dec]
cc Access, B'card/Visa; dep.

★★ Craigvrack, West Moulin Rd, PH16 5EQ ☎(0796) 2399 ♿

Stone and brick villa (with extensions), standing above road in outskirts. Putting.
🛏 19 bedrs, 14 en suite, 2 ba; TV; tcf
🏨 dogs, ns; P 22; child facs; con 30

★★ Dundarach, Perth Rd, PH16 5DJ ☎(0796) 2862 ♿
Large Victorian stone-built 2-storey hotel located on outskirts of town. Closed Feb. ⚒ Fr, Es
🛏 27 bedrs, 27 en suite; TV; tcf
🏨 ns; P 30, coach; con 30
✕ LD 8, bar meals only lunch
£ B&B £36, B&B (double) £55; HB weekly £220; D £12·50; [10% V]
cc Access, Amex, B'card/Visa, Diners.

Balrobin (Highly Acclaimed), Higher Oakfield, PH16 5HT ☎(0796) 2901. *Hotel.* Open Easter–Oct. ⚒ De, It
£ B&B £20–£22; HB weekly £175–£215; [10% V 16 May–Sep]

Knockendarroch House (Highly Acclaimed), Higher Oakfield, PH16 5HT ☎(0796) 3473. *Hotel.*

Well House (Acclaimed) 11 Toberargan Rd, PH16 5HG ☎(0796) 2239. *Private Hotel.* Open Mar–Oct.
£ B&B (double) £29–£31

PLOCKTON Highland (Ross & Cromarty). Map 53B4

Invergarry 69, London 576, Gairloch 67, Garve 45, Glasgow 189, Kyle of Lochalsh 15

★★ H C Haven, Innes St, IV52 8TW ☎(059 984) 223

Victorian residence tastefully modernised and extended. Closed 21 Dec–31 Jan.
🛏 13 bedrs, 13 en suite; TV; tcf
🏨 dogs, ns; P 7; no children under 7
✕ LD 8.30, nr lunch. Restrict lic
£ B&B £25–£28; HB weekly £217–£280; D £17·50
cc Access, B'card/Visa; dep.

POLMONT Central. Map 47B1

Pop 17,610. Armadale 7, London 394, M9 (jn 4) 1, Edinburgh 23, Glasgow 26, Kincardine 7, Lanark 24, Stirling 14.
EC Wed. **Golf** Polmont 9h. Polmonthill 18h.

★★★ Inchyra Grange, Grange Rd, FK2 0YB ☎(0324) 711911 Tx: 777693 Fax: (0324) 716134

In own grounds, 2-storey sandstone former private mansion; modern extensions. Additional 40 bedrooms planned for early 1991. Indoor swimming pool, sauna, solarium, gymnasium, billiards. ⚒ Fr, It. Gr
🛏 33 bedrs, 33 en suite; TV; tcf
🏨 dogs; P 160, coach; child facs; con 220
✕ LD 9.30, bar meals only Sat lunch
£ B&B £66–£72, B&B (double) £85–£95; L £9·50, D £14·50; WB £43 (HB); [10% V w/e]
cc Access, Amex, B'card/Visa, Diners.

PORT ASKAIG

See ISLE OF ISLAY.

PORTPATRICK Dumfries & Galloway (Wigtownshire). Map 42A2

Glenluce 13, London 395, Edinburgh 126, Gatehouse of Fleet 47, Glasgow 89½, New Galloway 47, Stranraer 7½.
EC Thur. **Golf** Dunskey 18h and 9h.

★★★ Fernhill, Heugh Rd, DG9 8TD ☎(077 681) 220 Fax: (077 681) 596
Attractive 19th-century building, with modern extension, on hill overlooking the sea,
🛏 16 bedrs, 14 en suite, 1 ba; annexe 4 bedrs, 4 en suite; TV; tcf
🏨 dogs, ns; P 50, coach; child facs; con 20
✕ LD 9
£ D £14·50; [10% V]
cc Access, Amex, B'card/Visa, Diners; dep.

★★ Mount Stewart, South Cres, DG9 8LE ☎(077 681) 291
Pleasing 2-storey building with a good view over the harbour.
🛏 8 bedrs, 3 en suite, 2 ba; TV; tcf
🏨 dogs; P 15; child facs
✕ LD 10
£ B&B £14–£17, B&B (double) £30–£40; L £3·45, D £8; WB
cc Access, B'card/Visa.

★★ Portpatrick, DG8 8TQ ☎(077 681) 333

Large turreted cliff-top hotel dominating north side of harbour. Swimming pool, golf, tennis, billiards. Open Mar–Nov. (MtCh)
🛏 57 bedrs, 57 en suite; TV; tcf
🏨 lift, dogs; P 60, coach; child facs; con 120
✕ LD 9, bar meals only lunch
£ B&B £37·50–£39·50, B&B (double) £59·50–£63·50; HB weekly £245–£259; D £11·50
cc Access, Amex, B'card/Visa, Diners; dep.

PORTREE

See ISLE OF SKYE.

PORT WILLIAM Dumfries & Galloway (Wigtownshire). Map 42C2

Pop 528. Wigtown 10, London 384, Edinburgh 118, Gatehouse of Fleet 35, Girvan 47, Glasgow 98, New Galloway 35, Stranraer 23.
EC Wed. **Golf** Monreith 9h.

★★★ R Corsemalzie House, DG8 9RL ☎(098 886) 254

Sc

19th century stone-built country mansion in magnificent wooded grounds. Private fishing. Putting. Closed 21 Jan–6 Mar. Fr
15 bedrs, 15 en suite; TV; tcf
dogs, P 35; child facs
LD 9.15
£ B&B £35·50–£43, B&B (double) £57–£67; HB weekly £231–£280; L £8·25, D £14·25; WB £36 (HB); [10% V]
cc Access, B'card/Visa; dep.

★★Monreith Arms, The Square, DG8 9SE
(098 87) 232

Pleasant 3-storey stone-built family-managed hotel overlooking the harbour.
12 bedrs, 11 en suite (1 sh), 1 ba; TV; tcf
TV, dogs; P 8, coach; child facs; con 50
LD 8.45
£ B&B £20, B&B (double) £38; HB weekly £192·50–£200; L £7, D £10; WB £55
cc Access, B'card/Visa; dep.

PRESTWICK Strathclyde (Ayrshire). Map 49B1
Pop 13,532. Ayr 2½, London 384, Edinburgh 70, Glasgow 30, Kilmarnock 9, Largs 28.
EC Wed. **Golf** Prestwick 18h, Prestwick St Cuthbert 18h, Prestwick St Nicholas 18h.
Boydfield Gdns (0292) 79946

★★★ Carlton Toby, 187 Ayr Rd, KA9 1TP
(0292) 76811 Fax: (0292) 76811

Purpose-built hotel convenient for Ayr and Prestwick. Large car park.
39 bedrs, 39 en suite; TV; tcf
TV, dogs, ns; P 200, coach; child facs

★★ North Beach, 5 Links Rd, KA9 1QG
(0292) 79069
Small hotel convenient for golf course, station and beach. Billiards.
12 bedrs, 12 en suite; TV; tcf
dogs; P 20, coach; child facs; con 20
LD 9.30
£ B&B £20; [10% V w/e]
cc Access, B'card/Visa; dep.

★★ St Nicholas, 41 Ayr Rd, KA9 1SY
(0292) 79568
Family-managed hotel in 3-storey Victorian building. Convenient for beach and town.
16 bedrs, 8 en suite, (1 sh), 3 ba; TV; tcf
TV; P 50, coach; child facs; con 122
(*See advertisement on p. 604*)

★ Auchencoyle, 13 Links Rd, KA9 1QG
(0292) 78316

Small hotel overlooking golf course. Close to sea.
6 bedrs, 3 en suite, 1 ba; tcf
TV, dogs; P 15, coach; child facs; con 40

Fernbank (Acclaimed), 213 Main St, KA9 1SU (0292) 75027. *Guest House.*

Braemar, 113 Ayr Rd, KA9 1TN (0292) 75820. *Private Hotel.*
Kincraig, 39 Ayr Rd, KA9 1SY (0292) 79480. *Private Hotel.*
£ B&B £13

RENFREW Strathclyde (Renfrewshire).
Map 46B2
Pop 21,759. Glasgow 5½, London 393, M8 (jn 26) 1, Dumbarton 9½, Edinburgh 50, Gourock 18, Paisley 2½.
EC Wed. **Golf** Renfrew 18h.

★★★★ Excelsior, Abbotsinch, PA3 2TR
041-887 1212 Tx: 777733
Fax: 041-887 3738

Modern soundproofed high-rise building, next to airport terminal. Solarium. (THF)
De, It
299 bedrs, 299 en suite; TV; tcf
lift, dogs, ns; P, coach; child facs; con 450
LD 10
£ B&B £87·60, B&B (double) £106·20; L £11·50, D £11·50; WB £64 (2 nts)
cc Access, Amex, B'card/Visa, CB, Diners.

★★★ Dean Park, Glasgow Rd, PA4 8YB
041-886 3771 Tx: 779032
Fax: 041-885 0681

Large modern hotel conveniently situated for Glasgow Airport. Solarium. (QMH) Fr, De, It
120 bedrs, 120 en suite; TV; tcf
dogs; P 200, coach; child facs; con 350
LD 9.45, bar meals only Sat lunch
£ B&B £65–£75 (w/e £34), B&B (double) £78–£88; L £10·50, D £12·95
cc Access, Amex, B'card/Visa, Diners.

★★★ Glynhill, Paisley Rd, PA4 8XB 041-886 5555 Tx: 779536
Fax: 041-885 2838

Extended and modernised former country mansion convenient for Glasgow Airport. Indoor swimming pool, sauna, solarium, gymnasium, billiards. Fr, De, It, Gr
125 bedrs, 125 en suite; TV; tcf
TV, dogs, ns; P 200, G 30, coach; child facs; con 450
LD 10.30
£ B&B £50–£80 (w/e £40), B&B (double) £60–£90; HB weekly £294–£504; L £8·25, D £12; WB £40 (HB); [10% V]
cc Access, Amex, B'card/Visa, Diners.
(*See advertisement on p. 604*)

★★★ Stakis Normandy, Inchinnan Rd, PA4 9EJ 041-886 4100 Tx: 778897
Fax: 041-885 2366
Modern hotel convenient for Airport. Bayeux tapestry feature in foyer. (Sk)
141 bedrs, 141 en suite; TV; tcf
lift, TV, dogs, ns; P 500, coach; child facs; con 1000
LD 10.30
£ B&B £75·50 (w/e £25), B&B (double) £91; L £9·50, D £14·95; WB £35
cc Amex, B'card/Visa, Diners.

RHU Strathclyde (Dunbartonshire).
Map 46A1
Pop 1,943. Helensburgh 2, London 412, Arrochar 15, Edinburgh 67, Glasgow 24.

★★ Ardencaple, Shore Rd, G84 8LS
(0436) 820200 Fax: (0436) 821099
An 18th century coaching inn by the shores of the Gare Loch.
15 bedrs, 15 en suite; TV; tcf
dogs; P 50, coach
LD 9.30, bar meals only lunch
£ B&B £40, B&B (double) £60–£66; D £10; [10% V]
cc Access, Amex, B'card/Visa, Diners.

ROCKCLIFFE Dumfries & Galloway (Kirkcudbrightshire). Map 43A2
Pop 100. Dalbeattie 6, London 347, Dumfries 20, Edinburgh 90, Gatehouse of Fleet 28.

★★★ Baron's Craig, DG5 4QF
(055 663) 225

EC *early closing* **MD** *market day* *country house hotel* *ns (NS) no smoking areas* *tcf tea/coffee facilities*

Imposing granite mansion (1880) in wooded grounds close to sea. Putting. Open 28 Mar –14 Oct.
🛏 27 bedrs, 20 en suite, 3 ba; TV
🏨 dogs; P 50; child facs
✕ LD 9
£ B&B £34–£52, B&B (double) £63–£94; D £18·50; WB
cc Access, B'card/Visa; dep.

★★ Clonyard House, Colvend, DG5 4QW ☎ (055 663) 372 ♿

Quiet hotel in own grounds, with modern bedroom extension. ✻ Fr, De
🛏 9 bedrs, 9 en suite; TV; tcf
🏨 TV, dogs; P 40; child facs
✕ LD 9, bar meals only lunch
£ B&B £30, B&B (double) £50, D £14; [5% V]
cc Access, B'card/Visa; dep.

ROSEBANK Strathclyde (Lanarkshire). Map 50A2
Pop 100. Abington 22, London 373, M74 (jn 7) 4, Edinburgh 36, Glasgow 17, Kilmarnock 29, Lanark 7, Stirling 31.

★★★ Popinjay, ML8 5QB ☎ Crossford (055 586) 441 Fax: (055 586) 204

On banks of the Clyde, a fine Tudor revival style (1900) building. Fishing. ✻ Fr, De, It
🛏 36 bedrs, 36 en suite; annexe 4 bedrs, 4 en suite; TV; tcf
🏨 dogs; P 100, coach; child facs; con 100
✕ LD 10
£ B&B £50, B&B (double) £65; L £7·95, D £12·50; WB £80
cc Access, Amex, B'card/Visa.

ROSYTH Fife. Map 47A2
Queensferry 4, London 384, M9 (spur) 6, M90 (jn 1) ½, Dunfermline 3, Edinburgh 13½, Glasgow 41.

★★ Gladyer Inn, Heath Rd, KY11 2BT ☎ (0383) 419977
Modern, white-painted, 2-storey hotel next to housing estate, close to M90. ✻ Fr
🛏 21 bedrs, 21 en suite; TV; tcf
🏨 TV, dogs, ns; P 81; child facs
✕ LD 9.30, bar meals only lunch
£ B&B £25, B&B (double) £35; D £11·75; WB £20; [10% V]
cc Access, Amex, B'card/Visa.
(See advertisement on p. 610)

ROTHES Grampian (Moray). Map 55A4
Pop 1,445. Craigellachie 3½, London 518, Banff 31, Edinburgh 143, Elgin 10, Glasgow 161.
EC Wed. **Golf** Dufftown 18h.

★★★ C Rothes Glen, IV33 7AH ☎ (034 03) 254
Splendid turreted stone-built Highland mansion in extensive grounds. Putting. Closed 1–15 Jan.
🛏 16 bedrs, 13 en suite; TV; tcf
🏨 TV, dogs; P 40, coach; child facs
✕ LD 9
£ B&B £56, B&B (double) £83; HB weekly £420; L £12, D £22; WB £30 (2 nts, Oct–Apr)
cc Access, Amex, B'card/Visa, Diners.

ROTHESAY *See* Isle of Bute

RUTHERGLEN Strathclyde (Lanarkshire). Map 46B3
Pop 24,732. M74 6, Hamilton 11, London 381, Edinburgh 44, Glasgow 2½, Lanark 23.

★★ Burnside, East Kilbride Rd, G73 5EA ☎ 041-634 1276 Fax: 041-634 1223 ♿

Purpose-built, long low hotel in quiet residential area, near station on Glasgow suburban railway. (BCB)
🛏 16 bedrs, 10 en suite, 2 ba; TV; tcf
🏨 ns; P 200, coach; child facs; con 150
✕ LD 10
£ B&B £42–£59·50, B&B (double) £58–£74·50; L £8·15, D £8·15; WB £27·50
cc Access, Amex, B'card/Visa, Diners.

ST ANDREWS Fife. Map 51A4
Pop 13,490. M90 27, Kirkcaldy 24, London 424, Dundee 12, Edinburgh 49, Glasgow 75, Kinross 35, Perth 32.
EC Thur. **Golf** Four 18h courses–Old, New, Eden and Jubilee, and 5 putting greens, open to visitors, St Andrews GC and New GC admit visitors as temp members, visitors to Royal and Ancient must be guests of members. **See** Cathedral ruins, Chapter House and Museum, St Rule's Church (Tower), Holy Trinity Church, University, Byre Theatre, Botanic Gdns, Castle ruins, The Pends, West Port, Sessions House.
ℹ South St. ☎ (0334) 72021

★★★★ Rusack's, Pilmour Links, KY16 9JQ ☎ (0334) 74321 Fax: (0334) 77896
Imposing 5-storey stone-built traditional Victorian style hotel in formal gardens. Sauna, solarium. (THF) ✻ Fr
🛏 50 bedrs, 50 en suite; TV; tcf
🏨 lift, dogs, ns; P 40, coach; child facs; con 100
✕ LD 10
£ room £81–£87, double room £119–£146; Bk £9·50, L £10·95, D £27
cc Access, Amex, B'card/Visa, CB, Diners.

★★★ R Rufflets, KY16 9TX ☎ (0334) 72594 Fax: (0334) 78703

Two-storey 1920s house in 10 acres of secluded grounds. Putting. Closed 16 Jan–13 Feb. ✻ De
🛏 18 bedrs, 18 en suite; annexe 3 bedrs, 3 en suite; TV; tcf
🏨 ns; P 80, G 6 (£2·50), coach; child facs; con 40
✕ LD 9.30
£ B&B £32–£60; HB weekly £245–£560; L £10.50, D £21
cc Access, Amex, B'card/Visa, Diners; dep.

★★★ H C St Andrews Golf, The Scores ☎ (0334) 72611 Tx: 94013267 Fax: (0334) 72188

Seafront hotel with fine views of the beach. Sauna, solarium. ✻ Fr, It
🛏 23 bedrs, 23 en suite; TV; tcf
🏨 lift, dogs, ns; P 6, coach; child facs; con 200
✕ LD 9.30
£ B&B £47–£58, B&B (double) £75–£105; HB weekly £343–£450; L £10·50, D £18; [10% V]
cc Access, Amex, B'card/Visa, Diners; dep.

★★★ Scores, The Scores, KY16 9BB ☎ (0334) 72451 Tx: 94012061 Fax: (0334) 73947
Seafront hotel conveniently located near to golf course. ✻ Fr, De
🛏 30 bedrs, 30 en suite; TV; tcf
🏨 lift, dogs; P 8; child facs; con 120
✕ LD 9.30, nr lunch
£ B&B £54–£60, B&B (double) £65–£110; HB weekly £266–£420; D £16·50; WB £42 (2 nts HB); [10% V Nov–Jan]
cc Access, Amex, B'card/Visa, Diners.

★★ Ardgowan, 2 Playfair Terr, KY16 9HX ☎ (0334) 72970
Small family-run hotel conveniently located for golf course. Open 15 Jan–23 Dec.
🛏 13 bedrs, 11 en suite, 1 ba; TV; tcf
🏨 TV, dogs; coach; child facs

Atlas Section
Consult the Atlas section at the back of the guide to find out which towns and villages have RAC Appointed and Listed hotels in them. They are shown on the maps by purple circles.

Sc

Rosyth (Scotland)

GLADYER INN

Heath Road/Ridley Drive, Rosyth KY11 2BT Scotland

Tel: (0383) 419977 Fax: (0383) 411728

Public Lounge & Cocktail Bar.
21 Twin-Double bedrooms, all en-suite with colour TV, direct dial telephone, tea and coffee making facilities.

Function suite also available.

We can quote reasonable rates to suit your requirements.

Lerwick (Shetland Islands)

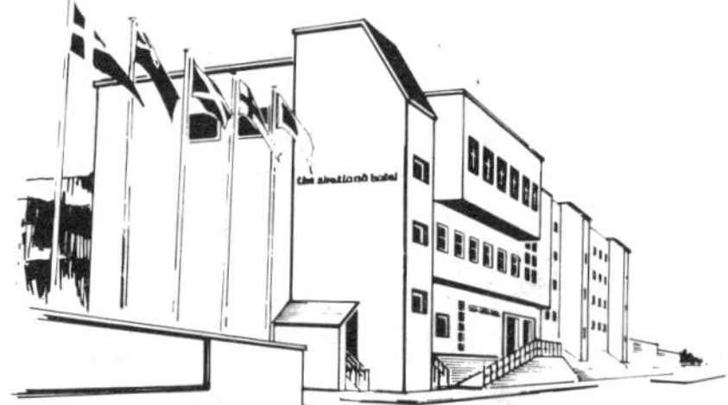

Situated opposite the ferry terminal, the Shetland Hotel offers modern luxury in a scenic island setting. All rooms en-suite with many accessories. Relax in our indoor heated swimming pool. Two fully equipped disabled bedrooms. Complimentary use of laundry facilities for those with young families.

TRAVEL AND CAR HIRE INCLUSIVE PACKAGES ARE AVAILABLE. FOR DETAILS PLEASE CONTACT US DIRECT.

the shetland hotel

Holmsgarth Road,
Lerwick, Shetland ZE1 0PW
Telephone: (0595) 5515
Telex: 75432 SHETEL G
Fax: (0595) 5828

Brae (Shetland Islands)

BUSTA HOUSE HOTEL***

Busta, Brae, Shetland ZE2 9QN

This 18th century former home of the Lairds of Busta combines old world charm with modern comfort. Good food, fine wines, peat fires and 120 malt whiskies await you at Busta.

Phone for details of our holiday package – Air/ Ferry and car hire

Tel: (080622) 506 or Fax: (080622) 588.

Family owned and run, Busta makes you welcome.

★★ **Parkland,** Kinburn Castle, Double Dykes Rd, KY16 9DS ☎(0334) 73620

Hotel in a late Victorian 'castle' in its own grounds in residential area of town.
15 bedrs, 9 en suite, 3 ba; TV; tcf
ns; P 15; child facs
LD 8.30
£ B&B £22·50–£33, B&B (double) £40–£57·50; HB weekly £255–£265; L £8, D £18·50; WB £65–£95 [Oct–May]
cc Access, B'card/Visa; dep.

Albany (Acclaimed), 56 North St, KY16 9AH ☎(0334) 77737. *Private Hotel.* Fr, De
£ B&B £12·50–£20; HB weekly £180–£220
Amberside (Acclaimed), 4 Murray Pk, KY16 9AW ☎(0334) 74644. *Guest House.* Open Feb–Nov.
£ B&B £16–£23.
Argyle (Acclaimed), 127 North St, KY16 9AG ☎(0334) 73387. *Hotel.* Open Mar–Nov.
£ B&B £18–£22
Arran House (Acclaimed), 5 Murray Park, KY16 9AW ☎(0334) 74724 Fax: 0334 72072. *Guest House.* Open Feb–Nov.
£ B&B £15–£25.
Beachway House (Acclaimed), 6 Murray Pk, KY16 9AW ☎(0334) 73319. *Guest House.* Open Mar–Dec.
£ B&B £20–£24; [10% V].
Bell Craig (Acclaimed), 8 Murray Park, KY16 9AW ☎(0334) 72962. *Guest House.*
Cleveden House (Acclaimed), 3 Murray Pk, KY16 9AP ☎(0334) 74212. *Guest House.*
£ B&B £12–£18; [5% V excl May–Sep].
Craigmore (Acclaimed), 3 Murray Park, KY16 9AW ☎(0334) 72142. *Guest House.*
Hazelbank (Acclaimed), 28 The Scores, KY16 9AS ☎(0334) 72466. *Private Hotel.*
Number Ten (Acclaimed), 10 Hope St, KY16 9HT ☎(0334) 74601. *Guest House.*
Sporting Laird (Acclaimed), 5 Playfair Terr, KY16 9HX ☎(0334) 75906. Fax: (0334) 73881 *Private Hotel.* Closed Feb.
£ B&B £24–£28; HB weekly £225–£250; [5% V]
West Park (Acclaimed), 5 St Mary's Pl, KY16 9UY ☎(0334) 75933. *Guest House.* Open Mar–Dec.
£ B&B £31–£37
Yorkston House (Acclaimed), 68 Argyle St, KY16 9BV ☎(0334) 72019. *Hotel.*
£ B&B £16–£20; HB weekly £160–£200

Cadzow, 58 North St, KY16 9AH ☎(0334) 76933. *Guest House.* Open Feb–Nov.
£ B&B (doublel) £23–£36

ST FILLANS Tayside (Perthshire). Map 50A4
Pop 250. Comrie 5, London 423, Crieff 12, Edinburgh 58, Glasgow 54, Lochearnhead 6½, Stirling 27.
EC Wed. **Golf** St Fillans 9h.

★★★ **Four Seasons,** PH6 2NF ☎(076 485) 333
Long, white-painted building with wonderful views of Loch Earn. Family owned and run.
12 bedrs, 12 en suite; TV; tcf
dogs; P 30, coach; child facs
LD 9.45; bar meals only Mon–Sat lunch
£ B&B £35–£45, B&B (double) £58–£70; HB weekly £270–£320; D £18; [10% V Mar–May, Oct–Nov]
cc Access, Amex, B'card/Visa.

SANDYHILLS Dumfries & Galloway (Kirkcudbrightshire). Map 43A2
Dumfries 18, London 345, Castle Douglas 11, Dalbeattie 5.

Craigbittern House (Acclaimed), nr Dalbeattie, DG5 4NZ. ☎ (0387) 78247 *Guest House.* Open Easter–Oct.
£ B&B £13; HB (weekly) £126–£154; dep.

SANQUHAR Dumfries & Galloway (Dumfriesshire). Map 43A4
Pop 2,070. Thornhill 12, London 353, Abington 16, Ayr 32, Dalmellington 21, Edinburgh 56, Glasgow 46, Lanark 29.
EC Thur. **Golf** Sanquhar 9h.
Tolbooth, High St ☎(0659) 50185

★ **Nithsdale,** High St, DG4 6DJ ☎(0659) 50506
Small and pleasant family-managed hotel situated on main street.
6 bedrs (1 sh), 2 ba; TV; tcf
dogs; coach; child facs; con 120
LD 10
£ B&B £15; L £7; D £10·50
cc B'card/Visa; dep.

SCONE Tayside (Perthshire). Map 50B4
Pop 3,830. Perth 2, London 418, Blairgowrie 15, Dundee 20, Edinburgh 43, Glasgow 59.
Golf Murrayshall House 18h.

★★★ H C R **Murrayshall House,** Tayside PH2 7PH ☎(0738) 51171 Tx: 76197 Fax: (0738) 52595
Country house in 400 acres of parkland. Golf, putting, tennis. Fr, Es
19 bedrs, 19 en suite; TV
dogs; P 90, coach; child facs; con 50
LD 9.30
£ B&B £70–£75, B&B (double) £105–£115; L £15, D £35; WB £75 (2 nts, Nov–Mar)
cc Access, Amex, B'card/Visa, Diners; dep.

SCOURIE Highland (Sutherland). Map 57C4
Pop 289. Lairg 43, London 620, Edinburgh 245, Glasgow 252, Tongue 59, Ullapool 43.
Golf Dornoch 18h.

★★ H **Scourie,** IV27 4SX ☎(0971) 2396 Fax: (0971) 2423

Dating from 1823, and in rugged scenery, hotel particularly caters for anglers. Fishing. Open 15 Mar–21 Oct.
18 bedrs, 16 en suite, 1 ba; annexe 2 bedrs, 2 en suite; tcf
TV, dogs; P 30; child facs
LD 8.30, nr Mon–Sat lunch
£ B&B £30–£35, B&B (double) £53–£60; HB weekly £245–£280; L £8, D £12; WB £72 (3 nts, low season only)
cc Access, Amex, B'card/Visa, Diners.

SELKIRK See ETTRICKBRIDGE.

SHETLAND ISLANDS

BRAE Mainland. Map 59C2
Lerwick 23, London (via Aberdeen) 515, Edinburgh (Fy) 140, Glasgow 153.

★★★ **Busta House,** ZE2 9QN ☎(080 622) 506 Tx: 9312100218 Fax: (080 622) 588

A fine 18th century mansion in spacious grounds overlooking its own private harbour and Busta Voe. Closed 23 Dec–2 Jan.
20 bedrs, 20 en suite; TV; tcf
dogs, ns; P 35, coach; child facs; con 25
LD 9.30, bar meals only lunch
£ B&B £45–£54, B&B (double) £65–£73; D £18·25
cc Access, Amex, B'card/Visa, Diners.
(*See advertisement on p. 610*)

LERWICK Mainland. Map 59C2
Pop 6,195. London (via Aberdeen) 492, Edinburgh (Fy) 117, Glasgow (Fy) 130.
EC Wed. **Golf** Dale 18h.
Market Cross. ☎(0595) 3434

★★★ **Shetland,** Holmsgarth Rd, ZE1 0PW ☎(0595) 5515 Tx: 75432 Fax: (0595) 5828
Modern 3-storey building with stone-faced buttresses. Overlooks harbour and bay. Indoor swimming pool, sauna, solarium.
66 bedrs, 66 en suite; TV; tcf
lift, dogs, ns; P 150, coach; child facs; con 300
LD 9.15
£ B&B £58 (w/e £16), B&B (double) £66; HB weekly £262·50; L £6, D £13·50
cc Access, Amex, B'card/Visa, Diners.
(*See advertisement on p. 610*)

Sc

★★ **Grand,** Commercial St, ☎(0595) 2826 Fax: (0595) 4048

Prominent building on main street in centre of town; hotel accommodation on first and second floors.
🛏 23 bedrs, 17 en suite; TV; tcf
🏨 dogs; coach; child facs
✕ LD 9
£ B&B £40, B&B (double) £55; HB weekly £315; L 4, D £10
cc Access, Amex, B'card/Visa, Diners.

★★ **Queens,** Commercial St, ZE1 0AB ☎(0595) 2826 Fax: (0595) 4048

Substantial stone-built hotel on water's edge by harbour.
🛏 26 bedrs, 26 en suite; TV; tcf
🏨 dogs; coach; child facs
✕ LD 9
£ B&B £40, B&B (double) £55; L £4, D £10
cc Access, Amex, B'card/Visa, Diners.

VIRKIE Mainland. Map 59C2
Lerwick 23, London (via Aberdeen) 514, Edinburgh (Fy) 140, Glasgow (Fy) 159.
Meadowvale (Acclaimed) ☎Sumburgh (0950) 60240

SKELMORLIE Strathclyde. Map 49B3
Pop 1,620. Greenock 9, London 417, Edinburgh 75, Glasgow 30, Gourock 8, Largs 5, Paisley 25.
🏰 ★★★ H C **Manor Park,** St Phillans, PA17 5HE ☎(0475) 520832

Country house, with extensive grounds and fine views of Firth of Clyde.
🛏 7 bedrs, 7 en suite; annexe 16 bedrs, 16 en suite; TV; tcf
🏨 P 25; no children under 7; con 70
✕ LD 9.15
£ B&B £35–£65, B&B (double) £60–£90; WB £155 (3 nts HB)
cc Access, Amex, B;card/Visa, Diners; dep.

SOUTH QUEENSFERRY Lothian. Map 47B2
Pop 5,000. Edinburgh 9½, London 384, M9 (jn 1) 2, Dunfermline 7½, Glasgow 39, Kincardine 14, Kinross 17, Kirkcaldy 15.
EC Wed. **Golf** Dundas 9h.
★★★ **Forth Bridges Moat House,** Forth Bridge Road, EH30 9SF ☎031-331 1199 Tx: 727430 Fax: 031-319 1733 ♿

Large, modern hotel overlooking Forth Bridges. Indoor swimming pool, squash, sauna, solarium, gymnasium, billiards. (QMH)
🛏 106 bedrs, 106 en suite; TV; tcf
🏨 lift, dogs, ns; P 180, coach; child facs; con 140
★★ R **Hawes Inn,** Newhalls Rd, EH30 9TE ☎031-331 1990
Attractive 2-storey white-painted 16th century inn with fine view of Forth Bridge.
🛏 8 bedrs, 3 ba; TV; tcf
🏨 dogs, ns; P 50, coach; child facs; con 60
✕ LD 10
£ B&B £35, B&B (double) £47·50; L £8·50, D £12; [10% V Oct–Mar, w/e Apr–Sep]
cc Access, Amex, B'card/Visa, Diners.

SPEAN BRIDGE Highland. Map 53C2
Pop 135. Fort William 9½, London 499, Dalwhinnie 35, Edinburgh 133, Glasgow 112, Invergarry 16, Kingussie 38.
EC Thur. **Golf** Spean Bridge 9h.
ℹ ☎ (039 781) 576
★★ H **Letterfinlay Lodge,** Letterfinlay, PH34 4DZ (7½ m N of Spean Bridge on A82) ☎(039 781) 622

Former coaching inn which has been modernised by the family owners. Fishing. Open Mar–Oct.
🛏 13 bedrs, 9 en suite, 4 ba
🏨 TV, dogs; P 100, coach; child facs
✕ LD 9.30, bar meals only lunch
£ B&B £25–£30, B&B (double) £36–£60, D £13·50; WB
cc Access, Amex, B'card/Visa, Diners.

★★ **Spean Bridge,** PH34 4ES ☎(039 781) 250 ♿
Modernised coaching inn steeped in history dating back to 1780. Billiards. Closed 24 Dec–2 Jan.
🛏 20 bedrs, 19 en suite, 2 ba; annexe 12 bedrs, 12 en suite; TV; tcf
🏨 TV, dogs; P 50, coach; child facs; con 40
✕ LD 9
£ B&B £23–£27, B&B (double) £45–£53; HB weekly £180–£245; D £12
cc Access, B'card/Visa, CB, Diners; dep.

STANLEY Tayside (Perthshire). Map 54C1
Perth 6, London 422, Burnam 6, Blairgowrie 7½, Edinburgh 47, Glasgow 63.
★★ **Tayside,** Mill St, PH2 0QL ☎(0738) 828249 Fax: (0738) 33449
Substantial stone-built Victorian house in centre of village. Fishing.
🛏 17 bedrs, 12 en suite, (2 sh) 2 ba; TV; tcf
🏨 dogs; P 50, U 4, coach; child facs; con 120
✕ LD 8.30
£ B&B £17–£29·50, B&B (double) £34–£49; HB weekly £192·50–£315; D fr £12·50; WB £24·50 (HB), [10% V excl Aug–Sep]
cc B'card/Visa, dep.

STEPPS Strathclyde (Lanarkshire). Map 46B4
Pop 1,791. M73 4, Hamilton 10, London 377, Edinburgh 42, Glasgow 4½, Kincardine 23, Stirling 54.
EC Wed. **Golf** Crow wood 18h.
★★★ **Garfield House,** Cumbernauld Rd, G33 6HW ☎041-779 2111 Fax: 041-779 2111
Converted house close to Glasgow-Stirling road. Conference facilities.
🛏 27 bedrs, 27 en suite; TV; tcf
🏨 dogs; P 70, coach; child facs; con 180

STIRLING Central (Stirlingshire). Map 50A3
Pop 29,776. Falkirk 10, London 395, M9 Motorway 2½, Dumbarton 34, Edinburgh 35, Glasgow 26, Kincardine 12, Kinross 23, Lochearnhead 30, Perth 33.
EC Wed. **MD** Thur. **Golf** King Park 18h. **See** Castle, Parliament Hall, Chapel Royal, S African Memorial, Museum and Art Gallery, Tolbooth (1701), Mercat Cross, Darnley's House, Argyll's Lodging, old Bridge, Church of Holy Rude, Mar's Work, Guildhall, Bruce's Statue, Abbey Craig with Wallace Monument 2 m NNE, Field of Bannockburn (Memorial), Cambuskenneth Abbey ruins 1 m E, Doune Castle and Doune Park Gardens, also Doune Motor Museum 6½ m NW.
ℹ Dumbarton Rd. ☎(0786) 75019
★★★ **Golden Lion,** King St, FK8 1BD ☎(0786) 75351 Fax: (0786) 72755

EC *early closing* **MD** *market day* 🏰 *country house hotel* *ns (NS) no smoking areas* *tcf tea/coffee facilities*

Five-storey stone-built hotel of 16th century origins, in town centre.
🛏 69 bedrs, 69 en suite; TV; tcf
🏨 lift, dogs; P 20, coach; child facs; con 250
✕ LD 9
£ B&B £48–£64, B&B (double) £72–£97; HB weekly £224–£315; L £7, D £14; WB £32; [10% V Nov–Apr w/e May–Jul, Sep–Oct]
cc Amex, Diners.

★★★ Terraces, 4 Melville Terr, FK8 2ND
📞(0786) 72268 Tx: 778025
Fax: (0786) 50314

Georgian-style building close to town centre now a family-run hotel. Fr, De, Da
🛏 15 bedrs, 15 en suite; TV; tcf
🏨 dogs; P 28, coach; child facs; con 100
✕ LD 9, bar meals only Sun lunch
£ B&B £44·50, B&B (double) £57·50; D £10·95; WB £62 (2 nts HB); [10% V]
cc Access, Amex, B'card/Visa, Diners.

★★ Garfield, Victoria Sq, FK8 2QZ 📞(0786) 73730
Two-storey stone building, with a conservatory; overlooking park.
🛏 8 bedrs, 5 en suite, 1 ba; TV; tcf
🏨 dogs; P 6; child facs
✕ LD 8.30; bar meals only lunch & Sun dinner
£ B&B £25–£35, B&B (double) £38–£50, D £12
cc Access, B'card/Visa.

Stirling Highland, Spittal St. 📞(Central reservations) 041-332 6538.
Hotel being built; completion expected Spring 1991.

STONEHAVEN
Grampian (Kincardineshire). Map 55C2
Pop 8,550. Brechin 24, London 478, Aberdeen 15, Braemar 56, Edinburgh 103, Glasgow 122, Montrose 23.
EC Wed. **Golf** Stonehaven 18h. **See** Restored 16th cent Tolbooth, Mercat Cross, Fireball Ceremony at Hogmanay, Dunnottar Castle ruins 1½ m S, Muchalls Castle.
ℹ The Square. 📞Stonehaven (0569) 62806

★★★ Commodore, Cowie Park, AB3 2PZ
📞(0569) 62936 Tx: 739111
Fax: (0569) 66179
A modern purpose-built hotel standing at roadside on edge of town.
🛏 40 bedrs, 40 en suite; TV; tcf
🏨 TV, dogs; P 280, coach; child facs; con 300

STONEYKIRK
Dumfries & Galloway (Wigtownshire). Map 42B2
Newton Stewart 16, London 383, Drummore 10, Glasgow 88, Stranraer 6.

★★ Torrs Warren, DG9 9DH 📞Sandhead (0776 83) 204
Two-storey white-painted hotel on the edge of the village with rural views. Fr, Es
🛏 7 bedrs, 2 en suite, 2 ba; TV; tcf
🏨 dogs; P 50; child facs
✕ LD 8.45, bar meals only lunch, Mon & Tue dinner
£ B&B £13, B&B (double) £26–£28

STRACHUR
Strathclyde (Argyll). Map 49A4
Pop 750. Arrochar 21, London 444, Dunoon 19, Edinburgh 98, Glasgow 56, Inveraray 21.

★★★ H R Creggans Inn, PA27 8BX
📞(036 986) 279 Tx: 777694
Fax: (036 986) 637 ♿

Charming lochside hotel with attractive decor and fine views. Fishing. Fr
🛏 21 bedrs, 17 en suite, 2 ba; TV
🏨 TV, dogs, ns; P 100, coach; child facs; con 120
✕ LD 9, bar meals only Mon–Fri lunch
£ B&B £34–£48, B&B (double) £68–£90; D £19
cc Access, Amex, B'card/Visa, Diners; dep.

STRANRAER
Dumfries & Galloway (Wigtownshire). Map 42B3. *See also* STONEYKIRK.
Pop 10,000. Glenluce 9½, London 391, Edinburgh 120, Gatehouse of Fleet 44, Girvan 30, Glasgow 82, New Galloway 44.
EC Wed. **Golf** Creachmore 18h. **See** Peel Tower (known as 'Stranraer Castle'), Old Town Hall, Lochinch and Castle, Kennedy Gdns 3 m E, Glenluce Abbey 7½ m E, Logan Botanic Garden 10 m S.
ℹ Port Rodie. 📞(0776) 2595

★★★★ North West Castle, Cairnryan Rd, DG9 8EH 📞(0776) 4413 Tx: 777088
Fax: (0776) 2646

Large white Regency building with sheltered garden (palm trees). Curling rink. Indoor swimming pool, sauna, solarium, gymnasium, billiards.
🛏 75 bedrs, 75 en suite; TV; tcf
🏨 lift, dogs; P 100; child facs; con 60
✕ LD 9.30
£ B&B £45–£50, B&B (double) £64–£80; HB weekly £259; D £18; WB £88
(See advertisement on p. 617)

STRATHAVEN
Strathclyde (Lanarkshire). Map 49C2
M74 (jn 8) 5; London 389, Cumnock 19, Kilmarnock 20, Glasgow 12, Edinburgh 32.

★★★ Strathaven, Hamilton Rd, ML10 6SZ
📞(0357) 21778 Tx: 776496
Fax: (0357) 20789
Three-storey Adam-designed house on outskirts of town convenient for M74.
🛏 10 bedrs, 10 en suite; TV; tcf
🏨 dogs; P 80, coach; child facs; con 180
✕ LD 10
£ WB £80
cc Access, Amex, B'card/Visa, Diners.

STRATHBLANE
Central (Stirlingshire). Map 46A3
Pop 835. Glasgow 11, London 398, Arrochar 33, Crianlarich 48, Dumbarton 20, Edinburgh 47, Lochearnhead 49, Stirling 27.
EC Wed. **Golf** Strathendrick 9h.

★★ Kirkhouse Inn, G63 9AA 📞(0360) 70621
Extended modernised coaching inn in village at foot of Campsie Hills.
🛏 15 bedrs, 15 en suite; TV; tcf
🏨 TV, dogs, ns; P 300, coach; child facs; con 30

STRATHPEFFER
Highland (Ross & Cromarty). Map 58A1
Pop 700. Contin 2½, London 548, Achnasheen 23, Beauly 11, Dingwall 4½, Edinburgh 173, Glasgow 177, Ullapool 40.
EC Thur. **Golf** Strathpeffer 18h.
ℹ The Square 📞(0997) 21415

★★ Highland, IV14 9AN 📞(0997) 21457
Tx: 75160
Large, modernised, tourist-orientated hotel in picturesque village.

★★ H R Holly Lodge, IV14 9AR
📞(0997) 21254

Small family-run Victorian hotel situated in own pleasant grounds. Sauna.
🛏 7 bedrs, 7 en suite; TV; tcf
🏨 dogs; P 15; child facs
✕ LD 9, bar meals only lunch
£ B&B £19–£21; HB weekly £180–£200; D £10

★★ Mackay's, The Square, IV14 9DC
📞(0997) 21542
Substantial 3-storey hotel set back from main street in town centre.

STRONTIAN
Highland (Argyll). Map 53B2
Pop 250. Loch Aline 20 (Fy to Oban), London 533 (Fy 497), Edinburgh 176 (Fy 140), Fort William 44, Glasgow 133 (Fy 110), Ballachulish (Fy) 20.
EC Wed, Thur. **See** Lead Mines.

♛ ★★ H C R **Kilcamb Lodge,** PH36 4HY ☎(0967) 2257

Small privately-owned mansion situated in own grounds beside Loch Sunart. Open Easter–20 Oct.
🛏 9 bedrs, 9 en suite; tcf
🏠 TV; P 20; child facs
✕ LD 7, bar meals only lunch
£ B&B £30; HB weekly £290·50; D £17

SYMINGTON Strathclyde (Lanarkshire). Map 50B2
Pop 1,192. Abington 9, London 360, Ayr 50, Edinburgh 32, Glasgow 34, Kincardine 41, Lanark 10, Peebles 21.
EC Wed. **Golf** Biggar 18h.

★★★ **Tinto,** ML12 6PQ ☎Tinto (089 93) 454 Fax: (089 93) 520
Charming white-painted building in attractive gardens at edge of small village on the A72. Solarium.
🛏 38 bedrs, 38 en suite; TV; tcf
🏠 dogs; P 100, coach; child facs; con 200
✕ LD 10
£ B&B £38, B&B (double) £56; L £6·50, D £9·50; [10% V]
cc Access, Amex, B'card/Visa, Diners
(*See advertisement below*)

♛ ★★★ **Wyndales House,** nr Biggar, ML12 6JU ☎Tinto (089 93) 207

At the foot of the Tinto Hills, a sandstone building in own grounds. ✱ Fr, It, Es
🛏 14 bedrs, 14 en suite; TV; tcf
🏠 dogs; P 50, coach; child facs; con 50
✕ LD 9.30
£ B&B £35–£38·50, B&B (double) £45–£50; HB weekly £245–£339·50; L £9, D £14·50; WB £38·50 (2 nts); [10% V]
cc Access, Amex, B'card/Visa.

TAIN Highland. Map 58B2
Pop 2,200. Alness 14, London 5462, Bonar Bridge 14, Dingwall 25, Edinburgh 187, Glasgow 194.

★★★ **Mansfield,** Scotsburn Rd, IV19 1PR ☎(0862) 2052

Turreted building situated in own well-kept grounds. Closed New Years Day.
🛏 18 bedrs, 18 en suite; TV; tcf
🏠 TV, dogs; P 40, coach; child facs; con 40
✕ LD 9
£ B&B £36–£38, B&B (double) £48–£56; L £5·50, D £8·50
cc Access, Amex, B'card/Visa.

★★★ H **Morangie House,** Morangie Rd, IV19 1PY ☎(0862) 2281
Sympathetically modernised Victorian mansion on northern side of town. ✱ Fr
🛏 11 bedrs, 11 en suite; TV; tcf
🏠 dogs; P 30, coach; child facs; con 25
✕ LD 10
£ B&B £30–£42, B&B (double) £45–£55; L £5·90, D £14·50
cc Access, Amex, B'card/Visa, Diners.

★★★ **Royal,** High St, IV19 1AB ☎(0862) 2013 Fax: (0862) 3450

Large privately-owned traditional hotel on corner site in centre of town.

TARBERT Strathclyde (Argyll). Map 49A3
Pop 226. Ardrishaig 11, London 481, Edinburgh 135, Glasgow 93, Lochgilphead 13, Whitehouse 8.
ℹ ☎(088 02) 429

♛ ★★★ **Stonefield Castle,** Loch Fyne, PA29 6YJ ☎(0880 820) 836 Tx: 776321 Fax: (0880 820) 929
Baronial building in wooded garden overlooking loch. Swimming pool, fishing, sauna, solarium, billiards.
🛏 32 bedrs, 31 en suite, 1 ba; TV; tcf
🏠 lift, TV, dogs, ns; P 30, coach; child facs; con 120
✕ LD 9
£ B&B £33–£50, B&B (double) £56–£84; HB weekly £224–£332; L £6, D £18; [10% V]
cc Access, Amex, B'card/Visa, Diners; dep.
(*See advertisement on p. 617*)

★★ **Anchor,** PA29 4YJ ☎(088 02) 577

White-painted hotel, close to harbour, with good views.

TAYNUILT Strathclyde (Argyll). Map 53B1
Pop 400. Dalmally 11, London 466, Ballachulish 40, Edinburgh 109, Fort William 50, Glasgow 79, Inveraray 26, Oban 12.

★★ **Brander Lodge,** Bridge of Awe, PA35 1HT ☎(086 62) 243 Fax: (086 62) 273
Modernised and extended hotel at entrance to historic Pass of Brander. ✱ Fr, De
🛏 20 bedrs, 20 en suite; TV; tcf
🏠 dogs; P 60, coach; child facs; con 50
✕ LD 8.30
£ B&B £22–£25; L £4; D £13·75; [10% V excl Jun–Sep]
cc Access, Amex, B'card/Visa, Diners; dep.

★★ **Polfearn,** PA35 1JQ ☎(086 62) 251 ♿
Modernised family-run hotel situated in quiet surroundings.

TEANGUE *See* ISLE OF SKYE.

THORNHILL Dumfries & Galloway (Dumfriesshire). Map 43A4
Pop 1,520. Dumfries 14, London 341, Ayr 44, Edinburgh 62, Glasgow 59, Moffat 31, New Galloway 22.
EC Thur. **Golf** Thornhill 18h.

★★ **Buccleuch & Queensberry,** Drumlanrig Rd, DG3 5LU ☎(0848) 30215
Attractive 3-storey Victorian stone-built hotel in centre of small town.
🛏 12 bedrs, 9 en suite, 2 ba; TV; tcf
🏠 TV, dogs; P, coach; child facs
✕ LD 9, bar meals only lunch
£ B&B £23·50, B&B (double) £44–£50; L £5·50, D £9
cc Access, B'card/Visa; dep.

★★ **George,** Drumlanrig Rd, DG3 5LU ☎(0848) 30326

 EC *early closing* **MD** *market day* ♛ *country house hotel* *ns (NS) no smoking areas* *tcf tea/coffee facilities*

Refurbished family-run hotel, once a coaching inn, on A76 in centre of town. Fr, Es
8 bedrs, 6 en suite, 1 ba; TV; tcf
TV, dogs; P 12, coach; child facs
LD 8.55, bar meals only lunch & Mon–Wed dinner
£ B&B £22·50–£25, B&B (double) £35–£45; D £9·50
cc Access, B'card/Visa; dep.

★★ R **Trigony House,** Closeburn, DG3 5EZ (0848) 31211

A 2-storey typical Scottish country house in own secluded grounds.
9 bedrs, 8 en suite, 1 ba; TV; tcf
P 80; no children under 8
LD 8.30, bar meals only lunch
£ B&B £29·50; B&B (double) £49–£53; D £12
cc Access, B'card/Visa; dep.

THURSO Highland (Caithness). Map 58C4
Pop 8,000. Helmsdale 41, London 644, Edinburgh 269, Glasgow 276, Melvich 16, Wick 20.
EC Thur. **MD** Tue. **Golf** Thurso 18h.
Car Park, Riverside. (0847) 62371

★★**Pentland,** Princes St, KW14 7AA (0847) 63202
Family-owned modernised stone and tile faced building on corner site.
53 bedrs, 36 en suite, 6 ba; TV
dogs; coach; child facs; con 150
LD 8.30
£ B&B £16–£21, B&B (double) £32–£38; L £3, D £6·50
cc Access, B'card/Visa.

★★ **Royal,** Traill St, KW14 8EH (0847) 63191

Large privately-owned hotel, within a terrace building, in town centre. Billiards

★★ **St Clair,** Sinclair St, KW14 7AJ (0847) 66481
Family-owned substantial stone-built hotel in main street in town centre.
35 bedrs, 26 en suite; (9 sh), 2 ba; TV; tcf
TV, dogs; U 6; coach; child facs

TONGUE Highland (Sutherland). Map 58A4
Pop 150. Lairg 36, London 613, Bettyhill 13, Durness 37, Edinburgh 238, Glasgow 245.
Golf Reay 18h.

★★ **Ben Loyal,** IV27 4XE (084 755) 216

Privately-owned stone-built tourist hotel situated in centre of village. Fr, De
13 bedrs, 6 en suite, 2 ba
TV, dogs, ns; P 19, coach; child facs
LD 7.45, bar meals only lunch
£ B&B £20–£26·50, B&B (double) £28–£53; HB weekly £126–£208; D £12·50; WB £50 (2 nts HB)
cc B'card/Visa; dep.

TROON Strathclyde (Ayrshire). Map 49B1
Pop 14,254. Monkton 4, London 389, Ayr 7, Edinburgh 69, Glasgow 29, Kilmarnock 9, Largs 24, Paisley 27.
EC Wed. **Golf** Darley 18h, Fullarton 18h, Lochgreen 18h, Royal Troon 18h (3).
Municipal Buildings, South Beach. (0292) 317696

★★★★ **Marine Highland,** Crosbie Rd, KA10 6HE (0292) 314444 Tx: 777595 Fax: (0292) 316922

Dignified Victorian sandstone building with views of sea and links. Indoor swimming pool, putting, squash, sauna, solarium, gymnasium, billiards. (SH). Fr, It, Du
72 bedrs, 72 en suite; TV; tcf
lift, dogs; P 200, coach; child facs; con 220
LD 11
£ B&B £70–£80 (w/e £45 HB), B&B (double) £105–£120; L £9·50, D £17·50; WB £90 (2nts HB)
cc Access, Amex, B'card/Visa, Diners.

★★★ **Piersland House,** Craig End Rd, KA10 6HD (0292) 314747 Fax: (0292) 365613
Privately-owned hotel near two golf courses and the beach. Putting.
15 bedrs, 15 en suite; annexe 4 bedrs, 4 en suite; TV; tcf
dogs; P 100, coach; child facs; con 60
LD 9.30
£ B&B £48–£74, B&B (double) £74–£95; D £17·50; WB £35 (2 nts HB)
cc Access, Amex, B'card/Visa.

★★ **Ardneil,** St Meddans St, KA10 6NU (0292) 311611
Victorian house with modern extension. Family-run hotel convenient for sea. Billiards.
9 bedrs, 3 en suite, 3 ba; TV; tcf
TV, dogs; P 100, coach; child facs; con 100
LD 9
£ B&B £23·50–£27·50, B&B (double) £43–£50; L £5, D £10; [5% V]
cc Access, Amex B'card/Visa; dep.

★★ **Craiglea,** South Beach, KA10 6EG (0292) 311366

A Victorian building with fine views of Firth of Clyde. It
20 bedrs, 10 en suite, 4 ba; TV; tcf
TV, dogs; P 14, coach; child facs; con 40
LD 8.45
£ B&B £28–£40, B&B (double) £44–£56; HB weekly £230–£365; L £7·50, D £11·50
cc Access, Amex, B'card/Visa, Diners.

★★ **South Beach,** South Beach, KA10 6EG (0292) 312033

White Victorian building of character with sun lounge facing sea. Putting, sauna, solarium, gymnasium.
27 bedrs, 27 en suite; TV; tcf
dogs, ns; P 45, coach; child facs; con 120
LD 8.30, bar meals only lunch
£ B&B £35–£50, B&B (double) £50–£95; D £14·50; WB £35 (HB); [5% V w/d excl May, June & Sep]
cc Access, Amex, B'card/Visa; dep.

TURNBERRY Strathclyde. Map 42B4
Pop 164. Maybole 7, London 386, Ayr 15, Dalmellington 20, Edinburgh 85, Girvan 5, Glasgow 47.

★★★★★ **Turnberry,** Maidens Rd, KA26 9LT (0655) 31000 Tx: 777779 Fax: (0655) 31706

Sc

Elegant Edwardian hotel with magnificent sea views. Indoor swimming pool, golf, putting, tennis, riding, sauna, solarium, billiards. Fr, De, It, Du.
115 bedrs, 115 en suite; TV
lift, dogs; P 200, coach; child facs; con 130
LD 9.30
£ B&B £105–£130, B&B (double) £115–£170; L £15, D £26·75; WB
cc Access, Amex, B'card/Visa, Diners.

★★★ H R **Malin Court,** KA26 9PB
(0655) 31457 Fax: (0655) 31072
Modern 2-storey hotel in pleasant rural site, close to sea. Fr, De, Es
8 bedrs, 8 en suite; TV; tcf
lift, dogs; P 50, coach; child facs; con 120
LD 9.30
£ B&B £41·95–£45·95, B&B (double) £72–£80; HB weekly £245–£275; L £7·95, D £13·50; WB £37·50 (HB); [10% V]
cc Access, Amex, B'card/Visa, Diners.

TWEEDSMUIR Borders (Peeblesshire) Map 50B1
Pop 60. Moffat 15, London 350, Abington 22, Beattock 16, Edinburgh 35, Glasgow 48, Lanark 25, Peebles 17.
Golf West Linton 18h. **See** Church.

★★ **Crook Inn,** ML12 6QN (089 97) 272
Distinctive 1930s 2-storey building beside road in Border hills.

ULLAPOOL Highland (Ross & Cromarty). Map 57C2
Pop 1,000. Garve 32, London 584, Achnasheen 48, Beauly 48, Durness 69, Edinburgh 209, Glasgow 213, Lairg 44.
EC Tue. **Golf** Gairloch 9h.
i West Shore St (0854) 2135

★★★ **Mercury,** North Rd, IV26 2UD
(0854) 2314

Modern motel on northern approach to this busy small town. Putting, sauna. Open Mar–Nov. (MtCh)
60 bedrs, 60 en suite; TV; tcf
dogs; P 60, coach; child facs; con 20
LD 8.45, bar meals only lunch
£ B&B £39·50 (w/e £33), B&B (double) £59·50; HB weekly £231; D £12·50; WB £25; [10% V]
cc Access, Amex, B'card/Visa, Diners; dep.

★★★ **Royal,** Garve St, IV26 2SY (0854) 2181 Fax; (0854) 2951

Large hotel conveniently situated by main southern approach road. Billiards. Fr
52 bedrs, 50 en suite; TV; tcf
TV, dogs; P 40, coach; child facs; con 100
LD 9, bar meals only lunch
£ B&B £38–£43, B&B (double) £60–£74; HB weekly £203–£252; D £14·50; WB £34; [5% V excl Jun–Sep]
cc Access, Amex, B'card/Visa, Diners; dep.

★★ **Harbour Lights,** Garve Rd, IV26 2SX
(0854) 2222
Attractive modern family-run hotel situated on southern approach to town.

UPHALL Lothian. Map 50B3
Edinburgh 18, London 393, M8 (jn. 3) 4, Glasgow 25, Linlithgow 7, Livingston 3.

★★★ **Houstoun House,** EH52 6JS
(0506) 853831 Fax: (0506) 854220

A 16th-century Laird's fortified house, with modern extension linking to converted ancilliary buildings, set in parkland off A89.
28 bedrs, 28 en suite; annexe 2 bedrs, 2 en suite; TV; tcf
dogs; P 120, coach; child facs; con 150
LD 9.30, bar meals only Sat lunch
£ B&B £75–£90, B&B (double) £110–£130; L £14, D £26; WB £50 (HB)
cc Access, Amex, B'card/Visa, Diners.

WALKERBURN Borders (Peeblesshire). Map 50C2
Pop 1,000. Galashiels 9, London 352, Edinburgh 29, Glasgow 58, Peebles 8, Selkirk 12.
EC Tue. **Golf** Innerleithen 9h.

★★★ H **Tweed Valley,** Galashiels Rd, EH43 6AA (089 687) 636
Fax: (089 687) 639

Overlooking Tweed Valley, attractive Victorian stone-built mansion. Putting, fishing, sauna, solarium, gymnasium. Fr
15 bedrs, 15 en suite; TV; tcf
dogs, ns; P 35, coach; child facs; con 40
LD 9.30
£ B&B £31·50–£38·50, B&B (double) £63–£66; HB weekly £275–£285; L £4·75, D £13·50; WB £39·50 (HB); [10% V excl Oct, Nov]
cc Access, B'card/Visa; dep.

WEST WEMYSS Fife. Map 50C3
Kirkcaldy 4, London 404, M90 (junc. 4) 10, Edinburgh 29, Glenrothes 6, Glasgow 43, St Andrews 19.

★★ **Belvedere,** Coxstool, KY1 4SL
(0592) 54167
Converted former Miners Institute on edge of village overlooking the Firth of Forth. Fr
5 bedrs, 5 en suite; annexe 16 bedrs, 16 en suite; TV; tcf
P 40, coach; child facs; con 20
LD 9, nr Sun
£ B&B £39, B&B (double) £50; L £10, D £13; [10% V]
cc Access, B/card/Visa

WHITEBRIDGE Highland (Inverness-shire). Map 54A3
Pop 620. Fort Augustus 9, London 530, Carrbridge 41, Edinburgh 164, Glasgow 143, Invergarry 17, Invermoriston 16.
Golf Fort Augustus 9h.

★★ **Whitebridge,** IV1 2UN Gorthleck (045 63) 226

Hotel in a quiet rural valley. Personal attention of proprietors. Fishing. Open Mar–Dec
12 bedrs, 10 en suite, 1 ba; TV; tcf
dogs; P 30, G 5, coach; child facs
LD 8.30, bar meals only lunch
£ B&B £25–£30, B&B (double) £40–£50; HB weekly £205; D £12·50; [10% V]
cc Access, Amex, B'card/Visa, Diners, dep.

WHITHORN Dumfries & Galloway (Wigtownshire). Map 42C2
Pop 1,000. Wigtown 10, London 384, Edinburgh 118, Gatehouse of Fleet 36, Glasgow 106, Stranraer 32.
EC Wed. **Golf** St Medan, Port William 9h.

★★ **Queen's Arms,** Isle of Whithorn, DG8 8LF (098 85) 369

Small charming 18th century building at head of fishing village.

WICK Highland (Caithness). Map 59A4
Pop 7,000. Helmsdale 35, London 638, Edinburgh 263, Glasgow 270, Thurso 20.
EC Wed. **MD** Thur. **Golf** Reiss 18h.
i Whitechapel Rd off High St. (0955) 2596

★★ **Mackays,** Union St, KW1 5ED
☎(0955) 2323
Purpose-built substantial Victorian hotel conveniently situated near town centre.
26 bedrs, 24 en suite, (2 sh); TV; tcf
lift, TV, dogs; P 20; child facs; con 150
LD 8.30
£ L £6; D £7·50
cc Access, B'card/Visa.

WISHAW Strathclyde (Lanarkshire). Map 50A2
Pop 30,540. Abington 26, London 377, M74 (jn 8) 4½, Ayr 40, Edinburgh 33, Glasgow 15, Kilmarnock 30, Lanark 10, Peebles 33. **EC** Wed. **Golf** Wishaw 18h, Colville Park 18h.

★ **Coltness,** Coltness Rd, ML2 7EX
☎(0698) 381616
A commercial-type hotel conveniently situated on outskirts of the town.
11 bedrs, 4 ba; tcf
TV, dogs, ns; P 80, coach; child facs; con 100
LD 9.30
£ B&B £22, B&B (double) £34; L £4, D £6; [10% V]
cc Access, Amex, B'card/Visa, Diners.

WORMIT Fife. Map 50C4
M90 24, Glenrothes 20, London 425, Edinburgh 51, Glasgow 71, Kinross 25, Kirkcaldy 26, St Andrews 11.

★★ **Sandford Hill,** Newport-on-Tay, DD6 8RG ☎Newport-on-Tay (0382) 541802
A 2-storey red-roofed English-style residence in own grounds. Tennis.

Closed 1&2 Jan. Es
15 bedrs, 13 en suite; 1 ba; TV; tcf
TV, dogs; P 50; child facs; con 30
LD 9
£ B&B £35·80–£44, B&B (double) £55–£66; HB weekly £252–£273; L £14, D £18; WB £36 (HB); [10% V]
cc Access, Amex, B'card/Visa, Diners; dep.

Stranraer (Dumfries & Galloway)

Tarbert (Argyll)

WALES

ABERCRAF Powys. Map 19A2
Aberdare 15, London 179, Ammanford 15, Merthyr Tydfil 17, Swansea 17.
i Dan yr Ogof Showcaves
☎(0639) 730284
Abercrave Inn, SA9 1XS ☎(0639) 730460

The river Craf runs through the garden of this traditional inn. Most bedrooms in motel-style building across road. Tennis.
2 bedrs, 2 en suite; annexe 7 bedrs, 7 en suite; TV; tcf
P 30, coach; con 30

ABERDARON Gwynedd. Map 28A2
Pop 375. Pwllheli 14, London 256, Caernarfon 33.
EC Wed. **Golf** Nefyn 18h, Abersoch 9h.
★★ Ty Newydd, LL53 8BE ☎(0758 86) 207
Small 3-storey white-painted hotel centrally placed next to beach.

ABERDYFI (ABERDOVEY) Gwynedd. Map 28B1
Pop 1,500. Newtown 39, London 215, Aberystwyth 28, Bala 39, Dolgellau 24.
EC Wed. **Golf** Aberdyfi 18h. **See** Happy Valley ("Bearded Lake"), Bird Rock 9 m, Dolgoch Falls 9 m, Cader Idris.
i The Wharf. ☎(065 472) 321
★★★ Trefeddian, LL35 0SB ☎(065 472) 213
Large seaside holiday hotel in gardens overlooking links and Bay. Indoor swimming pool, putting, tennis, solarium. Closed 2 Jan–17 Mar.
46 bedrs, 46 en suite; TV
lift, TV, dogs, ns; P 60, G 14 (80p); child facs
LD 8.45
£ B&B £26–£39; B&B (double) £52–£78; HB weekly £245–£273; L £7·50, D £12; WB fr £40 (HB)
cc Access, B'card/Visa; dep.
Bodfor (Acclaimed), Bodfor Ter, LL35 0EA ☎(0654) 767475. Fax: (0654) 767679. *Hotel.*
£ B&B £22–£26, HB weekly £203–£230; [10% V Nov–Mar]
Cartref (Acclaimed), LL35 0NR ☎(0654)767273. *Guest House.*
B&B £13; HB weekly £154.
Frondeg, Copperhill St, LL35 0HT ☎(065 472) 655. *Guest House.*

ABERGAVENNY Gwent. Map 19C2
Pop 12,000. Ross 22, London 143, Brecon 20, Chepstow 29, Hereford 23, Monmouth 15, Newport 18, Pontypool 10, Tredegar 11.
EC Thur. **MD** Tue, Fri. **Golf** Monmouthshire 18h. **See** Castle grounds and Museum, St Mary's Church, Sugar Loaf Mountain 4 m NW, Llanvihangel Court 4½ m NW, White Castle 5½ m E.
i Cross Street, ☎(0873) 77588
★★ Angel, Cross St, NP7 5EW ☎(0873) 7121 Fax: (0873) 78059
Renowned former coaching inn which is situated in the town centre. (THF)
29 bedrs, 29 en suite; TV; tcf
TV, dogs, ns; P 30, coach; child facs; con 200
LD 9.30
£ B&B £64–£66 (w/e £30); B&B (double) £80–£95; L £8·50, D £12·95; WB £50
cc Access, Amex, B'card/Visa, Diners.
★★ Llanwenarth Arms, Brecon Rd, NP8 1EP ☎Crickhowell (0873) 810550 Fax: (0873) 811880
16th century building with modern annexe. On A40 enjoying superb views.
18 bedrs, 18 en suite; TV; tcf
P 60, child facs;
LD 10
£ B&B £48, B&B (double) £58; L £8·95, D £8·95; B&B WB £23 (2 nts min)
cc Access, Amex, B'card/Visa, Diners.

ABERGELE Clwyd. Map 28C3
Pop 12,315. Mold 24, London 215, Colwyn Bay 7, Denbigh 8, Rhyl 5, Queensferry 26.
EC Thur. **MD** Mon. **Golf** Abergele 18h. **See** St Michael's Church 1 m W, Gwrych Castle.
★★ Kinmel Manor, St George Rd, LL22 9AS ☎(0745) 832014 ♿
Modernised Georgian style country house set in attractive gardens. Indoor swimming pool, sauna, solarium, gymnasium.
25 bedrs, 25 en suite; TV; tcf
dogs, P 120, coach; child facs; con 250
LD 9.30
£ B&B £45, B&B (double) £65; HB weekly £339·50; L £8, D £13·50; WB £37·50; [10% V]
cc Access, Amex, B'card/Visa, Diners.

ABERGYNOLWYN Gwynedd. Map 28B1
Newtown 41, London 218, Aberdyfi 11, Aberystwyth 30, Dolgellau 12.
Dolgoch Falls (Acclaimed), Tywyn, LL36 9UW ☎(0654 782258). Open Mar–Oct.
£ B&B £17·95–£20·95; HB weekly £150·50–£171·50

ABERPORTH Dyfed. Map 18B3
Pop 800. Lampeter 27, London 230, Aberystwyth 33, Cardigan 6½, Carmarthen 26.
★★★ Penrallt, Cardigan, SA43 2BS ☎(0239) 810227. Fax: (0239) 811375

A substantial building in some 40 acres of fields and woodlands. Swimming pool, golf, putting, tennis, sauna/solarium, gymnasium. Closed 25 Dec–27 Dec.
16 bedrs, 16 en suite; TV; tcf
dogs; P 100, child facs
LD 9, bar meals only lunch
£ B&B £44, B&B (double) £68; HB weekly £355; D £12·50
cc Access, Amex, B'card/Visa, Diners.

★★ Highcliffe, SA43 2DA ☎(0239) 810534

Small hotel attractively set near to a sandy beach. Fr
9 bedrs, 5 en suite; 3 ba; annexe 6 bedrs, 6 en suite; TV; tcf
TV, dogs, ns; P 18, coach; child facs
LD 8.30, bar meals only Mon–Sat lunch
£ B&B £26·50, B&B (double) £45; D £11; WB £29·50, [10% V]
cc Access, Amex, B'card/Visa; dep.

★★ Penbontbren Farm, Glynarthen, SA44 6PE ☎(0239) 810248 ♿

Imaginatively converted farm buildings, 3½ miles south-east of town. Riding.
10 bedrs, 10 en suite; TV; tcf
dogs, ns; P 50, coach; child facs; con 30

✕ LD 8.15, nr lunch. Resid & Rest lic
£ B&B £27–£30·45, B&B (double) £46–£52·90, WB £58·24
cc Access, B'card/Visa; dep.

ABERSOCH Gwynedd. Map 28A2

Pop 1,050. Pwllheli 6½, London 247, Aberdaron 10.
EC Wed. **Golf** Abersoch 9h.
ℹ Village Hall ☎(075 881) 2929.

★★★ **Harbour,** LL53 7HR ☎(075 881) 2406
Proprietor-run hotel enjoying fine view of harbour.
🛏 9 bedrs, 8 en suite, 1 ba; annexe 5 bedrs, 5 en suite; TV; tcf
🏠 dogs; P 50, coach; child facs; con 40
✕ LD 10
£ B&B £31–£54, B&B (double) £62–£108; L £12, D £12; [10% V Sep–Jul]
cc Access, Amex, B'card/Visa, dep.

★★★ **R** **Porth Tocyn,** LL53 7BU ☎(075 881) 3303. Fax: (075 881) 3538

Standing on own headland, attractive white-faced hotel with delightful bedrooms. Swimming pool, tennis. ⚒ Fr. Open Mar–15 Nov.
🛏 17 bedrs, 17 en suite; TV
🏠 dogs; P; child facs
✕ LD 9.30. Resid & Rest lic
£ B&B £36·50–£46, B&B (double) £57–£84; L £12·50, D £14·50–£21; WB
cc Access; dep.

★★★ **Riverside,** LL53 7HW ☎(075 881) 2419
Overlooking harbour, a cream-painted hotel with modern purpose-built extension. Indoor swimming pool. Open Feb–Nov.
🛏 12 bedrs, 12 en suite; TV; tcf
🏠 P 25; child facs
✕ LD 9, bar meals only lunch. Resid & Rest lic
cc Access, Amex, B'card/Visa.
(See advertisement on p. 621)

★★ **Deucoch,** Pwllheli, LL53 7LD ☎(075 881) 2680

Former farm house in grounds overlooking town. Well-equipped bedrooms. ⚒ Fr
🛏 10 bedrs, 9 en suite, 1 ba; TV; tcf
🏠 TV, dogs; P 50, coach; child facs
✕ LD 8.30, bar meals only lunch
£ B&B £20–£22, B&B (double) £40–£44; HB weekly £180–£195; D £11; [5% V w/d]
cc Access, Amex, B'card/Visa, Diners; dep.

★★ **Egryn,** Main St, LL53 7EE ☎(075 881) 2332.
Small white-painted hotel on main street, well maintained and run by caring owners.
🛏 7 bedrs, 5 en suite, 1 ba; TV; tcf
🏠 TV, dogs; P 20; child facs
✕ LD 9, nr lunch. Resid & Rest lic
£ B&B £20–£35; B&B £29–£50; [5% V Nov–Mar]
cc Access, B'card/Visa; dep.

★★ **H** **Neigwl,** Sarn Rd, LL53 7DY ☎(075 881) 2363
Attractive small white-faced hotel overlooking bay. Family-owned and run.
🛏 7 bedrs, 5 en suite, 1 ba; annexe 2 bedrs, 2 en suite; TV
🏠 TV; P 30; child facs
✕ LD 8.30, nr lunch Mon–Sat. Resid & Rest lic
£ B&B £30–£33, B&B (double) £50–£55; HB weekly £260–£285; L £9, D £15; [V]
cc Access, B'card/Visa, Diners; dep.

★★ **Tudor Court,** Lon Sarn Bach, LL53 7EB ☎(075 881) 3354

Small family-run hotel in Victorian house in a quiet location.
🛏 6 bedrs, 5 en suite, (1 sh), 1 ba; TV
🏠 dogs; P 12, coach; child facs
✕ LD 9.30. Resid & Rest lic
£ B&B £22·50–£29·50, B&B (double) £39–£55; HB weekly £200–£270; L £7·50, D £12·50; [5% V]
cc Access, B'card/Visa, Diners; dep.

Llysfor, LL53 7AL ☎(075 881) 2248. *Guest House.*

ABERYSTWYTH Dyfed. Map 18C4

Pop 15,300. Rhayader 34, London 211, Aberdyfi 28, Bala 47, Cardigan 38, Dolgellau 33, Lampeter 24, Newtown 43.
EC Wed. **MD** Mon. **Golf** Aberystwyth 18h.
See Castle ruins and Gorsedd Circle, National Library of Wales, University College of Wales, Plant Breeding Station, Vale of Rheidol Narrow Gauge Rly to Devil's Bridge, Nanteds Mansion.
ℹ Terrace Road ☎(0970) 612125

★★★ **Conrah,** Chancery, SY23 4DF ☎(0970) 617941 Tx: 35892 Fax: (0970) 624546

Pleasant Georgian country mansion enjoying good views. Indoor swimming pool, sauna.
🛏 13 bedrs, 11 en suite, 2 ba; annexe 9 bedrs, 9 en suite; TV; tcf
🏠 lift, ns; P 60, coach; no children under 5; con 40
✕ LD 9.30. Resid & Rest lic
£ B&B £43–£54, B&B (double) £60–£85; HB weekly £270–£324; L £11·50, D £17; WB £45 (min 2 nts)
cc Access, Amex, B'card/Visa, Diners; dep.

★★ **Bay,** 35–37 Marine Promenade, SY23 2BX ☎(0970) 617356 Fax: (0970) 612198
Substantial 4-storey Georgian building in fine position right on the Promenade.
🛏 32 bedrs, 18 en suite, 4 ba; TV; tcf
🏠 TV, dogs, P 20, coach; con 50
✕ LD 9, bar meals only Mon–Sat lunch & Sun dinner
£ B&B £18–£30; B&B (double) £50; HB weekly £172–£236, [10% V]
cc Access, Amex, B'card/Visa.

★★ **Belle Vue Royal,** Marine Ter, SY23 2BA ☎(0970) 617558 Fax: (0970) 612190

Large Victorian building in a commanding position overlooking Cardigan Bay. Closed 24–27 Dec.
🛏 42 bedrs, 22 en suite, (1 sh), 8 ba; TV; tcf
🏠 TV; P 8, G 9, coach; child facs; con 60
✕ LD 9.30
£ B&B £25–£34, B&B (double) £49–£65; HB weekly £234·50–£258; L £7·95, D £12·50; [10% V]
cc Access, Amex, B'card/Visa, Diners.

★★ **Cambrian,** Alexandra Rd, SY23 1LG ☎(0970) 612446
Pleasant 'mock Tudor' building close to town centre and opposite railway station.
🛏 11 bedrs, 7 en suite, 2 ba; TV; tcf
🏠 dogs; coach; child facs; con 20
✕ LD 9.30
£ B&B £26–£28, B&B (double) £48–£52; HB weekly £223–£235; L £7·25, D £9·25; WB £30; [10% V]
cc Access, B'card/Visa; dep.

★★ **Court Royale,** Eastgate, SY23 2AR ☎(0970) 611722
In town centre, 3-storey Georgian former coaching inn.
🛏 10 bedrs, 10 en suite; TV; tcf
🏠 TV, dogs; coach; child facs

★★ **Four Seasons,** 50–54 Portland St, SY23 2DX ☎(0970) 612120

Situated near centre of town, 3-storey hotel with patio garden. Closed 24 Dec–3 Jan.
14 bedrs, 14 en suite, 2 ba; TV; tcf
TV, dogs, ns; P 10, coach, child facs
LD 8.30, bar meals only Mon–Sat. Resid lic
£ B&B £28–£35, B&B (double) £45–£53; HB weekly £202–227; D £11·50; WB £72; [5% V]

★★ Groves, North Par, SY23 2NF (0970) 617623

Small hotel pleasantly situated near to town centre and beach. Fr
11 bedrs, 11 en suite; TV; tcf
ns; P 8; coach, child facs, con 20
LD 8.30, bar meals only lunch, Sun dinner
£ B&B £26, B&B (double) £44; L £6·25, D £9·50; [10% V w/e Oct–May]
cc Access, B'card/Visa.

★★ Queensbridge, Promenade, SY23 2BX (0970) 612343. Fax: (0970) 617452

Bay-windowed, Victorian building with panoramic views of Cardigan Bay.
15 bedrs, 15 en suite; TV; tcf
lift, TV, dogs; coach; child facs
LD 8, nr lunch. Resid lic
£ B&B £30, B&B (double) £42; D £9·50; WB £57
cc Access, Amex, B'card/Visa, Diners, dep.

Glyn Garth (Acclaimed), South Rd, SY23 1JS (0970) 615050. *Guest House.* Closed 23 Dec–3 Jan.
£ B&B £13·50–£25; [5% V Nov–Mar]

Shangri-La, 36 Portland St, SY23 2DX (0970) 617659. *Guest House.*
£ B&B £11

AMLWCH

Gwynedd. Map 28B4

Pop 4,000. Bangor 19, London 256, Caernarfon 25, Holyhead 20.
EC Wed. **MD** Fri. **Golf** Bull Bay 18h.

Residents only
Some Listed hotels only serve meals to residents. It is always wise to make a reservation for a meal in a hotel.

★★ Trecastell, Bull Bay, LL68 9SA (0407) 830651

Hotel in Edwardian building overlooking Bay. Personally supervised by proprietors.
12 bedrs, 11 en suite, (1 sh); TV; tcf
TV, dogs; P 50, coach; child facs; con
LD 8.30, bar meals only lunch
£ B&B £20–£22, B&B (double) £33–£35; D £8·95
cc Access, B'card/Visa.

AMMANFORD

Dyfed. Map 19A2

Pop 5,795. Neath 15, London 198, Carmarthen 17, Lampeter 20, Llandovery 20, Llanelli 13, Swansea 16.
EC Thur. **MD** Fri. **Golf** Glynhir (Llandeilo) 18h.

★★ The Mill at Glynhir, Llandybie, SA18 2TE Llandybie (0269) 850672
Converted mill with spacious gardens, in beautiful wooded countryside. Indoor swimming pool, fishing.
9 bedrs, 9 en suite; annexe 2 bedrs, 2 en suite; TV; tcf
dogs; P 20; no children under 11
LD 8.15. nr lunch, Resid & Rest lic
£ B&B £29, B&B (double) £58; D £12·50; WB £31
cc Access, B'card/Visa; dep.

BALA

Gwynedd. Map 28C2

Pop 1,850. Shrewsbury 44, London 199, Betws-y-Coed 23, Corwen 11, Dolgellau 18, Porthmadog 29, Welshpool 33.
EC Wed. **MD** Thur. **Golf** Bala Lakeside 9h.
High St. (0678) 520367

★★ Bala Lake, LL23 7BS (0678) 520344 Fax: (0678) 521193

Modern hotel with adjacent motel suites. Overlooking lake and golf course. Swimming pool, golf, putting. Fr
1 bedr, 1 en suite, annexe 12 bedrs, 12 en suite; ns, TV; tcf
dogs, ns; P 40, G 10; child facs
LD 8.30. Resid & Rest lic
£ B&B £37–£40, B&B (double) £50–£54; L £9, D £12; WB £70
cc Access, B'card/Visa, Diners.

★★ Plas Coch, High St, LL23 7AB (0678) 520309
Privately owned and run hotel on main wide tree-lined street.
10 bedrs, 10 en suite; TV; tcf
dogs; P 20; child facs; con 20
LD 8.30, Rest lic
£ B&B £29·50–£40, B&B (double) £47; HB weekly £171·50; L £5·50, D £10·50; WB £29·75; [10% V excl w/e summer]
cc Access, Amex, B'card/Visa, Diners; dep.

★★ White Lion Royal, High St, LL23 7AE (0678) 520314

Famous old coaching inn located in the High Street.
22 bedrs, 22 en suite; TV; tcf
TV, dogs; P 30, coach; child facs; con 100

Pen Isa'r Llan, Llanfor, LL23 7DW (0678) 520507. *Guest House. Sauna, solarium, gymnasium, riding.*

Plas Teg, 45 Tegid St, LL23 7EN (0678) 520268. *Guest House.*

BANGOR

Gwynedd. Map 28B3

Pop 14,558. Betws-y-Coed 20, London 237, Caernarfon 9, Colwyn Bay 20, Holyhead 23.
EC Wed. **MD** Fri. **Golf** St Deiniol, Bangor 18h. **See** Cathedral, University College of N Wales, Art Gallery, Museum, Menai Suspension Bridge, Penryhn Castle 1 m E.
Theatr Gwynedd, Deiniol Rd (0248) 352786

★★★ R Menai Court, Craig-y-Don Rd, LL57 2BG (0248) 354200

Renovated Victorian house, with Mansard roof, overlooking Menai Straits. Separate conference suite. Closed 26 Dec–8 Jan.
12 bedrs, 12 en suite; TV; tcf
dogs, ns; P 24, coach; child facs; con 60

★★ H Telford, Holyhead Rd. (0248) 352543
Converted private house, magnificently situated overlooking Menai Bridge.

★★ Ty Uchaf, Tal-y-Bont, LL57 3UR (0248) 352219

EC *early closing* **MD** *market day* *country house hotel* *ns (NS) no smoking areas* *tcf tea/coffee facilities*

Abersoch (Gwynedd)

RIVERSIDE HOTEL & RESTAURANT Abersoch

Telephone: Abersoch (075 881) 2419/2818

The Bakewells and their enthusiastic team welcome you to sample the hospitality of their delightful and luxurious hotel. The ever popular restaurant offers superb food, imaginative and creative dishes in a relaxing atmosphere. Twelve bedrooms all en-suite plus built this year our honeymoon suite where newly weds are welcomed with champagne and roses. Heated indoor pool with sun patio overlooking peaceful river Soch. All water sports close by. Safe, sandy beaches and several golf courses. Canoes & dinghies on the river.

Beddgelert (Gwynedd)

The Royal Goat Hotel

Beddgelert, Gwynedd, N. Wales, LL55 4YE
Telephone: 076-686 224 **RAC *** BTA 5 crowns**

Situated in the small mythical village of Beddgelert in the heart of the Snowdonia National Park stands this 18th century impressive hotel. Resident family owners. Salmon and trout fishing, golf, horse riding and other sporting activities. All rooms with private facilities. Magnificent views. Centrally heated. Two bars. Two restaurants table d'hôte and à la carte. Live entertainment on Saturday. Lift. Coral Chandelier Suite available for functions, banquets, conferences etc.

Completely modernised and extended, former coaching inn in own grounds. Closed 24 Dec–2 Jan.
🛏 9 bedrs, 9 en suite; TV; tcf
🏨 P 40, coach; children over 10
✕ LD 8.30, bar meals only lunch
£ B&B £27·50–£27·50, B&B (double) £37·50–£42·50; D £8·50–£12·50; WB £40 (2 nts)
cc Access, B'card/Visa, dep.

BARMOUTH Gwynedd. Map 28B1
Pop 2,200. Dolgellau 10, London 216, Betws-y-Coed 35, Caernarfon 37, Porthmadog 20.
EC Wed. **MD** Thur. **Golf** Royal St David's 18h. **See** St John's Church, Guild of St George Cottages, Dinas Oleu, Llanaber Church (1¾ m), Bontddu Gold Mines.
ℹ Old Library. ☎(0341) 280787

★★ **Panorama,** Panorama Rd, LL42 1DQ ☎(0341) 280550

High above town with magnificent views over the Mawddach Estuary to Cader Idris, a traditional stone-built hotel. Putting.
🛏 20 bedrs, 15 en suite, 2 ba; TV; tcf
🏨 TV, dogs; P 40, coach; no children under 2; con 50
✕ LD 9.30, bar meals only Mon–Sat lunch. Resid & Rest lic
£ B&B £17–£24, B&B (double) £34–£48; HB weekly £180–£230; L £7·50, D £10, WB £45; [10% V]
cc Access, B'card/Visa; dep.

★★ **Ty'r Graig Castle,** Llanaber Rd, LL42 1YN ☎(0341) 280470

Victorian building of character in premier position with fine views. Open Mar–Nov.
🛏 12 bedrs, 12 en suite, 2 ba; TV; tcf
🏨 ns; P 16; child facs
✕ LD 8.30, bar meals only Mon–Sat lunch. Resid & Rest lic
£ B&B £30–£40, B&B (double) £50–£60; HB weekly £240–£280; L £7·50, D £11·50; WB £70
cc Access, B'card/Visa; dep.

Licences
Establishments have a full licence unless shown as unlicensed or with the limitations listed on p 6.

★ **Bryn Melyn,** Panorama Rd, LL42 1DQ ☎(0341) 280556 Fax: (0341) 280990

Small well-appointed hotel in own grounds. Superb views across Mawddach estuary.
🛏 10 bedrs, 8 en suite, 1 ba; TV; tcf
🏨 dogs; P 10; child facs
✕ LD 8.30, bar meals only lunch. Resid & Rest lic
£ B&B £26·50–£27·50, B&B (double) £43–£46; HB weekly £199; D £10·95; WB £59 (2 nts HB); [10% V]
cc Access; B'card/Visa; dep.

★ **Marwyn,** 21 Marine Par, LL42 1NA ☎(0341) 280185
Small family-run hotel on sea front with views of bay and Mawddach estuary.
🛏 7 bedrs, 7 en suite; 1 ba; TV; tcf
🏨 TV; no children under 5

Tal-y-Don, St Anne's Sq, LL42 1DL ☎(0341) 280508. *Hotel.*

BARRY South Glamorgan. Map 4A4
Pop 43,000. Cardiff 9½, London 159, Bridgend 17.
ℹ Barry Island. ☎(0446) 747171

★★★ **Mount Sorrel,** Porthkerry Rd, CF6 8XY ☎(0446) 740069 Tx: 497819 Fax: (0446) 746600
Red-brick, 2-storey building in residential area. View of Bristol Channel.
🛏 46 bedrs, 46 en suite; annexe 4 bedrs, 4 en suite; TV; tcf
🏨 dogs; P 17, coach; child facs; con 150
✕ LD 10, bar meals only Sat lunch, Sun dinner
£ B&B £46–£57·50, B&B (double) £55–£72·50; HB weekly £235–£285; L £8·50, D £11·50; WB £79, [5% V]
cc Access, Amex, B'card/Visa, Diners; dep.

BEAUMARIS Gwynedd. Map 28B3
Pop 2,500. Bangor 7, London 244, Caernarfon 12, Holyhead 2.
EC Wed. **Golf** Baron Hill 18h.

★★★ **Bulkeley,** Castle St, LL58 8AW ☎(0248) 810415 ♿

Hotel built of traditional Welsh stone. Panoramic views of Snowdonia. Billiards. Under refurbishment, completion expected December 1990. Fr.
🛏 37 bedrs, 37 en suite; TV; tcf
🏨 lift, dogs; P 27, coach; child facs; con 120
✕ LD 10
£ B&B £33–£38, B&B (double) £52–£59; L £6·50, D £11·50; WB £70; [10% V Oct–Apr]
cc Access, Amex, B'card/Visa, Diners; dep.

★★ **Bishopsgate,** Castle St, LL58 8AB ☎(0248) 810302

Privately-owned Georgian town house, with Chinese Chippendale staircase. Open 14 Feb–20 Dec.
🛏 10 bedrs, 10 en suite, 1 ba; TV; tcf
🏨 dogs, ns; P 10; no children under 6
✕ LD 9, Resid & Rest lic
£ B&B £25–£27, B&B (double) £42–£46; L £7·50, D £11·50; WB £65; [5% V]
cc Access, B'card/Visa; dep.

★★ **Henllys Hall,** LL58 8HU ☎(0248) 810412 Fax: (0248) 811511
Set in 50 acres of woodland, an imposing 19th century mansion with distinctive clock tower. Swimming pool, tennis, sauna, solarium, gymnasium, billiards. Fr
🛏 22 bedrs, 22 en suite; TV; tcf
🏨 lift, TV, dogs; P 100, child facs; con 120
✕ LD 10, bar meals only Mon–Sat lunch
£ B&B £30–£42, B&B (double) £60–£74; HB weekly £210–£340; L £7·50, D £15; WB £80; [10%]
cc Access, Amex, B'card/Visa, Diners; dep.

BEDDGELERT Gwynedd. Map 28B2
Pop 320. Bala 30, London 230, Betws-y-Coed 17, Caernarfon 12, Dolgellau 27, Porthmadog 8, Pwllheli 19.
EC Wed. **Golf** Porthmadog 18h.
ℹ Llewellyn Cottage ☎(076 686) 293

★★★ **Royal Goat,** LL55 4YE ☎(076 686) 224
Georgian building, with modern extension, amidst spectacular natural beauty. Fishing.
🛏 31 bedrs, 31 en suite; TV; tcf
🏨 lift, dogs, ns; P 150, coach; child facs; con 150
✕ LD 9.30
£ B&B £41–£75, B&B (double) £78–£85; HB weekly £360–£420; L £9·50, D £16; [10% V]
cc Access, Amex, B'card/Visa, Diners; dep.
(*See advertisement on p. 621*)

★ **Tanronen,** LL55 4YB ☎(076 686) 347
Small, attractive, cosy hotel at head of magnificent Glaslyn Pass.
🛏 8 bedrs, 2 ba; TV; tcf
🏨 TV; P 8, U 3, coach; child facs
✕ LD 9
£ B&B £16, B&B (double) £32; HB weekly £156; L £6·50, D £11; WB £49·50 (2 nts)
c Access, B'card/Visa.

Sygun Fawr Country House (Acclaimed), LL55 4NE ☎(076 686) 258. *Sauna.*
£ B&B £15–£19; HB weekly £159–£183; [5% V]

BENLLECH BAY Gwynedd. Map 28B3

Pop 3,500. Bangor 10, London 248, Caernarfon 16, Holyhead 20.
EC Thur. **Golf** Bull Bay 18h.

★★ **Bay Court,** Beach Rd, LL74 8SW
☎ Tynygongl (0248) 852573

Family-run modern purpose-built hotel in delightful position overlooking sands.
🛏 19 bedrs, 4 en suite, 3 ba; annexe 4 bedrs, 4 en suite; TV; tcf
🏛 TV, dogs; P 50, child facs
✕ LD 8.30, Rest lic
£ B&B £16·50–£21·50; HB weekly £150–£160; L £7·50, D £7·50
cc Access, Amex, B'card/Visa, Diners; dep.

BETWS-Y-COED Gwynedd. Map 28C3

Pop 7,000. Corwen 22, London 216, Bala 22, Bangor 20, Caernarfon 23, Dolgellau 32, Llandudno 17, Porthmadog 23, Ruthin 25.
EC Thur. **Golf** Betws-y-Coed 9h.
ⓘ Royal Oak Stables. ☎ (069 02) 426

♣ ★★★ **Plas Hall,** Pont-y-Pant, LL25 0PJ
☎ (069 06) 206 Fax: (06906) 526 ♿

Attractive Victorian building with River Lledr flowing through wooded grounds. Fishing.
🛏 20 bedrs, 19 en suite; (1 sh); TV; tcf
🏛 P 24; coach; child facs; con 50
✕ LD 9. Resid lic
£ B&B £38·35–£51·35, £B&B double £59–£79; HB weekly fr £227·50; L £7·50, D 13·50; WB £59; [10% V]
cc Access, Amex, B'card/Visa, Diners; dep.
(*See advertisement on p. 624*)

Using RAC discount vouchers
Please tell the hotel when booking if you plan to use an RAC discount voucher (see p. 34) in part payment of your bill. Only one voucher will be accepted per party per stay. Discount vouchers will only be accepted in payment for accommodation, not for food.

★★★ **Royal Oak,** LL24 0AY ☎ (0690) 71021 Fax: (0690) 710433

Former coaching inn modernised to high standard; picturesque riverside setting.
🛏 27 bedrms, 27 en suite; TV; tcf
🏛 P 60, coach, child facs, con 25
✕ LD 9, bar meals only Mon–Sat lunch
£ B&B £37–£44, B&B (double) £50–£68; HB weekly £315; L £6·99, D £9; WB £90
cc Access, Amex, B'card/Visa, Diners, dep.
(*See advertisement on p. 624*)

★★★ **Waterloo,** LL24 0AR ☎ (069 02) 411
Purpose-built well-equipped modern complex surrounded by breathtaking scenery. Indoor swimming pool, sauna, solarium, gymnasium, billiards.
🛏 9 bedrs, 9 en suite; annexe 30 bedrs, 30 en suite; TV; tcf
🏛 dogs; P 200, coach; child facs
✕ LD 9.30, bar meals only Mon–Sat lunch
£ B&B £38·50–£45, B&B (double) £62–£67; HB weekly £316·75–£336; L £7·50, D £13·95; [10% V]
cc Access, Amex, B'card/Visa, Diners; dep.

★★ **Gwydyr**, LL24 0AB ☎ (0690) 710777
Family-run hotel in Victorian building in delightful surroundings. Fishing.
🛏 20 bedrs, 20 en suite, 2 ba; TV; tcf
🏛 dogs, ns; P 30, U 2, coach; child facs; con 20
✕ LD 8.30
£ B&B £21–£25; L £6, D £12; WB £55 (2 nts)
cc Access, B'card/Visa; dep.

★★ **H** **Park Hill,** Llanrwst Rd, LL24 0HD
☎ (069 02) 540

Converted Victorian house with modern well-equipped bedrooms. Own grounds. Indoor swimming pool, sauna.
🛏 11 bedrs, 9 en suite; 1 ba; TV; tcf
🏛 TV, ns; P 14; no children under 6
✕ LD 7.45, bar meals only lunch. Resid & Rest lic
£ B&B £16–£17, B&B (double) £62–£64; HB weekly £217–£224; L £6, D £12, WB £28
cc Access, Amex, B'card/Visa, Diners; dep.
(*See advertisement on p. 624*)

Please tell the manager if you chose your hotel through an advertisement in the guide.

★★ **H** **R** **Ty Gwyn,** LL24 0SG
☎ (069 02) 383 ♿

Charming stone-built former coaching inn with painted black and white features. Overlooks River Conwy.
🛏 13 bedrs, 9 en suite, 2 ba; TV; tcf
🏛 TV, dogs; P 14, coach; child facs
✕ LD 9.30. Resid & Rest lic
£ B&B £17–£30, B&B (double) £34–£60; HB weekly £209–£300; L £12·95, D £12·95; WB £59·50–£85·90; [10% V]
cc Access, B'card/Visa; dep.

★ **Fairy Glen,** Fairy Glen, LL24 0SH
☎ (069 02) 269

Stone-white hotel situated amongst some of the most magnificent scenery in Wales.
Open Feb–Nov.
🛏 10 bedrs, 7 en suite, 2 ba; TV, tcf
🏛 TV, dogs, ns; P 10; child facs
✕ LD 7.30, bar meals only lunch. Resid & Rest lic
£ B&B £16–£18; HB weekly £165–£180; D £10; WB £48 (2 nts)
cc Access, B'card/Visa, Diners; dep.

Tyn-y-Celyn House (Acclaimed), Llanrwst Rd, LL24 0HD ☎ (069 02) 202. *Guest House.* Open Easter–Jan.
£ B&B £20–£30; [5%]

BLACKWOOD Gwent. Map 19B1

Pop 7,000. Newport 13, London 150, Caerphilly 8, Hirwaun 19, Merthyr Tydfil 15, Pontypool 9, Pontypridd 12, Tredegar 8½.
EC Thur. **MD** Fri, Sat. **Golf** Blackwood 9h.
See St Margaret's Church.

★★★ **Maes Manor,** NP2 0AG ☎ (0495) 224551
Beautiful manor house set in 9 acres of wooded gardens, surrounded by magnificent views.
🛏 8 bedrs, 8 en suite, annexe 14 bedrs, 14 en suite; TV; tcf
🏛 dogs; P 100, coach; child facs; con 250
✕ LD 9.30, nr Sat lunch, Sun dinner
£ B&B £41, B&B (double) £55; L £7·95, D £10·95
cc Access, Amex, B'card/Visa, Diners.

BODEDERN Gwynedd Map 28A3

Bangor 20, London 257, Caernarfon 26, Holyhead 7.

Crown, Anglesey, LL65 3TU. ☎ Valley (0407) 740734. *Hotel.*

Betws-y-Coed (Gwynedd)

A BEAUTIFUL HALL IN A BEAUTIFUL SETTING

Old stone mullioned Hall specialising in fine food. With superbly appointed rooms amidst spectacular scenery. Please come to stay with us.

For reservations:

PLAS HALL HOTEL AND RESTAURANT ★★★
Pont-y-Pant,
Nr. Betws-y-Coed,
N. Wales.
Tel: Dolwyddelan (06906) 206
Fax: (06906) 526

plas hall

Betws y Coed (Gwynedd)

RAC ★★★

ROYAL OAK HOTEL

WTB 4 Crowns

Betws-y-Coed. Tel: 0690 710219

Picturesque former coaching inn overlooking River Llugwy with 27 luxury bedrooms, all en-suite. Our Grill is open daily 8am to 9pm offering varied menus, plus our excellent dining room specialising in fresh fish and meat delicacies. Our chef/manager is a member of the Chaine des Rotisseurs. Central for coast, mountains, waterfalls, fishing, golf and riding.

Double/twin B&B £25 per person per night min, £34 per person per night max.
Single B&B £37 per night min, £44 per night max.
Short breaks (min. 2 day stay) dinner, bed & breakfast.
Double/twin* £35 per person per night min, £45 per person per night max.
Single* £45 per night min, £54 per night max.
Breakfast £6.50 Lunch £6.99 Dinner £9.00 Grill – £16.00 Dining Room
**Dinner served in the Grill*

Betws-y-Coed (Gwynedd)

Park Hill Hotel

Betws-y-Coed, Gwynedd LL24 0HD. Tel: (069 02) 540

Nestling in own gardens with breathtaking views of Conwy Valley. Our magnificent indoor heated swimming pool and sauna complex is free and exclusively for our guests.

Builth Wells (Powys)

RAC ★★

The Lion Hotel

BROAD STREET, BUILTH WELLS, POWYS LD2 3DT Tel: (0982) 553570 Fax: (0982) 553999

Friendly family run hotel offering good food, from à la Carte to snacks, at reasonable prices. Extensive wine list. Comfortable en-suite bedrooms. Bargain breaks available.

BONTDDU Gwynedd. Map 28B1

Pop 200. Dolgellau 5, London 212, Betws-y-Coed 34, Caernarfon 42, Porthmadog 25. **EC** Sat. **Golf** Royal St David's, Harlech 18h.

★★★ Bontddu Hall, LL40 2SU (0341) 49661 Fax: (0341) 49284
Majestic Victorian baronial mansion in unforgettable setting overlooking Mawddach Estuary. Putting. Open Mar–Dec.
16 bedrs, 16 en suite; annexe 4 bedrs, 4 en suite; TV; tcf
TV, dogs, ns; P 50; child facs, con 120
LD 9.30
£ B&B £37·50–£42·50, B&B (double) £65–£70; HB weekly £295; L £7·95, D £17·95; WB £90; [5% V]
cc Access, Amex, B'card/Visa, Diners; dep.

Borthwnog Hall (Highly Acclaimed), LL40 2TT (0341) 49271
£ B&B £27–£30; HB weekly £240–£255

BORTH Dyfed. Map 19A4

Rhayader 37, London 214, Aberdovey 24, Aberystwyth 6½, Bala 44, Dolgellau 39, Newtown 42, Welshpool 51.

Glanmor, SY24 5UP (0970) 871689. *Hotel.*
£ B&B £14·50; HB weekly £136·15–£150·15; [V w/d Oct–Jun]

BRECON Powys. Map 19B2

Pop 7,000. Abergavenny 20, London 163, Builth Wells 16, Hereford 36, Leominster 37, Llandovery 21, Merthyr Tydfil 18. **EC** Wed. **MD** Tue, Fri. **Golf** Brecon 9h & 18h. **See** Cathedral (orig Priory Church), Norman castle remains, County Museum, Regimental Museum, Siddons Arms (birthplace of Sarah Siddons), Shire Hall, 13th cent Church.
[i] Watton Mount. (0874) 4437

★★ Aberclydach House, Aber, Talybont-on-Usk, LD3 7YS Talybont-on-Usk (087 487) 361. Fax: (087 487) 436
Tastefully converted Victorian mansion standing in 2½ acres of well-kept gardens.
11 bedrs, 11 en suite; TV; tcf
TV, ns; P 14, child facs; con 20
LD 8.30. Resid & Rest lic
£ B&B £34, B&B (double) £58; L £6·25, D £15·50; WB £72
cc Access, B'card/Visa, dep.

★★ Castle of Brecon, Castle Sq, LD3 9DB (0874) 4611 Tx: 57515

Stone-built hotel attached to castle ruins and overlooking River Usk.
34 bedrs, 34 en suite; annexe 12 bedrs, 12 en suite; TV; tcf
dogs; P 30, coach; child facs, con 150

★★ Nant Ddu Lodge, Cantref, Cwm Taf, Nr Storey Arms, CF48 2HY (0685) 79111 Fax: (0685) 77088

An attractive 2-storey building, with picturesque views of wooded valley and Brecon Beacons
15 bedrs, 15 en suite; TV; tcf
dogs; P 30, coach, child facs; con 45
LD 9.30
£ B&B £33, B&B (double) £45
cc Access, Amex, B'card/Visa, Diners; dep.

★★ Wellington, The Bulwark, LD3 OSL (0874) 5225

In town centre, a 3-storey white-painted Georgian hotel.
21 bedrs, 21 en suite; TV; tcf
ns; coach; child facs; con 250
LD 10

Coach (Highly Acclaimed), Orchard St, Llanfaes, LD3 8AN (0874) 3803. *Guest House.*
£ B&B £18–£20; dep.

Peterstone Court (Acclaimed), Llanhamlach, LD3 7YB Llanfrynach (0874 86) 666. *Guest House. Swimming pool.*

BRIDGEND Mid Glamorgan. Map 19B1

Pop. 28,000. Cardiff 19, London 169, Hirwaun 25, Neath 17, Pontypridd 17, Swansea 20.
EC Wed **Golf** Southerndown 18h
See 15th Century cottages (once hospice of Knights of St. John of Jerusalem) Eweny Priory 1½ m S. Old Bridge, Norman Gateway.

★★★ C Coed-y-Mwstwr, Coychurch, C36 6AF (0656) 860621. Fax: (0656) 8631222
Red-brick Victorian mansion in wooded gardens overlooking the Vale of Glamorgan. Conveniently placed about 1 mile from Junction 35 of M4. Fr, Po, Da
28 bedrs, 28 en suite; TV
lift, ns; P 65, coach, child facs, con 20
LD 10.15. Resid & Rest lic
£ B&B £79·50–£100, B&B (double) £90–£150; HB weekly £320; L £18·25, D £24·95; WB £120 (2 nts HB); [10% V]
cc Access, Amex, B'card/Visa, Diners

BROAD HAVEN Dyfed. Map 18A2

Pop 600. Haverfordwest 7, London 250, Pembroke 13, St David's 6.
[i] Car Park. (0437) 783412

Broad Haven (Acclaimed), SA62 3JN (0437) 781366. *Hotel. Swimming pool, solarium, billiards.*
£ B&B £22–£27; HB weekly £155–£185; [10% V]

BUILTH WELLS Powys. Map 19B3

Pop 1,500. Ross-on-Wye 49, London 171, Abergavenny 33, Brecon 16, Knighton 23, Leominster 34, Llandovery 24.
EC Wed. **MD** Mon. **Golf** Builth Wells 9h.
[i] Groe Car Park. (0982) 553307

★★ Pencerrig Country House, LD2 9XX (0982) 553226 Fax: (0982) 552347
Extended country house in 3 acres of lawns and trees.
20 bedrs, 20 en suite; TV; tcf
TV, dogs; coach; child facs; con 100
LD 9.30
£ B&B £39·50, B&B (double) £59; HB weekly £245; L £6·95, D £16·95, WB £70 (2 nts HB); [10% V]
cc Access, Amex, B'card/Visa, Diners.

★★ Lion, 2 Broad St, LD2 3DT (0982) 553670
Former coaching inn in a commanding position beside the River Wye. Fr
20 bedrs, 12 en suite; (2 sh), 4 ba; TV; tcf
dogs; P 14, coach; child facs; con 50
LD 9.30
£ B&B £26·50–£33, B&B (double) £42–£53; HB weekly £140–£199·50; L £6·25, D £9·50; WB £27·50; [10% V Sep–Jun]
cc Access, B'card/Visa, dep.
(*See advertisement on p. 624*)

BURTON Dyfed. Map 18B2

Pop 191. Pembroke Dock 2½, London 247, Haverfordwest 8½, Milford Haven 6½.

★★ Beggar's Reach, SA73 1PD Neyland (0646) 600700

Two-storey stone building with lawns and gardens close to Cleddau estuary.
10 bedrs, 10 en suite; TV; tcf
TV, dogs; P 30; child facs
LD 9.30, bar meals only Mon–Sat lunch, Sun dinner
£ B&B £21, B&B (double) £30; HB weekly £140; L £5·50, D £6·75; WB £38
cc Access, B'card/Visa.

CAERNARFON Gwynedd. Map 28B3

See also LLANRUG.
Pop 9,260. Betws-y-Coed 23, London 240, Aberdaron 33, Bangor 9, Dolgellau 39, Holyhead 29, Porthmadog 19, Pwllheli 20.
EC Thur. **MD** Sat. **Golf** Caernarfon 18h. **See** Medieval Castle, Town Walls, foundations of Segontium Roman Fort (Museum).
[i] Oriel Pendeitsh (0286) 672232

★ **Menai Bank,** North Rd, LL55 1BD
☎(0286) 673297

Privately-run converted 3-storey residence on A487 overlooking Menai Straits.
🛏 15 bedrs, 9 en suite, 3 ba; TV; tcf
🏨 TV, dogs; P 10, coach; child facs
✕ LD 7.30, bar meals only lunch. Resid & Rest lic
£ B&B £17–£19, B&B (double), £28–£32; HB weekly £136–£165; D £9·50; WB £40
cc Access, B'card/Visa; dep.

★ **Muriau Park,** Pwllheli Rd, LL55 2YS
☎(0286) 4647
Enjoying fine views of Snowdon range, 2–3 storey hotel with charming rose garden and spacious lawns.
🛏 6 bedrs, 2 en suite, 1 ba, TV
🏨 dogs; P 15; child facs
✕ LD 9.30, Resid & Res lic
£ B&B £14–£18, L £5, D £10; [5% V]
cc Access, B'card/Visa, Diners; dep.

Menai View, North Rd, LL55 1BD ☎(0286) 4602. *Hotel.*
£ B&B £14–£18; HB weekly £129·50–£143·50; [10% V]; dep.

CAERSWS Powys. Map 19B4

Pop 900. Newtown 6, London 183, Bala 48, Dolgellau 34, Rhayader 20.
Golf Newtown 18h. **See** Roman and British Camps.

♣ ★★ **Maesmawr Hall,** SY17 5SF
☎(068 684) 255

16th century house set in 5½ acres of wooded grounds. Fishing.
🛏 11 bedrs, 8 en suite, 2 ba; annexe 6 bedrs, 6 en suite; TV; tcf
🏨 TV, dogs; P 100, U 2 (£4), coach; child facs; con 135

CAPEL CURIG Gwynedd. Map 28C3

Pop 400. Betws-y Coed 5½, London 222, Bangor 15, Caernarfon 18, Porthmadog 19, Pwllheli 31.
EC Wed. **Golf** Betwys-y-Coed 9h. **See** Old Parish Church of St Julitta, St Curig Church (mosaic altar dome), The Ugly House.

★★ **Tyn-y-Coed,** LL24 0EE ☎(069 04) 331
Fax: (069 02) 777
Former residence with modern extensions. Features genuine stage coach. Fishing.
🛏 13 bedrs, 13 en suite; TV; tcf
🏨 TV, dogs; P 80, coach; child facs; con 100
✕ LD 9.30, bar meals only lunch
£ B&B £23–£25, B&B (double), £40–£46; HB weekly £185–£200; D £14; WB £28 (HB)
cc Access, B'card/Visa.

CARDIFF South Glamorgan. Map 19B1

See also PORTHKERRY
RAC Office, *202 Newport Rd, Cardiff, CF2 1YR* ☎(0222) 490959.
Pop 281,300. Newport 12, London 149, M4 Motorway 4½, Bridgend 19, Caerphilly 7½, Hirwaun 25, Merthyr Tydfil 23, Pontypridd 11.
See Plan, p. 627.
EC Wed. **P** See Plan. **Golf** Cardiff 18h. Llanishen 18h, Radyr 18h. **See** Castle (Medieval,Victorian additions with lavish rooms), Cathays Park (Civic Centre), St Fagan's Castle (Welsh Folk Museum), National Museum of Wales, University, City Hall, St John's Church, RC Cathedral, National Sport Centre, Llandaff Cathedral 2 m NW, Castell Coch 6 m NW.
ℹ 8–14 Bridge Street ☎(0222) 227281

★★★★ **Angel,** Castle St, CF1 2QZ ☎(0222) 232633 Tx: 498132 Fax: (0222) 396212

An impressive Victorian hotel, carefully restored, situated between the Castle and Cardiff Arms Park. Sauna, solarium, gymnasium, billiards, Fr, De, Es, Ar
🛏 91 bedrs, 91 en suite; TV; tcf
🏨 lift, dogs; ns; P 30, coach; child facs; con 300
✕ LD 10, nr Sat lunch
£ B&B £62·50–£92·50 (w/e £38·50), B&B (double) £85–£110; L £14·50, D £18·50; [10% w/e]
cc Access, Amex, B'card/Visa, Diners.
(See advertisement on p. 628)

★★★★ **Holiday Inn,** Mill La, CF1 1EZ
☎(0222) 399944 Tx: 497365
Fax: (0222) 395578 ♿

Tall, red-brick hotel in the city centre. Indoor swimming pool, squash, sauna, solarium, gymnasium. (CHIC).
🛏 182 bedrs, 182 en suite; TV; tcf
🏨 lift, dogs, ns; P 100, coach; child facs; con 300
✕ LD 10.30
£ B&B £98–£246 (w/e £40), B&B (double) £123–£256; L £11·95, D £13·95
cc Access, Amex, B'card/Visa, Diners

★★★★ **Park,** Park Pl, CF1 3UD ☎(0222) 383471 Tx: 497195 Fax: (0222) 399309

Luxury city centre hotel—a substantial Victorian building. (MtCh) Fr, Es, It
🛏 119 bedrs, 119 en suite; TV; tcf
🏨 lift, dogs, ns; P 60, coach, child facs, con 300
✕ LD 11
£ room £70–£80, double room £80–£90; L £8·50, D £13·95
cc Access, Amex, B'card/Visa, CB, Diners; dep.

★★★★ **Stakis Inn on the Avenue,** Circle Way East, Llanedeyrn, CF3 7XF ☎(0222) 732520 Tx: 497582 Fax: (0222) 549092
Luxury modern hotel of distinctive design. Set in own grounds. Indoor swimming pool, sauna, solarium, gymnasium. (Sk)
🛏 143 bedrs, 143 en suite; TV; tcf.
🏨 lift, TV, dogs, ns, P 350, coach, child facs, con 250
✕ LD 9.45, bar meals only Sat lunch
£ B&B £75·95 (w/e £45), B&B (double), £95·90; L £8·95, D £14·50; WB £41 (HB, min. 2 nts); [10% V]
cc Access, Amex, B'card/Visa, Diners.

★★★ **Crest,** Westgate St, CF1 1JB ☎(0222) 388681 Tx: 497258 Fax: (0222) 371495

Modern hotel with extensive conference facilities. Near the Castle. Snooker. (THF/Cr)
🛏 157 bedrs, 157 en suite; TV; tcf
🏨 lift, dogs, ns; P 120, coach, child facs, con 140
✕ LD 10
£ B&B £80·75, B&B (double) £99·50; L £9·50, D £13·50; WB £39·50 (HB); [10% V]
cc Access, Amex, B'card/Visa, Diners

★★★ **Manor Parc,** Thornhill Rd, Thornhill, CF4 5UA ☎(0222) 693723

EC *early closing* **MD** *market day* ♣ *country house hotel* *ns (NS) no smoking areas* *tcf tea/coffee facilities*

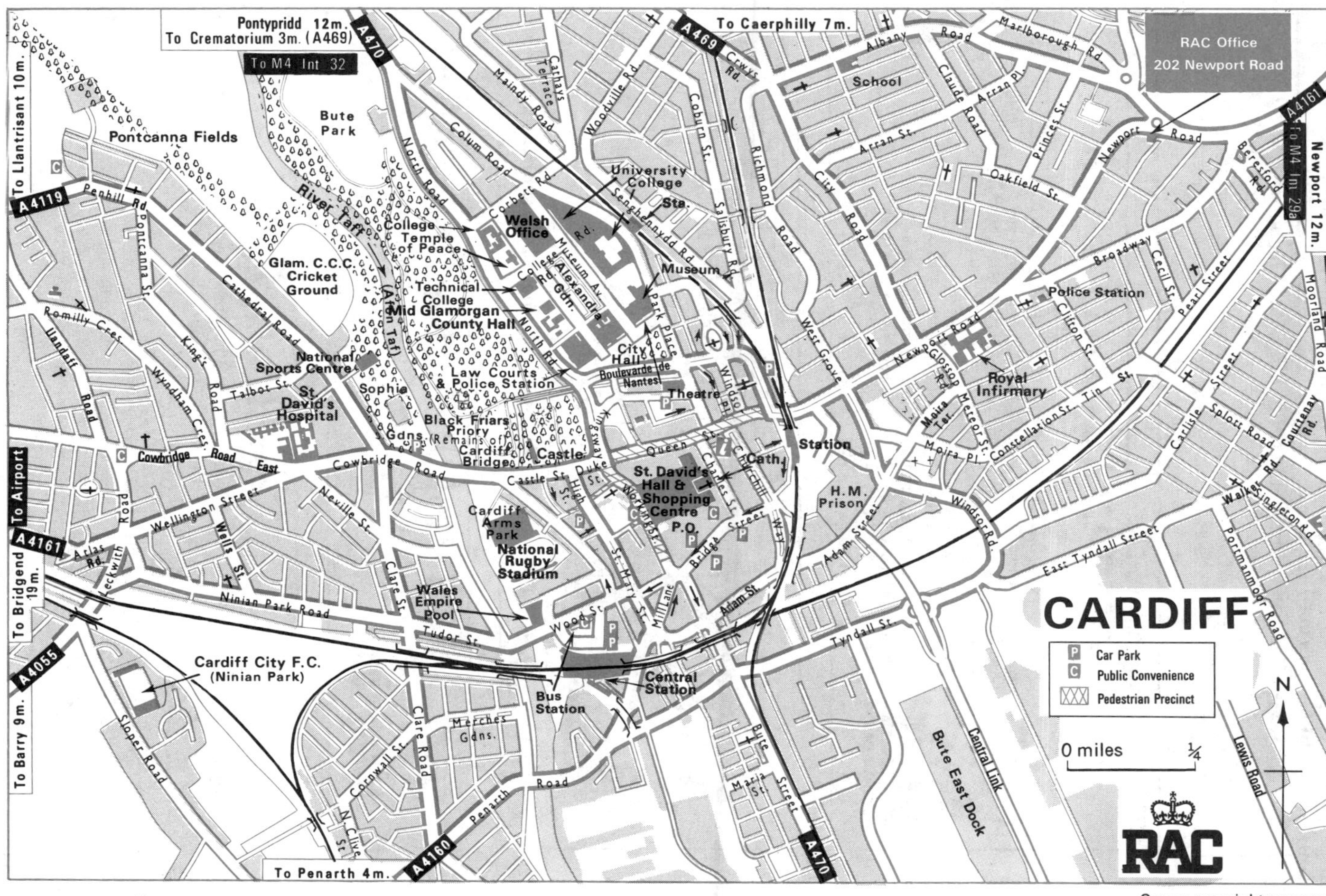

CARDIFF
Pontypridd 12m.
To Crematorium 3m. (A469)
To M4 Int 32
A470
To Caerphilly 7m.
A469
RAC Office
202 Newport Road
A4161
To M4 Int 29a
Newport 12m.
To Llantrisant 10m.
A4119
To Airport
A4161
To Bridgend 19m.
A4055
To Barry 9m.
To Penarth 4m.
A4160
Car Park
Public Convenience
Pedestrian Precinct
0 miles ¼
N
RAC
Lewis Road
Portmanmoor Road
East Tyndall Street
Central Link
Bute East Dock
Tyndall St.
Moorland Road
Courtenay Rd.
Walker Rd.
Singleton Rd.
Splott Road
Carlisle Street
Pearl Street
Beresford Rd.
Newport Road
Cecil St.
Broadway
Police Station
Clifton St.
Constellation St.
Tin St.
Royal Infirmary
Marlborough Rd.
Princes St.
Oakfield St.
Arran Pl.
Claude Road
Albany Road
School
Arran St.
City Road
Newport Road
Glossop Rd.
Meteor St.
Moira Ter.
Moira Pl.
Windsor Rd.
H.M. Prison
Adam Street
West Grove
Station
Richmond Road
Crwys Rd.
Salisbury Rd.
Coburn St.
Senghennydd Rd.
Museum
University College
Sta.
Woodville Rd.
Cathays Terrace
Maindy Road
Colum Road
Corbett Rd.
Welsh Office
Museum Av.
College Rd.
Alexandra Gdn.
City Hall
Park Place
Boulevarde de Nantes
Windsor Pl.
Theatre
Queen St.
Cath.
Churchill Way
Charles St.
St. David's Hall & Shopping Centre
P.O.
Bridge Street
Adam St.
Mill Lane
Central Station
Working St.
St. Mary St.
Kingsway
Duke St.
High St.
Castle St.
Castle
Wood St.
Bus Station
National Rugby Stadium
Cardiff Arms Park
North Rd.
Law Courts & Police Station
Mid Glamorgan County Hall
Technical College
Temple of Peace
College
North Road
Black Friars Priory
Cardiff Bridge
Wales Empire Pool
Tudor St.
Bute Street
Maria St.
Penarth Road
Merches Gdns.
Clare Road
Clare St.
Cornwall St.
N. Clive St.
Sophia Gdns.
River Taff (Afon Taf)
Bute Park
Glam. C.C.C. Cricket Ground
National Sports Centre
St. David's Hospital
Cowbridge Road
Neville St.
Ninian Park Road
Cardiff City F.C. (Ninian Park)
Sloper Road
Cathedral Road
Talbot St.
Cowbridge Road East
Wells St.
Wellington Street
King's Road
Wyndham Cres.
Pontcanna Fields
Pontcanna St.
Penhill Rd.
Romilly Cres.
Llandaff Road
Leckwith Road
Atlas Rd.

Wa

Cardiff (South Glamorgan)

Castle Street, Cardiff, South Glamorgan CF1 2QZ.
Tel: (0222) 232633. Telex: 498132. Fax: (0222) 396212

Cardiff's premier hotel situated in the heart of the city. 91 bedrooms, Leisure Club, Real Ale Pub, banqueting for 300. A la Carte restaurant, 24 hour service.

Cardiff (South Glamorgan)

THE CAMPANILE HOTEL – Cardiff

Restaurant
Hotel

Campanile

Caxton Place, Pentwyn, Cardiff CF2 7MA
Tel: (0222) 549044 Telex: 497553

Part of the international budget hotel chain "Campanile", the hotel offers 50 comfortable double or twin rooms with en-suite bathrooms, and tea/coffee making facilities, radio alarm, remote control colour TV, Sky TV and direct dial telephone at **competitive rates.**
Our informal restaurant provides a variety of home-cooked French/ Continental cuisine, and personal service at **affordable prices.**
Our seminar room is available for business meetings or small functions.

Your hosts: Alison & Michael Jago

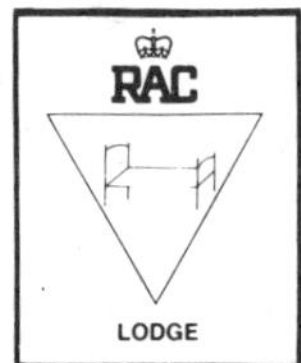

Chepstow (Gwent)

Castle View Hotel**

16 Bridge Street, Chepstow, Gwent NP6 5EZ
Tel: (02912) 70349 Fax: (0291) 627397

- All rooms with private bathroom, colour TV, radio, telephone, mini-bar, movies, hairdryer & tea tray.
- Commended restaurant and bar food.
- Short break and holiday terms
- Family rooms and suite available.
- Facing Chepstow Castle and Car Park.

'Our aim is to provide comfort, good food and personal attention in surroundings which retain the charm of the eighteenth century.'

Chepstow (Gwent)

THE FIRST HURDLE HOTEL

9–10 Upper Church Street, Chepstow, Gwent NP6 5EX Tel: (0291) 622189

12 bedroom family run hotel & licensed restaurant open all year. All rooms recently refurbished. All have colour TV, radio, tea/coffee facilities. Most en-suite. Period walled tea garden open in Summer and Autumn. 5 min M4 Severn Bridge, 15 min M5. St Pierre Golf Course 5 min, Forest of Dean 10 min. Families welcome. Highchairs & cots available.

Chepstow (Gwent)

Beaufort Hotel **

Beaufort Square, Chepstow, Gwent NP6 5EP
Telephone: (0291) 625074 (Reception) 622497 (Visitors)
Fax: (0291) 627389

Family run Hotel in town centre. 23 bedrooms, majority en suite. All with colour TV, telephone, coffee and tea making facilities. Centrally heated throughout.
Traditional restaurant offering comprehensive menu. Emphasis on fresh produce and home cooking.
Comfortably furnished bar. Small conference facilities with private car parking. Weekend breaks available.

Spacious Victorian building with full length windows, balconies and two bays. Set in well-kept grounds on northern edge of city. Tennis. Closed 24–26 Dec. Fr, De, It, Es
12 bedrs, 12 en suite; TV; tcf
TV; P 75, coach, child facs, con 100
LD 9.45, nr Sun dinner. Resid lic
£ B&B £50–£65, B&B (double) £75–£100; WB £70; [5% V]
cc Access, Amex, B'card/Visa.

★★★ **Post House,** Pentwyn Rd, Pentwyn, CF2 7XA (0222) 731212 Tx: 497633 Fax: (0222) 549147

Modern purpose-built hotel situated in outskirts near Pentwyn Interchange on A48. Indoor swimming pool, sauna, solarium, gymnasium. (THF)
140 bedrs, 140 en suite; TV; tcf
lift, dogs, ns; P 240, coach; child facs; con 140
LD 10, bar meals only Sat lunch
£ B&B £75 (w/e £39), B&B (double) £93·20; L £7·60, D £12·60
cc Access, Amex, B'card/Visa, CB, Diners.

★★★ **Royal,** St Mary's St, CF1 1LL (0222) 383321 Tx: 498062 Fax: (0222) 222238

City centre hotel dating from Victorian times, now renovated. Billiards. (Emb) Fr, Es, It
63 bedrs, 47 en suite, 5 ba; TV; tcf
lift; coach; child facs; con 300
LD 10, bar meals only Sat lunch
£ B&B £44–£80 (w/e £25), B&B (double) £58–£109; L £8·50, D £12·50; WB £32 (HB); [10% V Jun–Sep]
cc Access, Amex, B'card/Visa, Diners.

★★★ **St. Mellons,** St. Mellons, CF3 8XR Newport (0633) 680355 Fax: (0633) 680399

Modernised Victorian hotel between Cardiff and Newport. Indoor swimming pool, tennis, squash, sauna, solarium, gymnasium, billiards. Fr, Es
11 bedrs, 11 en suite; annexe 20 bedrs, 20 en suite; TV; tcf
dogs; P 500, coach; child facs; con 200
LD 9.45, bar meals only Sat lunch, Sun dinner
£ B&B £44–£48, B&B (double) £58; L £11·95; D £11·95; WB £69·50
cc Access, Amex, B'card/Visa.

★★★ **Wentloog Resort,** Castleton, CF3 8UQ Castleton (0633) 680591 Fax: (0633) 681287

An old house with a modern extension set in beautiful gardens. Sauna, solarium.
55 bedrs, 55 en suite; TV; tcf
dogs, ns; P 100, coach; child facs; con 100
LD 10
cc Access, Amex, B'card/Visa, Diners.

★★ **Campanile,** Caxton Pl, Pentwynn, CF2 7HA (0222) 549044
See Motor Lodge section.

★★ **Phoenix,** Fidlas Rd, Llanishen, CF4 5LZ (0222) 764615. Fax: (0222) 747812
Three-storied brick-built hotel with black and white gables; modern extension to rear. In residential suburb on northern side of city.
24 bedrs, 21 en suite, 2 ba; TV; tcf.
lift, TV, dogs, P 30, coach, child facs, con 110
LD 10
£ B&B £39, B&B (double) £51.50; L £7·95, D £7·95; WB £46·50 (2 nts); [V w/e]
cc Access, B'card/Visa.

★★ **Riverside,** 55–59 Despenser St, CF1 8RG (0222) 378866
Gabled stone-built hotel, pleasantly set in residential area on banks of River Taff.
36 bedrs, 36 en suite; TV; tcf
dogs; P 25, coach; child facs; con 80
LD 9.30. Resid & Club lic
£ B&B £38·50, B&B (double) £52; L £5, D £5; WB £40; [10% V]
cc Access, Amex, B'card/Visa, Diners.

★★ **Sandringham,** 21 St Mary St, CF1 2PL (0222) 232161
Four-storey hotel conveniently situated in the city centre.
28 bedrs, 28 en suite; TV; tcf
TV, dogs; ns; coach; child facs; con 100
LD 9.30, nr Sun
£ B&B £30–£45, B&B (double) £50–£60; L £7·50, D £7·50
cc Access, Amex, B'card/Visa, Diners.

Cardiff International, Mary Ann St (0222) 341441 Fax: (0222) 223742
Hotel under construction, opening expected September 1990

Clare Court (Acclaimed), 46–48 Clare Road, Grangetown, CF1 7QP (0222) 344839. *Hotel.*
£ B&B £22–£28; [5% V]

Balkan, 144 Newport Rd, CF2 1DT (0222) 463673. *Hotel.*
£ B&B £16–£20

Clayton, 65 Stacey Rd. CF2 1DS (0222) 492345. *Hotel.*

Domus, 201 Newport Rd, CF2 1AJ (0222) 473311 *Guest House.* Closed 21 Dec–8 Jan
£ B&B £16–£21

Imperial, 132 Newport Rd, CF2 1DJ (0222) 490032. *Private Hotel.*

Tane's, 148 Newport Rd, Roath, CF2 1DJ (0222) 491755. *Private Hotel.*
£ B&B £16; HB weekly £110 (5 nts); [5% V w/e]

Willows, 128 Cathedral Road, Pontcanna. CF1 9LQ (0222) 340881. *Hotel.* Es
£ B&B £16·50–£21·50; [5% V]

CARDIGAN Dyfed. Map 18B3

Pop 4,290. Lampeter 29, London 234, Aberystwyth 38, Carmarthen 25, Fishguard 17, Haverfordwest 26, Tenby 32.
EC Wed. **MD** Mon, Sat. **Golf** Cardigan 18h. **See** Castle ruins, St Mary's Church.
[i] Bath House Rd (0239) 613230

Highbury House (Acclaimed), North Rd, SA43 1JU (0239) 613403. *Guest House.*

Maes-y-Mor (Acclaimed), Gwbert Road, SA43 1AE (0239) 614929. *Guest House.*
£ B&B (double) £24–£30

Brynhyfryd, Gwbert Rd, SA43 1AE (0239) 612861. *Guest House.*
£ B&B £13; HB weekly £120–£134; [5% V]

CARMARTHEN Dyfed. Map 18C2

Pop 12,471. Llandovery 28, London 212, Cardigan 25, Haverfordwest 30, Lampeter 23, Llanelli 16, Swansea 27, Tenby 27.
EC Thur. **MD** Mon, Tues, Wed, Fri, Sat. **Golf** Carmarthen 18h. **See** St Peter's Church, County Museum, 14th cent Gatehouse.
[i] Lammas St. (0267) 231557

★★★ **Ivy Bush Royal**, Spilman St, SA31 1LG (0267) 235111
Pleasant hotel with a long history. Close to the town centre. Sauna. (THF)
77 bedrs, 77 en suite; TV; tcf
lift, dogs, ns; P 75, U 3 (£1), coach; child facs; con 200
LD 9.30
£ room £58 (w/e £32), double room £68; Bk £7·50, L £8·50, D £13·25
cc Access, Amex, B'card/Visa, Diners.

★ **Falcon,** Lammas St, SA31 3AP (0267) 234959
Of brick and stone construction, 2-storey building in town centre.

Ty Mawr (Highly Acclaimed), Brechfa, SAS32 7RA (0267) 202332. Fax: (0267) 202437
£ B&B £38; HB weekly £350; [10% V Nov–Jun]

CHEPSTOW Gwent. Map 20A1

Pop 10,000. Chippenham 32, London 123, M4 2, Abergavenny 29, Bath 25, Bristol 16, Gloucester 28, Monmouth 16, Newport 15, Pontypool 21, Ross-on-Wye 24, Swindon 48, Tetbury 29.
EC Wed. **Golf** St Pierre 18h. **See** Castle ruins, St Mary's Church.
[i] The Gatehouse, High St. (029 12) 3772

Wa

★★★ C **St Pierre,** St Pierre Park, NP6 6YA ☎(0291) 625261 Tx: 497562 Fax: (02912) 79975 ♿

14th century manor house set in parkland of 400 acres. Country club. Indoor swimming pool, golf, putting, tennis, squash, sauna/solarium, gymnasium, billiards. Fr, De, Es, It, Po
148 bedrs, 148 en suite; TV; tcf
dogs, ns; P 300, coach; child facs; con 250
✕ LD 9.30
£ B&B £86–£96 (w/e £55), B&B (double) £105–£120; D £15; [10% V]
cc Access, Amex, B'card/Visa, Diners; dep.

★★ **Beaufort,** Beaufort Sq, NP6 5EP ☎(0291) 622497 Fax: (0291) 627389
16th century coaching inn with elegant Georgian windows. De
18 bedrs, 16 en suite, 2 ba; TV; tcf
TV, ns; P 12; coach, child facs; con 35
✕ LD 9.15, bar meals only lunch
£ B&B £25–£30, B&B (double) £50; D £6·95–£12; [10% V w/e]
(*See advertisement on p. 628*)

★★ **Castle View,** 16 Bridge St, NP6 5PZ ☎(029 12) 70349 Fax: (0291) 627397

This ivy-covered building, opposite the Castle, dates back 300 years. Fr
9 bedrs, 9 en suite; annexe 2 bedrs, 2 en suite; TV; tcf
dogs, ns; coach; child facs; con 6
✕ LD 9
£ B&B £39·50–£46·50, B&B (double) £57·50–£60·50; L £9·25, D £13·50; WB £36 (HB); [10% V]
cc Access, Amex, B'card/Visa, Diners; dep.
(*See advertisement on p. 628*)

Atlas Section
Consult the Atlas section at the back of the guide to find out which towns and villages have RAC Appointed and Listed hotels in them. They are shown on the maps by purple circles.

★★ **First Hurdle,** 9 Upper Church St, NP6 5EX ☎(0291) 622189 ♿

In town centre, a 17th-century house full of antique furniture. Lawned garden to rear.
11 bedrs, 6 en suite, 2 ba; TV; tcf
TV, dogs, ns; coach; child facs; con
(*See advertisement on p. 628*)

★★ **George,** Moor St, NP6 5DB ☎(0291) 625363
An historic posting inn adjacent to 16th century town gate. (THF) Fr
15 bedrs, 15 en suite; TV; tcf
dogs, ns; P 20, coach; child facs; con 40
✕ LD 9.30, nr Mon–Sat lunch
£ B&B £60, B&B (double) £65; L £9·50, D £14; WB £42 (HB)
cc Access, Amex, B'card/Visa, Diners.

COLWYN BAY Clwyd. Map 28C3

See also OLD COLWYN.
Pop 25,500. Mold 30, London 222, Bangor 20, Betws-y-Coed 17, Chester 42, Denbigh 19, Llandudno 5½, Queensferry 34, Rhyl 11. **EC** Wed. **Golf** Old Colwyn 9h, Rhos-on-Sea 18h. **See** Welsh Mountain Zoo, Harlequin Puppet Theatre, Bodnant Gardens 5 m SW.
ℹ Station Road ☎(0492) 530478

★★★ **Hotel 70°,** Penmaenhead, LL29 9LD ☎(0492) 516555 Tx: 61362 Fax: (0492) 515565

Modern purpose-built clifftop hotel of striking design. Panoramic sea views.
43 bedrs, 43 en suite; TV; tcf
dogs, ns; P 90, coach; child facs; con 150
✕ LD 9.30
£ B&B £52–£57, B&B (double) £75–£85; HB weekly £297·50–£367·50; L £10·50, D £16; WB £42·50; [10% V]
cc Access, Amex, B'card/Visa, CB, Diners;
(*See advertisement on p. 632*)

★★★ **Norfolk House,** Princes Dr, LL29 8PF ☎(0492) 531757
Extensively modernised and enlarged Victorian house in own garden near Promenade. Putting. De
25 bedrs, 25 en suite; TV; tcf
lift, dogs, ns; P 30, coach; child facs; con 35
✕ LD 9, bar meals only lunch
£ B&B fr £39·50 (w/e £26), B&B (double) fr £55; HB weekly fr £220; WB £32·50 (HB); [10%]
cc Access, Amex, B'card/Visa, Diners.

★★ **Ashmount,** College Av, Rhos-on-Sea, LL28 4NT ☎(0492) 45479 ♿

Former private house, furnished to high standard. 125 yards from Promenade.
18 bedrs, 18 en suite; TV; tcf
dogs, ns; P 10, child facs
✕ LD 8.15. Rest lic
£ B&B £26–£32, B&B (double) £44–£52; L £6·25, D £10·25; WB £55·80 (2 nts HB); [V]
cc Access, Amex, B'card/Visa, Diners; dep.

★★ **Edelweiss,** Lawson Rd, LL29 8HD ☎(0492) 532314
An impressive 3-storey Victorian house in pleasant wooded garden. Sauna, solarium. Fr, Es
25 bedrs, 25 en suite; 1 ba; TV; tcf
dogs, ns; P 25, coach; child facs; con 40
✕ LD 8.30, bar meals only lunch
£ B&B £25, B&B (double) £42; D £11·50; WB £49 (2 nts HB); [10% V]
cc Access, Amex, B'card/Visa, Diners; dep.

★★ **Hopeside,** 63 Princes Dr, LL29 8PW ☎(0492) 533244

Attractively converted dwelling houses–a well-appointed holiday hotel. Solarium.
17 bedrs, 17 en suite; TV; tcf
TV, dogs, ns; P 20, no children under 5, con 50
✕ LD 9, bar meals only Sun lunch
£ B&B £19–£32·50, B&B (double) £38–£50; L £5, D £10·50
cc Access, Amex, B'card/Visa, CB, Diners

★★ **St Enoch's,** Marine Rd, LL28 4BL ☎(0492) 532031

A privately-owned white-faced hotel in a particularly attractive garden.
21 bedrs, 9 en suite, (1 sh), 3 ba; TV; tcf
TV, dogs; P 4, coach; child facs; con 30

★ **Melfort,** Llanerch Rd East, Rhos-on-Sea, LL28 4DF ☎(0492) 44390
Attractive privately-run hotel in residential district only minutes from Promenade.
🛏 18 bedrs, 8 en suite, (3 ba); TV; tcf.
lift, TV, dogs, P 20; coach, child facs
✕ LD 6.30, Resid lic
£ B&B £15, B&B (double) £30; HB weekly £140; L £5·50, D £6·50

★ **St Margarets,** Princes Dr, LL29 8RP ☎(0492) 532718
Modernised hotel two minutes walk from Promenade. Closed Nov.
🛏 13 bedrs, 10 en suite, 1 ba, TV; tcf
TV, dogs, ns; P 12; child facs
✕ LD 7, Resid & Rest lic
£ B&B £15–£18; HB weekly £115–£145; WB £40 (2 nts HB); L £5·50, D £6·95; [V]
cc Access, B'card/Visa;dep.

★ **West Point,** 102 Conwy Rd, LL29 7LE ☎(0492) 530331
Privately-owned Victorian building with landscaped gardens. Few minutes from centre. Closed Jan.
🛏 10 bedrs, 5 en suite, 2 ba; TV; tcf
TV, dogs, ns; P; child facs
✕ LD 7.30, bar meals only lunch. Resid lic
£ B&B £14·75–£17, B&B (double) £29·50–£34; HB weekly £130–£142; D £10; [5% V]
cc Access, B'card/Visa; dep.

★ **Whitehall,** Cayley Promenade, Rhos-on-Sea, LL28 4EP ☎(0492) 47296
Former private house with own garden. Enjoys views of Bay. Open Easter–Oct.
🛏 14 bedrs, 7 en suite, 3 ba; TV; tcf
TV, dogs, ns; P 5; child facs
✕ LD 7, bar meals only lunch. Resid & Rest lic
£ B&B £13·50–£15·50; HB weekly £120–£141
cc Access, B'card/Visa; dep.

Cabin Hill (Acclaimed), College Av, Rhos-on-Sea, LL28 4NT ☎(0492) 44568. *Hotel.* Open Mar–Oct.
£ B&B £15–£18; HB weekly £115–£131

Grosvenor, 106–108 Abergele Rd, LL29 7PS ☎(0492) 531586. *Hotel.*
£ B&B £14, HB weekly £120
Northwood, 47 Rhos Rd, Rhos-on-Sea, LL28 4RS ☎(0492) 49931
£ B&B £13–£15·50; HB weekly £107–£139; [5% V Oct–Apr]
Sunny Downs, 66 Abbey Road, Rhos-on-Sea, LL28 4NU. ☎(0492) 44256
£ B&B £17–£22; HB weekly £160; [5% V]

CONWY Gwynedd. Map 28C3

See also ROWEN
Pop 13,000. Colwyn Bay 5½, London 227, Bangor 16, Betws-y-Coed 14, Llandudno 4.
EC Wed. **MD** Tue, Sat. **Golf** Caernarfonshire 18h. **See** Castle (1284), St Mary's Church, Elizabethan Mansion (Plas Mawr), Telford's suspension Bridge.
ℹ Castle St. ☎(0492) 592248

> **Weekend breaks**
> Please consult the hotel for full details of weekend breaks; prices shown are an indication only. Many hotels offer mid week breaks as well

★★★ **Sychnant Pass,** LL32 8BJ ☎(0492) 596868 Tx: 61155 Fax: (0492) 870009

Edwardian country house, reminiscent of a Swiss chalet, in 3 acres of wooded grounds. Sauna, solarium. Fr
🛏 13 bedrs, 13 en suite; TV; tcf
TV, dogs, P 30, coach, child facs; con 20
✕ LD 9; Resid & Rest lic
£ B&B £26·50–£45, B&B (double) £43–£70; HB weekly £182–£252; L £7·95, D £13·95; WB £52 (HB); [5% V]
cc Access, Amex, B'card/Visa, Diners.

★★ **Caerlyr Hall,** Conwy Old Rd, Dwygyfylchi, LL34 6SW ☎(0492) 623518

Black and white gabled Victorian house, set in 2½ acres, with panoramic views. Next to golf course.
🛏 11 bedrs, 11 en suite; TV; tcf
TV, dogs; P 15, coach; child facs; con 25
✕ LD 9. Resid and Rest lic
£ B&B £22–£24, B&B (double) £44–£48; L £7·95, D £12·50; [5% V]
cc Access, B'card/Visa, dep.

★★ **Castle,** High St, LL32 8DB ☎(0492) 592324
17th century former coaching inn situated in the town centre. (THF)
🛏 29 bedrs, 29 en suite; TV; tcf
dogs, ns; P 30, coach; child facs; con 60

★★ **Castle Bank,** Mount Pleasant, LL32 8NY ☎(0492) 593888

Attractive building in peaceful grounds overlooking Conwy Estuary. Next to Castle. Open Feb–Dec.
🛏 9 bedrs, 8 en suite, 2 ba; TV; tcf
TV; P 12; child facs
✕ LD 8, nr Mon–Sat lunch. Resid & Rest lic
£ B&B £23–£27, B&B (double) £46; L £8·25, D £13; WB £59; [5% V w/d]
cc Access, B'card/Visa; dep.

★★ **Lodge,** Tal-y-Bont, LL32 8YX ☎Dalgarrog (049 269) 766

Modern purpose-built hotel set in an attractive garden.
🛏 10 bedrs, 10 en suite; TV; tcf
dogs, ns; P 60, coach; child facs; con 60

★★ **Park Hall,** Bangor Road, LL32 8DP. ☎(0492)592279

Gabled hotel with corner turret, set high up in 3½ acres of grounds about ½ mile from town centre. Distant views of Conwy Bay.
🛏 9 bdrs, 9 en suite, TV, tcf
dogs, P 20, coach, child facs.
✕ LD 9.30, nr Mon–Sat lunch
£ B&B £22·50–£25, B&B (double) £42–£45; D fr £10; [10% V]
cc Access, Amex, B'card/Visa, Diners, dep.

CORRIS Powys. Map 28C1

Machynlleth 53/4, London 211, Aberdyfi 14, Aberystwyth 22, Dolgellau 9¼, Welshpool 41.
ℹ Corris Craft Centre ☎(065 473) 244
Dulas Valley, Nr Machynlleth ☎(065 473) 688. *Hotel.*

COWBRIDGE S. Glamorgan. Map 19B1

Pop 4,360. Cardiff 12, London 162, Bridgend 6½, Caerphilly 16, Pontypridd 12.
EC Wed. **MD** Tue. **Golf** Southerndown 18h.

★★ **Bear,** High St, CF7 7AF ☎(044 63) 4814
Two-storey stone-built coaching inn situated in the High Street.
🛏 21 bedrs, 18 en suite, 1 ba; annexe 16 bedrs, 16 en suite; TV; tcf
dogs; P 80, G 2, coach; child facs; con 100

CRICCIETH Gwynedd. Map 28B2

Pop 1,530. Porthmadog 5, London 232, Caernarfon 17, Pwllheli 8½.
EC Wed. **Golf** Criccieth 18h. **See** Lloyd George Museum, Brynawelon.
ℹ 47 High Street ☎(0766) 523303

Colwyn Bay (Clwyd)

See ad for Maenen Abbey Hotel on page 630

Criccieth (Gwynedd)

Deganwy (Gwynedd)

⚘ ★★★ **Bron Eifion,** LL52 0SA ☏(0766) 522385. Fax: (0766) 522003

Large country house delightfully set in 5 acres of gardens on wooded estate. Fishing.
⚒ Fr, De, Es, It
🛏 19 bedrs, 19 en suite, TV; tcf
🏠 TV, dogs, P 80, coach, child facs; con 80
✕ LD 9.15
£ B&B £32–£45, B&B (double) £56–£70; L £7·50, D £14·50
cc Access, B'card/Visa; dep.

★★ **George IV,** High St, LL52 0BS ☏(0766) 522168
Imposing central hotel with spacious lounges, restaurant and grill room. (See advertisement on p. 632)

★★ **Gwyndy,** Llanystundwy. ☏(0766) 522720 ♿

Tastefully converted, 17th century farmhouse with modern bedroom wings. Open Feb–Nov.
🛏 10 bedrs, 10 en suite, TV, tcf
🏠 TV, dogs, ns; P 20, coach, child facs
✕ LD 9
£ B&B £24·50–£27, B&B (double) £40–£43; HB weekly £175–£180; L £7·50, D £10; dep.

★★ **Lion,** Y Maes, LL52 0AA ☏(0766) 522460
Charming old inn developed and extended. Faces the village green.
🛏 36 bedrs, 27 en suite, 5 ba; TV; tcf
🏠 lift, dogs; P 20, G 12, coach; child facs
✕ LD 8.15, bar meals only Mon–Sat lunch
£ B&B £18–£20·50, B&B (double) £35–£39; HB weekly £175–£190; L £5·50, D £11; WB £52; [5% V]
cc Access, Amex, B'card/Visa, Diners; dep.

⚘ ★★ **Parciau Mawr,** LL52 0RP ☏(0766) 522368 ♿
Small privately-owned country house in gardens with wonderful views. Open Mar–Oct. ⚒ Fr
🛏 6 bedrs, 6 en suite, annexe 6 bedrs, 6 en suite; TV; tcf
🏠 dogs; ns, P 30; no children under 5
✕ LD 8, Resid & Rest lic
£ B&B £21·50–£22·50, B&B (double) £43–£45; HB weekly £150–£210; D £8·50
cc Access, B'card/Visa.

★★ **Plas Isa,** Porthmadog Rd, LL52 0HP ☏(0766) 522443
Former private residence extensively modernised; overlooking Tremadog Bay.
🛏 14 bedrs, 14 en suite; TV; tcf
🏠 dogs; P 14, coach; child facs; con 30
✕ LD 9, bar meals only lunch, Sun dinner. Resid lic.
£ B&B £25–£35, B&B (double) £40–£45; L £5·50, D £8; WB £60; [5% V]
cc Access, B'card/Visa, Diners; dep.

★ **Abereistedd,** West Par, LL52 0EN ☏(0766) 522710
Small privately-owned hotel. Immediate access to the beach and fine sea view. Open 1 Mar–31 Oct.
🛏 12 bedrs, 8 en suite, 3 ba; TV; tcf
🏠 dogs, ns; P 12, coach; child facs
✕ LD 7. Resid & Rest lic
£ B&B £15·50–£17, B&B (double) £31–£34; HB weekly £144–£153; L £2, D £8·50; WB £44 (2 nts); [10% V Mar, Apr, Sep, Oct]
cc Access; dep.

★ C **Caerwylan,** Beach Bank, LL52 0HW ☏(0766) 522547

Large family hotel superbly situated within 30 yards of sea. Open Mar–Oct.
🛏 25 bedrs, 19 en suite, 5 ba; TV; tcf
🏠 lift, TV, dogs; P 8, U 8 (75p), G 7; coach, child facs
✕ LD 7.30, nr Mon–Sat lunch. Resid & Rest lic
£ B&B £16, B&B (double) £32; HB weekly £155; L £5·55, D £6·40; WB £44; dep.

★ C **Henfaes,** Porthmadog Rd, LL52 0HP ☏(0766) 522396
Attractive, modernised white-faced hotel. Panoramic views of Bay. Open Apr–Oct.
🛏 10 bedrs, 10 en suite; TV; tcf
🏠 U 3; no children under 5

Glyn-y-Coed, Porthmadog Rd, LL52 0HL ☏(0766) 522870. Fax: (0766) 523341 *Hotel.*
£ B&B £16–£17; HB weekly £165–£170
Min-y-Gaer, Porthmadog Rd, LL52 0HP ☏(0766) 522151. *Hotel.* Open 1 Mar–31 Oct.
£ B&B £13–£17; HB weekly £130–£156; [5% V Sep–Jul]
Mor Heli, Marine Ter, LL52 0EF ☏(0766) 522878.
Neptune, Marine Ter, LL52 0EF ☏(0766) 522794. Hotel. ⚒ Fr
£ B&B £13·50

CRICKHOWELL Powys. Map 19C2

Pop 2,000. Abergavenny 6½, London 150, Brecon 14, Builth Wells 27, Tredegar 10.
EC Wed. **MD** Thur. **Golf** Llangattock 9h.

⚘ ★★ **Gliffaes,** NP8 1RH ☏(0874) 730371 Fax: (0874) 730463

Victorian mansion with Italianate campaniles in a splendid position overlooking River Usk. Putting, tennis, fishing, snooker. ⚒ Fr, Es
🛏 19 bedrs, 18 en suite; 1 ba, annexe 3 bedrs, 3 en suite; TV; tcf
🏠 TV, dogs, ns; P 35, coach; child facs; con 15
✕ LD 9.15
£ B&B £27·50–£32, B&B (double) £55–£75; HB weekly £310–£370; L £9·60, D £15; WB £48·50 (FB)
cc Access, Amex, B'card/Visa, Diners.

Dragon House (Acclaimed), High St, NP8 1BE ☏(0873) 810362 Fax: (0873) 811868.
£ B&B £15–£30; HB weekly £140–175; [V]
Stables (Acclaimed), Llangattock, NP8 1LE ☏(0873) 810244. *Hotel. Riding.*
£ B&B £35

CROESGOCH Dyfed. Map 18A2

Haverfordwest 14, London 257, Fishguard 10, St David's 15.

Torbant Farm, SA62 5JN ☏(0348) 831276. *Guest House.* Open Easter–Oct ♿
£ B&B £12–£16; HB weekly £115–£140; [5% V Apr, May, Oct]
Trearched Farm, SA62 5JP ☏(0348) 831310. *Guest House.* Open Feb–Nov.
£ B&B £14–£15; HB weekly £132

CROSSGATES Powys. Map 19B3

Hereford 34, London 166, Newtown 23, Llandrindod Wells 3, Leominster 30.

★★ **Park,** Rhayader Rd, Llandrindod Wells, LD1 6RF ☏Penybont (059 787) 201

Former coaching inn with oak beams. Motel units attached. Swimming pool. Open 1 Feb –24 Dec
🛏 7 bedrs, 7 en suite; 2 ba; TV; tcf
🏠 TV, dogs; P 20; child facs
✕ LD 9.30. Resid & Rest lic
£ B&B £19–£22·50, B&B (double) £32–£38; L £3.35, D £3·95; dep.

Changes made after July 1990 are not included.

Wa

CWMBRAN Gwent. Map 19C1

Pop 47,013. Chepstow 19, London 141, M4 (jn 26) 4, Newport 5, Pontypool 4½.
EC Wed. **MD** Fri, Sat. **Golf** Pontnewydd 9h.

★★★★ **Parkway,** Cwmbran Dr, NP44 3UW ☎(0633) 871199
Modern hotel with single storied public rooms round a central courtyard, an attached two-storey bedroom block and an eye-catching flood-lit tower. Conference failities. Indoor swimming pool, sauna, solarium, gymnasium.
🛏 70 bedrs, 70 ensuite; TV; tcf.

★★★ **Commodore,** Mill Lane, Llanyrafon, NP4 2SH ☎(063 33) 4091 Tx: 57515 Fax: (063 33) 64831

Modern hotel in 5 acres of garden and woodland. Convenient for M4. Fr, De
🛏 60 bedrs, 60 en suite, 2 ba; TV; tcf
lift, TV, dogs, ns; P 250, G 8, coach; child facs; con 250
✕ LD 10
£ B&B £45–£55, B&B (double) £65; L £6·50, D £14·85; WB £27 (HB); [10% V]
cc Access, Amex, B'card/Visa, Diners; dep.

DEGANWY Gwynedd. Map 28C3

See also LLANDUDNO
Colwyn Bay 5½, London 227, Bangor 17, Betws-y-Coed 16, Llandudno 2½.

★★ C **Bryn Cregin Garden,** Ty Mawr Rd, LL31 9UR ☎(0492) 85266
Well-converted and modernised former private house set in gardens. Fr, Es
🛏 16 bedrs, 16 en suite; TV; tcf
dogs; P 30; child facs
✕ LD 8.30, nr lunch. Resid & Rest lic
£ B&B £48–£60, B&B (double) £62–£84; D £16; WB £85 (2 nts HB)
cc Access, B'card/Visa; dep.

★★ **Deganwy Castle,** Deganwy Rd, LL31 9DA ☎(0492) 83555 Tx: 61155
White-faced building with gardens, enjoying fine views of Conwy Estuary.
(*See advertisement on p. 632*)

DENBIGH Clwyd. Map 29A3

Pop 9,000. Ruthin 7½, London 204, Betws-y-Coed 23, Colwyn Bay 19, Mold 16, Rhyl 11.
EC Thur. **Golf** Denbigh 9h.

★★ **Bull,** Hall Sq, LL16 3NU ☎(074 571) 2582
16th century listed building with 17th century panelling in dining room.
🛏 13 bedrs, 7 en suite, 4 ba; TV
TV, P 12, coach; child facs
✕ LD 9
£ B&B £15–£17, B&B (double) £29–£31; [10% V]
cc Access, Amex, B'card/Visa, Diners.

DINAS MAWDDWY Gwynedd. Map 28C1

Pop 350. Welshpool 28, London 198, Aberdyfi 23, Bala 24, Dolgellau 10.
EC Thur. **Golf** Dolgellau 9h.

★★ **Buckley Pines,** SY20 9LP ☎(065 04) 261

Enjoying wonderful view over the Dovey, attractive 3-storey building. Fishing.
🛏 12 bedrs, 5 en suite, 2 ba; TV; tcf
dogs; P 40, coach

DOLGELLAU Gwynedd. Map 28C1

See also BONTDDU.
Pop 2,500. Welshpool 37, London 207, Aberdyfi 24, Aberystwyth 33, Bala 18, Betws-y-Coed 32, Caernarfon 39.
EC Wed. **MD** Fri. **Golf** Dolgellau 9h.
ⓘ The Bridge. ☎(0341) 422888

★★ **Dolserau Hall,** LL40 2AG ☎(0341) 422522

Well-appointed Victorian mansion quietly situated in five acres of grounds.
🛏 14 bedrs, 13 en suite; 1 ba, TV; tcf
lift, dogs; P 70, coach; child facs; con 50
✕ LD 8.30, nr lunch
£ B&B £35, B&B (double) £65; HB weekly £245–£265; L £15; WB £80
cc Access, B'card/Visa; dep.

★★ **George III,** Penmaenpool, LL40 1YD ☎(0341) 422525 Fax: (0341) 423565

Dramatically situated fine 17th century building, carefully restored and appointed. Fishing. Open 6 Jan–23 Dec.
🛏 6 bedrs, 4 en suite, (1 sh), 1 ba; annexe 6 bedrs, 6 en suite; TV; tcf
dogs, P 100, child facs
✕ LD 8.45, bar meals only Mon–Sat lunch, Sun dinner
£ B&B (double) £44–£88; L £7·70; WB £88 (2 nts, Nov–Apr)
cc Access, Amex, B'card/Visa; dep.

★★ **Royal Ship,** Queens Sq, LL40 1AR ☎(0341) 422209

Four-storey stone-built town centre hotel dating from the 18th century.
🛏 24 bedrs, 16 en suite, 5 ba; TV; tcf
lift, TV; P 8, coach; child facs
✕ LD 9
£ B&B £15·75–£26; HB weekly £154·50–£216; L £7, D £11·50; WB £49 (2 nts)
cc Access, B'card/Visa; dep.

★ **Clifton House,** Smithfield Sq, LL40 1ES ☎(0341) 422554
Impressive 18th century granite house, once the county gaol, in central position. Closed Jan.
🛏 7 bedrs, 3 en suite, 1 ba; TV; tcf
P 2
✕ LD 9.30, nr Mon lunch, also Tue–Sun lunch in winter. Resid & Rest lic
£ B&B £32–£44; HB weekly £182–£238; L £6·95, D £7·50; [10% V]
cc Access, B'card/Visa; dep.

DYFFRYN VALLEY Gwynedd. Map 28A3

Bangor 28, London 265, Amlwch 21, Holyhead 5.

★★ **Bull,** London Rd, LL65 3DP ☎(0407) 740351

Cream and green building on the A5 near centre of village. Secluded beer garden.
🛏 8 bedrs, 6 en suite, 1 ba; annexe 5 bedrs, 5 en suite; TV; tcf
dogs; P 200, coach; child facs; con 60
✕ LD 10, bar meals only Mon–Sat lunch
£ B&B £16·75–£24, B&B (double) £33·50; D £5·45, WB £45; [10% V]
cc Access, B'card/Visa, dep.
(*See advertisement on p. 637*)

EGLWYSFACH Dyfed (Powys). Map 28B1

Pop 120. Machynlleth 5, London 110, Aberystwyth 13.
Golf Ynyslas 18h. **See** Bird Sanctuary.

★★★ Ynyshir Hall, SY20 8TA
Glandyfi (065 474) 209

Elegant 16th century manor house with modern amenities. 12 acres of grounds.
9 bedrs, 9 en suite, TV
dogs; P 15; child facs, con 35
LD 8.30. Resid & Rest lic
£ B&B fr £30, B&B (double) fr £60; L fr £15, D fr £15; WB; [5% V Jan–Apr, Oct–Nov]
cc Access, Amex, B'card/Visa.

FISHGUARD Dyfed. Map 18A2

See also GOODWICK
Pop 4,980 (inc Goodwick). Lampeter 44, London 248, Cardigan 17, Haverfordwest 15, St David's 17.
EC Wed. **MD** Thur. **Golf** Newport 9h.
[i] 4 Hamilton Street. (0348) 873484

★★★ Fishguard Bay, Quay Rd, Goodwick, SA64 0BT (0348) 873571
Tx: 48602
Substantial Victorian building overlooking Fishguard Harbour; steep wooded hillside at rear. Swimming pool, billiards.

★★ Cartref, High St, SA65 9AW (0348) 872430

Attractive stone building set on main road in town centre. De, It, Yu, Es
12 bedrs, 6 en suite, 2 ba; TV; tcf
TV, dogs, ns; P 40, U 3, G 3, coach; child facs; con 40
Resid & Rest lic
£ B&B £19·50–£29, B&B (double) £32–£45; L £5·20, D £10·50; WB
cc Access, B'card/Visa; dep.

★ Manor House, Main St, SA65 9HJ
(0348) 873260
Pleasant compact hotel offering fine view across the harbour. De, Fr. Closed 24–28 Dec
7 bedrs, 1 en suite, 3 ba; TV; tcf
TV, dogs; child facs
LD 9.30, nr lunch
£ B&B £15–£17, B&B (double) £30–£38, HB weekly £245–£300; D £10
cc Access, B'card/Visa; dep.

FOUR MILE BRIDGE Gwynedd. Map 28A3

Pop 600. Bangor 21, London 258, Holyhead 4.
EC Thur. **Golf** Holyhead 18h.

★★★ Anchorage, LL65 2EZ Valley (0407) 740168

Attractive, white-faced, modern purpose-built hotel, 2 miles from Trearddur Bay.
17 bedrs, 17 en suite; TV; tcf
ns; P 100 coach; child facs
LD 9.30
£B&B £34–£39, B&B (double) £55–£59; L £7, D £12; WB £47·50
cc Access, Amex, B'card/Visa; dep.

GANLLWYD Gwynedd Map 28C2

Dolgellau 5½, London 213, Ffestiniog 13, Bala 23, Barmouth 23

★★★ Dolmelynllyn Hall, LL40 2HP
(034 140) 273

Mainly Victorian house furnished in restful country house style, in 3 acres of terraced gardens. Lovely views. Fishing.
11 bedrs, 11 en suite; TV; tcf.
dogs, ns; P 25, no children under 9
LD 8.30, nr lunch. Resid & Rest lic
£ B&B £30–£35, B&B (double) £60–£80; HB weekly £282·50–£332·50; D £16·25; WB £80 (2 nts); [5% V]
cc Access, Amex, B'card/Visa; dep.

★ Tyn-y-Groes, Dolgellau LL40 2HN
(034 140) 275

Attractively furnished former coaching inn with fishing on River Mawddach. Fr
8 bedrs, 7 en suite, 1 ba; TV; tcf
dogs; P 20, coach; child facs
LD 8.45, bar meals only Mon–Sat lunch
£ B&B £16–£22, B&B (double) £36–£45; HB weekly £146–£194; D £10·50; WB £43 [10% V]; dep.

GLYN CEIRIOG Clwyd. Map 29A2

Pop 821. Oswestry 8, London 181, Chester 28, Llangollen 4, Wrexham 16.
Golf Oswestry 18h. **See** 10th cent Church.

★★★ Golden Pheasant, Chirk, Llangollen, LL20 7BB (069 172) 281
Tx: 35664
Old black and white village inn with two new bedroom wings. Beautiful views in all directions. Riding.
18 bedrs, 18 en suite; TV; tcf
dogs; P 45, coach; child facs; con 60
LD 8.30
£ B&B £33·60, B&B (double) £63–£103; HB weekly £250–£280; L £9·50, D £16·85; [10% V w/d]
cc Access, Amex, B'card/Visa, Diners; dep.

GOODWICK Dyfed. Map 18A3

See also FISHGUARD
Fishguard 2, London 250, Cardigan 19, Haverfordwest 16, St Davids 16.

Siriole, Quay Rd, SA64 0BS Fishguard (0348) 873203. *Guest House.* De, Fr. Closed Xmas
£ B&B £11

GWAUN VALLEY Dyfed. Map 18B2

London 246, Cardigan 18, Carmarthen 34, Fishguard 5, Haverfordwest 16.

Tregynon Country (Acclaimed), nr Fishguard, SA65 9TU (0239) 820531.
Farm Fr, De
£ B&B (double) £59–£75; HB weekly £190–240

GWBERT-ON-SEA Dyfed. Map 18B3

Pop 150. Cardigan 3, London 237.
Golf Cardigan 18h.

★★★ Cliff, SA43 1PP Cardigan (0239) 613241 Tx: 48440

Holiday hotel on headland with panoramic views of Cardigan Bay. Swimming pool, golf, putting, fishing, squash, billiards.

HARLECH Gwynedd. Map 28B2

Pop 1,200. Dolgellau 20, London 226, Bala 31, Betwys-y-Coed 25, Caernarfon 27, Porthmadog 9½.
EC Wed. **Golf** Royal St David's 18h.
[i] High St. Harlech (0766) 780658

Castle Cottage (Acclaimed), LL46 2YL ☎(0766) 780479. *Private Hotel.*
£ B&B £17; [5% V]

St Davids (Acclaimed), LL46 2PT ☎(0766) 780366. *Hotel. Swimming pool, solarium, billiards.*
£ B&B £15–£25; HB weekly £120–£200; [10% V]

Byrdir, High St, LL46 2YN ☎(0766) 780316. *Guest House.*

HAVERFORDWEST Dyfed. Map 18A2

Pop 9,200. Carmarthen 30, London 243, Cardigan 26, Fishguard 15, Pembroke 11, St David's 15, Tenby 20.
EC Thur. **MD** Tue, Sat. **Golf** Haverfordwest 9h. **See** Norman castle remains, 12th cent St Martin's Church, Augustinian Priory ruins.
ℹ 40 High St. ☎(0437) 763110

★★ **Mariners,** Mariners Sq, SA61 2DU ☎(0437) 763353 Fax: (0437) 764258

Modernised 2-storey stone building ideally situated close to town centre. Fr
32 bedrs, 31 en suite, 1 ba; TV; tcf
dogs; P 40, coach; child facs; con 50
✕ LD 9.30
£ B&B £39–£45, B&B (double) £60–£74; HB weekly £247–£282; L £7, D £10; WB £33 (2 nts min)
cc Access, Amex, B'card/Visa, Diners.

★★ **Pembroke House,** 6 Spring Gdns, SA61 2EJ ☎(0437) 763652
Virginia creeper covered Georgian terrace house of architectural interest.
21 bedrs, 19 en suite, 1 ba; TV; tcf
TV, dogs; P 15, coach; child facs
✕ LD 9.30, nr lunch. Resid & Rest lic
£ B&B £35, B&B (double) £55; HB weekly £227·50 D £9·90; WB
cc Access, Amex, B'card/Visa, Diners; dep.
(*See advertisement on p. 637*)

HAY-ON-WYE Powys. Map 19C3

Hereford 21, London 153, Abergavenny 26, Brecon 13, Leominster 20.
EC Tue. **MD** Mon, Thur. **Golf** Brecon 18 h.
ℹ Car Park ☎(0497) 820144

★★★ **Swan,** Church St, HR3 5DQ ☎(0497) 821188 Fax: (0497) 821424
Elegant Georgian hotel in attractive gardens. Family owned and managed. Fishing.
14 bedrs, 14 en suite; TV; tcf
dogs, ns; P 18, coach; child facs; con 150
✕ LD 9.30, nr Mon–Sat lunch
£ B&B £35–£40, B&B (double) £50–£60; L £7·50, D £12·50; WB £45 (HB); [10% V Nov–Feb]
cc Access, Amex, B'card/Visa; dep.

★★ H R **Kilvert Country,** Bull Ring, via Hereford, HR3 5AG ☎(0497) 821042 Tx: 35315

Modernised stone-built hotel in centre of town.
15 bedrs, 15 en suite; TV, tcf.
lift, TV, dogs, P 15, coach, child facs, con 150
✕ LD 9.30
£ B&B £46–£59, B&B (double) £66–£76; HB weekly £275–£295; L £8·25, D £13; WB £83 (HB); [10% V]
cc Amex, B'card/Visa, Diners.

York House, Hardwicke Rd, Cusop, HR3 5QX ☎(0497) 820705. *Guest House.*
£ B&B £18–£28; HB weekly £154·35–£185·85

HOLYHEAD Gwynedd. Map 28A3

See DYFFRYN and TREARDDUR BAY
Pop 12,000. Bangor 23, London 261, Caernarfon 29.

HOLYWELL Clwyd. Map 29A3

Pop 9,000. Mold 9, London 200, Betws-y-Coed 35, Colwyn Bay 23, Denbigh 14, Queensferry 10, Rhyl 13, Ruthin 19.
EC Wed. **MD** Thur, Fri, Sat. **Golf** Holywell 9h. **See** St Winefride's Well and Church.

★★ **Stamford Gate,** Halkyn Rd, CH8 7SJ ☎(0352) 712942 Fax: (0352) 713309.
Modern purpose-built hotel conveniently situated on the A55. It
12 bedrs, 12 en suite; TV; tcf
P 100, coach; con 100
✕ LD 10
£ B&B £32, B&B (double) £46; L £8·25, D £11·85; [5% V w/e Jan–Feb]
cc Access, B'card/Visa.

Kinsale Hall, Llanerchymor, CH8 9DT ☎(0745) 560001
Awaiting inspection

Miners Arms, Rhes-y-Cae, CH8 8JG ☎Halkyn (0352) 780567

JOHNSTON Dyfed. Map 18A2

Pop 1,580. Haverfordwest 4, London 247, Pembroke 8, Tenby 16.
Golf Milford Haven 18h.

Redstock, SA62 3HW ☎(0437) 890287

KNIGHTON Powys. Map 19C4

Ludlow 15, London 158, Kington 13, Llandrindod Wells 18, Welshpool 34.
ℹ The Old School ☎(0547) 528753

★★★ **Knighton,** Broad St, LD7 1BL ☎(0547) 520530 Fax: (0547) 520529, ♿
Recently refurbished, 3-storied stone building and an adjacent black and white Tudor-style one in town centre. Billiards.

LAMPETER Dyfed. Map 18C3

Pop 2,700. Llandovery 19, London 203, Aberystwyth 23, Cardigan 29, Carmarthen 23, Newtown 53, Swansea 45.
EC Wed. **MD** Alt Tue. **Golf** Llangybi 9h.

★★★ **Falcondale,** SA48 7RX ☎(0570) 422910

On outskirts, substantial listed building with lawns, shrubs and meadows. Putting, tennis, fishing. Closed 6–19 Jan
21 bedrs, 21 en suite; TV; tcf
lift; P 80, coach; child facs; con 150
✕ LD 9.30, bar meals only Mon–Sat lunch
£ B&B £38–£48, B&B (double) £55–£65; HB weekly £225–£295; L £9, D £15; WB £85
cc Access, B'card/Visa, dep.
(*See advertisement on p. 637*)

★★ **Black Lion Royal,** High St, SA48 7BG ☎(0570) 422172
Pleasant Georgian coaching house in main shopping area of town.
16 bedrs, 15 en suite, 1 ba; TV; tcf
TV, dogs; P 50, coach; child facs

LANGLAND BAY West Glamorgan. Map 19A1

Swansea 5, London 193, Llanelli 16.
EC Wed. **Golf** Langland Bay 18h.

★★★ **Osborne,** Rotherslade Rd, SA3 4QL ☎(0792) 366274 Fax: (0792) 363100

Large modern hotel perched on clifftop overlooking Langland Bay. It (Emb)
36 bedrs, 32 en suite, 3 ba; TV; tcf
lift, dogs; P 45, coach; child facs; con 50
✕ LD 9
£ B&B £60–£75, B&B (double) £75–£95; HB weekly £276·50; L £10·50, D £13·50; WB £34 (HB)
cc Access, Amex, B'card/Visa, Diners.

 EC *early closing* **MD** *market day* *country house hotel* *ns (NS) no smoking areas* *tcf tea/coffee facilities*

Haverfordwest (Dyfed)

PEMBROKE HOUSE HOTEL**

Haverfordwest, Wales. Tel: 0437 763652

Set in a Georgian terraced house. Lounge bar. Restaurant. 21 bedrooms, 19 en-suite, Colour TV, tea & coffee in all rooms. Car Park. Weekend Breaks.

Holyhead (Gwynedd)

WTB ♛♛♛♛ **THE BULL HOTEL** RAC ★★

LONDON ROAD, VALLEY, HOLYHEAD, ISLE OF ANGLESEY Telephone: (0407) 740351

A special welcome to the magical island of Anglesey awaits you at The Bull. Situated on the A5 only 3½ miles from the ferry to Ireland. We have fifteen well-appointed bedrooms, most with en-suite facilities and all with colour TV, internal and external telephone, coffee and tea makers and radio alarms.

Our lounge bar with its beamed ceilings and stone walls has an olde worlde character. The friendly staff serve real ale and lagers. Delicious bar food is available both at lunch-time and in the evening. Our Bull Bach dining room with its flagged floors, check tablecloths and candle-light serves a wide variety of food at very competitive prices. Children's menus are always served.

Your hosts, David and Margaret Hall will do everything possible to make your stay enjoyable.

Double/Twin £35.50; Single £17.75; Short Breaks £45.00 per person, 2 nights, bed breakfast and evening meal.

Les Routiers recommended

Lampeter (Dyfed)

Telephone: (0570) 422 910

RAC ***

FALCONDALE HOTEL

Lampeter, Dyfed

Falcondale is a Victorian country mansion, set within 14 acres of mature parkland. Overlooking the university, market town of Lampeter, which is situated 9 miles from the coast.

All 22 individually designed bedrooms have bath/shower rooms, colour TV with film system, radio, tea and coffee makers, baby listening facility and central heating, direct dial telephone, hair dryers.

The restaurant offers both table d'hôte and very extensive à la carte menus, supported by a one acre walled kitchen garden, from which we produce our own fruit, vegetables and herbs as the seasons permit.

Services
2 bars — 2 lounges
Conservatory — Log fires
Lift — Restaurant for 50
Banqueting for 150
Full conference facilities and syndicate rooms

Sports Facilities
10 acre lake coarse fishing
Clay pigeon range
Tennis court
With:—Golf, pony trekking,
salmon and sea fishing. By arrangement.

Please write or telephone for brochure and tariff.

Wa

Llanbedr (Gwynedd)

TŶ MAWR HOTEL

LLANBEDR, GWYNEDD

Telephone: 034 123 440 ★★

Tŷ Mawr is a fully licensed country house situated in Snowdonia National Park near the sea and mountains. We have ten centrally heated bedrooms with bathrooms en-suite, colour television, and tea and coffee tray. Tastefully furnished and set in a lovely garden. Real ale, and excellent food served in the Restaurant or Bar, with open fire and central heating, ensure a warm and friendly stay.

Llanberis (Gwynedd)

Llanberis
Snowdonia
LL55 4SU

★★

Thinking of a holiday in Snowdonia?

. . . then the Padarn Lake Hotel in beautiful Llanberis has the answer. The perfect location for touring this wonderful countryside – with superb unspoilt beaches within easy driving distance.

The Hotel offers superb accommodation, all bedrooms are en-suite with colour TV, telephone, tea & coffee makers, radios and full central heating. Many rooms have either Lake or Mountain views. We have some family suites available with reductions for children under 12. The restaurant has extensive à la carte & table d'hôte menus. We also serve a high class range of bar meals in the large Welsh Lounge Bar & Ramblers Bar. Our intimate Cocktail Bar is open for residents and diners or anyone wanting a quiet relaxing drink.

We have special rates for short breaks or weekly stays.

Telephone now for full colour brochure & tariff

0286 870260

NEW FOR 1991

RAC Guide to Small Hotels, Guest Houses & Inns

- full details of over 2,000 RAC approved establishments
- pictures of Highly Acclaimed and Acclaimed hotels
- colour section of regional award winners

Great Value! — only £4.95

★★ **Langland Court,** Langland Court Rd, SA3 4TD ☎(0792) 361545 Tx: 498627 Fax: (0792) 362302

Substantial mock-Tudor building set in own pleasant grounds. Near to Bay. ✂ Fr
🛏 16 bedrs, 16 en suite, 1 ba; annexe 5 bedrs, 5 en suite; TV; tcf
🏨 dogs, ns, P 45, U 4 (£5), coach, child facs, con 150
✕ LD 9.30, bar meals only Mon–Sat lunch
£ B&B £46–£50, B&B (double) £64–£68; L £7·50, D £15·50; WB fr £42 (HB)
cc Access, Amex, B'card/Visa, Diners, dep.
(*See advertisement on p. 660*)

Wittenberg (Acclaimed), 2 Rotherslade Rd, SA3 4QN ☎Swansea (0792) 369696. *Private Hotel.* Closed Xmas.
£ B&B £30; HB weekly £190–£204; [5% V weekly bookings]

Brynteg, 1 Higher La, SA3 4NS ☎Swansea (0792) 366820. *Hotel.*

LANGSTONE Map 19C1

Chepstow 11, London 134, Cardiff 16, Newport 4½.

★★ **New Inn,** Chepstow Rd, NP6 2JN ☎(0633) 412426

18th century coaching inn with modern extension.
🛏 34 bedrs, 34 en suite; TV; tcf
🏨 TV; P 150, coach; child facs; con 150

LITTLE HAVEN Dyfed. Map 18A2

Pop 150. Haverfordwest 7, London 257, Pembroke 13, St David's 14, Tenby (Fy) 21. **Golf** Haverfordwest 18h. Milford Haven 18h.

Pendyffryn, SA62 3LA ☎(0437) 781337. *Private Hotel.* Open Apr–Sep.
£ B&B (double) £26–£34

LLANARMON-DYFFRYN-CEIRIOG

Clwyd. Map 29A2
Pop 100. Shrewsbury 26, London 183, Bala 23, Llangollen 17, Welshpool 22.

★★ **Hand,** LL20 7LD ☎(069 176) 666 Fax: (069 176) 262

Converted 16th century buildings offering modern comforts. Tennis.
🛏 14 bedrs, 14 en suite
🏨 TV, dogs, ns; P 30; coach; child facs; con 20
✕ LD 9, bar meals only Mon–Sat lunch
£ B&B £41, B&B (double) £64; HB weekly £280–£290; L £9·50, D £15·95; WB £45 (HB, min 2 nts)
cc Access, Amex, B'card/Visa, Diners.

★★ **West Arms,** Llangollen, LL20 7LD ☎(069 176) 665 Fax: (069 176) 264 ♿

400-year-old hotel–a place of character set in small village. Fishing.
🛏 14 bedrs, 14 en suite; TV
🏨 TV, dogs, ns; P 30, U 2; child facs; con 30
✕ LD 9, bar meals only Mon–Sat lunch
£ B&B £45–£50, B&B (double) £70–£80; HB weekly £310–£355; L £9·75, D £17·50; WB £50 (min 2 nts)
cc Access, Amex, B'card/Visa, Diners; dep.

LLANBEDR Gwynedd. Map 28B2

Pop 550. Dolgellau 16, London 219, Bala 35, Betws-y-Coed 28, Caernarfon 28, Porthmadog 12.

★★ **Ty Mawr,** LL45 2PX ☎(034 123) 440

Privately-owned, picturesque building in own grounds. Salmon and trout fishing.
🛏 10 bedrs, 10 en suite; TV; tcf
🏨 TV, dogs; P 28; child facs
(*See advertisement on p. 638*)

🍺🍺 **Victoria Inn,** LL45 2LD ☎(034 123) 213
Stone-built 18th century inn in village centre. Garden running down to River Artro.
🛏 5 bedrs, 5 en suite; TV; tcf
🏨 P 80, U 13, coach; child facs
✕ LD 9
£ B&B £20·50, B&B (double) £38; HB weekly £123; WB £37·50 (2 days), £54 (3 days)
cc Access, B'card/Visa.

LLANBERIS Gwynedd. Map 28B3

Pop 3,500. Betws-y-Coed 16, London 232, Bangor 10, Caernarfon 7, Porthmadog 23. **Golf** Caernarfon 18h. **See** Snowdon (Rack Rly to summit), Dolbardarn Castle.
ℹ Museum of the North ☎(0286) 870765

★★ C **Padarn Lake,** High St, LL55 4SU ☎(0286) 870260

Built 1820, privately-owned hotel in an attractive situation in Snowdonia.
🛏 20 bedrs, 20 en suite, 1 ba; TV; tcf
🏨 TV, dogs; P 50, coach; child facs
✕ LD 9.30
£ B&B £24, B&B (double) £43; HB weekly £170–£187; D £9·50; WB
cc Access, Amex, B'card/Visa, Diners; dep.
(*See advertisement on p. 638*)

Lake View (Acclaimed), Tan-y-Pant, LL55 4EL ☎(0286) 870422. *Hotel.*

LLANDEILO Dyfed. Map 19A2

Pop 2,000. Llandovery 12, London 197, Carmarthen 14, Lampeter 20, Swansea 22. **EC** Thur. **MD** Fri, Mon. **Golf** Glynhir 18h.

★★★ C **Cawdor Arms,** Rhosmaen St, SA19 6EN ☎(0558) 823500
Elegant 3-storey Georgian building of stone set in town centre.

Brynawel (Acclaimed), 19 New Road, SA19 6DD ☎(0558) 822925
Guest House. Closed 25–26 Dec.
£ B&B £16–£21; [5% V w/d]

LLANDELOY Dyfed. Map 18A2

Haverfordwest 12, London 255, Fishguard 10, St Davids 8.

Upper Vanley Farm (Acclaimed), Nr Solva ☎Croesgoch (034 83) 418. *Farm.* ♿

LLANDOGO Gwent. Map 20A1

Pop 350. Chepstow 8, London 131, Abergavenny 21, Gloucester 26, Monmouth 7, Pontypool 21.
Golf Monmouth 9h.

Brown's, NP5 4TW ☎(0594) 530262. *Guest House.*
Sloop, NP5 4TW ☎(0594) 530291. *Inn.*
£ B&B £25·50; [10% V]

LLANDOVERY Dyfed. Map 19A2

Pop 2,100. Brecon 21, London 184, Builth Wells 24, Carmarthen 28, Lampeter 19.

Wa

EC Thur. **MD** Fri. **Golf** Brecon 18h, Lampeter 18h.
🛈 Car Park, Broad St. ☎(0550) 20693

★★ Castle, Kings Rd, SA20 0AW ☎(0550) 20343
In 1802 Nelson stayed at this attractive Georgian coaching inn on A40 in town centre. Fishing.
🛏 24 bedrs, 17 en suite, 1 ba; TV; tcf
🏨 TV, dogs; P 18, coach; child facs; con 140

Llwyncelyn, Chain Bridge, SA20 0EP ☎(0550) 20566. *Guest House.*
£ B&B £16·80–£19·80; HB weekly £152·80–£180·80

LLANDRINDOD WELLS Powys. Map 19B3

See also CROSSGATES.
Pop 4,200. Hereford 41, London 171, Builth Wells 7, Knighton 18, Llandovery 27, Leominster 33, Newtown 24, Rhayader 10.
EC Wed. **MD** Fri. **Golf** Llandrindod Wells 18h.
🛈 Town Hall. ☎(0597) 2600

★★★ Metropole, Temple St, LD1 5DY ☎(0597) 822881 Tx: 35237 Fax (0597) 824828

Spacious, privately-owned Edwardian hotel near town centre. Indoor swimming pool, sauna, solarium. ✂ Fr, It
🛏 122 bedrs, 122 en suite; TV; tcf
🏨 lift, dogs, ns; P 150, coach, child facs, con 350.
✕ LD 9
£ B&B £45–£49·50, B&B (double) £62–£82; HB weekly £297·50–£327·25; L £9·15, D £15; WB £82; [10% V]
cc Access, Amex, B'card/Visa, Diners.

★★ Glen Usk, South Crescent, LD1 5DH ☎(0597) 822085 Tx: 61160

Elegant Victorian hotel in town centre. ✂ Fr. (MtCh)
🛏 79 bedrs, 79 en suite; TV; tcf
🏨 lift, dogs, ns, P 12, coach; child facs, con 150
✕ LD 9, nr lunch
£ B&B fr £38, B&B (double) fr £50; HB weekly fr £230; L £6, D £14; WB £32·50; [5% V]
cc Access, Amex B'card/Visa, Diners

Three Wells (Highly Acclaimed), Chapel Road, Howey, LD1 5PB ☎(0597) 824427. *Farm. Fishing.*
£ B&B £14–£19; HB weekly £130–£172

Charis (Acclaimed), Pentrosfa, LD1 5NL ☎(0597) 824732. *Guest House.* Open Mar–Nov.
£ B&B £15; HB weekly £120
Griffin Lodge (Acclaimed), Temple St, LD1 5HF ☎(0597) 822432. *Hotel.* Closed 24 Dec–Jan 31.
£ B&B £15·50–£19·50; HB weekly £130·50–£157·50; [15% V]

LLANDUDNO Gwynedd. Map 28C3

See also DEGANWY and LLANDUDNO JUNCTION.
Pop 20,000. Colwyn Bay 4½, London 227, Bangor 19, Betws-y-Coed 19.
EC Wed. **Golf** North Wales 18h, Llandudno (Maesdu) 18h, Rhos-on-Sea 18h.
🛈 Chapel St. ☎ (0492) 76413

♣ ★★★ Bodysgallen Hall, LL30 1RS ☎(0492) 584466 Tx: 617163 Fax: (0492) 582519

17th century mansion with antique furniture. Superb views from spacious grounds. Tennis. ✂ Ar, De, Fr
🛏 19 bedrs, 19 en suite; annexe 9 bedrs, 9 en suite; TV
🏨 dogs; P 60, coach, no children under 8; con 50
✕ LD 9.45
£ room £78–£98, double room £103–£135; Bk £8, L £15·25, D £25·75; WB £79; [10% V]
cc Access, Amex, B'card/Visa, Diners.

★★★ H C Empire, Church Walks, LL30 2HE ☎(0492) 860555 Tx: 617161 Fax: (0492) 860791

Modern family run hotel in central position with roof garden. Indoor & outdoor swimming pools, sauna, solarium. ✂ It
Closed 2 weeks Xmas & New Year.
🛏 56 bedrs, 56 en suite; 2 ba; annexe 8 bedrs, 8 en suite; TV; tcf
🏨 lift, dogs; P 30, G 5 (£5); coach, child facs; con 40
✕ LD 9.30
£ B&B £40–£55; B&B (double) £65–£90; HB weekly £175–£290; L £10·50, D £16·50, WB £64·50
cc Access, Amex, B'card/Visa, Diners; dep.

★★★ Gogarth Abbey, Abbey Rd, West Shore, LL30 2QY ☎(0492) 76211

Impressive building in sunny position on West Shore. Fine views. Indoor swimming pool, putting, sauna, solarium, gymnasium.
🛏 40 bedrs, 40 en suite; TV; tcf
🏨 dogs; ns; P 60, child facs; con 100
✕ LD 9
£ B&B £35; L £9, D £15; WB £85; [10% V w/d]
cc Access, Amex, B'card/Visa; Diners, dep.
(*See advertisement on p. 642*)

★★★ Imperial, Vaughan St, LL30 1AP ☎(0492) 77466 Tx: 61606 Fax: (0492) 78043

Classic Victorian building with wide sea views from sun lounge. Indoor swimming pool, sauna, solarium, gymnasium, billiards.
🛏 100 bedrs, 100 en suite; TV; tcf
🏨 lift, dogs, P 40, coach; child facs; con 350
✕ LD 9
£ B&B £45–£65, B&B (double) £75–£85; L £9·50, D £15·50; WB
cc Access, Amex, B'card/Visa, Diners; dep.

★★★ Risboro, Clement Av, LL30 2ED ☎(0492) 76343 (changing to (0492) 876343) Tx: 617117 Fax: (0492) 879881

Large elegant family hotel at foot of Great Orme. Indoor swimming pool, sauna/solarium, gymnasium, billiards. ✂ Fr
🛏 65 bedrs, 65 en suite; TV; tcf
🏨 lift, dogs; ns; P 40, coach; child facs; con 200
✕ LD 8.45
£ B&B £30–£33; HB weekly fr £250; L £8, D £15; WB £80; [10% V w/e]
cc Access, Amex, B'card/Visa, Diners; dep.
(*See advertisement on p. 642*)

EC *early closing* **MD** *market day* ♣ *country house hotel* *ns (NS) no smoking areas* *tcf tea/coffee facilities*

★★★ **H C R St Tudno,** North Par, LL30 2LP (0492) 874411 Tx: 61400 Fax: (0492) 860407

Beautifully refurbished, distinctive small luxury hotel with views of bay. Indoor swimming pool. Closed 27 Dec–11 Jan.
21 bedrs, 21 en suite; TV; tcf
lift, dogs, ns; P 4, G 2 (£3·50); child facs; con 30
LD 9.30. Resid & Rest lic
£ B&B £45–£63·50, B&B (double) £64–£106; HB weekly £271–£411; L £10·95, D £20·95; WB £99; [10% V w/d]
cc Access, Amex, B'card/Visa; dep.

★★ **Bedford,** Craig-y-Don Par, LL30 1BN (0492) 76647
Striking 4-storey building in Edwardian style in wonderful position on Promenade. It
27 bedrs, 27 en suite; TV; tcf
lift, TV, dogs; P 20, coach; child facs; con 40
LD 10.30, Resid & Rest lic
cc Access, B'card/Visa; dep.

★★ **Belle Vue,** North Par, LL30 2LP (0492) 879547
Attractive building with painted stucco. Sun terrace overlooks the Bay. Billiards. Es, Fr. Open Mar–Oct.
17 bedrs, 17 en suite; TV; tcf
lift, dogs; P 12; child facs
LD 8, bar meals only lunch. Resid & Rest lic
£ B&B £22–£26; HB weekly £189–£214; D fr £3.50; [10% V]
cc Access, B'card/Visa, Diners; dep.
(*See advertisement on p. 642*)

★★ **Bromwell Court,** The Promenade, LL30 1BG (0492) 78416
Victorian terrace on the Promenade with superb sea views.
11 bedrs, 11 en suite; TV; tcf
ns; coach; child facs
LD 8.30, bar meals only lunch, Resid & Rest lic
£ B&B £23, B&B (double) £42; HB weekly £195; D £9, WB £25 (HB 2nts min); [5% V]
cc Access, B'card/Visa; dep.

★★ **Castle,** Vaughan St, LL30 1AG, (0492) 77694

Attractive 4-storey building, cream rendered. Near shops and Promenade. Snooker. Closed 4 Jan–1 Feb
56 bedrs, 54 en suite; TV; tcf
lift, dogs, ns; P 30, coach, child facs, con 80
LD 8
£ B&B £20–£22, B&B (double) £49–£53; HB weekly £171·70; L £5·50, D £8·50
cc B'card/Visa; dep.
(*See advertisement on p. 642*)

★★ **Clarence,** Gloddaeth St, LL30 2DS (0492) 860193 Fax: (0492) 860308

Large impressive building, a short distance from Promenade. Conference facilities.
62 bedrs, 38 en suite; TV; tcf
lift, TV; dogs; ns, coach; child facs; con 10
LD 8.30, bar meals only Mon–Sat lunch
£ L £6·50, D £10; WB £50
cc Access, Amex, B'card/Visa, Diners; dep.

★★ **C Dunoon,** Gloddaeth St, LL30 2DW (0492) 860787 Fax: (0492) 860031

Impressive centrally-situated building–a well furnished and decorated hotel. Open mid-Mar–end Oct.
56 bedrs, 56 en suite; TV; tcf.
lift, dogs, P 24, coach, child facs.
LD 7.30. Resid & Rest lic
£ B&B £23–£29, B&B (double) £42–£58; L £6·50, D £9·50
cc Access, B'card/Visa.

★★ **Esplanade,** Central Promenade, LL30 2LL (0492) 860300 Tx: 61155 Fax: (0492) 860418

White-painted building with sun terrace overlooking the Promenade.
59 bedrs, 59 en suite; TV; tcf
lift, dogs; P 30, coach, child facs, con 120
LD 8.30, bar meals only lunch
£ B&B £27·50–£35, B&B (double) £57–£63; HB weekly £192·50–£259; D £9·50; WB £60 (2 nts HB); [5% V]
cc Access, Amex, B'card/Visa, Diners, dep.

★★ **Headlands,** Hill Terr, LL30 2LS (0492) 77485
Attractive Victorian hotel with conservatory and sun terrace overlooking Bay. Open Mar–Dec.
17 bedrs, 15 en suite, 2 ba; TV; tcf
TV, dogs; ns; P 7; no children under 5
LD 8.30, bar meals only lunch. Resid & Rest lic
£ B&B £23; HB weekly £189–£220; D £14·50; WB £55 (2 days); [10% V]
cc Access, B'card/Visa, Diners; dep.

★★ **Merrion,** Promenade, LL30 2LN (0492) 860022 Fax: (0492) 860378
Family-run hotel in a Victorian terraced building opposite the pier. Closed Feb.
65 bedrs, 65 en suite; TV; tcf
lift, dogs; P 15, G 25, coach; child facs
LD 8.30, bar meals only Mon–Sat lunch. Resid & Rest lic
£ B&B £39–£42, B&B (double) £54–£64; HB weekly £260–£300; L £9, D £14·50
cc Access, Amex, B'card/Visa.

★★ **Ormescliffe,** Promenade, LL30 1BE (0492) 77191. Fax: (0492) 860311

Family hotel with cream stucco façade and garden frontage on Promenade.
60 bedrs, 60 en suite, TV; tcf
lift, TV, ns; P 15, coach; child facs; con 120
LD 8.30, bar meals only lunch
£ B&B £22–£25; HB weekly £213–£230; D £9·50
cc Access, B'card/Visa; dep.

★★ **Royal,** Church Walks, LL30 2HW (0492) 76476

Impressive building standing in its own grounds facing South, Putting.
38 bedrs, 29 en suite, 3 ba; TV; tcf
lift, P 25, coach; child facs; con 80
LD 8, bar meals only lunch
£ B&B £19·50, B&B (double) £30–£48; HB weekly £179–£245; D £12·50; WB £50 (HB); [10% V]
cc Access, B'card/Visa; dep.

Wa

Llandudno (Gwynedd)

West Shore, Llandudno, Gwynedd LL30 2QY
Telephone: 0492 76211/2

Situated in the most famous resort in Wales, yet away from all the hustle and bustle, the 'Gogarth Abbey' is located on the West Shore facing South over the Snowdonia National Park and the Isle of Anglesey.

A superb Hotel in its own right, catering only in quality and comfort. Imaginative food and a fine collection of wine is complemented by bedrooms with every facility and a superb leisure complex. Croquet, putting and French boules are a regular event on our lawn.

Please telephone our Reception on **0492 76211/2**

Llandudno (Gwynedd)

W.T.B. ♣♣♣♣ commended

RAC ★★★

CLEMENT AVENUE, LLANDUDNO

LOOK WHAT WE HAVE – 65 Bedrooms all with Bath/Shower/WC, Colour TV, Tea/Coffee Making Facilities, Hair Dryers, Radio/Baby Listening, Direct line Telephones, Superb Heated Indoor Tropical Swimming Pool, Health Complex with Jacuzzi, Sauna, Solarium, Steam Room.

BALLROOM – with Dancing & Cabaret, Live Group
SNOOKER ROOM – with Full Size Snooker, Table Tennis
ROOF TOP Sun Garden & Patio
2 PASSENGER LIFTS – to all floors
CAR PARKING – in Hotel
WATER SKIING – from the hotel / lessons bookable
NIGHT PORTER – & Baby Listening

Excellent New Conference Facilities. You don't have to go out, we have most things to give you all your requirements for a HAPPY HOLIDAY. What about a Firm's Outing for a mini weekend this Autumn? *We do special rates for individual and groups.*

Give us a ring for Brochure & Details on LLANDUDNO (0492) 76343/4

AN IDEAL SITUATION FOR TOURING SNOWDONIA *Full 4 day Xmas and New Year programme.*

Fax: 879881 Telex: 617117

Llandudno (Gwynedd)

RAC ★★

Belle Vue Hotel

WTB ♣♣♣♣

26 North Parade, Llandudno, Gwynedd LL30 2LP
Telephone: (0492) 879547

This comfortable, family run hotel is ideally situated on the sea front, facing south, with delightful views of the bay. All rooms are en-suite with colour TV, video, radio, telephone, hairdryer and tea/coffee making facilities. Bar. Lift. Car park. Snooker and table tennis. Good food.

Brochure? With pleasure.

Llandudno (Gwynedd)

Castle Hotel

RAC ★★

(previously North Western Hotel)

Vaughan Street, Llandudno, Gwynedd LL30 1AG Tel: (0492) 77694 (Visitors) 76868

- Lift to all Floors
- Private Car Park
- Residents' Lounge Bar
- Non Residential Lounge & Restaurant
- Non Smoking Lounge
- Function & Conference Suite/Cocktail Lounge
- Full Central Heating
- All Bedrooms with colour TV and teamaking facilities
- Ideally situated near all amenities
- Large private car park at hotel
- Games Room

56 comfortable bedrooms – all en-suite.

For a copy of our brochure and moderate terms please telephone or write to the resident proprietors D. J. & L. W. Owen

★★ **Somerset,** Central Promenade, LL30 2LF ☎(0492) 76540

Family-run hotel. Classic building in superb position on Promenade. Open Mar–Nov.
🛏 37 bedrs, 37 en suite, 1 ba; TV; tcf
🏨 lift, dogs, ns; P 20, coach; child facs
✕ LD 8, bar meals only lunch. Rest lic
£ B&B £22–£26, B&B (double) & dinner £60–£68; D £9; WB £59
cc Access, B'card/Visa; dep.

★★ H **Tan Lan,** Great Orme's Rd, West Shore, LL30 2AR ☎(0492) 860221

Family hotel ideally situated on West Shore. Fine sea and mountain views. Fr, It. Open mid-Mar–end Oct.
🛏 18 bedrs, 18 en suite; TV; tcf
🏨 dogs; P 15; child facs
✕ LD 8, Resid lic
£ B&B £20–£22; HB weekly £178–£185; L £6·95, D £10; WB £53
cc Access, B'card/Visa; dep.
(*See advertisement on p. 645*)

★ **Branksome,** 62 Lloyd St, LL30 2YP ☎(0492) 75989
Formerly 3 houses–now a modern, well-equipped hotel. Between 2 bays.

★ **Bron Orme,** 53 Church Walks, LL30 2HL ☎(0492) 76735
Former residence with delightful garden facing south with fine views. Open Mar–Oct.
🛏 9 bedrs, 4 en suite, (1 sh), 2 ba; tcf
🏨 TV, ns; no children under 5
✕ LD 7, bar meals only lunch. Resid lic
£ B&B £11·50–£14, B&B (double) £21–£26; HB weekly £107–£126; L £6, D £10·50

★ **Clontarf,** Great Orme's Rd, West Shore, LL30 2AS ☎(0492) 77621
Privately-owned hotel in attractive early 20th century building near West Shore.

★ **Epperstone,** 15 Abbey Road, LL30 2EE ☎(0492) 78746. Open Mar–Dec.

Recently improved bay-windowed Victorian house retaining some period features. In quiet residential area.
🛏 8 bedrs, 7 en suite, 1 ba, TV, tcf
🏨 dogs, P 6, child facs
✕ LD 8.30, nr lunch. Resid lic
£ B&B £14–£16, B&B (double) £33–£37; D £8·50; WB fr £38; [5% V Nov–Apr]

★ **Hilbre Court,** Great Orme's Rd, LL30 2AR ☎(0492) 76632

Well-appointed and furnished converted house. Near West Shore. Open Mar–Oct & Xmas.
🛏 11 bedrs, 7 en suite, 2 ba; TV; tcf
🏨 TV, dogs; P 3; child facs
✕ LD 7.30, nr lunch. Resid lic
£ B&B £16–£17·50, B&B (double) £21–£22·50; D £7·50; [5% V]
cc Access, B'card/Visa; dep.

★ **Leamore,** 40 Lloyd St, LL30 2YG ☎(0492) 75552
Attractive building with stucco façade. On corner site, convenient for beach. Closed Dec 21–31
🛏 12 bedrs, 7 en suite, 2 ba; TV; tcf
🏨 TV, ns; P 4; coach; child facs
✕ LD 7.30, bar meals only lunch. Resid & Rest lic
£ B&B £16, B&B (double) £28–£33; HB weekly £140–£154; D £8; WB £24; [10% V Mar–June]

★ **Marlborough,** South Par, LL30 2LN ☎(0492) 75846 ♿
Pleasant 4-storey building in central position with view of pier. Open 1 Feb–30 Nov & 20 Dec–5 Jan.
🛏 41 bedrs, 32 en suite, 9 ba; TV, tcf
🏨 lift, TV, ns; P 4, coach, child facs
✕ LD 7.30. Resid & Rest lic
£ B&B £18–£21, B&B (double) £36–£40; HB weekly £175–£192; L £6·95, D £8·50; WB £50; [10% V w/d low season]
cc Access, B'card/Visa; dep.

★ **Min-y-Don,** North Par, LL30 2LP ☎(0492) 76511

Attractive stucco painted building with garden frontage opposite pier entrance. Open Mar–Oct.
🛏 28 bedrs, 19 en suite, 3 ba; TV; tcf
🏨 TV, ns; P 5, coach; child facs
✕ LD 7.30, bar meals only lunch. Resid & Rest lic
£ B&B £16–£17·70, HB weekly £130–£142; L £3·95, D £6·50; WB £39·95; [10% V Mar–mid Jul, Sept–Oct]
cc Access, B'card/Visa.

★ **Ravenhurst,** West Shore, LL30 2BB ☎(0492) 75525

Attractive holiday hotel with black and white gables. On West Shore. Open Feb– Nov.
🛏 23 bedrs, 23 en suite, 1 ba; annexe 1 bedr, 1 en suite; TV; tcf
🏨 dogs; P 15, coach; child facs
✕ LD 7. Resid & Rest lic
£ B&B £22–£23; HB weekly £192–£202; L £5, D £8; WB £58 (HB); [10% V]
cc Access, B'card/Visa, Diners; dep.

★ **Sandringham,** West Par, LL30 2BD ☎(0492) 76513
Two-storey hotel with outstanding sea view from attractive sun lounge. Closed Xmas.
🛏 18 bedrs, 18 en suite; TV; tcf
🏨 ns; P 6, coach; child facs; con 70
✕ LD 8.30
£ B&B £20–£23; HB weekly £185–£205; L £6·50, D £9; [5% V Nov–May]
cc Access, B'card/Visa; dep.

★ C **Sunnymede,** West Par, West Shore, LL30 2BD ☎(0492) 77130

White building with panelled bar-lounge. Sea and mountain views.
🛏 18 bedrs, 15 en suite, 1 ba; TV
🏨 dogs; P 18, child facs
✕ LD 7.30. Rest lic
£ B&B (double) £44–£57; HB weekly £144–£205; L £5, D £9·50; WB £22 (HB); [10% V]
cc Access, B'card/Visa; dep.

Grand, Happy Valley Road, LL30 2LR ☎(0492) 76245
Hotel awaiting inspection

St George's, St George's Pl, LL30 2LG ☎(0492) 77544 Tx: 61520
Hotel under refurbishment, awaiting inspection
(*See advertisement on p. 645*)

Banham House (Acclaimed), 2 St Davids Rd, LL30 2UL ☎(0492) 75680. *Hotel.*
£ B&B £14–£16; HB weekly £140–£154; [10% V Oct–Jun]

Britannia (Acclaimed), 15 Craig-y-Don Par, LL30 1BG ☎(0492) 77185. *Hotel.*

Bulle Hill (Acclaimed), 46 St Mary's Rd, LL30 2UE ☎(0492) 76972. *Private Hotel.* Open Mar–Dec.

Wa

£ B&B £13·50–£19·50; HB weekly £112–£147; [5% V]
Concord (Acclaimed), 35 Abbey Road, LL30 2EH, ☎(0492)75504. *Private Hotel*
Cornerways (Acclaimed), St David's Pl, LL30 2UG ☎(0492) 77334. *Hotel*. Open Easter–Oct.
£ B&B £23; HB weekly £175
Kinmel (Acclaimed), Central Promenade, LL30 1AR ☎(0492) 76171. *Hotel*. Es. Open 1 Mar–30 Oct & 23 Dec–1 Jan.
£ B&B £15–£18; HB weekly £140–£160; [10% V Mar–May]
Lynwood (Acclaimed), Clonmel St, LL30 2LE ☎(0492) 76613. *Hotel*.
£ B&B £22–£26; HB weekly £134–£165
Mayfair (Acclaimed), 4 Abbey Rd, LL30 2EA ☎(0492) 76170. *Private Hotel*. Open Easter–Oct.
£ B&B £16·50; HB weekly £160
Mayville (Acclaimed), 4 St David's Rd, LL30 2UL ☎(0492) 75406. *Private Hotel*.
£ B&B £24; HB weekly £150; [5% V w/d]
Northgate (Acclaimed), Central Promenade ☎(0492) 77701. *Hotel*.
Orotava (Acclaimed), 105 Glen-y-Mor Rd, Penrhyn Bay, LL30 3PH ☎(0492) 49780. *Private Hotel*. Fr
£ B&B £16·50–£19; [10% V]
Warwick (Acclaimed), 56 Church Walks, LL30 2HL ☎(0492) 76823. *Hotel*. Closed Jan & Dec.
£ B&B £14–£17·50; HB weekly £126–£150; [5% V mid Sep–mid Jul]
White Court (Acclaimed), 2 North Parade, LL30 2LP ☎(0492) 76719. *Hotel*.
White Lodge (Acclaimed), Central Promenade, LL30 1AT ☎(0492) 77713. *Hotel*. Open Mar–Nov.
£ B&B £17·50–£21·50; HB weekly £150·50–£175; [5% V Mar–Apr, Oct–Nov]
Wilton (Acclaimed), South Parade, LL30 2LN ☎(0492) 78343. *Hotel*.

Brannock, 36 St David's Rd, LL30 2UH ☎(0492) 77483. *Hotel*. Closed mid Dec–mid Jan.
£ B&B £11–£12; HB weekly £94–£102; [10% V]
Brigstock, 1 St David's Pl, LL30 2UG ☎(0492) 76416. *Private Hotel*. Closed Dec.
£ B&B £11–£12; HB weekly £109–£116; [10% V weekly, 5% V (3 nts)]
Carmel, 17 Craig-y-Don Par, LL30 1BG ☎(0492) 77643. *Hotel*. Open Easter–mid Oct
£ B&B £10·50–£16; HB weekly £105–£122·50
Cleave Court, 1 St Seiriol's Rd, LL30 2YY ☎(0492) 77849. *Private Hotel*.
Cumberland, North Par, LL30 2LP ☎(0492) 76379. *Hotel*.
Hen Dy, 10 North Pde, LL30 2LP ☎(0492) 76184. *Hotel*.
Karden, 16 Charlton St, LL30 2AN ☎(0492) 879347. *Hotel*.
£ B&B £10·50–£13; [5% V Oct–May]
Kenmore, 28 Trinity Ave, LL30 2SJ ☎(0492) 77774. *Private Hotel*. Open 1 April–31 Oct.
£ B&B £12·50–£15; HB weekly £114–£132; [10% V Apr–Jun & Oct]
Mayfield, 19 Curzon Rd, Craig-y-Don, LL30 1TB ☎(0492) 77427. *Hotel*.
Minion, 21 Carmen Sylva Rd, LL30 1EQ ☎(0492) 77740. *Hotel*. Open Easter–end Oct.
£ B&B £10–£12·50; HB weekly £108·50–£129·50; [5% V Apr–Oct]
Montclare, 4 North Par, LL30 2LP ☎(0492) 77061. *Hotel*. Open Mar–Nov.
£ B&B £13–£14·50; HB weekly £120–£130
Rosaire, 2 St Seiriols Rd, LL30 2YY ☎(0492) 77677. *Private Hotel*. Open Mar–Oct.
£ B&B £10·50–£13·50; HB weekly £92–£149; [5% V]
St Hilary, Craig-y-Don Par, Promenade, LL30 1BG ☎(0492) 75551. *Private Hotel*. Closed Dec.
£ B&B (double) £24–£29; HB weekly, £119–£136·50
Seaforth, 6 Neville Cres, Central Promenade, LL30 1AT ☎(0492) 76784. *Hotel. Snooker.*
Spindrift, 24 St David's Rd, LL30 2UL ☎(0492) 76490. *Guest House*. Closed Xmas.
£ B&B £16–£18 (£2 extra for 1 nt stay); HB weekly £140–£154; [10% V 2 nts min]
Tilstone, Carmen Sylva Rd, Craig-y-Don, LL30 1EQ ☎(0492) 75588. *Hotel*.
£ B&B £12; HB weekly £115
Wedgwood, 6 Deganwy Av, LL30 2YB ☎(0492) 77450. *Private Hotel*.
Westbourne, 8 Arvon Av, LL30 2DY ☎(0492) 77450. *Private Hotel*.
Westdale, 37 Abbey Rd, LL30 2EH ☎(0492) 77996. *Hotel*. Open Mar–Oct.
£ B&B fr £11; HB weekly fr £105

LLANDUDNO JUNCTION

Gwynedd. Map 28C3
Colwyn Bay 4, London 227, Bangor 16, Betws-y-Coed 16, Llandudno 3½.
EC Wed. **Golf** Caernarfon 18h, Conwy 18h.

★★ **Station,** Conwy Rd, LL31 9NE ☎Deganwy (0492) 81259
Beside A55, red brick hotel with black and white gables. Opposite station.

LLANELLI

Dyfed. Map 18C1
Pop 30,000. Neath 16, London 201, M4 Motorway 5, Carmarthen 16, Brecon 47, Llandovery 29, Swansea 11.
EC Tue. **MD** Thur, Sat. **Golf** Ashburnham 18h. **See** Parc Howard Mansion.

★★★ **Diplomat,** Ael-y-Bryn, Felin-Foel, SA15 3PJ ☎(0554) 756156
Fax: (0554) 751649
Well-furnished hotel in an attractive early 19th century building. Indoor swimming pool, sauna, solarium, gymnasium. It, Es
23 bedrs, 23 en suite; annexe 8 bedrs, 8 en suite; TV; tcf
lift, dogs; P 200, coach; child facs; con 250
✕ LD 9.45
£ B&B £46–£50 (w/e £32), B&B (double) £56–£60; L £10·95, D £14; WB; [10% V Jan–Nov]
cc Access, Amex, B'card/Visa, Diners.
(*See advertisement on p. 645*)

★★★ **Stradey Park,** Furnace, SA15 4HA ☎(0554) 758171 Tx: 48521
Elegant house set in a high position overlooking the town. Po (THF)
80 bedrs, 80 en suite; TV; tcf
lift, dogs, ns; P 120, coach; child facs; con 400
✕ LD 9.30
£ B&B £50, B&B (double) £55; HB weekly £203–£224; L £8·95, D £12·50; WB £32
cc Access, Amex, B'card/Visa, CB, Diners, dep.

★ **Miramar,** 158 Station Rd, SA15 1YU ☎(0554) 754726.
Two-storey hotel conveniently placed in town centre next to station. Es, Po
9 bedrs, 1 en suite; TV; tcf
P 6, coach, con 45
✕ LD 10, nr Mon–Sat lunch & Mon & Sun dinner.
£ B&B £14, B&B (double) £24; [10% V] dep.

LLANFAIRPWLLGWYNGYLL

Gwynedd. Map 28B3
Pop 2,840. Menai Bridge 2, London 242, Bangor 4, Caernarfon 7½, Holyhead 15.
EC Thur. **Golf** Bangor.

★★★ **Carreg Bran,** Church La, LL61 5YH ☎(0248) 714224 Tx: 61464
Fax: (0248) 715983
Elegant white house in the Welsh style. Magnificent woodland setting.
29 bedrs, 29 en suite, annexe 4 bedrs, 4 en suite; TV; tcf
TV, dogs; P 100, coach, child facs, con 150
✕ LD 10
£ B&B £46·20, B&B (double) £68·75; L £8·25, D £15·25; WB £90·20 (HB)
cc Access, Amex, B'card/Visa, Diners, dep.
(*See advertisement on p. 645*)

LLANFYLLIN

Powys. Map 29A1
Pop 1,252. Welshpool 11, London 181, Bala 21, Dolgellau 31, Shrewsbury 26.
Golf Welshpool 18h.
Council Offices ☎(069 184) 8868

★★ **Bodfach Hall,** Y-Parc, SY22 5HS ☎(069 184) 272

Small country house in 4 acres of gardens. Putting, fishing. Open Mar–Nov.
9 bedrs, 9 en suite; TV; tcf
dogs; P 20, child facs
✕ LD 8.45, bar meals only Mon–Sat lunch, Sun dinner
£ B&B £27·50, B&B (double) £55; HB weekly £225; L £8·75, D £13·50
cc Access, Amex, B'card/Visa, Diners; dep.

Cyfie Farm (Acclaimed), Llanfihangel, SY22 5JE. ☎(069 184) 451.
£ B&B £15–£18; HB weekly £126–£156

LLANGAMMARCH WELLS

Powys. Map 19B3
Pop 300. Builth Wells 8, London 179, Brecon 17, Llandovery 15, Rhayader 18.
EC Wed. **Golf** Builth Wells 9h. **See** Cefn Brith Farm.

Atlas Section
Consult the Atlas section at the back of the guide to find out which towns and villages have RAC Appointed and Listed hotels in them. They are shown on the maps by purple circles.

EC *early closing* **MD** *market day* *country house hotel* *ns (NS) no smoking areas* *tcf tea/coffee facilities*

Llandudno (Gwynedd)

H for Hospitality

TAN LAN

HOTEL

** RAC

Gt. Orme's Road
West Shore, Llandudno,
Gwynedd LL30 2AR
Tel: (0492) 860221

Elegant 2 star licensed hotel, all rooms at ground or first floor level with private facilities, colour TV, tea/coffee equipment. Central heating. Spacious lounges, Well stocked cocktail bar, fine dining room serving excellent cuisine. Private parking. Highly recommended.

Llandudno (Gwynedd)

LLANDUDNO,
GWYNEDD LL30 2LG
Tel:(0492) 77544
TELEX: 61520
FAX: 0492-78477

WE'RE NEARER THAN YOU THINK (1 hour Liverpool or Manchester Airport)

For you we have retained the elegance and style of a golden age and combined it with the needs of today's lifestyles to create the hotel we know you desire.

Sympathetically restored and elegantly furnished you can choose one of our suites or 87 en-suite bedrooms with satellite colour television, tea and coffee making facilities and 24 hour room service.

Our new à la Carte Restaurant offers the finest cuisine. With two separate bars, coffee shop and in-house Health Hair and Beauty Centre, you can be sure of a relaxing break.

SPECIAL DRAGON BREAKS AVAILABLE

Llanelli (Dyfed)

THE DIPLOMAT HOTEL

Felinfoel, Llanelli, Dyfed. Tel: 0554 756156 Fax: 0554 751649

Family owned and managed, this quality hotel with commendable rooms is very popular with businessmen. 31 bedrooms with private facilities. Recent upgrading has provided a new leisure and functions complex.

Wa

Llanfairpwllgwyngyll (Gwynedd)

CARREG BRAN HOTEL

Church Lane, Llanfairpwllgwyngyll, Isle of Anglesey, Gwynedd LL61 5YH. Tel: 0248 714224

Privately owned hotel situated in country setting close to banks of Menai Straits. Recently refurbished to high standard. 33 rooms en-suite with normal facilities. Functions/Conferences up to 150.
Centrally located for Anglesey and North Wales Coast Area.

⚘ ★★★ H C R Lake, LD4 4BS
☎(059 12) 202 Fax: (059 12) 457

Mock-Tudor style building in quiet surroundings, overlooking golf course. Tennis, fishing, billiards. ⚒ Fr. Open Feb–end Dec.
🛏 19 bedrs, 19 en suite; TV
🏠 dogs, ns; child facs; con 50
✕ LD 8.45, bar meals only Mon–Sat lunch. Resid lic
£ B&B £65, B&B (double) £85–£105; L £10·50, D £19·50
cc Access, Amex, B'card/Visa; dep.

LLANGEFNI Gwynedd. Map 28B3

Bangor 11, London 248, Amlwch 14, Beaumaris 12, Holyhead 16.

⚘ ★★★ H C Tre-ysgawen Hall, Capel Coch, LL77 7UR ☎(0248) 750750
Fax: (0248) 750035.

Victorian country mansion with spacious rooms carefully decorated and furnished in keeping, set in 3 acres of landscaped gardens. Indoor swimming pool. ⚒ Fr
🛏 19 bedrs, 19 en suite; TV
🏠 dogs, P 110, coach, child facs, con 120
✕ LD 9.30
£ B&B £52·75–£146, B&B (double) £105–£152; L £8·50, D £15·95
cc Access, Amex, B'card/Visa.
(*See advertisement on p. 647*)

★★ Nant yr Odyn, Llanfawr LL77 7YE
☎(0248) 723354

Converted 18th century farm buildings forming an L-shaped hotel and art centre complex.

LLANGOLLEN Clwyd. Map 29A2

Pop 3,117. Shrewsbury 29, London 184, Corwen 10, Mold 19, Ruthin 15, Welshpool 28, Whitchurch 23, Wrexham 11.
EC Thur. **Golf** Llangollen 18h. **See** Vale of Llangollen, Parish Church of St Collen, 14th cent bridge, Plas Newydd (home of "Ladies of Llangollen"), Pontcysyllte Aqueduct, Dinas Bran Castle ruins.
ℹ Town Hall. ☎(0978) 860828

⚘ ★★★ R Bryn Howel, LL20 7UW (2¾ m E on A539) ☎(0978) 860331
Imposing late-Victorian brick building with large modern extension. Superb views. Fishing, sauna/solarium.

★★★ Hand, Bridge St, LL20 8PL ☎(0978) 860303 Tx: 61160

Modernised 18th century coaching inn overlooking River Dee. Fishing. (MtCh)
🛏 59 bedrs, 59 en suite, TV, tcf
🏠 dogs, P 60, coach, child facs, con 100
✕ bar meals only Mon–Sat lunch
£ B&B £37·50, B&B (double) £60; HB weekly £225; L £6·50, D £10·50
cc Access, Amex, B'card/Visa, Diners.

★★★ Royal, Bridge St, LL20 8PG ☎(0978) 860202 Fax: (0978) 861824

17th century building in spectacular riverside setting. Fishing. (THF)
🛏 33 bedrs, 33 en suite; TV; tcf
🏠 dogs, ns; P 20, coach; child facs; con 60
✕ LD 9, bar meals only Mon–Sat lunch
£ B&B £43–£48, B&B (double) £49–£54; HB weekly £210–£275; L £7·50, D £10; WB £34
cc Access, Amex, B'card/Visa, Diners.

★★ Ty'n-y-Wern, Shrewsbury Rd, LL20 7PH ☎(0978) 860252

Pleasantly modernised hotel on A5. In own grounds amidst beautiful scenery. Fishing.
🛏 12 bedrs, 12 en suite, 1 ba; TV; tcf
🏠 dogs, ns; P 50, coach; child facs; con 25

LLANGURIG Powys. Map 19B4.

Pop 500. Rhayader 9½, London 186, Aberystwyth 25, Dolgellau 44, Newtown 18.
Golf Llanidloes 9h.

★★ R Glansevern Arms, Pant Mawr, SY18 6SY ☎(055 15) 240
Beautifully situated hotel with fine views of River Wye. Closed 10 days Xmas.
🛏 7 bedrs, 7 en suite; TV; tcf
🏠 dogs; P 30
✕ LD 8, bar meals only Mon–Sat lunch & Sun dinner
£ B&B £35–£40, B&B (double) £50–£55; HB weekly £230–£250; L £11 (Sun), D £16; WB (2 nts HB)

LLANGYNOG Powys. Map 29A2

Penybontfawr 3, London 186, Bala 13, Llanwddyn 9, Oswestry 17, Shrewsbury 32.

★ New Inn, Oswestry, SY10 0EX ☎Pennant (069 174) 229

Family-run country inn in beautiful mountain scenery; pony trekking arranged.
🛏 7 bedrs, 2 en suite, 2 ba
🏠 TV, dogs; P 20, coach; child facs

LLANIDLOES Powys. Map 19B4

Pop 2,381. Newtown 14, London 205, Aberystwyth 30, Dolgellau 39, Rhayader 12.
Golf St Idloes 9h.
ℹ Longbridge St. ☎ (055 12) 2605

★ Red Lion, Longbridge St, SY18 6EE
☎(055 12) 2270
Privately-owned and run, town centre public house with bedrooms.
🛏 6 bedrs, 6 en suite; TV; tcf.
🏠 dogs, ns; P 10, U2, coach, con
✕ LD 9
£ room £25, double room £40; Bk £3·50, L £5·50, D £7·50; [5% V]
cc Access, B'card/Visa.

LLANRUG Gwynedd. Map 28B3

Llanberis 3, London 235, Bangor 10, Betwys-y-Coed 19, Caernarfon 4, Porthmadog 18.

⚘ ★★★ C Seiont Manor, LL55 2AQ
☎(0286) 673366
A transformation has been wrought here. The original farm buildings are now a charming country house hotel. Indoor swimming pool, sauna, fishing.
🛏 28 bedrs, 28 en suite; TV; tcf
🏠 dogs, ns; P 60, coach, child facs; con 100
✕ LD 10
£ B&B £60, B&B £80–£125; L £9·50, D £14·50; WB £45 (HB); [10% V]
cc Access, Amex, B'card/Visa, Diners, dep.

EC *early closing* **MD** *market day* ⚘ *country house hotel* *ns (NS) no smoking areas* *tcf tea/coffee facilities*

Llangefni (Anglesey)

TRE-YSGAWEN HALL – THE ISLE OF ANGLESEY *Set in the heart of Anglesey sits a Pearl, surrounded by Woodland, Landscaped Gardens and having a magnificent view over the Mountains of Snowdonia, Tre-Ysgawen Hall oozes peace and tranquillity, yet under that cosy façade emits efficiency, wonderful food, caring service by a youthful and dedicated team of professional hoteliers.*

Deluxe bedrooms with every facility expected. As with the 19th century building goes 19th century service – a Shoe Cleaning service – put your shoes outside your door at night, Nightly Turn-down, Porters to carry bags to and from the car, a car parking facility. Fax, typing and secretarial service. Reception to take one, personally, to the room. 24 hour room service. **Food, French Style,** *skillfully created on a daily changing selection of menus, by an artistic and imaginative team of Chefs, producing generous portions of delectable food largely from locally grown produce ensuring freshness and quality enhanced by light, eye-catching sauces. A fine List of Wines, specially selected to complement the cuisine, and served by staff who care in the Conservatory Dining Room with its stunning black decor. Cocktail Bar with young ladies in Laura Ashley style dresses to attend to table service. Afternoon Teas served in the comfort of the Sitting Room. The magnificent Hall, in Winter with its large, open hearth fireplace. In Summer the light thrown through the huge glass dome above.*

For care and attention – **Tre-Ysgawen Hall –** ***The Country House of North Wales.***

TRE–YSGAWEN HALL

Capel Coch, Llangefni, Isle of Anglesey, North Wales, LL77 7UR

Telephone: 0248 750750 Fax: 0248 750035

RAC★★★, Wales Tourist Board 4 Crowns Highly Recommended, Egon Ronay, Ashley Courtenay, Signpost, Martell Collection.

Llanrwst (Gwynedd)

GOOD FOOD COSY LOG FIRES AMIDST A TRANQUIL SETTING

Idyllically located in the heart of the Conwy Valley, close to the Snowdonia National Park. ***Maenan Abbey*** *provides the perfect base for a relaxing break or overnight stay. With its 'olde worlde charm' winter log fires, cosy atmosphere and fine cuisine made from local fresh produce, the Abbey offers a welcome retreat from the pressures of modern life.*

Just beyond the relaxing gardens, you'll find no less than 7 golf courses, superb ramblers countryside, fishing, pony-trekking, shooting, dry-slope skiing and the famous ***Bodnant Gardens****. In fact, the whole area is steeped in history and fun to explore.*

Each of the charming bedrooms features private bathroom and all modern comforts. Our friendly caring staff make sure your stay is a pleasure from start to finish.

For a copy of our brochure and details of our ***super value rates****, write or phone today*

BARGAIN BREAKS ALL YEAR ROUND

MAENAN ABBEY HOTEL

★ ★ ★

Maenan, Llanrwst, Gwynedd, LL26 OUL

Telephone: **(0492 69) 247/230** Fax (0492 69) 734

FH

FEDRICK HOTELS *More than just hotels*

Also at: Hotel 70° Penmaenhead, Old Colwyn, Colwyn Bay, Clwyd. Telephone (0492) 516555

See ad for Hotel 70 on page 648

Wa

LLANRWST Gwynedd. Map 28C3

Pop 3,000. Corwen 23, London 218, Bala 24, Betws-y-Coed 4, Colwyn Bay 14, Denbigh 20, Llandudno 15, Rhyl 22, Ruthin 27.
EC Thur. **MD** Tue. **Golf** Betws-y-Coed 9h.

★★★ Maenan Abbey, Maenan, LL26 0UL Dolgarrog (049 269) 247

Historic stone building in magnificent Conwy Valley; all modern amenities. Fishing.
15 bedrs, 15 en suite; TV
P 50, coach; child facs; con
(*See advertisement on p. 647*)

★★★ Plas Maenan, Maenan, LL26 0YR Dolgarrog (0492) 660232

Large sensitively converted country house with well-equipped bedrooms. Mature grounds of 15 acres.
15 bedrs, 15 en suite; TV; tcf
dogs, P 80, coach; child facs; con 100
LD 9
£ B&B £24–£32, B&B (double) £44–£56; HB weekly £210–£230; L £6·95, D £13·50; WB £65; [5% V]
cc Access, B'card/Visa, dep.

★★ Eagles, Ancaster Sq, LL26 0LG (0492) 640454
Imposing building in the Market Place. Privately-owned and run hotel. Fishing, sauna, solarium, gymnasium, snooker.
12 bedrs, 12 en suite; TV; tcf
TV, dogs, ns; P 50, coach; child facs; con 150

★★ Meadowsweet, Station Rd, LL26 0DS (0492) 640732
Small hotel with well-equipped bedrooms. Overlooks Conwy Valley.
10 bedrs, 10 en suite, 2 ba; TV
dogs; ns; P 10; child facs
LD 9.30, nr lunch in low season. Resid & Rest lic
£ B&B £38–£50, B&B (double) £55–£80; L £9·95, D £19·75; WB £45 (HB); [10% V]
cc Access, B'card/Visa; dep.

LLANTWIT MAJOR South Glamorgan.

Map 4A4
Pop 8,776. Cardiff 15, London 164, Bridgend 9½, Caerphilly 21, Pontypridd 19.

★★ C West House, West St, CF6 9SP (0446) 792406

Well-maintained, traditional stone-built house close to castle ruins.
20 bedrs, 18 en suite, 2 ba; TV; tcf
dogs, ns; P 50, coach; child facs; con 70

LLANWNDA Gwynedd. Map 28B3

Caernarfon 3½, London 244, Betws-y-Coed 27, Holyhead 33, Porthmadog 17, Pwllheli 17.
Golf Caernarfon 18h. **See** Caernarfon Bay.

★★★ Stables, LL54 5SD (0286) 830711 Fax: (0286) 830413
Converted and extended stable block with well-equipped bedrooms. Swimming pool.
14 bedrs, 14 en suite; TV; tcf
dogs; P 40, child facs; con 100
LD 9.45. Resid & Rest lic
£ B&B £36–£41 (w/e £30), B&B (double) £54–£64; L £6·50, D £12·95
cc Access, Amex, B'card/Visa.

LLANWRTYD WELLS Powys. Map 19A3

Pop 500. Builth Wells 13, London 185, Brecon 24, Llandovery 11, Knighton 36, Newtown 44, Rhayader 21.
EC Wed. **Golf** Builth Wells 9h.

★ Neuadd Arms, LD5 4RB (059 13) 236
Attractive mid-19th century 3-storey inn set in centre of village.
18 bedrs, 8 en suite, 4 ba; TV; tcf
TV, dogs; P 10, coach; child facs
LD 9, bar meals only lunch
£ B&B £18; HB weekly £200; D £9·50; WB £52; [10% V]
cc B'card/Visa; dep.

Lasswade House (Highly Acclaimed), LD5 4RW (059 13) 515. *Hotel.*
£ B&B £32–£34; HB weekly £230–£240; WB; [10% V Oct–Apr]

LLANWYDDYN Powys. Map 29A1

Welshpool 19, London 191, Bala 17, Machynlleth 27, Oswestry 24.

★★★ Lake Vyrnwy, (Postal: via Oswestry, Shropshire), SY10 0LY (069 173) 692 Fax: (069 173) 259

Completely refurbished Victorian black and white timbered country house high up above Lake Vyrnwy. Fishing, tennis.
30 bedrs, 30 en suite; TV
dogs; P 70, coach; child facs; con 30
LD 9.15
£ B&B £39·75, B&B (double) £45·50–£95·50; L £8·25, D £16·75, WB £35·25
cc Access, Amex, B'card/Visa, Diners.

LLECHRYD Dyfed. Map 18B3

Newcastle Emlyn 7½, London 230, Cardigan 3, Fishguard 17.

★★★ Castell Malgwyn, Cardigan. SA43 2QA (023 987) 382

Georgian house set in 40 acres between two rivers. Swimming pool, putting, fishing.
23 bedrs, 22 en suite, 1 ba; TV; tcf
dogs, P 60, coach; child facs; con 200
LD 9
£ B&B £32–£33, B&B (double) £76–£78; HB weekly £243–£250; L £8·25, D £9·25
cc Access, Amex, B'card/Visa, Diners.
(*See advertisement on p. 650*)

LLYSWEN Powys. Map 19B3

Pop 150. Brecon 9, London 159, Abergavenny 21, Builth Wells 12, Hereford 29, Leominster 30.
Golf Brecon 9h, Cradoc 18h. **See** Church.

★★★★ Llangoed Hall, LD3 0YP (0874) 754525
A Grade 1 listed building, designed by Sir Clough Williams-Ellis, with panoramic views. Aims to re-create the atmosphere of an Edwardian country house. Tennis, fishing.
23 bedrs, 23 en suite; TV
£ B&B £85, B&B (double) £105–£195; L £15·50, D £32·50; WB fr £120 (HB)

MACHYNLLETH Powys. Map 28C1

See also EGLWYSFACH and PENNAL.
Pop 1,904. Newtown 28, London 205, Aberdyfi 10, Aberystwyth 17, Dolgellau 15.
EC Thur. **MD** Wed. **Golf** Machynlleth 9h.
See Owain Glyndwr Institute, Plas Machynlleth, Castlereagh Memorial Clock.
i Canolfan Owain Glyndwr. (0654) 2401

★★ Dolguog Hall, SY20 5UJ (0654) 702244

17th century building in beautiful grounds overlooking Dovey Valley. Fishing.
9 bedrs, 9 en suite, TV; tcf

EC *early closing* **MD** *market day* *country house hotel* *ns (NS) no smoking areas* *tcf tea/coffee facilities*

🏨 ns; P 50, coach; child facs; con 120
✕ LD 9, bar meals only Mon–Sat lunch
£ B&B £30–£36, B&B (double) £26–£31; D £12
cc Access, B'card/Visa, Diners; dep.

★★ **Wynnstay Arms,** Maengwyn St, SY80 8AE ☎(0654) 702941
New owners are updating this attractive white-faced building in prominent position in Market Place.
🛏 20 bedrs, 20 en suite; TV; tcf

🍺🍺 **White Lion,** Heol Pentrerhedyn, SY20 8ND ☎(0654) 703455. *Inn.*
Fax: (0654) 703746 ⚒ De
Charming old coaching inn right in the town centre by the clock tower.
🛏 9 bedrs, 6 en suite, 1 ba, TV; tcf
🏨 dogs, P 45, coach, child facs
✕ LD 9
£ B&B £20–£30, B&B (double) £37–£52; WB £55·95
cc Access, Amex, B'card/Visa, Diners.

Maenllwyd, Newton Rd, SY20 8EY ☎(0654) 702928. *Guest House.*
£ B&B £16·50–£18; [10% 5% V]

MANORBIER
Dyfed. Map 18B1

Pop 350. Tenby 5, London 244, Pembroke 6.
Golf Tenby 18h. **See** 12th cent Castle, 12th cent Parish Church.

★★ **Castle Mead,** SA70 7TA ☎(0834) 871358
Two-storey stone building in semi-rural surroundings; fronted by lawns and trees.
Open Mar–Oct. ⚒ Fr
🛏 5 bedrs, 5 en suite, annexe 3 bedrs, 3 en suite, TV; tcf.
🏨 dogs, ns; P 20; child facs
✕ LD 8. Resid & Rest lic
£ B&B £36; HB weekly £225; D £9; WB £65 (2 nts)
cc Access, Amex, B'card/Visa; dep.

MENAI BRIDGE
Gwynedd. Map 28B3

Pop 2,300. Bangor 2½, London 240, Caernarfon 8, Holyhead 21.
EC Wed. **MD** Mon. **Golf** Baron Hill, Beaumaris 9h.

★★ **Anglesey Arms,** LL59 5EA ☎(0248) 712305

Attractive gabled historic building set in secluded gardens. Fine views.

★★ **Gazelle,** Glyn Garth, LL59 5PD ☎(0248) 713364
Attractive white-faced building, beautifully situated on edge of Menai Straits.
🛏 9 bedrs, 5 en suite, 3 ba; TV; tcf
🏨 P 40, coach; child facs; con 25
✕ LD 9
£ B&B £25·50–£27·50, B&B (double) £38·50–£49
cc Access, B'card/Visa.

MERTHYR TYDFIL
Mid Glamorgan. Map 19B2

Pop 42,000. Tredegar 7½, London 162, Brecon 18, Caerphilly 16, Hirwaun 6, Llandovery 31, Newport 26, Pontypridd 12.
EC Thur. **MD** Tue, Sat. **Golf** Cilsanws 9h.
ℹ 14a Glebeland St ☎(0685) 79884

★★★ **Baverstock,** Heads of the Valley Rd, CF44 0LX ☎(0685) 6221 Fax: (0685) 723670

Stylish, purpose-built modern hotel overlooking the Brecon Beacons. Billiards.
🛏 53 bedrs, 53 en suite; TV; tcf
🏨 TV, P 100, coach; child facs, con 300
✕ LD 10. Resid & Rest lic
£ B&B £45 (w/e £34), B&B (double) £55; D £12·50
cc Access, Amex, B'card/Visa, Diners, dep.

★★ **Castle,** Castle St, CF47 8UX ☎(0685) 722327
Modern 5-storey hotel in town centre.
🛏 51 bedrs, 51 en suite; TV; tcf

★★ H C **Tregenna,** Park Terr, CF47 8RF ☎(0685) 723627 Fax: (0685) 721951 ♿

Family run hotel in residential area. White-painted building with modern extension.
🛏 14 bedrs, 14 en suite; annexe 7 bedrs, 7 en suite; TV; tcf
🏨 TV; dogs; P 25, coach; child facs; con 60
✕ LD 10
£ B&B £33–£35, B&B (double) £43–£46; L £7, D £8·50; WB £52; [10% V w/e]
cc Access, Amex, B'card/Visa; dep.

MILFORD HAVEN
Dyfed. Map 18A2

Pop 13,750. Haverfordwest 7, London 250, Pembroke 8, Tenby 17.
EC Thur. **MD** Fri. **Golf** Milford Haven 18h.

★★ **Lord Nelson,** Hamilton Terr; SA73 3AL ☎(0646) 695341 Tx: 48622
Fax: (0646) 692274
Overlooking the waterfront, a fine 3-storey Georgian hotel. Associations with Nelson.
🛏 26 bedrs, 26 en suite, annexe 5 bedrs, 5 en suite; TV; tcf
🏨 TV, dogs, ns; P 26, coach; child facs; con 40
✕ LD 9.30
£ B&B £41, B&B (double) £65; L £6·10, D £12·70; [10% V w/e]
cc Access, Amex, B'card/Visa, Diners.
(*See advertisement on p. 650*)

Belhaven House, 29 Hamilton Terr, SA73 3JJ ☎(0646) 695983. *Hotel.*
£ B&B £18·35–£26·45; HB weekly £176·30–£225·40; [10% V]

MISKIN
Mid Glamorgan. Map 19B1

M4 (jn 34) 1, London 155, Bridgend 11, Cardiff 8.

★★★ C **Miskin Manor,** CF7 8ND ☎(0443) 224204. Fax: (0443) 237606
Victorian manor house with spacious rooms, set in 20 acres of gardens and woodland overlooking the River Ely. Indoor swimming pool, squash, sauna, solarium, gymnasium, billiards.
🛏 32 bedrs, 32 en suite, TV.
🏨 dogs; ns, P 100, coach, child facs, con 150
✕ LD 9.45, nr Sat lunch. Resid & Rest lic
£ B&B £77–£92, B&B (double) £104–£109; [5% V w/d]
cc Access, Amex, B'card/Visa, Diners; dep.

MOLD
Clwyd. Map 29A3

Pop 8,860. Wrexham 11, London 191, Chester 11, Corwen 21, Denbigh 16, Llangollen 19, Queensferry 6½, Ruthin 10.
EC Thur. **MD** Wed, Sat. **Golf** Mold 18h.
ℹ Town Hall, Earl St. ☎(0352) 59331

★★★ **Arches,** Bryn Offa La, New Brighton, CH7 6RQ
Modern hotel, featuring an arched brick facade, 1½ miles NE of Mold, just off A494.
🛏 62 bedrs, 62 en suite; TV; tcf

★★ **Bryn Awel,** Denbigh Rd, CH7 1BL ☎(0352) 58622 Fax: (0352) 58625

Former dwelling house with purpose-built annexe; spacious lounge, bar and buttery.
🛏 7 bedrs, 7 en suite; annexe 10 bedrs, 10 en suite; TV; tcf
🏨 dogs, ns; P 40, coach; child facs; con 50
✕ LD 10.15, bar meals only Sun dinner
£ B&B £30, B&B (double) £44–£50; L £7·95, D £7·95; [10% V]
cc Access, B'card/Visa.

Old Mill (Acclaimed), Melin-y-Wern, Denbigh Road, Nannerch, CH7 5RH ☎(0352) 741542. *Guest House*
£ B&B £19·75–£28·60; [10% V Oct–Mar]

MONMOUTH
Gwent. Map 20A2

See also WHITEBROOK.
Pop 7,350. Gloucester 24, London 129, Abergavenny 15, Chepstow 16, Hereford 17, Newport 22, Pontypool 20, Ross-on-Wye 10.
EC Thur. **MD** Mon, Sat. **Golf** Monmouth 9h.
See Castle ruins (birthplace of Henry V).
ℹ Shire Hall ☎(0600) 3899

★★★ **King's Head,** Agincourt Sq, NP5 3DY ☎(0600) 2177 Tx: 497294
Fax: (0600) 3545

Llechryd (Dyfed)

Merthyr Tydfil (Mid-Glamorgan)

Milford Haven (Dyfed)

Mold (Clwyd)

Fine gabled building in town square. Dates from 17th century. Fr, De
29 bedrs, 27 en suite, (2 sh), 2 ba; TV
dogs; P 30, coach; child facs; con 200
LD 9
£ B&B £56, B&B (double) £80; D £12·50; WB £95 (HB); [10% V]
cc Access, Amex, B'card/Visa, Diners.

Queens Head, St James St., NP5 3DL
(0600) 2767 *Inn*.

MORFA NEFYN Gwynedd. Map 28A2

Pop 850. Porthmadog 19, London 247, Aberdaron 12, Caernarfon 21, Pwllheli 7.
EC Wed. **Golf** Morfa Nefyn 18h.

★★ Woodlands Hall, Edern, LL53 6JB
Nefyn (0758) 720425
In 7 acres of beautiful grounds, a small Georgian house. Billiards. Fr
13 bedrs, 7 en suite (2 sh), 2 ba, tcf
TV, dogs; ns; P 100, coach, child facs, con 90
LD 9. Resid lic
£ B&B £22; L £8, D £13; WB £56; [5% V]

MUMBLES West Glamorgan. Map 19A1

Pop 13,712. Swansea 3½, London 193, Carmarthen 29, Llanelli 13.
EC Wed. **Golf** Langland Bay 18h, Clyne 18h.

★★★ Norton House, Norton Rd, SA3 5TQ
(0792) 404891 Fax: (0792) 403210

Extended Georgian house with pillared entrance set in well-kept gardens. Views of Swansea Bay. Putting, sauna, solarium.
15 bedrs, 15 en suite; TV; tcf
P 40, no children under 8; con 20
LD 9.30, nr lunch
£ B&B £50–£60, B&B (double) £65–£75; D £17·50; [10% w/e]
cc Access, Amex, B'card/Visa, Diners.

★ Old School House, Nottage Road, Newton SA3 4TJ (0792) 361541

Charming stone building, once the school, in the village of Newton close to Langland Bay.
7 bedrs, 7 en suite, TV; tcf
dogs, P 30, coach, child facs, con 75
LD 10, bar meals only Sat. Resid & Rest lic
£ B&B £40, B&B (double) £50; HB weekly £200; D £12·95; WB £40 (HB) [10% V];
cc Access, Amex, B'card/Visa

★ St Anne's, Western La, SA3 4EY
Swansea (0792) 369147 Tx: 498450
Fax: (0222) 374671

A small modern hotel with a view over Swansea Bay. Snooker.
24 bedrs, 16 en suite, 2 ba; annexe 4 bedrs, 2 en suite, 1 ba; TV; tcf
TV, dogs; P 50, coach; child facs; con 100
LD 9, bar meals only Sun dinner. Resid lic
£ B&B £23–£28, B&B (double) £38–£42; L £7, D £7; WB £25; [10% V]
cc Access, B'card/Visa; dep.

Shoreline, 648 Mumbles Rd, Southend, SA3 4EA Swansea (0792) 366233

NEATH West Glamorgan. Map 19A1

Pop 15,125. Hirwaun 16, London 184, M4 3, Bridgend 17, Llandovery 16, Llanelli 16, Swansea 7½.
EC Thur. **MD** Wed. **Golf** Neath 18h.

★★ Castle, The Parade, SA11 1RB
(0639) 643581 Tx: 48119
Fax: (0639) 641624

Refurbished, 17th century coaching inn. In town centre. Sauna, solarium. (Lns)
28 bedrs, 28 en suite; TV; tcf
TV, dogs; ns; P 30, coach; child facs; con 120
LD 10.30
£ B&B £56, B&B (double) £69; L £8·50, D £13·50; WB £44; [10% V]
cc Access, Amex, B'card/Visa, Diners.

★★ Cimla Court, Cimla Rd, SA11 3TT
(0639) 645656
Converted mid-Victorian house, with modern hotel block. Small gardens.
24 bedrs, 24 en suite, TV; tcf
dogs; P 100; child facs; con 200
LD 9.30, nr Sat lunch & Sun dinner
£ B&B £35, B&B (double) £49; L £10·75, D £10·75
cc Access, Amex, B'card/Visa, Diners.

Europa, 32 Victoria Gdns, SA11 3BH
(0639) 635094. *Hotel*. Closed Xmas.
£ B&B £15; [5% V]

NEFYN Gwynedd. Map 28A2

Pop 1,150. Porthmadog 17, London 247, Aberdaron 13, Caernarfon 19, Pwllheli 6½.
EC Wed. **Golf** Morfa Nefyn 18h. **See** St Mary's Church, now Maritime Museum.

★★ C Nanhoron Arms, Ffordd, Dewi Scent, LL53 6EA (0758) 720203
Gabled town-centre hotel, recently refurbished with attractive furnishings and decor.
19 bedrs, 19 en suite, TV; tcf

★ Caeau Capel, Rhodfa'r Mor, LL53 6EB
(0758) 720240

Converted house in pleasant grounds close to beach. Putting, tennis. Open Easter–Oct.
20 bedrs, 10 en suite, 3 ba; tcf
TV, dogs; P, coach; child facs
LD 7.30, bar meals only lunch. Resid & Rest lic
£ B&B £15·25–£20; HB weekly £128–£170; D £10·25; WB £65·50
cc Access, B'card/Visa; dep.

NEWBRIDGE-ON-WYE Powys. Map 19B3

Pop 297. Hereford 45, London 175, Builth Wells 6½, Knighton 22, Leominster 37, Llandovery 23, Rhayader 7½.
EC Thur. **Golf** Llandrindod Wells 18h. **See** All Saints' Church, River Wye.

★ New Inn, LD1 6HY (059 789) 211
Attractive small Tudor inn set in a little village. Swimming pool.

NEWPORT Gwent. Map 19C1

Pop 135,000. Chepstow 15, London 137, M4 Motorway 1, Abergavenny 18, Caerphilly 11, Cardiff 12, Monmouth 22, Pontypool 9.
MD Weekdays. **Golf** Tredegar Park 18h, Caerleon 9h. **See** Norman Castle ruins (13th cent), St Woolos Cathedral, Museum and Art Gallery, Murals at Civic Centre, Transporter Bridge, Double View (Ridgeway), Roman Amphitheatre and relics in Museum at Caerleon 3m N, Caerleon Priory.
i Museum, John Frost Sq. (0633) 842962

★★★★ Celtic Manor, Coldra Woods, NP6 2YA (0633) 413000, Fax: (0633) 412910

19th century stone building, surrounded by well established lawns and trees. Indoor swimming pool, sauna, solarium, gymnasium. Fr
73 bedrs, 73 en suite; TV
lift, P 150, coach; child facs; con 350

Wa

✕ LD 10.30
£ L £14, D £18; WB £55 (HB); [10%]
cc Access, Amex, B'card/Visa, Diners.

★★★ **Hilton National,** The Coldra, NP6 2YG ☎ (0633) 412777 Tx: 497205 Fax: (0633) 413087

Modern hotel in a woodland setting just off the M4. Indoor swimming pool, sauna, gymnasium. (HN) Fr, Es
119 bedrs, 119 en suite; TV; tcf
dogs, ns; P 300, coach; child facs; con 500
✕ LD 11, bar meals only Sat lunch
£ B&B £78·25–£91·25, B&B (double) £103·50–£119·50; L £5·50, D £9·90; WB £37; [10% V]
cc Access, Amex, B'card/Visa, CB, Diners.

★★★ **Kings,** High St, NP9 1QU ☎ (0633) 842020 Tx: 497330 Fax: (0633) 244667

Opposite railway station, substantial1 5-storey building with a well-furnished and spacious lounge. Closed 26–31 Dec.
47 bedrs, 47 en suite; TV; tcf
lift, ns; P 20, G 10, coach; child facs; con 230
✕ LD 9.30, nr Sat lunch, Sun dinner
£ B&B £57 (w/e) £24; B&B (double) £67; L £8·95, D £11·45; WB £34; [5% V w/d]
cc Amex, B'card/Visa, Diners.
(*See advertisement below*)

★★★ **Westgate,** Commercial St, NP1 1TT, ☎ (0633) 244444
Jacobean inn–restored and modernised but retains character
69 bedrs, 69 en sute, TV; tcf.
lift; dogs, P 12, coach, child facs, con 150
✕ LD 10, bar meals only Sat lunch
£ B&B £55, B&B (double) £65; L £6·95, D £10·75
cc Access, Amex, B'card/Visa, CB, Diners

★★ **Newport Lodge,** 147 Bryn Bwan, NP9 5QN ☎ (0633) 821818
Three-storey, purpose-built hotel on hill overlooking M4 to west of town.
27 bedrs, 27 en suite; TV; tcf

NEW QUAY Dyfed. Map 18C3

Pop 1112. Lampeter 19, London 222, Aberystwyth 24, Cardigan 18, Carmarthen 29.
ℹ Church St ☎ (0545) 580865

Park Hall (Highly Acclaimed), Cwmtydu, Cardigan Bay, SA44 6LG ☎ (0545) 560306
£ B&B £25–£30; HB weekly £245–£280

Ty Hen Farm (Acclaimed), Llwyndafydd, Llandysul, SA44 6BZ ☎ (0545) 560346.
Guest House. Sauna, solarium, gymnasium. Open 14 Feb–15 Nov. Fr

NEWTOWN Powys. Map 19B4

Pop 5,517. Ludlow 32, London 175, Aberystwyth 43, Builth Wells 34, Rhayader 32, Welshpool 13.
EC Thur. **MD** Tue. **Golf** St Giles 9h. **See** Robt Owen's grave, Owen Memorial Museum, Textile Museum.
ℹ Central Car Park ☎ (0686) 625580

★★ **Elephant and Castle,** Broad St, SY16 2BQ ☎ (0686) 626271
Adjacent to River Severn, 3-storey building with attractive wrought iron balcony. Fishing.
25 bedrs, 25 en suite; TV; tcf
dogs; P 70, coach; child facs; con 250

NOLTON HAVEN Dyfed. Map 18A2

Haverfordwest 7, London 250, Fishguard 16, Pembroke 15, St David's 10.

★★ **Mariners,** Haverfordwest, SA62 3NH ☎ Camrose (0437) 710469

Across road from beach, 3-storey stone building with pleasant garden.

NORTHOP Clwyd. Map 29A3

Pop 2,600. Mold 3, London 194, Chester 12, Colwyn Bay 29, Queensferry 5, Rhyl 19.
Golf Mold 18h. **See** Parish Church.

★★★ **Gwesty Chequers,** Chester Rd, Northop Hall, CH7 6HJ ☎ (0244) 816181 Tx: 617112 Fax: (0244) 814661

Refurbished Victorian manor house with modern extension. In 40 acres of grounds.
27 bedrs, 27 en suite; TV; tcf
dogs; ns; P 100, U 2, G 2, coach; child facs; con 120
✕ LD 9.30

£ B&B £45–£50, B&B (double) £60–£80; L £5·50, D £13·50; WB £60 (HB); [10% V] cc Access, Amex, B'card/Visa.
(*See advertisement on p. 650*)

NOTTAGE Mid Glamorgan. Map 19A1

Bridgend 6, London 173, Cardiff 26, Swansea 17.

★★ Rose and Crown, Heol-y-Capel, CF36 3ST ☎ (065 671) 4850

Two-storey, stone-built traditional inn in centre of village. (BCB)
🛏 8 bedrs, 8 en suite; TV; tcf
🏠 ns; P 15, coach; child facs
✕ LD 9.15
£ B&B £41, B&B (double) £54·50; L £8·15, D £8·15; WB £27·50; [10% V]
cc Access, Amex, B'card/Visa, Diners.

OLD COLWYN Clwyd. Map 28C3

Mold 29, London 221, Colwyn Bay 1, Denbigh 18, Queenferry 33, Rhyl 10.

★★ Lyndale, Abergele Rd, LL29 9AB ☎ Colwyn Bay (0492) 515429

Hotel in attractive Edwardian building conveniently situated off A55. ✈ Fr, Es, Po
🛏 14 bedrs, 14 en suite, TV; tcf
🏠 dogs, ns P 20, coach, child facs, con 50
✕ LD 9.30, bar meals only Mon–Sat lunch
£ B&B £29·50, B&B (double) £47; D £12·50, WB £64·50; (HB); [10% V]
cc Access, Amex, B'card/Visa; dep

PEMBROKE Dyfed. Map 18B1

Pop 5,500. Carmarthen 32, London 244, Cardigan 37, Haverfordwest 19 (Fy 10), Tenby 10.
EC Wed. **Golf** South Pembrokeshire 9h.
ℹ Drill Hall ☎ (0646) 682148

★★★ Court, Lamphey, SA71 5NT ☎ (0646) 672273 Tx: 48587 Fax: (0646) 672480

Modernised country mansion with elegant portico. Set in 12 acres. Indoor swimming pool, sauna, solarium, gymnasium. ✈ Fr
🛏 22 bedrs, 22 en suite; annexe 8 bedrs, 8 en suite; TV; tcf
🏠 dogs; P 50, coach; child facs; con 100
✕ LD 9.45, bar meals only lunch
£ B&B £48–£58; B&B (double) £84–£95; HB weekly £294–£392; D £15; WB £42 (HB)
cc Access, Amex, B'card/Visa, Diners; dep.

★★ Coach House Inn, Main St, SA71 4HN ☎ (0646) 684602 Fax: (0646) 687456 ♿

Attractive black and white building situated on main road through town. Solarium.
🛏 14 bedrs, 14 en suite; TV; tcf
🏠 dogs, ns; P 8, coach; child facs; con 20
✕ LD 9, bar meals only lunch
£ B&B £33, B&B (double) £46; HB weekly £160–£175; D £12·50; WB £55 (2 nts); [10% V]
cc Access, Amex, B'card/Visa, Diners; dep.

★★ Hollyland Country House, Holyland Rd, SA71 4PP ☎ (0646) 681444
An attractive Georgian manor house in 5 acres of gardens on outskirts of town.
🛏 12 bedrs, 12 en suite, TV; tcf
🏠 dogs; P 50, coach; child facs; con 60
✕ LD 9.15. Resid & Rest lic
£ B&B £30, B&B (double) £50; L £6·75, D £10·95; WB £56; [5% V]
cc Access, B'card/Visa.

★★ Lamphey Hall, Lamphey, SA71 5NR ☎ (0646) 672394

Cream-painted period building with an attractive garden, 1½ miles west of town on road to Tenby.

★★ Milton Manor, Milton, SA70 8PG ☎ Carew (0646) 651398 Fax: (0646) 651897

Three-storey Georgian manor house in 2½ acres of secluded grounds. Putting.
🛏 18 bedrs, 18 en suite, TV; tcf
🏠 TV, dogs; P 40, G 4, coach; child facs, con 40
✕ LD 9. Resid & Rest lic
£ B&B £33·50–£39, B&B (double) £48·40–£54·40; HB weekly £387–£429; D £12; WB £58; [10% excl Jun–Aug]
cc Access, B'card/Visa; dep.

★★ Wheeler's Old Kings Arms, Main St, SA72 4UQ ☎ (0646) 683611
3-storey late Georgian coaching inn situated in town centre. Closed 25 Dec & 1 Jan.
🛏 20 bedrs, 20 en suite
🏠 dogs, P 21; child facs
✕ LD 10
£ B&B £25–£30, B&B (double) £38–40; L £8·50, D £10·50; [5% V]
cc Access, Amex, B'card/Visa.

PENARTH South Glamorgan. Map 4B4

Pop 22,500. Cardiff 4, London 153, Bridgend 22.
EC Wed. **Golf** Glamorganshire 18h. **See** Turner House Art Gallery, St Peter's Church, Penarth Head.

★ R Walton House, Victoria Rd, CF6 2HY ☎ (0222) 707782 Fax: (0222) 711012

Edwardian, mock-Tudor house in quiet residential area. ✈ Es
🛏 12 bedrs, 9 en suite, 2 ba; TV; tcf
🏠 P 16
✕ LD 9, nr Sun. Resid & Rest lic
£ B&B £21–£25·50, B&B (double) £35–£39; L £9·50, D £9·50
cc Access, B'card/Visa.

Westbourne, 8 Victoria Road, CF6 2EF ☎ (0222) 707268. *Hotel.*
£ B&B £17–£21; [5% V]

PENMAEN West Glamorgan. Map 18C1

M4 (jn 47) 9½, London 207, Horton 4, Swansea 7.

★★ Nicholaston House, Nicholaston, Gower, SA3 2HL ☎ (0792) 371317
Peaceful country hotel in own grounds with views over Oxwich Bay. Putting, snooker.
🛏 11 bedrs, 11 en suite; TV; tcf
🏠 TV, dogs, ns; P 30, coach; child facs; con 120
✕ LD 9, bar meals only lunch. Resid & Rest lic
£ B&B £16–£30, B&B (double) £32–£65; D £9·40
cc Access, B'card/Visa; dep.

PENNAL Gwynedd (Powys). Map 28C1

Pop 180. Machynlleth 4, London 209, Dolgellau 18.
EC Wed. **MD** Wed. **Golf** Aberdovey 18h. **See** Roman Fort.

Wa

🏠 ★★ **Llugwy Hall Country House,** SY20 9JX ☎(065 475) 228

Beautiful Elizabethan mansion in own grounds overlooking River Dovey.

PENYBONT Powys. Map 19B3

New Radnor 9, London 166, Builth Wells 12, Hereford 34, Rhayadar 10.
Golf Llandrindod Wells 18h. **See** Pottery.

★★ **Severn Arms,** LD1 5UA ☎(059 787) 224

'Olde worlde' coaching inn with oak beams. On main A44. Fishing. Closed Xmas week.
🛏 10 bedrs, 10 en suite; TV; tcf
🏠 TV, dogs; P 50, coach; child facs
✕ LD 9, bar meals only Mon–Sat lunch
£ B&B £24; HB weekly £180; D £9; [10% V]
cc Access, B'card/Visa.

PORTHCAWL Mid Glamorgan. Map 19A1

Pop 15,300. Bridgend 5½, London 174, Neath 16, Swansea 18.
EC Wed. **Golf** Royal Porthcawl 18h, Pyle and Kenfig 18h. **See** 13th cent St John's Church (Newton).
ℹ Old Police Station, John St. ☎(065 671) 6639

★★★ **Seabank,** The Promenade, CF36 3LU ☎(065 671) 2261 Tx: 497797 Fax: (065 671) 5363
Substantial building in prime position away from town centre. Fine sea views. Sauna, solarium, gymnasium.
🛏 62 bedrs, 62 en suite; TV; tcf
🏠 lift, TV, dogs, ns; P 150, coach; child facs; con 396
✕ LD 11
£ B&B £63, B&B (double) £76; L £8·95, D £14; WB £54; [10% V]
cc Access, Amex, B'card/Visa, Diners.

★★ **Brentwood,** Mary St, CF36 3YN ☎(065 671) 2725
Three-storey stone building pleasantly set in residential area near seafront.
🛏 22 bedrs, 22 en suite, TV; tcf
🏠 TV, dogs; P 12, coach; child facs; con 46
✕ LD 10, bar meals only Sun dinner
£ B&B £24–£30, B&B (double) £36–£42; HB weekly £150–£180; L £5·95, D £8·50; WB £46–£52 (HB); [5% V]
cc Access, Amex, B'card/Visa, Diners; dep.

★★ **Glenuab,** Mary St, CF36 3YA ☎(065 671) 8242

Privately-owned hotel offering modern accommodation. In pleasant residential area near seafront. 🎾, Fr, De
🛏 18 bedrs, 18 en suite; TV; tcf
🏠 TV, ns; P 12; child facs
✕ LD 10, nr Sun
£ B&B £37·50, B&B (double) £45·60; HB weekly £275; L £6·50, D £8·75; WB £51·75; [5% V]
cc Access, Amex, B'card/Visa, Diners.

★★ **Seaways,** Mary St, CF36 3YA ☎(065 671) 3510

Two-storey white stone building pleasantly situated off main promenade.
🛏 16 bedrs, 9 en suite, 2 ba; TV; tcf
🏠 TV, dogs; coach
✕ LD 9.45
£ B&B £15–£24, B&B (double) £30–£36; D £4–£10; WB £30 (2 nts)
cc Access, B'card/Visa; dep.

★ H **Lorelei,** Esplanade Av, CF36 3YU ☎(0656) 712683
Victorian-style building in a quiet road just off the Promenade.
🛏 15 bedrs, 15 en suite; TV; tcf
🏠 child facs, con 36

Collingwood, 40 Mary St, CF36 3YA ☎(065 671) 2899. *Hotel.*
Oakdale, 46 Mary St, CF36 3YA ☎(065 671) 3643
Penoyre, 29 Mary St, CF36 3YN ☎(065 671) 4550. *Private Hotel.*
£ B&B £13–£14; HB weekly £130–£140.
Summerfield, 44 Esplanade Av, ☎(0656) 715685
Villa, 27 Mary St, CF36 3YN ☎(065 671) 5074. *Guest House.*
£ B&B £13; HB weekly £112–£154

> **Residents only**
> Some Listed hotels only serve meals to residents. It is always wise to make a reservation for a meal in a hotel.

PORTHKERRY South Glamorgan. Map 4A4

Llandaff 11, London 160, Barry 4, Llantwit Major 8½.

🏠 ★★★ C **Egerton Grey,** CF6 9BZ ☎Barry (0446) 711666 Fax: (0446) 711690

Victorian rectory with some antique furniture set in 7 acres of gardens. Only 1 mile from Cardiff airport. Tennis. 🎾 Fr, De
🛏 10 bedrs, 10 en suite; TV; tcf
🏠 ns; P 40; con 30, children over 12.
✕ LD 9.45. Resid lic
£ B&B £45–£95 (w/e £27·50), B&B (double) £55–£110; HB weekly £295; L £14·75, D £24·50; WB £190; [10% V]
cc Access, Amex, B'card/Visa; dep.

PORTHMADOG Gwynedd. Map 28B2

Pop 2,000. Bala 29, London 228, Betws-y-Coed 23, Caernarfon 19, Dolgellau 20, Pwllheli 13.
EC Wed. **MD** Fri. **Golf** Porthmadog and Borth-y-Gest 18h. **See** Terminus of Ffestiniog Narrow Gauge Rly, Black Rock Sands.
ℹ High St. ☎(0766) 512981

★★ **Madoc** Market Sq, Tremadoc, LL49 9RB ☎(0766) 512021

Attractive period hotel dating back to 1770, situated on side of square.
🛏 21 bedrs, 4 en suite, (5 sh), 3 ba; tcf

★★ **Plasgwyn,** Pentrefelin, LL52 OPT ☎(0766) 522559 Fax: (0766) 523200
Privately owned converted house with modern extension
🛏 14 bedrs, 14 en suite, TV; tcf
🏠 TV, dogs; P 60, coach, child facs con 150
✕ LD 9. Resid & Rest lic
£ B&B £19·50–£21·50, B&B (double) £38–£42; L £7, D £11; WB £55
cc Access. Amex, B'card/Visa, Diners; dep.

★★ **Tyddyn Llwyn,** Black Rock Rd, LL49 9UR ☎(0766) 3903
Modern purpose-built, well-equipped hotel enjoying good views. Riding.

PORTMEIRION Gwynedd. Map 28B2

Penrhyndeudraeth 4, London 228, Betwys-y-Coed 24, Caernarfon 24, Dolgellau 26.

★★★ **C** **Portmeirion,** LL48 6RC ☎(0766) 7702281 Tx: 61540 Fax: (0766) 771331

Famous hotel in Sir Clough Williams-Ellis' Italian-style village, right beside the sea. Swimming pool, tennis. Fr, It. Closed 14 Jan–8 Feb
14 bedrs, 14 en suite, annexe 20 bedrs, 20 en suite, TV; tcf.
ns; P 100; child facs, con 100
✕ LD 9.30, coffee shop only Mon lunch
£ B&B £47·50–£92·50, B&B (double) £65–£110; HB weekly £371–£511; L £13·50, D £22·50
cc Access, Amex, B'card/Visa, Diners; dep.

PORT TALBOT W. Glamorgan. Map 19A1

Pop 42,143. Bridgend 12, London 180, M4 Motorway 2, Neath 5½, Swansea 8.
EC Wed. **MD** Tue, Sat. **Golf** Maesteg 9h.

★★★ **Aberafan Beach,** Aberavon SA12 6QP ☎(0639) 884949 ♿
On sea front, overlooking Swansea Bay, 3-storey modern brick building. Fr
66 bedrs, 66 en suite, TV; tcf
Lift, dogs, P 200, coach, child facs, con 500
✕ LD 10.15, bar meals only, Mon–Sat lunch
£ B&B £45 (w/e £21·50), B&B (double) £49; D £10; WB £63 (2 nts HB); [10% V]
cc Access, Amex, B'card/Visa, Diners, dep.

★★ **Twelve Knights,** Margam Rd, SA13 2DB ☎(0639) 882381
Small hotel conveniently located just off junction 38 of the M4.
11 bedrs, 11 en suite; TV; tcf
dogs, ns; P 100, coach; child facs; con 150

PRESTEIGNE Powys. Map 19C3

Pop 1,330. Leominster 12, London 151, Builth Wells 21, Hereford 23, Knighton 6, Ludlow 16, Rhayader 26.
EC Thur. **Golf** Knighton 9h.
i Old Market Hall ☎(0544) 260193

★★ **C** **Radnorshire Arms,** High St, LD8 2BE ☎(0544) 267406. Fax: (0544) 260418

Former private house, a fine example of Elizabethan magpie' architecture. (THF)
8 bedrs, 8 en suite; annexe 8 bedrs, 8 en suite; TV; tcf
dogs, ns; P 26, coach; child facs; con 30
✕ LD 9
£ B&B £59–£69, B&B (double) £81–£91; L £7·50, D £12·50; WB £47
cc Access, Amex, B'card/Visa, CB, Diners, dep.

RAGLAN Gwent. Map 19C2

Pop 1,800. Chepstow 13, London 136, Abergavenny 9, Monmouth 8, Newport 16, Pontypool 12.
Golf Monmouth 9h. **See** Ruins of Castle.

★★ **Beaufort Arms,** High St, NP5 2DY ☎(0291) 690412

Pleasant white-painted building, opposite the church.
10 bedrs, 10 en suite; TV; tcf
TV, P 80, coach; child facs; con 200

RED WHARF BAY Gwynedd. Map 28B3

Pop 1,080. Bangor 10, London 246, Caernarfon 15, Holyhead 22.
EC Thur. **Golf** Baron Hill 9h.

★★ **H** **Bryn Tirion,** LL75 8RZ ☎ (0248) 852366 ♿

Attractive gabled building in own grounds overlooking the bay. Open 1 Feb–3 Jan
19 bedrs, 19 en suite, TV; tcf
dogs, P 60, child facs, con 60
✕ LD 9; nr lunch. Resid & Rest lic
£ B&B £30, B&B (double) £50; HB weekly £203–£224; D £11, WB fr £62
cc Access, B'card/Visa; dep.
(*See advertisement on p. 657*)

★ **Min-y-Don,** LL75 8RJ ☎(0248) 852596
Attractive white-faced hotel of charm, beautifully positioned overlooking sandy bay. Open Mar–Oct & winter w/e
17 bedrs, 6 en suite (1 sh), 3 ba; TV; tcf
TV, dogs; P 60, coach; child facs
✕ LD 8.45, bar meals only lunch
cc Access, B'card/Visa; dep.

REYNOLDSTON West Glamorgan. Map 18C1

Swansea 11, London 199, Carmarthen 36, Llanelli 15.

★★ **R** **Fairyhill,** SA3 1BS ☎Swansea (0792) 390139.
18th century manor with own trout stream in 24 acres of parkland. Fishing, sauna. Closed Xmas
11 bedrs, 11 en suite, TV; tcf
dogs; P 50; child facs; con 22
✕ LD 9, nr Mon–Sat lunch & Sun dinner.
£ B&B £65–£75, B&B (double) £75–£85
cc Access, B'card/Visa.

RHOOSE South Glamorgan.

See BARRY.

RHOS-ON-SEA Clwyd.

See COLWYN BAY.

RHYL Clwyd. Map 29A3

Pop 23,000. Queensferry 22, London 212, Colwyn Bay 11, Denbigh 11, Mold 22.
EC Thur. **MD** Wed, Sat. **Golf** Rhyl 9h. **See** Royal Floral Hall, T'yn Rhyl–17th cent house, The Marine Lake Leisure Park, Rhuddlan Castle ruins 2½ m SE.
i Central Promenade. ☎(0745) 355068

★★ **Grange,** East Par, LL18 3AW ☎(0745) 353174 ♿
Attractive black and white gabled building on quiet residential East Promenade.
21 bedrs, 21 en suite; annexe 3 bedrs, 3 en suite; TV; tcf
dogs; P 6, coach; child facs; con 120
✕ LD 9.45
£ B&B £19, B&B (double) £35; HB weekly £140; L £5, D £6·50; WB £65; [10% V]
cc Access, Amex, B'card/Visa; dep.

Arncliffe, 100 Crescent Rd, LL18 1LY ☎(0745) 53634. *Hotel.*
Pier, 23 East Par, LL18 3AL ☎(0745) 350280. *Private Hotel.* De
£ B&B £12–£16; HB weekly £90–£130

ROSSETT Clwyd. Map 29B3

Whitchurch 18, London 181, Chester 7, Mold 11, Nantwich 21, Wrexham 5½

★★★ **Llyndir Hall,** Llyndir La, LL12 0AY ☎(0244) 571648

Early 19th century Strawberry Gothic country house in 2½ acres of gardens. Indoor swimming pool, solarium, gymnasium. De
38 bedrs, 38 en suite; TV
dogs, ns; P 80; coach; child facs; con 140
✕ LD 10
£ D £17·50; WB £98; [10% V]
cc Access, Amex, B'card/Visa, Diners.

ROWEN Gwynedd. Map 28C3

Betwys-y-Coed 12, London 228, Bangor 22, Caernarfon 28, Colwyn Bay 9½, Conway 5.

⚘ ★★ Tir-y-Coed, Conwy, LL32 8TP
☎Tyn-y-Groes (0492) 650219

Small black and white building in acre of landscaped garden. Open Mar–Oct. Restricted Nov–Feb.
🛏 7 bedrs, 7 en suite; TV; tcf
🏨 dogs, ns; P 8; child facs
✕ LD 7.30, nr lunch. Resid & Rest lic
£ B&B £19·25–££22·75, B&B (double) £36–£41·50; HB weekly £177·50–£207·25; D £9·25; WB £51 (2 nts HB, Oct–Apr); [10% V]

RUABON Clwyd. Map 29B2
Pop 5,500. Shrewsbury 27, London 181, Wrexham 5, Oswestry 10, Llangollen 6.
EC Sat. **Golf** Llangollen 18h.

★★ Wynnstay Arms, LL14 6BL ☎(0978) 822187

Stone-built Georgian house pleasantly set in town centre.
🛏 8 bedrs, 2 en suite, TV; tcf
🏨 TV; dogs; P 80, U 2, coach; con 120
✕ LD 9.30, nr Sun dinner
£ B&B £25 (w/e £23), B&B (double) £38; L £5·50, D £7·50; [10% V]
cc Access, Amex, B'card/Visa, Diners.

RUTHIN Clwyd. Map 29A3
Pop 4,338. Wrexham 18, London 196, Betws-y-Coed 25, Corwen 12, Denbigh 7½, Llangollen 15, Mold 10.
EC Thur. **MD** Tue, Thur, Fri. **Golf** Ruthin-Pwllglas 18h. **See** St Peter's Church (black oak roof of 500 panels), Castle.
ℹ Craft Centre. ☎ (082 42) 3992

★★★ Ruthin Castle, Corwen Rd, LL15 2NU ☎(082 42) 2664 Tx: 61169
Fax: (082 42) 5978

Historic (13th century) building offering modern comforts and medieval banquets. Fishing, billiards. ⚒ Fr. Es
🛏 58 bedrs, 58 en suite; TV; tcf
🏨 lift; P 200, coach; child facs; con 140
✕ LD 9.30, bar meals only Mon–Sat lunch
£ B&B £45–£64, B&B (double) £64–£94; HB weekly £269–£304; D £14, WB £82; [10% V]
cc Access, Amex, B'card/Visa, Diners; dep.

★★ Castle, St Peters Sq, LL15 1AA
☎(082 42) 2479

Fascinating Elizabethan and 18th century building offering modern comforts. ⚒ Fr. Closed 25 Dec–31 Jan.
🛏 16 bedrs, 16 en suite; TV; tcf
🏨 dogs; ns; P 16, coach, child facs, con 40
✕ LD 8.45, bar meals only lunch
£ B&B £32–£37, B&B (double) £48–£60; HB weekly £225; D £13; WB £70–£72; [10% V]
cc Access, Amex, B'card/Visa, Diners.

ST ASAPH Clwyd. Map 29A3
Pop 2,780. Mold 16, London 207, Betws-y-Coed 26, Colwyn Bay 11, Denbigh 5½, Rhyl 5½.
EC Thur. **MD** Thur. **Golf** Rhuddlan 18h.

★★★ Oriel House, Upper Denbigh Rd, LL17 0LW ☎(0745) 582716
Fax: (0745) 582716
Attractive Georgian house with large extension; in own grounds. Snooker. Closed Boxing Day. ⚒ Es
🛏 19 bedrs, 19 en suite; TV; tcf
🏨 dogs; P 200, coach; child facs; con 250
✕ LD 9.30
£ B&B £35–£38, B&B (double) £56–£65; HB weekly £309·40; L £8·50, D £11; WB £88·40
cc Access, Amex, B'card/Visa, Diners.

★★ Plas Elwy, The Roe, LL17 0LT ☎(0745) 582263

Black and white converted coaching inn. At junction of A55 and A525. Closed 26–31 Dec
🛏 7 bedrs, 7 en suite, annexe 6 bedrs, 6 en suite; TV; tcf.
🏨 TV, P 25; child facs
✕ LD 10, nr Mon–Sat lunch & Sun dinner
£ B&B £34·50–£37·50, B&B (double) £47–£53; D £12; WB £66; [10% V Sep–Apr]
cc Access, Amex, B'card/Visa, Diners.

ST CLEARS Dyfed. Map 18B2
Pop 1,170. Carmarthen 9, London 221, Cardigan 23, Haverfordwest 21, Pembroke 23, Tenby 17.
EC Wed. **MD** Tue. **Golf** Tenby 18h.

Black Lion, ☎(0994) 230700. *Hotel. Billiards.*

ST DAVID'S Dyfed. Map 18A2
Pop 1,759. Haverfordwest 15, London 259, Fishguard 17.
Golf St David's 9h. **See** Cathedral, Bishop's Palace ruins.
ℹ City Hall. ☎(0437) 720392.

⚘ ★★★ Warpool Court, SA62 6BN
☎(0437) 720300 Fax: (0437) 720676

Three-storey grey stone building, in extensive grounds. Views of sea. Swimming pool, tennis, sauna, gymnasium. ⚒ Fr, De
🛏 25 bedrs, 25 en suite, TV; tcf
🏨 dogs; P 100, coach; child facs; con 60
✕ LD 9.15
£ B&B £36–£50, B&B (double) £60–£96; L £12·50, D £20; WB £83 (2 nts HB)
cc Access, Amex, B'card/Visa, Diners.

★★ Old Cross, Cross Sq, SA62 6SP
☎(0437) 720387

In the square, a fine Georgian building with later extension. Open Mar–4 Nov.
🛏 17 bedrs, 17 en suite; TV; tcf
🏨 dogs, ns; P 20; child facs
✕ LD 8.30, bar meals only lunch
£ B&B £23–£28, HB weekly £205–£470; D £12; [10%]
cc Access, B'card/Visa, CB, Diners; dep.

★★ St Non's, Catherine St, SA62 6RJ
☎(0437) 720239. Fax: (0437) 721839

Charming 2-storey building in traditional Welsh style. Near to Cathedral. ⚒ Fr
🛏 24 bedrs, 24 en suite, TV; tcf

🏠 dogs, P 60, coach, child facs, con 100
✕ LD 9
£ B&B £33·50–£35·50; HB weekly £295–£325; L £10, D £14·85; WB £41; [10% V]
cc Access, Amex, B'card/Visa

★ **Ocean Haze,** Haverfordwest Rd, SA62 6QN ☎ (0437) 720826 ♿

Small family-run hotel set back from A487 on outskirts of town. Snooker.

Alandale, 43 Nun St, SA62 6NL ☎ (0437) 720333. *Guest House.*
Ramsey House, Lower Moor, SA62 6RP ☎ (0437) 720321. *Guest House.*
£ B&B £15·95–£18·80; HB weekly £136·20–£157·20; [5% V Oct–Apr]
Redcliffe House, 17 New St, SA62 6SW ☎ (0437) 720389. Open Apr–Oct
£ B&B (double) fr £24
Y Glennydd, 51 Nun St, SA62 6NU ☎ (0437) 720576. Open Mar–Dec.
£ B&B £13·50–£16; HB weekly £150·50–£168

SAUNDERSFOOT Dyfed. Map 18B1
Pop 2,500. Carmarthen 23, London 235, Cardigan 29, Fishguard 27, Haverfordwest 17, Pembroke 11, Tenby 3.
EC Wed. **Golf** Tenby 18h.
ℹ The Harbour ☎ (0834) 811411

★★★ **St Brides,** St Brides Hill, SA69 9NH ☎ (0834) 812304 Tx: 48350
Fax: (0834) 813303

Attractive 3-storey gabled building on cliff-top with dramatic sea views. Swimming pool. Closed 1–13 Jan. ⚒ Fr, De
🛏 45 bedrs, 45 en suite; TV; tcf
🏠 dogs; ns; P 70, coach; child facs; con 150
✕ LD 9.15
£ B&B £52–£70, B&B (double) £80–£110; HB weekly £300–£410; L £10·50, D £14·95; WB
cc Amex, B'card/Visa, Diners; dep.

★★ **C** **Cambrian,** Cambrian Terr, SA69 9ER ☎ (0834) 812448
Completely refurbished hotel, with feature conservatory lounge, situated on sea front.
🛏 28 bedrs, 28 en suite, TV, tcf
£ B&B fr £30

★★ **Glen Beach,** Swallow Tree Woods, SA69 9DE ☎ (0834) 813430
Originally a private residence in a woodland area, with outstanding sea view.
🛏 13 bedrs, 13 en suite; TV; tcf
🏠 TV, dogs; P 45, coach; child facs; con 100
✕ LD 8.30, bar meals only lunch
£ B&B £27 (w/e £18), B&B (double) £40–£50; HB weekly £125–£225; D £10; WB £40 (2 nts); [10% V]
cc Access, Amex, B'card/Visa, Diners; dep.

★★ **Rhodewood House,** St Brides Hill, SA69 9NU ☎ (0834) 812200
Fax: (0834) 811863

In 1½ acres overlooking the sea, a well-modernised hotel. Solarium, billiards.
🛏 34 bedrs, 34 en suite; TV; tcf
🏠 dogs, ns; P 50, coach; child facs; con 150
✕ LD 9.30, bar meals only lunch
£ B&B £27–£38, B&B (double) £44–£66; HB weekly £173–£252; D £8·25; WB £48 (2 nts); [10% V]
cc Access, Amex, B'card/Visa, Diners; dep.
(*See advertisement on p. 657*)

Bay View (Acclaimed), Pleasant Valley, Stepaside, SA67 8LR ☎ (0834) 813417. *Swimming pool, putting.* Open Apr–Oct
£ B&B £12–£15·95; HB weekly £110–£140
Gower (Acclaimed), Milford Terr, SA69 9EL ☎ (0834) 813452. *Private Hotel.*
Jalna (Acclaimed), Stammers Rd. SA69 9HH ☎ (0834) 812282. *Solarium.*
£ B&B £18–£20; HB weekly £142–167; [5% Mar–May & Sep]
Merlewood (Acclaimed), St Brides Hill, SA69 9NP ☎ (0834) 812421
Woodlands (Acclaimed) St Brides Hill, SA69 9NP ☎ (0834) 813338. *Private Hotel.*
£ B&B £18; HB weekly £138–£145.

Claremont, St Brides Hill, SA69 9NP ☎ (0834) 813231
Harbour Light, 2 High St, SA69 9EJ ☎ (0834) 813496. *Private Hotel.*
Malin House, St Brides Hill, SA69 9NP ☎ (0834) 812344. *Hotel. Indoor swimming pool.*
Sandy Hill, Tenby Rd, SA69 9DR ☎ (0834) 813165. *Guest House. Swimming pool.* Open Mar–Sep.
£ B&B £12·50; HB weekly £119; [5% V low season]
Springfield, St Brides Hill, SA69 9NP ☎ (0834) 813518. *Guest House.*

SOLVA Dyfed. Map 18A2
Haverfordwest 12, London 256, Fishguard 16, St. David's 3.

Lochmeyler Farm (Highly Acclaimed), Pen-y-Cwm, SA62 6LL ☎ (0348) 837724. *Guest House.* ♿
£ HB weekly £140–£150; [V]

SWANSEA West Glamorgan. Map 19A1
See also LANGLAND BAY and MUMBLES.
Pop 173,150. Neath 7½, London 188, M4 4, Bridgend 20, Brecon 39, Carmarthen 27, Llandovery 35, Llanelli 11.
See Plan, p. 659.
EC Thur. **MD** Sat. **P** See Plan. **Golf** Swansea Bay 18h, Clyne 18h. **See** Civic Centre, Royal Institute of S Wales (Museum), Guildhall, Law Courts, Brangwyn Hall (the British Empire Panels), Glynn Vivian Art Gallery, University, St Mary's Church.
ℹ Singleton St. ☎ (0792) 468321

★★★★ **Dragon,** 39 Kingsway Circle, SA1 5LS ☎ (0792) 651074 Tx: 48309
Fax: (0792) 456044

Imposing modern hotel adjacent to shopping area. Under refurbishment; completion expected March 1991. Indoor swimming pool, sauna, solarium, gymnasium. (THF)
🛏 99 bedrs, 99 en suite; TV; tcf
🏠 lift, dogs, ns; P 50, coach; child facs; con 300
✕ LD 10
£ room £85, double room £95
cc Access, Amex, B'card/Visa, CB, Diners.

★★★ **Dolphin,** Whitewalls, SA1 3AB ☎ (0792) 650011 Tx: 48128
Fax: (0792) 642871
A modern 3-storey stone building set in city centre. ⚒ Fr, Tu
🛏 66 bedrs, 66 en suite; TV; tcf
🏠 lift, dogs; coach; child facs; con 400
✕ LD 9.30, bar meals only Sun lunch
£ B&B £52–£62 (w/e £35), B&B (double) £69; L £5, D £11·50; [10% V w/e]
cc Access, Amex, B'card/Visa, Diners.
(*See advertisement on p. 657*)

★★★ **Fforest,** Pontardulais Rd, Fforestfach, SA5 4DA ☎ (0792) 588711
Tx: 48105 Fax: (0792) 586219
Modern red-brick hotel situated close to A483. Sauna, solarium. (Lns)
🛏 34 bedrs, 34 en suite; TV; tcf
🏠 TV, dogs, P 200, coach; child facs; con 200
✕ LD 11, nr Sat lunch
£ B&B £68, B&B (double) £82; L £8·95, D £14; WB £44; [10%]
cc Access, Amex, B'card/Visa, Diners.

★★★ **Hilton National,** Phoenix Way, Enterprise Park, SA7 9EG ☎ (0792) 310330
Tx: 48589 Fax: (0792) 797535 ♿
Beside lake in enterprise park, a modern hotel with charming garden. Indoor swimming pool, sauna, gymnasium. (HN)
🛏 120 bedrs, 120 en suite; TV; tcf
🏠 dogs, ns; P 150, coach, child facs, con 200
✕ LD 9.45, bar meals only Sat lunch
£ B&B £78–£90, B&B (double) £101–£105; L £8·50, D £13·50; WB £20; [10% V]
cc Access, Amex, B'card/Visa, Diners.

EC *early closing* **MD** *market day* 🏠 *country house hotel* *ns (NS) no smoking areas* *tcf tea/coffee facilities*

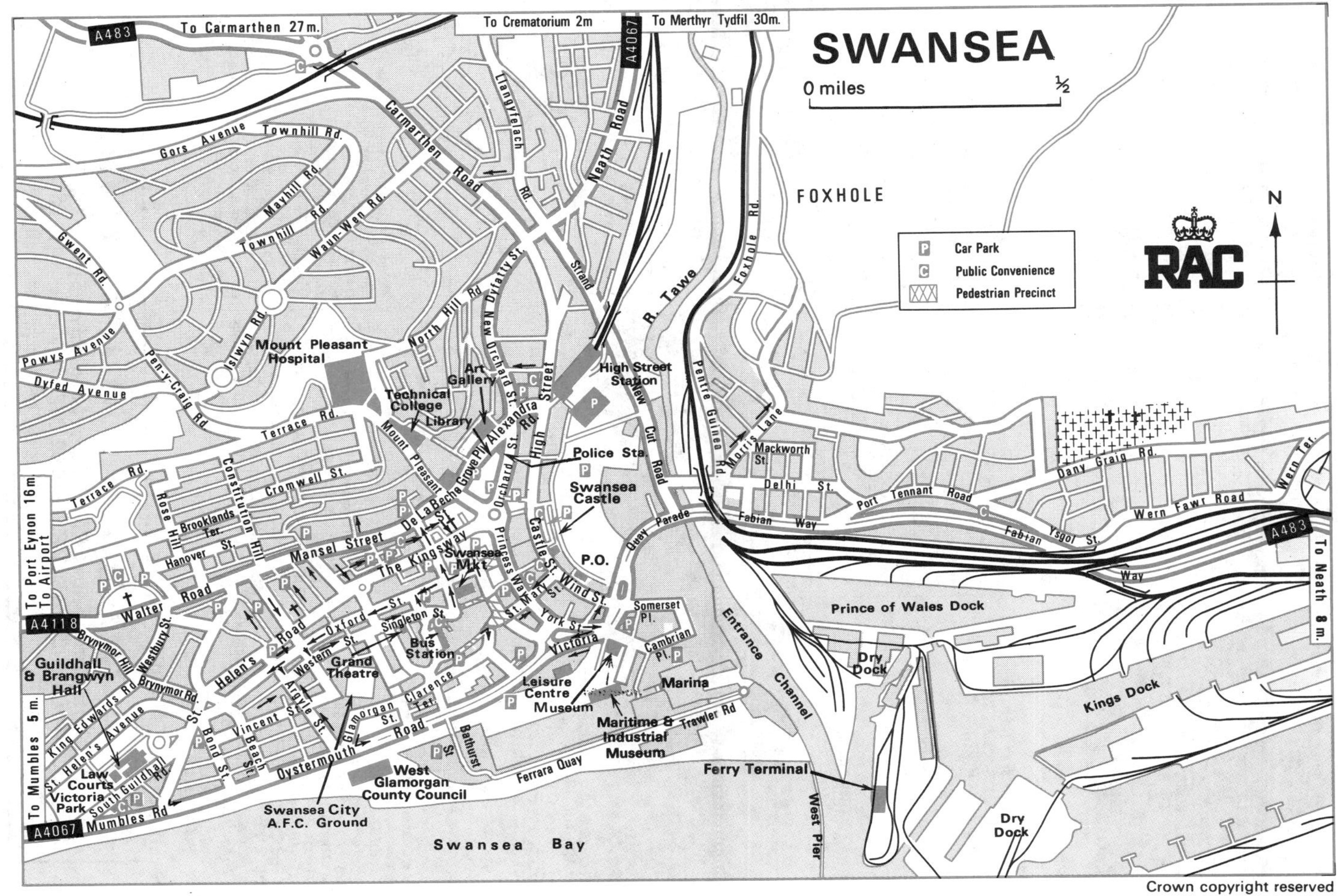

SWANSEA
0 miles
½
RAC
N
P Car Park
C Public Convenience
Pedestrian Precinct
FOXHOLE
To Carmarthen 27 m.
A483
To Crematorium 2m
A4067
To Merthyr Tydfil 30m.
To Neath 8 m.
A483
To Port Eynon 16 m
To Airport
A4118
To Mumbles 5 m.
A4067
Gors Avenue
Townhill Rd.
Carmarthen Road
Llangyfelach Rd.
Neath Road
Mayhill Rd.
Townhill Rd.
Waun-Wen Rd.
Gwent Rd
Islwyn Rd.
Powys Avenue
Dyfed Avenue
Pen-y-Craig Rd.
Mount Pleasant Hospital
North Hill Rd
Dyfatty St.
New Orchard St.
Strand
R. Tawe
Foxhole Rd.
Art Gallery
Technical College
Library
Alexandra Rd.
High Street
High Street Station
New Cut Road
Pentre Guinea Rd.
Morris Lane
Mackworth St.
Delhi St.
Dany Graig Rd.
Wern Ter.
Port Tennant Road
Wern Fawr Road
Fabian Way
Fabian Ysgol St.
Way
Terrace Rd.
Mount Pleasant
Grove Pl.
Orchard St.
Police Sta.
Swansea Castle
Terrace Rd.
Cromwell St.
Constitution Hill
Rose Hill
Brooklands Ter.
De La Beche St.
Hanover St.
Mansel Street
The Kingsway
Swansea Mkt
Princess Way
Castle St.
Quay Parade
P.O.
Wind St.
Walter Road
St. Mary St.
York St.
Somerset Pl.
Prince of Wales Dock
Entrance Channel
Brynymor Hill
Westbury St.
Oxford St.
Singleton St
Bus Station
Victoria
Cambrian Pl.
Dry Dock
Guildhall & Brangwyn Hall
King Edwards Rd
Brynymor Rd.
St. Helen's Road
Western St.
Grand Theatre
Clarence Ter.
Leisure Centre
Museum
Marina
Kings Dock
St. Helen's Avenue
Argyle St.
Glamorgan St.
Vincent St.
Bond St.
Beach St.
Oystermouth Road
Bathurst St
Maritime & Industrial Museum
Trawler Rd
Law Courts
Victoria Park
South Guildhall Rd.
Mumbles Rd
West Glamorgan County Council
Ferrara Quay
Ferry Terminal
Swansea City A.F.C. Ground
Swansea Bay
West Pier
Dry Dock
Crown copyright reserved

★★★ **Holiday Inn,** Maritime Quarter, SA1 3SS ☎(0792) 642020 Tx: 48395 Fax: (0792) 650345

With views over the marina and Swansea Bay, a new five-storey hotel in brown and yellow brickwork. Indoor swimming pool, solarium, gymnasium. (CHIC)
🛏 118 bedrs, 118 en suite, TV; tcf
🏠 lift, dogs, ns; P 122, coach, child facs, con 180
✕ LD 10.30. Resid lic
£ room £74, double room, £83; Bk £6·95, L £12·75, D £13·75; WB £40
cc Access, Amex, B'card/Visa, Diners; dep.

★★ H C **Beaumont,** Walter Rd, SA1 4QA ☎(0792) 643956 Fax: (0792) 643044

Four-storey white painted traditional hotel building in the main thoroughfare.
🛏 17 bedrs, 17 en suite, TV; tcf
🏠 dogs, ns; P 10; con 30
✕ LD 9.30. bar meals only lunch. Resid & Rest lic
£ B&B £45–£56, B&B (double) £55–£78; D £14·50
cc Access, Amex, B'card/Visa, Diners.

★★ **Oaktree Parc,** Birchgrove Rd, Birchgrove, SA7 9JR ☎(0792) 817781 Fax: (0792) 814542
Close to the M4, a red-brick building with bay windows set in a large garden.
🛏 10 bedrs, 10 en suite; TV; tcf
🏠 dogs, P 40, coach; child facs; con 50
✕ LD 10. Resid & Rest lic
£ B&B £37·50, B&B (double) £50; L £6·95, D £15; [5% V]
cc Access, Amex, B'card/Visa, Diners; dep.
(*See advertisement on p. 657*)

★★ H R **Windsor Lodge,** Mount Pleasant, SA1 6EG ☎(0792) 642158 Fax: (0792) 648996

An 18th century stone building situated close to town centre. Sauna. Fr
🛏 19 bedrs, 15 en suite, 4 ba; TV; tcf
🏠 dogs; P 25, U 1 (£2), child facs; con 25
✕ LD 9, nr lunch Sun & Mon dinner
£ B&B £28·75–£36·80, B&B (double) £42·55–£51·75; D £16·50; [5% V w/e]
cc Access, Amex, B'card/Visa, Diners.

★ **Parkway,** Cower Rd, Sketty, SA2 9JL ☎(0792) 201632

In quiet residential area on west side of city, a cream-rendered building on hill. Closed 25 Dec–1 Jan.
🛏 15 bedrs, 15 en suite, TV; tcf
🏠 TV, dogs, P 20, child facs
✕ LD 8, nr lunch. Rest lic
£ B&B £35, B&B (double) £44; HB weekly £170; D £7·50; WB £48 (2 nts HB); [5% V w/e]
cc Access, Amex, B'card/Visa, Diners; dep.

Campanile, Pentre Guinea Rd. *See Motor Lodge section*

Tredillion House (Highly Acclaimed), 26 Uplands Cres, Uplands, SA2 0PB ☎(0792) 470766. *Hotel.*
£ B&B £31–£35; HB weekly £212–£290; [5% V w/e]

Alexander (Acclaimed), 3 Sketty Rd, Uplands, SA2 0EU ☎(0792) 470045. *Private Hotel.*
The Guest House (Acclaimed), 4 Bryn Rd, Brynmill. SA2 OAR ☎(0792) 466947.
£ B&B £10
Winston (Acclaimed), 11 Church La, Bishopston Valley, Bishopston. SA3 3JT ☎Bishopston (044 128) 2074. *Private Hotel. Indoor swimming pool, sauna, billiards.*
£ B&B £17–£25

Coynant Farm, Felindre SA5 7PU ☎(0269) 5640. *Riding.*
Crescent, 132 Eaton Cres, Uplands, SA1 4QR ☎(0792) 466814. *Guest House.*
Tregare, 9 Sketty Rd, Uplands, SA2 0EU ☎(0792) 470608. *Hotel. Billiards.*
Uplands Court, 134 Eaton Crescent, Uplands, SA1 4QS ☎(0792) 473046.
Wittenberg, 2 Rotherslade Rd, SA3 4QN ☎(0792) 69696

TALSARNAU Gwynedd. Map 28B2

Dolgellau 28, London 235, Betws-y-Coed 26, Porthmadog 7

★★ H C **Maes-y-Neuadd,** LL47 6YA. ☎(0766) 780200
A centuries-old Welsh granite manor house tastefully decorated and furnished in period style. Set in 7½ acres of grounds.
🛏 16 bedrs, 16 en suite, TV
🏠 dogs, ns; P 50, no children under 7; con 14
✕ LD 9.15. Resid & Rest lic
£ B&B £40, B&B (double) £90–£118; HB weekly £430–£525; L £14, D £23·50; WB £57·50
cc Access, Amex, B'card/Visa, Diners; dep.

TAL-Y LLYN Gwynedd. Map 28C1

Pop 300. Newtown 38, London 215, Aberdyfi 13, Aberystwyth 27, Dolgellau 9.
See Talyllyn railway.

★★ **Tynycornel,** LL36 9AJ ☎Abergynolwyn (0654) 77282

Attractive modernised hotel on banks of lake. Swimming pool, fishing, sauna, solarium.
🛏 6 bedrs, 6 en suite; annexe 9 bedrs, 9 en suite; TV; tcf
🏠 dogs; P 60, child facs; con 30
✕ LD 9.30
£ B&B £34·50–£44·50, B&B (double) £69; HB weekly £329–£399; L £7·50, D £12·50
cc Access, Amex, B'card/Visa, Diners; dep.
(*See advertisement on p. 661*)

EC *early closing* **MD** *market day* *country house hotel* *ns (NS) no smoking areas* *tcf tea/coffee facilities*

Talyllyn (Gwynedd)

Talyllyn, Tywyn, Gwynedd LL36 9AJ
Tel: (0654) 77282
RAC ☆☆

The Tynycornel Hotel, situated in the magnificent Snowdonia National Park, looks out over its own natural 222 acre lake, in whose waters the majestic grandeur of Cader Idris is reflected.

★ Ideal for fishing – both for the novice and the experienced.
★ Quiet cosy bars and high standard of cuisine.
★ All 15 bedrooms have lakeside or garden views.
★ All rooms en-suite with TV and tea and coffee making facilities.
★ Warm welcoming atmosphere.
★ Outdoor heated swimming pool, sauna & solarium.

Tenby (Dyfed)

The Paragon, Tenby,
Dyfed, Wales SA70 7HR
Tel: (0834) 3737
Fax: (0834)4342

Magnificent clifftop location overlooking the South beach towards St Catherine's and Caldey Island. Luxurious bars, carvery and clifftop patios. Forty-five bedrooms, all en-suite, colour television, radio, telephone, tea/coffee making facilities, parking, lift to all floors, private steps to the beach, in-house laundry, games room. Superb facilities for sailing, windsurfing, fishing, riding, walking, golf and bowls. Warm friendly service. Just the place to stay.

Mid week and Weekend Breaks
Bargain Winter Breaks
Resident proprietor: Jan-Roelof Eggens.

Tenby (Dyfed)

Tenby's premier hotel exquisitely situated overlooking Tenby Harbour and Carmarthen Bay with all modern amenities. Central for town, beach and transport terminals. Adjacent parking facilities. Weekly, bargain breaks, mini weekends and mid week breaks. Terms on request. Mini sports complex with sauna, solarium, jacuzzi, squash courts, table tennis etc. Indoor swimming pool. Ideal centre for fishing, sailing, golf, skiing and riding.

For further information please contact Mr. Graham Fry.

The Royal Gate House Hotel

North Beach, Tenby, Dyfed, SA70 7ET. Telephone: Tenby (0834) 2255

Tenby (Dyfed)

ROYAL LION HOTEL

North Beach, Tenby, Dyfed   Tel: (0834) 2127

Situated close to the town centre and overlooking the beach. Private car park. All rooms with tea making facilities. TV. Lift to most floors. Cocktail bar.

Tintern (Gwent)

Wye Valley Hotel

Tintern, Nr. Chepstow, Gwent NP6 6SP
Telephone: Tintern (0291) 689441

A friendly family run inn offering en suite bedrooms, good food, fine wines, and well kept real ales. Village atmosphere, and good car parking in this lovely area. Suitable for day time conferences up to 70 people. From £15.50 per delegate to include coffee, tea, lunch, equipment and VAT.

Usk (Gwent)

Tredunnock, Nr Usk, Gwent NP5 1PG   Tel: 063349 521 Fax: 063349 220

Cwrt Bleddyn is set in pastoral, peaceful border country. Its history can be traced back to the 14th century, when Cwrt Bleddyn was a manor house. Thanks to an ambitious but sympathetic renovation, the past has been preserved within the present building. An elegantly gabled exterior holds many treasures, including an ancient staircase that leads nowhere and 17th century oak panelling.

The hotel's sense of history is particularly strong in the intimate restaurant. Here, guests can enjoy French-influenced cuisine, fine wines and attentive service. The hotel's commitment to classic country house comfort is also evident in the bedrooms, which are furnished to a very high standard indeed with all conceivable facilities. For something extra special, ask about the three period bedrooms or the suites with whirlpool baths. At the end of 1988 a new Health and Leisure Complex opened at the hotel providing a wealth of facilities – Swimming Pool, Saunas, Solarium, Squash, etc. Close by are a wealth of historic sites, including Roman Caerleon. Your host at this luxurious hotel is Andrew Cole.

Welshpool (Powys)

BWRDD CROESO CYMRU
WALES TOURIST BOARD

Edderton Hall

Forden, Welshpool (on Welshpool–Montgomery road) (0938 76) 339

Country House Hotel and Restaurant

Peaceful setting, superb views across to Powys Castle. 8 bedrooms, all en-suite, 2 four-posters.
'Taste of Wales'
RESTAURANT of the YEAR for this region

Wrexham (Clwyd)

Cefn Road, Wrexham, Clwyd LL13 0NY.
Tel: (0978) 261225

Seventeenth century manor house set in beautiful countryside. Thirteen bedrooms all with private facilities. Excellent cuisine, home grown fruit and vegetables. Open to non residents.

EC *early closing*   **MD** *market day*   *country house hotel*   *ns (NS) no smoking areas*   *tcf tea/coffee facilities*

★ **Minffordd,** LL36 9AJ ☎ (0654) 761665

Well-furnished former coaching inn full of character. A scenic gem.
7 bedrs, 7 en suite, tcf
ns; P 12; no children under 3
LD 8.30, nr lunch. Resid & Rest lic
£ B&B £36–£41, B&B (double) £52·50–£62·50; HB weekly £320–£350; D £14·75; WB £66–£72 [Mar-May & Oct-Dec]
cc Access, B'card/Visa, Diners.

TENBY Dyfed. Map 18B1

See also SAUNDERSFOOT.
Pop 4,950. Carmarthen 27, London 239, Haverfordwest 20, Pembroke 10.
EC Wed. **Golf** Tenby 18h.
The Croft ☎ (0834) 2402

★★★ **Imperial,** The Paragon, SA70 7HR ☎ (0834) 3737 Fax: (0834) 4342

Traditional seaside hotel in commanding clifftop position. De, Po, Du
46 bedrs, 46 en suite; TV; tcf
lift, dogs, P 18, G 16, coach, child facs; con 250
LD 9.30, bar meals only Mon–Sat lunch
£ B&B £25–£29, B&B (double) £46–£55; HB weekly £192·50–£240; D £12·50; [10% V]; WB £75 (HB)
cc Access, Amex, B'card/Visa, Diners; dep.

★★ H **Atlantic,** The Esplanade, SA70 7DU ☎ (0834) 2881
Hotel above South Beach with cliff gardens. Private access to beach. Indoor swimming pool, solarium.
35 bedrs, 35 en suite; TV; tcf
dogs, ns; P 30, coach; child facs
LD 8.30, bar meals only lunch
£ B&B £35–£38, B&B (double) £50–£70; WB £23
cc Access, B'card/Visa.

★★ **Esplanade,** The Esplanade, SA70 7DU ☎ (0834) 3333 Fax: (0834) 2391
Four-storey cream-painted hotel high above South Beach with superb views across the bay to Caldey Island.
16 bedrs, 16 en suite; TV; tcf
dogs; child facs
LD 9.30. Resid & Rest lic
£ B&B £17·50, B&B (double) £30–£75; L £7, D £10; [5% V]
cc Access, Amex, B'card/Visa, Diners.

★★ H **Fourcroft,** The Croft, SA70 8AP ☎ (0834) 2886 Fax: (0834) 2888

Clifftop hotel in Georgian terrace with gardens down to beach. Swimming pool, sauna, gymnasium, billiards. Open Easter–Nov. Fr
38 bedrs, 38 en suite, TV; tcf
lift, dogs, ns; P 6 (£1.50), coach; child facs; con 50
LD 8.30. Resid & Rest lic
£ B&B £35–£40, B&B (double) £62–£72; HB weekly £235–£255; D £13·50; WB £40 (HB)
cc Access, B'card/Visa; dep.

★★ **Royal Gate House,** North Beach, SA70 7ET ☎ (0834) 2255
Substantial 5-storey hotel high above harbour. Indoor swimming pool, squash, sauna, solarium, gymnasium, billiards.
62 bedrs, 62 en suite, TV, tcf
lift, TV, dogs, P 34, coach, child facs, con 10
LD 8.45
£ B&B £30–£37, B&B (double) £50–£60; L £6, D £13·50; [5% V excl Jul, Aug]
cc Access, Amex, B'card/Visa, Diners; dep.
(See advertisement on p. 661)

★★ **Royal Lion,** White Lion St, SA70 7EX ☎ (0834) 2127
White-painted 4-storey former coaching inn set in the High Street. Guests may use sports facilities at sister hotel, Royal Gate House.
36 bedrs, 15 en suite, 5 ba; TV; tcf
lift, TV, dogs, P 34, coach, child facs.
LD 8.30, bar meals only Mon–Sat lunch
£ B&B £22–£35, B&B £35–£65; D £11·50; [5% V excl. Jul, Aug]
cc Access, B'card/Visa, Diners; dep.
(See advertisement on p. 662)

★ **Buckingham,** The Esplanade, SA70 6DU ☎ (0834) 2622
Hotel overlooking South Beach and set high on the Esplanade.
21 bedrs, 17 en suite, 2 ba; TV, tcf
dogs; ns; child facs
LD 7.45, nr lunch
£ B&B £20–£22, B&B (double) £37–£40; HB weekly £180; D £9·50; [10% V]
cc Access, B'card/Visa; dep.

Harbour Heights (Highly Acclaimed), The Croft, SA70 8AP ☎ (0834) 2132. *Hotel.*

Heywood Lodge (Acclaimed), Heywood La, SA70 8BN ☎ (0834) 2684.
Ripley St. Marys (Acclaimed), St. Mary's St, SA70 7HN ☎ (0834) 2837. *Hotel.* Open Easter–Oct.
£ B&B £16–£20; HB weekly £145–£170; [10%]
Tall Ships (Acclaimed), 34 Victoria St, SA70 7DY ☎ (0834) 2055. *Hotel.* Open Mar–Oct.
£ B&B £12–£17·50; HB weekly £112–£150

Castle View, The Norton, SA70 8AA ☎ (0834) 2666. *Private Hotel.* Open Apr–Oct.
£ B&B £18; [5% V]
Myrtle House, St Mary's St, SA70 7HW ☎ (0834) 2508. *Hotel.* Open Mar–Nov.
£ B&B 13–£15
Sea Breezes, 18 The Norton, SA70 8AA ☎ (0834) 2753. *Private Hotel.* Open Mar–Nov.
£ B&B £15–£20; [5% V excl July–Sept]

THREE COCKS Powys. Map 19B3

Abergavenny 21, London 164, Brecon 10, Builth Wells 14, Hay-on-Wye 5.
Old Gwernyfed Manor (Acclaimed), Felindre, LD3 0SU ☎ (049 74) 376

TINTERN Gwent. Map 20A1

Pop 250. Monmouth 9½, London 138, Chepstow 6.
Tintern Abbey. ☎ (0291) 689431

★★★ **Beaufort,** NP6 6SF ☎ (0291) 689777 Fax: (0291) 689727

Small stone-built country inn, in part 15th century, overlooking Tintern Abbey. (Emb)
24 bedrs, 24 en suite; TV; tcf
dogs; P 60, coach; child facs; con 60
LD 9, bar meals only Mon–Sat lunch
£ B&B £60 (w/e £41), B&B (double) £80; D £15·95
cc Access, Amex, B'card/Visa, Diners.

★★ **Wye Valley,** NP6 6SP ☎ (0291) 689441

A purpose built hotel with excellent views on main A466
(See advertisement on p. 662)
Parva Farmhouse (Acclaimed), NP6 6SQ ☎ (0291) 689411
£ B&B £28–£40; [10% V w/d]

Wa

Fountain, Trellech Grange, NP6 6QW
☎(0291) 689303. *Inn.*
£ B&B £17; [10% V]

TREARDDUR BAY Gwynedd. Map 28A3

Pop 1,347. Bangor 22, London 259, Caernarfon 28, Holyhead 2.
EC Wed. **Golf** Holyhead 18h.

★★★ **Beach,** Lon St Ffraid, LL65 2YT
☎(0407) 860332 Tx: 61529
Fax: (0407) 861140
Attractive modern hotel near safe sandy beach. Tennis, squash, sauna, solarium, gymnasium, billiards.
🛏 26 bedrs, 26 en suite; TV; tcf
🏠 dogs; P, coach; child facs; con 100
✕ LD 9.15, nr Mon–Sat lunch, Sun dinner
£ B&B (double) £55–£70; HB weekly £300; D £12; WB £88 (2 nts HB)
cc Access, Amex, B'card/Visa, Diners, dep.

★★★ **Trearddur Bay,** Lon Isallt, LL65 2UW ☎(0407) 860301 Tx: 60609
Fax: (0407) 861181

Attractive and extensively-modernised white-faced hotel. Indoor swimming pool.
⚒ Es, No
🛏 27 bedrs, 27 en suite; TV; tcf
🏠 TV, dogs, P 250, coach, child facs; con 150
✕ LD 9.30, bar meals only Mon–Sat lunch
£ B&B £50–£75, B&B (double) £70–£90; HB weekly £345–£425; D £16; WB £85–£105 (HB); [5% V]
cc Access, Amex, B'card/Visa, Diners, dep.

★★ **Seacroft,** Ravenspoint Rd, LL65 2YU
☎(0407) 860348
Small, intimate hotel supervised by proprietors. Close to sandy beaches.

High Ground, off Ravenspoint Rd, LL65 2YY ☎(0407) 860078. *Hotel.*
£ B&B £14·50–£19·50; HB weekly £168–£196; [10% V excl. Jul–Sep]
Moranedd, Trearddur Rd, LL65 2UE
☎(0407) 860324. *Guest House.*
£ B&B £12–£16

TRECASTLE Powys. Map 19A2

Brecon 12, London 175, Carmarthen 36, Merthyr Tydfil 22, Swansea 29.

Castle (Acclaimed), LD3 8UH
☎Sennybridge (087 482) 354. *Hotel.*
£ B&B £29·50–£34; HB weekly £175; [5% V Oct–Jun]

TREFRIW Gwynedd. Map 28C3

Betws-y-Coed 4½, London 210, Conwy 8, Llanrwst 4.

★★ **C** **Hafod House,** LL27 0RQ ☎(0492) 640029 Fax: (0492) 641351

Skilfully converted 17th century farmhouse with views across the Conwy valley.
🛏 6 bedrs, 6 en suite; TV; tcf
🏠 P 25, coach; children over 11; con 24
✕ LD 9.30, nr Mon–Sat lunch. Resid & Rest lic
£ B&B £34–£39·50, B&B (double) £54–£65; HB weekly £198·50–£259·50; D £14; WB £65 (HB); [10% V]
cc Access, Amex, B'card/Visa, Diners; dep.

TREGARON Dyfed. Map 19A3

Pop 950. Rhyader 25, London 200, Aberystwyth 17, Lampeter 10, Newtown 42.

★ **Talbot,** The Square, SY25 6JL
☎(097 44) 208
Three-storey inn-type hotel conveniently situated in centre of town.

TRETOWER Powys. Map 19C2

Pop 650. Abergavenny 9, London 152, Brecon 11, Brynmawr 10, Talgarth 9.

Tretower Court, NP8 1RF ☎(0874) 730204

TYWYN Gwynedd. Map 28B1

Pop 2,800. Aberdyfi 4½, London 220, Dolgellau 19.
See Talyllyn railway.
ℹ Publicity Office, High St. ☎(0654) 710070

★ **Greenfield,** High St, LL36 9AD ☎(0654) 710354

Attractive converted terrace houses centrally situated. Few minutes from sea.
Closed Nov & Dec.
🛏 14 bedrs, 2 en suite, 4 ba
🏠 TV; coach; child facs
✕ LD 8. Resid & Rest lic
£ B&B £13·50–£16; HB weekly £127·50–£142·50; L £4·50, D £5·75

Arthur (Acclaimed), Marine Par, LL36 ODE.
☎(0654) 711863. *Hotel. Sauna.*
£ B&B £24; [5% V]

USK Gwent. Map 19C1

Pop 2,000. Chepstow 14, London 136, M4 Motorway 9½, Abergavenny 11, Monmouth 13, Newport 11, Pontypool 7.

★★★★ **Cwrt Bleddyn,** Llangybi, NP5 1PG
☎(063 349) 521 Fax: (063 349) 220
In 17 acres of grounds, a lovely manor house dating from 1329. Indoor swimming pool, tennis, squash, sauna, solarium, gymnasium, billiards. ⚒ Fr
🛏 29 bedrs, 29 en suite; annexe 7 bedrs, 7 en suite; TV; tcf
🏠 ns; P 150, coach, child facs, con 200
✕ LD 10.30
£ B&B £62·50–£115, B&B (double) £79·50–£115; L £17·95, D £17·95; WB £100 (2nts HB)
cc Access, Amex, B'card/Visa, Diners.
(*See advertisement on p. 662*)

♣ ★★ **Glen-yr-Afon House,** Pontypool Rd, NP5 1SY ☎(02913) 2302 ♿

Three-storey, turreted Victorian mansion in an acre of garden.
🛏 17 bedrs, 16 en suite, 1 ba; TV
🏠 TV, dogs, ns; P 60, coach; child facs; con 40
✕ LD 9
£ B&B £29·90–£40·25, B&B (double) £48·30–£51·75; L £9, D £12·50; WB £60; [5% V w/e Nov–Mar]
cc Access, B'card/Visa.

★★ **Three Salmons,** Porthycarne St, NP5 1BQ ☎(029 13) 2133
Well-restored 18th century former coaching inn. Set on corner site.
🛏 12 bedrs, 12 en suite, 1 ba; annexe 18 bedrs, 18 en suite; TV; tcf
🏠 dogs; P 40, coach; child facs; con 110

VALLEY See Dyffryn

WELSHPOOL Powys. Map 29A1

Pop 5,000. Shrewsbury 18, London 172, Bala 33, Dolgellau 37, Knighton 34, Llangollen 28, Ludlow 32, Newtown 13, Wrexham 31.
EC Thur. **MD** Mon. **Golf** Welshpool 18h.
ℹ Vicarage Gdns Car Park. ☎(0938) 552043

♣ ★★ **Edderton Hall,** Forden, SY21 8RZ
☎(0938 76) 339

EC *early closing* **MD** *market day* ♣ *country house hotel* *ns (NS) no smoking areas* *tcf tea/coffee facilities*

Georgian country house, with attractive bays and portico, in 2½ acres of grounds. Fishing.
8 bedrs, 8 en suite; TV; tcf
dogs; P 40, coach; con 80
(*See advertisement on p. 662*)

★★ C Golfa Hall, SY21 9AF (0938) 553399 Fax: (0938) 554777

Charming listed building, once a farmhouse, retaining many period features. Set in 8 acres of grounds with lovely country views.
10 bedrs, 10 en suite; TV; tcf.
dogs, ns; P 50, coach, child facs; con 60
LD 9; bar meals only Mon–Sat lunch. Resid & Rest lic
£ B&B £35–£39·50, B&B (double) £55–£70; HB weekly £255–£295; L £9·50, D £14·75; [5% V Nov–Mar]
cc Access, B'card/Visa, Diners.

★★ Royal Oak, The Cross, SY21 7DG (0938) 552217 Tx: 57515
Substantial 18th-century red brick hotel conveniently situated in town centre. Fr, It, Es
24 bedrs, 24 en suite; TV; tcf
TV, dogs; P 60, coach; child facs; con 120
LD 9
£ B&B £30–£34, B&B (double) £54–£60; HB weekly £280–£300; L £8·50, D £10; WB £32 (HB); [10% V]
cc Access, Amex, B'card/Visa; dep.

Tynllwyn, SY21 9BW (0938) 553175. *Farm.*
£ B&B £12, HB weekly £115, [10% V]

WHITEBROOK Gwent. Map 20A2

Chepstow 10, London 133, Abergavenny 20, Gloucester 24, Monmouth 5, Pontypool 23.

★★ Crown at Whitebrook, NP5 4TX (0600) 860254 Fax: (0600) 860607

White-stone building set high on a through road. Fine views. Closed 3–31 Jan: Fr
12 bedrs, 12 en suite; TV; tcf
dogs; P 40, child facs; con 12
LD 9. nr Sun dinner, Mon lunch
£ B&B £43–£48, B&B (double) £66–£76; HB weekly £300–£335; L £11·50, D £20·50; [5% V w/d, Nov–Mar]
cc Access, Amex, B'card/Visa, Diners.

WOLFSCASTLE Dyfed. Map 18A2

Pop 300. Haverfordwest 7, London 250, Fishguard 7, St Davids 15.

★★ Wolfscastle Country, SA62 5LZ Treffgarne (043 787) 225
Two-storey stone building with extension. Pleasant gardens. Tennis, squash.
15 bedrs, 15 en suite, TV; tcf
dogs, P 60, coach, child facs; con 180
LD 9.15, bar meals only Mon–Sat lunch. Resid lic
£ B&B £30, B&B (double) £50; L £10, D £12; WB (Oct–Jun)
cc Access, Amex, B'card/Visa.

Stone Hall (Acclaimed), Welsh Hook, SA62 5NS (0348) 840212. Fr
£ B&B £35; [5% V w/d]

WREXHAM Clwyd. Map 29B2

Pop 41,570. Whitchurch 15, London 178, Chester 11, Llangollen 11, Mold 11.
i Memorial Hall. (0978) 357845

★★★ Llwyn Onn Hall, Cefn Rd, LL13 0NY (0978) 261225
Cream coloured Georgian building with attractive verandah. In secluded gardens.
13 bedrs, 13 en suite; TV
dogs, P 50, coach, child facs, con 25
LD 9.30
£ B&B £52·50, B&B (double) £73–£85; L £9·50, D £13; WB £34·50; [5% V]
cc Access, Amex, B'card/Visa, Diners.
(*See advertisement on p. 662*)

Discount vouchers
RAC discount vouchers are on p. 34. Hotels with a [V] shown at the end of the price information will accept them in part payment for accommodation bills on the full, standard rate, not against bargain breaks or any other special offers. Please note the limitations shown in the entry: w/e for weekends, w/d for weekdays, and which months they are accepted.

★★★ Wynnstay Arms, York St, LL13 8LP (0978) 291010 Tx: 61674 Fax: (0978) 362138

Town centre hotel combining Georgian frontage with purpose-built modern wing.
74 bedrs, 74 en suite; TV; tcf
lift, TV, dogs, ns; P 50, G 20, coach; child facs; con 50

★★ C R Cross Lanes, Marchwiel, LL13 0TF (0978) 780555 Fax: (0978) 780568

19th century building with modern extensions in beautiful grounds. Indoor swimming pool, putting, fishing, sauna. It
18 bedrs, 18 en suite; TV; tcf
dogs, ns; P 80, coach; child facs, con 100
LD 9.30, bar meals only Sat lunch & Sun dinner
£ B&B £47, B&B (double) £70; L £7·95, D £12·95; WB £32·50 (HB low season); [5% V]
cc Access, Amex, B'card/Visa, Diners.

Atlas Section
Consult the Atlas section at the back of the guide to find out which towns and villages have RAC Appointed and Listed hotels in them. They are shown on the maps by purple circles.

ISLE OF MAN

CASTLETOWN
Map 42A1

Pop 3,000. Douglas 10, London 244, Peel 12.
EC Thur. **Golf** Castletown 18h. **See** Castle Rushen, Nautical Museum, Grammar School.
ℹ Commissioners' Office, Parliament Sq. ☎(0624) 823518

★★★ H C R **Castletown Golf Links,** Fort Island. ☎Douglas (0624) 822201 Tx: 627636 Fax: (0624) 824633 ♿

Magnificently situated hotel on Man's South coastline. Indoor swimming pool, sauna, solarium, golf, putting, billiards. ✱ Fr
🛏 58 bedrs, 58 en suite; TV; tcf
🏨 TV, dogs; P 100, coach; child facs; con 200
✕ LD 10
£ B&B £50–£90, B&B (double) £70–£160; L £9·75, D £14·50; WB £55 (HB); [10% V w/e]
cc Access, Amex, B'card/Visa, Diners; dep.

DOUGLAS
Map 42A1

Pop 19,897. Ferry service to Heysham and steamer service to Liverpool (peak season only). London 198, Castletown 10, Peel 11, Ramsey 15.
EC Thur. **Golf** Pulrose 18h. **See** Villa Marina Gdns, Lighthouse, Manx Museum and Art Gallery, House of Keys and Tynwald, Tower of Refuge, St George's Church, Derby Castle Aquadrome and Solarium. TT Races June, Manx Grand Prix Sept.
ℹ 13 Victoria St. ☎(0624) 74323

★★★ **Empress,** Central Promenade, ☎(0624) 661155 Tx: 627772 Fax: (0624) 73554
In a premier position on promenade, 6-storey cream stucco building. Indoor swimming pool, sauna, solarium, gymnasium, snooker. ✱ De
🛏 102 bedrs, 102 en suite; TV; tcf
🏨 lift, ns; child facs; con 180
✕ LD 11
£ B&B £62·50–£77·50, B&B (double) £95–£100; L fr £10, D fr £11
cc Access, Amex, B'card/Visa, Diners; dep.

★★★ **Palace,** Central Promenade. ☎(0624) 74521 Tx: 627742 Fax: (0624) 25535
Modern purpose-built hotel with 4 bars, night club, casino. Overlooks bay. Indoor swimming pool, sauna, solarium, gymnasium, snooker. ✱ Fr, It
🛏 135 bedrs, 135 en suite; TV; tcf
🏨 lift, dogs; P 100, coach; child facs; con 319
✕ LD 11
£ B&B £67–£77, B&B (double) £89–£99; L £5, D £13; WB £90
cc Access, Amex, B'card/Visa, Diners.

★★★ **Sefton,** Harris Promenade ☎(0624) 26011 Fax: (0624) 76004 ♿
Impressive 5-storey Victorian building in central position on Harris Promenade. Indoor swimming pool, sauna, solarium, gymnasium.
🛏 75 bedrs, 75 en suite; 2 ba; TV; tcf
🏨 lift, ns; P 40, coach; child facs; con 100
✕ LD 10
£ B&B £38·50 (w/e £20), B&B (double) £55; L £6·50, D £11
cc Access, Amex, B'card/Visa, Diners; dep.
(*See advertisement on p. 667*)

★★ **Ascot,** 7 Empire Ter ☎(0624) 75081, Fax: (0624) 661512

Four-storey red-brick building close to the Promenade.
🛏 45 bedrs, 45 en suite, TV, tcf
🏨 lift, coach; child facs, con 100
✕ LD 9, bar meals only lunch. Resid & Rest lic
£ B&B £20, B&B (double) £40; HB weekly £168; L £6·90; [10% V]
cc Access, B'card/Visa; dep.

★★ **Edelweiss,** Queen's Promenade ☎(0624) 75115
Four-storey white painted building set back from the Promenade.

★★ **Rutland,** Queen's Promenade, ☎(0624) 21218

Modernised family-run hotel on promenade with good views over the Bay.
🛏 73 bedrs, 47 en suite; 18 ba; TV; tcf
🏨 lift; coach; child facs

★★ **Welbeck,** Mona Dr ☎(0624) 75663. Fax: (0624) 661545
Victorian hotel in a corner position with good sea views. Solarium.
🛏 22 bedrs, 22 en suite; TV; tcf
🏨 lift, TV, coach, child facs
✕ LD 7.30, bar meals only lunch. Resid lic
£ B&B £23; D £10; [5% V]
cc Access, B'card/Visa.

Modwena (Acclaimed), 39 Loch Promenade ☎(0624) 75728. *Private Hotel.*

Dunvegan ☎(0624) 76635
Private Hotel. Open Apr–Sep, ✱ Fr, De
£ B&B £12–£14; HB weekly £96–£105; [10% V]

Hydro, Queen's Promenade. ☎(0624) 76870. *Hotel.* Open Easter–end Sep.
£ B&B £19–£26·50; HB weekly £140–£147

PORT ERIN
Map 42A1

Pop 1,800. Castletown 7, Douglas 13.

★★★ **Cherry Orchard,** Bridson St, ☎(0624) 833811 ♿
Modern hotel in town 5 minutes from beach. Disco and evening entertainment. Indoor swimming pool, sauna, solarium.
🛏 78 bedrs, 78 en suite; TV; tcf
🏨 lift; P 100, coach; child facs; con 300

Regent House (Highly Acclaimed), Promenade ☎(0624) 833454. *Guest House.*

RAMSEY
Map 42B1

Pop 6,000. Douglas 15, London 213, Peel 16.
EC Wed. **MD** Mon, Fri. **Golf** Ramsey 18h. **See** St Mary's Church, Albert Tower, Mooragh Park, Grove Rural Life Museum, Maughold Church 3 m, Snae Fell.
ℹ Town Hall, Parliament Sq. ☎(0624) 812228

★★★★ **Grand Island,** Bride Rd. ☎(0624) 812455 Tx: 629849 Fax: (0624) 815291 ♿
Looking straight out to sea, a large Victorian building in own attractive grounds. Indoor swimming pool, sauna, solarium, riding, putting, gymnasium, billiards. ✱ Fr, De
🛏 54 bedrs, 54 en suite; TV; tcf
🏨 lift, dogs, ns; P 150, child facs; con 200
✕ LD 10
£ B&B £54–£148, B&B (double) £74–£148; L £10·95, D £10·95; WB £40 (winter); [10% V]
cc Access, Amex, B'card/Visa, Diners; dep.
(*See advertisement on p. 000*)

Sulby Glen, ☎(0624) 897240. *Inn.* ✱ De
£ B&B £13·50–£15·50; [5% V]

EC *early closing* **MD** *market day* 🏠 *country house hotel* *ns (NS) no smoking areas* *tcf tea/coffee facilities*

Douglas (Isle of Man)

*** RAC
Isle of Man Tourist
graded 5 Keys Hotel.

SEFTON HOTEL

Open all year.
Private car park.

Harris Promenade, Douglas, Isle of Man Reservations Tel: 0624 626011 Fax: 0624 676004

Short break and special package hot line tel: 0624 663320

Tastefully renovated hotel ideally situated, the Sefton has a well earned reputation for style at affordable prices. All very attractive 80 bedrooms have bathroom, colour TV, tea and coffee making facilities, direct dial phones, radio, baby listening and hair dryers. The beautiful health club includes swimming pool, gym, steam rooms, saunas, poolside bar, sun bed rooms & spa pool. In the delightful setting of our new 'Far Pavilions' Restaurant residents enjoy a selection of dishes well known throughout the Island for their quality. Luxury coffee shop open 13 hours per day.

Suitable for the disabled. Ashley Courtenay recommended

Chris Robertshaw Manging Director

Ramsey (Isle of Man)

the GRAND ISLAND HOTEL

Ramsey, Isle of Man

Tel: 0624 812455 Telex: 629849 GIHMAN G
Fax: 0624 815291

The Island's only 4 star Hotel with panoramic views of Ramsey Bay and Snaefell Mountain. 55 luxuriously appointed rooms including 8 elegant suites. Extensive sport, health and leisure facilities including indoor wave-swimming pool, jacuzzi, sauna, solarium, snooker room, multi-gym, beauty therapist and ladies and gents hair salon. 6 croquet lawns and horse riding on site. Nearby golf, fishing and shooting. High quality international and country-style cuisine with choice of restaurants.

Full details of Short-Breaks and Special Packages available on request.

★★★★ RAC – Ashley Courtenay & Egon Ronay recommended – 5 Keys IOM

Castel (Guernsey, Channel Islands)

Hotel Hougue du Pommier

CASTEL, GUERNSEY. Tel: 56531/2 53904 (0481)

This 1712 Farmhouse now transformed into an elegant 2 star Hotel, which stands in its own 10 acres of ground, with a solar heated swimming pool, 18 hole putting green, 9 hole pitch and putt golf course offers pleasure and relaxation. Enjoy our famous Carvery luncheons in our Tudor Bar or superb Dining Room. An a la Carte candlelit dinner in this renowned Farm House Restaurant with its extensive wine menu is a must. We are looking forward to welcoming you here in Guernsey.

St Martin's (Guernsey, Channel Islands)

Saint Margaret's Lodge Hotel

Forest Road, St Martin's, Guernsey, Channel Islands
Tel: (0481) 35757 Fax: (0481) 37594 Telex: 4191664

Rural setting, country lanes and spectacular south coast beaches.
Family run, warm friendly atmosphere, all rooms completely refurbished, with remote control TVs, tea & coffee making facilities, hairdryers etc. Lift, courtesy shopping bus.
Residents & à la Carte garden room restaurants. Top quality fresh food expertly prepared.
Fully inclusive travel arrangements available.

IOM

CHANNEL ISLANDS

GUERNSEY

RAC Port Office, *St Julian's Pier, St Peter Port.* ☎ Guernsey (0481) 20822
Pop 55,000. Weymouth 75, Jersey 25.
EC Thur **MD** Thur. **P** Car Parks are indicated by "P" signs. Before using these parks, motorists **must** obtain parking "clocks" from the Police Station. Cars must not be parked on a public highway (except on a car park) other than for loading or unloading. **Golf** Royal Guernsey L'Ancresse 18h.
[i] Crown Pier, St Peter Port. ☎ (0481) 23552

CASTEL

★★ Hougue du Pommier ☎ (0481) 56531
Tx: 4191664. Fax: (0481) 56260
18th century granite farmhouse with extensions. In 10 acres of grounds. Swimming pool, golf, putting, solarium, gymnasium. Fr, De
39 bedrs, 39 en suite, 1 ba; TV; tcf
TV; P 70, coach; child facs; con 25
✕ LD 9.45, bar meals only lunch
cc Access, Amex, B'card/Visa; CB; dep.
(*See advertisement on p. 667*)

La Grande Mare, Vazon Bay
Hotel awaiting inspection

Le Galaad (Acclaimed), Rue des Francais ☎ (0481) 57233. *Hotel. Putting.* Open Mar–Oct.
£ room £17–£27; HB weekly £119–£189

FERMAIN-BAY

★★★ Le Chalet ☎ (0481) 35716
Tx: 4191342 Fax: (0481) 35718

Attractive chalet-style split-level hotel on woodedhillside overlooking Bay. Open mid Apr–Oct. De
46 bedrs, 46 en suite; annexe 2 bedrs, 2 en suite; TV; tcf
dogs; P 50; child facs
✕ LD 9.30, bar meals only Mon–Sat lunch
£ B&B £30·50–£35, B&B (double) £50–£69; L £8, D £12
cc Access, Amex, B'card/Visa, Diners.

> **Atlas Section**
> Consult the Atlas section at the back of the guide to find out which towns and villages have RAC Appointed and Listed hotels in them. They are shown on the maps by purple circles.

★★ [C] La Favorita ☎ (0481) 35666
Tx: 94016631 Fax: (0481) 354413

In a wooded valley, 3-storey former country house with modern wing. Fr, De. Open Mar–Nov.
30 bedrs, 30 en suite; TV; tcf
ns; P 30, coach; child facs
✕ LD 9
£ B&B £24–£60, B&B (double) £44–£66; HB weekly £189–£275; L £7·50, D £9·50; dep.

L'ANCRESSE

Lynton Park (Highly Acclaimed), Hacse La ☎ (0481) 45418. *Hotel. Putting.*
£ B&B £28–£35·50; HB weekly £188·50–£238

ST MARTINS

★★★ Green Acres, ☎ (0481) 35711
Fax: (0481) 35978

Attractive 2-storey 20th century building set in own grounds. Swimming pool, solarium.
48 bedrs, 48 en suite; TV; tcf
ns; P 75; child facs
✕ LD 8.30, bar meals only lunch
£ B&B £35–£60, B&B (double) £50–£80; L £8, D £10·50
cc Access, B'card/Visa; dep.

★★★ La Trelade, Forest Rd, ☎ (0481) 35454
Traditional, French influenced building with extensions in keeping. Set back from the road in lawned grounds. Swimming pool, putting. De, Es, Po
45 bedrs, 45 en suite; TV; tcf
lift, ns; P 120, coach, child facs, con 80
✕ LD 9, bar meals only lunch
£ B&B £21–33; L £6·50, D £7·50; [10% V]
cc Access, B'card/Visa; dep

★★★ [C] St Margaret's Lodge, Forest Rd ☎ (0481) 35757 Tx: 4191664
Fax: (0481) 37594

Modern hotel of 3 storeys in 1½ acres of lawns and gardens. Swimming pool, sauna, solarium. Fr, Es, Po
47 bedrs, 47 en suite, TV; tcf
lift; P 100, child facs; con 120
✕ LD 9.30
£ L £4·50, D £9·90
cc Access, Amex, B'card/Visa, Diners.
(*See advertisment on p. 667*)

★★★ St Martin's Country ☎ (0481) 35644

Large holiday hotel attractively set in its own grounds. Swimming pool, putting, tennis.

ST PETER PORT

★★★★ [H] Old Government House, Ann's Pl ☎ (0481) 24921 Tx: 4191144
Fax: (0481) 24429

Large Georgian building with modern extension. Magnificent views. Swimming pool, solarium. Fr, It, Po
73 bedrs, 73 en suite; TV
lift, dogs; P 20, coach; child facs; con 210
✕ LD 9.15
£ L £7·50, D £9
cc Access, Amex, B'card/Visa, CB, Diners; dep.

★★★★ **H** **R** **St Pierre Park** ☎ (0481) 28282 Tx: 4191662 Fax: (0481) 712041 ♿

Large modern hotel complex in landscaped grounds on town outskirts. Indoor swimming pool, golf, putting, tennis, sauna, solarium, gymnasium, snooker. Fr, It, Po
136 bedrs, 136 en suite; TV; tcf
lift; P 200, child facs; con
✕ LD 10.30, nr Sat lunch, Sun dinner
£ B&B £85–£145, B&B (double) £115–£145; L £11·50, D £16·50; WB £163·50 (2 nts HB)
cc Access, Amex, B'card/Visa, Diners; dep.

★★★ **De Havelet,** Havelet ☎ (0481) 22199 Fax: (0481) 714057

Gracious Georgian house with modern extension. Overlooks the harbour. De, It
34 bedrs, 34 en suite; TV; tcf
dogs, ns; P 50; child facs, con 20
✕ LD 9.30
£ B&B £32·50–£44·50, B&B (double) £53·50–£84; HB weekly £239·75–£325·50; L £8, D £12
cc Access, Amex, B'card/Visa, Diners.

★★★ **Moore's,** Pollet ☎ (0481) 24452 Tx: 4191342 Fax: (0481) 714037

Four-storey Georgian terrace building situated in town centre. Fr, De
48 bedrs, 48 en suite; 2 ba; TV; tcf
lift; dogs; child facs; con 20
✕ LD 9
£ B&B £23–£56, B&B (double) £36–£66; L £9, D £11
cc Access, Amex, B'card/Visa, Diners; dep.

★★★ **Royal,** Esplanade ☎ (0481) 23921 Tx: 4191221 ♿
Imposing 4-storey Georgian hotel on waterfront. Under refurbishment, awaiting inspection. Swimming pool.

★★ **Grange Lodge,** The Grange ☎ (0481) 25161 ♿
Compact, elegant 3-storey Georgian hotel with extensive garden to rear. Swimming pool, snooker.
31 bedrs, 31 en suite; TV
TV, dogs; P 30; child facs

★★ **Sunnycroft,** 5 Constitution Steps. ☎ (0481) 723008.

Small, friendly hotel in a peaceful area with magnificent views over harbour. Fr, Es Po
14 bedrs, 14 en suite, 1 ba; TV, tcf
TV, ns; no children under 14
✕ LD 8, bar meals only lunch
£ B&B £21–£25, B&B (double) £34–£50; HB weekly £147–£203; D £10; [5% V]
cc Access, B'card/Visa; dep.

Midhurst House (Highly Acclaimed), Candie Rd ☎ (0481) 24391. *Private Hotel.* Open mid Apr–mid Oct. Fr
£ B&B £25; HB weekly £210–£237

ST SAMPSONS

Ann-Dawn (Acclaimed), Route des Capelles ☎ (0481) 25606. *Private Hotel.* Open Easter–end Oct.
£ B&B £17–£22; HB weekly £157·50–£171·50; [5% V]

ST SAVIOURS

★★★ **H** **R** **L'Atlantique,** Perelle Bay ☎ (0481) 64056 Fax: (0481) 63800

Modern granite-built hotel in beautifully landscaped grounds. Close to beaches. Swimming pool. Fr, De, Po
21 bedrs, 21 en suite, TV; tcf
ns; P 70, child facs; con 25
✕ LD 10, bar meals only Mon–Sat lunch
£ B&B £20–£33, B&B (double) £40–£66; L £7·50, D £8·75; WB £50
cc Access, Amex, B'card/Visa, Diners.

La Girouette Country House (Highly Acclaimed), La Girouette ☎ (0481) 63269 Fax: (0481) 63023. Open end Apr–end Oct.
£ B&B £18–£39; [10% V]

Hotel locations
Hotel locations are shown on the maps at the back of the guide. All towns and villages containing an RAC Appointed or Listed hotel are ringed in purple.

VALE

★★★ **Novotel,** Les Dicqs ☎ (0481) 48400 Tx: 4191306 Fax: (0481) 48706 ♿

Modern hotel overlooking the Grand Havre Bay. Swimming pool, putting, gymnasium, snooker.
99 bedrs, 99 en suite; TV; tcf
lift, dogs; P 150, coach; child facs; con 200
(*See advertisement on p. 670*)

JERSEY

Pop 75,000. Guernsey 25, Weymouth 103. **EC** Thur.
Weighbridge, St Helier ☎ (0534) 78000

BEAUMONT

Bryn-y-Mor, Route de la Haule ☎ (0534) 20295 Tx: 4192638 Fax: (0354) 35231.

GOREY

★★★ **Les Arches,** Archirondel Bay ☎ (0534) 53839 Tx: 4192085 Fax: (0534) 56660

Modern granite white-rendered 3-storey building overlooking beautiful bay. Swimming pool, tennis, sauna, gymnasium. Fr, Es, It, Po
54 bedrs, 54 en suite; TV; tcf
TV, dogs; P 120; child facs; con 150
✕ LD 8.45
£ B&B £27·50–£39, B&B (double) £55–£78; L £9·50, D £11·50; [10% Nov–Apr]
cc Access, B'card/Visa; dep.

★★★ **Old Court House** ☎ (0534) 54444 Tx: 4192032 Fax: (0534) 53587

White building with distinctive verandahs. Incorporates 15th century court house. Swimming pool, sauna, solarium. Open Mar–Nov.

CI

Vale (Guernsey) Channel Islands

St Brelade (Jersey)

St Brelade (Jersey, Channel Islands)

🛏 58 bedrs, 58 en suite; TV
🏨 dogs, lift; P 40, coach; child facs
✕ LD 9
£ [10% V Mar, Apr, Oct]
cc Access, Amex, B'card/Visa, Diners; dep.

★★ **Dolphin,** Gorey Pier ☎ (0534) 53370
Tx: 4192085 Fax: (0534) 56660
Attractive 3-storey hotel overlooking picturesque Gorey Harbour. Fr, Es, Po
🛏 16 bedrs, 16 en suite; TV; tcf
🏨 TV, dogs; child facs; con 20
✕ LD 10.15
£ B&B £27·50–£39, B&B (double) £55–£78; L £9·25, D £12·50; [10% V Nov–Apr]
cc Access, B'card/Visa, CB; dep.

★★ **Maison Gorey** ☎ (0534) 57775
Fax: (0534) 57779

Recently refurbished, family-run hotel in centre of village. Po. Open Mar–Oct
🛏 30 bedrs, 30 en suite, TV; tcf
🏨 TV, dogs, P 6, coach, child facs
✕ LD 8.30, bar meals only Mon–Sat lunch. Resid & Rest lic
£ B&B £29–£42, B&B (double) £38–64; D £9
cc Access, Amex, B'card/Visa, Diners; dep.

★★ **Moorings,** Gorey Pier ☎ (0534) 53633
Tx: 4192085 Fax: (0534) 56660
Tucked between Mont Orgeuil castle and the harbour, a traditional hotel with lovely views. Fr, Es, Po
🛏 16 bedrs, 16 en suite; TV; tcf
🏨 TV, dogs; child facs; con 20
✕ LD 10.15
£ B&B £30–£39, B&B (double) £60–£78; L £9·25, D £13; [10% V]
cc Access, Amex, B'card/Visa, CB; dep.

ROZEL BAY

★★★ **Chateau la Chaire** ☎ (0534) 63354 Fax: (0534) 65137

Charming, multi-gabled Victorian house with conservatory extension on one side; in terraced, wooded gardens. Fr
🛏 13 bedrs, 13 en suite, TV
🏨 dogs; P 25, coach; no children under 7
✕ LD 10, Resid & Rest lic
£ B&B £52–£90, B&B (double) £74–£105; L £9·95
cc Access, Amex, B'card/Visa, Diners; dep.

ST BRELADE

★★★★ **Atlantic,** La Moye ☎ (0534) 44101
Tx: 4192405 Fax: (0534) 44102

Light, modern 3-storey luxury hotel with balconies overlooking pleasant gardens. Swimming pool, tennis, sauna, solarium, gymnasium. Open 9 Mar 3–Dec. Fr, De, It, Po
🛏 50 bedrs, 50 en suite; TV
🏨 lift; P 60; child facs; con 60
✕ LD 9.15
£ B&B £70–£100, B&B (double) £100–£170; HB weekly £472·50–£717·50; L £10·75, D £18·25; [V]
cc Access, Amex, B'card/Visa, Diners; dep.
(See advertisement on p. 670)

ST BRELADE'S BAY

★★★★ H C R **L'Horizon** ☎ (0534) 43101 Tx: 4192281 Fax: (0534) 46269 ♿
Elegant modern luxury hotel; a long building overlooking fine sandy beach. Indoor swimming pool, sauna, solarium.
🛏 104 bedrs, 104 en suite; TV
🏨 lift; P 125; child facs; con 180
✕ LD 10
£ B&B fr £65, B&B (double) fr £150; L fr £10·50, D fr £19·50; WB fr £195
cc Access, B'card/Visa.
(See advertisement on p. 670)

★★★★ **St Brelade's Bay** ☎ (0534) 46141
Tx: 4192519
Family-owned and managed, a white-painted luxury holiday hotel in lovely gardens beside the beach. Open May–Oct
🛏 72 bedrs, 72 ensuite; TV
🏨 lift; P 50; child facs
✕ LD 9

★★★ H R **Château de la Valeuse**
☎ (0534) 46281 Fax: (0534) 47110
4-storey white-painted hotel with fine views of long sandy beach. Swimming pool. Open Mar–Dec. Fr, De, It, Du
🛏 33 bedrs, 33 en suite, 1 ba; TV
🏨 P 50; no children under 5
✕ LD 9.15
£ B&B £32–£38, B&B (double) £64–£76; L £9·50, D £12; WB £32 (min 3 nts, Nov, Dec)
cc Access, B'card/Visa; dep.

★★ **Beau Rivage** ☎ (0534) 45983
Tx: 4192341

White-painted 4-storey building with sun terrace and verandahs overlooking picturesque bay.

ST CLEMENT

★★★ **Ambassadeur,** St Clements Bay
☎ (0534) 24455 Tx: 4192636
Fax: (0534) 30301

Modern 3-storey hotel on coastal road. Near extensive sandy beach. Swimming pool.
Fr, De, Es
🛏 41 bedrs, 41 en suite, 1 ba; TV; tcf
🏨 lift, dogs; P 50, coach; child facs; con 40
✕ LD 9.45
£ B&B £16·50–£35·75, B&B (double) £33–£71·50; HB weekly, £144–£285; L £6·50, D £7·50; [5% V]
cc Access, Amex, B'card/Visa, Diners; dep.

★★★ R **Shakespeare,** Samares ☎ (0534) 51915 Fax: (0534) 56269

Three-storey white-painted building with attractive terrace. Small private beach.
Open 2 Feb–30 Nov & 23 Dec–2 Jan
🛏 30 bedrs, 30 en suite; TV
🏨 lift, dogs; coach; child facs; con 20

ST HELIER

★★★★ **Grand,** Esplanade ☎ (0534) 22301
Tx: 4192104 Fax: (0534) 37815

Large and elegant luxury seafront hotel with distinctive gables. Overlooks Bay. Indoor swimming pool, sauna, solarium, gymnasium, billiards. (DeV) Fr, It
🛏 115 bedrs, 115 en suite, TV; tcf
🏨 lift, dogs; P 30, coach; child facs; con 200
✕ LD 10

CI

Apollo Hotel

St. Saviour's Rd., St. Helier, Jersey, Channel Islands
Telephone 0534:25441 Telex 4192086

Modern 3 Star Hotel with an Indoor Leisure Centre, built around a quiet courtyard in the middle of St. Helier.

85 rooms with bathroom en suite, colour television with satellite link, direct dial telephone, tea and coffee making facilities, trouser press and hairdryers.

Indoor swimming pool, jacuzzi, saunas, sun beds, gymnasium and games room. 'The Coffee Grove' overlooking the pool, 'Le Petit Jardin' for aperitifs and fine cuisine. 'Haughty Pigeon' bar for local atmosphere.

Centrally heated throughout.
Ample Car Parking.
Open all year.

Beaufort Hotel

St. Helier, Jersey, Channel Islands.
Telephone: 0534 - 76500
Telex: 4192160

Modern 3 Star Hotel well situated for shopping, business or beach in St. Helier's commercial centre. The Beaufort has been designed to offer every amenity for today's traveller. Brummels Bar for aperitifs. The Rib Room for fine cuisine. Ample car parking.

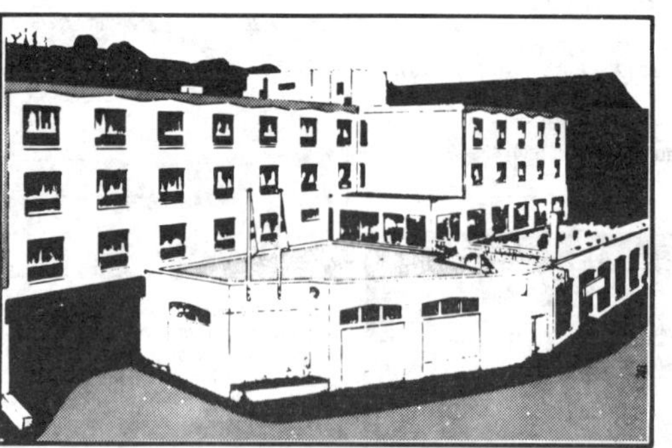

INDOOR SWIMMING POOL AND SPA

All bedrooms are equipped with

- Full Bathroom and Shower.
- Hairdryer and Trouser Press.
- Tea and Coffee making facilities.
- Direct Dial Telephones.
- Colour T.V. with Satellite Channels.
- Full Lounge Armchairs.
- Writing Desk.
- Mini Bars in De Luxe rooms.

First Register ☺☺☺

£ B&B £50–£75, B&B (double) £95–£140; HB weekly £409·50–£549·50; L fr £12·50, D Fr £13·50; WB £58·50 (HB); [10% V w/e] cc Access, Amex, B'card/Visa, Diners; dep.

★★★ C **Apollo,** St Saviour's Rd (0534) 25441 Tx: 4192086 Fax: (0534) 73545

Modern hotel conveniently situated near to town centre. Indoor swimming pool, sauna, solarium, gymnasium. Fr, De, Es, Po
85 bedrs, 85 en suite, TV; tcf
lift; ns; P 55, child facs; con 150
LD 9, nr lunch
£ B&B £42–£62, B&B (double) £69–£94; HB weekly £280–£329; L £8, D £9; WB £32 (HB, low season, 2 nts min)
cc Access, Amex, B'card/Visa, Diners; dep.
(*See advertisement on p. 672*)

★★★ **Beaufort,** Green St (0534) 76500 Tx: 4192160 Fax: (0534) 20371

Modern 4-storey hotel with sun terrace. Few minutes from sea. Indoor swimming pool. Fr, Es, It, Po
54 bedrs, 54 en suite, 1 ba; TV; tcf
lift, ns; P 27, coach; child facs; con 100
LD 9
£ B&B £45–£64·50, B&B (double) £73·50–£91; HB weekly £549·50–£672; L £7·50, D £9·50; WB £32 (2 nts min, low season)
cc Access, Amex, B'card/Visa, Diners; dep.
(*See advertisement on p. 672*)

★★★ **Ommaroo,** Havre des Pas, (0534) 23493 Tx: 4192225 Fax: (0534) 59912

A four-storey, white-painted hotel conveniently placed overlooking a bay east of St Helier.
85 bedrs, 63 en suite, 6 ba; TV
lift, TV, dogs; P 80, coach; child facs; con 100

★★★ **Pomme D'Or,** Liberation Sq (0534) 78644 Tx: 4192309 Fax: (0534) 37781

Cream painted building offering modern accommodation. Near town centre. Fr
150 bedrs, 150 en suite; TV; tcf
lift, ns; coach; child facs; con
LD 9, bar meals only lunch
£ B&B £50–£55, B&B (double) £70–£80; L fr £6·40, D £12·50; [10% V]
cc Access, Amex, B'card/Visa, Diners; dep.

★★ C **Laurels,** Route du Fort (0534) 36444 Tx: 4192193 Fax: (0534) 59904

Three-storey hotel on a main road close to town centre and not far from sea front. Swimming pool, sauna.
37 bedrs, 37 en suite; TV
dogs; P 35, coach; child facs

★★ **Mont Millais,** Mont Millais St (0534) 30281
Cream-painted 2- and 3-storey hotel with secluded suntrap garden.
44 bedrs, 44 en suite; TV
P 20; child facs; con 30

★★ **Royal Yacht,** (0534) 20511 Tx: 4192642 Fax: (0534) 67272

Five-storey Victorian building convenient for the ferries and town centre. Fr, Es, Po
45 bedrs, 45 en suite, 1 ba; TV; tcf
lift, TV, dogs; coach; child facs; con 30
LD 8.30
£ B&B £30–£34, B&B (double) £60–£72; HB weekly £255·50–£287; L £5·50, D £10·50; [10% V]
cc Access, Amex, B'card/Visa, CB; dep.

★★ **Sarum,** New St John's Rd, (0534) 58163 Tx: 4192341

Four-storey hotel in a quiet residential area close to town centre.

Runnymede Court (Highly Acclaimed), 46 Roseville St, (0534) 20044 *Hotel.* Open mid-Feb–mid Dec. Fr, De
£ B&B £16–£26; [10% V Feb–Apr, Sep–Dec]

Cornucopia (Acclaimed), Mont Pinel (0534) 32646 Fax: (0534) 66199 *Private Hotel*, Fr, Po, Yu. Closed Xmas
£ B&B £22–£30·50; HB weekly £164–£248; [V Oct–May]

Millbrook House (Acclaimed), Rue de Trachy, Millbrook (0534) 33036. *Hotel.* Open 25 Apr–8 Oct.
£ B&B £21·50–£30·50; HB weekly £150·50–£227–50

ST LAWRENCE

★★★ H R **Little Grove,** Rue de Haut (0534) 25321 Fax: (0534) 25325

In own secluded grounds, an attractive stone-built house. Swimming pool. Fr, Po
13 bedrs, 13 en suite; TV
P 24; children over 12; con 25
LD 9.30. Resid & Rest lic
£ B&B £74·50–£96, B&B (double) £99–£168; HB weekly £437·70–£538·65; L £11·50, D £22·50; [10% V Oct–Mar]
cc Access, Amex, B'card/Visa, Diners.

ST OUEN

★★★ C R **Lobster Pot,** L'Etacq (0534) 82888 Tx: 4192605 Fax: (0534) 81574
Pleasant long granite building with Georgian style windows. On St Ouen Bay. Fr, Po
13 bedrs, 13 en suite; TV; tcf
P 60; children over 14
LD 10.15
£ B&B £45–£63·50, B&B (double) £70–£107; HB weekly £437·50–£472·50; L £9·50, D £14; [10% V]
cc Access, Amex, B'card/Visa, Diners.
(*See advertisement on p. 674*)

Hotel des Pierres (Highly Acclaimed), Greve de Lecq Bay (0534) 81858 Fax: (0534) 85273. Open Mar–Dec. Fr, De
£ B&B £23–£28; HB weekly £175–£231

St Ouen (Jersey, Channel Islands)

For full details write to: The Manager, The Lobster Pot Hotel & Restaurant, L'Etacq, St. Ouen, Jersey, Channel Islands or Telephone: 0534 82888
Telex: 4192605 'LOBPOT'
Fax: 0534 81574

The Lobster Pot HOTEL & RESTAURANT
Jerseys' most famous restaurant for over a quarter of a century.

All bedrooms in this luxurious first register hotel have en suite bathrooms, central heating, hair dryers, razor points, colour television with video film channel, mini bar refrigerators, electric trouser presses, direct dial telephones and tea/coffee making facilities.
Situated only 75 yards from the beautiful St. Ouen's Bay (5 miles of golden sand), the Lobster Pot Hotel is open throughout the year and enjoys an internationally renowned reputation for excellent cuisine with full à la carte or table d'hôte menus available at all meals and the Coach House buffet bar open daily from 10.15am for lighter snacks. Dancing every evening (except Sunday) to our resident musician.
Recommended by Egon Ronay – The rest are waiting for you to discover!

St Peter's (Jersey)

Mermaid Hotel

First Register

St. Peter, Jersey, Channel Islands

Telephone : (0534) 41255 Telex : 4192249

Incorporating an original ancient Tavern and beautiful old granite Grill Room dating back to 1710 The Mermaid is a modern hotel built around a small natural lake.

The Mermaid has a superb Indoor Leisure Centre including a 44ft. swimming pool, jacuzzi, saunas, solarium sun beds and gymnasium. In the garden there are 2 tennis courts and an 18 hole putting green.

All bedrooms have bathrooms en suite and balconies. De Luxe rooms include minibar, trouserpress and hairdryer.

OPEN ALL YEAR

AMPLE PARKING

ST PETER'S

★★★ **Mermaid** ☎(0534) 41255
Tx: 4192249 Fax: (0534) 73543

Luxury, mainly modern, 2-storey hotel retaining historic tavern. Overlooks lake. Indoor swimming pool, putting, tennis, sauna, solarium, gymnasium. Fr, Es, Po
68 bedrs, 68 en suite, 2 ba; TV; tcf
ns; P 150; child facs; con 150
LD 9
£ B&B £39–£66, B&B (double) £68–£98; HB weekly £275–£357; L £7·50, D £9·50; WB £30 (HB low season)
cc Access, Amex, B'card/Visa, Diners; dep.
(*See advertisement on p. 674*)

Midvale, St Peter's Valley ☎(0534) 42498.
Private Hotel.

ST SAVIOUR'S

★★★★ **Longueville Manor** ☎(0534) 25501 Tx: 4192306
Fax: (0534) 31613

Gracious creeper-covered mansion in extensive gardens. Fine antique furnishings. Swimming pool. Fr, It, Po, No
33 bedrs, 33 en suite; 1 ba; TV
lift, dogs; ns; P 40; no children under 7; con 15
LD 9.30, Resid & Rest lic
£ B&B £68–£82, B&B (double) £104–£167; L £17, D £25; WB £55 (HB); [5% Nov–Mar]
cc Access, Amex, B'card/Visa, Diners; dep.

★★★ **L'Emeraude,** Longueville ☎(0534) 74512 Tx: 4192096

White-painted classical building with modern wings. Swimming pool.
51 bedrs, 47 en suite, 2 ba; TV
TV, dogs, ns; P 80; child facs; con 50

Please tell the manager if you chose your hotel through an advertisement in the guide.

CI

NORTHERN IRELAND

BALLYGALLY Co. Antrim. Map 61C4
Pop 2,245. Larne 3, Belfast 22, Antrim 22, Ballymena 18, Coleraine 40.
Golf Cairndhu 18h. **See** Ballygally Castle (now Hotel), sandy beach, Cairncastle Church.

★★★ **Ballygally Castle,** 274 Coast Rd, Larne, BT40 2QZ ☎ (0574) 83212
Fax: (0574) 83681
17th century castle, greatly extended and modernised, facing sandy beach. Tennis, fishing.
30 bedrs, 30 en suite; TV; tcf
TV, dogs; P 70, coach; child facs; con 100

★★ **Halfway,** Coast Rd, BT40 2RA ☎ (0574) 83265
Modern hotel in an attractive location on Antrim coast road.

BALLYMENA Co Antrim. Map 61B3
M2 1, M22 10, Antrim 11, Belfast 29, Coleraine 26, Larne 19.
80 Galgorm Rd ☎ (0266) 44111

★★★ **Adair Arms,** Ballymoney Rd, BT43 5BS ☎ (0266) 653674
Fax: (0266) 40436

Stone-built 3-storey Victorian hotel with modern extensions. In town centre. Fr
38 bedrs, 38 en suite; TV; tcf
TV, ns; dogs; P 70, coach; child facs; con 300
LD 9.30
£ B&B £45, B&B (double) £58; L £7·25, D £12·75; WB £53 (2 nts HB); [10% V]
cc Access, Amex, B'card/Visa, Diners.

BELFAST Co. Antrim and Co. Down. Map 61C3
See also NEWTOWN ABBEY.
RAC Office, *79 Chichester Street, Belfast, BT1 4JR* ☎ (General) Belfast (0232) 240261 (Rescue Service only) Belfast (0232) 323333
Pop 297,862. Antrim 14, Coleraine 4, Larne 19, Londonderry 74, Newry 38.
See Plan, p. 677.
MD Mon, Tue, Fri. **Golf** Royal Belfast (Craigavad) 18h, Balmoral 18h, Cliftonville 9h, Fortwilliam 18h, Belvoir Park 18h, Shandon Park 18h, The Knock 18h, Mahee Island 9h, Ormeau 9h. **See** University, Botanical Gardens, Museums, Cathedrals (St Anne's Protestant, St Peter's RC), Ormeau Park, City Hall, Art Gallery, *Titanic* Memorial, "Giants' Ring" one of the largest prehistoric earthworks in Ireland, Farrell's Fort, Belfast Castle, Cave Hill (1,182 ft), with McArt's fort on summit, Albert Memorial (tilted 5ft out of plumb).
52 High St. ☎ (0232) 246609

★★★★ **Europa,** Great Victoria St, BT2 7AP ☎ (0232) 327000 Tx: 74491
Fax: (0232) 327800

Luxury high-rise modern hotel right in the heart of Belfast. Fr, De, It, Ar
198 bedrs, 198 en suite; TV; tcf
lift, ns; coach; child facs; con 1100
LD 11.30
£ B&B £107·95, B&B (double) £155·90; L £9·95, D £17·75; [5% V w/e Jul, Aug, Dec, Jan]
cc Access, Amex, B'card/Visa; Diners.

★★★ **Stormont,** 587 Upper Newtonards Rd, BT4 1LP ☎ (0232) 658621 Tx: 748198
Fax: (0232) 480240
Former mansion house with modern extensions. Near Stormont Castle grounds.
67 bedrs, 67 en suite; TV; tcf
lift, P 600, coach; child facs; con 300
LD 9.45
£ L £10·50, D £14·50, WB £27·75
cc Access, Amex, B'card/Visa, Diners; dep.

BUSHMILLS Co. Antrim. Map 61B4
Portnish 7, Belfast 54, Ballycastle 10.
See Giant's Causeway.

★★★ **Bushmills Inn,** 25 Main St, BT57 8QA ☎ (026 57) 32339

Listed 19th-century coaching inn, restored and extended in keeping, now an attractive hotel. Fr
11 bedrs, 11 en suite; TV
dogs; P 35, coach; child facs; con 120
LD 9.30
£ B&B £38–£48, B&B (double) £58; HB weekly £235; L £8·50, D £14·50; WB £65 (2 nts HB)
cc Access, B'card/Visa.

CARNLOUGH Co. Antrim. Map 61C4
Pop 2,280. Larne 12, Belfast 31, Ballymena 14, Coleraine 34.
Golf Cairndhu 18h. **See** Glenarm Castle.
Post Office, Harbour Rd. ☎ (0574) 85210

★★ **Londonderry Arms,** BT44 0EU ☎ (0574) 885255 Fax: (0574) 885263
Fine 19th century building–former coaching inn withattractive furnishings. Fr, De
20 bedrs, 20 en suite; TV
ns; P 30, coach; child facs; con 50
LD 9
£ B&B £27, B&B (double) £48; HB weekly £210; L £8·95, D £11·95; WB £52·95 (2 nts); [5% V w/d]
cc Access, Amex, B'card/Visa, Diners; dep.

CARRICKFERGUS Co. Antrim. Map 61C3
Pop 19,000. Belfast 10, Antrim 17, Ballymena 23, Larne 14.
EC Wed. **MD** Thur. **Golf** Carrickfergus 18h, Bentra 9h, Greenisland 9h, Whitehead 18h.
See Castle, St Nicholas Church, Market Sq.
Castle Green. ☎ (096 03) 51604

★ **Dobbins Inn,** BT38 7AF ☎ (096 03) 51905

Charming historic building of 3 storeys on shores of Belfast Lough. Closed 25–26 Dec.
13 bedrs, 13 en suite; TV; tcf
TV, dogs; child facs; con 20
LD 9, bar meals only Mon–Sat lunch
£ B&B £33 (w/e £25), B&B (double) £52; L £3·50, D £5
cc Access, Amex, B'card/Visa, Diners.

CRAWFORDSBURN Co. Down. Map 61C3
Pop 2,904. Holywood 7, Belfast 11, Bangor 2, Newtownards 6.
EC Thur. **Golf** Holywood 18h, Carnalea 18h. **See** Ulster Folk Museum.

EC *early closing* **MD** *market day* *country house hotel* *ns (NS) no smoking areas* *tcf tea/coffee facilities*

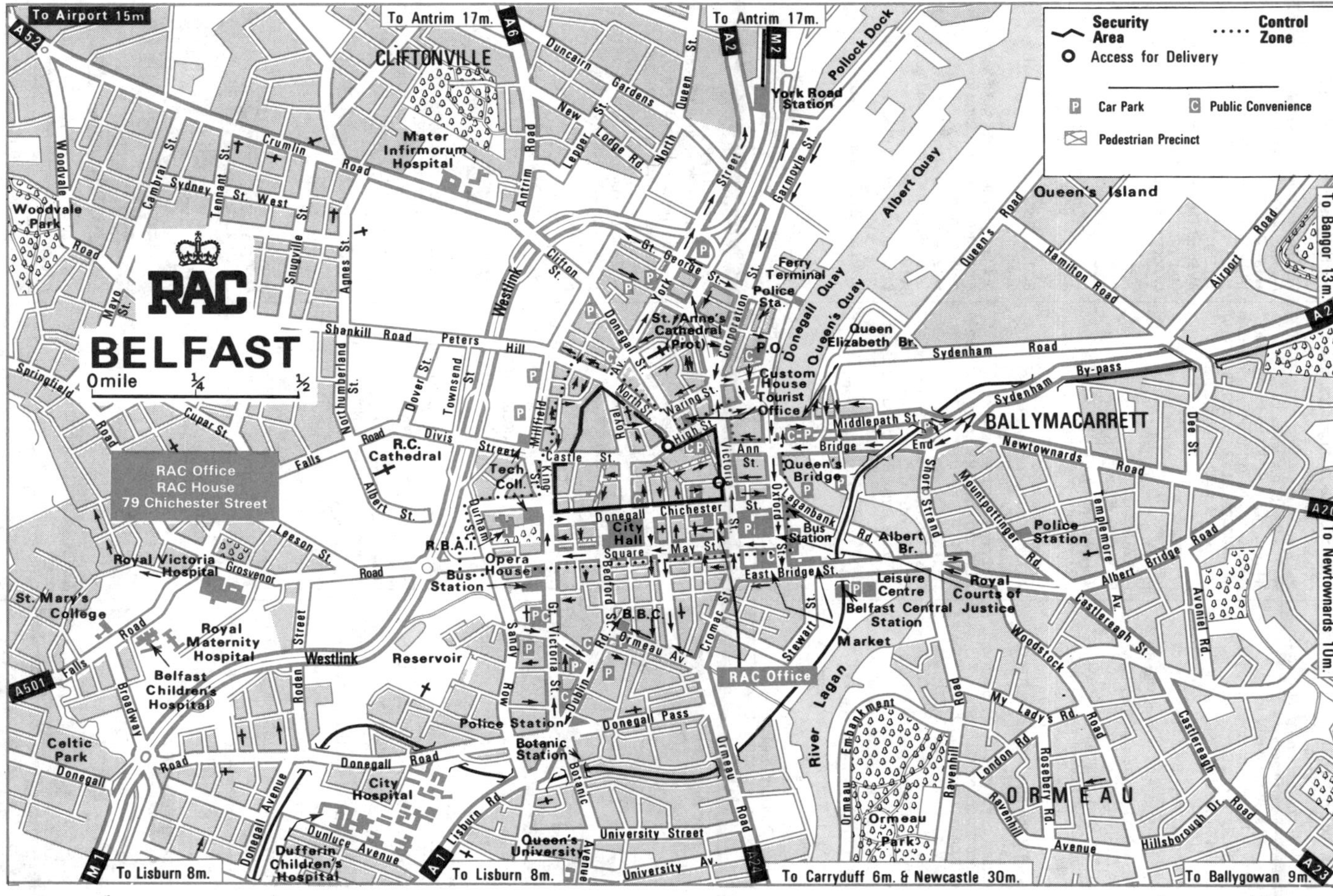
RAC
BELFAST
0 mile ¼ ½
RAC Office
RAC House
79 Chichester Street
Security Area
Control Zone
Access for Delivery
Car Park
Public Convenience
Pedestrian Precinct
To Airport 15m
To Antrim 17m.
To Antrim 17m.
To Bangor 13m.
To Newtownards 10m.
To Ballygowan 9m.
To Carryduff 6m. & Newcastle 30m.
To Lisburn 8m.
To Lisburn 8m.
CLIFTONVILLE
BALLYMACARRETT
ORMEAU
Queen's Island
Albert Quay
Pollock Dock
York Road Station
Mater Infirmorum Hospital
Woodvale Park
St. Anne's Cathedral (Prot)
Custom House
Tourist Office
City Hall
Bus Station
R.C. Cathedral
Tech Coll.
R.B.A.I.
Opera House
Bus Station
B.B.C.
Leisure Centre
Belfast Central Station
Royal Courts of Justice
Market
Police Station
RAC Office
River Lagan
Ormeau Park
Royal Victoria Hospital
Royal Maternity Hospital
Belfast Children's Hospital
St. Mary's College
Reservoir
Botanic Station
City Hospital
Queen's University
Dufferin Children's Hospital
Celtic Park

★★★ **Old Inn,** Main St, BT19 1JH ☎ Helen's Bay (0247) 853255 Fax: (0247) 852775
Mainly Georgian, charming "olde worlde" building—in part thatched.
🛏 32 bedrs, 32 en suite; TV; tcf
🏠 TV, P 76, child facs; con 120
✕ LD 9.30, HT only Sun dinner
£ B&B £60 (w/e £35), B&B (double) £75 (w/e £60); D £12
cc Access, Amex, B'card/Visa.

CUSHENDALL Co. Antrim. Map 61C4

Pop 1,100. Larne 24, Belfast 43, Ballymena 19, Coleraine 33.
EC Tue. **Golf** Cushendall 9h. **See** Glens of Antrim, Ossian's Grave, Forest Park, Curfew Tower.
ℹ Bridge St. ☎ (026 67) 71180

★★ **H** **Thornlea,** 6 Coast Rd, BT44 0RU ☎ (026 67) 71223
Attractive small white modern building adjacent to golf course.
🛏 13 bedrs, 9 en suite, (3 sh), 1 ba; TV; tcf
🏠 TV, dogs, P 35, coach; child facs
✕ LD 9.15
£ B&B £17·50, B&B (double) £32·50; L £6·50; WB £35
cc Access, Amex, B'card/Visa, Diners; dep.

DUNADRY Co. Antrim. Map 61B3

Pop 204. Belfast 12, M2 Motorway ½, Antrim 3, Ballymena 10, Larne 16.
EC Wed. **Golf** Massereene 18h.

★★★★ **Dunadry Inn,** BT41 2HA ☎ Templepatrick (084 94) 32474 Tx: 747245 Fax: (084 94) 33389

Traditional-style elegant modern building, beautifully furnished. Millstream in grounds. Fishing. ✂ Fr, Es, It. Closed 23–27 Dec.
🛏 64 bedrs, 64 en suite; TV
🏠 P 350, coach; child facs; con 350
✕ LD 9.45, bar meals only Sat lunch
£ B&B £67·50 (w/e £29·50), B&B (double) £82·50 (w/e £45); L £6, D £14
cc Access, Amex, B'card/Visa, CB, Diners.

DUNGANNON Co. Tyrone. Map 61B3

Pop 9,000. M1 Motorway 4, Belfast 42, Armagh 12, Cookstown 10, Monaghan 21, Portadown 16.
EC Wed. **MD** Tue, Thur. **Golf** Dungannon 18h.

★★★ **Inn on the Park,** Moy Rd, BT71 6BS ☎ (086 87) 25151 Fax: (086 87) 24953

In 7½ acres of secluded grounds, attractive modern 2-storey white building. Tennis, snooker.
🛏 15 bedrs, 15 en suite; TV; tcf
🏠 TV, dogs, ns; P 300, child facs; con 300
£ B&B £27·50 (w/e £15), B&B (double) £50; HB weekly £250; L £7·95, D £9·75; [10% V]
cc Access, B'card/Visa, Diners; dep.

DUNMURRY Co. Antrim. Map 61C3

Pop 3,700. Belfast 5, M1 2½, Antrim 20, Lisburn 3.
EC Wed. **Golf** Dunmurry 18h.

★★★★ **Conway,** BT17 9ES ☎ Belfast (0232) 612101 Tx: 74281 Fax: (0232) 626546
Elegant former residence in 14 acres of woodland. Swimming pool, squash, billiards. ✂ Fr, Re. (THF)
🛏 82 bedrs, 82 en suite; TV; tcf
🏠 lift, dogs, ns; P 300, coach; child facs; con 350
✕ LD 10
£ B&B £80, B&B (double) £98; L £7·50, D £12·50; WB £47 (2 nts); [10% V]
cc Access, Amex, B'card/Visa, CB, Diners.

ENNISKILLEN Co. Fermanagh. Map 61A3

Pop 10,429. Dungannon 37, Belfast 74, Donegal 31, Omagh 22, Sligo 34.
EC Wed. **MD** Thur. **Golf** Enniskillen 9h. **See** Castle, Lakes, Castle Coole (NT), Cathedral.
ℹ Lakeland Visitor Centre, Shore Rd. ☎ (0365) 23110

★★★ **Killyhevlin,** Dublin Rd, BT74 8JT ☎ (0365) 323481 Fax: (0365) 324726
Charmingly irregular, white-painted building in well-dept grounds near A4, east of town. Fine views over Lough Earn. Fishing.
🛏 23 bedrs, 23 en suite; TV; tcf
🏠 dogs, P 200, coach; child facs; con 550
✕ LD 9, nr Sun lunch
£ B&B £41·26–£45, B&B (double) £57·50–£62·50; L £6, D £14·50; WB £57·50; [5% V]
cc Access, Amex, B'card/Visa, Diners; dep.

★ **Railway,** BT74 6AJ ☎ (0365) 22084
Modern 3-storey hotel facing the market area in town.

HOLYWOOD Co. Down. Map 61C3

Pop 8,573. Belfast 5, Bangor 7, Newtownards 7.
EC Wed. **Golf** Holywood 18h. **See** Holywood Priory remains, Norman motte.

★★★★ **R** **Culloden,** Bangor Rd, Craigavad, BT18 0EX ☎ Holywood (023 17) 5223 Tx: 74617 Fax: (023 17) 6777 ♿
Fine 19th century Scottish baronial style mansion in 12 acres of grounds. Putting, tennis, squash, gymnasium, billiards. ✂ Fr, De
🛏 91 bedrs, 91 en suite; TV; tcf
🏠 lift, dogs; P 500, coach; child facs; con 550
✕ LD 9.30, nr Sat lunch
£ B&B £94, B&B (double) £120; L £13, D £13; WB £70
cc Access, Amex, B'card/Visa, Diners.

IRVINESTOWN Co. Fermanagh. Map 61A3

Pop 1,827. Dungannon 34, Belfast 71, Donegal 23, Omagh 15.
EC Thur. **MD** Wed. **Golf** Castlecoole 9h.

★★ **Mahons,** Enniskillen Rd, BT74 9XX ☎ (036 56) 21656
Victorian hotel with interesting touring relics. Near to Lough Erne. Solarium.
🛏 18 bedrs, 18 en suite; TV
🏠 TV, dogs; ns; P 20, G 10, child facs; con 150
✕ LD 9
£ L £6·50, D £9·50; WB £35; [5% V Oct–Apr]
cc Access, B'card/Visa.

KESH Co. Fermanagh. Map 61A3

Pop 2,607. Omagh 16, Belfast 74, Ballyshannon 19, Donegal 18, Enniskillen 13.
EC Thur. **Golf** Castle Coole 9h. **See** Boa Island.

★★ **Lough Erne,** Main St. ☎ (036 56) 31275
Attractive modern hotel of striking design near Lough Erne. Fishing.
🛏 12 bedrs, 12 en suite; TV; tcf
🏠 TV, dogs; P 100, coach; child facs
✕ LD 9
£ B&B £22, HB weekly £195; L fr £7; WB £46; [5% V]
cc Access, B'card/Visa, Diners; dep.

KILKEEL Co. Down. Map 61C2

Pop 5,000. Newry 16, Belfast 49, Downpatrick 22, Dundalk 27.
EC Thur. **MD** Wed. **Golf** Kilkeel 9h. **See** Harbour, Silent Valley Reservoir, Annalong Corn Mill and Marine Park.
ℹ Marine Esplanade. ☎ (069 37) 64666

★★ **Kilmorey Arms.** ☎ (069 37) 62220
Three-storey family hotel on corner site in delightful fishing port. ✂ Fr
🛏 12 bedrs, 12 en suite
🏠 TV, dogs, coach, child facs; con 30
✕ LD 8.30
£ B&B £18·50–£22·50, B&B (double) £34–£40; L £6·50, D £8; [5% V]
cc Access, B'card/Visa, Diners.

LONDONDERRY Co. Londonderry. Map 61A4

Pop 90,400. Dungiven 19, Belfast 70, Coleraine 30, Limavady 17, Strabane 14.
EC Thurs. **MD** Wed, Thur. **Golf** City of Derry 18h. **See** Cathedrals, Guildhall, City Walls.
ℹ Foyle St ☎ (0504) 267284

★★★★ **Everglades,** Prehen Rd, BT47 2PA ☎ (0504) 46722 Tx: 748005 Fax: (0504) 49200 ♿

Long, low-built modern hotel beside busy A5 on south side of city. Gymnasium.
🛏 56 bedrs, 56 en suite; TV; tcf
🏠 lift, dogs, ns; P 120, coach; child facs; con 250

MAGHERAMORNE Co. Antrim Map 61C3
Pop 300, Carrickfergus 10, Belfast 21, Antrim 28, Ballymena 24, Larne 4.
Golf Bentra, Whitehead 9h. **See** Nature Reserve (R.S.P.B.).

★★★ Magheramorne House, BT40 3HW Larne (0574) 79444
Carefully restored Victorian mansion in formal gardens and natural grounds.
23 bedrs, 23 en suite; TV; tcf
lift, dogs; P 150, coach; child facs; con 100

NEWCASTLE Co. Down. Map 61C2
Pop 4,647. Belfast 26, Armagh 32, Downpatrick 11, Newry 20.
EC Thur. **MD** Tue, Fri. **Golf** Royal County Down 18h (2).
Newcastle Centre, Central Promenade. (039 67) 22222

★★★ Slieve Donard, Downs Rd, BT33 0AG (039 67) 23681
Fax: (039 67) 24830
Glorious mansion in 6 acres with frontage on a private beach. Indoor swimming pool, putting, tennis, sauna, solarium, gymnasium.
100 bedrs, 100 en suite; TV; tcf
lift, TV, dogs; P 500, coach; child facs; con 1000
LD 9.30
£ B&B £52, B&B (double) £78; HB weekly £275; L £10·50, D £15·50; WB £75 (HB)
cc Access, Amex, B'card/Visa, Diners.

Brook Cottage (Acclaimed), 58 Bryansford Rd, BT33 0LD (039 67) 22204. *Hotel.*

NEWRY Co Down. Map 61B2
Pop 28,000. Belfast 38, Armagh 19, Banbridge 13, Dundalk 13, Rostrevor 9.
Bank Parade (0693) 61244

★★★ Mourne Country, 52 Belfast Rd, BT34 1TR (0693) 67922
Spacious, low-built modern hotel on the A1 one mile north of town.

NEWTOWNABBEY Co. Antrim. Map 61C3
Pop 71,917. Belfast 4, M2 Motorway 2, Antrim 13, Carrickfergus 5, Larne 15.
EC Wed. **MD** Mon. **Golf** Balleyclare 18h.

★★★ Chimney Corner, 630 Antrim Rd, BT36 8RH Glengormley (023 13) 44925
Tx: 748158
Large light modern hotel of attractive design. Just outside Belfast. Sauna, solarium, gymnasium.
63 bedrs, 63 en suite; TV; tcf
TV; P 320, coach; child facs; con 200

OMAGH Co. Tyrone. Map 61A3
Pop 15,000. Dungannon 23, Belfast 60, Enniskillen 22, Strabane 20.
EC Wed. **MD** Mon. **Golf** Omagh 9h. **See** Ulster American Folk Park, Gortin Glen Forest, Sloughan Glen.
1 Market St. (0662) 47831

★★ Royal Arms, 51 High St, BT78 1BA (0662) 243262 Fax: (0662) 245011

Fine 18th century building with pleasant garden at rear. Billiards. Closed 25 Dec.
21 bedrs, 21 en suite, TV; tcf
TV, dogs; ns; P 200, coach; child facs; con 250
LD 9.30
£ B&B £27·50, B&B (double) £49·50; L £8, D £10·50; WB £42·50; [10% V Wed–Sun, May–Jun]
cc Access, B'card/Visa; dep.

PORTADOWN Co Armagh. Map 61B3
Pop 24,000. M12 Motorway 3, Lurgan 6, Belfast 26, Armagh 10, Dungannon 16, Newry 18.
EC Thur. **MD** Fri, Sat. **Golf** Portadown 18h.

★★★ Seagoe, Upper Church La, BT63 5JE (0762) 333076
Extensively modernised hotel with lovely landscaped garden. In rural surroundings.

PORTBALLINTRAE Co Antrim. Map 61B4
Pop 600. Ballymoney 11, Belfast 51, Coleraine 6, Larne 44.
EC Thur. **Golf** Bushfoot 9h. **See** Giant's Causeway, Dunseverick Castle.
Beach Rd. (026 57) 31672

★★ Bayview, 2 Bayhead Rd, BT57 8RZ Bushmills (026 57) 31453
Fax: (026 57) 32360

Standing at roadside facing sea, an interesting mixture of buildings. Swimming pool, sauna, solarium, billiards.
16 bedrs, 16 en suite, TV; tcf.
TV; dogs; P 36, coach; child facs; con 150
LD 10
£ B&B £32, B&B (double) £52; HB weekly £180; L £6·95, D £11; WB £60
cc Access, B'card/Visa; dep.

STRABANE Co. Tyrone. Map 61A3
Belfast 96, Claudy 16, Letterkenny 17, Londonderry 14, Omagh 20, Stranorlar 14.
Abercorn Sq. (0504) 883735

★★★ Fir Trees, Melmount Rd, BT47 2NY (0504) 382382 Fax: (0504) 885932
Two-storey, L-shaped hotel, pleasantly situated on south side of town beside A5.
Fr. Closed 25 Dec.
30 bedrs, 30 en suite; TV; tcf
TV, dogs; P 100, coach; child facs; con 200
LD 9.30, bar meals only lunch
£ B&B £41·80–£43·70, B&B (double) £59·40–£66·70; HB weekly £362·60–£536·90; D £12; [5% V]
cc Access, Amex, B'card/Visa, Diners.

REPUBLIC OF IRELAND

The RAC does not currently inspect hotels in the Republic of Ireland. For the convenience of readers, and in order to make the Guide as comprehensive as possible, we include a number of selected establishments throughout the Republic.

The hotels have all been inspected and graded by Bord Fáilte—the Irish Tourist Board. The gradings are: A★, A, B★, B, C, and are very roughly equivalent to the RAC 5-star to 1-star classifications. For each hotel, we show the grading, the address, telephone and telex numbers, number of bedrooms, number en suite, prices and any sporting facilities owned by the hotel. In some cases we also give a short description of the hotel and its surroundings.

As well as hotels, we have included a selection from the bed and breakfast accommodation which has been visited and approved by Bord Fáilte. These premises are divided into Town, Country and Farm houses. Many will provide an evening meal, usually dinner but occasionally high tea, if notice is given.

Prices given for hotels in the Republic of Ireland are shown in Irish pounds (punts) and are those charged in 1990. Prices for 1991 may have increased.

ACHILL ISLAND Co. Mayo. Map 60A2

Mrs K. Sweeney, Aquila, Sraheens ☎(098) 45163. *Country.* Open May–Sep
🛏4 bedrs, 2 en suite
£ B&B IR£12–£13.

ADARE Co. Limerick. Map 62C3

A **Dunraven Arms,** ☎(061) 86209 Tx: 70202.
Attractive period building on the banks of the River Maigue.
🛏44 bedrs, 44 en suite; TV
£ room fr IR£42·50–£50, double room fr IR£70–£80; Bk IR£7, D IR£19·95
cc Access, Amex, B'card/Visa, Diners.

B **Woodlands House,** Knockanes ☎(061) 86118
One-storey modern hotel in 52 acres of grounds, 1½ miles from Adare.
Closed 21–31 Dec.
🛏12 bedrs, 12 en suite; TV
£ B&B IR£18–£19, B&B (double) IR £30–£32, D IR£9·95
cc Access, Amex, B'card/Visa, Diners.

Mrs M. Dundon, Abbey Villa, Kildimo Rd ☎(061) 86113. *Town.*
🛏6 bedrs, 6 en suite
£ B&B IR£15·50

Mrs K. Glavin, Castleview, Clonshire More, Croagh ☎(061) 86394. *Country.*
🛏4 bedrs, 3 en suite
£ B&B IR£15–£16; D IR£9·50.

ADRIGOLE Co. Cork. Map 62B1

Mrs J. Crowley, Forthill House ☎(027) 60034. *Farm.* Open Jun–Sep.
🛏5 bedrs
£ B&B (double) IR£20

ANNAGHDOWN Co. Galway. Map 60B1/62C4

Scott Family, Corrib View Farm ☎(091) 91114. *Farm.* Open 15 Apr–15 Sep.
🛏4 bedrs, 1 en suite
£ B&B (double) IR£24–£29, D IR£12·50

ARDARA Co. Donegal. Map 60C3

Mr & Mrs M. Bennett, Bayview Country House, Portnoo Rd ☎(075) 41145. *Country.* Open 1 Mar–15 Nov.
🛏7 bedrs, 7 en suite
£ B&B (double) IR£23, D IR£10

Vincent & Susan McConnell, Rose Wood Country House, Killybegs Rd ☎(075) 41168. *Country.* Open 1 Mar–31 Oct.
🛏3 bedrs, 3 en suite
£ B&B IR£15, B&B (double) IR£23

ARDEE Co. Louth. Map 61B2

B ★ **Gables House** ☎(041) 53789
🛏5 bedrs, 3 en suite; TV
£ B&B IR£18–£21, B&B (double) IR£28–£32, D IR£16·95
cc Access, Amex, B'card/Visa, Diners.

ARDMORE Co. Waterford. Map 63A2

B **Cliff House** ☎(024) 94106
Owner-run, family hotel on the cliffs with fine sea views. Open 29 Apr–3 Oct.
🛏20 bedrs, 13 en suite, tcf
£ B&B IR£17–£26·50, B&B (double) IR£40–£49
cc Access, Amex, B'card/Visa, Diners.

ARKLOW Co. Wicklow. Map 63C3

Mrs A. Nuzum, Ballykilty House, Coolgreany ☎(0402) 7111. *Farm. Tennis.* Open Mar–Oct.
🛏6 bedrs, 4 en suite
£ B&B IR£13–£15, D IR£10·50

ATHLONE Co. Westmeath. Map 60C1/63A4

B ★ **Prince of Wales,** Church St. ☎(0902) 72626 Fax: (0902) 75658
Modern hotel, reconstructed from a Victorian one, in centre of town.
🛏42 bedrs, 42 en suite, TV; tcf
£ B&B IR£35, B&B (double) IR£60; D IR£14·95
cc Access, Amex, B'card/Visa, Diners.

B ★ **Royal,** Mardyke Street. ☎(0902) 72924
🛏55 bedrs, 27 en suite, TV
£ B&B IR£22–£25·70, B&B (double) IR£42–£48; D IR£14·20.

Mrs N. Denby, Shelmalier House, Cartrontroy, Retreat Rd. ☎(0902) 72245. *Town.*
🛏7 bedrs, 6 en suite; tcf
£ B&B IR£15; D IR£10.

AUGHRIM Co. Wicklow. Map 63C3

B **Lawless's** ☎(0402) 36146
Small, family-run period hotel, recently modernised and refurbished. Fishing.
🛏12 bedrs
£ B&B IR£16; D IR£18
cc Access, Amex, B'card/Visa, Diners.

BALLINA Co. Mayo. Map 60B2

A **Downhill** ☎(096) 21033 Tx: 40796
Situated on the River Moy, 1 km outside town, this friendly hotel is set in spacious grounds. Fishing, golf, indoor swimming pool, squash, sauna, solarium, gymnasium, billiards.
🛏51 bedrs, 50 en suite; TV; tcf
£ B&B IR£52, B&B (double) IR£85
cc Access, Amex, B'card/Visa, Diners.

Mrs M. Dempsey, Whitestream House, Foxford Rd ☎(096) 21582. *Town.* Open Jan–Nov.
🛏6 bedrs, 5 en suite
£ B&B IR£13, B&B (double) IR£21–£23; D IR£10·50
cc B'card/Visa.

Mrs M O'Dowd, Cnoc Breandain, Quay Rd. ☎(096) 22145. *Country.* Open 1 May–30 Sep.
🛏4 bedrs, 3 en suite
£ B&B IR£13, B&B (double) IR£22; D IR£10

BALLINAKILL Co. Laois. Map 63A3

Mrs A. Dowling, The Glebe. ☎(0502) 33368. *Country. Fishing.*
🛏4 bedrs
£ B&B (double) IR£32; D IR£15

BALLINAMORE Co. Leitrim. Map 61A2

Thomas Family, Riversdale. ☎(078) 44122. *Farm. Fishing, indoor swimming pool, sauna, squash.*
🛏6 bedrs
£ B&B (double) IR£18; D IR£9.

BALLINASCARTHY Co. Cork. Map 62C1
A **Ardnavaha House** ☎ (023) 49135
Tx: 75702
Georgian house set amidst lawns, woods and meadows. Swimming pool, sauna, tennis, riding. Open 1 Apr–31 Oct
🛏 36 bedrs, 36 en suite
£ B&B IR£40–£46, B&B (double) IR£58–£70, HB weekly IR£283; D IR£15·50
cc Access, Amex, B'card/Visa, Diners.

BALLINASLOE Co. Galway. Map 62C4.
A **Hayden's**, Dunloe St ☎ (0905) 42347
Tx: 53947 Fax: (0905) 42895
Family owned and run hotel in landscaped gardens. Fishing
🛏 51 bedrs, 51 en suite, TV
£ room IR£23·50–£25·50, double room IR£41–£45, D IR£14·75
cc Access, Amex, B'card/Visa, Diners.

BALLINROBE Co. Mayo. Map 60B2
B **Lakeland** ☎ (092) 41020 Fax: (092) 41202
🛏 17 bedrs, 5 en suite; tcf
£ B&B IR£18–£23, B&B (double) IR£36–£46, D IR£12

BALLYBOFEY Co. Donegal. Map 61A3
B ★ **Jackson's** ☎ (074) 31021
Large family-run hotel on banks of River Finn overlooking woods of Drumboe.
🛏 39 bedrs, 39 en suite; TV
£ B&B IR£18–£19, B&B (double) IR£35–£36, D IR£13–£14
cc Access, Amex, B'card/Visa.

B ★ **Kee's**, Stranorlar ☎ (074) 31018
Recently modernised, family-run hotel with a cosy atmosphere. Fishing.
🛏 26 bedrs, 26 en suite; TV
£ B&B IR£20–£22·50; B&B (double) IR£35–£36; D IR£12
cc Access, Amex, B'card/Visa, Diners.

BALLYBUNION Co. Kerry. Map 62B3
B **Marine**, Sandhill Road ☎ (068) 27139
Open 15 Mar–31 Oct.
🛏 10 bedrs, 10 en suite; TV; tcf
£ B&B IR£29·50–£32·50, B&B (double) IR£45–£60; D IR£16–£18
cc Access, Amex, B'card/Visa,

BALLYCONNEELY Co. Galway. Map 60A1/62A4
Erriseask House ☎ (095) 23553. Open Apr–Oct
🛏 11 bedrs, 7 en suite
£ B&B IR£22–£28, B&B (double) IR£38–£42, D £14
cc Access, Amex, B'card/Visa, Diners.
Mrs. C. Joyce, Teach an Easard, ☎ (095) 23560. *Country.*
🛏 4 bedrs, 4 en suite
£ B&B IR£26; D IR£11.

BALLYDUFF Co. Waterford. Map 63A2
B **Blackwater Lodge**, Upper Ballyduff ☎ (058) 60235 Open 1 Feb–30 Sep.
🛏 21 bedrs, 8 en suite
£ B&B IR£26–£41, B&B (double) IR£38–£58, D IR£15

BALLYFERRITER Co. Kerry. Map 62A2
B ★ **Ostan Dun an Oir,** Dingle Peninsula ☎ (066) 56133 Tx: 73973
Swimming pool, tennis, golf, sauna. Open 23 Apr–26 Oct.
🛏 22 bedrs, 22 en suite; TV
£ B&B IR£28–£34, B&B (double) IR£46–60; D IR£14·75–£17·75
cc Access, Amex, B'card/Visa, Diners.

BALLYLICKEY Co. Cork. Map 62B1
A **Ballylickey Manor House** ☎ (027) 50071
Fishing, swimming pool. Open 1 Apr–2 Nov
🛏 11 bedrs, 11 en suite; TV
£ room IR£60, double room IR£61; D IR£19·50
cc Amex, B'card/Visa

B ★ **Sea View** ☎ (027) 50073
Owner-managed, country house hotel overlooking Bantry Bay. Open 1 Apr–31 Oct
🛏 13 bedrs, 13 en suite; tcf
£ B&B IR£35–£40, B&B (double) IR£60–£70, D IR£17·50
cc Access, Amex, B'card/Visa, Diners.

BALLYLIFFEN Co. Donegal. Map 61A4
B ★ **Strand** ☎ (077) 76107
Family-run village inn in beautiful gardens. Fine views.
🛏 12 bedrs, 12 en suite; TV; tcf
£ B&B IR£25–£30, B&B (double) IR£38–£45, D IR£15–£16
cc Access, B'card/Visa.

BALLYNAHINCH Co. Galway. Map 62B4
A **Ballynahinch Castle,** Ballinafad ☎ (095) 31006 Tx: 50809
Elegant country-house hotel beautifully situated at the foot of Bew Lettry and overlooking the River Owenmore. Tennis.
🛏 28 bedrs, 28 en suite
£ B&B IR£48–£55, B&B (double) IR£76–£90; D IR£16–£20
cc Access, Amex, B'card/Visa, Diners.

BALLYSHANNON Co. Donegal. Map 60C3
Mrs R. McCaffrey, Ardpatton House, Cavan Garden ☎ (072) 51546. *Farm. Riding.*
🛏 5 bedrs, 1 en suite
£ B&B IR£15, B&B (double) IR£24–£27; D IR£12
cc Amex B'card/Visa.
Mrs M.T. McGee, Killeadan, Bundoran Rd ☎ (072) 51377 Fax: (072) 51207 *Country.* Open 1 Jun–31 Jul.
🛏 4 bedrs, 3 en suite
£ B&B IR£13–£14·50, B&B (double) IR£22–£25

BALLYVAUGHAN Co. Clare. Map 62B4
A **Gregans Castle** ☎ (065) 77005
Fax: 77111
Owner-manager country-house hotel overlooking Galway Bay. Open 24 Mar–31 Oct
🛏 16 bedrs, 16 en suite
£ B&B IR£48–£58, B&B (double) IR£66–£74, D IR£20
cc B'card/Visa.

BANDON Co. Cork. Map 62C1
B ★ **Munster Arms** ☎ (023) 41562
🛏 30 bedrs, 25 en suite; TV
£ B&B IR£14·50–£20, B&B (double) IR£28–£37; D IR£12·50

Mrs E. Stone, Milton House ☎ (023) 41388. *Farm.* Open Easter–Sep.
🛏 6 bedrs
£ B&B IR£20, D IR£9·50.

BANTEER Co. Cork. Map 62C2
A **Clonmeen House** ☎ (029) 56008
Victorian mansion in park with a lake. Open 13 May–30 Sep.
🛏 12 bedrs, 12 en suite
£ B&B IR£35–£40, B&B (double) IR£54–£66, D IR£24.

BANTRY Co. Cork. Map 62B1
B ★ **Westlodge** ☎ (027) 50360 Tx: 75880
Modern hotel in grounds of 25 acres amidst scenic surroundings. Indoor swimming pool, tennis, squash, sauna, snooker.
🛏 90 bedrs, 90 en suite; TV
£ B&B IR£25·50–£34, B&B (double) IR£44–£55; D IR£17·50
cc Access, Amex, B'card/Visa, Diners.

Mrs K. O'Donovan, Ashling House, Cahir ☎ (027) 50616. *Country.* Open 1 Apr–15 Oct.
🛏 4 bedrs, 2 en suite
£ B&B IR£13·50–£15·50, B&B (double) IR£21–£25; D IR£10·50

BELMULLET Co. Mayo. Map 60A3
C **Western Strands** ☎ (097) 81096
🛏 10 bedrs
£ B&B IR£12, B&B (double) IR£20; D IR£10.

BIRR Co. Offaly. Map 60C1/63A3
B ★ **County Arms** ☎ (0509) 20791
Fax: (0509) 21234
Georgian mansion in delightful grounds. Squash, sauna.
🛏 18 bedrs, 18 en suite; TV; tcf
£ B&B IR£28–£32, B&B (double) IR£50–£54; D IR£13
cc Access, Amex, B'card/Visa, Diners.

B **Dooly's**, Emmet Sq. ☎ (0509) 20032
🛏 18 bedrs, 18 en suite, TV
£ B&B IR£24, B&B (double room) IR£44; D IR£13·95.

BLARNEY Co. Cork. Map 62C2
A **Blarney Park** ☎ (021) 385281 Tx: 75022
Closed 1 Jan–26 Feb.
🛏 70 bedrs, 70 en suite; TV
£ B&B IR£31–£34, B&B (double) IR£52–£55; D IR£15.
cc Access, Amex, B'card/Visa, Diners.

Callaghan Family, Ashlee Lodge, Tower ☎ (021) 385346. *Country.* Open Apr–Oct.
🛏 5 bedrs, 4 en suite
£ B&B (double) IR£22–£30

BLESSINGTON Co. Wicklow. Map 63B4
A **Downshire House** ☎ (045) 65199
Fax: (045) 65335
🛏 25 bedrs, 25 en suite
£ rooms IR£22, double room IR£36, Bk IR£5·50, D IR£18
Miss E. Beattie, Elbrook Manor, Kilbride ☎ (01) 582418. *Country.*
🛏 3 bedrs, 1 en suite
£ B&B (double) IR£20–£22, D IR£10

BORRIS IN OSSORY Co. Laois. Map 63A3

B ★ **Leix Country** ☎ (0505) 41213
🛏 19 bedrs, 19 en suite; TV; tcf
£ B&B IR£20, B&B (double) £38; D IR£13·65.
cc Access, Amex, B'card/Visa.

BOYLE Co. Roscommon. Map 60C2

B **Royal,** Bridge St ☎ (079) 62016 Tx: 80464
Family-run, 18th century hotel beside river in town centre. Closed 25 & 26 Dec.
🛏 16 bedrs, 16 en suite; TV; tcf
£ B&B IR£26·50, B&B (double) IR£46, D IR£14·75
cc Access, Amex, B'card/Visa, Diners.
Mrs E. Kelly, Forest Park House, Carrick-on-Shannon Rd ☎ (079) 62227. *Country.*
🛏 8 bedrs, 4 en suite.
£ B&B (double) IR£21–£24, D IR£9·50
Mr & Mrs Mitchell, Abbey House ☎ (079) 62385
🛏 6 bedrs, 5 en suite
£ B&B IR£13, B&B (double) IR£22–£24; D IR£10

BROADFORD Co. Clare. Map 62C3

Mrs N. O'Donnell, Lake View House, Doon Lake ☎ (061) 73125
🛏 3 bedrs
£ B&B (double) IR£22

BRITTAS BAY Co. Wicklow. Map 63C3

Mrs P. Tighe, Parkwood House, Jack White's Cross ☎ (0404) 7221. *Country.* Open Mar–31 Oct
🛏 5 bedrs, 1 en suite
£ B&B IR£15–£19, B&B (double) IR£22–£25; D IR£10

BRUCKLESS Co. Donegal. Map 60C3

Mrs J. Evans, Bruckless House ☎ (073) 37071. *Farm. Fishing.* Open Apr–Sep
🛏 5 bedrs
£ B&B IR£18; D IR£15.

BRUREE Co. Limerick. Map 62C2

Mrs E. McDonogh, Cooleen House ☎ (063) 90584. *Farm. Fishing.* Open May–Sep
🛏 4 bedrs
£ B&B (double) IR£22; D IR£11.

BUNBEG Co. Donegal. Map 60C4

A **Gweedore** ☎ (075) 31177
Large holiday hotel in superb position overlooking the beach. Open Easter, 1 May–31 Oct.
🛏 39 bedrs, 39 en suite; TV
£ B&B IR£27–£35, B&B (double) £45–£54, D IR£14·50
cc Access, B'card/Visa, Diners.

B ★ **Ostan Radharc Na Mara** (Seaview Hotel) ☎ (075) 31159
🛏 28 bedrs, 28 en suite
£ B&B IR£19·50–£25, B&B (double) IR£35–£45; D IR£12.

BUNCRANA Co. Donegal. Map 61A4

B ★ **Lake of Shadows,** Grianan Park ☎ (077) 61005
🛏 10 bedrs, 10 en suite; TV; tcf
£ B&B IR£21–£23, B&B (double) IR£40–£44, D IR£11
cc Access, B'card/Visa

B ★ **White Strand Motor Inn,** Railway Rd ☎ (077) 61059
🛏 12 bedrs, 12 en suite; TV; tcf
£ B&B IR£21–£22, B&B (double) IR£38–£44, D IR£11

BUNDORAN Co. Donegal. Map 60C3

A **Great Northern** ☎ (072) 41204 Tx: 40961
Indoor swimming pool, golf, tennis. Open Mar–Dec. ♿
🛏 96 bedrs, 96 en suite; TV
£ B&B IR £33–£38, B&B (double) IR£54–£64; D IR£16
cc Access, Amex, B'card/Visa, Diners

B ★ **Holyrood,** ☎ (072) 41232 Tx: 40961 Fax: (072) 41232
Family-run hotel in the centre of town. Evening entertainment. Tennis, golf.
🛏 61 bedrs, 61 en suite, TV
£ B&B IR£23–£24, B&B (double) £37·50–£39·50, D IR£13·50–£14·25
cc Access, Amex, B'card/Visa, Diners.

B ★ **Bayview**, Main St ☎ (072) 41296
🛏 15 bedrs, 14 en suite
£ B&B IR£11–£15, B&B (double) IR£22–£26, D IR£8·50.

BUNRATTY Co. Clare. Map 62C3

A **Fitzpatrick's Shannon Shamrock** ☎ (061) 361177 Tx: 72114 Fax: (061) 61252
Ranch-style hotel with attractive gardens in grounds of 15th century Bunratty Castle. Indoor swimming pool, sauna.
🛏 100 bedrs, 100 en suite; TV
£ room IR£49–£57, double room IR£62–£80, Bk IR£7, D IR£15
cc Access, Amex, B'card/Visa, Diners.
Mrs M. Browne, Bunratty Lodge ☎ (061) 72402 *Country*
🛏 9 bedrs, 9 en suite
£ B&B IR£17, B&B (double) IR£26.
Mrs M. Whyte, Palm Lodge, Hurlers Cross ☎ (061) 364682. *Country.* Open Apr–Oct
🛏 5 bedrs, 5 en suite
£ B&B IR£14, B&B (double) IR£22

BURREN Co. Clare. Map 62C4

Mrs A. Martin, Villa Maria, Leagh South ☎ (065) 78019. *Country.* Open 1 Feb–30 Nov.
🛏 5 bedrs, 3 en suite
£ B&B IR£13–£15, B&B (double) IR£21–£23, D IR£9 50

BUTLERS BRIDGE Co. Cavan. Map 61A2

Mrs P. Mundy, Ford House, Deredis ☎ (049) 31427. *Farm.* Open May–1 Oct
🛏 6 bedrs
£ B&B IR£10; D IR£9.

CAHIR Co. Tipperary. Map 63A2

Butler Family, Carrigeen Castle, Cork Rd ☎ (052) 41370. *Country.*
🛏 6 bedrs, 1 en suite
£ B&B IR£12·50; HT IR£9
Mrs B. Fitzgerald, Ashling, Dublin Rd ☎ (052) 41601. *Country.*
🛏 5 bedrs, 3 en suite
£ B&B IR£16

Changes made after July 1990 are not included.

CAHIRCIVEEN Co. Kerry. Map 62A2

Mrs B. Landers, San Antoine, Valentia Rd ☎ (0667) 2521. *Town.*
🛏 6 bedrs, 6 en suite
£ B&B IR£16, B&B (double) IR£24; D £11.
Mrs N. McKenna, Mount Rivers, Carhan Rd ☎ (0667) 2509. *Town.* Open 1 Apr–30 Sep.
🛏 5 bedrs, 4 en suite
£ B&B IR£13–£15, B&B (double) IR £21–£24.
Mrs A. Quill, Ard na Greine, Valentia Rd ☎ (0667) 2281. *Town.* Open 1 Mar–30 Nov.
🛏 3 bedrs
£ B&B IR£9, B&B (double) IR£20, D IR£9.

CARAGH LAKE Co. Kerry. Map 62A2

A **Ard Na Sidhe** ☎ (066) 69105
Well-kept, Victorian-style mansion situated in a delightful spot on Caragh Lake. Fishing. Open 1 May–30 Sep.
🛏 20 bedrs, 20 en suite
£ B&B IR£58, B&B (double) IR£76, D IR£21
cc Access, Amex, B'card/Visa, Diners.
A **Caragh Lodge** ☎ (066) 69115. *Fishing, tennis, sauna.* Open 15 Apr–31 Oct.
🛏 9 bedrs, 9 en suite
£ B&B IR£34, B&B (double) IR£60; D IR£18
cc Access, Amex, B'card/Visa.
Mrs H. Windecker, Carrig House ☎ (066) 69104. *Country*
🛏 5 bedrs, 5 en suite
£ B&B (double) IR£38, D IR£16

CARLINGFORD Co. Louth. Map 61B2

B ★ **Mc Kevitt's,** Market Sq ☎ (042) 73116
Family run hotel in centre of town.
🛏 10 bedrs, 10 en suite; TV
£ B&B IR£21–£26; D IR£14–£15
cc Access, Amex, B'card/Visa, Diners.

Mrs M. Woods, Viewpoint, Omeath Rd ☎ (042) 73149. *Town.* Open Mar–Oct
🛏 6 bedrs, 6 en suite; TV; tcf
£ B&B IR£15.

CARLOW Co. Carlow. Map 63B3

B ★ **Royal** ☎ (0503) 31621
Town-centre hotel in a walled garden.
🛏 30 bedrs, 26 en suite; TV
£ B&B IR£21–£33, B&B (double) IR££40–£58; D IR£14·95–£15·95
cc Access, Amex, B'card/Visa, Diners.

B ★ **Seven Oaks,** Athy Rd ☎ (0503) 31308
Modern hotel in landscaped grounds, 2 minutes walk from town centre.
🛏 16 bedrs. 12 en suite; TV; tcf
£ B&B IR £30–£33, B&B (double) IR£46–£52; D IR£13·50

Mrs M. Quinn, The Locks, Milford ☎ (0503) 46261. *Country. Fishing.*
🛏 6 bedrs, 1 en suite
£ B&B IR£12; D IR£8.

CARRICKMACROSS Co. Monaghan. Map 61B2

A **Nuremore** ☎ (042) 61438 Fax: (042) 61853
Family owned hotel in extensive wooded grounds with lakes. Fishing, golf, indoor swimming pool, squash, sauna, snooker.
🛏 51 bedrs, 51 en suite; TV
£ B&B IR£40–£60, B&B (double) IR£60–£100; D IR£17·50–£18·50
cc Access, Amex, B'card/Visa, Diners.

CARRICK-ON-SHANNON
Co. Leitrim. Map 60C2

B ★ **Bush,** Main St ☎ (078) 20014
Six generations of one family have run this 200-year-old hotel which has an interesting collection of pictures.
🛏 20 bedrs, 20 en suite; TV; tcf
£ B&B IR£17·50–£20, B&B (double) IR£29–£34; D IR£15
cc Access, Amex, B'card/Visa.

CARRICK-ON-SUIR
Co. Tipperary. Map 63A2

Cedarfield House, Waterford Rd ☎ (051) 40164. *Guest House.*
🛏 6 bedrs, 6 en suite; TV
£ B&B IR£23·50–£30; D IR£16·85

CASHEL
Co. Galway. Map 60C1

A **Cashel House** ☎ (095) 31001 Tx: 50812 Fax: (095) 31077
White-painted country-house hotel in award-winning gardens. Own harbour and tiny beach. Tennis, riding. Open 15 Feb–30 Nov
🛏 29 bedrs, 28 en suite
£ B&B IR£41–£44; D IR£21·50–£23·50
cc Access, Amex, B'card/Visa, Diners.

A **Zetland House** ☎ (095) 31111 Tx: 50853 Fax: (095) 31113
Old established country-house hotel with panoramic views over Cashel Bay.
Open 12 Apr–31 Oct
🛏 19 bedrs, 19 en suite
£ B&B IR£35–£55, B&B (double) IR£60–£80; D IR£21

Mrs M. M. Cloherty, Glynsh House, Cashel Bay ☎ (095) 32279
🛏 10 bedrs, 9 en suite
£ B&B IR£16–£18, B&B (double) IR£24–£48; D IR£13
cc Access, B'card/Visa

CASHEL
Co. Tipperary. Map 63A3

A **Cashel Palace,** ☎ (062) 61411 Tx: 70638 Fax: (062) 61521
Lovely Georgian mansion, once a Bishop's palace, in 20 acres of grounds next to the Rock of Cashel. Fishing.
🛏 20 bedrs, 20 en suite; TV
£ room IR£65–£87·50, D IR£19–£26
cc Access, Amex, B'card/Visa, Diners.

B ★ **Rectory House,** Dundrum ☎ (062) 71266 Tx: 93348
Fishing, riding.
🛏 11 bedrs, 11 en suite
£ B&B IR£25–£38, B&B (double) fr IR£42–£56; D IR£16·50

Mrs M. Foley, Rahard Lodge, Kilkenny Rd ☎ (062) 61052. *Farm.* Open Feb-Nov
🛏 6 bedrs, 4 en suite
£ B&B IR£22–£26; D IR£12
cc B'card/Visa.
Mrs M. A. Kennedy, Thornbrook House, Kilkenny/Dualla Rd ☎ (062) 61480. *Country.*
🛏 5 bedrs, 3 en suite
£ B&B IR£16, B&B (double) IR£22–£26
Mrs E. Moloney, Ros-Guil House, Kilkenny/Dualla Rd ☎ (062) 61507 *Country. Tennis.* Open Apr–Oct
🛏 5 bedrs, 3 en suite
£ B&B IR£16–£18, B&B (double) IR£22–£26
Mrs E. O'Brien, Knock Saint Lour House ☎ (062) 61172. *Farm.* Open Apr–Oct
🛏 8 bedrs, 4 en suite
£ B&B IR£14, B&B (double) IR£22–£26; D IR£11.

CASTLEBAR
Co. Mayo. Map 60B2

A **Breaffy House** ☎ (094) 22033 Tx: 53790
Stone-built mansion in 50 acres of parkland about 2 miles out of town.
🛏 40 bedrs, 40 en suite; TV; tcf
£ B&B IR£33·90–£35, B&B (double) fr IR£51·80–£54; D IR£14
cc Access, Amex, B'card/Visa, Diners.
Mrs M. Moran, Lakeview House, Westport Rd ☎ (094) 22374. *Country.*
🛏 4 bedrs, 2 en suite
£ B&B fr IR£10; HT IR£7.

CASTLEBLAYNEY
Co. Monaghan. Map 61B2

Mrs M. Fleming, Lochbeg, Corracloughan ☎ (042) 40664. *Country.*
🛏 3 bedrs
£ B&B fr IR£12, B&B (double) IR£21–£24.

CASTLECONNELL
Co. Limerick. Map 62C3

Mrs H. Wilson, Spa House ☎ (061) 377171. *Country.* Open Apr–Sep
🛏 5 bedrs, 3 en suite
£ B&B (double) IR£22–£25

CASTLEISLAND
Co. Kerry. Map 62B2

O'Mahony Family, Beach Grove, Camp Rd ☎ (066) 41217. *Farm.* Open 1 Apr–30 Sep
🛏 5 bedrs, 2 en suite
£ B&B IR£12; D IR£10.

CASTLEMAINE
Co. Kerry. Map 62B2

Mrs E. O'Connor, Tom & Eileen's Farm ☎ (066) 67373. *Farm.* Open 1 Apr–31 Oct.
🛏 5 bedrs, 1 en suite; tcf
£ B&B IR£13·50; D IR£10

CASTLETOWNBERE
Co. Cork. Map 62A1

B **Craigie's Cametringare House** ☎ (027) 70379
Modern hotel overlooking the harbour and close to Allihies beach. Tennis.
🛏 13 bedrs, 10 en suite; tcf
£ B&B IR£14–£20, D IR£14
cc Access, Amex, B'card/Visa, Diners.
Mrs M. Donegan, Realt-na-Mara ☎ (027) 70101. *Country.*
🛏 5 bedrs, 3 en suite
£ B&B IR£9·50–£10; D IR£9

CASTLETOWNSHEND
Co. Cork. Map 62B1

Mrs R. Vickery, Bow Hall ☎ (028) 36114. *Town.*
🛏 3 bedrs, 3 en suite
£ B&B IR£26; D IR£16.

CAVAN
Co. Cavan. Map 61A2

C **Farnham Arms,** Main St ☎ (049) 32577
🛏 18 bedrs, 18 en suite; TV
£ B&B IR£21·50–£23·50, B&B (double) IR£40–£44; D IR£13
cc Access, Amex, B'card/Visa, Diners.

CHARLESTOWN
Co. Mayo. Map 60C2

Mrs J. Keane, Hawthorne House ☎ (094) 54237. *Town.* Open May–Sep
🛏 5 bedrs
£ B&B (double) IR£21.
Mrs C. O'Gorman, Ashfort, Airport Rd ☎ (094) 54706. *Country.*
🛏 5 bedrs, 4 en suite
£ B&B IR£15, B&B (double) IR£22

CLAREMORRIS
Co. Mayo. Map 60B2

Basil & Cora Judge, Ashlawn, Brookhill ☎ (094) 71415. *Country.*
🛏 3 bedrs, 1 en suite
£ B&B IR£12–£13; D IR£6

CLIFDEN
Co. Galway. Map 60A1/62B4

A **Abbeyglen Castle,** Sky Rd ☎ (095) 21201 Tx: 50866 Fax: (095) 21797
Delightful mock castle set in beautiful gardens with views of the village and bay. Swimming pool, tennis, sauna, snooker. Open 1 Feb–22 Dec.
🛏 40 bedrs, 40 en suite, TV
£ room IR£40–£60, Bk IR£6, D IR£18
cc Access, Amex, B'card/Visa, Diners.

A **Hotel Ardagh,** Ballyconneely Rd ☎ (095) 21384
A family-run hotel beautifully located on the rocky edge of Ardbear Bay. Open 1 Mar–31 Oct.
🛏 17 bedrs, 17 en suite; TV
£ B&B IR£27–£32, B&B (double) IR£40–£50; D IR£15·50
cc Access, Amex, B'card/Visa, Diners.

A **Rock Glen Manor House** ☎ (095) 21035 Fax: 21737
A converted shooting lodge, built in 1815, now an owner-run hotel. Tennis, snooker.
Open mid Mar–end Oct
🛏 29 bedrs, 29 en suite
£ B&B IR£36–£41, B&B (double) IR£56–£66; D IR£18–£19
cc Access, Amex, B'card/Visa, Diners.

Mrs K. Hardman, Mallmore House ☎ (095) 21460. *Country.* Open Mar–Oct
🛏 6 bedrs, 4 en suite
£ B&B IR£22–£24.
Shanley-O'Toole Family, Rose Cottage, Rockfield, Moyard ☎ (095) 41082. *Farm. Fishing.*
🛏 6 bedrs, 6 en suite; tcf
£ B&B IR£24; D IR£12

CLONMEL
Co. Tipperary. Map 63A2

B **Clonmel Arms,** Sarsfield St ☎ (052) 21233 Fax: (052) 21526
🛏 34 bedrs, 26 en suite
£ B&B IR£28–£42; D IR£14
cc Access, Amex, B'card/Visa.

B **Hearn's** ☎ (052) 21611 Tx: 80464
Family-run hotel in town centre dating from 17th century, once a coaching inn. Closed 23–31 Dec & 2–9 Feb.
🛏 25 bedrs, 16 en suite; TV; tcf
£ room IR£20·75–£25, double room IR£30·50–£45, Bk IR£5·75; D IR£12·50
cc Access, Amex, B'card/Visa.
Mrs T. O'Callaghan, St Loman's, The Roundabout, Cahir Rd ☎ (052) 22916. *Town.*
🛏 3 bedrs, 1 en suite
£ B&B (double) IR£20–£26; D IR£10
Mrs B O'Connor, New Abbey, Marlfield ☎ (052) 22626. *Farm.* Open Apr–30 Sep
🛏 3 bedrs, 1 en suite
£ B&B (double) IR£22; D IR£10
Mrs O'Loughlin, Old Grange, Knocklofty ☎ (052)38232. *Farm*
🛏 3 bedrs

£ B&B IR£10, (double) IR£20; HT IR£6
Mrs J. Phelan, Cluain Ard, Melview ☎(052) 22413. *Town*
🛏3 bedrs
£ B&B IR£9; HT IR£7.
Mrs S. Phelan, Mullinarinka House ☎(052) 21374. *Farm, tennis*. Open Easter–Sep.
🛏5 bedrs
£ B&B (double) IR£24; D IR£12
Mrs M. Whelan, Amberville, Glenconner Rd (off Western Rd) ☎(052) 21470. *Town*.
🛏5 bedrs, 2 en suite
£ B&B IR£12·50; D IR£9·50

CONG Co. Mayo. Map 60B1

A ★ **Ashford Castle** ☎(092) 46003 Tx: 53749
Luxury hotel in a romantic castle dating from the 13th century and set on a lake. Fishing, golf, tennis, riding.
🛏83 bedrs, 83 en suite; TV
£ room IR£95–£170, Bk IR£10·50, D IR £29
cc Access, Amex, B'card/Visa, Diners.

COOTEHILL Co. Cavan. Map 61A2

B ★ **White Horse,** Main St ☎(049) 52124
🛏30 bedrs, 24 en suite; TV
£ B&B IR£12·50; D IR£11.
cc Amex, Access, B'card/Visa.

CORK Co Cork. Map 62C1–2

A ★ **Jurys**, Western Rd ☎(021) 276622 Tx: 76073 Fax: (021) 274477
Luxurious modern hotel in spacious grounds on River Lee, 5 minutes walk from city centre. Indoor/outdoor swimming pool, sauna, squash, gymnasium, tennis.
🛏185 bedrs, 185 en suite; TV
£ room IR£67·50–£71, double room IR£78·50–£81; Bk IR £7·50; D IR £16

A **Fitzpatrick Silver Springs,** Tivoli ☎(021) 507533 Tx: 76111 Fax: (021) 507641
Ultra-modern hotel on the main Dublin—Waterford Road, overlooking the River Lee. Tennis, indoor swimming pool, sauna, squash.
🛏110 bedrs, 110 en suite; TV
£ room IR£55–£65, double room IR£68–£84, Bk IR£7, D IR£15
cc Access, Amex, B'card/Visa, Diners.

A **Imperial,** South Mall ☎(021) 274040 Tx: 75126 Fax: (021) 274040
Modernised historic hotel in city centre.
🛏101 bedrs, 101 en suite; TV
£ B&B £58–£66, B&B (double) fr IR£90; D IR£15
cc Access, Amex, B'card/Visa, Diners.

B ★ **Arbutus Lodge,** Montenotte ☎(021) 501237 Tx: 75079 Fax: (021) 502893
Elegant town house in lovely gardens. Family owned and run. Collection of modern Irish art. Riding.
🛏20 bedrs, 20 en suite; TV
£ room IR£38·50, double room IR£68, D IR£19·95
cc Access, Amex, B'card/Visa, Diners.

B ★ **Country Club,** Montenotte ☎(021) 502922 Tx: 75262
Modern hotel overlooking River Lee.
🛏36 bedrs, 36 en suite; TV
£ B&B IR£36, B&B (double) IR£47; D IR£14·50
cc Access, Amex, B'card/Visa, Diners.

B ★ **Moore's,** Morrison's Island ☎(021) 271291 Tx: 80464
Traditional hotel in quiet area near city centre. Closed 25 & 26 Dec.
🛏39 bedrs, 36 en suite; TV
£ B&B IR£32–£38, B&B (double) IR£48–£60, D IR £13·50
cc Access, Amex, B'card/Visa, Diners.
Mrs N. Murray, Roserie Villa, Mardyke Walk, off Western Rd ☎(021) 272958. *Town*.
🛏7 bedrs, 5 en suite; TV
£ B&B IR£15–£20, B&B (double) IR£22–£35
cc Access, Amex, B'card/Visa, Diners.
Mrs M. Reddy, St Anthony's, Victoria Cross ☎(021) 541345. *Town*.
🛏6 bedrs
£ B&B IR£10·50.

COROFIN Co. Clare. Map 62B3

Kelleher Family, Fergus View, Kilnaboy ☎(065) 27606. *Farm. Fishing*. Open Apr–Sep
🛏6 bedrs, 3 en suite
£ B&B IR£14; B&B (double) IR£22–£26; D IR£10·50
John & Betty Kelleher, Inchiquin View Farm, Kilnaboy ☎(065) 27731. *Farm. Fishing*. Open Mar–Oct
🛏5 bedrs, 2 en suite
£ B&B IR£14; D IR£10·50

COURTOWN HARBOUR Co Wexford. Map 63C3

B ★ **Courtown** ☎(055) 25108
Friendly hotel in town. Indoor swimming pool, sauna. Open 24 Mar–30 Nov.
🛏21 bedrs, 21 en suite
£ B&B IR£20·50–£30, B&B (double) IR£41–£51; D IR£16·50
cc Access, Amex, B'card/Visa, Diners.

Miss B. Kinsella, Riverchapel House ☎(055) 25120
🛏7 bedrs
£ B&B (double) IR£20; D IR£9.

DINGLE Co Kerry. Map 62A2

A **Hotel Skellig** ☎(066) 51144 Fax: (066) 51501
Indoor swimming pool, sauna, tennis, snooker. Open Mar–Nov
🛏50 bedrs, 50 en suite; TV
£ B&B IR£37·50–£52, B&B (double) IR£55–£84, D IR£18·95
cc Access, Amex, B'card/Visa, Diners.

B ★ **Milltown House** ☎(066) 51372
A small white-painted guest house on the sea shore overlooking Dingle Harbour. Open 1 Apr–1 Oct
🛏7 bedrs, 7 en suite
£ B&B IR£18–£20, B&B (double) IR£24–£26
cc B'card/Visa.
Mrs R. Brosnan, Drom House, Coumgaugh ☎(066) 51134. *Country*.
🛏3 bedrs, 3 en suite; TV
£ B&B (double) IR£22; D IR£12
Mrs M. Devane, Lisdargan, Lispole ☎(066) 51418. *Farm*. Open 1 Jun–30 Sep.
🛏3 bedrs
£ B&B (double) IR£21; D IR£10
Mrs A. Murphy, Ard na Mara, Ballymore, Ventry ☎(066) 59072. *Country. Fishing*. Open 1 Mar–1 Dec
🛏5 bedrs, 4 en suite
£ B&B IR£12–£16, B&B (double) IR£21–£24.
Mrs A. Neligan, Duinin House, Conor Pass Rd ☎(066) 51335. *Country*. Open 1 Apr–31 Oct.
🛏5 bedrs, 4 en suite
£ B&B IR£14–£15, B&B (double) IR£22–£25
Mrs P. O'Connor, Knocknahow ☎(066) 51449. *Farm*. Open Apr–Oct
🛏4 bedrs, 2 en suite
£ B&B IR£12, B&B (double) IR£22–£23; HT IR£8.
Mrs C. O'Dowd, Knockarrogeen West ☎(066) 51307. *Farm. Riding, swimming pool, tennis, golf*. Open Mar–Nov
🛏6 bedrs, 6 en suite
£ B&B IR£16, B&B (double) IR£26; D IR£12
cc Access, Amex, B'card/Visa.

DONEGAL Co. Donegal. Map 60C3

A **Hyland Central,** The Diamond ☎(073) 21027 Tx: 40522
🛏72 bedrs, 72 en suite; TV; tcf
£ B&B IR£32–£38, B&B (double) IR£44–£54, D IR£15–£18
cc Access, Amex, B'card/Visa.

B ★ **Abbey,** The Diamond ☎(073) 21014
🛏43 bedrs, 43 en suite; TV
£ B&B IR£28–£31, B&B (double) IR£48–£52; D IR£13·50–£15·50.
cc Amex, Access, B'card/Visa, Diners.

B ★ **Mrs M. McGinty,** Ardeevin, Lough Eske, Barnesmore ☎(073) 21790. *Country*. Open Apr–Oct.
🛏5 bedrs, 4 en suite
£ B&B IR£15; B&B (double) IR£21–£24; D IR£9·50.
Mrs E. Murray, Glebe, Ballyshannon Rd ☎(073) 21223. *Town*. Open 1 May–30 Sep.
🛏4 bedrs, 3 en suite
£ B&B (double) IR£20–£22

DROGHEDA Co. Louth. Map 61B1/63C4

A **Boyne Valley,** Strameen ☎(041) 37737 Tx: 31334
Country mansion in own grounds, 2 km out of Drogheda.
🛏38 bedrs, 38 en suite; TV
£ B&B IR£38–£42, B&B (double) IR£65–IR£70; D IR£16
cc Access, Amex, B'card/Visa, Diners.

B ★ **Glenside,** Smithstown ☎(041) 29185 Open 1 Jan–18 Dec
🛏14 bedrs, 14 en suite; TV
£ B&B IR£26–£30, B&B (double) IR£36–£42, D IR£12·75

Mrs S. Dwyer, Harbour Villa, Mornington Rd ☎(041) 37441. *Country. Tennis*.
🛏4 bedrs
£ B&B IR£14, B&B (double) IR£22; D IR£10

DROICHEAD NUA (NEWBRIDGE) Co Kildare. Map 61B1/63B4

A **Keadeen** ☎(045) 31666 Tx: 60672
🛏37 bedrs, 37 en suite; TV
£ B&B fr IR£72, B&B (double) fr IR£80; D IR£20–£35

DRUMCLIFFE Co. Sligo. Map 60C3

McDonagh Family, Westway ☎(071) 63178. *Farm*. Open 15 May–31 Aug.
🛏3 bedrs
£ B&B IR£13, B&B (double) IR£22, D IR£11

DRUMSHANBO Co. Leitrim. Map 60C2

Mrs M. Costello, Forest View, Carrick Rd ☎(078) 41243. Open 1 Mar–30 Nov

EC *early closing* **MD** *market day* ♣♣ *country house hotel* *ns (NS) no smoking areas* *tcf tea/coffee facilities*

🛏 5 bedrs, 1 en suite
£ B&B (double) IR£20–£22; D IR£9·50

DUBLIN CITY Co. Dublin. Map 61B1/63C4
A ★ **Berkeley Court,** Lansdowne Road ☎ (01) 601711. Tx: 30554 Fax: (01) 617238
Elegant modern hotel with a mixture of up-to-date and antique furnishings. Indoor swimming pool, sauna.
🛏 210 bedrs, 210 en suite; TV
£ room IR£125, double room IR£135; Bk IR£8, D IR£18·50
cc Access, Amex, B'card/Visa, Diners.

A ★ **Jurys,** Pembroke Rd, Ballsbridge, 4 ☎ (01) 605000 Tx: 93723 Fax: (01) 605540
De luxe modern hotel close to main shopping area. Conference facilities. Indoor/outdoor swimming pool.
🛏 390 bedrs, 390 en suite; TV
£ room IR£82–£86, double room fr IR£94–£96; BkIR£7·75, D IR£16·75
cc Access, Amex, B'card/Visa, Diners.

A ★ **Shelbourne,** St. Stephen's Green, ☎ (01) 766471 Tx: 93653 Fax: (01) 616006
Luxury hotel in elegant period building in Dublin's most fashionable area. Sauna.
🛏 165 bedrs, 165 en suite; TV
£ room IR£110, (double) room IR£135; Bk IR£9·25; D IR£24
cc Access, Amex, B'card/Visa, Diners.

A ★ **Westbury**, off Grafton St, 2 ☎ (01) 791122 Tx: 91091 Fax: (01) 797078
Modern luxury hotel in a complex which includes a shopping mall.
🛏 200 bedrs, 200 en suite; TV
£ room IR£125, double room IR£135, Bk IR£8, D IR£18·50
cc Access, Amex, B'card/Visa, Diners.

A **Buswell's,** Molesworth St, 2 ☎ (01) 764013 Tx: 90622 Fax: (01) 762090
🛏 67 bedrs, 67 en suite; TV; tcf
£ room IR£47–£49, double room IR£74–£78; Bk IR£6·50, D IR£12·50
cc Access, Amex, B'card/Visa, Diners.

A **Montrose**, Stillurgan Rd, 4 ☎ (01) 693311 Telex: 91207 Fax: 691164
£ B&B IR£40–£44, B&B (double) IR£62–£72·60; Bk IR£5; D IR£14.
cc Access, Amex, B'card/Visa, Diners.

A **Tara Tower,** Merrion Road, 4 ☎ (01) 694666 Tx:90790 Fax: (01) 691027
Modern hotel 20 minutes drive from city centre on main coast road to ferry terminal at Dun Laoghaire.
🛏 84 bedrs, 84 en suite; TV
£ room IR£40–£44, double room IR£61–£74; Bk IR£5; D IR£14
cc Access, Amex, B'card/Visa, Diners.

B **Lansdowne,** Pembroke Rd, Ballsbridge, 4 ☎ (01) 684079 Tx: 80464 Fax: (055) 27398
Family-run hotel in heart of Georgian Dublin. Car parking.
🛏 28 bedrs, 21 en suite; TV
£ room IR£30–£45, double room IR£40–£70, Bk IR£5·75, D IR£18
cc Access, Amex, B'card/Visa, Diners.

C **Orwell Lodge,** Orwell Road, Rathgar 6 ☎ (01) 977256
Refurbished period house in quiet area.
🛏 10 bedrs, 10 en suite; TV
£ B&B IR£27·50; D IR£16·95
cc Access, Amex, B'card/Visa, Diners.

Mrs N. Doran, Wesley House, Anglesea Rd, Ballsbridge 4 ☎ (01) 681201
🛏 3 bedrs, 3 en suite; TV; tcf
£ B&B IR£18–£20, B&B (double) IR£30–£34; D IR£12·50
Mrs E. Kelly, 17 Seacourt, St Gabriel's Rd, off Seafield Rd, Clontarf ☎ (01) 332547.
🛏 3 bedrs, 2 en suite
£ B&B (double) IR£24–£28.
Mrs Mary Mooney, Aishling House, 20 St Lawrence Rd,Clontarf ☎ (01) 339097. Closed 24–31 Dec.
🛏 9 bedrs, 7 en suite
£ B&B IR£20–£25, B&B (double) IR£24–£28.
Mrs T. Ryan, Parknasilla, 15 Iona Dr, Drumcondra 9 ☎ (01) 305724
🛏 4 bedrs, 2 en suite
£ B&B IR£14, B&B (double) £24–£28.

DULEEK Co. Meath. Map 61B1/63C4
Mrs K. Sweetman, Annesbrook ☎ (041) 23293 *Country.* Open 15 May–15 Sep
🛏 3 bedrs, 3 en suite
£ B&B IR£19·50, B&B (double) IR£33; D IR£12·50.

DUNDALK Co. Louth. Map 61B2
A **Ballymascanlon** ☎ (042) 71124 Tx: 43735
Modernished and extended country mansion in extensive grounds. Indoor swimming pool, tennis, squash, sauna, solarium, gymnasium.
🛏 36 bedrs, 36 en suite; TV
£ B&B IR£35–£37, B&B (double) IR£58–£60; D IR£15·50.
cc Access, Amex, B'card/Visa, Diners.

B ★ **Carrickdale,** Ravensdale ☎ (042) 71397
🛏 31 bedrs, 25 en suite; TV
£ B&B IR£22, B&B (double) IR£35; D IR£13·50.
cc Access, Amex, B'card/Visa, Diners.

B ★ **Derryhale,** Carrick Road ☎ (042) 35471 Tx: 80464
Traditionally furnished, family-run hotel in spacious grounds.
🛏 23 bedrs, 17 en suite; TV
£ room IR£14–£29, double room IR£30–£36; Bk IR£6, D IR£14–£15
cc Access, Amex, B'card/Visa, Diners.

B ★ **Imperial,** Park St ☎ (042) 32241 Tx: 43735
🛏 47 bedrs, 47 en suite
£ B&B IR£31–£33, B&B (double) IR£44–£50; D IR£12·50.

Mrs M. Meehan, Rosemount, Dublin Rd ☎ (042) 35878. *Town.*
🛏 6 bedrs, 3 en suite
£ B&B IR£15, B&B (double) IR£22–£24

DUNFANAGHY Co. Donegal. Map 61A4
B ★ **Arnold's** ☎ (0704) 36208
Open Mar–Sep
🛏 34 bedrs, 34 en suite
£ B&B IR£26–£30, B&B (double) IR£40–£48; D IR£14
cc Access, Amex, B'card/Visa, Diners.

B ★ **Carrig-Rua** ☎ (074) 36133 Tx: 80464
Recently renovated old coaching inn with sea views. Open Easter, May–Sep
🛏 22 bedrs, 22 en suite; TV
£ B&B IR£22–£24, B&B (double) IR£44–£48; D IR£14
cc Amex, B'card/Visa.

DUNGARVAN Co. Waterford. Map 63A2
B ★ **Lawlor's,** T. F. Meagher St ☎ (058) 41056
Bustling town-centre hotel, recently refurbished.
🛏 52 bedrs, 52 en suite; TV
£ B&B IR£24–£26, B&B (double) IR£36–£39 weekly; D IR£14·50
cc Amex, B'card/Visa.

DUNGLOE Co. Donegal. Map 60C4
B **Óstán Na Rosann** ☎ (075) 21088
Family-run modern hotel overlooking Dungloe Bay. Indoor swimming pool, fishing. Open 27 May–30 Sep.
🛏 48 bedrs, 48 en suite
£ B&B IR£20–£25, B&B (double) IR£35–£42; D IR£12
cc Access, Amex, B'card/Visa, Diners.

DUN LAOGHAIRE Co. Dublin. Map 61B1/63C4
A **Royal Marine** ☎ (01) 801911 Tx: 91277 Fax: (01) 801089
Large grey stone hotel close to the ferry terminal and overlooking the sea.
🛏 104 bedrs, 104 en suite; TV
£ room IR£140–£170, double room IR£90–£140; Bk IR£7·50–£8·50, D IR£16
cc Access, Amex, B'card/Visa, Diners

B ★ **Victor,** Rochestown Av ☎ (01) 853555. Tx: 93366 Fax: (01) 853914 *Sauna.*
🛏 58 bedrs, 58 en suite; TV
£ B&B IR£37–£39, B&B (double) IR£56–£66; D IR£14·50.
cc Access, Amex, B'card/Visa, Diners.

DUNMORE EAST Co. Waterford. Map 63B2
Mrs M. Kent, Foxmount Farm, Half-way House ☎ (051) 74308 *Farm. Tennis, riding, snooker.* Open Apr–Oct
🛏 6 bedrs
£ B&B IR£16, B&B (double) IR£26; D IR£12

ENNIS Co. Clare. Map 62C3
A **Old Ground,** O'Connell St, ☎ (065) 28127 Tx: 70603
Well-modernised, part 18th century building in town. (THF)
🛏 60 bedrs, 60 en suite
£ room IR£51·15–£60·50, double room IR£69·30–£82·50; Bk fr IR£8·25–£8·80; D fr IR£17·60–£18·70
cc Access, Amex, B'card/Visa, Diners

B ★ **Queen's,** Abbey St ☎ (065) 28963 Fax: (065) 28628
Refurbished traditional hotel in town centre.
🛏 30 bedrs, 30 en suite; TV; tcf
£ B&B IR£25–£30, B&B (double) IR£40–£50; D IR£12–£13
cc Access, Amex, B'card/Visa, Diners.

Mrs M. Duggan, Woodquay House, Woodquay ☎ (065) 28320. *Town.* Open Mar–Oct.
🛏 4 bedrs, 1 en suite
£ B&B (double) £20–£22
Mrs T. O'Donohue, Sanborn House, Edenvale, Kilrush Rd ☎ (065) 24959. *Country.*
🛏 4 bedrs
£ B&B IR£13; HT IR£7·50.
Mrs M. O'Loughlin, Massabielle, Gaurus (Off Quin Rd) ☎ (065) 29363. *Country.*
🛏 5 bedrs, 4 en suite
£ B&B (double) IR£21–£24; D IR£11

ENNISCORTHY Co. Wexford. Map 63B2

B **Murphy-Floods,** 27 Main St ☎ (054) 33413 Tx: 80464 Fax: (055) 27398
Family-run hotel overlooking the Market Square.
22 bedrs, 16 en suite; TV; tcf
£ B&B IR£21·50–£22·50, B&B (double) IR£40–£44; D IR£13·50
cc Access, Amex, B'card/Visa, Diners.

ENNISKERRY Co. Wicklow. Map 63B4

Mrs K. Lynch, Cherbury, Monastery ☎ (01) 828679. *Country.*
3 bedrs, 3 en suite
£ B&B (double) IR£25

FANAD Co. Donegal. Map 61A4

B **Claggan House,** Ballyhernan ☎ (074) 59057. *Guest House. Fishing.* Open 16 Apr–30 Sep
6 bedrs
£ B&B IR£12; D IR£8·50.

FERMOY Co. Cork. Map 62C2

B **Grand,** Ashe Quay ☎ (025) 31444
Owner-managed hotel in an attractive terrace of 19th century houses on the banks of River Blackwater.
19 bedrs, 13 en suite; TV
£ B&B IR£23, B&B (double) IR£42; D IR£13
cc Access, Amex, B'card/Visa, Diners.

FERNS Co. Wexford. Map 63B3

Mrs Betty Breen, Clone House ☎ (054) 66113. *Farm. Fishing, tennis.* Open Apr–Sep.
4 bedrs, 3 en suite
£ B&B IR£15–£17, B&B double IR£24–£28; D IR£11

FURBO Co. Galway. Map 60B1/62C4

A **Connemara Coast** ☎ (091) 92108 Tx: 50905 Fax: (091) 82332
Traditional house with matching extensions in lovely position overlooking Galway Bay. Swimming pool. Open 1 Feb–31 Oct
83 bedrs, 83 en suite; TV
£ B&B IR£35–£49·75, B&B (double) IR£67·50–£77, D IR£16–£17

GALWAY AND SALTHILL Co. Galway. Map 60B1/62C4

A ★ **Great Southern,** Eyre Sq ☎ (091) 64041 Tx: 50164 Fax: (091) 66704
Large, mid 19th century hotel with a handsome facade in the heart of the city. Indoor swimming pool, sauna.
120 bedrs, 120 en suite; TV
£ room IR£51·50–£57, double room IR£73–£84; Bk IR£6, D IR£16
cc Access, Amex, B'card/Visa, Diners.

A **Ardilaun House,** Taylor's Hill ☎ (091) 21433 Tx: 50013 Fax: (091) 21546
Once a country mansion and situated in beautiful grounds, this hotel is half-way between Galway and Salthill.
91 bedrs, 91 en suite
£ B&B IR£31–£40, B&B (double) IR£50–£70; D IR£15·75–£17·50
cc Access, Amex, Bcard/Visa, Diners.

A **Corrib Great Southern,** Dublin Road ☎ (091) 55281 Tx: 50044 Fax: (091) 51390
Modern hotel with spectacular views of Galway Bay. Indoor swimming pool, sauna, snooker.
110 bedrs, 110 en suite; TV
£ room IR£37–£45·50, double room IR£50–£67; Bk IR£5·50; D IR£15
cc Access, Amex, B'card/Visa, Diners

A **Galway Ryan,** Dublin Rd, ☎ (091) 53181 Tx: 50149 Fax: (091) 53187
£ B&B IR£40–£53, B&B (double) IR£58–£74; D IR£14
cc Access, Amex, B'card/Visa, Diners.

Mrs S. Davy, Ross House, Whitestrand Av ☎ (091) 67431. *Town.*
4 bedrs, 2 en suite
£ B&B IR£15, B&B (double) IR£21–£24.

Mrs T. Cunningham, La Salette, Grattan Park ☎ (091) 65720. *Town.* Open Easter–Oct
4 bedrs, 3 en suite
£ B&B (double) IR£22–£24

Mrs J. Maher, Petra, Laurel Park, Newcastle ☎ (091) 21844. *Town.* Open 1 Apr–30 Sep.
4 bedrs, 1 en suite
£ B&B (double) IR£22–£24; D IR£10

Mrs M. Nolan, Glencree, 20 Whitestrand Av, Lower Salthill ☎ (091) 61061. *Town.*
4 bedrs, 4 en suite
£ B&B (double) IR£24.

Mrs O. Connolly, Seacrest, Roscam ☎ (091) 57975. *Town. Indoor swimming pool.*
6 bedrs, 5 en suite; tcf
£ B&B (double) IR£22–£26.

Tim & Carmel O'Halloran, Roncalli House, 24 Whitestrand Av, Lower Salthill ☎ (091) 64159. *Town.*
6 bedrs, 6 en suite
£ B&B (double) IR£24

Mrs B. Thomson, Rock Lodge, Whitestrand Rd ☎ (091) 63789. *Town.*
6 bedrs, 5 en suite
£ B&B IR£12, B&B (double) IR£24

Mr & Mrs Dermot & Margaret Walsh, De Sota, 54 Newcastle Rd ☎ (091) 65064. *Town.*
6 bedrs, 4 en suite
£ B&B (double) IR£21–£24.

GARRETTSTOWN Co. Cork. Map 62C1

B ★ **Coakley's Atlantic,** Ballinspittle ☎ (021) 778215
Family-run holiday hotel overlooking the sea.
22 bedrs, 22 en suite
£ B&B IR£24–£28, B&B (double) IR£34–£42; D IR£13–£13·50
cc Access, Amex, B'card/Visa, Diners.

GLENCOLUMBKILLE Co. Donegal. Map 60C3

B **Glencolmcille,** Malinmore ☎ (073) 30003
Two-storey, country-house-style hotel in rural area with magnificent sea and coast views. Open 1 Apr–1 Oct.
19 bedrs, 19 en suite; tcf
£ B&B IR£18·50–£22·50; B&B (double) IR£27–£33; D IR£13
cc B'card/Visa.

GLENGARRIFF Co. Cork. Map 62B1

B **Eccles,** Glengarriff Harbour ☎ (027) 63003 Fax: (027) 63319
Holiday hotel on shores of Bantry Bay. Hotel dinghies and windsurfers. Open May–Oct.
49 bedrs, 49 en suite; TV
£ B&B IR£19·25–£22, B&B (double) IR£38·50–£44; D IR£15·50
cc Access, Amex, B'card/Visa, Diners.

GLEN OF THE DOWNS Co. Wicklow. Map 63C3

A **Glenview** ☎ (01) 877029 Tx: 30638
Family-run hotel in lovely gardens overlooking the Glen.
23 bedrs, 23 en suite; TV
£ room IR£40, double room IR£60; Bk IR£6, D IR£13.

GORESBRIDGE Co. Kilkenny. Map 63B3

Mrs C. Lawlor, Mount Loftus ☎ (0503) 75228. *Country.* Open mid June–mid Sep
3 bedrs, 1 en suite
£ B&B IR£21–£25, D IR£10

GOREY Co. Wexford. Map 63C3

A **Marlfield House** ☎ (055) 21124 Tx: 80757 Fax: (055) 21572
Fine Regency country house hotel on the Gorey/Courtown road. Tennis, sauna.
19 bedrs, 19 en suite; TV
£ B&B (double) IR£250; D IR£26–£30

GRANGE Co. Sligo. Map 60C3

Mrs C. Anhold, Horse Holiday Farm, Mount Temple ☎ (071) 66152 Fax: (071) 66400. *Farm. Riding, sauna.* Open 15 Jan–15 Dec
4 bedrs, 4 en suite

Mrs U. Brennan, Armada Lodge, Mount Temple ☎ (071) 63250. *Country. Sauna, tennis.*
5 bedrs, 5 en suite
£ B&B IR£14–£15

HEADFORD Co. Galway. Map 60B1/62B4

McDonagh Family, Balrickard Farm ☎ (093) 35421. *Farm.* Open Mar–Nov
3 bedrs
£ B&B (double) IR£20–£25; D IR£10

HOWTH Co. Dublin. Map 61B1/63C4

Howth Lodge ☎ (01) 390288 Tx: 93348
Family owned hotel overlooking the sea and with direct access to the beach.
17 bedrs, 17 en suite; TV; tcf
£ room IR£32–£40, double room IR£41–£60; Bk IR£5·50, D IR£16·50
cc Access, Amex, B'card/Visa, Diners.

B **Deer Park Hotel** ☎ (01) 322624
Modern hotel with golf complex–four different courses–overlooking the sea. Famous rhododendron garden.
30 bedrs, 30 en suite; TV
£ B&B IR£28–£38, B&B (double) IR£48–£52; D IR£14
cc Access, Amex, B'card/Visa, Diners.

INNISCRONE Co. Sligo. Map 60B3

B **Atlantic** ☎ (096) 36119. *Tennis, snooker.* Open Mar–Oct.
10 bedrs, 6 en suite
£ B&B IR£13–£14·50, B&B (double) £26–£29, D IR£10

B **Castle Arms** ☎ (096) 36156
17 bedrs, 7 en suite
£ B&B IR£12–£14, B&B (double) £24–£30; D IR£9–£10

INNISHANNON Co. Cork. Map 62C1

B ★ **Innishannon House** ☎ (021) 775121 Fax: (021) 775609
🛏 13 bedrs, 13 en suite; TV
£ B&B IR£40–£55, B&B (double) IR£60–£75; D IR£17·50.
cc Access, Amex, B'card/Visa, Diners.

INVER Co. Donegal. Map 60C3

Mrs R.M. Boyd, Cranny House, ☎ (073) 36010. *Farm.* Open 1 Apr–31 Oct
🛏 3 bedrs, 1 en suite
£ B&B IR£12–£14; D IR£13·25.

KANTURK Co. Cork. Map 62C3

A **Assolas Country House** ☎ (029) 50015 Fax: (029) 50795
Charming 17th century family residence in lovely gardens. Tennis, fishing.
Open 1 Apr–31 Oct.
🛏 10 bedrs, 10 en suite
£ B&B IR£44–£55, B&B (double) £92–£118; D IR£22·50
cc Access, Amex, B'card/Visa, Diners.

KELLS Co. Meath. Map 61B2/63B4

B ★ **Headfort Arms** ☎ (046) 40063
🛏 15 bedrs, 15 en suite
£ B&B IR£28; D IR£14·95.

Mrs P. Mullan, Lennoxbrook, Carnacross ☎ (046) 45902. *Farm. Fishing.*
🛏 5 bedrs
£ B&B IR£14, B&B (double) IR£22; D IR£12

KENMARE Co. Kerry. Map 62B2

A ★ **Park Hotel Kenmare** ☎ (064) 41200 Tx: 73905 Fax: (064) 41402
Luxurious hotel, furnished with antiques in the public rooms, in spacious gardens overlooking the Kenmare Estuary. Golf, tennis, croquet, fishing, riding.
🛏 48 bedrs, 48 en suite
£ B&B IR£74–£86, B&B (double) IR£144–£180; D IR£33
cc Access, B'card/Visa.

B **Lansdowne Arms,** Main St ☎ (064) 41368
An 18th century inn next to the golf course on the shore of Kenmare Bay. Open 15 Mar–31 Dec
🛏 22 bedrs, 9 en suite
£ B&B (double) £26–£38; D IR£12·50

Mrs P. Dignam, Glendarragh ☎ (064) 41436. *Farm. Sauna.* Open Feb–15 Nov
🛏 6 bedrs, 6 en suite
£ B&B IR£12, B&B (double) IR£24; D IR£10.
Mrs T. Hayes, Ceann Mara, Killowen ☎ (064) 41220. *Farm. Tennis, fishing, private beach.* Open Apr–Oct
🛏 6 bedrs, 5 en suite; tcf
£ B&B IR£14–£15; D IR£11
O'Donnells of Ashgrove, Ashgrove ☎ (064) 41228. *Country.* Open 1 Mar–31 Oct.
🛏 4 bedrs, 3 en suite
£ B&B IR£11–£13, B&B (double) IR£20–£24; D IR£10.
Mrs M. O'Mahoney, The Arches, Blackwater Bridge ☎ (064) 82030. *Country.* Open Apr–Oct
🛏 5 bedrs, 5 en suite
£ B&B IR£17, B&B (double) IR£25
Mrs M. Whyte, Riverside, Killarney Rd ☎ (064) 41316. *Town.* Open Apr–Oct
🛏 3 bedrs
£ B&B IR£11.

KILDARE Co. Kildare. Map 61B1/63B4

Mrs A. Winters, St Mary's, Maddenstown, Curragh ☎ (045) 21243. *Farm.* Open Apr–Sep
🛏 3 bedrs
£ B&B IR£20; D IR£9

KILGARVAN Co. Kerry. Map 62B2

Eileen & Sean Dineen, Glenlea Farmhouse ☎ (064) 85314. *Farm. Fishing.* Open Feb–Nov
🛏 8 bedrs, 4 en suite
£ B&B (double) IR£23; D IR£10·50
Dineen Family, Hawthorn Farm ☎ (064) 85326. *Farm.* Open 1 Apr–31 Oct.
🛏 6 bedrs, 3 en suite
£ B&B IR£23–£25; D IR£10·50
Mrs J. McCarthy, Sillerdane Lodge, Coolnoohill ☎ (064) 85359. *Country. Swimming pool.*
🛏 6 bedrs, 6 en suite
£ B&B IR£14; D IR£10

KILKEE Co. Clare. Map 62B3

B **Victoria** ☎ (065) 56010
🛏 18 bedrs, 18 en suite; TV
£ B&B IR£18–£19, B&B (double) IR£32–£34; D IR£10

KILKENNY Co. Kilkenny. Map 63A3

A **Hotel Kilkenny,** College Road. ☎ (056) 62000 Tx: 80177 Fax: (056) 65984
Close to the city centre, a modern hotel built around an attractive mansion. Indoor swimming pool, tennis, sauna, solarium, gymnasium.
🛏 60 bedrs, 60 en suite; TV
£ room IR£37–£42, double room IR£62–64; Bk £6·25, D IR£14·95
cc Access, Amex, B'card/Visa.

A **Newpark,** Castlecomer Road ☎ (056) 22122 Tx: 80080 Fax: (056) 61111
Modern hotel set in over 30 acres of parkland. Indoor swimming pool, tennis, sauna, riding.
🛏 60 bedrs, 60 en suite; TV
£ room IR£30–£36, double room IR£49–£56; Bk IR£6·50; D IR£14–£15·50
cc Access, Amex, B'card/Visa, Diners.

B **Club House,** Patrick St ☎ (056) 21994 Tx: 80464
Originally the headquarters of the Foxhunters Club, this centrally placed hotel still has its traditional decor. Squash, sauna.
🛏 23 bedrs, 18 en suite; TV
£ room IR£21·50–£29·50, double room IR£38–£50; Bk IR£6·50, D IR£10·25

B **Lacken House,** Dublin Road ☎ (056) 65611
🛏 8 bedrs, 8 en suite; TV; tcf
£ room IR£24, double room IR£40; D IR£17
Mrs M. T. Neary, Tara Farm, off Freshford Rd ☎ (056) 67619. *Farm.* Open 1 Apr–31 Oct.
🛏 4 bedrs
£ B&B IR£22, D IR£9

KILLALOE Co. Clare. Map 62C3

B ★ **Lakeside** ☎ (061) 76122
Refurbished hotel on the shores of Lough Derg. Tennis, fishing, riding.
🛏 32 bedrs, 32 en suite
£ B&B IR£25–£28, B&B (double) IR£43–£48, D IR£15
cc Access, Amex, B'card/Visa, Diners.

Miss E. Coppen, Lantern House, Ogonnelloe, Tuamgraney ☎ (0619) 23034. *Country.* Closed Nov
🛏 6 bedrs, 6 en suite
£ B&B IR£15, B&B (double) IR£28; D IR£10.

KILLARNEY Co. Kerry. Map 62B2

A **Aghadoe Heights** ☎ (061) 31766 Tx: 73942 Fax: (064) 31345
Hotel awaiting RAC inspection Fishing, tennis.
🛏 61 bedrs, 61 en suite; TV
£ B&B IR£55–£75, B&B (double) IR£85–£110; L IR£14·50, D IR£23·50
cc Access, Amex, B'card/Visa, Diners.

A ★ **Dunloe Castle,** Beaufort, ☎ (064) 44111 Tx: 73833 Fax: (064) 32118
Indoor swimming pool, tennis, riding, sauna.
🛏 140 bedrs, 140 en suite; TV
£ B&B IR£42–£48, B&B (double) IR£65–£85; D IR£19·50–£21
cc Access, Amex, B'card/Visa, Diners.

A ★ **Europe,** Fossa ☎ (064) 31900 Tx: 73913 Fax: (064) 32118
Elegant modern hotel on the shores of Lough Leane and next to the golf course. Indoor swimming pool, riding, tennis, sauna, fishing. Open 1 Mar–31 Oct.
🛏 176 bedrs, 176 en suite; TV
£ B&B IR£56–£68, B&B (double) IR£80–£95; D IR£21

A ★ **Great Southern** ☎ (064) 31262 Tx: 73998 Fax: (064) 32118
Large mid 19th-century hotel set in beautiful grounds. Indoor swimming pool, sauna, tennis. Open 10 Mar–31 Dec.
🛏 180 bedrs, 180 en suite; TV
£ room IR£51·50–£57, double room IR£73–£84; Bk IR£6, D IR£16
cc Access, Amex, B'card/Visa, Diners.

A **Cahernane,** Muckross ☎ (064) 31895 Tx: 73823 Fax: (064) 33334. Open Apr–Oct.
🛏 50 bedrs, 50 en suite
£ B&B IR£50–£55, B&B (double) IR£75–£90; D IR£23·50

A **Torc Great Southern** ☎ (064) 31611 Tx: 73807
Swimming pool, tennis. Open 21 Apr–30 Sep
🛏 96 bedrs, 96 en suite; TV
£ room IR£37, double room IR£50; D IR£15
cc Access, Amex, B'card/Visa, Diners.

B ★ **Dromhall,** Muckross Rd ☎ (064) 31431
Low-built modern hotel in own grounds with large parking area. Open 24 Mar–31 Oct.
🛏 58 bedrs, 58 en suite
£ B&B IR£20–£32, B&B (double) IR£36–£50, D IR£12·50
cc Access, B'card/Visa.

B ★ **International,** Kenmare Place ☎ (064) 31816 Tx: 73825 Fax: (064) 33219
A centrally situated hotel with bar entertainment every night in season.
Open 1 Mar–31 Oct.
🛏 88 bedrs, 88 en suite; TV
£ room IR£23·50–£30·50, double room IR£31–£45, Bk IR£6, D IR£13·50

Mr & Mrs M. Beazley, Carriglea House, Muckcross Rd ☎ (064) 31116. *Farm.* Open Easter–Oct.
🛏 9 bedrs, 6 en suite
£ B&B IR£24–£27; D IR£9·50
Mrs M. Counihan, Villa Marias, Aghadoe ☎ (064) 32307. *Country.* Open Mar–Oct.

4 bedrs
£ B&B (double) IR£21

Mrs P. Cronin, St Ritas Villas, Mill Rd (off Muckcross Rd) (064) 31517. *Town.*
5 bedrs, 4 en suite
£ B&B IR£14–£15, B&B (double) IR£21–£24

Hannah & Dan Daly, Brookfield House, Coolgarrive, Aghadoe (064) 32077. *Farm.* Open Mar–Oct.
6 bedrs, 1 en suite
£ B&B (double) IR£24; D IR£9·50

Mrs N. Dineen, Manor House, 18 Whitebridge Manor, Ballycasheen (064) 32716. *Town.*
5 bedrs, 3 en suite
£ B&B IR£15, B&B (double) IR£22–£24; D IR£9·50

Mrs T. Doona, Hollybough House, Cappagh, Kilgobnet (064) 44255. *Country.* Open Easter–Oct.
4 bedrs, 2 en suite
£ B&B IR£14·50–£15, B&B (double) IR£21; D IR£10
cc Access.

Mrs M. Geaney, Pine Crest, Woodlawn Rd (off Muckcross Rd) (064) 31721. *Town.*
5 bedrs, 3 en suite
£ B&B IR£15, B&B double room IR£21–£23

Mrs K. Guerin, Irish Cottage, Muckcross Rd (064) 32443. *Town.*
5 bedrs, 1 en suite
£ B&B IR£14·50; D IR£10.

Mrs J. Horan, Knockane Farm, Ballyfinnane, Farranfore (066) 64324. *Farm. Riding, fishing.* Open 1 May–30 Sep.
3 bedrs, 1 en suite
£ B&B IR£12·50, D IR£12·50.

Mrs M.R. Kearney, Gap View Farm, Firies (via Ballyhar) (066) 64378. *Farm.* Open Easter–Oct.
6 bedrs, 2 en suite
£ B&B IR£10·50–£12; D IR£9·50

Mrs K. McAuliffe, Carrowmore House, Knockasarnett, Aghadoe (064) 33520. *Country.* Open Apr–Oct.
5 bedrs, 4 en suite
£ B&B IR£14·50–£16

Miss C. McSweeney, Emerville House, Muckcross Dr, Muckcross Rd (064) 33342. *Town.* Open Mar–Oct.
4 bedrs, (3 sh)
£ B&B (double) IR£22

Mrs C. O'Brien, Tara, Gap of Dunloe Rd (064) 44355. *Country.* Open 1 Apr–31 Oct.
5 bedrs, 4 en suite
£ B&B IR£14·50, B&B (double) IR£21–£24; D IR£10

Mrs N. O'Neill, Alderhaven, Ballycasheen (064) 31982. *Country.* Open 15 Mar–31 Oct.
5 bedrs, 4 en suite
£ B&B IR£16

Mrs C. Spillane, Beauty's Home, Tralee Rd (064) 31567. *Country.*
3 bedrs, 2 en suite; TV; tcf
£ B&B IR£14–£16·50, B&B (double) IR£22–£27

Mrs E. Spillane, Inveraray, Beaufort (064) 44224. *Farm. Fishing, riding.* Open Feb–Nov.
6 bedrs, 4 en suite
£ B&B IR£21–£24; D IR£9

Mrs A. Teahan, Fair Haven, Lissivigeen, Cork Rd (064) 32542. *Country.*
6 bedrs, 5 en suite
£ B&B (double) IR£21–£24.

KILLESHANDRA Co. Cavan. Map 61A2

B **Loughbawn** (O'Reilly's) (049) 34404
11 bedrs, 11 en suite
£ B&B IR£18–£20, B&B (double) IR£30–£34; D IR£13–£14

KILLINEY Co. Dublin. Map 61B1/63C4

A ★ **Fitzpatrick Castle** (01) 851533 Tx: 30353 Fax: (01) 850207
Luxury hotel in castle with modern extension. Spacious grounds. Indoor swimming pool, squash, tennis, sauna, solarium.
94 bedrs, 94 en suite, TV
£ room IR£53–£72, double room IR£70–£102; Bk IR£7, D IR£16
cc Access, Amex, B'card/Visa, Diners.

A **The Court** (01) 851622 Tx: 33244 Fax: (01) 852085
84 bedrs, 84 en suite, TV; tcf
£ room IR£40–£48, double room IR£55–£60; Bk IR£6, D IR£14·50

KILLORGLIN Co. Kerry. Map 62B2

Mrs M. Melia, Ashling, Sunhill (066) 61226. *Town.* Open Mar–Nov.
4 bedrs
£ B&B IR£10

KILLYBEGS Co. Donegal. Map 60C3

Mrs E. O'Keeney, Glenlee House, Fintra Rd (073) 31026. *Country.*
5 bedrs, 5 en suite; tcf
£ B&B IR£15, B&B (double) IR£24; D IR£10

KILMESSAN Co. Meath. Map 61B1/63B4

B **Kilmessan Station House** (046) 25239
Tennis, riding, fishing. Open 1 Jan–24 Dec
10 bedrs, 5 en suite; TV
£ B&B IR£24–£30; D IR£16·95
cc Amex, B'card/visa, Diners.

KILRUSH Co Clare. Map 62B3

B **Inis Cathaigh,** Francis St (065) 51036
15 bedrs, 9 en suite
£ B&B IR£15–£19·50, B&B (double) IR£26–£35
cc Access, B'card/Visa.

KILTEGAN Co. Wicklow. Map 63B3

Mrs E.F. Jackson, Beachlawn (0508) 73171. *Farm.* Open 1 Mar–31 Oct.
4 bedrs
£ B&B (double) IR£22; D IR£10

KILTIMAGH Co. Mayo. Map 60B2

Mrs M. Carney, Hillcrest, Kilkelly Rd (094) 81112. *Country.* Open Apr–Sep.
4 bedrs, 2 en suite
£ B&B (double) IR£20–£21; D IR£9·50

KINSALE Co. Cork. Map 62C1

A **Acton's** (021) 772135 Tx: 75443
Modernised hotel overlooking the picturesque harbour. Indoor swimming pool, sauna, billiards. (THF)
55 bedrs, 55 en suite; TV; tcf
£ B&B IR£42–£50, B&B (double) IR£60–£76, D fr IR£15
cc Access, Amex, B'card/Visa, Diners.

B ★ **Blue Haven** (021) 772209
Small, cosy owner-run hotel in the centre of town.
10 bedrs, 7 en suite; TV; tcf
£ B&B IR£28–£45, D IR£19
cc Access, Amex, B'card/Visa, Diners.

Griffin Family, Griffins, Hillside House, Camp Hill (021) 772315. *Country.*
6 bedrs, 3 en suite
£ B&B IR£10–£13; D IR£9·50.

Mr & Mrs A. Moran-Salinger, The Lighthouse, The Rock (021) 772734
6 bedrs, 3 en suite
£ B&B IR£17, B&B (double) IR£27; D IR£10

KNOCK Co. Mayo. Map 60B2

B **Knock International,** Main St (094) 88466 ♿
Single-storey modern hotel set in own gardens close to Knock shrine. Fishing.
10 bedrs, 10 en suite; TV
£ B&B IR£21–£24, B&B (double) IR£18–£21; D IR£12·95
cc Access, Amex, B'card/Visa.

KNOCKFERRY Co. Galway. Map 60B1

Mr Des Moran, Knockferry Lodge, Knockferry, Roscahill (091) 80122. *Farm.* Open May–Oct.
10 bedrs, 10 en suite
£ B&B IR£19, B&B (double) IR£32; D IR£13·50

KYLEMORE Co. Galway. Map 62B4

B **Kylemore Pass** (095) 41141 Tx: 80464
Beautifully situated small family-owned hotel overlooking Kylemore Lake. Fishing. Closed 22–31 Dec.
10 bedrs, 10 en suite; tcf
£ B&B IR£25–£27, B&B (double) IR£18–£20; D IR£18·50
cc Access, Amex, B'card/Visa, Diners.

LAHINCH Co. Clare. Map 62B3

A **Vaughans Aberdeen Arms** (065) 81100 Tx: 70132. Open 1 Mar–31 Dec.
55 bedrs, 55 en suite; TV; tcf
£ B&B IR£33–£37, B&B (double) IR£52–£60, D IR£16·50.

Mrs B. Fawl, Mulcarr House, Ennistymon Rd (065) 81123. *Town.* Open 17 Mar–31 Oct
4 bedrs, 3 en suite
£ B&B IR£14·50; B&B (double) IR£22–£24

LEENANE Co. Galway. Map 60B1–2/62B4

Mrs B. Daly, Portfinn Lodge (095) 42265. *Country. Fishing.* Open Apr–Sep.
4 bedrs, 4 en suite
£ B&B (double) IR£23; D IR£12·75
cc Access, B'card/Visa.

LEIXLIP Co. Kildare. Map 61B1/63B4

B **Springfield** (01) 244925
11 bedrs, 8 en suite; TV
£ B&B IR£19–£23, B&B (double) IR£37, D IR£14·50
cc Access, Amex, B'card/Visa.

LETTERFRACK Co. Galway. Map 60B2

A **Rosleague Manor** (095) 41101 Tx: 50906

Delightfully situated Georgian house in 25 acres of secluded gardens overlooking Ballinakill Bay. Tennis, sauna. Open 1 Apr–31 Oct.
🛏 13 bedrs, 13 en suite
£ B&B IR£45–£55, B&B (double) IR£70–£90; D IR£20
cc Access, Amex, B'card/Visa.

LETTERKENNY Co. Donegal. Map 61A4
A **Mount Errigal,** Ballyraine ☎(074) 22700 Tx: 42112. *Sauna.*
🛏 56 bedrs, 56 en suite; TV
£ B&B IR£28–£32, B&B (double) IR£50–£54; D fr IR£13

B ★ **Gallagher's,** 110 Upper Main St ☎(074) 22066 Fax: (074) 21016. Open 1 Jan–24 Dec.
🛏 27 bedrs, 27 en suite; TV
£ B&B IR£21·50, B&B (double) IR£37; D IR£12·50

LIMERICK Co. Limerick. Map 62C3
A **Greenhills,** Ennis Rd ☎(061) 53033 Tx: 70246
Modern Swiss-chalet-style hotel in over 4 acres of landscaped gardens just outside the city.
🛏 55 bedrs, 55 en suite; TV; tcf
£ room IR£40–£44, double room IR£60–£68; D IR16
cc Access, Amex, B'card/Visa, Diners.

A **Jurys,** Ennis Rd ☎(061) 55266 Tx: 70766 Fax: (061) 326400
Modern hotel in own grounds overlooking River Shannon.
🛏 96 bedrs, 96 en suite; TV
£ room IR£54–£56·50, double room IR£65–£66·50, Bk IR£7·25, D IR£10
cc Access, Amex, B'card/Visa, Diners.

A **Limerick Inn**, Ennis Rd, ☎(061) 51544 Tx: 70621 Fax: (061) 326281
🛏 153 bedrs, 153 en suite
£B&B IR£60–£65, B&B (double) IR£70–£80; Bk IR£6·50; D IR£19·50.
cc Access, Amex, B'card/Visa, Diners.

A **Two Mile Inn,** Ennis Rd ☎(061) 53122 Tx: 70157 ♿
🛏 125 bedrs, 125 en suite; TV
£ B&B IR£36–£46, B&B double room IR£51–£71; D IR£14.
cc Access, Amex, B'card/Visa, Diners.

Mrs B. Boylan, Trelawne House, Ennis Rd ☎(061) 54063. *Town.*
£ B&B IR£15–£16·50, B&B (double) IR£22–£25
Mrs M. Collins, St Anthony's, 8 Coolraine Ter, Ennis Rd ☎(061) 52607. *Town.*
🛏 3 bedrs
£ B&B (double) IR£19
Mrs C.A. Gavin, Shannonville, Ennis Rd ☎(061) 53690. *Town.* Open May–Sep.
🛏 3 bedrs
£ B&B (double) IR£19.
Mrs K. O'Reilly, Erris House, Fairs Rd, Meelick ☎(051) 54605. *Country.* Open May–1 Oct.
🛏 4 bedrs, 2 en suite
£ B&B IR£21–£24

LISDOONVARNA Co. Clare. Map 62B3
B ★ **Imperial** ☎(065) 74015 Fax: (065) 74406
Open 1 Mar–31 Oct.
🛏 60 bedrs, 60 en suite; TV; tcf
£ B&B IR£23–£25, B&B (double) IR£36–£40, D IR£10
cc Access, B'card/Visa.

B ★ **Sheedy's Spa View** ☎(065) 74026
Owner-managed modern hotel. Tennis. Open 1 Apr–5 Sep.
🛏 11 bedrs, 11 en suite
£ B&B IR£25, B&B (double) IR£40; D IR£15·50
cc Access, Amex, B'card/Visa, Diners.

LISTOWEL Co. Kerry. Map 62B3
Mrs J. Groarke, Burntwood House ☎(068) 21516. *Farm.* Open 1 Apr–1 Oct.
🛏 6 bedrs, 4 en suite
£ B&B IR£10; D IR£12.
Mrs T. Keane, Whispering Pines, Bedford ☎(068) 21503. *Country.*
🛏 4 bedrs
£ B&B (double) IR£22–£26; D IR£24.
Mrs N. O'Neill, Ashgrove House, Ballybunion Rd ☎(068) 21268. *Country.* Open Mar–Oct.
🛏 4 bedrs, 4 en suite
£ B&B IR£16; B&B (double) £22–£32.
Mrs K. Stack, Tralee Rd, Ballygrennane ☎(068) 21345. *Town.* Open Apr–Oct.
🛏 4 bedrs, 3 en suite
£ B&B (double) IR£21–£31.

LONGFORD Co. Longford. Map 61A2
B ★ **Longford Arms,** Main St ☎(043) 46296.
🛏 51 bedrs, 51 en suite; TV
£ B&B IR£21, B&B (double) IR£38; D IR£13·50.
cc Access, Amex, B'card/Visa, Diners.

LOUGHREA Co. Galway. Map 62C4
B **O'Dea's,** Bride St ☎(091) 41611
🛏 12 bedrs, 8 en suite
£ B&B IR£22·50–£25; B&B (double) IR£45; D IR£14·50
cc Access, Amex,

LOUISBURGH Co. Mayo. Map 60A2
B ★ **Old Head** ☎(098) 66021. Open 1 Jun–15 Sep.
🛏 12 bedrs, 12 en suite; TV; tcf
£ B&B IR£15–£20, D IR£14

MACROOM Co. Cork. Map 62B2
B ★ **Castle,** Main St ☎(026) 41074
Family owned and managed traditional hotel in town centre. Fishing.
🛏 16 bedrs, 16 en suite; TV
£ B&B IR£18, B&B (double) IR£32, D IR£13.
cc Amex, Access, B'card/Visa, Diners.

MALAHIDE Co. Dublin. Map 61B1/63C4
Mrs M. Farelly, Lynfar, Kinsealy La ☎(01) 463897. *Town.* Open Feb–Oct.
🛏 4 bedrs
£ B&B IR£15, B&B (double) IR£24

MALLOW Co. Cork. Map 62C2
A **Longueville House** ☎(022) 47156 Tx: 75498
Georgian mansion set in a wooded estate; now an owner-run hotel. Fishing.
🛏 17 bedrs, 17 en suite
£ B&B IR£50–£55, D fr IR£25–£27
cc Access, Amex, B'card/Visa, Diners.

Mrs B. Copplestone, Dawna, Navigation Rd ☎(022) 21479. *Country.* Open Mar–Oct.
🛏 3 bedrs, 3 en suite
£ B&B IR£15, B&B (double) IR£25, D IR£10.

RI

MAYNOOTH Co. Kildare. Map 61B1/63B4
A **Moyglare Manor** ☎(01) 286351 Tx: 90358
A Georgian country house in beautiful parkland. Swimming pool, tennis.
🛏 17 bedrs, 17 en suite
£ B&B IR£65, B&B (double) IR£100; D IR£18·50
cc Access, Amex, B'card/Visa, Diners.

MIDLETON Co. Cork. Map 62C1-2
A **Ballymaloe House,** Shanagarry ☎(021) 652531 Tx: 75208 Fax: (021) 652021
Gracious country house on the owner's farm only 1½ miles from the sea. Swimming pool, tennis, fishing.
🛏 29 bedrs, 29 en suite
£ room IR£46–£53, double room IR£60–£106; D IR£21–£24.
cc Access, Amex, B'card/Visa, Diners.

MILTOWN MALBAY Co. Clare. Map 62B3
B **Bay View,** Spanish Point ☎(065) 84006
🛏 8 bedrs, 4 en suite
£ B&B IR£9–£10; D IR£6·50.

MOUNTRATH Co. Laois. Map 63A3
Frank & Rosemarie Kennan, Roundwood House ☎(0502) 32120. *Country.*
🛏 6 bedrs, 6 en suite
£ B&B IR£30, B&B (double) IR£46; D IR£16.
cc Access, Amex

MOYARD Co. Galway. Map 60A1/62B4
A **Crocnaraw Country House** ☎(095) 41068. Open May–Oct.
🛏 6 bedrs, 4 en suite
£ B&B IR£28–£30, B&B (double) IR£50–£60, D IR£16·50.
cc Amex, B'card/Visa

MOYCULLEN Co. Galway. Map 60B1
B **Cloonabinnia House,** Ross Lake ☎(091) 85555. *Fishing.* Open Mar–Nov.
🛏 14 bedrs, 14 en suite
£ B&B IR£18–£20; HB weekly IR£185–£195; D IR£13·50.

MULLINAHONE Co. Tipperary. Map 63A2
Mrs R. E. Sherwood, Killaghy Castle ☎(052) 53112. *Farm.* Open mid Mar–mid Oct
🛏 4 bedrs, 2 en suite
£ B&B (double) IR£45–£50; D IR£14·50.

MULLINGAR Co. Westmeath. Map 61A1/63A4
B ★ **Greville Arms,** Pearse St ☎(044) 48563
Traditional town hotel with night club.

🛏 33 bedrs, 33 en suite; TV
£ B&B IR£28–£32, B&B (double) IR£46–£52; D IR£13·95.

Mr & Mrs S. Casey, Hilltop, Navan Rd, Rathconnell ☎(044) 48958. *Country.*
🛏 5 bedrs, 5 en suite
£ B&B IR£16, B&B (double) IR£24; D IR£11.

NAAS Co. Kildare. Map 61B1/63B4

B ★ **Curryhills House,** Prosperous Rd ☎(045) 68150
🛏 10 bedrs, 10 en suite; TV; tcf
£ B&B IR£30, B&B (double) IR£46, D IR£15.
cc Access, Amex, B'card/Visa, Diners.

NAVAN Co. Meath. Map 61B1/63B4

A **Ardboyne,** Dublin Rd ☎(046) 23119
Modern hotel in own grounds on outskirts of town.
🛏 26 bedrs, 26 en suite; TV
£ B&B IR£35·50–£65, B&B (double) IR£60–£110; D IR£17–£19·50.
cc Access, Amex, B'card/Visa, Diners

Mrs M. Reilly, Gainstown House ☎(046) 21448. *Farm.* Open Apr–Oct.
🛏 4 bedrs
£ B&B IR£14; D IR£8.

NENAGH Co. Tipperary. Map 62C3

Mrs K. Healy, Rathnaleen House, Golf Club Rd ☎(067) 32508. *Country.*
🛏 3 bedrs, 1 en suite
£ B&B IR£14, B&B (double) IR£22–£26; D IR£10
Mrs B. Lewis, Ballyartella Farmhouse ☎(067) 24219. *Farm. Fishing.* Open Mar–Oct.
🛏 4 bedrs
£ B&B (double) IR£22; D IR£9.
Mrs G. McAuliffe, Avondale, Tyone ☎(067) 31084. *Town.* Open Apr–Nov.
🛏 4 bedrs
£ B&B IR£14; D IR£10.

NEW BAWN Co. Wexford. Map 63B2

B ★ **Cedar Lodge,** Carrigbyrne ☎(051) 28386
Low-built modern hotel with views of Carrigbyrne Forest.
🛏 13 bedrs, 13 en suite; TV
£ B&B IR£30–£34, B&B (double) IR£50, D IR£18
cc Access, B'card/Visa.

NEWBLISS Co. Monaghan. Map 61A2

Mrs M. O'Grady, Glynch House ☎(047) 54045. *Farm.* Open Jan–mid Dec.
🛏 6 bedrs, 1 en suite
£ B&B IR£16, B&B (double) IR£26; D IR£11.

NEWMARKET-ON-FERGUS Co. Clare. Map 62C3

A ★ **Dromoland Castle** ☎(061) 71144
Tx: 70654 Fax: (061) 363355. *Tennis, golf.*
🛏 73 bedrs, 73 en suite; TV
£ room IR£95–£170, Bk IR£10·50, D IR£29.
cc Access, Amex, B'card/Visa, Diners.

Mrs P. O'Leary, Weavers Lodge ☎(061) 71348. *Farm.*
🛏 4 bedrs, 1 en suite
£ B&B IR£11, B&B (double) IR£21; D IR£9

NEWPORT Co. Mayo. Map 60B2

A **Newport House** ☎(098) 41222 Tx: 53740
Georgian house with some antique furniture. Set in gardens and park overlooking Newport River. Fishing, riding, billiards.
Open 15 Mar–30 Sep.
🛏 19 bedrs, 19 en suite
£ B&B IR£48–£49, B&B (double) IR£80–£86, D IR£23
cc Amex, B'card/Visa, Diners.

NEW ROSS Co. Wexford. Map 63B2

A **Five Counties** ☎(051) 21703 Tx: 80577 Fax: (051) 21567
Converted mansion in landscaped gardens overlooking River Barrow. Closed Xmas.
🛏 35 bedrs, 35 en suite; TV
£ B&B IR£33, B&B (double) IR£55; D IR£15
cc Access, Amex, B'card/Visa, Diners.

B **Old Rectory,** Rosbercon ☎(051) 22053
🛏 13 bedrs, 13 en suite; TV; tcf
£ B&B IR£21–£25, B&B (double) IR£36–£42; D IR£13·50.
cc Access, B'card/Visa, Diners.

OUGHTERARD Co. Galway. Map 60B1/62B4

A **Connemara Gateway** ☎(091) 82328
Tx: 50905 Fax: (091) 82332
Long, low modern hotel in well-tended gardens on N59. Swimming pool, tennis.
Open 1 Mar–31 Oct.
🛏 62 bedrs, 62 en suite; TV
£ B&B IR£35–£49·75, B&B (double) IR£67·50–£77; D IR£16–£17.
cc Access, Amex, B'card/Visa, CB, Diners.

A **Sweeney's Oughterard House** ☎(091) 82207
Delightful creeper-clad hotel, part Georgian, opposite the Owenriff River. Run by the Sweeney-Higgins family since 1913.
🛏 20 bedrs, 20 en suite
£ room IR£30–£37, room (double) IR£56–£70; Bk IR£7, D IR£17.
cc Access, B'card/Visa, Diners.

B ★ **Corrib** ☎(091) 82329
Friendly family-run hotel in centre of village.
🛏 26 bedrs, 26 en suite
£ B&B IR£25–£29·50, B&B (double) IR£41–£45; D IR£14·50
cc Access, Amex, B'card/Visa.

A **Currarevagh House** ☎(091) 82313
A mid 19th-century mansion beside Lough Corrib. Fishing, tennis. Open 23 Mar–31 Oct.
🛏 15 bedrs, 15 en suite
£ B&B IR£33–IR£66; D IR£15·25

Mr & Mrs M. Healy, Corrib Wave House, Portacarron ☎(091) 82147. *Farm.*
Open 1 Apr–15 Oct.
£ B&B IR£13–£14·50; D IR£11.
Mr & Mrs Lal Faherty, Lakeland Country House, Portacarron ☎(091) 82121. *Country.*
Open 2 Jun–mid Oct.
🛏 9 bedrs, 5 en suite
£ B&B IR£15–£17; HT IR£7.

PALLASKENRY Co. Limerick. Map 62C3

Mrs M. Walsh, Home Farm Stores ☎(061) 393142. *Town.*
🛏 4 bedrs
£ B&B IR£8·50; D IR£8.

PARKNASILLA Co. Kerry. Map 62A1

A ★ **Great Southern** ☎(064) 45122
Tx: 73899 Fax: (064) 45323
Graceful 19th-century mansion. Indoor salt-water swimming pool, sauna, golf, riding, tennis, fishing, snooker.
Open 10 Mar–31 Oct.
🛏 60 bedrs, 60 en suite, TV
£ room IR£57–£68·50, room (double) IR£84–£103; Bk IR£7, D IR£19·50
cc Access, Amex, B'card/Visa, Diners.

PATRICKSWELL Co. Limerick. Map 62C3

Mrs C. Geary, Carnlea, Caher Rd ☎(061) 27576. *Country.* Open Mar–Oct.
🛏 5 bedrs, 2 en suite
£ B&B IR£15, B&B (double) IR£21–£23.

PONTOON Co. Mayo. Map 60B2

A **Pontoon Bridge** ☎(094) 56120. *Tennis, fishing.* Open 1 May–30 Sep.
🛏 19 bedrs, 17 en suite; tcf
£ B&B IR£48–£58; D IR£17.
cc Access, Amex, B'card/Visa.

PORTLAOISE Co. Laois. Map 63A3

A **Montague,** Emo ☎(0502) 26154
Tx: 60036 ♿
🛏 70 bedrs, 70 en suite; TV
£ B&B IR£30–£32, B&B (double) IR£48–£52; D IR£14·75.

B ★ **Killieshin,** Dublin Rd ☎(0502) 21663
Tx: 60036
Riding, fishing.
🛏 44 bedrs, 44 en suite; TV
£ B&B IR£30–£32, B&B (double) IR£46–£50; D IR14·50

PORTMARNOCK Co. Dublin. Map 61B1/63C4

Mrs M. Creane, Robinia, 452 Strand Rd ☎(01) 462987. *Town.* Open Apr–Oct.
🛏 3 bedrs, 1 en suite
£ B&B IR£15, B&B (double) IR£24–£29.
Mrs A. Healy, Pine Lodge, Coast Rd ☎(01) 460097. *Town.* Open 15 Mar–31 Oct.
🛏 5 bedrs, 1 en suite
£ B&B IR£27–£33.

PORT NA BLAGH Co. Donegal. Map 61A4

A **Port Na Blagh** ☎(074) 36129. *Tennis.*
Open 24 Mar–18 Sep.
🛏 45 bedrs, 45 en suite
£ B&B IR£23·60–£28·60, B&B IR£47·40–£54·60; D IR£15·75.

RAMELTON Co. Donegal. Map 61A4

Mrs A. Campbell, Ardeen ☎(074) 51243. *Town. Tennis.* Open 23 Mar–30 Sep.
🛏 4 bedrs
£ B&B IR£12
cc Amex
Mrs F. Scott, The Manse ☎(074) 51047. *Town.* Open 1 Apr–30 Sep.
🛏 4 bedrs
£ B&B (double) IR£26; D IR£12.

RATHDRUM Co. Wicklow. Map 63C3

Mrs E. O'Brien, Abhainn Mor House, Corballis ☎(0404) 46330. *Country. Tennis.*
Open Feb–Nov.

6 bedrs, 4 en suite
£ B&B IR£16–£18, B&B (double) IR£22–£25; D IR£10.

RATHMULLAN Co. Donegal. Map 61A4

A **Rathmullan House** (074) 58188
A gracious country house by Lough Swilly. Tennis, fishing. Open 24 Mar–30 Oct.
18 bedrs, 16 en suite
£ B&B IR£20–£37·50; D IR£17·50
cc Access, Amex, B'card/Visa, Diners.

B ★ **Fort Royal** (074) 58100
A delightful country house hotel by Lough Swilly. Tennis, squash, golf.
Open Easter, 1 Jun–30 Sep.
18 bedrs, 13 en suite
£ B&B IR£35–£40, B&B (double) IR£60–£70; D IR£18.
cc Access, Amex, B'card/Visa, Diners.

RATHNEW Co. Wicklow. Map 63C3

A **Tinakilly House** (0404) 69274
Tx: 80412 Fax: (0404) 67806
Spacious Victorian mansion with period furnishings set in over 6 acres of gardens.
14 bedrs, 14 en suite; TV; tcf
£ B&B IR£60–£65, B&B (double) IR£70–£80, D IR£23–£26.
cc Access, Amex, B'card/Visa, Diners.

B ★ **Hunter's** (0404) 40106
An old coaching inn in lovely gardens along the banks of the River Vartry.
18 bedrs, 10 en suite
£ B&B IR£25·50–£27·50; D IR£16.

RENVYLE Co. Galway. Map 60A2/62B4

A **Renvyle House** (095) 43444 Tx: 50896
Fax: (095) 43515
*Swimming pool, riding, golf, fishing, sauna, tennis.*Open 11 Apr–31 Oct
40 bedrs, 40 en suite
£ room IR£33·50–£44·50, double room IR£43–£59; Bk IR£6·50; D IR£17·50.
cc Access, Amex, B'card/Visa, Diners.

RIVERSTOWN Co. Sligo. Map 60C2

Mr & Mrs B. C. O'Hara, Coopershill (071) 65108 Tx: 40301 Fax: (071) 65466. *Farm.*
Open 24 Mar–31 Oct.
6 bedrs, 6 en suite; tcf
£ B&B IR£38, D IR£16
cc Access, Amex; B'card/Visa.

ROSAPENNA Co. Donegal. Map 61A4

A **Rosapenna Golf** (074) 55301
Modern family-run hotel on Sheephaven Bay. Golf, tennis. Open 29 Mar–29 Oct.
40 bedrs, 40 en suite
£ B&B IR£25–£31, B&B (double) IR£45–£55; D IR£17.
cc Access, Amex, B'card/Visa, Diners.

ROSCOMMON Co. Roscommon. Map 60C1

Mrs D. Dolan, Munsboro House, Sligo Rd (0903) 26375. *Farm.* Open Mar–Nov.
4 bedrs
£ B&B (double) IR£22; D IR£11.

ROSCREA Co. Tipperary. Map 63A3

Mrs M. Fallon, Cregganbell, Birr Rd (0505) 21421. *Country.*
4 bedrs
£ B&B IR£10.

ROSSES POINT Co. Sligo. Map 60C3

A **Ballincar House** (071) 45361 Tx: 91297
Converted country house in 5 acres of mature gardens. Squash, tennis, sauna, fishing. Open 14 Mar–31 Oct.
20 bedrs, 20 en suite; TV
£ B&B IR£40–£45, B&B (double) IR£70–£80; D IR£19.
cc Access, Amex, B'card/Visa, Diners.

B ★ **Yeats Country Ryan** (071) 77211
Tx: 40403 Fax: (071) 77203
Large modern holiday hotel near sandy beaches. Tennis, putting. Open 14 Mar–31 Oct.
79 bedrs, 79 en suite
£ room IR£40–£53, room (double) IR£58–£74; Bk £7; D IR£14.
cc Access, Amex, B'card/Visa, Diners.

ROSSLARE Co. Wexford. Map 63B2

A **Casey's Cedars** (053) 32124 Tx: 80237
Fax: (053) 32243. Open 7 Feb–31 Dec.
34 bedrs, 34 en suite; TV
£ B&B IR£30–£41, B&B (double) IR£48–£64, D IR£20
cc Access, B'card/Visa.

A **Kellys** (053) 32114 Fax: (053) 32222
Leisure complex, indoor and outdoor swimming pool, Tennis, squash.
89 bedrs, 89 en suite
£ B&B IR£32, B&B (double) IR£58; D IR£17·95

ROSSLARE HARBOUR Co. Wexford. Map 63B2

A **Great Southern** (053) 33233 Tx: 80788
Fax: (053) 33543
Indoor swimming pool, sauna, tennis.
99 bedrs, 99 en suite; TV
£ room IR£74, room (double) IR£100; Bk IR£5·50, D IR£15
cc Access, Amex, B'card/Visa, Diners.

B ★ **Tuskar House,** St Martin's Rd, (053) 33363
20 bedrs, 20 en suite; TV
£ B&B IR£23–£26, B&B (double) IR£38–£44; D IR£15·50.
cc Access, Amex, B'card/Visa, Diners.

ROSSNOWLAGH Co. Donegal. Map 60C3

A **Sand House** (072) 51777 Tx: 40460
Large hotel on the edge of the Atlantic Ocean overlooking Donegal Bay. Tennis, water sports. Open 28 Mar–8 Oct
39 bedrs, 39 en suite
£ B&B IR£30–£45, B&B (double) IR£55–£75; D IR£16·50–£17·50.
cc Access, Amex, B'card/Visa, Diners.

B ★ **Manor House** (072) 51477
Open 2 Apr–30 Sep.
5 bedrs, 5 en suite
£ B&B IR£10–£16·25, D IR£8–£12·50.
cc Access, B'card/Visa

ROUNDSTONE Co. Galway. Map 60A1

Mrs M. King, High Trees, Errisbeg East (095) 35881. *Farm.* Open 1 Jun–30 Sep.
3 bedrs
£ B&B IR£10·50, D IR£10·50.

SHANNON AIRPORT Co. Clare. Map 62C3

A **Shannon International** (061) 61122
Tx: 72078
Long, low modern hotel close to Airport.
Open 1 Apr–31 Oct.
118 bedrs, 118 en suite; TV
£ B&B IR£32–£50, B&B (double) IR£48–£70; D IR£15
cc Access, Amex, B'card/Visa, Diners.

SKERRIES Co. Dublin. Map 61B1/63C4

B **Pier House,** Harbour Road (01) 491708
Family-run hotel right by the harbour and with views of the Mountains of Mourne.
10 bedrs, 7 en suite
£ B&B IR£22–£26, B&B (double) IR£40–£48, D IR£14·95.
cc Access, Amex, B'card/Visa, Diners.

SKIBBEREEN Co. Cork. Map 62B1

Mrs R. O'Byrne, Elysium Herb Farm, Lisheenroe, Castletownshend Rd (028) 21325. *Tennis.* Open 1 May–31 Aug.
4 bedrs, 1 en suite
£ B&B IR£16–£17·50; D IR£10.

SLANE Co. Meath. Map 61B1/63B4

B **Conyngham Arms** (041) 24155
Tx: 91297
Modernised mid 19th-century hotel in historic village.
12 bedrs, 11 en suite
£ B&B IR£23·50, B&B (double) IR£38–£44; D IR£13·95.

SLIGO Co. Sligo. Map 60C3

A **Sligo Park,** Pearse St (071) 60291
Tx: 40397 Fax: (071) 69556
Modern low-rise hotel in rural surroundings on edge of town.
60 bedrs, 60 en suite; TV
£ B&B IR£35–£40, B&B (double) IR£54–£64; D IR£16
cc Access, Amex, B'card/Visa, Diners.

B ★ **Silver Swan,** Hyde Bridge (071) 43231 Fax: (071) 42232
Family-run modern hotel by Garavogue river in centre of town.
24 bedrs, 16 en suite; TV
cc Access, Amex, B'card/Visa, Diners.

B ★ **Southern,** Lord Edward St (071) 62101 Fax: (071) 60328
Large modern hotel in award-winning gardens. Nightclub.
50 bedrs, 50 en suite; TV
£ B&B IR£30–£31, B&B (double) IR£46–£48; D IR£16.
cc Access, Amex, B'card/Visa, Diners.

Mrs C. Carr, St Martin's Cummeen, Strandhill Rd (071) 60614. Open Feb–Nov.
5 bedrs, 5 en suite; TV
£ B&B IR£15, B&B (double) IR£22–£24

Mrs L. Diamond, Lisadorn, Lisnalurg (071) 43417. *Country.*
5 bedrs, 5 en suite
£ B&B IR£13–£17·50, B&B (double) IR£27.

Mrs E. Fitzgerald, Lough Gill Lodge, Green Rd, Cairns (071) 60996. Open Apr–Sep.
3 bedrs, 1 en suite
£ B&B (double) IR£20–£22; HT IR£8.

Mrs D. MacEvilly, Tree Tops, Cleveragh Rd (off Dublin Rd) (071) 60160. *Town.*

RI

🛏 6 bedrs, 4 en suite
£ B&B IR£14·50–£15·50, B&B (double) IR£22–£24
Mrs A. McKiernan, Glenwood, Carrowmore ☎ (071) 61449. *Country*. Open Apr–Sep.
🛏 4 bedrs, 2 en suite
£ B&B IR£15–£17, B&B (double) IR£22–£26; D IR£11.

SNEEM Co. Kerry. Map 62A2

Mrs M. Teahan, Derry East Farmhouse, Waterville Rd ☎ (064) 45193. Open Mar–Nov.
🛏 4 bedrs, 1 en suite
£ B&B IR£15–£16; D IR£10.

SPIDDAL Co. Galway. Map 60B1/62B4

Mrs M. Feeney, Cala n'Uisce, Greenhill ☎ (091) 83324. *Country*. Open Apr–Oct.
🛏 6 bedrs, 4 en suite
£ B&B IR£14·50; D IR£10.
Mrs V. Feeney, Ardmor Country House, Greenhill ☎ (091) 83145. *Country*. Open 1 Mar–30 Nov.
🛏 8 bedrs, 7 en suite
£ B&B IR£13–£15, B&B (double) IR£21–£25; D IR£12·50.

STROKESTOWN Co. Roscommon. Map 60C2

Cox Family, Church View House ☎ (078) 33047. *Farm*. Open Feb–Nov.
🛏 6 bedrs, 2 en suite
£ B&B IR£12·50–£14·50; D IR£10–£11.

SWORDS Co. Dublin. Map 61B1/63C4

Mrs H. Dwyer, Greenogue House, Greenogue, Kilsallaghan ☎ (01) 350319.
🛏 3 bedrs
£ B&B (double) IR£24.

TAHILLA Co. Kerry. Map 62A1

A **Tahilla Cove** ☎ (064) 45204
Small family-run guest house on the sea shore. Private beach. Open 1 Apr–1 Oct.
🛏 9 bedrs, 8 en suite
£ B&B IR£22·50–£26, B&B (double) IR£40–£48; D IR£13.

TIPPERARY Co. Tipperary. Map 62C2

B ★ **The Glen,** Glen of Aherlow ☎ (062) 56146. *Riding*.
🛏 24 bedrs, 21 en suite; TV
£ B&B IR£30–£33, B&B (double) IR£49–£54; D IR£17.
cc Access, Amex, B'card/Visa, Diners.
Mr & Mrs J. Marnane, Bansha House, Bansha ☎ (062) 54194. Open Mar–Nov.
🛏 7 bedrs
£ B&B (double) IR£22; D IR£10.
Mrs M. Merrigan, Teach Gobnatan, Glen of Aherlow Rd ☎ (062) 51645. Open Mar–Oct.
🛏 4 bedrs, 3 en suite
£ B&B IR£11–£12; D IR£10.
Mrs N. O'Dwyer, Barronstown House, Emly Rd ☎ (062) 55130. *Farm*. Open May–Nov.
🛏 4 bedrs
£ B&B (double) IR£22; D IR£20.
Mrs M. O'Neill, Villa Maria, Bohercrowe, Limerick Rd ☎ (062) 51557. Open Jun–Sep.
🛏 3 bedrs
£ B&B IR£14, B&B (double) IR£21.
Mrs M. Quinn, Clonmore, Cork–Galbally Rd ☎ (062) 51637. *Country*. Open Apr–Oct.
🛏 4 bedrs, 4 en suite
£ B&B IR£15, B&B (double) IR£22.

TRALEE Co. Kerry. Map 62B2

B ★ **Ballygarry House,** Leebrook ☎ (066) 23305/23322
Refurbished hotel just outside town on the Killarney Road. Open 10 Jan–23 Dec.
🛏 16 bedrs, 16 en suite; TV
£ B&B fr IR£28·50–£30, B&B (double) fr IR£52; D IR£17·95.
cc Access, B'card/Visa.
Mrs B. Fitzgerald, Seaview House, Main Dingle Rd, Annagh ☎ (066) 21830. *Country*. Open Easter–Oct.
🛏 5 bedrs, 4 en suite
£ B&B IR£22–£26.
Mrs H. McCrohan, Woodview, Caherslee, Ardfert Rd ☎ (066) 22872. Open Easter–Oct.
🛏 3 bedrs
£ B&B IR£9.
Mrs M. McGrath, Kerria, Listellick North ☎ (066) 24451. *Country*. Open Easter–Oct.
🛏 5 bedrs
£ B&B IR£14, B&B (double) IR£22–£25; D IR£10·50.
Mrs C. Nealon, The Gables, Listowel Rd ☎ (066) 24396. *Town*. Open Jun–Sep.
🛏 4 bedrs, 1 en suite
£ B&B IR£12·50, B&B (double) IR£21–£25.
Mrs O'Sullivan, Knockanish House, The Spa ☎ (066) 36268. *Country*. Open Apr–Nov.
🛏 6 bedrs, 5 en suite; tcf
£ B&B (double) IR£26–£30; D IR£10
Misses N & K Prendergast, Caheerslee House, Caheerslee ☎ (066) 22616. *Town*.
🛏 5 bedrs £ B&B IR£12.

TRAMORE Co. Waterford. Map 63B2

B ★ **Grand** (051) 81414 Tx: 80141
Modern hotel overlooking Tramore Bay.
🛏 50 bedrs, 50 en suite; TV
£ B&B IR£26·50–£34, B&B (double) IR£47–£60, D IR£13·50
cc Access, Amex, B'card/Visa, Diners.

TRIM Co. Meath. Map 61B1/63B4

B ★ **Wellington Court** ☎ (046) 31516
🛏 18 bedrs, 18 en suite; TV; tcf
£ room IR£24–£26, double room IR£40–£44, Bk IR£4·50; D IR£11.
cc Access, Amex, B'card/Visa, Diners.

TUAM Co. Galway. Map 60B1

B **Imperial,** The Square ☎ (093) 24188
Family-run Georgian hotel in heart of town.
🛏 26 bedrs, 26 en suite; TV
£ B&B IR£21–£22·50, B&B (double IR£36–£40; D IR£11·50–£13·50.
cc Access, Amex, B'card/Visa, Diners.

C **Hermitage,** Dublin Rd ☎ (093) 24271.
🛏 12 bedrs, 12 en suite; tcf
£ B&B IR£15·50, B&B (double) IR£28; D IR£13·50.
cc Access, Amex, B'card/Visa, Diners.

TULLOW Co. Carlow. Map 63B3

B **Slaney,** Abbey St ☎ (0503) 51102.
🛏 10 bedrs, 4 en suite; tcf
£ B&B IR£16–£18, B&B (double) IR£31–£34; D IR£12.

TYRRELLSPASS Co. Westmeath. Map 61A1/63A4

The Village ☎ (044) 23171
Part of an elegant crescent of Georgian houses overlookingthe village green.
🛏 10 bedrs, 10 en suite; TV; tcf
£ B&B IR£23–£26, B&B (double) IR£38–£44; D IR£14·50–£16.
cc Access, Amex, B'card/Visa, Diners.

VIRGINIA Co. Cavan. Map 61A2

B ★ **Park** ☎ (049) 47235 Fax: (049) 47203.
Tennis, golf, sauna.
🛏 22 bedrs, 19 en suite; TV
£ B&B IR£39, B&B (double) IR£27·50; D IR£14.
cc Access, Amex, B'card/Visa, Diners.

Lake ☎ (049) 47561. *Fishing*.
🛏 13 bedrs, 6 en suite
£ B&B IR£17, B&B (double) IR£28; D IR£6·50.

WATERFORD Co. Waterford. Map 63B2

A **Ardree** ☎ (051) 32111 Fax: (051) 79316
Leisure complex, tennis, indoor swimming pool.
🛏 100 bedrs, 100 en suite
£ B&B IR£36·50–£49·50, B&B (double) IR£57–£73; D IR£16·50
cc Access, Amex, B'card/Visa, Diners.
A **Granville,** Meagher Quay ☎ (051) 55111
Town-centre hotel in tastefully restored period house. Closed Xmas.
🛏 74 bedrs, 74 en suite; TV
£ B&B IR£39·50–£43, B&B (double) IR£63–£70; D IR£15·50.
cc Access, Amex, B'card/Visa, Diners.

B ★ **Bridge,** The Quay ☎ (051) 77222 Tx: 80141
Large traditional hotel in town centre.
🛏 49 bedrs, 49 en suite; TV
£ B&B IR£32–£36, B&B (double) IR£53–£60; D IR£12·95–£13·95
cc Access, Amex, B'card/Visa, Diners.

B ★ **Diamond Hill,** Slieverue ☎ (051) 32855.
Guest House.
🛏 8 bedrs, 5 en suite
£ B&B IR£13–£16, B&B (double) IR£24–£30, D IR£10
cc B'card/Visa.

B ★ **Dooley's,** 30 The Quay ☎ (051) 73531 Fax: (051) 70262
Old-established, town-centre hotel.
🛏 37 bedrs, 34 en suite; TV
£ room IR£30–£32, double room IR£44–£54·60; Bk fr IR£4·50, D fr IR£12·50.
cc Access, Amex, B'card/Visa, Diners.
Mrs M. C. Fitzmaurice, Blenheim House, Blenheim Heights ☎ (051) 74115. *Country*.
🛏 6 bedrs, 6 en suite £ B&B IR£14·50
Mrs A Forrest, Ashbourne House, Slieverue ☎ (051) 32037. *Farm*. Open Apr–Oct.
🛏 7 bedrs, 6 en suite
£ B&B IR£14–£15·50, B&B (double) IR£22–£25; D IR£9.
Gough Family, Moat Farmhouse, Faithlegg, Cheekpoint Rd ☎ (051) 82166. *Farm*. 17 Mar–31 Oct.
🛏 3 bedrs
£ B&B IR£13; D IR£12.

WATERVILLE Co. Kerry. Map 62A2

A **Butler Arms** ☎ (0667) 4144 Tx: 73826
White-painted hotel overlooking the Atlantic. Tennis, riding. Open 15 Apr–12 Oct.
🛏 29 bedrs, 29 en suite

£ B&B IR£37–£43, B&B (double) IR£60–£70; D IR£18.
cc Access, Amex, B'card/Visa, Diners.

A **Waterville Lake Hotel** ☎(0667) 4133 Tx: 73806 Fax: (0667) 4482
Beautifully situated hotel. Fishing, golf, indoor swimming pool, sauna, solarium, tennis. Open 1 Apr–31 Oct.
🛏 50 bedrs, 50 en suite
£ B&B IR£48–£58, B&B (double) IR£72–£82; D IR£20.

Frank & Anne Donnelly, Lake Lands House, Lake Rd ☎(0667) 4303. *Farm.*
🛏 5 bedrs
£ B&B IR£13·50; D IR£10.

WESTPORT Co. Mayo. Map 60B2

A **Westport Ryan** ☎(098) 25811 Tx: 53757 Fax: (098) 26212
Long, low modern hotel in quiet woodland setting beside a lake. Tennis.
🛏 56 bedrs, 56 en suite; TV
£ room IR£40–£53, double room IR£58–£74; D IR£14.
cc Access, Amex, B'card/Visa, Diners.

B ★ **Olde Railway,** The Mall ☎(098) 25166 Tx: 80464 Fax: (098) 25605
Family-run 200-year-old inn overlooking the Carrowbeg River in town.
🛏 20 bedrs, 20 en suite; TV
£ B&B IR£32·50–£38, B&B (double) IR£44–£58; D IR£11·50–£12·50.
cc Access, Amex, B'card/Visa, Diners.

Mrs A. Cox, Sea River House, Mayour, Kilmeena ☎(098) 26536. *Farm.* Open May–mid Oct.
🛏 6 bedrs, 1 en suite
£ B&B IR£13·50–£14·50; D IR£11.

Mrs M. O'Brien, Rath a Rosa, Rossbeg ☎(098) 25348. *Farm.* Open 15 Mar–31 Oct.
🛏 4 bedrs, 3 en suite
£ B&B IR£16·50–£18; D IR£13.

O'Malley Family, Seapoint Ho., Kilmeena ☎(098) 41254. *Farm.* Open Mar–Oct.
🛏 7 bedrs, 5 en suite
£ B&B IR£15–£18; D IR£10·50

WEXFORD Co. Wexford. Map 63B2

A **Ferrycarrig,** Ferrycarrig Bridge ☎(053) 22999 Tx: 80147 Fax: (053) 41982
Modern hotel beside Estuary. Tennis.
🛏 40 bedrs, 40 en suite; TV
£ B&B IR£38·75–£45, B&B (double) £63–£83; D IR£21·75–£23.
cc Access, Amex, B'card/Visa, Diners.

A **Talbot,** Trinity St ☎(053) 22566 Tx: 80658 Fax: (053) 23377
Large town hotel with sea views. Indoor swimming pool, squash, sauna, snooker.
🛏 103 bedrs, 103 en suite; TV; tcf
£ room IR£29–£48·50, double room IR£41–£47; Bk IR£7; D IR£18.
cc Access, Amex, B'card/Visa.

Mrs E. Cuddihy, Rathaspeck Manor ☎(053) 42661. *Farm.* Open 1 Jun–31 Oct.
🛏 7 bedrs, 7 en suite; TV
£ B&B (double) IR£36–£40; D IR£12.

Mr & Mrs Hayes, Clonard Ho., Clonard Great ☎(053) 23141. Open 15 Apr–1 Nov.
🛏 9 bedrs, 9 en suite
£ B&B IR£16, B&B (double) IR£26–£28; D IR£11.

Mrs K. Mernagh, Killiane Castle, Drinagh ☎(053) 58885. *Farm.* Open Easter–Oct.
🛏 8 bedrs, 1 en suite
£ B&B IR£15–£17; D IR£12.

WICKLOW Co. Wicklow. Map 63C3

A **Old Rectory** ☎(0404) 67048
Lovingly restored Georgian house in quiet garden. Open 24 Mar–29 Oct.
🛏 5 bedrs, 5 en suite; TV; tcf
£ B&B IR£44; B&B (double) IR£68; D IR£20.

Mrs P. Klaue, Lissadell House, Ashtown ☎(0404) 67458. *Farm.* Open Mar–Nov.
🛏 4 bedrs, 2 en suite
£ B&B IR£24–£28; D IR£12.

YOUGHAL Co. Cork. Map 63A2

Miss S.O. Sullivan, Shalamar, Ballyvergan East ☎(024) 93398. Open May–Sep.
🛏 4 bedrs, 1 en suite
£ B&B (double) IR£19–£21.

Index of hotels by name

ENGLAND

Index of hotels by name

SCOTLAND

Index of hotels by name

WALES

Index of hotels by name

CHANNEL ISLANDS

GUERNSEY

JERSEY

Index of hotels by name

ISLE OF MAN

Index of hotels by name

NORTHERN IRELAND

RAC

DISCOUNT VOUCHER

10%

UP TO £50

off accommodation at hotels in this section
Only one voucher per visit
(for conditions see over)

RAC

DISCOUNT VOUCHER

5%

UP TO £25

off accommodation at hotels in this section
Only one voucher per visit
(for conditions see over)

RAC

DISCOUNT VOUCHER

10%

UP TO £50

off accommodation at hotels in this section
Only one voucher per visit
(for conditions see over)

RAC

DISCOUNT VOUCHER

5%

UP TO £25

off accommodation at hotels in this section
Only one voucher per visit
(for conditions see over)

CONDITIONS

1. Vouchers are only accepted for hotel accommodation at full tariff rates for the room and season, not against already discounted tariffs such as week-end breaks.
2. Only one voucher accepted per person or party per stay.
3. Hotels should be informed that an RAC voucher is to be used in part payment when a room is booked.
4. A copy of the RAC Hotel Guide 1991 must be produced when the voucher is used.
5. This voucher is not valid after 31 October 1991.

CONDITIONS

1. Vouchers are only accepted for hotel accommodation at full tariff rates for the room and season, not against already discounted tariffs such as week-end breaks.
2. Only one voucher accepted per person or party per stay.
3. Hotels should be informed that an RAC voucher is to be used in part payment when a room is booked.
4. A copy of the RAC Hotel Guide 1991 must be produced when the voucher is used.
5. This voucher is not valid after 31 October 1991.

CONDITIONS

1. Vouchers are only accepted for hotel accommodation at full tariff rates for the room and season, not against already discounted tariffs such as week-end breaks.
2. Only one voucher accepted per person or party per stay.
3. Hotels should be informed that an RAC voucher is to be used in part payment when a room is booked.
4. A copy of the RAC Hotel Guide 1991 must be produced when the voucher is used.
5. This voucher is not valid after 31 October 1991.

CONDITIONS

1. Vouchers are only accepted for hotel accommodation at full tariff rates for the room and season, not against already discounted tariffs such as week-end breaks.
2. Only one voucher accepted per person or party per stay.
3. Hotels should be informed that an RAC voucher is to be used in part payment when a room is booked.
4. A copy of the RAC Hotel Guide 1991 must be produced when the voucher is used.
5. This voucher is not valid after 31 October 1991.

ROAD ATLAS OF GREAT BRITAIN AND IRELAND

SYMBOLS COMMON TO ALL MAPS

RAC office

Town/village with RAC Hotel

RAC/AA Telephone

SLOUGH Primary Route Destination

International Airport

National Boundary

County Boundary

Ferry

Urban Area

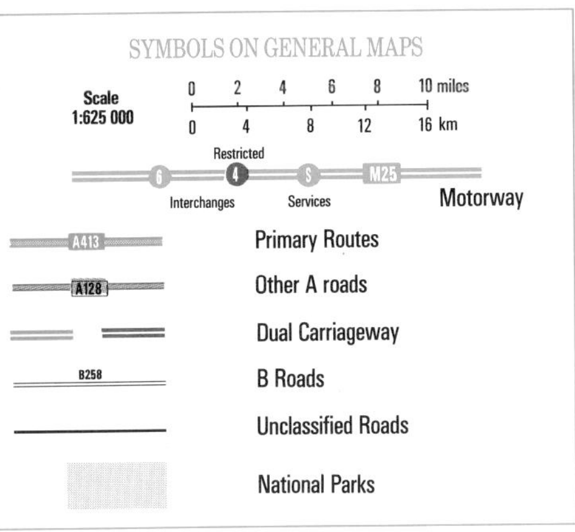

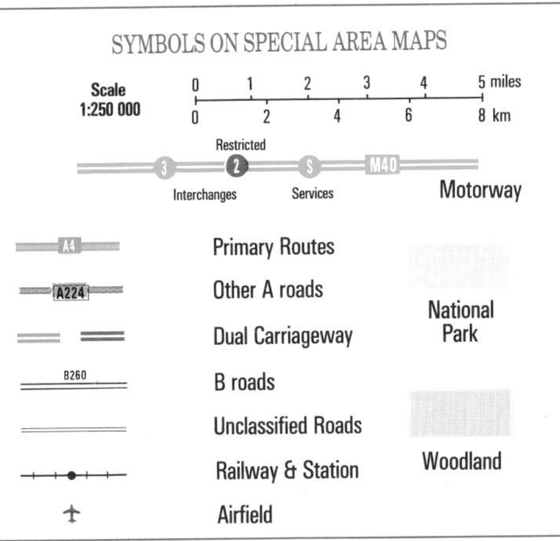

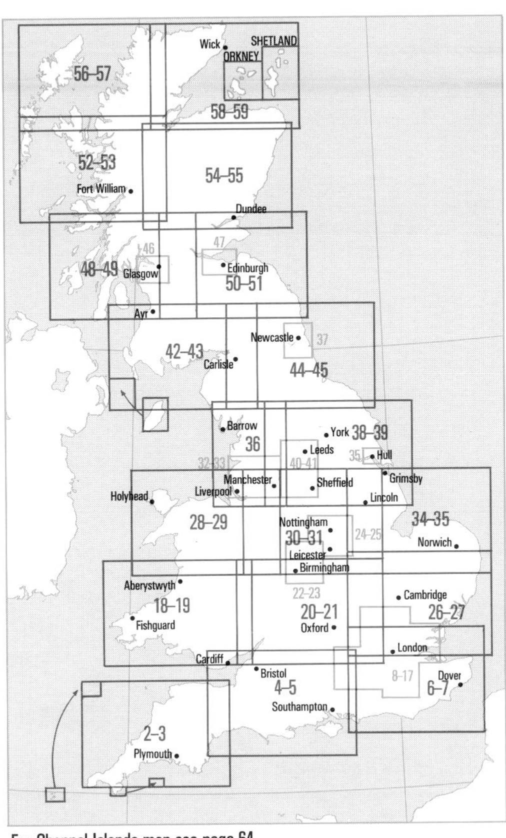

For Channel Islands map see page 64
Key to Ireland map is on page 60

Design & computerized cartography by Cook, Hammond & Kell Ltd

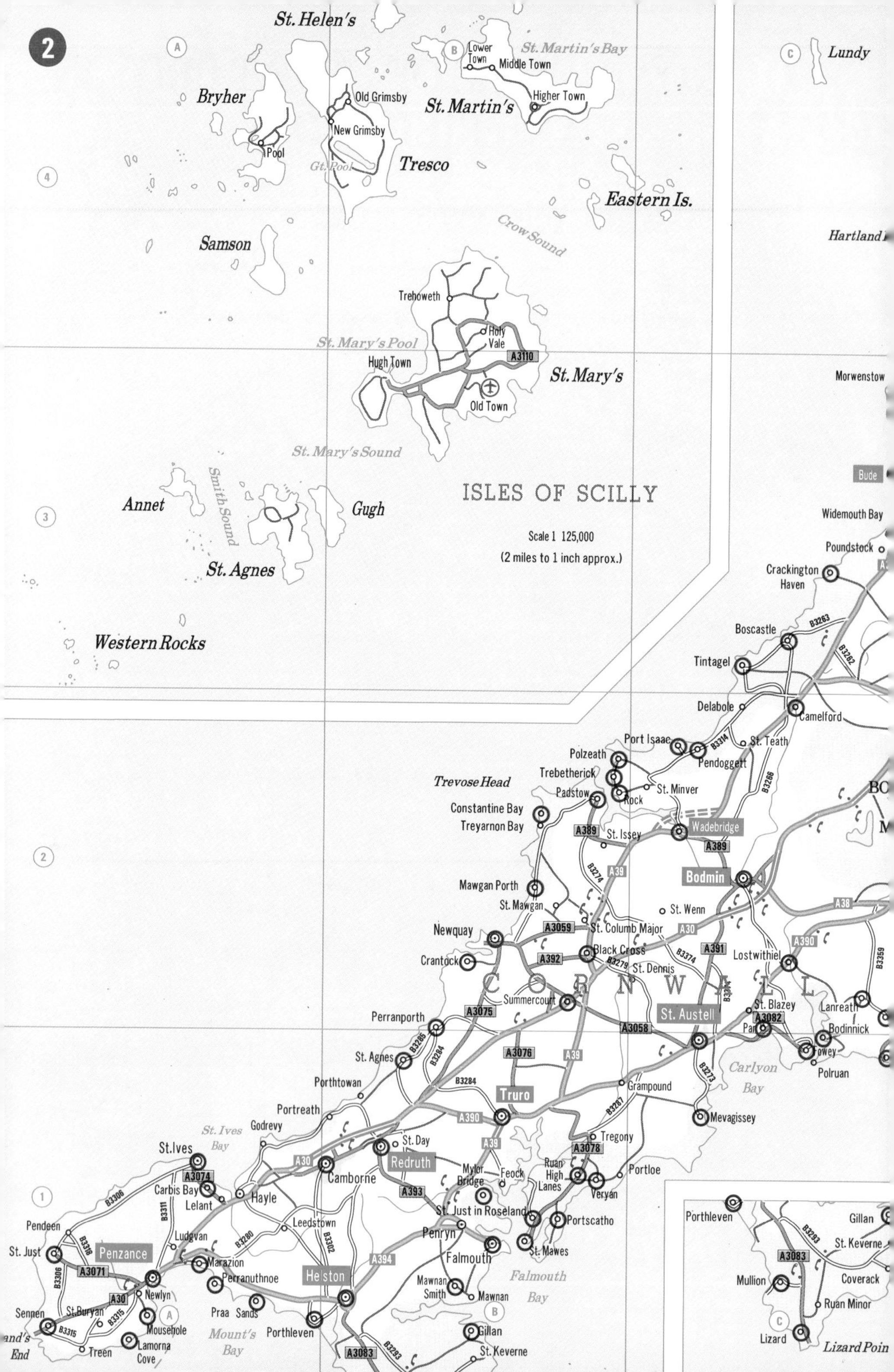
2
St. Helen's
Bryher
Pool
Old Grimsby
New Grimsby
Gt. Pool
Tresco
Lower Town
Middle Town
St. Martin's Bay
St. Martin's
Higher Town
Lundy
Eastern Is.
Crow Sound
Hartland
Samson
Trehoweth
Holy Vale
St. Mary's Pool
Hugh Town
A3110
St. Mary's
Old Town
St. Mary's Sound
Morwenstow
Annet
Smith Sound
Gugh
St. Agnes
ISLES OF SCILLY
Scale 1 125,000
(2 miles to 1 inch approx.)
Bude
Widemouth Bay
Poundstock
Crackington Haven
Western Rocks
Boscastle
Tintagel
Delabole
Camelford
Port Isaac
St. Teath
Pendoggett
Polzeath
Trebetherick
Trevose Head
Padstow
Rock
St. Minver
Constantine Bay
Treyarnon Bay
Wadebridge
St. Issey
Bodmin
Mawgan Porth
St. Mawgan
St. Wenn
Newquay
St. Columb Major
Crantock
Black Cross
St. Dennis
Lostwithiel
CORNWALL
Summercourt
St. Blazey
Lanreath
Perranporth
St. Austell
Par
Bodinnick
Fowey
Polruan
St. Agnes
Carlyon Bay
Porthtowan
Grampound
Truro
Portreath
Mevagissey
St. Ives Bay
Godrevy
St. Day
Tregony
St. Ives
Redruth
Camborne
Mylor Bridge
Feock
Ruan High Lanes
Portloe
Veryan
Carbis Bay
Lelant
Hayle
Leedstown
St. Just in Roseland
Portscatho
Porthleven
Gillan
Pendeen
Ludgvan
Penryn
St. Keverne
St. Just
Penzance
Marazion
Falmouth
St. Mawes
Mullion
Coverack
Newlyn
Perranuthnoe
Helston
Mawnan Smith
Mawnan
Falmouth Bay
Ruan Minor
Sennen
St. Buryan
Mousehole
Praa Sands
Lizard
Lizard Point
Land's End
Treen
Lamorna Cove
Mount's Bay
Porthleven
Gillan
St. Keverne
A30
A39
A389
A3059
A392
A3075
A3058
A3076
A390
A391
A38
A3082
A3078
A3074
A393
A3071
A394
A3083
B3263
B3262
B3314
B3266
B3274
B3279
B3374
B3285
B3284
B3287
B3273
B3359
B3306
B3311
B3318
B3280
B3302
B3315
B3293

Martinhoe
Lynmouth
Countisbury
Porlock Weir
Minehead
Ilfracombe
Woody Bay
Lynton
Brendon
A39
Porlock
Blue Anchor
4
3
A
Lee
Berrynarbor
Combe Martin
B
C
Luccombe
Mortehoe
Parracombe
B3223
Dunster
B3191
Watchet
Kilve
Woolacombe
B3343
B3343
EXMOOR
A39
Putsborough
B3231
West Down
Timberscombe
Bilbrock
Williton
Holford
B3358
EXMOOR NATIONAL PARK
A361
Bittadon
A39
Challacombe
Simonsbath
Weddon Cross
Luxborough
Washford
Croyde
Marwood
Exford
B3190
B3188
Braunton
SOMERSET
Bratton Fleming
B3224
Monksilver
A358
Saunton
Ashford
Withypool
Winsford
Exton
Brompton Ralph
Barnstaple
Brayford
4
West Bagborough
Bay
B3233
B3226
North Molton
B3223
Brompton Regis
B3224
Appledore
Instow
A361
A396
Huish Champflower
Bishops Lydeard
Westward Ho
Bishops Tawton
Swimbridge
Molland
Dulverton
B3190
Wiveliscombe
Northam
B3232
B3222
Abbotsham
A377
South Molton
Exebridge
Morebath
A361
Milverton
Bideford
Newton Tracey
Chittlehampton
B3227
B3227
Langford Budville
Clovelly
Oakfordbridge
Bampton
B3187
A386
B3227
Umberleigh
Oakford
Wellington
Horns Cross
Chittlehamholt
B3137
B3227
Buckland Brewer
King's Nympton
Meshaw
A38
Holcombe Rogus
Parkham
Great Torrington
B3217
Rackenford
Sampford Peverell
Torridge
Roborough
Burrington
B3391
Chulmleigh
B3137
A373
Bradworthy
Stibb Cross
Beaford
Witheridge
Tiverton
27
Culmstock
Dolton
B3042
Worlington
Milton Damerel
Merton
A377
Chawleigh
Uffculme
B3391
Shebbear
A386
Eggesford
Lapford
Morchard Bishop
Cheriton Fitzpaine
Cullompton
4
A388
Petrockstowe
Winkleigh
Bickleigh
28
A373
Black Torrington
B3220
DEVON
Bradninch
Broadhembury
Holsworthy
Hatherleigh
Honiton
B3176
A3072
Highampton
North Tawton
Copplestone
A3072
Silverton
M5
A3072
Crediton
B3181
Talaton
Clawton
Bow
Exe
A396
3
B3218
Yeoford
Broadclyst
Halwill
Northlew
Tedburn St. Mary
Stoke Canon
A30
Fenny Bridges
A388
B3215
Spreyton
Whitestone
Rockbeare
Ashwater
Tamar
Okehampton
Exeter
29
Exeter
Ottery St. Mary
Bratton Clovelly
A30
RAC
A375
South Zeal
30
Sidbury
B3178
A382
Dunsford
B3212
Topsham
Bridestowe
31
Newton Poppleford
Sidford
Moretonhampstead
Chagford
Woodbury
A376
Lewdown
A376
Sidmouth
Lewtrenchard
B3212
North Bovey
Otterton
Lydford
A38
Starcross
A30
Lifton
DARTMOOR NATIONAL PARK
Chillaton
A386
Budleigh Salterton
B3254
Chudleigh
North Brentor
Bovey Tracey
A380
Ideford
A379
A384
Milton Abbot
DARTMOOR
Exmouth
Mary Tavy
B3192
Dawlish
Haytor Vale
A388
Widecombe in the Moor
Bishopsteignton
B3257
Tavistock
Two Bridges
B3357
Teignmouth
Bickington
B3357
A390
A383
Newton Abbot
Shaldon
Princetown
B3212
Hexworthy
Callington
Horrabridge
Ashburton
A379
Gunnislake
Holne
2
Dousland
Buckfast
Yelverton
Kingskerswell
Bere Alston
Buckfastleigh
A388
A386
A384
St. Mellion
Cockington
Staverton
Torquay
Bere Ferrers
A3022
Hatt
Tor Bay
Tamerton Foliot
A385
A38
Plymouth
South Brent
Totnes
Paignton
Saltash
A381
PLYMOUTH
Plympton
Ivybridge
Stoke Gabriel
Polbathic
A38
B3210
Brixham
Harbertonford
A387
Torpoint
RAC
Halwell
A374
B3207
Dittisham
Seaton
Ermington
Crafthole
Plymstock
Brixton
Yealmpton
Modbury
Dartmouth
Kingswear
Millbrook
Rame
The Sound
Kingston
B3392
Newton Ferrers
A379
A379
Stoke Fleming
Bigbury-on-Sea
Kingsbridge
To Guernsey, Jersey and Alderney
Thurlestone
Frogmore
Torcross
A381
Chillington
Hope
Marlborough
Salcombe
East Portlemouth
Start Point
1
Bolt Head
Prawle Point
To Santander and Roscoff
A
B
C

4
19
20
3
GLAMORGAN
SOUTH
GLAMORGAN
Tonypandy
Maesteg
Nant-y-moel
Pontycymer
Ynysybwl
Porth
Cilfynydd
Senghenydd
Abercarn
Bedwas
Risca
Cwmbran
Caerleon
Llantrisant
Llangybi
Shirenewton
Langstone
Caerwent
Chepstow
Caldicot
Hill
Stone
Falfield
Thornbury
Alveston
Aust
Pontypridd
Llantrisant
Llanharan
Blackmill
Betws
Tondu
Aberkenfig
Pencoed
Bridgend
Llanharry
Caerphilly
St. Mellons
NEWPORT
Magor
Redwick
Goldcliff
Almondsbury
Easter Compton
Iron Acton
Yate
Avonmouth
Filton
Portishead
BRISTOL
Mangotsfield
Kingswood
Bonvilston
CARDIFF
St. Bride's Major
Cowbridge
Wick
St. Donat's
Llantwit Major
Llancarfan
Wenvoe
Dinas Powis
Penarth
Barry
Rhoose
Severn
Estuary
Clevedon
Nailsea
Failand
Oldland
Flax Bourton
Whitchurch
Keynsham
Kenn
Yatton
Chew Magna
Kingston Seymour
Congresbury
Kewstoke
A V O N
Hewish
Redhill
Pensford
Hunstrete
Marksbury
Weston-super-Mare
Sandford
Wrington
Chelwood
Bleadon
Winscombe
Shipham
Blagdon
Clutton
Radford
Brean
Lympsham
Brent Knoll
Axbridge
MENDIP HILLS
Cheddar
West Harptree
Chewton Mendip
Midsomer Norton
Draycott
Bristol
Channel
Bridgwater
Bay
East Brent
Burnham-on-Sea
Westbury-sub-Mendip
Emborough
Wells
Shepton Mallet
Porlock Weir
Porlock
Minehead
Luccombe
Blue Anchor
Watchet
Dunster
EXMOOR
Timberscombe
EXMOOR NATIONAL PARK
Exford
Williton
Kilve
Holford
Stockland Bristol
Cannington
Huntspill
Mark
Wedmore
Wookey
Coxley
Bilbrock
Washford
Luxborough
Monksilver
SOMERSET
Nether Stowey
Puriton
Shapwick
Glastonbury
Pilton
Evercreech
Weddon Cross
Winsford
Exton
Brompton Regis
Brompton Ralph
West Bagborough
Bridgwater
Moorlinch
Westonzoyland
Street
West Pennard
Baltonsborough
Dulverton
Huish Champflower
Wiveliscombe
Bishops Lydeard
North Petherton
Othery
Butleigh
High Ham
Castle Cary
Wincanton
Exebridge
Oakfordbridge
Oakford
Morebath
Bampton
Langford Budville
Milverton
Taunton
Norton Fitzwarren
North Curry
Langport
Somerton
Long Sutton
Sparkford
Charlton Horethorne
Ilchester
Wellington
Hatch Beauchamp
Kingsbury Episcopi
Marston Magna
Milborne Port
Rackenford
Holcombe Rogus
Corfe
Staple Fitzpaine
South Petherton
Martock
Trent
Sherborne
Yeovil
Sampford Peverell
Broadway
Ilminster
Montacute
Tiverton
Culmstock
Combe St. Nicholas
Merriott
East Chinnock
Yetminster
Cheriton Fitzpaine
Uffculme
Chard
Crewkerne
Cullompton
Bickleigh
Upottery
Yarcombe
Winsham
Bradninch
Stockland
Broadhembury
Evershot
D E V O N
Silverton
Chardstock
Thorncombe
Broadwindsor
Crediton
Talaton
Cotleigh
Wilmington
Hawkchurch
Beaminster
Maiden Newton
Cerne Abbas
Piddle
Stoke Canon
Broadclyst
Honiton
Axminster
Whitestone
Exeter
Fenny Bridges
Northleigh
Charmouth
Bridport
Powerstock
Frampton
Rockbeare
Ottery St. Mary
Colyton
Winterbourne Abbas
Sidbury
Lyme Regis
Chidcock
Topsham
Newton Poppleford
Sidford
Beer
Seaton
Burton Bradstock
Litton Cheney
Woodbury
Sidmouth
Branscombe
Portesham
Otterton
Abbotsbury
Starcross
Lyme
Bay
Chudleigh
Exmouth
Budleigh Salterton
Ideford
Dawlish
Bishopsteignton
Teignmouth
Newton Abbot
Shaldon
Fortuneswell
Kingskerswell

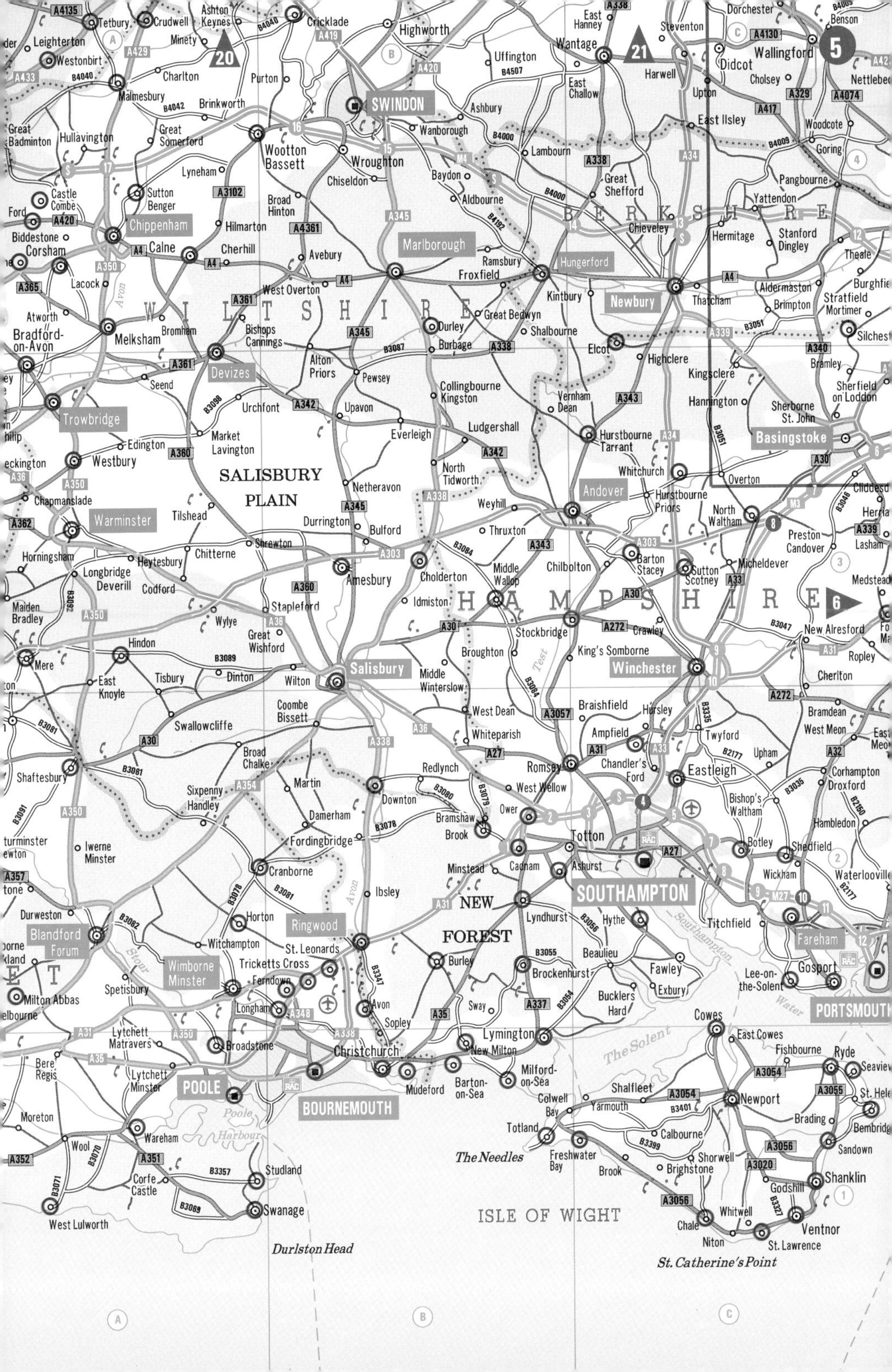

A4135
Tetbury
Crudwell
Ashton Keynes
B4040
Cricklade
Highworth
A338
East Hanney
Steventon
Dorchester
B4009
Benson
Leighterton
Minety
20
A419
B
Uffington
Wantage
21
C
Didcot
A4130
Wallingford
5
Westonbirt
A429
A420
B4507
Harwell
Cholsey
Nettlebed
A433
B4040
Charlton
Purton
East Challow
Upton
A329
A4074
Malmesbury
SWINDON
Ashbury
A417
B4042
Brinkworth
East Ilsley
Woodcote
Great Badminton
Hullavington
Great Somerford
Wootton Bassett
16
Wanborough
B4000
Lambourn
A34
B4009
Goring
15
Wroughton
M4
A338
4
17
Lyneham
Chiseldon
Baydon
Great Shefford
Pangbourne
Castle Combe
Sutton Benger
A3102
Broad Hinton
Aldbourne
B4000
Yattendon
Ford
A420
Chippenham
Hilmarton
A345
B4192
B E R K S H I R E
Biddestone
A4361
Chieveley
Hermitage
Stanford Dingley
12
Corsham
A4
Calne
Cherhill
Avebury
Marlborough
Ramsbury
Hungerford
14
13
Theale
A350
A4
Froxfield
A4
Lacock
Avon
West Overton
A4
Kintbury
Newbury
Thatcham
Aldermaston
Burghfield
A365
W I L T S H I R E
A361
Durley
Great Bedwyn
Brimpton
Stratfield Mortimer
Atworth
Bromham
Bishops Cannings
Shalbourne
A339
B3051
Bradford-on-Avon
Melksham
A345
B3087
Burbage
A338
Elcot
Silchester
Devizes
A361
Alton Priors
Pewsey
Highclere
Kingsclere
A340
Bramley
Seend
Collingbourne Kingston
Vernham Dean
Sherfield on Loddon
Trowbridge
B3098
Urchfont
A342
Upavon
A343
Hannington
Sherborne St. John
Market Lavington
Everleigh
Ludgershall
Hurstbourne Tarrant
A34
B3051
Basingstoke
Edington
A360
A342
Westbury
SALISBURY PLAIN
North Tidworth
Whitchurch
A30
6
A36
A350
Netheravon
A338
Andover
Overton
Cliddesden
Chapmanslade
Hurstbourne Priors
Warminster
Tilshead
A345
Weyhill
North Waltham
M3
B3046
Durrington
Bulford
Thruxton
8
Preston Candover
A339
A362
A303
B3084
A343
Barton Stacey
Lasham
Horningsham
Shrewton
Heytesbury
Chitterne
Amesbury
Chilbolton
Sutton Scotney
Micheldever
3
Longbridge Deverill
Codford
A360
Cholderton
Middle Wallop
A33
Medstead
B3092
Idmiston
H A M P S H I R E
A30
6
Maiden Bradley
A350
Wylye
Stapleford
A30
A272
Crawley
B3047
New Alresford
A36
Great Wishford
Stockbridge
Hindon
B3089
Broughton
Test
King's Somborne
A31
Ropley
Mere
Tisbury
Dinton
Wilton
Salisbury
Middle Winterslow
Winchester
9
East Knoyle
B3084
10
Cheriton
Coombe Bissett
West Dean
Braishfield
Hursley
A272
Bramdean
B3081
Swallowcliffe
A3057
B3335
Twyford
West Meon
A36
Whiteparish
Ampfield
A33
A30
A338
A31
B2177
Upham
A32
Shaftesbury
Broad Chalke
A27
Redlynch
Romsey
Chandler's Ford
Eastleigh
Corhampton
B3081
A354
Martin
B3080
B3079
West Wellow
S
Droxford
Sixpenny Handley
Downton
Bishop's Waltham
B3035
B2150
B3091
A350
Damerham
Bramshaw
Ower
Hambledon
B3078
Brook
Totton
Sturminster Newton
Fordingbridge
A27
Botley
Shedfield
Iwerne Minster
Cadnam
Ashurst
2
Minstead
Cranborne
Wickham
Waterlooville
A357
B3078
B3081
Ibsley
NEW FOREST
SOUTHAMPTON
M27
B2177
Avon
A31
Lyndhurst
B3056
Durweston
Horton
Hythe
Titchfield
Blandford Forum
B3082
Ringwood
FOREST
Southampton
Fareham
Witchampton
St. Leonards
B3055
Beaulieu
Stour
Wimborne Minster
Tricketts Cross
B3347
Burley
Brockenhurst
Fawley
Gosport
Spetisbury
Ferndown
Lee-on-the-Solent
Exbury
Milton Abbas
Avon
Sway
A337
B3054
Bucklers Hard
Longham
A348
Water
PORTSMOUTH
A35
Sopley
Cowes
A31
Lytchett Matravers
A350
A338
Lymington
East Cowes
A35
Broadstone
Christchurch
New Milton
The Solent
Fishbourne
Ryde
Bere Regis
Seaview
Lytchett Minster
Barton-on-Sea
Milford-on-Sea
A3054
POOLE
Mudeford
Shalfleet
A3054
Newport
A3055
St. Helens
BOURNEMOUTH
Colwell Bay
Yarmouth
B3401
Poole
Moreton
Brading
Harbour
Totland
Calbourne
Bembridge
Wareham
B3399
A3056
Sandown
Wool
Freshwater Bay
A352
A351
B3070
The Needles
Shorwell
B3357
Studland
Brook
Brighstone
A3020
Shanklin
Corfe Castle
Godshill
B3071
B3327
A3056
1
B3069
Swanage
West Lulworth
ISLE OF WIGHT
Whitwell
Chale
Ventnor
Niton
St. Lawrence
Durlston Head
St. Catherine's Point
A
B
C

6
SEE PAGES 12-13 FOR COVERAGE AT 4 MILES TO 1 INCH
SEE PAGES 12-13 FOR COVERAGE AT 4 MILES TO 1 INCH
SEE PAGES 10-11 FOR COV
Aylesbury
Long Crendon
Stone
Haddenham
Thame
Princes Risborough
Tetsworth
Chinnor
Wendover
Aston Clinton
Tring
Berkhamsted
Hemel Hempstead
St.Albans
Hertford
Harlow
Hatfield
Little Berkhamsted
Hoddesdon
Nazeing
Cheshunt
Waltham Abbey
Potters Bar
Great Hampden
Great Missenden
Chesham
Bovingdon
Kings Langley
WATFORD
Shenley
Stokenchurch
Little Missenden
Amersham
Chalfont St. Giles
Bushey
Loughton
Watlington
HIGH WYCOMBE
Rickmansworth
BARNET
Benson
Lane End
Beaconsfield
HARROW
Marlow
Gerrards Cross
Nettlebed
Bourne End
Cookham
Uxbridge
Henley-on-Thames
Maidenhead
SLOUGH
EALING
LONDON
Woodcote
Pangbourne
Wargrave
Eton
Windsor
Twyford
READING
Winkfield
Egham
London Heathrow Airport
HOUNSLOW
Theale
Wokingham
Bracknell
Ascot
Staines
Kingston
Burghfield
Sunningdale
Chertsey
BROMLEY
Stratfield Mortimer
Crowthorne
Bagshot
Weybridge
Esher
CROYDON
Silchester
Sandhurst
Bisley
Chobham
Epsom
Banstead
Warlingham
Bramley
Camberley
Woking
Leatherhead
Sherfield on Loddon
Hartley Wintney
Ripley
Tadworth
Caterham
Sherborne St. John
Hook
Fleet
Farnborough
Pirbright
Horsley
Basingstoke
Worplesdon
Westerham
ALDERSHOT
SURREY
Oxted
Godstone
Crockham
Odiham
Guildford
Dorking
Reigate
Redhill
Cliddesdon
Puttenham
Tongham
Leigh
Outwood
Edenbr
Herriard
South Warnborough
Farnham
Godalming
Wonersh
Horley
Bentley
Elstead
Milford
Lingfield
Preston Candover
Lasham
Frensham
Witley
Cranleigh
Ewhurst
Charlwood
Capel
London Gatwick Airport
East Grinstead
Alton
Ockley
Hindhead
Chiddingfold
Crawley
Turners Hill
Forest Row
Four Marks
Headley
Selborne
Rudgwick
Crowboro
Haslemere
Northchapel
Horsham
Balcombe
Ropley
Liphook
Fernhurst
Horsted Keynes
Bramdean
Liss
Lower Beeding
Wisborough Green
Billingshurst
Cuckfield
Haywards Heath
Petersfield
Rogate
Bolney
West Meon
Cowfold
Newick
East Meon
Trotton
Midhurst
Petworth
WEST
West Grinstead
Burgess Hill
South Harting
Fittleworth
Pulborough
Thakeham
Hurstpierpoint
Cocking
West Chiltington
Storrington
Henfield
Ditchling
Halland
Hambledon
Compton
Charlton
SUSSEX
Horndean
Washington
Ringme
Amberley
Steyning
Lewes
Waterlooville
SOUTH DOWNS
Havant
Goodwood
Slindon
Findon
Falmer
Arundel
Lancing
Chichester
Emsworth
BRIGHTON
Bosham
Climping
Rottingdean
Alfris
PORTSMOUTH
West Thorney
Littlehampton
Angmering-on-Sea
Shoreham-by-Sea
Hove
Newhave
Rustington
Worthing
Peacehaven
South Hayling
Middleton-on-Sea
Seaford
West Wittering
Bognor Regis
East Wittering
Selsey
Selsey Bill
Seaview
St. Helens
Bembridge
Arun
A
B
C
26
5

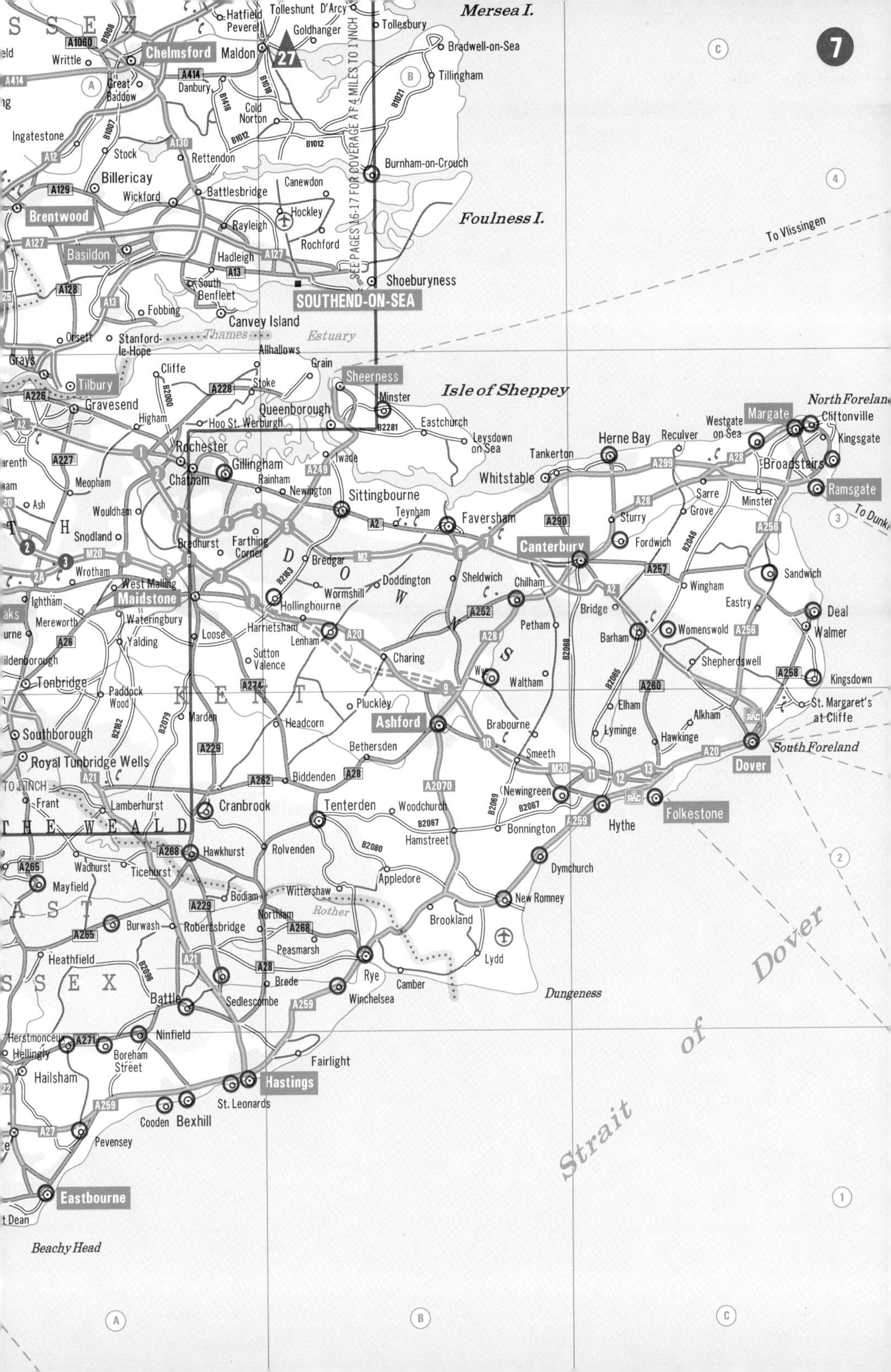
Mersea I.
Tolleshunt D'Arcy
Tollesbury
Hatfield Peverel
Goldhanger
Bradwell-on-Sea
Tillingham
Chelmsford
Maldon
27
Writtle
Great Baddow
Danbury
Cold Norton
Ingatestone
Stock
Rettendon
Burnham-on-Crouch
Billericay
Wickford
Battlesbridge
Canewdon
Hockley
Brentwood
Rayleigh
Foulness I.
To Vlissingen
Basildon
Rochford
Hadleigh
Shoeburyness
South Benfleet
SOUTHEND-ON-SEA
Fobbing
Canvey Island
Orsett
Stanford-le-Hope
Thames
Estuary
Allhallows
Grain
Grays
Tilbury
Cliffe
Stoke
Sheerness
Minster
Isle of Sheppey
Gravesend
Higham
Queenborough
Hoo St. Werburgh
Eastchurch
Leysdown on Sea
North Foreland
Margate
Cliftonville
Westgate on Sea
Kingsgate
Herne Bay
Reculver
Tankerton
Broadstairs
Rochester
Gillingham
Chatham
Rainham
Newington
Iwade
Whitstable
Ramsgate
Meopham
Sittingbourne
Teynham
Sarre
Minster
Grove
To Dunkirk
Wouldham
Faversham
Sturry
Snodland
Bredhurst
Farthing Corner
Canterbury
Fordwich
Wrotham
Bredgar
West Malling
Doddington
Sheldwich
Sandwich
Ightham
Maidstone
Wormshill
Chilham
Wingham
Hollingbourne
Eastry
Deal
Mereworth
Wateringbury
Harrietsham
Bridge
Walmer
Yalding
Loose
Lenham
Petham
Barham
Womenswold
Tonbridge
Sutton Valence
Charing
Shepherdswell
Paddock Wood
Wye
Waltham
Kingsdown
KENT
DOWNS
St. Margaret's at Cliffe
Pluckley
Elham
Alkham
Southborough
Marden
Headcorn
Ashford
Brabourne
Lyminge
Hawkinge
Royal Tunbridge Wells
Bethersden
Smeeth
Dover
South Foreland
Frant
Biddenden
Newingreen
Lamberhurst
Cranbrook
Tenterden
Woodchurch
Hythe
Folkestone
THE WEALD
Hamstreet
Bonnington
Hawkhurst
Rolvenden
Dymchurch
Wadhurst
Ticehurst
Mayfield
Appledore
Bodiam
Wittershaw
New Romney
Rother
Northiam
Brookland
Burwash
Robertsbridge
Peasmarsh
Heathfield
Lydd
Rye
Brede
Camber
Dungeness
Winchelsea
Battle
Sedlescombe
Strait of Dover
Herstmonceux
Ninfield
Hellingly
Boreham Street
Fairlight
Hailsham
Hastings
St. Leonards
Cooden
Bexhill
Pevensey
Eastbourne
Beachy Head
SEE PAGES 16-17 FOR COVERAGE AT 4 MILES TO 1 INCH

8
14
15
13
6
Lye Green
Bovingdon
Kings Langley
Bedmond
Abbots Langley
Bricket Wood
Colney Street
Shenley
Sherleybury
South Mimms
Northaw
Cuffley
Potters Bar
Waterside
Flaunden
Bucks Hill
Langleybury
Radlett
Ridge
Latimer
Sarratt
Chenies
WATFORD
Aldenham
Green Street
Wrotham Park
Botany Bay
Hadley Wood
Chandler's Cross
Cassiobury Park
Letchmore Heath
Little Chalfont
Chorleywood
Croxley Green
Borehamwood
Arkley
Monken Hadley
Cockfosters
Bushey
BARNET
Chalfont St Giles
Heronsgate
Rickmansworth
Elstree
Totteridge
East Barnet
Southgate
Horn Hill
Bushey Heath
South Oxhey
Chalfont Common
Chalfont St Peter
Maple Cross
Hatch End
Edgware
Mill Hill
Friern Barnet
Jordans
Eastbury
Stanmore
Gerrards Cross
West Hyde
Harefield
Harrow Weald
Finchley
Wood Green
Denham Green
Northwood
Pinner
HARROW
Wealdstone
Kingsbury
Hendon
Ruislip Common
Eastcote
Greenhill
Kenton
Golders Green
Hornsey
Gedgerley
Denham
Harrow on the Hill
Ruislip
Highgate
Fulmer
Ickenham
Hampstead
Camden Town
Islington
Northolt
WEMBLEY
Stoke Poges
Uxbridge
WILLESDEN
Hillingdon
Greenford
Harlesden
Paddington
Iver Heath
Yeading
Perivale
SLOUGH
EALING
Marylebone
City
Cowley
Iver
Yiewsley
Hayes
Southall
Acton
Upton
West Drayton
Hammersmith
Langley
Norwood Green
Brentford
Westminster
Kensington
Sipson
Chelsea
Longford
Cranford
Heston
Chiswick
Colnbrook
Fulham
Datchet
Barnes
Battersea
Poyle
London Heathrow Airport
HOUNSLOW
Horton
Mortlake
Clapham
Hatton
Wraysbury
Isleworth
Putney
Stanwell
Richmond
East Bedfont
Richmond Park
WANDSWORTH
Staines
FELTHAM
TWICKENHAM
Roehampton
Hythe End
Upper Tooting
Streatham
Ham
Englefield Green
Egham
Ashford
Hanworth
Teddington
Wimbledon
Sunbury
Kingston upon Thames
Hampton
Hampton Court
Merton
Littleton
Thorpe
East Molesey
Surbiton
Laleham
MITCHAM
Morden
Thames Ditton
Virginia Water
New Malden
Lyne
Walton-on-Thames
Shepperton
Chertsey
Long Ditton
Tolworth
Worchester Park
Carshalton
Beddington
Addlestone
Weybridge
Wallington
Esher
Hook
Cheam
Ottershaw
Hersham
Chessington
Burrowhill
Row Town
Sutton
Whiteley Village
Claygate
Ewell
Chobham
Woodham
Oxshott
Epsom
Byfleet
Cobham
Woodmansterne
Horsell
Stoke D'Abernon
Banstead
Pyrford
Woking
Ashtead
Burgh Heath
Coulsdon
Mayford
Ockham
SURREY
Chipstead
Ripley
Tadworth
Leatherhead
Kingswood
Send
Fetcham
Cheldon
East Horsley
Headley
Worplesdon
Great Bookham
Walton on the Hill
West Horsley
Mickleham
Pitch Place
East Clandon
The Hermitage
Merstham
Stoughton
Burpham
Effingham
Westhumble
M25
M1
M40
M4
M3
M23
M40(M)
M41
A404
A411
A4008
A4145
A4125
A4140
A410
A41
A5183
A1
A1081
A111
A1000
A1005
A413
A40
A412
A4180
A4006
A406
A5
A4007
A4020
A4
A30
A3044
A308
A320
A316
A3
A205
A24
A23
A217
A3050
A317
A318
A319
A244
A240
A245
A243
A246
A247
A237
A2022
A242
B4442
B416
B470
B376
B377
B386
B3121
B385
B365
B374
B382
B367
B280
B2039
B2033
B2032
B2219
B2030
B556
B5378
B156
B157
B466
B467
Grand Union
Chess
Thames
Wey
Mole

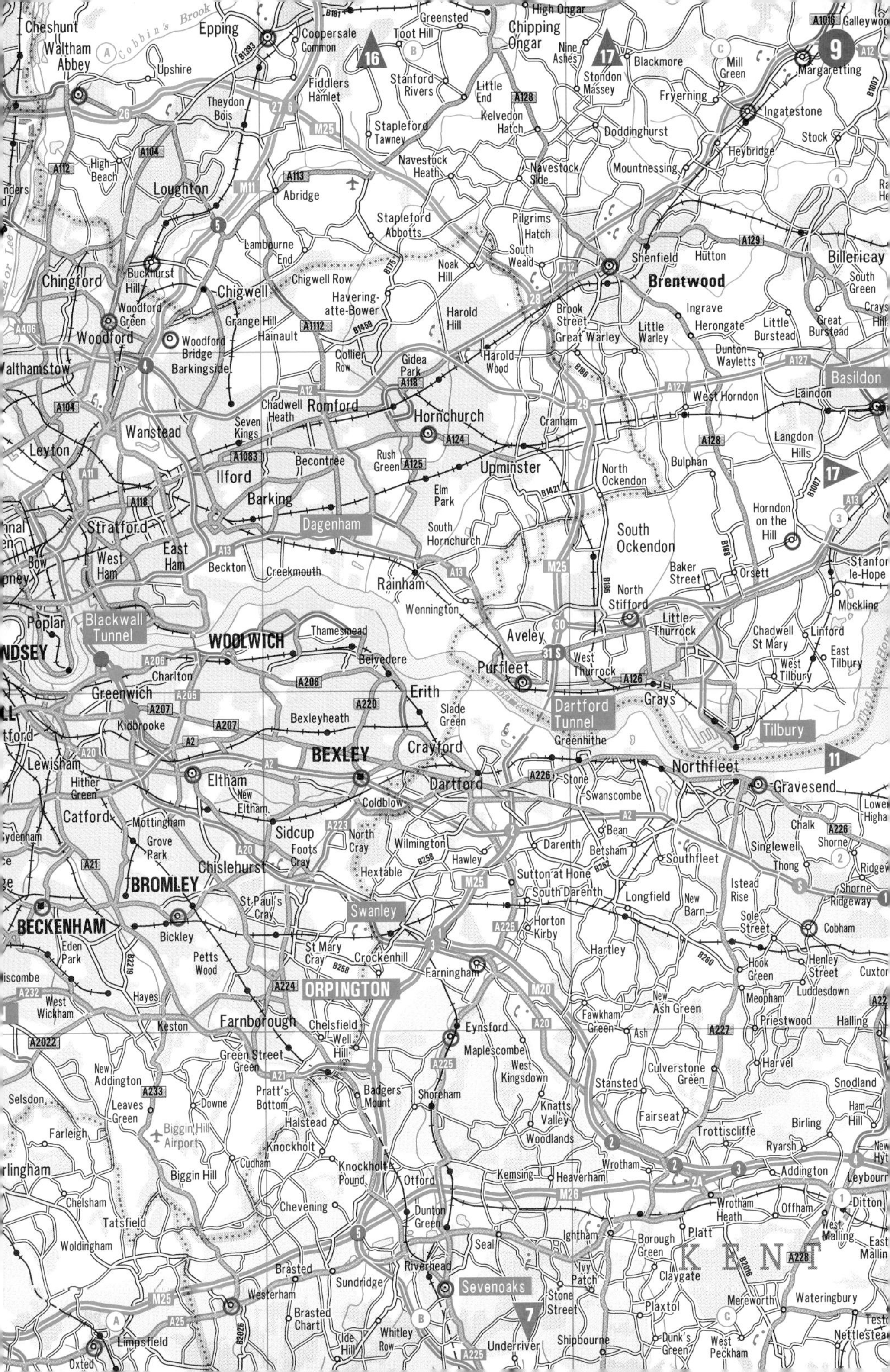

Cheshunt
Waltham Abbey
Cobbin's Brook
Epping
Coopersale Common
Greensted
High Ongar
Toot Hill
Chipping Ongar
Nine Ashes
Stondon Massey
Blackmore
Mill Green
Margaretting
Galleywood
A1016
B181
B1393
16
17
9
Upshire
Theydon Bois
Fiddlers Hamlet
Stanford Rivers
Little End
A128
Kelvedon Hatch
Fryerning
Ingatestone
B1007
A12
Stapleford Tawney
Doddinghurst
Stock
M25
26
27
6
A104
A112
High Beach
Loughton
M11
A113
Abridge
Navestock Heath
Navestock Side
Mountnessing
Heybridge
Stapleford Abbotts
Pilgrims Hatch
Lambourne End
5
Buckhurst Hill
Chingford
Chigwell
Chigwell Row
B175
Noak Hill
South Weald
Shenfield
Hutton
A129
Billericay
South Green
Brentwood
Havering-atte-Bower
Woodford Green
Woodford
Grange Hill
Hainault
A1112
B1459
Harold Hill
28
Brook Street
Great Warley
Little Warley
Ingrave
Herongate
Little Burstead
Great Burstead
A406
Woodford Bridge
Barkingside
Collier Row
Gidea Park
Harold Wood
B186
Dunton Wayletts
A127
Basildon
Walthamstow
4
A12
Romford
A118
Chadwell Heath
Seven Kings
Hornchurch
29
Cranham
West Horndon
Laindon
A104
Wanstead
A124
Leyton
A1083
Becontree
Rush Green
A125
Upminster
North Ockendon
Bulphan
A128
Langdon Hills
Ilford
Elm Park
B1421
A11
Barking
Horndon on the Hill
A118
Stratford
Dagenham
South Hornchurch
South Ockendon
B188
West Ham
East Ham
A13
Bow
Beckton
Creekmouth
M25
Baker Street
Orsett
Rainham
B186
North Stifford
Stanford-le-Hope
Mucking
Wennington
Poplar
Blackwall Tunnel
Thamesmead
Little Thurrock
Aveley
Chadwell St Mary
Linford
East Tilbury
30
31
WOOLWICH
A206
Charlton
Belvedere
West Thurrock
West Tilbury
Purfleet
A126
Greenwich
A205
A206
Erith
Grays
A207
A220
Slade Green
Dartford Tunnel
Tilbury
Kidbrooke
Bexleyheath
Greenhithe
A2
A207
Crayford
BEXLEY
A20
A2
Lewisham
Eltham
A226
Stone
Northfleet
Gravesend
11
Hither Green
New Eltham
Dartford
Swanscombe
Coldblow
Catford
Mottingham
Sidcup
A223
North Cray
Wilmington
Darenth
A2
Bean
Betsham
Southfleet
Chalk
A226
Shorne
Grove Park
A20
Foots Cray
B258
Hawley
Singlewell
Thong
A21
Chislehurst
Hextable
Sutton at Hone
B262
Istead Rise
Shorne Ridgeway
BROMLEY
M25
South Darenth
Longfield
New Barn
St Paul's Cray
Swanley
Horton Kirby
Sole Street
Cobham
BECKENHAM
Bickley
1
3
A225
Hartley
Eden Park
St Mary Cray
Crockenhill
B260
Henley Street
Hook Green
B2219
Petts Wood
B258
Farningham
Cuxton
A224
ORPINGTON
M20
Meopham
Luddesdown
A232
West Wickham
Hayes
New Ash Green
Keston
Farnborough
Chelsfield
Well Hill
Eynsford
Fawkham Green
Ash
A227
Priestwood
Halling
A2022
Green Street Green
A20
Maplescombe
West Kingsdown
Harvel
A225
New Addington
A21
Culverstone Green
Snodland
A233
Pratt's Bottom
Badgers Mount
Shoreham
Stansted
Selsdon
Leaves Green
Downe
Knatts Valley
Fairseat
Ham Hill
Biggin Hill Airport
Halstead
Trottiscliffe
Birling
Farleigh
Woodlands
Knockholt
Ryarsh
Cudham
Knockholt Pound
Wrotham
2
2A
3
Addington
Biggin Hill
Otford
Kemsing
Heaverham
Leybourne
M26
Chelsham
Chevening
Wrotham Heath
Offham
Ditton
Dunton Green
Platt
Tatsfield
Ighthan
West Malling
Woldingham
Seal
Borough Green
KENT
B2016
A228
Brasted
Riverhead
Ivy Patch
Claygate
Sundridge
Sevenoaks
Stone Street
Westerham
M25
Mereworth
Wateringbury
Brasted Chart
Plaxtol
A25
7
B2026
Limpsfield
Ide Hill
Whitley Row
Underriver
Shipbourne
Dunk's Green
West Peckham
Nettlestead
Oxted
A225

M25
10
Uxbridge
Hillingdon
Northolt
Greenford
Yeading
Cowley
Yiewsley
Hayes
Southall
Iver
West Drayton
13
Perivale
EALING
WEMBLEY
Harlesden
WILLESDEN
Acton
Brentford
Norwood Green
Hammersmith
Camden Town
Paddington
Marylebone
Finsbury
Bethnal Green
16
Shoreditch
Stepney
City of London
Westminster
Kensington
Chelsea
BERMONDSEY
Lambeth
CAMBERWELL
Battersea
Fulham
Chiswick
Barnes
Mortlake
Sipson
Cranford
Heston
Colnbrook
Longford
Poyle
London Heathrow Airport
HOUNSLOW
Hatton
Isleworth
Richmond
Richmond Park
Putney
Roehampton
Clapham
WANDSWORTH
Brixton
Deptford
Stanwell
East Bedfont
Staines
FELTHAM
TWICKENHAM
Ham
Teddington
Upper Tooting
Streatham
Dulwich
Sydenham
Ashford
Hanworth
Kingston upon Thames
Wimbledon
Crystal Palace
West Norwood
Penge
Sunbury
Littleton
Hampton
Hampton Court
East Molesey
Merton
MITCHAM
Thornton Heath
South Norwood
Laleham
Surbiton
Morden
New Malden
Thames Ditton
Walton-on-Thames
Shepperton
Chertsey
Long Ditton
Weybridge
Tolworth
Worchester Park
Carshalton
Beddington
CROYDON
Addiscombe
Esher
Hersham
Hook
Chessington
Cheam
Sutton
Wallington
Row Town
Whiteley Village
Claygate
Ewell
Purley
Selsdon
Sanderstead
Byfleet
Cobham
Oxshott
Epsom
Woodmansterne
Stoke D'Abernon
Banstead
Kenley
Warlingham
Pyrford
Ashtead
Burgh Heath
Coulsdon
Whyteleafe
Chipstead
Tadworth
Kingswood
Ripley
Ockham
Leatherhead
Fetcham
Cheldon
Caterham
East Horsley
West Horsley
Headley
Walton on the Hill
Great Bookham
Mickleham
East Clandon
West Clandon
Effingham
The Hermitage
Merstham
Godstone
Brewer St
Westhumble
Buckland
Redhill
SURREY
Dorking
Brockham
Betchworth
Reigate
South Nutfield
Nutfield
Bletchingley
Tandridge
Gomshall
Wotton
Westcott
Gadbrook
Earlswood
Ridge Green
Albury
Shere
Stonebridge
Doversgreen
Salfords
Childworth
Blackheath
Brook
Sutton Abinger
North Holmwood
Dowesgreen
Leigh
Nalderswood
Blindley Heath
Farley Green
Peaslake
Abinger Common
South Holmwood
Outwood
Wasp Green
Horne
Shamley Green
Holmbury St Mary
Coldharbour
Norwood Hill
Meath Green
Smallfield
Beare Green
Parkgate
Horley
Hookwood
Newchapel
Rowly
Newdigate
Burstow
Thorns Flush
Ewhurst
Forest Green
Jayes Park
Capel
Charlwood
London Gatwick Airport
Copthorne
Cranleigh
Ockley
County Oak
Pound Hill
Elmbridge
Walliswood
Crawley
Ifield
Three Bridges
Crawley Down
Oakwoodhill
Rusper
Kingsfold
Lambs Green
Worth
Turners Hill
Alford Crossways
Ellen's Green
WEST SUSSEX
Rowhook
Alford
Rudgwick
Bucks Green
Faygate
Warnham
Colgage
Broadfield
Pease Pottage
Worth Abbey
Selsfield Common
M4
M40(M)
M41
M23
A40
A4020
A3
A24
A23
A217
A25
A264
A22

Barking
Dagenham
East Ham
Beckton
Creekmouth
16
A13
Elm Park
South Hornchurch
Rainham
B1421
North Ockendon
South Ockendon
M25
B186
Horndon on the Hill
B1007
B188
Baker Street
Orsett
A13
Fobbing
Corringham
A1014
11
Stanford-le-Hope
Coryton
Thames Haven
Mucking
Thames Estuary
Wennington
North Stifford
Little Thurrock
Chadwell St Mary
Linford
East Tilbury
West Tilbury
WOOLWICH
Thamesmead
Belvedere
Charlton
A206
A205
A207
Aveley
30
31
Purfleet
West Thurrock
A126
Grays
Thames
The Lower Hope
Erith
A220
Bexleyheath
Slade Green
Dartford Tunnel
Tilbury
Cliffe
B2000
Cooling
A2
BEXLEY
Crayford
Greenhithe
Eltham
New Eltham
Coldblow
Dartford
A226
Stone
Swanscombe
Northfleet
Gravesend
Church Street
Cliffe Woods
Lower Higham
Sidcup
A223
North Cray
Foots Cray
Wilmington
B258
Hawley
Darenth
Bean
Betsham
B262
Southfleet
Chalk
A226
Singlewell
Shorne
Shorne Ridgeway
Thong
Wainscott
Higham
Upnor
Frindsbury
A20
Chislehurst
Hextable
M25
Sutton at Hone
South Darenth
Longfield
New Barn
Istead Rise
Sole Street
Cobham
Strood
Rochester
OMLEY
St Paul's Cray
Swanley
A225
Horton Kirby
Bickley
Petts Wood
St Mary Cray
Crockenhill
B258
Farningham
Hartley
B260
Hook Green
Henley Street
Cuxton
Borstal
Chatham
A229
ORPINGTON
A224
M20
Luddesdown
Meopham
A228
M2
Keston
Farnborough
Chelsfield
Well Hill
Eynsford
A20
Fawkham Green
Ash
New Ash Green
A227
Priestwood
Halling
Wouldham
Walderslade
Green Street Green
A21
Maplescombe
West Kingsdown
A225
Harvel
Culverstone Green
233
Downe
Pratt's Bottom
Badgers Mount
Shoreham
Stansted
Snodland
Burham
Halstead
Knatts Valley
Fairseat
Ham Hill
Biggin Hill Airport
Woodlands
Trottiscliffe
Birling
Eccles
Knockholt
Cudham
Knockholt Pound
Ryarsh
New Hythe
Aylesford
Biggin Hill
Otford
Kemsing
Heaverham
Wrotham
Addington
Leybourne
M26
2A
Chevening
Dunton Green
Wrotham Heath
Offham
Ditton
Royal British Legion Village
West Malling
East Malling
Maidstone
Sand
Seal
Ightham
Borough Green
Platt
B2016
A228
Brasted
Sundridge
Riverhead
Sevenoaks
Ivy Patch
Claygate
East Barming
Westerham
M25
Stone Street
Plaxtol
Mereworth
Wateringbury
Teston
A26
Tovil
A25
Brasted Chart
B2026
Whitley Row
Dunk's Green
West Peckham
Nettlestead
East Farleigh
West Farleigh
Loose
sfield
Shipbourne
A225
KENT
B2010
Coxheath
B2163
Crockham Hill
Toy's Hill
Ide Hill
B2042
Sevenoaks Weald
Underriver
A26
Nettlestead Green
Yalding
Linton
B269
Bough Beech Resr
Hildenborough
Hadlow
Hale Street
Hunton
Marlpit Hill
B2027
Four Elms
Chiddingstone Causeway
B245
Higham Wood
East Peckham
Benover
A229
Golden Green
Medway
Laddingford
Chainhurst
ch House Green
How Green
Bough Beech
B2027
Leigh
Tonbridge
B2015
Whetsted
Collier Street
Milebush
denbridge
Eden
Hever
Chiddingstone
A21
Tudeley
B2017
Five Oak Green
Paddock Wood
Marsh Green
Penshurst
B2176
A26
B2015
B2160
B2162
Marden Beech
Marden Thorn
B2028
Markbeech
B2188
Bidborough
Southborough
Matfield
B2079
ormansland
High Brooms
Brenchley
Winchet Hill
Cowden
Speldhurst
Rustall
Pembury
Horsmonden
Curtisden Green
B2026
Blackham
Fordcombe
Langton Green
A264
A21
A264
Ashurst
Royal Tunbridge Wells
t Grinstead
Ashurst Wood
EAST SUSSEX
Groombridge
Goudhurst
A262
Bells Yew Green
B2169
Lamberhurst
Hartfield
Withyham
A26
Eridge Green
Frant
Kilndown
Forest Row
B2110
Platt
Hartley
A22
Upper Hartfield
7
A267
Coleman's Hatch
Friar's Gate
Boarshead
Sparrow's Green
B2100
Cousley Wood
Bewl Water
A21

12
21
5
6
OXFORDSHIRE
BERKSHIRE
BU
HIGH WYCOMBE
READING
Basingstoke
Radley
Nuneham Courtenay
Marsh Baldon
Chiselhampton
Stadhampton
Stoke Talmage
Adwell
South Weston
Postcombe
Kingston Blount
Aston Rowant
Lewknor
Radnage
Bledlow Ridge
Speen
Walter's Ash
Naphill
Bradenham
The City
Stokenchurch
Beacon's Bottom
West Wycombe
Downley
Piddington
Clifton Hampden
Berinsfield
Drayton St Leonard
Chalgrove
Newington
Easington
Pyrton
Shirburn
Watlington
Christmas Common
Ibstone
Northend
Cadmore End
Lane End
Booker
Culham
Burcot
Long Wittenham
Dorchester
Warborough
Berrick Salome
Brightwell Baldwin
Cuxham
Britwell Salome
Greenfield
Turville Heath
Turville
Fingest
Appleford
Little Wittenham
Shillingford
Roke
Benson
Ewelme
Skirmett
Frieth
Pishill
Stonor
Parmoor
Chrisbridge Cross
Marlow Bottom
Rockwell End
Lower Woodend
Marlow
Didcot
North Moreton
Brightwell-cum-Sotwell
Wallingford
Crowmarsh Gifford
Cookley Green
Russell's Water
East Hagbourne
West Hagbourne
South Moreton
Cholsey
Aston Upthorpe
Aston Tirrold
Blewbury
Nuffield
Nettlebed
Fawley
Hambleden
Middle Assendon
Lower Assendon
Mill End
Medmenham
North Stoke
Ipsden
Bix
Moulsford
Stoke Row
Highmoor Cross
Shepherd's Green
Henley-on-Thames
Remenham
Aston
Remenham Hill
Hurley
South Stoke
Checkendon
Rotherfield Greys
Cockpole Green
Burchett's Green
Woodcote
Streatley
Goring
Cray's Pond
Sonning Common
Rotherfield Peppard
Harpsden
Warren Row
Compton
Aldworth
Cane End
Kidmore End
Lower Shiplake
Shiplake
Knowl Hill
Littlewick
Lower Basildon
Whitchurch Hill
Tokers Green
Binfield Heath
Wargrave
Hare Hatch
Waltham St. Lawrence
Hampstead Norris
Ashampstead
Whitchurch-on-Thames
Mapledurham
Emmer Green
Dunsden Green
Ruscombe
Twyford
Upper Basildon
Pangbourne
Purley on Thames
Caversham Heights
Play Patch
Sonning
Caversham
Whistley Green
Shurlock Row
Yattendon
Tidmarsh
Sulham
Tilehurst
Woodley
Hermitage
Frilsham
Bradfield
Calcot
Hurst
Stanford Dingley
Englefield
Theale
Winnersh
Binfield
The Slade
Bucklebury
Upper Bucklebury
South End
Sheffield Bottom
Whitley
Cold Ash
Chapel Row
Beenham
Sindlesham
Thatcham
Sulhamstead
Burghfield
Three Mile Cross
Arborfield
Wokingham
Brack
Midgham
Woolhampton
Ufton Nervet
Aldermaston Wharf
Burghfield Hill
Grazeley
Shinfield
Barkham
Aldermaston
Burghfield Common
Wokefield Park
Spencers Wood
Arborfield Cross
Arborfield Garrison
Brimpton
Padworth
Mortimer
Swallowfield
Farley Hill
Crookham
Wasing
Mortimer West End
Stratfield Mortimer
Beech Hill
Finchampstead
Crowthorne
Headley
Silchester
Riseley
Ashford Hill
Pamber Heath
West End Green
Stratfield Saye
Eversley
Plastow Green
Fair Oak
Heath End
Tadley
Fair oak Green
Bramshill
Eversley Cross
Sandhurst
Baughurst
Pamber Green
Little London
Stratfield Turgis
Heckfield
Yateley
Frogmore
Kingsclere
Bramley Green
Turgis Green
Hound Green
Hawley
Towns End
Charter Alley
Wolverton
Pamber End
Bramley
Sherfield on Loddon
Hazeley
Mattingley
Hartfordbridge
Fox Lane
Ramsdell
Monk Sherborne
Hartley Wespall
Lyde Green
Hartley Wintney
Minley Manor
Church End
West Green
Hannington
Rotherwick
Phoenix Green
Cove
Sherbourne St. John
North Oakley
Ibworth
Upper Wootton
Chineham
Newnham
Hook
Fleet
Wootton St Lawrence
Old Basing
Winchfield
Pondtail
Winklebury
Hatch
Up Nately
North Warnborough
Dogmersfield
Church Crookham
Quidhampton
Oakley
Mapledurwell
Greywell
Crookham Village
Deane
Kempshot
Odiham
Mill Lane
Heath End
Overton
East Oakley
Tunworth
Upton Grey
Crondall
Ewshot
Upper Hale
Steventon
Cliddesdon
Winslade
Thames
Pang
Kennet
Loddon
Blackwater
Hart
Basingstoke
M40
M4
M3
A423
A415
A329
A4130
A417
A4074
A340
A4
A339
A33
A30
A321
A4155
A404
A4010
A40
A329(M)
A327
A3095
A323
A287
B4015
B480
B4009
B4016
B481
B482
B471
B3024
B3018
B3034
B3030
B3349
B3430
B3051
B3016
B3011
B3104
B3400

Little Kingshill
Little Missenden
Chesham Bois
Latimer
Sarratt
Langleybury
Radlett
Aldenham
Green Street
13
Chenies
Chess
14
Chandler's Cross
WATFORD
Cassiobury Park
Letchmore Heath
Borehamwood
Arkley
BARNE
Totteridg
Amersham
Little Chalfont
Chorleywood
Croxley Green
Bushey
Elstree
Penn Street
Coleshill
Misbourne
Hazlemere
Tylers Green
Winchmore Hill
Chalfont St. Giles
Heronsgate
Rickmansworth
South Oxhey
Bushey Heath
Edgware
Mill Hill
Penn
Knotty Green
Seer Green
Chalfont Common
Jordans
Chalfont St Peter
Horn Hill
Maple Cross
Hatch End
Stanmore
Wycombe Marsh
Loudwater
Grand Union
West Hyde
Harefield
Eastbury
Harrow Weald
Beaconsfield
Gerrards Cross
Denham Green
Northwood
Pinner
Wealdstone
Kingsbury
Hend
HARROW
Bourne End
Wooburn Green
Wooburn
Ruislip Common
Eastcote
Greenhill
Kenton
Hedsor
Hedgerley
Denham
Harrow on the Hill
Ruislip
Fulmer
Burnham Beeches
Cookham
Farnham Common
Ickenham
Northolt
WEMBLEY
Cookham Rise
Stoke Poges
Uxbridge
Union
Hillingdon
Greenford
Harlesden
Taplow
Burnham
Farnham Royal
Iver Heath
Cowley
Yeading
Perivale
EALING
SLOUGH
Iver
Yiewsley
Hayes
Southall
Acton
Bray
Cippenham
West Drayton
Hammersmith
Dorney
Upton
Langley
Norwood Green
Brentford
Boveney
Eton
Sipson
Holyport
Longford
Cranford
Heston
Chiswick
Fulha
Colnbrook
Thames
Fifield
Datchet
Poyle
Barnes
Windsor
Oakley Green
Horton
London Heathrow Airport
Hatton
HOUNSLOW
Mortlake
Isleworth
Richmond
Putney
Wraysbury
Stanwell
Old Windsor
East Bedfont
Richmond Park
Roehampton
Winkfield
Windsor Great Park
Staines
FELTHAM
TWICKENHAM
Cranbourne
Hythe End
Ham
Winkfield Row
Englefield Green
Ashford
Hanworth
Teddington
Wimbledo
Woodside
Egham
Kingston upon Thames
North Ascot
Sunbury
Hampton Court
Hampton
Littleton
East Molesey
Thorpe
Laleham
Surbiton
Ascot
Sunningdale
Thames Ditton
New Malden
Sunninghill
Virginia Water
Walton-on-Thames
Lyne
Shepperton
Long Ditton
Chertsey
Tolworth
Worchester Park
Weybridge
Addlestone
Esher
Hook
Windlesham
Ottershaw
Hersham
Chessington
Bagshot
Burrowhill
Row Town
Whiteley Village
Claygate
Ewell
Lightwater
Woodham
Chobham
Oxshott
Epsom
Donkey Town
West End
Byfleet
Cobham
Mimbridge
Horsell
Stoke D'Abernon
Bisley
Pyrford
Mole
Burgh Heath
Knaphill
Woking
Ashtead
Deepcut
Brookwood
Wey
Firmley Green
Mayford
Ockham
Tadworth
Pirbright
Ripley
Leatherhead
Mytchett
Fetcham
Walton on the Hill
Send
East Horsley
Headley
Farnborough
Worplesdon
Great Bookham
Henley Park
West Horsley
Mickleham
Fairlands
Pitch Place
East Clandon
Effingham
The Hermitage
Ash Vale
Normandy
Wood Street
Stoughton
Burpham
West Clandon
Westhumble
Buckland
RSHOT
Wyke
Willow Green
SURREY
Brockham
Guildford
Betchworth
Ash
Flexford
Onslow Village
Westcott
Dorking
Albury
Gomshall
Stonebridge
Gadbrook
Puttenham

14
21
45
13
BEDFORD
SHIRE
BUCKINGHAM
SHIRE
Great Linford
A422
Willen
Broughton
Bradwell
Woolstone
Milton Keynes
Milton Keynes Village
M1
Moulsoe
Cranfield
Lower Shelton
Marston Moretaine
A421
Stewartby
How End
Houghton Conquest
Haynes
A600
Southill
Haynes West End
Haynes Church End
Chicksands
Shefford
Salford
Lidlington
Millbrook
B530
Mauldon
Water End
Beadlow
A507
Clifton
Brogborough
Ampthill
Clophill
Campton
Woughton-on-the-Green
A5130
Walton
Ridgmont
Meppershall
Upper Gravenhurst
Shenley Brook End
Simpson
Aspley Guise
Husborne Crawley
Steppingley
Flitton
Silsoe
Upper Stondon
Lower Stondon
Woburn Sands
Bow Brickhill
Flitwick
Greenfield
Pulloxhill
Hanscombe End
Bletchley
Fenny Stratford
A4012
Woburn
Froxfield
Eversholt
Tingrith
Higham Gobion
Shillington
Apsley End
Holwell
Little Brickhill
Ouzel or Lovat
Church End
Westoning
Barton-le-Clay
Pirton
Newton Longville
A5
Great Brickhill
Potsgrove
Milton Bryan
A5120
Harlington
Hexton
Pegsdon
Hitch
Drayton Parslow
Stoke Hammond
Battlesden
Toddington
Sharpenhoe
Streatley
B655
Mursley
Heath and Reach
Upper Sundon
A505
Soulbury
Hollingdon
A4146
Hockliffe
Tebworth
B579
Lower Sundon
Great Offley
Stewkley
B4032
Chalton
Wingfield
Sundon Park
Lilley
Offleyhoo
Littlecote
Linslade
Leighton Buzzard
Eggington
Tilsworth
Houghton Regis
Limbury
Ley Green
Burcote
Stanbridge
Stopsley
Dunton
Wing
Billington
Leagrave
Cockernhoe
Ledburn
Totternhoe
LUTON
Cublington
Eaton Bray
Dunstable
Luton Airport
Breachwood Green
Aston Abbotts
A418
Slapton
Church End
Edlesborough
Caddington
Grand Union
Mentmore
Wingrave
Horton
Ivinghoe Aston
Kensworth
A6
B653
Peter's Green
Rowsham
Cheddington
Whipsnade
B4540
Slip End
East Hyde
B652
Hulcott
B488
Dagnall
Studham
Markyate
A1081
Bierton
Long Marston
Pitstone
Ivinghoe
Marshalls Heath
Aylesbury
Puttenham
Marsworth
Ringshall
Flamstead
Harpenden
Wilstone
Wilstone Resr
Little Gaddesden
Hatching Green
A41
Buckland
New Mill
Aldbury
Trowley Bottom
Weston Turville
Aston Clinton
Tring
Great Gaddesden
Redbourn
Stoke Mandeville
B4506
Water End
Holtsmere End
Halton
Nettleden
B4443
A413
A4011
West Leith
A4146
Piccotts End
B487
Ver
A4010
Hastoe
Wigginton
Potten End
A4147
Nash Lee
Wendover
Northchurch
Berkhamsted
Warners End
A5183
Kimble
St Leonards
Cholesbury
Chaulden
Hemel Hempstead
Ellesborough
Buckland Common
Ashley Green
Bourne End
M10
St.A
Bellingdon
Whelpley Hill
Felden
Chiswell Green
Dunsmore
Lee Clump
B4505
Little Hampton
The Lee
Chartridge
A416
Bovingdon
Bedmond
Ballinger Common
Lye Green
M25
Great Hampden
Chesham
Chipperfield
Kings Langley
Abbots Langley
Colney Street
Prestwood
South Heath
B485
Botley
B556
Lacey Green
Great Missenden
Hyde Heath
Waterside
Flaunden
Bricket Wood
Radlett
Bucks Hill
Speen
Upper North Dean
Little Kingshill
Chesham Bois
Latimer
Sarratt
Langleybury
Aldenham
Walter's Ash
Great Kingshill
Little Missenden
Chenies
Chess
WATFORD
A404
Chandler's Cross
Letchmore Heath
Naphill
Amersham
Little Chalfont
Chorleywood
Cassiobury Park
A411
Hughenden Valley
Holmer Green
Penn Street
Croxley Green
A4008
Bushey
Downley
Hazlemere
Misbourne
Coleshill
B4442
A4128
A355
Tylers Green
Winchmore Hill
Chalfont St. Giles
Heronsgate
Rickmansworth
A4145
HIGH WYCOMBE
Totteridge
Penn
Horn Hill
A4125
Bushey Heath
B474
Chalfont Common
Maple Cross
South Oxhey
Hatch End
Wycombe Marsh
Knotty Green
Seer Green
A4140
Booker
Loudwater
Jordans
Chalfont St Peter
West Hyde
Harefield
Eastbury
Harrow Weald
A410
Stanm

HERTFORD
SHIRE
26
15
16
8
9
Steeple Morden
Litlington
Great Chesterford
Little Chesterford
Edworth
Hinxworth
Ashwell
Royston
Heydon
Great Chishill
Strethall
Elmdon
Saffron Walden
Littlebury
Caldecote
Newnham
Therfield
Reed End
Barley
Chrishall
Littlebury Green
Audley End
Bygrave
Kelshall
Reed
Duddenhoe End
Bridge Green
Wendens Ambo
Radwell
Norton
Baldock
Sandon
Barkway
Langley
Arkesden
Newport
Wallington
Roe Green
Mill End
Buckland
Nuthampstead
Wicken Bonhunt
Clothall
Chipping
Anstey
Meesden
Clavering
Widdington
Rushden
Wyddial
Brent Pelham
Rickling
Weston
Throcking
Buntingford
Berden
Quendon
Willian
Cumberlow Green
Hare Street
Great Hormead
Stocking Pelham
Great Wymondley
Hall's Green
Cottered
Little Wymondley
Graveley
Cromer
Aspenden
Furneux Pelham
Ugley
Ugley Green
Ardeley
Hay Street
East End
Manuden
Elsenham
Walkern
Westmill
Cherry Green
Wood End
Braughing
Farnham Green
Patmore Heath
Stansted Mountfitchet
Tye Green
Stevenage
Farnham
Burton End
Aston End
Great Munden
Nasty
Puckeridge
Albury
Little Hadham
Langley
Benington
Standon
Wellpond Green
Birchanger
Aston
Hadham Ford
Bishop's Stortford
London Stansted Airport
Old Knebworth
Bragbury End
Dane End
Colliers End
Bedlars Green
Knebworth
Sacombe
Datchworth
Much Hadham
Thorley
Great Hallingbury
Rableyheath
Watton at Stone
Wodmer Green
High Cross
Oaklands
Stapleford
Wadesmill
Hadham Cross
Perry Green
Spellbrook
Hatfield Broad Oak
Tonwell
Bakers End
Little Hallingbury
Burnham Green
Thundridge
Welwyn
Wareside
Widford
Hatfield Heath
Harmer Green
Bramfield
Waterford
Ware
Sawbridgeworth
Tewin
Hunsdon
High Wych
Sheering
Welwyn Garden City
Great Amwell
Matching
Hertford
Stanstead Abbots
Eastwick
Matching Tye
Hertingfordbury
Hertford Heath
Cole green
St Margarets
Hatfield
Nyde
Letty Green
Hailey
Harlow
Lea or Lee
Hoddesdon
Roydon
Potter Street
High Laver
Essendon
Bayford
Great Parndon
Foster Street
Magdalen Laver
Hatfield
West End
Brickdon
Roydon Hamlet
Woodside
Little Berkhamsted
Broxbourne
Broadley Common
Hastingwood
Lower Nazeing
Welham Green
Epping Green
Wormley West End
Nazeing
Epping Green
Bobbingworth
Brookmans Park
Wormley
Hammond Street
Newgate Street
Bumble's Green
Thornwood Common
North Weald Bassett
Water End
Goff's Oak
Greensted
Cheshunt
Epping
Coopersale Common
South Mimms
Northaw
Waltham Abbey
Chipping Ongar
Cuffley
Toot Hill
Potters Bar
Upshire
Stanford Rivers
Ridge
Waltham Cross
Fiddlers Hamlet
Crews Hill
Theydon Bois
Botany Bay
Hadley Wood
Forty Hill
Stapleford Tawney
Wrotham Park
High Beach
Navestock Heath
Enfield
Loughton
Monken Hadley
Cockfosters
Ponders End
Abridge
Arkley
Winchmore Hill
Stapleford Abbotts
BARNET
Totteridge
East Barnet
Southgate
Lambourne End
Noak Hill
Chingford
Buckhurst Hill
Chigwell
Chigwell Row
Edgware
Friern Barnet
Edmonton
Havering-atte-Bower
Harold Hill
Mill Hill
Woodford Green
Grange Hill
Wood Green
Woodford
Woodford Bridge
Finchley
Hainault
Cobbin's Brook
Quin
Rib
Ash
Stort
Cam or Granta
A1
A1(M)
A10
A505
A507
A120
A602
A1170
A119
A414
A1169
A1184
A1060
M11
M25
A1000
A1005
A1081
A111
A112
A104
A113
A1010
A406
A1112
B184
B1039
B1038
B1368
B1383
B1004
B158
B180
B181
B183
B194
B1000
B656
B197
B156
B157
B556
B5378
B1393
B1459
B175

Stevenage
16
15
Aston End
Great Munden
Nasty
Puckeridge
Little Hadham
Birchanger
Burton End
London Stansted Airport
Benington
Aston
Bragbury End
Wellpond Green
Standon
Hadham Ford
Bishop's Stortford
Takeley Street
Bedlars Green
Dane End
Colliers End
Sacombe
Knebworth
Datchworth
Watton at Stone
Much Hadham
Thorley
Great Hallingbury
Woolmer Green
Oaklands
High Cross
Stapleford
Wadesmill
Tonwell
Thundridge
Hadham Cross
Perry Green
Spellbrook
Little Hallingbury
Welwyn
Burnham Green
Harmer Green
Bakers End
Wareside
Widford
Hatfield Broad Oak
Hatfield Heath
Bramfield
Tewin
Waterford
Ware
Hunsdon
Sawbridgeworth
High Wych
Sheering
Welwyn Garden City
Hertford
Great Amwell
Stanstead Abbots
Eastwick
White Roothing or White Roding
Hatfield Nyde
Cole Green
Hertingfordbury
Hertford Heath
St Margarets
Matching Tye
Matching
Abbess Roding
Letty Green
Hailey
Harlow
Matching Green
Essendon
Hoddesdon
Roydon
Potter Street
Little Laver
Hatfield
Bayford
Brickdon
Great Parndon
Foster Street
High Laver
West End
Roydon Hamlet
Magdalen Laver
Woodside
Little Berkhamsted
Broxbourne
Broadley Common
Hastingwood
Fyfield
Epping Green
Wormley West End
Lower Nazeing
Nazeing
Welham Green
Wormley
Epping Green
Bobbingworth
Moreton
Brookmans Park
Newgate Street
Hammond Street
Bumble's Green
Thornwood Common
North Weald Bassett
Goff's Oak
Cheshunt
Greensted
Chipping Ongar
Northaw
Cuffley
Waltham Abbey
Epping
Coopersale Common
Potters Bar
Toot Hill
Waltham Cross
Upshire
Fiddlers Hamlet
Stanford River
Little End
Crews Hill
Botany Bay
Theydon Bois
Kelvedon Hatch
Wrotham Park
Hadley Wood
Forty Hill
Stapleford Tawney
Monken Hadley
Enfield
High Beach
Navestock Heath
Cockfosters
Ponders End
Loughton
Abridge
BARNET
Totteridge
East Barnet
Winchmore Hill
Southgate
Stapleford Abbotts
Pilgrims Hatch
Lambourne End
South Weald
Mill Hill
Friern Barnet
Edmonton
Chingford
Buckhurst Hill
Chigwell
Chigwell Row
Noak Hill
Havering-atte-Bower
Harold Hill
Finchley
Wood Green
Woodford Green
Woodford
Grange Hill
Hainault
Woodford Bridge
Barkingside
Collier Row
Gidea Park
Harold Wood
Hendon
Tottenham
Walthamstow
Golders Green
Hornsey
Chadwell Heath
Romford
Hornchurch
Wanstead
Seven Kings
Highgate
Stoke Newington
Leyton
Hampstead
Ilford
Becontree
Rush Green
Upminster
Camden Town
Islington
Hackney
Barking
Elm Park
Finsbury
Bethnal Green
Stratford
Dagenham
South Hornchurch
WILLESDEN
Paddington
Shoreditch
Bow
East Ham
West Ham
Stepney
Beckton
Creekmouth
Marylebone
City of London
Rainham
Wennington
Poplar
Blackwall Tunnel
Westminster
Thamesmead
Aveley
Kensington
Chelsea
BERMONDSEY
WOOLWICH
Belvedere
Purfleet
Lambeth
Charlton
Erith
Fulham
Greenwich
Battersea
CAMBERWELL
Kidbrooke
Bexleyheath
Slade Green
Deptford
Clapham
Brixton
Lewisham
BEXLEY
Crayford
Eltham
New Eltham
Hither Green
WANDSWORTH
Upper Tooting
Dulwich
Catford
Mottingham
Sidcup
Coldblow
North Cray
Dartford
Lea or Lee
Rib
Ash
Cobbin's Brook
Thames
M1
M11
M25
M40(M)
M41
A1
A5
A10
A11
A12
A13
A40
A41
A104
A107
A111
A112
A113
A118
A119
A120
A124
A125
A128
A142
A205
A206
A207
A220
A223
A226
A202
A406
A414
A602
A1000
A1005
A1010
A1060
A1081
A1083
A1112
A1169
A1170
A1184
B156
B157
B158
B180
B181
B183
B184
B194
B556
B1000
B1004
B1383
B1459
B175
A2
A3
A20
10
11
8

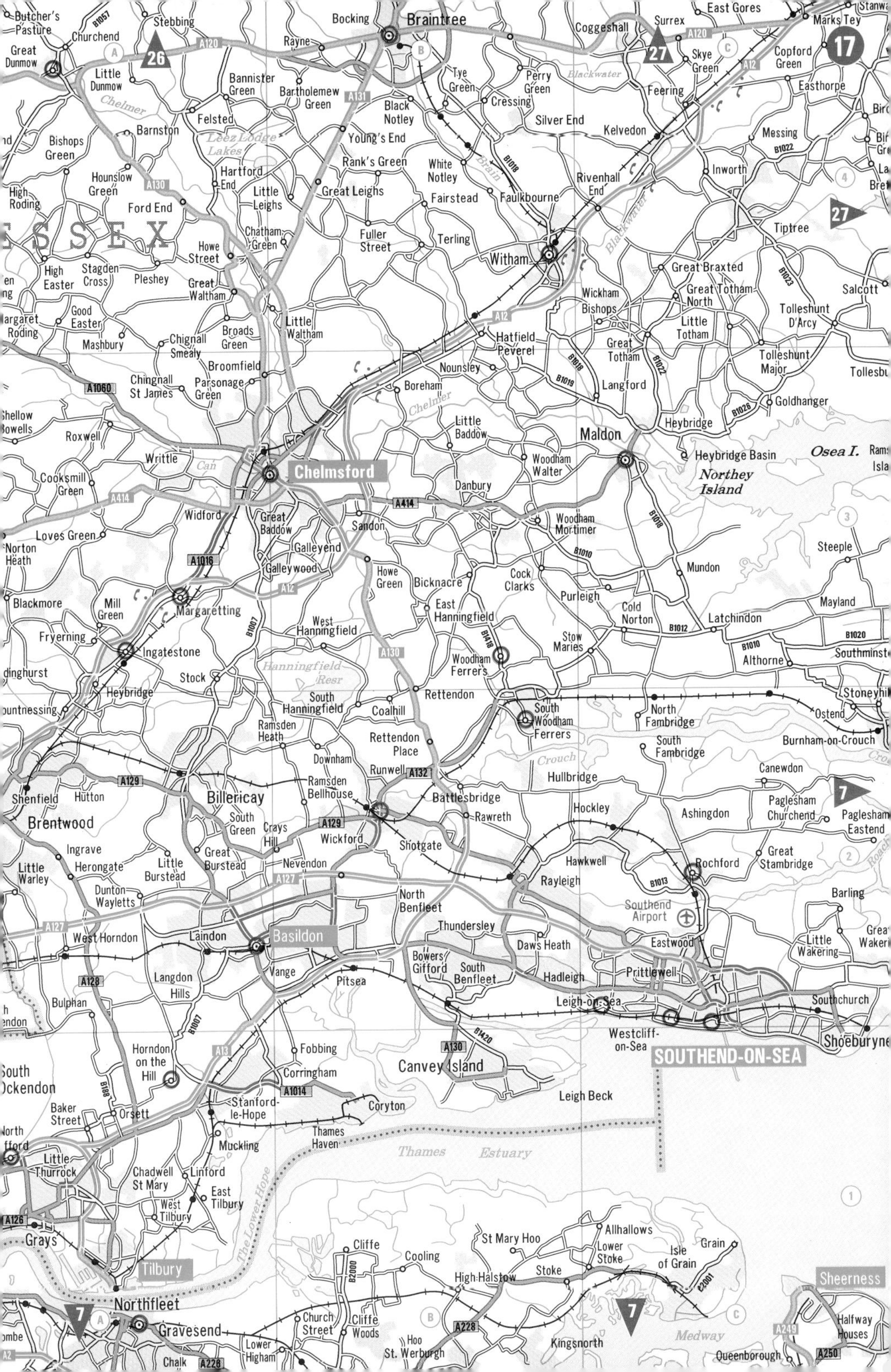

Butcher's Pasture
B1057
Churchend
Stebbing
Bocking
Braintree
Coggeshall
Surrex
East Gores
Marks Tey
Stanway
Great Dunmow
A
26
A120
Rayne
B
27
A120
C
Skye Green
Copford Green
17
Little Dunmow
Bannister Green
Bartholomew Green
A131
Tye Green
Perry Green
Blackwater
A12
Feering
Easthorpe
Chelmer
Felsted
Black Notley
Cressing
Silver End
Kelvedon
Bishops Green
Barnston
Leez Lodge Lakes
Young's End
Messing
B1022
Hounslow Green
Hartford End
Rank's Green
White Notley
Brain
B1018
Inworth
4
High Roding
A130
Little Leighs
Great Leighs
Fairstead
Faulkbourne
Rivenhall End
Ford End
27
ESSEX
Howe Street
Chatham Green
Fuller Street
Terling
Tiptree
Blackwater
Witham
High Easter
Stagden Cross
Pleshey
Great Waltham
Great Braxted
B1023
Salcott
Good Easter
Little Waltham
Wickham Bishops
Great Totham North
Margaret Roding
Mashbury
Chignall Smealy
Broads Green
A12
Little Totham
Tolleshunt D'Arcy
Hatfield Peverel
Great Totham
Broomfield
Nounsley
B1018
B1022
Tolleshunt Major
Chingnall St James
Parsonage Green
A1060
Boreham
B1019
Langford
Tollesbury
Shellow Bowells
Chelmer
Goldhanger
Roxwell
Little Baddow
B1026
Heybridge
Maldon
Writtle
Can
Woodham Walter
Heybridge Basin
Osea I.
Cooksmill Green
Chelmsford
Northey Island
Danbury
A414
A414
B1018
Widford
Great Baddow
Sandon
Woodham Mortimer
3
Loves Green
Galleyend
Norton Heath
A1016
Galleywood
Howe Green
B1010
Steeple
Cock Clarks
Mundon
A12
Bicknacre
Blackmore
Mill Green
Margaretting
Purleigh
East Hanningfield
Cold Norton
Mayland
Latchindon
West Hanningfield
B1007
B1012
Fryerning
Stow Maries
B1418
B1010
B1020
Ingatestone
A130
Woodham Ferrers
Althorne
Southminster
Hanningfield Resr
Stock
Rettendon
Stoneyhills
Heybridge
South Hanningfield
South Woodham Ferrers
North Fambridge
Ostend
Mountnessing
Coalhill
Ramsden Heath
Rettendon Place
South Fambridge
Burnham-on-Crouch
Downham
Crouch
Runwell
A132
Hullbridge
Canewdon
Shenfield
Hutton
A129
Ramsden Bellhouse
7
Billericay
Battlesbridge
Paglesham Churchend
Paglesham Eastend
Hockley
Ashingdon
Brentwood
South Green
Crays Hill
A129
Wickford
Rawreth
Ingrave
Shotgate
Great Stambridge
Great Burstead
Hawkwell
Rochford
2
Little Warley
Herongate
Little Burstead
Nevendon
Rayleigh
Barling
A127
Dunton Wayletts
North Benfleet
B1013
Southend Airport
A127
Thundersley
West Horndon
Laindon
Basildon
Daws Heath
Eastwood
Little Wakering
Great Wakering
Bowers Gifford
South Benfleet
Vange
Pitsea
Hadleigh
Prittlewell
A128
Langdon Hills
Bulphan
Leigh-on-Sea
Southchurch
B1007
B1420
Westcliff-on-Sea
Shoeburyness
Horndon on the Hill
A13
Fobbing
A130
Canvey Island
SOUTHEND-ON-SEA
South Ockendon
Corringham
B186
A1014
Leigh Beck
Baker Street
Orsett
Stanford-le-Hope
Coryton
Thames Haven
Muckling
Thames
Estuary
Little Thurrock
Chadwell St Mary
Linford
The Lower Hope
1
East Tilbury
West Tilbury
A126
Allhallows
Grays
St Mary Hoo
Lower Stoke
Grain
Cliffe
Isle of Grain
Cooling
B2000
Tilbury
Stoke
High Halstow
B2001
Sheerness
Northfleet
7
A
Church Street
Cliffe Woods
B
A228
7
C
Halfway Houses
Gravesend
Medway
A249
Hoo St. Werburgh
Lower Higham
Kingsnorth
Queenborough
A250
A2
Chalk
A226

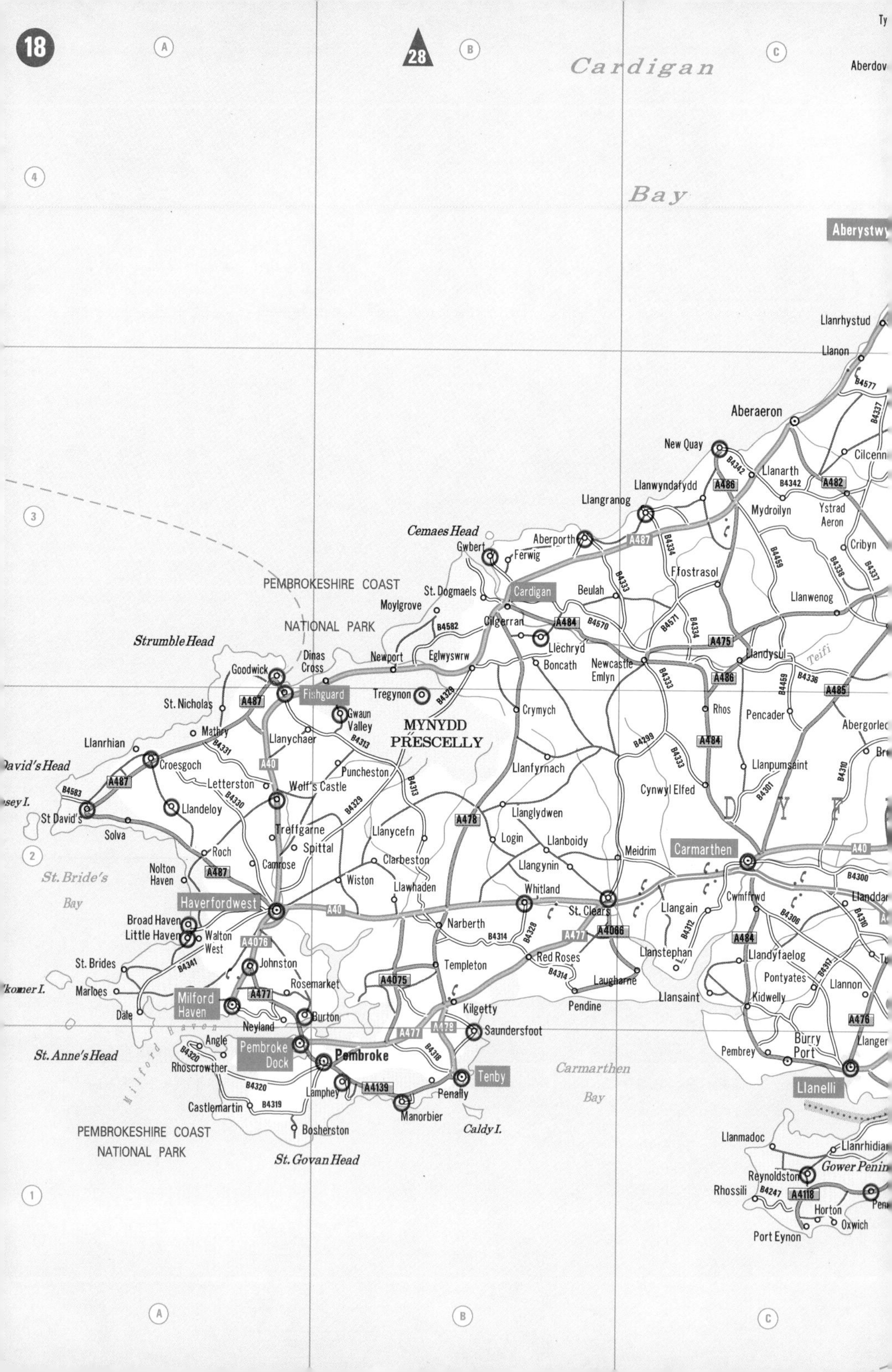
28
Cardigan Bay
PEMBROKESHIRE COAST NATIONAL PARK
MYNYDD PRESCELLY
Strumble Head
Cemaes Head
St. Bride's Bay
St. Anne's Head
St. Govan Head
Caldy I.
Carmarthen Bay
Gower Penin
Milford Haven
Teifi
Aberystwy
Aberaeron
New Quay
Llangranog
Aberporth
Cardigan
Fishguard
Goodwick
St David's
Haverfordwest
Milford Haven
Pembroke Dock
Pembroke
Tenby
Carmarthen
Llanelli
Newcastle Emlyn
Narberth
Whitland
St. Clears
Saundersfoot
Burry Port
Llanrhystud
Llanon
Llanarth
Llanwyndafydd
Mydroilyn
Ystrad Aeron
Cribyn
Llanwenog
Ffostrasol
Beulah
Gwbert
Ferwig
St. Dogmaels
Moylgrove
Cilgerran
Llechryd
Boncath
Newport
Eglwyswrw
Dinas Cross
Tregynon
Gwaun Valley
Crymych
Llandysul
Rhos
Pencader
Llanpumsaint
Cynwyl Elfed
Llanfyrnach
Llanglydwen
Login
Llanboidy
Llangynin
Meidrim
St. Nicholas
Mathry
Llanrhian
Croesgoch
Letterston
Llandeloy
Llanychaer
Puncheston
Wolf's Castle
Treffgarne
Spittal
Llanycefn
Clarbeston
Wiston
Llawhaden
Camrose
Roch
Nolton Haven
Solva
Broad Haven
Little Haven
Walton West
St. Brides
Marloes
Dale
Johnston
Rosemarket
Neyland
Burton
Angle
Rhoscrowther
Castlemartin
Bosherston
Lamphey
Manorbier
Penally
Templeton
Kilgetty
Red Roses
Laugharne
Pendine
Llangain
Llanstephan
Llansaint
Cwmffrwd
Llandyfaelog
Pontyates
Kidwelly
Llannon
Pembrey
Llangennech
Abergorlech
Llanddarog
Llanmadoc
Llanrhidian
Reynoldston
Rhossili
Horton
Oxwich
Port Eynon
Cilcennin
A40
A4076
A477
A478
A479
A4075
A4139
A487
A484
A475
A486
A485
A482
A4066
A476
A4118
B4583
B4331
B4330
B4329
B4313
B4341
B4320
B4319
B4318
B4314
B4328
B4582
B4570
B4571
B4334
B4333
B4299
B4312
B4306
B4317
B4300
B4310
B4301
B4459
B4336
B4338
B4337
B4342
B4577
B4247

A B C
1 2 3 4

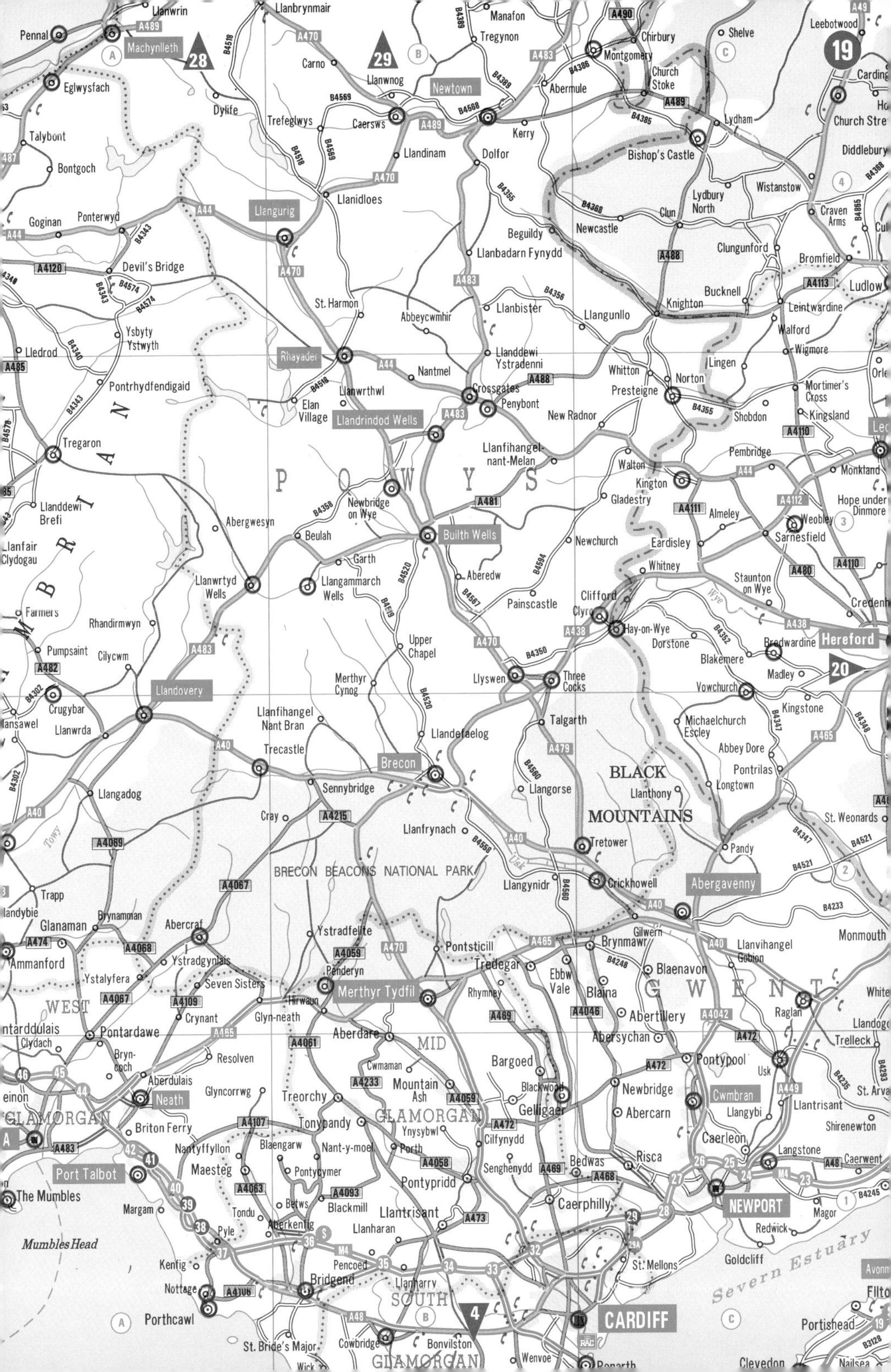

Llanwrin
Llanbrynmair
Manafon
A490
Chirbury
A49
Leebotwood
Pennal
A489
Machynlleth
28
A470
Carno
29
B4389
Tregynon
Montgomery
Shelve
19
Eglwysfach
Llanwnog
Newtown
A483
B4386
Abermule
Church Stoke
Carding
Dylife
B4518
B4569
Caersws
B4568
B4389
Kerry
A489
B4385
Lydham
Church Stre
Talybont
Trefeglwys
A489
Llandinam
Dolfor
Bishop's Castle
Diddlebury
Bontgoch
A470
Wistanstow
Llanidloes
B4355
Lydbury North
B4368
Craven Arms
Goginan
Ponterwyd
A44
Llangurig
B4368
Newcastle
Clun
B4343
Beguildy
Clungunford
Bromfield
A44
A4120
Devil's Bridge
Llanbadarn Fynydd
A488
Ludlow
B4574
B4343
A470
A483
B4356
Bucknell
A4113
St. Harmon
Abbeycwmhir
Llanbister
Knighton
Leintwardine
Ysbyty Ystwyth
Llangunllo
Walford
Lledrod
B4340
Rhayader
A44
Llanddewi Ystradenni
Lingen
Wigmore
A485
Nantmel
A488
Whitton
Norton
Pontrhydfendigaid
B4518
Llanwrthwl
Crossgates
Presteigne
Mortimer's Cross
Elan Village
Penybont
B4355
Shobdon
Kingsland
Llandrindod Wells
New Radnor
A4110
B4343
A483
Tregaron
Llanfihangel-nant-Melan
Pembridge
Walton
A44
Monkland
P O W Y S
Kington
Llanddewi Brefi
Newbridge on Wye
A481
Gladestry
A4111
A4112
Almeley
Hope under Dinmore
Weobley
B4358
Abergwesyn
Beulah
Builth Wells
Newchurch
Eardisley
Sarnesfield
Llanfair Clydogau
Garth
Aberedw
B4594
Whitney
A480
A4110
B4520
Llanwrtyd Wells
Llangammarch Wells
B4567
Staunton on Wye
Farmers
B4519
Painscastle
Clifford
Wye
Credenhill
Clyro
A438
Rhandirmwyn
Upper Chapel
A470
A438
Hay-on-Wye
B4352
Dorstone
Bredwardine
Hereford
Pumpsaint
Cilycwm
A483
B4350
Blakemere
A482
Merthyr Cynog
Llyswen
Three Cocks
Madley
20
B4302
Crugybar
Llandovery
Vowchurch
B4520
Talgarth
Michaelchurch Escley
Kingstone
Llanwrda
Llanfihangel Nant Bran
B4347
Llandefaelog
A479
A465
Trecastle
Abbey Dore
B4348
A40
Brecon
B4560
BLACK
Pontrilas
B4302
Sennybridge
Llangorse
Llanthony
Longtown
Llangadog
MOUNTAINS
St. Weonards
Cray
A4215
Llanfrynach
A40
A40
Towy
A4069
B4558
Tretower
Pandy
B4347
B4521
BRECON BEACONS NATIONAL PARK
Usk
B4521
Llangynidr
Crickhowell
Abergavenny
A4067
B4560
Trapp
A40
B4233
Llandybie
Brynamman
Gilwern
Glanaman
Abercraf
Ystradfellte
Monmouth
A474
A4068
A4059
A470
Pontsticill
A465
Brynmawr
A40
Llanvihangel Gobion
Ammanford
Ystradgynlais
Penderyn
Tredegar
Ebbw Vale
B4248
Blaenavon
Ystalyfera
Seven Sisters
Merthyr Tydfil
Rhymney
G W E N T
A4067
A4109
Hirwaun
Blaina
Raglan
WEST
A469
A4046
Abertillery
Llandogo
Crynant
Glyn-neath
Pontardawe
A465
Aberdare
A4042
Abersychan
A472
Trelleck
A4061
MID
Clydach
Resolven
Cwmaman
Bargoed
A472
Pontypool
Bryn-coch
B4293
Usk
46
45
Aberdulais
Mountain Ash
Blackwood
Newbridge
Cwmbran
B4235
A4233
A4059
A449
St. Arvans
44
Neath
Glyncorrwg
Treorchy
GLAMORGAN
Gelligaer
Abercarn
Llangybi
Llantrisant
GLAMORGAN
Briton Ferry
A4107
Tonypandy
Ynysybwl
A472
Shirenewton
Caerleon
Nantyffyllon
Blaengarw
Nant-y-moel
Porth
Cilfynydd
42
41
A483
A4058
Bedwas
Risca
Langstone
A48
Caerwent
Port Talbot
Maesteg
Pontycymer
Senghenydd
A469
A468
26
25
24
M4
23
40
A4063
A4093
Pontypridd
27
B4245
The Mumbles
39
Betws
Blackmill
Caerphilly
28
NEWPORT
Margam
Tondu
Llantrisant
Magor
38
Pyle
Aberkenfig
Llanharan
A473
29
Redwick
Mumbles Head
36
S
M4
32
29A
Severn Estuary
37
Kenfig
Pencoed
35
34
33
St. Mellons
Goldcliff
Avonm
Nottage
A4106
Bridgend
Llanharry
Filto
SOUTH
4
Porthcawl
A48
CARDIFF
Portishead
19
St. Bride's Major
Cowbridge
Bonvilston
GLAMORGAN
Wenvoe
RAC
Penarth
Clevedon
Nailsea
B3128
Wick

20
29
30
19
4
5
SHROPSHIRE
HEREFORD AND WORCESTER
GLOUCESTERSHIRE
WEST MIDLANDS
WARWICKSHIRE
COTSWOLDS
Ironbridge
Broseley
Much Wenlock
Leebotwood
Cardington
Hope Bowdler
Church Stretton
Morville
Bridgnorth
Ditton Priors
Diddlebury
Wistanstow
Craven Arms
Clungunford
Bromfield
Culmington
Clee St. Margaret
Billingsley
Aveley
Highley
Bitterley
Cleobury Mortimer
Ludlow
Cleehill
Leintwardine
Walford
Wigmore
Lingen
Orleton
Woofferton
Tenbury Wells
Mortimer's Cross
Kingsland
Hatfield
Leominster
Monkland
Weobley
Hope under Dinmore
Sarnesfield
Wellington
Credenhill
Bredwardine
Hereford
Madley
Kingstone
Abbey Dore
Much Birch
Carey
Fownhope
Mordiford
How Caple
Kings Caple
Peterstow
St. Weonards
Ross-on-Wye
Pencraig
Goodrich
Whitchurch
Symonds Yat
Monmouth
Staunton
Coleford
Clearwell
Whitebrook
Raglan
Llandogo
Trelleck
Tintern
Usk
St. Arvans
Llantrisant
Shirenewton
Chepstow
Langstone
Caerwent
Caldicot
Magor
Redwick
WOLVERHAMPTON
WALSALL
SUTTON COLDFIELD
Aldridge
Fazeley
WEST BROMWICH
Sedgley
Wombourne
Claverley
DUDLEY
Amblecote
Halesowen
Kinver
Stourbridge
Hagley
Belbroughton
BIRMINGHAM
Solihull
Knowle
Kidderminster
Bewdley
Stourport-on-Severn
Clows Top
Chaddesley Corbett
Bromsgrove
Alvechurch
Hockley Heath
Abberley
Great Witley
Shrawley
Ombersley
Droitwich
Stoke Prior
Redditch
Astwood Bank
Studley
Henley in-Arden
Clifton upon Teme
Holt Heath
Martley
Whitbourne
Bromyard
Worcester
Leigh
Powick
Great Malvern
Kempsey
Colwall
Malvern Wells
Wynds Point
Welland
Bosbury
Ledbury
Eastnor
Upton-upon-Severn
Longdon
Inkberrow
Crowle
Spetchley
Bishampton
Pershore
Defford
Harvington
Evesham
Alcester
Wootton Wawen
Bearley
Wilmcote
Billesley
Broom
Bidford on Avon
Dorsington
Long Marston
South Littleton
Alderminster
Mickleton
Willersey
Chipping Campden
Ashton under Hill
Broadway
Blockley
Bredon
Tewkesbury
Much Marcle
Dymock
Staunton
Newent
Hartpury
Tibberton
Huntley
Lea
Mitcheldean
Bishops Cleeve
Winchcombe
Stanway
Cleeve Hill
Southam
Guiting Power
Cheltenham
Norton
Staverton
Churchdown
GLOUCESTER
Andoversford
Upper Slaughter
Lower Slaughter
Bourton-on-the-Water
Great Rissington
Stow-on-the-Wold
Minsterworth
Cinderford
Newnham
Longney
Birdlip
Colesbourne
Withington
Northleach
Parkend
Blakeney
Bream
Lydney
St. Briavels
Frampton
Stonehouse
Painswick
Stroud
Winstone
North Cerney
Bisley
Daglingworth
Bibury
Aldsworth
Hatherop
Fairford
Barnsley
Eastington
Sharpness
Berkeley Road
Berkeley
Woodchester
Amberley
Nailsworth
Uley
Cirencester
Poulton
Lechlade
Dursley
Horsley
Avening
Kemble
Ewen
South Cerney
Ashton Keynes
Newport
Stone
Hill
Falfield
North Nibley
Tetbury
Crudwell
Cricklade
Thornbury
Wotton-under-Edge
Leighterton
Westonbirt
Minety
Charlton
Malmesbury
Purton
SWINDON
Aust
Alveston
Wickwar
Rangeworthy
Chipping Sodbury
Great Badminton
Hullavington
Brinkworth
Great Somerford
Wootton Bassett
Wroughton
Redwick
Almondsbury
Easter Compton
Iron Acton
Yate
Old Sodbury
Westerleigh
Avonmouth
Filton
Portishead
BRISTOL
Mangotsfield
Pucklechurch
Kingswood
Tormarton
Marshfield
Castle Combe
Sutton Benger
Lyneham
Hilmarton
Broad Hinton
Chiseldon
Chippenham
Ford
Biddestone
Cold Ashton
Severn Estuary
Severn
Avon

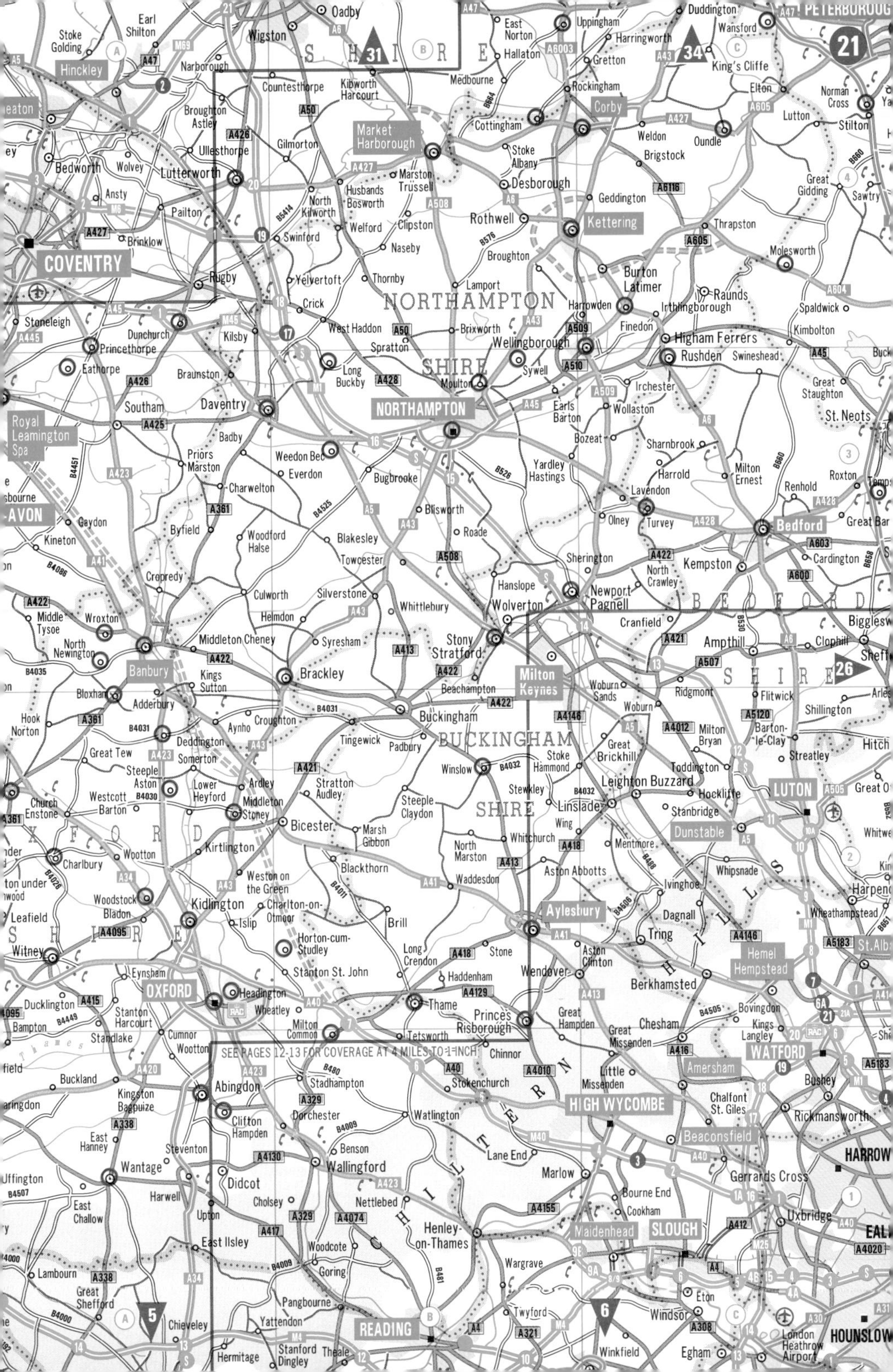

Oadby
Wigston
Earl Shilton
Stoke Golding
Hinckley
Narborough
Countesthorpe
Kibworth Harcourt
31
Medbourne
East Norton
Hallaton
Uppingham
Harringworth
Gretton
Duddington
Wansford
King's Cliffe
34
PETERBOROUGH
21
Rockingham
Corby
Elton
Norman Cross
Yaxley
Cottingham
Weldon
Oundle
Lutton
Stilton
Brigstock
Broughton Astley
Ullesthorpe
Gilmorton
Market Harborough
Stoke Albany
Desborough
Geddington
Great Gidding
Sawtry
Bedworth
Wolvey
Lutterworth
Marston Trussell
Husbands Bosworth
Nuneaton
Ansty
Pailton
North Kilworth
Welford
Clipston
Rothwell
Kettering
Thrapston
COVENTRY
Brinklow
Swinford
Naseby
Broughton
Molesworth
Rugby
Yelvertoft
Thornby
Lamport
Burton Latimer
Raunds
Crick
NORTHAMPTON
Harrowden
Irthlingborough
Spaldwick
Stoneleigh
Dunchurch
Kilsby
West Haddon
Brixworth
Finedon
Kimbolton
Princethorpe
Spratton
Wellingborough
Higham Ferrers
Rushden
Swineshead
Eathorpe
Braunston
Long Buckby
SHIRE
Moulton
Sywell
Great Staughton
Irchester
NORTHAMPTON
Southam
Daventry
Earls Barton
Wollaston
St. Neots
Royal Leamington Spa
Badby
Bozeat
Sharnbrook
Priors Marston
Weedon Bec
Everdon
Bugbrooke
Yardley Hastings
Harrold
Milton Ernest
Renhold
Roxton
Charwelton
Lavendon
Blisworth
Olney
Turvey
Bedford
Great Barford
AVON
Gaydon
Byfield
Woodford Halse
Blakesley
Roade
Kineton
Towcester
Sherington
Kempston
Cardington
Cropredy
North Crawley
Hanslope
Newport Pagnell
Culworth
Silverstone
Wolverton
Middle Tysoe
Wroxton
Helmdon
Whittlebury
Cranfield
BEDFORD
Biggleswade
North Newington
Middleton Cheney
Syresham
Stony Stratford
Ampthill
Clophill
Shefford
Banbury
Kings Sutton
Brackley
Milton Keynes
Woburn Sands
SHIRE
26
Bloxham
Adderbury
Beachampton
Ridgmont
Flitwick
Hook Norton
Aynho
Croughton
Buckingham
Woburn
Milton Bryan
Barton-le-Clay
Shillington
Deddington
Tingewick
Padbury
BUCKINGHAM
Great Brickhill
Hitchin
Great Tew
Somerton
Stoke Hammond
Toddington
Streatley
Steeple Aston
Ardley
Stratton Audley
Winslow
Leighton Buzzard
Hockliffe
LUTON
Great Offley
Westcott Barton
Lower Heyford
Middleton Stoney
Steeple Claydon
Stewkley
Linslade
Stanbridge
Church Enstone
Bicester
Marsh Gibbon
SHIRE
Wing
Dunstable
OXFORD
Wootton
Kirtlington
North Marston
Whitchurch
Mentmore
Whipsnade
Charlbury
Blackthorn
Waddesdon
Aston Abbotts
Ivinghoe
Harpenden
Weston on the Green
Woodstock
Bladon
Kidlington
Charlton-on-Otmoor
Dagnall
Wheathampstead
Leafield
Islip
Brill
Aylesbury
Tring
St. Albans
Witney
Horton-cum-Studley
Long Crendon
Stone
Aston Clinton
Hemel Hempstead
Eynsham
Stanton St. John
Haddenham
Wendover
Berkhamsted
OXFORD
Headington
Thame
Ducklington
Stanton Harcourt
Wheatley
Princes Risborough
Great Hampden
Chesham
Bovingdon
Kings Langley
Bampton
Standlake
Cumnor
Wootton
Milton Common
Tetsworth
Great Missenden
WATFORD
SEE PAGES 12-13 FOR COVERAGE AT 4 MILES TO 1 INCH
Chinnor
Little Missenden
Amersham
Bushey
Buckland
Abingdon
Stadhampton
Stokenchurch
Kingston Bagpuize
HIGH WYCOMBE
Chalfont St. Giles
Rickmansworth
Clifton Hampden
Dorchester
Watlington
Beaconsfield
East Hanney
Benson
Steventon
Lane End
HARROW
Wantage
Didcot
Wallingford
Marlow
Gerrards Cross
Uffington
Harwell
Cholsey
Nettlebed
Bourne End
Cookham
East Challow
Upton
Henley-on-Thames
Uxbridge
Maidenhead
SLOUGH
East Ilsley
Woodcote
Wargrave
Lambourn
Goring
Eton
Great Shefford
Pangbourne
Twyford
Windsor
Chieveley
Yattendon
READING
London Heathrow Airport
HOUNSLOW
Hermitage
Stanford Dingley
Theale
Winkfield
Egham
CHILTERN HILLS

22
Stafford
30
STAFFORDSHIRE
Lawnhead
Seighford
Ranton
Coton Clanford
Ranton Green
Knightly Dale
Oulton
Long Compton
Derrington
Shut Heath
Haughton
Gnosall
Gnosall Heath
Doxey
Ingeste
Tixall
Hixon
Newton
Blithfield Resr
Great Haywood
Little Haywood
Admaston
Abbots Bromley
Newborough
Hoar Cross
Weeping Cross
Walton-on-the-Hill
Milford
Colwich
Colton
Hamstall Ridware
Hill Ridware
Hadley End
Morrey
Coppenhall
Allimore Green
Bradley
Church Eaton
Dunston
Acton Trussell
Bednall
Brocton
Echinghill
Slittingmill
Rugeley
Mavesyn Ridware
Pipe Ridgeware
Bromstead Heath
High Onn
Levedale
Orslow
Great Chatwell
Mitton
Flaxley Green
Brereton
Armitage
Handsacre
Kings Bromley
Upper Longdon
Longdon
Rileyhill
Marston
Brineton
Wheaton Aston
Blymhill
Whiston
Penkridge
Huntington
Green Heath
Hazelslade
Cannock Wood
Longdon Green
Lapley
Stretton
Belvide Resr
Weston-under-Lizard
Gailey
High Town
Hednesford
Littleworth
Gentleshaw
Farewell
Curborough
Elmhurst
Bishop's Wood
Horesbrook
Kiddemore Green
Hatherton
Heath Hayes
Chorley
Chase Terrace
Stowe
Tong Norton
Tong
Brewood
Somerford
Four Crosses
Cannock
Norton Canes
Norton East
Lichfield
Burntwood
Chasetown
Hammerwich
Chasewater
Standeford
Bridgetown
Cheslyn Hay
Little Saredon
Shackerley
Park Lane
Coven
Great Wyrley
Landywood
Little Wyrley
Wall
Muckley Corner
Chesterfield
Shareshill
Featherstone
Cross Green
Codsall Wood
Codsall
Gunstone
Bilbrook
Brownhills
Shenstone
Albrighton
Essington
Pelsall
Clayhanger
Shire Oak
Walsall Wood
Stonnall
Little Hay
Boningale
Oaken
Lane Green
Oxley
Bushbury
Old Falling
Ashmore Park
Bloxwich
Shelfield
Footherley
Patshull Park
Wergs
Palmers Cross
Heath Town
Aldridge
Rushall
Shenstone Woodend
Tettenhall
Wednesfield
Coal Pool
Little Aston
WOLVERHAMPTON
WILLENHALL
WALSALL
WEST MIDLANDS
Four Oaks
Mere Green
Pattingham
Perton
Blakenhall
BILSTON
Darlaston
Streetly
Trescott
Shipley
Lower Penn
Orton
Great Barr
Wednesbury
Wylde Green
Seisdon
Coseley
Sedgley
Kingstanding
Trysull
Claverley
Wombourne
Hamstead
Short Heath
Heathton
Tipton
WEST BROMWICH
Handsworth
Perry Barr
Erdington
Halfpenny Green
Swindon
Himley
Gravelly Hill
Bobbington
The Village
DUDLEY
Winson Green
Aston
Six Ashes
Pensnett
Kingswinford
BRIERLEY HILL
Oldbury
SMETHWICK
Brockmoor
Rowley Regis
Enville
Wordsley
Bearwood
Coxgreen
Quarry Bank
Kitt's Green
BIRMINGHAM
Compton
Stourton
Amblecote
Silver End
Blackheath
Chad Valley
Yardley
Reddiffe
Potter's Cross
Cradley
Lye
Wollescote
Harborne
Acock's Green
Stourbridge
Kinver
Halesowen
Edgbaston
Moseley
Pedmore
Whittington
Illey
Woodgate
Selly Oak
Springfield
Olton
Kingsford
Blakeshall
Caunsall
Hagley
Hunnington
Bournville
Hall Green
Clent
Romsley
Frankley
King's Heath
Wolverley
Cookley
Trimpley
Franche
Churchill
Blakedown
Broome
Holy Cross
Dayhouse Bank
Longbridge
Northfield
King's Norton
Yardley Wood
Shirley
Bell End
Rubery
Major's Green
Kidderminster
Blakebrook
Belbroughton
Wildmoor
Hollywood
Drakes Cross
Whitlock's End
Wribbenhall
Stone
Mustow Green
Drayton
Broom Hill
Fairfield
Lickey
Crofton Hackett
Hopwood
Lea End
Wythall
Tidbury Green
Ribbesford
Shenstone
Bluntingdon
Catshill
Barnet Green
Eastwood
HEREFORD AND WORCESTER
20
RAC
M6
M5
M54
A5
A34
A38(M)
A449
A454
A513
A518
A51
A515
A5190
A461
A4124
A5127
A452
A41
A4031
A4041
A453
A463
A459
A457
A4101
A491
A458
A451
A442
A456
A441
A435
A47
B5405
B5013
B5234
B5014
B5012
B4161
B4176
B4151
B4124
B4128
B4188
B4551
B4096
B4102
Trent
Blithe
Church Eaton Brook
Shropshire Union Canal
Penk
Staffs and Worcs
Stour

Anslow
Horninglow
A5121
Burton-upon-Trent
Newton Solney
Melbourne
Sutton Bonington
Anslow Gate
30
25
Ticknall
A514
Wilson
Isley Walton
Diseworth
23
Rangemore
Winshill
Bretby
Staunton Harold Resr
Breedon on the Hill
Tonge
B5401
Long Whatton
Foremark Resr
A50
Tatenhill
Stapenhill
Hartshorne
Clake
A453
Hathern
Dunstall
Newhall
B5006
Staunton Harold Hall
Worthington
Belton
A6
Branston
Swadlincote
B5324
Thorpe Acre
A444
Smisby
Lount
Newbold
A447
Shepshed
Stanton
Woodville
Osgathorpe
Walton-on-Trent
Church Gresley
Castle Gresley
Ashby-de-la-Zouch
Coleorton
A512
Blackbrook Resr
Church Town
Caldwell
Blackfordby
Trent and Mersey
Rosliston
High Cross Bank
Norris Hill
Thringstone
Nanpantan
Linton
Swannington
Whitwick
Wychnor Bridge
Overseal
Moira
M1
B5350
A38
A50
Cotton in the Elms
B586
A453
B587
Snibstone
Short Heath
Donisthorpe
Packington
25
Coalville
Croxall
Oakthorpe
B5326
Ravenstone
Netherseal
Bardon
Copt Oak
Edingale
Lullington
Tame
Mease
Measham
Normanton le Heath
Donnington le Heath
Stretton en le Field
A447
Chilcote
B5002
B586
22
Haunton
B591
Ellistown
Newton Linford
Elford
Clifton Campville
Appleby Magna
Ibstock
Stanton under Bardon
Harlaston
Swepstone
Heather
Markfield
11
Field Head
No Man's Heath
Snarestone
Newton Burgoland
B585
Thorpe Constantine
A50
Whittington
Appleby Parva
Thornton
A513
A453
Bagworth
Hadmore
Seckington
Ashby
Odstone
Norton-Juxta-Twycross
Thornton Resr
Newton Regis
A444
Barton in the Beans
Nailstone
Comberford
Wigginton
Austrey
Shackerstone
Ratby
Barlestone
Shuttington
Congerstone
Bilstone
Botcheston
Hopwas
Perry Croft
Alvecote
M42
Coton
Anker
Twycross
Carlton
Osbaston
Market Bosworth
Amington
Warton
Orton-on-the-Hill
Tamworth
Newton Unthank
B5380
Glascote
Sence
Newbold Verdon
Desford
Bonehill
Kettlebrook
Polesworth
Wellsborough
Cadeby
Wilnecote
Sheepy Magna
Peckleton
Fazeley
Sheepy Parva
Dordon
B5000
Sibson
Kirkby Mallory
Drayton Bassett
Two Gates
Hackley
10
Grendon
Sutton Cheney
Thurlaston
A47
Dosthill
Coventry
Shenton
Ratcliffe Culey
Upton
Grendon Common
Whateley
A4091
Stapleton
Atherstone
Stoke Golding
M69
Wood End
A51
Baddesley Ensor
Witherley
A444
Barwell
Earl Shilton
Hunts Green
Dadlington
Allen End
A5
Kingsbury
Baxterley
Fenny Drayton
Elmesthorpe
Bodymoor Heath
Mancetter
Bentley
Higham on the Hill
A446
Marston
Hurley
Stoney Stanton
Wishaw
M42
A4097
Oldbury
A444
Ridge Lane
B4116
Hinckley
B4098
Hartshill
2
B4069
B581
Lea Marston
Caldecote
Weddington
Sapcote
Nether Whitacre
Church End
Galley Common
Whitacre Heath
B4114
Sketchley
Burbage
Cudworth
Whittleford
Aston Flamville
Tame
Over Whitacre
Ansley
Stockingford
Attleborough
Sharnford
Water Orton
B4112
Burton Hastings
Frolesworth
Smockington
8
Shustoke
Arley
Nuneaton
Shelford
4A
B4098
B4114
Wolvey Heath
Wibtoft
Claybrook Magna
Coleshill
Astley
Bramcote
M6
WARWICKSHIRE
Bedworth
Wolvey
B4455
M69
Ullesthorpe
Tile Cross
Maxstoke
Fillongley
7A
B4113
Coventry
Bulkington
7
Goodyers End
B4112
Marston Green
M6
Corley Ash
Blythe
Willey
Capel Green
Corley
Neal's Green
3
Shilton
Withybrook
Little Packington
Corley Moor
Longford
Barnacle
National Exhibition Centre
A45
Hawkes End
Keresley
Little Heath
Ansty
B4029
Monks Kirby
21
Bickenhill
6
Allesley
Foleshill
M6
Meriden
B4102
Rodforth
Great Heath
Pailton
Pickford
Churchover
Elmdon Heath
A452
Four Oaks
Eastern Green
Walsgrave on Sowe
Oxford
Stretton under Fosse
Hampton in Arden
Easenhall
COVENTRY
Berkswell
Eastcote
Whoberley
B4106
Brinklow
Harborough Magna
Copt Heath
Carol Green
B4029
Barston
Balsall Common
Tile Hill
Earlsdon
Binley
Binley Woods
Newbold on Avon
Knowle
Bretford
Canley
Sowe
Church Lawford
Long Lawford
Brandon
A428
B4102
Pinley
A41
20
Stivichall
Willenhall
21
Fen End
A429
Ryton-on-Dunsmore
Wolston
Burton Green
Coventry Airport
Dorridge
Meer End
Crackley
Baginton
A45
B4029
Rugby
A4071
Bilton

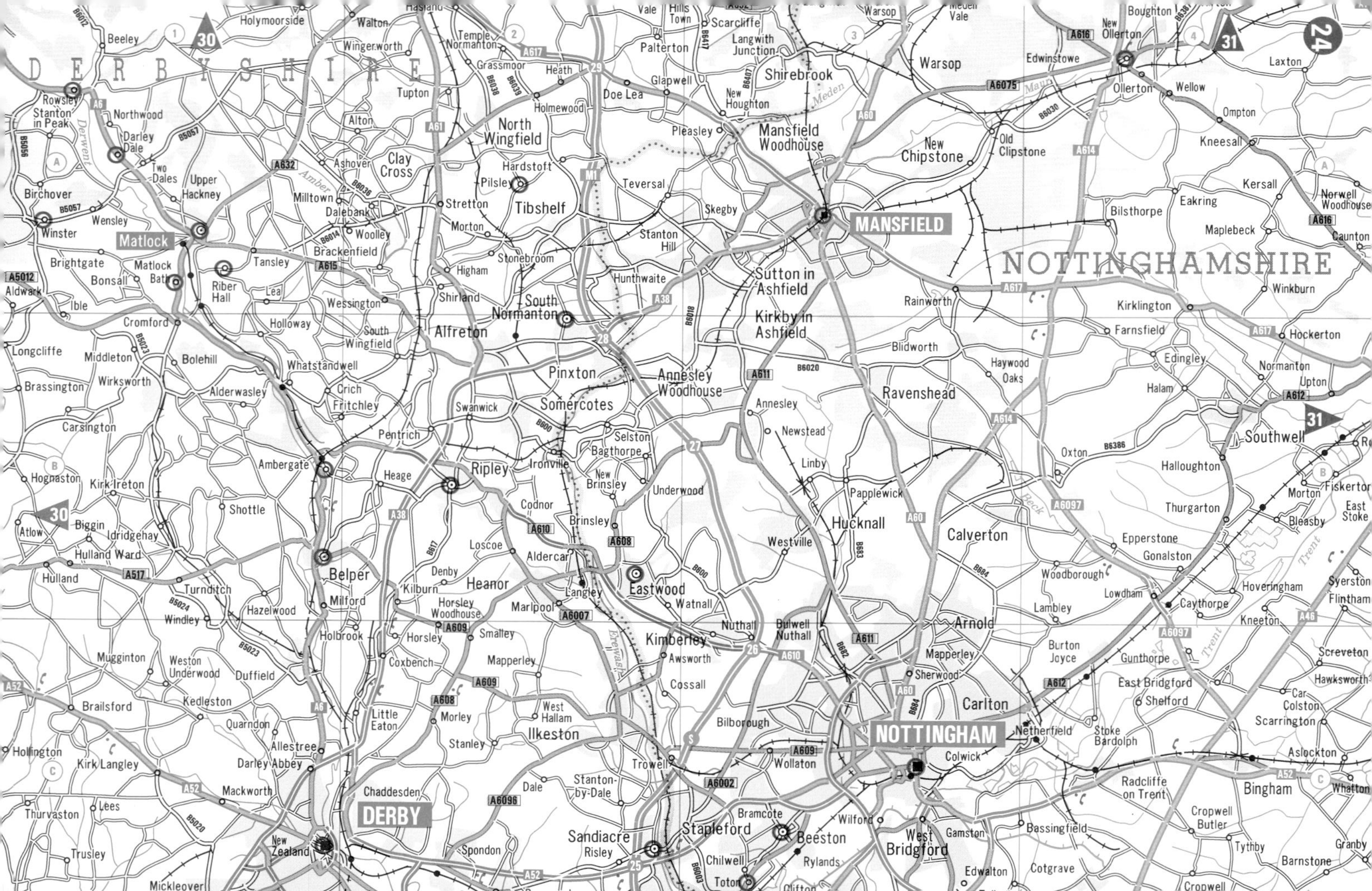

24
DERBYSHIRE
NOTTINGHAMSHIRE
MANSFIELD
NOTTINGHAM
DERBY
Matlock
Holymoorside
Walton
Beeley
Wingerworth
Temple Normanton
Grassmoor
Heath
Vale
Hills Town
Palterton
Scarcliffe
Langwith Junction
Warsop
Meden Vale
Boughton
New Ollerton
Laxton
Rowsley
Stanton in Peak
Northwood
Darley Dale
Two Dales
Tupton
North Wingfield
Holmewood
Doe Lea
Glapwell
Shirebrook
New Houghton
Edwinstowe
Ollerton
Wellow
Ompton
Kneesall
Alton
Clay Cross
Ashover
Hardstoft
Pilsley
Tibshelf
Teversal
Pleasley
Mansfield Woodhouse
New Chipstone
Old Clipstone
Kersall
Norwell Woodhouse
Eakring
Bilsthorpe
Maplebeck
Caunton
Birchover
Upper Hackney
Milltown
Dalebank
Woolley
Stretton
Morton
Skegby
Stanton Hill
Winster
Wensley
Brightgate
Matlock Bath
Bonsall
Tansley
Riber Hall
Brackenfield
Stonebroom
Higham
Shirland
Hunthwaite
Sutton in Ashfield
Winkburn
Aldwark
Ible
Lea
Wessington
South Normanton
Alfreton
Kirkby in Ashfield
Rainworth
Kirklington
Farnsfield
Hockerton
Cromford
Holloway
South Wingfield
Longcliffe
Middleton
Bolehill
Whatstandwell
Pinxton
Annesley Woodhouse
Bildworth
Haywood Oaks
Edingley
Normanton
Upton
Brassington
Wirksworth
Alderwasley
Crich
Fritchley
Somercotes
Annesley
Ravenshead
Halam
Carsington
Swanwick
Pentrich
Selston
Bagthorpe
Newstead
Southwell
Hognaston
Kirk Ireton
Ambergate
Heage
Ripley
Ironville
New Brinsley
Underwood
Linby
Papplewick
Oxton
Halloughton
Fiskerton
Morton
East Stoke
Atlow
Biggin
Idridgehay
Shottle
Codnor
Brinsley
Hucknall
Calverton
Thurgarton
Bleasby
Hulland Ward
Hulland
Belper
Loscoe
Aldercar
Eastwood
Westville
Epperstone
Gonalston
Denby
Heanor
Langley
Woodborough
Lowdham
Caythorpe
Hoveringham
Syerston
Flintham
Turnditch
Milford
Kilburn
Horsley Woodhouse
Marlpool
Watnall
Nuthall
Bulwell
Lambley
Kneeton
Windley
Hazelwood
Holbrook
Horsley
Smalley
Kimberley
Awsworth
Arnold
Burton Joyce
Gunthorpe
Screveton
Mugginton
Weston Underwood
Duffield
Coxbench
Mapperley
Cossall
Sherwood
East Bridgford
Hawksworth
Brailsford
Kedleston
Little Eaton
Morley
West Hallam
Ilkeston
Bilborough
Carlton
Shelford
Car Colston
Scarrington
Quarndon
Allestree
Stanley
Trowell
Wollaton
Netherfield
Stoke Bardolph
Aslockton
Hollington
Kirk Langley
Darley Abbey
Chaddesden
Stanton-by-Dale
Colwick
Radcliffe on Trent
Bingham
Whatton
Mackworth
Dale
Bramcote
Wilford
Cropwell Butler
Thurvaston
Lees
New Zealand
Spondon
Sandiacre
Risley
Stapleford
Beeston
West Bridgford
Gamston
Bassingfield
Tythby
Granby
Trusley
Chilwell
Rylands
Edwalton
Cotgrave
Barnstone
Mickleover
Toton
Clifton
Cropwell
Derwent
Amber
Meden
Maun
Erewash
Trent
Beck
M1
A6
A38
A52
A60
A61
A614
A616
A617
A632
A6075
A5012
A615
A517
A609
A608
A610
A6007
A611
A612
A6097
A6096
A6002
A46
B5056
B5057
B5023
B5024
B5020
B6012
B6014
B6036
B6038
B6039
B6417
B6407
B6030
B6018
B6020
B600
B617
B6386
B684
B683
B682
B6003

25
31
23
21
Melton Mowbray
Asfordby
Loughborough
Quorndon
Mountsorrel
Sileby
Syston
Birstall
Anstey
Glenfield
Braunstone
LEICESTER
Thurmaston
Thurnby
Oadby
Wigston
Earl Shilton
Keyworth
Castle Donington
Shepshed
Whitwick
Coalville
Ibstock
Ashby-de-la-Zouch
Swadlincote
Burton-upon-Trent
Atherstone
Market Bosworth
Kegworth
Melbourne
Hathern
Rothley
Groby
Markfield
Barwell
Measham
Kirby Muxloe
Enderby
Narborough
Blaby
Cropston Resr
Swithland Resr
Blackbrook Resr
Thornton Resr
Staunton Harold Resr
Foremark Resr
Soar
Trent
Trent and Mersey
Coventry

26
34
PETERBOROUGH
NORTHAMPTON
SHIRE
CAMBRIDGESHIRE
BEDFORD
SHIRE
HERTFORD
SHIRE
ESSEX
BUCKINGHAM
SHIRE
CHILTERN
HILLS
Kettering
Corby
Wellingborough
Huntingdon
Cambridge
Bedford
Milton Keynes
LUTON
Dunstable
Stevenage
Hertford
Harlow
Hemel Hempstead
St. Albans
Hatfield
WATFORD
Aylesbury
Amersham
HIGH WYCOMBE
Beaconsfield
Maidenhead
SLOUGH
Bishop's Stortford
March
Ely
LONDON
HARROW
BARNET
EALING
BARKING
BEXLEY
SEE PAGES 12-13 FOR COVERAGE AT 4 MILES TO 1 INCH
21
6

NORFOLK
35
27
Hillborough
Ashill
Watton
Caston
Hingham
Wymondham
Swardeston
Caister St. Edmunds
Brooke
Newton Flotman
Ashwellthorpe
Reedham
Belton
Gorleston on Sea
Hopton on Sea
Loddon
Hales
Haddiscoe
Corton
Oulton Broad
Lowestoft
Beccles
Carlton Colville
Kessingland
Mundford
Attleborough
Bunwell
Hempnall
Long Stratton
Denton
Bungay
East Wretham
Brandon
Thetford
East Harling
New Buckenham
Kenninghall
Pulham
Harleston
Diss
Dickleburgh
Metfield
Rumburgh
Wrentham
Frostenden
Wangford
Southwold
Walberswick
Elveden
Barnham
Garboldisham
Redgrave
Scole
Hoxne
Waveney
Fressingfield
Halesworth
Blythburgh
Bramfield
Icklingham
Tuddenham
Stanton
Barningham
Brome
Eye
Botesdale
Gislingham
Stradbroke
Laxfield
Heveningham
Ixworth
Ingham
Culford
Cavenham
Walsham le Willows
Finningham
Thorndon
Peasenhall
Yoxford
Dunwich
Westleton
Bury St. Edmunds
Mendlesham
Elmswell
SUFFOLK
Barrow
Beyton
Rattlesden
Stowmarket
Debenham
Earl Soham
Framlingham
Leiston
Saxmundham
Earl Stonham
Wickham Market
Otley
Needham Market
Coddenham
Aldeburgh
Tunstall
Lidgate
Hartest
Cockfield
Claydon
Grundisburgh
Ufford
Hitcham
Bildeston
Tuddenham
Offton
Woodbridge
Butley
Orford
Orford Ness
Glemsford
Lavenham
IPSWICH
Martlesham
Hundon
Long Melford
Cavendish
Bramford
Hintlesham
Hollesley
Ridgewell
Sudbury
Boxford
Hadleigh
Nacton
Kirton
Bawdsey
Assington
Stoke by Nayland
Holbrook
Sible Hedingham
East Bergholt
Shotley Gate
Felixstowe
Nayland
Dedham
Manningtree
Harwich
Bures
Stratford St.Mary
Halstead
Ramsey
Earls Colne
Wakes Colne
Mile End
Ardleigh
Wix
Great Oakley
Bocking Churchstreet
Colchester
Weeley
Thorpe-le-Soken
The Naze
Coggeshall
Marks Tey
Kelvedon
Wivenhoe
Thorrington
Walton-on-the-Naze
Frinton-on-Sea
White Notley
Layer de la Haye
Terling
Witham
Brightlingsea
Tiptree
St. Osyth
Holland-on-Sea
Clacton-on-Sea
Tolleshunt D'Arcy
Salcott
West Mersea
Hatfield Peverel
Goldhanger
Tollesbury
Mersea I.
Chelmsford
Maldon
Bradwell-on-Sea
Danbury
Tillingham
Cold Norton
Rettendon
Burnham-on-Crouch
Canewdon
Battlesbridge
Hockley
Southend
Rayleigh
Rochford
Foulness I.
Hadleigh
South Benfleet
Shoeburyness
SOUTHEND-ON-SEA
Fobbing
Canvey Island
Thames
Estuary
Allhallows
Grain
Cliffe
Stoke
Sheerness
Minster
Isle of Sheppey
7
SEE PAGES 16-17 FOR COVERAGE AT 4 MILES TO 1 INCH
To Oslo and Esbjerg
To Gothenburg and Kristiansand
To Hamburg
To Hook of Holland
To Zeebrugge
To Vlissingen
A11
A140
A146
A143
A144
A145
A12
A1075
A1066
A1065
A1088
A134
A1101
A1120
A45
A1049
A143
A152
A1141
A1092
A1071
A137
A120
A133
A604
A131
A414
A130
A127
A13
A228
RAC

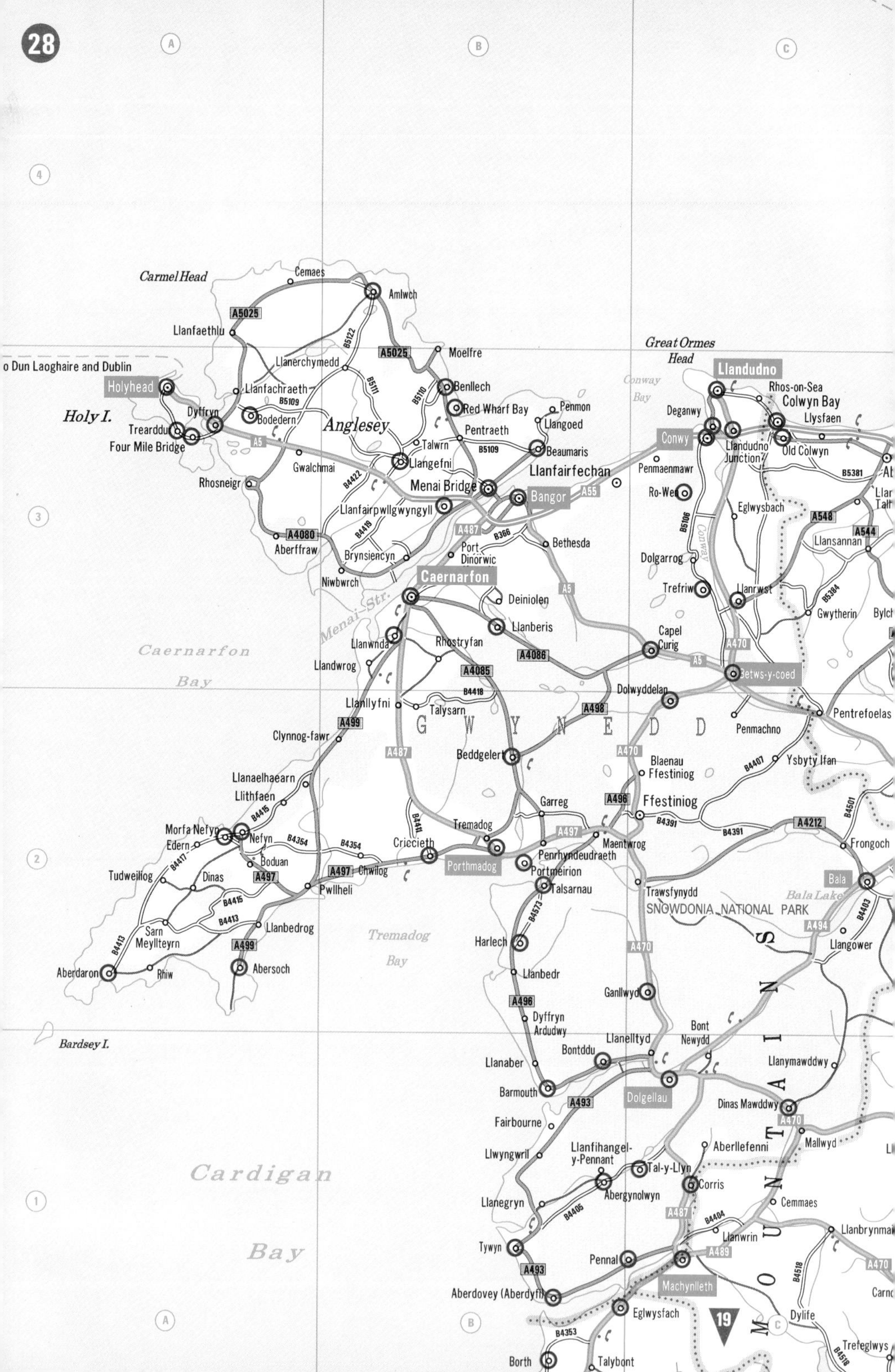
A
B
C
4
3
2
1
Carmel Head
Cemaes
Amlwch
A5025
Llanfaethlu
B5122
A5025
Moelfre
o Dun Laoghaire and Dublin
Llanerchymedd
B5111
Holyhead
Llanfachraeth
B5110
Benllech
B5109
Holy I.
Dyffryn
Bodedern
Anglesey
Red Wharf Bay
Penmon
Trearddur
Llangoed
Four Mile Bridge
Pentraeth
A5
Talwrn
B5109
Beaumaris
Llangefni
Gwalchmai
Llanfairfechan
Rhosneigr
B4422
Menai Bridge
Bangor
A55
Llanfairpwllgwyngyll
A4080
B4419
A487
B366
Bethesda
Aberffraw
Brynsiencyn
Port Dinorwic
Niwbwrch
Caernarfon
Deiniolen
Menai Str.
A5
Llanberis
Llanwnda
Caernarfon Bay
Rhostryfan
A4086
Llandwrog
A4085
B4418
Llanllyfni
Talysarn
A499
G W Y N E D D
Clynnog-fawr
A487
Beddgelert
A498
Llanaelhaearn
Llithfaen
Morfa Nefyn
Nefyn
B4415
B4354
B4354
B4411
Tremadog
Edern
Boduan
Criccieth
Porthmadog
B4417
Chwilog
A497
Tudweiliog
Dinas
A497
Pwllheli
B4415
B4413
Sarn Meyllteyrn
Llanbedrog
A499
B4413
Aberdaron
Rhiw
Abersoch
Bardsey I.
Tremadog Bay
Great Ormes Head
Llandudno
Conwy Bay
Rhos-on-Sea
Colwyn Bay
Deganwy
Llysfaen
Conwy
Llandudno Junction
Old Colwyn
Penmaenmawr
B5381
Ro-Wen
Eglwysbach
B5106
Conwy
A548
A544
Llansannan
Dolgarrog
Trefriw
Llanrwst
B5384
Gwytherin
Capel Curig
A470
A5
Betws-y-coed
Dolwyddelan
Pentrefoelas
Penmachno
A470
Blaenau Ffestiniog
B4407
Ysbyty Ifan
Garreg
A496
Ffestiniog
B4391
B4391
A4212
B4501
A497
Maentwrog
Frongoch
Penrhyndeudraeth
Portmeirion
Talsarnau
Trawsfynydd
Bala
Bala Lake
SNOWDONIA NATIONAL PARK
B4573
B4403
A494
Harlech
Llangower
Llanbedr
A470
A496
Ganllwyd
Dyffryn Ardudwy
Bont Newydd
Llanelltyd
Bontddu
Llanaber
Llanymawddwy
Barmouth
Dolgellau
A493
Dinas Mawddwy
Fairbourne
A470
Mallwyd
Llanfihangel-y-Pennant
Aberllefenni
Llwyngwril
Tal-y-Llyn
Corris
Abergynolwyn
Cemmaes
Llanegryn
B4405
A487
B4404
Llanwrin
Llanbrynmair
Tywyn
Pennal
A489
A470
A493
B4518
Machynlleth
Aberdovey (Aberdyfi)
Eglwysfach
Dylife
19
B4353
B4518
Trefeglwys
Borth
Talybont
Cardigan Bay
M O U N T A I N S

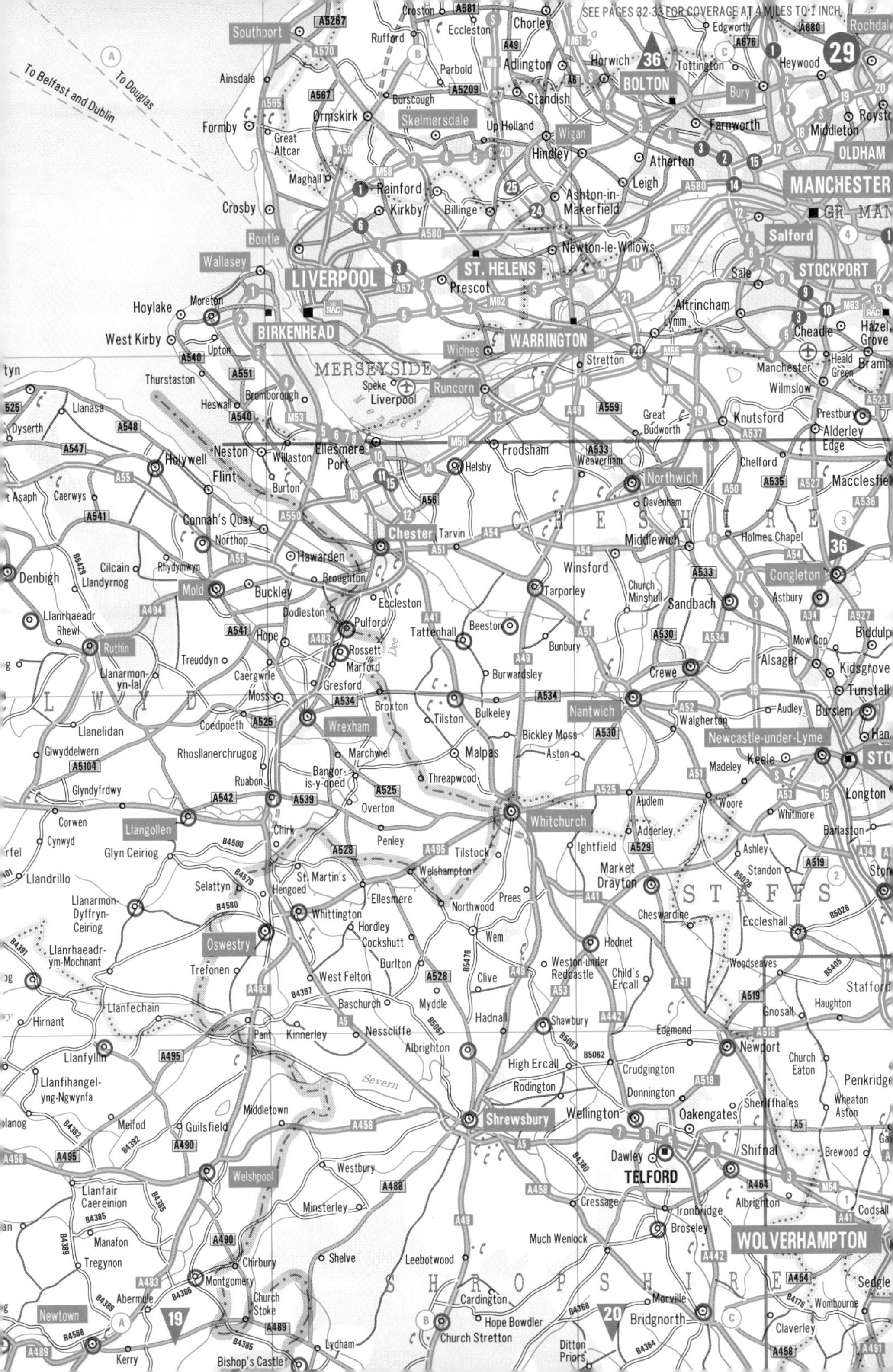

SEE PAGES 32-33 FOR COVERAGE AT 4 MILES TO 1 INCH
29
To Belfast and Dublin
To Douglas
Southport
Croston
Rufford
Eccleston
Chorley
Edgworth
Rochdale
Heywood
Ainsdale
Parbold
Adlington
Horwich
36
BOLTON
Tottington
Bury
Burscough
Standish
Formby
Ormskirk
Skelmersdale
Up Holland
Wigan
Farnworth
Middleton
Royton
Great Altcar
Hindley
Atherton
OLDHAM
Maghall
Rainford
Ashton-in-Makerfield
Leigh
MANCHESTER
Crosby
Kirkby
Billinge
GR MAN
Bootle
Salford
Newton-le-Willows
Wallasey
LIVERPOOL
ST. HELENS
Sale
STOCKPORT
Prescot
Altrincham
Hoylake
Moreton
Lymm
Hazel Grove
BIRKENHEAD
WARRINGTON
Cheadle
West Kirby
Upton
Widnes
Stretton
Manchester
Heald Green
Bramhall
MERSEYSIDE
Speke
Liverpool
Runcorn
Wilmslow
Thurstaston
Bromborough
Mersey
Heswall
Great Budworth
Knutsford
Prestbury
Llanasa
Alderley Edge
Dyserth
Neston
Willaston
Ellesmere Port
Frodsham
Weaverham
Holywell
Flint
Helsby
Chelford
Macclesfield
St Asaph
Caerwys
Burton
Northwich
Davenham
Connah's Quay
Chester
Tarvin
CHESHIRE
Northop
Hawarden
Middlewich
Holmes Chapel
36
Cilcain
Rhydymwyn
Winsford
Congleton
Denbigh
Llandyrnog
Broughton
Mold
Buckley
Tarporley
Church Minshull
Sandbach
Astbury
Llanrhaeadr
Eccleston
Biddulph
Rhewl
Dodleston
Pulford
Beeston
Hope
Tattenhall
Mow Cop
Ruthin
Rossett
Bunbury
Alsager
Treuddyn
Marford
Dee
Kidsgrove
Llanarmon-yn-Ial
Caergwrle
Burwardsley
Crewe
Tunstall
Gresford
Moss
Broxton
Bulkeley
Nantwich
Audley
Burslem
CLWYD
Coedpoeth
Tilston
Walgherton
Wrexham
Llanelidan
Bickley Moss
Newcastle-under-Lyme
Glwyddelwern
Marchwiel
Malpas
Aston
Keele
Rhosllanerchrugog
Madeley
Bangor-is-y-coed
Ruabon
Threapwood
Glyndyfrdwy
Overton
Audlem
Longton
Corwen
Whitchurch
Woore
Whitmore
Cynwyd
Llangollen
Chirk
Penley
Adderley
Barlaston
Glyn Ceiriog
Tilstock
Ightfield
Ashley
Llandrillo
Selattyn
St. Martin's
Welshampton
Market Drayton
Standon
Hengoed
Ellesmere
Prees
STAFFS
Llanarmon-Dyffryn-Ceiriog
Northwood
Cheswardine
Eccleshall
Whittington
Hordley
Wem
Oswestry
Cockshutt
Hodnet
Llanrhaeadr-ym-Mochnant
Burlton
Weston-under Redcastle
Woodseaves
Trefonen
Clive
Child's Ercall
Stafford
West Felton
Myddle
Gnosall
Haughton
Baschurch
Llanfechain
Hirnant
Hadnall
Shawbury
Pant
Kinnerley
Nesscliffe
Edgmond
Llanfyllin
Albrighton
Newport
Church Eaton
High Ercall
Llanfihangel-yng-Ngwynfa
Crudgington
Penkridge
Severn
Rodington
Donnington
Middletown
Sheriffhales
Wheaton Aston
Meifod
Guilsfield
Wellington
Oakengates
Shrewsbury
Dawley
Shifnal
Brewood
Welshpool
TELFORD
Westbury
Llanfair Caereinion
Cressage
Albrighton
Codsall
Minsterley
Ironbridge
Manafon
Broseley
WOLVERHAMPTON
Much Wenlock
Tregynon
Shelve
Leebotwood
Chirbury
Montgomery
SHROPSHIRE
Sedgley
Abermule
Church Stoke
Cardington
Morville
Wombourne
19
20
Newtown
Hope Bowdler
Bridgnorth
Claverley
Church Stretton
Ditton Priors
Kerry
Lydham
Bishop's Castle

30
36
38
29
20
Croston
Eccleston
Chorley
Edgworth
Whitworth
Littleborough
HUDDERSFIELD
Horbury
Golcar
Slaithwaite
Parbold
Adlington
Horwich
Tottington
Rochdale
Heywood
Denshaw
Meltham
Kirkburton
Denby Dale
Darton
Burscough
Standish
BOLTON
Bury
Shaw
Royston
Marsden
Holmfirth
Skelmersdale
Up Holland
Wigan
Farnworth
Middleton
OLDHAM
Dodworth
Hindley
Atherton
GR MAN
Lees
Mossley
Penistone
Dunford Bridge
Langsett
Rainford
Billinge
Ashton-in-Makerfield
Leigh
MANCHESTER
Ashton-under-Lyne
Stocksbridge
Salford
Hyde
Hollingworth
Glossop
High Bradfield
Newton-le-Willows
ST. HELENS
Prescot
Sale
Altrincham
STOCKPORT
Marple
PEAK DISTRICT
SHEFFIE
WARRINGTON
Widnes
Lymm
Cheadle
Hazel Grove
New Mills
Hayfield
Edale
Hope
Bamford
Stretton
Manchester
Heald Green
Bramhall
Chapel-en-le-Frith
Runcorn
Speke
Mersey
Wilmslow
Bollington
Whaley Bridge
Peak Forest
NATIONAL PARK
Bradwell
Hathersage
Great Budworth
Knutsford
Prestbury
Alderley Edge
Dove Holes
Eyam
Grindleford Bridge
Frodsham
Helsby
Weaverham
Northwich
Chelford
Macclesfield
Buxton
Tideswell
DERBY
Davenham
Taddington
Hassop
Baslow
Edensor
Tarvin
CHESHIRE
Middlewich
Holmes Chapel
Flash
Bakewell
Rowsley
SEE PAG
Winsford
Youlgreave
Tarporley
Church Minshull
Sandbach
Congleton
Bosley Wincle
Longnor
Astbury
Winster
Matlock Bath
Tattenhall
Beeston
Bunbury
Mow Cop
Biddulph
Leek
Hartington
Parwich
Brassington
Burwardsley
Crewe
Alsager
Kidsgrove
Wirksworth
Tunstall
Wetton
Dovedale
Tissington
Nantwich
Audley
Burslem
Ipstones
Kniveton
Bulkeley
Walgherton
Cellarhead
Kirk Ire
Bickley Moss
Newcastle-under-Lyme
Hanley
Ashbourne
Malpas
Aston
Keele
STOKE-ON-TRENT
Kingsley
Mayfield
Madeley
Alton
Threapwood
Longton
Cheadle
Upper Tean
Ellastone
Weston Underwood
Whitchurch
Audlem
Woore
Whitmore
Barlaston
Rocester
Alkmonton
Adderley
Kirk Langley
Tilstock
Ightfield
Ashley
Hilderstone
Longford
Welshampton
Standon
Stone
Uttoxeter
Doveridge
DER
Market Drayton
Sudbury
Prees
Northwood
Cheswardine
Draycott in the Clay
Etwall
Cockshutt
Wem
Eccleshall
STAFFORD
Tutbury
Burlton
Hodnet
Woodseaves
SEE PAGES 22-23 FOR COVERAGE AT 4 MILES TO 1 INCH
Burton-upo
Weston-under Redcastle
Child's Ercall
Abbots Bromley
Myddle
Clive
Stafford
Haughton
Hadnall
Gnosall
Swadlincote
Shawbury
Albrighton
Edgmond
Newport
SHIRE
Rugeley
Yoxall
Walton-on-Trent
High Ercall
Crudgington
Church Eaton
Rodington
Penkridge
Armitage
Kings Bromley
Overseal
Donnington
Alrewas
Wheaton Aston
Sheriffhales
Shrewsbury
Wellington
Oakengates
Cannock
Gailey
Lichfield
Whittington
Dawley
Shifnal
Brewood
TELFORD
Brownhills
Tamworth
Cressage
Ironbridge
Albrighton
Codsall
Aldridge
Fazeley
Polesworth
Broseley
Much Wenlock
WOLVERHAMPTON
WALSALL
SUTTON COLDFIELD
Kingsbury
eebotwood
HROPSHIRE
Sedgley
WEST BROMWICH
Atherstone
Cardington
Morville
Wombourne
Church Stretton
Hope Bowdler
Bridgnorth
Claverley
DUDLEY
Coleshill

38
39
31
34
20
21
26
Wentbridge
Ackworth
Barnsdale Bar
Askern
Sykehouse
Fishlake
Thorne
Eastoft
Crowle
Amcotts
Flixborough
Appleby
Winterton
Scunthorpe
Ulceby
Elsham
Worlaby
Immingham
Grimsby
Croxton
Keelby
Great Coates
Laceby
Humberside
Great Limber
Brigg
Bigby
Grasby
Waltham
Swallow
Cabourne
Caistor
Hemsworth
South Kirkby
Stainforth
Hatfield
Adwick le Street
Bentley
Dearne
Darfield
Mexborough
Doncaster
Armthorpe
Wroot
Belton
Epworth
Haxey
Messingham
Scawby
Hibaldstow
North Kelsey
South Kelsey
Thoresway
Binbrook
Wold Newton
Conisbrough
Rossington
Finningley
Owston Ferry
Scotter
Kirton in Lindsey
Waddingham
Wadworth
Braithwell
Bawtry
Misson
Misterton
Gringley on the Hill
Stockwith
Walkeringham
Blyton
Corringham
Glentham
Claxby
Tealby
Rotherham
Maltby
Tickhill
Ranskill
Beckingham
Gainsborough
West Rasen
Ludford
Market Rasen
Dinnington
Todwick
Carlton in Lindrick
Blyth
Sutton
Clayworth
Barnby Moor
Willingham by Stow
Spridlington
Faldingworth
Snelland
Barkwith
Killamarsh
Anston
Hayton
North Leverton
Marton
Sturton by Stow
Dunholme
Wragby
Eckington
Barlborough
Whitwell
Worksop
East Retford
Gamston
East Markham
Saxilby
Nettleham
Apley
Baumber
Staveley
Clowne
Cuckney
Tuxford
Kirton
Boughton
Newton on Trent
Harby
Reepham
Lincoln
Horncastle
Bolsover
Warsop
Laxton
North Scarle
Heighington
Bardney
Bucknall
Thimbleby
Shirebrook
Edwinstowe
Ollerton
Kneesall
Carlton-on-Trent
Thorpe on the Hill
Branston
Potterhanworth
Woodhall Spa
Mansfield Woodhouse
MANSFIELD
Eakring
Caunton
Swinderby
Collingham
Harmston
Dunston
Coningsby
Tibshelf
Sutton in Ashfield
Kirklington
North Muskham
Bassingham
LINCOLN
Alfreton
Blidworth
Farnsfield
Kelham
Newark-on-Trent
Navenby
Scopwick
Walcot
Billinghay
Kirkby in Ashfield
Southwell
Beckingham
Balderton
Leadenham
Ruskington
North Kyme
Witham
Ripley
Bleasby
Elston
Claypole
Cranwell
South Kyme
Langrick
Heanor
Eastwood
Hucknall
Oxton
Burton Joyce
Lowdham
Flintham
Caythorpe
Sleaford
Arnold
Carlton
East Bridgford
Honington
Heckington
Swineshead
Ilkeston
NOTTINGHAM
Bingham
Orston
Barkston
SHIRE
Stapleford
Beeston
West Bridgford
Radcliffe on Trent
Cotgrave
Bottesford
Redmile
Sedgebrook
Belvoir
Grantham
Welby
Osbournby
Helpringham
Bicker
Donington
Long Eaton
Ruddington
Plumtree
Colston Bassett
Harby
Stathern
Denton
Great Ponton
Folkingham
Billingborough
Gosberton
Castle Donington
Gotham
Kegworth
East Leake
Upper Broughton
Branston
Croxton Kerrial
Skillington
Ingoldsby
Dunsby
Pinchbeck West
Pinchbeck
East Midlands
Willoughby-on-the-Wolds
Wymeswold
Scalford
Waltham-on-the-Wolds
Colsterworth
Corby Glen
Morton
Spalding
Breedon on the Hill
Hathern
Saxelbye
Saxby
Swayfield
Castle Bytham
Edenham
Bourne
Shepshed
Loughborough
Frisby on the Wreake
Melton Mowbray
Wymondham
Stretton
Thurlby
Deeping St. Nicholas
Whitwick
Quorndon
Sileby
Great Dalby
Whissendine
Ashwell
Greetham
Essendine
Baston
Coalville
Mountsorrel
Rearsby
Cottesmore
Market Deeping
LEICESTER
Syston
Thurmaston
Twyford
Oakham
Empingham
Stamford
Helpston
Peakirk
Crowland
Barlestone
Groby
Knossington
North Luffenham
Ketton
Easton on the Hill
Ufford
Marholm
Eye
Desford
LEICESTER
Manton
Preston
Billesdon
Oadby
Uppingham
Duddington
Wansford
PETERBOROUGH
Earl Shilton
Wigston
East Norton
Harringworth
King's Cliffe
Whittlesey
Narborough
Hallaton
Gretton
Hinckley
Countesthorpe
Kibworth Harcourt
Medbourne
Rockingham
Elton
Norman Cross
Farcet
Yaxley
Broughton Astley
Market Harborough
Cottingham
Corby
Weldon
Oundle
Lutton
Stilton
Holme
NOTTINGHAMSHIRE
LINCOLN
LINCOLNSHIRE
LEICESTERSHIRE
Trent
Don
Welland
A19
A614
A161
A1077
A160
A180
A18
A46
M18
M180
M181
A638
A635
A633
A630
A631
A634
A60
A618
A57
A620
A1500
A159
A15
A1103
A1173
A1084
A158
A157
A638
A1
A614
A616
A6075
A617
A632
A619
A38
A608
A6095
A52
A453
A6006
A512
A447
A50
A6
A607
A606
A46
A612
A6097
A1133
A17
A153
A1121
A151
A6121
A47
A6003
A43
A605
A427
A426
A5
M1
M69
A16
A17
A153
B1398
B1400
B1205
B1434
B1203
B1202
B1399
B1190
B1241
B1191
B1188
B1189
B1429
B1174
B1176
B1397
B676
B668
B6047
B5380
B664
B1443
B1040
B6474
B6422
B6463
B6053
B6418
B6417
B1392
B1204
B1207
B1218
B1211

32
St Anne's
A587
Salter's Bank
Lytham St Anne's
Lytham
Warton
A584
B5259
Freckleton
RIBBLE
Banks Sands
36
Higher Penwortham
PRESTON
A582
Walton-le-Dale
Bamber Bridge
B6230
M6
Higher Walton
Gregson Lane
30
M61
A6
Hutton
Longton
New Longton
Farington
29
Walmer Bridge
Hesketh Bank
Becconsall
Much Hoole
Midge Hall
Leyland
28
Clayton-le-Woods
B5256
Whittle-le-Woods
B5248
Hundred End
Tarleton
A59
B5247
Bretherton
B5253
Runshaw Moor
Horse Bank
Crossens
Banks
A565
Marshside
Churchtown
Sollom
Mere Brow
Croston
A581
Newtown
Euxton
Hartwood
High Park
B5246
Holmeswood
Yarrow
Eccleston Green
Charnock Richard
Chorley
Southport
A5267
Birkdale
Rufford
Mawdesley
Heskin Green
Weld Bank
Carr Cross
Tarlscough
B5249
B5250
Bispham Green
Scarisbrick
New Lane
Wrightington Bar
Coppull
Adlington
B5243
Shirdley Hill
Ainsdale
Burscough Bridge
High Moor
Mossy Lea
A49
A5106
Pinfold
Douglas
Ribin Hood
Shevington Moor
Barton
Burscough
Parbold
A5209
Standish
Halsall
B5242
Appley Bridge
Black
A565
A570
A59
Newburgh
Leeds and Liverpool
Red Rock
A567
Shevington
Freshfield
Haskayne
Ormskirk
Dalton
Haigh
B5375
Formby
Great Altcar
Downland Cross
B5195
A577
Westhead
Gathurst
Crooke
Marylebone
Roby Mill
Scarth Hill
B5240
Skelmersdale
Orrell
Wigan
Aughton Park
Aughton
Alt
Up Holland
A506
3
4
Holt Green
5
Bickerstaffe
26
Ince-in-Makerfield
Lady Green
Lydiate
BELFAST
DOUGLAS
Ince Blundell
B5197
Higher End
Lamberhead Green
Hightown
M58
A59
Crawford
B5193
Homer Green
A565
Maghull
1
M6
Bryn
Bryn Gates
Lunt
B5206
25
Sefton
B5194
Melling
King's Moss
Billinge
CROSBY CHANNEL
Rainford
Netherton
Tower Hill
B5205
Crosby
Great Crosby
Ford
Kirkby
Crank
Garswood
Ashton-in-Makerfield
7
A5036
Moss Bank
24
A570
Litherland
Aintree
Waterloo
6
A58
Golborne
DUBLIN
Seaforth
A506
5
A580
23
Fazakerley
4
St Helens
Blackbrook
Haydock
Knowsley
New Brighton
Bootle
Walton-on-the-Hill
Eccleston
A572
Earlestown
M57
Peasley Cross
Newton-le-Willows
Wallasey
West Derby
3
Knowsley Hall
B5201
Thatto Heath
A58
B5204
A49
Everton
A5058
Huyton-with-Roby
2
Prescot
Sutton Leach
A59
Seacombe
Knotty Ash
A57
Whiston
RAC
Moreton
5
Rainhill Stoops
9
1
2
LIVERPOOL
6
M62
7
Bold Heath
A568
WARRINGTON
Upton
A5080
Cronton
Great Sankey
BIRKENHEAD
Toxteth
Childwall
Tarbock Green
A562
Hough Green
Farnworth
A57
29
Rock Ferry
B5178
Woolton
3
Allerton
A561
A562
Hunt's Cross
Ditton
New Ferry
Prenton
Storeton
Port Sunlight
Halewood
Irby
Thingwall
Bebington
Widnes
Moore
Higher Walton
Barnston
Garston
Hale Bank
A56
Pensby
1
A551
Speke
Runcorn
A558
Daresbury
Heswall
A5137
Liverpool Airport
Bromborough
Thornton Hough
A557
Norton
Halton
Hatton
Hale
MERSEY
A41
Preston Brook
Preston on the Hill
11
Gayton
M53
Brookhurst
Eastham
Weston
Raby
29
12
30
Sutton Weaver
Dutton
5
6
B
Ince Banks
Ship
Canal
A533
Willaston
Ellesmere Port
Frodsham
A56
Aston
Childer Thornton
Manchester
Weaver
Neston
7
8
Bradley
A
B
C
4
3
2
1

BURN
M65
Church
A56
Accrington
Clowbridge Resr
Walk Mill
Holme Chapel
Slack
Heptonstall
33
Mytholm
A674
36
B6234
Oswaldtwistle
Dunnockshaw
Baxenden
A646
38
A671
Portsmouth
Lydgate
Eastwood
A6062
Lower Darwen
Rising Bridge
Love Clough
Weir
Cornholme
B6231
Acre
Water
A646
Feniscowles
A677
Crawshawbooth
B6238
Lumb
Clough Foot
Withens Clough
Earcroft
Belthorn
Haslingden
Rawtenstall
A681
Todmorden
Haslingden Crane
Resr
ckholes
Sunnyhurst
bbey Village
Hoddlesden
B6232
Stacksteads
Bacup
Gorpley Resr
Mankinholes
Ogden Resr
Walsden
Ryal Fold
DARWEN
Blacksnape
Helmshore
Waterfoot
A6066
Brittania
Warland Resr
Shawforth
Warland
B6138
Rochdale
CASHIRE
Cown Resr
A6033
Edenfield
Whittlestone Head
Watergrove Resr
Whitworth
Calderbrook
Summit
A666
Crowthorn School
Stubbins
Belmont Resr
Spring Mill Resr
A58
40
Healey
Wardle
B6391
Ramsbottom
Naden Resr
Edgworth
Broadley
Littleborough
Chapeltown
Turton Bottoms
B6214
Ashworth Moor Resr
Belmont
Delph Resr
Greenbooth Resr
Syke
Egerton
Hollingworth Lake
Summerseat
Norden
Smallbridge
Tumbles Resr
A680
A676
Greenmount
22
B6213
Dunscar
Toppings
Walmersley
Firgrove
M66
Rochdale
Limefield
rwich
Milnrow
Bradshaw
Barrow Bridge
A675
Astley Bridge
B6222
Roch
Tottington
21
B6196
A640
B6226
A58
Newhey
Bury
Harwood
Denshaw
A58
2
A6052
BOLTON
M66
20
Ainsworth
Heywood
3
027
A673
Fishpool
A58
3
Shaw
Hollins
19
Lostock Junction
A676
B6209
Royton
Sholver
A672
Delph
GREATER
Birch
Moorside
es
Hunger Hill
Daubhill
Radcliffe
M62
Dobcross
5
Little Lever
Middleton
Farnworth
18
Uppermill
A6
B6199
A575
Whitefield
A6045
OLDHAM
Lees
Grasscroft
4
Kearsley
3
17
A664
Greenfield
Atherton
Prestwich
Chadderton
A579
2
A666
15
A56
Blackley
A627
Little Hulton
A6104
Failsworth
B6194
Walkden
1
Charlestown
Tyldsley
Pendlebury
Cheetham Hill
Bardsley
14
Broughton
A663
A670
Mossley
A6044
Harpurhey
Hurst
Swinton
A6
Leigh
A580
Boothstown
A62
13
Worsley
A576
Ashton-under-Lyne
Stalybridge
MANCHESTER
M62
Astley Green
12
Eccles
M602
Pendleton
Clayton
A662
Walkerwood Resr
Lately Common
A57
Droylsden
Dukinfield
Lowton Common
Salford
A5063
A635
A6018
2
Barton Moss
Trafford Park
Hulme
Gorton
Audenshaw
Glazebury
3
Stretford
1
2
Mottram in Longdendale
Culcheth
Irlam
Rusholme
A57
11
Urmston
4
Levenshulme
M67
Mose Side
Denton
Broadbottom
B5212
Flixton
M66
MANCHESTER
Haughton Green
Hyde
6
M62
Chorlton-cum-Hardy
A560
7
A6017
Etherow
Ashton upon Mersey
Withington
Burnage
Reddish
Bredbury
Gee Cross
Chisworth
11
Glazebrook
Carrington
A5145
8
A626
A574
M63
Heaton Moor
41
Cadishead
Romiley
A6
13
Didsbury
12
Hollinfare
9
A34
Partington
Sale
A5145
Compstall
A56
M6
12
STOCKPORT
A6144
A57
Warburton
Broadheath
A560
11
10
RAC
Mellor
21
Timperley
Marple
Heatley
3
2
Heaviley
Manchester Ship Canal
A626
Dunham Town
M56
Cheadle
Gatley
New Mills
B5166
Altrincham
Lymm
A5149
Hazel Grove
Bowdon
B6101
Bridgewater
4
A5102
High Lane
Hale
Heald Green
Halebarns
A34
Cheadle Hulme
A56
Bollington
A538
Bramhall
Broomedge
A6
8
7
Manchester International Airport
B5094
Poynton
Disley
Newtown
Ashley
20
9
Sworton Heath
High Legh
A556
Rosthere
Higher Poynton
Handforth
M56
A50
Bucklow Hill
Styal
Wood Lanes
A5034
New Mills
Morley Green
A5102
Woodford
Dean
Tatton Hall
M6
Mere
Arley
Wilmslow
Dean Row
Adlington
B5358
ESHIRE
A523
Bale Heath
Knolls Green
Kettleshulme
A538
Antrobus
30
Pott Shrigley
Mottram St Andrew
Mobberley
B5085
A559
Great Budworth
Knutsford
A5033
A5002
Alderley Edge
B5087
Prestbury
Bollington
Pickmere
B5391
A537

34
39
31
26
Scunthorpe
Burton upon Stather
Winterton
Flixborough
Appleby
Amcotts
Thornton Curtis
Ulceby
Elsham
Worlaby
Croxton
Humberside
Bigby
Brigg
Immingham
Grimsby
Keelby
Great Coates
Laceby
Great Limber
Cleethorpes
Humber Estuary
Sunk Island
Easington
Kilnsea
Spurn Head
Waltham
Humberston
Grasby
Swallow
Cabourne
Caistor
Hibaldstow
North Kelsey
South Kelsey
Messingham
Scawby
Scotter
Trent
Owston Ferry
Blyton
Kirton in Lindsey
Waddingham
Corringham
Glentham
Thoresway
Wold Newton
North Thoresby
Tetney
Marshchapel
Grainthorpe
North Somercotes
Fulstow
Ludborough
Saltfleet
Alvingham
Saltfleet by St. Peter
Binbrook
Claxby
Tealby
Ludford
Market Rasen
West Rasen
Gainsborough
Louth
Grimoldby
Great Carlton
Legbourne
Mablethorpe
Maltby le Marsh
Sutton on Sea
Willingham by Stow
Spridlington
Faldingworth
Marton
Sturton by Stow
Barkwith
Wragby
Dunholme
Snelland
Apley
Newton on Trent
Saxilby
Nettleham
Reepham
Lincoln
Baumber
Huttoft
Alford
Willoughby
Chapel St. Leonards
Tetford
Horncastle
Thimbleby
Harby
Ingoldmells
Partney
Spilsby
Burgh le Marsh
Skegness
Heighington
Branston
North Scarle
Thorpe on the Hill
Carlton-on-Trent
Swinderby
Collingham
Bardney
Bucknall
Potterhanworth
Old Bolingbroke
Keal
Woodhall Spa
Haltham
Harmston
Dunston
Revesby
Stickford
Coningsby
Wainfleet All Saints
Bassingham
North Muskham
Stickney
Eastville
Navenby
LINCOLNSHIRE
Walcot
Billinghay
Friskney
Newark-on-Trent
Scopwick
Ruskington
North Kyme
Witham
Beckingham
Leadenham
Balderton
Claypole
Cranwell
Wrangle
Caythorpe
South Kyme
Sibsey
Langrick
Sleaford
Butterwick
Boston
Honington
Heckington
Swineshead
Barkston
Helpringham
The Wash
Bicker
Donington
Kirton
Osbournby
Welby
Sutterton
Bottesford
Sedgebrook
Grantham
Belvoir
Billingborough
Gosberton
Fosdyke
Holbeach St. Matthew
Denton
Folkingham
Great Ponton
Ingoldsby
Knipton
Croxton Kerrial
Dunsby
Gedney Drove End
Lutton
Skillington
Corby Glen
Pinchbeck West
Pinchbeck
Whaplode
Long Sutton
Waltham-on-the-Wolds
Colsterworth
Morton
Spalding
Moulton
Holbeach
Sutton Bridge
Terrington St. Clement
Swayfield
Edenham
Bourne
Sutton St. James
Tydd St. Mary
Saxby
Castle Bytham
King's Lynn
Wymondham
Stretton
Thurlby
Deeping St. Nicholas
Cowbit
Holbeach St. Johns
Walpole
Whissendine
Ashwell
Greetham
Essendine
Baston
Welland
Tydd St. Giles
Wiggenhall St. Germans
Cottesmore
Market Deeping
Crowland
Wisbech
Gedney Hill
Oakham
Knossington
Empingham
Stamford
Helpston
Peakirk
Emneth
Downham Market
North Luffenham
Ketton
Manton
Easton on the Hill
Ufford
Murrow
Friday Bridge
Outwell
Preston
Marholm
Eye
Thorney
Guyhirn
Duddington
Upwell
East Norton
Uppingham
Wansford
PETERBOROUGH
Hallaton
Harringworth
King's Cliffe
Whittlesey
March
Christchurch
Hilgay
Gretton
Farcet
Yaxley
Wimblington
Cottingham
Rockingham
Elton
Norman Cross
Southery
Corby
Oundle
Lutton
Stilton
Benwick
Welney
Manea
Great Ouse
Hunstanton
Heacham
Snettisham
Wolferton
South Wootton
A161
A18
M181
M180
A159
A631
A15
A1103
A46
A1500
A57
A1133
A1077
A160
A180
A1173
A1084
A46
A16
A1031
A157
A1104
A1111
A153
A52
A1028
A158
A155
A607
A17
A1121
A52
A1
A151
A6121
A606
A6003
A43
A427
A605
A47
A141
A1073
A1101
A1122
A10
A6121

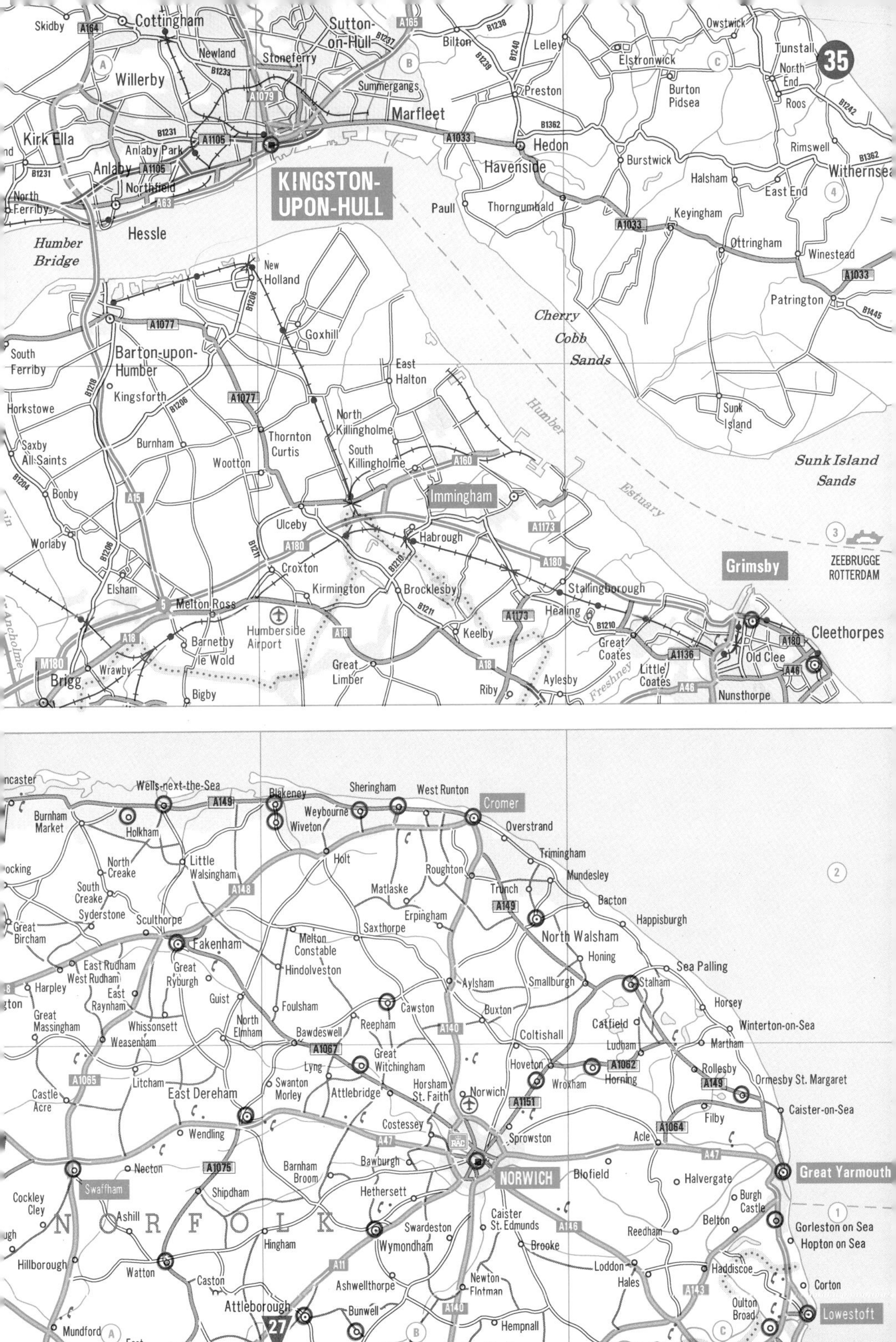
35
Skidby
A164
Cottingham
Sutton-on-Hull
A165
Bilton
B1238
Owstwick
Tunstall
Newland
Stoneferry
B1237
Lelley
Elstronwick
North End
Willerby
B1233
Summergangs
B1239
B1240
Preston
Burton Pidsea
Roos
B1242
A1079
Marfleet
B1362
Kirk Ella
B1231
A1105
A1033
Hedon
Rimswell
Anlaby Park
Havenside
Burstwick
B1362
Withernsea
Anlaby
A1105
Halsham
East End
Northfield
B1231
KINGSTON-UPON-HULL
North Ferriby
A63
Paull
Thorngumbald
Keyingham
Hessle
A1033
Ottringham
Winestead
Humber Bridge
A1033
New Holland
Patrington
B1206
B1445
Cherry Cobb Sands
A1077
Goxhill
South Ferriby
Barton-upon-Humber
East Halton
B1218
Kingsforth
A1077
Horkstowe
B1206
North Killingholme
Sunk Island
Humber
Saxby All Saints
Burnham
Thornton Curtis
South Killingholme
Sunk Island Sands
Wootton
A160
B1204
Bonby
Immingham
A15
Estuary
Ulceby
A1173
3
Worlaby
B1206
B1211
A180
Habrough
A180
ZEEBRUGGE
ROTTERDAM
Grimsby
Croxton
B1210
Elsham
Kirmington
Brocklesby
Stallingborough
Melton Ross
B1211
Healing
Cleethorpes
Humberside Airport
A1173
A18
Keelby
B1210
A180
Barnetby le Wold
A18
Great Coates
A1136
Old Clee
M180
A18
Little Coates
A46
Brigg
Wrawby
Great Limber
Riby
Aylesby
Freshney
A46
Bigby
Nunsthorpe
Ancholme
Brancaster
Wells-next-the-Sea
Blakeney
Sheringham
West Runton
Cromer
Burnham Market
A149
Weybourne
Holkham
Wiveton
Overstrand
Holt
Trimingham
North Creake
Little Walsingham
Roughton
Mundesley
Docking
2
South Creake
A148
Matlaske
Trunch
Bacton
Syderstone
A149
Erpingham
Happisburgh
Great Bircham
Sculthorpe
Saxthorpe
North Walsham
Fakenham
Melton Constable
East Rudham
Great Ryburgh
Honing
Sea Palling
West Rudham
Hindolveston
Harpley
East Raynham
Aylsham
Smallburgh
Stalham
Guist
Horsey
Foulsham
Cawston
Buxton
Great Massingham
North Elmham
Catfield
Winterton-on-Sea
Whissonsett
Reepham
A140
Coltishall
Weasenham
Bawdeswell
Ludham
Martham
A1067
Great Witchingham
Hoveton
A1062
Lyng
Horning
Rollesby
A1065
Litcham
Swanton Morley
Horsham St. Faith
Wroxham
A149
Ormesby St. Margaret
Castle Acre
East Dereham
Attlebridge
Norwich
A1151
Filby
Caister-on-Sea
Costessey
A1064
Wendling
Sprowston
Acle
RAC
A47
A47
Swaffham
Necton
A1075
Barnham Broom
Bawburgh
NORWICH
Blofield
Halvergate
Great Yarmouth
Cockley Cley
Shipdham
Hethersett
Caister St. Edmunds
Burgh Castle
1
NORFOLK
Ashill
Swardeston
A146
Reedham
Belton
Gorleston on Sea
Hingham
Wymondham
Brooke
Hopton on Sea
Hillborough
Watton
A11
Newton Flotman
Loddon
Hales
Haddiscoe
Corton
Caston
Ashwellthorpe
A143
Oulton Broad
Attleborough
Bunwell
A140
Lowestoft
Mundford
27
Hempnall
East Wretham
Long Stratton
Denton
Bungay
A1075
New Buckenham
Beccles
A146

36
43
44
29
30
LAKE DISTRICT
NATIONAL PARK
Ravenglass
Coniston
Hawkshead
Windermere
Bowness
Windermere
Grayrigg
Keld
Thwaite
Muker
Low Row
Seathwaite
Near Sawrey
Staveley
Burneside
Lowgill
Torver
Grizedale
Far Sawrey
Winster
Kendal
Sedbergh
Hardrow
Askrigg
Underbarrow
Broughton-in-Furness
Blawith
Satterthwaite
Cartmel Fell
Oxenholme
Hawes
Bainbridge
Bootle
Sedgwick
Stalling Busk
Grizebeck
Colton
Newby Bridge
Levens Bridge
Crooklands
Middleton
Dent
Whitbeck
The Hill
Haverthwaite
YORKSHIRE DALES NATIONAL PARK
Greenodd
Heversham
Old Town
Kirksanton
Soutergate
Milnthorpe
Lindale
Kirkby Lonsdale
Barbon
Millom
Cartmel
Beetham
Hubberholme
Haverigg
Askam-in-Furness
Ulverston
Arnside
Holme
Casterton
Cark
Grange-over-Sands
Burton
Halton Gill
Dalton-in-Furness
Bardsea
Flookburgh
Silverdale
Whittington
Horton in Ribblesdale
Litton
Borwick
Barrow-in-Furness
Warton
Burton in Lonsdale
Ingleton
Aldingham
Carnforth
Melling
Arncliffe
Vickerstown
Over Kellet
Hornby
Clapham
Morecambe Bay
Bolton-le-Sands
High Bentham
Austwick
Kilnsey
Wray
Claughton
Stainforth
Hest Bank
Caton
Settle
Malham
Grassington
Morecambe
Lancaster
Threshfield
Kirkby Malham
Isle of Walney
Heysham
Giggleswick
Airton
Long Preston
Rylstone
Overton
Hellifield
Wigglesworth
Glasson
Hampson Green
Gargrave
Slaidburn
Bolton by Bowland
Cockerham
Dolphinholme
Knott End
Pilling
Newton
Gisburn
Thornton-in-Craven
Winmarleigh
Fleetwood
LANCASHIRE
Barnoldswick
Grindleton
Rimington
Preesall
Garstang
Waddington
Chatburn
Hambleton
Chipping
Cleveleys
Thornton
Great Eccleston
Catterall
Hurst Green
Clitheroe
Foulridge
Bispham
Barley
Goosnargh
Longridge
Colne
Poulton-le-Fylde
Inskip
Great Mitton
Barrowford
Trawden
Broughton
BLACKPOOL
Great Harwood
Nelson
Ribchester
Elswick
Padiham
Ribble
Bartle
Rishton
Burnley
Kirkham
Wrea Green
Clayton-le-Moors
SEE PAGES 32-33 FOR COVERAGE AT 4 MILES TO 1 INCH
St. Anne's
Freckleton
PRESTON
Accrington
Lytham St. Anne's
Lytham
Oswaldtwistle
Longton
Faringdon
BLACKBURN
Todmorden
Hesketh Bank
Whittle-le-Woods
Withnell
Bacup
Leyland
DARWEN
Rawtenstall
Walsden
Banks
Tarleton
Haslingden
Croston
Whitworth
Edgworth
Littleborough
Southport
Eccleston
Chorley
Rufford
Rochdale
Horwich
Tottington
Adlington
Ainsdale
Heywood
Parbold
BOLTON
Bury
Shaw
Burscough
Standish
Royston
Formby
Ormskirk
Skelmersdale
Up Holland
Farnworth
Great Altcar
Wigan
Middleton
OLDHAM
Hindley
Atherton
GR MAN
Lees
Maghull
Rainford
MANCHESTER
Crosby
Leigh
Kirkby
Ashton-in-Makerfield
Billinge
Ashton-under-Lyne
Salford
Bootle
Newton-le-Willows
Hyde
Wallasey
ST. HELENS
LIVERPOOL
Prescot
Stockport
Hoylake
Moreton
Altrincham
Sale
West Kirby
Lymm
Hazel Grove
BIRKENHEAD
WARRINGTON
Cheadle
Upton
Heald Green
Widnes
Bramhall
Stretton
Thurstaston
MERSEYSIDE
Speke
Runcorn
Wilmslow
Heswall
Bromborough
Bollington
Llanasa
Great Budworth
Knutsford
Prestbury
Alderley Edge
Ellesmere Port
Neston
Holywell
Willaston
Frodsham
Chelford
Helsby
Weaverham
Macclesfield
Flint
Burton
Northwich
Caerwys
Davenham

Stanton
A697
A1
Hebron
Longhirst
B1337
45
A189
Woodhorn
Beacon Point
Pigdon
Pegswood
Ashington
Newbiggin-by-the-Sea
A197
Hirst
Throphill
Mitford
Morpeth
Bothal
Guide Post
North Seaton
Wansbeck
A196
Stakeford
Choppington
Scotland Gate
Cambois
A1
Hepscott
East Sleekburn
Clifton
Tranwell
Bedlington
Blyth
B6524
Bebside
Whalton
B1331
A192
A1068
B1505
Saltwick
East Hartford
Newsham
Stannington
A1061
Ogle
Blyth
Nelson Village
A1
Cramlington
A193
A696
Pont
New Hartley
A189
A192
Seaton Sluice
Higham Dykes
Berwick Hill
A1068
Seaton
Hartley
St. Mary's or Bait Island
GOTHENBURG
New Horton Grange
East Cramlington
B1325
Seaton Burn
A1
Seaton Delaval
Ponteland
Dinnington
Dudley
Seghill
Hazlerigg
Wide Open
Burradon
Prestwick
Earsdon
Whitley Bay
TYNE
Darras Hall
High Callerton
Newcastle Airport
A6125
Backworth
Shiremoor
Cullercoats
STAVANGER BERGEN
A191
Medburn
Woolsington
New York
Tynemouth
Black Callerton
Longbenton
A191
A1
ESBJERG
B6324
Gosforth
North Shields
Throckley
A1058
Willington
South Shields
Wallsend
A187
B6528
Heddon-on-the-Wall
NEWCASTLE UPON TYNE
Heaton
Harton
Marsden Bay
Newburn
Tyne
RAC
Walker
Jarrow
Ryton
Byker
Hebburn
Crawcrook
Monkton
A183
Blaydon
A695
A69
Dunston
Pelaw
Cleadon
Prudhoe
Gateshead
Boldon Colliery
Greenside
Felling
A1
Whitburn
Barlow
Whickham
Boldon
A108
B6315
AND
A692
WEAR
Fulwell
Wrekenton
Roker
High Spen
Highfield
Rowlands Gill
Sunniside
Southwick
Castletown
SUNDERLAND
Lamesley
South Hylton
Burnopfield
A6076
Kibblesworth
A1231
A694
Washington
Hobson
Hendon
Ebchester
Tanfield
Birtley
A183
New Silksworth
B6310
Ouston
Penshaw
Tantobie
Beamish
Herrington
A690
Ryhope
Dipton
Stanley
A693
Fatfield
B1286
Pelton
South Moor
Grange Villa
Silksworth
A692
A693
Shiney Row
A19
A183
Leadgate
Annfield Plain
B6313
Chester-le-Street
Bournmoor
Craghead
Fence Houses
Houghton-le-Spring
Seaham
Iveston
Waldridge
Maiden Law
Great Lumley
Edmondsley
B6532
Hetton-le-Hole
Dalton-le-Dale
Plawsworth
East Rainton
Murton
Burnhope
Lanchester
Sacriston
Kimblesworth
Cold Hesledon
B1285
B1432
A167
A1
West Rainton
Easington Lane
B6296
A691
Hawthorn
Langley Park
Witton Gilbert
Framwellgate Moor
Pittington
South Hetton
Butsfield
A690
A182
Quebec
Bearpark
Carrville
Easington Colliery
Cornsay
Esh
Littletown
Haswell
Satley
DURHAM
B6302
Esh Winning
Sherburn
Ushaw Moor
B1283
Shotton Colliery
Horden
New Brancepeth
Ludworth
Peterlee
Waterhouses
Shadforth
B1280
A177
A181
Thornley
B6301
East Hedleyhope
45
Shotton
Brandon
Wheatley Hill
Castle Eden
Tow Law
Sunniside
Wear
Bowburn
B1281

38
44
36
30
SEE PAGE 35 FOR COVERAGE AT 4 MILES TO 1 INCH
NORTH YORKSHIRE
YORKSHIRE DALES NATIONAL PARK
WEST YORKSHIRE
SOUTH YORKSHIRE
DERBYSHIRE
GR MAN
PEAK DISTRICT
PEAK FOREST NATIONAL PARK
Langthwaite
Keld
Thwaite
Muker
Low Row
Feetham
Reeth
Grinton
Marske
Marrick
Richmond
Catterick Garrison
Catterick
East Hauxwell
Welbury
Swainby
Osmotherly
Brompton
Northallerton
Great Langton
Scruton
Leeming Bar
Patrick Brompton
Bedale
Castle Bolton
Carperby
Redmire
Askrigg
Hardrow
Hawes
Bainbridge
Aysgarth
Wensley
Leyburn
West Witton
Middleham
Thornton Steward
Thornton Watlass
Burneston
South Otterington
Pickhill
Stalling Busk
Carlton
East Witton
Snape
Well
Thirsk
Hawnby
Boltby
Cold Kirby
Gillamoor
Kirkbymoorside
Helmsley
Harome
Kilburn
Ampleforth
Coxwold
Husthwaite
Gilling East
Horsehouse
Healey
Masham
West Tanfield
Skipton-on-Swale
Topcliffe
Sessay
Hubberholme
Buckden
Starbotton
Halton Gill
Litton
Middlesmoor
Mickley
Kirkby Malzeard
Winksley
Ripon
Dishforth
Brafferton
Brandsby
Horton in Ribblesdale
Kettlewell
Arncliffe
Ramsgill
Pateley Bridge
Bishop Monkton
Boroughbridge
Easingwold
Stillington
Sheriff Hutton
Sutton-on-the-Forest
Austwick
Kilnsey
Conistone
Stainforth
Settle
Malham
Kirkby Malham
Grassington
Threshfield
Linton
Burnsall
Summer Bridge
Burnt Yates
Staveley
Marton
Ripley
Strensall
Giggleswick
Long Preston
Airton
Rylstone
Hellifield
Wigglesworth
Gargrave
Embsay
Bolton Abbey
Blubberhouses
Hampsthwaite
Knaresborough
Green Hammerton
Newton on Ouse
Poppleton
Harrogate
Fewston
York
Bolton by Bowland
Gisburn
Thornton-in-Craven
Barnoldswick
Skipton
Spofforth
Kirkby Overblow
Tockwith
Long Marston
Wetherby
Addingham
Askwith
Otley
Weeton
Collingham
Tadcaster
Rimington
Chatburn
Glusburn
Silsden
Ilkley
Pool
Harewood
Boston Spa
Naburn
Bramham
Bolton Percy
Foulridge
Cowling
Keighley
Menston
Guiseley
Leeds/Bradford
Bardsey
Barley
Barrowford
Colne
Trawden
Nelson
Oakworth
Bingley
Shipley
Yeadon
Aberford
Church Fenton
Riccall
Cawood
Wistow
Padiham
Burnley
Haworth
Oxenhope
BRADFORD
LEEDS
Saxton
Sherburn in Elmet
Garforth
Selby
Pudsey
Queensbury
Rothwell
Castleford
Monk Fryston
Hemingbrough
Accrington
Hebden Bridge
Morley
Knottingley
Temple Hirst
Todmorden
Sowerby Bridge
Halifax
Brighouse
Dewsbury
Normanton
Bacup
Greetland
Wakefield
Pontefract
Darrington
Wentbridge
Rawtenstall
Walsden
Ripponden
Elland
Mirfield
Ossett
Sharlaston
Ackworth
Whitworth
HUDDERSFIELD
Horbury
Barnsdale Bar
Sykehouse
Littleborough
Golcar
Askern
Slaithwaite
Kirkburton
Hemsworth
Rochdale
Heywood
Denshaw
Denby Dale
Darton
Royston
Cudworth
South Kirkby
Stainforth
Hatfield
Meltham
Marsden
Holmfirth
Adwick le Street
Shaw
Royston
Dodworth
BARNSLEY
Bentley
Middleton
OLDHAM
Penistone
Wombwell
Darfield
Dearne
Lees
Mossley
Dunford Bridge
Langsett
Hoyland Nether
Mexborough
Doncaster
MANCHESTER
Ashton-under-Lyne
Conisbrough
Salford
Hyde
Stocksbridge
Rawmarsh
Wadworth
Rossington
Hollingworth
Glossop
Braithwell
High Bradfield
Ecclesfield
Rotherham
Tickhill
Maltby
STOCKPORT
Marple
SHEFFIELD
Dinnington
Cheadle
Hazel Grove
New Mills
Hayfield
Edale
Carlton in Lindrick
Todwick
Heald Green
Manchester
Bramhall
Chapel-en-le-Frith
Hope
Bamford
Killamarsh
Anston
Wilmslow
Bradwell
Hathersage
Bollington
Whaley Bridge
Dove Holes
Prestbury
Dronfield
Holmesfield
Eckington
Knutsford
Alderley Edge
Eyam
Grindleford Bridge
Barlborough
Whitwell
Worksop
Chelford
Macclesfield
Buxton
Tideswell
Baslow
Hassop
Chesterfield
Whittington
Staveley
Clowne
Cuckney
A684
A6108
A6136
A1
A19
A168
A167
A170
A61
A59
A65
A629
A6034
A658
A659
A661
A6055
A1237
A1036
A682
A56
A6068
A650
A6038
A64
A58
A642
A656
A63
A162
A644
A647
A646
A681
A6033
A672
A62
A640
A616
A637
A636
A628
A635
A6024
A629
A633
A6102
A6135
A630
A634
A60
A618
A57
A624
A6013
A625
A621
A623
A6
A523
A537
A535
A527
A619
A616
A1041
A645
A638
A18
M62
M63
M1
B6270
B6271
B1263
B1257
B6255
B6160
B6268
B6267
B6479
B6266
B6451
B6165
B6265
B6161
B6164
B1224
B1222
B1223
B1217
B6238
B6378
B6132
B6428
B6474
B6422
B6106
B6105
B6101
B6053
B6463
B6049
B6056
B5470
B6418
B6417
B1363

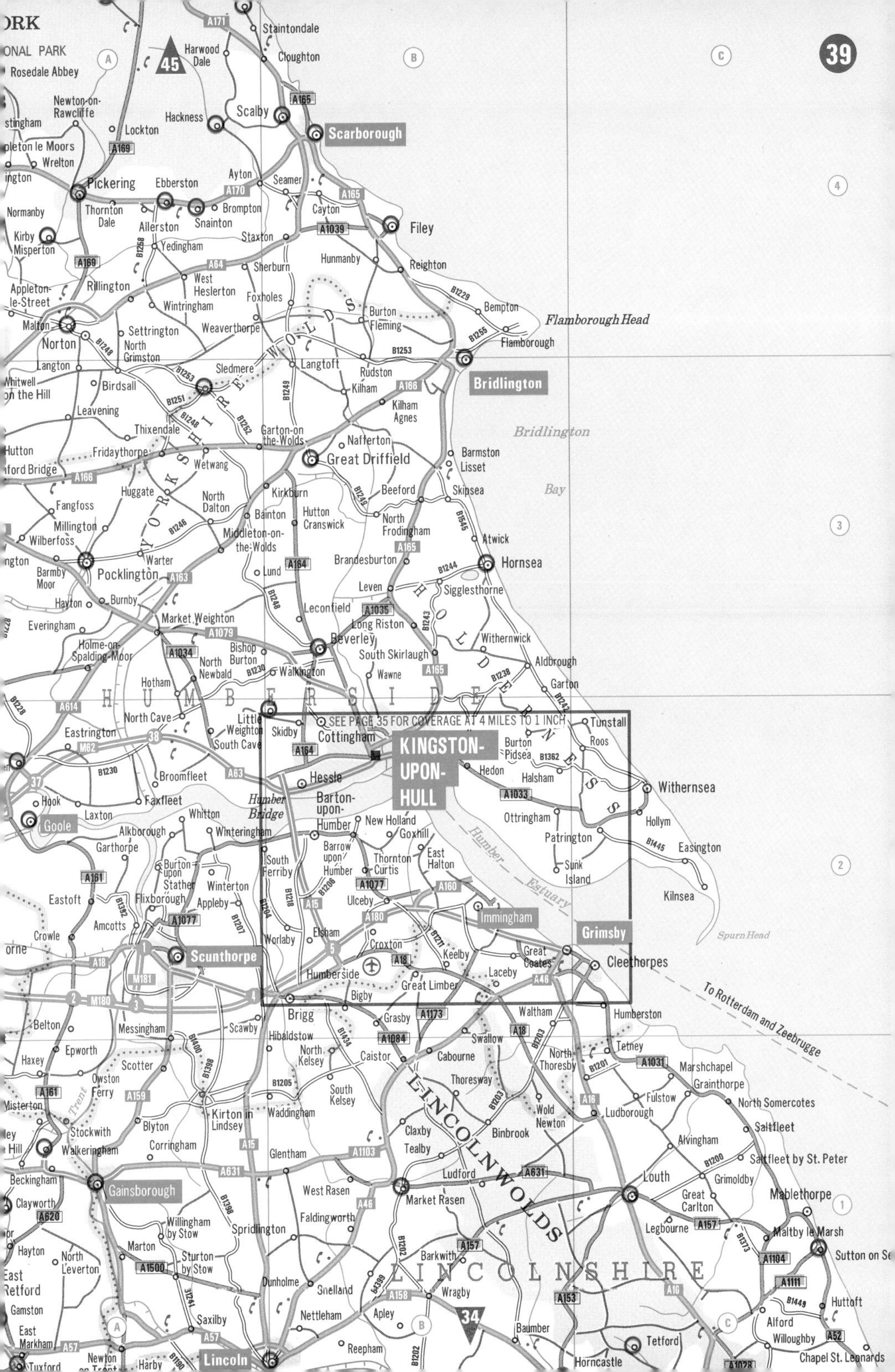

ORK
ONAL PARK
Rosedale Abbey
45
Harwood Dale
Staintondale
Cloughton
A171
A165
Newton-on-Rawcliffe
stingham
Lockton
Hackness
Scalby
Scarborough
pleton le Moors
Wrelton
A169
ington
Pickering
Ebberston
Ayton
Seamer
A170
Normanby
Thornton Dale
Allerston
Brompton
Snainton
Cayton
A165
Filey
Kirby Misperton
Yedingham
Staxton
A1039
B1258
A169
A64
Sherburn
Hunmanby
Reighton
Appleton-le-Street
Rillington
West Heslerton
Wintringham
Foxholes
B1229
Bempton
Flamborough Head
Malton
Norton
Settrington
North Grimston
Weaverthorpe
Burton Fleming
B1255
Flamborough
B1248
Langton
Sledmere
B1253
Langtoft
Rudston
B1253
Bridlington
Whitwell on the Hill
Birdsall
B1251
B1249
Kilham
A166
Kilham Agnes
Leavening
B1248
B1252
Thixendale
Garton-on the-Wolds
Nafferton
Bridlington
Hutton
Fridaythorpe
Great Driffield
Barmston
Lisset
ford Bridge
A166
Wetwang
Bay
Huggate
North Dalton
Kirkburn
B1249
Beeford
Skipsea
Fangfoss
Bainton
Hutton Cranswick
North Frodingham
B1545
Millington
B1246
Middleton-on-the-Wolds
Atwick
Wilberfoss
A165
ngton
Warter
Brandesburton
Hornsea
Barmby Moor
Pocklington
A163
Lund
A164
B1244
Leven
Sigglesthorne
Hayton
Burnby
B1248
Leconfield
A1035
Everingham
Market Weighton
Long Riston
B1243
A1079
Beverley
Withernwick
Holme-on-Spalding-Moor
A1034
Bishop Burton
South Skirlaugh
Aldbrough
North Newbald
B1230
Walkington
Wawne
A165
B1238
Garton
Hotham
YORKSHIRE WOLDS
HOLDERNESS
HUMBERSIDE
B1228
A614
North Cave
Little Weighton
Skidby
SEE PAGE 35 FOR COVERAGE AT 4 MILES TO 1 INCH
Tunstall
Eastrington
38
South Cave
Cottingham
KINGSTON-UPON-HULL
Burton Pidsea
Roos
M62
A164
B1362
B1230
Broomfield
A63
Hessle
Hedon
Halsham
Withernsea
37
Hook
Faxfleet
Humber Bridge
Barton-upon-Humber
A1033
Goole
Laxton
Whitton
Ottringham
Hollym
Winteringham
New Holland
Alkborough
Goxhill
Patrington
Garthorpe
Barrow upon Humber
Thornton Curtis
East Halton
Humber Estuary
B1445
Easington
Burton upon Stather
South Ferriby
Sunk Island
A161
Winterton
B1218
B1206
A1077
A160
Kilnsea
Eastoft
B1392
Flixborough
Appleby
Ulceby
Immingham
A15
Amcotts
A1077
B1207
B1204
A180
Spurn Head
Crowle
Worlaby
Elsham
B1211
Grimsby
orne
Scunthorpe
Croxton
Keelby
Great Coates
Cleethorpes
A18
M181
A18
Humberside
Laceby
To Rotterdam and Zeebrugge
2
M180
3
4
Great Limber
A46
Brigg
Bigby
Grasby
A1173
Waltham
Humberston
Belton
Messingham
Scawby
A18
B1400
Hibaldstow
B1434
A1084
Swallow
B1203
Tetney
Haxey
Epworth
Scotter
North Kelsey
Caistor
Cabourne
North Thoresby
A1031
B1398
B1201
Marshchapel
Owston Ferry
Thoresway
Grainthorpe
A161
Trent
A159
B1205
South Kelsey
B1203
Fulstow
North Somercotes
Misterton
Kirton in Lindsey
Waddingham
Wold Newton
A16
Ludborough
Saltfleet
Stockwith
Blyton
Claxby
LINCOLNWOLDS
Binbrook
Alvingham
Walkerington
Corringham
A15
Tealby
B1200
Saltfleet by St. Peter
Glentham
A1103
A631
Ludford
A631
Louth
Grimoldby
Beckingham
Gainsborough
West Rasen
Market Rasen
Great Carlton
Mablethorpe
Clayworth
A620
Willingham by Stow
Spridlington
Faldingworth
A46
Legbourne
A157
B1373
Maltby le Marsh
Hayton
Marton
B1202
A157
A1104
North Leverton
A1500
Sturton by Stow
Barkwith
Sutton on Se
East Retford
Dunholme
Snelland
B1399
LINCOLNSHIRE
A1111
Wragby
Gamston
B1241
A158
A153
A16
B1449
Huttoft
Saxilby
Nettleham
Apley
34
Alford
East Markham
A57
A57
Baumber
Willoughby
A52
Newton on Trent
Harby
B1190
Lincoln
Reepham
B1202
Horncastle
Tetford
A1028
Chapel St. Leonards
Tuxford

40
Wetherby
WEST YORKSHIRE
LEEDS
BRADFORD
HUDDERSFIELD
Halifax
Wakefield
Dewsbury
Brighouse
Pontefract
Carleton
Low Bradley
Addingham
Middleton
Denton
Askwith
Farnley
North Rigton
Stainburn
Kirkby Overblow
Sicklinghall
Bilton
Wighill
Cononley
Kildwick
Lothersdale
Silsden
Ilkley
Burley in Wharfedale
Weston
Otley
Leathley
Huby
Weeton
Linton
Collingham
Walton
Boston Spa
Thorp Arch
Newton Kyme
Glusburn
Sutton-in-Craven
Steeton
Cowling
Utley
Keighley
Riddlesden
Menston
Guiseley
East Carlton
Pool
Castley
Arthington
Weardley
Harewood
East Keswick
Bardsey
Clifford
Bramham
Bramhope
Eccup
Eccup Resr
Laycock
Fell Lane
East Morton
Eldwick
Hawksworth
Yeadon
Leeds/Bradford Airport
Tinshill
Alwoodley
Scarcroft
Thorner
Shadwell
Oakworth
Hareworth
Harden
Bingley
Baildon
Rawdon
Horsforth
Moortown
Moor Allerton
Chapel Allerton
Roundhay
Barwick in Elmet
Aberford
Saxton
Haworth
Cottingley
Cullingworth
Wilsden
Nab Wood
Shipley
Idle
Eccleshill
Calverley
Headingley
Kirkstall
Woodhouse
Potternewton
Scholes
Oxenhope
Denholme
Daisy Hill
Heaton
Thornton
Allerton
Farsley
Bramley
Upper Armley
Armley
Wortley
Sheepscar
Burmantofts
Osmondthorpe
Cross Gates
Manston
Whitkirt
Halton Moor
Garforth
Micklefield
Newthorpe
Tyeral
Pudsey
Denholme Gate
Clayton
Little Horton
Warley Moor Resr
Queensbury
Buttershaw
New Farnley
Beeston
Swillington
Kippax
Ledsham
Pecket Well
Slack
Heptonstall
Mytholm
Hebden Bridge
Wainstalls
Illingworth
Shelf
Low Moor
Birkenshaw
Drighlington
Churwell
Gildersome
Middleton
Robin Hood
Woodlesford
Oulton
Great Preston
Ledston
Fairburn
Mixenden
Ovenden
Northowram
Wyke
Oakenshaw
Morley
Rothwell
Carlton
Allerton Bywater
Methley
New Fryston
Midgley
Luddenden
Hipperholme
Cleckheaton
Gomersal
Birstall Smithies
Tingley
Ardsley East
Lofthouse Gate
Stanley
Brotherton
Castleford
Ferrybridge
Eastwood
Mytholmroyd
Withens Clough Resr
Cragg Vale
Sowerby
Sowerby Bridge
Southowram
Liversedge
Heckmondwike
Batley
Outwood
Altofts
Whitwood
Lumb
Mill Bank
Warland Resr
Greetland
Robertown
Kirkhamgate
Normanton
Ackton
Featherstone
Ripponden
Blackley
Barkisland
Stainland
Holywell Green
Elland
Rastrick
Deighton
Ravensthorpe
Earlsheaton
Ossett
Warmfield
Purston Jaglin
East Hardwick
Rishworth
Booth Wood Resr
Mirfield
Upper Hopton
Thornhill Edge
Thornhill
Horbury
Sharlston
West Hardwick
High Ackworth
Fartown
Scammonden Water
Golcar
Crosland Moor
Fenay Bridge
Kirkheaton
Grange Moor
Middlestown
Lepton
Netherton
Crigglestone
Hill Top
Walton
Crofton
Wintersett
Ryhill
Fitzwilliam
Ackworth Moor Top
Thorpe Audlin

Denshaw
Marsden
Meltham
Honley
Netherthong
Upperthong
Holmfirth
Thurstonland
Shepley
New Mill
Scholes
Skelmanthorpe
Denby Dale
High Hoyland
Kexbrough
Cawthorne
Darton
Staincross
Royston
Carlton
Shafton
Brierley
South Kirkby
Grimethorpe
Cudworth
Clayton
Great Houghton
Thurnscoe
Hickleton
BARNSLEY
Gawber
Ardsley
Darfield
Dearne
Goldthorpe
Billingley
Bolton upon Dearne
Adwick upon Dearne
Mexborough
Wath upon Dearne
Swinton
Kilnhurst
Delph
Diggle
Dobcross
Uppermill
Grasscroft
Greenfield
Mossley
Stalybridge
Butterley Resr
Dove Stone Resr
Chew Resr
Holme
Holmbridge
Hepworth
Upper Denby
Ingbirchworth
Ingbirchworth Resr
Silkstone
Dodworth
Silkstone Common
Hoyland Swaine
Worsbrough
Wombwell
Birdwell
Thurlstone
Carlecotes
Winscar Resr
Penistone
Oxspring
Thurgoland
Pilley
Tankersley
Brampton
Jump
Elsecar
Hoyland Nether
Dunford Bridge
Windleden Resrs
Langsett
Little Don
Wortley
Langsett Resr
Midhopestones
Stockbridge
Bolsterstone
Ewden Village
Broomhead Resr
Walkerwood Resr
Tintwhistle
Torside Resr
Hollingworth
Mottram Longdendale
Hadfield
Hyde
Broadbottom
Glossop
Charlesworth
Chisworth
Compstall
Chunal
PEAK DISTRICT
SOUTH YORKSHIRE
Derwent
Howden Resr
Abbey Brook
Alport
Derwent Resr
Dale Dike Resr
Strines Resr
Agden Resr
Wharncliffe Side
High Green
Chapeltown
Wentworth
Thorpe Hesley
Upper Haugh
Nether Haugh
Greasbrough
Rawmarsh
Thrybergh
Dalton
Grenoside
Ecclesfield
High Bradfield
Oughtbridge
Damflask Resr
Worrall
Low Bradfield
Parson Cross
ROTHERHAM
Wickersley
Moorgate
Whiston
Tinsley
Hillsborough
Owlerton
Brinsworth
DERBYSHIRE
Ashopton Woodlands
Ashop
Kinder Resr
Ladybower Resr
Loxley
Stannington
Catcliffe
Treeton
Ulley
Aughton
Aston
Mellor
New Mills
Birch Vale
Hayfield
NATIONAL PARK
Hallow Meadows
SHEFFIELD
RAC
Handsworth
Barber Booth
Edale
Noe
Low Leighton
Chinley Head
Fulwood
Redmires Resr
Woodhouse
Disley
Newtown
Hope
Aston
Bamford
Thornhill
Whirlow
Norton Woodseats
Beighton
Chinley
Castleton
Brough
Hathersage
Abbeydale
Sheaf
Gleadless
Waterthorpe
Wales
Whaley Bridge
Slackhall
Bradwell
Dore
Beauchief
Norton
Mosborough
Kettleshulme
Chapel-en-le-Frith
Sparrowpit
Abney
Greenhill
Coal Aston
Eckington
Killamarsh
Coombs Resr
Taxal
Peak Forest
Coplow Dale
Great Hucklow
Totley
Dronfield Woodhouse
Dronfield
Apperknowle
Fernilee
Fernilee Resr
Combs
Dove Holes
Little Hucklow
Windmill
Grindlow
Nether Padley
Barbrook Resr
Holmesfield
Unstone
West Handley
Renishaw
Peak Dale
Wheston
Foolow
Eyam
Grindleford
Froggatt
A640
A62
A6052
A672
A670
A635
A6024
A628
A636
A637
A633
A629
A61
M1
A616
A6018
M67
A560
A6016
A626
A57
A624
A6015
A625
A6013
A6102
A6135
A6101
A6123
A631
A618
A630
A616
A6102
A623
A6
A5002
A621
B6107
B6106
B6105
B6116
B6273
B6097
B6089
B6090
B6086
B6077
B6076
B6086
B6410
B6067
B6388
B6054
B6053
B6056
B6052
B6051
B6061
B6049
B6001
B6101
33
30
31
41
37
36
35
34
33
A
B
C
1
2
3
4

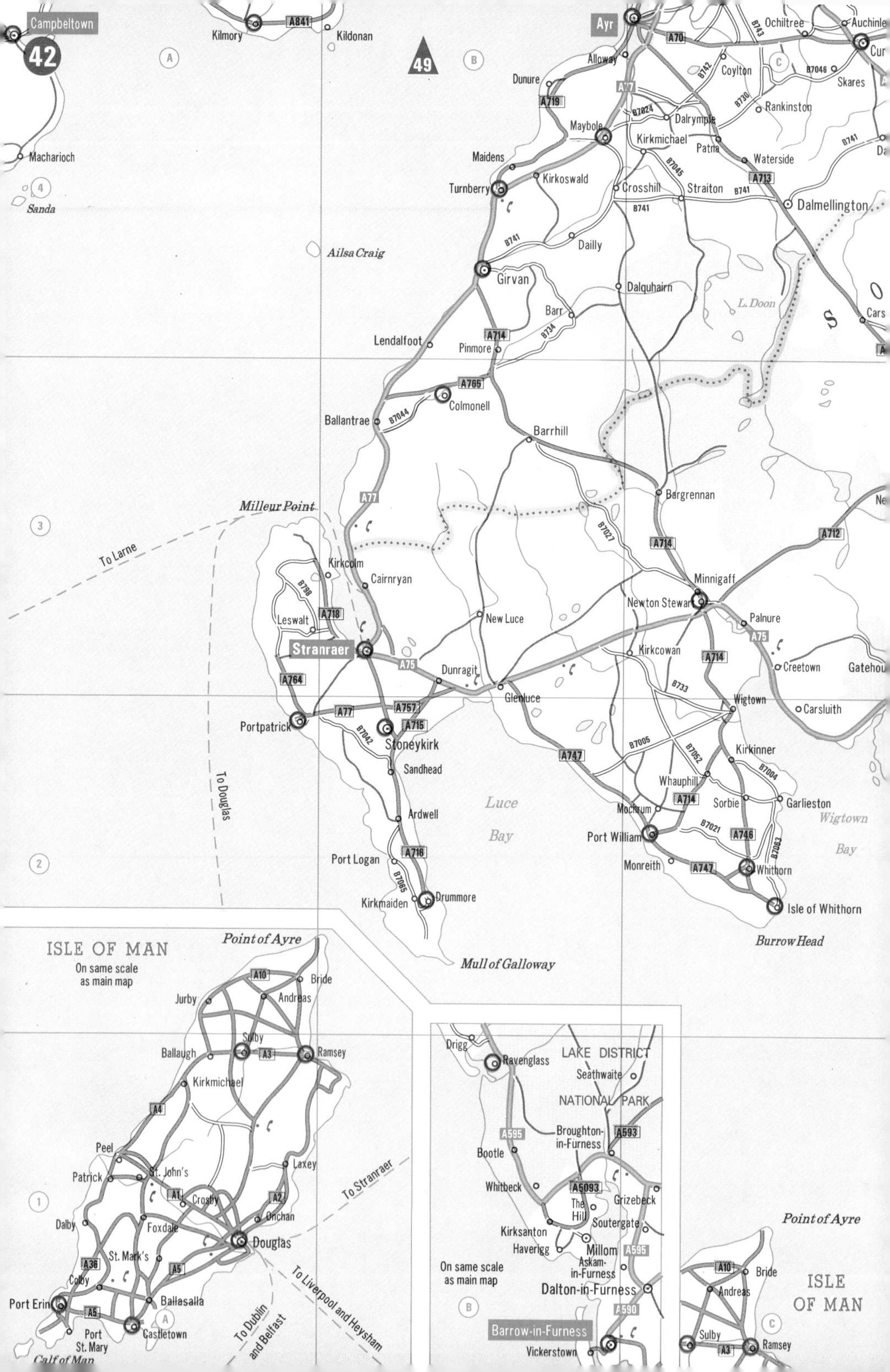

Campbeltown
42
Kilmory
A841
Kildonan
49
Ayr
A70
Ochiltree
Auchinleck
B743
Alloway
Coylton
B742
B7046
Skares
Dunure
A77
A719
B730
Rankinston
B7024
Dalrymple
Maybole
Kirkmichael
Patna
B741
Machrioch
Maidens
Waterside
B7045
A713
Turnberry
Kirkoswald
Crosshill
Straiton
B741
Sanda
Dalmellington
B741
Dailly
Ailsa Craig
Girvan
Dalquhairn
L. Doon
Barr
A714
B734
Lendalfoot
Pinmore
A765
Colmonell
Ballantrae
B7044
Barrhill
A77
Milleur Point
Bargrennan
To Larne
B7027
A714
A712
Kirkcolm
Cairnryan
B798
Minnigaff
A718
Newton Stewart
New Luce
Leswalt
Palnure
A75
Stranraer
Kirkcowan
A714
A75
Dunragit
Creetown
A764
Glenluce
B733
Wigtown
Carsluith
Portpatrick
A77
A757
A715
Stoneykirk
B7042
A747
B7005
B7052
Kirkinner
To Douglas
Sandhead
B7004
Whauphill
Luce
A714
Sorbie
Garlieston
Ardwell
Mochrum
Wigtown
Bay
Port William
B7021
A746
Bay
A716
B7063
Port Logan
Monreith
A747
Whithorn
B7065
Kirkmaiden
Drummore
Isle of Whithorn
Burrow Head
Mull of Galloway
ISLE OF MAN
On same scale as main map
Point of Ayre
A10
Bride
Andreas
Jurby
Sulby
Ballaugh
A3
Ramsey
Kirkmichael
A4
Peel
St. John's
Laxey
Patrick
A1
Crosby
A2
To Stranraer
Onchan
Dalby
Foxdale
Douglas
St. Mark's
A5
A36
To Liverpool and Heysham
Colby
Ballasalla
Port Erin
A5
To Dublin and Belfast
Castletown
Port St. Mary
Calf of Man
Drigg
Ravenglass
LAKE DISTRICT
Seathwaite
NATIONAL PARK
A595
Broughton-in-Furness
A593
Bootle
Whitbeck
A5093
The Hill
Grizebeck
Kirksanton
Soutergate
Haverigg
Millom
A595
On same scale as main map
Askam-in-Furness
Dalton-in-Furness
A590
Barrow-in-Furness
Vickerstown
Point of Ayre
A10
Bride
Andreas
ISLE OF MAN
Sulby
A3
Ramsey

Crawford
A708
BORDERS
Minto
43
Denholm
B740
B797
50
Ramseycleuch
B711
Roberton
Hawick
Kirkton
Leadhills
B7040
Elvanfoot
A702
Nith
Kirkconnel
Wanlockhead
A74
B719
A7
Newmill
B797
Sanquhar
Mennock
Davington
Teviothead
B709
Enterkinfoot
Moffat
Eskdalemuir
Durisdeer
Beattock
B723
B6399
Carronbridge
Locherben
Newton
Penpont
Thornhill
St. Ann's
Johnstonebridge
B709
DUMFRIES
Tynron
Closeburn
Boreland
Ewes
B7020
Moniaive
Kirkland
Parkgate
Bentpath
Newcastleton
A702
AND
A701
Templand
Corrie Common
Dalswinton
Dunscore
B729
Duncow
A76
Lochmaben
Lockerbie
Langholm
B6357
Kershopefoot
GALLOWAY
Tinwald
A709
B7068
Bankshill
Hightae
Annan
A7
Rowanburn
Balmaclellan
Dumfries
Torthorwald
Middlebie
B725
B6318
Catlowdy
A712
Corsock
Shawhead
Collin
B7020
Waterbeck
B6357
B722
Eaglesfield
Canonbie
Kingholm Quay
Dalton
Ecclefechan
A74
Milltown
Crocketford
A711
B724
Mouswald
Kirtlebridge
B722
B723
Kirkpatrick Fleming
Parton
B794
Kirkpatrick Durham
Clarencefield
Bankend
B725
A75
Brydekirk
B6357
Longtown
3
Beeswing
Haugh of Urr
Glencaple
Rigg
Hethersgill
Crossmichael
B795
New Abbey
Kirkgunzeon
Ruthwell
Cummertrees
Annan
Gretna
A6071
Smithfield
44
Walton
A75
Eastriggs
Scaleby
Brampton
Castle Douglas
B794
Dalbeattie
Bowness-on-Solway
Rockcliffe
Irthington
Bridge of Dee
B793
Burgh by Sands
Crosby
A69
Farlam
Gelston
Kirkbean
Drumburgh
Hayton
Castle Carrock
Ford
B736
Palnackie
Caulkerbush
Skinburness
Newton Arlosh
B5307
Carlisle
Warwick
A711
B727
A710
Solway Firth
Kirkbride
43
Faugh
Sandyhills
B5302
Great Orton
Wetheral
Cumwhitton
Tongland
A711
Rockliffe
Silloth
Aikton
Cummersdale
42
Eden
Cumrew
Abbeytown
Oulton
M6
Kirkcudbright
Auchencairn
Wigton
Dalston
Cotehill
B5300
Thursby
Wreay
Beckfoot
Croglin
Armathwaite
Dundrennan
B5301
Gaitsgill
Mawbray
A596
Waverton
High Hesket
Westnewton
Rosley
A6
A595
Sebergham
Kirkoswald
Allonby
B5299
Lazonby
Aspatria
B5305
Calthwaite
Mealsgate
B6413
Plumbland
Caldbeck
2
Great Salkeld
Bothel
Ireby
Gilcrux
Uldale
Lamonby
Maryport
Dearham
41
Newton Reigny
Flimby
Derwent
Penrith
Cockermouth
Mosedale
Broughton
Greystoke
A596
Bassenthwaite
B5288
A66
Mungrisdale
Workington
A591
Penruddock
Clifton
A66
Eaglesfield
Dacre
B5320
A66
Thornthwaite
Clifton
Harrington
B5292
Troutbeck
Dean
A5086
Lorton
Pooley Bridge
Threlkeld
A592
Distington
Ullock
A5091
Braithwaite
Watermillock
Keswick
A595
Lamplugh
Arlecdon
Dockray
Parton
Loweswater
Ullswater
CUMBRIAN
Howtown
Kirkland
Grange
Glenridding
Bampton
Cleator Moor
Whitehaven
B5295
Buttermere
CUMBRIA
B5289
Patterdale
St. Bees Head
Ennerdale Bridge
B5345
Cleator
A591
Borrowdale
St. Bees
Egremont
MOUNTAINS
A592
Grasmere
Wasdale Head
Sadgill
Great Langdale
Rydal
Haile
Elterwater
1
Ambleside
Beckermet
Calder Bridge
Kentmere
Little Langdale
Nether Wasdale
Skelwith Bridge
Troutbeck
Gosforth
LAKE DISTRICT
Windermere
Windermere
Seascale
Holmrook
Boot
Staveley
Coniston
B5285
Drigg
NATIONAL PARK
Burneside
Ravenglass
Hawkshead
Near Sawrey
Bowness
Seathwaite
36
A59
B5284
A
B
C
Far Sawrey
Grizedale
Torver
Winster
Kendal
A593
Underbarrow
A595
Blawith
Satterthwaite
A592

44
BORDERS
Ashkirk
Minto
Teviot
Lanton
Jedburgh
A698
Hownam
Oxnam
51
Ilderton
Wooperton
B6346
Denholm
B6358
Bedrule
B6357
Roberton
B711
Hawick
Ramseycleuch
Kirkton
A6088
Chesters
Bonchester Bridge
A68
Ingram
Glanton
Bolton
Prendwick
Whittingham
NORTHUMBERLAND
A697
Newmill
B709
Davington
A7
Teviothead
B6357
Alwinton
Netherton
NATIONAL
Harbottle
Snitter
Eskdalemuir
CHEVIOT HILLS
Holystone
Rothbury
Thropton
Hepple
PARK
B6344
B6399
A68
Rochester
B6341
Longhorsley
Kielder
Otterburn
Elsdon
B6342
Ewes
Newcastleton
NORTHUMBERLAND
A696
Bentpath
Falstone
Greenhaugh
West Woodburn
B6343
Hartburn
Langholm
B6357
Kirkwhelpington
Meldon
B7068
Kershopefoot
Kielder Water
Bellingham
Capheaton
Whalton
B722
A7
Rowanburn
Redesmouth
Kirkheaton
Belsay
B6318
Waterbeck
Catlowdy
Wark
Birtley
Hallington
Ryal
Eaglesfield
B6357
Bewcastle
B6320
Chollerton
B6309
Milltown
Canonbie
Simonburn
Humshaugh
Chollerford
Matfen
Great Whittington
Kirkpatrick Fleming
Walwick
Wall
A6079
B6318
B6357
Longtown
Hethersgill
Kirkcambeck
Gilsland
B5818
Newbrough
B6319
Acomb
Sandhoe
Gretna
A6071
Irthing
Haltwhistle
Horsley
Rigg
Smithfield
Banks
Greenhead
Bardon Mill
Haydon Bridge
B6305
Hexham
Corbridge
Tyne
Walton
A69
A695
Prudhoe
Scaleby
Irthington
Low Row
Plenmeller
Riding Mill
Chopwell
Rockcliffe
Brampton
B6309
Burgh by Sands
Crosby
A69
Whitfield
Whitley Chapel
Whittonstall
Drumburgh
B5307
Carlisle
Farlam
Lambley
Catton
Slaley
A68
Hayton
Kirkbride
Castle Carrock
A689
A686
Allendale Town
B6306
Shotley Bridge
43
Warwick
Faugh
Wetheral
Great Orton
Cumwhitton
Knarsdale
Edmundbyers
Aikton
Cummersdale
Eden
Slaggyford
Oulton
42
Cumrew
Blanchland
M6
Dalston
Wigton
Thursby
Wreay
Cotehill
B6143
Croglin
Alston
Carr Shield
B6278
Castleside
B6295
Gaitsgill
Armathwaite
Allenheads
A595
Rosley
High Hesket
Renwick
Leadgate
Nenthead
A689
Rookhope
A6
Kirkoswald
B5299
Sebergham
Garrigill
Calthwaite
Lazonby
Gamblesby
Eastgate
Stanhope
B6413
B5305
Caldbeck
Plumpton
Glassonby
B6277
Westgate
Wear
A689
Great Salkeld
A686
Uldale
Lamonby
B6412
St. John's Chapel
Frosterley
Wolsingham
Melmerby
Newton Reigny
41
Mosedale
Langwathby
B6278
Penrith
Skirwith
Bassenthwaite
Greystoke
Edenhall
DURHAM
Mungrisdale
Culgaith
A591
B5288
Penruddock
40
Temple Sowerby
Hamsterley
Woodland
A66
B5320
Clifton
Newbiggin
B6277
Dacre
Kirkby Thore
Thornthwaite
Troutbeck
Great Strickland
Middleton in Teesdale
Eggleston
B6282
Threlkeld
A592
Pooley Bridge
A66
Long Marton
B6279
A5091
Keswick
Watermillock
Morland
Newby
Murton
Romaldkirk
Dockray
M6
Hilton
B6276
B6278
Ullswater
Cotherstone
Barnard Castle
CUMBRIAN
Howtown
Appleby in Westmorland
Grange
Glenridding
Bampton
Little Strickland
B6277
CUMBRIA
Patterdale
A6
Crosby Ravensworth
Warcop
Shap
Brough
A66
A67
Bowes
Greta Bridge
Borrowdale
A591
B6260
Great Asby
B6259
A685
39
Soulby
Winton
Barningham
MOUNTAINS
A592
Grasmere
Crosby Garrett
Sadgill
Rydal
Kirkby Stephen
Great Langdale
Elterwater
Ambleside
38
Tebay
Kentmere
Nateby
Langthwaite
Little Langdale
Troutbeck
A59
Skelwith Bridge
Ravenstonedale
LAKE DISTRICT
Windermere
A6
Reeth
Marske
B6259
Keld
Feetham
NATIONAL
B5285
Windermere
Marrick
Coniston
A591
Staveley
Grayrigg
A683
Thwaite
B6270
PARK
Hawkshead
Near Sawrey
Bowness
Burneside
Lowgill
36
Muker
38
Low Row
Grinton
Satterthwaite
A685
B6257
Castle Bolton
Grizedale
Far Sawrey
B5284
Torver
Winster
Kendal
A684
Sedbergh
Carperby
Redmire
37
Askrigg
Underbarrow

51
Craster
Howick
Longhoughton
Boulmer
Lesbury
Alnmouth
Warkworth
Amble-by-the-Sea
Acklington
Broomhill
West Chevington
Widdrington
Cresswell
Ellington
Lynemouth
Longhirst
COVERAGE AT 4 MILES TO 1 INCH
Newbiggin-by-the-Sea
Ashington
Cambois
Bedlington
Blyth
Cramlington
Seaton Sluice
Seaton Delaval
Whitley Bay
NEWCASTLE UPON TYNE
Tynemouth
South Shields
Jarrow
Boldon
Whitburn
Whickham
Birtley
Washington
SUNDERLAND
Ryhope
Chester-le-Street
Houghton-le-Spring
Seaham
Hetton-le-Hole
Murton
Sacriston
Pittington
Easington
DURHAM
Haswell
Horden
Thornley
Peterlee
To Bergen, Gothenburg and Stavanger
To Esbjerg
TYNE AND WEAR
Tudhoe
Spennymoor
Trimdon
Ferryhill
Rushyford
Sedgefield
Hart
Hartlepool
Elwick
Seaton Carew
Greatham
Bishop Auckland
Newton Aycliffe
Wolviston
Thorpe Thewles
Billingham
TEESSIDE
MIDDLESBROUGH
Coatham
Redcar
Marske-by-the-Sea
Saltburn-by-the-Sea
Brotton
Kirkleatham
Grangetown
Eston
Guisborough
Skelton
Loftus
Staithes
Hinderwell
Heighington
Bishopton
Stockton-on-Tees
Sadberge
Thornaby-on-Tees
Darlington
Stainton
Teesside
Egglescliffe
Seamer
CLEVELAND
Commondale
Lythe
Whitby
Ugthorpe
Great Ayton
Croft-on-Tees
Hurworth
Tees
Stokesley
Crathorne
Castleton
Lealholme
Sleights
Ruswarp
Hawsker
Great Broughton
Westerdale
Glaisdale
Grosmont
Robin Hood's Bay
Ravenscar
Scotch Corner
Moulton
Great Smeaton
Rounton
Carlton
East Cowton
East Harsley
Swainby
NORTH YORKSHIRE
Goathland
Welbury
NORTH YORK
Staintondale
NORTH YORK MOORS NATIONAL PARK
Harwood Dale
Cloughton
Catterick
Usmotherly
Rosedale Abbey
Brompton
Great Langton
Northallerton
38
MOORS
Newton-on-Rawcliffe
Lockton
Hackness
39
Scalby
Patrick Brompton
Scruton
Hawnby
Gillamoor
Lastingham
A1068
B1337
A197
A192
A189
A1
A193
A187
A183
A19
A6076
A693
A690
A691
A182
B1283
B1280
A167
A177
B1278
A181
A1086
A689
A6072
A1M
A178
A1085
A174
A66
A135
A1044
A67
A173
B1366
B1266
A171
B1264
A172
B1257
B1416
B6275
B1263
B6271
A168
A165

CENTRAL
STRATHCLYDE
GLASGOW
Paisley
East Kilbride
Greenock
Erskine
Rhu
Helensburgh
Arden
Ballagan
Craighat
Dumgoyne
Carron Bridge
High Banton
Banton
Banknock
Kilsyth
Carron Valley Forest
Valley Resr
Carron
Gare Loch
Rosneath Point
Craigendoran
Colgran
Balloch
Auchencarroch
Jamestown
Alexandria
Bonhill
Renton
Geilston
Cardross
Castlehill
Brucehill
Kirktonhill
Dumbarton
Bellsmyre
Milton
Port Glasgow
Finlaystone
Lilybank
Woodhall
Langbank
Loch Thom
Gryfe Resrs
Bardrainney
Leperstone Resr
Auchendores Resr
Burncrooks Resr
Kilmannan Resr
Loch Humphrey
Cochno Loch
Jaw Resr
Greenside Resr
Mugdock Resr
Netherton
Blanefield
Strathblane
Clachan of Campsie
Balgrochan
Lennoxtown
Milton of Campsie
Queenzieburn
Castlecary
Dullatur
Croy
Twechar
Eastfield
Cumbernauld
Mugdock
Blairskaith
Birdston
Milngavie
Torrance
Bowling
Old Kilpatrick
Duntocher
Faifley
Bardowie
Balmore
Kirkintilloch
Waterside
Condorrat
Luggiebank
Bearsden
Drumchapel
Cadder
Lenzie
Mollinsburn
Bridgend
Bishopton
Rossland
Kilmacolm
Barochan Ho
Inchinnan
Clydebank
Yoker
Bishopbriggs
Temple
Auchinloch
Lumloch
Muirhead
Annathill
Riggend
Wattston
Marnock
Glenboig
Stepps
Springburn
Renfrew
Georgetown
Quarrier's Homes
Bridge of Weir
Glasgow Airport
Scotstoun
Patrick
Garnkirk
Ruchazie
Gartcosh
Lochwood
Glenmavis
Airdriehill
Carruth Ho
Houston
Crosslee
Coatbridge
Govan
Linwood
Ranfurly
Brookfield
Cardonald
Shettleston
Coatdyke
Old Monkland
Chapelhall
Kilbarchan
Elderslie
Johnstone
Charleston
Glenburn
Heathfield
Millikenpark
Pollokshields
Rutherglen
Baillieston
Birkenshaw
Calderbank
Carmyle
Viewpark
Newton
Mossend
Holytown
Cathcart
Waterside
Howwood
Nitshill
Pollokshaws
Muivend
Cambuslang
Uddingston
Bellshill
New Stevenston
Flemington
Castlemilk
Bothwell
Lochwinnoch
Newton of Beltrees
Nether Kirkton
Barrhead
Auchenbach
Thornliebank
Giffnock
Clarkston
Carmunnock
Blantyre
Motherwell
Muirhead Resr
Barcraigs Resr
Neilston
Busby
Rogerton
Nerston
Camphill Resr
Kilbirnie
Shilford
Uplawmoor
Neilston Pad
Netherplace
Newton Mearns
Thorntonhall
High Blantyre
Hamilton
Ferniegair
Waterfoot
Beith
Glengarnock
Gateside
Lugton
Halket
Barrmill
Jackton
Eaglesham
Meikle Earnock
Quarter
Larkhall
The Den
Earn Water
White Cart Water
Clyde
Forth and Clyde
Calder
Garnock
Leven
A770
A78
A814
A811
A813
A81
A809
A891
A803
A80
A8
A807
A879
A82
M8
A761
M73
A73
A726
A736
A737
A760
A749
A724
A725
M74
A723
A775
A77
B818
B822
B821
B8023
B8048
B757
B819
B812
B806
B804
B802
B786
B788
B789
B790
B775
B762
B766
B759
B776
B777
B784
B780
B769
B7001
B7078
B754
49
50

Kirkcaldy
Linktown
Kinghorn
Pettycur
Burntisland
Auchtertool
Cowdenbeath
Loch Gelly
Stenhouse Resr
Hill of Beath
Crossgates
Donibristle
Fordell
Aberdour
Dalgety Bay
Hillend
Inverkeithing
Inverkeithing Bay
North Queensferry
Mortimer's Deep
Inchcolm
Inchkeith
Firth of Forth
Inchmickery
Cramond Island
Dunfermline
FIFE
Loch Fitty
Bowershall
Kingseat
Townhill
Wellwood
Crossford
Pattiesmuir
Rosyth
Limekilns
Charlestown
Cowstrandburn
Blairhall
Comrie
Gowkhall
Carnock
Milesmark
Oakley
Shires Mill
Valleyfield
Caineyhill
Low Torry
Torryburn
Torry Bay
Culross
Moor Loch
Kincardine
South Alloa
Clackmannan
Kennet
Dunmore
Airth
Letham
Stenhousemuir
Skinflats
Carron
Grangemouth
Bo'ness
Grangepans
Carriden
Muirhouses
Blackness
St Margaret's Hope
Hopetoun Ho
Forth Bridge
Queensferry
Dalmeny
Newton
Bainsford
Falkirk
Glen Village
Redding
Reddingmuirhead
Shieldhill
California
Brightons
Maddiston
Linlithgow Bridge
Linlithgow
Champany
Philpstoun
Old Philpstoun
Bridgend
Whitecross
Winchburgh
Newbigging
Kirkliston
Cramond Bridge
Edinburgh Airport
Ingliston
Gogar
Newbridge
Ecclesmachan
Uphall
Broxburn
Burnside
Dechmont
Union
Loan
Standburn
Avonbridge
Westfield
Torphichen
Lochcote Resr
Bathgate
Boghall
Armadale
Whiteside
Westrigg
Blackridge
Eastfield
Harthill
Whitburn
East Whitburn
Longridge
Stoneyburn
Addiewell
Breich
Fauldhouse
Torbothie
Stane
Greenburn
Blackburn
Seafield
Livingston Village
Deans
Livingston
Craigshill
East Calder
Oakbank
Dedridge
Bellsquarry
Polbeth
West Calder
Murieston
Kirknewton
Wilkieston
Burnwynd
Bonnington
Ratho
Long Hermiston
Juniper Green
Currie
Balerno
Almond
Linhouse Water
Morton Resr
Water of Leith
Harperrig Resr
Cobbinshaw Resr
Crosswood
Harlaw Resr
Threipmuir Resr
Loganlea Resr
Glencorse Resr
LOTHIAN
EDINBURGH
Leith
Newhaven
Trinity
Granton
Cramond
Barnton
Blackhall
Corstorphine
Murrayfield
Sighthill
Morningside
Craiglockhart
Braid
Colinton
Liberton
Fairmilehead
Kaimes
Gilmerton
Danderhall
Millerhill
Craigmillar
Duddingston
Portobello
New Craighall
Musselburgh
Inveresk
Dolphinstone
Wallyford
Prestonpans
Cockenzie
Elphinstone
Whitecraig
Cousland
Dalkeith
Eskbank
Lasswade
Loanhead
Bonnyrigg
Mayfield
Easthouses
Newtongrange
Newlandrig
Arniston Engine
Gorebridge
Crichton
North Middleton
Middleton
Tynehead
Temple
Carrington
Rosewell
Polton
Roslin
Bilston
Auchendinny
Penicuik
Milton Bridge
Woodhouselee
Silverburn
Howgate
Edgelaw Resr
North Esk
Esk
Tyne Water
A977
A905
B9124
A876
A88
A907
A985
B9037
A823
A823(M)
M90
A910
A909
A921
A987
B925
B916
B981
B9156
B903
B924
A904
M9
A90
B9085
B701
A8
B8046
B9080
A801
A800
A899
B8047
B792
B825
B8084
B708
A89
A705
A71
M8
B7066
B7010
A706
B7015
B717
A704
B7008
A70
B7030
A720
A703
A702
A766
A701
A6094
A68
A7
A1
A199
A6093
B6414
B6372
B704
B7067
50
47
RAC

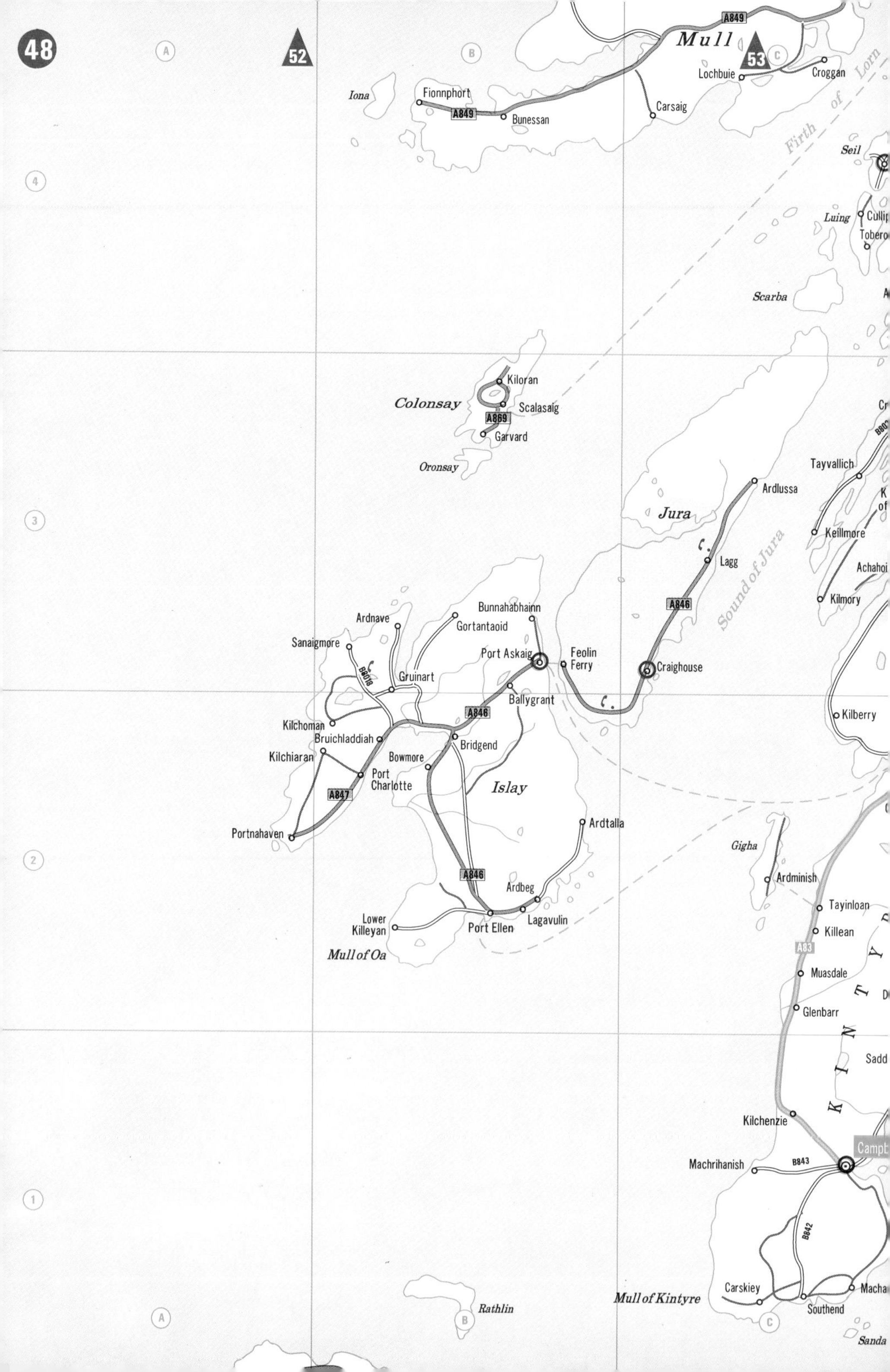

A
52
B
Mull
A849
53
C
Iona
Fionnphort
A849
Bunessan
Lochbuie
Croggan
Carsaig
Firth of Lorn
Seil
4
Luing
Cullip
Tobero
Scarba
Kiloran
Colonsay
Scalasaig
A869
Garvard
Oronsay
Tayvallich
Ardlussa
Jura
3
Keillmore
Lagg
Sound of Jura
Achahoi
Kilmory
A846
Bunnahabhainn
Ardnave
Gortantaoid
Sanaigmore
Port Askaig
Feolin
Ferry
Craighouse
B8018
Gruinart
Ballygrant
Kilberry
A846
Kilchoman
Bruichladdiah
Bridgend
Kilchiaran
Bowmore
Port
Charlotte
Islay
A847
Portnahaven
Ardtalla
Gigha
2
Ardminish
A846
Ardbeg
Tayinloan
Lower
Killeyan
Port Ellen
Lagavulin
Killean
Mull of Oa
A83
Muasdale
KINTYRE
Glenbarr
Sadd
Kilchenzie
Campt
Machrihanish
B843
1
B842
Carskiey
Macha
Mull of Kintyre
Southend
Rathlin
A
B
C
Sanda

Oban
Taynuilt
53
A85
Tyndrum
A85
54
49
Dalmally
Crianlarich
Lochearnhead
Balquhidder
Kingshouse
St. Fillans
L. Earn
Kilchrenan
Cladich
A82
L. Voil
A84
Strathyre
Dalchruin
B840
A819
Ardlui
L. Katrine
Kilmelford
Loch Awe
Cairndow
Stronachlachar
Inveraray
Inversnaid
Brig o' Turk
A821
Callander
B839
St. Catherines
B828
A83
Arrochar
Tarbet
B829
A81
B8032
A84
A815
Aberfoyle
Doune
Ford
Creggans
Lochgoilhead
Port of Menteith
A873
B822
Thornhill
A83
Furnace
Strachur
Newton
L. Long
B8034
Kilmartin
Minard
A814
CENTRAL
Gartmore
Buchlyvie
Garbhallt
Carnick Castle
Luss
Loch Lomond
Kippen
A811
Gargunnock
Bridgend
Balmaha
Lochgair
Garelochhead
Drymen
A875
B822
50
Cairnbaan
B8000
A886
Coulport
Balfron
B818
Lochgilphead
Ardentinny
B833
Shandon
B832
A82
Gartocharn
A811
Killearn
Fintry
Clachan of Glendaruel
A815
A880
SEE PAGE 46 FOR COVERAGE AT 4 MILES TO 1 INCH
Ardishaig
Rhu
Helensburgh
Balloch
A81
Otter Ferry
B836
Clachaig
Kilmun
Rosneath
Craigendoran
Jamestown
Blanefield
Clachan of Campsie
B822
Auchenbreck
Kilcreggan
Alexandria
Fyne
Sandbank
Hunter's Quay
Renton
Bonhill
A809
A891
Kilsyth
A886
A813
Strathblane
Kilfinan
Dunoon
Gourock
A770
Cardross
Dumbarton
Milngavie
A8003
Greenock
A807
Kirkintilloch
Loch
Tighna-Bruaich
Colintraive
Port Glasgow
A8
Lenzie
Bearsden
A879
Inverkip
M8
Bishopton
Innellan
Wemyss Bay
B788
Kilmacolm
Bishopbriggs
Tarbert
Kames
A886
A815
Glasgow
Clydebank
A82
West Tarbert
Port Bannatyne
Skelmorlie
Houston
Bridge of Weir
B786
A761
Paisley
GLASGOW
A844
Rothesay
Johnstone
A74
Kennacraig
B878
Ascog
A78
Kilbarchan
Bellshill
Whitehouse
A845
Howwood
A737
Barrhead
A749
A844
Largs
Lochwinnoch
A726
Bothwell
Skipness
B8001
Neilston
B775
Busby
A860
Kilbirnie
Newton Mearns
B767
Hamilton
Claonaig
Bute
Kingarth
A760
Beith
Uplawmoor
Eaglesham
East Kilbride
Millport
Fairlie
Kilchattan Bay
B706
Lugton
A77
A723
B769
A736
Lochranza
West Kilbride
B781
Dalry
Dunlop
B764
Auldhouse
Chapelton
B707
Glassford
Seamill
B780
Stewarton
Strathaven
B778
A78
Fenwick
Pirnmill
Corrie
Kilwinning
A735
A719
Ardrossan
Stevenston
Kilmaurs
B751
Blackwaterfoot
Lochranza
Arran
Saltcoats
Irvine
Kilmarnock
Newmilns
Drumclog
A841
A71
A71
Galston
Darvel
Clyde
High Dougarie
A78
A759
Brodick
B880
Dundonald
B730
B7037
A723
Lamlash
A77
Craigie
A719
Crosshands
Holy I.
Troon
Symington
B744
Mauchline
Sorn
B743
Muirkirk
Prestwick
Ayr
Whiting Bay
Tarbolton
Catrine
Prestwick
Kilbrannan Sound
Annbank
A76
Auchinleck
Kilmory
A841
Ayr
Ochiltree
B743
Kildonan
A70
Cumnock
Lugar
Alloway
Coylton
B742
B7046
Skares
Dunure
A77
B730
Rankinston
New Cumnock
A719
B7024
Dalrymple
Connel Park
Firth of Clyde
Maybole
Kirkmichael
Patna
B741
Dalleagles
Maidens
Waterside
B7045
A713
42
Turnberry
Kirkoswald
Crosshill
Straiton
B741
43
Dalmellington
B741
B741
Dailly

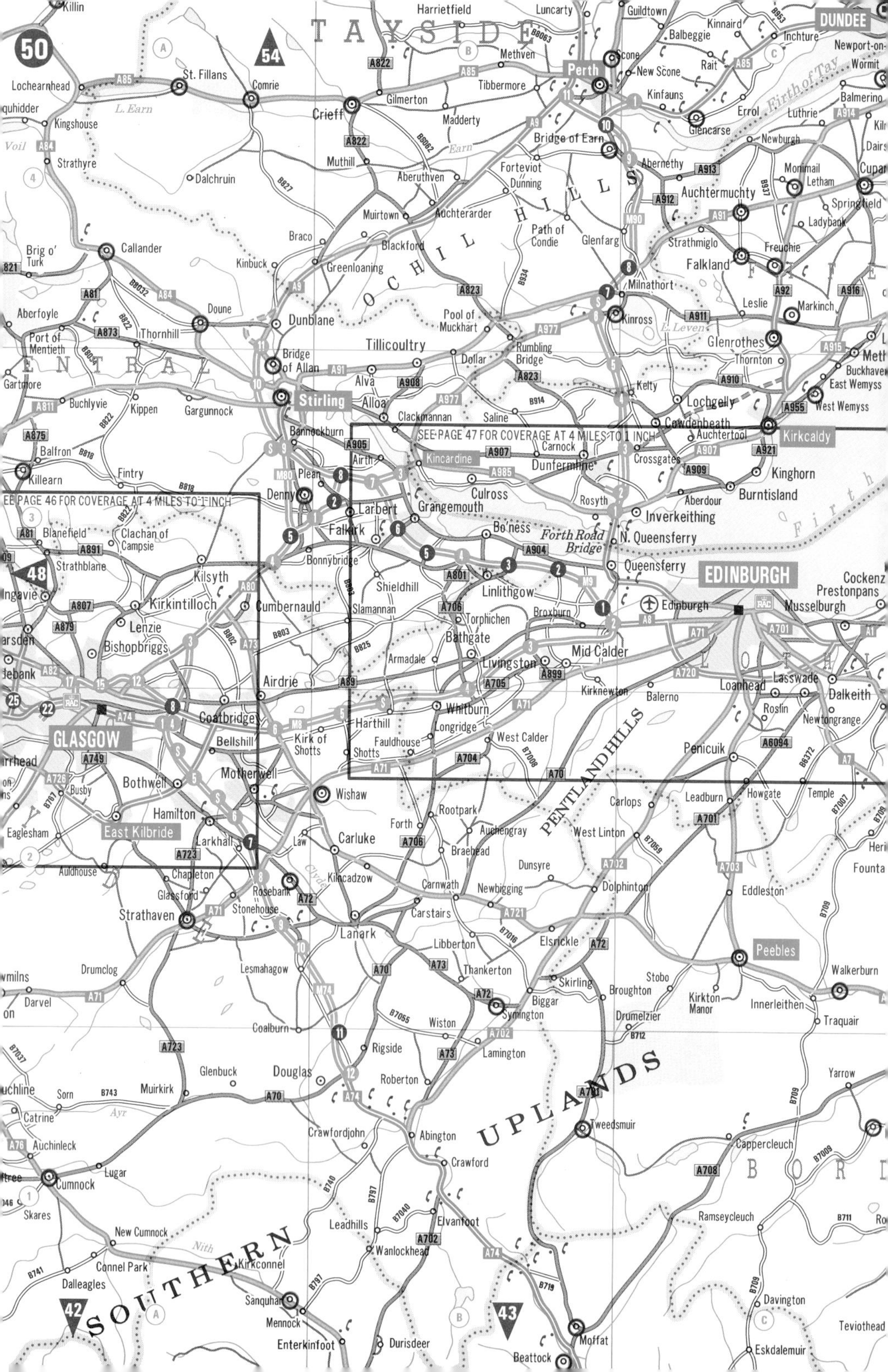

50
54
TAYSIDE
DUNDEE
Killin
Harrietfield
Luncarty
Guildtown
Kinnaird
Inchture
Newport-on-
Wormit
Balbeggie
Scone
Perth
New Scone
Rait
Firth of Tay
Methven
Tibbermore
Kinfauns
Errol
Balmerino
Luthrie
Lochearnhead
St. Fillans
Comrie
Crieff
Gilmerton
Madderty
Glencarse
Newburgh
L. Earn
Kingshouse
Strathyre
Dalchruin
Muthill
Aberuthven
Forteviot
Dunning
Bridge of Earn
Abernethy
Auchtermuchty
Monimail
Letham
Cupar
Springfield
Ladybank
Muirtown
Auchterarder
Path of Condie
Glenfarg
Strathmiglo
Freuchie
Falkland
OCHIL HILLS
Braco
Blackford
Greenloaning
Kinbuck
Callander
Brig o' Turk
Milnathort
Leslie
Markinch
Aberfoyle
Doune
Dunblane
Pool of Muckhart
Kinross
L. Leven
Glenrothes
Port of Menteith
Thornhill
Bridge of Allan
Tillicoultry
Dollar
Rumbling Bridge
Thornton
Buckhaven
East Wemyss
West Wemyss
CENTRAL
Gartmore
Alva
Alloa
Stirling
Kelty
Lochgelly
Cowdenbeath
Auchtertool
Kirkcaldy
Buchlyvie
Kippen
Gargunnock
Clackmannan
Saline
Balfron
Bannockburn
SEE PAGE 47 FOR COVERAGE AT 4 MILES TO 1 INCH
Kincardine
Carnock
Dunfermline
Crossgates
Kinghorn
Burntisland
Killearn
Fintry
Airth
Plean
Denny
Larbert
Falkirk
Grangemouth
Culross
Rosyth
Aberdour
Inverkeithing
SEE PAGE 46 FOR COVERAGE AT 4 MILES TO 1 INCH
Blanefield
Clachan of Campsie
Bo'ness
Forth Road Bridge
N. Queensferry
Firth
Strathblane
48
Bonnybridge
Queensferry
EDINBURGH
Cockenzie
Prestonpans
Kilsyth
Shieldhill
Linlithgow
Edinburgh
Musselburgh
Kirkintilloch
Cumbernauld
Slamannan
Torphichen
Broxburn
Lenzie
Bishopbriggs
Bathgate
Mid Calder
Armadale
Livingston
Lasswade
Dalkeith
Loanhead
Roslin
Newtongrange
Airdrie
Kirknewton
Balerno
Coatbridge
Whitburn
GLASGOW
Bellshill
Kirk of Shotts
Harthill
Longridge
Fauldhouse
Shotts
West Calder
Penicuik
PENTLAND HILLS
Motherwell
Bothwell
Busby
Hamilton
Wishaw
Eaglesham
East Kilbride
Larkhall
Carlops
Leadburn
Howgate
Temple
Rootpark
Forth
Auchengray
Braehead
West Linton
Law
Carluke
Auldhouse
Chapleton
Glassford
Kilncadzow
Rosebank
Stonehouse
Carnwath
Newbigging
Dunsyre
Dolphinton
Eddleston
Strathaven
Lanark
Carstairs
Libberton
Elsrickle
Thankerton
Peebles
Walkerburn
Drumclog
Lesmahagow
Skirling
Stobo
Broughton
Kirkton Manor
Innerleithen
Traquair
Darvel
Biggar
Symington
Drumelzier
Coalburn
Wiston
Lamington
Rigside
Glenbuck
Muirkirk
Douglas
Roberton
Sorn
UPLANDS
Yarrow
Catrine
Auchinleck
Crawfordjohn
Abington
Tweedsmuir
Cappercleuch
Crawford
Cumnock
Lugar
BORDERS
Skares
Leadhills
Elvanfoot
Ramseycleuch
New Cumnock
Wanlockhead
Nith
Kirkconnel
Connel Park
Dalleagles
SOUTHERN
Sanquhar
Mennock
Davington
42
43
Teviothead
Moffat
Enterkinfoot
Durisdeer
Beattock
Eskdalemuir

Buddon Ness
55
A
B
C
St. Andrews
Boarhills
A917
Kingsbarns
Dunino
Fife Ness
B940
Crail
B941
Kilrenny
Kilconquhar
Anstruther
Pittenweem
Elie
St. Monance
Earlsferry
Forth
North Berwick
Dirleton
A198
B1347
B1345
Whitekirk
B1377
East Linton
Dunbar
Drem
Athelstaneford
West Barns
Spott
A1
Haddington
Stenton
Innerwick
A6093
B6370
Garvald
Oldhamstocks
Cockburnspath
St. Abb's Head
St. Abbs
Gifford
A1107
Coldingham
East Saltoun
West Saltoun
B6355
Grantshouse
Eyemouth
Abbey St. Bathans
A6112
Humbie
Cranshaws
B6438
Reston
Burnmouth
Preston
B6355
Ayton
Chirnside
Longformacus
Foulden
A6105
Duns
Hutton
Berwick-upon-Tweed
Paxton
B6460
Whitsome
Carfraemill
B6456
A6112
B6461
Tweedmouth
Tweed
Westruther
Horncliffe
Polwarth
Norham
A698
Swinton
B6354
B6525
Cheswick
B6362
A697
Lauder
Greenlaw
Grindon
Ancroft
Goswick
Legerwood
Gordon
A68
Leitholm
Holy I.
A6105
Coldstream
Duddo
Bowsden
Beal
Holy Island
Eccles
Cornhill on Tweed
B6397
A6089
Langshaw
A698
B6353
Earlston
Stichill
Ross
Galashiels
Branxton
Etal
Birgham
Lowick
Ednam
Smailholm
Crookham
Warren Mill
Bamburgh
Ford
B7340
Sprouston
Melrose
Kelso
Flodden
Milfield
Belford
B6404
Seahouses
Doddington
B6396
St. Boswells
B6348
A699
A697
Lucker
B6352
Akeld
North Sunderland
B6348
Bowden
Maxton
Roxburgh
Kilham
B6351
Newham
Beadnell
Chatton
B6436
Kirknewton
Town Yetholm
Wooler
Chillingham
A68
Midlem
Chathill
Nisbet
Linton
B6401
A1
Lilliesleaf
Eckford
Ancrum
Ellingham
B6401
A7
Crailing
Middleton
North Charlton
Morebattle
B6347
Embleton
B6359
HILLS
Ilderton
B1340
Lanton
Minto
Teviot
B1339
Craster
S
R
A698
Jedburgh
Wooperton
B6346
Eglingham
Hownam
B6358
Rennington
Denholm
Oxnam
Howick
Hawick
Bedrule
B6357
Ingram
Glanton
Bolton
Longhoughton
Boulmer
Alnwick
Lesbury
Kirkton
Prendwick
A6088
NORTHUMBERLAND
Whittingham
Alnmouth
Chesters
A68
Edlingham
Bonchester Bridge
A697
Netherton
Shilbottle
CHEVIOT
NATIONAL
Alwinton
Newton on the Moor
Warkworth
44
B6341
45
B
Harbottle
Snitter
Amble-by-the-Se
B6357
PARK
Holystone
Rothbury
Longframlington
Acklington
Broomhill
Hepple
Thropton
B6344
Felton
B6345
A68
1
2
3
4

Benbecula
B892
Creagorry
Wiay
A865
Sandwick
West Gerinish
Stilligarry
Howmore
South Uist
Stoneybridge
Outer Hebrides
Daliburgh
Lochboisdale
Kilbride
Sound of Barra
Eriskay
A888
Borve
Barra
Castlebay
Vatersay
Sandray
Pabbay
Mingulay
Berneray
Barra Head
56
Borreraig
Milovaig
B884
Ramasaig
A850
Bernisdale
Skeabost Bridge
Dunvegan
Roag
Harlosh
A863
Skye
B885
Bracadale
Portnalong
B8009
Talisker
Carbost
Eynort
Canna
Kilmory
Rhum
Muck
Inner Hebrides
Ardnamurchan Point
Sorisdale
Coll
Ballyhaugh
Arinagour
Acha
Calgary
Kilninian
Caolas
Balevullin
Scarinish
Middleton
Tiree
Balemartine
Hynish
Ulva
STRA
48
Iona
Fionnphort
A
B
C
1
2
3
4

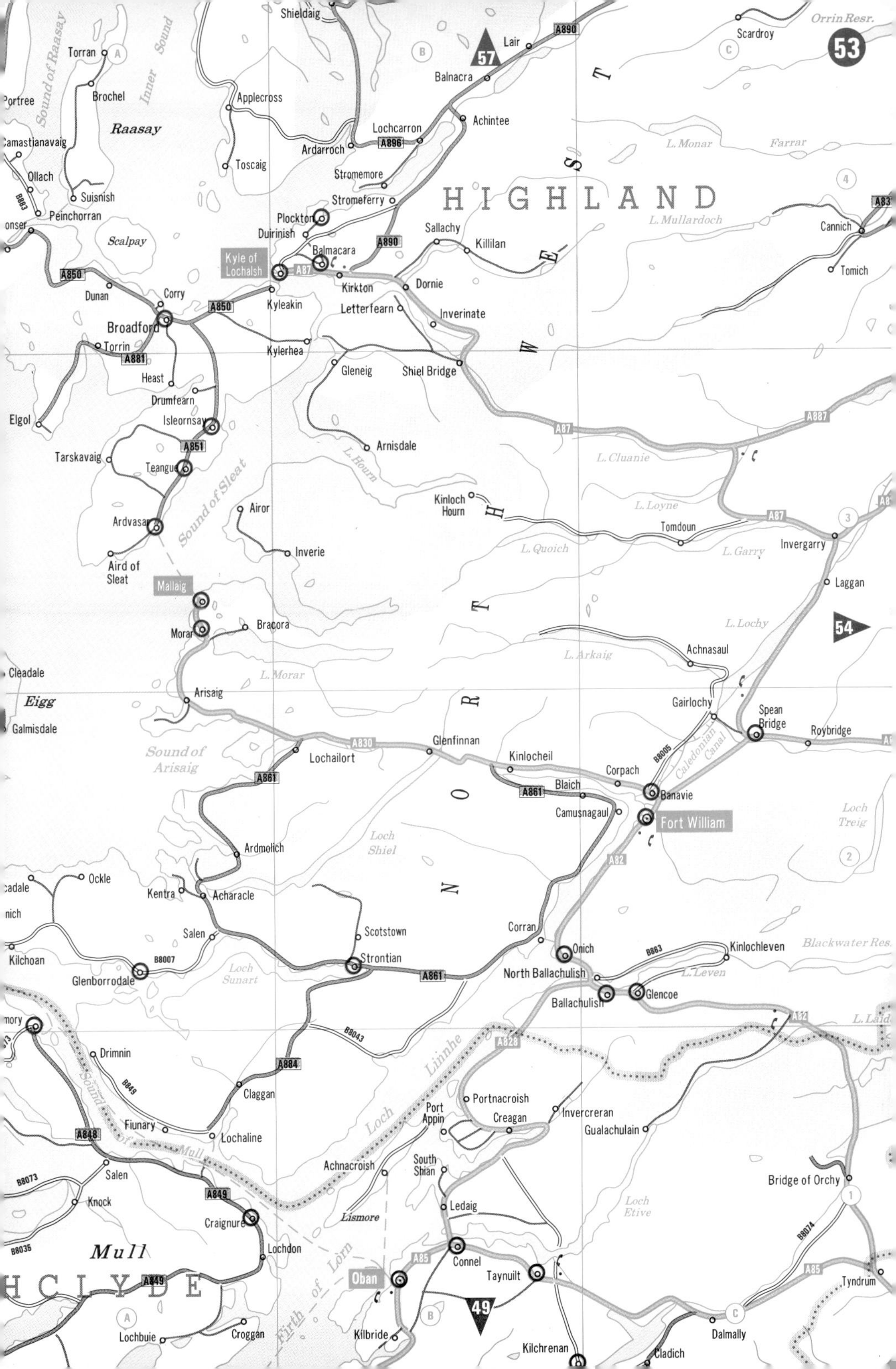

53
57
54
49
HIGHLAND
NORTH WEST
HCLYDE
Shieldaig
Lair
A890
Scardroy
Orrin Resr.
Torran
Brochel
Sound of Raasay
Inner Sound
Raasay
Portree
Applecross
Balnacra
Achintee
Lochcarron
A896
Ardarroch
Toscaig
Camastianavaig
Ollach
Suisnish
B883
Peinchorran
Stromemore
Stromeferry
Plockton
Duirinish
Balmacara
Kyle of Lochalsh
A87
A890
Sallachy
Killilan
L. Monar
Farrar
L. Mullardoch
Cannich
Tomich
Scalpay
A850
Dunan
Corry
Broadford
Kyleakin
Kirkton
Dornie
Letterfearn
Inverinate
Torrin
A881
Kylerhea
Gleneig
Shiel Bridge
Heast
Drumfearn
Isleornsay
A851
Elgol
Tarskavaig
Teangue
Ardvasar
Aird of Sleat
Sound of Sleat
Airor
Inverie
L. Hourn
Arnisdale
Kinloch Hourn
A87
A887
L. Cluanie
L. Loyne
Tomdoun
L. Quoich
L. Garry
Invergarry
Laggan
Mallaig
Morar
Bracora
L. Lochy
L. Arkaig
Achnasaul
Cleadale
Eigg
Galmisdale
Arisaig
L. Morar
Gairlochy
Spean Bridge
Roybridge
Caledonian Canal
B8005
Sound of Arisaig
A830
Lochailort
Glenfinnan
Kinlocheil
Corpach
Banavie
A861
Blaich
Camusnagaul
Fort William
Loch Treig
Loch Shiel
Ardmolich
A82
Ockle
Kentra
Acharacle
Salen
Scotstown
Corran
Onich
Kilchoan
B8007
Glenborrodale
Loch Sunart
Strontian
A861
North Ballachulish
B863
Kinlochleven
Blackwater Res.
L. Leven
Ballachulish
Glencoe
A82
L. Laidon
Drimnin
B8043
A828
Sound of Mull
B849
A884
Claggan
Loch Linnhe
Portnacroish
Port Appin
Creagan
Invercreran
Gualachulain
Fiunary
Lochaline
A848
Salen
B8073
Knock
Achnacroish
South Shian
Ledaig
Lismore
Loch Etive
Bridge of Orchy
B8074
A849
Craignure
Mull
B8035
Lochdon
A849
Connel
A85
Oban
Taynuilt
Firth of Lorn
A85
Tyndrum
Lochbuie
Croggan
Kilbride
Kilchrenan
Dalmally
Cladich

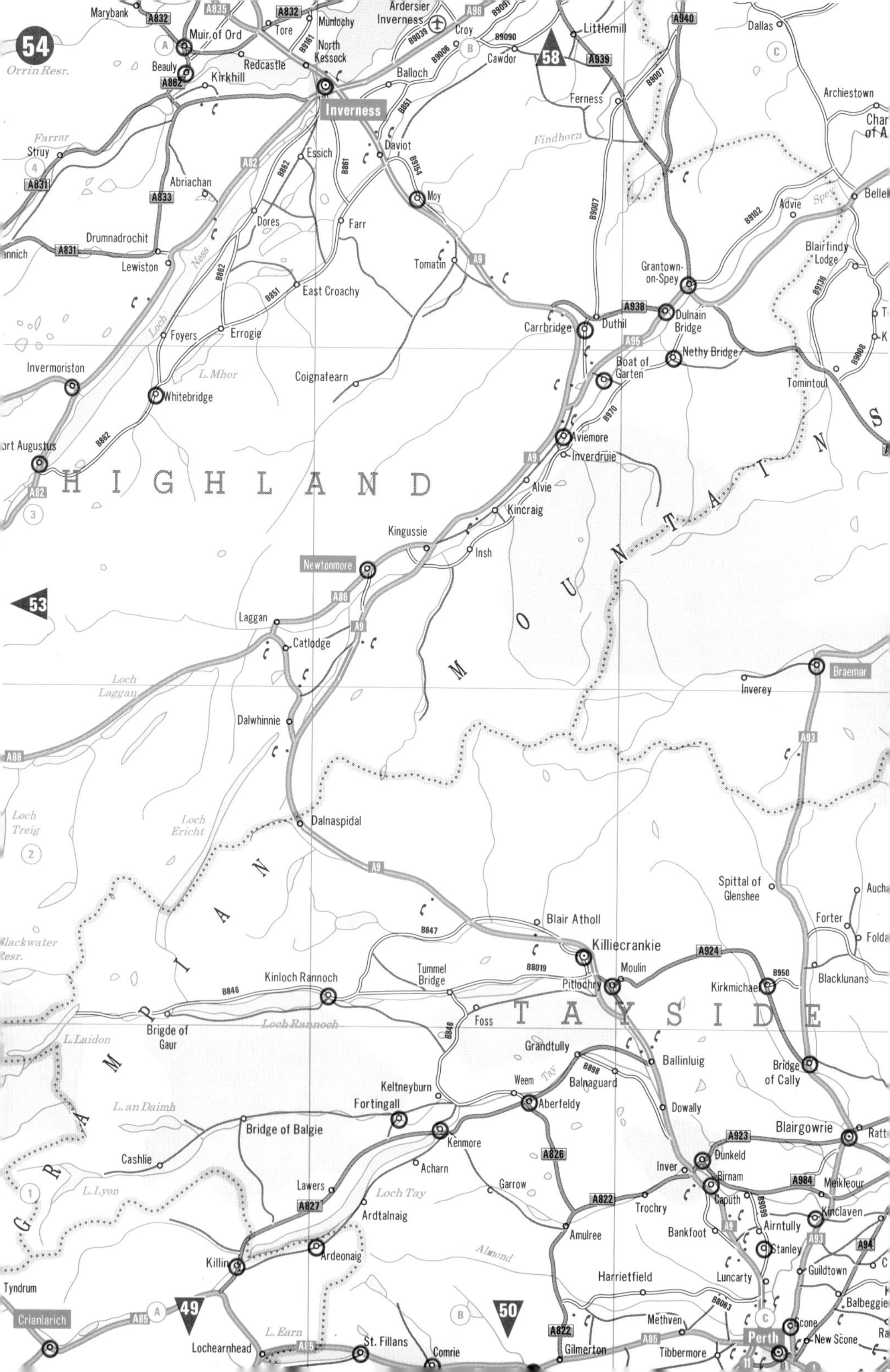
54
Orrin Resr.
Marybank
A832
A835
Muir of Ord
Beauly
A862
Tore
A832
Munlochy
North Kessock
Redcastle
Kirkhill
Ardersier
Inverness
A96
B9091
Croy
B9039
B9006
B9090
Cawdor
Balloch
Inverness
B851
58
Littlemill
A940
A939
Ferness
B9007
Dallas
Archiestown
Char of A
Farrar
Struy
A831
A82
B862
Essich
B861
Daviot
B9154
Moy
Abriachan
A833
Dores
Farr
Findhorn
B9007
Drumnadrochit
A831
Lewiston
Ness
B862
Tomatin
A9
B9102
Advie
Spey
Belle
Blairfindy Lodge
Grantown-on-Spey
B9136
B851
East Croachy
Loch
Foyers
Errogie
Carrbridge
Duthil
A938
Dulnain Bridge
A95
Boat of Garten
Nethy Bridge
B9008
Tomintoul
L. Mhor
Coignafearn
Invermoriston
Whitebridge
B970
Aviemore
Inverdruie
B862
Fort Augustus
A82
A9
Alvie
Kincraig
H I G H L A N D
Kingussie
Insh
Newtonmore
A86
53
Laggan
Catlodge
A9
Loch Laggan
Dalwhinnie
M O U N T A I N S
Inverey
Braemar
A93
A86
Loch Treig
Loch Ericht
Dalnaspidal
A9
Spittal of Glenshee
Aucha
Forter
Folda
Blackwater Resr.
B847
Blair Atholl
Killiecrankie
Moulin
A924
B950
Blacklunans
Kinloch Rannoch
B846
Tummel Bridge
B8019
Pitlochry
Kirkmichael
Bridge of Gaur
Loch Rannoch
Foss
B846
T A Y S I D E
L. Laidon
Grandtully
Ballinluig
Bridge of Cally
Weem
Tay
B898
Balnaguard
Keltneyburn
Aberfeldy
Dowally
L. an Daimh
Fortingall
Bridge of Balgie
Kenmore
A826
Blairgowrie
Ratt
A923
Dunkeld
Cashlie
Acharn
Inver
Birnam
A984
Meikleour
L. Lyon
Lawers
Loch Tay
Garrow
A822
Trochry
Caputh
B9099
A827
Ardtalnaig
Kinclaven
Airntully
Amulree
Bankfoot
A9
A93
A94
G R A M P I A N
Killin
Ardeonaig
Almond
Stanley
Tyndrum
Harrietfield
Luncarty
Guildtown
49
50
Balbeggie
Crianlarich
A85
L. Earn
B8063
Methven
Scone
A822
A85
Perth
New Scone
Lochearnhead
St. Fillans
Comrie
Gilmerton
Tibbermore

55
59
51
A
B
C
1
2
3
4
A96
Newmill
A95
Knock
B9023
B9025
Aberchirder
Turriff
Cuminestown
Fetterangus
A952
St. Fergus
B9103
Mulben
Keith
B9117
Deveron
Milltown of
Rothiemay
B9024
B9170
B9029
Mintlaw
Rora
Longside
Old Deer
A950
Peterhead
igellachie
B9014
B9115
B9022
Inverkeithny
New Deer
B9106
Stuartfield
Clola
Burnhaven
Boddam
Buchan
Ness
Kirktown of
Auchterless
B9030
Auchnagatt
A92
Dufftown
Huntly
Ythanwells
B992
Rothienorman
Methlick
A948
Hatton
A952
B9005
Cruden Bay
Fyvie
B9001
B9170
A96
A947
Kirktown of
Culsalmond
Ythanbank
A975
Bridgend
A97
Old Rayne
Meikle Wartle
Ellon
Kennethmont
Kirkton
of Rayne
Tarves
B999
Insch
A920
A920
Collieston
Cabrach
A941
B9002
Oldmeldrum
Pitmedden
Newburgh
B9002
Rhynie
Leslie
Oyne
Udny
Green
B9000
Foveran
Clatt
Auchleven
B992
B993
B999
Inverurie
Lumsden
Don
Newmachar
Badenyon
Tullynessle
Keig
Hatton
of Fintray
Balmedie
R A M P I A N
Kemnay
B977
Belhelvie
To Lerwick
Kintore
Kirkton of
Glenbuchat
Kildrummy
Monymusk
B993
A96
Aberdeen
Dyce
Alford
Towie
Blackburn
A92
A944
Strathdon
A980
Sauchen
B977
Dunecht
Bucksburn
A944
ABERDEEN
A97
Migvie
B993
B9119
Girdle Ness
Echt
Logie Coldstone
Tarland
Cults
Lumphanan
Torphins
B979
A956
A980
Ordie
B9094
B977
Peterculter
Cove Bay
B993
Kincardine
O'Neil
A93
Dinnet
Aboyne
Maryculter
Portlethen
A93
Banchory
A92
Downies
Ballater
Crathes
Kirkton
of Durris
Marywell
Dee
B979
Newtonhill
B976
Muchalls
Strachan
A957
Aucholzie
Stonehaven
Drumlithie
B974
A94
Tarfside
Auchenblae
Catterline
Roadside
of Kinneff
raedownie
B966
Arbuthnott
Kinneff
Fettercairn
Inverbervie
Clova
B966
Laurencekirk
Gourdon
B9120
Luthermuir
Bridgend
Edzell
A937
Kirkton of
Menmuir
A92
Johnshaven
rosen
illage
B955
Inchbare
A94
St. Cyrus
Marykirk
Fern
Hillside
Cortachy
Brechin
A935
Tannadice
A94
Bridge
of Dun
Montrose
South Esk
B957
B9134
Kirriemuir
Oathlaw
Aberlemno
Farnell
A934
Ferryden
B9113
A92
Kirkton of
Kingoldrum
Rescobie
Guthrie
A926
Forfar
Friockheim
Lunan Bay
Dean Water
A932
Letham
B9128
B961
Inverkeilor
A933
Glamis
B9127
Carmyllie
Colliston
Eassie
A928
B9127
St. Vigeans
A929
Inverarity
Newtyle
B978
B961
Arbirlot
Arbroath
Balgray
B954
Monikie
Muirdrum
Lundie
DUNDEE
Newbigging
A92
East Haven
Carnoustie
Barry
Muirhead
A930
Monifieth
Broughty
Ferry
Dundee
Buddon Ness
Inchture
B945
Newport-on-Tay
Firth of Tay
Wormit
Balmerino
A92

A
B
C
4
3
2
1
WESTERN
ISLES
Outer
Hebrides
Flannan Is.
Borve
Shader
Barvas
Arnol
Shawbost
Bragar
Garenin
A857
Gallan
Head
Carloway
Tolstachaolais
Great
Bernera
Valtos
Timsgarry
Miavaig
Breasclete
Callanish
Newmarket
Stornoway
A858
Cruliviq
Garynahine
B8011
Achmore
Islivig
Brenish
Lewis
Leurbost
Crossbo
Laxay
Keose
Balallan
Cromore
B8060
Marv
Arivruaich
Kershader
Loch
Langavat
Gravir
Scarp
A859
Hushinish
Ardvourlie
Eishken
Lemreway
B887
Amhuinnsuidhe
Govig
Meavaig
Taransay
Tarbert
Shiant Is.
Carnach
Scalpay
Grosebay
Harris
A859
Northton
Manish
Pabbay
Sound of Harris
Finsbay
Leverburgh
Berneray
Rodel
Renish Point
The Little Minch
Newtonferry
B893
Sollas
A865
Tigharry
Kilvaxter
North
Uist
A867
Lochmaddy
Waternish Point
Bayhead
Uig
Geary
Loch
Snizort
Earlish
Locheport
Carinish
Hallin
Dunvegan
Head
A856
Lusta
Balivanich
Ronay
Greshornish
Borreraig
52
Benbecula
A850
Bernisdale
Skye
B892
Skeabost
Bridge
Creagorry
Milovaig
B884
Dunvegan

57
A
B
C
Cape Wrath
Achiemore
Butt of Lewis
Port of Ness
Skigersta
Balchrick
Oldshoremore
Kinlochbervie
Rhiconich
North Tolsta
A894
Scourie
Badcall
Tiumpan Head
Port Nan Giuran
Shulishader
Garrabost
Bayble
Pt. of Stoer
Kylestrome
Loch More
Culkein
Drumbeg
B869
Clashnessie
Stoer
A894
A837
Loch Assynt
Lochinver
Inchnadamph
Inverkirkaig
58
Rubha Coigeach
Brae of Achnahaird
Reiff
Elphin
Polbain
Achiltibuie
A835
A837
The Minch
HIGHLAND
Strath Kanaird
Oykel Bridge
Mellon Udrigle
Badluarach
Ullapool
Mellon Charles
Laide
Badrallach
Leckmelm
Cove
L. Ewe
Aultbea
Camusnagaul
Ardcharnich
Dundonnell
Melvaig
A832
B8021
Naast
North Erradale
Poolewe
Loch Vaich
Gairloch
Badachro
A835
L. Maree
Opinan
A832
Talladale
Redpoint
L. Fannich
L. Torridon
Lower Diabaig
Kinlochewe
A832
L. Luichart
Inveralligin
Achnasheen
Rona
Torridon
A896
Sound of Raasay
Inner Sound
Shieldaig
Milton
Scardroy
Orrin Resr.
53
A890
Lair
Torran
1
2
3
4

58
A
B
C
Achiemore
Durness
Brough
Dunnet
Bridge of Forss
Scrabster
Thurso
Castletown
Dounreay
Portskerra
Armadale
Kirtomy
Farr
A836
Strathy
Melvich
Reay
Westfield
Shebster
Talmine
Skerray
Coldbackie
Bettyhill
4
Laid
A838
Tongue
Skelpick
Eriboll
Loch Hope
A836
Loch Calder
Halkirk
Dalhalvaig
Mybster
Westerdale
A897
Loch Loyal
Syre
Loch More
Thurso
A895
Achavanich
Forsinard
Loch More
Houstry
Altnaharra
Loch Naver
Kinbrace
Dunbeath
Braemore
3
Loch Choire
Borgue
HIGHLAND
A836
Berriedale
A897
A838
57
Helmsdale
Shinness
Loch Shin
A9
Balnacoil
Lairg
Dalreavoch
Muie
A837
Oykel Bridge
A839
Rogart
Brora
A839
Oykel
Altass
A836
Golspie
A837
Littleferry
2
Invershin
Culrain
Bonar Bridge
Embo
Croick
Ardgay
Dornoch
Kincardine
Clashmore
A9
Dornoch Firth
Wilkhaven
Edderton
Portmahomack
Tain
Inver
Hill of Fearn
Loch Vaich
A836
Kildary
Moray Firth
Hilton of Cadboll
Dalnavie
Boath
Balintore
Kilmuir
Nigg
Alness
Invergordon
A9
Hopeman
Nigg Ferry
Burghead
Cromarty Firth
Balblair
Cromarty
Garve
1
L. Luichart
Cullicudden
Jemimaville
Findhorn
Kinloss
A96
Alves
Dingwall
Strathpeffer
A834
Dyke
Culbokie
Rosemarkie
Forres
Contin
Fortrose
Nairn
Conon Bridge
Avoch
Rafford
Barnhill
Ardersier
Auldearn
Marybank
A835
A832
Inverness
A96
A940
Munlochy
54
Tore
Croy
Littlemill
Dallas
Muir of Ord
North Kessock
Cawdor
A939
Orrin Resr.
Beauly
Redcastle

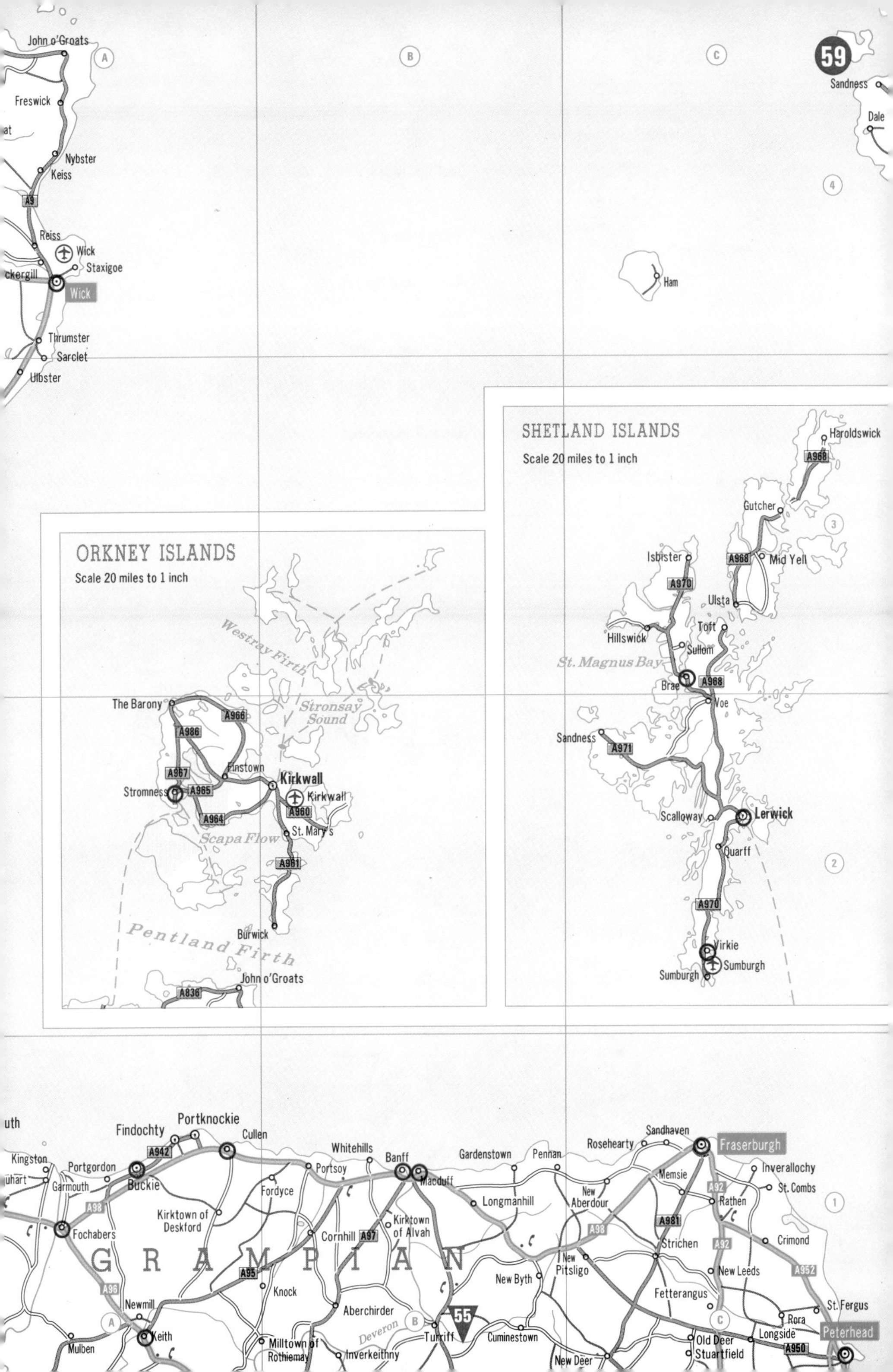

59
John o'Groats
Freswick
Nybster
Keiss
A9
Reiss
Wick
Staxigoe
Wick
Thrumster
Sarclet
Ulbster
Sandness
Dale
Ham
SHETLAND ISLANDS
Scale 20 miles to 1 inch
Haroldswick
A968
Gutcher
Isbister
A968
Mid Yell
A970
Ulsta
Toft
Hillswick
Sullom
St. Magnus Bay
Brae
A968
Voe
Sandness
A971
Scalloway
Lerwick
Quarff
A970
Virkie
Sumburgh
Sumburgh
ORKNEY ISLANDS
Scale 20 miles to 1 inch
Westray Firth
Stronsay Sound
The Barony
A966
A986
A967
Finstown
Kirkwall
Stromness
A965
Kirkwall
A960
A964
St. Mary's
Scapa Flow
A961
Burwick
Pentland Firth
John o'Groats
A836
Findochty
Portknockie
Cullen
Kingston
Portgordon
A942
Buckie
Garmouth
A98
Fochabers
Kirktown of Deskford
Fordyce
Portsoy
Whitehills
Banff
Macduff
Gardenstown
Pennan
Longmanhill
Rosehearty
Sandhaven
Fraserburgh
Inverallochy
St. Combs
Memsie
New Aberdour
A92
Rathen
A98
A981
Strichen
A92
Crimond
G R A M P I A N
Cornhill
A97
Kirktown of Alvah
A95
A96
Newmill
Knock
Aberchirder
Keith
Mulben
Milltown of Rothiemay
Inverkeithny
Deveron
Turriff
55
New Byth
New Pitsligo
New Leeds
A952
Cuminestown
Fetterangus
St. Fergus
Rora
Longside
Old Deer
Stuartfield
A950
Peterhead
New Deer

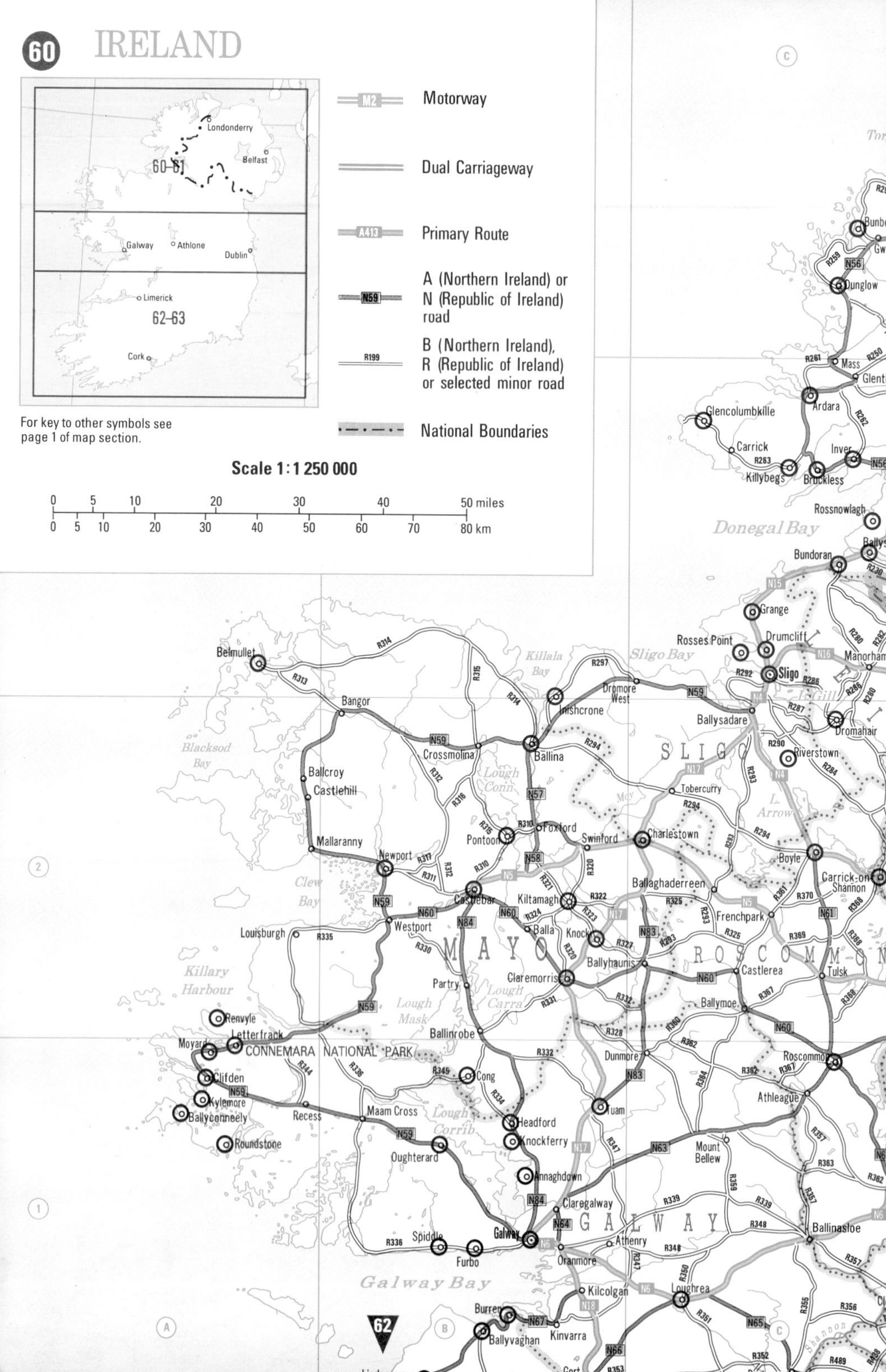
60
IRELAND
Londonderry
Belfast
60–61
Galway
Athlone
Dublin
Limerick
62–63
Cork
Motorway
Dual Carriageway
Primary Route
A (Northern Ireland) or N (Republic of Ireland) road
B (Northern Ireland), R (Republic of Ireland) or selected minor road
National Boundaries
M2
A413
N59
R199
For key to other symbols see page 1 of map section.
Scale 1:1 250 000
0 5 10 20 30 40 50 miles
0 5 10 20 30 40 50 60 70 80 km
Donegal Bay
Sligo Bay
Killala Bay
Blacksod Bay
Clew Bay
Killary Harbour
Galway Bay
Lough Conn
Lough Mask
Lough Carra
Lough Corrib
L. Arrow
L. Gill
Shannon
SLIGO
MAYO
ROSCOMMON
GALWAY
CONNEMARA NATIONAL PARK
Dunglow
Glencolumbkille
Ardara
Carrick
Killybegs
Bruckless
Inver
Mass
Rossnowlagh
Bundoran
Grange
Drumcliff
Rosses Point
Sligo
Manorhamilton
Dromahair
Riverstown
Ballysadare
Belmullet
Bangor
Crossmolina
Ballina
Inishcrone
Dromore West
Tobercurry
Ballcroy
Castlehill
Mallaranny
Newport
Pontoon
Foxford
Swinford
Charlestown
Boyle
Carrick-on-Shannon
Castlebar
Westport
Louisburgh
Kiltamagh
Balla
Knock
Ballaghaderreen
Frenchpark
Ballyhaunis
Claremorris
Castlerea
Tulsk
Partry
Ballinrobe
Ballymoe
Renvyle
Letterfrack
Moyard
Clifden
Kylemore
Ballyconneely
Roundstone
Recess
Maam Cross
Cong
Headford
Knockferry
Oughterard
Annaghdown
Dunmore
Tuam
Roscommon
Athleague
Mount Bellew
Claregalway
Galway
Spiddle
Furbo
Athenry
Oranmore
Ballinasloe
Kilcolgan
Loughrea
Burren
Ballyvaghan
Kinvarra
Gort
Portumna
62